SCIENCE FICTION
and
FANTASY REFERENCE INDEX
1992–1995

SCIENCE FICTION
and
FANTASY REFERENCE INDEX
1992–1995

An International Subject and Author Index
to History and Criticism

Edited by
HAL W. HALL
Head, Education and Audiovisual Services
Sterling C. Evans Library
Texas A&M University
College Station, Texas

1997
Libraries Unlimited, Inc.
Englewood, Colorado

LIBRARIES UNLIMITED, INC.
P.O. Box 6633
Englewood, CO 80155-6633
(800) 237-6124
www.lu.com

Library of Congress Cataloging-in-Publication Data

Science fiction and fantasy reference index 1992-1995 : an
  international subject and author index to history and criticism /
Hal W. Hall, editor.
    xxi, 503 p.   22x28 cm.
    Includes bibliographical references.
    ISBN 1-56308-527-5
    1. Science fiction--History and criticism--Indexes.   2. Fantastic
fiction--History and literature--Indexes.   I. Hall, Halbert W.
Z5917.S36S2974   1997
[PN3433.5]
016.8093'876--dc21   97-10057
                                                        CIP

For My Family:

Halbert Theon Hall
Edna Hall
Earl Oxford Hall
Vela Hall Evans
Edna Beth Hall Beckelhymer
Betty Gloff Hall
Julia Dauriece Hall Mundy
Sarah Anita Hall
Clark Simmons Mundy

They light up my life.

Contents

Preface

The *Science Fiction and Fantasy Reference Index* is by far the most comprehensive index yet published to the secondary literature dealing with science fiction and fantasy and related genres. *Science Fiction and Fantasy Reference Index, 1878-1985* indexed more than 19,000 individual books, articles, essays, news reports, and audiovisual items. Although the earliest entry is an 1878 item on Jules Verne, most of the entries date from 1945 through 1985. *Science Fiction and Fantasy Reference Index, 1985-1991* indexed more than 16,270 items. This volume, covering 1992 through 1995, with newly located earlier material, indexes 10,627 items. More than 95 percent of the items indexed were personally examined by the author; citations to the balance are based on secondary sources.

Scope

Fantastic literature is here defined as including science fiction, fantasy, and horror/supernatural/weird fiction. Science fiction generated the largest number of entries, followed by fantasy and horror. Approximately 90 percent of the indexed items are in English. Most of the citations to pre-1980 non-English material were supplied by David Samuelson, Professor of English at California State University, Long Beach, and supplemented by material from several European contributors, notably Luk de Vos of the Netherlands. Coverage of European material is representative, not comprehensive. The most significant non-English coverage is of French, German, and Italian material, but many other countries are represented. The non-English language entries are entered by author, with subject headings where subject analysis was possible. For a variety of reasons involving both the background of this segment of the project and the lack of a multilingual word processing program, diacritical marks are often omitted.

History

This index began in 1967 on 3x5-inch index cards, when no indexes to the secondary literature of science fiction and fantasy existed. In 1980, I published a preliminary computer-output microfiche bibliography, *The Science Fiction Index*, which contained 4,350 citations. In 1972, the first book-length bibliography of science fiction secondary literature was published, Thomas D. Clareson's *Science Fiction Criticism: An Annotated Checklist* (Kent State University Press), which descriptively annotated more than 800 items including book review columns from general magazines. Citations to reviews are contained in my *Science Fiction Book Review Index* and *Science Fiction and Fantasy Book Review Index*, published by Gale Research, covering over 85,000 reviews published from 1923–1991. The *Research Index* section of Charles N. Brown and William G. Contento's annual *Science Fiction, Fantasy, & Horror* supplemented and updated *Science Fiction and Fantasy Reference Index* from 1987–1991.

Methodology

A variety of methods were used to identify the items considered for indexing. A significant number were located by examination of my personal collection, and by intensive research in the Texas A&M University Library Science Fiction Research Collection. Bibliographic searching of published indexes, such as *Readers' Guide,* regular examination of almost 200 magazine titles, computer searches, citation analysis, help from fellow scholars, and good fortune were all significant tools in the growth of this index. Citation analysis proved to be one of the most fruitful methods. In effect, every scholar who wrote a footnote or provided a list of references became a contributor. More significantly, those citations led to other sources or hinted at new material in unexpected places. The value of citation analysis, and of such tools as *Arts and Humanities Citation Index*, cannot be overemphasized. Users should note that the outstanding author bibliographies published by Borgo Press and the older "Primary and Secondary Bibliographies" for individual authors published by G. K. Hall, are not fully analyzed in this index. Such author-specific bibliographies, which are cited here, will always be more inclusive than a general tool such as this one, and the scholar should always consult such specialty tools when researching a well-known writer.

Review of the historical files of magazines is a rewarding, if sometimes frustrating, activity. A new source, an uncited item, or a clue to a treasure trove of new material are the fruits of such labor. Missing issues are the bane of such effort; one never knows what might have been missed. In this volume, a gap in a sequential series of articles sometimes appears. While the existence of the item may be assumed, failure to verify the item sometimes precluded inclusion.

The coverage of news sources, particularly fan newspapers, deserves special notice. The issues of *Locus* and *Science Fiction Chronicle* are almost completely indexed and provide subject access to the fan newspapers for 1992 to 1995.

Scholars, critics, bibliographers, and librarians over the years have questioned the value of the material published in "fanzines." In his 1985 Pilgrim Award acceptance speech, Samuel R. Delany emphasized the value and importance of this material:

> Fanzines—to take only one manifestation of this reader/writer relationship— have created a vast, "informal critical system" around science fiction amounting to many, many hundreds of thousands of pages—possibly even exceeding the actual number of pages of science fiction written! This energetic dialogue has had its supportive and its destructive aspects, and any history of science fiction that does not research and theorize as to the scope and effect of this force on the way we read science fiction is ignoring an extraordinary historical influence on the field. (*SFRA Newsletter* No. 133: 7-15. August 1985)

The *Science Fiction and Fantasy Reference Series* indexes over 45,000 discrete bibliographic items. That total represents perhaps 50 to 60 percent of the directly applicable material published to date. The coverage of newspapers is significant but only touches on the information available in the nation's newspapers. Coverage of the "fanzines" is the most comprehensive ever attempted but is necessarily selective. The better fanzines of the 1930s and 1940s, in particular, are filled with valuable material, often the only critical commentary on many stories and books, yet these fanzines are essentially unindexed. Pavlat and Evan's *Fanzine Index* (Piser, 1965) lists hundreds of these unindexed fanzines published prior to 1952, and the majority of the "Fanzines" listed in the "Academic Periodicals and Major Fanzines" section of Tymn and Ashley's *Science Fiction, Fantasy and Weird Fiction Magazines* (Greenwood, 1985) are not indexed in any source.

Materials Indexed

Virtually all standard bibliographic sources were consulted in compiling *Science Fiction and Fantasy Reference Index*, such as *Readers' Guide, Humanities Index, Social Sciences Index, Arts and Humanities Citation Index*, the MLA bibliographies, *Library Literature, ERIC, NewsBank,* and many others. An ever-increasing variety of electronic indexes, abstracts, magazines and World Wide Web sites provided additional citations. Material from several thousand issues of magazines and newspapers was also indexed. The "List of Sources" indicates the titles that were systematically searched. The user should assume that coverage of the magazines listed is over 95 percent complete for each title noted. On occasion, issues were missing and will be included in supplements to this volume as they are located.

Arrangement

The *Science Fiction and Fantasy Reference Index* is divided into two sections. The Author Entries section provides access to authors and co-authors of all books, articles, and essays. By-lines of newspaper reports are not indexed by author. The Subject Entries section provides access by subject headings. In both sections, citations are printed in full, with no abbreviations, allowing the user immediate access to all information.

The *Science Fiction and Fantasy Reference Index* was compiled and sorted using computer sorting rules, essentially letter-by-letter. Numerical items are sorted and listed at the beginning of the alphabetical sequence. Items without authors are filed before author entries in the Subject Index. While this appears to result in repetitive alphabetical lists, the filing is consistent with the "nothing before something" standard commonly used in libraries and computers.

The following examples illustrate the filing order:

12:01 P.M. (Motion Picture)
18 Again (Motion Picture)
20,000 Leagues Under the Sea (Motion Picture)
2001: A Space Odyssey (Motion Picture)
4th Dimension (Motion Picture)
5,000 Fingers of Dr. T. (Motion Picture)
La Barre
Labare
New York
Newark
Newyorker
Mac Donald
Mace
MacGregor
Malone
McAuley

Conventions

In general, author names are used as published on the item. An attempt was made to combine author entries when name variations, such as Robert and Bob, could be attributable to the same individual; if that information could not be verified, the names were left as they appeared on the sources. **Book titles** appear in boldface type. *Magazine and newspaper titles* are italicized. ***Motion picture, radio, and television titles*** appear in bold italics. Partial titles of motion pictures, radio shows, or television shows are surrounded by single quotations, as in 'Return of the Jedi.'

Spelling is cited as presented in the source document, except for obvious errors. In particular, British spelling has been retained. Typographic oddities, where possible, have been retained, such as the use of symbols in titles.

During compilation of the data for this index, titles of books and articles were entered as presented in the source documents, resulting in wide variations in capitalization. Most titles have been regularized to a consistent style, but some have no doubt been overlooked. Book pagination and magazine page number citations have been regularized as much as possible for the convenience of the user.

Comments and suggestions from users are encouraged and should be directed to the editor:

H. W. Hall
3608 Meadow Oaks Lane
Bryan, TX 77802
Hal-Hall@TAMU.EDU

Sample Entries

Author Entries

Magazine article:

Author *Title of article*

ABBOTT, JOE
"Tolkien's Monsters: Concept and Function in the Lord of the Rings, Part III: Sauron,"
Mythlore 16(3): 51-59. Spring 1990 (No. 61)

Magazine title   *Volume no.*   *Issue no.*   *Pagination*   *Date*   *Whole no.*

Article in a book:

Author *Title of article*   *Book author or editor*

ALDISS, BRIAN W.
"Sturgeon: Mercury Plus X: Farewell to a Master," in: Aldiss, B. W. **And the Lurid Glare of the Comet.** Seattle: Serconia, 1986. pp.52-62.

Book title   *Book imprint*   *Pagination*

Edited book:

Editor's name   *Book title*   *Book imprint*

ALLEN, WILLIAM R.
(ed.) **Conversations With Kurt Vonnegut.** Jackson: University Press
of Mississippi, 1986. 160 pp.

Editor note   *Pagination*

Sample Entries

Monographs:

Author   *Book title*

ANDREW, MARTIN
   The Mask of the Prophet: The Extraordinary Fictions of Jules Verne. Oxford:
   Clarendon Press, 1990. 222pp.

   Book imprint   *Pagination*

Author   *Book Title*   *Joint authors*

SLUSSER, GEORGE E.
   Aliens: The Anthropology of Science Fiction, by George E. Slusser and Eric
   S. Rabkin. Carbondale: Southern Illinois University Press, 1987. 243pp.

      Book imprint   *Pagination*

Subject Entries

Subject heading   *Article title (anonymous work)*

                                  Magazine title Pagination Date

2001: A SPACE ODYSSEY (MOTION PICTURE)
   __"Sci-Fi Fans Judge 2001 Best Film at Rome Retro Event," *Variety* p.36. March 26,
   1974.
   __Sheldon, Robert. "Rendezvous with HAL: 2001/2010," *Extrapolation*
   28(3): 255-268. Fall 1987.
Author   *Title*   *Magazine title*

   Volume no.   Issue no. Pagination Date

BOOKS ANALYZED

The following books were systematically indexed for *Science Fiction and Fantasy Reference Index, 1992–1995*. Each pertinent essay or article in the books is individually entered in *Science Fiction and Fantasy Reference Index* by author and subject.

Aldiss, Brian W. *The Detached Retina: Aspects of SF and Fantasy*. Syracuse, NY: Syracuse University Press, 1995. 224pp.

Bloom, Harold. *Classic Fantasy Writers*. New York: Chelsea House, 1994. 187pp.

_____. *Classic Horror Writers*. New York: Chelsea House, 1994. 180pp.

_____. *George Orwell's 1984*. New York: Chelsea House, 1987. 135pp.

_____. *Modern Fantasy Writers*. New York: Chelsea House, 1995. 194pp.

_____. *Modern Horror Writers*. New York: Chelsea House, 1995. 185pp.

Bromwich, Rachel, Jarman, A. O. H., and Roberts, Brynley F., eds. *The Arthur of the Welsh: The Arthurian Legend in Medieval Welsh Literature*. Cardiff: University of Wales, 1991. 310pp.

Budd, Louis J. and Cady, Edwin H., eds. *On Poe: The Best From American Literature*. Durham, NC: Duke University Press, 1993. 270pp.

Busby, Keith, ed. *The Arthurian Yearbook I*. New York: Garland, 1991. 234pp.

Collins, Robert A. and Latham, Robert, eds. *Science Fiction and Fantasy Book Review Annual 1991*. Westport, CT: Greenwood, 1994. 880pp.

Delany, Samuel R. *Silent Interviews on Language, Race, Sex, Science Fiction and Some Comics*. Hanover, NH: Wesleyan University Press, 1994. 322pp.

Donawerth, Jane L. and Kolmerten, Carol A., eds. *Utopian and Science Fiction by Women: Worlds of Difference*. Syracuse, NY: Syracuse University Press, 1994. 260pp.

Elkins, Charles L. and Greenberg, Martin H., eds. *Robert Silverberg's Many Trapdoors: Critical Essays on His Science Fiction*. Westport, CT: Greenwood, 1992. 154pp.

Filmer, Kath, ed. *Twentieth-Century Fantasists: Essays on Culture, Society and Belief in Twentieth Century Mythopoeic Literature*. New York: St. Martin's, 1992. 222pp.

Fries, Maureen and Watson, Jeanie, eds. *Approaches to the Teaching of the Arthurian Tradition*. New York: Modern Language Association, 1992. 195pp.

Goldberg, Lee, Lofficier, Randy, Lofficier, Jean-Marc, and Rabkin, William, eds. *Science Fiction Filmmaking in the 1980s*. Jefferson, NC: McFarland, 1995. 267pp.

Golden, Christopher, ed. *Cut! Horror Writers on Horror Film*. New York: Berkley, 1992. 297pp.

Graham, Loren R. *Science and the Soviet Social Order*. Cambridge: Harvard University Press, 1990. 443pp.

Gray, Chris H., ed. *The Cyborg Handbook*. New York: Routledge, 1995. 540pp.

Greenberg, Mark L. and Schachterle, Lance, eds. *Literature and Technology*. Bethlehem, PA: Lehigh University Press, 1992. 322pp.

Greenberg, Martin H., Gorman, Ed, and Munster, Bill, eds. *The Dean Koontz Companion*. New York: Berkley, 1994. 311pp.

Gunn, James E. *Inside Science Fiction: Essays on Fantastic Literature*. San Bernardino, CA: Borgo Press, 1992. 176pp.

Hartwell, David G. and Cramer, Kathryn, eds. *The Ascent of Wonder: The Evolution of Hard SF*. New York: Tor, 1994. 990pp.

Harty, Kevin J., ed. *Cinema Arthuriana: Essays on Arthurian Film*. New York: Garland, 1991. 255pp.

Heuermann, Harmut, ed. *Der Science Fiction Roman in der angloamerikanischen Literatur*. Düsseldorf: Bagel, 1986. 399pp.

Heuermann, Hartmut and Lange, Bernd-Peter, eds. *Die Utopie in der angloamerikanischen Literatur: Interpretationen*. Düsseldorf: Bagel, 1984. 370pp.

Ingersoll, Earl G., ed. *Doris Lessing: Conversations*. Princeton, NJ: Ontario Review Press, 1994. 248pp.

Irons, Glenwood, ed. *Gender, Language and Myth: Essays on Popular Narrative*. Toronto: University of Toronto Press, 1992. 340pp.

Jakubowski, Maxim and James, Edward, eds. *The Profession of Science Fiction: SF Writers on Their Craft and Ideas*. New York: St. Martin's, 1993. 208pp.

Joshi, S. T., ed. *The Count of Thirty: A Tribute to Ramsey Campbell*. West Warwick, RI: Necronomicon, 1993. 54pp.

_____. *The H. P. Lovecraft Centennial Conference Proceedings*. West Warwick, RI: Necronomicon, 1991. 80pp.

Kondo, Yoji, ed. *Requiem: New Collected Works by Robert A. Heinlein and Tributes to the Grand Master*. New York: Tor, 1992. 341pp.

Kumar, Krishan and Bann, Stephen, eds. *Utopias and the Millennium*. London: Reaktion Books, 1993. 164pp.

Latham, Robert A. and Collins, Robert A., eds. *Modes of the Fantastic: Selected Essays from the Twelfth International Conference on the Fantastic in the Arts*. Westport, CT: Greenwood, 1995. 234pp.

Magistrale, Tony, ed. *The Dark Descent: Essays Defining Stephen King's Horrorscape*. Westport, CT: Greenwood, 1992. 227pp.

Murphy, Patrick D., ed. *Staging the Impossible: The Fantastic Mode in Modern Drama*. Westport, CT: Greenwood, 1992. 245pp.

Nicholson, Colin, ed. *Margaret Atwood: Writing and Subjectivity; New Critical Essays*. New York: St. Martin's, 1994. 261pp.

Price, Robert M., ed. *Black Forbidden Things: Cryptical Secrets from the Crypt of Cthulhu*. Mercer Island, WA: Starmont, 1992. 199pp.

Roberts, Sheila, ed. *Still the Frame Holds: Essays on Women Poets and Writers*. San Bernardino, CA: Borgo Press, 1993. 216pp.

Rose, Jonathan, ed. *The Revised Orwell*. East Lansing, MI: Michigan State University Press, 1992. 263pp.

Ruddick, Nicholas, ed. *State of the Fantastic: Studies in the Theory and Practice of Fantastic Literature and Film*. Westport, CT: Greenwood, 1992. 210pp.

Salwak, Dale, ed. *Kingsley Amis In Life and Letters*. New York: St. Martin's, 1990. 202pp.

Sanders, Joe, ed. *Functions of the Fantastic: Selected Essays from the Thirteenth International Conference on the Fantastic in the Arts*. Westport, CT: Greenwood, 1995. 230pp.

_____. *Science Fiction Fandom*. Westport, CT: Greenwood, 1994. 293pp.

Schweitzer, Darrell. *Speaking of Horror: Interviews With Writers of the Supernatural*. San Bernardino, CA: Borgo, 1994. 136pp.

Schweitzer, Darrell, ed. *Discovering Classic Horror Fiction I*. Mercer Island, WA: Starmont, 1992. 191pp.

Seed, David, ed. *Anticipations: Essays on Early Science Fiction and Its Precursors*. Liverpool: Liverpool University Press, 1995. 230pp.

Slocum, Sally K., ed. *Popular Arthurian Traditions*. Bowling Green, OH: Popular Press, 1992. 184pp.

Slusser, George and Rabkin, Eric S., eds. *Fights of Fancy: Armed Conflict in Science Fiction and Fantasy*. Athens, GA: University of Georgia Press, 1993. 224pp.

Slusser, George E. and Rabkin, Eric S., eds. *Styles of Creation: Aesthetic Technique and the Creation of Fictional Worlds*. Athens, GA: University of Georgia Press, 1992. 271pp.

Slusser, George E. and Shippey, Tom, eds. *Fiction 2000: Cyberpunk and the Future of Narrative*. Athens: University of Georgia Press, 1992. 303pp.

Stableford, Brian. *Opening Minds: Essays on Fantastic Literature*. San Bernardino, CA: Borgo Press, 1995. 144pp.

_____. *Outside the Human Aquarium: Masters of Science Fiction*. San Bernardino, CA: Borgo, 1995. 152pp.

Sullivan, C. W., III. *Science Fiction for Young Readers*. Westport, CT: Greenwood, 1993. 214pp.

Sullivan, E. D. S., ed. *The Utopian Vision: Seven Essays on the Quincentennial of Sir Thomas More*. San Diego, CA: San Diego State University Press, 1983. 265pp.

Tompkins, David G., ed. *Science Fiction Writer's Market Place and Sourcebook*. Cincinnati, OH: Writer's Digest Books, 1994. 486pp.

Umland, Samuel J., ed. *Philip K. Dick: Contemporary Critical Interpretations*. Westport, CT: Greenwood, 1995. 240pp.

Van Hise, James, ed. *Trek Celebration Two*. Las Vegas, NV: Pioneer, 1994. 166pp.

Watson, Jeanie and Fries, Maureen, eds. *The Figure of Merlin in the Nineteenth and Twentieth Centuries*. Lewiston, NY: Edwin Mellen Press, 1989. 197pp.

Weaver, Tom. *Attack of the Monster Movie Makers: Interviews with 20 Genre Giants*. Jefferson, NC: McFarland, 1994. 384pp.

_____. *They Fought the Creature Features: Interviews with 23 Classic Horror, Science Fiction and Serial Stars*. Jefferson, NC: McFarland, 1995. 318pp.

Wiater, Stanley. *Dark Visions: Conversations with the Masters of the Horror Film*. New York: Avon, 1992. 228pp.

Wober, J. Mallory, ed. *Television and Nuclear Power: Making the Public Mind*. Norwood, NJ: Ablex, 1992. 297pp.

Wolf, Milton T. and Mallett, Daryl F., eds. *Imaginative Futures: Proceedings of the 1993 Science Fiction Research Association Conference*. San Bernardino, CA: Jacob's Ladder Books/Borgo Press, 1995. 364pp.

Wolverton, Dave, ed. *Writers of the Future, Volume VIII*. Los Angeles, CA: Bridge, 1993. 396pp.

MAGAZINES INDEXED

The following magazines were systematically reviewed for *Science Fiction and Fantasy Reference Index, 1992–1995*. Titles marked by an asterisk (*) were indexed in depth, with coverage of all substantive material related to the fields of science fiction, fantasy and horror. Some issues of these titles were unavailable for indexing; any missing issues will be covered in a subsequent edition of *Science Fiction and Fantasy Reference Index*.

AB Bookman's Weekly (October SF issue
    only)*
Aboriginal Science Fiction*
Amazing*
America History and Life
American Cinematographer
American Film
American Literary History
American Quarterly
Analog*
Arizona Quarterly
Arthuriana (Formerly Quondam et Futurus)
Arts and Humanities Citation Index
Asimov's Science Fiction Magazine*
ATQ
Australian Science Fiction Review*
Bulletin of Bibliography
Burroughs Bulletin*
Cambridge Quarterly
CEA Critic
CEA Forum
Children's Literature Abstracts
Children's Literature Association Quarterly
Children's Literature in Education
Cimmaron Review
Cineaste
Cinefantastique*
Cinefex*
Cinema Journal
College English
Comparative Literature Studies
Contemporary Authors. New Revision Series.
Contemporary Literature
Critical Quarterly
Critique
CSL: The Bulletin of the New York C. S.
    Lewis Society
Current Biography
Current Contents

Dark Man: Journal of Robert E. Howard
    Studies*
Diacritics
Dissertation Abstracts
ELH
English Journal
English Language Notes
English Literature in Transition
English Studies
ERIC
Essays in Literature
Extrapolation*
Fantasy Commentator*
Filmfax
Focus (BSFA)
Foundation*
Futures
Futurist
Genders
Genre
Georgia Review
Hailing Frequencies (Waldenbooks)
Hollins Critic
Hudson Review
IAFA Newsletter*
Imagine
Inklings: Jahrbuch für Literatur und Ästhetik
    (Germany)*
Interzone*
Journal of Film and Video
Journal of Popular Culture
Journal of Popular Film and Television
Journal of the Fantastic in the Arts*
Journal of the William Morris Society
Journal of Youth Services in Libraries
Jump Cut
Kansas Quarterly
Kenyon Review
Language Arts

Lan's Lantern*
Library Literature
Lion and the Unicorn
Literary Research
Literary Review
Literature and Psychology
Literature/Film Quarterly
Locus*
Lovecraft Studies*
Lucasfilm Fan Club
Magazine of Fantasy and Science Fiction*
Magill's Cinema Annual
Marion Zimmer Bradley's Fantasy Magazine*
Matrix (BSFA)
Meanjin
Metaphysical Review
MLA Bibliography
Modern Fiction Studies
Monad*
Mosaic
Mythlore*
National Newspaper Index
New England Review
New York Review of Science Fiction*
NewsBank
NewsBank Names in the News
NewsBank Review of the Arts
Niekas
North Dakota Quarterly
Northwest Review
Notes on Contemporary Literature
Novel: A Forum on Fiction
Omni
Paradoxa
Periodical Abstracts
PKDS Newsletter*
PMLA
Postmodern Culture (On-Line Journal)
Prairie Schooner
Pulphouse: A Weekly Magazine*
Quantum (Formerly Thrust)*
Quarber Merkur*
Quondam et Futurus
Radio Free P K D*
Re Arts and Letters
Realms of Fantasy*
Renascence
Report, The: The Fiction Writer's Magazine*
Riverside Quarterly*
Rocky Mountain Review
Romanian Review
Science Fiction Age*

Science Fiction and Fantasy Forum*
Science Fiction Chronicle*
Science Fiction Eye*
Science Fiction News (Australia)*
Science Fiction Review*
Science Fiction Studies*
Science Fiction Times (Germany)*
Science Fiction: A Review of Speculative
   Fiction*
Sci-Fi Entertainment*
Sci-Fi Universe*
Sewanee Review
SF Commentary*
SFRA Review*
SFWA Bulletin*
Sight and Sound
Sol Rising (Toronto)
South Atlantic Quarterly
South Dakato Review
Southern Humanities Review
Southern Quarterly
Southern Review
Southwest Review
Star Trek: The Official Fan Club Magazine
Starlog*
Studies in American Fiction
Studies in Canadian Literature
Studies in Short Fiction
Studies in the Literary Imagination
Studies in the Novel
Studies in Weird Fiction*
Style
Substance
Tales of the Unanticipated
Teaching English in the Two Year College
Texas Studies in Literature and Language
Tomorrow Speculative Fiction*
Tulsa Studies in Women's Literature
Twentieth Century Literature
Utopian Studies*
Variety
Vector (BSFA)*
W-B (Waldenbooks)
Weird Tales*
Wide Angle
World SF Journal*
World SF Newsletter*
Worlds of Fantasy and Horror*
Writer
Writer's Digest
Yale Review

Acknowledgments

There are always more participants in a project such as this than anyone could imagine. The correspondents; the e-mail contributors; colleagues who direct material to me constantly; Interlibrary Loan Department staff who labor diligently and long to locate the rare, the fugitive, and the non-English items: to each of you a hearty Thank You, for your time, your interest and your professionalism.

There are also those who go "above and beyond" in their help, encouragement and time. Thank you
Rob Reginald, Daryl Mallett, James Harner, Rebecca Pedersen

Finally, there are those who contribute so much they must have special acknowledgement.
Bill Contento
and his unique, amazing, slightly arcane, and deeply appreciated computer program are the foundation upon which the current version of this index is built. Bill, Thank You so much for the program, your time, and your friendship.

Bill Page
the most effective reference person I have every worked with. He is a walking fount of information about the Evans Library, about "stuff" in general, and is able to track down the most esoteric information. Bill, Thank You for all the citations you have given me over the years, for the encouragement to continue, and for your friendship.

This index is only possible because of all of you!

Subject Index

12 MONKEYS (MOTION PICTURE)
___ Markowitz, Andy. "**Twelve Monkeys**: Preview," *Cinefantastique* 27(3): 8-9. December 1995.
___ Parks, Louis B. "**12 Monkeys**: Plenty of Style, Little Substance," *Houston (TX) Chronicle* January 4, 1996. (Cited from the Internet Edition.)
___ Stack, Peter. "**12 Monkeys** Is Not Exactly a Barrel of Laughs: Willis, Pitt in Grimy Futuristic Thriller about Killer Virus," *San Francisco (CA) Chronicle* February 5, 1996. (Cited from the Internet Edition.)

1984 (MOTION PICTURE)
___ "**1984** Pulled From Venice; Preem Off Until October," *Variety* p. 7. August 1, 1984.
___ "Atlantic Releasing Takes All U. S. Rights to **1984**," *Variety* p. 6. December 12, 1984.
___ "Death of Burton Spurs **1984** Sales," *Variety* p. 20. August 15, 1984.
___ "IVE Buys Homevid Rights to **1984** With Theatrical Shares Thrown In," *Variety* p. 24. December 26, 1984.
___ "Orwell's **1984** Rolls in London, First Project of Chi Film Buff," *Variety* p. 45. April 25, 1984.
___ Pitman, Jack. "But Who's Watching Big Brother?," *Variety* p. 2, 84. June 15, 1983.
___ Pitman, Jack. "Perry Sets Remake of Orwell's **1984**," *Variety* p. 4, 27. November 9, 1983.

20,000 LEAGUES UNDER THE SEA (1954) (MOTION PICTURE)
___ Maertens, James W. "Between Jules Verne and Walt Disney: Brains, Brawn, and Masculine Desire in **20,000 Leagues Under the Sea**," *Science Fiction Studies* 22(2): 209-225. July 1995.

2001: A SPACE ODYSSEY (MOTION PICTURE)
___ "**2001** Sequel: A Legal Odyssey? Metro Denies Phillips-Fox Rights," *Variety* p. 3, 25. December 22, 1982.
___ "Back to 70m, Six-Track Stereo, **2001** Displays Fast Legs With Young Mob," *Variety* p. 6. April 8, 1970.
___ "Fifth Time for **2001**; Metro Sees Benefit From Admen Lifts," *Variety* p. 5. March 18, 1970.
___ Bizony, Piers. "**2001** at 25," *Omni* 15(7): 42-50. May 1993.
___ Borgwald, James M. "Classroom Analysis of Rotating Space Vehicles in **2001: A Space Odyssey**," by James M. Borgwald and Serge Schreiner. *Physics Teacher* 31(7): 406-409. October 1993.
___ DeBellis, Jack. " 'The Awful Power': John Updike's Use of Kubrick's **2001: A Space Odyssey** in **Rabbit Redux**," *Literature/Film Quarterly* 21(3): 209-217. 1993.
___ Goldman, Lowell. "**2001: A Space Odyssey**: Gary Lockwood," *Cinefantastique* 25(3): 47. June 1994.
___ Goldman, Lowell. "**2001: A Space Odyssey**: Kier Dullea," *Cinefantastique* 25(3): 34. June 1994.
___ Gunn, James E. "Looking Backward at **2001**," in: Gunn, James E. **Inside Science Fiction: Essays on Fantastic Literature**. San Bernardino, CA: Borgo, 1992. pp.121-123.
___ Jongeward, Steven. "**2001: A Space Odyssey**: Arthur C. Clarke," *Cinefantastique* 25(3): 37. June 1994.
___ Larson, Randall D. "**2001: A Space Odyssey**: The Music," *Cinefantastique* 25(3): 40-42. June 1994.
___ Millar, Jeff. "A Movie That Made Us Dream," *Houston (TX) Chronicle* Sec. Z, p. 9. June 20, 1993.
___ Miller, Mark C. "**2001**: A Cold Descent," *Sight and Sound* 4(1): 18-25. January 1994.
___ Persons, Dan. "**2001: A Space Odyssey**: Post-Production Editing," *Cinefantastique* 25(3): 44-45. June 1994.

2001: A SPACE ODYSSEY (MOTION PICTURE) (continued)
___ Persons, Dan. "**2001: A Space Odyssey**," *Cinefantastique* 25(3): 32-47. June 1994.
___ Staggs, Jeffrey. "**2001**: Space Odyssey of the Mind," *Washington (DC) Times*. April 6, 1993. in: *NewsBank. Film & Television*. 40:A6. 1993.
___ Westbrook, Bruce. "**2001** Plus 25," *Houston (TX) Chronicle* Sec. Z, p. 8. June 20, 1993.
___ Wolff, Michael J. "Odysseys of the Mind," *Starlog* No. 194: 27-31, 82. September 1993.

2010: ODYSSEY TWO (MOTION PICTURE)
___ "**Dune, 2010** Pub Pushes Stir Source Novel Sales," *Variety* p. 22. January 23, 1985.
___ "Hyams Sets Precedent on **2010** By Wearing 4 Hats on Major Pic," *Variety* p. 18. November 14, 1984.
___ Goldberg, Lee. "**2010** (1984): Interview with Kier Dullea," in: Goldberg, Lee et al. **Science Fiction Filmmaking in the 1980s**. Jefferson, NC: McFarland, 1995. pp.237-252.

8 MAN (MOTION PICTURE)
___ Wilt, David. "**8 Man** (Review)," *Cinefantastique* 26(5): 59. August 1995.

A. BERTRAM CHANDLER AWARD, 1992
___ "A. Bertram Chandler Award," *Locus* 29(1): 69. July 1992.
___ "Van Ikin Wins A. Bertram Chandler Award," *Science Fiction Chronicle* 13(10): 8. July/August 1992.

ABBEY, EDWIN AUSTIN
___ O'Shaughnessey, Margaret. "Edwin Austin Abbey's Reinterpretation of the Grail Quest: The Boston Public Library Murals," *Arthuriana* 4(4): 298-312. Winter 1994.

ABBOTT, EDWIN A.
___ Gilbert, Elliott L. "Upward, Not Northward," *English Literature in Transition* 34(4): 391-404. 1991.

ABE, KOBO
___ "Abe, Kobo (Obituary)," *Locus* 30(2): 68. February 1993.
___ "Abe, Kobo (Obituary)," *Science Fiction Chronicle* 14(6): 16. March 1993.
___ Noetzel, Michael. "Kobo Abe: Eine betrachtung und posthume Würdigung des Avant-gardisten der modernen japanischen SF," *Quarber Merkur* 33(1): 39-53. June 1995. (No. 83)

ABIS, STEPHEN
___ "Abis, Stephen (Obituary)," *Locus* 28(2): 68. February 1992.

ABORIGINAL SF (MAGAZINE)
___ "*Aboriginal SF* Goes Quarterly," *Locus* 28(4): 6, 61. April 1992.
___ "*Aboriginal SF* Goes Quarterly," *Science Fiction Chronicle* 13(5): 4. February 1992.
___ "*Aboriginal SF* Granted Non-Profit Status," *Locus* 30(4): 7. April 1993.
___ "*Aboriginal SF* Suspends Publication," *Science Fiction Chronicle* 16(4): 4. February 1995.
___ "*Aboriginal SF, Amazing* for Sale," *Locus* 34(2): 8. February 1995.

ABYSS (MOTION PICTURE)
___ Abbott, Joe. "They Came From Beyond the Center: Ideology and Political Textuality in the Radical Science Fiction Films of James Cameron," *Literature/Film Quarterly* 22(1): 21-27. 1994.

ABYSS (MOTION PICTURE)

ABYSS (MOTION PICTURE) (continued)
___ Fein, David C. "Quick Cuts: Once More into the **Abyss**," *Cinefex* No. 55: 29-30. August 1993.
___ Lowe, Nick. "**The Abyss** (Review)," *Interzone* No. 75: 36. September 1993.
___ Lyle, Jody. "**The Abyss**: Like a Fish Out of Water," *Jump Cut* No. 38: 9-13. 1993.
___ Robley, Les P. "**The Abyss**: Special Edition (Review)," *Cinefantastique* 24(2): 59. August 1993.

ACADEMY OF SCIENCE FICTION, FANTASY AND HORROR FILM AWARDS, 1984
___ "**Gremlins** Sweeps Saturn Ceremony," *Variety* p.6. June 19, 1985.

ACADEMY OF SCIENCE FICTION, FANTASY AND HORROR FILM AWARDS, 1985
___ "**Gremlins** Grabs 9 Saturn Nominations," *Variety* p. 4, 32. February 27, 1985.

ACADEMY OF SCIENCE FICTION, FANTASY AND HORROR FILM AWARDS, 1986
___ " 'Future' Sweeps Sci-Fi Academy Nominations," *Variety* p. 6. February 12, 1986.

ACADEMY OF SCIENCE FICTION, FANTASY AND HORROR FILM AWARDS, 1992
___ "1992 Saturn Awards," *Locus* 28(6): 7. June 1992.
___ "Saturn Awards, 1992," *Science Fiction Chronicle* 13(9): 10. June 1992.

ACADEMY OF SCIENCE FICTION, FANTASY AND HORROR FILM AWARDS, 1993
___ "Saturn Awards, 1993," *Locus* 31(2): 62-63. August 1993.
___ "Saturn Awards, 1993," *Science Fiction Chronicle* 14(10): 8. July 1993.

ACCION MUTANTE (MOTION PICTURE)
___ Lowe, Nick. "**Accion Mutante** (Review)," *Interzone* No. 78: 34-35. December 1993.

ACE BOOKS
___ "Ace Revamped," *Locus* 34(2): 8. February 1995.

ACKER, KATHY
___ Brande, David J. **Technologies of Postmodernity: Ideology and Desire in Literature and Science (Pynchon, Thomas; Gibson, William; Butler, Octavia; Acker, Kathy).** Ph.D. Dissertation, University of Washington, 1995. 228pp. (DAI-A 56/07, p. 2677. January 1996.)
___ Latham, Robert A. "Collage as Critique and Invention in the Fiction of William S. Burroughs and Kathy Acker," *Journal of the Fantastic in the Arts* 5(3): 46-57. 1993. (No. 19)
___ Latham, Robert A. "Collage as Critique and Invention in the Fiction of William S. Burroughs and Kathy Acker," in: Latham, Robert A. and Collins, Robert A., eds. **Modes of the Fantastic**. Westport, CT: Greenwood, 1995. pp.29-37.
___ Peters, Greg L. "Dominance and Subversion: The Horizonal Sublime and Erotic Empowerment in the Works of Kathy Acker," in: Ruddick, Nicholas, ed. **State of the Fantastic**. Westport, CT: Greenwood, 1992. pp.149-156.

ACKERMAN, FORREST J
___ "Ackerman Memorabilia to Berlin," *Locus* 28(2): 6. February 1992.
___ Beyette, Beverly. "Monster Collection: Los Angeles Man, 75, Amasses Treasures of Horror and Sci-Fi Films," *Houston (TX) Chronicle* Sec. B, p. 3. January 4, 1993.
___ Booe, Martin. "The Monster Maven: Forrest Ackerman, Sci-Fi's Founding Fan," *Washington (DC) Post* Sec. G, p. 1. May 28, 1993.
___ Hatcher, Lint. "Enter: The Ackermansion," *Wonder* No. 7: 24-26. 1993.
___ Hatcher, Lint. "Inside Darkest Ackerman," by Lint Hatcher and Rod Bennett. *Wonder* No. 7: 4-11, 52-53. 1993.
___ Jones, Stephen. "The Man Who Bought Bela Lugosi's Trousers, or, Ghouls Just Want to Have Fun," *Science Fiction Chronicle* 14(12): 28-29. September 1993.
___ Kelley, Mike. "Monster Manse," *Grand Street* 13(1): 224-233. Summer 1994.

ADDAMS FAMILY (MOTION PICTURE)

ACKERMAN, FORREST J (continued)
___ Murphy, Suzanne. "The Godfather of Sci-Fi," *Westways* 79: 36-38. June 1987.

ADAMS, DOUGLAS
___ "Douglas Adams Takes the Road Again," *Hailing Frequencies* (Waldenbooks) No. 4: 4, 8, 10. 1992.
___ Morris, Anne. " 'Hitchhiker' Author Not Just Along for Ride," *Austin (TX) American Statesman* Sec. C, p. 1. March 4, 1994.
___ Nicholls, Stan. "Comedy Engineering," *Starlog* No. 188: 60-64. March 1993.
___ Nicholls, Stan. "Douglas Adams Will Never Say Never Again, Probably," in: Nicholls, Stan. **Wordsmiths of Wonder: Fifty Interviews with Writers of the Fantastic**. London: Orbit, 1993. pp.169-181.
___ Nicholls, Stan. "Zen and the Art of Never Saying Never Again: Douglas Adams," *Interzone* No. 66: 16-19. December 1992.
___ Pennington, John. "Shamanistic Mythmaking: From Civilization to Wilderness in **Watership Down**," *Journal of the Fantastic in the Arts* 6(1): 34-50. 1993.
___ Stableford, Brian. **Algebraic Fantasies and Realistic Romances: More Masters of Science Fiction.** San Bernardino, CA: Borgo Press, 1995 128pp.

ADAMS, GEORGIA F.
___ "Adams, Georgia F. (Obituary)," *Locus* 30(2): 69. February 1993.
___ "Adams, Georgia F. (Obituary)," *Science Fiction Chronicle* 14(4): 14. January 1993.

ADAMS, JULIE
___ Daniel, Dennis. "The Girl, the Gillman and the Great White One-Piece: An Interview with Julie Adams," *Filmfax* No. 37: 50-56. February/March 1993.
___ Weaver, Tom. "Julie Adams," in: Weaver, Tom. **They Fought the Creature Features: Interviews with 23 Classic Horror, Science Fiction and Serial Stars.** Jefferson, NC: McFarland, 1995. pp.1-11.
___ Zemnick, Diana J. "Creature Comfort: Julie Adams; The Beauty Recalls the Beast," *Cinefantastique* 27(3): 45-46. December 1995.

ADAMS, RICHARD
___ "Adams, Richard (George), 1920- ," in: Lesniak, James G., ed. **Contemporary Authors**. Detroit: Gale Research, 1992. New Revision Series, Vol. 35, pp.2-6
___ Anderson, Kathleen. "Shaping Self Through Spontaneous Oral Narration in Richard Adam's **Watership Down**," *Journal of the Fantastic in the Arts* 6(1): 25-33. 1993.
___ Bridgman, Joan. "The Significance of Myth in **Watership Down**," *Journal of the Fantastic in the Arts* 6(1): 7-24. 1993.
___ Meyer, Charles A. "The Efrafan Hunt for Immortality in **Watership Down**," *Journal of the Fantastic in the Arts* 6(1): 71-87. 1993.
___ Meyer, Charles A. "The Power of Myth and Rabbit Survival in Richard Adams' **Watership Down**," *Journal of the Fantastic in the Arts* 3(4): 139-150. 1994.
___ Miltner, Robert. "**Watership Down**: A Genre Study," *Journal of the Fantastic in the Arts* 6(1): 63-70. 1993.
___ Peters, John G. "Saturnalia and Sanctuary: The Role of the Tale in **Watership Down**," *Journal of the Fantastic in the Arts* 6(1): 51-62. 1993.
___ Schaaf, Barbara. "Richard Adams: The Early Years," *Chicago (IL) Sun Times*. August 4, 1991. in *NewsBank. Arts and Literature*. 28:A2. 1991

ADAMSON, AL
___ "Adamson, Al (Obituary)," *Science Fiction Chronicle* 16(9): 24. August/September 1995.

ADDAMS FAMILY (MOTION PICTURE)
___ "**The Addams Family** (Review)," *Cinefantastique* 22(5): 57. April 1992.
___ Arar, Yardena. " 'Addams Family's' Hired Hand," *Los Angeles (CA) Daily News*. November 30, 1991. in: *NewsBank. Film and Television*. 1: A6-A7. 1991
___ Biodrowski, Steve. "Slight of Hand: **The Addams Family**," *Cinefantastique* 22(5): 56. April 1992.
___ Ebert, Roger. " 'Addams': It's Creepy and It's Jokey, But Altogether Hokey," *Chicago (IL) Sun Times*. November 22, 1991. in: *NewsBank. Film and Television*. 1:A3. 1991

ADDAMS FAMILY (MOTION PICTURE) (continued)
___ Mahar, Ted. "They Really Are a Scream," (Portland, OR) *The Oregonian*. November 22, 1991. in: *NewsBank. Film and Television*. 1: A4-A5. 1991
___ Sragow, Michael. "It's Not Creepy or Kooky--Just Ooky," *San Francisco (CA) Examiner*. November 22, 1991. in: *NewsBank. Film and Television*. 1:A1-A2. 1991
___ Teitelbaum, Sheldon. "*The Addams Family*: Creating the Cartoon's Look," *Cinefantastique* 22(4): 50. February 1992.
___ Teitelbaum, Sheldon. "*The Addams Family*," *Cinefantastique* 22(4): 48-51. February 1992.

ADDAMS FAMILY (TV)
___ Cox, Stephen. **The Addams Chronicles: Everything You Ever Wanted to Know About the Addams Family.** New York: Harper Perennial, 1991. 205pp.

ADDAMS FAMILY VALUES (MOTION PICTURE)
___ Kutzera, Dale. "Quick Cuts: Digital Effects," *Cinefex* No. 57: 75-76. March 1994.
___ Lowe, Nick. "*Addams Family Values* (Review)," *Interzone* No. 81: 39. March 1994.
___ Neman, Daniel. "*Addams Family*: Not Much of Value (Review)," *Richmond (VA) Times-Dispatch*. November 20, 1993. in: *NewsBank. Art* 32:B2. 1993.
___ Newman, Kim. "*Addams Family Values* (Review)," *Sight and Sound* 4(2): 44-45. February 1994.
___ Vancheri, Barbara. "Altogether Ooky Sequel (Review)," *Pittsburgh (PA) Post-Gazette*. November 19, 1993. in: *NewsBank. Art*. 32:B3. 1993.

ADDING MACHINE (MOTION PICTURE)
___ "Universal's *Adding Machine* Strategy Intrigues Gotham Tradesters," *Variety* p. 8. September 10, 1969.

ADLERBERTH, ROLAND
___ "Adlerberth, Roland (Obituary)," *Locus* 31(4): 68. October 1993.

ADVENTURES OF BARON MUNCHAUSEN (MOTION PICTURE)
___ "Holder of Rights to 'Munchausen' Repeals Col Suit," *Variety* p. 7. February 10, 1988.
___ "'Munchausen' Producer Slams Attacks on Film as an 'Ishtar'," *Variety* p. 170. February 24, 1988.

ADVENTURES OF BRISCOE COUNTY, JR. (TV)
___ Shapiro, Marc. "The Adventures of Socrates Poole," *Starlog* No. 203: 55-58. June 1994.
___ Shapiro, Marc. "Bounty Hunter," *Starlog* No. 204: 27-30. July 1994.
___ Shapiro, Marc. "Cosmic Cowboy," *Starlog* No. 197: 63-66. December 1993.

ADVENTURES OF BUCKAROO BANZAI (MOTION PICTURE)
___ "*The Adventures of Buckaroo Banzai* (1984): Interviews with Earl Mac Rauch, W. D. Richter and Peter Weller," in: Goldberg, Lee, ed. **The Dreamweavers: Interviews With Fantasy Filmmakers of the 1980s.** Jefferson, NC: McFarland, 1995. pp.5-21.

ADVENTURES OF CAPTAIN ZOOM IN OUTER SPACE (TV)
___ Hiltbrand, David. "Picks and Pans: *The Adventures of Captain Zoom in Outer Space*," *People Weekly* 44(9): 14. August 28, 1995.

ADVENTURES OF SWORD AND SORCERY (MAGAZINE)
___ "New Fantasy Quarterly Planned," *Science Fiction Chronicle* 16(1): 5. October 1994.

ADVENTURES OF THE GALAXY RANGERS (TV)
___ "Mandell Back in Syndie Business With 'Galaxy Rangers' Kidvid," *Variety* p.68. June 12, 1985.

ADVERTISING
___ "Talk of the Town: Words Right Out of Their Mouths," *New Yorker* 71(5): 37. March 27, 1995.
___ Stanley, T. L. "NBC, Live Entertainment Link TV and Home Vid for Sci-Fi Synergy," *Brandweek* 36(3): 8. January 16, 1995.

AELITA (MOTION PICTURE)
___ Stanley, John. "Early Soviet Space-Race Victory," *San Francisco (CA) Chronicle* Sec. DAT, p. 34. April 12, 1992.

AFRAID OF THE DARK (MOTION PICTURE)
___ Campbell, Bob. "*Afraid of the Dark* Suffers Double Vision," *Newark (NJ) Star-Ledger*. July 24, 1992. in: *NewsBank. Film and Television*. 67: B1. 1992.
___ Chollet, Lawrence. "His Stories Operate on Several Levels," (Hackensack, NJ) *Record*. August 7, 1992. in: *NewsBank. Film and Television*. 76:A14. 1992
___ Jones, Alan. "High Class Horror: *Afraid of the Dark*," *Cinefantastique* 23(1): 4-5. August 1992.
___ Rosenberg, Scott. "A Psychological London Thriller Sheds Little Light on Its Subject," *San Francisco (CA) Examiner*. August 14, 1992. in: *NewsBank. Film and Television*. 76:B2. 1992
___ Strauss, Bob. "Peploe Fumbles in 'Dark' Trying to Illuminate Life's Fears," *Los Angeles (CA) Daily News*. August 7, 1992. in: *NewsBank. Film and Television*. 76:B1. 1992
___ Voedisch, Lynn. " 'Dark' Thriller Has More Than Just Murder in Mind," *Chicago (IL) Sun Times*. September 25, 1992. in: *NewsBank. Film and Television*. 87:A7. 1992

AFTERSHOCK (MOTION PICTURE)
___ Harris, Judith P. "*Aftershock* (Review)," *Cinefantastique* 22(6): 54. June 1992

AGAR, JOHN
___ Weaver, Tom. "John Agar," in: Weaver, Tom. **They Fought the Creature Features: Interviews with 23 Classic Horror, Science Fiction and Serial Stars.** Jefferson, NC: McFarland, 1995. pp.13-24.

AGENTS
___ "Agents vs. Publisher," *Locus* 33(6): 9, 79. December 1994.
___ "Curtis Goes Electronic," *Locus* 28(1): 7. January 1992.
___ "GEnie Round Table on Agents," *SFWA Bulletin* 27(1): 38-46. Spring 1993. (No. 119)
___ "Mass Exodus at Meredith," *Locus* 30(6): 6, 73. June 1993.
___ "Meredith Agency Cuts Back on SF Representation; Joshua Bilmes Forms New SF Agency," *Science Fiction Chronicle* 16(2): 4. November/December 1994.
___ "Meredith Agency Leaves SF Field," *Locus* 33(6): 8, 79. December 1994.
___ "Meredith Literary Agency Lets Its Authors Go," *Science Fiction Chronicle* 15(3): 5. January 1994.
___ "New Literary Agency," *Locus* 34(2): 9. February 1995.
___ "Scott Meredith Agency Sold," *Locus* 31(3): 6, 83. September 1993.
___ "Scott Meredith Literary Agency Sold," *Science Fiction Chronicle* 14(12): 4. September 1993.
___ "Scott Meredith/Scovil Chichak Galen Agreement," *Locus* 31(6): 7, 72. December 1993.
___ "Scovil Chichak Galen Literary Agency Opens," *Locus* 31(1): 6, 57. July 1993.
___ "Scovill, Chichak, Galen Quit Scott Meredith Agency," *Science Fiction Chronicle* 14(9): 4. June 1993.
___ Sperry, Ralph A. "Three Nasty Problems," *SFWA Bulletin* 26(3): 21-22. Fall 1992. (No. 117)

AGGIECON, 1992
___ Riecher, Anton. "AggieCon XXII Blasting Off," *Bryan-College Station Eagle* p. C1. March 19, 1992.

AICKMAN, ROBERT
___ Bloom, Harold. "Robert Aickman," in: Bloom, Harold. **Modern Horror Writers.** New York: Chelsea House, 1995. pp.1-15.
___ Briggs, Scott D. "Robert Aickman: Sojourns into the Unknown," *Studies in Weird Fiction* No. 12: 7-12. Spring 1993.

AIDS
___ Memmott, David. "The Witchdoctor and the Mad Scientist: Mechanical Models of Healing and the Challenge of AIDS," *Science Fiction Eye* No. 11: 53-59. December 1992.

AIKEN, JOAN
___ Rose, Anne. "Profile: Joan Aiken," *Language Arts* 66(7): 784-790. November 1989.

AKIRA (TV)

____ Hiltbrand, David. "Picks and Pans: *Akira*," *People Weekly* 44(8): 13. August 21, 1995.
____ Townsend, Emru. "*Akira*: Anime Comes of Age," *Sci-Fi Entertainment* 2(2): 38-40, 72. August 1995.

ALADDIN (MOTION PICTURE)

____ Harris, Judith P. "*Aladdin* (Review)," *Cinefantastique* 23(6): 60. April 1993.
____ Shaheen, Jack. "*Aladdin*: Animated Racism," *Cineaste* 20(1): 49. 1993.
____ Spelling, Ian. "Arabian Night Music," *Starlog* No. 186: 52-55. January 1993.
____ Teitelbaum, Sheldon. "Disney's *Aladdin*," *Cinefantastique* 23(4): 14-15. December 1992.

ALBANESE, MARY

____ Thomas, Margaret. "Flop Down With a Good Disk," *Juneau (AK) Empire*. January 13, 1994. in: *NewsBank. Film and Television*. 17:A14-B1. 1994.

ALDISS, BRIAN W.

____ "Aldiss Time Capsule Recovered," *Locus* 34(6): 9, 70. June 1995.
____ "Brian Aldiss: A Moderate Pursuit of Happiness," *Locus* 35(3): 5, 85. September 1993.
____ "Brian Aldiss: Arguing With the Subculture," *Locus* 29(1): 5, 74. July 1992.
____ Aldiss, Brian W. **The Detached Retina: Aspects of SF and Fantasy.** Syracuse, NY: Syracuse University Press, 1995. 224pp.
____ Aldiss, Brian W. "Remembrance of Lives Past," *Science Fiction Studies* 21(2): 129-133. July 1994.
____ Aldiss, Margaret. **The Work of Brian W. Aldiss: An Annotated Bibliography & Guide.** San Bernardino, CA: Borgo Press, 1992. 359pp.
____ Borgmeier, Raimund. "Brian W. Aldiss, **Frankenstein Unbound** (1973)," in: Heuermann, Harmut, ed. **Der Science Fiction Roman in der angloamerikanischen Literatur: Interpretationen.** Düsseldorf: Bagel, 1986. pp.331-345.
____ Hatherley, Frank. **A Is for Brian: A 65th Birthday Present for Brian W. Aldiss From His Family, Friends, Colleagues and Admirers.** London: Avernus, 1990. 122pp.
____ Jameson, Frederic. "Generic Discontinuities in SF: Brian Aldiss' **Starship**," *Chung Wai Literary Quarterly* 22(12): May 1994. (Issue not seen; pagination unavailable.)
____ McNelly, Willis E. "The First Time I Met Brian," in: Hatherley, Frank, ed. **A Is for Brian.** London: Avernus, 1990. pp.58-59.
____ Nicholls, Stan. "Brian Aldiss Buries His Heart on Far Andromeda," in: Nicholls, Stan. **Wordsmiths of Wonder: Fifty Interviews with Writers of the Fantastic.** London: Orbit, 1993. pp.12-24.

ALDRIDGE, RAY

____ "Eleventh Annual *S. F. Chronicle* Reader's Awards," *Science Fiction Chronicle* 13(11/12): 4. August 1992.

ALDRIN, BUZZ

____ "Astronaut Seeks Collaborator," *Science Fiction Chronicle* 13(5): 5. February 1992.

ALEXANDER, ELIZABETH

____ Chrissinger, Craig W. "Time Piece," *Starlog* No. 191: 32-34. June 1993.

ALEXANDER, LLOYD

____ Evans, Gwenth. "Harps and Harpers in Contemporary Fantasy," *Lion and the Unicorn* 16(2): 199-209. December 1992.

ALFONSI, ALICE

____ "Alice Alfonsi Out, Pat LaBrutto in at Zebra," *Science Fiction Chronicle* 14(10): 6. July 1993.

ALIEN CONTACT

____ Ore, Rebecca. "Aliens and the Artificial Other," *New York Review of Science Fiction* No. 56: 18-20. April 1993.

ALIEN FACTOR (MOTION PICTURE)

____ SEE: METAMORPHOSIS: THE ALIEN FACTOR (MOTION PICTURE).

ALIEN III (MOTION PICTURE)

____ "From Grim to Grimmer," *Seattle (WA) Times*. May 22, 1992. in: *NewsBank. Film and Television*. 49:C11. 1992.
____ **The Making of Alien 3.** Los Angeles, CA: Fox Video, 1992. Videocassette, VHS. 20 minutes.
____ Armstrong, David. "*Alien 3*: Meat the People," *San Francisco (CA) Examiner*. May 22, 1992. in: *NewsBank. Film and Television*. 49:B11-B12. 1992.
____ Arnold, Gary. "*Alien 3* Lost Is Foggy Plotting and Misdirection," *Washington (DC) Times*. May 22, 1992. in: *NewsBank. Film and Television*. 49:C10. 1992.
____ Bernard, Jami. "Nothing Alien to Her Is Human," *New York (NY) Post*. May 22, 1992. in: *NewsBank. Film and Television*. 49:C9. 1992.
____ Bernstein, Abbie. "Little John in Space," *Starlog* 179: 32-35, 89. June 1992.
____ Brandon, Carl. "*Alien 3*: A Review of the Work in Progress," *Cinefantastique* 22(6): 20-21. June 1992
____ Briggs, Bill. "*Aliens 3* Jumps Back on Treadmill," *Denver (CO) Post*. May 22, 1992. in: *NewsBank. Film and Television*. 49:B13. 1992.
____ Campbell, Bob. "*Alien 3* Environment Is No More Healthy for Humans This Time Around," *Newark (NJ) Star-Ledger*. May 22, 1992. in: *NewsBank. Film and Television*. 49:C7-C8. 1992.
____ DeChick, Joe. "*Alien 3*: Sci-Fi Shocker That Broke All of the Mainstream Rules Spawns a Third Thriller," *Cincinnati (OH) Enquirer*. May 20, 1992. in: *NewsBank. Film and Television*. 49:C12-C13. 1992.
____ Doense, Jan. "*Alien 3*: Design Genius H. R. Giger," *Cinefantastique* 22(6): 10. June 1992
____ Doherty, Thomas. "*Alien 3*," *Cinefantastique* 23(2/3): 6-7, 124. October 1992.
____ Hobby, Patrick. "*Alien 3*," *Cinefantastique* 22(6): 8-21. June 1992
____ Hunter, Stephen. "*Alien 3*: The Thrill Is Gone," *Baltimore (MD) Sun*. May 22, 1992. in: *NewsBank. Film and Television*. 49:C3-C4. 1992.
____ Johnson, Malcolm. "Terror Reigns, But the Beauty's Gone in *Alien 3*," *Hartford (CT) Courant*. May 22, 1992. in: *NewsBank. Film and Television*. 49:B14. 1992.
____ Kronke, David. "What's Scary Is How *Alien III* Fails to Deliver," *Los Angeles (CA) Daily News*. May 22, 1992. in: *NewsBank. Film and Television*. 49:B10. 1992.
____ Lowe, Nick. "*Alien 3* (Review)," *Interzone* No. 65: 32-33. November 1992.
____ Magid, Ron. "*Alien 3*: Space, They're Still Screaming," *American Cinematographer* 73(7): 52-58. July 1992.
____ Magid, Ron. "Speeding Up the Screams in *Alien 3*," *American Cinematographer* 73(12): 70-76. December 1992.
____ Murphy, Kathleen. "The Last Temptation of Sigourney Weaver," *Film Comment* 28(4): 17-20. July/August 1992.
____ Nicholls, Stan. "Alien Art," *Starlog* 179: 19-25. June 1992.
____ Norton, Bill. "Zealots and Xenomorphs," *Cinefex* No. 50: 26-53. May 1992.
____ Sachs, Lloyd. "Despite Riley's Heroics, *Alien 3* Lacks the Old Bite," *Chicago (IL) Sun Times*. May 22, 1992. in: *NewsBank. Film and Television*. 49:C1-C2. 1992.
____ Scobie, Stephen. "What's the Story, Mother?: The Mourning of the Alien," *Science Fiction Studies* 20(1): 80-93. March 1993.
____ Spelling, Ian. "An *Alien 3* Post-Mortem," *Starlog* No. 196: 71. November 1993.
____ Spelling, Ian. "Man of Many Parts," *Starlog* 180: 46-50. July 1992.
____ Strauss, Bob. "*Alien 3* Is Born: Long Difficult Gestation Finally Reaches an End," *Los Angeles (CA) Daily News*. May 21, 1992. in: *NewsBank. Film and Television*. 49:B7-B9. 1992.
____ Taubin, Amy. "Invading Bodies: *Alien 3* and the Trilogy," *Sight and Sound* 2(3): 8-10. 1992. [Not seen.]
____ Teitelbaum, Sheldon. "*Alien 3*: Development Hell," *Cinefantastique* 22(6): 15-18. June 1992
____ Teitelbaum, Sheldon. "*Alien 3*: William Gibson's 'Neuroaliens'," *Cinefantastique* 22(6): 12-13. June 1992
____ Verniere, James. "The Final Bleak Chapter of the *Alien* Sci-Fi Saga Gets Lost in Space Movies," *Boston (MA) Herald*. May 22, 1992. in: *NewsBank. Film and Television*. 49:C5-C6. 1992.
____ Verniere, James. "In Space, and In Reality, Aliens R Us," *Chicago (IL) Sun Times*. May 24, 1992. in: *NewsBank. Film and Television*. 62: A12-A13. 1992.

ALIEN INVASION

____ Ore, Rebecca. "Aliens and the Artificial Other," *New York Review of Science Fiction* No. 56: 18-20. April 1993.

ALIEN (MOTION PICTURE)

___ Greenberg, Harvey R. "Fembo: *Aliens'* Intentions," *Journal of Popular Film and Television* 15(4): 164-171. 1988.

___ Houghton, Hal. **Ripley, Believe It or Not: The 'Alien' Trilogy and the Image of Women in Science Fiction Film.** Master's Thesis, Mankato State University, 1993. 106pp.

___ Jones, Alan. "Queen of Outer Space," *Cinefantastique* 23(4): 6-9. December 1992.

___ Matheson, T. J. "Marcuse, Ellul, and the Science-Fiction Film: Negative Responses to Technology," *Science-Fiction Studies* 19(3): 326-339. November 1992.

___ Matheson, T. J. "Triumphant Technology and Minimal Man: **The Technological Society**, Science Fiction Films, and Ridley Scott's *Alien*," *Extrapolation* 33(3): 215-229. Fall 1992.

___ Murphy, Kathleen. "The Last Temptation of Sigourney Weaver," *Film Comment* 28(4): 17-20. July/August 1992.

___ Vaughn, Thomas. "Voices of Sexual Distortion: Rape, Birth, and Self-Annihilation Metaphors in the *Alien* Trilogy," *Quarterly Journal of Speech* 81(4): 423-435. November 1995.

ALIEN NATION: DARK HORIZON (TV)

___ Eby, Douglas. "*Alien Nation: Dark Horizon*: Effects," *Cinefantastique* 25(5): 51. October 1994.

___ Eby, Douglas. "*Alien Nation: Dark Horizon*," *Cinefantastique* 25(5): 48-51, 61. October 1994.

___ Harris, Judith P. "*Alien Nation: Dark Horizon* (Review)," *Cinefantastique* 26(3): 59. April 1995.

___ Richmond, Ray. "In Its Return, *Alien* not Alien to Success," *Los Angeles (CA) Times/Orange County Ed.*. Oct. 25, 1994. in: *NewsBank. Film and Television.* 107:A11. 1994.

___ Zurawik, David. "*Alien Nation* Worth Dropping in On," *(Baltimore, MD) Sun.* October 25, 1994. in: *NewsBank. Film and Television.* 107: A12. 1994.

ALIEN NATION (TV)

___ Eby, Douglas. "*Alien Nation: Dark Horizon*: The Original Series," *Cinefantastique* 25(5): 50. October 1994.

___ Greppi, Michele. "*Alien Nation* Lost in Space," *New York (NY) Post.* October 10, 1995. in: *NewsBank. Film and Television.* 92:A14. 1995.

___ Hiltbrand, David. "Picks and Pans: *Alien Nation*," *People Weekly* 42(17): 17, 15. October 24, 1994.

___ Nazzaro, Joe. "Newcomer Novels," *Starlog* No. 188: 36-37, 67. March 1993.

___ Peishel, Bob. "Video Beat: *Alien Nation* Revisited," *Cinefex* No. 59: 23-24. September 1994.

___ Shapiro, Marc. "Beyond the Dark," *Starlog* No. 207: 46-50, 72. October 1994.

ALIEN OUTLAW (MOTION PICTURE)

___ "Smoot, Larue Team for *Alien Outlaw*," *Variety* p.24. July 24, 1985.

ALIEN VS. PREDATOR (MOTION PICTURE)

___ SEE: HUNT: ALIEN VS. PREDATOR (MOTION PICTURE).

ALIEN WITHIN (MOTION PICTURE)

___ Harris, Judith P. "*Alien Within* (Review)," *Cinefantastique* 27(2): 59. November 1995.

ALIENS

___ Adams, John R. **Good, Evil and Alien: Outer Space and the New World in the European Enlightenment.** Ph.D. Dissertation, University of Texas, Austin, 1992. 275pp. (DAI-A 53/12. p. 4436. June 1993.)

___ Andrews, Arlan. "When Earth Has Its First Contact With Alien Beings, Will We Be Ready?," by Arlan Andrews, Yoji Kondo and Charles Sheffield. *Science Fiction Age* 3(2): 22, 24-28, 86. January 1995.

___ Braxton, T. S. "The 'Q' Question," in: Van Hise, James, ed. **Trek Celebration Two**. Las Vegas, NV: Pioneer, 1994. pp.57-70.

___ Brin, David. "Extraterrestrial Nightmares," *Omni* 16(9): 4. June 1994.

___ Clark, Stephen R. L. "Extraterrestrial Intelligence: The Neglected Experiment," *Foundation* No. 61: 50-65. Summer 1994.

___ Clement, Hal. "The Creation of Imaginary Beings," in: Dozois, Gardner, ed. **Writing Science Fiction and Fantasy**. New York: St. Martin's, 1991. pp.129-146.

___ Ferrell, Keith. "How to Build an Alien," *Omni* 14(9): 50-57, 111. October 1992.

ALIENS (continued)

___ Helford, Elyce R. **Reading Space Fictions: Representations of Gender, Race and Species in Popular Culture.** Ph.D. Dissertation, University of Iowa, 1993. (DAI-A 53/11, p. 3908. May 1993.)

___ Hixon, Celia. "Plotting Science into Science Fiction: Part Three, Alien Cultures," *Writers' Journal* 14(6): 9-10. 1993.

___ Hough, Peter. **Looking for the Aliens: A Psychological, Imaginative and Scientific Investigation**, by Peter Hough and Jenny Randles. London: Blandford, 1992. 241pp.

___ Jackson, Kevin. "The Good, the Bad, and the Ugly," *Sight and Sound* 2(3): 10-11. July 1992.

___ King, T. Jackson. "Creating Believable Aliens," *SFWA Bulletin* 27(4)/28(1): 32-39. Winter/Spring 1994. (No. 122/123)

___ Kuhn, Annette. "Border Crossing," *Sight and Sound* 2(3): 11-12. July 1992.

___ Malmgren, Carl D. "Self and Other in SF: Alien Encounters," *Science Fiction Studies* 20(1): 15-33. March 1993.

___ Ore, Rebecca. "Aliens and the Artificial Other," *New York Review of Science Fiction* No. 56: 18-20. April 1993.

___ Pfitzer, Gregory M. "The Only Good Alien Is a Dead Alien: Science Fiction and the Metaphysics of Indian-Hating on the High Frontier," *Journal of American Culture* 18(1): 51-67. Spring 1995.

___ Rovin, Jeff. **Aliens, Robots, and Spaceships**. New York: Facts on File, 1995. 372pp.

___ Salter, David I. "*Star Trek: Deep Space Nine*: Designing Aliens," *Cinefantastique* 24(3/4): 106. October 1993.

___ Van Hise, James. "The Major Alien Races of *Star Trek*," in: Van Hise, James, ed. **Trek Celebration Two**. Las Vegas, NV: Pioneer, 1994. pp.53-56.

___ Wolff, Michael J. "Universal Relations," *Starlog* No. 206: 35-39, 69. September 1994.

ALIENS: COLONIAL MARINES (COMIC)

___ Johnson, Kim H. "Bug Hunt," *Starlog* No. 189: 40-43, 64. April 1993.

ALIENS (MOTION PICTURE)

___ "Fox Sues Effects Outfit Over Work on *Aliens*," *Variety* p. 92. March 5, 1986.

___ Abbott, Joe. "They Came From Beyond the Center: Ideology and Political Textuality in the Radical Science Fiction Films of James Cameron," *Literature/Film Quarterly* 22(1): 21-27. 1994.

___ Cerone, Daniel H. "The Kindest Cut: Laser Discs Give Directors a Second Chance at Their Films," *Los Angeles (CA) Times*. December 18, 1991. in: *NewsBank. Film and Television.* 1:A8-A10. 1991

___ Fleury, Anthony G. **'Aliens' and Just-War Ideology: A Rhetorical Analysis**. Master's Thesis, Pennsylvania State University, 1992. 140pp. (Master's Abstracts 31/02, p. 506. Summer 1994.)

___ Greenberg, Harvey R. "Fembo: *Aliens'* Intentions," *Journal of Popular Film and Television* 15(4): 164-171. 1988.

___ Houghton, Hal. **Ripley, Believe It or Not: The 'Alien' Trilogy and the Image of Women in Science Fiction Film**. Master's Thesis, Mankato State University, 1993. 106pp.

___ Lofficier, Randy. "*Aliens* (1986): Interview with James Cameron and Gale Ann Hurd," by Randy Lofficier and Jean-Marc Lofficier. in: Goldberg, Lee et al. **Science Fiction Filmmaking in the 1980s**. Jefferson, NC: McFarland, 1995. pp.7-23.

___ Murphy, Kathleen. "The Last Temptation of Sigourney Weaver," *Film Comment* 28(4): 17-20. July/August 1992.

___ Pirani, Adam. "Alien Nemesis," by Adam Pirani and Ian Spelling. in: McDonnell, David, ed. **Starlog's Science Fiction Heroes and Heroines**. New York: Crescent Books, 1995. pp.9-11.

___ Spelling, Ian. "Man of Many Parts," *Starlog* 180: 46-50. July 1992.

___ Stephens, Bob. "*Aliens* Finally Busts Out," *San Francisco (CA) Examiner*. February 8, 1992 in: *NewsBank. Film and Television.* 17:A7. 1992

___ Vaughn, Thomas. "Voices of Sexual Distortion: Rape, Birth, and Self-Annihilation Metaphors in the *Alien* Trilogy," *Quarterly Journal of Speech* 81(4): 423-435. November 1995.

ALIVE (MOTION PICTURE)

___ Duncan, Jody. "Quick Cuts: A Crash in the Andes," *Cinefex* No. 55: 117-118. August 1993.

ALLAN, MABEL ESTHER

___ MacIlroy, Barry. "Those Magical Time-Slip Stories," *Souvenir* 21: 14-15. 1992. [Not seen.]

ALLAND, WILLIAM
___ Weaver, Tom. "The Producer From Lands Unknown (Part Three)," *Starlog* No. 219: 57-64. October 1995.
___ Weaver, Tom. "The Producer From Outer Space (Part One)," *Starlog* No. 217: 57-65. August 1995.
___ Weaver, Tom. "The Producer From the Black Lagoon (Part Two)," *Starlog* No. 218: 57-63, 65. September 1995.

ALLEGORY
___ Schlobin, Roger C. "The Craving for Meaning: Explicit Allegory in the Non-Implicit Age," *Journal of the Fantastic in the Arts* 5(1): 3-12. 1992. (No. 17)

ALLEN, DAVID
___ McGee, Mark T. "Full Moon's Effects Master," *Cinefantastique* 23(5): 47-49. February 1993.

ALLEN, IRWIN
___ Clark, Mike. "The Master of Disaster," *Starlog* No. 176: 58-61. March 1992.

ALLEN, ROGER McBRIDE
___ "Roger McBride Allen Explores a New Breed of Robots," *Hailing Frequencies* (Waldenbooks) No. 6: 7, 17. 1993.

ALLISON, SUSAN
___ "Ace Books' Susan Allison Promoted at Berkley," *Science Fiction Chronicle* 14(11): 4. August 1993.

ALMODOVAR, PEDRO
___ Jones, Alan. "Mutant Action: Science Fiction Splatter Boosted by Spain's Pedro Almodovar," *Cinefantastique* 24(5): 48-49. December 1993.

ALONZO, JOHN
___ Beeler, Michael. "*Star Trek: Generations*: John Alonzo," *Cinefantastique* 26(2): 27. February 1995.

ALPHAVILLE (MOTION PICTURE)
___ Darke, Chris. "It All Happened in Paris," *Sight and Sound* 4(7): 10-13. July 1994.

ALTERED STATES (MOTION PICTURE)
___ Bell-Metereau, Rebecca. "*Altered States* and the Popular Myth of Self-Discovery," *Journal of Popular Film and Television* 9(4): 171-179. 1982.

ALTERNATE HISTORY
___ Baxter, Stephen. "Cross-Reference and Context: Future Histories in SF," *Vector* No. 179: 26-27. June/July 1994.
___ Christopher, Joe R. "On Future History as a Basic S-F Literary Form," *Riverside Quarterly* 9(1): 26-31. August 1992. (No. 33)
___ Kincaid, Paul. "Cognitive Mapping 1: Alternate History," *Vector* No. 186: 3. December 1995.
___ Pollack, Andrew. "Fantasy Novels About WWII Becoming Popular in Japan," *Austin (TX) American Statesman* Sec. A, p. 17. March 19, 1995.
___ Teitelbaum, Sheldon. "Playing With History," *Los Angeles (CA) Times* Sec. E, p. 1. July 7, 1992.

AMANDA AND THE ALIEN (MOTION PICTURE)
___ Florence, Bill. "An Alien With Style," *Starlog* No. 219: 32-36, 66. October 1995.
___ Florence, Bill. "Robert Silverberg's Alien," *Starlog* No. 219: 34-35. October 1995.

AMAZING SCIENCE FICTION AND HORROR TRIVIA GAME (GAME)
___ Di Filippo, Paul. "Sci-Fi Goobers Invent an Intergalactic Game Show That's Anything But Trivial," *Science Fiction Age* 3(4): 94-97. May 1995.

AMAZING STORIES (MAGAZINE)
___ "*Aboriginal SF, Amazing* for Sale," *Locus* 34(2): 8. February 1995.
___ "*Amazing* Gets National Distributor," *Locus* 30(2): 7. February 1993.
___ "*Amazing* Reappears," *Locus* 32(6): 8. June 1994.
___ "*Amazing* Refunds Subscriptions," *Locus* 34(6): 9, 72. June 1995.
___ "*Amazing* Suspends Monthly Publication," *Locus* 31(6): 6. December 1993.

AMAZING STORIES (MAGAZINE) (continued)
___ "*Amazing* Temporarily Resumes Publication," *Locus* 32(2): 8. February 1994.
___ "*Amazing Stories* Signs New Retail Distributor," *Science Fiction Chronicle* 14(6): 4. March 1993.
___ "End of the Road for *Amazing Stories*," *Science Fiction Chronicle* 15(3): 4. January 1994.
___ "A Gallery of *Amazing* Art: Covers Through the Years," *Amazing Stories* 67(4): 52-56. July 1992.
___ "Same Cover on *Amazing, Analog*," *Science Fiction Chronicle* 14(10): 6-7. July 1993.
___ Ashley, Mike. "The *Amazing* Story: Part 1, The Twenties, By Radio to the Stars," *Amazing Stories* 66(9): 55-59. January 1992.
___ Ashley, Mike. "The *Amazing* Story: Part 2, The Thirties, Escape From Oblivion," *Amazing Stories* 66(10): 64-67. February 1992.
___ Ashley, Mike. "The *Amazing* Story: Part 3, The Forties, 'Gimme Bang-Bang' ," *Amazing Stories* 66(11): 58-63. March 1992.
___ Ashley, Mike. "The *Amazing* Story: Part 4, The Fifties, Dream Worlds," *Amazing Stories* 67(1): 49-54. April 1992.
___ Ashley, Mike. "The *Amazing* Story: Part 5, The Sixties; The Gooseflesh Factor," *Amazing Stories* 67(2): 59-64. May 1992.
___ Ashley, Mike. "The *Amazing* Story: Part 6, The Seventies: Sex and Drugs and Rock and Roll," *Amazing Stories* 67(3): 52-56. June 1992.
___ Ashley, Mike. "The *Amazing* Story: Part 7, The Eighties: Son of *Fantastic*," *Amazing Stories* 67(4): 47-56. July 1992.
___ Ashley, Mike. "A History of *Amazing Stories* Magazine," *Futures Past* No. 2: 6-11. April 1992.
___ Stone, Graham. "Beginning: Sixty Years of *Amazing Stories*, 1929-1930," *Science Fiction News* (Australia) No. 101: 2-12. February 1987.
___ Stone, Graham. "Beginning: Sixty Years of *Amazing Stories*, Part 1," *Science Fiction News* (Australia) No. 97: 2-16. April 1986.
___ Stone, Graham. "Beginning: Sixty Years of *Amazing Stories*, Part 2," *Science Fiction News* (Australia) No. 98: 1-12. May 1986.
___ Stone, Graham. "Beginning: Sixty Years of *Amazing Stories*, Part 3," *Science Fiction News* (Australia) No. 99: 2-12. June 1986.
___ Stone, Graham. "Sixty Years of *Amazing Stories*: 1930," *Science Fiction News* (Australia) No. 103: 2-12. March 1987.
___ Stone, Graham. "Sixty Years of *Amazing Stories*: 1931," *Science Fiction News* (Australia) No. 107: 1-8. 1988.
___ Stone, Graham. "Sixty Years of *Amazing Stories*: 1931 (Continued)," *Science Fiction News* (Australia) No. 109: 9-16. January 1990.
___ Stone, Graham. "Sixty Years of *Amazing Stories*: 1932," *Science Fiction News* (Australia) No. 110: 3-13, 16. April 1990.
___ Stone, Graham. "Sixty Years of *Amazing Stories*: 1933," *Science Fiction News* (Australia) No. 111: 7-16, 20. July 1990.
___ Stone, Graham. "Sixty Years of *Amazing Stories*: 1934," *Science Fiction News* (Australia) No. 112: 13-16. September 1990.
___ Stone, Graham. "Sixty Years of *Amazing Stories*: 1934, and The Quarterly, 1931-1934," *Science Fiction News* (Australia) No. 114: 6-23. December 1990.
___ Stone, Graham. "Sixty Years of *Amazing Stories*: 1935," *Science Fiction News* (Australia) No. 116: 21-24. October 1992.
___ Stone, Graham. "Sixty Years of *Amazing Stories*: 1935, Continued," *Science Fiction News* (Australia) No. 117: 11-14. December 1993.
___ Stone, Graham. "Sixty Years of *Amazing Stories*: The Quarterly, 1929-1930," *Science Fiction News* (Australia) No. 105: 8-20. October 1987.

AMAZING STORIES QUARTERLY (MAGAZINE)
___ Stone, Graham. "Sixty Years of *Amazing Stories*: 1934, and The Quarterly, 1931-1934," *Science Fiction News* (Australia) No. 114: 6-23. December 1990.
___ Stone, Graham. "Sixty Years of *Amazing Stories*: The Quarterly, 1929-1930," *Science Fiction News* (Australia) No. 105: 8-20. October 1987.

AMECHE, DON
___ "Ameche, Don (Obituary)," *Science Fiction Chronicle* 15(3): 14. January 1994.

AMERICAN BOOKSELLERS ASSOCIATION CONVENTION
___ "ABA Find Permanent Home in Chicago," *Locus* 31(6): 7, 72. December 1993.

AMERICAN BOOKSELLERS ASSOCIATION CONVENTION, 1992
___ "ABA 1992," *Locus* 28(2): 35-37. August 1992.
___ "ABA Draws 27,000," *Locus* 29(1): 6. July 1992.

ANDERS, MERRY
___ Weaver, Tom. "Merry Anders: Interview," in: Weaver, Tom, ed. **Attack of the Monster Movie Makers: Interviews with 20 Genre Giants.** Jefferson, NC: McFarland, 1994. pp.1-16.

ANDERSEN, HANS CHRISTIAN
___ Stecher-Hansen, Marianne. "Science Fiction in the Age of Romanticism: Hans Christian Andersen's Futuristic Tales," *Selecta* (Corvallis) 14: 74-78. 1993.

ANDERSON, GERRY
___ Bacal, Simon. "The Sci-Fi Worlds of Gerry Anderson," *Sci-Fi Entertainment* 2(2): 68-71. August 1995.

ANDERSON, GILLIAN
___ Counts, Kyle. "True Disbeliever," in: McDonnell, David, ed. **Starlog's Science Fiction Heroes and Heroines.** New York: Crescent Books, 1995. pp.70-72.
___ Lee, Julianne. "X Heroine," *Starlog* No. 213: 32-35. April 1995.
___ Vitaris, Paula. "**X-Files**: Mulder and Scully," *Cinefantastique* 26(6)/27(1): 23-24. October 1995.

ANDERSON, JOHN
___ Phillips, Mark. "Life in the **Twilight Zone**," *Starlog* No. 216: 58-61. July 1995.

ANDERSON, KEVIN J.
___ "Kevin J. Anderson: Flipping Burgers; Interview," *Locus* 35(6): 6, 84, 86. December 1995.
___ King, T. Jackson. "SFC Interviews: Kevin J. Anderson," *Science Fiction Chronicle* 15(5): 5, 28-30. March 1994.
___ Klein, Jay K. "Biolog: Kevin J. Anderson," *Analog* 112(13): 161, 169. November 1992.
___ Vester, John. "Dean of the Jedi Academy," *Starlog* No. 199: 50-53, 74. February 1994.

ANDERSON, POUL
___ "Other Awards," *Science Fiction Chronicle* 15(1): 4. October 1993.
___ Bloom, Harold. "Poul Anderson," in: Bloom, Harold, ed. **Science Fiction Writers of the Golden Age.** New York: Chelsea House, 1995. pp.1-16.
___ Jean, Lorraine A. "Poul Anderson," in: Bruccoli, Matthew J., ed. **Facts on File Bibliography of American Fiction 1919-1988.** New York: Facts on File, 1991. pp.53-55.
___ King, T. Jackson. "Interview: Poul Anderson," *Expanse* No. 3: 34-43. Summer 1994.

ANDERSON, RICHARD D.
___ Spelling, Ian. "**Legend** of the West," *Starlog* No. 216: 54-57. July 1995.
___ Weaver, Tom. "Richard Anderson," in: Weaver, Tom. **They Fought the Creature Features: Interviews with 23 Classic Horror, Science Fiction and Serial Stars.** Jefferson, NC: McFarland, 1995. pp.25-36.

ANDREWS, V. C.
___ "V. C. Andrews Imbroglio," *Locus* 31(1): 6. July 1993.
___ Kies, Cosette. **Presenting Young Adult Horror Fiction.** New York: Twayne, 1991. 203pp.
___ Streitfeld, David. "V. C. Andrews's Afterlife," *Washington (DC) Post Book World* p. 12. May 10, 1992.

ANDROIDS
___ SEE ALSO: CYBORGS, COMPUTERS.

ANDROMEDA STRAIN (MOTION PICTURE)
___ "'Strain' Rolls in Texas," *Variety* p. 25. March 4, 1970.

ANGEL HEART (MOTION PICTURE)
___ Ramsland, Katherine. "**Angel Heart**: The Journey to Self as the Ultimate Horror," in: Golden, Christopher, ed. **Cut! Horror Writers on Horror Film.** New York: Berkley, 1992. pp.189-198.

ANGEL, ALBALUCIA
___ Orozco-Allan, Gloria. "Lo fantástico y el discurso femenino en **Dos veces Alicia**, de Albalucia Angel," *Mester* (UCLA) 19(2): 137-144. Fall 1990.

ANIMAL MAKERS (COMPANY)
___ Keeney, Brian. "Company File: Animal Makers," *Cinefex* No. 59: 29-30. September 1994.

ANIMAL RIGHTS
___ Laurent, John. "C. S. Lewis and Animal Rights," *Mythlore* 19(1): 46-51. Winter 1993. (No. 71)

ANIMALS
___ Fowler, Judy. **Exploring How Animals Fare in Worlds Created by Feminist Science Fiction Writers.** Master's Thesis, University of Wisconsin, Whitewater, 1993. 71pp.
___ Martin, John. "C. S. Lewis and Animals: The Road to Whipsnade," *Bulletin of the New York C. S. Lewis Society* 24(11): 1-7. September 1993.
___ Scholtmeijer, Marian. "The Animal at the Door: Modern Works of Horror and the Natural Animal," in: Ruddick, Nicholas, ed. **State of the Fantastic.** Westport, CT: Greenwood, 1992. pp.189-198.

ANIMATION
___ Clements, Jonathan. "The Mechanics of the US Anime and Manga Industry," *Foundation* No. 64: 32-44. Summer 1995.
___ Hernandez, Lea. "Japanimation's Rising Sun," *Sci-Fi Entertainment* 1(1): 30-33. June 1994.
___ Sulski, Jim. "Japanimation, Kitsch Classics No Kids' Stuff," *Chicago Tribune* Sec. 7, p. 61. November 6, 1992.

ANSTEY, F.
___ Stableford, Brian. "Yesterday's Bestsellers, 15: F. Anstey and **Vice Versa**," *Interzone* No. 74: 57-60. August 1993.

ANTHONY, PATRICIA
___ "1994 *Locus* Awards," *Locus* 33(2): 7. August 1994.
___ "An Interview With Patricia Anthony," *Sense of Wonder* p. 11-12. February/March 1994.
___ "Patricia Anthony: A Voyage of Discovery," *Locus* 32(4): 5, 66. April 1994.

ANTHONY, PIERS
___ "Tor Books Pays $1 Million Advance for Four Piers Anthony Xanth Novels," *Science Fiction Chronicle* 13(4): 4. January 1992.
___ Anthony, Piers. "The Pun-derful Wizard of Xanth Takes a More Serious Look at Life," *Science Fiction Age* 2(4): 30-32. May 1994.
___ Starr, Richard. "SFC Interviews: Piers Anthony," *Science Fiction Chronicle* 15(10): 6, 32-36. September 1994.

ANTHROPOLOGY
___ Barnard, Alan. "Tarzan and the Lost Races: Parallels Between Anthropology and Early Science Fiction," in: Archetti, Eduardo P., ed. **Exploring the Written: Anthropology and the Multiplicity of Writing.** Stockholm: Scandinavian University Press, 1994. pp.231-257.

APOCALYPSE NOW (MOTION PICTURE)
___ Cahir, Linda C. "Narratological Parallels in Joseph Conrad's **Heart of Darkness** and Francis Ford Coppola's **Apocalypse Now**," *Literature/Film Quarterly* 20(3): 181-187. 1992.
___ Greiff, Louis K. "Soldier, Sailor, Surfer, Chef: Conrad's Ethics and the Margins of **Apocalypse Now**," *Literature/Film Quarterly* 20(3): 188-197. 1992.

APOLLO 11
___ "*Apollo* 11: 25 Years Later; Reports and Recollections," *Locus* 33(2): 46-51, 71-73. August 1994.

APOLLO 13 (MOTION PICTURE)
___ Baxter, Stephen. "**Apollo 13**," *Vector* No. 184: 8-9. Summer 1995.
___ Fisher, Bob. "**Apollo 13** Orbits Cinema's Outer Limits," *American Cinematographer* 76(6): 37-46. June 1995.
___ Franke, Lizzie. "**Apollo 13** (Review)," *Sight and Sound* 5(9): 42-43. September 1995.
___ Johnson, Kim H. "Mission Control," *Starlog* No. 217: 40-45, 66. August 1995.
___ Lowe, Nick. "**Apollo 13** (Review)," *Interzone* No. 102: 35-36. December 1995.
___ Maccarillo, Lisa. "Lost Moon," *Sci-Fi Entertainment* 2(2): 56-61, 81. August 1995.

APOLLO 13 (MOTION PICTURE)

APOLLO 13 (MOTION PICTURE) (continued)
___ Magid, Ron. "Digital Domain Provides Rocket Fuel for *Apollo 13*," *American Cinematographer* 76(6): 48-60. June 1995.
___ Prokop, Tim. "Launching *Apollo 13*," *Cinefex* No. 63: 85-85. September 1995.
___ Walker, Martin. "*Apollo* and Newt," *Sight and Sound* 5(9): 6-8. September 1995.

APPLEGATE, ROYCE D.

___ Warren, Bill. "Hail to the Chief," *Starlog* No. 207: 36-39, 70. October 1994.

APPLETON, VICTOR, PSEUD.

___ Molson, Francis J. "The Tom Swift Books," in: Sullivan, C. W., III. **Science Fiction for Young Readers**. Westport, CT: Greenwood, 1993. pp.3-20.

APRIL, JEAN-PIERRE

___ Eckern, Claude. "La Science-fiction de Jean-Pierre April," *Imagine* No. 61: 119-156. September 1992.

AQUIMANDA DE VACA, TIRSO

___ Dendle, Brian J. "Spain's First Novel of Science Fiction: A Nineteenth Century Voyage to Saturn," *Monographis Review* 3(1/2): 43-48. 1987.

ARABIC LITERATURE

___ Al-Raheb, Hani. "Five Patterns of the Fantastic in an Arabic Saga," *Journal of the Fantastic in the Arts* 5(4): 42-54. 1993. (No. 20)

ARAGON, LOUIS

___ Fickey, Pierrette. "Louis Aragon: The Fantastic in Collage and Poetry," in: Latham, Robert A. and Collins, Robert A., eds. **Modes of the Fantastic**. Westport, CT: Greenwood, 1995. pp.38-47.

ARCHAEOLOGY

___ Szarmach, Paul E. "Arthurian Archaeology," in: Fries, Maureen and Watson, Jeanie, eds. **Approaches to the Teaching of the Arthurian Tradition**. New York: Modern Language Association, 1992. pp.135-138.

ARCHER, JOHN

___ Weaver, Tom. "John Archer," in: Weaver, Tom. **They Fought the Creature Features: Interviews with 23 Classic Horror, Science Fiction and Serial Stars**. Jefferson, NC: McFarland, 1995. pp.37-49.
___ Weaver, Tom. "Lunar Destiny," *Starlog* No. 202: 60-65. May 1994.

ARCHITECTURE

___ Bliznakov, Milka. "The Dynamic Egalitarian City: Twentieth Century Designs for Urban Development in Russia and Their Utopian Sources," in: Saccaro Del Buffa, Giuseppa and Lewis, Arthur O., eds. **Utopia e Modernita: Teorie e prassi utopiche nell'eta moderna e postmoderna**. Rome: Gangemi Editore, 1989. pp.401-466.
___ Green, Ernest J. "The Social Functions of Utopian Architecture," *Utopian Studies* 4(1): 1-13. 1993.
___ Hatch, Richard C. "The Ideology of Work and the Architecture of Utopia," in: Saccaro Del Buffa, Giuseppa and Lewis, Arthur O., eds. **Utopia e Modernita: Teorie e prassi utopiche nell'eta moderna e postmoderna**. Rome: Gangemi Editore, 1989. pp.175-186.
___ Hovana, Ion. "Visioni urbanistiche ottocentesche in Romania," in: Saccaro Del Buffa, Giuseppa and Lewis, Arthur O., eds. **Utopia e Modernita: Teorie e prassi utopiche nell'eta moderna e postmoderna**. Rome: Gangemi Editore, 1989. pp.385-400.
___ Parapetti, Roberto. "Restauro e fortuna dell'immaginario: il caso della Torre di Babele," in: Saccaro Del Buffa, Giuseppa and Lewis, Arthur O., eds. **Utopia e Modernita: Teorie e prassi utopiche nell'eta moderna e postmoderna**. Rome: Gangemi Editore, 1989. pp.369-384.
___ Ramirez, Juan-Antonio. "La modernidad perfecta de la Isla-Maquina," in: Saccaro Del Buffa, Giuseppa and Lewis, Arthur O., eds. **Utopia e Modernita: Teorie e prassi utopiche nell'eta moderna e postmoderna**. Rome: Gangemi Editore, 1989. pp.467-500.
___ Raulet, Gerard. "360 Degrees in Time: Postmodern Architecture and the Question of Consensus," *Utopian Studies* 4(2): 57-65. 1993.

ARGENTINA

___ "Uncut 'Clockwork' Spurs Distrib-Exhib Heat in Argentina," *Variety* p. 44. September 15, 1982.

ARMY OF DARKNESS: EVIL DEAD III (MOTION PICTURE)

ARGENTINA (continued)
___ Dellepiane, Angela B. "Critical Notes on Argentinian Science Fiction Narrative," *Monographis Review* 3(1/2): 19-32. 1987.
___ García, Fernando. "Burroughs in Argentina," by Fernando García and Hernán Ostuni. *Burroughs Bulletin* NS. No. 17: 10-17. January 1994.
___ García, Fernando. "Tarzan, King of the Pampa," by Fernando García and Hernán Ostuni. *Burroughs Bulletin* NS. No. 18: 20-22. April 1994.
___ Kason, Nancy M. "The Dystopian Vision in **XYZ** by Clemente Palma," *Monographis Review* 3(1/2): 33-42. 1987.
___ Moreno, Horacio. "SF in Argentina," by Horacio Moreno and Roberto de Sousa Causo. *Locus* 33(1): 48-49. July 1994.

ARGENTO, DARIO

___ Winter, Douglas E. "Opera of Violence: The Films of Dario Argento," in: Golden, Christopher, ed. **Cut! Horror Writers on Horror Film**. New York: Berkley, 1992. pp.267-288.

ARGOSY (MAGAZINE)

___ Moskowitz, Sam. "Burroughs Returns to *Argosy*," *Burroughs Bulletin* NS. No. 20: 11-15. October 1994.

ARISTOPHANES

___ Smith, Nicholas D. "Political Activity and Ideal Economics: Two Related Utopian Themes in Aristophanic Comedy," *Utopian Studies* 3(1): 84-94. 1992.

ARISTOTLE

___ Depew, David J. "Aristotle's Critique of Plato's Ideal States," in: Saccaro Del Buffa, Giuseppa and Lewis, Arthur O., eds. **Utopia e Modernita: Teorie e prassi utopiche nell'eta moderna e postmoderna**. Rome: Gangemi Editore, 1989. pp.727-738.

ARMY OF DARKNESS: EVIL DEAD III (MOTION PICTURE)

___ Arnold, Gary. "The Farces of Darkness," *Washington (DC) Times*. February 19, 1993 in: *NewsBank. Film and Television*. 20:C14. 1993
___ Bernard, Jami. "Whisper a Happy Goon," *New York (NY) Post*. February 19, 1993 in: *NewsBank. Film and Television*. 20:C13. 1993
___ Biodrowski, Steve. "*Army of Darkness*," *Cinefantastique* 22(6): 22-23. June 1992
___ Biodrowski, Steve. "*Army of Darkness*," *Cinefantastique* 23(1): 24-52. August 1992.
___ Biodrowski, Steve. "*Evil Dead III*: Introvision Comes of Age," *Cinefantastique* 23(1): 44-45. August 1992.
___ Biodrowski, Steve. "*Evil Dead III*: KNB's Army of Darkness," *Cinefantastique* 23(1): 42. August 1992.
___ Biodrowski, Steve. "*Evil Dead III*: Production Design," *Cinefantastique* 23(1): 34. August 1992.
___ Biodrowski, Steve. "*Evil Dead III*: The Makeup World of Ash," *Cinefantastique* 23(1): 32-33. August 1992.
___ Biodrowski, Steve. "Sam Raimi's *Evil Dead III*," *Cinefantastique* 22(5): 4-5. April 1992.
___ Biodrowski, Steve. "Sam Raimi's *Evil Dead III*," *Cinefantastique* 23(5): 14-15. February 1993.
___ Campbell, Bob. "Grisly *Army of Darkness*: A Medieval Monster Mash," *Newark (NJ) Star-Ledger*. February 19, 1993 in: *NewsBank. Film and Television*. 30:D13. 1993
___ Hunter, Stephen. "Boys Play Soldier and Director in Raimi's Juvenile *Army of Darkness*," *Baltimore (MD) Sun*. February 19, 1993 in: *NewsBank. Film and Television*. 20:C12. 1993
___ Johnson, Malcolm. "Dark Ages Time-Travel Horror Film Brandishes Action Aplenty to Please 13-Year-Olds," *Hartford (CT) Courant*. February 19, 1993 in: *NewsBank. Film and Television*. 20:C11. 1993
___ Movshovitz, Howie. "*Army of Darkness* a Perfect Film for 14-Year Olds," *Denver (CO) Post*. February 19, 1993 in: *NewsBank. Film and Television*. 30:D11. 1993
___ Newman, Kim. "*Army of Darkness* (Review)," *Sight and Sound* 3(6): 46-47. June 1993.
___ Robley, Les P. "*Army of Darkness* (Review)," *Cinefantastique* 24(2): 59. August 1993.
___ Robley, Les P. "*Evil Dead III*: Stop-Motion Special Effects," *Cinefantastique* 23(1): 48-49. August 1992.
___ Robley, Les P. "Mobilizing *Army of Darkness* Via Go-Animation," *American Cinematographer* 74(3): 72-80. March 1993.

ARMY OF DARKNESS: EVIL DEAD III (MOTION PICTURE) (continued)
___ Rosenberg, Scott. "Knight and the Living Dead," *San Francisco (CA) Examiner.* February 19, 1993 in: *NewsBank. Film and Television.* 30:D9-D10. 1993
___ Stark, Susan. "The Darker Ages: Raimi's Campy **Army of Darkness** Supplies Special Effects by the Gross," *Detroit (MI) News.* February 19, 1993 in: *NewsBank. Film and Television.* 30:D12. 1993
___ Uram, Sue. "**Army of Darkness: Evil Dead III**," *Cinefantastique* 22(4): 41. February 1992.
___ Uram, Sue. "Bruce Campbell: Horror's Rambo," *Cinefantastique* 23(2/3): 31. October 1992.
___ Uram, Sue. "Dead Hero: Bruce Campbell: Actor/Producer," *Cinefantastique* 23(1): 36-37. August 1992.
___ Uram, Sue. "Evil Effects: Tom Sullivan, Gore Auteur," *Cinefantastique* 23(1): 50. August 1992.
___ Uram, Sue. "Sam Raimi's **Evil Dead III**," *Cinefantastique* 23(2/3): 28-30. October 1992.
___ Wuntch, Phillip. "**Army of Darkness**: Dark Ages Camp Has Relentlessly Messy Fun," *Dallas (TX) Morning News.* February 19, 1993 in: *NewsBank. Film and Television.* 30:D14. 1993

ARNASON, ELEANOR
___ "Arnason, Rushdie Win Mythopoeic Awards," *Science Fiction Chronicle* 14(1): 6. October 1992.
___ "Eleanor Arnason, Gwyneth Jones Win First James Tiptree, Jr. Award," *Science Fiction Chronicle* 13(7): 4. April 1992.
___ "James Tiptree, Jr. Award, 1991," *Locus* 28(5): 6, 65. May 1992.
___ "James Tiptree, Jr. Memorial Award Presented," *SFWA Bulletin* 26(2): 3-5. Summer 1992. (No. 116)
___ Arnason, Eleanor. "On Writing **A Woman of the Iron People**," *Monad* No. 3: 35-64. September 1993.

ARNOLD SCHWARZENEGGER
___ "1992 Saturn Awards," *Locus* 28(6): 7. June 1992.

ARNOLD, JACK
___ "Arnold, Jack; Made Popular Science Fiction, Horror Films (Obituary)," *Los Angeles (CA) Times* Sec. A, p. 26. March 20, 1992.
___ "Arnold, Jack, 1912-1992 (Obituary)," *Starlog* 181: 22-23. August 1992.
___ Newsom, Ted. "The Creature Remake That Never Got Made: An Afternoon with Jack Arnold and Nigel Kneale," *Filmfax* No. 37: 64-67, 82, 98. February/March 1993.

ARNOLD, MATTHEW
___ Roberts, Robin. "Matthew Arnold's 'Dover Beach', Gender, and Science Fiction," *Extrapolation* 33(3): 245-257. Fall 1992.

ARNOT, ROBIN PAGE
___ Roberts, Helen E. "Commemorating William Morris: Robin Page Arnot and the Early History of the William Morris Society," *Journal of the William Morris Society* 11(2): 33-37. Spring 1995.

ARNZEN, MICHAEL
___ "Bram Stoker Award Winners," *Science Fiction Chronicle* 16(7): 4. June/July 1995.

ARONICA, LOU
___ "Aronica Moves to Avon as Senior VP and Publisher," *Science Fiction Chronicle* 16(9): 5-6. August/September 1995.
___ "Aronica Moves to Berkley," *Locus* 32(2): 7. February 1994.
___ "Lou Aronica Moves to Avon," *Locus* 35(3): 8. September 1993.
___ "Lou Aronica Moves to Berkely," *Science Fiction Chronicle* 15(4): 6. February 1994.

ARROWFEATHER (MOTION PICTURE)
___ "Gas That Kills All Over Age 25: And That's AIP's Sci-Fi Satire," *Variety* p. 6. December 24, 1969.

ART AND ARTISTS
___ "1991 Chesley Awards Winners," *Locus* 29(4): 7, 73. October 1992
___ "1995 Chesley Awards," *Locus* 35(2): 8. August 1995.
___ "ASFA's Chesley Art Award Nominations, 1992," *Science Fiction Chronicle* 14(10): 5-6. July 1993.
___ "Association of SF and Fantasy Artists' Chesley Awards," *Science Fiction Chronicle* 14(1): 4. October 1992.

ART AND ARTISTS (continued)
___ "Chesley Award Nominations," *Science Fiction Chronicle* 15(9): 5. August 1994.
___ "Chesley Awards," *Science Fiction Chronicle* 15(1): 4. October 1993.
___ "Chesley Awards," *Science Fiction Chronicle* 15(10): 5. September 1994.
___ "Chesley Awards," *Science Fiction Chronicle* 16(9): 5. August/September 1995.
___ "Chesley Awards Nominations," *Locus* 31(1): 6, 57. July 1993.
___ "Chesley Awards Nominees," *Locus* 33(1): 7, 78. July 1994.
___ "Creative Explorations: An Interview With Michael Whelan," *Hailing Frequencies* (Waldenbooks) No. 9: 2-4. 1993.
___ "A Gallery of *Amazing* Art: Covers Through the Years," *Amazing Stories* 67(4): 52-56. July 1992.
___ "Interview: Robert Paul," *Futures Past* No. 3:31-32. September 1992.
___ "Maitz, Wurts Paintings Stolen," *Science Fiction Chronicle* 17(2): 5-6. December 1995/January 1996.
___ "Michael Whelan: Breathing Space," *Locus* 30(1): 4, 65. January 1993.
___ "Same Cover on *Amazing, Analog*," *Science Fiction Chronicle* 14(10): 6-7. July 1993.
___ "SF/Fantasy Art for Computers," *Locus* 32(6): 8, 76. June 1994.
___ "Space Art in Space," *Locus* 35(4): 9. October 1995.
___ "Spectrum Competition Open," *Locus* 33(5): 9, 73. November 1994.
___ "Valuable Artwork Missing," *Locus* 35(6): 8. December 1995.
___ Albert, Walter. "Science Fiction Illustration," by Walter Albert and Neil Barron. in: Barron, Neil, ed. **Anatomy of Wonder 4.** New York: Bowker, 1995. pp.651-672.
___ Alexander-Schaechtelin, Barbara F. "Eros and Thanatos: The Art of Alfred Kubin on the Edge of the Other Side," in: Morse, Donald E., ed. **The Celebration of the Fantastic.** Westport, CT: Greenwood, 1992. pp.165-182.
___ Barrett, Robert R. "Animal Fashion Plates: Charles Livingston Bull (1874-1932)," *Burroughs Bulletin* NS. No. 15: 22-25. July 1993.
___ Barrett, Robert R. "Edgar Rice Burroughs to Zane Grey: Stockton Mulford (1886-?)," *Burroughs Bulletin* NS. No. 16: 16-19. October 1993.
___ Barrett, Robert R. "Fortunino Mattania, R. I.: The Last Victorian," *Burroughs Bulletin* NS No. 10: 16-22. April 1992.
___ Barrett, Robert R. "The Indian Is Not an Apache!: Paul Stahr (1883-1953)," *Burroughs Bulletin* NS. No. 12: 15-18. October 1992.
___ Barrett, Robert R. "Richard Hescox: Penetrating the Cloud Cover," *Burroughs Bulletin* NS No. 9: 3-7. January 1992.
___ Barrett, Robert R. "To Bora-Bora and Back Again: The Story of Armstrong W. Sperry," *Burroughs Bulletin* NS No. 11: 3-8. July 1992.
___ Benford, Gregory. "Interplanetary Pioneer," *Science Fiction Age* 3(3): 86-91. March 1995.
___ Benford, Gregory. "A Lyrical Hardness," *Science Fiction Age* 2(4): 78-83. May 1994.
___ Bertha, Csilla. "Csontváry, the Painter of the 'Sun's Path'," in: Morse, Donald E., ed. **The Celebration of the Fantastic.** Westport, CT: Greenwood, 1992. pp.151-164.
___ Bertha, Csilla. "The Symbolic Versus the Fantastic: The Example of a Hungarian Painter," *Journal of the Fantastic in the Arts* 6(4): 295-311. 1995.
___ Borst, Ronald V., ed. **Graven Images: The Best of Horror, Fantasy, and Science Fiction Film Art from the Collection of Ronald V. Borst,** ed. by Ronald V. Borst, Keith Burns and Leith Adams. New York: Grove Press, 1992. 240pp.
___ Bova, Ben. "Future Di Fate," *Science Fiction Age* 2(3): 70-75. March 1994.
___ Bradbury, Ray. "Blueprinter of Our Future: Robert McCall," *Science Fiction Age* 1(1): 62-67. November 1992.
___ Bryant, Edward. "King Richard, Conqueror of Space," *Science Fiction Age* 3(6): 82-87. September 1995.
___ Brzezinski, Anthony. "Paulian Technique," *Futures Past* No. 3:33. September 1992.
___ Burnett, Cathy, ed. **Spectrum: The Best in Contemporary Fantastic Art (First Annual Collection),** ed. by Cathy Burnett, Arnie Fenner and Jim Loehr. Grass Valley, CA: Underwood Books, 1994. 204pp.
___ Canto, Christophe. **The History of the Future: Images of the 21st Century,** by Christophe Canto and Odile Faliu. New York and Paris: Flammarion, 1993. 159pp.

ART AND ARTISTS

ART AND ARTISTS (continued)

___ Cartier, Edd. "Notes to the New Artist," in: Wolverton, Dave, ed. **Writers of the Future, Vol. VIII.** Los Angeles, CA: Bridge, 1992. pp.167-175.

___ Clauson, Kathy. "The Veil of Time," *US Art* 11(4): 39-44. May/June 1992

___ Cole, Allan. "Magic Brush," *Science Fiction Age* 4(1): 84-89. November 1995.

___ Coombs, Charles I. "Martian Memories," *Burroughs Bulletin* NS No. 11: 21-23. July 1992.

___ Davidsmeyer, Jo. "An Illustrious Pair," *Strange New Worlds* No. 7: 6-8. April/May 1993.

___ Davidson, Jane P. "A Golem of Her Own: The Fantastic Art and Literature of Leilah Wendell," in: Wolf, Milton T. and Mallett, Daryl F., eds. **Imaginative Futures: Proceedings of the 1993 Science Fiction Research Association Conference.** San Bernardino, CA: Jacob's Ladder Books, 1995. pp.341-352.

___ Di Fate, Vincent. "Gadget Artists Return," by Vincent Di Fate and Roger Reed. *Science Fiction Age* 2(5): 70-75. July 1994.

___ Di Fate, Vincent. "A Short History of SF Art in Paperback," *Science Fiction Chronicle* 16(5): 12, 36-38. March/April 1995.

___ Di Fate, Vincent. "Sketches: Now Might Be the Right Time to Donate That Painting!," *Science Fiction Chronicle* 13(7): 25-26. April 1992.

___ Drake, David. "Hickmania," *Science Fiction Age* 2(1): 80-85. November 1993.

___ Eisenmann, Stephen. **Designing Utopia: The Art of William Morris and His Circle: Katonah Museum of Art, February 16 through April 12, 1992.** Katonah, NY: Katonah Museum of Art, 1992. 39pp.

___ Fenner, Arnie. "Punchatz: A Barnstormer in Texas," *Shayol* No. 6: 20-27. 1982.

___ Fenner, Arnie. "Roger Stine," *Shayol* No. 7: 24-31. 1985.

___ Frank, Jane. "Bio of a Space Artist," *Science Fiction Age* 1(5): 62-67. July 1993.

___ Freas, Frank K. "The Story Between the Words," *Analog* 112(5): 84-89. April 1992.

___ Freibert, Lucy M. "The Role of the Artist in the Commune," in: Saccaro Del Buffa, Giuseppa and Lewis, Arthur O., eds. **Utopie per gli Anni Ottana.** Rome: Gangemi Editore, 1986. pp.397-414.

___ French, Lawrence. "*Bram Stoker's Dracula*: Matte Artistry," *Cinefantastique* 23(6): 55-58. April 1993.

___ Friesner, Esther M. "One of the Good Guys," *Science Fiction Age* 3(5): 82-87. July 1995.

___ Gaughan, Jack. "An Apprenticeship: Artist," in: Sanders, Joe, ed. **Science Fiction Fandom.** Westport, CT: Greenwood, 1994. pp.207-210.

___ Graham, Douglas F. "Sci-Fi Art: No Alien Concept," *Washington (DC) Times* Sec. B, p. 1. July 4, 1992.

___ Hagenlocher, Will C. "Joe Jusko: An Interview," *Burroughs Bulletin* NS. No. 23: 19-23. July 1995.

___ Haldeman, Joe. "Architect of Space," *Science Fiction Age* 2(6): 78-83. September 1994.

___ Hammond, Wayne G. **J. R. R. Tolkien: Artist and Illustrator**, by Wayne G. Hammond and Christina Scull. Boston, MA: Houghton Mifflin, 1995. 208pp.

___ Heeszel, Marlys. **The Worlds of TSR: A Pictorial Journey Through the Landscape of the Imagination.** Lake Geneva, WI: TSR, 1994. 142pp.

___ Heller, Steven. **Jackets Required: An Illustrated History of American Book Jacket Design, 1920-1959,** by Steven Heller and Seymour Chwast. San Francisco, CA: Chronicle Books, 1995. 144pp.

___ Holländer, Hans. "Notizen zur Illustration 'phantastischer Literatur'. Anläßlich der Asgabe von MacDonalds **Phantastes** mit den Bildern von Fritz Hechelmann," in: Kranz, Gisbert, ed. **Inklings: Jahrbuch für Literatur und Ästhetik.** 1. Band. Lüdenscheid, Germany: Michael Claren, 1983. pp.139-149.

___ Jankus, Hank. "Interview: Thomas Blackshear," *Shayol* No. 7: 16-18. 1985.

___ Madsen, Dan. "The Art of Drew Struzan," *LucasFilms Fan Club* No. 18: 10-13. 1993.

___ McCaffrey, Anne. "Dragon-Master's Dialogue," *Science Fiction Age* 1(6): 78-83. September 1994.

___ McTigue, Maureen. "Man of Wonder: Michael Whelan," *Starlog* No. 197: 32-37, 68. December 1993.

___ McWhorter, George T. "Larry Schwinger: Ballantine Cover Artist," *Burroughs Bulletin* NS No. 11: 19-20. July 1992.

___ Melia, Sally-Ann. "Positively Dangerous to Stand Still: Artist Jim Burns Interviewed," *Interzone* No. 79: 20-24. January 1994.

ART AND ARTISTS (continued)

___ Miller, Ron. **The Dream Machines: An Illustrated History of the Spaceship in Art, Science and Literature.** Malabar, FL: Krieger, 1993. 714pp.

___ Morgan, Chris. "Neverending Visions of Space: David A. Hardy, Britain's Leading Space Artist," *Interzone* No. 69: 19-23. March 1993.

___ Murray, Will. "Heroic Artist," *Starlog* No. 198: 43-49, 82. January 1994.

___ Nazzaro, Joe. "Master Strokes," *Starlog* No. 195: 27-31, 72. October 1993.

___ Nisbet, Peter. "The Response to Science and Technology in the Visual Arts," in: Graham, Loren R., ed. **Science and the Soviet Social Order.** Cambridge: Harvard University Press, 1990. pp.341-358.

___ O'Shaughnessey, Margaret. "Edwin Austin Abbey's Reinterpretation of the Grail Quest: The Boston Public Library Murals," *Arthuriana* 4(4): 298-312. Winter 1994.

___ Paget, Stephen. "An Interview with Michael Whelan," *Sense of Wonder* (B. Dalton) pp.1-4. October/November 1993.

___ Peters, Jefferson M. **Art, Artists and Artistry in Science Fiction.** Ph.D. Dissertation, University of Michigan, 1993. (DAI-A 53/11, p. 3904. May 1993.)

___ Pohl, Frederik. "Extra-Terrestrial Michelangelo," *Science Fiction Age* 1(4): 54-59. May 1993.

___ Pujade, Robert. "Erotisme et fantastique en photographie," in: Bozzetto, Roger, ed. **Eros: Science & Fiction Fantastique.** Aix-en-Provence: Universite de Provence, 1991. pp.107-131.

___ Quinn, Julie. "Paul S. Farkas," *Nevada Magazine* 48: 58-50. March/April 1988.

___ Ravenscrot, Anthony. "Convention Art Shows: Seen as the East Wing of Hell," *Lan's Lantern* No. 40: 123-124. September 1992.

___ Resnick, Mike. "Visions and Voyages," *Science Fiction Age* 3(2): 70-75. January 1995.

___ Richardson, Darrell C. **J. Allen St. John: An Illustrated Bibliography.** Memphis, TN: Mid-America Publisher, 1991. 111pp.

___ Robertson, Andy. "Art and Metaphysics at Party-time: SMS Interviewed," by Andy Robertson and Jason Hurst. *Interzone* No. 100: 22-26. October 1995.

___ Schindler, Richard A. "Joseph Noel Paton's Fairy Paintings: Fantasy Art as Victorian Narrative," *Scotia: Interdisciplinary Journal of Scottish Studies* 14: 13-29. 1990.

___ Setiya, Kieran. "Two Notes on Lovecraft," *Lovecraft Studies* No. 26: 14-16. Spring 1992.

___ Simmons, Joe. "Fantasy Art and Warrior Women: An Aesthetic Critique of Feminine Images," *Mythlore* 21(1): 51-54, 65. Summer 1995. (No. 79)

___ Sinor, Bradley H. "Drawings in the Dark," *Starlog* No. 183: 50-53, 70. October 1992.

___ Steele, Allen. "SF's Cinematic Sentinel," *Science Fiction Age* 3(4): 82-87. May 1995.

___ Stephens, Bob. "Persistent Vision: Unforgettable Poster Art From the Golden Age of Science Fiction Movies," by Bob Stephens and Vincent Di Fate. *Sci-Fi Entertainment* 1(2): 48-51. August 1994.

___ Van Hise, James. "An Index to the Reed Crandall Illustrations From the Works of Edgar Rice Burroughs," *Burroughs Bulletin* NS. No. 20: 27-28. October 1994.

___ Van Hise, James. "Reed Crandall: Illustrator of Super Heroes," *Burroughs Bulletin* NS. No. 20: 17-28. October 1994.

___ Wachhorst, Wyn. "The Dream of Spaceflight: Nostalgia for a Bygone Future," *Massachusetts Review* 36(1): 7-32. Spring 1995.

___ Waterside, Pat. "Trek Gallery," *Sci-Fi Entertainment* 1(1): 48-51. June 1994.

___ Weinberg, Robert. "Profile: Frank R. Paul," *Futures Past* No. 3:30-32. September 1992. (Reprinted from: Weinberg, Robert. **A Biographical Dictionary of Science Fiction and Fantasy Artists.** 1988.)

___ Westwood, Frank. "Interview with Franco Matania," *Burroughs Bulletin* NS No. 10: 23-28. April 1992.

ART IN SF

___ Rampton, David. "Into the Secret Chamber: Art and the Artist in Kurt Vonnegut's **Bluebeard**," *Critique* 35(1): 16-26. Fall 1993.

ARTHUR C. CLARKE AWARD, 1991

___ "Arthur C. Clarke Award Nominees," *Locus* 28(3): 6. March 1992.

ARTHUR C. CLARKE AWARD, 1992

ARTHURIAN LEGEND (continued)

___ Pearcy, Roy J. "Fabliau Intervention in Some Mid-Thirteenth Century Arthurian Verse Romances," in: Busby, Keith, ed. **The Arthurian Yearbook I**. New York: Garland, 1991. pp.63-90.

___ Pigg, Daniel. "Language as Weapon: The Poetics of Plot in Malory's 'Tale of Sir Gareth'," *Quondam et Futurus* 2(1): 16-27. Spring 1992.

___ Purdon, Liam O. "Hollywood's Myopic Medievalism: *Excalibur* and Malory's **Morte d'Arthur**," by Liam O. Purdon and Robert J. Blanch. in: Slocum, Sally K., ed. **Popular Arthurian Traditions**. Bowling Green, OH: Popular Press, 1992. pp.156-161.

___ Raffel, Burton. "Translating **Yvain** and **Sir Gawain and the Green Knight** for Classroom Use," in: Fries, Maureen and Watson, Jeanie, eds. **Approaches to the Teaching of the Arthurian Tradition**. New York: Modern Language Association, 1992. pp.88-93.

___ Ragland, Ellie. "Psychoanalysis and Courtly Love," *Arthuriana* 5(1): 1-20. Spring 1995.

___ Reiss, Edmund. **Arthurian Legend and Literature: An Annotated Bibliography. Volume 1: The Middle Ages**, by Edmund Reiss, Louise H. Reiss and Beverly Taylor. New York: Garland, 1984. 467pp.

___ Reiss, Edmund. **Arthurian Legend and Literature: An Annotated Bibliography. Volume 2.**, by Edmund Reiss, Louise H. Reiss and Beverly Taylor. New York: Garland, 1995. [Not seen.]

___ Relihan, Constance C. "Vivien, Elaine, and the Model's Gaze: Cameron's Reading of **Idylls of the King**," in: Slocum, Sally K., ed. **Popular Arthurian Traditions**. Bowling Green, OH: Popular Press, 1992. pp.111-131.

___ Rewa, Michael P. "The Matter of Britain in English and American Popular Music (1966-1990)," in: Slocum, Sally K., ed. **Popular Arthurian Traditions**. Bowling Green, OH: Popular Press, 1992. pp.104-110.

___ Rider, Jeff. "The Arthurian Legend in French Cinema: *Lancelot du Lac* and *Perceval la Gallois*," by Jeff Rider, Richard Hull and Christopher Smith. in: Harty, Kevin J., ed. **Cinema Arthuriana: Essays on Arthurian Film**. New York: Garland, 1991. pp.41-56.

___ Roberts, Brynley F. "**Culhwch ac Olwen**, The Triads, Saint's Lives," in: Bromwich, Rachel, Jarman, A. O. H. and Roberts, Brynley F., eds. **The Arthur of the Welsh**. Cardiff: University of Wales Press, 1991. pp.73-96.

___ Roberts, Brynley F. "Geoffrey of Monmouth, **Historia Regum Britanniae** and **Brut y Brenhinedd**," in: Bromwich, Rachel, Jarman, A. O. H. and Roberts, Brynley F., eds. **The Arthur of the Welsh**. Cardiff: University of Wales Press, 1991. pp.97-116.

___ Rockwell, Paul V. "The Falsification of Resemblance: Reading the False Guinevere," in: Busby, Keith, ed. **The Arthurian Yearbook I**. New York: Garland, 1991. pp.27-42.

___ Rossignol, Rosalyn. "The Holiest Vessel: Maternal Aspects of the Grail," *Arthuriana* 5(1): 52-61. Spring 1995.

___ Roussineau, Gilles. "Tradition Littéraire et Culture Populaire dans L'Histoire de Troïlus et de Zellandine (**Perceforest**, Troisième partie), Version Ancienne du Conte de la Belle au Bois Dormant," *Arthuriana* 4(1): 30-45. Spring 1994.

___ Ruck, E. H. **An Index of Themes and Motifs in Twelfth-Century French Arthurian Poetry**. Rochester, NY: D. S. Brewer, 1991. 176pp. [Not seen.]

___ Rushing, James A., Jr. "Adventure and Iconography: Ywain Picture Cycles and the Literarization of Vernacular Narrative," in: Busby, Keith, ed. **The Arthurian Yearbook I**. New York: Garland, 1991. pp.91-106.

___ Ruud, Jay. "Teaching the 'Hoole' Tradition Through Parallel Passages," in: Fries, Maureen and Watson, Jeanie, eds. **Approaches to the Teaching of the Arthurian Tradition**. New York: Modern Language Association, 1992. pp.73-76.

___ Salda, Michael N. "Caxton's Print vs. the Winchester Manuscript: An Introduction to the Debate on Editing Malory's **Morte Darthur**," *Arthuriana* 5(2): 1-4. Summer 1995.

___ Salda, Michael N. "William Faulkner's Arthurian Tale: **Mayday**," *Arthuriana* 4(4): 348-375. Winter 1994.

___ Sandler, Florence F. "Family Romance in **The Once and Future King**," *Quondam et Futurus* 2(2): 72-80. Summer 1992.

___ Schneider, Angelika. "Zur Symbolik in Williams' Arthur-Dictung," in: Kranz, Gisbert, ed. **Inklings: Jahrbuch für Literatur und Ästhetik**. 3. Band. [Lüdenscheid, Germany: Stier], 1985. pp.49-70.

___ Schultz, James A. "Teaching Gottfried and Wolfram," in: Fries, Maureen and Watson, Jeanie, eds. **Approaches to the Teaching of the Arthurian Tradition**. New York: Modern Language Association, 1992. pp.94-99.

ARTHURIAN LEGEND (continued)

___ Shichtman, Martin B. "Wagner and the Arthurian Tradition," in: Fries, Maureen and Watson, Jeanie, eds. **Approaches to the Teaching of the Arthurian Tradition**. New York: Modern Language Association, 1992. pp.139-142.

___ Simpson, Roger. "Merlin and Hull: A Seventeenth Century Prophecy," *Quondam et Futurus* 3(1): 60-65. Spring 1993.

___ Simpson, Roger. "A Minor Road to Camelot: *Once A Week, 1859-1867*," *Arthuriana* 4(1): 46-69. Spring 1994.

___ Sims-Williams, Patrick. "The Early Welsh Arthurian Poems," in: Bromwich, Rachel, Jarman, A. O. H. and Roberts, Brynley F., eds. **The Arthur of the Welsh**. Cardiff: University of Wales Press, 1991. pp.33-72.

___ Sklar, Elizabeth S. "Thoroughly Modern Morgan: Morgan le Fey in Twentieth-Century Popular Arthuriana," in: Slocum, Sally K., ed. **Popular Arthurian Traditions**. Bowling Green, OH: Popular Press, 1992. pp.24-35.

___ Sleeth, Charles R. "Gawain's Judgment Day," *Arthuriana* 4(2): 175-183. Summer 1994.

___ Slocum, Sally K. "Arthur the Great Equalizer: Teaching a Course for Graduate and Undergraduate Students," in: Fries, Maureen and Watson, Jeanie, eds. **Approaches to the Teaching of the Arthurian Tradition**. New York: Modern Language Association, 1992. pp.127-130.

___ Slocum, Sally K. "Waxing Arthurian: **The Lyre of Orpheus** and **Cold Sassy Tree**," in: Slocum, Sally K., ed. **Popular Arthurian Traditions**. Bowling Green, OH: Popular Press, 1992. pp.96-103.

___ Slocum, Sally K., ed. **Popular Arthurian Traditions**. Bowling Green, OH: Bowling Green State University Popular Press, 1992. 184pp.

___ Smiley, Kathryn. "The Collectible King Arthur," *Firsts: Collecting Modern First Editions* 3(10): 39-41. October 1993.

___ Smith, Jeanette C. "The Role of Women in Contemporary Arthurian Fantasy," *Extrapolation* 35(2): 130-144. Summer 1994.

___ Speare, Mary J. "Wagnerian and Arthurian Elements in Chausson's **Le Roi Arthus**," in: Busby, Keith, ed. **The Arthurian Yearbook I**. New York: Garland, 1991. pp.195-214.

___ Spearing, A. C. "Public and Private Spaces in **Sir Gawain and the Green Knights**," *Arthuriana* 4(2): 138-145. Summer 1994.

___ Spivack, Charlotte. **The Company of Camelot: Arthurian Characters in Romance and Fantasy**, by Charlotte Spivack and Roberta L. Staple. Westport, CT: Greenwood, 1994. 161pp.

___ Spivack, Charlotte. "Morgan le Fey: Goddess or Witch?," in: Slocum, Sally K., ed. **Popular Arthurian Traditions**. Bowling Green, OH: Popular Press, 1992. pp.18-23.

___ Stephenson, Will. "Proto-Modernism in Tennyson's 'The Holy Grail'," by Will Stephenson and Stephenson Mimosa. *Quondam et Futurus* 2(4): 49-55. Winter 1992.

___ Sterling-Hellenbrand, Alexandra. "Women on the Edge in **Parzival**: A Study of the 'Grail Women'," *Quondam et Futurus* 3(2): 56-68. Summer 1993.

___ Stock, Lorraine K. "Arms and the (Wo)man in Medieval Romance: The Gendered Arming of Female Warriors in the **Roman d'Eneas** and Heldris's **Roman de Silence**," *Arthuriana* 5(4): 56-83. Winter 1995.

___ Sturges, Robert S. "Chrétien de Troyes in English Translation: A Guide to the Issues," *Arthuriana* 4(3): 205-223. Fall 1994.

___ Sutton, Anne F. "The Dark Dragon of the Normans: A Creation of Geoffrey of Monmouth, Stephen of Rouen, and Merlin Silvester," by Anne F. Sutton and Livia Visser-Fuchs. *Quondam et Futurus* 2(2): 1-20. Summer 1992.

___ Szarmach, Paul E. "Arthurian Archaeology," in: Fries, Maureen and Watson, Jeanie, eds. **Approaches to the Teaching of the Arthurian Tradition**. New York: Modern Language Association, 1992. pp.135-138.

___ Taylor, Beverly. "Using Nineteenth-Century Visual Arts in the Literature Classroom," in: Fries, Maureen and Watson, Jeanie, eds. **Approaches to the Teaching of the Arthurian Tradition**. New York: Modern Language Association, 1992. pp.143-146.

___ Thomas, Patrick M. "**Tristan** and the Avatars of the Lunar Goddess," *Quondam et Futurus* 2(3): 15-22. Fall 1992.

___ Thompson, Raymond H. "The Comic Sage: Merlin in Thomas Berger's **Arthur Rex**," in: Watson, Jeanie and Fries, Marueen, eds. **The Figure of Merlin in the Nineteenth and Twentieth Centuries**. Lewiston, NY: Mellen, 1989. pp.143-153.

___ Thompson, Raymond H. "The Ironic Tradition in Arthurian Films Since 1960," in: Harty, Kevin J., ed. **Cinema Arthuriana: Essays on Arthurian Film**. New York: Garland, 1991. pp.93-104.

___ Thompson, Raymond H. "Modern Visions and Revisions of the Matter of Britain," in: Fries, Maureen and Watson, Jeanie, eds. **Approaches to the Teaching of the Arthurian Tradition**. New York: Modern Language Association, 1992. pp.61-64.

ASIMOV, ISAAC   **ASIMOV, STANLEY**

ASPRIN, ROBERT
___ Lindskold, Jane M. "Robert Asprin: The Man Behind the Myths," *Extrapolation* 35(1): 60-67. Spring 1994.
___ Nicholls, Stan. "Hitting the Punchline: Robert Asprin Interviewed," *Interzone* No. 60: 23-25. June 1992.
___ Nicholls, Stan. "More Fine Myths," *Starlog* 182: 30-33, 71. September 1992.
___ Nicholls, Stan. "Robert Asprin Waits Two Beats Then Hits the Punchline," in: Nicholls, Stan. **Wordsmiths of Wonder: Fifty Interviews with Writers of the Fantastic**. London: Orbit, 1993. pp.276-284.

ASSOCIATION OF SCIENCE FICTION AND FANTASY ARTISTS
___ Guarino, Bettyann. "Things You Wanted to Know About the Chesleys: But Were Afraid to Ask," *ASFA Quarterly* 10(1): 6-13. Spring 1992.

ASTOR PICTURES
___ MacGillivray, Scott. "Astor Pictures," *Filmfax* No. 43: 36-41. February/March 1994.

ASTOUNDING (MAGAZINE)
___ Aldiss, Brian W. "Campbell's Soup," in: Aldiss, Brian W. **The Detached Retina: Aspects of SF and Fantasy**. Syracuse, NY: Syracuse University Press, 1995. pp.145-149.
___ Berger, Albert I. **The Magic That Works: John W. Campbell and the American Response to Technology**. San Bernardino, CA: Borgo Press, 1993. 231pp.
___ Moskowitz, Sam. "Correction re Desmond Hall," *Locus* 30(2): 69. February 1993.

ASTRO BOY (TV)
___ Perry, Joseph W. "Astro Boy: Happy 30th to That Mighty Mechanical Mite," *Filmfax* No. 42: 50-53. December 1993/January 1994.

ATHENEUM
___ "Paramount Drops Atheneum, Restructures Macmillan," *Locus* 32(3): 8, 69. March 1994.

ATKINS, PETER
___ Atkins, Peter. "Other Shelves, Other Shadows: A Conversation With Clive Barker," in: Golden, Christopher, ed. **Cut! Horror Writers on Horror Film**. New York: Berkley, 1992. pp.11-24.
___ Brown, Michael. "Raising Hell With Peter Atkins," in: Brown, Michael, ed. **Pandemonium: Further Explorations into the Worlds of Clive Barker**. Staten Island, NY: Eclise, 1991. pp.27-42.
___ Green, Steve. "The Shadow of the Torturer: Peter Atkins Interviewed," *Interzone* No. 81: 43-45. March 1994.
___ Nicholls, Stan. "Peter Atkins Makes a Pact With the Popcorn Eaters," in: Nicholls, Stan. **Wordsmiths of Wonder: Fifty Interviews with Writers of the Fantastic**. London: Orbit, 1993. pp.438-446.

ATOMIC WAR
___ Stone, Albert E. **Literary Aftershocks: American Writers, Readers, and the Bomb**. New York: Twayne, 1994. 204pp.
___ Wolff, Michael J. "In the Fields of the Fourth Horseman," *Starlog* No. 220: 27-31. November 1995.

ATTACK OF THE 50-FOOT WOMAN (MOTION PICTURE)
___ Francke, Lizzie. "***Attack of the 50 Ft. Woman*** (Review)," *Sight and Sound* 4(10): 35. October 1994.
___ Harris, Judith P. "***Attack of the 50-Ft. Woman*** (Review)," *Cinefantastique* 25(4): 59. August 1994.
___ Lowe, Nick. "***Attack of the Fifty Foot Woman*** (Review)," *Interzone* No. 88: 36. October 1994.
___ Prokop, Tim. "The Making of a 50-Foot Woman," *Cinefex* No. 57: 26-41. March 1994.

ATTACK OF THE PLEASURE PODS (MOTION PICTURE)
___ SEE: STAR WORMS II: ATTACK OF THE PLEASURE PODS (MOTION PICTURE).

ATWOOD, MARGARET
___ "Atwood's Voice Rings True in **Tips**," *Orlando (FL) Sentinel*. December 22, 1991. in *NewsBank. Literature*. 1:C7. 1992.

ATWOOD, MARGARET (continued)
___ Ahearn, Catherine. "An Archetype of Pain: From Plath to Atwood and Musgrave," in: Roberts, Sheila, ed. **Still the Frame Holds: Essays on Women Poets and Writers**. San Bernardino, CA: Borgo Press, 1993. pp.137-156.
___ Bargreen, Melinda. "Drawing on Memory Banks," *Seattle (WA) Times*. January 12, 1992. in *NewsBank. Literature*. 8:B2-B3. 1992.
___ Barr, Marleen S. **Lost in Space: Probing Feminist Science Fiction and Beyond**. Chapel Hill, NC: University of North Carolina Press, 1993. 231pp.
___ Bazin, Nancy T. "Women and Revolution in Dystopian Fiction: Nadine Gordimer's **July's People** and Margaret Atwood's **The Handmaid's Tale**," in: Crafton, John M., ed. **Selected Essays: International Conference on Representing Revolution, 1989**. n.p.: West Georgia College International Conference, 1991. pp.115-128.
___ Blackwood, Steven. "Atwood's **Wilderness** Has a Sense of Canada," *Milwaukee (WI) Journal*. January 5, 1992. in *NewsBank. Literature*. 8:B4. 1992.
___ Brady, Martin. "Dancing With Both Sexes, Atwood Style," *Chicago (IL) Sun Times*. December 8, 1991. in *NewsBank. Literature*. 1:C8-C9. 1992.
___ Brown, Julie. "Our Ladies of Perpetual Hell: Witches and Fantastic Virgins in Margaret Atwood's **Cat's Eye**," *Journal of the Fantastic in the Arts* 4(3): 40-52. 1991. (No. 15)
___ Caldwell, Larry W. "Wells, Orwell, and Atwood: (EPI)Logic and Eu/Utopia," *Extrapolation* 33(4): 333-345. Winter 1992.
___ Caminero-Santangelo, Marta. "Moving Beyond 'The Blank White Spaces': Atwood's Gilead, Postmodernism, and Strategic Resistance," *Studies in Canadian Literature* 19(1): 20-42. 1994.
___ Cheever, Leonard A. "Fantasies of Sexual Hell: Manuel Puig's **Pubis Angelical** and Margaret Atwood's **The Handmaid's Tale**," in: Latham, Robert A. and Collins, Robert A., eds. **Modes of the Fantastic**. Westport, CT: Greenwood, 1995. pp.110-121.
___ Cooley, Dennis. "Nearer by Far: The Upset 'I' in Margaret Atwood's Poetry," in: Nicholson, Colin, ed. **Margaret Atwood: Writing and Subjectivity: New Critical Essays**. New York: St. Martin's, 1994. pp.68-93.
___ Cowart, David. **History and the Contemporary Novel**. Carbondale: Southern Illinois University Press, 1989. 245pp.
___ Dopp, Jamie. "Subject-Position as Victim-Position in **The Handmaid's Tale**," *Studies in Canadian Literature* 19(1): 43-57. 1994.
___ Eder, Richard. "Atwood's Anger Shows in Explosive Short Stories," *Miami (FL) Herald*. December 15, 1991. in *NewsBank. Literature*. 1:C6. 1992.
___ Evans, Mark. "Versions of History: **The Handmaid's Tale** and Its Dedicatees," in: Nicholson, Colin, ed. **Margaret Atwood: Writing and Subjectivity: New Critical Essays**. New York: St. Martin's, 1994. pp.177-188.
___ Ferns, Chris. "The Value/s of Dystopia: **The Handmaid's Tale** and the Anti-Utopian Tradition," *Dalhousie Review* 69(3): 373-382. Fall 1989.
___ Gardner, Laurel J. "Pornography as a Matter of Power in **The Handmaid's Tale**," *Notes on Contemporary Literature* 24(5): 5-7. November 1994.
___ Garlick, Barbara. "**The Handmaid's Tale**: Narrative Voice and the Primacy of the Tale," in: Filmer, Kath, ed. **Twentieth-Century Fantasists: Essays in Culture, Society and Belief in Twentieth Century Mythopoeic Literature**. New York: St. Martin's, 1992. pp.161-171.
___ Govier, Katherine. "Q&Q Interview: Margaret Atwood; 'There's Nothing in the Book That Hasn't Already Happened'," *Quill and Quire* pp.66-67. September 1985.
___ Grace, Sherrill. "Gender as Genre: Atwood's Autobiographical 'I'," in: Nicholson, Colin, ed. **Margaret Atwood: Writing and Subjectivity: New Critical Essays**. New York: St. Martin's, 1994. pp.189-203.
___ Hansot, Elisabeth. "Selves, Survival and Resistance in **The Handmaid's Tale**," *Utopian Studies* 5(2): 56-69. 1994.
___ Hite, Molly P. "Optics and Autobiography in Margaret Atwood's **Cat's Eye**," *Twentieth Century Literature* 41(2): 135-159. Summer 1995.
___ Hoover, Bob. "Insights into Canadian Identity," *Pittsburgh (PA) Post Gazette*. January 27, 1992. in *NewsBank. Literature*. 9:E9. 1992.
___ Howells, Coral. "**Cat's Eye**: Elaine Risley's Retrospective Art," in: Nicholson, Colin, ed. **Margaret Atwood: Writing and Subjectivity: New Critical Essays**. New York: St. Martin's, 1994. pp.204-218.
___ Ingersoll, Earl G. "Margaret Atwood's **The Handmaid's Tale**: Echoes of Orwell," *Journal of the Fantastic in the Arts* 5(4): 64-72. 1993. (No. 20)

AUDIENCES (continued)
___ Tulloch, John. "It's Meant to Be Fantasy: Teenage Audiences and Genre," by John Tulloch and Marian Tulloch. in: Tulloch, John and Jenkins, Henry, eds. **Science Fiction Audiences: Watching Doctor Who and Star Trek.** New York: Routledge, 1995. pp.86-107.
___ Tulloch, John. "Positioning the SF Audience: *Star Trek*, *Doctor Who* and the Texts of Science Fiction," in: Tulloch, John and Jenkins, Henry, eds. **Science Fiction Audiences: Watching Doctor and Star Trek.** New York: Routledge, 1995. pp.25-49.
___ Tulloch, John. "Throwing a Little Bit of Poison into Future Generations: *Doctor Who* Audiences and Ideology," in: Tulloch, John and Jenkins, Henry, eds. **Science Fiction Audiences: Watching Doctor Who and Star Trek.** New York: Routledge, 1995. pp.67-85.
___ Tulloch, John. "We're Only a Speck in the Ocean: The Fans as Powerless Elite," in: Tulloch, John and Jenkins, Henry, eds. **Science Fiction Audiences: Watching Doctor Who and Star Trek.** New York: Routledge, 1995. pp.144-172.

AUDIOVISUAL
___ Rabkin, Eric S. **Science Fiction: The Literature of the Technological Imagination.** Springfield, VA: The Teaching Company, 1994. 2 videocassettes, 380 minutes.

AUEL, JEAN
___ Wilcox, Clyde. "The Not-So-Failed Feminism of Jean Auel," *Journal of Popular Culture* 28(3): 63-70. Winter 1994.

AUREALIS (MAGAZINE)
___ Ward, Ron B. "Review: *Aurealis*, No. 1," *Science Fiction News* (Australia) No. 113: 2-7. December 1990.

AURORA AWARDS
___ SEE: CANADIAN SF AND FANTASY AWARDS.

AUSTEN, JANE
___ Rowen, Norma. "Reinscribing **Cinderella**: Jane Austen and the Fairy Tale," in: Sanders, Joe, ed. **Functions of the Fantastic.** Westport, CT: Greenwood, 1995. pp.29-36.

AUSTIN, A. J.
___ Klein, Jay K. "Biolog: A. J. Austin," *Analog* 112(1/2): 75. January 1992.

AUSTRALIA
___ "A. Bertram Chandler Award," *Locus* 29(1): 69. July 1992.
___ " 'Oz' Gross in Talks With Cannon About 'Robot' Presale Deal," *Variety* p.30, 121. November 20, 1985.
___ "SF in Australia," *Locus* 28(1): 49. January 1992.
___ "SF in Australia," *Locus* 28(4): 40. April 1992.
___ "SF in Australia," *Locus* 29(1): 39, 71. July 1992.
___ "SF in Australia," *Locus* 30(4): 37. April 1993.
___ "SF in Australia," *Locus* 31(6): 41. December 1993.
___ "SF in Australia," *Locus* 35(2): 45. August 1995.
___ Buckrich, Judith R. "Past, Future and Present: Australian Science Fiction; An Interview with Sean McMullen and Lucy Sussex," *Overland* (Australia) 133: 8-14. Summer 1993.
___ Bull, Geoff. "Morning Comes Whether You Set the Alarm or Not: Science Fiction, a Genre for the Future," *Orana* (Australia) 31(3): 159-169. August 1995.
___ Congreve, Bill. "The Rise of Australian Fantasy," *Aurealis* No. 12: 43-48. 1993.
___ Dawson, W. H. "Forecasts of the Future in Modern Literature," *Science Fiction News* (Australia) No. 91: 2-12. July 1992.
___ Frost, Terry. "Four Days at Thylacon," *Metaphysical Review* No. 22/23: 49-51. November 1995.
___ Frost, Terry. "Four Days in Another Con," *Metaphysical Review* No. 22/23: 45-49. November 1995.
___ Ikin, Van. "Here There Be Monsters: Some Idiosyncrasies of Science Fiction Bibliography in Australia," *Bibliographical Society of Australia nad New Zealand Bulletin* 16(4): 149-153. Fourth Quarter 1992.
___ Mathews, Race. "Whirlaway to *Thrilling Wonder Stories*: Boyhood Reading in Wartime and Postwar Melbourne," *Metaphysical Review* No. 22/23: 5-16. November 1995.
___ McMullen, Sean. "The Golden Age of Australian Science Fiction," *Science Fiction: A Review of Speculative Literature* 12(3): 3-28. 1993(?). (No. 36)

AUSTRALIA (continued)
___ McMullen, Sean. "The Quest for Australian Fantasy," by Sean McMullen and Steven Paulsen. *Aurealis* No. 13: 35-42. 1994.
___ McMullen, Sean. "SF in Australia," by Sean McMullen and Terry Dowling. *Locus* 33(1): 46. July 1994.
___ McMullen, Sean. "SF in Australia," by Sean McMullen and Terry Dowling. *Locus* 34(1) 71. January 1995.
___ Stone, Graham. "Beginnings," *Science Fiction News* (Australia) No. 100: 2-12. November 1986.
___ Stone, Graham. "Chronology of Australian Science Fiction 1848-1992," *Science Fiction News* (Australia) No. 90: 3-10. July 1992.
___ Stone, Graham. "Early Days in Sydney SF Activities," *Science Fiction News* (Australia) No. 61: 6-13. June 1979.
___ Stone, Graham. "Eric North Again," *Science Fiction News* (Australia) No. 117: 10-11. December 1993.
___ Stone, Graham. "Fifty Years of Science Fiction Groups in Australia," *Science Fiction News* (Australia) No. 108: 2-8. November 1989.
___ Stone, Graham. "H. M. Crimp--And More," *Science Fiction News* (Australia) No. 116: 19-21. October 1992.
___ Stone, Graham. "Notes on Australian Science Fiction," *Science Fiction News* (Australia) No. 102: 2-5. March 1987.
___ Stone, Graham. "Notes on Australian Science Fiction," *Science Fiction News* (Australia) No. 105: 2-8. October 1987.
___ Stone, Graham. "Notes on Australian Science Fiction," *Science Fiction News* (Australia) No. 53: 2-5. February 1978.
___ Stone, Graham. "Notes on Australian Science Fiction," *Science Fiction News* (Australia) No. 67: 2-9. January 1983.
___ Stone, Graham. "Notes on Australian Science Fiction," *Science Fiction News* (Australia) No. 92: 2-8. February 1985.
___ Stone, Graham. "Notes on Australian Science Fiction," *Science Fiction News* (Australia) No. 93. 1985. (Not seen; pages not cited.)
___ Stone, Graham. "Notes on Australian Science Fiction," *Science Fiction News* (Australia) No. 93: 2-11. March 1985.
___ Stone, Graham. "Notes on Australian Science Fiction," *Science Fiction News* (Australia) No. 94: 2-11. January 1986.
___ Stone, Graham. "Notes on Australian Science Fiction," *Science Fiction News* (Australia) No. 95: 2-11. February 1986.
___ Stone, Graham. "Notes on Australian Science Fiction," *Science Fiction News* (Australia) No. 96: 5-9. March 1986.
___ Stone, Graham. "Notes on Australian Science Fiction: **Out of the Silence**, by Erle Cox," *Science Fiction News* (Australia) No. 62: 6-7. August 1979.
___ Stone, Graham. "Notes on Australian Science Fiction: **Out of the Silence**, by Erle Cox," *Science Fiction News* (Australia) No. 64: 2-7. 1980.
___ Stone, Graham. "Notes on Australian Science Fiction: **Out of the Silence**, by Erle Cox and J. Filmore Sherry," *Science Fiction News* (Australia) No. 66: 2-8. September 1982.
___ Stone, Graham. "Notes on Australian Science Fiction: **Out of the Silence**, by Erle Cox, Part 1," *Science Fiction News* (Australia) No. 58: 18-20. June 1978.
___ Stone, Graham. "Notes on Australian Science Fiction: **Out of the Silence**, by Erle Cox, Part 2," *Science Fiction News* (Australia) No. 59: 12-16. February 1979.
___ Stone, Graham. "Notes on Australian Science Fiction: **Out of the Silence**, by Erle Cox, Part 3," *Science Fiction News* (Australia) No. 60: 19-20. April 1979.
___ Stone, Graham. "Notes on Australian Science Fiction: *The Comet*," *Science Fiction News* (Australia) No. 54: 2-9. April 1978.
___ Stone, Graham. "Notes on Australian Science Fiction, Or Not, As the Case May Be," *Science Fiction News* (Australia) No. 102: 6-16. March 1987.
___ Stone, Graham. "Notes on Australian Science Fiction, Or Not, As the Case May Be," *Science Fiction News* (Australia) No. 68: 5-12. January 1983.
___ Stone, Graham. "Notes on Australian Science Fiction, Or Not, As the Case May Be," *Science Fiction News* (Australia) No. 92: 8-12. February 1985.
___ Stone, Graham. "Notes on Australian Science Fiction, Or Not, As the Case May Be," *Science Fiction News* (Australia) No. 93: 12. March 1985.
___ Stone, Graham. "Notes on Australian Science Fiction, Or Not, As the Case May Be," *Science Fiction News* (Australia) No. 94: 11-12. January 1986.
___ Stone, Graham. "Notes on Australian Science Fiction, Or Not, As the Case May Be," *Science Fiction News* (Australia) No. 95: 11-12. February 1986.

AUSTRALIA

AUSTRALIA (continued)
___ Stone, Graham. "Notes on Australian Science Fiction, Or Not, As the Case May Be," *Science Fiction News* (Australia) No. 96: 10-12. March 1986.
___ Stone, Graham. "Notes on Australian Science Fiction, Or Not, As the Case May Be, Part 2," *Science Fiction News* (Australia) No. 70: 5-12. April 1983.
___ Stone, Graham. "Notes on Australian Science Fiction, Or Not, As the Case May Be, Part 3," *Science Fiction News* (Australia) No. 71: 5-8. May 1983.
___ Stone, Graham. "Notes on Australian Science Fiction, Or Not, As the Case May Be, Part 4," *Science Fiction News* (Australia) No. 72: 6-8. June 1983.
___ Stone, Graham. "Notes on Australian Science Fiction, Or Not, As the Case May Be, Part 5," *Science Fiction News* (Australia) No. 77: 5-12. June 1983.
___ Stone, Graham. "**Out of the Silence** in Russian--Lost and Found," *Science Fiction News* (Australia) No. 115: 18-20. May 1992.
___ Stone, Graham. "Report on G. C. Bleeck, Australian Science Fiction Writer," *Science Fiction News* (Australia) No. 118: 1-16. 1995.
___ Stone, Graham. "Science Fiction in the *Man* Group of Magazines: A Checklist," *Science Fiction News* (Australia) No. 104: 1-18. May 1987. [Not seen.]
___ Yeoland, Sally. "Sally and John: The Early Years," by Sally Yeoland and John Bangsund. *Metaphysical Review* No. 22/23: 17-44. November 1995.

AUSTRALIAN SCIENCE FICTION ASSOCIATION
___ Stone, Graham. "Fifty Years of Science Fiction Groups in Australia," *Science Fiction News* (Australia) No. 108: 2-8. November 1989.

AUSTRALIAN SF ACHIEVEMENT AWARDS
___ SEE: DITMAR AWARDS.

AVENGERS (TV)
___ Shook, Karl. "Gentleman Avenger," *Starlog* No. 175: 77-81. February 1992.

AVICE, CLAUDE
___ "Avice, Claude (Obituary)," *Locus* 35(4): 70. October 1995.

AVON BOOKS
___ "Jennifer Brehl Joins Avon," *Locus* 35(6): 8, 81. December 1995.

AVON FANTASY READER (MAGAZINE)
___ Frazer, Roger. "A Guide to *The Avon Fantasy Reader*," *Wayfarer II* pp.17-35. n.d.

AVORIAZ FANTASTIC FILM FESTIVAL, 1981
___ "Avoriaz Fest Sked," *Variety* p. 7. December 23, 1981.

AVORIAZ FANTASTIC FILM FESTIVAL, 1982
___ "A Longer (10th) Avoriaz Will Reprise Winner and Repeat Jurors," *Variety* p. 20. November 11, 1981.
___ "**Mad Max 2** Wins Top Prize at Avoriaz Futuristic Film Fest," *Variety* p. 24, 26. February 3, 1982.

AVORIAZ FANTASTIC FILM FESTIVAL, 1983
___ "Avoriaz Fest Sets Fantasy Pic Slate," *Variety* p. 7, 30. December 7, 1983.
___ "Avoriaz Fest Sets Its Feature Slate," *Variety* p. 6. December 29, 1982.
___ "**Dark Crystal** Tops Avoriaz; Hershey, Furie, Coscarelli Wins," *Variety* p. 28. February 2, 1983.

AVORIAZ FANTASTIC FILM FESTIVAL, 1984
___ "Advisories from Avoriaz," *Variety* p. 6. February 1, 1984.
___ "Avoriaz Fest Was Dutch Treat But Otherwise Dullish for Auds; Tie-Ins, Mobile Cinema Irk CIC," *Variety* p. 7, 28. February 1, 1984.
___ "De Niro to Be a Judge at Avoriaz Film Festival," *Variety* p. 5. November 28, 1984.
___ "**Krull, Christine** into Avoriaz Fest," *Variety* p. 28. January 18, 1984.

AVORIAZ FANTASTIC FILM FESTIVAL, 1985
___ "Avoriaz Fantasy Fest Prizes," *Variety* p. 5. January 23, 1985.

AVORIAZ FANTASTIC FILM FESTIVAL, 1985 (continued)
___ "Avoriaz Fantasy Festival Sets Date for 14th Round," *Variety* p.6. January 1, 1986.
___ "Good Weather, Additional Venue Plusses at Avoriaz Fantasy Fest," *Variety* p. 5, 119. January 23, 1985.
___ " 'Lover' Takes Top Prize at Avoriaz," *Variety* p.5. January 22, 1986.

AVORIAZ FANTASTIC FILM FESTIVAL, 1988
___ "***Hidden*** a Winner at Avoriaz Festival of Fantasy Films," *Variety* p. 7, 24. January 27, 1988.

AWARDS
___ "1992 Prix Rosny Aîné Awards," *Locus* 29(5): 5. November 1992
___ "1992 Readercon Small Press Awards," *Locus* 29(5): 5. November 1992
___ "1993 Premio Italia Awards," *Science Fiction Chronicle* 15(8): 10. June 1994.
___ "1993 UPC Science Fiction Award," *Locus* 30(4): 40. April 1993.
___ "1994 European SF Society Awards," *Science Fiction Chronicle* 15(8): 10. June 1994.
___ "*Analog* MAFIA Threatens," *Locus* 33(5): 8. November 1994.
___ "Anne McCaffrey Wins '92, '93 SF Book Club Awards," *Science Fiction Chronicle* 15(7): 4-5. June 1994.
___ "Asimov Award Established," *Locus* 30(5): 8. May 1993.
___ "Eleventh Annual *S. F. Chronicle* Reader's Awards," *Science Fiction Chronicle* 13(11/12): 4. August 1992.
___ "Fine Awards to Bloch, Yarbro," *Locus* 30(4): 9. April 1993.
___ "Four Swords Awards," *Science Fiction Chronicle* 16(6): 5-6. May 1995.
___ "Lambda Literary Award SF/Fantasy Nominations," *Science Fiction Chronicle* 15(5): 5. March 1994.
___ "Octavia E. Butler Gets $295,000 MacArthur Grant," *Locus* 35(1): 8. July 1995.
___ "Readercon Small Press Award Judges Named," *Science Fiction Chronicle* 14(2): 4. November 1992.
___ "Spectrum Competition Open," *Locus* 33(5): 9, 73. November 1994.
___ "Writers/Artists of the Future Awards," *Science Fiction Chronicle* 14(2): 4. November 1992.
___ Clute, John. "On the Arthur C. Clarke Award 1993," *Vector* No. 173: 3-4. June/July 1993.
___ Guarino, Bettyann. "Things You Wanted to Know About the Chesleys: But Were Afraid to Ask," *ASFA Quarterly* 10(1): 6-13. Spring 1992.
___ Guillemette, Aurel. **The Best in Science Fiction: Winners and Nominees of the Major Awards in Science Fiction**. Aldershot, Eng.: Scolar Press, 1993. 379pp.
___ Mallett, Daryl F. **Reginald's Science Fiction and Fantasy Awards: A Comprehensive Guide to the Awards and Their Winners**. Third revised edition, by Daryl F. Mallett and Robert Reginald. San Bernardino, CA: Borgo Press, 1993. 248pp.

AWARDS, 1991
___ "Award Winners in 1991," in: Collins, Robert A. and Latham, Robert, eds. **Science Fiction and Fantasy Book Review Annual 1991**. Westport, CT: Greenwood, 1994. pp.240-242.
___ McGhan, Harlan. "SF Awards, 1991," in: Brown, Charles N. and Contento, William G. **Science Fiction, Fantasy, & Horror: 1991**. Oakland, CA: Locus Press, 1992. pp.457-476.

AWARDS, 1992
___ "1992 *Locus* Awards," *Locus* 28(2): 1, 42-45. August 1992.
___ "1992 Bram Stoker Awards Winners," *Locus* 28(2): 6, 68. August 1992.
___ "1992 Dell Reader's Awards," *Locus* 28(6): 6. June 1992.
___ "Compuserve HOMer Awards, 1992," *Science Fiction Chronicle* 14(9): 4-5. June 1993.
___ "Lambda Gay/Lesbian SF Award Nominations," *Science Fiction Chronicle* 13(9): 4. June 1992.
___ "McCaffrey Wins SFBC Award Again," *Locus* 33(1): 7, 78. July 1994.
___ "Robinson Wins Lambda Award," *Science Fiction Chronicle* 13(10): 8. July/August 1992.

AWARDS, 1993
___ "$1000 Susan Petrey SF Scholarships Awarded," *Science Fiction Chronicle* 14(11): 6-7. August 1993.

BANGSUND, JOHN
___ Yeoland, Sally. "Sally and John: The Early Years," by Sally Yeoland and John Bangsund. *Metaphysical Review* No. 22/23: 17-44. November 1995.

BANKS, IAIN M.
___ "BSFA Awards," *Locus* 34(6): 9. June 1995.
___ James, Martin. "Banks Statement," *Melody Maker* 72(37): 10. September 16, 1995.
___ Melia, Sally-Ann. "SFC Interviews: Iain Banks: 'Very likely impossible, but oh, the elegance...'," *Science Fiction Chronicle* 16(1): 7, 42-44. October 1994.
___ Nicholls, Stan. "Cultural Differences: Iain Banks Interviewed," *Interzone* No. 86: 22-24. August 1994.
___ Nicholls, Stan. "Iain M. Banks Makes Up Good Tunes," in: Nicholls, Stan. **Wordsmiths of Wonder: Fifty Interviews with Writers of the Fantastic**. London: Orbit, 1993. pp.137-142.
___ Nicholls, Stan. "Man of the Culture," *Starlog* No. 209: 76-79. December 1994.

BARBET, PIERRE
___ "Barbet, Pierre (Obituary)," *Locus* 35(5): 78. November 1995.
___ "Barbet, Pierre (Obituary)," *Science Fiction Chronicle* 17(1): 22. October/November 1995

BARCELO, ELIA
___ "Barcelo, Foster Win UPC Awards," *Science Fiction Chronicle* 15(4): 6-7. February 1994.
___ "UPC Award Presented," *Locus* 32(2): 9, 73. February 1994.

BARFIELD, OWEN
___ Diener, Astrid. "An Interview with Owen Barfield: Poetic Diction-- Between Conception and Publication," *Mythlore* 20(4): 14-19. Winter 1995. (Whole No. 78)
___ Duriez, Colin. "Tolkien and the Other Inklings," in: Reynolds, Patricia and GoodKnight, Glen H., eds. **Proceedings of the J. R. R. Tolkien Centenary Conference, Keble College, Oxford, 1992**. Altadena, CA: Mythopoeic Press, 1995. pp.360-363. (*Mythlore* Vol. 21, No. 2, Winter 1996, Whole No. 80)
___ Fulweiler, Howard W. "The Other Missing Link: Owen Barfield and the Scientific Imagination," *Renascence* 46(1): 39-54. Fall 1993.
___ Schenkel, Elmar. "Phantasie und Bewußtseinsgeschichte: Zur Philosophie von Owen Barfields," in: Kranz, Gisbert, ed. **Inklings: Jahrbuch für Literatur und Ästhetik**. 9. Band. Lüdenscheid, Germany: Stier, 1991. pp.111-126. [Not seen.]

BARKER, CLIVE
___ "Clive Barker: Love, Death, and the Whole Damned Thing," *Locus* 34(4): 4-5, 68-70. April 1995.
___ "The Films," in: Brown, Michael, ed. **Pandemonium: Further Explorations into the Worlds of Clive Barker**. Staten Island, NY: Eclise, 1991. pp.55-70.
___ "Pinhead Revisited," *New York (NY) Daily News*. September 10, 1992. in: *NewsBank. Film and Television*. 87:D1. 1992
___ Atkins, Peter. "Other Shelves, Other Shadows: A Conversation With Clive Barker," in: Golden, Christopher, ed. **Cut! Horror Writers on Horror Film**. New York: Berkley, 1992. pp.11-24.
___ Bacal, Simon. "Clive Barker's Triple Threat: *Lord of Illusions*, a Fable of Death and Resurrection," *Sci-Fi Entertainment* 1(5): 28-31. February 1995.
___ Barker, Clive. "At the Threshold: Some Thoughts on the Razorline Imprint," *Comics Buyer's Guide* No. 1024: 26-28, 32, 40. July 2, 1993.
___ Barker, Clive. "Trance of Innocence," *Sight and Sound* 5(12): 59. December 1995.
___ Beeler, Michael. "Clive Barker: Horror Visionary," *Cinefantastique* 26(3): 16-31. April 1995.
___ Beeler, Michael. "Clive Barker Producing Horror in Hollywood," *Cinefantastique* 26(3): 28-29. April 1995.
___ Beeler, Michael. "Clive Barker: Surrealist Artist," *Cinefantastique* 26(3): 18. April 1995.
___ Beeler, Michael. "Clive Barker: The Thief of Always," *Cinefantastique* 26(3): 20-21. April 1995.
___ Beeler, Michael. "Clive Barker's *Hellraiser IV: Bloodline*," *Cinefantastique* 26(2): 10-11, 60. February 1995.
___ Beeler, Michael. "Clive Barker's *Hellraiser IV: Bloodline*," *Cinefantastique* 26(3): 32-38. April 1995.

BARKER, CLIVE (continued)
___ Beeler, Michael. "Clive Barker's *Lord of Illusions*," *Cinefantastique* 26(2): 6-7. February 1995.
___ Beeler, Michael. "Clive Barker's *Lord of Illusions*," *Cinefantastique* 26(3): 23-26. April 1995.
___ Beeler, Michael. "*Lord of Illusions*," *Cinefantastique* 26(5): 12-13. August 1995.
___ Brown, Michael. "Raising Hell With Peter Atkins," in: Brown, Michael, ed. **Pandemonium: Further Explorations into the Worlds of Clive Barker**. Staten Island, NY: Eclise, 1991. pp.27-42.
___ Brown, Michael. "Revelations: Barker on Barker," in: Brown, Michael, ed. **Pandemonium: Further Explorations into the Worlds of Clive Barker**. Staten Island, NY: Eclise, 1991. pp.5-26.
___ Brown, Michael, ed. **Pandemonium: Further Explorations into the Worlds of Clive Barker**. Staten Island, NY: Eclipse Books, 1991. 018, LIV pp.
___ Burns, Craig W. " 'It's That Time of the Month': Representations of the Goddess in the Work of Clive Barker," *Journal of Popular Culture* 27(3): 35-40. Winter 1993.
___ Cowan, Ron. "Man Behind **Candyman**," *Salem (OR) Statesman-Journal*. December 8, 1992. in *NewsBank. Literature*. 1:C6. 1993.
___ Dumars, Denise. "Writer-Director Clive Barker on Launching Harry D'Amour as a Horror Hero Franchise," *Cinefantastique* 27(3): 55-56. December 1995.
___ French, Todd. "Clive Barker's *Candyman 2*," *Cinefantastique* 26(2): 8-9. February 1995.
___ French, Todd. "Clive Barker's *Candyman 2*," *Cinefantastique* 26(3): 40-43. April 1995.
___ Gore, Christian. "The Interview From Hell: Clive Barker," *Film Threat* No. 5: 39-41. August 1992.
___ Hoppenstand, Gary. **Clive Barker's Short Stories: Imagination as Metaphor in the Books of Blood and Other Works**. Jefferson, NC: McFarland, 1994. 231pp.
___ Hoppenstand, Gary. "The Secret Self in Clive Barker's Imaginative Fiction," in: Brown, Michael, ed. **Pandemonium: Further Explorations into the Worlds of Clive Barker**. Staten Island, NY: Eclise, 1991. pp.91-96.
___ Joshi, S. T. "Clive Barker: Sex, Death, and Fantasy," *Studies in Weird Fiction* No. 9: 2-13. Spring 1991.
___ Kronke, David. "Struck by Frightening: Barker Puts Own Spin on Scary Films, Kids' Book," *Los Angeles (CA) Daily News* October 19, 1992 in: *NewsBank. Film and Television*. 99:B12-B13. 1992
___ Leland, John. "Clive Barker: The Horror, the Horror," *Spin* 4: 82-83. December 1988.
___ Leydon, Joe. "The Man and the Myth: *Hellraiser* Creator Clive Barker's Horrific Demon Shows More Than the Average Pinhead," *Houston (TX) Post*. September 10, 1992. in: *NewsBank. Film and Television*. 87:D2-D3, 1992
___ Lipper, Hal. "Hooked on Horror," *St. Petersburg (FL) Times*. September 22, 1992. in: *NewsBank. Film and Television*. 87:C14. 1992
___ Mackenzie, Angus. "Brush Strokes in Blood: An Exclusive Interview with Alan Plent," in: Brown, Michael, ed. **Pandemonium: Further Explorations into the Worlds of Clive Barker**. Staten Island, NY: Eclipse, 1991. pp.43-51.
___ Marino, Frank P. "Sex, Death, and Comics," in: Brown, Michael, ed. **Pandemonium: Further Explorations into the Worlds of Clive Barker**. Staten Island, NY: Eclise, 1991. pp.99-104.
___ Nicholls, Stan. "Clive Barker Pulls Away the Veils," in: Nicholls, Stan. **Wordsmiths of Wonder: Fifty Interviews with Writers of the Fantastic**. London: Orbit, 1993. pp.379-389.
___ Piccoli, Sean. "Lock Up the Kids," *Washington (DC) Times*. December 16, 1992. in *NewsBank. Literature*. 1:C7-C8. 1993.
___ Proulx, Kevin. **Fear to the World: Eleven Voices in a Chorus of Horror**. Mercer Island, WA: Starmont, 1992. 243pp.
___ Shapiro, Marc. "Grand Illusionist," *Starlog* No. 212: 41-44. March 1995.
___ Sullivan, Jack. "Clive Barker and the End of the Horror Boom," *Studies in Weird Fiction* No. 14: 2-3. Winter 1994.
___ Van Hise, James. **Stephen King and Clive Barker: Masters of the Macabre II**. Las Vegas, NV: Pioneer Books, 1992. 144pp.
___ Vince, Nick. "Doug Bradley," in: Brown, Michael, ed. **Pandemonium: Further Explorations into the Worlds of Clive Barker**. Staten Island, NY: Eclise, 1991. pp.72-82.
___ Vince, Nick. "Simon Bamford," in: Brown, Michael, ed. **Pandemonium: Further Explorations into the Worlds of Clive Barker**. Staten Island, NY: Eclise, 1991. pp.87-89.

BARKER, CLIVE

BARKER, CLIVE (continued)
___ Welkos, Robert W. "A Spinner of (Horrific) Tales," *Los Angeles (CA) Times* October 11, 1992 in: *NewsBank. Film and Television.* 99:B9-B11. 1992

___ Wiater, Stanley. "Barker, Clive," in: Wiater, Stanley. **Dark Visions: Conversations with the Masters of the Horror Film.** New York: Avon, 1992. pp.9-18.

___ Winter, Douglas E. "The Great and Secret Show," in: Brown, Michael, ed. **Pandemonium: Further Explorations into the Worlds of Clive Barker.** Staten Island, NY: Eclise, 1991. pp.97-98.

___ Zeigler, Robert. "Fantasy's Timeless Feast in Clive Barker's **The Thief of Always**," *Notes on Contemporary Literature* 24(5): 7-9. November 1994.

___ Ziegler, Robert. "Fantasy's Timeless Feast in Clive Barker's **The Thief of Always**," *Notes on Contemporary Literature* 24(5): 7-9. November 1994.

BARLOW, ROBERT H.
___ Frenschkowski, Marco. " 'Alles is Ufer. Ewig ruft das Meer': Maritime Symbolik in zwei Ersählungen von R. H. Barlow und Ramsey Campbell," *Quarber Merkur* 33(2): 48-59. December 1995. (No. 84)

___ Humphreys, Brian. " 'The Night Ocean' and the Subtleties of Cosmicism," *Lovecraft Studies* No. 30: 14-21. Spring 1994.

BARLOWE, WAYNE
___ Pohl, Frederik. "Extra-Terrestrial Michelangelo," *Science Fiction Age* 1(4): 54-59. May 1993.

BARNES, CHRISTOPHER DANIEL
___ Jankiewicz, Pat. "Chris Barnes, the Spectacular Spiderman," *Starlog* No. 213: 52-55. April 1995.

BARNES, JOHN
___ "Tor Recalls, Reissues Barne's **Kaleidoscope Century**," *Science Fiction Chronicle* 16(7): 5. June/July 1995.

___ Starr, Richard. "SFC Interview: John Barnes," *Science Fiction Chronicle* 16(9): 6, 45-47. August/September 1995.

BARNES, STEVEN
___ Holliday, Liz. "SFC Interviews: Larry Niven and Steven Barnes," *Science Fiction Chronicle* 13(6): 6, 22, 24-25. March 1992.

___ Nicholls, Stan. "Larry Niven and Steve Barnes Lay out a Mental Playground," in: Nicholls, Stan. **Wordsmiths of Wonder: Fifty Interviews with Writers of the Fantastic.** London: Orbit, 1993. pp.192-201.

BARR, MIKE W.
___ Chrissinger, Craig W. "Station Log," *Starlog* No. 198: 52-55. January 1994.

BARRETT, MAJEL
___ Johnson, Kim H. "Universes Lost," *Starlog* No. 210: 27-31, 69. January 1995.

___ Magda, James. "Majel Barrett Nurses a Role," *Star Trek: The Official Fan Club* No. 94: 14-16, 41. February/March 1994.

BARRETT, NEAL, JR.
___ "Neal Barrett, Jr.: Life With Balloons," *Locus* 31(3): 4, 85. September 1993.

BARRIE, CHRIS
___ Nazzaro, Joe. "Working Class Hologram," *Starlog* No. 188: 78-81. March 1993.

BARRIE, J. M.
___ McQuade, Brett. "**Peter Pan**: Disney's Adaptation of J. M. Barrie's Original Work," *Mythlore* 20(1): 5-9. Winter 1994. (Whole No. 75)

___ Wullschläger, Jackie. **Inventing Wonderland: The Lives and Fantasies of Lewis Carroll, Edward Lear, J. M. Barrie, Kenneth Grahame and A. A. Milne.** New York: Free Press, 1995. 228pp.

BARRY R. LEVIN COLLECTORS AWARD, 1991
___ "Fourth Annual Collector's Award," *Locus* 28(5): 40. May 1992.

BARRY, JOHN
___ Soter, Tom. "License to Score," *Starlog* No. 199: 41-45. February 1994.

BASIC INSTINCT (MOTION PICTURE)

BARTH, JOHN
___ Strehle, Susan. **Fiction in the Quantum Universe.** Chapel Hill: University of North Carolina Press, 1992. 282pp.

BARTHELME, DONALD
___ Strehle, Susan. **Fiction in the Quantum Universe.** Chapel Hill: University of North Carolina Press, 1992. 282pp.

BASIC INSTINCT (MOTION PICTURE)
___ "Basically...Calling It Homophobic, Lesbophobic and Misogynist to the Core, Lesbians and Gay Men Engage in Hard Line Tactics Against **Basic Instinct**," *Oakland (CA) Tribune* March 19, 1992 in: *NewsBank. Film and Television.* 28:G8-G10. 1992.

___ Cady, Dick. "Instinct Overdoes the Thrills and Kills," *Indianapolis (IN) Star* March 20, 1992 in: *NewsBank. Film and Television.* 29:B4-B5. 1992.

___ Campbell, Bob. "**Basic Instinct** More Kinky Than Primal Thriller," *Newark (NJ) Star-Ledger* March 20, 1992 in: *NewsBank. Film and Television.* 29:B9-B10. 1992.

___ Corkery, P. J. "**Basic Instinct** Toned Down: Two Scenes Reportedly Cut From Costly, Controversial Film in Effort to Win R Rating," *San Francisco (CA) Examiner.* February 12, 1992 in: *NewsBank. Film and Television.* 17:D2. 1992.

___ Doherty, Thomas. "**Basic Instinct** (Review)," *Cinefantastique* 23(1): 60. August 1992.

___ Doherty, Thomas. "**Basic Instinct**," *Cinefantastique* 23(2/3): 4-5. October 1992.

___ Donnelly, Kathleen. "Out of the Closet, a Basic Backlash Hits the Streets," *San Jose (CA) Mercury News* March 20, 1992 in: *NewsBank. Film and Television.* 28:G13. 1992.

___ Ebert, Roger. "**Basic Instinct** Ends on a Disappointing Note," *Chicago (IL) Sun Times* March 20, 1992 in: *NewsBank. Film and Television.* 29:B2-B3. 1992.

___ Ebert, Roger. "The Same Old Insensitivity Makes Hollywood A Target," *Chicago (IL) Sun Times* March 22, 1992 in: *NewsBank. Film and Television.* 29:A1. 1992.

___ Fernandez, Elizabeth. "S. F. Furor Over Film Offensive to Gays," *San Francisco (CA) Examiner* March 18, 1992 in: *NewsBank. Film and Television.* 28:G11-G12. 1992.

___ Helm, Leslie. "Selling Hollywood in Japan," *Los Angeles (CA) Times.* September 21, 1992. in: *NewsBank. Film and Television.* 87:D6-D7. 1992

___ Hunter, Stephen. "Steamy Scenes Fail to Cover Very Thin Plot," *Baltimore (MD) Sun* March 20, 1992 in: *NewsBank. Film and Television.* 29:B6. 1992.

___ James, Michael. "Protest of **Basic Instinct** Silenced at the Rotunda," *Baltimore (MD) Sun* March 21, 1992 in: *NewsBank. Film and Television.* 29:A4. 1992.

___ Johnson, Barry. "**Basic Instinct**: Fast Cars, Hot Sex Spell Likely Profits, Lesbian Protests," *Portand (OR) The Oregonian.* March 20, 1992 in: *NewsBank. Film and Television.* 29:B11. 1992.

___ Johnson, Barry. "Protestors Will Follow Instinct," *Portland (OR) The Oregonian* March 21, 1992 in: *NewsBank. Film and Television.* 29:A8. 1992.

___ Johnson, Malcolm. "Hot, Heavy Instinct Can't Overcome Lack of Credibility, Humor," *Hartford (CT) Courant* March 20, 1992 in: *NewsBank. Film and Television.* 29:A14-B1. 1992.

___ Kirtzman, Andrew. "Gays Bare Film Plot," *New York (NY) Daily News* March 10, 1992 in: *NewsBank. Film and Television.* 29:A6. 1992.

___ Klinghoffer, David. "Murder Thriller a Muddle," *Washington (DC) Times.* March 20, 1992 in: *NewsBank. Film and Television.* 29:B14. 1992.

___ Kronke, David. "Instinct Delivers Compelling Roles," *Los Angeles (CA) Daily News* March 20, 1992 in: *NewsBank. Film and Television.* 29:A11. 1992.

___ Louie, Andrea. "Activists Say They'll Disrupt Film Showing," *Akron (OH) Beacon Journal* March 18, 1992 in: *NewsBank. Film and Television.* 29:A7. 1992.

___ Mullinax, Gary. "Film Angers Gay Groups," *Wilmington (DE) News Journal* March 19, 1992 in: *NewsBank. Film and Television.* 28:G14. 1992.

___ Sachs, Lloyd. "**Basic Instinct** Debate: Removing the Element of Risk from the Movies," *Chicago (IL) Sun Times* March 22, 1992 in: *NewsBank. Film and Television.* 29:A2-A3. 1992.

___ Schaeffer, Stephen. "An Instinct for Trouble," *Boston (MA) Herald* March 20, 1992 in: *NewsBank. Film and Television.* 29:A5. 1992.

BASIC INSTINCT (MOTION PICTURE) (continued)
___ Smith, Russell. "Gay Groups Tell Hollywood That *Basic Instinct* Is All Bad," *Dallas (TX) Morning News* March 15, 1992 in: *NewsBank. Film and Television*. 29:A9-A10. 1992.
___ Sragow, Michael. "Hype-Point of the Year in Film," *San Francisco (CA) Enquirer* March 20, 1992 in: *NewsBank. Film and Television*. 29: A12-A13. 1992.
___ Strauss, Bob. "*Basic Instinct*: Survival of the Grittiest?," *Los Angeles (CA) Daily News* March 20, 1992 in: *NewsBank. Film and Television*. 28:G6-G7. 1992.
___ Strauss, Bob. "Screenwriter Pleased With Director's Instinct," *Los Angeles (CA) Daily News* March 26, 1992 in: *NewsBank. Film and Television*. 28:G5. 1992.
___ Tobenkin, David. "Box-Office Boycotts: *Basic Instinct* Outcry Unlikely to Hurt Results," *Los Angeles (CA) Daily News* March 19, 1992. in: *NewsBank. Film and Television*. 28:G4. 1992.
___ Verniere, James. "Raw Energy Gives Spark to Weird and Wild Plot of *Basic Instinct*," *Boston (MA) Herald* March 20, 1992 in: *NewsBank. Film and Television*. 29:B7-B8. 1992.
___ Welkos, Robert W. "Director Trims *Basic Instinct* to Get R Rating," *Los Angeles (CA) Times*. February 11, 1992 in: *NewsBank. Film and Television*. 17:C14-D1. 1992.
___ Wuntch, Phillip. "*Basic Instinct* Drama's Cheap Thrills May Be Trashy and Even Campy, but They Do Satisfy," *Dallas (TX) Morning News*. March 20, 1992 in: *NewsBank. Film and Television*. 29:B12-B13. 1992.

BASKET CASE 3: THE PROGENY (MOTION PICTURE)
___ Biodrowski, Steve. "*Basket Case 3: The Progeny* (Review)," *Cinefantastique* 23(1): 60. August 1992.

BATANIDES, ARTHUR
___ Phillips, Mark. "Rocket Wrangler," *Starlog* No. 189: 60-62. April 1993.

BATES, H. E.
___ Hunt, Peter. " 'Coldtongue coldham coldbeef pickled gherkin salad frenchrolls cresssandwige spottedmeat gingerbeer lemonaide sodawater...' Fantastic Foods in the Books of Kenneth Grahame, Jerome K. Jerome, H. E. Bates, and Other Bakers of the Fantasy England," *Journal of the Fantastic in the Arts* 7(1): 5-22. 1996.

BATES, JEANNE
___ Weaver, Tom. "Jeanne Bates," in: Weaver, Tom. **They Fought the Creature Features: Interviews with 23 Classic Horror, Science Fiction and Serial Stars**. Jefferson, NC: McFarland, 1995. pp.50-60.

BATMAN
___ Nash, Jesse W. "Gotham's Dark Knight: The Postmodern Transformation of the Arthurian Mythos," in: Slocum, Sally K., ed. **Popular Arthurian Traditions**. Bowling Green, OH: Popular Press, 1992. pp.36-45.
___ Orr, Philip. "The Anoedipal Mythos of Batman and Catwoman," *Journal of Popular Culture* 27(4): 169-182. Spring 1994.

BATMAN FOREVER (MOTION PICTURE)
___ Biodrowski, Steve. "*Batman Forever* (Review)," *Cinefantastique* 27(3): 57. December 1995.
___ Biodrowski, Steve. "*Batman Forever*," *Cinefantastique* 26(4): 4-5, 61. June 1995.
___ Dargis, Manohla. "*Batman Forever* (Review)," *Sight and Sound* 5(7): 40-41. August 1995.
___ Lowe, Nick. "*Batman Forever* (Review)," *Interzone* No. 100: 35. October 1995.
___ Magid, Ron. "Effects Help Expand Batman's World," *American Cinematographer* 76(7): 45-55. July 1995.
___ Murray, Will. "Riddler of Forever?," *Starlog* No. 218: 27-30. September 1995.
___ Persons, Dan. "*Batman Forever* (Review)," *Cinefantastique* 27(2): 59. November 1995.
___ Pizzello, Stephen. "*Batman Forever* Mines Comic-Book Origins," *American Cinematographer* 76(7): 34-44. July 1995.
___ Roegger, Berthe. "Batman Reborn," *Sci-Fi Entertainment* 2(1): 40-47. June 1995.
___ Shapiro, Marc. "Knightmare Master," *Starlog* No. 216: 40-45. July 1995.

BATMAN FOREVER (MOTION PICTURE) (continued)
___ Shapiro, Marc. "Robin Forever," *Starlog* No. 217: 27-30. August 1995.
___ Vaz, Mark C. "Forever a Knight," *Cinefex* No. 63: 90-113. September 1995.
___ Warren, Bill. "Batman's Batman," *Starlog* No. 215: 50-53, 72. June 1995.
___ Weaver, Tom. "Gotham's Finest," *Starlog* No. 216: 46-49, 63. July 1995.

BATMAN III (MOTION PICTURE)
___ Altman, Mark A. "Dark Knight," *Cinefantastique* 24(6)/25(1): 64-66. February 1994.

BATMAN: MASK OF THE PHANTASM (MOTION PICTURE)
___ Garcia, Bob. "*Batman: Mask of the Phantasm*, the Animated Movie," *Cinefantastique* 24(6)/25(1): 71-74, 125. February 1994.

BATMAN: MASK OF THE PHANTASM (TV)
___ Persons, Dan. "*Batman: Mask of the Phantasm* (Review)," *Cinefantastique* 25(3): 60. June 1994.
___ Sachs, Lloyd. "Animated Batman Fights New Foe in *Mask of the Phantasm* (Review)," *Chicato (IL) Sun Times*. December 27, 1993. in: *NewsBank. Art* 36:G2. 1993.
___ Shulgasser, Barbara. "Batman's Happy Medium (Review)," *San Francisco (CA) Examiner*. December 27, 1993. in: *NewsBank. Art* 36: G3. 1993.
___ Vincent, Mal. "Amateurish Animation Fills Dark and Dull Batman (Review)," *Norfolk (VA) Virginian-Pilot*. December 29, 1993. in: *NewsBank. Art* 36:G1. 1993.

BATMAN (MOTION PICTURE)
___ Garcia, Bob. "*Batman*: Making the Original Movie," *Cinefantastique* 24(6)/25(1): 55-58. February 1994.
___ Lowentrout, Peter. "*Batman* Winging Through the Ruins of the American Baroque," *Extrapolation* 33(1): 25-31. Spring 1992.

BATMAN RETURNS (MOTION PICTURE)
___ Arar, Yardena. "All Ducky on *Batman* Set," *Los Angeles (CA) Daily News*. June 25, 1992. in: *NewsBank. Film and Television*. 67:E11. 1992.
___ Arnold, Gary. "Holy Sequel! Burton Lays an Egg Big as Gotham," *Washington (DC) Times*. June 19, 1992. in: *NewsBank. Film and Television*. 67:F7-F8. 1992.
___ Bernard, Jami. "Bat O' Nine Tales," *New York (NY) Post*. June 19, 1992. in: *NewsBank. Film and Television*. 62:F12-F13. 1992.
___ Bernardo, Susan M. "Recycling Victims and Villains in *Batman Returns*," *Literature/Film Quarterly* 22(1): 16-20. 1994.
___ Blanchard, Jayne M. "Bat Vibes: The Dark Comedy of Gotham City's Conflicted Crusader," *Washington (DC) Times*. June 14, 1992. in: *NewsBank. Film and Television*. 62:D10-D11. 1992.
___ Britton, Bonnie. "A Broody, Moody *Batman*," *Indianapolis (IN) Star*. June 19, 1992. in: *NewsBank. Film and Television*. 62:F6-F7. 1992.
___ Britton, Bonnie. "*Batman Returns* Generates Merchandising Flurry as Sequel of Gimmicky Movie Heads for Local Theaters," *Indianapolis (IN) Star*. June 17, 1992. in: *NewsBank. Film and Television*. 62:D14-E1. 1992.
___ Carter, Reon. "Holy Cow! *Batman* Booty Is Here Again," *Cincinnati (OH) Enquirer*. June 11, 1992. in: *NewsBank. Film and Television*. 62: E2. 1992.
___ Cavender, Charlotte. "Holy Cash Register! Batman Selling Out More Than the Movie," *Charleston (WV) Daily Mail*. June 19 1992. in: *NewsBank. Film and Television*. 62:E9-E10. 1992.
___ D'Orso, Mike. "*Batman* Movie Ain't Kids' Stuff," *Norfolk (VA) Virginian-Pilot*. June 23, 1992. in: *NewsBank. Film and Television*. 67: F3. 1992.
___ Dawidziak, Mark. "Native Clevelander Shaped Mysterious Return of Batman," *Akron (OH) Beacon Journal*. June 18, 1992. in: *NewsBank. Film and Television*. 62:D3-D4. 1992.
___ Doherty, Thomas. "*Batman Returns*," *Cinefantastique* 23(2/3): 8-11. October 1992.
___ Ebert, Roger. "The Batbrain Director," *New York (NY) Daily News*. June 21, 1992. in: *NewsBank. Film and Television*. 62:C13-D1. 1992.
___ Ebert, Roger. "*Batman Returns*...When Latex Meets Leather...," *Chicago (IL) Sun Times*. June 14, 1992. in: *NewsBank. Film and Television*. 62:C11-C12. 1992.

BATMAN RETURNS (MOTION PICTURE) (continued)

___ Ebert, Roger. "Knight of Darkness: Film Noir Foils the Caped Crusader in *Batman Returns*," *Chicago (IL) Sun Times*. June 19, 1992. in: *NewsBank. Film and Television*. 62:F5. 1992.

___ Flamm, Matthew. "*Batman* Tops, But It's Sliding," *New York (NY) Post*. July 7, 1992. in: *NewsBank. Film and Television*. 67:F2. 1992.

___ Hackett, Larry. "Feeding Hollywood's Kitty," *New York (NY) Daily News*. June 23, 1992. in: *NewsBank. Film and Television*. 62:D2. 1992.

___ Henterly, Meghan. "Kenner Banks on the Caped Crusader," *Cincinati (OH) Enquirer* June 22, 1992. in: *NewsBank. Film and Television*. 62:E3-E4. 1992.

___ James, Caryn. "*Batman Returns* With a Capeload of Angst and Ills," *New York Times* Sec. 2, pp.11, 14. June 28, 1992.

___ Johnson, Barry. "The Bat and the Cat," *Portland (OR) The Oregonian*. June 19, 1992. in: *NewsBank. Film and Television*. 62:F14-G1. 1992.

___ Johnson, Malcolm. "Two Plot Lines One Too Many, Spoil Bat Soup," *Hartford (CT) Courant*. June 19, 1992. in: *NewsBank. Film and Television*. 62:F2-F3. 1992.

___ Kronke, David. "He's Back: Is There Cloaked Violence in Caped Crusader's Sequel?," *Los Angeles (CA) Daily News*. June 19, 1992. in: *NewsBank. Film and Television*. 67:E12-E13. 1992.

___ Kronke, David. "Sometimes, It Does Pay to Be Villainous," *Los Angeles (CA) Daily News*. June 19, 1992. in: *NewsBank. Film and Television*. 67:E14-F1. 1992.

___ Krug, Justin. "*Batman Returns* Overrated, but It's Worth Seeing Anyway," *Portland (OR) The Oregonian*. June 24, 1992. in: *NewsBank. Film and Television*. 67:F6. 1992.

___ Lowe, Nick. "*Batman Returns* (Review)," *Interzone* No. 64: 31-32. October 1992.

___ Magid, Ron. "Back to Gotham: *Batman Returns*," *American Cinematographer* 73(7): 34-41. July 1992.

___ Magid, Ron. "Effects Army Mobilizes for Megasequel," *American Cinematographer* 73(7): 42-51. July 1992.

___ McKenna, Chris. "It's Lawman Against Batman," *New York (NY) Post*. June 18, 1992. in: *NewsBank. Film and Television*. 62:E11-E12. 1992.

___ Michael, Kay. "Parents Oppose Kid's Exposure to Sex on Screen," *Charleston (WV) Daily Mail*. July 20, 1992. in: *NewsBank. Film and Television*. 67:F4. 1992.

___ Movshovitz, Howie. "Holy Hit! *Batman Returns* Is a Stunner," *Denver (CO) Post*. June 19, 1992. in: *NewsBank. Film and Television*. 62:F1. 1992.

___ Mullinax, Gary. "Eager Fans Flip for *Batman Returns*," *Wilminton (DE) News-Journal*. June 20, 1992. in: *NewsBank. Film and Television*. 62:C10. 1992.

___ Parks, Louis B. "Meow! She's the Purr-fect Villain," *Houston (TX) Chronicle*. June 14, 1992. in: *NewsBank. Film and Television*. 62:D12-D13. 1992.

___ Pisik, Betsy. "Batmania! Merchandizers get on Bat-Wagon for Gotham City's Giddy Gold Rush," *Washington (DC) Times*. June 17, 1992. in: *NewsBank. Film and Television*. 62:E7-E8. 1992.

___ Ringel, Eleanor. "Pfeiffer's Feline Flair Steals the Spotlight in a Better Balanced and Wittier Sequel," *Atlanta (GA) Journal*. June 19, 1992. in: *NewsBank. Film and Television*. 62:F4. 1992.

___ Rosenberg, Scott. "Batman," *San Francisco (CA) Examiner*. June 19, 1992. in: *NewsBank. Film and Television*. 62:E13-E14. 1992.

___ Shapiro, Marc. "Dark Designs," *Starlog* 179: 27-31. June 1992.

___ Shapiro, Marc. "Dark Knight Director," *Starlog* 180: 40-45, 75. July 1992.

___ Shapiro, Marc. "Dark Knights in Gotham Again," *Starlog* 178: 40-46. May 1992.

___ Shapiro, Marc. "Demon in the Sewers," *Starlog* No. 183: 38-41. October 1992.

___ Shapiro, Marc. "Night of the Cat," *Starlog* No. 183: 42-45. October 1992.

___ Sharkey, Betsy. "Batman's City Gets a New Dose of Urban Blight," *New York Times* Sec. 2, pp.13, 14. June 14, 1992.

___ Spelling, Ian. "Mayor of Gotham," *Starlog* 181: 52-55. August 1992.

___ Spelling, Ian. "Merchant of Menace," *Starlog* No. 183: 46-49. October 1992.

___ Stark, Susan. "Hurt So Good: *Batman*'s Back, in a Spectacular Clash of Twisted Psyches," *Detroit (MI) News*. June 19, 1992. in: *NewsBank. Film and Television*. 62:F10-F11. 1992.

BATMAN RETURNS (MOTION PICTURE) (continued)

___ Strauss, Bob. "Finally, It's A-Bat Time: *Batman Returns*, But Don't Expect Too Much," *Los Angeles (CA) Daily News*. June 20, 1992. in: *NewsBank. Film and Television*. 67:F5. 1992.

___ Taylor, Michael. "Holy Product Tie-In: The Caped Crusader's New Movie Has Retailers All Aflutter," *Dallas (TX) Morning News*. June 13, 1992. in: *NewsBank. Film and Television*. 62:E5-E6. 1992.

___ Vaz, Mark C. "A Knight at the Zoo," *Cinefex* No. 51: 22-69. August 1992.

___ Verniere, James. "Pain and Pleasure in Gotham," *Boston (MA) Herald*. June 19, 1992. in: *NewsBank. Film and Television*. 62:F8-F9. 1992.

___ Warren, Bill. "The Vincent Schiavelli Story," *Starlog* No. 187: 36-39, 70. February 1993.

___ White, Taylor L. "*Batman Returns*," *Cinefantastique* 23(1): 8-11. August 1992.

___ White, Taylor L. "Creating Catwoman," *Cinefantastique* 23(2/3): 10. October 1992.

___ Wolley, John. "Tulsa Comics Artist Explodes into Big Time with *Batman Returns*," *Tulsa (OK) World*. September 4, 1992. in *NewsBank. Fine Arts and Architecture*. 49:A8-A9. 1992.

___ Wuntch, Phillip. "Get Ready for an Exhilarating Trip Back to Gotham," *Dallas (TX) Morning News*. June 19, 1992. in: *NewsBank. Film and Television*. 62:G2. 1992.

___ Wuntch, Phillip. "Walk on the Weird Side: Director Tim Burton Leads the Caped Crusader into a Dark, Sexy New Adventure Involving the Penguin and Catwoman," *Dallas (TX) Morning News*. June 14, 1992. in: *NewsBank. Film and Television*. 62:D5-D9. 1992.

BATMAN (TV)

___ Desris, Joe. "*Batman*: Comic Co-Creator Bill Finger," *Cinefantastique* 24(6)/25(1): 27. February 1994.

___ Desris, Joe. "*Batman*: Comic Creator Bob Kane," *Cinefantastique* 24(6)/25(1): 21. February 1994.

___ Desris, Joe. "*Batman*: Episode Guide," *Cinefantastique* 24(6)/25(1): 8-63. February 1994.

___ Desris, Joe. "*Batman*: From Comics to TV," *Cinefantastique* 24(6)/25(1): 62-63. February 1994.

___ Dreher, Ron. "Fox's Batman Pioneers a Genre: Toon Noir," *Washington (DC) Times*. September 5, 1992. in: *NewsBank. Film and Television*. 87:D8. 1992.

___ Garcia, Bob. "The Animated Adventures: *Batman*," *Cinefantastique* 24(6)/25(1): 68-70, 75-111. February 1994.

___ Garcia, Bob. "*Batman*: Alan Burnett, Script Supervisor," by Bob Garcia and Nancy Garcia. *Cinefantastique* 24(6)/25(1): 84-85. February 1994.

___ Garcia, Bob. "*Batman*: Andrea Romano, Voice Doctor," by Bob Garcia and Nancy Garcia. *Cinefantastique* 24(6)/25(1): 90-93, 125. February 1994.

___ Garcia, Bob. "*Batman*: Batmusic," *Cinefantastique* 24(6)/25(1): 37, 61. February 1994.

___ Garcia, Bob. "*Batman*: Bruce Timm, Series Co-Creator," by Bob Garcia and Nancy Garcia. *Cinefantastique* 24(6)/25(1): 79-80. February 1994.

___ Garcia, Bob. "*Batman*: Building the Batmobile," *Cinefantastique* 24(6)/25(1): 28-31. February 1994.

___ Garcia, Bob. "*Batman*: Catwoman," *Cinefantastique* 24(6)/25(1): 18-19. February 1994.

___ Garcia, Bob. "*Batman*: Composing Music for Animation," by Bob Garcia and Nancy Garcia. *Cinefantastique* 24(6)/25(1): 108-110. February 1994.

___ Garcia, Bob. "*Batman*: Costumes," *Cinefantastique* 24(6)/25(1): 38-40. February 1994.

___ Garcia, Bob. "*Batman*: Directing the Cartoon Action," by Bob Garcia and Nancy Garcia. *Cinefantastique* 24(6)/25(1): 95-97. February 1994.

___ Garcia, Bob. "*Batman*: Episode Guide," by Bob Garcia and Nancy Garcia. *Cinefantastique* 24(6)/25(1): 70-111. February 1994.

___ Garcia, Bob. "*Batman*: Eric Radomski, Series Co-Creator," by Bob Garcia and Nancy Garcia. *Cinefantastique* 24(6)/25(1): 76-77. February 1994.

___ Garcia, Bob. "*Batman*: Lorenzo Semple, Guru of Camp," *Cinefantastique* 24(6)/25(1): 44-45. February 1994.

___ Garcia, Bob. "*Batman*: Paul Dini, Cartoon Criminology," by Bob Garcia and Nancy Garcia. *Cinefantastique* 24(6)/25(1): 87-88. February 1994.

BATMAN (TV) (continued)
___ Garcia, Bob. "*Batman*: Producing the Presentation Reel," by Bob Garcia and Nancy Garcia. *Cinefantastique* 24(6)/25(1): 100-101. February 1994.
___ Garcia, Bob. "*Batman*: Series Creator," *Cinefantastique* 24(6)/25(1): 12-13. February 1994.
___ Garcia, Bob. "*Batman*: The Batcycle," *Cinefantastique* 24(6)/25(1): 60-61. February 1994.
___ Garcia, Bob. "*Batman*: The Joker," *Cinefantastique* 24(6)/25(1): 42. February 1994.
___ Garcia, Bob. "*Batman*: The Origin of Batgirl," *Cinefantastique* 24(6)/25(1): 32-34. February 1994.
___ Garcia, Bob. "*Batman*: The Origin of Egghead," *Cinefantastique* 24(6)/25(1): 52-53. February 1994.
___ Garcia, Bob. "*Batman*: The Penguin," *Cinefantastique* 24(6)/25(1): 10. February 1994.
___ Garcia, Bob. "*Batman*: The Riddler," *Cinefantastique* 24(6)/25(1): 15-16. February 1994.
___ Garcia, Bob. "*Batman*: Things to Come, Second Season," by Bob Garcia and Nancy Garcia. *Cinefantastique* 24(6)/25(1): 103-105. February 1994.
___ Garcia, Bob. "*Batman*: Comic Book Art Direction," *Cinefantastique* 24(6)/25(1): 22-25. February 1994.
___ Garcia, Bob. "*Batman*: Comic Book Makeup," *Cinefantastique* 24(6)/25(1): 48-50. February 1994.
___ Garcia, Bob. "*Batman*," *Cinefantastique* 24(6)/25(1): 8-63. February 1994.

BATTERIES NOT INCLUDED (MOTION PICTURE)
___ "Lower East Side 'Batteries' Shoot Upsets Residents," *Variety* p. 4, 25. August 13, 1986.

BATTLESTAR GALACTICA (COMIC)
___ Johnson, Kim H. "Galactica 1995," *Starlog* No. 220: 36-39. November 1995.

BATTLESTAR GALACTICA (TV)
___ Counts, Kyle. "Life Beyond the Battlestars," *Starlog* No. 196: 32-37. November 1993.
___ Van Hise, James. **Sci Fi TV: From Twilight Zone to Deep Space Nine.** Las Vegas, NV: Pioneer Books, 1993. 160pp. (Reprinted, HarperPrism, 1995. 258pp.)

BAUDINO, GAEL
___ Barrett, David V. "Music and Magic: Gael Baudino Interviewed," *Interzone* No. 90: 19-22. December 1994.

BAUDRILLARD, JEAN
___ Hollinger, Veronica. "Travels in Hyperreality: Jean Baudrillard's **America** and J. G. Ballard's **Hello America**," in: Sanders, Joe, ed. **Functions of the Fantastic.** Westport, CT: Greenwood, 1995. pp.185-194.

BAUM, L. FRANK
___ Bloom, Harold. "L. Frank Baum," in: Bloom, Harold. **Classic Fantasy Writers.** New York: Chelsea House, 1994. pp.1-13.
___ Earle, Neil. **The Wonderful Wizard of Oz in American Popular Culture: Uneasy in Eden.** Lewiston, NY: E. Mellen, 1993. 227pp.
___ Johnson, Michael. "An Ozdyssey in Plato," *Mythlore* 19(4): 22-27. Autumn 1993. (No. 74)

BAXTER, STEPHEN
___ Baxter, Stephen. "The Profession of Science Fiction, 47: Inspiration and Research," *Foundation* No. 63: 56-60. Spring 1995.

BAYLEY, BARRINGTON J.
___ Robertson, Andy. "Barrington J. Bayley: An Annotated Bibliography," *Interzone* No. 71: 52-53. May 1993.

BEACHAM, STEPHANIE
___ Warren, Bill. "Self-Made Woman," *Starlog* No. 202: 27-30, 68. May 1994.

BEAGLE, PETER S.
___ "1994 *Locus* Awards," *Locus* 33(2): 7. August 1994.
___ "Peter S. Beagle: Juggler on a Tightrope," *Locus* 31(1): 4, 63-64. July 1993.

BEAGLE, PETER S. (continued)
___ Bastien, Louis A. **Green Fire and the Legacy of the Dragon: Science Fiction, Fantasy and Cultural Ideology.** Ph.D. Dissertation, University of Connecticut, 1992. 238pp. (DAI-A 54/04. p. 1359. October 1993.)
___ Bittner, Drew. "The Storyteller's Song," *Starlog* No. 206: 54-58. September 1994.
___ Schweitzer, Darrell. "Interview With Peter Beagle," *Marion Zimmer Bradley's Fantasy Magazine* No. 23: 46-49. Spring 1994.

BEALE, DEBORAH
___ "Deborah Beale Quits Millennium; Caroline Oakley Becomes Editor," *Science Fiction Chronicle* 15(2): 4-5. November/December 1993.
___ "New Editor at Millennium," *Locus* 31(6): 6. December 1993.

BEAR, GREG
___ "13th Annual *Science Fiction Chronicle* Reader Awards," *Science Fiction Chronicle* 15(10): 4. September 1994.
___ "1994 Nebula Awards Winners," *Locus* 34(5): 7. May 1995.
___ "Bear, Greg(ory Dale), 1951- ," in: Lesniak, James G., ed. **Contemporary Authors.** Detroit: Gale Research, 1992. New Revision Series, Vol. 35, pp.30-31.
___ "Greg Bear: Planet Mover," *Locus* 33(3): 4-5, 85-86. September 1994.
___ "Nebula Award Winners," *Science Fiction Chronicle* 16(6): 4. May 1995.
___ "Other Awards at ConAdian," *Science Fiction Chronicle* 15(10): 5. September 1994.
___ Hatfield, Len. "Getting a Kick Out of Chaos: 'Fortunate Failure' in Greg Bear's Future Histories," in: Ruddick, Nicholas, ed. **State of the Fantastic.** Westport, CT: Greenwood, 1992. pp.133-140.
___ Hatfield, Len. "Growing Up in SF: A Profile of Greg Bear," in: Collins, Robert A. and Latham, Robert, eds. **Science Fiction and Fantasy Book Review Annual 1991.** Westport, CT: Greenwood, 1994. pp.36-48. (pp.44-48: Telephone interview with Bear, 1991.)
___ Hatfield, Len. "Legitimate Sequels: Character Structures and the Subject in Greg Bear's Sequence Novels," in: Morse, Donald E., ed. **The Celebration of the Fantastic.** Westport, CT: Greenwood, 1992. pp.237-250.
___ Nicholls, Stan. "Greg Bear Exposes the Dark Underside," in: Nicholls, Stan. **Wordsmiths of Wonder: Fifty Interviews with Writers of the Fantastic.** London: Orbit, 1993. pp.211-217.
___ Steele, Colin. "The Limits of Genre: Tad Williams and Greg Bear Interviewed," *SF Commentary* No. 71/72: 25-27. April 1992.
___ Vorda, Allan. "The Forging of Science Fiction: An Interview with Greg Bear," in: Vorda, Allan, ed. **Face to Face: Interviews with Contemporary Novelists.** Houston, TX: Rice University Press, 1993. pp.127-151.

BEARDSLEY, AUBREY VINCENT
___ Hughes, Linda K. "Illusion and Relation: Merlin as Image of the Artist in Tennyson, Doré, Burene-Jones, and Beardsley," in: Watson, Jeanie and Fries, Marueen, eds. **The Figure of Merlin in the Nineteenth and Twentieth Centuries.** Lewiston, NY: Mellen, 1989. pp.1-33.

BEASON, DOUG
___ Klein, Jay K. "Biolog: Doug Beason," *Analog* 112(14): 79. December 1992.

BEAST FROM 20,000 FATHOMS (MOTION PICTURE)
___ Weaver, Tom. "Eugene Lourie," in: Weaver, Tom. **They Fought the Creature Features: Interviews with 23 Classic Horror, Science Fiction and Serial Stars.** Jefferson, NC: McFarland, 1995. pp.201-210.

BEATTIE, GEORGE B.
___ Stone, Graham. "Notes on Australian Science Fiction," *Science Fiction News* (Australia) No. 67: 2-9. January 1983.

BEAUMONT, CHARLES
___ Dziemianowicz, Stefan. " 'Dark Music': The Macabre Fiction of Charles Beaumont," *Studies in Weird Fiction* No. 13: 28-34. Summer 1993. [Not seen.]

BEAUTY AND THE BEAST (COMIC)
___ Bittner, Drew. "Comics of the Beast," *Starlog* No. 188: 32-37, 67. March 1993.

BEAUTY AND THE BEAST (MOTION PICTURE)

BEAUTY AND THE BEAST (MOTION PICTURE)

___ "***Beauty and the Beast*** (Review)," *Cinefantastique* 22(5): 60. April 1992.

___ Teitelbaum, Sheldon. "***Beauty and the Beast***: The Story Behind the Making of the Fairy Tale," *Cinefantastique* 22(4): 42-43. February 1992.

BEAUTY AND THE BEAST (TV)

___ Erb, Cynthia. "Another World or the World of an Other? The Space of Romance in Recent Versions of ***Beauty and the Beast***," *Cinema Journal* 34(4): 50-70. Summer 1995.

___ Gross, Edward. "Fables of the Beast," *Starlog* 179: 62-65, 86. June 1992.

___ O'Brien, Dennis. "Shoring Fragments: How CBS's ***Beauty and the Beast*** Adapts Consensus Reality to Shape Its Magical World," in: Sanders, Joe, ed. **Functions of the Fantastic**. Westport, CT: Greenwood, 1995. pp.37-46.

___ Shapiro, Marc. "The Savage Beast," by Marc Shapiro and Edward Gross. in: McDonnell, David, ed. **Starlog's Science Fiction Heroes and Heroines**. New York: Crescent Books, 1995. pp.66-69.

___ Van Hise, James. **Sci Fi TV: From Twilight Zone to Deep Space Nine**. Las Vegas, NV: Pioneer Books, 1993. 160pp. (Reprinted, HarperPrism, 1995. 258pp.)

___ Vitaris, Paula. "Befriending ***Beauty and the Beast***," *Starlog* No. 212: 54-57, 69. March 1995.

BECKETT, SAMUEL

___ Olsen, Lance. "Beckett and the Horrific," in: Murphy, Patrick D., ed. **Staging the Impossible: The Fantastic Mode in Modern Drama**. Westport, CT: Greenwood, 1992. pp.116-126.

BECKFORD, WILLIAM

___ Bloom, Harold. "William Beckford," in: Bloom, Harold. **Classic Fantasy Writers**. New York: Chelsea House, 1994. pp.14-26.

BÉCQUER, G. A.

___ Marcone, Jorge. "La tradición oral y el cuento fantástico en 'La cruz del diablo' de G. A. Bécquer," *Mester* (UCLA) 19(2): 47-62. Fall 1990. [Not seen.]

___ Sebold, Russell P. **Bécquer en sus narraciones fantásticas**. Madrid: Taurus, 1989. 217pp.

BEEMAN, GREG

___ Warren, Bill. "Spengo's Greatest Director," *Starlog* 177: 63-66. April 1992.

BEETLEJUICE (MOTION PICTURE)

___ "***Beetlejuice*** (Review)," *Variety* p. 12. March 30, 1988.

BEHR, IRA STEPHEN

___ Altman, Mark A. "***Star Trek: Deep Space Nine***: Scripting the Adventures," *Cinefantastique* 23(6): 40-42. April 1993.

BELGIUM

___ Vanhecke, Johan. "Tolkien in Dutch: A Study of the Reception of Tolkien's Work in Belgium and the Netherlands," *Mythlore* 18(4): 53-60. Autumn 1992. (No. 70)

BELGIUM ROYAL OPERA

___ "Brussels Cancels Verne 'Trip to the Moon'; No Unity of Components--Huisman," *Variety* p. 30. February 4, 1970.

BELL, ERIC TEMPLE

___ Reid, Constance. **The Search for E. T. Bell, Also Known as John Taine**. Washington, DC: Mathematical Association of America, Aug. 1993. 372pp.

___ Robillard, Douglas. "Eric Temple Bell and John Taine," *Fantasy Commentator* 8(1/2): 17-21, 134. Winter 1993/1994. (Whole No. 45/46.)

BELLAIRS, JOHN

___ "Strickland Finishing Bellairs Books," *Locus* 29(3): 7. September 1992.

BELLAMY, EDWARD

___ Auerbach, Jonathan. "The Nation Organized: Utopian Importance in Edward Bellamy's **Looking Backward**," *American Literary History* 6(1): 24-47. Spring 1994.

BELLAMY, EDWARD (continued)

___ Geoghegan, Vincent. "The Utopian Past: Memory and History in Edward Bellamy's **Looking Backward** and William Morris's **News From Nowhere**," *Utopian Studies* 3(2): 75-90. 1992.

___ Hansen, Olaf. "Edward Bellamy: **Looking Backward: 2000-1887** (1888)," in: Heuermann, Hartmut and Lange, Bernd-Peter, eds. **Die Utopie in der angloamerikanischen Literatur: Interpretationen**. Düsseldorf: Bagel, 1984. pp.103-119.

___ Levitas, Ruth. "Who Holds the Hose: Domestic Labour in the Work of Bellamy, Gilman and Morris," *Utopian Studies* 6(1): 65-84. 1995.

___ Marion, David E. "Using Fiction to Expose a Fundamental Theme in American Public Policy," *Teaching Political Science* 15(2): 44-49. Winter 1988.

___ McClay, Wilfred M. "Reappraisal: Edward Bellamy and the Politics of Meaning," *American Scholar* 64(2): 264-271. Spring 1995.

___ Murdoch, Norman H. "Rose Culture and Social Reform: Edward Bellamy's **Looking Backward** (1888) and William Booth's **Darkest England and the Way Out** (1890)," *Utopian Studies* 3(2): 91-101. 1992.

___ Roemer, Kenneth M. "Domestic Nowheres and Androgynous Voices: The Sentimental Orgins of **Looking Backward**," in: Saccaro Del Buffa, Giuseppa and Lewis, Arthur O., eds. **Utopia e Modernita: Teorie e prassi utopiche nell'eta moderna e postmoderna**. Rome: Gangemi Editore, 1989. pp.641-654.

___ Segal, Howard P. **Future Imperfect: The Mixed Blessings of Technology in America**. Amherst: University of Massachusetts Press, 1994. 245pp.

___ Zauderer, Naomi B. "Charlotte Perkins Gilman's **Moving the Mountain**: A Response to **Looking Backward**," *Utopian Studies* 3(1): 53-69. 1992.

BELLAMY, RALPH

___ Niderost, Eric. "Always the Other Man," *Starlog* No. 176: 64-67. March 1992.

BENEDEK, TOM

___ Rabkin, William. "***Cocoon*** (1985): Interview with Tom Benedek," in: Goldberg, Lee et al. **Science Fiction Filmmaking in the 1980s**. Jefferson, NC: McFarland, 1995. pp.73-78.

BENEDICT, BILLY

___ Weaver, Tom. "Billy Benedict," in: Weaver, Tom. **They Fought the Creature Features: Interviews with 23 Classic Horror, Science Fiction and Serial Stars**. Jefferson, NC: McFarland, 1995. pp.61-72.

___ Weaver, Tom. "Captain Marvel's Pal," *Starlog* No. 199: 62-65, 74. February 1994.

BENET, STEPHEN VINCENT

___ Ursini, James. **More Things Than Are Dreamt Of: Masterpieces of Supernatural Horror, From Mary Shelley to Stephen King, in Literature and Film**, by James Ursini and Alain Silver. New York: Limelight, 1994. 226pp.

BENFORD, GREGORY

___ "Gregory Benford: Cross-Talk," *Locus* 31(5): 4, 68. November 1993.

___ Benford, Gregory. "Imagining the Real," *Magazine of Fantasy and Science Fiction* 84(1): 47-59. January 1993.

___ Benford, Gregory. "Time and **Timescape**," *Science Fiction Studies* 20(2): 184-190. July 1993.

___ Forshaw, Barry. "Freighting It In: Gregory Benford Interviewed," *Interzone* No. 102: 27-29. December 1995.

___ McLellan, Dennis. "The Forward Thinker: Gregory Benford," *Los Angeles (CA) Times* p.E1. September 25, 1994.

___ McLellan, Dennis. "Science Fiction, Full of Fact: Surfer-Astrophysicist Explains the Galaxy for the Rest of Us," *San Francisco (CA) Chronicle* October 30, 1994. (Cited from the Internet Edition.)

___ Preuss, Paul. "Loopholes in the Net: Ruminations on Hard SF; **Furious Gulf** by Gregory Benford," *New York Review of Science Fiction* No. 75: 1, 10-11. November 1994.

BENJAMIN, WALTER

___ Stewart, Elizabeth. **Destroying Angels: Messianic Rhetoric in Benjamin, Scholem, Psychoanalysis and Science Fiction**. Ph.D. Dissertation, New York University, 1994. 586pp. (DAI-A 55/09, p. 2820. March 1995.)

BENNETT, BRUCE
___ Ogden, D. Peter. "Herman Brix (a.k.a.) Bruce Bennett," *Filmfax* No. 32: 34-40. April/May 1992.

BENNETT, CHARLES
___ "Bennett, Charles (Obituary)," *Science Fiction Chronicle* 16(8): 21. July/August 1995
___ "Bennett, Charles, 1899-1995 (Obituary)," *Starlog* No. 220: 16-17. November 1995.
___ Weaver, Tom. "Charles Bennett: Interview," in: Weaver, Tom, ed. **Attack of the Monster Movie Makers: Interviews with 20 Genre Giants.** Jefferson, NC: McFarland, 1994. pp.17-30
___ Weaver, Tom. "The Oldest Living Screenwriter Explains All," *Starlog* No. 193: 57-62, 71. August 1993.

BENNETT, GREGORY R.
___ Klein, Jay K. "Biolog: Gregory R. Bennett," *Analog* 114(5): 115, 160. April 1994.

BENNETT, HARVE
___ Donlon, Brian. "Harve Bennett Makes 'Trax' With Sci-Fi Trek to the Past," *USA Today* Sec. D, p. 3. March 30, 1993.
___ Lofficier, Randy. "**Star Trek Movies** (1980-1988): Interviews with Jack Sowards, Nicholas Mayer, Harve Bennett; Leonard Nimoy and William Shatner," by Randy Lofficier and Jean-Marc Lofficier. in: Goldberg, Lee et al. **Science Fiction Filmmaking in the 1980s.** Jefferson, NC: McFarland, 1995. pp.189-236.
___ Shapiro, Marc. "School's Out," *Starlog* No. 189: 38-39, 68. April 1993.
___ Shapiro, Marc. "Time Keeper," *Starlog* No. 188: 27-31. March 1993.

BENNETT, NIGEL
___ Bloch-Hansen, Peter. "Unlife to Live," *Starlog* No. 215: 54-57. June 1995.

BENSON, ARTHUR CHRISTOPHER
___ Ashley, Mike. "Blood Brothers: The Supernatural Fiction of A. C., R. H., and E. F. Benson," in: Schweitzer, Darrell, ed. **Discovering Classic Horror Fiction I.** Mercer Island, WA: Starmont, 1992. pp.100-113.

BENSON, EDWARD FREDERICK
___ Ashley, Mike. "Blood Brothers: The Supernatural Fiction of A. C., R. H., and E. F. Benson," in: Schweitzer, Darrell, ed. **Discovering Classic Horror Fiction I.** Mercer Island, WA: Starmont, 1992. pp.100-113.
___ Bloom, Harold. "E. F. Benson," in: Bloom, Harold. **Modern Horror Writers.** New York: Chelsea House, 1995. pp.16-31.

BENSON, ROBERT HUGH
___ Ashley, Mike. "Blood Brothers: The Supernatural Fiction of A. C., R. H., and E. F. Benson," in: Schweitzer, Darrell, ed. **Discovering Classic Horror Fiction I.** Mercer Island, WA: Starmont, 1992. pp.100-113.

BENTCLIFFE, ERIC
___ "Bentcliffe, Eric (Obituary)," *Locus* 29(1): 67. July 1992.
___ "Bentcliffe, Eric (Obituary)," *Science Fiction Chronicle* 13(7): 14, 16. April 1992.
___ "Bentcliffe, Eric (Obituary)," *Science Fiction Chronicle* 13(8): 14, 16. May 1992.

BENTHAKE, BILL
___ "Benthake, Bill (Obituary)," *Science Fiction Chronicle* 16(2): 18. November/December 1994.

BEOWULF
___ Beach, Sarah. "Loss and Recompense: Responsibilities in **Beowulf**," *Mythlore* 18(2): 55-65. Spring 1992. (No. 68)

BERGER, BARBARA
___ Evans, Gwenth. "Harps and Harpers in Contemporary Fantasy," *Lion and the Unicorn* 16(2): 199-209. December 1992.

BERGER, THOMAS
___ Barr, Marleen S. **Lost in Space: Probing Feminist Science Fiction and Beyond.** Chapel Hill, NC: University of North Carolina Press, 1993. 231pp.

BERGER, THOMAS (continued)
___ Chapman, Edgar L. " 'Seeing' Invisibility: Or Invisibility as Metaphor in Thomas Berger's **Being Invisible**," *Journal of the Fantastic in the Arts* 4(2): 65-93. 1992. (No. 14)
___ Herman, Harold J. "Teaching White, Stewart, and Berger," in: Fries, Maureen and Watson, Jeanie, eds. **Approaches to the Teaching of the Arthurian Tradition.** New York: Modern Language Association, 1992. pp.113-117.
___ MacRae, Suzanne H. "Berger's Mythical **Arthur Rex**," in: Slocum, Sally K., ed. **Popular Arthurian Traditions.** Bowling Green, OH: Popular Press, 1992. pp.85-95.
___ Thompson, Raymond H. "The Comic Sage: Merlin in Thomas Berger's **Arthur Rex**," in: Watson, Jeanie and Fries, Maruuen, eds. **The Figure of Merlin in the Nineteenth and Twentieth Centuries.** Lewiston, NY: Mellen, 1989. pp.143-153.

BERKEY, JOHN
___ Haldeman, Joe. "Architect of Space," *Science Fiction Age* 2(6): 78-83. September 1994.

BERMAN, RICK
___ Altman, Mark A. "**Star Trek**: Rick Berman, Trek's New Great Bird," *Cinefantastique* 23(2/3): 36-37. October 1992.
___ Altman, Mark A. "**Star Trek: Deep Space Nine**: Rick Berman, Trek's Major Domo," *Cinefantastique* 23(6): 18. April 1993.
___ Altman, Mark A. "**Star Trek: The Next Generation**: Rick Berman, Keeper of the Flame," *Cinefantastique* 24(3/4): 20-21. October 1993.
___ Logan, Michael. "*TV Guide* Interview: Rick Berman," *TV Guide* 41(30): 10-13. July 24, 1993.
___ Madsen, Dan. "Rick Berman: Interview," *Star Trek: The Official Fan Club Magazine* No. 91: 2-6. May/June 1993.

BERTHA, ZOLTAN
___ Bertha, Csilla. "The Symbolic Versus the Fantastic: The Example of a Hungarian Painter," *Journal of the Fantastic in the Arts* 6(4): 295-311. 1995.

BESHER, ALEXANDER
___ " 'Virtual' Quake Echoes Reality," *Locus* 34(2): 8. February 1995.

BEST BOOKS LIST, INTERNET
___ "Internet Top 100 SF/Fantasy Titles," *Locus* 35(2): 8. August 1995.

BESTER, ALFRED
___ "The Priess/Bester Connection," *Locus* 31(4): 6, 70. October 1993.
___ Bloom, Harold. "Alfred Bester," in: Bloom, Harold, ed. **Science Fiction Writers of the Golden Age.** New York: Chelsea House, 1995. pp.47-62.
___ Haupt, Arthur. "Vanishing Stars: A Retrospective Look at Bester's **The Stars My Destination**," *Quantum* No. 42: 17-19. Summer/Fall 1992.
___ Kelleghan, Fiona. "Hell's My Destination: Imprisonment in the Works of Alfred Bester," *Science Fiction Studies* 21(3): 351-364. November 1994.
___ Langford, David. "The Editor My Destination," *Quantum* No. 43/44: 13, 15. Spring/Summer 1993.
___ Schwartz, Julius. "The Bester Years of My Life: Memoirs of a Time Traveller, Part 2," *Amazing Stories* 68(4): 55-59. July 1993.
___ Wendell, Carolyn H. "Alfred Bester," in: Bruccoli, Matthew J., ed. **Facts on File Bibliography of American Fiction 1919-1988.** New York: Facts on File, 1991. pp.89-90.

BESWICK, DOUG
___ Gilmer, Nance G. "Profile: Doug Beswick," *Cinefex* No. 53: 78. February 1993.

BEWITCHED (TV)
___ "Liz Montgomery Sealed by ABC; Foiling CBS Bid," *Variety* p. 24. December 24, 1969.

BEY, TUHAN
___ Weaver, Tom. "Tuhan Bey," in: Weaver, Tom. **They Fought the Creature Features: Interviews with 23 Classic Horror, Science Fiction and Serial Stars.** Jefferson, NC: McFarland, 1995. pp.73-83.

BEYOND BEDLAM (MOTION PICTURE)

BEYOND BEDLAM (MOTION PICTURE)
___ Lowe, Nick. "*Beyond Bedlam* (Review)," *Interzone* No. 85: 39-40. July 1994.

BIBLIOGRAPHY
___ "Bibliografía sobre la literatura fantástica en Iberoamérica," *Mester* (UCLA) 19(2): 145-164. Fall 1990.
___ "Canadian Fiction: 1991 and 1992," *Sol Rising* No. 9: 4-8. April 1993. (Newsletter of the Merril Collection, Toronto Public Library.)
___ Aldiss, Margaret. **The Work of Brian W. Aldiss: An Annotated Bibliography & Guide**. San Bernardino, CA: Borgo Press, 1992. 359pp.
___ Ashley, Mike. **The Work of William F. Temple: An Annotated Bibliography and Guide**. San Bernardino, CA: Borgo Press, 1994. 112pp.
___ Beghtol, Clare. **The Classification of Fiction: The Development of a System Based on Theoretical Principles**. Metuchen, NJ: Scarecrow, 1994. 365pp.
___ Bennett, James R. **Hiroshima, Nagazaki, and the Bomb: A Bibliography of Literature and the Arts**, by James R. Bennett and Karen Clark. Pullman, WA: International Society for the Study of Nuclear Texts and Contexts, 1989. 24pp. (Monograph Series, No. 1)
___ Bergen, James A., Jr. **Price and Reference Guide to Books Written by Edgar Rice Burroughs**. Beaverton, OR: Golden Lion Books, 1991. 214pp.
___ Biles, Jack I. "William Golding: Bibliography of Primary and Secondary Sources," in: Biles, Jack I. and Evans, Robert O., eds. **William Golding: Some Critical Considerations**. Lexington, KY: University Press of Kentucky, 1978. pp.237-280.
___ Boivin, Aurelien. **Bibliographie analytique de la science fiction et du fantastique Quebecois: 1960-1985**, by Aurelien Boivin, Maurice Emond and Michel Lord. Quebec: Nuit blanche editeur, 1992. 577pp.
___ Breuer, Hans-Peter. **Samuel Butler: An Annotated Bibliography of Writings About Him**. New York: Garland, 1990. 497pp.
___ Brown, Charles N. **Science Fiction, Fantasy, & Horror: 1991**, by Charles N. Brown and William G. Contento. Oakland, CA: Locus Press, 1992. 482pp.
___ Bruccoli, Matthew J., ed. **Facts on File Bibliography of American Fiction 1919-1988**, ed. by Matthew J. Bruccoli and Judith S. Baughman. New York: Facts on File, 1991. 2 v.
___ Burgess, Michael. **The Work of Robert Reginald: An Annotated Bibliography and Guide** 2nd ed., revised and enlarged. San Bernardino, CA: Borgo Press, 1992. 176pp.
___ Christopher, Joe R. "An Inklings Bibliography (45)," by Joe R. Christopher and Wayne G. Hammond. *Mythlore* 18(2): 28-33, 39-40. Spring 1992. (No. 68)
___ Christopher, Joe R. "An Inklings Bibliography (46)," by Joe R. Christopher and Wayne G. Hammond. *Mythlore* 18(3): 49-53. Summer 1992. (No. 69)
___ Christopher, Joe R. "An Inklings Bibliography (47)," by Joe R. Christopher and Wayne G. Hammond. *Mythlore* 18(4): 49-52. Autumn 1992. (No. 70)
___ Christopher, Joe R. "An Inklings Bibliography (48)," by Joe R. Christopher and Wayne G. Hammond. *Mythlore* 19(1): 56-64. Winter 1993. (No. 71)
___ Christopher, Joe R. "An Inklings Bibliography (49)," by Joe R. Christopher and Wayne G. Hammond. *Mythlore* 19(2): 61-65. Spring 1993. (No. 72)
___ Christopher, Joe R. "An Inklings Bibliography (50) (e.g. 51)," by Joe R. Christopher and Wayne G. Hammond. *Mythlore* 19(4): 60-65. Autumn 1993. (No. 74)
___ Christopher, Joe R. "An Inklings Bibliography (50)," by Joe R. Christopher and Wayne G. Hammond. *Mythlore* 19(3): 59-65. Summer 1993. (No. 73)
___ Christopher, Joe R. "An Inklings Bibliography (51)," by Joe R. Christopher and Wayne G. Hammond. *Mythlore* 20(1): 59-62. Winter 1994. (Whole No. 75)
___ Christopher, Joe R. "An Inklings Bibliography (52)," by Joe R. Christopher and Wayne G. Hammond. *Mythlore* 20(2): 32-34. Spring 1994. (Whole No. 76)
___ Christopher, Joe R. "An Inklings Bibliography (54)," by Joe R. Christopher and Wayne G. Hammond. *Mythlore* 20(4): 61-65. Winter 1995. (Whole No. 78)
___ Clarke, Boden. **The Work of Katherine Kurtz: An Annotated Bibliography & Guide**, by Boden Clarke and Mary A. Burgess. San Bernardino, CA: Borgo Press, 1993. 128pp.
___ Cox, Greg. **The Transylvanian Library: A Consumer's Guide to Vampire Fiction**. San Bernardino, CA: Borgo Press, 1993. 264pp.

BIBLIOGRAPHY (continued)
___ Crawford, Gary W. **J. Sheridan Le Fanu: A Bio-Bibliography**. Westport, CT: Greenwood, 1995. 155pp.
___ Day, Bradford M. **The Checklist of Fantastic Literature in Paperbound Books**. Revised and enlarged edition. Hillsville, VA: Bradford M. Day, 1994. 890pp.
___ Erlich, Richard D. **Clockworks: A Multimedia Bibliography of Works Useful for the Study of the Human/Machine Interface in SF**. Westport, CT: Greenwood Press, 1993. 344pp.
___ Frank, Frederick S. **Guide to the Gothic II: An Annotated Bibliography of Criticism, 1983-1993**. Lanham, MD: Scarecrow, 1995. 542pp.
___ Green, Scott E. **Isaac Asimov: An Annotated Bibliography of the Asimov Collection at Boston University**. Westport, CT: Greenwood Press, 1995. 146pp.
___ Greenberg, Mark L. "Selected Bibliography of Works Devoted to Literature and Technology," by Mark L. Greenberg and Lance Schachterle. in: Greenberg, Mark L. and Schachterle, Lance, eds. **Literature and Technology**. Bethlehem, PA: Lehigh University Press, 1992. pp.310-317.
___ Hall, Hal W. **Science Fiction and Fantasy Book Review Index, Volume 18, 1987**. San Bernardino, CA: Borgo Press, 1992. 70pp.
___ Hall, Hal W. **Science Fiction and Fantasy Book Review Index, Volume 19, 1988**. Bryan, TX: SFFBRI, 1992. 87pp.; San Bernardino, CA: Borgo Press, 1992. 85pp.
___ Hall, Hal W. **Science Fiction and Fantasy Book Review Index, Volume 20, 1989**. San Bernardino, CA: Borgo Press, 1993. 90pp.; Bryan, TX: SFFBRI, 1993. 90pp.
___ Hall, Hal W. **Science Fiction and Fantasy Book Review Index, Volume 21, 1990**. Bryan, TX: SFFBRI, 1994. 105pp.
___ Hall, Hal W. **Science Fiction and Fantasy Reference Index, 1985-1991: An International Author and Subject Index to History and Criticism**. Englewood, CO: Libraries Unlimited, 1993. 677pp.
___ Hall, Hal W. **Science Fiction and Fantasy Research Index, Volume 10**. San Bernardino, CA: Borgo Press, 1994. 153pp.
___ Hall, Hal W. **Science Fiction and Fantasy Research Index, Volume 9**. San Bernardino, CA: Borgo Press, 1992. 97pp.
___ Hammond, Wayne G. **J. R. R. Tolkien: A Descriptive Bibliography**, by Wayne G. Hammond and Douglas A. Anderson. Winchester, UK: St. Paul's Bibliographies, 1992. 434pp.; New Castle, DE: Oak Knoll Books, 1992. 434pp.
___ Harbottle, Philip. **British Science Fiction Paperbacks and Magazines, 1949-1956: An Annotated Bibliograhy and Guide**, by Philip Harbottle and Stephen Holland. San Bernardino, CA: Borgo Press, 1994. 232pp.
___ Haschak, Paul G. **Utopian/Dystopian Literature: A Bibliography of Literary Criticism**. Metuchen, NJ: Scarecrow, 1994. 370pp.
___ Hauck, Dennis W. **William Shatner: A Bio-Bibliography**. Westport, CT.: Greenwood Press, 1994. 324pp.
___ Hewett, Jerry. **The Work of Jack Vance: An Annotated Bibliography and Guide**, by Jerry Hewett and Daryl F. Mallett. San Bernardino, CA: Borgo Press, 1994. 293pp. (Issued simultaneously by Underwood-Miller.)
___ Holland, Stephen. **An Index to Mellifont Press: A Working Bibliography**. Leeds, Eng: Galactic Central, 1995. 76pp.
___ Jackson, Leslie. **65 Years in Science Fiction, 1928-1993: A Jack Williamson Bibliography**. Portales: NM: Golden Library, Eastern New Mexico University, 1993. 35pp.
___ Joshi, S. T. **Lord Dunsany: A Bibliography**, by S. T. Joshi and Darrell Schweitzer. Metuchen, NJ: Scarecrow, 1993. 389pp.
___ Knight, Damon. **An R. A. Lafferty Checklist**. New edition. Polk City, IA: Drumm, 1991. 28pp.
___ Kononenko, V. O. **Neznani svity fantastyky: rekomendattsiinyi bibliohrafichnyi pokazhchyk**, by V. O. Kononenko and V. M. Loi. Kyiv: Derzhavan biblioteke Ukrainy, 1992. 35pp. [Not seen.]
___ Koppel, T. **Chronography: A Chronological Bibliography of Books by Charles L. Harness**. Polk City, IA: Chris Drumm, 1993. 27pp.
___ Latham, David. **An Annotated Critical Bibliography of William Morris**, by David Latham and Sheila Latham. New York: St. Martin's, 1991. 423pp.
___ Latham, David. "William Morris: An Annotated Bibliography, 1992-1993," by David Latham and Sheila Latham. *Journal of the William Morris Society* 11(3): i-xx. Autumn 1995.
___ Lent, John A. **Comic Art of Europe: An International Comprehensive Bibliography**. Westport, CT: Greenwood, 1994. 663pp.

BIBLIOGRAPHY (continued)

___ Locke, George. **A Spectrum of Fantasy, Volume II: Acquistions to a Collection of Fantastic Literature, 1980-1993, Together with Additional Notes on Titles Covered in the First Volume**. London: Ferrett Fantasy, 1994. 156pp. [Not seen.]

___ Lynn, Ruth N. **Fantasy Literature for Children and Young Adults: An Annotated Bibliography**. 4th ed. New York: Bowker, 1995. 1092pp.

___ Mallett, Daryl F. **The Work of Elizabeth Chater: An Annotated Bibliography and Guide**, by Daryl F. Mallett and Annette Y. Mallett. San Bernardino, CA: Borgo Press, 1994. 80pp.

___ Moskowitz, Sam. "A Collector's Tale," *Fantasy Commentator* 8(1/2): 22-31. Winter 1993/1994. (Whole No. 45/46)

___ Pastourmatzi, Domna A. **Vivliogrphia epistemonikes phantasias, phantasias, kai tromou, 1960-1993** [Bibliography of Science Fiction, Fantasy and Horror, 1960-1993.]. Athens: Alien, 1995. 245pp.

___ Pringle, David. "SF, Fantasy & Horror Movie Novelizations," *Interzone* No. 80: 38-52. February 1994.

___ Reginald, Robert. **Science Fiction and Fantasy Literature 1975-1991: A Bibliography of Science Fiction, Fantasy and Horror Fiction Books and Nonfiction Monographs**. Detroit: Gale Research, 1992. 1512pp.

___ Reiss, Edmund. **Arthurian Legend and Literature: An Annotated Bibliography. Volume 1: The Middle Ages**, by Edmund Reiss, Louise H. Reiss and Beverly Taylor. New York: Garland, 1984. 467pp.

___ Reiss, Edmund. **Arthurian Legend and Literature: An Annotated Bibliography. Volume 2.**, by Edmund Reiss, Louise H. Reiss and Beverly Taylor. New York: Garland, 1995. [Not seen.]

___ Richardson, Darrell C. **J. Allen St. John: An Illustrated Bibliography**. Memphis, TN: Mid-America Publisher, 1991. 111pp.

___ Roberson, William H. **Walter M. Miller, Jr.: A Bio-Bibliography**, by William H. Roberson and Robert L. Battenfeld. Westport, CT: Greenwood, 1992. 149pp.

___ Ruddick, Nicholas. **British Science Fiction, 1478-1990: A Chronology**. Westport, CT: Greenwood, 1992. 296pp.

___ Salmonson, Jessica A. **Bibliography: Jessica Amanda Salmonson**. Polk City, IA: Drumm, 1992. [15pp.] [Bound with, inverted: her **Sorceries and Sorrows (Early Poems)**.] [21pp.]

___ Samuelson, David N. "On Hard Science Fiction: A Bibliography," *Science Fiction Studies* 20(2): 149-156. July 1993.

___ Sargent, Pamela. "Recommended Reading: Science Fiction by Women, 1979-1993," in: Sargent, Pamela, ed. **Women of Wonder: The Contemporary Years; Science Fiction by Women From the 1970s to the 1990s**. Orlando, FL: Harcourt Brace, 1995. pp.405-420.

___ Schlobin, Roger C. **Andre Norton: A Primary and Secondary Bibliography**. Revised edition, by Roger C. Schlobin and Irene R. Harrison. Framingham, MA: NESFA Press, 1994. 92pp.

___ Siclari, Joe. "Science Fiction Fandom: A Selected, Annotated Bibliography," in: Sanders, Joe, ed. **Science Fiction Fandom**. Westport, CT: Greenwood, 1994. pp.245-264.

___ Soanes, Paul A. **Daughter of the Night: A Tanith Lee Bibliography**, by Paul A. Soanes and Jim Pattison. Toronto: Gaffa Press, 1993. 44pp.

___ Stephens, Christopher P. **A Checklist of Fred Brown**. Hastings-on-Hudson, NY: Ultramarine, 1992. 83pp.

___ Stephens, Christopher P. **A Checklist of John Sladek**. Hastings-on-Hudson, NY: Ultramarine, 1992. 31pp. Revised ed.

___ Stephens, Christopher P. **A Checklist of Jonathan Carroll**. Hastings-on-Hudson, NY: Ultramarine, 1992. 11pp.

___ Stephens, Christopher P. **A Checklist of Roger Zelazny**. Hastings-on-Hudson, NY: Ultramarine, 1993. 47pp.

___ Stephens, Christopher P. **A Checklist of Ultramarine Press**. Hastings-on-Hudson, NY: Ultramarine, 1992. 13pp. Revised ed.

___ Stephensen-Payne, Phil. **Andre Norton: Grand Master of the Witch World, a Working Bibliography**, by Phil Stephensen-Payne and Gordon Benson, Jr. Albuquerque, NM: Galactic Central, 1992. 83pp.; San Bernardino, CA: Borgo Press, 1993. 83pp.

___ Stephensen-Payne, Phil. **Bob Shaw, Artist at Ground Zero: A Working Bibliography**. 5th Rev. Ed. Albuquerque, NM: Galactic Central, 1993. 51pp.

___ Stephensen-Payne, Phil. **C. J. Cherryh: A Working Bibliography**. Albuquerque, NM: Galactic Central, 1992. 36pp.

___ Stephensen-Payne, Phil. **Charles L. Harness: Attorney in Space, a Working Bibliography**. Albuquerque, NM: Galactic Central, 1992. 15pp.

___ Stephensen-Payne, Phil. **Edgar Pangborn: The Persistent Wonder, a Working Bibliography**, by Phil Stephensen-Payne and Gordon Benson, Jr. Albuquerque, NM: Galactic Central, 1993. 26pp.

BIBLIOGRAPHY (continued)

___ Stephensen-Payne, Phil. **Gene Wolfe: Urth-Man Extraordinary, a Working Bibliography**, by Phil Stephensen-Payne and Gordon Benson, Jr. Albuquerque, NM: Galactic Central, 1992. 62pp.

___ Stephensen-Payne, Phil. **H. Beam Piper, Emperor of Paratime: A Working Bibliography**. 4th edition, by Phil Stephensen-Payne and Gordon Benson, Jr. Albuquerque, NM: Galactic Central, 1994. 31pp.

___ Stephensen-Payne, Phil. **Keith Roberts: Master Craftsman, a Working Bibliography**. Albuquerque, NM: Galactic Central, 1993. 42pp.

___ Stephensen-Payne, Phil. **Michael Bishop: A Transfigured Talent, a Working Bibliography**. Albuquerque, NM: Galactic Central, 1992. 38pp.

___ Stephensen-Payne, Phil. **Robert Heinlein, Stormtrooping Guru: A Working Bibliography**. Albuquerque, NM: Galactic Central, 1993. 100pp.

___ Stephensen-Payne, Phil. **William Tenn: High Klass Talent, a Working Bibliography**, by Phil Stephensen-Payne and Gordon Benson, Jr. Albuquerque, NM: Galactic Central, 1993. 31pp.

___ Stephensen-Payne, Phil. **Wilson 'Bob' Tucker, Wild Talent: A Working Bibliography**, by Phil Stephensen-Payne and Gordon Benson, Jr. Albuquerque, NM: Galactic Central, 1994. 38pp. 4th. Edition.

___ Stone, Graham. "Chronology of Australian Science Fiction 1848-1992," *Science Fiction News* (Australia) No. 90: 3-10. July 1992.

___ Vegetti, Ernesto. **Fantascienza, Fantasy and Horror in Italia: 1990**, by Ernesto Vegetti and Piergiorgio Nicolazzini. Milano, Italy: Nicolazzini, 1992?. 142pp. [Not seen.]

___ Widder, William J. **The Fiction of L. Ron Hubbard: A Comprehensive Bibliography and Reference Guide to Published and Selected Unpublished Works**. Los Angeles, CA: Bridge Publications, 1994. 373pp.

BIBLIOGRAPHY, AUSTRALIA

___ Ikin, Van. "Here There Be Monsters: Some Idiosyncrasies of Science Fiction Bibliography in Australia," *Bibliographical Society of Australia nad New Zealand Bulletin* 16(4): 149-153. Fourth Quarter 1992.

BIDWELL, BENSON

___ Moskowitz, Sam. "A Collector's Tale," *Fantasy Commentator* 8(1/2): 22-31. Winter 1993/1994. (Whole No. 45/46)

BIEDERMANN, CAROLA

___ Simsa, Cyril. "The View From Olympus: Three Czech Women Writers Talk About SF," *Vector* No. 166: 14-16. April/May 1992.

BIERCE, AMBROSE

___ Bloom, Harold. "Ambrose Bierce," in: Bloom, Harold. **Classic Horror Writers**. New York: Chelsea House, 1994. pp.1-13.

___ Burleson, Donald R. "Bierce's 'The Damned Thing': A Nietzschean Allegory," *Studies in Weird Fiction* No. 13: 8-10. Summer 1993. [Not seen.]

___ Wandrei, Donald. "Bierce," *Studies in Weird Fiction* No. 10: 31-34. Fall 1991. (Reprinted from *Minnesota Quarterly*, Spring 1931.)

BIERKO, CRAIG

___ Hall, John S. "Lister, American Style," *Starlog* No. 221: 67-69. December 1995.

BIFFEL, TERRY

___ "Biffel, Terry (Obituary)," *Locus* 28(2): 68. February 1992.

BIG HEART AWARD, 1994

___ "Other Awards at ConAdian," *Science Fiction Chronicle* 15(10): 5. September 1994.

BIG TROUBLE IN LITTLE CHINA (MOTION PICTURE)

___ "*Big Trouble in Little China* (1986)," in: Goldberg, Lee, ed. **The Dreamweavers: Interviews With Fantasy Filmmakers of the 1980s**. Jefferson, NC: McFarland, 1995. pp.40-46.

BIGELOW, KATHRYN

___ Yakir, Dan. "*Strange Days*," *Starlog* No. 220: 32-35. November 1995.

BIGGLE, LLOYD, JR.

BIGGLE, LLOYD, JR.
___ "Biggle, Lloyd, Jr., 1923- ," in: Lesniak, James G., ed. **Contemporary Authors**. Detroit: Gale Research, 1992. New Revision Series, Vol. 35, pp.43-44.

BIGGLES (MOTION PICTURE)
___ "*Biggles* Rolling in U.K. After 9-Year Incubation Period," *Variety* p. 43. February 20, 1985.
___ "CBS/Fox Inks *Biggles* for U.K. Distribution," *Variety* p. 93. March 5, 1986.

BIGGLESTONE, HARRY C.
___ "Bigglestone, Clint (Obituary)," *Science Fiction Chronicle* 16(2): 20. November/December 1994.
___ "Bigglestone, Harry C. 'Clint' (Obituary)," *Locus* 33(6): 74. December 1994.

BIGGS, JOE BOB
___ Beeler, Michael. "*The Stand*: Joe Bob Biggs," *Cinefantastique* 25(3): 29. June 1994.

BIGGS-DAWSON, REXANN
___ Spelling, Ian. "Wildcat Heart," *Starlog* No. 214: 27-30. May 1995.

BILL AND TED'S BOGUS JOURNEY (MOTION PICTURE)
___ "Bill and Ted Journey Back for One Excellent Encore," *Chicago (IL) Sun Times*. July 19, 1991. in: *NewsBank. Film and Television*. 65:E14. 1991.
___ Arnold, Gary. "Nothing's Bogus in Bill and Ted's New Outing," *Washington (DC) Times*. July 19, 1991. in: *NewsBank. Film and Television*. 65:F7. 1991.
___ Farolino, Audrey. "Dud Dudes: Bill and Ted Get Bogus," *New York (NY) Post*. July 19, 1991. in: *NewsBank. Film and Television*. 65:F4. 1991.
___ Jacobs, Tom. "Bill & Ted Redux Is Certainly a Blast," *Los Angeles (CA) Daily News*. July 19, 1991. in: *NewsBank. Film and Television*. 65: E8. 1991.
___ Johnson, Malcolm. "Bill & Ted Yuk It Up With Grim Reaper," *Hartford (CT) Courant*. July 19, 1991. in: *NewsBank. Film and Television*. 65:E12. 1991.
___ Kronke, David. "Some Laughs, But Bill and Ted Still Bogus," *Dallas (TX) Times Herald*. July 19, 1991. in: *NewsBank. Film and Television*. 65:F6. 1991.
___ Mahar, Ted. "Bill & Ted's Adventure Definitely Bogus," *Portland (OR) Oregonian*. July 19, 1991. in: *NewsBank. Film and Television*. 65: F5. 1991.
___ Movshovitz, Howie. "Bogus Journey Strains If You're Over 14," *Denver (CO) Post*. July 19, 1991. in: *NewsBank. Film and Television*. 65:E11. 1991.
___ Murray, Steve. "Bill and Ted as Bogus as They Wanna Be," *Atlanta (GA) Journal*. July 19, 1991. in: *NewsBank. Film and Television*. 65: E13. 1991.
___ Shulgasser, Barbara. "Bill & Ted's Latest Is Bogus, But Its Better," *San Francisco (CA) Examiner*. July 19, 1991. in: *NewsBank. Film and Television*. 65:E9-10. 1991.
___ Stark, Susan. "Whoa, Dudes," *Detroit (MI) News*. July 19, 1991. in: *NewsBank. Film and Television*. 65:F2-F3. 1991.
___ Verniere, James. "Bill & Ted's Journey Is a Radical Cool Trip," *Boston (MA) Herald*. July 19, 1991. in: *NewsBank. Film and Television*. 65:F1. 1991.

BILL AND TED'S EXCELLENT ADVENTURES (MOTION PICTURE)
___ Shapiro, Marc. "Excellent Adventures?," *Starlog* 184: 80-81. November 1992.

BINDER, EANDO
___ Jones, Lauren. "Adam Link vs. **I, Robot**," *Science Fiction News* (Australia) No. 111: 2-6. July 1990. (Comments: No. 112, p.9-12; No. 113, p. 8-18; No. 114, p.3-6, 23.)

BIONIC EVERAFTER (MOTION PICTURE)
___ Spelling, Ian. "Bionic Breakdown," *Starlog* No. 211: 76-79. February 1995.

BIONIC WOMAN (TV)
___ Spelling, Ian. "Bionic Breakdown," *Starlog* No. 211: 76-79. February 1995.

BIOPUNK
___ Fiser, Miroslav. "A Few Notes About Biopunk," *Vector* No. 174: 17-18. August/September 1993.
___ Hauser, Eva. "Biopunk: A New Literary Movement for Post-Totalitarian Regimes," *Vector* No. 174: 15-16. August/September 1993.
___ Simsa, Cyril. "Two Short Articles About Biopunk," *Vector* No. 174: 12-14. August/September 1993.

BIRD, BETTINA
___ Stone, Graham. "Notes on Australian Science Fiction," *Science Fiction News* (Australia) No. 102: 2-5. March 1987.

BIRDS II: LAND'S END (MOTION PICTURE)
___ Faller, James M. "*Birds II: Land's End* (Review)," *Cinefantastique* 25(5): 59. October 1994.
___ Fischer, Dennis. "*The Birds II: Land's End* (Review)," *Cinefantastique* 26(4): 59. June 1995.
___ Goodson, William W., Jr. "*Birds II: Land's End*: Bird Wrangling," *Cinefantastique* 25(2): 49. April 1994.
___ Goodson, William W., Jr. "*Birds II: Land's End*: Remembering Hitchcock," *Cinefantastique* 25(2): 51. April 1994.
___ Goodson, William W., Jr. "*Birds II: Land's End*," *Cinefantastique* 25(2): 48-51. April 1994.

BIRDS, THE (MOTION PICTURE)
___ Swires, Steve. "Master of the *Time Machine*," in: McDonnell, David, ed. **Starlog's Science Fiction Heroes and Heroines**. New York: Crescent Books, 1995. pp.80-83.

BISHOP, MICHAEL
___ "1995 *Locus* Awards Winners," *Locus* 35(2): 7, 34-37. August 1995.
___ Bishop, Michael. "Goodbye Thrust, Farewell Quantum: A Personal Retrospective," *Quantum* No. 43/44: 49-50, 66. Spring/Summer 1993.
___ Currey, Lloyd W. "Work in Progress: Michael Bishop," *New York Review of Science Fiction* No. 42: 22-23. February 1992.
___ Stephensen-Payne, Phil. **Michael Bishop: A Transfigured Talent, a Working Bibliography**. Albuquerque, NM: Galactic Central, 1992. 38pp.
___ Tidmarsh, Andrew. "Michael Bishop: An Annotated Bibliography," *Interzone* No. 82: 57-58. April 1994.

BISSELL, TERRY
___ "Bissell, Terry (Obituary)," *Science Fiction Chronicle* 13(5): 14. February 1992.

BISSETTE, STEPHEN
___ "Bram Stoker Awards, 1993," *Science Fiction Chronicle* 14(10): 4. July 1993.

BISSON, TERRY
___ "Terry Bisson Collection Recalled," *Locus* 31(6): 6. December 1993.

BLACK KNIGHT (MOTION PICTURE)
___ Lupack, Alan. "An Enemy in Our Midst: *The Black Knight* and the American Dream," in: Harty, Kevin J., ed. **Cinema Arthuriana: Essays on Arthurian Film**. New York: Garland, 1991. pp.29-40.

BLACKS
___ Cox, Dan. "Rewriting the Rules," *Variety* 361(4): 6. November 27, 1995.
___ Dery, Mark. "Black to the Future: Interviews with Samuel R. Delany, Greg Tate, and Tricia Rose," *South Atlantic Quarterly* 92(4): 735-788. Fall 1993. (Reprinted in: Dery, Mark, Ed. **Flame Wars: The Discourse of Cyberculture**. Durham, NC: Duke University Press, 1994.)
___ Green, Carol A. "Women of Color: The Female Protagonists in the Novels of Octavia Butler," *Vector* No. 176: 14-15. December 1993/January 1994.
___ Gruesser, John. "Pauline Hopkin's **Of One Blood**: Creating an Afrocentric Fantasy for a Black Middle Class Audience," in: Latham, Robert A. and Collins, Robert A., eds. **Modes of the Fantastic**. Westport, CT: Greenwood, 1995. pp.74-83.
___ Hartnett, James R. "Black Power in Utopia," in: Saccaro Del Buffa, Giuseppa and Lewis, Arthur O., eds. **Utopie per gli Anni Ottana**. Rome: Gangemi Editore, 1986. pp.435-442.

BLACKS (continued)
___ Smith, Malaika D. **The African American Heroine in Octavia Butler's Wild Seed and Parable of the Sower**. Master's Thesis, UCLA, 1994. 66pp.

BLACKSHEAR, THOMAS
___ Jankus, Hank. "Interview: Thomas Blackshear," *Shayol* No. 7: 16-18. 1985.

BLACKWOOD, ALGERNON
___ Bloom, Harold. "Algernon Blackwood," in: Bloom, Harold. **Modern Horror Writers**. New York: Chelsea House, 1995. pp.32-47.
___ Murray, Will. "Lovecraft, Blackwood, and Chambers: A Colloquium of Ghosts," *Studies in Weird Fiction* No. 13: 2-7. Summer 1993. [Not seen.]
___ Reaver, J. Russell. "From Seed to Fruit: The Doubling of Psychic Landscapes in Algernon Blackwood's **The Centaur**," *The Romantist* No. 4-5: 55-58. 1982.

BLADE RUNNER (MOTION PICTURE)
___ "**Blade Runner** Stuck With Its 'R' Tag," *Variety* p. 42. May 19, 1982.
___ "**Blade Runner: The Director's Cut** (Review)," *Cinefantastique* 22(5): 60. April 1992.
___ Abbott, Joe. "The Monster Reconsidered: **Blade Runner's** Replicant as Romantic Hero," *Extrapolation* 34(4): 340-350. Winter 1993.
___ Albrecht, Donald. "**Blade Runner** Cuts Deep into American Culture," *New York Times* Sec. 2, p. 19. September 20, 1992.
___ Arnold, Gary. "Harder Edge and Well-Placed Cuts Make This **Blade Runner** Much Shaper," *Washington (DC) Times*. September 11, 1992. in: *NewsBank. Film and Television.* 87:F12-13. 1992.
___ Black, D. S. "**Blade Runner** Revisited," *PKDS Newsletter* No. 28: 7-8. March 1992.
___ Bukatman, Scott R. "Fractal Geographies," *Artforum* 31(4): 6-7. December 1992.
___ Bullaro, Grace R. "**Blade Runner**: The Subversion and Redefinition of Catagories," *Riverside Quarterly* 9(2): 102-108. August 1993. (Whole No. 34)
___ Doherty, Thomas. "**Blade Runner**," *Cinefantastique* 23(5): 56-57. February 1993.
___ Ebert, Roger. "Bleak New **Blade Runner**," *Chicago (IL) Sun Times*. September 11, 1992. in: *NewsBank. Film and Television.* 87:F9. 1992.
___ Fitting, Peter. "Futurecop: The Neutralization of Revolt in **Blade Runner**," in: Mullen, R. D., ed. **On Philip K. Dick: 40 Articles From Science-Fiction Studies**. Terre Haute, IN: SF-TH Inc., 1992. pp.132-144.
___ Friedman, Regien-Mihal. "Capitals of Sorrow: From **Metropolis** to **Brazil**," *Utopian Studies* 4(2): 35-43. 1993.
___ Heinze, Theodor T. "Science/Fiction, hin und zurück: Mensch, Maschine, Mythos im **Blade Runner**," in: Heinze, Theodor T., ed. **Subjektivität als Fiktion: Zur literarisch psychologischen Konstruktion des Modernen Menschen**. Pfaffenweiler: Gentaurus, 1993. pp.129-158.
___ Hunter, Stephen. "New Cut of **Blade Runner** Is as Provocative and Befuddling as Before," *Baltimore (MD) Sun*. September 11, 1992. in: *NewsBank. Film and Television.* 87:F10. 1992.
___ Kronke, David. "Re-released **Blade Runner** Is Original Work of Great Scott," *Los Angeles (CA) Daily News*. September 11, 1992. in: *NewsBank. Film and Television.* 87:F5. 1992.
___ Lofficier, Randy. "**Blade Runner** (1982): Interviews with Hampton Francher, David Peoples, Ridley Scott and Syd Mead," by Randy Lofficier and Jean-Marc Lofficier. in: Goldberg, Lee et al. **Science Fiction Filmmaking in the 1980s**. Jefferson, NC: McFarland, 1995. pp.23-58.
___ Lofficier, Randy. "Interview: David Peoples," by Randy Lofficier and Jean-Marc Lofficier. *Starlog* 184: 40-41. November 1992.
___ Lofficier, Randy. "Interview: Hamption Fancher," by Randy Lofficier and Jean-Marc Lofficier. *Starlog* 184: 35-39. November 1992.
___ Lofficier, Randy. "Interview: Lawrence G. Paull," by Randy Lofficier and Jean-Marc Lofficier. *Starlog* 184: 46-47, 70. November 1992.
___ Lofficier, Randy. "Interview: Ridley Scott," by Randy Lofficier and Jean-Marc Lofficier. *Starlog* 184: 48-51, 69. November 1992.
___ Lofficier, Randy. "Interview: Syd Mead," by Randy Lofficier and Jean-Marc Lofficier. *Starlog* 184: 42-45. November 1992.
___ Lowe, Nick. "**Blade Runner: The Director's Cut** (Review)," *Interzone* No. 69: 39-40. March 1993.

BLADE RUNNER (MOTION PICTURE) (continued)
___ Mahar, Ted. "Blade Gets Shorter, Sharper," *Portland (OR) The Oregonian*. September 11, 1992. in: *NewsBank. Film and Television.* 87:F11. 1992.
___ Murray, Steve. "Revisited Runner a Dazzler," *Atlata (GA) Journal*. September 11, 1992. in: *NewsBank. Film and Television.* 87:F8. 1992.
___ Rosenberg, Scott. "**Blade Runner**: Back to the Future," *San Francisco (CA) Examiner*. September 11, 1992. in: *NewsBank. Film and Television.* 87:F6-F7. 1992.
___ Turaji, Kenneth. "**Blade Runner**," *Los Angeles (CA) Times*. September 13, 1992. in: *NewsBank. Film and Television.* 87:E9-F4. 1992.
___ Turan, Kenneth. "**Blade Runner** 2," *Radio Free P.K.D.* No. 1: 2-3, 9. February 1993.
___ Wilmington, Michael. "The Rain People (On the Restored Version of **Blade Runner**)," *Film Comment* 28(1): 17-19. 1992.

BLAIR, DAVID
___ Tatsumi, Takayuki. "Eye to Eye With David Blair: An Interview," *Science Fiction Eye* No. 13: 54-61. Spring 1994.

BLAKE, WILLIAM
___ Hallab, Mary Y. "Carter and Blake: The Dangers of Innocence," in: Sanders, Joe, ed. **Functions of the Fantastic**. Westport, CT: Greenwood, 1995. pp.177-184.

BLANCHOT, MAURICE
___ Troiano, Maureen D. **New Physics and the Modern French Novel**. New York: Peter Lang, 1995. 276pp.

BLATTY, WILLIAM PETER
___ Briggs, Scott D. " 'So Much Mystery...': The Fiction of William Peter Blatty," *Studies in Weird Fiction* No. 9: 13-18. Spring 1991.
___ Geary, Robert F. "**The Exorcist**: Deep Horror?," *Journal of the Fantastic in the Arts* 5(4): 55-63. 1993. (No. 20)
___ Ursini, James. **More Things Than Are Dreamt Of: Masterpieces of Supernatural Horror, From Mary Shelley to Stephen King, in Literature and Film**, by James Ursini and Alain Silver. New York: Limelight, 1994. 226pp.

BLAYLOCK, JIM
___ Koontz, Dean R. "The Coming Blaylockian Age," in: Greenberg, Martin H., Ed Gorman and Bill Munster, eds. **The Dean Koontz Companion**. New York: Berkley, 1994. pp.177-179.

BLEECK, GORDON CLIVE
___ Stone, Graham. "Report on G. C. Bleeck, Australian Science Fiction Writer," *Science Fiction News* (Australia) No. 118: 1-16. 1995.

BLEILER, EVERETT F.
___ "1992 *Locus* Awards," *Locus* 28(2): 1, 42-45. August 1992.
___ "Norton Receives First Fandom Award," *Locus* 34(1) 8. January 1995.
___ "Other Awards at ConAdian," *Science Fiction Chronicle* 15(10): 5. September 1994.
___ Searles, A. Langley. "Anthology Days: An Interview with E. F. Bleiler," *Fantasy Commentator* 8(3/4): 204-213. Fall 1995. (Whole No. 47/48)

BLINK (MOTION PICTURE)
___ Kutzera, Dale. "Quick Cuts: Visionary Visuals," *Cinefex* No. 58: 17-18. June 1994.

BLISH, JAMES
___ Aldiss, Brian W. "Peep," in: Aldiss, Brian W. **The Detached Retina: Aspects of SF and Fantasy**. Syracuse, NY: Syracuse University Press, 1995. pp.101-105.
___ Blish, James. "The Development of a Science Fiction Writer," in: Jakubowski, Maxim and James, Edward, eds. **The Profession of Science Fiction**. New York: St. Martin's, 1992. pp.26-33.
___ Bloom, Harold. "James Blish," in: Bloom, Harold, ed. **Science Fiction Writers of the Golden Age**. New York: Chelsea House, 1995. pp.63-78.
___ Broich, Ulrich. "James Blish, **A Case of Conscience** (1958)," in: Heuermann, Harmut, ed. **Der Science Fiction Roman in der angloamerikanischen Literatur: Interpretationen**. Düsseldorf: Bagel, 1986. pp.166-181.

BLISH, JAMES (continued)

___ Tarrant, Desmond. "Cabell and James Blish (1921-1975)," *Kalki* 9(4): 133-136. 1991. (No. 36)

___ Wilson, Raymond J., III. "James Blish," in: Bruccoli, Matthew J., ed. **Facts on File Bibliography of American Fiction 1919-1988**. New York: Facts on File, 1991. pp.90-92.

___ Zebrowski, George. "Never Forget the Writers Who Helped Build Yesterday's Tomorrows," *Science Fiction Age* 3(6): 30-36, 100. 1995.

BLOB (MOTION PICTURE)

___ Weaver, Tom. "Birth of the *Blob*," *Starlog* No. 214: 59-65. May 1995.

___ Worcester, Kent. "Belle of the *Blob*," *Starlog* No. 214: 66-67, 70. May 1995.

BLOCH, ROBERT

___ "Bloch, Robert (1917-1994)(Obituary)," *Locus* 33(5): 6-7, 74-78. November 1994.

___ "Bloch, Robert (Obituary)," *Science Fiction Chronicle* 16(1): 16, 18. October 1994.

___ "Fine Awards to Bloch, Yarbro," *Locus* 30(4): 9. April 1993.

___ "Robert Bloch Gravely Ill," *Science Fiction Chronicle* 15(10): 4. September 1994.

___ "Robert Bloch, Author of *Psycho*, Dies at Age 77," *Radio Program: All Things Considered (NPR)* Program 1616. September 25, 1994.

___ Bloch, Robert. **Once Around the Bloch: An Unauthorized Autobiography**. New York: Tor, 1993. 416pp.

___ Bloom, Harold. "Robert Bloch," in: Bloom, Harold. **Modern Horror Writers**. New York: Chelsea House, 1995. pp.48-63.

___ Bradley, Matthew R. "Momma's Boy: A Conversation With Robert Bloch," *Filmfax* No. 40: 78-82. August/September 1993.

___ Burleson, Donald R. "Irony and Self-Difference in Robert Bloch's 'Beetles'," *Studies in Weird Fiction* No. 16: 25-28. Winter 1995.

___ Dziemianowicz, Stefan. "An Interview With Robert Bloch," *Studies in Weird Fiction* No. 16: 4-13. Winter 1995.

___ Harmon, Jim. "Harmony: Robert Bloch," *Riverside Quarterly* 9(3): 157-159. June 1995. (Whole No. 35)

___ Indick, Ben P. "Robert Bloch: A Personal Memory," *Studies in Weird Fiction* No. 16: 2-4. Winter 1995.

___ Joshi, S. T. "A Literary Tutelate: Robert Bloch and H. P. Lovecraft," *Studies in Weird Fiction* No. 16: 13-25. Winter 1995.

___ Kies, Cosette. **Presenting Young Adult Horror Fiction**. New York: Twayne, 1991. 203pp.

___ Matheson, Richard, ed. **Robert Bloch: Appreciations of the Master**, ed. by Richard Matheson and Ricia Mainhardt. New York: Tor, 1995. 382pp.

___ Schweitzer, Darrell. "Robert Bloch," in: Schweitzer, Darrell. **Speaking of Horror: Interviews With Writers of the Supernatural**. San Bernardino, CA: Borgo, 1994. pp.9-22.

BLOOD WINGS (MOTION PICTURE)

___ SEE: PUMPKINHEAD II: BLOOD WINGS (MOTION PICTURE).

BLOODLINES (MOTION PICTURE)

___ SEE: HELLRAISER IV: BLOODLINES (MOTION PICTURE).

BLOODSTONE: SUBSPECIES II (MOTION PICTURE)

___ Altman, Mark A. "*Bloodstone: Subspecies II* (Review)," *Cinefantastique* 24(3/4): 123. October 1993.

BLUE BOOK (MAGAZINE)

___ Moskowitz, Sam. "Edgar Rice Burroughs and *Blue Book*," *Burroughs Bulletin* NS. No. 15: 11-20. July 1993.

BLUE LIGHT RED LIGHT (MAGAZINE)

___ Katz, Bill. "Magazines: *Blue Light Red Light: A Periodical of Speculative Fiction and the Arts*," *Library Journal* p.144. July 1991.

BLUE THUNDER (MOTION PICTURE)

___ Lofficier, Randy. "*Blue Thunder* (1983): Interview with John Badham," by Randy Lofficier and Jean-Marc Lofficier. in: Goldberg, Lee et al. **Science Fiction Filmmaking in the 1980s**. Jefferson, NC: McFarland, 1995. pp.59-72.

BODY BAGS (MOTION PICTURE)

___ Biodrowski, Steve. "*Body Bags*: The Horror Games," *Cinefantastique* 24(3/4): 114. October 1993.

BODY BAGS (MOTION PICTURE) (continued)

___ Biodrowski, Steve. "*Body Bags*," *Cinefantastique* 24(3/4): 112-115. October 1993.

BODY MELT (MOTION PICTURE)

___ Harris, Judith P. "*Body Melt* (Review)," *Cinefantastique* 25(5): 59. October 1994.

BODY PUZZLE (MOTION PICTURE)

___ Harris, Judith P. "*Body Puzzle* (Review)," *Cinefantastique* 26(4): 59. June 1995.

BODY SNATCHERS (MOTION PICTURE)

___ Benn, Alvin. "Tilley Gets Leading Role in Selma Filming," *Montgomery (AL) Journal and Advertiser*. February 4, 1992. in: *NewsBank. Film and Television*. 17:G2. 1992.

BODY SNATCHERS (MOTION PICTURE)

___ Arnold, Gary. "*Body Snatchers*: Just a Lifeless Remake," *Washington (DC) Times*. February 19, 1994. in: *NewsBank. Film and Television*. 21: C3. 1994.

___ Campbell, Bob. "Not Creepy Enough to Be a Classic," *Newark (NJ) Star-Ledger*. February 4, 1994. in: *NewsBank. Film and Television*. 21: B14. 1994.

___ Holder, Keith. "*Body Snatchers*: The New Invasion," *Cinefantastique* 23(4): 10-11. December 1992.

___ Holder, Keith. "*Body Snatchers*," *Cinefantastique* 24(1): 4-5. June 1993.

___ Holder, Keith. "*Body Snatchers*," *Cinefantastique* 24(2): 56. August 1993.

___ Holder, Keith. "*The New Invasion*," *Cinefantastique* 24(1): 5. June 1993.

___ Johnson, Kim H. "*Body Snatchers*," *Starlog* 185: 50-53, 72. December 1992.

___ Johnson, Kim H. "The Human Touch," *Starlog* No. 192: 48-57. July 1993.

___ Johnson, Kim H. "Sleep No More," *Starlog* No. 189: 75-77. April 1993.

___ Johnson, Stephen. "Timeless Terror: *Body Snatchers* Stands Up to Third Interpretation," *(Baltimore, MD) Sun*. February 25, 1994. in: *NewsBank. Film and Television*. 21:B12. 1994.

___ Lowe, Nick. "*Body Snatchers* (Review)," *Interzone* No. 83: 36. May 1994.

___ Marr, Madeleine. "Don't Lose Sleep Over 'Snatchers' (Review)," *San Juan (Puerto Rico) Star* November 18, 1993. in: *NewsBank. Film and Television*. 124:F3. 1993.

___ Meyers, Joe. "Sharp Acting Saves Second Remake of *Body Snatchers*," *(Bridgeport, CT) Connecticut Post*. August 14, 1994. in: *NewsBank. Film and Television*. 87:B12. 1994.

___ Persons, Dan. "*Body Snatchers* (Review)," *Cinefantastique* 25(3): 60. June 1994.

___ Verniere, James. "Snatchers Is a Good Update of Attack of the Mod Pod," *Boston (MA) Herald*. February 25, 1994. in: *NewsBank. Film and Television*. 21:B13. 1994.

___ Weiskind, Ron. "Only Shell Is Left," *Pittsburgh (PA) Post Gazette*. February 25, 1994. in: *NewsBank. Film and Television*. 21: C1. 1994.

___ Wuntch, Phillip. "The Pod People Make a Witty Comeback," *Dallas (TX) Morning News*. February 18, 1994. in: *NewsBank. Film and Television*. 21: C2. 1994.

BODY STEALERS (MOTION PICTURE)

___ "Close to Lucky Title: AA's New *Body Stealers* Recalls Its *Body Snatchers*," *Variety* p. 20. May 20, 1970.

BOEX, SERAPHIM J. F.

___ SEE: ROSNY, J. H.

BOGERT, JEAN

___ "Bogert, Jean (Obituary)," *Science Fiction Chronicle* 15(5): 12. March 1994.

BOHNHOFF, MAYA KAATHRYN

___ Vester, John. "In Silken Steel," *Starlog* No. 221: 60-63. December 1995.

BONANNO, MARGARET WANDER
___ "*Star Trek* Author Complains Her Book Was Rewritten," *Science Fiction Chronicle* 13(7): 4. April 1992.
___ "*Star Trek*: Problem," *Locus* 28(3): 7. March 1992.

BOND, JAMES
___ "*James Bond* Films (1980-1989): Interviews with Timothy Dalton, George Lazenby, Barry Nelson, Richard Maibaum, Tom Mankiewicz, Roger Moore, and Michael Wilson," in: Goldberg, Lee, ed. **The Dreamweavers: Interviews With Fantasy Filmmakers of the 1980s**. Jefferson, NC: McFarland, 1995. pp.163-191.

BOND, NANCY
___ Evans, Gwenth. "Harps and Harpers in Contemporary Fantasy," *Lion and the Unicorn* 16(2): 199-209. December 1992.

BONESTELL, CHESLEY
___ Benford, Gregory. "Interplanetary Pioneer," *Science Fiction Age* 3(3): 86-91. March 1995.
___ Wachhorst, Wyn. "The Dream of Spaceflight: Nostalgia for a Bygone Future," *Massachusetts Review* 36(1): 7-32. Spring 1995.

BONSALL, BRIAN
___ Jankiewicz, Pat. "Most Wanted: The Klingon Kid," *Starlog* No. 194: 58-61. September 1993.

BOOK COLLECTING
___ SEE: COLLECTING SF.

BOOK JACKETS
___ Heller, Steven. **Jackets Required: An Illustrated History of American Book Jacket Design, 1920-1959**, by Steven Heller and Seymour Chwast. San Francisco, CA: Chronicle Books, 1995. 144pp.
___ Moskowitz, Sam. "A Remedy in Book Jackets," *Fantasy Commentator* 8(3/4): 173-181. Fall 1995. (Whole No. 47/48)

BOOK LIST
___ D'Ammassa, Don. "Before the Hugos: The H. G. Awards (1921-1956)," *Science Fiction Chronicle* 13(10): 30-31. July/August 1992.
___ Kessel, John. "It's Time to Load the Canon With SF's Most Influential Books," *Science Fiction Age* 3(2): 32-35. January 1995.

BOOK LIST, 1990
___ "Best SF/Fantasy/Horror List," *Voice of Youth Advocates* 13(1): 11-16. April 1990.
___ de Lint, Charles. "Recommended Reading for 1990 and 1991," *Pulphouse* 1(12/13): 70-71. September/October 1992.

BOOK LIST, 1991
___ "*Publishers Weekly* 1991 Best Sellers," *Locus* 28(5): 7, 66. May 1992.
___ "Recommended Reading, 1991," *Locus* 28(2): 32-40. February 1992.
___ "Recommended Reading, 1991," in: Brown, Charles N. and Contento, William G. **Science Fiction, Fantasy, & Horror: 1991**. Oakland, CA: Locus Press, 1992. pp.440-456.
___ Amies, Chris. "Reviewer's Choice: The Best Books of 1991," *Vector* No. 166: 6-9. April/May 1992.
___ D'Ammassa, Don. "The Best SF, Fantasy and Horror Novels of 1991," *Science Fiction Chronicle* 13(6): 20, 22. March 1992.
___ de Lint, Charles. "Recommended Reading for 1990 and 1991," *Pulphouse* 1(12/13): 70-71. September/October 1992.

BOOK LIST, 1992
___ "Recommended Reading: 1992," *Locus* 30(2): 34-40, 71-73. February 1993.
___ "The Reviewer's Poll 1992: The Best Books," *Vector* No. 172: 13-15. April/May 1992.
___ D'Ammassa, Don. "The Best SF, Fantasy, and Horror Novels of the Year, 1992," *Science Fiction Chronicle* 14(5): 5, 22-24. February 1993.

BOOK LIST, 1993
___ "Best Science Fiction, Fantasy and Horror, 1992," *Voice of Youth Advocates* 16(1): 9-10. April 1993.
___ "The NYRSF Recommended Reading List for 1993: Part the First: Things Bound as Books," *New York Review of Science Fiction* No. 65: 24, 23. January 1994.

BOOK LIST, 1993 (continued)
___ "The NYRSF Recommended Reading List for 1993: Part the Second: Short Fiction," *New York Review of Science Fiction* No. 66: 24, 23. February 1994.
___ "Recommended Reading: 1993," *Locus* 32(2): 36-42, 74-76. February 1994.
___ "Reviewer's Poll, 1993: The Best Books," *Vector* No. 179: 5-11. June/July 1994.
___ "Unjustly Neglected Works of Science Fiction: A Survey," *Science Fiction Studies* 20(3): 422-432. November 1993.
___ D'Ammassa, Don. "The Best SF, Fantasy and Horror Novels of the Year," *Science Fiction Chronicle* 15(4): 5, 28-30. February 1994.

BOOK LIST, 1994
___ "Books of the Year, 1994," *Vector* No. 183: 3-7. July/August 1995.
___ "(Not Necessarily) The Best Books of 1994," *New York Review of Science Fiction* No. 77: 24, 23. January 1995.
___ "Recommended Reading, 1994," *Locus* 34(2): 34-42, 76-77. February 1995.
___ D'Ammassa, Don. "The Best SF, Fantasy and Horror Novels of 1994," *Science Fiction Chronicle* 16(4): 7, 29-30. February 1995.
___ Lerner, Fred. "Concerning Purely Personal Preferences," *Voice of Youth Advocates* 17(4): 200-201. October 1994.

BOOK REVIEWING
___ SEE: REVIEWING.

BOOK REVIEWS, INDEXES
___ SEE: INDEXES.

BOOKNET (CABLE CHANNEL)
___ "Book Cable TV Channel Planned," *Science Fiction Chronicle* 14(12): 5. September 1993.

BOOKSELLING
___ "1993 Salon du Livre," *Locus* 31(6): 39-40. December 1993.
___ "B. Dalton's *Sense of Wonder*," *Locus* 30(1): 6. January 1993.
___ "Baker and Taylor Sold," *Locus* 28(1): 6. January 1992.
___ "B&N/B. Dalton '94 Top Sellers," *Locus* 34(2): 9, 73. February 1995.
___ "Bookstores Account for Only Half of Books Sold," *Locus* 28(2): 7. February 1992.
___ "Britain's Book Club Associates Seeking 50 More Retail Sites," *Science Fiction Chronicle* 15(6): 6-7. April/May 1994.
___ "Burning Brite," *Locus* 33(4): 9, 76. October 1994.
___ "Chain Bookstores Take Lead," *Locus* 35(2): 9, 70. August 1995.
___ "Chain Financial Figures," *Locus* 34(1) 7. January 1995.
___ "Chain Sales Way Up Again," *Locus* 35(4): 8. October 1995.
___ "Chain SF Buyers Change," *Locus* 34(2): 8. February 1995.
___ "Chains Have a Bigger Piece of the Action," *Locus* 32(6): 7, 76. June 1994.
___ "Chains Increase Market Share," *Locus* 32(1): 6. January 1994.
___ "Dillons Bankruptcy," *Locus* 34(4): 9. April 1995.
___ "Inland Files for Bankruptcy," *Locus* 35(3): 9. September 1993.
___ "KMart Kills Walden Book Company Name," *Locus* 34(1) 7. January 1995.
___ "Lauriat's Buys Encore," *Locus* 34(1) 7. January 1995.
___ "National Coverage for 'Burned Flesh' Book," *Science Fiction Chronicle* 16(1): 4-5. October 1994.
___ "On-Line Bookselling a Successful Experiment," *Locus* 32(6): 9, 75. June 1994.
___ "Quake Damages Book Trade," *Locus* 32(3): 7. March 1994.
___ "Record Number Top Sellers for Fourth Year," *Locus* 32(4): 9, 62-63. April 1994.
___ "Reorganization in the Chains," *Locus* 31(3): 6, 83. September 1993.
___ "SF at the San Francisco Book Festival," *Locus* 28(1): 9. January 1992.
___ "SF Bookstore Crime Wave," *Locus* 31(1): 6, 63. July 1993.
___ "SF in French," *Locus* 31(6): 40. December 1993.
___ "SF Tops 1993 UK Bestsellers," *Science Fiction Chronicle* 15(4): 6. February 1994.
___ "SF Tumbles on British List of 1994 Paperback Bestsellers," *Science Fiction Chronicle* 16(4): 5. February 1995.
___ "UK Book Clubs Open Bookstores," *Science Fiction Chronicle* 14(12): 5. September 1993.
___ "Waldenbooks '94 Top Sellers," *Locus* 34(3): 8, 77. March 1995.

BOOKSELLING

BOOKSELLING (continued)
___ "Where Books Are Bought," *Locus* 34(4): 8. April 1995.
___ Cox, Glen E. "Pulped! How Books Die an Early Death," *SFWA Bulletin* 25(4): 3-6. Winter 1992. (No. 114)
___ Currey, Lloyd W. "Facing Troubled Times: The Science Fiction Specialist Dealer," *AB Bookman's Weekly* 92(16): 1449-1460. October 18, 1993.
___ Di Filippo, Paul. "Selling Books, Touching Lives," *Science Fiction Eye* No. 10: 22-26. June 1992.
___ Heller, Steven. **Jackets Required: An Illustrated History of American Book Jacket Design, 1920-1959,** by Steven Heller and Seymour Chwast. San Francisco, CA: Chronicle Books, 1995. 144pp.

BOOKSTORES
___ "B. Dalton Hugo Winners Promotion," *Locus* 33(4): 8, 76. October 1994.
___ "B. Dalton's *Sense of Wonder,*" *Locus* 30(1): 6. January 1993.
___ "Bookstores Account for Only Half of Books Sold," *Locus* 28(2): 7. February 1992.
___ "Britain's Book Club Associates Seeking 50 More Retail Sites," *Science Fiction Chronicle* 15(6): 6-7. April/May 1994.
___ "Chains Have a Bigger Piece of the Action," *Locus* 32(6): 7, 76. June 1994.
___ "Chicago Bookstore Celebrates Fifth Anniversary," *Locus* 31(1): 9. July 1993.
___ "**Fahrenheit 451** in Trouble," *Locus* 32(5): 8, 66. May 1994.
___ "Flight of Fantasy Opens in LA Area," *Science Fiction Chronicle* 14(11): 7. August 1993.
___ "Hugo's (and Edgar's) Awards to Firefighters," *Locus* 28(3): 4, 78. March 1992.
___ "LA Earthquake Hits Bookstores, Writers," *Locus* 32(2): 7. February 1994.
___ "Minneapolis SF Bookstore Escapes the Flames," *Science Fiction Chronicle* 13(6): 4-5. March 1992.
___ "New Mass. SF/Mystery Bookstore," *Science Fiction Chronicle* 17(1): 8. October/November 1995
___ "New SF Store in San Diego," *Science Fiction Chronicle* 14(8): 5. May 1993.
___ "New Specialty Stores Opening," *Locus* 30(5): 9. May 1993.
___ "Planet 10 Bankruptcy," *Locus* 30(2): 5. February 1993.
___ "Quake Damages Book Trade," *Locus* 32(3): 7. March 1994.
___ "Reorganization in the Chains," *Locus* 31(3): 6, 83. September 1993.
___ "SF Store Opens in Texas," *Science Fiction Chronicle* 17(2): 6. December 1995/January 1996.
___ "*Starlog* Launching Nationwide Comics/SF Bookstore Chain," *Science Fiction Chronicle* 15(3): 6. January 1994.
___ "Superstore Wars Escalate," *Locus* 29(5): 4. November 1992
___ "Waldenbooks and Borders Merge," *Locus* 32(2): 8, 73. February 1994.
___ King, T. Jackson. "Bookstore Signings: The Good, the Bad, the Ugly," *SFWA Bulletin* 26(3): 10-14. Fall 1992. (No. 117)
___ Tannenbaum, Jeffrey A. "Focus on Franchising: Outer Space," *Wall Street Journal* Sec. B, p. 2. April 26, 1993.

BOOTH, WILLIAM
___ Murdoch, Norman H. "Rose Culture and Social Reform: Edward Bellamy's **Looking Backward** (1888) and William Booth's **Darkest England and the Way Out** (1890)," *Utopian Studies* 3(2): 91-101. 1992.

BORDEN, GAVIN G.
___ "Borden, Gavin G. (Obituary)," *Science Fiction Chronicle* 13(5): 14. February 1992.

BORGES, JORGE LUIS
___ **The Inner World of J. L. Borges**. Princeton, NJ: Films for the Humanities, 1991. 1 videocassette, 28 minutes.
___ Balderson, Daniel. **Out of Context: Historical Reference and the Representation of Reality in Borges**. Durham, NC: Duke University Press, 1993. 216pp.
___ Barnstone, Willis. **With Borges on an Ordinary Evening in Buenos Aires: A Memoir**. Urbana: University of Illinois Press, 1993. 198pp.
___ Irwin, John T. "A Clew to the Clue: Locked Rooms and Labyrinths in Poe and Borges," in: Rosenheim, Shawn and Rachman, Stephen, ed. **The American Face of Edgar Allan Poe**. Baltimore: Johns Hopkins University Press, 1995. pp.139-154.

BORGES, JORGE LUIS (continued)
___ Maier, Linda S. **Borges and the European Avant-garde**. New York: P. Lang, 1992. 186pp. [Not seen.]
___ Mosher, Mark R. "Atemporal Labyrinths in Time: J. L. Borges and the New Physicists," *Symposium* 48(1): 51-61. Spring 1994.
___ Mosher, Mark R. **Jorge Luis Borges and the New Physics: The Literature of Modern Science and the Science of Modern Literature**. Ph.D. Dissertation, State University of New York, Albany, 1992. (DAI 53: 2392A.)
___ Read, Malcolm K. **Jorge Luis Borges and His Predecessors, or Notes Towards a Materialist History of Linguistic Idealism**. Chapel Hill: University of North Carolina, Dept. of Romance Languages, 1993. 152pp.
___ Rodríguez-Luis, Julio. **The Contemporary Praxis of the Fantastic: Borges and Cortazar**. New York: Garland, 1991. 131pp.
___ Slusser, George E. "Spacetime Geometries: Time Travel and the Modern Geometrical Narrative," by George E. Slusser and Daniele Chatelain. *Science Fiction Studies* 22(2): 161-186. July 1995.
___ Smith, Evans L. "The Golem and the Garland in Borges and Broch," *Journal of the Fantastic in the Arts* 7(2/3): 177-190. 1995.

BORGO PRESS
___ "Starmont Ceases Publishing, Passes Titles to Borgo," *Science Fiction Chronicle* 14(7): 4. April 1993.
___ "Starmont House Suspends Publication," *Locus* 30(3): 6. March 1993.

BORIS AND NATASHA (MOTION PICTURE)
___ Flynn, Rochelle O. "**Boris and Natasha** Is Just Bad Enough," *Boston (MA) Herald*. April 17, 1992. in: *NewsBank. Film and Television*. 39:B10. 1992.
___ Harris, Judith P. "**Boris and Natasha** (Review)," *Cinefantastique* 23(2/3): 122. October 1992.
___ McClain, Buzz. "**Boris and Natasha** Is Nogoodnik Update," *Washington (DC) Times*. April 17, 1992. in: *NewsBank. Film and Television*. 39:B12. 1992.
___ Millman, Joyce. "Boris Is Badenov to Be Buried," *San Francisco (CA) Examiner*. April 2, 1992. in: *NewsBank. Film and Television*. 39: B8-B9. 1992.
___ Perkins, Ken Parrish. "**Boris and Natasha** Bombs," *Dallas (TX) Morning News*. April 17, 1992. in: *NewsBank. Film and Television*. 39: B11. 1992.

BOUCHER, ANTHONY
___ Anderson, Poul. "Beer Mutterings: John W. Campbell and Anthony Boucher," *Quantum* No. 43/44: 5-6. Spring/Summer 1993.
___ Dick, Philip K. "A Letter to Anthony Boucher/A Letter From Anne Dick," *PKDS Newsletter* No. 30: 1-4. December 1992.

BOULLE, PIERRE
___ "Boulle, Pierre (Obituary)," *Locus* 32(3): 68. March 1994.
___ "Boulle, Pierre (Obituary)," *Science Fiction Chronicle* 15(4): 16. February 1994.
___ Becker, Lucille F. "Science and Detective Fiction: Complementary Genres on the Margins of French Literature," *French Literature Series* 20: 119-125. 1993.

BOVA, BEN
___ "Interview: Ben Bova," *Hailing Frequencies* (Waldenbooks) No. 2: 1, 3, 15. 1992.
___ Nicholls, Stan. "The Promise of Space," *Starlog* No. 200: 68-71, 82. March 1994.
___ Nicholls, Stan. "Scouting Ahead: Ben Bova Interviewed," *Interzone* No. 82: 23-27. April 1994.

BOWMAN, JEANNE
___ "Jeanne Bowman Wins TAFF," *Science Fiction Chronicle* 13(6): 26. March 1992.

BOWMAN, ROB
___ Vitaris, Paula. "**X-Files**: Rob Bowman," *Cinefantastique* 26(6)/27(1): 83. October 1995.

BOXING HELENA (MOTION PICTURE)
___ Ross, Patricia. "**Boxing Helena**," *Cinefantastique* 24(1): 6-7. June 1993.

BOXLIETNER, BRUCE

___ Nazzaro, Joe. "Pressures of Command," *Starlog* No. 213: 27-31, 69. April 1995.

BOY AND HIS DOG (MOTION PICTURE)

___ Moore, Patty. "Jones-Dog's Ghostwriter," *Dallas Morning News* Sec. D, p. 5. June 26, 1975.

BOYLE, ROBERT

___ Markley, Robert. "Robert Boyle, Peter Shaw, and the Reinscription of Technology: Inventing and Reinventing the Air Pump," in: Greenberg, Mark L. and Schachterle, Lance, eds. **Literature and Technology**. Bethlehem, PA: Lehigh University Press, 1992. pp.125-153.

BRACKETT, LEIGH

___ "Brackett, Leigh (Obituary)," *Science Fiction News* (Australia) No. 55: 11-12. June 1978.

___ Stableford, Brian. "Edmond Hamilton and Leigh Brackett: An Appreciation," in: Stableford, Brian. **Outside the Human Aquarium: Masters of Science Fiction**. San Bernardino, CA: Borgo, 1995. pp.7-17.

BRADBURY AWARD FOR BEST SCRIPT, 1992

___ "**Terminator II** Wins SFWA's First Bradbury Script Award," *Science Fiction Chronicle* 13(9): 4. June 1992.

BRADBURY, MALCOLM

___ Fiedler, Heiko. "Magie und Realität in Malcolm Bradburys Roman **Rates of Exchange**," *Quarber Merkur* 33(1): 15-26. June 1995. (No. 83)

BRADBURY, RAY

___ "The Essential Bradbury," *Wonder* No. 8: 7. 1992.

___ "First L. A. Imax Site Begins; Bradbury Pens Wide-Screen Properties," *Variety* p. 8. September 28, 1983.

___ "**Philip Marlowe, Bradbury Theater** Picked Up by HBO," *Variety* p.55, 64. September 11, 1985.

___ "**Something Wicked This Way Comes** (1983): Interview with Ray Bradbury and Jack Clayton," in: Goldberg, Lee, ed. **The Dreamweavers: Interviews With Fantasy Filmmakers of the 1980s**. Jefferson, NC: McFarland, 1995. pp.241-278.

___ "Talking with...Ray Bradbury: Men Are from Mars," *People Weekly* 4(22): 45. November 27, 1995.

___ Bloom, Harold. "Ray Bradbury," in: Bloom, Harold, ed. **Modern Fantasy Writers**. New York: Chelsea House, 1995. pp.1-15.

___ Bloom, Harold. "Ray Bradbury," in: Bloom, Harold, ed. **Science Fiction Writers of the Golden Age**. New York: Chelsea House, 1995. pp.78-93.

___ Bradbury, Ray. "Burning Bright: A Foreword," in: Bradbury, Ray. **Fahrenheit 451: The 40th Anniversary Edition**. New York: Simon & Schuster, 1993. pp.11-21.

___ Bradbury, Ray. **Green Shadows, White Whale**. New York: Knopf, 1992. 271pp.

___ Burleson, Donald R. "Connings: Bradbury/Oates," *Studies in Weird Fiction* No. 11: 24-29. Spring 1992.

___ DeArmond, William D. **Ray Bradbury and Oral Interpretation: An Interpreters Theatre Adaptation of Fahrenheit 451**. Ph.D. Dissertation, Southern Illinois University, Carbondale, 1981. 193pp.

___ Eller, Jon R. "The Stories of Ray Bradbury: An Annotated Finding List (1938-1991)," *Bulletin of Bibliography* 49(1): 72-51. March 1992.

___ Engelberger, Joseph F. "Commentary: Robotics in the 21st Century," *Scientific American* 273(3): 166. September 1995.

___ Eyman, Scott. "Bradbury Goes for Blarney," *West Palm Beach (FL) Post*. June 26, 1992. in: *NewsBank. Literature*. 64:E12. 1992

___ Felgenhauer, H. S. "Bradbury at Harper," *Fantasy Commentator* 8(3/4): 182-185. Fall 1995. (Whole No. 47/48)

___ Gross, Edward. "The New Illustrated Man," *Starlog* 185: 75-79. December 1992.

___ Heuermann, Hartmut. "Ray Bradbury: **Fahrenheit 451** (1953)," in: Heuermann, Hartmut and Lange, Bernd-Peter, eds. **Die Utopie in der angloamerikanischen Literatur: Interpretationen**. Düsseldorf: Bagel, 1984. pp.259-282.

___ Hoskinson, Kevin. "**The Martian Chronicles** and **Fahrenheit 451**: Ray Bradbury's Cold War Novels," *Extrapolation* 36(4): 345-359. Winter 1995.

BRADBURY, RAY (continued)

___ Kagle, Steven E. "Homage to Melville: Ray Bradbury and the Nineteenth-Century American Romance," in: Morse, Donald E., ed. **The Celebration of the Fantastic**. Westport, CT: Greenwood, 1992. pp.279-289.

___ Linaweaver, Brad. "I Sing the Image Electric: Ray Bradbury Goes to Hollywood," by Brad Linaweaver and Rod Bennett. *Wonder: The Children's Magazine for Grown-Ups* No. 8: 10-17. 1995.

___ Linaweaver, Brad. "Ray Bradbury This Way Comes," *Wonder: The Children's Magazine for Grown-Ups* No. 8: 3-6. 1995. (Reprinted from the **World Science Fiction Convention Program Book**, 1986.)

___ Lipp, Linda. "Bradbury Chronicles," *Chicago Tribune* p. 18L. June 20, 1993.

___ Lipp, Linda. "Ray Bradbury Joins Fight for Library," *Chicago Tribune* Sec. 2C, p. 1. March 9, 1992. [Not seen.]

___ Martin, Rick. "**Fahrenheit 451** Burns Even Brighter," *Washington (DC) Times*. May 10, 1992. in: *NewsBank. Literature*. 45:F7-F8. 1992

___ McGuire, Patrick. "Ray Bradbury's IQ Unnecessary," *Australian Science Fiction Review* 5(3): 11. Spring 1990. (Whole No. 25)

___ Newlove, Donald. "Ray Bradbury Is Back in Top Form, Reclaiming Fans With Refreshed Style," *Philadelphia (PA) Inquirer*. July 26, 1992. in: *NewsBank. Literature*. 56:E10. 1992

___ Nicholls, Stan. "Ray Bradbury Celebrates the Eye," in: Nicholls, Stan. **Wordsmiths of Wonder: Fifty Interviews with Writers of the Fantastic**. London: Orbit, 1993. pp.125-136.

___ Ramey, Anthony H. **Postmodernism and the Apocalyptic in Bradbury's Fiction Exposing the Eroding Aesthetic**. Master's Thesis, Marshall University, 1995. 73pp.

___ Saccaro Del Buffa, Giuseppa. "Un'utopia dell'autorigenerazione: 'La Crisalide' di Bradbury," in: Saccaro Del Buffa, Giuseppa and Lewis, Arthur O., eds. **Utopie per gli Anni Ottana**. Rome: Gangemi Editore, 1986. pp.427-434.

___ Schleier, Curt. "Bradbury's Irish Stew of a Story Is Flavored Just Right," *Detroit (MI) News*. May 6, 1992. in: *NewsBank. Literature*. 45: F9. 1992

___ Schlossberg, Howard. "Science Fiction Writer Has Bad News From the Front," *Marketing News* 26(9): 15. April 27, 1992.

___ Schwartz, Julius. "Quoth Ray Bradbury: Thank God for Julie: Memoirs of a Time Traveller, Part 3," *Amazing Stories* 68(6): 59-65. September 1993.

___ Welsh, James L. "Ray Bradbury," in: Bruccoli, Matthew J., ed. **Facts on File Bibliography of American Fiction 1919-1988**. New York: Facts on File, 1991. pp.101-103.

BRADLEY, DOUG

___ Beeler, Michael. "**Hellraiser IV: Bloodline**: Pin Head Speaks," *Cinefantastique* 26(3): 36-37. April 1995.

___ Stone, Lisa. "All Actor: Doug Bradley Is Not Pinhead," *Sci-Fi Entertainment* 1(5): 30-31. February 1995.

___ Vince, Nick. "Doug Bradley," in: Brown, Michael, ed. **Pandemonium: Further Explorations into the Worlds of Clive Barker**. Staten Island, NY: Eclise, 1991. pp.72-82.

BRADLEY, MARION ZIMMER

___ Fry, Carrol L. "The Goddess Ascending: Feminist Neo-Pagan Witchcraft in Marion Zimmer Bradley's Novels," *Journal of Popular Culture* 27(1): 67-80. Summer 1993.

___ Green, Carol A. "Only a Girl: Heroines in the Work of Anne McCaffrey and Marion Zimmer Bradley," *Vector* No. 172: 16-17. April/May 1993.

___ Hughes, Melinda. "Dark Sisters and Light Sisters: Sister Doubles and the Search for Sisterhood in **The Mists of Avalon** and **The White Raven**," *Mythlore* 19(1): 24-28. Winter 1993. (No. 71)

___ Tobin, Lee A. "Why Change the Arthur Story? Marion Zimmer Bradley's **The Mists of Avalon**," *Extrapolation* 34(2): 147-157. Summer 1993.

___ Vaughn, Sue F. "The Female Hero in Science Fiction and Fantasy: 'Carrier Bag' to 'No-Road'," *Journal of the Fantastic in the Arts* 4(4): 82-96. 1991. (No. 16)

BRADSHAW, BOOKER

___ Phillips, Mark. "Journeys to Strange Country," *Starlog* No. 206: 66-67. September 1994.

BRAGA, BRANNON

___ Altman, Mark A. "**Star Trek: The Next Generation**: Ron Moore and Brannon Braga," *Cinefantastique* 24(3/4): 60-61. October 1993.

BRAGA, BRANNON

BRAGA, BRANNON (continued)
___ Hull, Peter R. "Brannon Braga: First Best Destiny," *Star Trek: The Official Fan Club Magazine* No. 92: 30-31, 34. July/August 1993.

BRAIN DEAD (MOTION PICTURE)
___ Jones, Alan. "***Brain Dead***," *Cinefantastique* 23(6): 50-51. April 1993.
___ Schweiger, Daniel. "***Brain Dead*** (Review)," *Cinefantastique* 23(5): 59. February 1993.

BRAINS
___ Wolff, Michael J. "Brain Food," *Starlog* No. 198: 27-31. January 1994.

BRAINSCAN (MOTION PICTURE)
___ Arar, Yardena. "High-Tech Horror No Help in Awkward ***Brainscan***," *Los Angeles (CA) Daily News.* April 22, 1994. in: *NewsBank. Film and Television.* 51:F3. 1994.
___ Campbell, Bob. "Brooding Teen Turns into Mega Hitman on Computer," *(Newark, NJ) Star-Ledger.* April 22, 1994. in: *NewsBank. Film and Television.* 41:B8. 1994.
___ DeChick, Joe. "***Brainscan*** Tries to Deliver Too Much," *Cincinnati (OH) Enquirer.* April 22, 1994. in: *NewsBank. Film and Television.* 41: B9. 1994.
___ Ebert, Roger. "***Brainscan*** Updates Only-A-Dream Plots," *Denver (CO) Post.* April 22, 1994. in: *NewsBank. Film and Television.* 41:B5. 1994.
___ Faller, James M. "***Brainscan*** (Review)," *Cinefantastique* 25(5): 59. October 1994.
___ Hunter, Stephen. "***Brainscan*** Is a No-Brainer: Don't Bother," *(Baltimore, MD) Sun.* April 22, 1994. in: *NewsBank. Film and Television.* 41:B7. 1994.
___ Johnson, Malcolm. "Low-Budget Splatter Hits High-Tech Fan in ***Brainscan***," *Hartford (CT) Courant.* April 22, 1994. in: *NewsBank. Film and Television.* 41:B6. 1994.
___ Lovell, Glenn. "It Came from Cyberspace," *San Jose (CA) Mercury News.* April 22, 1994. in: *NewsBank. Film and Television.* 51:F5. 1994.
___ Lowe, Nick. "***Brainscan*** (Review)," *Interzone* No. 90: 30-32. December 1994.
___ McClain, Buzz. "Brain-Dead ***Brainscan*** Clicks Twice on Cliche," *Washington (DC) Times.* April 24, 1994. in: *NewsBank. Film and Television.* 41:B13. 1994.
___ Montesano, Anthony P. "***Brainscan***: Computer Graphics," *Cinefantastique* 25(3): 50. June 1994.
___ Montesano, Anthony P. "***Brainscan***," *Cinefantastique* 25(3): 48-51. June 1994.
___ Mosley, Ed. "Virtual Reality Bites," *Pittsburgh (PA) Post Gazette.* April 22, 1994. in: *NewsBank. Film and Television.* 41:B11. 1994.
___ Neman, Daniel. "***Brainscan*** Is Mostly a Brain-Dead Bore," *Richmond (VA) Times-Dispatch.* April 22, 1994. in: *NewsBank. Film and Television.* 41:B12. 1994.
___ Newman, Kim. "***Brainscan*** (Review)," *Sight and Sound* 4(11): 40-41. November 1994.
___ Pierce, Susan. "Despite Standard Shock Tactics, ***Brainscan*** Disturbingly Realistic," *(Little Rock, AR) Arkansas Democrat-Gazette.* April 27, 1994. in: *NewsBank. Film and Television.* 41:B4. 1994.
___ Rosenberg, Scott. "Virtual Banality," *San Francisco (CA) Examiner.* April 22, 1994. in: *NewsBank. Film and Television.* 51:F4. 1994.
___ Ryan, Desmond. "Could Violent Games Make Teens Kill?," *Philadelphia (PA) Inquirer.* April 23, 1994. in: *NewsBank. Film and Television.* 41:B10. 1994.
___ Vincent, Mal. "More Technological Brawn With No Brains," *Norfolk (VA) Virginian-Pilot.* April 27, 1994. in: *NewsBank. Film and Television.* 51:F6. 1994.

BRAM STOKER AWARDS
___ "Stoker Awards Revamped," *Locus* 34(3): 8. March 1995.

BRAM STOKER AWARDS, 1992
___ "1992 Bram Stoker Awards Winners," *Locus* 28(2): 6, 68. August 1992.
___ "Bram Stoker Awards," *Science Fiction Chronicle* 13(10): 4. July/August 1992.
___ "Bram Stoker Awards Nominations," *Locus* 28(5): 6, 65. May 1992.
___ "HWA's Bram Stoker Award Nominations," *Science Fiction Chronicle* 13(8): 4. May 1992.

BRAM STOKER'S DRACULA (MOTION PICTURE)

BRAM STOKER AWARDS, 1992 (continued)
___ "John Carpenter Keynoting NYC Bram Stoker Weekend," *Science Fiction Chronicle* 14(9): 5. June 1993.

BRAM STOKER AWARDS, 1993
___ "1994 Bram Stoker Nominations," *Locus* 32(5): 8. May 1994.
___ "Bram Stoker Awards," *Science Fiction Chronicle* 15(8): 5. June 1994.
___ "Bram Stoker Awards, 1993," *Science Fiction Chronicle* 14(10): 4. July 1993.
___ "Ellison Ties for Stoker Award After HWA Miscount Discovered," *Science Fiction Chronicle* 15(9): 4-5. August 1994.
___ "HWA Stoker Awards Winners," *Locus* 31(2): 6, 62. August 1993.
___ "HWA's Bram Stoker Award Nominations," *Science Fiction Chronicle* 14(9): 4. June 1993.
___ "Stoker Award Nomination," *Locus* 30(6): 6, 73. June 1993.
___ Hautala, Rick. "Bram Stoker Weekend," *Science Fiction Chronicle* 14(12): 26-28. September 1993.

BRAM STOKER AWARDS, 1994
___ "Bram Stoker Awards Nominees," *Locus* 34(5): 8. May 1995.
___ "Ellison Wins Delayed Stoker," *Locus* 33(4): 8, 75. October 1994.
___ "HWA Stoker Awards Winners," *Locus* 33(1): 7. July 1994.
___ "HWA's Bram Stoker Award Nominations," *Science Fiction Chronicle* 15(6): 5. April/May 1994.
___ "Preliminary Stoker Award Ballot Issued," *Locus* 34(4): 8, 66. April 1995.

BRAM STOKER AWARDS, 1995
___ "Bram Stoker Award Finalists," *Science Fiction Chronicle* 16(6): 4. May 1995.
___ "Bram Stoker Award Winners," *Science Fiction Chronicle* 16(7): 4. June/July 1995.
___ "HWA Annual Meeting and Stoker Awards Banquet," *Science Fiction Chronicle* 16(9): 4145 August/September 1995.
___ "HWA Preliminary Ballot," *Science Fiction Chronicle* 16(5): 4-5. March/April 1995.
___ "HWA Stoker Awards," *Locus* 35(1): 9. July 1995.

BRAM STOKER'S DRACULA (MOTION PICTURE)
___ Arnold, Gary. "***Dracula*** Anemic Offspring in the Bloodline," *Washington (DC) Times.* November 13, 1992. in: *NewsBank. Film and Television.* 111:B13-B14. 1992.
___ Bernard, Jami. "Out for the Count," *New York (NY) Post.* November 13, 1992. in: *NewsBank. Film and Television.* 111:B10. 1992.
___ Biodrowski, Steve. "***Bram Stoker's Dracula***: Francis Ford Coppola on Adapting Stoker's Gothic Masterpiece for the '90s," *Cinefantastique* 23(6): 54. April 1993.
___ Biodrowski, Steve. "Coppola's ***Dracula***: Adapting Bram Stoker," *Cinefantastique* 23(4): 36-38. December 1992.
___ Biodrowski, Steve. "Coppola's ***Dracula***: Directing the Horror Epic," *Cinefantastique* 23(4): 32-34. December 1992.
___ Biodrowski, Steve. "Coppola's ***Dracula***: Filming Lo-Tech Gothic," *Cinefantastique* 23(4): 52-54. December 1992.
___ Biodrowski, Steve. "Coppola's ***Dracula***: The Vampire Brides," *Cinefantastique* 23(4): 48-49. December 1992.
___ Biodrowski, Steve. "Coppola's ***Dracula***: Vampire Effects," *Cinefantastique* 23(4): 40-42. December 1992.
___ Biodrowski, Steve. "Coppola's ***Dracula***," *Cinefantastique* 23(4): 24-55. December 1992.
___ Biodrowski, Steve. "***Dracula***: The Untold Story," *Cinefantastique* 23(2/3): 12-13. October 1992.
___ Campbell, Bob. "***Bram Stoker's Dracula*** a Shocker to Count On," *Newark (NJ) Star-Ledger.* November 13, 1992. in: *NewsBank. Film and Television.* 111:B9. 1992.
___ Cook, Pam. "***Dracula*** (Review)," *Sight and Sound* 3(2): 47-48. February 1993.
___ Doherty, Thomas. "***Bram Stoker's Dracula***: Reviving an Undead Career," *Cinefantastique* 23(6): 59. April 1993.
___ Ebert, Roger. "Despite Overbite, ***Dracula*** Looks Good," *Chicago (IL) Sun Times.* November 13, 1992. in: *NewsBank. Film and Television.* 111:B3-B4. 1992.
___ Ehrenstein, David. "One From the Art," *Film Comment* 29(1): 27-30. January/February 1993.
___ French, Lawrence. "***Bram Stoker's Dracula***: Matte Artistry," *Cinefantastique* 23(6): 55-58. April 1993.

BRAM STOKER'S DRACULA (MOTION PICTURE) (continued)
___ Hunter, Stephen. "*Dracula*: The Old Boy Never Looked So Good," *Baltimore (MD) Sun*. November 13, 1992. in: *NewsBank. Film and Television*. 111:B5-B6. 1992.
___ Johnson, Malcolm. "Coppola's *Dracula* a Flashy but Hollow Version of a Classic," *Hartford (CT) Courant*. November 13, 1992. in: *NewsBank. Film and Television*. 111:A13-A14. 1992.
___ Kronke, David. "*Dracula*'s Problem: All Show and No Tell," *Los Angeles (CA) Daily News*. November 13, 1992. in: *NewsBank. Film and Television*. 111:A8-A9. 1992.
___ Lowe, Nick. "*Bram Stoker's Dracula* (Review)," *Interzone* No. 70: 59-60. April 1993.
___ Magid, Ron. "Effects Add Bite to *Bram Stoker's Dracula*," *American Cinematographer* 73(12): 56-64. December 1992.
___ Mahar, Ted. "Down for the Count: A Dreary *Dracula*," *Portland (OR) The Oregonian*. November 13, 1992. in: *NewsBank. Film and Television*. 111:B11. 1992.
___ Mills, Michael. "Undead and a Hit (Review)," *West Palm Beach (FL) Post*. November 15, 1992. in: *NewsBank. Film and Television*. 112:E6-E7. 1992.
___ Movshovitz, Howie. "A Taste for the Bizarre," *Denver (CO) Post*. November 13, 1992. in: *NewsBank. Film and Television*. 111:A12. 1992.
___ Pourroy, Janine. "Heart of Darkness," *Cinefex* No. 53: 22-53. February 1993.
___ Ringel, Eleanor. "New Blood," *Atlanta (GA) Journal*. November 13, 1992. in: *NewsBank. Film and Television*. 111:B1-B2. 1992.
___ Rosenberg, Scott. "Carnal Gnawledge," *San Francisco (CA) Examiner*. November 13, 1992. in: *NewsBank. Film and Television*. 111:A10-A11. 1992.
___ Shapiro, Marc. "Blood & Shadows," *Starlog* 185: 40-43, 72. December 1992.
___ Turner, George. "*Bram Stoker's Dracula*: A Happening Vampire," *American Cinematographer* 73(11): 36-45. November 1992.
___ Turner, George. "*Dracula* Meets the Son of Coppola," *American Cinematographer* 73(11): 46-52. November 1992.
___ Verniere, James. "Visual Feast," *Boston (MA) Herald*. November 13, 1992. in: *NewsBank. Film and Television*. 111:B7-B8. 1992.
___ Wilmington, Michael. "A Shtick Through the Heart," *Los Angeles (CA) Times*. November 15, 1992. in: *NewsBank. Film and Television*. 111:A5-A7. 1992.
___ Wuntch, Phillip. "*Bram Stoker's Dracula* Coppola's Opulence Revives a Classic," *Dallas (TX) Morning News*. November 13, 1992. in: *NewsBank. Film and Television*. 111:B12. 1992.

BRANAGH, KENNETH
___ Spelling, Ian. "Horrors of *Frankenstein*," *Starlog* No. 211: 32-35, 70. February 1995.

BRANDIS, JONATHAN
___ Warren, Bill. "Sub Teen," *Starlog* No. 197: 55-57, 82. December 1993.

BRANDNER, GARY
___ Wood, Martine. **The Work of Gary Brandner: An Annotated Bibiography and Guide**. San Bernardino, CA: Borgo Press, 1995. 112pp.

BRAVESTARR (TV)
___ "Filmation Prepping *Bravestarr* Film, Syndie TV Series," *Variety* p. 7, 26. June 11, 1986.
___ "High Tech Kidvid Cowboys Are the Latest to Ride Syndie Trail," *Variety* p. 47, 74. June 18, 1986.

BRAZIL
___ de Sousa Causo, Roberto. "Science Fiction, a Global Community: Brazil," *Locus* 32(4): 40-41. April 1994.
___ de Sousa Causo, Roberto. "SF in Brazil," *Locus* 28(4): 37, 65. April 1992.
___ de Sousa Causo, Roberto. "SF in Brazil," *Locus* 29(6): 48. December 1992.
___ de Sousa Causo, Roberto. "SF in Brazil," *Locus* 31(6): 36, 70. December 1993.
___ de Sousa Causo, Roberto. "SF in Brazil," *Locus* 33(1): 47. July 1994.
___ de Sousa Causo, Roberto. "SF in Brazil," *Locus* 34(1) 72. January 1995.

BRAZIL (continued)
___ de Sousa Causo, Roberto. "SF in Brazil," *Locus* 34(4): 35, 38. April 1995.
___ de Sousa Causo, Roberto. "SF in Brazil," *Locus* 35(3): 52-53. September 1993.
___ Nascimento, R. C., ed. **Catálogo de Ficção Científica Em Língua Portuguesa (1921-1993)**. Sao Paulo, Brazil: Nasciemento, 1994. Part 1 of 6, 80pp. [Not seen.]
___ Tavares, Braulio, ed. **Fantastic, Fantasy and Science Fiction Literature Catalog**. Rio de Janeiro, Brasil: Biblioteca Nacional, n.d., ca. 1993. 78pp. (International Publications Series No. 2)

BRAZIL (MOTION PICTURE)
___ "*Brazil* Makers Vow to Fight Universal Over Stateside Cuts," *Variety* p.4, 22. September 25, 1985.
___ "Universal Scrambles to Place *N. Y. Times Brazil* Ads," *Variety* p.6. December 25, 1985.
___ Erickson, John. "The Ghost in the Machine: Gilliam's Postmodern Response in *Brazil* to the Orwellian Dystopia of **Nineteen Eighty-Four**," *Utopian Studies* 4(2): 26-34. 1993.
___ Friedman, Regien-Mihal. "Capitals of Sorrow: From **Metropolis** to *Brazil*," *Utopian Studies* 4(2): 35-43. 1993.

BREEN, WALTER
___ "Breen, Walter (Obituary)," *Locus* 30(6): 72. June 1993.
___ "Breen, Walter (Obituary)," *Science Fiction Chronicle* 14(9): 16. June 1993.
___ "Walter Breen Charged With Child Molestation," *Science Fiction Chronicle* 13(5): 27. February 1992.

BREHL, JENNIFER
___ "Jennifer Brehl Joins Avon," *Locus* 35(6): 8, 81. December 1995.
___ "John Douglas Moves to HarperPrism; Jennifer Brehl Is New Avonova Editor," *Science Fiction Chronicle* 17(2): 4. December 1995/January 1996.

BRENNAN, JOSEPH PAYNE
___ Dziemianowicz, Stefan. "Darkness Come to Life: The Weird Fiction of Joseph Payne Brennan," *Studies in Weird Fiction* No. 9: 18-26. Spring 1991.

BRENNERT, ALAN
___ Florence, Bill. "His Pilgrim Soul," *Starlog* No. 215: 75-81. June 1995.

BRETNOR, REGINALD
___ "Bretnor, Reginald (Obituary)," *Locus* 29(3): 76-77. September 1992.
___ "Bretnor, Reginald (Obituary)," *Science Fiction Chronicle* 13(11/12): 18. August 1992.

BRIDE OF FRANKENSTEIN (MOTION PICTURE)
___ Bennett, Rod. "One Man's Passion, or, How I Got My Tape of *The Bride of Frankenstein*," *Wonder: The Children's Magazine for Grown-Ups* No. 8: 32-39, 51-54. 1995.
___ Sevastakis, Michael. **Songs of Love and Death: The Classical American Horror Film of the 1930s**. Westport, CT: Greenwood, 1993. 232pp.

BRIDGE PUBLICATIONS
___ "Bridge Helps L. A. Libraries," *Locus* 32(1): 9. January 1994.

BRIDGES, JEFF
___ Lowry, Brian. "Beloved *Starman*," by Brian Lowry and Christine C. Menefee. in: McDonnell, David, ed. **Starlog's Science Fiction Heroes and Heroines**. New York: Crescent Books, 1995. pp.55-57.

BRIDGES, LLOYD
___ Weaver, Tom. "Lloyd Bridges," in: Weaver, Tom. **They Fought the Creature Features: Interviews with 23 Classic Horror, Science Fiction and Serial Stars**. Jefferson, NC: McFarland, 1995. pp.85-96.
___ Weaver, Tom. "Man of the Seas," *Starlog* 182: 25-29, 66. September 1992.

BRIEF HISTORY OF TIME (MOTION PICTURE)

BROOKS, TERRY

BRIEF HISTORY OF TIME (MOTION PICTURE)
___ Rosenheim, Shawn. "Extraterrestrial: Science Fictions in *A Brief History of Time* and *The Incredible Shrinking Man*," *Film Quartrely* 48(4): 15-21. Summer 1995.

BRIGGS, PETER
___ Jones, Alan. "*Alien vs. Predator*," *Cinefantastique* 25(4): 4-5. August 1994.

BRIGGS, RAYMOND
___ Lenz, Millicent. "Raymond Brigg's **When the Wind Blows**: Toward an Ecology of the Mind for Young Readers," in: Sullivan, C. W., III. **Science Fiction for Young Readers**. Westport, CT: Greenwood, 1993. pp.197-204.

BRIN, DAVID
___ "David Brin Takes a Fresh Look at an Old SF Theme with His Latest Book, **The Glory Season**," *Hailing Frequencies* (Waldenbooks) No. 7: 3-6, 20. 1993.
___ "On Technology: Sci-Fi Vision of Things to Come: Authors Brin and Gibson Depict Opposing Future Outcomes for the Evolving Internet," *San Francisco (CA) Chronicle* February 20, 1996. (Cited from the Internet Edition.)
___ Brin, David. "A Shaman's View," in: Jakubowski, Maxim and James, Edward, eds. **The Profession of Science Fiction**. New York: St. Martin's, 1992. pp.161-168.
___ Nicholls, Stan. "David Brin Won't Cop the Rap," in: Nicholls, Stan. **Wordsmiths of Wonder: Fifty Interviews with Writers of the Fantastic**. London: Orbit, 1993. pp.33-42.

BRINKLEY, WILLIAM C.
___ "Brinkley, William C. (Obituary)," *Locus* 32(1): 61. January 1994.

BRISBANE, COUTTS
___ Stone, Graham. "Notes on Australian Science Fiction," *Science Fiction News* (Australia) No. 53: 2-5. February 1978.
___ Stone, Graham. "Notes on Australian Science Fiction," *Science Fiction News* (Australia) No. 67: 2-9. January 1983.

BRITE, POPPY Z.
___ "British Fantasy Awards," *Science Fiction Chronicle* 16(1): 5. October 1994.
___ "Interview: Poppy Z. Brite," *Journal of the Dark* No. 6: 7-8. Spring 1995.
___ "Poppy Z. Brite: Taking the Plunge," *Locus* 30(5): 4, 73. May 1993.
___ Fowler, Christopher J. "Brite Now! Poppy Z. Brite Interviewed," *Interzone* No. 84: 23-27. June 1994.
___ MacCulloch, Simon. "Popacateptl Purple: Poppy Z. Brite's **Lost Souls**," *Studies in Weird Fiction* No. 15: 5-12. Summer 1994.

BRITISH FANTASY AWARDS, 1992
___ "British Fantasy Awards," *Science Fiction Chronicle* 14(3): 4. December 1992.
___ "British Fantasy Awards, 1992," *Locus* 28(2): 7. February 1992.
___ "British Fantasy Awards, 1992," *Locus* 29(5): 5. November 1992

BRITISH FANTASY AWARDS, 1993
___ "British Fantasy Awards," *Science Fiction Chronicle* 15(2): 4. November/December 1993.

BRITISH FANTASY AWARDS, 1994
___ "British Fantasy Awards," *Science Fiction Chronicle* 16(1): 5. October 1994.

BRITISH FANTASY AWARDS, 1995
___ "British Fantasy Awards, 1995," *Locus* 35(6): 9. December 1995.
___ "British Fantasy Awards, 1995," *Science Fiction Chronicle* 17(2): 5. December 1995/January 1996.

BRITISH SCIENCE FICTION ASSOCIATION AWARDS, 1992
___ "BSFA Awards," *Locus* 28(6): 7. June 1992.
___ "Dan Simmons, Molly Brown Win BSFA Awards," *Science Fiction Chronicle* 13(8): 4. May 1992.

BRITISH SCIENCE FICTION ASSOCIATION AWARDS, 1993
___ "British SF Awards, 1993," *Science Fiction Chronicle* 14(10): 8. July 1993.

BRITISH SCIENCE FICTION ASSOCIATION AWARDS, 1993 (continued)
___ "BSFA Awards Winners," *Locus* 31(2): 6. August 1993.
___ "BSFA Awards, 1993," *Locus* 32(5): 8, 66. May 1994.

BRITISH SCIENCE FICTION ASSOCIATION AWARDS, 1994
___ "BSFA Awards," *Locus* 34(6): 9. June 1995.
___ "BSFA Awards Nominations," *Locus* 34(5): 9, 75. May 1995.

BRITTON, DAVID
___ "SF Author Jailed," *Locus* 30(5): 9. May 1993.

BROADCASTING
___ "New Media Giant: Time Warner/Turner Merge," *Locus* 35(4): 9. October 1995.

BROBST, HARRY
___ "An Interview With Harry Brobst," in: Joshi, S. T., ed. **The H. P. Lovecraft Centennial Conference Proceedings**. West Warwick, RI: Necronomicon, 1991. pp.22-23.

BROCH, HERMANN
___ Smith, Evans L. "The Golem and the Garland in Borges and Broch," *Journal of the Fantastic in the Arts* 7(2/3): 177-190. 1995.

BROCKSMITH, ROY
___ Warren, Bill. "Real Truths," *Starlog* No. 195: 58-61, 72. October 1993.

BRODERICK, DAMIEN
___ Blackford, Russell. "Tiger in the Prison House: Damien Broderick," *Science Fiction: A Review of Speculative Literature* 13(1): 3-9. 1995(?). (No. 37)
___ Broderick, Damien. "The Profession of Science Fiction, 44: The Semi-Detached Sci-Fi Life of an Almost Famous Writer," *Foundation* No. 59: 5-16. Autumn 1993.

BRODY, LARRY
___ Florence, Bill. "The Magic Man," *Starlog* No. 189: 30-33, 68. April 1993.

BROKEN ARROW (MOTION PICTURE)
___ Duncan, Jody. "*Broken Arrow*: Stealth Effects," *Cinefex* No. 64: 13-14. December 1995.

BROKEN VICTORY (MOTION PICTURE)
___ "*Broken Victory* (Review)," *Variety* p. 16. May 18, 1988.

BROMLEY-DAVENPORT, HARRY
___ van Hise, James. "*Xtro-3: Watch the Skies*: Series Auteur," *Cinefantastique* 27(2): 50. November 1995.

BROOKHOUSE, CHRISTOPHER
___ Harkins, Patricia. "Speaking Dead in the Medieval Romance **Sir Amadace and the White Knight**," *Journal of the Fantastic in the Arts* 3(3): 62-71. 1994.

BROOKS, AVERY
___ Spelling, Ian. "In Command," *Starlog* No. 207: 41-44, 70. October 1994.

BROOKS, CONRAD
___ Kaltenbach, Chris. "A Maryland Actor Saw His Spaceship Come in in an Awful 1959 Film," (Baltimore, MD) Sun. July 7, 1994. in: *NewsBank. Film and Television.* 62:E8. 1994.

BROOKS, TERRY
___ "Terry Brooks: Telling a Story," *Locus* 32(2): 4-5, 71. February 1994.
___ Lyke, M. L. "Terry Brooks and the Importance of Success," *Seattle Post-Intelligencer* Sec. C, p. 1, 3. April 5, 1993.
___ Nicholls, Stan. "The Nature of the Beast: Terry Brooks Interviewed," *Interzone* No. 60: 40-42. June 1992.
___ Nicholls, Stan. "Terry Brooks Majors in Myth," in: Nicholls, Stan. **Wordsmiths of Wonder: Fifty Interviews with Writers of the Fantastic**. London: Orbit, 1993. pp.303-310.

BROPHY, BRIGID

BROPHY, BRIGID
___ "Brophy, Brigid (Obituary)," *Locus* 35(4): 70. October 1995.

BROTHER FROM ANOTHER PLANET (MOTION PICTURE)
___ "Sayles Holds Back U.S. Rights to His Comedy for Cannes Bids," *Variety* p. 284. May 9, 1984.

BROWN, CHARLES BROCKDEN
___ Bloom, Harold. "Charles Brockden Brown," in: Bloom, Harold. **Classic Horror Writers**. New York: Chelsea House, 1994. pp.14-26.
___ Christophersen, Bill. **The Apparition in the Glass: Charles Brockden Brown's American Gothic**. Athens: University of Georgia Press, 1994. 208pp.
___ Clemit, Pamela. **The Godwinian Novel: The Rational Fictions of Godwin, Brockden Brown, Mary Shelley**. Oxford: Clarendon Press, 1993. 254pp.

BROWN, CHARLES N.
___ Brown, Charles N. "25 Years of *Locus*," *Locus* 30(4): 34-35. April 1993.

BROWN, CLAIRE PARMAN
___ "Brown, Claire (Obituary)," *Science Fiction Chronicle* 15(3): 14. January 1994.
___ "Brown, Claire Parman (Obituary)," *Locus* 31(6): 68. December 1993.

BROWN, CLANCY
___ Chrissinger, Craig W. "Mechanically Inclined," *Starlog* No. 210: 32-35, 66. January 1995.

BROWN, FREDRIC
___ Seabrook, Jack. **Martians and Misplaced Clues: The Life and Work of Fredric Brown**. Bowling Green, OH: Popular Press, 1994. 312pp.
___ Stephens, Christopher P. **A Checklist of Fred Brown**. Hastings-on-Hudson, NY: Ultramarine, 1992. 83pp.

BROWNING, RICOU
___ Weaver, Tom. "Ricou Browning," in: Weaver, Tom. **They Fought the Creature Features: Interviews with 23 Classic Horror, Science Fiction and Serial Stars**. Jefferson, NC: McFarland, 1995. pp.97-109.

BROWNING, TOD
___ Blake, Michael F. "The Dark Duo: Tod Browning and Lon Chaney, Sr.," *Filmfax* No. 43: 50-57, 97. February/March 1994.
___ Skal, David J. "Dark Carnival: The Secret World of Tod Browning (Book Excerpt)," by David J. Skal and Elias Savada. *Cinefantastique* 27(3): 36-38. December 1995.

BRUCE DIET (MOTION PICTURE)
___ Persons, Dan. "*The Bruce Diet* (Review)," *Cinefantastique* 23(2/3): 122. October 1992.

BRUNNER, JOHN
___ "Brunner, John: Tomorrow May Be Even Worse: John Kilian Houston Brunner (1934-1995) (Obituary)," *Vector* No. 185: 4. September/October 1995.
___ "Brunner, John (Obituary)," *Locus* 35(4): 5, 70-73. October 1995.
___ "Brunner, John (Obituary)," *Locus* 35(5): 78-79. November 1995.
___ "Brunner, John (Obituary)," *Science Fiction Chronicle* 17(1): 22. October/November 1995
___ Ashley, Mike. "Behind the Realities: The Fantasies of John Brunner," *Weird Tales* 53(3): 80-84. Spring 1992. (No. 304)
___ Brunner, John. "Sometime in the Recent Future...," *New Scientist* 138(1868): 28-31. April 10, 1993.
___ Brunner, John. "Sometime in the Recent Future...," *Science Fiction Chronicle* 15(5): 30-31. March 1994.
___ Edgar, Robert. "The Nature of Survival in the 21st Century: The Survival of Concern in 1995," *Vector* No. 185: 5-8. September/October 1995.
___ Melia, Sally-Ann. "Power Corrupts: John Brunner Interviewed," *Interzone* No. 97: 18-21. July 1995.
___ Puschmann-Nalenz, Barbara. **Science Fiction and Postmodern Fiction: A Genre Study**. New York: Peter Lang, 1992. 268pp. (Trans. of **Science Fiction und Ihre Grenzbereieche**.)

BUFFY THE VAMPIRE SLAYER (MOTION PICTURE)

BRUNNER, JOHN (continued)
___ Zajac, Ronald J. **The Dystopian City in British and United States Science Fiction, 1960-1975: Urban Chronotopes as Models of Historical Closure**. Master's Thesis, McGill University, 1992. 104pp. (Master's Abstracts 31/03, p. 1020. Fall 1993.)

BRUST, STEVEN
___ "Steven Brust: The Cool Theory of Literature," *Locus* 32(3): 4, 73. March 1994.
___ Ringel, Faye. "The Scribblies: A Shared World," *Extrapolation* 35(3): 201-210. Fall 1994.
___ Sinor, Bradley H. "Rapier's Edge," *Starlog* No. 203: 49-51. June 1994.

BUCHANAN, LARRY
___ Goodsell, Greg. "The Weird and Wacky World of Larry Buchanan," *Filmfax* No. 38: 60-66. April/May 1993.

BUCK ROGERS (TV)
___ "MCA Back in Space With Salvage Plan for *Buck Rogers*," *Variety* p. 50. January 6, 1982.

BUCKLIN, NATHAN
___ Ringel, Faye. "The Scribblies: A Shared World," *Extrapolation* 35(3): 201-210. Fall 1994.

BUDRYS, ALGIS
___ "Algis Budrys Buys *Tomorrow* SF From Pulphouse," *Science Fiction Chronicle* 14(4): 4. January 1993.
___ "Budrys Buys *Tomorrow*," *Locus* 30(1): 6. January 1993.
___ "Budrys Drops Review Columns," *Locus* 29(6): 6. December 1992.
___ Beggs, Delores G. "Algis Budrys Talks About Science Fiction," *Quantum* No. 43/44: 9-11. Spring/Summer 1993.
___ Blackmore, Tim. "The Hunchbacked Hero in the Fiction of A. J. Budrys," *Extrapolation* 33(3): 230-244. Fall 1992.
___ Melia, Sally-Ann. "I Write and I Write Good--And That's the Way of It: Algis Budrys Interviewed," *Interzone* No. 95: 23-26. May 1995.
___ Patrouch, Joe. "Rogue Moon and Me," *Lan's Lantern* No. 41: 69-72. July 1993.

BUFFY THE VAMPIRE SLAYER (MOTION PICTURE)
___ "Whimsical Buffy Passes Blood Test," *Washington (DC) Times*. July 31, 1992. in: *NewsBank. Film and Television*. 68:A14. 1992
___ Bernard, Jami. "Buffy: Rough Fluff Just Enough," *New York (NY) Post*. July 31, 1992. in: *NewsBank. Film and Television*. 68:A13. 1992
___ Campbell, Bob. "*Buffy the Vampire Slayer* Plays Its Horror Tooth in Cheek as Wry Reanimated Feature," *Newark (NJ) Star-Ledger*. July 31, 1992. in: *NewsBank. Film and Television*. 68:A12. 1992
___ Hunter, Stephen. "The Vampire Hasn't Been Born Whose Fangs Are a Match for a Valley Girl," *Baltimore (MD) Sun*. July 31, 1992. in: *NewsBank. Film and Television*. 77:C3. 1992
___ Johnson, Malcolm. "Promising Vampire Slayer Evaporates," *Hartford (CT) Courant*. July 31, 1992. in: *NewsBank. Film and Television*. 68:A9. 1992
___ Mahar, Ted. "Buffy Goes for the Jugular," *Portland (OR) The Oregonian*. July 31, 1992. in: *NewsBank. Film and Television*. 77:C4. 1992
___ Mosvshovitz, Howie. "Vampires vs. Valley Girls Comedy Clever But Disjointed," *Denver (CO) Post*. July 31, 1992. in: *NewsBank. Film and Television*. 77:B14. 1992
___ Persons, Dan. "*Buffy the Vampire Slayer* (Review)," *Cinefantastique* 23(4): 60. December 1992.
___ Rhodes, Joe. "Eeeeyew. . . Gross. Where's My Wooden Stake," *Los Angeles (CA) Times*. July 31, 1992. in: *NewsBank. Film and Television*. 63:A6-A8. 1992
___ Rosenberg, Scott. "Saved By the Belle," *San Francisco (CA) Examiner*. July 31, 1992. in: *NewsBank. Film and Television*. 77:B12-13. 1992
___ Stark, Susan. "Blood Lite: Buffy Sends a Valley Girl on a Comic Sleigh Ride," *Detroit (MI) News*. July 31, 1992. in: *NewsBank. Film and Television*. 68:A11. 1992
___ Strauss, Bob. "So Much Wrong With Buffy It Plays Like a Suicide Attempt," *Los Angeles (CA) Daily News*. July 31, 1992. in: *NewsBank. Film and Television*. 77:B11. 1992
___ Tucker, Ernest. "Lifeless Buffy Lacks the Bite of a Good Spoof," *Chicago (IL) Sun Times*. July 31, 1992. in: *NewsBank. Film and Television*. 77:C1-C2. 1992

BUFFY THE VAMPIRE SLAYER (MOTION PICTURE)

BUFFY THE VAMPIRE SLAYER (MOTION PICTURE) (continued)
___ Verniere, James. "Buffy Stakes Her Claim," *Boston (MA) Herald*. July 31, 1992. in: *NewsBank. Film and Television*. 68:A10. 1992

BUJOLD, LOIS McMASTER
___ "1992 *Locus* Awards," *Locus* 28(2): 1, 42-45. August 1992.
___ "1992 Hugo Awards Winners," *Locus* 29(4): 6, 42-47. October 1992.
___ "1995 *Locus* Awards Winners," *Locus* 35(2): 7, 34-37. August 1995.
___ "1995 Hugo Winners," *Locus* 35(3): 7. September 1993.
___ "The Hugos (Or, the Empire Strikes Back)," *Science Fiction Chronicle* 17(2): 55-56. December 1995/January 1996.
___ "Lois McMaster Bujold: No-Fault Series," *Locus* 35(2): 4-5, 70-71. August 1995.
___ "World Science Fiction Convention Hugo Awards, 1995," *Science Fiction Chronicle* 17(1): 5. October/November 1995
___ "World SF Convention Hugo Awards," *Science Fiction Chronicle* 14(1): 4. October 1992.
___ Counihan, Elizabeth. "The Worst Possible Thing: Lois McMaster Bujold Interviewed," *Interzone* No. 101: 20-23. November 1995.
___ Kemper, Bart. "Dancing on the Edge," *Writer's Digest* 74(7): 6-7. July 1994.
___ Kemper, Bart. "Touching the Reader: An Interview With Lois McMaster Bujold," *Quantum* No. 43/44: 17-18. Spring/Summer 1993.
___ Lake, Ken. "Lois McMaster Bujold Interviewed," *Vector* No. 171: 7-11. February/March 1993.
___ Levy, Michael M. "A Certain Inherent Kindness: An Interview With Lois McMaster Bujold," *SFRA Review* No. 220: 15-32. November/December 1995.
___ Rand, Ken. "SFC Interview: Talking With the Real Lois McMaster Bujold," *Science Fiction Chronicle* 17(1): 7, 37-40. October/November 1995
___ Shwartz, Susan. "An Interview With Lois McMaster Bujold," *Marion Zimmer Bradley's Fantasy Magazine* No. 16: 14-18. Spring/Summer 1992.

BULGARIA
___ "Science Fiction, a Global Community: Bulgaria," *Locus* 32(4): 39-40. April 1994.
___ "SF in Bulgaria," *Locus* 28(4): 40. April 1992.
___ "SF in Bulgaria," *Locus* 30(4): 37, 62. April 1993.

BULGARIN, FADDEI VENEDIKTOVICH
___ Pospisil, Ivo. "Horce ironicka science fiction Faddeje Bulgarina," *Svet Literatury: Casopis pro Novoveke Zahranicni Literatury* (Amsterdam, Netherlands) 5: 22-28. 1993.

BULL, CHARLES LIVINGSTON
___ Barrett, Robert R. "Animal Fashion Plates: Charles Livingston Bull (1874-1932)," *Burroughs Bulletin* NS. No. 15: 22-25. July 1993.

BULL, EMMA
___ "Emma Bull: Interpreting the World," *Locus* 28(4): 4, 65. April 1992.
___ Ringel, Faye. "The Scribblies: A Shared World," *Extrapolation* 35(3): 201-210. Fall 1994.

BULLETIN OF THE SCIENCE FICTION WRITERS OF AMERICA
___ SEE: SFWA BULLETIN.

BULLOCH, JEREMY
___ Nensi, Salman A. "Exclusive Interview: Jeremy Bulloch, Behind the Mask of Boba Fett," *Lucasfilm Fan Club* No. 21: 2-3. Winter 1994.

BULWER-LYTTON, EDWARD
___ Lange, Bernd-Peter. "Edward Bulwer-Lytton, **The Coming Race** (1871)," in: Heuermann, Harmut, ed. **Der Science Fiction Roman in der angloamerikanischen Literatur: Interpretationen**. Düsseldorf: Bagel, 1986. pp.31-46.

BULYCHEV, KIR
___ "Russian Author's Dacha Firebombed," *Locus* 32(6): 8, 76. June 1994.
___ Rudishina, T. "O trudnykh i legkikh voposakn zhezni," *Detskaya Literatura* 5: 74-76. May 1991. [Not seen.]

BUNCH, CHRIS
___ "Allen Cole and Chris Bunch: The Accidental Series," *Locus* 34(2): 5, 75. February 1995.

BUNIN, LOU
___ "Bunin, Lou (Obituary)," *Science Fiction Chronicle* 15(5): 12. March 1994.

BURDEKIN, KATHERINE
___ McKay, George. "Metapropaganda: Self-reading Dystopian Fiction: Burdekin's **Swastika Night** and Orwell's **Nineteen Eighty-Four**," *Science Fiction Studies* 21(3): 302-314. November 1994.
___ Russell, Elizabeth. "Katherine Burdekin's **Swastika Night**: The Search for Truths and Texts," *Foundation* No. 55: 36-43. Summer 1992.

BURGESS, ANTHONY
___ "Burgess, Anthony (Obituary)," *Locus* 32(1): 60-61. January 1994.
___ "Burgess, Anthony (Obituary)," *Newsweek* 122(23): 84. December 6, 1993.
___ "Burgess, Anthony: The Last Man of Letters (Obituary)," *Washington (DC) Post Book World* p. 15. December 12, 1993.
___ Atlas, James. "Burgeoning Burgess," *Vanity Fair* 50: 110-111. March 1987.
___ Bly, James I. **Structure and Theme in Burgess's *Honey for the Bears*, *A Clockwork Orange*, and *Tremor of Intent***. Ph.D. Dissertation, University of Northern Colorado, 1978. 372pp. (DAI 39:4954A. Feb. 1979.)
___ Brady, Charles A. "A Vaudeville for Mozart," *Buffalo (NY) News*. January 19, 1992. in: *NewsBank. Literature*. 8:G9. 1992
___ Dexter, Bruce. "Burgess Celebrates Mozart's Life With Keen Delight," *San Diego (CA) Union*. January 12, 1992. in: *NewsBank. Literature*. 8:G8. 1992
___ Guinn, John. "Genius Comes in Multiple Servings," *Detroit (MI) News and Free Press*. December 15, 1991. in: *NewsBank. Literature*. 2: A8. 1992
___ Heller, Arno. "Anthony Burgess, *A Clockwork Orange* (1962)," in: Heuermann, Harmut, ed. **Der Science Fiction Roman in der angloamerikanischen Literatur: Interpretationen**. Düsseldorf: Bagel, 1986. pp.236-252.
___ Mentzer, Thomas L. "The Ethics of Behavior Modification: **A Clockwork Orange** Revisited," *Essays in Arts and Sciences* 9(1): 93-105. May 1980.
___ Roth, Ellen S. **The Rhetoric of First-Person Point of View in the Novel and Film Forms: A Study of Anthony Burgess' A Clockwork Orange and Henry James' A Turn of the Screw and Their Film Adaptations**. Ph.D. Dissertation, New York University, 1978. 308pp. (DAI 39: 4558A. Feb. 1979.)
___ Sage, Lorna. "In Full Spate: The Fertility and Generosity of Anthony Burgess," *Times Literary Supplement* No. 4733: 26. December 17, 1993.
___ Sisk, David W. **Claiming Mastery over the Word: Transformations of Language in Six Twentieth Century Dystopias**. Ph.D. Dissertation, University of North Carolina, Chapel Hill, 1994. 405pp. (DAI-A 55/07, p. 1972. January 1995.)
___ Steffen, Nancy L. **Burgess' World of Words**. Ph.D. Dissertation, Brandeis University, 1977. 469pp. (DAI-A 38(5): 2781. November 1977.)

BURGESS, MICHAEL
___ Burgess, Michael. **The Work of Robert Reginald: An Annotated Bibliography and Guide** 2nd ed., revised and enlarged. San Bernardino, CA: Borgo Press, 1992. 176pp.

BURKETT, LARRY
___ Sterling, Bruce. "Sneaking for Jesus 2001," *Science Fiction Eye* No. 11: 13-17. December 1992.

BURLESON, DONALD R.
___ Deleault, Arthur R. "Perceptions: Campbell/Burleson," *Studies in Weird Fiction* No. 15: 18-19. Summer 1994.

BURNETT, ALAN
___ Garcia, Bob. "***Batman*: Alan Burnett, Script Supervisor," by Bob Garcia and Nancy Garcia. *Cinefantastique* 24(6)/25(1): 84-85. February 1994.

BURNETT, FRANCES HODGSON

___ Stolzenbach, Mary M. "Braid Yorkshire: The Language of Myth? An Appreciation of **The Secret Garden** by Frances Hodgson Burnett," *Mythlore* 20(4): 25-29. Winter 1995. (Whole No. 78)

BURNS, BOB

___ Voger, Mark. "Gorilla My Screams; Or, How My Life With Movie Monsters Made a Monkey out of Me," *Filmfax* No. 36: 43-48, 98. December 1992/January 1993.

BURNS, JIM

___ Frank, Jane. "Bio of a Space Artist," *Science Fiction Age* 1(5): 62-67. July 1993.

___ Melia, Sally-Ann. "Positively Dangerous to Stand Still: Artist Jim Burns Interviewed," *Interzone* No. 79: 20-24. January 1994.

BURNS, OLIVE ANN

___ Slocum, Sally K. "Waxing Arthurian: **The Lyre of Orpheus** and **Cold Sassy Tree**," in: Slocum, Sally K., ed. **Popular Arthurian Traditions**. Bowling Green, OH: Popular Press, 1992. pp.96-103.

BURNS, RICHARD

___ "Burns, Richard (Obituary)," *Locus* 29(4): 66. October 1992

___ "Burns, Richard (Obituary)," *Science Fiction Chronicle* 14(2): 12. November 1992.

BURNS, STEPHEN L.

___ Klein, Jay K. "Biolog: Stephen L. Burns," *Analog* 113(1/2): 53-54. January 1993.

BURROUGHS, EDGAR RICE

___ "Bibliographer's Corner: **Beyond Thirty**," *Burroughs Bulletin* NS. No. 20: 34. October 1994.

___ "Bibliographer's Corner: **Tarzan and the Jewels of Opar**," *Burroughs Bulletin* NS. No. 21: 33. January 1995.

___ "Bibliographer's Corner: **The Beasts of Tarzan**," *Burroughs Bulletin* NS. No. 13: 36-37. January 1993.

___ "Bibliographer's Corner: **The Eternal Lover**," *Burroughs Bulletin* NS. No. 12: 20. October 1992.

___ "Bibliographer's Corner: **The Girl From Farris's**," *Burroughs Bulletin* NS. No. 15: 37. July 1993.

___ "Bibliographer's Corner: **The Lad and the Lion**," *Burroughs Bulletin* NS. No. 14: 33. April 1993.

___ "Bibliographer's Corner: **The Son of Tarzan**," *Burroughs Bulletin* NS. No. 18: 32-32. April 1994.

___ "Bibliographer's Corner: **Thuvia, Maid of Mars**," *Burroughs Bulletin* NS. No. 16: 25. October 1993.

___ "Bibliographer's Corner: H. R. H., the Rider," *Burroughs Bulletin* NS. No. 22: 33. April 1995.

___ "Bibliographer's Corner: The New Stories of Tarzan," *Burroughs Bulletin* NS. No. 23: 34. July 1995.

___ "Book on Tarzan of Films, Etc. Provokes Estate Suit in France," *Variety* p. 22. June 16, 1982.

___ "Burroughs Appeal Nixed; Uphold MGM on Bo's **Tarzan** Retread," *Variety* p. 7, 28. June 2, 1982.

___ "The Complete Works of Edgar Rice Burroughs," *Futures Past* No. 3:20-24. September 1992.

___ "Edgar Rice Burroughs," in: Bloom, Harold, ed. **Classic Science Fiction Writers**. New York: Chelsea House, 1995. pp.15-30.

___ Adams, David A. "Carnivora, or, Lord Greystoke, Cooked and Raw in **Tarzan & the Jewels of Opar**," *Burroughs Bulletin* NS. No. 21: 10-15. January 1995.

___ Adams, David A. "Jungle Tales of Tarzan," *Burroughs Bulletin* NS. No. 23: 13-17. July 1995.

___ Adams, David A. "Major Burroughs in a Minor Gothic Tale: A Study of **The Oakdale Affair**," *Burroughs Bulletin* NS. No. 24: 3-7. October 1995.

___ Alonso, George. "Tarzan Still Lives at McLaughlin, South Dakota," *Burroughs Bulletin* NS. No. 24: 26-27. October 1995.

___ Barrett, Robert R. "Animal Fashion Plates: Charles Livingston Bull (1874-1932)," *Burroughs Bulletin* NS. No. 15: 22-25. July 1993.

___ Barrett, Robert R. "Burroughs, Kline and Henry Herbert Knibbs: Another Opinion," *Burroughs Bulletin* NS No. 9: 27-32. January 1992.

___ Barrett, Robert R. "Edgar Rice Burroughs to Zane Grey: Stockton Mulford (1886-?)," *Burroughs Bulletin* NS. No. 16: 16-19. October 1993.

___ Barrett, Robert R. "ERB's Ur: A Speculation," *Burroughs Bulletin* NS. No. 24: 8-14. October 1995.

BURROUGHS, EDGAR RICE (continued)

___ Barrett, Robert R. "Joe Jusko's Edgar Rice Burroughs Collection," *Burroughs Bulletin* NS. No. 22: 3-5. April 1995.

___ Barrett, Robert R. "Tarzan's Third Great Comic Strip Artist: Russell G. Manning (1929-1981)," *Burroughs Bulletin* NS. No. 13: 11-21. January 1993.

___ Bergen, James A., Jr. **Price and Reference Guide to Books Written by Edgar Rice Burroughs**. Beaverton, OR: Golden Lion Books, 1991. 214pp.

___ Burger, Phillip R. "ERB and the Educated Man: A Reply," *Burroughs Bulletin* NS. No. 24: 15-17. October 1995.

___ Burger, Phillip R. **Glimpses of a World Past: Edgar Rice Burroughs, the West, and the Birth of an American Writer**. Master's Thesis, Utah State University, 1987. 158pp.

___ Burger, Phillip R. "Knocking About the Neocene: Some Thoughts on **The Eternal Lover**," *Burroughs Bulletin* NS. No. 12: 3-9. October 1992.

___ Burger, Phillip R. "Mesas, Mormons, and Martians: The Possible Origins of Barsoomian History," *Burroughs Bulletin* NS. No. 16: 3-7. October 1993.

___ Burger, Phillip R. "Of Burroughs and Businessmen," *Burroughs Bulletin* NS. No. 18: 12-15. April 1994.

___ Burger, Phillip R. "Whatever Happened to Perry Rhodan, Riding the Space Trails Alone?," *Burroughs Bulletin* NS. No. 22: 12-17. April 1995.

___ Burger, Phillip R. " 'Whatever It Is It Gets You and Me': Some Thoughts on **The Return of the Mucker**," *Burroughs Bulletin* NS No. 10: 3-7. April 1992.

___ Casella, Elaine. "Apeman, Arab, Ancient Alien: A Synopsis of Gene Roddenberry's Tarzan Script," *Burroughs Bulletin* NS. No. 22: 26-31. April 1995.

___ Casella, Elaine. "A Lion Is Still a Lion," *Burroughs Bulletin* NS. No. 23: 24-30. July 1995.

___ Casella, Elaine. "Two Sequels to **Greystoke**," *Burroughs Bulletin* NS. No. 14: 34-38. April 1993.

___ Chapman, Mike. "Glenn Morris: Tarzan Number Eight," *Burroughs Bulletin* NS. No. 16: 8-15. October 1993.

___ Coriell, Rita. "The Coriell Years of Burroughs Fandom," *Burroughs Bulletin* NS. No. 12: 31-33. October 1992.

___ Currie, Philip J. "Dinosaurs of Pellucidar," *Burroughs Bulletin* NS. No. 17: 5-9. January 1994.

___ Currie, Philip J. "On Mahars, Gryfs and the Paleontology of ERB," *Burroughs Bulletin* NS. No. 16: 21-24. October 1993.

___ Fulwiler, William. "E. R. B. and H. P. L.," in: Price, Robert M., ed. **Black Forbidden Things**. Mercer Island, WA: Starmont, 1992. pp.60-65.

___ Fury, David. "Burroughs Spotlight on Rudy Sigmund," *Burroughs Bulletin* NS. No. 21: 24-26. January 1995.

___ Fury, David. "Interview with the Tarzan Man, Mr. Denny Miller," *Burroughs Bulletin* NS. No. 17: 25-29. January 1994.

___ Fury, David. "Maureen O'Sullivan: A Jewel of a Jane," *Burroughs Bulletin* NS. No. 15: 3-10. July 1993.

___ García, Fernando. "Burroughs in Argentina," by Fernando García and Hernán Ostuni. *Burroughs Bulletin* NS. No. 17: 10-17. January 1994.

___ García, Fernando. "Tarzan, King of the Pampa," by Fernando García and Hernán Ostuni. *Burroughs Bulletin* NS. No. 18: 20-22. April 1994.

___ Graham, Harry L. "How the Gaonas Flew With Tarzan in the Comics," *Burroughs Bulletin* NS. No. 18: 17-19. April 1994.

___ Griffin, Scott T. "Why Do We Need Tarzan?," *Burroughs Bulletin* NS. No. 20: 32-33. October 1994.

___ Griffin, Scott T. "Woody Strode: An Epic Life Remembered," *Burroughs Bulletin* NS. No. 22: 18-25. April 1995.

___ Hanson, Alan. "The Edgar Rice Burroughs Amateur Press Association," *Burroughs Bulletin* NS No. 11: 27-30. July 1992.

___ Hanson, Alan. "ERB and the Educated Man," *Burroughs Bulletin* NS. No. 17: 19-24. January 1994.

___ Harrison, Mitchell. "The Burroughs Pre-Pubs," *Burroughs Bulletin* NS. No. 14: 29-32. April 1993.

___ Hofmann, Roberta. "Realism in the Tarzan Novels," *Burroughs Bulletin* NS. No. 20: 29-31. October 1994.

___ Holtsmark, Erling B. "Tarzan: Projects Past and Future," *Burroughs Bulletin* NS No. 9: 8-14. January 1992.

___ Lacassin, Francis. **Tarzan ou le Chevalier crispe**. Paris: H. Veyrier, 1982. 223pp. [Revised edition].

___ Lacassin, Francis. **Tarzan ou le Chevalier crispe**. Paris: Union Generale d'editions, 1971. 511pp.

___ Lupoff, Richard A. "Edgar & Otis & Sam & Bob: Consider the Possibilities," *Burroughs Bulletin* NS No. 11: 24-26. July 1992.

BURROUGHS, EDGAR RICE

BURROUGHS, EDGAR RICE (continued)
___ Lupoff, Richard A. "Edgar Rice Burroughs and the Maxwell Perkins Syndrome," *Burroughs Bulletin* NS. No. 13: 3-10. January 1993.
___ Mandell, Paul. "Tarzan of the Paperbacks," *Life* 55(22): 11-12. November 29, 1963.
___ Mason, Richard. "We Meet Jane!," *Burroughs Bulletin* NS. No. 24: 32-33. October 1995.
___ McWhorter, George T. "Fire!: A Report on the Fire at ERB, Inc., May 8, 1958," *Burroughs Bulletin* NS. No. 18: 24-26. April 1994.
___ McWhorter, George T. "Historiated Initials in **The Son of Tarzan**," *Burroughs Bulletin* NS. No. 18: 30-31. April 1994.
___ Moskowitz, Sam. "Burroughs Returns to *Argosy*," *Burroughs Bulletin* NS. No. 20: 11-15. October 1994.
___ Moskowitz, Sam. "Burroughs, Kline, Knibbs: A Reply," *Burroughs Bulletin* NS No. 9: 34-39. January 1992.
___ Moskowitz, Sam. "Edgar Rice Burroughs and *Blue Book*," *Burroughs Bulletin* NS. No. 15: 11-20. July 1993.
___ Moskowitz, Sam. "Hugo Gernsback and Edgar Rice Burroughs," *Burroughs Bulletin* NS. No. 21: 3-9. January 1995.
___ Moskowitz, Sam. "To Barsoom and Back With Edgar Rice Burroughs, Part 1," *Futures Past* No. 3:14-19. September 1992. (Reprinted from: Moskowitz, Sam. **Explorers of the Infinite**. 1958.)
___ Musso, Joseph. "Forty Acres: A History of the RKO Backlot Films," *Burroughs Bulletin* NS. No. 14: 11-16. April 1993.
___ Pohl, Frederik. "Edgar Rice Burroughs and the Development of Science Fiction," *Burroughs Bulletin* NS No. 10: 8-14. April 1992.
___ Price, Robert M. "Randolph Carter, Warlord of Mars," in: Price, Robert M., ed. **Black Forbidden Things**. Mercer Island, WA: Starmont, 1992. pp.66-68.
___ Roberts, Tom. "Tarzan: The Marvel Way! An Interview with John Buscema," *Burroughs Bulletin* NS. No. 15: 26-32. July 1993.
___ Ross, Bill. "The 1995 ERB Chain of Friendship Gathering," *Burroughs Bulletin* NS. No. 24: 28-31. October 1995.
___ Ross, Bill. "The Tenth Annual E. C. O. F. Gathering," *Burroughs Bulletin* NS. No. 12: 21-30. October 1992.
___ Roy, John F. "The Many Tongues of Pellucidar," *Wayfarer II* pp.4-6. n.d.
___ Sarnya, Count. "***The Lad and the Lion*** in Films: 1917-1937," *Burroughs Bulletin* NS. No. 14: 3-10. April 1993.
___ Schneider, Jerry L. "On Location at the Arboretum, Part II," *Burroughs Bulletin* NS. No. 12: 10-14. October 1992.
___ Schneider, Jerry L. "On Location at the Iverson Movie Ranch," *Burroughs Bulletin* NS. No. 20: 3-10. October 1994.
___ Spurlock, Duane. "Hail and Farewell, Pellucidar: An Interview with Allan Gross," *Burroughs Bulletin* NS. No. 16: 27-31. October 1993.
___ Spurlock, Duane. "Where Have All the Fans Gone?: An Interview with Henning Kure," *Burroughs Bulletin* NS. No. 13: 23-35. January 1993.
___ Thomas, Roy. "Tarz and the Apes," *Burroughs Bulletin* NS. No. 21: 16-23. January 1995.
___ Toelle, Kevin. "Tarzan: The Least Adventure?," *Burroughs Bulletin* NS. No. 23: 31-33. July 1995.
___ Van Hise, James. "An Index to the Reed Crandall Illustrations From the Works of Edgar Rice Burroughs," *Burroughs Bulletin* NS. No. 20: 27-28. October 1994.
___ Van Hise, James. "Jungle Tales of Tarzan: A Closer Look," *Burroughs Bulletin* NS. No. 23: 3-12. July 1995.
___ Van Hise, James. "Reed Crandall: Illustrator of Super Heroes," *Burroughs Bulletin* NS. No. 20: 17-28. October 1994.
___ Warren, Bill. "Tarzan the Magnificent," *Starlog* No. 187: 27-31. February 1993.
___ Webber, Ken. "Interview With Mike Richardson, Publisher of Dark Horse Comics," *Burroughs Bulletin* NS. No. 21: 27-32. January 1995.
___ Zeuschner, Bob. "ERB Is Alive and Well on the Information Highway," *Burroughs Bulletin* NS. No. 24: 19-25. October 1995.
___ Ziemann, Irvin H. "Tarzan in the Dell...And Gold Key," *Burroughs Bulletin* NS. No. 22: 6-11. April 1995.

BURROUGHS, JOHN COLEMAN
___ Coombs, Charles I. "Martian Memories," *Burroughs Bulletin* NS No. 11: 21-23. July 1992.

BURROUGHS, WILLIAM
___ Bozzetto, Roger. "William Burroughs, le scribe étasunien halluciné," in: Terramorsi, Bernard, ed. **Américana**. Paris: Université de la Réunion/Éditions l'Harmattan, 1994. pp.201-215. (*Cahiers CRLH Ciraoi* No. 9, 1994)

BURROUGHS, WILLIAM S.
___ Ayers, David. " 'Politics Here Is Death': William Burroughs's **Cities of the Red Night**," in: Kumar, Krishan and Bann, Stephen, eds. **Utopias and the Millennium**. London: Reaktion Books, 1993. pp.90-106.
___ Goodman, Michael B. "William S. Burroughs," in: Bruccoli, Matthew J., ed. **Facts on File Bibliography of American Fiction 1919-1988**. New York: Facts on File, 1991. pp.111-114.
___ Goodman, Michael B. **William S. Burroughs: A Reference Guide**. New York: Garland, 1990. 270pp.
___ Harris, Oliver, ed. **The Letters of William S. Burroughs: 1945-1959**. New York: Viking, 1993. 472pp.
___ Kimber, Gary. "***Naked Lunch***: William S. Burroughs, Possessed by Genius," *Cinefantastique* 22(5): 12-14. April 1992.
___ Latham, Robert A. "Collage as Critique and Invention in the Fiction of William S. Burroughs and Kathy Acker," *Journal of the Fantastic in the Arts* 5(3): 46-57. 1993. (No. 19)
___ Latham, Robert A. "Collage as Critique and Invention in the Fiction of William S. Burroughs and Kathy Acker," in: Latham, Robert A. and Collins, Robert A., eds. **Modes of the Fantastic**. Westport, CT: Greenwood, 1995. pp.29-37.
___ Miles, Barry. **William Burroughs: El Hombre Invisible**. New York: Hyperion, 1993. 263pp.
___ Puschmann-Nalenz, Barbara. **Science Fiction and Postmodern Fiction: A Genre Study**. New York: Peter Lang, 1992. 268pp. (Trans. of **Science Fiction und Ihre Grenzberieche**.)
___ Schrage, Michael. "The Naked Scene: The Spirit of Burroughs Permeates the Software Scence," *Washington (DC) Post* Sec. F, p. 3. February 21, 1992.
___ Ward, Geoff. "William Burroughs: A Literary Outlaw?," *Cambridge Quarterly* 22(4): 339-354. 1993.
___ Wu, Duncan. "Wordsmith in Space: The Fantasies of William S. Burroughs," in: Filmer, Kath, ed. **Twentieth-Century Fantasists: Essays in Culture, Society and Belief in Twentieth Century Mythopoeic Literature**. New York: St. Martin's, 1992. pp.121-134.

BURSTEIN, MICHAEL
___ "1994 Donald A. Wollheim Memorial Scholarship," *Science Fiction Chronicle* 15(9): 8. August 1994.

BURTON, LeVAR
___ Cohen, Amy J. "LeVar Burton: The Vision of Georgi LaForge," *Star Trek: The Official Fan Club* No. 94: C-D, 1. November/December 1993.

BURTON, RICHARD
___ "Death of Burton Spurs *1984* Sales," *Variety* p. 20. August 15, 1984.

BURTON, TIM
___ Jones, Alan. "Tim Burton's **Edward Scissorhands**," *Cinefantastique* 25(5): 12-18. October 1994.
___ Mitchell, James. "Master of Nightmares," *Starlog* No. 200: 58-61. March 1994.
___ Shapiro, Marc. "Dark Knight Director," *Starlog* 180: 40-45, 75. July 1992.

BUSBY, F. M.
___ King, T. Jackson. "SFC Interviews: F. M. Busby," *Science Fiction Chronicle* 15(3): 5, 24-26. January 1994.

BUSCEMA, JOHN
___ Roberts, Tom. "Tarzan: The Marvel Way! An Interview with John Buscema," *Burroughs Bulletin* NS. No. 15: 26-32. July 1993.

BUSINESS IN SF
___ Stableford, Brian. "Utopia--And Afterwards: Socioeconomic Speculation in the SF of Mack Reynolds," in: Stableford, Brian. **Outside the Human Aquarium: Masters of Science Fiction**. San Bernardino, CA: Borgo, 1995. pp.49-75.

BUTLER, OCTAVIA E.
___ "Butler Book to Be Warner Lead," *Locus* 32(4): 8. April 1994.
___ "Octavia E. Butler Gets $295,000 MacArthur Grant," *Locus* 35(1): 8. July 1995.
___ "Octavia E. Butler Receives $295,000 MacArthur Foundation Grant," *Science Fiction Chronicle* 16(8): 4. July/August 1995

BUTLER, OCTAVIA E. (continued)

___ Allison, Dorothy. "The Future of Female: Octavia Butler's Mother Lode," in: Gates, Henry L., Jr., ed. **Reading Black, Reading Feminist: A Critical Anthology.** New York: Meridian, 1990. pp.471-478.

___ Barr, Marleen S. **Lost in Space: Probing Feminist Science Fiction and Beyond.** Chapel Hill, NC: University of North Carolina Press, 1993. 231pp.

___ Bogstad, Janice M. **Gender, Power and Reversal in Contemporary Anglo-American and French Feminist Science Fiction.** Ph.D. Dissertation, University of Wisconsin, Madison, 1992. 229pp. (DAI-A 54/02, p. 509. August 1993.)

___ Brande, David J. **Technologies of Postmodernity: Ideology and Desire in Literature and Science (Pynchon, Thomas; Gibson, William; Butler, Octavia; Acker, Kathy).** Ph.D. Dissertation, University of Washington, 1995. 228pp. (DAI-A 56/07, p. 2677. January 1996.)

___ Davis, Ben. **History, Race and Gender in the Science Fiction of Octavia Estelle Butler.** Master's Thesis, Ohio State University, 1992. 89pp.

___ Green, Carol A. "Women of Color: The Female Protagonists in the Novels of Octavia Butler," *Vector* No. 176: 14-15. December 1993/ January 1994.

___ Green, Michelle G. "There Goes the Neighborhood: Octavia Butler's Demand for Diversity in Utopias," in: Donawerth, Jane L. and Kolmerten, Carol A., eds. **Utopian and Science Fiction by Women: Worlds of Difference.** Syracuse, NY: Syracuse University Press, 1994. pp.166-189.

___ Hall, Debra K. **A New Synthesis for Science Fiction: The Fiction of Octavia Butler.** Master's Thesis, Eastern New Mexico University, 1992. 75pp.

___ Hayes, Nancy V. "An Interview With Octavia E. Butler," *Science Fiction Eye* No. 13: 99-100. Spring 1994.

___ Helford, Elyce R. **Reading Space Fictions: Representations of Gender, Race and Species in Popular Culture.** Ph.D. Dissertation, University of Iowa, 1993. (DAI-A 53/11, p. 3908. May 1993.)

___ Helford, Elyce R. " 'Would You Really Rather Die Than Bear My Young?': The Construction of Gender, Race, and Species in Octavia E. Butler's **Bloodchild**," *African American Review* 28(2): 259-271. Summer 1994.

___ Hodgson, Jeffrey. "FEATURE-Sci-Fi Writer Wins Awards With Focus on Human Soul," *Reuters* August 12, 1996. (Cited from **The Electric Library** on-line service.)

___ Jackson, H. Jerome. "Sci-Fi Tales From Octavia E. Butler," *Crisis (NAACP)* 101(3): 4-5. April 1994.

___ Johnson, Rebecca O. "Adapt to Your Circumstances," *Sojourner* 19(6): 12-13. February 1994.

___ Johnson, Rebecca O. "African American Feminist Science Fiction," *Sojourner* 19(6): 12-13. February 1994.

___ Kempen, Bernhard. "Eine Lektion in Misanthropie: Über Octavia Butlers 'schwarze' SF," *Science Fiction Times* (Germany) 34(1): 4-9. January 1992.

___ McTyre, Robert E. "Octavia Butler: Black America's First Lady of Science Fiction," *Michigan Chronicle* pp.PG. April 26, 1994. (Cited from **The Electric Library** on-line service.)

___ Peppers, Cathy. "Dialogic Origins and Alien Identities in Butler's **Xenogenesis**," *Science Fiction Studies* 22(1): 47-62. March 1995.

___ Raffel, Burton. "Genre to the Rear, Race and Gender to the Fore: The Novels of Octavia E. Butler," *Literary Review* 38(3): 454-461. Spring 1995.

___ Rusdy, Ashraf H. A. "Families of Orphans: Relation and Disrelation in Octavia Butler's **Kindred**," *College English* 55(2): 135-157. February 1993.

___ See, Lisa. "PW Interviews: Octavia E. Butler," *Publishers Weekly* 240(50): 50-51. December 13, 1993.

___ Smith, Malaika D. **The African American Heroine in Octavia Butler's Wild Seed and Parable of the Sower.** Master's Thesis, UCLA, 1994. 66pp.

___ Smith, Stephanie A. "Morphing, Materialism, and the Marketing of **Xenogenesis**," *Genders* No. 18: 67-86. Winter 1993.

___ White, Eric. "The Erotics of Becoming: **Xenogenesis** and **The Thing**," *Science Fiction Studies* 20(3): 394-408. November 1993.

___ Wolmark, Jenny. **Aliens and Others: Science Fiction, Feminism, and Postmodernism.** London: Harester Wheatsheaf, 1993. 167pp.; Iowa City: University of Iowa Press, 1994. 167pp.

___ Yancy, George. "Black Woman Pioneers Science Fiction Writing," *Philadelphia Tribune* pp.PG. January 16, 1996. (Cited from **The Electric Library** on-line service.)

BUTLER, SAMUEL

___ Breuer, Hans-Peter. **Samuel Butler: An Annotated Bibliography of Writings About Him.** New York: Garland, 1990. 497pp.

___ Garrett, John C. **Hope or Disillusion: Three Versions of Utopia: Nathaniel Hawthorne, Samuel Butler, George Orwell.** Christchurch, NZ: University of Canterbury Publications Committee, 1984. 69pp.

___ Klein, Jürgen. "Samuel Butler **Erewhon** (1872)," by Jürgen Klein and Klaus Zöllner. in: Heuermann, Hartmut and Lange, Bernd-Peter, eds. **Die Utopie in der angloamerikanischen Literatur: Interpretationen.** Düsseldorf: Bagel, 1984. pp.80-102.

___ Raby, Peter. **Samuel Butler: A Biography.** Iowa City: University of Iowa Press, 1991. 334pp.

CABELL, JAMES BRANCH

___ Bloom, Harold. "James Branch Cabell," in: Bloom, Harold. **Classic Fantasy Writers.** New York: Chelsea House, 1994. pp.27-39.

___ Jordan, A. M. "Three Masterpieces by Cabell," *Lan's Lantern* No. 40: 36-37. September 1992.

___ MacDonald, Edgar. **James Branch Cabell and Richmond-in-Virginia.** Jackson: University of Mississippi Press, 1993. 373pp.

___ Riemer, James D. **The Fantasies of James Branch Cabell.** Ph.D. Dissertation, Bowling Green State University, 1982. 179pp.

___ Tarrant, Desmond. "Cabell and James Blish (1921-1975)," *Kalki* 9(4): 133-136. 1991. (No. 36)

CABINET OF DR. CALIGARI (MOTION PICTURE)

___ Murphy, Richard J. "Carnival Desire and the Sideshow of Fantasy: Dream, Duplicity and Representational Instability in **The Cabinet of Dr. Caligari**," *Germanic Review* 66(1): 48-56. Winter 1991.

CADBURY CHOCOLATE (COMPANY)

___ "Cadbury Chocolate Links with 'Future'," *Variety* p.7. July 10, 1985.

CADIGAN, PAT

___ "Cadigan Wins Clarke Award," *Locus* 29(3): 6, 79. September 1992.

___ "Cadigan Wins Clarke Award," *Locus* 34(6): 8. June 1995.

___ "Pat Cadigan: A Bibliography," *Nova Express* 3(1): 20-21. Fall 1989. (Whole No. 9)

___ "Pat Cadigan: Technofeminist," *Locus* 29(5): 2, 74. November 1992

___ "Pat Cadigan: Transforming the Familiar," *Locus* 35(1): 4, 68-69. July 1995.

___ "Pat Cadigan Wins Arthur C. Clarke Award," *Science Fiction Chronicle* 16(6): 5. May 1995.

___ "Pat Cadigan's **Synners** Wins Arthur C. Clarke Award," *Science Fiction Chronicle* 13(11/12): 4. August 1992.

___ Balsamo, Anne. "Feminism for the Incurably Informed," *South Atlantic Quarterly* 92(4): 681-712. Fall 1993.

___ Brown, Dwight. "The Cadigan Interviews: Interviews with, Yup, Pat Cadigan," *Nova Express* 3(1): 9-19. Fall 1989. (Whole No. 9)

___ Farr, Russell B. "An Interview With Pat Cadigan and Ellen Datlow," *Science Fiction: A Review of Speculative Literature* 13(1): 13-18. 1995(?). (No. 37)

___ Harper, Mary C. "Incurably Alien Other: A Case for Feminist Cyborg Writers," *Science Fiction Studies* 22(3): 399-420. November 1995

___ Wolmark, Jenny. **Aliens and Others: Science Fiction, Feminism, and Postmodernism.** London: Harester Wheatsheaf, 1993. 167pp.; Iowa City: University of Iowa Press, 1994. 167pp.

CADY, JACK

___ "13th Annual *Science Fiction Chronicle* Reader Awards," *Science Fiction Chronicle* 15(10): 4. September 1994.

___ "1993 Nebula Awards Winners," *Locus* 32(5): 8. May 1994.

___ "Bram Stoker Awards," *Science Fiction Chronicle* 15(8): 5. June 1994.

___ "HWA Stoker Awards Winners," *Locus* 33(1): 7. July 1994.

___ "Nebula Awards," *Science Fiction Chronicle* 15(7): 4. June 1994.

CALLENBACH, ERNEST

___ Tschachler, Heinz. "Ernest Callenbach: **Ecotopia: A Novel about Ecology, People, and Politics in 1999** (1975)," in: Heuermann, Hartmut and Lange, Bernd-Peter, eds. **Die Utopie in der angloamerikanischen Literatur: Interpretationen.** Düsseldorf: Bagel, 1984. pp.328-348.

CALVINO, ITALO

___ Cannon, Joann. "Literary Signification: An Analysis of Calvino's Trilogy," *Symposium* 34(1): 3-12. Spring 1980.

___ Hume, Kathryn. "Calvino's Fictions: Cogito and Cosmos," Oxford: Clarendon, 1992. 212pp.

___ Hume, Kathryn. "Science and Imagination in Calvino's **Cosmicomics**," *Mosaic* 15(4): 47-58. December 1982.

___ Koebel, Chuck. "Fantasy in the Mainstream: The Fiction of Italo Calvino," *OtherRealms* No. 24: 7-8. Spring 1989.

___ Sbragia, Albert. "Italo Calvino's Ordering of Chaos," *Modern Fiction Studies* 39(2): 283-306. Summer 1993.

CAMELOT (MOTION PICTURE)

___ Grellner, Mary A. "Two Films That Sparkle: *The Sword in the Stone* and *Camelot*," in: Harty, Kevin J., ed. **Cinema Arthuriana: Essays on Arthurian Film**. New York: Garland, 1991. pp.71-83.

CAMERON, JAMES

___ Abbott, Joe. "They Came From Beyond the Center: Ideology and Political Textuality in the Radical Science Fiction Films of James Cameron," *Literature/Film Quarterly* 22(1): 21-27. 1994.

___ Lofficier, Randy. "*Aliens* (1986): Interview with James Cameron and Gale Ann Hurd," by Randy Lofficier and Jean-Marc Lofficier. in: Goldberg, Lee et al. **Science Fiction Filmmaking in the 1980s**. Jefferson, NC: McFarland, 1995. pp.7-23.

CAMERON, JULIA MARGARET

___ Relihan, Constance C. "Vivien, Elaine, and the Model's Gaze: Cameron's Reading of **Idylls of the King**," in: Slocum, Sally K., ed. **Popular Arthurian Traditions**. Bowling Green, OH: Popular Press, 1992. pp.111-131.

CAMPBELL, BRUCE

___ Shapiro, Marc. "Cosmic Cowboy," *Starlog* No. 197: 63-66. December 1993.

___ Uram, Sue. "Bruce Campbell: Horror's Rambo," *Cinefantastique* 23(2/3): 31. October 1992.

___ Uram, Sue. "Dead Hero: Bruce Campbell: Actor/Producer," *Cinefantastique* 23(1): 36-37. August 1992.

CAMPBELL, JOHN W., JR.

___ Aldiss, Brian W. "Campbell's Soup," in: Aldiss, Brian W. **The Detached Retina: Aspects of SF and Fantasy**. Syracuse, NY: Syracuse University Press, 1995. pp.145-149.

___ Anderson, Poul. "Beer Mutterings: John W. Campbell and Anthony Boucher," *Quantum* No. 43/44: 5-6. Spring/Summer 1993.

___ Berger, Albert I. **The Magic That Works: John W. Campbell and the American Response to Technology**. San Bernardino, CA: Borgo Press, 1993. 231pp.

___ Campbell, John W. **Collected Editorial From Analog**. Garden City, NY: Doubleday, 1996. 251pp.

___ Moskowitz, Sam. "Correction re Desmond Hall," *Locus* 30(2): 69. February 1993.

___ Westfahl, Gary. "A Convenient Analog System: John W. Campbell, Jr.'s Theory of Science Fiction," *Foundation* No. 54: 52-70. Spring 1992.

___ Westfahl, Gary. "Dictatorial, Authoritarian, Uncooperative: The Case Against John W. Campbell," *Foundation* No. 56: 36-60. Autumn 1992. (Letter of comment: Alexei Panshin, *Foundation* No. 58: 87-91. Summer 1993; Rejoiner, Westfahl, *Foundation* No. 58: 93-94.)

CAMPBELL, JOSEPH

___ Day, Mildred L. "Joseph Campbell and the Power of Arthurian Myth," in: Slocum, Sally K., ed. **Popular Arthurian Traditions**. Bowling Green, OH: Popular Press, 1992. pp.80-84.

CAMPBELL, RAMSEY

___ "British Fantasy Awards," *Science Fiction Chronicle* 16(1): 5. October 1994.

___ "British Fantasy Awards, 1992," *Locus* 28(2): 7. February 1992.

___ Deleault, Arthur R. "Perceptions: Campbell/Burleson," *Studies in Weird Fiction* No. 15: 18-19. Summer 1994.

___ Dziemianowicz, Stefan. "An Interview With Ramsey Campbell," in: Joshi, S. T., ed. **The Count of Thirty: A Tribute to Ramsey Campbell**. West Warwick, RI: Necronomicon, 1993. pp.7-26.

CAMPBELL, RAMSEY (continued)

___ Frenschkowski, Marco. " 'Alles is Ufer. Ewig ruft das Meer': Maritime Symbolik in zwei Ersählungen von R. H. Barlow und Ramsey Campbell," *Quarber Merkur* 33(2): 48-59. December 1995. (No. 84)

___ Joshi, S. T. "Campbell: Before and After Lovecraft," in: Joshi, S. T., ed. **The Count of Thirty: A Tribute to Ramsey Campbell**. West Warwick, RI: Necronomicon, 1993. pp.27-31.

___ Joshi, S. T. "Ramsey Campbell: The Fiction of Paranoia," *Studies in Weird Fiction* No. 17: 22-33. Summer 1995.

___ Joshi, S. T., ed. **The Count of Thirty: A Tribute to Ramsey Campbell**. West Warwick, RI: Necronomicon, 1993. 54pp.

___ Lane, Joel. "Beyond the Light: The Recent Novels of Ramsey Campbell," in: Joshi, S. T., ed. **The Count of Thirty: A Tribute to Ramsey Campbell**. West Warwick, RI: Necronomicon, 1993. pp.46-50.

___ Lane, Joel. "Negatives in Print: The Early Novels of Ramsey Campbell," in: Joshi, S. T., ed. **The Count of Thirty: A Tribute to Ramsey Campbell**. West Warwick, RI: Necronomicon, 1993. pp.38-45.

___ MacCulloch, Simon. "Glimpses of Absolute Power: Ramsey Campbell's Concept of Evil," in: Joshi, S. T., ed. **The Count of Thirty: A Tribute to Ramsey Campbell**. West Warwick, RI: Necronomicon, 1993. pp.32-37.

___ Menegaldo, Gilles. "Quelques substituts et simulacres d'Eros dans le recit fantastique moderne," in: Bozzetto, Roger, ed. **Eros: Science & Fiction Fantastique**. Aix-en-Provence: Universite de Provence, 1991. pp.43-57.

___ Nicholls, Stan. "Ramsey Campbell Finds Dreaming on the Page Bloody Hard Work," in: Nicholls, Stan. **Wordsmiths of Wonder: Fifty Interviews with Writers of the Fantastic**. London: Orbit, 1993. pp.397-403.

___ Proulx, Kevin. **Fear to the World: Eleven Voices in a Chorus of Horror**. Mercer Island, WA: Starmont, 1992. 243pp.

___ Schweitzer, Darrell. "Ramsey Campbell," in: Schweitzer, Darrell. **Speaking of Horror: Interviews With Writers of the Supernatural**. San Bernardino, CA: Borgo, 1994. pp.23-36.

CAMPERT, JAN REMCO

___ Lehmann, L. "Science Fiction," *Maatstaf* (Amsterdam, Netherlands) 39(7): 35-36. July 1991.

CANADA

___ "1995 Prix Aurora Awards," *Locus* 34(6): 8. June 1995.

___ "Aurora Awards," *Science Fiction Chronicle* 13(11/12): 12. August 1992.

___ "Aurora Awards," *Science Fiction Chronicle* 15(10): 5. September 1994.

___ "Aurora Awards," *Science Fiction Chronicle* 16(7): 4. June/July 1995.

___ "Aurora Awards Winners, 1992," *Locus* 30(4): 6, 64. April 1993.

___ "Canadian Fiction: 1991 and 1992," *Sol Rising* No. 9: 4-8. April 1993. (Newsletter of the Merril Collection, Toronto Public Library.)

___ "Science Fiction, a Global Community: Canada," *Locus* 32(4): 39. April 1994.

___ "SF in French," *Locus* 31(6): 40. December 1993.

___ Boivin, Aurelien. **Bibliographie analytique de la science fiction et du fantastique Quebecois: 1960-1985**, by Aurelien Boivin, Maurice Emond and Michel Lord. Quebec: Nuit blanche editeur, 1992. 577pp.

___ Colas-Charpentier, Helene. "Four Quebecois Dystopias, 1963-1972," *Science Fiction Studies* 20(3): 383-393. November 1993.

___ Colombo, John R. "Favorite Canadian Works," *Sol Rising* (Toronto) No. 10: 3-4. May 1994.

___ Ketterer, David. **Canadian Science Fiction and Fantasy**. Bloomington: Indiana University Press, 1991. 206pp.

___ Ketterer, David. "The Establishment of Canadian Science Fiction (1958-1983), Part 1," *New York Review of Science Fiction* No. 42: 1, 8-14. February 1992.

___ Ketterer, David. "The Establishment of Canadian Science Fiction (1958-1983), Part 2," *New York Review of Science Fiction* No. 43: 17-22. March 1992.

___ Trudel, Jean-Louis. "Science Fiction in Francophone Canada (1839-1989)," *Sol Rising* No. 8: 1-5. February 1992.

___ Winston, Iris. "Speaking From...Out of This World," *National Library News* (Canada) 27(5): 2-4. May 1995.

___ Woods, Randy. **A Typological Analysis of Canadian Science Fiction**. Master's Thesis, Carleton University, 1993. 167pp. (Master's Abstracts 32/03, p. 811. June 1994.)

CANADIAN SF AND FANTASY AWARDS, 1992
___ "Aurora Awards," *Science Fiction Chronicle* 13(11/12): 12. August 1992.
___ "Aurora Awards Winners," *Locus* 28(2): 7. August 1992.
___ "Aurora Awards Winners, 1992," *Locus* 30(4): 6, 64. April 1993.

CANADIAN SF AND FANTASY AWARDS, 1993
___ "Aurora Canadian SF and Fantasy Awards, 1993," *Science Fiction Chronicle* 14(7): 4. April 1993.

CANADIAN SF AND FANTASY AWARDS, 1994
___ "1994 Aurora Winners," *Locus* 33(4): 8, 76. October 1994.
___ "Aurora Awards," *Science Fiction Chronicle* 15(10): 5. September 1994.

CANADIAN SF AND FANTASY AWARDS, 1995
___ "1995 Aurora Award Nominations," *Science Fiction Chronicle* 16(6): 4-5. May 1995.
___ "Aurora Awards," *Science Fiction Chronicle* 16(7): 4. June/July 1995.

CANDYMAN 2: FAREWELL TO THE FLESH (MOTION PICTURE)
___ "*Candyman 2: Farewell to the Flesh*," *Sci-Fi Entertainment* 1(5): 32-33. February 1995.
___ French, Todd. "*Candyman 2*: Interview with the Master," *Cinefantastique* 26(3): 42. April 1995.
___ French, Todd. "Clive Barker's *Candyman 2*," *Cinefantastique* 26(2): 8-9. February 1995.
___ French, Todd. "Clive Barker's *Candyman 2*," *Cinefantastique* 26(3): 40-43. April 1995.
___ Newman, Kim. "*Candyman 2: Farewell to the Flesh* (Review)," *Sight and Sound* 5(12): 42-43. December 1995.

CANDYMAN (MOTION PICTURE)
___ Scapperotti, Dan. "*Candyman*," *Cinefantastique* 23(4): 18-19. December 1992.

CANETTI, ELIAS
___ Willingham, Ralph A. "Dystopian Vision in the Plays of Elias Canetti," *Science Fiction Studies* 19(1): 69-74. March 1992.

CANNIBALISM
___ Ptacek, Kathryn. "You Are What You Eat/Watch: Cannibalism in Movies," in: Golden, Christopher, ed. **Cut! Horror Writers on Horror Film**. New York: Berkley, 1992. pp.183-188.

CANNON, DANNY
___ Nazzaro, Joe. "Chief Justice," *Starlog* No. 217: 47-51. August 1995.
___ Roegger, Berthe. "Building a World of Dredd," *Sci-Fi Entertainment* 2(2): 42-49. August 1995.

CAPEK, KAREL
___ Clute, John. "Karel Capek," in: Clute, John. **Look at the Evidence: Essays and Reviews**. Liverpool: Liverpool University Press, 1995. pp.427-430.
___ Comrada, Norma. "Golem and Robot: The Search for Connections," *Journal of the Fantastic in the Arts* 7(2/3): 244-254. 1995.

CAPRA, FRANK
___ "Capra, Frank, 1897-1991 (Obituary)," *Starlog* No. 174: 22. January 1992.

CAPTAIN POWER AND THE SOLDIERS OF THE FUTURE (TV)
___ Altman, Mark A. "*Babylon 5*: Captain Power," *Cinefantastique* 25(2): 47, 61. April 1994.
___ Chrissinger, Craig W. "Warrior Pilot," *Starlog* No. 213: 50-52. April 1995.

CAPTAIN POWER (TV)
___ "Mattell **Capt. Power** Looking for Distrib to Keep Show Going," *Variety* p. 49. February 17, 1988.

CAPTAIN ZOOM (MOTION PICTURE)
___ Winikoff, Kenneth. "*Captain Zoom*," *Cinefantastique* 27(2): 38-39, 61. November 1995.

CARADUCCI, MARK
___ Scapperotti, Dan. "The Plan 9 Companion," *Cinefantastique* 25(5): 43. October 1994.

CARD, ORSON SCOTT
___ "Orson Scott Card: Creative Chaos," *Locus* 28(1): 4, 75. January 1992.
___ "Orson Scott Card Draws Gay Protest," *Science Fiction Chronicle* 13(6): 4. March 1992.
___ Attebery, Brian. "Godmaking in the Heartland: The Backgrounds of Orson Scott Card's American Fantasy," in: Morse, Donald E., ed. **The Celebration of the Fantastic**. Westport, CT: Greenwood, 1992. pp.61-69.
___ Jeapes, Ben. "Orson Scott Card: An Appreciation," *Vector* No. 168: 8-11. August/September 1992.
___ Johnston, Jerry. "Orson Scott Card," *Salt Lake City (UT) Deseret News*. November 8, 1992. in: *NewsBank. Literature*. 99:E7-E8. 1992
___ Jordan, Anne D. "**Ender's Game**," *Teaching and Learning Literature* 4(5): 26-28. May/June 1995.
___ McNally, Joel. "Sci-Fi Novelist Dips His Hand in the Mainstream," *Milwaukee (WI) Journal*. October 25, 1992. in: *NewsBank. Literature*. 89:D1. 1992
___ Townsend, Johnny. "Passion vs. Will: Homosexuality in Orson Scott Card's **Wyrms**," *Riverside Quarterly* 9(1): 48-55. August 1992. (No. 33)

CARDIGAN, JAKE
___ Bloch-Hansen, Peter. "Tek Hero," *Starlog* No. 213: 44-47. April 1995.

CAREFUL (MOTION PICTURE)
___ Persons, Dan. "*Careful* (Review)," *Cinefantastique* 24(6)/25(1): 123. February 1994.
___ Persons, Dan. "*Careful*," *Cinefantastique* 25(2): 54-55, 61. April 1994.

CAREY, KEN
___ Davis, Erik. "Techgnosis: Magic, Memory and the Angel of Information," *South Atlantic Quarterly* 92(4): 585-616. Fall 1993. (Reprinted in: Dery, Mark, ed. **Flame Wars: The Discourse of Cyberculture**. Durham, NC: Duke University Press, 1994.)

CARLYLE, THOMAS
___ Mason, Michael. "A Clearing of Vision: 1843-1962. The Evolution of the Utopian Ideal in Carlyle, Shaw and Huxley," in: Saccaro Del Buffa, Giuseppa and Lewis, Arthur O., eds. **Utopia e Modernita: Teorie e prassi utopiche nell'eta moderna e postmoderna**. Rome: Gangemi Editore, 1989. pp.931-944.

CARNIVAL
___ Erisan, Wendy E. "Inverting the Ideal World: Carnival and the Carnivalesque in Contemporary Utopian Science Fiction," *Extrapolation* 36(4): 331-344. Winter 1995.

CARNOSAUR II (MOTION PICTURE)
___ Harris, Judith P. "*Carnosaur II* (Review)," *Cinefantastique* 26(5): 59. August 1995.
___ Wilt, David. "*Carnosaur II* (Review)," *Cinefantastique* 27(2): 59. November 1995.

CARNOSAUR (MOTION PICTURE)
___ Biodrowski, Steve. "*Jurassic Park*: *Carnosaur*," *Cinefantastique* 24(2): 23, 60. August 1993.

CARPAL TUNNEL SYNDROME
___ Anderson, Kevin J. "Carpal Tunnel Syndrome: When Writing Gets on Your Nerves," by Kevin J. Anderson and Rebecca M. Anderson. *SFWA Bulletin* 26(3): 5-9. Fall 1992. (No. 117)
___ Platt, Charles. "Wrist Voodoo," *Interzone* No. 83: 41-43. May 1994.

CARPENTER, JOHN
___ "John Carpenter Keynoting NYC Bram Stoker Weekend," *Science Fiction Chronicle* 14(9): 5. June 1993.
___ Jones, Alan. "John Carpenter: Directing **In the Mouth of Madness** a la H. P. Lovecraft," *Cinefantastique* 26(2): 44-45. February 1995.
___ Martin, Robert. "Mounting Madness," *Sci-Fi Entertainment* 1(6): 48-50. April 1995.

CARPENTER, JOHN (continued)
___ Wiater, Stanley. "Carpenter, John," in: Wiater, Stanley. **Dark Visions: Conversations with the Masters of the Horror Film.** New York: Avon, 1992. pp.19-28.

CARR, JOHN DICKSON
___ Greene, Douglas G. **John Dickson Carr: The Man Who Explained Miracles.** New York: Penzler, 1995. 537pp.

CARRERAS, MICHAEL
___ "Carreras, Michael (Obituary)," *Science Fiction Chronicle* 15(9): 16. August 1994.

CARREY, JIM
___ Murray, Will. "Riddler of Forever?," *Starlog* No. 218: 27-30. September 1995.

CARROLL, JONATHAN
___ "British Fantasy Awards," *Science Fiction Chronicle* 14(3): 4. December 1992.
___ "British Fantasy Awards, 1992," *Locus* 29(5): 5. November 1992.
___ Gillespie, Bruce. "Jonathan Carroll, Storyteller," *SF Commentary* No. 71/72: 28-33. April 1992.
___ Olson, D. H. "An Interview With Jonathan Carroll," *Tales of the Unanticipated* No. 9: 28-34. Fall/Winter 1991/1992.
___ Stephens, Christopher P. **A Checklist of Jonathan Carroll.** Hastings-on-Hudson, NY: Ultramarine, 1992. 11pp.

CARROLL, LEWIS
___ Bloom, Harold. "Lewis Carroll," in: Bloom, Harold. **Classic Fantasy Writers.** New York: Chelsea House, 1994. pp.40-55.
___ Deleuze, Gilles. **The Logic of Sense.** New York: Columbia University Press, 1990. 393pp.
___ Pennington, John. "Alice at the Back of the North Wind, or the Metafictions of Lewis Carroll and George MacDonald," *Extrapolation* 33(1): 59-72. Spring 1992.
___ Pennington, John. "Reader Response and Fantasy Literature: The Use and Abuses of Interpretation in **Queen Victoria's Alice in Wonderland**," in: Sanders, Joe, ed. **Functions of the Fantastic.** Westport, CT: Greenwood, 1995. pp.55-66.
___ Stableford, Brian. "Yesterday's Bestsellers, 16: Lewis Carroll's Alice Books," *Interzone* No. 76: 56-59. October 1993.
___ Wullschläger, Jackie. **Inventing Wonderland: The Lives and Fantasies of Lewis Carroll, Edward Lear, J. M. Barrie, Kenneth Grahame and A. A. Milne.** New York: Free Press, 1995. 228pp.

CARRY, JULIUS
___ Shapiro, Marc. "Bounty Hunter," *Starlog* No. 204: 27-30. July 1994.

CARSON, DAVID
___ Nazzaro, Joe. "Generations Gap," *Starlog* No. 210: 40-45. January 1995.

CARTER, ANGELA
___ "Carter, Angela (Obituary)," *Locus* 28(3): 72. March 1992.
___ "Carter, Angela (Obituary)," *Science Fiction Chronicle* 13(6): 12. March 1992.
___ "Carter, Angela: Wise Child, Wayward Woman (Obituary)," *Vector* No. 166: 10-12. April/May 1992.
___ Clark, Robert. "Angela Carter's Desire Machine," *Women's Studies* 14(2): 147-162. 1987.
___ Gordon, Joan. "The Moebius Fiction of Angela Carter," *New York Review of Science Fiction* No. 59: 1, 3-5. July 1993.
___ Hallab, Mary Y. "Carter and Blake: The Dangers of Innocence," in: Sanders, Joe, ed. **Functions of the Fantastic.** Westport, CT: Greenwood, 1995. pp.177-184.
___ Kaveney, Roz. "New New World Dreams: Angela Carter and Science Fiction," in: Sage, Lorna, ed. **Flesh and the Mirror: Essays on the Art of Angela Carter.** London: Virago, 1994. pp.171-188.
___ Ledwon, Lenora. "The Passion of the Phallus and Angela Carter's **The Passion of New Eve**," *Journal of the Fantastic in the Arts* 5(4): 26-41. 1993. (No. 20)

CARTER, ANGELA (continued)
___ Manlove, C. N. "In the Demythologising Business: Angela Carter's **The Infernal Desire Machines of Dr. Hoffman** (1972)," in: Filmer, Kath, ed. **Twentieth-Century Fantasists: Essays in Culture, Society and Belief in Twentieth Century Mythopoeic Literature.** New York: St. Martin's, 1992. pp.148-160.
___ Romano, Carlin. "Show Biz Sisters From a Nutty Family Tree," *Philadelphia (PA) Inquirer.* January 12, 1992. in: *NewsBank. Literature.* 9:B4-B5. 1992
___ Rushdie, Salman. "Angela Carter, 1940-1992: A Very Good Wizard, a Very Dear Friend," *New York Times Book Review* p. 5. March 8, 1992.
___ Sage, Lorna, ed. **Flesh and the Mirror: Essays on the Art of Angela Carter.** London: Virago, 1994. 358pp.
___ Teissl, Verena. "Der tod in drei asugewählten phantastischen texten der Moderne," *Quarber Merkur* 33(2): 34-46. December 1995. (No. 84)
___ Upchurch, Michael. "**Wise Children**," *Seattle (WA) Times.* March 1, 1992. in: *NewsBank. Literature.* 26:B10. 1992
___ Vallorani, Nicoletta. "The Body of the City: Angela Carter's **The Passion of the New Eve**," *Science Fiction Studies* 21(3): 365-379. November 1994.

CARTER, CHRIS
___ Kutzera, Dale. "**X-Files**," *Cinefantastique* 26(2): 52-53. February 1995.
___ Maccarillo, Lisa. "**X-Files**," *Sci-Fi Entertainment* 1(4): 74-77. December 1994.
___ Swallow, James. "X-aminations," *Starlog* No. 221: 30-33, 64. December 1995.
___ Vitaris, Paula. "**X-Files**: Chris Carter, Creator," *Cinefantastique* 26(6)/27(1): 19-20. October 1995.

CARTER, HELENA BONHAM
___ Stephens, Lynne. "Bride of Frankenstein," *Starlog* No. 209: 27-30, 68. December 1994.

CARTER, LIN
___ Price, Robert M. **Lin Carter: A Look Behind His Imaginary Worlds.** Mercer Island, WA: Starmont, 1992. 172pp.

CARTIER, EDD
___ "1992 World Fantasy Awards Winners," *Locus* 29(6): 6. December 1992.
___ "World Fantasy Awards," *Science Fiction Chronicle* 14(3): 4. December 1992.

CARTIER, RUDOLPH
___ "Cartier, Rudolph (Obituary)," *Science Fiction Chronicle* 15(9): 16. August 1994.

CARTOONS
___ "High Tech Kidvid Cowboys Are the Latest to Ride Syndie Trail," *Variety* p. 47, 74. June 18, 1986.
___ Beeler, Michael. "Clive Barker: The Thief of Always," *Cinefantastique* 26(3): 20-21. April 1995.
___ Garcia, Bob. "The Animated Adventures: **Batman**," *Cinefantastique* 24(6)/25(1): 68-70, 75-111. February 1994.
___ Garcia, Bob. "**Batman**: Alan Burnett, Script Supervisor," by Bob Garcia and Nancy Garcia. *Cinefantastique* 24(6)/25(1): 84-85. February 1994.
___ Garcia, Bob. "**Batman**: Andrea Romano, Voice Doctor," by Bob Garcia and Nancy Garcia. *Cinefantastique* 24(6)/25(1): 90-93, 125. February 1994.
___ Garcia, Bob. "**Batman**: Bruce Timm, Series Co-Creator," by Bob Garcia and Nancy Garcia. *Cinefantastique* 24(6)/25(1): 79-80. February 1994.
___ Garcia, Bob. "**Batman**: Composing Music for Animation," by Bob Garcia and Nancy Garcia. *Cinefantastique* 24(6)/25(1): 108-110. February 1994.
___ Garcia, Bob. "**Batman**: Directing the Cartoon Action," by Bob Garcia and Nancy Garcia. *Cinefantastique* 24(6)/25(1): 95-97. February 1994.
___ Garcia, Bob. "**Batman**: Episode Guide," by Bob Garcia and Nancy Garcia. *Cinefantastique* 24(6)/25(1): 70-111. February 1994.
___ Garcia, Bob. "**Batman**: Eric Radomski, Series Co-Creator," by Bob Garcia and Nancy Garcia. *Cinefantastique* 24(6)/25(1): 76-77. February 1994.

CARTOONS (continued)
___ Garcia, Bob. "*Batman*: Paul Dini, Cartoon Criminology," by Bob Garcia and Nancy Garcia. *Cinefantastique* 24(6)/25(1): 87-88. February 1994.
___ Garcia, Bob. "*Batman*: Producing the Presentation Reel," by Bob Garcia and Nancy Garcia. *Cinefantastique* 24(6)/25(1): 100-101. February 1994.
___ Garcia, Bob. "*Batman*: Things to Come, Second Season," by Bob Garcia and Nancy Garcia. *Cinefantastique* 24(6)/25(1): 103-105. February 1994.
___ Garcia, Bob. "*Batman: Mask of the Phantasm*, the Animated Movie," *Cinefantastique* 24(6)/25(1): 71-74, 125. February 1994.
___ Kaufman, Dave. "Lucas Producing Two ABC Cartoons on Ewoks and R2D2," *Variety* p. 145. January 16, 1985.
___ Sulski, Jim. "Japanimation, Kitsch Classics No Kids' Stuff," *Chicago Tribune* Sec. 7, p. 61. November 6, 1992.

CASARES, ADOLFO BIOY
___ Bach, Caleb. "The Inventions of Adolfo Bioy Casares," *Americas* 45(6): 14-19. November 1993.

CASINO (MOTION PICTURE)
___ Vaz, Mark C. "*Casino*: The Lights of Las Vegas," *Cinefex* No. 64: 37-38, 140. December 1995.

CASPER AWARDS
___ SEE: CANADIAN SF AND FANTASY AWARDS.

CASPER (MOTION PICTURE)
___ Biodrowski, Steve. "*Casper* (Review)," *Cinefantastique* 27(3): 52. December 1995.
___ Duncan, Jody. "Quickcuts: The Ghost and Mr. Muren," *Cinefex* No. 63: 13-16. September 1995.
___ Jankiewicz, Pat. "Ghost, the Rapist," *Starlog* No. 216: 36-39. July 1995.
___ Lowe, Nick. "*Casper* (Review)," *Interzone* No. 99: 34. September 1995.
___ Persons, Dan. "*Casper*," *Cinefantastique* 26(4): 14-15, 61. June 1995.
___ Wells, Curt. "*Casper* Has Risen From the Grave," *Sci-Fi Entertainment* 2(1): 50-53. June 1995.

CASTLE FREAK (MOTION PICTURE)
___ Fischer, Dennis. "Full Moon Preview: *Castle Freak*," *Cinefantastique* 26(4): 32-34. June 1995.

CAT PEOPLE (MOTION PICTURE)
___ Berks, John. "What Alice Does: Looking Otherwise at *The Cat People*," *Cinema Journal* 32(1): 26-42. Fall 1992.
___ Garton, Ray. "On Kids and *Cat People*," in: Golden, Christopher, ed. **Cut! Horror Writers on Horror Film**. New York: Berkley, 1992. pp.101-112.

CAT WOMEN OF THE MOON (MOTION PICTURE)
___ Hogan, David J. "*Cat Women of the Moon* (Review)," *Filmfax* No. 34: 18, 20. August/September 1992.

CATASTROPHES
___ Broderick, Mick. "Surviving Armageddon: Beyond the Imagination of Disaster," *Science Fiction Studies* 20(3): 342-382. November 1993.
___ Innerhofer, Roland. "Katastrophenbilder," *Quarber Merkur* 31(1): 53-71. June 1993. (No. 79)
___ Schafer, William J. "The Imagination of Catastrophe," *North American Review* 268(3): 61-66. September 1983.
___ Stableford, Brian. "The Mythology of Man-Made Catastrophe," in: Stableford, Brian. **Opening Minds: Essays on Fantastic Literature**. San Bernardino, CA: Borgo Press, 1995. pp.53-90.
___ Wolff, Michael J. "In the Fields of the Fourth Horseman," *Starlog* No. 220: 27-31. November 1995.

CATHOLICISM
___ Wilson, Patricia A. **Conflict and Resolution: The Divergent Roles of Catholic Men of Faith in Science Fiction**. Master's Thesis, University of Regina (Canada), 1992. 108pp. (Master's Abstracts 32/03, p. 805. June 1993.)

CATMULL, EDWIN E.
___ French, Lawrence. "*Toy Story*: Renderman," *Cinefantastique* 27(2): 18-19. November 1995.

CATWOMAN
___ Orr, Philip. "The Anoedipal Mythos of Batman and Catwoman," *Journal of Popular Culture* 27(4): 169-182. Spring 1994.

CAULTON, DAVID
___ "Caulton, David (Obituary)," *Locus* 31(6): 68. December 1993.
___ "Caulton, David (Obituary)," *Science Fiction Chronicle* 15(2): 16. November/December 1993.

CAVE, HUGH B.
___ Cave, Hugh B. **Magazines I Remember: Some Pulps, Their Editors, and What It Was Like to Write for Them**. Chicago, IL: Tattered Pages Press, 1994. 174pp.

CAVELOS, JEANNE
___ "Cavelos Launches Editorial Service," *Locus* 33(6): 8, 79. December 1994.
___ "Cavelos Quits Dell," *Locus* 33(2): 8. August 1994.
___ "Jeanne Cavelos Quits Abyss for Academic Life," *Science Fiction Chronicle* 15(9): 4. August 1994.

CAVENDISH, MARGARET
___ Jacobs, Naomi. "The Frozen Landscape in Women's Utopian and Science Fiction," in: Donawerth, Jane L. and Kolmerten, Carol A., eds. **Utopian and Science Fiction by Women: Worlds of Difference**. Syracuse, NY: Syracuse University Press, 1994. pp.190-202.
___ Trubowitz, Rachel. "The Reenchantment of Utopia and the Female Monarchial Self: Margaret Cavendish's **Blazing World**," *Tulsa Studies in Women's Literature* 11(2): 229-245. Fall 1992.

CAZOTTE, JACQUES
___ Gilman, Juliette. "Shades of the Fantastic: The Forest in Jacques Cazotte's 'Aventure du pelerin' and George Sand's 'La Mare au diable'," in: Latham, Robert A. and Collins, Robert A., eds. **Modes of the Fantastic**. Westport, CT: Greenwood, 1995. pp.137-142.

CeLUCCHIO, PATRIZIA
___ "$1000 Susan Petrey SF Scholarships Awarded," *Science Fiction Chronicle* 14(11): 6-7. August 1993.

CENSORSHIP
___ " 'Clockwork' Ban Still Enforced," *Locus* 30(3): 6, 72. March 1993.
___ "Comics Fanzine Ruled Obscene," *Locus* 32(5): 9. May 1994.
___ " 'Jones' PG Focus of TV Violence Group," *Variety* p. 3, 123. May 30, 1984.
___ "Seeing Nuke Panic, Germans Dump Pic From TV Schedule," *Variety* p. 116, 124. March 21, 1984.
___ "Uncut 'Clockwork' Spurs Distrib-Exhib Heat in Argentina," *Variety* p. 44. September 15, 1982.
___ Hennessy, Joan. "King Books 'Off Limits' for Middle School Kids," *Jacksonville (FL) Times-Union*. March 12, 1992. in: *NewsBank. Literature.* 29:D14. 1992.
___ Langford, David. "Banned in New York," *Quantum* No. 41: 15. Winter/Spring 1992.
___ Norman, John. "How Far Is Too Far? An Open Letter From John Norman," *New York Review of Science Fiction* No. 83: 1, 10-15. July 1995.
___ Salmonson, Jessica A. "Journal Notes on Censorship," *Quantum* No. 43/44: 14-15. Spring/Summer 1993.
___ Tunnell, Michael O. "The Double-Edged Sword: Fantasy and Censorship," *Language Arts* 71(8): 606-612. December 1994.
___ Tusher, Will. " 'Jones' Criticism Prompts Valenti to Defend MPAA Rating System," *Variety* p. 5, 24. June 6, 1984.
___ Wingrove, David. "Letter to Catie, with Responses," *Vector* No. 165: 9-15, 23. February/March 1992. (Response to editorial, *Vector* No. 164: 3. December 1991/January 1992.)

CENTURY (MAGAZINE)
___ "*Century* Is New SF Magazine," *Science Fiction Chronicle* 15(8): 6. June 1994.
___ Bryant, Eric. "*Century*," *Library Journal* 120(13): 127. August 1995.

CHAING, TED
___ "1992 Hugo Awards Winners," *Locus* 29(4): 6, 42-47. October 1992.

CHAMBERS, ROBERT WILLIAM
___ Murray, Will. "Lovecraft, Blackwood, and Chambers: A Colloquium of Ghosts," *Studies in Weird Fiction* No. 13: 2-7. Summer 1993. [Not seen.]
___ Weinstein, Lee. "Chambers and **The King in Yellow**," in: Schweitzer, Darrell, ed. **Discovering Classic Horror Fiction I**. Mercer Island, WA: Starmont, 1992. pp.57-72.

CHAMBERS, WHITTAKER
___ Sarrocco, Clara. "Whittaker Chambers on Christians," *CSL: The Bulletin of the New York C. S. Lewis Society* 23(7): 6-7. May 1992.

CHAMPETIER, JOEL
___ "1995 Prix Aurora Awards," *Locus* 34(6): 8. June 1995.
___ "Aurora Awards," *Science Fiction Chronicle* 16(7): 4. June/July 1995.

CHANDLER, A. BERTRAM
___ McMullen, Sean. "A. Bertram Chandler: A Survey," *Science Fiction: A Review of Speculative Literature* 11(1): 3-9. 1991. (No. 31)

CHANDLER, HELEN
___ Bowman, David. "The Strange Odyssey of Helen Chandler," *Filmfax* No. 35: 67-72. October/November 1992.

CHANDLER, RAYMOND
___ Bruccoli, Matthew J. "Raymond Chandler," in: Bruccoli, Matthew J., ed. **Facts on File Bibliography of American Fiction 1919-1988**. New York: Facts on File, 1991. pp.126-127.

CHANEY, LON
___ Blake, Michael F. "The Dark Duo: Tod Browning and Lon Chaney, Sr.," *Filmfax* No. 43: 50-57, 97. February/March 1994.
___ Blake, Michael F. **Lon Chaney: The Man Behind the Thousand Faces**. Vestal, NY: Vestal Press, 1990. 394pp.
___ Blake, Michael F. "The Man Behind the Thousand Faces," *Filmfax* No. 38: 42-49, 78-82, 94-96. April/May 1993.
___ Blake, Michael F. "Master of Early Movie Makeup: Lon Chaney," *Filmfax* No. 39: 85-63, 98. June/July 1993.
___ Smith, Don G. **Lon Chaney, Jr.: Horror Film Star, 1906-1993**. Jefferson, NC: McFarland, 1995. 272pp.

CHANG HSI-KUO
___ Wong, Kin-yuen. "Rhetoric, History and Interpretation in Chang Hsi-Kuo's The Star Cloud Suite," *Modern Chinese Literature* (Boulder, CO) 6(1/2): 115-132. Spring-Fall 1992.

CHAPMAN, BEN
___ Weaver, Tom. "Ben Chapman: Interview," in: Weaver, Tom, ed. **Attack of the Monster Movie Makers: Interviews with 20 Genre Giants**. Jefferson, NC: McFarland, 1994. pp.31-44.
___ Weaver, Tom. "Creature King: From Out of the Black Lagoon, Ben Chapman Walked," by Tom Weaver and Paul Parla. *Starlog* 180: 59-64, 73. July 1992.

CHAPPELL, FRED
___ "1994 World Fantasy Awards," *Locus* 33(6): 7, 49. December 1994.
___ "World Fantasy Awards," *Science Fiction Chronicle* 16(2): 4. November/December 1994.
___ Schweitzer, Darrell. "A Talk With Fred Chappell," *Worlds of Fantasy and Horror* 1(1): 40-43. Summer 1994. (No. 1)

CHARACTERIZATION
___ "Forum: Characters," *Focus* (BSFA) No. 24: 7-11. June/July 1993.
___ Budrys, Algis. "Naming Characters and Why," in: Wolverton, Dave, ed. **Writers of the Future, Vol. VIII**. Los Angeles, CA: Bridge, 1992. pp.107-111.
___ Card, Orson S. "Characters in Science Fiction," in: Thompkins, David G., ed. **Science Fiction Writer's Market Place and Source Book**. Cincinnati, OH: Writer's Digest Books, 1994. pp.18-24.
___ Clement, Hal. "The Creation of Imaginary Beings," in: Dozois, Gardner, ed. **Writing Science Fiction and Fantasy**. New York: St. Martin's, 1991. pp.129-146.

CHARACTERIZATION (continued)
___ Ferrell, Keith. "How to Build an Alien," *Omni* 14(9): 50-57, 111. October 1992.
___ Kelly, James P. "You and Your Characters," in: Dozois, Gardner, ed. **Writing Science Fiction and Fantasy**. New York: St. Martin's, 1991. pp.38-49.

CHARNAS, SUZY McKEE
___ "1994 Mythopoeic Fantasy Awards," *Locus* 33(4): 72. October 1994.
___ "Mythopoeic Awards, 1994," *Science Fiction Chronicle* 16(1): 8. October 1994.
___ "Suzy McKee Charnas: Functional Schizophrenia," *Locus* 29(3): 4, 80-81. September 1992.
___ Barr, Marleen S. **Lost in Space: Probing Feminist Science Fiction and Beyond**. Chapel Hill, NC: University of North Carolina Press, 1993. 231pp.
___ Charnas, Suzy M. "A Case for Fantasy," *ALAN Review* 19(3): 20-22. Spring 1992.
___ King, Maureen. "Contemporary Women Writers and the 'New Evil': The Vampires of Anne Rice and Suzy McKee Charnas," *Journal of the Fantastic in the Arts* 5(3): 75-84. 1993. (No. 19)
___ Wolmark, Jenny. **Aliens and Others: Science Fiction, Feminism, and Postmodernism**. London: Harester Wheatsheaf, 1993. 167pp.; Iowa City: University of Iowa Press, 1994. 167pp.

CHARNO, SARA
___ Vitaris, Paula. "**X-Files**: Boy's Club," *Cinefantastique* 26(6)/27(1): 88. October 1995.

CHARTERIS, LESLIE
___ "Charteris, Leslie (Obituary)," *Locus* 30(6): 71. June 1993.
___ "Charteris, Leslie (Obituary)," *Science Fiction Chronicle* 14(9): 16. June 1993.

CHATER, ELIZABETH
___ Mallett, Daryl F. **The Work of Elizabeth Chater: An Annotated Bibliography and Guide**, by Daryl F. Mallett and Annette Y. Mallett. San Bernardino, CA: Borgo Press, 1994. 80pp.

CHAUSSON, ERNEST
___ Speare, Mary J. "Wagnerian and Arthurian Elements in Chausson's **Le Roi Arthus**," in: Busby, Keith, ed. **The Arthurian Yearbook I**. New York: Garland, 1991. pp.195-214.

CHEMISTRY
___ Foster, Natalie. "Science and the Final Frontier: Chemistry and *Star Trek*," *Chemistry and Industry* No. 24: 18-20. December 21, 1992.

CHERNOBYL
___ "Chernobyl Nuke Fire Stokes Sales Action on Atlas' **Nuclear Conspiracy**," *Variety* p. 1, 98. May 21, 1986.

CHERRY 2000 (MOTION PICTURE)
___ "**Cherry 2000** (Review)," *Variety* p. 12, 14. July 20, 1988.

CHERRYH, C. J.
___ "C. J. Cherryh: Adjusting the Language," *Locus* 30(1): 5, 66. January 1993.
___ Beal, Rebecca S. "C. J. Cherryh's Arthurian Humanism," in: Slocum, Sally K., ed. **Popular Arthurian Traditions**. Bowling Green, OH: Popular Press, 1992. pp.56-67.
___ Hayles, N. Katherine. "The Life Cycle of Cyborgs: Writing the Posthuman," in: Gray, Chris H., ed. **The Cyborg Handbook**. New York: Routledge, 1995. pp.321-335.
___ Hayles, N. Katherine. "The Life Cycle of Cyborgs: Writing the Posthuman," in: Benjamin, Marina, ed. **A Question of Identity: Women, Science, and Literature**. New Brunswick, NJ: Rutgers University Press, 1993. pp.152-170.
___ Hyde, Paul N. "Dances With Dusei: A Personal Response to C. J. Cherryh's **The Faded Sun**," *Mythlore* 18(2): 45-53. Spring 1992. (No. 68)
___ Jones, Neil. "C. J. Cherryh: An Annotated Bibliography," *Interzone* No. 55: 47-49. January 1992.
___ Nicholls, Stan. "C. J. Cherryh Clears Out the Dead Wood," in: Nicholls, Stan. **Wordsmiths of Wonder: Fifty Interviews with Writers of the Fantastic**. London: Orbit, 1993. pp.43-54.

CHERRYH, C. J. (continued)
___ Stephensen-Payne, Phil. **C. J. Cherryh: A Working Bibliography**. Albuquerque, NM: Galactic Central, 1992. 36pp.
___ Wolmark, Jenny. **Aliens and Others: Science Fiction, Feminism, and Postmodernism**. London: Harester Wheatsheaf, 1993. 167pp.; Iowa City: University of Iowa Press, 1994. 167pp.

CHESLEY AWARDS
___ Guarino, Bettyann. "Things You Wanted to Know About the Chesleys: But Were Afraid to Ask," *ASFA Quarterly* 10(1): 6-13. Spring 1992.

CHESLEY AWARDS, 1991
___ "1991 Chesley Awards Winners," *Locus* 29(4): 7, 73. October 1992

CHESLEY AWARDS, 1992
___ "1992 Chesley Award Winners," *Locus* 31(4): 6. October 1993.
___ "ASFA's Chesley Art Award Nominations, 1992," *Science Fiction Chronicle* 14(10): 5-6. July 1993.
___ "Association of SF and Fantasy Artists' Chesley Awards," *Science Fiction Chronicle* 14(1): 4. October 1992.

CHESLEY AWARDS, 1993
___ "Chesley Awards," *Science Fiction Chronicle* 15(1): 4. October 1993.
___ "Chesley Awards," *Science Fiction Chronicle* 15(10): 5. September 1994.
___ "Chesley Awards Nominations," *Locus* 31(1): 6, 57. July 1993.

CHESLEY AWARDS, 1994
___ "Chesley Award Nominations," *Science Fiction Chronicle* 15(9): 5. August 1994.
___ "Chesley Awards Nominees," *Locus* 33(1): 7, 78. July 1994.

CHESLEY AWARDS, 1995
___ "1995 Chesley Awards," *Locus* 35(2): 8. August 1995.
___ "Chesley Awards," *Science Fiction Chronicle* 16(9): 5. August/ September 1995.

CHESNEY, GEORGE TOMKYNS
___ Stableford, Brian. "Yesterday's Bestsellers, 19: **The Battle of Dorking** and Its Aftermath," *Interzone* No. 83: 52-56. May 1994.

CHESTERTON, G. K.
___ Conlon, D. J., ed. **G. K. Chesterton: The Critical Judgments, Part 1: 1900-1937**. Antwerp, Belgium: Antwerp Studies in English Literature, 1976. 555pp. [Not seen.]
___ Crowther, Ian. **G. K. Chesterton**. London: Claridge Press, 1991. 101pp. [Not seen.]
___ Mackey, Aidan. "The Christian Influence of G. K. Chesterton on C. S. Lewis," in: Walker, Andrew and Patric, James, eds. **A Christian for All Christians**. Washington, DC: Regnery, 1992. pp.68-82.
___ Schenkel, Elmar. "Visions From the Verge: Terror and Play in G. K. Chesterton's Imagination," in: Filmer, Kath, ed. **Twentieth-Century Fantasists: Essays in Culture, Society and Belief in Twentieth Century Mythopoeic Literature**. New York: St. Martin's, 1992. pp.34-46.
___ Walczuk, Anna. "The Permanent in Lewis and Chesterton," *Chesterton Review* 17(3/4): 313-321. August/November 1991.

CHIANG, TED
___ "World SF Convention Hugo Awards," *Science Fiction Chronicle* 14(1): 4. October 1992.

CHILDREN
___ Cantor, Joanne. "Children's Emotional Reactions to Technological Disasters Conveyed by the Mass Media," in: Wober, J. Mallory, ed. **Television and Nuclear Power: Making the Public Mind**. Norwood, NJ: Ablex, 1992. pp.31-54.

CHILDREN OF CORN II: DEADLY HARVEST (MOTION PICTURE)
___ Goodson, William W., Jr. "Stephen King: **Children of Corn II: Deadly Harvest**," *Cinefantastique* 23(4): 13. December 1992.

CHILDREN OF THE NIGHT (MOTION PICTURE)
___ Harris, Judith P. "**Children of the Night** (Review)," *Cinefantastique* 25(5): 59. October 1994.

CHILDREN OF THE NIGHT (MOTION PICTURE) (continued)
___ Wilt, David. "**Children of the Night** (Review)," *Cinefantastique* 23(6): 60. April 1993.

CHILDREN'S SF AND FANTASY
___ Apseloff, Marilyn F. "The British Science Fiction of Louise Lawrence," in: Sullivan, C. W., III. **Science Fiction for Young Readers**. Westport, CT: Greenwood, 1993. pp.133-144.
___ Bailey, K. V. "Masters, Slaves, and Rebels: Dystopia as Defined and Defied by John Christopher," in: Sullivan, C. W., III. **Science Fiction for Young Readers**. 1993. Westport, CT: Greenwood, 1993. pp.97-112.
___ Bull, Geoff. "Morning Comes Whether You Set the Alarm or Not: Science Fiction, a Genre for the Future," *Orana* (Australia) 31(3): 159-169. August 1995.
___ Callahan, Tim. "Censoring the World Riddle," *Mythlore* 20(1): 15-21. Winter 1994. (Whole No. 75)
___ Colin, Mariella. "Du fantastique en tant que genre litteraire pour les enfants in Italie," in: Perrot, Jean, ed. **Culture, texte et Juene Lecteur. Actes du Xe Congres de l'International Research Society for Children's Literature, Paris, September 1991**. Nancy: Presses Universitaires, 1993. pp.43-49
___ Coville, Bruce. "About Tomorrow: Learning with Literature," *Instructor* 101(9): 20, 22-23. May/June 1992.
___ Crisler, Jesse. "Fantasy: A Welcome Alternative," in: Canham, Stephen, ed. **Literature and Hawaii's Children**. Honolulu, HI: University of Hawaii Manoa, 1992. pp.69-75
___ Dowd, Frances A. "Is There a Typical YA Fantasy? A Content Analysis," by Frances A. Dowd and Lisa C. Taylor. *Journal of Youth Services in Libraries* 5(2): 175-183. Winter 1992.
___ Dunn, Thom. "Growing Home: The Triumph of Youth in the Novels of H. M. Hoover," by Thom Dunn and Karl Hiller. in: Sullivan, C. W., III. **Science Fiction for Young Readers**. Westport, CT: Greenwood, 1993. pp.121-131.
___ Goderham, David. "Children's Fantasy Literature: Toward an Anatomy," *Children's Literature in Education* 26(3): 171-183. September 1995.
___ Golden, Joanne M. **A Schema for Analyzing Response to Literature Applied to the Responses of Fifth and Eighth Graders to Realistic and Fantasy Short Stories**. Ph.D. Dissertation, Ohio State University, 1978. 195pp. (DAI 39: 5996A. Apr. 1978.)
___ Gooderham, David. "Children's Fantasy Literature: Toward an Anatomy," *Children's Literature in Education* 26(3): 171-183. September 1995.
___ Goodknight, Glen H. "Is Children's Literature Childish?," *Mythlore* 19(4): 4-5. Autumn 1993. (No. 74)
___ Harkins, Patricia. "Myth in Action: The Trials and Transformation of Menolly," in: Sullivan, C. W., III. **Science Fiction for Young Readers**. Westport, CT: Greenwood, 1993. pp.157-166.
___ Hendrix, Howard V. "The Things of a Child: Coming Full Circle With Alan E. Nourse's **Raiders From the Rings**," in: Sullivan, C. W., III. **Science Fiction for Young Readers**. Westport, CT: Greenwood, 1993. pp.87-96.
___ Hill, Douglas. "Writing SF for Kids," *Books for Keeps* 83: 24-25. 1993.
___ Hull, Elizabeth A. "Asimov: Man Thinking," in: Sullivan, C. W., III. **Science Fiction for Young Readers**. Westport, CT: Greenwood, 1993. pp.47-64.
___ Jones, Gwyneth. "C. S. Lewis and Tolkien: Writers for Children?," *New York Review of Science Fiction* No. 87: 1, 8-12. November 1995.
___ Jones, Raymond E. "True Myth: Female Archetypes in Monica Hughes's **The Keeper of the Isis Light**," in: Sullivan, C. W., III. **Science Fiction for Young Readers**. Westport, CT: Greenwood, 1993. pp.169-178.
___ Lance, Donna. "Science Fiction and Mythology: Creatures of Light and Darkness," in: Kellogg, Judith and Crisler, Jesse, eds. **Literature & Hawaii's Children: Stories as Bridges to Many Realms**. Honolulu, HI: University of Hawaii at Manoa, 1994. pp.125-132.
___ Le Guin, Ursula K. **Earthsea Revisioned**. Madison, NJ: Children's Literature New England, 1993. 26pp.
___ Lehnert, Gertrud. "Trauma, Fluchten, Utopien: Wirklichkeit im Spiegel der phantistischen Kinder- und Jungendliteratur," *Fundevogel* No. 88/89: 11-18. 1991.
___ Lehr, Susan. "Fantasy: Inner Journeys for Today's Child," *Publishing Research Quarterly* 7(3): 91-101. Fall 1991. [Not seen.]

CHILDREN'S SF AND FANTASY (continued)

___ Lenz, Millicent. "**Danger Quotient, Fiskadoro, Riddley Walker**, and the Failure of the Campbellian Monomyth," in: Sullivan, C. W., III. **Science Fiction for Young Readers**. Westport, CT: Greenwood, 1993. pp.113-119.

___ Lenz, Millicent. "Raymond Brigg's **When the Wind Blows**: Toward an Ecology of the Mind for Young Readers," in: Sullivan, C. W., III. **Science Fiction for Young Readers**. Westport, CT: Greenwood, 1993. pp.197-204.

___ Lepage, Francoise. "Pour une rhetorique de la representation fantastique (In Search of a Theory of Illustration of Fantastique)," *Canadian Children's Literature* 60: 97-107. 1990. [Not seen.]

___ Lynn, Ruth N. **Fantasy Literature for Children and Young Adults: An Annotated Bibliography**. 4th ed. New York: Bowker, 1995. 1092pp.

___ Masson, Sophie. "The Medieval and the Fantastic," *Magpies: Talking About Books for Children* 10(4): 8-9. September 1995.

___ May, Jill P. "The Year in Children's Science Fiction and Fantasy, 1990," in: Collins, Robert A. and Latham, Robert, eds. **Science Fiction and Fantasy Book Review Annual 1991**. Westport, CT: Greenwood, 1994. pp.178-204.

___ Milner, Joseph O. "Captain Kirk and Dr. Who: Meliorist and Spenglerian World Views in Science Fiction for Young Adults," in: Sullivan, C. W., III. **Science Fiction for Young Readers**. Westport, CT: Greenwood, 1993. pp.187-196.

___ Mitchell, Judith N. "Neo-Gnostic Elements in Louise Lawrence's **Moonwind**," in: Sullivan, C. W., III. **Science Fiction for Young Readers**. Westport, CT: Greenwood, 1993. pp.179-185.

___ Molson, Francis J. "The Tom Swift Books," in: Sullivan, C. W., III. **Science Fiction for Young Readers**. Westport, CT: Greenwood, 1993. pp.3-20.

___ Nauman, Ann K. "Sci-Fi Science," by Ann K. Nauman and Edward L. Shaw. *Science Activities* 31(3): 18-20. Fall 1994.

___ Nelson, Craig A. **A Content Analysis of Female and Male Authors' Portrayals of Sex Roles in Science Fiction for Children From 1970 to 1990**. Ph.D. Disseration, University of Minnesota, 1991. 235pp.

___ Newsinger, John. "Futuretracks: The Juvenile Science Fiction of Robert Westall," *Foundation* No. 63: 61-67. Spring 1995.

___ Payson, Patricia. **Science Fiction: Imagining Worlds**. Tucson, AZ: Zephyr Press, 1994. 84pp. (Zephyr Press Learning Packet)

___ Petzold, Dieter. "Tolkien als Kinderbuchautor," in: Kranz, Gisbert, ed. **Inklings: Jahrbuch für Literatur und Ästhetik**. 8. Band. Lüdenscheid, Germany: Stier, 1990. pp.53-70. [Not seen.]

___ Pratchett, Terry. "Let There Be Dragons," *Science Fiction Chronicle* 15(1): 5, 28-29. October 1993.

___ Sammons, Todd H. "Science Fiction and Mythology: An Overview," in: Kellogg, Judith and Crisler, Jesse, eds. **Literature & Hawaii's Children: Stories as Bridges to Many Realms**. Honolulu, HI: University of Hawaii at Manoa, 1994. pp.117-124.

___ Sarjeant, William A. S. "A Forgotten Children's Fantasy: Philip Woodruff's **The Sword of Northumbria**," *Mythlore* 20(4): 30-35. Winter 1995. (Whole No. 78)

___ Schlobin, Roger C. "The Formulaic and Rites of Transformation in Andre Norton's Magic Series," in: Sullivan, C. W., III. **Science Fiction for Young Readers**. Westport, CT: Greenwood, 1993. pp.37-45.

___ Sircar, Sanjay. "Children's Fantasy Fiction in English: Early Generic Discriminations and Our Modern Critical Inheritance," *Merveilles & Contes* 7(2): 423-449. December 1993.

___ Smedman, M. Sarah. "The 'Terrible Journey' Past 'Dragons in the Waters' to a 'House Like a Lotus': Faces of Love in the Fiction of Madeleine L'Engle," in: Sullivan, C. W., III. **Science Fiction for Young Readers**. Westport, CT: Greenwood, 1993. pp.65-82.

___ Smith, Sherwood. "Writing for Adults vs. Writing for Children," *Focus* (BSFA) No. 29: 13-14. December 1995/January 1996.

___ Stewig, John W. "The Witch Woman: A Recurring Motif in Recent Fantasy Writing for Young Readers," *Mythlore* 20(1): 48-52. Winter 1994. (Whole No. 75) (Reprinted: *Children's Literature in Education* 26(2): 119-133. June 1995.)

___ Sullivan, C. W., III. "Heinlein's Juveniles: Growing Up in Outer Space," in: Sullivan, C. W., III. **Science Fiction for Young Readers**. Westport, CT: Greenwood, 1993. pp.21-35.

___ Sullivan, C. W., III. **Science Fiction for Young Readers**. Westport, CT: Greenwood, 1993. 214pp.

___ Tunnell, Michael O. "The Double-Edged Sword: Fantasy and Censorship," *Language Arts* 71(8): 606-612. December 1994.

___ Vollprecht, Sabine. **Science-Fiction fur Kinder in der DDR**. Stuttgart: H.-D. Heinz, 1994. 135pp.

CHILDREN'S SF AND FANTASY (continued)

___ Westfahl, Gary. "The Genre That Evolved: On Science Fiction as Children's Literature," *Foundation* No. 62: 70-74. Winter 1994/1995.

___ Whitaker, Muriel. "Arthur for Children," in: Fries, Maureen and Watson, Jeanie, eds. **Approaches to the Teaching of the Arthurian Tradition**. New York: Modern Language Association, 1992. pp.151-154.

___ Wytenbroek, J. R. "The Debate Continues: Technology or Nature--A Study of Monica Hughes's Science Fiction Novels," in: Sullivan, C. W., III. **Science Fiction for Young Readers**. Westport, CT: Greenwood, 1993. pp.145-155.

___ Yates, Jessica. "Children's Fantasy: A Roundup Review," *Vector* No. 179: 18-22. June/July 1994.

___ Yates, Jessica. "Journeys into Inner Space," *Books For Keeps* No. 83: 26-29. November 1993.

CHILE

___ Bell, Andrea. "**Desde Júpiter**: Chile's Earliest Science Fiction Novel," *Science Fiction Studies* 22(2): 187-197. July 1995.

___ Mora, Gabriela. "**De repente los Lugares Desaparecen** de Patricio Manns: Ciencia Ficción a la Latinoamericana?," *Revista Iberoamericana* 60(No. 168/169): 1039-1049. July/December 1994.

CHINA

___ "Chinese SF Outside the Mainland," *Locus* 28(2): 45. August 1992.

___ "Harrison Awards, 1994," *Locus* 34(2): 9. February 1995.

___ "Harrison Science Fiction Prize, 1995," *Locus* 34(3): 76. March 1995.

___ "Science Fiction, a Global Community: China," *Locus* 32(4): 41. April 1994.

___ "SF in China," *Locus* 28(1): 43-44. January 1992.

___ "SF in China," *Locus* 29(1): 39, 72. July 1992.

___ "SF in China," *Locus* 30(4): 39. April 1993.

___ Clements, Jonathan. "Flesh and Metal: Marriage and Female Emancipation in the Science Fiction of Wei Yahua," *Foundation* No. 65: 61-80. Autumn 1995.

___ Dingbo, Wu. "Fandom in China," in: Sanders, Joe, ed. **Science Fiction Fandom**. Westport, CT: Greenwood, 1994. pp.133-136.

___ Ke, Fan. "Science Fiction Film Calls for Environmental Protection: *Legend of the Celestial Sphere* Directed by Wei Judang," *Beijing Review* 38(37): 34. September 11, 1995.

___ Squires, John D. "Some Contemporary Themes in Shiel's Early Novels: The Dragon's Tale; M. P. Shiel on the Emergence of Modern China," in: **Shiel in Diverse Hands: A Collection of Essays**. Cleveland, OH: Reynolds Morse Foundation, 1983. pp.249-301.

___ Wu, Quingyun. **Female Rule in Chinese and English Literary Utopias**. Syracuse, NY: Syracuse University Press, 1995. 225pp.; London: Liverpool University Press, 1995. 225pp.

___ Yan, Wu. "SF in China: A Special Report," *Locus* 33(1): 45. July 1994.

CHLEBNIKOV, VELIMIR

___ Solivetti, Carla. "L'utopia linguistica di Velimir Chlebnikov," in: Saccaro Del Buffa, Giuseppa and Lewis, Arthur O., eds. **Utopie per gli Anni Ottana**. Rome: Gangemi Editore, 1986. pp.51-70.

CHOI, ERIC

___ "First Asimov SF Award," *Science Fiction Chronicle* 15(6): 4. April/May 1994.

___ Williams, Sheila. "Isaac Asimov Award Winners," *Asimov's Science Fiction Magazine* 18(12/13): 152-153. November 1994.

CHRÉTIEN DE TROYES

___ Brumlik, Joan. "The Knight, The Lady, and The Dwarf in Chrétien's **Erec**," *Quondam et Futurus* 2(2): 54-72. Summer 1992.

___ Furtado, Antonio L. "A Source in Babylon," *Quondam et Futurus* 3(1): 38-59. Spring 1993.

___ Kimsey, John. "Dolorous Strokes, or Balin at the Bat: Malamud, Malory and Chrétien," in: Morse, Donald E., ed. **The Celebration of the Fantastic**. Westport, CT: Greenwood, 1992. pp.103-112.

___ Raffel, Burton. "Translating **Yvain** and **Sir Gawain and the Green Knight** for Classroom Use," in: Fries, Maureen and Watson, Jeanie, eds. **Approaches to the Teaching of the Arthurian Tradition**. New York: Modern Language Association, 1992. pp.88-93.

___ Ryan, J. S. "Uncouth Innocence: Some Links Between Chrétien de Troyes, Wolfram von Eschenbach and J. R. R. Tolkien," in: Kranz, Gisbert, ed. **Inklings: Jahrbuch für Literatur und Ästhetik**. 2. Band. [Lüdensceid, Germany, Stier], 1984. pp.25-41.

CLARKE, ARTHUR C. (continued)
___ "Arthur C. Clarke Receives Degree via Satellite," *Science Fiction Chronicle* 16(4): 5. February 1995.
___ "Arthur C. Clarke Tours Florida," *Locus* 33(4): 46. October 1994.
___ "Clarke Takes Plunge," *Locus* 29(1): 6. July 1992.
___ "Clarke Treasure Shown," *Locus* 29(5): 4. November 1992
___ "Minehead Space Festival to Celebrate Arthur C. Clarke's 75th Birthday," *Science Fiction Chronicle* 13(6): 6. March 1992.
___ "Right on the Money: Arthur C. Clarke Receives Honorary Degree from Liverpool University," *Los Angeles (CA) Times* p.M4. February 12, 1995.
___ Bloom, Harold. "Arthur C. Clarke," in: Bloom, Harold, ed. **Science Fiction Writers of the Golden Age.** New York: Chelsea House, 1995. pp.94-109.
___ Burns, John F. "A Science Fiction Writer's Long-ago Voyage to a Quieter World, Far Away," *New York Times* p. A4. November 28, 1994.
___ Coll, Steve. "Arthur C. Clarke's Red Thumb," *Washington (DC) Post* Sec. B, p. 1. March 9, 1992.
___ Connolly, John. "A Progressive End: Arthur C. Clarke and Teilhard de Chardin," *Foundation* No. 61: 66-76. Summer 1994.
___ Fineman, Mark. "Arthur C. Clarke's Space Odyssey Didn't End With 2001--His New Dream Is Gardening on Mars," *Los Angeles (CA) Times* p. E1, E4. January 24, 1992.
___ Fineman, Mark. "Out of This World," *Los Angeles (CA) Times* Sec. E, p. 1. January 24, 1992.
___ Gargan, Edward A. "For Arthur Clarke, Sri Lanka Is a Link to Space," *New York Times* Sec. C, p. 13. April 7, 1993.
___ Goizet, Annette. "A. C. Clarke **Childhood's End** (1953)," in: Le Bouille, Lucien, ed. **Fins de Romans: Aspects de la conclusion dans lo latterature anglaise.** Caen: PU de Caen, 1993. pp57-68.
___ Guy, Pat. "*Time* Special Issue Includes Fiction," *USA Today* Sec. B, p. 4. September 28, 1992.
___ Holliday, Liz. "Last of the Old Guard? Liz Holliday Meets Arthur C. Clarke and His Biographer, Neil McAleer," *Interzone* No. 66: 43-46. December 1992.
___ Ikin, Van. "Clarke as Constructor: Thoughts About Arthur C. Clarke's **Astounding Days** and **The Ghost From the Grand Banks**," *Science Fiction: A Review of Speculative Literature* 12(1): 9-14. 1993. (Whole No. 34)
___ Jongeward, Steven. "**2001: A Space Odyssey**: Arthur C. Clarke," *Cinefantastique* 25(3): 37. June 1994.
___ Mantell, Suzanne. "Back to the Future With Arthur C. Clarke," *Publishers Weekly* 240(7): 18-19. February 15, 1993.
___ Martin-Diaz, M. J. "Science Fiction Comes to the Classroom: Maelstrom II," by M. J. Martin-Diaz, A. Pizarro, P. Bacas, J. P. Garcia and F. Perera. *Physics Education* 27(1): 18-23. January 1992.
___ McAleer, Neil. **Odyssey: The Authorised Biography of Arthur C. Clarke.** London: Gollancz, 1992. 430pp. (As: **Arthur C. Clarke: The Authorized Biography.** New York: Contemporary Books, 1992. 430pp.)
___ Nicholls, Stan. "Author of Odysseys," *Starlog* No. 200: 27-31. March 1994.
___ Nicholls, Stan. "A Blip on the Way to the Big Crunch: Arthur C. Clarke Interviewed," *Interzone* No. 78: 23-26. December 1993.
___ Schütz, Helmut. "Arthur C. Clarke, **Childhood's End** (1953)," in: Heuermann, Harmut, ed. **Der Science Fiction Roman in der angloamerikanischen Literatur: Interpretationen.** Düsseldorf: Bagel, 1986. pp.144-165.
___ Westfahl, Gary. "Good Physics, Lousy Engineering: Arthur C. Clarke's **A Fall of Moondust**," *Monad* No. 3: 65-90. September 1993.

CLARKE, NORM
___ "Clarke, Norm (Obituary)," *Locus* 34(6): 67. June 1995.
___ "Clarke, Norm (Obituary)," *Science Fiction Chronicle* 16(7): 19. June/July 1995.

CLARKE, ROBERT
___ Clarke, Robert. "The Actor From Planet X," *Starlog* No. 219: 27-31, 66. October 1995.

CLASSIC SCI-FI AND FANTASY (MAGAZINE)
___ "Classic Sci-Fi and Fantasy," *Science Fiction Chronicle* 16(8): 10. July/August 1995

CLASSIFICATION
___ Beghtol, Clare. **The Classification of Fiction: The Development of a System Based on Theoretical Principles.** Metuchen, NJ: Scarecrow, 1994. 365pp.

CLAUDEL, PAUL
___ Kranz, Gisbert. "Stellvertretung bei Williams, Claudel und G. v. le Fort," in: Kranz, Gisbert, ed. **Inklings: Jahrbuch für Literatur und Ästhetik.** 3. Band. [Lüdenscheid, Germany: Stier], 1985. pp.87-108.

CLAVELL, JAMES
___ "Clavell, James (Obituary)," *Locus* 33(4): 70. October 1994.

CLAYTON, JACK
___ "Clayton, Jack (Obituary)," *Science Fiction Chronicle* 16(5): 18. March/April 1995.

CLEATOR, PHILIP E.
___ "Cleator, Philip E. (Obituary)," *Locus* 34(4): 62. April 1995.
___ "Cleator, Philip E. (Obituary)," *Science Fiction Chronicle* 16(4): 14-16. February 1995.
___ Ashley, Mike. "The Rocket Man: Memories of Philip Cleator," *Fantasy Commentator* 8(3/4): 166-172. Fall 1995. (Whole No. 47/48)

CLEAVER, DIANE
___ "Cleaver, Diane (Obituary)," *Locus* 34(5): 72. May 1995.
___ "Cleaver, Diane (Obituary)," *Science Fiction Chronicle* 16(6): 20, 22. May 1995.

CLEMENSON, CHRISTIAN
___ Shapiro, Marc. "The Adventures of Socrates Poole," *Starlog* No. 203: 55-58. June 1994.

CLEMENT, HAL
___ Weiss, Allan. "An Interview With Hal Clement," *Sol Rising* (Toronto) No. 10: 4-5. May 1994.

CLEREMONT, CHRIS
___ Johnson, Kim H. "In the Light of **The Shadow Moon**," *Starlog* No. 219: 38-41. October 1995.

CLIFFHANGER (MOTION PICTURE)
___ Kaufman, Debra. "Effects in the Vertical Realm," *Cinefex* No. 54: 30-53. May 1993.

CLIVE, COLIN
___ Mank, Gregory W. "Colin Clive: Tragic Victim of His Own Monsters," *Filmfax* No. 35: 40-49, 94. October/November 1992.

CLOCKWORK ORANGE (MOTION PICTURE)
___ " 'Clockwork' Ban Still Enforced," *Locus* 30(3): 6, 72. March 1993.
___ "Uncut 'Clockwork' Spurs Distrib-Exhib Heat in Argentina," *Variety* p. 44. September 15, 1982.
___ Roth, Ellen S. **The Rhetoric of First-Person Point of View in the Novel and Film Forms: A Study of Anthony Burgess' A Clockwork Orange and Henry James' A Turn of the Screw and Their Film Adaptations.** Ph.D. Dissertation, New York University, 1978. 308pp. (DAI 39: 4558A. Feb. 1979.)

CLONING OF JOANNA MAY (MOTION PICTURE)
___ Millman, Joyce. "**Joanna May**: Send in the Clones (Review)," *San Francisco (CA) Examiner.* February 29, 1992. in: *NewsBank. Film and Television.* 30:C4. 1992.
___ Persons, Dan. "**The Cloning of Joanna May** (Review)," *Cinefantastique* 23(1): 60. August 1992.

CLOSE ENCOUNTERS OF THE THIRD KIND (MOTION PICTURE)
___ Fairchild, B. H. "An Event Sociologique: **Close Encounters**," *Journal of Popular Film and Television* 6(4): 342-349. 1978.
___ Rubin, Steven J. "When Saucers Were Young," *Sci-Fi Entertainment* 1(1): 34-37. June 1994.

CLOTHING
___ Altman, Mark A. "**Star Trek**: Fashion in the 24th Century," *Cinefantastique* 23(2/3): 76-77. October 1992.

CLUB, THE (MOTION PICTURE)
___ Wilt, David. "**The Club** (Review)," *Cinefantastique* 25(6)/26(1): 122. December 1994.

CLUBS
___ SEE: ORGANIZATIONS.

CLUTE, JOHN
___ "John Clute: The Passage of the Knot," *Locus* 35(1): 5, 69. July 1995.
___ **No Great Endeavor: Presentation of the Pilgrim and Pioneer Awards**. Ann Arbor, MI: Tucker Video, 1994. 1 videocassette, 67 minutes. (Presentation at the 1994 Science Fiction Research Association Conference. Sheri S. Tepper, John Clute, Takayuki Tatsumi, Larry McCaffery, speakers.)
___ "Pilgrim Award, 1994," *Science Fiction Chronicle* 15(10): 8. September 1994.
___ Clute, John. "Something About an Old Encyclopedia, and a Word About a New," *Foundation* No. 58: 96-99. Summer 1993.

CLYNES, MANFRED E.
___ Gray, Chris H. "An Interview With Manfred E. Clynes," in: Gray, Chris H., ed. **The Cyborg Handbook**. New York: Routledge, 1995. pp.43-53.

COAD, BRIAN C.
___ Klein, Jay K. "Biolog: Brian C. Coad," *Analog* 112(11): 73. September 1992.

COATES, PHYLLIS
___ McDowell, Rider. "More Than Just *Superman*'s Serious Sidekick: A Conversation with Phyllis Coates," *Filmfax* No. 36: 70-73. December 1992/January 1993

COBLENTZ, STANTON A.
___ Coblentz, Stanton A. **Adventures of a Freelancer: The Literary Exploits and Autobiography of Stanton A. Coblentz**, by Stanton A. Coblentz and Jeffrey M. Elliot. San Bernardino, CA: Borgo Press, 1993. 160pp.

COCK, SAMUEL
___ Lewes, Darby. "Nudes From Nowhere: Pornography, Empire, and Utopia," *Utopian Studies* 4(2): 66-73. 1993.

COCOMAN, TRACY
___ "Fourth Annual Collector's Award," *Locus* 28(5): 40. May 1992.

COCOON (MOTION PICTURE)
___ "Fox Moves *Cocoon* to Summer Release," *Variety* p. 4, 21. December 26, 1984.
___ Rabkin, William. "*Cocoon* (1985): Interview with Tom Benedek," in: Goldberg, Lee et al. **Science Fiction Filmmaking in the 1980s**. Jefferson, NC: McFarland, 1995. pp.73-78.

COCTEAU, JEAN
___ Yarrow, Ralph. "Ambiguity and the Supernatural in Cocteau's **La machine infernale**," in: Murphy, Patrick D., ed. **Staging the Impossible: The Fantastic Mode in Modern Drama**. Westport, CT: Greenwood, 1992. pp.108-115.

COHEN, HERMAN
___ Galbraith, Stuart, IV. "The How to of Making a Monster Movie: An Interview with AIP Producer Herman Cohen," *Filmfax* No. 37: 43-49. February/March 1993.
___ Weaver, Tom. "Herman Cohen: Interview," in: Weaver, Tom, ed. **Attack of the Monster Movie Makers: Interviews with 20 Genre Giants**. Jefferson, NC: McFarland, 1994. pp.45-84.

COHEN, LARRY
___ Wiater, Stanley. "Cohen, Larry," in: Wiater, Stanley. **Dark Visions: Conversations with the Masters of the Horror Film**. New York: Avon, 1992. pp.29-38.

COLBERT, ROBERT
___ Counts, Kyle. "Time Traveler," *Starlog* 179: 38-41, 84. June 1992.

COLBY, RICK
___ Peterson, Don E. "**Star Trek: Voyager**: Rick Colby at the Helm of the Latest Starship," *Sci-Fi Entertainment* 1(5): 38-41, 45. February 1995.

COLD WAR
___ Worland, Rick. "Captain Kirk: Cold Warrior," *Journal of Popular Film and Television* 16(3): 109-117. 1988.

COLE, ALLEN
___ "Allen Cole and Chris Bunch: The Accidental Series," *Locus* 34(2): 5, 75. February 1995.

COLLAS, PHIL
___ Stone, Graham. "Notes on Australian Science Fiction," *Science Fiction News* (Australia) No. 53: 2-5. February 1978.

COLLECTING SF AND FANTASY
___ Barrett, Robert R. "Joe Jusko's Edgar Rice Burroughs Collection," *Burroughs Bulletin* NS. No. 22: 3-5. April 1995.
___ Bleiler, Everett F. "In the Early, Early Days: Collecting and Dealing in Science Fiction," *AB Bookmans Weekly* 94(17): 1638-1644. October 24, 1994.
___ Currey, Lloyd W. "Facing Troubled Times: The Science Fiction Specialist Dealer," *AB Bookman's Weekly* 92(16): 1449-1460. October 18, 1993.
___ Davis, Kerra. "Out of This World (*Star Wars* Collectibles)," *Antiques & Collecting Hobbies* 97: 24-25. July 1992. [Not seen.]
___ DeVore, Howard. "A Science Fiction Collector," in: Sanders, Joe, ed. **Science Fiction Fandom**. Westport, CT: Greenwood, 1994. pp.221-228.
___ Felchner, William J. "Science Fiction Movie Posters," *Antiques & Collecting Magazine* 99(9): 40-43. November 1994.
___ Frank, Jane. "Should I Buy It?," *Strange New Worlds* No. 7: 4-5, 13. April/May 1993.
___ Fury, David. "Burroughs Spotlight on Rudy Sigmund," *Burroughs Bulletin* NS. No. 21: 24-26. January 1995.
___ Gentry, Chris. **Greenberg's Guide to Star Trek Collectibles**, by Chris Gentry and Sally Gibson-Downs. Sykesville, MD: Greenberg, 1992. 3 vols.; 190, 172, 192pp.
___ Kelley, Mike. "Monster Manse," *Grand Street* 13(1): 224-233. Summer 1994.
___ Kingston, F. Colin. "Dreams for Sale," *Starlog* No. 198: 62-65. January 1994.
___ Locke, George. **A Spectrum of Fantasy, Volume II: Acqusitions to a Collection of Fantastic Literature, 1980-1993, Together with Additional Notes on Titles Covered in the First Volume**. London: Ferret Fantasy, 1994. 156pp. [Not seen.]
___ Marchese, John. "Cosmic Collectibles," *TV Guide* 41(30): 32-33. July 24, 1993.
___ Moskowitz, Sam. "Collecting: A Form of Residual Research," *Foundation* No. 60: 13-20. Spring 1994.
___ Moskowitz, Sam. "A Collector's Tale," *Fantasy Commentator* 8(1/2): 22-31. Winter 1993/1994. (Whole No. 45/46)
___ Moskowitz, Sam. "A Remedy in Book Jackets," *Fantasy Commentator* 8(3/4): 173-181. Fall 1995. (Whole No. 47/48)
___ Mossberg, S. M. "Eccentric Classics of Modern Science Fiction and Fantasy," *Firsts: Collecting Modern First Editions* 3(10): 16-21. October 1993.
___ Osborne, Elizabeth A. "Collecting," *Lan's Lantern* No. 40: 10. September 1992.
___ Overstreet, Robert M. **The Overstreet Comic Book Grading Guide**. First edition, by Robert M. Overstreet and Gary M. Carter. New York: Avon, 1992. 303pp.
___ Sansweet, Stephen J. "Scouting the Galaxy: Collecting *Star Wars* Memoribilia," *Lucasfilm Fan Club* No. 21: 30-31. Winter 1994.
___ Sansweet, Stephen J. **Star Wars: From Concept to Screen to Collectible**. San Francisco, CA: Chronicle Books, 1992. 131pp.
___ Seels, James T. "Collecting Dean Koontz," *Firsts: Collecting Modern First Editions* 3(10): 28-36. October 1993.
___ Smiley, Kathryn. "The Collectible King Arthur," *Firsts: Collecting Modern First Editions* 3(10): 39-41. October 1993.
___ Stevens, Kevin. "Star Wares," *Sci-Fi Universe* No. 3: 96-97. October/November 1994.
___ Voger, Mark. "Gorilla My Screams; Or, How My Life With Movie Monsters Made a Monkey out of Me," *Filmfax* No. 36: 43-48, 98. December 1992/January 1993.
___ White, Jonathan. "Collectible Science Fiction Magazines," *AB Bookman's Weekly* pp.2109-2130. October 1, 1984.
___ Woods, Larry D. "Speculating on Speculative Fiction," *AB Bookman's Weekly* pp.2153-2154. October 1, 1984.

COLLEGE
___ James, Edward. "Science Fiction Courses in Higher Education in Great Britain: A Preliminary Guide," by Edward James and Farah Mendlesohn. *Foundation* No. 59: 59-69. Autumn 1993.

COLLIER, JOHN

___ Bloom, Harold. "John Collier," in: Bloom, Harold, ed. **Modern Fantasy Writers**. New York: Chelsea House, 1995. pp.16-28.

COLLINS, NANCY

___ "Nancy Collins: Small Apocalypses," *Locus* 33(6): 4, 80-81. December 1994.

COLLINS, WILKIE

___ Heller, Tamar. **Dead Secrets: Wilkie Collins and the Female Gothic**. New Haven, CT: Yale University Press, 1992. 201pp.

___ Peters, Catherine. **The King of Inventors: A Life of Wilkie Collins**. Princeton, NJ: Princeton University Press, 1993. 502pp.

___ Taylor, Jenny B. **In the Secret Theatre of Home: Wilkie Collins, Sensation Narrative, and Nineteenth Century Psychology**. London, New York: Routledge, 1988. 306pp.

COLOSSUS: THE FORBIN PROJECT (MOTION PICTURE)

___ Matheson, T. J. "Marcuse, Ellul, and the Science-Fiction Film: Negative Responses to Technology," *Science-Fiction Studies* 19(3): 326-339. November 1992.

COMEDY

___ Willis, Connie. "Learning to Write Comedy, or Why It's Impossible and How to Do It," in: Dozois, Gardner, ed. **Writing Science Fiction and Fantasy**. New York: St. Martin's, 1991. pp.76-88.

COMET (MAGAZINE)

___ Stone, Graham. "Notes on Australian Science Fiction: The Comet," *Science Fiction News* (Australia) No. 54: 2-9. April 1978.

COMIC STRIPS

___ Alonso, George. "Tarzan Still Lives at McLaughlin, South Dakota," *Burroughs Bulletin* NS. No. 24: 26-27. October 1995.

COMICS

___ "Big Entertainment Lures Big Names," *Locus* 32(1): 6. January 1994.

___ "Comic Book Kiosks?," *Science Fiction Chronicle* 15(3): 6. January 1994.

___ "Comic Fan From Childhood, Shooter Is Man Behind Those Superheroes," *Variety* p. 82. September 17, 1986.

___ "Comics Fanzine Ruled Obscene," *Locus* 32(5): 9. May 1994.

___ "Diamond Comics Buys Titan Distributors," *Science Fiction Chronicle* 14(3): 5. December 1992.

___ "Ellison Goes Two-Dimensional," *Locus* 33(6): 8. December 1994.

___ "French Marvel Maniacs Can Plug into Info About Comics Via Teletext Net," *Variety* p. 84. September 17, 1986.

___ **Space Aces: Comic Book Heroes from the Forties and the Fifties**. London: Green Wood, 1992. 96pp.

___ "*Spider-Man* Departs Web of Italian Newsstands as Chief Shareholder Exits," *Variety* p. 84. September 17, 1986.

___ "'Superheroes' Head for Homevid Via Marvel Comics Video Library; DC Comics in WHV's July Lineup," *Variety* p.85. May 22, 1985.

___ "Upheaval in Comics Distribution," *Locus* 34(6): 9. June 1995.

___ Atkinson, Mike. "Delirious Inventions," *Sight and Sound* 5(7): 12-16. July 1995.

___ Barker, Clive. "At the Threshold: Some Thoughts on the Razorline Imprint," *Comics Buyer's Guide* No. 1024: 26-28, 32, 40. July 2, 1993.

___ Barker, Martin. "Seeing How Far You Can See: On Being a Fan of 2000 A.D.," in: Buckingham, D., ed. **Reading Audiences: Young People and the Media**. Manchester, Eng.: Manchester University Press, 1993. pp.159-183.

___ Barrett, Robert R. "Tarzan's Third Great Comic Strip Artist: Russell G. Manning (1929-1981)," *Burroughs Bulletin* NS. No. 13: 11-21. January 1993.

___ Barshay, Robert. "Ethnic Stereotypes in *Flash Gordon*," *Journal of Popular Film and Television* 3(1): 15-30. 1974.

___ Benton, Mike. **Masters of Imagination: The Comic Book Artists Hall of Fame**. Dallas, TX: Taylor, 1994. 176pp.

___ Benton, Mike. **Science Fiction Comics: The Illustrated History**. Dallas, TX: Taylor, 1992. 150pp.

___ Benton, Mike. **Superhero Comics: The Illustrated History**. Dallas, TX: Taylor, 1992. 224pp. (Spine title: **Superhero Comics of the Silver Age**.)

___ Bierbaum, Tom. "Stan Lee's Imperfect Heroes Lifted Marvel to Top of the Heap," *Variety* p. 81, 88. September 17, 1986.

COMICS (continued)

___ Bisson, Terry. "Kitchen Sink's *Flesh Crawlers* Brings Back SF's Bug-eyed Monsters," *Science Fiction Age* 2(1): 86-89. November 1993.

___ Casella, Elaine. "A Lion Is Still a Lion," *Burroughs Bulletin* NS. No. 23: 24-30. July 1995.

___ Castro, Adam-Troy. "Barry Windsor-Smith Trades in a Barbarian for an Alien Vampire," *Science Fiction Age* 2(3): 76-78. March 1994.

___ Chalin, Michael. "Shazam! Comic Book Heroes Invade the Electronic Frontier," *PC Novice* 5(8): 60-62. August 1994.

___ Chrissinger, Craig W. "Station Log," *Starlog* No. 198: 52-55. January 1994.

___ Clements, Jonathan. "The Mechanics of the US Anime and Manga Industry," *Foundation* No. 64: 32-44. Summer 1995.

___ Coogan, Peter M. "Science Fiction Comics," in: Barron, Neil, ed. **Anatomy of Wonder 4**. New York: Bowker, 1995. pp.673-689.

___ Cooper, Bob. "How a Classic Newspaper Strip Became a Comic Book Series: The Story Behind a Comic Book Series," *Lucasfilm Fan Club* No. 20: 6, 32. Fall 1993.

___ Coopman, Jeremy. "Sales of Marvel Comics Move Up Fast in Britain," *Variety* p. 83. September 17, 1986.

___ Cziraky, Dan. "**Guyver**," *Cinefantastique* 22(4): 46. February 1992.

___ Daniels, Les. **DC Comics: Sixty Years of the World's Favorite Comic Book Heroes**. Boston, MA: Little, Brown, 1995. 256pp.

___ Desris, Joe. "**Batman**: Comic Co-Creator Bill Finger," *Cinefantastique* 24(6)/25(1): 27. February 1994.

___ Desris, Joe. "**Batman**: Comic Creator Bob Kane," *Cinefantastique* 24(6)/25(1): 21. February 1994.

___ Desris, Joe. "**Batman**: From Comics to TV," *Cinefantastique* 24(6)/25(1): 62-63. February 1994.

___ Di Filippo, Paul. "Hugo Winner Alan Moore Takes a Genre-Bending Time Warp Back to 1963," *Science Fiction Age* 1(6): 84-86. September 1993.

___ Di Filippo, Paul. "Topps Returns to Its Cult Classic as *Mars Attacks...Again*," *Science Fiction Age* 2(5): 82-84. July 1994.

___ Gabilliet, Jean-Paul. "Cultural and Mythical Aspects of a Superhero: The Silver Surfer 1968-1970," *Journal of Popular Culture* 28(2): 203-213. Fall 1994.

___ Galvan, Dave. "Comic Book Heroes: From Panel to Screen," *Sci-Fi Entertainment* 1(6): 42-47, 73. April 1995.

___ Garcia, Bob. "**Batman**: Comic Book Art Direction," *Cinefantastique* 24(6)/25(1): 22-25. February 1994.

___ Garcia, Bob. "**Batman**: Comic Book Makeup," *Cinefantastique* 24(6)/25(1): 48-50. February 1994.

___ Gelman, Morrie. "Sunbow Takes to Marvel Like Duck to Water in Animation," *Variety* p. 81, 98. September 17, 1986.

___ Gerber, Ernst. **The Photo Journal Guide to Comic Books**, by Ernst Gerber and Mary Gerber. Minden, NV: Gerber Publishing, 1989. 856pp.

___ Gilroy, Dan. "Marvel Now $100 Million a Year Hulk," *Variety* p. 81, 92. September 17, 1986.

___ Gordon, Joan. "Surviving the Survivor: Art Spiegelman's **Maus**," *Journal of the Fantastic in the Arts* 5(2): 80-89. 1993. (No. 18)

___ Green, Steve. "All in Colour for a Dime: A Profile of Stan Lee," *Interzone* No. 59: 43-47. May 1992.

___ Greenberger, Robert. "The Roots of Dredd," *Sci-Fi Entertainment* 2(1): 34-35. June 1995.

___ Gross, Edward. "The New Illustrated Man," *Starlog* 185: 75-79. December 1992.

___ Hirsch, Connie. "Amidst Endless Superheroes, *Illegal Alien* Is as Ambitious as the Best SF," *Science Fiction Age* 3(1): 84-87. November 1994.

___ Hirsch, Connie. "Harlan Ellison Rides a Dark Horse to Invade His Personal *Dream Corridors*," *Science Fiction Age* 3(3): 18. March 1995.

___ Hofstede, David. **Hollywood and the Comics: Film Adaptations of Comic Books and Scripts**. Las Vegas, NV: Zanne-3, 1991. 198pp.

___ Johnson, Kim H. "Bug Hunt," *Starlog* No. 189: 40-43, 64. April 1993.

___ Johnson, Kim H. "Conehead Comics," *Starlog* No. 202: 38-39, 68. May 1994.

___ Johnson, Kim H. "*Mars Attacks Again*," *Starlog* No. 203: 38-41. June 1994.

___ Johnson, Kim H. "Tarzan," *Starlog* 177: 25-27, 71. April 1992.

___ Jones, Alan. "Fumetti Inspiration," *Cinefantastique* 25(5): 54. October 1994.

___ Jones, Alan. "**Judge Dredd**: Comic Book Origins," *Cinefantastique* 26(5): 20-22. August 1995.

COMPUTERS (continued)
___ Radin, Darlene M. **The Human and Computer Relationship: A Vehicle for Character Metamorphosis in Fictive Literature**. Ph.D. Dissertation, University of Massachusetts, Amherst, 1992. 167pp.
___ Stockwell, Peter J. **The Thinking Machine: Metaphoric Patterns in the Discourse of Science Fiction**. Ph.D. Dissertation, University of Liverpool, 1993. (DAI BRDX97757; 53: 3210A.)

CONAN THE BARBARIAN (MOTION PICTURE)
___ "Charge Universal and DeLaurentiis Used Spain to Enjoy Lax Animal Law," *Variety* p. 6. May 26, 1982.

CONAN THE DESTROYER (MOTION PICTURE)
___ "**Conan the Destroyer** (1984): Interview with Arnold Schwarzenegger," in: Goldberg, Lee, ed. **The Dreamweavers: Interviews With Fantasy Filmmakers of the 1980s**. Jefferson, NC: McFarland, 1995. pp.47-57.

CONEHEADS (COMIC)
___ Johnson, Kim H. "Conehead Comics," *Starlog* No. 202: 38-39, 68. May 1994.

CONEHEADS (MOTION PICTURE)
___ Kutzera, Dale. "**Coneheads**: Stop Motion Garthok," *Cinefantastique* 24(6)/25(1): 121-122. February 1994.
___ Kutzera, Dale. "**Coneheads**," *Cinefantastique* 24(6)/25(1): 118-119. February 1994.
___ Shapiro, Marc. "**Coneheads**," *Starlog* No. 194: 43-48. September 1993.

CONEY, MICHAEL
___ Coney, Michael. "Thank You for the Music," in: Jakubowski, Maxim and James, Edward, eds. **The Profession of Science Fiction**. New York: St. Martin's, 1992. pp.120-130.

CONFESSIONS OF A SERIAL KILLER (MOTION PICTURE)
___ Wilt, David. "**Confessions of a Serial Killer** (Review)," *Cinefantastique* 24(1): 60. June 1993.

CONGO (MOTION PICTURE)
___ Duncan, Jody. "Gorilla Warfare," *Cinefex* No. 62: 34-53. June 1995.
___ Fischer, Dennis. "**Congo**: Director Frank Marshall on Filming the Bestseller," *Cinefantastique* 26(5): 56-57, 61. August 1995.
___ Fischer, Dennis. "**Congo** (Review)," *Cinefantastique* 26(6)/27(1): 123. October 1995.
___ Fischer, Dennis. "**Congo**," *Cinefantastique* 26(4): 12-13. June 1995.
___ Lowe, Nick. "**Congo** (Review)," *Interzone* No. 99: 32-33. September 1995.
___ Warren, Bill. "Gorilla Warfare," *Starlog* No. 215: 40-45, 72. June 1995.
___ Warren, Bill. "Gorillas by Winston," *Starlog* No. 218: 46-49, 66. September 1995.
___ Warren, Bill. "Jungle Heroine," *Starlog* No. 216: 32-35, 64. July 1995.
___ Warren, Bill. "Jungle Wizard," *Starlog* No. 217: 35-39, 66. August 1995.

CONRAD, JOSEPH
___ Cahir, Linda C. "Narratological Parallels in Joseph Conrad's **Heart of Darkness** and Francis Ford Coppola's **Apocalypse Now**," *Literature/Film Quarterly* 20(3): 181-187. 1992.
___ Greiff, Louis K. "Soldier, Sailor, Surfer, Chef: Conrad's Ethics and the Margins of **Apocalypse Now**," *Literature/Film Quarterly* 20(3): 188-197. 1992.

CONRAD, WILLIAM
___ "Conrad, William (Obituary)," *Science Fiction Chronicle* 15(5): 12. March 1994.

CONSCIOUSNESS
___ Stableford, Brian. "The Concept of Mind in Science Fiction," in: Stableford, Brian. **Opening Minds: Essays on Fantastic Literature**. San Bernardino, CA: Borgo Press, 1995. pp.37-52.

CONSERVATISM
___ Sharrett, Christopher. "The Horror Film in Neoconservative Culture," *Journal of Popular Film and Television* 21(3): 100-110. Fall 1993.

CONSTANTINE, STORM
___ Joyce, Graham. "SFC Interviews: Storm Constantine," *Science Fiction Chronicle* 13(10): 5, 28-30. July/August 1992.
___ Nicholls, Stan. "Ripping Yarns: Storm Constantine Interviewed," *Interzone* No. 58: 46-49. April 1992.
___ Nicholls, Stan. "Storm Constantine Is Still Waiting for the Earth to Move," in: Nicholls, Stan. **Wordsmiths of Wonder: Fifty Interviews with Writers of the Fantastic**. London: Orbit, 1993. pp.227-236.

CONTESTS
___ "Baen Books $1,000.00 Podkayne Essay Contest," *Science Fiction Chronicle* 14(9): 4. June 1993.

CONTRACTS
___ "Agents vs. Publisher," *Locus* 33(6): 9, 79. December 1994.
___ "Writers and Electronic Rights," *Locus* 33(6): 9, 79. December 1994.
___ Brin, David. "Agent-Author (Pre-Nuptial) Agreements," *SFWA Bulletin* 26(1): 34-35. Spring 1992. (No. 115)
___ Feist, Raymond E. "Contract Article IV: Advances, Payment & Royalties, and a Few Other Things," *SFWA Bulletin* 25(4): 15-20. Winter 1992. (No. 114)
___ Feist, Raymond E. "Contract Article IX: Editorial Courtesy," *SFWA Bulletin* 27(1): 47-53. Spring 1993. (No. 119)
___ Feist, Raymond E. "Contract Article V: A Little More Money; Sub-Rights," *SFWA Bulletin* 26(1): 50-57. Spring 1992. (No. 115)
___ Feist, Raymond E. "Contract Article VI: Options and Miscellany," *SFWA Bulletin* 26(2): 20-27. Summer 1992. (No. 116)
___ Feist, Raymond E. "Contract Article VII: Agency Clause, Agents, and Other Writers," *SFWA Bulletin* 26(3): 23-28. Fall 1992. (No. 117)
___ Feist, Raymond E. "Contract Article VIII: Negotiations," *SFWA Bulletin* 26(4): 12-15. Winter 1993. (No. 118)
___ Feist, Raymond E. "Contract Article X: Packagers," *SFWA Bulletin* 27(2): 19-24. Summer 1993. (No. 120)
___ Feist, Raymond E. "Contract Article XI: The Law Is an Ass," *SFWA Bulletin* 27(3): 19-25. Fall 1993. (No. 121)
___ Feist, Raymond E. "Contract Article XII: Changes, Part 1," *SFWA Bulletin* 28(2): 21-26. Summer 1994. (No. 124)
___ Feist, Raymond E. "Contract Article XIII: Changes, Part 2," *SFWA Bulletin* 28(3): 23-27. Winter 1994. (No. 125)
___ Feist, Raymond E. "Contract Article XIV: Model Contracts," *SFWA Bulletin* 29(1): 44-52. Spring 1995. (No. 126)
___ Knight, Damon. "Dell Magazine Contract," *SFWA Bulletin* 28(2): 2-4. Summer 1994. (No. 124)
___ Knight, Damon. "Dell Magazines Contract Update," *SFWA Bulletin* 28(3): 2. Winter 1994. (No. 125)
___ Stith, John E. "SFWA Model Author-Agent Contract, First Cut," *SFWA Bulletin* 27(4)/28(1): 40-43. Winter/Spring 1994. (No. 122/123)

CONVENTIONS
___ "1992 Eurocon and World SF Meeting Relocate," *Locus* 28(3): 7, 74. March 1992.
___ "**Dr. Who** Jamboree Attracts 40,000 Fans," *Variety* p. 2. April 6, 1983.
___ "Étonnants Voyageurs Festival," *Locus* 31(6): 41. December 1993.
___ Banks, Michael A. "Attending Science Fiction Conventions for Fun and Profit," in: **1991 Novel and Short Story Writers Market**. Cinncinati, OH: Writer's Digest Books, 1991. pp.55-58.
___ Bond, Jonathan. "Sexual Etiquette at Conventions," by Jonathan Bond and Jak Koke. *The Report: The Fiction Writer's Magazine* No. 7: 11-12. June 1992.
___ Bradley, Marion Z. "Essay: Science Fiction Conventions," *Science Fiction Age* 1(2): 22, 71. January 1993.
___ Eskin, Leah. "Sci-fi's a Smash," *Chicago Tribune* Sec. 7, p. 18. July 23, 1993.
___ Hull, Peter R. "Creation Salutes **Star Trek**, the Grand Slam Show," *Star Trek: The Official Fan Club Magazine* No. 92: 32-33. July/August 1993.
___ Karlen, Neal. "Sci-Fi Schlock Is Turned on Its Ear at Convention of Fans," *New York Times* p.B1. September 19, 1994.
___ Luttrell, Hank. "The Science Fiction Convention Scene," in: Sanders, Joe, ed. **Science Fiction Fandom**. Westport, CT: Greenwood, 1994. pp.149-160.

COPYRIGHT (continued)
___ Yarbro, Chelsea Q. "A Matter of Willful Copyright Infringement," *SFWA Bulletin* 26(2): 11-13. Summer 1992. (No. 116)

CORBETT, ELIZABETH BURGOYNE
___ Suksang, Duangrudi. "Overtaking Patriarchy: Crobett's and Dixie's Visions of Women," *Utopian Studies* 4(2): 74-93. 1993.

CORIELL, RITA
___ Coriell, Rita. "The Coriell Years of Burroughs Fandom," *Burroughs Bulletin* NS. No. 12: 31-33. October 1992.

CORIELL, VERNELL
___ Coriell, Rita. "The Coriell Years of Burroughs Fandom," *Burroughs Bulletin* NS. No. 12: 31-33. October 1992.

CORMAN, ROGER
___ "Corman, Harryhausen San Jose Fest Honorees," *Variety* p. 7. April 10, 1985.
___ Kenny, Glenn. "It's Showtime for Corman," *TV Guide* 43(23): 50. June 10, 1995.
___ Liberti, Fabrizio. "Pe regie de Roger Corman in vista della *Factory*" [Roger Corman and Science Fiction in *Factory*]. *Cineforum* 31(9): 18-21. 1991.
___ Linaweaver, Brad. "Corman Unwound," *Wonder* No. 7: 36-38. 1993.
___ Persons, Dan. "*Silence of the Lambs*: The Corman Connection," *Cinefantastique* 22(4): 20-22. February 1992.
___ Peterson, Don E. "It Came From Hollywood," *Sci-Fi Entertainment* 1(2): 56-61. August 1994.
___ Pharr, Mary. "Different Shops of Horrors: From Roger Corman's Cult Classic to Frank Oz's Mainstream Musical," in: Latham, Robert A. and Collins, Robert A., eds. **Modes of the Fantastic**. Westport, CT: Greenwood, 1995. pp.212-220.
___ Wiater, Stanley. "Corman, Roger," in: Wiater, Stanley. **Dark Visions: Conversations with the Masters of the Horror Film**. New York: Avon, 1992. pp.39-46.

CORNTHWAITE, ROBERT
___ Weaver, Tom. "Robert Cornthwaite," in: Weaver, Tom. **They Fought the Creature Features: Interviews with 23 Classic Horror, Science Fiction and Serial Stars**. Jefferson, NC: McFarland, 1995. pp.111-130.

CORSAUT, ANETA
___ Worcester, Kent. "Belle of the *Blob*," *Starlog* No. 214: 66-67, 70. May 1995.

CORTAZAR, JULIO
___ Rodríguez-Luis, Julio. **The Contemporary Praxis of the Fantastic: Borges and Cortazar**. New York: Garland, 1991. 131pp.

COSMIC SLOP (TV)
___ Charles, Nick. "Cosmic Relief," *(New York, NY) Daily News*. November 8, 1994. in: *NewsBank. Film and Television*. 119:D3. 1994.

COSTELLO, MATT
___ Gagliano, William D. "SFC Interviews: Matt Costello's Journey," *Science Fiction Chronicle* 14(9): 5, 29-30. June 1993.

COSTIKYAN, GREG
___ Pedersen, Martin. "Serial From Prodigy to Be Hardcover Book," *Publishers Weekly* 240(7): 18. February 15, 1993.

COSTNER, KEVIN
___ Lovell, Glenn. "*Waterworld*: Kevin Costner, Auteur," *Cinefantastique* 26(5): 8. August 1995.
___ Shapiro, Marc. "Storm Gathering," *Starlog* No. 219: 50-53. October 1995.
___ Warren, Bill. "Deadly Gamesters," *Starlog* No. 219: 45-49. October 1995.

COSTUMES
___ Boswell, Thom. **The Costumemaker's Art: Cloaks of Fantasy, Masks of Revelation**. Asheville, NC: Lark Books, 1992. 144pp.
___ Calhoun, John. "*The Journey Inside*," *TCI* 28(8): 78. October 1994.

COSTUMES (continued)
___ Salter, David I. "*Babylon 5*: Costume Design," *Cinefantastique* 23(5): 34. February 1993.

COTO, MANNY
___ Kutzera, Dale. "*Dr. Giggles*: Horror Director Manny Coto," *Cinefantastique* 23(4): 23. December 1992.

COTTEN, JOSEPH
___ "Cotten, Joseph (Obituary)," *Science Fiction Chronicle* 15(5): 12. March 1994.

COUNSELMAN, MARY ELIZABETH
___ Burleson, Donald R. "On Mary Elizabeth Counselman's 'Twister'," *Studies in Weird Fiction* No. 15: 16-18. Summer 1994.

COURSES IN SF
___ James, Edward. "Science Fiction Courses in Higher Education in Great Britain: A Preliminary Guide," by Edward James and Farah Mendlesohn. *Foundation* No. 59: 59-69. Autumn 1993.

COWPER, RICHARD
___ Cowper, Richard. "Backwards Across the Frontier," in: Jakubowski, Maxim and James, Edward, eds. **The Profession of Science Fiction**. New York: St. Martin's, 1992. pp.78-94.

COX, ERLE
___ Stone, Graham. "Notes on Australian Science Fiction: **Out of the Silence**, by Erle Cox," *Science Fiction News* (Australia) No. 62: 6-7. August 1979.
___ Stone, Graham. "Notes on Australian Science Fiction: **Out of the Silence**, by Erle Cox," *Science Fiction News* (Australia) No. 64: 2-7. 1980.
___ Stone, Graham. "Notes on Australian Science Fiction: **Out of the Silence**, by Erle Cox and J. Filmore Sherry," *Science Fiction News* (Australia) No. 66: 2-8. September 1982.
___ Stone, Graham. "Notes on Australian Science Fiction: **Out of the Silence**, by Erle Cox, Part 1," *Science Fiction News* (Australia) No. 58: 18-20. June 1978.
___ Stone, Graham. "Notes on Australian Science Fiction: **Out of the Silence**, by Erle Cox, Part 2," *Science Fiction News* (Australia) No. 59: 12-16. February 1979.
___ Stone, Graham. "Notes on Australian Science Fiction: **Out of the Silence**, by Erle Cox, Part 3," *Science Fiction News* (Australia) No. 60: 19-20. April 1979.
___ Stone, Graham. "**Out of the Silence** in Russian--Lost and Found," *Science Fiction News* (Australia) No. 115: 18-20. May 1992.

CRAIG, YVONNE
___ Garcia, Bob. "*Batman*: The Origin of Batgirl," *Cinefantastique* 24(6)/25(1): 32-34. February 1994.

CRANDALL, REED
___ Van Hise, James. "An Index to the Reed Crandall Illustrations From the Works of Edgar Rice Burroughs," *Burroughs Bulletin* NS. No. 20: 27-28. October 1994.
___ Van Hise, James. "Reed Crandall: Illustrator of Super Heroes," *Burroughs Bulletin* NS. No. 20: 17-28. October 1994.

CRANK! (MAGAZINE)
___ "*Crank!*," *Locus* 31(3): 7. September 1993.
___ "*Crank!, Non-Stop* Are New Science Fiction Magazine Titles," *Science Fiction Chronicle* 15(1): 6. October 1993.
___ Katz, Bill. "Magazines: *Crank!*," *Library Journal* 119(5): 107. March 15, 1994.

CRAVEN, WES
___ Gorman, Ed. "Several Hundred Words About Wes Craven," in: Golden, Christopher, ed. **Cut! Horror Writers on Horror Film**. New York: Berkley, 1992. pp.113-116.
___ Wiater, Stanley. "Craven, Wes," in: Wiater, Stanley. **Dark Visions: Conversations with the Masters of the Horror Film**. New York: Avon, 1992. pp.47-56.

CRAWFORD AWARD, 1991
___ "Crawford Award," *Locus* 28(4): 7. April 1992.

CREATURE FROM THE BLACK LAGOON (MOTION PICTURE)

CRITICISM

CREATURE FROM THE BLACK LAGOON (MOTION PICTURE)
___ Daniel, Dennis. "The Girl, the Gillman and the Great White One-Piece: An Interview with Julie Adams," *Filmfax* No. 37: 50-56. February/March 1993.
___ Jankiewicz, Pat. "Bard of the Black Lagoon," *Starlog* No. 197: 21-24, 81. December 1993.
___ Newsom, Ted. "The Creature Remake That Never Got Made: An Afternoon with Jack Arnold and Nigel Kneale," *Filmfax* No. 37: 64-67, 82, 98. February/March 1993.
___ Weaver, Tom. "Creature King: From Out of the Black Lagoon, Ben Chapman Walked," by Tom Weaver and Paul Parla. *Starlog* 180: 59-64, 73. July 1992.
___ Weaver, Tom. "Julie Adams," in: Weaver, Tom. **They Fought the Creature Features: Interviews with 23 Classic Horror, Science Fiction and Serial Stars.** Jefferson, NC: McFarland, 1995. pp.1-11.
___ Weaver, Tom. **MagicImage Filmbooks Presents Creature From the Black Lagoon.** Absecon, NJ: MagicImage Filmbooks, 1992. [195pp.]
___ Weaver, Tom. "The Other Creature," by Tom Weaver and Paul Parla. *Starlog* No. 206: 61-65. September 1994.
___ Weaver, Tom. "Ricou Browning," in: Weaver, Tom. **They Fought the Creature Features: Interviews with 23 Classic Horror, Science Fiction and Serial Stars.** Jefferson, NC: McFarland, 1995. pp.97-109.
___ Weaver, Tom, ed. **Creature From the Black Lagoon.** Absecon, NJ: MagicImage Filmbooks, 1992. unpaged.
___ Zemnick, Diana J. "Creature Comfort: Julie Adams; The Beauty Recalls the Beast," *Cinefantastique* 27(3): 45-46. December 1995.
___ Zemnick, Diana J. "*The Creature From the Black Lagoon*," *Cinefantastique* 27(3): 44-47, 61. December 1995.

CREATURES OF DARKNESS (MOTION PICTURE)
___ "Chorvinsky Digging for More Dollars in 'Creatures' Aid," *Variety* p. 156. May 7, 1986.

CREEPERS (MOTION PICTURE)
___ "Wide N. Y. Bread Eyed for *Creepers*," *Variety* p.6, 26. August 28, 1985.

CREEPSHOW (MOTION PICTURE)
___ "*Creepshow* Big Buck Exception to Rubinstein, Romero Mini-Pix," *Variety* p. 22, 24. December 23, 1981.

CREESE, IRENE
___ "Creese, Irene (Obituary)," *Science Fiction Chronicle* 15(4): 16. February 1994.

CRESCENDO (MOTION PICTURE)
___ "Hammer Ends Longtime Taboo--Mates Sex to Its *Crescendo* Horror Pic," *Variety* p. 1, 92. May 6, 1970.

CRICHTON, MICHAEL
___ Biodrowski, Steve. "*Jurassic Park*: Michael Crichton," *Cinefantastique* 24(2): 11-13. August 1993.
___ Dutka, Elaine. "Crichton Stays Busy Straddling Worlds of Film, Fiction," *Austin (TX) American Statesman* Sec. B, p. 9. June 14, 1993.
___ Romano, Carlin. "Novelist Makes an Unusual Rewrite," *Philadelphia (PA) Inquirer.* January 10, 1992. in: *NewsBank. Literature.* 9:D12-D13. 1992.
___ Seago, Kate. " 'Jurassic' Sells Well at Bookstores, Too," *Los Angeles (CA) Daily News.* May 19, 1993. in: *NewsBank. Literature.* 45: B2. 1993.
___ Telotte, J. P. "*Westworld, Futureworld*, and the World's Obscenity," in: Ruddick, Nicholas, ed. **State of the Fantastic.** Westport, CT: Greenwood, 1992. pp.179-188.
___ Warren, Bill. "The Curator of *Jurassic Park*," *Starlog* No. 192: 32-37, 74. July 1993.

CRIME IN SF
___ Borchardt, Edith. "Criminal Artists and Artisans in Mysteries by E. T. A. Hoffman, Dorothy Sayers, Ernesto Sábato, Patrick Süskind, and Thomas Harris," in: Sanders, Joe, ed. **Functions of the Fantastic.** Westport, CT: Greenwood, 1995. pp.125-134.

CRIMP, H. M.
___ Stone, Graham. "H. M. Crimp--And More," *Science Fiction News* (Australia) No. 116: 19-21. October 1992.

CRIMP, H. M. (continued)
___ Stone, Graham. "Notes on Australian Science Fiction," *Science Fiction News* (Australia) No. 53: 2-5. February 1978.

CRIMSON TIDE (MOTION PICTURE)
___ Shay, Estelle. "Quick Cuts: Sub Plots," *Cinefex* No. 62: 11-12. June 1995.
___ Wrathall, John. "*Crimson Tide* (Review)," *Sight and Sound* 5(12): 43-44. December 1995.

CRISPIN, EDMUND
___ "Crispin, Edmund, 1921-1978 (Obituary)," *Science Fiction News* (Australia) No. 60: 4. April 1979.

CRITICISM
___ **Beyond Cyberpunk: A Do-It-Yourself Guide to the Future.** Louisa, VA: The Computer Lab, 1992. 5 computer disks, minicomic. Macintosh program, with essays, reviews, etc.. (Cf. OCLC, not seen.) Alternate title: **Kata Sutra in Beyond Cyberpunk.**
___ Aldiss, Brian W. **The Detached Retina: Aspects of SF and Fantasy.** Syracuse, NY: Syracuse University Press, 1995. 224pp.
___ Anderson, Poul. "Quatrolude: Epistle to the SFRAns," in: Wolf, Milton T. and Mallett, Daryl F., eds. **Imaginative Futures: Proceedings of the 1993 Science Fiction Research Association Conference.** San Bernardino, CA: Jacob's Ladder Books, 1995. pp.249-262.
___ Angenot, Marc. "The Absent Paradigm: An Introduction to the Semiotics of Science Fiction," *Chung Wai Literary Quarterly* 22(12): May 1994. (Issue not seen; pagination unavailable.) (Reprinted from *Science Fiction Studies.*)
___ Attebery, Brian. "The Closing of the Final Frontier: Science Fiction After 1960," in: Sanders, Joe, ed. **Functions of the Fantastic.** Westport, CT: Greenwood, 1995. pp.205-213.
___ Attebery, Brian. **Strategies of Fantasy.** Bloomington: University of Indiana Press, 1992. 152pp.
___ Bachman, Debbie. **The Outsider in '50s' Science Fiction.** Master's Thesis, S. U. N. Y. College at Brockport, 1994. 119pp.
___ Baggesen, Soren. **Natur/videnskab/fortælling: Om science fiction som civilisationskritik.** s.l.: Odense Universitetsforlag, 1993. 120pp.
___ Bailey, K. V. "Bright Day-Dreadful Night: Metaphoric Polarities in Fantasy and Science Fiction," *Foundation* No. 54: 36-52. Spring 1992.
___ Balsamo, Anne. "Signal to Noise: On the Meaning of Cyberpunk Subculture," in: Wolf, Milton T. and Mallett, Daryl F., eds. **Imaginative Futures: Proceedings of the 1993 Science Fiction Research Association Conference.** San Bernardino, CA: Jacob's Ladder Books, 1995. pp.217-228.
___ Barr, Marleen S. **Feminist Fabulation: Space/Postmodern Fiction.** Iowa City, IA: University of Iowa Press, 1993. 312pp.
___ Barron, Neil, ed. **Anatomy of Wonder 4: A Critical Guide to Science Fiction.** New York: Bowker, 1995. 912pp.
___ Baugh, E. Susan. "The Electronic Book in Future Information Access," in: Wolf, Milton T. and Mallett, Daryl F., eds. **Imaginative Futures: Proceedings of the 1993 Science Fiction Research Association Conference.** San Bernardino, CA: Jacob's Ladder Books, 1995. pp.53-60.
___ Becker, Allienne R. **The Lost Worlds Romance: From Dawn Till Dusk.** Westport, CT: Greenwood, 1992. 184pp.
___ Beghtol, Clare. **The Classification of Fiction: The Development of a System Based on Theoretical Principles.** Metuchen, NJ: Scarecrow, 1994. 365pp.
___ Ben-Tov, Sharona. **The Artificial Paradise: Science Fiction and American Reality.** Ann Arbor: University of Michigan Press, 1995. 201pp.
___ Benford, Gregory. "Style, Substance, and Other Illusions," in: Slusser, George E. and Rabkin, Eric S., eds. **Styles of Creation: Aesthetic Technique and the Creation of Fictional Worlds.** Athens: University of Georgia Press, 1992. pp.47-57.
___ Biederman, Marcia. "Genre Writing: It's Entertaining, But Is It Art?," *Poets and Writers Magazine* 20(1): 21-25. January/February 1992.
___ Bisson, Terry. "Science Fiction and the Post-*Apollo* Blues," *Locus* 32(1): 38-40, 59. January 1994.
___ Booker, M. Keith. **Dystopian Literature: A Theory and Research Guide.** Westport, CT: Greenwood Press, 1994. 424pp.
___ Bouchard, Guy. **Les 42210 univers de la science-fiction.** Sainte-Foy, Quebec: Le Passeur, 1993. 338pp.
___ Bozzetto, Roger. **L'Obscur Objet d'un Savoir: Fantastique et Science-fiction: deux litteratures de l'imagination.** Marseille, France: Universite de Provence, 1991. 280pp.

CRITICISM (continued)

___ Brigg, Peter. "Maggots, Tropes, and Metafictional Challenge: John Fowles' **A Maggot**," in: Wolf, Milton T. and Mallett, Daryl F., eds. **Imaginative Futures: Proceedings of the 1993 Science Fiction Research Association Conference**. San Bernardino, CA: Jacob's Ladder Books, 1995. pp.293-306.

___ Brin, David. "Waging War With Reality," in: Slusser, George E. and Rabkin, Eric S., eds. **Styles of Creation: Aesthetic Technique and the Creation of Fictional Worlds**. Athens: University of Georgia Press, 1992. pp.24-29.

___ Broderick, Damien. "The Object of Science Fiction," *New York Review of Science Fiction* No. 59: 16-18. July 1993.

___ Broderick, Damien. **Reading By Starlight: Postmodern Science Fiction**. London and New York: Routledge, 1995. 197pp.

___ Broderick, Damien. "Reading by Starlight: Science Fiction as a Reading Protocol," *Science Fiction: A Review of Speculative Literature* 11(2): 5-16. 1991. (No. 32)

___ Broderick, Damien. "Reading SF as a Mega-Text," *New York Review of Science Fiction* No. 47: 1, 8-11. July 1992.

___ Broderick, Damien. "SF as Genetic Engineering," *Foundation* No. 59: 16-28. Autumn 1993.

___ Broderick, Damien. "SF as Modular Calculus," *Southern Review: Literary and Interdisciplinary Essays (Australia)* 24(1): 43-53. March 1991.

___ Bukatman, Scott R. "Amidst These Fields of Data: Allegory, Rhetoric, and the Paraspace," *Critique* 33(3): 199-219. Spring 1992.

___ Bukatman, Scott R. **Terminal Identity: The Virtual Subject in Postmodern Science Fiction**. Durham, NC: Duke University Press, 1993. 404pp.

___ Burgess, Thomas. **Take Me Under the Sea: The Dream Merchants of the Deep**. Salem, OR: Ocean Archives, 1994. 259pp.

___ Burmeister, Klaus, ed. **Streifzuge ins Übermorgen: Science Fiction und Zukunftsforschung**, ed. by Klaus Burmeister and Karlheinz Steinmüller. Weinheim: Beltz, 1992. 328pp.

___ Capanna, Pablo. **El mundo de la ciencia ficcion: Sentido e historia**. Buenos Aires: Ediciones Letra Buena, 1992. 192pp.

___ Carter, Paul A. "From 'Nat' to 'Nathan': The Liberal Arts Odyssey of a Pulpmaster," in: Slusser, George E. and Rabkin, Eric S., eds. **Styles of Creation: Aesthetic Technique and the Creation of Fictional Worlds**. Athens: University of Georgia Press, 1992. pp.58-78.

___ Cherniak, Laura R. **Calling in Question: Science Fiction and Cultural Studies**. Ph.D. Dissertation, University of California, Santa Cruz, 1995. 257pp. (DAI-A 56/04, p. 1554. October 1995.)

___ Clark, John R. **The Modern Satiric Grotesque and Its Traditions**. Lexington, KY: University Press of Kentucky, 1991. 212pp.

___ Clark, Stephen R. L. **How to Live Forever: Science Fiction and Philosophy**. London, New York: Routledge, 1995. 223pp.

___ Cogswell, Theodore R., ed. **PITFCS: Proceedings of the Institute for Twenty-First Century Studies**. Chicago: Advent: Publishers, 1992. 374pp.

___ Cooke, Brett. "Sociobiology, Science Fiction and the Future," *Foundation* No. 60: 42-51. Spring 1994.

___ Crossley, Robert. "In the Palace of Green Porcelain: Artifacts from the Museum of Science Fiction," in: Slusser, George E. and Rabkin, Eric S., eds. **Styles of Creation: Aesthetic Technique and the Creation of Fictional Worlds**. Athens: University of Georgia Press, 1992. pp.205-220.

___ Cupp, Jeff. "Do Science Fiction and Fantasy Writers Have Postmodern Dreams?," by Jeff Cupp and Charles Avinger. *LIT: Literature Interpretation Theory* 4(3): 175-184. 1993.

___ Davidson, Howard L. "Virtual Reality and Other Electronic Intimacies," in: Wolf, Milton T. and Mallett, Daryl F., eds. **Imaginative Futures: Proceedings of the 1993 Science Fiction Research Association Conference**. San Bernardino, CA: Jacob's Ladder Books, 1995. pp.15-30.

___ Dawson, W. H. "Forecasts of the Future in Modern Literature," *Science Fiction News (Australia)* No. 91: 2-12. July 1992.

___ Delany, Samuel R. "Reading Modern American Science Fiction," in: Kostelanetz, Richard, ed. **American Writing Today**. Troy, NY: Whitston, 1991. pp.517-528.

___ Delmendo, Sharon. "'Born of **Misery**': Stephen King's (En)Gendered Text," in: Slusser, George E. and Rabkin, Eric S., eds. **Styles of Creation: Aesthetic Technique and the Creation of Fictional Worlds**. Athens: University of Georgia Press, 1992. pp.172-180.

___ Disch, Thomas M. "Big Ideas and Dead-End Thrills," *Atlantic* 269(2): 86-94. February 1992.

CRITICISM (continued)

___ Donahoo, Robert. "Moving With the Mainstream: A View of Postmodern American Science Fiction," in: Trachtenberg, Stanley, ed. **Critical Essays on American Postmodernism**. New York: G. K. Hall, 1995. pp.152-165.

___ Filmer, Kath. **Scepticism and Hope in Twentieth Century Fantasy Literature**. Bowling Green, OH: Bowling Green State University Popular Press, 1992. 160pp.

___ Fitting, Peter. "Utopian Effects/Utopian Pleasure," in: Slusser, George E. and Rabkin, Eric S., eds. **Styles of Creation: Aesthetic Technique and the Creation of Fictional Worlds**. Athens: University of Georgia Press, 1992. pp.153-165.

___ Franklin, H. Bruce. "The Vietnam War as American Science Fiction and Fantasy," in: Irons, Glenwood, ed. **Gender, Language and Myth: Essays on Popular Narrative**. Toronto: University of Toronto Press, 1992. pp.208-230.

___ Freedman, Carl. "Style, Fiction, Science Fiction: The Case of Philip K. Dick," in: Slusser, George E. and Rabkin, Eric S., eds. **Styles of Creation: Aesthetic Technique and the Creation of Fictional Worlds**. Athens: University of Georgia Press, 1992. pp.30-45.

___ Friedrich, Hans-Edwin. **Science Fiction in der deutschsprachigen Literatur: Ein Referat zur Forschung bis 1993**. Tubigen: Max Niemeyer Verlag, 1995. 493pp.

___ Gattegno, Jean. **La Science-Fiction**. Paris: Presses Universitaires de France, 1992. 128pp. 5th ed.

___ Gilmore, Chris. "Why Is Science Fiction?," *Interzone* No. 62: 48-49. August 1992.

___ Goldstine, Lisa. "Bilude: The Imaginative Future," in: Wolf, Milton T. and Mallett, Daryl F., eds. **Imaginative Futures: Proceedings of the 1993 Science Fiction Research Association Conference**. San Bernardino, CA: Jacob's Ladder Books, 1995. pp.75-82.

___ Gough, Noel. **Body and Narrative as Cultural Text: Toward a Curriculum of Continuity and Connection**, by Noel Gough and Kathleen Kesson. ERIC ED 347544. 9pp. 1992. Paper presented at the Annual Meeting of the American Educational Research Association, San Francisco, CA, April 20-24, 1992.

___ Grenier, Christian. **La science-fiction, lectures d'avenir?**. Nancy: Presses Universitaires de Nancy, 1994. 169pp.

___ Grivet, Charles. **Fantastique-Fiction**. Paris: Presses universitaires francaises, 1993. 255pp.

___ Gunn, James E. **Inside Science Fiction: Essays on Fantastic Literature**. San Bernardino, CA: Borgo Press, 1992. 176pp.

___ Gunn, James E. "Science Fiction Scholarship Revisited," *Foundation* No. 60: 5-9. Spring 1994.

___ Gunn, James E. "Trilude: Imagining the Future," in: Wolf, Milton T. and Mallett, Daryl F., eds. **Imaginative Futures: Proceedings of the 1993 Science Fiction Research Association Conference**. San Bernardino, CA: Jacob's Ladder Books, 1995. pp.125-135.

___ Gunn, James E. "The Worldview of Science Fiction," *Extrapolation* 36(2): 91-95. Summer 1995.

___ Halbert, Martin. "Database Visualization and Future Innovations in Information Retrieval," in: Wolf, Milton T. and Mallett, Daryl F., eds. **Imaginative Futures: Proceedings of the 1993 Science Fiction Research Association Conference**. San Bernardino, CA: Jacob's Ladder Books, 1995. pp.31-52.

___ Hammer, Stephanie. "Camouflage and Sabotage: Satiric Maneuvers in the Fantastic Fiction of the German Democratic Republic," in: Slusser, George E. and Rabkin, Eric S., eds. **Styles of Creation: Aesthetic Technique and the Creation of Fictional Worlds**. Athens: University of Georgia Press, 1992. pp.143-152.

___ Haschak, Paul G. **Utopian/Dystopian Literature: A Bibliography of Literary Criticism**. Metuchen, NJ: Scarecrow, 1994. 370pp.

___ Hassler, Donald M. "Machen, Williams, and Autobiography: Fantasy and Decadence," in: Wolf, Milton T. and Mallett, Daryl F., eds. **Imaginative Futures: Proceedings of the 1993 Science Fiction Research Association Conference**. San Bernardino, CA: Jacob's Ladder Books, 1995. pp.319-328.

___ Hassler, Donald M. "Working on SF: Observation With Extensive View," *Foundation* No. 60: 10-13. Spring 1994.

___ Heinze, Theodor T., ed. **Subjektivität als Fiktion: zur literarisch psychologischen Konstruktion des modernen Menschen**. Pfaffenweiler: Centaurus, 1993. 172pp.

___ Hendrix, Howard V. "Memories of the Sun, Perceptions of Eclipse," *New York Review of Science Fiction* No. 46: 13-15. June 1992.

___ Heuermann, Hartmut, ed. **Der Science Fiction Roman in der angloamerikanischen Literatur**. Düsseldorf: Bagel, 1986. 399pp.

CRITICISM (continued)

___ Heyne, Eric. "**Gateway** to an Erotics of Narrative," *Extrapolation* 35(4): 298-311. Winter 1994.

___ Hohne, Karen A. "The Voice of Cthulhu: Language Interaction in Contemporary Horror Fiction," in: Slusser, George E. and Rabkin, Eric S., eds. **Styles of Creation: Aesthetic Technique and the Creation of Fictional Worlds**. Athens: University of Georgia Press, 1992. pp.79-87.

___ Hollinger, Veronica. **Future Presence: Intersections of Science Fiction and Postmodernism**. Ph.D. Dissertation, Concordia University, 1994. 248pp. (DAI-A 56/07, p. 2676. January 1996.)

___ Hollinger, Veronica. "Specular SF: Postmodern Allegory," in: Ruddick, Nicholas, ed. **State of the Fantastic**. Westport, CT: Greenwood, 1992. pp.29-39.

___ Irwin, Robert. "Fantasy Without God," *Times Literary Supplement* 4770: 7. September 2, 1994.

___ James, Edward. **Science Fiction in the 20th Century**. Oxford, New York: Oxford University Press, 1994. 250pp.

___ Joseph, Paul. "Perry Mason in Space: A Call for More Inventive Lawyers in Television Science Fiction Series," by Paul Joseph and Sharon Carton. in: Wolf, Milton T. and Mallett, Daryl F., eds. **Imaginative Futures: Proceedings of the 1993 Science Fiction Research Association Conference**. San Bernardino, CA: Jacob's Ladder Books, 1995. pp.307-318.

___ Kahl, Nathan W. **The Meeting of Parallel Lines: Science and Fiction and Science Fiction**. Honor's Paper, Duke University, 1992. 76pp.

___ Kearns, Martha. "Postmodern Images of Sexuality in Vampire Literature," in: Wolf, Milton T. and Mallett, Daryl F., eds. **Imaginative Futures: Proceedings of the 1993 Science Fiction Research Association Conference**. San Bernardino, CA: Jacob's Ladder Books, 1995. pp.147-160.

___ Kelleghan, Fiona. "Humor in Science Fiction," in: Wolf, Milton T. and Mallett, Daryl F., eds. **Imaginative Futures: Proceedings of the 1993 Science Fiction Research Association Conference**. San Bernardino, CA: Jacob's Ladder Books, 1995. pp.263-278.

___ Klein, Gérard. "Discontent in American Science Fiction," *Chung Wai Literary Quarterly* 22(12): May 1994. (Issue not seen; pagination unavailable.) (Reprinted from *Science Fiction Studies*.)

___ Kleinschmidt, Erich. " 'Begreif-Weit': Zur fiktionalen Raumregahrung in der deutschen Literatur des 18. Jahrhunderts," *Germanisch-Romanische Monatsschrift* (Berlin) 41(2): 145-152. 1991.

___ Kolker, Robert P. "The Moving Image Reclaimed," *Postmodern Culture* 5(1): [6pp., with imbedded motion picture full-motion clips in MPEG]. September 1994. (Electronic Journal: pmc@jefferson.village.virginia.edu).

___ Kordigel, Metka. "Poskus Literarnoteoreticne definicije znanstvene fantastike," *Slavisticna Revija* (Slovenia) 40(3): 291-308. July/September 1992. [Not seen.]

___ Kotani, Mari. **Joseijo Muishiki: tekunogaineshisu, josei SF-ron josetsu**. [Techno-gynesis: The Political Unconscious of Feminist Science Fiction]. Tokyo: Keiso Shobo, 1994. 283pp. [In Japanese, not seen. cf. OCLC.]

___ Kramer, Reinhold. "Im/maculate: Some Instances of Gnostic Science Fiction," in: Ruddick, Nicholas, ed. **State of the Fantastic**. Westport, CT: Greenwood, 1992. pp.49-58.

___ Landon, Brooks. "Styles of Invisibility: Sustaining the Transparent in Contemporary Prose Semblances," in: Slusser, George E. and Rabkin, Eric S., eds. **Styles of Creation: Aesthetic Technique and the Creation of Fictional Worlds**. Athens: University of Georgia Press, 1992. pp.245-258.

___ Latham, Robert A. "Some Thoughts on Modernism and Science Fiction (Suggested by Robert Silverberg's **Downward to the Earth**)," in: Morse, Donald E., ed. **The Celebration of the Fantastic**. Westport, CT: Greenwood, 1992. pp.49-60.

___ Latham, Robert A. "Youth Culture and Cybernetic Technologies," in: Wolf, Milton T. and Mallett, Daryl F., eds. **Imaginative Futures: Proceedings of the 1993 Science Fiction Research Association Conference**. San Bernardino, CA: Jacob's Ladder Books, 1995. pp.191-202.

___ Latham, Robert A., ed. **Modes of the Fantastic: Selected Essays from the Twelfth International Conference on the Fantastic in the Arts**, ed. by Robert A. Latham and Robert A. Collins. Athens: Greenwood, 1995. 234pp.

___ Le Guin, Ursula K. "American SF and the Other," *Chung Wai Literary Quarterly* 22(12): May 1994. (Issue not seen; pagination unavailable.) (Reprinted from *Science Fiction Studies*.)

CRITICISM (continued)

___ Letson, Russell. "Contributions to the Critical Dialogue: As an Academic Sees It," in: Sanders, Joe, ed. **Science Fiction Fandom**. Westport, CT: Greenwood, 1994. pp.229-234.

___ Livia, Anna. "Putting the Abortion Controversy into Deep Freeze," in: Wolf, Milton T. and Mallett, Daryl F., eds. **Imaginative Futures: Proceedings of the 1993 Science Fiction Research Association Conference**. San Bernardino, CA: Jacob's Ladder Books, 1995. pp.245-248.

___ Loney, Mark. "SF, Genre, and Conservatism," *Science Fiction: A Review of Speculative Literature* 12(1): 3-8. 1993. (Whole No. 34)

___ Luckhurst, Roger. "The Many Deaths of Science Fiction: A Polemic," *Science Fiction Studies* 21(1): 35-50. March 1994.

___ Lutz, Reinhart. "Styles Within Styles, or 'Death of a Hack Writer': **Herovit's World** Reconsidered," in: Slusser, George E. and Rabkin, Eric S., eds. **Styles of Creation: Aesthetic Technique and the Creation of Fictional Worlds**. Athens: University of Georgia Press, 1992. pp.181-191.

___ Malekin, Peter. "Knowing about Knowing: Paradigms of Knowledge in the Postmodern Fantastic," in: Ruddick, Nicholas, ed. **State of the Fantastic**. Westport, CT: Greenwood, 1992. pp.41-47.

___ McGuirk, Carol. "Nowhere Man: Towards a Poetics of Post-Utopian Characterization," *Science Fiction Studies* 21(2): 141-154. July 1994.

___ McHale, Brian. **Constructing Postmodernism**. London: Routledge, 1992. 342pp.

___ McKay, George. "It's Not 'About' Science, It's 'About' Fiction and It's 'About' About," *Foundation* No. 60: 51-57. Spring 1994.

___ McKay, George. " 'Time Way Back': 'Motivation' and Speculative Fiction," *Critical Quarterly* 34(1): 102-116. Spring 1992.

___ Melara, Miriella. "Science, Fiction and Artificial Paradise: Villiers de l'Isle-Adam's **Future Eve**," in: Wolf, Milton T. and Mallett, Daryl F., eds. **Imaginative Futures: Proceedings of the 1993 Science Fiction Research Association Conference**. San Bernardino, CA: Jacob's Ladder Books, 1995. pp.203-216.

___ Miesel, Sandra. "The Fan as Critic," in: Sanders, Joe, ed. **Science Fiction Fandom**. Westport, CT: Greenwood, 1994. pp.235-242.

___ Miller, B. Diane. "Claims-Making in Artificial Intelligence Research," in: Wolf, Milton T. and Mallett, Daryl F., eds. **Imaginative Futures: Proceedings of the 1993 Science Fiction Research Association Conference**. San Bernardino, CA: Jacob's Ladder Books, 1995. pp.61-74.

___ Miller, Joseph D. "Just How Frumious Is a Bandersnatch? The Exotic and the Ambiguous in Imaginative Literature," in: Slusser, George E. and Rabkin, Eric S., eds. **Styles of Creation: Aesthetic Technique and the Creation of Fictional Worlds**. Athens: University of Georgia Press, 1992. pp.128-142.

___ Mogen, David. **Wilderness Visions: The Western Theme in Science Fiction Literature**. 2nd ed., Revised and Expanded. San Bernardino, CA: Borgo Press, 1994. 128pp.

___ Montgomery, Marion. "The Prophetic Poet and the Loss of Middle Earth," *Georgia Review* 33(1): 66-83. Spring 1979.

___ Morgan, Gwendolyn A. "Dualism and Mirror Imagery in Anglo-Saxon Riddles," *Journal of the Fantastic in the Arts* 5(1): 74-85. 1992. (No. 17)

___ Morris, David. **The Masks of Lucifer: Technology and the Occult in Twentieth Century Popular Literature**. London: Batsford, 1992. 223pp.

___ Morrison, Michael A. "Author Studies," by Michael A. Morrison and Neil Barron. in: Barron, Neil, ed. **Anatomy of Wonder 4**. New York: Bowker, 1995. pp.547-611.

___ Morse, Donald E. "Masterpieces or Garbage: Martin Tropp and Science Fiction," *The CEA Critic* 43(3): 14-17. March 1981.

___ Moylan, Thomas P. "Science Fiction Since 1980: Utopia, Dystopia, Cyberpunk, and Beyond," *Chung Wai Literary Quarterly* 22(12): May 1994. (Issue not seen; pagination unavailable.)

___ Mullen, R. D. "A Few Words About Science Fiction Criticism," *Foundation* No. 60: 9. Spring 1994.

___ Muñóz, Gabriel T. **La Ciencia Ficción: Conocimiento y Literatura**. Mexicali, B. C.: Instituto de Cultura de Baja California, 1991. 349pp. [Not seen.]

___ Navarette, Susan J. "The Soul of the Plot: The Aesthetics of Fin de Siècle Literature of Horror," in: Slusser, George E. and Rabkin, Eric S., eds. **Styles of Creation: Aesthetic Technique and the Creation of Fictional Worlds**. Athens: University of Georgia Press, 1992. pp.88-115.

___ Niewiadowski, Andrzej. **Literatura fantastycznonaukowa**. Warsaw: Wydawn. Naukowe PWN, 1992. 371pp. [Not seen.]

___ Nilson, Peter. **Rymdljus: en bok om katastrofer och underverk**. Stockholm: Norstedt, 1992. 266pp. [Not seen.]

CRITICISM (continued)

___ Ormes, Marie G. "Surprises in the Heinlein Bibliography," in: Wolf, Milton T. and Mallett, Daryl F., eds. **Imaginative Futures: Proceedings of the 1993 Science Fiction Research Association Conference**. San Bernardino, CA: Jacob's Ladder Books, 1995. pp.95-114.

___ Panshin, Alexei. "Greater Work and Lesser Work," *New York Review of Science Fiction* No. 42: 16-19. February 1992.

___ Panshin, Alexei. "The Sound of Light's Footsteps," *New York Review of Science Fiction* No. 49: 19-23. September 1992.

___ Parrinder, Patrick. "Landscapes of British Science Fiction," in: Slusser, George E. and Rabkin, Eric S., eds. **Styles of Creation: Aesthetic Technique and the Creation of Fictional Worlds**. Athens: University of Georgia Press, 1992. pp.193-204.

___ Peters, Jefferson M. "Persuasive Worlds and the Rhetorics of Art and Science in Science Fiction," in: Slusser, George E. and Rabkin, Eric S., eds. **Styles of Creation: Aesthetic Technique and the Creation of Fictional Worlds**. Athens: University of Georgia Press, 1992. pp.117-127.

___ Pierce, John J. **Odd Genre: A Study in Imagination and Evolution**. Westport, CT: Greenwood, 1994. 222pp.

___ Platt, Charles. "The 'Missing Middle' of Science Fiction," in: Slusser, George E. and Rabkin, Eric S., eds. **Styles of Creation: Aesthetic Technique and the Creation of Fictional Worlds**. Athens: University of Georgia Press, 1992. pp.167-171.

___ Pohl, Frederik. "Monolide: The Imaginative Future," in: Wolf, Milton T. and Mallett, Daryl F., eds. **Imaginative Futures: Proceedings of the 1993 Science Fiction Research Association Conference**. San Bernardino, CA: Jacob's Ladder Books, 1995. pp.9-14.

___ Pollvogt, Susannah W. **A Different Sort of Pussycat: Cyborg Subjectivities in Science Fiction Narratives and Their Promise for Feminist Politics**. Thesis (B.A.), Williams College, 1994. 196pp.

___ Pransky, Joanne. "Social Adjustments to a Robotic Future," in: Wolf, Milton T. and Mallett, Daryl F., eds. **Imaginative Futures: Proceedings of the 1993 Science Fiction Research Association Conference**. San Bernardino, CA: Jacob's Ladder Books, 1995. pp.137-146.

___ Puschmann-Nalenz, Barbara. **Science Fiction and Postmodern Fiction: A Genre Study**. New York: Peter Lang, 1992. 268pp. (Trans. of **Science Fiction und Ihre Grenzberieche**.)

___ Rabkin, Eric S. "Forms of Future Fiction," *ANQ* 5(4): 236-239. November 1992.

___ Rabkin, Eric S. "Imagination and Survival: The Case of Fantastic Literature," *Foundation* No. 56: 84-98. Autumn 1992. (Letter of comment: K. V. Bailey, *Foundation* No. 58: 85-87. Summer 1993.)

___ Reid, Constance. "New Light on the Work of John Taine," in: Wolf, Milton T. and Mallett, Daryl F., eds. **Imaginative Futures: Proceedings of the 1993 Science Fiction Research Association Conference**. San Bernardino, CA: Jacob's Ladder Books, 1995. pp.115-124.

___ Reynolds, Patricia, ed. **Proceedings of the J. R. R. Tolkien Centenary Conference, Keble College, Oxford, 1992**, ed. by Patricia Reynolds and Glen H. Goodknight. Altadena, CA: Mythopoeic Press, 1995. 458pp.

___ Roberts, Robin. "It's Still Science Fiction: Strategies of Feminist Science Fiction Criticism," *Extrapolation* 36(3): 184-197. Fall 1995.

___ Robinson, Kim S. "Pentalude: Science Fiction as Fantasy," in: Wolf, Milton T. and Mallett, Daryl F., eds. **Imaginative Futures: Proceedings of the 1993 Science Fiction Research Association Conference**. San Bernardino, CA: Jacob's Ladder Books, 1995. pp.353-358.

___ Ruddick, Nicholas, ed. **State of the Fantastic: Studies in the Theory and Practice of Fantastic Literature and Film**. Westport, CT: Greenwood, 1992. 210pp.

___ Russ, Joanna. **To Write Like a Woman: Essays in Feminism and Science Fiction**. Bloomington: Indiana University Press, 1995. 181pp.

___ Samuelson, David N. "Necessary Constraints: Samuel R. Delany on Science Fiction," *Foundation* No. 60: 21-41. Spring 1994.

___ Sanders, Joe L. **Functions of the Fantastic: Selected Essays from the Thirteenth International Conference on the Fantastic in the Arts**. Westport, CT: Greenwood, 1995. 230pp.

___ Seed, David, ed. **Anticipations: Essays on Early Science Fiction and Its Precursors**. Liverpool: Liverpool University Press, 1995. 225pp.

___ Seesholtz, Mel. "*Homo Electronicus*: Futures of Human-Enhancement, a Pictorial Primer of Probable Possibilities," in: Wolf, Milton T. and Mallett, Daryl F., eds. **Imaginative Futures: Proceedings of the 1993 Science Fiction Research Association Conference**. San Bernardino, CA: Jacob's Ladder Books, 1995. pp.229-244.

CRITICISM (continued)

___ Senior, William. "Oliphaunts in the Perilous Realm: The Function of Internal Wonder in Fantasy," in: Sanders, Joe, ed. **Functions of the Fantastic**. Westport, CT: Greenwood, 1995. pp.115-124.

___ Slethaug, Gordon E. **The Play of the Double in Postmodern American Fiction**. Carbondale: Southern Illinois University Press, 1993. 247pp.

___ Slusser, George E. "Reflections on Style and Science Fiction," in: Slusser, George E. and Rabkin, Eric S., eds. **Styles of Creation: Aesthetic Technique and the Creation of Fictional Worlds**. Athens: University of Georgia Press, 1992. pp.3-23.

___ Slusser, George E., ed. **Styles of Creation: Aesthetic Technique and the Creation of Fictional Worlds**, ed. by George E. Slusser and Eric S. Rabkin. Athens: University of Georgia Press, 1992. 271pp.

___ Spinrad, Norman. "If You Love Science Fiction, Then It's Time to Fight Back Against Anti-SF," *Science Fiction Age* 2(1): 32-36. November 1993.

___ Stableford, Brian. "How Should a Science Fiction Story End?," *New York Review of Science Fiction* No. 78: 1, 8-15. February 1995.

___ Stableford, Brian. **Opening Minds: Essays on Fantastic Literature**. San Bernardino, CA: Borgo Press, 1995. 144pp.

___ Stableford, Brian. **Outside the Human Aquarium: Masters of Science Fiction**. 2nd ed., Revised and Exanded. San Bernardino, CA: Borgo, 1995. 152pp.

___ Stableford, Brian. "The Redemption of the Infimal," *New York Review of Science Fiction* No. 52: 1-8. December 1992.

___ Stableford, Brian. "SF: The Nature of the Medium," in: Stableford, Brian. **Opening Minds: Essays on Fantastic Literature**. San Bernardino, CA: Borgo Press, 1995. pp.9-14.

___ Stockton, Sharon. "The Self Regained: Cyberpunk's Retreat to the Imperium," *Contemporary Literature* 36(4): 588-612. Winter 1995.

___ Stone-Blackburn, Susan. "Feminist Nurturers and Psychic Healers," in: Wolf, Milton T. and Mallett, Daryl F., eds. **Imaginative Futures: Proceedings of the 1993 Science Fiction Research Association Conference**. San Bernardino, CA: Jacob's Ladder Books, 1995. pp.167-178.

___ Suvin, Darko. "SF and the Novum," *Chung Wai Literary Quarterly* 22(12): May 1994. (Issue not seen; pagination unavailable.)

___ Tatsumi, Takayuki. **Gendai SF no retorikku**. [The Rhetoric of Contemporary Science Fiction.]. Tokyo: Iwaanami Shoten, 1992. 266pp. [Not seen.]

___ Tatsumi, Takayuki. **Japanoido sengen: gendai Nihon Sfo yomu tameni**. Tokyo: Hayakawa Shobo, 1993. 246pp. [Not seen.]

___ Telotte, J. P. "*The World of Tomorrow* and the 'Secret Goal' of Science Fiction," *Journal of Film and Video* 45(1): 27-39. Spring 1993.

___ Veldman, Meredith. **Fantasy, the Bomb, and the Greening of Britain: Romantic Protest, 1945-1980**. Cambridge: Cambridge University Press, 1994. 325pp.

___ Vonarburg, Elisabeth. "The Reproduction of the Body in Space," in: Ruddick, Nicholas, ed. **State of the Fantastic**. Westport, CT: Greenwood, 1992. pp.59-72.

___ Weiner, Andrew. "SF--NOT," *New York Review of Science Fiction* No. 57: 20-22. May 1993.

___ Weisenburger, Steven. **Fables of Subversion: Satire and the American Novel, 1930-1980**. Athens, GA: University of Georgia Press, 1995. 320pp.

___ Westfahl, Gary. "Academic Criticism of Science Fiction: What It Is, What It Should Be," *Monad* No. 2: 75-96. March 1992.

___ Westfahl, Gary. "Beyond Logic and Literacy: The Strange Case of Space Opera," *Extrapolation* 35(3): 176-185. Fall 1994.

___ Westfahl, Gary. "In Research of Wonder: The Future of Science Fiction Criticism," in: Wolf, Milton T. and Mallett, Daryl F., eds. **Imaginative Futures: Proceedings of the 1993 Science Fiction Research Association Conference**. San Bernardino, CA: Jacob's Ladder Books, 1995. pp.83-94.

___ Westfahl, Gary. "'Man Against Man, Brain Against Brain': The Transformation of Melodrama in Science Fiction," in: Redmond, James, ed. **Melodrama**. Cambridge: Cambridge University Press, 1992. pp.193-211.

___ Westfahl, Gary. "A New Campaign for Science Fiction," *Extrapolation* 33(1): 6-24. Spring 1992.

___ Westfahl, Gary. "The Undiscovered Country: The Finished and Unfinished Business of Science Fiction Research and Criticism," *Foundation* No. 60: 84-94. Spring 1994.

CRITICISM

CRITICISM (continued)
___ Westfahl, Gary. "Words of Wishdom: The Neologisms of Science Fiction," in: Slusser, George E. and Rabkin, Eric S., eds. **Styles of Creation: Aesthetic Technique and the Creation of Fictional Worlds**. Athens: University of Georgia Press, 1992. pp.221-244.
___ White, Linda. "Wildmen, Witches, and Wanderlust: No Basque Science Fiction?," in: Wolf, Milton T. and Mallett, Daryl F., eds. **Imaginative Futures: Proceedings of the 1993 Science Fiction Research Association Conference**. San Bernardino, CA: Jacob's Ladder Books, 1995. pp.279-292.
___ Williams, Joseph M. **An Analysis of the Human/Non-Human Opposition in Science Fiction Films: A Research Project**. Master's Thesis, Emerson College, 1988. 67pp.
___ Williams, Madawc. "Tales of Wonder: Science Fiction and Fantasy in the Age of Jane Austen," in: Reynolds, Patricia and GoodKnight, Glen H., eds. **Proceedings of the J. R. R. Tolkien Centenary Conference, Keble College, Oxford, 1992**. Altadena, CA: Mythopoeic Press, 1995. pp.419-430. (*Mythlore* Vol. 21, No. 2, Winter 1996, Whole No. 80)
___ Wishnia, Kenneth. "Science Fiction and Magic Realism: Two Openings, Same Space," *Foundation* No. 59: 29-41. Autumn 1993.
___ Wolf, Milton T., ed. **Imaginative Futures: Proceedings of the 1993 Science Fiction Research Association Conference**, ed. by Milton T. Wolf and Daryl F. Mallett. San Bernardino, CA: Jacob's Ladder Books/ Borgo Press, 1995. 364pp.
___ Wolfe, Gary K. "History and Criticism," in: Barron, Neil, ed. **Anatomy of Wonder 4**. New York: Bowker, 1995. pp.483-546.
___ Wolmark, Jenny. **Aliens and Others: Science Fiction, Feminism, and Postmodernism**. London: Harester Wheatsheaf, 1993. 167pp.; Iowa City: University of Iowa Press, 1994. 167pp.
___ Zaki, Hoda M. **Phoenix Renewed: The Survival and Mutation of Utopian Thought in North American Science Fiction 1965-1982**. Rev. ed. San Bernardino, CA: Borgo Press, 1994. 151pp.

CRITTERS 2: THE MAIN COURSE (MOTION PICTURE)
___ "**Critters 2: The Main Course** (Review)," *Variety* p. 10. May 4, 1988.

CRITTERS 3 (MOTION PICTURE)
___ Wilt, David. "**Critters 3** (Review)," *Cinefantastique* 22(6): 54. June 1992

CRITTERS 4 (MOTION PICTURE)
___ Wilt, David. "**Critters 4** (Review)," *Cinefantastique* 23(6): 60. April 1993.

CRITTERS (MOTION PICTURE)
___ " 'Critters' First Pic in New Line's Coventure with RCA/Col Homevid," *Variety* p.31. May 15, 1985.

CROATIA
___ Mrkocki, Igor. "SF in Croatia," *Locus* 34(1) 71. January 1995.

CRONENBERG, DAVID
___ Beard, William. "The Canadianness of David Cronenberg," *Mosaic* 27(2): 113-133. June 1994.
___ Rodley, Chris, ed. **Cronenberg on Cronenberg**. London, Boston: Faber and Faber, 1992. 197pp.
___ Wiater, Stanley. "Cronenberg, David," in: Wiater, Stanley. **Dark Visions: Conversations with the Masters of the Horror Film**. New York: Avon, 1992. pp.57-66.

CRONOS (MOTION PICTURE)
___ Faller, James M. "**Cronos** (Review)," *Cinefantastique* 25(4): 59. August 1994.

CROSBY, DENISE
___ Altman, Mark A. "**The Next Generation**: Reincarnating Denise Crosby," *Cinefantastique* 23(2/3): 34. October 1992.
___ Spelling, Ian. "Like a Phoenix," *Starlog* No. 218: 52-55, 66. September 1995.

CROW (MOTION PICTURE)
___ Duncan, Jody. "Quick Cuts: Making the Crow Fly," *Cinefex* No. 58: 23-24. June 1994.
___ Lowe, Nick. "**The Crow** (Review)," *Interzone* No. 84: 38-39. June 1994.

CURSE OF THE FLY (MOTION PICTURE)

CROW (MOTION PICTURE) (continued)
___ Scapperotti, Dan. "**The Crow** (Review)," *Cinefantastique* 25(4): 59. August 1994.

CROWE, CATHERINE
___ Geary, Robert F. "The Corpse in the Dung Cart: *The Night Side of Nature* and the Victorian Supernatural Tale," in: Sanders, Joe, ed. **Functions of the Fantastic**. Westport, CT: Greenwood, 1995. pp.47-54.

CROWLEY, JOHN
___ "John Crowley: The Writing on the Wall," *Locus* 32(3): 4, 72-73. March 1994.
___ Ellis, Mark. **Philosophical Romance: Theories of Time and Their Relationship to Genre in the Fiction of John Crowley**. Master's Thesis, University of Manitoba (Canada), 1990. 101pp. (Master's Abstracts 31/02, p. 566. Summer 1993.)
___ Killheffer, Robert K. J. "PW Interview: John Crowley," *Publishers Weekly* 241(35): 53-54. August 29, 1994.

CROWLEY, KATHLEEN
___ Weaver, Tom. "Target Earthwoman," *Starlog* No. 201: 59-63. April 1994.

CRUMB (MOTION PICTURE)
___ Persons, Dan. "**Crumb** (Review)," *Cinefantastique* 26(6)/27(1): 123. October 1995.

CRUSHER, WESLEY
___ Altman, Mark A. "**The Next Generation**: The Making of 'The First Duty'," *Cinefantastique* 23(2/3): 52-53. October 1992.

CRYOGENICS
___ Platt, Charles. "Freeze!," *Science Fiction Eye* No. 11: 61-64. December 1992.

CSICSERY-RONAY, ISTVAN
___ Gordon, Joan. "1992 Pioneer Award Presentation and Acceptance," *SFRA Review* No. 199: 9-11. July/August/September 1992.

CTHULHU MANSION (MOTION PICTURE)
___ Wilt, David. "**Cthulhu Mansion** (Review)," *Cinefantastique* 23(2/3): 122. October 1992.

CUMMINGS, RAY
___ Ladd, Thyril L. "Ray Cummings: A Meeting," in: Cummings, Ray. **The Girl in the Golden Atom**. Westport, CT: Hyperion, 1974. [8 pp., unpaged]. (Originally published in *Fantasy Commentator*, Winter 1948, as 'This Is About Ray Cummings.')

CUNNINGHAM, SEAN
___ Crisafulli, Chuck. "Mr. Friday Night," *Cinefantastique* 24(3/4): 118-119. October 1993.

CUNQUEIRO, ALVARO
___ Gonzáles-Millán, Juan. "Fantasía y parodia: la subversión del texto narrativo en **Las crónicas del sochantre**," *Monographis Review* 3(1/2): 81-99. 1987.

CURRIE, LOUISE
___ Weaver, Tom. "Louise Currie," in: Weaver, Tom. **They Fought the Creature Features: Interviews with 23 Classic Horror, Science Fiction and Serial Stars**. Jefferson, NC: McFarland, 1995. pp.131-143.

CURRY, DAN
___ Prokop, Tim. "**Star Trek: The Next Generation**: Curry's Heroes," *Cinefantastique* 25(6)/26(1): 92-93. December 1994.
___ Rubinstein, Mitchell. "**The Next Generation**: Special Visual Effects," *Cinefantastique* 23(2/3): 38-41. October 1992.

CURSE OF MICHAEL MEYERS (MOTION PICTURE)
___ SEE: HALLOWEEN VI: THE CURSE OF MICHAEL MEYERS (MOTION PICTURE).

CURSE OF THE FLY (MOTION PICTURE)
___ Henenlotter, Frank. "Films From Under the Floorboards," *Sci-Fi Entertainment* 1(6): 52-57. April 1995.

CUSHING, PETER

___ "Cushing, Peter (Obituary)," *Science Fiction Chronicle* 15(10): 19. September 1994.

___ "Cushing, Peter, 1913-1994 (Obituary)," *Starlog* No. 208: 76-77. November 1994.

___ Del Vecchio, Deborah. **Peter Cushing: The Gentle Man of Horror and His 91 Films**, by Deborah Del Vecchio and Tom Johnson. Jefferson, NC: McFarland, 1992. 496pp.

CUTTHROAT ISLAND (MOTION PICTURE)

___ Hatch, Jim. "*Cutthroat Island*: Getting Away With Murder," *Cinefex* No. 64: 49-50, 133. December 1995.

CYBER NINJA (MOTION PICTURE)

___ Whitty, Stephen. "Run For Your Life! It's Your Inner Godzilla," *San Jose (CA) Mercury News*. July 8, 1994. in: *NewsBank. Film and Television*. 81:C14. 1994.

___ Wilt, David. "*Cyber Ninja* (Review)," *Cinefantastique* 27(2): 59. November 1995.

CYBER TRACKER (MOTION PICTURE)

___ Wilt, David. "*Cyber Tracker* (Review)," *Cinefantastique* 26(3): 59. April 1995.

CYBERPUNK

___ "Cyberpunk Era: Interviews With William Gibson," *Whole Earth Review* No. 63: 78-82. Summer 1989.

___ Alkon, Paul. "Deus Ex Machina in William Gibson's Cyberpunk Trilogy," in: Slusser, George E. and Shippey, Tom, eds. **Fiction 2000: Cyberpunk and the Future of Narrative**. Athens: University of Georgia Press, 1992. pp.75-87.

___ Balsamo, Anne. "Feminism for the Incurably Informed," *South Atlantic Quarterly* 92(4): 681-712. Fall 1993.

___ Balsamo, Anne. "Signal to Noise: On the Meaning of Cyberpunk Subculture," in: Wolf, Milton T. and Mallett, Daryl F., eds. **Imaginative Futures: Proceedings of the 1993 Science Fiction Research Association Conference**. San Bernardino, CA: Jacob's Ladder Books, 1995. pp.217-228.

___ Benford, Gregory. "Science Fiction, Rhetoric, and Realities: Words to the Critic," in: Slusser, George E. and Shippey, Tom, eds. **Fiction 2000: Cyberpunk and the Future of Narrative**. Athens: University of Georgia Press, 1992. pp.223-229.

___ Bethke, Bruce. "The Contrapunk Manifesto," *OtherRealms* No. 24: 18. Spring 1989.

___ Biddick, Kathleen. "Humanist History and the Haunting of Virtual Worlds: Problems of Memory and Rememoration," *Genders* No. 18: 47-66. Winter 1993.

___ Bonner, Frances J. "Separate Development: Cyberpunk in Film and TV," in: Slusser, George E. and Shippey, Tom, eds. **Fiction 2000: Cyberpunk and the Future of Narrative**. Athens: University of Georgia Press, 1992. pp.191-207.

___ Branwyn, Gareth. "Compu-sex: Erotica for Cybernauts," *South Atlantic Quarterly* 92(4): 779-791. Fall 1993.

___ Bukatman, Scott R. "Gibson's Typewriter," *South Atlantic Quarterly* 92(4): 627-645. Fall 1993.

___ Cadora, Karen. "Feminist Cyberpunk," *Science Fiction Studies* 22(3): 357-372. November 1995

___ Caywood, Carolyn. "Cyberpunk," *Voice of Youth Advocates* 15(1): 14. April 1992.

___ Cherniavsky, Eva. "(En)gendering Cyberspace in **Neuromancer**: Postmodern Subjectivity and Virtual Motherhood," *Genders* No. 18: 32-46. Winter 1993.

___ Christie, John. "Of AIs and Others: William Gibson's Transit," in: Slusser, George E. and Shippey, Tom, eds. **Fiction 2000: Cyberpunk and the Future of Narrative**. Athens: University of Georgia Press, 1992. pp.171-182.

___ Csicsery-Ronay, Istvan, Jr. "Futuristic Flu, or, The Revenge of the Future," in: Slusser, George E. and Shippey, Tom, eds. **Fiction 2000: Cyberpunk and the Future of Narrative**. Athens: University of Georgia Press, 1992. pp.26-45.

___ Csicsery-Ronay, Istvan, Jr. "The Sentimental Futurist: Cybernetics and Art in William Gibson's **Neuromancer**," *Critique* 33(3): 221-240. Spring 1992.

___ Curl, Robert. "The Metaphors of Cyberpunk: Ontology, Epistemology, and Science Fiction," in: Slusser, George E. and Shippey, Tom, eds. **Fiction 2000: Cyberpunk and the Future of Narrative**. Athens: University of Georgia Press, 1992. pp.230-245.

CYBERPUNK (continued)

___ Davis, Erik. "Techgnosis: Magic, Memory and the Angel of Information," *South Atlantic Quarterly* 92(4): 585-616. Fall 1993. (Reprinted in: Dery, Mark, ed. **Flame Wars: The Discourse of Cyberculture**. Durham, NC: Duke University Press, 1994.)

___ Dery, Mark. "Cyberculture," *South Atlantic Quarterly* 91(3): 501-523. Summer 1992.

___ Donahoo, Robert. "Lewis Shiner and the 'Good' Anarchist," by Robert Donahoo and Chuck Etheridge. in: Slusser, George E. and Shippey, Tom, eds. **Fiction 2000: Cyberpunk and the Future of Narrative**. Athens: University of Georgia Press, 1992. pp.183-190.

___ Easterbrook, Neil. "The Arc of Our Destruction: Reversal and Erasure in Cyberpunk," *Science-Fiction Studies* 19(3): 378-394. November 1992.

___ Elmer-Dewitt, Philip. "Cyberpunk," *Time* 141(6): 59-65. February 8, 1993.

___ Foster, Thomas. "Incurably Informed: The Pleasures and Dangers of Cyberpunk," *Genders* No. 18: 1-10. Winter 1993.

___ Foster, Thomas. "Meat Puppets or Robopaths? Cyberpunk and the Question of Embodiment," *Genders* No. 18: 11-31. Winter 1993.

___ Frongia, Terri. "'We're on the Eve of 2000': Writers and Critics Speak Out on Cyberpunk, Hypercard, and the (New?) Nature," by Terri Frongia and Alida Allision. in: Slusser, George E. and Shippey, Tom, eds. **Fiction 2000: Cyberpunk and the Future of Narrative**. Athens: University of Georgia Press, 1992. pp.279-292.

___ Fuchs, Cynthia J. "'Death Is Irrelevant': Cyborgs, Reproduction, and the Future of Male Hysteria," *Genders* No. 18: 113-133. Winter 1993. Also in: Gray, Chris H., ed. **The Cyborg Handbook**. New York: Routledge, 1995. pp.281-300.

___ Gordon, Joan. "Joe Haldeman: Cyberpunk Before Cyberpunk Was Cool?," in: Morse, Donald E., ed. **The Celebration of the Fantastic**. Westport, CT: Greenwood, 1992. pp.251-257.

___ Gough, Noel. "Neuromancing the Stones: Experience, Intertextuality and Cyberpunk Science Fiction," *Journal of Experiential Education* 16(3): 9-17. December 1993.

___ Harper, Mary C. "Incurably Alien Other: A Case for Feminist Cyborg Writers," *Science Fiction Studies* 22(3): 399-420. November 1995

___ Howarth, David A. **The Technoculture of Cyberpunk Science Fiction and Its Publics: A Grounded Theory Analysis**. Master's Thesis, University of Delaware, 1995. 162pp.

___ Huntington, John. "Newness, **Neuromancer**, and the End of Narrative," in: Slusser, George E. and Shippey, Tom, eds. **Fiction 2000: Cyberpunk and the Future of Narrative**. Athens: University of Georgia Press, 1992. pp.133-141.

___ Jones, Steve. "Hyper-Punk: Cyberpunk and Information Technology," *Journal of Popular Culture* 28(2): 81-92. Fall 1994.

___ Landon, Brooks. "Not What It Used to Be: The Overloading of Memory in Digital Narrative," in: Slusser, George E. and Shippey, Tom, eds. **Fiction 2000: Cyberpunk and the Future of Narrative**. Athens: University of Georgia Press, 1992. pp.153-167.

___ Liu, Albert. "The Last Days of Arnold Schwarzenegger," *Genders* No. 18: 102-112. Winter 1993.

___ McGuirk, Carol. "The 'New' Romancers: Science Fiction Innovators From Gernsback to Gibson," in: Slusser, George E. and Shippey, Tom, eds. **Fiction 2000: Cyberpunk and the Future of Narrative**. Athens: University of Georgia Press, 1992. pp.109-129.

___ McHale, Brian. **Constructing Postmodernism**. London: Routledge, 1992. 342pp.

___ McHale, Brian. "Elements of a Poetics in Cyberpunk," *Critique* 33(3): 149-175. Spring 1992.

___ Nixon, Nicola. "Cyberpunk: Preparing the Ground for Revolution or Keeping the Boys Satisfied?," *Science-Fiction Studies* 19(2): 219-235. July 1992.

___ Olsen, Lance. "Cyberpunk and the Crisis of Postmodernity," in: Slusser, George E. and Shippey, Tom, eds. **Fiction 2000: Cyberpunk and the Future of Narrative**. Athens: University of Georgia Press, 1992. pp.142-152.

___ Porush, David. "Frothing the Synaptic Bath: What Puts the Punk in Cyberpunk?," in: Slusser, George E. and Shippey, Tom, eds. **Fiction 2000: Cyberpunk and the Future of Narrative**. Athens: University of Georgia Press, 1992. pp.246-261.

___ Rabkin, Eric S. "Undecidability and Oxymoronism," in: Slusser, George E. and Shippey, Tom, eds. **Fiction 2000: Cyberpunk and the Future of Narrative**. Athens: University of Georgia Press, 1992. pp.262-278.

___ Schmitt, Ronald E. "Mythology and Technology: The Novels of William Gibson," *Extrapolation* 34(1): 64-78. Spring 1993.

CYBERPUNK (continued)
___ Schroeder, Ralph. "Cyberculture, Cyborg Post-Modernism and the Sociology of Virtual Reality Technologies," *Futures* 26(5): 519-528. June 1994.
___ Sey, James A. "Trashing the Millenium: Subjectivity and Technology in Cyberpunk Science Fiction," *Liberator: Tydskrif vir Besondere en Vergelykende Taal- en Literatuurstudie* (South Africa) 13(1): 111-117. April 1992.
___ Shannon, L. R. "Science Times: I Left My Heart in the Land of Cyberpunk," *New York Times* Sec. C, p. 8. May 12, 1992.
___ Sherman, Paul. "Cyberpunk Film Festival Is Pure Sci-Fi Splendor," *Boston (MA) Herald*. March 15, 1994. in: *NewsBank. Film and Television*. 31:G5. 1994.
___ Shiner, Lewis. "Inside the Movement: Past, Present, and Future," in: Slusser, George E. and Shippey, Tom, eds. **Fiction 2000: Cyberpunk and the Future of Narrative**. Athens: University of Georgia Press, 1992. pp.17-25.
___ Shippey, Tom. "Semiotic Ghosts and Ghostliness in the Work of Bruce Sterling," in: Slusser, George E. and Shippey, Tom, eds. **Fiction 2000: Cyberpunk and the Future of Narrative**. Athens: University of Georgia Press, 1992. pp.208-220.
___ Slusser, George E. "The Frankenstein Barrier," in: Slusser, George E. and Shippey, Tom, eds. **Fiction 2000: Cyberpunk and the Future of Narrative**. Athens: University of Georgia Press, 1992. pp.46-71.
___ Slusser, George E. "Introduction," in: Slusser, George E. and Shippey, Tom, eds. **Fiction 2000: Cyberpunk and the Future of Narrative**. Athens: University of Georgia Press, 1992. pp.1-14.
___ Slusser, George E., ed. **Fiction 2000: Cyberpunk and the Future of Narrative**, ed. by George E. Slusser and Tom Shippey. Athens: University of Georgia Press, 1992. 303pp.
___ Smith, Stephanie A. "Morphing, Materialism, and the Marketing of **Xenogenesis**," *Genders* No. 18: 67-86. Winter 1993.
___ Sobchack, Vivian. "New Age Mutant Ninja Hackers: Reading *Mondo 2000*," *South Atlantic Quarterly* 92(4): 569-584. Fall 1993.
___ Sponsler, Claire. "Beyond the Ruins: The Geopolitics of Urban Decay and Cybernetic Play," *Science Fiction Studies* 20(2): 251-265. July 1993.
___ Sponsler, Claire. "Cyberpunk and the Dilemmas of Postmodern Narrative: The Example of William Gibson," *Contemporary Literature* 33(4): 625-644. December 1992.
___ Sponsler, Claire. "William Gibson and the Death of Cyberpunk," in: Latham, Robert A. and Collins, Robert A., eds. **Modes of the Fantastic**. Westport, CT: Greenwood, 1995. pp.47-55.
___ Springer, Claudia. "Muscular Circuitry: The Invincible Armored Cyborg in Cinema," *Genders* No. 18: 87-101. Winter 1993.
___ Springer, Claudia. "Sex, Memories, and Angry Women," *South Atlantic Quarterly* 92(4): 713-734. Fall 1993.
___ Stewart, Elizabeth. **Destroying Angels: Messianic Rhetoric in Benjamin, Scholem, Psychoanalysis and Science Fiction**. Ph.D. Dissertation, New York University, 1994. 586pp. (DAI-A 55/09, p. 2820. March 1995.)
___ Stockton, Sharon. "The Self Regained: Cyberpunk's Retreat to the Imperium," *Contemporary Literature* 36(4): 588-612. Winter 1995.
___ Voller, Jack G. "Neuromanticism: Cyberspace and the Sublime," *Extrapolation* 34(1): 18-29. Spring 1993.
___ Warsh, David. "Cyberspace: What Is in It for You?," *Boston (MA) Globe* p. 65. May 30, 1993.
___ Westfahl, Gary. " 'The Gernsback Continuum': William Gibson in the Context of Science Fiction," in: Slusser, George E. and Shippey, Tom, eds. **Fiction 2000: Cyberpunk and the Future of Narrative**. Athens: University of Georgia Press, 1992. pp.88-108.
___ Whalen, Terence. "The Future of a Commodity: Notes Toward a Critique of Cyberpunk and the Information Age," *Science Fiction Studies* 19(1): 75-88. March 1992.
___ Wolmark, Jenny. "Space, Time and Gender: The Impact of Cybernetics on the Feminist Utopia," *Foundation* No. 62: 22-30. Winter 1994/1995.

CYBERPUNK 2020 (GAME)
___ Baker, Eric T. "The Worlds of Williams and Effinger Come Alive in *Cyberpunk 2020*," *Science Fiction Age* 1(6): 90-92. September 1993.

CYBERRACE (GAME)
___ Weaver, Steven. "**Blade Runner**'s Designer Brings His Magic to Your Home Computer With *CyberRace*," *Science Fiction Age* 2(3): 82-85. March 1994.

CYBERSPACE
___ Bukatman, Scott R. "Amidst These Fields of Data: Allegory, Rhetoric, and the Paraspace," *Critique* 33(3): 199-219. Spring 1992.
___ Warsh, David. "Cyberspace: What Is in It for You?," *Boston (MA) Globe* p. 65. May 30, 1993.

CYBERTECH P. D. (MOTION PICTURE)
___ Bloch-Hansen, Peter. "**Cybertech P. D.**," *Starlog* No. 221: 70-73. December 1995.

CYBORG SOLDIER (MOTION PICTURE)
___ Wilt, David. "**Cyborg Soldier** (Review)," *Cinefantastique* 27(2): 60. November 1995.

CYBORGS
___ "Pilot's Associate," in: Gray, Chris H., ed. **The Cyborg Handbook**. New York: Routledge, 1995. pp.101-103.
___ Annas, George J. "Minerva v. National Health Agency," in: Gray, Chris H., ed. **The Cyborg Handbook**. New York: Routledge, 1995. pp.169-181.
___ Casper, Monica J. "Fetal Cyborgs and Technomoms on the Reproductive Frontier: Which Way to the Carnival?," in: Gray, Chris H., ed. **The Cyborg Handbook**. New York: Routledge, 1995. pp.183-201.
___ Clarke, Adele. "Modernity, Postmodernity and Reproductive Processes, ca. 1890-1990, or, 'Mommy, Where Do Cyborgs Come From Anyway?'," in: Gray, Chris H., ed. **The Cyborg Handbook**. New York: Routledge, 1995. pp.139-155.
___ Clynes, Manfred E. "Cyborg II: Sentic Space Travel," in: Gray, Chris H., ed. **The Cyborg Handbook**. New York: Routledge, 1995. pp.35-41.
___ Clynes, Manfred E. "Cyborgs and Space," by Manfred E. Clynes and Nathan S. Kline. in: Gray, Chris H., ed. **The Cyborg Handbook**. New York: Routledge, 1995. pp.29-33.
___ Dery, Mark. "Cyberculture," *South Atlantic Quarterly* 91(3): 501-523. Summer 1992.
___ Downey, Gary L. "Cyborg Anthropology," by Gary L. Downey, Joseph Dumit and Sarah Williams. in: Gray, Chris H., ed. **The Cyborg Handbook**. New York: Routledge, 1995. pp.341-346.
___ Downey, Gary L. "Human Agency in CAD/CAM Technology," in: Gray, Chris H., ed. **The Cyborg Handbook**. New York: Routledge, 1995. pp.363-370.
___ Driscoll, Robert W. "Engineering Man for Space: The Cyborg Study," in: Gray, Chris H., ed. **The Cyborg Handbook**. New York: Routledge, 1995. pp.75-81.
___ Dumit, Joseph. "Brain-Mind Machines and American Technological Dream Marketing: Towards an Ethnography of Cyborg Envy," in: Gray, Chris H., ed. **The Cyborg Handbook**. New York: Routledge, 1995. pp.347-362.
___ Eglash, Ron. "African Influences in Cybernetics," in: Gray, Chris H., ed. **The Cyborg Handbook**. New York: Routledge, 1995. pp.17-27.
___ Eglash, Ron. "An Interview With Patricia Cowings," in: Gray, Chris H., ed. **The Cyborg Handbook**. New York: Routledge, 1995. pp.93-99.
___ Figueroa-Sarriera, Heidi J. "Children of the Mind With Disposable Bodies: Metaphors of Self in a Text on Artificial Intelligence and Robotics," in: Gray, Chris H., ed. **The Cyborg Handbook**. New York: Routledge, 1995. pp.127-135.
___ Friedman, Eli A. "ISAO Proffers a Marvelous Cover for Acting out Fantasies," in: Gray, Chris H., ed. **The Cyborg Handbook**. New York: Routledge, 1995. pp.167-168.
___ Fuchs, Cynthia J. " 'Death Is Irrelevant': Cyborgs, Reproduction, and the Future of Male Hysteria," *Genders* No. 18: 113-133. Winter 1993. Also in: Gray, Chris H., ed. **The Cyborg Handbook**. New York: Routledge, 1995. pp.281-300.
___ Gabilondo, Joseba. "Postcolonial Cyborgs: Subjectivity in the Age of Cybernetic Reproduction," in: Gray, Chris H., ed. **The Cyborg Handbook**. New York: Routledge, 1995. pp.423-432.
___ Gaffney, F. Andrew. "Barney B. Clark, DDS: A View From the Medical Service," by F. Andrew Gaffney and Barry J. Fenton. in: Gray, Chris H., ed. **The Cyborg Handbook**. New York: Routledge, 1995. pp.157-160.
___ Goldberg, Jonathan. "Recalling Totalities: The Mirrored Stages of Arnold Schwarzenegger," in: Gray, Chris H., ed. **The Cyborg Handbook**. New York: Routledge, 1995. pp.233-254.
___ Gonzales, Jennifer. "Envisioning Cyborg Bodies: Notes From Current Research," in: Gray, Chris H., ed. **The Cyborg Handbook**. New York: Routledge, 1995. pp.267-279.

CYBORGS (continued)

___ Gray, Chris H. "The Cyborg Body Politic: Version 1.2," by Chris H. Gray and Steven Mentor. in: Gray, Chris H., ed. **The Cyborg Handbook.** New York: Routledge, 1995. pp.453-467.

___ Gray, Chris H. "An Interview With Jack E. Steele," in: Gray, Chris H., ed. **The Cyborg Handbook.** New York: Routledge, 1995. pp.61-69.

___ Gray, Chris H. "An Interview With Manfred E. Clynes," in: Gray, Chris H., ed. **The Cyborg Handbook.** New York: Routledge, 1995. pp.43-53.

___ Gray, Chris H. "Introduction: Constructing the Knowledge of Cybernetic Organisms," by Chris H. Gray, Steven Mentor and Heidi J. Figueroa-Sarriera. in: Gray, Chris H., ed. **The Cyborg Handbook.** New York: Routledge, 1995. pp.1-14.

___ Gray, Chris H. "Science Fiction Becomes Science Fact," in: Gray, Chris H., ed. **The Cyborg Handbook.** New York: Routledge, 1995. pp.104-106.

___ Gray, Chris H., ed. **The Cyborg Handbook.** New York: Routledge, 1995. 540pp.

___ Gusterson, Hugh. "*Short Circuit*: Watching Television With a Nuclear-Weapons Scientist," in: Gray, Chris H., ed. **The Cyborg Handbook.** New York: Routledge, 1995. pp.107-117.

___ Hardaway, Donna J. "Cyborgs and Symbionts: Living Together in the New World Order," in: Gray, Chris H., ed. **The Cyborg Handbook.** New York: Routledge, 1995. pp.xi-xx.

___ Hayles, N. Katherine. "The Life Cycle of Cyborgs: Writing the Posthuman," in: Gray, Chris H., ed. **The Cyborg Handbook.** New York: Routledge, 1995. pp.321-335.

___ Hayles, N. Katherine. "The Life Cycle of Cyborgs: Writing the Posthuman," in: Benjamin, Marina, ed. **A Question of Identity: Women, Science, and Literature.** New Brunswick, NJ: Rutgers University Press, 1993. pp.152-170.

___ Hogle, Linda F. "Tales From the Cryptic: Technology Meets Organism in the Living Cadaver," in: Gray, Chris H., ed. **The Cyborg Handbook.** New York: Routledge, 1995. pp.203-216.

___ Hori, Motokazu. "Artificial Liver: Present and Future," in: Gray, Chris H., ed. **The Cyborg Handbook.** New York: Routledge, 1995. pp.163-166.

___ Jankiewicz, Pat. "Borg to Be Wild," *Starlog* No. 201: 36-39. April 1994.

___ Jess, David J. "On Low-Tech Cyborgs," in: Gray, Chris H., ed. **The Cyborg Handbook.** New York: Routledge, 1995. pp.371-377.

___ Johnson, Edwin G. "Teleoperators and Human Augmentation," by Edwin G. Johnson and William R. Corliss. in: Gray, Chris H., ed. **The Cyborg Handbook.** New York: Routledge, 1995. pp.83-92.

___ Johnson, Victoria. "The Politics of Morphing: Michael Jackson as Science Fiction Border Text," *Velvet Light Trap* (Austin, TX) 32: 58-65. 1993.

___ Macauley, William R. "From Cognitive Pyschologies to Mythologies: Advancing Cyborg Textualities for a Narrative of Resistance," by William R. Macauley and Angel J. Gordo-Lopez. in: Gray, Chris H., ed. **The Cyborg Handbook.** New York: Routledge, 1995. pp.433-443.

___ Oehlert, Mark. "From Captain America to Wolverine: Cyborgs in Comic Books, Alternative Images of Cybernetic Heroes and Villains," in: Gray, Chris H., ed. **The Cyborg Handbook.** New York: Routledge, 1995. pp.219-231.

___ Robins, Ken. "Socializing the Cyborg Self: The Gulf War and Beyond," by Ken Robins and Les Levidow. in: Gray, Chris H., ed. **The Cyborg Handbook.** New York: Routledge, 1995. pp.119-125.

___ Sandoval, Chela. "New Sciences: Cyborg Feminism and the Methodology of the Oppressed," in: Gray, Chris H., ed. **The Cyborg Handbook.** New York: Routledge, 1995. pp.407-421.

___ Schroeder, Ralph. "Cyberculture, Cyborg Post-Modernism and the Sociology of Virtual Reality Technologies," *Futures* 26(5): 519-528. June 1994.

___ Springer, Claudia. "Muscular Circuitry: The Invincible Armored Cyborg in Cinema," *Genders* No. 18: 87-101. Winter 1993.

___ Steele, Jack E. "How Do We Get There?," in: Gray, Chris H., ed. **The Cyborg Handbook.** New York: Routledge, 1995. pp.55-59.

___ Stone, Sandy. "Split Subjects, Not Atoms: or, How I Fell In Love With My Prosthesis," in: Gray, Chris H., ed. **The Cyborg Handbook.** New York: Routledge, 1995. pp.393-406.

___ Tomas, David. "Art, Psychasthenic Assimilation, and the Cybernetic Automation," in: Gray, Chris H., ed. **The Cyborg Handbook.** New York: Routledge, 1995. pp.255-266.

___ Van Citters, Robert L. "Artificial Heart and Assist Devices: Directions, Needs, Costs, Societal and Ethical Issues (Abstract)," in: Gray, Chris H., ed. **The Cyborg Handbook.** New York: Routledge, 1995. pp.161-162.

CYBORGS (continued)

___ Williams, Sarah. " 'Perhaps Images at One With the World Are Already Lost Forever': Visions of Cyborg Anthropology in Post-Cultural Worlds," in: Gray, Chris H., ed. **The Cyborg Handbook.** New York: Routledge, 1995. pp.379-390.

___ Wood, Brent D. **Cyborgs and Soft Machines: Control and Chaos in Technological Evolution.** Master's Thesis, Trent University, 1995. 263pp. (Master's Abstracts 34/01, p. 124. Feb. 1996.)

CZECH REPUBLIC

___ "Science Fiction, a Global Community: Czech Republic," *Locus* 32(4): 42. April 1994.

___ "SF in the Czech Republic," *Locus* 31(6): 38. December 1993.

___ Adamovic, Ivan. **Encyklopedie fantastického filmu.** Praha: Cinema, 1994. 224pp. [Not seen; OCLC record.]

___ Adamovic, Ivan. "SF in the Czech Republic," *Locus* 34(4): 38-39. April 1995.

___ Adamovic, Ivan. "SF in the Czech Republic in 1993," *Locus* 33(1): 45-46. July 1994.

___ Hauser, Eva. "Science Fiction in the Czech Republic and the Former Czechoslovakia: The Pleasures and the Disappointments of the New Cosmopolitanism," *Science Fiction Studies* 21(2): 133-140. July 1994.

___ Pospisil, Ivo. "Horce ironicka science fiction Faddeje Bulgarina," *Svet Literatury: Casopis pro Novoveke Zahranicni Literatury* (Amsterdam, Netherlands) 5: 22-28. 1993.

___ Rampas, Zdenek. **Kdo je Kdo v ceské a slovenské science fiction,** by Zdenek Rampas and Pavel Kosatik. Praha, CZ: Ceskoslovenského fandomu, 1994. 84pp. [Not seen.]

CZECHOSLOVAKIA

___ Adamovic, Ivan. "Jan Weiss (1892-1972), Karel Capek's Overlooked Contemporary," *Extrapolation* 36(4): 285-291. Winter 1995.

___ Hauser, Eva. "Science Fiction in the Czech Republic and the Former Czechoslovakia: The Pleasures and the Disappointments of the New Cosmopolitanism," *Science Fiction Studies* 21(2): 133-140. July 1994.

___ Simsa, Cyril. "The View From Olympus: Three Czech Women Writers Talk About SF," *Vector* No. 166: 14-16. April/May 1992.

CZYNSKI, JOE

___ Stone, Graham. "H. M. Crimp--And More," *Science Fiction News* (Australia) No. 116: 19-21. October 1992.

D'AMATO, BRIAN

___ Hughes, Dave. "The Golden Age of Plastic: Brian D'Amato Interview," *Interzone* No. 72: 39-41. June 1993.

D'ANNUNZIO, GABRIELE

___ Hoffman, Donald L. "Isotta di Rimini: Gabriele D'Annunzio's Use of the Tristan Legend in His **Da Rimini**," *Quondam et Futurus* 2(3): 46-54. Fall 1992.

D'AQUINO, JOHN

___ Warren, Bill. "Underwater Journeyman," *Starlog* No. 199: 37-40, 74. February 1994.

DA CRUZ, DANIEL

___ "Da Cruz, Daniel (Obituary)," *Locus* 29(4): 66. October 1992

DAEDALUS ENCOUNTER (GAME)

___ Perry, Clark. "*The Daedalus Encounter* Moves Big-Budget Special Effects Inside Your PC," *Science Fiction Age* 4(1): 100-101. November 1995.

DAHL, ROALD

___ Treglown, Jeremy. **Roald Dahl: A Biography.** New York: Farrar, 1994. 322pp.

DALKEY, KARA

___ Ringel, Faye. "The Scribblies: A Shared World," *Extrapolation* 35(3): 201-210. Fall 1994.

DANN, JACK

___ Dann, Jack. "**The Memory Cathedral**," *New York Review of Science Fiction* No. 82: 1, 8-10. June 1995.

___ Dann, Jack. "The Profession of Science Fiction, 45: Sparks in the Dark," *Foundation* No. 61: 5-35. Summer 1994.

DANTE, JOE
___ "Terror Master: Joe Dante," *Sight and Sound* 3(6): 7-9. June 1993.
___ Crisafulli, Chuck. "A Fan Turned Pro: A Guy Named Joe," *Filmfax* No. 38: 36-41, 72. April/May 1993.
___ McDonagh, Maitland. "The Ultimate Joe Dante Interview," *Sci-Fi Entertainment* 1(1): 42-46, 62. June 1994.
___ Warren, Bill. "Other People's Dreams," *Starlog* No. 200: 36-39, 90. March 1994.

DANTE, MICHAEL
___ Phillips, Mark. "Good Warrior," *Starlog* No. 174: 68-69. January 1992.

DARK CRYSTAL (MOTION PICTURE)
___ "*Dark Crystal* Tops Avoriaz; Hershey, Furie, Coscarelli Wins," *Variety* p. 28. February 2, 1983.
___ "Initial *Dark Crystal* Sell to Be Soft; Unusual Tie-Ins," *Variety* p. 27. September 1, 1982.
___ "Madrid Sci-Fi Prizes," *Variety* p. 23. April 6, 1983.

DARK HALF (MOTION PICTURE)
___ Leayman, Charles D. "*The Dark Half*: Makeup Effects," *Cinefantastique* 24(1): 18. June 1993.
___ Leayman, Charles D. "*The Dark Half*: Stephen King," *Cinefantastique* 24(1): 21. June 1993.
___ Leayman, Charles D. "*The Dark Half*: Visual Effects by V. C. E.," *Cinefantastique* 24(1): 23. June 1993.
___ Leayman, Charles D. "*The Dark Half*," *Cinefantastique* 24(1): 16-23. June 1993.
___ Leayman, Charles D. "Stephen King's *The Dark Half*," *Cinefantastique* 22(4): 5. February 1992.
___ Robley, Les P. "*The Dark Half* (Review)," *Cinefantastique* 24(3/4): 123. October 1993.

DARK INTRUDER (MOTION PICTURE)
___ Leeper, Mark R. "*Dark Intruder* (Review)," *Lan's Lantern* No. 42: 106. May 1994.

DARK SHADOWS (MOTION PICTURE)
___ "Theatricalize ABC-TV *Dark Shadows* for MGM," *Variety* p. 28. February 11, 1970.
___ "TV's *Dark Shadows*'s Theatre Feature," *Variety* p. 17. April 1, 1970.

DARK SHADOWS (TV)
___ "Theatricalize ABC-TV *Dark Shadows* for MGM," *Variety* p. 28. February 11, 1970.
___ "TV's *Dark Shadows*'s Theatre Feature," *Variety* p. 17. April 1, 1970.
___ Van Hise, James. **Sci Fi TV: From Twilight Zone to Deep Space Nine**. Las Vegas, NV: Pioneer Books, 1993. 160pp. (Reprinted, HarperPrism, 1995. 258pp.)

DARK, THE (MOTION PICTURE)
___ Harris, Judith P. "*The Dark* (Review)," *Cinefantastique* 25(6)/26(1): 122. December 1994.

DARKMAN II: DURANT RETURNS (MOTION PICTURE)
___ Szebin, Frederick C. "*Darkman II: Durant Returns*," *Cinefantastique* 25(6)/26(1): 36-37, 125. December 1994.

DARKMAN III: DIE, DARKMAN, DIE (MOTION PICTURE)
___ Szebin, Frederick C. "*Darkman III: Die, Darkman, Die*," *Cinefantastique* 26(6)/27(1): 92-93, 125. October 1995.

DARKSEED (GAME)
___ Hautala, Rick. "H. R. Giger's Alien Nightmares Invade Your Computer in *Darkseed*," *Science Fiction Age* 1(5): 74, 80. July 1993.

DARREN, JAMES
___ Counts, Kyle. "A Time to Remember," *Starlog* 180: 32-35, 66. July 1992.

DATLOW, ELLEN
___ "1995 World Fantasy Awards," *Locus* 35(6): 4, 81. December 1995.

DATLOW, ELLEN (continued)
___ "Editor Interview: Ellen Datlow, Fiction Editor, *Omni* Magazine, Part 2," *The Report: The Fiction Writer's Magazine* No. 10: 17-19. Summer 1993.
___ "Editor Interviews: Ellen Datlow, Fiction Editor, *Omni* Magazine, Part 1," *The Report: The Fiction Writer's Magazine* No. 9: 15-16. March 1993.
___ "World Fantasy Awards, 1995," *Science Fiction Chronicle* 17(2): 5. December 1995/January 1996.
___ Errera, Robert. "Ellen Datlow Interview," *2AM Magazine* 5(3): 45-46, 50. Spring 1992.
___ Farr, Russell B. "An Interview With Pat Cadigan and Ellen Datlow," *Science Fiction: A Review of Speculative Literature* 13(1): 13-18. 1995(?). (No. 37)

DAVE (MOTION PICTURE)
___ Pieshel, Bob. "Quick Cuts: Hail to the Imposter," *Cinefex* No. 55: 35-36. August 1993.

DAVID, REBECCA HARDING
___ Rose, Jane A. "Images of Self: The Example of Rebecca Harding Davis and Charlotte Perkins Gilman," *English Language Notes* 29(4): 70-78. June 1992.

DAVID-NEEL, ALEXANDRA
___ Schweitzer, Darrell. "When Is a Fantasy Novel Not a Fantasy Novel?," *Studies in Weird Fiction* No. 11: 29-31. Spring 1992.

DAVIDMAN, JOY
___ Ben-Chorin, Schalom. "Joy Davidman und C. S. Lewis zu alttestamentlichen Texten," in: Kranz, Gisbert, ed. **Inklings: Jahrbuch für Literatur und Ästhetik**. 1. Band. Lüdenscheid, Germany: Michael Claren, 1983. pp.89-102.

DAVIDSON, AVRAM
___ "Davidson, Avram: In Memorium (Obituary)," *Locus* 31(1): 60-61. July 1993.
___ "Davidson, Avram (Obituary)," *Science Fiction Chronicle* 14(9): 16. June 1993.
___ "Davidson, Avram, 1923 - 1993 (Obituary)," *Magazine of Fantasy and Science Fiction* 85(3): 4. September 1992.
___ "Davidson, Avram, Dies (Obituary)," *Locus* 30(6): 5, 69-71. June 1993.

DAVIES, GERAINT WYN
___ Bloch-Hansen, Peter. "Forever and a Knight," *Starlog* No. 212: 50-53, 72. March 1995.

DAVIES, ROBERTSON
___ Slocum, Sally K. "Waxing Arthurian: **The Lyre of Orpheus** and **Cold Sassy Tree**," in: Slocum, Sally K., ed. **Popular Arthurian Traditions**. Bowling Green, OH: Popular Press, 1992. pp.96-103.

DAVIS, ANTHONY
___ Delany, Samuel R. "Anthony Davis, a Conversation," in: Delany, Samuel R. **Silent Interviews on Language, Race, Sex, Science Fiction and Some Comics**. Hanover, NH: Wesleyan University Press, 1994. pp.289-311.

DAVIS, DANIEL
___ Stephens, Lynne. "A Study in Starflight," *Starlog* No. 190: 27-29, 69. May 1993.

DAVIS, GEENA
___ Timpone, Anthony. "Bride of the Fly," by Anthony Timpone and Carr D'Angelo. in: McDonnell, David, ed. **Starlog's Science Fiction Heroes and Heroines**. New York: Crescent Books, 1995. pp.47-49.

DAVIS, WILLIAM
___ Vitaris, Paula. "*X-Files*: Cancer Man," *Cinefantastique* 26(6)/27(1): 67-68. October 1995.

DAY AFTER (MOTION PICTURE)
___ "ABC TV's Nuclear Disaster Pic: Too Hot to Handle or Blockbuster?," *Variety* p. 63. October 26, 1983.
___ "*The Day After* Axed in Poland; Further Queries," *Variety* p. 1, 68. December 21, 1983.

DAY AFTER (MOTION PICTURE)

DAY AFTER (MOTION PICTURE) (continued)
___ "*Day After* Reaction Mixed From Advertisers & Viewers; CBS Runs Tape, ABC Fumes," *Variety* p. 90, 104. November 22, 1983.
___ "*Day After* Record in Wide Italo Run," *Variety* p. 42. February 15, 1984.
___ "*Day After* Scores on Euro Screenings; Italo Sale Pending," *Variety* p. 5, 13. December 14, 1983.
___ "*Day After, Last Unicorn* Hit Big in Germany, Campaigns Help," *Variety* p. 123. January 25, 1984.
___ "'Day' Big in Japan," *Variety* p. 123. February 1, 1984.
___ "Nuke War Telepic to Be Tough Sale for ABC Peddlers," *Variety* p. 69, 86. September 14, 1983.
___ "Poland to Air *Day After* Pic," *Variety* p. 2. January 25, 1984.
___ Cantor, Joanne. "Children's Emotional Reactions to Technological Disasters Conveyed by the Mass Media," in: Wober, J. Mallory, ed. **Television and Nuclear Power: Making the Public Mind.** Norwood, NJ: Ablex, 1992. pp.31-54.
___ Greenberg, James. "ABC Pics Expects *Day After* to Hit Top 10 Foreign Grossers in 1984; Estimates $50-Mil B. O.," *Variety* p. 3, 38. April 4, 1984.
___ Gunter, Barrie. "The Impact of Nuclear Fiction in Britain: *The Day After* and *Threads*," by Barrie Gunter and M. Svennevig. in: Wober, J. Mallory, ed. **Television and Nuclear Power: Making the Public Mind.** Norwood, NJ: Ablex, 1992. pp.55-66.
___ Iwao, Sumiko. "*The Day After* in Japan," in: Wober, J. Mallory, ed. **Television and Nuclear Power: Making the Public Mind.** Norwood, NJ: Ablex, 1992. pp.67-76.
___ Kubey, Robert W. "U.S. Opinion and Politics Before and After *The Day After*: Television Movie as Rorschach," in: Wober, J. Mallory, ed. **Television and Nuclear Power: Making the Public Mind.** Norwood, NJ: Ablex, 1992. pp.19-30.
___ Lometti, Guy E. "Broadcast Preparations for and Consequences of *The Day After*," in: Wober, J. Mallory, ed. **Television and Nuclear Power: Making the Public Mind.** Norwood, NJ: Ablex, 1992. pp.3-18.
___ Wober, J. Mallory, ed. **Television and Nuclear Power: Making the Public Mind.** Norwood, NJ: Ablex, 1992. 297pp.

DAY BEFORE (MOTION PICTURE)
___ "Seeing Nuke Panic, Germans Dump Pic From TV Schedule," *Variety* p. 116, 124. March 21, 1984.

DAY MARS INVADED EARTH (MOTION PICTURE)
___ Henenlotter, Frank. "Films From Under the Floorboards," *Sci-Fi Entertainment* 1(6): 52-57. April 1995.

DAY OF THE DOLPHIN (MOTION PICTURE)
___ "Schaffner's 'Dolphin'," *Variety* p. 24. May 24, 1970.

DAY THE EARTH STOOD STILL (MOTION PICTURE)
___ Kenny, Glenn. "New Life for a '50s Classic," *TV Guide* 43(35): 20. September 2, 1995.
___ Weaver, Tom. "Years After Stillness," *Starlog* No. 211: 24-27, 69. February 1995.
___ Wolff, Michael J. "After the Earth Stood Still," *Starlog* No. 211: 19-23, 69. February 1995.

DAY, DONALD B.
___ "Day, Donald B. (Obituary)," *Science Fiction News* (Australia) No. 54: 10. April 1978.

DAY, ROBERT
___ Weaver, Tom. "Robert Day: Interview," in: Weaver, Tom, ed. **Attack of the Monster Movie Makers: Interviews with 20 Genre Giants.** Jefferson, NC: McFarland, 1994. pp.85-97.

DE BERGERAC, CYRANO
___ Pleithner, Regina. "Zwei Mondreisen des 17. Jahrhunderts: Voyages imaginaires oder Reiseutopien? Beitrage zum Kolloquium der Arbeitsgruppe Kultrugeschichte des Barockzeitalters an der Herzog-August-Bibliothek Wolfenbuttle von 10. Bis 12. Juli 1989," in: Pleithner, Regina, ed. **Reisen des Barock: Selbst- und Fremderfahrung und ihre Darstellung.** Bonn: Romanistischer, 1991. pp.75-87.

DE CAMP, L. SPRAGUE
___ Bloom, Harold. "L. Sprague de Camp and Fletcher Pratt," in: Bloom, Harold, ed. **Modern Fantasy Writers.** New York: Chelsea House, 1995. pp.29-42.

DEAD AGAIN (MOTION PICTURE)

DE CHAIR, SOMERSET
___ "de Chair, Somerset (Obituary)," *Science Fiction Chronicle* 16(4): 16. February 1995.

DE HAAS, TIMOTHY
___ Florence, Bill. "Alien Dreams," *Starlog* No. 194: 50-53. September 1993.

DE L'ISLE-ADAM, VILLIERS
___ Melara, Miriella. "Science, Fiction and Artificial Paradise: Villiers de l'Isle-Adam's **Future Eve**," in: Wolf, Milton T. and Mallett, Daryl F., eds. **Imaginative Futures: Proceedings of the 1993 Science Fiction Research Association Conference.** San Bernardino, CA: Jacob's Ladder Books, 1995. pp.203-216.

DE LA MARE, WALTER
___ Bloom, Harold. "Walter de la Mare," in: Bloom, Harold. **Modern Horror Writers.** New York: Chelsea House, 1995. pp.64-78.
___ Crawford, Gary W. "Over the Edge: The Ghost Stories of Walter de la Mare," in: Schweitzer, Darrell, ed. **Discovering Classic Horror Fiction I.** Mercer Island, WA: Starmont, 1992. pp.53-57.

DE LA REE, GERRY
___ "de la Ree, Gerry (Obituary)," *Locus* 30(2): 68. February 1993.
___ "de la Ree, Gerry (Obituary)," *Science Fiction Chronicle* 14(5): 10, 12. February 1993.

DE LANCIE, JOHN
___ Nazzaro, Joe. "Heroic Passings," *Starlog* No. 221: 35-37. December 1995.
___ Spelling, Ian. "Q & A," by Ian Spelling and David McDonnell. *Starlog* No. 206: 47-51, 70. September 1994.

DE LAURENTIIS, RAFFAELLA
___ Lofficier, Randy. "*Dune* (1984): Interviews with David Lynch, Raffaella de Laurentiis and Kyle MacLachlan," by Randy Lofficier and Jean-Marc Lofficier. in: Goldberg, Lee et al. **Science Fiction Filmmaking in the 1980s.** Jefferson, NC: McFarland, 1995. pp.79-110.

DE LILLO, DON
___ Atwill, William D. **Fire and Power: The American Space Program as Postmodern Narrative.** Athens, GA: The University of Georgia Press, 1994. 172pp.

DE LINT, CHARLES
___ Caven, Patricia. "A Talk With Charles de Lint," *Worlds of Fantasy and Horror* 1(2): 51-55. Spring 1995. (No. 2)
___ Toolis, Lorna. "Charles de Lint: On the Border," by Lorna Toolis and Michael Skeet. in: Collins, Robert A. and Latham, Robert, eds. **Science Fiction and Fantasy Book Review Annual 1991.** Westport, CT: Greenwood, 1994. pp.79-86.

DE NIRO, ROBERT
___ "De Niro to Be a Judge at Avoriaz Film Festival," *Variety* p. 5. November 28, 1984.
___ Jones, Alan. "Making Up DeNiro," *Cinefantastique* 25(6)/26(1): 8. December 1994.

DE PALMA, BRIAN
___ Von Gunden, Kenneth. **Postmodern Auteurs: Coppola, Lucas, De Palma, Spielberg and Scorcese.** Jefferson, NC: McFarland, 1991. 200pp.

DE VEGA, LOPE
___ de Armas, Frederick A. "Gyges' Ring: Invisibility in Plato, Tolkien, and Lope de Vega," *Journal of the Fantastic in the Arts* 3(4): 120-138. 1994.

DEAD AGAIN (MOTION PICTURE)
___ Gire, Dann. "Director Kenneth Branagh on *Dead Again*, Sending-Up Sir Alfred Hitchcock," *Cinefantastique* 22(4): 58, 61. February 1992.
___ Leayman, Charles D. "*Dead Again* (Review)," *Cinefantastique* 22(4): 59, 61. February 1992.

DEAD AT 21 (TV)

___ Adalian, Josef. "Dead Pretending to Be Lively Drama," *Washington (DC) Times*. June 9, 1994. in: *NewsBank. Film and Television*. 64:D12. 1994.

___ Griffin, Dominic. "Brain Dead at 21," *Sci-Fi Universe* No. 3: 44-46. October/November 1994.

___ Kenny, Glenn. "MTV's Dead-End Kid," *TV Guide* 42(24): 31. June 11, 1994.

___ Kenny, Glenn. "Teleporting Teens and a Generation X Hero," *TV Guide* 42(9): 41. February 26, 1994.

DEAD MAN WALKING (MOTION PICTURE)

___ "*Dead Man Walking* (Review)," *Variety* p. 17. July 13, 1988.

DEAD ZONE (MOTION PICTURE)

___ "*The Dead Zone* (1983)/*Videodrome* (1984): Interview with David Cronenberg," in: Goldberg, Lee, ed. **The Dreamweavers: Interviews With Fantasy Filmmakers of the 1980s**. Jefferson, NC: McFarland, 1995. pp.58-74.

DEADLY GAMES (MOTION PICTURE)

___ Warren, Bill. "Deadly Gamesters," *Starlog* No. 219: 45-49. October 1995.

___ Warren, Bill. "Deadly Rose," *Starlog* No. 221: 52-55. December 1995.

___ Warren, Bill. "Playing Games," *Starlog* No. 220: 46-49. November 1995.

DEADLY GAMES (TV)

___ Bierbaum, Tom. "TV Reviews: *Deadly Games*," *Variety* 360(5): 31. September 4, 1995.

___ Richmond, Ray. "It Plays 'Games' With Logic But Scores Big in Nuttiness," *Los Angeles (CA) Daily News*. September 5, 1995. in: *NewsBank. Film and Television*. 84:D2. 1995.

DEADLY HARVEST (MOTION PICTURE)

___ SEE: CHILDREN OF CORN II: DEADLY HARVEST (MOTION PICTURE).

DEAN, PAMELA

___ Ringel, Faye. "The Scribblies: A Shared World," *Extrapolation* 35(3): 201-210. Fall 1994.

DEATH

___ Hadomi, Leah. "Islands of the Living: Death and Dying in Utopian Fiction," *Utopian Studies* 6(1): 85-101. 1995.

___ Teissl, Verena. "Der tod in drei asugewählten phantastischen texten der Moderne," *Quarber Merkur* 33(2): 34-46. December 1995. (No. 84)

___ Teissl, Verena. "Die Todestehmatik als ein grundlegendes Muster der Phantastik," *Quarber Merkur* 33(1): 54-65. June 1995. (No. 83)

DEATH BECOMES HER (MOTION PICTURE)

___ Arnold, Gary. "*Death*: Plot Sickens While It Thickens (Review)," *Washington (DC) Times*. July 31, 1992. in: *NewsBank. Film and Television*. 68:G4. 1992.

___ Bernard, Jami. "*Death* Is Full of Femmes Fatales (Review)," *New York (NY) Post*. July 31, 1992. in: *NewsBank. Film and Television*. 68:G3. 1992.

___ Biodrowski, Steve. "*Death Becomes Her* (Review)," *Cinefantastique* 23(4): 60. December 1992.

___ Campbell, Bob. "*Death Becomes Her* Falls Victim to Overkill (Review)," *Newark (NJ) Star-Ledger*. July 31, 1992. in: *NewsBank. Film and Television*. 68:G2. 1992.

___ Demaline, Jackie. "Body Language (Review)," *Albany (NY) Times Union*. July 26, 1992. in: *NewsBank. Film and Television*. 68:F9-F10. 1992.

___ Falk, Sally. "Talent and Death Take a Holiday in Oddball Film (Review)," *Indianapolis (IN) Star*. July 31, 1992. in: *NewsBank. Film and Television*. 78:D6-D7. 1992.

___ Hunter, Stephen. "Streep, Hawn Laugh in the Face of Death (Review)," *Baltimore (MD) Sun*. July 31, 1992. in: *NewsBank. Film and Television*. 78:D8. 1992.

___ Johnson, Malcolm. "Despite Good Makeup Job, *Death Becomes Her* an Unflattering Concept (Review)," *Hartford (CT) Courant*. July 31, 1992. in: *NewsBank. Film and Television*. 68:F11-F12. 1992.

___ Lowe, Nick. "*Death Becomes Her* (Review)," *Interzone* No. 69: 38-39. March 1993.

DEATH BECOMES HER (MOTION PICTURE) (continued)

___ Mahar, Ted. " 'Death' Deserves a Proper Burial (Review)," *Portland (OR) The Oregonian*. July 31, 1992. in: *NewsBank. Film and Television*. 78:D9. 1992.

___ Martin, Kevin H. "Life Everlasting," *Cinefex* No. 52: 54-78. November 1992.

___ Movshovitz, Howie. "Streep Adds Life to *Death*, But It's Too Late (Review)," *Denver (CO) Post*. July 31, 1992. in: *NewsBank. Film and Television*. 78:D3. 1992.

___ O'Sullivan, Eleanor. "Streep Smarts," *Neptune (NJ) Asbury Park Press*. July 30, 1992. in: *NewsBank. Film and Television*. 68:F7-F8. 1992.

___ Ringel, Eleanor. "Just Call It Her 'Death' By Vanity (Review)," *Atlanta (GA) Journal*. July 31, 1992. in: *NewsBank. Film and Television*. 78:D4. 1992.

___ Rosenberg, Scott. "Read My Liposuction: *Death Becomes Her* Goes for Vanity Fare (Review)," *San Francisco (CA) Examiner*. July 31, 1992. in: *NewsBank. Film and Television*. 78:D1-D2. 1992.

___ Sachs, Lloyd. " 'Death' Has Grave Flaws (Review)," *Chicago (IL) Sun Times*. July 31, 1992. in: *NewsBank. Film and Television*. 78:D5. 1992.

___ Stark, Susan. "Steep's Spirit Puts Some Life into *Death* (Review)," *Detroit (MI) News*. July 31, 1992. in: *NewsBank. Film and Television*. 68:G1. 1992.

___ Strauss, Bob. "If Only 'Death' Were as Good as Its Looks (Review)," *Los Angeles (CA) Daily News*. July 31, 1992. in: *NewsBank. Film and Television*. 78:C14. 1992.

___ Verniere, James. "Death Trap (Review)," *Boston (MA) Herald*. July 31, 1992. in: *NewsBank. Film and Television*. 68:F13-F14. 1992.

___ Yakir, Dan. "Eternal Beauties," *Starlog* 185: 36-39, 66. December 1992.

DEATH MACHINE (MOTION PICTURE)

___ Jones, Alan. "*Death Machine*," *Cinefantastique* 26(6)/27(1): 94-95, 125. October 1995.

DECAPITRON (MOTION PICTURE)

___ "*Decapitron* Biggest Empire Production Ever, Set for May Start," *Variety* p.4, 38. September 18, 1985.

DECEIT (MOTION PICTURE)

___ Thonen, John. "*Deceit* (Review)," *Cinefantastique* 25(2): 59. April 1994.

DEFINITIONS

___ Bull, Geoff. "Morning Comes Whether You Set the Alarm or Not: Science Fiction, a Genre for the Future," *Orana* (Australia) 31(3): 159-169. August 1995.

___ Disch, Thomas M. "Big Ideas and Dead-End Thrills," *Atlantic* 269(2): 86-94. February 1992.

___ Dyck, Axel. "*Phantastik* oder *phantastische Literatur?*," *Quarber Merkur* 30(2): 61-63. December 1992. (No. 78)

___ Gunn, James E. "The Gatekeepers," in: Gunn, James E. **Inside Science Fiction: Essays on Fantastic Literature**. San Bernardino, CA: Borgo, 1992. pp.52-59.

___ Gunn, James E. "The Worldview of Science Fiction," *Extrapolation* 36(2): 91-95. Summer 1995.

___ Jordan, Anne D. "Future Reading: Science Fiction," *Teaching and Learning Literature* 4(5): 17-23. May/June 1995.

___ Loney, Mark. "SF, Genre, and Conservatism," *Science Fiction: A Review of Speculative Literature* 12(1): 3-8. 1993. (Whole No. 34)

___ McKay, George. "It's Not 'About' Science, It's 'About' Fiction and It's 'About' About," *Foundation* No. 60: 51-57. Spring 1994.

___ Stableford, Brian. "SF: The Nature of the Medium," in: Stableford, Brian. **Opening Minds: Essays on Fantastic Literature**. San Bernardino, CA: Borgo Press, 1995. pp.9-14.

___ Terrel, Denise. "L'Erotisme, un paramètre de définition de la science fiction," in: Bozzetto, Roger, ed. **Eros: Science & Fiction Fantastique**. Aix-en-Provence: Universite de Provence, 1991. pp.191-199.

___ Tiedemann, Mark W. "Science Fiction vs. Fantasy: Part IV: Process and Precept: Natural Differences Between Science Fiction and Fantasy," *Quantum* No. 43/44: 43-38. Spring/Summer 1993.

DEKKER, FRED

___ Johnson, Kim H. "Robodirector," *Starlog* 181: 56-58. August 1992.

DEL ARCO, JONATHAN
___ Jankiewicz, Pat. "Borg to Be Wild," *Starlog* No. 201: 36-39. April 1994.
___ Madsen, Dan. "Jonathan Del Arco: I, Borg," *Star Trek: The Official Fan Club* No. 93: 33-34. September/October 1993.

DEL REY, LESTER
___ "del Rey, Lester (1915-1993) (Obituary)," *Analog* 113(13): 110. November 1993.
___ "del Rey, Lester (Obituary)," *Science Fiction Chronicle* 14(9): 17. June 1993.
___ "del Rey, Lester: Science Fiction Author (Obituary)," *Los Angeles (CA) Times* Sec. A, p. 26. May 14, 1993.
___ "del Rey, Lester, 1915-1993 (Obituary)," *Starlog* No. 196: 22. November 1993.
___ "del Rey, Lester, Dies (Obituary)," *Locus* 30(6): 4, 67-69. June 1993.
___ "Lester del Rey: In Memorium," *Locus* 31(1): 58-59. July 1993.
___ Grace, Dominick M. "Rereading Lester del Rey's 'Helen O'Loy'," *Science Fiction Studies* 20(1): 45-51. March 1993.
___ Pourteau, Chris. "Lester del Rey," in: Bruccoli, Matthew J., ed. **Facts on File Bibliography of American Fiction 1919-1988.** New York: Facts on File, 1991. pp.142-143.

DeLANCIE, JOHN
___ Altman, Mark A. "*Star Trek: The Next Generation*: Guess Q's Coming to Dinner?," *Cinefantastique* 24(3/4): 47-49. October 1993.

DELANY, BESSIE
___ "Delany, Bessie (Obituary)," *Locus* 35(5): 78. November 1995.

DELANY, SAMUEL R.
___ "Delany Back in Print," *Locus* 31(4): 6, 70. October 1993.
___ "Delany Novel to Launch Small Press," *Locus* 28(2): 6, 68. August 1992.
___ "Paradoxa Interview: Samuel R. Delany," *Paradoxa* 1(3): 257-286. 1995.
___ "Samuel R. Delany: Teaching and Writing," *Locus* 35(5): 4-5, 82, 84. November 1995.
___ Bartlett, Karen J. "Subversive Desire: Sex and Ethics in Delany's **Dahlgren**," *New York Review of Science Fiction* No. 75: 1, 3-7. November 1994.
___ Blackford, Russell. "Hi-Tech, Samuel R. Delany, and the Transhuman Condition," *New York Review of Science Fiction* No. 74: 1, 3-6. October 1994.
___ Broderick, Damien. "The Multiplicity of Worlds, of Others," *Foundation* No. 55: 66-81. Summer 1992.
___ Broderick, Damien. "SF as Modular Calculus," *Southern Review: Literary and Interdisciplinary Essays* (Australia) 24(1): 43-53. March 1991.
___ Clayton, David. "The Apocalyptic Mirage: Violence and Eschatology in **Dhalgren**," in: Slusser, George and Eric S. Rabkin, eds. **Fights of Fancy: Armed Conflict in Science Fiction and Fantasy.** Athens, GA: University of Georgia Press, 1993. pp.132-144.
___ Davis, Ray. "Delany's Dirt," *New York Review of Science Fiction* No. 84: 1, 8-13. August 1995.
___ Delany, Samuel R. "Anthony Davis, a Conversation," in: Delany, Samuel R. **Silent Interviews on Language, Race, Sex, Science Fiction and Some Comics.** Hanover, NH: Wesleyan University Press, 1994. pp.289-311.
___ Delany, Samuel R. "Introduction: Reading and the Written Interview," in: Delany, Samuel R. **Silent Interviews on Language, Race, Sex, Science Fiction and Some Comics.** Hanover, NH: Wesleyan University Press, 1994. pp.1-20.
___ Delany, Samuel R. **Silent Interviews on Language, Race, Sex, Science Fiction and Some Comics.** Hanover, NH: Wesleyan University Press, 1994. 322pp.
___ Dery, Mark. "Black to the Future: Interviews with Samuel R. Delany, Greg Tate, and Tricia Rose," *South Atlantic Quarterly* 92(4): 735-788. Fall 1993. (Reprinted in: Dery, Mark, Ed. **Flame Wars: The Discourse of Cyberculture.** Durham, NC: Duke University Press, 1994.)
___ Fox, Robert E. **The Mirrors of Caliban: A Study of the Fiction of LeRoi Jones (Imamu Amiri Baraka), Ishmael Reed, and Samuel R. Delany.** Ph.D. Dissertation, State University of New York at Buffalo, 1974. 407pp. (DAI 37: 5121A.)

DELANY, SAMUEL R. (continued)
___ Gregory, Sinda. "The Semiology of Silence: The *Science Fiction Studies* Interview," by Sinda Gregory and Larry McCaffery. in: Delany, Samuel R. **Silent Interviews on Language, Race, Sex, Science Fiction and Some Comics.** Hanover, NH: Wesleyan University Press, 1994. pp.21-58.
___ Grossman, Susan. "The Susan Grossman Interview," in: Delany, Samuel R. **Silent Interviews on Language, Race, Sex, Science Fiction and Some Comics.** Hanover, NH: Wesleyan University Press, 1994. pp.250-268.
___ Hassler, Donald M. "Urban Pastoral and Labored Ease of Samuel R. Delany," in: Hakutani, Yoshinobu and Butler, Robert, eds. **The City in African-American Literature.** Rutherford, NJ: Fairleigh Dickinson University Press, 1995. pp.227-235.
___ Hemingway, Lloyd. "Toto, We're Back: The *Cottonwood Review* Interview," by Lloyd Hemingway and Johan Heye. in: Delany, Samuel R. **Silent Interviews on Language, Race, Sex, Science Fiction and Some Comics.** Hanover, NH: Wesleyan University Press, 1994. pp.59-82.
___ James, Kenneth. "The Kenneth James Interview," in: Delany, Samuel R. **Silent Interviews on Language, Race, Sex, Science Fiction and Some Comics.** Hanover, NH: Wesleyan University Press, 1994. pp.233-249.
___ Kincaid, Paul. "A Perfectly Mysterious Process: Samuel R. Delany Interviewed," *Vector* No. 186: 8-14. December 1995.
___ Malmgren, Carl D. "The Languages of Science Fiction: Samuel Delaney's **Babel 17**," *Extrapolation* 34(1): 5-17. Spring 1993.
___ O'Neill, Dennis. "Refractions of Empire: The *Comics Journal* Interview," in: Delany, Samuel R. **Silent Interviews on Language, Race, Sex, Science Fiction and Some Comics.** Hanover, NH: Wesleyan University Press, 1994. pp.83-126.
___ Penley, Constance. "Sword & Sorcery, S/M, and the Economics of Inadequation: The *Camera Obscura* Interview," by Constance Penley and Sharon Willis. in: Delany, Samuel R. **Silent Interviews on Language, Race, Sex, Science Fiction and Some Comics.** Hanover, NH: Wesleyan University Press, 1994. pp.127-163.
___ Reed-Pharrr, Robert F. "Sex, Race, and Science Fiction: The *Callaloo* Interview," in: Delany, Samuel R. **Silent Interviews on Language, Race, Sex, Science Fiction and Some Comics.** Hanover, NH: Wesleyan University Press, 1994. pp.216-229.
___ Samuelson, David N. "Necessary Constraints: Samuel R. Delany on Science Fiction," *Foundation* No. 60: 21-41. Spring 1994.
___ Steiner, K. Leslie. "The K. Leslie Steiner Interview," in: Delany, Samuel R. **Silent Interviews on Language, Race, Sex, Science Fiction and Some Comics.** Hanover, NH: Wesleyan University Press, 1994. pp.269-288.
___ Tate, Greg. "Ghetto in the Sky: Samuel Delany's Black Whole," in: Tate, Greg. **Flyboy in the Buttermilk: Essays on Contemporary America.** New York: Simon & Schuster, 1992. pp.159-167.
___ Tatsumi, Takayuki. "Science Fiction and Criticism: The *Diacritics* Interview," in: Delany, Samuel R. **Silent Interviews on Language, Race, Sex, Science Fiction and Some Comics.** Hanover, NH: Wesleyan University Press, 1994. pp.186-215.
___ Tatsumi, Takayuki. "Some Real Mothers: The *SF Eye* Interview," in: Delany, Samuel R. **Silent Interviews on Language, Race, Sex, Science Fiction and Some Comics.** Hanover, NH: Wesleyan University Press, 1994. pp.164-185.
___ Zajac, Ronald J. **The Dystopian City in British and United States Science Fiction, 1960-1975: Urban Chronotopes as Models of Historical Closure.** Master's Thesis, McGill University, 1992. 104pp. (Master's Abstracts 31/03, p. 1020. Fall 1993.)
___ Zaldivar, Marc. "Delany's **Neveryona**: Re(textu)ality," *New York Review of Science Fiction* No. 78: 16-20. February 1995.

DELAPLACE, BARBARA
___ "Compuserve HOMer Awards, 1992," *Science Fiction Chronicle* 14(9): 4-5. June 1993.

DELGADO, RICHARD
___ Salter, David I. "*Star Trek: Deep Space Nine*: Conceptual Artist Richard Delgado," *Cinefantastique* 23(6): 36-37. April 1993.

DELICATESSEN (MOTION PICTURE)
___ "Homme on Wry From Comic Deli (Review)," *Washington (DC) Times*. April 17, 1992. in: *NewsBank. Film and Television.* 40:G2. 1992.

DELICATESSEN (MOTION PICTURE) (continued)
___ Bernard, Jami. "Glad to Meet Chew (Review)," *New York (NY) Post.* April 3, 1992. in: *NewsBank. Film and Television.* 40:G1. 1992.
___ Johnson, Barry. "*Delicatessen* a Good Film to Gobble Up (Review)," *Portland (OR) The Oregonian.* May 8, 1992. in: *NewsBank. Film and Television.* 51:G1. 1992.
___ Johnson, Malcolm. "A Delicious Vision of the Future (Review)," *Hartford (CT) Courant.* June 19, 1992. in: *NewsBank. Film and Television.* 63:E3. 1992.
___ Meyers, Joe. "*Delicatessen*: Python-Lovers Will Eat It Up (Review)," *Bridgeport (CT) Post.* July 10, 1992. in: *NewsBank. Film and Television.* 68:G5-G6. 1992.
___ Movshovitz, Howie. "*Delicatessen* Bizarre, Original (Review)," *Denver (CO) Post.* May 8, 1992. in: *NewsBank. Film and Television.* 51: F12. 1992.
___ Persons, Dan. "*Delicatessen* (Review)," *Cinefantastique* 23(2/3): 122. October 1992.
___ Persons, Dan. "*Delicatessen* (Review)," *Cinefantastique* 23(4): 59. December 1992.
___ Persons, Dan. "Dominique Pinon on Clowning in *Delicatessen*," *Cinefantastique* 23(4): 58-59. December 1992.
___ Ringel, Eleanor. "Cannibal House: This *Delicatessen* Dishes Up Hilarious Helpings of Dark Farce (Review)," *Atlanta (GA) Journal.* May 29, 1992. in: *NewsBank. Film and Television.* 51:F13-F14. 1992.
___ Sherman, Paul. "*Delicatessen* a Juicy Delight (Review)," *Boston (MA) Herald.* April 17, 1992. in: *NewsBank. Film and Television.* 40: F14. 1992.
___ Shulgasser, Barbara. "Guess Who We're Having for Dinner: French Co-Directors' *Delicatessen* Is a Mouthful, and Full of Belly Laughs (Review)," *San Francisco (CA) Examiner.* April 10, 1992. in: *NewsBank. Film and Television.* 40:F13. 1992.
___ Strauss, Bob. "Ham on Wry at *Deli* (Review)," *Los Angeles (CA) Daily News.* April 10, 1992. in: *NewsBank. Film and Television.* 51:F11. 1992.

DeLISSER, HERBERT
___ Harkins, Patricia. " 'Spells of Darkness': Invisibility in **The White Witch of Rosehall**," *Journal of the Fantastic in the Arts* 4(2): 49-64. 1992. (No. 14)

DELIVER US FROM EVIL (MOTION PICTURE)
___ SEE: PROM NIGHT IV: DELIVER US FROM EVIL (MOTION PICTURE).

DELL MAGAZINES
___ Knight, Damon. "Dell Magazine Contract," *SFWA Bulletin* 28(2): 2-4. Summer 1994. (No. 124)
___ Knight, Damon. "Dell Magazines Contract Update," *SFWA Bulletin* 28(3): 2. Winter 1994. (No. 125)

DELLAMORTE DELLAMORE (MOTION PICTURE)
___ Jones, Alan. "*Dellamorte Dellamore*," *Cinefantastique* 25(5): 52-55. October 1994.
___ Jones, Alan. "Fumetti Inspiration," *Cinefantastique* 25(5): 54. October 1994.

DeLUISE, MICHAEL
___ Wilson, Bill. "Gill Man," *Starlog* No. 211: 46-49. February 1995.

DeLUISE, PETER
___ Wilson, Bill. "Mutant Hero," *Starlog* No. 214: 50-52, 69. May 1995.

DEMOGRAPHICS
___ Robins, J. Max. "Gen X Marks the Spot," by J. Max Robins and Brian Lowry. *Variety* 358(7): 1, 63. March 20, 1995.

DEMOLITION MAN (MOTION PICTURE)
___ Altman, Mark A. "*Demolition Man* (Review)," *Cinefantastique* 25(2): 59. April 1994.
___ Arar, Yardena. "Snipes, Stallone Duke It Out in Engaging 'Demolition' (Review)," *Los Angeles (CA) Daily News* October 8, 1993. in: *NewsBank. Film and Television.* 114:G4. 1993.
___ Biodrowski, Steve. "Stallone: *Demolition Man*," *Cinefantastique* 24(3/4): 4-6. October 1993.
___ Bowman, Jon. "*Demolition Man* Movie Version of an Action-Packed Comic Book (Review)," *(Santa Fe, NM) New Mexican* October 15, 1993. in: *NewsBank. Film and Television.* 115:A3. 1993.

DEMOLITION MAN (MOTION PICTURE) (continued)
___ Caine, Barry. "Stallone's *Demolition Man* Pretty Bizarre, But Fascinating (Review)," *Oakland (CA) Tribune* October 9, 1993. in: *NewsBank. Film and Television.* 114:G5-G6. 1993.
___ Campbell, Bob. "*Demolition Man* Self Destructs Before Our Eyes (Review)," *Newark (NJ) Star-Ledger* October 8, 1993. in: *NewsBank. Art.* 28:B14. 1993.
___ Counts, Kyle. "Join *Demolition Man* Sylvester Stallone on the Set of His Near Future SF Thriller," *Science Fiction Age* 2(1): 20-22, 90. November 1993.
___ Duncan, Jody. "Fire and Ice," *Cinefex* No. 57: 42-69. March 1994.
___ Johnson, Malcolm. " 'Demolition' Roll to a Crash Finish (Review)," *Hartford (CT) Courant.* October 9, 1993. in: *NewsBank. Art.* 28:B13. 1993.
___ Leydon, Joe. " 'Demo Man' Full of Surprises (Review)," *Houston (TX) Post.* October 9, 1993. in: *NewsBank. Film and Television.* 115:A6. 1993.
___ Lowe, Nick. "*Demolition Man* (Review)," *Interzone* No. 81: 38-39. March 1994.
___ Lyman, David. "Wit, Violence Smashing Hits in 'Demo Man' (Review)," *Cincinnati (OH) Enquirer* October 8, 1993. in: *NewsBank. Art.* 28:C1. 1993.
___ McKerrow, Steve. "*Demolition Man* Looks Awfully Familiar (Review)," *Baltimore (MD) Sun* October 9, 1993. in: *NewsBank. Film and Television.* 114:G12. 1993.
___ Pierce, Susan. "Giggles, Thrills, a la Stallone," *(Little Rock) Arkasas Democrat.* October 13, 1993. in: *NewsBank. Film and Television.* 114: G2-G3. 1993.
___ Shapiro, Marc. "*Demolition Man*," *Starlog* No. 195: 32-37, 72. October 1993.
___ Shapiro, Marc. "Sleeper Cop," *Starlog* No. 196: 27-30. November 1993.
___ Sheehan, Henry. "*Demolition Man* Makes Lots of Noise (Review)," *Santa Ana (CA) Orange County Register* October 8, 1993. in: *NewsBank. Film and Television.* 114:G9-G10. 1993.
___ Shipiro, Marc. "Some Kind of Mutant," *Starlog* No. 197: 27-30. December 1993.
___ Shulgasser, Barbara. "An Old-Fashioned Cop in the Future (Review)," *San Francisco (CA) Examiner* October 8, 1993. in: *NewsBank. Film and Television.* 114:G7. 1993.
___ Terry, Clifford. "I Thought I Thaw a Rambo (Review)," *San Jose (CA) Mercury News* October 9, 1993. in: *NewsBank. Film and Television.* 114:G8. 1993.
___ Wuntch, Phillip. "Blasting Subtley Off the Screen (Review)," *Dallas (TX) Morning News.* October 9, 1993. in: *NewsBank. Film and Television.* 115:A5. 1993.
___ Wuntch, Phillip. "It's Funny; It's Smart; It's Splashy (Review)" (Reprinted from *Dallas Morning News*). *Richmond (VA) Times-Dispatch* October 9, 1993. in: *NewsBank. Film and Television.* 115:A7. 1993.

DEMON KNIGHT (MOTION PICTURE)
___ SEE: TALES FROM THE CRYPT: DEMON KNIGHT (MOTION PICTURE).

DEMONS
___ Noll, Richard. **Vampires, Werewolves, and Demons: Twentieth Century Reports in the Psychiatric Literature.** New York: Brunner, 1992. 244pp.

DEMONWARP (MOTION PICTURE)
___ "*Demonwarp* (Review)," *Variety* p. 13. March 30, 1988.

DENMARK
___ "*Valhalla* First Danish Animation to Go Feature Length Since War," *Variety* p. 43. February 27, 1985.
___ Engholm, Ahrvid. "SF in the Nordic Countries," *Locus* 34(4): 39. April 1995.

DENNING, RICHARD
___ Weaver, Tom. "Richard Denning," in: Weaver, Tom. **They Fought the Creature Features: Interviews with 23 Classic Horror, Science Fiction and Serial Stars.** Jefferson, NC: McFarland, 1995. pp.145-160.

DENSHAM, PENRAY
___ Garcia, Frank. "*The Outer Limits*," *Starlog* No. 214: 54-57. May 1995.

DENT, LESTER
___ Cannady, Marilyn. **Bigger Than Life: The Creator of Doc Savage**. Bowling Green, OH: Popular Press, 1990. 201pp.

DENTON, BRADLEY
___ "Denton, Kessel Win Campbell, Sturgeon Awards," *Locus* 29(3): 6. September 1992.
___ "Denton, Kessel Win Campbell, Sturgeon Awards," *Science Fiction Chronicle* 14(1): 5. October 1992.
___ Sinor, Bradley H. "Greetings From Ganymede," *Starlog* No. 207: 75-77. October 1994.

DERLETH, AUGUST
___ Price, Robert M. "August Derleth: Myth-Maker," in: Price, Robert M., ed. **Black Forbidden Things**. Mercer Island, WA: Starmont, 1992. pp.72-73.
___ Price, Robert M. "The Last Vestige of the Derleth Mythos," *Lovecraft Studies* No. 24: 20-21. Spring 1991.
___ Spencer, Paul. "The Shadow Over Derleth," in: Schweitzer, Darrell, ed. **Discovering Classic Horror Fiction I**. Mercer Island, WA: Starmont, 1992. pp.114-119.

DERN, LAURA
___ Warren, Bill. "Dinosaur Huntress," in: McDonnell, David, ed. **Starlog's Science Fiction Heroes and Heroines**. New York: Crescent Books, 1995. pp.73-76.

DERR, RICHARD
___ Williams, Wade. "Behind the Scenes with Richard Derr, **When Worlds Collide**," *Filmfax* No. 30: 50-59. December 1991/January 1992.

DESTINATION MOON (MOTION PICTURE)
___ "Docu a Highlight of George Pal Tribute," *Variety* p. 2, 108. August 27, 1986.
___ Heinlein, Robert A. "Shooting **Destination Moon**," in: Kondo, Yoji, ed. **Requiem: New Collected Works by Robert A. Heinlein and Tributes to the Grand Master**. New York: Tor, 1992. pp.117-131.
___ Weaver, Tom. "Lunar Destiny," *Starlog* No. 202: 60-65. May 1994.

DETECTIVE FICTION
___ Becker, Lucille F. "Science and Detective Fiction: Complementary Genres on the Margins of French Literature," *French Literature Series* 20: 119-125. 1993.
___ Gomel, Elana. "Mystery, Apocalypse and Utopia: The Case of the Ontological Detective Story," *Science Fiction Studies* 22(3): 343-356. November 1995.
___ Guillaud, Lauric. "Paranormal Detectives: Sherlock Holmes in the House of Usher," *Paradoxa* 1(3): 301-319. 1995.

DETECTIVES IN SF
___ Gray, W. Russell. "Science Fiction Detectives, (or, Stick 'em Up! I Picked Your Pocket With My Invisible Third Hand After You Handcuffed Me)," *Mid-Atlantic Almanack: Journal of the Mid Atlantic Popular American Culture Association* 2: 46-53. 1993.
___ Guillaud, Lauric. "Paranormal Detectives: Sherlock Holmes in the House of Usher," *Paradoxa* 1(3): 301-319. 1995.

DEVIL
___ Testa, Carlo. **Desire and the Devil: Demonic Contracts in French and European Literature**. New York: Peter Lang, 1991. 192pp.

DEVIL DOLL (MOTION PICTURE)
___ Sevastakis, Michael. **Songs of Love and Death: The Classical American Horror Film of the 1930s**. Westport, CT: Greenwood, 1993. 232pp.

DEVIL'S DAUGHTER (MOTION PICTURE)
___ Harris, Judith P. "**The Devil's Daughter** (Review)," *Cinefantastique* 23(2/3): 122. October 1992.

DI FATE, VINCENT
___ "Vincent Di Fate: The Mind's Eye," *Locus* 30(2): 4, 70. February 1993.
___ Bova, Ben. "Future Di Fate," *Science Fiction Age* 2(3): 70-75. March 1994.

DIALOGUE
___ Asimov, Isaac. "Dialog," in: Dozois, Gardner, ed. **Writing Science Fiction and Fantasy**. New York: St. Martin's, 1991. pp.33-37.
___ Barnes, John. "Demand, Response, Reaction: A Troubleshooting Technique for Dialogue," *The Report: The Fiction Writer's Magazine* No. 10: 5-7. Summer 1993.

DICK AND MARGE SAVE THE WORLD (MOTION PICTURE)
___ Warren, Bill. "Some Call Him Tod," *Starlog* No. 176: 46-49. March 1992.
___ Warren, Bill. "Spengo's Greatest Director," *Starlog* 177: 63-66. April 1992.

DICK, ANNE
___ Dick, Philip K. "A Letter to Anthony Boucher/A Letter From Anne Dick," *PKDS Newsletter* No. 30: 1-4. December 1992.

DICK, KAY
___ McKay, George. "Kay Dick's **They** and Rudyard Kipling's **They**: Intertextual Politicisation and the Grand End of Narrative," *Foundation* No. 58: 62-75. Summer 1993.

DICK, PHILIP K.
___ "Flow My Tears: The Correspondence," *PKDS Newsletter* No. 28: 6, 9. March 1992.
___ "An Interview With Paul Williams: Reflection on Phil Dick, Part 1," *Radio Free P.K.D.* No. 1: 4-5, 10. February 1993.
___ "Memories and Visions: Fans and Fellow Writers Remember Philip K. Dick," *New York Review of Science Fiction* No. 70: 4-7. June 1994.
___ "Philip K. Dick: The Greatest Novels," *New York Review of Science Fiction* No. 70: 1, 3-4. June 1994.
___ "Philip K. Dick: The Mainstream Novels," *New York Review of Science Fiction* No. 74: 12-18. October 1994.
___ "Philip K. Dick Told FBI Disch Novel Contained Codes," *Science Fiction Chronicle* 15(4): 6. February 1994.
___ "Philip K. Dick Weekend," *Locus* 28(1): 39. January 1992.
___ "The Religious Visions of Philip K. Dick," *New York Review of Science Fiction* No. 77: 12-16. January 1995.
___ Abrash, Merritt. "Dick and SF Scholarship: A Failure of Scholarship," in: Mullen, R. D., ed. **On Philip K. Dick: 40 Articles From Science-Fiction Studies**. Terre Haute, IN: SF-TH Inc., 1992. pp.123-124.
___ Abrash, Merritt. "Dick and SF Scholarship: In Response to George Slusser," in: Mullen, R. D., ed. **On Philip K. Dick: 40 Articles From Science-Fiction Studies**. Terre Haute, IN: SF-TH Inc., 1992. pp.129-130.
___ Abrash, Merritt. " 'Man Everywhere in Chains': Dick, Rousseau, and **The Penultimate Truth**," in: Umland, Samuel J., ed. **Philip K. Dick: Contemporary Critical Interpretations**. Westport, CT: Greenwood, 1995. pp.157-168.
___ Aldiss, Brian W. "Dick's Maledictory Web: About and Around **The Martian Time-Slip**," in: Mullen, R. D., ed. **On Philip K. Dick: 40 Articles From Science-Fiction Studies**. Terre Haute, IN: SF-TH Inc., 1992. pp.37-40.
___ Aldiss, Brian W. "What Did the Policeman Say? In Memoriam PKD," *PKDS Newsletter* No. 29: 1. September 1992.
___ Aldiss, Brian W. "A Whole New Can of Worms," in: Aldiss, Brian W. **The Detached Retina: Aspects of SF and Fantasy**. Syracuse, NY: Syracuse University Press, 1995. pp.44-51.
___ Barricelli, Jean-Pierre. "Afterword: The Morigny Conference," in: Mullen, R. D., ed. **On Philip K. Dick: 40 Articles From Science-Fiction Studies**. Terre Haute, IN: SF-TH Inc., 1992. pp.236.
___ Black, D. S. "**Blade Runner** Revisited," *PKDS Newsletter* No. 28: 7-8. March 1992.
___ Bozzetto, Roger. "Dick in France: A Love Story," in: Mullen, R. D., ed. **On Philip K. Dick: 40 Articles From Science-Fiction Studies**. Terre Haute, IN: SF-TH Inc., 1992. pp.153-160.
___ Burgheim, Manfred G. "Philip K. Dicks **Ubik** und Thomas Pynchons **Die Versteigerung von No. 49**: Zwei romane, ein epistemologisches Modell," *Quarber Merkur* 33(2): 25-29. December 1995. (No. 84)
___ Campbell, Laura E. "Dickian Time in **The Man in the High Castle**," *Extrapolation* 33(3): 190-201. Fall 1992.
___ Carrere, Emmanuel. **Je suis vivant et vous etes morts: Philip K. Dick, 1928-1982**. Paris: Editions du Seuil, 1993. 358pp.
___ Carter, Cassie. "The Metacolonization of Dick's **The Man in the High Castle**: Mimicry, Parasitism, and Americanism in the PSA," *Science Fiction Studies* 22(3): 333-342. November 1995

DICK, PHILIP K.

DICK, PHILIP K. (continued)
___ Perez, Dan. "Dan O'Bannon Brings Philip K. Dick's Nightmare Visions to Life in **Screamers**," *Science Fiction Age* 3(6): 18-22, 101. 1995.
___ Philmus, Robert M. "The Two Faces of Philip K. Dick," *Science Fiction Studies* 18(1): 91-103. March 1991.
___ Philmus, Robert M. "The Two Faces of Philip K. Dick," in: Mullen, R. D., ed. **On Philip K. Dick: 40 Articles From Science-Fiction Studies**. Terre Haute, IN: SF-TH Inc., 1992. pp.246-256.
___ Pierce, Hazel. "Philip K. Dick," in: Bruccoli, Matthew J., ed. **Facts on File Bibliography of American Fiction 1919-1988**. New York: Facts on File, 1991. pp.146-149.
___ Pinsky, Michael. **Paradise Deferred: Autobiography as Metaphor and the Effacement of Structure in Philip K. Dick**. Master's Thesis, University of South Florida, 1992. 36pp.
___ Rabkin, Eric S. "Irrational Expectations: Or, How Economics and the Post-Industrial World Failed Philip K. Dick," in: Mullen, R. D., ed. **On Philip K. Dick: 40 Articles From Science-Fiction Studies**. Terre Haute, IN: SF-TH Inc., 1992. pp.178-187.
___ Rickman, Gregg. "Dick, Deception, and Dissociation: A Comment on 'The Two Faces of Philip K. Dick'," in: Mullen, R. D., ed. **On Philip K. Dick: 40 Articles From Science-Fiction Studies**. Terre Haute, IN: SF-TH Inc., 1992. pp.262-264.
___ Rickman, Gregg. "The Nature of Dick's Fantasies," in: Mullen, R. D., ed. **On Philip K. Dick: 40 Articles From Science-Fiction Studies**. Terre Haute, IN: SF-TH Inc., 1992. pp.275-277.
___ Rickman, Gregg. " 'What Is This Sickness?': 'Schizophrenia' and **We Can Build You**," in: Umland, Samuel J., ed. **Philip K. Dick: Contemporary Critical Interpretations**. Westport, CT: Greenwood, 1995. pp.143-156.
___ Rieder, John. "The Metafictive World of **The Man in the High Castle**: Hermeneutics, Ethics, and Political Ideology," in: Mullen, R. D., ed. **On Philip K. Dick: 40 Articles From Science-Fiction Studies**. Terre Haute, IN: SF-TH Inc., 1992. pp.223-231.
___ Robinson, Kim S. "Dick and SF Scholarship: Whose Failure of Scholarship?," in: Mullen, R. D., ed. **On Philip K. Dick: 40 Articles From Science-Fiction Studies**. Terre Haute, IN: SF-TH Inc., 1992. pp.125-126.
___ Slusser, George E. "Dick and SF Scholarship: Scholars and Pedants," in: Mullen, R. D., ed. **On Philip K. Dick: 40 Articles From Science-Fiction Studies**. Terre Haute, IN: SF-TH Inc., 1992. pp.127-128.
___ Slusser, George E. "History, Historicity, Story," in: Mullen, R. D., ed. **On Philip K. Dick: 40 Articles From Science-Fiction Studies**. Terre Haute, IN: SF-TH Inc., 1992. pp.199-222.
___ Spinelli, Ernesto. "Philip K. Dick and the Philosophy of Uncertainty," *PKDS Newsletter* No. 28: 19-22. March 1992.
___ Stableford, Brian. "The Creators of Science Fiction, 4: Philip K. Dick," *Interzone* No. 101: 54-57. November 1995.
___ Stableford, Brian. "Little Victories: The Heartfelt Fiction of Philip K. Dick," in: Stableford, Brian. **Outside the Human Aquarium: Masters of Science Fiction**. San Bernardino, CA: Borgo, 1995. pp.99-107.
___ Stanley, John. "The Fantastic Life of an Ordinary Man, Philip K. Dick," *San Francisco (CA) Chronicle. Datebook.* pp.27-30. September 19, 1993.
___ Stephensen-Payne, Phil. **Philip Kindred Dick: Metaphysical Conjurer, a Working Bibliography**, by Phil Stephensen-Payne and Gordon Benson, Jr. Albuquerque, NM: Galactic Central, 1995. 154pp. (4th Revised Ed.)
___ Sutin, Lawrence, ed. **The Shifting Realities of Philip K. Dick: Selected Literary and Philosophical Writings**. New York: Pantheon, 1995. 350pp.
___ Suvin, Darko. "The Opus: Artifice as Refuge and World View (Introductory Reflections)," in: Mullen, R. D., ed. **On Philip K. Dick: 40 Articles From Science-Fiction Studies**. Terre Haute, IN: SF-TH Inc., 1992. pp.2-15.
___ Teissl, Verena. "Der tod in drei asugewählten phantastischen texten der Moderne," *Quarber Merkur* 33(2): 34-46. December 1995. (No. 84)
___ Tiptree, James, Jr. "A Genius Darkly: A Letter to Ted White on Philip K. Dick," *New York Review of Science Fiction* No. 63: 16. November 1993.
___ Trokhachev, Sergei. "Escape to **The High Castle**," *Radio Free P K D* No. 5: 1, 9-11. August 1995.
___ Truchlar, Leo. "Philip K. Dick, **Ubik** (1969)," in: Heuermann, Harmut, ed. **Der Science Fiction Roman in der angloamerikanischen Literatur: Interpretationen**. Düsseldorf: Bagel, 1986. pp.315-330.

DICK, PHILIP K. (continued)
___ Tumey, Paul C. "The First Annual Philip K. Dick Convention: Opening Address," *New York Review of Science Fiction* No. 70: 1, 3-4. June 1994.
___ Turan, Kenneth. "**Blade Runner** 2," *Radio Free P.K.D.* No. 1: 2-3, 9. February 1993.
___ Umland, Rebecca A. "Unrequited Love in **We Can Build You**," in: Umland, Samuel J., ed. **Philip K. Dick: Contemporary Critical Interpretations**. Westport, CT: Greenwood, 1995. pp.127-142.
___ Umland, Samuel J. " 'Faith of Our Fathers': A Comparison of the Original Manuscript with the Published Text," *PKDS Newsletter* No. 29: 12-14. September 1992.
___ Umland, Samuel J. "Introduction," in: Umland, Samuel J., ed. **Philip K. Dick: Contemporary Critical Interpretations**. Westport, CT: Greenwood, 1995. pp.1-6.
___ Umland, Samuel J. "To Flee From Dionysus: *Euthousiasmos* From 'Upon the Dull Earth' to **VALIS**," in: Umland, Samuel J., ed. **Philip K. Dick: Contemporary Critical Interpretations**. Westport, CT: Greenwood, 1995. pp.81-100.
___ Umland, Samuel J., ed. **Philip K. Dick: Contemporary Critical Interpretations**. Westport, CT: Greenwood, 1995. 240pp.
___ Warrick, Patricia S. "The Encounter of Taoism and Fascism in **The Man in the High Castle**," in: Mullen, R. D., ed. **On Philip K. Dick: 40 Articles From Science-Fiction Studies**. Terre Haute, IN: SF-TH Inc., 1992. pp.74-79.
___ Warrick, Patricia S. "In Memory of Philip K. Dick," in: Mullen, R. D., ed. **On Philip K. Dick: 40 Articles From Science-Fiction Studies**. Terre Haute, IN: SF-TH Inc., 1992. pp.80-91.
___ Watson, Ian. "Le Guin's **Lathe of Heaven** and the Role of Dick: The False Reality as Mediator," in: Mullen, R. D., ed. **On Philip K. Dick: 40 Articles From Science-Fiction Studies**. Terre Haute, IN: SF-TH Inc., 1992. pp.63-72.
___ Wessel, Karl. "Worlds of Chance and Counterfeit: Dick, Lem, and the Preestablished Cacaphony," in: Umland, Samuel J., ed. **Philip K. Dick: Contemporary Critical Interpretations**. Westport, CT: Greenwood, 1995. pp.43-60.
___ Wolfe, Gary K. "Not Quite Coming to Terms," in: Mullen, R. D., ed. **On Philip K. Dick: 40 Articles From Science-Fiction Studies**. Terre Haute, IN: SF-TH Inc., 1992. pp.237-239.
___ Wolk, Anthony. "The Swiss Connection: Psychological Systems in the Novels of Philip K. Dick," in: Umland, Samuel J., ed. **Philip K. Dick: Contemporary Critical Interpretations**. Westport, CT: Greenwood, 1995. pp.101-126.
___ Zajac, Ronald J. **The Dystopian City in British and United States Science Fiction, 1960-1975: Urban Chronotopes as Models of Historical Closure**. Master's Thesis, McGill University, 1992. 104pp. (Master's Abstracts 31/03, p. 1020. Fall 1993.)
___ Zhu, Jianjiong. "Reality, Fiction, and *Wu* in **The Man in the High Castle**," *Journal of the Fantastic in the Arts* 5(3): 36-45. 1993. (No. 19)
___ Zhu, Jianjiong. "Reality, Fiction, and *Wu* in **The Man in the High Castle**," in: Ruddick, Nicholas, ed. **State of the Fantastic**. Westport, CT: Greenwood, 1992. pp.107-114.
___ Zoreda, Margaret L. "Bakhtin, Blobels and Philip K. Dick," *Journal of Popular Culture* 28(3): 55-61. Winter 1994.

DICKSON, GORDON R.
___ Butvin, Susan M. "**The Final Encyclopedia** Gordon R. Dickson's Creative Universe," *Extrapolation* 36(4): 360-368. Winter 1995.

DIE WATCHING (MOTION PICTURE)
___ Wilt, David. "**Die Watching** (Review)," *Cinefantastique* 24(6)/25(1): 123. February 1994.

DIE, DARKMAN, DIE (MOTION PICTURE)
___ SEE: DARKMAN III: DIE, DARKMAN, DIE (MOTION PICTURE).

DILLARD, ANNIE
___ Bicchieri, Sarah N. **Quantum Physics and Annie Dillard: Parallels in Science and Literature**. Master's Thesis, Central Washington University, 1993. 85pp.

DIME NOVELS
___ Bleiler, Everett F. "Dime Novel Science-Fiction," *AB Bookmans Weekly* 96(17): 1542-1550. October 23, 1995.

DOCTOR WHO (TV)

DOCTOR WHO (TV) (continued)
___ Tulloch, John. "Positioning the SF Audience: *Star Trek*, *Doctor Who* and the Texts of Science Fiction," in: Tulloch, John and Jenkins, Henry, eds. **Science Fiction Audiences: Watching Doctor Who and Star Trek.** New York: Routledge, 1995. pp.25-49.
___ Tulloch, John. **Science Fiction Audiences: Doctor Who, Star Trek, and Their Fans.** London: Routledge, 1994. 294pp.
___ Tulloch, John. "Throwing a Little Bit of Poison into Future Generations: *Doctor Who* Audiences and Ideology," in: Tulloch, John and Jenkins, Henry, eds. **Science Fiction Audiences: Watching Doctor Who and Star Trek.** New York: Routledge, 1995. pp.67-85.
___ Tulloch, John. "We're Only a Speck in the Ocean: The Fans as Powerless Elite," in: Tulloch, John and Jenkins, Henry, eds. **Science Fiction Audiences: Watching Doctor Who and Star Trek.** New York: Routledge, 1995. pp.144-172.

DOLLENS, MORRIS SCOTT
___ "Dollens, Morris Scott (Obituary)," *Locus* 33(3): 78. September 1994.
___ "Dollens, Morris Scott (Obituary)," *Locus* 33(4): 70. October 1994.
___ "Dollens, Morris Scott (Obituary)," *Science Fiction Chronicle* 15(10): 19-20. September 1994.

DOLLMAN (MOTION PICTURE)
___ "*Dollman* (Review)," *Cinefantastique* 22(5): 60. April 1992.

DOLLY DEAREST (MOTION PICTURE)
___ "*Dolly Dearest* (Review)," *Cinefantastique* 22(5): 60. April 1992.

DOLPHINS
___ Wytenbroek, J. R. "Cetacean Consciousness in Katz's **Whalesinger** and L'Engle's **A Ring of Endless Light**," in: Reynolds, Patricia and GoodKnight, Glen H., eds. **Proceedings of the J. R. R. Tolkien Centenary Conference, Keble College, Oxford, 1992.** Altadena, CA: Mythopoeic Press, 1995. pp.435-438. (*Mythlore* Vol. 21, No. 2, Winter 1996, Whole No. 80)

DONALD A. WOLLHEIM MEMORIAL SCHOLARSHIP, 1994
___ "1994 Donald A. Wollheim Memorial Scholarship," *Science Fiction Chronicle* 15(9): 8. August 1994.

DONALDSON, ROGER
___ "**Species**: MGM Leases Giger's Titular Creature to Be Directed by Roger Donaldson," *Cinefantastique* 25(4): 51. August 1994.
___ Martin, Robert. "The Evolution of **Species**," *Sci-Fi Entertainment* 2(1): 36-39, 64. June 1995.
___ Warren, Bill. "The Deadliest of **Species**," *Starlog* No. 217: 52-56. August 1995.

DONALDSON, STEPHEN R.
___ Fike, Matthew A. "Nature as Supernature: Donaldson's Revision of Spenser," *Mythlore* 18(2): 17-20, 22. Spring 1992. (No. 68)
___ Hendrix, Laurel L. "A World of Glass: The Heroine's Quest for Identity in Spenser's **Faerie Queene** and Stephen R. Donaldson's **Mirror of Her Dreams**," in: Sanders, Joe, ed. **Functions of the Fantastic.** Westport, CT: Greenwood, 1995. pp.91-100
___ Langford, David. "The Dragonhiker's Guide to Battlefield Covenant at Dune's Edge: Odyssey Two," *Australian Science Fiction Review* 5(3): 3-11. Spring 1990. (Whole No. 25)
___ Nicholls, Stan. "The Donaldson Chronicles: Stephen Donaldson Interviewed," *Interzone* No. 60: 43-45. June 1992.
___ Nicholls, Stan. "Stephen Donaldson Writes for Love, Sells for Money," in: Nicholls, Stan. **Wordsmiths of Wonder: Fifty Interviews with Writers of the Fantastic.** London: Orbit, 1993. pp.259-267.
___ Nicholls, Stan. "Writing for Love, Selling for Money," *Starlog* 184: 76-79. November 1992.
___ Senior, W. A. **Stephen R. Donaldson's Chronicles of Thomas Covenant: Variations on the Fantasy Tradition.** Kent, OH: Kent State University Press, 1995. 275pp.
___ Senior, William. "Donaldson and Tolkien," *Mythlore* 18(4): 37-43. Autumn 1992. (No. 70)
___ Slethaug, Gordon E. " 'The Discourse of Arrogance,' Popular Power, and Anarchy: The (First) Chronicles of Thomas Covenant the Unbeliever," *Extrapolation* 34(1): 48-63. Spring 1993.
___ Stableford, Brian. **Algebraic Fantasies and Realistic Romances: More Masters of Science Fiction.** San Bernardino, CA: Borgo Press, 1995 128pp.

DONAT, PETER
___ Warren, Bill. "Time Killer," *Starlog* No. 190: 46-48, 69. May 1993.

DONNELLY, IGNATIUS
___ Lang, Hans-Joachim. "Ignatius Donnelly: **Caesar's Column: A Story of the Twentieth Century** (1890)," in: Heuermann, Hartmut and Lange, Bernd-Peter, eds. **Die Utopie in der angloamerikanischen Literatur: Interpretationen.** Düsseldorf: Bagel, 1984. pp.139-160.

DONNER, JILL SHERMAN
___ Jankiewicz, Pat. "Time of the Green," *Starlog* No. 204: 72-76. July 1994.

DOOHAN, JIMMY
___ Hogan, Jeanne. "Where Faith and Glory Lead: *U. S. S. Enterprise* (CVAN/CN-65) Association Honors Jimmy Doohan for World War II Heroism," *Star Trek: The Official Fan Club* No. 94: 42. February/March 1994.

DOORWAYS (MOTION PICTURE)
___ Valada, M. C. "Step Through George R. R. Martin's **Doorways** into Alternate Worlds," *Science Fiction Age* 1(4): 18-21, 72. May 1993.
___ Warren, Bill. "Portals to Elsewhen," *Starlog* No. 189: 78-81. April 1993.

DOPPELGANGER (MOTION PICTURE)
___ Teitelbaum, Sheldon. "**Doppelganger**," *Cinefantastique* 23(5): 40-41. February 1993.

DORN, MICHAEL
___ McDonnell, David. "Klingon Warrior," by David McDonnell and Ian Spelling. in: McDonnell, David, ed. **Starlog's Science Fiction Heroes and Heroines.** New York: Crescent Books, 1995. pp.58-61.
___ Spelling, Ian. "Cry of the Warrior," *Starlog* No. 175: 27-31. February 1992.
___ Spelling, Ian. "Klingon Again," *Starlog* No. 219: 42-43. October 1995.

DORRINGTON, ALBERT
___ Stone, Graham. "Notes on Australian Science Fiction," *Science Fiction News* (Australia) No. 102: 2-5. March 1987.

DOSTOEVSKY, F. M.
___ Noble, Andrew A. J. "Dostoevsky's Anti-Utopianism," in: Butt, J. and Clarke, I. F., eds. **The Victorians and Social Protest: A Symposium.** New York: David and Charles, 1973. pp.133-155.

DOUBLE DRAGON (MOTION PICTURE)
___ Shamray, Gerry. "**Double Dragon**," *Cinefantastique* 25(3): 54-55. June 1994.

DOUBLE DRAGON (VIDEO GAME)
___ Fletcher, Tanya A. "Deadly Games," *Sci-Fi Entertainment* 1(4): 78-84. December 1994.

DOUBLE IN LITERATURE
___ Blackmore, Tim. "Talking the Talk, Walking the Walk: The Role of Discourse in Joe Haldeman's 'The Monster' and Lucius Shepard's 'Delta Sly Honey'," *Journal of the Fantastic in the Arts* 6(2/3): 191-202. 1994.
___ Casebeer, Edwin F. "The Ecological System of Stephen King's **The Dark Half**," *Journal of the Fantastic in the Arts* 6(2/3): 126-142. 1994.
___ Francavualla, Joseph. "The Concept of the Divided Self and Harlan Ellison's 'I Have No Mouth and I Must Scream' and 'Shatterday'," *Journal of the Fantastic in the Arts* 6(2/3): 107-125. 1994.
___ Hassold, Cris. "The Double and Doubling in Modern and Postmodern Art," *Journal of the Fantastic in the Arts* 6(2/3): 253-274. 1994.
___ Jurich, Marilyn. " 'A Woman's a Two-faced,' or the *Doppelgängerin* Unveiled," *Journal of the Fantastic in the Arts* 6(2/3): 143-165. 1994.
___ Larsen, Michael J. "Selected Bibliography (The Double)," *Journal of the Fantastic in the Arts* 6(2/3): 275-277. 1994.
___ Mabee, Barbara. "The Witch as Double: Feminist Doubles in German Literature and Irmtraud Morgner's **Amanda**," *Journal of the Fantastic in the Arts* 6(2/3): 166-190. 1994.
___ Pennington, John. "Textual Doubling and Divided Selves: The Strange Case of Dr. Jekyll and Mary Reilly," *Journal of the Fantastic in the Arts* 6(2/3): 203-216. 1994.

DOUBLE IN LITERATURE

DOUBLE IN LITERATURE (continued)
___ Sanders, Joe L. "**Raising Arizona**: Not Quite Ozzie and Harriet Meet the Biker From Hell," *Journal of the Fantastic in the Arts* 6(2/3): 217-233. 1994.
___ Telotte, J. P. "In the Realm of the Revealing: The Technological Double in the Contemporary Science Fiction Film," *Journal of the Fantastic in the Arts* 6(2/3): 234-252. 1994.

DOUGLAS, JOHN
___ "John Douglas Joins HarperPrism," *Locus* 35(6): 8, 81. December 1995.
___ "John Douglas Moves to HarperPrism; Jennifer Brehl Is New Avonova Editor," *Science Fiction Chronicle* 17(2): 4. December 1995/ January 1996.

DOVE, TONI
___ Fischlin, Daniel. "Cybertheater, Postmodernism, and Virtual Reality: An Interview With Toni Dove and Michael Mackenzie," by Daniel Fischlin and Andrew Taylor. *Science Fiction Studies* 21(1): 1-23. March 1994.

DOWLING, TERRY
___ "Terry Dowling: Australian Talespinner," *Locus* 32(6): 4, 76-77. June 1994.

DOWN UNDER FAN FUND, 1993
___ "DUFF's Roger Weddell Dies, Complicating New DUFF Race," *Science Fiction Chronicle* 14(4): 4. January 1993.

DOWN UNDER FAN FUND, 1994
___ "Alan Stewart Wins DUFF," *Science Fiction Chronicle* 15(9): 38-39. August 1994.

DOWN UNDER FAN FUND, 1995
___ "Pat and Roger Sims Win DUFF," *Science Fiction Chronicle* 16(6): 42. May 1995.

DOWNING, PAULA E.
___ King, T. Jackson. "Pros and Cons of Being a Writer Couple," by T. Jackson King and Paula E. Downing. *SFWA Bulletin* 25(4): 7-14. Winter 1992. (No. 114)

DOYLE, ARTHUR CONAN
___ "Sir Arthur Conan Doyle," in: Bloom, Harold, ed. **Classic Science Fiction Writers**. New York: Chelsea House, 1995. pp.31-45.
___ Darlington, Andrew. "Our Eyes Have Seen Great Wonders: The Lost World of Arthur Conan Doyle," *Fantasy Commentator* 7(3): 181-188. Spring 1992. (No. 43)
___ Lindensmith, Gerhard. **Arthur Conan Doyle. Eine illustrierte Bibliographie der Veroffentlichungen in deutschen Sprachraum**. Amsterdam-Giessen: Verlag Munniksma, 1994. 236pp. [Not seen.]
___ Orel, Harold, ed. **Critical Essays on Sir Arthur Conan Doyle**. New York: G. K. Hall, 1992. 290pp.

DOYLE, DEBRA
___ "1993 Mythopoeic Fiction Awards," *Locus* 31(3): 77. September 1993.

DOYLE, JERRY
___ Nazzaro, Joe. "Babylon's Finest," *Starlog* No. 203: 77-79. June 1994.

DOZIER, WILLIAM
___ Garcia, Bob. "**Batman**: Series Creator," *Cinefantastique* 24(6)/ 25(1): 12-13. February 1994.

DOZOIS, GARDNER
___ Nicholls, Stan. "Gardner Dozois Turns Off the TV," in: Nicholls, Stan. **Wordsmiths of Wonder: Fifty Interviews with Writers of the Fantastic**. London: Orbit, 1993. pp.61-70.
___ Nicholls, Stan. "White Noise & Razor Endings: Gardner Dozois," *Starlog* 177: 18-20, 68. April 1992.

DR. GIGGLES (MOTION PICTURE)
___ Arnold, Gary. "**Dr. Giggles** Proves to Be a Real Cut-Up (Review)," *Washington (DC) Times*. October 26, 1992. in: *NewsBank. Film and Television*. 101:A5. 1992.

DR. GIGGLES (MOTION PICTURE) (continued)
___ Campbell, Bob. "Jokey Creepshow Guilty of Cinematic Malpractice (Review)," *Newark (NJ) Star-Ledger*. October 27, 1992. in: *NewsBank. Film and Television*. 101:A3. 1992.
___ Hemphill, Jim. "**Dr. Giggle** (Review)," *Cinefantastique* 23(6): 60. April 1993.
___ Johnson, Malcolm. "**Giggles** So Stupid, It's Not Funny (Review)," *Hartford (CT) Courant*. October 24, 1992. in: *NewsBank. Film and Television*. 101:A1. 1992.
___ Kutzera, Dale. "**Dr. Giggles**: Horror Director Manny Coto," *Cinefantastique* 23(4): 23. December 1992.
___ Kutzera, Dale. "**Dr. Giggles**: Queasy Mix of Humor and Horror Toplines Larry Drake," *Cinefantastique* 23(4): 20-22. December 1992.
___ Lloyd, Sachs. "Witless, Dreary Pulse Drags **Dr. Giggles** to Horror Lows (Review)," *Chicago (IL) Sun Times*. October 26, 1992. in: *NewsBank. Film and Television*. 101:A2. 1992.
___ Mahar, Ted. "**Dr. Giggles** Brings Nothing But Yawns (Review)," *Portland (OR) The Oregonian*. October 27, 1992. in: *NewsBank. Film and Television*. 101:A4. 1992.
___ Shulgasser, Barbara. "'Giggles' Not Much of a Cutup (Review)," *San Francisco (CA) Examiner*. October 24, 1992. in: *NewsBank. Film and Television*. 100:G14. 1992.

DR. JEKYLL AND MR. HYDE (MOTION PICTURE)
___ Sevastakis, Michael. **Songs of Love and Death: The Classical American Horror Film of the 1930s**. Westport, CT: Greenwood, 1993. 232pp.

DR. JEKYLL AND MS. HYDE (MOTION PICTURE)
___ Newman, Kim. "**Dr. Jekyll and Ms. Hyde** (Review)," *Sight and Sound* 5(12): 44-45. December 1995.
___ Scapperotti, Dan. "**Dr. Jekyll and Ms. Hyde**," *Cinefantastique* 26(3): 10-11. April 1995.

DRACULA
___ McNally, Raymond T. **In Search of Dracula: The History of Dracula and Vampires**. Rev. Ed., by Raymond T. McNally and Radu Florescu. Boston, MA: Houghton Mifflin, 1994. 297pp.
___ Newman, Kim. "Bloodlines," *Sight and Sound* 3(1): 12-13. January 1993.
___ Sheehan, Henry. "Trust the Teller," *Sight and Sound* 3(1): 14. January 1993.
___ Sinclair, Iain. "Invasion of the Blood," *Sight and Sound* 3(1): 15. January 1993.
___ Treptow, Kurt W., ed. **Dracula: Essays on the Life and Times of Vlad Tepes**. New York: Columbia University Press, 1991. 336pp.

DRACULA (1931) (MOTION PICTURE)
___ Riley, Philip J. **MagicImage Filmbooks Presents Dracula: The Original 1931 Shooting Script**. Absecon, NJ: MagicImage Filmbooks, 1990. 287pp.

DRACULA (1931, SPANISH) (MOTION PICTURE)
___ Harris, Judith P. "**Dracula** (Spanish, 1931) (Review)," *Cinefantastique* 23(6): 60. April 1993.
___ Skal, David J. "The Spanish **Dracula**," *American Film* 15(12): 38-41. September 1990.

DRACULA (MOTION PICTURE)
___ Dyer, Richard. "**Dracula** and Desire," *Sight and Sound* 3(1): 8-12. January 1993.
___ Flynn, John L. **Cinematic Vampires: The Living Dead on Film and Televison, From** *The Devil's Castle* **(1896) to** *Bram Stoker's Dracula* **(1992)**. Jefferson, NC: McFarland, 1992. 328pp.
___ Maslin, Janet. "Neither **Dracula** Nor Rumor Frightens Coppola," *New York Times* p. 15, 24. November 15, 1992.
___ Sevastakis, Michael. **Songs of Love and Death: The Classical American Horror Film of the 1930s**. Westport, CT: Greenwood, 1993. 232pp.
___ Whalen, Tom. "Romancing Film: Coppola's **Dracula**," *Literature/ Film Quarterly* 23(2): 99-101. 1995.

DRACULA'S DAUGHTER (MOTION PICTURE)
___ Sevastakis, Michael. **Songs of Love and Death: The Classical American Horror Film of the 1930s**. Westport, CT: Greenwood, 1993. 232pp.

DRAGONHEART (MOTION PICTURE)

DUNSTAN, FREDERICK

DRAGONHEART (MOTION PICTURE)
___ van Hise, James. "*Dragonheart*: Preview," *Cinefantastique* 27(3): 7. December 1995.

DRAGONLANCE SERIES
___ Weis, Margaret, ed. **Leaves From the Inn of the Last Home: The Complete Krynn Source Book**, ed. by Margaret Weis and Tracy Hickman. Lake Geneva, WI: TSR, 1993. 255pp.

DRAKE, LARRY
___ Kutzera, Dale. "*Dr. Giggles*: Queasy Mix of Humor and Horror Toplines Larry Drake," *Cinefantastique* 23(4): 20-22. December 1992.

DRAMA
___ SEE: PLAYS.

DREAM CORRIDOR (COMIC)
___ Hirsch, Connie. "Harlan Ellison Rides a Dark Horse to Invade His Personal *Dream Corridors*," *Science Fiction Age* 3(3): 18. March 1995.

DREAM LOVER (MOTION PICTURE)
___ "'Lover' Takes Top Prize at Avoriaz," *Variety* p.5. January 22, 1986.

DREAMS
___ Brewer, William D. "Mary Shelley on Dreams," *Southern Humanities Review* 29(2): 105-126. Spring 1995.

DROIDS: THE ADVENTURES OF R2D2 AND C3P0 (TV)
___ Kaufman, Dave. "Lucas Producing Two ABC Cartoons on Ewoks and R2D2," *Variety* p. 145. January 16, 1985.

DRUILLET, PHILIPPE
___ Radisich, Paula R. "Evolution and Salvation: The Iconic Origins of Druillet's Monstrous Combatants of the Night," in: Slusser, George and Eric S. Rabkin, eds. **Fights of Fancy: Armed Conflict in Science Fiction and Fantasy**. Athens, GA: University of Georgia Press, 1993. pp.103-113.

DU BOIS, WILLIAM PENÉ
___ "du Bois, William Pené (Obituary)," *Locus* 30(3): 70. March 1993.

DuBOIS, GAYLORD
___ Ziemann, Irvin H. "Tarzan in the Dell...And Gold Key," *Burroughs Bulletin* NS. No. 22: 6-11. April 1995.

DUCHOVNY, DAVID
___ Grant, James. "Red Hot Right Now: David Duchovny," *Cosmopolitan* 219(4): 144. October 1995.
___ Lee, Julianne. "X-Symbol," *Starlog* No. 215: 27-30, 71. June 1995.
___ Shapiro, Marc. "Devil's Advocate," *Starlog* No. 202: 46-49. May 1994.
___ Vitaris, Paula. "*X-Files*: Mulder and Scully," *Cinefantastique* 26(6)/ 27(1): 23-24. October 1995.

DUFF
___ SEE: DOWN UNDER FAN FUND.

DUGAN, JOHN T.
___ Florence, Bill. "Tomorrow's Story," *Starlog* No. 194: 62-64, 81. September 1993.

DUGUAY, CHRISTIAN
___ Flixman, Ed. "Man and Machine," *Sci-Fi Entertainment* 2(3): 48-53. October 1995.

DULLEA, KIER
___ Goldberg, Lee. "*2010* (1984): Interview with Kier Dullea," in: Goldberg, Lee et al. **Science Fiction Filmmaking in the 1980s**. Jefferson, NC: McFarland, 1995. pp.237-252.
___ Goldman, Lowell. "*2001: A Space Odyssey*: Kier Dullea," *Cinefantastique* 25(3): 34. June 1994.

DUNCAN, DAVE
___ "Dave Duncan: From Oil to Fantasy," *Locus* 30(4): 5, 66. April 1993.

DUNCAN, ROBERT
___ Spelling, Ian. "The Colors of Loyalty," *Starlog* No. 213: 36-39, 72. April 1995.

DUNE II: THE BUILDING OF A DYNASTY (GAME)
___ Castro, Adam-Troy. "Conquer the Desert Planet Arrakis as Frank Herbert's **Dune** Novels Come to Life," *Science Fiction Age* 2(1): 92-95. November 1993.

DUNE (MOTION PICTURE)
___ "De Lauretiis Presents $42-Mil **Dune** Offering," *Variety* p. 13. November 7, 1984.
___ "**Dune** Finally on Launch Pad After Convoluted 11-Year Saga," *Variety* p. 31. March 16, 1983.
___ "**Dune** Release Will Test Print Coding to Hinder Pirates," *Variety* p. 1, 141. December 12, 1984.
___ "**Dune**, 2010 Pub Pushes Stir Source Novel Sales," *Variety* p. 22. January 23, 1985.
___ "Licensee to Presell 250,000 Posters for **Dune** Sight Unseen," *Variety* p. 7, 34. November 7, 1984.
___ "Massive **Dune** Promo Includes Book and Department Store Tie-Ins," *Variety* p. 6, 26. November 21, 1984.
___ "Redone **Dune**, Sans Lynch Signature, Will Work on Air, MCA Sez," *Variety* p. 83. June 1, 1988.
___ "Universal Limits Advance **Dune** Screenings," *Variety* p. 6. December 12, 1984.
___ Lofficier, Randy. "**Dune** (1984): Interviews with David Lynch, Raffaella de Laurentiis and Kyle MacLachlan," by Randy Lofficier and Jean-Marc Lofficier. in: Goldberg, Lee et al. **Science Fiction Filmmaking in the 1980s**. Jefferson, NC: McFarland, 1995. pp.79-110.

DUNN, DAWN PAULINE
___ "Two Pauline Dunn Horror Novels Plagiarized Dean R. Koontz's **Phantoms**," *Science Fiction Chronicle* 13(10): 4. July/August 1992.
___ "Zebra Withdraws Two Novels for Plagiarism," *Locus* 28(2): 6. August 1992.

DUNNE, J. W.
___ Flieger, Verlyn. "Tolkien's Experiment With Time: The Lost Road, 'The Notion Club Papers' and J. W. Dunne," in: Reynolds, Patricia and GoodKnight, Glen H., eds. **Proceedings of the J. R. R. Tolkien Centenary Conference, Keble College, Oxford, 1992**. Altadena, CA: Mythopoeic Press, 1995. pp.39-44. (*Mythlore* Vol. 21, No. 2, Winter 1996, Whole No. 80)

DUNSANY, LORD
___ Bloom, Harold. "Lord Dunsany," in: Bloom, Harold. **Classic Fantasy Writers**. New York: Chelsea House, 1994. pp.56-70.
___ Burleson, Donald R. "On Dunsany's 'Probable Adventure of the Three Literary Men'," *Studies in Weird Fiction* No. 10: 23-26. Fall 1991.
___ Duperray, Max. "Lord Dunsany Revisited," *Studies in Weird Fiction* No. 13: 10-14. Summer 1993. [Not seen.]
___ Joshi, S. T. **Lord Dunsany: A Bibliography**, by S. T. Joshi and Darrell Schweitzer. Metuchen, NJ: Scarecrow, 1993. 389pp.
___ Joshi, S. T. **Lord Dunsany: Master of the Anglo-Irish Imagination**. Westport, CT: Greenwood, 1995. 230pp.
___ Lobdell, Jared C. "The Man Who Didn't Write Fantasy: Lord Dunsany and the Self-Deprecatory Tradition in English Light Fiction," *Extrapolation* 35(1): 33-42. Spring 1994.
___ Lovecraft, H. P. "Lord Dunsany and His Work (1922)," in: Joshi, S. T., ed. **Miscellaneous Writings: H. P. Lovecraft**. Sauk City, WI: Arkham House, 1995. pp.104-112.
___ Pashka, Linda. "'Hunting for Allegories' in the Prose Fantasy of Lord Dunsany," *Studies in Weird Fiction* No. 12: 19-24. Spring 1993.
___ Schweitzer, Darrell. "How Much of Dunsany Is Worth Reading?," *Studies in Weird Fiction* No. 10: 19-23. Fall 1991.

DUNSTAN, ANDREW
___ Stone, Graham. "Notes on Australian Science Fiction," *Science Fiction News* (Australia) No. 94: 2-11. January 1986.

DUNSTAN, FREDERICK
___ Langford, David. "The Dragonhiker's Guide to Battlefield Covenant at Dune's Edge: Odyssey Two," *Australian Science Fiction Review* 5(3): 3-11. Spring 1990. (Whole No. 25)

DUPREE, TOM

___ "Betsy Mitchell Moves to Warner's Questar SF; Tom Dupree to Head Bantam Spectra," *Science Fiction Chronicle* 14(11): 4. August 1993.

___ "Silbersack to Start New SF Line at HarperCollins; Mitchell Moves to Warner; Bantam Promotes From Within," *Locus* 31(2): 6, 61. August 1993.

DURANT RETURNS (MOTION PICTURE)

___ SEE: DARKMAN II: DURANT RETURNS (MOTION PICTURE).

DUST DEVIL (MOTION PICTURE)

___ Jones, Alan. "*Dust Devil*: The Final Cut," *Cinefantastique* 24(3/4): 15. October 1993.

___ Jones, Alan. "*Dust Devil*," *Cinefantastique* 24(3/4): 12-14. October 1993.

DUTRA, RANDAL M.

___ Shay, Estelle. "Profile: Randal M. Dutra," *Cinefex* No. 59: 117-118. September 1994.

DYING

___ Hadomi, Leah. "Islands of the Living: Death and Dying in Utopian Fiction," *Utopian Studies* 6(1): 85-101. 1995.

DYSON, MARIANNE J.

___ Klein, Jay K. "Biolog: Marianne J. Dyson," *Analog* 114(7): 157, 168. June 1994.

DYSTOPIA

___ Baldini, Enzo. **Utopia e distopia.** Nuova ed., by Enzo Baldini and Arrigo Colombo. Bari: Edizioni Dedalo, 1993. 373pp. [Not seen.]

___ Bazin, Nancy T. "Women and Revolution in Dystopian Fiction: Nadine Gordimer's **July's People** and Margaret Atwood's **The Handmaid's Tale**," in: Crafton, John M., ed. **Selected Essays: International Conference on Representing Revolution, 1989.** n.p.: West Georgia College International Conference, 1991. pp.115-128.

___ Bertinetti, Roberto. **L'infondazione di Babele: l'antiutopia.** Milan: F. Angeli, 1983. 164pp.

___ Booker, M. Keith. **The Dystopian Impulse in Modern Literature: Fiction as Social Criticism.** Westport, CT: Greenwood, 1994. 197pp.

___ Booker, M. Keith. **Dystopian Literature: A Theory and Research Guide.** Westport, CT: Greenwood Press, 1994. 424pp.

___ Booker, M. Keith. "Woman on the Edge of a Genre: The Feminist Dystopias of Marge Piercy," *Science Fiction Studies* 21(3): 337-350. November 1994.

___ Bouchard, Guy. **Images feministes du futur.** Quebec: Groupe de recherches en analyse des discours de l'Universite Laval, 1992. 153pp.

___ Browning, William G. **Anti-Utopian Fiction: Definition and Standards for Evaluation.** Ph.D. Dissertation, Louisiana State University, 1966. 145pp.

___ Caywood, Carolyn. "Tales of the Dark Side," *School Library Journal* 41(7): 31. July 1995.

___ Chalpin, Lila. **Dystopias as Viewed by Social Scientists and Novelists.** Ph.D. Dissertation, Boston University, 1977. 232pp. (DAI 38: 5383A.)

___ Chien, Ying-Ying. "From Utopian to Dystopian World: Two Faces of Feminism in Contemporary Taiwanese Women's Fiction," *World Literature Today* 68(1): 35-42. Winter 1994.

___ Colas-Charpentier, Helene. "Four Quebecois Dystopias, 1963-1972," *Science Fiction Studies* 20(3): 383-393. November 1993.

___ Dietz, Frank. "Robert Silverberg's **The World Inside** as an Ambiguous Dystopia," in: Elkins, Charles L. and Greenberg, Martin H., eds. **Robert Silverberg's Many Trapdoors: Critical Essays on His Science Fiction.** Westport, CT: Greenwood, 1992. pp.95-105.

___ Ferns, Chris. "The Value/s of Dystopia: **The Handmaid's Tale** and the Anti-Utopian Tradition," *Dalhousie Review* 69(3): 373-382. Fall 1989.

___ Filmer, Kath. **Scepticism and Hope in Twentieth Century Fantasy Literature.** Bowling Green, OH: Bowling Green State University Popular Press, 1992. 160pp.

___ Foote, Bud. "Verne's **Paris in the Twentieth Century**: The First Science Fiction Dystopia?," *New York Review of Science Fiction* No. 88: 1, 8-10. December 1995.

___ Grossman, Kathryn M. "Woman as Temptress: The Way to (Br)otherhood in Science Fiction Dystopias," *Women's Studies* 14(2): 135-146. 1987.

DYSTOPIA (continued)

___ Grossman, Kathryn M. "Woman as Temptress: The Way to (Br)otherhood in Science Fiction Dystopias," in: Saccaro Del Buffa, Giuseppa and Lewis, Arthur O., eds. **Utopie per gli Anni Ottana.** Rome: Gangemi Editore, 1986. pp.489-498.

___ Guardamagna, Daniela. **Analisi dell'incubo: l'utopia negativa da Swift alla fantascienza.** Roma: Bulzoni, 1980. 237pp. [Not seen.]

___ Haschak, Paul G. **Utopian/Dystopian Literature: A Bibliography of Literary Criticism.** Metuchen, NJ: Scarecrow, 1994. 370pp.

___ Jackson, Kevin. "The Trappings of Disaster: Sci-Fi's Bygone Dystopias," *Sight and Sound* 3(5): 38-39. May 1993.

___ Kason, Nancy M. "The Dystopian Vision in **XYZ** by Clemente Palma," *Monographis Review* 3(1/2): 33-42. 1987.

___ Keough, Trent. "The Dystopia Factor: Industrial Capitalism in **Sybil** and **The Grapes of Wrath**," *Utopian Studies* 4(1): 38-54. 1993.

___ Lassner, Phyllis. "A New World Indeed: Feminist Critique and Power Relations in British Anti-Utopian Literature of the 1930s," *Extrapolation* 36(3): 259-272. Fall 1995.

___ Maurstad, Tom. "Future Tense," *Dallas (TX) Morning News.* July 30, 1995. in: *NewsBank. Film and Television.* 80:E9-E11. 1995.

___ McKay, George. "Metapropaganda: Self-reading Dystopian Fiction: Burdekin's **Swastika Night** and Orwell's **Nineteen Eighty-Four**," *Science Fiction Studies* 21(3): 302-314. November 1994.

___ Noble, Andrew A. J. "Dostoevsky's Anti-Utopianism," in: Butt, J. and Clarke, I. F., eds. **The Victorians and Social Protest: A Symposium.** New York: David and Charles, 1973. pp.133-155.

___ Sisk, David W. **Claiming Mastery over the Word: Transformations of Language in Six Twentieth Century Dystopias.** Ph.D. Dissertation, University of North Carolina, Chapel Hill, 1994. 405pp. (DAI-A 55/07, p. 1972. January 1995.)

___ Snodgrass, Mary E. **Encyclopedia of Utopian Literature.** Santa Barbara, CA: ABC-CLIO, 1995. 644pp.

___ Swirski, Peter. **Dystopia or Dischtopia: An Analysis of the SF Paradigms in Thomas M. Disch.** Master's Thesis, McGill University, 1990. 123pp. (Master's Abstracts 31/03, p. 1019. Fall 1993.)

___ Tiger, Virginia. " 'The words had been right and necessary': Doris Lessing's Transformations of Utopian and Dystopian Modalities in **The Marriages Between Zones Three, Four and Five**," *Style* 27(1): 63-80. Spring 1993.

___ Willingham, Ralph A. "Dystopian Vision in the Plays of Elias Canetti," *Science Fiction Studies* 19(1): 69-74. March 1992.

E. T.: THE EXTRATERRESTRIAL (MOTION PICTURE)

___ " *E. T.* Script Absolved," *Variety* p. 2. June 29, 1983.

___ " *E. T.* Social Comment," *Variety* p. 7. July 14, 1982.

___ "Open Letter From MCA to Spielberg and Stock Owners About *E.T.* Pic," *Variety* p. 7, 32. June 2, 1982.

___ "Paris *E. T.* Record," *Variety* p. 7. January 5, 1983.

___ "Pitt Subrun Claims Universal's Longrun *E. T.* Violates Bid Rules," *Variety* p. 7. September 15, 1982.

___ "Spielberg's *E. T.* Out In June With 11 Kiddie Licensing Deals Tied In," *Variety* p. 26. April 11, 1982.

___ "Sweden Bans *E. T.* to Under-elevens; May Cost Film 10%," *Variety* p. 9. January 12, 1983.

___ Bick, Ilsa J. "The Look Back in *E. T.* ," *Cinema Journal* 31(4): 25-41. Summer 1992.

EARTH 2 (TV)

___ Adalian, Josef. "Stereotypes Populate **Earth 2** Series," *Washington (DC) Times.* November 6, 1994. in: *NewsBank. Film and Television.* 119:F11. 1994.

___ Bark, Ed. "Light Years From Genius," *Dallas (TX) Morning News.* November 6, 1994. in: *NewsBank. Film and Television.* 119:F9. 1994.

___ Chrissinger, Craig W. "Brave New World," *Starlog* No. 209: 42-47. December 1994.

___ Chrissinger, Craig W. "Company Man," *Starlog* No. 212: 76-79. March 1995.

___ Chrissinger, Craig W. "Earth Mother," *Starlog* No. 214: 36-39, 69. May 1995.

___ Chrissinger, Craig W. "Frontier Doctor," *Starlog* No. 213: 48-51, 70. April 1995.

___ Chrissinger, Craig W. "Lessons of Life," *Starlog* No. 215: 46-49. June 1995.

___ Chrissinger, Craig W. "Mechanically Inclined," *Starlog* No. 210: 32-35, 66. January 1995.

___ Chrissinger, Craig W. "Sky Pilot," *Starlog* No. 216: 67-70. July 1995.

EARTH 2 (TV) (continued)

___ Chrissinger, Craig W. "Wilderness Leader," *Starlog* No. 211: 36-39, 70. February 1995.

___ Hilbrand, David. "Picks and Pans: *Earth 2*," *People Weekly* 42(21): 17, 19. November 21, 1994.

___ Jarvis, Jeff. "The Couch Critic: *Earth 2*," *TV Guide* 42(50): 12. December 10, 1994.

___ Kenny, Glenn. "Lost in Space, Again," *TV Guide* 42(42): 42. October 15, 1994.

___ Littlefield, Kinney. "*Earth 2*? Not Stellar, But Don't Abort Mission Yet," *(Santa Ana, CA) Orange County Register.* Nov. 4, 1994. in: *NewsBank. Film and Television.* 119:F8. 1994.

___ Mangioni, Gino. "Spielberg Team Picks N.M. for Sci-Fi TV Series," by Gino Mangioni and Chuck Mittelstadt. *Albuquerque (NM) Tribune.* April 28, 1994. in: *NewsBank. Film and Television.* 53:F5. 1994.

___ Martin, Ed. "Science Fiction, By the Numbers: *Earth 2* and *Babylon 5* on Course for Programming's Black Hole," *Inside Media* p. 58. November 30, 1994. (Cited from *IAC Insite* on-line service.)

___ Norton, Bill. "Video Beat: Piloting to *Earth 2*," *Cinefex* No. 60: 13-14. December 1994.

___ Obsatz, Sharyn. "*Earth 2* to Leave Santa Fe," *(Santa Fe, NM) New Mexican.* March 18, 1995. in: *NewsBank. Film and Television.* 33:D9. 1995.

___ Sandrin, Kathleen. "*Wagon Train* of the Future Keeps on Rolling," *(Santa Fe, NM) New Mexican.* January 27, 1995. in: *NewsBank. Film and Television.* 25:E10. 1995.

___ Stanley, T. L. "NBC, Live Entertainment Link TV and Home Vid for Sci-Fi Synergy," *Brandweek* 36(3): 8. January 16, 1995.

___ Walker, Hollis. "*Earth 2* Lands in SF," *(Santa Fe, NM) New Mexican.* September 3, 1994. in: *NewsBank. Film and Television.* 97:C12-c13. 1994.

EARTH STAR VOYAGER (MOTION PICTURE)

___ "*Earth Star Voyager* (Review)," *Variety* p. 76. January 27, 1988.

EATING

___ Parker, Emma. "You Are What You Eat: The Politics of Eating in the Novels of Margaret Atwood," *Twentieth Century Literature* 41(3): 349-368. Fall 1995.

ECOLOGY

___ Alier, Juan M. "Ecological Economics and Concrete Utopias," *Utopian Studies* 3(1): 39-52. 1992.

___ Juhren, Marcella. "The Ecology of Middle-Earth," *Mythlore* 20(2): 5-9. Spring 1994. (Whole No. 76)

___ Keller, Chester Z. "Human Nature: Ecosystemic Limits and Techne. Some Utopian Implications," in: Saccaro Del Buffa, Giuseppa and Lewis, Arthur O., eds. **Utopia e Modernita: Teorie e prassi utopiche nell'eta moderna e postmoderna.** Rome: Gangemi Editore, 1989. pp.131-142.

___ McLoughlin, Maryann. "Female Utopian Writers and the Environment," *CEA Forum* 22(1): 3-6. Winter 1992.

___ Stapleton, Amy L. **Utopias for a Dying World: Contemporary German Science Fiction's Plea for a New Ecological Awareness.** New York: Peter Lang, 1993. 158pp.

___ Tramson, Jacques. "L'ecologie dans la letterature de science fiction," *La Revue des Livres pour Enfants* 147: 96-102. Autumn 1992. [Not seen.]

ECONOMICS IN SF

___ Adorisio, Ilio. "L'utopia ed i segni dell'economia," in: Saccaro Del Buffa, Giuseppa and Lewis, Arthur O., eds. **Utopie per gli Anni Ottana.** Rome: Gangemi Editore, 1986. pp.185-195.

___ Adorisio, Ilio. "Ucronia in Oiconomia. Considerazioni sulla cronofagia della societa industriale," in: Saccaro Del Buffa, Giuseppa and Lewis, Arthur O., eds. **Utopia e Modernita: Teorie e prassi utopiche nell'eta moderna e postmoderna.** Rome: Gangemi Editore, 1989. pp.237-276.

___ Coats, Gary. "Stone Soup: Utopia, Gift Exchange, and the Aesthetics of the Self-Consuming Artifact," in: Saccaro Del Buffa, Giuseppa and Lewis, Arthur O., eds. **Utopia e Modernita: Teorie e prassi utopiche nell'eta moderna e postmoderna.** Rome: Gangemi Editore, 1989. pp.287-310.

___ Lanza, Luciano. "Al di la dell'economia: primi appunti per una concezione utopica dell'economia," in: Saccaro Del Buffa, Giuseppa and Lewis, Arthur O., eds. **Utopie per gli Anni Ottana.** Rome: Gangemi Editore, 1986. pp.167-184.

ECONOMICS IN SF (continued)

___ Lanza, Luciano. "Utopia, domminio, economia," in: Saccaro Del Buffa, Giuseppa and Lewis, Arthur O., eds. **Utopia e Modernita: Teorie e prassi utopiche nell'eta moderna e postmoderna.** Rome: Gangemi Editore, 1989. pp.225-236.

___ Perotti, Stefano. "Spazio e utopia nelle societa post-industriali," in: Saccaro Del Buffa, Giuseppa and Lewis, Arthur O., eds. **Utopia e Modernita: Teorie e prassi utopiche nell'eta moderna e postmoderna.** Rome: Gangemi Editore, 1989. pp.277-286.

___ Stableford, Brian. "Utopia--And Afterwards: Socioeconomic Speculation in the SF of Mack Reynolds," in: Stableford, Brian. **Outside the Human Aquarium: Masters of Science Fiction.** San Bernardino, CA: Borgo, 1995. pp.49-75.

___ Trezza, Bruno. "Economia e utopia," in: Saccaro Del Buffa, Giuseppa and Lewis, Arthur O., eds. **Utopia e Modernita: Teorie e prassi utopiche nell'eta moderna e postmoderna.** Rome: Gangemi Editore, 1989. pp.217-224.

ECONOMICS OF SF

___ Sedgewick, Cristina. "The Fork in the Road: Can Science Fiction Survive in Postmodern, Megacorporate America?," *Science Fiction Studies* 18(1): 11-52. March 1991.

ED AND HIS DEAD MOTHER (MOTION PICTURE)

___ Harris, Judith P. "*Ed and His Dead Mother* (Review)," *Cinefantastique* 26(3): 59. April 1995.

ED WOOD (MOTION PICTURE)

___ Carducci, Mark. "*Ed Wood* Cult Legend," *Cinefantastique* 25(5): 20-45. October 1994.

___ Carducci, Mark. "*Ed Wood*: Deadringer for Tor," *Cinefantastique* 25(5): 26-27. October 1994.

___ Carducci, Mark. "*Ed Wood*: Flying Saucer Myths," *Cinefantastique* 25(5): 31. October 1994.

___ Carducci, Mark. "*Ed Wood*: Hollywood Rat Race," *Cinefantastique* 25(5): 38-39. October 1994.

___ Carducci, Mark. "*Ed Wood*: Makeup," *Cinefantastique* 25(5): 28-29, 61. October 1994.

___ Carducci, Mark. "*Ed Wood*," *Cinefantastique* 25(2): 4-5. April 1994.

___ French, Lawrence. "*Ed Wood*: Cinematography," *Cinefantastique* 25(6)/26(1): 16-17. December 1994.

___ French, Lawrence. "*Ed Wood*: Lugosi's Makeup," *Cinefantastique* 25(6)/26(1): 112-113. December 1994.

___ French, Lawrence. "*Ed Wood*: Playing Bela Lugosi," *Cinefantastique* 25(5): 34-35. October 1994.

___ French, Lawrence. "*Ed Wood*: Production Design," *Cinefantastique* 25(6)/26(1): 116-117. December 1994.

___ French, Lawrence. "*Ed Wood*: Writing the Script," *Cinefantastique* 25(6)/26(1): 12-13. December 1994.

___ French, Lawrence. "*Ed Wood: The Haunted World of Edward D. Wood, Jr.*," *Cinefantastique* 25(6)/26(1): 120-121. December 1994.

___ French, Lawrence. "Tim Burton's *Ed Wood*," *Cinefantastique* 25(5): 32-34. October 1994.

___ French, Lawrence. "Tim Burton's *Ed Wood*," *Cinefantastique* 25(6)/26(1): 10-18, 112-121. December 1994.

___ Lowe, Nick. "*Ed Wood* (Review)," *Interzone* No. 96: 36-38. June 1995.

___ Persons, Dan. "*Ed Wood* (Review)," *Cinefantastique* 26(3): 59. April 1995.

___ Ryan, Al. "*Ed Wood*: Vampira," by Al Ryan and Dan Cziraky. *Cinefantastique* 25(5): 40-41, 61. October 1994.

___ Sammon, Paul M. "Quick Cuts: Wood Works," *Cinefex* No. 61: 107-110. March 1995.

___ Shay, Don. "Quick Cuts: The Return of the Vampire," *Cinefex* No. 60: 117-118. December 1994.

___ Thonen, John. "*Ed Wood*: 'Plan 9' Movie Mogul," *Cinefantastique* 25(5): 22. October 1994.

EDDINGS, DAVID

___ "Eddings, David, 1931- ," in: Lesniak, James G., ed. **Contemporary Authors.** Detroit: Gale Research, 1992. New Revision Series, Vol. 35, pp.145-146.

___ Nicholls, Stan. "Prime U.S. Beef: David Eddings Interviewed," *Interzone* No. 85: 25-30. July 1994.

___ Nicholls, Stan. "Ring Bearer," *Starlog* No. 210: 76-81. January 1995.

EDDISON, E. R.
___ Bloom, Harold. "E. R. Eddison," in: Bloom, Harold, ed. **Modern Fantasy Writers**. New York: Chelsea House, 1995. pp.43-56.

EDGAR ALLAN POE AWARDS, 1983
___ "Disney's 'Something Wicked' Tops National Horror Assn. Awards," *Variety* p. 29, 31. June 6, 1984.

EDGAR RICE BURROUGHS AMATEUR PRESS ASSOCIATION
___ Hanson, Alan. "The Edgar Rice Burroughs Amateur Press Association," *Burroughs Bulletin* NS No. 11: 27-30. July 1992.

EDGE CITY (GAME)
___ Honigsberg, David M. "*RoboRally* and *Edge City* Transport Board Games to an Exciting Tomorrow," *Science Fiction Age* 3(3): 98-101. March 1995.

EDGE OF DARKNESS (TV)
___ Sanders, Joe L. "*Edge of Darkness* as Transhuman Thriller," *Journal of the Fantastic in the Arts* 5(4): 83-91. 1993. (No. 20)

EDISON, THOMAS
___ Harty, Kevin J. "**The Knights of the Square Table**: The Boy Scouts and Thomas Edison Make an Arthurian Film," *Arthuriana* 4(4): 313-323. Winter 1994.

EDITORS AND EDITING
___ Cook, Sebastian. "Editing the Stars: An Interview With Jane Johnson," *Focus* (BSFA) No. 26: 15-16. June/July 1994.
___ Gunn, James E. "The Gatekeepers," in: Gunn, James E. **Inside Science Fiction: Essays on Fantastic Literature**. San Bernardino, CA: Borgo, 1992. pp.52-59.
___ Platt, Charles. "The Selling of Science Fiction," *Interzone* No. 89: 46-47. November 1994.
___ Schmidt, Stanley. "Authors vs. Editors," in: Dozois, Gardner, ed. **Writing Science Fiction and Fantasy**. New York: St. Martin's, 1991. pp.236-249.
___ Sperry, Ralph A. "Three Nasty Problems," *SFWA Bulletin* 26(3): 21-22. Fall 1992. (No. 117)
___ Van Belkom, Edo. "Editing Anthologies," *SFWA Bulletin* 28(3): 18-21. Winter 1994. (No. 125)
___ Westfahl, Gary. "Dictatorial, Authoritarian, Uncooperative: The Case Against John W. Campbell," *Foundation* No. 56: 36-60. Autumn 1992. (Letter of comment: Alexei Panshin, *Foundation* No. 58: 87-91. Summer 1993; Rejoiner, Westfahl, *Foundation* No. 58: 93-94.)

EDLUND, RICHARD
___ Warren, Bill. "Building the Perfect Beast," *Starlog* No. 214: 41-45, 70. May 1995.

EDUCATION
___ Coleman, Stephen. "William Morris and Education Toward Revolution," *Journal of the William Morris Society* 11(1): 49-58. Autumn 1994.
___ Faulkner, Peter. "Morris and the Study of English," *Journal of the William Morris Society* 11(1): 26-30. Autumn 1994.
___ Harvey, Charles. "William Morris and the Royal Commission on Technical Instruction, 1881-84," by Charles Harvey and Jon Press. *Journal of the William Morris Society* 11(1): 31-43. Autumn 1994.
___ Kay, Ann. "William Morris and the National Curriculum," by Ann Kay and John Kay. *Journal of the William Morris Society* 11(1): 44-48. Autumn 1994.
___ Mineo, Ady. "The Reverse of Salem House: The 'Holistic' Process of Education in **News From Nowhere**," *Journal of the William Morris Society* 11(1): 6-15. Autumn 1994.
___ Mohideen, Kerima. "Morris and Literacy," *Journal of the William Morris Society* 11(1): 19-25. Autumn 1994.
___ Morris, William. "Thoughts and Education Under Capitalism," *Journal of the William Morris Society* 11(1): 3-5. Autumn 1994.

EDWARD SCISSORHANDS (MOTION PICTURE)
___ "1992 Saturn Awards," *Locus* 28(6): 7. June 1992.
___ "Saturn Awards, 1992," *Science Fiction Chronicle* 13(9): 10. June 1992.
___ Jones, Alan. "Tim Burton's **Edward Scissorhands**," *Cinefantastique* 25(5): 12-18. October 1994.

EFFINGER, GEORGE ALEC
___ "Effinger Fund Auction Held at Worldcon," *Locus* 29(5): 4. November 1992
___ "Effinger Medical Fund Established," *Locus* 28(2): 6. February 1992.
___ "George Alec Effinger Medical Fund Established," *Science Fiction Chronicle* 13(5): 4-5. February 1992.
___ Bell, Lydia. "Writer Stumbled into Success," *New Orleans (LA) Times-Picayune* Sec. OTL, p. 1. May 20, 1993.
___ Indick, Ben P. **George Alec Effinger: From Entrophy to Buyadeen**. San Bernardino, CA: Borgo Press, 1994. 96pp.

EGAN, GREG
___ "Campbell and Sturgeon Award Winners," *Locus* 35(2): 8. August 1995.
___ "Ditmar Awards, 1992," *Science Fiction Chronicle* 14(9): 6. June 1993.
___ "Greg Egan Wins Campbell Memorial Award; Sturgeon Award to Ursula K. Le Guin," *Science Fiction Chronicle* 16(9): 5. August/September 1995.

EGGERT, NICOLE
___ Florence, Bill. "An Alien With Style," *Starlog* No. 219: 32-36, 66. October 1995.

EGGLETON, BOB
___ "Bob Eggleton: Making It Real," *Locus* 30(5): 5, 73. May 1993.
___ Benford, Gregory. "A Lyrical Hardness," *Science Fiction Age* 2(4): 78-83. May 1994.

EIDELMAN, CLIFF
___ Hirsch, David. "Symphony for Klingon," *Starlog* 180: 76-80. July 1992.

EISELEY, LOREN
___ Christianson, Gale E. "Autobiography as Science Fiction: The Strange Case of Loren Eiseley," in: Morse, Donald E., ed. **The Celebration of the Fantastic**. Westport, CT: Greenwood, 1992. pp.113-119.

EL FADIL, SIDDIG
___ Spelling, Ian. "Bashir Grows Up," *Starlog* No. 201: 50-53. April 1994.

ELDRIDGE, PAUL
___ Stableford, Brian. "Yesterday's Bestsellers, 20: **My First Two Thousand Years** by George Viereck and Paul Eldridge," *Interzone* No. 86: 48-52. August 1994.

ELECTONIC PUBLISHING
___ "*Galaxy* Follows *Omni* into the Great Unknown," *Locus* 35(1): 9. July 1995.

ELECTRONIC FICTION
___ Gess, Richard. "Notes on Hypertext: One Artist's Slate, 1992-1994," *New York Review of Science Fiction* No. 72: 1, 8-9. August 1994.
___ McDaid, John. "Luddism, SF, and the Aesthetics of Electronic Fiction," *New York Review of Science Fiction* No. 69: 1, 8-11. May 1994.
___ Moulthrop, Stuart. "Electronic Fictions and 'The Lost Game of Self'," *New York Review of Science Fiction* No. 66: 1, 8-14. February 1994.
___ Platt, Charles. "Why Hypertext Doesn't Really Work," *New York Review of Science Fiction* No. 72: 1, 3-5. August 1994.
___ Smith, Sarah. "Electronic Fictions: The State of the Art," *New York Review of Science Fiction* No. 63: 1, 8-11. November 1993.

ELECTRONIC GAMES
___ Chalin, Michael. "Shazam! Comic Book Heroes Invade the Electronic Frontier," *PC Novice* 5(8): 60-62. August 1994.
___ May, Scott A. "Science Fiction CD-ROMs," *Compute* 16(6): 66-70. June 1994.

ELECTRONIC MAGAZINES
___ "*Galaxy* Follows *Omni* into the Great Unknown," *Locus* 35(1): 9. July 1995.

ELECTRONIC PUBLISHING
___ "Electronic Gibsons," *Locus* 28(6): 7. June 1992.

ELECTRONIC PUBLISHING

ELECTRONIC PUBLISHING (continued)
___ Maddox, Tom. "Reports From the Electronic Frontier: Cyberspace, Freedom and the Law," *Locus* 30(1): 11, 49-50. January 1993.
___ Maddox, Tom. "Reports From the Electronic Frontier: I Sing the Text Electric, Part 2, Reading Hypertext," *Locus* 29(6): 11-12. December 1992.
___ Maddox, Tom. "Reports from the Electronic Frontier: Life on the Internet, Part 2; Exploring the Datasphere," *Locus* 30(3): 11, 58. March 1993.
___ Maddox, Tom. "Reports From the Electronic Frontier: Someone to Watch Over Me," *Locus* 30(5): 13, 53-54. May 1993.

ELECTRONIC RIGHTS
___ "Writers and Electronic Rights," *Locus* 33(6): 9, 79. December 1994.

ELGIN, SUZETTE HADEN
___ Sisk, David W. **Claiming Mastery over the Word: Transformations of Language in Six Twentieth Century Dystopias.** Ph.D. Dissertation, University of North Carolina, Chapel Hill, 1994. 405pp. (DAI-A 55/07, p. 1972. January 1995.)

ELIOT, GEORGE
___ Seeber, Hans-Ulrich. "Utopian Mentality in George Eliot's **Middlemarch** (1871/72) and in D. H. Lawrence's **The Rainbow**," *Utopian Studies* 6(1): 30-39. 1995.

ELIOT, T. S.
___ Airaudi, Jesse T. "Fantasia for Sewercovers and Drainpipes: T. S. Eliot, Abram Tertz, and the Surreal Quest for Pravda," in: Latham, Robert A. and Collins, Robert A., eds. **Modes of the Fantastic.** Westport, CT: Greenwood, 1995. pp.21-27.

ELLIOTT, DENHOLM
___ "Elliott, Denholm (Obituary)," *Science Fiction Chronicle* 14(3): 14. December 1992.

ELLIOTT, JANICE
___ "Elliott, Janice (Obituary)," *Science Fiction Chronicle* 17(1): 24. October/November 1995

ELLIOTT, KATE
___ King, T. Jackson. "Kate Elliott: The Writer as Anthropological Historian," *Mindsparks* 2(1): 29-34. 1994. (Whole No. 4)

ELLIOTT, TED
___ Warren, Bill. "Pulling the Strings," *Starlog* No. 208: 46-51, 72. November 1994.

ELLIS, JOHN
___ Mayo, Mike. "Successful Low-Budget SF Film-making Is Itself an Act of Science Fiction," *Science Fiction Age* 2(4): 20-23, 33-34. May 1994.

ELLISON, HARLAN
___ "1993 World Fantasy Awards Winners," *Locus* 31(6): 6. December 1993.
___ "1994 *Locus* Awards," *Locus* 33(2): 7. August 1994.
___ "Ellison Explains Internet Actions," *Science Fiction Chronicle* 17(1): 7-8. October/November 1995
___ "Ellison Goes Two-Dimensional," *Locus* 33(6): 8. December 1994.
___ "Ellison Recovering," *Locus* 28(2): 6. August 1992.
___ "Ellison Ties for Stoker Award After HWA Miscount Discovered," *Science Fiction Chronicle* 15(9): 4-5. August 1994.
___ "Ellison Wins Delayed Stoker," *Locus* 33(4): 8, 75. October 1994.
___ "Ellison's **Slippage** Slips," *Science Fiction Chronicle* 16(9): 6. August/September 1995.
___ "Ellsion Appeals for On-Line Input for **I, Robot** Graphics Novel," *Science Fiction Chronicle* 16(5): 4. March/April 1995.
___ "Harlan Ellison Attacks SFC Editor on National Cable TV Show," *Science Fiction Chronicle* 14(11): 4-6. August 1993.
___ "Longmeadow Options Ellison," *Locus* 33(3): 8, 79. September 1994.
___ "Longmeadow Press to Do Ellison," *Science Fiction Chronicle* 15(8): 6. June 1994.
___ "White Wolf to Publish Ellison Backlist," *Locus* 34(3): 8. March 1995.

ENCINO MAN (MOTION PICTURE)

ELLISON, HARLAN (continued)
___ "World Fantasy Awards," *Science Fiction Chronicle* 15(2): 4. November/December 1993.
___ Curry, Jayson. "Formal Synthesis in **Deathbird Stories**: Harlan Ellison's Stacked Deck," *Foundation* No. 56: 23-35. Autumn 1992.
___ Ellison, Harlan. **The Harlan Ellison Hornbook.** New York: Penzler, 1990. 418pp.
___ Ellison, Harlan. **Sleepless Nights in a Procrustean Bed.** San Bernardino, CA: Borgo, 1990. 192pp.
___ Francavualla, Joseph. "The Concept of the Divided Self and Harlan Ellison's 'I Have No Mouth and I Must Scream' and 'Shatterday'," *Journal of the Fantastic in the Arts* 6(2/3): 107-125. 1994.
___ Hirsch, Connie. "Harlan Ellison Rides a Dark Horse to Invade His Personal *Dream Corridors*," *Science Fiction Age* 3(3): 18. March 1995.
___ Kenny, Glenn. "Harlan Ellison Sounds Off," *TV Guide* 42(8): 26. February 19, 1994.
___ Paget, Stephen. "An Interview With Harlan Ellison," *Sense of Wonder* (B. Dalton) pp.10-12. October/November 1993.
___ Platt, Charles. **My Love Affair With Harlan Ellison.** New York: Interactive Systems, 1994. 36pp.

ELLISON, RALPH
___ Fleissner, Robert F. "H. G. Wells and Ralph Ellison: Need the Effect of One Invisible Man on Another Be *Itself* Invisible?," *Extrapolation* 33(4): 346-350. Winter 1992.

ELLUL, JACQUES
___ Matheson, T. J. "Triumphant Technology and Minimal Man: **The Technological Society**, Science Fiction Films, and Ridley Scott's **Alien**," *Extrapolation* 33(3): 215-229. Fall 1992.

ELROD, P. N.
___ Paget, Stephen. "An Interview With P. N. Elrod," *Sense of Wonder* (B. Dalton) pp.2-4. August/September 1993.

EMPIRE OF THE DARK (MOTION PICTURE)
___ Szebin, Frederick C. "**Empire of the Dark** (Review)," *Cinefantastique* 25(2): 59. April 1994.

EMPIRE STRIKES BACK (MOTION PICTURE)
___ SEE: STAR WARS: THE EMPIRE STRIKES BACK (MOTION PICTURE).

EMSHWILLER, CAROL
___ Holliday, Liz. "SFC Interviews: Carol Emshwiller," *Science Fiction Chronicle* 14(4): 5, 26-27. January 1993.

ENCINO MAN (MOTION PICTURE)
___ "***Encino Man***: Lowbrow Breakdown (Review)," *Washington (DC) Times.* May 22, 1992. in: *NewsBank. Film and Television.* 52:D5. 1992.
___ Burden, Martin. "***Encino Man*** Belongs Back on Ice (Review)," *New York (NY) Post.* May 22, 1992. in: *NewsBank. Film and Television.* 52: D2. 1992.
___ Hunter, Stephen. "***Encino Man*** Is Primitive Entertainment, From Plot to Message (Review)," *Baltimore (MD) Sun.* May 22, 1992. in: *NewsBank. Film and Television.* 52:C13. 1992.
___ Johnson, Barry. "***Encino Man*** Is Like Totally Bogus (Review)," *Portland (OR) The Oregonian.* May 25, 1992. in: *NewsBank. Film and Television.* 52:D3. 1992.
___ Johnson, Malcolm. "***Encino Man***: Just Hope There's Never a Sequel (Review)," *Hartford (CT) Courant.* May 22, 1992. in: *NewsBank. Film and Television.* 52:C11. 1992.
___ Kronke, David. "Tossing Caution, Geography to the Wind: ***Encino Man*** Neatly Sidesteps Namesake City (Review)," *Los Angeles (CA) Daily News.* February 12, 1992. in: *NewsBank. Film and Television.* 30:G13-G14. 1992.
___ Martin, Carrie. "Crusty ***Encino Man*** Totally, Like, Major, Mediocre (Review)," *Denver (CO) Post.* May 22, 1992. in: *NewsBank. Film and Television.* 52:C10. 1992.
___ Robley, Les P. "***Encino Man*** (Review)," *Cinefantastique* 23(2/3): 123. October 1992.
___ Sachs, Lloyd. "Timid ***Encino Man*** Skimps on Teen Spirit (Review)," *Chicago (IL) Sun Times.* May 22, 1992. in: *NewsBank. Film and Television.* 52:C12. 1992.
___ Shannon, Jeff. "***Encino Man***: Might As Well Roll It Back to the Stone Age (Review)," *Seattle (WA) Times.* May 22, 1992. in: *NewsBank. Film and Television.* 52:D6. 1992.

ENCINO MAN (MOTION PICTURE) (continued)
___ Sherman, Paul. "*Encino Man* Is Predictable Teen Comedy (Review)," *Boston (MA) Herald.* May 22, 1992. in: *NewsBank. Film and Television.* 52:C14. 1992.
___ Stark, Susan. "*Encino Man*'s Missing Links Are Plot and Quality Acting (Review)," *Detroit (MI) News.* May 22, 1992. in: *NewsBank. Film and Television.* 52:D1. 1992.
___ Wuntch, Phillip. "*Encino Man*: To Find This No-Brainer Funny, You'd Need a Neanderthal Sense of Humor (Review)," *Dallas (TX) Morning News.* May 22, 1992. in: *NewsBank. Film and Television.* 52:D4. 1992.

ENDE, MICHAEL
___ "Ende, Michael (Obituary)," *Locus* 35(4): 70. October 1995.
___ "Ende, Michael (Obituary)," *Science Fiction Chronicle* 17(1): 22. October/November 1995
___ Filmer, Kath. **Scepticism and Hope in Twentieth Century Fantasy Literature.** Bowling Green, OH: Bowling Green State University Popular Press, 1992. 160pp.

ENDFIELD, CY
___ Aldiss, Brian W. "Cy Endfield: An Appreciation," *Locus* 34(6): 66-67. June 1995.

ENDORE, GUY
___ Ball, Jerry L. "Guy Endore's **The Werewolf of Paris**: The Definitive Werewolf Novel?," *Studies in Weird Fiction* No. 17: 2-12. Summer 1995.

ENEMY MINE (MOTION PICTURE)
___ "*Enemy Mine* Back on Track for Fox," *Variety* p. 7. November 28, 1984.
___ "Petersen Lures Runaway to Bavaria," *Variety* p. 7, 38. January 23, 1985.
___ "Petersen Replaces Loncraine on 'Enemy'," *Variety* p. 4, 137. May 16, 1984.
___ Rabkin, William. "*Enemy Mine* (1985): Interview with Wolfgang Petersen," in: Goldberg, Lee et al. **Science Fiction Filmmaking in the 1980s.** Jefferson, NC: McFarland, 1995. pp.111-132.

ENGLAND, GEORGE ALLAN
___ Pittenger, Mark. "Imagining Genocide in the Progressive Era: The Socialist Science Fiction of George Allan England," *American Studies* 35(1): 91-108. Spring 1994.

ENGLUND, ROBERT
___ Wiater, Stanley. "Englund, Robert," in: Wiater, Stanley. **Dark Visions: Conversations with the Masters of the Horror Film.** New York: Avon, 1992. pp.67-76.

ENO, BRIAN
___ Joy, Dan. "Eye to Eye With Brian Eno," *Science Fiction Eye* No. 12: 60-67. Summer 1993.

ENVIRONMENT
___ McDowell, Elizabeth J. **Power and Environment in Recent Writings by Barbara Kingsolver, Ursula K. Le Guin, Alice Walker and Terry Tempest Williams.** Master's Thesis, University of Oregon, 1992. [Not seen.]
___ McLoughlin, Maryann. "Female Utopian Writers and the Environment," *CEA Forum* 22(1): 3-6. Winter 1992.

EQUINOX (MOTION PICTURE)
___ Wilt, David. "*Equinox* (Review)," *Cinefantastique* 25(4): 59. August 1994.

ERASERHEAD (MOTION PICTURE)
___ Lowe, Nick. "*Eraserhead* (Review)," *Interzone* No. 78: 35-36. December 1993.

ERB, INC.
___ McWhorter, George T. "Fire!: A Report on the Fire at ERB, Inc., May 8, 1958," *Burroughs Bulletin* NS. No. 18: 24-26. April 1994.

ERICKSON, STEVE
___ Drummond, Ron. "Steve Erickson...," *Science Fiction Eye* No. 12: 69-73. Summer 1993.

ERICKSON, STEVE (continued)
___ Erickson, Steve. "Arc d'X," *Science Fiction Eye* No. 12: 74-76. Summer 1993.
___ Kincaid, Paul. "Defying Rational Chronology: Time and Identity in the Work of Steve Erickson," *Foundation* No. 58: 27-42. Summer 1993.
___ Kincaid, Paul. "Secret Maps: The Topography of Fantasy and Morality in the Work of Steve Erickson," *Foundation* No. 57: 26-48. Spring 1993.

ESCAPE FROM FANTASIA (MOTION PICTURE)
___ SEE: NEVERENDING STORY III: ESCAPE FROM FANTASIA (MOTION PICTURE).

ESCHEVARRIA, RENE
___ Altman, Mark A. "*Star Trek: The Next Generation*: Rene Eschevarria, Waiter Cum Writer," *Cinefantastique* 24(3/4): 68-69. October 1993.
___ Chrissinger, Craig W. "Alien Ideas," *Starlog* No. 189: 54-58, 64. April 1993.

ESHBACH, LLOYD
___ Davin, Eric L. "Pioneer Publisher: An Interview With Lloyd Eshbach," *Fantasy Commentator* 8(1/2): 121-134. Winter 1993/1994. (Whole No. 45/46)

ESP
___ SEE: EXTRASENSORY PERCEPTION.

ESSEX, HARRY
___ Jankiewicz, Pat. "Bard of the Black Lagoon," *Starlog* No. 197: 21-24, 81. December 1993.

ESTES, ROSE
___ Attebery, Jennifer E. "The Trolls of Fiction: Ogres or Warm Fuzzies," *Journal of the Fantastic in the Arts* 7(1): 61-74. 1996.

ESTONIA
___ "SF in Estonia: 1992," *Locus* 29(1): 41. July 1992.

ETCHISON, DENNIS
___ "British Fantasy Awards," *Science Fiction Chronicle* 16(1): 5. October 1994.
___ Joshi, S. T. "Dennis Etchison: Spanning the Genres," *Studies in Weird Fiction* No. 15: 30-36. Summer 1994.
___ Schweitzer, Darrell. "Dennis Etchison," in: Schweitzer, Darrell. **Speaking of Horror: Interviews With Writers of the Supernatural.** San Bernardino, CA: Borgo, 1994. pp.37-46.

ETHICS
___ Milam, Michael C. "Science Fiction and Human Nature," *Humanist* 55(2): 29-32. March/April 1995.

EUROCON
___ SEE: EUROPEAN SCIENCE FICTION CONGRESS.

EUROCON, 1992
___ "1992 Eurocon and World SF Meeting Relocate," *Locus* 28(3): 7, 74. March 1992.

EUROCON, 1994
___ "Eurocon 1994," *Locus* 34(1) 44. January 1995.

EUROPE
___ Goudriaan, Roelof. "The European Echo: Science Fiction Fandom as a European Movement," in: Sanders, Joe, ed. **Science Fiction Fandom.** Westport, CT: Greenwood, 1994. pp.127-132.
___ Hordern, Kate. "Selling SF and Fantasy Translation Rights in Eastern Europe and Russia," *SFWA Bulletin* 29(2): 28-31. Summer 1995. (No. 127)
___ Lent, John A. **Comic Art of Europe: An International Comprehensive Bibliography.** Westport, CT: Greenwood, 1994. 663pp.

EUROPEAN SF SOCIETY AWARDS, 1994
___ "1994 European SF Society Awards," *Science Fiction Chronicle* 15(8): 10. June 1994.

EVANS, A. C.
___ Sneyd, Steve. "Space Opera: An Interview With A. C. Evans," *Fantasy Commentator* 8(3/4): 253-256. Fall 1995. (Whole No. 47/48)

EVANS, CHRISTOPHER
___ "BSFA Awards, 1993," *Locus* 32(5): 8, 66. May 1994.
___ Evans, Christopher. "On the Receiving End," *Interzone* No. 92: 31-33. February 1995.

EVANS, MONTGOMERY
___ Hassler, Sue S., ed. **Arthur Machen and Montgomery Evans: Letters of a Literary Friendship, 1923-1947**, ed. by Sue S. Hassler and Donald M. Hassler. Kent, OH: Kent State University Press, 1994. 195pp.

EVIL DEAD (MOTION PICTURE)
___ Uram, Sue. "*Evil Dead*: 8mm Amateur Origins," *Cinefantastique* 23(1): 26. August 1992.
___ Uram, Sue. "*Evil Dead*: The Original 16mm Horror," *Cinefantastique* 23(1): 31. August 1992.

EVIL DEAD II (MOTION PICTURE)
___ Uram, Sue. "*Evil Dead II*: Making the First Sequel," *Cinefantastique* 23(1): 39-41. August 1992.
___ Uram, Sue. "*Evil Dead II*: Working With Sam Raimi," *Cinefantastique* 23(1): 47. August 1992.

EVIL DEAD III: ARMY OF DARKNESS (MOTION PICTURE)
___ SEE: ARMY OF DARKNESS: EVIL DEAD III (MOTION PICTURE).

EVIL TOONS (MOTION PICTURE)
___ Thonen, John. "*Evil Toons* (Review)," *Cinefantastique* 23(1): 60. August 1992.

EVISON, KATHY
___ Wilson, Bill. "Mistress of the Sea," *Starlog* No. 216: 74-77. July 1995.

EVOLUTION
___ Ower, John. "Theology and Evolution in the Short Fiction of Walter M. Miller, Jr.," *Cithara* 25(2): 57-74. May 1986.

EWOKS (TV)
___ Kaufman, Dave. "Lucas Producing Two ABC Cartoons on Ewoks and R2D2," *Variety* p. 145. January 16, 1985.

EXCALIBUR (MOTION PICTURE)
___ Bartone, Richard C. "Variations on Arthurian Legend in **Lancelot du Lac** and **Excalibur**," in: Slocum, Sally K., ed. **Popular Arthurian Traditions**. Bowling Green, OH: Popular Press, 1992. pp.144-155.
___ Blanch, Robert J. "Gawain on Film," by Robert J. Blanch and Julian N. Wasserman. in: Harty, Kevin J., ed. **Cinema Arthuriana: Essays on Arthurian Film**. New York: Garland, 1991. pp.57-74.
___ Lacy, Norris J. "Mythopoeia in **Excalibur**," in: Harty, Kevin J., ed. **Cinema Arthuriana: Essays on Arthurian Film**. New York: Garland, 1991. pp.121-134.
___ Purdon, Liam O. "Hollywood's Myopic Medievalism: **Excalibur** and Malory's **Morte d'Arthur**," by Liam O. Purdon and Robert J. Blanch. in: Slocum, Sally K., ed. **Popular Arthurian Traditions**. Bowling Green, OH: Popular Press, 1992. pp.156-161.
___ Whitaker, Muriel. "Fire, Water, Rock: Elements of Setting in **Excalibur**," in: Harty, Kevin J., ed. **Cinema Arthuriana: Essays on Arthurian Film**. New York: Garland, 1991. pp.135-144.

EXHIBITIONS, 1992
___ "SF to Science Fact Exhibit in New York City," *Science Fiction Chronicle* 13(4): 5. January 1992.

EXHIBITIONS, 1993
___ Thrasher, Paula C. "*Star Trek* Exhibit Beams You Out of This World," *Atlanta Journal Constitution* Sec. WL, p. 1. January 30, 1993. [Not seen.]

EXHIBITIONS, 1995
___ McTaggart, Maureen. "It's Life, Jim, but Not as We've Known It," *Times Educational Supplement* 4139: SS21. October 27, 1995.
___ Paradis, Andrea. "New Dimensions at the National Library," *National Library News* 27(9): 11-14. September 1995.

EXHIBITIONS, 1995 (continued)
___ Winston, Iris. "Speaking From...Out of This World," *National Library News* (Canada) 27(5): 2-4. May 1995.

EXORCIST (MOTION PICTURE)
___ Willson, Robert F., Jr. "**The Exorcist** and Multi-Cinema Aesthetics," *Journal of Popular Film and Television* 3(2): 183-187. 1974.

EXTRASENSORY PERCEPTION
___ Guillaud, Lauric. "Paranormal Detectives: Sherlock Holmes in the House of Usher," *Paradoxa* 1(3): 301-319. 1995.
___ Stone-Blackburn, Susan. "Consciousness Evolution and Early Telepathic Tales," *Science Fiction Studies* 20(2): 241-250. July 1993.

EXTRATERRESTRIALS
___ Clark, Stephen R. L. "Extraterrestrial Intelligence: The Neglected Experiment," *Foundation* No. 61: 50-65. Summer 1994.

EXTROPY
___ Platt, Charles. "Taking the N out of Entropy," *Science Fiction Eye* No. 13: 30-35. Spring 1994.

FADS, HOBBIES
___ DeSmet, Kate. "Trekkers Chase Future with a Religious Zeal," *Detroit (MI) News*. March 13, 1995. in: *NewsBank. Film and Television*. 38:E7. 1995.

FAIRBAIRNS, ZOE
___ Barr, Marleen S. **Lost in Space: Probing Feminist Science Fiction and Beyond**. Chapel Hill, NC: University of North Carolina Press, 1993. 231pp.

FAIRMAN, PAUL W.
___ "Fairman, Paul W. (Obituary)," *Science Fiction News* (Australia) No. 54: 10. April 1978.

FAIRY TALES
___ Canaan, Howard. "All Hell into His Knapsack: The Spirit of Play in Two Fairy Tales," *Mythlore* 19(4): 41-45. Autumn 1993. (No. 74)
___ Curran, Ronald T. "Complex, Archetype, and Primal Fear: King's Use of Fairy Tales in **The Shining**," in: Magistrale, Tony, ed. **The Dark Descent: Essays Defining Stephen King's Horrorscape**. Westport, CT: Greenwood, 1992. pp.33-46.
___ Hess, Kathleen. "The Bittersweet Vine: Fairy Tales and Nursery Rhymes," *Mythlore* 19(2): 54-56, 60. Spring 1993. (No. 72)
___ Hruschka, John. "Anne Sexton and Anima Transformations: Transformations as a Critique of the Psychology of Love in Grimm's Fairy Tales," *Mythlore* 20(1): 45-47. Winter 1994. (Whole No. 75)
___ King, James R. **Old Tales and New Truths: Charting the Bright-Shadow World**. Albany: State University of New York Press, 1992. 267pp.
___ Rowen, Norma. "Reinscribing **Cinderella**: Jane Austen and the Fairy Tale," in: Sanders, Joe, ed. **Functions of the Fantastic**. Westport, CT: Greenwood, 1995. pp.29-36.
___ Sprug, Joseph W. **Index to Fairy Tales, 1987-1992: Including 310 Collections of Fairy Tales, Myths and Legends With Significant Pre-1987 Titles Not Previously Indexed**. Metuchen, NJ: Scarecrow, 1994. 587pp.
___ Stein, Murray, ed. **Psyche's Stories: Modern Jungian Interpretations of Fairy Tales**, ed. by Murray Stein and Lionel Corbett. Wilmette, IL: Chiron, 1991. 166pp.
___ Tatar, Maria. **Off With Their Heads: Fairy Tales and the Culture of Childhood**. Princeton, NJ: Princeton University Press, 1992. 295pp.
___ Taves, Brian. "**Adventures of the Rat Family**: A Verne Expert Brings Fairy Tale to English-Speaking Public," *Library of Congress Information Bulletin* 53(1): 7-11. January 10, 1994.
___ von Franz, Marie-Louise. **The Feminine in Fairy Tales**. New York: Shambala, 1993. 224pp. (Revised edition of **Problems of the Feminine in Fairy Tales**, 1972.)
___ Zipes, Jack. **Fairy Tale as Myth / Myth as Fairy Tale**. Lexington, KY: University Press of Kentucky, 1994. 192pp.
___ Zipes, Jack. "Recent Trends in the Contemporary American Fairy Tale," *Journal of the Fantastic in the Arts* 5(1): 13-41. 1992. (No. 17)
___ Zipes, Jack. "Recent Trends in the Contemporary American Fairy Tale," in: Sanders, Joe, ed. **Functions of the Fantastic**. Westport, CT: Greenwood, 1995. pp.1-18.

FAMILY

___ Christensen, Bryce J. "The Family in Utopia," *Renascence* 44(1): 31-44. Fall 1991.

___ Gordon, Andrew. "You'll Never Get out of Bedford Falls: The Inescapable Family in American Science Fiction and Fantasy Films," *Journal of Popular Film and Television* 20(2): 2-8. Summer 1992.

___ Palmer, Christopher. "Philip K. Dick and the Nuclear Family," in: Umland, Samuel J., ed. **Philip K. Dick: Contemporary Critical Interpretations**. Westport, CT: Greenwood, 1995. pp.61-80.

___ Sargent, Pamela. "Writing, Science Fiction, and Family Values," *Amazing Stories* 69(1): 100-111. Spring 1994.

FAMILY DOG (TV)

___ Persons, Dan. "*Family Dog* (Review)," *Cinefantastique* 25(2): 59. April 1994.

FAMOUS MONSTERS OF FILMLAND (MAGAZINE)

___ Jones, Stephen. "The Man Who Bought Bela Lugosi's Trousers, or, Ghouls Just Want to Have Fun," *Science Fiction Chronicle* 14(12): 28-29. September 1993.

FANCHER, HAMPTON

___ Lofficier, Randy. "Interview: Hamption Fancher," by Randy Lofficier and Jean-Marc Lofficier. *Starlog* 184: 35-39. November 1992.

FANGS (MOTION PICTURE)

___ Hogan, David J. "*Fangs* (Review)," *Filmfax* No. 35: 18, 20. October/November 1992.

FANS

___ "1992 *Locus* Survey Results," *Locus* 29(3): 52-53, 78. September 1992.

___ "1994 *Locus* Survey," *Locus* 33(3): 56-58, 84-85. September 1994.

___ "Ashley, Berry, Frost, Watkins in TAFF Race," *Science Fiction Chronicle* 14(4): 27. January 1993.

___ "*Dr. Who* Jamboree Attracts 40,000 Fans," *Variety* p. 2. April 6, 1983.

___ "DUFF's Roger Weddell Dies, Complicating New DUFF Race," *Science Fiction Chronicle* 14(4): 4. January 1993.

___ "Fan Club Listing," in: Hopkins, Mariane S., ed. **Fandom Directory No. 14**. Springfield, VA: Fandata, 1992. pp.97-137.

___ "Fan Publications Index," in: Hopkins, Mariane S., ed. **Fandom Directory No. 14**. Springfield, VA: Fandata, 1992. pp.23-69.

___ "First Fandom Reunion at Archon," *Locus* 35(6): 11. December 1995.

___ "From Berkeley's Greyhaven, a Fannish Fantasy Band," *Science Fiction Chronicle* 14(4): 27. January 1993.

___ **Preliminary Status Passage of the Science Fiction Fan Becoming a Member of the Science Fiction Fan Subculture**. Ann Arbor, MI: Tucker Video, 1994. 1 videocassette, 84 minutes. (Panel Presentation on SF fans at the 1994 Science Fiction Research Association Conference. Panelists: Diane Miller, Frederik Pohl, Alex Eisenstein, Leah Zeldes Smith, and Beverly Friend.)

___ "Results of the *Science Fiction Chronicle* Reader Survey," *Science Fiction Chronicle* 14(3): 30-31. December 1992.

___ "Roger Weddall Wins DUFF," *Science Fiction Chronicle* 13(10): 31. July/August 1992.

___ "Timebinders Preserving Fan History," *Science Fiction Chronicle* 17(2): 8. December 1995/January 1996.

___ Altman, Mark A. "Talking Trek," *Star Trek: The Official Fan Club* No. 94: 4-5. November/December 1993.

___ Baker, Wayne. "Community Service, the Final Frontier for the Klingon Fleet," *Chicago Tribune* p. 18D. January 31, 1993.

___ Berkman, Meredith. "Trek's Appeal," *Mademoiselle* 100(12): 85. December 1994.

___ Bick, Ilsa J. "Boys in Space: *Star Trek*, Latency, and the Neverending Story," *Cinema Journal* 35(2): 43-60. Winter 1996.

___ Bloch, Robert. **The Eighth Stage of Fandom**. Newark, NJ: Wildside Press, 1992. 208pp. (Reprint of the 1962 edition.)

___ Bosky, Bernadette L. "Amateur Press Associations: Intellectual Society and Social Intellectualism," in: Sanders, Joe, ed. **Science Fiction Fandom**. Westport, CT: Greenwood, 1994. pp.181-196.

___ Brown, Rich. "Post-Sputnik Fandom (1957-1990)," in: Sanders, Joe, ed. **Science Fiction Fandom**. Westport, CT: Greenwood, 1994. pp.75-102.

___ Busby, F. M. "Fan Clubs: An Example," in: Sanders, Joe, ed. **Science Fiction Fandom**. Westport, CT: Greenwood, 1994. pp.143-148.

FANS (continued)

___ Coriell, Rita. "The Coriell Years of Burroughs Fandom," *Burroughs Bulletin* NS. No. 12: 31-33. October 1992.

___ Coulson, Juanita. "Why Is a Fan?," in: Sanders, Joe, ed. **Science Fiction Fandom**. Westport, CT: Greenwood, 1994. pp.1-10.

___ Coulson, Robert. "Fandom as a Way of Life," in: Sanders, Joe, ed. **Science Fiction Fandom**. Westport, CT: Greenwood, 1994. pp.11-14.

___ Davis, Erik. "The Imperial Race," *Village Voice* 38(47): 35-40. November 23, 1993.

___ DeCarlo, Tessa. "Style: Costuming at the World Con," *Omni* 16(12): 22. September 1994.

___ DeVore, Howard. "A Science Fiction Collector," in: Sanders, Joe, ed. **Science Fiction Fandom**. Westport, CT: Greenwood, 1994. pp.221-228.

___ Dewey, Patrick R. **Fan Club Directory: 2000 Fan Clubs and Fan Mail Addresses in the United States and Abroad**. Jefferson, NC: McFarland, 1993. 104pp.

___ Dingbo, Wu. "Fandom in China," in: Sanders, Joe, ed. **Science Fiction Fandom**. Westport, CT: Greenwood, 1994. pp.133-136.

___ Eskin, Leah. "Sci-fi's a Smash," *Chicago Tribune* Sec. 7, p. 18. July 23, 1993.

___ Fratz, Doug. "The Twenty-Year Spree: A Personal History of *Thrust/Quantum*," *Quantum* No. 43/44: 51-66. Spring/Summer 1993.

___ Gamboa, Suzanne. "Guest of Honor at *Star Trek* Event Urges Support for NASA Space Station," *Austin (TX) American Statesman* Sec. B, p. 1, 3. June 7, 1993.

___ Gaughan, Jack. "An Apprenticeship: Artist," in: Sanders, Joe, ed. **Science Fiction Fandom**. Westport, CT: Greenwood, 1994. pp.207-210.

___ Goudriaan, Roelof. "The European Echo: Science Fiction Fandom as a European Movement," in: Sanders, Joe, ed. **Science Fiction Fandom**. Westport, CT: Greenwood, 1994. pp.127-132.

___ Gunderloy, Mike. **The World of Zines: A Guide to the Independent Magazine Revolution**. New York: Penguin Books, 1992. 181pp.

___ Hanson, Alan. "The Edgar Rice Burroughs Amateur Press Association," *Burroughs Bulletin* NS No. 11: 27-30. July 1992.

___ Hatcher, Lint. "Monster Fan 2000," by Lint Hatcher and Rod Bennett. *Wonder* No. 7: 39-43, 54-56. 1993.

___ Hogan, Jeanne. "Operation Enterprise," *Star Trek: The Official Fan Club Magazine* No. 92: 1, 34. July/August 1993.

___ Hopkins, Mariane S., ed. **Fandom Directory, No. 14: 1992-1993 Edition**. Springfield, VA: Fandata, 1992. 544pp.

___ Hopkins, Mariane S., ed. **Fandom Directory, No. 15, 1995-1996**. Springfield, VA: Fandata Publications, 1995. 607pp.

___ Hutchison, David. "Rescues at Sea Trek," *Starlog* No. 196: 50-51. November 1993.

___ Jeeves, Terry. "British Fandom," in: Sanders, Joe, ed. **Science Fiction Fandom**. Westport, CT: Greenwood, 1994. pp.113-118.

___ Jenkins, Henry. "At Other Times, Like Females: Gender and *Star Trek* Fiction," in: Tulloch, John and Jenkins, Henry, eds. **Science Fiction Audiences: Watching Doctor Who and Star Trek**. New York: Routledge, 1995. pp.196-212.

___ Jenkins, Henry. "Beyond the *Star Trek* Phenomenon: Reconceptualizing the Science Fiction Audience," by Henry Jenkins and John Tulloch. in: Tulloch, John and Jenkins, Henry, eds. **Science Fiction Audiences: Watching Doctor Who and Star Trek**. New York: Routledge, 1995. pp.3-24.

___ Jenkins, Henry. "How Many Starfleet Officers Does It Take to Change a Lightbulb?: *Star Trek* at MIT," by Henry Jenkins and Greg Dancer. in: Tulloch, John and Jenkins, Henry, eds. **Science Fiction Audiences: Watching Doctor Who and Star Trek**. New York: Routledge, 1995. pp.213-236.

___ Jenkins, Henry. "Infinite Diversity in Infinite Combinations: Genre and Authorship in *Star Trek*," in: Tulloch, John and Jenkins, Henry, eds. **Science Fiction Audiences: Watching Doctor Who and Star Trek**. New York: Routledge, 1995. pp.175-195.

___ Jenkins, Henry. "Out of the Closet and into the Universe: Queers and *Star Trek*," in: Tulloch, John and Jenkins, Henry, eds. **Science Fiction Audiences: Watching Doctor Who and Star Trek**. New York: Routledge, 1995. pp.237-265.

___ Leeper, Mark R. "Commando Cody and His Lost Science Fiction Fan," *Lan's Lantern* No. 40: 8-9. September 1992.

___ Letson, Russell. "Contributions to the Critical Dialogue: As an Academic Sees It," in: Sanders, Joe, ed. **Science Fiction Fandom**. Westport, CT: Greenwood, 1994. pp.229-234.

___ Lichtenberg, Jacqueline. **Star Trek Lives!**, by Jacqueline Lichtenberg, Sandra Marshak and Jean Winston. New York: Bantam, 1975. 274pp.

FANS (continued)

___ Lofton, S. C. "Under the Influence," *Lan's Lantern* No. 40: 120-122. September 1992.

___ Lupoff, Richard A. "Into the Aether, Junior Spacepersons!," in: Sanders, Joe, ed. **Science Fiction Fandom**. Westport, CT: Greenwood, 1994. pp.197-206.

___ Luttrell, Hank. "The Science Fiction Convention Scene," in: Sanders, Joe, ed. **Science Fiction Fandom**. Westport, CT: Greenwood, 1994. pp.149-160.

___ Madle, Robert A. "Fandom up to World War II," in: Sanders, Joe, ed. **Science Fiction Fandom**. Westport, CT: Greenwood, 1994. pp.37-54.

___ Mathews, Race. "Whirlaway to *Thrilling Wonder Stories*: Boyhood Reading in Wartime and Postwar Melbourne," *Metaphysical Review* No. 22/23: 5-16. November 1995.

___ Miesel, Sandra. "The Fan as Critic," in: Sanders, Joe, ed. **Science Fiction Fandom**. Westport, CT: Greenwood, 1994. pp.235-242.

___ Moskowitz, Sam. "The Immortal Storm II: A History of Science Fiction Fandom, Part One," *Fantasy Commentator* 8(1/2): 107-120, 13. Winter 1993/1994. (Whole No. 45/46)

___ Moskowitz, Sam. "The Immortal Storm II: A History of Science Fiction Fandom, Part Two," *Fantasy Commentator* 8(3/4): 278-288. Fall 1995. (Whole No. 47/48)

___ Moskowitz, Sam. "The Origins of Science Fiction Fandom: A Reconstruction," in: Sanders, Joe, ed. **Science Fiction Fandom**. Westport, CT: Greenwood, 1994. pp.17-36.

___ Osako, Masamichi. "Science Fiction Fandom in Japan," in: Sanders, Joe, ed. **Science Fiction Fandom**. Westport, CT: Greenwood, 1994. pp.137-140.

___ Peet, Judy. "2000 'Philes' Trek to Convention," *Newark (NJ) Star-Ledger*. November 25, 1995. in: *NewsBank. Film and Television*. 107: C12. 1995.

___ Platt, Charles. **My Love Affair With Harlan Ellison**. New York: Interactive Systems, 1994. 36pp.

___ Point, Michael. "Business on an Astronomical Scale," *Austin (TX) American Statesman* Time Out, p. 5. June 15, 1993.

___ Pratchett, Terry. "Kevins," *The Author* pp.132-133. Winter 1993.

___ Rampas, Zdenek. **Kdo je Kdo v ceské a slovenské science fiction**, by Zdenek Rampas and Pavel Kosatik. Praha, CZ: Ceskoslovenského fandomu, 1994. 84pp. [Not seen.]

___ Reed, Jilly. "What's a Convention For, Mummy?," *Matrix* No. 116: 10-11. August/September 1995.

___ Riddell, Paul T. **Squashed Armadillocon: Or 'Fear and Loathing in Austin: A Savage Journey into the Heart of the Fanboy Dream'**. Eugene, OR: Hillybilly Press, 1993. 151pp. [Not seen.]

___ Ross, Bill. "The Tenth Annual E. C. O. F. Gathering," *Burroughs Bulletin* NS. No. 12: 21-30. October 1992.

___ Rusch, Kristine K. "Editorial: Magazine Readership," *Magazine of Fantasy and Science Fiction* 89(1): 6-8. July 1995.

___ Rusch, Kristine K. "Editorial: New Readers," *Magazine of Fantasy and Science Fiction* 87(2): 5-7. August 1994.

___ Sanders, Joe L. "Glossary of Fanspeak," by Joe L. Sanders and Rich Brown. in: Sanders, Joe, ed. **Science Fiction Fandom**. Westport, CT: Greenwood, 1994. pp.265-270.

___ Sanders, Joe L., ed. **Science Fiction Fandom**. Westport, CT: Greenwood, 1994. 293pp.

___ Schelly, Bill. **The Golden Age of Comic Fandom**. Seattle, WA: Hamster Press, 1995. 144pp.

___ Siclari, Joe. "Science Fiction Fandom: A Selected, Annotated Bibliography," in: Sanders, Joe, ed. **Science Fiction Fandom**. Westport, CT: Greenwood, 1994. pp.245-264.

___ Speer, Jack. **Up to Now: A History of Fandom as Jack Speer Sees It**. Brooklyn, NY: Richard Newsome, [1996?]. 48pp. (Reprint, originally published in 1939.) [Not seen.]

___ Steele, Allen. "SF vs. The Thing," *New York Review of Science Fiction* No. 86: 13-16. October 1995.

___ Stone, Graham. "Beginnings," *Science Fiction News* (Australia) No. 100: 2-12. November 1986.

___ Stone, Graham. "Early Days in Sydney SF Activities," *Science Fiction News* (Australia) No. 61: 6-13. June 1979.

___ Stone, Graham. "Fifty Years of Science Fiction Groups in Australia," *Science Fiction News* (Australia) No. 108: 2-8. November 1989.

___ Thomas, Pascal J. "Science Fiction Fandom in Western Europe: A French Perspective," in: Sanders, Joe, ed. **Science Fiction Fandom**. Westport, CT: Greenwood, 1994. pp.119-126.

FANS (continued)

___ Trimble, John. "Alternative Fandoms," by John Trimble and Bjo Trimble. in: Sanders, Joe, ed. **Science Fiction Fandom**. Westport, CT: Greenwood, 1994. pp.103-109.

___ Tulloch, John. "But He's a Time Lord! He's a Time Lord!: Reading Formations, Followers, and Fans," in: Tulloch, John and Jenkins, Henry, eds. **Science Fiction Audiences: Watching Doctor Who and Star Trek**. New York: Routledge, 1995. pp.125-143.

___ Tulloch, John. "But Why Is *Doctor Who* So Attractive?: Negotiating Ideology and Pleasure," in: Tulloch, John and Jenkins, Henry, eds. **Science Fiction Audiences: Watching Doctor Who and Star Trek**. New York: Routledge, 1995. pp.108-124.

___ Tulloch, John. "The Changing Audiences of Science Fiction," in: Tulloch, John and Jenkins, Henry, eds. **Science Fiction Audiences: Watching Doctor Who and Star Trek**. New York: Routledge, 1995. pp.50-63.

___ Tulloch, John. "It's Meant to Be Fantasy: Teenage Audiences and Genre," by John Tulloch and Marian Tulloch. in: Tulloch, John and Jenkins, Henry, eds. **Science Fiction Audiences: Watching Doctor Who and Star Trek**. New York: Routledge, 1995. pp.86-107.

___ Tulloch, John. "Positioning the SF Audience: *Star Trek*, *Doctor Who* and the Texts of Science Fiction," in: Tulloch, John and Jenkins, Henry, eds. **Science Fiction Audiences: Watching Doctor Who and Star Trek**. New York: Routledge, 1995. pp.25-49.

___ Tulloch, John. **Science Fiction Audiences: Doctor Who, Star Trek, and Their Fans**. London: Routledge, 1994. 294pp.

___ Tulloch, John. "Throwing a Little Bit of Poison into Future Generations: *Doctor Who* Audiences and Ideology," in: Tulloch, John and Jenkins, Henry, eds. **Science Fiction Audiences: Watching Doctor Who and Star Trek**. New York: Routledge, 1995. pp.67-85.

___ Tulloch, John. "We're Only a Speck in the Ocean: The Fans as Powerless Elite," in: Tulloch, John and Jenkins, Henry, eds. **Science Fiction Audiences: Watching Doctor Who and Star Trek**. New York: Routledge, 1995. pp.144-172.

___ Verba, Joan M. **Boldly Writing: A Trekker Fan and Zine History, 1967-1987**. Minnetonka, MN: FTL Publications, 1996. 100pp.

___ Warner, Harry, Jr. "Fandom Between World War II and *Sputnik*," in: Sanders, Joe, ed. **Science Fiction Fandom**. Westport, CT: Greenwood, 1994. pp.65-74.

___ Warner, Harry, Jr. "A History of Fanzines," in: Sanders, Joe, ed. **Science Fiction Fandom**. Westport, CT: Greenwood, 1994. pp.175-180.

___ Warner, Harry, Jr. **A Wealth of Fable: An Informal History of Science Fiction Fandom in the 1950s**. Van Nuys, CA: SCIFI Press, 1992. 456pp.

___ Weinberg, Robert. "The Fan Presses," in: Sanders, Joe, ed. **Science Fiction Fandom**. Westport, CT: Greenwood, 1994. pp.211-220.

___ Whitmore, Tom. "Science Fiction Conventions: Behind the Scenes," by Tom Whitmore and Debbie Notkin. in: Sanders, Joe, ed. **Science Fiction Fandom**. Westport, CT: Greenwood, 1994. pp.161-171.

___ Widner, Art. "Wartime Fandom," in: Sanders, Joe, ed. **Science Fiction Fandom**. Westport, CT: Greenwood, 1994. pp.55-64.

___ Yeoland, Sally. "Sally and John: The Early Years," by Sally Yeoland and John Bangsund. *Metaphysical Review* No. 22/23: 17-44. November 1995.

FANTASIA (MOTION PICTURE)

___ "30-Year Old Disney-Sikowski Film Hopefully Seen as Roper for Today's Fantasy Fancying Youth Market," *Variety* p. 5. November 26, 1969.

___ "*Fantasia*: 30 Years After, Now Red Hot at B. O.," *Variety* p. 3. June 24, 1970.

___ "Technique of *Fantasia* Gets New Buff Breed," *Variety* p. 7. February 25, 1970.

FANTASPORTO FANTASY FILM FESTIVAL, 1986

___ "100 Films Scheduled for Fantasporto Fest," *Variety* p. 7. January 22, 1986.

FANTASTIC FOUR (MOTION PICTURE)

___ Biodrowski, Steve. "*Fantastic Four*: Optic Nerve Makeups," *Cinefantastique* 24(3/4): 10. October 1993.

___ Biodrowski, Steve. "*Fantastic Four*," *Cinefantastique* 24(3/4): 8-11. October 1993.

___ Shapiro, Marc. "Man on Fire," *Starlog* No. 195: 63-65. October 1993.

FANTASTIC PLANET (MOTION PICTURE)

___ Hannaham, James. "Wild Planet," *Village Voice* 39(3): 56-57. January 18, 1994.

FANTASY

___ "Helmer-Distrib Chung Says Fantasy Pics Don't Make It in South Korea," *Variety* p.44. October 9, 1985.

___ Airaudi, Jesse T. "Fantasia for Sewercovers and Drainpipes: T. S. Eliot, Abram Tertz, and the Surreal Quest for Pravda," in: Latham, Robert A. and Collins, Robert A., eds. **Modes of the Fantastic**. Westport, CT: Greenwood, 1995. pp.21-27.

___ Alazraki, Jaime. "Qué es lo neofantástico?," *Mester* (UCLA) 19(2): 21-34. Fall 1990. [Not seen.]

___ Aldiss, Brian W. "Fantasy: U.S. Versus U.K.," *Monad* No. 2: 17-24. March 1992.

___ Aldiss, Brian W. "One Hump or Two?," in: Aldiss, Brian W. **The Detached Retina: Aspects of SF and Fantasy**. Syracuse, NY: Syracuse University Press, 1995. pp.133-136.

___ Alexander, Lloyd. "Fantasy and the Human Condition," *New Advocate* 1(2): 75-83. Spring 1988.

___ Andriano, Joseph. "The Masks of Gödel: Math and Myth in Thomas Pynchon's **Gravity's Rainbow**," in: Latham, Robert A. and Collins, Robert A., eds. **Modes of the Fantastic**. Westport, CT: Greenwood, 1995. pp.14-20.

___ Arbuckle, Nan. "That Hidden Strength: C. S. Lewis' Merlin as Modern Grail," in: Watson, Jeanie and Fries, Marueen, eds. **The Figure of Merlin in the Nineteenth and Twentieth Centuries**. Lewiston, NY: Mellen, 1989. pp.79-99.

___ Attebery, Brian. "Fantasy and the Narrative Transaction," in: Ruddick, Nicholas, ed. **State of the Fantastic**. Westport, CT: Greenwood, 1992. pp.15-27.

___ Attebery, Brian. "The Politics of Fantasy," in: Latham, Robert A. and Collins, Robert A., eds. **Modes of the Fantastic**. Westport, CT: Greenwood, 1995. pp.1-13.

___ Attebery, Brian. **Strategies of Fantasy**. Bloomington: University of Indiana Press, 1992. 152pp.

___ Auerbach, Nina, ed. **Forbidden Journeys: Fairy Tales and Fantasies**, ed. by Nina Auerbach and U. C. Knoepflmacher. Chicago: University of Chicago Press, 1992. 373pp.

___ Bilija, Ksenija. "From Golem to Plastisex: An Analytical Survey of Spanish American Fantastic Literature," *Journal of the Fantastic in the Arts* 7(2/3): 201-214. 1995.

___ Bloom, Harold, ed. **Classic Fantasy Writers**. New York: Chelsea House, 1994. 187pp.

___ Bloom, Harold, ed. **Modern Fantasy Writers**. New York: Chelsea House, 1995. 194pp.

___ Boyers, Robert H. "Introduction: Classic Fantasy," by Robert H. Boyers and Kenneth J. Zahorski. in: Boyer, Robert H. and Zahorski, Kenneth J., eds. **Visions and Imaginings: Classic Fantasy Fiction**. Chicago: Academy Chicago, 1992. pp.xiii-xxvi.

___ Butsch, Richard J. **Personal Perception in Scientific and Medieval World Views: A Comparative Study of Fantasy Literature**. Ph.D. Dissertation, Rutgers University, 1975. 95pp. (DAI 35: 2518B.)

___ Caswell, Brian. "The Fantasy Phenomenon," *Orana* 30(4): 256-267. November 1994.

___ Caywood, Carolyn. "The Quest for Character," *School Library Journal* 41(3): 152. March 1995.

___ Charnas, Suzy M. "A Case for Fantasy," *ALAN Review* 19(3): 20-22. Spring 1992.

___ Chichester, Ana G. "Metamorphosis in Two Short Stories of the Fantastic by Virgilio Peñera and Felisberto Hernández," *Studies in Short Fiction* 31(3): 385-395. Summer 1994.

___ Congreve, Bill. "The Rise of Australian Fantasy," *Aurealis* No. 12: 43-48. 1993.

___ Dingley, Robert. "Meaning Everything: The Image of Pan at the Turn of the Century," in: Filmer, Kath, ed. **Twentieth-Century Fantasists: Essays in Culture, Society and Belief in Twentieth Century Mythopoeic Literature**. New York: St. Martin's, 1992. pp.47-59.

___ Ensor, Allison. "The Magic of Fol-de-Rol: Mark Twain's Merlin," in: Watson, Jeanie and Fries, Marueen, eds. **The Figure of Merlin in the Nineteenth and Twentieth Centuries**. Lewiston, NY: Mellen, 1989. pp.51-63.

___ Fickey, Pierrette. "Louis Aragon: The Fantastic in Collage and Poetry," in: Latham, Robert A. and Collins, Robert A., eds. **Modes of the Fantastic**. Westport, CT: Greenwood, 1995. pp.38-47.

FANTASY (continued)

___ Filmer, Kath. "Atseiniau O Ddyddiau Gynt: Welsh Myth and Culture in Contemporary Fantasy," in: Filmer, Kath, ed. **Twentieth-Century Fantasists: Essays in Culture, Society and Belief in Twentieth Century Mythopoeic Literature**. New York: St. Martin's, 1992. pp.108-120.

___ Filmer, Kath. "Dreaming Each Other: The Discourse of Fantasy in Contemporary News Media," in: Filmer, Kath, ed. **Twentieth-Century Fantasists: Essays in Culture, Society and Belief in Twentieth Century Mythopoeic Literature**. New York: St. Martin's, 1992. pp.193-206.

___ Filmer, Kath. "Introduction," in: Filmer, Kath, ed. **Twentieth-Century Fantasists: Essays in Culture, Society and Belief in Twentieth Century Mythopoeic Literature**. New York: St. Martin's, 1992. pp.1-7.

___ Filmer, Kath. **Scepticism and Hope in Twentieth Century Fantasy Literature**. Bowling Green, OH: Bowling Green State University Popular Press, 1992. 160pp.

___ Filmer, Kath, ed. **Twentieth-Century Fantasists: Essays on Culture, Society and Belief in Twentieth Century Mythopoeic Literature**. New York: St. Martin's, 1992. 212pp.

___ Forrest, Linda A. "Young Adult Fantasy and the Search for Gender-Fair Genres," *Journal of Youth Services in Libraries* 7(1): 37-42. Fall 1993.

___ Freeman, Judy. "In the Realm of Fantasy," *Instructor* 104(8): 77-82. May 1995.

___ Frongia, Terri. "Merlin's Fathers: The Sacred and the Profane," *Children's Literature Association Quarterly* 18(3): 120-125. Fall 1993.

___ Goderham, David. "Children's Fantasy Literature: Toward an Anatomy," *Children's Literature in Education* 26(3): 171-183. September 1995.

___ Golden, Joanne M. **A Schema for Analyzing Response to Literature Applied to the Responses of Fifth and Eighth Graders to Realistic and Fantasy Short Stories**. Ph.D. Dissertation, Ohio State University, 1978. 195pp. (DAI 39: 5996A. Apr. 1978.)

___ Goodrich, Peter. "Modern Merlins: An Aeriel Survey (Bibliographic Essay)," in: Watson, Jeanie and Fries, Marueen, eds. **The Figure of Merlin in the Nineteenth and Twentieth Centuries**. Lewiston, NY: Mellen, 1989. pp.175-197.

___ Goodrich, Peter. "The New Age Mage: Merlin as Contemporary Occult Icon," *Journal of the Fantastic in the Arts* 5(1): 42-73. 1992. (No. 17)

___ Gordon, Joan. "Surviving the Survivor: Art Spiegelman's **Maus**," *Journal of the Fantastic in the Arts* 5(2): 80-89. 1993. (No. 18)

___ Goslee, David F. "Lost in the Siege Perilous: The Merlin of Tennyson's Idylls," in: Watson, Jeanie and Fries, Maureen, eds. **The Figure of Merlin in the Nineteenth and Twentieth Centuries**. Lewiston, NY: Mellen, 1989. pp.35-50.

___ Grivet, Charles. **Fantastique-Fiction**. Paris: Presses universitaires francaises, 1993. 255pp.

___ Grixti, Joseph. "Consumed Identities: Heroic Fantasy and the Trivialization of Selfhood," *Journal of Popular Culture* 28(3): 207-227. Winter 1994.

___ Hahm, Oscar. "Trayectoria del cuento fantástico hispanoamericano," *Mester* (UCLA) 19(2): 35-46. Fall 1990.

___ Hanks, D. Thomas, Jr. "T. H. White's Merlin: More Than Malory Made Him," in: Watson, Jeanie and Fries, Marueen, eds. **The Figure of Merlin in the Nineteenth and Twentieth Centuries**. Lewiston, NY: Mellen, 1989. pp.100-120.

___ Harger-Grinling, Virginia, ed. **Robbe-Grillet and the Fantastic: A Collection of Essays**, ed. by Virginia Harger-Grinling and Tony Chadwick. Westport, CT: Greenwood, 1994. 168pp.

___ Hughes, Linda K. "Illusion and Relation: Merlin as Image of the Artist in Tennyson, Doré, Burene-Jones, and Beardsley," in: Watson, Jeanie and Fries, Marueen, eds. **The Figure of Merlin in the Nineteenth and Twentieth Centuries**. Lewiston, NY: Mellen, 1989. pp.1-33.

___ Irving, James A. **The World Makers: Techniques of Fantasy in J. R. R. Tolkien's The Lord of the Rings and Ursula K. Le Guin's Earthsea Trilogy**. Master's Thesis, Acadia University, 1976. 128pp.

___ Irwin, Robert. "Fantasy Without God," *Times Literary Supplement* 4770: 7. September 2, 1994.

___ Jordan, Anne D. "Tell Me Where Is Fancy Bred: Fantasy," *Teaching and Learning Literature* 4(4): 16-20. March/April 1995.

___ Kalade, Linas. "Weaving a Colourful Tapestry," *Viewpoint on Books for Young Adults* 1(2): 8-9. Winter 1993.

FANTASY

FANTASY (continued)

___ Kenny, Virginia C. "The Eternal Feminine Reclaimed: Ford Madox Ford's Medieval Fantasies," in: Filmer, Kath, ed. **Twentieth-Century Fantasists: Essays in Culture, Society and Belief in Twentieth Century Mythopoeic Literature**. New York: St. Martin's, 1992. pp.60-70.

___ Kerman, Judith B. "Uses of the Fantastic in Literature of the Holocaust," *Journal of the Fantastic in the Arts* 5(2): 14-31. 1993. (No. 18)

___ Kilworth, Garry. "On Animal Fantasy," *Million* 11: 11-15. 1992. [Not seen.]

___ Kimsey, John. "Dolorous Strokes, or Balin at the Bat: Malamud, Malory and Chrétien," in: Morse, Donald E., ed. **The Celebration of the Fantastic**. Westport, CT: Greenwood, 1992. pp.103-112.

___ King, Roma A., Jr. "Charles William's Merlin: Worker in Time of the Images of Eternity," in: Watson, Jeanie and Fries, Marueen, eds. **The Figure of Merlin in the Nineteenth and Twentieth Centuries**. Lewiston, NY: Mellen, 1989. pp.65-77.

___ Kordeski, Stanley. **Anatomy of Fantasy: An Examination of Works of J. R. R. Tolkien and C. S. Lewis**. Master's Thesis, University of Vermont, 1975. 67pp.

___ Kramer, Reinhold. "Im/maculate: Some Instances of Gnostic Science Fiction," in: Ruddick, Nicholas, ed. **State of the Fantastic**. Westport, CT: Greenwood, 1992. pp.49-58.

___ Latham, Robert A. "Collage as Critique and Invention in the Fiction of William S. Burroughs and Kathy Acker," in: Latham, Robert A. and Collins, Robert A., eds. **Modes of the Fantastic**. Westport, CT: Greenwood, 1995. pp.29-37.

___ Latham, Robert A., ed. **Modes of the Fantastic: Selected Essays from the Twelfth International Conference on the Fantastic in the Arts**, ed. by Robert A. Latham and Robert A. Collins. Westport, CT: Greenwood, 1995. 234pp.

___ Lehr, Susan. "Fantasy: Inner Journeys for Today's Child," *Publishing Research Quarterly* 7(3): 91-101. Fall 1991. [Not seen.]

___ Lepage, Francoise. "Pour une rhetorique de la representation fantastique (In Search of a Theory of Illustration of Fantastique)," *Canadian Children's Literature* 60: 97-107. 1990. [Not seen.]

___ Malekin, Peter. "Knowing about Knowing: Paradigms of Knowledge in the Postmodern Fantastic," in: Ruddick, Nicholas, ed. **State of the Fantastic**. Westport, CT: Greenwood, 1992. pp.41-47.

___ Manlove, C. N. **Christian Fantasy From 1200 to the Present**. Notre Dame, IN: University of Notre Dame Press, 1992. 356pp.

___ Manlove, C. N. "Scottish Fantasy," *Extrapolation* 35(1): 15-32. Spring 1994.

___ Manlove, C. N. **Scottish Fantasy Literature: A Critical Survey**. Edinburgh: Canongate Academic, 1994. 263pp.

___ Manlove, C. N. "Victorian and Modern Fantasy: Some Contrasts," in: Morse, Donald E., ed. **The Celebration of the Fantastic**. Westport, CT: Greenwood, 1992. pp.9-22.

___ Mappin, Alf. "A Core List: Fantasy," *Literature Base* 3(2): 16-17. June 1992.

___ Mappin, Alf. "Defining Fantasy," *Literature Base* 3(2): 12-15. June 1992.

___ Marcone, Jorge. "La tradición oral y el cuento fantástico en 'La cruz del diablo' de G. A. Bécquer," *Mester* (UCLA) 19(2): 47-62. Fall 1990. [Not seen.]

___ McKillip, Patricia A. "Once Upon a Time Too Often," *Writer* 105(8): 18-20, 44. August 1992.

___ Michalson, Karen. **Victorian Fantasy Literature: Literary Battles with Church and Empire**. Lewiston, NY: Edwin Mellen Press, 1990. 292pp.

___ Miller, Miriam Y. "J. R. R. Tolkien's Merlin--An Old Man With a Staff: Galdalf and the Magus Tradition," in: Watson, Jeanie and Fries, Marueen, eds. **The Figure of Merlin in the Nineteenth and Twentieth Centuries**. Lewiston, NY: Mellen, 1989. pp.121-142.

___ Morin, Lise. "Deux frères siamois: le fantastique canonique et le néo-fantastique," *Imagine* No. 61: 59-68. September 1992.

___ Morse, Donald E., ed. **The Celebration of the Fantastic: Selected Papers From the Tenth Anniversary International Conference on the Fantastic in the Arts**, ed. by Donald E. Morse, Marshall B. Tymn and Csilla Bertha. Westport, CT: Greenwood, 1992. 309pp.

___ Morse, Donald E., ed. **More Real Than Reality: The Fantastic in Irish Literature and the Arts**, ed. by Donald E. Morse and Csilla Bertha. Westport, CT: Greenwood, 1992. 266pp.

___ Naddaff, Sandra. **Arabesque: Narrative Structure and the Aesthetics of Repetition in the '1001 Nights'**. Evanston, IL: Northwestern University Press, 1991. 156pp.

FANTASY (continued)

___ Noll, Richard. **Vampires, Werewolves, and Demons: Twentieth Century Reports in the Psychiatric Literature**. New York: Brunner, 1992. 244pp.

___ Orozco-Allan, Gloria. "Lo fantástico y el discurso femenino en **Dos veces Alicia**, de Albalucia Angel," *Mester* (UCLA) 19(2): 137-144. Fall 1990.

___ Palwick, Susan. "Never Going Home: Failed Fantasy Logic in Kathleen Sidney's **Michael and the Magic Man** and Robert Irwin's **The Limits of Vision**," *New York Review of Science Fiction* No. 11: 15-17. July 1989.

___ Pierce, Tamora. "Fantasy: Why Kids Read It, Why Kids Need It," *School Library Journal* 39(10): 50-51. October 1993.

___ Platt, Charles. "News From the Ghetto: The Teflon Fantasist," *Quantum* No. 43/44: 19-20. Spring/Summer 1993.

___ Pollack, Andrew. "Fantasy Novels About WWII Becoming Popular in Japan," *Austin (TX) American Statesman* Sec. A, p. 17. March 19, 1995.

___ Pratchett, Terry. "Let There Be Dragons," *Science Fiction Chronicle* 15(1): 5, 28-29. October 1993.

___ Prickett, Stephen. "Centering the Margins: Postmodernism and Fantasy," in: Filmer, Kath, ed. **Twentieth-Century Fantasists: Essays in Culture, Society and Belief in Twentieth Century Mythopoeic Literature**. New York: St. Martin's, 1992. pp.183-192.

___ Rangel, Javier. "De lo fantástico a lo alegórico: El llamado a la resistencia en **The Shrunken Head of Pancho Villa**," *Mester* (UCLA) 19(2): 123-136. Fall 1990.

___ Risco, Antonio. "Los autómatas de Holmberg," *Mester* (UCLA) 19(2): 63-70. Fall 1990.

___ Rodríguez-Luis, Julio. **The Contemporary Praxis of the Fantastic: Borges and Cortazar**. New York: Garland, 1991. 131pp.

___ Rovano, Marcelaine W. "The Angel as a Fantasy Figure in Classic and Contemporary Film," *Journal of the Fantastic in the Arts* 5(3): 56-74. 1993. (No. 19)

___ Ruddick, Nicholas, ed. **State of the Fantastic: Studies in the Theory and Practice of Fantastic Literature and Film**. Westport, CT: Greenwood, 1992. 210pp.

___ Sandor, Andras. "Myths and the Fantastic," *New Literary History* 22(2): 339-358. Spring 1991.

___ Schakel, Peter J. "Elusive Birds and Narrative Nets: The Appeal of Story in C. S. Lewis' **Chronicles of Narnia**," in: Walker, Andrew and Patric, James, eds. **A Christian for All Christians**. Washington, DC: Regnery, 1992. pp.116-131.

___ Schlobin, Roger C. "The Artisan in Modern Fantasy," *Journal of the Fantastic in the Arts* 6(4): 285-294. 1995.

___ Schlobin, Roger C. "Pagan Survival: Why the Shaman in Modern Fantasy?," in: Morse, Donald E., ed. **The Celebration of the Fantastic**. Westport, CT: Greenwood, 1992. pp.39-48.

___ Schuessler, Michael. "Un espejo en la oscuridad: 'la escritura del Dios' y la ontologia del Verbo," *Mester* (UCLA) 19(2): 83-96. Fall 1990.

___ Schweitzer, Darrell. "When Is a Fantasy Novel Not a Fantasy Novel?," *Studies in Weird Fiction* No. 11: 29-31. Spring 1992.

___ Scoffham, S. "Realms of Fantasy," *Junior Education* pp.22-23. June 1992. [Not seen.]

___ Sellin, Bernard. "Journeys into Fantasy: The Fiction of David Lindsay and C. S. Lewis," in: Walker, Andrew and Patric, James, eds. **A Christian for All Christians**. Washington, DC: Regnery, 1992. pp.98-115.

___ Senior, W. A. "Medieval Literature and Modern Fantasy: Toward a Common Metaphysics," *Journal of the Fantastic in the Arts* 3(3): 32-49. 1994.

___ Sherman, Josepha. "An Open Letter to Fantasy Writers," *Writer* 106(5): 13-15. May 1993.

___ Smith, Karen P. **The Fabulous Realm: A Literary-Historical Approach to British Fantasy, 1780-1990**. Metuchen, NJ: Scarecrow, 1993. 532pp.

___ Spaemann, Cordelia. "Phantastische Literatur," in: Kranz, Gisbert, ed. **Jahrbuch für Literatur und Ästhetik**. Lüdenscheid, Germany: Stier, 1992. Band 10, pp.293-308.

___ Stavans, Ilan. "El arte de la memoria," *Mester* (UCLA) 19(2): 97-108. Fall 1990.

___ Stein, Leon. "A Holocaust Education in Reverse: Stephen King's 'The Summer of Corruption: Apt Pupil'," *Journal of the Fantastic in the Arts* 5(2): 60-79. 1993. (No. 18)

___ Stewig, John W. "The Witch Woman: A Recurring Motif in Recent Fantasy Writing for Young Readers," *Mythlore* 20(1): 48-52. Winter 1994. (Whole No. 75) (Reprinted: *Children's Literature in Education* 26(2): 119-133. June 1995.)

FANTASY

FANTASY (continued)
___ Strugnell, John. "Hammering the Demons: Sword, Sorcery and Contemporary Society," in: Filmer, Kath, ed. **Twentieth-Century Fantasists: Essays in Culture, Society and Belief in Twentieth Century Mythopoeic Literature**. New York: St. Martin's, 1992. pp.172-182.
___ Sullivan, C. W., III. "Cultural Worldview: Marginalizing the Fantastic in the Seventeenth Century," *Paradoxa* 1(3): 287-300. 1995.
___ Sullivan, C. W., III. **The Influence of Celtic Myth and Legend on Modern Imaginative Fantasy**. Ph.D. Dissertation, University of Oregon, 1976. 213pp. (DAI 37: 5979A. Mar. 1977.)
___ Swanwick, Michael. "Viewpoint: In the Tradition...," *Asimov's Science Fiction Magazine* 18(12/13): 74-101. November 1994.
___ Talbot, Norman. " 'Escape!': That Dirty Word in Modern Fantasy: Le Guin's Earthsea," in: Filmer, Kath, ed. **Twentieth-Century Fantasists: Essays in Culture, Society and Belief in Twentieth Century Mythopoeic Literature**. New York: St. Martin's, 1992. pp.135-147.
___ Thompson, Raymond H. "The Comic Sage: Merlin in Thomas Berger's **Arthur Rex**," in: Watson, Jeanie and Fries, Marueen, eds. **The Figure of Merlin in the Nineteenth and Twentieth Centuries**. Lewiston, NY: Mellen, 1989. pp.143-153.
___ Tunnell, Michael O. "The Double-Edged Sword: Fantasy and Censorship," *Language Arts* 71(8): 606-612. December 1994.
___ Velasco, Juan. "Lo fantástico y la historia: La polémica entre **La sombra del caudillo y Tirano Banderas**," *Mester* (UCLA) 19(2): 71-82. Fall 1990.
___ Vonarburg, Elisabeth. "The Reproduction of the Body in Space," in: Ruddick, Nicholas, ed. **State of the Fantastic**. Westport, CT: Greenwood, 1992. pp.59-72.
___ Watson, Jeanie. "Mary Stewart's Merlin: Word of Power," in: Watson, Jeanie and Fries, Marueen, eds. **The Figure of Merlin in the Nineteenth and Twentieth Centuries**. Lewiston, NY: Edwin Mellen Press, 1989. pp.155-174.
___ Watson, Jeanie, ed. **The Figure of Merlin in the Nineteenth and Twentieth Centuries**, ed. by Jeanie Watson and Maureen Fries. Lewiston, NY: Edwin Mellin Press, 1989. 197pp.
___ Weil, Ellen R. "The Door to Lilith's Cave: Memory and Imagination in Jane Yolen's Holocaust Novels," *Journal of the Fantastic in the Arts* 5(2): 90-104. 1993. (No. 18)
___ Wolfe, Gary K. "Introduction: Fantasy as Testimony," *Journal of the Fantastic in the Arts* 5(2): 3-10. 1993. (No. 18)
___ Wu, Duncan. "Wordsmith in Space: The Fantasies of William S. Burroughs," in: Filmer, Kath, ed. **Twentieth-Century Fantasists: Essays in Culture, Society and Belief in Twentieth Century Mythopoeic Literature**. New York: St. Martin's, 1992. pp.121-134.
___ Yogev, Michael P. "The Fantastic in Holocaust Literature: Writing and Unwriting the Unbearable," *Journal of the Fantastic in the Arts* 5(2): 32-48. 1993. (No. 18)
___ Yolen, Jane. "Dark Mirrors: The Scholar Guest of Honor Address From the 1993 Mythopoeic Conference," *Mythlore* 20(4): 38-40. Winter 1995. (Whole No. 78)
___ Yolen, Jane. "Foreword: The Rumpelstiltskin Factor," *Journal of the Fantastic in the Arts* 5(2): 11-14. 1993. (No. 18)
___ Zanelli, Carmela. "Las aspiraciones de Tlön," *Mester* (UCLA) 19(2): 109-122. Fall 1990.
___ Zanger, Jules. "**The Last of the Just**: Lifting Moloch to Heaven," *Journal of the Fantastic in the Arts* 5(2): 49-59. 1993. (No. 18)

FANTASY TALES (MAGAZINE)
___ "UK's *Fantasy Tales* Ceasing Publication," *Science Fiction Chronicle* 15(1): 5-6. October 1993.

FANTASY WORLDS OF GEORGE PAL (MOTION PICTURE)
___ "Docu a Highlight of George Pal Tribute," *Variety* p. 2, 108. August 27, 1986.

FANZINES
___ "Fan Publications Index," in: Hopkins, Mariane S., ed. **Fandom Directory No. 14**. Springfield, VA: Fandata, 1992. pp.23-69.
___ Bosky, Bernadette L. "Amateur Press Associations: Intellectual Society and Social Intellectualism," in: Sanders, Joe, ed. **Science Fiction Fandom**. Westport, CT: Greenwood, 1994. pp.181-196.
___ Lupoff, Richard A. "Into the Aether, Junior Spacepersons!," in: Sanders, Joe, ed. **Science Fiction Fandom**. Westport, CT: Greenwood, 1994. pp.197-206.
___ Moskowitz, Sam. "The Origin of the Term 'Fanzine'," *Fantasy Commentator* 8(3/4): 200-202. Fall 1995. (Whole No. 47/48)

FANZINES (continued)
___ Warner, Harry, Jr. "A History of Fanzines," in: Sanders, Joe, ed. **Science Fiction Fandom**. Westport, CT: Greenwood, 1994. pp.175-180.

FARENTINO, DEBRAH
___ Chrissinger, Craig W. "Wilderness Leader," *Starlog* No. 211: 36-39, 70. February 1995.

FAREWELL TO THE FLESH (MOTION PICTURE)
___ SEE: CANDYMAN 2: FAREWELL TO THE FLESH (MOTION PICTURE).

FARKAS, PAUL S.
___ Quinn, Julie. "Paul S. Farkas," *Nevada Magazine* 48: 58-50. March/April 1988.

FARMER, PHILIP JOSE
___ Dudley, Joseph M. "Transformational SF Religions: Philip Jose Farmer's **Night of Light** and Robert Silverberg's **Downward to the Earth**," *Extrapolation* 35(4): 342-351. Winter 1994.
___ Goizet, Annette. "Amour, sexualité, érotisme dans **The Lovers** (**Les amants étrangers**) de P. J. Farmer," in: Bozzetto, Roger, ed. **Eros: Science & Fiction Fantastique**. Aix-en-Provence: Universite de Provence, 1991. pp.201-218.
___ Westfahl, Gary. "The Sequelizer, Or, The Farmer Gone to Hell," *Science Fiction Eye* No. 11: 23-27. December 1992.
___ Wolfe, Gary K. "The Dawn Patriot: Sex, Technology, and Irony in Farmer and Ballard," in: Ruddick, Nicholas, ed. **State of the Fantastic**. Westport, CT: Greenwood, 1992. pp.159-167.

FARRELL, TERRY
___ Spelling, Ian. "The Trill of It All," *Starlog* No. 188: 42-45, 64. March 1993.

FARRIS, JOHN
___ Proulx, Kevin. **Fear to the World: Eleven Voices in a Chorus of Horror**. Mercer Island, WA: Starmont, 1992. 243pp.

FATAL ATTRACTION (MOTION PICTURE)
___ Bernard, Jami. "**Fatal Attraction**(s) (Review)," *New York (NY) Post*. March 12, 1992. in: *NewsBank. Film and Television*. 31:B2. 1992.
___ Cerone, Daniel H. "Why Director Adrian Lyne Went for the Jugular," *Los Angeles (CA) Times*. February 18, 1992. in: *NewsBank. Film and Television*. 19:E4. 1992.
___ Hall, Mia M. "Love Kills: Another Look at **Fatal Attraction**," in: Golden, Christopher, ed. **Cut! Horror Writers on Horror Film**. New York: Berkley, 1992. pp.123-130.
___ Westbrook, David. "Video Series Looks Behind the Cameras," *Houston (TX) Chronicle*. March 11, 1992. in: *NewsBank. Film and Television*. 31:B3-B4. 1992.

FATHER'S DAY (MOTION PICTURE)
___ SEE: STEPFATHER III: FATHER'S DAY (MOTION PICTURE).

FAULKNER, WILLIAM
___ Salda, Michael N. "William Faulkner's Arthurian Tale: **Mayday**," *Arthuriana* 4(4): 348-375. Winter 1994.
___ Wagner, Vivian. "Gender, Technology and Utopia in Faulkner's Airplane Tales," *Arizona Quarterly* 49(4): 79-97. Winter 1993.

FAUST (MOTION PICTURE)
___ Faller, James M. "**Faust** (Review)," *Cinefantastique* 26(4): 59. June 1995.

FAWCETT, EDGAR
___ Stableford, Brian. **Algebraic Fantasies and Realistic Romances: More Masters of Science Fiction**. San Bernardino, CA: Borgo Press, 1995 128pp.

FAWCETT, GORDON W.
___ "Fawcett, Gordon W. (Obituary)," *Locus* 30(3): 70-71. March 1993.

FEELEY, GREGORY
___ Wolfe, Gene. "A Critic at the Crossroads: Gregory Feeley's 'How Far to th' End of the World'," *New York Review of Science Fiction* No. 86: 6-7. October 1995.

FEINBERG, GERALD
___ "Feinberg, Gerald (Obituary)," *Locus* 28(6): 67. June 1992.
___ "Feinberg, Gerald (Obituary)," *Science Fiction Chronicle* 13(9): 14. June 1992.

FELDMAN, DENNIS
___ Warren, Bill. "In the Blood," *Starlog* No. 218: 78-81, 66. September 1995.

FELICE, CYNTHIA
___ Bogstad, Janice M. **Gender, Power and Reversal in Contemporary Anglo-American and French Feminist Science Fiction.** Ph.D. Dissertation, University of Wisconsin, Madison, 1992. 229pp. (DAI-A 54/02, p. 509. August 1993.)

FERNANDEZ CUBAS, CRISTINA
___ Zatlin, Phyllis. "Tales from Fernández Cubas: Adventure in the Fantastic," *Monographis Review* 3(1/2): 107-118. 1987.

FERRARA, ABLE
___ Johnson, Kim H. "Matters of Identity," *Starlog* No. 190: 60-61. May 1993.

FICKE, ARTHUR DAVISON
___ Searles, A. Langley. "Forgotten Fantasy Verse: I, Arthur Davison Ficke," *Fantasy Commentator* 8(1/2): 14-16. Winter 1993/1994. (Whole No. 45/46.)

FIELDS, PETER ALLEN
___ Altman, Mark A. "**Star Trek: Deep Space Nine**: Scripting the Adventures," *Cinefantastique* 23(6): 40-42. April 1993.

FILASTO, NINO
___ "Premio Italia 1992 Awards," *Science Fiction Chronicle* 13(10): 8. July/August 1992.

FILM FESTIVALS
___ Sherman, Paul. "Cyberpunk Film Festival Is Pure Sci-Fi Splendor," *Boston (MA) Herald*. March 15, 1994. in: *NewsBank. Film and Television.* 31:G5. 1994.

FILM POSTERS
___ Borst, Ronald V., ed. **Graven Images: The Best of Horror, Fantasy, and Science Fiction Film Art from the Collection of Ronald V. Borst,** ed. by Ronald V. Borst, Keith Burns and Leith Adams. New York: Grove Press, 1992. 240pp.

FILMER, KATH
___ "Mythopoeic Awards, 1994," *Science Fiction Chronicle* 16(1): 8. October 1994.

FINAL FRONTIER (MOTION PICTURE)
___ SEE: STAR TREK V: THE FINAL FRONTIER (MOTION PICTURE).

FINDLEY, NIGEL D.
___ "Findley, Nigel D. (Obituary)," *Locus* 34(4): 62-63. April 1995.

FINE FOUNDATION AWARDS, 1992
___ "Fine Awards to Bloch, Yarbro," *Locus* 30(4): 9. April 1993.

FINGER, JOE
___ Desris, Joe. "**Batman**: Comic Co-Creator Bill Finger," *Cinefantastique* 24(6)/25(1): 27. February 1994.

FINLAND
___ "Finnish Radio Drama About **The Next War** Causes a Civil Upset," *Variety* p.1, 145. January 1, 1986.
___ Engholm, Ahrvid. "SF in the Nordic Countries," *Locus* 34(4): 39. April 1995.

FINNERMAN, GERALD PERRY
___ Fisher, Bob. "**Star Trek** Meets **The Next Generation**," *American Cinematographer* 75(10): 74-82. October 1994.

FINNEY, CHARLES G.
___ Whyde, Janet M. "Fantastic Disillusionment: Rupturing Narrative and Rewriting Reality in **The Circus of Dr. Lao**," *Extrapolation* 35(3): 230-240. Fall 1994.

FINNEY, JACK
___ "Finney, Jack (Obituary)," *Locus* 35(6): 79. December 1995.
___ "Finney, Jack (Obituary)," *Science Fiction Chronicle* 17(2): 24. December 1995/January 1996.
___ Oliver, Myrna. "Finney, Jack: *Body Snatchers* Author Jack Finney, 84, Dies," *Houston (TX) Chronicle* November 16, 1995. (Cited from the Internet Edition.)

FIRE IN THE SKY (MOTION PICTURE)
___ Altman, Mark A. "*Fire in the Sky*," *Cinefantastique* 23(6): 4-5. April 1993.
___ Johnson, Kim H. "True Documentation," *Starlog* No. 189: 52-53. April 1993.
___ Lowe, Nick. "*Fire in the Sky* (Review)," *Interzone* No. 76: 37. October 1993.
___ Pourroy, Janine. "Quick Cuts: Unfriendly Skies," *Cinefex* No. 54: 9-10. May 1993.

FIRE MAIDENS OF OUTER SPACE (MOTION PICTURE)
___ Henenlotter, Frank. "Films From Under the Floorboards," *Sci-Fi Entertainment* 1(6): 52-57. April 1995.

FIRE NEXT TIME (MOTION PICTURE)
___ Fischer, Dennis. "*The Fire Next Time* (Review)," *Cinefantastique* 24(3/4): 123. October 1993.

FIRE WALK WITH ME (MOTION PICTURE)
___ SEE: TWIN PEAKS: FIRE WALK WITH ME (MOTION PICTURE).

FIRESTARTER (MOTION PICTURE)
___ "Universal Tables *Firestarter* at $17.5-Mil Budget," *Variety* p. 15. August 25, 1982.

FIRST CONTACT
___ SEE ALSO: INTERSPECIES COMMUNICATION.
___ Andrews, Arlan. "When Earth Has Its First Contact With Alien Beings, Will We Be Ready?," by Arlan Andrews, Yoji Kondo and Charles Sheffield. *Science Fiction Age* 3(2): 22, 24-28, 86. January 1995.
___ Hough, Peter. **Looking for the Aliens: A Psychological, Imaginative and Scientific Investigation,** by Peter Hough and Jenny Randles. London: Blandford, 1992. 241pp.
___ Malmgren, Carl D. "Self and Other in SF: Alien Encounters," *Science Fiction Studies* 20(1): 15-33. March 1993.
___ Wolff, Michael J. "Universal Relations," *Starlog* No. 206: 35-39, 69. September 1994.

FIRST FANDOM HALL OF FAME AWARD, 1994
___ "Norton Receives First Fandom Award," *Locus* 34(1) 8. January 1995.
___ "Other Awards at ConAdian," *Science Fiction Chronicle* 15(10): 5. September 1994.

FIRST MEN IN THE MOON (MOTION PICTURE)
___ Renzi, Thomas C. **H. G. Wells: Six Scientific Romances Adapted for Film.** Metuchen, NJ: Scarecrow, 1992. 249pp.
___ Swires, Steve. "*First Men in the Moon*," *Starlog* No. 205: 62-67. August 1994.

FISHER, CARRIE
___ Greenberger, Robert. "Rebel Princess," in: McDonnell, David, ed. **Starlog's Science Fiction Heroes and Heroines.** New York: Crescent Books, 1995. pp.15-18.

FISHER, M. F. K.
___ "Fisher, M. F. K. (Obituary)," *Locus* 29(3): 78. September 1992.

FIST OF THE NORTH STAR (MOTION PICTURE)
___ Stevenson, Jay. "*Fist of the North Star* (Review)," *Cinefantastique* 27(3): 29. December 1995.

FITZGERALD, F. SCOTT
___ Baldwin, Marc. "F. Scott Fitzgerald's 'One Trip Abroad': A Metafantasy of the Divided Self," *Journal of the Fantastic in the Arts* 4(3): 69-78. 1991. (No. 15)
___ Lupack, Barbara T. "F. Scott Fitzgerald's 'Following of a Grail'," *Arthuriana* 4(4): 324-347. Winter 1994.

FLANERY, SEAN PATRICK
___ Madsen, Dan. "Exclusive Interview: Sean Patrick Flanery; The Further Adventures of *Young Indiana Jones*," *Lucasfilm Fan Club Magazine* No. 16: 2-6. 1992.

FLASH GORDON
___ Kohl, Leonard. "Flash Back to the Future: From Cosmic Comic Strip to Serial Sci-Fi," *Filmfax* No. 45: 47-58. June/July 1994.

FLASH GORDON (MOTION PICTURE)
___ Barshay, Robert. "Ethnic Stereotypes in *Flash Gordon*," *Journal of Popular Film and Television* 3(1): 15-30. 1974.

FLESH CRAWLERS (COMIC)
___ Bisson, Terry. "Kitchen Sink's *Flesh Crawlers* Brings Back SF's Bug-eyed Monsters," *Science Fiction Age* 2(1): 86-89. November 1993.

FLESH GORDON MEETS THE COSMIC CHEERLEADERS (MOTION PICTURE)
___ Scapperotti, Dan. "*Flesh Gordon Meets the Cosmic Cheerleaders* (Review)," *Cinefantastique* 25(2): 59-60. April 1994.

FLIGHT OF THE NAVIGATOR (MOTION PICTURE)
___ Keller, J. R. Keith. " 'Navigator' to Wrap in Norway March 1," *Variety* p. 43. February 26, 1986.

FLINN, DENNY MARTIN
___ Chrissinger, Craig W. "Undiscovered Writer," *Starlog* No. 205: 76-81. August 1994.

FLINT, HOMER EON
___ Ashley, Mike. "The Galactic Emancipator: Remembering Homer Eon Flint," *Fantasy Commentator* 8(3/4): 258-267. Fall 1995. (Whole No. 47/48)

FLINTSTONES (MOTION PICTURE)
___ Beeler, Michael. "*The Flintstones*: Building Bedrock," *Cinefantastique* 25(3): 23. June 1994.
___ Beeler, Michael. "*The Flintstones*: Jim Henson's Creature Shop," *Cinefantastique* 25(3): 15-18. June 1994.
___ Beeler, Michael. "*The Flintstones*: The Script Debacle," *Cinefantastique* 25(3): 10. June 1994.
___ Beeler, Michael. "*The Flintstones*," *Cinefantastique* 25(3): 8-23. June 1994.
___ Duncan, Jody. "The Making of a Blockbuster," *Cinefex* No. 58: 34-65. June 1994.
___ Faller, James M. "*The Flintstones* (Review)," *Cinefantastique* 25(6)/26(1): 122. December 1994.
___ Lowe, Nick. "*Flintstones* (Review)," *Interzone* No. 88: 35-36. October 1994.

FLORA
___ Schulp, J. A. "The Flora of Middle Earth," in: Kranz, Gisbert, ed. **Inklings: Jahrbuch für Literatur und Ästhetik**. 3. Band. [Lüdenscheid, Germany: Stier], 1985. pp.129-186.

FLUKE (MOTION PICTURE)
___ Wells, Curt. "James Herbert Is No *Fluke*," *Sci-Fi Entertainment* 1(6): 58-29, 72. April 1995.

FLY, THE (1958) (MOTION PICTURE)
___ Knee, Adam. "Metamorphosis of *The Fly*," *Wide Angle* 14(1): 20-35. January 1992.

FLY, THE (1986) (MOTION PICTURE)
___ Knee, Adam. "Metamorphosis of *The Fly*," *Wide Angle* 14(1): 20-35. January 1992.
___ Timpone, Anthony. "Bride of the Fly," by Anthony Timpone and Carr D'Angelo. in: McDonnell, David, ed. **Starlog's Science Fiction Heroes and Heroines**. New York: Crescent Books, 1995. pp.47-49.

FLYING SAUCERS OVER HOLLYWOOD: THE PLAN 9 COMPANION (MOTION PICTURE)
___ Scapperotti, Dan. "The Plan 9 Companion," *Cinefantastique* 25(5): 43. October 1994.

FOLKLORE
___ Bullard, Thomas E. "UFO Abduction Reports: The Supernatural Kidnap Narrative Returns in Technological Guise," *Journal of American Folklore* 102(404): 147-170. April/June 1989.
___ Gilet, P. "Folk Tales and Science Fiction: Testing a Thesis," *Australian Folklore* 8: 142-145. August 1993.
___ Weist, Andrew. **The Function of Folklore in the Science Fiction of Cordwainer Smith**. Master's Thesis, Bowling Green State University, 1992. 43pp.

FOLKTALES
___ Röhrich, Lutz. **Folktales and Reality**. Bloomington: Indiana University Press, 1991. 290pp.
___ Sandow, Sandra J. "Touch Magic: The Importance of Teaching Folktales to Emotionally Disturbed, Disabled Readers," *Mythlore* 19(4): 56-59. Autumn 1993. (No. 74)

FOOD
___ Hunt, Peter. " 'Coldtongue coldham coldbeef pickled gherkin salad frenchrolls cresssandwige spottedmeat gingerbeer lemonaide sodawater...' Fantastic Foods in the Books of Kenneth Grahame, Jerome K. Jerome, H. E. Bates, and Other Bakers of the Fantasy England," *Journal of the Fantastic in the Arts* 7(1): 5-22. 1996.

FOOD OF THE GODS (1976) (MOTION PICTURE)
___ Renzi, Thomas C. **H. G. Wells: Six Scientific Romances Adapted for Film**. Metuchen, NJ: Scarecrow, 1992. 249pp.

FOR THE CAUSE (MOTION PICTURE)
___ Cox, Dan. "Cause and Effect," *Variety* 360(8): 12. September 25, 1995.

FORBES, MICHELLE
___ Altman, Mark A. "*The Next Generation*: Ensign Ro Laren," *Cinefantastique* 23(2/3): 96-98. October 1992.
___ Spelling, Ian. "Actress With Attitude," *Starlog* No. 205: 53-56, 70. August 1994.

FORBIDDEN PLANET (COMIC)
___ Weaver, Tom. "*Forbidden Planet*," *Starlog* No. 176: 38-41. March 1992.

FORBIDDEN PLANET (MOTION PICTURE)
___ Matheson, T. J. "Marcuse, Ellul, and the Science-Fiction Film: Negative Responses to Technology," *Science-Fiction Studies* 19(3): 326-339. November 1992.
___ Trushell, John. "Return of *Forbidden Planet*?," *Foundation* No. 64: 82-89. Summer 1995.
___ Weaver, Tom. "Anne Francis," in: Weaver, Tom. **They Fought the Creature Features: Interviews with 23 Classic Horror, Science Fiction and Serial Stars**. Jefferson, NC: McFarland, 1995. pp.161-172.
___ Weaver, Tom. "Woman of the *Forbidden Planet*," *Starlog* No. 186: 27-31. January 1993. Also in: McDonnell, David, ed. **Starlog's Science Fiction Heroes and Heroines**. New York: Crescent Books, 1995. pp.41-43.

FORBIN PROJECT (MOTION PICTURE)
___ "Computer-as-Dictator Beats Sabotage: Universal Sales Slant: Science-Fact," *Variety* p. 17. May 6, 1970.
___ "Universal Alters Ballyhoo on 'Forbin' Hoping for Hypo in B. O.," *Variety* p. 6. May 20, 1970.

FORD, FORD MADOX
___ Kenny, Virginia C. "The Eternal Feminine Reclaimed: Ford Madox Ford's Medieval Fantasies," in: Filmer, Kath, ed. **Twentieth-Century Fantasists: Essays in Culture, Society and Belief in Twentieth Century Mythopoeic Literature**. New York: St. Martin's, 1992. pp.60-70.

FORD, JOHN M.
___ "Philip K. Dick Award Winners, 1993," *Locus* 32(5): 8. May 1994.

FORD, JOHN M. (continued)
___ "Womack and Ford Tie for Philip K. Dick Award," *Science Fiction Chronicle* 15(6): 4. April/May 1994.

FORECASTING
___ Carlson, Richard C. **2020 Visions: Long View of a Changing World**, by Richard C. Carlson and Bruce Goldman. Stanford, CA: Stanford Alumni Association, 1991. 252pp.
___ De Canio, Stephen J. "The Future Through Yesterday: Long-Term Forecasting in the Novels of H. G. Wells and Jules Verne," *Centennial Review* 75(1): 75-93. Winter 1994.
___ Heilbroner, Robert. **Visions of the Future: The Distant Past, Yesterday, Today, Tomorrow**. New York: Oxford University Press, 1995. 133pp.

FOREVER KNIGHT (MOTION PICTURE)
___ Stone, Lisa. "**Forever Knight** Has Risen From the Grave," *Sci-Fi Entertainment* 1(5): 34-37, 55. February 1995.

FOREVER KNIGHT (TV)
___ Bloch-Hansen, Peter. "Forever and a Knight," *Starlog* No. 212: 50-53, 72. March 1995.
___ Bloch-Hansen, Peter. "Unlife to Live," *Starlog* No. 215: 54-57. June 1995.
___ Johnson, Kim H. "Knight Shift," *Starlog* No. 214: 78-81. May 1995.
___ Kenny, Glenn. "Knight Moves," *TV Guide* 42(46): 44. November 12, 1994.
___ Mahoney, Eve. "A **Forever Knight** Episode Guide," *Journal of the Dark* No. 4: 35-37. Fall 1995.
___ Mahoney, Eve. "A **Forever Knight** Episode Guide," *Journal of the Dark* No. 5: 28-30. Winter 1995/1996.
___ Mahoney, Eve. "A **Forever Knight** Episode Guide," *Journal of the Dark* No. 6: 16-18. Spring 1995.

FOREVER YOUNG (MOTION PICTURE)
___ Johnson, Kim H. "**Forever Young**," *Starlog* No. 186: 44-47. January 1993.

FORREST GUMP (MOTION PICTURE)
___ Pourroy, Janine. "Making Gump Happen," *Cinefex* No. 60: 90-107. December 1994.

FORSTCHEN, WILLIAM
___ Piccoli, Sean. "How to Run for Congress and Write Sexy Thrillers-- Get a Coauthor," *Insight on the News* 11(18): 24. May 8, 1995.

FORSTER, E. M.
___ Loney, Douglas. "C. S. Lewis' Debt to E. M. Forster's **The Celestial Omnibus and Other Stories**," *Mythlore* 21(1): 14-22. Summer 1995. (No. 79)

FORTRESS (MOTION PICTURE)
___ Lehti, Steven J. "**Fortress** (Review)," *Cinefantastique* 24(6)/25(1): 123. February 1994.
___ Lowe, Nick. "**Fortress** (Review)," *Interzone* No. 88: 36. October 1994.
___ Scapperotti, Dan. "**Fortress**," *Cinefantastique* 24(2): 4-5. August 1993.

FORTUNINO MATANIA, R. I.
___ Westwood, Frank. "Interview with Franco Matania," *Burroughs Bulletin* NS No. 10: 23-28. April 1992.

FORTUNINO MATTANIA, R. I.
___ Barrett, Robert R. "Fortunino Mattania, R. I.: The Last Victorian," *Burroughs Bulletin* NS No. 10: 16-22. April 1992.

FOSTER, ALAN DEAN
___ Larson, Randall D. "A Movie Novelizer Speaks: Alan Dean Foster Interviewed," *Interzone* No. 80: 53-55. February 1994.
___ Patton, Charles. **On Writing Science Fiction and Screenplays**, by Charles Patton and Alan D. Foster. Alexandria, VA: PBS Adult Learning Satellite Service, 1994. 1 Videocassette, 30 minutes.

FOUNDATION IMAGING (COMPANY)
___ Altman, Mark A. "**Babylon 5**: Foundation Imaging," *Cinefantastique* 25(2): 32-34. April 1994.

FOUNDATION IMAGING (COMPANY) (continued)
___ Altman, Mark A. "**Babylon 5**: It Came From the Video Toaster," *Cinefantastique* 25(2): 29. April 1994.

FOUR-SIDED TRIANGLE (MOTION PICTURE)
___ Hogan, David J. "**Four-Sided Triangle** (1953) (Review)," *Filmfax* No. 33: 18, 20. June/July 1992.

FOWLER, CHRISTOPHER
___ Hughes, Dave. "Talking Fowler Language: Christopher Fowler Interview," *Interzone* No. 55: 19-22. January 1992.
___ Nicholls, Stan. "Christopher Fowler Won't Breathe Anything He Can't See," in: Nicholls, Stan. **Wordsmiths of Wonder: Fifty Interviews with Writers of the Fantastic**. London: Orbit, 1993. pp.425-431.

FOWLER, KAREN JOY
___ "Karen Joy Fowler: A Question of Identity," *Locus* 31(3): 5, 85-86. September 1993.

FOWLER, SHANNON
___ "1995 Isaac Asimov Award," *Science Fiction Chronicle* 16(6): 12. May 1995.
___ Williams, Sheila. "The 1995 Isaac Asimov Award," *Isaac Asimov's Science Fiction Magazine* 19(9): 44-45. August 1995.

FOWLES, JOHN
___ Brigg, Peter. "Maggots, Tropes, and Metafictional Challenge: John Fowles' **A Maggot**," in: Wolf, Milton T. and Mallett, Daryl F., eds. **Imaginative Futures: Proceedings of the 1993 Science Fiction Research Association Conference**. San Bernardino, CA: Jacob's Ladder Books, 1995. pp.293-306.
___ Svoboda, Randall A. **Between Private and Public Space: The Problem of Writing Personal History in the Novels of Lessing, Lawrence, Joyce and Fowles**. Ph.D. Dissertation, University of Iowa, 1995. 313pp. (DAI-A 56/06, p. 2253. December 1995.)

FOX, MICHAEL J.
___ Goldberg, Lee. "Time Tripper," by Lee Goldberg and Marc Shapiro. in: McDonnell, David, ed. **Starlog's Science Fiction Heroes and Heroines**. New York: Crescent Books, 1995. pp.84-86.
___ Weaver, Tom. "Man of **The Lost Planet**: Michael Fox Interviewed," *Starlog* No. 198: 67-70, 72. January 1994.

FRAHM, LEANNE
___ "1994 Ditmar Awards," *Locus* 32(5): 9, 64. May 1994.

FRAKES, JONATHAN
___ Altman, Mark A. "**Star Trek: The Next Generation**: Will Riker, to Be or Not to Be?," *Cinefantastique* 24(3/4): 58. October 1993.
___ Collins, Diana. "Jonathan Frakes: Will Riker Speaks," in: Van Hise, James, ed. **Trek Celebration Two**. Las Vegas, NV: Pioneer, 1994. pp.122-133.
___ Spelling, Ian. "Directorial Enterprise," *Starlog* No. 204: 40-45. July 1994.

FRANCE
___ "1992 Prix Rosny Aîné Awards," *Locus* 29(5): 5. November 1992
___ "1993 Salon du Livre," *Locus* 31(6): 39-40. December 1993.
___ "Dancer Clones Self by Hologram in Diamant-Berger's Hi-Tech Pic," *Variety* p.367. October 16, 1985.
___ "French Marvel Maniacs Can Plug into Info About Comics Via Teletext Net," *Variety* p. 84. September 17, 1986.
___ "French Try to Crack Sci-Fi Feature Film Field," *Variety* p. 53. February 3, 1982.
___ "Quest Fires Spate of Prehistoric Pix," *Variety* p. 48. February 3, 1982.
___ "Sci-fi Pen and Inker on Way From Laloux in Coprod With Spain," *Variety* p.366, 380. October 16, 1985.
___ "Science Fiction, a Global Community: France," *Locus* 32(4): 38-39. April 1994.
___ "SF in France," *Locus* 28(1): 45-47. January 1992.
___ "SF in France," *Locus* 30(4): 38-39, 62. April 1993.
___ "SF in French," *Locus* 31(6): 40. December 1993.
___ "Étonnants Voyageurs Festival," *Locus* 31(6): 41. December 1993.
___ Becker, Lucille F. "Science and Detective Fiction: Complementary Genres on the Margins of French Literature," *French Literature Series* 20: 119-125. 1993.

FRANCE (continued)

___ Bogstad, Janice M. **Gender, Power and Reversal in Contemporary Anglo-American and French Feminist Science Fiction.** Ph.D. Dissertation, University of Wisconsin, Madison, 1992. 229pp. (DAI-A 54/02, p. 509. August 1993.)

___ Bozzetto, Roger. "Dick in France: A Love Story," in: Mullen, R. D., ed. **On Philip K. Dick: 40 Articles From Science-Fiction Studies.** Terre Haute, IN: SF-TH Inc., 1992. pp.153-160.

___ Brown, Gregory S. "Critical Responses to Utopian Writings in the French Enlightenment: Three Periodicals as Case Studies," *Utopian Studies* 5(1): 48-71. 1994.

___ Capasso, Ruth C. "Islands of Felicity: Women Seeing Utopia in Seventeenth Century France," in: Donawerth, Jane L. and Kolmerten, Carol A., eds. **Utopian and Science Fiction by Women: Worlds of Difference.** Syracuse, NY: Syracuse University Press, 1994. pp.35-53.

___ Cummiskey, Gary. **The Changing Face of Horror: A Study of the Nineteenth Century French Fantastic Short Story.** New York: Peter Lang, 1992. 170pp.

___ Dover, Carol. "The Split-Shield Motif in the Old French Prose **Lancelot**," in: Busby, Keith, ed. **The Arthurian Yearbook I.** New York: Garland, 1991. pp.43-62.

___ Evans, Arthur B. "The Fantastic Science Fiction of Maurice Renard," *Science Fiction Studies* 21(3): 380-396. November 1994.

___ Fitting, Peter. "Philip K. Dick in France," in: Mullen, R. D., ed. **On Philip K. Dick: 40 Articles From Science-Fiction Studies.** Terre Haute, IN: SF-TH Inc., 1992. pp.131.

___ Fulton, Helen. "A Woman's Place: Guinevere in the Welsh and French Romances," *Quondam et Futurus* 3(2): 1-25. Summer 1993.

___ Gallardo Torrano, Pedro. "**Frankenstein's** French Counterpart: Villiers de l'Isle-Adam's **L'Eve Future**," *Foundation* No. 63: 74-80. Spring 1995.

___ Gardiner, Michael. "Utopia and Everyday Life in French Social Thought," *Utopian Studies* 6(2): 90-123. 1995.

___ Grivet, Charles. **Fantastique-Fiction.** Paris: Presses universitaires francaises, 1993. 255pp.

___ Jouanne, Emmanuel. "How 'Dickian' Is the New French Science Fiction?," in: Mullen, R. D., ed. **On Philip K. Dick: 40 Articles From Science-Fiction Studies.** Terre Haute, IN: SF-TH Inc., 1992. pp.232-235.

___ Marcoin, Francis. "**Les Exiles de la terre** d'Andre Laurie," *La Revue des Livres pour Enfants* 146: 61-65. Summer 1992.

___ Monet, Jack. "Gallic Live of Comics Lends Marvel French Licensees a Hand," *Variety* p. 83, 88. September 17, 1986.

___ Murray, Timothy. "Philosophical Antibodies: Grotesque Fantasy in a French Stoic Fiction," *Yale French Studies* 86: 143-163. 1994.

___ Ransom, Amy J. **The Feminine as Fantastic in the Conte Fantastique: Visions of the Other.** New York: P. Lang, 1995. 280pp.

___ Ransom, Amy J. **Visions of the Other: The Feminine as Fantastic in the Conte Fantastique.** Ph.D. Dissertation, University of Minnesota, 1993. 286pp.

___ Rhodes, Randall. "Death in **Natures Mortes: Vanitas** in French Still Lifes of the Seventeenth Century," in: Latham, Robert A. and Collins, Robert A., eds. **Modes of the Fantastic.** Westport, CT: Greenwood, 1995. pp.161-172.

___ Ruaud, André. "Between Entropy and Renaissance: SF in France," by André Ruaud and Jean-Daniel Brèque. *Vector* No. 168: 28-29. August/September 1992.

___ Thomas, Pascal J. "Science Fiction Fandom in Western Europe: A French Perspective," in: Sanders, Joe, ed. **Science Fiction Fandom.** Westport, CT: Greenwood, 1994. pp.119-126.

___ Thomas, Pascal J. "SF in France," *Locus* 34(4): 34-35. April 1995.

___ Troiano, Maureen D. **New Physics and the Modern French Novel.** New York: Peter Lang, 1995. 276pp.

___ Trudel, Jean-Louis. "French SF and SF in French: A Primer," *New York Review of Science Fiction* No. 88: 12-17. December 1995.

___ Trudel, Jean-Louis. "SF in France," *Locus* 33(1): 47-48. July 1994.

___ Walters, Lori. "The Creation of a Super Romance: Paris, Bibliotheque Nationale, fond francais, MS 1433," in: Busby, Keith, ed. **The Arthurian Yearbook I.** New York: Garland, 1991. pp.3-26.

FRANCE, ANATOLE

___ Gilman, Juliette. "The Craft of the Fantastic in Anatole France's **La Révolte des anges**," in: Sanders, Joe, ed. **Functions of the Fantastic.** Westport, CT: Greenwood, 1995. pp.135-142.

FRANCHER, HAMPTON

___ Lofficier, Randy. "**Blade Runner** (1982): Interviews with Hampton Francher, David Peoples, Ridley Scott and Syd Mead," by Randy Lofficier and Jean-Marc Lofficier. in: Goldberg, Lee et al. **Science Fiction Filmmaking in the 1980s.** Jefferson, NC: McFarland, 1995. pp.23-58.

FRANCIS, ANNE

___ Weaver, Tom. "Anne Francis," in: Weaver, Tom. **They Fought the Creature Features: Interviews with 23 Classic Horror, Science Fiction and Serial Stars.** Jefferson, NC: McFarland, 1995. pp.161-172.

___ Weaver, Tom. "Woman of the **Forbidden Planet**," *Starlog* No. 186: 27-31. January 1993. Also in: McDonnell, David, ed. **Starlog's Science Fiction Heroes and Heroines.** New York: Crescent Books, 1995. pp.41-43.

FRANK, ANNE

___ Chiarello, Barbara. "The Utopian Space of a Nightmare: **The Diary of Anne Frank**," *Utopian Studies* 5(1): 128-140. 1994.

FRANKENSTEIN (1931) (MOTION PICTURE)

___ Holt, Wesley G. "**Frankenstein** (1931) (Review)," *Filmfax* No. 35: 24, 26, 30. October/November 1992.

FRANKENSTEIN (MOTION PICTURE)

___ Leeper, Mark R. "**Frankenstein** (Review)," *Lan's Lantern* No. 42: 109. May 1994.

___ Mauceri, J. B. "Rebuilding **Frankenstein**," *Sci-Fi Entertainment* 1(4): 68-73, 86-88. December 1994.

___ Sevastakis, Michael. **Songs of Love and Death: The Classical American Horror Film of the 1930s.** Westport, CT: Greenwood, 1993. 232pp.

___ Vaz, Mark C. "Haunting Creation," *Cinefex* No. 60: 70-85. December 1994.

FRANKENSTEIN: THE COLLEGE YEARS (MOTION PICTURE)

___ "**Frankenstein: The College Years** (Review)," *Cinefantastique* 22(5): 60. April 1992.

FRANZ KAFKA'S IT'S A WONDERFUL LIFE (MOTION PICTURE)

___ Biodrowski, Steve. "Directors Dave Borthwick and Peter Capladi on **The Secret Adventures of Tom Thumb** and **Franz Kafka's It's a Wonderful Life**," *Cinefantastique* 27(3): 58-59. December 1995.

___ Biodrowski, Steve. "**Franz Kafka's It's a Wonderful Life** (Review)," *Cinefantastique* 27(3): 59. December 1995.

FRATZ, DOUG

___ Fratz, Doug. "The Twenty-Year Spree: A Personal History of *Thrust/Quantum*," *Quantum* No. 43/44: 51-66. Spring/Summer 1993.

FRAZER, JAMES GEORGE

___ Van Calenbergh, Hubert. "The Roots of Horror in **The Golden Bough**," *Lovecraft Studies* No. 26: 21-23. Spring 1992.

FREAKED (MOTION PICTURE)

___ Harris, Judith P. "**Freaked** (Review)," *Cinefantastique* 25(2): 60. April 1994.

FREAKS (MOTION PICTURE)

___ Yarbro, Chelsea Q. "On **Freaks**," in: Golden, Christopher, ed. **Cut! Horror Writers on Horror Film.** New York: Berkley, 1992. pp.289-298.

FREAS, FRANK KELLY

___ Davidsmeyer, Jo. "An Illustrious Pair," *Strange New Worlds* No. 7: 6-8. April/May 1993.

FREDDY'S DEAD: THE FINAL NIGHTMARE (MOTION PICTURE)

___ Biodrowski, Steve. "**Freddy's Dead**," *Cinefantastique* 22(4): 56, 60. February 1992.

___ Doherty, Thomas. "**Freddy's Dead: The Final Nightmare** (Review)," *Cinefantastique* 22(4): 57. February 1992.

FREDDY'S REVENGE (MOTION PICTURE)

___ SEE: NIGHTMARE ON ELM STREET, PART 2: FREDDY'S REVENGE (MOTION PICTURE).

FREE WILLY (MOTION PICTURE)

FREE WILLY (MOTION PICTURE)
___ Shannon, John. "Quick Cuts: Under Heavy Cetacean," *Cinefex* No. 55: 17-18. August 1993.

FREED, BERT
___ "Freed, Bert (Obituary)," *Science Fiction Chronicle* 15(10): 20. September 1994.

FREEJACK (MOTION PICTURE)
___ Campbell, Bob. "Jagger's Edge Sharpens Dull Script of *Freejack* (Review)," *Newark (NJ) Star-Ledger.* January 21, 1992. in: *NewsBank. Film and Television.* 11:D9. 1992.
___ Farolino, Audrey. "Jumpin' *Freejack* Flash (Review)," *New York (NY) Post.* January 21, 1992. in: *NewsBank. Film and Television.* 11: D10. 1992.
___ Hunter, Stephen. "More Jagger, Less Estevez Might Have Pumped More Life into Feeble *Freejack* (Review)," *Baltimore (MD) Sun.* January 21, 1992. in: *NewsBank. Film and Television.* 11:D7. 1992.
___ Klinghoffer, David. "*Freejack*: Movie Is Born Brain-Dead (Review)," *Washington (DC) Times.* January 20, 1992. in: *NewsBank. Film and Television.* 11:D12. 1992.
___ Mahar, Ted. "*Freejack*: A Ho-Hum Mix of Old Sci-Fi Tricks (Review)," *Portland (OR) The Oregonian.* January 20, 1992. in: *NewsBank. Film and Television.* 11:D11. 1992.
___ McNally, Owen. "Futuristic *Freejack* Fizzles By a Furlong (Review)," *Hartfort (CT) Courant.* January 18, 1992. in: *NewsBank. Film and Television.* 11:D4-D5. 1992.
___ Murray, Steve. "Predictable *Freejack* Goes Back to the Future (Review)," *Atlanta (GA) Journal.* January 20, 1992. in: *NewsBank. Film and Television.* 11:D6. 1992.
___ Murray, Will. "The Quiet Future," *Starlog* No. 175: 70-74. February 1992.
___ Peterseim, Locke. "*Freejack* (Review)," *Cinefantastique* 22(6): 57. June 1992
___ Ross, Patricia. "*Freejack*," *Cinefantastique* 22(6): 56, 61. June 1992
___ Sherman, Paul. "Futuristic *Freejack* Falls Flat on Face (Review)," *Boston (MA) Herald.* January 18, 1992. in: *NewsBank. Film and Television.* 11:D8. 1992.
___ Spelling, Ian. "Jack on the Run," *Starlog* No. 176: 30-33. March 1992.
___ Sragow, Michael. "*Freejack*: If It Only Had a Brain (Review)," *San Francisco (CA) Examiner.* January 18, 1992. in: *NewsBank. Film and Television.* 11:D3. 1992.
___ Strauss, Bob. "*Freejack*: Back to the Future? (Review)," *Los Angeles (CA) Daily News.* January 19, 1992. in: *NewsBank. Film and Television.* 11:D2. 1992.
___ Wood, Gary L. "*Freejack*: Filming 'Immortality Delivered'," *Cinefantastique* 22(4): 14-15. February 1992.

FREEMAN, MARY WILKINS
___ Reichardt, Mary R. **A Web of Relationship: Women in the Short Stories of Mary Wilkins Freeman.** Jackson: University Press of Mississippi, 1992. 186pp.

FREEMAN, PAUL
___ Nazzaro, Joe. "Sophisticated Evil," *Starlog* No. 218: 72-75, 65. September 1995.

FRELENG, FRITZ
___ "Freleng, Fritz (Obituary)," *Science Fiction Chronicle* 16(8): 21. July/August 1995

FRENKEL, JAMES
___ **Breaking into Writing**. Ann Arbor, MI: Tucker Video, 1994. 1 videocassette, 98 minutes. (Panel Presentation at the 1994 Science Fiction Research Association Conference.)

FRIDAY THE 13TH IX: JASON GOES TO HELL (MOTION PICTURE)
___ Crisafulli, Chuck. "*Friday the 13th IX: Jason Goes to Hell*," *Cinefantastique* 23(6): 44-45. April 1993.
___ Crisafulli, Chuck. "*Friday the 13th: Jason Goes to Hell*," *Cinefantastique* 24(2): 50-55. August 1993.
___ Crisafulli, Chuck. "Jason's 13th: KNB Makeup Effects," *Cinefantastique* 24(2): 55. August 1993.
___ Crisafulli, Chuck. "Jason's 13th: The Man Behind the Mask," *Cinefantastique* 24(2): 53. August 1993.

FRIDAY THE 13TH IX: JASON GOES TO HELL (MOTION PICTURE) (continued)
___ Crisafulli, Chuck. "Mr. Friday Night," *Cinefantastique* 24(3/4): 118-119. October 1993.

FRIDAY THE 13TH (MOTION PICTURE)
___ "Suit Seeks Royalties for 'Friday' Director, Writer," *Variety* p.8. October 2, 1985.

FRIDAY THE 13TH: THE SERIES (TV)
___ "*Friday the 13th: The Series* Big Surprise; Station Interest Running High," *Variety* p. 42. June 29, 1988.
___ "Paramount Rises From the *Amerika* Debacle with 'Trek' and 'Friday'," *Variety* p. 155, 167. October 15, 1986.

FRIDAY THE 13TH VII: THE NEW BLOOD (MOTION PICTURE)
___ "*Friday the 13th Part VII: The New Blood* (Review)," *Variety* p. 16. May 18, 1988.

FRIESNER, ESTER
___ Starr, Richard. "SFC Interviews: A Conversation With Ester Friesner," *Science Fiction Chronicle* 16(4): 5, 30-32. February 1995.

FROST, LINDSAY
___ Jankiewicz, Pat. "Detective Story," *Starlog* No. 198: 50-51. January 1994.

FRYE, DWIGHT D.
___ Bowman, David. "A Tragically Miscast Comedian: Dwight Frye," *Filmfax* No. 35: 73-78. October/November 1992.
___ Ford, Ron. "The Next Generation Speaks: Dwight D. Frye, the Son of Dracula's Servant," *Filmfax* No. 35: 78-81. October/November 1992.

FUENTES, CARLOS
___ Stavans, Ilan. "Carlos Fuentes and the Future," *Science Fiction Studies* 20(3): 409-413. November 1993.

FUGITIVE (TV)
___ Proctor, Mel. **The Official Fan's Guide to The Fugitive**. Stamford, CT: Longmeadow, 1994. 185pp.

FULL ECLIPSE (MOTION PICTURE)
___ Wilt, David. "*Full Eclipse* (Review)," *Cinefantastique* 25(5): 59. October 1994.

FULL MOON ENTERTAINMENT (COMPANY)
___ Fischer, Dennis. "Charles Band: Full Moon Mogul," *Cinefantastique* 26(4): 16-49. June 1995.
___ Fischer, Dennis. "Full Moon Effects: Creature Creators," *Cinefantastique* 26(4): 47-49. June 1995.
___ Gire, Dann. "Band on the Run," *Cinefantastique* 23(5): 46, 61. February 1993.
___ McGee, Mark T. "Full Moon's Effects Master," *Cinefantastique* 23(5): 47-49. February 1993.
___ Robley, Les P. "Full Moon Effects: Low Budget Magic," *Cinefantastique* 26(4): 40-42, 61. June 1995.
___ Willens, Michelle. "Making Films That Go Straight to Video--By Design," *New York Times* Sec. 2, p. 22. September 19, 1993.

FULLER, THOMAS
___ Schwartzkopff, Frances. "Sci-Fi Writer Stretches Outer Limits of Sound," *Atlanta Constitution* Sec. XJ, p. 1. April 1, 1992. [Not seen.]

FUNERALS
___ Reynolds, Patricia. "Funeral Customs in Tolkien's Fiction," *Mythlore* 19(2): 45-53. Spring 1993. (No. 72)

FUNNY BONES (MOTION PICTURE)
___ Stevenson, Jay. "*Funny Bones* (Review)," *Cinefantastique* 27(3): 52. December 1995.

FUREY, MAGGIE
___ "British Fantasy Awards, 1995," *Science Fiction Chronicle* 17(2): 5. December 1995/January 1996.

FURLAN, MIRA
___ Nazzaro, Joe. "Alien Ambassador," *Starlog* No. 202: 41-44, 70. May 1994.

FURST, ANTON
___ "Furst, Anton (Obituary)," *Science Fiction Chronicle* 13(4): 12. January 1992.
___ "Furst, Anton, 1944-1992 (Obituary)," *Starlog* 182: 69. September 1992.

FURST, STEPHEN
___ Nazzaro, Joe. "Honorable Diplomat," *Starlog* No. 219: 76-79. October 1995.

FUTURE HISTORY
___ SEE: ALTERNATE HISTORY.

FUTURE OF SF
___ Platt, Charles. "Upstream," *Science Fiction Eye* No. 12: 29-34. Summer 1993.

FUTURE SHOCK (MOTION PICTURE)
___ Wilt, David. "***Future Shock*** (Review)," *Cinefantastique* 25(4): 59. August 1994.

FUTURE STUDIES
___ Aiex, Patrick K. **Reflections on Science Fiction in Light of Today's Global Concerns**. Position Paper, ERIC ED 364 904. 7pp.
___ Burmeister, Klaus, ed. **Streifzuge ins Übermorgen: Science Fiction und Zukunftsforschung**, ed. by Klaus Burmeister and Karlheinz Steinmüller. Weinheim: Beltz, 1992. 328pp.
___ Miles, Ian. "Stranger Than Fiction: How Important Is Science Fiction for Futures Studies?," *Futures* 25(3): 315-321. April 1993. (Reprinted: *Engineering Management Review* 21(4): 49-52. Winter 1993.)
___ Pohl, Frederik. "The Uses of the Future," *Futurist* 27(2): 9-12. March-April 1993.
___ Wagar, W. Warren. **The Next Three Futures: Paradigms of Things to Come**. Westport, CT: Greenwood, 1991. 164pp.

FUTURE WAR
___ Cooper, Kenneth D. **Fables of the Nuclear Age: Fifty Years of World War III**. Ph.D. Dissertation, Vanderbilt University, 1992. 352pp. (DAI-A 54/01. p. 176. July 1993.)

FUTURES PAST (MAGAZINE)
___ Anderson, Kevin J. "*Futures Past* Magazine," *SFWA Bulletin* 26(4): 16. Winter 1993. (No. 118)

FUTUREWORLD (MOTION PICTURE)
___ Telotte, J. P. "***Westworld*, *Futureworld*, and the World's Obscenity,**" in: Ruddick, Nicholas, ed. **State of the Fantastic**. Westport, CT: Greenwood, 1992. pp.179-188.

FUTURIAN SOCIETY OF SYDNEY (AUSTRALIA)
___ Stone, Graham. "Fifty Years of Science Fiction Groups in Australia," *Science Fiction News* (Australia) No. 108: 2-8. November 1989.

GADDIS, WILLIAM
___ Strehle, Susan. **Fiction in the Quantum Universe**. Chapel Hill: University of North Carolina Press, 1992. 282pp.

GAINES, WILLIAM M.
___ "Gaines, William M. (Obituary)," *Locus* 29(1): 67. July 1992.
___ "Gaines, William (Obituary)," *Science Fiction Chronicle* 13(10): 14, 16. July/August 1992.

GALACTIC GIGOLO (MOTION PICTURE)
___ "***Galactic Gigolo*** (Review)," *Variety* p. 18. February 3, 1988.

GALAXY (MAGAZINE)
___ "*Galaxy* Follows *Omni* into the Great Unknown," *Locus* 35(1): 9. July 1995.
___ "*Galaxy* Giving Up Magazine Format, to Be Available Only Electronically," *Science Fiction Chronicle* 16(9): 6. August/September 1995.
___ "*Galaxy* Resurrected," *Locus* 32(2): 8, 74. February 1994.

GALAXY (MAGAZINE) (continued)
___ "*Galaxy Magazine* Revived," *Science Fiction Chronicle* 15(3): 4-5. January 1994.

GALLAGHER, STEPHEN
___ Nicholls, Stan. "Stephen Gallagher Peeps into the Abyss," in: Nicholls, Stan. **Wordsmiths of Wonder: Fifty Interviews with Writers of the Fantastic**. London: Orbit, 1993. pp.417-424.

GALLUN, RAYMOND Z.
___ "Gallun, Raymond Z. (Obituary)," *Locus* 32(5): 62. May 1994.
___ "Gallun, Raymond Z. (Obituary)," *Science Fiction Chronicle* 15(6): 24. April/May 1994.

GAMES
___ "*King's Quest* Moves to Books," *Locus* 32(1): 6. January 1994.
___ Baker, Eric T. "With a Roll of the Dice, *Metascape* Provides Superior Space Opera Thrills," *Science Fiction Age* 2(4): 84-86. May 1994.
___ Baker, Eric T. "The Worlds of Williams and Effinger Come Alive in *Cyberpunk 2020*," *Science Fiction Age* 1(6): 90-92. September 1993.
___ Betancourt, John G. "*Shadowrun's* Second Edition Cyberfantasy Is Bigger and Better Than Ever," *Science Fiction Age* 1(4): 66, 71. May 1993.
___ Castro, Adam-Troy. "Conquer the Desert Planet Arrakis as Frank Herbert's **Dune** Novels Come to Life," *Science Fiction Age* 2(1): 92-95. November 1993.
___ Di Filippo, Paul. "Sci-Fi Goobers Invent an Intergalactic Game Show That's Anything But Trivial," *Science Fiction Age* 3(4): 94-97. May 1995.
___ Hautala, Rick. "H. R. Giger's Alien Nightmares Invade Your Computer in *Darkseed*," *Science Fiction Age* 1(5): 74, 80. July 1993.
___ Honigsberg, David M. "*RoboRally* and *Edge City* Transport Board Games to an Exciting Tomorrow," *Science Fiction Age* 3(3): 98-101. March 1995.
___ Honigsberg, David M. "*Star Riders* Sends up SF With Serious Space Opera Silliness," *Science Fiction Age* 2(6): 90-93. September 1994.
___ Kelley, Robert. "A Maze of Twisty Little Passages All Alike: Aesthetics and Teleology in Interactive Computer Fictional Elements," *Science Fiction Studies* 20(1): 52-68. March 1993.
___ Perry, Clark. "*The Daedalus Encounter* Moves Big-Budget Special Effects Inside Your PC," *Science Fiction Age* 4(1): 100-101. November 1995.
___ Platt, Charles. "The Tenacity of Fiction," *Interzone* No. 91: 44-45. January 1995.
___ Rothman, Chuck. "Larry Niven's Ringworld Novels Spawn a Fun and Challenging Computer Sequel," *Science Fiction Age* 3(1): 88-91. November 1994.
___ Schimel, Lawrence. "Be Prepared to Save Tomorrow's Ecology in *Jump Raven's* Complex Future," *Science Fiction Age* 2(5): 76-78. July 1994.
___ Soukup, Martha. "Climb Aboard an *Iron Dragon* for a Railroad Journey to Adventure," *Science Fiction Age* 3(5): 98-100. July 1995.
___ Thomas, G. W. "The Gaming Market: Writing Role-Playing Games," in: Thompkins, David G., ed. **Science Fiction Writer's Market Place and Source Book**. Cincinnati, OH: Writer's Digest Books, 1994. pp.276-283.
___ Thomas, G. W. "An Untapped Market: Writing Role-Playing Games," *Writer's Digest* 73(6): 38-41. June 1993.
___ Thompson, Tom. "Interactive Science Fiction for the Mac," *Byte* 19(12): 34-35. December 1994.
___ Weaver, Steven. "*Blade Runner's* Designer Brings His Magic to Your Home Computer With *CyberRace*," *Science Fiction Age* 2(3): 82-85. March 1994.

GANN, ERNEST
___ "Gann, Ernest (Obituary)," *Locus* 28(2): 68. February 1992.

GARBER, ERIC
___ "Garber, Eric (Obituary)," *Locus* 35(5): 78. November 1995.

GARCIA MARQUEZ, GABRIEL
___ Hood, Edward W. **La ficción de Gabriel García Márquez: Repetición e intertextualidad**. New York: Peter Lang, 1994. 229pp.

GARDNER, CRAIG SHAW
___ Schweitzer, Darrell. "SFC Interviews: Craig Shaw Gardner," *Science Fiction Chronicle* 15(8): 7, 35-36. June 1994.

GARDNER, JOHN
___ Payne, Craig. "The Cycle of the Zodiac in John Gardner's Grendel," *Mythlore* 18(4): 61-65. Autumn 1992. (No. 70)
___ Payne, Craig. "The Redemption of Cain in John Gardner's Grendel," *Mythlore* 18(2): 12-16. Spring 1992. (No. 68)

GARNER, ALAN
___ Beach, Sarah. "Breaking the Pattern: Alan Garner's **The Owl Service** and the **Mabinogion**," *Mythlore* 20(1): 10-14. Winter 1994. (Whole No. 75)
___ Cameron, Eleanor. "**The Owl Service**: A Study," *Wilson Library Bulletin* 44(4): 425-433. December 1969.
___ Gillies, Carolyn. "Possession and Structure in the Novels of Alan Garner," *Children's Literature in Education* 18: 107-117. Fall 1975.
___ Lockwood, Michael. "A Sense of the Spoken: Language in **The Owl Service**," *Children's Literature in Education* 23(2): 83-92. June 1992.
___ McMahon, Patricia. "A Second Look: **Elidor**," *Horn Book* 56(3): 328-331. June 1980.
___ Rees, David. "Alan Garner: Some Doubts," *Horn Book* 55(3): 282-289. June 1979.
___ Taylor, Andrew. "Polishing Up the Pattern: The Ending of **The Owl Service**," *Children's Literature in Education* 23(2): 93-100. June 1992.

GARNETT, DAVID
___ Nicholls, Stan. "Spaceships & Solicitors: David Garnett Interviewed," *Interzone* No. 93: 19-22. March 1995.

GARRIS, MICK
___ Beeler, Michael. "**The Stand**: Working With Stephen King," *Cinefantastique* 25(3): 30-31. June 1994.

GASKELL, ELIZABETH
___ Rosenthal, Rae. "Gaskell's Feminist Utopia: The Cranfordians and the Reign of Goodwill," in: Donawerth, Jane L. and Kolmerten, Carol A., eds. **Utopian and Science Fiction by Women: Worlds of Difference**. Syracuse, NY: Syracuse University Press, 1994. pp.73-92.

GAUTIER, THEOPHILE
___ Crichfield, Grant. "Bakhtin's Chronotope and the Fantastic: Gautier's 'Jettatura' and 'Arria Marcella'," *Journal of the Fantastic in the Arts* 4(3): 25-39. 1991. (No. 15)

GAWAIN AND THE GREEN KNIGHT (MOTION PICTURE)
___ Blanch, Robert J. "Gawain on Film," by Robert J. Blanch and Julian N. Wasserman. in: Harty, Kevin J., ed. **Cinema Arthuriana: Essays on Arthurian Film**. New York: Garland, 1991. pp.57-70.

GAY, ANNE
___ Melia, Sally-Ann. "The Bells of Hell Go Ting-a-Ling-a-Ling: Anne Gay Interviewed," *Interzone* No. 92: 20-23. February 1995.

GAYHEART, REBECCA
___ Chrissinger, Craig W. "Earth Mother," *Starlog* No. 214: 36-39, 69. May 1995.

GEARHART, SALLY MILLER
___ Barr, Marleen S. **Lost in Space: Probing Feminist Science Fiction and Beyond**. Chapel Hill, NC: University of North Carolina Press, 1993. 231pp.
___ Kuelen, Margarete. **Radical Imagination: Feminist Conceptions of the Future in Ursula Le Guin, Marge Piercy and Sally Miller Gearhart**. Frankfurt-am-Main/New York: Peter Lang, 1991. 122pp.

GEGENHUBER, JOHN
___ Chrissinger, Craig W. "Company Man," *Starlog* No. 212: 76-79. March 1995.

GEMMELL, DAVID
___ Nicholls, Stan. "David Gemmell Won't Get Out of This Life Alive," in: Nicholls, Stan. **Wordsmiths of Wonder: Fifty Interviews with Writers of the Fantastic**. London: Orbit, 1993. pp.364-376.

GENDER
___ Attebery, Brian. "Gender, Fantasy, and the Authority of Tradition," *Journal of the Fantastic in the Arts* 7(1): 51-60. 1996.

GENDER (continued)
___ Bogstad, Janice M. **Gender, Power and Reversal in Contemporary Anglo-American and French Feminist Science Fiction**. Ph.D. Dissertation, University of Wisconsin, Madison, 1992. 229pp. (DAI-A 54/02, p. 509. August 1993.)
___ Burleson, Donald R. "Lovecraft and Gender," *Lovecraft Studies* No. 27: 21-25. Fall 1992.
___ Deery, June. "Technology and Gender in Aldous Huxley's Alternative (?) Worlds," *Extrapolation* 33(3): 258-273. Fall 1992.
___ Doughan, David. "Tolkien, Sayers, Sex and Gender," in: Reynolds, Patricia and GoodKnight, Glen H., eds. **Proceedings of the J. R. R. Tolkien Centenary Conference, Keble College, Oxford, 1992**. Altadena, CA: Mythopoeic Press, 1995. pp.356-359. (*Mythlore* Vol. 21, No. 2, Winter 1996, Whole No. 80)
___ Helford, Elyce R. "Reading Masculinities in the 'Postpatriarchal' Space of *Red Dwarf*," *Foundation* No. 64: 20-31. Summer 1995.
___ Jenkins, Henry. "At Other Times, Like Females: Gender and *Star Trek* Fiction," in: Tulloch, John and Jenkins, Henry, eds. **Science Fiction Audiences: Watching Doctor Who and Star Trek**. New York: Routledge, 1995. pp.196-212.
___ McKee, Alan. "Intentional Phalluses: The Male 'Sex' in J. G. Ballard," *Foundation* No. 57: 58-67. Spring 1993.
___ Roberts, Robin. "Matthew Arnold's 'Dover Beach', Gender, and Science Fiction," *Extrapolation* 33(3): 245-257. Fall 1992.

GENDER IN FILM
___ Clover, Carol J. "Her Body, Himself: Gender in the Slasher Film," in: Irons, Glenwood, ed. **Gender, Language and Myth: Essays on Popular Narrative**. Toronto: University of Toronto Press, 1992. pp.253-302.

GENE RODDENBERRY'S LOST UNIVERSE (COMIC)
___ Johnson, Kim H. "Universes Lost," *Starlog* No. 210: 27-31, 69. January 1995.

GENERATIONS (MOTION PICTURE)
___ SEE: STAR TREK GENERATIONS (MOTION PICTURE).

GENRE
___ Malzberg, Barry N. "A Formal Feeling Comes," *Amazing Stories* 68(7): 61-63. November 1993.

GEOLOGY
___ Brice, William C. "Geology Teaching and Science Fiction," *Journal of Geological Education* 29(2): 105-107. March 1980.

GEORGE LUCAS
___ Cerone, Daniel H. "Interactive Jones: George Lucas Dreams of Multimedia Adventures for **Young Indiana Jones**," *Los Angeles (CA) Times*. March 4, 1992. in: *NewsBank. Film and Television*. 33:B10. 1992.
___ Davis, Sally O. "George Lucas Goes for Broke in His TV Debut--the Time Traveling, Globe-Trotting **Young Indiana Jones Chronicles** (Review)," *Boston (MA) Herald*. March 1, 1992. in: *NewsBank. Film and Television*. 37:G10-G11. 1992. also in: *NewsBank. Names in the News* 71:G2-G3. 1992.
___ Klinghoffer, David. "Will Young Indy Jones Grow Up to Be Himself? (Review)," *Washington (DC) Times*. March 4, 1992. in: *NewsBank. Film and Television*. 27:C4-C5. 1992.
___ Laurence, Robert P. "Jones Chronicles Is Lavish, Yet Shallow (Review)," *San Diego (CA) Union*. March 3, 1992. in: *NewsBank. Film and Television*. 27:C2. 1992.
___ Laurence, Robert P. "Series Explores Future Hero's Coming of Age (Review)," *San Diego (CA) Union*. March 3, 1992. in: *NewsBank. Film and Television*. 27:B14-C1. 1992.
___ Rosenthal, Phil. "No Feeling of Doom for Young Indy (Review)," *Los Angeles (CA) Daily News*. March 1, 1992. in: *NewsBank. Film and Television*. 37:G7-G8. 1992.
___ Rosenthal, Phil. "**Young Indiana Jones** Doesn't Live Up to Big Screen Brother (Review)," *Los Angeles (CA) Daily News*. March 1, 1992. in: *NewsBank. Film and Television*. 37:G9. 1992.
___ Zurawik, David. "Young Indy Explodes onto the Small Screen in a Sprawling, Exciting Yarn (Review)," *Baltimore (MD) Sun*. March 4, 1992. in: *NewsBank. Film and Television*. 27:C3. 1992.

GEORGE PAL MEMORIAL AWARD, 1992
___ "1992 Saturn Awards," *Locus* 28(6): 7. June 1992.

GERMANY

___ "**Day After**, **Last Unicorn** Hit Big in Germany, Campaigns Help," *Variety* p. 123. January 25, 1984.

___ "German Encyclopedia of Horror to Appear," *Locus* 33(6): 9, 79. December 1994.

___ "Hold Back the 'Dawn'," *Variety* p. 37. January 9, 1985.

___ "**Neverending Story** Big Marks Gamble for Germany, But Film Has All Elements for Solid Hit," *Variety* p. 277, 299. March 2, 1983.

___ "Reconstruction of Original Score Gave **Nosferatu** Gloss at Berlin," *Variety* p. 348. May 9, 1984.

___ "Seeing Nuke Panic, Germans Dump Pic From TV Schedule," *Variety* p. 116, 124. March 21, 1984.

___ "SF in Germany," *Locus* 28(1): 47. January 1992.

___ "SF in Germany," *Locus* 30(4): 36, 62. April 1993.

___ Becker, Siegfried. "Konjunkturen des Phantastischen: Anmerkungen zu den Karrieren von Science Fiction, Fantasy und Marchen sowie verwandtne Formen," by Siegfried Becker and Gerd Hallenberger. *Zeitschrift fur Literaturwissenschaft und Linguistik* No. 92: 141-155. 1993.

___ Castein, Hanne. "Mit der Reichbahn ins Weltall: Zur Science-Fiction der DDR," in: Goodbody, Axel and Tate, Dennis, eds. **Geist und Macht: Writers and the State in the DDR**. Amsterdam and Atlanta, GA: Rodopi, 1992. pp.81-89. (German Monitor, No. 29)

___ Dickens, David B. "Rings, Belts, and a Bird's Nest: Invisibility in German Literature," *Journal of the Fantastic in the Arts* 4(2): 29-48. 1992. (No. 14)

___ Dyck, Axel. "*Phantastik* oder *phantastische Literatur*?," *Quarber Merkur* 30(2): 61-63. December 1992. (No. 78)

___ Friedrich, Hans-Edwin. **Science Fiction in der deutschsprachigen Literatur: Ein Referat zur Forschung bis 1993**. Tubigen: Max Niemeyer Verlag, 1995. 493pp.

___ Gottwald, Ulrike. **Science Fiction (SF) als Literatur in der Bundesrepublik der siebziger und achtziger Jahre**. Frankfurt: Peter Lang, 1990. 308pp.

___ Hammer, Stephanie. "Camouflage and Sabotage: Satiric Maneuvers in the Fantastic Fiction of the German Democratic Republic," in: Slusser, George E. and Rabkin, Eric S., eds. **Styles of Creation: Aesthetic Technique and the Creation of Fictional Worlds**. Athens: University of Georgia Press, 1992. pp.143-152.

___ Heinze, Theodor T., ed. **Subjektivität als Fiktion: zur literarisch psychologischen Konstruktion des modernen Menschen.** Pfaffenweiler: Centaurus, 1993. 172pp.

___ Hornigk, Frank. "Die Literatur bleibt zuständig: Ein Versuch über das Verhältnis von Literatur, Utopie und Politik in der DDR--am Ende der DDR," *Germanic Review* 67(3): 99-105. Summer 1992.

___ Kempen, Bernhard. "Perry Rhodan--Our Man in Space: Transformations of a German SF Phenomenon," *Foundation* No. 56: 5-22. Autumn 1992.

___ Kleinschmidt, Erich. " 'Begreif-Welt': Zur fiktionalen Raumregahrung in der deutschen Literatur im 18. Jahrhunderts," *Germanisch-Romanische Monatsschrift* (Berlin) 41(2): 145-152. 1991.

___ Lehnert, Gertrud. "Trauma, Fluchten, Utopien: Wirklichkeit im Spiegel der phantistischen Kinder- und Jungendliteratur," *Fundevogel* No. 88/89: 11-18. 1991.

___ Mabee, Barbara. "Astronauts, Angels, and Time Machines: The Fantastic in Recent German Democratic Republic Literature," in: Morse, Donald E., ed. **The Celebration of the Fantastic**. Westport, CT: Greenwood, 1992. pp.221-236.

___ Mabee, Barbara. "The Witch as Double: Feminist Doubles in German Literature and Irmtraud Morgner's **Amanda**," *Journal of the Fantastic in the Arts* 6(2/3): 166-190. 1994.

___ McDonald, William C. **Arthur and Tristan: On the Intersection of Legends in German Medieval Literature**. Lewiston, NY: Mellen, 1991. 296pp.

___ Müller, Hans-Harald. **Leo Perutz**. München: Beck, 1992. 138pp.

___ Müller, Ulrich. "Blank, Syberberg, and the German Arthurian Tradition," in: Harty, Kevin J., ed. **Cinema Arthuriana: Essays on Arthurian Film**. New York: Garland, 1991. pp.157-168.

___ Myers, Michael. "Visions of Tomorrow: German Science Fiction and Socialist Utopian Novels of the Late Nineteenth Century," *Selecta* (Corvallis) 14: 63-69. 1993.

___ Rode, Silvia A. **Franz Werfels 'Stern der Ungeborenen': die Utopie als Fiktionaler Genrediskurs und Ideengeschichte**. Ph.D. Dissertation, University of California, Los Angeles, 1993. 304pp. (DAI-A 54/03, p. 943. September 1993.)

GERMANY (continued)

___ Schultz, James A. "Teaching Gottfried and Wolfram," in: Fries, Maureen and Watson, Jeanie, eds. **Approaches to the Teaching of the Arthurian Tradition**. New York: Modern Language Association, 1992. pp.94-99.

___ Smith, Arden R. "Duzen and Ihrzen in the German Translation of **The Lord of the Rings**," *Mythlore* 21(1): 33-40. Summer 1995. (No. 79)

___ Spies, Bernhard. "Der Anteil der sozialistischen Utopie an der Beendigung der DDR-Literatur. Am Beispiel Christoph Heins," *Germanic Review* 67(3): 112-118. Summer 1992.

___ Springman, Luke. **Comrades, Friends and Companions: Utopian Projections and Social Action in German Literature for Young People, 1926-1934**. New York: P. Lang, 1989. 242pp. [Not seen.]

___ Springman, Luke. **Comrades, Friends and Companions: Utopian Projections and Social Action in German Literature for Young People, 1926-1934**. Ph.D. Dissertation, Ohio State University, 1988. 338pp.

___ Stapleton, Amy L. **Future Perspectives: Contemporary German Science Fiction's Contribution to an Ecological Bewesstseinswandel**. Ph.D. Dissertation, University of Wisconsin, Madison, 1992. (DAI-A 52,/ 11, p. 3947. May 1992.)

___ Stapleton, Amy L. **Utopias for a Dying World: Contemporary German Science Fiction's Plea for a New Ecological Awareness**. New York: Peter Lang, 1993. 158pp.

___ Steinmüller, Karlheinz. "Das Ende der Utopischen Literatur: Ein themengeschichtlicher Nachruf auf der DDR-Science-Fiction," *Germanic Review* 67(4): 166-173. Fall 1992.

___ Troster, Horst G. **Science Fiction im Horspiel, 1947-1987**. Frankfurt-am-Main: Rundfunkarchiv, 1993. 750pp.

___ Vollprecht, Sabine. **Science-Fiction fur Kinder in der DDR**. Stuttgart: H.-D. Heinz, 1994. 135pp.

GERNSBACK, HUGO

___ Moskowitz, Sam. "Hugo Gernsback and Edgar Rice Burroughs," *Burroughs Bulletin* NS. No. 21: 3-9. January 1995.

___ Ross, Andrew. **Strange Weather: Culture, Science, and Technology in the Age of Limits**. London: Verso, 1991. 275pp.

___ Westfahl, Gary. "The Jules Verne, H. G. Wells, Edgar Allan Poe Type of Story: Hugo Gernsback's History of Science Fiction," *Science-Fiction Studies* 19(3): 340-353. November 1992.

___ Westfahl, Gary. " 'Man Against Man, Brain Against Brain': The Transformation of Melodrama in Science Fiction," in: Redmond, James, ed. **Melodrama**. Cambridge: Cambridge University Press, 1992. pp.193-211.

___ Westfahl, Gary. " 'This Unique Document': Hugo Gernsback's **Ralph 124C 41 +** and the Genres of Science Fiction," *Extrapolation* 35(2): 95-119. Summer 1994.

GERROLD, DAVID

___ "1994 Nebula Awards Winners," *Locus* 34(5): 7. May 1995.

___ "1995 Hugo Winners," *Locus* 35(3): 7. September 1993.

___ "David Gerrold: A Growing Experience," *Locus* 31(1): 5, 65-66. July 1993.

___ "The Hugos (Or, the Empire Strikes Back)," *Science Fiction Chronicle* 17(2): 55-56. December 1995/January 1996.

___ "Nebula Award Winners," *Science Fiction Chronicle* 16(6): 4. May 1995.

___ "World Science Fiction Convention Hugo Awards, 1995," *Science Fiction Chronicle* 17(1): 5. October/November 1995

GHISLAZONI, ANTONIA

___ Roda, Vittorio. "La fantascienza umoristica de Antonia Ghislazoni," *Studi e Problemi de Critica Testuale* 49: 121-152. October 1994.

GHOST IN THE MACHINE (MOTION PICTURE)

___ Beeler, Michael. "**Ghost in the Machine**," *Cinefantastique* 24(2): 6-7. August 1993.

___ Beeler, Michael. "**Ghost in the Machine**," *Cinefantastique* 25(2): 56-57. April 1994.

___ Harris, Judith P. "**Ghost in the Machine** (Review)," *Cinefantastique* 25(4): 59-60. August 1994.

___ Kliewer, Brent. "Eek, There's a **Ghost in the Machine**," (Santa Fe, NM) *New Mexican* January 7, 1994. in: *NewsBank. Film and Television* 12: A9. 1994.

___ Pierce, Susan. " 'Ghost' Full of Used Spooks," (Little Rock) *Arkansas Democrat* pp.1F, 8F. January 5, 1994. in: *NewsBank. Film and Television* 12: A5-A6. 1994.

GHOST STORY (MOTION PICTURE)

GHOST STORY (MOTION PICTURE)

___ "Fall Trial Is Expected for 3 Teamsters Over *Ghost Story* Practices," *Variety* p. 1, 109. August 27, 1986.

___ "*Ghost Story* Trial Underway in N.Y.," *Variety* p. 4, 30. September 24, 1986.

___ "Trial of Teamsters on Universal's *Ghost Story* Underway in Albany," *Variety* p. 1, 112. October 1, 1986.

GHOSTBUSTER (GROUP W) (TV)

___ Dempsey, John. "Hey! That's My Ghost, Buster," *Variety* p.65. August 28, 1985.

GHOSTBUSTERS (MOTION PICTURE)

___ "Col Claims Major Win With Piracy Settlement of *Ghostbusters* Items," *Variety* p. 4. October 31, 1984.

___ "Columbia Calls Harvey Comics 'Ghost' Suit Baseless," *Variety* p. 3, 30. November 28, 1984.

___ "Columbia's *Ghostbuster* a Grossbuster in First Foreign Dates," *Variety* p. 4, 28. November 28, 1984.

___ "*Ghostbusters* (1984): Interviews with Ivan Reitman, Richard Edlund, Michael Gross, and John Bruno," in: Goldberg, Lee, ed. **The Dreamweavers: Interviews With Fantasy Filmmakers of the 1980s.** Jefferson, NC: McFarland, 1995. pp.75-105.

___ "*Gremlins* Sweeps Saturn Ceremony," *Variety* p.6. June 19, 1985.

___ "Harey Comics Sues Columbia Pics Over *Ghostbusters* Logo," *Variety* p. 4. November 21, 1984.

___ Dempsey, John. "Hey! That's My Ghost, Buster," *Variety* p.65. August 28, 1985.

GHOULIES GO TO COLLEGE (MOTION PICTURE)

___ "*Ghoulies Go to College* (Review)," *Cinefantastique* 22(5): 60. April 1992.

GHOULIES IV (MOTION PICTURE)

___ Wilt, David. "*Ghoulies IV* (Review)," *Cinefantastique* 26(3): 59. April 1995.

GIBB, CYNTHIA

___ Warren, Bill. "Deadly Rose," *Starlog* No. 221: 52-55. December 1995.

GIBSON, MEL

___ Lofficier, Randy. "*Mad Max* Movies (1979-1985): Interview with George Miller, Terry Hayes, George Ogilvie and Mel Gibson," by Randy Lofficier and Jean-Marc Lofficier. in: Goldberg, Lee et al. **Science Fiction Filmmaking in the 1980s.** Jefferson, NC: McFarland, 1995. pp.133-174.

___ Lofficier, Randy. "Road Warrior," by Randy Lofficier and Jean-Marc Lofficier. in: McDonnell, David, ed. **Starlog's Science Fiction Heroes and Heroines.** New York: Crescent Books, 1995. pp.12-14.

GIBSON, WILLIAM

___ "1995 Prix Aurora Awards," *Locus* 34(6): 8. June 1995.

___ "$850,000+ for New William Gibson Novel," *Science Fiction Chronicle* 15(7): 4. June 1994.

___ "Aurora Awards," *Science Fiction Chronicle* 16(7): 4. June/July 1995.

___ "Cyberpunk Era: Interviews With William Gibson," *Whole Earth Review* No. 63: 78-82. Summer 1989.

___ "Electronic Gibsons," *Locus* 28(6): 7. June 1992.

___ "Gibson Moves to Putnam/Berkley," *Locus* 32(6): 7. June 1994.

___ "Gibson Novelization to Pocket Books for $200,000," *Science Fiction Chronicle* 15(9): 4. August 1994.

___ "On Technology: Sci-Fi Vision of Things to Come: Authors Brin and Gibson Depict Opposing Future Outcomes for the Evolving Internet," *San Francisco (CA) Chronicle* February 20, 1996. (Cited from the Internet Edition.)

___ "William Gibson: New Futures, Just on the Horizon," *Hailing Frequencies* (Waldenbooks) No. 8: 1, 3-5, 13. 1993.

___ Alkon, Paul. "Deus Ex Machina in William Gibson's Cyberpunk Trilogy," in: Slusser, George E. and Shippey, Tom, eds. **Fiction 2000: Cyberpunk and the Future of Narrative.** Athens: University of Georgia Press, 1992. pp.75-87.

___ Angulo, Michael M. **Random Access Memories: Mechanism and Metaphor in the Fiction of William Gibson.** Ph.D. Dissertation, University of Illinois, Urbana-Champaign, 1993. 345pp. (DAI-A 54/11, p. 4086. May 1994.)

GIBSON, WILLIAM (continued)

___ Annis, Ethan. **The Utility of Information in William Gibson's Futuristic Science Fiction.** Master's Thesis, University of North Carolina, Chapel Hill, 1992. 38pp.

___ Biddick, Kathleen. "Humanist History and the Haunting of Virtual Worlds: Problems of Memory and Rememoration," *Genders* No. 18: 47-66. Winter 1993.

___ Bolhafner, J. Stephen. "Guide to Cyberspace," *Starlog* No. 200: 72-74, 87. March 1994.

___ Booker, M. Keith. "Technology, History, and the Postmodern Imagination: The Cyberpunk Fiction of William Gibson," *Arizona Quarterly* 50(4): 63-87. Winter 1994.

___ Brande, David J. **Technologies of Postmodernity: Ideology and Desire in Literature and Science (Pynchon, Thomas; Gibson, William; Butler, Octavia; Acker, Kathy).** Ph.D. Dissertation, University of Washington, 1995. 228pp. (DAI-A 56/07, p. 2677. January 1996.)

___ Bredehoft, Thomas A. "The Gibson Continuum: Cyberspace and Gibson's Mervyn Kihn Stories," *Science Fiction Studies* 22(2): 252-263. July 1995.

___ Bukatman, Scott R. "Gibson's Typewriter," *South Atlantic Quarterly* 92(4): 627-645. Fall 1993.

___ Cherniavsky, Eva. "(En)gendering Cyberspace in **Neuromancer**: Postmodern Subjectivity and Virtual Motherhood," *Genders* No. 18: 32-46. Winter 1993.

___ Christie, John. "Of Als and Others: William Gibson's Transit," in: Slusser, George E. and Shippey, Tom, eds. **Fiction 2000: Cyberpunk and the Future of Narrative.** Athens: University of Georgia Press, 1992. pp.171-182.

___ Csicsery-Ronay, Istvan, Jr. "Antimancere: Cybernetics and Art in Gibson's **Count Zero**," *Science Fiction Studies* 22(1): 63-86. March 1995.

___ Csicsery-Ronay, Istvan, Jr. "The Sentimental Futurist: Cybernetics and Art in William Gibson's **Neuromancer**," *Critique* 33(3): 221-240. Spring 1992.

___ Dargis, Manohla. "Cyber Johnny," *Sight and Sound* 5(7): 6-7. July 1995.

___ Delany, Samuel R. "Zelazny/Varley/Gibson--and Quality, Part 1," *New York Review of Science Fiction* No. 48: 1, 10-13. August 1992.

___ Delany, Samuel R. "Zelazny/Varley/Gibson--and Quality, Part 2," *New York Review of Science Fiction* No. 49: 1, 3-7. September 1992.

___ Dever, Sean. "Quick Cuts: Cinematic Cyberspace," *Cinefex* No. 62: 17-18. June 1995.

___ Dolphin, Ric. "Master of the Virtual World," *Maclean's* 105: 44. December 14, 1992. [Not seen.]

___ Fischlin, Daniel. "The Charisma Leak: A Conversation With William Gibson and Bruce Sterling," by Daniel Fischlin, Veronica Hollinger and Andrew Taylor. *Science Fiction Studies* 19(1): 1-16. March 1992.

___ Garreau, Joel. "Cyberspaceman: Sci-Fi Writer William Gibson, Far Flung and Back Again," *Washington (DC) Post* p.D1. October 18, 1993.

___ Gibson, William. "Notes on a Process: Novel into Film," *Wired* 3(6): 157-159. June 1995.

___ Greenfield, Adam. "New Romancer: Interview with William Gibson," *Spin* 4: 96-99, 119. December 1988.

___ Hamburg, Victoria. "The King of Cyberpunk," *Interview* 19: 84-86, 91-92. January 1989.

___ Harmon, Amy. "Crossing Cyberpunk's Threshold: William Gibson," *Los Angeles (CA) Times* p.D1. May 24, 1995.

___ Huntington, John. "Newness, **Neuromancer**, and the End of Narrative," in: Slusser, George E. and Shippey, Tom, eds. **Fiction 2000: Cyberpunk and the Future of Narrative.** Athens: University of Georgia Press, 1992. pp.133-141.

___ Johnson, Brian D. "Mind Games With William Gibson," *Maclean's* 108(23): 60-64. June 5, 1995.

___ Johnson, Kim H. "Memories Can't Wait," *Starlog* No. 216: 50-53, 64. July 1995.

___ Killheffer, Robert K. J. "PW Interview: William Gibson," *Publishers Weekly* 240(36):70-71. September 6, 1993.

___ Leonard, Andrew. "Cyberpunks and Techno-hicks: Surfing the Matrix of Novelist William Gibson," *San Francisco (CA) Bay Guardian* 27(46): 31-33. August 18, 1993.

___ Maccarillo, Lisa. "Hardwired Hero," *Sci-Fi Entertainment* 1(5): 46-50, 72. February 1995.

___ Masters, John. "Hollywood Strains SF Writer's Imagination," *Financial Post* p. S19. August 28, 1993. (Cited from *IAC Insite* on-line service.)

GIBSON, WILLIAM (continued)

___ Mayrhofer, Maximilian. "William Gibsons Cyberspace Trilogie. 2. Teil: Abenteuer -- Science Fiction--Krimi. Struktur in Gibsons Werk," *Quarber Merkur* 31(2): 34-54. Dezember 1993. (No. 80)

___ Mayrhofer, Maximilian. "William Gibsons Cyberspace-Trilogie. 3. Teil: Thematik und Bausteine einer fiktiven Welt," *Quarber Merkur* 32(1): 21-39. June 1994. (Whole No. 81)

___ Mayrhofer, Maximilian. "William Gibsons Cyberspace-Trilogie. 4. Teil und Schluß: Sprache bei Gibson und die Sprache Gibsons," *Quarber Merkur* 32(2): 3-23. December 1994. (Whole No. 82)

___ Mayrhofer, Maximilian. "William Gibsons Cyberspace-Trilogie. I: Handlungsverlauf und Charaktere," *Quarber Merkur* 31(1): 41-52. June 1993. (No. 79)

___ McHale, Brian. "Difference Engines," *ANQ* 5(4): 220-223. November 1992.

___ McQuiddy, A. P. "William Gibson: Hallucinating on the Present: An Interview," *Texas SF Inquirer* No. 22: 2-7. October/November 1987.

___ Olsen, Lance. **William Gibson**. Mercer Island, WA: Starmont, 1992. 131pp. (Starmont Reader's Guide, 58)

___ Ruddick, Nicholas. "Putting the Bits Together: Information Theory, **Neuromancer**, and Science Fiction," *Journal of the Fantastic in the Arts* 3(4): 84-92. 1994.

___ Schmitt, Ronald E. "Mythology and Technology: The Novels of William Gibson," *Extrapolation* 34(1): 64-78. Spring 1993.

___ Schroeder, Randy. "Determinancy, Indeterminacy, and the Romantic in William Gibson," *Science Fiction Studies* 21(2): 155-163. July 1994.

___ Schroeder, Randy. "Neu-Criticizing William Gibson," *Extrapolation* 35(4): 330-341. Winter 1994.

___ Sims, Michael. "William Gibson: The Day After Tomorrow Meets Film Noir in the Imagination of This Writer, Interview," *BookPage* p. 3. August 1993.

___ Snead, Elizabeth. "His Future Is Closer Than You Think," *USA Today* Sec. D, p. 1. September 2, 1993.

___ Speller, Maureen. "Horribly Real: A Conversation With William Gibson," *Vector* No. 179: 12-17. June/July 1994.

___ Sponsler, Claire. "Cyberpunk and the Dilemmas of Postmodern Narrative: The Example of William Gibson," *Contemporary Literature* 33(4): 625-644. December 1992.

___ Sponsler, Claire. "William Gibson and the Death of Cyberpunk," in: Latham, Robert A. and Collins, Robert A., eds. **Modes of the Fantastic**. Westport, CT: Greenwood, 1995. pp.47-55.

___ Stone, Linda. "A Glimpse of Cyberspace," *Sci-Fi Entertainment* 1(5): 51. February 1995.

___ Teitelbaum, Sheldon. "**Alien 3**: William Gibson's 'Neuroaliens'," *Cinefantastique* 22(6): 12-13. June 1992

___ van Bakel, Rogier. "Remembering Johnny," *Wired* 3(6): 154-157. June 1995.

___ Voller, Jack G. "Neuromanticism: Cyberspace and the Sublime," *Extrapolation* 34(1): 18-29. Spring 1993.

___ Wahl, Wendy. "Bodies and Technologies: **Dora**, **Neuromancer**, and Strategies of Resistance," *Postmodern Culture* 3(2): [17pp.]. January 1993. (Electronic Journal: pmc@jefferson.village.virginia.edu).

___ Warsh, David. "Cyberspace: What Is in It for You?," *Boston (MA) Globe* p. 65. May 30, 1993.

___ Westfahl, Gary. " 'The Gernsback Continuum': William Gibson in the Context of Science Fiction," in: Slusser, George E. and Shippey, Tom, eds. **Fiction 2000: Cyberpunk and the Future of Narrative**. Athens: University of Georgia Press, 1992. pp.88-108.

___ White, Tim. "William Gibson: Exploring the Newest Frontier," *Mindsparks* 2(1): 35-36. 1994. (Whole No. 4)

___ Yule, Jeffrey. "The Marginalized Short Stories of William Gibson: 'Hinterlands' and 'The Winter Market'," *Foundation* No. 58: 76-84. Summer 1994.

___ Zuckerman, Edward. "William Gibson," *People Weekly* 35(22): 103-108. June 10, 1991.

GIGER, H. R.

___ "**Species**: MGM Leases Giger's Titular Creature to Be Directed by Roger Donaldson," *Cinefantastique* 25(4): 51. August 1994.

___ Doense, Jan. "**Alien 3**: Design Genius H. R. Giger," *Cinefantastique* 22(6): 10. June 1992

___ Warren, Bill. "Building the Perfect Beast," *Starlog* No. 214: 41-45, 70. May 1995.

GILBERT, ROBERT ERNEST

___ "Gilbert, Robert E. (Obituary)," *Science Fiction Chronicle* 14(8): 16. May 1993.

GILBERT, ROBERT ERNEST (continued)

___ "Gilbert, Robert E(rnest) (Obituary)," *Locus* 30(6): 72. June 1993.

GILLIAM, TERRY

___ Bernhardt, Peter. "Theatre of the Fantastic: Genius Squashed?," *Riverside Quarterly* 9(2): 94-95. August 1993. (Whole No. 34)

___ Johnson, Kim H. "The Fantastic Realist," *Starlog* No. 200: 44-47, 90. March 1994.

GILLILAND, E. DOROTHEA

___ "Gilliland, Doll (Obituary)," *Science Fiction Chronicle* 13(4): 12. January 1992.

___ "Gilliland, E. Dorothea (Obituary)," *Locus* 28(1): 72. January 1992.

GILLMORE, INEZ HAYNES

___ Axsom, Margo. "Border Crossings: The Emergence of Feminist Science Fiction as a Genre. Chapter 3: Frankenstein Evolves," [9 pp.] 1996. (Cited from the Internet. (http: //www-admrec. sonoma.edu /A&R / STAFF /axsom .dissertation.html)). (Chapter 3 of a dissertation in progress.)

GILMAN, CHARLOTTE PERKINS

___ Allen, Polly W. **Building Domestic Liberty: Charlotte Perkins Gilman's Architectural Feminism**. Amherst: University of Massachusetts Press, 1988. 195pp.

___ Crewe, Jonathan. "Queering 'The Yellow Wallpaper'? Clarlotte Perkins Gilman and the Politics of Form," *Tulsa Studies in Women's Literature* 14(2): 273-294. Fall 1995.

___ Gilman, Charlotte P. **The Diaries of Charlotte Perkins Gilman**. Charlottesville: University Press of Virginia, 1994. 943pp.

___ Golden, Catherine. **The Captive Imagination: A Casebook on 'The Yellow Wallpaper'**. New York: Feminist Press, 1992. 341pp.

___ Gough, Val. "Lesbians and Virgins: The New Motherhood in **Herland**," in: Seed, David, ed. **Anticipations: Essays on Early Science Fiction and Its Precursors**. Liverpool: Liverpool University Press, 1995. pp.195-215.

___ Hill, Mary A. **Charlotte Perkins Gilman: A Feminist Paradox**. Ph.D. Dissertation, McGill University, 1975. 273pp.

___ Hill, Mary A. **Charlotte Perkins Gilman: The Making of a Radical Feminist, 1860-1896**. Philadelphia, PA: Temple University Press, 1980. 362pp.

___ Kessler, Carol F. **Charlotte Perkins Gilman: Her Progress Toward Utopia With Selected Writings**. Liverpool: Liverpool University Press, 1995. 316pp.

___ Kessler, Carol F. "Consider Her Ways: The Cultural Work of Charlotte Perkins Gilman's Pragmatopian Stories, 1908-1913," in: Donawerth, Jane L. and Kolmerten, Carol A., eds. **Utopian and Science Fiction by Women: Worlds of Difference**. Syracuse, NY: Syracuse University Press, 1994. pp.126-136.

___ Lancaster, Jane. " 'I Could Easily Have Been an Acrobat': Charlotte Perkins Gilman and the Providence Ladies' Gymnasium 1881-1884," *ATQ* 8(1): 33-52. March 1994.

___ Levitas, Ruth. "Who Holds the Hose: Domestic Labour in the Work of Bellamy, Gilman and Morris," *Utopian Studies* 6(1): 65-84. 1995.

___ Peyser, Thomas G. "Reproducing Utopia: Charlotte Perkins Gilman and **Herland**," *Studies in American Fiction* 20(1): 1-16. Spring 1992.

___ Rose, Jane A. "Images of Self: The Example of Rebecca Harding Davis and Charlotte Perkins Gilman," *English Language Notes* 29(4): 70-78. June 1992.

___ Walker, Sue. "Undiscovered Countries: **Milledgeville, Herland** and Beyond," *Connecticut Review* 16(2): 91-100. Fall 1994.

___ Zauderer, Naomi B. "Charlotte Perkins Gilman's **Moving the Mountain**: A Response to **Looking Backward**," *Utopian Studies* 3(1): 53-69. 1992.

GILMAN, GREER ILENE

___ "Crawford Award," *Locus* 28(4): 7. April 1992.

GINGRICH, NEWT

___ "SF Writing Is Safer," *Locus* 34(2): 7, 72. February 1995.

___ Disch, Thomas M. "Newt's Futurist Brain Trust," by Thomas M. Disch and Micah I. Sifry. *Nation* 260(8): 266-270. February 27, 1995.

___ Dowd, Maureen. "Newt's Potboiler," *New York Times Magazine* pp.44-46. December 4, 1994.

___ Hertzberg, Hendrik. "Cookie Monster," *New Yorker* 71(20): 6-7. July 17, 1995.

GINGRICH, NEWT (continued)
___ Piccoli, Sean. "How to Run for Congress and Write Sexy Thrillers-- Get a Coauthor," *Insight on the News* 11(18): 24. May 8, 1995.

GLADIATORS (MOTION PICTURE)
___ "Computer a Hero (Natch) at Trieste's Festival of Science Fiction Films," *Variety* p. 6. August 5, 1970.

GLOAG, JOHN
___ Stableford, Brian. **Algebraic Fantasies and Realistic Romances: More Masters of Science Fiction**. San Bernardino, CA: Borgo Press, 1995 128pp.

GNOME NAMED GNORM (MOTION PICTURE)
___ Harris, Judith P. "*A Gnome Named Gnorm* (Review)," *Cinefantastique* 25(5): 59. October 1994.

GNOSTICISM
___ Kramer, Reinhold. "Im/maculate: Some Instances of Gnostic Science Fiction," in: Ruddick, Nicholas, ed. **State of the Fantastic**. Westport, CT: Greenwood, 1992. pp.49-58.

GNP-CRESCENDO RECORDS
___ Kenny, Glenn. "The Sounds of Science," *TV Guide* 43(6): 28. February 11, 1995.

GOD IN SF
___ Kosko, Bart. "The Future of God," *Free Inquiry* 15(3): 43-44. Summer 1995.

GODDARD, MARK
___ Voger, Mark. "Mark Goddard: Interview," *Filmfax* No. 33: 72-76. June/July 1992.
___ Weaver, Tom. "Mark Goddard," in: Weaver, Tom. **They Fought the Creature Features: Interviews with 23 Classic Horror, Science Fiction and Serial Stars**. Jefferson, NC: McFarland, 1995. pp.173-186.
___ Weaver, Tom. "Space Duty," *Starlog* No. 190: 30-35, 72. May 1993.

GODWIN, FRANCIS
___ Pleithner, Regina. "Zwei Mondreisen des 17. Jahrhunderts: Voyages imaginaires oder Reiseutopien? Beitrage zum Kolloquium der Arbeitsgruppe Kultrugeschichte des Barockzeitalters an der Herzog-August-Bibliothek Wolfenbuttle von 10. Bis 12. Juli 1989," in: Pleithner, Regina, ed. **Reisen des Barock: Selbst- und Fremderfahrung und ihre Darstellung**. Bonn: Romanistischer, 1991. pp.75-87.

GODWIN, PARKE
___ Falsani, Teresa B. "Parke Godwin's Guenevere: An Archetypal Transformation," *Quondam et Futurus* 3(3): 55-65. Fall 1993.
___ Hoberg, Tom. "In Her Own Right: The Guenevere of Parke Godwin," in: Slocum, Sally K., ed. **Popular Arthurian Traditions**. Bowling Green, OH: Popular Press, 1992. pp.68-79.

GODWIN, WILLIAM
___ Clemit, Pamela. **The Godwinian Novel: The Rational Fictions of Godwin, Brockden Brown, Mary Shelley**. Oxford: Clarendon Press, 1993. 254pp.

GODZILLA
___ Anisfield, Nancy. "*Godzilla*/Gojiro: Evolution of the Nuclear Metaphor," *Journal of Popular Culture* 29(3): 53-62. Winter 1995.
___ Henderson, Ed. "The Big Green Guy," *Starlog* 180: 29-31, 73. July 1992.
___ Jankiewicz, Pat. "*Godzilla*, American Style," *Starlog* No. 193: 55. August 1993.
___ Maslin, Janet. "*Godzilla* Clomp! Bestrides the Ages," *New York Times* p.H13. March 14, 1993.
___ Reid, T. R. "A Monster Hit (Review)," *Washington (DC) Post*. February 2, 1992. in: *NewsBank. Film and Television*. 20:F8-F9. 1992.

GODZILLA VS MECHA-GODZILLA (MOTION PICTURE)
___ "*Godzilla* Alive, Well and Attacking Japan Again (Review)," *Boston (MA) Herald)* October 30, 1993. in: NewsBank. Film and Television.) 117:C1. 1993.

GOFF, HARPER
___ "Goff, Harper, 1912-1993 (Obituary)," *Starlog* No. 196: 23. November 1993.

GOLDBARTH, ALFRED
___ "Campbell and Sturgeon Award Winners," *Locus* 35(2): 8. August 1995.

GOLDEN AGE OF SCIENCE FICTION THRILLERS, VOL. 2 (MOTION PICTURE)
___ Stephens, Bob. "Pre-tinsel Science Fiction Tales," *San Francisco (CA) Examiner* November 25, 1995. (Cited from the Internet Edition.)

GOLDEN ASTEROID AWARD, 1970
___ "Computer a Hero (Natch) at Trieste's Festival of Science Fiction Films," *Variety* p. 6. August 5, 1970.

GOLDEN CHILD (MOTION PICTURE)
___ "*Golden Child* (1986): Interview with Michael Richie," in: Goldberg, Lee, ed. **The Dreamweavers: Interviews With Fantasy Filmmakers of the 1980s**. Jefferson, NC: McFarland, 1995. pp.106-114.

GOLDEN DUCK AWARDS, 1993
___ "Other Awards at ConAdian," *Science Fiction Chronicle* 15(10): 5. September 1994.

GOLDEN FLEECE (MAGAZINE)
___ Cockcroft, T. G. L. "An Index to 'The Eyrie'," *Fantasy Commentator* 8(3/4): 217-229. Fall 1995. (Whole No. 47/48)

GOLDEN SCROLL AWARDS
___ SEE: ACADEMY OF SCIENCE FICTION, FANTASY AND HORROR FILMS AWARDS.

GOLDENEYE (MOTION PICTURE)
___ Jones, Alan. "*Goldeneye*: Bond Villains," *Cinefantastique* 27(3): 18-19. December 1995.
___ Jones, Alan. "*Goldeneye*: Directing Bond," *Cinefantastique* 27(3): 22-24. December 1995.
___ Jones, Alan. "*Goldeneye*: Production Design," *Cinefantastique* 27(3): 24-25. December 1995.
___ Jones, Alan. "*Goldeneye*," *Cinefantastique* 26(6)/27(1): 6-7. October 1995.
___ Jones, Alan. "*Goldeneye*," *Cinefantastique* 27(2): 6-7. November 1995.
___ Jones, Alan. "*Goldeneye*," *Cinefantastique* 27(3): 14-17. December 1995.
___ Rubin, Steven J. "*Goldeneye*: Recreating Bond for the '90s," *Cinefantastique* 27(3): 19-20. December 1995.

GOLDING, WILLIAM
___ "Golding, William: **Lord of the Flies** Author Golding Dies (Obituary)," *Austin (TX) American Statesman* Sec. C, p. 2. June 20, 1993.
___ "Golding, William (Obituary)," *Locus* 31(2): 58. August 1993.
___ "Golding, William (Obituary)," *Science Fiction Chronicle* 14(10): 16. July 1993.
___ "Novelist Golding Wins Knighthood," *Variety* p. 71. June 22, 1988.
___ Anderson, David. "Is Golding's Theology Christian?," in: Biles, Jack I. and Evans, Robert O., eds. **William Golding: Some Critical Considerations**. Lexington, KY: University Press of Kentucky, 1978. pp.1-20.
___ Biles, Jack I. "William Golding: Bibliography of Primary and Secondary Sources," in: Biles, Jack I. and Evans, Robert O., eds. **William Golding: Some Critical Considerations**. Lexington, KY: University Press of Kentucky, 1978. pp.237-280.
___ Biles, Jack I., ed. **William Golding: Some Critical Considerations**, ed. by Jack I. Biles and Robert O. Evans. Lexington, KY: University Press of Kentucky, 1978. 283pp.
___ Boyle, Ted E. "Golding's Existential Vision," in: Biles, Jack I. and Evans, Robert O., eds. **William Golding: Some Critical Considerations**. Lexington, KY: University Press of Kentucky, 1978. pp.21-38.
___ Bufkin, E. C. "**The Spire**: The Image of the Book," in: Biles, Jack I. and Evans, Robert O., eds. **William Golding: Some Critical Considerations**. Lexington, KY: University Press of Kentucky, 1978. pp.136-150.

GOLDING, WILLIAM (continued)

_____ Cammarota, Richard S. "**The Spire**: A Symbolic Analysis," in: Biles, Jack I. and Evans, Robert O., eds. **William Golding: Some Critical Considerations**. Lexington, KY: University Press of Kentucky, 1978. pp.151-175.

_____ Delbaere-Garant, Jeanne. "Rhythm and Expansion in **Lord of the Flies**," in: Biles, Jack I. and Evans, Robert O., eds. **William Golding: Some Critical Considerations**. Lexington, KY: University Press of Kentucky, 1978. pp.72-86.

_____ Dickson, L. L. **The Modern Allegories of William Golding**. Tampa: University of South Florida Press, 1990. 163pp.

_____ Evans, Robert O. "**The Inheritors**: Some Inversions," in: Biles, Jack I. and Evans, Robert O., eds. **William Golding: Some Critical Considerations**. Lexington, KY: University Press of Kentucky, 1978. pp.87-102.

_____ Fitzgerald, John F. "Golding's **Lord of the Flies**: Pride as Original Sin," by John F. Fitzgerald and John R. Kayser. _Studies in the Novel_ 24(1): 78-88. Spring 1992.

_____ Friedman, Lawrence S. **William Golding**. New York: Continuum, 1993. 191pp.

_____ Halio, Jay L. "**Free Fall**: Golding's Modern Novel," in: Biles, Jack I. and Evans, Robert O., eds. **William Golding: Some Critical Considerations**. Lexington, KY: University Press of Kentucky, 1978. pp.117-136.

_____ Hodson, Leighton. "**The Scorpion God**: Clarity, Technique, and Communication," in: Biles, Jack I. and Evans, Robert O., eds. **William Golding: Some Critical Considerations**. Lexington, KY: University Press of Kentucky, 1978. pp.188-202.

_____ Johnston, Arnold. "The Miscasting of Pincher Martin," in: Biles, Jack I. and Evans, Robert O., eds. **William Golding: Some Critical Considerations**. Lexington, KY: University Press of Kentucky, 1978. pp.103-116.

_____ McCullen, Maurice L. "**Lord of the Flies**: The Critical Quest," in: Biles, Jack I. and Evans, Robert O., eds. **William Golding: Some Critical Considerations**. Lexington, KY: University Press of Kentucky, 1978. pp.203-236.

_____ Reilly, Patrick. **Lord of the Flies: Fathers and Sons**. New York: Twayne, 1992. 153pp.

_____ Skilton, David. "**The Pyramid** and Comic Social Fiction," in: Biles, Jack I. and Evans, Robert O., eds. **William Golding: Some Critical Considerations**. Lexington, KY: University Press of Kentucky, 1978. pp.176-187.

_____ Tebbutt, Glorie. "Reading and Righting: Metafiction and Metaphysics in William Golding's **Darkness Visible**," _Twentieth Century Literature_ 39(1): 47-58. Spring 1993.

_____ Tristram, Philippa. "Golding and the Language of Caliban," in: Biles, Jack I. and Evans, Robert O., eds. **William Golding: Some Critical Considerations**. Lexington, KY: University Press of Kentucky, 1978. pp.39-55.

_____ Wolfe, Peter. "The Brass Butterfly: Formula for Slow Change.," in: Biles, Jack I. and Evans, Robert O., eds. **William Golding: Some Critical Considerations**. Lexington, KY: University Press of Kentucky, 1978. pp.56-71.

GOLDSTEIN, LISA

_____ Brandenburg, Sandra. "Things in That Forest: A Profile of Lisa Goldstein," by Sandra Brandenburg and Debora Hill. _Science Fiction Eye_ No. 11: 110-113.113. December 1992.

GOLDSWORTHY, PETER

_____ Goldsworthy, Peter. "Honk If You Love Science," _Island Magazine_ 54: 40-43. Fall 1993.

GOLEM

_____ Bilija, Ksenija. "From Golem to Plastisex: An Analytical Survey of Spanish American Fantastic Literature," _Journal of the Fantastic in the Arts_ 7(2/3): 201-214. 1995.

_____ Christensen, Peter G. "Abraham Rothberg's **The Sword of the Golem**: The Use of the Fantastic in Defense of Judaism," _Journal of the Fantastic in the Arts_ 7(2/3): 163-176. 1995.

_____ Comrada, Norma. "Golem and Robot: The Search for Connections," _Journal of the Fantastic in the Arts_ 7(2/3): 244-254. 1995.

_____ Davidson, Jane P. "Golem--**Frankenstein**--Golem of Your Own," _Journal of the Fantastic in the Arts_ 7(2/3): 228-243. 1995.

_____ Frongia, Terri. "Tales of Old Prague: Of Ghettos, Passover, and the Blood Libel," _Journal of the Fantastic in the Arts_ 7(2/3): 146-162. 1995.

GOLEM (continued)

_____ Honigsberg, David M. "Rava's Golem," _Journal of the Fantastic in the Arts_ 7(2/3): 137-145. 1995.

_____ Krause, Maureen T. "Appendix: Selective Glossary," _Journal of the Fantastic in the Arts_ 7(2/3): 269-271. 1995.

_____ Krause, Maureen T. "_Bereshit bara Elohim_: A Survey of the Genesis and Evolution of the Golem," _Journal of the Fantastic in the Arts_ 7(2/3): 113-136. 1995.

_____ Pinsky, Mike. "The Mistaken Mistake: Permutations of the Golem Legend," _Journal of the Fantastic in the Arts_ 7(2/3): 215-227. 1995.

_____ Sautter, Diane. "Erotic and Existential Paradoxes of the Golem: Marge Piercy's **He, She and It**," _Journal of the Fantastic in the Arts_ 7(2/3): 255-268. 1995.

_____ Schaffer, Carl. "Leivick's **The Golem** and the Golem Legend," in: Murphy, Patrick D., ed. **Staging the Impossible: The Fantastic Mode in Modern Drama**. Westport, CT: Greenwood, 1992. pp.137-149.

_____ Smith, Evans L. "The Golem and the Garland in Borges and Broch," _Journal of the Fantastic in the Arts_ 7(2/3): 177-190. 1995.

_____ Strauss, Walter A. "The Golem on the Operatic Stage: Nature's Warning," _Journal of the Fantastic in the Arts_ 7(2/3): 191-200. 1995.

GOLLANCZ (PUBLISHER)

_____ "Houghton Mifflin Sells Gollancz," _Science Fiction Chronicle_ 14(3): 5. December 1992.

GOODMAN, MARTIN

_____ "Goodman, Martin (Obituary)," _Science Fiction Chronicle_ 13(10): 16. July/August 1992.

GOODWIN, R. W.

_____ Vitaris, Paula. "**X-Files**: R. W. Goodwin," _Cinefantastique_ 26(6)/27(1): 21-22. October 1995.

GOONAN, KATHLEEN ANN

_____ "Kathleen Ann Goonan: Running to Queen City," _Locus_ 35(3): 4, 84-85. September 1993.

GOONIES (MOTION PICTURE)

_____ "**Goonies** (1985): Interview with Richard Donner," in: Goldberg, Lee, ed. **The Dreamweavers: Interviews With Fantasy Filmmakers of the 1980s**. Jefferson, NC: McFarland, 1995. pp.115-120.

GORDIMER, NADINE

_____ Bazin, Nancy T. "Madness, Mysticism, and Fantasy: Shifting Perspectives of the Novels of Doris Lessing, Bessie Head, and Nadine Gordimer," _Extrapolation_ 33(1): 73-87. Spring 1992.

_____ Bazin, Nancy T. "Women and Revolution in Dystopian Fiction: Nadine Gordimer's **July's People** and Margaret Atwood's **The Handmaid's Tale**," in: Crafton, John M., ed. **Selected Essays: International Conference on Representing Revolution, 1989**. n.p.: West Georgia College International Conference, 1991. pp.115-128.

GORDON, HOWARD

_____ Vitaris, Paula. "**X-Files**: Howard Gordon," _Cinefantastique_ 26(6)/27(1): 48-49. October 1995.

GORDON, STUART

_____ Jankiewicz, Pat. "Baby Boomer," _Starlog_ 181: 48-51, 69. August 1992.

_____ Wiater, Stanley. "Gordon, Stuart," in: Wiater, Stanley. **Dark Visions: Conversations with the Masters of the Horror Film**. New York: Avon, 1992. pp.77-88.

GORMAN, ED

_____ Koontz, Dean R. "Oh, to Be in Cedar Rapids When the Hog Blood Flows," in: Greenberg, Martin H., Ed Gorman and Bill Munster, eds. **The Dean Koontz Companion**. New York: Berkley, 1994. pp.155-162.

GORODISCHER, ANGELICA

_____ Urraca, Beatriz. "Angelica Gorodischer's Voyages of Discovery: Sexuality and Historical Allegory in Science Fiction's Cross-Cultural Encounters," _Latin American Literary Review_ 23(45): 85-102. January 1995.

GORSHIN, FRANK

_____ Garcia, Bob. "**Batman**: The Riddler," _Cinefantastique_ 24(6)/25(1): 15-16. February 1994.

GOTHIC GENRE

___ Christophersen, Bill. **The Apparition in the Glass: Charles Brockden Brown's American Gothic.** Athens: University of Georgia Press, 1994. 208pp.

___ Frank, Frederick S. **Guide to the Gothic II: An Annotated Bibliography of Criticism, 1983-1993.** Lanham, MD: Scarecrow, 1995. 542pp.

___ Geary, Robert F. "The Corpse in the Dung Cart: *The Night Side of Nature* and the Victorian Supernatural Tale," in: Sanders, Joe, ed. **Functions of the Fantastic.** Westport, CT: Greenwood, 1995. pp.47-54.

___ Geary, Robert F. "M. G. Lewis and Later Gothic Fiction: The Numinous Dissipated," in: Ruddick, Nicholas, ed. **State of the Fantastic.** Westport, CT: Greenwood, 1992. pp.75-81.

___ Geary, Robert F. **The Supernatural in Gothic Fiction: Horror, Belief and Literary Change.** Lewiston, NY: Mellen, 1992. 151pp.

___ Graff, Bennett. **Horror in Evolution: Determinism, Materialism, and Darwinism in the American Gothic (Edgar Allan Poe, Frank Norris, Jack London, H. P. Lovecraft).** Ph.D. Dissertation, City University of New York, 1995. 282pp. (DAI-A 56/05, p. 1777. November 1995.)

___ Haggerty, George E. **Gothic Fiction/Gothic Form.** University Park: Pennsylvania State University Press, 1989. 194pp.

___ Kilgour, Maggie. **The Rise of the Gothic Novel.** New York: Routledge, 1995. 280pp.

___ Massé, Michelle A. **In the Name of Love: Women, Masochism and the Gothic.** Ithaca, NY: Cornell University Press, 1992. 301pp.

___ Winter, Kari J. **Subjects of Slavery, Agents of Change: Women and Power in Gothic Novels and Slave Narratives, 1790-1865.** Athens: University of Georgia Press, 1992. 172pp.

___ Wolstenholme, Susan. **Gothic (Re) Visions: Writing Women as Readers.** Albany: State University of New York Press, 1993. 201pp.

___ Wright, Bruce L. **Nightwalkers: Gothic Horror Movies, The Modern Era.** Dallas, TX: Taylor Publishing Co., 9195. 171pp.

GOTLIEB, PHYLLIS

___ Gotlieb, Phyllis. "How I Became a Science Fiction Writer," *Communique* 5(1): 1, 6-7. January/February 1993.

GOULART, RON

___ "Ron Goulart: Stand-Up Writing," *Locus* 30(2): 4, 70. February 1993.

GRADISNIK, BRANKO

___ Lubej-Longyka, Marjeta. "Prvine Znanstvene fantastike v noveli Jona Brnak Gradisnika," *Jezik in Slovstvo* (Slovenia) 38(7/8): 261-266. May 1992/1993. [Not seen.]

GRAHAM, RONALD EDWARD

___ "Graham, Ronald Edward (Obituary)," *Science Fiction News* (Australia) No. 59: 10. February 1979.

GRAHAME, KENNETH

___ Bloom, Harold. "Kenneth Grahame," in: Bloom, Harold. **Classic Fantasy Writers.** New York: Chelsea House, 1994. pp.71-81.

___ Hunt, Peter. " 'Coldtongue coldham coldbeef pickled gherkin salad frenchrolls cresssandwige spottedmeat gingerbeer lemonaide sodawater...' Fantastic Foods in the Books of Kenneth Grahame, Jerome K. Jerome, H. E. Bates, and Other Bakers of the Fantasy England," *Journal of the Fantastic in the Arts* 7(1): 5-22. 1996.

___ Wullschläger, Jackie. **Inventing Wonderland: The Lives and Fantasies of Lewis Carroll, Edward Lear, J. M. Barrie, Kenneth Grahame and A. A. Milne.** New York: Free Press, 1995. 228pp.

___ Wytenbroek, J. R. "Natural Mysticism in Kenneth Grahame's **The Wind in the Willows**," in: Reynolds, Patricia and GoodKnight, Glen H., eds. **Proceedings of the J. R. R. Tolkien Centenary Conference, Keble College, Oxford, 1992.** Altadena, CA: Mythopoeic Press, 1995. pp.431-434. (*Mythlore* Vol. 21, No. 2, Winter 1996, Whole No. 80)

GRANT, CHARLES L.

___ Schweitzer, Darrell. "Charles L. Grant," in: Schweitzer, Darrell. **Speaking of Horror: Interviews With Writers of the Supernatural.** San Bernardino, CA: Borgo, 1994. pp.47-58.

GRANT, RICHARD

___ "Philip K. Dick Award Winner, 1992," *Locus* 30(4): 6. April 1993.

___ "Richard Grant Wins Philip K. Dick Award," *Science Fiction Chronicle* 14(7): 4. April 1993.

GRANT, RICHARD (continued)

___ Grant, Richard. "Get Along, Little Robot," in: Jakubowski, Maxim and James, Edward, eds. **The Profession of Science Fiction.** New York: St. Martin's, 1992. pp.182-199.

GRAVES, ROBERT

___ Seymour, Miranda. **Robert Graves: Life on the Edge.** New York: Holt, 1995. 524pp.

GRAY, SPALDING

___ Prinz, Jessica. "Spalding Gray's **Swimming to Cambodia**: A Performance Gesture," in: Murphy, Patrick D., ed. **Staging the Impossible: The Fantastic Mode in Modern Drama.** Westport, CT: Greenwood, 1992. pp.156-168.

GREAT BRITAIN

___ "Anthony Cheeham Buys Weidenfeld; Deborah Beale to Head New Genre List," *Science Fiction Chronicle* 13(4): 4. January 1992.

___ "Baen Invades United Kingdom," *Locus* 31(1): 7. July 1993.

___ "BBC's **The Tripods** Starts Second Season, Clears 41 U.S. Markets," *Variety* p.58. August 7, 1985.

___ "Britain's Radnor Rolling 65 Segs of TV Drama on the Supernatural," *Variety* p. 240. April 23, 1986.

___ "British Book Summary: 1991," *Locus* 28(3): 6, 76. March 1992.

___ "British Book Summary: 1992," *Locus* 30(4): 6, 64. April 1993.

___ "British Book Summary: 1993," *Locus* 32(4): 8, 63-64. April 1994.

___ "British Book Summary: 1994," *Locus* 34(4): 7, 66. April 1995.

___ "British Publishing Problems," *Locus* 31(1): 7, 63. July 1993.

___ "CBS/Fox Inks **Biggles** for U.K. Distribution," *Variety* p. 93. March 5, 1986.

___ " 'Clockwork' Ban Still Enforced," *Locus* 30(3): 6, 72. March 1993.

___ "**Dr. Who** Under Stethoscope," *Variety* p. 88. September 17, 1986.

___ "Fantasycon XVI," *Science Fiction Chronicle* 13(5): 23-25. February 1992.

___ "Gollancz Sold Again," *Locus* 29(5): 4. November 1992

___ "Hammer Ends Longtime Taboo--Mates Sex to Its **Crescendo** Horror Pic," *Variety* p. 1, 92. May 6, 1970.

___ "HarperCollins and Penguin Streamline UK Publishing," *Locus* 35(2): 8. August 1995.

___ "HarperCollins UK SF & Fantasy Imprint," *Locus* 30(5): 9. May 1993.

___ "Hodder & Stoughton, Headline Merge," *Locus* 31(1): 7. July 1993.

___ "Millenium Launched Early," *Locus* 29(5): 4. November 1992

___ "Orion Books New British Publisher," *Locus* 28(1): 6. January 1992.

___ "Raven Books Is New UK Fantasy/Horror Line," *Science Fiction Chronicle* 15(9): 4. August 1994.

___ "Raven Books New Robinson Imprint," *Locus* 31(5): 6. November 1993.

___ "Reprieve for UK's Ringpull Press," *Science Fiction Chronicle* 16(7): 5. June/July 1995.

___ "SF Foundation Settles at University of Liverpool," *Science Fiction Chronicle* 15(2): 6. November/December 1993.

___ "SF Tops 1993 UK Bestsellers," *Science Fiction Chronicle* 15(4): 6. February 1994.

___ "SF Tumbles on British List of 1994 Paperback Bestsellers," *Science Fiction Chronicle* 16(4): 5. February 1995.

___ **Space Aces: Comic Book Heroes from the Forties and the Fifties.** London: Green Wood, 1992. 96pp.

___ "UK Book Clubs Open Bookstores," *Science Fiction Chronicle* 14(12): 5. September 1993.

___ "UK Net Book Agreement Dies," *Locus* 35(5): 8. November 1995.

___ "UK Publishing Financial Picture Mixed," *Locus* 30(5): 9. May 1993.

___ "UK's **Fantasy Tales** Ceasing Publication," *Science Fiction Chronicle* 15(1): 5-6. October 1993.

___ "UK's GW Books, Boxtree Publishers Sue Transworld," *Science Fiction Chronicle* 14(4): 4. January 1993.

___ "UK's Net Book Agreement Dies," *Science Fiction Chronicle* 17(1): 6-7. October/November 1995

___ Aldiss, Brian W. "Fantasy: U.S. Versus U.K.," *Monad* No. 2: 17-24. March 1992.

___ Apseloff, Marilyn F. "The British Science Fiction of Louise Lawrence," in: Sullivan, C. W., III. **Science Fiction for Young Readers.** Westport, CT: Greenwood, 1993. pp.133-144.

___ Coopman, Jeremy. "Sales of Marvel Comics Move Up Fast in Britain," *Variety* p. 83. September 17, 1986.

GREAT BRITAIN (continued)
___ Green, Steve. "Of Midwich, Moonmen and Monoliths: A Brief Guide to British SF & F Cinema in the Sixties," *Lan's Lantern* No. 41: 64-68. July 1993.
___ Gunn, James E. "SF the British Way," *Amazing* 68(2): 54-60. May 1993.
___ Gunter, Barrie. "The Impact of Nuclear Fiction in Britain: *The Day After* and *Threads*," by Barrie Gunter and M. Svennevig. in: Wober, J. Mallory, ed. **Television and Nuclear Power: Making the Public Mind.** Norwood, NJ: Ablex, 1992. pp.55-66.
___ Hanke, Ken. "Tod Slaughter: Demon Barber of Great Britain," *Filmfax* No. 45: 31-35, 98. June/July 1994.
___ Harbottle, Philip. **British Science Fiction Paperbacks and Magazines, 1949-1956: An Annotated Bibliograhy and Guide**, by Philip Harbottle and Stephen Holland. San Bernardino, CA: Borgo Press, 1994. 232pp.
___ Harbottle, Philip. **Vultures of the Void: A History of British Science Fiction Publishing 1946-1956**, by Philip Harbottle and Stephen Holland. San Bernardino, CA: Borgo Press, 1992. 128pp.
___ Holland, Stephen. **The Mushroom Jungle: A History of Postwar Paperback Publishing**. Westbury, Eng.: Zeon Books, 1993. 196pp.
___ James, Edward. "Science Fiction Courses in Higher Education in Great Britain: A Preliminary Guide," by Edward James and Farah Mendlesohn. *Foundation* No. 59: 59-69. Autumn 1993.
___ Jeeves, Terry. "British Fandom," in: Sanders, Joe, ed. **Science Fiction Fandom**. Westport, CT: Greenwood, 1994. pp.113-118.
___ Jones, Alan. "The Return of Hammer's Horror," *Cinefantastique* 24(6)/25(1): 4-5, 125. February 1994.
___ Kincaid, Paul. "British SF: An Obituary," *Vector* No. 176: 12. December 1993/January 1994.
___ Lassner, Phyllis. "A New World Indeed: Feminist Critique and Power Relations in British Anti-Utopian Literature of the 1930s," *Extrapolation* 36(3): 259-272. Fall 1995.
___ Lewes, Darby. "Nudes From Nowhere: Pornography, Empire, and Utopia," *Utopian Studies* 4(2): 66-73. 1993.
___ Mendlesohn, Farah. "Audio Books: A New Medium for SF?," *Foundation* No. 64: 90-96. Summer 1995.
___ Moskowitz, Sam. "The Immortal Storm II: A History of Science Fiction Fandom, Part Two," *Fantasy Commentator* 8(3/4): 278-288. Fall 1995. (Whole No. 47/48)
___ Nicholls, Stan. "Dance of the Supermarionettes," *Starlog* 184: 52-55, 70. November 1992.
___ Nicholls, Stan. "*Thunderbirds*: The Next Generation," *Starlog* 182: 64-65, 71. September 1992.
___ Parrinder, Patrick. "Landscapes of British Science Fiction," in: Slusser, George E. and Rabkin, Eric S., eds. **Styles of Creation: Aesthetic Technique and the Creation of Fictional Worlds**. Athens: University of Georgia Press, 1992. pp.193-204.
___ Ruddick, Nicholas. **British Science Fiction, 1478-1990: A Chronology**. Westport, CT: Greenwood, 1992. 296pp.
___ Ruddick, Nicholas. **Ultimate Island: On the Nature of British Science Fiction**. Westport, CT: Greenwood, 1993. 202pp.
___ Schmitt, Ronald E. **The Reclamation of the Future Dream: Dreams in British Science Fiction (Mary Shelley, H. G. Wells, George Orwell, Michael Moorcock)**. Ph.D. Dissertation, University of Rhode Island, 1995. 182pp. (DAI-A 56/09, p. 3598. March 1996.)
___ Smith, Karen P. **The Fabulous Realm: A Literary-Historical Approach to British Fantasy, 1780-1990**. Metuchen, NJ: Scarecrow, 1993. 532pp.
___ Stableford, Brian. "Adolf Hitler: His Part in Our Struggle; A Brief Economic History of British SF Magazines," *Interzone* No. 57: 17-20. March 1992.
___ Stephensen-Payne, Phil. "U.K. Year in SF, 1991," in: Brown, Charles N. and Contento, William G. **Science Fiction, Fantasy, & Horror: 1991**. Oakland, CA: Locus Press, 1992. pp.437-439.
___ Veldman, Meredith. **Fantasy, the Bomb, and the Greening of Britain: Romantic Protest, 1945-1980**. Cambridge: Cambridge University Press, 1994. 325pp.
___ Watson, Ian. "Negentrophy Rules OK: The Refloating of *New Worlds*," *Amazing* 68(1): 48-52. April 1993.

GREAT MARVEL (SERIES)
___ Molson, Francis J. "Great Marvel: The First American Hardcover Science Fiction Series," *Extrapolation* 34(2): 101-122. Summer 1993.

GREECE
___ Pastourmatzi, Domna A. **Vivliogrphia epistemonikes phantasias, phantasias, kai tromou, 1960-1993** [Bibliography of Science Fiction, Fantasy and Horror, 1960-1993.]. Athens: Alien, 1995. 245pp.
___ Smith, Nicholas D. "Political Activity and Ideal Economics: Two Related Utopian Themes in Aristophanic Comedy," *Utopian Studies* 3(1): 84-94. 1992.

GREEN, SIMON
___ Melia, Sally-Ann. "Fifteen Years of Nothing, Then an Overnight Dose of Success: Simon Green interviewed," *Interzone* No. 74: 26-29. August 1993.
___ Melia, Sally-Ann. "SFC Interviews: Simon Green: 15 Years of Nothing, Then Overnight Success," *Science Fiction Chronicle* 16(6): 5, 42-45. May 1995.

GREENLAND, COLIN
___ Nicholls, Stan. "Colin Greenland Brings Back Plenty," in: Nicholls, Stan. **Wordsmiths of Wonder: Fifty Interviews with Writers of the Fantastic**. London: Orbit, 1993. pp.71-79.
___ Nicholls, Stan. "Plenty of Space: Colin Greenland Interviewed," *Interzone* No. 63: 24-26. September 1992.

GREMLINS (MOTION PICTURE)
___ "*Gremlins* (1984): Interview with Joe Dante," in: Goldberg, Lee, ed. **The Dreamweavers: Interviews With Fantasy Filmmakers of the 1980s**. Jefferson, NC: McFarland, 1995. pp.121-142.
___ "*Gremlins* Grabs 9 Saturn Nominations," *Variety* p. 4, 32. February 27, 1985.
___ "*Gremlins* Promo Biggest in Warner Bros. History," *Variety* p. 6. June 6, 1984.
___ "*Gremlins* Sweeps Saturn Ceremony," *Variety* p.6. June 19, 1985.
___ "WB Enlists Govt. to Fight Gremlins," *Variety* p. 3, 27. August 1, 1984.
___ Smetak, Jacqueline R. "Summer at the Movies: Steven Spielberg: Gore, Guts, and PG-13," *Journal of Popular Film and Television* 14(1): 4-13. 1986.

GRIBBIN, JOHN
___ Gribbin, John. "Fact 'n Fiction 'n Me," *Concatenation* No. 7: 10. 1993.
___ Melia, Sally-Ann. " 'What If All Science Is Wrong': John Gribbin Interviewed," *Interzone* No. 84: 43-47. June 1994.

GRID RUNNERS (VIDEO GAME)
___ Fletcher, Tanya A. "Deadly Games," *Sci-Fi Entertainment* 1 (4): 78-84. December 1994.

GRIFFITH, NICOLA
___ "Griffith Wins Tiptree Award," *Locus* 33(1): 7, 78. July 1994.
___ "Nicola Griffith Wins Tiptree Award," *Science Fiction Chronicle* 15(8): 5. June 1994.
___ Green, Carol A. "Pretty Bloody Happy! Nicola Griffith Interviewed," *Vector* No. 173: 7-10 June/July 1993.

GRODENCHIK, MAX
___ Altman, Mark A. "Just the Facts, Max," *Star Trek: The Official Fan Club* No. 96: 50-52. April/May 1994.

GROSS, ALLAN
___ Spurlock, Duane. "Hail and Farewell, Pellucidar: An Interview with Allan Gross," *Burroughs Bulletin* NS. No. 16: 27-31. October 1993.

GROSSMAN, ROBERTA BENDER
___ "Grossman, Roberta Bender (Obituary)," *Locus* 28(5): 59. May 1992.

GROUNDHOG DAY (MOTION PICTURE)
___ Doherty, Thomas. "*Groundhog Day* (Review)," *Cinefantastique* 24(2): 57. August 1993.
___ Lowe, Nick. "*Groundhog Day* (Review)," *Interzone* No. 74: 38-40. August 1993.

GROVE, FREDERICK PHILIP
___ Proietti, Salvator. "Frederick Philip Grove's Version of Pastoral Utopianism," *Science-Fiction Studies* 19(3): 361-377. November 1992.

GRYPHON AWARD, 1992
___ "World SF Convention Hugo Awards," *Science Fiction Chronicle* 14(1): 4. October 1992.

GUEST, VAL
___ Weaver, Tom. "Val Guest: Interview," in: Weaver, Tom, ed. **Attack of the Monster Movie Makers: Interviews with 20 Genre Giants.** Jefferson, NC: McFarland, 1994. pp.99-126.

GUILTY AS CHARGED (MOTION PICTURE)
___ Biodrowski, Steve. "*Guilty as Charged*," *Cinefantastique* 22(4): 52-53. February 1992.
___ Burden, Martin. "Current Event Tale Fizzles (Review)," *New York (NY) Post.* January 29, 1992. in: *NewsBank. Film and Television.* 12: A13. 1992.
___ Strauss, Bob. "*Charged* Lacks Juice to Pull Off Effective Death Penalty Satire (Review)," *Los Angeles (CA) Daily News.* February 7, 1992. in: *NewsBank. Film and Television.* 21:A9. 1992.

GULF WAR
___ Robins, Ken. "Socializing the Cyborg Self: The Gulf War and Beyond," by Ken Robins and Les Levidow. in: Gray, Chris H., ed. **The Cyborg Handbook.** New York: Routledge, 1995. pp.119-125.

GUNHED (MOTION PICTURE)
___ Lowe, Nick. "*Gunhed* (Review)," *Interzone* No. 84: 39. June 1994.

GUNN, JAMES E.
___ "Gunn Center," *Locus* 28(5): 7. May 1992.
___ Bourassa, Alain. "Deaths of **The Immortal**, Part Two," by Alain Bourassa and Mark Phillips. *Starlog* No. 186: 67-72, 74. January 1993.
___ McKitterick, Christopher. "James Gunn and **The Dreamers**: Epitomes of an Evolving Science Fiction," *Extrapolation* 36(4): 316-330. Winter 1995.
___ Phillips, Mark. "Lives of **The Immortal**, Part One," by Mark Phillips and Alain Bourassa. *Starlog* 185: 58-62. December 1992.
___ Zebrowski, George. "Never Forget the Writers Who Helped Build Yesterday's Tomorrows," *Science Fiction Age* 3(6): 30-36, 100. 1995.

GUNNARSSON, THORARINN
___ Vester, John. "Dragonsmith," *Starlog* No. 206: 76-79. September 1994.

GURNEY, JAMES
___ "1992 Chesley Award Winners," *Locus* 31(4): 6. October 1993.

GUSTAFSON, JON
___ King, T. Jackson. "Pros and Cons of Being a Writer Couple," by T. Jackson King and Paula E. Downing. *SFWA Bulletin* 25(4): 7-14. Winter 1992. (No. 114)

GUYVER (MOTION PICTURE)
___ Cziraky, Dan. "*Guyver*," *Cinefantastique* 22(4): 46. February 1992.
___ Merriwether, Chip. "Effects Hero," *Cinefantastique* 22(4): 47, 60. February 1992.

GUZMAN, MARTIN L.
___ Velasco, Juan. "Lo fantástico y la historia: La polémica entre **La sombra del caudillo y Tirano Banderas**," *Mester* (UCLA) 19(2): 71-82. Fall 1990.

GWYNNE, FRED
___ "Gwynne, Fred (Obituary)," *Science Fiction Chronicle* 14(11): 14. August 1993.

H. G. WELLS CONFERENCE, 1995
___ "H. G. Wells Conference," *Locus* 35(4): 8. October 1995.

H. P. LOVECRAFT'S THE UNNAMABLE II: THE STATEMENT OF RANDOLPH CARTER (MOTION PICTURE)
___ Harris, Judith P. "*H. P. Lovecraft's The Unnamable II: The Statement of Randolph Carter* (Review)," *Cinefantastique* 24(2): 59. August 1993.

HAGGARD, H. RIDER
___ Bloom, Harold. "H. Rider Haggard," in: Bloom, Harold. **Classic Fantasy Writers.** New York: Chelsea House, 1994. pp.82-95.

HAGGARD, H. RIDER (continued)
___ Gold, Barri J. "Embracing the Corpse: Discursive Recycling in H. Rider Haggard's **She**," *English Literature in Transition* 38(3): 305-327. 1995.
___ Liebfred, Philip. "The Cinema Legacy of a Literary Legend: H. Rider Haggard," *Filmfax* No. 30: 67-71. December 1991/January 1992.
___ Liebfred, Philip. "H. Rider Haggard on the Screen," *Films in Review* 46(7/8): 20-29. September/October 1995.

HAINES, JOHN FRANCIS
___ Haines, John F. "Confessions of a Fantasy Versaholic," *Fantasy Commentator* 7(4): 304-306. Fall 1992. (Whole No. 44)

HALAS, JOHN
___ "Halas, John (Obituary)," *Science Fiction Chronicle* 16(5): 16, 18. March/April 1995.

HALDEMAN, JOE
___ "1993 Nebula Awards Winners," *Locus* 32(5): 8. May 1994.
___ "1995 Hugo Winners," *Locus* 35(3): 7. September 1993.
___ "The Hugos (Or, the Empire Strikes Back)," *Science Fiction Chronicle* 17(2): 55-56. December 1995/January 1996.
___ "Joe Haldeman: A Different Universe," *Locus* 29(5): 3, 74-75. November 1992.
___ "Joe Haldeman: A Lost Year," *Locus* 32(5): 4, 67-68. May 1994.
___ "Nebula Awards," *Science Fiction Chronicle* 15(7): 4. June 1994.
___ "World Fantasy Awards," *Science Fiction Chronicle* 15(2): 4. November/December 1993.
___ Blackmore, Tim. "Talking the Talk, Walking the Walk: The Role of Discourse in Joe Haldeman's 'The Monster' and Lucius Shepard's 'Delta Sly Honey'," *Journal of the Fantastic in the Arts* 6(2/3): 191-202. 1994.
___ Blackmore, Tim. "Warring Stories: Fighting for Truth in the Science Fiction of Joe Haldeman," *Extrapolation* 34(2): 131-146. Summer 1993.
___ Gordon, Joan. "Joe Haldeman: Cyberpunk Before Cyberpunk Was Cool?," in: Morse, Donald E., ed. **The Celebration of the Fantastic.** Westport, CT: Greenwood, 1992. pp.251-257.
___ Nicholls, Stan. "Joe Haldeman Frees Something Up," in: Nicholls, Stan. **Wordsmiths of Wonder: Fifty Interviews with Writers of the Fantastic.** London: Orbit, 1993. pp.80-91.

HALE, EDWARD EVERETT
___ Moskowitz, Sam. "Voyagers Through Eternity: A History of Science Fiction From the Beginnings to H. G. Wells," *Fantasy Commentator* 8(1/2): 135-144. Winter 1993/1994. (Whole No. 45/46)

HALL, DESMOND W.
___ "Hall, Desmond W. (Obituary)," *Locus* 29(6): 68. December 1992.
___ "Hall, Desmond W. (Obituary)," *Science Fiction Chronicle* 14(3): 14-15. December 1992.
___ Moskowitz, Sam. "Correction re Desmond Hall," *Locus* 30(2): 69. February 1993.

HALLOWEEN VI: THE CURSE OF MICHAEL MEYERS (MOTION PICTURE)
___ Adams, Max. "*Halloween VI*," *Cinefantastique* 26(6)/27(1): 10-15, 125. October 1995.

HAMBLY, BARBARA
___ Monk, Patricia. "Dragonsaver: The Female Hero in Barbara Hambly's **Dragonsbane**," *Journal of the Fantastic in the Arts* 4(4): 60-81. 1991. (No. 16)

HAMILTON, EDMOND
___ Stableford, Brian. "Edmond Hamilton and Leigh Brackett: An Appreciation," in: Stableford, Brian. **Outside the Human Aquarium: Masters of Science Fiction.** San Bernardino, CA: Borgo, 1995. pp.7-17.

HAMILTON, MARGARET
___ Catsos, Gregory J. M. "The Wonderful Witch: A Lost Interview with Margaret Hamilton," *Filmfax* No. 41: 50-57. October/November 1993.

HAMILTON, PETER F.
___ Lovegrove, James. "From Rutland to the Universe: Peter F. Hamilton Interviewed," *Interzone* No. 96: 28-31. June 1995.

HAMM, THELMA D.
___ "Hamm, Thelma D. (Obituary)," *Locus* 33(1): 74. July 1994.
___ "Hamm, Thelma D. (Obituary)," *Science Fiction Chronicle* 15(7): 16. June 1994.

HAMMER FILMS
___ "Hammer Ends Longtime Taboo--Mates Sex to Its *Crescendo* Horror Pic," *Variety* p. 1, 92. May 6, 1970.
___ Jones, Alan. "The Return of Hammer's Horror," *Cinefantastique* 24(6)/25(1): 4-5, 125. February 1994.
___ McDonald, T. Liam. "The Horrors of Hammer: The House That Blood Built," in: Golden, Christopher, ed. **Cut! Horror Writers on Horror Film**. New York: Berkley, 1992. pp.151-160.
___ Plamer, Randy. "Hinds Horrors: Forging the Fright Fantastic," *Filmfax* No. 37: 76-81. February/March 1993.

HAMMOND, WAYNE G.
___ "1994 Mythopoeic Fantasy Awards," *Locus* 33(4): 72. October 1994.
___ "Mythopoeic Awards, 1994," *Science Fiction Chronicle* 16(1): 8. October 1994.

HAND THAT ROCKS THE CRADLE (MOTION PICTURE)
___ "Cradle Rocks as Subtle Turns Suspenseful (Review)," *Washington (DC) Times*. January 10, 1992. in: *NewsBank. Film and Television*. 12: C2. 1992.
___ Armstrong, David. "Violent Nanny Really Knows How to Rock the Cradle (Review)," *San Francisco (CA) Examiner*. January 10, 1992. in: *NewsBank. Film and Television*. 12:B9. 1992.
___ Arnold, Gary. "Rebecca DeMornay: Right at Home in Peyton('s) Place (Review)," *Washington (DC) Times*. January 17, 1992. in: *NewsBank. Film and Television*. 12:B7. 1992.
___ Bernard, Jami. "The Invasion of the Family Snatcher (Review)," *New York (NY) Post*. January 10, 1992. in: *NewsBank. Film and Television*. 12:B14. 1992.
___ Hartl, John. "Their Looks Rock Cradle (Review)," *New York (NY) Daily News*. January 5, 1992. in: *NewsBank. Film and Television*. 12: B5-B6. 1992.
___ Hunter, Stephen. *The Hand That Rocks the Cradle* (Review)," *Chicago (IL) Sun Times*. January 10, 1992. in: *NewsBank. Film and Television*. 12:B12-B13. 1992.
___ Johnson, Malcolm. "Suspenseless Cradle Rocks to Standstill (Review)," *Hartford (CT) Courant*. January 10, 1992. in: *NewsBank. Film and Television*. 12:B10. 1992.
___ Lipper, Hal. "Victim and Villain (Review)," *St. Petersburg (FL) Times*. January 13, 1992. in: *NewsBank. Film and Television*. 12:B1-B2. 1992.
___ Mahar, Ted. "Contrived *Hand That Rocks the Cradle* Offers Thrills by the Number (Review)," *Portand (OR) The Oregonian*. January 10, 1992. in: *NewsBank. Film and Television*. 12:C1. 1992.
___ Marbella, Jean. "Nanny Dearest: *Hand That Rocks the Cradle* Strikes a Nerve Among Nannies, Working Mothers (Review)," *Baltimore (MD) Sun*. January 15, 1992. in: *NewsBank. Film and Television*. 12: B3-B4. 1992.
___ Ringel, Eleanor. "Au Pair Scare: Frightening Cradle Really Rocks (Review)," *Atlanta (GA) Journal*. January 10, 1992. in: *NewsBank. Film and Television*. 12:B11. 1992.
___ Schweiger, Daniel. *The Hand That Rocks the Cradle* (Review)," *Cinefantastique* 22(6): 54. June 1992
___ Strauss, Bob. "Cradle's Prurient Fun Weakened By Credibility Factor (Review)," *Los Angeles (CA) Daily News*. January 10, 1992. in: *NewsBank. Film and Television*. 12:B8. 1992.

HAND, ELIZABETH
___ "1995 World Fantasy Awards," *Locus* 35(6): 4, 81. December 1995.
___ "Elizabeth Hand: Reflections of a Catholic School Girl," *Locus* 35(4): 6-7, 76, 78. October 1995.
___ "World Fantasy Awards, 1995," *Science Fiction Chronicle* 17(2): 5. December 1995/January 1996.
___ Harper, Mary C. "Being a Boundary: The Abject Subjects of Elizabeth Hand's HEL Trilogy," *Extrapolation* 36(3): 222-243. Fall 1995.
___ von Malder, Tom. "Writer Creates a Brave New World," *The Republican Journal* (Maine) Sec. B, p. 2. September 3, 1992.

HANDMAID'S TALE (MOTION PICTURE)
___ "Wilson, Cinetudes Option 'Tale' for Screen; Pinter to Script, Reisz to Helm," *Variety* p. 6, 38. October 15, 1986.

HANLEY, FLORENCE
___ "Hanley, Florence (Obituary)," *Locus* 31(2): 59. August 1993.
___ "Hanley, Florence (Obituary)," *Science Fiction Chronicle* 14(11): 14. August 1993.

HARD SCIENCE FICTION
___ Benford, Gregory. "Imagining the Real," *Magazine of Fantasy and Science Fiction* 84(1): 47-59. January 1993.
___ Benford, Gregory. "Real Science, Imaginary Worlds," in: Hartwell, David G. and Kathryn Cramer, eds. **The Ascent of Wonder: The Evolution of Hard SF**. New York: Tor, 1994. pp.15-23.
___ Benford, Gregory. "Time and **Timescape**," *Science Fiction Studies* 20(2): 184-190. July 1993.
___ Browning, Tonya J. **Mapping the Unknown and Leaving No Footprints: Feminism and Hard Science Fiction**. Master's Report, The University of Texas at Austin, 1993. 87pp.
___ Cramer, Kathryn. "On Science and Science Fiction," in: Hartwell, David G. and Kathryn Cramer, eds. **The Ascent of Wonder: The Evolution of Hard SF**. New York: Tor, 1994. pp.24-29.
___ Feinberg, Gerald. "Discussing Hard SF," by Gerald Feinberg, Hal Clement, Kathryn Cramer and David G. Hartwell. *New York Review of Science Fiction* No. 46: 19-21. June 1992.
___ Gadallah, Leslie. "On Hard SF," *ON SPEC* 6(1): 89-90. Spring 1994.
___ Hartwell, David G. "Aspects of Hard Science Fiction," *New York Review of Science Fiction* No. 66: 11-21. February 1994.
___ Hartwell, David G. "Hard Science Fiction," *New York Review of Science Fiction* No. 62: 1, 8-13. October 1993.
___ Hartwell, David G. "Hard Science Fiction," in: Hartwell, David G. and Kathryn Cramer, eds. **The Ascent of Wonder: The Evolution of Hard SF**. New York: Tor, 1994. pp.30-40.
___ Kincaid, Paul. "How Hard Is SF?," *Vector* No. 182: 5-13. Spring 1995.
___ Pierce, John J. "The Literary Experience of Hard Science Fiction," *Science Fiction Studies* 20(2): 176-183. July 1993.
___ Preuss, Paul. "Loopholes in the Net: Ruminations on Hard SF; **Furious Gulf** by Gregory Benford," *New York Review of Science Fiction* No. 75: 1, 10-11. November 1994.
___ Samuelson, David N. "Modes of Extrapolation: The Formulas of Hard Science Fiction," *Science Fiction Studies* 20(2): 191-240. July 1993.
___ Samuelson, David N. "On Hard Science Fiction: A Bibliography," *Science Fiction Studies* 20(2): 149-156. July 1993.
___ Samuelson, David N. "On Hard Science Fiction: Introduction," *Science Fiction Studies* 20(2): 145-148. July 1993.
___ Stableford, Brian. "The Last Chocolate Bar and the Majesty of Truth: Reflections on the Concept of 'Hardness' in Science Fiction, Part 1," *New York Review of Science Fiction* No. 71: 1, 8-12. July 1994.
___ Stableford, Brian. "The Last Chocolate Bar and the Majesty of Truth: Reflections on the Concept of 'Hardness' in Science Fiction, Part 2," *New York Review of Science Fiction* No. 72: 10-16. August 1994.
___ Steele, Allen. "Hard Again," *New York Review of Science Fiction* No. 46: 1, 3-5. June 1992.
___ Westfahl, Gary. "The Closely Reasoned Technological Story: The Critical History of Hard Science Fiction," *Science Fiction Studies* 20(2): 157-175. July 1993.

HARD TO BE A GOD (MOTION PICTURE)
___ "Fleischmann Firms Lotsa Presales for **Hard to Be a God**," *Variety* p. 46, 148. October 15, 1986.

HARDIN, JERRY
___ Vitaris, Paula. "**X-Files**: Deep Throat," *Cinefantastique* 26(6)/27(1): 45-46. October 1995.

HARDWARE (MOTION PICTURE)
___ Telotte, J. P. "Enframing the Self: The Hardware and Software of **Hardware**," *Science Fiction Studies* 22(3): 323-332. November 1995

HARDY, DAVID A.
___ Morgan, Chris. "Neverending Visions of Space: David A. Hardy, Britain's Leading Space Artist," *Interzone* No. 69: 19-23. March 1993.

HARMON, JIM
___ Harmon, Jim. "Harmony: Getting Personal," *Riverside Quarterly* 9(2): 82-85. August 1993. (Whole No. 34)

HARNESS, CHARLES L.
___ Koppel, T. **Chronography: A Chronological Bibliography of Books by Charles L. Harness.** Polk City, IA: Chris Drumm, 1993. 27pp.
___ Stephensen-Payne, Phil. **Charles L. Harness: Attorney in Space, a Working Bibliography.** Albuquerque, NM: Galactic Central, 1992. 15pp.
___ Zebrowski, George. "Never Forget the Writers Who Helped Build Yesterday's Tomorrows," *Science Fiction Age* 3(6): 30-36, 100. 1995.

HARPERPRISM
___ "John Douglas Joins HarperPrism," *Locus* 35(6): 8, 81. December 1995.

HARPS
___ Evans, Gwenth. "Harps and Harpers in Contemporary Fantasy," *Lion and the Unicorn* 16(2): 199-209. December 1992.

HARRIS, JONATHAN
___ Voger, Mark. "The Wily Wit of Jonathan Harris," *Filmfax* No. 32: 44-49, 94. April/May 1992.

HARRIS, NAOMIE
___ Eramo, Steven. "Girl of Tomorrow," *Starlog* No. 219: 54-55. October 1995.

HARRIS, THOMAS
___ Borchardt, Edith. "Criminal Artists and Artisans in Mysteries by E. T. A. Hoffman, Dorothy Sayers, Ernesto Sábato, Patrick Süskind, and Thomas Harris," in: Sanders, Joe, ed. **Functions of the Fantastic.** Westport, CT: Greenwood, 1995. pp.125-134.

HARRISON BERGERON (MOTION PICTURE)
___ Droesch, Paul. "Hits and Misses: Kurt Vonnegut's *Harrison Bergeron*," *TV Guide* 43(32): 41. August 12, 1995.
___ Goudas, John N. "Showtime Adapts the Biting Satire of Vonnegut's *Harrison Bergeron*," *Buffalo (NY) News.* August 13, 1995. in: *NewsBank. Film and Television.* 77:D13. 1995.
___ Kenny, Glenn. "Kurt Vonnegut's Law of Averages," *TV Guide* 43(32): 31. August 12, 1995.
___ Lee, Luaine. "Welcome to the Monkey House," *San Francisco (CA) Examiner* August 12, 1995. (Cited from the Internet Edition.)
___ Solomon, Harvey. "Showtime Expands on Vonnegut Satire," *Boston (MA) Herald.* August 12, 1995. in: *NewsBank. Film and Television.* 86:A1. 1995.

HARRISON SCIENCE FICTION AWARD, 1994
___ "Harrison Awards, 1994," *Locus* 34(2): 9. February 1995.

HARRISON SCIENCE FICTION AWARD, 1995
___ "Harrison Science Fiction Prize, 1995," *Locus* 34(3): 76. March 1995.

HARRISON, HARRY
___ Davidson, Clive. "Catch up on Minsky's Missing Chapters," *Guardian* Sec. 2, p. 17. March 25, 1993. [Not seen.]
___ Nicholls, Stan. "Harry Harrison Catches the Rapture," in: Nicholls, Stan. **Wordsmiths of Wonder: Fifty Interviews with Writers of the Fantastic.** London: Orbit, 1993. pp.55-60.
___ Paget, Stephen. "An Interview With Harry Harrison," *Sense of Wonder* (B. Dalton) pp.10-12. August/September 1993.
___ Shreeve, John. "A Stainless Steel Rap: Harry Harrison Interviewed," *Interzone* No. 72: 23-26. June 1993.

HARRISON, LINDA
___ Weaver, Tom. "Woman of the Apes," *Starlog* No. 213: 57-63. April 1995.

HARRISON, M. JOHN
___ Clute, John. "M. John Harrison," in: Clute, John. **Look at the Evidence: Essays and Reviews.** Liverpool: Liverpool University Press, 1995. pp.430-435.
___ Fowler, Christopher J. "A Detective Fiction of the Heart: The First London Interview with M. John Harrison," *Foundation* No. 58: 5-26. Summer 1993.
___ Fowler, Christopher J. "On the Edge: The Last Holmfirth Interview with M. John Harrison," *Foundation* No. 57: 7-25. Spring 1993.

HARRISON, M. JOHN (continued)
___ Harrison, M. John. "The Profession of Fiction," in: Jakubowski, Maxim and James, Edward, eds. **The Profession of Science Fiction.** New York: St. Martin's, 1992. pp.140-153.

HARRYHAUSEN, RAY
___ "1992 Saturn Awards," *Locus* 28(6): 7. June 1992.
___ "Berlin Fantasy Fest Unspools 70 Films; Harryhausen Laud," *Variety* p. 6, 52. May 11, 1983.
___ "Corman, Harryhausen San Jose Fest Honorees," *Variety* p. 7. April 10, 1985.
___ Fein, David C. "Laser Revolution: Harryhausen Cornucopia," *Cinefex* No. 53: 81-82. February 1993.
___ Leeper, Mark R. "An Annotated Filmography of Ray Harryhausen," *Lan's Lantern* No. 41: 33-35. July 1993.
___ Mandell, Paul. "Harryhausen Animates Annual Sci-Tech Awards," *American Cinematographer* 73(5): 73-74. May 1992.
___ Mandell, Paul. "Of Genies and Dragons: The Career of Ray Harryhausen," *American Cinematographer* 73(12): 77-81. December 1992.
___ Smith, Russell. "Tribute to a Maker of Monsters," *Dallas (TX) Morning News.* August 7, 1992. in: *NewsBank. Film and Television.* 80: F13-F14. 1992.

HART, SUSAN
___ Weaver, Tom. "Susan Hart: Interview," in: Weaver, Tom, ed. **Attack of the Monster Movie Makers: Interviews with 20 Genre Giants.** Jefferson, NC: McFarland, 1994. pp.127-144

HARTLEY, L. P.
___ Bloom, Harold. "L. P. Hartley," in: Bloom, Harold. **Modern Horror Writers.** New York: Chelsea House, 1995. pp.79-92.

HARTLEY, MARIETTE
___ Goldberg, Lee. "The Face of Television," *Starlog* 180: 36-39, 73. July 1992.

HARTWELL, DAVID G.
___ Schaeffer, Sirikanya B. "Award Winning Science Fiction Editor Speaks at LC," *Library of Congress Information Bulletin* 51(13): 289. June 29, 1992.

HARTZELL, SUSAN
___ "Two Pauline Dunn Horror Novels Plagiarized Dean R. Koontz's **Phantoms**," *Science Fiction Chronicle* 13(10): 4. July/August 1992.
___ "Zebra Withdraws Two Novels for Plagiarism," *Locus* 28(2): 6. August 1992.

HASFORD, GUSTAV
___ "Hasford, Gustav (Obituary)," *Locus* 30(3): 70. March 1993.

HASSLER, DONALD M.
___ "1993 J. Lloyd Eaton Memorial Award," *Locus* 30(6): 72. June 1993.

HATLEW, BURTON
___ Davis, Jonathan. **Stephen King's America.** Mercer Island, WA: Starmont House, 1992.

HAUNTED (MOTION PICTURE)
___ Wells, Curt. "James Herbert Is No *Fluke*," *Sci-Fi Entertainment* 1(6): 58-29, 72. April 1995.

HAUNTING (MOTION PICTURE)
___ Holder, Nancy. "Why *The Haunting* Is So Damn Scary," in: Golden, Christopher, ed. **Cut! Horror Writers on Horror Film.** New York: Berkley, 1992. pp.131-140.

HAUSER, EVA
___ Fiser, Miroslav. "A Few Notes About Biopunk," *Vector* No. 174: 17-18. August/September 1993.
___ Hauser, Eva. "Biopunk: A New Literary Movement for Post-Totalitarian Regimes," *Vector* No. 174: 15-16. August/September 1993.
___ Simsa, Cyril. "The View From Olympus: Three Czech Women Writers Talk About SF," *Vector* No. 166: 14-16. April/May 1992.

HAWKING, STEPHEN

___ Altman, Mark A. "*Star Trek: The Next Generation*: Stephen Hawking's *Star Trek* cameo," *Cinefantastique* 24(3/4): 63. October 1993.

___ Rosenheim, Shawn. "Extraterrestrial: Science Fictions in *A Brief History of Time* and *The Incredible Shrinking Man*," *Film Quartrely* 48(4): 15-21. Summer 1995.

HAWTHORNE, NATHANIEL

___ Burleson, Donald R. "Sabbats: Hawthorne/Wharton," *Studies in Weird Fiction* No. 12: 12-16. Spring 1993.

___ Garrett, John C. **Hope or Disillusion: Three Versions of Utopia: Nathaniel Hawthorne, Samuel Butler, George Orwell**. Christchurch, NZ: University of Canterbury Publications Committee, 1984. 69pp.

___ Miller, Edwin H. **Salem Is My Dwelling Place: A Life of Nathaniel Hawthorne**. Ames: University of Iowa Press, 1992. 596pp.

HAYAKAWA, KIYOSHI

___ "Hayakawa, Kiyoshi (Obituary)," *Locus* 31(3): 81-82. September 1993.

___ "Hayakawa, Kiyoshi (Obituary)," *Science Fiction Chronicle* 14(12): 12. September 1993.

HAYES, TERRY

___ Lofficier, Randy. "*Mad Max* Movies (1979-1985): Interview with George Miller, Terry Hayes, George Ogilvie and Mel Gibson," by Randy Lofficier and Jean-Marc Lofficier. in: Goldberg, Lee et al. **Science Fiction Filmmaking in the 1980s**. Jefferson, NC: McFarland, 1995. pp.133-174.

HE-MAN AND MASTERS OF THE UNIVERSE (TV)

___ " 'He-Man' a Commercial?," *Variety* p. 66. April 11, 1984.

HEAD, BESSIE

___ Bazin, Nancy T. "Madness, Mysticism, and Fantasy: Shifting Perspectives of the Novels of Doris Lessing, Bessie Head, and Nadine Gordimer," *Extrapolation* 33(1): 73-87. Spring 1992.

HEARN, LAFCADIO

___ Bloom, Harold. "Lafcadio Hearn," in: Bloom, Harold. **Classic Fantasy Writers**. New York: Chelsea House, 1994. pp.96-109

___ Dawson, Carl. **Lafcadio Hearn and the Vision of Japan**. Baltimore: Johns Hopkins University Press, 1992. 187pp.

___ Umemoto, Junko. "Lafcadio Hearn and Christianity," *Comparitive Literature Studies* 30(4): 388-396. 1993.

HEARTSTOPPER (MOTION PICTURE)

___ Wilt, David. "*Heartstopper* (Review)," *Cinefantastique* 24(2): 59. August 1993.

HEAVEN SENT (MOTION PICTURE)

___ Leydon, Joe. "*Heaven Sent* (Review)," *Variety* 359(2): 68. May 8, 1995.

HEAVENLY CREATURES (MOTION PICTURE)

___ Faller, James M. "*Heavenly Creatures* (Review)," *Cinefantastique* 26(4): 59. June 1995.

___ Jones, Alan. "*Heavenly Creatures*," *Cinefantastique* 26(2): 42-43, 60. February 1995.

HECHELMANN, FRITZ

___ Holländer, Hans. "Notizen zur Illustration 'phantastischer Literatur'. Anläßlich der Asgabe von MacDonalds **Phantastes** mit den Bildern von Fritz Hechelmann," in: Kranz, Gisbert, ed. **Inklings: Jahrbuch für Literatur und Ästhetik**. 1. Band. Lüdenscheid, Germany: Michael Claren, 1983. pp.139-149.

HEGEL, GEORG WILHELM FRIEDRICH

___ Stillman, Peter S. "A Critique of Ideal Worlds: Hegel and Marx on Modern Utopian Thought," in: Saccaro Del Buffa, Giuseppa and Lewis, Arthur O., eds. **Utopie per gli Anni Ottana**. Rome: Gangemi Editore, 1986. pp.635-674.

HEIN, CHRISTOPH

___ Spies, Bernhard. "Der Anteil der sozialistischen Utopie an der Beendigung der DDR-Literatur. Am Beispiel Christoph Heins," *Germanic Review* 67(3): 112-118. Summer 1992.

HEINLEIN, ROBERT A.

___ "Baen Books $1,000.00 Podkayne Essay Contest," *Science Fiction Chronicle* 14(9): 4. June 1993.

___ "Heinlein on Mars (...and in Hollywood)," *Locus* 33(5): 8. November 1994.

___ "Martian Crater to Bear Heinlein's Name; Asteroid Named for Zappa," *Science Fiction Chronicle* 16(2): 5. November/December 1994.

___ "NASA Medal for Distinguished Public Service to Robert A. Heinlein," in: Kondo, Yoji, ed. **Requiem: New Collected Works by Robert A. Heinlein and Tributes to the Grand Master**. New York: Tor, 1992. pp.217-218.

___ "Warner Brothers Buys Heinlein's Book," *Variety* p. 6. October 15, 1969.

___ Anderson, Poul. "RAH: A Memoir," in: Kondo, Yoji, ed. **Requiem: New Collected Works by Robert A. Heinlein and Tributes to the Grand Master**. New York: Tor, 1992. pp.243-251.

___ Baen, Jim. "Jim Baen's RAH Story," in: Kondo, Yoji, ed. **Requiem: New Collected Works by Robert A. Heinlein and Tributes to the Grand Master**. New York: Tor, 1992. pp.252-254.

___ Bastien, Louis A. **Green Fire and the Legacy of the Dragon: Science Fiction, Fantasy and Cultural Ideology**. Ph.D. Dissertation, University of Connecticut, 1992. 238pp. (DAI-A 54/04. p. 1359. October 1993.)

___ Bear, Greg. "Remembering Robert Heinlein," in: Kondo, Yoji, ed. **Requiem: New Collected Works by Robert A. Heinlein and Tributes to the Grand Master**. New York: Tor, 1992. pp.255-258.

___ Black, D. S. **The Man Who Sold America: Heinlein in Dementia**. San Francisco, CA: Atlantis Express, 1988. 28pp.

___ Blackmore, Tim. "Talking with *Strangers*: Interrogating the Many Texts That Became Heinlein's **Stranger in a Strange Land**," *Extrapolation* 36(2): 136-150. Summer 1995.

___ Bloom, Harold. "Robert A. Heinlein," in: Bloom, Harold, ed. **Science Fiction Writers of the Golden Age**. New York: Chelsea House, 1995. pp.110-125.

___ Bouchard, Alexander J. L. "Robert A. Heinlein: An Appreciation," *Lan's Lantern* No. 38: 31-32. July 1992.

___ Bowen, J. Hartley, Jr. "Recalling Robert Anson Heinlein," in: Kondo, Yoji, ed. **Requiem: New Collected Works by Robert A. Heinlein and Tributes to the Grand Master**. New York: Tor, 1992. pp.259-260.

___ Clancy, Tom. "Speech: Robert A. Heinlein," in: Kondo, Yoji, ed. **Requiem: New Collected Works by Robert A. Heinlein and Tributes to the Grand Master**. New York: Tor, 1992. pp.220-223.

___ Clarke, Arthur C. "Robert Heinlein," in: Kondo, Yoji, ed. **Requiem: New Collected Works by Robert A. Heinlein and Tributes to the Grand Master**. New York: Tor, 1992. pp.261-264.

___ de Camp, Catherine Crook. "Speech: Robert A. Heinlein," in: Kondo, Yoji, ed. **Requiem: New Collected Works by Robert A. Heinlein and Tributes to the Grand Master**. New York: Tor, 1992. pp.235-238.

___ de Camp, L. Sprague. "Speech: Robert A. Heinlein," in: Kondo, Yoji, ed. **Requiem: New Collected Works by Robert A. Heinlein and Tributes to the Grand Master**. New York: Tor, 1992. pp.224-226.

___ Dickson, Gordon R. "Robert Heinlein," in: Kondo, Yoji, ed. **Requiem: New Collected Works by Robert A. Heinlein and Tributes to the Grand Master**. New York: Tor, 1992. pp.265-271.

___ Garcia, Robert T. "Robert A. Heinlein," *Cinefantastique* 25(6)/26(1): 42, 125. December 1994.

___ Haldeman, Joe. "Robert A. Heinlein and Us," in: Kondo, Yoji, ed. **Requiem: New Collected Works by Robert A. Heinlein and Tributes to the Grand Master**. New York: Tor, 1992. pp.272-274.

___ Heinlein, Robert A. "Guest of Honor Speech at the Third World Science Fiction Convention, Denver, 1941," in: Kondo, Yoji, ed. **Requiem: New Collected Works by Robert A. Heinlein and Tributes to the Grand Master**. New York: Tor, 1992. pp.153-167.

___ Heinlein, Robert A. "Guest of Honor Speech at the XIXth World Science Fiction Convention, Seattle, 1961," in: Kondo, Yoji, ed. **Requiem: New Collected Works by Robert A. Heinlein and Tributes to the Grand Master**. New York: Tor, 1992. pp.168-197.

___ Heinlein, Robert A. "Guest of Honor Speech at the XXXIVth World Science Fiction Convention, Kansas City, 1976," in: Kondo, Yoji, ed. **Requiem: New Collected Works by Robert A. Heinlein and Tributes to the Grand Master**. New York: Tor, 1992. pp.205-213.

___ Heinlein, Robert A. "Guest of Honor Speech: Rio de Janeiro Movie Festival, 1969," in: Kondo, Yoji, ed. **Requiem: New Collected Works by Robert A. Heinlein and Tributes to the Grand Master**. New York: Tor, 1992. pp.198-204.

HEINLEIN, ROBERT A.

HEINLEIN, ROBERT A. (continued)

___ Heinlein, Robert A. "Letter to Theodore Sturgeon, February 11, 1955," *New York Review of Science Fiction* No. 84: 1, 3-5. August 1995.

___ Heinlein, Robert A. "Shooting *Destination Moon*," in: Kondo, Yoji, ed. **Requiem: New Collected Works by Robert A. Heinlein and Tributes to the Grand Master.** New York: Tor, 1992. pp.117-131.

___ Heinlein, Robert A. "This I Believe," in: Kondo, Yoji, ed. **Requiem: New Collected Works by Robert A. Heinlein and Tributes to the Grand Master.** New York: Tor, 1992. pp.218-220.

___ Heinlein, Robert A. **Tramp Royale.** New York: Ace, 1992. 372pp.

___ Heinlein, Virginia. "Preface: Requiem," in: Kondo, Yoji, ed. **Requiem: New Collected Works by Robert A. Heinlein and Tributes to the Grand Master.** New York: Tor, 1992. pp.1-5.

___ Ingebretson, Edward J. "Robert A. Heinlein," in: Bruccoli, Matthew J., ed. **Facts on File Bibliography of American Fiction 1919-1988.** New York: Facts on File, 1991. pp.235-237.

___ Kondo, Yoji. "Farewell to the Master," by Yoji Kondo and Charles Sheffield. in: Kondo, Yoji, ed. **Requiem: New Collected Works by Robert A. Heinlein and Tributes to the Grand Master.** New York: Tor, 1992. pp.337-341.

___ Kondo, Yoji, ed. **Requiem: New Collected Works by Robert A. Heinlein and Tributes to the Grand Master.** New York: Tor, 1992. 341pp.

___ Lerner, Fred. "The Posthumous Heinlein," *Voice of Youth Advocates* 17(1): 15-16. April 1994.

___ Major, Joseph T. "Star Soldiers Are for Star Wars," *Lan's Lantern* No. 38: 33-41. July 1992.

___ McBride, Jon. "Speech: Robert A. Heinlein," in: Kondo, Yoji, ed. **Requiem: New Collected Works by Robert A. Heinlein and Tributes to the Grand Master.** New York: Tor, 1992. pp.233-234.

___ Mercier-Davis, Helen E. "Heinlein's Influence," *Lan's Lantern* No. 38: 42-43. July 1992.

___ Niven, Larry. "The Return of William Proxmire," in: Kondo, Yoji, ed. **Requiem: New Collected Works by Robert A. Heinlein and Tributes to the Grand Master.** New York: Tor, 1992. pp.275-285.

___ Ormes, Marie G. **Robert A. Heinlein: A Bibliographical Research Guide to Heinlein's Complete Works.** Ph.D. Dissertation, University of Kentucky, 1993. 272pp. (DAI 54/11, p. 4095. May 1994.)

___ Ormes, Marie G. "Surprises in the Heinlein Bibliography," in: Wolf, Milton T. and Mallett, Daryl F., eds. **Imaginative Futures: Proceedings of the 1993 Science Fiction Research Association Conference.** San Bernardino, CA: Jacob's Ladder Books, 1995. pp.95-114.

___ Parkin-Speer, Diane. "Almost a Feminist: Robert A. Heinlein," *Extrapolation* 36(2): 113-125. Summer 1995.

___ Perry, Thomas. "Ham and Eggs and Heinlein," *Monad* No. 3: 91-128. September 1993.

___ Perry, Thomas. "Who Broke the Chronoviatmeter," *Monad* No. 2: 51-64. March 1992.

___ Pournelle, Jerry. "Speech: Robert A. Heinlein," in: Kondo, Yoji, ed. **Requiem: New Collected Works by Robert A. Heinlein and Tributes to the Grand Master.** New York: Tor, 1992. pp.227-228.

___ Reno, Shaun. "The Zuni Indian Tribe: A Model for **Stranger in a Strange Land**'s Martian Culture," *Extrapolation* 36(2): 151-158. Summer 1995.

___ Robinson, Spider. "Rah Rah RAH!," in: Kondo, Yoji, ed. **Requiem: New Collected Works by Robert A. Heinlein and Tributes to the Grand Master.** New York: Tor, 1992. pp.286-309.

___ Robinson, Spider. "Robert," in: Kondo, Yoji, ed. **Requiem: New Collected Works by Robert A. Heinlein and Tributes to the Grand Master.** New York: Tor, 1992. pp.310-321.

___ Rodenberg, Hans-Peter. "Robert A. Heinlein, **Stranger in a Strange Land** (1961)," in: Heuermann, Harmut, ed. **Der Science Fiction Roman in der angloamerikanischen Literatur: Interpretationen.** Düsseldorf: Bagel, 1986. pp.220-236.

___ Sanders, Joe L. "Breaking the Circle: Heinlein's **The Door into Summer**," *New York Review of Science Fiction* No. 60: 1, 10-13. August 1993.

___ Sheffield, Charles. "Speech: Robert A. Heinlein," in: Kondo, Yoji, ed. **Requiem: New Collected Works by Robert A. Heinlein and Tributes to the Grand Master.** New York: Tor, 1992. pp.229-232.

___ Silverberg, Robert. "Heinlein," in: Kondo, Yoji, ed. **Requiem: New Collected Works by Robert A. Heinlein and Tributes to the Grand Master.** New York: Tor, 1992. pp.322-327.

___ Slusser, George E. "Heinlein's Fallen Futures," *Extrapolation* 36(2): 96-112. Summer 1995.

HELLRAISER IV: BLOODLINE (MOTION PICTURE)

HEINLEIN, ROBERT A. (continued)

___ Slusser, George E. "Spacetime Geometries: Time Travel and the Modern Geometrical Narrative," by George E. Slusser and Daniele Chatelain. *Science Fiction Studies* 22(2): 161-186. July 1995.

___ Stephensen-Payne, Phil. **Robert Heinlein, Stormtrooping Guru: A Working Bibliography.** Albuquerque, NM: Galactic Central, 1993. 100pp.

___ Sullivan, C. W., III. "Heinlein's Juveniles: Growing Up in Outer Space," in: Sullivan, C. W., III. **Science Fiction for Young Readers.** Westport, CT: Greenwood, 1993. pp.21-35.

___ Tiptree, James, Jr. "From a Spoken Journal: Thinking About Heinlein, et al., 1971," *New York Review of Science Fiction* No. 60: 1, 3-6. August 1993. (Edited by David G. Hartwell.)

___ Turtledove, Harry. "Thank You," in: Kondo, Yoji, ed. **Requiem: New Collected Works by Robert A. Heinlein and Tributes to the Grand Master.** New York: Tor, 1992. pp.328-332.

___ Usher, Robin L. "Robert A. Heinlein: Theologist?," *Foundation* No. 54: 70-86. Spring 1992.

___ Wells, Curt. "Robert Heinlein's Classic **The Puppet Masters** Leaps From Page to Screen at Last!," *Science Fiction Age* 2(5): 18-22, 34. July 1994.

___ Wells, Earl. "Robert A. Heinlein: EPIC Crusader," *New York Review of Science Fiction* No. 56: 1, 3-7. April 1993.

___ Westfahl, Gary. "The Dark Side of the Moon: Robert A. Heinlein's **Project Moonbase**," *Extrapolation* 36(2): 126-135. Summer 1995.

___ Williams, Donna G. "The Moons of Le Guin and Heinlein," *Science Fiction Studies* 21(2): 164-172. July 1994.

___ Williamson, Jack. "Who Was Robert Heinlein?," in: Kondo, Yoji, ed. **Requiem: New Collected Works by Robert A. Heinlein and Tributes to the Grand Master.** New York: Tor, 1992. pp.333-336.

___ Yano, Tetsu. "Speech: Robert A. Heinlein," in: Kondo, Yoji, ed. **Requiem: New Collected Works by Robert A. Heinlein and Tributes to the Grand Master.** New York: Tor, 1992. pp.238-239.

HELL ON EARTH (MOTION PICTURE)
___ SEE: HELLRAISER III: HELL ON EARTH (MOTION PICTURE).

HELLMASTER (MOTION PICTURE)
___ Harris, Judith P. "**Hellmaster** (Review)," *Cinefantastique* 24(6)/25(1): 123. February 1994.

HELLRAISER III: HELL ON EARTH (MOTION PICTURE)
___ Goodson, William W., Jr. "**Hellraiser III: Hell on Earth**: The Origin of Pinhead," *Cinefantastique* 22(6): 26. June 1992.

___ Goodson, William W., Jr. "**Hellraiser III: Hell on Earth**," *Cinefantastique* 22(6): 24-27, 61. June 1992

___ Hunter, Stephen. "TV Reporter Saves the World from **Hellraiser**s in NYC (Review)," *Baltimore (MD) Sun.* September 12, 1992. in: *NewsBank. Film and Television.* 91:A9. 1992.

___ Jones, Alan. "**Hellraiser III**: Pinhead's Apotheosis," *Cinefantastique* 23(2/3): 18. October 1992.

___ Jones, Alan. "**Hellraiser III**: The Politics of Hell," *Cinefantastique* 23(2/3): 21. October 1992.

___ Jones, Alan. "**Hellraiser III: Hell on Earth**," *Cinefantastique* 23(2/3): 16-20. October 1992.

___ Newman, Kim. "**Hellraiser III: Hell on Earth** (Review)," *Sight and Sound* 3(2): 46-47. February 1993.

___ Pearlman, Cindy. "Third **Hellraiser** Saga Is a Film for Pinheads (Review)," *Chicago (IL) Sun Times.* September 22, 1992. in: *NewsBank. Film and Television.* 91:A8. 1992.

___ Sherman, Paul. "**Hellraiser III** Goes Down In Flames (Review)," *Boston (MA) Herald.* September 12, 1992. in: *NewsBank. Film and Television.* 91:A10. 1992.

HELLRAISER IV: BLOODLINE (MOTION PICTURE)
___ Beeler, Michael. "Clive Barker's **Hellraiser IV: Bloodline**," *Cinefantastique* 26(2): 10-11, 60. February 1995.

___ Beeler, Michael. "Clive Barker's **Hellraiser IV: Bloodline**," *Cinefantastique* 26(3): 32-38. April 1995.

___ Beeler, Michael. "Clive Barker's **Hellraiser IV: Bloodline**," *Cinefantastique* 27(2): 14-15. November 1995.

___ Beeler, Michael. "**Hellraiser IV: Bloodline**: Kevin Yagher, Director," *Cinefantastique* 26(3): 34. April 1995.

___ Beeler, Michael. "**Hellraiser IV: Bloodline**: Makeup Effects," *Cinefantastique* 26(3): 39. April 1995.

___ Beeler, Michael. "**Hellraiser IV: Bloodline**: Pin Head Speaks," *Cinefantastique* 26(3): 36-37. April 1995.

HENDERSON, GEORGE
___ "Henderson, George (Obituary)," *Locus* 28(6): 68. June 1992.
___ "Henderson, George (Obituary)," *Science Fiction Chronicle* 13(8): 16. May 1992.

HENDERSON, ZENNA
___ Erisman, Fred. "Zenna Henderson and the Not-So-Final Frontier," *Western American Literature* 30(3): 275-285. November 1995.
___ Mendlesohn, Farah. "Gender, Power, and Conflict Resolution: 'Subcommittee' by Zenna Henderson," *Extrapolation* 35(2): 120-129. Summer 1994.

HENNESY, TOM
___ Weaver, Tom. "The Other Creature," by Tom Weaver and Paul Parla. *Starlog* No. 206: 61-65. September 1994.

HENRIKSEN, LANCE
___ Spelling, Ian. "Man of Many Parts," *Starlog* 180: 46-50. July 1992.

HENSON, BRIAN
___ Beeler, Michael. "Henson's New, Lean, Mean Green Machine," *Cinefantastique* 23(5): 10-11. February 1993.

HENSTRIDGE, NATASHA
___ "The Beauty Is a Beast," *People Weekly* 44(4): 164-165. July 24, 1995.

HERBERT, BENSON
___ "Herbert, Benson (Obituary)," *Locus* 29(4): 66. October 1992

HERBERT, BRIAN
___ Hendee, J. C. "The Race for Success: An Interview With Brian Herbert," *Quantum* No. 43/44: 24-26. Spring/Summer 1993.

HERBERT, BRUCE C.
___ "Herbert, Bruce C. (Obituary)," *Locus* 31(3): 82. September 1993.

HERBERT, FRANK
___ DiTommaso, Lorenzo. "History and Historical Effect in Frank Herbert's **Dune**," *Science-Fiction Studies* 19(3): 311-325. November 1992.
___ Feehan, Ellen. "Frank Herbert and the Making of Myths: Irish History, Celtic Mythology, and IRA Ideology in **The White Plague**," *Science-Fiction Studies* 19(3): 289-310. November 1992.
___ McNelly, Willis E. "The Science Fiction Collection," in: Vogeler, Albert R. and Arthur A. Hansen, eds. **Very Special Collections: Essays on Library Holdings at California State University, Fullerton.** Fullerton, CA: Patron of the Library, 1992. pp.17-62.
___ Seeber, Hans-Ulrich. "Frank Herbert, **Dune-Trilogie** (1965ff)," in: Heuermann, Harmut, ed. **Der Science Fiction Roman in der angloamerikanischen Literatur: Interpretationen.** Düsseldorf: Bagel, 1986. pp.253-274.
___ Smith, Mary R. **Dune: More Than Genre Fiction.** Master's Thesis, East Carolina University, 1992. 48pp.
___ Tobin, Jean. "Frank Herbert's **The Heaven Makers**: A Reconsideration, Part 1," *New York Review of Science Fiction* No. 46: 21-23. June 1992.
___ Tobin, Jean. "Frank Herbert's **The Heaven Makers**: A Reconsideration, Part 2," *New York Review of Science Fiction* No. 47: 16-19. July 1992.
___ Touponce, William F. "Frank Herbert," in: Bruccoli, Matthew J., ed. **Facts on File Bibliography of American Fiction 1919-1988.** New York: Facts on File, 1991. pp.247-248.
___ Zeender, Marie-Noelle. "The Moi-Peau of Leto II in Herbert's Atreides Saga," *Science Fiction Studies* 22(2): 226-233. July 1995.

HERBERT, GEORGE
___ Hill, Darci. " 'The Church Militant' Resurrected: Mythic Elements in George Herbert's **The Temple**," *Mythlore* 21(1): 29-32. Summer 1995. (No. 79)

HERBERT, JAMES
___ "James Herbert: A Working Bibliography," in: Jones, Stephen, ed. **James Herbert: By Horror Haunted.** London: New English Library, 1992. pp.302-317.

HERBERT, JAMES (continued)
___ Ashley, Mike. "Castaway," in: Jones, Stephen, ed. **James Herbert: By Horror Haunted.** London: New English Library, 1992. pp.69-74.
___ Barker, Clive. "James Herbert: Afterword," in: Jones, Stephen, ed. **James Herbert: By Horror Haunted.** London: New English Library, 1992. pp.299-301.
___ Campbell, Ramsey. "Notes Towards a Reappraisal," in: Jones, Stephen, ed. **James Herbert: By Horror Haunted.** London: New English Library, 1992. pp.289-298.
___ Cole, Adrian. "Season of the Rat," in: Jones, Stephen, ed. **James Herbert: By Horror Haunted.** London: New English Library, 1992. pp.99-104.
___ Fletcher, Jo. "The Curious Case of 'The Spear'," in: Jones, Stephen, ed. **James Herbert: By Horror Haunted.** London: New English Library, 1992. pp.113-121.
___ Fraser, John. "The Dark Domain," in: Jones, Stephen, ed. **James Herbert: By Horror Haunted.** London: New English Library, 1992. pp.151-159.
___ Gaiman, Neil. "The Craft," in: Jones, Stephen, ed. **James Herbert: By Horror Haunted.** London: New English Library, 1992. pp.79-91.
___ Gallagher, Stephen. "Herbert, **Haunted**, and the Integrity of Bestsellerdom," in: Jones, Stephen, ed. **James Herbert: By Horror Haunted.** London: New English Library, 1992. pp.181-188.
___ Gilbert, John. "The Devil You Know," in: Jones, Stephen, ed. **James Herbert: By Horror Haunted.** London: New English Library, 1992. pp.235-241.
___ Gilbert, John. "Haunted by Success," in: Jones, Stephen, ed. **James Herbert: By Horror Haunted.** London: New English Library, 1992. pp.189-198.
___ Gilbert, John. "Horror of **The Rats**," in: Jones, Stephen, ed. **James Herbert: By Horror Haunted.** London: New English Library, 1992. pp.105-107.
___ Herbert, James. "Bowled Over by the Beast: Me and My Car," in: Jones, Stephen, ed. **James Herbert: By Horror Haunted.** London: New English Library, 1992. pp.39-42.
___ Herbert, James. "Comic Relief," in: Jones, Stephen, ed. **James Herbert: By Horror Haunted.** London: New English Library, 1992. pp.65-67.
___ Herbert, James. "The Fog," in: Jones, Stephen, ed. **James Herbert: By Horror Haunted.** London: New English Library, 1992. pp.109-111.
___ Herbert, James. **James Herbert's Dark Places: Locations and Legends.** London: HarperCollins, 1993. 168pp.
___ Herbert, James. "My Ten Favorite Books," in: Jones, Stephen, ed. **James Herbert: By Horror Haunted.** London: New English Library, 1992. pp.75-78.
___ Herbert, James. "Swamp Thing," in: Jones, Stephen, ed. **James Herbert: By Horror Haunted.** London: New English Library, 1992. pp.231-233.
___ Howe, David J. "A British Phenomenon," in: Jones, Stephen, ed. **James Herbert: By Horror Haunted.** London: New English Library, 1992. pp.169-180.
___ Howe, David J. " 'Creed': The Advertisement," in: Jones, Stephen, ed. **James Herbert: By Horror Haunted.** London: New English Library, 1992. pp.243-247.
___ Hughes, Dave. "At Home With James Herbert," in: Jones, Stephen, ed. **James Herbert: By Horror Haunted.** London: New English Library, 1992. pp.43-46.
___ Hughes, Dave. "Jim Meets Gray," in: Jones, Stephen, ed. **James Herbert: By Horror Haunted.** London: New English Library, 1992. pp.267-270.
___ Jaworzyn, Stefan. "Big Climaxes and Movie Bullshit," in: Jones, Stephen, ed. **James Herbert: By Horror Haunted.** London: New English Library, 1992. pp.249-266.
___ Jones, Stephen. "A Category to Himself," in: Jones, Stephen, ed. **James Herbert: By Horror Haunted.** London: New English Library, 1992. pp.19-32.
___ Jones, Stephen, ed. **James Herbert: By Horror Haunted.** London: New English Library, 1992. 320pp.
___ King, Stephen. "James Herbert: Introduction," in: Jones, Stephen, ed. **James Herbert: By Horror Haunted.** London: New English Library, 1992. pp.9-17.
___ Laws, Stephen. "Breaking the Mould," in: Jones, Stephen, ed. **James Herbert: By Horror Haunted.** London: New English Library, 1992. pp.161-164.

HERBERT, JAMES (continued)
___ Morrison, Michael A. "The Eidetic Image," in: Jones, Stephen, ed. **James Herbert: By Horror Haunted**. London: New English Library, 1992. pp.165-168.
___ Morrison, Michael A. "James Herbert and Science Fiction," in: Jones, Stephen, ed. **James Herbert: By Horror Haunted**. London: New English Library, 1992. pp.137-150.
___ Nicholls, Stan. "James Herbert Pricks a Few Balloons," in: Nicholls, Stan. **Wordsmiths of Wonder: Fifty Interviews with Writers of the Fantastic**. London: Orbit, 1993. pp.432-437.
___ Olliver, Victor. "A Life in the Day of James Herbert," in: Jones, Stephen, ed. **James Herbert: By Horror Haunted**. London: New English Library, 1992. pp.33-37.
___ Pouncey, Edwin. "In the Hall of the Monster King: Music and the Maestro of Horror," in: Jones, Stephen, ed. **James Herbert: By Horror Haunted**. London: New English Library, 1992. pp.209-216.
___ Sayers, Nick. "Selling a Bestseller," by Nick Sayers, Ian Hughes, David Singer and Tony Hammond. in: Jones, Stephen, ed. **James Herbert: By Horror Haunted**. London: New English Library, 1992. pp.199-207.
___ Talbot, Mary. " 'It Felt Good to Kill': Schoolboy Dreams in the Novels of James Herbert," *Foundation* No. 62: 47-63. Winter 1994/1995.
___ Wells, Curt. "James Herbert Is No *Fluke*," *Sci-Fi Entertainment* 1(6): 58-29, 72. April 1995.
___ Wiater, Stanley. "Dark Dreamer," in: Jones, Stephen, ed. **James Herbert: By Horror Haunted**. London: New English Library, 1992. pp.271-282.
___ Winter, Douglas E. "Doing It With Style," in: Jones, Stephen, ed. **James Herbert: By Horror Haunted**. London: New English Library, 1992. pp.47-63.

HERCULES (TV)
___ Bufalino, Jamie. "Coming on Strong," *TV Guide* 43(28): 16-18. July 16, 1995.
___ Kenny, Glenn. "Coming on Strong," *TV Guide* 42(47): 42. November 19, 1994.
___ Szebin, Frederick C. "The New Adventures of *Hercules*," *Cinefantastique* 26(2): 46-51. February 1995.
___ Szebin, Frederick C. "The Special Effects of *Hercules*," *Cinefantastique* 26(2): 49-50, 60. February 1995.

HERNANDEZ, FELISBERTO
___ Chichester, Ana G. "Metamorphosis in Two Short Stories of the Fantastic by Virgilio Peñera and Felisberto Hernández," *Studies in Short Fiction* 31(3): 385-395. Summer 1994.

HEROIC FANTASY
___ Grixti, Joseph. "Consumed Identities: Heroic Fantasy and the Trivialization of Selfhood," *Journal of Popular Culture* 28(3): 207-227. Winter 1994.

HERSEY, JOHN
___ "Hersey, John (Obituary)," *Locus* 30(5): 66. May 1993.
___ "Hersey, John (Obituary)," *Science Fiction Chronicle* 14(8): 16. May 1993.

HERSHEY, JENNIFER
___ "Hershey Leaves Bantam for Avon," *Locus* 35(4): 8. October 1995.
___ "Hershey Moves up at Bantam," *Locus* 32(3): 8. March 1994.
___ "Jennifer Hershey to Avon Books," *Science Fiction Chronicle* 17(1): 6. October/November 1995
___ "Silbersack to Start New SF Line at HarperCollins; Mitchell Moves to Warner; Bantam Promotes From Within," *Locus* 31(2): 6, 61. August 1993.

HESCOX, RICHARD
___ Barrett, Robert R. "Richard Hescox: Penetrating the Cloud Cover," *Burroughs Bulletin* NS No. 9: 3-7. January 1992.
___ Bryant, Edward. "King Richard, Conqueror of Space," *Science Fiction Age* 3(6): 82-87. September 1995.

HESSE, HERMANN
___ Antosik, Stanley. "Utopian Machines: Liebniz's 'Computer' and Hesse's **Glass Bead Game**," *Germanic Review* 67(1): 35-45. Spring 1992.

HETRICK, JENNIFER
___ Florence, Bill. "Captain's Lady," *Starlog* No. 220: 54-57. November 1995.

HIBBERT, ELEANOR
___ "Hibbert, Eleanor (Obituary)," *Locus* 30(2): 68. February 1993.

HICKMAN, STEVE
___ Drake, David. "Hickmania," *Science Fiction Age* 2(1): 80-85. November 1993.

HICKMAN, TRACY
___ "An Interview With Margaret Weis and Tracy Hickman," *Sense of Wonder* p. 1-4. February/March 1994.
___ "Weis and Hickman All Over," *Locus* 33(4): 8, 75. October 1994.
___ Weis, Margaret, ed. **Leaves From the Inn of the Last Home: The Complete Krynn Source Book**, ed. by Margaret Weis and Tracy Hickman. Lake Geneva, WI: TSR, 1993. 255pp.

HICKS, WILLIAM PLUMMER
___ "Profile: William Plummer Hicks," *Burroughs Bulletin* NS. No. 22: 32. April 1995.

HIDDEN (MOTION PICTURE)
___ "*Hidden* a Winner at Avoriaz Festival of Fantasy Films," *Variety* p. 7, 24. January 27, 1988.

HIDDEN II (MOTION PICTURE)
___ Harris, Judith P. "*The Hidden II* (Review)," *Cinefantastique* 26(2): 59. February 1995.

HIDEAWAY (MOTION PICTURE)
___ Duncan, Jody. "Quick Cuts: Bonnie and Clyde," *Cinefex* No. 63: 53-54. September 1995.
___ Winikoff, Kenneth. "*Hideaway*," *Cinefantastique* 26(3): 14-15, 61. April 1995.

HIDEOUS MUTANT FREEKZ (MOTION PICTURE)
___ Biodrowski, Steve. "*Hideous Mutant Freekz*," *Cinefantastique* 23(6): 14-15. April 1993.

HIDER IN THE HOUSE (MOTION PICTURE)
___ Harris, Judith P. "*Hider in the House* (Review)," *Cinefantastique* 22(6): 54. June 1992

HIERRO, JOSE
___ de Torre Gracia, Emilio E. "La ciencia ficción en la poesía de José Hierro," *Monographis Review* 3(1/2): 100-106. 1987.

HIGHLANDER (MOTION PICTURE)
___ "*Highlander* (1986): Interview with Greg Widen," in: Goldberg, Lee, ed. **The Dreamweavers: Interviews With Fantasy Filmmakers of the 1980s**. Jefferson, NC: McFarland, 1995. pp.143-149.
___ "Roof of Gotham Studio Employed as Location Site for *Highlander*," *Variety* p.29. July 17, 1985.

HIGHLANDER (TV)
___ Bloch-Hansen, Peter. "Heroic Immortal," *Starlog* No. 186: 48-51. January 1993.
___ Shapiro, Marc. "Battle of the Immortals," *Starlog* 185: 32-35. December 1992.

HIGHLANDER II: THE QUICKENING (MOTION PICTURE)
___ Shapiro, Marc. "The Immortal Man," *Starlog* No. 174: 48-51, 71. January 1992.

HIGHLANDER: THE FINAL DIMENSION (MOTION PICTURE)
___ Hunter, Stephen. "Swords Keep Clanking, But Third Time for *Highlander* Is No Charm," (Baltimore, MD) Sun. January 28, 1995. in: *NewsBank. Film and Television*. 17:C11. 1995.
___ Neman, Daniel. "*Highlander III*: The Final Sequel, Please?," *Richmond (VA) Times-Dispatch*. January 28, 1995. in: *NewsBank. Film and Television*. 17:C13. 1995.
___ Sherman, Paul. "Lowest *Highlander*," *Boston (MA) Herald*. January 28, 1995. in: *NewsBank. Film and Television*. 17:C12. 1995.
___ Yakir, Dan. "Higher Ground," *Starlog* No. 212: 46-49, 72. March 1995.

HIGHLANDER: THE FINAL DIMENSION (MOTION PICTURE) (continued)
___ Yakir, Dan. "Raising Kane," *Starlog* No. 210: 36-39, 66. January 1995.

HIGHLANDER: THE MAGICIAN (MOTION PICTURE)
___ Scapperotti, Dan. "**Highlander III: The Magician**," *Cinefantastique* 26(2): 54-55, 60. February 1995.

HIGHLANDER: THE SORCERER (MOTION PICTURE)
___ Tunney, Tom. "**Highlander III: The Sorcerer** (Review)'". *Sight and Sound* 5(3): 37-38. March 1995.

HIGHSMITH, PATRICIA
___ "Highsmith, Patricia (Obituary)," *Locus* 34(3): 74. March 1995.

HILDEBRANDT, EVELYN BEHESHTI
___ "Hildebrandt, Evelyn Beheshti (Obituary)," *Locus* 34(5): 72. May 1995.

HILLEGAS, MARK R.
___ Lewis, Arthur O. "1992 Pilgrim Award Presentation and Acceptance," *SFRA Review* No. 199: 11-14. July/August/September 1992.

HILLIGOSS, CANDACE
___ Weaver, Tom. "Candace Hilligoss: Interview," in: Weaver, Tom, ed. **Attack of the Monster Movie Makers: Interviews with 20 Genre Giants**. Jefferson, NC: McFarland, 1994. pp.145-156.

HINDS, ANTHONY
___ Plamer, Randy. "Hinds Horrors: Forging the Fright Fantastic," *Filmfax* No. 37: 76-81. February/March 1993.

HINGLE, PAT
___ Weaver, Tom. "Gotham's Finest," *Starlog* No. 216: 46-49, 63. July 1995.

HISTORICAL ADVENTURE (MAGAZINE)
___ Cockcroft, T. G. L. "An Index to 'The Eyrie'," *Fantasy Commentator* 8(3/4): 217-229. Fall 1995. (Whole No. 47/48)

HISTORY IN SF
___ DiTommaso, Lorenzo. "History and Historical Effect in Frank Herbert's **Dune**," *Science-Fiction Studies* 19(3): 311-325. November 1992.

HISTORY OF SF
___ "A Gallery of *Amazing* Art: Covers Through the Years," *Amazing Stories* 67(4): 52-56. July 1992.
___ "**Metropolis** Stills Exhibit Now on Display in Paris," *Variety* p.30. June 26, 1985.
___ Adamovic, Ivan. "Jan Weiss (1892-1972), Karel Capek's Overlooked Contemporary," *Extrapolation* 36(4): 285-291. Winter 1995.
___ Adams, John R. **Good, Evil and Alien: Outer Space and the New World in the European Enlightenment**. Ph.D. Dissertation, University of Texas, Austin, 1992. 275pp. (DAI-A 53/12. p. 4436. June 1993.)
___ Albinski, Nan B. "Utopia Reconsidered: Women Novelists and Nineteenth-Century Utopian Visions," *Signs: Journal of Women in Culture and Society* 13(4): 830-841. Summer 1988.
___ Aldiss, Brian W. "Science Fiction's Mother Figure," in: Aldiss, Brian W. **The Detached Retina: Aspects of SF and Fantasy**. Syracuse, NY: Syracuse University Press, 1995. pp.52-86.
___ Aldiss, Brian W. "Some Early Men in the Moon," in: Aldiss, Brian W. **The Detached Retina: Aspects of SF and Fantasy**. Syracuse, NY: Syracuse University Press, 1995. pp.150-158.
___ Alkon, Paul. **Science Fiction Before 1900: Imagination Discovers Technology**. New York: Macmillan Twayne, 1994. 177pp.
___ Allessio, Dominic. "Document in the History of Science Fiction: Dominic Allessio, ed. The Great Romance, by The Inhabitant," *Science Fiction Studies* 20(3): 305-340. November 1993.
___ Ashley, Mike. "The *Amazing* Story: Part 1, The Twenties, By Radio to the Stars," *Amazing Stories* 66(9): 55-59. January 1992.
___ Ashley, Mike. "The *Amazing* Story: Part 2, The Thirties, Escape From Oblivion," *Amazing Stories* 66(10): 64-67. February 1992.
___ Ashley, Mike. "The *Amazing* Story: Part 3, The Forties, 'Gimme Bang-Bang' ," *Amazing Stories* 66(11): 58-63. March 1992.
___ Ashley, Mike. "The *Amazing* Story: Part 4, The Fifties, Dream Worlds," *Amazing Stories* 67(1): 49-54. April 1992.

HISTORY OF SF (continued)
___ Ashley, Mike. "The *Amazing* Story: Part 5, The Sixties; The Gooseflesh Factor," *Amazing Stories* 67(2): 59-64. May 1992.
___ Ashley, Mike. "The *Amazing* Story: Part 6, The Seventies: Sex and Drugs and Rock and Roll," *Amazing Stories* 67(3): 52-56. June 1992.
___ Ashley, Mike. "The *Amazing* Story: Part 7, The Eighties: Son of *Fantastic*," *Amazing Stories* 67(4): 47-56. July 1992.
___ Ashley, Mike. "A History of *Amazing Stories* Magazine," *Futures Past* No. 2: 6-11. April 1992.
___ Ashley, Mike. "Science Fiction in the Depression," *Fantasy Commentator* 8(1/2): 95-102. Winter 1993/1994. (Whole No. 45/46)
___ Attebery, Brian. "The Closing of the Final Frontier: Science Fiction After 1960," in: Sanders, Joe, ed. **Functions of the Fantastic**. Westport, CT: Greenwood, 1995. pp.205-213.
___ Auerbach, Nina, ed. **Forbidden Journeys: Fairy Tales and Fantasies**, ed. by Nina Auerbach and U. C. Knoepflmacher. Chicago: University of Chicago Press, 1992. 373pp.
___ Baines, Paul. " 'Able Mechanick': **The Life and Adventures of Peter Wilkins** and the Eighteenth Century Fantastic Voyage," in: Seed, David, ed. **Anticipations: Essays on Early Science Fiction and Its Precursors**. Liverpool: Liverpool University Press, 1995. pp.1-25.
___ Barker, Lynn. "Klushantsev: Russia's Wizard of **Fantastika**, Part One," by Lynn Barker and Robert Skotak. *American Cinematographer* 75(6): 78-83. June 1994.
___ Barker, Lynn. "Klushantsev: Russia's Wizard of **Fantastika**, Part Two," by Lynn Barker and Robert Skotak. *American Cinematographer* 75(7): 77-82. July 1994.
___ Barrett, Robert R. "Burroughs, Kline and Henry Herbert Knibbs: Another Opinion," *Burroughs Bulletin* NS No. 9: 27-32. January 1992.
___ Becker, Allienne R. **The Lost Worlds Romance: From Dawn Till Dusk**. Westport, CT: Greenwood, 1992. 184pp.
___ Bell, Andrea. "**Desde Júpiter**: Chile's Earliest Science Fiction Novel," *Science Fiction Studies* 22(2): 187-197. July 1995.
___ Berger, Albert I. **The Magic That Works: John W. Campbell and the American Response to Technology**. San Bernardino, CA: Borgo Press, 1993. 231pp.
___ Bleiler, Everett F. "Dime Novel Science-Fiction," *AB Bookmans Weekly* 96(17): 1542-1550. October 23, 1995.
___ Bleiler, Everett F. "In the Early, Early Days: Collecting and Dealing in Science Fiction," *AB Bookmans Weekly* 94(17): 1638-1644. October 24, 1994.
___ Brown, Charles N. "25 Years of *Locus*," *Locus* 30(4): 34-35. April 1993.
___ Brown, Rich. "Post-Sputnik Fandom (1957-1990)," in: Sanders, Joe, ed. **Science Fiction Fandom**. Westport, CT: Greenwood, 1994. pp.75-102.
___ Capasso, Ruth C. "Islands of Felicity: Women Seeing Utopia in Seventeenth Century France," in: Donawerth, Jane L. and Kolmerten, Carol A., eds. **Utopian and Science Fiction by Women: Worlds of Difference**. Syracuse, NY: Syracuse University Press, 1994. pp.35-53.
___ Carter, Paul A. "From 'Nat' to 'Nathan': The Liberal Arts Odyssey of a Pulpmaster," in: Slusser, George E. and Rabkin, Eric S., eds. **Styles of Creation: Aesthetic Technique and the Creation of Fictional Worlds**. Athens: University of Georgia Press, 1992. pp.58-78.
___ Carter, Paul A. "From the Golden Age to the Atomic Age: 1940-1963," in: Barron, Neil, ed. **Anatomy of Wonder 4**. New York: Bowker, 1995. pp.115-221.
___ Cave, Hugh B. **Magazines I Remember: Some Pulps, Their Editors, and What It Was Like to Write for Them**. Chicago, IL: Tattered Pages Press, 1994. 174pp.
___ Chalker, Jack L. **The Science Fantasy Publishers: A Critical and Bibliographic History**, by Jack L. Chalker and Mark Owings. Westminster, MD: Mirage, 1992. 744pp. (Revised Fourth Printing)
___ Chalker, Jack L. **The Science Fantasy Publishers: Supplement One, July 1991-June 1992**, by Jack L. Chalker and Mark Owings. Westminster, MD: Mirage Press, 1992. 130pp.
___ Chandler, Dixon H. **The Sounds of Dissension: Science Fiction Programming on American Popular Radio Through Dimension X (1950/1)**. Master's Thesis, Bowling Green State University, 1992. 194pp.
___ Clareson, Thomas D. "The Emergence of Science Fiction: The Beginnings Through 1915," in: Barron, Neil, ed. **Anatomy of Wonder 4**. New York: Bowker, 1995. pp.3-61.
___ Clark, Stephen R. L. "Alien Dreams: Kipling," in: Seed, David, ed. **Anticipations: Essays on Early Science Fiction and Its Precursors**. Liverpool: Liverpool University Press, 1995. pp.172-194.
___ Clarke, I. F. "20th Century Future-Think: All Our Yesterdays," *Futures* 24(3): 251-260. April 1992.

HISTORY OF SF (continued)

___ Clarke, I. F. "20th Century Future-Think: And Now for the Good News," *Futures* 25(9): 898-996. November 1993.

___ Clarke, I. F. "20th Century Future-Think: From the Flame Deluge to the Bad Time," *Futures* 24(6): 605-614. July/August 1992.

___ Clarke, I. F. "20th Century Future-Think: Infinite Space and Life Everlasting," *Futures* 24(7): 821-830. September 1992.

___ Clarke, I. F. "20th Century Future-Think: Rediscovering Original Sins," *Futures* 24(4): 388-396. May 1992.

___ Clarke, I. F. "20th Century Future-Think: The City: Heaven on Earth or the Hell to Come?," *Futures* 24(7): 701-710. September 1992.

___ Clarke, I. F. "20th Century Future-Think: The Future Formula; or, Are There Lessons in History?," *Futures* 25(10): 1094-1102. December 1993.

___ Clarke, I. F. "20th Century Future-Think: The Future Is Not What It Used to Be," *Futures* 25(7): 792-800. September 1993.

___ Clarke, I. F. "20th Century Future-Think: The Shape of Wars to Come," *Futures* 24(5): 483-492. June 1992.

___ Clarke, I. F. "20th Century Future-Think: World War II; or, What Did the Future Hold?," *Futures* 26(3): 335-344. April 1994.

___ Clarke, I. F. **The Tale of the Next Great War, 1871-1914: Fictions of Future Warefare and Battles Still-to-Come.** Liverpool: Liverpool University Press, 1995. 382pp.

___ Clery, E. J. **The Rise of Supernatural Fiction, 1762-1800.** Cambridge: Cambridge University Press, 1995. 222pp.

___ Cogswell, Theodore R., ed. **PITFCS: Proceedings of the Institute for Twenty-First Century Studies.** Chicago: Advent: Publishers, 1992. 374pp.

___ Colin, Mariella. "Du fantastique en tant que genre litteraire pour les enfants in Italie," in: Perrot, Jean, ed. **Culture, texte et Juene Lecteur. Actes du Xe Congres de l'International Research Society for Children's Literature, Paris, September 1991.** Nancy: Presses Universitaires, 1993. pp.43-49

___ Davies, Eric L. "Inspector Zadig: Voltaire and the Birth of the Scientific Detective Story," *Fantasy Commentator* 8(3/4): 214-216, 172. Fall 1995. (Whole No. 47/48)

___ Davies, Eric L. "Remembering R. F. Starzl: A Conversation with Dr. Thomas E. Starzl," *Fantasy Commentator* 8(3/4): 150-160, 163-165. Fall 1995. (Whole No. 47/48)

___ Davin, Eric L. "Pioneer Publisher: An Interview With Lloyd Eshbach," *Fantasy Commentator* 8(1/2): 121-134. Winter 1993/1994. (Whole No. 45/46)

___ Dawson, W. H. "Forecasts of the Future in Modern Literature," *Science Fiction News* (Australia) No. 91: 2-12. July 1992.

___ Dendle, Brian J. "Spain's First Novel of Science Fiction: A Nineteenth Century Voyage to Saturn," *Monographis Review* 3(1/2): 43-48. 1987.

___ Donawerth, Jane L. "Science Fiction by Women in the Early Pulps, 1926-1930," in: Donawerth, Jane L. and Kolmerten, Carol A., eds. **Utopian and Science Fiction by Women: Worlds of Difference.** Syracuse, NY: Syracuse University Press, 1994. pp.137-152.

___ Finney, Kathe D. "Science Fiction and the Discourse of Power: The American Failure 1910-1930," *European Contributions to American Studies* [Netherlands] 10: 178-188. 1986.

___ Foote, Bud. "Verne's **Paris in the Twentieth Century**: The First Science Fiction Dystopia?," *New York Review of Science Fiction* No. 88: 1, 8-10. December 1995.

___ Frank, Lyndsey M. **From Nautilus to Neuromancer: The Human-Machine Relationship in Science Fiction Literature From the Victorian Era to the 1980s.** Honor's Thesis, Linfield College, 1995. 80pp.

___ Fratz, Doug. "The Twenty-Year Spree: A Personal History of *Thrust/ Quantum*," *Quantum* No. 43/44: 51-66. Spring/Summer 1993.

___ Gernsback, Hugo. "How to Write 'Science' Stories," *Science Fiction Studies* 21(2): 268-272. July 1994. (Reprinted from *Writer's Digest* 10: 27-29. February 1930.)

___ Gunn, James E. "From the Pulps to the Classroom: The Strange Journey of Science Fiction," in: Gunn, James E. **Inside Science Fiction: Essays on Fantastic Literature.** San Bernardino, CA: Borgo, 1992. pp.16-29.

___ Gunn, James E. "SF the British Way," *Amazing* 68(2): 54-60. May 1993.

___ Hammerton, M. "Verne's Amazing Journeys," in: Seed, David, ed. **Anticipations: Essays on Early Science Fiction and Its Precursors.** Liverpool: Liverpool University Press, 1995. pp.98-110.

HISTORY OF SF (continued)

___ Harbottle, Philip. **British Science Fiction Paperbacks and Magazines, 1949-1956: An Annotated Bibliograhy and Guide,** by Philip Harbottle and Stephen Holland. San Bernardino, CA: Borgo Press, 1994. 232pp.

___ Harbottle, Philip. **Vultures of the Void: A History of British Science Fiction Publishing 1946-1956,** by Philip Harbottle and Stephen Holland. San Bernardino, CA: Borgo Press, 1992. 128pp.

___ Hartwell, David G. "The Golden Age of Science Fiction Is Twelve (Excerpt from **Age of Wonders**)," *Futures Past* No. 2: 49-57. April 1992.

___ James, Edward. "Science Fiction by Gaslight: An Introduction to English-Language Science Fiction in the Nineteenth Century," in: Seed, David, ed. **Anticipations: Essays on Early Science Fiction and Its Precursors.** Liverpool: Liverpool University Press, 1995. pp.26-45.

___ James, Edward. **Science Fiction in the 20th Century.** Oxford, New York: Oxford University Press, 1994. 250pp.

___ Kessler, Carol F. "Annotated Bibliography: United States Women's Utopian Fiction, 1836-1983," in: Kessler, Carol K., ed. **Daring to Dream: Utopian Stories by United States Women, 1836-1919.** Boston, MA: Pandora Press, 1984. pp.233-266.

___ Kessler, Carol F. "Consider Her Ways: The Cultural Work of Charlotte Perkins Gilman's Pragmatopian Stories, 1908-1913," in: Donawerth, Jane L. and Kolmerten, Carol A., eds. **Utopian and Science Fiction by Women: Worlds of Difference.** Syracuse, NY: Syracuse University Press, 1994. pp.126-136.

___ Kessler, Carol F. **Daring to Dream: Utopian Fiction by United States Women, 1836-1919.** 2nd ed. Syracuse, NY: Syracuse University Press, 1995. 326pp.

___ Kessler, Carol F. "Introduction: Feminist Utopias by United States Women," in: Kessler, Carol K., ed. **Daring to Dream: Utopian Stories by United States Women, 1836-1919.** Boston, MA: Pandora Press, 1984. pp.1-25.

___ Ketterer, David. **Canadian Science Fiction and Fantasy.** Bloomington: Indiana University Press, 1991. 206pp.

___ Ketterer, David. "The Establishment of Canadian Science Fiction (1958-1983), Part 1," *New York Review of Science Fiction* No. 42: 1, 8-14. February 1992.

___ Ketterer, David. "The Establishment of Canadian Science Fiction (1958-1983), Part 2," *New York Review of Science Fiction* No. 43: 17-22. March 1992.

___ Kleinschmidt, Erich. "'Begreif-Weit': Zur fiktionalen Raumregahrung in der deutschen Literatur des 18. Jahrhunderts," *Germanisch-Romanische Monatsschrift* (Berlin) 41(2): 145-152. 1991.

___ Knight, Damon. "The History of the SFWA 1965-1967," *SFWA Bulletin* 26(3): 3-4. Fall 1992. (No. 117)

___ Kolmerten, Carol A. "Texts and Contexts: American Women Envision Utopia, 1890-1920," in: Donawerth, Jane L. and Kolmerten, Carol A., eds. **Utopian and Science Fiction by Women: Worlds of Difference.** Syracuse, NY: Syracuse University Press, 1994. pp.107-125.

___ Kotani, Mari. **Joseijo Muishiki: tekunogaineshisu, josei SF-ron josetsu.** [Techno-gynesis: The Political Unconscious of Feminist Science Fiction]. Tokyo: Keiso Shobo, 1994. 283pp. [In Japanese, not seen. cf. OCLC.]

___ Lerner, Fred. "Master of Our Art: Rudyard Kipling," *Voice of Youth Advocates* 16(4): 211-213. October 1993.

___ Levy, Michael M. "The New Wave, Cyberpunk, and Beyond: 1963-1994," by Michael M. Levy and Brian Stableford. in: Barron, Neil, ed. **Anatomy of Wonder 4.** New York: Bowker, 1995. pp.222-377.

___ Lewes, Darby. "Gynotopia: A Checklist of Nineteenth Century Utopias by American Women," *Legacy* 6(2): 29-41. Fall 1989.

___ Liberti, Fabrizio. "I grandi classici della fantascienza," *Cineforum* 34(4): 90-92. 1994.

___ MacKillop, Ian. "Fly Me to the Moon," *New Scientist* 144(1948): 51-52. October 22, 1994.

___ Madle, Robert A. "Fandom up to World War II," in: Sanders, Joe, ed. **Science Fiction Fandom.** Westport, CT: Greenwood, 1994. pp.37-54.

___ Mathews, Race. "Whirlaway to *Thrilling Wonder Stories*: Boyhood Reading in Wartime and Postwar Melbourne," *Metaphysical Review* No. 22/23: 5-16. November 1995.

___ Matics, Mark A. **Louder Than Bombs: Science Fiction and Nuclear Weapons, 1945-1965.** Master's Thesis, Marshall University, 1992. 86pp.

___ McMullen, Sean. "The Golden Age of Australian Science Fiction," *Science Fiction: A Review of Speculative Literature* 12(3): 3-28. 1993(?). (No. 36)

HISTORY OF SF (continued)

___ McMullen, Sean. "The Quest for Australian Fantasy," by Sean McMullen and Steven Paulsen. *Aurealis* No. 13: 35-42. 1994.

___ Michalson, Karen. **Victorian Fantasy Literature: Literary Battles with Church and Empire.** Lewiston, NY: Edwin Mellen Press, 1990. 292pp.

___ Molson, Francis J. "Great Marvel: The First American Hardcover Science Fiction Series," *Extrapolation* 34(2): 101-122. Summer 1993.

___ Moskowitz, Sam. "Bernarr Macfadden and His Obsession With Science Fiction, Part VII: Conclusion," *Fantasy Commentator* 7(3): 189-203. Spring 1992. (No. 43)

___ Moskowitz, Sam. "Burroughs, Kline, Knibbs: A Reply," *Burroughs Bulletin* NS No. 9: 34-39. January 1992.

___ Moskowitz, Sam. "A Collector's Tale," *Fantasy Commentator* 8(1/2): 22-31. Winter 1993/1994. (Whole No. 45/46)

___ Moskowitz, Sam. "The Immortal Storm II: A History of Science Fiction Fandom, Part One," *Fantasy Commentator* 8(1/2): 107-120, 13. Winter 1993/1994. (Whole No. 45/46)

___ Moskowitz, Sam. "The Immortal Storm II: A History of Science Fiction Fandom, Part Two," *Fantasy Commentator* 8(3/4): 278-288. Fall 1995. (Whole No. 47/48)

___ Moskowitz, Sam. "The Origin of the Term 'Fanzine'," *Fantasy Commentator* 8(3/4): 200-202. Fall 1995. (Whole No. 47/48)

___ Moskowitz, Sam. "The Origins of Science Fiction Fandom: A Reconstruction," in: Sanders, Joe, ed. **Science Fiction Fandom.** Westport, CT: Greenwood, 1994. pp.17-36.

___ Moskowitz, Sam. "The Science Fiction of Nat Schachner, Part 1," *Fantasy Commentator* 7(3): 160-179. Spring 1992. (No. 43)

___ Moskowitz, Sam. "Voyagers Through Eternity: A History of Science Fiction From the Beginnings to H. G. Wells," *Fantasy Commentator* 8(1/2): 135-144. Winter 1993/1994. (Whole No. 45/46)

___ Moskowitz, Sam. "Voyagers Through Eternity: A History of Science Fiction From the Beginnings to H. G. Wells; Part XIII, Verne's Greatest Work," *Fantasy Commentator* 7(3): 232-236. Spring 1992. (No. 43)

___ Moskowitz, Sam. "Voyagers Through Eternity: A History of Science Fiction From the Beginnings to H. G. Wells, Part XV," *Fantasy Commentator* 8(3/4): 230-242. Fall 1995. (Whole No. 47/48)

___ Myers, Michael. "Visions of Tomorrow: German Science Fiction and Socialist Utopian Novels of the Late Nineteenth Century," *Selecta* (Corvallis) 14: 63-69. 1993.

___ Nellist, Brian. "Imagining the Future: Predictive Fiction in the Nineteenth Century," in: Seed, David, ed. **Anticipations: Essays on Early Science Fiction and Its Precursors.** Liverpool: Liverpool University Press, 1995. pp.111-136.

___ Nevers, Kevin L. **Immovable Objects, Irresistible Forces: The Sublime and the Technological in the Eighteenth Century.** Ph.D. Dissertation, University of Virginia, 1993. 473pp. (DAI-A 54/08, p. 3044. February 1994.)

___ Niewiadowski, Andrzej. **Literatura fantastycznonaukowa.** Warsaw: Wydawn. Naukowe PWN, 1992. 371pp. [Not seen.]

___ Paris, Michael. "Fear of Flying: The Fiction of War, 1886-1916," *History Today* 43: 29-35. June 1993.

___ Parrinder, Patrick. "From Mary Shelley to **The War of the Worlds:** The Thames Valley Catastrophe," in: Seed, David, ed. **Anticipations: Essays on Early Science Fiction and Its Precursors.** Liverpool: Liverpool University Press, 1995. pp.58-74.

___ Parrinder, Patrick. **Shadows of the Future: H. G. Wells, Science Fiction and Prophecy.** Liverpool: Liverpool University Press, 1995. 170pp.

___ Pastourmatzi, Domna A. **Vivliogrphia epistemonikes phantasias, phantasias, kai tromou, 1960-1993** [Bibliography of Science Fiction, Fantasy and Horror, 1960-1993.]. Athens: Alien, 1995. 245pp.

___ Pedrotti, Louis. "Warfare Celestial and Terrestrial: Osip Senkovsky's 1833 Russian Science Fantasy," in: Slusser, George and Eric S. Rabkin, eds. **Fights of Fancy: Armed Conflict in Science Fiction and Fantasy.** Athens, GA: University of Georgia Press, 1993. pp.49-58.

___ Pierce, John J. **Odd Genre: A Study in Imagination and Evolution.** Westport, CT: Greenwood, 1994. 222pp.

___ Pleithner, Regina. "Zwei Mondreisen des 17. Jahrhunderts: Voyages imaginaires oder Reiseutopien? Beitrage zum Kolloquium der Arbeitsgruppe Kultrugeschichte des Barockzeitalters an der Herzog-August-Bibliothek Wolfenbuttle von 10. Bis 12. Juli 1989," in: Pleithner, Regina, ed. **Reisen des Barock: Selbst- und Fremderfahrung und ihre Darstellung.** Bonn: Romanistischer, 1991. pp.75-87.

___ Pohl, Frederik. "Edgar Rice Burroughs and the Development of Science Fiction," *Burroughs Bulletin* NS No. 10: 8-14. April 1992.

HISTORY OF SF (continued)

___ Putzier, Mary G. **Mary Wollstonecraft Shelley and the Creation of Science Fiction.** Master's Thesis, Eastern Washington University, 1995. 113pp.

___ Rees, Christine. **Utopian Imagination and Eighteenth Century Fiction.** London: Longman, 1995. 296pp.

___ Renaud, Maurice. "Document in the History of Science Fiction: On the Scientific-Marvellous Novel and Its Influence on the Understanding of Progress," *Science Fiction Studies* 21(3): 397-405. November 1994.

___ Rovin, Jeff. **Aliens, Robots, and Spaceships.** New York: Facts on File, 1995. 372pp.

___ Ruddick, Nicholas. **British Science Fiction, 1478-1990: A Chronology.** Westport, CT: Greenwood, 1992. 296pp.

___ Ruddick, Nicholas. **Ultimate Island: On the Nature of British Science Fiction.** Westport, CT: Greenwood, 1993. 202pp.

___ Sawyer, Andy. "More Than Metaphor: Double Vision in Lang's *Metropolis*," *Foundation* No. 64: 70-81. Summer 1995.

___ Seed, David. "Breaking the Bounds: The Rhetoric of Limits in the Works of Edgar Allan Poe, His Contemporaries, and Adaptors," in: Seed, David, ed. **Anticipations: Essays on Early Science Fiction and Its Precursors.** Liverpool: Liverpool University Press, 1995. pp.75-97.

___ Server, Lee. **Danger Is My Business: An Illustrated History of the Fabulous Pulp Magazines 1896-1953.** San Francisco, CA: Chronicle Books, 1993. 144pp.

___ Sheckley, Robert. "Memories of the 50s," *New York Review of Science Fiction* No. 48: 19-20. August 1992.

___ Silverberg, Robert. "The History of the SFWA 1967-1968," *SFWA Bulletin* 27(1): 28-29. Spring 1993. (No. 119)

___ Sircar, Sanjay. "Children's Fantasy Fiction in English: Early Generic Discriminations and Our Modern Critical Inheritance," *Merveilles & Contes* 7(2): 423-449. December 1993.

___ Skal, David J. "Drive-Ins Are a Ghoul's Best Friend: Horror in the Fifties," *New York Review of Science Fiction* No. 53: 1, 8-16. January 1993.

___ Sneyd, Steve. "Empress of the Stars: A Reassessment of Lilith Lorraine, Pioneering Fantasy Poetess," *Fantasy Commentator* 7(3): 206-229. Spring 1992. (No. 43)

___ Speer, Jack. **Up to Now: A History of Fandom as Jack Speer Sees It.** Brooklyn, NY: Richard Newsome, [1996?]. 48pp. (Reprint, originally published in 1939.) [Not seen.]

___ Stableford, Brian. "**Frankenstein** and the Origins of Science Fiction," in: Seed, David, ed. **Anticipations: Essays on Early Science Fiction and Its Precursors.** Liverpool: Liverpool University Press, 1995. pp.46-57.

___ Stableford, Brian. "Future Wars, 1890-1950," in: Stableford, Brian. **Opening Minds: Essays on Fantastic Literature.** San Bernardino, CA: Borgo Press, 1995. pp.111-134.

___ Stableford, Brian. "Science Fiction Between the Wars: 1916-1939," in: Barron, Neil, ed. **Anatomy of Wonder 4.** New York: Bowker, 1995. pp.62-114.

___ Stableford, Brian. "William Wilson's Prospectus for Science Fiction, 1851," in: Stableford, Brian. **Opening Minds: Essays on Fantastic Literature.** San Bernardino, CA: Borgo Press, 1995. pp.15-22.

___ Stableford, Brian. "Yesterday's Bestsellers, 15: F. Anstey and **Vice Versa**," *Interzone* No. 74: 57-60. August 1993.

___ Stableford, Brian. "Yesterday's Bestsellers, 19: **The Battle of Dorking** and Its Aftermath," *Interzone* No. 83: 52-56. May 1994.

___ Starzl, R. F. "The Fantastic Science Market," *Fantasy Commentator* 8(3/4): 161-165, 257. Fall 1995. (Whole No. 47/48)

___ Stone, Graham. "Beginning: Sixty Years of *Amazing Stories*, 1929-1930," *Science Fiction News* (Australia) No. 101: 2-12. February 1987.

___ Stone, Graham. "Beginning: Sixty Years of *Amazing Stories*, Part 1," *Science Fiction News* (Australia) No. 97: 2-16. April 1986.

___ Stone, Graham. "Beginning: Sixty Years of *Amazing Stories*, Part 2," *Science Fiction News* (Australia) No. 98: 1-12. May 1986.

___ Stone, Graham. "Beginning: Sixty Years of *Amazing Stories*, Part 3," *Science Fiction News* (Australia) No. 99: 2-12. June 1986.

___ Stone, Graham. "Beginnings," *Science Fiction News* (Australia) No. 100: 2-12. November 1986.

___ Stone, Graham. "Chronology of Australian Science Fiction 1848-1992," *Science Fiction News* (Australia) No. 90: 3-10. July 1992.

___ Stone, Graham. "Early Days in Sydney SF Activities," *Science Fiction News* (Australia) No. 61: 6-13. June 1979.

___ Stone, Graham. "Fifty Years of Science Fiction Groups in Australia," *Science Fiction News* (Australia) No. 108: 2-8. November 1989.

___ Stone, Graham. "H. M. Crimp--And More," *Science Fiction News* (Australia) No. 116: 19-21. October 1992.

HISTORY OF SF (continued)

___ Stone, Graham. "Looking Backward," *Science Fiction News* (Australia) No. 63: 5-7. 1979.

___ Stone, Graham. "Notes on Australian Science Fiction," *Science Fiction News* (Australia) No. 102: 2-5. March 1987.

___ Stone, Graham. "Notes on Australian Science Fiction," *Science Fiction News* (Australia) No. 105: 2-8. October 1987.

___ Stone, Graham. "Notes on Australian Science Fiction," *Science Fiction News* (Australia) No. 67: 2-9. January 1983.

___ Stone, Graham. "Notes on Australian Science Fiction," *Science Fiction News* (Australia) No. 92: 2-8. February 1985.

___ Stone, Graham. "Notes on Australian Science Fiction," *Science Fiction News* (Australia) No. 93: 2-11. March 1985.

___ Stone, Graham. "Notes on Australian Science Fiction," *Science Fiction News* (Australia) No. 94: 2-11. January 1986.

___ Stone, Graham. "Notes on Australian Science Fiction," *Science Fiction News* (Australia) No. 95: 2-11. February 1986.

___ Stone, Graham. "Notes on Australian Science Fiction," *Science Fiction News* (Australia) No. 96: 5-9. March 1986.

___ Stone, Graham. "Notes on Australian Science Fiction: **Out of the Silence**, by Erle Cox," *Science Fiction News* (Australia) No. 62: 6-7. August 1979.

___ Stone, Graham. "Notes on Australian Science Fiction: **Out of the Silence**, by Erle Cox," *Science Fiction News* (Australia) No. 64: 2-7. 1980.

___ Stone, Graham. "Notes on Australian Science Fiction: **Out of the Silence**, by Erle Cox and J. Filmore Sherry," *Science Fiction News* (Australia) No. 66: 2-8. September 1982.

___ Stone, Graham. "Notes on Australian Science Fiction, Or Not, As the Case May Be," *Science Fiction News* (Australia) No. 102: 6-16. March 1987.

___ Stone, Graham. "Notes on Australian Science Fiction, Or Not, As the Case May Be," *Science Fiction News* (Australia) No. 68: 5-12. January 1983.

___ Stone, Graham. "Notes on Australian Science Fiction, Or Not, As the Case May Be," *Science Fiction News* (Australia) No. 92: 8-12. February 1985.

___ Stone, Graham. "Notes on Australian Science Fiction, Or Not, As the Case May Be," *Science Fiction News* (Australia) No. 93: 12. March 1985.

___ Stone, Graham. "Notes on Australian Science Fiction, Or Not, As the Case May Be," *Science Fiction News* (Australia) No. 94: 11-12. January 1986.

___ Stone, Graham. "Notes on Australian Science Fiction, Or Not, As the Case May Be," *Science Fiction News* (Australia) No. 95: 11-12. February 1986.

___ Stone, Graham. "Notes on Australian Science Fiction, Or Not, As the Case May Be," *Science Fiction News* (Australia) No. 96: 10-12. March 1986.

___ Stone, Graham. "Notes on Australian Science Fiction, Or Not, As the Case May Be, Part 2," *Science Fiction News* (Australia) No. 70: 5-12. April 1983.

___ Stone, Graham. "Notes on Australian Science Fiction, Or Not, As the Case May Be, Part 3," *Science Fiction News* (Australia) No. 71: 5-8. May 1983.

___ Stone, Graham. "Notes on Australian Science Fiction, Or Not, As the Case May Be, Part 4," *Science Fiction News* (Australia) No. 72: 6-8. June 1983.

___ Stone, Graham. "Notes on Australian Science Fiction, Or Not, As the Case May Be, Part 5," *Science Fiction News* (Australia) No. 77: 5-12. June 1983.

___ Stone, Graham. "**Out of the Silence** in Russian--Lost and Found," *Science Fiction News* (Australia) No. 115: 18-20. May 1992.

___ Stone, Graham. "Sixty Years of *Amazing Stories*: 1930," *Science Fiction News* (Australia) No. 103: 2-12. March 1987.

___ Stone, Graham. "Sixty Years of *Amazing Stories*: 1931," *Science Fiction News* (Australia) No. 107: 1-8. 1988.

___ Stone, Graham. "Sixty Years of *Amazing Stories*: 1931 (Continued)," *Science Fiction News* (Australia) No. 109: 9-16. January 1990.

___ Stone, Graham. "Sixty Years of *Amazing Stories*: 1932," *Science Fiction News* (Australia) No. 110: 3-13, 16. April 1990.

___ Stone, Graham. "Sixty Years of *Amazing Stories*: 1933," *Science Fiction News* (Australia) No. 111: 7-16, 20. July 1990.

___ Stone, Graham. "Sixty Years of *Amazing Stories*: 1934," *Science Fiction News* (Australia) No. 112: 13-16. September 1990.

HISTORY OF SF (continued)

___ Stone, Graham. "Sixty Years of *Amazing Stories*: 1934, and The Quarterly, 1931-1934," *Science Fiction News* (Australia) No. 114: 6-23. December 1990.

___ Stone, Graham. "Sixty Years of *Amazing Stories*: 1935," *Science Fiction News* (Australia) No. 116: 21-24. October 1992.

___ Stone, Graham. "Sixty Years of *Amazing Stories*: 1935, Continued," *Science Fiction News* (Australia) No. 117: 11-14. December 1993.

___ Stone, Graham. "Sixty Years of *Amazing Stories*: The Quarterly, 1929-1930," *Science Fiction News* (Australia) No. 105: 8-20. October 1987.

___ Stone-Blackburn, Susan. "Consciousness Evolution and Early Telepathic Tales," *Science Fiction Studies* 20(2): 241-250. July 1993.

___ Sullivan, C. W., III. "Cultural Worldview: Marginalizing the Fantastic in the Seventeenth Century," *Paradoxa* 1(3): 287-300. 1995.

___ Taves, Brian. "**Adventures of the Rat Family**: A Verne Expert Brings Fairy Tale to English-Speaking Public," *Library of Congress Information Bulletin* 53(1): 7-11. January 10, 1994.

___ Van Hise, James, ed. **Pulp Heroes of the Thirties**. Yucca Valley, CA: Midnight Graffiti, 1994. 168pp.

___ Vedder, Catherine M. **New Woman, Old Science: Readings in Late Victorian Fiction**. Ph.D. Dissertation, Cornell University, 1993. (DAI 54: 537A-538A.)

___ Walters, Lori. "The Creation of a Super Romance: Paris, Bibliotheque Nationale, fond francais, MS 1433," in: Busby, Keith, ed. **The Arthurian Yearbook I**. New York: Garland, 1991. pp.3-26.

___ Warner, Harry, Jr. "Fandom Between World War II and *Sputnik*," in: Sanders, Joe, ed. **Science Fiction Fandom**. Westport, CT: Greenwood, 1994. pp.65-74.

___ Warner, Harry, Jr. **A Wealth of Fable: An Informal History of Science Fiction Fandom in the 1950s**. Van Nuys, CA: SCIFI Press, 1992. 456pp.

___ Westfahl, Gary. "A Convenient Analog System: John W. Campbell, Jr.'s Theory of Science Fiction," *Foundation* No. 54: 52-70. Spring 1992.

___ Westfahl, Gary. "Dictatorial, Authoritarian, Uncooperative: The Case Against John W. Campbell," *Foundation* No. 56: 36-60. Autumn 1992. (Letter of comment: Alexei Panshin, *Foundation* No. 58: 87-91. Summer 1993; Rejoiner, Westfahl, *Foundation* No. 58: 93-94.)

___ Westfahl, Gary. "The Jules Verne, H. G. Wells, Edgar Allan Poe Type of Story: Hugo Gernsback's History of Science Fiction," *Science-Fiction Studies* 19(3): 340-353. November 1992.

___ Westfahl, Gary. " 'Man Against Man, Brain Against Brain': The Transformation of Melodrama in Science Fiction," in: Redmond, James, ed. **Melodrama**. Cambridge: Cambridge University Press, 1992. pp.193-211.

___ Westfahl, Gary. " 'This Unique Document': Hugo Gernsback's **Ralph 124C 41 +** and the Genres of Science Fiction," *Extrapolation* 35(2): 95-119. Summer 1994.

___ Westfahl, Gary. "Wanted: A Symbol for Science Fiction," *Science Fiction Studies* 22(1): 1-21. March 1995.

___ Widner, Art. "Wartime Fandom," in: Sanders, Joe, ed. **Science Fiction Fandom**. Westport, CT: Greenwood, 1994. pp.55-64.

___ Wiemer, Annegret J. **The Feminist Science Fiction Utopia: Faces of a Genre, 1820-1897**. Ph.D. Dissertation, University of Alberta, 1991. (Ottawa: National Library of Canada, 1992. 5 microfiche) (DAI-A 53/08, p. 2811. Feb. 1993.)

___ Williams, Madawc. "Tales of Wonder: Science Fiction and Fantasy in the Age of Jane Austen," in: Reynolds, Patricia and GoodKnight, Glen H., eds. **Proceedings of the J. R. R. Tolkien Centenary Conference, Keble College, Oxford, 1992**. Altadena, CA: Mythopoeic Press, 1995. pp.419-430. (*Mythlore* Vol. 21, No. 2, Winter 1996, Whole No. 80)

___ Williamson, Jack. "A Long Time Ago, in a Galaxy Not That Far Away, Science Fiction Was Born," *Science Fiction Age* 2(3): 30, 86. March 1994.

___ Williamson, Jack. "The Way It Was, 1933-1937," in: Jakubowski, Maxim and James, Edward, eds. **The Profession of Science Fiction**. New York: St. Martin's, 1992. pp.12-25.

___ Williamson, Jack. "Wonder Remembered," *Amazing* 68(9): 27-28. Winter 1994.

___ Willis, Connie. "The Women SF Doesn't See," *Isaac Asimov's Science Fiction Magazine* 16(11): 4-8. October 1992.

___ Wolfe, Gary K. "History and Criticism," in: Barron, Neil, ed. **Anatomy of Wonder 4**. New York: Bowker, 1995. pp.483-546.

___ Yeoland, Sally. "Sally and John: The Early Years," by Sally Yeoland and John Bangsund. *Metaphysical Review* No. 22/23: 17-44. November 1995.

HISTORY OF SF (continued)
___ Zebrowski, George. "Never Forget the Writers Who Helped Build Yesterday's Tomorrows," *Science Fiction Age* 3(6): 30-36, 100. 1995.
___ Zebrowski, George. "*The Shadow*: Radio and Pulp Origins," *Cinefantastique* 25(4): 20-21. August 1994.

HISTORY OF UTOPIAN THOUGHT
___ Widdicombe, Richard T. "Early Histories of Utopian Thought (to 1950)," *Utopian Studies* 3(1): 1-38. 1992.

HITCHCOCK, ALFRED
___ Goodson, William W., Jr. "*Birds II: Land's End*: Remembering Hitchcock," *Cinefantastique* 25(2): 51. April 1994.
___ Williams, Linda. "Learning to Scream," *Sight and Sound* 4(12): 14-17. December 1994.

HJORTSBERG, WILLIAM
___ Singer, Robert. "Hellish Contexts: A Study of Hjortsberg's **Falling Angel**," *Studies in Weird Fiction* No. 10: 2-5. Fall 1991.

HOBAN, RUSSELL
___ Filmer, Kath. **Scepticism and Hope in Twentieth Century Fantasy Literature**. Bowling Green, OH: Bowling Green State University Popular Press, 1992. 160pp.
___ Lenz, Millicent. "**Danger Quotient, Fiskadoro, Riddley Walker**, and the Failure of the Campbellian Monomyth," in: Sullivan, C. W., III. **Science Fiction for Young Readers**. Westport, CT: Greenwood, 1993. pp.113-119.
___ Sisk, David W. **Claiming Mastery over the Word: Transformations of Language in Six Twentieth Century Dystopias**. Ph.D. Dissertation, University of North Carolina, Chapel Hill, 1994. 405pp. (DAI-A 55/07, p. 1972. January 1995.)

HOBART, ROSE
___ Weaver, Tom. "Rose Hobart: Interview," in: Weaver, Tom, ed. **Attack of the Monster Movie Makers: Interviews with 20 Genre Giants**. Jefferson, NC: McFarland, 1994. pp.157-174.

HOCUS POCUS (MOTION PICTURE)
___ Counts, Kyle. "Magic Time," *Starlog* No. 194: 32-37. September 1993.
___ Peishel, Bob. "Quick Cuts: Feline Fabrication," *Cinefex* No. 56: 17-18. November 1993.

HODDER-WILLIAMS, CHRISTOPHER
___ "Hodder-Williams, Christopher (Obituary)," *Locus* 34(6): 66. June 1995.
___ "Hodder-Williams, Christopher (Obituary)," *Science Fiction Chronicle* 16(7): 19. June/July 1995.

HODGSON, WILLIAM HOPE
___ Behrends, Steve. "Spinning in the Night Land: A Footnote to William Hope Hodgson," *Studies in Weird Fiction* No. 13: 35-36. Summer 1993. [Not seen.]
___ Bloom, Harold. "William Hope Hodgson," in: Bloom, Harold. **Modern Horror Writers**. New York: Chelsea House, 1995. pp.93-107.
___ Frenschkowski, Marco. "Bis ins dunkelste Herz des Meeres. Maritime Symbolik als Ausdruck des Unheimlichen in Erzählungen von W. H. Hodgson und H. P. Lovecraft," *Quarber Merkur* 32(2): 42-69. December 1994. (Whole No. 82)
___ Gafford, Sam. "Writing Backward: The Novels of William Hope Hodgson," *Studies in Weird Fiction* No. 11: 12-15. Spring 1992.
___ Warren, Alan. "Full Fathom Five: The Supernatural Fiction of William Hope Hodgson," in: Schweitzer, Darrell, ed. **Discovering Classic Horror Fiction I**. Mercer Island, WA: Starmont, 1992. pp.41-52.

HOFFMAN, E. T. A.
___ Borchardt, Edith. "Criminal Artists and Artisans in Mysteries by E. T. A. Hoffman, Dorothy Sayers, Ernesto Sábato, Patrick Süskind, and Thomas Harris," in: Sanders, Joe, ed. **Functions of the Fantastic**. Westport, CT: Greenwood, 1995. pp.125-134.
___ Jennings, Lee B. "Woman as Reality Demarcator in Three Tales of E. T. A. Hoffman," in: Latham, Robert A. and Collins, Robert A., eds. **Modes of the Fantastic**. Westport, CT: Greenwood, 1995. pp.122-127.
___ Nikolchina, Miglena. "Love and Automata: From Hoffman to Lem and From Freud to Kristeva," in: Sanders, Joe, ed. **Functions of the Fantastic**. Westport, CT: Greenwood, 1995. pp.77-82.

HOFFMAN, E. T. A. (continued)
___ Willis, Martin T. "Scientific Portraits in Magical Frames: The Construction of Preternatural Narrative in the Work of E. T. A. Hoffman and Arthur Machen," *Extrapolation* 35(3): 186-200. Fall 1994.

HOFFMAN, NINA KIRIKI
___ "HWA Stoker Awards Winners," *Locus* 33(1): 7. July 1994.
___ "Nina Kiriki Hoffman: Bedtime Stories," *Locus* 33(4): 4-5, 77. October 1994.
___ Schweitzer, Darrell. "*Weird Tales* Talks With Nina Kiriki Hoffman," *Weird Tales* 54(1): 60-64. Spring 1993. (No. 306)

HOGAN, JAMES P.
___ "Other Awards at ConAdian," *Science Fiction Chronicle* 15(10): 5. September 1994.

HOLDER, NANCY
___ "Bram Stoker Award Winners," *Science Fiction Chronicle* 16(7): 4. June/July 1995.
___ "Bram Stoker Awards," *Science Fiction Chronicle* 15(8): 5. June 1994.
___ "HWA Stoker Awards," *Locus* 35(1): 9. July 1995.
___ "HWA Stoker Awards Winners," *Locus* 33(1): 7. July 1994.

HOLDSTOCK, ROBERT
___ "BSFA Awards, 1993," *Locus* 32(5): 8, 66. May 1994.
___ Brown, Carroll. "The Flame in the Heart of the Wood: The Integration of Myth and Science in Robert Holdstock's **Mythago Wood**," *Extrapolation* 34(2): 158-172. Summer 1993.
___ Brown, Carroll. "SFC Interviews: Robert Holdstock," *Science Fiction Chronicle* 16(2): 5, 44-48. November/December 1994.
___ Cary, Catie. "Robert Holdstock: Interviewed," *Vector* No. 175: 3-6. October/November 1993.
___ Kincaid, Paul. "Touching the Earth: The Fiction of Robert Holdstock," *Vector* No. 175: 7-9. October/November 1993.
___ Melia, Sally-Ann. "Mythago-Mania: A Journey into Robert Holdstock's **Mythago Wood**," *Vector* No. 175: 10-11. October/November 1993.
___ Nicholls, Stan. "Robert Holdstock Plays With His Cerebral Cortex," in: Nicholls, Stan. **Wordsmiths of Wonder: Fifty Interviews with Writers of the Fantastic**. London: Orbit, 1993. pp.99-110.

HOLLAND
___ Poldervaart, Saskia. "Utopian Socialism in Holland Around 1900: Strategies and Gender," *Utopian Studies* 6(1): 51-64. 1995.
___ van Rossenberg, Rene. "Tolkien's Exceptional Visit to Holland: A Reconstruction," in: Reynolds, Patricia and GoodKnight, Glen H., eds. **Proceedings of the J. R. R. Tolkien Centenary Conference, Keble College, Oxford, 1992**. Altadena, CA: Mythopoeic Press, 1995. pp.301-309. (*Mythlore* Vol. 21, No. 2, Winter 1996, Whole No. 80)

HOLLAND, CECELIA
___ "British Author Accused of Copying," *Locus* 32(4): 8. April 1994.
___ "Orbit Withdraws William James Books," *Science Fiction Chronicle* 16(3): 4. January 1995.

HOLLAND, TOM
___ Eby, Douglas. "Tom Holland: Directing Stephen King," *Cinefantastique* 26(5): 52-53. August 1995.

HOLMBERG, E. L.
___ Risco, Antonio. "Los autómatas de Holmberg," *Mester* (UCLA) 19(2): 63-70. Fall 1990.

HOLMES, RON
___ "Holmes, Ron (Obituary)," *Science Fiction Chronicle* 15(3): 14. January 1994.

HOLOCAUST
___ Gomoll, Jeanne. "Out of Context: Post-Holocaust Themes in Feminist Science Fiction," *Janus* 6(2): 14-17. Winter 1980. (Whole No. 18)
___ Gordon, Joan. "Surviving the Survivor: Art Spiegelman's **Maus**," *Journal of the Fantastic in the Arts* 5(2): 80-89. 1993. (No. 18)
___ Kerman, Judith B. "Uses of the Fantastic in Literature of the Holocaust," *Journal of the Fantastic in the Arts* 5(2): 14-31. 1993. (No. 18)

HOOK (MOTION PICTURE) (continued)

___ Hunter, Stephen. "Spielberg's Revisonist Look at Peter Pan Isn't Enough *Hook* to Hang a New Movie On (Review)," *Baltimore (MD) Sun.* December 11, 1991. in: *NewsBank. Film and Television.* 3:F7. 1992.

___ Jacobs, Tom. "*Hook* and the Child Within Spielberg (Review)," *Los Angeles (CA) Daily News.* December 11, 1991. in: *NewsBank. Film and Television.* 3:E12. 1992.

___ Johnson, Malcolm. "High-Flown *Hook* Oft Suffers for Spielberg's Excess (Review)," *Hartford (CT) Courant.* December 11, 1991. in: *NewsBank. Film and Television.* 3:F1. 1992.

___ Mahar, Ted. "A Heavy *Hook* (Review)," *Portland (OR) The Oregonian.* December 11, 1991. in: *NewsBank. ilm and Television.* 3:F12-13. 1992.

___ Pintarich, Paul. "Peter Pan Appeal Springs From Ultimate Escape," *Portland (OR) The Oregonian.* December 13, 1991. in: *NewsBank. Film and Television.* 3:E11. 1992.

___ Ringel, Eleanor. "*Hook*, Line and Stinker (Review)," *Atlanta (GA) Journal.* December 11, 1991. in: *NewsBank. Film and Television.* 3:F2-F3. 1992.

___ Rosenfeld, Megan. "Spielberg in Neverland: Where the Movies Cost Millions and the Moguls Never Grow Up," *Washington (DC) Post.* December 15, 1991. in: *NewsBank. Film and Television.* 7:B13-C3. 1992. also in: *NewsBank. Names in the News* 8:B9. 1992.

___ Shapiro, Marc. "World Builder," *Starlog* No. 175: 66-69, 85. February 1992.

___ Spelling, Ian. "Hook's Mate," *Starlog* No. 174: 38-42, 72. January 1992.

___ Sragow, Michael. "*Hook*, Whine and Sinker (Review)," *San Francisco (CA) Examiner.* December 11, 1991. in: *NewsBank. Film and Television.* 3:E13-E14. 1992.

___ Stark, Susan. "*Hook*'s Delightful Magic Forgives a Pushy Message (Review)," *Detroit (MI) News.* December 11, 1991. in: *NewsBank. Film and Television.* 3:F9-F10. 1992.

___ Stephens, Lynne. "Designing *Hook*," *Starlog* No. 175: 61-65, 85. February 1992.

___ Strauss, Bob. "*Hook* Stays Afloat at No. 1, But Being Scuttled By Slow Sales," *Los Angeles (CA) Daily News.* December 24, 1991. in: *NewsBank. Film and Television.* 3:E8. 1992.

___ Strauss, Bob. "Peter Pan Takes a Flying Leap: Spielberg Indulges His Love of Flight In New Film," *Los Angeles (CA) Daily News.* December 8, 1991. in: *NewsBank. Film and Television.* 3:E3. 1992.

___ Strauss, Bob. "Spielberg Panning for Gold in *Hook*," *Los Angeles (CA) Daily News.* December 8, 1991. in: *NewsBank. Film and Television.* 3:E4-E7. 1992.

___ Vaz, Mark C. "Return to Neverland," *Cinefex* No. 49: 4-23. February 1992.

___ Verniere, James. "*Hook* Should Get the Hook in Neverland Reunion (Review)," *Boston (MA) Herald.* December 11, 1991. in: *NewsBank. Film and Television.* 3:F8. 1992.

___ Verniere, James. "Spielberg Hopes to Recapture Magic Touch," *Boston (MA) Herald.* December 13, 1991. in: *NewsBank. Film and Television.* 7:B12. 1992.

___ Verniere, James. "Who Took the Wonder out of the Wunderkind," *Boston (MA) Herald.* December 15, 1991. in: *NewsBank. Film and Television.* 7:C7-C8. 1992.

HOOVER, H. M.

___ Dunn, Thom. "Growing Home: The Triumph of Youth in the Novels of H. M. Hoover," by Thom Dunn and Karl Hiller. in: Sullivan, C. W., III. **Science Fiction for Young Readers.** Westport, CT: Greenwood, 1993. pp.121-131.

HOPKINS, ANTHONY

___ Pirani, Adam. "An Actor's Life," *Starlog* No. 176: 25-29, 68. March 1992.

HOPKINS, PAULINE

___ Gruesser, John. "Pauline Hopkin's **Of One Blood**: Creating an Afrocentric Fantasy for a Black Middle Class Audience," in: Latham, Robert A. and Collins, Robert A., eds. **Modes of the Fantastic.** Westport, CT: Greenwood, 1995. pp.74-83.

HOPPENSTAND, GARY

___ Davis, Jonathan. **Stephen King's America.** Mercer Island, WA: Starmont House, 1992.

HORROR GENRE

___ "Bloody Good Times Just Around the Coroner," *New York (NY) Daily News.* January 24, 1993. in: *NewsBank. Film and Television.* 14:E12. 1993.

___ "A Creed for the Future," *Science Fiction Chronicle* 15(10): 4-5. September 1994.

___ "Dell Abyss, Zebra Books Still Horror Publishers," *Science Fiction Chronicle* 15(10): 4. September 1994.

___ "Fear 'Stalk & Slash' Horror Saturation," *Variety* p. 7, 36. May 26, 1982.

___ "German Encyclopedia of Horror to Appear," *Locus* 33(6): 9, 79. December 1994.

___ "Hammer Ends Longtime Taboo--Mates Sex to Its **Crescendo** Horror Pic," *Variety* p. 1, 92. May 6, 1970.

___ "High Cost of Horror," *Variety* p. 35. January 9, 1985.

___ "Horror With Some Sexy Scenes Seen Cashable by Omen-Reading Mishkin," *Variety* p. 7. December 10, 1969.

___ "HWA's Bram Stoker Award Nominations," *Science Fiction Chronicle* 14(9): 4. June 1993.

___ "Incredible Shrinking Horror Market: Hi-Cost Scarepix Hurt; Output Down," *Variety* p. 7, 24. February 16, 1983.

___ "Movie Nightmares," *Sight and Sound* 3(5): 30-39. May 1993.

___ "Others Take Porno; Kirt Staying With Low-Cost Screams," *Variety* p. 6. July 22, 1970.

___ "Strange Matter Gets Goosebumps," *Locus* 35(3): 9. September 1993.

___ "Terror Master: Joe Dante," *Sight and Sound* 3(6): 7-9. June 1993.

___ "Young Adult Horror Bright Spot in Market," *Locus* 31(3): 7, 83. September 1993.

___ "Zebra Drops Pinnacle Horror Titles," *Locus* 31(6): 6. December 1993.

___ Arnzen, Michael A. "Who's Laughing Now? The Postmodern Splatter Film," *Journal of Popular Film and Television* 21(4): 176-814. Winter 1993.

___ Ashley, Mike. "Blood Brothers: The Supernatural Fiction of A. C., R. H., and E. F. Benson," in: Schweitzer, Darrell, ed. **Discovering Classic Horror Fiction I.** Mercer Island, WA: Starmont, 1992. pp.100-113.

___ Ashley, Mike. "Oliver Onions: The Man at the Edge," in: Schweitzer, Darrell, ed. **Discovering Classic Horror Fiction I.** Mercer Island, WA: Starmont, 1992. pp.120-126.

___ Ashley, Mike. **The Supernatural Index: A Listing of Fantasy, Supernatural, Weird, and Horror Anthologies.** Westport, CT: Greenwood Press, 1995. 952pp.

___ Atkins, Peter. "Other Shelves, Other Shadows: A Conversation With Clive Barker," in: Golden, Christopher, ed. **Cut! Horror Writers on Horror Film.** New York: Berkley, 1992. pp.11-24.

___ Badley, Linda. **Film, Horror, and the Body Fantastic.** Westport, CT: Greenwood, 1995. 199pp.

___ Bansak, Edmund G. **Fearing the Dark: The Val Lewton Career.** Jefferson, NC: McFarland, 1995. 571pp.

___ Barker, Clive. "At the Threshold: Some Thoughts on the Razorline Imprint," *Comics Buyer's Guide* No. 1024: 26-28, 32, 40. July 2, 1993.

___ Baumbold, Julie. "A Graveyard Smash," *Esquire* 123(1): 120, 118. January 1995.

___ Beeler, Michael. "Clive Barker: Horror Visionary," *Cinefantastique* 26(3): 16-31. April 1995.

___ Beeler, Michael. "Clive Barker Producing Horror in Hollywood," *Cinefantastique* 26(3): 28-29. April 1995.

___ Beeler, Michael. "Clive Barker: Surrealist Artist," *Cinefantastique* 26(3): 18. April 1995.

___ Beeler, Michael. "Clive Barker: The Thief of Always," *Cinefantastique* 26(3): 20-21. April 1995.

___ Berkenkamp, Lauri. "Reading, Writing and Interpreting: Stephen King's **Misery**," in: Magistrale, Tony, ed. **The Dark Descent: Essays Defining Stephen King's Horrorscape.** Westport, CT: Greenwood, 1992. pp.203-211.

___ Bianco, Robert. "A Good Night for Good Fright," *Boston (MA) Herald.* October 30, 1993. in: *NewsBank. Film and Television,* 123:A6. 1993.

___ Biddle, Arthur W. "The Mythic Journey in 'The Body'," in: Magistrale, Tony, ed. **The Dark Descent: Essays Defining Stephen King's Horrorscape.** Westport, CT: Greenwood, 1992. pp.83-97.

___ Bishop, Michael. "Children Who Survive: An Autobiographical Meditation on Horror Fiction," *Quantum* No. 41: 5-8. Winter/Spring 1992.

HORROR GENRE

HORROR GENRE (continued)

___ Bissette, Stephen R. "Higher Ground: Moral Transgressions, Tanscendent Fantasies," in: Golden, Christopher, ed. **Cut! Horror Writers on Horror Film.** New York: Berkley, 1992. pp.25-56.

___ Bloom, Harold, ed. **Classic Horror Writers.** New York: Chelsea House, 1994. 180pp.

___ Bloom, Harold, ed. **Modern Horror Writers.** New York: Chelsea House, 1995. 185pp.

___ Bosky, Bernadette L. "Playing the Heavy: Weight, Appetite, and Embodiment in Three Novels by Stephen King," in: Magistrale, Tony, ed. **The Dark Descent: Essays Defining Stephen King's Horrorscape.** Westport, CT: Greenwood, 1992. pp.137-156.

___ Brandner, Gary. "No, But I Saw the Movie," in: Golden, Christopher, ed. **Cut! Horror Writers on Horror Film.** New York: Berkley, 1992. pp.57-66.

___ Campbell, Patty. "The Sand in the Oyster," *Horn Book* 70(2): 234-238. March/April 1994.

___ Campbell, Ramsey. "The Quality of Terror," in: Golden, Christopher, ed. **Cut! Horror Writers on Horror Film.** New York: Berkley, 1992. pp.67-74.

___ Casebeer, Edwin F. "The Three Genres of The Stand," in: Magistrale, Tony, ed. **The Dark Descent: Essays Defining Stephen King's Horrorscape.** Westport, CT: Greenwood, 1992. pp.47-59.

___ Cerasini, Marc A. **How to Write Horror and Get It Published.** Brooklyn Heights, NY: Romantic Times, 1989. 210pp.

___ Christophersen, Bill. **The Apparition in the Glass: Charles Brockden Brown's American Gothic.** Athens: University of Georgia Press, 1994. 208pp.

___ Citro, Joseph A. "Foreword: *The King and I*," in: Magistrale, Tony, ed. **The Dark Descent: Essays Defining Stephen King's Horrorscape.** Westport, CT: Greenwood, 1992. pp.xi-xiv.

___ Clover, Carol J. **Men, Women, and Chain Saws: Gender in the Modern Horror Film.** Princeton, NJ: Princeton University Press, 1992. 260pp.

___ Cohn, Lawrence. "Filmers Resort to Old Scare Tactics: Horror Film Resurgence Boosted by Video," *Variety* p. 1, 24. June 8, 1988.

___ Cohn, Lawrence. "Horrid Year for Horror Pix at B. O.," *Variety* p. 3, 36. January 25, 1984.

___ Collins, Michael J. "The Body in the Work of the Body: Physio-Textuality in Contemporary Horror," *Journal of the Fantastic in the Arts* 5(3): 28-35. 1993. (No. 19)

___ Collins, Nancy A. "The Place of Dreams," in: Golden, Christopher, ed. **Cut! Horror Writers on Horror Film.** New York: Berkley, 1992. pp.75-82.

___ Crane, Jonathan L. **Terror and Everyday Life: A History of Horror.** Ph.D. Dissertation, University of Illinois at Urbana-Champaign, 1991. 297pp.

___ Crane, Jonathan L. **Terror and Everyday Life: Singular Moments in the History of the Horror Film.** Thousand Oaks, CA: Sage, 1994. 183pp.

___ Crawford, Gary W. "The Landscape of Sin: The Ghost Stories of J. Sheridan LeFanu," in: Schweitzer, Darrell, ed. **Discovering Classic Horror Fiction I.** Mercer Island, WA: Starmont, 1992. pp.74-99.

___ Crawford, Gary W. "Over the Edge: The Ghost Stories of Walter de la Mare," in: Schweitzer, Darrell, ed. **Discovering Classic Horror Fiction I.** Mercer Island, WA: Starmont, 1992. pp.53-57.

___ Cummiskey, Gary. **The Changing Face of Horror: A Study of the Nineteenth Century French Fantastic Short Story.** New York: Peter Lang, 1992. 170pp.

___ Curran, Ronald T. "Complex, Archetype, and Primal Fear: King's Use of Fairy Tales in The Shining," in: Magistrale, Tony, ed. **The Dark Descent: Essays Defining Stephen King's Horrorscape.** Westport, CT: Greenwood, 1992. pp.33-46.

___ Deist, Thomas. "Laßt die Puppen tanzen! Eine möglicher neuer Impuls im Horror-Genre und seine Geschichte," *Science Fiction Times* (Germany) 34(1): 12-16. January 1992.

___ Del Vecchio, Deborah. **Peter Cushing: The Gentle Man of Horror and His 91 Films,** by Deborah Del Vecchio and Tom Johnson. Jefferson, NC: McFarland, 1992. 496pp.

___ Dickerson, Mary J. "Stephen King Reading William Faulkner: Memory, Desire, and Time in the Making of IT," in: Magistrale, Tony, ed. **The Dark Descent: Essays Defining Stephen King's Horrorscape.** Westport, CT: Greenwood, 1992. pp.171-186.

___ Dobbs, G. Michael. "Stanley Wiater: A Conversation with the Interviewer," in: Wiater, Stanley. **Dark Visions: Conversations with the Masters of the Horror Film.** New York: Avon, 1992. pp.1-7.

HORROR GENRE (continued)

___ Doty, Gene. "A Clockwork Evil: Guilt and Coincidence in 'The Monkey'," in: Magistrale, Tony, ed. **The Dark Descent: Essays Defining Stephen King's Horrorscape.** Westport, CT: Greenwood, 1992. pp.129-136.

___ Druse, Judy. "Easy Talking: Horror," *Voice of Youth Advocates* 16(1): 11-15, 21. April 1993.

___ Dumars, Denise. "Writer-Director Clive Barker on Launching Harry D'Amour as a Horror Hero Franchise," *Cinefantastique* 27(3): 55-56. December 1995.

___ Evans, Walter. "Monster Movies and Rites of Initiation," *Journal of Popular Film and Television* 4(2): 124-142. 1975.

___ Farris, John. "A User's Guide to Hollywood Horror (As Told to Kelley Wilde)," in: Golden, Christopher, ed. **Cut! Horror Writers on Horror Film.** New York: Berkley, 1992. pp.83-90.

___ Flynn, John L. **Cinematic Vampires: The Living Dead on Film and Televison, From** *The Devil's Castle* **(1896) to** *Bram Stoker's Dracula* **(1992).** Jefferson, NC: McFarland, 1992. 328pp.

___ Gardner, Craig S. "Blood and Laughter: The Humor in Horror Film," in: Golden, Christopher, ed. **Cut! Horror Writers on Horror Film.** New York: Berkley, 1992. pp.91-100.

___ Garton, Ray. "On Kids and *Cat People*," in: Golden, Christopher, ed. **Cut! Horror Writers on Horror Film.** New York: Berkley, 1992. pp.101-112.

___ Geary, Robert F. "The Exorcist: Deep Horror?," *Journal of the Fantastic in the Arts* 5(4): 55-63. 1993. (No. 20)

___ Geary, Robert F. **The Supernatural in Gothic Fiction: Horror, Belief and Literary Change.** Lewiston, NY: Mellen, 1992. 151pp.

___ Golden, Christopher. "Introduction: First Cut," in: Golden, Christopher, ed. **Cut! Horror Writers on Horror Film.** New York: Berkley, 1992. pp.1-9.

___ Golden, Christopher, ed. **Cut! Horror Writers on Horror Film.** New York: Berkley, 1992. 297pp.

___ Gorman, Ed. "Several Hundred Words About Wes Craven," in: Golden, Christopher, ed. **Cut! Horror Writers on Horror Film.** New York: Berkley, 1992. pp.113-116.

___ Graff, Bennett. **Horror in Evolution: Determinism, Materialism, and Darwinism in the American Gothic (Edgar Allan Poe, Frank Norris, Jack London, H. P. Lovecraft).** Ph.D. Dissertation, City University of New York, 1995. 282pp. (DAI-A 56/05, p. 1777. November 1995.)

___ Grant, Barry K. "Taking Back *The Night of the Living Dead*: George Romero, Feminism and the Horror Film," *Wide Angle* 14(1): 64-77. January 1992.

___ Grant, Charles L. "Black and White, in Color," in: Golden, Christopher, ed. **Cut! Horror Writers on Horror Film.** New York: Berkley, 1992. pp.117-122.

___ Guttmacher, Peter. **Legendary Horror Films: Essential Genre History; Offscreen Anecdotes; Special Effects Secrets; Ghoulish Facts and Photographs.** New York: Metro Books, 1995. 128pp.

___ Hall, Mia M. "Love Kills: Another Look at *Fatal Attraction*," in: Golden, Christopher, ed. **Cut! Horror Writers on Horror Film.** New York: Berkley, 1992. pp.123-130.

___ Hanke, Ken. **A Critical Guide to Horror Film Series.** New York: Garland, 1991. 341pp.

___ Hanke, Ken. "Tod Slaughter: Demon Barber of Great Britain," *Filmfax* No. 45: 31-35, 98. June/July 1994.

___ Hanson, Philip. "Horror and Ethnic Identity in 'The Jewbird'," *Studies in Short Fiction* 30(3): 359-366. Summer 1993.

___ Hardy, Phil, ed. **The Overlook Film Encyclopedia: Horror.** Second edition. Woodstock, NY: Overlook, 1994. 496pp.

___ Hartwell, David G. "Introduction," in: Hartwell, David G., ed. **The Dark Descent.** New York: Tor, 1987. pp.1-11.

___ Hatcher, Lint. "Monster Fan 2000," by Lint Hatcher and Rod Bennett. *Wonder* No. 7: 39-43, 54-56. 1993.

___ Hohne, Karen A. "The Voice of Cthulhu: Language Interaction in Contemporary Horror Fiction," in: Slusser, George E. and Rabkin, Eric S., eds. **Styles of Creation: Aesthetic Technique and the Creation of Fictional Worlds.** Athens: University of Georgia Press, 1992. pp.79-87.

___ Holder, Nancy. "Why *The Haunting* Is So Damn Scary," in: Golden, Christopher, ed. **Cut! Horror Writers on Horror Film.** New York: Berkley, 1992. pp.131-140.

___ Horne, Philip. "I Shopped With a Zombie," *Critical Quarterly* 34(4): 97-110. Winter 1992.

___ Iaccino, James F. **Psychological Reflections on Cinematic Terror: Jungian Archetypes in Horror Films.** Westport, CT: Praeger, 1994. 217pp.

HORROR GENRE (continued)

___ Indick, Ben P. "H. Russell Wakefield: The Man Who Believed in Ghosts," in: Schweitzer, Darrell, ed. **Discovering Classic Horror Fiction I**. Mercer Island, WA: Starmont, 1992. pp.73-93.

___ James, Caryn. "Old Hollywood Horror, But With Depth and Flair," *New York Times* Sec. C, p. 3. July 2, 1993.

___ Jancovich, Mark. **Horror**. London: Batsford, 1992. 128pp.

___ Jones, Alan. "The Return of Hammer's Horror," *Cinefantastique* 24(6)/25(1): 4-5, 125. February 1994.

___ Jones, Stephen, ed. **Horror: 100 Best Books**. Revised and updated edition, ed. by Stephen Jones and Kim Newman. London: Hodder/New English Library, 1992. 368pp.

___ Joshi, S. T. "Arthur Machen: Philosophy and Fiction," in: Schweitzer, Darrell, ed. **Discovering Classic Horror Fiction I**. Mercer Island, WA: Starmont, 1992. pp.1-33.

___ Keesey, Douglas. " 'The Face of Mr. Flip': Homophobia in the Horror of Stephen King," in: Magistrale, Tony, ed. **The Dark Descent: Essays Defining Stephen King's Horrorscape**. Westport, CT: Greenwood, 1992. pp.187-201.

___ Kermode, Mark. "Ghoul School: The Horror Genre," *Sight and Sound* 3(6): 10-12. June 1993.

___ Kies, Cosette. "Eeek! They Just Keep Coming! YA Horror Series," *Voice of Youth Advocates* 17(1): 17-19. April 1994.

___ Kies, Cosette. "The Humor in Horror," *Voice of Youth Advocates* 18(3): 143-144. August 1995.

___ Kies, Cosette. **Presenting Young Adult Horror Fiction**. New York: Twayne, 1991. 203pp.

___ Killheffer, Robert K. J. "Rising From the Grave: Horror," *Publishers Weekly* 240(38): 43-47. September 20, 1993.

___ Kinnard, Roy. **Horror in the Silent Films: A Filmography, 1896-1929**. Jefferson, NC: McFarland, 1995. 256pp.

___ Koontz, Dean R. "A Genre in Crisis," in: Greenberg, Martin H., Ed Gorman and Bill Munster, eds. **The Dean Koontz Companion**. New York: Berkley, 1994. pp.206-215.

___ Lansdale, Joe R. "A Hard-On for Horror: Low-Budget Excitement," in: Golden, Christopher, ed. **Cut! Horror Writers on Horror Film**. New York: Berkley, 1992. pp.141-150.

___ Latham, Rod. "Inside Outside: Horror in SF Novels, 1960 to the Present," *Scream Factory: The Magazine of Horrors Past, Present and Future* 13: 20-27. Spring 1994.

___ Linaweaver, Brad. "The Monster God of Dreams," *Riverside Quarterly* 9(3): 164-173. June 1995. (Whole No. 35)

___ Lloyd, Ann. **The Films of Stephen King**. New York: St. Martin's, 1993. 96pp.

___ Lovecraft, H. P. **Supernatural Horror in Literature**. Chislehurst, Kent, Eng.: Gothic Society, 1994. 32pp.

___ Maass, Donald. "Is Horror Dead, or Just Resting?," *Science Fiction Chronicle* 13(6): 25-26. March 1992.

___ MacCulloch, Simon. "The Dead Line: Horror and Tragedy," *Studies in Weird Fiction* No. 10: 26-31. Fall 1991.

___ Magistrale, Tony. "Defining Stephen King's Horrorscape: An Introduction," in: Magistrale, Tony, ed. **The Dark Descent: Essays Defining Stephen King's Horrorscape**. Westport, CT: Greenwood, 1992. pp.1-4.

___ Magistrale, Tony. "Science, Politics, and the Epic Imagination: **The Talisman**," in: Magistrale, Tony, ed. **The Dark Descent: Essays Defining Stephen King's Horrorscape**. Westport, CT: Greenwood, 1992. pp.113-127.

___ Magistrale, Tony, ed. **The Dark Descent: Essays Defining Stephen King's Horrorscape**. Westport, CT: Greenwood, 1992. 227pp.

___ Mank, Gregory W. **Hollywood Cauldron: Thirteen Horror Films From the Genre's Golden Age**. Jefferson, NC: McFarland, 1993. 384pp.

___ Massé, Michelle A. **In the Name of Love: Women, Masochism and the Gothic**. Ithaca, NY: Cornell University Press, 1992. 301pp.

___ Masterson, Graham. "Why Horror?," *Writer* 107(7): 7-9. July 1994.

___ McCarty, John. **John McCarty's Official Splatter Movie Guide, Vol. II**. New York: St. Martin's, 1992. 199pp.

___ McCarty, John. **Movie Psychos and Madmen: Film Psychopaths From Jekyll and Hyde to Hannibal Lecter**. Secaucus, NJ: Carol, 1993. 255pp.

___ McCarty, John. **Psychos: Eighty Years of Mad Movies, Maniacs, and Murderous Deeds**. New York: St. Martin's, 1986. 211pp.

___ McDonald, T. Liam. "The Horrors of Hammer: The House That Blood Built," in: Golden, Christopher, ed. **Cut! Horror Writers on Horror Film**. New York: Berkley, 1992. pp.151-160.

HORROR GENRE (continued)

___ Monteleone, Thomas F. "A Double Feature and a Cartoon for 35 Cents," in: Golden, Christopher, ed. **Cut! Horror Writers on Horror Film**. New York: Berkley, 1992. pp.161-170.

___ Morrison, Michael A. "After the Danse: Horror at the End of the Century," *New York Review of Science Fiction* No. 79: 1, 8-14. March 1995.

___ Morrison, Michael A. "Horror at the End of the Century: A Reading List," *New York Review of Science Fiction* No. 79: 10-12. March 1995.

___ Moskowitz, Sam. "W. C. Morrow: Forgotten Master of Horror; First Phase," in: Schweitzer, Darrell, ed. **Discovering Classic Horror Fiction I**. Mercer Island, WA: Starmont, 1992. pp.127-173.

___ Murphy, Brian. "Monster Movies: They Came From Beneath the Fifties," *Journal of Popular Film and Television* 1(1): 31-44. 1972.

___ Mustazza, Leonard. "Fear and Pity: Tragic Horror in King's **Pet Sematary**," in: Magistrale, Tony, ed. **The Dark Descent: Essays Defining Stephen King's Horrorscape**. Westport, CT: Greenwood, 1992. pp.73-82.

___ Navarette, Susan J. "The Soul of the Plot: The Aesthetics of Fin de Siècle Literature of Horror," in: Slusser, George E. and Rabkin, Eric S., eds. **Styles of Creation: Aesthetic Technique and the Creation of Fictional Worlds**. Athens: University of Georgia Press, 1992. pp.88-115.

___ Nottridge, Rhoda. **Horror Films**. New York: Crestwood House, 1991. 32pp.

___ Nutman, Philip. "The Exploding Family," in: Golden, Christopher, ed. **Cut! Horror Writers on Horror Film**. New York: Berkley, 1992. pp.171-182.

___ Oates, Joyce C. "Reflections on the Grotesque," *New York Review of Science Fiction* No. 66: 1, 3-5. February 1994.

___ Pharr, Mary. "Partners in the Danse: Women in Stephen King's Fiction," in: Magistrale, Tony, ed. **The Dark Descent: Essays Defining Stephen King's Horrorscape**. Westport, CT: Greenwood, 1992. pp.19-32.

___ Pierce, Dale. "Horror With a Spanish Twist: Paul Naschy," *Filmfax* No. 33: 68-71, 98. June/July 1992.

___ Proulx, Kevin. **Fear to the World: Eleven Voices in a Chorus of Horror**. Mercer Island, WA: Starmont, 1992. 243pp.

___ Ptacek, Kathryn. "You Are What You Eat/Watch: Cannibalism in Movies," in: Golden, Christopher, ed. **Cut! Horror Writers on Horror Film**. New York: Berkley, 1992. pp.183-188.

___ Radice, Sophie. "A Horror Story at Bedtime," *Guardian* p. G2, G8. January 4, 1994. [Not seen.]

___ Ramsland, Katherine. "*Angel Heart*: The Journey to Self as the Ultimate Horror," in: Golden, Christopher, ed. **Cut! Horror Writers on Horror Film**. New York: Berkley, 1992. pp.189-198.

___ Reesman, Jeanne C. "Riddle Game: Stephen King's Metafictive Dialogue," in: Magistrale, Tony, ed. **The Dark Descent: Essays Defining Stephen King's Horrorscape**. Westport, CT: Greenwood, 1992. pp.157-170.

___ Rice, Anne. "The Art of Horror in Film (As Told to Katherine Ramsland)," in: Golden, Christopher, ed. **Cut! Horror Writers on Horror Film**. New York: Berkley, 1992. pp.199-210.

___ Roberts, Jack. "Voices of Terror," *Filmfax* No. 45: 36-45, 96-97. June/July 1994.

___ Rule, Patty. "Monsters Take over TNT Saturdays," *USA Today* Sec. D, p. 3. June 4, 1993.

___ Russo, John. **Scare Tactics: The Art, Craft, and Trade Secrets of Writing, Producing, and Directing Chillers and Thrillers**. New York: Dell, 1992. 241pp.

___ Ruthner, Clemens. "Phänomenologie des Schreckens," by Clemens Ruthner and Michael Koseler. *Quarber Merkur* 33(2): 30-34. December 1995. (No. 84)

___ Salmonson, Jessica A. "A True Tale of Horror: Striving to Break the Rules of the Genre Game," *Quantum* No. 42: 13-14. Summer/Fall 1992.

___ Sammon, Paul M. "The Salacious Gaze: Sex, the Erotic Trilogy and the Decline of David Lynch," in: Golden, Christopher, ed. **Cut! Horror Writers on Horror Film**. New York: Berkley, 1992. pp.211-236.

___ Sanjek, David. "The Hysterical Imagination: The Horror Films of Oliver Stone," *Post Script* 12(1): 47-60. Fall 1992.

___ Sarracino, Carmine. "Natural Law and the Monster," *Connecticut Review* 15(1): 23-32. Spring 1993.

___ Schaeffer, Stephen. "Hollywood Goes to Hell," *Boston (MA) Herald*. August 29, 1993. in: *NewsBank. Film and Television*. 104:F1-F2. 1993.

HORROR GENRE (continued)
___ Winter, Douglas E. "Opera of Violence: The Films of Dario Argento," in: Golden, Christopher, ed. **Cut! Horror Writers on Horror Film**. New York: Berkley, 1992. pp.267-288.
___ Winter, Douglas E. "Shadowings: By Any Other Name," *Worlds of Fantasy and Horror* 1(1): 10-14. Summer 1994. (No. 1)
___ Wolstenholme, Susan. **Gothic (Re) Visions: Writing Women as Readers**. Albany: State University of New York Press, 1993. 201pp.
___ Wood, Martine. **The Work of Gary Brandner: An Annotated Bibliography and Guide**. San Bernardino, CA: Borgo Press, 1995. 112pp.
___ Wood, Robin. "Cat and Dog: Lewis Teague's Stephen King Movies," in: Irons, Glenwood, ed. **Gender, Language and Myth: Essays on Popular Narrative**. Toronto: University of Toronto Press, 1992. pp.303-318.
___ Yarbro, Chelsea Q. "On *Freaks*," in: Golden, Christopher, ed. **Cut! Horror Writers on Horror Film**. New York: Berkley, 1992. pp.289-298.
___ Zancanella, Don. "The Horror, the Horror," *English Journal* 83(2): 9-11. February 1994.

HORROR (MAGAZINE)
___ "*Horror* Newsmagazine Dead," *Science Fiction Chronicle* 17(2): 58. December 1995/January 1996.
___ "New Horror, SF Magazines Due," *Science Fiction Chronicle* 14(10): 6. July 1993.

HORROR WRITERS ASSOCIATION
___ "HWA Annual Meeting," *Locus* 32(1): 6. January 1994.
___ "HWA Changes," *Locus* 31(4): 6. October 1993.

HORROR WRITERS OF AMERICA
___ "Gahan Wilson to Be Honored at HWA's Bram Stoker Awards," *Science Fiction Chronicle* 13(8): 4-5. May 1992.
___ "Groundswell for Change in HWA," *Science Fiction Chronicle* 15(9): 5-6. August 1994.
___ "HWA Annual Meeting and Stoker Awards Banquet," *Science Fiction Chronicle* 16(9): 4145 August/September 1995.
___ "HWA Changes," *Locus* 31(4): 6. October 1993.
___ "HWA Election," *Locus* 33(6): 8, 79. December 1994.
___ "HWA Stoker Awards," *Locus* 35(1): 9. July 1995.
___ "HWA Stoker Awards Winners," *Locus* 31(2): 6, 62. August 1993.
___ Jones, Stephen. "1992 Horror Writers of America Meeting," by Stephen Jones and Jo Fletcher. *Science Fiction Chronicle* 13(11/12): 34-38. August 1992.
___ Willems, S. F. "Lawrence Watt-Evans Discusses HWA," *Genre Writer's News* 1(7): 11-14. May/June 1995.

HOUSE IV (MOTION PICTURE)
___ Biodrowski, Steve. "*House IV* (Review)," *Cinefantastique* 22(6): 54-55. June 1992

HOWARD THE DUCK (MOTION PICTURE)
___ "*Howard the Duck* (1986): Steve Gerber and Gloria Katz," in: Goldberg, Lee, ed. **The Dreamweavers: Interviews With Fantasy Filmmakers of the 1980s**. Jefferson, NC: McFarland, 1995. pp.150-163.

HOWARD, ROBERT E.
___ "Conan in the Courts," *Locus* 34(5): 9, 75. May 1995.
___ " 'Conan' Rights Holders Sue Mail Order House Over Sale of Posters," *Variety* p. 22. November 28, 1984.
___ "The Robert E. Howard Home," *The Dark Man: The Journal of Robert E. Howard Studies* No. 2: 40. July 1991.
___ "Robert E. Howard Winner of Essay Medal While in High School," *The Dark Man: The Journal of Robert E. Howard Studies* No. 3: 17-21. April 1993.
___ Biffle, Kent. "Canonizing the Creator of Conan," *Dallas Morning News* p. 41A, 43A. June 21, 1992.
___ Bloom, Harold. "Robert E. Howard," in: Bloom, Harold, ed. **Modern Fantasy Writers**. New York: Chelsea House, 1995. pp.57-70.
___ Blosser, Fred. "From Cross Plains to the Stars: Robert E. Howard's Science Fiction," *The Dark Man: The Journal of Robert E. Howard Studies* No. 3: 1-8. April 1993.
___ Burke, Rusty. "The Active Voice: Robert E. Howard's Personae," *The Dark Man: The Journal of Robert E. Howard Studies* No. 3: 22-26. April 1993.

HOWARD, ROBERT E. (continued)
___ Burke, Rusty. "The Old Deserted House: Images of the South in Howard's Fiction," *The Dark Man: The Journal of Robert E. Howard Studies* No. 2: 13-22. July 1991.
___ Cerasini, Marc A. " 'Come Back to Valusia Ag'in, Kull Honey!': Robert E. Howard and Mainstream American Literature," *The Dark Man: The Journal of Robert E. Howard Studies* No. 2: 22-23. July 1991.
___ Herron, Don. On Howardian Fairyland. *The Dark Man: The Journal of Robert E. Howard Studies* No. 2: 24. July 1991.
___ Hoffman, Charles. "Cosmic Filth: Howard's View of Evil," *The Dark Man: The Journal of Robert E. Howard Studies* No. 3: 9-16. April 1993.
___ Howard, Robert E. "Bill Smalley and the Power of the Human Eye," *The Dark Man: The Journal of Robert E. Howard Studies* No. 2: 25-30. July 1991.
___ Kellar, Michael. "Solomon and Sorcery," *The Dark Man: The Journal of Robert E. Howard Studies* No. 2: 11-13. July 1991.
___ Lord, Glenn. "The Mystery Titles of Robert E. Howard," *Wayfarer II* pp.13-16. n.d.
___ Lovecraft, H. P. "In Memoriam: Robert Ervin Howard (1936)," in: Joshi, S. T., ed. **Miscellaneous Writings: H. P. Lovecraft**. Sauk City, WI: Arkham House, 1995. pp.123-126.
___ Reid, Thomas R. "Cultural Trends in Literature," *The Dark Man: The Journal of Robert E. Howard Studies* No. 2: 30-32. July 1991.
___ Spencer, Paul. "A Voice From the Past," *The Dark Man: The Journal of Robert E. Howard Studies* No. 2: 32-33. July 1991.
___ Trout, Steven R. "The Expurgated Solomon Kane," *The Dark Man: The Journal of Robert E. Howard Studies* No. 2: 33-37. July 1991.
___ Trout, Steven R. "The Horror Fiction of Robert E. Howard," *The Dark Man: The Journal of Robert E. Howard Studies* No. 2: 2-11. July 1991.

HOWARD, RON
___ Johnson, Kim H. "Mission Control," *Starlog* No. 217: 40-45, 66. August 1995.

HOWLING II (MOTION PICTURE)
___ "*Howling II* Shortcomings Push Mora to Try Harder on 3d Part," *Variety* p. 4, 22. August 20, 1986.

HOWLING III: THE MARSUPIALS (MOTION PICTURE)
___ "*Howling II* Shortcomings Push Mora to Try Harder on 3d Part," *Variety* p. 4, 22. August 20, 1986.

HOWLING (MOTION PICTURE)
___ Brandner, Gary. "No, But I Saw the Movie," in: Golden, Christopher, ed. **Cut! Horror Writers on Horror Film**. New York: Berkley, 1992. pp.57-66.

HOYT, JOHN
___ "Hoyt, John, 1904-1991 (Obituary)," *Starlog* No. 174: 22-23. January 1992.

HUBBARD, L. RON
___ Corydon, Bent. **L. Ron Hubbard: Messiah or Madman?**. (Revised, expanded and updated edition). Fort Lee, NJ: Barricade Books, 1992. 459pp.
___ Langford, David. "The Dragonhiker's Guide to Battlefield Covenant at Dune's Edge: Odyssey Two," *Australian Science Fiction Review* 5(3): 3-11. Spring 1990. (Whole No. 25)
___ Widder, William J. **The Fiction of L. Ron Hubbard: A Comprehensive Bibliography and Reference Guide to Published and Selected Unpublished Works**. Los Angeles, CA: Bridge Publications, 1994. 373pp.

HUDLIN, REGINALD
___ Cox, Dan. "Rewriting the Rules," *Variety* 361(4): 6. November 27, 1995.

HUDSON, ERNIE
___ Spelling, Ian. "Intimate Insider," *Starlog* No. 202: 32-36. May 1994.

HUDSUCKER PROXY (MOTION PICTURE)
___ Odien, W. C. "The Rise and Fall of Norville Barnes," *Cinefex* No. 58: 66-81. June 1994.
___ Persons, Dan. "*The Hudsucker Proxy* (Review)," *Cinefantastique* 25(4): 60. August 1994.

HUFF, TANYA

___ Shaver, Stephanie D. "Interview With Tanya Huff," *Marion Zimmer Bradley's Fantasy Magazine* No. 29: 42-45. Fall 1995.

HUGHES, MONICA

___ Hughes, Monica. "Science Fiction as Myth and Metaphor," *ALAN Review* 19(3): 2-5. Spring 1992.

___ Jones, Raymond E. "True Myth: Female Archetypes in Monica Hughes's **The Keeper of the Isis Light**," in: Sullivan, C. W., III. **Science Fiction for Young Readers**. Westport, CT: Greenwood, 1993. pp.169-178.

___ Wytenbroek, J. R. "The Debate Continues: Technology or Nature--A Study of Monica Hughes's Science Fiction Novels," in: Sullivan, C. W., III. **Science Fiction for Young Readers**. Westport, CT: Greenwood, 1993. pp.145-155.

HUGO AWARDS, 1992

___ "1992 Hugo Awards Nominations," *Locus* 28(6): 5. June 1992.

___ "1992 Hugo Awards Winners," *Locus* 29(4): 6, 42-47. October 1992.

___ "1993 Hugo Awards," *Science Fiction Chronicle* 15(1): 4. October 1993.

___ "Hugo Award Nomination Statistics," *Science Fiction Chronicle* 14(2): 5, 10-11. November 1992.

___ "Hugo Award Nominations," *Science Fiction Chronicle* 13(9): 4. June 1992.

___ "Hugo Award Nominations, 1992," *Science Fiction Chronicle* 14(8): 4. May 1993.

___ "World SF Convention Hugo Awards," *Science Fiction Chronicle* 14(1): 4. October 1992.

HUGO AWARDS, 1993

___ "1993 Hugo Awards Ceremony," *Locus* 31(4): 38-39. October 1993.

___ "1993 Hugo Awards Nominations," *Locus* 30(5): 7. May 1993.

___ "1993 Hugo Awards Winners," *Locus* 31(4): 5, 70. October 1993.

___ "1993 Hugo Nominations Ballot," *Locus* 30(2): 7. February 1993.

___ "Complete Hugo Voting, 1993," *Locus* 31(4): 36-37. October 1993.

___ "Hugo Award Nominations," *Science Fiction Chronicle* 15(7): 4. June 1994.

___ "Hugo Award Voting Statistics, 1993," *Science Fiction Chronicle* 15(1): 10-14, 33-34. October 1993.

___ Resnick, Mike. "The Hugo Awards," *Science Fiction Chronicle* 16(2): 50-51. November/December 1994.

HUGO AWARDS, 1994

___ "1994 Hugo Award," *Science Fiction Chronicle* 15(10): 5. September 1994.

___ "1994 Hugo Awards Nominating Ballots," *Locus* 32(3): 8. March 1994.

___ "1994 Hugo Awards Nominations," *Locus* 32(5): 7. May 1994.

___ "1994 Hugo Awards Winners," *Locus* 33(4): 7, 38-41. October 1994.

___ "Hugo Award Voting Statistics," *Science Fiction Chronicle* 16(1): 39-41. October 1994.

HUGO AWARDS, 1995

___ "1995 Hugo Awards Nominees," *Locus* 34(6): 7. June 1995.

___ "1995 Hugo Winners," *Locus* 35(3): 7. September 1993.

___ "Brits Dominate Hugo Awards," *Science Fiction Chronicle* 17(1): 5. October/November 1995

___ "Complete Hugo Voting, 1995," *Locus* 35(4): 38-40. October 1995.

___ "Hugo Award Nominations," *Science Fiction Chronicle* 16(6): 36. May 1995.

___ "Hugo Award Nominations," *Science Fiction Chronicle* 16(7): 4. June/July 1995.

___ "Hugo/Campbell Award Nominees and Voting," *Science Fiction Chronicle* 17(1): 17, 43-45. October/November 1995

___ "World Science Fiction Convention Hugo Awards, 1995," *Science Fiction Chronicle* 17(1): 5. October/November 1995

___ Brown, Charles N. "Hugo Awards Ceremony, 1995," *Locus* 35(4): 40-42. October 1995.

HUMANISM

___ Marsalek, Kenneth. " **Star Trek**: Humanism of the Future," *Free Inquiry* 12(4): 53-57. Fall 1992.

HUMOR

___ Di Filippo, Paul. "Plumage From Pegasus: Not the Encyclopedia of Science Fiction," *Magazine of Fantasy and Science Fiction* 87(3): 73-79. September 1994.

___ Friesner, Esther M. "There's Nothing Funny About Mixing Humor and SF," *Science Fiction Age* 4(1): 36-40. November 1995.

___ Gardner, Craig S. "Blood and Laughter: The Humor in Horror Film," in: Golden, Christopher, ed. **Cut! Horror Writers on Horror Film**. New York: Berkley, 1992. pp.91-100.

___ Kelleghan, Fiona. "Humor in Science Fiction," in: Wolf, Milton T. and Mallett, Daryl F., eds. **Imaginative Futures: Proceedings of the 1993 Science Fiction Research Association Conference**. San Bernardino, CA: Jacob's Ladder Books, 1995. pp.263-278.

___ Kies, Cosette. "The Humor in Horror," *Voice of Youth Advocates* 18(3): 143-144. August 1995.

___ Zaharoff, Howard. "The Four Rules of SF Humor," *Amazing Stories* 67(10): 60-61. January 1993.

HUNT: ALIEN VS. PREDATOR (MOTION PICTURE)

___ Jones, Alan. "**Alien vs. Predator**," *Cinefantastique* 25(4): 4-5. August 1994.

HUNT, ALAN

___ Phillips, Mark. "The Life of Riley," *Starlog* No. 196: 65-69, 79. November 1993.

HUNTED (MOTION PICTURE)

___ Biodrowski, Steve. "**The Hunted** (Review)," *Cinefantastique* 27(3): 52-53. December 1995.

HURD, GALE ANN

___ Lofficier, Randy. "**Aliens** (1986): Interview with James Cameron and Gale Ann Hurd," by Randy Lofficier and Jean-Marc Lofficier. in: Goldberg, Lee et al. **Science Fiction Filmmaking in the 1980s**. Jefferson, NC: McFarland, 1995. pp.7-23.

___ Shapiro, Marc. "Boss of the **Penal Colony**," *Starlog* No. 200: 48-51. March 1994.

___ Wiater, Stanley. "Hurd, Gale Ann," in: Wiater, Stanley. **Dark Visions: Conversations with the Masters of the Horror Film**. New York: Avon, 1992. pp.89-100.

HUTCHISON, DOUG

___ Vitaris, Paula. "**X-Files**: Serial Killer," *Cinefantastique* 26(6)/27(1): 53-54. October 1995.

HUTSON, SHAUN

___ Nicholls, Stan. "Shaun Hutson Doesn't Give a Toss," in: Nicholls, Stan. **Wordsmiths of Wonder: Fifty Interviews with Writers of the Fantastic**. London: Orbit, 1993. pp.454-461.

HUXLEY, ALDOUS

___ "Aldous Huxley," in: Bloom, Harold, ed. **Classic Science Fiction Writers**. New York: Chelsea House, 1995. pp.46-61.

___ Aldiss, Brian W. "Between Privy and Universe: Aldous Huxley (1894-1963)," *New York Review of Science Fiction* No. 74: 19-21. October 1994.

___ Aldiss, Brian W. "Between Privy and Universe: Aldous Huxley (1894-1963)," in: Aldiss, Brian W. **The Detached Retina: Aspects of SF and Fantasy**. Syracuse, NY: Syracuse University Press, 1995. pp.31-36.

___ Bertinetti, Roberto. **L'infondazione di Babele: l'antiutopia**. Milan: F. Angeli, 1983. 164pp.

___ Bhat, Yashoda. **Aldous Huxley and George Orwell: A Comparative Study of Satire in Their Novels**. New Delhi: Sterling, 1991. 172pp.

___ Booker, M. Keith. **The Dystopian Impulse in Modern Literature: Fiction as Social Criticism**. Westport, CT: Greenwood, 1994. 197pp.

___ Bradshaw, David. "A New Bibliography of Aldous Huxley's Work and Its Reception, 1912-1937," *Bulletin of Bibliography* 51(3): 237-256. September 1994.

___ Browning, William G. **Anti-Utopian Fiction: Definition and Standards for Evaluation**. Ph.D. Dissertation, Louisiana State University, 1966. 145pp.

___ Calcraft, L. G. A. "Aldous Huxley and the Sheldonian Hypothesis," *Annals of Science* 37657-671. 1980.

___ Clute, John. "Aldous Huxley," in: Clute, John. **Look at the Evidence: Essays and Reviews**. Liverpool: Liverpool University Press, 1995. pp.435-438.

HUXLEY, ALDOUS (continued)

___ Clute, John. "When the Wheel Stops," *New Statesman and Society* 6(283): 61-62. December 17, 1993.

___ Corrado, Adriana. **Da un'isola all'altra: il pensiero utopico nella narrativa inglese da Thomas More ad Aldous Huxley.** Napoli: Scientifiche Italiane, 1988. 189pp. [Not seen.]

___ Deery, June. "Technology and Gender in Aldous Huxley's Alternative (?) Worlds," *Extrapolation* 33(3): 258-273. Fall 1992.

___ Dunaway, David K. **Aldous Huxley Recollected: An Oral History.** New York: Carroll & Graf, 1995. 225pp.

___ Erzgräber, Willi. "Aldous Huxley: **Brave New World** (1932)," in: Heuermann, Hartmut and Lange, Bernd-Peter, eds. **Die Utopie in der angloamerikanischen Literatur: Interpretationen.** Düsseldorf: Bagel, 1984. pp.196-218.

___ Guardamagna, Daniela. **La Narrativa di Aldous Huxley.** Bari: Adriatica Editrice, 1989. 252pp. [Not seen.]

___ Jehmlich, Reimer. "Aldous Huxley, **Ape and Essence** (1948)," in: Heuermann, Hartmut, ed. **Der Science Fiction Roman in der angloamerikanischen Literatur: Interpretationen.** Düsseldorf: Bagel, 1986. pp.101-117.

___ Kranz, Gisbert. "Aldous Huxley und C. S. Lewis: Eine vergleichende Studie," in: Kranz, Gisbert, ed. **Inklings: Jahrbuch für Literatur und Ästhetik.** 2. Band. [Lüdenscheid, Germany: Stier], 1984. pp.112-153.

___ Mason, Michael. "A Clearing of Vision: 1843-1962. The Evolution of the Utopian Ideal in Carlyle, Shaw and Huxley," in: Saccaro Del Buffa, Giuseppa and Lewis, Arthur O., eds. **Utopia e Modernita: Teorie e prassi utopiche nell'eta moderna e postmoderna.** Rome: Gangemi Editore, 1989. pp.931-944.

___ Sisk, David W. **Claiming Mastery over the Word: Transformations of Language in Six Twentieth Century Dystopias.** Ph.D. Dissertation, University of North Carolina, Chapel Hill, 1994. 405pp. (DAI-A 55/07, p. 1972. January 1995.)

HYDE-WHITE, WILFRED

___ "Hyde-White, Wilfred, 1903-1991 (Obituary)," *Starlog* No. 174: 23. January 1992.

HYPERFICTION

___ McDaid, John. "Luddism, SF, and the Aesthetics of Electronic Fiction," *New York Review of Science Fiction* No. 69: 1, 8-11. May 1994.

___ Moulthrop, Stuart. "Electronic Fictions and 'The Lost Game of Self'," *New York Review of Science Fiction* No. 66: 1, 8-14. February 1994.

___ Smith, Sarah. "Electronic Fictions: The State of the Art," *New York Review of Science Fiction* No. 63: 1, 8-11. November 1993.

HYPERSPACE

___ Kaku, Michio. **Hyperspace: A Scientific Odyssey Through Parallel Universes, Time Warps, and the Tenth Dimension.** New York: Oxford University Press, 1994. 359pp.

HYPERTEXT

___ Gess, Richard. "Notes on Hypertext: One Artist's Slate, 1992-1994," *New York Review of Science Fiction* No. 72: 1, 8-9. August 1994.

___ Maddox, Tom. "Reports From the Electronic Frontier: I Sing the Text Electric, Part 2, Reading Hypertext," *Locus* 29(6): 11-12. December 1992.

___ Platt, Charles. "Why Hypertext Doesn't Really Work," *New York Review of Science Fiction* No. 72: 1, 3-5. August 1994.

___ Schmidt, Stanley. "Hypertext as a Writing Tool," *SFWA Bulletin* 26(2): 6-10. Summer 1992. (No. 116)

I AM LEGEND (MOTION PICTURE)

___ "Repeat of Matheson: WB's **I Am Legend** Done Before in '64 by AIP," *Variety* p. 3. May 13, 1970.

I, ROBOT (MOTION PICTURE SCRIPT)

___ Ellison, Harlan. "Me 'N' Isaac at the Movies: A Brief Memoir of Citizen Calvin," *Science Fiction Age* 3(1): 78-83. November 1994.

ICELAND

___ Driscoll, Matthew J. "The Cloak of Fidelity: **Skikkjurimur,** a Late-Medieval Icelandic Version of **Le Mantel Mautaillie,**" in: Busby, Keith, ed. **The Arthurian Yearbook I.** New York: Garland, 1991. pp.107-134.

___ Engholm, Ahrvid. "SF in the Nordic Countries," *Locus* 34(4): 39. April 1995.

ICON (COMIC)

___ Kilby, Damian. "With Science Fictional Abilities, the Alien Icon Seeks to Bring Racial Harmony to Earth," *Science Fiction Age* 1(4): 68-69. May 1993.

IKIN, VAN

___ "A. Bertram Chandler Award," *Locus* 29(1): 69. July 1992.

___ "Van Ikin Wins A. Bertram Chandler Award," *Science Fiction Chronicle* 13(10): 8. July/August 1992.

ILLEGAL ALIEN (COMIC)

___ Hirsch, Connie. "Amidst Endless Superheroes, *Illegal Alien* Is as Ambitious as the Best SF," *Science Fiction Age* 3(1): 84-87. November 1994.

ILLUSTRATION

___ SEE: ART AND ARTISTS.

IMAGINARY VOYAGES

___ Fausett, David. **Writing the New World: Imaginary Voyages and Utopias of the Great Southern Land.** Syracuse, NY: Syracuse University Press, 1993. 237pp.

IMMORTAL (MOTION PICTURE)

___ Bourassa, Alain. "Deaths of **The Immortal**, Part Two," by Alain Bourassa and Mark Phillips. *Starlog* No. 186: 67-72, 74. January 1993.

___ Gunn, James E. "Television and **The Immortal**," in: Gunn, James E. **Inside Science Fiction: Essays on Fantastic Literature.** San Bernardino, CA: Borgo, 1992. pp.113-117.

___ Phillips, Mark. "Lives of **The Immortal**, Part One," by Mark Phillips and Alain Bourassa. *Starlog* 185: 58-62. December 1992.

IMMORTAL (TV)

___ Bourassa, Alain. "Deaths of **The Immortal**, Part Two," by Alain Bourassa and Mark Phillips. *Starlog* No. 186: 67-72, 74. January 1993.

___ Phillips, Mark. "**Immortal** Chaser," *Starlog* No. 188: 20-22, 66. March 1993.

___ Phillips, Mark. "Lives of **The Immortal**, Part One," by Mark Phillips and Alain Bourassa. *Starlog* 185: 58-62. December 1992.

IMMORTALITY

___ Bowman, Tanya F. "Cautionary Tales of Immortality," *Science Fiction: A Review of Speculative Literature* 13(1): 19-21. 1995(?). (No. 37)

___ Meyer, Charles A. "The Efrafan Hunt for Immortality in **Watership Down**," *Journal of the Fantastic in the Arts* 6(1): 71-87. 1993.

___ Wolff, Michael J. "Extended Engagement," *Starlog* 185: 27-33, 66. December 1992.

IMPRISONMENT

___ Kelleghan, Fiona. "Hell's My Destination: Imprisonment in the Works of Alfred Bester," *Science Fiction Studies* 21(3): 351-364. November 1994.

IN THE FOLD (TV)

___ Meza, Ed. "First Command," *Starlog* No. 217: 32-33. August 1995.

IN THE MOUTH OF MADNESS (MOTION PICTURE)

___ Harris, Judith P. "**In the Mouth of Madness** (Review)," *Cinefantastique* 26(5): 59. August 1995.

___ Jones, Alan. "John Carpenter: Directing **In the Mouth of Madness** a la H. P. Lovecraft," *Cinefantastique* 26(2): 44-45. February 1995.

___ Lowe, Nick. "**In the Mouth of Madness** (Review)," *Interzone* No. 99: 33. September 1995.

___ Martin, Robert. "Mounting Madness," *Sci-Fi Entertainment* 1(6): 48-50. April 1995.

___ Moir, Patricia. "**In the Mouth of Madness** (Review)," *Cinefantastique* 27(3): 42. December 1995.

___ Schwartzberg, Shlomo. "**In the Mouth of Madness**," *Cinefantastique* 25(5): 8-9. October 1994.

___ Schwartzberg, Shlomo. "KNB EFX Madness," *Cinefantastique* 25(5): 11. October 1994.

INCREDIBLE HULK RETURNS (MOTION PICTURE)

___ "**Incredible Hulk Returns** (Review)," *Variety* p. 53, 56. June 8, 1988.

INCREDIBLE HULK (TV)

INCREDIBLE HULK (TV)
___ Jankiewicz, Pat. "Time of the Green," *Starlog* No. 204: 72-76. July 1994.

INCREDIBLE SHRINKING MAN (MOTION PICTURE)
___ Rosenheim, Shawn. "Extraterrestrial: Science Fictions in *A Brief History of Time* and *The Incredible Shrinking Man*," *Film Quartrely* 48(4): 15-21. Summer 1995.

INDEPENDENCE DAY (MOTION PICTURE)
___ Rohan, Virginia. "Extra! Extra!," *(Hackensack, NJ) Record.* September 10, 1995. in: *NewsBank. Film and Television.* 86:B13-B14. 1995.

INDEXES
___ "Index: *Cinefex* No. 1-50," *Cinefex* No. 50: 90-106. May 1992.
___ "Index to *Analog*, Vol. 114, 1994," *Analog* 115(1/2): 315-318. January 1995.
___ "Index to *Lovecraft Studies* 1-25," *Lovecraft Studies* No. 26: 35-39. Spring 1992.
___ "Index to Society for Utopian Studies Publications Prior to *Utopian Studies*," *Utopian Studies* 6(1): 191-205. 1995.
___ "Index to the *PKDS Newsletter*, No. 1-30," *PKDS Newsletter* No. 30: 5-13. December 1992.
___ "Index, Volume 15," *Isaac Asimov's Science Fiction Magazine* 16(1): 168-171. January 1992.
___ Cockcroft, T. G. L. "An Index to 'The Eyrie'," *Fantasy Commentator* 8(3/4): 217-229. Fall 1995. (Whole No. 47/48)
___ Hall, Hal W. **Science Fiction and Fantasy Book Review Index, Volume 18, 1987.** San Bernardino, CA: Borgo Press, 1992. 70pp.
___ Hall, Hal W. **Science Fiction and Fantasy Book Review Index, Volume 19, 1988.** Bryan, TX: SFFBRI, 1992. 87pp.; San Bernardino, CA: Borgo Press, 1992. 85pp.
___ Hall, Hal W. **Science Fiction and Fantasy Book Review Index, Volume 20, 1989.** San Bernardino, CA: Borgo Press, 1993. 90pp.; Bryan, TX: SFFBRI, 1993. 90pp.
___ Hall, Hal W. **Science Fiction and Fantasy Book Review Index, Volume 21, 1990.** Bryan, TX: SFFBRI, 1994. 105pp.
___ Hall, Hal W. **Science Fiction and Fantasy Research Index, Volume 10.** San Bernardino, CA: Borgo Press, 1994. 153pp.
___ Hall, Hal W. **Science Fiction and Fantasy Research Index, Volume 9.** San Bernardino, CA: Borgo Press, 1992. 97pp.
___ Holland, Stephen. **An Index to Mellifont Press: A Working Bibliography.** Leeds, Eng: Galactic Central, 1995. 76pp.
___ Joshi, S. T. **An Index to the Fiction and Poetry of H. P. Lovecraft.** West Warwick, RI: Necronomicon Press, 1992. 42pp.
___ Reynolds, Trevor. "Index to J. R. R. Tolkien in *Mythlore* Issues 1-68," *Mythlore* 18(3): 70-77. Summer 1992. (No. 69)
___ Ruck, E. H. **An Index of Themes and Motifs in Twelfth-Century French Arthurian Poetry.** Rochester, NY: D. S. Brewer, 1991. 176pp. [Not seen.]
___ Senn, Bryan. **Fantastic Cinema Subject Guide: A Topical Index to 2500 Horror, Science Fiction, and Fantasy Films**, by Bryan Senn and John Johnson. Jefferson, NC: McFarland, 1992. 682pp.
___ Sprug, Joseph W. **Index to Fairy Tales, 1987-1992: Including 310 Collections of Fairy Tales, Myths and Legends With Significant Pre-1987 Titles Not Previously Indexed.** Metuchen, NJ: Scarecrow, 1994. 587pp.
___ Stone, Graham. "Index to *Science Fiction News* Nos. 59-106, 1979-1987," *Science Fiction News* (Australia) No. 106: 8-17. December 1987.
___ Van Hise, James. "An Index to the Reed Crandall Illustrations From the Works of Edgar Rice Burroughs," *Burroughs Bulletin* NS. No. 20: 27-28. October 1994.

INDIAN IN THE CUPBOARD (MOTION PICTURE)
___ Duncan, Jody. "Quick Cuts: Cowboys and Indians," *Cinefex* No. 63: 27-28. September 1995.
___ Fischer, Dennis. "*Indian in the Cupboard*," *Cinefantastique* 26(5): 46-47. August 1995.
___ Harris, Judith P. "*Indian in the Cupboard* (Review)," *Cinefantastique* 27(2): 60. November 1995.
___ Magid, Ron. "Incredible Shrinking 'Indian' Effects," by Ron Magid and Chris Probst. *American Cinematographer* 76(8): 68-69. August 1995.
___ Probst, Chris. "*Indian in the Cupboard*'s Cinematic Intimacy," *American Cinematographer* 76(8): 62-67. August 1995.

INTERNATIONAL CONFERENCE ON THE FANTASTIC

INDIANA JONES AND THE TEMPLE OF DOOM (MOTION PICTURE)
___ " 'Jones' PG Focus of TV Violence Group," *Variety* p. 3, 123. May 30, 1984.
___ "Par Demands Long 'Jones' Playtimes," *Variety* p. 3. April 25, 1984.
___ Aronstein, Susan. " 'Not Exactly a Knight': Arthurian Narrative and Recuperative Politics in the *Indiana Jones* Trilogy," *Cinema Journal* 34(4): 3-30. Summer 1995.
___ Smetak, Jacqueline R. "Summer at the Movies: Steven Spielberg: Gore, Guts, and PG-13," *Journal of Popular Film and Television* 14(1): 4-13. 1986.
___ Tusher, Will. " 'Jones' Criticism Prompts Valenti to Defend MPAA Rating System," *Variety* p. 5, 24. June 6, 1984.

INDIANS, AMERICAN
___ Mercier, Andree. "L'Indien de la Science/Fiction (The Indian in Science/Fiction)," *Recerches Amerindiennes au Quebec* (Canada) 17(3): 53-63. 1987.

INDONESIA
___ Olsa, Jaroslav, Jr. "SF in Southeast Asia," *Locus* 34(1) 70. January 1995.

INDUSTRIAL LIGHT & MAGIC (COMPANY)
___ Magid, Ron. "ILM Magic Is Organized Mayhem," *American Cinematographer* 75(12): 50-56. December 1994.
___ Magid, Ron. "ILM's Digital Dinosaurs Tear up Effects Jungle," *American Cinematographer* 74(12): 46-57. December 1993.

INFLUENCES
___ Burger, Phillip R. "Mesas, Mormons, and Martians: The Possible Origins of Barsoomian History," *Burroughs Bulletin* NS. No. 16: 3-7. October 1993.
___ Reno, Shaun. "The Zuni Indian Tribe: A Model for **Stranger in a Strange Land**'s Martian Culture," *Extrapolation* 36(2): 151-158. Summer 1995.

INFORMATION HIGHWAY
___ Zeuschner, Bob. "ERB Is Alive and Well on the Information Highway," *Burroughs Bulletin* NS. No. 24: 19-25. October 1995.

INFORMATION RETRIEVAL
___ Baugh, E. Susan. "The Electronic Book in Future Information Access," in: Wolf, Milton T. and Mallett, Daryl F., eds. **Imaginative Futures: Proceedings of the 1993 Science Fiction Research Association Conference.** San Bernardino, CA: Jacob's Ladder Books, 1995. pp.53-60.
___ Halbert, Martin. "Database Visualization and Future Innovations in Information Retrieval," in: Wolf, Milton T. and Mallett, Daryl F., eds. **Imaginative Futures: Proceedings of the 1993 Science Fiction Research Association Conference.** San Bernardino, CA: Jacob's Ladder Books, 1995. pp.31-52.

INGALLS, DON
___ Goldberg, Lee. "Paladin in Blue," *Starlog* 179: 36-37, 84. June 1992.

INNOCENT BLOOD (MOTION PICTURE)
___ Biodrowski, Steve. "Guilty Director," *Cinefantastique* 23(6): 53. April 1993.
___ Doherty, Thomas. "*Innocent Blood*," *Cinefantastique* 23(6): 52-53. April 1993.
___ Fischer, Dennis. "*Innocent Blood* (Review)," *Cinefantastique* 23(5): 59. February 1993.

INTERACTIVE FICTION
___ Kelley, Robert. "A Maze of Twisty Little Passages All Alike: Aesthetics and Teleology in Interactive Computer Fictional Elements," *Science Fiction Studies* 20(1): 52-68. March 1993.

INTERACTIVE GAMES
___ Stevens, Kevin. "On a Wing and a Prayer: The Making of *Wing Commander III*," *Sci-Fi Universe* No. 3: 82-83. October/November 1994.

INTERNATIONAL CONFERENCE ON THE FANTASTIC IN THE ARTS, 1992
___ "Conference on the Fantastic, 1992," *Locus* 28(6): 50-51. June 1992.

INTERNATIONAL CONFERENCE ON THE FANTASTIC IN THE ARTS, 1992 (continued)

___ Heldreth, Leonard G. "Conference Report, ICFA XIII," *IAFA Newsletter* 5(2): 7-20. Summer 1992.

INTERNATIONAL CONFERENCE ON THE FANTASTIC IN THE ARTS, 1993

___ "1993 Conference on the Fantastic," *Locus* 30(5): 40-41, 72. May 1993.

INTERNATIONAL CONFERENCE ON THE FANTASTIC IN THE ARTS, 1994

___ "1994 International Conference on the Fantastic in the Arts," *Locus* 32(5): 36-37, 66. May 1994.

INTERNATIONAL CONFERENCE ON THE FANTASTIC IN THE ARTS, 1995

___ "International Conference on the Fantastic in the Arts, 1995," *Locus* 34(5): 38-42. May 1995.

INTERNATIONAL FANTASY AND SCIENCE FICTION FILM FESTIVAL (ROME), 1988

___ "Sci-Fi and Fantasy Fest Celebrates 8th Anniversary," *Variety* p.313. May 4, 1988.

INTERNATIONAL FANTASY AND SCIENCE FICTION FILM FESTIVAL (ROME), 1992

___ Martani, Marco. "Horror party con brididi a basso costo [Fantafestival 1992: The 12th International Rome Film Festival of Science Fiction and Horror]," *Cineforum* 32(9): 38-39. 1992.

INTERNATIONAL FESTIVAL OF FANTASTIC AND SCIENCE FICTION FILMS (PARIS), 1981

___ "Paris Sci-Fi Fest Has Full Agenda; Vinny Price Salute," *Variety* p. 43, 45. November 4, 1981.

___ "Paris Sci-Fi Fest's Grand Prix Goes to Aussie 'Mad Max'," *Variety* p. 7, 30. December 2, 1981.

INTERNATIONAL FESTIVAL OF FANTASTIC AND SCIENCE FICTION FILMS (PARIS), 1982

___ "Paris Sci-Fi Entries," *Variety* p. 5. July 28, 1982.

___ "Paris Sci-Fi Fest Boasts 15 Features in Chiller Mold," *Variety* p. 6, 92. November 10, 1982.

INTERNATIONAL FESTIVAL OF FANTASTIC AND SCIENCE FICTION FILMS (PARIS), 1983

___ "Paris Sci-Fi Fest Sets 10-day Slate," *Variety* p. 6. November 9, 1983.

___ "*Xtro* Wins Paris Sci-Fi Fest," *Variety* p. 7. December 7, 1983.

INTERNATIONAL FESTIVAL OF FANTASTIC AND SCIENCE FICTION FILMS (PARIS), 1984

___ "28 Pics Slated for Paris Sci-Fi Fest," *Variety* p. 6. November 21, 1984.

___ "Paris Sci-Fi Fest Winners," *Variety* p. 5. December 12, 1984.

INTERNATIONAL FESTIVAL OF FANTASTIC AND SCIENCE FICTION FILMS (PARIS), 1986

___ "Paris Fantasy Fest Streamlined for '86," *Variety* p. 5, 26. February 5, 1986.

INTERNATIONAL FESTIVAL OF FANTASTIC AND SCIENCE FICTION FILMS (PARIS), 1988

___ "*Near Dark* Tops Sci Fest Nods," *Variety* p. 33. July 6, 1988.

___ "Seventeenth Paris Festival of Sci-Fi/Fantasy Fields International Lineup," *Variety* p. 16. June 15, 1988.

INTERNATIONAL FESTIVAL OF FANTASTIC FILMS (BERLIN), 1982

___ "Berlin Fantasy Fest Unspools 70 Films; Harryhausen Laud," *Variety* p. 6, 52. May 11, 1983.

INTERNET RESOURCES

___ "Internet Top 100 SF/Fantasy Titles," *Locus* 35(2): 8. August 1995.

___ "Library of Congress Starts Online SF Forum," *Locus* 34(3): 9. March 1995.

___ "Online SF," *Locus* 34(1) 8. January 1995.

INTERNET RESOURCES (continued)

___ Maddox, Tom. "Reports From the Electronic Frontier: 1994, The Year in Review," *Locus* 34(1) 13, 53. January 1995.

INTERSPECIES COMMUNICATION

___ SEE ALSO: FIRST CONTACT.

INTERVIEW WITH THE VAMPIRE (MOTION PICTURE)

___ Jones, Alan. "*Interview With the Vampire*," *Cinefantastique* 25(6)/26(1): 24-26. December 1994.

___ Lowe, Nick. "*Interview With the Vampire* (Review)," *Interzone* No. 92: 28-29. February 1995.

___ Magid, Ron. "Digital Domain Arranges an *Interview With the Vampire*," *American Cinematographer* 76(1): 53-61. January 1995.

___ Newman, Kim. "*Interview With the Vampire* (Review)," *Sight and Sound* 5(2): 46-47. February 1995.

___ Persons, Dan. "The State of Lestat," *Sci-Fi Entertainment* 1(4): 62-67. December 1994.

___ Pizzello, Stephen. "*Interview With the Vampire* Taps New Vein," *American Cinematographer* 76(1): 43-52. January 1995.

___ Shay, Estelle. "Immortal Images," *Cinefex* No. 61: 38-57. March 1995.

INTERZONE (MAGAZINE)

___ "*Interzone* Incorporates *Million*," *Science Fiction Chronicle* 14(12): 4-5. September 1993.

___ "*Interzone* to Incorporate *Million*," *Locus* 31(2): 7. August 1993.

___ Ashley, Mike. "*Interzone*: A Bridge So Far," *Interzone* No. 57: 45-47. March 1992.

___ Dalkin, Gary. "Happy Centenary, *Interzone*," *Vector* No. 185: 3. September/October 1995.

INTRUDERS (MOTION PICTURE)

___ Crisafulli, Chuck. "*Intruders*," *Cinefantastique* 23(4): 56. December 1992.

___ Harris, Judith P. "*Intruders* (Review)," *Cinefantastique* 23(2/3): 122. October 1992.

___ Shannon, John. "Short Intruders," *Cinefex* No. 51: 79-80. August 1992.

INVADERS FROM MARS (MOTION PICTURE)

___ Latham, Robert A. "Subterranean Suburbia: Underneath the Smalltown Myth in Two Versions of *Invaders From Mars*," *Science Fiction Studies* 22(2): 198-208. July 1995.

INVADERS (MOTION PICTURE)

___ Droesch, Paul. "Hits and Misses' *The Invaders*," *TV Guide* 43(45): 55. November 11, 1995.

___ Mayo, Mike. "Successful Low-Budget SF Film-making Is Itself an Act of Science Fiction," *Science Fiction Age* 2(4): 20-23, 33-34. May 1994.

___ Nollinger, Mark. "They Came From Outer Space (Again!)," *TV Guide* 43(45): 24-26. November 11, 1995.

INVADERS (TV)

___ Phillips, Mark. "Unmasked *Invaders*, Part Two," *Starlog* No. 207: 59-66. October 1994.

___ Phillips, Mark. "Unseen *Invaders*, Part One," *Starlog* No. 206: 21-26, 69. September 1994.

INVASION OF THE BODY SNATCHERS (MOTION PICTURE)

___ Hoberman, J. "Paranoia and the Pods," *Sight and Sound* 4(5): 28-31. May 1994.

___ Horne, Philip. "I Shopped With a Zombie," *Critical Quarterly* 34(4): 97-110. Winter 1992.

___ Johnson, Kim H. "Matters of Identity," *Starlog* No. 190: 60-61. May 1993.

___ Wolff, Michael J. "Nine-Tenths of the Law," *Starlog* No. 190: 56-59. May 1993.

INVASION OF THE SAUCER-MEN (MOTION PICTURE)

___ Di Fate, Vincent. "Creature Capsules," *Science Fiction Chronicle* 13(11/12): 38-42. August 1992.

INVISIBILITY

___ Chapman, Edgar L. " 'Seeing' Invisibility: Or Invisibility as Metaphor in Thomas Berger's **Being Invisible**," *Journal of the Fantastic in the Arts* 4(2): 65-93. 1992. (No. 14)

IT'S ABOUT TIME (MOTION PICTURE)
___ SEE: AMITYVILLE 1992: IT'S ABOUT TIME (MOTION PICTURE).

ITALY
___ "*1984* Pulled From Venice; Preem Off Until October," *Variety* p. 7. August 1, 1984.
___ "1993 Premio Italia Awards," *Science Fiction Chronicle* 15(8): 10. June 1994.
___ "*Day After* Record in Wide Italo Run," *Variety* p. 42. February 15, 1984.
___ "Premio Italia Award, 1992," *Locus* 29(1): 69. July 1992.
___ "Premio Italia, 1993," *Locus* 31(2): 62. August 1993.
___ " *Spider-Man* Departs Web of Italian Newsstands as Chief Shareholder Exits," *Variety* p. 84. September 17, 1986.
___ Bruschini, Antonio. **Mondi Incredibili: Il Cinema Fantastico-Avvneturoso Italiano**, by Antonio Bruschini and Antonio Tentori. Bologna: Granta Press, 1995. 173pp.
___ Colin, Mariella. "Du fantastique en tant que genre litteraire pour les enfants en Italie," in: Perrot, Jean, ed. **Culture, texte et Juene Lecteur. Actes du Xe Congres de l'International Research Society for Children's Literature, Paris, September 1991**. Nancy: Presses Universitaires, 1993. pp.43-49
___ Dellavalle, Renato. "Horror a basso costo," *Cineforum* 30(11): 67-78. 1990.
___ Dinallo, Antonella. " 'I racconti di Samuele Weller': di Guiseppe Mezzanotte: le fantasie scientifiche (Con inedito). [Guiseppe Mezzanotte i 'Racconti de Samuele Weller': Science Fiction Including a Previously Unpublished Text, gli 'Amanti Siderati'," *Critica Letteraria* 21(3): 537-562. 1993.
___ Hunt, Leon. "A (Sadistic) Night at the Opera: Notes on the Italian Horror Film," *Velvet Light Trap* 30: 65-75. 1992.
___ Martani, Marco. "Horror party con brididi a basso costo [Fantafestival 1992: The 12th International Rome Film Festival of Science Fiction and Horror]," *Cineforum* 32(9): 38-39. 1992.
___ Martani, Marco. "Roma: Fantafestival; Concorso d'autore senza l'orrore," *Cineforum* 30(7/8): 31-33. 1990.
___ Parisi, Luciano. "Per una storia della fantascienza italiana: Flavia Steno," *Stanford Italian Review* 9(1/2): 105-113. 1990.
___ Roda, Vittorio. "La fantascienza umoristica de Antonia Ghislazoni," *Studi e Problemi de Critica Testuale* 49: 121-152. October 1994.
___ Roda, Vittorio. "Tra scienza e fantascienza: il cervello umano in alcuni scrittori postunitari. [Between Science and Science-Fiction: The Human Brain as Depicted in Post-Unification Italian Literature]," *Otto-Novecento* 19(5): 35-64. September/October 1995.
___ Spina, Giorgio. "The Inklings in Italy," in: Kranz, Gisbert, ed. **Inklings: Jahrbuch für Literatur und Ästhetik**. 7. Band. Lüdenscheid, Germany: Stier, 1989. pp.83-92. [Not seen.]
___ Vegetti, Ernesto. **Fantascienza, Fantasy and Horror in Italia: 1990**, by Ernesto Vegetti and Piergiorgio Nicolazzini. Milano, Italy: Nicolazzini, 1992?. 142pp. [Not seen.]

J. LLOYD EATON MEMORIAL AWARD, 1993
___ "1993 J. Lloyd Eaton Memorial Award," *Locus* 30(6): 72. June 1993.
___ "J. Lloyd Eaton Memorial Award, 1993," *Science Fiction Chronicle* 14(9): 6. June 1993.

JABLOKOV, ALEXANDER
___ "Alexander Jablokov: The Literary Lab Bench," *Locus* 28(3): 4, 77. March 1992.

JACK OF SWORDS (MOTION PICTURE)
___ SEE: TRANCERS 4: JACK OF SWORDS (MOTION PICTURE).

JACKSON, MICHAEL
___ Johnson, Victoria. "The Politics of Morphing: Michael Jackson as Science Fiction Border Text," *Velvet Light Trap* (Austin, TX) 32: 58-65. 1993.
___ Stableford, Brian. **Algebraic Fantasies and Realistic Romances: More Masters of Science Fiction**. San Bernardino, CA: Borgo Press, 1995 128pp.

JACKSON, SHIRLEY
___ Bloom, Harold. "Shirley Jackson," in: Bloom, Harold. **Modern Horror Writers**. New York: Chelsea House, 1995. pp.108-123.
___ Joshi, S. T. "Shirley Jackson: Domestic Horror," *Studies in Weird Fiction* No. 14: 9-28. Winter 1994.

JACKSON, SHIRLEY (continued)
___ Morrison, Michael A. "Journey's End: **The Haunting**: From Book to Film," *Studies in Weird Fiction* No. 12: 25-30. Spring 1993.
___ Ursini, James. **More Things Than Are Dreamt Of: Masterpieces of Supernatural Horror, From Mary Shelley to Stephen King, in Literature and Film**, by James Ursini and Alain Silver. New York: Limelight, 1994. 226pp.

JACKSON, STEVE
___ "Steve Jackson Collects Damages," *Locus* 32(6): 8, 75. June 1994.
___ "Steve Jackson Wins Lawsuit," *Locus* 30(4): 6. April 1993.

JACOBI, CARL
___ Cave, Hugh B. **Magazines I Remember: Some Pulps, Their Editors, and What It Was Like to Write for Them**. Chicago, IL: Tattered Pages Press, 1994. 174pp.

JACQUES, BRIAN
___ "Brian Jacques: Rodent Warrior," *Locus* 35(5): 5, 84. November 1995.

JAMES TIPTREE, JR. MEMORIAL AWARD, 1991
___ "James Tiptree, Jr. Award, 1991," *Locus* 28(5): 6, 65. May 1992.
___ "Tiptree Award," *Locus* 28(4): 6. April 1992.

JAMES TIPTREE, JR. MEMORIAL AWARD, 1992
___ "Eleanor Arnason, Gwyneth Jones Win First James Tiptree, Jr. Award," *Science Fiction Chronicle* 13(7): 4. April 1992.
___ "James Tiptree, Jr. Memorial Award Presented," *SFWA Bulletin* 26(2): 3-5. Summer 1992. (No. 116)
___ "Maureen F. McHugh Wins Tiptree Award," *Science Fiction Chronicle* 14(6): 4. March 1993.
___ "Tiptree Award Presented," *Locus* 30(5): 8. May 1993.
___ "Tiptree Award Winner, 1992," *Locus* 30(3): 7. March 1993.

JAMES TIPTREE, JR. MEMORIAL AWARD, 1993
___ "Griffith Wins Tiptree Award," *Locus* 33(1): 7, 78. July 1994.
___ "Nicola Griffith Wins Tiptree Award," *Science Fiction Chronicle* 15(8): 5. June 1994.

JAMES TIPTREE, JR. MEMORIAL AWARD, 1995
___ "1995 Tiptree Award Presented," *Locus* 34(3): 7. March 1995.
___ "Nancy Springer, Ursula K. Le Guin Win Tiptree Award," *Science Fiction Chronicle* 16(5): 4. March/April 1995.

JAMES, HENRY
___ Allen, Virginia. "Ethos and Marginalization in the Henry James/H. G. Wells Affair," *Extrapolation* 33(4): 317-332. Winter 1992.
___ Allen, Virginia. "The Ethos of English Departments: Henry James and H. G. Wells, Continued," *Extrapolation* 34(4): 305-328. Winter 1993.
___ Bloom, Harold. "Henry James," in: Bloom, Harold. **Classic Horror Writers**. New York: Chelsea House, 1994. pp.27-42.
___ Cramer, Kathryn. "Possession and 'The Jolly Corner'," *New York Review of Science Fiction* No. 65: 19-22. January 1994.
___ Heldreth, Leonard G. "The Ghost and the Self: The Supernatural Fiction of Henry James," in: Morse, Donald E., ed. **The Celebration of the Fantastic**. Westport, CT: Greenwood, 1992. pp.133-140.
___ Roth, Ellen S. **The Rhetoric of First-Person Point of View in the Novel and Film Forms: A Study of Anthony Burgess' A Clockwork Orange and Henry James' A Turn of the Screw and Their Film Adaptations**. Ph.D. Dissertation, New York University, 1978. 308pp. (DAI 39: 4558A. Feb. 1979.)

JAMES, JOHN
___ "James, John (Obituary)," *Locus* 32(3): 68. March 1994.

JAMES, M. R.
___ Bloom, Harold. "M. R. James," in: Bloom, Harold. **Modern Horror Writers**. New York: Chelsea House, 1995. pp.124-137.
___ Schweitzer, Darrell. "M. R. James and H. P. Lovecraft: The Ghostly and the Cosmic," *Studies in Weird Fiction* No. 15: 12-16. Summer 1994.

JAMES, P. D.
___ Young, Susan. "Author P. D. James Boldly Goes Where She Hasn't Gone Before," *Oakland (CA) Tribune* Sec. C, p. 4. March 15, 1993.

JAMES, PETER

___ Webb, Martin R. "Tailor-Made: An Interview With Peter James," *Vector* No. 182: 3-4. Spring 1995.

JAMES, WILLIAM

___ "British Author Accused of Copying," *Locus* 32(4): 8. April 1994.
___ "Orbit Withdraws William James Books," *Science Fiction Chronicle* 16(3): 4. January 1995.

JANEWAY, KATHRYN

___ Spelling, Ian. "Voyager Captain," in: McDonnell, David, ed. **Starlog's Science Fiction Heroes and Heroines**. New York: Crescent Books, 1995. pp.34-37.

JANSSEN, FAMKE

___ Bloch-Hansen, Peter. "Perfect Mating," *Starlog* No. 197: 58-61. December 1993.

JAPAN

___ "Comic Book Types, TV Push Yields Japan's Sci-Fi Cat Hit," *Variety* p. 328. May 12, 1982.
___ "'Day' Big in Japan," *Variety* p. 123. February 1, 1984.
___ "Japanese Audiences Prefer Sci-Fi, Action Drama," *Variety* p. 346. May 4, 1982.
___ "SF in Japan," *Locus* 28(1): 49. January 1992.
___ "SF in Japan," *Locus* 29(6): 48. December 1992.
___ "Shochiku to Herald Spacey 'Yamato' Pack," *Variety* p. 290. May 4, 1988.
___ Anisfield, Nancy. "**Godzilla**/Gojiro: Evolution of the Nuclear Metaphor," *Journal of Popular Culture* 29(3): 53-62. Winter 1995.
___ Clements, Jonathan. "The Mechanics of the US Anime and Manga Industry," *Foundation* No. 64: 32-44. Summer 1995.
___ Cramer, John G. "Science and SF in Japan," *Analog* 113(5): 108-112. April 1993.
___ Cziraky, Dan. "**Guyver**," *Cinefantastique* 22(4): 46. February 1992.
___ Dawson, Carl. **Lafcadio Hearn and the Vision of Japan**. Baltimore: Johns Hopkins University Press, 1992. 187pp.
___ Galbraith, Stuart, IV. **Japanese Science Fiction, Fantasy and Horror Films: A Critical Analysis and Filmography of 103 Features Released in the United States, 1950-1992**. Jefferson, NC: McFarland, 1994. 424pp.
___ Hernandez, Lea. "Japanimation's Rising Sun," *Sci-Fi Entertainment* 1(1): 30-33. June 1994.
___ Iwao, Sumiko. "**The Day After** in Japan," in: Wober, J. Mallory, ed. **Television and Nuclear Power: Making the Public Mind**. Norwood, NJ: Ablex, 1992. pp.67-76.
___ Kenny, Glenn. "Animania," *TV Guide* 42(21): 42. May 21, 1994.
___ Matthew, Robert. **Japanese Science Fiction: A View of a Changing Society**. New York: Routledge, 1989. 259pp.
___ Noetzel, Michael. "Kobo Abe: Eine betrachtung und posthume Würdigung des Avant-gardisten der modernen japanischen SF," *Quarber Merkur* 33(1): 39-53. June 1995. (No. 83)
___ Osako, Masamichi. "Science Fiction Fandom in Japan," in: Sanders, Joe, ed. **Science Fiction Fandom**. Westport, CT: Greenwood, 1994. pp.137-140.
___ Perry, Joseph W. "Astro Boy: Happy 30th to That Mighty Mechanical Mite," *Filmfax* No. 42: 50-53. December 1993/January 1994.
___ Persons, Dan. "Cheap Genius," *Cinefantastique* 23(5): 53. February 1993.
___ Persons, Dan. "**Tetsuo: The Iron Man**," *Cinefantastique* 23(5): 50-52. February 1993.
___ Pollack, Andrew. "Fantasy Novels About WWII Becoming Popular in Japan," *Austin (TX) American Statesman* Sec. A, p. 17. March 19, 1995.
___ Poulton, Cody. "The Grotesque and the Gothic: Izumi Kyoka's Japan," *Japan Quarterly* 41(3): 324-35. July 1994.
___ Tanner, Ron. "Toy Robots in America, 1955-75: How Japan Really Won the War," *Journal of Popular Culture* 28(3): 125-154. Winter 1994.
___ Tatsumi, Takayuki. **Japanoido sengen: gendai Nihon Sfo yomu tameni**. Tokyo: Hayakawa Shobo, 1993. 246pp. [Not seen.]
___ Turner, George. "**Terabyss** Takes Audience on Suboceanic Thrill Mission," by George Turner and Nora Lee. *American Cinematographer* 74(8): 59-65. August 1993.
___ Wharton, Lawrence. "**Godzilla** to **Latitude Zero**: The Cycle of the Technological Monster," *Journal of Popular Film and Television* 3(1): 31-38. 1974.

JAPAN (continued)

___ Whitty, Stephen. "A Journey to No Place Special," *San Jose (CA) Mercury News*. December 2, 1994. in: *NewsBank. Film and Television.* 9:E14. 1995.
___ Whitty, Stephen. "Run For Your Life! It's Your Inner Godzilla," *San Jose (CA) Mercury News*. July 8, 1994. in: *NewsBank. Film and Television.* 81:C14. 1994.
___ Yamano, Koichi. "Japanese SF, Its Originality and Orientation," *Science Fiction Studies* 21(1): 67-80. March 1994. Also in: *Chung Wai Literary Quarterly* 22(12): May 1994. (Issue not seen. Pagination not available.)
___ Yamano, Koichi. "Japanese SF, Its Originality and Orientation (1969)," *Chung Wai Literary Quarterly* 22(12): May 1994. (Issue not seen; pagination unavailable.)

JARRY, ALFRED

___ Stableford, Brian. "Opening Minds," in: Stableford, Brian. **Opening Minds: Essays on Fantastic Literature**. San Bernardino, CA: Borgo Press, 1995. pp.23-28.

JASON GOES TO HELL (MOTION PICTURE)

___ SEE: FRIDAY THE 13TH IX: JASON GOES TO HELL (MOTION PICTURE).

JEFFERIES, MIKE

___ McVeigh, Kev. "Mike Jefferies Interviewed," *Vector* No. 167: 14-16. June/July 1992

JEFFRIES, LIONEL

___ Swires, Steve. "**First Men in the Moon**," *Starlog* No. 205: 62-67. August 1994.

JEROME, JEROME K.

___ Hunt, Peter. " 'Coldtongue coldham coldbeef pickled gherkin salad frenchrolls cresssandwige spottedmeat gingerbeer lemonaide sodawater...' Fantastic Foods in the Books of Kenneth Grahame, Jerome K. Jerome, H. E. Bates, and Other Bakers of the Fantasy England," *Journal of the Fantastic in the Arts* 7(1): 5-22. 1996.

JETER, K. W.

___ Cappio, James. "A Long Guide to K. W. Jeter," *New York Review of Science Fiction* No. 44: 1, 8-14. April 1992.

JEWISH MYTHOLOGY

___ Troen, Saul B. **Science Fiction and the Reemergence of Jewish Mythology in a Contemporary Literary Genre**. Ph.D. Dissertation, New York University, 1995. 336pp. (DAI-A 56/05, p. 1762. November 1995.)

JOHN W. CAMPBELL AWARD FOR BEST NEW SF WRITER, 1991-1992

___ "1993 Hugo Awards Winners," *Locus* 31(4): 5, 70. October 1993.
___ "Other Awards," *Science Fiction Chronicle* 15(1): 4. October 1993.

JOHN W. CAMPBELL AWARD FOR BEST NEW SF WRITER, 1992-1993

___ "1994 Hugo Award," *Science Fiction Chronicle* 15(10): 5. September 1994.

JOHN W. CAMPBELL AWARD FOR BEST NEW SF WRITER, 1992-93

___ "1994 Hugo Awards Winners," *Locus* 33(4): 7, 38-41. October 1994.

JOHN W. CAMPBELL AWARD FOR BEST NEW SF WRITER, 1994-1995

___ "1995 Hugo Winners," *Locus* 35(3): 7. September 1993.

JOHN W. CAMPBELL MEMORIAL AWARD, 1992

___ "1992 Hugo Awards Winners," *Locus* 29(4): 6, 42-47. October 1992.
___ "Denton, Kessel Win Campbell, Sturgeon Awards," *Locus* 29(3): 6. September 1992.
___ "Denton, Kessel Win Campbell, Sturgeon Awards," *Science Fiction Chronicle* 14(1): 5. October 1992.
___ "World SF Convention Hugo Awards," *Science Fiction Chronicle* 14(1): 4. October 1992.

JOHN W. CAMPBELL MEMORIAL AWARD, 1993

___ "Sheffield, Simmons Win Campbell, Sturgeon Awards," *Locus* 31(3): 6, 83. September 1993.

JOHN W. CAMPBELL MEMORIAL AWARD, 1993 (continued)
___ "Sheffield, Simmons, Win Campbell, Sturgeon Awards," *Science Fiction Chronicle* 14(11): 4. August 1993.

JOHN W. CAMPBELL MEMORIAL AWARD, 1994
___ "Kij Johnson Wins Sturgeon Award; 'No Award' First for Campbell Award," *Science Fiction Chronicle* 15(9): 4. August 1994.
___ "No Campbell Winner; Johnson Wins Sturgeon Award," *Locus* 33(2): 8. August 1994.

JOHN W. CAMPBELL MEMORIAL AWARD, 1995
___ "Campbell and Sturgeon Award Winners," *Locus* 35(2): 8. August 1995.
___ "Greg Egan Wins Campbell Memorial Award; Sturgeon Award to Ursula K. Le Guin," *Science Fiction Chronicle* 16(9): 5. August/ September 1995.
___ "Hugo/Campbell Award Nominees and Voting," *Science Fiction Chronicle* 17(1): 17, 43-45. October/November 1995
___ "The Hugos (Or, the Empire Strikes Back)," *Science Fiction Chronicle* 17(2): 55-56. December 1995/January 1996.
___ "World Science Fiction Convention Hugo Awards, 1995," *Science Fiction Chronicle* 17(1): 5. October/November 1995

JOHN, CAROLINE
___ Eramo, Steven. "Beautiful Companion," *Starlog* No. 221: 56-58. December 1995.

JOHNNY MNEMONIC (MOTION PICTURE)
___ Arar, Yardena. "Mnemonic More Than a Johnny-Come-Lately Thriller," *Los Angeles (CA) Daily News*. May 26, 1995. in: *NewsBank. Film and Television.* 63:A4. 1995.
___ Arnold, Gary. "Erase From Memory *Johnny Mnemonic*," *Washington (DC) Times*. May 26, 1995. in: *NewsBank. Film and Television.* 55:B8. 1995.
___ Campbell, Bob. "*Johnny Mnemonic* Plays Mind Games in Cyberspace," *(Newark, NJ) Star-Ledger*. May 26, 1995. in: *NewsBank. Film and Television.* 55:B6. 1995.
___ Dargis, Manohla. "Cyber Johnny," *Sight and Sound* 5(7): 6-7. July 1995.
___ Dever, Sean. "Quick Cuts: Cinematic Cyberspace," *Cinefex* No. 62: 17-18. June 1995.
___ Gibson, William. "Notes on a Process: Novel into Film," *Wired* 3(6): 157-159. June 1995.
___ Goldman, Michael R. "Big Bucks Planted in 'Mnemonic'," *Variety* 357(4): 83. November 21, 1994.
___ Johnson, Kim H. "Memories Can't Wait," *Starlog* No. 216: 50-53, 64. July 1995.
___ Johnson, Malcolm. "*Johnny Mnemonic* Is a Movie That You Could Remember to Miss," *Hartford (CT) Courant*. May 27, 1995. in: *NewsBank. Film and Television.* 55:B3. 1995.
___ Kridler, Chris. "*Johnny Mnemonic* Boggles Mind," *(Baltimore, MD) Sun*. May 27, 1995. in: *NewsBank. Film and Television.* 55:B4. 1995.
___ Longo, Robert. "Cyber Johnny," *Sight and Sound* 5(7): 6-7. July 1995.
___ Maccarillo, Lisa. "Hardwired Hero," *Sci-Fi Entertainment* 1(5): 46-50, 72. February 1995.
___ Maccarillo, Lisa. "William Gibson's Cyberpunk Future Is Made Real in *Johnny Mnemonic*," *Science Fiction Age* 3(2): 18, 20, 81. January 1995.
___ Maurstad, Tom. "An On-Line Uplink to Adventure," *Dallas (TX) Morning News*. May 26, 1995. in: *NewsBank. Film and Television.* 63: A7. 1995.
___ Medved, Michael. "Techno-Tale's Wires Crossed," *New York (NY) Post*. May 26, 1995. in: *NewsBank. Film and Television.* 55:B7. 1995.
___ Montesano, Anthony P. "*Johnny Mnemonic*," *Cinefantastique* 26(2): 14-15. February 1995.
___ Montesano, Anthony P. "*Johnny Mnemonic*," *Cinefantastique* 26(3): 44-46. April 1995.
___ Montesano, Anthony P. "Mnemonic Design," *Cinefantastique* 26(3): 46-47. April 1995.
___ Persons, Dan. "*Johnny Mnemonic* (Review)," *Cinefantastique* 26(6)/27(1): 123. October 1995.
___ Rizzo, Frank. "Director Learns to Make Art Move in Mnemonic," *Hartford (CT) Courant*. May 21, 1995. in: *NewsBank. Film and Television.* 55:B1-B2. 1995.

JOHNNY MNEMONIC (MOTION PICTURE) (continued)
___ Rosenberg, Scott. "Johnny Aims High, Almost Hits Mark," *San Francisco (CA) Examiner*. May 26, 1995. in: *NewsBank. Film and Television.* 63:A5. 1995.
___ Schaeffer, Stephen. "*Johnny Mnemonic*," *Boston (MA) Herald*. May 26, 1995. in: *NewsBank. Film and Television.* 55:B5. 1995.
___ Sheehan, Henry. "Mnemonic Device Doesn't Help Johnny," *(Santa Ana, CA) Orange County Register*. May 26, 1995. in: *NewsBank. Film and Television.* 63:A6. 1995.
___ Stone, Linda. "A Glimpse of Cyberspace," *Sci-Fi Entertainment* 1(5): 51. February 1995.
___ van Bakel, Rogier. "Remembering Johnny," *Wired* 3(6): 154-157. June 1995.

JOHNSON, ANNABEL
___ Lenz, Millicent. "**Danger Quotient, Fiskadoro, Riddley Walker,** and the Failure of the Campbellian Monomyth," in: Sullivan, C. W., III. **Science Fiction for Young Readers**. Westport, CT: Greenwood, 1993. pp.113-119.

JOHNSON, DENIS
___ Lenz, Millicent. "**Danger Quotient, Fiskadoro, Riddley Walker,** and the Failure of the Campbellian Monomyth," in: Sullivan, C. W., III. **Science Fiction for Young Readers**. Westport, CT: Greenwood, 1993. pp.113-119.

JOHNSON, EDGAR
___ Lenz, Millicent. "**Danger Quotient, Fiskadoro, Riddley Walker,** and the Failure of the Campbellian Monomyth," in: Sullivan, C. W., III. **Science Fiction for Young Readers**. Westport, CT: Greenwood, 1993. pp.113-119.

JOHNSON, GEORGE CLAYTON
___ Warren, Bill. "His Own Man," *Starlog* No. 174: 63-69. January 1992.

JOHNSON, JANE
___ Cook, Sebastian. "Editing the Stars: An Interview With Jane Johnson," *Focus* (BSFA) No. 26: 15-16. June/July 1994.

JOHNSON, KIJ
___ "Kij Johnson Wins Sturgeon Award," *Locus* 33(3): 7. September 1994.
___ "Kij Johnson Wins Sturgeon Award; 'No Award' First for Campbell Award," *Science Fiction Chronicle* 15(9): 4. August 1994.
___ "No Campbell Winner; Johnson Wins Sturgeon Award," *Locus* 33(2): 8. August 1994.

JOHNSON, MICHAEL
___ "$1000 Susan Petrey SF Scholarships Awarded," *Science Fiction Chronicle* 14(11): 6-7. August 1993.

JOHNSON, RUSSELL
___ Sanford, Jay A. "An Interview with Russell Johnson," *Filmfax* No. 33: 62-67, 77. June/July 1992.

JOHNSON, SALLY
___ Joiner, Dorothy. "Sally Johnson: Paperworks," in: Sanders, Joe, ed. **Functions of the Fantastic**. Westport, CT: Greenwood, 1995. pp.143-154.

JOHNSON, SHANE
___ "Death Star Days," *Starlog* No. 204: 52-53, 69. July 1994.

JOHNSON, STEVE
___ Warren, Bill. "Building the Perfect Beast," *Starlog* No. 214: 41-45, 70. May 1995.

JOHNSON, W. RYERSON
___ "Johnson, W. Ryerson (Obituary)," *Science Fiction Chronicle* 16(8): 21. July/August 1995

JOHNSTONE, ANNA
___ "Johnstone, Anna (Obituary)," *Science Fiction Chronicle* 14(3): 15. December 1992.

JONES, CLAUDE EARL
___ Jankiewicz, Pat. "Mr. Expendable," *Starlog* No. 191: 62-64. June 1993.

JONES, DAVID
___ Beresford, Anne. "Memories of David Jones," in: Kranz, Gisbert, ed. **Inklings: Jahrbuch für Literatur und Ästhetik.** 9. Band. Lüdenscheid, Germany: Stier, 1991. pp.187-192. [Not seen.]

JONES, DIANA WYNNE
___ Gross, Roslyn K. "Diana Wynne Jones: An Overview," *SF Commentary* No. 71/72: 34-37. April 1992.
___ Jones, Diana W. "Aiming for the Moon," *Focus* (BSFA) No. 25: 14-16. December/January 1994.
___ Jones, Diana W. "Why Don't You Write Real Books?," *Reading Time* 37(2): 9-11. May 1993.

JONES, GWYNETH
___ "Eleanor Arnason, Gwyneth Jones Win First James Tiptree, Jr. Award," *Science Fiction Chronicle* 13(7): 4. April 1992.
___ "Gwyneth Jones: Simple Pressures; Interview," *Locus* 35(6): 5, 83-84. December 1995.
___ "James Tiptree, Jr. Award, 1991," *Locus* 28(5): 6, 65. May 1992.
___ "James Tiptree, Jr. Memorial Award Presented," *SFWA Bulletin* 26(2): 3-5. Summer 1992. (No. 116)
___ "Tiptree Award," *Locus* 28(4): 6. April 1992.
___ Jones, Gwyneth. "The Journey Through Sumatra," *New York Review of Science Fiction* No. 77: 1, 8-11. January 1995.
___ Jones, Gwyneth. "The North Wind Read This," *New York Review of Science Fiction* No. 71: 17-19. July 1994.
___ Jones, Gwyneth. "Riddles in the Dark," in: Jakubowski, Maxim and James, Edward, eds. **The Profession of Science Fiction.** New York: St. Martin's, 1992. pp.169-181.
___ Wolmark, Jenny. **Aliens and Others: Science Fiction, Feminism, and Postmodernism.** London: Harester Wheatsheaf, 1993. 167pp.; Iowa City: University of Iowa Press, 1994. 167pp.

JONES, RAYMOND F.
___ "Jones, Raymond F. (Obituary)," *Locus* 32(5): 62. May 1994.
___ "Jones, Raymond F. (Obituary)," *Science Fiction Chronicle* 15(7): 16. June 1994.

JONES-DIGGS, BARBARA
___ "Jones-Diggs, Barbara (Obituary)," *Locus* 34(2): 70. February 1995.

JONES-MORELAND, BETSY
___ Weaver, Tom. "Betsy Jones-Moreland: Interview," in: Weaver, Tom, ed. **Attack of the Monster Movie Makers: Interviews with 20 Genre Giants.** Jefferson, NC: McFarland, 1994. pp.175-194.

JORDAN, ROBERT
___ "Robert Jordan Spins His Fourth 'Wheel of Time' Yarn," *Hailing Frequencies* (Waldenbooks) No. 4: 1, 3, 12. 1992.

JOSH KIRBY: TIME WARRIOR (MOTION PICTURE)
___ Fischer, Dennis. "Moonbeam Preview: *Josh Kirby, Time Warrior*," *Cinefantastique* 26(4): 24-26. June 1995.

JOURNEY TO THE CENTER OF THE EARTH (MOTION PICTURE)
___ "Cannon Rolls 'Journey' for Christmas Release," *Variety* p. 6. July 2, 1986.

JOYCE, GRAHAM
___ "British Fantasy Awards," *Science Fiction Chronicle* 15(2): 4. November/December 1993.
___ Cary, Catie. "A Conversation With Graham Joyce," *Vector* No. 180: 5-11. August/September 1994.

JOYCE, JAMES
___ Svoboda, Randall A. **Between Private and Public Space: The Problem of Writing Personal History in the Novels of Lessing, Lawrence, Joyce and Fowles.** Ph.D. Dissertation, University of Iowa, 1995. 313pp. (DAI-A 56/06, p. 2253. December 1995.)

JUDGE DREDD (MOTION PICTURE)
___ "Sly Slugs it out For PG-13 Rating," *New York (NY) Post.* June 20, 1995. in: *NewsBank. Film and Television.* 70:B2. 1995.
___ Barker, Martin. "Waiting for Dredd," by Martin Barker and Kate Brooks. *Sight and Sound* 5(8): 16-19. August 1995.
___ Campbell, Bob. "Stodgy, Droning Parody," *(Newark, NJ) Star-Ledger.* June 30, 1995. in: *NewsBank. Film and Television.* 63:A14. 1995.
___ Denerstein, Robert. "Dredd Yawningly Familiar," *(Denver, CO) Rocky Mountain News.* June 30, 1995. in: *NewsBank. Film and Television.* 70:B3. 1995.
___ Ebert, Roger. "Judge Lacks Conviction," *Chicago (IL) Sun Times.* June 30, 1995. in: *NewsBank. Film and Television.* 70:B5. 1995.
___ Greenberger, Robert. "The Roots of Dredd," *Sci-Fi Entertainment* 2(1): 34-35. June 1995.
___ Hunter, Stephen. "Stallone's Newest Isn't That Good, But Isn't Dreadful," *(Baltimore, MD) Sun.* June 30, 1995. in: *NewsBank. Film and Television.* 63:A13. 1995.
___ James, Nick. "*Judge Dredd* (Review)," *Sight and Sound* 5(9): 55-56. September 1995.
___ Johnson, Malcolm. "Snarling, Cartoonishly Heroic Stallone Gives Fine Comic Turn in *Judge Dredd*," *Hartford (CT) Courant.* June 30, 1995. in: *NewsBank. Film and Television.* 70:B4. 1995.
___ Jones, Alan. "*Judge Dredd*: Comedy Relief," *Cinefantastique* 26(5): 37. August 1995.
___ Jones, Alan. "*Judge Dredd*: Comic Book Origins," *Cinefantastique* 26(5): 20-22. August 1995.
___ Jones, Alan. "*Judge Dredd*: Deadly Diane Lane," *Cinefantastique* 26(5): 26-27. August 1995.
___ Jones, Alan. "*Judge Dredd*: Line Producer Beau Marks," *Cinefantastique* 26(5): 38-39. August 1995.
___ Jones, Alan. "*Judge Dredd*: Makeup Design and Effects," *Cinefantastique* 26(5): 23-25, 61. August 1995.
___ Jones, Alan. "*Judge Dredd*: Production Design," *Cinefantastique* 26(5): 29-31. August 1995.
___ Jones, Alan. "*Judge Dredd*: Special Visual Effects," *Cinefantastique* 26(5): 32-34. August 1995.
___ Jones, Alan. "*Judge Dredd*: Sylvester Stallone," *Cinefantastique* 26(5): 18-19. August 1995.
___ Jones, Alan. "*Judge Dredd*: Wertham Revisited," *Cinefantastique* 26(5): 36. August 1995.
___ Jones, Alan. "*Judge Dredd*," *Cinefantastique* 26(4): 6-7. June 1995.
___ Jones, Alan. "*Judge Dredd*," *Cinefantastique* 26(5): 16-38. August 1995.
___ Killick, Jane. **The Making of *Judge Dredd*,** by Jane Killick, David Chute and Charles M. Lippincott. London: Boxtree, 1995; New York: Hyperion, 1995. 192pp.
___ Lowe, Nick. "*Judge Dredd* (Review)," *Interzone* No. 100: 34-35. October 1995.
___ Magid, Ron. " 'Mega City' Architects," *American Cinematographer* 76(12): 69-72. December 1995.
___ Nazzaro, Joe. "Chief Justice," *Starlog* No. 217: 47-51. August 1995.
___ Peterson, Don E. "22nd Century Law," *Sci-Fi Entertainment* 2(1): 30-35, 68. June 1995.
___ Peterson, Don E. "Sylvester Stallone Takes on Tomorrow as Britain's Cult Anti-Hero, *Judge Dredd*," *Science Fiction Age* 3(5): 18-23, 63. July 1995.
___ Roegger, Berthe. "Building a World of Dredd," *Sci-Fi Entertainment* 2(2): 42-49. August 1995.
___ Shulgasser, Barbara. "*Judge Dredd*: It's the (Arm)Pits," *San Francisco (CA) Examiner.* June 30, 1995. in: *NewsBank. Film and Television.* 63:A12. 1995.
___ Vaz, Mark C. "Dredd World," *Cinefex* No. 62: 58-73. June 1995.
___ Verniere, James. "Dreadful 'Judge' Is Violent, Dumb," *Boston (MA) Herald.* June 30, 1995. in: *NewsBank. Film and Television.* 70:B6. 1995.

JUDGE (MOTION PICTURE)
___ Persons, Dan. "*Judge* (Review)," *Cinefantastique* 26(3): 59-60. April 1995.

JUDGEMENT DAY (MOTION PICTURE)
___ SEE: TERMINATOR II: JUDGEMENT DAY (MOTION PICTURE).

KADLECKOVA, VILMA
___ Simsa, Cyril. "The View From Olympus: Three Czech Women Writers Talk About SF," *Vector* No. 166: 14-16. April/May 1992.

KAFKA (MOTION PICTURE)
___ Persons, Dan. "***Kafka***: Steven Soderbergh on Directing," *Cinefantastique* 22(6): 58-59. June 1992
___ Persons, Dan. "***Kafka***," *Cinefantastique* 22(6): 59. June 1992

KAFKA, FRANZ
___ Gross, Ruth V., ed. **Critical Essays on Franz Kafka**. Boston, MA: G. K. Hall, 1990. 281pp.
___ Thiher, Allen. **Franz Kafka: A Study of the Short Fiction**. Boston, MA: Twayne, 1990. 171pp.

KAGAN, JANET
___ "1993 Hugo Awards," *Science Fiction Chronicle* 15(1): 4. October 1993.

KANDEL, ABEN
___ "Kandel, Aben (Obituary)," *Science Fiction Chronicle* 14(6): 16. March 1993.

KANDINSKY, WASSILY
___ Hooper, Kent W. "Wassily Kandinsky's Stage Composition **Yellow Sound**: The Fantastic and the Symbolic Mode of Communication," in: Murphy, Patrick D., ed. **Staging the Impossible: The Fantastic Mode in Modern Drama**. Westport, CT: Greenwood, 1992. pp.56-86.

KANE, ROBERT
___ Desris, Joe. "***Batman***: Comic Creator Bob Kane," *Cinefantastique* 24(6)/25(1): 21. February 1994.

KARLOFF, BORIS
___ Karloff, Boris. "Houses I Have Haunted," *Wonder* No. 7: 22-23. 1993.
___ Sanford, Jay A. "Boris Korloff's Classic TV Series ***Thriller***, Part Two," *Filmfax* No. 30: 79-85. 1992.
___ Vivona, Stephen T. "The Films of Val Lewton and Boris Karloff," *Filmfax* No. 44: 50-56. April/May 1994.

KATSULAS, ANDREAS
___ Airey, Jean. "Alien Aboard," *Starlog* No. 188: 38-41, 68. March 1993.

KATZ, WELWYN WILTON
___ Jenkinson, Dave. "Portrait: Welwyn Wilton Katz," *Emergency Librarian* 21(2): 61-62. November/December 1993.
___ Jenkinson, Dave. "Welwyn Wilton Katz: Author of Award Winning Fantasy," *Emergency Librarian* 21(2): 61-65. November/December 1993.
___ Wytenbroek, J. R. "Cetacean Consciousness in Katz's **Whalesinger** and L'Engle's **A Ring of Endless Light**," in: Reynolds, Patricia and GoodKnight, Glen H., eds. **Proceedings of the J. R. R. Tolkien Centenary Conference, Keble College, Oxford, 1992**. Altadena, CA: Mythopoeic Press, 1995. pp.435-438. (*Mythlore* Vol. 21, No. 2, Winter 1996, Whole No. 80)

KAY, GUY GAVRIEL
___ Webb, Janeen. "Post-Romantic Romance: Guy Gavriel Kay's **Tigana** and **A Song for Arbonne**," *New York Review of Science Fiction* No. 77: 17-19. January 1995.

KAYE, MARVIN
___ Schweitzer, Darrell. "SFC Interviews: Marvin Kaye," *Science Fiction Chronicle* 14(2): 5, 27-28. November 1992.

KEAN, KATHERINE
___ Duncan, Jody. "Profile: Katherine Kean," *Cinefex* No. 51: 12. August 1992.

KEANE, GLEN
___ Lyons, Michael. "***Pocahontas***: Animator Glen Keane on the Renaissance of Disney Animation," *Cinefantastique* 27(3): 50. December 1995.

KEARNEY, PAUL
___ Melia, Sally-Ann. "Leaving Reality Behind: Paul Kearney Interviewed," *Interzone* No. 87: 16-19. September 1994.

KELLER, DAVID H.
___ Stableford, Brian. "The Creators of Science Fiction, 3: David H. Keller," *Interzone* No. 97: 54-57. July 1995.
___ Stableford, Brian. "Gernsback's Pessimist: The Futuristic Fantasies of David H. Keller," in: Stableford, Brian. **Outside the Human Aquarium: Masters of Science Fiction**. San Bernardino, CA: Borgo, 1995. pp.108-116.

KELLERMAN, JONATHAN
___ Koontz, Dean R. "Mister Bizarro," in: Greenberg, Martin H., Ed Gorman and Bill Munster, eds. **The Dean Koontz Companion**. New York: Berkley, 1994. pp.182-186.

KELLEY, GEORGE
___ "Alum's Pulp Gift out of This World With Rare SF Titles, Fanzines," *Wilson Library Bulletin* 69(5): 16. January 1995.

KELLOGG, MARJORIE BRADLEY
___ Walker, Charlotte Z. "Marjorie Bradley Kellogg: Creating Spaces, Creating Worlds," *Ms.* 6(3): 91. November 1995.

KELLY, JAMES PATRICK
___ Cox, F. Brett. "We Mean It, Man: Nancy Kress's 'Out of All Them Bright Stars' and James Patrick Kelly's 'Rat'," *New York Review of Science Fiction* No. 50: 15-17. October 1992.

KENIN, MILLEA
___ "Kenin, Millea (Obituary)," *Locus* 29(4): 66. October 1992
___ "Kenin, Millea (Obituary)," *Science Fiction Chronicle* 14(2): 12. November 1992.

KENNEALY, PATRICIA
___ Nicholls, Stan. "Patricia Kennealy Likes to Say She's Just the Typist," in: Nicholls, Stan. **Wordsmiths of Wonder: Fifty Interviews with Writers of the Fantastic**. London: Orbit, 1993. pp.356-363.
___ Skublics, Heather A. **Naming and Vocation in the Novels of J. R. R. Tolkien, Patricia Kennealy and Anne McCaffrey**. Master's Thesis, McGill University, 1994. 154pp. (Master's Abstracts 33/04, p. 1078. August 1995.)

KENNEDY, KATHLEEN
___ Warren, Bill. "Producer in the Cupboard," *Starlog* No. 218: 36-39. September 1995.

KENWITH, HERBERT
___ Jankiewicz, Pat. "Auteur of Zetar," *Starlog* 179: 92-95. June 1992.

KERR, EDWARD
___ Wilson, Bill. "Underwater Cowboy," *Starlog* No. 215: 36-39. June 1995.

KERR, KATHARINE
___ Brandenburg, Sandra. "A Time of Fantasies," by Sandra Brandenburg and Debora Hill. *Starlog* 179: 70-72, 90. June 1992.
___ Cary, Catie. "Katharine Kerr Interviewed," *Vector* No. 168: 16. August/September 1992.
___ King, T. Jackson. "SFC Interviews: Katharine Kerr," *Science Fiction Chronicle* 14(11): 5, 31-34. August 1993.
___ Nicholls, Stan. "Katharine Kerr Has Something Nasty in the Closet," in: Nicholls, Stan. **Wordsmiths of Wonder: Fifty Interviews with Writers of the Fantastic**. London: Orbit, 1993. pp.268-275.
___ Nicholls, Stan. "The Same Place You Get Your Dreams: Interview with Katharine Kerr," *Interzone* No. 71: 18-21. May 1993.

KESSEL, JOHN
___ "Denton, Kessel Win Campbell, Sturgeon Awards," *Locus* 29(3): 6. September 1992.
___ "Denton, Kessel Win Campbell, Sturgeon Awards," *Science Fiction Chronicle* 14(1): 5. October 1992.
___ "John Kessel: Between Two Worlds," *Locus* 31(2): 4, 64-65. August 1993.

KESSEL, JOHN

KESSEL, JOHN (continued)
___ Cox, F. Brett. "Epiphanies of the Mind and Heart: John Kessel's **Meeting in Infinity** and Bruce Sterling's **Globalhead**," *New York Review of Science Fiction* No. 86: 1, 3-5. October 1995.
___ Feehan, Ellen. "An Interview With John Kessel," *Science Fiction Studies* 20(1): 94-107. March 1993.
___ Kelleghan, Fiona. "Ambiguous News From the Heartland: John Kessel's **Good News From Outer Space**," *Extrapolation* 35(4): 281-297. Winter 1994.

KEYES, DANIEL

___ Heuermann, Hartmut. "Daniel Keyes, **Flowers for Algernon** (1966)," in: Heuermann, Harmut, ed. **Der Science Fiction Roman in der angloamerikanischen Literatur: Interpretationen**. Düsseldorf: Bagel, 1986. pp.275-294.

KIDD, TOM

___ Cole, Allan. "Magic Brush," *Science Fiction Age* 4(1): 84-89. November 1995.

KILLER KLOWNS FROM OUTER SPACE (MOTION PICTURE)

___ "**Killer Klowns From Outer Space** (Review)," *Variety* p. 13. June 8, 1988.

KILLER TOMATOES STRIKE BACK (MOTION PICTURE)

___ Harris, Judith P. "**Killer Tomatoes Strike Back** (Review)," *Cinefantastique* 22(6): 55. June 1992

KILLOUGH, PAT

___ "Killough, Pat (Obituary)," *Locus* 33(6): 74. December 1994.
___ "Killough, Pat (Obituary)," *Science Fiction Chronicle* 16(2): 18, 20. November/December 1994.

KILPATRICK, NANCY

___ "Interview: Nancy Kilpatrick," *Journal of the Dark* No. 4: 7-10. Fall 1995.

KILWORTH, GARRY

___ "BSFA Awards, 1993," *Locus* 32(5): 8, 66. May 1994.
___ Gomel, Elana. "Mystery, Apocalypse and Utopia: The Case of the Ontological Detective Story," *Science Fiction Studies* 22(3): 343-356. November 1995
___ Jones, Gwyneth. "The Mystique of Landscape: An Interview With Garry Kilworth," *Interzone* No. 62: 24-28, 47. August 1992.
___ Kilworth, Garry. "Confessions of a Bradbury Eater," in: Jakubowski, Maxim and James, Edward, eds. **The Profession of Science Fiction**. New York: St. Martin's, 1992. pp.154-160.

KINCAID, JAMAICA

___ Harkins, Patricia. "Family Magic: Invisibility in Jamaica Kincaid's **Lucy**," *Journal of the Fantastic in the Arts* 4(3): 53-68. 1991. (No. 15)

KING KONG (MOTION PICTURE)

___ Harmetz, Aljean. "Kong and Wray: 60 Years of Love," *New York Times* Sec. 2, p. 13. February 28, 1993.
___ Kinnard, Roy. "Queen of Screams," *Starlog* No. 194: 66-69. September 1993.
___ Kinnard, Roy. "Queen of Screams," in: McDonnell, David, ed. **Starlog's Science Fiction Heroes and Heroines**. New York: Crescent Books, 1995. pp.38-40.
___ Mandell, Paul. "Commercial Spot: Kong Reenergized," *Cinefex* No. 58: 97-98. June 1994.
___ Pizzello, Stephen. "Energizer Ad Recharges **King Kong**," *American Cinematographer* 75(3): 66-71. March 1994.
___ Torry, Robert. " 'You Can't Look Away': Spectacle and Transgression in **King Kong**," *Arizona Quarterly* 49(4): 61-78. Winter 1993.
___ Weaver, Tom. "Kong Conversations," *Starlog* No. 194: 70-73. September 1993.

KING, STEPHEN

___ "1995 World Fantasy Awards," *Locus* 35(6): 4, 81. December 1995.
___ "King of the 1996 Serials," *Locus* 35(6): 8, 82. December 1995.
___ "King of the Road," *Locus* 33(3): 9. September 1994.
___ "King Tour Plans Progress," *Locus* 33(2): 9. August 1994.
___ "King Wins Case Against Movie Company, Again," *Locus* 32(6): 8. June 1994.

KING, STEPHEN (continued)
___ "King's Independent Tour," *Locus* 33(1): 9, 75. July 1994.
___ "Lots of Stephen King Due in 1996," *Science Fiction Chronicle* 17(2): 6. December 1995/January 1996.
___ "A Stephen King Bibliography," in: Magistrale, Tony, ed. **The Dark Descent: Essays Defining Stephen King's Horrorscape**. Westport, CT: Greenwood, 1992. pp.213-220.
___ "Stephen King Chronology," in: Magistrale, Tony, ed. **The Dark Descent: Essays Defining Stephen King's Horrorscape**. Westport, CT: Greenwood, 1992. pp.xvii-xix.
___ "Stephen King Is the King of Rock 'N' Roll!," *Science Fiction Chronicle* 13(10): 5. July/August 1992.
___ "Stephen King's Newest Is Ziesing Limited Edition," *Science Fiction Chronicle* 15(6): 4-5. April/May 1994.
___ "Ties With King Led to Laurel's **Pet Sematary**," *Variety* p.81, 90. July 17, 1985.
___ "World Fantasy Awards, 1995," *Science Fiction Chronicle* 17(2): 5. December 1995/January 1996.
___ "Ziesing to Publish King First Edition," *Locus* 32(4): 8. April 1994.
___ Arnold, Gary. "Mower Cuts Swath of Diabolical Silliness (Review)," *Washington (DC) Times*. March 7, 1992. in: *NewsBank. Film and Television.* 33:A10. 1992.
___ Beahm, George. **The Stephen King Companion**. Revised edition. Kansas City, MO.: Andrews and McMeel, 1995. 3112pp.
___ Beeler, Michael. "The Horror Meister," *Cinefantastique* 25(2): 12-13. April 1994.
___ Beeler, Michael. "**The Stand**: Working With Stephen King," *Cinefantastique* 25(2): 16-17. April 1994.
___ Beeler, Michael. "**The Stand**: The Book vs. the Miniseries," *Cinefantastique* 25(2): 10-11. April 1994.
___ Beeler, Michael. "**The Stand**: Working With Stephen King," *Cinefantastique* 25(3): 30-31. June 1994.
___ Beeler, Michael. "Stephen King: **The Stand**," *Cinefantastique* 25(3): 24-30. June 1994.
___ Berkenkamp, Lauri. "Reading, Writing and Interpreting: Stephen King's **Misery**," in: Magistrale, Tony, ed. **The Dark Descent: Essays Defining Stephen King's Horrorscape**. Westport, CT: Greenwood, 1992. pp.203-211.
___ Biddle, Arthur W. "The Mythic Journey in 'The Body'," in: Magistrale, Tony, ed. **The Dark Descent: Essays Defining Stephen King's Horrorscape**. Westport, CT: Greenwood, 1992. pp.83-97.
___ Bosky, Bernadette L. "Choice, Sacrifice, Destiny, and Nature in **The Stand**," in: Magistrale, Tony, ed. **A Casebook on The Stand**. San Bernardino, CA: Borgo Press, 1992. pp.123-142.
___ Bosky, Bernadette L. "Playing the Heavy: Weight, Appetite, and Embodiment in Three Novels by Stephen King," in: Magistrale, Tony, ed. **The Dark Descent: Essays Defining Stephen King's Horrorscape**. Westport, CT: Greenwood, 1992. pp.137-156.
___ Burden, Martin. "The Cutting Edge for Sci-Fi Fans (Review)," *New York (NY) Post*. March 6, 1992. in: *NewsBank. Film and Television.* 43: A11. 1992.
___ Casebeer, Edwin F. "Dialogue Within the Archetypal Community of **The Stand**," in: Magistrale, Tony, ed. **A Casebook on The Stand**. San Bernardino, CA: Borgo Press, 1992. pp.173-188.
___ Casebeer, Edwin F. "The Ecological System of Stephen King's **The Dark Half**," *Journal of the Fantastic in the Arts* 6(2/3): 126-142. 1994.
___ Casebeer, Edwin F. "The Three Genres of **The Stand**," in: Magistrale, Tony, ed. **The Dark Descent: Essays Defining Stephen King's Horrorscape**. Westport, CT: Greenwood, 1992. pp.47-59.
___ Cassuto, Leonard. "The 'Power of Blackness' in **The Stand**," in: Magistrale, Tony, ed. **A Casebook on The Stand**. San Bernardino, CA: Borgo Press, 1992. pp.69-88.
___ Citro, Joseph A. "Foreword: **The King and I**," in: Magistrale, Tony, ed. **The Dark Descent: Essays Defining Stephen King's Horrorscape**. Westport, CT: Greenwood, 1992. pp.xi-xiv.
___ Corliss, Richard. "The King of Creep," *Time* 139(17): 62-63. April 27, 1992.
___ Counihan, Elizabeth. "The Film or the Book?," *Vector* No. 166: 13. April/May 1992.
___ Coven, Laurence. "King Turns to Other Worlds for Epic Tales," *Los Angeles (CA) Daily News*. January 5, 1992. in: *NewsBank. Literature.* 11:B6. 1992.
___ Curran, Ronald T. "Complex, Archetype, and Primal Fear: King's Use of Fairy Tales in **The Shining**," in: Magistrale, Tony, ed. **The Dark Descent: Essays Defining Stephen King's Horrorscape**. Westport, CT: Greenwood, 1992. pp.33-46.

KING, STEPHEN

KING, STEPHEN (continued)

___ Davis, Jonathan. **Stephen King's America.** Mercer Island, WA: Starmont House, 1992.

___ Delmendo, Sharon. " 'Born of **Misery**': Stephen King's (En)Gendered Text," in: Slusser, George E. and Rabkin, Eric S., eds. **Styles of Creation: Aesthetic Technique and the Creation of Fictional Worlds.** Athens: University of Georgia Press, 1992. pp.172-180.

___ Dickerson, Mary J. "Stephen King Reading William Faulkner: Memory, Desire, and Time in the Making of **IT**," in: Magistrale, Tony, ed. **The Dark Descent: Essays Defining Stephen King's Horrorscape.** Westport, CT: Greenwood, 1992. pp.171-186.

___ Doty, Gene. "A Clockwork Evil: Guilt and Coincidence in 'The Monkey'," in: Magistrale, Tony, ed. **The Dark Descent: Essays Defining Stephen King's Horrorscape.** Westport, CT: Greenwood, 1992. pp.129-136.

___ Eby, Douglas. "Tom Holland: Directing Stephen King," *Cinefantastique* 26(5): 52-53. August 1995.

___ Goodman, Denise. "Creator of Strange Tale Haunts Stephen King," *Boston (MA) Globe.* August 21, 1992. in: *NewsBank. Literature.* 74:G8-G9. 1992.

___ Goodson, William W., Jr. "Stephen King: **Children of Corn II: Deadly Harvest**," *Cinefantastique* 23(4): 13. December 1992.

___ Hennessy, Joan. "King Books 'Off Limits' for Middle School Kids," *Jacksonville (FL) Times-Union.* March 12, 1992. in: *NewsBank. Literature.* 29:D14. 1992.

___ Hohne, Karen A. "The Power of the Spoken Word in the Works of Stephen King," *Journal of Popular Culture* 28(2): 93-103. Fall 1994.

___ Holland-Toll, Linda J. "Contemporary Tragedy: Stephen King's **Pet Sematary**," *Studies in Weird Fiction* No. 16: 28-33. Winter 1995.

___ Hunter, Stephen. "**Lawnmower Man** Is a Visual Treat (Review)," *Baltimore (MD) Sun.* March 7, 1992. in: *NewsBank. Film and Television.* 33:A5. 1992.

___ Jankus, Hank. "Has Success Spoiled Stephen King?," *Shayol* No. 6: 17-19. 1982.

___ Kagle, Steven E. "Beyond Armageddon: Stephen King's **The Stand** and the Post Catastrophic World in Speculative Fiction," in: Magistrale, Tony, ed. **A Casebook on The Stand.** San Bernardino, CA: Borgo Press, 1992. pp.189-209.

___ Keesey, Douglas. " 'The Face of Mr. Flip': Homophobia in the Horror of Stephen King," in: Magistrale, Tony, ed. **The Dark Descent: Essays Defining Stephen King's Horrorscape.** Westport, CT: Greenwood, 1992. pp.187-201.

___ Keesey, Douglas. " 'I Think the Government Stinks!': Stephen King's **Stand** on Politics," in: Magistrale, Tony, ed. **A Casebook on The Stand.** San Bernardino, CA: Borgo Press, 1992. pp.21-36.

___ Kent, Brian. "Stephen King and His Readers: A Dirty, Compelling Romance," in: Magistrale, Tony, ed. **A Casebook on The Stand.** San Bernardino, CA: Borgo Press, 1992. pp.37-68.

___ Kies, Cosette. **Presenting Young Adult Horror Fiction.** New York: Twayne, 1991. 203pp.

___ Kronke, David. "King's Latest Victim May Be the Viewer With This Dumb Plot (Review)," *Los Angeles (CA) Daily News.* April 11, 1992. in: *NewsBank. Film and Television.* 46:C7. 1992.

___ Leayman, Charles D. "**The Dark Half**: Stephen King," *Cinefantastique* 24(1): 21. June 1993.

___ Leayman, Charles D. "Stephen King's **The Dark Half**," *Cinefantastique* 22(4): 5. February 1992.

___ Lloyd, Ann. **The Films of Stephen King.** New York: St. Martin's, 1993. 96pp.

___ Lovett, Verena. "Bodily Symbolism and the Fiction of Stephen King," in: Longhurst, Derek, ed. **Gender, Genre and Narrative Pleasure.** Boston, MA: Unwin Hyman, 1989. pp.157-176.

___ Magistrale, Tony. "Art Versus Madness in Stephen King's **Misery**," in: Morse, Donald E., ed. **The Celebration of the Fantastic.** Westport, CT: Greenwood, 1992. pp.271-278.

___ Magistrale, Tony. **A Casebook on The Stand.** Mercer Island, WA: Starmont, 1992. 210pp.

___ Magistrale, Tony. "Defining Stephen King's Horrorscape: An Introduction," in: Magistrale, Tony, ed. **The Dark Descent: Essays Defining Stephen King's Horrorscape.** Westport, CT: Greenwood, 1992. pp.1-4.

___ Magistrale, Tony. "Free Will and Sexual Choice in **The Stand**," *Extrapolation* 34(1): 30-38. Spring 1993.

___ Magistrale, Tony. "Free Will and Sexual Choice in **The Stand**," in: Magistrale, Tony, ed. **A Casebook on The Stand.** San Bernardino, CA: Borgo Press, 1992. pp.109-122.

KING, STEPHEN (continued)

___ Magistrale, Tony. "Science, Politics, and the Epic Imagination: **The Talisman**," in: Magistrale, Tony, ed. **The Dark Descent: Essays Defining Stephen King's Horrorscape.** Westport, CT: Greenwood, 1992. pp.113-127.

___ Magistrale, Tony. **Stephen King, the Second Decade: Danse Macabre to The Dark Half.** New York: Twayne, 1992. 186pp.

___ Magistrale, Tony, ed. **The Dark Descent: Essays Defining Stephen King's Horrorscape.** Westport, CT: Greenwood, 1992. 227pp.

___ Mahar, Ted. "A Little Clipping Here and There Wouldn't Hurt **Lawnmower Man** (Review)," *Portland (OR) The Oregonian.* March 14, 1992. in: *NewsBank. Film and Television.* 33:A9. 1992.

___ McGuire, Karen. "Of Artists, Vampires and Creativity," *Studies in Weird Fiction* No. 11: 2-4. Spring 1992.

___ Morrison, Michael A. "Dark Streets and Bright Dreams: Rationalism, Technology, and 'Impossible Knowledge' in Stephen King's **The Stand**," in: Magistrale, Tony, ed. **A Casebook on The Stand.** San Bernardino, CA: Borgo Press, 1992. pp.143-172.

___ Murray, Steve. "**Sleepwalkers** Isn't Likely to Be King's Sleeper Hit (Review)," *Atlanta (GA) Journal.* April 13, 1992. in: *NewsBank. Film and Television.* 46:C9. 1992.

___ Mustazza, Leonard. "Fear and Pity: Tragic Horror in King's **Pet Sematary**," in: Magistrale, Tony, ed. **The Dark Descent: Essays Defining Stephen King's Horrorscape.** Westport, CT: Greenwood, 1992. pp.73-82.

___ Mustazza, Leonard. "The Power of Symbols and the Failure of Virtue: Catholicism in Stephen King's **Salem's Lot**," *Journal of the Fantastic in the Arts* 3(4): 107-119. 1994.

___ Mustazza, Leonard. "Repaying Service With Pain: The Role of God in **The Stand**," in: Magistrale, Tony, ed. **A Casebook on The Stand.** San Bernardino, CA: Borgo Press, 1992. pp.89-108.

___ Pharr, Mary. "Almost Better: Surviving the Plague in Stephen King's **The Stand**," in: Magistrale, Tony, ed. **A Casebook on The Stand.** San Bernardino, CA: Borgo Press, 1992. pp.1-20.

___ Pharr, Mary. "Partners in the Danse: Women in Stephen King's Fiction," in: Magistrale, Tony, ed. **The Dark Descent: Essays Defining Stephen King's Horrorscape.** Westport, CT: Greenwood, 1992. pp.19-32.

___ Pollin, Burton R. "Stephen King's Fiction and the Legacy of Poe," *Journal of the Fantastic in the Arts* 5(4): 2-25. 1993. (No. 20)

___ Pourteau, Chris. "The Individual and Society: Narrative Structure and Thematic Unity in Stephen King's **Rage**," *Journal of Popular Culture* 27(1): 171-178. Summer 1993.

___ Reesman, Jeanne C. "Riddle Game: Stephen King's Metafictive Dialogue," in: Magistrale, Tony, ed. **The Dark Descent: Essays Defining Stephen King's Horrorscape.** Westport, CT: Greenwood, 1992. pp.157-170.

___ Rodriguez, Rene. "Stephen King as the Movies: Just Frightful," *Miami (FL) Herald.* September 13, 1992. in: *NewsBank. Film and Television.* 92:A4-A5. 1992.

___ Rodriguez, Rene. "Stephen King Sees Horror Story in Movie Adaptations," *Austin (TX) American Statesman* Sec. B, p. 9. November 2, 1992.

___ Roegger, Berthe. "**The Langoliers**," *Sci-Fi Entertainment* 2(1): 54-57, 65. June 1995.

___ Ross, Patricia. "**Pet Sematary II**: Makeup Effects," *Cinefantastique* 23(2/3): 26. October 1992.

___ Ross, Patricia. "**Pet Sematary II**," *Cinefantastique* 23(1): 6-7. August 1992.

___ Ross, Patricia. "**Pet Sematary II**," *Cinefantastique* 23(2/3): 24-26. October 1992.

___ Rudell, Michael I. "Entertainment Law: Possessory and 'Based Upon' Credits," *New York Law Journal* p. 2, 4. October 23, 1992.

___ Saidman, Anne. **Stephen King: Master of Horror.** Minneapolis, MN: Lerner, 1992. 56pp.

___ Schaeffer, Stephen. "Hollywood Goes to Hell," *Boston (MA) Herald.* August 29, 1993. in: *NewsBank. Film and Television.* 104:F1-F2. 1993.

___ Sherman, Paul. "**Lawnmower Man** Is a Seedy Sci-Fi Flick (Review)," *Boston (MA) Herald.* March 6, 1992. in: *NewsBank. Film and Television.* 33:A6. 1992.

___ Sherman, Paul. "Stephen King's Latest Yarn, **Sleepwalkers**, Is a Yawner (Review)," *Boston (MA) Herald.* April 11, 1992. in: *NewsBank. Film and Television.* 46:C10. 1992.

___ Shulgasser, Barbara. "King's **Sleepwalkers** Falls Down (Review)," *San Francisco (CA) Examiner.* April 10, 1992. in: *NewsBank. Film and Television.* 46:C8. 1992.

KING, STEPHEN (continued)

___ Smith, James F. " 'Everybody Pays. . . Even for Things They Didn't Do': Stephen King's Pay-out in the Bachman Novels," in: Magistrale, Tony, ed. **The Dark Descent: Essays Defining Stephen King's Horrorscape**. Westport, CT: Greenwood, 1992. pp.99-112.

___ Stanton, Michael N. "Some Ways of Reading **The Dead Zone**," in: Magistrale, Tony, ed. **The Dark Descent: Essays Defining Stephen King's Horrorscape**. Westport, CT: Greenwood, 1992. pp.61-72.

___ Stein, Leon. "A Holocaust Education in Reverse: Stephen King's 'The Summer of Corruption: Apt Pupil'," *Journal of the Fantastic in the Arts* 5(2): 60-79. 1993. (No. 18)

___ Strauss, Bob. "**Lawnmower Man** Is Not Exactly Cutting Edge (Review)," *Los Angeles (CA) Daily News*. March 6, 1992. in: *NewsBank. Film and Television*. 33:A4. 1992.

___ Strauss, Bob. "**Pet Sematary II** Comes Alive With No Help From King," *Austin (TX) American Statesman* Sec. B, p.5. August 31, 1992.

___ Strickler, Jeff. "**Lawnmower Man** Is Just a Cut Above Average Sci-Fi Movies (Review)," *Minneapolis (MN) Star and Tribune*. March 6, 1992. in: *NewsBank. Film and Television*. 33:A7. 1992.

___ Stroby, W. C. "Digging Up Stories With Stephen King," *Writer's Digest* 72(3): 22-27. March 1992.

___ Terrell, Carroll. **Stephen King: Man and Artist**. Orono, ME: Northern Lights, 1991. 274pp.

___ Ullrich, Allan. "Here's Reality: Mower Is Less (Review)," *San Francisco (CA) Examiner*. March 7, 1992. in: *NewsBank. Film and Television*. 33:A8. 1992.

___ Ursini, James. **More Things Than Are Dreamt Of: Masterpieces of Supernatural Horror, From Mary Shelley to Stephen King, in Literature and Film**, by James Ursini and Alain Silver. New York: Limelight, 1994. 226pp.

___ Van Hise, James. **Stephen King and Clive Barker: Masters of the Macabre II**. Las Vegas, NV: Pioneer Books, 1992. 144pp.

___ Vancheri, Barbara. "The Devil Disappoints: **Needful Things** Fails to Shiver (Review)," *Pittsburgh (PA) Post Gazette*. August 27, 1993. in: *NewsBank. Art*. 18:E6. 1993.

___ Weller, Greg. "The Masks of the Goddess: The Unfolding of the Female Archetype in Stephen King's **Carrie**," in: Magistrale, Tony, ed. **The Dark Descent: Essays Defining Stephen King's Horrorscape**. Westport, CT: Greenwood, 1992. pp.5-17.

___ Wohleber, Curt. "The Man Who Can Scare Stephen King," *American Heritage* 46(8): 82-90. December 1995.

___ Wood, Gary L. "**The Stand**: Development Movie Hell," *Cinefantastique* 25(2): 19-21. April 1994.

___ Wood, Gary L. "**The Stand**: Stephen King: The Horror Franchise," *Cinefantastique* 25(2): 22-23. April 1994.

___ Wood, Gary L. "Stephen King on Film," *Cinefantastique* 23(4): 12. December 1992.

___ Wood, Gary L. "Stephen King Strikes Again," *Cinefantastique* 22(4): 4-6. February 1992.

___ Wood, Gary L. "Stephen King's **Sleepwalkers**," *Cinefantastique* 22(4): 6. February 1992.

___ Wood, Gary L. "Stephen King's **Sleepwalkers**," *Cinefantastique* 22(5): 20-21. April 1992.

___ Wood, Gary L. "Stephen King's **Sleepwalkers**," *Cinefantastique* 23(2/3): 120. October 1992.

___ Wood, Gary L. "Stephen King's **The Lawnmower Man**," *Cinefantastique* 22(4): 7, 60. February 1992.

___ Wood, Gary L. "Stephen King, Computer Graphic," *Cinefantastique* 22(5): 6-7. April 1992.

___ Wood, Robin. "Cat and Dog: Lewis Teague's Stephen King Movies," in: Irons, Glenwood, ed. **Gender, Language and Myth: Essays on Popular Narrative**. Toronto: University of Toronto Press, 1992. pp.303-318.

KING, T. JACKSON

___ King, T. Jackson. "Pros and Cons of Being a Writer Couple," by T. Jackson King and Paula E. Downing. *SFWA Bulletin* 25(4): 7-14. Winter 1992. (No. 114)

KINGDOM (RIGET) (TV)

___ Harris, Judith P. "**The Kingdom (Riget)** (Review)," *Cinefantastique* 26(4): 59. June 1995.

KINGSOLVER, BARBARA

___ McDowell, Elizabeth J. **Power and Environment in Recent Writings by Barbara Kingsolver, Ursula K. Le Guin, Alice Walker and Terry Tempest Williams**. Master's Thesis, University of Oregon, 1992. [Not seen.]

KINSKI, KLAUS

___ "Kinski, Klaus (Obituary)," *Science Fiction Chronicle* 13(4): 12. January 1992.

KIPLING, RUDYARD

___ Bloom, Harold. "Rudyard Kipling," in: Bloom, Harold. **Classic Fantasy Writers**. New York: Chelsea House, 1994. pp.110-123.

___ Clark, Stephen R. L. "Alien Dreams: Kipling," in: Seed, David, ed. **Anticipations: Essays on Early Science Fiction and Its Precursors**. Liverpool: Liverpool University Press, 1995. pp.172-194.

___ Lerner, Fred. "Master of Our Art: Rudyard Kipling," *Voice of Youth Advocates* 16(4): 211-213. October 1993.

___ McKay, George. "Kay Dick's **They** and Rudyard Kipling's *They*: Intertextual Politicisation and the Grand End of Narrative," *Foundation* No. 58: 62-75. Summer 1993.

___ Voller, Jack G. "Kipling's Myth of Making: Creation and Contradiction in **Puck of Pook's Hill**," in: Morse, Donald E., ed. **The Celebration of the Fantastic**. Westport, CT: Greenwood, 1992. pp.81-90.

KIRBY, JACK

___ "Kirby, Jack (Obituary)," *Locus* 32(3): 68. March 1994.

___ "Kirby, Jack (Obituary)," *Science Fiction Chronicle* 15(5): 12. March 1994.

KIRIKI, NINA

___ "Bram Stoker Awards," *Science Fiction Chronicle* 15(8): 5. June 1994.

KIRK, GEORGE WILLARD

___ Hart, Mara K. "Walkers in the City: George Willard Kirk and Howard Phillips Lovecraft in New York City, 1924-1926," *Lovecraft Studies* No. 28: 2-17. Fall 1992.

KIRK, RUSSELL

___ "Kirk, Russell (Obituary)," *Locus* 32(6): 72. June 1994.

KIRKPATRICK, JOHN

___ McMahan, Robert Y. "John Kirkpatrick: A Personal Remembrance of His Last Nine Years, 1983-1991," *CSL: The Bulletin of the New York C. S. Lewis Society* 23(1): 1-8. November 1991.

KISS OF THE SPIDER WOMAN (MOTION PICTURE)

___ Heldreth, Leonard G. "Films, Film Fantasies, and Fantasies: Spinning Reality From the Self in **Kiss of the Spider Woman**," *Journal of the Fantastic in the Arts* 3(4): 93-106. 1994.

KLEIN, T. E. D.

___ Joshi, S. T. "T. E. D. Klein: Urban Horror," *Studies in Weird Fiction* No. 10: 6-18. Fall 1991.

KLEISER, RANDAL

___ Warren, Bill. "Kid Stuff," *Starlog* 181: 40-43, 69. August 1992.

KLIEST, HEINRICH VON

___ Rhiel, Mary. "The Taming of the Screw: Rohmer's Filming of Kliest's 'Die Marquise von O...'," in: Ruddick, Nicholas, ed. **State of the Fantastic**. Westport, CT: Greenwood, 1992. pp.83-90.

KLINE, OTIS ADELBERT

___ Barrett, Robert R. "Burroughs, Kline and Henry Herbert Knibbs: Another Opinion," *Burroughs Bulletin* NS No. 9: 27-32. January 1992.

___ Lupoff, Richard A. "Edgar & Otis & Sam & Bob: Consider the Possibilities," *Burroughs Bulletin* NS No. 11: 24-26. July 1992.

___ Moskowitz, Sam. "Burroughs, Kline, Knibbs: A Reply," *Burroughs Bulletin* NS No. 9: 34-39. January 1992.

KLINGONS

___ Davis, Erik. "The Imperial Race," *Village Voice* 38(47): 35-40. November 23, 1993.

KLINGONS (continued)
___ Pearlman, Cindy. "Captains Quirk," *Chicago* 44(12): December 1995.

KLUSHANTSEV, PAVEL
___ Barker, Lynn. "Klushantsev: Russia's Wizard of *Fantastika*, Part One," by Lynn Barker and Robert Skotak. *American Cinematographer* 75(6): 78-83. June 1994.
___ Barker, Lynn. "Klushantsev: Russia's Wizard of *Fantastika*, Part Two," by Lynn Barker and Robert Skotak. *American Cinematographer* 75(7): 77-82. July 1994.

KNEALE, NIGEL
___ Newsom, Ted. "The Creature Remake That Never Got Made: An Afternoon with Jack Arnold and Nigel Kneale," *Filmfax* No. 37: 64-67, 82, 98. February/March 1993.

KNEBEL, FLETCHER
___ "Knebel, Fletcher (Obituary)," *Locus* 30(4): 60. April 1993.
___ "Knebel, Fletcher (Obituary)," *Science Fiction Chronicle* 14(7): 18. April 1993.

KNIBBS, HENRY HERBERT
___ Barrett, Robert R. "Burroughs, Kline and Henry Herbert Knibbs: Another Opinion," *Burroughs Bulletin* NS No. 9: 27-32. January 1992.
___ Moskowitz, Sam. "Burroughs, Kline, Knibbs: A Reply," *Burroughs Bulletin* NS No. 9: 34-39. January 1992.

KNIGHT, DAMON
___ "Damon Knight Honored," *Science Fiction Chronicle* 17(1): 7. October/November 1995
___ "Nebula Award Winners," *Science Fiction Chronicle* 16(6): 4. May 1995.

KNIGHT, DAN
___ Chalker, Jack L. "On Publishing and Personalities," *Pulphouse* No. 11: 53-57. August 1992.

KNIGHT, WAYNE
___ Warren, Bill. "Dinosaur Lunch," *Starlog* No. 194: 38-41, 82. September 1993.

KNIGHTRIDERS (MOTION PICTURE)
___ Harty, Kevin J. "Camelot Twice Removed: *Knightriders* and the Film Versions of **A Connecticut Yankee in King Arthur's Court**," in: Harty, Kevin J., ed. **Cinema Arthuriana: Essays on Arthurian Film**. New York: Garland, 1991. pp.105-120.

KNIGHTS (MOTION PICTURE)
___ Harris, Judith P. "**Knights** (Review)," *Cinefantastique* 25(6)/26(1): 122. December 1994.
___ Hawkins, Robert J. "**Knights** in Shining, Cyborg Armor (Review)," *San Diego (CA) Union* November 25, 1993. in: *NewsBank. Film and Television.* 128:F12-F13. 1993.

KOCH, HOWARD W.
___ "Koch, Howard (Obituary)," *Locus* 35(3): 78. September 1993.
___ "Koch, Howard W. (Obituary)," *Science Fiction Chronicle* 17(1): 22, 24. October/November 1995

KOENIG, WALTER
___ Stephens, Lynne. "*Raver*," *Starlog* No. 190: 24-26. May 1993.
___ Uram, Sue. "**Star Trek: Generations**: Chekov Makes Captain," *Cinefantastique* 26(2): 32-33. February 1995.

KOEPP, DAVID
___ Altman, Mark A. "**The Shadow**: Screenwriter David Koepp," *Cinefantastique* 25(4): 23. August 1994.

KOJA, KATHE
___ "1992 *Locus* Awards," *Locus* 28(2): 1, 42-45. August 1992.
___ "1992 Bram Stoker Awards Winners," *Locus* 28(2): 6, 68. August 1992.
___ "Bram Stoker Awards," *Science Fiction Chronicle* 13(10): 4. July/August 1992.
___ "Kathe Koja: Through the Back Door," *Locus* 28(1): 4, 77. January 1992.

KOJA, KATHE (continued)
___ Arnzen, Michael A. "Behold the Funhole: Post-Structuralist Theory and Kathe Koja's **The Cipher**," *Paradoxa* 1(3): 342-351. 1995.

KOOISTRA, JEFFERY D.
___ Klein, Jay K. "Biolog: Jeffery D. Kooistra," *Analog* 113(14): 89, 110. December 1993.

KOONTZ, DEAN R.
___ "Dean Koontz: A Comedian in Hell," *Locus* 33(5): 4-5, 81-82. November 1994.
___ "Dean R. Koontz: Annotated Bibliography," in: Greenberg, Martin H., Ed Gorman and Bill Munster, eds. **The Dean Koontz Companion**. New York: Berkley, 1994. pp.283-312.
___ "Koontz Moves to Random House," *Science Fiction Chronicle* 13(11/12): 6. August 1992.
___ "Koontz to Knopf in Super Deal," *Locus* 29(3): 6, 79. September 1992.
___ "Koontz vs. TriStar," *Locus* 34(4): 8, 68. April 1995.
___ "The Ten Questions Readers Most Often Ask Dean Koontz," in: Greenberg, Martin H., Ed Gorman and Bill Munster, eds. **The Dean Koontz Companion**. New York: Berkley, 1994. pp.265-282.
___ "Two Pauline Dunn Horror Novels Plagiarized Dean R. Koontz's **Phantoms**," *Science Fiction Chronicle* 13(10): 4. July/August 1992.
___ "Zebra Withdraws Two Novels for Plagiarism," *Locus* 28(2): 6. August 1992.
___ Costello, Matthew J. "Films, Television, and Dean Koontz," in: Greenberg, Martin H., Ed Gorman and Bill Munster, eds. **The Dean Koontz Companion**. New York: Berkley, 1994. pp.101-146.
___ de Lint, Charles. "The Heart of the Ticktock Man," in: Greenberg, Martin H., Ed Gorman and Bill Munster, eds. **The Dean Koontz Companion**. New York: Berkley, 1994. pp.75-100.
___ Gorman, Ed. "Interview With Dean Koontz," in: Greenberg, Martin H., Ed Gorman and Bill Munster, eds. **The Dean Koontz Companion**. New York: Berkley, 1994. pp.1-56
___ Greenberg, Martin H., ed. **The Dean Koontz Companion**, ed. by Martin H. Greenberg, Ed Gorman and Bill Munster. New York: Berkley, 1994. 312pp.
___ Kies, Cosette. **Presenting Young Adult Horror Fiction**. New York: Twayne, 1991. 203pp.
___ Koontz, Dean R. "Koontzramble," in: Greenberg, Martin H., Ed Gorman and Bill Munster, eds. **The Dean Koontz Companion**. New York: Berkley, 1994. pp.149-154.
___ Koontz, Dean R. "My First Short Story," in: Greenberg, Martin H., Ed Gorman and Bill Munster, eds. **The Dean Koontz Companion**. New York: Berkley, 1994. pp.187-192.
___ Seels, James T. "Collecting Dean Koontz," *Firsts: Collecting Modern First Editions* 3(10): 28-36. October 1993.
___ Silva, David B. "Keeping Pace With the Master," in: Greenberg, Martin H., Ed Gorman and Bill Munster, eds. **The Dean Koontz Companion**. New York: Berkley, 1994. pp.57-74

KORNBLUTH, CYRIL M.
___ Hassler, Donald M. "Swift, Pohl, and Kornbluth: Publicists Anatomize Newness," *Extrapolation* 34(3): 245-250. Fall 1993.
___ Rich, Mark. " 'It Was a Wonderful Time': Outtakes: Kornblume: Kronbluthiana: Issues One Through Nine, 13 August 94 to 13 April 95," *New York Review of Science Fiction* No. 88: 1, 3-7. December 1995.
___ Seed, David. "Take-over Bids: The Power Fantasies of Frederik Pohl and Cyril Kornbluth," *Foundation* No. 59: 42-58. Autumn 1993.

KOSTAL, IRWIN
___ "Kostal, Irwin (Obituary)," *Science Fiction Chronicle* 16(3): 16. January 1995.

KOSZTKA, TIVADAR CSONTVARY
___ Bertha, Csilla. "Csontváry, the Painter of the 'Sun's Path'," in: Morse, Donald E., ed. **The Celebration of the Fantastic**. Westport, CT: Greenwood, 1992. pp.151-164.

KOTZWINKLE, WILLIAM
___ Schumacher, Michael. "The Inner Worlds of William Kotzwinkle," *Writer's Digest* 72(7): 34-39. July 1992.

KRAMER, ERIC
___ "Kramer, Eric (Obituary)," *Locus* 29(6): 68. December 1992.

KRAMER, ERIC (continued)
___ "Kramer, Eric (Obituary)," *Science Fiction Chronicle* 14(2): 12. November 1992.

KRESS, NANCY
___ "13th Annual *Science Fiction Chronicle* Reader Awards," *Science Fiction Chronicle* 15(10): 4. September 1994.
___ "Eighth Annual Reader's Awards Results," *Asimov's Science Fiction Magazine* 18(10): 166-167. September 1994.
___ "Eleventh Annual *S. F. Chronicle* Reader's Awards," *Science Fiction Chronicle* 13(11/12): 4. August 1992.
___ "An Interview With Nancy Kress," *Sense of Wonder* p. 5, 10. February/March 1994.
___ "Nancy Kress: The Children's Hour," *Locus* 29(6): 5, 74. December 1992.
___ "World SF Convention Hugo Awards," *Science Fiction Chronicle* 14(1): 4. October 1992.
___ Cox, F. Brett. "We Mean It, Man: Nancy Kress's 'Out of All Them Bright Stars' and James Patrick Kelly's 'Rat'," *New York Review of Science Fiction* No. 50: 15-17. October 1992.
___ Trull, Anthony. "Atlas in Spain: Comparing Nancy Kress' 'Beggars in Spain' with Ayn Rand's **Atlas Shrugged**," *Quantum* No. 42: 31-32. Summer/Fall 1992.

KRICFALUS, JOHN
___ Persons, Dan. "Spumco: This Is Your Life, John Kricfalus," *Cinefantastique* 24(1): 35-37. June 1993.

KRIZMAN, SERGE
___ Garcia, Bob. "*Batman*: Comic Book Art Direction," *Cinefantastique* 24(6)/25(1): 22-25. February 1994.

KUBE-McDOWELL, MICHAEL
___ Kube-McDowell, Michael P. "The Quiet Pools," *OtherRealms* No. 27: 4-5. Spring 1990.

KUBILIUS, WALTER
___ "Kubilius, Walter (Obituary)," *Locus* 31(5): 64. November 1993.
___ "Kubilius, Walter (Obituary)," *Science Fiction Chronicle* 15(2): 16-18. November/December 1993.

KUBIN, ALFRED
___ Alexander-Schaechtelin, Barbara F. "Eros and Thanatos: The Art of Alfred Kubin on the Edge of the Other Side," in: Morse, Donald E., ed. **The Celebration of the Fantastic**. Westport, CT: Greenwood, 1992. pp.165-182.

KUBRICK, STANLEY
___ DeBellis, Jack. " 'The Awful Power': John Updike's Use of Kubrick's **2001: A Space Odyssey** in **Rabbit Redux**," *Literature/Film Quarterly* 21(3): 209-217. 1993.
___ Deer, Harriet. "Kubrick and the Structures of Popular Culture," by Harriet Deer and Irving Deer. *Journal of Popular Film and Television* 3(3): 232-244. 1974.
___ Macklin, F. Anthony. "Understanding Kubrick: **The Shining**," *Journal of Popular Film and Television* 9(2): 93-95. 1981.
___ Manchel, Frank. "What About Jack? Another Perspective on Family Relationships in Stanley Kubrick's **The Shining**," *Literature/Film Quarterly* 23(1): 68-78. 1995.
___ Titterington, P. L. "Kubrick and **The Shining**," *Sight and Sound* 50(2): 117-121. Spring 1981.

KURAN, PETER
___ Duncan, Jody. "Profile: Peter Kuran," *Cinefex* No. 54: 88. May 1993.

KURE, HENNING
___ Spurlock, Duane. "Where Have All the Fans Gone?: An Interview with Henning Kure," *Burroughs Bulletin* NS. No. 13: 23-35. January 1993.

KURT VONNEGUT'S HARRISON BERGERON (MOTION PICTURE)
___ SEE: HARRISON BERGERON (MOTION PICTURE).

KURTZ, KATHERINE
___ Clarke, Boden. **The Work of Katherine Kurtz: An Annotated Bibliography & Guide**, by Boden Clarke and Mary A. Burgess. San Bernardino, CA: Borgo Press, 1993. 128pp.
___ Holmen, Rachel E. "Interview With Katherine Kurtz," *Marion Zimmer Bradley's Fantasy Magazine* No. 24: 40-44. Summer 1994.

KURTZMAN, HARVEY
___ "Kurtzman, Harvey (Obituary)," *Locus* 30(4): 60. April 1993.
___ "Kurtzman, Harvey (Obituary)," *Science Fiction Chronicle* 14(7): 18. April 1993.

KUSHNER, ELLEN
___ "Ellen Kushner: True Fantasy," *Locus* 28(4): 5, 65-66. April 1992.

KUTTNER, HENRY
___ Bloom, Harold. "C. L. Moore & Henry Kuttner," in: Bloom, Harold, ed. **Science Fiction Writers of the Golden Age**. New York: Chelsea House, 1995. pp.141-156.
___ Mueller, Allen. "A Wild Surmise," *Fantasy Commentator* 7(4): 282-285. Fall 1992. (Whole No. 44)

KYOKA, IZUMI
___ Poulton, Cody. "The Grotesque and the Gothic: Izumi Kyoka's Japan," *Japan Quarterly* 41(3): 324-35. July 1994.

L'ENGLE, MADELEINE
___ **Madeleine L'Engle: Star Gazer**. Patterson, NY: Ishtar Films, 1989. 30 min.
___ Arfken, Deborah E. "Madeleine L'Engle," in: Bruccoli, Matthew J., ed. **Facts on File Bibliography of American Fiction 1919-1988**. New York: Facts on File, 1991. pp.293-294.
___ Edge, Peggy. "WLB Biography: Madeleine L'Engle," *Wilson Library Bulletin* 36(9): 766. May 1962.
___ Garrison, Greg. "Storyteller Sees Religion in Many Hues," *Birmingham (AL) News*. January 31, 1992. in: *NewsBank. Names in the News*. 37:D10-D11. 1992.
___ Glass, Rona. "**A Wrinkle in Time** and **The High King**: Two Couples, Two Perspectives," *Children's Literature Association. Quarterly* 6(3): 15-18. Fall 1981.
___ Gonzales, Doreen. **Madeleine L'Engle: Author of A Wrinkle in Time**. New York: Dillon Press, 1991. 112pp.
___ Hammond, Wayne G. "Seraphim, Cherubim and Virtual Unicorns: Order and Being in Madeline L'Engle's Time Quartet," *Mythlore* 20(4): 41-45. Winter 1995. (Whole No. 78)
___ Hettinga, Donald R. **Presenting Madeleine L'Engle**. New York: Macmillan/Twayne, 1993. 169pp.
___ Jones, Kellie F. C. **A Pentaperceptual Analysis of Social and Philosophical Commentary in A Wrinkle in Time by Madeleine L'Engle**. Ph.D. Dissertation, University of Mississippi, 1977. 177pp. (DAI-A 38(12): 7325. June 1978.)
___ Mehren, Elizabeth. "Children's Author? Christian Author? Don't Try to Label Madeleine L'Engle. At 73, She's Still. . .Following Her Heart," *Los Angeles (CA) Times*. October 12, 1992. in: *NewsBank. Literature*. 92:G3-G5. 1992.
___ Perry, Barbara. "Profile: Madeleine L'Engle, a Real Person," *Language Arts* 812-816. October 1977.
___ Sadler, Glenn E. "**A Wrinkle in Time**: A Life-Fantasy of Tessering Through Space," *Teaching and Learning Literature* 4(5): 29-33. May/June 1995.
___ Smedman, M. Sarah. "The 'Terrible Journey' Past 'Dragons in the Waters' to a 'House Like a Lotus': Faces of Love in the Fiction of Madeleine L'Engle," in: Sullivan, C. W., III. **Science Fiction for Young Readers**. Westport, CT: Greenwood, 1993. pp.65-82.
___ Weber, Katharine. "Tessering Through Time," *Connecticut* 51: 76-85. November 1988.
___ Wytenbroek, J. R. "Cetacean Consciousness in Katz's **Whalesinger** and L'Engle's **A Ring of Endless Light**," in: Reynolds, Patricia and GoodKnight, Glen H., eds. **Proceedings of the J. R. R. Tolkien Centenary Conference, Keble College, Oxford, 1992**. Altadena, CA: Mythopoeic Press, 1995. pp.435-438. (*Mythlore* Vol. 21, No. 2, Winter 1996, Whole No. 80)

LA BLUE GIRL (TV)
___ Persons, Dan. "**La Blue Girl** (Review)," *Cinefantastique* 27(2): 59. November 1995.

LaBRUTTO, PAT
___ "Alice Alfonsi Out, Pat LaBrutto in at Zebra," *Science Fiction Chronicle* 14(10): 6. July 1993.

LABYRINTH
___ Baker, Rob. "Tangent: A Modern Metaphor," *Parabola* 17(2): 83-87. May 1992.

LACKEY, MERCEDES
___ "Mercedes Lackey: From Bardo to Brainships," *Hailing Frequencies* (Waldenbooks) No. 2: 4, 6-7. 1992.
___ Taylor, Rececca. "Interview with Mercedes," by Rececca Taylor, Gayle Keresey and Margaret Miles. *Voice of Youth Advocates* 15(4): 213-217. October 1992.
___ Waters, Elizabeth. "Interview With Mercedes Lackey," *Marion Zimmer Bradley's Fantasy Magazine* No. 19: 50-52. Spring 1993.

LAD AND THE LION (MOTION PICTURE)
___ Sarnya, Count. "*The Lad and the Lion* in Films: 1917-1937," *Burroughs Bulletin* NS. No. 14: 3-10. April 1993.

LADY IN WHITE (MOTION PICTURE)
___ "*Lady in White* (Review)," *Variety* p. 20. April 13, 1988.

LADYHAWKE (MOTION PICTURE)
___ "*Ladyhawke* (1985): Interviews Richard Donner, Michelle Pfeiffer, and Rutger Hauer," in: Goldberg, Lee, ed. **The Dreamweavers: Interviews With Fantasy Filmmakers of the 1980s.** Jefferson, NC: McFarland, 1995. pp.192-212.

LAFFERTY, R. A.
___ "Other Awards," *Science Fiction Chronicle* 15(1): 4. October 1993.
___ Knight, Damon. **An R. A. Lafferty Checklist.** New edition. Polk City, IA: Drumm, 1991. 28pp.
___ Lafferty, R. A. **It's Down the Slippery Cellar Stairs: Essays and Speeches on Fantastic Literature.** San Bernardino, CA: Borgo, 1995. 104pp.
___ Swanwick, Michael. "The Strange Case of Raphael Aloysius Lafferty," *Amazing* 68(7): 51-57. October 1993.
___ Tidmarsh, Andrew. "R. A. Lafferty: An Annotated Bibliography," *Interzone* No. 64: 44-47. October 1992.
___ Zebrowski, George. "Never Forget the Writers Who Helped Build Yesterday's Tomorrows," *Science Fiction Age* 3(6): 30-36, 100. 1995.

LAIDLAW, MARC
___ Zebrowski, George. "Laidlaw Rising," *Amazing Stories* 67(9): 54-57. December 1992.

LAING, RONALD
___ Caretti, Vincenzo. "Ronald Laing e la demistificazione della famiglia interiorizzata," in: Colombo, Arrigo and Quarta, Cosimo, eds. **Il Destino della Famiglia nell'Utopia.** Bari: Edizione Dedalo, 1991. pp.309-320.

LAMBDA LITERARY AWARD, 1993
___ "Lambda Literary Award SF/Fantasy Nominations," *Science Fiction Chronicle* 15(5): 5. March 1994.

LAMBERT, CHRISTOPHER
___ Fletcher, Tanya A. "Christopher Lambert: There Is Only One," *Sci-Fi Entertainment* 1(6): 38-41. April 1995.
___ Yakir, Dan. "Higher Ground," *Starlog* No. 212: 46-49, 72. March 1995.

LAMBERT, MARY
___ Ross, Patricia. "*Pet Sematary II*," *Cinefantastique* 23(5): 55. February 1993.

LAMSLEY, TERRY
___ "1994 World Fantasy Awards," *Locus* 33(6): 7, 49. December 1994.

LANCE, LANCELOT
___ Stone, Graham. "Notes on Australian Science Fiction," *Science Fiction News* (Australia) No. 94: 2-11. January 1986.

LANCELOT DU LAC (MOTION PICTURE)
___ Bartone, Richard C. "Variations on Arthurian Legend in **Lancelot du Lac** and **Excalibur**," in: Slocum, Sally K., ed. **Popular Arthurian Traditions.** Bowling Green, OH: Popular Press, 1992. pp.144-155.
___ Rider, Jeff. "The Arthurian Legend in French Cinema: **Lancelot du Lac** and **Perceval la Gallois**," by Jeff Rider, Richard Hull and Christopher Smith. in: Harty, Kevin J., ed. **Cinema Arthuriana: Essays on Arthurian Film.** New York: Garland, 1991. pp.41-56.

LAND OF THE GIANTS (TV)
___ Counts, Kyle. "Living Doll in Giant Land," *Starlog* 181: 27-31, 60. August 1992.

LAND OF THE LOST (TV)
___ Shapiro, Marc. "Dinosaur Safari," *Starlog* No. 175: 94-97. February 1992.

LAND UNKNOWN (MOTION PICTURE)
___ Stephens, Bob. "Pre-tinsel Science Fiction Tales," *San Francisco (CA) Examiner* November 25, 1995. (Cited from the Internet Edition.)

LAND'S END (MOTION PICTURE)
___ SEE: BIRDS II: LAND'S END (MOTION PICTURE).

LANDAU, MARTIN
___ French, Lawrence. "*Ed Wood*: Playing Bela Lugosi," *Cinefantastique* 25(5): 34-35. October 1994.

LANDIS, GEOFFREY A.
___ "World SF Convention Hugo Awards," *Science Fiction Chronicle* 14(1): 4. October 1992.

LANE, DIANE
___ Jones, Alan. "*Judge Dredd*: Deadly Diane Lane," *Cinefantastique* 26(5): 26-27. August 1995.

LANE, JOEL
___ "British Fantasy Awards, 1995," *Science Fiction Chronicle* 17(2): 5. December 1995/January 1996.

LANE, MARY E. BRADLEY
___ Jacobs, Naomi. "The Frozen Landscape in Women's Utopian and Science Fiction," in: Donawerth, Jane L. and Kolmerten, Carol A., eds. **Utopian and Science Fiction by Women: Worlds of Difference.** Syracuse, NY: Syracuse University Press, 1994. pp.190-202.
___ Segal, Howard P. **Future Imperfect: The Mixed Blessings of Technology in America.** Amherst: University of Massachusetts Press, 1994. 245pp.

LANG, ANDREW
___ Bloom, Harold. "Andrew Lang," in: Bloom, Harold. **Classic Fantasy Writers.** New York: Chelsea House, 1994. pp.124-136.

LANG, FRITZ
___ "Profile: Fritz Lang: The Genius Behind **Metropolis**," *Futures Past* No. 2: 24-25. April 1992.
___ Sawyer, Andy. "More Than Metaphor: Double Vision in Lang's **Metropolis**," *Foundation* No. 64: 70-81. Summer 1995.

LANGOLIERS (TV)
___ Eby, Douglas. "Tom Holland: Directing Stephen King," *Cinefantastique* 26(5): 52-53. August 1995.
___ Gadberry, Greg. "The Making of a Miniseries: *The Langoliers*," *(Portland, ME) Maine Sunday Telegram*. September 4, 1994. in: *NewsBank. Film and Television.* 100:D4. 1994.
___ Roegger, Berthe. "*The Langoliers*," *Sci-Fi Entertainment* 2(1): 54-57, 65. June 1995.
___ Scapperotti, Dan. "King Effect: Computer Graphics by Image Design," *Cinefantastique* 26(5): 55. August 1995.
___ Scapperotti, Dan. "Stephen King's *The Langoliers*," *Cinefantastique* 26(5): 50-54, 61. August 1995.
___ Soriano, Cesar G. "*Langoliers* Just Languishes in Its Time Warp," *Washington (DC) Times*. May 13, 1995. in: *NewsBank. Film and Television.* 55:C10. 1995.

LANGSTAFF, LYDIA

___ "Langstaff, Lydia (Obituary)," *Science Fiction Chronicle* 16(2): 20. November/December 1994.

LANGUAGE

___ Bailey, Richard W. **Images of English: A Cultural History of the Language.** Ann Arbor: University of Michigan Press, 1992. 329pp. (See section: 'Imaginary English,' pp.215-176.)

___ Dorfles, Gillo. "L'utopia della omoglossia e il ritorno a un linguaggio prebabelico," in: Saccaro Del Buffa, Giuseppa and Lewis, Arthur O., eds. **Utopie per gli Anni Ottana.** Rome: Gangemi Editore, 1986. pp.45-50.

___ Elgin, Suzette H. "Women's Language and Near Future Science Fiction: A Reply," *Women's Studies* 14(2): 175-182. 1987.

___ Glennon, Dorinda. **Creative Philology: The Use of Language in J. R. R. Tolkien's The Lord of the Rings.** Master's Thesis, Idaho State University, 1977. 55pp.

___ Keene, Louise E. "The Restoration of Language in Middle-Earth," *Mythlore* 20(4): 6-13. Winter 1995. (Whole No. 78)

___ Kramarae, Cheris. "Present Problems With the Language of the Future," *Women's Studies* 14(2): 183-186. 1987.

___ Malmgren, Carl D. "The Languages of Science Fiction: Samuel Delaney's **Babel 17**," *Extrapolation* 34(1): 5-17. Spring 1993.

___ Marik, Jaroslav. "Planlingvo kaj scienca fikcio," *Starto* 4(145): 4-6. 1991.

___ Marrone, Caterina. "Lingue universali e utopie nel pensiero linguistico del secolo XVII," in: Saccaro Del Buffa, Giuseppa and Lewis, Arthur O., eds. **Utopia e Modernita: Teorie e prassi utopiche nell'eta moderna e postmoderna.** Rome: Gangemi Editore, 1989. pp.505-518.

___ Padol, Lisa. "Whose English?: Language in the Modern Arthurian Novel," *Mythlore* 20(4): 20-24. Winter 1995. (Whole No. 78)

___ Roy, John F. "The Many Tongues of Pellucidar," *Wayfarer II* pp.4-6. n.d.

___ Sisk, David W. **Claiming Mastery over the Word: Transformations of Language in Six Twentieth Century Dystopias.** Ph.D. Dissertation, University of North Carolina, Chapel Hill, 1994. 405pp. (DAI-A 55/07, p. 1972. January 1995.)

___ Solivetti, Carla. "L'utopia linguistica di Velimir Chlebnikov," in: Saccaro Del Buffa, Giuseppa and Lewis, Arthur O., eds. **Utopie per gli Anni Ottana.** Rome: Gangemi Editore, 1986. pp.51-70.

___ Tompson, Ricky L. "Tolkien's Word-Hoard Onleac," *Mythlore* 20(1): 22-40. Winter 1994. (Whole No. 75)

___ Van Matre, Lynn. "Trekkers Say 'HISlaH' to Klingon Language Lessons," *Austin (TX) American Statesman* Sec. D, p. 6. March 6, 1993.

___ Vonarburg, Elisabeth. "The Reproduction of the Body in Space," in: Ruddick, Nicholas, ed. **State of the Fantastic.** Westport, CT: Greenwood, 1992. pp.59-72.

___ Wiemer, Annegret J. "Foreign L(anguish), Mother Tongue: Concepts of Language in Contemporary Feminist Science Fiction," *Women's Studies* 14(2): 163-174. 1987.

___ Young, John W. **Orwell's Newspeak and Totalitarian Language: Its Nazi and Communist Antecedents.** Charlottesville: University Press of Virginia, 1991. 335pp.

LANSDALE, JOE R.

___ "Bram Stoker Awards, 1993," *Science Fiction Chronicle* 14(10): 4. July 1993.

___ Koontz, Dean R. "Tater Bacon," in: Greenberg, Martin H., Ed Gorman and Bill Munster, eds. **The Dean Koontz Companion.** New York: Berkley, 1994. pp.173-176.

___ MacColloch, Simon. "Joe R. Lansdale's 'The Nightrunners': The Art of Violence," *Studies in Weird Fiction* No. 12: 2-6. Spring 1993.

___ Proulx, Kevin. **Fear to the World: Eleven Voices in a Chorus of Horror.** Mercer Island, WA: Starmont, 1992. 243pp.

___ Wade, Susan. "Author Stays Close to Home in East Texas," *Austin (TX) American Statesman* Sec. E, p. 1, 7. September 15, 1995.

LANSING, ROBERT

___ "Lansing, Robert, 1929-1994 (Obituary)," *Starlog* No. 212: 20. March 1995.

LANTZ, WALTER

___ "Lantz, Walter (Obituary)," *Science Fiction Chronicle* 15(6): 24. April/May 1994.

LARNACH, STANLEY LORIN

___ "Larnach, Stanley Lorin (Obituary)," *Science Fiction News* (Australia) No. 59: 8-10. February 1979.

LARSON, DOUG

___ Klein, Jay K. "Biolog: Doug Larson," *Analog* 114(1/2): 225, 300. January 1994.

___ Larsen, T. E. "From Fiction to Fact: A Technology Postscript to 'Only the Weatherman'," *Analog* 114(4): 74-79. March 1994.

LAS VEGAS

___ Brill, Louis M. "Special Venues: Inside the Luxor Pyramid," *Cinefex* No. 61: 23-28. March 1995.

LASKY, KATHRYN

___ Lasky, Kathryn. "Shuttling Through Realities: The Warp and the Weft of Fantasy and Nonfiction Writing," *The New Advocate* 6(4): 235-242. Fall 1993.

LASSETER, JOHN

___ French, Lawrence. "**Toy Story**: CGI Director," *Cinefantastique* 27(2): 20-21. November 1995.

LAST ACTION HERO (MOTION PICTURE)

___ Lowe, Nick. "**Last Action Hero** (Review)," *Interzone* No. 76: 36-37. October 1993.

___ Norton, Bill. "Pandora's Paintbox," *Cinefex* No. 56: 54-69. November 1993.

___ Shapiro, Marc. "**Last Action Hero**," *Starlog* No. 192: 39-46. July 1993.

___ Shapiro, Marc. "Last Action Man," *Starlog* No. 194: 55-57. September 1993.

___ Shapiro, Marc. "To Be or Not to Be?," *Starlog* No. 193: 42-46. August 1993.

LAST HALLOWEEN (MOTION PICTURE)

___ "**The Last Halloween** (Review)," *Cinefantastique* 22(5): 61. April 1992.

LAST ONE (COMIC)

___ Kilby, Damian. "Vertigo's *Last One* Shows That Immortality May Not Be All It's Cracked Up to Be," *Science Fiction Age* 1(5): 76-78. July 1993.

LAST STARFIGHTER (MOTION PICTURE)

___ "Lorimar Given Overseas Rights to 'Starfighter'," *Variety* p. 5, 28. June 20, 1984.

LAST UNICORN (MOTION PICTURE)

___ "**Day After**, **Last Unicorn** Hit Big in Germany, Campaigns Help," *Variety* p. 123. January 25, 1984.

LATE FOR DINNER (MOTION PICTURE)

___ "**Late for Dinner** (Review)," *Cinefantastique* 22(5): 61. April 1992.

LATIN AMERICA

___ Robinett, Jane. **This Rough Magic: Technology in Latin American Fiction.** New York: P. Lang, 1993. 284pp.

___ Stavans, Ilan. "Introduction: Private Eyes and Time Travelers," *Literary Review* 38(1): 5-20. Fall 1994.

LATIN AMERICANS

___ del Olmo, Frank. "Donde muy pocos Latinos han ido," *Los Angeles (CA) Times* p.M5. March 19, 1995.

LAUMER, KEITH

___ "Laumer, Keith (Obituary)," *Locus* 30(3): 69-70. March 1993.

___ "Laumer, Keith (Obituary)," *Science Fiction Chronicle* 14(6): 16. March 1993.

___ Andrews, Graham. "Keith Laumer: An Annotated Bibliography," *Interzone* No. 79: 56-60. January 1994.

___ Stephensen-Payne, Phil. **Keith Laumer: Ambassador to Space, a Working Bibliography.** 2nd revised edition, by Phil Stephensen-Payne and Gordon Benson, Jr. Albuquerque, NM: Galactic Central, 1990. 41pp.

LAURIE, ANDRE

___ Marcoin, Francis. "**Les Exiles de la terre** d'Andre Laurie," *La Revue des Livres pour Enfants* 146: 61-65. Summer 1992.
___ Stone, Graham. "Notes on Australian Science Fiction," *Science Fiction News* (Australia) No. 105: 2-8. October 1987.

LAWNMOWER MAN (MOTION PICTURE)

___ Arnold, Gary. "Mower Cuts Swath of Diabolical Silliness (Review)," *Washington (DC) Times*. March 7, 1992. in: *NewsBank. Film and Television*. 33:A10. 1992.
___ Burden, Martin. "The Cutting Edge for Sci-Fi Fans (Review)," *New York (NY) Post*. March 6, 1992. in: *NewsBank. Film and Television*. 43: A11. 1992.
___ Doherty, Thomas. "**Lawnmower Man** (Review)," *Cinefantastique* 23(1): 57. August 1992.
___ Hunter, Stephen. "**Lawnmower Man** Is a Visual Treat (Review)," *Baltimore (MD) Sun*. March 7, 1992. in: *NewsBank. Film and Television*. 33:A5. 1992.
___ Mahar, Ted. "A Little Clipping Here and There Wouldn't Hurt **Lawnmower Man** (Review)," *Portland (OR) The Oregonian*. March 14, 1992. in: *NewsBank. Film and Television*. 33:A9. 1992.
___ Michelini, Alex. "**Lawnmower** Trim: Stephen King Gets Himself Cut From Film," *New York (NY) Daily News*. July 7, 1992. in: *NewsBank. Film and Television*. 71:B1. 1992.
___ Murray, Steve. "**Lawnmower Man**: A Cut Below the Average Thriller (Review)," *Atlanta (GA) Journal*. March 6, 1992. in: *NewsBank. Film and Television*. 22:D8. 1992.
___ Sherman, Paul. "**Lawnmower Man** Is a Seedy Sci-Fi Flick (Review)," *Boston (MA) Herald*. March 6, 1992. in: *NewsBank. Film and Television*. 33:A6. 1992.
___ Sorensen, Peter. "Cyberworld," *Cinefex* No. 50: 54-76. May 1992.
___ Strauss, Bob. "**Lawnmower Man** Is Not Exactly Cutting Edge (Review)," *Los Angeles (CA) Daily News*. March 6, 1992. in: *NewsBank. Film and Television*. 33:A4. 1992.
___ Strickler, Jeff. "**Lawnmower Man** Is Just a Cut Above Average Sci-Fi Movies (Review)," *Minneapolis (MN) Star and Tribune*. March 6, 1992. in: *NewsBank. Film and Television*. 33:A7. 1992.
___ Ullrich, Allan. "Here's Reality: Mower Is Less (Review)," *San Francisco (CA) Examiner*. March 7, 1992. in: *NewsBank. Film and Television*. 33:A8. 1992.
___ Wood, Gary L. "**Lawnmower Man**: Effects by Angel Studios and Xaos, Inc.," *Cinefantastique* 23(1): 56. August 1992.
___ Wood, Gary L. "Stephen King's **The Lawnmower Man**," *Cinefantastique* 22(4): 7, 60. February 1992.
___ Wood, Gary L. "Stephen King, Computer Graphic," *Cinefantastique* 22(5): 6-7. April 1992.

LAWRENCE, D. H.

___ Seeber, Hans-Ulrich. "Utopian Mentality in George Eliot's **Middlemarch** (1871/72) and in D. H. Lawrence's **The Rainbow**," *Utopian Studies* 6(1): 30-39. 1995.
___ Svoboda, Randall A. **Between Private and Public Space: The Problem of Writing Personal History in the Novels of Lessing, Lawrence, Joyce and Fowles**. Ph.D. Dissertation, University of Iowa, 1995. 313pp. (DAI-A 56/06, p. 2253. December 1995.)

LAWRENCE, LOUISE

___ Apseloff, Marilyn F. "The British Science Fiction of Louise Lawrence," in: Sullivan, C. W., III. **Science Fiction for Young Readers**. Westport, CT: Greenwood, 1993. pp.133-144.
___ Mitchell, Judith N. "Neo-Gnostic Elements in Louise Lawrence's **Moonwind**," in: Sullivan, C. W., III. **Science Fiction for Young Readers**. Westport, CT: Greenwood, 1993. pp.179-185.

LAWRENCE, T. E.

___ Seyer, Geoffrey. " 'Morris Was a Giant': The Quest of T. E. Lawrence," *Journal of the William Morris Society* 10(4): 48-52. Spring 1994.

LAWS AND LEGISLATION

___ Altman, Mark A. "UFP Law: The Legal Quagmires of the Federation," *Star Trek: The Official Fan Club* No. 93: 2-5. September/October 1993.
___ Corcos, Christine. **Women's Rights and Women's Images in Science Fiction: A Selected Bibliography**. Cleveland, OH: Case Western Reserve University, Law Library, 1994. 17pp.

LAWS AND LEGISLATION (continued)

___ Joseph, Paul. "The Law of the Federation: Images of Law, Lawyers, and the Legal System in **Star Trek: The Next Generation**," by Paul Joseph and Sharon Carton. *University of Toledo Law Review* 24(1): 43-85. Fall 1992.
___ Lyall, Francis. "Law in Science Fiction: An Introduction," *Foundation* No. 55: 36-57. Summer 1992.

LAWYERS

___ Joseph, Paul. "The Law of the Federation: Images of Law, Lawyers, and the Legal System in **Star Trek: The Next Generation**," by Paul Joseph and Sharon Carton. *University of Toledo Law Review* 24(1): 43-85. Fall 1992.
___ Joseph, Paul. "Perry Mason in Space: A Call for More Inventive Lawyers in Television Science Fiction Series," by Paul Joseph and Sharon Carton. in: Wolf, Milton T. and Mallett, Daryl F., eds. **Imaginative Futures: Proceedings of the 1993 Science Fiction Research Association Conference**. San Bernardino, CA: Jacob's Ladder Books, 1995. pp.307-318.

LE GUIN, URSULA K.

___ "1995 Tiptree Award Presented," *Locus* 34(3): 7. March 1995.
___ "1995 World Fantasy Awards," *Locus* 35(6): 4, 81. December 1995.
___ "Campbell and Sturgeon Award Winners," *Locus* 35(2): 8. August 1995.
___ "Greg Egan Wins Campbell Memorial Award; Sturgeon Award to Ursula K. Le Guin," *Science Fiction Chronicle* 16(9): 5. August/ September 1995.
___ "Nancy Springer, Ursula K. Le Guin Win Tiptree Award," *Science Fiction Chronicle* 16(5): 4. March/April 1995.
___ "Ursula K. Le Guin: Looking Back," *Locus* 30(5): 6, 73-74. May 1993.
___ "World Fantasy Awards, 1995," *Science Fiction Chronicle* 17(2): 5. December 1995/January 1996.
___ Attebery, Brian. "Gender, Fantasy, and the Authority of Tradition," *Journal of the Fantastic in the Arts* 7(1): 51-60. 1996.
___ Attebery, Jennifer E. "The Trolls of Fiction: Ogres or Warm Fuzzies," *Journal of the Fantastic in the Arts* 7(1): 61-74. 1996.
___ Baldry, Cherith. "A Hand Held out in the Dark: Some Relationships in the Science Fiction of Ursula Le Guin," *Vector* No. 168: 6-8. August/ September 1992.
___ Barr, Marleen S. **Lost in Space: Probing Feminist Science Fiction and Beyond**. Chapel Hill, NC: University of North Carolina Press, 1993. 231pp.
___ Barr, Marleen S. "**Searoad Chronicles of Klatsand** as a Pathway Toward New Directions in Feminist Science Fiction: Or, Who's Afraid of Connecting Ursula Le Guin to Virginia Woolf?," *Foundation* No. 60: 58-67. Spring 1994.
___ Barry, Nora. "Beyond Words: The Impact of Rhythm as Narrative Technique in **The Left Hand of Darkness**," by Nora Barry and Mary Prescott. *Extrapolation* 33(2): 154-165. Summer 1992.
___ Bastien, Louis A. **Green Fire and the Legacy of the Dragon: Science Fiction, Fantasy and Cultural Ideology**. Ph.D. Dissertation, University of Connecticut, 1992. 238pp. (DAI-A 54/04. p. 1359. October 1993.)
___ Clarke, Amy M. **A Woman Writing: Feminist Awareness in the Work of Ursula K. Le Guin**. Ph.D. Dissertation, University of California, Davis, 1992. 290pp. (DAI-A 54/01. p. 176. July 1993.)
___ Damico, Natalie W. **The Other: Duality in the Science Fiction of Ursula K. Le Guin**. Master's Thesis, Indiana University of Pennsylvania, 1977. 82pp.
___ Dooley, Patricia. "Earthsea Patterns," *Children's Literature Association. Quarterly* 4(2): 1-4. Summer 1979.
___ Drake, Barbara. "Two Utopias: Marge Piercy's **Women on the Edge of Time** and Ursula K. Le Guin's **The Dispossessed**," in: Roberts, Sheila, ed. **Still the Frame Holds: Essays on Women Poets and Writers**. San Bernardino, CA: Borgo Press, 1993. pp.109-128.
___ Feimer, Joel N. "Biblical Typology in Le Guin's **The Eye of the Heron**: Character, Structure and Theme," *Mythlore* 19(4): 13-19. Autumn 1993. (No. 74)
___ Filmer, Kath. **Scepticism and Hope in Twentieth Century Fantasy Literature**. Bowling Green, OH: Bowling Green State University Popular Press, 1992. 160pp.
___ Hatfield, Len. "From Master to Brother: Shifting the Balance of Authority in Ursula K. Le Guin's **Farthest Shore** and **Tehanu**," *Children's Literature* 21: 43-65. 1993.

LE GUIN, URSULA K. (continued)

___ Heldreth, Leonard G. "ICFA Converses With 1992 G. O. H. Ursula K. Le Guin," *IAFA Newsletter* 5(2): 24-27. Summer 1992.

___ Holway, Lowell H. "Ursula K. Le Guin at SJSU: The Future Is a Metaphor," *San Jose Studies* 20(1): 54-71. Winter 1994.

___ Huff, Marjorie L. **The Monomyth Pattern in Ursula K. Le Guin's Earthsea Trilogy.** Master's Thesis, Middle Tennessee State University, 1977. 164pp.

___ Irving, James A. **The World Makers: Techniques of Fantasy in J. R. R. Tolkien's The Lord of the Rings and Ursula K. Le Guin's Earthsea Trilogy.** Master's Thesis, Acadia University, 1976. 128pp.

___ Jacobs, Naomi. "The Frozen Landscape in Women's Utopian and Science Fiction," in: Donawerth, Jane L. and Kolmerten, Carol A., eds. **Utopian and Science Fiction by Women: Worlds of Difference.** Syracuse, NY: Syracuse University Press, 1994. pp.190-202.

___ Jago, Wendy. "**A Wizard of Earthsea** and the Charge of Escapism," *Children's Literature in Education* 8: 21-29. July 1972.

___ Jameson, Sara. "Ursula K. Le Guin: A Galaxy of Books and Laurels," *Publishers Weekly* 242(39): 32-33. September 25, 1995.

___ Jean, Lorraine A. "Ursula K. Le Guin," in: Bruccoli, Matthew J., ed. **Facts on File Bibliography of American Fiction 1919-1988.** New York: Facts on File, 1991. pp.288-290.

___ Klarer, Mario. "Gender and 'The Simultaniety Principle': Ursula K. Le Guin's **The Dispossessed**," *Mosaic* 25(2): 107-121. Spring 1992.

___ Kuelen, Margarete. **Radical Imagination: Feminist Conceptions of the Future in Ursula Le Guin, Marge Piercy and Sally Miller Gearhart.** Frankfurt-am-Main/New York: Peter Lang, 1991. 122pp.

___ Le Guin, Ursula K. "A Citizen of Mondath," in: Jakubowski, Maxim and James, Edward, eds. **The Profession of Science Fiction.** New York: St. Martin's, 1992. pp.73-77.

___ Le Guin, Ursula K. **Earthsea Revisioned.** Madison, NJ: Children's Literature New England, 1993. 26pp.

___ Le Guin, Ursula K. "Talking About Writing," *Writer* 105(12): 9-11, 41. December 1992.

___ Littlefield, Holly. "Unlearning Patriarchy: Ursula Le Guin's Feminist Consciousness in **The Tombs of Atuan** and **Tehanu**," *Extrapolation* 36(3): 244-258. Fall 1995.

___ Madrigal, Alix. "A Specialist in the Unexpected," *San Francisco (CA) Chronicle.* Review p. 5. February 2, 1992.

___ Malkki, Tarya. "The Marriage Metaphor in the Works of Ursula K. Le Guin," in: Latham, Robert A. and Collins, Robert A., eds. **Modes of the Fantastic.** Westport, CT: Greenwood, 1995. pp.100-109.

___ McDowell, Elizabeth J. **Power and Environment in Recent Writings by Barbara Kingsolver, Ursula K. Le Guin, Alice Walker and Terry Tempest Williams.** Master's Thesis, University of Oregon, 1992. [Not seen.]

___ Mills, Alice. "Burning Women in Ursula K. Le Guin's **Tehanu: The Last Book of Earthsea**," *New York Review of Science Fiction* No. 79: 1, 3-7. March 1995.

___ Moore, John. "An Archaeology of the Future: Ursula K. Le Guin and Anarcho-Primitivism," *Foundation* No. 63: 32-39. Spring 1995.

___ Nodelman, Perry. "Reinventing the Past: Gender in Ursula K. Le Guin's **Tehanu** and the Earthsea Trilogy," *Children's Literature* 23: 179-201. 1995.

___ Pegg, Barry. "Down to Earth: Terrain, Territory, and the Language of Realism in Ursula K. Le Guin's **The Left Hand of Darkness** and **The Dispossessed**," *Michigan Academician* 27(4): 481-492. August 1995.

___ Platt, Charles. "News From the Ghetto: The Teflon Fantasist," *Quantum* No. 43/44: 19-20. Spring/Summer 1993.

___ Reinking, Victor. "A Conversation with Ursula K. Le Guin," by Victor Reinking and David Willingham. *Paradoxa* 1(1): 39-57. 1995.

___ Schicke, Ulrike. "Individuum und gesellschaft in Ursula K. Le Guins **The Dispossessed**, 1. Teil," *Quarber Merkur* 31(1): 23-34. June 1993. (No. 79)

___ Schicke, Ulrike. "Individuum und Gesellschaft in Ursula K. Le Guins **The Dispossessed**, 2. Teil," *Quarber Merkur* 31(2): 3-13. Dezember 1993. (No. 80)

___ Schicke, Ulrike. "Individuum und Gesellschaft in Ursula Le Guins **The Dispossessed**. 3. Teil und Schluß," *Quarber Merkur* 32(1): 3-20. June 1994. (Whole No. 81)

___ Simon, Erik. "Das Quartum Comparatur. Eine Beogbachtung zu Ursula Le Guins Erdsee-Zyklus," *Quarber Merkur* 32(1): 39-41. June 1994. (Whole No. 81)

___ Slusser, George E. "The Politically Correct Book of Science Fiction: Le Guin's Norton Collection," *Foundation* No. 60: 67-84. Spring 1994.

LE GUIN, URSULA K. (continued)

___ Talbot, Norman. " 'Escape!': That Dirty Word in Modern Fantasy: Le Guin's Earthsea," in: Filmer, Kath, ed. **Twentieth-Century Fantasists: Essays in Culture, Society and Belief in Twentieth Century Mythopoeic Literature.** New York: St. Martin's, 1992. pp.135-147.

___ Tiptree, James, Jr. "From a Spoken Journal: Thinking About Heinlein, et al., 1971," *New York Review of Science Fiction* No. 60: 1, 3-6. August 1993. (Edited by David G. Hartwell.)

___ Tschachler, Heinz. "Ursula K. Le Guin, **The Left Hand of Darkness** (1969)," in: Heuermann, Harmut, ed. **Der Science Fiction Roman in der angloamerikanischen Literatur: Interpretationen.** Düsseldorf: Bagel, 1986. pp.295-314.

___ Vinge, Joan D. "Introduction to **The Left Hand of Darkness**," *New York Review of Science Fiction* No. 43: 14-16. March 1992.

___ Watson, Ian. "Le Guin's **Lathe of Heaven** and the Role of Dick: The False Reality as Mediator," in: Mullen, R. D., ed. **On Philip K. Dick: 40 Articles From Science-Fiction Studies.** Terre Haute, IN: SF-TH Inc., 1992. pp.63-72.

___ Webb, Sarah Jo. "Culture as Spiritual Metaphor in Le Guin's **Always Coming Home**," in: Sanders, Joe, ed. **Functions of the Fantastic.** Westport, CT: Greenwood, 1995. pp.155-160.

___ Welton, Ann. "Earthsea Revisited: Tehanu and Feminism," *Voice of Youth Advocates* 14(1): 14-16, 18. April 1991.

___ Williams, Donna G. "The Moons of Le Guin and Heinlein," *Science Fiction Studies* 21(2): 164-172. July 1994.

___ Wilson, Mary. **Balancing Polar Opposites in the Novels of Ursula K. Le Guin.** Master's Thesis, Tennessee Technological University, 1992. 61pp.

___ Wilson, Mary. "The Earthsea Series of Ursula Le Guin: A Successful Example of Modern Fantasy," *Papers: Explorations into Children's Literature* 3(2): 60-74. August 1992. [Not seen.]

___ Yamano, Koichi. "Ursula K. Le Guin: Das Mittelalter der Frauenzivilisation," *Quarber Merkur* 33(1): 26-33. June 1995. (No. 83)

___ Zaki, Hoda M. **Phoenix Renewed: The Survival and Mutation of Utopian Thought in North American Science Fiction 1965-1982.** Rev. ed. San Bernardino, CA: Borgo Press, 1994. 151pp.

LEA, NICHOLAS

___ Vitaris, Paula. "**X-Files**: F. B. I. Judas," *Cinefantastique* 26(6)/27(1): 75-76. October 1995.

LEAR, EDWARD

___ Wullschläger, Jackie. **Inventing Wonderland: The Lives and Fantasies of Lewis Carroll, Edward Lear, J. M. Barrie, Kenneth Grahame and A. A. Milne.** New York: Free Press, 1995. 228pp.

LEE, BRANDON

___ "Actor Dies on Horror Film Set," *Science Fiction Chronicle* 14(8): 5. May 1993.

LEE, CHRISTOPHER

___ "Bram Stoker Award Winners," *Science Fiction Chronicle* 16(7): 4. June/July 1995.

___ "HWA Stoker Awards," *Locus* 35(1): 9. July 1995.

LEE, ELAINE

___ "Interview: Elaine Lee," *Journal of the Dark* No. 5: 7-11. Winter 1995/1996.

LEE, STAN

___ Bierbaum, Tom. "Stan Lee's Imperfect Heroes Lifted Marvel to Top of the Heap," *Variety* p. 81, 88. September 17, 1986.

___ Green, Steve. "All in Colour for a Dime: A Profile of Stan Lee," *Interzone* No. 59: 43-47. May 1992.

LEE, TANITH

___ Garratt, Peter. "Unstoppable Fate: Tanith Lee Interview," *Interzone* No. 64: 23-25. October 1992.

___ Lefanu, Sarah. "Robots and Romance: The Science Fiction and Fantasy of Tanith Lee," in: Radstone, Susannah, ed. **Sweet Dreams: Sexuality, Gender and Popular Fiction.** London: Lawrence & Wishart, 1988. pp.121-136.

___ Nicholls, Stan. "Tanith Lee Has an Art Deco Radio Box in Her Head," in: Nicholls, Stan. **Wordsmiths of Wonder: Fifty Interviews with Writers of the Fantastic.** London: Orbit, 1993. pp.348-355.

LEE, TANITH

LEE, TANITH (continued)
___ Schweitzer, Darrell. "Tanith Lee," in: Schweitzer, Darrell. **Speaking of Horror: Interviews With Writers of the Supernatural.** San Bernardino, CA: Borgo, 1994. pp.59-66.
___ Soanes, Paul A. **Daughter of the Night: A Tanith Lee Bibliography**, by Paul A. Soanes and Jim Pattison. Toronto: Gaffa Press, 1993. 44pp.

LEE, TINA
___ Klein, Jay K. "Biolog: Tina Lee," *Analog* 115(12): 129, 161. October 1995.

LEECH WOMAN (MOTION PICTURE)
___ Stephens, Bob. "Pre-tinsel Science Fiction Tales," *San Francisco (CA) Examiner* November 25, 1995. (Cited from the Internet Edition.)

LEEVES, JANE
___ Nazzaro, Joe. "Little Lost Holly," *Starlog* No. 221: 68-69. December 1995.

LeFANU, J. SHERIDAN
___ Bloom, Harold. "Joseph Sheridan LeFanu," in: Bloom, Harold. **Classic Horror Writers.** New York: Chelsea House, 1994. pp.43-58.
___ Crawford, Gary W. **J. Sheridan Le Fanu: A Bio-Bibliography**. Westport, CT: Greenwood, 1995. 155pp.
___ Crawford, Gary W. "The Landscape of Sin: The Ghost Stories of J. Sheridan LeFanu," in: Schweitzer, Darrell, ed. **Discovering Classic Horror Fiction I.** Mercer Island, WA: Starmont, 1992. pp.74-99.

LEGATO, ROB
___ Rubinstein, Mitchell. "*The Next Generation*: Special Visual Effects," *Cinefantastique* 23(2/3): 38-41. October 1992.

LEGEND (MOTION PICTURE)
___ Nazzaro, Joe. "Heroic Passings," *Starlog* No. 221: 35-37. December 1995.
___ Spelling, Ian. "*Legend* of the West," *Starlog* No. 216: 54-57. July 1995.
___ Spelling, Ian. "Under Western Skies," *Starlog* No. 217: 76-79. August 1995.

LEGEND OF THE CELESTIAL SPHERE (MOTION PICTURE)
___ Ke, Fan. "Science Fiction Film Calls for Environmental Protection: *Legend of the Celestial Sphere* Directed by Wei Judang," *Beijing Review* 38(37): 34. September 11, 1995.

LEGENDARY JOURNEYS OF HERCULES (TV)
___ Shapiro, Marc. "The Labors of Hercules," *Starlog* No. 211: 55-58. February 1995.

LEGGETT, JOHN HAROLD
___ "Leggett, John Harold (Obituary)," *Science Fiction News* (Australia) No. 59: 11. February 1979.

LEIBER, FRITZ
___ "Authors Fritz Leiber, Mary Norton Dead," *Science Fiction Chronicle* 14(1): 4. October 1992.
___ "Fritz Leiber at 81," *Locus* 28(3): 9. March 1992.
___ "Fritz Leiber: In Memoriam," *Locus* 29(5): 46-49, 73-74. November 1992
___ "Fritz Leiber Loves Margo Skinner," *Locus* 29(1): 6. July 1992.
___ **Fritz Leiber Remembered.** San Francisco, CA: Familiar Productions, 1992. one videocassette, 55 minutes. [Not seen.]
___ "Leiber, Fritz: 1910-1992 (Obituary)," *Locus* 29(4): 4-5, 68-72. October 1992.
___ "Leiber, Fritz (Obituary)," *Science Fiction Chronicle* 14(2): 12. November 1992.
___ "Leiber, Fritz: Science Fiction Writer Fritz Leiber, 81 (Obituary)," *Chicago Tribune* Sec. C, p. 10. September 10, 1992.
___ "Leiber, Fritz, 1910-1992 (Obituary)," *Starlog* No. 189: 22-23. April 1993.
___ "Time Capsule Discovered at Tor," *Locus* 28(2): 6. February 1992.
___ Bloom, Harold. "Fritz Leiber," in: Bloom, Harold, ed. **Modern Fantasy Writers.** New York: Chelsea House, 1995. pp.71-84.
___ Bloom, Harold. "Fritz Leiber," in: Bloom, Harold, ed. **Science Fiction Writers of the Golden Age.** New York: Chelsea House, 1995. pp.126-140.

LEIBER, FRITZ (continued)
___ Brandt, Richard. "Fritzish Thoughts," *Lan's Lantern* No. 38: 14-16. July 1992.
___ Byfield, Bruce. "Fritz Leiber," in: Bruccoli, Matthew J., ed. **Facts on File Bibliography of American Fiction 1919-1988.** New York: Facts on File, 1991. pp.291-292.
___ Heideman, Eric M. "Fritz Leiber," *Lan's Lantern* No. 38: 6-7. July 1992.
___ Laskowski, George. "Fritz Leiber: A Bibliography," *Lan's Lantern* No. 38: 8-13. July 1992.
___ Laskowski, George. "Modern Demons and a Twisted Mind: The Fantastic Fiction of Fritz Leiber," *Lan's Lantern* No. 38: 19-25. July 1992.
___ Leiber, Justin. "Fritz Leiber at Bay," *Locus* 29(5): 47-49. November 1992
___ Leiber, Justin. "Fritz Leiber: Swordsman and Philosopher, Part Two, Philosophical Dramatizations," *Riverside Quarterly* 9(1): 36-44. August 1992. (No. 33)
___ Moorcock, Michael. "Fritz Leiber," *Paradoxa* 1(3): 320-324. 1995.
___ Sabella, Robert. "Fritz Leiber: A Chronology," *Lan's Lantern* No. 38: 17. July 1992.
___ Sadler, Tom. "An Appreciation of Fritz Leiber's Fiction," *Lan's Lantern* No. 38: 3-5. July 1992.
___ Sadler, Tom. "Thoughts on Fritz Leiber," *Lan's Lantern* No. 38: 26. July 1992.
___ Schweitzer, Darrell. "An Interview With Fritz Leiber," *Marion Zimmer Bradley's Fantasy Magazine* No. 15: 7-10. Winter 1992.
___ Thiel, John. "Fritz Leiber: A Man of Variety," *Lan's Lantern* No. 38: 18. July 1992.
___ Ursini, James. **More Things Than Are Dreamt Of: Masterpieces of Supernatural Horror, From Mary Shelley to Stephen King, in Literature and Film,** by James Ursini and Alain Silver. New York: Limelight, 1994. 226pp.

LEIBNIZ, WILHELM
___ Antosik, Stanley. "Utopian Machines: Liebniz's 'Computer' and Hesse's **Glass Bead Game,**" *Germanic Review* 67(1): 35-45. Spring 1992.

LEINSTER, MURRAY
___ Sabella, Robert. "The Lost Worlds of Science Fiction: Murray Leinster," *Lan's Lantern* No. 42: 32-33. May 1994.

LEIVICK, HALPER
___ Schaffer, Carl. "Leivick's **The Golem** and the Golem Legend," in: Murphy, Patrick D., ed. **Staging the Impossible: The Fantastic Mode in Modern Drama.** Westport, CT: Greenwood, 1992. pp.137-149.

LEM, STANISLAW
___ Balczerzak, Ewa. **Stanislaw Lem.** Warsaw: Pantswowy Instytut Wydawniczy, 1973. (Not seen. Cf. *Science-Fiction Studies*, Nov. 1992.)
___ Beres, Stanislaw. **Rozmony ze Stanislawem Lemem** (Conversations with Stanislaw Lem). Cracow: Wydawnictwo Literackie, 1987. (Not seen. Cf. *Science-Fiction Studies, Nov. 1992.*)
___ Cheever, Leonard A. "Epistemological Chagrin: The Literary and Philosophical Antecedents of Stanislaw Lem's Romantic Misanthrope," *Extrapolation* 35(4): 319-329. Winter 1994.
___ Ciesl14, Anna B. "Stanislaw Lems **Solaris** in deutschen Übersetzungen. Eine sprachliche Analyse aus polnischer Sicht, 2. Teil," *Quarber Merkur* 30(1): 3-17. June 1992. (No. 77)
___ Dick, Philip K. "A Clarification," in: Mullen, R. D., ed. **On Philip K. Dick: 40 Articles From Science-Fiction Studies.** Terre Haute, IN: SF-TH Inc., 1992. pp.73.
___ Easterbrook, Neil. "The Sublime Simulacra: Repetition, Reversal, and Re-covery in Lem's **Solaris,**" *Critique* 36(3): 177-194. Spring 1995.
___ Ende, Dagmar. "Untersuchungen zum Menschen- und Gesellschaftsbild in ausgewählten Science-Fiction-Werken Stanislaw Lems und zu deren Aufnahme durch del Literaturkritik der DDR 1954-1990," *Quarber Merkur* 30(2): 3-13. December 1992. (No. 78)
___ Ferchland, Jutta. "**Solaris.** Der Film von Andrej Tarkovskij im Vergleich zu Lems roman," *Quarber Merkur* 32(2): 34-42. December 1994. (Whole No. 82)
___ Flessner, Bernd. **Weltprothesen und Prothesenwelten: zu den technischen Prognosen Arno Schmidts und Stanislaw Lems.** Frankfurt-am-Main: P. Lang, 1991. 343pp.

LEM, STANISLAW (continued)

___ Geier, Manfred. "Stanislaw Lem's Fantastic Ocean: Toward a Semantic Interpretation of **Solaris**," *Science-Fiction Studies* 19(2): 192-218. July 1992.

___ Helford, Elyce R. "We Are Only Seeking Man: Gender, Psychoanalysis, and Stanislaw Lem's **Solaris**," *Science-Fiction Studies* 19(2): 167-177. July 1992.

___ Jarzebski, Jerzy, ed. **Lem w oczach krytyki swiatowej** (Lem in the Eyes of World Criticism). Cracow: Wydawnictwo Literackie, 1989. (Not seen. Cf. *Science-Fiction Studies*, Nov. 1992.)

___ Krabbenhoft, Kenneth. "Lem as Moral Theologian," *Science Fiction Studies* 21(2): 212-224. July 1994.

___ Krywak, Piotr. **Stanislaw Lem**. Cracow: Panswowe Wydawnictwo Naukowe, 1974. (Not seen. Cf. *Science-Fiction Studies*, Nov. 1992.)

___ Nikolchina, Miglena. "Love and Automata: From Hoffman to Lem and From Freud to Kristeva," in: Sanders, Joe, ed. **Functions of the Fantastic**. Westport, CT: Greenwood, 1995. pp.77-82.

___ Parker, Jo A. "Gendering the Robot: Stanislaw Lem's 'The Mask'," *Science-Fiction Studies* 19(2): 178-191. July 1992.

___ Stoff, Andrzej. **Krytyka o pierwszych utworach Stanislawa Lema** (Critical Opinion on the First Works of Stanislaw Lem). Torun: Acta Universitatis Nicolai Copernick, 1975. (Not seen. Cf. *Science-Fiction Studies*, Nov. 1992.)

___ Stoff, Andrzej. **Lem i inni: Szkice o Polskiej science fiction** (Lem and Others: Sketches on Polish Science Fiction). Bydgoszcz: Pomorze, 1990. (Not seen. Cf. *Science-Fiction Studies*, Nov. 1992.)

___ Stoff, Andrzej. **Powiesci fantasryczno-naukowe Stanislawa Lema** (The Science Fiction Novels of Stanislaw Lem). Warsaw: Panstwowe Wydawnictwo Naukowe, 1983. (Not seen. Cf. *Science-Fiction Studies*, Nov. 1992.)

___ Swirski, Peter. "On Games With the Universe: Preconceptions of Science in Stanislaw Lem's **The Invincible**," *Contemporary Literature* 35(2): 324-342. Summer 1994.

___ Swirski, Peter. "Playing a Game of Ontology: A Postmodern Reading of **The Futurological Congress**," *Extrapolation* 33(1): 32-40. Spring 1992.

___ Weinstone, Ann. "Resisting Monsters: Notes on **Solaris**," *Science Fiction Studies* 21(2): 173-190. July 1994.

___ Weissert, Thomas P. "Stanislaw Lem and a Topology of Mind," *Science-Fiction Studies* 19(2): 161-166. July 1992.

___ Wessel, Karl. "Worlds of Chance and Counterfeit: Dick, Lem, and the Preestablished Cacaphony," in: Umland, Samuel J., ed. **Philip K. Dick: Contemporary Critical Interpretations**. Westport, CT: Greenwood, 1995. pp.43-60.

LEONARD, BRETT

___ Maccarillo, Lisa. "More Than Human," *Sci-Fi Entertainment* 2(2): 62-67, 81. August 1995.

___ Shapiro, Marc. "Virtual Virtuoso," *Starlog* No. 218: 32-35. September 1995.

LEPPINS, PAUL

___ Teissl, Verena. "Paul Leppins **Severins Gang in die Finsternis**. Ein Prager Gespensterroman," *Quarber Merkur* 32(2): 28-32. December 1994. (Whole No. 82)

LEPRECHAUN (MOTION PICTURE)

___ Jones, Alan. "**Leprechaun**," *Cinefantastique* 23(5): 42-43. February 1993.

LEPRECHAUN 2 (MOTION PICTURE)

___ Faller, James M. "**Leprechaun 2** (Review)," *Cinefantastique* 25(5): 60. October 1994.

___ Sawicki, Stephen. "**Leprechaun 2** (Review)," *Cinefantastique* 27(2): 60. November 1995.

LEPRECHAUN 3 (MOTION PICTURE)

___ Kingston, F. Colin. "**Leprechaun 3**," *Cinefantastique* 26(4): 52-53. June 1995.

LESSING, DORIS

___ Adams, Marueen B. **Feminine Mythic Patterns in Doris Lessing's The Summer Before the Dark and The Memoirs of a Survivor**. Master's Thesis, Lehigh University, 1977. 114pp.

___ Aldiss, Brian W. "Living in Catastrophe (Interview, 1988)," in: Ingersoll, Earl G., ed. **Doris Lessing: Conversations**. Princeton, NJ: Ontario Review Press, 1994. pp.169-172.

LESSING, DORIS (continued)

___ Bazin, Nancy T. "Madness, Mysticism, and Fantasy: Shifting Perspectives of the Novels of Doris Lessing, Bessie Head, and Nadine Gordimer," *Extrapolation* 33(1): 73-87. Spring 1992.

___ Bertelsen, Eve. "Acknowledging a New Frontier (Interview, 1984)," in: Ingersoll, Earl G., ed. **Doris Lessing: Conversations**. Princeton, NJ: Ontario Review Press, 1994. pp.120-145.

___ Bigsby, Christopher. "The Need to Tell Stories (Interview, 1980)," in: Ingersoll, Earl G., ed. **Doris Lessing: Conversations**. Princeton, NJ: Ontario Review Press, 1994. pp.70-85.

___ Bikman, Minda. "Creating Your Own Demand (Interview, 1980)," in: Ingersoll, Earl G., ed. **Doris Lessing: Conversations**. Princeton, NJ: Ontario Review Press, 1994. pp.57-63.

___ de Montremy, Jean-Maurice. "A Writer Is Not a Professor (Interview, 1990)," in: Ingersoll, Earl G., ed. **Doris Lessing: Conversations**. Princeton, NJ: Ontario Review Press, 1994. pp.193-199.

___ Dean, Michael. "Writing as Time Runs Out (Interview, 1980)," in: Ingersoll, Earl G., ed. **Doris Lessing: Conversations**. Princeton, NJ: Ontario Review Press, 1994. pp.86-93.

___ DuPlessis, Rachel B. "The Feminist Apologies of Lessing, Piercy, and Russ," *Frontiers* 4(1): 1-8. 1979.

___ Ean, Tan Gim. "The Older I Get, The Less I Believe (Interview, 1991)," in: Ingersoll, Earl G., ed. **Doris Lessing: Conversations**. Princeton, NJ: Ontario Review Press, 1994. pp.200-203.

___ Field, Michele. "PW Interviews: Doris Lessing," *Publishers Weekly* 241(38): 47-48. September 19, 1994.

___ Flynn, Caroline. "Doris Lessing: An Overview," *Science Fiction: A Review of Speculative Literature* 11(2): 17-22. 1991. (No. 32)

___ Forde, Nigel. "Reporting From the Terrain of the Mind (Interview, 1992)," in: Ingersoll, Earl G., ed. **Doris Lessing: Conversations**. Princeton, NJ: Ontario Review Press, 1994. pp.214-218.

___ Frick, Thomas. "Caged by the Experts (Interview, 1987)," in: Ingersoll, Earl G., ed. **Doris Lessing: Conversations**. Princeton, NJ: Ontario Review Press, 1994. pp.155-168.

___ Gardiner, Judith K. **Rhys, Stead, Lessing, and the Politics of Empathy**. Bloomington: Indiana University Press, 1989. 186pp.

___ Gray, Stephen. "Breaking Down These Forms (Interview, 1983)," in: Ingersoll, Earl G., ed. **Doris Lessing: Conversations**. Princeton, NJ: Ontario Review Press, 1994. pp.109-119.

___ Greene, Gayle. **Doris Lessing: The Poetics of Change**. Ann Arbor: University of Michigan Press, 1994. 283pp.

___ Greene, Gayle. "Doris Lessing's **Landlocked**: A New Kind of Knowledge," *Contemporary Literature* 28(1): 82-103. Spring 1987.

___ Güth, Gudrun. "Doris Lessing, **Canopus in Argos: Archives** (1979ff)," by Gudrun Güth and Jürgen Schmidt-Güth. in: Heuermann, Harmut, ed. **Der Science Fiction Roman in der angloamerikanischen Literatur: Interpretationen**. Düsseldorf: Bagel, 1986. pp.375-399.

___ Hendin, Josephine. "The Capacity to Look at a Situation Coolly (Interview, 1972)," in: Ingersoll, Earl G., ed. **Doris Lessing: Conversations**. Princeton, NJ: Ontario Review Press, 1994. pp.41-56.

___ Hynes, Joseph. "Doris Lessing's Briefing as Structural Life and Death," *Renascence* 46(4): 225-246. Summer 1994.

___ Ingersoll, Earl G. "Describing This Beautiful and Nasty Planet (Interview, 1994)," in: Ingersoll, Earl G., ed. **Doris Lessing: Conversations**. Princeton, NJ: Ontario Review Press, 1994. pp.228-240.

___ Ingersoll, Earl G., ed. **Doris Lessing: Conversations**. Princeton, NJ: Ontario Review Press, 1994. 248pp.

___ Jacobs, Naomi. "The Frozen Landscape in Women's Utopian and Science Fiction," in: Donawerth, Jane L. and Kolmerten, Carol A., eds. **Utopian and Science Fiction by Women: Worlds of Difference**. Syracuse, NY: Syracuse University Press, 1994. pp.190-202.

___ Kauffman, Linda S. **Special Delivery: Epistolary Modes in Modern Fiction**. Chicago: University of Chicago Press, 1992. 278pp.

___ King, Jeanette. **Doris Lessing**. New York: Edward Arnold, 1990. 117pp. [Not seen.]

___ Kurzweil, Edith. "Unexamined Mental Attitudes Left Behind by Communism (Interview, 1992)," in: Ingersoll, Earl G., ed. **Doris Lessing: Conversations**. Princeton, NJ: Ontario Review Press, 1994. pp.204-213.

___ Lessing, Doris. **Under My Skin: Volume One of My Autobiography, to 1949**. New York: HarperCollins, 1994. 419pp.

___ Malekin, Peter. "'What Dreams May Come?': Relativity of Perception in Doris Lessing's **Briefing for a Descent into Hell**," in: Morse, Donald E., ed. **The Celebration of the Fantastic**. Westport, CT: Greenwood, 1992. pp.73-80.

LESSING, DORIS (continued)

___ Newquist, Roy. "Talking as a Person (Interview, 1964)," in: Ingersoll, Earl G., ed. **Doris Lessing: Conversations**. Princeton, NJ: Ontario Review Press, 1994. pp.3-12.

___ Oates, Joyce C. "One Keeps Coming (Interview, 1972)," in: Ingersoll, Earl G., ed. **Doris Lessing: Conversations**. Princeton, NJ: Ontario Review Press, 1994. pp.33-40.

___ Pifer, Ellen. "**The Fifth Child**: Lessing's Subversion of the Pastoral," in: Morse, Donald E., ed. **The Celebration of the Fantastic**. Westport, CT: Greenwood, 1992. pp.123-132.

___ Raskin, Jonah. "The Inadequacy of the Imagination (Interview, 1970)," in: Ingersoll, Earl G., ed. **Doris Lessing: Conversations**. Princeton, NJ: Ontario Review Press, 1994. pp.13-18.

___ Rousseau, Francois-Olivier. "The Habit of Observing (Interview, 1985)," in: Ingersoll, Earl G., ed. **Doris Lessing: Conversations**. Princeton, NJ: Ontario Review Press, 1994. pp.146-154.

___ Rowe, Margaret M. **Doris Lessing**. New York: St. Martin's, 1994. 137pp.

___ Sage, Lorna. "Doris Lessing," in: Sage, Lorna. **Women in the House of Fiction: Post-War Women Novelists**. New York: Routledge, 1992. pp.13-23.

___ Schültz-Güth, Gudrun. "Doris Lessing: **The Memoirs of a Survivor** (1974)," in: Heuermann, Hartmut and Lange, Bernd-Peter, eds. **Die Utopie in der angloamerikanischen Literatur: Interpretationen**. Düsseldorf: Bagel, 1984. pp.310-327.

___ Shaw, Deborah A. **The Marriage Quest in 'Canopus': A Study of Doris Lessing's 'The Marriages Between Zones Three, Four and Five'**. Master's Thesis, University of Victoria (Canada), 1992. 111pp. (Master's Abstracts 32/01, p. 61. February 1994.)

___ Svoboda, Randall A. **Between Private and Public Space: The Problem of Writing Personal History in the Novels of Lessing, Lawrence, Joyce and Fowles**. Ph.D. Dissertation, University of Iowa, 1995. 313pp. (DAI-A 56/06, p. 2253. December 1995.)

___ Terkel, Studs. "Learning to Put the Questions Differently (Interview, 1969)," in: Ingersoll, Earl G., ed. **Doris Lessing: Conversations**. Princeton, NJ: Ontario Review Press, 1994. pp.19-32.

___ Thomson, Sedge. "Drawn to a Type of Landscape (Interview, 1989)," in: Ingersoll, Earl G., ed. **Doris Lessing: Conversations**. Princeton, NJ: Ontario Review Press, 1994. pp.178-192.

___ Thorpe, Michael. "Running Through Stories in My Mind (Interview, 1980)," in: Ingersoll, Earl G., ed. **Doris Lessing: Conversations**. Princeton, NJ: Ontario Review Press, 1994. pp.94-101.

___ Tiger, Virginia. " 'The words had been right and necessary': Doris Lessing's Transformations of Utopian and Dystopian Modalities in **The Marriages Between Zones Three, Four and Five**," *Style* 27(1): 63-80. Spring 1993.

___ Tomalin, Claire. "Watching the Angry and Destructive Hordes Go By (Interview, 1988)," in: Ingersoll, Earl G., ed. **Doris Lessing: Conversations**. Princeton, NJ: Ontario Review Press, 1994. pp.173-177.

___ Torrents, Nissa. "Testimony of Mysticism (Interview, 1980)," in: Ingersoll, Earl G., ed. **Doris Lessing: Conversations**. Princeton, NJ: Ontario Review Press, 1994. pp.64-69.

___ Turner, Martha A. **Mechanism and the Novel: Science in the Narrative Process**. Cambridge: Cambridge University Press, 1993. 199pp.

___ Twiste, Regina. **Die Evolutionasthematik in Doris Lessings 'Space Fiction'**. Frankfurt-am-Main: P. Lang, 1994. 357pp.

___ Upchurch, Michael. "Voice of England, Voice of Africa (Interview, 1992)," in: Ingersoll, Earl G., ed. **Doris Lessing: Conversations**. Princeton, NJ: Ontario Review Press, 1994. pp.219-227.

___ von Schwarzkopf, Margarete. "Placing Their Fingers on the Wounds of Our Times (Interview, 1981)," in: Ingersoll, Earl G., ed. **Doris Lessing: Conversations**. Princeton, NJ: Ontario Review Press, 1994. pp.102-108.

LETHEM, JONATHAN

___ "1994 William L. Crawford Memorial Award," *Science Fiction Chronicle* 16(6): 12. May 1995.

___ "1995 *Locus* Awards Winners," *Locus* 35(2): 7, 34-37. August 1995.

___ "Lethem Wins Crawford," *Locus* 34(4): 9. April 1995.

LEVENTHAL, STAN

___ "Leventhal, Stan (Obituary)," *Locus* 34(3): 74. March 1995.

LEVIATHAN (MOTION PICTURE)

___ "Producers Call Off 6-Day Filming on **Leviathan** Following Protests," *Variety* p. 7. May 11, 1988.

LEVIN, BARRY R.

___ "Fourth Annual Collector's Award," *Locus* 28(5): 40. May 1992.

LEVIN, IRA

___ Ursini, James. **More Things Than Are Dreamt Of: Masterpieces of Supernatural Horror, From Mary Shelley to Stephen King, in Literature and Film**, by James Ursini and Alain Silver. New York: Limelight, 1994. 226pp.

LEWIN, ROBERT

___ Jankiewicz, Pat. "Present at the Creation," *Starlog* No. 191: 75-79. June 1993.

LEWIS, AL

___ Voger, Mark. "Clown Prince of Darkness: The Biting Brooklyn Wit of Al Lewis," *Filmfax* No. 41: 70-72. October/November 1993.

LEWIS, C. S.

___ "C. S. Lewis," in: Bloom, Harold, ed. **Classic Science Fiction Writers**. New York: Chelsea House, 1995. pp.62-75.

___ "C. S. Lewis's House in Oxford Being Restored as Study Center," *Science Fiction Chronicle* 15(6): 6. April/May 1994.

___ "HarperCollins Captures Narnia," *Locus* 33(1): 8. July 1994.

___ "HarperCollins to Publish Narnia Books," *Science Fiction Chronicle* 15(8): 5. June 1994.

___ "In Memoriam: C. S. Lewis," in: Watson, George, ed. **Critical Essays on C. S. Lewis**. Hants, Eng.: Scolar Press, 1992. pp.22-23.

___ "Lewis 'Hoax' Goes on and on...," *Locus* 29(4): 7, 72. October 1992

___ "Libel Charge Against Lindskoog Book," *Locus* 34(2): 8, 72. February 1995.

___ "**Wonderworks** has 'Narnia' as 9-Hour Coprod," *Variety* p. 45. June 15, 1988.

___ Arbuckle, Nan. "That Hidden Strength: C. S. Lewis' Merlin as Modern Grail," in: Watson, Jeanie and Fries, Marueen, eds. **The Figure of Merlin in the Nineteenth and Twentieth Centuries**. Lewiston, NY: Mellen, 1989. pp.79-99.

___ Baker, Rob. "Tangent: A Modern Metaphor," *Parabola* 17(2): 83-87. May 1992.

___ Baldry, Cherith. "Magic in Narnia," *Vector* No. 176: 16-17. December 1993/January 1994.

___ Beach, Charles F. "C. S. Lewis, Courtly Love, and Chaucer's **Troilus and Criseyde**," *Bulletin of the New York C. S. Lewis Society* 26(4/5): 1-10. February/March 1995.

___ Beach, Charles F. "Courtesy and Self in the Thought of Charles Williams and C. S. Lewis," *Bulletin of the New York C. S. Lewis Society* 25(3/4): 1-11. January/February 1994.

___ Ben-Chorin, Schalom. "Joy Davidman und C. S. Lewis zu alttestamentlichen Texten," in: Kranz, Gisbert, ed. **Inklings: Jahrbuch für Literatur und Ästhetik**. 1. Band. Lüdenscheid, Germany: Michael Claren, 1983. pp.89-102.

___ Bennett, J. A. W. "From: **The Humane Medievalist**," in: Watson, George, ed. **Critical Essays on C. S. Lewis**. Hants, Eng.: Scolar Press, 1992. pp.52-76.

___ Bernhardt, Peter. "Theatre of the Fantastic: A Choice of Shadows," *Riverside Quarterly* 9(3): 151-153. June 1995. (Whole No. 35)

___ Beversluis, John. "Surprised by Freud: A Critical Appraisal of A. N. Wilson's Biography of C. S. Lewis," *Christianity and Literature* 41(2): 179-195. Winter 1992.

___ Bloom, Harold. "C. S. Lewis," in: Bloom, Harold, ed. **Modern Fantasy Writers**. New York: Chelsea House, 1995. pp.85-97.

___ Branson, David A. "Arthurian Elements in **That Hideous Strength**," *Mythlore* 19(4): 20-21. Autumn 1993. (No. 74)

___ Cantor, Norman F. **Inventing the Middle Ages: The Lives, Works and Ideas of the Great Medievalists of the Twentieth Century**. New York: Morrow, 1991. 477pp.

___ Christopher, Joe R. "Biographies and Bibliographies on C. S. Lewis," in: Walker, Andrew and Patric, James, eds. **A Christian for All Christians**. Washington, DC: Regnery, 1992. pp.216-222.

___ Christopher, Joe R. "C. S. Lewis' Linguistic Myth," *Mythlore* 21(1): 41-50. Summer 1995. (No. 79)

___ Christopher, Joe R. "An Inklings Bibliography (45)," by Joe R. Christopher and Wayne G. Hammond. *Mythlore* 18(2): 28-33, 39-40. Spring 1992. (No. 68)

___ Christopher, Joe R. "An Inklings Bibliography (46)," by Joe R. Christopher and Wayne G. Hammond. *Mythlore* 18(3): 49-53. Summer 1992. (No. 69)

LEWIS, C. S. (continued)

___ Christopher, Joe R. "An Inklings Bibliography (47)," by Joe R. Christopher and Wayne G. Hammond. *Mythlore* 18(4): 49-52. Autumn 1992. (No. 70)

___ Christopher, Joe R. "An Inklings Bibliography (48)," by Joe R. Christopher and Wayne G. Hammond. *Mythlore* 19(1): 56-64. Winter 1993. (No. 71)

___ Christopher, Joe R. "An Inklings Bibliography (49)," by Joe R. Christopher and Wayne G. Hammond. *Mythlore* 19(2): 61-65. Spring 1993. (No. 72)

___ Christopher, Joe R. "An Inklings Bibliography (50) (e.g. 51)," by Joe R. Christopher and Wayne G. Hammond. *Mythlore* 19(4): 60-65. Autumn 1993. (No. 74)

___ Christopher, Joe R. "An Inklings Bibliography (50)," by Joe R. Christopher and Wayne G. Hammond. *Mythlore* 19(3): 59-65. Summer 1993. (No. 73)

___ Christopher, Joe R. "An Inklings Bibliography (51)," by Joe R. Christopher and Wayne G. Hammond. *Mythlore* 20(1): 59-62. Winter 1994. (Whole No. 75)

___ Christopher, Joe R. "An Inklings Bibliography (52)," by Joe R. Christopher and Wayne G. Hammond. *Mythlore* 20(2): 32-34. Spring 1994. (Whole No. 76)

___ Christopher, Joe R. "An Inklings Bibliography (54)," by Joe R. Christopher and Wayne G. Hammond. *Mythlore* 20(4): 61-65. Winter 1995. (Whole No. 78)

___ Christopher, Joe R. "An Inklings Bibliography (55)," by Joe R. Christopher and Wayne G. Hammond. *Mythlore* 21(1): 61-65. Summer 1995. (No. 79)

___ Christopher, Joe R. "No Fish for the Phoenix," *CSL: The Bulletin of the New York C. S. Lewis Society* 23(9): 1-7. July 1992.

___ Como, James. "The Centrality of Rhetoric to an Understanding of C. S. Lewis," *Bulletin of the New York C. S. Lewis Society* 25(1): 1-7. November 1993.

___ Como, James. "A Seeing Eye," *Bulletin of the New York C. S. Lewis Society* 25(9/11): 3-6. July/September 1994.

___ Como, James. "Shadowlands IV," *CSL: The Bulletin of the New York C. S. Lewis Society* 24(6): 1-7. April 1993.

___ Constable, John. "C. S. Lewis: From Magdalen to Magdalene," in: Watson, George, ed. **Critical Essays on C. S. Lewis**. Hants, Eng.: Scolar Press, 1992. pp.47-51.

___ Coren, Michael. **The Man Who Created Narnia: The Story of C. S. Lewis**. Toronto: Lester, 1994. 140pp.

___ Daniel, Jerry. "The Taste of the Pineapple: A Basis for Literary Criticism," *CSL: The Bulletin of the New York C. S. Lewis Society* 23(2): 1-12. December 1991.

___ Dorsett, Lyle W. "Researching C. S. Lewis," in: Walker, Andrew and Patric, James, eds. **A Christian for All Christians**. Washington, DC: Regnery, 1992. pp.213-215.

___ Downing, David C. **Planets in Peril: A Critical Study of C. S. Lewis's Ransom Trilogy**. Amherst: University of Massachusetts Press, 1992. 186pp.

___ Duriez, Colin. "Tolkien and the Other Inklings," in: Reynolds, Patricia and GoodKnight, Glen H., eds. **Proceedings of the J. R. R. Tolkien Centenary Conference, Keble College, Oxford, 1992**. Altadena, CA: Mythopoeic Press, 1995. pp.360-363. (*Mythlore* Vol. 21, No. 2, Winter 1996, Whole No. 80)

___ Fiddes, Paul S. "C. S. Lewis the Myth-Maker," in: Walker, Andrew and Patric, James, eds. **A Christian for All Christians**. Washington, DC: Regnery, 1992. pp.132-155.

___ Filmer, Kath. **The Fiction of C. S. Lewis: Mask and Mirror**. New York: St. Martin's, 1992. 153pp.; Basingstoke: Macmillan, 1993. 153pp. [Not seen; cf. OCLC.]

___ Filmer, Kath. "A Place in Deep Heaven: Figurative Language in **Out of the Silent Planet**," in: Kranz, Gisbert, ed. **Inklings: Jahrbuch für Literatur und Ästhetik**. 3. Band. [Lüdenscheid, Germany: Stier], 1985. pp.187-196.

___ Filmer, Kath. **Scepticism and Hope in Twentieth Century Fantasy Literature**. Bowling Green, OH: Bowling Green State University Popular Press, 1992. 160pp.

___ Ford, Paul F. **Companion to Narnia**. 4th ed. San Francisco, CA: Harper, 1994. 460pp.

___ Fuller, Edward. "The Christian Spaceman--C. S. Lewis," *Bulletin of the New York C. S. Lewis Society* 27(1/2): 9-15. November/December 1995. (Reprinted from *Horizon* Vol. 1, No. 5, May, 1959.)

___ Gammons, Neil G. "**Till We Have Faces**: A Key-Word Concordance, Part 1," *CSL: The Bulletin of the New York C. S. Lewis Society* 23(10/11): 11-16. August/September 1992.

LEWIS, C. S. (continued)

___ Gammons, Neil G. "**Till We Have Faces**: A Key-Word Concordance, Part 2," *CSL: The Bulletin of the New York C. S. Lewis Society* 23/24(No.12/No. 1): 11-16. October/November 1992.

___ Gardner, Helen. "British Academy Obituary: C. S. Lewis," in: Watson, George, ed. **Critical Essays on C. S. Lewis**. Hants, Eng.: Scolar Press, 1992. pp.10-21.

___ Gatling, Clover H. "Echoes of Epic in Lewis' **The Great Divorce**," *Bulletin of the New York C. S. Lewis Society* 26(3): 1-8. January 1995.

___ Goodman, Margaret. "Posthumous Journeys: **The Great Divorce** and Other Travels to Eternity," *Bulletin of the New York C. S. Lewis Society* 27(1/2): 1-8. November/December 1995.

___ Green, Roger L. **C. S. Lewis: A Biography**. Revised Edition, by Roger L. Green and Walter Hooper. San Diego, CA: Harcourt Brace, 1994. 320pp.

___ Griffin, William. "In Search of the Real C. S. Lewis," *Bulletin of the New York C. S. Lewis Society* 25(9/11): 18-26. July/September 1994.

___ Gussman, Neil. "Translations of Latin, Greek and French Phrases From **Studies in Medieval and Renaissance Literature** and **The Pilgrim's Regress**," *Bulletin of the New York C. S. Lewis Society* 25(12): 1-5. October 1994.

___ Hannay, Margaret. "The Mythology of **Out of the Silent Planet**," *Mythlore* 20(2): 20-22. Spring 1994. (Whole No. 76)

___ Hardie, Colin. "Inklings: British at Oxford and German at Aachen," in: Kranz, Gisbert, ed. **Inklings: Jahrbuch für Literatur und Ästhetik**. 1. Band. Lüdenscheid, Germany: Michael Claren, 1983. pp.15-19.

___ Heiser, James. "C. S. Lewis as Media Critic," *Intercollegiate Review* 27(2): 51-54. Spring 1992.

___ Herrick, Jim. "C. S. Lewis and Narrative Argument in **Out of the Silent Planet**," *Mythlore* 18(4): 15-22. Autumn 1992. (No. 70)

___ Hopkins, Lisa. "Female Authority Figures in the Works of Tolkien, C. S. Lewis, and Charles Williams," in: Reynolds, Patricia and GoodKnight, Glen H., eds. **Proceedings of the J. R. R. Tolkien Centenary Conference, Keble College, Oxford, 1992**. Altadena, CA: Mythopoeic Press, 1995. pp.364-366. (*Mythlore* Vol. 21, No. 2, Winter 1996, Whole No. 80)

___ Horne, Brian. "A Peculiar Debt: The Influence of Charles Williams on C. S. Lewis," in: Walker, Andrew and Patric, James, eds. **A Christian for All Christians**. Washington, DC: Regnery, 1992. pp.83-97.

___ Howell, Cynthia M. **C. S. Lewis and the Twentieth Century: An Analysis of Out of the Silent Planet, Perelandra and That Hideous Strength**. Master's Thesis, Vanderbilt University, 1975. 78pp.

___ Jones, Gwyneth. "C. S. Lewis and Tolkien: Writers for Children?," *New York Review of Science Fiction* No. 87: 1, 8-12. November 1995.

___ Kastor, Frank S. "C. S. Lewis's John Milton: Influence, Presence and Beyond," *Bulletin of the New York C. S. Lewis Society* 24(9/10): 1-11. July/August 1993.

___ Keffer, Sarah L. "Work-Writing to Create the Fictional Portrait: Tolkien's Inclusion of Lewis in **The Lord of the Rings**," *English Studies in Canada* 18(2): 181-198. June 1992.

___ Kern, Raimund B. "Von der Werklichkeit zum Phantastischen und zurück: Natur und Kultur in den Narnia-büchern von C. S. Lewis," in: Kranz, Gisbert, ed. **Inklings: Jahrbuch für Literatur und Ästhetik**. 8. Band. Lüdenscheid, Germany: Stier, 1990. pp.71-102. [Not seen.]

___ Knecht, William R. "C. S. Lewis and the Apotheosis," *CSL: The Bulletin of the New York C. S. Lewis Society* 23(8): 1-4. June 1992.

___ Kordeski, Stanley. **Anatomy of Fantasy: An Examination of Works of J. R. R. Tolkien and C. S. Lewis**. Master's Thesis, University of Vermont, 1975. 67pp.

___ Koterski, Joseph W. "C. S. Lewis and Natural Law," *Bulletin of the New York C. S. Lewis Society* 26(6): 1-7. April 1995.

___ Kranz, Gisbert. "Aldous Huxley und C. S. Lewis: Eine vergleichende Studie," in: Kranz, Gisbert, ed. **Inklings: Jahrbuch für Literatur und Ästhetik**. 2. Band. [Lüdenscheid, Germany: Stier], 1984. pp.112-153.

___ Kranz, Gisbert. "Ein Dinosaurier? C. S. Lewis und die moderne Literatur," in: Kranz, Gisbert, ed. **Inklings: Jahrbuch für Literatur und Ästhetik**. 7. Band. Lüdenscheid, Germany: Stier, 1989. pp.53-62. [Not seen.]

___ Kranz, Gisbert, ed. **Inklings: Jahrbuch für Literatur und Ästhetik**. 1.Band. Lüdenscheid: Michael Claren, 1983. 185pp.

___ Kreeft, Peter. **C. S. Lewis for the Third Millennium: Six Essays on The Abolition of Man**. San Francisco, CA: Ignatius, 1994. 193pp.

___ Kreeft, Peter. "How to Save Western Civilisation: C. S. Lewis as Prophet," in: Walker, Andrew and Patric, James, eds. **A Christian for All Christians**. Washington, DC: Regnery, 1992. pp.190-212.

LEWIS, C. S.

LEWIS, C. S. (continued)

___ Kreeft, Peter. "Walker Percy's **Lost in the Cosmos: The Abolition of Man** in Late-night Comedy Format," in: Kreeft, Peter. **C. S. Lewis for the Third Millenium**. San Francisco, CA: Ignatius, 1994. pp.131-164.

___ Lake, David. "Wells, **The First Men in the Moon**, and Lewis's Ransom Trilogy," in: Filmer, Kath, ed. **Twentieth-Century Fantasists: Essays in Culture, Society and Belief in Twentieth Century Mythopoeic Literature**. New York: St. Martin's, 1992. pp.23-33.

___ Lambarski, Tim. "Homeliness, Strangeness, and Receptivity: Paths to Aslan's Country in **The Voyage of the Dawn Treader**," *Bulletin of the New York C. S. Lewis Society* 25(5/6): 6-11. March/April 1994.

___ Laurent, John. "C. S. Lewis and Animal Rights," *Mythlore* 19(1): 46-51. Winter 1993. (No. 71)

___ Lewis, C. S. **The Letters of C. S. Lewis to Arthur Greeves (1914-1963)**, ed. by Walter Hooper. New York: Collier, 1986. 592pp. (Reissue of **They Stand Together**, 1979.)

___ Lewis, C. S. "Two New Letters from C. S. Lewis," *Bulletin of the New York C. S. Lewis Society* 25(9/11): 14-15. July/September 1994.

___ Lindskoog, Kathryn. "The Dark Scandal: Science Fiction Forgery," *Quantum* No. 42: 29-30. Summer/Fall 1992.

___ Lindskoog, Kathryn. **Light in the Shadow Lands: Protecting the Real C. S. Lewis**. Sisters, OR: Multnomah Press, 1994. 345pp.

___ Loney, Douglas. "C. S. Lewis' Debt to E. M. Forster's **The Celestial Omnibus and Other Stories**," *Mythlore* 21(1): 14-22. Summer 1995. (No. 79)

___ Lowenberg, Susan. **C. S. Lewis: A Reference Guide, 1972-1988**. New York: G. K. Hall, 1993. 319pp.

___ Mackey, Aidan. "The Christian Influence of G. K. Chesterton on C. S. Lewis," in: Walker, Andrew and Patric, James, eds. **A Christian for All Christians**. Washington, DC: Regnery, 1992. pp.68-82.

___ Manlove, C. N. **The Chronicles of Narnia: The Patterning of a Fantastic World**. New York: Twayne, 1993. 136pp.

___ Martin, John. "C. S. Lewis and Animals: The Road to Whipsnade," *Bulletin of the New York C. S. Lewis Society* 24(11): 1-7. September 1993.

___ McBride, Sam. "C. S. Lewis's **A Preface to Paradise Lost**, the Milton Controversy, and Lewis Scholarship," *Bulletin of Bibliography* 52(4): 317-332. Decenber 1995.

___ McGovern, Eugene. "The Greeves Letters as Seen by Arthur Greeves," *Bulletin of the New York C. S. Lewis Society* 25(9/11): 9-13. July/September 1994.

___ McGovern, Eugene. "Lewis and Modern Christian Novels," *CSL: The Bulletin of the New York C. S. Lewis Society* 23(5): 5-8. March 1992.

___ McGovern, Eugene. "Lewis and Winston Churchill: A Note Necessarily Short," *CSL: The Bulletin of the New York C. S. Lewis Society* 23(3): 6-7. January 1992.

___ McGovern, Eugene. "Lewis, Columbus, and the Discovery of New Worlds," *CSL: The Bulletin of the New York C. S. Lewis Society* 23/24(No.12/No. 1): 1-7. October/November 1992.

___ McGrew, Lydia M. "Action and the Passionate Patient in **That Hideous Strength**," *CSL: The Bulletin of the New York C. S. Lewis Society* 23(7): 1-6. May 1992.

___ McKim, Mark G. "C. S. Lewis on the Disappearance of the Individual," *CSL: The Bulletin of the New York C. S. Lewis Society* 23(5): 1-5. March 1992.

___ McKim, Mark G. "The Poison Brewed in the West," *Bulletin of the New York C. S. Lewis Society* 26(11/12): 1-6. September/October 1995.

___ McLaughlin, Sara P. "**The City of God** Revisited: C. S. Lewis's Debt to Saint Augustine," *CSL: The Bulletin of the New York C. S. Lewis Society* 23(6): 1-9. April 1992.

___ McLaughlin, Sara P. "A Legacy of Truth: The Influence of George MacDonald's **Unspoken Sermons** on C. S. Lewis's **Mere Christianity**," *CSL: The Bulletin of the New York C. S. Lewis Society* 24(4): 1-6. February 1993.

___ Merchant, Robert. "Pope, Council, Bible and/or Self: Lewis and the Question of Authority," *CSL: The Bulletin of the New York C. S. Lewis Society* 23(10/11): 1-10. August/September 1992.

___ Moynihan, Martin. "C. S. Lewis and the Arthurian Tradition," in: Kranz, Gisbert, ed. **Inklings: Jahrbuch für Literatur und Ästhetik**. 1. Band. Lüdenscheid, Germany: Michael Claren, 1983. pp.21-41.

___ Myers, Doris T. **C. S. Lewis in Context**. Kent, OH: Kent State University Press, 1994. 248pp.

___ Myers, Doris T. "Law and Disorder: Two Settings in **That Hideous Strength**," *Mythlore* 19(1): 9-14. Winter 1993. (No. 71)

___ Nicholson, Mervyn. "Bram Stoker and C. S. Lewis: **Dracula** as a Source for **That Hideous Strength**," *Mythlore* 19(3): 16-22. Summer 1993. (No. 73)

LEWIS, C. S. (continued)

___ Nuttall, A. D. "Jack the Giant-Killer," *CSL: The Bulletin of the New York C. S. Lewis Society* 24(2/3): 1-14. December 1992/January 1993.

___ Patrick, James. "C. S. Lewis and Idealism," in: Walker, Andrew and Patric, James, eds. **A Christian for All Christians**. Washington, DC: Regnery, 1992. pp.156-173.

___ Perrin, Noel. "A C. S. Lewis Miscellany," *CSL: The Bulletin of the New York C. S. Lewis Society* 23(3): 1-3. January 1992.

___ Prothero, James. "Lewis's Poetry: A Preliminary Exploration," *Bulletin of the New York C. S. Lewis Society* 25(5/6): 2-6. March/April 1994.

___ Purtill, Richard L. "Did C. S. Lewis Lose His Faith?," in: Walker, Andrew and Patric, James, eds. **A Christian for All Christians**. Washington, DC: Regnery, 1992. pp.27-62.

___ Sarrocco, Clara. "Whittaker Chambers on Christians," *CSL: The Bulletin of the New York C. S. Lewis Society* 23(7): 6-7. May 1992.

___ Sayer, George. **Jack: A Life of C. S. Lewis**. 2nd ed. Wheaton, IL: Crossway, 1994. 457pp.

___ Sayer, George. "Recollections of J. R. R. Tolkien," in: Reynolds, Patricia and GoodKnight, Glen H., eds. **Proceedings of the J. R. R. Tolkien Centenary Conference, Keble College, Oxford, 1992**. Altadena, CA: Mythopoeic Press, 1995. pp.21-25. (*Mythlore* Vol. 21, No. 2, Winter 1996, Whole No. 80)

___ Schakel, Peter J. "Elusive Birds and Narrative Nets: The Appeal of Story in C. S. Lewis' **Chronicles of Narnia**," in: Walker, Andrew and Patric, James, eds. **A Christian for All Christians**. Washington, DC: Regnery, 1992. pp.116-131.

___ Schrey, Helmut. "Von **Paradise Lost** zu **Perelandra**," in: Kranz, Gisbert, ed. **Inklings: Jahrbuch für Literatur und Ästhetik**. 1. Band. Lüdenscheid, Germany: Michael Claren, 1983. pp.67-88.

___ Sellin, Bernard. "Journeys into Fantasy: The Fiction of David Lindsay and C. S. Lewis," in: Walker, Andrew and Patric, James, eds. **A Christian for All Christians**. Washington, DC: Regnery, 1992. pp.98-115.

___ Shaw, Luci N. "Looking Back to Eden: The Poetry of C. S. Lewis," *CSL: The Bulletin of the New York C. S. Lewis Society* 23(4): 1-7. February 1992.

___ Shippey, Tom. "Tolkien as a Post-War Writer," in: Reynolds, Patricia and GoodKnight, Glen H., eds. **Proceedings of the J. R. R. Tolkien Centenary Conference, Keble College, Oxford, 1992**. Altadena, CA: Mythopoeic Press, 1995. pp.84-93. (*Mythlore* Vol. 21, No. 2, Winter 1996, Whole No. 80)

___ Splett, Jörg. "Der Schmerz und die Freude. C. S. Lewis' christliche Perspektiv," in: Kranz, Gisbert, ed. **Inklings: Jahrbuch für Literatur und Ästhetik**. 1. Band. Lüdenscheid, Germany: Michael Claren, 1983. pp.43-66.

___ Stableford, Brian. "C. S. Lewis and the Decline of Scientific Romances," *New York Review of Science Fiction* No. 45: 1, 8-12. May 1992.

___ Swift, Catherine. **C. S. Lewis**. Minneapolis, MN: Bethany House, 1989. 127pp.

___ Sys, Jacques. " 'Look Out! It's Alive!: C. S. Lewis on Doctrine," in: Walker, Andrew and Patric, James, eds. **A Christian for All Christians**. Washington, DC: Regnery, 1992. pp.174-189.

___ Taylor, A. J. P. "Intellectual Gaiety," in: Watson, George, ed. **Critical Essays on C. S. Lewis**. Hants, Eng.: Scolar Press, 1992. pp.37-47.

___ Tolkien, J. R. R. "Letter to Anne Barrett, Houghton Mifflin Co., 30 August 1964, No. 261," in: Watson, George, ed. **Critical Essays on C. S. Lewis**. Hants, Eng.: Scolar Press, 1992. pp.9-10.

___ Totaro, Rebecca. "Regaining Perception: The Ransom Trilogy as a Re-embodiment of the Neoplatonic Model," *CSL: The Bulletin of the New York C. S. Lewis Society* 22(10): 1-11. August 1991.

___ Trupia, Robert C. "Learning Christian Behavior: The Path of Virtue in **The Chronicles of Narnia**," *Bulletin of the New York C. S. Lewis Society* 24(7/8): 1-5. May/June 1993.

___ Veldman, Meredith. **Fantasy, the Bomb, and the Greening of Britain: Romantic Protest, 1945-1980**. Cambridge: Cambridge University Press, 1994. 325pp.

___ Wain, John. "C. S. Lewis," in: Watson, George, ed. **Critical Essays on C. S. Lewis**. Hants, Eng.: Scolar Press, 1992. pp.24-36.

___ Walczuk, Anna. "The Permanent in Lewis and Chesterton," *Chesterton Review* 17(3/4): 313-321. August/November 1991.

___ Walker, Andrew. **A Christian for All Christians: Essays in Honor of C. S. Lewis**, by Andrew Walker and James Patrick. Washington, DC: Regnery, 1992. 255pp.

LEWIS, C. S. (continued)
___ Walker, Andrew. "Reflections on C. S. Lewis, Apologetics, and the Moral Tradition," by Andrew Walker and Basil Mitchell. in: Walker, Andrew and Patric, James, eds. **A Christian for All Christians.** Washington, DC: Regnery, 1992. pp.7-26.
___ Walker, Andrew. "Under the Russian Cross: A Research Note on C. S. Lewis and the Eastern Orthodox Church," in: Walker, Andrew and Patric, James, eds. **A Christian for All Christians.** Washington, DC: Regnery, 1992. pp.63-67.
___ Washick, James. "The Framed Narrative in **Perelandra,**" *Bulletin of the New York C. S. Lewis Society* 25(7/8): 1-4. May/June 1994.
___ Watson, George. "Introduction: **Critical Essays on C. S. Lewis,**" *CSL: The Bulletin of the New York C. S. Lewis Society* 24(5): 1-7. March 1993.
___ Watson, George, ed. **Critical Essays on C. S. Lewis.** Hants, Eng.: Scolar Press, 1992. 284pp. (Critical Thought Series: 1)
___ Watson, Thomas R. "Enlarging Augustinian Systems: C. S. Lewis' **The Great Divorce** and **Till We Have Faces,**" *Renascence* 46(3): 163-174. Spring 1994.
___ Watson, Victor. "Snobberies, Sneers, and Narnia: On the Narrowness of C. S. Lewis," *Books for Keeps* 83: 21. November 1994.

LEWIS, MATTHEW GREGORY
___ Bloom, Harold. "Matthew Gregory Lewis," in: Bloom, Harold. **Classic Horror Writers.** New York: Chelsea House, 1994. pp.59-72.
___ Ethridge, Gareth M. "The Company We Keep: Comic Function in M. G. Lewis's **The Monk,**" in: Sanders, Joe, ed. **Functions of the Fantastic.** Westport, CT: Greenwood, 1995. pp.63-90.
___ Geary, Robert F. "M. G. Lewis and Later Gothic Fiction: The Numinous Dissipated," in: Ruddick, Nicholas, ed. **State of the Fantastic.** Westport, CT: Greenwood, 1992. pp.75-81.

LEWIS, OSCAR
___ "Lewis, Oscar (Obituary)," *Locus* 29(3): 78. September 1992.

LEWTON, VAL
___ Bansak, Edmund G. **Fearing the Dark: The Val Lewton Career.** Jefferson, NC: McFarland, 1995. 571pp.
___ James, Caryn. "Old Hollywood Horror, But With Depth and Flair," *New York Times* Sec. C, p. 3. July 2, 1993.
___ Vivona, Stephen T. "The Films of Val Lewton and Boris Karloff," *Filmfax* No. 44: 50-56. April/May 1994.

LIBERTARIANS
___ Lerner, Fred. "The Libertarian Ideal in Science Fiction," *Voice of Youth Advocates* 13(1): 17-18. April 1990.

LIBRARIES IN SF
___ Barnes, John. "Information and Unfictionable Science," *Information Technology and Libraries* 14(4): 247-250. December 1995. (Cited from IAC Insite on-line service.)
___ Gunn, James E. "Dreams Written Out: Libraries in Science Fiction," *Wilson Library Bulletin* 69(6): 26-29. February 1995.
___ Wiseman, Gillian. "Visions of the Future: The Library in Science Fiction," *Journal of Youth Services in Libraries* 7(2): 191-198. Winter 1994.

LIBRARY COLLECTIONS OF SF AND FANTASY
___ "Alum's Pulp Gift out of This World With Rare SF Titles, Fanzines," *Wilson Library Bulletin* 69(5): 16. January 1995.
___ "Eric Frank Russell, Wyndam Collections to UK's SF Foundation," *Science Fiction Chronicle* 15(6): 5-6. April/May 1994.
___ "Last H. G. Wells Papers Acquired by the H. G. Wells Archives at Illinois," *Locus* 30(2): 7, 74. February 1993.
___ "Maison d'Ailleurs; A House of Elsewhere," *Locus* 32(1): 40. January 1994.
___ "Merrill Collection in Trouble Again," *Locus* 33(4): 9. October 1994.
___ Barron, Neil. "Science Fiction Publishing and Libraries," in: Barron, Neil, ed. **Anatomy of Wonder 4.** New York: Bowker, 1995. pp.455-461.
___ Covington, Veronica. "The Science Fiction Research Collection at Texas A&M University," *Popular Culture in Libraries* 2(1): 81-87. 1994.
___ Dowlin, C. Edwin. "The Wondrous Williamson Collection," *Popular Culture in Libraries* 1 (2): 79-85. 1993.
___ Gold, Mici. "The Merril Collection, a Rare Jewel," *Sol Rising* (Toronto) No. 10: 1-2. May 1994.

LIBRARY COLLECTIONS OF SF AND FANTASY (continued)
___ McNelly, Willis E. "The Science Fiction Collection," in: Vogeler, Albert R. and Arthur A. Hansen, eds. **Very Special Collections: Essays on Library Holdings at California State University, Fullerton.** Fullerton, CA: Patron of the Library, 1992. pp.17-62.
___ Schramm, Susan. "7 Years of TV Scripts Make Long Trek to IU's Lilly Library," *Indianapolis (IN) Star.* November 28, 1994. in: *NewsBank. Film and Television.* FTV 21: D5. 1995.
___ Scott, Randall W. **Comics Librarianship: A Handbook.** Jefferson, NC: McFarland, 1990. 188pp.
___ Scott, Randall W. "Research Libraries of Interest to Fandom," in: Hopkins, Mariane S., ed. **Fandom Directory No. 14.** Springfield, VA: Fandata, 1992. pp.138-148.
___ Scott, Randall W. "Research Library Collections of Science Fiction," in: Barron, Neil, ed. **Anatomy of Wonder 4.** New York: Bowker, 1995. pp.738-764.
___ Winchester, Mark D. "Comic Strip Theatricals in Public and Private Collections," *Popular Culture in Libraries* 1(1): 67-76. 1993.

LIFEPOD (MOTION PICTURE)
___ Altman, Mark A. "*Lifepod*: An Outer Space Version of Hitchcock's *Lifeboat* Becomes a Fox TV Movie," *Cinefantastique* 24(3/4): 116-117. October 1993.

LIGHT YEARS (MOTION PICTURE)
___ Burden, Martin. "After 390 Books, Sci-Fi's Isaac Asimov Tries a Movie," in: *NewsBank. Literature* LIT 56: C4-C5. 1988.
___ Taylor, Clarke. "Animated Asimov: Mr. Sci-Fi (Momentarily) Abandons Books for Film," in: *NewsBank. Film and Television* FTV 27: F4-F5. 1988.

LIGOTTI, THOMAS
___ Dziemianowicz, Stefan. "The Weird Fiction of Thomas Ligotti: **Grimscribe** and **Songs of a Dead Dreamer,**" *New York Review of Science Fiction* No. 54: 1, 3-4. February 1993.
___ Joshi, S. T. "Thomas Ligotti: The Escape From Life," *Studies in Weird Fiction* No. 12: 30-36. Spring 1993.
___ Price, Robert M. "Thomas Ligotti's Gnostic Quest," *Studies in Weird Fiction* No. 9: 27-31. Spring 1991.
___ Schweitzer, Darrell. "Thomas Ligotti," in: Schweitzer, Darrell. **Speaking of Horror: Interviews With Writers of the Supernatural.** San Bernardino, CA: Borgo, 1994. pp.67-74.

LINDALA, TOBY
___ Vitaris, Paula. "*X-Files*: Monster Maker," *Cinefantastique* 26(6)/27(1): 39-40. October 1995.

LINDBERGH, ANNE SPENCER
___ "Lindbergh, Anne Spencer (Obituary)," *Science Fiction Chronicle* 15(3): 14. January 1994.

LINDSAY, DAVID
___ Bloom, Harold. "David Lindsay," in: Bloom, Harold, ed. **Modern Fantasy Writers.** New York: Chelsea House, 1995. pp.98-109.
___ Elflandsson, Galad. "Arcturus Revisited: David Lindsay and the Quest for Muspel-Fire," *AB Bookman's Weekly* pp.2131-2146. October 1, 1984.
___ Kegler, Adelheid. "Encountering Darkness: The Black Platonism of David Lindsay," *Mythlore* 19(2): 24-33. Spring 1993. (No. 72)
___ Power, David. **David Lindsay's Vision.** Nottingham: Pauper's Press, 1991. 36pp.
___ Raff, Melvin. "The Structure of **A Voyage to Arcturus,**" *Studies in Scottish Literature* 15: 262-268. 1980.
___ Sellin, Bernard. "Journeys into Fantasy: The Fiction of David Lindsay and C. S. Lewis," in: Walker, Andrew and Patric, James, eds. **A Christian for All Christians.** Washington, DC: Regnery, 1992. pp.98-115.

LINDSKOOG, KATHRYN
___ "Libel Charge Against Lindskoog Book," *Locus* 34(2): 8, 72. February 1995.

LINGUISTICS
___ Dorfles, Gillo. "L'utopia della omoglossia e il ritorno a un linguaggio prebabelico," in: Saccaro Del Buffa, Giuseppa and Lewis, Arthur O., eds. **Utopie per gli Anni Ottana.** Rome: Gangemi Editore, 1986. pp.45-50.

LINGUISTICS

LINGUISTICS (continued)
___ Marik, Jaroslav. "Planlingvo kaj scienca fikcio," *Starto* 4(145): 4-6. 1991.

___ Marrone, Caterina. "Lingue universali e utopie nel pensiero linguistico del secolo XVII," in: Saccaro Del Buffa, Giuseppa and Lewis, Arthur O., eds. **Utopia e Modernita: Teorie e prassi utopiche nell'eta moderna e postmoderna.** Rome: Gangemi Editore, 1989. pp.505-518.

___ Solivetti, Carla. "L'utopia linguistica di Velimir Chlebnikov," in: Saccaro Del Buffa, Giuseppa and Lewis, Arthur O., eds. **Utopie per gli Anni Ottana.** Rome: Gangemi Editore, 1986. pp.51-70.

___ Tompson, Ricky L. "Tolkien's Word-Hoard Onleac," *Mythlore* 20(1): 22-40. Winter 1994. (Whole No. 75)

___ Westfahl, Gary. "Wrangling Conversation: Linguistic Patterns in the Dialogue of Heroes and Villains," in: Slusser, George and Eric S. Rabkin, eds. **Fights of Fancy: Armed Conflict in Science Fiction and Fantasy.** Athens, GA: University of Georgia Press, 1993. pp.35-48.

LINNEY, LAURA
___ Warren, Bill. "Jungle Heroine," *Starlog* No. 216: 32-35, 64. July 1995.

LION KING (MOTION PICTURE)
___ Ferrante, A. C. "Jungle Fever: *The Lion King* (Review)," *Sci-Fi Universe* No. 3: 72-73. October/November 1994.

___ Myers, Caren. "*Lion King* (Review)," *Sight and Sound* 4(10): 47-48. October 1994.

___ Persons, Dan. "*The Lion King* (Review)," *Cinefantastique* 25(6)/26(1): 122. December 1994.

___ Wells, Curt. "*The Lion King*," *Sci-Fi Entertainment* 1(2): 34-37. August 1994.

LIOTTA, RAY
___ Spelling, Ian. "The Hero This Time," *Starlog* No. 203: 43-48. June 1994.

LIQUID DREAMS (MOTION PICTURE)
___ Bernard, Jami. "*Dreams* Is a Nightmare (Review)," *New York (NY) Post.* April 15, 1992. in: *NewsBank. Film and Television.* 43:B10. 1992.

___ Persons, Dan. "*Liquid Dreams* (Review)," *Cinefantastique* 23(2/3): 123. October 1992.

___ Strauss, Bob. "Skyscraper Sex Thriller With Plot Gives *Dreams* a Lift (Review)," *Los Angeles (CA) Daily News.* June 5, 1992. in: *NewsBank. Film and Television.* 64:F9. 1992.

LISLE, HOLLY
___ "Holly Lisle: Drums in the Jungle," *Hailing Frequencies* (Waldenbooks) No. 6: 12-13. 1993.

LITERATURE AND SOCIETY
___ Cherniak, Laura R. **Calling in Question: Science Fiction and Cultural Studies.** Ph.D. Dissertation, University of California, Santa Cruz, 1995. 257pp. (DAI-A 56/04, p. 1554. October 1995.)

LITTLE NEMO: ADVENTURES IN SLUMBERLAND (MOTION PICTURE)
___ Goodson, William W., Jr. "*Little Nemo: Adventures in Slumberland* (Review)," *Cinefantastique* 23(6): 60. April 1993.

LITTLE SHOP OF HORRORS (MOTION PICTURE)
___ "Corman, WB Ink 'Little Shop' Deal," *Variety* p. 7, 14. January 22, 1986.

___ "Horizon Targets Illegal 'Horrors'," *Variety* p.31. July 3, 1985.

___ "*Little Shop of Horrors* Filmusical Rolls Monday," *Variety* p.6. October 15, 1985.

___ Pharr, Mary. "Different Shops of Horrors: From Roger Corman's Cult Classic to Frank Oz's Mainstream Musical," in: Latham, Robert A. and Collins, Robert A., eds. **Modes of the Fantastic.** Westport, CT: Greenwood, 1995. pp.212-220.

LIVERPOOL UNIVERSITY (UK)
___ Gardiner, Josephine. "Forward With the Masters of the Sci-Fi Universe," *Times Educational Supplement* 4061: SS2. April 29, 1994.

LLOYD, CHRISTOPHER
___ Warren, Bill. "The Many Faces of Christoper Lloyd," *Starlog* No. 193: 32-36. August 1993.

LLUESMA, JORGE
___ "Lluesma, Jorge, 28, Madrid Fest Director, Dies (Obituary)," *Variety* p. 6, 34. January 30, 1985.

LOCKHART, JUNE
___ Weaver, Tom. "June Lockhart," in: Weaver, Tom. **They Fought the Creature Features: Interviews with 23 Classic Horror, Science Fiction and Serial Stars.** Jefferson, NC: McFarland, 1995. pp.187-199.

___ Weaver, Tom. "Outrageous Original," *Starlog* No. 198: 32-37, 82. January 1994.

___ Weaver, Tom. "Space Mom," by Tom Weaver and Steve Swires. in: McDonnell, David, ed. **Starlog's Science Fiction Heroes and Heroines.** New York: Crescent Books, 1995. pp.44-46.

LOCKWOOD, GARY
___ Goldman, Lowell. "*2001: A Space Odyssey*: Gary Lockwood," *Cinefantastique* 25(3): 47. June 1994.

LOCUS AWARDS, 1992
___ "1992 *Locus* Awards," *Locus* 28(2): 1, 42-45. August 1992.

LOCUS AWARDS, 1993
___ "1993 *Locus* Awards," *Locus* 31(2): 1, 38-41 August 1993.

LOCUS AWARDS, 1994
___ "1994 *Locus* Awards," *Locus* 33(2): 7. August 1994.

LOCUS AWARDS, 1995
___ "1995 *Locus* Awards Winners," *Locus* 35(2): 7, 34-37. August 1995.

LOCUS (MAGAZINE)
___ "*Locus* Court Case," *Locus* 30(4): 6. April 1993.

___ "*Locus* Magazine: Silver Anniversary Letters; 25 Years and Counting," *Locus* 31(3): 52-59. September 1993.

___ Brown, Charles N. "25 Years of *Locus*," *Locus* 30(4): 34-35. April 1993.

LOCUS SURVEY, 1992
___ "1992 *Locus* Survey Results," *Locus* 29(3): 52-53, 78. September 1992.

LOCUS SURVEY, 1993
___ "1993 *Locus* Survey Results," *Locus* 31(3): 60-62, 84. September 1993.

LOCUS SURVEY, 1995
___ Cushman, Carolyn. "1995 *Locus* Survey Results," *Locus* 35(3): 56-58, 84. September 1993.

LOGAN'S RUN (MOTION PICTURE)
___ Nolan, William F. "Introduction: Logan, a Media History," in: Nolan, William F. **William F. Nolan's Logan: A Trilogy.** Baltimore, MD: Maclay, 1986. pp.7-19.

___ Wuntch, Phillip. "On the Move With *Logan's Run*," *Dallas Morning News* Sec. C, p. 4. July 1, 1975.

LOIS AND CLARK (TV)
___ Derro, Marc. "Video Beat: Midair Morphing," *Cinefex* No. 58: 29-30. June 1994.

___ Harris, Judith P. "*Lois & Clark* (Review)," *Cinefantastique* 24(6)/25(1): 123. February 1994.

___ Schwed, Mark. "On the Horizon: Whole New Worlds," *TV Guide* 41(30): 29-31. July 24, 1993.

LONDON, JACK
___ "Jack London," in: Bloom, Harold, ed. **Classic Science Fiction Writers.** New York: Chelsea House, 1995. pp.76-90.

___ Barley, Tony. "Prediction, Programme and Fantasy in Jack London's *The Iron Heel*," in: Seed, David, ed. **Anticipations: Essays on Early Science Fiction and Its Precursors.** Liverpool: Liverpool University Press, 1995. pp.153-171.

___ Graff, Bennett. **Horror in Evolution: Determinism, Materialism, and Darwinism in the American Gothic (Edgar Allan Poe, Frank Norris, Jack London, H. P. Lovecraft).** Ph.D. Dissertation, City University of New York, 1995. 282pp. (DAI-A 56/05, p. 1777. November 1995.)

LONDON, JACK (continued)
___ Karter, Wolfgang. "Jack London: **The Iron Heel** (1908)," in: Heuermann, Hartmut and Lange, Bernd-Peter, eds. **Die Utopie in der angloamerikanischen Literatur: Interpretationen**. Düsseldorf: Bagel, 1984. pp.176-195.
___ Labor, Earle. **Jack London**. Revised edition. New York: Twayne, 1994. 186pp.
___ London, Joan. **Jack London and His Daughters**. Berkeley, CA: Heyday Books, 1990. 184pp.
___ Shor, Francis. "**The Iron Heel**'s Marginal(ized) Utopia," *Extrapolation* 35(3): 211-229. Fall 1994.

LONG, FRANK BELKNAP
___ "Long, Frank Belknap (Obituary)," *Locus* 32(2): 72. February 1994.
___ "Long, Frank Belknap (Obituary)," *Science Fiction Chronicle* 15(4): 16. February 1994.
___ Cannon, Peter. "Frank Belknap Long: When Was He Born and Why Was Lovecraft Wrong?," *Studies in Weird Fiction* No. 17: 33-34. Summer 1995.
___ Indick, Ben P. "Long, Frank Belknap: In Memoriam," *Lovecraft Studies* No. 30: 3-4. Spring 1994.

LONG, KARAWYNN
___ "$4,000 for Karawynn Long in Writers of the Future Contest," *Science Fiction Chronicle* 15(2): 6. November/December 1993.

LONGO, ROBERT
___ Johnson, Kim H. "Memories Can't Wait," *Starlog* No. 216: 50-53, 64. July 1995.

LORD OF ILLUSIONS (MOTION PICTURE)
___ Bacal, Simon. "Clive Barker's Triple Threat: *Lord of Illusions*, a Fable of Death and Resurrection," *Sci-Fi Entertainment* 1(5): 28-31. February 1995.
___ Beeler, Michael. "Clive Barker's *Lord of Illusions*," *Cinefantastique* 26(2): 6-7. February 1995.
___ Beeler, Michael. "Clive Barker's *Lord of Illusions*," *Cinefantastique* 26(3): 23-26. April 1995.
___ Beeler, Michael. "*Lord of Illusions*," *Cinefantastique* 26(5): 12-13. August 1995.
___ Beeler, Michael. "*Lord of Illusions*," *Cinefantastique* 26(6)/27(1): 90-91. October 1995.
___ Biodrowski, Steve. "*Lord of Illusions* (Review)," *Cinefantastique* 27(3): 55-56, 60. December 1995.
___ Shapiro, Marc. "Grand Illusionist," *Starlog* No. 212: 41-44. March 1995.

LORD OF THE DEAD (MOTION PICTURE)
___ SEE: PHANTASMS III: LORD OF THE DEAD (MOTION PICTURE).

LORDS, TRACI
___ "Corman's 'Earth' Remake to Feature Traci Lords," *Variety* p. 1, 34. February 10, 1988.

LORENZ, A. F.
___ Lovecraft, H. P. "Notes on 'Alias Peter Marchall' by A. F. Lorenz," *Lovecraft Studies* No. 28: 20-21. Fall 1992.

LORRAINE, LILITH
___ Sneyd, Steve. "Empress of the Stars: A Reassessment of Lilith Lorraine, Pioneering Fantasy Poetess," *Fantasy Commentator* 7(3): 206-229. Spring 1992. (No. 43)

LOST BOYS (MOTION PICTURE)
___ "*Lost Boys* (1987): Interivews with Jamie Gertz and Corey Feldman," in: Goldberg, Lee, ed. **The Dreamweavers: Interviews With Fantasy Filmmakers of the 1980s**. Jefferson, NC: McFarland, 1995. pp.213-223.

LOST HORIZON (MOTION PICTURE)
___ "Col Classics Issuing Restored 'Horizon'," *Variety* p. 4, 24. June 4, 1986.

LOST IN SPACE (TV)
___ Phillips, Mark. "Space Families Found, Part Two," *Starlog* No. 220: 67-72. November 1995.
___ Phillips, Mark. "Space Families Lost, Part One," *Starlog* No. 219: 69-74. October 1995.

LOST IN SPACE (TV) (continued)
___ Van Hise, James. **Sci Fi TV: From Twilight Zone to Deep Space Nine**. Las Vegas, NV: Pioneer Books, 1993. 160pp. (Reprinted, HarperPrism, 1995. 258pp.)
___ Voger, Mark. "Mark Goddard: Interview," *Filmfax* No. 33: 72-76. June/July 1992.
___ Voger, Mark. "The Wily Wit of Jonathan Harris," *Filmfax* No. 32: 44-49, 94. April/May 1992.
___ Weaver, Tom. "The Man in the Bubble-Headed Mask," *Starlog* No. 201: 32-35, 66. April 1994.
___ Weaver, Tom. "Outrageous Original," *Starlog* No. 198: 32-37, 82. January 1994.
___ Weaver, Tom. "Space Duty," *Starlog* No. 190: 30-35, 72. May 1993.
___ Weaver, Tom. "Space Mom," by Tom Weaver and Steve Swires. in: McDonnell, David, ed. **Starlog's Science Fiction Heroes and Heroines**. New York: Crescent Books, 1995. pp.44-46.

LOST IN TIME (MOTION PICTURE)
___ SEE: WAXWORKS II: LOST IN TIME (MOTION PICTURE).

LOST RACES
___ Barnard, Alan. "Tarzan and the Lost Races: Parallels Between Anthropology and Early Science Fiction," in: Archetti, Eduardo P., ed. **Exploring the Written: Anthropology and the Multiplicity of Writing**. Stockholm: Scandinavian University Press, 1994. pp.231-257.

LOST WORLD (1925) (MOTION PICTURE)
___ "*The Lost World* (1925) (Review)," *Cinefex* No. 52: 92. November 1992.
___ Kinnard, Roy, ed. **The Lost World** of Willis O'Brien: The Original Shooting Script of the 1925 Landmark Special Effects Dinosaur Film, with Photographs. Jefferson, NC: McFarland, 1993. 176pp.
___ MacQueen, Scott. "Effects Scene: Cinematic Archaeology," *Cinefex* No. 55: 123-124. August 1993.

LOST WORLD (MOTION PICTURE)
___ MacQueen, Scott. "*The Lost World*: Merely Misplaced?," *American Cinematographer* 73(6): 37-44. June 1992.

LOST WORLDS
___ "Dinosaurs and Lost Worlds," *Literature Base* 3(4): 22-25. October 1992.
___ Becker, Allienne R. **The Lost Worlds Romance: From Dawn Till Dusk**. Westport, CT: Greenwood, 1992. 184pp.

LOTT, DOUG
___ "Lott, Doug (Obituary)," *Science Fiction Chronicle* 15(7): 16. June 1994.

LOURIE, EUGENE
___ Weaver, Tom. "Director of Dinosaurs," *Starlog* No. 193: 63-68. August 1993.
___ Weaver, Tom. "Eugene Lourie," in: Weaver, Tom. **They Fought the Creature Features: Interviews with 23 Classic Horror, Science Fiction and Serial Stars**. Jefferson, NC: McFarland, 1995. pp.201-210.

LOVE
___ Palmer, Steve. "Head over Wheels: Love in SF," *Vector* No. 165: 6-8. February/March 1992

LOVECRAFT STUDIES (MAGAZINE)
___ "Index to *Lovecraft Studies* 1-25," *Lovecraft Studies* No. 26: 35-39. Spring 1992.

LOVECRAFT, H. P.
___ "H. P. Lovecraft," in: Bloom, Harold, ed. **Classic Science Fiction Writers**. New York: Chelsea House, 1995. pp.91-105.
___ "Index to *Lovecraft Studies* 1-25," *Lovecraft Studies* No. 26: 35-39. Spring 1992.
___ "The Last Days of H. P. Lovecraft: Four Documents," *Lovecraft Studies* No. 28: 36. Fall 1992.
___ "Medical Record of Winfield Scott Lovecraft," *Lovecraft Studies* No. 24: 15-17. Spring 1991.

LOVECRAFT, H. P. (continued)

___ Anderson, James A. **Out of the Shadows: A Structuralist Approach to Understanding the Fiction of H. P. Lovecraft**. Ph.D. Dissertation, University of Rhode Island, 1992. 187pp. (DAI-A 53/08. p. 2811. February 1993.)

___ Barlow, Robert H. **On Lovecraft and Life**. West Warwick, RI: Necronomicon, 1992. 25pp.

___ Beckwith, Henry L. P. "Lovecraft's Xenophobia and Providence Between the Wars," in: Joshi, S. T., ed. **The H. P. Lovecraft Centennial Conference Proceedings**. West Warwick, RI: Necronomicon, 1991. pp.10.

___ Biodrowski, Steve. "H. P. Lovecraft's *The Resurrected*," *Cinefantastique* 22(6): 4-6. June 1992

___ Biodrowski, Steve. "Lovecraft Special Effects," *Cinefantastique* 22(6): 7. June 1992

___ Blake, Ian. "Lovecraft and the Dark Grail," *Lovecraft Studies* No. 26: 16-18. Spring 1992.

___ Bloch, Robert. "Introduction: An Open Letter to H. P. Lovecraft," in: Weinberg, Robert E. and Greenberg, Martin H., eds. **Lovecraft's Legacy**. New York: TOR, 1996. pp.ix-xvi.

___ Bloom, Harold. "H. P. Lovecraft," in: Bloom, Harold. **Modern Horror Writers**. New York: Chelsea House, 1995. pp.138-154.

___ Boerem, R. "Other Elements in 'The Color out of Space'," in: Joshi, S. T., ed. **The H. P. Lovecraft Centennial Conference Proceedings**. West Warwick, RI: Necronomicon, 1991. pp.37-39.

___ Buchanan, Carl. " 'The Music of Erich Zann': A Psychological Interpretation (Or Two)," *Lovecraft Studies* No. 27: 10-13. Fall 1992.

___ Buchanan, Carl. " 'The Outsider' as an Homage to Poe," *Lovecraft Studies* No. 31: 12-14. Fall 1994.

___ Buchanan, Carl. " 'The Terrible Old Man': A Myth of the Devouring Father," *Lovecraft Studies* No. 29: 19-30. Fall 1993. [Not seen.]

___ Buettner, John A. "H. P. Lovecraft: The Mythos of Scientific Materialism," *Strange Magazine* No. 11: 8-9, 51. Spring/Summer 1993.

___ Burleson, Donald R. "Lovecraft and Adjectivitis: A Deconstructionist View," *Lovecraft Studies* No. 31: 22-24. Fall 1994.

___ Burleson, Donald R. "Lovecraft and Gender," *Lovecraft Studies* No. 27: 21-25. Fall 1992.

___ Burleson, Donald R. "Lovecraft: Textual Keys," *Lovecraft Studies* No. 32: 27-30. Spring 1995.

___ Burleson, Donald R. "Lovecraft's **The Color out of Space**," *Explicator* 52(1): 48-50. Fall 1993.

___ Burleson, Donald R. "Lovecraft's 'The Unknown': A Sort of Runic Rhyme," *Lovecraft Studies* No. 26: 19-21. Spring 1992.

___ Burleson, Donald R. "On Lovecraft's 'The Ancient Track'," *Lovecraft Studies* No. 28: 17-20. Fall 1992.

___ Burleson, Donald R. "Prismatic Heroes: The Colour out of Dunwich," *Lovecraft Studies* No. 25: 13-18. Fall 1991.

___ Burleson, Donald R. "Providence and Lovecraft's Fiction," in: Joshi, S. T., ed. **The H. P. Lovecraft Centennial Conference Proceedings**. West Warwick, RI: Necronomicon, 1991. pp.10-12.

___ Burleson, Donald R. "Scansion Problems in Lovecraft's 'Mirage'," *Lovecraft Studies* No. 24: 18-19, 21. Spring 1991.

___ Burleson, Donald R. "The Thing: On the Doorstep," *Lovecraft Studies* No. 33: 14-18. Fall 1995.

___ Burleson, Mollie L. "Mirror, Mirror: Sylvia Plath's 'Mirror' and Lovecraft's 'The Outsider'," *Lovecraft Studies* No. 31: 10-12. Fall 1994.

___ Cannon, Peter. "Frank Belknap Long: When Was He Born and Why Was Lovecraft Wrong?," *Studies in Weird Fiction* No. 17: 33-34. Summer 1995.

___ Carter, Lin. **Lovecraft: A Look Behind the Cthulhu Mythos; The Background of a Myth That Has Captured a Generation**. San Bernardino, CA: Borgo Press, 1992. 198pp.

___ Chorvinsky, Mark. "The Lovecraft Paradox," by Mark Chorvinsky and Douglas Chapman. *Strange Magazine* No. 11: 4-7, 52-53. Spring/Summer 1993.

___ Clore, Dan. "Metonyms of Alterity: A Semiotic Interpretation of **Fungi From Yuggoth**," *Lovecraft Studies* No. 30: 21-32. Spring 1994.

___ Dansky, Richard E. "Transgression, Spheres of Influence, and the Use of the Utterly Other in Lovecraft," *Lovecraft Studies* No. 30: 5-14. Spring 1994.

___ Drewer, Cecelia. "Symbolism of Style in 'The Strange High House in the Mist'," *Lovecraft Studies* No. 31: 17-21. Fall 1994.

___ Dziemianowicz, Stefan. "On 'The Call of Cthulhu'," *Lovecraft Studies* No. 33: 30-35. Fall 1995.

LOVECRAFT, H. P. (continued)

___ Estren, Mark J. **Horrors Within and Without: A Psychoanalytic Study of Edgar Allan Poe and Howard Phillips Lovecraft**. Ph.D. Dissertation, State University of New York at Buffalo, 1978. 250pp. (DAI 39: 1565A.)

___ Faig, Kenneth W., Jr. "Lovecraft's Parents," in: Joshi, S. T., ed. **The H. P. Lovecraft Centennial Conference Proceedings**. West Warwick, RI: Necronomicon, 1991. pp.24-25.

___ Frenschkowski, Marco. "Bis ins dunkelste Herz des Meeres. Maritime Symbolik als Ausdruck des Unheimlichen in Erzählungen von W. H. Hodgson und H. P. Lovecraft," *Quarber Merkur* 32(2): 42-69. December 1994. (Whole No. 82)

___ Frenschkowski, Marco. "H. P. Lovecrafts 'The Transition of Juan Romero': eine Interpretation," *Quarber Merkur* 32(1): 43-50. June 1994. (Whole No. 81)

___ Fulwiler, William. "E. R. B. and H. P. L.," in: Price, Robert M., ed. **Black Forbidden Things**. Mercer Island, WA: Starmont, 1992. pp.60-65.

___ Gafford, Sam. " 'The Shadow Over Innsmouth': Lovecraft's Melting Pot," *Lovecraft Studies* No. 24: 6-13. Spring 1991.

___ Gayford, Norman R. "Lovecraft's Narrators," in: Joshi, S. T., ed. **The H. P. Lovecraft Centennial Conference Proceedings**. West Warwick, RI: Necronomicon, 1991. pp.32-33.

___ Graff, Bennett. **Horror in Evolution: Determinism, Materialism, and Darwinism in the American Gothic (Edgar Allan Poe, Frank Norris, Jack London, H. P. Lovecraft)**. Ph.D. Dissertation, City University of New York, 1995. 282pp. (DAI-A 56/05, p. 1777. November 1995.)

___ Hart, Mara K. "Walkers in the City: George Willard Kirk and Howard Phillips Lovecraft in New York City, 1924-1926," *Lovecraft Studies* No. 28: 2-17. Fall 1992.

___ Hazel, Faye R. "Some Strange New England Mortuary Practices: Lovecraft Was Right," *Lovecraft Studies* No. 29: 13-18. Fall 1993. [Not seen.]

___ Hohne, Karen A. "The Voice of Cthulhu: Language Interaction in Contemporary Horror Fiction," in: Slusser, George E. and Rabkin, Eric S., eds. **Styles of Creation: Aesthetic Technique and the Creation of Fictional Worlds**. Athens: University of Georgia Press, 1992. pp.79-87.

___ Humphreys, Brian. " 'The Night Ocean' and the Subtleties of Cosmicism," *Lovecraft Studies* No. 30: 14-21. Spring 1994.

___ Humphreys, Brian. "Who or What Was Iranon?," *Lovecraft Studies* No. 25: 10-13. Fall 1992.

___ Joshi, S. T. "Campbell: Before and After Lovecraft," in: Joshi, S. T., ed. **The Count of Thirty: A Tribute to Ramsey Campbell**. West Warwick, RI: Necronomicon, 1993. pp.27-31.

___ Joshi, S. T. "The Genesis of 'The Shadow out of Time'," *Lovecraft Studies* No. 33: 24-29. Fall 1995.

___ Joshi, S. T. "H. P. Lovecraft and **The Dream-Quest of Unknown Kadath**," in: Price, Robert M., ed. **Black Forbidden Things**. Mercer Island, WA: Starmont, 1992. pp.7-17.

___ Joshi, S. T. **An Index to the Fiction and Poetry of H. P. Lovecraft**. West Warwick, RI: Necronomicon Press, 1992. 42pp.

___ Joshi, S. T. "A Literary Tutelate: Robert Bloch and H. P. Lovecraft," *Studies in Weird Fiction* No. 16: 13-25. Winter 1995.

___ Joshi, S. T. "Lovecraft and the **Regnum Congo**," in: Price, Robert M., ed. **Black Forbidden Things**. Mercer Island, WA: Starmont, 1992. pp.24-29.

___ Joshi, S. T. "Lovecraft's Aesthetic Development: From Classicism to Decadence," *Lovecraft Studies* No. 31: 24-34. Fall 1994.

___ Joshi, S. T. "The Sources for 'From Beyond'," in: Price, Robert M., ed. **Black Forbidden Things**. Mercer Island, WA: Starmont, 1992. pp.18-23.

___ Joshi, S. T. "Who Wrote 'The Mound'?," in: Price, Robert M., ed. **Black Forbidden Things**. Mercer Island, WA: Starmont, 1992. pp.3-6.

___ Joshi, S. T., ed. **The H. P. Lovecraft Centennial Conference Proceedings**. West Warwick, RI: Necronomicon, 1991. 80pp.

___ Joshi, S. T., ed. **Miscellaneous Writings: H. P. Lovecraft**. Sauk City, WI: Arkham House, 1995. 568pp.

___ Kleiner, Rheinhart. "After a Decade and the Kalem Club," *Lovecraft Studies* No. 28: 34-35. Fall 1992. (Reprinted from *The Californian*, Fall 1936.)

___ Lippi, Giuseppe. "Lovecraft's Dreamworld Revisited," *Lovecraft Studies* No. 26: 23-25. Spring 1992.

___ Llopis, Rafael. "The Cthulhu Mythos," *Lovecraft Studies* No. 27: 13-21. Fall 1992.

___ Long, Frank B. "Lovecraft the Man," in: Joshi, S. T., ed. **The H. P. Lovecraft Centennial Conference Proceedings**. West Warwick, RI: Necronomicon, 1991. pp.29-30.

LOVECRAFT, H. P. (continued)
___ Lovecraft, H. P. **H. P. Lovecraft: Letters to Richard F. Searight**, edited by S. T. Joshi. West Warwick, RI: Necronomicon, 1992. 90pp.
___ Lovecraft, H. P. "A Letter from Lovecraft: On the Philosophy of Religion," *The Generalist Papers* 4(6): 1-4. February 1994.
___ Lovecraft, H. P. "Letter to Myrta Alice Little," *Lovecraft Studies* No. 26: 26-30. Spring 1992.
___ Lovecraft, H. P. "Notes on Writing Weird Fiction (1932/33)," in: Joshi, S. T., ed. **Miscellaneous Writings: H. P. Lovecraft**. Sauk City, WI: Arkham House, 1995. pp.113-116.
___ Lovecraft, H. P. "Plaster-all [Unpublished poem]," *Lovecraft Studies* No. 27: 30-31. Fall 1992.
___ Lovecraft, H. P. "Some Notes on Interplanetary Fiction (1934)," in: Joshi, S. T., ed. **Miscellaneous Writings: H. P. Lovecraft**. Sauk City, WI: Arkham House, 1995. pp.117-122.
___ Lovecraft, H. P. **Supernatural Horror in Literature**. Chislehurst, Kent, Eng.: Gothic Society, 1994. 32pp.
___ Lovett-Graff, Bennett. "Lovecraft: Reproduction and Its Discontents: Degeneration and Detection in 'The Lurking Fear'," *Paradoxa* 1(3): 325-341. 1995.
___ Mariconda, Steven J. " 'Expect Great Revelations': Lovecraft Criticism in His Centennial Year," *Lovecraft Studies* No. 24: 24-29. Spring 1991.
___ Mariconda, Steven J. "H. P. Lovecraft: Art, Artifact, and Reality," *Lovecraft Studies* No. 29: 2-12. Fall 1993. [Not seen.]
___ Mariconda, Steven J. "Introduction: Style and Imagery in Lovecraft," in: Joshi, S. T., ed. **The H. P. Lovecraft Centennial Conference Proceedings**. West Warwick, RI: Necronomicon, 1991. p.31.
___ Mariconda, Steven J. "Tightening the Coil: The Revision of 'The Whisperer in Darkness'," *Lovecraft Studies* No. 32: 12-17. Spring 1995.
___ McInnis, John. "The Call of Cthulhu: An Analysis," *Fantasy Commentator* 7(4): 268-281. Fall 1992. (Whole No. 44)
___ McInnis, John. " 'The Color out of Space' as the History of H. P. Lovecraft's Immediate Family," in: Joshi, S. T., ed. **The H. P. Lovecraft Centennial Conference Proceedings**. West Warwick, RI: Necronomicon, 1991. pp.35-37.
___ McNamara, M. Eileen. "Lovecraft's Medical History," in: Joshi, S. T., ed. **The H. P. Lovecraft Centennial Conference Proceedings**. West Warwick, RI: Necronomicon, 1991. pp.26-27.
___ McNamara, M. Eileen. "Winfield Scott Lovecraft's Final Illness," *Lovecraft Studies* No. 24: 14. Spring 1991.
___ Monteleone, Paul. " 'Ex Ovlivione': The Contemplative Lovecraft," *Lovecraft Studies* No. 33: 2-14. Fall 1995.
___ Monteleone, Paul. " 'The Rats in the Walls': A Study in Pessimism," *Lovecraft Studies* No. 32: 18-26. Spring 1995.
___ Morrison, Michael A. "From the Bygone Ashes: The Legacy of Howard Phillips Lovecraft," by Michael A. Morrison and Stefan Dziemianowicz. *Lovecraft Studies* No. 27: 2-9. Fall 1992.
___ Morrison, Michael A. "The Legacy of Howard Phillips Lovecraft," by Michael A. Morrison and Stefan Dziemianowicz. in: Collins, Robert A. and Latham, Robert, eds. **Science Fiction and Fantasy Book Review Annual 1991**. Westport, CT: Greenwood, 1994. pp.117-129.
___ Murray, Will. "Behind the Mask of Nyarlathotep," *Lovecraft Studies* No. 25: 25-29. Fall 1991.
___ Murray, Will. "The First Cthulhu Mythos Poem," in: Price, Robert M., ed. **Black Forbidden Things**. Mercer Island, WA: Starmont, 1992. pp.37-40.
___ Murray, Will. "Lovecraft's Arkham Country," in: Joshi, S. T., ed. **The H. P. Lovecraft Centennial Conference Proceedings**. West Warwick, RI: Necronomicon, 1991. pp.15-16.
___ Murray, Will. "Lovecraft, Blackwood, and Chambers: A Colloquium of Ghosts," *Studies in Weird Fiction* No. 13: 2-7. Summer 1993. [Not seen.]
___ Murray, Will. "Prehuman Language in Lovecraft," in: Price, Robert M., ed. **Black Forbidden Things**. Mercer Island, WA: Starmont, 1992. pp.41-45.
___ Murray, Will. "Self-Parody in Lovecraft's Revisions," in: Price, Robert M., ed. **Black Forbidden Things**. Mercer Island, WA: Starmont, 1992. pp.34-36.
___ Murray, Will. "Tentacles in Dreamland: Cthulhu Mythos Elements in the Dunsanian Stories," in: Price, Robert M., ed. **Black Forbidden Things**. Mercer Island, WA: Starmont, 1992. pp.30-33.
___ Murray, Will. "Where Was Foxfield?," *Lovecraft Studies* No. 33: 18-23. Fall 1995.
___ Nelson, Dale J. "Lovecraft and the Burkean Sublime," *Lovecraft Studies* No. 24: 2-6. Spring 1991.

LOVECRAFT, H. P. (continued)
___ Price, Robert M. "A Biblical Antecedent for 'The Colour out of Space'," *Lovecraft Studies* No. 25: 23-25. Fall 1991.
___ Price, Robert M. "Cosmic Fear and the Fear of the Lord: Lovecraft's Religious Vision," in: Price, Robert M., ed. **Black Forbidden Things**. Mercer Island, WA: Starmont, 1992. pp.78-85.
___ Price, Robert M. "The Last Vestige of the Derleth Mythos," *Lovecraft Studies* No. 24: 20-21. Spring 1991.
___ Price, Robert M. "Lovecraft and 'Ligeia'," *Lovecraft Studies* No. 31: 15-17. Fall 1994.
___ Price, Robert M. "Lovecraftianity and the Pagan Revival," in: Price, Robert M., ed. **Black Forbidden Things**. Mercer Island, WA: Starmont, 1992. pp.74-77.
___ Price, Robert M. "Randolph Carter, Warlord of Mars," in: Price, Robert M., ed. **Black Forbidden Things**. Mercer Island, WA: Starmont, 1992. pp.66-68.
___ Reid, Thomas R. "Cultural Trends in Literature," *The Dark Man: The Journal of Robert E. Howard Studies* No. 2: 30-32. July 1991.
___ Sánchez Ron, José M. "Lovecraft, la ciencia y los terrores espacio-temporales," *Revista de Occidente* No. 115: 57-76. December 1990.
___ Schultz, David E. "Lovecraft's New York Exile," in: Price, Robert M., ed. **Black Forbidden Things**. Mercer Island, WA: Starmont, 1992. pp.46-51.
___ Schultz, David E. "Personal Elements in Lovecraft's Writings," in: Joshi, S. T., ed. **The H. P. Lovecraft Centennial Conference Proceedings**. West Warwick, RI: Necronomicon, 1991. pp.27-28.
___ Schultz, David E., ed. **H. P. Lovecraft Letters to Robert Bloch**, ed. by David E. Schultz and S. T. Joshi. West Warrick, RI: Necronomicon, 1993. 91pp.
___ Schweitzer, Darrell. "About 'The Whisperer in Darkness'," *Lovecraft Studies* No. 32: 8-11. Spring 1995.
___ Schweitzer, Darrell. "M. R. James and H. P. Lovecraft: The Ghostly and the Cosmic," *Studies in Weird Fiction* No. 15: 12-16. Summer 1994.
___ Setiya, Kieran. "Empiricism and the Limits of Knowledge in Lovecraft," *Lovecraft Studies* No. 25: 18-22. Fall 1991.
___ Setiya, Kieran. "Lovecraft on Human Knowledge: An Exchange," by Kieran Setiya and S. T. Joshi. *Lovecraft Studies* No. 24: 22-23. Spring 1991.
___ Setiya, Kieran. "Lovecraft's Semantics," *Lovecraft Studies* No. 27: 26-30. Fall 1992.
___ Setiya, Kieran. "Two Notes on Lovecraft," *Lovecraft Studies* No. 26: 14-16. Spring 1992.
___ Sigurdson, Kirk. "A Gothic Approach to Lovecraft's Sense of Outsideness," *Lovecraft Studies* No. 28: 22-34. Fall 1992.
___ Squires, Richard D. **Stern Fathers 'neath the Mould: The Lovecraft Family in Rochester**. West Warwick, RI: Necronomicon Press, 1995. 60pp.
___ St. Armand, Barton L. "Roots of Horror in New England," in: Joshi, S. T., ed. **The H. P. Lovecraft Centennial Conference Proceedings**. West Warwick, RI: Necronomicon, 1991. pp.12-14.
___ Ursini, James. **More Things Than Are Dreamt Of: Masterpieces of Supernatural Horror, From Mary Shelley to Stephen King, in Literature and Film**, by James Ursini and Alain Silver. New York: Limelight, 1994. 226pp.
___ Van Calenbergh, Hubert. "The Roots of Horror in **The Golden Bough**," *Lovecraft Studies* No. 26: 21-23. Spring 1992.
___ Waugh, Robert H. "Documents, Creatures, and History in H. P. Lovecraft," *Lovecraft Studies* No. 25: 2-10. Fall 1991.
___ Waugh, Robert H. "Dr. Margaret Murray and H. P. Lovecraft: The Witch-Cult in New England," *Lovecraft Studies* No. 31: 2-10. Fall 1994.
___ Waugh, Robert H. "Lovecraft's Documentary Style," in: Joshi, S. T., ed. **The H. P. Lovecraft Centennial Conference Proceedings**. West Warwick, RI: Necronomicon, 1991. pp.34-35.
___ Waugh, Robert H. " 'The Picture in the House': Images of Complicity," *Lovecraft Studies* No. 32: 2-8. Spring 1995.
___ Waugh, Robert H. "The Structural and Thematic Unity of **Fungi From Yuggoth**," *Lovecraft Studies* No. 26: 2-14. Spring 1992.
___ Wilson, Colin. "The **Necronomicon**: The Origin of a Spoof," in: Price, Robert M., ed. **Black Forbidden Things**. Mercer Island, WA: Starmont, 1992. pp.88-90.
___ Wohleber, Curt. "The Man Who Can Scare Stephen King," *American Heritage* 46(8): 82-90. December 1995.

LOVECRAFT, WINFIELD SCOTT
___ McNamara, M. Eileen. "Winfield Scott Lovecraft's Final Illness," *Lovecraft Studies* No. 24: 14. Spring 1991.

MacDONALD, GEORGE (continued)
___ Pennington, John. "Alice at the Back of the North Wind, or the Metafictions of Lewis Carroll and George MacDonald," *Extrapolation* 33(1): 59-72. Spring 1992.
___ Petzold, Dieter. "Reifen und Erziehen in George MacDonalds Mächen," in: Kranz, Gisbert, ed. **Inklings: Jahrbuch für Literatur und Ästhetik**. 9. Band. Lüdenscheid, Germany: Stier, 1991. pp.92-110. [Not seen.]
___ Risco, Mary. "Awakening In Fairyland: The Journey of a Soul in George MacDonald's **The Golden Key**," *Mythlore* 20(4): 46-51. Winter 1995. (Whole No. 78)
___ Shaberman, Raphael B. **George MacDonald: A Bibliographical Study**. Detroit: Omnigraphics, 1990. 176pp.

MacDONALD, JAMES D.
___ "1993 Mythopoeic Fiction Awards," *Locus* 31(3): 77. September 1993.

MacDONNELL, J. E.
___ Stone, Graham. "Notes on Australian Science Fiction," *Science Fiction News* (Australia) No. 92: 2-8. February 1985.

MACFADDEN, BERNARR
___ Moskowitz, Sam. "Bernarr Macfadden and His Obsession With Science Fiction, Part VII: Conclusion," *Fantasy Commentator* 7(3): 189-203. Spring 1992. (No. 43)

MACHEN, ARTHUR
___ "On Arthur Machen's **The House of Souls**," *Studies in Weird Fiction* No. 16: 33-35. Winter 1995. (Reprinted from *Academy* August 11, 1906.)
___ Bloom, Harold. "Arthur Machen," in: Bloom, Harold. **Modern Horror Writers**. New York: Chelsea House, 1995. pp.155-170.
___ Eckersley, Adrian. "A Theme in the Early Work of Arthur Machen: 'Degeneration'," *English Literature in Transition* 35(3): 277-287. 1992.
___ Eng, Steve. "M. P. Shiel and Arthur Machen," in: **Shiel in Diverse Hands: A Collection of Essays**. Cleveland, OH: Reynolds Morse Foundation, 1983. pp.233-247.
___ Frenschkowski, Marco. "Machenalia. Neue Veröffentlichungen von und über Arthur Machen," *Quarber Merkur* 31(1): 35-40. June 1993. (No. 79)
___ Hassler, Donald M. "Arthur Machen and Genre: Filial and Fannish Alternatives," *Extrapolation* 33(2): 115-127. Summer 1992.
___ Hassler, Donald M. "Machen, Williams, and Autobiography: Fantasy and Decadence," in: Wolf, Milton T. and Mallett, Daryl F., eds. **Imaginative Futures: Proceedings of the 1993 Science Fiction Research Association Conference**. San Bernardino, CA: Jacob's Ladder Books, 1995. pp.319-328.
___ Hassler, Sue S., ed. **Arthur Machen and Montgomery Evans: Letters of a Literary Friendship, 1923-1947**, ed. by Sue S. Hassler and Donald M. Hassler. Kent, OH: Kent State University Press, 1994. 195pp.
___ Joshi, S. T. "Arthur Machen: Philosophy and Fiction," in: Schweitzer, Darrell, ed. **Discovering Classic Horror Fiction I**. Mercer Island, WA: Starmont, 1992. pp.1-33.
___ Russell, R. B. "Alterative Lives in Arthur Machen's 'A Fragment of Life' and Sylvia Townsend Warner's **Lolly Willowes**," *Studies in Weird Fiction* No. 12: 17-19. Spring 1993.
___ Ursini, James. **More Things Than Are Dreamt Of: Masterpieces of Supernatural Horror, From Mary Shelley to Stephen King, in Literature and Film**, by James Ursini and Alain Silver. New York: Limelight, 1994. 226pp.
___ Valentine, Mark. **Arthur Machen**. Bridgend, Wales: Seren, 1995. 147pp.
___ Wandrei, Donald. "Arthur Machen and **The Hill of Dreams**," *Studies in Weird Fiction* No. 15: 27-30. Summer 1994. (Reprinted from *Minnesota Quarterly*, Spring 1926.)
___ Willis, Martin T. "Scientific Portraits in Magical Frames: The Construction of Preternatural Narrative in the Work of E. T. A. Hoffman and Arthur Machen," *Extrapolation* 35(3): 186-200. Fall 1994.

MACKENZIE, MICHAEL
___ Fischlin, Daniel. "Cybertheater, Postmodernism, and Virtual Reality: An Interview With Toni Dove and Michael Mackenzie," by Daniel Fischlin and Andrew Taylor. *Science Fiction Studies* 21(1): 1-23. March 1994.

MacLACHLAN
___ Lofficier, Randy. "**Dune** (1984): Interviews with David Lynch, Raffaella de Laurentiis and Kyle MacLachlan," by Randy Lofficier and Jean-Marc Lofficier. in: Goldberg, Lee et al. **Science Fiction Filmmaking in the 1980s**. Jefferson, NC: McFarland, 1995. pp.79-110.

MacLEAN, KATHERINE
___ Klein, Jay K. "Biolog: Katherine MacLean," *Analog* 115(1/2): 215, 245. January 1995.

MACMILLAN
___ "Paramount Drops Atheneum, Restructures Macmillan," *Locus* 32(3): 8, 69. March 1994.

MAD LOVE (MOTION PICTURE)
___ Sevastakis, Michael. **Songs of Love and Death: The Classical American Horror Film of the 1930s**. Westport, CT: Greenwood, 1993. 232pp.

MAD MAX 2: THE ROAD WARRIOR (MOTION PICTURE)
___ "**Mad Max 2** Preems in Japan; No. 1 Was Earner for Australia," *Variety* p. 33. December 9, 1981.
___ "**Mad Max 2** Wins Top Prize at Avoriaz Futuristic Film Fest," *Variety* p. 24, 26. February 3, 1982.

MAD MAX BEYOND THUNDERDOME (MOTION PICTURE)
___ "Big 'Thunderdome' Push Includes Docu to Air on 88 TV Stations," *Variety* p.4, 81. July 3, 1985.
___ "Near $13-Mil 'Mad Max 3' Set to Roll With Gibson, Tina Turner," *Variety* p. 7, 30. September 5, 1984.
___ "Third 'Mad Max' May Be Last, But Miller Said That Before," *Variety* p.7. July 24, 1985.
___ Lofficier, Randy. "Road Warrior," by Randy Lofficier and Jean-Marc Lofficier. in: McDonnell, David, ed. **Starlog's Science Fiction Heroes and Heroines**. New York: Crescent Books, 1995. pp.12-14.

MAD MAX (MOTION PICTURE)
___ "Paris Sci-Fi Fest's Grand Prix Goes to Aussie 'Mad Max'," *Variety* p. 7, 30. December 2, 1981.
___ Lofficier, Randy. "**Mad Max** Movies (1979-1985): Interview with George Miller, Terry Hayes, George Ogilvie and Mel Gibson," by Randy Lofficier and Jean-Marc Lofficier. in: Goldberg, Lee et al. **Science Fiction Filmmaking in the 1980s**. Jefferson, NC: McFarland, 1995. pp.133-174.

MADALONE, DENNIS
___ Roller, Pamela E. "Lights! Camera! Dennis Madalone Delivers the Action," *Star Trek: The Official Fan Club* No. 96: 13-16. April/May 1994.

MADRID FESTIVAL OF IMAGINATIVE AND SCIENCE FICTION FILMS, 1982
___ "Madrid Sci-Fi Fest (3d) Readying for April 16; No Culture Aid," *Variety* p. 48, 78. February 24, 1982.
___ "Madrid's Sci-Fi Fest Improved But Peckinpah, Reed Vex-Prone," *Variety* p. 6, 25. April 28, 1982.
___ "Polish Pic Prized Four Ways; Other Madrid Scifi Nods," *Variety* p. 6. April 28, 1982.

MADRID FESTIVAL OF IMAGINATIVE AND SCIENCE FICTION FILMS, 1983
___ "Madrid Sci-Fi Fest Tributes Corman, Price, Russo Fantasies," *Variety* p. 14. March 16, 1983.
___ "Madrid Sci-Fi Prizes," *Variety* p. 23. April 6, 1983.

MADRID FESTIVAL OF IMAGINATIVE AND SCIENCE FICTION FILMS, 1984
___ "Madrid's 4th Sci-Fi Fest Shapes As a Winner, UIP Has 5 Films," *Variety* p. 7, 36. February 1, 1984.
___ "Madrid's Sci-Fi Fest Kicks Off; Marathon Sked; Price Is Honored," *Variety* p. 32. April 4, 1984.
___ "Spain's Imagfic Sci-Fi Fest Finally a Hit in Its 5th Try," *Variety* p. 6, 215. April 18, 1984.
___ "'Zone' Tops Spanish Sci-Fi Fest," *Variety* p. 20. April 18, 1984.

MADRID FESTIVAL OF IMAGINATIVE AND SCIENCE...

MADRID FESTIVAL OF IMAGINATIVE AND SCIENCE FICTION FILMS, 1985
___ "Features Set for Imagfic Fest; Budget Doubled From 1984 Level," *Variety* p. 6, 34. January 30, 1985.
___ "Imagic, Now Madrid Fest, Seeks World Status with Broader Fare," *Variety* p. 5, 34. April 3, 1985.
___ "Lluesma, Jorge, 28, Madrid Fest Director, Dies (Obituary)," *Variety* p. 6, 34. January 30, 1985.

MADRID FESTIVAL OF IMAGINATIVE AND SCIENCE FICTION FILMS, 1986
___ "Madrid Fest Strays From Sci-Fi Roots; Auds Thin, Critics Happy," *Variety* p. 7, 34. March 26, 1986.
___ "Spain's Imagic Widening Scope; Commercial Pics, 100,000 Festees," *Variety* p. 6, 28. January 29, 1986.

MAGAZINES
___ "*Aboriginal SF* Suspends Publication," *Science Fiction Chronicle* 16(4): 4. February 1995.
___ "*Aboriginal SF, Amazing* for Sale," *Locus* 34(2): 8. February 1995.
___ "*Amazing* Gets National Distributor," *Locus* 30(2): 7. February 1993.
___ "*Amazing* Reappears," *Locus* 32(6): 8. June 1994.
___ "*Amazing* Refunds Subscriptions," *Locus* 34(6): 9, 72. June 1995.
___ "*Amazing* Suspends Monthly Publication," *Locus* 31(6): 6. December 1993.
___ "*Amazing* Temporarily Resumes Publication," *Locus* 32(2): 8. February 1994.
___ "*Amazing Stories* Signs New Retail Distributor," *Science Fiction Chronicle* 14(6): 4. March 1993.
___ "*Analog/Asimov's* Changes and Problems," *Locus* 35(6): 9, 83. December 1995.
___ "*Asimov's/Analog* Redesign," *Locus* 28(6): 7. June 1992.
___ "*Century* Is New SF Magazine," *Science Fiction Chronicle* 15(8): 6. June 1994.
___ "*Classic Sci-Fi and Fantasy*," *Science Fiction Chronicle* 16(8): 10. July/August 1995
___ "*Crank!*," *Locus* 31(3): 7. September 1993.
___ "*Crank!, Non-Stop* Are New Science Fiction Magazine Titles," *Science Fiction Chronicle* 15(1): 6. October 1993.
___ "Davis Publications Sells *Analog, Asimov's* SF Magazines to Dell Magazines," *Science Fiction Chronicle* 13(5): 4. February 1992.
___ "Dean Wesley Smith Fiction Editor for Programming Magazine," *Science Fiction Chronicle* 16(6): 6. May 1995.
___ "Dell Magazine Copyright Change," *Locus* 33(4): 9, 76. October 1994.
___ "End of the Road for *Amazing Stories*," *Science Fiction Chronicle* 15(3): 4. January 1994.
___ "*Galaxy* Follows *Omni* into the Great Unknown," *Locus* 35(1): 9. July 1995.
___ "*Galaxy* Giving Up Magazine Format, to Be Available Only Electronically," *Science Fiction Chronicle* 16(9): 6. August/September 1995.
___ "*Galaxy* Resurrected," *Locus* 32(2): 8, 74. February 1994.
___ "*Galaxy Magazine* Revived," *Science Fiction Chronicle* 15(3): 4-5. January 1994.
___ "A Gallery of *Amazing* Art: Covers Through the Years," *Amazing Stories* 67(4): 52-56. July 1992.
___ "*Horror* Newsmagazine Dead," *Science Fiction Chronicle* 17(2): 58. December 1995/January 1996.
___ "Index: *Cinefex* No. 1-50," *Cinefex* No. 50: 90-106. May 1992.
___ "*Interzone* Incorporates *Million*," *Science Fiction Chronicle* 14(12): 4-5. September 1993.
___ "*Interzone* to Incorporate *Million*," *Locus* 31(2): 7. August 1993.
___ "Magazine Warehouse Burns," *Locus* 30(3): 6. March 1993.
___ "New Fantasy Quarterly Planned," *Science Fiction Chronicle* 16(1): 5. October 1994.
___ "New Horror, SF Magazines Due," *Science Fiction Chronicle* 14(10): 6. July 1993.
___ "November 'Relaunch' for *Analog, Asimov's SF*," *Science Fiction Chronicle* 13(10): 4. July/August 1992.
___ "*Omni* Ceases Monthly Publication'". *Locus* 34(4): 7. April 1995.
___ "*Omni* for Sale?," *Science Fiction Chronicle* 14(7): 4. April 1993.
___ "*Omni Magazine* Goes Quarterly, With Monthly On-Line Presence," *Science Fiction Chronicle* 16(5): 4. March/April 1995.
___ "Possible Sale Looms for *Analog* and *Asimov's SF*, as Rising Costs Force Frequency, Size Changes," *Science Fiction Chronicle* 17(2): 4-5. December 1995/January 1996.

MAGAZINES (continued)
___ "*Pulphouse* Publishing Plans Magazine Distribution Service," *Science Fiction Chronicle* 13(10): 6. July/August 1992.
___ "*Realms of Fantasy* Advances," *Science Fiction Chronicle* 15(4): 5. February 1994.
___ "*Realms of Fantasy* New Magazine," *Locus* 32(4): 7. April 1994.
___ "Same Cover on *Amazing, Analog*," *Science Fiction Chronicle* 14(10): 6-7. July 1993.
___ "*Science Fiction Age* Launched," *Locus* 29(4): 7. October 1992
___ "*Science Fiction Age*, New Bimonthly, to Start Publication This Summer," *Science Fiction Chronicle* 13(6): 4. March 1992.
___ "*SF Age* Goes Forward," *Locus* 28(2): 6. August 1992.
___ "*SF Age* Subscriber List for Sale," *Science Fiction Chronicle* 13(10): 6. July/August 1992.
___ "SF Magazines Raise Cover Prices," *Locus* 31(3): 7. September 1993.
___ "SF Media Magazine Explosion," *Locus* 32(3): 8, 69. March 1994.
___ "*Sirius Visions* Folds," *Science Fiction Chronicle* 17(1): 6. October/November 1995
___ "*Sirius Visions* Is New Magazine," *Science Fiction Chronicle* 15(3): 6-7. January 1994.
___ "Sovereign Media Moves Two Magazines Forward," *Science Fiction Chronicle* 15(5): 4. March 1994.
___ "*Tomorrow* SF Is Latest Magazine From Pulphouse," *Science Fiction Chronicle* 13(11/12): 4. August 1992.
___ "UK's *Fantasy Tales* Ceasing Publication," *Science Fiction Chronicle* 15(1): 5-6. October 1993.
___ "*Visions: The Magazine of Fantasy TV, Home Video and New Media*," *Science Fiction Chronicle* 16(8): 10. July/August 1995
___ "*Weird Tales* Changes Names," *Locus* 32(4): 8. April 1994.
___ "*Weird Tales* Reformats; Other Magazine Changes," *Locus* 29(3): 7, 79. September 1992.
___ Ashley, Mike. "The *Amazing* Story: Part 6, The Seventies: Sex and Drugs and Rock and Roll," *Amazing Stories* 67(3): 52-56. June 1992.
___ Ashley, Mike. "The *Amazing* Story: Part 7, The Eighties: Son of *Fantastic*," *Amazing Stories* 67(4): 47-56. July 1992.
___ Bosky, Bernadette L. "Amateur Press Associations: Intellectual Society and Social Intellectualism," in: Sanders, Joe, ed. **Science Fiction Fandom**. Westport, CT: Greenwood, 1994. pp.181-196.
___ Brown, Charles N. "25 Years of *Locus*," *Locus* 30(4): 34-35. April 1993.
___ Carmody, Deirdre. "Dell Buys Four Noted Fiction Magazines," *New York Times* Sec. D, p. 5. January 24, 1992.
___ Cave, Hugh B. **Magazines I Remember: Some Pulps, Their Editors, and What It Was Like to Write for Them**. Chicago, IL: Tattered Pages Press, 1994. 174pp.
___ Donaton, Scott. "New Sci Fi Magazine Will Launch This Fall," *Advertising Age* 63(35): 29. August 31, 1992.
___ Donawerth, Jane L. "Science Fiction by Women in the Early Pulps, 1926-1930," in: Donawerth, Jane L. and Kolmerten, Carol A., eds. **Utopian and Science Fiction by Women: Worlds of Difference**. Syracuse, NY: Syracuse University Press, 1994. pp.137-152.
___ Fratz, Doug. "Index: *Thrust/Quantum*, No. 1, February 1973-No. 43/44, May 1993," *Quantum* No. 43/44: 67-69. Spring/Summer 1993.
___ Fratz, Doug. "The Twenty-Year Spree: A Personal History of *Thrust/Quantum*," *Quantum* No. 43/44: 51-66. Spring/Summer 1993.
___ Frazer, Roger. "A Guide to *The Avon Fantasy Reader*," *Wayfarer II* pp.17-35. n.d.
___ Gunderloy, Mike. **The World of Zines: A Guide to the Independent Magazine Revolution**. New York: Penguin Books, 1992. 181pp.
___ Gunn, James E. "Fifty Amazing, Astounding, Wonderful Years," in: Gunn, James E. **Inside Science Fiction: Essays on Fantastic Literature**. San Bernardino, CA: Borgo, 1992. pp.60-64.
___ Harbottle, Philip. **British Science Fiction Paperbacks and Magazines, 1949-1956: An Annotated Bibliograhy and Guide**, by Philip Harbottle and Stephen Holland. San Bernardino, CA: Borgo Press, 1994. 232pp.
___ Katz, Bill. "Magazines: *Blue Light Red Light: A Periodical of Speculative Fiction and the Arts*," *Library Journal* p.144. July 1991.
___ Klossner, Michael. "Word and Image: A Survey of Fantastic Film & TV Magazines," *SFRA Newsletter* No. 194: 10-15. January/February 1992.
___ Lupoff, Richard A. "Into the Aether, Junior Spacepersons!," in: Sanders, Joe, ed. **Science Fiction Fandom**. Westport, CT: Greenwood, 1994. pp.197-206.
___ Moskowitz, Sam. "Burroughs Returns to *Argosy*," *Burroughs Bulletin* NS. No. 20: 11-15. October 1994.

MAGAZINES (continued)

___ Moskowitz, Sam. "Hugo Gernsback and Edgar Rice Burroughs," *Burroughs Bulletin* NS. No. 21: 3-9. January 1995.

___ Mullen, R. D. "From Standard Magazines to Pulps and Big Slicks: A Note on the History of US General and Fiction Magazines," *Science Fiction Studies* 22(1): 144-156. March 1995.

___ Rusch, Kristine K. "Editorial: Magazine Readership," *Magazine of Fantasy and Science Fiction* 89(1): 6-8. July 1995.

___ Rusch, Kristine K. "Editorial: Science Fiction Readership," *Magazine of Fantasy and Science Fiction* 89(3): 5-7. September 1995.

___ Sanders, Joe L. "Science Fiction Magazines," in: Barron, Neil, ed. **Anatomy of Wonder 4**. New York: Bowker, 1995. pp.690-714.

___ Server, Lee. **Danger Is My Business: An Illustrated History of the Fabulous Pulp Magazines 1896-1953**. San Francisco, CA: Chronicle Books, 1993. 144pp.

___ Stableford, Brian. "Adolf Hitler: His Part in Our Struggle; A Brief Economic History of British SF Magazines," *Interzone* No. 57: 17-20. March 1992.

___ Stone, Graham. "Index to *Science Fiction News* Nos. 59-106, 1979-1987," *Science Fiction News* (Australia) No. 106: 8-17. December 1987.

___ Stone, Graham. "Looking Backward," *Science Fiction News* (Australia) No. 63: 5-7. 1979.

___ Stone, Graham. "Notes on Australian Science Fiction: *The Comet*," *Science Fiction News* (Australia) No. 54: 2-9. April 1978.

___ Stone, Graham. "Science Fiction in the *Man* Group of Magazines: A Checklist," *Science Fiction News* (Australia) No. 104: 1-18. May 1987. [Not seen.]

___ Stone, Graham. "Sixty Years of *Amazing Stories*: 1931," *Science Fiction News* (Australia) No. 107: 1-8. 1988.

___ Stone, Graham. "Sixty Years of *Amazing Stories*: 1931 (Continued)," *Science Fiction News* (Australia) No. 109: 9-16. January 1990.

___ Stone, Graham. "Sixty Years of *Amazing Stories*: 1932," *Science Fiction News* (Australia) No. 110: 3-13, 16. April 1990.

___ Stone, Graham. "Sixty Years of *Amazing Stories*: 1933," *Science Fiction News* (Australia) No. 111: 7-16, 20. July 1990.

___ Stone, Graham. "Sixty Years of *Amazing Stories*: 1934," *Science Fiction News* (Australia) No. 112: 13-16. September 1990.

___ Stone, Graham. "Sixty Years of *Amazing Stories*: 1934, and The Quarterly, 1931-1934," *Science Fiction News* (Australia) No. 114: 6-23. December 1990.

___ Swain, Alex. "Zine Scene: Sci-Fi Circuit," *Internet World* 6(9): 50. September 1995.

___ Verba, Joan M. **Boldly Writing: A Trekker Fan and Zine History, 1967-1987**. Minnetonka, MN: FTL Publications, 1996. 100pp.

___ Ward, Ron B. "Review: *Aurealis*, No. 1," *Science Fiction News* (Australia) No. 113: 2-7. December 1990.

___ Warner, Harry, Jr. "A History of Fanzines," in: Sanders, Joe, ed. **Science Fiction Fandom**. Westport, CT: Greenwood, 1994. pp.175-180.

___ Westfahl, Gary. "Dictatorial, Authoritarian, Uncooperative: The Case Against John W. Campbell," *Foundation* No. 56: 36-60. Autumn 1992. (Letter of comment: Alexei Panshin, *Foundation* No. 58: 87-91. Summer 1993; Rejoiner, Westfahl, *Foundation* No. 58: 93-94.)

___ White, Jonathan. "Collectible Science Fiction Magazines," *AB Bookman's Weekly* pp.2109-2130. October 1, 1984.

___ Zebrowski, George. "*The Shadow*: Radio and Pulp Origins," *Cinefantastique* 25(4): 20-21. August 1994.

MAGAZINES, 1991

___ "1991 Magazine Summary," *Locus* 28(2): 44-47, 74. February 1992.

___ Winnett, Scott. "1991 Magazine Summary," by Scott Winnett and Charles N. Brown. in: Brown, Charles N. and Contento, William G. **Science Fiction, Fantasy, & Horror: 1991**. Oakland, CA: Locus Press, 1992. pp.428-432.

MAGAZINES, 1992

___ Winnett, Scott. "1992 Magazine Summary," by Scott Winnett and Charles N. Brown. *Locus* 30(2): 44-46. February 1993.

MAGAZINES, 1993

___ Winnett, Scott. "1993 Magazine Summary," by Scott Winnett and Charles N. Brown. *Locus* 32(2): 44-48, 51. February 1994.

MAGAZINES, 1994

___ "1994 Magazine Summary," *Locus* 34(2): 46-48, 76. February 1995.

MAGIC

___ Dodds, David L. "Magic in the Myths of J. R. R. Tolkien and Charles Williams," in: Kranz, Gisbert, ed. **Jahrbuch für Literatur und Ästhetik**. Lüdenscheid, Germany: Stier, 1992. Band 10, pp.37-60.

MAGIC CARPET MAGAZINE

___ Cockcroft, T. G. L. "An Index to 'The Eyrie'," *Fantasy Commentator* 8(3/4): 217-229. Fall 1995. (Whole No. 47/48)

MAGIC ISLAND (MOTION PICTURE)

___ Fischer, Dennis. "Moonbeam Preview: **Magic Island**," *Cinefantastique* 26(4): 36-37. June 1995.

MAGISTRALE, TONY

___ Davis, Jonathan. **Stephen King's America**. Mercer Island, WA: Starmont House, 1992.

MAHR, KURT

___ "Mahr, Kurt (Obituary)," *Locus* 31(4): 68. October 1993.

MAILER, NORMAN

___ Atwill, William D. **Fire and Power: The American Space Program as Postmodern Narrative**. Athens, GA: The University of Georgia Press, 1994. 172pp.

MAIN COURSE (MOTION PICTURE)

___ SEE: CRITTERS II: THE MAIN COURSE (MOTION PICTURE).

MAISON D'AILLEURS

___ "Maison d'Ailleurs; A House of Elsewhere," *Locus* 32(1): 40. January 1994.

MAITZ, DON

___ "Maitz, Wurts Paintings Stolen," *Science Fiction Chronicle* 17(2): 5-6. December 1995/January 1996.

___ "Valuable Artwork Missing," *Locus* 35(6): 8. December 1995.

MAJORS, LEE

___ Spelling, Ian. "Bionic Breakdown," *Starlog* No. 211: 76-79. February 1995.

MAKEUP

___ Blake, Michael F. "Master of Early Movie Makeup: Lon Chaney," *Filmfax* No. 39: 85-63, 98. June/July 1993.

___ Crisafulli, Chuck. "The Way out World of Dick Smith," *Filmfax* No. 41: 58-64. October/November 1993.

MAKEUP & SPECIAL EFFECTS LABORATORIES (COMPANY)

___ Shay, Estelle. "Company File: Makeup and Special Effects Laboratories," *Cinefex* No. 59: 111-112. September 1994.

MAKING OF MAD MAX BEYOND THUNDERDOME (MOTION PICTURE)

___ "Big 'Thunderdome' Push Includes Docu to Air on 88 TV Stations," *Variety* p.4, 81. July 3, 1985.

MALAMUD, BERNARD

___ Freese, Peter. "Surviving the End: Apocalypse, Evolution, and Entropy in Bernard Malamud, Kurt Vonnegut and Thomas Pynchon," *Critique* 36(3): 163-176. Spring 1995.

___ Hanson, Philip. "Horror and Ethnic Identity in 'The Jewbird'," *Studies in Short Fiction* 30(3): 359-366. Summer 1993.

___ Kimsey, John. "Dolorous Strokes, or Balin at the Bat: Malamud, Malory and Chrétien," in: Morse, Donald E., ed. **The Celebration of the Fantastic**. Westport, CT: Greenwood, 1992. pp.103-112.

MALES IN SF

___ Rabkin, Eric S. "The Male Body in Science Fiction," *Michigan Quarterly Review* 33(1): 203-216. Winter 1994.

MALORY, THOMAS

___ Fehrenbacher, Richard. "The Domestication of Merlin in Malory's **Morte Dauthur**," *Quondam et Futurus* 3(4): 1-16. Winter 1993.

___ Goyne, Jo. "Parataxis and Causality in the Tale of Sir Launcelot du Lake," *Quondam et Futurus* 2(4): 36-48. Winter 1992.

___ Grimm, Kevin T. "The Reception of Malory's **Morte D'Arthur** Medieval and Modern," *Quondam et Futurus* 2(3): 1-14. Fall 1992.

MALORY, THOMAS (continued)

___ Hanks, D. Thomas, Jr. "Foil and Forecast: Dinadan in **The Book of Sir Tristam**," in: Busby, Keith, ed. **The Arthurian Yearbook I**. New York: Garland, 1991. pp.149-164.

___ Hanks, D. Thomas, Jr. "Malory's **Book of Sir Tristram**: Focusing on **Le Morte Dearthur**," *Quondam et Futurus* 3(1): 14-31. Spring 1993.

___ Hanks, D. Thomas, Jr. "Malory, Dialogue and Style," *Quondam et Futurus* 3(3): 24-35. Fall 1993.

___ Hodges, Laura F. "Steinbeck's Adaptation of Malory's Launcelot: A Triumph of Realism over Supernaturalism," *Quondam et Futurus* 2(1): 69-81. Spring 1992.

___ Keiser, George R. "Malory and the Middle English Romance: A Graduate Course," in: Fries, Maureen and Watson, Jeanie, eds. **Approaches to the Teaching of the Arthurian Tradition**. New York: Modern Language Association, 1992. pp.131-134.

___ Kimsey, John. "Dolorous Strokes, or Balin at the Bat: Malamud, Malory and Chrétien," in: Morse, Donald E., ed. **The Celebration of the Fantastic**. Westport, CT: Greenwood, 1992. pp.103-112.

___ Kindrick, Robert L. "Which Malory Should I Teach?," in: Fries, Maureen and Watson, Jeanie, eds. **Approaches to the Teaching of the Arthurian Tradition**. New York: Modern Language Association, 1992. pp.100-105.

___ Macbain, Danielle M. "Love Versus Politics: Competing Paradigms of Chivalry in Malory's **Morte D'Arthur**," *Quondam et Futurus* 2(3): 22-31. Fall 1992.

___ Mahoney, Dhira B. "Malory's **Tale of Gareth** and the Comedy of Class," in: Busby, Keith, ed. **The Arthurian Yearbook I**. New York: Garland, 1991. pp.165-194.

___ Morse, Ruth. "Sterile Queens and Questing Orphans," *Quondam et Futurus* 2(2): 41-53. Summer 1992.

___ Pigg, Daniel. "Language as Weapon: The Poetics of Plot in Malory's 'Tale of Sir Gareth'," *Quondam et Futurus* 2(1): 16-27. Spring 1992.

___ Thornton, Ginger. "The Weakening of the King: Arthur's Disintegration in **The Book of Sir Tristam**," in: Busby, Keith, ed. **The Arthurian Yearbook I**. New York: Garland, 1991. pp.135-148.

___ Wirthington, John. "'He telleth the number of the stars; he calleth them all by their names': The Lesser Knights of Sir Thomas Malory's **Morte Dauthur**," *Quondam et Futurus* 3(4): 17-27. Winter 1993.

MALZBERG, BARRY N.

___ Layton, David A. "The Barriers of Inner and Outer Space: The Science Fiction of Barry N. Malzberg," *Science Fiction Studies* 18(1): 71-90. March 1991.

___ Lutz, Reinhart. "Styles Within Styles, or 'Death of a Hack Writer': **Herovit's World** Reconsidered," in: Slusser, George E. and Rabkin, Eric S., eds. **Styles of Creation: Aesthetic Technique and the Creation of Fictional Worlds**. Athens: University of Georgia Press, 1992. pp.181-191.

___ Stableford, Brian. "Insoluble Problems: Barry Malzberg's Career in Science Fiction," in: Stableford, Brian. **Outside the Human Aquarium: Masters of Science Fiction**. San Bernardino, CA: Borgo, 1995. pp.28-36.

___ Tidmarsh, Andrew. "Barry N. Malzberg: An Annotated Bibliography," *Interzone* No. 61: 50-52. July 1992

MAN FROM PLANET X (MOTION PICTURE)

___ Clarke, Robert. "The Actor From Planet X," *Starlog* No. 219: 27-31, 66. October 1995.

___ Stephens, Bob. "United Artists **Sci-Fi Matinee**," *Films in Review* 46(9/10): 54-60. November/December 1995.

MAN'S BEST FRIEND (MOTION PICTURE)

___ Crisafulli, Chuck. "**Man's Best Friend**," *Cinefantastique* 25(4): 44-45, 61. August 1994.

MANCINI, HENRY

___ "Mancini, Henry (Obituary)," *Science Fiction Chronicle* 15(8): 20. June 1994.

MANGLER (MOTION PICTURE)

___ Harris, Judith P. "**Mangler** (Review)," *Cinefantastique* 26(5): 59. August 1995.

___ Lowe, Nick. "**Mangler** (Review)," *Interzone* No. 98: 31-32. August 1995.

___ Martin, Robert. "**The Mangler**," *Sci-Fi Entertainment* 1(6): 34-37. April 1995.

MANIAC COP 3: BADGE OF SILENCE (MOTION PICTURE)

___ Harris, Judith P. "**Maniac Cop 3: Badge of Silence** (Review)," *Cinefantastique* 24(1): 60. June 1993.

MANKIEWICZ, DON

___ Florence, Bill. "Trials and Errors," *Starlog* 177: 42-45, 68. April 1992.

MANN, PHILLIP

___ Holliday, Liz. "Master of the Alien: Phillip Mann," *Interzone* No. 68: 41-43. February 1993.

MANNING, RUSSELL G.

___ Barrett, Robert R. "Tarzan's Third Great Comic Strip Artist: Russell G. Manning (1929-1981)," *Burroughs Bulletin* NS. No. 13: 11-21. January 1993.

MANNS, PATRICIO

___ Mora, Gabriela. "**De repente los Lugares Desaparecen** de Patricio Manns: Ciencia Ficción a la Latinoamericana?," *Revista Iberoamericana* 60(No. 168/169): 1039-1049. July/December 1994.

MANT (MOTION PICTURE)

___ Biodrowski, Steve. "**Mant**," *Cinefantastique* 24(1): 58. June 1993.

MARCUSE, KATHERINE

___ Barr, Marleen S. **Lost in Space: Probing Feminist Science Fiction and Beyond**. Chapel Hill, NC: University of North Carolina Press, 1993. 231pp.

MARKETING

___ "Canandian 'Trek' Promo Reaps Free Ad Space," *Variety* p. 23. September 1, 1982.

___ "**Day After**, **Last Unicorn** Hit Big in Germany, Campaigns Help," *Variety* p. 123. January 25, 1984.

___ "Dealers Ecstatic as Paramount Halves 'Trek II' Tape Tab," *Variety* p. 56. September 1, 1982.

___ "Initial **Dark Crystal** Sell to Be Soft; Unusual Tie-Ins," *Variety* p. 27. September 1, 1982.

___ "Lucasfilms Execs Outline 'Star Wars,' 'Raiders' Segs to Come; 'Jedi' Teasers," *Variety* p. 5. September 1, 1982.

___ "Pic Marketing Seminar to Create 'Campaign' for Vintage Sci-Fier," *Variety* p. 12, 30. February 8, 1984.

___ "Pitt Subrun Claims Universal's Longrun **E. T.** Violates Bid Rules," *Variety* p. 7. September 15, 1982.

___ "Spielberg's **E. T.** Out In June With 11 Kiddie Licensing Deals Tied In," *Variety* p. 26. April 11, 1982.

___ "**Star Trek** TV Episode Released by Paramount at $30," *Variety* p. 37. June 2, 1982.

___ "**Star Trek II**: Sales Vs. Rental Fulcrum," *Variety* p. 31-32. October 6, 1982.

___ Burger, Phillip R. "Whatever Happened to Perry Rhodan, Riding the Space Trails Alone?," *Burroughs Bulletin* NS. No. 22: 12-17. April 1995.

___ Jensen, Jeff. "Invasion of the Sci-Fi Marketers," *Advertising Age* 65(49): 1-2. November 21, 1994.

___ Stanley, T. L. "NBC, Live Entertainment Link TV and Home Vid for Sci-Fi Synergy," *Brandweek* 36(3): 8. January 16, 1995.

___ Underwood, Elaine. "Spencer Tests Sci-Fi On-Site TV," *Brandweek* 36(23): 3. June 5, 1995.

MARKS, BEAU

___ Jones, Alan. "**Judge Dredd**: Line Producer Beau Marks," *Cinefantastique* 26(5): 38-39. August 1995.

MARLOWE, CHRISTOPHER

___ Bartlett, Sally A. "Fantasy and Mimesis in **Doctor Faustus**," *Journal of the Fantastic in the Arts* 5(3): 18-27. 1993. (No. 19)

MAROONED (MOTION PICTURE)

___ "Columbia's Soiree for **Marooned**: A Captive Audience," *Variety* p. 7, 38. November 12, 1969.

___ "Nix **Marooned** Exploit of Near Space Tragedy," *Variety* p. 22. April 22, 1970.

___ "Nowadays Anything's a Boxoffice Plus or Minus; Columbia's **Marooned** Sensitive re Moonshot; Shares Rise," *Variety* p. 6. September 3, 1969.

MAROONED (MOTION PICTURE)

MAROONED (MOTION PICTURE) (continued)
___ "Promo Ammo Load for Col's **Marooned**," *Variety* p. 13. April 1, 1970.

MARQUAND, RICHARD
___ Goldberg, Lee. "**Return of the Jedi** (1983): Interview with Richard Marquand," in: Goldberg, Lee et al. **Science Fiction Filmmaking in the 1980s**. Jefferson, NC: McFarland, 1995. pp.175-182.

MARQUETTE, JACQUES
___ Weaver, Tom. "Jacques Marquette: Interview," in: Weaver, Tom, ed. **Attack of the Monster Movie Makers: Interviews with 20 Genre Giants**. Jefferson, NC: McFarland, 1994. pp.195-208.
___ Weaver, Tom. "Killer Brains and Giant Women," *Starlog* No. 187: 57-61, 69. February 1993.

MARQUISE OF O (MOTION PICTURE)
___ Rhiel, Mary. "The Taming of the Screw: Rohmer's Filming of Kliest's 'Die Marquise von O...'," in: Ruddick, Nicholas, ed. **State of the Fantastic**. Westport, CT: Greenwood, 1992. pp.83-90.

MARRIAGE
___ Malkki, Tarya. "The Marriage Metaphor in the Works of Ursula K. Le Guin," in: Latham, Robert A. and Collins, Robert A., eds. **Modes of the Fantastic**. Westport, CT: Greenwood, 1995. pp.100-109.

MARS
___ Menefee, Christine C. "Imagining Mars: The New Chronicles," *School Library Journal* 40(12): 38-39. December 1994.
___ Terra, Richard. "Shades of Rose and Red: Nostalgic and Visionary Images of the Human Exploration of Mars," *New York Review of Science Fiction* No. 54: 1, 8-11. February 1993.

MARS ATTACKS (COMIC)
___ Di Filippo, Paul. "Topps Returns to Its Cult Classic as *Mars Attacks...Again*," *Science Fiction Age* 2(5): 82-84. July 1994.
___ Johnson, Kim H. "*Mars Attacks* Again," *Starlog* No. 203: 38-41. June 1994.

MARS NEEDS WOMEN (MOTION PICTURE)
___ Hogan, David J. "**Mars Needs Women** (1956) (Review)," *Filmfax* No. 38: 20, 30. April/May 1993.

MARSHALL, FRANK
___ Fischer, Dennis. "**Congo**: Director Frank Marshall on Filming the Bestseller," *Cinefantastique* 26(5): 56-57, 61. August 1995.
___ Warren, Bill. "Gorilla Warfare," *Starlog* No. 215: 40-45, 72. June 1995.
___ Warren, Bill. "Jungle Wizard," *Starlog* No. 217: 35-39, 66. August 1995.

MARSUPIALS (MOTION PICTURE)
___ SEE: HOWLING III: THE MARSUPIALS (MOTION PICTURE).

MARTIN, GEORGE R. R.
___ "George R. R. Martin: Running the Show," *Locus* 34(5): 4-5, 77-78. May 1995.
___ Holliday, Liz. "On the Sharing of Worlds: George R. R. Martin Interviewed," *Interzone* No. 70: 44-47. April 1993.
___ Proulx, Kevin. **Fear to the World: Eleven Voices in a Chorus of Horror**. Mercer Island, WA: Starmont, 1992. 243pp.
___ Stephensen-Payne, Phil. **George R. R. Martin: The Ace From New Jersey**. Albuquerque, NM: Galactic Central, 1989. 22pp. (2nd Revised Edition)
___ Valada, M. C. "Step Through George R. R. Martin's **Doorways** into Alternate Worlds," *Science Fiction Age* 1(4): 18-21, 72. May 1993.

MARTIN, KENNETH JOSEPH
___ "Martin, Kenneth Joseph (Obituary)," *Science Fiction News* (Australia) No. 59: 10-11. February 1979.

MARTIN, LARRY W.
___ "Martin, Larry W. (Obituary)," *Locus* 30(3): 71. March 1993.
___ "Martin, Larry W. (Obituary)," *Science Fiction Chronicle* 14(7): 18. April 1993.

MARTIN, VALERIE
___ Roberts, Bette B. "The Strange Case of **Mary Reilly**," *Extrapolation* 34(1): 39-47. Spring 1993.

MARTINE-BARNES, ADRIENNE
___ Holmen, Rachel E. "Interview With Diana L. Paxson and Adrienne Martine-Barnes," *Marion Zimmer Bradley's Fantasy Magazine* No. 28: 47-50. Summer 1995.

MARTINSON, HARRY
___ "Martinson, Harry (Obituary)," *Science Fiction News* (Australia) No. 55: 12. June 1978.

MARVEL COMICS
___ Gelman, Morrie. "Sunbow Takes to Marvel Like Duck to Water in Animation," *Variety* p. 81, 98. September 17, 1986.
___ Gilroy, Dan. "Marvel Now $100 Million a Year Hulk," *Variety* p. 81, 92. September 17, 1986.

MARVEL COMICS VIDEO LIBRARY
___ "'Superheroes' Head for Homevid Via Marvel Comics Video Library; DC Comics in WHV's July Lineup," *Variety* p.85. May 22, 1985.

MARX, KARL
___ Stableford, Brian. "Marxism, Science Fiction, and the Poverty of Prophecy: Some Comparisons and Contrasts," in: Stableford, Brian. **Opening Minds: Essays on Fantastic Literature**. San Bernardino, CA: Borgo Press, 1995. pp.99-110.
___ Stillman, Peter S. "A Critique of Ideal Worlds: Hegel and Marx on Modern Utopian Thought," in: Saccaro Del Buffa, Giuseppa and Lewis, Arthur O., eds. **Utopie per gli Anni Ottana**. Rome: Gangemi Editore, 1986. pp.635-674.

MARY REILLY (MOTION PICTURE)
___ Jones, Alan. "Dr. Jekyll and the Maid," *Cinefantastique* 26(3): 12-13, 61. April 1995.

MARY SHELLEY'S FRANKENSTEIN (MOTION PICTURE)
___ Harris, Judith P. "**Mary Shelley's Frankenstein** (Review)," *Cinefantastique* 26(3): 59. April 1995.
___ Hochman, David. "Playing Doctor," *US* 200: 66-67. September 1994.
___ Jones, Alan. "**Mary Shelley's Frankenstein**," *Cinefantastique* 25(6)/26(1): 6-9. December 1994.
___ Kirkham, Pat. "Making Frankenstein and the Monster," *Sight and Sound* 4(11): 6-11. November 1994.
___ Lipman, Amanda. "**Mary Shelley's Frankenstein** (Review)," *Sight and Sound* 4(12): 51-52. December 1994.
___ Lowe, Nick. "**Mary Shelley's Frankenstein** (Review)," *Interzone* No. 91: 37-39. January 1995.
___ Magid, Ron. "CFC's Effects Give Life to **Mary Shelley's Frankenstein**," *American Cinematographer* 75(12): 42-48. December 1994.
___ Magid, Ron. "New Look for a Classic Creature," *American Cinematographer* 75(12): 34-40. December 1994.
___ Spelling, Ian. "Horrors of **Frankenstein**," *Starlog* No. 211: 32-35, 70. February 1995.
___ Stephens, Lynne. "Bride of Frankenstein," *Starlog* No. 209: 27-30, 68. December 1994.
___ Vaz, Mark C. "Haunting Creation," *Cinefex* No. 60: 70-85. December 1994.

MASK (MOTION PICTURE)
___ Atkinson, Michael. "**The Mask** (Review)," *Sight and Sound* 4(10): 48-49. October 1994.
___ Crisafulli, Chuck. "**The Mask**: Computer Graphics," *Cinefantastique* 25(4): 11. August 1994.
___ Crisafulli, Chuck. "**The Mask**," *Cinefantastique* 25(4): 8-11. August 1994.
___ Duncan, Jody. "From Zero to Hero," *Cinefex* No. 60: 46-65. December 1994.
___ Jankiewicz, Pat. "Masks of Time," *Starlog* No. 206: 40-45. September 1994.
___ Lowe, Nick. "**The Mask** (Review)," *Interzone* No. 89: 38-39. November 1994.
___ Magid, Ron. "Dream Quest Adds Lunatic Fringes," *American Cinematographer* 75(12): 57-58. December 1994.

MASK (MOTION PICTURE)

MASK (MOTION PICTURE) (continued)
___ Magid, Ron. "ILM Magic Is Organized Mayhem," *American Cinematographer* 75(12): 50-56. December 1994.
___ Magid, Ron. "Making Strange Faces," *American Cinematographer* 75(12): 59-60. December 1994.
___ Peterson, Don E. "***The Mask***," *Sci-Fi Entertainment* 1(1): 38-41, 63. June 1994.
___ Shapiro, Marc. "***Mask*** Maker," *Starlog* No. 205: 32-35. August 1994.

MASK OF THE PHANTOM (MOTION PICTURE)
___ SEE: BATMAN: MASK OF THE PHANTOM (MOTION PICTURE).

MASKE, SUSAN GUDELIS
___ "Maske, Susan Gudelis (Obituary)," *Locus* 34(3): 74. March 1995.

MASON, COLIN
___ Stone, Graham. "Notes on Australian Science Fiction," *Science Fiction News* (Australia) No. 53: 2-5. February 1978.

MASON, LISA
___ "Lisa Mason: Politics and Ecstasy," *Locus* 32(5): 5, 68-70. May 1994.
___ Harper, Mary C. "Incurably Alien Other: A Case for Feminist Cyborg Writers," *Science Fiction Studies* 22(3): 399-420. November 1995
___ Hill, Debora. "Image of the Spider," by Debora Hill and Sandra Brandenburg. *Starlog* 182: 40-41. September 1992.

MASSIE, ELIZABETH
___ "Bram Stoker Awards, 1993," *Science Fiction Chronicle* 14(10): 4. July 1993.
___ "HWA Stoker Awards Winners," *Locus* 31(2): 6, 62. August 1993.

MASTERS OF THE UNIVERSE (MOTION PICTURE)
___ "'Masters,' Pressman & RKO's 3d, to Roll at Churubusco Studios," *Variety* p.22. July 31, 1985.

MASTERTON, GRAHAM
___ Nicholls, Stan. "Graham Masterton Deals With the Incongruity," in: Nicholls, Stan. **Wordsmiths of Wonder: Fifty Interviews with Writers of the Fantastic.** London: Orbit, 1993. pp.390-396.

MATAKOVICH, JEFF
___ Mason, Mary C. "Profile: Jeff Matakovich," *Cinefex* No. 62: 29. June 1995.

MATHESON, RICHARD C.
___ "Repeat of Matheson: WB's *I Am Legend* Done Before in '64 by AIP," *Variety* p. 3. May 13, 1970.
___ "Richard C. Matheson's House Burns in Los Angeles Fires," *Science Fiction Chronicle* 15(2): 5. November/December 1993.
___ Bloom, Harold. "Richard Matheson," in: Bloom, Harold. **Modern Horror Writers.** New York: Chelsea House, 1995. pp.171-185.
___ Bradley, Matthew R. "And in the Beginning Was the Word...: An Interview With Screenwriter Richard Matheson," *Filmfax* No. 42: 40-44, 78-80, 98. December 1993/January 1994.
___ Dziemianowicz, Stefan. "Horror Begins at Home: Richard Matheson's Fear of the Familiar," *Studies in Weird Fiction* No. 14: 29-36. Winter 1994.
___ Proulx, Kevin. **Fear to the World: Eleven Voices in a Chorus of Horror.** Mercer Island, WA: Starmont, 1992. 243pp.
___ Weaver, tom. "Twilight Testaments," *Starlog* No. 203: 32. June 1994.

MATINEE (MOTION PICTURE)
___ Biodrowski, Steve. "***Mant***," *Cinefantastique* 24(1): 58. June 1993.
___ Biodrowski, Steve. "***Matinee***," *Cinefantastique* 23(6): 46-47. April 1993.
___ Doherty, Thomas. "***Matinee*** (Review)," *Cinefantastique* 24(1): 59. June 1993.
___ Lowe, Nick. "***Matinee*** (Review)," *Interzone* No. 74: 40. August 1993.

MATTINGLY, DAVID B.
___ Friesner, Esther M. "One of the Good Guys," *Science Fiction Age* 3(5): 82-87. July 1995.

MATTINGLY, DAVID B. (continued)
___ Nazzaro, Joe. "Master Strokes," *Starlog* No. 195: 27-31, 72. October 1993.

MATURIN, CHARLES ROBERT
___ Bloom, Harold. "Charles Robert Maturin," in: Bloom, Harold. **Classic Horror Writers.** New York: Chelsea House, 1994. pp.73-85.

MAXX (TV)
___ Kenny, Glenn. "***Maxx***-ed Out," *TV Guide* 43(8): 42. February 25, 1995.
___ Persons, Dan. "The ***Maxx*** (Review)," *Cinefantastique* 26(6)/27(1): 123. October 1995.

MAY, BOB
___ Weaver, Tom. "The Man in the Bubble-Headed Mask," *Starlog* No. 201: 32-35, 66. April 1994.

MAYER, GERALD
___ Spelling, Ian. "My Uncle, the Director," *Starlog* No. 204: 64-67. July 1994.

MAYER, NICHOLAS
___ Lofficier, Randy. "***Star Trek Movies*** (1980-1988): Interviews with Jack Sowards, Nicholas Mayer, Harve Bennett; Leonard Nimoy and William Shatner," by Randy Lofficier and Jean-Marc Lofficier. in: Goldberg, Lee et al. **Science Fiction Filmmaking in the 1980s.** Jefferson, NC: McFarland, 1995. pp.189-236.

MAYHAR, ARDATH
___ Mayhar, Ardath. "***Golden Dreams***: Odyssey of an Alien," *Paperback Parade* No. 35: 45-47. August 1993.

MAYNARD, YVES;
___ "Aurora Awards," *Science Fiction Chronicle* 15(10): 5. September 1994.

McAULEY, PAUL J.
___ "British Fantasy Awards, 1995," *Locus* 35(6): 9. December 1995.
___ "British Fantasy Awards, 1995," *Science Fiction Chronicle* 17(2): 5. December 1995/January 1996.
___ "Paul J. McAuley: Not a Movement," *Locus* 28(2): 4. February 1992.
___ Holliday, Liz. "SFC Interviews: Paul J. McAuley," *Science Fiction Chronicle* 13(9): 5, 27-28. June 1992.
___ Lovegrove, James. "Mythic Templates: Paul McAuley Interviewed," *Interzone* No. 98: 18-21. August 1995.

McBAIN, GORDON D., III
___ "McBain, Gordon D., III (Obituary)," *Locus* 29(4): 66. October 1992
___ "McBain, Gordon D., III (Obituary)," *Science Fiction Chronicle* 14(2): 12, 14. November 1992.

McCAFFERY, LARRY
___ **No Great Endeavor: Presentation of the Pilgrim and Pioneer Awards.** Ann Arbor, MI: Tucker Video, 1994. 1 videocassette, 67 minutes. (Presentation at the 1994 Science Fiction Research Association Conference. Sheri S. Tepper, John Clute, Takayuki Tatsumi, Larry McCaffery, speakers.)

McCAFFREY, ANNE
___ "Anne McCaffrey: Life With Dragons," *Locus* 30(3): 5, 74. March 1993.
___ "Anne McCaffrey Wins '92, '93 SF Book Club Awards," *Science Fiction Chronicle* 15(7): 4-5. June 1994.
___ "Anne McCaffrey Wins SFBC Book of the Year Award," *Science Fiction Chronicle* 14(11): 5. August 1993.
___ "McCaffrey Wins SFBC Award Again," *Locus* 33(1): 7, 78. July 1994.
___ "McCaffrey, Anne (Inez), 1926- ," in: Lesniak, James G., ed. **Contemporary Authors.** Detroit: Gale Research, 1992. New Revision Series, Vol. 35, pp.307-309.
___ "Science Fiction's Brave New Worlds: Anne McCaffrey," *Library Journal* 119(3): 123. February 15, 1994.
___ Barr, Marleen S. **Lost in Space: Probing Feminist Science Fiction and Beyond.** Chapel Hill, NC: University of North Carolina Press, 1993. 231pp.

McCAFFREY, ANNE

McCAFFREY, ANNE (continued)
___ Bittner, Drew. "Dragonlady of Pern," *Starlog* No. 190: 40-45. May 1993.

___ Evans, Gwenth. "Harps and Harpers in Contemporary Fantasy," *Lion and the Unicorn* 16(2): 199-209. December 1992.

___ Green, Carol A. "Only a Girl: Heroines in the Work of Anne McCaffrey and Marion Zimmer Bradley," *Vector* No. 172: 16-17. April/May 1993.

___ Hargreaves, Mathew D. **Anne Inez McCaffrey: Forty Years of Publishing, An International Bibliograpy**. Seattle, WA: Mathew Hargreaves, 1992. 338pp.

___ Harkins, Patricia. "Myth in Action: The Trials and Transformation of Menolly," in: Sullivan, C. W., III. **Science Fiction for Young Readers**. Westport, CT: Greenwood, 1993. pp.157-166.

___ Hayles, N. Katherine. "The Life Cycle of Cyborgs: Writing the Posthuman," in: Gray, Chris H., ed. **The Cyborg Handbook**. New York: Routledge, 1995. pp.321-335.

___ Hayles, N. Katherine. "The Life Cycle of Cyborgs: Writing the Posthuman," in: Benjamin, Marina, ed. **A Question of Identity: Women, Science, and Literature**. New Brunswick, NJ: Rutgers University Press, 1993. pp.152-170.

___ Langford, David. "The Dragonhiker's Guide to Battlefield Covenant at Dune's Edge: Odyssey Two," *Australian Science Fiction Review* 5(3): 3-11. Spring 1990. (Whole No. 25)

___ McCaffrey, Anne. **[Anne McCaffrey; Voting Rights of Women in Canada; Sandy Wimer]**. (Collected interviews: Supplied title.). Troy, NY: WAMC Public Radio, 1993. 1 cassette, 25 minutes.

___ Monaghan, Pat. "Booklist Interview: Anne McCaffrey," *Booklist* 90(14): 1300-1301. March 15, 1994.

___ Salmonson, Jessica A. "Gender Structuring of Shell Persons in **The Ship Who Sang**," *New York Review of Science Fiction* No. 10: 15-18. June 1989.

___ Skublics, Heather A. **Naming and Vocation in the Novels of J. R. R. Tolkien, Patricia Kennealy and Anne McCaffrey**. Master's Thesis, McGill University, 1994. 154pp. (Master's Abstracts 33/04, p. 1078. August 1995.)

___ Slotkin, Alan R. "A Back-(To the Future)-Formation," by Alan R. Slotkin and Robert F. Bode. *American Speech* 68(3): 323-327. Fall 1993.

___ Talbot, Norman. "Fair Dinkum at Dragonsdawn: Or, How to Turn Australians, and Especially, Australian SF Readers, into Paranoid Androids," by Norman Talbot and Clare Fennessy. *Australian Science Fiction Review* 5(3): 12-15. Spring 1990. (Whole No. 25)

___ Thompson, Raymond H. "Anne McCaffrey," in: Bruccoli, Matthew J., ed. **Facts on File Bibliography of American Fiction 1919-1988**. New York: Facts on File, 1991. pp.334-335.

___ Wytenbroek, J. R. "The Child as Creature Creator in McCaffrey's **Dragonsong** and **Dragonsinger**," *Lion and the Unicorn* 16(2): 210-214. December 1992.

___ Yoo, Paula. "Science Fiction Author Cranks out Books as If There Were No Tomorrow," *Seattle (WA) Times*. July 14, 1992. in: *NewsBank*. Names in the News. 174:A14-B1. 1992.

McCALL, ROBERT
___ Bradbury, Ray. "Blueprinter of Our Future: Robert McCall," *Science Fiction Age* 1(1): 62-67. November 1992.

McCAMMON, ROBERT R.
___ "1992 Bram Stoker Awards Winners," *Locus* 28(2): 6, 68. August 1992.

___ "1992 World Fantasy Awards Winners," *Locus* 29(6): 6. December 1992.

___ "Bram Stoker Awards," *Science Fiction Chronicle* 13(10): 4. July/August 1992.

___ "World Fantasy Awards," *Science Fiction Chronicle* 14(3): 4. December 1992.

___ Kies, Cosette. **Presenting Young Adult Horror Fiction**. New York: Twayne, 1991. 203pp.

McCARTHY, SHAWNA
___ "McCarthy Joins Meredith," *Locus* 30(3): 6. March 1993.

___ "*Realms of Fantasy* New Magazine," *Locus* 32(4): 7. April 1994.

McCOMAS, ANNETTE PELZ
___ "McComas, Annette Pelz (Obituary)," *Locus* 33(5): 71. November 1994.

McCOMAS, ANNETTE PELZ (continued)
___ "McComas, Annette Pelz (Obituary)," *Science Fiction Chronicle* 16(2): 20. November/December 1994.

McCOMAS, J. FRANCIS
___ "McComas, J. Francis (Obituary)," *Science Fiction News* (Australia) No. 55: 12. June 1978.

McCONNELL, ASHLEY
___ Chrissinger, Craig W. "Leaps and Bounds," *Starlog* No. 199: 34-36. February 1994.

McCONNELL, FRANK
___ "J. Lloyd Eaton Memorial Award, 1993," *Science Fiction Chronicle* 14(9): 6. June 1993.

McCONNELL, JAMES V.
___ "McConnell, James V. (1925-1990) (Obituary)," *American Psychologist* 46(6): 650. June 1991.

McCRUMB, SHARYN
___ Dellinger, Paul. "Bimbos, Zombies & Fans," *Starlog* 182: 50-51. September 1992.

McDEVITT, JACK
___ "1993 UPC Science Fiction Award," *Locus* 30(4): 40. April 1993.

___ "Jack McDevitt: Big Questions," *Locus* 34(2): 4-5, 74-75. February 1995.

___ "Jack McDevitt Wins Spanish Novella Contest," *Science Fiction Chronicle* 14(7): 4. April 1993.

McDONALD, IAN
___ "British SF Awards, 1993," *Science Fiction Chronicle* 14(10): 8. July 1993.

___ "Ian McDonald Wins Philip K. Dick Award," *Science Fiction Chronicle* 13(8): 4. May 1992.

___ "McDonald Wins Philip K. Dick Award," *Locus* 28(5): 6, 65. May 1992.

McDOWELL, MALCOLM
___ Beeler, Michael. "O Lucky Man: Malcolm McDowell on His Career Revival," *Cinefantastique* 27(3): 26-29. December 1995.

___ Spelling, Ian. "The Man Who Killed Kirk," *Starlog* No. 213: 75-79, 72. April 1995.

McDOWELL, MICHAEL
___ Wiater, Stanley. "McDowell, Michael," in: Wiater, Stanley. **Dark Visions: Conversations with the Masters of the Horror Film**. New York: Avon, 1992. pp.101-110.

McEWNA, IAN
___ Menegaldo, Gilles. "Quelques substituts et simulacres d'Eros dans le recit fantastique moderne," in: Bozzetto, Roger, ed. **Eros: Science & Fiction Fantastique**. Aix-en-Provence: Universite de Provence, 1991. pp.43-57.

McFADDEN, GATES
___ Buck, Jerry. "**Star Trek** Opened Gates for McFadden," *Austin (TX) American Statesman*. Show World p. 8. July 12, 1992.

___ Cohen, Amy J. "More Than Just a Country Doctor," *Star Trek: The Official Fan Club* No. 96: 41-45. April/May 1994.

___ Kutzera, Dale. "**Star Trek: The Next Generation**: Doctor Turns Director," *Cinefantastique* 25(6)/26(1): 83. December 1994.

McGARRY, TERRY
___ "World SF Convention Hugo Awards," *Science Fiction Chronicle* 14(1): 4. October 1992.

McGEE, JACK
___ Shapiro, Marc. "Cosmic Mechanic," *Starlog* No. 189: 27-29, 67. April 1993.

McHUGH, MAUREEN F.
___ "Compuserve HOMer Awards, 1992," *Science Fiction Chronicle* 14(9): 4-5. June 1993.

___ "Maureen F. McHugh: Fan Dancing in Public," *Locus* 31(6): 4, 72, 74. December 1993.

McHUGH, MAUREEN F.

McHUGH, MAUREEN F. (continued)

___ "Maureen F. McHugh Wins Tiptree Award," *Science Fiction Chronicle* 14(6): 4. March 1993.

___ "Tiptree Award Presented," *Locus* 30(5): 8. May 1993.

___ "Tiptree Award Winner, 1992," *Locus* 30(3): 7. March 1993.

___ Kandel, Michael. "Twelve Thoughts, Not All Equally Important, on Reading Maureen F. McHugh's **China Mountain Zhang** and **Half the Day Is Night**," *New York Review of Science Fiction* No. 77: 21-22. January 1995.

McINTYRE, VONDA N.

___ "Pocket Does McIntyre Alternate History," *Locus* 35(3): 8. September 1993.

___ King, T. Jackson. "SFC Interviews: Vonda N. McIntyre," *Science Fiction Chronicle* 14(8): 5, 30-32. May 1993.

___ Wolmark, Jenny. **Aliens and Others: Science Fiction, Feminism, and Postmodernism**. London: Harester Wheatsheaf, 1993. 167pp.; Iowa City: University of Iowa Press, 1994. 167pp.

McKILLIP, PATRICIA A.

___ "1995 Mythopoeic Fantasy Awards," *Locus* 35(3): 9. September 1995.

___ "Patricia A. McKillip: Moving Forward," *Locus* 28(2): 4, 69. August 1992.

McKINLEY, ROBIN

___ Cadden, Michael. "The Illusion of Control: Narrative Authority in Robin McKinley's **Beauty** and **The Blue Sword**," *Mythlore* 20(2): 16-19, 31. Spring 1994. (Whole No. 76)

McMULLEN, SEAN

___ Buckrich, Judith R. "Past, Future and Present: Australian Science Fiction; An Interview with Sean McMullen and Lucy Sussex," *Overland* (Australia) 133: 8-14. Summer 1993.

McNAIL, STANLEY D.

___ "McNail, Stanley D. (Obituary)," *Locus* 34(6): 66. June 1995.

McQUAY, MIKE

___ "McQuay, Mike (Obituary)," *Locus* 35(1): 62-63. July 1995.

___ "McQuay, Mike (Obituary)," *Science Fiction Chronicle* 16(7): 18-19. June/July 1995.

McQUINN, DONALD E.

___ "Donald E. McQuinn: Luck of the Irish," *Locus* 34(5): 5, 76. May 1995.

McTIERNAN, JOHN

___ Shapiro, Marc. "Last Action Man," *Starlog* No. 194: 55-57. September 1993.

MEAD, SYD

___ Lofficier, Randy. "**Blade Runner** (1982): Interviews with Hampton Francher, David Peoples, Ridley Scott and Syd Mead," by Randy Lofficier and Jean-Marc Lofficier. in: Goldberg, Lee et al. **Science Fiction Filmmaking in the 1980s**. Jefferson, NC: McFarland, 1995. pp.23-58.

___ Lofficier, Randy. "Interview: Syd Mead," by Randy Lofficier and Jean-Marc Lofficier. *Starlog* 184: 42-45. November 1992.

___ Steele, Allen. "SF's Cinematic Sentinel," *Science Fiction Age* 3(4): 82-87. May 1995.

MEDICINE

___ Brunner, John. "In Our Pharmaceutical Future, the Cure May Be Worse Than the Disease," *Science Fiction Age* 3(1): 34-40. November 1994.

___ Thompson, Linda W. **The Image of Nursing in Science Fiction Literature**. Thesis (D.S.N.), University of Alabama at Birmingham School of Nursing, 1993. 297pp. (DAI-B 54/07, p. 3554. January 1994.)

___ Van Hise, James. "Exobiology: Space Medicine at the Time of **Star Trek**," in: Van Hise, James, ed. **Trek Celebration Two**. Las Vegas, NV: Pioneer, 1994. pp.102-110.

MEGAZONE 23: PART I (ANIMATION)

___ Whitty, Stephen. "Run For Your Life! It's Your Inner Godzilla," *San Jose (CA) Mercury News*. July 8, 1994. in: *NewsBank. Film and Television*. 81:C14. 1994.

MELBOURNE SCIENCE FICTION CLUB

___ Mathews, Race. "Whirlaway to *Thrilling Wonder Stories*: Boyhood Reading in Wartime and Postwar Melbourne," *Metaphysical Review* No. 22/23: 5-16. November 1995.

MELLIFONT PRESS

___ Holland, Stephen. **An Index to Mellifont Press: A Working Bibliography**. Leeds, Eng: Galactic Central, 1995. 76pp.

MELODRAMA

___ Westfahl, Gary. " 'Man Against Man, Brain Against Brain': The Transformation of Melodrama in Science Fiction," in: Redmond, James, ed. **Melodrama**. Cambridge: Cambridge University Press, 1992. pp.193-211.

MELTZER, DAVID

___ "Meltzer, David, 1937- ," in: Lesniak, James G., ed. **Contemporary Authors**. Detroit: Gale Research, 1992. New Revision Series, Vol. 35, pp.313-315.

MEMOIRS OF AN INVISIBLE MAN (MOTION PICTURE)

___ "*Invisible Man* Really Should Stay Incognito (Review)," *Washington (DC) Times*. February 28, 1992. in: *NewsBank. Film and Television*. 23: D11. 1992.

___ Biodrowski, Steve. "**Memoirs of an Invisible Man**," *Cinefantastique* 22(4): 10-11. February 1992.

___ Burden, Martin. "*Invisible* Sight Gags (Review)," *New York (NY) Post*. February 28, 1992. in: *NewsBank. Film and Television*. 23:D9. 1992.

___ Campbell, Bob. "Invisible Man Fantasies Have Seen Better Days (Review)," *Newark (NJ) Star Ledger*. February 28, 1992. in: *NewsBank. Film and Television*. 23:D8. 1992.

___ Campbell, Bob. "No Laughs to Be Seen in *Invisible Man*; It's Depressingly Dull (Review)," *Minneapolis (MN) Star and Tribune*. February 28, 1992. in: *NewsBank. Film and Television*. 23:D7. 1992.

___ Ebert, Roger. "Transparent Plot Foils 'Man' (Review)," *Chicago (IL) Sun Times*. February 28, 1992. in: *NewsBank. Film and Television*. 23: D3. 1992.

___ Johnson, Malcolm. "*Invisible* Special Effects Would Best Be Left Unseen (Review)," *Hartford (CT) Courant*. February 28, 1992. in: *NewsBank. Film and Television*. 23:D1. 1992.

___ Mahar, Ted. "Clearly *Invisible Man* Is Something to See (Review)," *Portland (OR) The Oregonian*. March 2, 1992. in: *NewsBank. Film and Television*. 23:D10. 1992.

___ Murray, Steve. "Chevy Transparently Chases Good Fun in *Invisible Man* (Review)," *Atlanta (GA) Journal*. February 28, 1992. in: *NewsBank. Film and Television*. 23:D2. 1992.

___ Shapiro, Marc. "I'm Invisible and You're Not," *Starlog* 178: 7-9. May 1992.

___ Stark, Susan. "Vanishing Interest: A Transparent Comedy, *Invisible Man* Displays and Excess of F/X, But Little Else (Review)," *Detroit (MI) News*. February 28, 1992. in: *NewsBank. Film and Television*. 23:D6. 1992.

___ Swires, Steve. "John Carpenter's Guide to Hollywood (In)Visibility," *Starlog* 177: 28-33, 71. April 1992.

___ Verniere, James. "Chevy Chase Mixes Laughs, Love in *Invisible Man* (Review)," *Boston (MA) Herald*. February 28, 1992. in: *NewsBank. Film and Television*. 23:D4-D5. 1992.

MEN IN BLACK (MOTION PICTURE)

___ "Will Smith Inks $5 Million Movie Deal With Columbia," *Jet* 88(23): 46. October 16, 1995.

MENKEN, ALAN

___ Spelling, Ian. "Arabian Night Music," *Starlog* No. 186: 52-55. January 1993.

MERCIER, LOUIS SÉBASTIEN

___ Ludlow, Gregory. "Imagining the Future: Mercier's **L'an 2440** and Morris' **News From Nowhere**," *Comparative Literature Studies* 29(1): 20-38. 1992.

MEREDITH, BURGESS

___ Garcia, Bob. "**Batman**: The Penguin," *Cinefantastique* 24(6)/25(1): 10. February 1994.

MEREDITH, SCOTT
___ "Meredith, Scott (Obituary)," *Locus* 30(5): 66, 68. May 1993.
___ "Meredith, Scott (Obituary)," *Locus* 30(3): 68-69. March 1993.
___ "Meredith, Scott (Obituary)," *Science Fiction Chronicle* 14(6): 16. March 1993.

MEREDITH, SIDNEY
___ "Meredith, Sidney (Obituary)," *Locus* 29(3): 78. September 1992.
___ "Meredith, Sidney (Obituary)," *Science Fiction Chronicle* 13(11/12): 18, 20. August 1992.

MERINO, JOSE MARIA
___ Glenn, Kathleen M. "Recapturing the Past: José María Merino's **El caldero de oro**," *Monographis Review* 3(1/2): 119-128. 1987.

MERLE, ROBERT
___ "Schaffner's 'Dolphin'," *Variety* p. 24. May 24, 1970.

MERLIN
___ Arbuckle, Nan. "That Hidden Strength: C. S. Lewis' Merlin as Modern Grail," in: Watson, Jeanie and Fries, Marueen, eds. **The Figure of Merlin in the Nineteenth and Twentieth Centuries.** Lewiston, NY: Mellen, 1989. pp.79-99.
___ Ensor, Allison. "The Magic of Fol-de-Rol: Mark Twain's Merlin," in: Watson, Jeanie and Fries, Marueen, eds. **The Figure of Merlin in the Nineteenth and Twentieth Centuries.** Lewiston, NY: Mellen, 1989. pp.51-63.
___ Goodrich, Peter. "Modern Merlins: An Aeriel Survey (Bibliographic Essay)," in: Watson, Jeanie and Fries, Marueen, eds. **The Figure of Merlin in the Nineteenth and Twentieth Centuries.** Lewiston, NY: Mellen, 1989. pp.175-197.
___ Goodrich, Peter. "The New Age Mage: Merlin as Contemporary Occult Icon," *Journal of the Fantastic in the Arts* 5(1): 42-73. 1992. (No. 17)
___ Goslee, David F. "Lost in the Siege Perilous: The Merlin of Tennyson's Idylls," in: Watson, Jeanie and Fries, Maureen, eds. **The Figure of Merlin in the Nineteenth and Twentieth Centuries.** Lewiston, NY: Mellen, 1989. pp.35-50.
___ Hanks, D. Thomas, Jr. "T. H. White's Merlin: More Than Malory Made Him," in: Watson, Jeanie and Fries, Marueen, eds. **The Figure of Merlin in the Nineteenth and Twentieth Centuries.** Lewiston, NY: Mellen, 1989. pp.100-120.
___ Hughes, Linda K. "Illusion and Relation: Merlin as Image of the Artist in Tennyson, Doré, Burene-Jones, and Beardsley," in: Watson, Jeanie and Fries, Marueen, eds. **The Figure of Merlin in the Nineteenth and Twentieth Centuries.** Lewiston, NY: Mellen, 1989. pp.1-33.
___ Jarman, A. O. H. "The Merlin Legend and the Welsh Tradition of Prophecy," in: Bromwich, Rachel, Jarman, A. O. H. and Roberts, Brynley F., eds. **The Arthur of the Welsh.** Cardiff: University of Wales Press, 1991. pp.117-146.
___ King, Roma A., Jr. "Charles William's Merlin: Worker in Time of the Images of Eternity," in: Watson, Jeanie and Fries, Marueen, eds. **The Figure of Merlin in the Nineteenth and Twentieth Centuries.** Lewiston, NY: Mellen, 1989. pp.65-77.
___ Miller, Miriam Y. "J. R. R. Tolkien's Merlin--An Old Man With a Staff: Galdalf and the Magus Tradition," in: Watson, Jeanie and Fries, Marueen, eds. **The Figure of Merlin in the Nineteenth and Twentieth Centuries.** Lewiston, NY: Mellen, 1989. pp.121-142.
___ Thompson, Raymond H. "The Comic Sage: Merlin in Thomas Berger's **Arthur Rex**," in: Watson, Jeanie and Fries, Marueen, eds. **The Figure of Merlin in the Nineteenth and Twentieth Centuries.** Lewiston, NY: Mellen, 1989. pp.143-153.
___ Watson, Jeanie. "Mary Stewart's Merlin: Word of Power," in: Watson, Jeanie and Fries, Marueen, eds. **The Figure of Merlin in the Nineteenth and Twentieth Centuries.** Lewiston, NY: Edwin Mellen Press, 1989. pp.155-174.
___ Watson, Jeanie, ed. **The Figure of Merlin in the Nineteenth and Twentieth Centuries**, ed. by Jeanie Watson and Maureen Fries. Lewiston, NY: Edwin Mellin Press, 1989. 197pp.

MERLIN, JAN
___ Phillips, Mark. "Space Cadet," *Starlog* No. 212: 62-67. March 1995.

MERRIL, JUDITH
___ "Merrill Collection in Trouble Again," *Locus* 33(4): 9. October 1994.

MERRIL, JUDITH (continued)
___ Aldiss, Brian W. "When Things Changed--A Little," *Aloud* (Toronto) 2(7): 1-2. October 1992.
___ Asakura, Hisashi. "Judith Merril in Japan," *Aloud* (Toronto) 2(7): 3. October 1992.
___ Atwood, Margaret. "Ode to Judith Merril," *Aloud* (Toronto) 2(7): 3. October 1992.
___ Ballard, J. G. "The Widest Windows onto the New," *Aloud* (Toronto) 2(7): 12. October 1992.
___ Beer, Stafford. "Hi-Fi Sci-Fi," *Aloud* (Toronto) 2(7): 11. October 1992.
___ Cummins, Elizabeth. "Judith Merril: A Link With the New Wave, Then and Now," *Extrapolation* 36(3): 198-209. Fall 1995.
___ Cummins, Elizabeth. "Judith Merril: Scouting SF," *Extrapolation* 35(1): 5-14. Spring 1994.
___ Cummins, Elizabeth. "Short Fiction by Judith Merril," *Extrapolation* 33(3): 202-214. Fall 1992.
___ Dorsey, Candas J. "All This--And Also Dancing," *Aloud* (Toronto) 2(7): 5, 10. October 1992.
___ Gotlieb, Phyllis. "A Woman of the Future," *Aloud* (Toronto) 2(7): 8. October 1992.
___ Kidd, Virginia. "The Expatriate," *Aloud* (Toronto) 2(7): 9. October 1992.
___ Lee, Dennis. "Judith Merril Meets Rochdale College," *Aloud* (Toronto) 2(7): 4-5. October 1992.
___ Lomberg, Jon. "What Limits," *Aloud* (Toronto) 2(7): 8. October 1992.
___ MacLean, Katherine. "Judith Merril vs. Plotto," *Aloud* (Toronto) 2(7): 6. October 1992.
___ Marshall, Joyce. "A Romantic Realist," *Aloud* (Toronto) 2(7): 7. October 1992.
___ Merril, Judith. "Better to Have Loved: From a Memoir-in-Progress, Part 1," *New York Review of Science Fiction* No. 59: 1, 8-14. July 1993.
___ Vonarburg, Elisabeth. "So Many Children," *Aloud* (Toronto) 2(7): 10. October 1992.

MERRITT, A.
___ Bloom, Harold. "A. Merritt," in: Bloom, Harold, ed. **Modern Fantasy Writers.** New York: Chelsea House, 1995. pp.110-122.
___ Sabella, Robert. "The Lost Worlds of Science Fiction: A. Merritt," *Lan's Lantern* No. 40: 34-35. September 1992.

MESKYS, EDMOND R.
___ "Maske, Susan Gudelis (Obituary)," *Locus* 34(3): 74. March 1995.

METALBEAST (MOTION PICTURE)
___ Harris, Judith P. "**Metalbeast** (Review)," *Cinefantastique* 26(6)/27(1): 123. October 1995.

METAMORPHOSIS: THE ALIEN FACTOR (MOTION PICTURE)
___ Harris, Judith P. "**Metamorphosis: The Alien Factor** (Review)," *Cinefantastique* 25(3): 60. June 1994.

METASCAPE (GAME)
___ Baker, Eric T. "With a Roll of the Dice, *Metascape* Provides Superior Space Opera Thrills," *Science Fiction Age* 2(4): 84-86. May 1994.

METEOR MAN (MOTION PICTURE)
___ Campbell, Bob. "**Meteor Man** a Starry-Eyed Ghetto Fantasy (Review)," *Newark (NJ) Star-Ledger.* August 6, 1993. in: *NewsBank. Art.* 18:E3. 1993.
___ Fisher, Bob. "**Meteor Man** Gets His Digital Wings," *American Cinematographer* 74(4): 42-45. April 1993.
___ Fisher, Bob. "**Meteor Man**: Rock and Hard Place Produce a Hero," *American Cinematographer* 74(4): 34-38, 40. April 1993.
___ Gray, Louise. "**Meteor Man** (Review)," *Sight and Sound* 4(2): 57-58. February 1994.
___ Lowe, Nick. "**Meteor Man** (Review)," *Interzone* No. 82: 31. April 1994.
___ Persons, Dan. "**Meteor Man**," *Cinefantastique* 23(6): 12-13. April 1993.
___ Sherman, Paul. "**Meteor Man** a Blast (Review)," *Boston (MA) Herald.* August 6, 1993. in: *NewsBank. Art.* 18:E5. 1993.
___ Wuntch, Phillip. "**Meteor Man**: There's a Lot to Like About This Action Hero (Review)," *Dallas (TX) Morning News.* August 6, 1993. in: *NewsBank. Art.* 18:E4. 1993.

METROPOLIS (MOTION PICTURE)
___ "Film Classics: *Metropolis*," *Futures Past* No. 2: 20-23. April 1992.
___ "*Metropolis* Stills Exhibit Now on Display in Paris," *Variety* p.30. June 26, 1985.
___ "Profile: Fritz Lang: The Genius Behind *Metropolis*," *Futures Past* No. 2: 24-25. April 1992.
___ Friedman, Regien-Mihal. "Capitals of Sorrow: From *Metropolis* to *Brazil*," *Utopian Studies* 4(2): 35-43. 1993.
___ McCarthy, Todd. "Moroder's Redo of *Metropolis* Sparks Spirited Cannes Talk," *Variety* p. 5, 137. May 16, 1984.
___ Sawyer, Andy. "More Than Metaphor: Double Vision in Lang's *Metropolis*," *Foundation* No. 64: 70-81. Summer 1995.

MEYNARD, YVES
___ "1994 Aurora Winners," *Locus* 33(4): 8, 76. October 1994.

MEYRINK, GUSTAV
___ Clute, John. "Gustav Meyrink," in: Clute, John. **Look at the Evidence: Essays and Reviews**. Liverpool: Liverpool University Press, 1995. pp.438-443.

MIAMI HORROR (MOTION PICTURE)
___ "*Miami Horror* (Review)," *Variety* p. 34. April 20, 1988.

MIDDLETON, RICHARD
___ Schweitzer, Darrell. "Richard Middleton: Beauty, Sadness, and Terror," in: Schweitzer, Darrell, ed. **Discovering Classic Horror Fiction I**. Mercer Island, WA: Starmont, 1992. pp.34-40.

MIDDLETON, THOMAS
___ Keller, James R. "Middleton's **The Witch**: Witchcraft and the Domestic Female Hero," *Journal of the Fantastic in the Arts* 4(4): 37-59. 1991. (No. 16)

MIDKIFF, DALE
___ Chrissinger, Craig W. "Man of Time," *Starlog* No. 189: 34-37. April 1993.

MIDNIGHT 2: SEX, DEATH AND VIDEOTAPE (MOTION PICTURE)
___ Wilt, David. "*Midnight 2: Sex, Death and Videotape* (Review)," *Cinefantastique* 24(2): 59. August 1993.

MIDNIGHT KISS (MOTION PICTURE)
___ Scapperotti, Dan. "*Midnight Kiss* (Review)," *Cinefantastique* 24(6)/25(1): 123-124. February 1994.

MIDNIGHT'S CHILD (MOTION PICTURE)
___ Wilt, David. "*Midnight's Child* (Review)," *Cinefantastique* 23(6): 60. April 1993.

MILLAR, MARGARET
___ "Millar, Margaret (Obituary)," *Locus* 32(5): 63. May 1994.

MILLENNIUM (MOTION PICTURE)
___ Fischer, Dennis. "**Millennium**: Novel vs. Film," *Lan's Lantern* No. 35: 75-78. December 1990.

MILLER, DENNY
___ Fury, David. "Interview with the Tarzan Man, Mr. Denny Miller," *Burroughs Bulletin* NS. No. 17: 25-29. January 1994.

MILLER, GEORGE
___ Lofficier, Randy. "**Mad Max** Movies (1979-1985): Interview with George Miller, Terry Hayes, George Ogilvie and Mel Gibson," by Randy Lofficier and Jean-Marc Lofficier. in: Goldberg, Lee et al. **Science Fiction Filmmaking in the 1980s**. Jefferson, NC: McFarland, 1995. pp.133-174.

MILLER, WALTER M., JR.
___ Dalmyn, Tony. "Some Thoughts on Walter Miller's **A Canticle for Leibowitz**," *Winding Numbers* No. 2: 4-8. Winter 1975-1976.
___ Horstmann, Ulrich. "Walter M. Miller, **A Canticle for Leibowitz** (1959)," in: Heuermann, Harmut, ed. **Der Science Fiction Roman in der angloamerikanischen Literatur: Interpretationen**. Düsseldorf: Bagel, 1986. pp.182-195.
___ Ower, John. "Theology and Evolution in the Short Fiction of Walter M. Miller, Jr.," *Cithara* 25(2): 57-74. May 1986.

MILLER, WALTER M., JR. (continued)
___ Percy, Walker. "Walker Percy on Walter M. Miller, Jr.'s **A Canticle for Leibowitz**," in: Madden, David, ed. **Rediscoveries**. New York: Crown, 1971. pp.262-269.
___ Roberson, William H. **Walter M. Miller, Jr.: A Bio-Bibliography**, by William H. Roberson and Robert L. Battenfeld. Westport, CT: Greenwood, 1992. 149pp.
___ Schroth, Raymond A. "**Canticle for Leibowitz**," *America* 118(3): 79. January 20, 1968.
___ Senior, W. A. "From the Begetting of Monsters: Distortion as Unifier in **A Canticle for Liebowitz**," *Extrapolation* 34(4): 329-339. Winter 1993.
___ Spector, Judith A. "Walter Miller's **A Canticle for Leibowitz**: A Parable for Our Time?," *Midwest Quarterly* 22(4): 337-345. Summer 1981.
___ Stoler, John A. "Christian Lore and Characters' Names in **A Canticle for Leibowitz**," *Literary Onomastics Studies* 11: 77-91. 1984.

MILNE, A. A.
___ Wullschläger, Jackie. **Inventing Wonderland: The Lives and Fantasies of Lewis Carroll, Edward Lear, J. M. Barrie, Kenneth Grahame and A. A. Milne**. New York: Free Press, 1995. 228pp.

MIND
___ Stableford, Brian. "The Concept of Mind in Science Fiction," in: Stableford, Brian. **Opening Minds: Essays on Fantastic Literature**. San Bernardino, CA: Borgo Press, 1995. pp.37-52.

MIND BENDERS (MOTION PICTURE)
___ Leeper, Mark R. "*Mind Benders* (Review)," *Lan's Lantern* No. 42: 105-106. May 1994.

MINNETT, CORA
___ Stone, Graham. "Notes on Australian Science Fiction," *Science Fiction News* (Australia) No. 92: 2-8. February 1985.

MINSKY, MARVIN
___ Davidson, Clive. "Catch up on Minsky's Missing Chapters," *Guardian* Sec. 2, p. 17. March 25, 1993. [Not seen.]

MIRALLES, FRANCISCO
___ Bell, Andrea. "**Desde Júpiter**: Chile's Earliest Science Fiction Novel," *Science Fiction Studies* 22(2): 187-197. July 1995.

MIRAMAX FILMS
___ Evans, Greg. "Indies Head of Genre Pic Middle Ground," *Variety* 359(4): 7, 22. May 22, 1995.

MIRANDA, VINCENT
___ "Miranda, Vincent (Obituary)," *Locus* 28(3): 72-73. March 1992.

MISCEGENATION
___ Wilcox, Rhonda V. "Dating Data: Miscegenation in **Star Trek: The Next Generation**," *Extrapolation* 34(3): 265-277. Fall 1993.

MISHKIN, WILLIAM
___ "Horror With Some Sexy Scenes Seen Cashable by Omen-Reading Mishkin," *Variety* p. 7. December 10, 1969.

MITCHELL, BETSY
___ "Betsy Mitchell Moves to Warner's Questar SF; Tom Dupree to Head Bantam Spectra," *Science Fiction Chronicle* 14(11): 4. August 1993.
___ "Silbersack to Start New SF Line at HarperCollins; Mitchell Moves to Warner; Bantam Promotes From Within," *Locus* 31(2): 6, 61. August 1993.

MITCHELL, CAMERON
___ "Mitchell, Cameron (Obituary)," *Science Fiction Chronicle* 15(10): 20. September 1994.
___ Weaver, Tom. "Cameron Mitchell: Interview," in: Weaver, Tom, ed. **Attack of the Monster Movie Makers: Interviews with 20 Genre Giants**. Jefferson, NC: McFarland, 1994. pp.209-228.

MITCHELL, V. E.
___ King, T. Jackson. "Pros and Cons of Being a Writer Couple," by T. Jackson King and Paula E. Downing. *SFWA Bulletin* 25(4): 7-14. Winter 1992. (No. 114)

MITCHISON, NAOMI

___ Benton, Jill. **Naomi Mitchison: A Century of Experiment in Life and Letters**. London: Pandora, 1992. 192pp.

___ Lefanu, Sarah. "Difference and Sexual Politics in Naomi Mitchison's **Solution Three**," in: Donawerth, Jane L. and Kolmerten, Carol A., eds. **Utopian and Science Fiction by Women: Worlds of Difference**. Syracuse, NY: Syracuse University Press, 1994. pp.153-165.

___ Mitchison, Naomi. "Wonderful Deathless Ditties," in: Jakubowski, Maxim and James, Edward, eds. **The Profession of Science Fiction**. New York: St. Martin's, 1992. pp.34-43.

___ Squier, Susan M. "Naomi Mitchison: The Feminist Art of Making Things Difficult," in: Mitchison, Naomi. **Solution Three**. New York: Feminist Press, 1995. pp.161-183.

MIXON, LAURA J.

___ Harper, Mary C. "Incurably Alien Other: A Case for Feminist Cyborg Writers," *Science Fiction Studies* 22(3): 399-420. November 1995

MODEL BY DAY (MOTION PICTURE)

___ Scapperotti, Dan. "**Model By Day** (Review)," *Cinefantastique* 25(3): 60. June 1994.

MOFFETT, JUDITH

___ Mendlesohn, Farah. "The Profession of Science Fiction, 46: Grinding Axes," *Foundation* No. 62: 10-21. Winter 1994/1995.

___ Moffett, Judith. "Confessions of a Metamorph," *Kenyon Review* 15(4): 112-122. Fall 1993.

MOLL, RICHARD

___ Counts, Kyle. "Serious Heavy," *Starlog* No. 188: 54-58, 68. March 1993.

MOM AND DAD SAVE THE WORLD (MOTION PICTURE)

___ "Here's Hoping Mom and Dad Won't Procreate (Review)," *Los Angeles (CA) Daily News*. July 25, 1992. in: *NewsBank. Film and Television*. 82:C11. 1992.

___ Armstrong, David. "Mom, Dad Can't Save This Movie (Review)," *San Francisco (CA) Examiner*. July 27, 1992. in: *NewsBank. Film and Television*. 72:B5. 1992.

___ Biodrowski, Steve. "**Mom and Dad Save the World**," *Cinefantastique* 23(2/3): 22-23. October 1992.

___ Campbell, Bob. "Review," *Newark (NJ) Star-Ledger*. July 29, 1992. in: *NewsBank. Film and Television*. 72:B8. 1992.

___ Johnson, Malcolm. "They Want to Save the World, But They Can't Save the Movie (Review)," *Hartford (CT) Courant*. July 25, 1992. in: *NewsBank. Film and Television*. 72:B6. 1992.

___ Sherman, Paul. "**Mom/Dad** Is Just A **Bill and Ted** Reject (Review)," *Boston (MA) Herald*. July 25, 1992. in: *NewsBank. Film and Television*. 72:B7. 1992.

___ Torson, John. "**Mom and Dad Save the World** (Review)," *Cinefantastique* 23(4): 61. December 1992.

MOMMY (MOTION PICTURE)

___ Lundin, Steven J. "**Mommy** (Review)," *Cinefantastique* 27(3): 30-31. December 1995.

MONDO 2000 (MAGAZINE)

___ Sobchack, Vivian. "New Age Mutant Ninja Hackers: Reading *Mondo 2000*," *South Atlantic Quarterly* 92(4): 569-584. Fall 1993.

MONEY TRAIN (MOTION PICTURE)

___ Duncan, Jody. "**Money Train**: Training Film," *Cinefex* No. 64: 25-30, 134. December 1995.

MONITORS (MOTION PICTURE)

___ "Enter 2 U.S. Pix in Trieste's International Sci-Fi Film Fest," *Variety* p. 24. June 10, 1970.

MONOLITH MONSTERS (MOTION PICTURE)

___ Stephens, Bob. "Pre-tinsel Science Fiction Tales," *San Francisco (CA) Examiner* November 25, 1995. (Cited from the Internet Edition.)

MONOLITH (MOTION PICTURE)

___ Harris, Judith P. "**Monolith** (Review)," *Cinefantastique* 25(4): 60. August 1994.

MONSTER ON CAMPUS (MOTION PICTURE)

___ Stephens, Bob. "Pre-tinsel Science Fiction Tales," *San Francisco (CA) Examiner* November 25, 1995. (Cited from the Internet Edition.)

MONSTER THAT CHALLENGED THE WORLD (MOTION PICTURE)

___ Stephens, Bob. "United Artists **Sci-Fi Matinee**," *Films in Review* 46(9/10): 54-60. November/December 1995.

MONSTERS

___ Sarracino, Carmine. "Natural Law and the Monster," *Connecticut Review* 15(1): 23-32. Spring 1993.

MONTEITH, CHARLES

___ "Monteith, Charles (Obituary)," *Locus* 34(6): 66. June 1995.

MONTELEONE, THOMAS F.

___ "Bram Stoker Awards, 1993," *Science Fiction Chronicle* 14(10): 4. July 1993.

___ "HWA Stoker Awards Winners," *Locus* 31(2): 6, 62. August 1993.

MONTY PYTHON AND THE HOLY GRAIL (MOTION PICTURE)

___ Blanch, Robert J. "Gawain on Film," by Robert J. Blanch and Julian N. Wasserman. in: Harty, Kevin J., ed. **Cinema Arthuriana: Essays on Arthurian Film**. New York: Garland, 1991. pp.57-70.

___ Day, David D. "Monty Python and the Medieval Other," in: Harty, Kevin J., ed. **Cinema Arthuriana: Essays on Arthurian Film**. New York: Garland, 1991. pp.83-92.

MOON

___ MacKillop, Ian. "Fly Me to the Moon," *New Scientist* 144(1948): 51-52. October 22, 1994.

___ Wolff, Michael J. "Shooting for the Moon," *Starlog* No. 205: 41-45. August 1994.

MOON SHOT (TV)

___ Jarvis, Jeff. "Moon Struck," by Jeff Jarvis, James Reston, Jr., Glenn Kenny and Penelope Patsuris. *TV Guide* 42(29): 10-16. July 16, 1994.

MOON, ELIZABETH

___ "Elizabeth Moon: Question Assumptions," *Locus* 34(3): 4, 80-81. March 1995.

___ "Elizabeth Moon's Hunting Party: Space Opera With a Bit of Mystery," *Hailing Frequencies* (Waldenbooks) No. 7: 16-17, 19. 1993.

___ Jones, Katy H. "Interview With Elizabeth Moon," *Marion Zimmer Bradley's Fantasy Magazine* No. 22: 36-40. Winter 1994.

MOONSHADOW (COMIC)

___ Kilby, Damian. "Freed From a Cosmic Zoo, *Moonshadow* Seeks the Secrets of the Universe," *Science Fiction Age* 2(6): 84-86. September 1994.

MOORCOCK, MICHAEL

___ "British Fantasy Awards," *Science Fiction Chronicle* 15(2): 4. November/December 1993.

___ "Michael Moorcock: An Ongoing Dialog," *Locus* 31(4): 4, 73-74. October 1993.

___ Davey, John. **Michael Moorcock: A Reader's Guide**. London: John Davey, 1992. 35pp. Revised and Updated Edition.

___ Delville, Michel. "The Moorcock/Hawkwind Connection: Science Fiction and Rock'n'Roll Culture," *Foundation* No. 62: 64-63. Winter 1994/1995.

___ Greenland, Colin. **Michael Moorcock: Death Is No Obstacle**. Manchester, Eng.: Savoy, 1992. 146pp.

___ Nicholls, Stan. "Facing the Demons," *Starlog* No. 207: 52-57, 72. October 1994.

___ Nicholls, Stan. "Michael Moorcock Could Dignify It All," in: Nicholls, Stan. **Wordsmiths of Wonder: Fifty Interviews with Writers of the Fantastic**. London: Orbit, 1993. pp.111-124.

___ Nicholls, Stan. "Vegetable Love, Vaster Than Empires: Michael Moorcock and Tad Williams Interviewed," *Interzone* No. 91: 24-30. January 1995.

___ Schmitt, Ronald E. **The Reclamation of the Future Dream: Dreams in British Science Fiction (Mary Shelley, H. G. Wells, George Orwell, Michael Moorcock)**. Ph.D. Dissertation, University of Rhode Island, 1995. 182pp. (DAI-A 56/09, p. 3598. March 1996.)

___ Sneyd, Steve. "Michael Moorcock: Interview," *Star Line* 15(1): 3-5. 1992.

MOORE, ALAN
___ Winterton, Ian. "Yeti vs. The Bloodsuckers: Alan Moore Interviewed," *Interzone* No. 89: 28-30. November 1994.

MOORE, C. L.
___ Bloom, Harold. "C. L. Moore & Henry Kuttner," in: Bloom, Harold, ed. **Science Fiction Writers of the Golden Age**. New York: Chelsea House, 1995. pp.141-156.
___ Mueller, Allen. "A Wild Surmise," *Fantasy Commentator* 7(4): 282-285. Fall 1992. (Whole No. 44)

MOORE, CHRIS
___ Resnick, Mike. "Visions and Voyages," *Science Fiction Age* 3(2): 70-75. January 1995.

MOORE, HARRY B.
___ "Moore, Harry B. (Obituary)," *Science Fiction Chronicle* 17(1): 24. October/November 1995

MOORE, RON
___ Altman, Mark A. "*Star Trek: The Next Generation*: Ron Moore and Brannon Braga," *Cinefantastique* 24(3/4): 60-61. October 1993.

MOORE, TERRY
___ Weaver, Tom. "Monkey Business," *Starlog* No. 220: 59-63. November 1995.

MOORE, WARD
___ "Moore, Ward (Obituary)," *Science Fiction News* (Australia) No. 54: 10-11. April 1978.
___ Zebrowski, George. "Never Forget the Writers Who Helped Build Yesterday's Tomorrows," *Science Fiction Age* 3(6): 30-36, 100. 1995.

MORALITY
___ Lloyd, Donald G. "Renegade Robots and Hard-Wired Heroes: Technology and Morality in Contemporary Science Fiction Films," in: Loukides, Paul and Fuller, Linda K., eds. **Beyond the Stars III: The Material World in American Popular Film**. Bowling Green, OH: Popular Press, 1993. pp.216-228.

MORE, MAX
___ Platt, Charles. "Taking the N out of Entropy," *Science Fiction Eye* No. 13: 30-35. Spring 1994.

MORE, THOMAS
___ Baker-Smith, Dominic. **More's Utopia**. New York: HarperCollins Academic, 1991. 269pp.
___ Boswell, Jackson C. **Sir Thomas More in the English Renaissance: An Annotated Catalogue**. Binghamton, NY: Medieval & Renaissance Texts & Studies, 1994. 362pp.
___ Cantu, Francesca. "Scoperta del nuovo Mondo e visiione utopica nel cinquecento," in: Saccaro Del Buffa, Giuseppa and Lewis, Arthur O., eds. **Utopia e Modernita: Teorie e prassi utopiche nell'eta moderna e postmoderna**. Rome: Gangemi Editore, 1989. pp.749-775.
___ Corrado, Adriana. **Da un'isola all'altra: il pensiero utopico nella narrativa inglese da Thomas More ad Aldous Huxley**. Napoli: Scientifiche Italiane, 1988. 189pp. [Not seen.]
___ Freeman, John. "Discourse on More's **Utopia**: Pretext/Postscript," *ELH* 59(2): 289-312. Summer 1992.
___ Freeman, John. "More's Place in 'No Place': The Self-Fashioning Transaction in **Utopia**," *Texas Studies in Literature and Language* 34(2): 197-217. Summer 1992.
___ Gordon, Walter M. "Dialogue, Myth and More's Utopian Drama," *Cithara* 25(1): 19-34. November 1985.
___ Lange, Bernd-Peter. "Thomas More: **Utopia** (1516)," in: Heuermann, Hartmut and Lange, Bernd-Peter, eds. **Die Utopie in der angloamerikanischen Literatur: Interpretationen**. Düsseldorf: Bagel, 1984. pp.11-31.
___ Ludacer, Kenneth. "The Heaven and Hell of More's **Utopia**," *CEA Critic* 56(3): 66-73. Spring/Summer 1995.
___ Martz, Louis L. **Thomas More: The Search for the Inner Man**. New Haven, CT: Yale University Press, 1990. 112pp.
___ McCutcheon, Elizabeth. "Ten English Translations: Editions of Thomas More's **Utopia**," *Utopian Studies* 3(2): 102-120. 1992.
___ Pavkovic, Aleksandar. "Prosperity and Intellectual Needs: The Credibility and Coherence of More's **Utopia**," *Utopian Studies* 4(1): 26-37. 1993.

MORE, THOMAS (continued)
___ Quarta, Cosimo. "Le regioni della conservazione: Thomas More," in: Colombo, Arrigo and Quarta, Cosimo, eds. **Il Destino della Famiglia nell'Utopia**. Bari: Edizione Dedalo, 1991. pp.193-221.
___ Quarta, Cosimo. **Thomas More: Testimone della pace e della coscienza**. n.p.: Edizioni Cultura dell Pace, 1993. 231pp. [Not seen.]
___ Quarta, Cosimo. **Tommaso Moro: una reinterpretazone dell''Utopia'**. Bari: Edizioni Dedalo, 1991. 434pp. [Not seen.]
___ Renna, Thomas. "More's **Utopia** and English Medieval Traditions," in: Saccaro Del Buffa, Giuseppa and Lewis, Arthur O., eds. **Utopia e Modernita: Teorie e prassi utopiche nell'eta moderna e postmoderna**. Rome: Gangemi Editore, 1989. pp.739-748.
___ Rielly, Edward J. "Irony in **Gulliver's Travels** and **Utopia**," *Utopian Studies* 3(1): 70-83. 1992.
___ Wegemer, Gerald. "The City of God in Thomas More's **Utopia**," *Renascence* 44(2): 115-136. Winter 1992.

MORGAN, GLEN
___ Spelling, Ian. "**Space: Above and Beyond**," *Starlog* No. 220: 40-45. November 1995.
___ Vitaris, Paula. "Writers," *Starlog* No. 210: 61-64. January 1995.
___ Vitaris, Paula. "**X-Files**: Morgan and Wong," *Cinefantastique* 26(6)/27(1): 62. October 1995.

MORGNER, IRMTRAUD
___ Mabee, Barbara. "The Witch as Double: Feminist Doubles in German Literature and Irmtraud Morgner's **Amanda**," *Journal of the Fantastic in the Arts* 6(2/3): 166-190. 1994.

MORRIS, GLENN
___ Chapman, Mike. "Glenn Morris: Tarzan Number Eight," *Burroughs Bulletin* NS. No. 16: 8-15. October 1993.

MORRIS, JANET
___ "Morris, Janet (Ellen), 1946- ," in: Lesniak, James G., ed. **Contemporary Authors**. Detroit: Gale Research, 1992. New Revision Series, Vol. 35, pp.320-321.

MORRIS, KENNETH
___ Killheffer, Robert K. J. "The Legacy of Columbus: The Lost Races of Edward Myers and Kenneth Morris," *New York Review of Science Fiction* No. 44: 1, 3-6. April 1992.

MORRIS, WILLIAM
___ Baker, Leslie. "Morris and Music," *Journal of the William Morris Society* 10(3): 6-9. Autumn 1993.
___ Baker, Leslie. "Romantic Realities," *Journal of the William Morris Society* 10(1): 10-13. Autumn 1992.
___ Bloom, Harold. "William Morris," in: Bloom, Harold. **Classic Fantasy Writers**. New York: Chelsea House, 1994. pp.150-163.
___ Burns, Marjorie J. "Echoes of William Morris's **Icelandic Journals** in J. R. R. Tolkien," *Studies in Medievalism* 3(3): 367-373. Winter 1991.
___ Coleman, Stephen. "William Morris and Education Toward Revolution," *Journal of the William Morris Society* 11(1): 49-58. Autumn 1994.
___ Coote, Stephen. **William Morris: His Life and Work**. Godalming, U.K.: Sutton, 1995. 224pp.
___ Corrado, Adriana. **William Morris, News From Nowhere: cent'anni dopo**. Napoli: Guida Editori, 1992. 133pp. [Not seen.]
___ Davis, Virginia. "Morris and Indigo Darkness," *Journal of the William Morris Society* 11(3): 8-18. Autumn 1995.
___ Dewan, Pauline. "Patterns of Enclosure in Morris' Early Stories," *Journal of the William Morris Society* 11(2): 9-10. Spring 1995.
___ Eckert, Hans. "The Impact of Morris and the Kelmscott Press in Germany," *Journal of the William Morris Society* 11(2): 20-23. Spring 1995.
___ Eisenmann, Stephen. **Designing Utopia: The Art of William Morris and His Circle: Katonah Museum of Art, February 16 through April 12, 1992**. Katonah, NY: Katonah Museum of Art, 1992. 39pp.
___ Ellison, Ruth. "The Saga of Jón Jónsson Saddelsmith of Lithend-Cot," *Journal of the William Morris Society* 10(1): 21-30. Autumn 1992.
___ Faulkner, Peter. "Dark Days in Hammersmith: Lily Yates and the Morrises," *Journal of the William Morris Society* 11(3): 22-25. Autumn 1995.
___ Faulkner, Peter. "Morris and the Study of English," *Journal of the William Morris Society* 11(1): 26-30. Autumn 1994.

MORRIS, WILLIAM (continued)

___ Frow, Edmund. "Morris on Working Folk and the Future of Art," by Edmund Frow and Ruth Frow. *Journal of the William Morris Society* 11(3): 2-5. Autumn 1995.

___ Geoghegan, Vincent. "The Utopian Past: Memory and History in Edward Bellamy's **Looking Backward** and William Morris's **News From Nowhere**," *Utopian Studies* 3(2): 75-90. 1992.

___ Hansen, Regina. "Forms of Friendship in **The Roots of the Mountains**," *Journal of the William Morris Society* 11(3): 19-21. Autumn 1995.

___ Hartley, Eeyan. "Morris & Co. in a Baroque Setting," *Journal of the William Morris Society* 11(2): 5-8. Spring 1995.

___ Harvey, Charles. "William Morris and the Royal Commission on Technical Instruction, 1881-84," by Charles Harvey and Jon Press. *Journal of the William Morris Society* 11(1): 31-43. Autumn 1994.

___ Herbert, Isolde K. "Nature and Art: Morris's Conception of Progress," *Journal of the William Morris Society* 10(1): 4-9. Autumn 1992.

___ Heywood, Andrew. "Morris and Early Music: The Shaw/Dolmetsch Connection," *Journal of the William Morris Society* 10(4): 13-19. Spring 1994.

___ Hillgärtner, Rüdiger. "William Morris: **News from Nowhere; Or, an Epoch of Rest, Being Some Chapters from a Utopian Romance** (1890)," in: Heuermann, Hartmut and Lange, Bernd-Peter, eds. **Die Utopie in der angloamerikanischen Literatur: Interpretationen.** Düsseldorf: Bagel, 1984. pp.120-138.

___ Hollamby, Edward. "Address at the Birthday Party, 1993," *Journal of the William Morris Society* 10(3): 10-12. Autumn 1993.

___ Holm, Jan. "The Old Grumbler of Runnymede," *Journal of the William Morris Society* 10(2): 17-21. Spring 1993.

___ Kay, Ann. "William Morris and the National Curriculum," by Ann Kay and John Kay. *Journal of the William Morris Society* 11(1): 44-48. Autumn 1994.

___ Kumar, Krishan. "A Pilgrimage of Hope: William Morris's Journey to Utopia," *Utopian Studies* 5(1): 89-107. 1994.

___ Latham, David. **An Annotated Critical Bibliography of William Morris,** by David Latham and Sheila Latham. New York: St. Martin's, 1991. 423pp.

___ Latham, David. "William Morris: An Annotated Bibliography, 1990-1991," by David Latham and Sheila Latham. *Journal of the William Morris Society* 10(3): i-xxvii. Autumn 1993.

___ Latham, David. "William Morris: An Annotated Bibliography, 1992-1993," by David Latham and Sheila Latham. *Journal of the William Morris Society* 11(3): i-xx. Autumn 1995.

___ Ledger, Sally. "William Morris, Philip Webb, and Mark Rutherford," *Journal of the William Morris Society* 10(1): 14-20. Autumn 1992.

___ Levitas, Ruth. "Who Holds the Hose: Domestic Labour in the Work of Bellamy, Gilman and Morris," *Utopian Studies* 6(1): 65-84. 1995.

___ Londraville, Janis. "May Morris's Editing of 'So Many Stories Written Here'," *Journal of the William Morris Society* 10(1): 31-34. Autumn 1992.

___ Ludlow, Gregory. "Imagining the Future: Mercier's **L'an 2440** and Morris' **News From Nowhere**," *Comparative Literature Studies* 29(1): 20-38. 1992.

___ MacCarthy, Fiona. **William Morris: A Life for Our Times.** New York: Knopf, 1995. 780pp.

___ MacDonald, Alexander. "The Liveliness of **News From Nowhere**: Structure, Language, and Allusion," *Journal of the William Morris Society* 10(2): 22-26. Spring 1993.

___ Mackenzie, Jim. "Reminiscences of Cotswold Craftsmen," *Journal of the William Morris Society* 11(2): 27-31. Spring 1995.

___ Marsh, Jan. "A Note on Morris and Van Eyck," *Journal of the William Morris Society* 11(3): 6-7. Autumn 1995.

___ Mendelson, Michael. "**The Wood Beyond the World** and the Politics of Desire," *Essays in Literature* 18(2): 211-234. Fall 1991.

___ Mineo, Ady. "The Reverse of Salem House: The 'Holistic' Process of Education in **News From Nowhere**," *Journal of the William Morris Society* 11(1): 6-15. Autumn 1994.

___ Mohideen, Kerima. "Morris and Literacy," *Journal of the William Morris Society* 11(1): 19-25. Autumn 1994.

___ Mooney, Sue. "Self-Revelation in Morris's Unfinished Novel," *Journal of the William Morris Society* 10(2): 2-8. Spring 1993.

___ Morris, William. "Thoughts and Education Under Capitalism," *Journal of the William Morris Society* 11(1): 3-5. Autumn 1994.

___ Nichols, Ashton. "Liberationist Sexuality and Non-Violent Resistance: The Legacy of Blake and Shelley in Morris's **News From Nowhere**," *Journal of the William Morris Society* 10(4): 20-27. Spring 1994.

MORRIS, WILLIAM (continued)

___ Pendery, David. "Ernest Gimson's Works in Kelmscott," *Journal of the William Morris Society* 10(3): 13-18. Autumn 1993.

___ Purkis, John. "Morris and Traditional Storytelling," *Journal of the William Morris Society* 11(1): 16-18. Autumn 1994.

___ Redmond, James. "William Morris or Bernard Shaw: Two Faces of Victorian Socialism," in: Butt, J. and Clarke, I. F., eds. **The Victorians and Social Protest: A Symposium.** New York: David and Charles, 1973. pp.156-176.

___ Roberts, Helen E. "Commemorating William Morris: Robin Page Arnot and the Early History of the William Morris Society," *Journal of the William Morris Society* 11(2): 33-37. Spring 1995.

___ Rubens, Godfrey. "A Response to Godfrey Rubens," *Journal of the William Morris Society* 11(2): 26-27. Spring 1995.

___ Salmon, Nicholas. "The Revision of **A Dream of John Ball**," *Journal of the William Morris Society* 10(2): 15-16. Spring 1993.

___ Salmon, Nicholas. "Tropical Realism in **The Tables Turned**," *Journal of the William Morris Society* 11(2): 11-19. Spring 1995.

___ Seyer, Geoffrey. "'Morris Was a Giant': The Quest of T. E. Lawrence," *Journal of the William Morris Society* 10(4): 48-52. Spring 1994.

___ Sharp, Frank C. "A Lesson in International Relations: Morris and the SPAB," *Journal of the William Morris Society* 10(2): 9-14. Spring 1993.

___ Skoblow, Jeffrey. **Paradise Dislocated: Morris, Politics, Art.** Charlottesville: University Press of Virginia, 1993. 221pp.

___ Talbot, Norman. "'But He Were King, or Kinges Eyr...': Morris's Retelling of **Havelok**," *Journal of the William Morris Society* 10(4): 28-39. Spring 1994.

___ Thompson, Paul. **The Work of William Morris.** Third Edition. New York: Viking, 1991. 400pp.

___ Tyler, Wat. "An Interview with William Morris," *Journal of the William Morris Society* 10(3): 2-5. Autumn 1993.

___ Wingate, Arthur. "Working for Morris & Co.," *Journal of the William Morris Society* 11(2): 31-32. Spring 1995.

MORRISON, TONI

___ "Morrison, Rushdie Win Major Prizes," *Locus* 31(5): 6. November 1993.

___ Daily, Gary W. "Toni Morrison's **Beloved**: Rememory, History, and the Fantastic," in: Morse, Donald E., ed. **The Celebration of the Fantastic.** Westport, CT: Greenwood, 1992. pp.141-148.

___ Epstein, Grace A. "Out of the Blue Water: Dream Flight and Narrative Construction in the Novels of Toni Morrison," in: Ruddick, Nicholas, ed. **State of the Fantastic.** Westport, CT: Greenwood, 1992. pp.141-148.

MORROW, JAMES

___ "1995 World Fantasy Awards," *Locus* 35(6): 4, 81. December 1995.

___ "Nebula Award Winners, 1992," *Science Fiction Chronicle* 14(8): 4. May 1993.

___ "World Fantasy Awards, 1995," *Science Fiction Chronicle* 17(2): 5. December 1995/January 1996.

___ Bishop, Michael. "James Morrow and **Towing Jehovah**," *New York Review of Science Fiction* No. 67: 1, 8-11. March 1994.

MORROW, JEFF

___ Weaver, Tom. "Jeff Morrow," in: Weaver, Tom. **They Fought the Creature Features: Interviews with 23 Classic Horror, Science Fiction and Serial Stars.** Jefferson, NC: McFarland, 1995. pp.211-219.

MORROW, WILLIAM CHAMBERS

___ Moskowitz, Sam. "W. C. Morrow: Forgotten Master of Horror; First Phase," in: Schweitzer, Darrell, ed. **Discovering Classic Horror Fiction I.** Mercer Island, WA: Starmont, 1992. pp.127-173.

MORSE, BARRY

___ Eramo, Steven. "Space Refugee," *Starlog* No. 221: 47-51, 64. December 1995.

MORTAL KOMBAT (MOTION PICTURE)

___ Eby, Douglas. "**Mortal Kombat**: The Movie," *Cinefantastique* 26(5): 42. August 1995.

___ Eby, Douglas. "**Mortal Kombat**," *Cinefantastique* 26(4): 8-11. June 1995.

___ Felperin, Leslie. "**Mortal Kombat** (Review)," *Sight and Sound* 5(11): 47-48. November 1995.

MORTAL KOMBAT (MOTION PICTURE) (continued)
___ Griest, Stephanie. "***Mortal Kombat***'s Bloodless Coup," *Washington (DC) Post*. August 28, 1995. in: *NewsBank. Film and Television*. 79: B12-B13. 1995.
___ Hunter, Stephen. "As Cosmic Battles Go, Kombat's Merely Mortal," *(Baltimore, MD) Sun*. August 19, 1995. in: *NewsBank. Film and Television*. 79:B14. 1995.
___ Millar, Jeff. "It's Kombat," *Houston (TX) Chronicle*. August 21, 1995. in: *NewsBank. Film and Television*. 79:C1. 1995.
___ Riemenschneider, Chris. "Kombat Set to Battle New Terrain--And Critics," *Los Angeles (CA) Times*. August 24, 1995. in: *NewsBank. Film and Television*. 79:B8. 1995.
___ Weeks, Janet. "Is Faux Violence Less Violent?," *Los Angeles (CA) Daily News*. August 19, 1995. in: *NewsBank. Film and Television*. 79: B10-B11. 1995.

MORTAL KOMBAT: THE JOURNEY BEGINS (MOTION PICTURE)
___ Montesano, Anthony P. "***Mortal Kombat: The Journey Begins***," *Cinefantastique* 26(4): 10. June 1995.

MORTAL KOMBAT (VIDEO GAME)
___ Fletcher, Tanya A. "Deadly Games," *Sci-Fi Entertainment* 1(4): 78-84. December 1994.
___ Garcia, Robert T. "*Mortal Kombat*," *Cinefantastique* 26(5): 40-44. August 1995.

MORTE D'ARTHUR (MOTION PICTURE)
___ Purdon, Liam O. "Hollywood's Myopic Medievalism: ***Excalibur*** and Malory's **Morte d'Arthur**," by Liam O. Purdon and Robert J. Blanch. in: Slocum, Sally K., ed. **Popular Arthurian Traditions**. Bowling Green, OH: Popular Press, 1992. pp.156-161.

MOSCOE, MIKE
___ Klein, Jay K. "Biolog: Mike Moscoe," *Analog* 115(3): 93, 103. February 1995.

MOSKOWITZ, SAM
___ Moskowitz, Sam. "Collecting: A Form of Residual Research," *Foundation* No. 60: 13-20. Spring 1994.

MOTHERING
___ Laperriere, Maureen C. **The Evolution of Mothering: Images and Impact of the Mother-Figure in Feminist Utopian Science Fiction**. Master's Thesis, McGill University, 1994. 130pp. (Master's Abstracts. 33/04, p. 1076. August 1995.)

MOTION PICTURES
___ "Actor Dies on Horror Film Set," *Science Fiction Chronicle* 14(8): 5. May 1993.
___ "Arnold, Jack; Made Popular Science Fiction, Horror Films (Obituary)," *Los Angeles (CA) Times* Sec. A, p. 26. March 20, 1992.
___ "Bloody Good Times Just Around the Coroner," *New York (NY) Daily News*. January 24, 1993. in: *NewsBank. Film and Television*. 14:E12. 1993.
___ "Comic Book Types, TV Push Yields Japan's Sci-Fi Cat Hit," *Variety* p. 328. May 12, 1982.
___ "Cornel Wilde at MGM; Will Produce-Direct **Blade of Grass** Novel," *Variety* p. 4. November 5, 1969.
___ "Dancer Clones Self by Hologram in Diamant-Berger's Hi-Tech Pic," *Variety* p.367. October 16, 1985.
___ "Fear 'Stalk & Slash' Horror Saturation," *Variety* p. 7, 36. May 26, 1982.
___ "FHE, Harmony Pact for 'Robotech' Ani Series, Pic," *Variety* p.48. October 30, 1985.
___ "The Films," in: Brown, Michael, ed. **Pandemonium: Further Explorations into the Worlds of Clive Barker**. Staten Island, NY: Eclise, 1991. pp.55-70.
___ "French Try to Crack Sci-Fi Feature Film Field," *Variety* p. 53. February 3, 1982.
___ "Furst, Anton (Obituary)," *Science Fiction Chronicle* 13(4): 12. January 1992.
___ "***Gremlins*** Sweeps Saturn Ceremony," *Variety* p.6. June 19, 1985.
___ "Grim Fairy Tales: Universal Studios, 1931-1954," *Wonder* No. 7: 13-21. 1993.
___ "Helmer-Distrib Chung Says Fantasy Pics Don't Make It in South Korea," *Variety* p.44. October 9, 1985.

MOTION PICTURES (continued)
___ **Hoffman's Guide to SF, Horror and Fantasy Movies 1991-1992**. London: Corgi, 1991. 432pp. [Not seen.]
___ "Horror With Some Sexy Scenes Seen Cashable by Omen-Reading Mishkin," *Variety* p. 7. December 10, 1969.
___ "Incredible Shrinking Horror Market: Hi-Cost Scarepix Hurt; Output Down," *Variety* p. 7, 24. February 16, 1983.
___ "Israeli Poet's Pic Due at Trieste Sci-Fi Fest," *Variety* p. 36. May 5, 1982.
___ "Japanese Audiences Prefer Sci-Fi, Action Drama," *Variety* p. 346. May 4, 1982.
___ "Koontz vs. TriStar," *Locus* 34(4): 8, 68. April 1995.
___ "Lucasfilms Execs Outline 'Star Wars,' 'Raiders' Segs to Come; 'Jedi' Teasers," *Variety* p. 5. September 1, 1982.
___ "***Mad Max 2*** Preems in Japan; No. 1 Was Earner for Australia," *Variety* p. 33. December 9, 1981.
___ "Mantley Sues WB over Asimov Rights," *Variety* p. 6. September 5, 1984.
___ "Movie Nightmares," *Sight and Sound* 3(5): 30-39. May 1993.
___ "***Neverending Story*** Big Marks Gamble for Germany, But Film Has All Elements for Solid Hit," *Variety* p. 277, 299. March 2, 1983.
___ "Others Take Porno; Kirt Staying With Low-Cost Screams," *Variety* p. 6. July 22, 1970.
___ " 'Oz' Gross in Talks With Cannon About 'Robot' Presale Deal," *Variety* p.30, 121. November 20, 1985.
___ "Paramount: Defeats and Victories," *Locus* 32(1): 7, 64. January 1994.
___ "Phillips Plans 'Foundation Trilogy' for Back-to-Back Exhibition," *Variety* p. 6, 21. December 16, 1981.
___ "Pic Marketing Seminar to Create 'Campaign' for Vintage Sci-Fier," *Variety* p. 12, 30. February 8, 1984.
___ "Quest Fires Spate of Prehistoric Pix," *Variety* p. 48. February 3, 1982.
___ "Saturn Awards, 1993," *Locus* 31(2): 62-63. August 1993.
___ "Sci-fi Pen and Inker on Way From Laloux in Coprod With Spain," *Variety* p.366, 380. October 16, 1985.
___ "Seeing Nuke Panic, Germans Dump Pic From TV Schedule," *Variety* p. 116, 124. March 21, 1984.
___ "Shochiku to Herald Spacey 'Yamato' Pack," *Variety* p. 290. May 4, 1988.
___ "***Star Trek***: The Next Movie," *TV Guide* 41(30): 15. July 24, 1993.
___ "Survey Says Public Likes Sci-Fi, But Really Loves Comedy," *Variety* p. 22. September 22, 1982.
___ "Tackle 3-Level Tale; Geller Accepts Writing Challenge of 'Slaughterhouse'," *Variety* p. 5. May 13, 1970.
___ "Terror Master: Joe Dante," *Sight and Sound* 3(6): 7-9. June 1993.
___ "Tim Sullivan: SF Writer and Movie Mogul," *Science Fiction Age* 2(4): 22-23. May 1994.
___ "United Artists Grabs Kids' Tolkien," *Variety* p. 5. October 29, 1969.
___ "Upper-Teen 'Hobbits' As Boorman Feature for UA; Director Co-Scripting," *Variety* p. 22. July 1, 1970.
___ "***Valhalla*** First Danish Animation to Go Feature Length Since War," *Variety* p. 43. February 27, 1985.
___ "Wall Street Report: ***Star Trek***," *Wall Street Report* Program 636. December 3, 1994. (Transcript available.)
___ "Warner Brothers Buys Heinlein's Book," *Variety* p. 6. October 15, 1969.
___ "Yet to Roll 'Star Trek II' Seeks Six Weeks, 90-10, for June 1982," *Variety* p. 7, 37. November 18, 1981.
___ Abbott, Joe. "They Came From Beyond the Center: Ideology and Political Textuality in the Radical Science Fiction Films of James Cameron," *Literature/Film Quarterly* 22(1): 21-27. 1994.
___ Abrams, Janet. "Escape From Gravity," *Sight and Sound* 5(5): 14-19. May 1995.
___ Ackerman, Forrest J. **Famous Monsters of Filmland, Vol. 2 (Issues 51-100)**. Universal City, CA: Hollywood Publishing, 1991. 162pp.
___ Adamovic, Ivan. **Encyklopedie fantastického filmu**. Praha: Cinema, 1994. 224pp. [Not seen; OCLC record.]
___ Alexander, David. **Star Trek Creator: The Authorized Biography of Gene Roddenberry**. New York: Penguin/Roc, 1994. 599pp.
___ Altman, Mark A. "***Star Trek***: Paramount Turned Down Captain Kirk's Spec Script," *Cinefantastique* 23(4): 5. December 1992.
___ Anisfield, Nancy. "***Godzilla***/Gojiro: Evolution of the Nuclear Metaphor," *Journal of Popular Culture* 29(3): 53-62. Winter 1995.
___ Archer, Steve. **Willis O'Brien: Special Effects Genius**. Jefferson, NC: McFarland, 1993. 239pp.

MOTION PICTURES (continued)

___ Arnzen, Michael A. "Who's Laughing Now? The Postmodern Splatter Film," *Journal of Popular Film and Television* 21(4): 176-814. Winter 1993.

___ Aronstein, Susan. " 'Not Exactly a Knight': Arthurian Narrative and Recuperative Politics in the *Indiana Jones* Trilogy," *Cinema Journal* 34(4): 3-30. Summer 1995.

___ Atkins, Peter. **The Hellraiser Chronicles**. London: Titan, 1992. unpaged.

___ Atkins, Peter. "Other Shelves, Other Shadows: A Conversation With Clive Barker," in: Golden, Christopher, ed. **Cut! Horror Writers on Horror Film**. New York: Berkley, 1992. pp.11-24.

___ Atkinson, Mike. "Delirious Inventions," *Sight and Sound* 5(7): 12-16. July 1995.

___ Badley, Linda. **Film, Horror, and the Body Fantastic**. Westport, CT: Greenwood, 1995. 199pp.

___ Baillou, Charles. "Two Black Film Makers Ripped Off?," *Amsterdam News* p. 72. October 3, 1992.

___ Bansak, Edmund G. **Fearing the Dark: The Val Lewton Career**. Jefferson, NC: McFarland, 1995. 571pp.

___ Barker, Clive. "Trance of Innocence," *Sight and Sound* 5(12): 59. December 1995.

___ Barker, Lynn. "Klushantsev: Russia's Wizard of *Fantastika*, Part One," by Lynn Barker and Robert Skotak. *American Cinematographer* 75(6): 78-83. June 1994.

___ Barker, Lynn. "Klushantsev: Russia's Wizard of *Fantastika*, Part Two," by Lynn Barker and Robert Skotak. *American Cinematographer* 75(7): 77-82. July 1994.

___ Bartone, Richard C. "Variations on Arthurian Legend in **Lancelot du Lac** and **Excalibur**," in: Slocum, Sally K., ed. **Popular Arthurian Traditions**. Bowling Green, OH: Popular Press, 1992. pp.144-155.

___ Baumbold, Julie. "A Graveyard Smash," *Esquire* 123(1): 120, 118. January 1995.

___ Beard, William. "The Canadianness of David Cronenberg," *Mosaic* 27(2): 113-133. June 1994.

___ Beeler, Michael. "Clive Barker: Horror Visionary," *Cinefantastique* 26(3): 16-31. April 1995.

___ Beeler, Michael. "Clive Barker Producing Horror in Hollywood," *Cinefantastique* 26(3): 28-29. April 1995.

___ Berenbaum, May R. "Life History Strategies and Population Biology in Science Fiction Films," by May R. Berenbaum and Richard J. Leskosky. *Bulletin of the Ecological Society of America* 73(4): 236-240. December 1992.

___ Bernard, Jami. "Film Forum Fest Fulfills Fantasy, Horror, and Sci-Fi," *The New York (NY) National*. August 5, 1994. in: *NewsBank. Film and Television*. 93:C8. 1994.

___ Bernhardt, Peter. "Theatre of the Fantastic: Genius Squashed?," *Riverside Quarterly* 9(2): 94-95. August 1993. (Whole No. 34)

___ Bianco, Robert. "A Good Night for Good Fright," *Boston (MA) Herald*. October 30, 1993. in: *NewsBank. Film and Television,* 123:A6. 1993.

___ Bissette, Stephen R. "Higher Ground: Moral Transgressions, Tanscendent Fantasies," in: Golden, Christopher, ed. **Cut! Horror Writers on Horror Film**. New York: Berkley, 1992. pp.25-56.

___ Blake, Michael F. "The Dark Duo: Tod Browning and Lon Chaney, Sr.," *Filmfax* No. 43: 50-57, 97. February/March 1994.

___ Blake, Michael F. **Lon Chaney: The Man Behind the Thousand Faces**. Vestal, NY: Vestal Press, 1990. 394pp.

___ Blanch, Robert J. "Gawain on Film," by Robert J. Blanch and Julian N. Wasserman. in: Harty, Kevin J., ed. **Cinema Arthuriana: Essays on Arthurian Film**. New York: Garland, 1991. pp.57-70.

___ Bojarski, Richard. **The Complete Films of Bela Lugosi**. New York: Carol Publishing, 1992. 256pp. (Reissue of **The Films of Bela Lugosi**, 1980.)

___ Bonner, Frances J. "Separate Development: Cyberpunk in Film and TV," in: Slusser, George E. and Shippey, Tom, eds. **Fiction 2000: Cyberpunk and the Future of Narrative**. Athens: University of Georgia Press, 1992. pp.191-207.

___ Bonner, Frances J. **Stories of What Is to Come: The Future in Film and Television, 1959-1989**. Ph.D. Dissertation, Open University (Great Britain), 1991. 284pp. (DAI-A 53/09, p. 3028. March 1993.)

___ Borst, Ronald V., ed. **Graven Images: The Best of Horror, Fantasy, and Science Fiction Film Art from the Collection of Ronald V. Borst**, ed. by Ronald V. Borst, Keith Burns and Leith Adams. New York: Grove Press, 1992. 240pp.

___ Boswell, Thom. **The Costumemaker's Art: Cloaks of Fantasy, Masks of Revelation**. Asheville, NC: Lark Books, 1992. 144pp.

MOTION PICTURES (continued)

___ Bowman, David. "The Strange Odyssey of Helen Chandler," *Filmfax* No. 35: 67-72. October/November 1992.

___ Bowman, David. "They Called Him 'Herr Doktor': Edward Van Sloan," *Filmfax* No. 35: 63-66. October/November 1992.

___ Bowman, David. "A Tragically Miscast Comedian: Dwight Frye," *Filmfax* No. 35: 73-78. October/November 1992.

___ Bradley, Matthew R. "And in the Beginning Was the Word...: An Interview With Screenwriter Richard Matheson," *Filmfax* No. 42: 40-44, 78-80, 98. December 1993/January 1994.

___ Brandner, Gary. "No, But I Saw the Movie," in: Golden, Christopher, ed. **Cut! Horror Writers on Horror Film**. New York: Berkley, 1992. pp.57-66.

___ Broderick, Mick. "Surviving Armageddon: Beyond the Imagination of Disaster," *Science Fiction Studies* 20(3): 342-382. November 1993.

___ Brosch, Robert. **Horror Science Fiction Fantasy Movie Posters & Lobby Cards**. Allen Park, MI: Archival Photography, 1993. 79pp.

___ Bruschini, Antonio. **Mondi Incredibili: Il Cinema Fantastico-Avvneturoso Italiano**, by Antonio Bruschini and Antonio Tentori. Bologna: Granta Press, 1995. 173pp.

___ Cahir, Linda C. "Narratological Parallels in Joseph Conrad's **Heart of Darkness** and Francis Ford Coppola's **Apocalypse Now**," *Literature/ Film Quarterly* 20(3): 181-187. 1992.

___ Calhoun, John. "*The Journey Inside*," *TCI* 28(8): 78. October 1994.

___ Campbell, Ramsey. "The Quality of Terror," in: Golden, Christopher, ed. **Cut! Horror Writers on Horror Film**. New York: Berkley, 1992. pp.67-74.

___ Cantor, Joanne. "Children's Emotional Reactions to Technological Disasters Conveyed by the Mass Media," in: Wober, J. Mallory, ed. **Television and Nuclear Power: Making the Public Mind**. Norwood, NJ: Ablex, 1992. pp.31-54.

___ Caputi, Jane. "Films of the Nuclear Age," *Journal of Popular Film and Television* 16(3): 100-107. 1988.

___ Casella, Elaine. "Apeman, Arab, Ancient Alien: A Synopsis of Gene Roddenberry's Tarzan Script," *Burroughs Bulletin* NS. No. 22: 26-31. April 1995.

___ Casella, Elaine. "Two Sequels to **Greystoke**," *Burroughs Bulletin* NS. No. 14: 34-38. April 1993.

___ Catsos, Gregory J. M. "Priceless: A Farewell Interview With Vincent Price," *Filmfax* No. 42: 45-49. December 1993/January 1994.

___ Champlin, Charles. **George Lucas, the Creative Impulse: Lucasfilm's First Twenty Years**. New York: Abrams, 1992. 207pp.

___ Chang, Kenny. "Capitalism and the Concept of the Other: The Social Significance of Contemporary Hollywood Science Fiction Cinema," *Chung Wai Literary Quarterly* 22(12): May 1994. (Issue not seen; pagination unavailable.)

___ Chapman, Mike. "Glenn Morris: Tarzan Number Eight," *Burroughs Bulletin* NS. No. 16: 8-15. October 1993.

___ Clark, Mike. "The Master of Disaster," *Starlog* No. 176: 58-61. March 1992.

___ Clover, Carol J. "Her Body, Himself: Gender in the Slasher Film," in: Irons, Glenwood, ed. **Gender, Language and Myth: Essays on Popular Narrative**. Toronto: University of Toronto Press, 1992. pp.253-302.

___ Clover, Carol J. **Men, Women, and Chain Saws: Gender in the Modern Horror Film**. Princeton, NJ: Princeton University Press, 1992. 260pp.

___ Cohn, Lawrence. "Filmers Resort to Old Scare Tactics: Horror Film Resurgence Boosted by Video," *Variety* p. 1, 24. June 8, 1988.

___ Cohn, Lawrence. "Horrid Year for Horror Pix at B. O.," *Variety* p. 3, 36. January 25, 1984.

___ Collins, Nancy A. "The Place of Dreams," in: Golden, Christopher, ed. **Cut! Horror Writers on Horror Film**. New York: Berkley, 1992. pp.75-82.

___ Corbett, J. Martin. "Celluloid Projections: Images of Technology and Organizational Futures in Contemporary Science Fiction Film," *Organization* 2(3/4): 467-488. August/November 1995

___ Coriell, Vernell. "*The Son of Tarzan*: The Movie," *Burroughs Bulletin* NS. No. 18: 3-5. April 1994.

___ Costello, Matthew J. "Films, Television, and Dean Koontz," in: Greenberg, Martin H., Ed Gorman and Bill Munster, eds. **The Dean Koontz Companion**. New York: Berkley, 1994. pp.101-146.

___ Counts, Kyle. "Character Music," *Starlog* No. 183: 55-57, 70. October 1992.

___ Cox, Dan. "Rewriting the Rules," *Variety* 361(4): 6. November 27, 1995.

MOTION PICTURES (continued)

___ Crane, Jonathan L. **Terror and Everyday Life: A History of Horror.** Ph.D. Dissertation, University of Illinois at Urbana-Champaign, 1991. 297pp.

___ Crane, Jonathan L. **Terror and Everyday Life: Singular Moments in the History of the Horror Film.** Thousand Oaks, CA: Sage, 1994. 183pp.

___ Crisafulli, Chuck. "A Fan Turned Pro: A Guy Named Joe," *Filmfax* No. 38: 36-41, 72. April/May 1993.

___ Crisafulli, Chuck. "The Monstrous Genius of Jack Pierce," *Filmfax* No. 35: 36-39, 80-81. October/November 1992.

___ D'Alessandro, Kathryn C. **Mixed Competence: The Tendency Toward Hybridization in Post-1976 Science Fiction Films.** Ph.D. Dissertation, University of Wisconsin, Madison, 1992. 308pp. (DAI-A 3/03, p. 649-650. 1992.)

___ Davidson, Jim. "*The Thing* About Filmmaker Christian Nyby," *Filmfax* No. 34: 36-46. August/September 1992.

___ Day, David D. "Monty Python and the Medieval Other," in: Harty, Kevin J., ed. **Cinema Arthuriana: Essays on Arthurian Film.** New York: Garland, 1991. pp.83-92.

___ de Weever, Jacqueline. "Morgan and the Problem of Incest," in: Harty, Kevin J., ed. **Cinema Arthuriana: Essays on Arthurian Film.** New York: Garland, 1991. pp.145-156.

___ Deist, Thomas. "Laßt die Puppen tanzen! Eine möglicher neuer Impuls im Horror-Genre und seine Geschichte," *Science Fiction Times* (Germany) 34(1): 12-16. January 1992.

___ Del Vecchio, Deborah. **Peter Cushing: The Gentle Man of Horror and His 91 Films**, by Deborah Del Vecchio and Tom Johnson. Jefferson, NC: McFarland, 1992. 496pp.

___ Dellavalle, Renato. "Horror a basso costo," *Cineforum* 30(11): 67-78. 1990.

___ Dery, Mark. "Cyberculture," *South Atlantic Quarterly* 91(3): 501-523. Summer 1992.

___ Dettman, Bruce. "Children and Chills," *Filmfax* No. 31: 34-37. February/March 1992.

___ Di Fate, Vincent. "Creature Capsules," *Science Fiction Chronicle* 13(11/12): 38-42. August 1992.

___ Dick, Philip K. "Universe Makers... and Breakers," *Radio Free P.K.D.* No. 1: 1,8. February 1993.

___ Dobbs, G. Michael. "Stanley Wiater: A Conversation with the Interviewer," in: Wiater, Stanley. **Dark Visions: Conversations with the Masters of the Horror Film.** New York: Avon, 1992. pp.1-7.

___ Donald, Ralph R. "The *Mary Ann*, the *Ruptured Duck* and the *Enterprise*: Character Relationships with Air and Space Craft as Metaphors for Human Affinities," in: Loukides, Paul and Fuller, Linda K., eds. **Beyond the Stars III: The Material World in American Popular Film.** Bowling Green, OH: Popular Press, 1993. pp.123-133.

___ Dubeck, Leroy W. **Fantastic Voyages: Learning Science Through Science Fiction Films.** New York: American Institute of Physics, 1994. 327pp.

___ Dubeck, Leroy W. "Finding the Facts in Science Fiction Films," by Leroy W. Dubeck, Suzanne E. Moshier, Matthew H. Bruce and Judith E. Boss. *Science Teacher* 60(4): 46-48. April 1993.

___ Ellerbee, Linda. "Movie Offers a Dose of Reality," *Austin (TX) American Statesman* Sec. A, p. 13. June 18, 1993.

___ Ellison, Harlan. "Me 'N' Isaac at the Movies: A Brief Memoir of Citizen Calvin," *Science Fiction Age* 3(1): 78-83. November 1994.

___ Erickson, John. "The Ghost in the Machine: Gilliam's Postmodern Response in *Brazil* to the Orwellian Dystopia of **Nineteen Eighty-Four**," *Utopian Studies* 4(2): 26-34. 1993.

___ Evans, Greg. "Indies Head of Genre Pic Middle Ground," *Variety* 359(4): 7, 22. May 22, 1995.

___ Evans, Walter. "Monster Movies and Rites of Initiation," *Journal of Popular Film and Television* 4(2): 124-142. 1975.

___ Evans-Karastamatis, Joyce A. **Celluloid Mushroom Clouds: Hollywood and the Atomic Bomb.** Ph.D. Dissertation, University of California, San Diego, 1993. 432pp. (DAI-A 54/06, p. 1986. December 1993.)

___ Everman, Welch D. **Cult Science Fiction Films: From the Amazing Colossal Man to Yog, the Monster From Space.** Secaucus, NJ: Carol Publishing Group, 1995. 255pp.

___ Farinotti, Pino. **Dizionarion dei film de fantascienza e horror.** Carnago, Italy: SugarCo, 1993. 174pp.

___ Farris, John. "A User's Guide to Hollywood Horror (As Told to Kelley Wilde)," in: Golden, Christopher, ed. **Cut! Horror Writers on Horror Film.** New York: Berkley, 1992. pp.83-90.

MOTION PICTURES (continued)

___ Felchner, William J. "Science Fiction Movie Posters," *Antiques & Collecting Magazine* 99(9): 40-43. November 1994.

___ Fischer, Dennis. "The Amicus Empire: An Interview With Milton Subotsky," *Filmfax* No. 42: 54-61, 96-97. December 1993/January 1994.

___ Fischer, Dennis. "Charles Band: Full Moon Mogul," *Cinefantastique* 26(4): 16-49. June 1995.

___ Fitting, Peter. "What Is Utopian Film? An Introductory Taxonomy," *Utopian Studies* 4(2): 1-17. 1993.

___ Fitting, Peter. "You're History, Buddy: Postapocalyptic Visions in Recent Science Fiction Film," in: Slusser, George and Eric S. Rabkin, eds. **Fights of Fancy: Armed Conflict in Science Fiction and Fantasy.** Athens, GA: University of Georgia Press, 1993. pp.114-131.

___ Fletcher, Tanya A. "Deadly Games," *Sci-Fi Entertainment* 1(4): 78-84. December 1994.

___ Flinn, Caryl. **Strains of Utopia: Gender, Nostalgia, and Hollywood Film Music.** Princeton, NJ: Princeton University Press, 1992. 195pp.

___ Flixman, Ed. "*Judge Dredd*, *Casper*, and *Congo* Top a Bumper Crop of Genre Blockbusters," *Science Fiction Age* 3(4): 18-23. May 1995.

___ Flynn, John L. **Cinematic Vampires: The Living Dead on Film and Televison, From *The Devil's Castle* (1896) to *Bram Stoker's Dracula* (1992).** Jefferson, NC: McFarland, 1992. 328pp.

___ Friedman, Regien-Mihal. "Capitals of Sorrow: From *Metropolis* to *Brazil*," *Utopian Studies* 4(2): 35-43. 1993.

___ Fuchs, Cynthia J. "Death Is Irrelevant': Cyborgs, Reproduction, and the Future of Male Hysteria," *Genders* No. 18: 113-133. Winter 1993. Also in: Gray, Chris H., ed. **The Cyborg Handbook.** New York: Routledge, 1995. pp.281-300.

___ Fury, David. "Johnny Weissmuller...The Two Career Star," *Burroughs Bulletin* NS. No. 14: 19-28. April 1993.

___ Fury, David. **Kings of the Jungle: An Illustrated Reference to 'Tarzan' on Screen and Television.** Jefferson, NC: McFarland, 1993. 272pp.

___ Fury, David. "Maureen O'Sullivan: A Jewel of a Jane," *Burroughs Bulletin* NS. No. 15: 3-10. July 1993.

___ Gabilondo, Joseba. **Cinematic Hyperspace: New Hollywood Cinema and Science Fiction Film: Image Commodification in Late Capitalism.** Ph.D. Dissertation, University of California, San Diego, 1992. (DAI-A 53/01, p. 5. July 1992.)

___ Galbraith, Stuart, IV. "*Godzilla*'s American Cousin: The Eclectic Career of Henry G. Saperstein," *Filmfax* No. 45: 59-63. June/July 1994.

___ Galbraith, Stuart, IV. "The How to of Making a Monster Movie: An Interview with AIP Producer Herman Cohen," *Filmfax* No. 37: 43-49. February/March 1993.

___ Galbraith, Stuart, IV. **Japanese Science Fiction, Fantasy and Horror Films: A Critical Analysis and Filmography of 103 Features Released in the United States, 1950-1992.** Jefferson, NC: McFarland, 1994. 424pp.

___ Galligan, John. "They Came From Outer Space--And Moved to the 'Burbs," by John Galligan and Jon Haber. *Boston (MA) Globe* Sec. B, p. 29. July 25, 1993.

___ Galvan, Dave. "Comic Book Heroes: From Panel to Screen," *Sci-Fi Entertainment* 1(6): 42-47, 73. April 1995.

___ Garcia, Robert T. "The Amazing Colossal Movies: Inspiration and Legal Hassles," *Cinefantastique* 23(1): 21. August 1992.

___ Gardner, Craig S. "Blood and Laughter: The Humor in Horror Film," in: Golden, Christopher, ed. **Cut! Horror Writers on Horror Film.** New York: Berkley, 1992. pp.91-100.

___ Garton, Ray. "On Kids and *Cat People*," in: Golden, Christopher, ed. **Cut! Horror Writers on Horror Film.** New York: Berkley, 1992. pp.101-112.

___ Gelman, Morrie. "Sunbow Takes to Marvel Like Duck to Water in Animation," *Variety* p. 81, 98. September 17, 1986.

___ Gire, Dann. "Band on the Run," *Cinefantastique* 23(5): 46, 61. February 1993.

___ Goldberg, Lee. **The Dreamweavers: Interviews with Fantasy Filmmakers of the 1980s**, by Lee Goldberg, Randy Lofficier, Jean-Marc Lofficier and William Rabkin. Jefferson, NC: McFarland, 1995. 320pp.

___ Goldberg, Lee, ed. **Science Fiction Filmmaking in the 1980s: Interviews with Actors, Directors, Producers and Writers**, ed. by Lee Goldberg, Randy Lofficier, Jean-Marc Lofficier and William Rabkin. Jefferson, NC: McFarland, 1995. 279pp.

___ Golden, Christopher. "Introduction: First Cut," in: Golden, Christopher, ed. **Cut! Horror Writers on Horror Film.** New York: Berkley, 1992. pp.1-9.

MOTION PICTURES (continued)

___ Golden, Christopher, ed. **Cut! Horror Writers on Horror Film.** New York: Berkley, 1992. 297pp.

___ Goodsell, Greg. "The Weird and Wacky World of Larry Buchanan," *Filmfax* No. 38: 60-66. April/May 1993.

___ Gordon, Andrew. "You'll Never Get out of Bedford Falls: The Inescapable Family in American Science Fiction and Fantasy Films," *Journal of Popular Film and Television* 20(2): 2-8. Summer 1992.

___ Gorman, Ed. "Several Hundred Words About Wes Craven," in: Golden, Christopher, ed. **Cut! Horror Writers on Horror Film.** New York: Berkley, 1992. pp.113-116.

___ Grant, Barry K. "Looking Upwards: Reason and the Visible in Science Fiction Film," in: Irons, Glenwood, ed. **Gender, Language and Myth: Essays on Popular Narrative.** Toronto: University of Toronto Press, 1992. pp.185-207.

___ Grant, Barry K. "Taking Back *The Night of the Living Dead*: George Romero, Feminism and the Horror Film," *Wide Angle* 14(1): 64-77. January 1992.

___ Grant, Charles L. "Black and White, in Color," in: Golden, Christopher, ed. **Cut! Horror Writers on Horror Film.** New York: Berkley, 1992. pp.117-122.

___ Grebe, Coralee. "Tarot Card Symbolism in the *Star Wars* Films," *Mythlore* 20(2): 27-31. Spring 1994. (Whole No. 76)

___ Green, Steve. "Of Midwich, Moonmen and Monoliths: A Brief Guide to British SF & F Cinema in the Sixties," *Lan's Lantern* No. 41: 64-68. July 1993.

___ Greene, Eric. **Planet of the Apes as American Myth: Race and Politics in the Films and Television Series.** Jefferson, NC: McFarland, 1995. 264pp.

___ Greiff, Louis K. "Soldier, Sailor, Surfer, Chef: Conrad's Ethics and the Margins of *Apocalypse Now*," *Literature/Film Quarterly* 20(3): 188-197. 1992.

___ Grellner, Mary A. "Two Films That Sparkle: *The Sword in the Stone* and *Camelot*," in: Harty, Kevin J., ed. **Cinema Arthuriana: Essays on Arthurian Film.** New York: Garland, 1991. pp.71-83.

___ Grey, Rudolph. **Nightmare of Ecstasy: The Life and Art of Edward D. Wood, Jr.** Los Angeles, CA: Feral House Press, 1992. 231pp.

___ Griffin, Scott T. "Woody Strode: An Epic Life Remembered," *Burroughs Bulletin* NS. No. 22: 18-25. April 1995.

___ Gross, Edward. **The Making of the Trek Films.** 2nd rev. ed., by Edward Gross and Mark A. Altman. East Meadow, NY: Image Publishing, 1992. 162pp.

___ Gross, Larry. "Big and Loud," *Sight and Sound* 5(8): 6-11. August 1995.

___ Gunn, James E. "Television and *The Immortal*," in: Gunn, James E. **Inside Science Fiction: Essays on Fantastic Literature.** San Bernardino, CA: Borgo, 1992. pp.113-117.

___ Gunn, James E. "The Tinsel Screen," in: Gunn, James E. **Inside Science Fiction: Essays on Fantastic Literature.** San Bernardino, CA: Borgo, 1992. pp.101-112.

___ Gunter, Barrie. "The Impact of Nuclear Fiction in Britain: *The Day After* and *Threads*," by Barrie Gunter and M. Svennevig. in: Wober, J. Mallory, ed. **Television and Nuclear Power: Making the Public Mind.** Norwood, NJ: Ablex, 1992. pp.55-66.

___ Guttmacher, Peter. **Legendary Horror Films: Essential Genre History; Offscreen Anecdotes; Special Effects Secrets; Ghoulish Facts and Photographs.** New York: Metro Books, 1995. 128pp.

___ Hall, Mia M. "Love Kills: Another Look at *Fatal Attraction*," in: Golden, Christopher, ed. **Cut! Horror Writers on Horror Film.** New York: Berkley, 1992. pp.123-130.

___ Hanke, Ken. **A Critical Guide to Horror Film Series.** New York: Garland, 1991. 341pp.

___ Hanke, Ken. "Tod Slaughter: Demon Barber of Great Britain," *Filmfax* No. 45: 31-35, 98. June/July 1994.

___ Hardy, Phil. **The Overlook Film Encyclopedia: Science Fiction.** Woodstock, NY: Overlook Press, 1994. 478pp.

___ Hardy, Phil, ed. **The Overlook Film Encyclopedia: Science Fiction.** Third edition. Woodstock, NY: Overlook, 1995. 512pp.

___ Harty, Kevin J. "Appendix: An Alphabetical Filmography," in: Harty, Kevin J., ed. **Cinema Arthuriana: Essays on Arthurian Film.** New York: Garland, 1991. pp.245-247.

___ Harty, Kevin J. "A Bibliography on Arthurian Film," in: Harty, Kevin J., ed. **Cinema Arthuriana: Essays on Arthurian Film.** New York: Garland, 1991. pp.203-243.

MOTION PICTURES (continued)

___ Harty, Kevin J. "Camelot Twice Removed: *Knightriders* and the Film Versions of **A Connecticut Yankee in King Arthur's Court**," in: Harty, Kevin J., ed. **Cinema Arthuriana: Essays on Arthurian Film.** New York: Garland, 1991. pp.105-120.

___ Harty, Kevin J. "Teaching Arthurian Film," in: Fries, Maureen and Watson, Jeanie, eds. **Approaches to the Teaching of the Arthurian Tradition.** New York: Modern Language Association, 1992. pp.147-150.

___ Harty, Kevin J., ed. "The Arthurian Legend on Film: An Overview," in: Harty, Kevin J., ed. **Cinema Arthuriana: Essays on Arthurian Film.** New York: Garland, 1991. pp.3-28.

___ Harty, Kevin J., ed. **Cinema Arthuriana: Essays on Arthurian Film.** New York: Garland, 1991. 255pp.

___ Hasumi, Shigehiko. "Über die Nichtexistenz des SF-Films," *Quarber Merkur* 33(2): 21-24. December 1995. (No. 84)

___ Hatcher, Lint. "Monster Fan 2000," by Lint Hatcher and Rod Bennett. *Wonder* No. 7: 39-43, 54-56. 1993.

___ Haycock, Kate. **Science Fiction Films.** New York: Crestwood House, 1992. 32pp.

___ Henderson, Ed. "The Big Green Guy," *Starlog* 180: 29-31, 73. July 1992.

___ Henenlotter, Frank. "Films From Under the Floorboards," *Sci-Fi Entertainment* 1(6): 52-57. April 1995.

___ Hofstede, David. **Hollywood and the Comics: Film Adaptations of Comic Books and Scripts.** Las Vegas, NV: Zanne-3, 1991. 198pp.

___ Hogan, David J. "Art of the Fright: Celebrating the Life of Vincent Price," *Filmfax* No. 42: 32-39, 94-95. December 1993/January 1994.

___ Holder, Nancy. "Why *The Haunting* Is So Damn Scary," in: Golden, Christopher, ed. **Cut! Horror Writers on Horror Film.** New York: Berkley, 1992. pp.131-140.

___ Horne, Philip. "I Shopped With a Zombie," *Critical Quarterly* 34(4): 97-110. Winter 1992.

___ Hornig, Susanna. "Digital Delusions: Intelligent Computers in Science Fiction Film," in: Loukides, Paul and Fuller, Linda K., eds. **Beyond the Stars III: The Material World in American Popular Film.** Bowling Green, OH: Popular Press, 1993. pp.207-215.

___ Houghton, Hal. **Ripley, Believe It or Not: The 'Alien' Trilogy and the Image of Women in Science Fiction Film.** Master's Thesis, Mankato State University, 1993. 106pp.

___ Hougron, Alexandra. "La couleur de l'Autre: Le rouge et le vert dans les films de science fiction," *Positif* no. 375: 143-146. May 1992.

___ Hunt, Leon. "A (Sadistic) Night at the Opera: Notes on the Italian Horror Film," *Velvet Light Trap* 30: 65-75. 1992.

___ Iaccino, James F. **Psychological Reflections on Cinematic Terror: Jungian Archetypes in Horror Films.** Westport, CT: Praeger, 1994. 217pp.

___ Iwao, Sumiko. "*The Day After* in Japan," in: Wober, J. Mallory, ed. **Television and Nuclear Power: Making the Public Mind.** Norwood, NJ: Ablex, 1992. pp.67-76.

___ Jackson, Kevin. "The Good, the Bad, and the Ugly," *Sight and Sound* 2(3): 10-11. July 1992.

___ Jackson, Kevin. "Gothic Shadows," *Sight and Sound* 2(7): 16-19. 1992. [Not seen.]

___ Jackson, Kevin. "The Trappings of Disaster: Sci-Fi's Bygone Dystopias," *Sight and Sound* 3(5): 38-39. May 1993.

___ James, Caryn. "Old Hollywood Horror, But With Depth and Flair," *New York Times* Sec. C, p. 3. July 2, 1993.

___ Jancovich, Mark. **Horror.** London: Batsford, 1992. 128pp.

___ Jankiewicz, Pat. "*Godzilla*, American Style," *Starlog* No. 193: 55. August 1993.

___ Jones, Alan. "Mutant Action: Science Fiction Splatter Boosted by Spain's Pedro Almodovar," *Cinefantastique* 24(5): 48-49. December 1993.

___ Jones, Stephen. **The Illustrated Dinosaur Movie Guide.** London: Titan, 1993. 144pp.

___ Kaspersen, Flemming. "Tech Noir: blod, teknologi og fremtidsvisioner fra 2001 til Sidste Udkald," *Kosmorama* 36(No. 194): 12-16. 1990.

___ Katovich, Michael A. "The Stories Told in Science Fiction and Social Science: Reading *The Thing* and Other Remakes From Two Eras," by Michael A. Katovich and Patrick T. Kinkade. *Sociological Quarterly* 34(4): 619-651. 1993.

___ Katz, Ephriam. **The Film Encyclopedia.** 2nd Ed. New York: Harper Perennial, 1994. 1496pp.

___ Ke, Fan. "Science Fiction Film Calls for Environmental Protection: *Legend of the Celestial Sphere* Directed by Wei Judang," *Beijing Review* 38(37): 34. September 11, 1995.

MOTION PICTURES (continued)

___ Kenny, Glenn. "OscarVision," *TV Guide* 42(12): 58. March 19, 1994.

___ Kerman, Judith B. "Virtual Space and Its Boundaries in Science Fiction Film and Television: *Tron, Max Headroom, War Games*," in: Morse, Donald E., ed. **The Celebration of the Fantastic.** Westport, CT: Greenwood, 1992. pp.191-204.

___ Kermode, Mark. "Endnotes," *Sight and Sound* 4(6): 71. June 1994.

___ Kermode, Mark. "Ghoul School: The Horror Genre," *Sight and Sound* 3(6): 10-12. June 1993.

___ Kimmel, Dan. "Sci-Fi Festival Is a Giant Sit for Mankind," *Variety* 354(4): 38. February 26, 1994.

___ Kinnard, Roy. **Horror in the Silent Films: A Filmography, 1896-1929.** Jefferson, NC: McFarland, 1995. 256pp.

___ Kinnard, Roy, ed. **The Lost World of Willis O'Brien: The Original Shooting Script of the 1925 Landmark Special Effects Dinosaur Film, with Photographs.** Jefferson, NC: McFarland, 1993. 176pp.

___ Klossner, Michael. "Science Fiction in Film, Television, and Radio," in: Barron, Neil, ed. **Anatomy of Wonder 4.** New York: Bowker, 1995. pp.612-650.

___ Klossner, Michael. "Word and Image: A Survey of Fantastic Film & TV Magazines," *SFRA Newsletter* No. 194: 10-15. January/February 1992.

___ Kolker, Robert P. "The Moving Image Reclaimed," *Postmodern Culture* 5(1): [6pp., with imbedded motion picture full-motion clips in MPEG]. September 1994. (Electronic Journal: pmc@jefferson.village.virginia.edu).

___ Kozloff, Sarah R. "Superman as Saviour: Christian Allegory in the Superman Movies," *Journal of Popular Film and Television* 9(2): 78-82. 1981.

___ Kubey, Robert W. "U.S. Opinion and Politics Before and After **The Day After**: Television Movie as Rorschach," in: Wober, J. Mallory, ed. **Television and Nuclear Power: Making the Public Mind.** Norwood, NJ: Ablex, 1992. pp.19-30.

___ Kuhn, Annette. "Border Crossing," *Sight and Sound* 2(3): 11-12. July 1992.

___ Lacy, Norris J. "Mythopoeia in *Excalibur*," in: Harty, Kevin J., ed. **Cinema Arthuriana: Essays on Arthurian Film.** New York: Garland, 1991. pp.121-134.

___ Landon, Brooks. **The Aesthetics of Ambivalence: Rethinking Science Fiction Film in the Age of Electronic (Re) Production.** Westport, CT: Greenwood, 1992. 224pp.

___ Lansdale, Joe R. "A Hard-On for Horror: Low-Budget Excitement," in: Golden, Christopher, ed. **Cut! Horror Writers on Horror Film.** New York: Berkley, 1992. pp.141-150.

___ Larson, Randall D. **Film into Books: An Analytical Bibliography of Film Novelizations, Movie and TV Tie-Ins.** Metuchen, NJ: Scarecrow Press, 1995. 608pp.

___ Latham, Robert A. "Subterranean Suburbia: Underneath the Smalltown Myth in Two Versions of *Invaders From Mars*," *Science Fiction Studies* 22(2): 198-208. July 1995.

___ Leeper, Mark R. "An Analytical Filmography of Ray Harryhausen," *Lan's Lantern* No. 41: 33-35. July 1993.

___ Leeper, Mark R. "A Brief Filmography of Arthurian Films," *Lan's Lantern* No. 43: 40-42. March 1995.

___ Lenihan, John H. "Superweapons From the Past," in: Loukides, Paul, ed. **The Material World in American Popular Film.** Bowling Green, OH: Popular Press, 1993. pp.164-174.

___ Lentz, Harris M., III. **Science Fiction, Horror & Fantasy Film and Television Credits Supplement 2: Through 1993.** Jefferson, NC: McFarland, 1994. 854pp.

___ Lerner, Jesse. "Face the Nation: The Filmic Formulation of National Identity," *Afterimage* 21(5): 8-10. December 1993.

___ Liberti, Fabrizio. "I grandi classici della fantascienza," *Cineforum* 34(4): 90-92. 1994.

___ Liberti, Fabrizio. "Pe regie de Roger Corman in vista della *Factory*" [Roger Corman and Science Fiction in *Factory*]. *Cineforum* 31(9): 18-21. 1991.

___ Liebfred, Philip. "The Cinema Legacy of a Literary Legend: H. Rider Haggard," *Filmfax* No. 30: 67-71. December 1991/January 1992.

___ Liebfred, Philip. "H. Rider Haggard on the Screen," *Films in Review* 46(7/8): 20-29. September/October 1995.

___ Linaweaver, Brad. "I Sing the Image Electric: Ray Bradbury Goes to Hollywood," by Brad Linaweaver and Rod Bennett. *Wonder: The Children's Magazine for Grown-Ups* No. 8: 10-17. 1995.

___ Liu, Albert. "The Last Days of Arnold Schwarzenegger," *Genders* No. 18: 102-112. Winter 1993.

MOTION PICTURES (continued)

___ Lloyd, Ann. **The Films of Stephen King.** New York: St. Martin's, 1993. 96pp.

___ Lloyd, Donald G. "Renegade Robots and Hard-Wired Heroes: Technology and Morality in Contemporary Science Fiction Films," in: Loukides, Paul and Fuller, Linda K., eds. **Beyond the Stars III: The Material World in American Popular Film.** Bowling Green, OH: Popular Press, 1993. pp.216-228.

___ Lometti, Guy E. "Broadcast Preparations for and Consequences of *The Day After*," in: Wober, J. Mallory, ed. **Television and Nuclear Power: Making the Public Mind.** Norwood, NJ: Ablex, 1992. pp.3-18.

___ Lopez, Daniel. **Films by Genre: 775 Categories, Styles, Trends and Movements Defined, with a Filmography for Each.** Jefferson, NC: McFarland, 1993. 519pp.

___ Lovece, Frank. "Filmmakers See Future: Science Fiction," *Los Angeles (CA) Times* p.F1. November 9, 1994.

___ Lupack, Alan. "An Enemy in Our Midst: *The Black Knight* and the American Dream," in: Harty, Kevin J., ed. **Cinema Arthuriana: Essays on Arthurian Film.** New York: Garland, 1991. pp.29-40.

___ MacGillivray, Scott. "Astor Pictures," *Filmfax* No. 43: 36-41. February/March 1994.

___ Maertens, James W. "Between Jules Verne and Walt Disney: Brains, Brawn, and Masculine Desire in **20,000 Leagues Under the Sea**," *Science Fiction Studies* 22(2): 209-225. July 1995.

___ Mandell, Paul. "Harryhausen Animates Annual Sci-Tech Awards," *American Cinematographer* 73(5): 73-74. May 1992.

___ Manels, Andy. **Star Wars: The Essential Guide to Characters.** New York: Del Rey, 1995. 199pp.

___ Mank, Gregory W. **Hollywood Cauldron: Thirteen Horror Films From the Genre's Golden Age.** Jefferson, NC: McFarland, 1993. 384pp.

___ Martani, Marco. "Horror party con brididi a basso costo [Fantafestival 1992: The 12th International Rome Film Festival of Science Fiction and Horror]," *Cineforum* 32(9): 38-39. 1992.

___ Martani, Marco. "Roma: Fantafestival; Concorso d'autore senza l'orrore," *Cineforum* 30(7/8): 31-33. 1990.

___ Martinez Montalban, Jorge L. "Entre la ciencia y la ficcion: avatares de un genero cinematografico [Between Science and Fiction: Transformations of a Cinematic Genre (The Science Fiction Film)]," *Arbor - Ciencia Pensamiento y Cultura* 145(569): 39-54. May 1993.

___ Maslin, Janet. "*Godzilla Clomp!* Bestrides the Ages," *New York Times* p.H13. March 14, 1993.

___ Matheson, T. J. "Marcuse, Ellul, and the Science-Fiction Film: Negative Responses to Technology," *Science-Fiction Studies* 19(3): 326-339. November 1992.

___ Matheson, T. J. "Triumphant Technology and Minimal Man: **The Technological Society**, Science Fiction Films, and Ridley Scott's **Alien**," *Extrapolation* 33(3): 215-229. Fall 1992.

___ Maurstad, Tom. "Future Tense," *Dallas (TX) Morning News.* July 30, 1995. in: *NewsBank. Film and Television.* 80:E9-E11. 1995.

___ Mayer, Peter C. "Film, Ontology and the Structure of a Novel," *Film Literature Quarterly* 8(3): 204-208. 1980.

___ Mayo, Mike. "Successful Low-Budget SF Film-making Is Itself an Act of Science Fiction," *Science Fiction Age* 2(4): 20-23, 33-34. May 1994.

___ McCarty, John. **John McCarty's Official Splatter Movie Guide, Vol. II.** New York: St. Martin's, 1992. 199pp.

___ McCarty, John. **Movie Psychos and Madmen: Film Psychopaths From Jekyll and Hyde to Hannibal Lecter.** Secaucus, NJ: Carol, 1993. 255pp.

___ McCarty, John. **Psychos: Eighty Years of Mad Movies, Maniacs, and Murderous Deeds.** New York: St. Martin's, 1986. 211pp.

___ McDonagh, Maitland. "The Ultimate Joe Dante Interview," *Sci-Fi Entertainment* 1(1): 42-46, 62. June 1994.

___ McDonald, T. Liam. "The Horrors of Hammer: The House That Blood Built," in: Golden, Christopher, ed. **Cut! Horror Writers on Horror Film.** New York: Berkley, 1992. pp.151-160.

___ McDonnell, David. **Starlog's Science Fiction Heroes and Heroines.** New York: Crescent Books, 1995. 93pp.

___ McGee, Mark T. "Full Moon's Effects Master," *Cinefantastique* 23(5): 47-49. February 1993.

___ McMunn, Meradith T. "Filming the Tristan Myth: From Text to Icon," in: Harty, Kevin J., ed. **Cinema Arthuriana: Essays on Arthurian Film.** New York: Garland, 1991. pp.169-180.

___ Melehy, Hassan. "Images Without: Deleuzian Becoming, Science Fiction Cinema in the Eighties," *Postmodern Culture* 5(2): [19pp.] January 1995. (Electronic Journal: pmc@jefferson.village.virginia.edu).

MOTION PICTURES (continued)

___ Shelton, Robert. "The Utopian Film Genre: Putting Shadows on the Silver Screen," *Utopian Studies* 4(2): 18-25. 1993.

___ Sherman, Paul. "Cyberpunk Film Festival Is Pure Sci-Fi Splendor," *Boston (MA) Herald*. March 15, 1994. in: *NewsBank. Film and Television*. 31:G5. 1994.

___ Skal, David J. "Drive-Ins Are a Ghoul's Best Friend: Horror in the Fifties," *New York Review of Science Fiction* No. 53: 1, 8-16. January 1993.

___ Skal, David J. "The Graveyard Bash: Horror in the Sixties," *New York Review of Science Fiction* No. 56: 1, 8-13. April 1993. (From: **The Monster Show: A Cultural History of Horror**. New York: Norton, 1993.)

___ Skipp, John. "Death's Rich Pageantry, or Skipp and Spector's Handy-Dandy Splatterpunk Guide to the Horrors of Non-Horror Film," by John Skipp and Craig Spector. in: Golden, Christopher, ed. **Cut! Horror Writers on Horror Film.** New York: Berkley, 1992. pp.237-254.

___ Smetak, Jacqueline R. "Summer at the Movies: Steven Spielberg: Gore, Guts, and PG-13," *Journal of Popular Film and Television* 14(1): 4-13. 1986.

___ Smith, Don G. **Lon Chaney, Jr.: Horror Film Star, 1906-1993.** Jefferson, NC: McFarland, 1995. 272pp.

___ Smith, Starita. "Horror Flicks of Today May Mar Kids Tomorrow," *Austin (TX) American Statesman* Sec. B, p. 1, 8. June 16, 1993.

___ Solman, Gregory. "The Illusion of a Future," *Film Comment* 28(2): 32-41. March/April 1992.

___ Springer, Claudia. "Muscular Circuitry: The Invincible Armored Cyborg in Cinema," *Genders* No. 18: 87-101. Winter 1993.

___ Stanley, John. **The Creature Features Movie Guide Strikes Again: Fourth Revised Edition.** Pacifica, CA: Large Press, 1994. 454pp.

___ Stanley, John. "Early Soviet Space-Race Victory," *San Francisco (CA) Chronicle* Sec. DAT, p. 34. April 12, 1992.

___ Stanley, John. "An Evening of Androids, Humanoids and Robots," *San Francisco (CA) Chronicle* Sec. C, p. 3. March 13, 1993.

___ Staskowski, Andrea. **Science Fiction Movies.** Minneapolis MN: Lerner, 1992. 80pp.

___ Stephens, Bob. "Persistent Vision: Unforgettable Poster Art From the Golden Age of Science Fiction Movies," by Bob Stephens and Vincent Di Fate. *Sci-Fi Entertainment* 1(2): 48-51. August 1994.

___ Stud Brothers. "Sci-Fi Fidelity: The Best and Worst SF Motion Pictures," *Melody Maker* 72(32): 36. August 12, 1995.

___ Sulski, Jim. "False Futures," *Chicago Tribune* Sec. 5, p. 6. January 7, 1993.

___ Swires, Steve. "Quartermaster," *Starlog* No. 183: 58-62, 70. October 1992.

___ Taubin, Amy. "Bloody Tales," *Sight and Sound* 5(1): 8-11. January 1995.

___ Taubin, Amy. "Invading Bodies: **Alien 3** and the Trilogy," *Sight and Sound* 2(3): 8-10. 1992. [Not seen.]

___ Tautkus, Marjorie R. **Salvation at the Cinema: Religious References in American Science Fiction Films of the 1980's.** Master's Thesis, Old Dominion University, 1992. 93pp. (Master's Abstracts, 31/04, p. 1413. Winter 1993.)

___ Taylor, Philip M. **Steven Spielberg: The Man, His Movies, and Their Meaning.** New York: Continuum, 1992. 176pp.

___ Telotte, J. P. "In the Realm of the Revealing: The Technological Double in the Contemporary Science Fiction Film," *Journal of the Fantastic in the Arts* 6(2/3): 234-252. 1994.

___ Telotte, J. P. **Replications: A Robotic History of the Science Fiction Film.** Champaign: University of Illinois Press, 1995. 222pp.

___ Telotte, J. P. "**The Terminator, Terminator 2**, and the Expanded Body," *Journal of Popular Film and Television* 20(2): 26-34. Summer 1992.

___ Telotte, J. P. "**The World of Tomorrow** and the 'Secret Goal' of Science Fiction," *Journal of Film and Video* 45(1): 27-39. Spring 1993.

___ Thomas, Tony. **The Best of Universal.** Vestal, NY: Vestal Press, 1990. 102pp.

___ Thompson, Raymond H. "The Ironic Tradition in Arthurian Films Since 1960," in: Harty, Kevin J., ed. **Cinema Arthuriana: Essays on Arthurian Film.** New York: Garland, 1991. pp.93-104.

___ Tohill, Cathal. **Immoral Tales: European Sex and Horror Movies, 1956-1984**, by Cathal Tohill and Pete Tombs. New York: St. Martin's Griffin, 1995. 272pp.

___ Travers, Peter. "Reel Projections: When Movie-Makers Imagine the Future, the Ending Is Rarely Happy," *House and Garden* 164(1): 94-95. January 1992.

___ Turan, Kenneth. "**Blade Runner** 2," *Radio Free P.K.D.* No. 1: 2-3, 9. February 1993.

MOTION PICTURES (continued)

___ Tushnet, Rebecca L. **Fire With Firepower: Women in Recent Science Fiction Blockbuster Movies.** Thesis, A. B. Honors in Social Studies, Harvard University, 1995. 153pp.

___ Uram, Sue. "Dead Auteur: Sam Raimi, Tyro Director," *Cinefantastique* 23(1): 28-29. August 1992.

___ Ursini, James. **More Things Than Are Dreamt Of: Masterpieces of Supernatural Horror, From Mary Shelley to Stephen King, in Literature and Film**, by James Ursini and Alain Silver. New York: Limelight, 1994. 226pp.

___ Van Hise, James. **Hot Blooded Dinosaur Movies.** Las Vegas, NV: Pioneer, 1993. 179pp.

___ Van Hise, James. **The Man Who Created Star Trek: Gene Roddenberry.** Las Vegas, NV: Pioneer Books, 1992. 156pp.

___ Vaughn, Thomas. "Voices of Sexual Distortion: Rape, Birth, and Self-Annihilation Metaphors in the **Alien** Trilogy," *Quarterly Journal of Speech* 81(4): 423-435. November 1995.

___ Vince, Nick. "More Than a Face," in: Brown, Michael, ed. **Pandemonium: Further Explorations into the Worlds of Clive Barker.** Staten Island, NY: Eclise, 1991. pp.83-86.

___ Vivona, Stephen T. "The Films of Val Lewton and Boris Karloff," *Filmfax* No. 44: 50-56. April/May 1994.

___ Voger, Mark. "Gorilla My Screams; Or, How My Life With Movie Monsters Made a Monkey out of Me," *Filmfax* No. 36: 43-48, 98. December 1992/January 1993.

___ Von Gunden, Kenneth. **Postmodern Auteurs: Coppola, Lucas, De Palma, Spielberg and Scorcese.** Jefferson, NC: McFarland, 1991. 200pp.

___ Wachhorst, Wyn. "The Dream of Spaceflight: Nostalgia for a Bygone Future," *Massachusetts Review* 36(1): 7-32. Spring 1995.

___ Warren, Bill. "Other People's Dreams," *Starlog* No. 200: 36-39, 90. March 1994.

___ Warren, Bill. "Producer in the Cupboard," *Starlog* No. 218: 36-39. September 1995.

___ Warren, Bill. "Spengo's Greatest Director," *Starlog* 177: 63-66. April 1992.

___ Watt-Evans, Lawrence. "The Movies Invented Typecasting, But SF Made It an Art," *Science Fiction Age* 3(3): 34-36. March 1995.

___ Weaver, Tom. "Ann Robinson: Interview," in: Weaver, Tom, ed. **Attack of the Monster Movie Makers: Interviews with 20 Genre Giants.** Jefferson, NC: McFarland, 1994. pp.289-308.

___ Weaver, Tom. "Anne Francis," in: Weaver, Tom. **They Fought the Creature Features: Interviews with 23 Classic Horror, Science Fiction and Serial Stars.** Jefferson, NC: McFarland, 1995. pp.161-172.

___ Weaver, Tom. "Ben Chapman: Interview," in: Weaver, Tom, ed. **Attack of the Monster Movie Makers: Interviews with 20 Genre Giants.** Jefferson, NC: McFarland, 1994. pp.31-44.

___ Weaver, Tom. "Betsy Jones-Moreland: Interview," in: Weaver, Tom, ed. **Attack of the Monster Movie Makers: Interviews with 20 Genre Giants.** Jefferson, NC: McFarland, 1994. pp.175-194.

___ Weaver, Tom. "Billy Benedict," in: Weaver, Tom. **They Fought the Creature Features: Interviews with 23 Classic Horror, Science Fiction and Serial Stars.** Jefferson, NC: McFarland, 1995. pp.61-72.

___ Weaver, Tom. "Cameron Mitchell: Interview," in: Weaver, Tom, ed. **Attack of the Monster Movie Makers: Interviews with 20 Genre Giants.** Jefferson, NC: McFarland, 1994. pp.209-228.

___ Weaver, Tom. "Candace Hilligoss: Interview," in: Weaver, Tom, ed. **Attack of the Monster Movie Makers: Interviews with 20 Genre Giants.** Jefferson, NC: McFarland, 1994. pp.145-156.

___ Weaver, Tom. "Charles Bennett: Interview," in: Weaver, Tom, ed. **Attack of the Monster Movie Makers: Interviews with 20 Genre Giants.** Jefferson, NC: McFarland, 1994. pp.17-30

___ Weaver, Tom. "Director of Dinosaurs," *Starlog* No. 193: 63-68. August 1993.

___ Weaver, Tom. "Don Taylor," in: Weaver, Tom. **They Fought the Creature Features: Interviews with 23 Classic Horror, Science Fiction and Serial Stars.** Jefferson, NC: McFarland, 1995. pp.263-276.

___ Weaver, Tom. "Ed Nelson: Interview," in: Weaver, Tom, ed. **Attack of the Monster Movie Makers: Interviews with 20 Genre Giants.** Jefferson, NC: McFarland, 1994. pp.229-248.

___ Weaver, Tom. "Eugene Lourie," in: Weaver, Tom. **They Fought the Creature Features: Interviews with 23 Classic Horror, Science Fiction and Serial Stars.** Jefferson, NC: McFarland, 1995. pp.201-210.

___ Weaver, Tom. "George Wallace," in: Weaver, Tom. **They Fought the Creature Features: Interviews with 23 Classic Horror, Science Fiction and Serial Stars.** Jefferson, NC: McFarland, 1995. pp.277-287.

MOTION PICTURES (continued)

___ Weaver, Tom. "Harry Spalding: Interview," in: Weaver, Tom, ed. **Attack of the Monster Movie Makers: Interviews with 20 Genre Giants**. Jefferson, NC: McFarland, 1994. pp.319-338.

___ Weaver, Tom. "Herbert Rudley: Interview," in: Weaver, Tom, ed. **Attack of the Monster Movie Makers: Interviews with 20 Genre Giants**. Jefferson, NC: McFarland, 1994. pp.309-318.

___ Weaver, Tom. "Herman Cohen: Interview," in: Weaver, Tom, ed. **Attack of the Monster Movie Makers: Interviews with 20 Genre Giants**. Jefferson, NC: McFarland, 1994. pp.45-84.

___ Weaver, Tom. "Jacques Marquette: Interview," in: Weaver, Tom, ed. **Attack of the Monster Movie Makers: Interviews with 20 Genre Giants**. Jefferson, NC: McFarland, 1994. pp.195-208.

___ Weaver, Tom. "Jane Wyatt," in: Weaver, Tom. **They Fought the Creature Features: Interviews with 23 Classic Horror, Science Fiction and Serial Stars**. Jefferson, NC: McFarland, 1995. pp.289-302.

___ Weaver, Tom. "Jeanne Bates," in: Weaver, Tom. **They Fought the Creature Features: Interviews with 23 Classic Horror, Science Fiction and Serial Stars**. Jefferson, NC: McFarland, 1995. pp.50-60.

___ Weaver, Tom. "Jeff Morrow," in: Weaver, Tom. **They Fought the Creature Features: Interviews with 23 Classic Horror, Science Fiction and Serial Stars**. Jefferson, NC: McFarland, 1995. pp.211-219.

___ Weaver, Tom. "John Agar," in: Weaver, Tom. **They Fought the Creature Features: Interviews with 23 Classic Horror, Science Fiction and Serial Stars**. Jefferson, NC: McFarland, 1995. pp.13-24.

___ Weaver, Tom. "John Archer," in: Weaver, Tom. **They Fought the Creature Features: Interviews with 23 Classic Horror, Science Fiction and Serial Stars**. Jefferson, NC: McFarland, 1995. pp.37-49.

___ Weaver, Tom. "Julie Adams," in: Weaver, Tom. **They Fought the Creature Features: Interviews with 23 Classic Horror, Science Fiction and Serial Stars**. Jefferson, NC: McFarland, 1995. pp.1-11.

___ Weaver, Tom. "June Lockhart," in: Weaver, Tom. **They Fought the Creature Features: Interviews with 23 Classic Horror, Science Fiction and Serial Stars**. Jefferson, NC: McFarland, 1995. pp.187-199.

___ Weaver, Tom. "Kenneth Tobey: Interview," in: Weaver, Tom, ed. **Attack of the Monster Movie Makers: Interviews with 20 Genre Giants**. Jefferson, NC: McFarland, 1994. pp.339-356.

___ Weaver, Tom. "Killer Brains and Giant Women," *Starlog* No. 187: 57-61, 69. February 1993.

___ Weaver, Tom. "Lloyd Bridges," in: Weaver, Tom. **They Fought the Creature Features: Interviews with 23 Classic Horror, Science Fiction and Serial Stars**. Jefferson, NC: McFarland, 1995. pp.85-96.

___ Weaver, Tom. "Lori Nelson," in: Weaver, Tom. **They Fought the Creature Features: Interviews with 23 Classic Horror, Science Fiction and Serial Stars**. Jefferson, NC: McFarland, 1995. pp.221-232.

___ Weaver, Tom. "Louise Currie," in: Weaver, Tom. **They Fought the Creature Features: Interviews with 23 Classic Horror, Science Fiction and Serial Stars**. Jefferson, NC: McFarland, 1995. pp.131-143.

___ Weaver, Tom. "Lupita Tovar: Interview," in: Weaver, Tom, ed. **Attack of the Monster Movie Makers: Interviews with 20 Genre Giants**. Jefferson, NC: McFarland, 1994. pp.357-365.

___ Weaver, Tom. "Man With a Plan (9)," *Starlog* No. 208: 59-67. November 1994.

___ Weaver, Tom. "Mark Goddard," in: Weaver, Tom. **They Fought the Creature Features: Interviews with 23 Classic Horror, Science Fiction and Serial Stars**. Jefferson, NC: McFarland, 1995. pp.173-186.

___ Weaver, Tom. "Merry Anders: Interview," in: Weaver, Tom, ed. **Attack of the Monster Movie Makers: Interviews with 20 Genre Giants**. Jefferson, NC: McFarland, 1994. pp.1-16.

___ Weaver, Tom. "Monkey Business," *Starlog* No. 220: 59-63. November 1995.

___ Weaver, Tom. "The Oldest Living Screenwriter Explains All," *Starlog* No. 193: 57-62, 71. August 1993.

___ Weaver, Tom. **Poverty Row Horrors! Monogram, PRC and Republic Horror Films of the Forties**. Jefferson, NC: McFarland, 1993. 376pp.

___ Weaver, Tom. "The Producer From Lands Unknown (Part Three)," *Starlog* No. 219: 57-64. October 1995.

___ Weaver, Tom. "The Producer From Outer Space (Part One)," *Starlog* No. 217: 57-65. August 1995.

___ Weaver, Tom. "The Producer From the Black Lagoon (Part Two)," *Starlog* No. 218: 57-63, 65. September 1995.

___ Weaver, Tom. "Rex Reason," in: Weaver, Tom. **They Fought the Creature Features: Interviews with 23 Classic Horror, Science Fiction and Serial Stars**. Jefferson, NC: McFarland, 1995. pp.233-243.

MOTION PICTURES (continued)

___ Weaver, Tom. "Richard Anderson," in: Weaver, Tom. **They Fought the Creature Features: Interviews with 23 Classic Horror, Science Fiction and Serial Stars**. Jefferson, NC: McFarland, 1995. pp.25-36.

___ Weaver, Tom. "Richard Denning," in: Weaver, Tom. **They Fought the Creature Features: Interviews with 23 Classic Horror, Science Fiction and Serial Stars**. Jefferson, NC: McFarland, 1995. pp.145-160.

___ Weaver, Tom. "Ricou Browning," in: Weaver, Tom. **They Fought the Creature Features: Interviews with 23 Classic Horror, Science Fiction and Serial Stars**. Jefferson, NC: McFarland, 1995. pp.97-109.

___ Weaver, Tom. "Robert Cornthwaite," in: Weaver, Tom. **They Fought the Creature Features: Interviews with 23 Classic Horror, Science Fiction and Serial Stars**. Jefferson, NC: McFarland, 1995. pp.111-130.

___ Weaver, Tom. "Robert Day: Interview," in: Weaver, Tom, ed. **Attack of the Monster Movie Makers: Interviews with 20 Genre Giants**. Jefferson, NC: McFarland, 1994. pp.85-97.

___ Weaver, Tom. "Rose Hobart: Interview," in: Weaver, Tom, ed. **Attack of the Monster Movie Makers: Interviews with 20 Genre Giants**. Jefferson, NC: McFarland, 1994. pp.157-174.

___ Weaver, Tom. "Susan Hart: Interview," in: Weaver, Tom, ed. **Attack of the Monster Movie Makers: Interviews with 20 Genre Giants**. Jefferson, NC: McFarland, 1994. pp.127-144

___ Weaver, Tom. **They Fought in the Creature Features: Interviews with 23 Classic Horror, Science Fiction and Serial Stars**. Jefferson, NC: McFarland, 1995. 328pp.

___ Weaver, Tom. "Tuhan Bey," in: Weaver, Tom. **They Fought the Creature Features: Interviews with 23 Classic Horror, Science Fiction and Serial Stars**. Jefferson, NC: McFarland, 1995. pp.73-83.

___ Weaver, Tom. "Val Guest: Interview," in: Weaver, Tom, ed. **Attack of the Monster Movie Makers: Interviews with 20 Genre Giants**. Jefferson, NC: McFarland, 1994. pp.99-126.

___ Weaver, Tom. "Vincent Price: Interview," in: Weaver, Tom, ed. **Attack of the Monster Movie Makers: Interviews with 20 Genre Giants**. Jefferson, NC: McFarland, 1994. pp.267-288.

___ Weaver, Tom. "William Phipps: Interview," in: Weaver, Tom, ed. **Attack of the Monster Movie Makers: Interviews with 20 Genre Giants**. Jefferson, NC: McFarland, 1994. pp.249-266.

___ Weaver, Tom. "William Schallert," in: Weaver, Tom. **They Fought the Creature Features: Interviews with 23 Classic Horror, Science Fiction and Serial Stars**. Jefferson, NC: McFarland, 1995. pp.245-262.

___ Weaver, Tom, ed. **Attack of the Monster Movie Makers: Interviews With 20 Genre Giants**. Jefferson, NC: McFarland, 1994. 384pp.

___ Wells, Paul. "The Invisible Man: Shrinking Masculinity in the 1950s Science Fiction B-Movie," in: Kirkham, Pat, and Thumim, Janet, ed. **You Tarzan: Masculinity, Movies, and Men**. New York: St. Martin's, 1993. pp.181-199.

___ Westfahl, Gary. "Extracts From the **The Biographical Encyclopedia of Science Fiction Film**," *Foundation* No. 64: 45-69. Summer 1995.

___ Westfahl, Gary. " 'Man Against Man, Brain Against Brain': The Transformation of Melodrama in Science Fiction," in: Redmond, James, ed. **Melodrama**. Cambridge: Cambridge University Press, 1992. pp.193-211.

___ Wharton, Lawrence. "**Godzilla** to **Latitude Zero**: The Cycle of the Technological Monster," *Journal of Popular Film and Television* 3(1): 31-38. 1974.

___ Whitaker, Muriel. "Fire, Water, Rock: Elements of Setting in **Excalibur**," in: Harty, Kevin J., ed. **Cinema Arthuriana: Essays on Arthurian Film**. New York: Garland, 1991. pp.135-144.

___ Whitty, Stephen. "Run For Your Life! It's Your Inner Godzilla," *San Jose (CA) Mercury News*. July 8, 1994. in: *NewsBank. Film and Television*. 81:C14. 1994.

___ Wiater, Stanley. "Barker, Clive," in: Wiater, Stanley. **Dark Visions: Conversations with the Masters of the Horror Film**. New York: Avon, 1992. pp.9-18.

___ Wiater, Stanley. "Carpenter, John," in: Wiater, Stanley. **Dark Visions: Conversations with the Masters of the Horror Film**. New York: Avon, 1992. pp.19-28.

___ Wiater, Stanley. "Cohen, Larry," in: Wiater, Stanley. **Dark Visions: Conversations with the Masters of the Horror Film**. New York: Avon, 1992. pp.29-38.

___ Wiater, Stanley. "Corman, Roger," in: Wiater, Stanley. **Dark Visions: Conversations with the Masters of the Horror Film**. New York: Avon, 1992. pp.39-46.

MOTION PICTURES

MOTION PICTURES (continued)
___ Wiater, Stanley. "Craven, Wes," in: Wiater, Stanley. **Dark Visions: Conversations with the Masters of the Horror Film.** New York: Avon, 1992. pp.47-56.
___ Wiater, Stanley. "Cronenberg, David," in: Wiater, Stanley. **Dark Visions: Conversations with the Masters of the Horror Film.** New York: Avon, 1992. pp.57-66.
___ Wiater, Stanley. **Dark Visions: Conversations with the Masters of the Horror Film.** New York: Avon, 1992. 228pp.
___ Wiater, Stanley. "Disturbo 13: The Most Disturbing Horror Films Ever Made," in: Golden, Christopher, ed. **Cut! Horror Writers on Horror Film.** New York: Berkley, 1992. pp.255-266.
___ Wiater, Stanley. "Englund, Robert," in: Wiater, Stanley. **Dark Visions: Conversations with the Masters of the Horror Film.** New York: Avon, 1992. pp.67-76.
___ Wiater, Stanley. "Gordon, Stuart," in: Wiater, Stanley. **Dark Visions: Conversations with the Masters of the Horror Film.** New York: Avon, 1992. pp.77-88.
___ Wiater, Stanley. "Hurd, Gale Ann," in: Wiater, Stanley. **Dark Visions: Conversations with the Masters of the Horror Film.** New York: Avon, 1992. pp.89-100.
___ Wiater, Stanley. "McDowell, Michael," in: Wiater, Stanley. **Dark Visions: Conversations with the Masters of the Horror Film.** New York: Avon, 1992. pp.101-110.
___ Wiater, Stanley. "Munro, Caroline," in: Wiater, Stanley. **Dark Visions: Conversations with the Masters of the Horror Film.** New York: Avon, 1992. pp.111-118.
___ Wiater, Stanley. "Nolan, William F.," in: Wiater, Stanley. **Dark Visions: Conversations with the Masters of the Horror Film.** New York: Avon, 1992. pp.119-128.
___ Wiater, Stanley. "Price, Vincent," in: Wiater, Stanley. **Dark Visions: Conversations with the Masters of the Horror Film.** New York: Avon, 1992. pp.129-136.
___ Wiater, Stanley. "Raimi, Sam," in: Wiater, Stanley. **Dark Visions: Conversations with the Masters of the Horror Film.** New York: Avon, 1992. pp.137-146.
___ Wiater, Stanley. "Romero, George A.," in: Wiater, Stanley. **Dark Visions: Conversations with the Masters of the Horror Film.** New York: Avon, 1992. pp.147-158.
___ Wiater, Stanley. "Sammon, Paul M.," in: Wiater, Stanley. **Dark Visions: Conversations with the Masters of the Horror Film.** New York: Avon, 1992. pp.219-226.
___ Wiater, Stanley. "Savini, Tom," in: Wiater, Stanley. **Dark Visions: Conversations with the Masters of the Horror Film.** New York: Avon, 1992. pp.159-166.
___ Wiater, Stanley. "Smith, Dick," in: Wiater, Stanley. **Dark Visions: Conversations with the Masters of the Horror Film.** New York: Avon, 1992. pp.167-178.
___ Wiater, Stanley. "Stefano, Joseph," in: Wiater, Stanley. **Dark Visions: Conversations with the Masters of the Horror Film.** New York: Avon, 1992. pp.179-188.
___ Wiater, Stanley. "Winston, Stan," in: Wiater, Stanley. **Dark Visions: Conversations with the Masters of the Horror Film.** New York: Avon, 1992. pp.189-198.
___ Wiater, Stanley. "Yagher, Kevin," in: Wiater, Stanley. **Dark Visions: Conversations with the Masters of the Horror Film.** New York: Avon, 1992. pp.199-208.
___ Wiater, Stanley. "Yuzna, Brian," in: Wiater, Stanley. **Dark Visions: Conversations with the Masters of the Horror Film.** New York: Avon, 1992. pp.209-218.
___ Willens, Michelle. "Making Films That Go Straight to Video--By Design," *New York Times* Sec. 2, p. 22. September 19, 1993.
___ Williams, Linda. "Learning to Scream," *Sight and Sound* 4(12): 14-17. December 1994.
___ Williams, Lucy C. **The Complete Films of Vincent Price.** New York: Citadel, 1995. 287pp.
___ Winter, Douglas E. "Opera of Violence: The Films of Dario Argento," in: Golden, Christopher, ed. **Cut! Horror Writers on Horror Film.** New York: Berkley, 1992. pp.267-288.
___ Wober, J. Mallory, ed. **Television and Nuclear Power: Making the Public Mind.** Norwood, NJ: Ablex, 1992. 297pp.
___ Wolff, Michael J. "Gifts of the New Magi," *Starlog* No. 174: 56-60. January 1992.
___ Wolff, Michael J. "Nine-Tenths of the Law," *Starlog* No. 190: 56-59. May 1993.
___ Wollen, Peter. "Theme Park and Variations," *Sight and Sound* 3(7): 7-10. August 1993.

MOTION PICTURES (continued)
___ Wood, Gary L. "Stephen King on Film," *Cinefantastique* 23(4): 12. December 1992.
___ Wood, Gary L. "Stephen King Strikes Again," *Cinefantastique* 22(4): 4-6. February 1992.
___ Wood, Robin. "Cat and Dog: Lewis Teague's Stephen King Movies," in: Irons, Glenwood, ed. **Gender, Language and Myth: Essays on Popular Narrative.** Toronto: University of Toronto Press, 1992. pp.303-318.
___ Wright, Bruce L. **Nightwalkers: Gothic Horror Movies, The Modern Era.** Dallas, TX: Taylor Publishing Co., 9195. 171pp.
___ Wright, Bruce L. **Yesterday's Tomorrows: The Golden Age of the Science Fiction Movie Poster, 1950-1964.** Dallas, TX: Taylor, 1993. 184pp.
___ Wright, Nolan. "Where's *Star Wars* 4?," *Cinefantastique* 22(6): 28-29. June 1992
___ Wuntch, Phillip. "Former TV Tarzan Makes Strong 'Doc'," *Dallas Morning News* Sec. A, p. 27. June 6, 1975.
___ Yarbro, Chelsea Q. "On *Freaks*," in: Golden, Christopher, ed. **Cut! Horror Writers on Horror Film.** New York: Berkley, 1992. pp.289-298.

MOTION PICTURES, 1991
___ Robinson, Frank M. "Cinema Summary 1991," in: Brown, Charles N. and Contento, William G. **Science Fiction, Fantasy, & Horror: 1991.** Oakland, CA: Locus Press, 1992. pp.433-436.
___ Robinson, Frank M. "Cinema Summary, 1991," *Locus* 28(2): 40, 72-73. February 1992.

MOTION PICTURES, 1993
___ Robinson, Frank M. "Cinema Summary, 1993," *Locus* 32(2): 49-51. February 1994.

MOTION PICTURES, 1994
___ "Cinema Summary, 1994," *Locus* 34(2): 49-51, 73. February 1995.

MR. PAYBACK (MOTION PICTURE)
___ Persons, Dan. "*Mr. Payback* (Review)," *Cinefantastique* 26(5): 59-60. August 1995.

MRS. DOUBTFIRE (MOTION PICTURE)
___ Loren, Christalene. "Quick Cuts: A Lady in Disguise," *Cinefex* No. 58: 91-92. June 1994.

MUGNAINI, JOSEPH
___ "Mugnaini, Joe (Obituary)," *Science Fiction Chronicle* 13(8): 16. May 1992.
___ "Mugnaini, Joseph (Obituary)," *Locus* 28(4): 60. April 1992.

MULCAHY, RUSSELL
___ Altman, Mark A. "*The Shadow*: Russell Mulcahy, Genre Stylist," *Cinefantastique* 25(4): 18. August 1994.
___ Murray, Will. "Master of Death," *Starlog* No. 205: 27-31. August 1994.

MULFORD, STOCKTON
___ Barrett, Robert R. "Edgar Rice Burroughs to Zane Grey: Stockton Mulford (1886-?)," *Burroughs Bulletin* NS. No. 16: 16-19. October 1993.

MULGREW, KATE
___ Spelling, Ian. "Voyager Captain," *Starlog* No. 212: 27-31, 72. March 1995.
___ Westbrook, Bruce. "The Next Voyage: Kate Mulgrew Takes Command of *Star Trek* Role," *Houston (TX) Chronicle TV Chronilog* p. 3-4. January 15-21, 1995.

MULTIMEDIA
___ "Multimedia Update," *Locus* 31(5): 6, 64. November 1993.

MUMMY (MOTION PICTURE)
___ Sevastakis, Michael. **Songs of Love and Death: The Classical American Horror Film of the 1930s.** Westport, CT: Greenwood, 1993. 232pp.

MUMY, BILL
___ Airey, Jean. "Lost in Babylon," by Jean Airey and Kim H. Johnson. *Starlog* No. 214: 32-35, 70. May 1995.

MUNRO, ALAN

___ Linton, Richard. "Profile: Alan Munro," *Cinefex* No. 52: 84. November 1992.

MUNRO, CAROLINE

___ Wiater, Stanley. "Munro, Caroline," in: Wiater, Stanley. **Dark Visions: Conversations with the Masters of the Horror Film.** New York: Avon, 1992. pp.111-118.

MUNSTERS (TV)

___ Hogan, David J. "*The Munsters*: 'My Fair Munster' (Review)," *Filmfax* No. 33: 18. June/July 1992.

MUPPET'S CHRISTMAS CAROL (MOTION PICTURE)

___ Hutchison, David. "*The Muppet's Christmas Carol*," *Starlog* No. 186: 32-34. January 1993.

___ Jones, Alan. "Those Little Dickens, the Muppets," *Cinefantastique* 23(5): 8-11. February 1993.

___ Sellin, Christine. "Quick Cuts: Muppetized Dickens," *Cinefex* No. 53: 9-10. February 1993.

MUREN, DENNIS

___ French, Lawrence. "*Jurassic Park*: Dennis Muren," *Cinefantastique* 24(2): 26-28. August 1993.

MURPHY, JOE

___ Jankiewicz, Pat. "Stunt Alien," *Starlog* No. 209: 64-65. December 1994.

MURPHY, MICHAEL

___ Spelling, Ian. "Mayor of Gotham," *Starlog* 181: 52-55. August 1992.

MURPHY-GIBB, DWINA

___ Nicholls, Stan. "Dwina Murphy-Gibb Is on the Greatest High in the World," in: Nicholls, Stan. **Wordsmiths of Wonder: Fifty Interviews with Writers of the Fantastic.** London: Orbit, 1993. pp.332-339.

MURRAY, G. G. A.

___ Stone, Graham. "Notes on Australian Science Fiction," *Science Fiction News* (Australia) No. 102: 2-5. March 1987.

MURRAY, MARGARET ALICE

___ Waugh, Robert H. "Dr. Margaret Murray and H. P. Lovecraft: The Witch-Cult in New England," *Lovecraft Studies* No. 31: 2-10. Fall 1994.

MUSEUMS

___ "Smithsonian Beams Up 'Trek' Exhibit," *Austin (TX) American Statesman* p. A2. February 28, 1992.

MUSGRAVE, SUSAN

___ Ahearn, Catherine. "An Archetype of Pain: From Plath to Atwood and Musgrave," in: Roberts, Sheila, ed. **Still the Frame Holds: Essays on Women Poets and Writers.** San Bernardino, CA: Borgo Press, 1993. pp.137-156.

MUSIC

___ **Back to the Future: Great Science Fiction Film Themes.** Holland: Star Music, 1995. one compact disc, 35 minutes.

___ "'Jedi' Disk Spinoffs Outsell Soundtrack," *Variety* p. 5, 37. June 27, 1983.

___ "Reconstruction of Original Score Gave *Nosferatu* Gloss at Berlin," *Variety* p. 348. May 9, 1984.

___ Baker, Leslie. "Morris and Music," *Journal of the William Morris Society* 10(3): 6-9. Autumn 1993.

___ Bishop, Norma. "Utopia and Dystopia in American Folksongs," in: Saccaro Del Buffa, Giuseppa and Lewis, Arthur O., eds. **Utopia e Modernita: Teorie e prassi utopiche nell'eta moderna e postmoderna.** Rome: Gangemi Editore, 1989. pp.1003-1012.

___ Callahan, Tim. "Censoring the World Riddle," *Mythlore* 20(1): 15-21. Winter 1994. (Whole No. 75)

___ DeCarlo, Tessa. "Tomorrow's Songs Today," *Wall Street Journal* p.A15. November 1, 1993.

___ Delville, Michel. "The Moorcock/Hawkwind Connection: Science Fiction and Rock'n'Roll Culture," *Foundation* No. 62: 64-63. Winter 1994/1995.

MUSIC (continued)

___ Evans, Gwenth. "Harps and Harpers in Contemporary Fantasy," *Lion and the Unicorn* 16(2): 199-209. December 1992.

___ Flinn, Caryl. **Strains of Utopia: Gender, Nostalgia, and Hollywood Film Music.** Princeton, NJ: Princeton University Press, 1992. 195pp.

___ Garcia, Bob. "*Batman*: Batmusic," *Cinefantastique* 24(6)/25(1): 37, 61. February 1994.

___ Garcia, Bob. "*Batman*: Composing Music for Animation," by Bob Garcia and Nancy Garcia. *Cinefantastique* 24(6)/25(1): 108-110. February 1994.

___ Giltz, Michael. "Sci-Fi Highs," *Premiere* 7(6): 98. February 1994.

___ Grubbs, Pete. "Rock Music as Science Fiction," *Lan's Lantern* No. 42: 20-29. May 1994.

___ Heywood, Andrew. "Morris and Early Music: The Shaw/Dolmetsch Connection," *Journal of the William Morris Society* 10(4): 13-19. Spring 1994.

___ Hirsch, David. "Music for *Robocop*," *Starlog* No. 196: 58-63. November 1993.

___ Hirsch, David. "Symphony for Klingon," *Starlog* 180: 76-80. July 1992.

___ Kendall, Lukas. "*Star Trek*: Scoring the Final Frontier," *Cinefantastique* 23(2/3): 100-102, 124. October 1992.

___ Kendall, Lukas. "*Star Trek: The Next Generation*: The Final Frontier's Musical Discord," *Cinefantastique* 24(3/4): 84-85. October 1993.

___ Kenny, Glenn. "The Sounds of Science," *TV Guide* 43(6): 28. February 11, 1995.

___ Kermode, Mark. "Endnotes," *Sight and Sound* 4(6): 71. June 1994.

___ Larson, Randall D. "*2001: A Space Odyssey*: The Music," *Cinefantastique* 25(3): 40-42. June 1994.

___ Pouncey, Edwin. "In the Hall of the Monster King: Music and the Maestro of Horror," in: Jones, Stephen, ed. **James Herbert: By Horror Haunted.** London: New English Library, 1992. pp.209-216.

___ Prevos, Andre J. M. "A Comment About the Utopian Character of the Afro-American Blues," in: Saccaro Del Buffa, Giuseppa and Lewis, Arthur O., eds. **Utopia e Modernita: Teorie e prassi utopiche nell'eta moderna e postmoderna.** Rome: Gangemi Editore, 1989. pp.1013-1018.

___ Rewa, Michael P. "The Matter of Britain in English and American Popular Music (1966-1990)," in: Slocum, Sally K., ed. **Popular Arthurian Traditions.** Bowling Green, OH: Popular Press, 1992. pp.104-110.

___ Soter, Tom. "License to Score," *Starlog* No. 199: 41-45. February 1994.

___ Speare, Mary J. "Wagnerian and Arthurian Elements in Chausson's **Le Roi Arthus**," in: Busby, Keith, ed. **The Arthurian Yearbook I.** New York: Garland, 1991. pp.195-214.

___ Spelling, Ian. "Arabian Night Music," *Starlog* No. 186: 52-55. January 1993.

___ Van Hise, James. "The Music of *The Next Generation*," in: Van Hise, James, ed. **Trek Celebration Two.** Las Vegas, NV: Pioneer, 1994. pp.134-141.

___ Vitaris, Paula. "*X-Files*: Music of the Night," *Cinefantastique* 26(6)/27(1): 79-81. October 1995.

MUSICAL COMEDY

___ "Brussels Cancels Verne 'Trip to the Moon'; No Unity of Components--Huisman," *Variety* p. 30. February 4, 1970.

MUSTCHIN, CHARLES

___ "Mustchin, Charles (Obituary)," *Science Fiction Chronicle* 17(1): 24. October/November 1995

MY BEST FRIEND IS A VAMPIRE (MOTION PICTURE)

___ "*My Best Friend Is a Vampire* (Review)," *Variety* p. 558. May 4, 1988.

MY LIVING DOLL (TV)

___ Hogan, David J. "*My Living Doll* (Review)," *Filmfax* No. 31: 20, 22. February/March 1992.

MYERS, EDWARD

___ Killheffer, Robert K. J. "The Legacy of Columbus: The Lost Races of Edward Myers and Kenneth Morris," *New York Review of Science Fiction* No. 44: 1, 3-6. April 1992.

MYSTERIES

___ Becker, Lucille F. "Science and Detective Fiction: Complementary Genres on the Margins of French Literature," *French Literature Series* 20: 119-125. 1993.

___ Borchardt, Edith. "Criminal Artists and Artisans in Mysteries by E. T. A. Hoffman, Dorothy Sayers, Ernesto Sábato, Patrick Süskind, and Thomas Harris," in: Sanders, Joe, ed. **Functions of the Fantastic**. Westport, CT: Greenwood, 1995. pp.125-134.

MYSTERY GENRE

___ Gray, W. Russell. "Science Fiction Detectives, (or, Stick 'em Up! I Picked Your Pocket With My Invisible Third Hand After You Handcuffed Me)," *Mid-Atlantic Almanack: Journal of the Mid Atlantic Popular American Culture Association* 2: 46-53. 1993.

MYSTERY OF RAMPO (MOTION PICTURE)

___ Fischer, Dennis. "***Mystery of Rampo*** (Review)," *Cinefantastique* 26(6)/27(1): 123. October 1995.

MYSTERY SCIENCE THEATER 3000 (MOTION PICTURE)

___ Bream, Jon. "Mystery Science Project," *TV Guide* 43(28): 19-21. July 15, 1995.

MYSTERY SCIENCE THEATER 3000 (TV)

___ Bream, Jon. "***Mystery Science Theater 3000*** Switcheroo," *TV Guide* 41(30): 26-28. July 24, 1993.

___ Corliss, Richard. "Play MST for Me," *Film Comment* 31(4): 26-35. July 1995.

___ Johnson, Kim H. "Down in Front," *Starlog* No. 210: 54-58. January 1995.

___ Karlen, Neal. "Sci-Fi Schlock Is Turned on Its Ear at Convention of Fans," *New York Times* p.B1. September 19, 1994.

___ Kenny, Glenn. "MST3K's Conventional Wisdom," *TV Guide* 42(30): 28. July 23, 1994.

MYTHOLOGY

___ Aveni, Anthony F. **Conversing with the Planets: How Science and Myth Invented the Cosmos**. New York: Times Books, 1992. 255pp.

___ Bridgman, Joan. "The Significance of Myth in **Watership Down**," *Journal of the Fantastic in the Arts* 6(1): 7-24. 1993.

___ Carlin, Russell. "The Hero Who Was Thursday: A Modern Myth," *Mythlore* 19(3): 27-30. Summer 1993. (No. 73)

___ Filmer, Kath. "Atseiniau O Ddyddiau Gynt: Welsh Myth and Culture in Contemporary Fantasy," in: Filmer, Kath, ed. **Twentieth-Century Fantasists: Essays in Culture, Society and Belief in Twentieth Century Mythopoeic Literature**. New York: St. Martin's, 1992. pp.108-120.

___ Filmer-Davies, Kath. "Chwedl Gymaeg a Llenyddiaeth Gyfoesol: Welsh Myth and Comtempory Literature," *Mythlore* 19(3): 53-58. Summer 1993. (No. 73)

___ Huttar, Charles A. "Tolkien, Epic Traditions and Golden Age Myths," in: Filmer, Kath, ed. **Twentieth-Century Fantasists: Essays in Culture, Society and Belief in Twentieth Century Mythopoeic Literature**. New York: St. Martin's, 1992. pp.92-107.

___ Lance, Donna. "Science Fiction and Mythology: Creatures of Light and Darkness," in: Kellogg, Judith and Crisler, Jesse, eds. **Literature & Hawaii's Children: Stories as Bridges to Many Realms**. Honolulu, HI: University of Hawaii at Manoa, 1994. pp.125-132.

___ Pennington, John. "Shamanistic Mythmaking: From Civilization to Wilderness in **Watership Down**," *Journal of the Fantastic in the Arts* 6(1): 34-50. 1993.

___ Sammons, Todd H. "Science Fiction and Mythology: An Overview," in: Kellogg, Judith and Crisler, Jesse, eds. **Literature & Hawaii's Children: Stories as Bridges to Many Realms**. Honolulu, HI: University of Hawaii at Manoa, 1994. pp.117-124.

___ Sherman, Josepha. **Once Upon a Galaxy**. Little Rock, AR: August House, 1994. 251pp.

___ St. Clair, Gloriana. "An Overview of the Northern Influences on Tolkien's Work," in: Reynolds, Patricia and GoodKnight, Glen H., eds. **Proceedings of the J. R. R. Tolkien Centenary Conference, Keble College, Oxford, 1992**. Altadena, CA: Mythopoeic Press, 1995. pp.63-67. (Mythlore Vol. 21, No. 2, Winter 1996, Whole No. 80)

___ Sullivan, C. W., III. " 'The Northern Thing' Reconsidered," *Journal of the Fantastic in the Arts* 3(3): 21-31. 1994.

___ Troen, Saul B. **Science Fiction and the Reemergence of Jewish Mythology in a Contemporary Literary Genre**. Ph.D. Dissertation, New York University, 1995. 336pp. (DAI-A 56/05, p. 1762. November 1995.)

MYTHOPOEIC FANTASY AWARDS, 1992

___ "Arnason, Rushdie Win Mythopoeic Awards," *Science Fiction Chronicle* 14(1): 6. October 1992.

MYTHOPOEIC FANTASY AWARDS, 1993

___ "1993 Mythopoeic Fiction Awards," *Locus* 31(3): 77. September 1993.

MYTHOPOEIC FANTASY AWARDS, 1994

___ "1994 Mythopoeic Fantasy Awards," *Locus* 33(4): 72. October 1994.

___ "Mythopoeic Award Nominations," *Science Fiction Chronicle* 15(8): 7-8. June 1994.

___ "Mythopoeic Awards, 1994," *Science Fiction Chronicle* 16(1): 8. October 1994.

MYTHOPOEIC FANTASY AWARDS, 1995

___ "1995 Mythopoeic Fantasy Awards," *Locus* 35(3): 9. September 1995.

___ "Mythopieic Award Nominations," *Science Fiction Chronicle* 16(8): 5. July/August 1995

MYTHOPOEIC SOCIETY

___ "Twenty-Five Years: The Mythopoeic Society: Appreciations," *Mythlore* 19(1): 31-36. Winter 1993. (No. 71)

___ Goodknight, Glen H. "Twenty-Five Years With the Mythopoeic Society: A Personal Reprise," *Mythlore* 19(1): 29-30. Winter 1993. (No. 71)

NADJA (MOTION PICTURE)

___ French, Lawrence. "Vampire Girl," *Cinefantastique* 27(2): 44-45, 61. November 1995.

NAKED LUNCH (MOTION PICTURE)

___ "Lunch Is Served. Bon Appetit (Review)," *Washington (DC) Times*. January 10, 1992. in: *NewsBank. Film and Television*. 14:A4-A5. 1992.

___ "Naked Out To Serious Lunch (Review)," *New York (NY) Post*. December 27, 1991. in: *NewsBank. Film and Television*. 5:F2. 1992.

___ Armstrong, David. "Burrough-ing to Hell (Review)," *San Francisco (CA) Examiner*. January 10, 1992. in: *NewsBank. Film and Television*. 13:G8-G9. 1992.

___ Duncan, Jody. "Borrowed Flesh," *Cinefex* No. 49: 24-39. February 1992.

___ Ebert, Roger. "***Naked Lunch*** Plumbs Depths of Writer's Mind (Review)," *Chicago (IL) Sun Times*. January 10, 1992. in: *NewsBank. Film and Television*. 14:A1. 1992

___ French, Lawrence. "***Naked Lunch***: Special Effects," *Cinefantastique* 22(5): 15-19. April 1992.

___ Hunter, Stephen. "***Naked Lunch*** Celebrates the Un-hip in a Plain Brown Suit (Review)," *Baltimore (MD) Sun*. February 13, 1992. in: *NewsBank. Film and Television*. 23:G8. 1992.

___ Johnson, Malcolm. "Cronenberg's ***Lunch*** Is Intriguing But Mechanical (Review)," *Hartford (CT) Courant*. January 10, 1992. in: *NewsBank. Film and Television*. 13:G12. 1992.

___ Kimber, Gary. "Cronenberg: ***Naked Lunch***," *Cinefantastique* 22(5): 8-9. April 1992.

___ Kimber, Gary. "***Naked Lunch***: Production Design," *Cinefantastique* 22(5): 18. April 1992.

___ Kimber, Gary. "***Naked Lunch***: William S. Burroughs, Possessed by Genius," *Cinefantastique* 22(5): 12-14. April 1992.

___ Kimber, Gary. "***The Naked Lunch***," *Cinefantastique* 22(4): 12-13, 60. February 1992.

___ Mahar, Ted. "Brilliant ***Naked Lunch*** Only for Stout Hearted (Review)," *Portland (OR) The Oregonian*. January 17, 1992. in: *NewsBank. Film and Television*. 23:G10. 1992.

___ Movshovitz, Howie. "Events, Sights, Actors All Off-Center in ***Naked Lunch*** (Review)," *Denver (CO) Post*. January 10, 1992. in: *NewsBank. Film and Television*. 13:G10-G11. 1992.

___ Persons, Dan. "***Naked Lunch***: Cronenberg's Impossible Dream," *Cinefantastique* 22(5): 10-11. April 1992.

___ Ringel, Eleanor. "Biting into ***Naked Lunch*** (Review)," *Atlanta (GA) Journal*. January 10, 1992. in: *NewsBank. Film and Television*. 13:G13-G14. 1992

___ Silverberg, Ira, ed. **Everything Is Permitted: The Making of Naked Lunch**. London: Grafton, 1992. 128pp.

NAKED LUNCH (MOTION PICTURE)   **NEOLOGISMS**

NAKED LUNCH (MOTION PICTURE) (continued)
___ Strauss, Bob. "*Naked Lunch* Lays Bare Compulsions and Psychic Powers (Review)," *Los Angeles (CA) Daily News*. December 27, 1991. in: *NewsBank. Film and Television*. 5:F1. 1992.
___ Strickler, Jeff. "*Naked Lunch* Is a Bizarre Mindbender (Review)," *Minneapolis (MN) Star and Tribune*. February 7, 1992. in: *NewsBank. Film and Television*. 23:G9. 1992.
___ Verniere, James. "*Naked Lunch* a Descent into Drugged-Out Hysteria (Review)," *Boston (MA) Herald*. January 10, 1992. in: *NewsBank. Film and Television*. 14:A2-A3. 1992.

NANCE, RON
___ "Nance, Ron (Obituary)," *Locus* 31(2): 59. August 1993.

NASCHY, PAUL
___ Pierce, Dale. "Horror With a Spanish Twist: Paul Naschy," *Filmfax* No. 33: 68-71, 98. June/July 1992.

NATIONAL ACADEMY OF TV ARTS AND SCIENCES
___ "Rod Serling Sees TV Academy Kaput," *Variety* p. 36. October 1, 1969.

NATIONAL AIR AND SPACE MUSEUM
___ "*Star Trek* Exhibit Opens," *Locus* 28(4): 7. April 1992.

NATIONAL LAMPOON'S FAVORITE DEADLY SINS (MOTION PICTURE)
___ Bark, Ed. "Vice-Nasty But Nice," *Dallas (TX) Morning News*. November 12, 1995. in: *NewsBank. Film and Television*. 104:G2. 1995.

NATURAL LAW
___ Koterski, Joseph W. "C. S. Lewis and Natural Law," *Bulletin of the New York C. S. Lewis Society* 26(6): 1-7. April 1995.

NEAR DARK (MOTION PICTURE)
___ "*Near Dark* Tops Sci Fest Nods," *Variety* p. 33. July 6, 1988.

NEBULA AWARDS
___ Kube-McDowell, Michael P. "The Encyclopedic Article of Nebula Lists," *SFWA Bulletin* 27(4)/28(1): 23-31. Winter/Spring 1994. (No. 122/123)

NEBULA AWARDS, 1991
___ "1991 Nebula Awards Nominations," *Locus* 28(3): 6. March 1992.
___ "1991 Nebula Awards Winners," *Locus* 28(5): 6. May 1992.

NEBULA AWARDS, 1992
___ "1992 Nebula Awards Jury Selected," *Science Fiction Chronicle* 13(4): 4-5. January 1992.
___ "1992 Nebula Awards Nominations," *Locus* 30(3): 6. March 1993.
___ "1992 Nebula Awards Winners," *Locus* 30(5): 8. May 1993.
___ "1992 Nebula Banquet," *Locus* 28(6): 48-49, 71-72. June 1992.
___ "1992 Nebula Jury," *Locus* 28(1): 6. January 1992.
___ "1992 Preliminary Nebula Ballot," *Locus* 30(2): 5. February 1993.
___ "Nebula Award Winners, 1992," *Science Fiction Chronicle* 14(8): 4. May 1993.
___ "Nebula Banquet Redux," *Locus* 30(2): 5. February 1993.
___ "SFWA's Nebula Award Winners," *Science Fiction Chronicle* 13(8): 4. May 1992.

NEBULA AWARDS, 1993
___ "1993 Nebula Awards Final Ballot," *Locus* 32(3): 7. March 1994.
___ "1993 Nebula Awards Preliminary Ballot," *Locus* 32(2): 8. February 1994.
___ "1993 Nebula Awards Winners," *Locus* 32(5): 8. May 1994.
___ "1993 Nebula Banquet," *Locus* 30(6): 46-48, 74. June 1993.
___ "1993 Nebula Banquet, Nebula Jury Announced," *Locus* 29(6): 7. December 1992.
___ "Nebula Award Nominations," *Science Fiction Chronicle* 13(6): 4. March 1992.
___ "Nebula Awards," *Science Fiction Chronicle* 15(7): 4. June 1994.
___ "Nebula, World Fantasy, Philip K. Dick Award Juries Established," *Science Fiction Chronicle* 14(3): 4-5. December 1992.

NEBULA AWARDS, 1994
___ "1994 Nebula Award Judges Named," *Locus* 31(6): 7. December 1993.
___ "1994 Nebula Awards Final Ballot," *Locus* 34(3): 7. March 1995.

NEBULA AWARDS, 1994 (continued)
___ "1994 Nebula Awards Preliminary Ballot," *Locus* 34(2): 72. February 1995.
___ "1994 Nebula Awards Winners," *Locus* 34(5): 7. May 1995.
___ "1994 Nebula Jury Chosen," *Science Fiction Chronicle* 15(2): 6. November/December 1993.
___ "1994 Nebula Preliminary Ballot," *Science Fiction Chronicle* 16(4): 4. February 1995.
___ "1994 Nebula Weekend," *Locus* 32(6): 51-53. June 1994.
___ "Final Nebula Award Nominations," *Science Fiction Chronicle* 16(4): 4. February 1995.
___ "Nebula Award Nominations," *Science Fiction Chronicle* 15(5): 4. March 1994.
___ "Nebula Awards Weekend 1994," *Locus* 31(4): 6. October 1993.

NEBULA AWARDS, 1995
___ "1995 Nebula Award Novel, Short Story Juries Chosen," *Science Fiction Chronicle* 16(3): 4-5. January 1995.
___ "1995 Nebula Judges Named," *Locus* 34(1) 8, 73. January 1995.
___ "1995 Nebula Weekend," *Locus* 34(6): 42-45, 72. June 1995.
___ "1995 Nebula Weekend Set For New York City," *Science Fiction Chronicle* 16(3): 4. January 1995.
___ "Nebula Award Winners," *Science Fiction Chronicle* 16(6): 4. May 1995.
___ "Nebula Awards Weekend," *Science Fiction Chronicle* 16(7): 33-34. June/July 1995.
___ "Nebula Awards Weekend 1995," *Locus* 33(5): 9. November 1994.

NECRONOMICON (MOTION PICTURE)
___ Kermode, Mark. "*Necronomicon* (Review)," *Sight and Sound* 4(9): 42-43. September 1994.
___ Lowe, Nick. "*Necronomicon* (Review)," *Interzone* No. 89: 39. November 1994.

NEEDFUL THINGS (MOTION PICTURE)
___ Persons, Dan. "*Needful Things* (Review)," *Cinefantastique* 24(6)/25(1): 124. February 1994.
___ Schaeffer, Stephen. "Hollywood Goes to Hell," *Boston (MA) Herald*. August 29, 1993. in: *NewsBank. Film and Television*. 104:F1-F2. 1993.
___ Vancheri, Barbara. "The Devil Disappoints: *Needful Things* Fails to Shiver (Review)," *Pittsburgh (PA) Post Gazette*. August 27, 1993. in: *NewsBank. Art*. 18:E6. 1993.

NELSON, ED
___ Weaver, Tom. "Ed Nelson: Interview," in: Weaver, Tom, ed. **Attack of the Monster Movie Makers: Interviews with 20 Genre Giants**. Jefferson, NC: McFarland, 1994. pp.229-248.

NELSON, GENE
___ Jankiewicz, Pat. "The Gamesters People Play," *Starlog* 180: 51-55. July 1992.

NELSON, LORI
___ Weaver, Tom. "Lori Nelson," in: Weaver, Tom. **They Fought the Creature Features: Interviews with 23 Classic Horror, Science Fiction and Serial Stars**. Jefferson, NC: McFarland, 1995. pp.221-232.

NELSON, RAY
___ Schweitzer, Darrell. "Interview With Ray Nelson," *Marion Zimmer Bradley's Fantasy Magazine* No. 25: 40-44. Fall 1994.

NEMEC, JOE, III
___ Altman, Mark A. "*The Shadow*: Production Design by Joe Nemec III," *Cinefantastique* 25(4): 31, 61. August 1994.

NEMESIS (MOTION PICTURE)
___ Harris, Judith P. "*Nemesis* (Review)," *Cinefantastique* 25(5): 60. October 1994.

NEOLOGISMS
___ Westfahl, Gary. "The Words That Could Happen: Science Fiction Neologisms and the Creation of Future Worlds," *Extrapolation* 34(4): 290-304. Winter 1993.

NESBIT, E.
___ Schenkel, Elmar. "Utopie und Phantastik in den Kinderbüchern von E. Nesbit," in: Kranz, Gisbert, ed. **Inklings: Jahrbuch für Literatur und Ästhetik.** 8. Band. Lüdenscheid, Germany: Stier, 1990. pp.103-124. [Not seen.]

NEST (MOTION PICTURE)
___ "*The Nest* (Review)," *Variety* p. 18. February 3, 1988.

NET (MOTION PICTURE)
___ Biodrowski, Steve. "*The Net* (Review)," *Cinefantastique* 27(3): 53. December 1995.

NETHERLANDS
___ "Meulenhoff to Do Paperbacks, Including SF/Fantasy Titles," *Science Fiction Chronicle* 16(7): 5. June/July 1995.
___ Lehmann, L. "Science Fiction," *Maatstaf* (Amsterdam, Netherlands) 39(7): 35-36. July 1991.
___ Rossenberg, René van. **Hobbits in Holland: Leven en werk van J. R. R. Tolkien (1892-1973)**. Den Hag: Koninklijke Bibliotheek, 1992. 99pp. [Not seen.]
___ Vanhecke, Johan. "Tolkien in Dutch: A Study of the Reception of Tolkien's Work in Belgium and the Netherlands," *Mythlore* 18(4): 53-60. Autumn 1992. (No. 70)

NETHERWORLD (MOTION PICTURE)
___ Wilt, David. "*Netherworld* (Review)," *Cinefantastique* 23(4): 61. December 1992.

NEUBE, RICK
___ "Neube, Resnick, McDevitt Win 1994 UPC Awards," *Science Fiction Chronicle* 16(3): 5. January 1995.

NEUROMANCER (MOTION PICTURE)
___ Harris, Judith P. "*Neuromancer* (Review)," *Cinefantastique* 24(1): 60. June 1993.

NEVERENDING STORY III: ESCAPE FROM FANTASIA (MOTION PICTURE)
___ Felperin, Leslie. "*Neverending Story III* (Review)," *Sight and Sound* 5(1): 50-51. January 1995.

NEVERENDING STORY (MOTION PICTURE)
___ "*Neverending Story* Big Marks Gamble for Germany, But Film Has All Elements for Solid Hit," *Variety* p. 277, 299. March 2, 1983.

NEW ADVENTURES OF GIGANTOR (TV)
___ Schwed, Mark. "On the Horizon: Whole New Worlds," *TV Guide* 41(30): 29-31. July 24, 1993.

NEW BLOOD (MOTION PICTURE)
___ SEE: FRIDAY THE 13TH VII: THE NEW BLOOD (MOTION PICTURE).

NEW EDEN (MOTION PICTURE)
___ Fischer, Dennis. "*New Eden* (Review)," *Cinefantastique* 26(2): 59. February 1995.

NEW EXPLORERS: THE SCIENCE OF STAR TREK (TV)
___ Droesch, Paul. "Hits and Misses: The New Explorers," *TV Guide* 43(2): 45. January 14, 1995.

NEW NIGHTMARE (MOTION PICTURE)
___ SEE: WES CRAVEN'S NEW NIGHTMARE (MOTION PICTURE).

NEW ROSE HOTEL (MOTION PICTURE)
___ Montesano, Anthony P. "*New Rose Hotel*," *Cinefantastique* 26(3): 44-45. April 1995.

NEW WAVE
___ Cummins, Elizabeth. "Judith Merril: A Link With the New Wave, Then and Now," *Extrapolation* 36(3): 198-209. Fall 1995.
___ Stewart, Elizabeth. **Destroying Angels: Messianic Rhetoric in Benjamin, Scholem, Psychoanalysis and Science Fiction**. Ph.D. Dissertation, New York University, 1994. 586pp. (DAI-A 55/09, p. 2820. March 1995.)

NEW WORLDS (MAGAZINE)
___ Watson, Ian. "Negentrophy Rules OK: The Refloating of *New Worlds*," *Amazing* 68(1): 48-52. April 1993.

NEW ZEALAND
___ Horne, Linnette. "SF in New Zealand," *Locus* 34(1) 72. January 1995.

NEWMAN, JOHN
___ "Newman, John (Obituary)," *Science Fiction Chronicle* 14(1): 12. October 1992.

NEWMAN, KIM
___ Nicholls, Stan. "Kim Newman Is a Velcro Man," in: Nicholls, Stan. **Wordsmiths of Wonder: Fifty Interviews with Writers of the Fantastic.** London: Orbit, 1993. pp.410-416.
___ Schweitzer, Darrell. "SFC Interview: Kim Newman," *Science Fiction Chronicle* 17(2): 6, 44, 46, 48. December 1995/January 1996.

NEWMAR, JULIE
___ Garcia, Bob. "*Batman*: Catwoman," *Cinefantastique* 24(6)/25(1): 18-19. February 1994.

NEXT GENERATION (TV)
___ SEE: STAR TREK: THE NEXT GENERATION (TV).

NEXT PHASE (MAGAZINE)
___ Katz, Bill. "*Next Phase*," *Library Journal* 119(13): 144. August 1994.

NEXT WAR (RADIO)
___ "Finnish Radio Drama About *The Next War* Causes a Civil Upset," *Variety* p.1, 145. January 1, 1986.

NIBELUNGENLIED
___ Bahn, Linda B. **A Comparative Study Between The Lord of the Rings and Das Nibelungenlied.** Master's Thesis, Pennsylvania State University, 1977. 131pp.

NICHOLLS, PETER
___ Clute, John. "Something About an Old Encyclopedia, and a Word About a New," *Foundation* No. 58: 96-99. Summer 1993.

NICHOLS, NICHELLE
___ Lowry, Brian. "Starfleet Siren," by Brian Lowry and Ian Spelling. in: McDonnell, David, ed. **Starlog's Science Fiction Heroes and Heroines**. New York: Crescent Books, 1995. pp.77-79.
___ Nichols, Nichelle. **Beyond Uhura: Star Trek and Other Memories**. New York: Putnam, 1995. 323pp.
___ Spelling, Ian. "Uhura and Beyond," *Starlog* No. 210: 47-49. January 1995.
___ Spelling, Ian. "Uhura's Mission," *Starlog* No. 175: 36-39, 82. February 1992.
___ Uram, Sue. "Beyond Uhura," *Cinefantastique* 26(2): 31. February 1995.

NIER, LENORE MARIE
___ "Nier, Lenore Marie (Obituary)," *Locus* 31(5): 64. November 1993.

NIGHT OF THE DEMONS 2 (MOTION PICTURE)
___ Harris, Judith P. "*Night of the Demons 2* (Review)," *Cinefantastique* 26(4): 59-60. June 1995.

NIGHT OF THE LIVING DEAD (MOTION PICTURE)
___ Grant, Barry K. "Taking Back *The Night of the Living Dead*: George Romero, Feminism and the Horror Film," *Wide Angle* 14(1): 64-77. January 1992.
___ Horne, Philip. "I Shopped With a Zombie," *Critical Quarterly* 34(4): 97-110. Winter 1992.

NIGHT TIDE (MOTION PICTURE)
___ Hogan, David J. "*Night Tide* (Review)," *Filmfax* No. 34: 18. August/September 1992.

NIGHTMARE BEFORE CHRISTMAS (MOTION PICTURE)
___ Kozachik, Pete. "Stop Motion Without Compromise: *The Nightmare Before Christmas*," *American Cinematographer* 74(12): 37-43. December 1993.

NIGHTMARE BEFORE CHRISTMAS (MOTION PICTURE)

NIGHTMARE BEFORE CHRISTMAS (MOTION PICTURE) (continued)
___ Lowe, Nick. "*Nightmare Before Christmas* (Review)," *Interzone* No. 92: 30. February 1995.
___ Mitchell, James. "Master of Nightmares," *Starlog* No. 200: 58-61. March 1994.
___ Newman, Kim. "*Nightmare Before Christmas* (Review)," *Sight and Sound* 4(12): 53-54. December 1994.
___ Persons, Dan. "*Nightmare Before Christmas* (Review)," *Cinefantastique* 25(2): 60. April 1994.
___ Vaz, Mark C. "Animation in the Third Dimension," *Cinefex* No. 56: 30-53. November 1993.
___ Yakir, Dan. " 'Twas the Night Before Halloween," *Starlog* No. 197: 43-48. December 1993.

NIGHTMARE CAFE (MOTION PICTURE)
___ Davis, Ivor. "The Maitre'd of Limbo (Review)," *Boston (MA) Herald.* February 27, 1992. in: *NewsBank. Film and Television.* 24:B10. 1992.
___ Dawidziak, Mark. "*Nightmare Cafe*," *Cinefantastique* 22(6): 46-47, 61. June 1992

NIGHTMARE ON ELM STREET (MOTION PICTURE)
___ "*Nightmare on Elm Street* (1984): Interview with Wes Craven," in: Goldberg, Lee, ed. **The Dreamweavers: Interviews With Fantasy Filmmakers of the 1980s.** Jefferson, NC: McFarland, 1995. pp.224-240.

NIGHTMARE ON ELM STREET, PART 2: FREDDY'S REVENGE (MOTION PICTURE)
___ "Cardinal Files Suit Over 'Elm Street 2'," *Variety* p.3, 140. January 1, 1986.

NIGHTSWARM (MOTION PICTURE)
___ Uram, Sue. "*Nightswarm*," *Cinefantastique* 25(5): 56-58. October 1994.

NIMOY, LEONARD
___ Cohn, Lawrence. "Par Backs Nimoy, 'Trek' to Hilt; Talks Going Re Possible Part IV," *Variety* p. 5, 26. June 6, 1984.
___ Lofficier, Randy. "*Star Trek Movies* (1980-1988): Interviews with Jack Sowards, Nicholas Mayer, Harve Bennett; Leonard Nimoy and William Shatner," by Randy Lofficier and Jean-Marc Lofficier. in: Goldberg, Lee et al. **Science Fiction Filmmaking in the 1980s.** Jefferson, NC: McFarland, 1995. pp.189-236.
___ Nimoy, Leonard. **I Am Spock.** New York: Hyperion, 1995. 342pp.
___ Price, Michael. "Nimoy Starts Comics Series," *San Francisco (CA) Chronicle* November 19, 1994. (Cited from the Internet Edition.)
___ Rhodes, Joe. "Nimoy and Son (and a Robot)," *TV Guide* 43(28): 13-14. July 16, 1995.
___ Rice, Lynette. "Boldly Going into Comics: Leonard Nimoy Is Exploring a New Role," *San Francisco (CA) Chronicle* November 14, 1994. (Cited from the Internet Edition.)
___ Schaeffer, Stephen. "Nimoy Ready to Pack Up His Pointed Ears," *Boston (MA) Herald.* December 6, 1991. in: *NewsBank. Names in the News.* 1:D6. 1992.
___ Spelling, Ian. "I, Nimoy," *Starlog* No. 217: 72-73. August 1995.
___ Strauss, Bob. "Star Finale: Nimoy Turns in His Ears After 25 Years As Spock," *Los Angeles (CA) Daily News.* December 6, 1991. in: *NewsBank. Names in the News.* 1:D7-D8. 1992.
___ Swires, Steve. "Vulcan Legend," in: McDonnell, David, ed. **Starlog's Science Fiction Heroes and Heroines.** New York: Crescent Books, 1995. pp.50-54.
___ Uram, Sue. "*Star Trek: Generations*: Spock Speaks," *Cinefantastique* 26(2): 20-21. February 1995.
___ Van Hise, James. **The Man Between the Ears: Star Trek's Leonard Nimoy.** Las Vegas, NV: Pioneer, 1992. 154pp.
___ Warren, Bill. "Deadly Gamesters," *Starlog* No. 219: 45-49. October 1995.

NINE (MOTION PICTURE)
___ Jankiewicz, Pat. "Incident of the Nine," *Starlog* No. 192: 76-80. July 1993.

NIPAR, YVETTE
___ Bloch-Hansen, Peter. "Robo Partner," *Starlog* No. 204: 36-39. July 1994.

NO ESCAPE (MOTION PICTURE)

NIRVANA (MOTION PICTURE)
___ Rooney, David. "Eye on the Future," *Variety* 358(5): 47. March 6, 1995.

NIVEN, LARRY
___ "Larry Niven and Jerry Pournelle: Master Collaborators," *Hailing Frequencies* (Waldenbooks) No. 5: 1-5. 1992.
___ Bowman, Tanya F. "Cautionary Tales of Immortality," *Science Fiction: A Review of Speculative Literature* 13(1): 19-21. 1995(?). (No. 37)
___ Holliday, Liz. "SFC Interviews: Larry Niven and Steven Barnes," *Science Fiction Chronicle* 13(6): 6, 22, 24-25. March 1992.
___ Nicholls, Stan. "Larry Niven and Steve Barnes Lay out a Mental Playground," in: Nicholls, Stan. **Wordsmiths of Wonder: Fifty Interviews with Writers of the Fantastic.** London: Orbit, 1993. pp.192-201.
___ Rothman, Chuck. "Larry Niven's Ringworld Novels Spawn a Fun and Challenging Computer Sequel," *Science Fiction Age* 3(1): 88-91. November 1994.
___ Stein, Kevin. **The Guide to Larry Niven's Ringworld.** New York: Baen, 1994. 188pp.

NO BLADE OF GRASS (MOTION PICTURE)
___ "*Grass* First British Pic via New Netro Regime," *Variety* p. 31. February 4, 1970.
___ "MGM's Topical 'Grass' Lensing on U.K. Location," *Variety* p. 24. June 3, 1970.

NO ESCAPE (MOTION PICTURE)
___ Baron, David. "Future Shocker," *New Orleans (LA) Times-Picayune.* May 7, 1994. in: *NewsBank. Film and Television.* 58:A12. 1994.
___ Caine, Barry. "*No Escape* Full of Comic-Book Action, Violence," *Oakland (CA) Tribune.* April 29, 1994. in: *NewsBank. Film and Television.* 58:A9. 1994.
___ Campbell, Bob. "*No Escape* Traps Itself in Outdated Sci-Fi Plot," *(Newark, NJ) Star-Ledger.* April 29, 1994. in: *NewsBank. Film and Television.* 46:E6. 1994.
___ Duncan, Jody. "Quick Cuts: Crime and Banishment," *Cinefex* No. 58: 11-12. June 1994.
___ Elliott, David. "*No Escape* Is One Action Fest Fully in Touch With Its Male Side," *San Diego (CA) Union.* April 28, 1994. in: *NewsBank. Film and Television.* 46:E1. 1994.
___ Faller, James M. "*No Escape* (Review)," *Cinefantastique* 25(6)/26(1): 122. December 1994.
___ Hunter, Stephen. "*No Escape* Is a Mad Mix of Too Many Future Fantasy Movie Styles," *(Baltimore, MD) Sun.* April 29, 1994. in: *NewsBank. Film and Television.* 46:E3. 1994.
___ Johnson, Malcolm. "Raw Future Awaits in *No Escape*," *Hartford (CT) Courant.* April 29, 1994. in: *NewsBank. Film and Television.* 46:E2. 1994.
___ Lovell, Glenn. "Van Dammed: *No Escape* from Gruesomly Familiar Territory," *San Jose (CA) Mercury News.* April 29, 1994. in: *NewsBank. Film and Television.* 58:A10. 1994.
___ Lowe, Nick. "*No Escape* (Review)," *Interzone* No. 85: 38-39. July 1994.
___ Movshovitz, Howie. "Yelling Overpowers *No Escape*," *Denver (CO) Post.* April 29, 1994. in: *NewsBank. Film and Television.* 58:A11. 1994.
___ Pierce, Susan. "Not Even Liotta's Charm, Skill Can Rescue Violent *No Escape*," *(Little Rock, AR) Arkansas Democrat-Gazette.* May 4, 1994. in: *NewsBank. Film and Television.* 58:A8. 1994.
___ Sherman, Paul. "No Escaping It: *No Escape* Is Just a Generic Action Flick," *Boston (MA) Herald.* April 29, 1994. in: *NewsBank. Film and Television.* 46:E4-E5. 1994.
___ Spelling, Ian. "The Hero This Time," *Starlog* No. 203: 43-48. June 1994.
___ Spelling, Ian. "Intimate Insider," *Starlog* No. 202: 32-36. May 1994.
___ Staggs, Jeffrey. "*No Escape*, Except for the Audience," *Washington (DC) Times.* April 29, 1994. in: *NewsBank. Film and Television.* 58:B1. 1994.
___ Strauss, Bob. "Just Call *No Escape* an Apocalypse Man," *Los Angeles (CA) Daily News.* April 29, 1994. in: *NewsBank. Film and Television.* 46:D14. 1994.
___ Terry, Clifford. "Set Outperforms Script in 'Escape'," *Richmond (VA) Times-Dispatch.* April 30, 1994. in: *NewsBank. Film and Television.* 58: A14. 1994.
___ Toots, J. M. "There Is *No Escape*," *Sci-Fi Entertainment* 1(1): 52-55. June 1994.

NO ESCAPE (MOTION PICTURE) (continued)
___ Vancheri, Barbara. "Lost in the Jungle," *Pittsburgh (PA) Post Gazette*. April 29, 1994. in: *NewsBank. Film and Television*. 58:A13. 1994.
___ Wuntch, Phillip. "**No Escape**: Action Thriller's Characters Seem Familiar," *Dallas (TX) Morning News*. April 29, 1994. in: *NewsBank. Film and Television*. 46:E7-E8. 1994.

NOLAN, WILLIAM F.
___ Schweitzer, Darrell. "William F. Nolan," in: Schweitzer, Darrell. **Speaking of Horror: Interviews With Writers of the Supernatural**. San Bernardino, CA: Borgo, 1994. pp.81-92.
___ Wiater, Stanley. "Nolan, William F.," in: Wiater, Stanley. **Dark Visions: Conversations with the Masters of the Horror Film**. New York: Avon, 1992. pp.119-128.

NON-STOP (MAGAZINE)
___ "*Crank!, Non-Stop* Are New Science Fiction Magazine Titles," *Science Fiction Chronicle* 15(1): 6. October 1993.

NOON, JEFF
___ "The Hugos (Or, the Empire Strikes Back)," *Science Fiction Chronicle* 17(2): 55-56. December 1995/January 1996.
___ "Noon Wins Clarke Award," *Locus* 32(6): 8, 76. June 1994.
___ "**Vurt** Brings Ringpull Recognition," *Science Fiction Chronicle* 15(8): 6. June 1994.
___ "World Science Fiction Convention Hugo Awards, 1995," *Science Fiction Chronicle* 17(1): 5. October/November 1995
___ Evenson, Laura. "Author Jeff Noon's Psychedelic Visions," *San Francisco (CA) Chronicle* February 15, 1996. (Cited from the Internet Edition.)
___ Ryman, Geoff. "High Noon: Jeff Noon Interviewed," *Interzone* No. 88: 25-27. October 1994.

NORDLEY, GERALD DAVID
___ Klein, Jay K. "Biolog: Gerald David Nordley," *Analog* 114(3): 94, 158. February 1994.

NORMAN, JOHN
___ Laidlaw, Marc. "An Open Letter to John Norman From a Reader He Lost Long Ago," *New York Review of Science Fiction* No. 87: 22. November 1995.
___ Norman, John. "How Far Is Too Far? An Open Letter From John Norman," *New York Review of Science Fiction* No. 83: 1, 10-15. July 1995.

NORRIS, FRANK
___ Graff, Bennett. **Horror in Evolution: Determinism, Materialism, and Darwinism in the American Gothic (Edgar Allan Poe, Frank Norris, Jack London, H. P. Lovecraft)**. Ph.D. Dissertation, City University of New York, 1995. 282pp. (DAI-A 56/05, p. 1777. November 1995.)

NORTH AMERICAN SCIENCE FICTION CONVENTION, 1995
___ Brown, Charles N. "NASFIC/Dragon Con," *Locus* 35(3): 50-51. September 1993.

NORTH (MOTION PICTURE)
___ Persons, Dan. "**North** (Review)," *Cinefantastique* 25(6)/26(1): 122-123. December 1994.

NORTH, ERIC
___ Stone, Graham. "Eric North Again," *Science Fiction News* (Australia) No. 117: 10-11. December 1993.

NORTON, ANDRE
___ "Andre Norton at 80," *Locus* 28(4): 6. April 1992.
___ "Andre Norton Scholarship," *Locus* 33(1): 8. July 1994.
___ "Andre Norton Scholarship Award," *Locus* 31(1): 6. July 1993.
___ "'High Hallack' Is Andre Norton's Dream Genre Writers Retreat," *Science Fiction Chronicle* 15(9): 6. August 1994.
___ "Norton Receives First Fandom Award," *Locus* 34(1) 8. January 1995.
___ "Other Awards at ConAdian," *Science Fiction Chronicle* 15(10): 5. September 1994.

NORTON, ANDRE (continued)
___ Schlobin, Roger C. "Andre Norton," in: Bruccoli, Matthew J., ed. **Facts on File Bibliography of American Fiction 1919-1988**. New York: Facts on File, 1991. pp.382-384.
___ Schlobin, Roger C. **Andre Norton: A Primary and Secondary Bibliography**. Revised edition, by Roger C. Schlobin and Irene R. Harrison. Framingham, MA: NESFA Press, 1994. 92pp.
___ Schlobin, Roger C. "Andre Norton: The Author Becomes Her Fiction and Creates Life," in: Collins, Robert A. and Latham, Robert, eds. **Science Fiction and Fantasy Book Review Annual 1991**. Westport, CT: Greenwood, 1994. pp.172-177.
___ Schlobin, Roger C. "The Formulaic and Rites of Transformation in Andre Norton's Magic Series," in: Sullivan, C. W., III. **Science Fiction for Young Readers**. Westport, CT: Greenwood, 1993. pp.37-45.
___ Stephensen-Payne, Phil. **Andre Norton: Grand Master of the Witch World, a Working Bibliography**, by Phil Stephensen-Payne and Gordon Benson, Jr. Albuquerque, NM: Galactic Central, 1992. 83pp.; San Bernardino, CA: Borgo Press, 1993. 83pp.
___ Yoke, Carl B. "Slaying the Dragon Within: Andre Norton's Female Heroes," *Journal of the Fantastic in the Arts* 4(3): 79-92. 1991. (No. 15)

NORTON, MARY
___ "Authors Fritz Leiber, Mary Norton Dead," *Science Fiction Chronicle* 14(1): 4. October 1992.
___ "Norton, Mary (Obituary)," *Locus* 29(4): 66. October 1992
___ "Norton, Mary (Obituary)," *Science Fiction Chronicle* 14(2): 14. November 1992.

NORWAY
___ Engholm, Ahrvid. "SF in the Nordic Countries," *Locus* 34(4): 39. April 1995.
___ St. Clair, Gloriana. "An Overview of the Northern Influences on Tolkien's Work," in: Reynolds, Patricia and GoodKnight, Glen H., eds. **Proceedings of the J. R. R. Tolkien Centenary Conference, Keble College, Oxford, 1992**. Altadena, CA: Mythopoeic Press, 1995. pp.63-67. (*Mythlore* Vol. 21, No. 2, Winter 1996, Whole No. 80)

NOSFERATU (MOTION PICTURE)
___ "Reconstruction of Original Score Gave **Nosferatu** Gloss at Berlin," *Variety* p. 348. May 9, 1984.
___ Holt, Wesley G. "**Nosferatu** (Prana Films, 1922) (Review)," *Filmfax* No. 38: 25-26. April/May 1993.

NOT OF THIS EARTH (MOTION PICTURE)
___ "Corman's 'Earth' Remake to Feature Traci Lords," *Variety* p. 1, 34. February 10, 1988.
___ "**Not of This Earth** (Review)," *Variety* p. 16. May 25, 1988.

NOTO, CLAIR
___ Szebin, Frederick C. "**The Tourist**: The Hollywood Horror Story of Writer Clair Noto's Unfilmed Masterpiece," *Cinefantastique* 25(4): 46-55. August 1994.

NOURSE, ALAN E.
___ "Nourse, Alan E. (Obituary)," *Locus* 29(3): 76. September 1992.
___ "Nourse, Alan E. (Obituary)," *Science Fiction Chronicle* 13(11/12): 20. August 1992.
___ Harrison, Harry. "Allen E. Nourse: An Appreciation," *Locus* 29(4): 66. October 1992
___ Hendrix, Howard V. "The Things of a Child: Coming Full Circle With Alan E. Nourse's **Raiders From the Rings**," in: Sullivan, C. W., III. **Science Fiction for Young Readers**. Westport, CT: Greenwood, 1993. pp.87-96.

NOVELIZATIONS, MOTION PICTURES
___ Larson, Randall D. "A Movie Novelizer Speaks: Alan Dean Foster Interviewed," *Interzone* No. 80: 53-55. February 1994.
___ Pringle, David. "SF, Fantasy & Horror Movie Novelizations," *Interzone* No. 80: 38-52. February 1994.

NOWHERE MAN (TV)
___ Kenny, Glenn. "He's a Real **Nowhere Man**," *TV Guide* 43(34): 28. August 26, 1995.
___ Zuccola, Dianne. "Hits and Misses: **Nowhere Man**," *TV Guide* 43(34): 37. August 26, 1995.

NOYES, ALFRED
___ Burleson, Donald R. " 'Midnight Express': Alfred Noyes at the Borderlands of Self-Reference," *Studies in Weird Fiction* No. 17: 18-22. Summer 1995.

NUCLEAR CONSPIRACY (MOTION PICTURE)
___ "Chernobyl Nuke Fire Stokes Sales Action on Atlas' *Nuclear Conspiracy*," *Variety* p. 1, 98. May 21, 1986.

NUCLEAR WAR
___ Bartter, Martha A. "The Hidden Agenda," in: Slusser, George and Eric S. Rabkin, eds. **Fights of Fancy: Armed Conflict in Science Fiction and Fantasy**. Athens, GA: University of Georgia Press, 1993. pp.155-169.
___ Bennett, James R. **Hiroshima, Nagazaki, and the Bomb: A Bibliography of Literature and the Arts**, by James R. Bennett and Karen Clark. Pullman, WA: International Society for the Study of Nuclear Texts and Contexts, 1989. 24pp. (Monograph Series, No. 1)
___ Burns, Grant. **The Nuclear Present: A Guide to Recent Books on Nuclear War, Weapons, the Peace Movement, and Related Issues, With a Chronology of Nuclear Events, 1789-1991**. Metuchen, NJ: Scarecrow, 1992. 654pp.
___ Cantor, Joanne. "Children's Emotional Reactions to Technological Disasters Conveyed by the Mass Media," in: Wober, J. Mallory, ed. **Television and Nuclear Power: Making the Public Mind**. Norwood, NJ: Ablex, 1992. pp.31-54.
___ Cooper, Kenneth D. **Fables of the Nuclear Age: Fifty Years of World War III**. Ph.D. Dissertation, Vanderbilt University, 1992. 352pp. (DAI-A 54/01. p. 176. July 1993.)
___ Evans-Karastamatis, Joyce A. **Celluloid Mushroom Clouds: Hollywood and the Atomic Bomb**. Ph.D. Dissertation, University of California, San Diego, 1993. 432pp. (DAI-A 54/06, p. 1986. December 1993.)
___ Gunter, Barrie. "The Impact of Nuclear Fiction in Britain: *The Day After* and *Threads*," by Barrie Gunter and M. Svennevig. in: Wober, J. Mallory, ed. **Television and Nuclear Power: Making the Public Mind**. Norwood, NJ: Ablex, 1992. pp.55-66.
___ Iwao, Sumiko. "*The Day After* in Japan," in: Wober, J. Mallory, ed. **Television and Nuclear Power: Making the Public Mind**. Norwood, NJ: Ablex, 1992. pp.67-76.
___ Kubey, Robert W. "U.S. Opinion and Politics Before and After *The Day After*: Television Movie as Rorschach," in: Wober, J. Mallory, ed. **Television and Nuclear Power: Making the Public Mind**. Norwood, NJ: Ablex, 1992. pp.19-30.
___ Lometti, Guy E. "Broadcast Preparations for and Consequences of *The Day After*," in: Wober, J. Mallory, ed. **Television and Nuclear Power: Making the Public Mind**. Norwood, NJ: Ablex, 1992. pp.3-18.
___ Matics, Mark A. **Louder Than Bombs: Science Fiction and Nuclear Weapons, 1945-1965**. Master's Thesis, Marshall University, 1992. 86pp.
___ Seed, David. "Push-Button Holocaust: Mordecai Roshwald's **Level 7**," *Foundation* No. 57: 68-86. Spring 1993.
___ Wober, J. Mallory, ed. **Television and Nuclear Power: Making the Public Mind**. Norwood, NJ: Ablex, 1992. 297pp.

NUCLEAR WEAPONS
___ Matics, Mark A. **Louder Than Bombs: Science Fiction and Nuclear Weapons, 1945-1965**. Master's Thesis, Marshall University, 1992. 86pp.

NURMI, MAILA
___ Ryan, Al. "*Ed Wood*: Vampira," by Al Ryan and Dan Cziraky. *Cinefantastique* 25(5): 40-41, 61. October 1994.

NURSERY RHYMES
___ Hess, Kathleen. "The Bittersweet Vine: Fairy Tales and Nursery Rhymes," *Mythlore* 19(2): 54-56, 60. Spring 1993. (No. 72)

NURSING
___ Thompson, Linda W. **The Image of Nursing in Science Fiction Literature**. Thesis (D.S.N.), University of Alabama at Birmingham School of Nursing, 1993. 297pp. (DAI-B 54/07, p. 3554. January 1994.)

NUTTER, DAVID
___ Vitaris, Paula. "*X-Files*: David Nutter," *Cinefantastique* 26(6)/27(1): 29-30. October 1995.

NYBY, CHRISTIAN
___ Davidson, Jim. " *The Thing* About Filmmaker Christian Nyby," *Filmfax* No. 34: 36-46. August/September 1992.

O'BANNON, ROCKNE S.
___ Nazzaro, Joe. "Underwater Thoughts," *Starlog* No. 204: 54-58. July 1994.

O'BRIEN, FITZ-JAMES
___ Hoppenstand, Gary. "Robots of the Past: Fitz-james O'Brien's 'The Wondersmith'," *Journal of Popular Culture* 27(4): 13-30. Spring 1994.

O'BRIEN, WILLIS
___ Archer, Steve. **Willis O'Brien: Special Effects Genius**. Jefferson, NC: McFarland, 1993. 239pp.
___ Jones, Alan. "*Jurassic Park*: O'Brien's *Oso Si-Papu*," *Cinefantastique* 24(2): 24-25. August 1993.
___ Kinnard, Roy, ed. **The Lost World of Willis O'Brien: The Original Shooting Script of the 1925 Landmark Special Effects Dinosaur Film, with Photographs**. Jefferson, NC: McFarland, 1993. 176pp.

O'CONNELL, JERRY
___ Johnson, Kim H. "Parallel Excitement," *Starlog* No. 215: 32-35. June 1995.

O'CONNER, FLANNERY
___ Walker, Sue. "Undiscovered Countries: **Milledgeville, Herland** and Beyond," *Connecticut Review* 16(2): 91-100. Fall 1994.

O'DONNELL, CHRIS
___ Shapiro, Marc. "Robin Forever," *Starlog* No. 217: 27-30. August 1995.

O'DONNELL, KEVIN, JR.
___ King, T. Jackson. "SFC Interviews: Kevin O'Donnell, Jr.," *Science Fiction Chronicle* 15(9): 7, 30-32. August 1994.

O'HARE, MICHAEL
___ Nazzaro, Joe. "Once a Commander," by Joe Nazzaro and Sheelagh J. Wells. *Starlog* No. 208: 53-57, 69. November 1994.

O'NEILL, GERARD K.
___ "O'Neill, Gerard K. (Obituary)," *Locus* 28(6): 67. June 1992.

O'REILLY, JOHN BOYLE
___ Stone, Graham. "Notes on Australian Science Fiction," *Science Fiction News* (Australia) No. 92: 2-8. February 1985.

O'SULLIVAN, MAUREEN
___ Fury, David. "Maureen O'Sullivan: A Jewel of a Jane," *Burroughs Bulletin* NS. No. 15: 3-10. July 1993.

OAKLEY, CAROLINE
___ "Deborah Beale Quits Millennium; Caroline Oakley Becomes Editor," *Science Fiction Chronicle* 15(2): 4-5. November/December 1993.
___ "New Editor at Millennium," *Locus* 31(6): 6. December 1993.

OATES, JOYCE CAROL
___ "Bram Stoker Awards," *Science Fiction Chronicle* 15(8): 5. June 1994.
___ "HWA Stoker Awards Winners," *Locus* 33(1): 7. July 1994.
___ Burleson, Donald R. "Connings: Bradbury/Oates," *Studies in Weird Fiction* No. 11: 24-29. Spring 1992.

OBITUARIES
___ "Abe, Kobo," *Locus* 30(2): 68. February 1993.
___ "Abe, Kobo," *Science Fiction Chronicle* 14(6): 16. March 1993.
___ "Abis, Stephen," *Locus* 28(2): 68. February 1992.
___ "Adams, Georgia F.," *Locus* 30(2): 69. February 1993.
___ "Adams, Georgia F.," *Science Fiction Chronicle* 14(4): 14. January 1993.
___ "Adamson, Al," *Science Fiction Chronicle* 16(9): 24. August/September 1995.
___ "Adlerberth, Roland," *Locus* 31(4): 68. October 1993.
___ "Ameche, Don," *Science Fiction Chronicle* 15(3): 14. January 1994.
___ "Amis, Kingsley," *Locus* 35(6): 78. December 1995.

OBITUARIES (continued)

___ "Amis, Kingsley," *Science Fiction Chronicle* 17(2): 24, 26. December 1995/January 1996.

___ "Arnold, Jack; Made Popular Science Fiction, Horror Films," *Los Angeles (CA) Times* Sec. A, p. 26. March 20, 1992.

___ "Arnold, Jack, 1912-1992," *Starlog* 181: 22-23. August 1992.

___ "Ashton, Roy," *Science Fiction Chronicle* 16(5): 16. March/April 1995.

___ "Asimov, Isaac," *Current Biography* 53(5): 60. May 1992.

___ "Asimov, Isaac," *Science Fiction Chronicle* 13(8): 13-14. May 1992.

___ "Asimov, Isaac," *Wall Street Journal* Sec. A, p. 1. April 7, 1992.

___ "Asimov, Isaac. A Visionary Author," *Miami (FL) Herald* April 7, 1992. in: *NewsBank. Names in the News* NIN 84: G13. 1992.

___ "Asimov, Isaac. Sci-Fi King Dead at 72," *Boston (MA) Herald* April 7, 1992. in: *NewsBank. Names in the News* NIN 84: G12. 1992.

___ "Asimov, Isaac: Science Fiction Author Isaac Asimov Dead at 72," *New York (NY) Post.* April 7, 1992. in *NewsBank. Names in the News.* 105:E14. 1992.

___ "Asimov, Isaac: 1920-1992," *Locus* 28(5): 4-5, 59-64. May 1992.

___ "Asimov, Isaac (1920-1992)," *Nature* 357(6374): 113. May 14, 1992.

___ "Asimov, Isaac: Asimov's Golden Age of Science Fiction," *Detroit News & Free Press* Sec. C, p. 12. April 11, 1992.

___ "Asimov, Isaac: Author Asimov Dead at Age 72," *Austin (TX) American Statesman* p. A1, A6. April 7, 1992.

___ "Asimov, Isaac: Celebration of Isaac Asimov," *New York Times* Sec. 3, p. 8. April 12, 1992.

___ "Asimov, Isaac Dies," *Science Fiction Chronicle* 13(7): 8. April 1992.

___ "Asimov, Isaac Dies; A Visionary Author," *Miami (FL) Herald* April 7, 1992. in *NewsBank. Names in the News.* 84:G13. 1992.

___ "Asimov, Isaac Dies at 72; Master of Science Fiction," *Washington (DC) Post* Sec. B, p. 6. April 7, 1992.

___ "Asimov, Isaac Dies at 72 of Heart, Kidney Failure," *Bryan-College Station Eagle* p. A1. April 7, 1992.

___ "Asimov, Isaac: In Memoriam," *Locus* 28(6): 1, 44-47, 69-71. June 1992.

___ "Asimov, Isaac: Lavish Curiosity on Future Worlds," *Guardian* p. 39. April 7, 1992.

___ "Asimov, Isaac: Laws of Asimov," *Denver (CO) Post* Sec. B, p. 6. April 7, 1992.

___ "Asimov, Isaac: Never an Unwritten Idea," *St. Louis Post-Dispatch* Sec. B, p. 2. April 11, 1992.

___ "Asimov, Isaac: Nightfall," *Economist* 323(7754): 87. April 11, 1992.

___ "Asimov, Isaac. Passing of the Most Golden Period in Science Fiction," *Atlanta (GA) Journal* Sec. B, p. 1. April 7, 1992. in: *NewsBank. Literature* LIT 35: C1-C2. 1992.

___ "Asimov, Isaac: Prolific Science Fiction Writer Isaac Asimov Dies at Age 72 (AP)," *Battalion* (Texas A&M University) p. 1. April 7, 1992.

___ "Asimov, Isaac: Sci-Fi King Asimov Dead at 72," *Boston (MA) Herald.* April 7, 1992. in *NewsBank. Literature.* 35:C3. 1992.

___ "Asimov, Isaac: Science Fiction Author Dead at 72," *New York (NY) Post* April 7, 1992. in: *NewsBank. Names in the News* NIN 105: E14. 1992.

___ "Asimov, Isaac: Storyteller Who Explored Many Worlds," *USA Today* Sec. D, p. 1. April 7, 1992.

___ "Asimov, Isaac's Fanciful Foundation," *Washington (DC) Times* Sec. E, p. 1. April 7, 1992.

___ "Asimov, Isaac, 1920-1992," *Fantasy Commentator* 7(4): 242-244. Fall 1992. (Whole No. 44)

___ "Asimov, Isaac, 1920-1992," *Interzone* No. 61: 35-37. July 1992

___ "Asimov, Isaac, 1920-1992: In Memoriam," *Isaac Asimov's Science Fiction Magazine* 16(12/13): 4-31. November 1992.

___ "Asimov, Isaac, 2 January 1920 - 6 April 1992," *Magazine of Fantasy and Science Fiction* 83(2): 5-8. August 1992.

___ "Asimov, Isaac, 72, Leaves Vast Written Legacy in Many Disciplines," *Houston (TX) Post* p. A2. April 7, 1992.

___ "Asimov, Isaac, Artist of SF, Dies," *Guardian* p. 22. April 7, 1992.

___ "Asimov, Isaac, Prolific Author of Science Fiction and Fact, Dies," *Boston (MA) Globe* p. 27. April 7, 1992.

___ "Asimov, Isaac, Sci-Fi Writer, Dead at 72," *Sacramento (CA) Bee.* April 7, 1992. in: *NewsBank. Names in the News.* 105:E13. 1992.

___ "Asimov, Isaac, Science Fiction Virtuoso, Dies," *Los Angeles (CA) Times* Sec. A, p. 1. April 7, 1992. also in: *NewsBank. Literature* 35:B13-B14. 1992.; *Newsbank. Names in the News* NIN 105: F1. 1992.

___ "Asimov, Isaac, Whose Thoughts and Books Traveled the Universe, Is Dead at 72," *New York Times* p. A16. April 7, 1992.

OBITUARIES (continued)

___ "Asimov, Isaac--Requiem: Isaac Asimov 1920-1992," *Omni* 14(9): 22. June 1992.

___ "Asimov, Stanley," *Locus* 35(3): 78. September 1993.

___ "Asimov, Stanley," *Science Fiction Chronicle* 17(1): 24. October/November 1995

___ "Avice, Claude," *Locus* 35(4): 70. October 1995.

___ "Bacon, Francis," *Locus* 28(6): 68. June 1992.

___ "Ballantine, Ian," *Locus* 34(4): 60-62. April 1995.

___ "Ballantine, Ian," *Science Fiction Chronicle* 16(5): 5. March/April 1995.

___ "Ballantine, Ian," *Science Fiction Chronicle* 16(6): 20. May 1995.

___ "Barbet, Pierre," *Locus* 35(5): 78. November 1995.

___ "Barbet, Pierre," *Science Fiction Chronicle* 17(1): 22. October/November 1995

___ "Bennett, Charles," *Science Fiction Chronicle* 16(8): 21. July/August 1995

___ "Bennett, Charles, 1899-1995," *Starlog* No. 220: 16-17. November 1995.

___ "Bentcliffe, Eric," *Locus* 29(1): 67. July 1992.

___ "Bentcliffe, Eric," *Science Fiction Chronicle* 13(7): 14, 16. April 1992.

___ "Bentcliffe, Eric," *Science Fiction Chronicle* 13(8): 14, 16. May 1992.

___ "Benthake, Bill," *Science Fiction Chronicle* 16(2): 18. November/December 1994.

___ "Biffel, Terry," *Locus* 28(2): 68. February 1992.

___ "Bigglestone, Clint," *Science Fiction Chronicle* 16(2): 20. November/December 1994.

___ "Bigglestone, Harry C. 'Clint'," *Locus* 33(6): 74. December 1994.

___ "Bissell, Terry," *Science Fiction Chronicle* 13(5): 14. February 1992.

___ "Bloch, Robert," *Science Fiction Chronicle* 16(1): 16, 18. October 1994.

___ "Bloch, Robert (1917-1994)," *Locus* 33(5): 6-7, 74-78. November 1994.

___ "Bogert, Jean," *Science Fiction Chronicle* 15(5): 12. March 1994.

___ "Borden, Gavin G.," *Science Fiction Chronicle* 13(5): 14. February 1992.

___ "Boulle, Pierre," *Locus* 32(3): 68. March 1994.

___ "Boulle, Pierre," *Science Fiction Chronicle* 15(4): 16. February 1994.

___ "Brackett, Leigh," *Science Fiction News* (Australia) No. 55: 11-12. June 1978.

___ "Breen, Walter," *Locus* 30(6): 72. June 1993.

___ "Breen, Walter," *Science Fiction Chronicle* 14(9): 16. June 1993.

___ "Bretnor, Reginald," *Locus* 29(3): 76-77. September 1992.

___ "Bretnor, Reginald," *Science Fiction Chronicle* 13(11/12): 18. August 1992.

___ "Brinkley, William C.," *Locus* 32(1): 61. January 1994.

___ "Brophy, Brigid," *Locus* 35(4): 70. October 1995.

___ "Brown, Claire," *Science Fiction Chronicle* 15(3): 14. January 1994.

___ "Brown, Claire Parman," *Locus* 31(6): 68. December 1993.

___ "Brunner, John," *Locus* 35(4): 5, 70-73. October 1995.

___ "Brunner, John," *Locus* 35(5): 78-79. November 1995.

___ "Brunner, John," *Science Fiction Chronicle* 17(1): 22. October/November 1995

___ "Brunner, John: Tomorrow May Be Even Worse: John Kilian Houston Brunner (1934-1995)," *Vector* No. 185: 4. September/October 1995.

___ "Bunin, Lou," *Science Fiction Chronicle* 15(5): 12. March 1994.

___ "Burgess, Anthony," *Locus* 32(1): 60-61. January 1994.

___ "Burgess, Anthony," *Newsweek* 122(23): 84. December 6, 1993.

___ "Burgess, Anthony: The Last Man of Letters," *Washington (DC) Post Book World* p. 15. December 12, 1993.

___ "Burns, Richard," *Locus* 29(4): 66. October 1992.

___ "Burns, Richard," *Science Fiction Chronicle* 14(2): 12. November 1992.

___ "Capra, Frank, 1897-1991," *Starlog* No. 174: 22. January 1992.

___ "Carreras, Michael," *Science Fiction Chronicle* 15(9): 16. August 1994.

___ "Carter, Angela," *Locus* 28(3): 72. March 1992.

___ "Carter, Angela," *Science Fiction Chronicle* 13(6): 12. March 1992.

___ "Carter, Angela: Wise Child, Wayward Woman," *Vector* No. 166: 10-12. April/May 1992.

___ "Cartier, Rudolph," *Science Fiction Chronicle* 15(9): 16. August 1994.

___ "Caulton, David," *Locus* 31(6): 68. December 1993.

OBITUARIES (continued)
___ "Caulton, David," *Science Fiction Chronicle* 15(2): 16. November/December 1993.
___ "Charteris, Leslie," *Locus* 30(6): 71. June 1993.
___ "Charteris, Leslie," *Science Fiction Chronicle* 14(9): 16. June 1993.
___ "Clareson, T. D., 66, a Leading Scholar on Science Fiction," *New York Times* Sec. D, p. 18. July 9, 1993.
___ "Clareson, Thomas D.," *Locus* 31(2): 58-59. August 1993.
___ "Clareson, Thomas D., 1926-1993," *Extrapolation* 35(1): 3-4. Spring 1994.
___ "Clareson, Thomas D., 1926-1993.," *Science Fiction Studies* 20(3): 486. November 1993.
___ "Clareson, Thomas Dean," *Science Fiction Chronicle* 14(11): 14. August 1993.
___ "Clarke, Norm," *Locus* 34(6): 67. June 1995.
___ "Clarke, Norm," *Science Fiction Chronicle* 16(7): 19. June/July 1995.
___ "Clavell, James," *Locus* 33(4): 70. October 1994.
___ "Clayton, Jack," *Science Fiction Chronicle* 16(5): 18. March/April 1995.
___ "Cleator, Philip E.," *Locus* 34(4): 62. April 1995.
___ "Cleator, Philip E.," *Science Fiction Chronicle* 16(4): 14-16. February 1995.
___ "Cleaver, Diane," *Locus* 34(5): 72. May 1995.
___ "Cleaver, Diane," *Science Fiction Chronicle* 16(6): 20, 22. May 1995.
___ "Conrad, William," *Science Fiction Chronicle* 15(5): 12. March 1994.
___ "Cook, Robin," *Locus* 33(3): 78. September 1994.
___ "Cotten, Joseph," *Science Fiction Chronicle* 15(5): 12. March 1994.
___ "Creese, Irene," *Science Fiction Chronicle* 15(4): 16. February 1994.
___ "Crispin, Edmund, 1921-1978," *Science Fiction News* (Australia) No. 60: 4. April 1979.
___ "Cushing, Peter," *Science Fiction Chronicle* 15(10): 19. September 1994.
___ "Cushing, Peter, 1913-1994," *Starlog* No. 208: 76-77. November 1994.
___ "Da Cruz, Daniel," *Locus* 29(4): 66. October 1992
___ "Davidson, Avram," *Science Fiction Chronicle* 14(9): 16. June 1993.
___ "Davidson, Avram: In Memorium," *Locus* 31(1): 60-61. July 1993.
___ "Davidson, Avram, 1923 - 1993," *Magazine of Fantasy and Science Fiction* 85(3): 4. September 1992.
___ "Davidson, Avram, Dies," *Locus* 30(6): 5, 69-71. June 1993.
___ "Day, Donald B.," *Science Fiction News* (Australia) No. 54: 10. April 1978.
___ "de Chair, Somerset," *Science Fiction Chronicle* 16(4): 16. February 1995.
___ "de la Ree, Gerry," *Locus* 30(2): 68. February 1993.
___ "de la Ree, Gerry," *Science Fiction Chronicle* 14(5): 10, 12. February 1993.
___ "del Rey, Lester," *Science Fiction Chronicle* 14(9): 17. June 1993.
___ "del Rey, Lester (1915-1993)," *Analog* 113(13): 110. November 1993.
___ "del Rey, Lester: Science Fiction Author," *Los Angeles (CA) Times* Sec. A, p. 26. May 14, 1993.
___ "del Rey, Lester, 1915-1993," *Starlog* No. 196: 22. November 1993.
___ "del Rey, Lester, Dies," *Locus* 30(6): 4, 67-69. June 1993.
___ "Delany, Bessie," *Locus* 35(5): 78. November 1995.
___ "Dollens, Morris Scott," *Locus* 33(3): 78. September 1994.
___ "Dollens, Morris Scott," *Locus* 33(4): 70. October 1994.
___ "Dollens, Morris Scott," *Science Fiction Chronicle* 15(10): 19-20. September 1994.
___ "du Bois, William Pené," *Locus* 30(3): 70. March 1993.
___ "Elliott, Denholm," *Science Fiction Chronicle* 14(3): 14. December 1992.
___ "Elliott, Janice," *Science Fiction Chronicle* 17(1): 24. October/November 1995
___ "Ende, Michael," *Locus* 35(4): 70. October 1995.
___ "Ende, Michael," *Science Fiction Chronicle* 17(1): 22. October/November 1995
___ "Fairman, Paul W.," *Science Fiction News* (Australia) No. 54: 10. April 1978.
___ "Fawcett, Gordon W.," *Locus* 30(3): 70-71. March 1993.
___ "Feinberg, Gerald," *Locus* 28(6): 67. June 1992.

OBITUARIES (continued)
___ "Feinberg, Gerald," *Science Fiction Chronicle* 13(9): 14. June 1992.
___ "Findley, Nigel D.," *Locus* 34(4): 62-63. April 1995.
___ "Finney, Jack," *Locus* 35(6): 79. December 1995.
___ "Finney, Jack," *Science Fiction Chronicle* 17(2): 24. December 1995/January 1996.
___ "Fisher, M. F. K.," *Locus* 29(3): 78. September 1992.
___ "Freed, Bert," *Science Fiction Chronicle* 15(10): 20. September 1994.
___ "Freleng, Fritz," *Science Fiction Chronicle* 16(8): 21. July/August 1995
___ "Furst, Anton," *Science Fiction Chronicle* 13(4): 12. January 1992.
___ "Furst, Anton, 1944-1992," *Starlog* 182: 69. September 1992.
___ "Gaines, William," *Science Fiction Chronicle* 13(10): 14, 16. July/August 1992.
___ "Gaines, William M.," *Locus* 29(1): 67. July 1992.
___ "Gallun, Raymond Z.," *Locus* 32(5): 62. May 1994.
___ "Gallun, Raymond Z.," *Science Fiction Chronicle* 15(6): 24. April/May 1994.
___ "Gann, Ernest," *Locus* 28(2): 68. February 1992.
___ "Garber, Eric," *Locus* 35(5): 78. November 1995.
___ "Gilbert, Robert E.," *Science Fiction Chronicle* 14(8): 16. May 1993.
___ "Gilbert, Robert E(rnest)," *Locus* 30(6): 72. June 1993.
___ "Gilliland, Doll," *Science Fiction Chronicle* 13(4): 12. January 1992.
___ "Gilliland, E. Dorothea," *Locus* 28(1): 72. January 1992.
___ "Goff, Harper, 1912-1993," *Starlog* No. 196: 23. November 1993.
___ "Golding, William," *Locus* 31(2): 58. August 1993.
___ "Golding, William," *Science Fiction Chronicle* 14(10): 16. July 1993.
___ "Golding, William: **Lord of the Flies** Author Golding Dies," *Austin (TX) American Statesman* Sec. C, p. 2. June 20, 1993.
___ "Goodman, Martin," *Science Fiction Chronicle* 13(10): 16. July/August 1992.
___ "Graham, Ronald Edward," *Science Fiction News* (Australia) No. 59: 10. February 1979.
___ "Grossman, Roberta Bender," *Locus* 28(5): 59. May 1992.
___ "Gwynne, Fred," *Science Fiction Chronicle* 14(11): 14. August 1993.
___ "Halas, John," *Science Fiction Chronicle* 16(5): 16, 18. March/April 1995.
___ "Hall, Desmond W.," *Locus* 29(6): 68. December 1992.
___ "Hall, Desmond W.," *Science Fiction Chronicle* 14(3): 14-15. December 1992.
___ "Hamm, Thelma D.," *Locus* 33(1): 74. July 1994.
___ "Hamm, Thelma D.," *Science Fiction Chronicle* 15(7): 16. June 1994.
___ "Hanley, Florence," *Locus* 31(2): 59. August 1993.
___ "Hanley, Florence," *Science Fiction Chronicle* 14(11): 14. August 1993.
___ "Hasford, Gustav," *Locus* 30(3): 70. March 1993.
___ "Hayakawa, Kiyoshi," *Locus* 31(3): 81-82. September 1993.
___ "Hayakawa, Kiyoshi," *Science Fiction Chronicle* 14(12): 12. September 1993.
___ "Henderson, George," *Locus* 28(6): 68. June 1992.
___ "Henderson, George," *Science Fiction Chronicle* 13(8): 16. May 1992.
___ "Herbert, Benson," *Locus* 29(4): 66. October 1992
___ "Herbert, Bruce C.," *Locus* 31(3): 82. September 1993.
___ "Hersey, John," *Locus* 30(5): 66. May 1993.
___ "Hersey, John," *Science Fiction Chronicle* 14(8): 16. May 1993.
___ "Hibbert, Eleanor," *Locus* 30(2): 68. February 1993.
___ "Highsmith, Patricia," *Locus* 34(3): 74. March 1995.
___ "Hildebrandt, Evelyn Beheshti," *Locus* 34(5): 72. May 1995.
___ "Hodder-Williams, Christopher," *Locus* 34(6): 66. June 1995.
___ "Hodder-Williams, Christopher," *Science Fiction Chronicle* 16(7): 19. June/July 1995.
___ "Holmes, Ron," *Science Fiction Chronicle* 15(3): 14. January 1994.
___ "Honda, Inishiro," *Science Fiction Chronicle* 14(7): 18. April 1993.
___ "Honda, Ishiro," *Locus* 30(4): 60. April 1993.
___ "Hoyt, John, 1904-1991," *Starlog* No. 174: 22-23. January 1992.
___ "Hyde-White, Wilfred, 1903-1991," *Starlog* No. 174: 23. January 1992.
___ "Ionesco, Eugene," *Locus* 32(5): 63. May 1994.
___ "James, John," *Locus* 32(3): 68. March 1994.
___ "Johnson, W. Ryerson," *Science Fiction Chronicle* 16(8): 21. July/August 1995

OBITUARIES

OBITUARIES (continued)

___ "Johnstone, Anna," *Science Fiction Chronicle* 14(3): 15. December 1992.

___ "Jones, Raymond F.," *Locus* 32(5): 62. May 1994.

___ "Jones, Raymond F.," *Science Fiction Chronicle* 15(7): 16. June 1994.

___ "Jones-Diggs, Barbara," *Locus* 34(2): 70. February 1995.

___ "Julia, Raul," *Science Fiction Chronicle* 16(2): 20. November/December 1994.

___ "Kandel, Aben," *Science Fiction Chronicle* 14(6): 16. March 1993.

___ "Kenin, Millea," *Locus* 29(4): 66. October 1992

___ "Kenin, Millea," *Science Fiction Chronicle* 14(2): 12. November 1992.

___ "Killough, Pat," *Locus* 33(6): 74. December 1994.

___ "Killough, Pat," *Science Fiction Chronicle* 16(2): 18, 20. November/December 1994.

___ "Kinski, Klaus," *Science Fiction Chronicle* 13(4): 12. January 1992.

___ "Kirby, Jack," *Locus* 32(3): 68. March 1994.

___ "Kirby, Jack," *Science Fiction Chronicle* 15(5): 12. March 1994.

___ "Kirk, Russell," *Locus* 32(6): 72. June 1994.

___ "Knebel, Fletcher," *Locus* 30(4): 60. April 1993.

___ "Knebel, Fletcher," *Science Fiction Chronicle* 14(7): 18. April 1993.

___ "Koch, Howard," *Locus* 35(3): 78. September 1993.

___ "Koch, Howard W.," *Science Fiction Chronicle* 17(1): 22, 24. October/November 1995

___ "Kostal, Irwin," *Science Fiction Chronicle* 16(3): 16. January 1995.

___ "Kramer, Eric," *Locus* 29(6): 68. December 1992.

___ "Kramer, Eric," *Science Fiction Chronicle* 14(2): 12. November 1992.

___ "Kubilius, Walter," *Locus* 31(5): 64. November 1993.

___ "Kubilius, Walter," *Science Fiction Chronicle* 15(2): 16-18. November/December 1993.

___ "Kurtzman, Harvey," *Locus* 30(4): 60. April 1993.

___ "Kurtzman, Harvey," *Science Fiction Chronicle* 14(7): 18. April 1993.

___ "Langstaff, Lydia," *Science Fiction Chronicle* 16(2): 20. November/December 1994.

___ "Lansing, Robert, 1929-1994," *Starlog* No. 212: 20. March 1995.

___ "Lantz, Walter," *Science Fiction Chronicle* 15(6): 24. April/May 1994.

___ "Larnach, Stanley Lorin," *Science Fiction News* (Australia) No. 59: 8-10. February 1979.

___ "Laumer, Keith," *Science Fiction Chronicle* 14(6): 16. March 1993.

___ "Leggett, John Harold," *Science Fiction News* (Australia) No. 59: 11. February 1979.

___ "Leiber, Fritz," *Science Fiction Chronicle* 14(2): 12. November 1992.

___ "Leiber, Fritz: 1910-1992," *Locus* 29(4): 4-5, 68-72. October 1992.

___ "Leiber, Fritz: Science Fiction Writer Fritz Leiber, 81," *Chicago Tribune* Sec. C, p. 10. September 10, 1992.

___ "Leiber, Fritz, 1910-1992," *Starlog* No. 189: 22-23. April 1993.

___ "Leventhal, Stan," *Locus* 34(3): 74. March 1995.

___ "Lewis, Oscar," *Locus* 29(3): 78. September 1992.

___ "Lindbergh, Anne Spencer," *Science Fiction Chronicle* 15(3): 14. January 1994.

___ "Lluesma, Jorge, 28, Madrid Fest Director, Dies," *Variety* p. 6, 34. January 30, 1985.

___ "Long, Frank Belknap," *Locus* 32(2): 72. February 1994.

___ "Long, Frank Belknap," *Science Fiction Chronicle* 15(4): 16. February 1994.

___ "Lott, Doug," *Science Fiction Chronicle* 15(7): 16. June 1994.

___ "Lubin, Arthur," *Science Fiction Chronicle* 16(7): 19. June/July 1995.

___ "Macauley, Robie," *Science Fiction Chronicle* 17(2): 26. December 1995/January 1996.

___ "MacBeth, George," *Locus* 28(3): 73. March 1992.

___ "MacBeth, George Mann, 1932-1992," *Vector* No. 166: 12. April/May 1992.

___ "Mahr, Kurt," *Locus* 31(4): 68. October 1993.

___ "Mancini, Henry," *Science Fiction Chronicle* 15(8): 20. June 1994.

___ "Martin, Kenneth Joseph," *Science Fiction News* (Australia) No. 59: 10-11. February 1979.

___ "Martin, Larry W.," *Locus* 30(3): 71. March 1993.

___ "Martin, Larry W.," *Science Fiction Chronicle* 14(7): 18. April 1993.

___ "Martinson, Harry," *Science Fiction News* (Australia) No. 55: 12. June 1978.

___ "Maske, Susan Gudelis," *Locus* 34(3): 74. March 1995.

OBITUARIES (continued)

___ "McBain, Gordon D., III," *Locus* 29(4): 66. October 1992

___ "McBain, Gordon D., III," *Science Fiction Chronicle* 14(2): 12, 14. November 1992.

___ "McComas, Annette Pelz," *Locus* 33(5): 71. November 1994.

___ "McComas, Annette Pelz," *Science Fiction Chronicle* 16(2): 20. November/December 1994.

___ "McComas, J. Francis," *Science Fiction News* (Australia) No. 55: 12. June 1978.

___ "McConnell, James V. (1925-1990)," *American Psychologist* 46(6): 650. June 1991.

___ "McNail, Stanley D.," *Locus* 34(6): 66. June 1995.

___ "McQuay, Mike," *Locus* 35(1): 62-63. July 1995.

___ "McQuay, Mike," *Science Fiction Chronicle* 16(7): 18-19. June/July 1995.

___ "Meredith, Scott," *Locus* 30(5): 66, 68. May 1993.

___ "Meredith, Scott," *Locus* 30(3): 68-69. March 1993.

___ "Meredith, Scott," *Science Fiction Chronicle* 14(6): 16. March 1993.

___ "Meredith, Sidney," *Locus* 29(3): 78. September 1992.

___ "Meredith, Sidney," *Science Fiction Chronicle* 13(11/12): 18, 20. August 1992.

___ "Millar, Margaret," *Locus* 32(5): 63. May 1994.

___ "Miranda, Vincent," *Locus* 28(3): 72-73. March 1992.

___ "Mitchell, Cameron," *Science Fiction Chronicle* 15(10): 20. September 1994.

___ "Monteith, Charles," *Locus* 34(6): 66. June 1995.

___ "Moore, Harry B.," *Science Fiction Chronicle* 17(1): 24. October/November 1995

___ "Moore, Ward," *Science Fiction News* (Australia) No. 54: 10-11. April 1978.

___ "Mugnaini, Joe," *Science Fiction Chronicle* 13(8): 16. May 1992.

___ "Mugnaini, Joseph," *Locus* 28(4): 60. April 1992.

___ "Mustchin, Charles," *Science Fiction Chronicle* 17(1): 24. October/November 1995

___ "Nance, Ron," *Locus* 31(2): 59. August 1993.

___ "Newman, John," *Science Fiction Chronicle* 14(1): 12. October 1992.

___ "Nier, Lenore Marie," *Locus* 31(5): 64. November 1993.

___ "Norton, Mary," *Locus* 29(4): 66. October 1992

___ "Norton, Mary," *Science Fiction Chronicle* 14(2): 14. November 1992.

___ "Nourse, Alan E.," *Locus* 29(3): 76. September 1992.

___ "Nourse, Alan E.," *Science Fiction Chronicle* 13(11/12): 20. August 1992.

___ "O'Neill, Gerard K.," *Locus* 28(6): 67. June 1992.

___ "Oliver, Chad," *Locus* 31(3): 80-81. September 1993.

___ "Oliver, Chad," *Matrix* (BSFA) No. 108: 8. November 1993.

___ "Oliver, Chad," *Science Fiction Chronicle* 14(12): 12. September 1993.

___ "Oliver, Chad, 1928-1993," *Starlog* No. 202: 77. May 1994.

___ "Oliver, Symmes Chadwick (1928-1993)," *Austin (TX) American Statesman* Sec. B, p. 4. August 15, 1993.

___ "Pargeter, Edith," *Locus* 35(6): 79. December 1995.

___ "Parker, Ella," *Science Fiction Chronicle* 15(4): 16, 18. February 1994.

___ "Parker, Ella," *Science Fiction Chronicle* 15(5): 12. March 1994.

___ "Parkinson, Terry Lee," *Locus* 30(2): 69. February 1993.

___ "Patterson, Kent R.," *Locus* 34(5): 72. May 1995.

___ "Peak, Bob," *Science Fiction Chronicle* 14(1): 12. October 1992.

___ "Peak, Robert," *Locus* 29(4): 66. October 1992

___ "Pelton, Lee," *Science Fiction Chronicle* 16(4): 16. February 1995.

___ "Pendleton, Don," *Science Fiction Chronicle* 17(2): 26. December 1995/January 1996.

___ "Pendleton, Donald Eugene," *Locus* 35(6): 79. December 1995.

___ "Perkins, Anthony," *Science Fiction Chronicle* 14(2): 14. November 1992.

___ "Phelps, Gilbert," *Locus* 31(2): 59. August 1993.

___ "Phoenix, River, 1970-1993," *Starlog* No. 202: 77. May 1994.

___ "Pleasence, Donald," *Science Fiction Chronicle* 16(5): 18. March/April 1995.

___ "Pollack, James," *Locus* 33(2): 70. August 1994.

___ "Pollack, James," *Science Fiction Chronicle* 15(8): 20. June 1994.

___ "Pope, Doyle," *Locus* 28(1): 72. January 1992.

___ "Possony, Stefan T.," *Locus* 34(6): 66. June 1995.

___ "Postal, Julius," *Science Fiction Chronicle* 14(7): 18. April 1993.

___ "Potter, Dennis," *Science Fiction Chronicle* 15(8): 20. June 1994.

___ "Preston, John," *Locus* 32(6): 72. June 1994.

OBITUARIES

OBLIVION (MOTION PICTURE)

OCCULT
___ Morris, David. **The Masks of Lucifer: Technology and the Occult in Twentieth Century Popular Literature.** London: Batsford, 1992. 223pp.

OCEANS
___ Burgess, Thomas. **Take Me Under the Sea: The Dream Merchants of the Deep.** Salem, OR: Ocean Archives, 1994. 259pp.
___ Frenschkowski, Marco. " 'Alles is Ufer. Ewig ruft das Meer': Maritime Symbolik in zwei Ersählungen von R. H. Barlow und Ramsey Campbell," *Quarber Merkur* 33(2): 48-59. December 1995. (No. 84)
___ Frenschkowski, Marco. "Bis ins dunkelste Herz des Meeres. Maritime Symbolik als Ausdruck des Unheimlichen in Erzählungen von W. H. Hodgson und H. P. Lovecraft," *Quarber Merkur* 32(2): 42-69. December 1994. (Whole No. 82)

OGILVIE, GEORGE
___ Lofficier, Randy. "***Mad Max*** Movies (1979-1985): Interview with George Miller, Terry Hayes, George Ogilvie and Mel Gibson," by Randy Lofficier and Jean-Marc Lofficier. in: Goldberg, Lee et al. **Science Fiction Filmmaking in the 1980s.** Jefferson, NC: McFarland, 1995. pp.133-174.

OKUDA, DENISE
___ Nensi, Salman A. "Revealing the History of the Future," *Star Trek: The Official Fan Club Magazine* No. 91: 1, 8. May/June 1993.

OKUDA, MIKE
___ Nensi, Salman A. "Revealing the History of the Future," *Star Trek: The Official Fan Club Magazine* No. 91: 1, 8. May/June 1993.

OLIPHANT, MARGARET
___ Shuttleworth, Sally. "Science and the Supernatural in the Stories of Margaret Oliphant," in: Benjamin, Marina, ed. **A Question of Identity: Women, Science, and Literature.** New Brunswick, NJ: Rutgers University Press, 1993. pp.173-191.

OLIVER, CHAD
___ "Oliver, Chad (Obituary)," *Locus* 31(3): 80-81. September 1993.
___ "Oliver, Chad (Obituary)," *Matrix* (BSFA) No. 108: 8. November 1993.
___ "Oliver, Chad (Obituary)," *Science Fiction Chronicle* 14(12): 12. September 1993.
___ "Oliver, Chad, 1928-1993 (Obituary)," *Starlog* No. 202: 77. May 1994.
___ "Oliver, Symmes Chadwick (1928-1993) (Obituary)," *Austin (TX) American Statesman* Sec. B, p. 4. August 15, 1993.
___ Knowles, Tom W., II. "Writing from the Heart of Time," *Starlog* No. 183: 27-31, 70. October 1992.
___ Zebrowski, George. "Never Forget the Writers Who Helped Build Yesterday's Tomorrows," *Science Fiction Age* 3(6): 30-36, 100. 1995.

OMNI (MAGAZINE)
___ "*Galaxy* Follows *Omni* into the Great Unknown," *Locus* 35(1): 9. July 1995.
___ "*Omni* Ceases Monthly Publication'". *Locus* 34(4): 7. April 1995.
___ "*Omni* for Sale?," *Science Fiction Chronicle* 14(7): 4. April 1993.
___ "*Omni* to Publish Trade Paperback SF Anthologies," *Science Fiction Chronicle* 13(9): 4-5. June 1992.
___ "*Omni Magazine* Goes Quarterly, With Monthly On-Line Presence," *Science Fiction Chronicle* 16(5): 4. March/April 1995.

ONIONS, OLIVER
___ Ashley, Mike. "Oliver Onions: The Man at the Edge," in: Schweitzer, Darrell, ed. **Discovering Classic Horror Fiction I.** Mercer Island, WA: Starmont, 1992. pp.120-126.
___ Menegaldo, Gilles. "Quelques substituts et simulacres d'Eros dans le recit fantastique moderne," in: Bozzetto, Roger, ed. **Eros: Science & Fiction Fantastique.** Aix-en-Provence: Universite de Provence, 1991. pp.43-57.

OPERA
___ "Brussels Cancels Verne 'Trip to the Moon'; No Unity of Components--Huisman," *Variety* p. 30. February 4, 1970.
___ Strauss, Walter A. "The Golem on the Operatic Stage: Nature's Warning," *Journal of the Fantastic in the Arts* 7(2/3): 191-200. 1995.

OPERATION DUMBO DROP (MOTION PICTURE)
___ Shay, Estelle. "***Operation Dumbo Drop***: Pachyderms and Parachutes," *Cinefex* No. 64: 121-122, 140. December 1995.

ORE, REBECCA
___ Ore, Rebecca. "The First Time," *New York Review of Science Fiction* No. 88: 15. December 1995.
___ Wolmark, Jenny. **Aliens and Others: Science Fiction, Feminism, and Postmodernism.** London: Harester Wheatsheaf, 1993. 167pp.; Iowa City: University of Iowa Press, 1994. 167pp.

ORGANIZATIONAL STRUCTURES
___ Corbett, J. Martin. "Celluloid Projections: Images of Technology and Organizational Futures in Contemporary Science Fiction Film," *Organization* 2(3/4): 467-488. August/November 1995

ORGANIZATIONS
___ Busby, F. M. "Fan Clubs: An Example," in: Sanders, Joe, ed. **Science Fiction Fandom.** Westport, CT: Greenwood, 1994. pp.143-148.
___ Luttrell, Hank. "The Science Fiction Convention Scene," in: Sanders, Joe, ed. **Science Fiction Fandom.** Westport, CT: Greenwood, 1994. pp.149-160.
___ Whitmore, Tom. "Science Fiction Conventions: Behind the Scenes," by Tom Whitmore and Debbie Notkin. in: Sanders, Joe, ed. **Science Fiction Fandom.** Westport, CT: Greenwood, 1994. pp.161-171.

ORIENTAL STORIES (MAGAZINE)
___ Cockcroft, T. G. L. "An Index to 'The Eyrie'," *Fantasy Commentator* 8(3/4): 217-229. Fall 1995. (Whole No. 47/48)

ORION BOOKS
___ "Orion Books New British Publisher," *Locus* 28(1): 6. January 1992.

ORSON WELLES' GHOST STORY (MOTION PICTURE)
___ Persons, Dan. "***Orson Welles' Ghost Story*** (Review)," *Cinefantastique* 26(2): 59. February 1995.

ORWELL, GEORGE
___ "George Orwell," in: Bloom, Harold, ed. **Classic Science Fiction Writers.** New York: Chelsea House, 1995. pp.106-121.
___ Aldiss, Brian W. "The Downward Journey: Orwell's **1984**," in: Aldiss, Brian W. **The Detached Retina: Aspects of SF and Fantasy.** Syracuse, NY: Syracuse University Press, 1995. pp.92-100.
___ Argyros, Alexander J. "Chaos Versus Contingency Theory: Epistemological Issues in Orwell's **1984**," *Mosaic* 26(1): 109-120. Winter 1993.
___ Bertinetti, Roberto. **L'infondazione di Babele: l'antiutopia.** Milan: F. Angeli, 1983. 164pp.
___ Bhat, Yashoda. **Aldous Huxley and George Orwell: A Comparative Study of Satire in Their Novels.** New Delhi: Sterling, 1991. 172pp.
___ Bloom, Harold. "Introduction," in: Bloom, Harold, ed. **George Orwell's 1984.** New York: Chelsea House, 1987. pp.1-8.
___ Bloom, Harold, ed. **George Orwell's 1984.** New York: Chelsea House, 1987. 135pp.
___ Booker, M. Keith. **The Dystopian Impulse in Modern Literature: Fiction as Social Criticism.** Westport, CT: Greenwood, 1994. 197pp.
___ Browning, William G. **Anti-Utopian Fiction: Definition and Standards for Evaluation.** Ph.D. Dissertation, Louisiana State University, 1966. 145pp.
___ Burgess, Anthony. "Ingsoc Considered," in: Bloom, Harold, ed. **George Orwell's 1984.** New York: Chelsea House, 1987. pp.35-46.
___ Caldwell, Larry W. "Wells, Orwell, and Atwood: (EPI)Logic and Eu/Utopia," *Extrapolation* 33(4): 333-345. Winter 1992.
___ Chalikova, Victoria. "A Russian Preface to George Orwell," in: Rose, Jonathan, ed. **The Revised Orwell.** East Lansing, MI: Michigan State University Press, 1992. pp.5-12.
___ Davison, Peter. "George Orwell: Dates and Origins," *The Library* 13(2): 137-150. June 1991. [Not seen.]
___ Eckstein, Arthur M. "The Classic Heritage of Airstrip One," in: Rose, Jonathan, ed. **The Revised Orwell.** East Lansing, MI: Michigan State University Press, 1992. pp.97-116.
___ Eckstein, Arthur M. "George Orwell's Second Thoughts on Capitalism," in: Rose, Jonathan, ed. **The Revised Orwell.** East Lansing, MI: Michigan State University Press, 1992. pp.191-206.

OUTER LIMITS (TV) (continued)

___ Scott, Tony. "TV Reviews: *The Outer Limits*," *Variety* 358(7): 30. March 20, 1995.

___ Spelling, Ian. "I, Nimoy," *Starlog* No. 217: 72-73. August 1995.

___ Van Hise, James. **Sci Fi TV: From Twilight Zone to Deep Space Nine.** Las Vegas, NV: Pioneer Books, 1993. 160pp. (Reprinted, HarperPrism, 1995. 258pp.)

___ Winikoff, Kenneth. "*Outer Limits*," *Cinefantastique* 26(3): 6-7, 61. April 1995.

OUTLAND (MOTION PICTURE)

___ Marcus, Steven J. "Tunnel Vision in Space," *Technology Review* 84(1): 2. October 1981.

OZ, FRANK

___ Pharr, Mary. "Different Shops of Horrors: From Roger Corman's Cult Classic to Frank Oz's Mainstream Musical," in: Latham, Robert A. and Collins, Robert A., eds. **Modes of the Fantastic.** Westport, CT: Greenwood, 1995. pp.212-220.

PAGEL, STEVE

___ "Barnes and Noble Genre Buyer Steve Pagel Moves to White Wolf; New SF/Fantasy Publisher," *Science Fiction Chronicle* 16(3): 4. January 1995.

___ "Pagel Leaving Barnes & Noble/B. Dalton," *Locus* 34(1) 7. January 1995.

___ "Steve Pagel Interview," *SFWA Bulletin* 27(2): 16-18. Summer 1993. (No. 120)

PAGEMASTER (MOTION PICTURE)

___ Crisafulli, Chuck. "*The Pagemaster*," *Cinefantastique* 25(3): 6-7, 61. June 1994.

___ Crisafulli, Chuck. "*Pagemaster*," *Cinefantastique* 25(6)/26(1): 38-39. December 1994.

___ Felperin, Leslie. "*Pagemaster* (Review)," *Sight and Sound* 5(2): 49-50. February 1995.

___ Lowe, Nick. "*The Pagemaster* (Review)," *Interzone* No. 92: 29-30. February 1995.

PAL, GEORGE

___ "Docu a Highlight of George Pal Tribute," *Variety* p. 2, 108. August 27, 1986.

___ Palumbo, Donald E. "The Politics of Entropy: Revolution vs. Evolution in George Pal's 1960 Film Version of H. G. Wells's **The Time Machine,**" in: Latham, Robert A. and Collins, Robert A., eds. **Modes of the Fantastic.** Westport, CT: Greenwood, 1995. pp.204-211.

PALE BLOOD (MOTION PICTURE)

___ Harris, Judith P. "*Pale Blood* (Review)," *Cinefantastique* 23(6): 60-61. April 1993.

PALMA, CLEMENTE

___ Kason, Nancy M. "The Dystopian Vision in **XYZ** by Clemente Palma," *Monographis Review* 3(1/2): 33-42. 1987.

PALTOCK, ROBERT

___ Baines, Paul. " 'Able Mechanick': **The Life and Adventures of Peter Wilkins** and the Eighteenth Century Fantastic Voyage," in: Seed, David, ed. **Anticipations: Essays on Early Science Fiction and Its Precursors.** Liverpool: Liverpool University Press, 1995. pp.1-25.

PALWICK, SUSAN

___ "Crawford Award Winners," *Locus* 30(3): 7. March 1993.

PAN

___ Dingley, Robert. "Meaning Everything: The Image of Pan at the Turn of the Century," in: Filmer, Kath, ed. **Twentieth-Century Fantasists: Essays in Culture, Society and Belief in Twentieth Century Mythopoeic Literature.** New York: St. Martin's, 1992. pp.47-59.

PANGBORN, EDGAR

___ Stephensen-Payne, Phil. **Edgar Pangborn: The Persistent Wonder, a Working Bibliography,** by Phil Stephensen-Payne and Gordon Benson, Jr. Albuquerque, NM: Galactic Central, 1993. 26pp.

___ Zebrowski, George. "Never Forget the Writers Who Helped Build Yesterday's Tomorrows," *Science Fiction Age* 3(6): 30-36, 100. 1995.

PAON, PAUL

___ Yaari, Monique. "Paul Paon's Sur-surreal Chimera," *Utopian Studies* 5(1): 108-127. 1994.

PARAMOUNT COMMUNICATIONS

___ "Bidding War for Paramount," *Locus* 31(4): 7. October 1993.

___ "Paramount Soap Opera," *Locus* 32(2): 8, 73. February 1994.

___ "Paramount Sold (Finally)," *Locus* 32(3): 8. March 1994.

___ "Paramount Under Siege; Acquires Macmillan," *Locus* 31(6): 6, 72. December 1993.

PARAMOUNT STUDIOS

___ "Wall Street Report: **Star Trek,**" *Wall Street Report* Program 636. December 3, 1994. (Transcript available.)

PARANORMAL

___ Guillaud, Lauric. "Paranormal Detectives: Sherlock Holmes in the House of Usher," *Paradoxa* 1(3): 301-319. 1995.

PARASITE (MOTION PICTURE)

___ "Sci-Fi **Parasite** Goes to Avemb Co.; Irv Yablan's 3-D'er," *Variety* p. 7, 39. November 4, 1981.

PARGETER, EDITH

___ "Pargeter, Edith (Obituary)," *Locus* 35(6): 79. December 1995.

PARK, PAUL

___ "Paul Park: Finding a Genre," *Locus* 28(6): 4, 74. June 1992.

___ Griffiths, Nick. "The Cult of Loving Kindness: Paul Park Interview," *Interzone* No. 61: 18-21. July 1992

PARKER, ELLA

___ "Parker, Ella (Obituary)," *Science Fiction Chronicle* 15(4): 16, 18. February 1994.

___ "Parker, Ella (Obituary)," *Science Fiction Chronicle* 15(5): 12. March 1994.

PARKINSON, TERRY LEE

___ "Parkinson, Terry Lee (Obituary)," *Locus* 30(2): 69. February 1993.

PATON, JOSEPH NOEL

___ Schindler, Richard A. "Joseph Noel Paton's Fairy Paintings: Fantasy Art as Victorian Narrative," *Scotia: Interdisciplinary Journal of Scottish Studies* 14: 13-29. 1990.

PATRICK, BUTCH

___ Voger, Mark. "The Boy Who Cried 'Woof Woof': An Interview with Butch Patrick," *Filmfax* No. 41: 73-76. October/November 1993.

PATRICK, ROBERT

___ Spelling, Ian. "True Believer," *Starlog* No. 189: 50-53, 67. April 1993.

PATROUCH, JOE

___ Patrouch, Joe. "Rogue Moon and Me," *Lan's Lantern* No. 41: 69-72. July 1993.

PATTERSON, KENT R.

___ "Patterson, Kent R. (Obituary)," *Locus* 34(5): 72. May 1995.

___ Klein, Jay K. "Biolog: Kent Patterson," *Analog* 115(10): 161, 174. August 1995.

PATTY, ANN

___ "Ann Patty Leaves S&S: Poseidon Eliminated," *Locus* 31(3): 6. September 1993.

PAUL, FRANK R.

___ "Interview: Robert Paul," *Futures Past* No. 3:31-32. September 1992.

___ Brzezinski, Anthony. "Paulian Technique," *Futures Past* No. 3:33. September 1992.

___ Weinberg, Robert. "Profile: Frank R. Paul," *Futures Past* No. 3:30-32. September 1992. (Reprinted from: Weinberg, Robert. **A Biographical Dictionary of Science Fiction and Fantasy Artists.** 1988.)

PAULL, LAWRENCE G.
___ Lofficier, Randy. "Interview: Lawrence G. Paull," by Randy Lofficier and Jean-Marc Lofficier. *Starlog* 184: 46-47, 70. November 1992.

PAXSON, DIANA L.
___ Holmen, Rachel E. "Interview With Diana L. Paxson and Adrienne Martine-Barnes," *Marion Zimmer Bradley's Fantasy Magazine* No. 28: 47-50. Summer 1995.
___ Hughes, Melinda. "Dark Sisters and Light Sisters: Sister Doubles and the Search for Sisterhood in **The Mists of Avalon** and **The White Raven**," *Mythlore* 19(1): 24-28. Winter 1993. (No. 71)
___ Nicholls, Stan. "Diana Paxson Invents Her Own Religion," in: Nicholls, Stan. **Wordsmiths of Wonder: Fifty Interviews with Writers of the Fantastic.** London: Orbit, 1993. pp.295-302.
___ Nicholls, Stan. "Writing and Ritual: Diana Paxson Interviewed," *Interzone* No. 76: 26-28. October 1993.

PEAK, ROBERT
___ "Peak, Bob (Obituary)," *Science Fiction Chronicle* 14(1): 12. October 1992.
___ "Peak, Robert (Obituary)," *Locus* 29(4): 66. October 1992

PEAKE, MERVYN
___ Bloom, Harold. "Mervyn Peake," in: Bloom, Harold, ed. **Modern Fantasy Writers.** New York: Chelsea House, 1995. pp.123-136.

PELTON, LEE
___ "Pelton, Lee (Obituary)," *Science Fiction Chronicle* 16(4): 16. February 1995.

PENAL COLONY (MOTION PICTURE)
___ Shapiro, Marc. "Boss of the **Penal Colony**," *Starlog* No. 200: 48-51. March 1994.

PENDLETON, DONALD EUGENE
___ "Pendleton, Don (Obituary)," *Science Fiction Chronicle* 17(2): 26. December 1995/January 1996.
___ "Pendleton, Donald Eugene (Obituary)," *Locus* 35(6): 79. December 1995.

PENERA, VIRGILIO
___ Chichester, Ana G. "Metamorphosis in Two Short Stories of the Fantastic by Virgilio Peñera and Felisberto Hernández," *Studies in Short Fiction* 31(3): 385-395. Summer 1994.

PENGUIN BOOKS
___ "Oldest Living Penguin Turns 60," *Locus* 34(5): 7. May 1995.

PENN, LEO
___ Jankiewicz, Pat. "Captain of Television," *Starlog* 179: 73-76. June 1992.

PEOPLE UNDER THE STAIRS (MOTION PICTURE)
___ "**The People Under the Stairs** (Review)," *Cinefantastique* 22(5): 59. April 1992.
___ Biodrowski, Steve. "Director Wes Craven on the Politics of Horror," *Cinefantastique* 22(5): 58. April 1992.

PEOPLES, DAVID
___ Lofficier, Randy. "**Blade Runner** (1982): Interviews with Hampton Francher, David Peoples, Ridley Scott and Syd Mead," by Randy Lofficier and Jean-Marc Lofficier. in: Goldberg, Lee et al. **Science Fiction Filmmaking in the 1980s.** Jefferson, NC: McFarland, 1995. pp.23-58.
___ Lofficier, Randy. "Interview: David Peoples," by Randy Lofficier and Jean-Marc Lofficier. *Starlog* 184: 40-41. November 1992.

PERCEVAL LE GALLOIS (MOTION PICTURE)
___ Rider, Jeff. "The Arthurian Legend in French Cinema: **Lancelot du Lac** and **Perceval la Gallois**," by Jeff Rider, Richard Hull and Christopher Smith. in: Harty, Kevin J., ed. **Cinema Arthuriana: Essays on Arthurian Film.** New York: Garland, 1991. pp.41-56.

PERCY, WALKER
___ Bizup, Joseph. "Hopkins' Influence on Percy's **Love in the Ruins**," *Renascence* 46(4): 247-260. Summer 1994.

PERCY, WALKER (continued)
___ Desmond, John E. "Walker Percy's Triad: Science, Literature, and Religion," *Renascence* 47(1): 3-10. Fall 1994.
___ Hobson, Linda W. "Walker Percy," in: Bruccoli, Matthew J., ed. **Facts on File Bibliography of American Fiction 1919-1988.** New York: Facts on File, 1991. pp.398-400.
___ Kreeft, Peter. **C. S. Lewis for the Third Millennium: Six Essays on The Abolition of Man.** San Francisco, CA: Ignatius, 1994. 193pp.
___ Kreeft, Peter. "Walker Percy's **Lost in the Cosmos: The Abolition of Man** in Late-night Comedy Format," in: Kreeft, Peter. **C. S. Lewis for the Third Millenium.** San Francisco, CA: Ignatius, 1994. pp.131-164.
___ Oleksy, Elzbieta H. "From Silence and Madness to the Exchange That Multiplies: Walker Percy and the Woman Question," *Southern Quarterly* 31(3): 58-68. Spring 1993.
___ Tolson, Jay. **Pilgrim in the Ruins: A Life of Walker Percy.** New York: Simon & Schuster, 1992. 544pp.
___ Westarp, Karlheinz. "Message to the Lost Self: Percy's Analysis of the Human Situation," *Renascence* 44(3): 215-224. Spring 1992.

PEREZ GALDOS, BENITO
___ García-Sánchez, Franklin B. "Ubicación genérica de **El Caballero Encantado** (1909) de Benito Pérez Galdós," *Monographis Review* 3(1/2): 71-80. 1987.

PERKINS, ANTHONY
___ "Perkins, Anthony (Obituary)," *Science Fiction Chronicle* 14(2): 14. November 1992.

PERKINS, GIL
___ Weaver, Tom. "Kong Conversations," *Starlog* No. 194: 70-73. September 1993.

PERKINS, MAXWELL
___ Lupoff, Richard A. "Edgar Rice Burroughs and the Maxwell Perkins Syndrome," *Burroughs Bulletin* NS. No. 13: 3-10. January 1993.

PERLMAN, RON
___ Shapiro, Marc. "The Savage Beast," by Marc Shapiro and Edward Gross. in: McDonnell, David, ed. **Starlog's Science Fiction Heroes and Heroines.** New York: Crescent Books, 1995. pp.66-69.

PERRY RHODAN
___ Kempen, Bernhard. "Perry Rhodan--Our Man in Space: Transformations of a German SF Phenomenon," *Foundation* No. 56: 5-22. Autumn 1992.

PERSONALITIES
___ "The 200 Most Important People in Science Fiction and Fantasy," *Starlog* No. 200: 6-23, 32-35, 40-43, 52-57, 62-67, 76-81. March 1994.

PERUCHO, JOAN
___ McSorley, Bonnie S. "Revamping the Vampire in Joan Perucho's **Natural History**," *Studies in Weird Fiction* No. 15: 2-5. Summer 1994.

PERUTZ, LEO
___ **Leo Perutz, 1882-1957: eine Ausstellung der Deutschen Bibliothek, Frankfurt-am-Main.** Wein: P. Zsolnay, 1989. 451pp.
___ Koseler, Michael. "Leo Perutz' **Der Meister des Jüngsten Tages**: Detektion und Verrätselung," *Quarber Merkur* 33(1): 3-15. June 1995. (No. 83)
___ Müller, Hans-Harald. **Leo Perutz.** München: Beck, 1992. 138pp.
___ Müller, Hans-Harald. **Leo Perutz: eine bibliographie.** Frankfurt-am-Main: P. Lang, 1991. 153pp.
___ Viaud, Didier. "Zeit und Phantastik. Die Zeit als Mittel des Phantastischen in den Romanen von Leo Perutz **Zwischen neun und neun** und **Sankt Petri-Schnee.** 2. Teil," *Quarber Merkur* 30(2): 47-60. December 1992. (No. 78)
___ Viaud, Didier. "Zeit und Phantastik. Die Zeit als Mittel des Phantastischen in den Romanen von Leo Perutz **Zwischen neun und neun** und **Sankt Petri-Schnee,** 1. Teil," *Quarber Merkur* 30(1): 28-46. June 1992. (No. 77)

PET SEMATARY II (MOTION PICTURE)
___ "**Sematary II**: Zombie Flick's Humor Surprises (Review)," *Washington (DC) Times.* August 31, 1992. in: *NewsBank. Film and Television.* 94:D12. 1992.

PET SEMATARY II (MOTION PICTURE)

PET SEMATARY II (MOTION PICTURE) (continued)
___ Doherty, Thomas. "*Pet Sematary Two* (Review)," *Cinefantastique* 23(5): 54, 61. February 1993.
___ McNally, Owen. "Gore Aplenty Splatters Screen in *Sematary* (Review)," *Hartford (CT) Courant*. August 29, 1992. in: *NewsBank. Film and Television*. 82:G10. 1992.
___ Ross, Patricia. "*Pet Sematary II*: Makeup Effects," *Cinefantastique* 23(2/3): 26. October 1992.
___ Ross, Patricia. "*Pet Sematary II*," *Cinefantastique* 23(1): 6-7. August 1992.
___ Ross, Patricia. "*Pet Sematary II*," *Cinefantastique* 23(2/3): 24-26. October 1992.
___ Ross, Patricia. "*Pet Sematary II*," *Cinefantastique* 23(5): 55. February 1993.
___ Stephens, Bob. "*Pet Sematary* Returns Like a Curse (Review)," *San Francisco (CA) Examiner*. August 29, 1992. in: *NewsBank. Film and Television*. 94:D10. 1992.
___ Strauss, Bob. "*Pet Sematary II* Comes Alive With No Help From King," *Austin (TX) American Statesman* Sec. B, p.5. August 31, 1992.
___ Thomas, Kevin. "Scare Tactics Don't Work Well in *Pet Sematary II* (Review)," *Newark (NJ) Star-Ledger*. September 1, 1992. in: *NewsBank. Film and Television*. 94:D11. 1992.

PET SEMATARY (MOTION PICTURE)
___ "Ties With King Led to Laurel's *Pet Sematary*," *Variety* p.81, 90. July 17, 1985.

PETER PAN (1924) (MOTION PICTURE)
___ Tetewsky, Lawrence. "*Peter Pan*: The Silent Film Version," *Cinefantastique* 22(6): 36-37. June 1992

PETER PAN (MOTION PICTURE)
___ McQuade, Brett. "*Peter Pan*: Disney's Adaptation of J. M. Barrie's Original Work," *Mythlore* 20(1): 5-9. Winter 1994. (Whole No. 75)
___ White, Taylor L. "Making the Cartoon Classic: Walt Disney's *Peter Pan*," *Cinefantastique* 22(6): 34-45. June 1992

PETERS, ELLIS, PSEUD.
___ "Pargeter, Edith (Obituary)," *Locus* 35(6): 79. December 1995.

PETERSEN, WOLFGANG
___ Rabkin, William. "*Enemy Mine* (1985): Interview with Wolfgang Petersen," in: Goldberg, Lee et al. **Science Fiction Filmmaking in the 1980s**. Jefferson, NC: McFarland, 1995. pp.111-132.

PETRUCHA, STEFAN
___ Florence, Bill. "The X-Comics," *Starlog* No. 212: 58-60. March 1995.

PETTY, LORI
___ Johnson, Kim H. "*Tank Girl*," *Starlog* No. 213: 40-43. April 1995.

PHANTASM II (MOTION PICTURE)
___ "*Phantasm II* (Review)," *Variety* p. 16. July 13, 1988.

PHANTASM III: LORD OF THE DEAD (MOTION PICTURE)
___ Fischer, Dennis. "*Phantasm: Lord of the Dead* (Review)," *Cinefantastique* 26(3): 60. April 1995.
___ Harris, Judith P. "*Phantasm III: Lord of the Dead* (Review)," *Cinefantastique* 26(4): 60. June 1995.

PHANTOM OF THE OPERA (1943) (MOTION PICTURE)
___ MacQueen, Scott. " '43 Phantom Found New Formula for Classic Tale," *American Cinematographer* 74(9): 80-85. September 1993.

PHANTOM OF THE OPERA (PLAY)
___ "*The Phantom of the Opera* (Review)," *Variety* p. 100. January 27, 1988.

PHELPS, GILBERT
___ "Phelps, Gilbert (Obituary)," *Locus* 31(2): 59. August 1993.

PHELPS, NIGEL
___ Roeger, Berthe. "Building a World of Dredd," *Sci-Fi Entertainment* 2(2): 42-49. August 1995.

PHILADELPHIA EXPERIMENT II (MOTION PICTURE)
___ Wilt, David. "*Philadelphia Experiment II* (Review)," *Cinefantastique* 25(6)/26(1): 123. December 1994.

PHILIP K. DICK MEMORIAL AWARD, 1992
___ "Ian McDonald Wins Philip K. Dick Award," *Science Fiction Chronicle* 13(8): 4. May 1992.
___ "McDonald Wins Philip K. Dick Award," *Locus* 28(5): 6, 65. May 1992.
___ "Philip K. Dick Award Nominees," *Locus* 28(2): 6. February 1992.
___ "Philip K. Dick Award Nominees," *Locus* 30(2): 5. February 1993.
___ "Philip K. Dick Award Nominees," *Science Fiction Chronicle* 13(5): 4. February 1992.
___ "Philip K. Dick Award Winner, 1992," *Locus* 30(4): 6. April 1993.
___ "Richard Grant Wins Philip K. Dick Award," *Science Fiction Chronicle* 14(7): 4. April 1993.

PHILIP K. DICK MEMORIAL AWARD, 1993
___ "Judges Announced for Philip K. Dick Award," *Locus* 29(5): 4. November 1992.
___ "Nebula, World Fantasy, Philip K. Dick Award Juries Established," *Science Fiction Chronicle* 14(3): 4-5. December 1992.
___ "Philip K. Dick Award Nominations," *Science Fiction Chronicle* 14(5): 4. February 1993.
___ "Philip K. Dick Award Nominations," *Science Fiction Chronicle* 15(5): 4-5. March 1994.
___ "Philip K. Dick Award Nominees," *Locus* 32(2): 9. February 1994.
___ "Philip K. Dick Award Winners, 1993," *Locus* 32(5): 8. May 1994.
___ "Womack and Ford Tie for Philip K. Dick Award," *Science Fiction Chronicle* 15(6): 4. April/May 1994.

PHILIP K. DICK MEMORIAL AWARD, 1994
___ "Philip K. Dick Award Nominees," *Locus* 34(2): 8. February 1995.
___ "Philip K. Dick Awards Judges," *Locus* 31(1): 6. July 1993.
___ "Philip K. Dick Awards Nominations," *Science Fiction Chronicle* 16(4): 4. February 1995.
___ "Wilson Wins Philip K. Dick Award," *Locus* 34(5): 8. May 1995.

PHILIP K. DICK MEMORIAL AWARD, 1995
___ "Robert Charles Wilson Wins Philip K. Dick Award," *Science Fiction Chronicle* 16(6): 4. May 1995.

PHILIP K. DICK SOCIETY NEWSLETTER (MAGAZINE)
___ "Index to the *PKDS* Newsletter, No. 1-30," *PKDS Newsletter* No. 30: 5-13. December 1992.

PHILIPPINES
___ Olsa, Jaroslav, Jr. "SF in Southeast Asia," *Locus* 34(1) 70. January 1995.

PHILOSOPHY
___ Clark, Stephen R. L. **How to Live Forever: Science Fiction and Philosophy**. London, New York: Routledge, 1995. 223pp.

PHIPPS, WILLIAM
___ Weaver, Tom. "William Phipps: Interview," in: Weaver, Tom, ed. **Attack of the Monster Movie Makers: Interviews with 20 Genre Giants**. Jefferson, NC: McFarland, 1994. pp.249-266.

PHOENIX THE WARRIOR (MOTION PICTURE)
___ "*Phoenix the Warrior* (Review)," *Variety* p. 28. May 25, 1988.

PHOENIX, RIVER
___ "Phoenix, River, 1970-1993 (Obituary)," *Starlog* No. 202: 77. May 1994.

PHOTOGRAPHY
___ Kelley, Scott. "Photo-Utopia and Poetic Representations of the Impossible: The Utopic Figure in Modern Poetic and Photographic Discourse," *Utopian Studies* 6(1): 1-18. 1995.

PHYSICS
___ Bicchieri, Sarah N. **Quantum Physics and Annie Dillard: Parallels in Science and Literature**. Master's Thesis, Central Washington University, 1993. 85pp.
___ Krauss, Lawrence M. **The Physics of Star Trek**. New York: Basic Books, 1995. 188pp.

PHYSICS

PHYSICS (continued)
___ Martin-Diaz, M. J. "Science Fiction Comes to the Classroom: Maelstrom II," by M. J. Martin-Diaz, A. Pizarro, P. Bacas, J. P. Garcia and F. Perera. *Physics Education* 27(1): 18-23. January 1992.
___ Nahin, Paul J. **Time Machines: Time Travel in Physics, Metaphysics, and Science Fiction**. New York: American Institute of Physics, 1993. 408pp.

PHYSICS IN LITERATURE
___ Troiano, Maureen D. **New Physics and the Modern French Novel**. New York: Peter Lang, 1995. 276pp.

PICARA
___ Kaler, Anne K. **The Picara: From Hera to Fantasy Heroine**. Bowling Green, OH: Popular Press, 1991. 215pp.

PICARDO, ROBERT
___ Fletcher, Tanya A. "Interview With the Hologram," *Sci-Fi Entertainment* 1(5): 42-44. February 1995.
___ Spelling, Ian. "Smoke and Mirrors," *Starlog* No. 216: 27-30, 64. July 1995.

PICNIC AT HANGING ROCK (MOTION PICTURE)
___ Callahan, Tim. "Censoring the World Riddle," *Mythlore* 20(1): 15-21. Winter 1994. (Whole No. 75)

PIERCE, JACK
___ Crisafulli, Chuck. "The Monstrous Genius of Jack Pierce," *Filmfax* No. 35: 36-39, 80-81. October/November 1992.

PIERCY, MARGE
___ "Arthur C. Clarke Award," *Locus* 30(5): 8. May 1993.
___ "Marge Piercy Wins Arthur C. Clarke Award," *Science Fiction Chronicle* 14(8): 4. May 1993.
___ Barr, Marleen S. **Lost in Space: Probing Feminist Science Fiction and Beyond**. Chapel Hill, NC: University of North Carolina Press, 1993. 231pp.
___ Booker, M. Keith. "Woman on the Edge of a Genre: The Feminist Dystopias of Marge Piercy," *Science Fiction Studies* 21(3): 337-350. November 1994.
___ Deery, June. "Ectopic and Utopic Reproduction: **He, She and It**," *Utopian Studies* 5(2): 36-49. 1994.
___ Drake, Barbara. "Two Utopias: Marge Piercy's **Women on the Edge of Time** and Ursula K. Le Guin's **The Dispossessed**," in: Roberts, Sheila, ed. **Still the Frame Holds: Essays on Women Poets and Writers**. San Bernardino, CA: Borgo Press, 1993. pp.109-128.
___ DuPlessis, Rachel B. "The Feminist Apologies of Lessing, Piercy, and Russ," *Frontiers* 4(1): 1-8. 1979.
___ Fitting, Peter. "Beyond the Wasteland: A Feminist in Cyberspace," *Utopian Studies* 5(2): 4-15. 1994.
___ Kuelen, Margarete. **Radical Imagination: Feminist Conceptions of the Future in Ursula Le Guin, Marge Piercy and Sally Miller Gearhart**. Frankfurt-am-Main/New York: Peter Lang, 1991. 122pp.
___ Kuryllo, Helen A. "Cyborgs, Sorcery, and the Struggle for Utopia," *Utopian Studies* 5(2): 50-55. 1994.
___ Macklin, Lisa A. **Feminism in the Selected Science Fiction Novels of Margaret Atwood and Marge Piercy**. Master's Thesis, Texas Woman's University, 1993. 105pp. (Master's Abstracts 32/03, p. 805. June 1994.)
___ Neverow, Vara. "The Politics of Incorporation and Embodiment: **Woman on the Edge of Time** and **He, She and It** as Feminist Epistemologies of Resistance," *Utopian Studies* 5(2): 16-35. 1994.
___ Piercy, Marge. "Telling Stories About Stories," *Utopian Studies* 5(2): 1-3. 1994.
___ Sauter-Baillet, Theresia. "Marge Piercy: **Woman on the Edge of Time** (1976)," in: Heuermann, Hartmut and Lange, Bernd-Peter, eds. **Die Utopie in der angloamerikanischen Literatur: Interpretationen**. Düsseldorf: Bagel, 1984. pp.349-370.
___ Sautter, Diane. "Erotic and Existential Paradoxes of the Golem: Marge Piercy's **He, She and It**," *Journal of the Fantastic in the Arts* 7(2/3): 255-268. 1995.
___ Wolmark, Jenny. **Aliens and Others: Science Fiction, Feminism, and Postmodernism**. London: Harester Wheatsheaf, 1993. 167pp.; Iowa City: University of Iowa Press, 1994. 167pp.

PILEGGI, MITCH
___ Vitaris, Paula. "**X-Files**: F. B. I. Box Skinner," *Cinefantastique* 26(6)/27(1): 77-78. October 1995.

PILGRIM AWARD (SFRA), 1992
___ Lewis, Arthur O. "1992 Pilgrim Award Presentation and Acceptance," *SFRA Review* No. 199: 11-14. July/August/September 1992.

PILGRIM AWARD (SFRA), 1994
___ **No Great Endeavor: Presentation of the Pilgrim and Pioneer Awards**. Ann Arbor, MI: Tucker Video, 1994. 1 videocassette, 67 minutes. (Presentation at the 1994 Science Fiction Research Association Conference. Sheri S. Tepper, John Clute, Takayuki Tatsumi, Larry McCaffery, speakers.)
___ "Pilgrim Award, 1994," *Science Fiction Chronicle* 15(10): 8. September 1994.
___ Clute, John. "Pilgrim Award Acceptance Speech," in: Clute, John. **Look at the Evidence: Essays and Reviews**. Liverpool: Liverpool University Press, 1995. pp.8-11.

PILGRIM AWARD (SFRA), 1995
___ Attebery, Brian. "Pilgrim Award Presentation Speech, 1995," *SFRA Review* No. 219: 25-27. September/October 1995.
___ Sobchack, Vivian. "Pilgrim Award Acceptance Speech, 1995," *SFRA Review* No. 219: 27-29. September/October 1995.

PILLER, MICHAEL
___ Altman, Mark A. "**The Next Generation**: Next Generation's Piller of Strength," *Cinefantastique* 23(2/3): 44-45. October 1992.
___ Altman, Mark A. "**Star Trek: Deep Space Nine**: Michael Piller, Series Co-Creator," *Cinefantastique* 23(6): 23. April 1993.
___ Altman, Mark A. "**Star Trek: The Next Generation**: Michael Piller, Trek's Secret Weapon," *Cinefantastique* 24(3/4): 28-29. October 1993.
___ Kutzera, Dale. "**Star Trek: Voyager**," *Cinefantastique* 26(2): 28-29. February 1995.
___ Spelling, Ian. "Under Western Skies," *Starlog* No. 217: 76-79. August 1995.

PILOT'S ASSOCIATE
___ "Pilot's Associate," in: Gray, Chris H., ed. **The Cyborg Handbook**. New York: Routledge, 1995. pp.101-103.
___ Gray, Chris H. "Science Fiction Becomes Science Fact," in: Gray, Chris H., ed. **The Cyborg Handbook**. New York: Routledge, 1995. pp.104-106.

PINOCCHIO
___ Wunderlich, Richard. "De-Radicalizing **Pinocchio**," in: Sanders, Joe, ed. **Functions of the Fantastic**. Westport, CT: Greenwood, 1995. pp.19-28.

PIONEER AWARD (SFRA), 1992
___ Gordon, Joan. "1992 Pioneer Award Presentation and Acceptance," *SFRA Review* No. 199: 9-11 . July/August/September 1992.

PIONEER AWARD (SFRA), 1994
___ **No Great Endeavor: Presentation of the Pilgrim and Pioneer Awards**. Ann Arbor, MI: Tucker Video, 1994. 1 videocassette, 67 minutes. (Presentation at the 1994 Science Fiction Research Association Conference. Sheri S. Tepper, John Clute, Takayuki Tatsumi, Larry McCaffery, speakers.)

PIONEER AWARD (SFRA), 1995
___ Sanders, Joe L. "Pioneer Award Presentation Speech, 1995," *SFRA Review* No. 219: 23-25. September/October 1995.

PIPER, H. BEAM
___ Lovisi, Gary. "H. Beam Piper in Paperback," *Paperback Parade* No. 35: 50-58. August 1993.
___ Lovisi, Gary. "**Little Fuzzy**: The 8th Printing," *Paperback Parade* No. 35: 48-49. August 1993.
___ Lovisi, Gary. "The Long Lost Fuzzy," *Paperback Parade* No. 35: 40-44. August 1993.
___ Major, Joseph T. "Lord Kalvan of Otherwriters," *Paperback Parade* No. 35: 72-100. August 1993.
___ Mayhar, Ardath. "**Golden Dreams**: Odyssey of an Alien," *Paperback Parade* No. 35: 45-47. August 1993.

PIPER, H. BEAM

PIPER, H. BEAM (continued)

___ Stephensen-Payne, Phil. **H. Beam Piper, Emperor of Paratime: A Working Bibliography**. 4th edition, by Phil Stephensen-Payne and Gordon Benson, Jr. Albuquerque, NM: Galactic Central, 1994. 31pp.

PIRACY

___ "**Dune** Release Will Test Print Coding to Hinder Pirates," *Variety* p. 1, 141. December 12, 1984.

___ "Uncut 'Clockwork' Spurs Distrib-Exhib Heat in Argentina," *Variety* p. 44. September 15, 1982.

PIXAR (COMPANY)

___ French, Lawrence. "*Toy Story*: CGI Production," *Cinefantastique* 27(2): 28-29 November 1995.

___ French, Lawrence. "*Toy Story*: Pixar," *Cinefantastique* 27(2): 23-25. November 1995.

___ French, Lawrence. "*Toy Story*: Renderman," *Cinefantastique* 27(2): 18-19. November 1995.

___ Shay, Estelle. "Company File: Pixar," *Cinefex* No. 55: 23-24. August 1993.

PLAGIARISM

___ "Cuckoo in Wrong Nest," *Locus* 33(1): 9, 75. July 1994.

___ "Orbit Withdraws William James Books," *Science Fiction Chronicle* 16(3): 4. January 1995.

___ "Two Pauline Dunn Horror Novels Plagiarized Dean R. Koontz's **Phantoms**," *Science Fiction Chronicle* 13(10): 4. July/August 1992.

___ "Zebra Withdraws Two Novels for Plagiarism," *Locus* 28(2): 6. August 1992.

___ Yarbro, Chelsea Q. "A Matter of Willful Copyright Infringement," *SFWA Bulletin* 26(2): 11-13. Summer 1992. (No. 116)

PLAN 10 FROM OUTER SPACE (MOTION PICTURE)

___ Adams, Max. "**Ed Wood**: **Plan 10 From Outer Space**," *Cinefantastique* 25(5): 45. October 1994.

___ Means, Sean P. "**Plan 10 From Outer Space**: Utah's Alien Invasion," *Salt Lake City (UT) Tribune*. October 30, 1994. in: *NewsBank. Film and Television*. 123:F2-F4. 1994.

PLAN 9 FROM OUTER SPACE (MOTION PICTURE)

___ Kaltenbach, Chris. "A Maryland Actor Saw His Spaceship Come in in an Awful 1959 Film," *(Baltimore, MD) Sun*. July 7, 1994. in: *NewsBank. Film and Television*. 62:E8. 1994.

PLAN 9 FROM OUTER SPACE: THE MUSICAL (PLAY)

___ Thonen, John. "**Ed Wood**: Plan 9 Alive! The Musical," *Cinefantastique* 25(5): 36-37. October 1994.

PLANET OF THE APES (MOTION PICTURE)

___ Atkinson, Michael. "Son of Apes," *Film Comment* 31(5): 62-66. September/October 1995.

___ Greene, Eric. **Planet of the Apes as American Myth: Race and Politics in the Films and Television Series**. Jefferson, NC: McFarland, 1995. 264pp.

___ Weaver, Tom. "Woman of the Apes," *Starlog* No. 213: 57-63. April 1995.

PLANTS

___ Schulp, J. A. "The Flora of Middle Earth," in: Kranz, Gisbert, ed. **Inklings: Jahrbuch für Literatur und Ästhetik**. 3. Band. [Lüdenscheid, Germany: Stier], 1985. pp.129-186.

PLATH, SYLVIA

___ Ahearn, Catherine. "An Archetype of Pain: From Plath to Atwood and Musgrave," in: Roberts, Sheila, ed. **Still the Frame Holds: Essays on Women Poets and Writers**. San Bernardino, CA: Borgo Press, 1993. pp.137-156.

___ Burleson, Mollie L. "Mirror, Mirror: Sylvia Plath's 'Mirror' and Lovecraft's 'The Outsider'," *Lovecraft Studies* No. 31: 10-12. Fall 1994.

PLATO

___ Bertelli, Lucio. "Platone," in: Colombo, Arrigo and Quarta, Cosimo, eds. **Il Destino della Famiglia nell'Utopia**. Bari: Edizione Dedalo, 1991. pp.33-48.

___ de Armas, Frederick A. "Gyges' Ring: Invisibility in Plato, Tolkien, and Lope de Vega," *Journal of the Fantastic in the Arts* 3(4): 120-138. 1994.

PLATO (continued)

___ Depew, David J. "Aristotle's Critique of Plato's Ideal States," in: Saccaro Del Buffa, Giuseppa and Lewis, Arthur O., eds. **Utopia e Modernita: Teorie e prassi utopiche nell'eta moderna e postmoderna**. Rome: Gangemi Editore, 1989. pp.727-738.

___ Smith, Nicholas D. "Political Activity and Ideal Economics: Two Related Utopian Themes in Aristophanic Comedy," *Utopian Studies* 3(1): 84-94. 1992.

PLATT, CHARLES

___ Platt, Charles. "The Carnival of Angst," *Interzone* No. 87: 31-33. September 1994.

___ Platt, Charles. **My Love Affair With Harlan Ellison**. New York: Interactive Systems, 1994. 36pp.

PLAYS

___ Bertha, Csilla. "The Harmony of Reality and Fantasy: The Fantastic in Irish Drama," *Journal of the Fantastic in the Arts* 4(3): 2-24. 1991. (No. 15)

___ Frazier, Paul M. **Patterns in Recent Science Fiction Drama**. Ph.D. Dissertation, Bowling Green State University, 1992. 196pp.

___ Gordon, Mel. "A History of the Theater of the Future (to 1984)," *Theater* 26(1/2): 12-32. 1995.

___ Heck, Peter J. "Three Views of Two Guys: *Two Guys From the Future* and Other Plays; An Evening of Science Fiction Theater," by Peter J. Heck, Greg Cox and Shira Daemon. *New York Review of Science Fiction* No. 47: 1, 3-6. July 1992.

___ Hollinger, Veronica. "Playing at the End of the World: Postmodern Theater," in: Murphy, Patrick D., ed. **Staging the Impossible: The Fantastic Mode in Modern Drama**. Westport, CT: Greenwood, 1992. pp.182-196.

___ Krupnik, Joseph. "Infinity in a Cigar Box: The Problem of Science Fiction on Stage," in: Murphy, Patrick D., ed. **Staging the Impossible: The Fantastic Mode in Modern Drama**. Westport, CT: Greenwood, 1992. pp.197-219.

___ Murphy, Patrick D. "Introduction," in: Murphy, Patrick D., ed. **Staging the Impossible: The Fantastic Mode in Modern Drama**. Westport, CT: Greenwood, 1992. pp.1-14.

___ Murphy, Patrick D., ed. **Staging the Impossible: The Fantastic Mode in Modern Drama**. Westport, CT: Greenwood, 1992. 245pp.

___ Schenkel, Elmar. "Visions From the Verge: Terror and Play in G. K. Chesterton's Imagination," in: Filmer, Kath, ed. **Twentieth-Century Fantasists: Essays in Culture, Society and Belief in Twentieth Century Mythopoeic Literature**. New York: St. Martin's, 1992. pp.34-46.

___ Shank, Theodore. "The Shock of the Actual: Disrupting the Theatrical Illusion," in: Murphy, Patrick D., ed. **Staging the Impossible: The Fantastic Mode in Modern Drama**. Westport, CT: Greenwood, 1992. pp.169-181.

___ Willingham, Ralph A. "Dystopian Vision in the Plays of Elias Canetti," *Science Fiction Studies* 19(1): 69-74. March 1992.

___ Willingham, Ralph A. **Science Fiction and the Theatre**. Ph.D. Dissertation, University of Illinois, Urbana-Champaign, 1991. 382pp.

___ Willingham, Ralph A. **Science Fiction and the Theatre**. Westport, CT: Greenwood, 1994. 213pp.

PLEASENCE, DONALD

___ "Pleasence, Donald (Obituary)," *Science Fiction Chronicle* 16(5): 18. March/April 1995.

___ Maronie, Sam. "Some Gentle Evil," *Starlog* No. 215: 63-67. June 1995.

PLENT, ALAN

___ Mackenzie, Angus. "Brush Strokes in Blood: An Exclusive Interview with Alan Plent," in: Brown, Michael, ed. **Pandemonium: Further Explorations into the Worlds of Clive Barker**. Staten Island, NY: Eclipse, 1991. pp.43-51.

PLOT

___ Asimov, Isaac. "Plotting," in: Dozois, Gardner, ed. **Writing Science Fiction and Fantasy**. New York: St. Martin's, 1991. pp.28-32.

___ Kress, Nancy. "Plot: Using Coincidence in Your Fiction," in: Thompkins, David G., ed. **Science Fiction Writer's Market Place and Source Book**. Cincinnati, OH: Writer's Digest Books, 1994. pp.30-33.

PLUGHEAD REWIRED (MOTION PICTURE)
___ SEE: CIRCUITRY MAN II: PLUGHEAD REWIRED (MOTION PICTURE).

POCAHONTAS (MOTION PICTURE)
___ Lyons, Michael. "*Pocahontas*: Animator Glen Keane on the Renaissance of Disney Animation," *Cinefantastique* 27(3): 50. December 1995.
___ Lyons, Michael. "*Pocahontas* (Review)," *Cinefantastique* 27(3): 49. December 1995.
___ Lyons, Michael. "*Pocahontas*," *Cinefantastique* 27(3): 48, 50, 60. December 1995.
___ Malmquist, Allen. "*Pocahontas*," *Cinefantastique* 26(5): 14-15. August 1995.
___ Malmquist, Allen. "*Pocahontas*," *Cinefantastique* 26(6)/27(1): 118-121. October 1995.

POCKET BOOKS
___ "Pocket Does McIntyre Alternate History," *Locus* 35(3): 8. September 1993.

POE, EDGAR ALLAN
___ "Edgar Allan Poe," in: Bloom, Harold, ed. **Classic Science Fiction Writers**. New York: Chelsea House, 1995. pp.122-136.
___ "Edgar Allan Poe Special Puts AI Pictures into Production for TV; Eye Web Sale," *Variety* p. 34. February 18, 1970.
___ Badenhausen, Richard. "Fear and Trembling in Literature of the Fantastic: Edgar Allan Poe's 'The Black Cat'," *Studies in Short Fiction* 29(4): 487-498. Fall 1992.
___ Bloom, Harold. "Edgar Allan Poe," in: Bloom, Harold. **Classic Horror Writers**. New York: Chelsea House, 1994. pp.86-106.
___ Brown, Gillian. "The Poetics of Extinction," in: Rosenheim, Shawn and Rachman, Stephen, ed. **The American Face of Edgar Allan Poe**. Baltimore: Johns Hopkins University Press, 1995. pp.330-344.
___ Budd, Louis J., ed. **On Poe: The Best From *American Literature***, ed. by Louis J. Budd and Edwin H. Cady. Durham, NC: Duke University Press, 1993. 270pp.
___ Butler, David W. "Usher's Hypochondriasis: Mental Alienation and Romantic Idealism in Poe's Gothic Tales (1976)," in: Budd, Louis J. and Cady, Edwin H., eds. **On Poe**. Durham, NC: Duke University Press, 1993. pp.185-196.
___ Capek, Karel. "Edgar Allan Poe: The Unparalleled Adventure of One Hans Pfall," *Studies in Weird Fiction* No. 14: 8-9. Winter 1994.
___ Caputi, Anthony. "The Refrain in Poe's Poetry (1953)," in: Budd, Louis J. and Cady, Edwin H., eds. **On Poe**. Durham, NC: Duke University Press, 1993. pp.92-101.
___ Cavell, Stanley. "Being Odd, Getting Even (Descartes, Emerson, Poe)," in: Rosenheim, Shawn and Rachman, Stephen, ed. **The American Face of Edgar Allan Poe**. Baltimore: Johns Hopkins University Press, 1995. pp.3-37.
___ Cersowsky, Peter. "Varianten phantastischer Lyrik: Edgar Allan Poe und Georg Trakl," in: Kranz, Gisbert, ed. **Inklings: Jahrbuch für Literatur und Ästhetik**. 9. Band. Lüdenscheid, Germany: Stier, 1991. pp.165-186. [Not seen.]
___ Cherniavsky, Eva. "Revivification and Utopian Time: Poe Versus Stowe," in: Rosenheim, Shawn and Rachman, Stephen, ed. **The American Face of Edgar Allan Poe**. Baltimore: Johns Hopkins University Press, 1995. pp.121-139.
___ Dameron, J. Lasley. "Poe's Pym and Scoresby on Polar Cataracts," *Resources for American Literary Study* 21(2): 258-260. 1995.
___ Dayan, Joan. "Amorous Bondage: Poe, Ladies, and Slaves," in: Rosenheim, Shawn and Rachman, Stephen, ed. **The American Face of Edgar Allan Poe**. Baltimore: Johns Hopkins University Press, 1995. pp.179-210.
___ Eakin, Paul J. "Poe's Sense of an Ending (1973)," in: Budd, Louis J. and Cady, Edwin H., eds. **On Poe**. Durham, NC: Duke University Press, 1993. pp.150-171.
___ Elmer, Jonathan. "Terminate or Liquidate? Poe, Sensationalism, and the Sentimental Tradition," in: Rosenheim, Shawn and Rachman, Stephen, ed. **The American Face of Edgar Allan Poe**. Baltimore: Johns Hopkins University Press, 1995. pp.91-120.
___ Estren, Mark J. **Horrors Within and Without: A Psychoanalytic Study of Edgar Allan Poe and Howard Phillips Lovecraft**. Ph.D. Dissertation, State University of New York at Buffalo, 1978. 250pp. (DAI 39: 1565A.)

POE, EDGAR ALLAN (continued)
___ Fisher, Benjamin F. "Poe's 'Metzengerstein': Not a Hoax (1971)," in: Budd, Louis J. and Cady, Edwin H., eds. **On Poe**. Durham, NC: Duke University Press, 1993. pp.142-149.
___ Friedman, William F. "Edgar Allan Poe, Cryptographer (1936)," in: Budd, Louis J. and Cady, Edwin H., eds. **On Poe**. Durham, NC: Duke University Press, 1993. pp.40-54.
___ Graff, Bennett. **Horror in Evolution: Determinism, Materialism, and Darwinism in the American Gothic (Edgar Allan Poe, Frank Norris, Jack London, H. P. Lovecraft)**. Ph.D. Dissertation, City University of New York, 1995. 282pp. (DAI-A 56/05, p. 1777. November 1995.)
___ Hart, Alden W. **The Poetry of Edgar Allan Poe**. Ph.D. Dissertation, University of Oregon, 1972. 260pp. (DAI 33: 2326A. Nov/Dec. 1972.)
___ Hungerford, Edward. "Poe and Phrenology (1930)," in: Budd, Louis J. and Cady, Edwin H., eds. **On Poe**. Durham, NC: Duke University Press, 1993. pp.1-23.
___ Irwin, John T. "A Clew to the Clue: Locked Rooms and Labyrinths in Poe and Borges," in: Rosenheim, Shawn and Rachman, Stephen, ed. **The American Face of Edgar Allan Poe**. Baltimore: Johns Hopkins University Press, 1995. pp.139-154.
___ Johnson, Barbara. "Strange Fits: Poe and Wordsworth on the Nature of Poetic Language," in: Rosenheim, Shawn and Rachman, Stephen, ed. **The American Face of Edgar Allan Poe**. Baltimore: Johns Hopkins University Press, 1995. pp.37-48.
___ Jordan, Cynthia S. "Poe's Re-Vision: The Recovery of the Second Story (1987)," in: Budd, Louis J. and Cady, Edwin H., eds. **On Poe**. Durham, NC: Duke University Press, 1993. pp.247-266.
___ Kennedy, J. Gerald. "The Limits of Reason: Poe's Deluded Detectives (1975)," in: Budd, Louis J. and Cady, Edwin H., eds. **On Poe**. Durham, NC: Duke University Press, 1993. pp.172-184.
___ Lemay, J. A. Leo. "The Psychology of 'The Murders in the Rue Morgue' (1982)," in: Budd, Louis J. and Cady, Edwin H., eds. **On Poe**. Durham, NC: Duke University Press, 1993. pp.223-246.
___ Leverenz, David. "Poe and Gentry Virginia," in: Rosenheim, Shawn and Rachman, Stephen, ed. **The American Face of Edgar Allan Poe**. Baltimore: Johns Hopkins University Press, 1995. pp.210-236.
___ Ljungquist, Kent P. "Prospects for the Study of Edgar Allan Poe," *Resources for American Literary Study* 21(2): 173-188. 1995.
___ Marchand, Ernest. "Poe as Social Critic (1934)," in: Budd, Louis J. and Cady, Edwin H., eds. **On Poe**. Durham, NC: Duke University Press, 1993. pp.24-39.
___ Marks, Emerson R. "Poe as Literary Theorist: A Reappraisal (1961)," in: Budd, Louis J. and Cady, Edwin H., eds. **On Poe**. Durham, NC: Duke University Press, 1993. pp.122-132.
___ McGill, Meridith L. "Poe, Literary Nationalism, and Authorial Identity," in: Rosenheim, Shawn and Rachman, Stephen, ed. **The American Face of Edgar Allan Poe**. Baltimore: Johns Hopkins University Press, 1995. pp.271-305.
___ Meyers, Jeffrey. **Edgar Allan Poe: His Life and Legacy**. New York: Macmillan, 1992. 348pp.
___ Mooney, Stephen L. "The Comic in Poe's Fiction (1962)," in: Budd, Louis J. and Cady, Edwin H., eds. **On Poe**. Durham, NC: Duke University Press, 1993. pp.133-141.
___ Moss, Sidney P. "Poe and His Nemesis: Lewis Gaylord Clark (1956)," in: Budd, Louis J. and Cady, Edwin H., eds. **On Poe**. Durham, NC: Duke University Press, 1993. pp.102-121.
___ Pollin, Burton R. "Stephen King's Fiction and the Legacy of Poe," *Journal of the Fantastic in the Arts* 5(4): 2-25. 1993. (No. 20)
___ Price, Robert M. "Lovecraft and 'Ligeia'," *Lovecraft Studies* No. 31: 15-17. Fall 1994.
___ Rachman, Stephen. " 'Es lasst sich nicht scrieben': Plagiarism and 'The Man in the Crowd'," in: Rosenheim, Shawn and Rachman, Stephen, ed. **The American Face of Edgar Allan Poe**. Baltimore: Johns Hopkins University Press, 1995. pp.49-90.
___ Renza, Louis A. "Ut Pictura Poe: Poetic Politics in 'The Island of the Fay' and 'Morning on the Wissahiccon'," in: Rosenheim, Shawn and Rachman, Stephen, ed. **The American Face of Edgar Allan Poe**. Baltimore: Johns Hopkins University Press, 1995. pp.305-329.
___ Rosenheim, Shawn. "Detective Fiction, Psychoanalysis, and the Analytic Sublime," in: Rosenheim, Shawn and Rachman, Stephen, ed. **The American Face of Edgar Allan Poe**. Baltimore: Johns Hopkins University Press, 1995. pp.153-178.
___ Rosenheim, Shawn. "Introduction: Beyond 'The Problem of Poe'," by Shawn Rosenheim and Stephen Rachman. in: Rosenheim, Shawn and Rachman, Stephen, eds. **The American Face of Edgar Allan Poe**. Baltimore, MD: Johns Hopkins University Press, 1995. pp.ix-xx.

POE, EDGAR ALLAN (continued)

___ Rosenheim, Shawn, ed. **The American Face of Edgar Allan Poe**, ed. by Shawn Rosenheim and Stephen Rachman. Baltimore, MD: Johns Hopkins University Press, 1995. 364pp.

___ Seed, David. "Breaking the Bounds: The Rhetoric of Limits in the Works of Edgar Allan Poe, His Contemporaries, and Adaptors," in: Seed, David, ed. **Anticipations: Essays on Early Science Fiction and Its Precursors.** Liverpool: Liverpool University Press, 1995. pp.75-97.

___ Slatz, Laura. " '(Horrible to Relate)': Recovering the Body of Marie Roget," in: Rosenheim, Shawn and Rachman, Stephen, ed. **The American Face of Edgar Allan Poe**. Baltimore: Johns Hopkins University Press, 1995. pp.237-270.

___ Smith, Dave. "Edgar Allan Poe and the Nightmare Ode," *Southern Humanities Review* 29(1): 1-14. Winter 1995.

___ Ursini, James. **More Things Than Are Dreamt Of: Masterpieces of Supernatural Horror, From Mary Shelley to Stephen King, in Literature and Film,** by James Ursini and Alain Silver. New York: Limelight, 1994. 226pp.

___ Williams, Michael. "The 'Language of the Cipher': Interpretation in 'The Gold Bug' (1982)," in: Budd, Louis J. and Cady, Edwin H., eds. **On Poe**. Durham, NC: Duke University Press, 1993. pp.208-222.

___ Wimsatt, W. K., Jr. "Poe and the Chess Automaton (1939)," in: Budd, Louis J. and Cady, Edwin H., eds. **On Poe**. Durham, NC: Duke University Press, 1993. pp.78-91.

___ Winters, Yvor. "Edgar Allan Poe: A Crisis in the History of American Obscurantism (1937)," in: Budd, Louis J. and Cady, Edwin H., eds. **On Poe**. Durham, NC: Duke University Press, 1993. pp.55-77.

___ Zanger, Jules. "Poe and the Theme of Forbidden Knowledge (1978)," in: Budd, Louis J. and Cady, Edwin H., eds. **On Poe**. Durham, NC: Duke University Press, 1993. pp.197-207.

POETRY

___ "1992 Rhysling Awards," *Locus* 30(1): 7. January 1993.

___ "1994 Rhysling Awards," *Locus* 33(4): 72. October 1994.

___ "Rhysling Awards, 1994," *Science Fiction Chronicle* 16(1): 8. October 1994.

___ Bailey, K. V. "Alien or Kin? Science Fiction and Poetry," *Fantasy Commentator* 8(1/2): 32-39. Winter 1993/1994. (Whole No. 45/46)

___ Cooley, Dennis. "Nearer by Far: The Upset 'I' in Margaret Atwood's Poetry," in: Nicholson, Colin, ed. **Margaret Atwood: Writing and Subjectivity: New Critical Essays**. New York: St. Martin's, 1994. pp.68-93.

___ Curtis, Jan. "Byzantium and the Matter of Britain: The Narrative Framework of Charles Williams's Later Arthurian Poems," *Quondam et Futurus* 2(1): 28-54. Spring 1992.

___ de Torre Gracia, Emilio E. "La ciencia ficción en la poesía de José Hierro," *Monographis Review* 3(1/2): 100-106. 1987.

___ Eng, Steve. "The Speculative Muse: An Introduction to Science Fiction Poetry," in: Barron, Neil, ed. **Anatomy of Wonder 4**. New York: Bowker, 1995. pp.378-392.

___ Fickey, Pierrette. "Louis Aragon: The Fantastic in Collage and Poetry," in: Latham, Robert A. and Collins, Robert A., eds. **Modes of the Fantastic**. Westport, CT: Greenwood, 1995. pp.38-47.

___ Göller, Karl H. "Die Modernität von Williams' Arthur-Dichtung," in: Kranz, Gisbert, ed. **Inklings: Jahrbuch für Literatur und Ästhetik**. 3. Band. [Lüdenscheid, Germany: Stier], 1985. pp.37-48.

___ Haines, John F. "Confessions of a Fantasy Versaholic," *Fantasy Commentator* 7(4): 304-306. Fall 1992. (Whole No. 44)

___ Kokot, Joanna. "Cultural Functions Motivating Art: Poems and Their Contexts in **The Lord of the Rings**," in: Kranz, Gisbert, ed. **Jahrbuch für Literatur und Ästhetik**. Lüdenscheid, Germany: Stier, 1992. Band 10, pp.191-207.

___ Lindskold, Jane M. "Pervasive Influence of Poetry in the Works of Roger Zelazny," *Extrapolation* 33(1): 41-58. Spring 1992.

___ Mintz, Catherine. "Poetry, Poets and the Rest of the World: An Interview with Steve Sneyd," *Foundation* No. 63: 68-73. Spring 1995.

___ Nicholson, Colin. "Living on the Edges: Constructions of Post-Colonial Subjectivity in Atwood's Early Poetry," in: Nicholson, Colin, ed. **Margaret Atwood: Writing and Subjectivity: New Critical Essays**. New York: St. Martin's, 1994. pp.11-50.

___ Prothero, James. "Lewis's Poetry: A Preliminary Exploration," *Bulletin of the New York C. S. Lewis Society* 25(5/6): 2-6. March/April 1994.

___ Rawls, Melanie A. "The Verse of J. R. R. Tolkien," *Mythlore* 19(1): 4-8. Winter 1993. (No. 71)

POETRY (continued)

___ Schneider, Angelika. "Zur Symbolik in Williams' Arthur-Dictung," in: Kranz, Gisbert, ed. **Inklings: Jahrbuch für Literatur und Ästhetik**. 3. Band. [Lüdenscheid, Germany: Stier], 1985. pp.49-70.

___ Searles, A. Langley. "Forgotten Fantasy Verse: I, Arthur Davison Ficke," *Fantasy Commentator* 8(1/2): 14-16. Winter 1993/1994. (Whole No. 45/46.)

___ Shaw, Luci N. "Looking Back to Eden: The Poetry of C. S. Lewis," *CSL: The Bulletin of the New York C. S. Lewis Society* 23(4): 1-7. February 1992.

___ Sneyd, Steve. "Empress of the Stars: A Reassessment of Lilith Lorraine, Pioneering Fantasy Poetess," *Fantasy Commentator* 7(3): 206-229. Spring 1992. (No. 43)

___ Sneyd, Steve. "Hearing From the Ion Engineers: A Quarter Century of SF Poetry," *Vector* No. 180: 12-14. August/September 1994.

___ Sneyd, Steve. "Michael Moorcock: Interview," *Star Line* 15(1): 3-5. 1992.

___ Sneyd, Steve. "Science Fiction and Poetry: An Interview With Duncan Lunan," *Fantasy Commentator* 8(1/2): 84-92. Winter 1993/1994. (Whole No. 45/46)

___ Zimmer, Paul E. "Another Opinion of the Verse of J. R. R. Tolkien," *Mythlore* 19(2): 16-23. Spring 1993. (No. 72)

POHL, FREDERIK

___ "1992 Nebula Awards Winners," *Locus* 30(5): 8. May 1993.

___ **Breaking into Writing**. Ann Arbor, MI: Tucker Video, 1994. 1 videocassette, 98 minutes. (Panel Presentation at the 1994 Science Fiction Research Association Conference.)

___ "Nebula Award Winners, 1992," *Science Fiction Chronicle* 14(8): 4. May 1993.

___ Bailey, K. V. "Spindly Mazes, Dead Men and Doppels: Frederik Pohl's Gateway Creations," *Foundation* No. 63: 40-55. Spring 1995.

___ Bloom, Harold. "Frederik Pohl," in: Bloom, Harold, ed. **Science Fiction Writers of the Golden Age**. New York: Chelsea House, 1995. pp.157-172.

___ Felgenhauer, H. S. "Pages and Pages of Pohl," *Fantasy Commentator* 8(1/2): 4-13. Winter 1993/1994. (Whole No. 45/46.)

___ Goldman, Stephen H. "Frederik Pohl," in: Bruccoli, Matthew J., ed. **Facts on File Bibliography of American Fiction 1919-1988**. New York: Facts on File, 1991. pp.403-405.

___ Hassler, Donald M. "Swift, Pohl, and Kornbluth: Publicists Anatomize Newness," *Extrapolation* 34(3): 245-250. Fall 1993.

___ Heyne, Eric. "**Gateway** to an Erotics of Narrative," *Extrapolation* 35(4): 298-311. Winter 1994.

___ Kening, Dan. "Gatekeeper to the Universe," *Chicago Tribune* Sec. 18 (Tempo Northwest), p. 1, 4. October 4, 1992.

___ Nicholls, Stan. "Frederik Pohl Just Wants Everyone to Play Nicely Together," in: Nicholls, Stan. **Wordsmiths of Wonder: Fifty Interviews with Writers of the Fantastic**. London: Orbit, 1993. pp.3-11.

___ Nicholls, Stan. "Playing Nicely Together: Frederik Pohl," *Interzone* No. 68: 22-25. February 1993.

___ Nicholls, Stan. "The View From a Distant Star," by Stan Nicholls and Michael McCarty. *Starlog* No. 192: 59-69. July 1993.

___ Pohl, Frederik. "Essay: A SF Grandmaster Explains How Good Ideas Build Better Stories," *Science Fiction Age* 2(6): 34-37. September 1994.

___ Pohl, Frederik. "Pohl Declares a War of the Words," *Chicago Tribune* Sec. 13, p. 5. May 17, 1992.

___ Seed, David. "Take-over Bids: The Power Fantasies of Frederik Pohl and Cyril Kornbluth," *Foundation* No. 59: 42-58. Autumn 1993.

POLAND

___ "Poland to Air **Day After** Pic," *Variety* p. 2. January 25, 1984.

___ "Polish Pic Prized Four Ways; Other Madrid Scifi Nods," *Variety* p. 6. April 28, 1982.

___ Tokarczyk, Roman A. "Polish Utopian Thought: A Historical Survey," *Utopian Studies* 4(2): 128-143. 1993.

POLITICS AND GOVERNMENT

___ Abbott, Joe. "They Came From Beyond the Center: Ideology and Political Textuality in the Radical Science Fiction Films of James Cameron," *Literature/Film Quarterly* 22(1): 21-27. 1994.

___ Airaudi, Jesse T. "Fantasia for Sewercovers and Drainpipes: T. S. Eliot, Abram Tertz, and the Surreal Quest for Pravda," in: Latham, Robert A. and Collins, Robert A., eds. **Modes of the Fantastic**. Westport, CT: Greenwood, 1995. pp.21-27.

POLITICS AND GOVERNMENT

POLITICS AND GOVERNMENT (continued)
___ Andriano, Joseph. "The Masks of Gödel: Math and Myth in Thomas Pynchon's **Gravity's Rainbow**," in: Latham, Robert A. and Collins, Robert A., eds. **Modes of the Fantastic**. Westport, CT: Greenwood, 1995. pp.14-20.
___ Attebery, Brian. "The Politics of Fantasy," in: Latham, Robert A. and Collins, Robert A., eds. **Modes of the Fantastic**. Westport, CT: Greenwood, 1995. pp.1-13.
___ Barton-Kriese, Paul. "Exploring Divergent Realities: Using Science Fiction to Teach Introductory Political Science," Extrapolation 34(3): 209-215. Fall 1993.
___ Bertolo, Amedeo. "L'immaginario sovversivo. Considerazioni anarchiche sull'utopia," in: Saccaro Del Buffa, Giuseppa and Lewis, Arthur O., eds. **Utopie per gli Anni Ottana**. Rome: Gangemi Editore, 1986. pp.145-166.
___ Cummings, Michael S. "Practicing Utopia in the Twilight of Capitalism," in: Saccaro Del Buffa, Giuseppa and Lewis, Arthur O., eds. **Utopie per gli Anni Ottana**. Rome: Gangemi Editore, 1986. pp.125-144.
___ Ecker, Gisela. "The Politics of Fantasy in Recent American Women's Novels," Englishch-Amerikanische Studien 3: 503-510. 1984.
___ Keesey, Douglas. " 'I Think the Government Stinks!': Stephen King's **Stand** on Politics," in: Magistrale, Tony, ed. **A Casebook on The Stand**. San Bernardino, CA: Borgo Press, 1992. pp.21-36.
___ Kuelen, Margarete. **Radical Imagination: Feminist Conceptions of the Future in Ursula Le Guin, Marge Piercy and Sally Miller Gearhart**. Frankfurt-am-Main/New York: Peter Lang, 1991. 122pp.
___ Lagon, Mark P. " 'We Owe It to Them to Interfere': **Star Trek** and U.S. Statecraft in the 1960s and 1990s," Extrapolation 34(3): 251-264. Fall 1993.
___ Lerner, Fred. "The Libertarian Ideal in Science Fiction," Voice of Youth Advocates 13(1): 17-18. April 1990.
___ Lyall, Francis. "Law in Science Fiction: An Introduction," Foundation No. 55: 36-57. Summer 1992.
___ Marion, David E. "Using Fiction to Expose a Fundamental Theme in American Public Policy," Teaching Political Science 15(2): 44-49. Winter 1988.
___ Meyer, David S. "Star Wars, **Star Wars**, and American Political Culture," Journal of Popular Culture 26(2): 99-115. Fall 1992.
___ Pohl, Frederik. "Political Science Fiction," Locus 30(1): 32-33, 63-65. January 1993.
___ Pohl, Frederik. "The Politics of Prophecy," Extrapolation 34(3): 199-208. Fall 1993.
___ Slade, Margot. "Ross Perot or Superstoe? Science Fiction Got There First," New York Times Sec. 4, p. 4. October 4, 1992.
___ Winter, Michael. "Utopia in Everyday Politics: Blessing or Nightmare?," in: Saccaro Del Buffa, Giuseppa and Lewis, Arthur O., eds. **Utopia e Modernita: Teorie e prassi utopiche nell'eta moderna e postmoderna**. Rome: Gangemi Editore, 1989. pp.77-86.

POLLACK, JAMES
___ "Pollack, James (Obituary)," Locus 33(2): 70. August 1994.
___ "Pollack, James (Obituary)," Science Fiction Chronicle 15(8): 20. June 1994.

POLLS AND SURVEYS, 1982
___ "Survey Says Public Likes Sci-Fi, But Really Loves Comedy," Variety p. 22. September 22, 1982.

POLLS AND SURVEYS, 1991
___ Kube-McDowell, Michael P. "Report on the 1991 SFWA Membership Profile Project," SFWA Bulletin 26(1): 39-42. Spring 1992. (No. 115)

POLLS AND SURVEYS, 1992
___ "1992 Locus Survey Results," Locus 29(3): 52-53, 78. September 1992.
___ "Results of the Science Fiction Chronicle Reader Survey," Science Fiction Chronicle 14(3): 30-31. December 1992.

POLLS AND SURVEYS, 1993
___ "1993 Locus Survey Results," Locus 31(3): 60-62, 84. September 1993.

POLLS AND SURVEYS, 1994
___ "1994 Locus Survey," Locus 33(3): 56-58, 84-85. September 1994.
___ "Locus Poll Results," Locus 33(2): 42-45. August 1994.

POLLS AND SURVEYS, 1995
___ "1995 Locus Awards Winners," Locus 35(2): 7, 34-37. August 1995.
___ Cushman, Carolyn. "1995 Locus Survey Results," Locus 35(3): 56-58, 84. September 1993.
___ Rusch, Kristine K. "Editorial: Reader Survey," Magazine of Fantasy and Science Fiction 88(2): 5-7. February 1995.

POLTERGEIST II: THE OTHER SIDE (MOTION PICTURE)
___ "Fields Slates 'Poltergeist' Sequel With Original Cast for May Start," Variety p. 8, 232. April 17, 1985.

POLTERGEIST III (MOTION PICTURE)
___ "**Poltergeist III** (Review)," Variety p. 12. June 15, 1988.

POLTERGEIST (MOTION PICTURE)
___ "DGA Arbitrates on **Poltergeist**: Who's Angry at Whom?," Variety p. 3, 35. June 16, 1982.

POPE, DOYLE
___ "Pope, Doyle (Obituary)," Locus 28(1): 72. January 1992.

POPPER, KARL R.
___ Stableford, Brian. "Marxism, Science Fiction, and the Poverty of Prophecy: Some Comparisons and Contrasts," in: Stableford, Brian. **Opening Minds: Essays on Fantastic Literature**. San Bernardino, CA: Borgo Press, 1995. pp.99-110.

POPULATION BIOLOGY
___ Berenbaum, May R. "Life History Strategies and Population Biology in Science Fiction Films," by May R. Berenbaum and Richard J. Leskosky. Bulletin of the Ecological Society of America 73(4): 236-240. December 1992.

PORNOGRAPHY
___ Lewes, Darby. "Nudes From Nowhere: Pornography, Empire, and Utopia," Utopian Studies 4(2): 66-73. 1993.
___ Wingrove, David. "Letter to Catie, with Responses," Vector No. 165: 9-15, 23. February/March 1992. (Response to editorial, Vector No. 164: 3. December 1991/January 1992.)

PORTER, ANDREW
___ "Harlan Ellison Attacks SFC Editor on National Cable TV Show," Science Fiction Chronicle 14(11): 4-6. August 1993.

PORTUGAL
___ "Science Fiction, a Global Community: Portugal," Locus 32(4): 42. April 1994.
___ Almeida, Teresa Sousa de. "Estranha viagem ao mundo da ficçao científica em protuguês," Vertice: Revista de Cultura e Arte 41: 7-17. August 1991.
___ Nascimento, R. C. , ed. **Catálogo de Ficçáo Científica Em Língua Portuguesa (1921-1993)**. Sao Paulo, Brazil: Nasciemento, 1994. Part 1 of 6, 80pp. [Not seen.]
___ Silva, Lous F. "SF in Portugal," Locus 35(3): 53. September 1993.

POSSONY, STEFAN T.
___ "Possony, Stefan T. (Obituary)," Locus 34(6): 66. June 1995.

POST, JONATHAN V.
___ "SF Writer Jailed," Locus 32(5): 9. May 1994.

POSTAL, JULIUS
___ "Postal, Julius (Obituary)," Science Fiction Chronicle 14(7): 18. April 1993.

POSTERS
___ Felchner, William J. "Science Fiction Movie Posters," Antiques & Collecting Magazine 99(9): 40-43. November 1994.
___ Stephens, Bob. "Persistent Vision: Unforgettable Poster Art From the Golden Age of Science Fiction Movies," by Bob Stephens and Vincent Di Fate. Sci-Fi Entertainment 1(2): 48-51. August 1994.

POSTMODERNISM
___ Cupp, Jeff. "Do Science Fiction and Fantasy Writers Have Postmodern Dreams?," by Jeff Cupp and Charles Avinger. LIT: Literature Interpretation Theory 4(3): 175-184. 1993.

POSTMODERNISM (continued)
___ Hollinger, Veronica. **Future Presence: Intersections of Science Fiction and Postmodernism.** Ph.D. Dissertation, Concordia University, 1994. 248pp. (DAI-A 56/07, p. 2676. January 1996.)

POTTER, BEATRIX
___ Bloom, Harold. "Beatrix Potter," in: Bloom, Harold. **Classic Fantasy Writers.** New York: Chelsea House, 1994. pp.164-174.

POTTER, DENNIS
___ "Potter, Dennis (Obituary)," *Science Fiction Chronicle* 15(8): 20. June 1994.

POTTER, J.K.
___ King, Stephen. "On J. K. Potter: The Art of the Morph," *Interzone* No. 77: 23-24. November 1993.

POTTER, ROBERT
___ Stone, Graham. "Notes on Australian Science Fiction," *Science Fiction News* (Australia) No. 67: 2-9. January 1983.

POTTS, STEPHEN W.
___ "1993 J. Lloyd Eaton Memorial Award," *Locus* 30(6): 72. June 1993.
___ "J. Lloyd Eaton Memorial Award, 1993," *Science Fiction Chronicle* 14(9): 6. June 1993.

POURNELLE, JERRY
___ "Larry Niven and Jerry Pournelle: Master Collaborators," *Hailing Frequencies* (Waldenbooks) No. 5: 1-5. 1992.

POWDER (MOTION PICTURE)
___ "Mythic Claims Turn to Dust in *Powder*," *Washington (DC) Times.* October 27, 1995. in: *NewsBank. Film and Television.* 97:G5. 1995.
___ Adams, Thelma. "Don't Take a *Powder*," *New York (NY) Post.* October 27, 1995. in: *NewsBank. Film and Television.* 97:G2. 1995.
___ Cardwell, Annette. "Positive Message Found in *Powder*," *Boston (MA) Herald.* October 27, 1995. in: *NewsBank. Film and Television.* 97: F14. 1995.
___ Kaltenbach, Chris. "Disney's *Powder* Is Predictable," *(Baltimore, MD) Sun.* October 27, 1995. in: *NewsBank. Film and Television.* 97: F13. 1995.
___ Lawson, Terry. "*Powder* Means Well, But Veers Out of Control," *Detroit (MI) Free Press.* October 27, 1995. in: *NewsBank. Film and Television.* 97:G1. 1995.
___ Millar, Jeff. "*Powder*: It's Hard to Like, Hard to Resist," *Houston (TX) Chronicle.* October 27, 1995. in: *NewsBank. Film and Television.* 97: G4. 1995.
___ Pinsker, Beth. "*Powder*: Offbeat Flick Misses Too Many Beats," *Dallas (TX) Morning News.* October 27, 1995. in: *NewsBank. Film and Television.* 97:G3. 1995.
___ Shulgasser, Barbara. "*Powder* Is an Inane *E. T.*," *San Francisco (CA) Examiner.* October 27, 1995. in: *NewsBank. Film and Television.* 97:F12. 1995.

POWERS OF MATTHEW STAR (TV)
___ "Powers of Star Preem Is Delayed," *Variety* p. 35. October 28, 1981.

POWERS, RICHARD
___ Berube, Michael. "Urban Renewal," *Village Voice* 40(23): SS8-SS10. June 6, 1995.

POWERS, TIM
___ "1993 World Fantasy Awards Winners," *Locus* 31(6): 6. December 1993.
___ "Powers Buys Book Back," *Locus* 33(6): 8. December 1994.
___ "Tim Powers: Joke Booths on the Way In," *Locus* 32(1): 5, 65-66. January 1994.
___ "World Fantasy Awards," *Science Fiction Chronicle* 15(2): 4. November/December 1993.
___ Koontz, Dean R. "The Man Who Knows All About Hippodurkees," in: Greenberg, Martin H., Ed Gorman and Bill Munster, eds. **The Dean Koontz Companion.** New York: Berkley, 1994. pp.163-166.
___ Sinor, Bradley H. "Drawings in the Dark," *Starlog* No. 183: 50-53, 70. October 1992.
___ Starr, Richard. "SFC Interviews: A Conversation With Tim Powers," *Science Fiction Chronicle* 15(6): 40-44. April/May 1994.

POWYS, JOHN COWPER
___ Schenkel, Elmar. "John Cowper Powys und die Ursprünge der Phantasie," in: Kranz, Gisbert, ed. **Inklings: Jahrbuch für Literatur und Ästhetik.** 7. Band. Lüdenscheid, Germany: Stier, 1989. pp.121-138. [Not seen.]

PRAED, MICHAEL
___ Airey, Jean. "Students of Sherwood," *Starlog* No. 195: 39-42. October 1993.

PRAMOJ, MOM RAJAWONGSE KUKRIT
___ "Cuckoo in Wrong Nest," *Locus* 33(1): 9, 75. July 1994.

PRATCHETT, TERRY
___ English, George. "Tripping the Light Fantastic: Terry Pratchett," *Language and Learning* pp.33-35. September/October 1994.
___ Hargreaves, Stella. "The SF Kick: Terry Pratchett Interviewed," *Interzone* No. 81: 25-28. March 1994.
___ Holliday, Liz. "SFC Interviews: Terry Pratchett," *Science Fiction Chronicle* 13(7): 5, 26-27. April 1992.
___ Nicholls, Stan. "Terry Pratchett Leaves the Furniture Alone," in: Nicholls, Stan. **Wordsmiths of Wonder: Fifty Interviews with Writers of the Fantastic.** London: Orbit, 1993. pp.340-347.
___ Pratchett, Terry. "Kevins," *The Author* pp.132-133. Winter 1993.
___ Pratchett, Terry. "Let There Be Dragons," *The Bookseller* p. 60-62. June 11, 1993.
___ Stone, Grant. "Know the Author: Terry Pratchett," *Magpies* 8(1): 19. March 1993.
___ Watson, Ian. "Pratchett Job," *Melody Maker* 72(7): 15. February 18, 1995.
___ Young, Elizabeth. "Funny Old World: From the Mind of Terry Pratchett," *The Guardian Weekend* 23: 6, 9-10. October 23, 1993.

PRATT, FLETCHER
___ Bloom, Harold. "L. Sprague de Camp and Fletcher Pratt," in: Bloom, Harold, ed. **Modern Fantasy Writers.** New York: Chelsea House, 1995. pp.29-42.

PREDICTION
___ Schmitt, Ronald E. **The Reclamation of the Future Dream: Dreams in British Science Fiction (Mary Shelley, H. G. Wells, George Orwell, Michael Moorcock).** Ph.D. Dissertation, University of Rhode Island, 1995. 182pp. (DAI-A 56/09, p. 3598. March 1996.)
___ Sulski, Jim. "False Futures," *Chicago Tribune* Sec. 5, p. 6. January 7, 1993.
___ Wagar, W. Warren. **The Next Three Futures: Paradigms of Things to Come.** Westport, CT: Greenwood, 1991. 164pp.

PREHISTORY
___ Hammerton, M. "Prehistoric Science Fiction," *Foundation* No. 54: 87-88. Spring 1992.

PREHYSTERIA (MOTION PICTURE)
___ Crisafulli, Chuck. "*Jurassic Park*: Prehysteria," *Cinefantastique* 24(2): 31, 60. August 1993.

PRELUDE TO A KISS (MOTION PICTURE)
___ "A Loving Kiss: *Prelude* Proves Surprisingly Thoughtful (Review)," *Chicago (IL) Sun Times.* July 10, 1992. in: *NewsBank. Film and Television.* 73:C4. 1992.
___ "Lucas' *Prelude to a Kiss*: Soul-searching, Whimsically (Review)," *Washington (DC) Times.* July 10, 1992. in: *NewsBank. Film and Television.* 73:C12. 1992.
___ Campbell, Bob. "Modern Fairy Tale's a Rehumanizing Experience (Review)," *Mewark (NJ) Star-Ledger.* July 10, 1992. in: *NewsBank. Film and Television.* 73:C10. 1992.
___ Doherty, Thomas. "*Prelude to a Kiss* (Review)," *Cinefantastique* 23(4): 57. December 1992.
___ Johnson, Malcolm. "*Prelude* Poignant Yet Boring (Review)," *Hartford (CT) Courant.* July 10, 1992. in: *NewsBank. Film and Television.* 73:C3. 1992.
___ Kronke, David. "Prelude to an Overly Worked But Slightly Funny Comedy (Review)," *Los Angeles (CA) Daily News.* July 10, 1992. in: *NewsBank. Film and Television.* 73:B14. 1992.
___ Mahar, Ted. "Unbelievably, *Prelude to a Kiss* Works (Review)," *Portland (OR) The Oregonian.* July 10, 1992. in: *NewsBank. Film and Television.* 73:C11. 1992.

PRELUDE TO A KISS (MOTION PICTURE) (continued)
___ Rosenberg, Scott. "*Prelude to a Kiss*: She's Not the Woman He Married, But There's More Here Than Meets the Eye (Review)," *San Francisco (CA) Examiner*. July 10, 1992. in: *NewsBank. Film and Television*. 73:C1-C2. 1992.
___ Strickler, Jeff. "Charming Moments Make the Moments in *Prelude to a Kiss* (Review)," *Minneapolis (MN) Star and Tribune*. July 10, 1992. in: *NewsBank. Film and Television*. 73:C9. 1992.
___ Verniere, James. "Odd Couple: Light, Romantic Comedy Turns Dark in *Prelude to a Kiss* (Review)," *Boston (MA) Herald*. July 10, 1992. in: *NewsBank. Film and Television*. 73:C7-C8. 1992.
___ Wingler, Stephen. "Prelude to a Dull Movie (Review)," *Baltimore (MD) Sun*. July 10, 1992. in: *NewsBank. Film and Television*. 73:C5-C6. 1992.

PREMIO ITALIA AWARDS, 1992
___ "Premio Italia 1992 Awards," *Science Fiction Chronicle* 13(10): 8. July/August 1992.
___ "Premio Italia Award, 1992," *Locus* 29(1): 69. July 1992.

PREMIO ITALIA AWARDS, 1993
___ "1993 Premio Italia Awards," *Science Fiction Chronicle* 15(8): 10. June 1994.
___ "Premio Italia, 1993," *Locus* 31(2): 62. August 1993.

PRESTON, JOHN
___ "Preston, John (Obituary)," *Locus* 32(6): 72. June 1994.

PREYING MANTIS (MOTION PICTURE)
___ Scapperotti, Dan. "*Preying Mantis* (Review)," *Cinefantastique* 24(6)/25(1): 124. February 1994.

PRICE, VINCENT
___ "Madrid's Sci-Fi Fest Kicks Off; Marathon Sked; Price Is Honored," *Variety* p. 32. April 4, 1984.
___ "Price, Vincent (Obituary)," *Locus* 31(6): 68. December 1993.
___ "Price, Vincent (Obituary)," *Science Fiction Chronicle* 15(2): 18. November/December 1993.
___ "Price, Vincent, 1911-1993 (Obituary)," *Starlog* No. 202: 76. May 1994.
___ Catsos, Gregory J. M. "Priceless: A Farewell Interview With Vincent Price," *Filmfax* No. 42: 45-49. December 1993/January 1994.
___ Garcia, Bob. "*Batman*: The Origin of Egghead," *Cinefantastique* 24(6)/25(1): 52-53. February 1994.
___ Hogan, David J. "Art of the Fright: Celebrating the Life of Vincent Price," *Filmfax* No. 42: 32-39, 94-95. December 1993/January 1994.
___ Weaver, Tom. "Vincent Price: Interview," in: Weaver, Tom, ed. **Attack of the Monster Movie Makers: Interviews with 20 Genre Giants**. Jefferson, NC: McFarland, 1994. pp.267-288.
___ Wiater, Stanley. "Price, Vincent," in: Wiater, Stanley. **Dark Visions: Conversations with the Masters of the Horror Film**. New York: Avon, 1992. pp.129-136.
___ Williams, Lucy C. **The Complete Films of Vincent Price**. New York: Citadel, 1995. 287pp.

PRIEST, CHRISTOPHER
___ Gomel, Elana. "Mystery, Apocalypse and Utopia: The Case of the Ontological Detective Story," *Science Fiction Studies* 22(3): 343-356. November 1995
___ Priest, Christopher. "Pax Ortygia," *Interzone* No. 88: 52. October 1994.
___ Roche, Alan. "Outward From the Centre: Christopher Priest Interviewed," *Interzone* No. 99: 18-20. September 1995.
___ Tuttle, Lisa. "Memories of Ortygia House," *Interzone* No. 88: 48-51. October 1994.

PRIMEDALS (MOTION PICTURE)
___ Fischer, Dennis. "Full Moon Preview: *The Primedals*," *Cinefantastique* 26(4): 20-22. June 1995.

PRIMORTALS (COMIC)
___ Price, Michael. "Nimoy Starts Comics Series," *San Francisco (CA) Chronicle* November 19, 1994. (Cited from the Internet Edition.)
___ Rice, Lynette. "Boldly Going into Comics: Leonard Nimoy Is Exploring a New Role," *San Francisco (CA) Chronicle* November 14, 1994. (Cited from the Internet Edition.)

PRINCE OF DARKNESS (MOTION PICTURE)
___ Dietrich, Bryan. "*Prince of Darkness*, Prince of Light: From Faust to Physicist," *Journal of Popular Film and Television* 19(2): 91-96. 1991.

PRINCE VALIANT (MOTION PICTURE)
___ Blanch, Robert J. "Gawain on Film," by Robert J. Blanch and Julian N. Wasserman. in: Harty, Kevin J., ed. **Cinema Arthuriana: Essays on Arthurian Film**. New York: Garland, 1991. pp.57-70.

PRISON
___ Kelleghan, Fiona. "Hell's My Destination: Imprisonment in the Works of Alfred Bester," *Science Fiction Studies* 21(3): 351-364. November 1994.

PRISONER OF GRAVITY (TV)
___ "*Prisoner of Gravity* Canceled," *Science Fiction Chronicle* 15(8): 8. June 1994.

PRISONER (TV)
___ Van Hise, James. **Sci Fi TV: From Twilight Zone to Deep Space Nine**. Las Vegas, NV: Pioneer Books, 1993. 160pp. (Reprinted, HarperPrism, 1995. 258pp.)

PRIX AURORA AWARDS, 1995
___ "1995 Prix Aurora Awards," *Locus* 34(6): 8. June 1995.

PRIX ROSNY AINE AWARDS, 1992
___ "1992 Prix Rosny Aîné Awards," *Locus* 29(5): 5. November 1992

PROGENY (MOTION PICTURE)
___ SEE: BASKET CASE 3 THE PROGENY (MOTION PICTURE).

PROJECT A-KO 2: PLOT OF THE DAITOKUJI FINANCIAL GROUP (TV)
___ Persons, Dan. "*Project A-KO 2: Plot of the Daitokuji Financial Group* (Review)," *Cinefantastique* 25(4): 60. August 1994.

PROJECT MOONBASE (MOTION PICTURE)
___ Westfahl, Gary. "The Dark Side of the Moon: Robert A. Heinlein's *Project Moonbase*," *Extrapolation* 36(2): 126-135. Summer 1995.

PROJECT: SHADOWCHASER (MOTION PICTURE)
___ Wilt, David. "*Project: Shadowchaser* (Review)," *Cinefantastique* 23(6): 61. April 1993.

PROKOP, GERD
___ "Prokop, Gerd (Obituary)," *Locus* 33(2): 70. August 1994.

PROM NIGHT IV: DELIVER US FROM EVIL (MOTION PICTURE)
___ Harris, Judith P. "*Prom Night IV: Deliver Us From Evil* (Review)," *Cinefantastique* 23(5): 59. February 1993.

PROMETHEUS AWARDS, 1993
___ "Other Awards at ConAdian," *Science Fiction Chronicle* 15(10): 5. September 1994.

PROPHECY
___ Schmitt, Ronald E. **The Reclamation of the Future Dream: Dreams in British Science Fiction (Mary Shelley, H. G. Wells, George Orwell, Michael Moorcock)**. Ph.D. Dissertation, University of Rhode Island, 1995. 182pp. (DAI-A 56/09, p. 3598. March 1996.)
___ Stableford, Brian. "Marxism, Science Fiction, and the Poverty of Prophecy: Some Comparisons and Contrasts," in: Stableford, Brian. **Opening Minds: Essays on Fantastic Literature**. San Bernardino, CA: Borgo Press, 1995. pp.99-110.

PROPHECY (MOTION PICTURE)
___ Biodrowski, Steve. "*The Prophecy* (Review)," *Cinefantastique* 27(3): 53. December 1995.
___ Saunders, Matthew F. "God's Army," *Cinefantastique* 27(2): 52-53. November 1995.

PROSPERO'S BOOKS (MOTION PICTURE)
___ "Stormy Weather for Greenaway's Prurient *Prospero* (Review)," *Washington (DC) Times*. November 27, 1991. in: *NewsBank. Film and Television*. 6:D8. 1992.

PUBLISHING

PUBLISHING (continued)

___ "Tesseract SF Imprint Sold," *Science Fiction Chronicle* 16(3): 4. January 1995.

___ "Thomsen Moves to TSR," *Locus* 28(2): 7. August 1992.

___ "Time Capsule Discovered at Tor," *Locus* 28(2): 6. February 1992.

___ "Time Warner Buys Macdonald," *Locus* 28(3): 6. March 1992.

___ "Tor Begets Forge and Orb," *Locus* 30(6): 6, 73. June 1993.

___ "Tor Books Pays $1 Million Advance for Four Piers Anthony Xanth Novels," *Science Fiction Chronicle* 13(4): 4. January 1992.

___ "Tor Recalls, Reissues Barne's **Kaleidoscope Century**," *Science Fiction Chronicle* 16(7): 5. June/July 1995.

___ "Tor Starts Forge Mass Market List," *Locus* 32(3): 8, 69. March 1994.

___ "Tor/St. Martin's Sold," *Locus* 34(5): 8. May 1995.

___ "Two Pauline Dunn Horror Novels Plagiarized Dean R. Koontz's **Phantoms**," *Science Fiction Chronicle* 13(10): 4. July/August 1992.

___ "UK Net Book Agreement Dies," *Locus* 35(5): 8. November 1995.

___ "UK Publishing Financial Picture Mixed," *Locus* 30(5): 9. May 1993.

___ "UK's GW Books, Boxtree Publishers Sue Transworld," *Science Fiction Chronicle* 14(4): 4. January 1993.

___ "UK's Net Book Agreement Dies," *Science Fiction Chronicle* 17(1): 6-7. October/November 1995

___ "UK's Pan Kills Book of Horror; Series Reborn at Gollancz," *Science Fiction Chronicle* 16(6): 6. May 1995.

___ "Underwood-Miller Splits," *Locus* 33(1): 8, 75. July 1994.

___ "Underwood-Miller Splits in Two," *Science Fiction Chronicle* 15(8): 5-6. June 1994.

___ "US Dominates World Book Market," *Locus* 33(6): 9. December 1994.

___ "US HarperCollins Sets SF and Fantasy Paperbacks," *Science Fiction Chronicle* 14(8): 4-5. May 1993.

___ "V. C. Andrews Gets Refund," *Locus* 33(1): 9. July 1994.

___ "V. C. Andrews Imbroglio," *Locus* 31(1): 6. July 1993.

___ "V. C. Andrews Triumphant," *Locus* 34(4): 8. April 1995.

___ "Viacom Fires Snyder; S&S Speculation," *Locus* 33(2): 8, 76. August 1994.

___ "**Vurt** Brings Ringpull Recognition," *Science Fiction Chronicle* 15(8): 6. June 1994.

___ "**Vurt** Publisher Ringpull Press Forced into Receivership," *Science Fiction Chronicle* 16(6): 4. May 1995.

___ "Waldenbooks Presentation," *Locus* 28(4): 7. April 1992.

___ "Warner Decides Ripper Didn't Write Diary," *Science Fiction Chronicle* 15(1): 6. October 1993.

___ "Warner Science Fiction Relaunch," *Locus* 31(5): 6. November 1993.

___ "Warner's Questar Imprint to Relaunch as Aspect SF," *Science Fiction Chronicle* 15(2): 4. November/December 1993.

___ "Warner/Tekno Tie-Ins," *Locus* 34(3): 9. March 1995.

___ "White Wolf to Publish Ellison Backlist," *Locus* 34(3): 8. March 1995.

___ "Wildstar Is New Agency/Packager," *Science Fiction Chronicle* 15(2): 6. November/December 1993.

___ "William Morrow, Avon Books for Sale?," *Science Fiction Chronicle* 14(10): 5. July 1993.

___ "Wizards Hire Silverstein for New Imprint," *Locus* 33(4): 8, 76. October 1994.

___ "Wizards of the Coast Kills SF Publishing Program," *Science Fiction Chronicle* 17(2): 58. December 1995/January 1996.

___ "Wyatt Quits Ballantine Books," *Locus* 29(1): 7. July 1992.

___ "Young Adult Horror Bright Spot in Market," *Locus* 31(3): 7, 83. September 1993.

___ "Zebra Drops Pinnacle Horror Titles," *Locus* 31(6): 6. December 1993.

___ "Zebra Sale to Harlequin Falls Through," *Locus* 28(2): 6. August 1992.

___ "Zebra Sale to Harlequin Off," *Science Fiction Chronicle* 13(11/12): 6. August 1992.

___ "Zebra's Z-Wave Books Coming in August," *Science Fiction Chronicle* 14(7): 4. April 1993.

___ "Ziesing to Publish King First Edition," *Locus* 32(4): 8. April 1994.

___ Arbitman, Roman. "Vzglyad s 'tsentral 'nogo energoatrona," *Detskaya Lietatura* 5: 6-10. 1993.

___ Barnes, John. "Publications in the Bucket: Threat, Menace, Hidden Subsidy, or Just a Thing?," *SFWA Bulletin* 28(2): 6-13. Summer 1994. (No. 124)

___ Barron, Neil. "Science Fiction Publishing and Libraries," in: Barron, Neil, ed. **Anatomy of Wonder 4**. New York: Bowker, 1995. pp.455-461.

PUBLISHING (continued)

___ Burger, Phillip R. "Whatever Happened to Perry Rhodan, Riding the Space Trails Alone?," *Burroughs Bulletin* NS. No. 22: 12-17. April 1995.

___ Carmody, Deirdre. "Dell Buys Four Noted Fiction Magazines," *New York Times* Sec. D, p. 5. January 24, 1992.

___ Chalker, Jack L. "On Publishing and Personalities," *Pulphouse* No. 10: 42-45. July 1992.

___ Chalker, Jack L. "On Publishing and Personalities," *Pulphouse* No. 11: 53-57. August 1992.

___ Chalker, Jack L. **The Science Fantasy Publishers: A Critical and Bibliographic History**, by Jack L. Chalker and Mark Owings. Westminster, MD: Mirage, 1992. 744pp. (Revised Fourth Printing)

___ Chalker, Jack L. **The Science Fantasy Publishers: Supplement One, July 1991-June 1992**, by Jack L. Chalker and Mark Owings. Westminster, MD: Mirage Press, 1992. 130pp.

___ Cholfin, Bryan G. "No One Will Be Watching Us: The Complaints of a Small Press Publisher," *New York Review of Science Fiction* No. 57: 17-20. May 1993.

___ Cogswell, Theodore R., ed. **PITFCS: Proceedings of the Institute for Twenty-First Century Studies**. Chicago: Advent: Publishers, 1992. 374pp.

___ Cook, Sebastian. "Editing the Stars: An Interview With Jane Johnson," *Focus* (BSFA) No. 26: 15-16. June/July 1994.

___ Copobianco, Michael. "Interview With Paul Rosenzweig," *SFWA Bulletin* 28(2): 19-20. Summer 1994. (No. 124)

___ Costello, John H. "American SF in Russian," *Locus* 35(3): 54. September 1993.

___ Cox, Glen E. "Pulped! How Books Die an Early Death," *SFWA Bulletin* 25(4): 3-6. Winter 1992. (No. 114)

___ Curtis, Richard. "Agent's Corner: Last Chance," *Locus* 28(1): 11, 13, 61. January 1992.

___ Davin, Eric L. "Pioneer Publisher: An Interview With Lloyd Eshbach," *Fantasy Commentator* 8(1/2): 121-134. Winter 1993/1994. (Whole No. 45/46)

___ Di Fate, Vincent. "A Short History of SF Art in Paperback," *Science Fiction Chronicle* 16(5): 12, 36-38. March/April 1995.

___ Donaton, Scott. "New Sci Fi Magazine Will Launch This Fall," *Advertising Age* 63(35): 29. August 31, 1992.

___ Harbottle, Philip. **British Science Fiction Paperbacks and Magazines, 1949-1956: An Annotated Bibliograhy and Guide**, by Philip Harbottle and Stephen Holland. San Bernardino, CA: Borgo Press, 1994. 232pp.

___ Harbottle, Philip. **Vultures of the Void: A History of British Science Fiction Publishing 1946-1956**, by Philip Harbottle and Stephen Holland. San Bernardino, CA: Borgo Press, 1992. 128pp.

___ Harrison, Mitchell. "The Burroughs Pre-Pubs," *Burroughs Bulletin* NS. No. 14: 29-32. April 1993.

___ Harvey, Rich. "Indiana Jones and the Paperback Crusades," *Starlog* 179: 59-61, 90. June 1992.

___ Heller, Steven. **Jackets Required: An Illustrated History of American Book Jacket Design, 1920-1959**, by Steven Heller and Seymour Chwast. San Francisco, CA: Chronicle Books, 1995. 144pp.

___ Holland, Stephen. **The Mushroom Jungle: A History of Postwar Paperback Publishing**. Westbury, Eng.: Zeon Books, 1993. 196pp.

___ James, E. R. "Shake the Invisible Hand," *Vector* No. 166: 17. April/May 1992.

___ Ketterer, David. "The Establishment of Canadian Science Fiction (1958-1983), Part 1," *New York Review of Science Fiction* No. 42: 1, 8-14. February 1992.

___ Ketterer, David. "The Establishment of Canadian Science Fiction (1958-1983), Part 2," *New York Review of Science Fiction* No. 43: 17-22. March 1992.

___ Killheffer, Robert K. J. "Category Close-Up: Science Fiction, Exploring Alternative Worlds," *Publishers Weekly* 240(31):53-56. August 2, 1993. (Reprinted, *Science Fiction Chronicle*, May 1994, pp.44-46.)

___ Killheffer, Robert K. J. "Category Closeup: Science Fiction: Exploring New Worlds," *Publishers Weekly* 241(9): 56-60. February 28, 1994.

___ Killheffer, Robert K. J. "Inter-Galactic Licensing," *Publishers Weekly* 242(39): 27-31. September 25, 1995.

___ Killheffer, Robert K. J. "Mainstreaming the Millennium," *Publishers Weekly* 241(34): 33-38. August 22, 1994.

___ Killheffer, Robert K. J. "The Quest for Future Authors," *Publishers Weekly* 240(6): 25-27. February 8, 1993.

___ Killheffer, Robert K. J. "Rising From the Grave: Horror," *Publishers Weekly* 240(38): 43-47. September 20, 1993.

PUBLISHING

PUBLISHING (continued)

___ Killheffer, Robert K. J. "When Opportunity Knocks: SF and Fantasy Small Presses Find New Niches in a Changing Marketplace," *Science Fiction Chronicle* 16(1): 33-38. October 1994. (Revised from original *Publishers Weekly* publication.)

___ Kolker, Robert P. "The Moving Image Reclaimed," *Postmodern Culture* 5(1): [6pp., with imbedded motion picture full-motion clips in MPEG]. September 1994. (Electronic Journal: pmc@jefferson.village.virginia.edu).

___ Kuschnik, Anne. "Zur Neuübersetzung zweier Tolkien-Gedichte," in: Kranz, Gisbert, ed. **Jahrbuch für Literatur und Ästhetik**. Lüdenscheid, Germany: Stier, 1992. Band 10, pp.209-220.

___ Larson, Randall D. **Film into Books: An Analytical Bibliography of Film Novelizations, Movie and TV Tie-Ins**. Metuchen, NJ: Scarecrow Press, 1995. 608pp.

___ Lerner, Fred. "Small Is Beautiful: SF Small Press Publishing," *Voice of Youth Advocates* 14(1): 17-18. April 1991.

___ Lindskoog, Kathryn. "The Dark Scandal: Science Fiction Forgery," *Quantum* No. 42: 29-30. Summer/Fall 1992.

___ Lupoff, Richard A. "Edgar Rice Burroughs and the Maxwell Perkins Syndrome," *Burroughs Bulletin* NS. No. 13: 3-10. January 1993.

___ Maass, Donald. "Is Horror Dead, or Just Resting?," *Science Fiction Chronicle* 13(6): 25-26. March 1992.

___ Maddox, Tom. "Reports From the Electronic Frontier: Cyberspace, Freedom and the Law," *Locus* 30(1): 11, 49-50. January 1993.

___ Maddox, Tom. "Reports From the Electronic Frontier: I Sing the Text Electric, Part 1, Hypertext Local and General," *Locus* 29(5): 11, 58. November 1992

___ Maddox, Tom. "Reports From the Electronic Frontier: I Sing the Text Electric, Part 2, Reading Hypertext," *Locus* 29(6): 11-12. December 1992.

___ Mandell, Paul. "Tarzan of the Paperbacks," *Life* 55(22): 11-12. November 29, 1963.

___ McMullen, Sean. "The Golden Age of Australian Science Fiction," *Science Fiction: A Review of Speculative Literature* 12(3): 3-28. 1993(?). (No. 36)

___ Mendlesohn, Farah. "Audio Books: A New Medium for SF?," *Foundation* No. 64: 90-96. Summer 1995.

___ Miller, Chuck. "1983-84: The Market of SF&F: An Overview," *AB Bookman's Weekly* pp.2149-2152. October 1, 1984.

___ Molson, Francis J. "Great Marvel: The First American Hardcover Science Fiction Series," *Extrapolation* 34(2): 101-122. Summer 1993.

___ Morrish, Bob. "Small Press," *Twilight Zone* 8(2): 12-13, 92-93. June 1988.

___ Moskowitz, Sam. "Burroughs Returns to *Argosy*," *Burroughs Bulletin* NS. No. 20: 11-15. October 1994.

___ Moskowitz, Sam. "Edgar Rice Burroughs and *Blue Book*," *Burroughs Bulletin* NS. No. 15: 11-20. July 1993.

___ Moskowitz, Sam. "Hugo Gernsback and Edgar Rice Burroughs," *Burroughs Bulletin* NS. No. 21: 3-9. January 1995.

___ Moskowitz, Sam. "A Remedy in Book Jackets," *Fantasy Commentator* 8(3/4): 173-181. Fall 1995. (Whole No. 47/48)

___ Nascimento, R. C., ed. **Catálogo de Ficção Científica Em Língua Portuguesa (1921-1993)**. Sao Paulo, Brazil: Nasciemento, 1994. Part 1 of 6, 80pp. [Not seen.]

___ Nazzaro, Joe. "Newcomer Novels," *Starlog* No. 188: 36-37, 67. March 1993.

___ O'Brien, Maureen. "Christian Publishing SF/F," *Lan's Lantern* No. 43: 43-46. March 1995.

___ O'Donnell, Kevin, Jr. "How Thor Power Hammered Publishing," *SFWA Bulletin* 27(1): 30-37. Spring 1993. (No. 119)

___ Pastourmatzi, Domna A. **Vivliogrphia epistemonikes phantasias, phantasias, kai tromou, 1960-1993** [Bibliography of Science Fiction, Fantasy and Horror, 1960-1993.]. Athens: Alien, 1995. 245pp.

___ Pedersen, Martin. "Serial From Prodigy to Be Hardcover Book," *Publishers Weekly* 240(7): 18. February 15, 1993.

___ Platt, Charles. "The Selling of Science Fiction," *Interzone* No. 89: 46-47. November 1994.

___ Platt, Charles. "The Tenacity of Fiction," *Interzone* No. 91: 44-45. January 1995.

___ Reginald, Robert. "A Requiem for Starmont House (1976-1993)," *Science Fiction Studies* 20(3): 414-421. November 1993.

___ Roller, Pamela E. "*Star Wars* Young Reader's Series: A New Generation of Fans Discovers the 'Force'," *The LucasFilm Fan Club* No. 17: 8-9. 1993.

___ Ruddick, Nicholas. **British Science Fiction, 1478-1990: A Chronology**. Westport, CT: Greenwood, 1992. 296pp.

PUBLISHING (continued)

___ Schmidt, Stanley. "Editorial: The Manuscript That Never Was," *Analog* 113(3): 4-12. February 1993.

___ Sedgewick, Cristina. "The Fork in the Road: Can Science Fiction Survive in Postmodern, Megacorporate America?," *Science Fiction Studies* 18(1): 11-52. March 1991.

___ Server, Lee. **Over My Dead Body: The Sensational Age of American Paperbacks 1945-1955**. San Francisco, CA: Chronicle Books, 1994. 108pp.

___ Sperry, Ralph A. "Three Nasty Problems," *SFWA Bulletin* 26(3): 21-22. Fall 1992. (No. 117)

___ Spinrad, Norman. "If You Love Science Fiction, Then It's Time to Fight Back Against Anti-SF," *Science Fiction Age* 2(1): 32-36. November 1993.

___ Stephensen-Payne, Phil. "U.K. Year in SF, 1991," in: Brown, Charles N. and Contento, William G. **Science Fiction, Fantasy, & Horror: 1991**. Oakland, CA: Locus Press, 1992. pp.437-439.

___ Stone, Graham. "Science Fiction in the *Man* Group of Magazines: A Checklist," *Science Fiction News* (Australia) No. 104: 1-18. May 1987. [Not seen.]

___ Streitfeld, David. "V. C. Andrews's Afterlife," *Washington (DC) Post Book World* p. 12. May 10, 1992.

___ Summer, Bob. "Graphics Go Literary: Comics Aren't Just for Superheroes Anymore," *Publishers Weekly* 241(38): 20-21. September 19, 1994.

___ Thomas, Margaret. "Flop Down With a Good Disk," *Juneau (AK) Empire*. January 13, 1994. in: *NewsBank. Film and Television*. 17:A14-B1. 1994.

___ Trudel, Jean-Louis. "Science Fiction in Francophone Canada (1839-1989)," *Sol Rising* No. 8: 1-5. February 1992.

___ Unwin, Rayner. "Publishing Tolkien," in: Reynolds, Patricia and GoodKnight, Glen H., eds. **Proceedings of the J. R. R. Tolkien Centenary Conference, Keble College, Oxford, 1992**. Altadena, CA: Mythopoeic Press, 1995. pp.26-29. (*Mythlore* Vol. 21, No. 2, Winter 1996, Whole No. 80)

___ Weinberg, Robert. "The Fan Presses," in: Sanders, Joe, ed. **Science Fiction Fandom**. Westport, CT: Greenwood, 1994. pp.211-220.

___ Weiner, Andrew. "SF--NOT," *New York Review of Science Fiction* No. 57: 20-22. May 1993.

___ Westfahl, Gary. "Wanted: A Symbol for Science Fiction," *Science Fiction Studies* 22(1): 1-21. March 1995.

___ Winnett, Scott. "1991 Book Summary," in: Brown, Charles N. and Contento, William G. **Science Fiction, Fantasy, & Horror: 1991**. Oakland, CA: Locus Press, 1992. pp.423-427.

___ Winnett, Scott. "1991 Magazine Summary," by Scott Winnett and Charles N. Brown. in: Brown, Charles N. and Contento, William G. **Science Fiction, Fantasy, & Horror: 1991**. Oakland, CA: Locus Press, 1992. pp.428-432.

___ Winnett, Scott. "1992 Magazine Summary," by Scott Winnett and Charles N. Brown. *Locus* 30(2): 44-46. February 1993.

___ Winnett, Scott. "1993 Book Summary," by Scott Winnett and Charles N. Brown. *Locus* 32(2): 43-45, 73-76. February 1994.

___ Winnett, Scott. "1993 Magazine Summary," by Scott Winnett and Charles N. Brown. *Locus* 32(2): 44-48, 51. February 1994.

PUIG, MANUEL

___ Cheever, Leonard A. "Fantasies of Sexual Hell: Manuel Puig's **Pubis Angelical** and Margaret Atwood's **The Handmaid's Tale**," in: Latham, Robert A. and Collins, Robert A., eds. **Modes of the Fantastic**. Westport, CT: Greenwood, 1995. pp.110-121.

PULLMAN, BILL

___ Jankiewicz, Pat. "Ghost, the Rapist," *Starlog* No. 216: 36-39. July 1995.

PULPHOUSE (MAGAZINE)

___ "*Pulphouse* Goes Monthly," *Science Fiction Chronicle* 13(6): 5. March 1992.

PUMPING IRON (MOTION PICTURE)

___ Goldberg, Jonathan. "Recalling Totalities: The Mirrored Stages of Arnold Schwarzenegger," in: Gray, Chris H., ed. **The Cyborg Handbook**. New York: Routledge, 1995. pp.233-254.

PUMPKINHEAD II: BLOOD WINGS (MOTION PICTURE)

___ Crisafulli, Chuck. "**Pumpkinhead II**," *Cinefantastique* 25(3): 52-53, 61. June 1994.

PUMPKINHEAD II: BLOOD WINGS (MOTION PICTURE) (continued)
___ Harris, Judith P. "*Pumpkinhead II: Blood Wings* (Review)," *Cinefantastique* 26(3): 60. April 1995.

PUNCHATZ, DON IVAN
___ Fenner, Arnie. "Punchatz: A Barnstormer in Texas," *Shayol* No. 6: 20-27. 1982.

PUPP, JULIUS
___ "Materialien zu Julius Pupp und **Freinacht**," *Quarber Merkur* 32(2): 23-28. December 1994. (Whole No. 82)

PUPPET MASTERS III: TOULON'S REVENGE (MOTION PICTURE)
___ Harris, Judith P. "*Puppet Masters III: Toulon's Revenge* (Review)," *Cinefantastique* 22(6): 55. June 1992

PUPPET MASTERS (MOTION PICTURE)
___ SEE: ROBERT A. HEINLEIN'S THE PUPPET MASTERS (MOTION PICTURE).

PURVES, PETER
___ Eramo, Steven. "Traveling Man," *Starlog* No. 215: 58-61. June 1995.

PYLE, HOWARD
___ Lupack, Alan. "Beyond the Model: Howard Pyle's Arthurian Books," in: Busby, Keith, ed. **The Arthurian Yearbook I**. New York: Garland, 1991. pp.215-234.

PYNCHON, THOMAS
___ Andriano, Joseph. "The Masks of Gödel: Math and Myth in Thomas Pynchon's **Gravity's Rainbow**," in: Latham, Robert A. and Collins, Robert A., eds. **Modes of the Fantastic**. Westport, CT: Greenwood, 1995. pp.14-20.
___ Atwill, William D. **Fire and Power: The American Space Program as Postmodern Narrative**. Athens, GA: The University of Georgia Press, 1994. 172pp.
___ Berressem, Hanjo. **Pynchon's Poetics: Interfacing Theory and Text**. Urbana: University of Illinois Press, 1993. 273pp.
___ Brande, David J. **Technologies of Postmodernity: Ideology and Desire in Literature and Science (Pynchon, Thomas; Gibson, William; Butler, Octavia; Acker, Kathy)**. Ph.D. Dissertation, University of Washington, 1995. 228pp. (DAI-A 56/07, p. 2677. January 1996.)
___ Bumas, E. Shaskan. "The Utopian States of America: The People, the Republic, and Rock and Roll in Thomas Pynchon's **Vineland**," *Arizona Quarterly* 51(3): 149-175. Autumn 1995.
___ Burgheim, Manfred G. "Philip K. Dicks **Ubik** und Thomas Pynchons **Die Versteigerung von No. 49**: Zwei romane, ein epistemologisches Modell," *Quarber Merkur* 33(2): 25-29. December 1995. (No. 84)
___ Cowart, David. "Attenuated Postmodernism: Pynchon's **Vineland**," in: Trachtenberg, Stanley, ed. **Critical Essays on American Postmodernism**. New York: G. K. Hall, 1995. pp.182-191.
___ Cullen, Robert J. **Words and a Yarn: Language and Narrative Technique in the Works of Thomas Pynchon**. Ph.D. Dissertation, University of California, Los Angeles, 1981. 222pp.
___ Freese, Peter. "Surviving the End: Apocalypse, Evolution, and Entropy in Bernard Malamud, Kurt Vonnegut and Thomas Pynchon," *Critique* 36(3): 163-176. Spring 1995.
___ Gorman, Lawrence J. **Gravity's Rainbow: The Promise and Trap of Mythology**. Ph.D. Dissertation, Northern Illinois University, 1981. 262pp.
___ Hite, Molly P. **Ideas of Order in the Novels of Thomas Pynchon**. Ph.D. Dissertation, University of Washington, 1981. 269pp.
___ Hume, Kathryn. "Repetition and the Construction of Character in **Gravity's Rainbow**," *Critique* 33(4): 243-254. Summer 1992.
___ Kappel, Lawrence. "Psychic Geography in **Gravity's Rainbow**," *Contemporary Literature* 21(1): 225-251. Winter 1980.
___ Melley, Timothy. "Bodies Incorporated: Scenes of Agency Panic in **Gravity's Rainbow**," *Contemporary Literature* 25(4): 709-738. Winter 1994.
___ Newman, Robert D. "Thomas Pynchon," in: Bruccoli, Matthew J., ed. **Facts on File Bibliography of American Fiction 1919-1988**. New York: Facts on File, 1991. pp.413-414.
___ Puschmann-Nalenz, Barbara. **Science Fiction and Postmodern Fiction: A Genre Study**. New York: Peter Lang, 1992. 268pp. (Trans. of **Science Fiction und Ihre Grenzberieche**.)

PYNCHON, THOMAS (continued)
___ Schachterle, Lance. "Pynchon and the Civil Wars of Technology," in: Greenberg, Mark L. and Schachterle, Lance, eds. **Literature and Technology**. Bethlehem, PA: Lehigh University Press, 1992. pp.253-274.
___ Strehle, Susan. **Fiction in the Quantum Universe**. Chapel Hill: University of North Carolina Press, 1992. 282pp.
___ Weisenburger, Steven. "Hysteron Proteron in **Gravity's Rainbow**," *Texas Studies in Language and Literature* 34(1): 87-105. Spring 1992.

QUANTUM LEAP (MOTION PICTURE)
___ Spelling, Ian. "Quantum Leaper," by Ian Spelling and Marc Shapiro. in: McDonnell, David, ed. **Starlog's Science Fiction Heroes and Heroines**. New York: Crescent Books, 1995. pp.87-89.

QUANTUM LEAP (TV)
___ Goldberg, Lee. "Leap Years," *Starlog* 184: 30-33, 70. November 1992.
___ Lomartire, Paul. "West Palm Native **Leaps** into 1968," *West Palm Beach (FL) Post*. October 6, 1992. in: *NewsBank. Film and Television*. 106:B5. 1992.
___ Shapiro, Marc. "Grand Illusionist," *Starlog* No. 212: 41-44. March 1995.
___ Van Hise, James. **Sci Fi TV: From Twilight Zone to Deep Space Nine**. Las Vegas, NV: Pioneer Books, 1993. 160pp. (Reprinted, HarperPrism, 1995. 258pp.)
___ Wiggins, Kayla M. "Epic Heroes, Ethical Issues, and Time Paradoxes in **Quantum Leap**," *Journal of Popular Film and Television* 21(3): 111-120. Fall 1993.

QUANTUM (MAGAZINE)
___ "Quantum Quits," *Locus* 29(4): 8, 73. October 1992
___ Fratz, Doug. "Index: *Thrust/Quantum*, No. 1, February 1973-No. 43/44, May 1993," *Quantum* No. 43/44: 67-69. Spring/Summer 1993.
___ Fratz, Doug. "The Twenty-Year Spree: A Personal History of *Thrust/Quantum*," *Quantum* No. 43/44: 51-66. Spring/Summer 1993.

QUATERMASS 2 (MOTION PICTURE)
___ Palmer, Randy. "Serious Sci-Fi From the British Front: The Quatermass Experience," *Filmfax* No. 37: 68-75. February/March 1993.

QUATERMASS AND THE PIT (MOTION PICTURE)
___ Hogan, David J. "*Quatermass and the Pit* (Review)," *Filmfax* No. 37: 19-20. February/March 1993.

QUATERMASS EXPERIMENT (MOTION PICTURE)
___ Hogan, David J. "*The Quatermass Experiment* (Review)," *Filmfax* No. 37: 18-19. February/March 1993.
___ Palmer, Randy. "Serious Sci-Fi From the British Front: The Quatermass Experience," *Filmfax* No. 37: 68-75. February/March 1993.

QUEST FOR FIRE (MOTION PICTURE)
___ "Quest Fires Spate of Prehistoric Pix," *Variety* p. 48. February 3, 1982.
___ "A Shuffleboard of Producers, Other **Quest for Fire** Lessons," *Variety* p. 5, 42. February 17, 1982.

QUEST FOR LOVE (MOTION PICTURE)
___ Leeper, Mark R. "*Quest for Love* (Review)," *Lan's Lantern* No. 42: 106. May 1994.

RACE
___ Barshay, Robert. "Ethnic Stereotypes in **Flash Gordon**," *Journal of Popular Film and Television* 3(1): 15-30. 1974.
___ Helford, Elyce R. **Reading Space Fictions: Representations of Gender, Race and Species in Popular Culture**. Ph.D. Dissertation, University of Iowa, 1993. (DAI-A 53/11, p. 3908. May 1993.)
___ Jakaitis, Jake. "Two Cases of Conscience: Loyalty and Race in **The Crack in Space** and **Counter-Clock World**," in: Umland, Samuel J., ed. **Philip K. Dick: Contemporary Critical Interpretations**. Westport, CT: Greenwood, 1995. pp.169-196.
___ Reed-Pharrr, Robert F. "Sex, Race, and Science Fiction: The *Callaloo* Interview," in: Delany, Samuel R. **Silent Interviews on Language, Race, Sex, Science Fiction and Some Comics**. Hanover, NH: Wesleyan University Press, 1994. pp.216-229.

RACE RELATIONS

RACE RELATIONS

___ Bernardi, Daniel. "Infinite Diversity in Infinite Combinations: Diegetic Logics and Racial Articulations in the Originial **Star Trek**," *Film & History* 24(1/2): 60-74. February/May 1994.

RADCLIFFE, ANN

___ Bloom, Harold. "Ann Radcliffe," in: Bloom, Harold. **Classic Horror Writers**. New York: Chelsea House, 1994. pp.107-120.

RADER, PETER

___ Johnson, Kim H. "Rime of the Future Mariner," *Starlog* No. 218: 40-44. September 1995.

RADIO

___ "Finnish Radio Drama About **The Next War** Causes a Civil Upset," *Variety* p.1, 145. January 1, 1986.

___ "Public Radio Strikes Back With 'Empire'," *Variety* p. 38. April 21, 1982.

___ "Radio Caracas to Roll Sci-Fi Series," *Variety* p. 56. February 23, 1983.

___ "Welles' 'War' Replayed: Police Alerted, But 31 Years Have Tamed the Drama," *Variety* p. 32. November 5, 1969.

___ Chandler, Dixon H. **The Sounds of Dissension: Science Fiction Programming on American Popular Radio Through Dimension X (1950/1)**. Master's Thesis, Bowling Green State University, 1992. 194pp.

___ Daley, Brian. **Star Wars: The National Public Radio Dramatization**. New York: Del Rey, 1994. 346pp.

___ Fontrodona, Mariano. "El dia que marte invadio la tierra [The Day That Mars Invaded Earth]," *Historia y Vida* 21(249): 104-109. 1988.

___ Gunn, James E. "The Great Science Fiction Radio Show," in: Gunn, James E. **Inside Science Fiction: Essays on Fantastic Literature**. San Bernardino, CA: Borgo, 1992. pp.118-120.

___ Klossner, Michael. "Science Fiction in Film, Television, and Radio," in: Barron, Neil, ed. **Anatomy of Wonder 4**. New York: Bowker, 1995. pp.612-650.

___ Roberts, Jack. "Voices of Terror," *Filmfax* No. 45: 36-45, 96-97. June/July 1994.

___ Troster, Horst G. **Science Fiction im Horspiel, 1947-1987**. Frankfurt-am-Main: Rundfunkarchiv, 1993. 750pp.

RADIO FLYER (MOTION PICTURE)

___ "Dull **Radio Flyer** Never Takes Off (Review)," *Washington (DC) Times*. February 21, 1992. in: *NewsBank. Film and Television*. 24:G8. 1992.

___ Bacal, Simon. "The Giant Buffalo of Rick Lazzarini's Character Shop," *Cinefantastique* 23(1): 58-59. August 1992.

___ Burden, Martin. "Boys and a Hood (Review)," *New York (NY) Post*. February 21, 1992. in: *NewsBank. Film and Television*. 24:G7. 1992.

___ Campbell, Bob. "Confused **Radio Flyer** Lands Short of Runway (Review)," *Newark (NJ) Star-Ledger*. February 21, 1992. in: *NewsBank. Film and Television*. 24:G6. 1992.

___ Doherty, Thomas. "**Radio Flyer** (Review)," *Cinefantastique* 23(1): 58-59. August 1992.

___ Ebert, Roger. "Child Abuse Meets Peter Pan in **Radio Flyer** (Review)," *Denver (CO) Post*. February 21, 1992. in: *NewsBank. Film and Television*. 24:G2. 1992.

___ Johnson, Malcolm. "**Radio Flyer** a Fantasy Without Any Direction (Review)," *Hartford (CT) Courant*. February 21, 1992. in: *NewsBank. Film and Television*. 24:G3. 1992.

___ Kunk, Deborah J. "Through a Child's Eyes (Review)," *St. Paul (MN) Pioneer Press-Dispatch*. March 3, 1992. in: *NewsBank. Film and Television*. 24:F13. 1992

___ Shulgasser, Barbara. "Overcome By Gravity: **Radio Flyer** Never Takes Off (Review)," *San Francisco (CA) Examiner*. February 21, 1992. in: *NewsBank. Film and Television*. 24:G1. 1992

___ Strauss, Bob. "**Flyer** Is Finally Given Its Wings (Review)," *Los Angeles (CA) Daily News*. February 21, 1992. in: *NewsBank. Film and Television*. 24:F11-F12. 1992

___ Strauss, Bob. "**Radio Flyer** Has Solid Roles But Never Really Takes Off (Review)," *Los Angeles (CA) Daily News*. February 21, 1992. in: *NewsBank. Film and Television*. 24:F14. 1992

___ Verniere, James. "**Radio Flyer's** Attempt at a Childhood Adventure Story Turns into a Fractured Fairy Tale (Review)," *Boston (MA) Herald*. February 21, 1992. in: *NewsBank. Film and Television*. 24:G4-G5. 1992.

RADOMSKI, ERIC

___ Garcia, Bob. "**Batman**: Eric Radomski, Series Co-Creator," by Bob Garcia and Nancy Garcia. *Cinefantastique* 24(6)/25(1): 76-77. February 1994.

RAIDERS OF THE LOST ARK (MOTION PICTURE)

___ "Court of Appeals Upholds 'Raiders' Ruling for Paramount," *Variety* p.20. December 18, 1985.

___ " 'Raiders' Sweeps 7 Sci-Fi Pic Awards," *Variety* p. 7, 28. August 11, 1982.

___ "Scripter's 'Raiders' Suit Against Paramount Dismissed," *Variety* p.22. July 31, 1985.

___ Nazzaro, Joe. "Sophisticated Evil," *Starlog* No. 218: 72-75, 65. September 1995.

___ Seideman, Tony. " 'Raiders' Setting Sales Marks, Paramount Claims 500,000 in Route," *Variety* p. 27-28. November 23, 1983.

RAIMI, SAM

___ Uram, Sue. "Dead Auteur: Sam Raimi, Tyro Director," *Cinefantastique* 23(1): 28-29. August 1992.

___ Uram, Sue. "**Evil Dead**: College Filmmakers Turn Professional," *Cinefantastique* 23(1): 52-53. August 1992.

___ Uram, Sue. "**Evil Dead II**: Working With Sam Raimi," *Cinefantastique* 23(1): 47. August 1992.

___ Wiater, Stanley. "Raimi, Sam," in: Wiater, Stanley. **Dark Visions: Conversations with the Masters of the Horror Film**. New York: Avon, 1992. pp.137-146.

RAIMI, TED

___ Warren, Bill. "The Young Ted Raimi," *Starlog* No. 198: 38-41. January 1994.

RAIN WITHOUT THUNDER (MOTION PICTURE)

___ Rosenberg, Scott. "A Feminist Nightmare in the Year 2042 (Review)," *San Francisco (CA) Examiner*. February 12, 1993. in: *NewsBank. Art.* 7:C4-C5. 1993.

RAISING ARIZONA (MOTION PICTURE)

___ Sanders, Joe L. "**Raising Arizona**: Not Quite Ozzie and Harriet Meet the Biker From Hell," *Journal of the Fantastic in the Arts* 6(2/3): 217-233. 1994.

RAISING CAIN (MOTION PICTURE)

___ "Not Very Able **Cain** on Hollywood's Schiz Row (Review)," *Washingotn (D.C.) Times*. August 7, 1992. in: *NewsBank. Film and Television*. 83:B2. 1992.

___ Campbell, Bob. "A Dizzy, Dire Delirium Puts Mind-Blowing Spin on De Palma's **Raising Cain** (Review)," *Newark (NJ) Star-Ledger*. August 7, 1992. in: *NewsBank. Film and Television*. 83:A14. 1992.

___ Doherty, Thomas. "**Raising Cain** (Review)," *Cinefantastique* 23(4): 61. December 1992.

___ Johnson, Malcolm. "**Cain** Is a Mixed-up Movie About One Confused Guy (Review)," *Hartford (CT) Courant*. August 7, 1992. in: *NewsBank. Film and Television*. 83:A10. 1992.

___ Mahar, Ted. "**Raising Cain** Quickly Sinks to Absurd Levels of Contrivance (Review)," *Portland (OR) The Oregonian*. August 7, 1992. in: *NewsBank. Film and Television*. 83:B1. 1992.

___ Ringel, Eleanor. "**Cain** Not So Able; De Palma Can't Get Back on Track (Review)," *Atlanta (GA) Journal*. August 7, 1992. in: *NewsBank. Film and Television*. 83:A11. 1992.

___ Rosen, Stephen. "De Palma's **Raising Cain** Is De-lightful (Review)," *Denver (CO) Post*. August 7, 1992. in: *NewsBank. Film and Television*. 83:A9. 1992.

___ Rosenberg, Scott. "Unable to Raise **Cain** (Review)," *San Francisco (CA) Examiner*. August 7, 1992. in: *NewsBank. Film and Television*. 83: A7-A8. 1992.

___ Sachs, Lloyd. "**Raising Cain** Isn't Able to Save De Palma (Review)," *Chicago (IL) Sun Times*. August 7, 1992. in: *NewsBank. Film and Television*. 83:A12. 1992.

___ Verniere, James. "De Palma Rebounds With **Raising Cain** (Review)," *Boston (MA) Herald*. August 7, 1992. in: *NewsBank. Film and Television*. 83:A13. 1992.

RAND, AYN

___ Trull, Anthony. "Atlas in Spain: Comparing Nancy Kress' 'Beggars in Spain' with Ayn Rand's **Atlas Shrugged**," *Quantum* No. 42: 31-32. Summer/Fall 1992.

RANSOM, BILL
___ Rain, Lenora. "Interview: Bill Ransom," by Lenora Rain and Lee Good. *Westwind* No. 183: 13-16. December 1993.

RAPHAEL, RICK
___ "Raphael, Rick (Obituary)," *Locus* 32(3): 68. March 1994.
___ "Raphael, Rick (Obituary)," *Science Fiction Chronicle* 15(6): 24-26. April/May 1994.

RAPTURE (MOTION PICTURE)
___ Lowe, Nick. "***The Rapture*** (Review)," *Interzone* No. 64: 30-31. October 1992.
___ Masley, Ed. "***The Rapture*** Mixes Sex and Religion and Comes Up Looking Blurred (Review)," *Pittsburgh (PA) Press.* February 14, 1992. in: *NewsBank. Film and Television.* 24:G9. 1992.

RAVER (COMIC)
___ Stephens, Lynne. "*Raver*," *Starlog* No. 190: 24-26. May 1993.

RAWN, MELANIE
___ "Melanie Rawn: Recycling History," *Hailing Frequencies* (Waldenbooks) No. 5: 6-7. 1992.
___ "Rawn Sell to Avon," *Locus* 35(5): 8. November 1995.

RAY BRADBURY THEATER III (TV)
___ "***Ray Bradbury Theater III*** (Review)," *Variety* p. 113. May 11, 1988.

RAY BRADBURY THEATER (TV)
___ "***Philip Marlowe, Bradbury Theater*** Picked Up by HBO," *Variety* p.55, 64. September 11, 1985.

RAY, N.
___ Stone, Graham. "Notes on Australian Science Fiction," *Science Fiction News* (Australia) No. 92: 2-8. February 1985.

RAY, SATYAJIT
___ "Ray, Satyajit (Obituary)," *Locus* 28(6): 67. June 1992.

READERCON SMALL PRESS AWARDS, 1992
___ "1992 Readercon Small Press Awards," *Locus* 29(5): 5. November 1992

REAL GHOSTBUSTERS (TV)
___ "Columbia's ***Real Ghostbusters*** Haunts Web and Syndie Markets," *Variety* p. 52. January 29, 1986.

REALMS OF FANTASY (MAGAZINE)
___ "*Realms of Fantasy* Advances," *Science Fiction Chronicle* 15(4): 5. February 1994.
___ "*Realms of Fantasy* New Magazine," *Locus* 32(4): 7. April 1994.
___ "Sovereign Media Moves Two Magazines Forward," *Science Fiction Chronicle* 15(5): 4. March 1994.

REANIMATOR (MOTION PICTURE)
___ "Edited ***Re-Animator*** Garners an R Rating," *Variety* p. 7, 17. June 18, 1986.
___ "***Re-Animator*** Ads Rejected Because of Unrated Status," *Variety* p.4, 38. October 30, 1985.

REASON, REX
___ Weaver, Tom. "Rex Reason," in: Weaver, Tom. **They Fought the Creature Features: Interviews with 23 Classic Horror, Science Fiction and Serial Stars.** Jefferson, NC: McFarland, 1995. pp.233-243.

REAVER, HERBERT R., JR.
___ "Reaver, Herbert R., Jr. (Obituary)," *Locus* 30(3): 71. March 1993.

REBEL ASSAULT (CD-ROM)
___ SEE: STAR WARS: REBEL ASSAULT (CD-ROM).

REBOOT (MOTION PICTURE)
___ Hammell, Tim. "***Reboot*** (Review)," *Cinefantastique* 26(4): 60. June 1995.

RECORDED BOOKS
___ Mendlesohn, Farah. "Audio Books: A New Medium for SF?," *Foundation* No. 64: 90-96. Summer 1995.

RED DAWN (MOTION PICTURE)
___ " 'Dawn' Called Reagan Propaganda by Pickets," *Variety* p. 30. August 29, 1984.
___ "Hold Back the 'Dawn'," *Variety* p. 37. January 9, 1985.
___ "Oversight in ***Red Dawn*** Campaign Riles Alaskan," *Variety* p. 3, 40. September 19, 1984.

RED DWARF (TV)
___ Hall, John S. "Lister, American Sty!e," *Starlog* No. 221: 67-69. December 1995.
___ Helford, Elyce R. "Reading Masculinities in the 'Postpatriarchal' Space of ***Red Dwarf***," *Foundation* No. 64: 20-31. Summer 1995.
___ Nassaro, Joe. "***Red Dwarf***," *Starlog* No. 186: 75-80. January 1993.
___ Nazzaro, Joe. "Cats Tale," *Starlog* No. 190: 78-81. May 1993.
___ Nazzaro, Joe. "Computer Print-Out," *Starlog* No. 189: 48-49. April 1993.
___ Nazzaro, Joe. "Face of Metal," *Starlog* No. 196: 39-42. November 1993.
___ Nazzaro, Joe. "Little Lost Holly," *Starlog* No. 221: 68-69. December 1995.
___ Nazzaro, Joe. "Recession Dwarf," *Starlog* No. 201: 46-49. April 1994.
___ Nazzaro, Joe. "Slob of the Spaceways," *Starlog* No. 187: 50-53. February 1993.
___ Nazzaro, Joe. "Working Class Hologram," *Starlog* No. 188: 78-81. March 1993.

RED PLANET MARS (MOTION PICTURE)
___ Stephens, Bob. "United Artists ***Sci-Fi Matinee***," *Films in Review* 46(9/10): 54-60. November/December 1995.

RED PLANET (TV)
___ Fischer, Dennis. "***Red Planet*** (Review)," *Cinefantastique* 25(6)/26(1): 123. December 1994.

RED SONJA (MOTION PICTURE)
___ "***Red Sonja*** Completing Shooting, Presages Revival of Dinocitta," *Variety* p. 69. December 19, 1984.

REFERENCE
___ Ashley, Mike. **The Supernatural Index: A Listing of Fantasy, Supernatural, Weird, and Horror Anthologies.** Westport, CT: Greenwood Press, 1995. 952pp.
___ Barron, Neil. "General Reference Works," in: Barron, Neil, ed. **Anatomy of Wonder 4.** New York: Bowker, 1995. pp.462-482.
___ Barron, Neil, ed. **Anatomy of Wonder 4: A Critical Guide to Science Fiction.** New York: Bowker, 1995. 912pp.
___ Barron, Neil, ed. **What Do I Read Next? A Reader's Guide to Current Genre Fiction.** Detroit: Gale Research, 1992. 608pp.
___ Bloom, Harold, ed. **Classic Science Fiction Writers.** New York: Chelsea House, 1995. 186pp.
___ Brown, Charles N. **Science Fiction, Fantasy, & Horror: 1991,** by Charles N. Brown and William G. Contento. Oakland, CA: Locus Press, 1992. 482pp.
___ Bruccoli, Matthew J., ed. **Facts on File Bibliography of American Fiction 1919-1988,** ed. by Matthew J. Bruccoli and Judith S. Baughman. New York: Facts on File, 1991. 2 v.
___ Bunson, Matthew. **The Vampire Encyclopedia.** New York: Crown, 1993. 303pp.
___ Burgess, Michael. **Reference Guide to Science Fiction, Fantasy, and Horror.** Littleton, CO: Libraries Unlimited, 1992. 403pp.
___ Cassiday, Bruce. **Modern Mystery, Fantasy and Science Fiction Writers.** New York: Continuum, 1993. 673pp.
___ Clute, John. **The Encyclopedia of Science Fiction.** CD-ROM Edition. New York: Grolier, 1995. 1 CD-ROM.
___ Clute, John. **The Encyclopedia of Science Fiction,** by John Clute and Peter Nicholls. New York: St. Martin's, 1993. 1370pp.
___ Clute, John. **Science Fiction: The Illustrated Encyclopedia.** London: Dorling, 1995. 312pp.
___ Cox, Greg. **The Transylvanian Library: A Consumer's Guide to Vampire Fiction.** San Bernardino, CA: Borgo Press, 1993. 264pp.
___ Currey, Lloyd W. "A Select List of Reference Books: Science Fiction, Fantasy and Horror Literature," *AB Bookmans Weekly* 94(17): 1648-1657. October 24, 1994.
___ Day, Bradford M. **The Checklist of Fantastic Literature in Paperbound Books.** Revised and enlarged edition. Hillsville, VA: Bradford M. Day, 1994. 890pp.

REPP, ED EARL
___ "Repp, Ed Earl, 1901-1979 (Obituary)," *Science Fiction News* (Australia) No. 60: 4. April 1979.

RESNICK, LAURA
___ "1993 Hugo Awards Winners," *Locus* 31(4): 5, 70. October 1993.
___ "Other Awards," *Science Fiction Chronicle* 15(1): 4. October 1993.

RESNICK, MIKE
___ "1994 Nebula Awards Winners," *Locus* 34(5): 7. May 1995.
___ "1995 Hugo Winners," *Locus* 35(3): 7. September 1993.
___ "Compuserve HOMer Awards, 1992," *Science Fiction Chronicle* 14(9): 4-5. June 1993.
___ "The Hugos (Or, the Empire Strikes Back)," *Science Fiction Chronicle* 17(2): 55-56. December 1995/January 1996.
___ "Nebula Award Winners," *Science Fiction Chronicle* 16(6): 4. May 1995.
___ "Neube, Resnick, McDevitt Win 1994 UPC Awards," *Science Fiction Chronicle* 16(3): 5. January 1995.
___ "World Science Fiction Convention Hugo Awards, 1995," *Science Fiction Chronicle* 17(1): 5. October/November 1995
___ Resnick, Mike. "It's Not That Long a Road From New Fan to SF Elder Statesman," *Science Fiction Age* 3(5): 34-36, 101. July 1995.
___ Resnick, Mike. "A Look at Paradise," *OtherRealms* No. 24: 11-12. Spring 1989.
___ Schweitzer, Darrell. "An Interview With Mike Resnick," *Marion Zimmer Bradley's Fantasy Magazine* No. 17: 53-58. Fall 1992.
___ Tilton, Lois. "Strangling the Baby: Cultural Relativism in Mike Resnick's 'Kirinyaga'," *New York Review of Science Fiction* No. 9: 11-12. May 1989.
___ Van Gelder, Gordon. "Let's Go Look at the Natives: Conflicts of Culture in Mike Resnick's 'Kirinyaga'," *New York Review of Science Fiction* No. 9: 11-14. May 1989.

RESURRECTED (MOTION PICTURE)
___ Biodrowski, Steve. "H. P. Lovecraft's *The Resurrected*," *Cinefantastique* 22(6): 4-6. June 1992
___ Biodrowski, Steve. "Lovecraft Special Effects," *Cinefantastique* 22(6): 7. June 1992
___ Harris, Judith P. "*The Resurrected* (Review)," *Cinefantastique* 23(2/3): 123. October 1992.

RETAILING
___ Underwood, Elaine. "Spencer Tests Sci-Fi On-Site TV," *Brandweek* 36(23): 3. June 5, 1995.

RETURN OF JACK DETH (MOTION PICTURE)
___ SEE: TRANCERS II: RETURN OF JACK DETH (MOTION PICTURE).

RETURN OF THE JEDI (MOTION PICTURE)
___ SEE: STAR WARS: RETURN OF THE JEDI (MOTION PICTURE).

RETURN OF THE TEXAS CHAINSAW MASSACRE (MOTION PICTURE)
___ Frost, Gordon W. "*Return of the Texas Chainsaw Massacre*," *Cinefantastique* 27(3): 12-13. December 1995.

RETURN TO RINGWORLD (GAME)
___ Rothman, Chuck. "Larry Niven's Ringworld Novels Spawn a Fun and Challenging Computer Sequel," *Science Fiction Age* 3(1): 88-91. November 1994.

RETURN TO THE LOST WORLD (MOTION PICTURE)
___ Harris, Judith P. "*Return to the Lost World* (Review)," *Cinefantastique* 25(5): 60. October 1994.

REUSS, GUSTAV MARURICIUS
___ Srpon, Vlado. "Dr Gustav Maruricius Reuss: The First Slovak Literary Fantasist," *Foundation* No. 63: 81-84. Spring 1995.

REVENGE OF THE CREATURE (MOTION PICTURE)
___ Weaver, Tom. "Lori Nelson," in: Weaver, Tom. **They Fought the Creature Features: Interviews with 23 Classic Horror, Science Fiction and Serial Stars**. Jefferson, NC: McFarland, 1995. pp.221-232.

REVIEWING
___ "Budrys Drops Review Columns," *Locus* 29(6): 6. December 1992.

REVIEWING (continued)
___ Clute, John. "Necessary Golems," in: Clute, John. **Look at the Evidence: Essays and Reviews**. Liverpool: Liverpool University Press, 1995. pp.3-7.
___ Collins, Robert A., ed. **Science Fiction and Fantasy Book Review Annual 1991**, ed. by Robert A. Collins and Robert A. Latham. Westport, CT: Greenwood, 1994. 880pp.
___ Easton, Thomas A. "Book Reviewing: A Matter of Opinion," *SFWA Bulletin* 26(1): 29-31. Spring 1992. (No. 115)
___ Feeley, Gregory. "Raters of the Graustark: Science Fiction Criticism and Its Critics," *SFWA Bulletin* 29(1): 35-39. Spring 1995. (No. 126)
___ Hall, Hal W. **Science Fiction and Fantasy Book Review Index, Volume 18, 1987**. San Bernardino, CA: Borgo Press, 1992. 70pp.
___ Hall, Hal W. **Science Fiction and Fantasy Book Review Index, Volume 19, 1988**. Bryan, TX: SFFBRI, 1992. 87pp.; San Bernardino, CA: Borgo Press, 1992. 85pp.
___ Hall, Hal W. **Science Fiction and Fantasy Book Review Index, Volume 20, 1989**. San Bernardino, CA: Borgo Press, 1993. 90pp.; Bryan, TX: SFFBRI, 1993. 90pp.
___ Hall, Hal W. **Science Fiction and Fantasy Book Review Index, Volume 21, 1990**. Bryan, TX: SFFBRI, 1994. 105pp.
___ Harrison, Mitchell. "The Burroughs Pre-Pubs," *Burroughs Bulletin* NS. No. 14: 29-32. April 1993.
___ Kincaid, Paul. "The Art of Reading a Review," *Focus* (BSFA) No. 24: 18. June/July 1993.
___ Langford, David. "The Dragonhiker's Guide to Battlefield Covenant at Dune's Edge: Odyssey Two," *Australian Science Fiction Review* 5(3): 3-11. Spring 1990. (Whole No. 25)
___ Von Rospach, Chuq. "Reviewing the Reviewers: A Survey of Science Fiction Critics," *OtherRealms* No. 23: 5-7. Winter 1989.
___ Wells, Earl. "The Rule of the Game," *New York Review of Science Fiction* No. 47: 6-7. July 1992.
___ Whitmore, Tom. "The Care and Feeding of Reviewers," *The Report: The Fiction Writer's Magazine* 2(6): 22. April 1992. (No. 59)

REVISION
___ "Forum: Revision," *Focus* (BSFA) No. 26: 5-9. June/July 1994.

REYNOLDS, MACK
___ Smith, Curtis C. "The Legacy of Mack Reynolds," *Journal of the Fantastic in the Arts* 5(4): 73-82. 1993. (No. 20)
___ Smith, Curtis C. **Welcome to the Revolution: The Literary Legacy of Mack Reynolds**. San Bernardino, CA: Borgo, 1995. 136pp.
___ Stableford, Brian. "Utopia--And Afterwards: Socioeconomic Speculation in the SF of Mack Reynolds," in: Stableford, Brian. **Outside the Human Aquarium: Masters of Science Fiction**. San Bernardino, CA: Borgo, 1995. pp.49-75.

RHODES, WILLIAM HENRY
___ Moskowitz, Sam. "Voyagers Through Eternity: A History of Science Fiction From the Beginnings to H. G. Wells," *Fantasy Commentator* 8(1/2): 135-144. Winter 1993/1994. (Whole No. 45/46)

RHOMER, ERIC
___ Rhiel, Mary. "The Taming of the Screw: Rohmer's Filming of Kliest's 'Die Marquise von O...'," in: Ruddick, Nicholas, ed. **State of the Fantastic**. Westport, CT: Greenwood, 1992. pp.83-90.

RHYSLING AWARD
___ SEE ALSO: POETRY.

RHYSLING AWARDS, 1992
___ "1992 Rhysling Awards," *Locus* 30(1): 7. January 1993.

RHYSLING AWARDS, 1994
___ "1994 Rhysling Awards," *Locus* 33(4): 72. October 1994.
___ "Rhysling Awards, 1994," *Science Fiction Chronicle* 16(1): 8. October 1994.

RICE, ANNE
___ "Par, Author Suing Trio over Pic Rights to Novel," *Variety* p. 3. October 3, 1984.
___ "Playboy Interview: Anne Rice," *Playboy* 40(3): 53-64. March 1993.
___ "Rice Recants re Vampire Cruise," *Locus* 33(5): 8. November 1994.
___ Dawidziak, Mark. "Anne Rice: The Universe Interview," *Sci-Fi Universe* No. 3: 19-27. October/November 1994.

RICE, ANNE

RICE, ANNE (continued)
___ DiGiacomo, Frank. "Naughty and Rice: Author Porn to Be Wild," *New York (NY) Post*. November 24, 1992. in: *NewsBank. Literature*. 105:C7-C8. 1992.
___ Due, Tananarive. "Anne Rice: Queen of the Night (Interview)," *Miami (FL) Herald*. November 19, 1992. in: *NewsBank. Literature*. 105: C5-C6. 1992.
___ Fasolino, Greg. "Lestat of the Art: The Dark Gift Discussed," *Reflex* No. 29: 42-46. 1992.
___ Joshi, S. T. "Anne Rice: The Philosophy of Vampirism," *Interzone* No. 75: 47-50, 61. September 1993.
___ Kendrick, Walter. "Better Undead Than Unread: Have Vampires Lost Their Bite?," *New York Times Book Review* p. 55. October 18, 1992.
___ Kies, Cosette. **Presenting Young Adult Horror Fiction**. New York: Twayne, 1991. 203pp.
___ King, Maureen. "Contemporary Women Writers and the 'New Evil': The Vampires of Anne Rice and Suzy McKee Charnas," *Journal of the Fantastic in the Arts* 5(3): 75-84. 1993. (No. 19)
___ Leopold, Glenn. "New Vampire Saga Has Certain Bite to It," *Los Angeles (CA) Daily News*. October 25, 1992. in *NewsBank. Literature*. 95:C1-C2. 1992.
___ Marigny, Jean. "The Different Faces of Eros in the Vampire Chronicles of Anne Rice," *Paradoxa* 1(3): 352-362. 1995.
___ Marigny, Jean. "Les différents visages d'Eros dans la trilogie d'Anne Rice, the Vampire Chronicles," in: Bozzetto, Roger, ed. **Eros: Science & Fiction Fantastique**. Aix-en-Provence: Universite de Provence, 1991. pp.71-83.
___ Ramsland, Katherine. **The Anne Rice Trivia Book**. New York: Ballantine, 1994. 244pp.
___ Ramsland, Katherine. **The Vampire Companion: The Official Guide to Anne Rice's The Vampire Chronicles**. Revised edition. New York: Ballantine, 1995. 581pp.
___ Ramsland, Katherine. **The Vampire Companion: The Official Guide to Anne Rice's The Vampire Chronicles**. New York: Ballantine, 1993. 512pp.
___ Ramsland, Katherine. **The Witches' Companion: The Official Guide to Anne Rice's Lives of the Mayfair Witches**. New York: Ballantine, 1994. 540pp.
___ Rice, Dale. "Imagination: Anne Rice," *Austin (TX) American Statesman* Sec. C, p. 1, 3. October 15, 1993.
___ Rice, Dale. "Leaving Old Haunts," *Austin (TX) American Statesman* Sec. F, p. 1, 8. August 18, 1995.
___ Sumner, Jane. "Rice Has Biting Words for Hollywood (Interview)," *Dallas (TX) Morning News*. November 25, 1992. in: *NewsBank. Literature*. 105:C9-C10. 1992.
___ Waxman, Barbara F. "Postextentialism in the Neo-Gothic Mode: Anne Rice's **Interview With the Vampire**," *Mosaic* 25(3): 79-97. Summer 1992.
___ Yoo, Paula. "Rice Didn't Become a Nun, But She Did Get the Writing Habit (Interview)," *Seattle (WA) Times*. November 5, 1992. in: *NewsBank. Literature*. 105:C11-C12. 1992.

RICH, MARK
___ Klein, Jay K. "Biolog: Mark Rich," *Analog* 114(13): 99, 108. November 1994.

RICHARDSON, MIKE
___ Webber, Ken. "Interview With Mike Richardson, Publisher of Dark Horse Comics," *Burroughs Bulletin* NS. No. 21: 27-32. January 1995.

RIDLEY, FRANK
___ "Ridley, Frank (Obituary)," *Locus* 32(5): 62. May 1994.

RIDLEY, PHILIP
___ Stanley, John. "Philip Ridley," *Cinefantastique* 23(2/3): 114-119. October 1992.

RIO DE JANEIRO MOVIE FESTIVAL, 1969
___ Heinlein, Robert A. "Guest of Honor Speech: Rio de Janeiro Movie Festival, 1969," in: Kondo, Yoji, ed. **Requiem: New Collected Works by Robert A. Heinlein and Tributes to the Grand Master**. New York: Tor, 1992. pp.198-204.

ROACH, HAL
___ "Roach, Hal (Obituary)," *Science Fiction Chronicle* 14(3): 15. December 1992.

ROAD WARRIOR (MOTION PICTURE)
___ SEE: MAD MAX 2: THE ROAD WARRIOR (MOTION PICTURE).

ROBBE-GRILLET, ALAIN
___ Chadwick, Tony. "Alain Robbe-Grillet and the Fantastic," by Tony Chadwick and Virginia Harger-Grinling. in: Ruddick, Nicholas, ed. **State of the Fantastic**. Westport, CT: Greenwood, 1992. pp.91-96.
___ Chadwick, Tony. "The Fantastic Robbe-Grillet," by Tony Chadwick and Virginia Harger-Grinling. in: Harger-Grinling, Virginia and Chadwick, Tony, eds. **Robbe-Grillet and the Fantastic**. Westport, CT: Greenwood, 1994. pp.1-10.
___ Harger-Grinling, Virginia, ed. **Robbe-Grillet and the Fantastic: A Collection of Essays**, ed. by Virginia Harger-Grinling and Tony Chadwick. Westport, CT: Greenwood, 1994. 168pp.
___ Havercroft, Barbara. "Fluctuations of Fantasy: The Combination and Subversion of Literary Genres in **Djinn**," in: Harger-Grinling, Virginia and Chadwick, Tony, eds. **Robbe-Grillet and the Fantastic**. Westport, CT: Greenwood, 1994. pp.101-124.
___ Houppermans, Sjef. "Fantastique Angélique," in: Harger-Grinling, Virginia and Chadwick, Tony, eds. **Robbe-Grillet and the Fantastic**. Westport, CT: Greenwood, 1994. pp.77-100.
___ Jost, François. "Fragmented Representation," in: Harger-Grinling, Virginia and Chadwick, Tony, eds. **Robbe-Grillet and the Fantastic**. Westport, CT: Greenwood, 1994. pp.125-138.
___ Spear, Thomas. "Staging the Elusive Self," in: Harger-Grinling, Virginia and Chadwick, Tony, eds. **Robbe-Grillet and the Fantastic**. Westport, CT: Greenwood, 1994. pp.55-76.
___ Stoltzfus, Ben. "Fantasy, Metafiction and Desire," in: Harger-Grinling, Virginia and Chadwick, Tony, eds. **Robbe-Grillet and the Fantastic**. Westport, CT: Greenwood, 1994. pp.11-34.
___ Troiano, Maureen D. **New Physics and the Modern French Novel**. New York: Peter Lang, 1995. 276pp.
___ Yarrow, Ralph. "Traces of the Trickster," in: Harger-Grinling, Virginia and Chadwick, Tony, eds. **Robbe-Grillet and the Fantastic**. Westport, CT: Greenwood, 1994. pp.35-54.

ROBERSON, JENNIFER
___ King, Tom, Jr. "SFC Interviews: Jennifer Roberson," *Science Fiction Chronicle* 14(1): 5, 29-30. October 1992.
___ Shaver, Stephanie D. "Interview With Jennifer Roberson," *Marion Zimmer Bradley's Fantasy Magazine* No. 26: 44-48. Winter 1995.

ROBERT A. HEINLEIN'S THE PUPPET MASTERS (MOTION PICTURE)
___ Beeler, Michael. "**The Puppet Masters**," *Cinefantastique* 25(6)/26(1): 40-43. December 1994.
___ Bernard, Jami. "**Puppet Masters** Is UFOh So Entertaining," *(New York, NY) Daily News*. October 21, 1994. in: *NewsBank. Film and Television*. 114:F10. 1994.
___ Bokamper, Jerry. "**Puppet Masters** Terror Is Too Predictable," *Dallas (TX) Morning News*. October 24, 1994. in: *NewsBank. Film and Television*. 114:F11. 1994.
___ Campbell, Bob. "Heinlein's Vintage Sci-Fi Still Gives the Chills," *(Newark, NJ) Star-Ledger*. October 21, 1994. in: *NewsBank. Film and Television*. 124:B10. 1994.
___ Harris, Judith P. "**Puppet Masters** (Review)," *Cinefantastique* 26(3): 60. April 1995.
___ Hunter, Stephen. "**The Puppet Masters** Has the Soul of a 1950s Monster B-Movie," *(Baltimore, MD) Sun*. October 25, 1994. in: *NewsBank. Film and Television*. 114:F8. 1994.
___ Johnson, Malcolm. "Strung Along for a While by Masters," *Hartford (CT) Courant*. October 22, 1994. in: *NewsBank. Film and Television*. 124:B9. 1994.
___ Sherman, Paul. "**The Puppet Masters** Is a No Brainer of Sci-Fi," *Boston (MA) Herald*. October 22, 1994. in: *NewsBank. Film and Television*. 114:F9. 1994.
___ Teitelbaum, Sheldon. "The Mouse Who Sold the Moon: Disney Does Heinlein's **Puppet Masters**," *Sci-Fi Universe* No. 3: 38-43. October/November 1994.
___ Warren, Bill. "Pulling the Strings," *Starlog* No. 208: 46-51, 72. November 1994.
___ Wells, Curt. "Robert Heinlein's Classic **The Puppet Masters** Leaps From Page to Screen at Last!," *Science Fiction Age* 2(5): 18-22, 34. July 1994.

ROSE, TRICIA
___ Dery, Mark. "Black to the Future: Interviews with Samuel R. Delany, Greg Tate, and Tricia Rose," *South Atlantic Quarterly* 92(4): 735-788. Fall 1993. (Reprinted in: Dery, Mark, Ed. **Flame Wars: The Discourse of Cyberculture**. Durham, NC: Duke University Press, 1994.)

ROSEMARY'S BABY (MOTION PICTURE)
___ Fischer, Lucy. "Birth Traumas: Parturition and Horror in *Rosemary's Baby*," *Cinema Journal* 31(3): 3-18. Spring 1992.

ROSENBAUM, J. MICHAEL
___ "Rosenbaum, J. Michael (Obituary)," *Science Fiction News* (Australia) No. 58: 16-17. June 1978.

ROSENBLUM, MARY
___ "Mary Rosenblum: A Chameleon Life," *Locus* 32(4): 4, 64-65. April 1994.
___ "Mary Rosenblum Wins Compton Crook Award," *Locus* 32(5): 8. May 1994.
___ King, T. Jackson. "SFC Interview: Mary Rosenblum," *Science Fiction Chronicle* 16(8): 5, 34-36. July/August 1995

ROSENDORFER, HERBERT
___ Clute, John. "Herbert Rosendorfer," in: Clute, John. **Look at the Evidence: Essays and Reviews**. Liverpool: Liverpool University Press, 1995. pp.443-447.
___ Teissl, Verena. "Der tod in drei asugewählten phantastischen texten der Moderne," *Quarber Merkur* 33(2): 34-46. December 1995. (No. 84)

ROSHWALD, MORDECAI
___ Seed, David. "Push-Button Holocaust: Mordecai Roshwald's **Level 7**," *Foundation* No. 57: 68-86. Spring 1993.

ROSSIO, TERRY
___ Warren, Bill. "Pulling the Strings," *Starlog* No. 208: 46-51, 72. November 1994.

ROSWELL (MOTION PICTURE)
___ Counts, Kyle. "The UFO Incident," *Starlog* No. 206: 28-32, 69. September 1994.
___ Ogier, Mark. "*Roswell* (Review)," *Matrix* No. 115: 13. June/July 1995.
___ Teitelbaum, Sheldon. "U. F. O. Crash at Roswell," *Cinefantastique* 25(4): 12-13, 61. August 1994.

ROTHBERG, ABRAHAM
___ Christensen, Peter G. "Abraham Rothberg's **The Sword of the Golem**: The Use of the Fantastic in Defense of Judaism," *Journal of the Fantastic in the Arts* 7(2/3): 163-176. 1995.

ROTHMAN, STEPHANIE
___ Williams, Tony. "Feminism, Fantasy and Violence: An Interview With Stephanie Rothman," *Journal of Popular Film and Television* 9(2): 84-90. 1981. ('Letter of Correction': 10(3): 137. 1982.)

ROUJIN Z (MOTION PICTURE)
___ Lowe, Nick. "*Roujin Z* (Review)," *Interzone* No. 87: 25. September 1994.

ROYAL SPACE FORCE: THE WINGS OF HONNEAMISE (MOTION PICTURE)
___ Whitty, Stephen. "A Journey to No Place Special," *San Jose (CA) Mercury News*. December 2, 1994. in: *NewsBank. Film and Television.* 9:E14. 1995.

ROYLE, NICHOLAS
___ "British Fantasy Awards," *Science Fiction Chronicle* 15(2): 4. November/December 1993.
___ Kenworthy, Chris. "Toy Cars, Teaspoons and Scissors: Nicholas Royle Interviewed," *Interzone* No. 77: 48-51. November 1993.

ROZSA, MIKLOS
___ "Rozsa, Miklos (Obituary)," *Science Fiction Chronicle* 16(9): 24. August/September 1995.

RUDLEY, HERBERT
___ Weaver, Tom. "Herbert Rudley: Interview," in: Weaver, Tom, ed. **Attack of the Monster Movie Makers: Interviews with 20 Genre Giants**. Jefferson, NC: McFarland, 1994. pp.309-318.

RUNE (COMIC)
___ Castro, Adam-Troy. "Barry Windsor-Smith Trades in a Barbarian for an Alien Vampire," *Science Fiction Age* 2(3): 76-78. March 1994.

RUNNING MAN (MOTION PICTURE)
___ "*Running Man* Production Nixes Plans to Location in Edmonton," *Variety* p. 35. April 9, 1986.

RUSH, MARVIN
___ Altman, Mark A. "*Star Trek*: Cinematographer Marvin Rush," *Cinefantastique* 23(2/3): 68-69. October 1992.
___ Fisher, Bob. "*Star Trek* Meets *The Next Generation*," *American Cinematographer* 75(10): 74-82. October 1994.

RUSHDIE, SALMAN
___ "Arnason, Rushdie Win Mythopoeic Awards," *Science Fiction Chronicle* 14(1): 6. October 1992.
___ "Morrison, Rushdie Win Major Prizes," *Locus* 31(5): 6. November 1993.
___ "Rushdie Speaks Out," *Locus* 28(1): 7. January 1992.
___ "Salman Rushdie Four Years Later," *Locus* 30(3): 6. March 1993.
___ "**Satanic Verses** Paperback Appears," *Locus* 28(5): 7, 66. May 1992.
___ Al-Raheb, Hani. "Religious Satire in Rushdie's **Satanic Verses**," *Journal of the Fantastic in the Arts* 6(4): 330-340. 1995.
___ Harrison, James. **Salman Rushie**. Boston, MA: Twayne, 1992. 147pp.
___ MacDonogh, Steve, ed. **The Rushdie Letters: Freedom to Speak, Freedom to Write**. Dingle, Ireland: Brandon, 1993. 189pp.

RUSKIN, JOHN
___ Phillips, Mark. "Untouchable Evil," *Starlog* No. 188: 50-53. March 1993.

RUSS, JOANNA
___ Ayres, Susan. "The Straight Mind in Russ's **The Female Man**," *Science Fiction Studies* 22(1): 22-34. March 1995.
___ Barr, Marleen S. **Lost in Space: Probing Feminist Science Fiction and Beyond**. Chapel Hill, NC: University of North Carolina Press, 1993. 231pp.
___ Brownworth, Victoria A. "Battling Back," *Lambda Book Report* 4(7): 6-7. November/December 1994. [Not seen.]
___ DuPlessis, Rachel B. "The Feminist Apologies of Lessing, Piercy, and Russ," *Frontiers* 4(1): 1-8. 1979.
___ Murphy, Patrick D. "Suicide, Murder, Culture, and Catastrophe: Joanna Russ's **We Who Are About to...**," in: Ruddick, Nicholas, ed. **State of the Fantastic**. Westport, CT: Greenwood, 1992. pp.121-132.
___ Parkin-Speer, Diane. "Joanna Russ," in: Bruccoli, Matthew J., ed. **Facts on File Bibliography of American Fiction 1919-1988**. New York: Facts on File, 1991. pp.433-434.
___ Sauter-Bailliet, Theresia. "Joanna Russ, **The Female Man** (1975)," in: Heuermann, Harmut, ed. **Der Science Fiction Roman in der angloamerikanischen Literatur: Interpretationen**. Düsseldorf: Bagel, 1986. pp.355-374.
___ Wills, Deborah. "The Madwoman in the Matrix: Joanna Russ's **The Two of Them** and the Psychiatric Postmodern," in: Latham, Robert A. and Collins, Robert A., eds. **Modes of the Fantastic**. Westport, CT: Greenwood, 1995. pp.93-99.

RUSSELL, CHARLES
___ Shapiro, Marc. "*Mask* Maker," *Starlog* No. 205: 32-35. August 1994.

RUSSELL, ERIC FRANK
___ "Eric Frank Russell, Wyndam Collections to UK's SF Foundation," *Science Fiction Chronicle* 15(6): 5-6. April/May 1994.
___ "Russell, Eric Frank (Obituary)," *Science Fiction News* (Australia) No. 55: 10-11. June 1978.

RUSSELL, KURT
___ Yakir, Dan. "Two-Fisted Hero," *Starlog* No. 211: 50-53. February 1995.

RUSSELL, RAY
___ "Bram Stoker Awards, 1993," *Science Fiction Chronicle* 14(10): 4. July 1993.
___ "HWA Stoker Awards Winners," *Locus* 31(2): 6, 62. August 1993.

RUSSIA
___ "Four Swords Awards," *Science Fiction Chronicle* 16(6): 5-6. May 1995.
___ "Russian Author's Dacha Firebombed," *Locus* 32(6): 8, 76. June 1994.
___ "Russian Publishing Crisis," *Locus* 30(6): 7, 73. June 1993.
___ Arbitman, Roman. "Vzglyad s 'tsentral 'nogo energoatrona," *Detskaya Lietatura* 5: 6-10. 1993.
___ Baehr, Stephen L. **The Paradise Myth in Eighteenth-Century Russia: Utopian Patterns in Early Secular Russian Literature and Culture**. Stanford, CA: Stanford University Press, 1991. 308pp.
___ Barker, Lynn. "Klushantsev: Russia's Wizard of *Fantastika*, Part One," by Lynn Barker and Robert Skotak. *American Cinematographer* 75(6): 78-83. June 1994.
___ Barker, Lynn. "Klushantsev: Russia's Wizard of *Fantastika*, Part Two," by Lynn Barker and Robert Skotak. *American Cinematographer* 75(7): 77-82. July 1994.
___ Bartholomew, Frank M. "The Russian Utopia," in: Sullivan, E. D. S., ed. **The Utopian Vision**. San Diego, CA: San Diego University Press, 1983. pp.69-92.
___ Bulychev, Kir. "Letter From Moscow," *Locus* 31(6): 37-38, 44. December 1993.
___ Costello, John H. "American SF in Russian," *Locus* 35(3): 54. September 1993.
___ Giles, Stacie L. M. **Russian Science Fiction: Window into Which Future?**. Master's Thesis, University of California, Los Angeles, 1995. 126pp.
___ Grigorieva, Natalia. "Problems of Translating into Russian," in: Reynolds, Patricia and GoodKnight, Glen H., eds. **Proceedings of the J. R. R. Tolkien Centenary Conference, Keble College, Oxford, 1992**. Altadena, CA: Mythopoeic Press, 1995. pp.200-205. (*Mythlore* Vol. 21, No. 2, Winter 1996, Whole No. 80).
___ Grushetskiy, Vladimir. "How Russians See Tolkien," in: Reynolds, Patricia and GoodKnight, Glen H., eds. **Proceedings of the J. R. R. Tolkien Centenary Conference, Keble College, Oxford, 1992**. Altadena, CA: Mythopoeic Press, 1995. pp.221-225. (*Mythlore* Vol. 21, No. 2, Winter 1996, Whole No. 80)
___ Hartley, Matthew R. **The Image of Space in Soviet Literature**. Master's Thesis, University of Massachusetts at Amherst, 1993. 71pp.
___ Hordern, Kate. "Selling SF and Fantasy Translation Rights in Eastern Europe and Russia," *SFWA Bulletin* 29(2): 28-31. Summer 1995. (No. 127)
___ Shervatykh, Yuri. "SF in Russia," by Yuri Shervatykh and Boris Ivanov. *Locus* 35(3): 54. September 1993.

RYMAN, GEOFF
___ McVeigh, Kev. "And He Was... Geoff Ryman: Interview," *Vector* No. 174: 8-11. August/September 1993.
___ Youmans, Brian. "An Hour With Geoff Ryman," *Quantum* No. 41: 9-13. Winter/Spring 1992.

SABAROFF, ROBERT
___ Phillips, Mark. "Biology Amok," *Starlog* No. 203: 52-54. June 1994.

SABATO, ANTONIO, JR.
___ Chrissinger, Craig W. "Sky Pilot," *Starlog* No. 216: 67-70. July 1995.

SÄBATO, ERNESTO
___ Borchardt, Edith. "Criminal Artists and Artisans in Mysteries by E. T. A. Hoffman, Dorothy Sayers, Ernesto Sábato, Patrick Süskind, and Thomas Harris," in: Sanders, Joe, ed. **Functions of the Fantastic**. Westport, CT: Greenwood, 1995. pp.125-134.

SABER RIDERS & THE STAR SHERIFFS (TV)
___ "High Tech Kidvid Cowboys Are the Latest to Ride Syndie Trail," *Variety* p. 47, 74. June 18, 1986.

SAGARA, MICHELLE
___ Gold, Mici. "Michelle Sagara: Motherhood and the Writing Muse," *Sol Rising* (Toronto) No. 10: 6-7. May 1994.

SALMONSON, JESSICA AMANDA
___ Barr, Marleen S. **Lost in Space: Probing Feminist Science Fiction and Beyond**. Chapel Hill, NC: University of North Carolina Press, 1993. 231pp.
___ Salmonson, Jessica A. **Bibliography: Jessica Amanda Salmonson**. Polk City, IA: Drumm, 1992. [15pp.] [Bound with, inverted: her **Sorceries and Sorrows (Early Poems)**.] [21pp.]
___ Salmonson, Jessica A. "Fanciful Dreams of the Author," *Science Fiction Eye* No. 13: 101. Spring 1994.

SALTER, HANS J.
___ "Salter, Hans J. (Obituary)," *Science Fiction Chronicle* 15(9): 16. August 1994.

SALVATORE, R. A.
___ "R. A. Salvatore Books to Del Rey," *Locus* 32(4): 8, 63. April 1994.
___ "R. A. Salvatore's Fantastic Legacy," *Hailing Frequencies* (Waldenbooks) No. 3: 1, 3, 8, 10. 1992.

SALVATORES, GABRIELE
___ Rooney, David. "Eye on the Future," *Variety* 358(5): 47. March 6, 1995.

SAMMON, PAUL M.
___ Wiater, Stanley. "Sammon, Paul M.," in: Wiater, Stanley. **Dark Visions: Conversations with the Masters of the Horror Film**. New York: Avon, 1992. pp.219-226.

SAMPSON, ROBERT
___ "Sampson, Robert (Obituary)," *Locus* 30(2): 68. February 1993.
___ "Sampson, Robert (Obituary)," *Science Fiction Chronicle* 14(4): 14. January 1993.

SAN JOSE FILM FESTIVAL, 1985
___ "Corman, Harryhausen San Jose Fest Honorees," *Variety* p. 7. April 10, 1985.

SANCHEZ, MARCO
___ Warren, Bill. "Longhair at Sea," *Starlog* No. 203: 34-37, 66. June 1994.

SAND, GEORGE
___ Gilman, Juliette. "Shades of the Fantastic: The Forest in Jacques Cazotte's 'Aventure du pelerin' and George Sand's 'La Mare au diable'," in: Latham, Robert A. and Collins, Robert A., eds. **Modes of the Fantastic**. Westport, CT: Greenwood, 1995. pp.137-142.
___ Grossman, Kathryn M. "The Ideal Community of George Sand's **La Petite Fadette**," *Utopian Studies* 6(1): 19-29. 1995.

SANDERSON, HAROLD PETER
___ "Sanderson, Harold Peter 'Sandy' (Obituary)," *Locus* 31(2): 59. August 1993.

SANDERSON, SANDY
___ "Sanderson, Sandy (Obituary)," *Science Fiction Chronicle* 14(9): 17. June 1993.

SANTA CLAUSE (MOTION PICTURE)
___ Duncan, Jody. "Quick Cuts: Clause and Effects," *Cinefex* No. 61: 17-18. March 1995.
___ Shay, Estelle. "Quick Cuts: Santa's Helpers," *Cinefex* No. 61: 33-34. March 1995.

SAPERSTEIN, HENRY G.
___ Galbraith, Stuart, IV. "**Godzilla**'s American Cousin: The Eclectic Career of Henry G. Saperstein," *Filmfax* No. 45: 59-63. June/July 1994.

SARGENT, PAMELA
___ "Nebula Award Winners, 1992," *Science Fiction Chronicle* 14(8): 4. May 1993.
___ Fitting, Peter. "Reconsiderations of the Separatist Paradigm in Recent Feminist Science Fiction," *Science Fiction Studies* 19(1): 32-48. March 1992.
___ Sargent, Pamela. "The Writer as Nomad," in: Jakubowski, Maxim and James, Edward, eds. **The Profession of Science Fiction**. New York: St. Martin's, 1992. pp.111-119.

SARGENT, PAMELA (continued)
___ Wolmark, Jenny. **Aliens and Others: Science Fiction, Feminism, and Postmodernism**. London: Harester Wheatsheaf, 1993. 167pp.; Iowa City: University of Iowa Press, 1994. 167pp.

SATURN AWARD
___ SEE: ACADEMY OF SCIENCE FICTION, FANTASY AND HORROR FILM AWARDS.

SAUL, JOHN
___ Kies, Cosette. **Presenting Young Adult Horror Fiction**. New York: Twayne, 1991. 203pp.

SAVINI, TOM
___ Wiater, Stanley. "Savini, Tom," in: Wiater, Stanley. **Dark Visions: Conversations with the Masters of the Horror Film**. New York: Avon, 1992. pp.159-166.

SAWYER, ROBERT J.
___ "1994 Aurora Winners," *Locus* 33(4): 8, 76. October 1994.
___ "Aurora Awards," *Science Fiction Chronicle* 13(11/12): 12. August 1992.
___ "Aurora Awards," *Science Fiction Chronicle* 15(10): 5. September 1994.
___ "Aurora Awards Winners," *Locus* 28(2): 7. August 1992.
___ "Compuserve HOMer Awards, 1992," *Science Fiction Chronicle* 14(9): 4-5. June 1993.
___ King, T. Jackson. "SFC Interview: Robert J. Sawyer," *Science Fiction Chronicle* 14(12): 5, 30-31. September 1993.
___ Klein, Jay K. "Biolog: Robert J. Sawyer," *Analog* 114(15): 69, 112. mid-December 1994.
___ Levinson, Paul. "Punctuated Equilibria in Dinosaurs and Trilogies," *New York Review of Science Fiction* No. 81: 14-16. May 1995.

SAYERS, DOROTHY L.
___ Aird, Catherine. "It Was the Cat!," in: Dale, Alzina S., ed. **Dorothy L. Sayers: The Centenary Celebration**. New York: Walker, 1993. pp.79-86.
___ Beach, Sarah. "Harriet in Rehearsal: Hilary Thorpe in **The Nine Tailors**," *Mythlore* 19(3): 37-39, 65. Summer 1993. (No. 73)
___ Borchardt, Edith. "Criminal Artists and Artisans in Mysteries by E. T. A. Hoffman, Dorothy Sayers, Ernesto Sábato, Patrick Süskind, and Thomas Harris," in: Sanders, Joe, ed. **Functions of the Fantastic**. Westport, CT: Greenwood, 1995. pp.125-134.
___ Brunsdale, Mitzi. **Dorothy L. Sayers: Solving the Mystery of Wickedness**. Dover, NH: Berg, 1991. 256pp.
___ Christopher, Joe R. "The Fragmentary Lord Peter," *Mythlore* 19(3): 23-26. Summer 1993. (No. 73)
___ Dale, Alzina S. "A Brief Biography of Dorothy L. Sayers," in: Dale, Alzina S., ed. **Dorothy L. Sayers: The Centenary Celebration**. New York: Walker, 1993. pp.151-152.
___ Dale, Alzina S. "**Thrones, Dominations**: Unfinished Testament to Friendship?," in: Dale, Alzina S., ed. **Dorothy L. Sayers: The Centenary Celebration**. New York: Walker, 1993. pp.67-78.
___ Dale, Alzina S., ed. **Dorothy L. Sayers: The Centenary Celebration**. New York: Walker, 1993. 167pp.
___ Doughan, David. "Tolkien, Sayers, Sex and Gender," in: Reynolds, Patricia and GoodKnight, Glen H., eds. **Proceedings of the J. R. R. Tolkien Centenary Conference, Keble College, Oxford, 1992**. Altadena, CA: Mythopoeic Press, 1995. pp.356-359. (*Mythlore* Vol. 21, No. 2, Winter 1996, Whole No. 80)
___ Elkins, Aaron. "The Art of Framing Lies: Dorothy L. Sayers on Mystery Fiction," in: Dale, Alzina S., ed. **Dorothy L. Sayers: The Centenary Celebration**. New York: Walker, 1993. pp.99-108.
___ Gilbert, Michael. "A Personal Memoir: Dorothy L. Sayers," in: Dale, Alzina S., ed. **Dorothy L. Sayers: The Centenary Celebration**. New York: Walker, 1993. pp.15-22.
___ Hart, Carolyn G. "**Gaudy Night**: Quintessential Sayers," in: Dale, Alzina S., ed. **Dorothy L. Sayers: The Centenary Celebration**. New York: Walker, 1993. pp.45-50.
___ Heilbrun, Carolyn G. "Dorothy L. Sayers: Biography Between the Lines," in: Dale, Alzina S., ed. **Dorothy L. Sayers: The Centenary Celebration**. New York: Walker, 1993. pp.1-14.
___ Keating, H. R. F. "Dorothy L.'s Mickey Finn," in: Dale, Alzina S., ed. **Dorothy L. Sayers: The Centenary Celebration**. New York: Walker, 1993. pp.129-138.

SAYERS, DOROTHY L. (continued)
___ Kenney, Catherine M. "The Comedy of Dorothy L. Sayers," in: Dale, Alzina S., ed. **Dorothy L. Sayers: The Centenary Celebration**. New York: Walker, 1993. pp.139-150.
___ Kenney, Catherine M. **The Remarkable Case of Dorothy L. Sayers**. Kent, OH: Kent State University Press, 1990. 309pp.
___ Love, William F. "Butler, Dabbler, Spy: Jeeves to Wimsey to Bond," in: Dale, Alzina S., ed. **Dorothy L. Sayers: The Centenary Celebration**. New York: Walker, 1993. pp.31-44.
___ McCrumb, Sharyn. "Where the Bodies Are Buried: The Real Murder Cases in the Crime Novels of Dorothy L. Sayers," in: Dale, Alzina S., ed. **Dorothy L. Sayers: The Centenary Celebration**. New York: Walker, 1993. pp.87-98.
___ McInerny, Ralph. "Unsoothing Sayers," in: Dale, Alzina S., ed. **Dorothy L. Sayers: The Centenary Celebration**. New York: Walker, 1993. pp.123-128.
___ Patterson, Nancy-Lou. "A Bloomsbury Blue-Stocking: Dorothy L. Sayers' Bloomsbury Years in Their 'Spatial and Temporal Content'," *Mythlore* 19(3): 6-15. Summer 1993. (No. 73)
___ Patterson, Nancy-Lou. "Why We Honor the Centenary of Dorothy L. Sayers (1893-1957)," *Mythlore* 19(3): 4-5. Summer 1993. (No. 73)
___ Perry, Anne. "Dorothy L. Sayers on Dante," in: Dale, Alzina S., ed. **Dorothy L. Sayers: The Centenary Celebration**. New York: Walker, 1993. pp.109-122.
___ Rahn, B. J. "Marriage of True Minds," in: Dale, Alzina S., ed. **Dorothy L. Sayers: The Centenary Celebration**. New York: Walker, 1993. pp.51-66.
___ Reynolds, Barbara. **Dorothy L. Sayers: Her Life and Soul**. New York: St. Martin's Press, 1993. 398pp.
___ Stuart, Ian. "D. L. S.: An Unsteady Throne?," in: Dale, Alzina S., ed. **Dorothy L. Sayers: The Centenary Celebration**. New York: Walker, 1993. pp.23-30.
___ Vink, Renée. "Tolkien und Dorothy L. Sayers," in: Kranz, Gisbert, ed. **Jahrbuch für Literatur und Ästhetik**. Lüdenscheid, Germany: Stier, 1992. Band 10, pp.61-76.

SCANNER CAP (MOTION PICTURE)
___ Harris, Judith P. "**Scanner Cap** (Review)," *Cinefantastique* 26(2): 59. February 1995.

SCANNER III: THE TAKEOVER (MOTION PICTURE)
___ Harris, Judith P. "**Scanner III: The Takeover** (Review)," *Cinefantastique* 24(1): 60-61. June 1993.

SCANNERS: THE SHOWDOWN (MOTION PICTURE)
___ Wilt, David. "**Scanners: The Showdown** (Review)," *Cinefantastique* 27(2): 60. November 1995.

SCARBOROUGH, ELIZABETH ANN
___ Holmen, Rachel E. "Interview With Elizabeth Ann Scarborough," *Marion Zimmer Bradley's Fantasy Magazine* No. 21: 42-47. Fall 1993.

SCHACHNER, NATHAN
___ Carter, Paul A. "From 'Nat' to 'Nathan': The Liberal Arts Odyssey of a Pulpmaster," in: Slusser, George E. and Rabkin, Eric S., eds. **Styles of Creation: Aesthetic Technique and the Creation of Fictional Worlds**. Athens: University of Georgia Press, 1992. pp.58-78.
___ Moskowitz, Sam. "The Science Fiction of Nat Schachner, Part 1," *Fantasy Commentator* 7(3): 160-179. Spring 1992. (No. 43)
___ Moskowitz, Sam. "The Science Fiction of Nat Schachner, Part 2," *Fantasy Commentator* 7(4): 292-303. Fall 1992. (Whole No. 44)
___ Moskowitz, Sam. "The Science Fiction of Nat Schachner, Part 3," *Fantasy Commentator* 8(1/2): 52-73. Winter 1993/1994. (Whole No. 45/46)

SCHALLERT, WILLIAM
___ Vaughn, Donald. "A. K. A. Mr. TV: An Interview With William Schallert," *Filmfax* No. 42: 62-69, 98. December 1993/January 1994.
___ Weaver, Tom. "Character Star," *Starlog* 184: 57-62, 72. November 1992.
___ Weaver, Tom. "William Schallert," in: Weaver, Tom. **They Fought the Creature Features: Interviews with 23 Classic Horror, Science Fiction and Serial Stars**. Jefferson, NC: McFarland, 1995. pp.245-262.

SCHEETZ, HARVEY D.
___ Crum, Richard M. "News Flash: Alien From Another Planet?," *National Geographic World* 231: 17-91. November 1994.

SCHELLING, CHRISTOPHER
___ "Chris Schelling out, Amy Stout up at Roc," *Science Fiction Chronicle* 15(4): 4-5. February 1994.
___ "HarperPrism Launch Announced; Schelling Hired," *Locus* 32(4): 7. April 1994.
___ "Schelling Leaves HarperPrism," *Locus* 35(5): 8. November 1995.
___ "Schelling out at Roc, Stout Promoted," *Locus* 32(3): 8. March 1994.

SCHIAVELLI, VINCENT
___ Warren, Bill. "The Vincent Schiavelli Story," *Starlog* No. 187: 36-39, 70. February 1993.

SCHMERER, JAMES
___ Florence, Bill. "Colors of a Chameleon," *Starlog* No. 191: 56-57. June 1993.

SCHMID, KRISTIAN
___ Eramo, Steven. "Teenager of Tomorrow," *Starlog* No. 221: 76-78. December 1995.

SCHMIDT, ARNO
___ Flessner, Bernd. **Weltprothesen und Prothesenwelten: zu den technischen Prognosen Arno Schmidts und Stanislaw Lems**. Frankfurt-am-Main: P. Lang, 1991. 343pp.

SCHMIDT, STANLEY
___ "Stanley Schmidt Interview, Part 2," *The Report: The Fiction Writer's Magazine* 2(6): 17-18. April 1992. (No. 59)

SCHMITZ, JAMES H.
___ Kagan, Janet. "Mischief in the Spaceways," in: Olson, Mark L., ed. **The Best of James H. Schmitz**. Cambridge, MA: NESFA Press, 1991. pp.v-xi.

SCHNAUBELT, FRANZ JOSEPH
___ "Schnaubelt, Franz J. (Obituary)," *Science Fiction Chronicle* 15(9): 16, 18. August 1994.
___ "Schnaubelt, Franz Joseph (Obituary)," *Locus* 33(2): 70. August 1994.

SCHOLEM, GERSHOM
___ Stewart, Elizabeth. **Destroying Angels: Messianic Rhetoric in Benjamin, Scholem, Psychoanalysis and Science Fiction**. Ph.D. Dissertation, New York University, 1994. 586pp. (DAI-A 55/09, p. 2820. March 1995.)

SCHOW, DAVID J.
___ Joshi, S. T. "David J. Schow and Splatterpunk," *Studies in Weird Fiction* No. 13: 21-27. Summer 1993. [Not seen.]
___ Michaels, Richard. "Night Bloomer: The Defiant Fiction of David J. Schow," in: Collins, Robert A. and Latham, Robert, eds. **Science Fiction and Fantasy Book Review Annual 1991**. Westport, CT: Greenwood, 1994. pp.130-137.

SCHUMACHER, JOEL
___ Shapiro, Marc. "Knightmare Master," *Starlog* No. 216: 40-45. July 1995.

SCHWARTZ, ALVIN
___ "Schwartz, Alvin (Obituary)," *Locus* 28(5): 59. May 1992.
___ "Schwartz, Alvin (Obituary)," *Science Fiction Chronicle* 13(7): 16. April 1992.

SCHWARTZ, DAVID
___ Vitaris, Paula. "Befriending **Beauty and the Beast**," *Starlog* No. 212: 54-57, 69. March 1995.

SCHWARTZ, JULIUS
___ Maggin, Elliot S. "My Amazing Stories: Memoirs of a Time Traveller, Part 1, by Julius Schwartz," *Amazing* 68(2): 48-53. May 1993.
___ Schwartz, Julius. "The Bester Years of My Life: Memoirs of a Time Traveller, Part 2," *Amazing Stories* 68(4): 55-59. July 1993.

SCHWARTZ-BART, ANDRE
___ Zanger, Jules. "**The Last of the Just**: Lifting Moloch to Heaven," *Journal of the Fantastic in the Arts* 5(2): 49-59. 1993. (No. 18)

SCHWARZENEGGER, ARNOLD
___ Liu, Albert. "The Last Days of Arnold Schwarzenegger," *Genders* No. 18: 102-112. Winter 1993.
___ Lowry, Brian. "Science Fiction Hero," in: McDonnell, David, ed. **Starlog's Science Fiction Heroes and Heroines**. New York: Crescent Books, 1995. pp.19-23.
___ Shapiro, Marc. "**Last Action Hero**," *Starlog* No. 192: 39-46. July 1993.

SCHWEITZER, DARRELL
___ "World Fantasy Awards," *Science Fiction Chronicle* 14(3): 4. December 1992.

SCHWINGER, LARRY
___ McWhorter, George T. "Larry Schwinger: Ballantine Cover Artist," *Burroughs Bulletin* NS No. 11: 19-20. July 1992.

SCI-FI BUZZ (TV)
___ Rusch, Kristine K. "Editorial: **Sci-Fi Buzz**," *Magazine of Fantasy and Science Fiction* 86(6): 5-8. June 1994.

SCI-FI CHANNEL MAGAZINE (MAGAZINE)
___ "SF Media Magazine Explosion," *Locus* 32(3): 8, 69. March 1994.

SCI-FI CHANNEL (TV)
___ "Sci-Fi Channel Tentative Schedule," *Science Fiction Chronicle* 13(11/12): 10. August 1992.
___ "Science Fiction Channel Is Continuing to Grow, Despite Fact That Largest MSO Hasn't Yet Agreed to Carry It," *Communications Daily* 15(89): 6. May 9, 1995. (Cited from *IAC Insite* on-line service.)
___ "USA Cable Network Acquires Sci-Fi Channel," *Science Fiction Chronicle* 13(8): 4. May 1992.
___ "USA Network Buys Sci-Fi Channel," *Locus* 28(5): 7, 65. May 1992.
___ "USA Network to Launch Its New Sci-Fi Channel," *Bryan-College Station Eagle* p. C3. May 14, 1992.
___ Brown, Rich. "Sci-Fi Unveils Schedule for September Debut," *Broadcasting* p. 21. July 20, 1992.
___ Cerone, Daniel H. "Sci-Fi Channel on the Launching Pad," *Los Angeles (CA) Times* Sec. F, p. 16. September 5, 1992.
___ Donlon, Brian. "Sci-Fi Channel Nears a Full Launch," *USA Today* Sec. D., p. 1. May 4, 1992.
___ Grossman, Laurie M. "Marketing: Well, It's in Orbit, But Will It Fly?," *Wall Street Journal* Sec. B, p. 1. September 25, 1992.
___ Jensen, Elizabeth. "Sci-Fi Channel Will Debut in the Fall," by Elizabeth Jensen and George Maksian. *Austin (TX) American Statesman* Sec. B, p. 4. April 2, 1992.
___ Kenny, Glenn. "Phantasia," *TV Guide* 43(11): 36. March 18, 1995.
___ Kenny, Glenn. "Sci-Fi Central," *TV Guide* 43(28): 15. July 16, 1995.
___ Martin, Kevin H. "Video Beat: Order out of Xaos," *Cinefex* No. 57: 21-22. March 1994.
___ McConville, Jim. "Sci-Fi Goes Hi-Tech for Fall," *Broadcasting and Cable* 125(33): 20-21. August 14, 1995.
___ Menagh, Melanie. "A Channel for Science Fiction," by Melanie Menagh and Stephen Mills. *Omni* 14(9): 76-82, 112. October 1992.
___ Point, Michael. "The Incredible Shrinking Expectations: The Sci-Fi Channel," *Austin (TX) American Statesman*. October 23, 1995. in: *NewsBank. Film and Television*. 98:E10-E11. 1995.
___ Wilson, Bill. "I Want My SF-TV," *Starlog* No. 176: 17-21, 71. March 1992.
___ Winfrey, Lee. "Going Where No Network Has Gone Before: Sci-Fi Channel Debuting Today," *Bryan-College Station Eagle* p. B4. September 24, 1992.

SCI-FI MATINEE (MOTION PICTURE)
___ Stephens, Bob. "United Artists **Sci-Fi Matinee**," *Films in Review* 46(9/10): 54-60. November/December 1995.

SCI-FI UNIVERSE (MAGAZINE)
___ "SF Media Magazine Explosion," *Locus* 32(3): 8, 69. March 1994.
___ Krieger, Todd. "Street Creed: *Sci-Fi Universe*," *Wired* 3(2): 144. February 1995.

SCIENCE FICTION: A JOURNEY INTO THE UNKNOWN (TV)
___ Droesch, Paul. "Hits and Misses: **Science Fiction: A Journey into the Unknown**," *TV Guide* 42(50): 53. December 10, 1994.
___ Lowry, Brian. "TV Reviews: **Science Fiction: A Journey into the Unknown**," *Variety* 357(7): 38. December 12, 1994.

SCIENCE FICTION AGE (MAGAZINE)
___ "*Science Fiction Age* Debut," *Locus* 28(5): 6. May 1992.
___ "*Science Fiction Age* Launched," *Locus* 29(4): 7. October 1992
___ "*Science Fiction Age*, New Bimonthly, to Start Publication This Summer," *Science Fiction Chronicle* 13(6): 4. March 1992.
___ "*SF Age* Goes Forward," *Locus* 28(2): 6. August 1992.
___ "*SF Age* Subscriber List for Sale," *Science Fiction Chronicle* 13(10): 6. July/August 1992.
___ "Sovereign Media Moves Two Magazines Forward," *Science Fiction Chronicle* 15(5): 4. March 1994.
___ Donaton, Scott. "New Sci Fi Magazine Will Launch This Fall," *Advertising Age* 63(35): 29. August 31, 1992.

SCIENCE FICTION AND FANTASY WRITERS OF AMERICA
___ "By-Laws of Science Fiction and Fantasy Writers of America, Inc.," *SFWA Bulletin* 27(1): 60-64. Spring 1993. (No. 119)
___ "Nebula Awards Weekend," *Science Fiction Chronicle* 16(7): 33-34. June/July 1995.
___ "New Orleans Hosting SFWA's Nebula Banquet," *Science Fiction Chronicle* 14(5): 4. February 1993.
___ "Newt Gingrich Opposed as Nebula Banquet Speaker," *Science Fiction Chronicle* 13(8): 4. May 1992.
___ "SFWA Changes Name," *Locus* 28(2): 6. February 1992.
___ Knight, Damon. "The History of the SFWA 1965-1967," *SFWA Bulletin* 26(3): 3-4. Fall 1992. (No. 117)
___ Kube-McDowell, Michael P. "Report on the 1991 SFWA Membership Profile Project," *SFWA Bulletin* 26(1): 39-42. Spring 1992. (No. 115)
___ Nourse, Alan E. "The History of the SFWA, 1967-1968," *SFWA Bulletin* 27(2): 4. Summer 1993. (No. 120)
___ Silverberg, Robert. "The History of the SFWA 1967-1968," *SFWA Bulletin* 27(1): 28-29. Spring 1993. (No. 119)

SCIENCE FICTION BOOK CLUB
___ "SFBC at 40," *Locus* 30(1): 6. January 1993.

SCIENCE FICTION BOOK CLUB AWARD, 1992
___ "McCaffrey Wins SFBC Award Again," *Locus* 33(1): 7, 78. July 1994.

SCIENCE FICTION BOOK CLUB AWARD, 1993
___ "Anne McCaffrey Wins SFBC Book of the Year Award," *Science Fiction Chronicle* 14(11): 5. August 1993.

SCIENCE FICTION CHRONICLE (MAGAZINE)
___ "Harlan Ellison Attacks SFC Editor on National Cable TV Show," *Science Fiction Chronicle* 14(11): 4-6. August 1993.

SCIENCE FICTION CHRONICLE READER AWARDS, 1992
___ "Eleventh Annual *S. F. Chronicle* Reader's Awards," *Science Fiction Chronicle* 13(11/12): 4. August 1992.

SCIENCE FICTION CHRONICLE READER AWARDS, 1993
___ "12th Annual *S. F. Chronicle* Reader Awards," *Science Fiction Chronicle* 14(12): 4. September 1993.

SCIENCE FICTION CHRONICLE READER AWARDS, 1994
___ "13th Annual *Science Fiction Chronicle* Reader Awards," *Science Fiction Chronicle* 15(10): 4. September 1994.

SCIENCE FICTION CHRONICLE READER AWARDS, 1995
___ "14th Annual *Science Fiction Chronicle* Reader Awards," *Science Fiction Chronicle* 16(8): 4. July/August 1995

SCIENCE FICTION FOUNDATION
___ "SF Foundation in Trouble," *Locus* 28(5): 7, 66. May 1992.
___ "SF Foundation Moving," *Locus* 30(1): 6, 61. January 1993.
___ "SF Foundation Settles at University of Liverpool," *Science Fiction Chronicle* 15(2): 6. November/December 1993.

SCIENCE FICTION NEWS (AUSTRALIA) (MAGAZINE)
___ Stone, Graham. "Index to *Science Fiction News* Nos. 59-106, 1979-1987," *Science Fiction News* (Australia) No. 106: 8-17. December 1987.

SCIENCE FICTION RESEARCH ASSOCIATION CONFERENCE, 1994
___ "1994 Science Fiction Research Association Conference," *Locus* 33(4): 42. October 1994.

SCIENCE FICTION RESEARCH ASSOCIATION CONFERENCE, 1995
___ "1995 Science Fiction Research Association Conference," *Locus* 35(2): 68-69. August 1995.
___ "Special Feature: The 1995 SFRA Conference," *SFRA Review* No. 219: 15-23. September/October 1995.

SCIENCE FICTION REVIEW (MAGAZINE)
___ "*Weird Tales* Reformats; Other Magazine Changes," *Locus* 29(3): 7, 79. September 1992.

SCIENCE FICTION, COLLEGE
___ Gardiner, Josephine. "Forward With the Masters of the Sci-Fi Universe," *Times Educational Supplement* 4061: SS2. April 29, 1994.

SCIENCE FICTION, DEGREES
___ Gardiner, Josephine. "Forward With the Masters of the Sci-Fi Universe," *Times Educational Supplement* 4061: SS2. April 29, 1994.

SCIENCE IN ART
___ Miller, Ron. **The Dream Machines: An Illustrated History of the Spaceship in Art, Science and Literature**. Malabar, FL: Krieger, 1993. 714pp.
___ Nisbet, Peter. "The Response to Science and Technology in the Visual Arts," in: Graham, Loren R., ed. **Science and the Soviet Social Order**. Cambridge: Harvard University Press, 1990. pp.341-358.

SCIENCE IN FICTION
___ Segal, Howard P. **Future Imperfect: The Mixed Blessings of Technology in America**. Amherst: University of Massachusetts Press, 1994. 245pp.

SCIENCE IN LITERATURE
___ Alkon, Paul. **Science Fiction Before 1900: Imagination Discovers Technology**. New York: Macmillan Twayne, 1994. 177pp.
___ Allen, Glen S. "Master Mechanics and Evil Wizards: Science and the American Imagination from Frankenstein to Sputnik," *Massachusetts Review* 33(4): 505-558. Winter 1992/93.
___ Clark, Katerina. "The Changing Image of Science and Technology in Soviet Literature," in: Graham, Loren R., ed. **Science and the Soviet Social Order**. Cambridge: Harvard University Press, 1990. pp.259-298.
___ Fulweiler, Howard W. "The Other Missing Link: Owen Barfield and the Scientific Imagination," *Renascence* 46(1): 39-54. Fall 1993.
___ Goldbort, Robert C. "Science, Technology, and Popular Literature: (Re)visionary Symbioses," *National Forum: Phi Kappa Phi Journal* 74(4): 5-6. Fall 1994.
___ Greenberg, Mark L. "Introduction: Literature and Technology," by Mark L. Greenberg and Lance Schachterle. in: Greenberg, Mark L. and Schachterle, Lance, eds. **Literature and Technology**. Bethlehem, PA: Lehigh University Press, 1992. pp.13-24.
___ Greenberg, Mark L. "Romantic Technology: Books, Printing, and Blake's **Marriage of Heaven and Hell**," in: Greenberg, Mark L. and Schachterle, Lance, eds. **Literature and Technology**. Bethlehem, PA: Lehigh University Press, 1992. pp.154-176.
___ Greenberg, Mark L. "Selected Bibliography of Works Devoted to Literature and Technology," by Mark L. Greenberg and Lance Schachterle. in: Greenberg, Mark L. and Schachterle, Lance, eds. **Literature and Technology**. Bethlehem, PA: Lehigh University Press, 1992. pp.310-317.
___ Greenberg, Mark L., ed. **Literature and Technology**, ed. by Mark L. Greenberg and Lance Schachterle. Bethlehem, PA: Lehigh University Press, 1992. 322pp.
___ Hartley, Matthew R. **The Image of Space in Soviet Literature**. Master's Thesis, University of Massachusetts at Amherst, 1993. 71pp.
___ Knoespel, Kenneth J. "Gazing on Technology: *Theatrum Mechanorum* and the Assimilation of Renaissance Machinery," in: Greenberg, Mark L. and Schachterle, Lance, eds. **Literature and Technology**. Bethlehem, PA: Lehigh University Press, 1992. pp.99-124.
___ Krasner, James. **The Entangled Eye: Visual Perception and the Representation of Nature in Post-Darwinian Narrative**. New York: Oxford University Press, 1992. 191pp.
___ Kuchment, Mark. "Bridging the Two Cultures: The Emergence of Scientific Prose," in: Graham, Loren R., ed. **Science and the Soviet Social Order**. Cambridge: Harvard University Press, 1990. pp.335-340.
___ Layton, David A. "Approaching the Limits: Science in Postmodernist Fiction," Ph.D. Dissertation, University of California, Santa Barbara, 1994. 571pp.

SCIENCE IN LITERATURE (continued)
___ Lee, Judith Y. "The Feminization of Technology: Mechanical Characters in Picture Books," in: Greenberg, Mark L. and Schachterle, Lance, eds. **Literature and Technology.** Bethlehem, PA: Lehigh University Press, 1992. pp.206-224.
___ Levy-Leblond, Jean-Marc. "The Mirror, the Beauty and the Touchstone: Or, What Can Literature Do for Science?," *Substance* No. 71/72: 7-26. 1993.
___ Markley, Robert. "Robert Boyle, Peter Shaw, and the Reinscription of Technology: Inventing and Reinventing the Air Pump," in: Greenberg, Mark L. and Schachterle, Lance, eds. **Literature and Technology.** Bethlehem, PA: Lehigh University Press, 1992. pp.125-153.
___ Mendelsohn, James R. **The Brute Fact: The Cultural Authority of Science in Twentieth Century American Literature.** Ph.D. Dissertation, University of Washington, 1992. (DAI 53: 2372A.)
___ Miller, Ron. **The Dream Machines: An Illustrated History of the Spaceship in Art, Science and Literature.** Malabar, FL: Krieger, 1993. 714pp.
___ Mitcham, Carl. "Selected Basic References in the Philosophy of Technology," by Carl Mitcham and Timothy Casey. in: Greenberg, Mark L. and Schachterle, Lance, eds. **Literature and Technology.** Bethlehem, PA: Lehigh University Press, 1992. pp.307-309.
___ Mitcham, Carl. "Toward an Archeology of the Philosophy of Technology and Relations with Imaginative Literature," by Carl Mitcham and Timothy Casey. in: Greenberg, Mark L. and Schachterle, Lance, eds. **Literature and Technology.** Bethlehem, PA: Lehigh University Press, 1992. pp.31-64.
___ Morris, David. **The Masks of Lucifer: Technology and the Occult in Twentieth Century Popular Literature.** London: Batsford, 1992. 223pp.
___ Mosher, Mark R. **Jorge Luis Borges and the New Physics: The Literature of Modern Science and the Science of Modern Literature.** Ph.D. Dissertation, State University of New York, Albany, 1992. (DAI 53: 2392A.)
___ Nahin, Paul J. **Time Machines: Time Travel in Physics, Metaphysics, and Science Fiction.** New York: American Institute of Physics, 1993. 408pp.
___ Ordway, Frederick I., III, ed. **Blueprint for Space: Science Fiction to Science Fact,** ed. by Frederick I. Ordway, III and Randy Liebermann. Washington, DC: Smithsonian Institution Press, 1992. 224pp.
___ Porush, David. "Literature as Dissipative Structure: Prigogine's Theory and the Postmodern 'Chaos' Machine," in: Greenberg, Mark L. and Schachterle, Lance, eds. **Literature and Technology.** Bethlehem, PA: Lehigh University Press, 1992. pp.275-306.
___ Roda, Vittorio. "Tra scienza e fantascienza: il cervello umano in alcuni scrittori postunitari. [Between Science and Science-Fiction: The Human Brain as Depicted in Post-Unification Italian Literature]," *Otto-Novecento* 19(5): 35-64. September/October 1995.
___ Ross, Andrew. **Strange Weather: Culture, Science, and Technology in the Age of Limits.** London: Verso, 1991. 275pp.
___ Schachterle, Lance. "Pynchon and the Civil Wars of Technology," in: Greenberg, Mark L. and Schachterle, Lance, eds. **Literature and Technology.** Bethlehem, PA: Lehigh University Press, 1992. pp.253-274.
___ Scholnick, Robert J., ed. **American Literature and Science.** Lexington, KY: University Press of Kentucky, 1992. 287pp.
___ Shuttleworth, Sally. "Science and the Supernatural in the Stories of Margaret Oliphant," in: Benjamin, Marina, ed. **A Question of Identity: Women, Science, and Literature.** New Brunswick, NJ: Rutgers University Press, 1993. pp.173-191.
___ Slade, Joseph W. "Technology and the Spy Novel," in: Greenberg, Mark L. and Schachterle, Lance, eds. **Literature and Technology.** Bethlehem, PA: Lehigh University Press, 1992. pp.225-252.
___ Terpening, Jon. **Science in Literature: Exploring Fiction, Poetry and Non-Fiction.** Toronto: Harcourt Canada, 1994.
___ Tomasch, Sylvia. "**Mappae Mundi** and 'The Knight's Tale': The Geography of Power, the Technology of Control," in: Greenberg, Mark L. and Schachterle, Lance, eds. **Literature and Technology.** Bethlehem, PA: Lehigh University Press, 1992. pp.66-98.
___ Troiano, Maureen D. **New Physics and the Modern French Novel.** New York: Peter Lang, 1995. 276pp.
___ Turner, Martha A. **Mechanism and the Novel: Science in the Narrative Process.** Cambridge: Cambridge University Press, 1993. 199pp.

SCIENCE IN LITERATURE (continued)
___ van Sant, Ann J. **Eighteenth-Century Sensibility and the Novel: The Senses in Social Context.** Cambridge, Eng.: Cambridge University Press, 1993. 143pp.
___ Williams, Rosalind H. "Jules Romains, **Unanimisme,** and the Poetics of Urban Systems," in: Greenberg, Mark L. and Schachterle, Lance, eds. **Literature and Technology.** Bethlehem, PA: Lehigh University Press, 1992. pp.177-205.

SCIENCE IN SF
___ "But It's *Star Trek* to the Rescue," *New Scientist* 141(1908): 6. January 15, 1994.
___ "SF Prediction on the Money," *Locus* 28(2): 7. February 1992.
___ "Warp Speed and Wormholes," *San Francisco (CA) Examiner* August 21, 1995. (Cited from the Internet edition.)
___ Aldiss, Brian W. "The Pale Shadow of Science," in: Aldiss, Brian W. **The Detached Retina: Aspects of SF and Fantasy.** Syracuse, NY: Syracuse University Press, 1995. pp.177-186.
___ Appleyard, Bryan. **Understanding the Present: Science and the Soul of Modern Man.** New York: Doubleday, 1992. 269pp.
___ Atkin, Denny. "The Science of *Star Trek,*" *Omni* 17(8): 46-53. Fall 1995.
___ Banks, Iain. "Escape From the Laws of Physics," *New Scientist* 138(1865): 38-39. March 20, 1993.
___ Beauchamp, Gorman. "Biotechnics and Utopia," in: Saccaro Del Buffa, Giuseppa and Lewis, Arthur O., eds. **Utopie per gli Anni Ottana.** Rome: Gangemi Editore, 1986. pp.73-88.
___ Begley, Sharon. "Here Come the DNAsaurs," *Newsweek* 121(24): 56-61. June 14, 1993.
___ Benford, Gregory. "Real Science, Imaginary Worlds," *New York Review of Science Fiction* No. 65: 1, 8-12. January 1994.
___ Benford, Gregory. "Real Science, Imaginary Worlds," in: Hartwell, David G. and Kathryn Cramer, eds. **The Ascent of Wonder: The Evolution of Hard SF.** New York: Tor, 1994. pp.15-23.
___ Berenbaum, May R. "Life History Strategies and Population Biology in Science Fiction Films," by May R. Berenbaum and Richard J. Leskosky. *Bulletin of the Ecological Society of America* 73(4): 236-240. December 1992.
___ Beswick, Norman. "The Machineries of Hokum, in Space Opera and Elsewhere," *Vector* No. 171: 16-18. February/March 1993.
___ Bianco, Lucio. "Scienza e tecnologia per lo sviluppo," in: Saccaro Del Buffa, Giuseppa and Lewis, Arthur O., eds. **Utopia e Modernita: Teorie e prassi utopiche nell'eta moderna e postmoderna.** Rome: Gangemi Editore, 1989. pp.187-198.
___ Bicchieri, Sarah N. **Quantum Physics and Annie Dillard: Parallels in Science and Literature.** Master's Thesis, Central Washington University, 1993. 85pp.
___ Borgwald, James M. "Classroom Analysis of Rotating Space Vehicles in *2001: A Space Odyssey,*" by James M. Borgwald and Serge Schreiner. *Physics Teacher* 31(7): 406-409. October 1993.
___ Bova, Ben. "Why *Science* Fiction?," *Amazing Stories* 67(11): 62-65. February 1993.
___ Braine, F. S. "Technological Utopias: The Future of the Next Generation," *Film & History* 24(1/2): 1-18. February/May 1994.
___ Brande, David J. **Technologies of Postmodernity: Ideology and Desire in Literature and Science (Pynchon, Thomas; Gibson, William; Butler, Octavia; Acker, Kathy).** Ph.D. Dissertation, University of Washington, 1995. 228pp. (DAI-A 56/07, p. 2677. January 1996.)
___ Browne, Malcolm W. "Chemists Succumb to Fantasy's Lure," *New York Times* p. 21. April 12, 1992.
___ Browne, Malcolm W. "Scientists Fret About *Jurassic Park* Message," *New York Times* p.B1. May 11, 1993.
___ Burns, John E. "One for the Books: Using Literature-Based Science Lessons," *Science Teacher* 61(7): 38-41. October 1994.
___ Carter, Steven. "Avatars of the Turtles," *Journal of Popular Film and Television* 18(3): 94-102. 1990.
___ Ceccato, Silvio. "Utopia, futurologia e scienza. L'utopia e l'uomo del futuro," in: Saccaro Del Buffa, Giuseppa and Lewis, Arthur O., eds. **Utopia e Modernita: Teorie e prassi utopiche nell'eta moderna e postmoderna.** Rome: Gangemi Editore, 1989. pp.199-204.
___ Clark, Katerina. "The Changing Image of Science and Technology in Soviet Literature," in: Graham, Loren R., ed. **Science and the Soviet Social Order.** Cambridge: Harvard University Press, 1990. pp.259-298.
___ Clement, Hal. "Whatever Happened to the Science in Science Fiction?," *Science Fiction Age* 1(6): 30-33. September 1993.
___ Cramer, Kathryn. "On Science and Science Fiction," *New York Review of Science Fiction* No. 63: 1, 3-5. November 1993.

SCIENCE IN SF (continued)

___ Cramer, Kathryn. "On Science and Science Fiction," in: Hartwell, David G. and Kathryn Cramer, eds. **The Ascent of Wonder: The Evolution of Hard SF**. New York: Tor, 1994. pp.24-29.

___ Delany, Samuel R. "The Future of the Body: And Science Fiction and Technology," *New York Review of Science Fiction* No. 51: 1, 3-5. November 1992.

___ Dietrich, Bryan. "***Prince of Darkness***, Prince of Light: From Faust to Physicist," *Journal of Popular Film and Television* 19(2): 91-96. 1991.

___ Dolgoff, Stephanie. "What Do Hieroglyphs Really Sound Like," *New York Times* p.H24. October 23, 1994.

___ Droesch, Paul. "Hits and Misses: The New Explorers," *TV Guide* 43(2): 45. January 14, 1995.

___ Dubeck, Leroy W. **Fantastic Voyages: Learning Science Through Science Fiction Films**. New York: American Institute of Physics, 1994. 327pp.

___ Dubeck, Leroy W. "Finding the Facts in Science Fiction Films," by Leroy W. Dubeck, Suzanne E. Moshier, Matthew H. Bruce and Judith E. Boss. *Science Teacher* 60(4): 46-48. April 1993.

___ Dubeck, Leroy W. "Using Science Fiction Films to Teach Science at the College Level," by Leroy W. Dubeck, Suzanne E. Moshier and Judith E. Boss. *Journal of College Science Teaching* 25(1): 46-50. September/October 1995.

___ Erlich, Richard D. **Clockworks: A Multimedia Bibliography of Works Useful for the Study of the Human/Machine Interface in SF**. Westport, CT: Greenwood Press, 1993. 344pp.

___ Evans, Arthur B. "Optograms and Fiction: Photo in a Dead Man's Eye," *Science Fiction Studies* 20(3): 341-361. November 1993.

___ Favret, Mary A. "A Woman Writes the Fiction of Science: The Body in **Frankenstein**," *Genders* No. 14: 50-65. Fall 1992.

___ Feinberg, Gerald. "Discussing Hard SF," by Gerald Feinberg, Hal Clement, Kathryn Cramer and David G. Hartwell. *New York Review of Science Fiction* No. 46: 19-21. June 1992.

___ Frank, Lyndsey M. **From Nautilus to Neuromancer: The Human-Machine Relationship in Science Fiction Literature From the Victorian Era to the 1980s**. Honor's Thesis, Linfield College, 1995. 80pp.

___ Gadallah, Leslie. "On Hard SF," *ON SPEC* 6(1): 89-90. Spring 1994.

___ Gillett, Stephen L. "Beyond Prometheus," *Analog* 113(14): 66-77. December 1993.

___ Goldbort, Robert C. "Science, Technology, and Popular Literature: (Re)visionary Symbioses," *National Forum: Phi Kappa Phi Journal* 74(4): 5-6. Fall 1994.

___ Gould, Donald. "Letting Poetry Loose in the Laboratory," *New Scientist* 135(1836): 50-51. August 29, 1992.

___ Hartwell, David G. "Hard Science Fiction," in: Hartwell, David G. and Kathryn Cramer, eds. **The Ascent of Wonder: The Evolution of Hard SF**. New York: Tor, 1994. pp.30-40.

___ Haynes, Roslynn D. **From Faust to Strangelove: Representations of the Scientist in Western Literature**. Baltimore: Johns Hopkins University Press, 1994. 417pp.

___ Haynes, Roslynn D. "Science, Myth and Utopia," in: Filmer, Kath, ed. **Twentieth-Century Fantasists: Essays in Culture, Society and Belief in Twentieth Century Mythopoeic Literature**. New York: St. Martin's, 1992. pp.8-22.

___ Hoffman, Donald L. "Mark's Merlin: Magic vs. Technology in **A Connecticut Yankee in King Arthur's Court**," in: Slocum, Sally K., ed. **Popular Arthurian Traditions**. Bowling Green, OH: Popular Press, 1992. pp.46-55.

___ Holden, Constance. "Bringing More Reality to Fiction," *Science* 263(5144): 176-177. January 14, 1994.

___ Hood, Leroy. "Could **Jurassic Park** Happen?," *Atlanta Constitution* Sec. A, p. 15. June 23, 1993.

___ Hubert, Hal. "Orbital Mechanics for Science Fiction Writers," *SFWA Bulletin* 26(4): 2-6. Winter 1993. (No. 118)

___ Hubert, Hal. "Orbits, Quibbles, Maps, and Drawing With Satellites," *SFWA Bulletin* 27(2): 6-9. Summer 1993. (No. 120)

___ Kahl, Nathan W. **The Meeting of Parallel Lines: Science and Fiction and Science Fiction**. Honor's Paper, Duke University, 1992. 76pp.

___ Keller, Chester Z. "Human Nature: Ecosystemic Limits and Techne. Some Utopian Implications," in: Saccaro Del Buffa, Giuseppa and Lewis, Arthur O., eds. **Utopia e Modernita: Teorie e prassi utopiche nell'eta moderna e postmoderna**. Rome: Gangemi Editore, 1989. pp.131-142.

SCIENCE IN SF (continued)

___ Keller, Chester Z. "Imitations of Utopia: Some Readings From Nature," in: Saccaro Del Buffa, Giuseppa and Lewis, Arthur O., eds. **Utopie per gli Anni Ottana**. Rome: Gangemi Editore, 1986. pp.89-98.

___ Kelner, Steve. "Mind and Brain: SF and Fact," *Science Fiction Eye* No. 13: 73-81. Spring 1994.

___ King, T. Jackson. "Habitable Stars Within 100 Light Years," *The Report: The Fiction Writer's Magazine* No. 9: 9-11. March 1993.

___ Kraczmarek, Nancy. "Collaboration: The Science in Science Fiction," *The English Record* 42(3): 13-15. 1992.

___ Krauss, Lawrence M. "Beam Me Up an Einstein, Scotty," *Wired* 3(11): 16-130. November 1995.

___ Krauss, Lawrence M. **The Physics of Star Trek**. New York: Basic Books, 1995. 188pp.

___ Krueger, Richard J. **Science and Fiction**. Thesis (M.F.A), University of Notre Dame, 1994. 32pp.

___ Kurtis, Bill. **The Science of Star Trek**. Chicago, IL: Public Media Video, 1995. 1 videocassette, 60 minutes.

___ Langberg, Mike. "Star Tech," *Austin (TX) American Statesman* Sec. D., p. 1, 3. July 12, 1992.

___ Langsberg, Mike. "Treknology," *Star Trek: The Official Fan Club* No. 94: 32-35. November/December 1993.

___ Larsen, T. E. "From Fiction to Fact: A Technology Postscript to 'Only the Weatherman'," *Analog* 114(4): 74-79. March 1994.

___ Latham, Robert A. "The Men Who Walked on the Moon: Images of America in the 'New Wave' Science Fiction of the 1960s and 1970s," in: Sanders, Joe, ed. **Functions of the Fantastic**. Westport, CT: Greenwood, 1995. pp.195-204.

___ Layton, David A. "Approaching the Limits: Science in Postmodernist Fiction," Ph.D. Dissertation, University of California, Santa Barbara, 1994. 571pp.

___ Levine, Richard S. "The Sustainable City: A Necessary Utopia," in: Saccaro Del Buffa, Giuseppa and Lewis, Arthur O., eds. **Utopia e Modernita: Teorie e prassi utopiche nell'eta moderna e postmoderna**. Rome: Gangemi Editore, 1989. pp.157-174.

___ Lloyd, Donald G. "Renegade Robots and Hard-Wired Heroes: Technology and Morality in Contemporary Science Fiction Films," in: Loukides, Paul and Fuller, Linda K., eds. **Beyond the Stars III: The Material World in American Popular Film**. Bowling Green, OH: Popular Press, 1993. pp.216-228.

___ Martin-Diaz, M. J. "Science Fiction Comes to the Classroom: Maelstrom II," by M. J. Martin-Diaz, A. Pizarro, P. Bacas, J. P. Garcia and F. Perera. *Physics Education* 27(1): 18-23. January 1992.

___ McKee, J. S. C. "Science Fact and Science Fiction: Are They Indistinguishable?," *Physics in Canada* 48(4): 247-250. July 1992.

___ Nahin, Paul J. **Time Machines: Time Travel in Physics, Metaphysics, and Science Fiction**. New York: American Institute of Physics, 1993. 408pp.

___ Nicholls, Stan. "The Promise of Space," *Starlog* No. 200: 68-71, 82. March 1994.

___ Oehlert, Mark. "From Captain America to Wolverine: Cyborgs in Comic Books, Alternative Images of Cybernetic Heroes and Villains," in: Gray, Chris H., ed. **The Cyborg Handbook**. New York: Routledge, 1995. pp.219-231.

___ Ordway, Frederick I., III, ed. **Blueprint for Space: Science Fiction to Science Fact**, ed. by Frederick I. Ordway, III and Randy Liebermann. Washington, DC: Smithsonian Institution Press, 1992. 224pp.

___ Parrinder, Patrick. "Scientists in Science Fiction: Enlightenment and After," *Chung Wai Literary Quarterly* 22(12): May 1994. (Issue not seen; pagination unavailable.) (Reprinted from Garrett, Rhys, ed. **Science Fiction Roots and Branches**. 1990.)

___ Pohl, Frederik. "Pohlemic: Chasing Science," *Science Fiction Chronicle* 14(5): 30-32. February 1993.

___ Pohl, Frederik. "Science Fiction: Stepchild of Science," *Technology Review* 97(7): 57-61. October 1994.

___ Pohl, Frederik. "Two-Way Look at the Literature of Change," *New Scientist* 138(1874): 48-49. May 22, 1993

___ Robinett, Jane. **This Rough Magic: Technology in Latin American Fiction**. New York: P. Lang, 1993. 284pp.

___ Ross, Andrew. **Strange Weather: Culture, Science, and Technology in the Age of Limits**. London: Verso, 1991. 275pp.

___ Schelde, Per. **Androids, Humanoids, and Other Science Fiction Monsters: Science and Soul in Science Fiction Films**. New York: New York University Press, 1993. 279pp.

___ Scholz, Carter. "Dance of Shadows," *New York Review of Science Fiction* No. 81: 1, 3-6. May 1995.

SCIENCE IN SF (continued)

___ Setiya, Kieran. "Two Notes on Lovecraft," *Lovecraft Studies* No. 26: 14-16. Spring 1992.

___ Siegel, Lee. "Scientists Have a Bone to Pick with Dinosaur-Cloning Theory," *Austin (TX) American Statesman* Sec. B, p. 10. June 7, 1993.

___ Slonczewski, Joan. "Science in Science Fiction: Making It Work," *Writer* 107(4): 14-17. April 1994.

___ Steele, Allen. "Hard Again," *New York Review of Science Fiction* No. 46: 1, 3-5. June 1992.

___ Stein, Ben P. "*Star Trek*: Science on the Edge," *Science World* 51(3): 9-13. October 7, 1994.

___ Stites, Richard. "World Outlook and Inner Fears in Soviet Science Fiction," in: Graham, Loren R., ed. **Science and the Soviet Social Order**. Cambridge: Harvard University Press, 1990. pp.299-324.

___ Strehle, Susan. **Fiction in the Quantum Universe**. Chapel Hill: University of North Carolina Press, 1992. 282pp.

___ Swirski, Peter. "On Games With the Universe: Preconceptions of Science in Stanislaw Lem's **The Invincible**," *Contemporary Literature* 35(2): 324-342. Summer 1994.

___ Teitelbaum, Sheldon. "Scientists Say Asimov Put the Stars in Their Eyes," *Los Angeles (CA) Times.* Sec. E, p. 1. April 8, 1992. in *NewsBank. Literature.* 35:B11-B12. 1992.

___ Toumey, Christopher P. "The Moral Character of Mad Scientists: A Cultural Critique of Science," *Science, Technology and Human Values* 17(4): 411-437. Autumn 1992.

___ Westfahl, Gary. "Good Physics, Lousy Engineering: Arthur C. Clarke's **A Fall of Moondust**," *Monad* No. 3: 65-90. September 1993.

___ Weyland, Jack. **Megapowers: Science Fact vs. Science Fiction**. Toronto: Kids Can Press, 1992. 78pp. (Cf. OCLC)

___ Wicken, Jeffrey S. "Evolutionary Constraints on Utopian Thought," in: Saccaro Del Buffa, Giuseppa and Lewis, Arthur O., eds. **Utopia e Modernita: Teorie e prassi utopiche nell'eta moderna e postmoderna**. Rome: Gangemi Editore, 1989. pp.143-156.

___ Wolansky, Taras. "Fantasy vs. Science Fiction: Part III," *Quantum* No. 41: 21-22. Winter/Spring 1992.

___ Wolfe, Gary K. "The Dawn Patrol: Sex, Technology, and Irony in Farmer and Ballard," in: Ruddick, Nicholas, ed. **State of the Fantastic**. Westport, CT: Greenwood, 1992. pp.159-167.

SCIENCE-FICTION STUDIES (MAGAZINE)

___ Zook, Jim. "Daring Journal of 'SF' Theory," *Chronicle of Higher Education* 40(39): A8. June 1, 1994.

SCIENTISTS

___ Allen, Glen S. "Master Mechanics and Evil Wizards: Science and the American Imagination from Frankenstein to Sputnik," *Massachusetts Review* 33(4): 505-558. Winter 1992/93.

___ Dietrich, Bryan. "**Prince of Darkness**, Prince of Light: From Faust to Physicist," *Journal of Popular Film and Television* 19(2): 91-96. 1991.

___ Gould, Donald. "Letting Poetry Loose in the Laboratory," *New Scientist* 135(1836): 50-51. August 29, 1992.

___ Haynes, Roslynn D. **From Faust to Strangelove: Representations of the Scientist in Western Literature**. Baltimore: Johns Hopkins University Press, 1994. 417pp.

___ Parrinder, Patrick. "Scientists in Science Fiction: Enlightenment and After," *Chung Wai Literary Quarterly* 22(12): May 1994. (Issue not seen; pagination unavailable.) (Reprinted from Garrett, Rhys, ed. **Science Fiction Roots and Branches**. 1990.)

___ Toumey, Christopher P. "The Moral Character of Mad Scientists: A Cultural Critique of Science," *Science, Technology and Human Values* 17(4): 411-437. Autumn 1992.

SCITHERS, GEORGE

___ "World Fantasy Awards," *Science Fiction Chronicle* 14(3): 4. December 1992.

SCORCESE, MARTIN

___ Rose, Charles J. **The Passionate Observer: Martin Scorcese.** Master's Thesis, University of Southern California, 1980. 175pp.

___ Von Gunden, Kenneth. **Postmodern Auteurs: Coppola, Lucas, De Palma, Spielberg and Scorcese**. Jefferson, NC: McFarland, 1991. 200pp.

SCOTLAND

___ Manlove, C. N. "Scottish Fantasy," *Extrapolation* 35(1): 15-32. Spring 1994.

SCOTLAND (continued)

___ Manlove, C. N. **Scottish Fantasy Literature: A Critical Survey**. Edinburgh: Canongate Academic, 1994. 263pp.

SCOTT, G. FIRTH

___ Stone, Graham. "Notes on Australian Science Fiction," *Science Fiction News* (Australia) No. 67: 2-9. January 1983.

SCOTT, MELISSA

___ Schleifer, Paul C. "Fear of the 'Other' in Melissa Scott's **Dreamships**," *Extrapolation* 35(4): 312-318. Winter 1994.

SCOTT, RIDLEY

___ Jakaitis, Jake. "Ridley Scott and Philip K. Dick," in: Mullen, R. D., ed. **On Philip K. Dick: 40 Articles From Science-Fiction Studies**. Terre Haute, IN: SF-TH Inc., 1992. pp.278-282.

___ Lofficier, Randy. "**Blade Runner** (1982): Interviews with Hampton Francher, David Peoples, Ridley Scott and Syd Mead," by Randy Lofficier and Jean-Marc Lofficier. in: Goldberg, Lee et al. **Science Fiction Filmmaking in the 1980s**. Jefferson, NC: McFarland, 1995. pp.23-58.

___ Lofficier, Randy. "Interview: Ridley Scott," by Randy Lofficier and Jean-Marc Lofficier. *Starlog* 184: 48-51, 69. November 1992.

SCOTT, SARAH ROBINSON

___ Dunne, Linda. "Mothers and Monsters in Sarah Robinson Scott's **Millenium Hall**," in: Donawerth, Jane L. and Kolmerten, Carol A., eds. **Utopian and Science Fiction by Women: Worlds of Difference**. Syracuse, NY: Syracuse University Press, 1994. pp.54-72.

SCREAM AND SCREAM AGAIN (MOTION PICTURE)

___ "Enter 2 U.S. Pix in Trieste's International Sci-Fi Film Fest," *Variety* p. 24. June 10, 1970.

SCREAMERS (MOTION PICTURE)

___ Flixman, Ed. "Man and Machine," *Sci-Fi Entertainment* 2(3): 48-53. October 1995.

___ Perez, Dan. "Dan O'Bannon Brings Philip K. Dick's Nightmare Visions to Life in **Screamers**," *Science Fiction Age* 3(6): 18-22, 101. 1995.

___ Thonen, John. "**Screamers** EFX," *Cinefantastique* 27(2): 42. November 1995.

___ Thonen, John. "**Screamers**," *Cinefantastique* 27(2): 40-43. November 1995.

SCRIBNERS

___ "Paramount Drops Atheneum, Restructures Macmillan," *Locus* 32(3): 8, 69. March 1994.

SEAQUEST DSV (TV)

___ Burnfield, Steve. "The Butt From Another Planet," *New York (NY) Post.* May 3, 1994. in: *NewsBank. Film and Television.* 58:G2. 1994.

___ Carlson, Timothy. "The Universe Is Expanding All over the Dial," by Timothy Carlson and Mark Schwed. *TV Guide* 41(1): 16-19. January 2, 1993. (Issue 2075)

___ Cerone, Daniel H. "**Seaquest** Comes Up for Repairs," *Los Angeles (CA) Times.* April 30, 1994. in: *NewsBank. Film and Television.* 58:F14-G1. 1994.

___ Lorando, Mark. "Shock Cousteau Scheider Makes More Waves," *New Orleans (LA) Times-Picayune.* September 19, 1994. in: *NewsBank. Film and Television.* 103:E12. 1994.

___ Nazzaro, Joe. "Underwater Thoughts," *Starlog* No. 204: 54-58. July 1994.

___ Rosenthal, Bruce. "**Sea Quest's** Spin-off," *Sea Frontiers* 40(1): 8. January 1994.

___ Schwed, Mark. "On the Horizon: Whole New Worlds," *TV Guide* 41(30): 29-31. July 24, 1993.

___ Warren, Bill. "Altered Voyages," *Starlog* No. 208: 32-36, 72. November 1994.

___ Warren, Bill. "Hail to the Chief," *Starlog* No. 207: 36-39, 70. October 1994.

___ Warren, Bill. "Longhair at Sea," *Starlog* No. 203: 34-37, 66. June 1994.

___ Warren, Bill. "Prepare to Submerge," *Starlog* No. 196: 44-49, 72. November 1993.

___ Warren, Bill. "Self-Made Woman," *Starlog* No. 202: 27-30, 68. May 1994.

SEAQUEST DSV (TV)

SEAQUEST DSV (TV) (continued)
___ Warren, Bill. "Sub Teen," *Starlog* No. 197: 55-57, 82. December 1993.
___ Warren, Bill. "Underwater Journeyman," *Starlog* No. 199: 37-40, 74. February 1994.
___ Warren, Bill. "The Young Ted Raimi," *Starlog* No. 198: 38-41. January 1994.
___ Wilson, Bill. "Gill Man," *Starlog* No. 211: 46-49. February 1995.
___ Wilson, Bill. "Mistress of the Sea," *Starlog* No. 216: 74-77. July 1995.
___ Wilson, Bill. "Mutant Hero," *Starlog* No. 214: 50-52, 69. May 1995.
___ Wilson, Bill. "Underwater Cowboy," *Starlog* No. 215: 36-39. June 1995.

SEARCH FOR SPOCK (MOTION PICTURE)
___ SEE: STAR TREK III: THE SEARCH FOR SPOCK (MOTION PICTURE).

SEARLE, RONALD
___ Davies, Russell. **Ronald Searle: A Biography**. London: Sinclair-Stevenson, 1990. 192pp.

SEARLE, SAMUEL COOPER
___ Coriell, Vernell. "**The Son of Tarzan**: The Movie," *Burroughs Bulletin* NS. No. 18: 3-5. April 1994.

SEARLES, BAIRD
___ "Searles, Baird (Obituary)," *Locus* 30(5): 66. May 1993.
___ "Searles, Baird (Obituary)," *Science Fiction Chronicle* 14(8): 16. May 1993.
___ "Searles, Baird, 1936-1993: In Memoriam (Obituary)," *Isaac Asimov's Science Fiction Magazine* 17(11): 164. October 1993.

SECOND ENCOUNTER (MOTION PICTURE)
___ SEE: XTRO II: THE SECOND ENCOUNTER (MOTION PICTURE).

SECRET ADVENTURES OF TOM THUMB (MOTION PICTURE)
___ Biodrowski, Steve. "Directors Dave Borthwick and Peter Capladi on **The Secret Adventures of Tom Thumb** and **Franz Kafka's It's a Wonderful Life**," *Cinefantastique* 27(3): 58-59. December 1995.
___ Biodrowski, Steve. "**The Secret Adventures of Tom Thumb** (Review)," *Cinefantastique* 27(3): 59. December 1995.
___ Persons, Dan. "**The Secret Adventures of Tom Thumb** (Review)," *Cinefantastique* 25(4): 60. August 1994.
___ Sharman, Leslie F. "**Secret Adventures of Tom Thumb** (Review)," *Sight and Sound* 4(1): 52-53. January 1994.

SECRET OF ROAN INISH (MOTION PICTURE)
___ Biodrowski, Steve. "**The Secret of Roan Inish** (Review)," *Cinefantastique* 27(3): 34. December 1995.
___ Scapperotti, Dan. "**The Secret of Roan Inish** (Review)," *Cinefantastique* 26(5): 60. August 1995.
___ Scapperotti, Dan. "**The Secret of Roan Inish**," *Cinefantastique* 27(3): 3235. December 1995.

SECRETS OF STARGATE (CD-ROM)
___ Korman, Ken. "**Secrets of Stargate** (Review)," *Video Magazine* 18(10): 65. January 1995.

SECT (MOTION PICTURE)
___ Jones, Alan. "**The Sect**," *Cinefantastique* 22(6): 50-51. June 1992

SEIUN AWARDS, 1993
___ "Other Awards," *Science Fiction Chronicle* 15(1): 4. October 1993.

SEIUN AWARDS, 1994
___ "Other Awards at ConAdian," *Science Fiction Chronicle* 15(10): 5. September 1994.

SEIUN AWARDS, 1995
___ "The Hugos (Or, the Empire Strikes Back)," *Science Fiction Chronicle* 17(2): 55-56. December 1995/January 1996.

SELICK, HENRY
___ Felperin, Leslie. "Animated Dreams," *Sight and Sound* 4(12): 26-29. December 1994.

SELLERS, CONNIE L.
___ "Sellers, Connie L. (Obituary)," *Locus* 28(3): 73. March 1992.

SEMPLE, LORENZO
___ Garcia, Bob. "**Batman**: Lorenzo Semple, Guru of Camp," *Cinefantastique* 24(6)/25(1): 44-45. February 1994.

SENDAK, MAURICE
___ Sullivan, C. W., III. "Fantasy According to **Mister Roger's Neighborhood** and **In the Night Kitchen**," in: Morse, Donald E., ed. **The Celebration of the Fantastic**. Westport, CT: Greenwood, 1992. pp.183-190.

SENKOVSKY, OSIP
___ Pedrotti, Louis. "Warfare Celestial and Terrestrial: Osip Senkovsky's 1833 Russian Science Fantasy," in: Slusser, George and Eric S. Rabkin, eds. **Fights of Fancy: Armed Conflict in Science Fiction and Fantasy**. Athens, GA: University of Georgia Press, 1993. pp.49-58.

SENSE OF WONDER (MAGAZINE)
___ "B. Dalton's *Sense of Wonder*," *Locus* 30(1): 6. January 1993.
___ "*Sense of Wonder* Is B. Dalton SF/Fantasy Newsletter," *Science Fiction Chronicle* 14(5): 4. February 1993.

SEPULCHRE HOUSE (MAGAZINE)
___ "Whither *Sepulchre House*?," *Science Fiction Chronicle* 13(6): 5. March 1992.

SERIES AND SEQUELS
___ Gilmore, C. N. "Some Notes on the Pitfalls Attendant on Universal Creation," *Foundation* No. 61: 77-84. Summer 1994.
___ Kan, Katharine L. **Mindscapes II: Science Fiction and Fantasy in Series**. Honolulu, HI: Hawaii State Public Library System, 1993. 37pp.
___ Westfahl, Gary. "Sequel and Ye Shall Find Well: Book Two in the Chronicles of Westfahl the Critic," *Monad* No. 2: 25-42. March 1992.

SERLING, ROD
___ "Rod Serling Sees TV Academy Kaput," *Variety* p. 36. October 1, 1969.
___ Busby, Laurie. "Serling's Intensity Drove Him into a Twilight Zone in His Personal Life," *Santa Ana (CA) Orange County Register*. November 26, 1992. in: *NewsBank. Film and Television.* 118:G10. 1992.
___ Hughes, Mike. "Serling's Tales Continue to Haunt Us," *Boston (MA) Herald*. May 19, 1994. in: *NewsBank. Film and Television.* 60:B12. 1994.
___ Lofficier, Jean-Marc. **Into the Twilight Zone: The Rod Serling Programme Guide**, by Jean-Marc Lofficier and Randy Lofficier. London: Virgin, 1995. 296pp.
___ Rees, Robert R. "Driving Rod Serling," *Starlog* No. 203: 27-29. June 1994.
___ Rees, Robert R. "Master in Twilight," *Starlog* No. 203: 30-31. June 1994.
___ Richmond, Ray. "Serling's 'Lost' Tales Lose Something in 90s Transition," *Los Angeles (CA) Daily News*. May 19, 1994. in: *NewsBank. Film and Television.* 60: B13. 1994.
___ Sander, Gordon. **Serling: The Rise and Twilight of Television's Last Angry Man**. New York: Penguin/Dutton, 1992. 284pp.
___ Weaver, tom. "Twilight Testaments," *Starlog* No. 203: 32. June 1994.
___ Westbrook, Bruce. "Re-entering Serling's **Twilight Zone**," *Houston (TX) Chronicle* Sec. C, p. 3. September 4, 1992.

SERNINE, DANIEL
___ "1994 Aurora Winners," *Locus* 33(4): 8, 76. October 1994.
___ "Aurora Awards," *Science Fiction Chronicle* 15(10): 5. September 1994.

SERVICE, PAMELA F.
___ Service, Pamela F. "On Writing Sci Fi and Fantasy for Kids," *ALAN Review* 19(3): 16-18. Spring 1992.

SETTING
___ SEE: BACKGROUND.

SEVERANCE, CAROL
___ "Compton Crook Memorial Award, 1991," *Locus* 28(6): 6. June 1992.

SEVERN, DAVID
___ MacIlroy, Barry. "Those Magical Time-Slip Stories," *Souvenir* 21: 14-15. 1992. [Not seen.]

SEX
___ Bartlett, Karen J. "Subversive Desire: Sex and Ethics in Delany's **Dahlgren**," *New York Review of Science Fiction* No. 75: 1, 3-7. November 1994.
___ Doughan, David. "Tolkien, Sayers, Sex and Gender," in: Reynolds, Patricia and GoodKnight, Glen H., eds. **Proceedings of the J. R. R. Tolkien Centenary Conference, Keble College, Oxford, 1992**. Altadena, CA: Mythopoeic Press, 1995. pp.356-359. (*Mythlore* Vol. 21, No. 2, Winter 1996, Whole No. 80)
___ Haldeman, Joe. "Sex and Violence in SF," *The Report: The Fiction Writer's Magazine* No. 9: 1, 3. March 1993.
___ Kalien, Ben. "Lust in Space," in: Van Hise, James, ed. **Trek Celebration Two**. Las Vegas, NV: Pioneer, 1994. pp.111-116.
___ McKee, Alan. "Intentional Phalluses: The Male 'Sex' in J. G. Ballard," *Foundation* No. 57: 58-67. Spring 1993.
___ Springer, Claudia. "Sex, Memories, and Angry Women," *South Atlantic Quarterly* 92(4): 713-734. Fall 1993.

SEX IN SF
___ Rabkin, Eric S. "The Male Body in Science Fiction," *Michigan Quarterly Review* 33(1): 203-216. Winter 1994.
___ Reed-Pharrr, Robert F. "Sex, Race, and Science Fiction: The *Callaloo* Interview," in: Delany, Samuel R. **Silent Interviews on Language, Race, Sex, Science Fiction and Some Comics.** Hanover, NH: Wesleyan University Press, 1994. pp.216-229.
___ Wolfe, Gary K. "The Dawn Patrol: Sex, Technology, and Irony in Farmer and Ballard," in: Ruddick, Nicholas, ed. **State of the Fantastic**. Westport, CT: Greenwood, 1992. pp.159-167.

SEX ROLES
___ Harvey, Jessica G. **Are We Not Men Too? Women and the Sex-Gender Role Reversal Motif in Science Fiction**. Master's Thesis, Acadia University, 1993. 160pp. (Master's Abstracts 32/03, p. 804. June 1994.)
___ Helford, Elyce R. "Reading Masculinities in the 'Postpatriarchal' Space of **Red Dwarf**," *Foundation* No. 64: 20-31. Summer 1995.
___ Kuelen, Margarete. **Radical Imagination: Feminist Conceptions of the Future in Ursula Le Guin, Marge Piercy and Sally Miller Gearhart**. Frankfurt-am-Main/New York: Peter Lang, 1991. 122pp.
___ Nelson, Craig A. **A Content Analysis of Female and Male Authors' Portrayals of Sex Roles in Science Fiction for Children From 1970 to 1990**. Ph.D. Dissertation, University of Minnesota, 1991. 235pp.
___ Salmonson, Jessica A. "Gender Structuring of Shell Persons in **The Ship Who Sang**," *New York Review of Science Fiction* No. 10: 15-18. June 1989.

SEX, DEATH AND VIDEOTAPE (MOTION PICTURE)
___ SEE: MIDNIGHT 2: SEX, DEATH AND VIDEOTAPE (MOTION PICTURE).

SEXUALITY
___ Kearns, Martha. "Postmodern Images of Sexuality in Vampire Literature," in: Wolf, Milton T. and Mallett, Daryl F., eds. **Imaginative Futures: Proceedings of the 1993 Science Fiction Research Association Conference**. San Bernardino, CA: Jacob's Ladder Books, 1995. pp.147-160.
___ McKee, Alan. "Intentional Phalluses: The Male 'Sex' in J. G. Ballard," *Foundation* No. 57: 58-67. Spring 1993.

SF INSIDER (MAGAZINE)
___ "New Horror, SF Magazines Due," *Science Fiction Chronicle* 14(10): 6. July 1993.

SHADOW (CHARACTER)
___ "The Shadow Chronology," *Sci-Fi Entertainment* 1(2): 31. August 1994.

SHADOW (MAGAZINE)
___ Zebrowski, George. "**The Shadow**: Radio and Pulp Origins," *Cinefantastique* 25(4): 20-21. August 1994.

SHADOW MOON (MOTION PICTURE)
___ Johnson, Kim H. "In the Light of **The Shadow Moon**," *Starlog* No. 219: 38-41. October 1995.

SHADOW (MOTION PICTURE)
___ Altman, Mark A. "Dark Man: **The Shadow** (Review)," *Sci-Fi Universe* No. 3: 70-71. October/November 1994.
___ Altman, Mark A. "**The Shadow**: Production Design by Joe Nemec III," *Cinefantastique* 25(4): 31, 61. August 1994.
___ Altman, Mark A. "**The Shadow**: Russell Mulcahy, Genre Stylist," *Cinefantastique* 25(4): 18. August 1994.
___ Altman, Mark A. "**The Shadow**: Screenwriter David Koepp," *Cinefantastique* 25(4): 23. August 1994.
___ Altman, Mark A. "**The Shadow**: The Origin of the Shadow," *Cinefantastique* 25(4): 19. August 1994.
___ Altman, Mark A. "**The Shadow**," *Cinefantastique* 25(4): 16-43. August 1994.
___ Faller, James M. "**The Shadow** (Review)," *Cinefantastique* 25(6)/26(1): 123. December 1994.
___ Jones, Alan. "**The Shadow**," *Cinefantastique* 25(3): 4-5, 61. June 1994.
___ Murray, Will. "Master of Death," *Starlog* No. 205: 27-31. August 1994.
___ Newman, Kim. "**The Shadow** (Review)," *Sight and Sound* 4(11): 52. November 1994.
___ Peterson, Don E. "**The Shadow** Takes Shape," *Sci-Fi Entertainment* 1(2): 26-32. August 1994.
___ Prokop, Tim. "**The Shadow**: Making Mr. Shadow," *Cinefantastique* 25(4): 24-25. August 1994.
___ Prokop, Tim. "**The Shadow**: Matte Painting Beyond the Backlot," *Cinefantastique* 25(4): 40-41. August 1994.
___ Prokop, Tim. "**The Shadow**: Miniaturizing New York," *Cinefantastique* 25(4): 42-43. August 1994.
___ Prokop, Tim. "**The Shadow**: Special Effects Computer Graphics," *Cinefantastique* 25(4): 32-32. August 1994.
___ Prokop, Tim. "**The Shadow**: Superhero Merchandising," *Cinefantastique* 25(4): 39. August 1994.
___ Prokop, Tim. "**The Shadow**: The Art of Makeup," *Cinefantastique* 25(4): 36-37. August 1994.
___ Scapperotti, Dan. "**The Shadow**: Movie and Serial Adventures," *Cinefantastique* 25(4): 27-29. August 1994.
___ Vaz, Mark C. "Quick Cuts: Shadow World," *Cinefex* No. 60: 33-34. December 1994.
___ Zebrowski, George. "**The Shadow**: Radio and Pulp Origins," *Cinefantastique* 25(4): 20-21. August 1994.

SHADOWCHASER (MOTION PICTURE)
___ Pirani, Adam. "**Shadowchaser**," *Starlog* 178: 36-39. May 1992.

SHADOWLANDS (MOTION PICTURE)
___ Como, James. "Shadowlands IV," *CSL: The Bulletin of the New York C. S. Lewis Society* 24(6): 1-7. April 1993.

SHADOWRUN (GAME)
___ Betancourt, John G. "**Shadowrun's** Second Edition Cyberfantasy Is Bigger and Better Than Ever," *Science Fiction Age* 1(4): 66, 71. May 1993.

SHAKESPEARE, WILLIAM
___ Buhler, Stephen M. " 'Who Calls Me Villian?': Blank Verse and the Black Hat," *Extrapolation* 36(1): 18-27. Spring 1995.
___ Bulger, Thomas. "The Utopic Structure of **The Tempest**," *Utopian Studies* 5(1): 38-47. 1994.
___ Burelback, Frederick M. "Totemic Animals in Some Shakespeare Plays," in: Latham, Robert A. and Collins, Robert A., eds. **Modes of the Fantastic**. Westport, CT: Greenwood, 1995. pp.155-160.
___ Dutta, Mary B. " 'Very Bad Poetry, Captain': Shakespeare in **Star Trek**," *Extrapolation* 36(1): 38-45. Spring 1995.
___ Hegarty, Emily. "Some Suspect of Ill: Shakespeare's Sonnets and 'The Perfect Mate'," *Extrapolation* 36(1): 55-64. Spring 1995.
___ Houlahan, Mark. "Cosmic Hamlets? Contesting Shakespeare in Federation Space," *Extrapolation* 36(1): 28-37. Spring 1995.
___ Pendergast, John S. "A Nation of Hamlets: Shakespeare and Cultural Politics," *Extrapolation* 36(1): 10-17. Spring 1995.
___ Prouty, William. " **The Tempest**: Shakespeare's Anti-Utopia Tract," in: Saccaro Del Buffa, Giuseppa and Lewis, Arthur O., eds. **Utopie per gli Anni Ottana**. Rome: Gangemi Editore, 1986. pp.579-586.

SHAKESPEARE, WILLIAM (continued)

___ Reinheimer, David. "Ontological and Ethical Allusion: Shakespeare in *The Next Generation*," *Extrapolation* 36(1): 46-54. Spring 1995.

SHAMANISM

___ Pennington, John. "Shamanistic Mythmaking: From Civilization to Wilderness in **Watership Down**," *Journal of the Fantastic in the Arts* 6(1): 34-50. 1993.

___ Stewig, John W. "The Witch Woman: A Recurring Motif in Recent Fantasy Writing for Young Readers," *Mythlore* 20(1): 48-52. Winter 1994. (Whole No. 75) (Reprinted: *Children's Literature in Education* 26(2): 119-133. June 1995.)

SHARKEY, JACK

___ "Sharkey, Jack (Obituary)," *Locus* 29(6): 68. December 1992.

___ "Sharkey, Jack (Obituary)," *Science Fiction Chronicle* 14(4): 14. January 1993.

SHATNER, WILLIAM

___ "Shatner Ends Holdout, Joins Cast of 'Trek IV'," *Variety* p. 23. February 6, 1985.

___ Altman, Mark A. "**Star Trek**: Paramount Turned Down Captain Kirk's Spec Script," *Cinefantastique* 23(4): 5. December 1992.

___ Altman, Mark A. "William Shatner," *Cinefantastique* 22(4): 44-45. February 1992.

___ Bloch-Hansen, Peter. "Classic Captain," by Peter Bloch-Hansen and Ian Spelling. *Starlog* No. 212: 36-37, 70. March 1995.

___ Bloch-Hansen, Peter. "Declaring **TekWar**," *Starlog* No. 199: 46-49, 73. February 1994.

___ Campbell, Bob. "Dauntless Captain Kirk Claims Humor Has Kept Starship *Enterprise* in Orbit," *Newark (NJ) Star-Ledger*. December 15, 1991. in: *NewsBank. Film and Television.* 7:A12-A13. 1992.

___ Cohen, Charles E. "The Trek to Tek," *TV Guide* 42(3): 16-17. January 15, 1994.

___ Flixman, Ed. "The Once and Future Kirk," *Sci-Fi Entertainment* 1(4): 47. December 1994.

___ Flixman, Ed. "William Shatner: Back to the Future," *Sci-Fi Entertainment* 1(5): 56-59, 72. February 1995.

___ Florence, Bill. "Trek World," *Starlog* 182: 56-58, 72. September 1992.

___ Hauck, Dennis W. **Captain Quirk: The Unauthorized Biography of William Shatner**. New York: Pinnacle, 1995. 298pp.

___ Hauck, Dennis W. **William Shatner: A Bio-Bibliography**. Westport, CT.: Greenwood Press, 1994. 324pp.

___ Lofficier, Randy. "**Star Trek Movies** (1980-1988): Interviews with Jack Sowards, Nicholas Mayer, Harve Bennett; Leonard Nimoy and William Shatner," by Randy Lofficier and Jean-Marc Lofficier. in: Goldberg, Lee et al. **Science Fiction Filmmaking in the 1980s**. Jefferson, NC: McFarland, 1995. pp.189-236.

___ Madsen, Dan. "Exclusive Interview: William Shatner: The Final Voyage of Captain Kirk," *Star Trek: The Official Fan Club Magazine* No. 85: 2-4. May/June 1992.

___ Marin, Rick. "Warp Speed Ahead," *TV Guide* 41(30): 21-24. July 24, 1993.

___ Ryan, Desmond. "Off the Beaten Trek," *Philadelphia (PA) Inquirer.* December 8, 1991. in: *NewsBank. Film and Television.* 7:A14-B1. 1992. also in: *NewsBank. Names in the News.* 1:F13-F14. 1992.

___ Shatner, William. **Shatner: Where No Man, the Authorized Biography of William Shatner**. New York: Grosset & Dunlap, 1979. 327pp.

___ Shatner, William. **Star Trek Movie Memories: Behind the Scenes Coverage of All Seven Star Trek Films, Including Star Trek VII**. New York: HarperCollins, 1994. 357pp.

___ Strauss, Bob. "Captain Doesn't Want to Go Down With His Starship," *Los Angeles (CA) Daily News.* December 6, 1991. in: *NewsBank. Film and Television.* 7:A10-A11. 1992.; *NewsBank. Names in the News.* NIN 1: F11-F12. 1992.

___ Witchel, Alex. "Boldly Contemplating Death and the Sequel," *New York Times* p.B1. November 23, 1994.

___ Yakir, Dan. "The Undiscovered Kirk," *Starlog* No. 175: 6-10, 82. February 1992.

SHATTER DEAD (MOTION PICTURE)

___ Wilt, David. "**Shatter Dead** (Review)," *Cinefantastique* 26(3): 60. April 1995.

SHATTERWORLD (TV)

___ Spelling, Ian. "Welcome to **Shatterworld**," *Starlog* No. 205: 58-60. August 1994.

SHAW, BERNARD

___ Mason, Michael. "A Clearing of Vision: 1843-1962. The Evolution of the Utopian Ideal in Carlyle, Shaw and Huxley," in: Saccaro Del Buffa, Giuseppa and Lewis, Arthur O., eds. **Utopia e Modernita: Teorie e prassi utopiche nell'eta moderna e postmoderna**. Rome: Gangemi Editore, 1989. pp.931-944.

___ Redmond, James. "William Morris or Bernard Shaw: Two Faces of Victorian Socialism," in: Butt, J. and Clarke, I. F., eds. **The Victorians and Social Protest: A Symposium**. New York: David and Charles, 1973. pp.156-176.

___ Smith, J. Percy , ed. **Bernard Shaw and H. G. Wells**. Toronto: University of Toronto Press, 1995. 242pp.

SHAW, BOB

___ Pringle, David. "Bob Shaw: An Annotated Bibliography," *Interzone* No. 67: 4-5. January 1993.

___ Stableford, Brian. **Algebraic Fantasies and Realistic Romances: More Masters of Science Fiction**. San Bernardino, CA: Borgo Press, 1995 128pp.

___ Stableford, Brian. "Escape to Reality: A Profile of Bob Shaw," *Interzone* No. 67: 40-43. January 1993.

___ Stephensen-Payne, Phil. **Bob Shaw, Artist at Ground Zero: A Working Bibliography**. 5th Rev. Ed. Albuquerque, NM: Galactic Central, 1993. 51pp.

___ Wake, Helen. "Glad to Be of Use: Bob Shaw Interview," *Interzone* No. 67: 13-16. January 1993.

SHAW, PETER

___ Markley, Robert. "Robert Boyle, Peter Shaw, and the Reinscription of Technology: Inventing and Reinventing the Air Pump," in: Greenberg, Mark L. and Schachterle, Lance, eds. **Literature and Technology**. Bethlehem, PA: Lehigh University Press, 1992. pp.125-153.

SHAYNE, ROBERT

___ "Shayne, Robert, 1900-1992 (Obituary)," *Starlog* No. 189: 22-23. April 1993.

SHE (1935) (MOTION PICTURE)

___ Turner, George. "**She**: Empire of the Imagination," *American Cinematographer* 76(6): 103-108. June 1995.

SHE-CREATURE (MOTION PICTURE)

___ Di Fate, Vincent. "Creature Capsules," *Science Fiction Chronicle* 13(11/12): 38-42. August 1992.

___ Henenlotter, Frank. "Films From Under the Floorboards," *Sci-Fi Entertainment* 1(6): 52-57. April 1995.

SHEA, ROBERT JOSEPH

___ "Shea, Robert (Appreciation)," *Locus* 32(5): 63. May 1994.

___ "Shea, Robert Joseph (Obituary)," *Science Fiction Chronicle* 15(6): 26. April/May 1994.

___ "Shea, Robert (Obituary)," *Locus* 32(4): 60. April 1994.

SHECKLEY, ROBERT

___ Marx, Doug. "The Indeterminate Man," *Oregon* 17: 32-34, 93, 96. December 1987.

___ Nicholls, Stan. "Dreaming Boy: Robert Sheckley Interviewed," *Interzone* No. 63: 47-49. September 1992.

___ Nicholls, Stan. "His Mad Universe," *Starlog* 185: 54-56, 72. December 1992.

___ Nicholls, Stan. "Robert Sheckley Is a Dreaming Boy," in: Nicholls, Stan. **Wordsmiths of Wonder: Fifty Interviews with Writers of the Fantastic**. London: Orbit, 1993. pp.25-32.

___ Wood, Gary L. "**Freejack**: Filming 'Immortality Delivered'," *Cinefantastique* 22(4): 14-15. February 1992.

SHEFFIELD, CHARLES

___ "1993 Nebula Awards Winners," *Locus* 32(5): 8. May 1994.

___ "1994 Hugo Award," *Science Fiction Chronicle* 15(10): 5. September 1994.

___ "1994 Hugo Awards Winners," *Locus* 33(4): 7, 38-41. October 1994.

SHEFFIELD, CHARLES (continued)

___ "Charles Sheffield: Future Nightmares, Future Dreams," *Locus* 33(2): 4-5, 76, 78. August 1994.

___ "Nebula Awards," *Science Fiction Chronicle* 15(7): 4. June 1994.

___ "Sheffield, Simmons Win Campbell, Sturgeon Awards," *Locus* 31(3): 6, 83. September 1993.

___ "Sheffield, Simmons, Win Campbell, Sturgeon Awards," *Science Fiction Chronicle* 14(11): 4. August 1993.

SHELDRAKE, RUPERT

___ Di Filippo, Paul. "You Are Not Your Genes!," *Science Fiction Eye* No. 11: 18-22. December 1992.

SHELLEY, MARY

___ "Mary Shelley," in: Bloom, Harold, ed. **Classic Science Fiction Writers**. New York: Chelsea House, 1995. pp.137-151.

___ "Revisiting **Frankenstein**: A Study in Reading and Education," *English Journal* 83(4): 33-35. April 1994.

___ Aldiss, Brian W. "Science Fiction's Mother Figure," in: Aldiss, Brian W. **The Detached Retina: Aspects of SF and Fantasy**. Syracuse, NY: Syracuse University Press, 1995. pp.52-86.

___ Bennett, Betty T., ed. **Selected Letters of Mary Wollstonecraft Shelley**. Baltimore, MD: Johns Hopkins University Press, 1995. 391pp.

___ Bloom, Harold. "Mary Shelley," in: Bloom, Harold. **Classic Horror Writers**. New York: Chelsea House, 1994. pp.121-137.

___ Blumberg, Jane. **Mary Shelley's Early Novels**. Iowa City: University of Iowa Press, 1993. 257pp.

___ Bochm, Gudrun. "Mary W. Shelley, **Frankenstein, or the Modern Prometheus** (1818)," in: Heuermann, Harmut, ed. **Der Science Fiction Roman in der angloamerikanischen Literatur: Interpretationen**. Düsseldorf: Bagel, 1986. pp.15-30.

___ Brewer, William D. "Mary Shelley on Dreams," *Southern Humanities Review* 29(2): 105-126. Spring 1995.

___ Clemit, Pamela. **The Godwinian Novel: The Rational Fictions of Godwin, Brockden Brown, Mary Shelley**. Oxford: Clarendon Press, 1993. 254pp.

___ Conger, Syndy M. **Mary Wollstonecraft and the Language of Sensibility**. Rutherford, NJ: Fairleigh Dickinson University Press, 1994. 214pp.

___ Davidson, Jane P. "Golem--**Frankenstein**--Golem of Your Own," *Journal of the Fantastic in the Arts* 7(2/3): 228-243. 1995.

___ Dickerson, Vanessa D. "The Ghost of a Self: Female Identity in Mary Shelley's **Frankenstein**," *Journal of Popular Culture* 27(3): 79-91. Winter 1993.

___ Duyfhuizen, Bernard. "Periphrastic Naming in Mary Shelley's **Frankenstein**," *Studies in the Novel* 27(4): 477-492. Winter 1995.

___ Favret, Mary A. "A Woman Writes the Fiction of Science: The Body in **Frankenstein**," *Genders* No. 14: 50-65. Fall 1992.

___ Forry, Steven E. **Hideous Progenies: Dramatizations of Frankenstein From Mary Shelley to the Present**. Philadelphia: University of Pennsylvania Press, 1990. 311pp.

___ Hobbs, Colleen. "Reading the Symptoms: An Exploration of Repression and Hysteria in Mary Shelley's **Frankenstein**," *Studies in the Novel* 25(2): 152-169. Summer 1993.

___ Jacobs, Naomi. "The Frozen Landscape in Women's Utopian and Science Fiction," in: Donawerth, Jane L. and Kolmerten, Carol A., eds. **Utopian and Science Fiction by Women: Worlds of Difference**. Syracuse, NY: Syracuse University Press, 1994. pp.190-202.

___ Ketterer, David. "The Corrected **Frankenstein**: Twelve Preferred Readings in the Last Draft," *English Language Notes* 33(1): 23-34. September 1995.

___ Ketterer, David. "**Frankenstein**: The Source of a Name," *Science Fiction Studies* 22(3): 455-456. November 1995

___ Lamb, John B. "Mary Shelley's **Frankenstein** and Milton's Monstrous Myth," *Nineteenth Century Literature* 47(3): [7pp.] 1995. (Cited from the electronic edition, NCL-E, 47(3), 1995. [http: //sunsite. berkeley. edu:8080/ scan/ncle.473/ articles/ lamb.art473.html]).

___ Lehman, Steven. "The Motherless Child in Science Fiction: **Frankenstein** and Moreau," *Science Fiction Studies* 19(1): 49-58. March 1992.

___ London, Bette. "Mary Shelley, **Frankenstein**, and the Spectacle of Masculinity," *PMLA* 108(2): 253-267. March 1993.

___ Manson, Michael. "Heroes and Hideousness: **Frankenstein** and Failed Unity," by Michael Manson and Robert S. Stewart. *Substance* No. 71/72: 228-242. 1993.

SHELLEY, MARY (continued)

___ Nellist, Brian. "Imagining the Future: Predictive Fiction in the Nineteenth Century," in: Seed, David, ed. **Anticipations: Essays on Early Science Fiction and Its Precursors**. Liverpool: Liverpool University Press, 1995. pp.111-136.

___ Palmer, Lorraine. "Tracking the Monster: **Frankenstein** in an Academic Library," *RSF: Reference Services Review* 20(3): 25-31. Fall 1992.

___ Parrinder, Patrick. "From Mary Shelley to **The War of the Worlds**: The Thames Valley Catastrophe," in: Seed, David, ed. **Anticipations: Essays on Early Science Fiction and Its Precursors**. Liverpool: Liverpool University Press, 1995. pp.58-74.

___ Purinton, Marjean D. "Ideological Revision: Cross-Gender Characterization in Mary Shelley's **Frankenstein**," *CEA Critic* 56(1): 53-64. Fall 1993.

___ Putzier, Mary G. **Mary Wollstonecraft Shelley and the Creation of Science Fiction**. Master's Thesis, Eastern Washington University, 1995. 113pp.

___ Roberts, Marie M. "The Male Scientist, Man-Midwife, and Female Monster: Appropriation and Transmutation in **Frankenstein**," in: Benjamin, Marina, ed. **A Question of Identity: Women, Science, and Literature**. New Brunswick, NJ: Rutgers University Press, 1993. pp.59-73.

___ Rowen, Norma. "The Making of Frankenstein's Monster: Post-Golem, Pre-Robot," in: Ruddick, Nicholas, ed. **State of the Fantastic**. Westport, CT: Greenwood, 1992. pp.169-177.

___ Schmitt, Ronald E. **The Reclamation of the Future Dream: Dreams in British Science Fiction (Mary Shelley, H. G. Wells, George Orwell, Michael Moorcock)**. Ph.D. Dissertation, University of Rhode Island, 1995. 182pp. (DAI-A 56/09, p. 3598. March 1996.)

___ Stableford, Brian. "**Frankenstein** and the Origins of Science Fiction," in: Seed, David, ed. **Anticipations: Essays on Early Science Fiction and Its Precursors**. Liverpool: Liverpool University Press, 1995. pp.46-57.

___ Stableford, Brian. "Yesterday's Bestsellers, 17: Mary Shelley's **Frankenstein**," *Interzone* No. 78: 56-58, 68. December 1993.

___ Ursini, James. **More Things Than Are Dreamt Of: Masterpieces of Supernatural Horror, From Mary Shelley to Stephen King, in Literature and Film**, by James Ursini and Alain Silver. New York: Limelight, 1994. 226pp.

___ Waldo, Mark L. "Mary Shelley's Machines in the Garden: Victor Frankenstein and His Monster," in: Wolf, Milton T. and Mallett, Daryl F., eds. **Imaginative Futures: Proceedings of the 1993 Science Fiction Research Association Conference**. San Bernardino, CA: Jacob's Ladder Books, 1995. pp.179-190.

___ Weinstone, Ann. "Resisting Monsters: Notes on **Solaris**," *Science Fiction Studies* 21(2): 173-190. July 1994.

___ Wolstenholme, Susan. **Gothic (Re) Visions: Writing Women as Readers**. Albany: State University of New York Press, 1993. 201pp.

SHEPARD, LUCIUS

___ "12th Annual *S. F. Chronicle* Reader Awards," *Science Fiction Chronicle* 14(12): 4. September 1993.

___ "1993 Hugo Awards," *Science Fiction Chronicle* 15(1): 4. October 1993.

___ "Lucius Shepard: The Cockroach Syndrome," *Locus* 29(6): 4, 71. December 1992.

___ Blackmore, Tim. "Talking the Talk, Walking the Walk: The Role of Discourse in Joe Haldeman's 'The Monster' and Lucius Shepard's 'Delta Sly Honey'," *Journal of the Fantastic in the Arts* 6(2/3): 191-202. 1994.

SHERLOCK HOLMES AND THE INCIDENT AT VICTORIA FALLS (MOTION PICTURE)

___ Scapperotti, Dan. "**Sherlock Holmes and the Incident at Victoria Falls** (Review)," *Cinefantastique* 23(1): 60. August 1992.

SHERMAN, DELIA

___ "1994 Mythopoeic Fantasy Awards," *Locus* 33(4): 72. October 1994.

___ "Delia Sherman: The Other Aliens," *Locus* 33(4): 4-5, 77-78. October 1994.

___ "Mythopoeic Awards, 1994," *Science Fiction Chronicle* 16(1): 8. October 1994.

___ Attebery, Brian. "Gender, Fantasy, and the Authority of Tradition," *Journal of the Fantastic in the Arts* 7(1): 51-60. 1996.

SHERRY, J. FILMORE

___ Stone, Graham. "Notes on Australian Science Fiction: **Out of the Silence**, by Erle Cox and J. Filmore Sherry," *Science Fiction News* (Australia) No. 66: 2-8. September 1982.

SHETTERLY, WILL

___ Ringel, Faye. "The Scribblies: A Shared World," *Extrapolation* 35(3): 201-210. Fall 1994.

SHIBANO, TAKUMI

___ "Other Awards," *Science Fiction Chronicle* 15(1): 4. October 1993.

SHIEL, MATTHEW PHIPPS

___ "**Man Abroad** Chapter IX 'Henrygeorgia'," in: **Shiel in Diverse Hands: A Collection of Essays**. Cleveland, OH: Reynolds Morse Foundation, 1983. pp.485-490.

___ **Shiel in Diverse Hands: A Collection of Essays**. Cleveland, OH: Reynolds Morse Foundation, 1983. 491pp.

___ Arrington, Robert. "The Illustrated Shiel," in: **Shiel in Diverse Hands: A Collection of Essays**. Cleveland, OH: Reynolds Morse Foundation, 1983. pp.171-174.

___ Barrett, Mike. "A Primate of Pure Prose (With: The Short Stories of M. P. Shiel: A Chronological Listing)," in: **Shiel in Diverse Hands: A Collection of Essays**. Cleveland, OH: Reynolds Morse Foundation, 1983. pp.133-143.

___ Billings, Harold. "The Shape of Shiel (Notes on the Early Years)," in: **Shiel in Diverse Hands: A Collection of Essays**. Cleveland, OH: Reynolds Morse Foundation, 1983. pp.77-108.

___ Bleiler, Everett F. "M. P. Shiel 1865-1947," in: **Shiel in Diverse Hands: A Collection of Essays**. Cleveland, OH: Reynolds Morse Foundation, 1983. pp.123-131.

___ Bleiler, Everett F. "M. P. Shiel: Humorist?," in: **Shiel in Diverse Hands: A Collection of Essays**. Cleveland, OH: Reynolds Morse Foundation, 1983. pp.132.

___ Bloom, Harold. "M. P. Shiel," in: Bloom, Harold, ed. **Modern Fantasy Writers**. New York: Chelsea House, 1995. pp.137-150.

___ Derleth, August. "Two Notes on Shiel's Style," in: **Shiel in Diverse Hands: A Collection of Essays**. Cleveland, OH: Reynolds Morse Foundation, 1983. pp.145-146.

___ Drake, David A. "**The New King** (Shiel's Final Novel): An Appreciation," in: **Shiel in Diverse Hands: A Collection of Essays**. Cleveland, OH: Reynolds Morse Foundation, 1983. pp.329-330.

___ Eng, Steve. "John Gawsworth...on M. P. Shiel: A Selection," in: **Shiel in Diverse Hands: A Collection of Essays**. Cleveland, OH: Reynolds Morse Foundation, 1983. pp.395-405.

___ Eng, Steve. "M. P. Shiel and Arthur Machen," in: **Shiel in Diverse Hands: A Collection of Essays**. Cleveland, OH: Reynolds Morse Foundation, 1983. pp.233-247.

___ Eng, Steve. "M. P. Shiel and Secret Societies," in: **Shiel in Diverse Hands: A Collection of Essays**. Cleveland, OH: Reynolds Morse Foundation, 1983. pp.223-232.

___ Ferguson, Malcolm. "On Digging Shiel," in: **Shiel in Diverse Hands: A Collection of Essays**. Cleveland, OH: Reynolds Morse Foundation, 1983. pp.69-74.

___ Foster, Stephen W. "Prince Zaleski and Count Stenbock," in: **Shiel in Diverse Hands: A Collection of Essays**. Cleveland, OH: Reynolds Morse Foundation, 1983. pp.175-177.

___ Goldwater, Walter. "Shiel, Van Vechten and the Question of Color," in: **Shiel in Diverse Hands: A Collection of Essays**. Cleveland, OH: Reynolds Morse Foundation, 1983. pp.75-76.

___ Hartwell, David G. "Introduction to **The Purple Cloud**," in: **Shiel in Diverse Hands: A Collection of Essays**. Cleveland, OH: Reynolds Morse Foundation, 1983. pp.115-122.

___ Hay, George. "Shiel Versus the Renegade Romantic," in: **Shiel in Diverse Hands: A Collection of Essays**. Cleveland, OH: Reynolds Morse Foundation, 1983. pp.109-113.

___ Herron, Don. "The Mysteries of M. P. Shiel," in: **Shiel in Diverse Hands: A Collection of Essays**. Cleveland, OH: Reynolds Morse Foundation, 1983. pp.179-194.

___ Home, W. Scott. "The Rose Beyond the Thunders and the Whirlpools," in: **Shiel in Diverse Hands: A Collection of Essays**. Cleveland, OH: Reynolds Morse Foundation, 1983. pp.343-355.

___ Indick, Ben P. "Villain, Vaudevillian and Saint," in: **Shiel in Diverse Hands: A Collection of Essays**. Cleveland, OH: Reynolds Morse Foundation, 1983. pp.357-368.

SHIEL, MATTHEW PHIPPS (continued)

___ Locke, George. "The Book Collector and M. P. Shiel," in: **Shiel in Diverse Hands: A Collection of Essays**. Cleveland, OH: Reynolds Morse Foundation, 1983. pp.159-170.

___ Lofts, W. O. G. "My Search for Elusive Shiel Material (With: Magazines Containing Works of M. P. Shiel)," in: **Shiel in Diverse Hands: A Collection of Essays**. Cleveland, OH: Reynolds Morse Foundation, 1983. pp.147-157.

___ Morse, A. Reynolds. "M. P. Shiel the Author--Still Unknown," in: **Shiel in Diverse Hands: A Collection of Essays**. Cleveland, OH: Reynolds Morse Foundation, 1983. pp.331-342.

___ Moskowitz, Sam. "The Dark Plots of One Shiel," in: **Shiel in Diverse Hands: A Collection of Essays**. Cleveland, OH: Reynolds Morse Foundation, 1983. pp.57-68.

___ Shanks, Edward. "**The Purple Cloud** and Its Author (1929)," in: **Shiel in Diverse Hands: A Collection of Essays**. Cleveland, OH: Reynolds Morse Foundation, 1983. pp.23-29.

___ Shiel, M. P. "On Printing," in: **Shiel in Diverse Hands: A Collection of Essays**. Cleveland, OH: Reynolds Morse Foundation, 1983. pp.406.

___ Shiel, M. P. "On Reading and Writing (Revised Version, 1950)," in: **Shiel in Diverse Hands: A Collection of Essays**. Cleveland, OH: Reynolds Morse Foundation, 1983. pp.449-483.

___ Shiel, M. P. "On Reading (First Version, 1909)," in: **Shiel in Diverse Hands: A Collection of Essays**. Cleveland, OH: Reynolds Morse Foundation, 1983. pp.406-447.

___ Spencer, Paul. "Shiel Versus Shiel," in: **Shiel in Diverse Hands: A Collection of Essays**. Cleveland, OH: Reynolds Morse Foundation, 1983. pp.31-55.

___ Squires, John D. "Some Contemporary Themes in Shiel's Early Novels: Steel Afloat; M. P. Shiel on Naval Warfare," in: **Shiel in Diverse Hands: A Collection of Essays**. Cleveland, OH: Reynolds Morse Foundation, 1983. pp.303-328.

___ Squires, John D. "Some Contemporary Themes in Shiel's Early Novels: The Dragon's Tale; M. P. Shiel on the Emergence of Modern China," in: **Shiel in Diverse Hands: A Collection of Essays**. Cleveland, OH: Reynolds Morse Foundation, 1983. pp.249-301.

___ Stableford, Brian. **Algebraic Fantasies and Realistic Romances: More Masters of Science Fiction**. San Bernardino, CA: Borgo Press, 1995 128pp.

___ Stableford, Brian. "The Politics of Evolution," in: **Shiel in Diverse Hands: A Collection of Essays**. Cleveland, OH: Reynolds Morse Foundation, 1983. pp.369-394.

___ Tytheridge, Alan. "An Uncrowned Lord of Language (1924)," in: **Shiel in Diverse Hands: A Collection of Essays**. Cleveland, OH: Reynolds Morse Foundation, 1983. pp.1-14.

___ Van Vechten, Carl. "A Prolegomenon (Introduction to **The Lord of the Sea**, 1924)," in: **Shiel in Diverse Hands: A Collection of Essays**. Cleveland, OH: Reynolds Morse Foundation, 1983. pp.15-21.

___ Wade, James. "You Can't Get There From Here: 'How the Old Woman Got Home' and M. P. Shiel as Thinker," in: **Shiel in Diverse Hands: A Collection of Essays**. Cleveland, OH: Reynolds Morse Foundation, 1983. pp.195-203.

___ Wilson, Colin. "Why Is Shiel Neglected?," in: **Shiel in Diverse Hands: A Collection of Essays**. Cleveland, OH: Reynolds Morse Foundation, 1983. pp.213-222.

___ Wynne-Tyson, Jon. "M. P. Shiel: Right Royal Fantasist," in: **Shiel in Diverse Hands: A Collection of Essays**. Cleveland, OH: Reynolds Morse Foundation, 1983. pp.208-212.

___ Wynne-Tyson, Jon. "A Reluctant Monarch," in: **Shiel in Diverse Hands: A Collection of Essays**. Cleveland, OH: Reynolds Morse Foundation, 1983. pp.205-207.

SHIMERMAN, ARMIN

___ Altman, Mark A. "*Star Trek: Deep Space Nine*: Quark," *Cinefantastique* 24(3/4): 90. October 1993.

___ Snyder, Sharon. "Another Fine Ferengi," by Sharon Snyder and Marc Shapiro. *Starlog* No. 190: 36-39. May 1993.

SHINER, LEWIS

___ "1994 World Fantasy Awards," *Locus* 33(6): 7, 49. December 1994.

___ "World Fantasy Awards," *Science Fiction Chronicle* 16(2): 4. November/December 1994.

___ Donahoo, Robert. "Lewis Shiner and the 'Good' Anarchist," by Robert Donahoo and Chuck Etheridge. in: Slusser, George E. and Shippey, Tom, eds. **Fiction 2000: Cyberpunk and the Future of Narrative**. Athens: University of Georgia Press, 1992. pp.183-190.

SHINER, LEWIS (continued)
___ McCaffery, Larry. "Skating Across Cyberpunk's Brave New Worlds: An Interview with Lewis Shiner," *Critique* 33(3): 177-196. Spring 1992.
___ McQuiddy, A. P. "Eyeball Kicks, Prigogine's Theory and Re-Thinking the World: An Interview With Bruce Sterling and Lewis Shiner," *Texas SF Inquirer* No. 19: 5-26. December 1986.

SHINING (MOTION PICTURE)
___ Keeler, Greg. "**The Shining**: Ted Kramer Has a Nightmare," *Journal of Popular Film and Television* 8(4): 2-8. 1981.
___ Macklin, F. Anthony. "Understanding Kubrick: **The Shining**," *Journal of Popular Film and Television* 9(2): 93-95. 1981.
___ Manchel, Frank. "What About Jack? Another Perspective on Family Relationships in Stanley Kubrick's **The Shining**," *Literature/Film Quarterly* 23(1): 68-78. 1995.
___ Titterington, P. L. "Kubrick and **The Shining**," *Sight and Sound* 50(2): 117-121. Spring 1981.

SHIPPEY, TOM
___ "Tom Shippey: A Man of Many Parts," *Locus* 33(1): 5, 81-82. July 1994.

SHORT CIRCUIT 2 (MOTION PICTURE)
___ "**Short Circuit 2** (Review)," *Variety* p. 10. July 6, 1988.

SHORT CIRCUIT (MOTION PICTURE)
___ Gusterson, Hugh. "**Short Circuit**: Watching Television With a Nuclear-Weapons Scientist," in: Gray, Chris H., ed. **The Cyborg Handbook**. New York: Routledge, 1995. pp.107-117.

SHORT FORM (MAGAZINE)
___ "Final *Short Form* in Sight," *Science Fiction Chronicle* 13(6): 6. March 1992.

SHOWDOWN (MOTION PICTURE)
___ SEE: SCANNERS: THE SHOWDOWN (MOTION PICTURE).

SHRUNKEN HEADS (MOTION PICTURE)
___ Harris, Judith P. "**Shrunken Heads** (Review)," *Cinefantastique* 26(3): 60. April 1995.

SHUSTER, JOE
___ "Shuster, Joe (Obituary)," *Locus* 29(3): 77-78. September 1992.
___ "Shuster, Joe (Obituary)," *Science Fiction Chronicle* 14(1): 12. October 1992.
___ Washington, Julie. "*Superman* Creator Joe Schuster Dies," *Lan's Lantern* No. 41: 3. July 1993.

SHUTAN, JAN
___ Jankiewicz, Pat. "Star of Zetar," *Starlog* No. 199: 58-60. February 1994.

SHWARTZ, SUSAN
___ "12th Annual *S. F. Chronicle* Reader Awards," *Science Fiction Chronicle* 14(12): 4. September 1993.
___ King, T. Jackson. "SFC Interview: Susan Shwartz," *Science Fiction Chronicle* 16(7): 5, 30-33. June/July 1995.

SIDNEY, KATHLEEN
___ Palwick, Susan. "Never Going Home: Failed Fantasy Logic in Kathleen Sidney's **Michael and the Magic Man** and Robert Irwin's **The Limits of Vision**," *New York Review of Science Fiction* No. 11: 15-17. July 1989.

SIEGEL, DON
___ "Siegel, Don, 1912-1991 (Obituary)," *Starlog* No. 174: 23. January 1992.

SIGMUND, RUDY
___ Fury, David. "Burroughs Spotlight on Rudy Sigmund," *Burroughs Bulletin* NS. No. 21: 24-26. January 1995.

SILBERSACK, JOHN
___ "John Silbersack Heading Warner's Questar Line," *Science Fiction Chronicle* 14(1): 4-5. October 1992.
___ "Questar's John Silbersack Leaves to Head HarperCollins SF and Fantasy Imprint," *Science Fiction Chronicle* 14(10): 4. July 1993.

SILBERSACK, JOHN (continued)
___ "Silbersack New Warner Editor," *Locus* 29(3): 6. September 1992.
___ "Silbersack to Start New SF Line at HarperCollins; Mitchell Moves to Warner; Bantam Promotes From Within," *Locus* 31(2): 6, 61. August 1993.

SILENCE OF THE LAMBS (MOTION PICTURE)
___ "1992 Saturn Awards," *Locus* 28(6): 7. June 1992.
___ "Saturn Awards, 1992," *Science Fiction Chronicle* 13(9): 10. June 1992.
___ Doherty, Thomas. "**Silence of the Lambs**: Hannibal Lector's Horror Pedigree," *Cinefantastique* 22(4): 36-37. February 1992.
___ Garrett, Greg. "Objecting to Objectification: Re-viewing the Feminine in **The Silence of the Lambs**," *Journal of Popular Culture* 27(4): 1-12. Spring 1994.
___ Gire, Dann. "**Silence of the Lambs**: Anthony Hopkins on Hannibal Lecter," *Cinefantastique* 23(2/3): 108-109. October 1992.
___ Lyman, David. "**Silence of the Lambs** Wins Chicago Awards," *Cincinnati (OH) Post*. March 16, 1992. in: *NewsBank. Film and Television*. 36:C2. 1992.
___ Persons, Dan. "**Silence of the Lambs**: Confessions of a 'Moth Wrangler'," *Cinefantastique* 22(4): 28-29. February 1992.
___ Persons, Dan. "**Silence of the Lambs**: Jonathan Demme on Horror," *Cinefantastique* 22(4): 39. February 1992.
___ Persons, Dan. "**Silence of the Lambs**: Makeup Effects Behind-the-Scenes," *Cinefantastique* 22(4): 32-34. February 1992.
___ Persons, Dan. "**Silence of the Lambs**: Perfecting Performance," *Cinefantastique* 22(4): 18. February 1992.
___ Persons, Dan. "**Silence of the Lambs**: Production Design, Visualizing the Nightmare," *Cinefantastique* 22(4): 24-26. February 1992.
___ Persons, Dan. "**Silence of the Lambs**: Scripting the Bestseller," *Cinefantastique* 22(4): 31. February 1992.
___ Persons, Dan. "**Silence of the Lambs**: The Corman Connection," *Cinefantastique* 22(4): 20-22. February 1992.
___ Persons, Dan. "**Silence of the Lambs**," *Cinefantastique* 22(4): 16-23, 27, 30, 35-38. February 1992.
___ Persons, Dan. "**Silence of the Lambs**," *Cinefantastique* 23(2/3): 106-111. October 1992.
___ Sundelson, David. "The Dream Therapist and Other Dangers: Jonathan Demme's **The Silence of the Lambs**," *Journal of Popular Film and Television* 21(1): 12-18. Spring 1993.
___ Tharp, Julie. "The Transvestite as Monster: Gender Horror in **The Silence of the Lambs** and **Psycho**," *Journal of Popular Film and Television* 19(3): 106-113. 1991.
___ Willman, David. "Lambs Stew: Battle Over 'Silence' Sequel May Change Hollywood Deal Making," *Los Angeles (CA) Times*. May 29, 1992. in: *NewsBank. Film and Television*. 58:E8-E9. 1992.

SILENT FILMS
___ Kinnard, Roy. **Horror in the Silent Films: A Filmography, 1896-1929**. Jefferson, NC: McFarland, 1995. 256pp.

SILENT NIGHT, DEADLY NIGHT: THE TOYMAKER (MOTION PICTURE)
___ Wilt, David. "**Silent Night, Deadly Night: The Toymaker**," *Cinefantastique* 23(1): 60. August 1992.

SILVERBERG, HELEN
___ "Silverberg, Helen (Obituary)," *Locus* 29(1): 67. July 1992.

SILVERBERG, ROBERT
___ "Moving Majipoor," *Locus* 33(3): 8. September 1994.
___ "Robert Silverberg's 'Majipoor' Series Returning to Its First Publisher," *Science Fiction Chronicle* 15(9): 5. August 1994.
___ "Silverberg, Helen (Obituary)," *Locus* 29(1): 67. July 1992.
___ Chapman, Edgar L. "An Ironic Deflation of the Superman Myth: Literary Influence and Science Fiction Tradition in **Dying Inside**," in: Elkins, Charles L. and Greenberg, Martin H., eds. **Robert Silverberg's Many Trapdoors: Critical Essays on His Science Fiction**. Westport, CT: Greenwood, 1992. pp.39-57.
___ Clareson, Thomas D. "Introduction," in: Elkins, Charles L. and Greenberg, Martin H., eds. **Robert Silverberg's Many Trapdoors: Critical Essays on His Science Fiction**. Westport, CT: Greenwood, 1992. pp.1-13.
___ Dean, John. "The Sick Hero Reborn: Two Versions of the Philoctetes Myth," *Comparative Literature Studies* 17(3): 334-340. September 1980.

SILVERBERG, ROBERT (continued)

___ Dietz, Frank. "Robert Silverberg's **The World Inside** as an Ambiguous Dystopia," in: Elkins, Charles L. and Greenberg, Martin H., eds. **Robert Silverberg's Many Trapdoors: Critical Essays on His Science Fiction**. Westport, CT: Greenwood, 1992. pp.95-105.

___ Dudley, Joseph M. "Transformational SF Religions: Philip Jose Farmer's **Night of Light** and Robert Silverberg's **Downward to the Earth**," *Extrapolation* 35(4): 342-351. Winter 1994.

___ Elkins, Charles L., ed. **Robert Silverberg's Many Trapdoors: Critical Essays on His Science Fiction**, ed. by Charles L. Elkins and Martin H. Greenberg. Westport, CT: Greenwood, 1992. 154pp.

___ Flodstrom, John H. "Personal Identity in the Majipoor Trilogy, **To Live Again**, and **Downward to Earth**," in: Elkins, Charles L. and Greenberg, Martin H., eds. **Robert Silverberg's Many Trapdoors: Critical Essays on His Science Fiction**. Westport, CT: Greenwood, 1992. pp.73-94.

___ Florence, Bill. "Robert Silverberg's Alien," *Starlog* No. 219: 34-35. October 1995.

___ Francavilla, Joseph. "Repetition With Reversal: Robert Silverberg's Ironic Twist Endings," in: Elkins, Charles L. and Greenberg, Martin H., eds. **Robert Silverberg's Many Trapdoors: Critical Essays on His Science Fiction**. Westport, CT: Greenwood, 1992. pp.59-72.

___ Killheffer, Robert K. J. "Striking a Balance: Robert Silverberg's **Lord of Darkness, Dying Inside** and Others," *New York Review of Science Fiction* No. 12: 1, 12-14. August 1989.

___ Latham, Robert A. "Some Thoughts on Modernism and Science Fiction (Suggested by Robert Silverberg's **Downward to the Earth**)," in: Morse, Donald E., ed. **The Celebration of the Fantastic**. Westport, CT: Greenwood, 1992. pp.49-60.

___ Letson, Russell. "Robert Silverberg: An Overview," in: Elkins, Charles L. and Greenberg, Martin H., eds. **Robert Silverberg's Many Trapdoors: Critical Essays on His Science Fiction**. Westport, CT: Greenwood, 1992. pp.15-38.

___ Manlove, C. N. "On Silverberg's **Tom O'Bedlam**," in: Elkins, Charles L. and Greenberg, Martin H., eds. **Robert Silverberg's Many Trapdoors: Critical Essays on His Science Fiction**. Westport, CT: Greenwood, 1992. pp.121-139.

___ Nicholls, Stan. "Robert Silverberg Keeps Coming Back," in: Nicholls, Stan. **Wordsmiths of Wonder: Fifty Interviews with Writers of the Fantastic**. London: Orbit, 1993. pp.202-210.

___ Reilly, Robert. "Silverberg's Ambiguous Transcendence," in: Elkins, Charles L. and Greenberg, Martin H., eds. **Robert Silverberg's Many Trapdoors: Critical Essays on His Science Fiction**. Westport, CT: Greenwood, 1992. pp.107-119.

___ Silverberg, Robert. "Introduction," in: Silverberg, Robert. **The Collected Stories of Robert Silverberg**. New York: Bantam, 1992. pp.xi-xviii.

___ Silverberg, Robert. "The Silverberg Papers: The Time of the Great Freeze," *Science Fiction Chronicle* 14(4): 28-29. January 1993.

___ Silverberg, Robert. "The Silverberg Papers: The Time of the Great Freeze," *Science Fiction Chronicle* 14(5): 28-29. February 1993.

___ Stableford, Brian. "The Metamorphosis of Robert Silverberg," in: Stableford, Brian. **Outside the Human Aquarium: Masters of Science Fiction**. San Bernardino, CA: Borgo, 1995. pp.37-48.

SILVERSTEIN, JANNA

___ "Wizards Hire Silverstein for New Imprint," *Locus* 33(4): 8, 76. October 1994.

SIMAK, CLIFFORD D.

___ "Simak, Clifford D(onald), 1904-1988," in: Lesniak, James G., ed. **Contemporary Authors**. Detroit: Gale Research, 1992. New Revision Series, Vol. 35, pp.423-425.

___ Becker, Muriel R. "Clifford D. Simak," in: Bruccoli, Matthew J., ed. **Facts on File Bibliography of American Fiction 1919-1988**. New York: Facts on File, 1991. pp.457-458.

SIMMONS, DAN

___ "1992 *Locus* Awards," *Locus* 28(2): 1, 42-45. August 1992.

___ "1994 *Locus* Awards," *Locus* 33(2): 7. August 1994.

___ "1995 *Locus* Awards Winners," *Locus* 35(2): 7, 34-37. August 1995.

___ "Bram Stoker Awards, 1993," *Science Fiction Chronicle* 14(10): 4. July 1993.

___ "BSFA Awards," *Locus* 28(6): 7. June 1992.

___ "Dan Simmons: Hangin' Around the Ruins...," *Locus* 32(6): 5, 77-78. June 1994.

SIMMONS, DAN (continued)

___ "Dan Simmons: Mining the Classics for Inspiration," *Hailing Frequencies* (Waldenbooks) No. 3: 4, 7, 10. 1992.

___ "Dan Simmons, Molly Brown Win BSFA Awards," *Science Fiction Chronicle* 13(8): 4. May 1992.

___ "The Hugos (Or, the Empire Strikes Back)," *Science Fiction Chronicle* 17(2): 55-56. December 1995/January 1996.

___ "HWA Stoker Awards Winners," *Locus* 33(1): 7. July 1994.

___ "Sheffield, Simmons Win Campbell, Sturgeon Awards," *Locus* 31(3): 6, 83. September 1993.

___ "Sheffield, Simmons, Win Campbell, Sturgeon Awards," *Science Fiction Chronicle* 14(11): 4. August 1993.

___ "World Fantasy Awards," *Science Fiction Chronicle* 15(2): 4. November/December 1993.

___ Currey, Lloyd W. "Work in Progress: Dan Simmons," *New York Review of Science Fiction* No. 41: 23. January 1992.

___ Nicholls, Stan. "Chewing the Raccoon: Dan Simmons Interviewed," *Interzone* No. 59: 24-26. May 1992.

___ Nicholls, Stan. "Dan Simmons Chews on the Raccoon," in: Nicholls, Stan. **Wordsmiths of Wonder: Fifty Interviews with Writers of the Fantastic**. London: Orbit, 1993. pp.143-154.

SIMMONS, JACK

___ "Bram Stoker Awards," *Science Fiction Chronicle* 15(8): 5. June 1994.

SIMON, CLAUDE

___ Troiano, Maureen D. **New Physics and the Modern French Novel**. New York: Peter Lang, 1995. 276pp.

SIMON, SHERIDAN A.

___ "Simon, Sheridan A. (Obituary)," *Locus* 32(6): 72. June 1994.

SIMS, PAT

___ "Pat and Roger Sims Win DUFF," *Science Fiction Chronicle* 16(6): 42. May 1995.

SIMS, ROGER

___ "Pat and Roger Sims Win DUFF," *Science Fiction Chronicle* 16(6): 42. May 1995.

SINGLE WHITE FEMALE (MOTION PICTURE)

___ Doherty, Thomas. "**Single White Female** (Review)," *Cinefantastique* 23(4): 61. December 1992.

SIR GAWAIN AND THE GREEN KNIGHT

___ Kline, Barbara. "Duality, Reality and Magic in **Sir Gawain and the Green Knight**," in: Sanders, Joe, ed. **Functions of the Fantastic**. Westport, CT: Greenwood, 1995. pp.107-114.

SIRIUS VISIONS (MAGAZINE)

___ "*Sirius Visions* Folds," *Science Fiction Chronicle* 17(1): 6. October/November 1995

___ "*Sirius Visions* Is New Magazine," *Science Fiction Chronicle* 15(3): 6-7. January 1994.

SIRTIS, MARINA

___ Altman, Mark A. "**Star Trek: The Next Generation**: Marina Sirtis, Betazoid Beauty," *Cinefantastique* 24(3/4): 64-66. October 1993.

___ Kutzera, Dale. "**Star Trek: The Next Generation**: Troi's Marina Sirtis," *Cinefantastique* 25(6)/26(1): 88-89. December 1994.

___ Spelling, Ian. "Beloved Betazoid," *Starlog* No. 196: 52-57, 80. November 1993.

SISTERHOOD (MOTION PICTURE)

___ "**Sisterhood** (Review)," *Variety* p. 16. July 13, 1988.

SITGES INTERNATIONAL FANTASY AND HORROR FESTIVAL, 1981

___ "Sitges Sci-Fi Fest Prizes for Best," *Variety* p. 7, 48. October 21, 1981.

SITGES INTERNATIONAL FANTASY AND HORROR FESTIVAL, 1982

___ "Sitges Horror Fest Targets Major Pix; Local Subsidy Spells Upgrade," *Variety* p. 15. August 18, 1982.

___ "Sitges Terrorfest Set for Oct. 2 Features 'Parasite'," *Variety* p. 22, 25. September 22, 1982.

SITGES INTERNATIONAL FANTASY AND HORROR FESTIVAL, 1982 (continued)
___ "Transitional Sitges Terror Fest Wraps, See Some Improvement," *Variety* p. 7. October 27, 1982.

SITGES INTERNATIONAL FANTASY AND HORROR FESTIVAL, 1983
___ "Local Gov't Aid Boosts Status of Spain's Sitges Fest," *Variety* p. 6, 31. September 14, 1983.
___ "Sitges Festival Up a Bit as Luis Goas Takes over Control," *Variety* p. 7, 34. October 12, 1983.

SITGES INTERNATIONAL FANTASY AND HORROR FESTIVAL, 1984
___ Besas, Peter. "Sitges Fest Stays on Course for Quality Pic; Financial Woes Felt," *Variety* p. 4, 18. October 17, 1984.

SITGES INTERNATIONAL FANTASY AND HORROR FESTIVAL, 1985
___ "Last-Minute Changes in Sitges Fest Sked," *Variety* p.402. October 16, 1985.
___ "Sitges Fantasy Fest Sets Bulk of Fare," *Variety* p.5, 24. September 25, 1985.

SITGES INTERNATIONAL FANTASY AND HORROR FESTIVAL, 1986
___ "Strong Celeb Turnout for Sitges; More Trade Types Show, Too," *Variety* p. 7, 502. October 22, 1986.
___ Besas, Peter. "Full Roster of New Pics; Retros Set for Sitges Fantasy Festival," *Variety* p. 7. September 24, 1986.

SITGES INTERNATIONAL FANTASY AND HORROR FESTIVAL, 1994
___ Giuffrida, Sergiio. "Sitges: al supermarket dell'orrore quotidiano [Sitges: At the Daily Horror Supermarket, the 27th International Science Fiction Film Festival]," by Sergiio Giuffrida and Luisella Angiari. *Cineforum* 34(11): 7-9. 1994.

SIX MILLION DOLLAR MAN (TV)
___ Spelling, Ian. "Bionic Breakdown," *Starlog* No. 211: 76-79. February 1995.

SKAL, DAVID J.
___ Foster, Thomas. "Meat Puppets or Robopaths? Cyberpunk and the Question of Embodiment," *Genders* No. 18: 11-31. Winter 1993.

SKEETER (MOTION PICTURE)
___ Harris, Judith P. "*Skeeter* (Review)," *Cinefantastique* 25(5): 60. October 1994.

SKINNER (MOTION PICTURE)
___ Salter, David I. "*Skinner*," *Cinefantastique* 25(2): 52-53. April 1994.

SKINNER, B. F.
___ Marion, David E. "Using Fiction to Expose a Fundamental Theme in American Public Policy," *Teaching Political Science* 15(2): 44-49. Winter 1988.
___ Schaller, Hans-Wolfgang. "B. F. Skinner: **Walden Two** (1948)," in: Heuermann, Hartmut and Lange, Bernd-Peter, eds. **Die Utopie in der angloamerikanischen Literatur: Interpretationen**. Düsseldorf: Bagel, 1984. pp.219-234.
___ Wolfe, Peter. "**Walden Two** Twenty-Five Years Later: A Retrospective Look," *Studies in the Literary Imagination* 6(2): 11-26. Fall 1973.

SKINNER, MARGO
___ "Skinner, Margo (Obituary)," *Locus* 30(2): 68. February 1993.

SLADEK, JOHN
___ Stephens, Christopher P. **A Checklist of John Sladek**. Hastings-on-Hudson, NY: Ultramarine, 1992. 31pp. Revised ed.

SLATER, JOYCE
___ "Slater, Joyce (Obituary)," *Locus* 34(4): 62. April 1995.
___ "Slater, Joyce (Obituary)," *Science Fiction Chronicle* 16(5): 18. March/April 1995.

SLAUGHTER, TOD
___ Hanke, Ken. "Tod Slaughter: Demon Barber of Great Britain," *Filmfax* No. 45: 31-35, 98. June/July 1994.

SLAUGHTERHOUSE FIVE (MOTION PICTURE)
___ "Tackle 3-Level Tale; Geller Accepts Writing Challenge of 'Slaughterhouse'," *Variety* p. 5. May 13, 1970.
___ Mayer, Peter C. "Film, Ontology and the Structure of a Novel," *Film Literature Quarterly* 8(3): 204-208. 1980.

SLAUGHTERHOUSE ROCK (MOTION PICTURE)
___ "**Slaughterhouse Rock** (Review)," *Variety* p. 11, 22. March 9, 1988.

SLAVATORE, R. A.
___ Hall, John T. "Bestselling Fantasies," *Starlog* No. 209: 38-41, 68. December 1994.

SLAYTON, DEKE
___ "Forge to Publish Deke Slayton Memoirs," *Locus* 31(2): 7. August 1993.

SLEATOR, WILLIAM
___ Davis, James E. "Attracting Middle-School Readers With William Sleator's **Strange Attractors**," by James E. Davis and Alison Smalley. *College English* 55(2): 76-77. February 1993.
___ Davis, James E., ed. **Presenting William Sleator**, ed. by James E. Davis and Hazel K. Davis. New York: Twayne, 1992. 131pp.
___ Sleator, William. "From Interstellar Pigs to Spirit Houses," *ALAN Review* 19(3): 10-12, 15. Spring 1992.

SLEEPWALKERS (MOTION PICTURE)
___ Biodrowski, Steve. "**Sleepwalkers** (Review)," *Cinefantastique* 23(1): 61. August 1992.
___ Doherty, Thomas. "**Sleepwalkers** (Review)," *Cinefantastique* 23(2/3): 121. October 1992.
___ Kronke, David. "King's Latest Victim May Be the Viewer With This Dumb Plot (Review)," *Los Angeles (CA) Daily News*. April 11, 1992. in: *NewsBank. Film and Television*. 46:C7. 1992.
___ Murray, Steve. "**Sleepwalkers** Isn't Likely to Be King's Sleeper Hit (Review)," *Atlanta (GA) Journal*. April 13, 1992. in: *NewsBank. Film and Television*. 46:C9. 1992.
___ Sherman, Paul. "Stephen King's Latest Yarn, **Sleepwalkers**, Is a Yawner (Review)," *Boston (MA) Herald*. April 11, 1992. in: *NewsBank. Film and Television*. 46:C10. 1992.
___ Shulgasser, Barbara. "King's **Sleepwalkers** Falls Down (Review)," *San Francisco (CA) Examiner*. April 10, 1992. in: *NewsBank. Film and Television*. 46:C8. 1992.
___ Wood, Gary L. "Stephen King's **Sleepwalkers**," *Cinefantastique* 22(4): 6. February 1992.
___ Wood, Gary L. "Stephen King's **Sleepwalkers**," *Cinefantastique* 22(5): 20-21. April 1992.
___ Wood, Gary L. "Stephen King's **Sleepwalkers**," *Cinefantastique* 23(2/3): 120. October 1992.

SLEIGH, BARBARA
___ Stone, Graham. "Notes on Australian Science Fiction," *Science Fiction News* (Australia) No. 94: 2-11. January 1986.

SLESAR, HENRY
___ Simsa, Cyril. "The Short Fiction of Henry Slesar," *Foundation* No. 59: 78-87. Autumn 1993.

SLIDERS (TV)
___ "Winter Preview: **Sliders**," *TV Guide* 43(3): 18-19. January 21, 1995.
___ Bacal, Simon. "The Cosmic Slide," *Sci-Fi Entertainment* 2(1): 48-49. June 1995.
___ Harris, Judith P. "**Sliders** (Review)," *Cinefantastique* 26(6)/27(1): 123. October 1995.
___ Johnson, Kim H. "Parallel Excitement," *Starlog* No. 215: 32-35. June 1995.
___ Kenny, Glenn. "Sci-Fi/Fantasy: Earth 2, 3, 4...," *TV Guide* 43(10): 30. March 11, 1995.
___ Rochmond, Roy. "Smart-Alecky **Sliders** in No 'Quantum'," *Los Angeles (CA) Daily News*. March 22, 1995. in: *NewsBank. Film and Television*. 49:F8. 1995.
___ Sandler, Adam. "TV Reviews: **Sliders**," *Variety* 358(7): 30. March 20, 1995.

SLOAN, EDWARD VAN
___ Bowman, David. "They Called Him 'Herr Doktor': Edward Van Sloan," *Filmfax* No. 35: 63-66. October/November 1992.

SLONCZEWSKI, JOAN
___ **Breaking into Writing**. Ann Arbor, MI: Tucker Video, 1994. 1 videocassette, 98 minutes. (Panel Presentation at the 1994 Science Fiction Research Association Conference.)
___ Bogstad, Janice M. **Gender, Power and Reversal in Contemporary Anglo-American and French Feminist Science Fiction**. Ph.D. Dissertation, University of Wisconsin, Madison, 1992. 229pp. (DAI-A 54/02, p. 509. August 1993.)
___ Fitting, Peter. "Reconsiderations of the Separatist Paradigm in Recent Feminist Science Fiction," *Science Fiction Studies* 19(1): 32-48. March 1992.

SLOVAK REPUBLIC
___ Adamovic, Ivan. **Encyklopedie fantastického filmu**. Praha: Cinema, 1994. 224pp. [Not seen; OCLC record.]
___ Kordigel, Metka. "Nastansk in razvoj termina znanstvena fantastike na Slovenskem," *Slavisticna Revija* 41(4): 571-580. 1993. [Not seen.]
___ Rampas, Zdenek. **Kdo je Kdo v ceské a slovenské science fiction**, by Zdenek Rampas and Pavel Kosatik. Praha, CZ: Ceskoslovenského fandomu, 1994. 84pp. [Not seen.]
___ Srpon, Vlado. "Dr Gustav Maruricius Reuss: The First Slovak Literary Fantasist," *Foundation* No. 63: 81-84. Spring 1995.

SLUGS (MOTION PICTURE)
___ "*Slugs* (Review)," *Variety* p. 13. April 6, 1988.

SLUMBER PARTY MASSACRE 3 (MOTION PICTURE)
___ Wilt, David. "*Slumber Party Massacre 3* (Review)," *Cinefantastique* 23(1): 61. August 1992.

SMALL PRESSES
___ "Delany Novel to Launch Small Press," *Locus* 28(2): 6, 68. August 1992.
___ Cholfin, Bryan G. "No One Will Be Watching Us: The Complaints of a Small Press Publisher," *New York Review of Science Fiction* No. 57: 17-20. May 1993.
___ Lerner, Fred. "Small Is Beautiful: SF Small Press Publishing," *Voice of Youth Advocates* 14(1): 17-18. April 1991.
___ Morrish, Bob. "Small Press," *Twilight Zone* 8(2): 12-13, 92-93. June 1988.

SMITH, CLARK ASHTON
___ Bloom, Harold. "Clark Ashton Smith," in: Bloom, Harold, ed. **Modern Fantasy Writers**. New York: Chelsea House, 1995. pp.151-164.
___ Clore, Dan. "Loss and Recuperation: A Model for Reading Clark Ashton Smith's 'Xeethra'," *Studies in Weird Fiction* No. 13: 15-17. Summer 1993. [Not seen.]
___ Stableford, Brian. "Outside the Human Aquarium: The Fantastic Imagination of Clark Ashton Smith," in: Stableford, Brian. **Outside the Human Aquarium: Masters of Science Fiction**. San Bernardino, CA: Borgo, 1995. pp.76-98.

SMITH, CORDWAINER
___ "The Hugos (Or, the Empire Strikes Back)," *Science Fiction Chronicle* 17(2): 55-56. December 1995/January 1996.
___ Elms, Alan C. "Cordwainer Smith," in: Bruccoli, Matthew J., ed. **Facts on File Bibliography of American Fiction 1919-1988**. New York: Facts on File, 1991. pp.461-462.
___ Hellekson, Karen. "Never Never Underpeople: Cordwainer Smith's Humanity," *Extrapolation* 34(2): 123-130. Summer 1993.
___ Pierce, John J. "Introduction: Cordwainer Smith," in: Smith, Cordwainer. **The Rediscovery of Man: The Complete Short Science Fiction of Cordwainer Smith**, ed. by James A. Mann. Framingham, MA: NESFA Press, 1993. pp.viii-xv.
___ Weist, Andrew. **The Function of Folklore in the Science Fiction of Cordwainer Smith**. Master's Thesis, Bowling Green State University, 1992. 43pp.

SMITH, DAVID ALEXANDER
___ Smith, David A. "How I Write," *Quantum* No. 42: 15-16. Summer/Fall 1992.

SMITH, DICK
___ Crisafulli, Chuck. "The Way out World of Dick Smith," *Filmfax* No. 41: 58-64. October/November 1993.
___ Shay, Don. "Dick Smith: 50 Years in Makeup," *Cinefex* No. 62: 78-135. June 1995.

SMITH, DICK (continued)
___ Wiater, Stanley. "Smith, Dick," in: Wiater, Stanley. **Dark Visions: Conversations with the Masters of the Horror Film**. New York: Avon, 1992. pp.167-178.

SMITH, GORDON
___ Sandoval, Christine. "Gordon Smith: Seeking Silicone Solutions," *Cinefex* No. 64: 19-20, 128. December 1995.

SMITH, GUY N.
___ Nicholls, Stan. "Guy N. Smith Writes by Moonlight," in: Nicholls, Stan. **Wordsmiths of Wonder: Fifty Interviews with Writers of the Fantastic**. London: Orbit, 1993. pp.404-409.

SMITH, MICHAEL MARSHALL
___ "British Fantasy Awards, 1995," *Locus* 35(6): 9. December 1995.
___ "British Fantasy Awards, 1995," *Science Fiction Chronicle* 17(2): 5. December 1995/January 1996.

SMITH, WESLEY DEAN
___ "Dean Wesley Smith Fiction Editor for Programming Magazine," *Science Fiction Chronicle* 16(6): 6. May 1995.

SMITH, WILL
___ "Will Smith Inks $5 Million Movie Deal With Columbia," *Jet* 88(23): 46. October 16, 1995.

SMITHSON, ROBERT
___ Tsai, Eugenie M. **Reconstructing Robert Smithson (Sculpture, Science Fiction)**. Ph.D. Dissertation, Columbia University, 1995. 314pp. (DAI-A 56/06, p. 2022. Dec. 1995.)

SNEAKERS (MOTION PICTURE)
___ "*Sneakers* Hacks It (Review)," *New York (NY) Post*. September 9, 1992. in: *NewsBank. Film and Television*. 96:D9. 1992.
___ Arnold, Gary. "*Sneakers* Moves With Playfulness and Bounce (Review)," *Washington (DC) Times*. September 10, 1992. in: *NewsBank. Film and Television*. 96:D11. 1992.
___ Black, Kent. "The Operatives Behind *Sneakers*," *Los Angeles (CA) Times*. September 15, 1992. in: *NewsBank. Film and Television*. 96: C13-C14. 1992.
___ Campbell, Bob. "Redford and Company Keep *Sneakers* in Stride (Review)," *Newark (NJ) Star-Ledger*. September 11, 1992. in: *NewsBank. Film and Television*. 96:D8. 1992.
___ Ebert, Roger. "*Sneakers* Recycles Old Film Formulas (Review)," *Chicago (IL) Sun Times*. September 9, 1992. in: *NewsBank. Film and Television*. 96:D5. 1992.
___ Kronke, David. "For All Its Gadgetry, *Sneakers* Never Accelerates into High Gear (Review)," *Los Angeles (CA) Daily News*. September 9, 1992. in: *NewsBank. Film and Television*. 96:D1. 1992.
___ Mahar, Ted. "*Sneakers* Romps Through High-Tech Fun (Review)," *Portland (OR) The Oregonian*. September 11, 1992. in: *NewsBank. Film and Television*. 96:D10. 1992.
___ McNally, Owen. "*Sneakers* Trips as High-Tech Thriller (Review)," *Hartford (CT) Courant*. September 11, 1992. in: *NewsBank. Film and Television*. 96:D2. 1992.
___ Ringel, Eleanor. "*Sneakers* Hits All the Right Buttons (Review)," *Atlanta (GA) Journal*. September 11, 1992. in: *NewsBank. Film and Television*. 96:D3-D4. 1992.
___ Sterling, Bruce. "Sneaking for Jesus 2001," *Science Fiction Eye* No. 11: 13-17. December 1992.
___ Verniere, James. "Redford's *Sneakers* Comes Untied (Review)," *Boston (MA) Herald*. September 11, 1992. in: *NewsBank. Film and Television*. 96:D6-D7. 1992.

SNEYD, STEVE
___ Mintz, Catherine. "Poetry, Poets and the Rest of the World: An Interview with Steve Sneyd," *Foundation* No. 63: 68-73. Spring 1995.

SNIPES, WESLEY
___ Shipiro, Marc. "Some Kind of Mutant," *Starlog* No. 197: 27-30. December 1993.

SNODGRASS, MELISSA
___ Meza, Ed. "First Command," *Starlog* No. 217: 32-33. August 1995.

SOCIOLOGY OF SF (continued)

___ Jenkins, Henry. "How Many Starfleet Officers Does It Take to Change a Lightbulb?: *Star Trek* at MIT," by Henry Jenkins and Greg Dancer. in: Tulloch, John and Jenkins, Henry, eds. **Science Fiction Audiences: Watching Doctor Who and Star Trek.** New York: Routledge, 1995. pp.213-236.

___ Jenkins, Henry. "Infinite Diversity in Infinite Combinations: Genre and Authorship in *Star Trek*," in: Tulloch, John and Jenkins, Henry, eds. **Science Fiction Audiences: Watching Doctor Who and Star Trek.** New York: Routledge, 1995. pp.175-195.

___ Jenkins, Henry. "Out of the Closet and into the Universe: Queers and *Star Trek*," in: Tulloch, John and Jenkins, Henry, eds. **Science Fiction Audiences: Watching Doctor Who and Star Trek.** New York: Routledge, 1995. pp.237-265.

___ Jones, Alan. "*Judge Dredd*: Wertham Revisited," *Cinefantastique* 26(5): 36. August 1995.

___ Kessel, John. "The Brother From Another Planet: Science Fiction vs. Mainstream Short Stories," *New York Review of Science Fiction* No. 55: 1, 8-11. March 1993. (Responses: No. 56: 22-23.)

___ Kilgore, De Witt D. **Beyond Earth: Popular Science, Science Fiction, and the Cultural Construction of an American Future in Space.** Ph.D. Dissertation, Brown University, 1994. 414pp. (DAI-A 55/07, p. 2018. January 1995.)

___ Kronke, David. "The Marketing of a Monster," *Dallas Morning News* Sec. C., p. 5, 11. June 12, 1993.

___ Lagon, Mark P. "'We Owe It to Them to Interfere': *Star Trek* and U.S. Statecraft in the 1960s and 1990s," *Extrapolation* 34(3): 251-264. Fall 1993.

___ Lagorio, Valerie M. "King Arthur and Camelot, U.S.A. in the Twentieth Century," in: Rosenthal, Bernard and Szarmach, Paul E., eds. **Medievalism in American Culture.** Binghamton, NY: Medieval & Renaissance Texts and Studies, 1989. pp.151-169.

___ Le Guin, Ursula K. **Earthsea Revisioned.** Madison, NJ: Children's Literature New England, 1993. 26pp.

___ Letson, Russell. "Contributions to the Critical Dialogue: As an Academic Sees It," in: Sanders, Joe, ed. **Science Fiction Fandom.** Westport, CT: Greenwood, 1994. pp.229-234.

___ Lichtenberg, Jacqueline. **Star Trek Lives!,** by Jacqueline Lichtenberg, Sandra Marshak and Jean Winston. New York: Bantam, 1975. 274pp.

___ Lofton, S. C. "Under the Influence," *Lan's Lantern* No. 40: 120-122. September 1992.

___ Lupoff, Richard A. "Into the Aether, Junior Spacepersons!," in: Sanders, Joe, ed. **Science Fiction Fandom.** Westport, CT: Greenwood, 1994. pp.197-206.

___ Luttrell, Hank. "The Science Fiction Convention Scene," in: Sanders, Joe, ed. **Science Fiction Fandom.** Westport, CT: Greenwood, 1994. pp.149-160.

___ Madle, Robert A. "Fandom up to World War II," in: Sanders, Joe, ed. **Science Fiction Fandom.** Westport, CT: Greenwood, 1994. pp.37-54.

___ Malzberg, Barry N. "Thus Our Words Unspoken," *Amazing Stories* 67(6): 62-64. September 1992.

___ Marsalek, Kenneth. "Humanism, Science Fiction and Fairy Tales," *Free Inquiry* 15(3): 39-42. Summer 1995.

___ Mason, Marilynne S. "Today's Problems Tomorrow: Television's Growing Fleet of Science Fiction Dramas Paint a Brighter--or Darker-- Future," *Christian Science Monitor* p. 12-13. March 2, 1993.

___ McKinley, Marlene M. "Tolkien's Influence in America," in: Kranz, Gisbert, ed. **Jahrbuch für Literatur und Ästhetik.** Lüdenscheid, Germany: Stier, 1992. Band 10, pp.261-274.

___ Meyer, David S. "Star Wars, *Star Wars*, and American Political Culture," *Journal of Popular Culture* 26(2): 99-115. Fall 1992.

___ Miesel, Sandra. "The Fan as Critic," in: Sanders, Joe, ed. **Science Fiction Fandom.** Westport, CT: Greenwood, 1994. pp.235-242.

___ Moir, Patricia. "Real vs. Reel Terror," *Cinefantastique* 27(3): 40-43. December 1995.

___ Moskowitz, Sam. "The Origins of Science Fiction Fandom: A Reconstruction," in: Sanders, Joe, ed. **Science Fiction Fandom.** Westport, CT: Greenwood, 1994. pp.17-36.

___ Ordway, Frederick I., III, ed. **Blueprint for Space: Science Fiction to Science Fact,** ed. by Frederick I. Ordway, III and Randy Liebermann. Washington, DC: Smithsonian Institution Press, 1992. 224pp.

___ Osako, Masamichi. "Science Fiction Fandom in Japan," in: Sanders, Joe, ed. **Science Fiction Fandom.** Westport, CT: Greenwood, 1994. pp.137-140.

SOCIOLOGY OF SF (continued)

___ Petzold, Dieter. "Zwölf Jahre Tolkien-Rezeption in Deutschland, 1980-1991," in: Kranz, Gisbert, ed. **Jahrbuch für Literatur und Ästhetik.** Lüdenscheid, Germany: Stier, 1992. Band 10, pp.241-259.

___ Platt, Charles. "Upstream," *Science Fiction Eye* No. 12: 29-34. Summer 1993.

___ Pohl, Frederik. "The Politics of Prophecy," *Extrapolation* 34(3): 199-208. Fall 1993.

___ Rabkin, Eric S. "The Male Body in Science Fiction," *Michigan Quarterly Review* 33(1): 203-216. Winter 1994.

___ Renaud, Maurice. "Document in the History of Science Fiction: On the Scientific-Marvellous Novel and Its Influence on the Understanding of Progress," *Science Fiction Studies* 21(3): 397-405. November 1994.

___ Robins, J. Max. "Gen X Marks the Spot," by J. Max Robins and Brian Lowry. *Variety* 358(7): 1, 63. March 20, 1995.

___ Ross, Andrew. **Strange Weather: Culture, Science, and Technology in the Age of Limits.** London: Verso, 1991. 275pp.

___ Rusch, Kristine K. "Editorial: Magazine Readership," *Magazine of Fantasy and Science Fiction* 89(1): 6-8. July 1995.

___ Sanders, Joe L., ed. **Science Fiction Fandom.** Westport, CT: Greenwood, 1994. 293pp.

___ Sargent, Pamela. "Writing, Science Fiction, and Family Values," *Amazing Stories* 69(1): 100-111. Spring 1994.

___ Shippey, Tom. "The Critique of America in Contemporary Science Fiction," *Interzone* No. 88: 12-17. October 1994.

___ Shirley, John. "Violence," *Science Fiction Eye* No. 13: 47-53. Spring 1994.

___ Siclari, Joe. "Science Fiction Fandom: A Selected, Annotated Bibliography," in: Sanders, Joe, ed. **Science Fiction Fandom.** Westport, CT: Greenwood, 1994. pp.245-264.

___ Stapleton, Amy L. **Utopias for a Dying World: Contemporary German Science Fiction's Plea for a New Ecological Awareness.** New York: Peter Lang, 1993. 158pp.

___ Teitelbaum, Sheldon. "Scientists Say Asimov Put the Stars in Their Eyes," *Los Angeles (CA) Times.* Sec. E, p. 1. April 8, 1992. in *NewsBank. Literature.* 35:B11-B12. 1992.

___ Thomas, Pascal J. "Science Fiction Fandom in Western Europe: A French Perspective," in: Sanders, Joe, ed. **Science Fiction Fandom.** Westport, CT: Greenwood, 1994. pp.119-126.

___ Trimble, John. "Alternative Fandoms," by John Trimble and Bjo Trimble. in: Sanders, Joe, ed. **Science Fiction Fandom.** Westport, CT: Greenwood, 1994. pp.103-109.

___ Tulloch, John. "But He's a Time Lord! He's a Time Lord!: Reading Formations, Followers, and Fans," in: Tulloch, John and Jenkins, Henry, eds. **Science Fiction Audiences: Watching Doctor Who and Star Trek.** New York: Routledge, 1995. pp.125-143.

___ Tulloch, John. "But Why Is *Doctor Who* So Attractive?: Negotiating Ideology and Pleasure," in: Tulloch, John and Jenkins, Henry, eds. **Science Fiction Audiences: Watching Doctor Who and Star Trek.** New York: Routledge, 1995. pp.108-124.

___ Tulloch, John. "The Changing Audiences of Science Fiction," in: Tulloch, John and Jenkins, Henry, eds. **Science Fiction Audiences: Watching Doctor Who and Star Trek.** New York: Routledge, 1995. pp.50-63.

___ Tulloch, John. "It's Meant to Be Fantasy: Teenage Audiences and Genre," by John Tulloch and Marian Tulloch. in: Tulloch, John and Jenkins, Henry, eds. **Science Fiction Audiences: Watching Doctor Who and Star Trek.** New York: Routledge, 1995. pp.86-107.

___ Tulloch, John. "Positioning the SF Audience: *Star Trek, Doctor Who* and the Texts of Science Fiction," in: Tulloch, John and Jenkins, Henry, eds. **Science Fiction Audiences: Watching Doctor Who and Star Trek.** New York: Routledge, 1995. pp.25-49.

___ Tulloch, John. "Throwing a Little Bit of Poison into Future Generations: *Doctor Who* Audiences and Ideology," in: Tulloch, John and Jenkins, Henry, eds. **Science Fiction Audiences: Watching Doctor Who and Star Trek.** New York: Routledge, 1995. pp.67-85.

___ Tulloch, John. "We're Only a Speck in the Ocean: The Fans as Powerless Elite," in: Tulloch, John and Jenkins, Henry, eds. **Science Fiction Audiences: Watching Doctor Who and Star Trek.** New York: Routledge, 1995. pp.144-172.

___ Warner, Harry, Jr. "Fandom Between World War II and *Sputnik*," in: Sanders, Joe, ed. **Science Fiction Fandom.** Westport, CT: Greenwood, 1994. pp.65-74.

___ Warner, Harry, Jr. "A History of Fanzines," in: Sanders, Joe, ed. **Science Fiction Fandom.** Westport, CT: Greenwood, 1994. pp.175-180.

___ Webb, Don. "The Mysterious," *Science Fiction Eye* No. 13: 62-66. Spring 1994.

SOCIOLOGY OF SF

SOCIOLOGY OF SF (continued)
___ Weinberg, Robert. "The Fan Presses," in: Sanders, Joe, ed. **Science Fiction Fandom**. Westport, CT: Greenwood, 1994. pp.211-220.
___ Westfahl, Gary. "Wanted: A Symbol for Science Fiction," *Science Fiction Studies* 22(1): 1-21. March 1995.
___ Whitmore, Tom. "Science Fiction Conventions: Behind the Scenes," by Tom Whitmore and Debbie Notkin. in: Sanders, Joe, ed. **Science Fiction Fandom**. Westport, CT: Greenwood, 1994. pp.161-171.
___ Widner, Art. "Wartime Fandom," in: Sanders, Joe, ed. **Science Fiction Fandom**. Westport, CT: Greenwood, 1994. pp.55-64.
___ Williams, Rosalind H. **Notes on the Underground: an Essay on Technology, Society, and the Imaginagion**. Cambridge, Mass.: MIT Press, 1990. 265pp. [Not seen.]

SOCRATES
___ Brickhouse, Thomas C. "Socrates the Anti-Utopian," by Thomas C. Brickhouse and Nicholas D. Smith. in: Saccaro Del Buffa, Giuseppa and Lewis, Arthur O., eds. **Utopia e Modernita: Teorie e prassi utopiche nell'eta moderna e postmoderna**. Rome: Gangemi Editore, 1989. pp.717-726.

SOHUS, LINDA MAYFIELD
___ "Missing Fan Artist Involved in Murder," *Locus* 33(1): 9, 75. July 1994.

SOLARBABIES (MOTION PICTURE)
___ "MGM/UA Picks Up **Solarbabies**," *Variety* p.5. January 22, 1986.

SOLARIS (MOTION PICTURE)
___ Ferchland, Jutta. "**Solaris**. Der Film von Andrej Tarkovskij im Vergleich zu Lems roman," *Quarber Merkur* 32(2): 34-42. December 1994. (Whole No. 82)

SOMETHING IS OUT THERE (MOTION PICTURE)
___ "**Something Is Out There** (Review)," *Variety* p. 112. May 11, 1988.

SOMETHING WICKED THIS WAY COMES (MOTION PICTURE)
___ "Disney's 'Something Wicked' Tops National Horror Assn. Awards," *Variety* p. 29, 31. June 6, 1984.
___ "**Something Wicked This Way Comes** (1983): Interview with Ray Bradbury and Jack Clayton," in: Goldberg, Lee, ed. **The Dreamweavers: Interviews With Fantasy Filmmakers of the 1980s**. Jefferson, NC: McFarland, 1995. pp.241-278.

SOMETIMES THEY COME BACK (MOTION PICTURE)
___ Wilt, David. "Stephen King's **Sometimes They Come Back** (Review)," *Cinefantastique* 24(3/4): 123. October 1993.

SON OF KONG (MOTION PICTURE)
___ Turner, George. "Sailing Back to Skull Island: **The Son of Kong**," *American Cinematographer* 73(8): 67-71. August 1992.

SON OF TARZAN (MOTION PICTURE)
___ Coriell, Vernell. "**The Son of Tarzan**: The Movie," *Burroughs Bulletin* NS. No. 18: 3-5. April 1994.

SORBO, KEVIN
___ Shapiro, Marc. "The Labors of Hercules," *Starlog* No. 211: 55-58. February 1995.

SORORITY HOUSE MASSACRE II (MOTION PICTURE)
___ Wilt, David. "**Sorority House Massacre II** (Review)," *Cinefantastique* 24(1): 61. June 1993.

SOUKUP, MARTHA
___ "1994 Nebula Awards Winners," *Locus* 34(5): 7. May 1995.
___ "Nebula Award Winners," *Science Fiction Chronicle* 16(6): 4. May 1995.
___ Davis, Ray. "Five Stories by Martha Soukup," *New York Review of Science Fiction* No. 60: 15-17. August 1993.
___ King, T. Jackson. "SFC Interviews: Martha Soukup," *Science Fiction Chronicle* 15(7): 5, 34-38. June 1994.

SOUTH KOREA
___ "Helmer-Distrib Chung Says Fantasy Pics Don't Make It in South Korea," *Variety* p.44. October 9, 1985.

SOUTHERN, TERRY
___ "Southern, Terry (Obituary)," *Locus* 35(6): 79. December 1995.
___ "Southern, Terry (Obituary)," *Science Fiction Chronicle* 17(2): 26. December 1995/January 1996.

SOWARDS, JACK
___ Lofficier, Randy. "**Star Trek Movies** (1980-1988): Interviews with Jack Sowards, Nicholas Mayer, Harve Bennett; Leonard Nimoy and William Shatner," by Randy Lofficier and Jean-Marc Lofficier. in: Goldberg, Lee et al. **Science Fiction Filmmaking in the 1980s**. Jefferson, NC: McFarland, 1995. pp.189-236.

SPACE: 1999 (TV)
___ Eramo, Steven. "Space Refugee," *Starlog* No. 221: 47-51, 64. December 1995.
___ Gore, Christian. "Space: $19.99: **Space 1999** (Review)," *Sci-Fi Universe* No. 3: 74. October/November 1994.
___ Van Hise, James. **Sci Fi TV: From Twilight Zone to Deep Space Nine**. Las Vegas, NV: Pioneer Books, 1993. 160pp. (Reprinted, HarperPrism, 1995. 258pp.)

SPACE: ABOVE AND BEYOND (TV)
___ Jarvis, Jeff. "The Couch Critic: Space," *TV Guide* 43(38): 8. September 23, 1995.
___ Perenson, Melissa J. "Space War," *Sci-Fi Entertainment* 2(3): 66-70. October 1995.
___ Perez, Dan. "The **X-Files** Producers Declare Interstellar War With **Space: Above and Beyond**," *Science Fiction Age* 4(1): 22-24, 104. November 1995.
___ Spelling, Ian. "**Space: Above and Beyond**," *Starlog* No. 220: 40-45. November 1995.
___ Vitaris, Paula. "**Space: Above and Beyond**," *Cinefantastique* 27(2): 54-55. November 1995.

SPACE AND TIME (MAGAZINE)
___ "**Weird Tales** Reformats; Other Magazine Changes," *Locus* 29(3): 7, 79. September 1992.

SPACE FLIGHT
___ **Blue Print for Space: Science Fiction to Science Fact**. Whittier, CA: Holiday Video Library, 1993. 1 videocassette, 60 minutes.
___ Bruzzi, Stella. "Space Looks: Space Costumes," *Sight and Sound* 5(9): 10-11. September 1995.
___ Kilgore, De Witt D. **Beyond Earth: Popular Science, Science Fiction, and the Cultural Construction of an American Future in Space**. Ph.D. Dissertation, Brown University, 1994. 414pp. (DAI-A 55/07, p. 2018. January 1995.)
___ Lind, Michael. "New York Diarist: The Nerd Frontier," *New Republic* 213(5): 42. July 31, 1995.
___ Wolff, Michael J. "Shooting for the Moon," *Starlog* No. 205: 41-45. August 1994.

SPACE GHOST: COAST TO COAST (TV)
___ Kenny, Glenn. "The Ghost With the Most," *TV Guide* 42(25): 40. June 18, 1994.
___ Persons, Dan. "**Space Ghost: Coast to Coast** (Review)," *Cinefantastique* 26(4): 60. June 1995.

SPACE IN LITERATURE
___ Hartley, Matthew R. **The Image of Space in Soviet Literature**. Master's Thesis, University of Massachusetts at Amherst, 1993. 71pp.

SPACE OPERA
___ Monk, Patricia. "Not Just 'Cosmic Skullduggery': A Partial Reconsideration of Space Opera," *Extrapolation* 33(4): 295-316. Winter 1992.
___ Sanders, Joe L. "Space Opera Reconsidered," *New York Review of Science Fiction* No. 82: 1, 3-6. June 1995.
___ Westfahl, Gary. "Beyond Logic and Literacy: The Strange Case of Space Opera," *Extrapolation* 35(3): 176-185. Fall 1994.

SPACE PATROL (COMIC)
___ Weaver, Tom. "**Space Patrol**," *Starlog* No. 187: 20-22. February 1993.

SPACE PATROL (TV)
___ Weaver, Tom. "*Space Patrol*," *Starlog* No. 187: 20-22. February 1993.

SPACE POLICE (TV)
___ Clark, Mike. "Space Station Blues," *Starlog* No. 205: 48-51, 70. August 1994.

SPACE PRECINCT (TV)
___ Harris, Judith P. "**Space Precinct** (Review)," *Cinefantastique* 26(3): 60. April 1995.
___ Nazzaro, Joe. "Intergalactic Blue," *Starlog* No. 208: 37-40. November 1994.

SPACE PROGRAM
___ "Apollo 11: 25 Years Later; Reports and Recollections," *Locus* 33(2): 46-51, 71-73. August 1994.

SPACE RANGERS (TV)
___ Altman, Mark A. "**Space Rangers**," *Cinefantastique* 23(6): 48-49. April 1993.
___ Carlson, Timothy. "The Universe Is Expanding All over the Dial," by Timothy Carlson and Mark Schwed. *TV Guide* 41(1): 16-19. January 2, 1993. (Issue 2075)
___ Cerone, Daniel H. "Space Team Shooting for the Moon," *Los Angeles (CA) Times* Sec. F, p. 1. December 8, 1992.
___ Masson, Charles. "Jeff Kaake: Boss in Space," *New Orleans (LA) Times-Picayune* Sec. TV, p. 6. January 3, 1993.
___ Shapiro, Marc. "Cosmic Mechanic," *Starlog* No. 189: 27-29, 67. April 1993.
___ Shapiro, Marc. "Ranger of Fortune," *Starlog* No. 190: 49-51. May 1993.
___ Westbrook, Bruce. "Star Wars," *Houston (TX) Chronicle* Sec. D, p. 1, 6. January 6, 1993.

SPACE SUITS
___ Bruzzi, Stella. "Space Looks: Space Costumes," *Sight and Sound* 5(9): 10-11. September 1995.

SPACE TRAVEL
___ Innerhofer, Roland. "Flugphantasien. Die Luftfahrt bei Jules Verne und im deutschen technischen Zukunftsroman vom ausgehenden 19. Jahrhundert bis 1914. 1. Teil," *Quarber Merkur* 30(1): 47-68. June 1992. (No. 77)
___ Innerhofer, Roland. "Flugphantasien. Die Luftfahrt bei Jules Verne und im deutschen technischen Zukunftsroman vom ausgehenden 19. Jahrhundert bis 1914. 2. Teil und Schluß," *Quarber Merkur* 30(2): 14-46. December 1992. (No. 78)
___ Pohl, Frederik. "Where Space Travel Went Wrong," *Amazing Stories* 69(1): 88-99. Spring 1994.

SPACE TRUCKERS (MOTION PICTURE)
___ Fischer, Dennis. "**Space Truckers**," *Cinefantastique* 26(4): 54-57. June 1995.

SPACEFLIGHT
___ Wachhorst, Wyn. "The Dream of Spaceflight: Nostalgia for a Bygone Future," *Massachusetts Review* 36(1): 7-32. Spring 1995.

SPACESHIPS
___ Donald, Ralph R. "The *Mary Ann*, the *Ruptured Duck* and the *Enterprise*: Character Relationships with Air and Space Craft as Metaphors for Human Affinities," in: Loukides, Paul and Fuller, Linda K., eds. **Beyond the Stars III: The Material World in American Popular Film**. Bowling Green, OH: Popular Press, 1993. pp.123-133.
___ Miller, Ron. **The Dream Machines: An Illustrated History of the Spaceship in Art, Science and Literature**. Malabar, FL: Krieger, 1993. 714pp.
___ Rovin, Jeff. **Aliens, Robots, and Spaceships**. New York: Facts on File, 1995. 372pp.

SPAIN
___ "1993 UPC Science Fiction Award," *Locus* 30(4): 40. April 1993.
___ "Jack McDevitt Wins Spanish Novella Contest," *Science Fiction Chronicle* 14(7): 4. April 1993.
___ "One Million Paseta ($10,000) SF Novella Contest," *Science Fiction Chronicle* 13(10): 4-5. July/August 1992.

SPAIN (continued)
___ "Science Fiction, a Global Community: Spain," *Locus* 32(4): 40. April 1994.
___ "SF in Spain," *Locus* 29(6): 47. December 1992.
___ "SF in Spain," *Locus* 30(4): 40, 62. April 1993.
___ Charnon-Deutsch, Lou. "**Las Vírgenes Locas** as Product of the Unconscious," *Monographis Review* 3(1/2): 49-57. 1987.
___ de Torre Gracia, Emilio E. "La ciencia ficción en la poesía de José Hierro," *Monographis Review* 3(1/2): 100-106. 1987.
___ Dendle, Brian J. "Spain's First Novel of Science Fiction: A Nineteenth Century Voyage to Saturn," *Monographis Review* 3(1/2): 43-48. 1987.
___ García-Sánchez, Franklin B. "Ubicación genérica de **El Caballero Encantado** (1909) de Benito Pérez Galdós," *Monographis Review* 3(1/2): 71-80. 1987.
___ Glenn, Kathleen M. "Recapturing the Past: José María Merino's **El caldero de oro**," *Monographis Review* 3(1/2): 119-128. 1987.
___ Gonzáles-Millán, Juan. "Fantasía y parodia: la subversión del texto narrativo en **Las crónicas del sochantre**," *Monographis Review* 3(1/2): 81-99. 1987.
___ Jones, Alan. "Mutant Action: Science Fiction Splatter Boosted by Spain's Pedro Almodovar," *Cinefantastique* 24(5): 48-49. December 1993.
___ Pope, Randolph D. "Una brecha sobrenatural en **Theoría del conocimiento** de Luis Goytisolo," *Monographis Review* 3(1/2): 129-139. 1987.
___ Risco, Antonio. "Notas para un estudio de la leteratura fantástica hispánica del siglo XX," *Monographis Review* 3(1/2): 58-70. 1987.
___ Zatlin, Phyllis. "Tales from Fernández Cubas: Adventure in the Fantastic," *Monographis Review* 3(1/2): 107-118. 1987.

SPALDING, HARRY
___ Weaver, Tom. "Harry Spalding: Interview," in: Weaver, Tom, ed. **Attack of the Monster Movie Makers: Interviews with 20 Genre Giants**. Jefferson, NC: McFarland, 1994. pp.319-338.

SPANISH
___ Bilija, Ksenija. "From Golem to Plastisex: An Analytical Survey of Spanish American Fantastic Literature," *Journal of the Fantastic in the Arts* 7(2/3): 201-214. 1995.

SPARHAWK, BUD
___ Klein, Jay K. "Biolog: Bud Sparhawk," *Analog* 114(6): 92, 97. May 1994.

SPECIAL EFFECTS
___ "Death Star Days," *Starlog* No. 204: 52-53, 69. July 1994.
___ "Fox Sues Effects Outfit Over Work on **Aliens**," *Variety* p. 92. March 5, 1986.
___ Abrams, Janet. "Escape From Gravity," *Sight and Sound* 5(5): 14-19. May 1995.
___ Altman, Mark A. "**Babylon 5**: Designing the Future," *Cinefantastique* 23(5): 31. February 1993.
___ Altman, Mark A. "**Babylon 5**: Designing the Future," *Cinefantastique* 25(2): 43-45. April 1994.
___ Altman, Mark A. "**Babylon 5**: Foundation Imaging," *Cinefantastique* 25(2): 32-34. April 1994.
___ Altman, Mark A. "**Babylon 5**: It Came From the Video Toaster," *Cinefantastique* 25(2): 29. April 1994.
___ Altman, Mark A. "**Babylon 5**: Makeup Effects," *Cinefantastique* 25(2): 40-41, 61. April 1994.
___ Altman, Mark A. "**Star Trek: Deep Space Nine**: Herman Zimmerman, Production Designer," *Cinefantastique* 23(6): 28-29. April 1993.
___ Archer, Steve. **Willis O'Brien: Special Effects Genius**. Jefferson, NC: McFarland, 1993. 239pp.
___ Beeler, Michael. "**The Flintstones**: Building Bedrock," *Cinefantastique* 25(3): 23. June 1994.
___ Beeler, Michael. "**The Flintstones**: Jim Henson's Creature Shop," *Cinefantastique* 25(3): 15-18. June 1994.
___ Beeler, Michael. "**Hellraiser IV: Bloodline**: Makeup Effects," *Cinefantastique* 26(3): 39. April 1995.
___ Biodrowski, Steve. "Coppola's **Dracula**: Filming Lo-Tech Gothic," *Cinefantastique* 23(4): 52-54. December 1992.
___ Biodrowski, Steve. "**Evil Dead III**: The Makeup World of Ash," *Cinefantastique* 23(1): 32-33. August 1992.

SPECIAL EFFECTS (continued)

___ Biodrowski, Steve. "***Fantastic Four***: Optic Nerve Makeups," *Cinefantastique* 24(3/4): 10. October 1993.

___ Biodrowski, Steve. "***Jurassic Park***: Coordinating the Effects," *Cinefantastique* 24(2): 18-19. August 1993.

___ Biodrowski, Steve. "***Jurassic Park***: Filming the Dinosaurs," *Cinefantastique* 24(2): 14-16. August 1993.

___ Biodrowski, Steve. "***Jurassic Park***: Stop Motion's Extinction," *Cinefantastique* 24(2): 13. August 1993.

___ Blake, Michael F. "Master of Early Movie Makeup: Lon Chaney," *Filmfax* No. 39: 85-63, 98. June/July 1993.

___ Boswell, Thom. **The Costumemaker's Art: Cloaks of Fantasy, Masks of Revelation.** Asheville, NC: Lark Books, 1992. 144pp.

___ Brill, Louis M. "Special Venues: Inside the Luxor Pyramid," *Cinefex* No. 61: 23-28. March 1995.

___ Bruzzi, Stella. "Space Looks: Space Costumes," *Sight and Sound* 5(9): 10-11. September 1995.

___ Calhoun, John. "***The Journey Inside***," *TCI* 28(8): 78. October 1994.

___ Cameron, James. "Effects Scene: Technology and Magic," *Cinefex* No. 51: 5-7. August 1992.

___ Carpenter, Phil. "Commercial Spot: Cola Bears," *Cinefex* No. 60: 27-28. December 1994.

___ Carpenter, Phil. "Commercial Spot: Sci-Fi Pest Control," *Cinefex* No. 53: 73-74. February 1993.

___ Carpenter, Phil. "***Robocop*** Redux," *Cinefex* No. 56: 70-83. November 1993.

___ Clark, Mike. "Designing Man," *Starlog* No. 187: 75-81, 69. February 1993.

___ Cox, Vic. "Effects Scene: Full Moon Rising," *Cinefex* No. 53: 17-18. February 1993.

___ Crisafulli, Chuck. "Jason's 13th: KNB Makeup Effects," *Cinefantastique* 24(2): 55. August 1993.

___ Crisafulli, Chuck. "***The Mask***: Computer Graphics," *Cinefantastique* 25(4): 11. August 1994.

___ Crisafulli, Chuck. "The Monstrous Genius of Jack Pierce," *Filmfax* No. 35: 36-39, 80-81. October/November 1992.

___ Crisafulli, Chuck. "The Way out World of Dick Smith," *Filmfax* No. 41: 58-64. October/November 1993.

___ Derro, Marc. "Profile: Kevin Yagher," *Cinefex* No. 58: 103-104. June 1994.

___ Derro, Marc. "Quick Cuts: Animal House," *Cinefex* No. 61: 101-102. March 1995.

___ Derro, Marc. "Video Beat: Midair Morphing," *Cinefex* No. 58: 29-30. June 1994.

___ Dever, Sean. "Quick Cuts: Cinematic Cyberspace," *Cinefex* No. 62: 17-18. June 1995.

___ Duncan, Jody. "The Beauty in the Beasts," *Cinefex* No. 55: 42-95. August 1993.

___ Duncan, Jody. "Blowing Up Baby," *Cinefex* No. 52: 22-53. November 1992.

___ Duncan, Jody. "Borrowed Flesh," *Cinefex* No. 49: 24-39. February 1992.

___ Duncan, Jody. "***Broken Arrow***: Stealth Effects," *Cinefex* No. 64: 13-14. December 1995.

___ Duncan, Jody. "Commercial Spot: Evolutionary Auto," *Cinefex* No. 55: 105-106. August 1993.

___ Duncan, Jody. "Commercial Spot: They Keep Going and Going," *Cinefex* No. 59: 83-84. September 1994.

___ Duncan, Jody. "Commercial Spot: Thoroughbred Animation," *Cinefex* No. 54: 15-16. May 1993.

___ Duncan, Jody. "Fire and Ice," *Cinefex* No. 57: 42-69. March 1994.

___ Duncan, Jody. "From Zero to Hero," *Cinefex* No. 60: 46-65. December 1994.

___ Duncan, Jody. "Gorilla Warfare," *Cinefex* No. 62: 34-53. June 1995.

___ Duncan, Jody. "The Making of a Blockbuster," *Cinefex* No. 58: 34-65. June 1994.

___ Duncan, Jody. "***Money Train***: Training Film," *Cinefex* No. 64: 25-30, 134. December 1995.

___ Duncan, Jody. "Profile: Peter Kuran," *Cinefex* No. 54: 88. May 1993.

___ Duncan, Jody. "Quick Cuts: A Crash in the Andes," *Cinefex* No. 55: 117-118. August 1993.

___ Duncan, Jody. "Quick Cuts: Clause and Effects," *Cinefex* No. 61: 17-18. March 1995.

SPECIAL EFFECTS (continued)

___ Duncan, Jody. "Quick Cuts: Crime and Banishment," *Cinefex* No. 58: 11-12. June 1994.

___ Duncan, Jody. "Quick Cuts: Making the Crow Fly," *Cinefex* No. 58: 23-24. June 1994.

___ Duncan, Jody. "Quick Cuts: Maximum Speed," *Cinefex* No. 59: 89-92. September 1994.

___ Duncan, Jody. "Quick Cuts: Terminal Effects," *Cinefex* No. 59: 17-18. September 1994.

___ Duncan, Jody. "Special Venues: MGM's Grand EFX," *Cinefex* No. 63: 21-22. September 1995.

___ Duncan, Jody. "Special Venues: Moon Shot," *Cinefex* No. 59: 11-12. September 1994.

___ Duncan, Jody. "Video Beat: Making Movie Magic," *Cinefex* No. 56: 97-98. November 1993.

___ Eby, Douglas. "***Star Trek: Deep Space Nine***: The Wormhole," *Cinefantastique* 24(3/4): 111. October 1993.

___ Fein, David C. "Laser Revolution: Harryhausen Cornucopia," *Cinefex* No. 53: 81-82. February 1993.

___ Fein, David C. "Quick Cuts: Once More into the ***Abyss***," *Cinefex* No. 55: 29-30. August 1993.

___ Fischer, Dennis. "Full Moon Effects: Creature Creators," *Cinefantastique* 26(4): 47-49. June 1995.

___ Fisher, Bob. "***Apollo 13*** Orbits Cinema's Outer Limits," *American Cinematographer* 76(6): 37-46. June 1995.

___ Fisher, Bob. "***Jurassic Park***: When Dinosaurs Rule the Box Office," *American Cinematographer* 74(6): 37-44. June 1993.

___ Fisher, Bob. "***Meteor Man*** Gets His Digital Wings," *American Cinematographer* 74(4): 42-45. April 1993.

___ French, Lawrence. "***Bram Stoker's Dracula***: Matte Artistry," *Cinefantastique* 23(6): 55-58. April 1993.

___ French, Lawrence. "***Ed Wood***: Lugosi's Makeup," *Cinefantastique* 25(6)/26(1): 112-113. December 1994.

___ French, Lawrence. "***Jurassic Park***: Dennis Muren," *Cinefantastique* 24(2): 26-28. August 1993.

___ French, Lawrence. "***Jurassic Park***: Dinosaur Movements," *Cinefantastique* 24(2): 20-21. August 1993.

___ French, Lawrence. "***Jurassic Park***: Phil Tippett, Dinosaur," *Cinefantastique* 24(2): 16-17. August 1993.

___ French, Lawrence. "***Naked Lunch***: Special Effects," *Cinefantastique* 22(5): 15-19. April 1992.

___ French, Lawrence. "***Toy Story***: CGI Director," *Cinefantastique* 27(2): 20-21. November 1995.

___ French, Lawrence. "***Toy Story***: CGI Production," *Cinefantastique* 27(2): 28-29 November 1995.

___ French, Lawrence. "***Toy Story***: Pixar," *Cinefantastique* 27(2): 23-25. November 1995.

___ French, Lawrence. "***Toy Story***: Renderman," *Cinefantastique* 27(2): 18-19. November 1995.

___ French, Lawrence. "***Toy Story***: Scanning," *Cinefantastique* 27(2): 34-35. November 1995.

___ Gilmer, Nance G. "Profile: Doug Beswick," *Cinefex* No. 53: 78. February 1993.

___ Hatch, Jim. "***Cutthroat Island***: Getting Away With Murder," *Cinefex* No. 64: 49-50, 133. December 1995.

___ Hubbard, Janice. "Commercial Spot: Reflects of the Dead," *Cinefex* No. 50: 82-83. May 1992.

___ Hubbard, Janice. "Commercial Spot: Simian Simulation," *Cinefex* No. 52: 9-10. November 1992.

___ Hubbard, Janice. "Commercial Spot: True Colors," *Cinefex* No. 53: 14-15. February 1993.

___ Jones, Alan. "***Judge Dredd***: Makeup Design and Effects," *Cinefantastique* 26(5): 23-25, 61. August 1995.

___ Jones, Alan. "***Judge Dredd***: Special Visual Effects," *Cinefantastique* 26(5): 32-34. August 1995.

___ Kapland, David A. "Believe in Magic," *Newsweek* 121(24): 60-61. June 14, 1993.

___ Kaufman, Debra. "Effects in the Vertical Realm," *Cinefex* No. 54: 30-53. May 1993.

___ Keeney, Brian. "Company File: Animal Makers," *Cinefex* No. 59: 29-30. September 1994.

___ Kenny, Glenn. "OscarVision," *TV Guide* 42(12): 58. March 19, 1994.

___ Kinnard, Roy, ed. **The Lost World of Willis O'Brien: The Original Shooting Script of the 1925 Landmark Special Effects Dinosaur Film, with Photographs.** Jefferson, NC: McFarland, 1993. 176pp.

SPECIAL EFFECTS (continued)

___ Korman, Ken. "Building a Better Beast," *Video Magazine* 17(8): 56-57, 98, 108. November 1994.

___ Kozachik, Pete. "Stop Motion Without Compromise: *The Nightmare Before Christmas*," *American Cinematographer* 74(12): 37-43. December 1993.

___ Kutzera, Dale. "***Coneheads***: Stop Motion Garthok," *Cinefantastique* 24(6)/25(1): 121-122. February 1994.

___ Kutzera, Dale. "Quick Cuts: Digital Effects," *Cinefex* No. 57: 75-76. March 1994.

___ Kutzera, Dale. "Quick Cuts: Visionary Visuals," *Cinefex* No. 58: 17-18. June 1994.

___ Leayman, Charles D. "*The Dark Half*: Visual Effects by V. C. E.," *Cinefantastique* 24(1): 23. June 1993.

___ Loren, Christalene. "Quick Cuts: A Lady in Disguise," *Cinefex* No. 58: 91-92. June 1994.

___ Loren, Christalene. "Video Beat: *Deep Space Nine* Miniatures," *Cinefex* No. 54: 21-22. May 1993.

___ Loren, Christalene. "Video Beat: Deep Space Wormholes," *Cinefex* No. 55: 11-12. August 1993.

___ Loren, Christalene. "Video Beat: Toasting *Babylon 5*," *Cinefex* No. 57: 11-12. March 1994.

___ Maccarillo, Lisa. "In the Lab of the Imagination with Michael Westmore," *Sci-Fi Entertainment* 1(2): 52-54. August 1994.

___ Maccarillo, Lisa. "Renaissance Man: An Afternoon With Stan Winston," *Sci-Fi Entertainment* 2(1): 58-63. June 1995

___ MacQueen, Scott. " '43 Phantom Found New Formula for Classic Tale," *American Cinematographer* 74(9): 80-85. September 1993.

___ Magid, Ron. "After *Jurassic Park*, Traditional Techniques May Become Fossils," *American Cinematographer* 74(12): 58-65. December 1993.

___ Magid, Ron. "CGI Spearheads Brave New World of Special Effects," *American Cinematographer* 74(12): 26-36. December 1993.

___ Magid, Ron. "Digital Domain Provides Rocket Fuel for *Apollo 13*," *American Cinematographer* 76(6): 48-60. June 1995.

___ Magid, Ron. "Dream Quest Adds Lunatic Fringes," *American Cinematographer* 75(12): 57-58. December 1994.

___ Magid, Ron. "Effects Add Bite to *Bram Stoker's Dracula*," *American Cinematographer* 73(12): 56-64. December 1992.

___ Magid, Ron. "Effects Army Mobilizes for Megasequel," *American Cinematographer* 73(7): 42-51. July 1992.

___ Magid, Ron. "Effects Team Brings Dinosaurs Back from Extinction," *American Cinematographer* 74(6): 46-52. June 1993.

___ Magid, Ron. "Exploring the Future of Special Effects," *American Cinematographer* 75(2): 26-33. February 1994.

___ Magid, Ron. "ILM Creates New Universe of Effects for *Star Trek: Generations*," *American Cinematographer* 76(4): 78-88. April 1995.

___ Magid, Ron. "ILM Magic Is Organized Mayhem," *American Cinematographer* 75(12): 50-56. December 1994.

___ Magid, Ron. "ILM's Digital Dinosaurs Tear up Effects Jungle," *American Cinematographer* 74(12): 46-57. December 1993.

___ Magid, Ron. "Incredible Shrinking 'Indian' Effects," by Ron Magid and Chris Probst. *American Cinematographer* 76(8): 68-69. August 1995.

___ Magid, Ron. "Making Strange Faces," *American Cinematographer* 75(12): 59-60. December 1994.

___ Magid, Ron. "Speeding Up the Screams in *Alien 3*," *American Cinematographer* 73(12): 70-76. December 1992.

___ Magid, Ron. "*Star Trek VI: The Undiscovered Country*: Director Meyer Explores Familiar Country," *American Cinematographer* 73(1): 51-57. January 1992.

___ Magid, Ron. "*Star Trek VI: The Undiscovered Country*: ILM Gets a Piece of the Action," *American Cinematographer* 73(1): 58-65. January 1992.

___ Magid, Ron. "*Star Trek VI: The Undiscovered Country*: Narita Leads *Enterprise* Camera Crew," *American Cinematographer* 73(1): 42-50. January 1992.

___ Magid, Ron. "*Star Trek VI: The Undiscovered Country*: Specialized Departments Add Artistic Touches," *American Cinematographer* 73(1): 66-75. January 1992.

___ Mandell, Paul. "Commercial Spot: Byte-Size Cookies," *Cinefex* No. 60: 129-130. December 1994.

___ Mandell, Paul. "Commercial Spot: Kong Reenergized," *Cinefex* No. 58: 97-98. June 1994.

___ Mandell, Paul. "Harryhausen Animates Annual Sci-Tech Awards," *American Cinematographer* 73(5): 73-74. May 1992.

SPECIAL EFFECTS (continued)

___ Mandell, Paul. "Of Genies and Dragons: The Career of Ray Harryhausen," *American Cinematographer* 73(12): 77-81. December 1992.

___ Manson, Chris. "Video Beat: Chronicling Young Indy," *Cinefex* No. 54: 77-78. May 1993.

___ Martin, Kevin H. "Commercial Spot: Track Sold Separately," *Cinefex* No. 56: 23-24. November 1993.

___ Martin, Kevin H. "Kirk Out," *Cinefex* No. 61: 62-77. March 1995.

___ Martin, Kevin H. "Letting Slip the Dogs of War," *Cinefex* No. 49: 40-59. February 1992.

___ Martin, Kevin H. "Life Everlasting," *Cinefex* No. 52: 54-78. November 1992.

___ Martin, Kevin H. "Video Beat: Order out of Xaos," *Cinefex* No. 57: 21-22. March 1994.

___ Martinez, Cal. "Future Special Effects: Recent Advances in *Star Trek*," in: Van Hise, James, ed. **Trek Celebration Two**. Las Vegas, NV: Pioneer, 1994. pp.148-151.

___ Mason, Mary C. "Effects Scene: The Last Hurrah," *Cinefex* No. 63: 117-118. September 1995.

___ Mason, Mary C. "Profile: Jeff Matakovich," *Cinefex* No. 62: 29. June 1995.

___ Mason, Mary C. "Video Beat: Cannon Creations," *Cinefex* No. 62: 139-140. June 1995.

___ McGee, Mark T. "Full Moon's Effects Master," *Cinefantastique* 23(5): 47-49. February 1993.

___ Miller, Jeff T. "Commercial Spot: Chevy Hulk," *Cinefex* No. 57: 79-80. March 1994.

___ Miller, Marcus. "Video Beat: Attack of the 80-Foot Stones," *Cinefex* No. 60: 111-112. December 1994.

___ Montesano, Anthony P. "*Brainscan*: Computer Graphics," *Cinefantastique* 25(3): 50. June 1994.

___ Nensi, Salman A. "The Special Effects of *Jurassic Park*," *Lucasfilm Fan Club* No. 20: 28-30. Fall 1993.

___ Norton, Bill. "Pandora's Paintbox," *Cinefex* No. 56: 54-69. November 1993.

___ Norton, Bill. "Zealots and Xenomorphs," *Cinefex* No. 50: 26-53. May 1992.

___ Odien, Jeff. "On the Water Front," *Cinefex* No. 64: 96-117. December 1995.

___ Odien, W. C. "The Rise and Fall of Norville Barnes," *Cinefex* No. 58: 66-81. June 1994.

___ Parisi, Paula. "Long Nights and *Strange Days*," *American Cinematographer* 76(11): 64-68. November 1995.

___ Peishel, Bob. "Commercial Spot: Elevator to the Stars," *Cinefex* No. 52: 14-15. November 1992.

___ Peishel, Bob. "Commercial Spot: What's Up, Nike?," *Cinefex* No. 54: 25-26. May 1993.

___ Peishel, Bob. "Quick Cuts: Feline Fabrication," *Cinefex* No. 56: 17-18. November 1993.

___ Peishel, Bob. "Video Beat: *Alien Nation* Revisited," *Cinefex* No. 59: 23-24. September 1994.

___ Persons, Dan. "*Robocop 3*: CGI Effects," *Cinefantastique* 24(2): 42. August 1993.

___ Persons, Dan. "*Robocop 3*: Optical Effects," *Cinefantastique* 24(2): 47. August 1993.

___ Persons, Dan. "*Robocop 3*: Special Effects," *Cinefantastique* 24(2): 34. August 1993.

___ Persons, Dan. "*Silence of the Lambs*: Confessions of a 'Moth Wrangler'," *Cinefantastique* 22(4): 28-29. February 1992.

___ Persons, Dan. "*Silence of the Lambs*: Makeup Effects Behind-the-Scenes," *Cinefantastique* 22(4): 32-34. February 1992.

___ Phillips, Mark. "Biology Amok," *Starlog* No. 203: 52-54. June 1994.

___ Pieshel, Bob. "Quick Cuts: Hail to the Imposter," *Cinefex* No. 55: 35-36. August 1993.

___ Pieshel, Bob. "Video Beat: *Viper* Sheds Its Skin," *Cinefex* No. 58: 85-86. June 1994.

___ Pizzello, Stephen. "*Batman Forever* Mines Comic-Book Origins," *American Cinematographer* 76(7): 34-44. July 1995.

___ Pourroy, Janine. "The Board Game Jungle," *Cinefex* No. 64: 54-71. December 1995.

___ Pourroy, Janine. "Heart of Darkness," *Cinefex* No. 53: 22-53. February 1993.

___ Pourroy, Janine. "Making Gump Happen," *Cinefex* No. 60: 90-107. December 1994.

___ Pourroy, Janine. "Quick Cuts: Unfriendly Skies," *Cinefex* No. 54: 9-10. May 1993.

SPECIAL EFFECTS

SPECIAL EFFECTS (continued)

___ Probst, Chris. "Cyberthriller Comes of Age," *American Cinematographer* 76(10): 88-96. October 1995.

___ Probst, Chris. "Darkness Descends on *The X-Files*," *American Cinematographer* 76(6): 28-32. June 1995.

___ Probst, Chris. "*Indian in the Cupboard*'s Cinematic Intimacy," *American Cinematographer* 76(8): 62-67. August 1995.

___ Prokop, Tim. "Closeup: Adding Teeth to *Wolf*," *Cinefex* No. 59: 97-106. September 1994.

___ Prokop, Tim. "Launching *Apollo 13*," *Cinefex* No. 63: 85-85. September 1995.

___ Prokop, Tim. "The Making of a 50-Foot Woman," *Cinefex* No. 57: 26-41. March 1994.

___ Prokop, Tim. "Quick Cuts: A New Twist on Tornadoes," *Cinefex* No. 61: 11-12. March 1995.

___ Prokop, Tim. "*The Shadow*: Miniaturizing New York," *Cinefantastique* 25(4): 42-43. August 1994.

___ Prokop, Tim. "*The Shadow*: Special Effects Computer Graphics," *Cinefantastique* 25(4): 32-32. August 1994.

___ Prokop, Tim. "*The Shadow*: The Art of Makeup," *Cinefantastique* 25(4): 36-37. August 1994.

___ Prokop, Tim. "*Star Trek: Deep Space Nine*: Special Effects," *Cinefantastique* 25(6)/26(1): 99-102. December 1994.

___ Prokop, Tim. "*Star Trek: The Next Generation*: Low Tech Effects," *Cinefantastique* 25(6)/26(1): 90-91. December 1994.

___ Prokop, Tim. "*Star Trek: The Next Generation*: Painting for the Future," *Cinefantastique* 25(6)/26(1): 70-73. December 1994.

___ Prokop, Tim. "*Star Trek: The Next Generation*: Shot by Shot," *Cinefantastique* 25(6)/26(1): 64-69. December 1994.

___ Prokop, Tim. "*Star Trek: The Next Generation*: Special Visual Effects," *Cinefantastique* 25(6)/26(1): 52-63, 124. December 1994.

___ Prokop, Tim. "*Stargate*: CGI Effects," *Cinefantastique* 26(3): 50. April 1995.

___ Prokop, Tim. "*Stargate*: Makeup Design," *Cinefantastique* 25(6)/26(1): 30. December 1994.

___ Prokop, Tim. "*Stargate*: Special Effects," *Cinefantastique* 25(6)/26(1): 35. December 1994.

___ Robley, Les P. "*Babylon 5*: Foundation Imaging," *Cinefantastique* 23(5): 23-26. February 1993.

___ Robley, Les P. "*Evil Dead III*: Stop-Motion Special Effects," *Cinefantastique* 23(1): 48-49. August 1992.

___ Robley, Les P. "Full Moon Effects: Low Budget Magic," *Cinefantastique* 26(4): 40-42, 61. June 1995.

___ Robley, Les P. "The Making of a Beautiful Monster," *American Cinematographer* 76(12): 62-68. December 1995.

___ Robley, Les P. "Mobilizing *Army of Darkness* Via Go-Animation," *American Cinematographer* 74(3): 72-80. March 1993.

___ Ross, Patricia. "*Pet Sematary II*: Makeup Effects," *Cinefantastique* 23(2/3): 26. October 1992.

___ Rubinstein, Mitchell. "*The Next Generation*: Special Visual Effects," *Cinefantastique* 23(2/3): 38-41. October 1992.

___ Salter, David I. "*Babylon 5*: Alien Makeups," *Cinefantastique* 23(5): 32-33. February 1993.

___ Salter, David I. "*Babylon 5*: Costume Design," *Cinefantastique* 23(5): 34. February 1993.

___ Salter, David I. "*Babylon 5*: The Future of CGI," *Cinefantastique* 23(5): 39. February 1993.

___ Salter, David I. "*The Next Generation*: Alien Makeups," *Cinefantastique* 23(2/3): 103-105. October 1992.

___ Salter, David I. "*The Next Generation*: Building the *U. S. S. Enterprise*," *Cinefantastique* 23(2/3): 95. October 1992.

___ Salter, David I. "*Star Trek: Deep Space Nine*: Alien Makeups," *Cinefantastique* 23(6): 31. April 1993.

___ Salter, David I. "*Star Trek: Deep Space Nine*: Conceptual Artist Richard Delgado," *Cinefantastique* 23(6): 36-37. April 1993.

___ Salter, David I. "*Star Trek: Deep Space Nine*: Designing Aliens," *Cinefantastique* 24(3/4): 106. October 1993.

___ Salter, David I. "*Star Trek: Deep Space Nine*: Effects," *Cinefantastique* 24(3/4): 105. October 1993.

___ Salter, David I. "*Star Trek: The Next Generation*: Alien Makeups," *Cinefantastique* 24(3/4): 50. October 1993.

___ Salter, David I. "*Star Trek: The Next Generation*: Special Visual Effects," *Cinefantastique* 24(3/4): 79-82. October 1993.

___ Sammon, Paul M. "Effects Scene: The Perigee of Apogee," *Cinefex* No. 54: 83-84. May 1993.

___ Sammon, Paul M. "Quick Cuts: That Other T-rex," *Cinefex* No. 56: 87-88. November 1993.

SPECIAL EFFECTS (continued)

___ Sammon, Paul M. "Quick Cuts: Wood Works," *Cinefex* No. 61: 107-110. March 1995.

___ Sandoval, Christine. "Gordon Smith: Seeking Silicone Solutions," *Cinefex* No. 64: 19-20, 128. December 1995.

___ Scapperotti, Dan. "King Effect: Computer Graphics by Image Design," *Cinefantastique* 26(5): 55. August 1995.

___ Schweiger, Daniel. "The Amazing Colossal Kid: Low Rent Movie Magic," *Cinefantastique* 23(1): 23. August 1992.

___ Scott, Elaine. **Movie Magic: Behind the Scenes with Special Effects**. New York: William Morrow, 1995. 95pp.

___ Shannon, John. "Panic on Liberty Island," *Cinefex* No. 52: 79-80. November 1992.

___ Shannon, John. "Quick Cuts: Under Heavy Cetacean," *Cinefex* No. 55: 17-18. August 1993.

___ Shannon, John. "Short Intruders," *Cinefex* No. 51: 79-80. August 1992.

___ Shay, Don. "Dick Smith: 50 Years in Makeup," *Cinefex* No. 62: 78-135. June 1995.

___ Shay, Don. "Effects Scene: In the Digital Domain," *Cinefex* No. 55: 111-112. August 1993.

___ Shay, Don. **The Making of Jurassic Park**, by Don Shay and Jody Duncan. New York: Ballantine, 1993. 195pp.

___ Shay, Don. "Mayhem over Miami," *Cinefex* No. 59: 34-79. September 1994.

___ Shay, Don. "Quick Cuts: The Return of the Vampire," *Cinefex* No. 60: 117-118. December 1994.

___ Shay, Estelle. "*Babe*: From the Mouth of Babe," *Cinefex* No. 64: 31-32, 130. December 1995.

___ Shay, Estelle. "Commercial Spot: Batteries Included," *Cinefex* No. 63: 129-130. September 1995.

___ Shay, Estelle. "Commercial Spot: Bear Necessities," *Cinefex* No. 63: 33-34. September 1995.

___ Shay, Estelle. "Commercial Spot: Light and Liberty," *Cinefex* No. 60: 39-40. December 1994.

___ Shay, Estelle. "Commercial Spot: This Frog's for You," *Cinefex* No. 63: 123-124. September 1995.

___ Shay, Estelle. "Company File: Makeup and Special Effects Laboratories," *Cinefex* No. 59: 111-112. September 1994.

___ Shay, Estelle. "Company File: Pixar," *Cinefex* No. 55: 23-24. August 1993.

___ Shay, Estelle. "Immortal Images," *Cinefex* No. 61: 38-57. March 1995.

___ Shay, Estelle. "*Operation Dumbo Drop*: Pachyderms and Parachutes," *Cinefex* No. 64: 121-122, 140. December 1995.

___ Shay, Estelle. "Profile: Pete Romano," *Cinefex* No. 56: 93. November 1993.

___ Shay, Estelle. "Profile: Randal M. Dutra," *Cinefex* No. 59: 117-118. September 1994.

___ Shay, Estelle. "Quick Cuts: Digital Soul Searching," *Cinefex* No. 56: 11-12. November 1993.

___ Shay, Estelle. "Quick Cuts: Santa's Helpers," *Cinefex* No. 61: 33-34. March 1995.

___ Shay, Estelle. "Quick Cuts: Sub Plots," *Cinefex* No. 62: 11-12. June 1995.

___ Shay, Estelle. "Quick Cuts: Thirty Seconds over Zaire," *Cinefex* No. 62: 23-24. June 1995.

___ Shay, Estelle. "*Three Wishes*: Making Wishes Come True," *Cinefex* No. 64: 43-44, 127. December 1995.

___ Shay, Estelle. "Video Beat: Casting Another Spell," *Cinefex* No. 60: 123-124. December 1994.

___ Skotak, Robert. "Creating the Metaluna Mutant," *Filmfax* No. 33: 56-59. June/July 1992.

___ Skotak, Robert. "Creating the Special FX for *This Island Earth*," *Filmfax* No. 33: 78-82, 94-97. June/July 1992.

___ Solman, Gregory. "The Illusion of a Future," *Film Comment* 28(2): 32-41. March/April 1992.

___ Sorensen, Peter. "Cyberworld," *Cinefex* No. 50: 54-76. May 1992.

___ Street, Rita. "Toys Will Be Toys," *Cinefex* No. 64: 76-91. December 1995.

___ Szebin, Frederick C. "The Special Effects of *Hercules*," *Cinefantastique* 26(2): 49-50, 60. February 1995.

___ Uram, Sue. "Evil Effects: Tom Sullivan, Gore Auteur," *Cinefantastique* 23(1): 50. August 1992.

___ Vaz, Mark C. "Animation in the Third Dimension," *Cinefex* No. 56: 30-53. November 1993.

SPECIAL EFFECTS (continued)

___ Vaz, Mark C. "*Casino*: The Lights of Las Vegas," *Cinefex* No. 64: 37-38, 140. December 1995.

___ Vaz, Mark C. "Dredd World," *Cinefex* No. 62: 58-73. June 1995.

___ Vaz, Mark C. "Effects Scene: From Tatooine to Endor," *Cinefex* No. 61: 115-116. March 1995.

___ Vaz, Mark C. "Forever a Knight," *Cinefex* No. 63: 90-113. September 1995.

___ Vaz, Mark C. "Haunting Creation," *Cinefex* No. 60: 70-85. December 1994.

___ Vaz, Mark C. "A Knight at the Zoo," *Cinefex* No. 51: 22-69. August 1992.

___ Vaz, Mark C. "Return to Neverland," *Cinefex* No. 49: 4-23. February 1992.

___ Vaz, Mark C. "Special Venues: Deep Earth, Dark Ride," *Cinefex* No. 57: 16-17. March 1994.

___ Vaz, Mark C. "Through the *Stargate*," *Cinefex* No. 61: 82-97. March 1995.

___ Vaz, Mark C. "Toy Wars," *Cinefex* No. 54: 54-73. May 1993.

___ Vaz, Mark C. "Video Beat: McCartney Takes Wing," *Cinefex* No. 57: 85-86. March 1994.

___ Vitaris, Paula. "*X-Files*: Computer Graphics," *Cinefantastique* 26(6)/27(1): 71-72. October 1995.

___ Vitaris, Paula. "*X-Files*: Monster Maker," *Cinefantastique* 26(6)/27(1): 39-40. October 1995.

___ Vitaris, Paula. "*X-Files*: Special Effects," *Cinefantastique* 26(6)/27(1): 55-56. October 1995.

___ Warren, Bill. "Gorillas by Winston," *Starlog* No. 218: 46-49, 66. September 1995.

___ Williams, David E. "An Oceanic Odyssey," *American Cinematographer* 76(8): 40-51. August 1995.

SPECIALTY PUBLISHING
___ SEE: SMALL PRESSES.

SPECIES (MOTION PICTURE)

___ "The Beauty Is a Beast," *People Weekly* 44(4): 164-165. July 24, 1995.

___ "*Species*: MGM Leases Giger's Titular Creature to Be Directed by Roger Donaldson," *Cinefantastique* 25(4): 51. August 1994.

___ Arnold, Gary. "Defective Alien Has Origin in Bad Taste," *Washington (DC) Times*. July 7, 1995. in: *NewsBank. Film and Television*. 81:A8. 1995.

___ Biodrowski, Steve. "*Species* (Review)," *Cinefantastique* 27(3): 53. December 1995.

___ Ebert, Roger. "*Species* Follows Old Formula," *Chicago (IL) Sun Times*. July 7, 1995. in: *NewsBank. Film and Television*. 72:A3. 1995.

___ Fristoe, Roger. "Designs on Hollywood," *(Louisville, KY) Courier-Journal*. July 2, 1995. in: *NewsBank. Film and Television*. 71:G13. 1995.

___ Holter, Rick. "Sci-Fi Film's Promise Turns into a Poor Excuse," *Dallas (TX) Morning News*. July 7, 1995. in: *NewsBank. Film and Television*. 72:A5. 1995.

___ Johnson, Malcolm. "Barren *Species* Barely Fit for Survival," *Hartford (CT) Courant*. July 7, 1995. in: *NewsBank. Film and Television*. 72:A2. 1995.

___ Kemp, Philip. "*Species* (Review)," *Sight and Sound* 5(10): 60-61. October 1995.

___ Lowe, Nick. "*Species* (Review)," *Interzone* No. 102: 34-35. December 1995.

___ Martin, Robert. "The Evolution of *Species*," *Sci-Fi Entertainment* 2(1): 36-39, 64. June 1995.

___ Medved, Michael. "Gore-geous Alien," *New York (NY) Post*. July 7, 1995. in: *NewsBank. Film and Television*. 81:A7. 1995.

___ Robley, Les P. "The Making of a Beautiful Monster," *American Cinematographer* 76(12): 62-68. December 1995.

___ Ryan, James. "Designing a Deadly Alien Who's Both Beauty, Beast," *Los Angeles (CA) Daily News*. July 7, 1995. in: *NewsBank. Film and Television*. 81:A4-A5. 1995.

___ Shay, Estelle. "Quick Cuts: An Endangering Species," *Cinefex* No. 63: 39-40. September 1995.

___ Shay, Estelle. "Quick Cuts: Capturing an Alien Species," *Cinefex* No. 63: 45-48. September 1995.

___ Shulgasser, Barbara. "*Species*: Return to Sender," *San Francisco (CA) Examiner*. July 7, 1995. in: *NewsBank. Film and Television*. 72:A1. 1995.

SPECIES (MOTION PICTURE) (continued)

___ Strauss, Bob. "Specious *Species* But Old-Fashioned Film," *Los Angeles (CA) Daily News*. July 7, 1995. in: *NewsBank. Film and Television*. 81:A6. 1995.

___ Verniere, James. "Top-Notch Cast Can't Save *Species* From Itself," *Boston (MA) Herald*. July 7, 1995. in: *NewsBank. Film and Television*. 72:A4. 1995.

___ Warren, Bill. "Building the Perfect Beast," *Starlog* No. 214: 41-45, 70. May 1995.

___ Warren, Bill. "The Deadliest of *Species*," *Starlog* No. 217: 52-56. August 1995.

___ Warren, Bill. "In the Blood," *Starlog* No. 218: 78-81, 66. September 1995.

SPEED (MOTION PICTURE)

___ Duncan, Jody. "Quick Cuts: Maximum Speed," *Cinefex* No. 59: 89-92. September 1994.

SPEER, JACK

___ "The Hugos (Or, the Empire Strikes Back)," *Science Fiction Chronicle* 17(2): 55-56. December 1995/January 1996.

SPENCE, THOMAS

___ Klaus, H. Gustav. "Thomas Spence: **Description of Spensonia** (1795)," in: Heuermann, Hartmut and Lange, Bernd-Peter, eds. **Die Utopie in der angloamerikanischen Literatur: Interpretationen**. Düsseldorf: Bagel, 1984. pp.60-79.

SPENCER GIFTS (STORE)

___ Underwood, Elaine. "Spencer Tests Sci-Fi On-Site TV," *Brandweek* 36(23): 3. June 5, 1995.

SPENCER, WILLIAM

___ Pringle, David. "The Sonic Sculptor: William Spencer Interviewed," *Interzone* No. 79: 42-46. January 1994.

SPERRY, ARMSTRONG W.

___ Barrett, Robert R. "To Bora-Bora and Back Again: The Story of Armstrong W. Sperry," *Burroughs Bulletin* NS No. 11: 3-8. July 1992.

SPIDERMAN (TV)

___ Jankiewicz, Pat. "Chris Barnes, the Spectacular Spiderman," *Starlog* No. 213: 52-55. April 1995.

SPIEGELMAN, ART

___ Gordon, Joan. "Surviving the Survivor: Art Spiegelman's **Maus**," *Journal of the Fantastic in the Arts* 5(2): 80-89. 1993. (No. 18)

SPIELBERG, STEVEN

___ "Open Letter From MCA to Spielberg and Stock Owners About *E.T.* Pic," *Variety* p. 7, 32. June 2, 1982.

___ "Spielberg Defers to Prophet Lucas," *Variety* p. 5, 36. June 2, 1982.

___ Andrews, Suzanna. "The Man Who Would Be Walt," *New York Times* Sec. 2, p. 1, 20-21. January 26, 1992.

___ Baltake, Joe. "Raider of Our Lost Youth: With *Hook*, Steven Spielberg Charts His Return to the World of Childhood Fantasy," *Sacramento (CA) Bee*. December 15, 1991. in: *NewsBank. Film and Television*. 7:C4-C6. 1992. also in: *NewsBank. Names in the News*. NIN 8: B6-B8. 1992.

___ Rosenfeld, Megan. "Spielberg in Neverland: Where the Movies Cost Millions and the Moguls Never Grow Up," *Washington (DC) Post*. December 15, 1991. in: *NewsBank. Film and Television*. 7:B13-C3. 1992. also in: *NewsBank. Names in the News* 8:B9. 1992.

___ Shay, Don. "A Close Encounter with Stephen Spielberg: Interview," *Cinefex* No. 53: 54-69. February 1993.

___ Sheehan, Henry. "The Fears of Children," *Sight and Sound* 3(7): 10. August 1993.

___ Slade, Darren. **Supernatural Spielberg**, by Darren Slade and Nigel Watson. London: Valis, 1992. 136pp.

___ Taylor, Philip M. **Steven Spielberg: The Man, His Movies, and Their Meaning**. New York: Continuum, 1992. 176pp.

___ Verniere, James. "Spielberg Hopes to Recapture Magic Touch," *Boston (MA) Herald*. December 13, 1991. in: *NewsBank. Film and Television*. 7:B12. 1992.

___ Verniere, James. "Who Took the Wonder out of the Wunderkind," *Boston (MA) Herald*. December 15, 1991. in: *NewsBank. Film and Television*. 7:C7-C8. 1992.

STAR TREK

STAR TREK (continued)

___ Lagon, Mark P. " 'We Owe It to Them to Interfere': *Star Trek* and U.S. Statecraft in the 1960s and 1990s," *Extrapolation* 34(3): 251-264. Fall 1993.

___ Langberg, Mike. "Star Tech," *Austin (TX) American Statesman* Sec. D., p. 1, 3. July 12, 1992.

___ Langsberg, Mike. "Treknology," *Star Trek: The Official Fan Club* No. 94: 32-35. November/December 1993.

___ Lees, Stella. "Morality Lesson or Hornblower in Space," *Viewpoint on Books for Young Adults* 1(2): 12-13. Winter 1993.

___ Lovett, Richard A. "*Star Trek* Science Exhibit Tours Country," *Science Fiction Age* 1(6): 20-21. September 1993.

___ Maccarillo, Lisa. "In the Lab of the Imagination with Michael Westmore," *Sci-Fi Entertainment* 1(2): 52-54. August 1994.

___ Madsen, Dan. "Designing *Deep Space Nine*," *Star Trek: The Official Fan Club* No. 89: 2-6. January/February 1993.

___ Madsen, Dan. "Exclusive Interview: William Shatner: The Final Voyage of Captain Kirk," *Star Trek: The Official Fan Club Magazine* No. 85: 2-4. May/June 1992.

___ Madsen, Dan. "The Future of *Star Trek*," *Star Trek: The Official Fan Club Magazine* No. 85: 7-9. May/June 1992.

___ Madsen, Dan. "Rick Berman: Interview," *Star Trek: The Official Fan Club Magazine* No. 91: 2-6. May/June 1993.

___ Magda, James. "Majel Barrett Nurses a Role," *Star Trek: The Official Fan Club* No. 94: 14-16, 41. February/March 1994.

___ Maloni, Kelly. **NetTrek: Your Guide to Trek Life in Cyberspace.** New York: Random House, 1995. 383pp.

___ Marin, Rick. "Warp Speed Ahead," *TV Guide* 41(30): 21-24. July 24, 1993.

___ Marinaccio, Dave. **All I Really Need to Know I Learned From Watching Star Trek.** New York: Crown, 1994. 128pp.

___ Martinez, Cal. "Future Special Effects: Recent Advances in *Star Trek*," in: Van Hise, James, ed. **Trek Celebration Two.** Las Vegas, NV: Pioneer, 1994. pp.148-151.

___ Meisler, Andy. "New *Star Trek* Adrift After Captain Abandons Ship," *Austin (TX) American Statesman* Sec. B, p. 6. September 17, 1994.

___ Nazzaro, Joe. "Reunifications," *Starlog* No. 208: 42-45. November 1994.

___ Nensi, Salman A. "Revealing the History of the Future," *Star Trek: The Official Fan Club Magazine* No. 91: 1, 8. May/June 1993.

___ Nichols, Nichelle. **Beyond Uhura: Star Trek and Other Memories.** New York: Putnam, 1995. 323pp.

___ Nimoy, Leonard. **I Am Spock.** New York: Hyperion, 1995. 342pp.

___ Okuda, Michael. **Star Trek Chronology: The History of the Future,** by Michael Okuda and Denise Okuda. New York: Pocket Books, 1993. 184pp.

___ Okuda, Michael. **The Star Trek Encyclopedia: A Reference Guide to the Future,** by Michael Okuda, Denise Okuda, Debbie Mirek and Doug Drexler. New York: Pocket Books, 1994. 396pp.

___ Parks, Louis B. "The Long, Great Trek," *Houston (TX) Chronicle* Sec. D, p. 1, 5. September 1, 1992.

___ Pearlman, Cindy. "Captains Quirk," *Chicago* 44(12): December 1995.

___ Pendergast, John S. "A Nation of Hamlets: Shakespeare and Cultural Politics," *Extrapolation* 36(1): 10-17. Spring 1995.

___ Perez, Dan. "*Star Trek*: The Saga Continues," *Science Fiction Age* 2(3): 22-23. March 1994.

___ Peterson, Don E. "*Star Trek*: Generations Gap," *Sci-Fi Entertainment* 1(4): 44-55, 96. December 1994.

___ Phillips, Mark. "Journeys to Strange Country," *Starlog* No. 206: 66-67. September 1994.

___ Plotsky, Richard. "News From the Front: The Penultimate Season," in: Van Hise, James, ed. **Trek Celebration Two.** Las Vegas, NV: Pioneer, 1994. pp.156-164.

___ Point, Michael. "Business on an Astronomical Scale," *Austin (TX) American Statesman* Time Out, p. 5. June 15, 1993.

___ Reinheimer, David. "Ontological and Ethical Allusion: Shakespeare in *The Next Generation*," *Extrapolation* 36(1): 46-54. Spring 1995.

___ Rivera, C. J. "Props to the Stars," in: Van Hise, James, ed. **Trek Celebration Two.** Las Vegas, NV: Pioneer, 1994. pp.152-155.

___ Roddenberry, Majel B. "The Legacy of *Star Trek*," *Humanist* 55(4): 9-11. July 1995.

___ Roller, Pamela E. "Lights! Camera! Dennis Madalone Delivers the Action," *Star Trek: The Official Fan Club* No. 96: 13-16. April/May 1994.

___ Saunders, Matthew F. **Star Trek as Modern Myth.** Master's Thesis, Colorado State University, 1994. 142pp.

STAR TREK (continued)

___ Schuster, Hal. **Trek: The Encyclopedia.** 'Unofficial and Uncensored,' by Hal Schuster and Wendy Rathbone. Las Vegas, NV: Pioneer, 1994. 229pp.

___ Schuster, Hal. **Trek: The Unauthorized A-Z,** by Hal Schuster and Wendy Rathbone. New York: Harper Prism, 1995. 576pp. (Mass market edition of the 1994 Pioneer Books title **Trek: The Encyclopedia**).

___ Shatner, William. **Shatner: Where No Man, the Authorized Biography of William Shatner.** New York: Grosset & Dunlap, 1979. 327pp.

___ Shatner, William. **Star Trek Movie Memories: Behind the Scenes Coverage of All Seven Star Trek Films, Including Star Trek VII.** New York: HarperCollins, 1994. 357pp.

___ Spelling, Ian. "Guest Star," *Starlog* No. 176: 50-53. March 1992.

___ Stanley, Dick. "Philosophy Teacher Hits Warp Speed; *Star Trek* Boldly Explored in Class," *Austin (TX) American Statesman* Sec. B, pp.1, 6. March 7, 1993.

___ Sulski, Jim. "Moonlighting," *Chicago Tribune* Sec. 5, p. 3. January 12, 1993.

___ Takei, George. **To the Stars: The Autobiography of George Takei, Star Trek's Mr. Sulu.** New York: Pocket Books, 1994. 406pp.

___ Takei, George. **To the Stars: The Autobiography of Star Trek's Mr. Sulu.** New York: Simon & Schuster Audio, 1994. 2 audiocassettes, 3 hours.

___ Tharsher, Paula C. "*Star Trek* Exhibit Beams You Out of This World," *Atlanta Journal. Leisure Magazine* p. 6. January 30, 1993.

___ Thrasher, Paula C. "*Star Trek* Exhibit Beams You Out of This World," *Atlanta Journal Constitution* Sec. WL, p. 1. January 30, 1993. [Not seen.]

___ Uram, Sue. "Beyond Uhura," *Cinefantastique* 26(2): 31. February 1995.

___ Van Hise, James. "Exobiology: Space Medicine at the Time of *Star Trek*," in: Van Hise, James, ed. **Trek Celebration Two.** Las Vegas, NV: Pioneer, 1994. pp.102-110.

___ Van Hise, James. "Foundation Is *Star Trek*," in: Van Hise, James, ed. **Trek Celebration Two.** Las Vegas, NV: Pioneer, 1994. pp.16-23.

___ Van Hise, James. **Let's Trek: The Budget Guide to the Klingons 1995.** Las Vegas, NV: Pioneer, 1994. 161pp.

___ Van Hise, James. "Life in the Mirror Universe," in: Van Hise, James, ed. **Trek Celebration Two.** Las Vegas, NV: Pioneer, 1994. pp.117-121.

___ Van Hise, James. "A Look at *The Next Generation*," in: Van Hise, James, ed. **Trek Celebration Two.** Las Vegas, NV: Pioneer, 1994. pp.24-28.

___ Van Hise, James. "The Major Alien Races of *Star Trek*," in: Van Hise, James, ed. **Trek Celebration Two.** Las Vegas, NV: Pioneer, 1994. pp.53-56.

___ Van Hise, James. **The Man Between the Ears: Star Trek's Leonard Nimoy.** Las Vegas, NV: Pioneer, 1992. 154pp.

___ Van Hise, James. **The Man Who Created Star Trek: Gene Roddenberry.** Las Vegas, NV: Pioneer Books, 1992. 156pp.

___ Van Hise, James. "The Music of *The Next Generation*," in: Van Hise, James, ed. **Trek Celebration Two.** Las Vegas, NV: Pioneer, 1994. pp.134-141.

___ Van Hise, James. "The Secondary Bridge Crews of the *Enterprise*," in: Van Hise, James, ed. **Trek Celebration Two.** Las Vegas, NV: Pioneer, 1994. pp.89-101.

___ Van Hise, James. **The Trek Celebration Two.** Las Vegas: Pioneer, 1994. 166pp.

___ Van Hise, James. **Trek: The Unauthorized Story of the Movies,** by James Van Hise and Hal Schuster. Las Vegas, NV: Pioneer Books, 1995. 208pp.

___ Van Matre, Lynn. "Trekkers Say 'HISlaH' to Klingon Language Lessons," *Austin (TX) American Statesman* Sec. D, p. 6. March 6, 1993.

___ Verba, Joan M. **Boldly Writing: A Trekker Fan and Zine History, 1967-1987.** Minnetonka, MN: FTL Publications, 1996. 100pp.

___ Walden, Justine. "The Political Aesthetic: Nation and Narrativity on the Starship *Enterprise*," [17 pp.] 1994. (Cited from the Internet. HTTP: //remarque.berkeley. edu:8001 /[tilde]xcohen /Papers /Walden / walden.toc.html.) (Note: Insert tilde character, delete spaces to use on-line. Typography requirements required these changes.)

___ Waterside, Pat. "Trek Gallery," *Sci-Fi Entertainment* 1(1): 48-51. June 1994.

___ Witchel, Alex. "Boldly Contemplating Death and the Sequel," *New York Times* p.B1. November 23, 1994.

___ Woods, Louis A. "Jung and *Star Trek*: The Coincidentia Oppositorum and Images of the Shadow," by Louis A. Woods and Gary L. Harmon. *Journal of Popular Culture* 28(2): 169-183. Fall 1994.

STAR TREK

STAR TREK (continued)

___ Worland, Rick. "From the New Frontier to the Final Frontier: *Star Trek* From Kennedy to Gorbachev," *Film & History* 24(1/2): 19-35. February/May 1994.

___ Zoglin, Richard. "Trekking Onward," by Richard Zoglin and Michael Walsh. *Time* 144(22): 72-79. November 28, 1994.

STAR TREK: DEEP SPACE NINE (COMIC)

___ Altman, Mark A. "Deep Space Four-Color," *Star Trek: The Official Fan Club* No. 94: 50-51. February/March 1994.

___ Chrissinger, Craig W. "Station Log," *Starlog* No. 198: 52-55. January 1994.

STAR TREK: DEEP SPACE NINE (TV)

___ "*Star Trek*: The Next Season," *TV Guide* 41(30): 13. July 24, 1993.

___ Airey, Jean. "Alien Aboard," *Starlog* No. 188: 38-41, 68. March 1993.

___ Altman, Mark A. "Deep and Confused: Can *Deep Space Nine* Replace *Next Generation*?," *Sci-Fi Universe* No. 3: 47-63. October/November 1994.

___ Altman, Mark A. "*Deep Space Nine* Second Season Episode Guide," *Sci-Fi Universe* No. 3: 50-63. October/November 1994.

___ Altman, Mark A. "*Star Trek: Deep Space Nine*: Behind the Scenes, A Day on the Set," *Cinefantastique* 24(3/4): 96-98. October 1993.

___ Altman, Mark A. "*Star Trek: Deep Space Nine*: Casting the Space Station Ensemble," *Cinefantastique* 23(6): 20-21. April 1993.

___ Altman, Mark A. "*Star Trek: Deep Space Nine*: 'Emissary': Creating the Pilot," *Cinefantastique* 24(3/4): 100-101. October 1993.

___ Altman, Mark A. "*Star Trek: Deep Space Nine*: Episode Guide, the First Season," *Cinefantastique* 24(3/4): 91-110. October 1993.

___ Altman, Mark A. "*Star Trek: Deep Space Nine*: Filming on the New Frontier," *Cinefantastique* 23(6): 24-25. April 1993.

___ Altman, Mark A. "*Star Trek: Deep Space Nine*: Herman Zimmerman, Production Designer," *Cinefantastique* 23(6): 28-29. April 1993.

___ Altman, Mark A. "*Star Trek: Deep Space Nine*: Major Kira," *Cinefantastique* 24(3/4): 103. October 1993.

___ Altman, Mark A. "*Star Trek: Deep Space Nine*: Michael Piller, Series Co-Creator," *Cinefantastique* 23(6): 23. April 1993.

___ Altman, Mark A. "*Star Trek: Deep Space Nine*: Odo," *Cinefantastique* 24(3/4): 95. October 1993.

___ Altman, Mark A. "*Star Trek: Deep Space Nine*: Quark," *Cinefantastique* 24(3/4): 90. October 1993.

___ Altman, Mark A. "*Star Trek: Deep Space Nine*: Rick Berman, Trek's Major Domo," *Cinefantastique* 23(6): 18. April 1993.

___ Altman, Mark A. "*Star Trek: Deep Space Nine*: Scripting the Adventures," *Cinefantastique* 23(6): 40-42. April 1993.

___ Altman, Mark A. "*Star Trek: Deep Space Nine*: Shooting on the New Space Station," *Cinefantastique* 24(3/4): 92-93. October 1993.

___ Altman, Mark A. "*Star Trek: Deep Space Nine*: Spin-Off Series Preview," *Cinefantastique* 23(2/3): 80-83. October 1992.

___ Altman, Mark A. "*Star Trek: Deep Space Nine*: The Pilot, Behind the Scenes," *Cinefantastique* 23(6): 32-34. April 1993.

___ Altman, Mark A. "*Star Trek: Deep Space Nine*: Visitor on Board," *Cinefantastique* 23(6): 26. April 1993.

___ Altman, Mark A. "*Star Trek: Deep Space Nine*," *Cinefantastique* 23(4): 4-5. December 1992.

___ Altman, Mark A. "*Star Trek: Deep Space Nine*," *Cinefantastique* 23(6): 16-43. April 1993.

___ Altman, Mark A. "*Star Trek: Deep Space Nine*," *Cinefantastique* 24(3/4): 88-110. October 1993.

___ Bischoff, David. "Behind the Scenes of *Star Trek: Deep Space Nine*," *Omni* 15(5): 34-40, 84-85. February/March 1993.

___ Carone, Daniel. "Roddenberry Spirit Molds Latest Spinoff, *Deep Space Nine*," *Austin (TX) American Statesman* Sec. B, p. 4. January 5, 1993.

___ Cohen, Amy J. "Rene Auberjonois, the Morphing Man," *Star Trek: The Official Fan Club Magazine* No. 92: 2-6. July/August 1993.

___ Dreher, Ron. "Be Sure to Beam Yourself up to *Deep Space Nine* (Review)," *Washington (DC) Times*. January 4, 1993. in: *NewsBank. Art.* 1:C4. 1993.

___ Eby, Douglas. "*Star Trek: Deep Space Nine*: The Wormhole," *Cinefantastique* 24(3/4): 111. October 1993.

___ Fisher, Bob. "*Star Trek* Meets *The Next Generation*," *American Cinematographer* 75(10): 74-82. October 1994.

___ Flixman, Ed. "*Star Trek: Deep Space Nine*; Beyond the Wormhole," *Sci-Fi Entertainment* 1(4): 56-61. December 1994.

STAR TREK: DEEP SPACE NINE (TV) (continued)

___ Jankiewicz, Pat. "Time of the Green," *Starlog* No. 204: 72-76. July 1994.

___ Jensen, Elizabeth. "Latest *Star Trek* Spinoff of Spinoff Starts at Warp Speed," *Wall Street Journal* p. B7. January 7, 1993.

___ Jonas, Gerald. "Stop the Spaceship, I Want to Get Off," *New York Times* Sec. 2, p. 26. January 31, 1993.

___ Kenny, Glenn. "Double Time on DS9," *TV Guide* 43(11): 36. March 18, 1995.

___ Kenny, Glenn. "The Facts About Dax," *TV Guide* 42(34): 30. August 20, 1994.

___ Kutzera, Dale. "*Star Trek: Deep Space Nine*: Episode Guide, Second Season," *Cinefantastique* 25(6)/26(1): 96-111. December 1994.

___ Kutzera, Dale. "*Star Trek: Deep Space Nine*," *Cinefantastique* 25(6)/26(1): 94-98. December 1994.

___ Logan, Michael. "Deep Dish," *TV Guide* 41(1): 10-15. January 2, 1993. (Issue 2075)

___ Logan, Michael. "*TV Guide* Interview: Rick Berman," *TV Guide* 41(30): 10-13. July 24, 1993.

___ Logan, Michael. "What's Happening With the Hits: Introducing the Defiant," *TV Guide* 42(39): 24-25. September 24, 1994.

___ Lorando, Mark. "Trekkies Headed for Deep Space," *New Orleans (LA) Times-Picayune* Sec. A, p. 9. January 21, 1992.

___ Loren, Christalene. "Video Beat: *Deep Space Nine* Miniatures," *Cinefex* No. 54: 21-22. May 1993.

___ Loren, Christalene. "Video Beat: Deep Space Wormholes," *Cinefex* No. 55: 11-12. August 1993.

___ Madsen, Dan. "Designing *Deep Space Nine*," *Star Trek: The Official Fan Club* No. 89: 2-6. January/February 1993.

___ Madsen, Dan. "*Star Trek* Update," *Star Trek: The Official Fan Club* No. 93: 29-31. September/October 1993.

___ Madsen, Dan. "Welcome to *Deep Space Nine*, Part 1," *Star Trek: The Official Fan Club* No. 89: 10-13. January/February 1993.

___ Madsen, Dan. "Welcome to *Deep Space Nine*, Part 2," *Star Trek: The Official Fan Club* No. 90: 11-13. March/April 1993.

___ Madsen, Dan. "Welcome to *Deep Space Nine*, Part 3," *Star Trek: The Official Fan Club Magazine* No. 91: 10-12. May/June 1993.

___ Mae, James. "A Labor of Love: The Making of 'Relics'," *Star Trek: The Official Fan Club* No. 90: 2-4. March/April 1993.

___ Mitchard, Jacquelyn. "The Best Young Teen Shows: *Star Trek: Deep Space Nine*," *TV Guide* 42(11): 16. March 12, 1994.

___ Nance, Scott. **Trek: Deep Space Nine**. Las Vegas: Pioneer Books, 1993. 127pp.

___ Parks, Louis B. "Starfleet Finds New Commander for Series," *Houston (TX) Chronicle* Sec. D, p. 1, 5. September 1, 1992.

___ Prokop, Tim. "*Star Trek: Deep Space Nine*: Ferengi Stardom," *Cinefantastique* 25(6)/26(1): 110. December 1994.

___ Prokop, Tim. "*Star Trek: Deep Space Nine*: Special Effects," *Cinefantastique* 25(6)/26(1): 99-102. December 1994.

___ Prokop, Tim. "*Star Trek: Deep Space Nine*: The Alternate," *Cinefantastique* 25(6)/26(1): 106-107. December 1994.

___ Prokop, Tim. "*Star Trek: Deep Space Nine*: The Jem'Hadar," *Cinefantastique* 25(6)/26(1): 106-107. December 1994.

___ Reeves-Stevens, Judith. **The Making of Star Trek: Deep Space Nine**, by Judith Reeves-Stevens and Garfield Reeves-Stevens. New York: Pocket Books, 1994. 319pp.

___ Salter, David I. "*Star Trek: Deep Space Nine*: Alien Makeups," *Cinefantastique* 23(6): 31. April 1993.

___ Salter, David I. "*Star Trek: Deep Space Nine*: Conceptual Artist Richard Delgado," *Cinefantastique* 23(6): 36-37. April 1993.

___ Salter, David I. "*Star Trek: Deep Space Nine*: Designing Aliens," *Cinefantastique* 24(3/4): 106. October 1993.

___ Salter, David I. "*Star Trek: Deep Space Nine*: Effects," *Cinefantastique* 24(3/4): 105. October 1993.

___ Salter, David I. "*Star Trek: Deep Space Nine*: Shape-Shifting Security Chief," *Cinefantastique* 23(6): 39. April 1993.

___ Shapiro, Marc. "*Star Trek: Deep Space Nine*," *Starlog* No. 186: 40-43. January 1993.

___ Snyder, Sharon. "Another Fine Ferengi," by Sharon Snyder and Marc Shapiro. *Starlog* No. 190: 36-39. May 1993.

___ Spelling, Ian. "Bashir Grows Up," *Starlog* No. 201: 50-53. April 1994.

___ Spelling, Ian. "Constable Morph," *Starlog* No. 191: 27-31. June 1993.

___ Spelling, Ian. "Deep Thoughts," *Starlog* No. 189: 44-47, 64. April 1993.

STAR TREK: DEEP SPACE NINE (TV)

STAR TREK: DEEP SPACE NINE (TV) (continued)
___ Spelling, Ian. " 'DS9' Pals Live out a Tom Sawyer Fantasy," *Houston (TX) Chronicle* Sec. C, p. 2. June 4, 1994.
___ Spelling, Ian. "In Command," *Starlog* No. 207: 41-44, 70. October 1994.
___ Spelling, Ian. "Klingon Again," *Starlog* No. 219: 42-43. October 1995.
___ Spelling, Ian. "Leader of the Space Station," *Starlog* No. 187: 40-45, 70. February 1993.
___ Spelling, Ian. "Major Player," *Starlog* No. 199: 27-33. February 1994.
___ Spelling, Ian. "Major Player," in: McDonnell, David, ed. **Starlog's Science Fiction Heroes and Heroines**. New York: Crescent Books, 1995. pp.62-65.
___ Spelling, Ian. "The Trill of It All," *Starlog* No. 188: 42-45, 64. March 1993.
___ Van Hise, James. **The Deep Space Celebration**. Las Vegas, NV: Pioneer, 1994. 190pp.
___ Van Hise, James. **The Deep Space Crew Book**. Las Vegas, NV: Pioneer, 1994. 193pp.
___ Van Hise, James. **Sci Fi TV: From Twilight Zone to Deep Space Nine**. Las Vegas, NV: Pioneer Books, 1993. 160pp. (Reprinted, HarperPrism, 1995. 258pp.)
___ Van Hise, James. **Trek in the 24th Century: The Next Generation and Deep Space Nine**. 'Unofficial and Uncensored'. Las Vagas, NV: Pioneer, 1994. 164pp.
___ Van Hise, James. **The Unauthorized Trek: Deep Space, The Voyage Continues**. Las Vegas, NV: Pioneer, 1994. 198pp.
___ Westbrook, Bruce. "DS9 Takes a Fresh Approach: Klingon Worf Joins the Crew," *Houston (TX) Chronicle*. October 4, 1995. in: *NewsBank. Film and Television*. 99:B5. 1995.
___ Westbrook, Bruce. "Third Time's the Charm: Newest **Star Trek** Offers TV Universe a 'Real' Good Time," *Houston (TX) Chronicle*. TV Chronilog pp.3-4. January 3, 1993.
___ Zimmerman, Herman. "Architect of Illusion: Designing **Deep Space Nine**," *Omni* 15(5): 42-46, 86. February/March 1993.

STAR TREK: EXHIBITION
___ McTaggart, Maureen. "It's Life, Jim, but Not as We've Known It," *Times Educational Supplement* 4139: SS21. October 27, 1995.

STAR TREK GENERATIONS (MOTION PICTURE)
___ "Generations: The Baton Is Passed to **The Next Generation**," *Sci-Fi Universe* No. 3: 64. October/November 1994.
___ "Seeing the Future," *Sci-Fi Entertainment* 1(4): 54-55. December 1994.
___ Altman, Mark A. "**Star Trek: The Next Generation**: Heading for the Big Screen," *Cinefantastique* 24(3/4): 31-34. October 1993.
___ Arnold, Gary. "Picard and Co. Engage the Cinema," *Washington (DC) Times*. November 18, 1994. in: *NewsBank. Film and Television*. 125:D14. 1994.
___ Bark, Ed. "If Not Excellent, At Least It's Entertaining," *Dallas (TX) Morning News*. November 18, 1994. in: *NewsBank. Film and Television*. 125:D11-12. 1994.
___ Beeler, Michael. "**Star Trek: Generations**: El-Curian Heavy," *Cinefantastique* 26(2): 23. February 1995.
___ Beeler, Michael. "**Star Trek: Generations**: Feature vs. Series," *Cinefantastique* 26(2): 24-25. February 1995.
___ Beeler, Michael. "**Star Trek: Generations**: John Alonzo," *Cinefantastique* 26(2): 27. February 1995.
___ Beeler, Michael. "**Star Trek: Generations**: The Star Trek Curse," *Cinefantastique* 26(2): 26. February 1995.
___ Beeler, Michael. "**Star Trek: Generations**: Two Captains," *Cinefantastique* 26(2): 18. February 1995.
___ Beeler, Michael. "**Star Trek: Generations**," *Cinefantastique* 25(5): 4-5. October 1994.
___ Beeler, Michael. "**Star Trek: Generations**," *Cinefantastique* 25(6)/26(1): 20-23. December 1994.
___ Beeler, Michael. "**Star Trek: Generations**," *Cinefantastique* 26(2): 16-30, 40. February 1995.
___ Berkman, Meredith. "Trek's Appeal," *Mademoiselle* 100(12): 85. December 1994.
___ Bonko, Larry. "Final Trek," *Norfolk (VA) Virginian-Pilot*. May 28, 1994. in: *NewsBank. Film and Television*. 59:B6-B8. 1994.
___ Britton, Bonnie. "**Next Generation** Cast Inherits Big-Screen Time," *Indianapolis (IN) Star*. November 18, 1994. in: *NewsBank. Film and Television*. 125:D4-D5. 1994.

STAR TREK II: THE WRATH OF KHAN (MOTION PICTURE)

STAR TREK GENERATIONS (MOTION PICTURE) (continued)
___ Campbell, Bob. "Latest Star Trek Mission to Save the World (or 2)," *(Newark, NJ) Star-Ledger*. November 18, 1994. in: *NewsBank. Film and Television*. 125:D7. 1994.
___ Cerone, Daniel H. "Star Trek Only a Show? Is This Guy Serious?," *Los Angeles (CA) Times*. November 13, 1994. in: *NewsBank. Film and Television*. 10:D8-D12. 1995.
___ Flixman, Ed. "The Once and Future Kirk," *Sci-Fi Entertainment* 1(4): 47. December 1994.
___ Hulbert, Dan. "Film Passes Baton to *Enterprise's* Heirs," *(Atlanta, GA) Journal*. November 17, 1994. in: *NewsBank. Film and Television*. 125:C12-C13. 1994.
___ Hunter, Stephen. "Generations Has Gaps, But Picard and Co. Are Stellar," *(Baltimore, MD) Sun*. November 18, 1994. in: *NewsBank. Film and Television*. 125:D6. 1994.
___ Johnson, Barry. "Captains Courageous," *Portland (OR) The Oregonian*. November 18, 1994. in: *NewsBank. Film and Television*. 125:D9-D10. 1994.
___ Johnson, Malcolm. "Universal Appeal," *Hartford (CT) Courant*. November 18, 1994. in: *NewsBank. Film and Television*. 125:D2-D3. 1994.
___ Katz, Francis. "Sell-Out Has Trekkies Weeping in the Rain," *Boston (MA) Herald*. November 19, 1994. in: *NewsBank. Film and Television*. 125:C14. 1994.
___ Lowe, Nick. "**Star Trek: Generations** (Review)," *Interzone* No. 95: 35-36. May 1995.
___ Madsen, Dan. "Movie Update," *Star Trek: The Official Fan Club* No. 94: 30-31. November/December 1993.
___ Magid, Ron. "ILM Creates New Universe of Effects for **Star Trek: Generations**," *American Cinematographer* 76(4): 78-88. April 1995.
___ Martin, Kevin H. "Kirk Out," *Cinefex* No. 61: 62-77. March 1995.
___ Medved, Michael. "Star-Crossed Mission," *New York (NY) Post*. November 18, 1994. in: *NewsBank. Film and Television*. 125:D8. 1994.
___ Nazzaro, Joe. "Generations Gap," *Starlog* No. 210: 40-45. January 1995.
___ Parks, Louis B. "Kirk and Picard Unite for Stellar Enterprise," *Houston (TX) Chronicle*. November 18, 1994. in: *NewsBank. Film and Television*. 125:D13. 1994.
___ Peterson, Don E. "**Star Trek**: Generations Gap," *Sci-Fi Entertainment* 1(4): 44-55, 96. December 1994.
___ Smith, Russell. "Bridging the Generations Gap," *Austin (TX) American Statesman* p. E1, E8. November 18, 1994.
___ Spelling, Ian. "The Man Who Killed Kirk," *Starlog* No. 213: 75-79, 72. April 1995.
___ Spelling, Ian. "Spanning Generations," *Starlog* No. 209: 48-53. December 1994.
___ Stein, Ben P. "**Star Trek**: Science on the Edge," *Science World* 51(3): 9-13. October 7, 1994.
___ Strauss, Bob. "Generations," *Los Angeles (CA) Daily News*. November 18, 1994. in: *NewsBank. Film and Television*. 125:C10-C11. 1994.
___ Strauss, Bob. "Generations Sends Originals into Final Frontier," *Los Angeles (CA) Daily News*. November 18, 1994. in: *NewsBank. Film and Television*. 125:D1. 1994.
___ Strauss, Bob. "Kirk Out?," *Los Angeles (CA) Daily News*. November 26, 1994. in: *NewsBank. Film and Television*. 10:D6-D7. 1995.
___ Strick, Philip. "**Star Trek: Generations** (Review)," *Sight and Sound* 5(3): 55-56. March 1995.
___ Uram, Sue. "**Star Trek: Generations**: Chekov Makes Captain," *Cinefantastique* 26(2): 32-33. February 1995.
___ Uram, Sue. "**Star Trek: Generations**: Roddenberry's Legacy," *Cinefantastique* 26(2): 34-39. February 1995.
___ Uram, Sue. "**Star Trek: Generations**: Spock Speaks," *Cinefantastique* 26(2): 20-21. February 1995.
___ Uram, Sue. "**Star Trek: Generations**: Where's Captain Sulu," *Cinefantastique* 25(6)/26(1): 22. December 1994.
___ Uram, Sue. "**Star Trek: Generations**: You're Dead, Jim," *Cinefantastique* 25(6)/26(1): 23. December 1994.
___ Zoglin, Richard. "Trekking Onward," by Richard Zoglin and Michael Walsh. *Time* 144(22): 72-79. November 28, 1994.

STAR TREK II: THE WRATH OF KHAN (MOTION PICTURE)
___ "Canadian 'Trek' Promo Reaps Free Ad Space," *Variety* p. 23. September 1, 1982.
___ "Dealers Ecstatic as Paramount Halves 'Trek II' Tape Tab," *Variety* p. 56. September 1, 1982.

STAR TREK II: THE WRATH OF KHAN (MOTION PICTURE) (continued)

___ "Paramount Revises Its 'Star Trek 2' Tag; 'Vengeance' Now 'Wrath'," *Variety* p. 5, 25. April 14, 1982.

___ "*Star Trek II*: Sales Vs. Rental Fulcrum," *Variety* p. 31-32. October 6, 1982.

___ Hodges, Shari. "A Pedagogically Useful Comparison of *Star Trek II* and *Paradise Lost*," *CEA Forum* 24(2): 4-7. Summer 1994.

STAR TREK III: THE SEARCH FOR SPOCK (MOTION PICTURE)

___ Cohn, Lawrence. "Par Backs Nimoy, 'Trek' to Hilt; Talks Going Re Possible Part IV," *Variety* p. 5, 26. June 6, 1984.

STAR TREK IV: THE VOYAGE HOME (MOTION PICTURE)

___ "Shatner Ends Holdout, Joins Cast of 'Trek IV'," *Variety* p. 23. February 6, 1985.

STAR TREK (MOTION PICTURE)

___ "Yet to Roll 'Star Trek II' Seeks Six Weeks, 90-10, for June 1982," *Variety* p. 7, 37. November 18, 1981.

___ Lofficier, Randy. "*Star Trek Movies* (1980-1988): Interviews with Jack Sowards, Nicholas Mayer, Harve Bennett; Leonard Nimoy and William Shatner," by Randy Lofficier and Jean-Marc Lofficier. in: Goldberg, Lee et al. **Science Fiction Filmmaking in the 1980s**. Jefferson, NC: McFarland, 1995. pp.189-236.

___ Shapiro, Marc. "School's Out," *Starlog* No. 189: 38-39, 68. April 1993.

___ Sherman, Paul. "For Trek Merchandisers, the Sky's No Limit," *Boston (MA) Herald*. November 17, 1994. in: *NewsBank. Film and Television*. 10:A1. 1995.

STAR TREK: THE NEXT GENERATION (TV)

___ "Best of Generation: Readers Name the Top 25 Episodes of *Star Trek: The Next Generation*," *Starlog* No. 195: 44-49. October 1993.

___ "Galactic Series Ends With a Stellar Show," *Washington (DC) Times*. May 22, 1994. in: *NewsBank. Film and Television*. 59:C8. 1994.

___ "Paramount Rises From the *Amerika* Debacle with 'Trek' and 'Friday'," *Variety* p. 155, 167. October 15, 1986.

___ "Saying Goodbye to Another Starfleet Generation," *Radio Program: Weekend Edition (NPR)* Program 1071. May 15, 1994. (Transcript available)

___ "*Star Trek*: The Next Season," *TV Guide* 41(30): 13. July 24, 1993.

___ " 'Trek' A Trip Worth Taking: Show's Optimistic Message Not Just for Fanatics (Review)," *Boston (MA) Herald*. January 24, 1992. in: *NewsBank. Film and Television*. 15:C3-C4. 1992.

___ Adalian, Josef. "Nixed Generation," *Washington (DC) Times*. May 22, 1994. in: *NewsBank. Film and Television*. 59:B9-B11. 1994.

___ Altman, Mark A. "Just the Facts, Max," *Star Trek: The Official Fan Club* No. 96: 50-52. April/May 1994.

___ Altman, Mark A. "*The Next Generation: Star Trek*'s Unification," *Cinefantastique* 23(2/3): 47-50. October 1992.

___ Altman, Mark A. "*The Next Generation*: Data Entry," *Cinefantastique* 23(2/3): 64-66. October 1992.

___ Altman, Mark A. "*The Next Generation*: Ensign Ro Laren," *Cinefantastique* 23(2/3): 96-98. October 1992.

___ Altman, Mark A. "*The Next Generation*: Inside the Writing Staff," *Cinefantastique* 23(2/3): 42. October 1992.

___ Altman, Mark A. "*The Next Generation*: Next Generation's Piller of Strength," *Cinefantastique* 23(2/3): 44-45. October 1992.

___ Altman, Mark A. "*The Next Generation*: Q-Where?," *Cinefantastique* 23(2/3): 63, 125. October 1992.

___ Altman, Mark A. "*The Next Generation*: Quiet on the Set," *Cinefantastique* 23(2/3): 87-89. October 1992.

___ Altman, Mark A. "*The Next Generation*: Reincarnating Denise Crosby," *Cinefantastique* 23(2/3): 34. October 1992.

___ Altman, Mark A. "*The Next Generation*: Shooting *Star Trek*," *Cinefantastique* 23(2/3): 55-58. October 1992.

___ Altman, Mark A. "*The Next Generation*: Tackling Gay Rights," *Cinefantastique* 23(2/3): 71-74. October 1992.

___ Altman, Mark A. "*The Next Generation*: The Making of 'The First Duty'," *Cinefantastique* 23(2/3): 52-53. October 1992.

___ Altman, Mark A. "*Star Trek*: Building for the Future," *Cinefantastique* 23(2/3): 84-85. October 1992.

___ Altman, Mark A. "*Star Trek*: Cinematographer Marvin Rush," *Cinefantastique* 23(2/3): 68-69. October 1992.

___ Altman, Mark A. "*Star Trek*: Fashion in the 24th Century," *Cinefantastique* 23(2/3): 76-77. October 1992.

STAR TREK: THE NEXT GENERATION (TV) (continued)

___ Altman, Mark A. "*Star Trek*: Rick Berman, Trek's New Great Bird," *Cinefantastique* 23(2/3): 36-37. October 1992.

___ Altman, Mark A. "*Star Trek*: Two Wrights Don't Make a Wrong," *Cinefantastique* 23(2/3): 60-61. October 1992.

___ Altman, Mark A. "*Star Trek: The Next Generation: Star Trek*'s Next Spin-Off," *Cinefantastique* 24(3/4): 18. October 1993.

___ Altman, Mark A. "*Star Trek: The Next Generation*: Brent Spiner on Data," *Cinefantastique* 24(3/4): 42. October 1993.

___ Altman, Mark A. "*Star Trek: The Next Generation*: Chain of Command," *Cinefantastique* 24(3/4): 39-41. October 1993.

___ Altman, Mark A. "*Star Trek: The Next Generation*: Episode Guide, Sixth Season," *Cinefantastique* 24(3/4): 16-87. October 1993.

___ Altman, Mark A. "*Star Trek: The Next Generation*: Guess Q's Coming to Dinner?," *Cinefantastique* 24(3/4): 47-49. October 1993.

___ Altman, Mark A. "*Star Trek: The Next Generation*: Heading for the Big Screen," *Cinefantastique* 24(3/4): 31-34. October 1993.

___ Altman, Mark A. "*Star Trek: The Next Generation*: Jeri Taylor, Script Supervisor," *Cinefantastique* 24(3/4): 36-37. October 1993.

___ Altman, Mark A. "*Star Trek: The Next Generation*: Marina Sirtis, Betazoid Beauty," *Cinefantastique* 24(3/4): 64-66. October 1993.

___ Altman, Mark A. "*Star Trek: The Next Generation*: Michael Piller, Trek's Secret Weapon," *Cinefantastique* 24(3/4): 28-29. October 1993.

___ Altman, Mark A. "*Star Trek: The Next Generation*: Rene Eschevarria, Waiter Cum Writer," *Cinefantastique* 24(3/4): 68-69. October 1993.

___ Altman, Mark A. "*Star Trek: The Next Generation*: Rick Berman, Keeper of the Flame," *Cinefantastique* 24(3/4): 20-21. October 1993.

___ Altman, Mark A. "*Star Trek: The Next Generation*: Ron Moore and Brannon Braga," *Cinefantastique* 24(3/4): 60-61. October 1993.

___ Altman, Mark A. "*Star Trek: The Next Generation*: Stephen Hawking's *Star Trek* cameo," *Cinefantastique* 24(3/4): 63. October 1993.

___ Altman, Mark A. "*Star Trek: The Next Generation*: Technobabble's Main Man," *Cinefantastique* 24(3/4): 76-77. October 1993.

___ Altman, Mark A. "*Star Trek: The Next Generation*: The Acting Ensemble," *Cinefantastique* 24(3/4): 44-45. October 1993.

___ Altman, Mark A. "*Star Trek: The Next Generation*: The Board and the Art of the Pitch," *Cinefantastique* 24(3/4): 52-55. October 1993.

___ Altman, Mark A. "*Star Trek: The Next Generation*: The Making of 'Birthright'," *Cinefantastique* 24(3/4): 71-74. October 1993.

___ Altman, Mark A. "*Star Trek: The Next Generation*: The Making of 'Relics'," *Cinefantastique* 24(3/4): 22-27. October 1993.

___ Altman, Mark A. "*Star Trek: The Next Generation*: The Making of 'Tapestry'," *Cinefantastique* 24(3/4): 56-57. October 1993.

___ Altman, Mark A. "*Star Trek: The Next Generation*: Will Riker, to Be or Not to Be?," *Cinefantastique* 24(3/4): 58. October 1993.

___ Altman, Mark A. "*Star Trek: The Next Generation*," *Cinefantastique* 23(2/3): 32-102. October 1992.

___ Altman, Mark A. "*Star Trek: The Next Generation*," *Cinefantastique* 24(3/4): 16-87. October 1993.

___ Antonucci, Mike. "The Final Frontier," *San Jose (CA) Mercury News*. May 22, 1994. in: *NewsBank. Film and Television*. 59:C4. 1994.

___ Bloch-Hansen, Peter. "Perfect Mating," *Starlog* No. 197: 58-61. December 1993.

___ Bonko, Larry. "Final Trek," *Norfolk (VA) Virginian-Pilot*. May 28, 1994. in: *NewsBank. Film and Television*. 59:B6-B8. 1994.

___ Brady, James. "In Step With: Patrick Stewart," *Austin (TX) American Statesman. Parade Magazine* p. 12. April 5, 1992.

___ Cerone, Daniel H. "Ending of *Next Generation* Spawns New Films, Series," *Austin (TX) American Statesman* Sec. B, p. 6. April 7, 1994.

___ Chrissinger, Craig W. "Alien Ideas," *Starlog* No. 189: 54-58, 64. April 1993.

___ Cohen, Amy J. "LeVar Burton: The Vision of Georgi LaForge," *Star Trek: The Official Fan Club* No. 94: C-D, 1. November/December 1993.

___ Cohen, Amy J. "More Than Just a Country Doctor," *Star Trek: The Official Fan Club* No. 96: 41-45. April/May 1994.

___ Collins, Diana. "Guy Vardaman: Standing in for Data," in: Van Hise, James, ed. **Trek Celebration Two**. Las Vegas, NV: Pioneer, 1994. pp.142-147.

___ Doty, Kay. "Sarek of Vulcan," in: Van Hise, James, ed. **Trek Celebration Two**. Las Vegas, NV: Pioneer, 1994. pp.40-52.

___ Fisher, Bob. "*Star Trek* Meets *The Next Generation*," *American Cinematographer* 75(10): 74-82. October 1994.

___ Florence, Bill. "Alien Dreams," *Starlog* No. 194: 50-53. September 1993.

STAR TREK: THE NEXT GENERATION (TV) (continued)

___ Florence, Bill. "Captain's Lady," *Starlog* No. 220: 54-57. November 1995.

___ Grant, Glenn. "Channeling Horny Jellyfish in an Anyon Field," *New York Review of Science Fiction* No. 67: 7. March 1994.

___ Hackleton, Matt. "Season Six: A Quick Look Back," in: Van Hise, James, ed. **Trek Celebration Two**. Las Vegas, NV: Pioneer, 1994. pp.29-39.

___ Jankiewicz, Pat. "Borg to Be Wild," *Starlog* No. 201: 36-39. April 1994.

___ Jankiewicz, Pat. "Man and Pakled," *Starlog* No. 187: 54-56, 72. February 1993.

___ Jankiewicz, Pat. "Most Wanted: The Klingon Kid," *Starlog* No. 194: 58-61. September 1993.

___ Jankiewicz, Pat. "Present at the Creation," *Starlog* No. 191: 75-79. June 1993.

___ Kendall, Lukas. "*Star Trek*: Scoring the Final Frontier," *Cinefantastique* 23(2/3): 100-102, 124. October 1992.

___ Kendall, Lukas. "*Star Trek: The Next Generation*: The Final Frontier's Musical Discord," *Cinefantastique* 24(3/4): 84-85. October 1993.

___ Keveney, Bill. "Until the Next Voyage," *Hartford (CT) Courant*. May 27, 1994. in: *NewsBank. Film and Television*. 59:C5-C6. 1994.

___ Kutzera, Dale. "*Star Trek: The Next Generation*: All Things Good," *Cinefantastique* 25(6)/26(1): 74-76. December 1994.

___ Kutzera, Dale. "*Star Trek: The Next Generation*: Doctor Turns Director," *Cinefantastique* 25(6)/26(1): 83. December 1994.

___ Kutzera, Dale. "*Star Trek: The Next Generation*: Episode Guide, 7th Season," *Cinefantastique* 25(6)/26(1): 47-93. December 1994.

___ Kutzera, Dale. "*Star Trek: The Next Generation*: Freelance Writers," *Cinefantastique* 25(6)/26(1): 81-82. December 1994.

___ Kutzera, Dale. "*Star Trek: The Next Generation*: Making 'Lower Decks'," *Cinefantastique* 25(6)/26(1): 77-80. December 1994.

___ Kutzera, Dale. "*Star Trek: The Next Generation*: Troi's Marina Sirtis," *Cinefantastique* 25(6)/26(1): 88-89. December 1994.

___ Kutzera, Dale. "*Star Trek: The Next Generation*," *Cinefantastique* 25(6)/26(1): 44-93, 124. December 1994.

___ Le Guin, Ursula K. "My Appointment With the *Enterprise*: An Appreciation," *TV Guide* 42(20): 31-32. May 14, 1994.

___ Logan, Michael. "*TV Guide* Interview: Rick Berman," *TV Guide* 41(30): 10-13. July 24, 1993.

___ Madsen, Dan. "Jonathan Del Arco: I, Borg," *Star Trek: The Official Fan Club* No. 93: 33-34. September/October 1993.

___ Madsen, Dan. "*Star Trek* Update," *Star Trek: The Official Fan Club* No. 93: 29-31. September/October 1993.

___ Mason, Marilynne S. "Today's Problems Tomorrow: Television's Growing Fleet of Science Fiction Dramas Paint a Brighter--or Darker–Future," *Christian Science Monitor* p. 12-13. March 2, 1993.

___ McDonnell, David. "Klingon Warrior," by David McDonnell and Ian Spelling. in: McDonnell, David, ed. **Starlog's Science Fiction Heroes and Heroines**. New York: Crescent Books, 1995. pp.58-61.

___ McDonnell, David. "Starship Captain," in: McDonnell, David, ed. **Starlog's Science Fiction Heroes and Heroines**. New York: Crescent Books, 1995. pp.24-27.

___ Nazzaro, Joe. "Android Ideas," *Starlog* No. 192: 27-31. July 1993.

___ Nazzaro, Joe. "Heroic Android," by Joe Nazzaro and Marc Shapiro. in: McDonnell, David, ed. **Starlog's Science Fiction Heroes and Heroines**. New York: Crescent Books, 1995. pp.28-30.

___ Nemecek, Larry. **The Star Trek: The Next Generation Companion**. Revised and Updated. New York: Pocket Books, 1995. 339pp.

___ Nemecek, Larry. **The Star Trek: The Next Generation Companion**. New York: Pocket Books, 1992. 213pp.

___ Perigard, Mark A. "'TNG' Mission Accomplished," *Boston (MA) Herald*. May 23, 1994. in: *NewsBank. Film and Television*. 59:B4-B5. 1994.

___ Pizzello, Stephen. "TV Sci-Fi Hits Warp Speed With *The Next Generation*," *American Cinematographer* 73(1): 76-87. January 1992.

___ Plotsky, Richard. "News From the Front: The Penultimate Season," in: Van Hise, James, ed. **Trek Celebration Two**. Las Vegas, NV: Pioneer, 1994. pp.156-164.

___ Prokop, Tim. "*Star Trek: The Next Generation*: Curry's Heroes," *Cinefantastique* 25(6)/26(1): 92-93. December 1994.

___ Prokop, Tim. "*Star Trek: The Next Generation*: Low Tech Effects," *Cinefantastique* 25(6)/26(1): 90-91. December 1994.

___ Prokop, Tim. "*Star Trek: The Next Generation*: Painting for the Future," *Cinefantastique* 25(6)/26(1): 70-73. December 1994.

STAR TREK: THE NEXT GENERATION (TV) (continued)

___ Prokop, Tim. "*Star Trek: The Next Generation*: Shot by Shot," *Cinefantastique* 25(6)/26(1): 64-69. December 1994.

___ Prokop, Tim. "*Star Trek: The Next Generation*: Special Visual Effects," *Cinefantastique* 25(6)/26(1): 52-63, 124. December 1994.

___ Richmond, Ray. "Its Final Frontier: *The Next Generation* Heads Off to Film Just Like *Star Trek*," *Los Angeles (CA) Daily News*. May 23, 1994. in: *NewsBank. Film and Television*. 59:B2-B3. 1994.

___ Richmond, Ray. "Not for the Uninitiated," *Los Angeles (CA) Daily News*. May 23, 1994. in: *NewsBank. Film and Television*. 59:C3. 1994.

___ Rios, Delia M. "Brent Spiner Explores His and Data's Future," *Dallas (TX) Morning News*. September 14, 1992. in: *NewsBank. Film and Television*. 96:E4-E6. 1992.

___ Rosenberg, Alan. "Journey's End," *(Providence, RI) Journal-Bulletin*. May 22, 1994. in: *NewsBank. Film and Television*. 59:B12-B13. 1994.

___ Rubinstein, Mitchell. "*The Next Generation*: Special Visual Effects," *Cinefantastique* 23(2/3): 38-41. October 1992.

___ Salter, David I. "*The Next Generation*: Alien Makeups," *Cinefantastique* 23(2/3): 103-105. October 1992.

___ Salter, David I. "*The Next Generation*: Building the *U. S. S. Enterprise*," *Cinefantastique* 23(2/3): 95. October 1992.

___ Salter, David I. "*Star Trek*: 24th-Century Techs," *Cinefantastique* 23(2/3): 92-93. October 1992.

___ Salter, David I. "*Star Trek: The Next Generation*: Alien Makeups," *Cinefantastique* 24(3/4): 50. October 1993.

___ Salter, David I. "*Star Trek: The Next Generation*: Special Visual Effects," *Cinefantastique* 24(3/4): 79-82. October 1993.

___ Shapiro, Marc. "Independent Data," *Starlog* No. 221: 27-29. December 1995.

___ Spelling, Ian. "Actress With Attitude," *Starlog* No. 205: 53-56, 70. August 1994.

___ Spelling, Ian. "Beloved Betazoid," *Starlog* No. 196: 52-57, 80. November 1993.

___ Spelling, Ian. "Cry of the Warrior," *Starlog* No. 175: 27-31. February 1992.

___ Spelling, Ian. "Directorial Enterprise," *Starlog* No. 204: 40-45. July 1994.

___ Spelling, Ian. "Guide to a New Generation," *Starlog* No. 195: 50-57. October 1993.

___ Spelling, Ian. "Like a Phoenix," *Starlog* No. 218: 52-55, 66. September 1995.

___ Spelling, Ian. "The Once and Future Captain," *Starlog* No. 212: 32-35, 70. March 1995.

___ Spelling, Ian. "Q & A," by Ian Spelling and David McDonnell. *Starlog* No. 206: 47-51, 70. September 1994.

___ Spelling, Ian. "Star Quarters," *Starlog* 178: 56-58. May 1992.

___ Spelling, Ian. "Swan Songs," *Starlog* No. 204: 32-34. July 1994.

___ Stephens, Lynne. "A Captain's Carol," *Starlog* No. 174: 25-29. January 1992.

___ Stephens, Lynne. "Captain's Holiday," *Starlog* No. 186: 35-39, 74. January 1993.

___ Stephens, Lynne. "A Study in Starflight," *Starlog* No. 190: 27-29, 69. May 1993.

___ Van Hise, James. "A Look at *The Next Generation*," in: Van Hise, James, ed. **Trek Celebration Two**. Las Vegas, NV: Pioneer, 1994. pp.24-28.

___ Van Hise, James. "The Music of *The Next Generation*," in: Van Hise, James, ed. **Trek Celebration Two**. Las Vegas, NV: Pioneer, 1994. pp.134-141.

___ Van Hise, James. **The Next Generation Tribute Book Two**. 'Unauthorized and Uncensored'. Las Vegas, NV: Pioneer, 1994. 171pp.

___ Van Hise, James. **Sci Fi TV: From Twilight Zone to Deep Space Nine**. Las Vegas, NV: Pioneer Books, 1993. 160pp. (Reprinted, HarperPrism, 1995. 258pp.)

___ Van Hise, James. **Trek in the 24th Century: The Next Generation and Deep Space Nine**. 'Unofficial and Uncensored'. Las Vagas, NV: Pioneer, 1994. 164pp.

___ Van Hise, James. **Trek: The Next Generation Crew Book**. Las Vegas: Pioneer Books, 1993. 155pp.

___ Van Hise, James. **Trek: The Next Generation: Third Edition**. Las Vegas: Pioneer, 1994. 268pp.

___ Van Hise, James, ed. **Trek: The Unauthorized Behind-the-Scenes Story of Trek: The Next Generation**. Las Vegas, NV: Pioneer Books, 1993. 132pp.

___ Warren, Bill. "Real Truths," *Starlog* No. 195: 58-61, 72. October 1993.

STAR TREK: THE NEXT GENERATION (TV) (continued)

___ Westbrook, Bruce. "Tonight Marks Series Finale, But Memories Linger," *Houston (TX) Chronicle*. May 23, 1994. in: *NewsBank. Film and Television*. 59:C7. 1994.

___ Westbrook, Bruce. "Trekkers Plan Farewell Parties," *Houston (TX) Chronicle*. May 23, 1994. in: *NewsBank. Film and Television*. 59:B14. 1994.

___ Wilcox, Rhonda V. "Dating Data: Miscegenation in **Star Trek: The Next Generation**," *Extrapolation* 34(3): 265-277. Fall 1993.

___ Zurawik, David. "A Time Warp," *(Baltimore, MD) The Evening Sun*. May 23, 1994. in: *NewsBank. Film and Television*. 59:C1-C2. 1994.

STAR TREK (TV)

___ "Par Puts TV 'Trek' In HV Warp Drive," *Variety* p. 41-42. April 10, 1985.

___ "**Star Trek** Going Where No Syndie Has Gone Before," *Variety* p. 46-50. June 11, 1986.

___ "**Star Trek** TV Episode Released by Paramount at $30," *Variety* p. 37. June 2, 1982.

___ Altman, Mark A. "UFP Law: The Legal Quagmires of the Federation," *Star Trek: The Official Fan Club* No. 93: 2-5. September/October 1993.

___ Baker, Wayne. "Community Service, the Final Frontier for the Klingon Fleet," *Chicago Tribune* p. 18D. January 31, 1993.

___ Bernardi, Daniel. "Infinite Diversity in Infinite Combinations: Diegetic Logics and Racial Articulations in the Originial **Star Trek**," *Film & History* 24(1/2): 60-74. February/May 1994.

___ Davidson, Keay. "To Fly in the Face of Physics," *San Francisco (CA) Examiner*. December 10, 1991. in: *NewsBank. Film and Television*. 7:D1-D3. 1992.

___ DeSmet, Kate. "Trekkers Chase Future with a Religious Zeal," *Detroit (MI) News*. March 13, 1995. in: *NewsBank. Film and Television*. 38:E7. 1995.

___ Dillard, J. M. **Star Trek: Where No One Has Gone Before, a History in Pictures**. New York: Pocket Books, 1994. 239pp.

___ Durden, Douglas. "**Star Trek** Brings Message of Hope," *Richmond (VA) Times-Dispatch*. February 27, 1992. in: *NewsBank. Film and Television*. 26:A3. 1992.

___ Ebert, Bruce C. "Beam Back to **Star Trek**: Watershed TV Show Celebrated in Galactic Smithsonian Exhibit," *Newport News (VA) Daily Press*. March 27, 1992. in: *NewsBank. Film and Television*. 46:B14-C2. 1992.

___ Epstein, Warren. "Beam 'em Up, Scotty: **Star Trek** Convention Puts Ardent Fans into a World of Their Own," *Colorado Springs (CO) Gazette Telegraph*. May 8, 1992. in: *NewsBank. Film and Television*. 59:A4-A5. 1992.

___ Farrell, John Aloysius. "The Smithsonian Goes Trekkie," *Boston (MA) Globe*. February 29, 1992. in: *NewsBank. Film and Television*. 26: A2. 1992.

___ Fisher, Bob. "**Star Trek** Meets **The Next Generation**," *American Cinematographer* 75(10): 74-82. October 1994.

___ Foote, Stephanie. "Annals of Humanism: We Have Met the Alien and It Is Us," *Humanist* 52(2):21-24, 33. March/April 1992.

___ Franklin, H. Bruce. "**Star Trek** in the Vietnam Era," *Science Fiction Studies* 21(1): 24-34. March 1994.

___ Gross, Edward. **Captain's Logs: The Complete Star Trek Voyages**, by Edward Gross and Mark A. Altman. London: Boxtree, 1993. 269pp. [Not seen.]

___ Henderson, Jan A. "Where No Show Has Gone Before," *American Cinematographer* 73(1): 34-40. January 1992.

___ Jenkins, Henry. "At Other Times, Like Females: Gender and **Star Trek** Fiction," in: Tulloch, John and Jenkins, Henry, eds. **Science Fiction Audiences: Watching Doctor Who and Star Trek**. New York: Routledge, 1995. pp.196-212.

___ Jenkins, Henry. "How Many Starfleet Officers Does It Take to Change a Lightbulb?: **Star Trek** at MIT," by Henry Jenkins and Greg Dancer. in: Tulloch, John and Jenkins, Henry, eds. **Science Fiction Audiences: Watching Doctor Who and Star Trek**. New York: Routledge, 1995. pp.213-236.

___ Jenkins, Henry. "Infinite Diversity in Infinite Combinations: Genre and Authorship in **Star Trek**," in: Tulloch, John and Jenkins, Henry, eds. **Science Fiction Audiences: Watching Doctor Who and Star Trek**. New York: Routledge, 1995. pp.175-195.

___ Jenkins, Henry. "Out of the Closet and into the Universe: Queers and **Star Trek**," in: Tulloch, John and Jenkins, Henry, eds. **Science Fiction Audiences: Watching Doctor Who and Star Trek**. New York: Routledge, 1995. pp.237-265.

STAR TREK (TV) (continued)

___ Joseph, Paul. "The Law of the Federation: Images of Law, Lawyers, and the Legal System in **Star Trek: The Next Generation**," by Paul Joseph and Sharon Carton. *University of Toledo Law Review* 24(1): 43-85. Fall 1992.

___ Kahn, Joseph P. "Beamed up in Boston," *Boston (MA) Globe*. October 3, 1992. in: *NewsBank. Film and Television*. 108:A3-A4. 1992.

___ Kohler, Vince. "OMSI Exhibit Goes Where No Museum Has Gone Before," *Portland (OR) The Oregonian*. January 24, 1992. in: *NewsBank. Film and Television*. 15:C6. 1992.

___ Kohler, Vince. "**Star Trek**: An American Icon at Work," *Portland (OR) The Oregonian*. January 24, 1992. in: *NewsBank. Film and Television*. 15:C5. 1992.

___ Kurtis, Bill. **The Science of Star Trek**. Chicago, IL: Public Media Video, 1995. 1 videocassette, 60 minutes.

___ Lichtenberg, Jacqueline. **Star Trek Lives!**, by Jacqueline Lichtenberg, Sandra Marshak and Jean Winston. New York: Bantam, 1975. 274pp.

___ Lowry, Brian. "Starfleet Siren," by Brian Lowry and Ian Spelling. in: McDonnell, David, ed. **Starlog's Science Fiction Heroes and Heroines**. New York: Crescent Books, 1995. pp.77-79.

___ Madsen, Dan. "Syndicating **Star Trek**," *Star Trek: The Official Fan Club* No. 93: 1. September/October 1993.

___ Mae, James. "Discovering the Dyson Sphere," *Star Trek: The Official Fan Club* No. 90: 10-11. March/April 1993.

___ Mae, James. "Return to Yesterday: Recreating the Classic *Enterprise* Bridge," *Star Trek: The Official Fan Club* No. 90: 5-7. March/April 1993.

___ Marsalek, Kenneth. "**Star Trek**: Humanism of the Future," *Free Inquiry* 12(4): 53-57. Fall 1992.

___ Mestel, Rosie. "Education: The Final Frontier," *New Scientist* 141(1914): 11. February 26, 1994.

___ Miller, Nick. "Fans Remain Avid As Ever," *Cincinnati (OH) Post*. December 6, 1991. in: *NewsBank. Film and Television*. 7:D6. 1992.

___ Milner, Joseph O. "Captain Kirk and Dr. Who: Meliorist and Spenglerian World Views in Science Fiction for Young Adults," in: Sullivan, C. W., III. **Science Fiction for Young Readers**. Westport, CT: Greenwood, 1993. pp.187-196.

___ Osborne, Elizabeth A. "Collecting," *Lan's Lantern* No. 40: 10. September 1992.

___ Parks, Louis B. "Adventure Began 30 Years Ago," *Houston (TX) Chronicle*. November 13, 1994. in: *NewsBank. Film and Television*. 125: E1-E2. 1994.

___ Phillips, Mark. "Biology Amok," *Starlog* No. 203: 52-54. June 1994.

___ Romanko, Karen A. "Where No Librarian Has Gone Before: The 10 Best **Star Trek** Episodes," *Emergency Librarian* 21(2): 24-26. November/December 1993.

___ Saunders, Michael. "The Parallel Universes of **Star Trek**," *Boston (MA) Globe*. November 13, 1994. in: *NewsBank. Film and Television*. 10:E1-E4. 1995.

___ Schramm, Susan. "7 Years of TV Scripts Make Long Trek to IU's Lilly Library," *Indianapolis (IN) Star*. November 28, 1994. in: *NewsBank. Film and Television*. FTV 21: D5. 1995.

___ Shapiro, Marc. "Farewell to Spock," *Starlog* No. 174: 30-33, 71. January 1992.

___ Sherman, Paul. "What a Long, Strange **Trek** It's Been," *Boston (MA) Herald*. December 6, 1991. in: *NewsBank. Film and Television*. 7:D4-D5. 1992.

___ Spelling, Ian. "Captain Sulu," *Starlog* No. 174: 43-47. January 1992.

___ Spelling, Ian. "Uhura and Beyond," *Starlog* No. 210: 47-49. January 1995.

___ Spelling, Ian. "Uhura's Mission," *Starlog* No. 175: 36-39, 82. February 1992.

___ Stewart, Patrick (a.k.a. Picard, Jean-Luc). "A Deep Space Diary: Picard Ponders **Star Trek**'s Next Step," *TV Guide* 41(1): 9-10. January 2, 1993. (Issue 2075)

___ Swires, Steve. "Vulcan Legend," in: McDonnell, David, ed. **Starlog's Science Fiction Heroes and Heroines**. New York: Crescent Books, 1995. pp.50-54.

___ Tulloch, John. "Positioning the SF Audience: **Star Trek**, **Doctor Who** and the Texts of Science Fiction," in: Tulloch, John and Jenkins, Henry, eds. **Science Fiction Audiences: Watching Doctor Who and Star Trek**. New York: Routledge, 1995. pp.25-49.

___ Tulloch, John. **Science Fiction Audiences: Doctor Who, Star Trek, and Their Fans**. London: Routledge, 1994. 294pp.

STARGATE (MOTION PICTURE)

STAY TUNED (MOTION PICTURE)

STARGATE (MOTION PICTURE) (continued)

___ Arar, Yardena. "*Stargate* Porthole to Thrilling Time Travel," *Los Angeles (CA) Daily News*. October 28, 1994. in: *NewsBank. Film and Television*. 115: G3-G4. 1994.

___ Arnold, Gary. "Sci-Fi Film Gets by on Allusion, Illusions," *Washington (DC) Times*. October 28, 1994. in: *NewsBank. Film and Television*. 115: G14. 1994.

___ Campbell, Bob. "*Stargate* Version of Sci-Fi an Earthbound Melodrama," *Newark (NJ) Star-Ledger*. October 28, 1994. in: *NewsBank. Film and Television*. 115: G13. 1994.

___ Cunneff, Tom. "Star Trip," *People Weekly* 42(17): 37. October 24, 1994.

___ Dolgoff, Stephanie. "What Do Hieroglyphs Really Sound Like," *New York Times* p.H24. October 23, 1994.

___ Ebert, Roger. "*Stargate* World Bizarre Yet Barren," *Chicago (IL) Sun Times*. October 28, 1994. in: *NewsBank. Film and Television*. 115: G8. 1994.

___ Ferrante, A. C. "Roland's Gate," *Sci-Fi Universe* No. 3: 28-37. October/November 1994.

___ Fischer, Dennis. "*Lawrence of Arabia* Meets *Star Wars* in *Stargate*," *Science Fiction Age* 2(6): 18-24. September 1994.

___ Fischer, Dennis. "*Stargate* (Review)," *Science Fiction Age* 2(6): 18-24. September 1994

___ Hunter, Stephen. "The Small-Minded *Stargate* Goes Nowhere Fast," *Baltimore (MD) Sun*. October 29, 1994. in: *NewsBank. Film and Television*. 115: G9. 1994.

___ Johnson, Barry. "Journey to Nowhere," *Portland (OR) The Oregonian*. October 28, 1994. in: *NewsBank. Film and Television*. 125: E3. 1994.

___ Korman, Ken. "*Secrets of Stargate* (Review)," *Video Magazine* 18(10): 65. January 1995.

___ Lowe, Nick. "*Stargate* (Review)," *Interzone* No. 93: 31-32. March 1995.

___ McNally, Owen. "*Stargate* a Barren Desert Trek," *Hartford (CT) Courant*. October 29, 1994. in: *NewsBank. Film and Television*. 115: G7. 1994.

___ Movshovitz, Howie. "*Stargate* Needs 50s Spirit," *Denver (CO) Post*. October 28, 1994. in: *NewsBank. Film and Television*. 115: G6. 1994.

___ Newman, Kim. "*Stargate* (Review)," *Sight and Sound* 5(2): 53-54. February 1995.

___ Oppenheimer, Jean. "*Stargate*: Adding Layers in the Outer Limits," *American Cinematographer* 75(12): 30-32. December 1994.

___ Prokop, Tim. "*Stargate*: CGI Effects," *Cinefantastique* 26(3): 50. April 1995.

___ Prokop, Tim. "*Stargate*: Makeup Design," *Cinefantastique* 25(6)/26(1): 30. December 1994.

___ Prokop, Tim. "*Stargate*: Production Design," *Cinefantastique* 25(6)/26(1): 32-33. December 1994.

___ Prokop, Tim. "*Stargate*: Production Design," *Cinefantastique* 26(3): 52-53. April 1995.

___ Prokop, Tim. "*Stargate*: Special Effects," *Cinefantastique* 25(6)/26(1): 35. December 1994.

___ Prokop, Tim. "*Stargate*," *Cinefantastique* 25(5): 46-47. October 1994.

___ Prokop, Tim. "*Stargate*," *Cinefantastique* 25(6)/26(1): 28-35, 125. December 1994.

___ Prokop, Tim. "*Stargate*," *Cinefantastique* 26(3): 48-53. April 1995.

___ Rodriguez, Rene. "On the Other Side of *Stargate* Is a World That's Cliched, Silly," *Miami (FL) Herald*. October 28, 1994. in: *NewsBank. Film and Television*. 33:F8. 1994.

___ Rosenberg, Scott. "*Stargate* Open Portal to a Confusing Universe," *San Francisco (CA) Examiner*. October 28, 1994. in: *NewsBank. Film and Television*. 115: G5. 1994.

___ Shapiro, Marc. "*Stargate*," *Starlog* No. 209: 32-37. December 1994.

___ Stanley, T. L. "NBC, Live Entertainment Link TV and Home Vid for Sci-Fi Synergy," *Brandweek* 36(3): 8. January 16, 1995.

___ Stark, Susan. "*Stargate* Shoots for the Moon--and Misses," *Detroit (MI) News*. October 28, 1994. in: *NewsBank. Film and Television*. 115: G12. 1994.

___ Vaz, Mark C. "Through the *Stargate*," *Cinefex* No. 61: 82-97. March 1995.

___ Verniere, James. "Space Camp," *Boston (MA) Herald*. October 28, 1994. in: *NewsBank. Film and Television*. 115: G10-G11. 1994.

___ Vincent, Mal. "A Dune Deal," *Norfolk (VA) Virginian-Pilot*. October 29, 1994. in: *NewsBank. Film and Television*. 115: G1-G2. 1994.

STARGATE (MOTION PICTURE) (continued)

___ Yakir, Dan. "Two-Fisted Hero," *Starlog* No. 211: 50-53. February 1995.

STARLOG (MAGAZINE)

___ "*Starlog* Launching Nationwide Comics/SF Bookstore Chain," *Science Fiction Chronicle* 15(3): 6. January 1994.

STARMAN (MOTION PICTURE)

___ Lowry, Brian. "Beloved *Starman*," by Brian Lowry and Christine C. Menefee. in: McDonnell, David, ed. **Starlog's Science Fiction Heroes and Heroines**. New York: Crescent Books, 1995. pp.55-57.

STARMAN (TV)

___ "Grassroots Campaign Paying Off: ABC Is Mulling *Starman* Revival," *Variety* p. 48, 86. January 27, 1988.

STARMONT HOUSE

___ "Starmont Ceases Publishing, Passes Titles to Borgo," *Science Fiction Chronicle* 14(7): 4. April 1993.

___ "Starmont House Suspends Publication," *Locus* 30(3): 6. March 1993.

___ Reginald, Robert. "A Requiem for Starmont House (1976-1993)," *Science Fiction Studies* 20(3): 414-421. November 1993.

STARS

___ King, T. Jackson. "Habitable Stars Within 100 Light Years," *The Report: The Fiction Writer's Magazine* No. 9: 9-11. March 1993.

STARZL, R. F.

___ Davies, Eric L. "Remembering R. F. Starzl: A Conversation with Dr. Thomas E. Starzl," *Fantasy Commentator* 8(3/4): 150-160, 163-165. Fall 1995. (Whole No. 47/48)

___ Starzl, R. F. "The Fantastic Science Market," *Fantasy Commentator* 8(3/4): 161-165, 257. Fall 1995. (Whole No. 47/48)

STATISTICS, 1991

___ "1991 Book Summary," *Locus* 28(2): 41-43, 73. February 1992.

___ "1991 Magazine Summary," *Locus* 28(2): 44-47, 74. February 1992.

___ Winnett, Scott. "1991 Book Summary," in: Brown, Charles N. and Contento, William G. **Science Fiction, Fantasy, & Horror: 1991**. Oakland, CA: Locus Press, 1992. pp.423-427.

___ Winnett, Scott. "1991 Magazine Summary," by Scott Winnett and Charles N. Brown. in: Brown, Charles N. and Contento, William G. **Science Fiction, Fantasy, & Horror: 1991**. Oakland, CA: Locus Press, 1992. pp.428-432.

STATISTICS, 1992

___ "1992 Book Summary," *Locus* 30(2): 41-43, 73. February 1993.

___ Winnett, Scott. "1992 Magazine Summary," by Scott Winnett and Charles N. Brown. *Locus* 30(2): 44-46. February 1993.

STATISTICS, 1993

___ Winnett, Scott. "1993 Book Summary," by Scott Winnett and Charles N. Brown. *Locus* 32(2): 43-45, 73-76. February 1994.

___ Winnett, Scott. "1993 Magazine Summary," by Scott Winnett and Charles N. Brown. *Locus* 32(2): 44-48, 51. February 1994.

STATISTICS, 1994

___ "1994 *Locus* Survey," *Locus* 33(3): 56-58, 84-85. September 1994.

___ "1994 Book Summary," *Locus* 34(2): 43-45, 75. February 1995.

___ "1994 Magazine Summary," *Locus* 34(2): 46-48, 76. February 1995.

STAY TUNED (MOTION PICTURE)

___ "Hell Bent for Parody, *Tuned* Stuck in Limbo (Review)," *Washington (DC) Times*. August 18, 1992. in: *NewsBank. Film and Television*. 84: A11. 1992.

___ Brunet, Robin. "Stay Tooned, Chuck Jones," *Cinefantastique* 23(2/3): 112-113. October 1992.

___ Brunet, Robin. "*Stay Tuned*," *Cinefantastique* 23(1): 14-15. August 1992.

___ Grahnke, Lon. "*Stay Tuned* Mocks TV, But the Joke's on Ritter (Review)," *Chicago (IL) Sun Times*. August 17, 1992. in: *NewsBank. Film and Television*. 84:A7. 1992.

___ Hunter, Stephen. "Devilishly Bad Movie Gives No Reason to *Stay Tuned* (Review)," *Baltimore (MD) Sun*. August 15, 1992. in: *NewsBank. Film and Television*. 84:A8. 1992.

STAY TUNED (MOTION PICTURE) (continued)
___ Kronke, David. "As Far as Idiocy Goes, *Tuned* Matches Up With the Year's Best (Review)," *Los Angeles (CA) Daily News*. August 15, 1992. in: *NewsBank. Film and Television*. 84:A5. 1992.
___ Lowe, Nick. "*Stay Tuned* (Review)," *Interzone* No. 72: 34. June 1993.
___ Shapiro, Marc. "Hellvision," *Starlog* 181: 76-80. August 1992.
___ Shapiro, Marc. "A Passion for Moviemaking," *Starlog* 182: 46-49. September 1992.
___ Sherman, Paul. "*Stay Tuned* Is out of Focus on TV Parody (Review)," *Boston (MA) Herald*. August 15, 1992. in: *NewsBank. Film and Television*. 84:A9. 1992.
___ Shulgasser, Barbara. "*Stay Tuned*: Most Won't to This 3rd-rate Putdown of Television (Review)," *San Francisco (CA) Examiner*. August 15, 1992. in: *NewsBank. Film and Television*. 84:A6. 1992.
___ Wuntch, Phillip. "*Stay Tuned*? On Second Thought, Don't (Review)," *Dallas (TX) Morning News*. August 15, 1992. in: *NewsBank. Film and Television*. 84:A10. 1992.

STEELE, ALLEN
___ "Allen Steele: Back to Space," *Locus* 28(2): 5. February 1992.

STEELE, GEORGE
___ Carducci, Mark. "*Ed Wood*: Deadringer for Tor," *Cinefantastique* 25(5): 26-27. October 1994.

STEELE, JACK E.
___ Gray, Chris H. "An Interview With Jack E. Steele," in: Gray, Chris H., ed. **The Cyborg Handbook**. New York: Routledge, 1995. pp.61-69.

STEEN, JESSICA
___ Chrissinger, Craig W. "Frontier Doctor," *Starlog* No. 213: 48-51, 70. April 1995.
___ Chrissinger, Craig W. "Warrior Pilot," *Starlog* No. 213: 50-52. April 1995.

STEFANO, JOSEPH
___ Phillips, Mark. "Nightmares in Color," *Starlog* No. 217: 70-73. August 1995.
___ Wiater, Stanley. "Stefano, Joseph," in: Wiater, Stanley. **Dark Visions: Conversations with the Masters of the Horror Film**. New York: Avon, 1992. pp.179-188.

STEFFAN, DAN
___ "Dan Steffan Wins TAFF," *Science Fiction Chronicle* 16(7): 30. June/July 1995.

STEFKO, JOE
___ "Fourth Annual Collector's Award," *Locus* 28(5): 40. May 1992.

STEINBECK, JOHN
___ Hodges, Laura F. "Steinbeck's Adaptation of Malory's Launcelot: A Triumph of Realism over Supernaturalism," *Quondam et Futurus* 2(1): 69-81. Spring 1992.
___ Keough, Trent. "The Dystopia Factor: Industrial Capitalism in **Sybil** and **The Grapes of Wrath**," *Utopian Studies* 4(1): 38-54. 1993.

STEINBRUNNER, CHRIS
___ "Steinbrunner, Chris (Obituary)," *Locus* 31(3): 82. September 1993.
___ "Steinbrunner, Chris (Obituary)," *Science Fiction Chronicle* 14(11): 14. August 1993.

STENO, FLAVIA
___ Parisi, Luciano. "Per una storia della fantascienza italiana: Flavia Steno," *Stanford Italian Review* 9(1/2): 105-113. 1990.

STEPFATHER III: FATHER'S DAY (MOTION PICTURE)
___ Brooks, Lawrence. "*Stepfather III: Father's Day*," *Cinefantastique* 22(5): 22-23. April 1992.

STEPHENSON, NEAL
___ Carroll, Jerry. "Tapping Dickens for Clues for the Future: New Sci-Fi Master Neal Stephenson Pens a Follow-Up to Cult Hit **Snow Crash**," *San Francisco (CA) Chronicle* February 1, 1995. (Cited from the Internet edition.)

STEPHENSON, NEAL (continued)
___ Eisenhart, Mary. "Text: The Ultimate VR Tool? An Electronic Interview with **Snow Crash** Author Neal Stephenson," *Microtimes* No. 112: 91, 231-233. August 23, 1993.
___ Schwartz, John. "On the Net's Cutting Edge: **The Diamond Age**, Neal Stephenson's New Science Fiction Novel, Is Turning Him into a Cyber-lebrity," *Washington (DC) Post* p.D1. February 21, 1995.

STEREOTYPES
___ Barshay, Robert. "Ethnic Stereotypes in **Flash Gordon**," *Journal of Popular Film and Television* 3(1): 15-30. 1974.

STERLING, BRUCE
___ Concannon, Tim. "The Cops and Hackers Can Go to Hell: Bruce Sterling Interviewed," *Interzone* No. 83: 25-29. May 1994.
___ Cox, F. Brett. "Epiphanies of the Mind and Heart: John Kessel's **Meeting in Infinity** and Bruce Sterling's **Globalhead**," *New York Review of Science Fiction* No. 86: 1, 3-5. October 1995.
___ Dingus, Anne. "Br-u-u-cel!," *Texas.Monthly* 23(12): 28. December 1995.
___ Fischlin, Daniel. "The Charisma Leak: A Conversation With William Gibson and Bruce Sterling," by Daniel Fischlin, Veronica Hollinger and Andrew Taylor. *Science Fiction Studies* 19(1): 1-16. March 1992.
___ Marvel, Bill. "Sam Houston Meets the Cyberpunks," *Dallas (TX) Morning News*. January 12, 1992. in: *NewsBank. Literature*. 13:G4-G6. 1992.
___ McQuiddy, A. P. "Eyeball Kicks, Prigogine's Theory and Re-Thinking the World: An Interview With Bruce Sterling and Lewis Shiner," *Texas SF Inquirer* No. 19: 5-26. December 1986.
___ Schuster, Judy. "Technology Fashion Victims," *Electronic Learning* 14(1): 28-29. September 1994.
___ Shippey, Tom. "Semiotic Ghosts and Ghostliness in the Work of Bruce Sterling," in: Slusser, George E. and Shippey, Tom, eds. **Fiction 2000: Cyberpunk and the Future of Narrative**. Athens: University of Georgia Press, 1992. pp.208-220.

STERLING, KENNETH
___ "Sterling, Kenneth (Obituary)," *Locus* 34(3): 74. March 1995.
___ "Sterling, Kenneth (Obituary)," *Science Fiction Chronicle* 16(4): 16. February 1995.
___ "Sterling, Kenneth (Obituary)," *Science Fiction Chronicle* 16(5): 18. March/April 1995.

STEVE JACKSON GAMES (COMPANY)
___ "Steve Jackson Wins Lawsuit," *Locus* 30(4): 6. April 1993.

STEVENSON, ROBERT LOUIS
___ Bloom, Harold. "Robert Louis Stevenson," in: Bloom, Harold. **Classic Horror Writers**. New York: Chelsea House, 1994. pp.138-151.
___ Pennington, John. "Textual Doubling and Divided Selves: The Strange Case of Dr. Jekyll and Mary Reilly," *Journal of the Fantastic in the Arts* 6(2/3): 203-216. 1994.
___ Terry, R. C. **Robert Louis Stevenson: Interviews and Recollections**. Iowa City: University of Iowa Press, 1995. 216pp.
___ Ursini, James. **More Things Than Are Dreamt Of: Masterpieces of Supernatural Horror, From Mary Shelley to Stephen King, in Literature and Film**, by James Ursini and Alain Silver. New York: Limelight, 1994. 226pp.

STEWART, ALAN
___ "Alan Stewart Wins DUFF," *Science Fiction Chronicle* 15(9): 38-39. August 1994.

STEWART, J. I. M.
___ "Stewart, J. I. M. (Obituary)," *Locus* 34(1) 66. January 1995.

STEWART, MARY
___ Herman, Harold J. "Teaching White, Stewart, and Berger," in: Fries, Maureen and Watson, Jeanie, eds. **Approaches to the Teaching of the Arthurian Tradition**. New York: Modern Language Association, 1992. pp.113-117.
___ Jurich, Marilyn. "Mithraic Aspects of Merlin in Mary Stewart's **The Crystal Cave**," in: Morse, Donald E., ed. **The Celebration of the Fantastic**. Westport, CT: Greenwood, 1992. pp.91-102.

STEWART, MARY (continued)
___ Watson, Jeanie. "Mary Stewart's Merlin: Word of Power," in: Watson, Jeanie and Fries, Marueen, eds. **The Figure of Merlin in the Nineteenth and Twentieth Centuries.** Lewiston, NY: Edwin Mellen Press, 1989. pp.155-174.

STEWART, PATRICK
___ Brady, James. "In Step With: Patrick Stewart," *Austin (TX) American Statesman. Parade Magazine* p. 12. April 5, 1992.
___ McDonnell, David. "Starship Captain," in: McDonnell, David, ed. **Starlog's Science Fiction Heroes and Heroines.** New York: Crescent Books, 1995. pp.24-27.
___ Spelling, Ian. "The Once and Future Captain," *Starlog* No. 212: 32-35, 70. March 1995.
___ Stephens, Lynne. "A Captain's Carol," *Starlog* No. 174: 25-29. January 1992.
___ Stephens, Lynne. "Captain's Holiday," *Starlog* No. 186: 35-39, 74. January 1993.
___ Stewart, Patrick (a.k.a. Picard, Jean-Luc). "A Deep Space Diary: Picard Ponders *Star Trek*'s Next Step," *TV Guide* 41(1): 9-10. January 2, 1993. (Issue 2075)

STEWART, SEAN
___ "1994 Aurora Winners," *Locus* 33(4): 8, 76. October 1994.
___ "Aurora Awards," *Science Fiction Chronicle* 15(10): 5. September 1994.
___ "Aurora Awards Winners, 1992," *Locus* 30(4): 6, 64. April 1993.
___ "Sean Stewart: Growing up Ambitious," *Locus* 33(6): 5, 81-82. December 1994.

STIERS, DAVID OGDEN
___ Counts, Kyle. "Character Music," *Starlog* No. 183: 55-57, 70. October 1992.

STINE, ROGER
___ Fenner, Arnie. "Roger Stine," *Shayol* No. 7: 24-31. 1985.

STITH, JOHN E.
___ Kennedy, John. "SFC Interviews: John E. Stith," *Science Fiction Chronicle* 14(10): 5, 27-29. July 1993.

STOKER, BRAM
___ Appleby, Robin S. "**Dracula** and Dora: The Diagnosis and Treatment of Alternative Narratives," *Literature and Psychology* 39(3): 16-37. 1993.
___ Biodrowski, Steve. "**Dracula**: The Oft-Told Story," *Cinefantastique* 23(4): 27-30. December 1992.
___ Bloom, Harold. "Bram Stoker," in: Bloom, Harold. **Classic Horror Writers.** New York: Chelsea House, 1994. pp.152-167.
___ Boone, Troy. "He Is English and Therefore Adventurous: Politics, Decadence and **Dracula**," *Studies in the Novel* 25(1): 76-91. Spring 1993.
___ Croley, Laura S. "The Rhetoric of Reform in Stoker's **Dracula**: Depravity, Decline, and the Fin-de-siècle Residuum," *Criticism* 37(1): 85-108. Winter 1995.
___ Gutjahr, Paul. "Stoker's **Dracula**," *Explicator* 52(1): 36-38. Fall 1993.
___ Laurent, Diane M. "Bram Stoker's **Dracula**: The Ultimate Victorian Novel," *Journal of the Dark* No. 5: 40-42. Winter 1995/1996.
___ McDonald, Beth E. "The Vampire as Trickster Figure in Bram Stoker's **Dracula**," *Extrapolation* 33(2): 128-144. Summer 1992.
___ McGuire, Karen. "Of Artists, Vampires and Creativity," *Studies in Weird Fiction* No. 11: 2-4. Spring 1992.
___ Nicholson, Mervyn. "Bram Stoker and C. S. Lewis: **Dracula** as a Source for **That Hideous Strength**," *Mythlore* 19(3): 16-22. Summer 1993. (No. 73)
___ O'Brien, Edward W., Jr. "Bram Stoker's **Dracula**: Eros or Agape?," *Fantasy Commentator* 8(1/2): 75-79. Winter 1993/1994. (Whole No. 45/46)
___ Schweitzer, Darrell. "Will the Real Dracula Please Stand Up?," *Sci-Fi Entertainment* 1(1): 56-61, 72. June 1994.
___ Senf, Carol A. **The Critical Response to Bram Stoker.** Westport, CT: Greenwood Press, 1993. 216pp.
___ Ursini, James. **More Things Than Are Dreamt Of: Masterpieces of Supernatural Horror, From Mary Shelley to Stephen King, in Literature and Film**, by James Ursini and Alain Silver. New York: Limelight, 1994. 226pp.

STOKER, BRAM (continued)
___ Wicke, Jennifer. "Vampiric Typewriting: Dracula and Its Media," *ELH* 59(2): 467-494. Summer 1992.
___ Zeender, Marie-Noelle. "L'érotisme et la mort: images de la mère dans trois oeuvres de Bram Stoker," in: Bozzetto, Roger, ed. **Eros: Science & Fiction Fantastique.** Aix-en-Provence: Universite de Provence, 1991. pp.59-70.

STONE, LESLIE F.
___ "Stone, Leslie F. (Obituary)," *Science Fiction Chronicle* 14(8): 16. May 1993.

STONE, OLIVER
___ Sanjek, David. "The Hysterical Imagination: The Horror Films of Oliver Stone," *Post Script* 12(1): 47-60. Fall 1992.

STOPPARD, TOM
___ Chetta, Peter N. "Multiplicities of Illusion in Tom Stoppard's Plays," in: Murphy, Patrick D., ed. **Staging the Impossible: The Fantastic Mode in Modern Drama.** Westport, CT: Greenwood, 1992. pp.127-136.

STOUT, AMY
___ "Amy Stout Joins Roc Books," *Science Fiction Chronicle* 14(3): 5. December 1992.
___ "Chris Schelling out, Amy Stout up at Roc," *Science Fiction Chronicle* 15(4): 4-5. February 1994.
___ "Schelling out at Roc, Stout Promoted," *Locus* 32(3): 8. March 1994.

STOUT, REX
___ Koontz, Dean R. "Rex Stout and Nero Wolfe," in: Greenberg, Martin H., Ed Gorman and Bill Munster, eds. **The Dean Koontz Companion.** New York: Berkley, 1994. pp.167-172.

STRACZYNSKI, J. MICHAEL
___ "Let There Be Light, Let There Be Shadows: Joe Straczynski on **Babylon 5**," *Sci-Fi Entertainment* 2(3): 61-65, 72. October 1995.
___ Altman, Mark A. "**Babylon 5**: Creating the Series," *Cinefantastique* 23(5): 20. February 1993.
___ Straczynski, J. Michael. "The Profession of Science Fiction, 48: Approaching Babylon," *Foundation* No. 64: 5-19. Summer 1995.

STRANGE DAYS (MOTION PICTURE)
___ "Revolting **Strange Days** Is Much Worse," *Washington (DC) Times.* October 14, 1995. in: *NewsBank. Film and Television.* 99:D2. 1995.
___ "**Strange Days** Cautions Against What Could Happen," *Television Program: Showbiz Today (CNN)* Program Number 924. October 13, 1995. (Transcript available.)
___ Adams, Thelma. "A Fiennes Madness," *New York (NY) Post.* October 6, 1995. in: *NewsBank. Film and Television.* 99:C13. 1995.
___ Carr, Jay. "A Walk on the Wired Side," *Boston (MA) Globe.* October 13, 1995. in: *NewsBank. Film and Television.* 99:C7-C8. 1995.
___ Covert, Collin. "Days a Reach That Loses Its Grasp," *Minneapolis (MN) Star And Tribune.* October 13, 1995. in: *NewsBank. Film and Television.* 99:C12.1995.
___ Dawes, Amy. "It's Just a Movie...Or Is It?," *Los Angeles (CA) Daily News.* October 15, 1995. in: *NewsBank. Film and Television.* 99:B13-B14. 1995.
___ Ebert, Roger. "Virtual Voyeurism," *Chicago (IL) Sun Times.* October 13, 1995. in: *NewsBank. Film and Television.* 99:C3-C4. 1995.
___ Franke, Lizzie. "Virtual Fears," *Sight and Sound* 5(12): 6-9. December 1995.
___ Hartl, John. "Lots of Bang for a Plot That Fizzles," *Seattle (WA) Times.* October 13, 1995. in: *NewsBank. Film and Television.* 99:D3. 1995.
___ Hunter, Stephen. "The End Is Not Near Enough," *(Baltimore, MD) Sun.* October 13, 1995. in: *NewsBank. Film and Television.* 99:C5-C6. 1995.
___ Maccarillo, Lisa. "Brave New World," *Sci-Fi Entertainment* 2(3): 38-41. October 1995.
___ Millar, Jeff. "**Strange Days** Full of Thrills," *Houston (TX) Chronicle.* October 13, 1995. in: *NewsBank. Film and Television.* 99:D1. 1995.
___ Parisi, Paula. "Long Nights and **Strange Days**," *American Cinematographer* 76(11): 64-68. November 1995.
___ Stark, Susan. "It's Not All in Your Head: Cyberthrills Add Byte to Terrifying **Strange Days**," *Detroit (MI) News.* October 13, 1995. in: *NewsBank. Film and Television.* 99:C11. 1995.

STRANGE DAYS (MOTION PICTURE) (continued)
___ Strauss, Bob. "New Level of Intensity Makes *Strange Days* Strange," *Los Angeles (CA) Daily News*. October 13, 1995. in: *NewsBank. Film and Television*. 99:B12. 1995.
___ Verniere, James. "Bleak to the Future," *Boston (MA) Herald*. October 13, 1995. in: *NewsBank. Film and Television*. 99:C9-C10. 1995.
___ Wuntch, Phillip. "*Strange Days*: Futuristic Thriller a Strong Dose of Unreality," *Dallas (TX) Morning News*. October 13, 1995. in: *NewsBank. Film and Television*. 99:C14. 1995.
___ Yakir, Dan. "*Strange Days*," *Starlog* No. 220: 32-35. November 1995.

STRANGE STORIES (MAGAZINE)
___ Cockcroft, T. G. L. "An Index to 'The Eyrie'," *Fantasy Commentator* 8(3/4): 217-229. Fall 1995. (Whole No. 47/48)

STRANGE TALES OF MYSTERY AND TERROR (MAGAZINE)
___ Cockcroft, T. G. L. "An Index to 'The Eyrie'," *Fantasy Commentator* 8(3/4): 217-229. Fall 1995. (Whole No. 47/48)

STRATEMEYER, EDWARD
___ Molson, Francis J. "Great Marvel: The First American Hardcover Science Fiction Series," *Extrapolation* 34(2): 101-122. Summer 1993.

STRAUB, PETER
___ "Bram Stoker Awards," *Science Fiction Chronicle* 15(8): 5. June 1994.
___ "HWA Stoker Awards Winners," *Locus* 33(1): 7. July 1994.
___ "Peter Straub: The Path of Extremity," *Locus* 32(1): 4, 65. January 1994.
___ "World Fantasy Awards," *Science Fiction Chronicle* 15(2): 4. November/December 1993.
___ Bosky, Bernadette L. "Haunting and Healing: Memory and Guilt in the Fiction of Peter Straub," *New York Review of Science Fiction* No. 73: 1, 8-13. September 1994.

STREET FIGHTER (MOTION PICTURE)
___ Brandt, James B. "*Street Fighter*," *Cinefantastique* 26(2): 56-57. February 1995.

STREET FIGHTER (VIDEO GAME)
___ Fletcher, Tanya A. "Deadly Games," *Sci-Fi Entertainment* 1(4): 78-84. December 1994.

STRETSER, THOMAS
___ Lewes, Darby. "Nudes From Nowhere: Pornography, Empire, and Utopia," *Utopian Studies* 4(2): 66-73. 1993.

STRICKLAND, BRAD
___ "Strickland Finishing Bellairs Books," *Locus* 29(3): 7. September 1992.

STRODE, WOODY
___ Griffin, Scott T. "Woody Strode: An Epic Life Remembered," *Burroughs Bulletin* NS. No. 22: 18-25. April 1995.

STRUGATSKY, ARKADY
___ "SF in the (Former) Soviet Union," *Locus* 28(1): 42, 73. January 1992.
___ "Strugatskii, Arkadii Natanovich," in: Vronskaya, Jeanne, ed. **A Biographical Dictionary of the Soviet Union 1917-1988**. London: K. G. Sauer, 1989. pp.424.
___ "Strugatsky, Arkady (Obituary)," *Science Fiction Chronicle* 13(4): 12. January 1992.
___ Garsault, A. "Strougakski, Arcadi and Strougatski, Boris, Russian Science Fiction Writers," *Positif* No. 247: 15. October 1981.
___ Gomel, Elana. "The Poetics of Censorship: Allegory as Form and Ideology in the Novels of Arkady and Boris Strugatsky," *Science Fiction Studies* 22(1): 87-105. March 1995.
___ Gopman, Vladimir. "Science Fiction Teaches the Civic Virtues: An Interview with Arkadii Strugatsky," *Science Fiction Studies* 18(1): 1-10. March 1991.
___ Howell, Yvonne H. **Apocalyptic Realism: The Science Fiction of Arkady and Boris Strugatsky**. New York: Peter Lang, 1994. 184pp.

STRUGATSKY, ARKADY (continued)
___ Howell, Yvonne H. **Apocalyptic Realism: The Science Fiction of Arkady and Boris Strugatsky**. Ph.D. Dissertation, University of Michigan, 1990. 232pp.

STRUGATSKY, BORIS
___ "Strugatskii, Boris Natanovich," in: Vronskaya, Jeanne, ed. **A Biographical Dictionary of the Soviet Union 1917-1988**. London: K. G. Sauer, 1989. pp.424.
___ Garsault, A. "Strougakski, Arcadi and Strougatski, Boris, Russian Science Fiction Writers," *Positif* No. 247: 15. October 1981.
___ Gomel, Elana. "The Poetics of Censorship: Allegory as Form and Ideology in the Novels of Arkady and Boris Strugatsky," *Science Fiction Studies* 22(1): 87-105. March 1995.
___ Howell, Yvonne H. **Apocalyptic Realism: The Science Fiction of Arkady and Boris Strugatsky**. New York: Peter Lang, 1994. 184pp.
___ Howell, Yvonne H. **Apocalyptic Realism: The Science Fiction of Arkady and Boris Strugatsky**. Ph.D. Dissertation, University of Michigan, 1990. 232pp.

STRUMFELS, DAVID J.
___ Klein, Jay K. "Biolog: David J. Strumfels," *Analog* 114(8/9): 158, 178. July 1994.

STRUZAN, DREW
___ Madsen, Dan. "The Art of Drew Struzan," *LucasFilms Fan Club* No. 18: 10-13. 1993.

STURGEON AWARD
___ SEE: THEODORE STURGEON MEMORIAL AWARD.

STURGEON, THEODORE
___ Aldiss, Brian W. "Sturgeon: The Cruelty of the Gods," in: Aldiss, Brian W. **The Detached Retina: Aspects of SF and Fantasy**. Syracuse, NY: Syracuse University Press, 1995. pp.87-91.
___ Bloom, Harold. "Theodore Sturgeon," in: Bloom, Harold, ed. **Science Fiction Writers of the Golden Age**. New York: Chelsea House, 1995. pp.173-187.
___ Bradbury, Ray. "About Theodore Sturgeon," in: Sturgeon, Theodore. **The Ultimate Egoist, Vol. 1: The Complete Stories of Theodore Sturgeon**, ed. by Paul Williams. Berkeley, CA: North Atlantic Books, 1994. pp.ix-xii.
___ Clarke, Arthur C. "About Theodore Sturgeon," in: Sturgeon, Theodore. **The Ultimate Egoist, Vol. 1: The Complete Stories of Theodore Sturgeon**, ed. by Paul Williams. Berkeley, CA: North Atlantic Books, 1994. pp.xii-xiv.
___ Stableford, Brian. "The Creators of Science Fiction, 2: Theodore Sturgeon," *Interzone* No. 93: 43-45, 55. March 1995.
___ Stableford, Brian. "Schemes of Salvation: The Literary Explorations of Theodore Sturgeon," in: Stableford, Brian. **Outside the Human Aquarium: Masters of Science Fiction**. San Bernardino, CA: Borgo, 1995. pp.117-125.
___ Sturgeon, Theodore. **Argyll: A Memoir**. Glen Ellen, CA: Paul Williams, 1993. 84pp. [Not seen.]
___ Wolfe, Gene. "About Theodore Sturgeon," in: Sturgeon, Theodore. **The Ultimate Egoist, Vol. 1: The Complete Stories of Theodore Sturgeon**, ed. by Paul Williams. Berkeley, CA: North Atlantic Books, 1994. pp.xiv-xvi.

STYLE
___ Benford, Gregory. "Style, Substance, and Other Illusions," in: Slusser, George E. and Rabkin, Eric S., eds. **Styles of Creation: Aesthetic Technique and the Creation of Fictional Worlds**. Athens: University of Georgia Press, 1992. pp.47-57.
___ Brin, David. "Waging War With Reality," in: Slusser, George E. and Rabkin, Eric S., eds. **Styles of Creation: Aesthetic Technique and the Creation of Fictional Worlds**. Athens: University of Georgia Press, 1992. pp.24-29.
___ Carter, Paul A. "From 'Nat' to 'Nathan': The Liberal Arts Odyssey of a Pulpmaster," in: Slusser, George E. and Rabkin, Eric S., eds. **Styles of Creation: Aesthetic Technique and the Creation of Fictional Worlds**. Athens: University of Georgia Press, 1992. pp.58-78.
___ Freedman, Carl. "Style, Fiction, Science Fiction: The Case of Philip K. Dick," in: Slusser, George E. and Rabkin, Eric S., eds. **Styles of Creation: Aesthetic Technique and the Creation of Fictional Worlds**. Athens: University of Georgia Press, 1992. pp.30-45.

STYLE (continued)
___ Hohne, Karen A. "The Voice of Cthulhu: Language Interaction in Contemporary Horror Fiction," in: Slusser, George E. and Rabkin, Eric S., eds. **Styles of Creation: Aesthetic Technique and the Creation of Fictional Worlds.** Athens: University of Georgia Press, 1992. pp.79-87.
___ Navarette, Susan J. "The Soul of the Plot: The Aesthetics of Fin de Siècle Literature of Horror," in: Slusser, George E. and Rabkin, Eric S., eds. **Styles of Creation: Aesthetic Technique and the Creation of Fictional Worlds.** Athens: University of Georgia Press, 1992. pp.88-115.
___ Slusser, George E. "Reflections on Style and Science Fiction," in: Slusser, George E. and Rabkin, Eric S., eds. **Styles of Creation: Aesthetic Technique and the Creation of Fictional Worlds.** Athens: University of Georgia Press, 1992. pp.3-23.

SUBOTSKY, MILTON
___ Fischer, Dennis. "The Amicus Empire: An Interview With Milton Subotsky," *Filmfax* No. 42: 54-61, 96-97. December 1993/January 1994.

SUBSPECIES II (MOTION PICTURE)
___ SEE: BLOODSTONE: SUBSPECIES II (MOTION PICTURE).

SUBSPECIES (MOTION PICTURE)
___ Wilt, David. "**Subspecies** (Review)," *Cinefantastique* 22(6): 55. June 1992

SULLIVAN, TIM
___ "Tim Sullivan: SF Writer and Movie Mogul," *Science Fiction Age* 2(4): 22-23. May 1994.

SULLIVAN, TOM
___ Uram, Sue. "Evil Effects: Tom Sullivan, Gore Auteur," *Cinefantastique* 23(1): 50. August 1992.

SUMMER FESTIVAL OF FANTASY, HORROR AND SCIENCE FICTION, 1994
___ Bernard, Jami. "Film Forum Fest Fulfills Fantasy, Horror, and Sci-Fi," *The New York (NY) National.* August 5, 1994. in: *NewsBank. Film and Television.* 93:C8. 1994.

SUMMONED BY SHADOWS (MOTION PICTURE)
___ Selander, Victoria. "Comes the Stranger," *Starlog* No. 188: 75-77. March 1993.

SUNDOWN (MOTION PICTURE)
___ Wilt, David. "**Sundown** (Review)," *Cinefantastique* 22(6): 55. June 1992

SUPER FORCE (TV)
___ Wilson, Bill. "Future Cops," *Starlog* No. 174: 52-55. January 1992.

SUPER MARIO BROS. (MOTION PICTURE)
___ Goodson, William W., Jr. "**Super Mario Bros.**," *Cinefantastique* 24(1): 8-15. June 1993.
___ Goodson, William W., Jr. "**Super Mario Bros.**: Designing Dinohattan," *Cinefantastique* 24(1): 13. June 1993.
___ Goodson, William W., Jr. "**Super Mario Bros.**: Dinosaur Creations," *Cinefantastique* 24(1): 10. June 1993.
___ Goodson, William W., Jr. "**Super Mario Bros.**: Special Visual Effects," *Cinefantastique* 24(1): 15. June 1993.
___ Lowe, Nick. "**Super Mario Bros.** (Review)," *Interzone* No. 75: 35-36. September 1993.
___ Sammon, Paul M. "Quick Cuts: That Other T-rex," *Cinefex* No. 56: 87-88. November 1993.
___ Yakir, Dan. "**Super Mario Bros.**," *Starlog* No. 192: 53-58. July 1993.

SUPERBOY (TV)
___ "It's a Bird, It's a Plane, Actually It's Viacom's Superboy Spinoff," *Variety* p. 83. March 2, 1988.

SUPERHEROES
___ Sherman, Josepha. "Creating Superheroes in Science Fiction and Fantasy," *Writer* 108(7): 13-14. July 1995.

SUPERMAN
___ "Shuster, Joe (Obituary)," *Locus* 29(3): 77-78. September 1992.

SUPERMAN (continued)
___ Kozloff, Sarah R. "Superman as Saviour: Christian Allegory in the Superman Movies," *Journal of Popular Film and Television* 9(2): 78-82. 1981.
___ Rich, Frank. "Term Limit for the Man of Steel: Yes, It's Time for Him to Go," *New York Times* Sec. 4, p. 1-2. November 22, 1992

SUPERMAN (COMICS)
___ "Look! It's a Bird! It's a Plane! It's Curtains for the Man of Steel!," *New York Times* p. 25. November 15, 1992.

SUPERMAN III (MOTION PICTURE)
___ "**Superman** Lands in Calgary," *Variety* p. 4, 32. September 1, 1982.

SUPERMAN (MOTION PICTURE)
___ Lederman, Marie J. "**Superman**, Oedipus and the Myth of the Birth of the Hero," *Journal of Popular Film and Television* 7(3): 235-245. 1979.

SUPERMAN (TV)
___ McDowell, Rider. "More Than Just **Superman**'s Serious Sidekick: A Conversation with Phyllis Coates," *Filmfax* No. 36: 70-73. December 1992/January 1993

SUPERMAN'S 50TH ANNIVERSARY: A CELEBRATION OF THE MAN OF STEEL (TV)
___ "**Superman's 50th Anniversary: A Celebration of the Man of Steel** (Review)," *Variety* p. 60. April 13, 1988.

SUPERNATURAL FICTION
___ Cavaliero, Glen. **The Supernatural and English Fiction.** Oxford: Oxford University Press, 1995. 273pp.
___ Clery, E. J. **The Rise of Supernatural Fiction, 1762-1800.** Cambridge: Cambridge University Press, 1995. 222pp.
___ Geary, Robert F. **The Supernatural in Gothic Fiction: Horror, Belief and Literary Change.** Lewiston, NY: Mellen, 1992. 151pp.

SUPERNATURAL (MOTION PICTURE)
___ Henenlotter, Frank. "Films From Under the Floorboards," *Sci-Fi Entertainment* 1(6): 52-57. April 1995.

SURVEY
___ "Favorite Writers of Science Fiction and Fantasy," *English Journal* 82(6): 83-85. October 1993.

SURVEY, 1987
___ Clute, John. "Year Roundup from **The Orbit Science Fiction Yearbook 1**," in: Clute, John. **Look at the Evidence: Essays and Reviews.** Liverpool: Liverpool University Press, 1995. pp.17-27.

SURVEY, 1988
___ Clute, John. "Year Roundup from **The Orbit Science Fiction Yearbook 2**," in: Clute, John. **Look at the Evidence: Essays and Reviews.** Liverpool: Liverpool University Press, 1995. pp.75-84.

SURVEY, 1989
___ Clute, John. "Year Roundup from **The Orbit Science Fiction Yearbook 3**," in: Clute, John. **Look at the Evidence: Essays and Reviews.** Liverpool: Liverpool University Press, 1995. pp.139-148.

SURVEY, 1990
___ "**VOYA's** Best Science Fiction, Fantasy and Horror," *Voice of Youth Advocates* 14(1): 9-13. April 1991.
___ Barron, Neil. "A Critical Survey of Fantastic Literature and Film Scholarship in 1990," by Neil Barron and Michael Klossner. in: Collins, Robert A. and Latham, Robert, eds. **Science Fiction and Fantasy Book Review Annual 1991.** Westport, CT: Greenwood, 1994. pp.205-239.
___ Becker, Muriel R. "The Year in Young Adult Science Fiction, Fantasy and Horror: 1990," in: Collins, Robert A. and Latham, Robert, eds. **Science Fiction and Fantasy Book Review Annual 1991.** Westport, CT: Greenwood, 1994. pp.138-168.
___ Clute, John. "Year Roundup from **New Worlds 1**," in: Clute, John. **Look at the Evidence: Essays and Reviews.** Liverpool: Liverpool University Press, 1995. pp.195-205.
___ Cramer, Kathryn. "Democrazy, the Personal Planetarium, and the American Way: The Year 1990 in Science Fiction," *New York Review of Science Fiction* No. 45: 18-22. May 1992.

SURVEY, 1990 (continued)
___ Dziemianowicz, Stefan. "Horror Enters the '90s," by Stefan Dziemianowicz and Michael A. Morrison. in: Collins, Robert A. and Latham, Robert, eds. **Science Fiction and Fantasy Book Review Annual 1991**. Westport, CT: Greenwood, 1994. pp.87-116.
___ Levy, Michael M. "The Year in Science Fiction, 1990," in: Collins, Robert A. and Latham, Robert, eds. **Science Fiction and Fantasy Book Review Annual 1991**. Westport, CT: Greenwood, 1994. pp.1-26.
___ May, Jill P. "The Year in Children's Science Fiction and Fantasy, 1990," in: Collins, Robert A. and Latham, Robert, eds. **Science Fiction and Fantasy Book Review Annual 1991**. Westport, CT: Greenwood, 1994. pp.178-204.
___ Senior, William. "New Fantasy Writers in 1990," in: Collins, Robert A. and Latham, Robert, eds. **Science Fiction and Fantasy Book Review Annual 1991**. Westport, CT: Greenwood, 1994. pp.70-78.
___ Senior, William. "The Year in Fantasy Literature, 1990," by William Senior and C. W. Sullivan, III. in: Collins, Robert A. and Latham, Robert, eds. **Science Fiction and Fantasy Book Review Annual 1991**. Westport, CT: Greenwood, 1994. pp.49-69.

SURVEY, 1991
___ "Best Science Fiction, Fantasy and Horror, 1991," *Voice of Youth Advocates* 15(1): 9-13. April 1992.
___ Clute, John. "Year Roundup from **New Worlds 3**," in: Clute, John. **Look at the Evidence: Essays and Reviews**. Liverpool: Liverpool University Press, 1995. pp.275-287.
___ D'Ammassa, Don. "The Best SF, Fantasy and Horror Novels of 1991," *Science Fiction Chronicle* 13(6): 20, 22. March 1992.
___ Lerner, Fred. "Science Fiction With Rivets," *Voice of Youth Advocates* 15(1): 19-20. April 1992.

SURVEY, 1992
___ Clute, John. "Marrying Out: The Year in SF, 1992," *New York Review of Science Fiction* No. 64: 1, 8-10. December 1993.
___ Clute, John. "Year Roundup from **Nebula Awards 28**," in: Clute, John. **Look at the Evidence: Essays and Reviews**. Liverpool: Liverpool University Press, 1995. pp.355-361.
___ D'Ammassa, Don. "The Best SF, Fantasy, and Horror Novels of the Year, 1992," *Science Fiction Chronicle* 14(5): 5, 22-24. February 1993.
___ Dozois, Gardner. "Summation 1992," in: Dozois, Gardner, ed. **The Year's Best Science Fiction: Tenth Annual Collection**. New York: St. Martin's, 1993. pp.xi-xxxvi.
___ Miller, Chuck. "Science Fiction, Fantasy & Horror: The Year in Review," *AB Bookman's Weekly* 90(17): 1448-1450. October 26, 1992.

SURVEY, 1993
___ "Best Science Fiction, Fantasy, & Horror: 1993," *Voice of Youth Advocates* 17(1): 7-10. April 1994.
___ Winnett, Scott. "1993 Book Summary," by Scott Winnett and Charles N. Brown. *Locus* 32(2): 43-45, 73-76. February 1994.
___ Winnett, Scott. "1993 Magazine Summary," by Scott Winnett and Charles N. Brown. *Locus* 32(2): 44-48, 51. February 1994.

SUSAN PETREY CLARION SCHOLARSHIPS, 1993
___ "$1000 Susan Petrey SF Scholarships Awarded," *Science Fiction Chronicle* 14(11): 6-7. August 1993.

SÜSKIND, PATRICK
___ Borchardt, Edith. "Caricature, Parody, Satire: Narrative Masks as Subversion of the Picaro in Patrick Süskind's **Perfume**," in: Ruddick, Nicholas, ed. **State of the Fantastic**. Westport, CT: Greenwood, 1992. pp.97-103.
___ Borchardt, Edith. "Criminal Artists and Artisans in Mysteries by E. T. A. Hoffman, Dorothy Sayers, Ernesto Sábato, Patrick Süskind, and Thomas Harris," in: Sanders, Joe, ed. **Functions of the Fantastic**. Westport, CT: Greenwood, 1995. pp.125-134.

SUSPENSION OF DISBELIEF
___ Stableford, Brian. "The Plausibility of the Impossible," in: Stableford, Brian. **Opening Minds: Essays on Fantastic Literature**. San Bernardino, CA: Borgo Press, 1995. pp.91-98.

SUSSEX, LUCY
___ Buckrich, Judith R. "Past, Future and Present: Australian Science Fiction; An Interview with Sean McMullen and Lucy Sussex," *Overland* (Australia) 133: 8-14. Summer 1993.

SUTCLIFF, ROSEMARY
___ "Sutcliff, Rosemary (Obituary)," *Locus* 29(4): 66. October 1992

SUTIN, LAWRENCE
___ Kincaid, Paul. "The Entire Enchilada: Lawrence Sutin Interviewed," *Vector* No. 168: 9-12. August/September 1992.
___ Tidmarsh, Andrew. "Lawrence Sutin: Interview," *Interzone* No. 56: 26-28. February 1992.

SUTTON, DAVID
___ "British Fantasy Awards," *Science Fiction Chronicle* 16(1): 5. October 1994.

SVANKMAJER, JAN
___ Clarke, Jeremy. "Jan Svankmajer Puppetry's Dark Poet," *Cinefantastique* 26(3): 54-57. April 1995.
___ Persons, Dan. "Svankmajer: A Retrospective Look at the Amazing Oeuvre of the Czech Fabulist," *Cinefantastique* 26(3): 56. April 1995.

SWAIN, DWIGHT V.
___ "Swain, Dwight V. (Obituary)," *Locus* 28(4): 60. April 1992.
___ "Swain, Dwight V. (Obituary)," *Science Fiction Chronicle* 13(7): 16. April 1992.

SWAN PRINCESS (MOTION PICTURE)
___ Persons, Dan. "**Swan Princess** (Review)," *Cinefantastique* 26(3): 60. April 1995.

SWANN, DONALD
___ "Swann, Donald (Obituary)," *Locus* 32(5): 62-63. May 1994.
___ "Swann, Donald (Obituary)," *Science Fiction Chronicle* 15(6): 26. April/May 1994.

SWANWICK, MICHAEL
___ "1991 Nebula Awards Winners," *Locus* 28(5): 6. May 1992.
___ "Eleventh Annual *S. F. Chronicle* Reader's Awards," *Science Fiction Chronicle* 13(11/12): 4. August 1992.
___ "Michael Swanwick: Writing at Last," *Locus* 29(3): 5, 81. September 1992.
___ "SFWA's Nebula Award Winners," *Science Fiction Chronicle* 13(8): 4. May 1992.
___ Nicholls, Stan. "Michael Swanwick Has Strange Notions," in: Nicholls, Stan. **Wordsmiths of Wonder: Fifty Interviews with Writers of the Fantastic**. London: Orbit, 1993. pp.92-98.
___ Nicholls, Stan. "Strange Notions: An Interview With Michael Swanwick," *Interzone* No. 62: 45-47. August 1992.
___ Schweitzer, Darrell. "SFC Interviews: Michael Swanwick," *Science Fiction Chronicle* 16(5): 5, 34-36. March/April 1995.

SWEDEN
___ Engholm, Ahrvid. "SF in the Nordic Countries," *Locus* 34(4): 39. April 1995.
___ Holmbert, John-Henri. "Letter From Sweden," *Science Fiction Chronicle* 17(2): 6. December 1995/January 1996.
___ Stenström, Beregond A. "Tolkien in Swedish," in: Kranz, Gisbert, ed. **Inklings: Jahrbuch für Literatur und Ästhetik**. 2. Band. [Lüdenscheid, Germany: Stier], 1984. pp.43-49.

SWIFT, JONATHAN
___ Chalmers, Alan D. **Jonathan Swift and the Burden of the Future**. Newark, NJ: University of Delaware Press, 1995. 175pp.
___ Forster, Jean-Paul. **Jonathan Swift: The Fictions of the Satirist**. New York: Peter Lang, 1991. 248pp.
___ Hassler, Donald M. "Swift, Pohl, and Kornbluth: Publicists Anatomize Newness," *Extrapolation* 34(3): 245-250. Fall 1993.
___ Pujia, Roberto. "Scienza, Utopia scientista e satira nell'Inghilterra dell'eta augustea: l'antifilosofia di J. Swift," in: Saccaro Del Buffa, Giuseppa and Lewis, Arthur O., eds. **Utopia e Modernita: Teorie e prassi utopiche nell'eta moderna e postmoderna**. Rome: Gangemi Editore, 1989. pp.877-890.
___ Radner, John B. "The Fall and Decline: **Gulliver's Travels** and the Failure of Utopia," *Utopian Studies* 3(2): 50-74. 1992.
___ Rielly, Edward J. "Irony in **Gulliver's Travels** and Utopia," *Utopian Studies* 3(1): 70-83. 1992.

SWIFT, TOM
___ Molson, Francis J. "The Tom Swift Books," in: Sullivan, C. W., III. **Science Fiction for Young Readers**. Westport, CT: Greenwood, 1993. pp.3-20.

SWINBURNE, ALGERNON CHARLES
___ Lambdin, Laura. "Swinburne's Early Arthurian Poems: Shadows of His Mature Vision," *Quondam et Futurus* 3(4): 63-76. Winter 1993.

SWITZERLAND
___ "Science Fiction, a Global Community: Switzerland," *Locus* 32(4): 39. April 1994.
___ "SF in French," *Locus* 31(6): 40. December 1993.
___ "SF in Switzerland," *Locus* 28(1): 48. January 1992.

SWORD AND SORCERER (MOTION PICTURE)
___ "*Sword and Sorcerer* A Whammo; Tho Anguish Alley Getting There," *Variety* p. 8, 444. May 12, 1982.

SWORD IN THE STONE (MOTION PICTURE)
___ Grellner, Mary A. "Two Films That Sparkle: *The Sword in the Stone* and *Camelot*," in: Harty, Kevin J., ed. **Cinema Arthuriana: Essays on Arthurian Film**. New York: Garland, 1991. pp.71-83.

SWORD OF THE VALIANT (MOTION PICTURE)
___ Blanch, Robert J. "Gawain on Film," by Robert J. Blanch and Julian N. Wasserman. in: Harty, Kevin J., ed. **Cinema Arthuriana: Essays on Arthurian Film**. New York: Garland, 1991. pp.57-70.

SWYCAFFER, JEFFERSON P.
___ Mintz, Catherine. "Rules of the Game," *Starlog* No. 203: 61-63. June 1994.

SYKORA, WILL
___ "Sykora, Will (Obituary)," *Locus* 34(2): 70. February 1995.
___ "Sykora, Will (Obituary)," *Science Fiction Chronicle* 16(2): 20. November/December 1994.

SYMONS, JULIAN
___ "Symons, Julian (Obituary)," *Locus* 34(1) 66. January 1995.

TAFF
___ SEE: TRANSATLANTIC FAN FUND.

TAINE, JOHN
___ Reid, Constance. "New Light on the Work of John Taine," in: Wolf, Milton T. and Mallett, Daryl F., eds. **Imaginative Futures: Proceedings of the 1993 Science Fiction Research Association Conference**. San Bernardino, CA: Jacob's Ladder Books, 1995. pp.115-124.
___ Reid, Constance. **The Search for E. T. Bell, Also Known as John Taine**. Washington, DC: Mathematical Association of America, Aug. 1993. 372pp.

TAINTED BLOOD (MOTION PICTURE)
___ Scapperotti, Dan. "*Tainted Blood* (Review)," *Cinefantastique* 24(2): 59. August 1993.

TAIWAN
___ Chien, Ying-Ying. "From Utopian to Dystopian World: Two Faces of Feminism in Contemporary Taiwanese Women's Fiction," *World Literature Today* 68(1): 35-42. Winter 1994.
___ Wong, Kin-yuen. "Rhetoric, History and Interpretation in Chang Hsi-Kuo's The Star Cloud Suite," *Modern Chinese Literature* (Boulder, CO) 6(1/2): 115-132. Spring-Fall 1992.

TAKEI, GEORGE
___ Fischer, Dennis. "*Oblivion*," *Cinefantastique* 25(4): 56-57, 61. August 1994.
___ Goldsmith, Steven. "Takei Takes Helm in Autobiography," *Austin (TX) American Statesman* Sec. E, p. 11. October 15, 1994.
___ Spelling, Ian. "Captain Sulu," *Starlog* No. 174: 43-47. January 1992.
___ Takei, George. **To the Stars: The Autobiography of George Takei, Star Trek's Mr. Sulu**. New York: Pocket Books, 1994. 406pp.
___ Takei, George. **To the Stars: The Autobiography of Star Trek's Mr. Sulu**. New York: Simon & Schuster Audio, 1994. 2 audiocassettes, 3 hours.

TAKEI, GEORGE (continued)
___ Uram, Sue. "*Star Trek: Generations*: Where's Captain Sulu," *Cinefantastique* 25(6)/26(1): 22. December 1994.

TAKEOVER (MOTION PICTURE)
___ SEE: SCANNERS III: THE TAKEOVER (MOTION PICTURE).

TALALAY, RACHEL
___ Johnson, Kim H. "Tank Mechanic," *Starlog* No. 214: 46-49. May 1995.

TALBOT, MICHAEL
___ "Talbot, Michael (Obituary)," *Locus* 29(1): 67. July 1992.
___ "Talbot, Michael (Obiturary)," *Science Fiction Chronicle* 13(10): 16. July/August 1992.

TALE OF A VAMPIRE (MOTION PICTURE)
___ Jones, Alan. "*Tale of a Vampire*," *Cinefantastique* 24(6)/25(1): 116-117. February 1994.

TALES FROM THE CRYPT: DEMON KNIGHT (MOTION PICTURE)
___ Eby, Douglas. "*Demon Knight*," *Cinefantastique* 26(2): 12-13. February 1995.
___ Newman, Kim. "*Tales From the Crypt: Demon Knight* (Review)," *Sight and Sound* 5(6): 54-55. June 1995.

TALES FROM THE HOOD (MOTION PICTURE)
___ Harris, Judith P. "*Tales From the Hood* (Review)," *Cinefantastique* 26(6)/27(1): 123-124. October 1995.

TALES OF THE DARKSIDE (TV)
___ "LBS & Tribune Sharing Profits From 'Darkside'," *Variety* p. 23, 101. February 15, 1984.

TALL TALES (MOTION PICTURE)
___ French, Lawrence. "*Tall Tales*," *Cinefantastique* 26(3): 8-9. April 1995.
___ Prokop, Tim. "Quick Cuts: A New Twist on Tornadoes," *Cinefex* No. 61: 11-12. March 1995.

TALLMAN, PATRICIA
___ Jankiewicz, Pat. "Bloody Double," *Starlog* No. 209: 59-62. December 1994.

TANGENTS (MOTION PICTURE)
___ Edelstein, Art. "Vermont Struggles with Film Policy," *Vermont Business Magazine (Brattleboro, VT)*. February 1,1994. in: *NewsBank. Film and Television*. 23:D6-D9. 1994.

TANK GIRL (MOTION PICTURE)
___ Adams, Thelma. "You'll 'Tank' Yourself," *New York (NY) Post*. March 31, 1995. in: *NewsBank. Film and Television*. 39:A1. 1995.
___ Arnold, Gary. "*Tank Girl* Flattens All Potential," *Washington (DC) Times*. March 31, 1995. in: *NewsBank. Film and Television*. 50:C7. 1995.
___ Britton, Bonnie. "Lori Petty Best Part of *Tank Girl*," *Indianapolis (IN) Star*. March 31, 1995. in: *NewsBank. Film and Television*. 50:C2. 1995.
___ Campbell, Bob. "*Tank Girl* Comes Loaded With Macho Swagger," *(Newark, NJ) Star-Ledger*. March 31, 1995. in: *NewsBank. Film and Television*. 38:G14. 1995.
___ Considine, J. B. "English Comics *Tank Girl* May Have Most Yanks Yawning," *(Baltimore, MD) Sun*. March 31, 1995. in: *NewsBank. Film and Television*. 50:B12. 1995.
___ Felperin, Leslie. "*Tank Girl* (Review)," *Sight and Sound* 5(7): 54-55. July 1995.
___ Gubbins, Teresa. "*Tank Girl*: Generation X Marks the Spot, But This One Missed by a Mile," *Dallas (TX) Morning News*. March 31, 1995. in: *NewsBank. Film and Television*. 50:C6. 1995.
___ Hunter, Stephen. "Bring on the Apocalypse, But Spare Us the Travail of *Tank Girl*," *(Baltimore, MD) Sun*. March 31, 1995. in: *NewsBank. Film and Television*. 50:C3. 1995.
___ Johnson, Kim H. "*Tank Girl*," *Starlog* No. 213: 40-43. April 1995.
___ Johnson, Kim H. "Tank Mechanic," *Starlog* No. 214: 46-49. May 1995.
___ Johnson, Malcolm. "*Tank Girl* Terribly Hip, But Comic Book Was Better," *Hartford (CT) Courant*. April 1, 1995. in: *NewsBank. Film and Television*. 50:B14. 1995.

TANK GIRL (MOTION PICTURE) (continued)

___ Kipen, David. "Petty Can't Save Horribly Misconceived *Tank Girl*," *Boston (MA) Herald*. March 31, 1995. in: *NewsBank. Film and Television*. 50:C5. 1995.

___ Lowe, Nick. "*Tank Girl* (Review)," *Interzone* No. 98: 30-31. August 1995.

___ Maccarillo, Lisa. "Cyberpunk Heroine *Tank Girl* Plays Tour Guide to a Gritty Tomorrow," *Science Fiction Age* 3(3): 20-22, 92. March 1995.

___ Maccarillo, Lisa. "Cyberpunk Heroine *Tank Girl*," *Sci-Fi Entertainment* 1(6): 28-33. April 1995.

___ Murray, Steve. "*Tank Girl* Is Road Warrior in Fishnet Hose," *(Atlanta, GA) Journal*. March 31, 1995. in: *NewsBank. Film and Television*. 50:C1. 1995.

___ Rosenberg, Scott. "Punk Heroine Hits Screen With a Bang," *San Francisco (CA) Examiner*. March 31, 1995. in: *NewsBank. Film and Television*. 50:B13. 1995.

___ Scapperotti, Dan. "*Tank Girl*," *Cinefantastique* 26(4): 50-51. June 1995.

___ Sherman, Paul. "Punk Apocalypse Saga Doesn't Always Hit Its Target," *Boston (MA) Herald*. March 31, 1995. in: *NewsBank. Film and Television*. 50:C4. 1995.

___ Wynne, Frank. **The Making of Tank Girl**. London: Titan, 1995. 96pp.

TANNEN, JACK

___ "Tannen, Jack (Obituary)," *Locus* 28(2): 68. February 1992.

___ "Tannen, Jack (Obituary)," *Science Fiction Chronicle* 13(4): 12. January 1992.

TAROT CARDS

___ Grebe, Coralee. "Tarot Card Symbolism in the *Star Wars* Films," *Mythlore* 20(2): 27-31. Spring 1994. (Whole No. 76)

TARR, JUDITH

___ King, T. Jackson. "SFC Interviews: Judith Tarr," *Science Fiction Chronicle* 14(7): 5, 27-29. April 1993.

TARZAN

___ Chapman, Mike. "Glenn Morris: Tarzan Number Eight," *Burroughs Bulletin* NS. No. 16: 8-15. October 1993.

___ Fury, David. **Kings of the Jungle: An Illustrated Reference to 'Tarzan' on Screen and Television**. Jefferson, NC: McFarland, 1993. 272pp.

___ Lacassin, Francis. **Tarzan ou le Chevalier crispe**. Paris: H. Veyrier, 1982. 223pp. [Revised edition].

___ Lacassin, Francis. **Tarzan ou le Chevalier crispe**. Paris: Union Generale d'editions, 1971. 511pp.

___ Warren, Bill. "Tarzan the Magnificent," *Starlog* No. 187: 27-31. February 1993.

TARZAN (COMIC)

___ Graham, Harry L. "How the Gaonas Flew With Tarzan in the Comics," *Burroughs Bulletin* NS. No. 18: 17-19. April 1994.

TARZAN (RADIO)

___ García, Fernando. "Tarzan, King of the Pampa," by Fernando García and Hernán Ostuni. *Burroughs Bulletin* NS. No. 18: 20-22. April 1994.

TARZAN, THE APE MAN (1959) (MOTION PICTURE)

___ Fury, David. "Interview with the Tarzan Man, Mr. Denny Miller," *Burroughs Bulletin* NS. No. 17: 25-29. January 1994.

TARZAN, THE APE MAN (1981) (MOTION PICTURE)

___ "Burroughs Appeal Nixed; Uphold MGM on Bo's *Tarzan* Retread," *Variety* p. 7, 28. June 2, 1982.

TATE, GREG

___ Dery, Mark. "Black to the Future: Interviews with Samuel R. Delany, Greg Tate, and Tricia Rose," *South Atlantic Quarterly* 92(4): 735-788. Fall 1993. (Reprinted in: Dery, Mark, Ed. **Flame Wars: The Discourse of Cyberculture**. Durham, NC: Duke University Press, 1994.)

TATSUMI, TAKAYUKI

___ **No Great Endeavor: Presentation of the Pilgrim and Pioneer Awards**. Ann Arbor, MI: Tucker Video, 1994. 1 videocassette, 67 minutes. (Presentation at the 1994 Science Fiction Research Association Conference. Sheri S. Tepper, John Clute, Takayuki Tatsumi, Larry McCaffery, speakers.)

TAYLOR, DON

___ Weaver, Tom. "Don Taylor," in: Weaver, Tom. **They Fought the Creature Features: Interviews with 23 Classic Horror, Science Fiction and Serial Stars**. Jefferson, NC: McFarland, 1995. pp.263-276.

TAYLOR, JERI

___ Altman, Mark A. "*Star Trek: The Next Generation*: Jeri Taylor, Script Supervisor," *Cinefantastique* 24(3/4): 36-37. October 1993.

___ Hull, Peter R. "The Voice of Jeri Taylor: Multipart Harmony," *Star Trek: The Official Fan Club* No. 94: 44-45. February/March 1994.

TAYLOR, ROD

___ Swires, Steve. "Master of the *Time Machine*," in: McDonnell, David, ed. **Starlog's Science Fiction Heroes and Heroines**. New York: Crescent Books, 1995. pp.80-83.

TEACHING

___ Dubeck, Leroy W. "Using Science Fiction Films to Teach Science at the College Level," by Leroy W. Dubeck, Suzanne E. Moshier and Judith E. Boss. *Journal of College Science Teaching* 25(1): 46-50. September/October 1995

TEACHING PHYSICS

___ Dubeck, Leroy W. "Science and Science Fiction Films," *Journal of College Science Teaching* 11(2): 111-113. November 1981.

TEACHING SF AND FANTASY

___ "*Star Trek* 101," *San Francisco (CA) Chronicle* January 17, 1995. (Cited from the Internet Edition.)

___ Attebery, Brian. **Teacher's Guide to the Norton Book of Science Fiction**. New York: Norton, 1993. 129pp.

___ Beaudry, Mary L. "Lignum Vitae in the Two-Year College," in: Fries, Maureen and Watson, Jeanie, eds. **Approaches to the Teaching of the Arthurian Tradition**. New York: Modern Language Association, 1992. pp.122-126.

___ Boardman, Phillip C. "Teaching the Moderns in an Arthurian Course," in: Fries, Maureen and Watson, Jeanie, eds. **Approaches to the Teaching of the Arthurian Tradition**. New York: Modern Language Association, 1992. pp.81-87.

___ Brice, William C. "Geology Teaching and Science Fiction," *Journal of Geological Education* 29(2): 105-107. March 1980.

___ Dubeck, Leroy W. "Science and Science Fiction Films," *Journal of College Science Teaching* 11(2): 111-113. November 1981.

___ Fries, Maureen. "The Labyrinthine Ways: Teaching the Arthurian Tradition," in: Fries, Maureen and Watson, Jeanie, eds. **Approaches to the Teaching of the Arthurian Tradition**. New York: Modern Language Association, 1992. pp.33-50.

___ Fries, Maureen. "Readings for Students and Teachers," in: Fries, Maureen and Watson, Jeanie, eds. **Approaches to the Teaching of the Arthurian Tradition**. New York: Modern Language Association, 1992. pp.18-30.

___ Fries, Maureen. "Texts for Teaching," in: Fries, Maureen and Watson, Jeanie, eds. **Approaches to the Teaching of the Arthurian Tradition**. New York: Modern Language Association, 1992. pp.3-18.

___ Fries, Maureen. "Women in Arthurian Literature," in: Fries, Maureen and Watson, Jeanie, eds. **Approaches to the Teaching of the Arthurian Tradition**. New York: Modern Language Association, 1992. pp.155-158.

___ Fries, Maureen, ed. **Approaches to the Teaching of the Arthurian Tradition**, ed. by Maureen Fries and Jeanie Watson. New York: Modern Language Association, 1992. 195pp.

___ Gaylord, Alan T. "Arthur and the Green World," in: Fries, Maureen and Watson, Jeanie, eds. **Approaches to the Teaching of the Arthurian Tradition**. New York: Modern Language Association, 1992. pp.56-60.

___ Gough, Noel. **Laboratories in Fiction: Science Education and Popular Media**. Geelong: Deakin University, 1993. 137pp.

TEACHING SF AND FANTASY

TEACHING SF AND FANTASY (continued)
___ Grellner, Mary A. "Arthuriana and Popular Culture," in: Fries, Maureen and Watson, Jeanie, eds. **Approaches to the Teaching of the Arthurian Tradition.** New York: Modern Language Association, 1992. pp.159-162.
___ Gunn, James E. "The Academic Viewpoint," in: Gunn, James E. **Inside Science Fiction: Essays on Fantastic Literature.** San Bernardino, CA: Borgo, 1992. pp.73-78.
___ Gunn, James E. "The City and the Critics," in: Gunn, James E. **Inside Science Fiction: Essays on Fantastic Literature.** San Bernardino, CA: Borgo, 1992. pp.92-98.
___ Gunn, James E. "The Education of a Science Fiction Teacher," in: Gunn, James E. **Inside Science Fiction: Essays on Fantastic Literature.** San Bernardino, CA: Borgo, 1992. pp.9-15.
___ Gunn, James E. "From the Pulps to the Classroom: The Strange Journey of Science Fiction," in: Gunn, James E. **Inside Science Fiction: Essays on Fantastic Literature.** San Bernardino, CA: Borgo, 1992. pp.16-29.
___ Gunn, James E. "Science Fiction as Literature," in: Gunn, James E. **Inside Science Fiction: Essays on Fantastic Literature.** San Bernardino, CA: Borgo, 1992. pp.79-91.
___ Gunn, James E. "Teaching Science Fiction Revisited," in: Gunn, James E. **Inside Science Fiction: Essays on Fantastic Literature.** San Bernardino, CA: Borgo, 1992. pp.67-72.
___ Hamilton, Ruth E. "Teaching Arthur at a Summer Institute for Secondary School Teachers," in: Fries, Maureen and Watson, Jeanie, eds. **Approaches to the Teaching of the Arthurian Tradition.** New York: Modern Language Association, 1992. pp.118-121.
___ Harty, Kevin J. "Teaching Arthurian Film," in: Fries, Maureen and Watson, Jeanie, eds. **Approaches to the Teaching of the Arthurian Tradition.** New York: Modern Language Association, 1992. pp.147-150.
___ Herman, Harold J. "Teaching White, Stewart, and Berger," in: Fries, Maureen and Watson, Jeanie, eds. **Approaches to the Teaching of the Arthurian Tradition.** New York: Modern Language Association, 1992. pp.113-117.
___ Hughes, Linda K. "Teaching Tennyson: **Idylls of the King** as a Serial Poem," in: Fries, Maureen and Watson, Jeanie, eds. **Approaches to the Teaching of the Arthurian Tradition.** New York: Modern Language Association, 1992. pp.106-112.
___ James, Edward. "Science Fiction Courses in Higher Education in Great Britain: A Preliminary Guide," by Edward James and Farah Mendlesohn. *Foundation* No. 59: 59-69. Autumn 1993.
___ Jordan, Anne D. "Future Reading: Science Fiction," *Teaching and Learning Literature* 4(5): 17-23. May/June 1995.
___ Keiser, George R. "Malory and the Middle English Romance: A Graduate Course," in: Fries, Maureen and Watson, Jeanie, eds. **Approaches to the Teaching of the Arthurian Tradition.** New York: Modern Language Association, 1992. pp.131-134.
___ Kelly, Thomas. "The World of King Arthur: An Interdisciplinary Course," by Thomas Kelly and Thomas Ohlgren. in: Fries, Maureen and Watson, Jeanie, eds. **Approaches to the Teaching of the Arthurian Tradition.** New York: Modern Language Association, 1992. pp.77-80.
___ Kindrick, Robert L. "Which Malory Should I Teach?," in: Fries, Maureen and Watson, Jeanie, eds. **Approaches to the Teaching of the Arthurian Tradition.** New York: Modern Language Association, 1992. pp.100-105.
___ Kraczmarek, Nancy. "Collaboration: The Science in Science Fiction," *The English Record* 42(3): 13-15. 1992.
___ Kratz, Dennis M. "Teaching Science Fiction," in: Barron, Neil, ed. **Anatomy of Wonder 4.** New York: Bowker, 1995. pp.715-737.
___ Lacy, Norris J. "Teaching the King Arthur of History and Chronicle," in: Fries, Maureen and Watson, Jeanie, eds. **Approaches to the Teaching of the Arthurian Tradition.** New York: Modern Language Association, 1992. pp.51-55.
___ Lynch, Kathryn L. "Implementing an Interdisciplinary Course," in: Fries, Maureen and Watson, Jeanie, eds. **Approaches to the Teaching of the Arthurian Tradition.** New York: Modern Language Association, 1992. pp.65-69.
___ McClatchey, Joseph. "Teaching Individual Characters and Motifs," in: Fries, Maureen and Watson, Jeanie, eds. **Approaches to the Teaching of the Arthurian Tradition.** New York: Modern Language Association, 1992. pp.70-72.
___ Norton, Mary F. "Visions of the Future: Utopian and Apocalyptic Designs," *CEA Forum* 23(2)/24(1): 15-20. Summer/Winter 1993/1994.
___ Payson, Patricia. **Science Fiction: Imagining Worlds.** Tucson, AZ: Zephyr Press, 1994. 84pp. (Zephyr Press Learning Packet)

TEACHING SF AND FANTASY (continued)
___ Rabkin, Eric S. **Science Fiction: The Literature of the Technological Imagination.** Springfield, VA: The Teaching Company, 1994. 2 videocassettes, 380 minutes.
___ Raffel, Burton. "Translating **Yvain** and **Sir Gawain and the Green Knight** for Classroom Use," in: Fries, Maureen and Watson, Jeanie, eds. **Approaches to the Teaching of the Arthurian Tradition.** New York: Modern Language Association, 1992. pp.88-93.
___ Ruud, Jay. "Teaching the 'Hoole' Tradition Through Parallel Passages," in: Fries, Maureen and Watson, Jeanie, eds. **Approaches to the Teaching of the Arthurian Tradition.** New York: Modern Language Association, 1992. pp.73-76.
___ Schultz, James A. "Teaching Gottfried and Wolfram," in: Fries, Maureen and Watson, Jeanie, eds. **Approaches to the Teaching of the Arthurian Tradition.** New York: Modern Language Association, 1992. pp.94-99.
___ Shichtman, Martin B. "Wagner and the Arthurian Tradition," in: Fries, Maureen and Watson, Jeanie, eds. **Approaches to the Teaching of the Arthurian Tradition.** New York: Modern Language Association, 1992. pp.139-142.
___ Slocum, Sally K. "Arthur the Great Equalizer: Teaching a Course for Graduate and Undergraduate Students," in: Fries, Maureen and Watson, Jeanie, eds. **Approaches to the Teaching of the Arthurian Tradition.** New York: Modern Language Association, 1992. pp.127-130.
___ Szarmach, Paul E. "Arthurian Archaeology," in: Fries, Maureen and Watson, Jeanie, eds. **Approaches to the Teaching of the Arthurian Tradition.** New York: Modern Language Association, 1992. pp.135-138.
___ Taylor, Beverly. "Using Nineteenth-Century Visual Arts in the Literature Classroom," in: Fries, Maureen and Watson, Jeanie, eds. **Approaches to the Teaching of the Arthurian Tradition.** New York: Modern Language Association, 1992. pp.143-146.
___ Thompson, Raymond H. "Modern Visions and Revisions of the Matter of Britain," in: Fries, Maureen and Watson, Jeanie, eds. **Approaches to the Teaching of the Arthurian Tradition.** New York: Modern Language Association, 1992. pp.61-64.
___ Westfahl, Gary. "Nonsense of Wonder: On Teaching Science Fiction," *Science Fiction Eye* No. 13: 67-71. Spring 1994.
___ Whitaker, Muriel. "Arthur for Children," in: Fries, Maureen and Watson, Jeanie, eds. **Approaches to the Teaching of the Arthurian Tradition.** New York: Modern Language Association, 1992. pp.151-154.

TEACHING SF AND FANTASY, UNIVERSITY COURSES
___ "MA in SF Offered," *Locus* 31(6): 7. December 1993.

TEACHING, ELEMENTARY AND MIDDLE SCHOOL
___ Coville, Bruce. "About Tomorrow: Learning with Literature," *Instructor* 101(9): 20, 22-23. May/June 1992.

TEACHING, POLITICAL SCIENCE
___ Barton-Kriese, Paul. "Exploring Divergent Realities: Using Science Fiction to Teach Introductory Political Science," *Extrapolation* 34(3): 209-215. Fall 1993.

TEACHING, USE OF SF
___ Bear, Greg. "State of the Art: Contact in the Classroom," *Analog* 112(1/2): 228-237. January 1992.
___ Burns, John E. "One for the Books: Using Literature-Based Science Lessons," *Science Teacher* 61(7): 38-41. October 1994.
___ Dubeck, Leroy W. **Fantastic Voyages: Learning Science Through Science Fiction Films.** New York: American Institute of Physics, 1994. 327pp.
___ Dubeck, Leroy W. "Finding the Facts in Science Fiction Films," by Leroy W. Dubeck, Suzanne E. Moshier, Matthew H. Bruce and Judith E. Boss. *Science Teacher* 60(4): 46-48. April 1993.
___ Laz, Cheryl. "Science Fiction and Introductory Sociology: The Handmaid in the Classroom," *Teaching Sociology* 24(1): 54-63. January 1995.
___ Osif, Bonnie A. "Teaching Tough Stuff: Science Fiction Futures and Bibliographic Instruction," *Research Strategies* 11(2): 116-119. Spring 1993.

TEAGUE, LEWIS
___ Wood, Robin. "Cat and Dog: Lewis Teague's Stephen King Movies," in: Irons, Glenwood, ed. **Gender, Language and Myth: Essays on Popular Narrative.** Toronto: University of Toronto Press, 1992. pp.303-318.

TECHNOLOGY IN FILM

TECHNOLOGY IN FILM
___ Matheson, T. J. "Marcuse, Ellul, and the Science-Fiction Film: Negative Responses to Technology," *Science-Fiction Studies* 19(3): 326-339. November 1992.
___ Matheson, T. J. "Triumphant Technology and Minimal Man: **The Technological Society**, Science Fiction Films, and Ridley Scott's **Alien**," *Extrapolation* 33(3): 215-229. Fall 1992.

TECHNOLOGY IN LITERATURE
___ Greenberg, Mark L. "Introduction: Literature and Technology," by Mark L. Greenberg and Lance Schachterle. in: Greenberg, Mark L. and Schachterle, Lance, eds. **Literature and Technology**. Bethlehem, PA: Lehigh University Press, 1992. pp.13-24.
___ Greenberg, Mark L. "Selected Bibliography of Works Devoted to Literature and Technology," by Mark L. Greenberg and Lance Schachterle. in: Greenberg, Mark L. and Schachterle, Lance, eds. **Literature and Technology**. Bethlehem, PA: Lehigh University Press, 1992. pp.310-317.
___ Knoespel, Kenneth J. "Gazing on Technology: *Theatrum Mechanorum* and the Assimilation of Renaissance Machinery," in: Greenberg, Mark L. and Schachterle, Lance, eds. **Literature and Technology**. Bethlehem, PA: Lehigh University Press, 1992. pp.99-124.
___ Lee, Judith Y. "The Feminization of Technology: Mechanical Characters in Picture Books," in: Greenberg, Mark L. and Schachterle, Lance, eds. **Literature and Technology**. Bethlehem, PA: Lehigh University Press, 1992. pp.206-224.
___ Manlove, C. N. "Charles Kingsley, H. G. Wells, and the Machine in Victorian Fiction," *Nineteenth Century Literature* 48(2): [10pp.] 1995. (Cited from the electronic edition, NCL-E, 48(2), 1995. (http: //sunsite. berkeley. edu:8080/ scan/ncle.482/ articles/ manlove.art482.html)).
___ Markley, Robert. "Robert Boyle, Peter Shaw, and the Reinscription of Technology: Inventing and Reinventing the Air Pump," in: Greenberg, Mark L. and Schachterle, Lance, eds. **Literature and Technology**. Bethlehem, PA: Lehigh University Press, 1992. pp.125-153.
___ Mitcham, Carl. "Selected Basic References in the Philosophy of Technology," by Carl Mitcham and Timothy Casey. in: Greenberg, Mark L. and Schachterle, Lance, eds. **Literature and Technology**. Bethlehem, PA: Lehigh University Press, 1992. pp.307-309.
___ Mitcham, Carl. "Toward an Archeology of the Philosophy of Technology and Relations with Imaginative Literature," by Carl Mitcham and Timothy Casey. in: Greenberg, Mark L. and Schachterle, Lance, eds. **Literature and Technology**. Bethlehem, PA: Lehigh University Press, 1992. pp.31-64.
___ Porush, David. "Literature as Dissipative Structure: Prigogine's Theory and the Postmodern 'Chaos' Machine," in: Greenberg, Mark L. and Schachterle, Lance, eds. **Literature and Technology**. Bethlehem, PA: Lehigh University Press, 1992. pp.275-306.
___ Schachterle, Lance. "Pynchon and the Civil Wars of Technology," in: Greenberg, Mark L. and Schachterle, Lance, eds. **Literature and Technology**. Bethlehem, PA: Lehigh University Press, 1992. pp.253-274.
___ Segal, Howard P. **Future Imperfect: The Mixed Blessings of Technology in America**. Amherst: University of Massachusetts Press, 1994. 245pp.
___ Slade, Joseph W. "Technology and the Spy Novel," in: Greenberg, Mark L. and Schachterle, Lance, eds. **Literature and Technology**. Bethlehem, PA: Lehigh University Press, 1992. pp.225-252.
___ Tomasch, Sylvia. "**Mappae Mundi** and 'The Knight's Tale': The Geography of Power, the Technology of Control," in: Greenberg, Mark L. and Schachterle, Lance, eds. **Literature and Technology**. Bethlehem, PA: Lehigh University Press, 1992. pp.66-98.
___ Wagner, Vivian. "Gender, Technology and Utopia in Faulkner's Airplane Tales," *Arizona Quarterly* 49(4): 79-97. Winter 1993.
___ Williams, Rosalind H. "Jules Romains, **Unanimisme**, and the Poetics of Urban Systems," in: Greenberg, Mark L. and Schachterle, Lance, eds. **Literature and Technology**. Bethlehem, PA: Lehigh University Press, 1992. pp.177-205.

TECHNOLOGY IN SF
___ Antosik, Stanley. "Utopian Machines: Liebniz's 'Computer' and Hesse's **Glass Bead Game**," *Germanic Review* 67(1): 35-45. Spring 1992.
___ Beauchamp, Gorman. "Biotechnics and Utopia," in: Saccaro Del Buffa, Giuseppa and Lewis, Arthur O., eds. **Utopie per gli Anni Ottana**. Rome: Gangemi Editore, 1986. pp.73-88.

TECHNOLOGY IN SF (continued)
___ Bianco, Lucio. "Scienza e tecnologia per lo sviluppo," in: Saccaro Del Buffa, Giuseppa and Lewis, Arthur O., eds. **Utopia e Modernita: Teorie e prassi utopiche nell'eta moderna e postmoderna**. Rome: Gangemi Editore, 1989. pp.187-198.
___ Carter, Steven. "Avatars of the Turtles," *Journal of Popular Film and Television* 18(3): 94-102. 1990.
___ Ceccato, Silvio. "Utopia, futurologia e scienza. L'utopia e l'uomo del futuro," in: Saccaro Del Buffa, Giuseppa and Lewis, Arthur O., eds. **Utopia e Modernita: Teorie e prassi utopiche nell'eta moderna e postmoderna**. Rome: Gangemi Editore, 1989. pp.199-204.
___ Corbett, J. Martin. "Celluloid Projections: Images of Technology and Organizational Futures in Contemporary Science Fiction Film," *Organization* 2(3/4): 467-488. August/November 1995.
___ Delany, Samuel R. "The Future of the Body: And Science Fiction and Technology," *New York Review of Science Fiction* No. 51: 1, 3-5. November 1992.
___ Erlich, Richard D. **Clockworks: A Multimedia Bibliography of Works Useful for the Study of the Human/Machine Interface in SF**. Westport, CT: Greenwood Press, 1993. 344pp.
___ Guillaud, Lauric. "From Bachelor Machines to 'Cybernetic Fiction': 'Eternity Machines' in Science Fiction and Fantasy," *New York Review of Science Fiction* No. 75: 12-17. November 1994.
___ Keller, Chester Z. "Imitations of Utopia: Some Readings From Nature," in: Saccaro Del Buffa, Giuseppa and Lewis, Arthur O., eds. **Utopie per gli Anni Ottana**. Rome: Gangemi Editore, 1986. pp.89-98.
___ Langberg, Mike. "Star Tech," *Austin (TX) American Statesman* Sec. D., p. 1, 3. July 12, 1992.
___ Langsberg, Mike. "Treknology," *Star Trek: The Official Fan Club* No. 94: 32-35. November/December 1993.
___ Lloyd, Donald G. "Renegade Robots and Hard-Wired Heroes: Technology and Morality in Contemporary Science Fiction Films," in: Loukides, Paul and Fuller, Linda K., eds. **Beyond the Stars III: The Material World in American Popular Film**. Bowling Green, OH: Popular Press, 1993. pp.216-228.
___ Matheson, T. J. "Marcuse, Ellul, and the Science-Fiction Film: Negative Responses to Technology," *Science-Fiction Studies* 19(3): 326-339. November 1992.
___ Matteoli, Lorenzo. "Utopia, Technology and the Future," [9 pp.] 1996 (?). (Cited from the Internet. (http://www. geocities.com/ Athens/ 3019/)).
___ Sirianni, Carmen J. "Work and Technology in a Complex Utopia," in: Saccaro Del Buffa, Giuseppa and Lewis, Arthur O., eds. **Utopie per gli Anni Ottana**. Rome: Gangemi Editore, 1986. pp.225-235.
___ Spreen, Dierk. "Technotext und Technokörper: Visionen eines neuen Heils," *Quarber Merkur* 33(2): 3-16. December 1995. (No. 84)
___ Wolfe, Gary K. "The Dawn Patrol: Sex, Technology, and Irony in Farmer and Ballard," in: Ruddick, Nicholas, ed. **State of the Fantastic**. Westport, CT: Greenwood, 1992. pp.159-167.

TEENAGE CATGIRLS IN HEAT (MOTION PICTURE)
___ Harris, Judith P. "**Teenage Catgirls in Heat** (Review)," *Cinefantastique* 25(6)/26(1): 123. December 1994.

TEENAGE MUTANT NINJA TURTLES III (MOTION PICTURE)
___ Kutzera, Dale. "The Mutant Ninja Turtles Movie Mutiny," *Cinefantastique* 23(6): 8-11. April 1993.
___ Kutzera, Dale. "**Teenage Mutant Ninja Turtles III**," *Cinefantastique* 23(5): 6-7. February 1993.
___ Kutzera, Dale. "Turtles III: Fixing the Franchise," *Cinefantastique* 23(6): 10. April 1993.

TEKWAR (MOTION PICTURE)
___ Bloch-Hansen, Peter. "Declaring **TekWar**," *Starlog* No. 199: 46-49, 73. February 1994.
___ Harris, Judith P. "**Tekwar** (Review)," *Cinefantastique* 25(3): 60. June 1994.

TEKWAR (TV)
___ Bloch-Hansen, Peter. "Classic Captain," by Peter Bloch-Hansen and Ian Spelling. *Starlog* No. 212: 36-37, 70. March 1995.
___ Bloch-Hansen, Peter. "Tek Hero," *Starlog* No. 213: 44-47. April 1995.
___ Bloch-Hansen, Peter. "TekNologies," *Starlog* No. 212: 38-39. March 1995.
___ Cohen, Charles E. "The Trek to Tek," *TV Guide* 42(3): 16-17. January 15, 1994.

TEKWAR (TV)

TELEVISION (continued)

___ Jenkins, Henry. "How Many Starfleet Officers Does It Take to Change a Lightbulb?: *Star Trek* at MIT," by Henry Jenkins and Greg Dancer. in: Tulloch, John and Jenkins, Henry, eds. **Science Fiction Audiences: Watching Doctor Who and Star Trek**. New York: Routledge, 1995. pp.213-236.

___ Jenkins, Henry. "Infinite Diversity in Infinite Combinations: Genre and Authorship in *Star Trek*," in: Tulloch, John and Jenkins, Henry, eds. **Science Fiction Audiences: Watching Doctor Who and Star Trek**. New York: Routledge, 1995. pp.175-195.

___ Jenkins, Henry. "Out of the Closet and into the Universe: Queers and *Star Trek*," in: Tulloch, John and Jenkins, Henry, eds. **Science Fiction Audiences: Watching Doctor Who and Star Trek**. New York: Routledge, 1995. pp.237-265.

___ Jensen, Elizabeth. "Sci-Fi Channel Will Debut in the Fall," by Elizabeth Jensen and George Maksian. *Austin (TX) American Statesman* Sec. B, p. 4. April 2, 1992.

___ Joseph, Gary. "Inside the Dahl House of Horror," by Gary Joseph and Martin H. Friedenthal. *Filmfax* No. 41: 65-69. October/November 1993.

___ Joseph, Paul. "Perry Mason in Space: A Call for More Inventive Lawyers in Television Science Fiction Series," by Paul Joseph and Sharon Carton. in: Wolf, Milton T. and Mallett, Daryl F., eds. **Imaginative Futures: Proceedings of the 1993 Science Fiction Research Association Conference**. San Bernardino, CA: Jacob's Ladder Books, 1995. pp.307-318.

___ Kaufman, Dave. "Lucas Producing Two ABC Cartoons on Ewoks and R2D2," *Variety* p. 145. January 16, 1985.

___ Kenny, Glenn. "Double Time on DS9," *TV Guide* 43(11): 36. March 18, 1995.

___ Kenny, Glenn. "MTV's Dead-End Kid," *TV Guide* 42(24): 31. June 11, 1994.

___ Kenny, Glenn. "Phantasia," *TV Guide* 43(11): 36. March 18, 1995.

___ Kenny, Glenn. "Sci-Fi/Fantasy: Earth 2, 3, 4...," *TV Guide* 43(10): 30. March 11, 1995.

___ Kenny, Glenn. "TV's Brave New Worlds," *TV Guide* 42(3): 22-24. January 15, 1994.

___ Kerman, Judith B. "Virtual Space and Its Boundaries in Science Fiction Film and Television: *Tron*, *Max Headroom*, *War Games*," in: Morse, Donald E., ed. **The Celebration of the Fantastic**. Westport, CT: Greenwood, 1992. pp.191-204.

___ Klossner, Michael. "Science Fiction in Film, Television, and Radio," in: Barron, Neil, ed. **Anatomy of Wonder 4**. New York: Bowker, 1995. pp.612-650.

___ Klossner, Michael. "Word and Image: A Survey of Fantastic Film & TV Magazines," *SFRA Newsletter* No. 194: 10-15. January/February 1992.

___ Layton, David A. "Closed Circuits and Monitored Lives: Television as Power in *Doctor Who*," *Extrapolation* 35(3): 241-251. Fall 1994.

___ Lentz, Harris M., III. **Science Fiction, Horror & Fantasy Film and Television Credits Supplement 2: Through 1993**. Jefferson, NC: McFarland, 1994. 854pp.

___ Littleton, Cynthia. "Television of the Weird: First-run Faces Unreality," *Broadcasting and Cable* 125(44): 57-58. October 30, 1995.

___ Lofficier, Jean-Marc. **The Doctor Who Programme Guide**. London: Target, 1989. 177pp.

___ Logan, Michael. "Close Encounters With the Cast of Voyagers," *TV Guide* 43(28): 6-10. July 16, 1995.

___ Logan, Michael. "Deep Dish," *TV Guide* 41(1): 10-15. January 2, 1993. (Issue 2075)

___ Lorando, Mark. "Trekkies Headed for Deep Space," *New Orleans (LA) Times-Picayune* Sec. A, p. 9. January 21, 1992.

___ Madracki, John. "Twilight's Last Gleaming: A Historical Survey of TV SF," *Vector* No. 179: 28-35. June/July 1994.

___ Martin, Kevin H. "Video Beat: Order out of Xaos," *Cinefex* No. 57: 21-22. March 1994.

___ Martin, Rick. "Tripping in the Fantasy Zone," *Newsweek* 125(11): 70. March 13, 1995.

___ Masello, Robert. "The Write Stuff: Sci-Fi Authors on Sci-Fi TV," *TV Guide* 41(30): 16-19. July 24, 1993.

___ Mason, Marilynne S. "Today's Problems Tomorrow: Television's Growing Fleet of Science Fiction Dramas Paint a Brighter--or Darker-- Future," *Christian Science Monitor* p. 12-13. March 2, 1993.

___ McConville, Jim. "Sci-Fi Goes Hi-Tech for Fall," *Broadcasting and Cable* 125(33): 20-21. August 14, 1995.

___ McDonnell, David. **Starlog's Science Fiction Heroes and Heroines**. New York: Crescent Books, 1995. 93pp.

TELEVISION (continued)

___ Menagh, Melanie. "A Channel for Science Fiction," by Melanie Menagh and Stephen Mills. *Omni* 14(9): 76-82, 112. October 1992.

___ Milner, Joseph O. "Captain Kirk and Dr. Who: Meliorist and Spenglerian World Views in Science Fiction for Young Adults," in: Sullivan, C. W., III. **Science Fiction for Young Readers**. Westport, CT: Greenwood, 1993. pp.187-196.

___ O'Brien, Dennis. "Shoring Fragments: How CBS's *Beauty and the Beast* Adapts Consensus Reality to Shape Its Magical World," in: Sanders, Joe, ed. **Functions of the Fantastic**. Westport, CT: Greenwood, 1995. pp.37-46.

___ Okuda, Michael. **Star Trek Chronology: The History of the Future**, by Michael Okuda and Denise Okuda. New York: Pocket Books, 1993. 184pp.

___ Perez, Dan. "Spielberg, Ellison, and a New Trek Series Will Bring More SF to TV Viewers," *Science Fiction Age* 1(6): 18-21, 36. September 1993.

___ Perry, Joseph W. "Astro Boy: Happy 30th to That Mighty Mechanical Mite," *Filmfax* No. 42: 50-53. December 1993/January 1994.

___ Point, Michael. "The Incredible Shrinking Expectations: The Sci-Fi Channel," *Austin (TX) American Statesman*. October 23, 1995. in: *NewsBank. Film and Television*. 98:E10-E11. 1995.

___ Reeves-Stevens, Judith. **The Making of Star Trek: Deep Space Nine**, by Judith Reeves-Stevens and Garfield Reeves-Stevens. New York: Pocket Books, 1994. 319pp.

___ Robins, J. Max. "Gen X Marks the Spot," by J. Max Robins and Brian Lowry. *Variety* 358(7): 1, 63. March 20, 1995.

___ Rubenstein, Steve. "Scotty, Beam Up Some New Aliens," *San Francisco (CA) Chronicle* Sec. C, p. 20. September 12, 1992.

___ Rule, Patty. "Monsters Take over TNT Saturdays," *USA Today* Sec. D, p. 3. June 4, 1993.

___ Sander, Gordon. **Serling: The Rise and Twilight of Television's Last Angry Man**. New York: Penguin/Dutton, 1992. 284pp.

___ Sanders, Joe L. "*Edge of Darkness* as Transhuman Thriller," *Journal of the Fantastic in the Arts* 5(4): 83-91. 1993. (No. 20)

___ Sansweet, Stephen J. **The World of Star Wars: The Creation of a Phenomenon**. San Francisco, CA: Chronicle Books, 1992. [Not seen.]

___ Schwed, Mark. "On the Horizon: Whole New Worlds," *TV Guide* 41(30): 29-31. July 24, 1993.

___ Skal, David J. "The Graveyard Bash: Horror in the Sixties," *New York Review of Science Fiction* No. 56: 1, 8-13. April 1993. (From: **The Monster Show: A Cultural History of Horror**. New York: Norton, 1993.)

___ Spelling, Ian. "'DS9' Pals Live out a Tom Sawyer Fantasy," *Houston (TX) Chronicle* Sec. C, p. 2. June 4, 1994.

___ Sullivan, C. W., III. "Fantasy According to *Mister Roger's Neighborhood* and *In the Night Kitchen*," in: Morse, Donald E., ed. **The Celebration of the Fantastic**. Westport, CT: Greenwood, 1992. pp.183-190.

___ Sulski, Jim. "Japanimation, Kitsch Classics No Kids' Stuff," *Chicago Tribune* Sec. 7, p. 61. November 6, 1992.

___ Tulloch, John. "But He's a Time Lord! He's a Time Lord!: Reading Formations, Followers, and Fans," in: Tulloch, John and Jenkins, Henry, eds. **Science Fiction Audiences: Watching Doctor Who and Star Trek**. New York: Routledge, 1995. pp.125-143.

___ Tulloch, John. "But Why Is *Doctor Who* So Attractive?: Negotiating Ideology and Pleasure," in: Tulloch, John and Jenkins, Henry, eds. **Science Fiction Audiences: Watching Doctor Who and Star Trek**. New York: Routledge, 1995. pp.108-124.

___ Tulloch, John. "The Changing Audiences of Science Fiction," in: Tulloch, John and Jenkins, Henry, eds. **Science Fiction Audiences: Watching Doctor Who and Star Trek**. New York: Routledge, 1995. pp.50-63.

___ Tulloch, John. "It's Meant to Be Fantasy: Teenage Audiences and Genre," by John Tulloch and Marian Tulloch. in: Tulloch, John and Jenkins, Henry, eds. **Science Fiction Audiences: Watching Doctor Who and Star Trek**. New York: Routledge, 1995. pp.86-107.

___ Tulloch, John. "Positioning the SF Audience: *Star Trek*, *Doctor Who* and the Texts of Science Fiction," in: Tulloch, John and Jenkins, Henry, eds. **Science Fiction Audiences: Watching Doctor Who and Star Trek**. New York: Routledge, 1995. pp.25-49.

___ Tulloch, John. "Throwing a Little Bit of Poison into Future Generations: *Doctor Who* Audiences and Ideology," in: Tulloch, John and Jenkins, Henry, eds. **Science Fiction Audiences: Watching Doctor Who and Star Trek**. New York: Routledge, 1995. pp.67-85.

TELEVISION

TELEVISION (continued)

___ Tulloch, John. "We're Only a Speck in the Ocean: The Fans as Powerless Elite," in: Tulloch, John and Jenkins, Henry, eds. **Science Fiction Audiences: Watching Doctor Who and Star Trek**. New York: Routledge, 1995. pp.144-172.

___ Valada, M. C. "Step Through George R. R. Martin's **Doorways** into Alternate Worlds," *Science Fiction Age* 1(4): 18-21, 72. May 1993.

___ Van Hise, James. **The Man Who Created Star Trek: Gene Roddenberry**. Las Vegas, NV: Pioneer Books, 1992. 156pp.

___ Van Hise, James. **The New Sci Fi TV**. Las Vegas, NV: Pioneer, 1994. 182pp.

___ Van Hise, James. **Sci Fi TV: From Twilight Zone to Deep Space Nine**. Las Vegas, NV: Pioneer Books, 1993. 160pp. (Reprinted, HarperPrism, 1995. 258pp.)

___ Warren, Bill. "Back in Time," *Starlog* No. 198: 56-59. January 1994.

___ Warren, Bill. "Time Killer," *Starlog* No. 190: 46-48, 69. May 1993.

___ Westbrook, Bruce. "Bold Journeys: **Wagon Train** Provided a Guide for **Star Trek**," *Houston (TX) Chronicle TV Chronilog* p. 7. January 15-21, 1995.

___ Westbrook, Bruce. "Star Wars," *Houston (TX) Chronicle* Sec. D, p. 1, 6. January 6, 1993.

___ Westbrook, Bruce. "Third Time's the Charm: Newest **Star Trek** Offers TV Universe a 'Real' Good Time," *Houston (TX) Chronicle. TV Chronilog* pp.3-4. January 3, 1993.

___ Wilcox, Clyde. "To Boldly Return Where Others Have Gone Before: Cultural Change and the Old and New **Star Trek**s'," *Extrapolation* 33(1): 88-100. Spring 1992.

___ Williams, Scott. "Science Fiction Hottest TV Trend," *Bryan College Station Eagle* p. A12. January 22, 1993.

___ Wilson, Bill. "I Want My SF-TV," *Starlog* No. 176: 17-21, 71. March 1992.

___ Winfrey, Lee. "Going Where No Network Has Gone Before: Sci-Fi Channel Debuting Today," *Bryan-College Station Eagle* p. B4. September 24, 1992.

TEM, MELANIE

___ "1992 Bram Stoker Awards Winners," *Locus* 28(2): 6, 68. August 1992.

___ "Bram Stoker Awards," *Science Fiction Chronicle* 13(10): 4. July/August 1992.

TEM, STEVE RASNIC

___ Proulx, Kevin. **Fear to the World: Eleven Voices in a Chorus of Horror**. Mercer Island, WA: Starmont, 1992. 243pp.

TEMPLE, WILLIAM F.

___ "Temple, William F.: Crystal Ball Gazing Through Science Fiction (Obituary)," *Times* (London) p. 16. July 18, 1989.

___ "Temple, William F. (Obituary)," *Manchester Guardian* p. 47. July 19, 1989.

___ Ashley, Mike. "Tell Them I Meant Well: A Tribute to William F. Temple," *Foundation* No. 55: 5-24. Summer 1992.

___ Ashley, Mike. **The Work of William F. Temple: An Annotated Bibliography and Guide**. San Bernardino, CA: Borgo Press, 1994. 112pp.

___ Warren, Alan. **Roald Dahl: From the Gremlins to the Chocolate Factory**. 2nd ed., revised and expanded. San Bernardino, CA: Borgo Press, 1994. 128pp.

TENN, WILLIAM

___ Stephensen-Payne, Phil. **William Tenn: High Klass Talent, a Working Bibliography**, by Phil Stephensen-Payne and Gordon Benson, Jr. Albuquerque, NM: Galactic Central, 1993. 31pp.

___ Zebrowski, George. "Never Forget the Writers Who Helped Build Yesterday's Tomorrows," *Science Fiction Age* 3(6): 30-36, 100. 1995.

TENNYSON, ALFRED LORD

___ Goslee, David F. "Lost in the Siege Perilous: The Merlin of Tennyson's Idylls," in: Watson, Jeanie and Fries, Maureen, eds. **The Figure of Merlin in the Nineteenth and Twentieth Centuries**. Lewiston, NY: Mellen, 1989. pp.35-50.

___ Hughes, Linda K. "Illusion and Relation: Merlin as Image of the Artist in Tennyson, Doré, Burene-Jones, and Beardsley," in: Watson, Jeanie and Fries, Marueen, eds. **The Figure of Merlin in the Nineteenth and Twentieth Centuries**. Lewiston, NY: Mellen, 1989. pp.1-33.

TENNYSON, ALFRED LORD (continued)

___ Hughes, Linda K. "Teaching Tennyson: **Idylls of the King** as a Serial Poem," in: Fries, Maureen and Watson, Jeanie, eds. **Approaches to the Teaching of the Arthurian Tradition**. New York: Modern Language Association, 1992. pp.106-112.

___ Stephenson, Will. "Proto-Modernism in Tennyson's 'The Holy Grail'," by Will Stephenson and Stephenson Mimosa. *Quondam et Futurus* 2(4): 49-55. Winter 1992.

TEPPER, SHERI S.

___ "1992 *Locus* Awards," *Locus* 28(2): 1, 42-45. August 1992.

___ "Sheri S. Tepper: Fiction, Farming and Other Rare Breeds," *Locus* 33(1): 4, 80-81. July 1994.

___ Attebery, Brian. "Gender, Fantasy, and the Authority of Tradition," *Journal of the Fantastic in the Arts* 7(1): 51-60. 1996.

___ Bogstad, Janice M. **Gender, Power and Reversal in Contemporary Anglo-American and French Feminist Science Fiction**. Ph.D. Dissertation, University of Wisconsin, Madison, 1992. 229pp. (DAI-A 54/02, p. 509. August 1993.)

___ Clois, William L. "An Interview with Sheri S. Tepper," by William L. Clois and Catherine Mintz. *Quantum* No. 43/44: 35-38. Spring/Summer 1993.

___ Fitting, Peter. "Reconsiderations of the Separatist Paradigm in Recent Feminist Science Fiction," *Science Fiction Studies* 19(1): 32-48. March 1992.

___ Price, Beverly. "Sheri S. Tepper and Feminism's Future," *Mythlore* 18(2): 41-44. Spring 1992. (No. 68)

___ Wolmark, Jenny. **Aliens and Others: Science Fiction, Feminism, and Postmodernism**. London: Harester Wheatsheaf, 1993. 167pp.; Iowa City: University of Iowa Press, 1994. 167pp.

TERABYSS (MOTION PICTURE)

___ Turner, George. "**Terabyss** Takes Audience on Suboceanic Thrill Mission," by George Turner and Nora Lee. *American Cinematographer* 74(8): 59-65. August 1993.

TERMINATOR II: JUDGEMENT DAY (MOTION PICTURE)

___ "1992 Saturn Awards," *Locus* 28(6): 7. June 1992.

___ "Saturn Awards, 1992," *Science Fiction Chronicle* 13(9): 10. June 1992.

___ "**Terminator II** Wins SFWA's First Bradbury Script Award," *Science Fiction Chronicle* 13(9): 4. June 1992.

___ Mooney, Josh. "Arnold's T2 Due on Video," *Boston (MA) Herald*. November 28, 1991. in: *NewsBank. Film and Television*. 8:B7. 1992.

___ Sey, James A. "The **Terminator** Syndrome: Science Fiction, Cinema, and Contemporary Culture," *Liberator: Tydskrif vir Besondere en Vergelykende Taal- en Literatuurstudie* (South Africa) 13(3): 13-19. November 1992.

___ Telotte, J. P. "**The Terminator**, **Terminator 2**, and the Expanded Body," *Journal of Popular Film and Television* 20(2): 26-34. Summer 1992.

TERMINATOR (MOTION PICTURE)

___ "Corman Alumni Cameron, Hurd Joined Forces for **Terminator**," *Variety* p. 6. October 31, 1984.

___ "**Gremlins** Sweeps Saturn Ceremony," *Variety* p.6. June 19, 1985.

___ Abbott, Joe. "They Came From Beyond the Center: Ideology and Political Textuality in the Radical Science Fiction Films of James Cameron," *Literature/Film Quarterly* 22(1): 21-27. 1994.

___ Goldberg, Jonathan. "Recalling Totalities: The Mirrored Stages of Arnold Schwarzenegger," in: Gray, Chris H., ed. **The Cyborg Handbook**. New York: Routledge, 1995. pp.233-254.

___ Jancovich, Mark. "Modernity and Subjectivity in **The Terminator**," *Velvet Light Trap* 30: 3-17. 1992. [Not seen.]

___ Sey, James A. "The **Terminator** Syndrome: Science Fiction, Cinema, and Contemporary Culture," *Liberator: Tydskrif vir Besondere en Vergelykende Taal- en Literatuurstudie* (South Africa) 13(3): 13-19. November 1992.

___ Telotte, J. P. "**The Terminator**, **Terminator 2**, and the Expanded Body," *Journal of Popular Film and Television* 20(2): 26-34. Summer 1992.

TERRELL, CARROLL

___ Davis, Jonathan. **Stephen King's America**. Mercer Island, WA: Starmont House, 1992.

TERROR FROM THE YEAR 5000 (MOTION PICTURE)
___ Henenlotter, Frank. "Films From Under the Floorboards," *Sci-Fi Entertainment* 1(6): 52-57. April 1995.

TERTZ, ABRAM
___ Airaudi, Jesse T. "Fantasia for Sewercovers and Drainpipes: T. S. Eliot, Abram Tertz, and the Surreal Quest for Pravda," in: Latham, Robert A. and Collins, Robert A., eds. **Modes of the Fantastic**. Westport, CT: Greenwood, 1995. pp.21-27.

TETSUO: THE IRON MAN (MOTION PICTURE)
___ Persons, Dan. "Cheap Genius," *Cinefantastique* 23(5): 53. February 1993.
___ Persons, Dan. "***Tetsuo: The Iron Man***," *Cinefantastique* 23(5): 50-52. February 1993.

TEXAS
___ Riecher, Anton. "AggieCon XXII Blasting Off," *Bryan-College Station Eagle* p. C1. March 19, 1992.

THAILAND
___ Olsa, Jaroslav, Jr. "SF in Southeast Asia," *Locus* 34(1) 70. January 1995.

THEATER
___ Gordon, Mel. "A History of the Theater of the Future (to 1984)," *Theater* 26(1/2): 12-32. 1995.

THELMA AND LOUISE (MOTION PICTURE)
___ Barr, Marleen S. **Lost in Space: Probing Feminist Science Fiction and Beyond**. Chapel Hill, NC: University of North Carolina Press, 1993. 231pp.
___ Metzer, David. "Rhetoric and Death in **Thelma and Louise**: Notes Toward a Logic of the Fantastic," *Journal of the Fantastic in the Arts* 4(4): 9-18. 1991. (No. 16)
___ Rose, Rita. "Controversial **Thelma** Is Sexist? Nah. (Review)," *Indianapolis (IN) Star*. January 10, 1992. in: *NewsBank. Film and Television*. 15:F6-F7. 1992.

THEM (MOTION PICTURE)
___ Murphy, Brian. "Monster Movies: They Came From Beneath the Fifties," *Journal of Popular Film and Television* 1(1): 31-44. 1972.

THEODORE STURGEON MEMORIAL AWARD
___ "Sturgeon Award Revamped," *Locus* 34(3): 8, 77. March 1995.

THEODORE STURGEON MEMORIAL AWARD, 1992
___ "Denton, Kessel Win Campbell, Sturgeon Awards," *Locus* 29(3): 6. September 1992.
___ "Denton, Kessel Win Campbell, Sturgeon Awards," *Science Fiction Chronicle* 14(1): 5. October 1992.

THEODORE STURGEON MEMORIAL AWARD, 1993
___ "Kij Johnson Wins Sturgeon Award," *Locus* 33(3): 7. September 1994.
___ "Kij Johnson Wins Sturgeon Award; 'No Award' First for Campbell Award," *Science Fiction Chronicle* 15(9): 4. August 1994.
___ "Sheffield, Simmons Win Campbell, Sturgeon Awards," *Locus* 31(3): 6, 83. September 1993.
___ "Sheffield, Simmons, Win Campbell, Sturgeon Awards," *Science Fiction Chronicle* 14(11): 4. August 1993.

THEODORE STURGEON MEMORIAL AWARD, 1994
___ "No Campbell Winner; Johnson Wins Sturgeon Award," *Locus* 33(2): 8. August 1994.

THEODORE STURGEON MEMORIAL AWARD, 1995
___ "Campbell and Sturgeon Award Winners," *Locus* 35(2): 8. August 1995.
___ "Greg Egan Wins Campbell Memorial Award; Sturgeon Award to Ursula K. Le Guin," *Science Fiction Chronicle* 16(9): 5. August/September 1995.
___ "Sturgeon Award Nominees," *Science Fiction Chronicle* 16(7): 5-6. June/July 1995.

THEOLOGY
___ SEE: RELIGION.

THING (1951) (MOTION PICTURE)
___ Katovich, Michael A. "The Stories Told in Science Fiction and Social Science: Reading **The Thing** and Other Remakes From Two Eras," by Michael A. Katovich and Patrick T. Kinkade. *Sociological Quarterly* 34(4): 619-651. 1993.
___ Weaver, Tom. "Friend of **The Thing**," *Starlog* 178: 61-69. May 1992.
___ Weaver, Tom. "Robert Cornthwaite," in: Weaver, Tom. **They Fought the Creature Features: Interviews with 23 Classic Horror, Science Fiction and Serial Stars**. Jefferson, NC: McFarland, 1995. pp.111-130.
___ White, Eric. "The Erotics of Becoming: **Xenogenesis** and **The Thing**," *Science Fiction Studies* 20(3): 394-408. November 1993.

THING (1982) (MOTION PICTURE)
___ "Track New Interest in Foster's **Thing**," *Variety* p. 8, 28. March 10, 1982.
___ Katovich, Michael A. "The Stories Told in Science Fiction and Social Science: Reading **The Thing** and Other Remakes From Two Eras," by Michael A. Katovich and Patrick T. Kinkade. *Sociological Quarterly* 34(4): 619-651. 1993.

THING (COMIC)
___ Weaver, Tom. "Things Change," *Starlog* No. 174: 35-37, 72. January 1992.

THIS ISLAND EARTH (MOTION PICTURE)
___ Skotak, Robert. "Creating the Metaluna Mutant," *Filmfax* No. 33: 56-59. June/July 1992.
___ Skotak, Robert. "Creating the Special FX for **This Island Earth**," *Filmfax* No. 33: 78-82, 94-97. June/July 1992.
___ Skotak, Robert. "**This Island Earth**," *Filmfax* No. 33: 50-61. June/July 1992.
___ Weaver, Tom. "Jeff Morrow," in: Weaver, Tom. **They Fought the Creature Features: Interviews with 23 Classic Horror, Science Fiction and Serial Stars**. Jefferson, NC: McFarland, 1995. pp.211-219.
___ Weaver, Tom. "Lori Nelson," in: Weaver, Tom. **They Fought the Creature Features: Interviews with 23 Classic Horror, Science Fiction and Serial Stars**. Jefferson, NC: McFarland, 1995. pp.221-232.
___ Weaver, Tom. "Rex Reason," in: Weaver, Tom. **They Fought the Creature Features: Interviews with 23 Classic Horror, Science Fiction and Serial Stars**. Jefferson, NC: McFarland, 1995. pp.233-243.

THOMAS, D. M.
___ Vieira, Gregory C. "No Place for Utopia: Postmodern Theory and **The White Hotel**," *Utopian Studies* 4(2): 117-127. 1993.

THOMAS, SUE
___ Harper, Mary C. "Incurably Alien Other: A Case for Feminist Cyborg Writers," *Science Fiction Studies* 22(3): 399-420. November 1995
___ Sawyer, Andy. "Correspondence Course: Sue Thomas Interviewed," *Vector* No. 167: 10-11. June/July 1992

THOMERSON, TIM
___ Shapiro, Marc. "SF's Video Hero," *Starlog* 179: 66-69, 84. June 1992.

THOMPSON, ANDREA
___ Chrissinger, Craig W. "Mind Reader," *Starlog* No. 209: 55-58, 66. December 1994.

THOMPSON, DON
___ "Thompson, Don (Obituary)," *Locus* 33(1): 74. July 1994.
___ "Thompson, Don (Obituary)," *Science Fiction Chronicle* 15(8): 20. June 1994.

THOMSEN, BRIAN
___ "Brian Thomsen Leaves Questar for TSR," *Science Fiction Chronicle* 13(11/12): 4-5. August 1992.

THOMSON, AMY
___ "1994 Hugo Award," *Science Fiction Chronicle* 15(10): 5. September 1994.
___ "1994 Hugo Awards Winners," *Locus* 33(4): 7, 38-41. October 1994.

THREADS (MOTION PICTURE)

THREADS (MOTION PICTURE)
___ "BBC Readies Nuke War Pic for '84 Airing," *Variety* p. 43, 80. December 14, 1983.
___ "*Threads* Sales Record for World Vid Pictures," *Variety* p. 39. August 20, 1986.
___ "*Threads* SRO in D. C.," *Variety* p.48. June 26, 1985.
___ Gunter, Barrie. "The Impact of Nuclear Fiction in Britain: *The Day After* and *Threads*," by Barrie Gunter and M. Svennevig. in: Wober, J. Mallory, ed. **Television and Nuclear Power: Making the Public Mind.** Norwood, NJ: Ablex, 1992. pp.55-66.

THREE WISHES (MOTION PICTURE)
___ Shay, Estelle. "*Three Wishes*: Making Wishes Come True," *Cinefex* No. 64: 43-44, 127. December 1995.

THRILLER (TV)
___ Sanford, Jay A. "Boris Korloff's Classic TV Series *Thriller*, Part Two," *Filmfax* No. 30: 79-85. 1992.

THRONE, MALACHI
___ Eisner, Joel. "Throne of Villainy," *Starlog* No. 190: 52-55, 72. May 1993.

THRUST (MAGAZINE)
___ Fratz, Doug. "Index: *Thrust/Quantum*, No. 1, February 1973-No. 43/44, May 1993," *Quantum* No. 43/44: 67-69. Spring/Summer 1993.
___ Fratz, Doug. "The Twenty-Year Spree: A Personal History of *Thrust/Quantum*," *Quantum* No. 43/44: 51-66. Spring/Summer 1993.

THUCYDIDES
___ Smith, Nicholas D. "Political Activity and Ideal Economics: Two Related Utopian Themes in Aristophanic Comedy," *Utopian Studies* 3(1): 84-94. 1992.

THUNDERBIRDS (TV)
___ Nicholls, Stan. "Dance of the Supermarionettes," *Starlog* 184: 52-55, 70. November 1992.
___ Nicholls, Stan. "*Thunderbirds*: The Next Generation," *Starlog* 182: 64-65, 71. September 1992.

TICKS (MOTION PICTURE)
___ Wilt, David. "*Ticks* (Review)," *Cinefantastique* 26(5): 60. August 1995.

TIME
___ Ellis, Mark. **Philosophical Romance: Theories of Time and Their Relationship to Genre in the Fiction of John Crowley.** Master's Thesis, University of Manitoba (Canada), 1990. 101pp. (Master's Abstracts 31/02, p. 566. Summer 1993.)
___ Russell, W. M. S. "Time Before and After **The Time Machine**," *Foundation* No. 65: 24-40. Autumn 1995.

TIME AFTER TIME (1979) (MOTION PICTURE)
___ Renzi, Thomas C. **H. G. Wells: Six Scientific Romances Adapted for Film.** Metuchen, NJ: Scarecrow, 1992. 249pp.

TIME MACHINE (MOTION PICTURE)
___ Swires, Steve. "Master of the *Time Machine*," in: McDonnell, David, ed. **Starlog's Science Fiction Heroes and Heroines.** New York: Crescent Books, 1995. pp.80-83.

TIME MACHINE (1960) (MOTION PICTURE)
___ Palumbo, Donald E. "The Politics of Entropy: Revolution vs. Evolution in George Pal's 1960 Film Version of H. G. Wells's **The Time Machine**," in: Latham, Robert A. and Collins, Robert A., eds. **Modes of the Fantastic.** Westport, CT: Greenwood, 1995. pp.204-211.
___ Renzi, Thomas C. **H. G. Wells: Six Scientific Romances Adapted for Film.** Metuchen, NJ: Scarecrow, 1992. 249pp.

TIME MACHINE (1978) (MOTION PICTURE)
___ Renzi, Thomas C. **H. G. Wells: Six Scientific Romances Adapted for Film.** Metuchen, NJ: Scarecrow, 1992. 249pp.

TIME MACHINE: THE WAY BACK (TV DOCUMENTARY)
___ Warren, Bill. "Back in Time," *Starlog* No. 198: 56-59. January 1994.

TIME MAGAZINE
___ Guy, Pat. "*Time* Special Issue Includes Fiction," *USA Today* Sec. B, p. 4. September 28, 1992.

TIME RUNNER (MOTION PICTURE)
___ Harris, Judith P. "*Time Runner* (Review)," *Cinefantastique* 24(6)/25(1): 124. February 1994.

TIME TRAVEL
___ Benford, Gregory. "Time and **Timescape**," *Science Fiction Studies* 20(2): 184-190. July 1993.
___ Imdieke, Sandra A. **Characters in Time Travel as Historical Guides,** by Sandra A. Imdieke and Lynn Madaus. ERIC ED 305601. 9pp. 1992.
___ Nahin, Paul J. **Time Machines: Time Travel in Physics, Metaphysics, and Science Fiction.** New York: American Institute of Physics, 1993. 408pp.
___ Palumbo, Donald E. "The Monomyth in Time Travel Films," in: Morse, Donald E., ed. **The Celebration of the Fantastic.** Westport, CT: Greenwood, 1992. pp.211-218.
___ Slusser, George E. "Spacetime Geometries: Time Travel and the Modern Geometrical Narrative," by George E. Slusser and Daniele Chatelain. *Science Fiction Studies* 22(2): 161-186. July 1995.
___ Wiggins, Kayla M. "Epic Heroes, Ethical Issues, and Time Paradoxes in **Quantum Leap**," *Journal of Popular Film and Television* 21(3): 111-120. Fall 1993.
___ Wolff, Michael J. "Time Without Fools," *Starlog* No. 207: 27-30, 69. October 1994.

TIME TRAX (TV)
___ Altman, Mark A. "*Time Trax*," *Cinefantastique* 23(5): 44-45. February 1993.
___ Carlson, Timothy. "The Universe Is Expanding All over the Dial," by Timothy Carlson and Mark Schwed. *TV Guide* 41(1): 16-19. January 2, 1993. (Issue 2075)
___ Chrissinger, Craig W. "Man of Time," *Starlog* No. 189: 34-37. April 1993.
___ Chrissinger, Craig W. "Time Piece," *Starlog* No. 191: 32-34. June 1993.
___ Chrissinger, Craig W. "Time Police," *Starlog* No. 187: 32-35, 72. February 1993.
___ Donlon, Brian. "Harve Bennett Makes 'Trax' With Sci-Fi Trek to the Past," *USA Today* Sec. D, p. 3. March 30, 1993.
___ Kenny, Glenn. "Time and Again," *TV Guide* 42(19): 33. May 7, 1994.
___ Shapiro, Marc. "Time Keeper," *Starlog* No. 188: 27-31. March 1993.
___ Warren, Bill. "Time Killer," *Starlog* No. 190: 46-48, 69. May 1993.

TIME TUNNEL (TV)
___ Counts, Kyle. "A Time to Remember," *Starlog* 180: 32-35, 66. July 1992.
___ Counts, Kyle. "Time Traveler," *Starlog* 179: 38-41, 84. June 1992.

TIMEBINDERS
___ "Timebinders Preserving Fan History," *Science Fiction Chronicle* 17(2): 8. December 1995/January 1996.

TIMECOP (MOTION PICTURE)
___ Arar, Yardena. "*Timecop* Takes a Creative Sci-Fi Cue," *Los Angeles (CA) Daily News*. September 16, 1994. in: *NewsBank. Film and Television.* 105:C6. 1994.
___ Baron, David. "*Timecop* Stands Still as Van Damme Star Vehicle," *New Orleans (LA) Times-Picayune.* September 16, 1994. in: *NewsBank. Film and Television.* 105:D2. 1994.
___ Bowman, Jon. "Van Damme Gets His Kicks in *Timecop*," *(Santa Fe, NM) New Mexican.* September 23, 1994. in: *NewsBank. Film and Television.* 105:D7. 1994.
___ Britton, Bonnie. "Van Damme Lives in Past as *Timecop*," *Indianapolis (IN) Star.* September 16, 1994. in: *NewsBank. Film and Television.* 105:D1. 1994.
___ Brunet, Robin. "*Timecop*," *Cinefantastique* 25(4): 14-15, 61. August 1994.
___ Brunet, Robin. "*Timecop*," *Cinefantastique* 25(5): 6-7. October 1994.

TOLKIEN, J. R. R. (continued)

___ Basney, Lionel. "Tolkien and the Ethical Function of 'Escape' Literature," *Mosaic* 13(2): 24-35. 1980.

___ Bastien, Louis A. **Green Fire and the Legacy of the Dragon: Science Fiction, Fantasy and Cultural Ideology.** Ph.D. Dissertation, University of Connecticut, 1992. 238pp. (DAI-A 54/04. p. 1359. October 1993.)

___ Bauer, Hannspeter. "Anmerkungen zu Tolkiens Wortschatz," in: Kranz, Gisbert, ed. **Jahrbuch für Literatur und Ästhetik.** Lüdenscheid, Germany: Stier, 1992. Band 10, pp.103-109.

___ Bloom, Harold. "J. R. R. Tolkien," in: Bloom, Harold, ed. **Modern Fantasy Writers.** New York: Chelsea House, 1995. pp.165-179.

___ Bosse, Jan. "Unquendor, Its Sense and Nonsense," *Lembas Extra.* [Leiden]: Tolkien Genootschap Unquendor, 1991. [Not seen, cf. *Mythlore*.]

___ Bratman, David. "A Corrigenda to the **Lord of the Rings**," *The Tolkien Collector* 6: 17-25. 1994.

___ Burns, Marjorie J. "Eating, Devouring, Sacrifice and Ultimate Just Desserts," in: Reynolds, Patricia and GoodKnight, Glen H., eds. **Proceedings of the J. R. R. Tolkien Centenary Conference, Keble College, Oxford, 1992.** Altadena, CA: Mythopoeic Press, 1995. pp.108-114. (*Mythlore* Vol. 21, No. 2, Winter 1996, Whole No. 80)

___ Burns, Marjorie J. "Echoes of William Morris's **Icelandic Journals** in J. R. R. Tolkien," *Studies in Medievalism* 3(3): 367-373. Winter 1991.

___ Cantor, Norman F. **Inventing the Middle Ages: The Lives, Works and Ideas of the Great Medievalists of the Twentieth Century.** New York: Morrow, 1991. 477pp.

___ Chance, Jane. **The Lord of the Rings: The Mythology of Power.** New York: Twayne, 1992. 130pp.

___ Chance, Jane. "Power and Knowledge in Tolkien: The Problem of Difference in 'The Birthday Party'," in: Reynolds, Patricia and GoodKnight, Glen H., eds. **Proceedings of the J. R. R. Tolkien Centenary Conference, Keble College, Oxford, 1992.** Altadena, CA: Mythopoeic Press, 1995. pp.115-120. (*Mythlore* Vol. 21, No. 2, Winter 1996, Whole No. 80)

___ Chapman, Vera. "Reminiscences: Oxford in 1920, Meeting Tolkien and Becoming an Author at 77," in: Reynolds, Patricia and GoodKnight, Glen H., eds. **Proceedings of the J. R. R. Tolkien Centenary Conference, Keble College, Oxford, 1992.** Altadena, CA: Mythopoeic Press, 1995. pp.12-14. (*Mythlore* Vol. 21, No. 2, Winter 1996, Whole No. 80)

___ Christopher, Joe R. "An Inklings Bibliography (45)," by Joe R. Christopher and Wayne G. Hammond. *Mythlore* 18(2): 28-33, 39-40. Spring 1992. (No. 68)

___ Christopher, Joe R. "An Inklings Bibliography (46)," by Joe R. Christopher and Wayne G. Hammond. *Mythlore* 18(3): 49-53. Summer 1992. (No. 69)

___ Christopher, Joe R. "An Inklings Bibliography (47)," by Joe R. Christopher and Wayne G. Hammond. *Mythlore* 18(4): 49-52. Autumn 1992. (No. 70)

___ Christopher, Joe R. "An Inklings Bibliography (48)," by Joe R. Christopher and Wayne G. Hammond. *Mythlore* 19(1): 56-64. Winter 1993. (No. 71)

___ Christopher, Joe R. "An Inklings Bibliography (49)," by Joe R. Christopher and Wayne G. Hammond. *Mythlore* 19(2): 61-65. Spring 1993. (No. 72)

___ Christopher, Joe R. "An Inklings Bibliography (50) (e.g. 51)," by Joe R. Christopher and Wayne G. Hammond. *Mythlore* 19(4): 60-65. Autumn 1993. (No. 74)

___ Christopher, Joe R. "An Inklings Bibliography (50)," by Joe R. Christopher and Wayne G. Hammond. *Mythlore* 19(3): 59-65. Summer 1993. (No. 73)

___ Christopher, Joe R. "An Inklings Bibliography (51)," by Joe R. Christopher and Wayne G. Hammond. *Mythlore* 20(1): 59-62. Winter 1994. (Whole No. 75)

___ Christopher, Joe R. "An Inklings Bibliography (52)," by Joe R. Christopher and Wayne G. Hammond. *Mythlore* 20(2): 32-34. Spring 1994. (Whole No. 76)

___ Christopher, Joe R. "An Inklings Bibliography (54)," by Joe R. Christopher and Wayne G. Hammond. *Mythlore* 20(4): 61-65. Winter 1995. (Whole No. 78)

___ Christopher, Joe R. "An Inklings Bibliography (55)," by Joe R. Christopher and Wayne G. Hammond. *Mythlore* 21(1): 61-65. Summer 1995. (No. 79)

TOLKIEN, J. R. R. (continued)

___ Christopher, Joe R. "J. R. R. Tolkien and the Clerihew," in: Reynolds, Patricia and GoodKnight, Glen H., eds. **Proceedings of the J. R. R. Tolkien Centenary Conference, Keble College, Oxford, 1992.** Altadena, CA: Mythopoeic Press, 1995. pp.263-271. (*Mythlore* Vol. 21, No. 2, Winter 1996, Whole No. 80)

___ Christopher, Joe R. "The Moral Epiphanies in **The Lord of the Rings**," in: Reynolds, Patricia and GoodKnight, Glen H., eds. **Proceedings of the J. R. R. Tolkien Centenary Conference, Keble College, Oxford, 1992.** Altadena, CA: Mythopoeic Press, 1995. pp.121-125. (*Mythlore* Vol. 21, No. 2, Winter 1996, Whole No. 80)

___ Colebatch, Hal. "Patterns of Epic: The Re-Affirmation of Western Values in *Star Wars* and **The Lord of the Rings**," *Science Fiction: A Review of Speculative Literature* 11(3): 5-16. 1992. (No. 33)

___ Colebatch, Hal. **Return of the Heroes: The Lord of the Rings, Star Wars, and Contemporary Culture.** Perth, Aust.: Australian Institute for Public Policy, 1990. 104pp.

___ Collins, David. **J. R. R. Tolkien: Master of Fantasy.** Minneapolis, MN: Lerner/First Avenue Editions, 1993. 112pp.

___ Coombs, Jenny. "A Physics of Middle-Earth," by Jenny Coombs and Marc Read. in: Reynolds, Patricia and GoodKnight, Glen H., eds. **Proceedings of the J. R. R. Tolkien Centenary Conference, Keble College, Oxford, 1992.** Altadena, CA: Mythopoeic Press, 1995. pp.323-329. (*Mythlore* Vol. 21, No. 2, Winter 1996, Whole No. 80)

___ Coulombe, Charles A. "Hermetic Imagination: The Effects of the Golden Dawn on Fantasy Literature," in: Reynolds, Patricia and GoodKnight, Glen H., eds. **Proceedings of the J. R. R. Tolkien Centenary Conference, Keble College, Oxford, 1992.** Altadena, CA: Mythopoeic Press, 1995. pp.345-356. (*Mythlore* Vol. 21, No. 2, Winter 1996, Whole No. 80)

___ Crowe, Edith L. "Power in Arda: Sources, Uses and Misuses," in: Reynolds, Patricia and GoodKnight, Glen H., eds. **Proceedings of the J. R. R. Tolkien Centenary Conference, Keble College, Oxford, 1992.** Altadena, CA: Mythopoeic Press, 1995. pp.272-277. (*Mythlore* Vol. 21, No. 2, Winter 1996, Whole No. 80)

___ Curry, Patrick. "'Less Noise and More Green': Tolkien's Ideology for England," in: Reynolds, Patricia and GoodKnight, Glen H., eds. **Proceedings of the J. R. R. Tolkien Centenary Conference, Keble College, Oxford, 1992.** Altadena, CA: Mythopoeic Press, 1995. pp.126-138. (*Mythlore* Vol. 21, No. 2, Winter 1996, Whole No. 80)

___ Daem, Alexandre O. "Gedanken über die stille beim lesen: Die künstlichen Schricten in Tolkiens *Herrn der Ringe*: Versuch einer Beschreibung," in: Kranz, Gisbert, ed. **Jahrbuch für Literatur und Ästhetik.** Lüdenscheid, Germany: Stier, 1992. Band 10, pp.177-189.

___ Davis, William A. "Hobbit Forming," *Boston (MA) Globe.* December 29, 1991. in: *NewsBank. Names in the News.* 18:E7-E10. 1992.

___ de Armas, Frederick A. "Gyges' Ring: Invisibility in Plato, Tolkien, and Lope de Vega," *Journal of the Fantastic in the Arts* 3(4): 120-138. 1994.

___ Dodds, David L. "Magic in the Myths of J. R. R. Tolkien and Charles Williams," in: Kranz, Gisbert, ed. **Jahrbuch für Literatur und Ästhetik.** Lüdenscheid, Germany: Stier, 1992. Band 10, pp.37-60.

___ Doughan, David. "Tolkien, Sayers, Sex and Gender," in: Reynolds, Patricia and GoodKnight, Glen H., eds. **Proceedings of the J. R. R. Tolkien Centenary Conference, Keble College, Oxford, 1992.** Altadena, CA: Mythopoeic Press, 1995. pp.356-359. (*Mythlore* Vol. 21, No. 2, Winter 1996, Whole No. 80)

___ Duriez, Colin. **The J. R. R. Tolkien Handbook.** Grand Rapids, MI: Baker House, 1992. 316pp.

___ Duriez, Colin. **The Tolkien and Middle Earth Handbook.** Tunbridge Wells, U.K.: Monarch, 1992. 316pp.

___ Duriez, Colin. "Tolkien and the Other Inklings," in: Reynolds, Patricia and GoodKnight, Glen H., eds. **Proceedings of the J. R. R. Tolkien Centenary Conference, Keble College, Oxford, 1992.** Altadena, CA: Mythopoeic Press, 1995. pp.360-363. (*Mythlore* Vol. 21, No. 2, Winter 1996, Whole No. 80)

___ Ellison, John. "Baggins Remembered," in: Reynolds, Patricia and GoodKnight, Glen H., eds. **Proceedings of the J. R. R. Tolkien Centenary Conference, Keble College, Oxford, 1992.** Altadena, CA: Mythopoeic Press, 1995. pp.394-395. (*Mythlore* Vol. 21, No. 2, Winter 1996, Whole No. 80)

___ Evans, Gwenth. "Harps and Harpers in Contemporary Fantasy," *Lion and the Unicorn* 16(2): 199-209. December 1992.

___ Filmer, Kath. **Scepticism and Hope in Twentieth Century Fantasy Literature.** Bowling Green, OH: Bowling Green State University Popular Press, 1992. 160pp.

TOLKIEN, J. R. R. (continued)
___ Flieger, Verlyn. "Elves, Eden, and Utopia: Tolkien's Impossible Dream," in: Saccaro Del Buffa, Giuseppa and Lewis, Arthur O., eds. **Utopie per gli Anni Ottana**. Rome: Gangemi Editore, 1986. pp.419-426.
___ Flieger, Verlyn. "Time and Dream in 'The Lost Road' and **The Lord of the Rings**," in: Kranz, Gisbert, ed. **Jahrbuch für Literatur und Ästhetik**. Lüdenscheid, Germany: Stier, 1992. Band 10, pp.111-134.
___ Flieger, Verlyn. "Tolkien's Experiment With Time: The Lost Road, 'The Notion Club Papers' and J. W. Dunne," in: Reynolds, Patricia and GoodKnight, Glen H., eds. **Proceedings of the J. R. R. Tolkien Centenary Conference, Keble College, Oxford, 1992**. Altadena, CA: Mythopoeic Press, 1995. pp.39-44. (*Mythlore* Vol. 21, No. 2, Winter 1996, Whole No. 80)
___ Fonstad, Karen W. **The Atlas of Middle-Earth** Rev. ed. New York: Houghton Mifflin, 1992. 210pp.
___ Funk, David A. "Explorations into the Psyche of Dwarves," in: Reynolds, Patricia and GoodKnight, Glen H., eds. **Proceedings of the J. R. R. Tolkien Centenary Conference, Keble College, Oxford, 1992**. Altadena, CA: Mythopoeic Press, 1995. pp.330-334. (*Mythlore* Vol. 21, No. 2, Winter 1996, Whole No. 80)
___ Gardner, John. "**The Silmarillion**, by J. R. R. Tolkien," in: Gardner, John. **On Writers and Writing**. Reading, MA: Addison-Wesley, 1994. pp.140-144.
___ Gilliver, Peter M. "At the Wordface: J. R. R. Tolkien's Work on the **Oxford English Dictionary**," in: Reynolds, Patricia and GoodKnight, Glen H., eds. **Proceedings of the J. R. R. Tolkien Centenary Conference, Keble College, Oxford, 1992**. Altadena, CA: Mythopoeic Press, 1995. pp.173-186. (*Mythlore* Vol. 21, No. 2, Winter 1996, Whole No. 80)
___ Gilson, Christopher. "The Growth of Grammar in the Elven Tongues," by Christopher Gilson and Patrick Wynne. in: Reynolds, Patricia and GoodKnight, Glen H., eds. **Proceedings of the J. R. R. Tolkien Centenary Conference, Keble College, Oxford, 1992**. Altadena, CA: Mythopoeic Press, 1995. pp.187-194. (*Mythlore* Vol. 21, No. 2, Winter 1996, Whole No. 80)
___ Glennon, Dorinda. **Creative Philology: The Use of Language in J. R. R. Tolkien's The Lord of the Rings**. Master's Thesis, Idaho State University, 1977. 55pp.
___ Goodknight, Glen H. "J. R. R. Tolkien in Translation," *Mythlore* 18(3): 61-69. Summer 1992. (No. 69)
___ Goodknight, Glen H. "Tolkien Centenary Banquet Address," in: Reynolds, Patricia and GoodKnight, Glen H., eds. **Proceedings of the J. R. R. Tolkien Centenary Conference, Keble College, Oxford, 1992**. Altadena, CA: Mythopoeic Press, 1995. pp.15-16. (*Mythlore* Vol. 21, No. 2, Winter 1996, Whole No. 80)
___ Gorman, Anita G. "J. R. R. Tolkien's 'Leaf by Niggle': Word Pairs and Paradoxes," *Mythlore* 20(4): 52-55. Winter 1995. (Whole No. 78)
___ Graff, Eric S. "The Three Faces of Faërie in Tolkien's Shorter Fiction: Niggle, Smith and Giles," *Mythlore* 18(3): 15-18. Summer 1992. (No. 69)
___ Greene, Deidre. "Higher Argument: Tolkien and the Tradition of Vision, Epic and Prophecy," in: Reynolds, Patricia and GoodKnight, Glen H., eds. **Proceedings of the J. R. R. Tolkien Centenary Conference, Keble College, Oxford, 1992**. Altadena, CA: Mythopoeic Press, 1995. pp.45-52. (*Mythlore* Vol. 21, No. 2, Winter 1996, Whole No. 80)
___ Greene, Deidre. "Tolkien's Dictionary Poetics: The Influence of the OED's Defining Style on Tolkien's Fiction," in: Reynolds, Patricia and GoodKnight, Glen H., eds. **Proceedings of the J. R. R. Tolkien Centenary Conference, Keble College, Oxford, 1992**. Altadena, CA: Mythopoeic Press, 1995. pp.195-199. (*Mythlore* Vol. 21, No. 2, Winter 1996, Whole No. 80)
___ Greenman, David. "Aeneidic and Odyssean Pattern of Escape and Return in Tolkien's 'Fall of Gondolin' and **The Return of the King**," *Mythlore* 18(2): 4-9. Spring 1992. (No. 68)
___ Grigorieva, Natalia. "Problems of Translating into Russian," in: Reynolds, Patricia and GoodKnight, Glen H., eds. **Proceedings of the J. R. R. Tolkien Centenary Conference, Keble College, Oxford, 1992**. Altadena, CA: Mythopoeic Press, 1995. pp.200-205. (*Mythlore* Vol. 21, No. 2, Winter 1996, Whole No. 80)
___ Grotta, Daniel. **The Biography of J. R. R. Tolkien: Architect of Middle-Earth**. Philadelphia, PA: Running Press, 1992. 197pp.
___ Grushetskiy, Vladimir. "How Russians See Tolkien," in: Reynolds, Patricia and GoodKnight, Glen H., eds. **Proceedings of the J. R. R. Tolkien Centenary Conference, Keble College, Oxford, 1992**. Altadena, CA: Mythopoeic Press, 1995. pp.221-225. (*Mythlore* Vol. 21, No. 2, Winter 1996, Whole No. 80)

TOLKIEN, J. R. R. (continued)
___ Haefer, Todd. "Happy 100th, J. R. R.," *Oshkosh (WI) Northwestern*. January 30, 1992. in: *NewsBank. Names in the News*. 59:D2-D3. 1992.
___ Hammond, Wayne G. "The Critical Response to Tolkien's Fiction," in: Reynolds, Patricia and GoodKnight, Glen H., eds. **Proceedings of the J. R. R. Tolkien Centenary Conference, Keble College, Oxford, 1992**. Altadena, CA: Mythopoeic Press, 1995. pp.226-232. (*Mythlore* Vol. 21, No. 2, Winter 1996, Whole No. 80)
___ Hammond, Wayne G. **J. R. R. Tolkien: A Descriptive Bibliography**, by Wayne G. Hammond and Douglas A. Anderson. Winchester, UK: St. Paul's Bibliographies, 1992. 434pp.; New Castle, DE: Oak Knoll Books, 1992. 434pp.
___ Hammond, Wayne G. **J. R. R. Tolkien: Artist and Illustrator**, by Wayne G. Hammond and Christina Scull. Boston, MA: Houghton Mifflin, 1995. 208pp.
___ Hardie, Colin. "Inklings: British at Oxford and German at Aachen," in: Kranz, Gisbert, ed. **Inklings: Jahrbuch für Literatur und Ästhetik**. 1. Band. Lüdenscheid, Germany: Michael Claren, 1983. pp.15-19.
___ Hood, Gwenyth. "The Earthly Paradise in Tolkien's **The Lord of the Rings**," in: Reynolds, Patricia and GoodKnight, Glen H., eds. **Proceedings of the J. R. R. Tolkien Centenary Conference, Keble College, Oxford, 1992**. Altadena, CA: Mythopoeic Press, 1995. pp.139-144. (*Mythlore* Vol. 21, No. 2, Winter 1996, Whole No. 80)
___ Hood, Gwenyth. "Nature and Technology: Angelic and Sacrificial Strategies in Tolkien's **The Lord of the Rings**," *Mythlore* 19(4): 6-12. Autumn 1993. (No. 74)
___ Hopkins, Chris. "Tolkien and Englishness," in: Reynolds, Patricia and GoodKnight, Glen H., eds. **Proceedings of the J. R. R. Tolkien Centenary Conference, Keble College, Oxford, 1992**. Altadena, CA: Mythopoeic Press, 1995. pp.278-280. (*Mythlore* Vol. 21, No. 2, Winter 1996, Whole No. 80)
___ Hopkins, Lisa. "Bilbo Baggins as a Burglar," in: Kranz, Gisbert, ed. **Jahrbuch für Literatur und Ästhetik**. Lüdenscheid, Germany: Stier, 1992. Band 10, pp.93-101.
___ Hopkins, Lisa. "Female Authority Figures in the Works of Tolkien, C. S. Lewis, and Charles Williams," in: Reynolds, Patricia and GoodKnight, Glen H., eds. **Proceedings of the J. R. R. Tolkien Centenary Conference, Keble College, Oxford, 1992**. Altadena, CA: Mythopoeic Press, 1995. pp.364-366. (*Mythlore* Vol. 21, No. 2, Winter 1996, Whole No. 80)
___ Hostetter, Carl F. "A Mythology for England," by Carl F. Hostetter and Arden R. Smith. in: Reynolds, Patricia and GoodKnight, Glen H., eds. **Proceedings of the J. R. R. Tolkien Centenary Conference, Keble College, Oxford, 1992**. Altadena, CA: Mythopoeic Press, 1995. pp.281-290. (*Mythlore* Vol. 21, No. 2, Winter 1996, Whole No. 80)
___ Hostetter, Carl F. "Stone Towers," by Carl F. Hostetter and Patrick Wynne. *Mythlore* 19(4): 47-55, 65. Autumn 1993. (No. 74)
___ Huttar, Charles A. "Tolkien, Epic Traditions and Golden Age Myths," in: Filmer, Kath, ed. **Twentieth-Century Fantasists: Essays in Culture, Society and Belief in Twentieth Century Mythopoeic Literature**. New York: St. Martin's, 1992. pp.92-107.
___ Hyde, Paul N. "Quenti Lambardillion: Snuffling out Footsteps; A Translation at Risk," *Mythlore* 18(2): 23-27. Spring 1992. (No. 68)
___ Hyde, Paul N. "Quenti Lambardillion: The Gondolinic Runes: Another Picture," *Mythlore* 18(3): 20-25. Summer 1992. (No. 69)
___ Irving, James A. **The World Makers: Techniques of Fantasy in J. R. R. Tolkien's The Lord of the Rings and Ursula K. Le Guin's Earthsea Trilogy**. Master's Thesis, Acadia University, 1976. 128pp.
___ Irwin, Robert. "From Science Future to a Fantasy Past," *Antiquity* 69(263): June 1995.
___ Jones, Gwyneth. "C. S. Lewis and Tolkien: Writers for Children?," *New York Review of Science Fiction* No. 87: 1, 8-12. November 1995.
___ Juhren, Marcella. "The Ecology of Middle-Earth," *Mythlore* 20(2): 5-9. Spring 1994. (Whole No. 76)
___ Keene, Louise E. "The Restoration of Language in Middle-Earth," *Mythlore* 20(4): 6-13. Winter 1995. (Whole No. 78)
___ Keffer, Sarah L. "Work-Writing to Create the Fictional Portrait: Tolkien's Inclusion of Lewis in **The Lord of the Rings**," *English Studies in Canada* 18(2): 181-198. June 1992.
___ Kilby, Clyde S. "Mythic and Christian Elements in Tolkien," in: Kranz, Gisbert, ed. **Inklings: Jahrbuch für Literatur und Ästhetik**. 1. Band. Lüdenscheid, Germany: Michael Claren, 1983. pp.103-120.
___ Kokot, Joanna. "Cultural Functions Motivating Art: Poems and Their Contexts in **The Lord of the Rings**," in: Kranz, Gisbert, ed. **Jahrbuch für Literatur und Ästhetik**. Lüdenscheid, Germany: Stier, 1992. Band 10, pp.191-207.

TOLKIEN, J. R. R.

TOLKIEN, J. R. R.

TOLKIEN, J. R. R. (continued)

___ Kondratiev, Alexei. "Tales Newly Told: Tolkien," *Mythlore* 18(2): 10-11. Spring 1992. (No. 68)

___ Kordeski, Stanley. **Anatomy of Fantasy: An Examination of Works of J. R. R. Tolkien and C. S. Lewis**. Master's Thesis, University of Vermont, 1975. 67pp.

___ Kotowski, Nathalie. "Frodo, Sam and Aragorn in the Light of C. G. Jung," in: Kranz, Gisbert, ed. **Jahrbuch für Literatur und Ästhetik**. Lüdenscheid, Germany: Stier, 1992. Band 10, pp.145-159.

___ Kranz, Gisbert. "Der heilende Aragorn," in: Kranz, Gisbert, ed. **Inklings: Jahrbuch für Literatur und Ästhetik**. 2. Band. [Lüdenscheid, Germany: Stier], 1984. pp.11-24.

___ Kranz, Gisbert. **Tolkien in aller Welt: Eine Ausustellung der Inklings-Gesellschaft anlässlich des 100. Geburtstags von J. R. R. Tolkien und des Internationalen Tolkien-Symposions in Aachen**. Aachen: Öffentliche Bibliothek der Stadt Aachen, 1992. 67pp.

___ Kranz, Gisbert. "Tolkien und sein sohn Michael," in: Kranz, Gisbert, ed. **Jahrbuch für Literatur und Ästhetik**. Lüdenscheid, Germany: Stier, 1992. Band 10, pp.11-23.

___ Kranz, Gisbert. "Tolkine und den Inklings auf der Spur," in: Kranz, Gisbert, ed. **Jahrbuch für Literatur und Ästhetik**. Lüdenscheid, Germany: Stier, 1992. Band 10, pp.283-292.

___ Kranz, Gisbert, ed. **Inklings: Jahrbuch für Literatur und Ästhetik. 1.Band**. Lüdenscheid: Michael Claren, 1983. 185pp.

___ Kubinski, Wojciech. "Comprehending the Incomprehensible: On the Pragmatic Analysis of Elvish Texts in **The Lord of the Rings**," in: Kranz, Gisbert, ed. **Inklings: Jahrbuch für Literatur und Ästhetik**. 7. Band. Lüdenscheid, Germany: Stier, 1989. pp.63-82. [Not seen.]

___ Kuschnik, Anne. "Zur Neuübersetzung zweier Tolkien-Gedichte," in: Kranz, Gisbert, ed. **Jahrbuch für Literatur und Ästhetik**. Lüdenscheid, Germany: Stier, 1992. Band 10, pp.209-220.

___ Lenz, Millicent. "Archetypal Images of Otherworlds in Singer's 'Menaseh's Dream' and Tolkien's 'Leaf by Niggle'," *Children's Literature Association Quarterly* 19(1): 3-7. Spring 1994.

___ Lewis, Alex. "Boromir's Journey," in: Kranz, Gisbert, ed. **Jahrbuch für Literatur und Ästhetik**. Lüdenscheid, Germany: Stier, 1992. Band 10, pp.135-144.

___ Lewis, Alex. "Historical Bias in the Making of **The Silmarillion**," in: Reynolds, Patricia and GoodKnight, Glen H., eds. **Proceedings of the J. R. R. Tolkien Centenary Conference, Keble College, Oxford, 1992**. Altadena, CA: Mythopoeic Press, 1995. pp.158-166. (*Mythlore* Vol. 21, No. 2, Winter 1996, Whole No. 80)

___ Luling, Virginia. "An Anthropologist in Middle-Earth," in: Reynolds, Patricia and GoodKnight, Glen H., eds. **Proceedings of the J. R. R. Tolkien Centenary Conference, Keble College, Oxford, 1992**. Altadena, CA: Mythopoeic Press, 1995. pp.53-57. (*Mythlore* Vol. 21, No. 2, Winter 1996, Whole No. 80)

___ Maganiello, Dominic. "The Neverending Story: Textual Happiness in **The Lord of the Rings**," *Mythlore* 18(3): 5-14. Summer 1992. (No. 69)

___ Marginter, Peter. "Tolkiens Phantastik," in: Kranz, Gisbert, ed. **Inklings: Jahrbuch für Literatur und Ästhetik**. 1. Band. Lüdenscheid, Germany: Michael Claren, 1983. pp.121-138.

___ Martsch, Nancy. "A Tolkien Chronology," in: Reynolds, Patricia and GoodKnight, Glen H., eds. **Proceedings of the J. R. R. Tolkien Centenary Conference, Keble College, Oxford, 1992**. Altadena, CA: Mythopoeic Press, 1995. pp.291-297. (*Mythlore* Vol. 21, No. 2, Winter 1996, Whole No. 80)

___ Martsch, Nancy, ed. **List of Tolkienalia**. Sherman Oaks, CA: Beyond Bree, 1992. 56pp.

___ Mathews, Richard. "The Edges of Reality in Tolkien's Tale of Aldarion and Erendis," *Mythlore* 18(3): 27-31. Summer 1992. (No. 69)

___ McComas, Alan. "Negating and Affirming Spirit Through Language: The Integration of Character, Magic and Story in **The Lord of the Rings**, Part 1," *Mythlore* 19(2): 4-14. Spring 1993. (No. 72)

___ McComas, Alan. "Negating and Affirming Spirit Through Language: The Integration of Character, Magic, and Story in **The Lord of the Rings**, Part 2," *Mythlore* 19(3): 40-49. Summer 1993. (No. 73)

___ McKinley, Marlene M. "Tolkien's Influence in America," in: Kranz, Gisbert, ed. **Jahrbuch für Literatur und Ästhetik**. Lüdenscheid, Germany: Stier, 1992. Band 10, pp.261-274.

___ Miller, Miriam Y. "J. R. R. Tolkien's Merlin--An Old Man With a Staff: Galdalf and the Magus Tradition," in: Watson, Jeanie and Fries, Marueen, eds. **The Figure of Merlin in the Nineteenth and Twentieth Centuries**. Lewiston, NY: Mellen, 1989. pp.121-142.

___ Miller, Miriam Y. "'Of sum mayn merualye, bat he mygt trawe': **The Lord of the Rings** and **Sir Gawain and the Green Knight**," *Studies in Medievalism* 3(3): 345-365. Winter 1991.

TOLKIEN, J. R. R. (continued)

___ Mitchell, Bruce. "J. R. R. Tolkien and Old English Studies: An Appreciation," in: Reynolds, Patricia and GoodKnight, Glen H., eds. **Proceedings of the J. R. R. Tolkien Centenary Conference, Keble College, Oxford, 1992**. Altadena, CA: Mythopoeic Press, 1995. pp.206-212. (*Mythlore* Vol. 21, No. 2, Winter 1996, Whole No. 80)

___ Modlmayr, Hans-Jörg. "Fantasy Makes Strange Bedfellows: Mien Besuch bei Tolkien und die Folgen," in: Kranz, Gisbert, ed. **Jahrbuch für Literatur und Ästhetik**. Lüdenscheid, Germany: Stier, 1992. Band 10, pp.275-282.

___ Murray, Robert. "Sermon at Thanksgiving Service, Keble College Chapel, 23rd August 1992," in: Reynolds, Patricia and GoodKnight, Glen H., eds. **Proceedings of the J. R. R. Tolkien Centenary Conference, Keble College, Oxford, 1992**. Altadena, CA: Mythopoeic Press, 1995. pp.17-20. (*Mythlore* Vol. 21, No. 2, Winter 1996, Whole No. 80)

___ Nelson, Charles W. "But Who Is Rose Cotton? Love and Romance in **The Lord of the Rings**," *Journal of the Fantastic in the Arts* 3(3): 6-20. 1994.

___ Noad, Charles E. "Frodo and His Spectre: Blakean Resonances in Tolkien," in: Reynolds, Patricia and GoodKnight, Glen H., eds. **Proceedings of the J. R. R. Tolkien Centenary Conference, Keble College, Oxford, 1992**. Altadena, CA: Mythopoeic Press, 1995. pp.58-62. (*Mythlore* Vol. 21, No. 2, Winter 1996, Whole No. 80)

___ Norman, Felicity. "J. R. R. Tolkien's **The Hobbit**," *Literature Base* 3(3): 12-13. August 1992.

___ Obertino, James. "Moria and Hades: Underworld Journeys in Tolkien and Virgil," *Comparative Literature Studies* 30(2): 153-169. 1993.

___ Olszanski, Tadeusz A. "Evil and the Evil One in Tolkien's Theology," in: Reynolds, Patricia and GoodKnight, Glen H., eds. **Proceedings of the J. R. R. Tolkien Centenary Conference, Keble College, Oxford, 1992**. Altadena, CA: Mythopoeic Press, 1995. pp.298-300. (*Mythlore* Vol. 21, No. 2, Winter 1996, Whole No. 80)

___ Papajewski, Helmut. "Tolkiens Briefe," in: Kranz, Gisbert, ed. **Inklings: Jahrbuch für Literatur und Ästhetik**. 3. Band. [Lüdenscheid, Germany: Stier], 1985. pp.109-128.

___ Pavlac, Diana L. "More Than a Bandersnatch: Tolkien as a Collaborative Writer," in: Reynolds, Patricia and GoodKnight, Glen H., eds. **Proceedings of the J. R. R. Tolkien Centenary Conference, Keble College, Oxford, 1992**. Altadena, CA: Mythopoeic Press, 1995. pp.367-374. (*Mythlore* Vol. 21, No. 2, Winter 1996, Whole No. 80)

___ Petzold, Dieter. "Tolkien als Kinderbuchautor," in: Kranz, Gisbert, ed. **Inklings: Jahrbuch für Literatur und Ästhetik**. 8. Band. Lüdenscheid, Germany: Stier, 1990. pp.53-70. [Not seen.]

___ Petzold, Dieter. "Zwölf Jahre Tolkien-Rezeption in Deutschland, 1980-1991," in: Kranz, Gisbert, ed. **Jahrbuch für Literatur und Ästhetik**. Lüdenscheid, Germany: Stier, 1992. Band 10, pp.241-259.

___ Plotz, Richard. "Tolkien and I: A Brief Memoir," *Mythlore* 19(1): 41-42. Winter 1993. (No. 71)

___ Ponsen, Arti. "In a Hole in the Ground: Tolkien and the Emancipation of Fantasy," *Lembas Extra*. [Leiden]: Tolkien Genootschap Unquendor, 1991. [Not seen, cf. *Mythlore*.]

___ Priestman, Judith. **J. R. R. Tolkien: Life and Legend**. Oxford: Bodleian Library, 1992. 96pp.

___ Rawls, Melanie A. "The Verse of J. R. R. Tolkien," *Mythlore* 19(1): 4-8. Winter 1993. (No. 71)

___ Reynolds, Patricia. "Funeral Customs in Tolkien's Fiction," *Mythlore* 19(2): 45-53. Spring 1993. (No. 72)

___ Reynolds, Patricia, ed. **Proceedings of the J. R. R. Tolkien Centenary Conference, Keble College, Oxford, 1992**, ed. by Patricia Reynolds and Glen H. Goodknight. Altadena, CA: Mythopoeic Press, 1995. 458pp.

___ Reynolds, Trevor. "Index to J. R. R. Tolkien in *Mythlore* Issues 1-68," *Mythlore* 18(3): 70-77. Summer 1992. (No. 69)

___ Rosebury, Brian. **Tolkien: A Critical Assessment**. London: Macmillan, 1992. 167pp.; New York: St. Martin's, 1993. 167pp.

___ Rossenberg, René van. **Hobbits in Holland: Leven en werk van J. R. R. Tolkien (1892-1973)**. Den Hag: Koninklijke Bibliotheek, 1992. 99pp. [Not seen.]

___ Russell, Peter. "Tolkien and the Imagination," in: Kranz, Gisbert, ed. **Jahrbuch für Literatur und Ästhetik**. Lüdenscheid, Germany: Stier, 1992. Band 10, pp.77-91.

___ Ryan, J. S. "Uncouth Innocence: Some Links Between Chrétien de Troyes, Wolfram von Eschenbach and J. R. R. Tolkien," in: Kranz, Gisbert, ed. **Inklings: Jahrbuch für Literatur und Ästhetik**. 2. Band. [Lüdensceid, Germany, Stier], 1984. pp.25-41.

TOLKIEN, J. R. R. (continued)

___ Sarjeant, William A. S. "The Geology of Middle-Earth," in: Reynolds, Patricia and GoodKnight, Glen H., eds. **Proceedings of the J. R. R. Tolkien Centenary Conference, Keble College, Oxford, 1992.** Altadena, CA: Mythopoeic Press, 1995. pp.334-339. (*Mythlore* Vol. 21, No. 2, Winter 1996, Whole No. 80)

___ Sarjeant, William A. S. "Where Did the Dwarves Come From?," *Mythlore* 19(1): 43, 64. Winter 1993. (No. 71)

___ Sawa, Hubert. "Short History of the Territorial Development of the Dwarves' Kingdom in the Second and Third Ages of Middle-Earth," in: Reynolds, Patricia and GoodKnight, Glen H., eds. **Proceedings of the J. R. R. Tolkien Centenary Conference, Keble College, Oxford, 1992.** Altadena, CA: Mythopoeic Press, 1995. pp.396-410. (*Mythlore* Vol. 21, No. 2, Winter 1996, Whole No. 80)

___ Sayer, George. "Recollections of J. R. R. Tolkien," in: Reynolds, Patricia and GoodKnight, Glen H., eds. **Proceedings of the J. R. R. Tolkien Centenary Conference, Keble College, Oxford, 1992.** Altadena, CA: Mythopoeic Press, 1995. pp.21-25. (*Mythlore* Vol. 21, No. 2, Winter 1996, Whole No. 80)

___ Schreier, Josef. "Sprache und Sein: Hermeneutische und ontologische Reflexionen zu den Inklings-Autoren," in: Kranz, Gisbert, ed. **Inklings: Jahrbuch für Literatur und Ästhetik.** 2. Band. [Lüdenscheid, Germany: Stier], 1984. pp.51-63.

___ Schrey, Helmut. "Fluchtwege? Science Fiction und Fantasy Literatur," in: Kranz, Gisbert, ed. **Inklings: Jahrbuch für Literatur und Ästhetik.** 2. Band. [Lüdenscheid, Germany: Stier], 1984. pp.65-83.

___ Schulp, J. A. "The Flora of Middle Earth," in: Kranz, Gisbert, ed. **Inklings: Jahrbuch für Literatur und Ästhetik.** 3. Band. [Lüdenscheid, Germany: Stier], 1985. pp.129-186.

___ Schweicher, Eric. "Aspects of the Fall in **The Silmarillion**," in: Reynolds, Patricia and GoodKnight, Glen H., eds. **Proceedings of the J. R. R. Tolkien Centenary Conference, Keble College, Oxford, 1992.** Altadena, CA: Mythopoeic Press, 1995. pp.167-171. (*Mythlore* Vol. 21, No. 2, Winter 1996, Whole No. 80)

___ Scull, Christina. "Open Minds, Closed Minds in the **Lord of the Rings**," in: Reynolds, Patricia and GoodKnight, Glen H., eds. **Proceedings of the J. R. R. Tolkien Centenary Conference, Keble College, Oxford, 1992.** Altadena, CA: Mythopoeic Press, 1995. pp.151-157. (*Mythlore* Vol. 21, No. 2, Winter 1996, Whole No. 80)

___ Seeman, Chris. "Tolkien's Revision of the Romantic Tradition," in: Reynolds, Patricia and GoodKnight, Glen H., eds. **Proceedings of the J. R. R. Tolkien Centenary Conference, Keble College, Oxford, 1992.** Altadena, CA: Mythopoeic Press, 1995. pp.73-83. (*Mythlore* Vol. 21, No. 2, Winter 1996, Whole No. 80)

___ Senior, William. "Donaldson and Tolkien," *Mythlore* 18(4): 37-43. Autumn 1992. (No. 70)

___ Shippey, Tom. "Heroes and Heroism: Tolkien's Problems, Tolkien's Solutions," *Lembas Extra.* [Leiden]: Tolkien Genootschap Unquendor, 1991. pp.5-17. [Not Seen, cf. *Mythlore*.]

___ Shippey, Tom. **The Road to Middle Earth.** 2nd ed. London: Grafton, 1992. 337pp.

___ Shippey, Tom. "Tolkien and the Gawain-Poet," in: Reynolds, Patricia and GoodKnight, Glen H., eds. **Proceedings of the J. R. R. Tolkien Centenary Conference, Keble College, Oxford, 1992.** Altadena, CA: Mythopoeic Press, 1995. pp.213-220. (*Mythlore* Vol. 21, No. 2, Winter 1996, Whole No. 80)

___ Shippey, Tom. "Tolkien as a Post-War Writer," in: Reynolds, Patricia and GoodKnight, Glen H., eds. **Proceedings of the J. R. R. Tolkien Centenary Conference, Keble College, Oxford, 1992.** Altadena, CA: Mythopoeic Press, 1995. pp.84-93. (*Mythlore* Vol. 21, No. 2, Winter 1996, Whole No. 80)

___ Simons, Lester E. "Writing and Allied Technologies in Middle-Earth," in: Reynolds, Patricia and GoodKnight, Glen H., eds. **Proceedings of the J. R. R. Tolkien Centenary Conference, Keble College, Oxford, 1992.** Altadena, CA: Mythopoeic Press, 1995. pp.340-343. (*Mythlore* Vol. 21, No. 2, Winter 1996, Whole No. 80)

___ Skublics, Heather A. **Naming and Vocation in the Novels of J. R. R. Tolkien, Patricia Kennealy and Anne McCaffrey.** Master's Thesis, McGill University, 1994. 154pp. (Master's Abstracts 33/04, p. 1078. August 1995.)

___ Smith, Arden R. "Duzen and Ihrzen in the German Translation of **The Lord of the Rings**," *Mythlore* 21(1): 33-40. Summer 1995. (No. 79)

___ Spivack, Charlotte. "Tolkien's Images of Evil," in: Kranz, Gisbert, ed. **Jahrbuch für Literatur und Ästhetik.** Lüdenscheid, Germany: Stier, 1992. Band 10, pp.23-36.

TOLKIEN, J. R. R. (continued)

___ St. Clair, Gloriana. "An Overview of the Northern Influences on Tolkien's Work," in: Reynolds, Patricia and GoodKnight, Glen H., eds. **Proceedings of the J. R. R. Tolkien Centenary Conference, Keble College, Oxford, 1992.** Altadena, CA: Mythopoeic Press, 1995. pp.63-67. (*Mythlore* Vol. 21, No. 2, Winter 1996, Whole No. 80)

___ St. Clair, Gloriana. "Tolkien as Reviser: A Case Study," in: Reynolds, Patricia and GoodKnight, Glen H., eds. **Proceedings of the J. R. R. Tolkien Centenary Conference, Keble College, Oxford, 1992.** Altadena, CA: Mythopoeic Press, 1995. pp.145-150. (*Mythlore* Vol. 21, No. 2, Winter 1996, Whole No. 80)

___ St. Clair, Gloriana. "Volsunga Saga and Narn: Some Analogies," in: Reynolds, Patricia and GoodKnight, Glen H., eds. **Proceedings of the J. R. R. Tolkien Centenary Conference, Keble College, Oxford, 1992.** Altadena, CA: Mythopoeic Press, 1995. pp.68-72. (*Mythlore* Vol. 21, No. 2, Winter 1996, Whole No. 80)

___ Stenström, Anders. "A Mythology? for England," in: Reynolds, Patricia and GoodKnight, Glen H., eds. **Proceedings of the J. R. R. Tolkien Centenary Conference, Keble College, Oxford, 1992.** Altadena, CA: Mythopoeic Press, 1995. pp.310-314. (*Mythlore* Vol. 21, No. 2, Winter 1996, Whole No. 80)

___ Stenström, Beregond A. "Tolkien in Swedish," in: Kranz, Gisbert, ed. **Inklings: Jahrbuch für Literatur und Ästhetik.** 2. Band. [Lüdenscheid, Germany: Stier], 1984. pp.43-49.

___ Stevens, David. **J. R. R. Tolkien,** by David Stevens and Carol D. Stevens. Mercer Island, WA: Starmont, 1992. 178pp. (Starmont Reader's Guide, 54)

___ Stevens, David. **J. R. R. Tolkien: The Art of the Myth-Maker.** Revised Ed., by David Stevens and Carol D. Stevens. San Bernardino, CA: Borgo Press, 1993. 178pp.

___ Stoddard, William H. "Law and Institutions in the Shire," *Mythlore* 18(4): 4-8. Autumn 1992. (No. 70)

___ Sullivan, C. W., III. "Tolkien and the Telling of a Traditional Narrative," *Journal of the Fantastic in the Arts* 7(1): 75-82. 1996.

___ Surtees, Angela. "The Mechanics of Dragons: An Introduction to the Study of Their 'Ologies," by Angela Surtees and Steve Gardner. in: Reynolds, Patricia and GoodKnight, Glen H., eds. **Proceedings of the J. R. R. Tolkien Centenary Conference, Keble College, Oxford, 1992.** Altadena, CA: Mythopoeic Press, 1995. pp.411-418. (*Mythlore* Vol. 21, No. 2, Winter 1996, Whole No. 80)

___ Talbot, Norman. "Where Do Elves Go To? Tolkien and a Fantasy Tradition," in: Reynolds, Patricia and GoodKnight, Glen H., eds. **Proceedings of the J. R. R. Tolkien Centenary Conference, Keble College, Oxford, 1992.** Altadena, CA: Mythopoeic Press, 1995. pp.94-106. (*Mythlore* Vol. 21, No. 2, Winter 1996, Whole No. 80)

___ Thorpe, Dwayne. "Tolkien's Elvish Craft," in: Reynolds, Patricia and GoodKnight, Glen H., eds. **Proceedings of the J. R. R. Tolkien Centenary Conference, Keble College, Oxford, 1992.** Altadena, CA: Mythopoeic Press, 1995. pp.315-321. (*Mythlore* Vol. 21, No. 2, Winter 1996, Whole No. 80)

___ Tolkien, John. **The Tolkien Family Album,** by John Tolkien and Priscilla Tolkien. Boston, MA: Houghton Mifflin, 1992. 90pp.

___ Tolley, Clive. "Tolkien's 'Essay on Man': A Look at *Mythopoeia*," in: Kranz, Gisbert, ed. **Jahrbuch für Literatur und Ästhetik.** Lüdenscheid, Germany: Stier, 1992. Band 10, pp.221-240.

___ Tompson, Ricky L. "Tolkien's Word-Hoard Onleac," *Mythlore* 20(1): 22-40. Winter 1994. (Whole No. 75)

___ Unwin, Rayner. "Publishing Tolkien," in: Reynolds, Patricia and GoodKnight, Glen H., eds. **Proceedings of the J. R. R. Tolkien Centenary Conference, Keble College, Oxford, 1992.** Altadena, CA: Mythopoeic Press, 1995. pp.26-29. (*Mythlore* Vol. 21, No. 2, Winter 1996, Whole No. 80)

___ van Rossenberg, Rene. "Tolkien's Exceptional Visit to Holland: A Reconstruction," in: Reynolds, Patricia and GoodKnight, Glen H., eds. **Proceedings of the J. R. R. Tolkien Centenary Conference, Keble College, Oxford, 1992.** Altadena, CA: Mythopoeic Press, 1995. pp.301-309. (*Mythlore* Vol. 21, No. 2, Winter 1996, Whole No. 80)

___ Vanhecke, Johan. "Aspects of Christ in Gandalf," *Lembas Extra.* [Leiden]: Tolkien Genootschap Unquendor, 1991. pp.63-75. [Not seen, cf. *Mythlore*.]

___ Vanhecke, Johan. "Tolkien in Dutch: A Study of the Reception of Tolkien's Work in Belgium and the Netherlands," *Mythlore* 18(4): 53-60. Autumn 1992. (No. 70)

___ Veldman, Meredith. **Fantasy, the Bomb, and the Greening of Britain: Romantic Protest, 1945-1980.** Cambridge: Cambridge University Press, 1994. 325pp.

TOLKIEN, J. R. R.

TOLKIEN, J. R. R. (continued)

___ Vink, Renée. "Tolkien und Dorothy L. Sayers," in: Kranz, Gisbert, ed. **Jahrbuch für Literatur und Ästhetik**. Lüdenscheid, Germany: Stier, 1992. Band 10, pp.61-76.

___ Waugh, Robert H. "Perilous Faërie: J. R. R. Tolkien in the Selva Oscura," *Studies in Weird Fiction* No. 15: 20-27. Summer 1994.

___ Webb, Janeen. "The Quests for Middle-Earth," in: Kranz, Gisbert, ed. **Jahrbuch für Literatur und Ästhetik**. Lüdenscheid, Germany: Stier, 1992. Band 10, pp.161-175.

___ Williams, Lynn F. "Tolkien of Our Esteem," *Austin (TX) American Statesman* Sec. G, p. 1, 9. January 12, 1992.

___ Williams, Madawc. "Tales of Wonder: Science Fiction and Fantasy in the Age of Jane Austen," in: Reynolds, Patricia and GoodKnight, Glen H., eds. **Proceedings of the J. R. R. Tolkien Centenary Conference, Keble College, Oxford, 1992**. Altadena, CA: Mythopoeic Press, 1995. pp.419-430. (*Mythlore* Vol. 21, No. 2, Winter 1996, Whole No. 80)

___ Wood, Ralph C. "Traveling the One Road: **The Lord of the Rings** as a 'Pre-Christian' Classic," *Christian Century* 110(6): 208-211. February 24, 1993.

___ Yandell, Stephen. "A Pattern Which Our Nature Cries out For: The Medieval Tradition of the Ordered Four in the Fiction of J. R. R. Tolkien," in: Reynolds, Patricia and GoodKnight, Glen H., eds. **Proceedings of the J. R. R. Tolkien Centenary Conference, Keble College, Oxford, 1992**. Altadena, CA: Mythopoeic Press, 1995. pp.375-392. (*Mythlore* Vol. 21, No. 2, Winter 1996, Whole No. 80)

___ Yates, Jessica. "Tolkien the Anti-totalitarian," in: Reynolds, Patricia and GoodKnight, Glen H., eds. **Proceedings of the J. R. R. Tolkien Centenary Conference, Keble College, Oxford, 1992**. Altadena, CA: Mythopoeic Press, 1995. pp.233-245. (*Mythlore* Vol. 21, No. 2, Winter 1996, Whole No. 80)

___ Zgorzelski, Andrzej. "Does Tolkien Provoke Us to Comprehend Elvish Texts," in: Kranz, Gisbert. ed. **Inklings: Jahrbuch für Literatur und Ästhetik**. 8. Band. Lüdenscheid, Germany: Stier, 1990. pp.47-52. [Not seen.]

___ Zgorzelski, Andrzej. "A Fairy Tale Modified: Time and Space as Syncretic Factors in J. R. R. Tolkien's Trilogy," *Zeitschrift fur Literaturwissenschaft und Linguistik* No. 92: 126-140. 1993.

___ Zimmer, Paul E. "Another Opinion of the Verse of J. R. R. Tolkien," *Mythlore* 19(2): 16-23. Spring 1993. (No. 72)

TOM CORBETT, SPACE CADET (TV)

___ Phillips, Mark. "Space Cadet," *Starlog* No. 212: 62-67. March 1995.

TOMMYKNOCKERS (MOTION PICTURE)

___ Harris, Judith P. "**Tommyknockers** (Review)," *Cinefantastique* 24(3/4): 123. October 1993.

TOMORROW (MAGAZINE)

___ "Algis Budrys Buys *Tomorrow* SF From Pulphouse," *Science Fiction Chronicle* 14(4): 4. January 1993.

___ "Budrys Buys *Tomorrow*," *Locus* 30(1): 6. January 1993.

___ "*Tomorrow* at Worldcon," *Locus* 29(3): 7. September 1992.

___ "*Tomorrow* SF Is Latest Magazine From Pulphouse," *Science Fiction Chronicle* 13(11/12): 4. August 1992.

TOMORROW PEOPLE (TV)

___ Bradley, Wendy. "**The Tomorrow People** (Review)," *Interzone* No. 69: 40, 49. March 1993.

___ Eramo, Steven. "Girl of Tomorrow," *Starlog* No. 219: 54-55. October 1995.

___ Eramo, Steven. "Teenager of Tomorrow," *Starlog* No. 221: 76-78. December 1995.

___ Kenny, Glenn. "Teleporting Teens and a Generation X Hero," *TV Guide* 42(9): 41. February 26, 1994.

TOR BOOKS

___ "Tor Books Pays $1 Million Advance for Four Piers Anthony Xanth Novels," *Science Fiction Chronicle* 13(4): 4. January 1992.

TOTAL RECALL (MOTION PICTURE)

___ Ellis, R. J. "Are You a Fucking Mutant?: **Total Recall**'s Fantastic Hesitations," *Foundation* No. 65: 81-97. Autumn 1995.

___ Mizejewski, Linda. "Total Recoil: The Schwarzenegger Body on Postmodern Mars," *Post Script* 12(3): 25-33. Summer 1993.

___ Murray, Will. "Absolute Recall," *Starlog* 177: 34-37, 68. April 1992.

TOTAL RECALL (MOTION PICTURE) (continued)

___ Schmertz, Johanna. "On Reading the Politics of **Total Recall**," *Post Script* 12(3): 34-42. Summer 1993.

TOULON'S REVENGE (MOTION PICTURE)

___ SEE: PUPPET MASTERS III: TOULON'S REVENGE (MOTION PICTURE).

TOURIST, THE (SCRIPT)

___ Szebin, Frederick C. "**The Tourist**: The Hollywood Horror Story of Writer Clair Noto's Unfilmed Masterpiece," *Cinefantastique* 25(4): 46-55. August 1994.

TOURNIER, MICHEL

___ Koopman Thurlings, Mariska. "Fantastique ludique et érotisme inquiétant dans l'oeuvre de Michel Tournier," in: Bozzetto, Roger, ed. **Eros: Science & Fiction Fantastique**. Aix-en-Provence: Universite de Provence, 1991. pp.135-153.

TOVAR, LUPITA

___ Weaver, Tom. "Lupita Tovar: Interview," in: Weaver, Tom, ed. **Attack of the Monster Movie Makers: Interviews with 20 Genre Giants**. Jefferson, NC: McFarland, 1994. pp.357-365.

TOXIC AVENGER (MOTION PICTURE)

___ "Ontario's Censors Ban Troxma's **Toxic Avenger**," *Variety* p. 6, 32. June 18, 1986.

TOY STORY (MOTION PICTURE)

___ French, Lawrence. "**Toy Story**: Art Direction," *Cinefantastique* 27(2): 32-33. November 1995.

___ French, Lawrence. "**Toy Story**: Beginnings," *Cinefantastique* 27(2): 36. November 1995.

___ French, Lawrence. "**Toy Story**: CGI Director," *Cinefantastique* 27(2): 20-21. November 1995.

___ French, Lawrence. "**Toy Story**: CGI Production," *Cinefantastique* 27(2): 28-29 November 1995.

___ French, Lawrence. "**Toy Story**: Licensing," *Cinefantastique* 27(2): 26. November 1995.

___ French, Lawrence. "**Toy Story**: Pixar," *Cinefantastique* 27(2): 23-25. November 1995.

___ French, Lawrence. "**Toy Story**: Renderman," *Cinefantastique* 27(2): 18-19. November 1995.

___ French, Lawrence. "**Toy Story**: Scanning," *Cinefantastique* 27(2): 34-35. November 1995.

___ French, Lawrence. "**Toy Story**: Voices," *Cinefantastique* 27(2): 31. November 1995.

___ French, Lawrence. "**Toy Story**," *Cinefantastique* 26(6)/27(1): 8-9, 125. October 1995.

___ French, Lawrence. "**Toy Story**," *Cinefantastique* 27(2): 16-37. November 1995.

___ Street, Rita. "Toys Will Be Toys," *Cinefex* No. 64: 76-91. December 1995.

___ Sullivan, Darcy. "**Toy Story**," *Starlog* No. 221: 38-45. December 1995.

TOYMAKER (MOTION PICTURE)

___ SEE: SILENT NIGHT, DEADLY NIGHT: THE TOYMAKER (MOTION PICTURE).

TOYS

___ Jankiewicz, Pat. "The Good, the Bad, and the Plastic," *Starlog* No. 218: 50-51. September 1995.

___ Tanner, Ron. "Toy Robots in America, 1955-75: How Japan Really Won the War," *Journal of Popular Culture* 28(3): 125-154. Winter 1994.

TOYS (MOTION PICTURE)

___ Lowe, Nick. "**Toys** (Review)," *Interzone* No. 72: 34. June 1993.

___ Vaz, Mark C. "Toy Wars," *Cinefex* No. 54: 54-73. May 1993.

TRADING CARDS

___ Counts, Kyle. "Views of the Wars," *Starlog* No. 191: 41-45. June 1993.

___ Johnson, Kim H. "*Mars Attacks* Again," *Starlog* No. 203: 38-41. June 1994.

___ Maschi, Bob. "Cardboard Spacecraft," *Starlog* No. 191: 35-40. June 1993.

TRAKL, GEORG
___ Cersowsky, Peter. "Varianten phantastischer Lyrik: Edgar Allan Poe und Georg Trakl," in: Kranz, Gisbert, ed. **Inklings: Jahrbuch für Literatur und Ästhetik**. 9. Band. Lüdenscheid, Germany: Stier, 1991. pp.165-186. [Not seen.]

TRANCERS 4: JACK OF SWORDS (MOTION PICTURE)
___ Wilt, David. "***Trancers 4: Jack of Swords*** (Review)," *Cinefantastique* 25(4): 60. August 1994.

TRANCERS II: THE RETURN OF JACK DETH (MOTION PICTURE)
___ Lehti, Steven J. "***Trancers II*** (Review)," *Cinefantastique* 23(2/3): 123. October 1992.
___ Shapiro, Marc. "SF's Video Hero," *Starlog* 179: 66-69, 84. June 1992.

TRANS-ATLANTIC FAN FUND
___ "Abigail Frost Wins TAFF," *Science Fiction Chronicle* 14(9): 30. June 1993.
___ "Dan Steffan Wins TAFF," *Science Fiction Chronicle* 16(7): 30. June/July 1995.
___ "Jeanne Bowman Wins TAFF," *Science Fiction Chronicle* 13(6): 26. March 1992.
___ "Three Running in '95 TAFF Race," *Science Fiction Chronicle* 16(2): 36. November/December 1994.

TRANSFORMERS (TV)
___ "Intl. Video Lines Up N. American Rights to ***Transformers***," *Variety* p. 35-36. March 27, 1985.
___ "***Transformers*** Pic 1st Feature Effort by Animation Firm," *Variety* p. 16. March 13, 1985.

TRANSLATIONS
___ Grigorieva, Natalia. "Problems of Translating into Russian," in: Reynolds, Patricia and GoodKnight, Glen H., eds. **Proceedings of the J. R. R. Tolkien Centenary Conference, Keble College, Oxford, 1992**. Altadena, CA: Mythopoeic Press, 1995. pp.200-205. (*Mythlore* Vol. 21, No. 2, Winter 1996, Whole No. 80)
___ Smith, Arden R. "Duzen and Ihrzen in the German Translation of **The Lord of the Rings**," *Mythlore* 21(1): 33-40. Summer 1995. (No. 79)

TRANSNATIONALISM
___ Cherniak, Laura R. **Calling in Question: Science Fiction and Cultural Studies**. Ph.D. Dissertation, University of California, Santa Cruz, 1995. 257pp. (DAI-A 56/04, p. 1554. October 1995.)

TRANSVESTITES
___ Tharp, Julie. "The Transvestite as Monster: Gender Horror in **The Silence of the Lambs** and **Psycho**," *Journal of Popular Film and Television* 19(3): 106-113. 1991.

TRAUMA (MOTION PICTURE)
___ Harris, Judith P. "***Trauma*** (Review)," *Cinefantastique* 25(5): 60. October 1994.

TREECE, HENRY
___ Bailey, K. V. "We, Old as History Now...," *Vector* No. 180: 15-16. August/September 1994.

TRESTRAIL, VERNA SMITH
___ "Trestrail, Verna Smith (Obituary)," *Science Fiction Chronicle* 15(6): 26. April/May 1994.

TREVARTHEN, HAL P.
___ Stone, Graham. "Notes on Australian Science Fiction," *Science Fiction News* (Australia) No. 94: 2-11. January 1986.

TREVOR, ELLESTON
___ "Trevor, Elleston (Obituary)," *Locus* 35(3): 78. September 1993.
___ "Trevor, Elleston (Obituary)," *Science Fiction Chronicle* 16(9): 24. August/September 1995.

TRIESTE FILM FESTIVAL, 1970
___ "Computer a Hero (Natch) at Trieste's Festival of Science Fiction Films," *Variety* p. 6. August 5, 1970.
___ "Enter 2 U.S. Pix in Trieste's International Sci-Fi Film Fest," *Variety* p. 24. June 10, 1970.

TRIESTE FILM FESTIVAL, 1982
___ "Israeli Poet's Pic Due at Trieste Sci-Fi Fest," *Variety* p. 36. May 5, 1982.
___ "Trieste Festival Features 12 Pictures, Lotsa Effects," *Variety* p. 6, 30. July 28, 1982.

TRIPODS (TV)
___ "BBC's **The Tripods** Starts Second Season, Clears 41 U.S. Markets," *Variety* p.58. August 7, 1985.

TROLLS
___ Attebery, Jennifer E. "The Trolls of Fiction: Ogres or Warm Fuzzies," *Journal of the Fantastic in the Arts* 7(1): 61-74. 1996.

TRON (MOTION PICTURE)
___ "Disney's Megabuck **Tron** Has More Than Cash Riding on It," *Variety* p. 5, 20. February 10, 1982.
___ "**Tron** Suit Dismissed," *Variety* p. 24. November 7, 1984.
___ Kerman, Judith B. "Virtual Space and Its Boundaries in Science Fiction Film and Television: **Tron**, **Max Headroom**, **War Games**," in: Morse, Donald E., ed. **The Celebration of the Fantastic**. Westport, CT: Greenwood, 1992. pp.191-204.

TROPP, MARTIN
___ Morse, Donald E. "Masterpieces or Garbage: Martin Tropp and Science Fiction," *The CEA Critic* 43(3): 14-17. March 1981.

TROTT, JUDI
___ Airey, Jean. "Marian of Sherwood," *Starlog* 180: 56-58. July 1992.

TRUE LIES (MOTION PICTURE)
___ Shay, Don. "Mayhem over Miami," *Cinefex* No. 59: 34-79. September 1994.

TRUMBULL, DOUGLAS
___ Abrams, Janet. "Escape From Gravity," *Sight and Sound* 5(5): 14-19. May 1995.
___ Pizzello, Chris. "Riding the Movies with Doug Trumbull," *American Cinematographer* 74(8): 53-58. August 1993.

TSUKAMOTO, SHINYA
___ Persons, Dan. "Cheap Genius," *Cinefantastique* 23(5): 53. February 1993.
___ Persons, Dan. "**Tetsuo: The Iron Man**," *Cinefantastique* 23(5): 50-52. February 1993.

TUCKER, WILSON 'BOB'
___ Stephensen-Payne, Phil. **Wilson 'Bob' Tucker, Wild Talent: A Working Bibliography**, by Phil Stephensen-Payne and Gordon Benson, Jr. Albuquerque, NM: Galactic Central, 1994. 38pp. 4th. Edition.

TUFAYL, ABU IBN
___ Farmer, Philip J. "**Hayy ibn Yaqzan**, by Abu ibn Tufayl: An Arabic Mowgli," *Journal of the Fantastic in the Arts* 3(3): 72-78. 1994.

TURNER, FREDERICK
___ O'Sullivan, Gerry. "Inventing Arcadia: An Interview With Frederick Turner," by Gerry O'Sullivan and Carl Pletsch. *Humanist* 53(6): 9-18. November/December 1993.

TURNER, GEORGE
___ "1994 Ditmar Awards," *Locus* 32(5): 9, 64. May 1994.
___ "Ditmar Awards," *Science Fiction Chronicle* 15(9): 8. August 1994.

TURTLEDOVE, HARRY
___ "1994 Hugo Award," *Science Fiction Chronicle* 15(10): 5. September 1994.
___ "1994 Hugo Awards Winners," *Locus* 33(4): 7, 38-41. October 1994.
___ "Harry Turtledove: The Real Thing," *Locus* 30(4): 4, 66. April 1993.
___ King, T. Jackson. "Pros and Cons of Being a Writer Couple," by T. Jackson King and Paula E. Downing. *SFWA Bulletin* 25(4): 7-14. Winter 1992. (No. 114)
___ Teitelbaum, Sheldon. "Playing With History," *Los Angeles (CA) Times* Sec. E, p. 1. July 7, 1992.

TURTLEDOVE, LAURA

___ King, T. Jackson. "Pros and Cons of Being a Writer Couple," by T. Jackson King and Paula E. Downing. *SFWA Bulletin* 25(4): 7-14. Winter 1992. (No. 114)

TUTTLE, LISA

___ Cary, Catie. "Magic in the Real World: Lisa Tuttle Interviewed," *Vector* No. 168: 16-19. August/September 1992.

___ Nicholls, Stan. "Lisa Tuttle Thinks It World Be Nice to Have a Proper Job," in: Nicholls, Stan. **Wordsmiths of Wonder: Fifty Interviews with Writers of the Fantastic**. London: Orbit, 1993. pp.155-163.

___ Tuttle, Lisa. "Memories of Ortygia House," *Interzone* No. 88: 48-51. October 1994.

TWAIN, MARK

___ Ensor, Allison. "The Magic of Fol-de-Rol: Mark Twain's Merlin," in: Watson, Jeanie and Fries, Marueen, eds. **The Figure of Merlin in the Nineteenth and Twentieth Centuries**. Lewiston, NY: Mellen, 1989. pp.51-63.

___ Fulton, Valerie. "The Other Frontier: Voyaging West with Mark Twain and *Star Trek*'s Imperial Subject," *Postmodern Culture* 4(3): [14pp.]. May 1994. (Electronic Journal: pmc@jefferson.village.virginia.edu).

___ Hoffman, Donald L. "Mark's Merlin: Magic vs. Technology in **A Connecticut Yankee in King Arthur's Court**," in: Slocum, Sally K., ed. **Popular Arthurian Traditions**. Bowling Green, OH: Popular Press, 1992. pp.46-55.

___ Michaelson, Scott. "Twain's **The American Claimant** and the Figure of Frankenstein: A Reading of the Rhetorical Hermeneutics," in: Latham, Robert A. and Collins, Robert A., eds. **Modes of the Fantastic**. Westport, CT: Greenwood, 1995. pp.195-203.

TWILIGHT OF THE DOGS (MOTION PICTURE)

___ Mayo, Mike. "Successful Low-Budget SF Film-making Is Itself an Act of Science Fiction," *Science Fiction Age* 2(4): 20-23, 33-34. May 1994.

TWILIGHT ZONE: ROD SERLING'S LOST CLASSICS (TV)

___ Hughes, Mike. "Serling's Tales Continue to Haunt Us," *Boston (MA) Herald*. May 19, 1994. in: *NewsBank. Film and Television*. 60:B12. 1994.

___ Richmond, Ray. "Serling's 'Lost' Tales Lose Something in 90s Transition," *Los Angeles (CA) Daily News*. May 19, 1994. in: *NewsBank. Film and Television*. 60: B13. 1994.

TWILIGHT ZONE (THEME PARK)

___ Schellbach, Richard J. "The Twilight Zone: Tower of Terror," *Sci-Fi Entertainment* 1(5): 52-53, 55. February 1995.

TWILIGHT ZONE (TV)

___ Lofficier, Jean-Marc. **Into the Twilight Zone: The Rod Serling Programme Guide**, by Jean-Marc Lofficier and Randy Lofficier. London: Virgin, 1995. 296pp.

___ Van Hise, James. **Sci Fi TV: From Twilight Zone to Deep Space Nine**. Las Vegas, NV: Pioneer Books, 1993. 160pp. (Reprinted, HarperPrism, 1995. 258pp.)

___ Westbrook, Bruce. "Re-entering Serling's *Twilight Zone*," *Houston (TX) Chronicle* Sec. C, p. 3. September 4, 1992.

TWIN PEAKS: FIRE WALK WITH ME (MOTION PICTURE)

___ Corsaletti, Louis T. "Television Show 'Peaks' Interest," *Seattle (WA) Times*. April 7, 1992. in: *NewsBank. Film and Television*. 47:D3. 1992.

___ Lewis, Dana. "They Really Care Who Killed Laura Palmer," *Los Angeles (CA) Times*. June 21, 1992. in: *NewsBank. Film and Television*. 66:E13-E14. 1992.

___ Pally, Marcia. "Moralizing Mars Film's Fantasy (Review)," *Boston (MA) Herald*. May 18, 1992. in: *NewsBank. Film and Television*. 50:E6. 1992.

___ Persons, Dan. "*Twin Peaks: Fire Walk With Me* (Review)," *Cinefantastique* 23(5): 59. February 1993.

___ Persons, David. "Son of *Twin Peaks*," *Cinefantastique* 23(2/3): 14-15. October 1992.

TWIN PEAKS (TV)

___ Buffington, Nancy. "What About Bob? Doubles and Demons in *Twin Peaks*," in: Sanders, Joe, ed. **Functions of the Fantastic**. Westport, CT: Greenwood, 1995. pp.101-106.

TWO EVIL EYES (MOTION PICTURE)

___ "*Two Evil Eyes* (Review)," *Cinefantastique* 22(5): 61. April 1992.

___ Baltake, Joe. "Poe's Subtle Horror Shines in *Evil Eyes* (Review)," *Sacramento (CA) Bee*. December 12, 1991. in: *NewsBank. Film and Television*. 8:E3. 1992.

___ Blank, Ed. "*Two Evil Eyes* Could be Good with Poe Stories, But Just Too Cheesy (Review)," *Pittsburgh (PA) Press*. December 7, 1991. in: *NewsBank. Film and Television*. 8:E4. 1992.

TYERS, KATHY

___ "Bozeman Author Continues *Star Wars* Saga," *Great Falls (MT) Tribune* November 6, 1993. in: *NewsBank. Literature*. 99:F4. 1993.

___ Cowan, Lisa. "Kathy Tyers' Most Enjoyable Assignment: **Star Wars: The Mission at Bakura**," *Lucasfilm Fan Club* No. 21: 32-33. Winter 1994.

___ Mintz, Catherine. "SFC Interviews: Kathy Tyers," *Science Fiction Chronicle* 15(2): 5, 39-40. November/December 1993.

TYMN, MARSHALL B.

___ "Marshall Tymn's Family Sues After Car Crash," *Science Fiction Chronicle* 13(4): 5. January 1992.

TYRON, THOMAS

___ Joshi, S. T. "Thomas Tyron: Rural Horror," *Studies in Weird Fiction* No. 11: 5-12. Spring 1992.

U. F. O.: THE MOVIE (MOTION PICTURE)

___ Lowe, Nick. "*UFO--The Movie* (Review)," *Interzone* No. 82: 30. April 1994.

___ Macnab, Geoffrey. "*U.F.O.* (Review)," *Sight and Sound* 4(2): 60-61. February 1994.

U. S. S. ENTERPRISE (AIRCRAFT CARRIER)

___ Hogan, Jeanne. "Operation *Enterprise*," *Star Trek: The Official Fan Club Magazine* No. 92: 1, 34. July/August 1993.

UFOS

___ Szewczyk, Stacey. "Something Is Out There...Maybe," *Sci-Fi Universe* No. 3: 94-95. October/November 1994.

UKRAINE

___ "SF in Ukraine: 1992," *Locus* 29(1): 41. July 1992.

___ "Ukrainian SF: Past & Future," *Locus* 28(2): 48-49. August 1992.

___ Kononenko, V. O. **Neznani svity fantastyky: rekomendattsiinyi bibliohrafichnyi pokazhchyk**, by V. O. Kononenko and V. M. Loi. Kylv: Derzhavan biblioteke Ukrainy, 1992. 35pp. [Not seen.]

___ McKenney, Michael. "Chumatsky Shlyah: The Ukrainian National SF Convention," *Lan's Lantern* No. 42: 30-31. May 1994.

ULTRAMARINE PRESS

___ Stephens, Christopher P. **A Checklist of Ultramarine Press**. Hastings-on-Hudson, NY: Ultramarine, 1992. 13pp. Revised ed.

UNBORN II (MOTION PICTURE)

___ Faller, James M. "*Unborn II* (Review)," *Cinefantastique* 26(2): 59. February 1995.

UNDERWOOD, JAY

___ Shapiro, Marc. "Man on Fire," *Starlog* No. 195: 63-65. October 1993.

UNDISCOVERED COUNTRY (MOTION PICTURE)

___ SEE: STAR TREK VI: THE UNDISCOVERED COUNTRY (MOTION PICTURE).

UNEARTHLY STRANGER (MOTION PICTURE)

___ Leeper, Mark R. "*Unearthly Stranger* (Review)," *Lan's Lantern* No. 42: 106. May 1994.

UNIDENTIFIED FLYING OBJECTS

___ Pfluger, Carl. "God vs. the Flying Saucers," *Southwest Review* 78(4): 555-571. Autumn 1993.

UNITED MYTHOLOGIES PRESS

___ Chalker, Jack L. "On Publishing and Personalities," *Pulphouse* No. 11: 53-57. August 1992.

UNIVERSAL SOLDIER (MOTION PICTURE)

___ "*Universal Soldier* Misfires (Review)," *Washington (DC) Times*. July 12, 1992. in: *NewsBank. Film and Television*. 74:G8. 1992.

___ Backman, Lisa. "Movie's Story Line Disputed," *Tampa (FL) Tribune*. July 28, 1992. in: *NewsBank. Film and Television*. 74:F14. 1992.

___ Biodrowski, Steve. "Futuristic Musclemen: Jean Claude Van Damme, Dolph Lundgren Flex It in Carolco's *Universal Soldier*," *Cinefantastique* 23(1): 12-13. August 1992.

___ Biodrowski, Steve. "*Universal Soldier* (Review)," *Cinefantastique* 23(4): 61. December 1992.

___ Campbell, Bob. "GI Corpse Tries to Escape Second Hitch as Robot Soldier (Review)," *Newark (NJ) Star-Ledger*. July 10, 1992. in: *NewsBank. Film and Television*. 74:G6. 1992.

___ Ebert, Roger. "*Universal Soldier* Loses Battle Against Monotony (Review)," *Chicago (IL) Sun Times*. July 10, 1992. in: *NewsBank. Film and Television*. 74:G4. 1992.

___ Johnson, Kim H. "Drill Sergeant to the Stars," *Starlog* 182: 52-55. September 1992.

___ Johnson, Kim H. "Resurrected Warriors," *Starlog* 178: 75-81. May 1992.

___ Johnson, Kim H. "Rogue Trooper," *Starlog* 182: 42-45. September 1992.

___ Johnson, Kim H. "Super-Soldier," *Starlog* 181: 36-39. August 1992.

___ Kronke, David. "*Soldier* Surrenders All Pretense of Plot, Credibility (Review)," *Los Angeles (CA) Daily News*. July 28, 1992. in: *NewsBank. Film and Television*. 74:G1. 1992.

___ Lowe, Nick. "*Universal Soldier* (Review)," *Interzone* No. 65: 33. November 1992.

___ Mahar, Ted. "Blood-Splattering Mayhem Spurts Out Unintended Satire in *Universal Soldier* (Review)," *Portland (OR) The Oregonian*. July 11, 1992. in: *NewsBank. Film and Television*. 74:G7. 1992.

___ McNally, Owen. "*Soldier* Is No More Than Bloodbath (Review)," *Hartford (CT) Courant*. July 10, 1992. in: *NewsBank. Film and Television*. 74:G3. 1992.

___ Shulgasser, Barbara. "The Fight of the Living Dead: *Universal Soldier* Delivers a Blow to Recycling Programs (Review)," *San Francisco (CA) Examiner*. July 10, 1992. in: *NewsBank. Film and Television*. 74: G2. 1992.

___ Verniere, James. "*Terminator* Ripoff Is a Universal Bore (Review)," *Boston (MA) Herald*. July 10, 1992. in: *NewsBank. Film and Television*. 74:G5. 1992.

UNIVERSAL STUDIOS

___ "Grim Fairy Tales: Universal Studios, 1931-1954," *Wonder* No. 7: 13-21. 1993.

UNIVERSITY OF BUFFALO

___ "Alum's Pulp Gift out of This World With Rare SF Titles, Fanzines," *Wilson Library Bulletin* 69(5): 16. January 1995.

UNKNOWN TERROR (MOTION PICTURE)

___ Henenlotter, Frank. "Films From Under the Floorboards," *Sci-Fi Entertainment* 1(6): 52-57. April 1995.

UNNAMABLE (MOTION PICTURE)

___ "*Unnamable* (Review)," *Variety* p. 13. June 15, 1988.

UNTIL THE END OF THE WORLD (MOTION PICTURE)

___ "*End* Comes Too Late to Save Story (Review)," *Washington (DC) Times*. January 17, 1992. in: *NewsBank. Film and Television*. 16:C1. 1992.

___ Bernard, Jami. "Island of Ah! In Sea of Blah (Review)," *New York (NY) Post*. December 24, 1991. in: *NewsBank. Film and Television*. 8: E6. 1992.

___ Campbell, Bob. "Spacey Sci-Fi Odyssey Is Metaphysically Far Out (Review)," *Newark (NJ) Star-Ledger*. December 26, 1991. in: *NewsBank. Film and Television*. 8:E5. 1992.

___ Ebert, Roger. "Story Keeps Wandering Until the End of 'World' (Review)," *Chicago (IL) Sun Times*. January 17, 1992. in: *NewsBank. Film and Television*. 16:B12-B13. 1992.

___ Freeman, Paul. "Ears Have it as Rock Stars Roll In *End of the World* Film (Review)," *Washington (DC) Times*. February 16, 1992. in: *NewsBank. Film and Television*. 26:F13. 1992.

___ Mahar, Ted. "Wim Wender's Work to Open Film Festival," *Portland (OR) The Oregonian*. February 13, 1992. in: *NewsBank. Film and Television*. 24:F4. 1992.

UNTIL THE END OF THE WORLD (MOTION PICTURE) (continued)

___ Movshovitz, Howie. "*End of World* Explores Technologies of the Future (Review)," *Denver (CO) Post*. February 7, 1992. in: *NewsBank. Film and Television*. 26:G2-G3. 1992.

___ Ringel, Eleanor. "This Lasts *Until the End of the World* (Review)," *Atlanta (GA) Journal*. March 20, 1992. in: *NewsBank. Film and Television*. 37:D5. 1992.

___ Robley, Les P. "*Until the End of the World* (Review)," *Cinefantastique* 22(6): 55. June 1992

___ Shulgasser, Barbara. "Not With a Bang But a Wenders (Review)," *San Francisco (CA) Examiner*. January 24, 1992. in: *NewsBank. Film and Television*. 26:F14-G1. 1992.

___ Verniere, James. "*Until the End of the World* an Overindulged Megathud (Review)," *Boston (MA) Herald*. January 17, 1992. in: *NewsBank. Film and Television*. 16:B14. 1992.

___ Wuntch, Phillip. "Road Movie Breaks Down, But Scenery's Great (Review)," *Dallas (TX) Morning News*. March 6, 1992. in: *NewsBank. Film and Television*. 37:D6. 1992.

___ Yakir, Dan. "To the Ends of the Dream World," *Starlog* 177: 38-40, 77. April 1992.

___ Yakir, Dan. "Wenders' *End* Looks to Justify the Means (Review)," *Boston (MA) Globe*. January 12, 1992. in: *NewsBank. Film and Television*. 16:B10-B11. 1992.

UPC AWARDS (UNIVERSITAT POLITECNIA DE CATALUNYA INTERNATIONAL AWARD), 1992

___ "1993 UPC Science Fiction Award," *Locus* 30(4): 40. April 1993.

UPC AWARDS (UNIVERSITAT POLITECNIA DE CATALUNYA INTERNATIONAL AWARD), 1993

___ "UPC Award Presented," *Locus* 32(2): 9, 73. February 1994.

UPC AWARDS (UNIVERSITAT POLITECNIA DE CATALUNYA INTERNATIONAL AWARD), 1994

___ "1994 UPC Award Contest Opens," *Locus* 32(5): 8, 66. May 1994.

___ "Barcelo, Foster Win UPC Awards," *Science Fiction Chronicle* 15(4): 6-7. February 1994.

___ "Neube, Resnick, McDevitt Win 1994 UPC Awards," *Science Fiction Chronicle* 16(3): 5. January 1995.

UPDIKE, JOHN

___ Atwill, William D. **Fire and Power: The American Space Program as Postmodern Narrative**. Athens, GA: The University of Georgia Press, 1994. 172pp.

___ DeBellis, Jack. " 'The Awful Power': John Updike's Use of Kubrick's *2001: A Space Odyssey* in **Rabbit Redux**," *Literature/Film Quarterly* 21(3): 209-217. 1993.

___ Jurkiewicz, Kenneth. "Giving the Devil More Than His Due: *The Witches of Eastwick* as Fiction and Film," in: Morse, Donald E., ed. **The Celebration of the Fantastic**. Westport, CT: Greenwood, 1992. pp.205-210.

USE OF SF

___ "A Modest Proposal From 'The Killer Bees'," *Science Fiction Chronicle* 17(2): 5. December 1995/January 1996.

___ Bear, Greg. "State of the Art: Contact in the Classroom," *Analog* 112(1/2): 228-237. January 1992.

___ Booker, M. Keith. **The Dystopian Impulse in Modern Literature: Fiction as Social Criticism**. Westport, CT: Greenwood, 1994. 197pp.

___ Borgwald, James M. "Classroom Analysis of Rotating Space Vehicles in *2001: A Space Odyssey*," by James M. Borgwald and Serge Schreiner. *Physics Teacher* 31(7): 406-409. October 1993.

___ Brice, William C. "Geology Teaching and Science Fiction," *Journal of Geological Education* 29(2): 105-107. March 1980.

___ Bull, Geoff. "Morning Comes Whether You Set the Alarm or Not: Science Fiction, a Genre for the Future," *Orana* (Australia) 31(3): 159-169. August 1995.

___ Burns, John E. "One for the Books: Using Literature-Based Science Lessons," *Science Teacher* 61(7): 38-41. October 1994.

___ Coville, Bruce. "About Tomorrow: Learning with Literature," *Instructor* 101(9): 20, 22-23. May/June 1992.

___ Crisler, Jesse. "Fantasy: A Welcome Alternative," in: Canham, Stephen, ed. **Literature and Hawaii's Children**. Honolulu, HI: University of Hawaii Manoa, 1992. pp.69-75

___ Dubeck, Leroy W. **Fantastic Voyages: Learning Science Through Science Fiction Films**. New York: American Institute of Physics, 1994. 327pp.

USE OF SF (continued)
___ Dubeck, Leroy W. "Finding the Facts in Science Fiction Films," by Leroy W. Dubeck, Suzanne E. Moshier, Matthew H. Bruce and Judith E. Boss. *Science Teacher* 60(4): 46-48. April 1993.

___ Dubeck, Leroy W. "Science and Science Fiction Films," *Journal of College Science Teaching* 11(2): 111-113. November 1981.

___ Dubeck, Leroy W. "Using Science Fiction Films to Teach Science at the College Level," by Leroy W. Dubeck, Suzanne E. Moshier and Judith E. Boss. *Journal of College Science Teaching* 25(1): 46-50. September/October 1995

___ Freeman, Judy. "In the Realm of Fantasy," *Instructor* 104(8): 77-82. May 1995.

___ Gough, Noel. "Environmental Education, Narrative Complexity and Postmodern Science/Fiction," *International Journal of Science Education* 15(5): 607-625. 1993.

___ Gough, Noel. "Neuromancing the Stones: Experience, Intertextuality and Cyberpunk Science Fiction," *Journal of Experiential Education* 16(3): 9-17. December 1993.

___ Harris, June. "How to Tell the Schlock from the Good Stuff in Science Fiction," *ALAN Review* 19(3): 38-40. Spring 1992.

___ Henly, Carolyn P. "Escape From the *Twilight Zone*: Reading and Writing 'At-Risk' Students," *ALAN Review* 19(3): 31-32, 35, 37. Spring 1992.

___ Imdieke, Sandra A. **Characters in Time Travel as Historical Guides**, by Sandra A. Imdieke and Lynn Madaus. ERIC ED 305601. 9pp. 1994.

___ Jordan, Anne D. "Science Fiction: Something for Everyone," *Teaching and Learning Literature* 4(5): 24-25. May/June 1995.

___ Lackey, Chad. "Social Science Fiction: Writing Sociological Short Stories to Learn About Social Issues," *Teaching Sociology* 22(2): 166-173. April 1994.

___ Laz, Cheryl. "Science Fiction and Introductory Sociology: The Handmaid in the Classroom," *Teaching Sociology* 24(1): 54-63. January 1995.

___ Magyar, Miki. "Science Fiction for Technical Communicators," in: **International Professional Communication Conference 93 Proceedings: The New Face of Technical Communication: People, Processes, Products.** New York: IEEE, 1993. pp.107-111.

___ Marchesani, Joseph J. "Constellation Prizes: Using Science Fiction for Lesbian, Gay, and Bisexual Issues in College Classes," ED 370 117 (Paper presented at the Annual Meeting of the Conference on College Composition and Communication, 45th, Nashville, TN, March 16-19, 1994.) 1 microfiche.

___ Marion, David E. "Using Fiction to Expose a Fundamental Theme in American Public Policy," *Teaching Political Science* 15(2): 44-49. Winter 1988.

___ Miles, Ian. "Stranger Than Fiction: How Important Is Science Fiction for Futures Studies?," *Futures* 25(3): 315-321. April 1993. (Reprinted: *Engineering Management Review* 21(4): 49-52. Winter 1993.)

___ Nauman, Ann K. "Sci-Fi Science," by Ann K. Nauman and Edward L. Shaw. *Science Activities* 31(3): 18-20. Fall 1994.

___ Perry, Phyllis J. **The World of Water: Linking Fiction to Nonfiction.** Englewood, CO: Teacher Ideas Press, 1995. 149pp.

___ Pohl, Frederik. "The Uses of the Future," *Futurist* 27(2): 9-12. March-April 1993.

___ Rusch, Kristine K. "Editorial: Science Fiction in the Mainstream," *Magazine of Fantasy and Science Fiction* 87(4/5): 8-10. October 1994.

___ Service, Pamela F. "On Writing Sci Fi and Fantasy for Kids," *ALAN Review* 19(3): 16-18. Spring 1992.

___ Stanley, Dick. "Philosophy Teacher Hits Warp Speed; *Star Trek* Boldly Explored in Class," *Austin (TX) American Statesman* Sec. B, pp.1, 6. March 7, 1993.

___ Sutin, Lawrence. "The Case for Science Fiction," *Hungry Mind Review* pp.22-23. Winter 1995/1996.

___ Underwood, Elaine. "Spencer Tests Sci-Fi On-Site TV," *Brandweek* 36(23): 3. June 5, 1995.

___ Weyland, Jack. **Megapowers: Science Fact vs. Science Fiction.** Toronto: Kids Can Press, 1992. 78pp. (Cf. OCLC)

USSR
___ "The Book Market in the Former USSR, Part One, 1976-1987," *Locus* 29(1): 40-41, 71. July 1992.

___ *Fear* in Moscow," *Locus* 28(2): 49. August 1992.

___ "(Russian) Agent's Corner," *Locus* 28(2): 46, 49. August 1992.

___ "SF in Estonia: 1992," *Locus* 29(1): 41. July 1992.

___ "SF in Russia," *Locus* 29(6): 48. December 1992.

USSR (continued)
___ "SF in the (Former) Soviet Union," *Locus* 28(1): 42, 73. January 1992.

___ "SF in Ukraine: 1992," *Locus* 29(1): 41. July 1992.

___ "Strugatsky, Arkady (Obituary)," *Science Fiction Chronicle* 13(4): 12. January 1992.

___ "Zamiatin, Evangii Ivanovich," in: Vronskaya, Jeanne, ed. **A Biographical Dictionary of the Soviet Union 1917-1988.** London: K. G. Sauer, 1989. pp.482.

___ Baehr, Stephen L. **The Paradise Myth in Eighteenth-Century Russia: Utopian Patterns in Early Secular Russian Literature and Culture.** Stanford, CA: Stanford University Press, 1991. 308pp.

___ Bartholomew, Frank M. "The Russian Utopia," in: Sullivan, E. D. S., ed. **The Utopian Vision.** San Diego, CA: San Diego University Press, 1983. pp.69-92.

___ Booker, M. Keith. **The Dystopian Impulse in Modern Literature: Fiction as Social Criticism.** Westport, CT: Greenwood, 1994. 197pp.

___ Bulychev, Kir. "Letter From Moscow," *Locus* 28(2): 47-48. August 1992.

___ Bulychev, Kir. "Letter From Moscow," *Locus* 30(4): 41-43, 62. April 1993.

___ Clark, Katerina. "The Changing Image of Science and Technology in Soviet Literature," in: Graham, Loren R., ed. **Science and the Soviet Social Order.** Cambridge: Harvard University Press, 1990. pp.259-298.

___ Gomel, Elana. "The Poetics of Censorship: Allegory as Form and Ideology in the Novels of Arkady and Boris Strugatsky," *Science Fiction Studies* 22(1): 87-105. March 1995.

___ Howell, Yvonne H. **Apocalyptic Realism: The Science Fiction of Arkady and Boris Strugatsky.** Ph.D. Dissertation, University of Michigan, 1990. 232pp.

___ Kononenko, V. O. **Neznani svity fantastyky: rekomendattsiinyi bibliohrafichnyi pokazhchyk**, by V. O. Kononenko and V. M. Loi. Kylv: Derzhavan biblioteke Ukrainy, 1992. 35pp. [Not seen.]

___ Kuchment, Mark. "Bridging the Two Cultures: The Emergence of Scientific Prose," in: Graham, Loren R., ed. **Science and the Soviet Social Order.** Cambridge: Harvard University Press, 1990. pp.335-340.

___ Nisbet, Peter. "The Response to Science and Technology in the Visual Arts," in: Graham, Loren R., ed. **Science and the Soviet Social Order.** Cambridge: Harvard University Press, 1990. pp.341-358.

___ Oswald, Ingrid. "Sowjetische Science Fiction Literatur als soziologisches Erkenntnismittel," *Osteuropa* 41(4): 393-405. 1991.

___ Pedrotti, Louis. "Warfare Celestial and Terrestrial: Osip Senkovsky's 1833 Russian Science Fantasy," in: Slusser, George and Eric S. Rabkin, eds. **Fights of Fancy: Armed Conflict in Science Fiction and Fantasy.** Athens, GA: University of Georgia Press, 1993. pp.49-58.

___ Ryurikov, Yury. "Depicting the New Communist World in Science Fiction," *Current Digest of the Soviet Press* 12(10):13-17. April 6, 1990. (Abstracted from *Novy Mir* No. 12, December 1959, pp.228-245.)

___ Stanley, John. "Early Soviet Space-Race Victory," *San Francisco (CA) Chronicle* Sec. DAT, p. 34. April 12, 1992.

___ Stites, Richard. "World Outlook and Inner Fears in Soviet Science Fiction," in: Graham, Loren R., ed. **Science and the Soviet Social Order.** Cambridge: Harvard University Press, 1990. pp.299-324.

UTOPIA
___ "Dinosaurs and Lost Worlds," *Literature Base* 3(4): 22-25. October 1992.

___ Adorisio, Ilio. "L'utopia ed i segni dell'economia," in: Saccaro Del Buffa, Giuseppa and Lewis, Arthur O., eds. **Utopie per gli Anni Ottana.** Rome: Gangemi Editore, 1986. pp.185-195.

___ Adorisio, Ilio. "Ucronia in Oiconomia. Considerazioni sulla cronofagia della societa industriale," in: Saccaro Del Buffa, Giuseppa and Lewis, Arthur O., eds. **Utopia e Modernita: Teorie e prassi utopiche nell'eta moderna e postmoderna.** Rome: Gangemi Editore, 1989. pp.237-276.

___ Albinski, Nan B. "Australia in the 1890s; Depression, Socialism, Utopia," in: Saccaro Del Buffa, Giuseppa and Lewis, Arthur O., eds. **Utopia e Modernita: Teorie e prassi utopiche nell'eta moderna e postmoderna.** Rome: Gangemi Editore, 1989. pp.1019-1032.

___ Albinski, Nan B. "Utopia Reconsidered: Women Novelists and Nineteenth-Century Utopian Visions," *Signs: Journal of Women in Culture and Society* 13(4): 830-841. Summer 1988.

___ Aldiss, Brian W. "Utopia: Dream or Pipe Dream?," *Locus* 32(5): 41, 66. May 1994.

___ Alier, Juan M. "Ecological Economics and Concrete Utopias," *Utopian Studies* 3(1): 39-52. 1992.

UTOPIA (continued)

___ Dunne, Linda. "Mothers and Monsters in Sarah Robinson Scott's **Millenium Hall**," in: Donaworth, Jane L. and Kolmerten, Carol A., eds. **Utopian and Science Fiction by Women: Worlds of Difference.** Syracuse, NY: Syracuse University Press, 1994. pp.54-72.

___ Eisenmann, Stephen. **Designing Utopia: The Art of William Morris and His Circle: Katonah Museum of Art, February 16 through April 12, 1992.** Katonah, NY: Katonah Museum of Art, 1992. 39pp.

___ Erickson, John. "The Ghost in the Machine: Gilliam's Postmodern Response in **Brazil** to the Orwellian Dystopia of **Nineteen Eighty-Four**," *Utopian Studies* 4(2): 26-34. 1993.

___ Erisan, Wendy E. "Inverting the Ideal World: Carnival and the Carnivalesque in Contemporary Utopian Science Fiction," *Extrapolation* 36(4): 331-344. Winter 1995.

___ Erzgräber, Willi. "Aldous Huxley: **Brave New World** (1932)," in: Heuermann, Hartmut and Lange, Bernd-Peter, eds. **Die Utopie in der angloamerikanischen Literatur: Interpretationen.** Düsseldorf: Bagel, 1984. pp.196-218.

___ Fausett, David. **Writing the New World: Imaginary Voyages and Utopias of the Great Southern Land.** Syracuse, NY: Syracuse University Press, 1993. 237pp.

___ Firpo, Luigi. "Per una definizione de Utopia," in: Saccaro Del Buffa, Giuseppa and Lewis, Arthur O., eds. **Utopie per gli Anni Ottana.** Rome: Gangemi Editore, 1986. pp.801-811.

___ Fitting, Peter. "Beyond the Wasteland: A Feminist in Cyberspace," *Utopian Studies* 5(2): 4-15. 1994.

___ Fitting, Peter. "Ideological Foreclosure and Utopian Discourse," in: Saccaro Del Buffa, Giuseppa and Lewis, Arthur O., eds. **Utopia e Modernita: Teorie e prassi utopiche nell'eta moderna e postmoderna.** Rome: Gangemi Editore, 1989. pp.541-552.

___ Fitting, Peter. "Reconsiderations of the Separatist Paradigm in Recent Feminist Science Fiction," *Science Fiction Studies* 19(1): 32-48. March 1992.

___ Fitting, Peter. "Utopian Effects/Utopian Pleasure," in: Slusser, George E. and Rabkin, Eric S., eds. **Styles of Creation: Aesthetic Technique and the Creation of Fictional Worlds.** Athens: University of Georgia Press, 1992. pp.153-165.

___ Fitting, Peter. "What Is Utopian Film? An Introductory Taxonomy," *Utopian Studies* 4(2): 1-17. 1993.

___ Flieger, Verlyn. "Elves, Eden, and Utopia: Tolkien's Impossible Dream," in: Saccaro Del Buffa, Giuseppa and Lewis, Arthur O., eds. **Utopie per gli Anni Ottana.** Rome: Gangemi Editore, 1986. pp.419-426.

___ Flinn, Caryl. **Strains of Utopia: Gender, Nostalgia, and Hollywood Film Music.** Princeton, NJ: Princeton University Press, 1992. 195pp.

___ Formichetti, G. "Manoscritti ed immagini di Tommaso Campanella. Orientamenti de recerca," by G. Formichetti, O. Lucchesi, P. Sagi and F. Troncarelli. in: Saccaro Del Buffa, Giuseppa and Lewis, Arthur O., eds. **Utopie per gli Anni Ottana.** Rome: Gangemi Editore, 1986. pp.587-590.

___ Fortunati, Vita. "The Metamorphosis of the Apocalyptic Myth: From Utopia to Science Fiction," in: Kumar, Krishan and Bann, Stephen, eds. **Utopias and the Millennium.** London: Reaktion Books, 1993. pp.81-89.

___ Francescato, Donata. "Le comuni familiari: riflessioni dopo un decennio," in: Colombo, Arrigo and Quarta, Cosimo, eds. **Il Destino della Famiglia nell'Utopia.** Bari: Edizione Dedalo, 1991. pp.399-404.

___ Franko, Carol. "Working the 'In Between': Kim Stanley Robinson's Utopian Fiction," *Science Fiction Studies* 21(2): 191-211. July 1994.

___ Freeman, John. "Discourse on More's **Utopia**: Pretext/Postscript," *ELH* 59(2): 289-312. Summer 1992.

___ Freeman, John. "More's Place in 'No Place': The Self-Fashioning Transaction in **Utopia**," *Texas Studies in Literature and Language* 34(2): 197-217. Summer 1992.

___ Freese, Peter. "Kurt Vonnegut: **Cat's Cradle** (1963)," in: Heuermann, Hartmut and Lange, Bernd-Peter, eds. **Die Utopie in der angloamerikanischen Literatur: Interpretationen.** Düsseldorf: Bagel, 1984. pp.283-309.

___ Freibert, Lucy M. "The Role of the Artist in the Commune," in: Saccaro Del Buffa, Giuseppa and Lewis, Arthur O., eds. **Utopie per gli Anni Ottana.** Rome: Gangemi Editore, 1986. pp.397-414.

___ Friedman, Regien-Mihal. "Capitals of Sorrow: From **Metropolis** to **Brazil**," *Utopian Studies* 4(2): 35-43. 1993.

___ Gaillard, Roger. **Bienvenue en Utopie**, by Roger Gaillard and Felicie Girardin. Yverdon-les-Bains, Switzerland: Maison d'Ailleurs, 1991. 183pp. [Not seen.]

___ Gardiner, Michael. "Bakhtin's Carnival: Utopia as Critique," *Utopian Studies* 3(2): 21-49. 1992.

___ Gardiner, Michael. "Utopia and Everyday Life in French Social Thought," *Utopian Studies* 6(2): 90-123. 1995.

UTOPIA (continued)

___ Garno, Diana M. "Gender Dilemmas: Equality and Rights for Icarian Women," *Utopian Studies* 6(2): 52-74. 1995.

___ Garrett, John C. **Hope or Disillusion: Three Versions of Utopia: Nathaniel Hawthorne, Samuel Butler, George Orwell.** Christchurch, NZ: University of Canterbury Publications Committee, 1984. 69pp.

___ Gasparini, Alberto. "Utopia e carisma nell'organizzazione. Discorsi sulle asimmetrie tra ambiente e Nomadelfia e sulla loro proiezioine al futuro," in: Saccaro Del Buffa, Giuseppa and Lewis, Arthur O., eds. **Utopia e Modernita: Teorie e prassi utopiche nell'eta moderna e postmoderna.** Rome: Gangemi Editore, 1989. pp.1087-1124.

___ Genovese, E. N. "Paradise and the Golden Age: Ancient Origins of the Heavenly Utopia," in: Sullivan, E. D. S., ed. **The Utopian Vision.** San Diego, CA: San Diego University Press, 1983. pp.9-28.

___ Geoghegan, Vincent. "The Utopian Past: Memory and History in Edward Bellamy's **Looking Backward** and William Morris's **News From Nowhere**," *Utopian Studies* 3(2): 75-90. 1992.

___ Gies, Joseph. "Looking Forward to Utopia," *VocEd* 57(1): 30-31. January/February 1982.

___ Golffing, Francis. **Possibility: An Essay in Utopian Vision.** New York: P. Lang, 1991. 157pp. [Not seen.]

___ Gordon, Walter M. "Dialogue, Myth and More's Utopian Drama," *Cithara* 25(1): 19-34. November 1985.

___ Green, Ernest J. "The Social Functions of Utopian Architecture," *Utopian Studies* 4(1): 1-13. 1993.

___ Green, Michelle G. "There Goes the Neighborhood: Octavia Butler's Demand for Diversity in Utopias," in: Donawerth, Jane L. and Kolmerten, Carol A., eds. **Utopian and Science Fiction by Women: Worlds of Difference.** Syracuse, NY: Syracuse University Press, 1994. pp.166-189.

___ Groeben, Norbert. "Frauen--Science Fiction--Utopie: Vom Ende aller Utopie(n) zue Neugeburt einer literarischen Gattung?," *Internationales Archiv für Sozialgeschicte der Deutschen Literatur* 19(2): 173-206. 1994.

___ Grossman, Kathryn M. "The Ideal Community of George Sand's **La Petite Fadette**," *Utopian Studies* 6(1): 19-29. 1995.

___ Grossman, Kathryn M. "Woman as Temptress: The Way to (Br)otherhood in Science Fiction Dystopias," in: Saccaro Del Buffa, Giuseppa and Lewis, Arthur O., eds. **Utopie per gli Anni Ottana.** Rome: Gangemi Editore, 1986. pp.489-498.

___ Guardamagna, Daniela. **Analisi dell'incubo: l'utopia negativa da Swift alla fantascienza.** Roma: Bulzoni, 1980. 237pp. [Not seen.]

___ Guarneri, Carl J. "The Americanization of Utopia: Fourierism and the Dilemma of Utopian Dissent in the United States," *Utopian Studies* 5(1): 72-88. 1994.

___ Guillerme, Jacques. "Teleghaphe el territoire; notes sur l'imaginaire del reseaux," in: Saccaro Del Buffa, Giuseppa and Lewis, Arthur O., eds. **Utopie per gli Anni Ottana.** Rome: Gangemi Editore, 1986. pp.329-342.

___ Hadomi, Leah. **[Between Hope and Doubt: The Story of Utopia].** Israel: Hakibbutz Hameuchad Publishing House, 1989. 208pp. (In Hebrew) [Not seen.]

___ Hadomi, Leah. "Islands of the Living: Death and Dying in Utopian Fiction," *Utopian Studies* 6(1): 85-101. 1995.

___ Hansen, Olaf. "Edward Bellamy: **Looking Backward: 2000-1887** (1888)," in: Heuermann, Hartmut and Lange, Bernd-Peter, eds. **Die Utopie in der angloamerikanischen Literatur: Interpretationen.** Düsseldorf: Bagel, 1984. pp.103-119.

___ Hansot, Elisabeth. "Selves, Survival and Resistance in **The Handmaid's Tale**," *Utopian Studies* 5(2): 56-69. 1994.

___ Hardesty, John J. "Illusions of Endless Affluence," in: Sullivan, E. D. S., ed. **The Utopian Vision.** San Diego, CA: San Diego University Press, 1983. pp.51-68.

___ Hartnett, James R. "Black Power in Utopia," in: Saccaro Del Buffa, Giuseppa and Lewis, Arthur O., eds. **Utopie per gli Anni Ottana.** Rome: Gangemi Editore, 1986. pp.435-442.

___ Haschak, Paul G. **Utopian/Dystopian Literature: A Bibliography of Literary Criticism.** Metuchen, NJ: Scarecrow, 1994. 370pp.

___ Hatch, Richard C. "The Ideology of Work and the Architecture of Utopia," in: Saccaro Del Buffa, Giuseppa and Lewis, Arthur O., eds. **Utopia e Modernita: Teorie e prassi utopiche nell'eta moderna e postmoderna.** Rome: Gangemi Editore, 1989. pp.175-186.

___ Haynes, Roslynn D. "Science, Myth and Utopia," in: Filmer, Kath, ed. **Twentieth-Century Fantasists: Essays in Culture, Society and Belief in Twentieth Century Mythopoeic Literature.** New York: St. Martin's, 1992. pp.8-22.

UTOPIA

UTOPIA (continued)

___ Heuermann, Hartmut. "Ray Bradbury: **Fahrenheit 451** (1953)," in: Heuermann, Hartmut and Lange, Bernd-Peter, eds. **Die Utopie in der angloamerikanischen Literatur: Interpretationen.** Düsseldorf: Bagel, 1984. pp.259-282.

___ Heuermann, Hartmut, ed. **Die Utopie in der Angloamerikanischen Literatur: Interpretationen,** ed. by Hartmut Heuermann and Bernd-Peter Lange. Düsseldorf: Bagel, 1984. 370pp.

___ Hillgärtner, Rüdiger. "William Morris: **News from Nowhere; Or, an Epoch of Rest, Being Some Chapters from a Utopian Romance** (1890)," in: Heuermann, Hartmut and Lange, Bernd-Peter, eds. **Die Utopie in der angloamerikanischen Literatur: Interpretationen.** Düsseldorf: Bagel, 1984. pp.120-138.

___ Hoover, Kenneth R. "Mondragon's Answers to Utopia's Problems," *Utopian Studies* 3(2): 1-20. 1992.

___ Hornigk, Frank. "Die Literatur bleibt zuständig: Ein Versuch über das Verhältnis on Literatur, Utopie und Politik in der DDR--am Ende der DDR," *Germanic Review* 67(3): 99-105. Summer 1992.

___ Hottois, Gilbert. " 'Language et technique' ou 'Du site philosophique de la Science-Fiction contemporaine'," in: Saccaro Del Buffa, Giuseppa and Lewis, Arthur O., eds. **Utopia e Modernita: Teorie e prassi utopiche nell'eta moderna e postmoderna.** Rome: Gangemi Editore, 1989. pp.519-528.

___ Hovana, Ion. "Visioni urbanistiche ottocentesche in Romania," in: Saccaro Del Buffa, Giuseppa and Lewis, Arthur O., eds. **Utopia e Modernita: Teorie e prassi utopiche nell'eta moderna e postmoderna.** Rome: Gangemi Editore, 1989. pp.385-400.

___ Huckle, Patricia. "Women in Utopia," in: Sullivan, E. D. S., ed. **The Utopian Vision.** San Diego, CA: San Diego University Press, 1983. pp.115-136.

___ Imbroscio, Carmelina. "Elementi de rovesciamento speculare nella narrativa utopica del settecento francese," in: Saccaro Del Buffa, Giuseppa and Lewis, Arthur O., eds. **Utopia e Modernita: Teorie e prassi utopiche nell'eta moderna e postmoderna.** Rome: Gangemi Editore, 1989. pp.533-540.

___ Jacobs, Naomi. "The Frozen Landscape in Women's Utopian and Science Fiction," in: Donawerth, Jane L. and Kolmerten, Carol A., eds. **Utopian and Science Fiction by Women: Worlds of Difference.** Syracuse, NY: Syracuse University Press, 1994. pp.190-202.

___ Jacobs, Naomi. "**Islandia:** Plotting Utopian Desire," *Utopian Studies* 6(2): 75-89. 1996.

___ James, Louis. "From Robinson to Robina, and Beyond: **Robinson Crusoe** as a Utopian Concept," in: Kumar, Krishan and Bann, Stephen, eds. **Utopias and the Millennium.** London: Reaktion Books, 1993. pp.33-45.

___ Johnson, Judith E. "Women and Vampires: Nightmare or Utopia?," *Kenyon Review* 15(1): 72-80. Winter 1993.

___ Karp, Andrew. "The Need for Boundries: Homer's Critique of the Phaeakian Utopia in the **Odyssey**," *Utopian Studies* 6(2): 25-34. 1995.

___ Karter, Wolfgang. "Jack London: **The Iron Heel** (1908)," in: Heuermann, Hartmut and Lange, Bernd-Peter, eds. **Die Utopie in der angloamerikanischen Literatur: Interpretationen.** Düsseldorf: Bagel, 1984. pp.176-195.

___ Keinhorst, Annette. "Emancipatory Projection: An Introduction to Women's Critical Utopias," *Women's Studies* 14(2): 91-100. 1987.

___ Keinhorst, Annette. **Utopien von Frauen in der zeitgenössischen Literatur der USA.** Frankfurt-am-Main: Peter Lang, 1985. 230pp.

___ Keller, Chester Z. "Human Nature: Ecosystemic Limits and Techne. Some Utopian Implications," in: Saccaro Del Buffa, Giuseppa and Lewis, Arthur O., eds. **Utopia e Modernita: Teorie e prassi utopiche nell'eta moderna e postmoderna.** Rome: Gangemi Editore, 1989. pp.131-142.

___ Keller, Chester Z. "Imitations of Utopia: Some Readings From Nature," in: Saccaro Del Buffa, Giuseppa and Lewis, Arthur O., eds. **Utopie per gli Anni Ottana.** Rome: Gangemi Editore, 1986. pp.89-98.

___ Kelley, Scott. "Photo-Utopia and Poetic Representations of the Impossible: The Utopic Figure in Modern Poetic and Photographic Discourse," *Utopian Studies* 6(1): 1-18. 1995.

___ Kessler, Carol F. "Annotated Bibliography of U.S. Women's Utopian Fiction, 1836-1988," in: Kessler, Carol F., ed. **Daring to Dream: Utopian Fiction by United States Women Before 1950.** Second Edition. Syracuse, NY: Syracuse University Press, 1995. pp.247-304.

___ Kessler, Carol F. "Annotated Bibliography: United States Women's Utopian Fiction, 1836-1983," in: Kessler, Carol K., ed. **Daring to Dream: Utopian Stories by United States Women, 1836-1919.** Boston, MA: Pandora Press, 1984. pp.233-266.

UTOPIA (continued)

___ Kessler, Carol F. **Charlotte Perkins Gilman: Her Progress Toward Utopia With Selected Writings.** Liverpool: Liverpool University Press, 1995. 316pp.

___ Kessler, Carol F. "Consider Her Ways: The Cultural Work of Charlotte Perkins Gilman's Pragmatopian Stories, 1908-1913," in: Donawerth, Jane L. and Kolmerten, Carol A., eds. **Utopian and Science Fiction by Women: Worlds of Difference.** Syracuse, NY: Syracuse University Press, 1994. pp.126-136.

___ Kessler, Carol F. "Daring to Dream: Utopian Fiction by United States Women," in: Saccaro Del Buffa, Giuseppa and Lewis, Arthur O., eds. **Utopie per gli Anni Ottana.** Rome: Gangemi Editore, 1986. pp.455-466.

___ Kessler, Carol F. **Daring to Dream: Utopian Fiction by United States Women, 1836-1919.** 2nd ed. Syracuse, NY: Syracuse University Press, 1995. 326pp.

___ Kessler, Carol F. "Introduction," in: Kessler, Carol F., ed. **Daring to Dream: Utopian Fiction by United States Women Before 1950.** Second Edition. Syracuse, NY: Syracuse University Press, 1995. pp.xiii-xxviii.

___ Kessler, Carol F. "Introduction: Feminist Utopias by United States Women," in: Kessler, Carol K., ed. **Daring to Dream: Utopian Stories by United States Women, 1836-1919.** Boston, MA: Pandora Press, 1984. pp.1-25.

___ Khanna, Lee C. "Contemporary Utopian Fiction: New Strategies for Change," in: Saccaro Del Buffa, Giuseppa and Lewis, Arthur O., eds. **Utopia e Modernita: Teorie e prassi utopiche nell'eta moderna e postmoderna.** Rome: Gangemi Editore, 1989. pp.587-595.

___ Khanna, Lee C. "Frontiers of Imagination: Women's World," in: Saccaro Del Buffa, Giuseppa and Lewis, Arthur O., eds. **Utopie per gli Anni Ottana.** Rome: Gangemi Editore, 1986. pp.467-476.

___ Khanna, Lee C. "The Subject of Utopia," in: Donawerth, Jane L. and Kolmerten, Carol A., eds. **Utopian and Science Fiction by Women: Worlds of Difference.** Syracuse, NY: Syracuse University Press, 1994. pp.15-34.

___ Klarer, Mario. **Frau und Utopie: feministische Literaturtheorie und utopischer Diskurs im angloamerikanischen Roman.** Darmstadt: Wissenschaftliche Buchgesellschaft, 1993. 164pp. [Not seen.]

___ Klaus, H. Gustav. "Thomas Spence: **Description of Spensonia** (1795)," in: Heuermann, Hartmut and Lange, Bernd-Peter, eds. **Die Utopie in der angloamerikanischen Literatur: Interpretationen.** Düsseldorf: Bagel, 1984. pp.60-79.

___ Klein, Jürgen. "Samuel Butler **Erewhon** (1872)," by Jürgen Klein and Klaus Zöllner. in: Heuermann, Hartmut and Lange, Bernd-Peter, eds. **Die Utopie in der angloamerikanischen Literatur: Interpretationen.** Düsseldorf: Bagel, 1984. pp.80-102.

___ Klinger, Cornelia. "Radikalfeminismus, Science Fiction und das Verhältnis zur Natur," in: Grabher, Gudrun M. and Devine, Marureen, eds. **Women in Search of Literary Space.** Tübingen: Gunter Narr Verlag, 1992. pp.180-197.

___ Knapp, Jeffrey. **An Empire Nowhere: England, America, and Literature from Utopia to The Tempest.** Berkeley: University of California Press, 1992. 387pp.

___ Kolmerten, Carol A. "Frances Wright and the Search for Equality," in: Saccaro Del Buffa, Giuseppa and Lewis, Arthur O., eds. **Utopia e Modernita: Teorie e prassi utopiche nell'eta moderna e postmoderna.** Rome: Gangemi Editore, 1989. pp.987-1002.

___ Kolmerten, Carol A. "Texts and Contexts: American Women Envision Utopia, 1890-1920," in: Donawerth, Jane L. and Kolmerten, Carol A., eds. **Utopian and Science Fiction by Women: Worlds of Difference.** Syracuse, NY: Syracuse University Press, 1994. pp.107-125.

___ Kolmerten, Carol A. "Women Seeing Utopia: Patterns in Utopian Literature, 1880-1915," in: Saccaro Del Buffa, Giuseppa and Lewis, Arthur O., eds. **Utopie per gli Anni Ottana.** Rome: Gangemi Editore, 1986. pp.499-510.

___ Kraiski, Giorgio. "Aspetti dell'utopia dostoievskiana," in: Saccaro Del Buffa, Giuseppa and Lewis, Arthur O., eds. **Utopie per gli Anni Ottana.** Rome: Gangemi Editore, 1986. pp.675-678.

___ Kuelen, Margarete. **Radical Imagination: Feminist Conceptions of the Future in Ursula Le Guin, Marge Piercy and Sally Miller Gearhart.** Frankfurt-am-Main/New York: Peter Lang, 1991. 122pp.

___ Kumar, Krishan. "The End of Socialism? The End of Utopia? The End of History?," in: Kumar, Krishan and Bann, Stephen, eds. **Utopias and the Millennium.** London: Reaktion Books, 1993. pp.63-80.

___ Kumar, Krishan. "A Pilgrimage of Hope: William Morris's Journey to Utopia," *Utopian Studies* 5(1): 89-107. 1994.

___ Kumar, Krishan, ed. **Utopias and the Millennium,** ed. by Krishan Kumar and Stephen Bann. London: Reaktion Books, 1993. 164pp.

UTOPIA (continued)

___ Moylan, Thomas P. **Figures of Hope: The Critical Utopia of the 1970s. The Revival, Destruction, and Transformation of Utopian Writing in the United States: A Study of the Ideology, Structure , and Historical Context of Representative Texts.** Ph.D. Dissertation, University of Wisconsin, Milwaukee, 1981. 290pp.

___ Moylan, Thomas P. "Utopia Is When Our Lives Matter: Reading Kim Stanley Robinson's **Pacific Edge**," *Utopian Studies* 6(2): 1-25. 1995.

___ Mucci, Egidio. "Utopia e immaginario nell'architettura degli anni '60," in: Saccaro Del Buffa, Giuseppa and Lewis, Arthur O., eds. **Utopie per gli Anni Ottana.** Rome: Gangemi Editore, 1986. pp.387-394.

___ Mucillo, Maria. "Aristotelismo, platonismo ed ermetismo ne 'La citta felice' de Francesco patrizi da Cherso," in: Saccaro Del Buffa, Giuseppa and Lewis, Arthur O., eds. **Utopie per gli Anni Ottana.** Rome: Gangemi Editore, 1986. pp.553-578.

___ Mucillo, Maria. "Eta dell'Oro e tempo ciclico in Francesco Partizi," in: Saccaro Del Buffa, Giuseppa and Lewis, Arthur O., eds. **Utopia e Modernita: Teorie e prassi utopiche nell'eta moderna e postmoderna.** Rome: Gangemi Editore, 1989. pp.785-826.

___ Murdoch, Norman H. "Rose Culture and Social Reform: Edward Bellamy's **Looking Backward** (1888) and William Booth's **Darkest England and the Way Out** (1890)," *Utopian Studies* 3(2): 91-101. 1992.

___ Muzzarelli, Maria G. "Christine de Pizan," in: Colombo, Arrigo and Quarta, Cosimo, eds. **Il Destino della Famiglia nell'Utopia.** Bari: Edizione Dedalo, 1991. pp.125-143.

___ Myers, Michael. "Visions of Tomorrow: German Science Fiction and Socialist Utopian Novels of the Late Nineteenth Century," *Selecta* (Corvallis) 14: 63-69. 1993.

___ Nebuloni, Roberto. "I Francofortesi: Pro e contro la freddezza borghese," in: Colombo, Arrigo and Quarta, Cosimo, eds. **Il Destino della Famiglia nell'Utopia.** Bari: Edizione Dedalo, 1991. pp.285-307.

___ Neustadter, Roger. "Back From the Future: Childhood as Utopia," *Extrapolation* 35(2): 145-154. Summer 1994.

___ Neverow, Vara. "The Politics of Incorporation and Embodiment: **Woman on the Edge of Time** and **He, She and It** as Feminist Epistemologies of Resistance," *Utopian Studies* 5(2): 16-35. 1994.

___ Norton, Mary F. "Visions of the Future: Utopian and Apocalyptic Designs," *CEA Forum* 23(2)/24(1): 15-20. Summer/Winter 1993/1994.

___ O'Neill, John. "*McTopia*: Eating Time," in: Kumar, Krishan and Bann, Stephen, eds. **Utopias and the Millennium.** London: Reaktion Books, 1993. pp.129-137.

___ Otten, Kurt. **Der englische Roman: Entwurfe der Gegenwart: Ideenroman und Utopie.** Berlin: E. Schmidt, 1990. 243pp. [Not seen.]

___ Paccini, Riccardo. "La 'Fabbrica del Grande Albergo Generale dei Poveri' a Modena (1764-71)," in: Saccaro Del Buffa, Giuseppa and Lewis, Arthur O., eds. **Utopie per gli Anni Ottana.** Rome: Gangemi Editore, 1986. pp.263-274.

___ Paolini, Lorenzo. "L'ereria medevale," in: Colombo, Arrigo and Quarta, Cosimo, eds. **Il Destino della Famiglia nell'Utopia.** Bari: Edizione Dedalo, 1991. pp.79-124.

___ Parapetti, Roberto. "Restauro e fortuna dell'immaginario: il caso della Torre di Babele," in: Saccaro Del Buffa, Giuseppa and Lewis, Arthur O., eds. **Utopia e Modernita: Teorie e prassi utopiche nell'eta moderna e postmoderna.** Rome: Gangemi Editore, 1989. pp.369-384.

___ Pavia, Rosario. "Dall'utopia dell'edilizia pubblica: Orgini della cooperazione de abatazione in Italia," in: Saccaro Del Buffa, Giuseppa and Lewis, Arthur O., eds. **Utopie per gli Anni Ottana.** Rome: Gangemi Editore, 1986. pp.379-386.

___ Pavkovic, Aleksandar. "Prosperity and Intellectual Needs: The Credibility and Coherence of More's **Utopia**," *Utopian Studies* 4(1): 26-37. 1993.

___ Perez, Ysidore R. "The Value of Utopian Thought: A Platonic View," in: Saccaro Del Buffa, Giuseppa and Lewis, Arthur O., eds. **Utopie per gli Anni Ottana.** Rome: Gangemi Editore, 1986. pp.543-552.

___ Perotti, Stefano. "Spazio e utopia nelle societa post-industriale," in: Saccaro Del Buffa, Giuseppa and Lewis, Arthur O., eds. **Utopia e Modernita: Teorie e prassi utopiche nell'eta moderna e postmoderna.** Rome: Gangemi Editore, 1989. pp.277-286.

___ Peyser, Thomas G. "Reproducing Utopia: Charlotte Perkins Gilman and **Herland**," *Studies in American Fiction* 20(1): 1-16. Spring 1992.

___ Pfaelzer, Jean. "Subjectivity as Feminist Utopia," in: Donawerth, Jane L. and Kolmerten, Carol A., eds. **Utopian and Science Fiction by Women: Worlds of Difference.** Syracuse, NY: Syracuse University Press, 1994. pp.93-106.

UTOPIA (continued)

___ Piccaluga, Gabriella F. "Il pauperismo a Milano nell'eta de Maria Teresa: Utopia e realita," in: Saccaro Del Buffa, Giuseppa and Lewis, Arthur O., eds. **Utopie per gli Anni Ottana.** Rome: Gangemi Editore, 1986. pp.247-262.

___ Pleithner, Regina. "Zwei Mondreisen des 17. Jahrhunderts: Voyages imaginaires oder Reiseutopien? Beitrage zum Kolloquium der Arbeitsgruppe Kultrugeschichte des Barockzeitalters an der Herzog-August-Bibliothek Wolfenbuttle von 10. Bis 12. Juli 1989," in: Pleithner, Regina, ed. **Reisen des Barock: Selbst- und Fremderfahrung und ihre Darstellung.** Bonn: Romanistischer, 1991. pp.75-87.

___ Poldervaart, Saskia. "Utopian Socialism in Holland Around 1900: Strategies and Gender," *Utopian Studies* 6(1): 51-64. 1995.

___ Popescu, Grigore A. "Concezioni utopiche verso la meta del l'Ottocento nei Principati Romeni," in: Saccaro Del Buffa, Giuseppa and Lewis, Arthur O., eds. **Utopia e Modernita: Teorie e prassi utopiche nell'eta moderna e postmoderna.** Rome: Gangemi Editore, 1989. pp.919-930.

___ Prevos, Andre J. M. "A Comment About the Utopian Character of the Afro-American Blues," in: Saccaro Del Buffa, Giuseppa and Lewis, Arthur O., eds. **Utopia e Modernita: Teorie e prassi utopiche nell'eta moderna e postmoderna.** Rome: Gangemi Editore, 1989. pp.1013-1018.

___ Prevos, Andre J. M. "Planning and Building the Utopian Village: The Icarian Settlements in Iowa, 1853-1898," in: Saccaro Del Buffa, Giuseppa and Lewis, Arthur O., eds. **Utopia e Modernita: Teorie e prassi utopiche nell'eta moderna e postmoderna.** Rome: Gangemi Editore, 1989. pp.971-986.

___ Proietti, Salvator. "Frederick Philip Grove's Version of Pastoral Utopianism," *Science-Fiction Studies* 19(3): 361-377. November 1992.

___ Prouty, William. "**The Tempest**: Shakespeare's Anti-Utopia Tract," in: Saccaro Del Buffa, Giuseppa and Lewis, Arthur O., eds. **Utopie per gli Anni Ottana.** Rome: Gangemi Editore, 1986. pp.579-586.

___ Pujia, Roberto. "La scienza luciferian. Monismo metodologico ed utopia nella epistemologia moderna," in: Saccaro Del Buffa, Giuseppa and Lewis, Arthur O., eds. **Utopie per gli Anni Ottana.** Rome: Gangemi Editore, 1986. pp.107-121.

___ Pujia, Roberto. "Scienza, Utopia scientista e satira nell'Inghilterra dell'eta augustea: l'antifilosofia di J. Swift," in: Saccaro Del Buffa, Giuseppa and Lewis, Arthur O., eds. **Utopia e Modernita: Teorie e prassi utopiche nell'eta moderna e postmoderna.** Rome: Gangemi Editore, 1989. pp.877-890.

___ Quarta, Cosimo. "Le regioni della conservazione: Thomas More," in: Colombo, Arrigo and Quarta, Cosimo, eds. **Il Destino della Famiglia nell'Utopia.** Bari: Edizione Dedalo, 1991. pp.193-221.

___ Quarta, Cosimo. **Tommaso Moro: una reinterpretazone dell'Utopia'.** Bari: Edizioni Dedalo, 1991. 434pp. [Not seen.]

___ Quistelli, Antonio. "L'utopia nella condizione post-moderna: un commento con immagini di Soleri e di Moebius," in: Saccaro Del Buffa, Giuseppa and Lewis, Arthur O., eds. **Utopie per gli Anni Ottana.** Rome: Gangemi Editore, 1986. pp.11-14.

___ Quistelli, Antonio. "Una pietra per il futuro," in: Saccaro Del Buffa, Giuseppa and Lewis, Arthur O., eds. **Utopia e Modernita: Teorie e prassi utopiche nell'eta moderna e postmoderna.** Rome: Gangemi Editore, 1989. pp.11-12.

___ Rabkin, Eric S. "The Utopian Paradox: On the Necessity of an Impossible Dream," *Foundation* No. 55: 57-65. Summer 1992.

___ Radner, John B. "The Fall and Decline: **Gulliver's Travels** and the Failure of Utopia," *Utopian Studies* 3(2): 50-74. 1992.

___ Rak, Michele. "Il modello sporco: la sociata letteraria tra l'invenzione del libro a stampa e i media elettronici," in: Saccaro Del Buffa, Giuseppa and Lewis, Arthur O., eds. **Utopia e Modernita: Teorie e prassi utopiche nell'eta moderna e postmoderna.** Rome: Gangemi Editore, 1989. pp.569-586.

___ Ramirez, Juan-Antonio. "La modernidad perfecta de la Isla-Maquina," in: Saccaro Del Buffa, Giuseppa and Lewis, Arthur O., eds. **Utopia e Modernita: Teorie e prassi utopiche nell'eta moderna e postmoderna.** Rome: Gangemi Editore, 1989. pp.467-484.

___ Rapisarda, Giusi M. L. "I'Utopia del saggismo, l'immagine della stanza chiara'". in: Saccaro Del Buffa, Giuseppa and Lewis, Arthur O., eds. **Utopia e Modernita: Teorie e prassi utopiche nell'eta moderna e postmoderna.** Rome: Gangemi Editore, 1989. pp.945-950.

___ Rapisarda, Giusi M. L. "Superuomisnmo macchinista, utopie e mito del moderno nella letteratura europea inizio Novecento," in: Saccaro Del Buffa, Giuseppa and Lewis, Arthur O., eds. **Utopie per gli Anni Ottana.** Rome: Gangemi Editore, 1986. pp.693-704.

UTOPIA (continued)

___ Raulet, Gerard. "360 Degrees in Time: Postmodern Architecture and the Question of Consensus," *Utopian Studies* 4(2): 57-65. 1993.

___ Raulet, Gerard. "Fin de l'utopie ou nouvelle utopie? Reflexions sur la condition post-moderne," in: Saccaro Del Buffa, Giuseppa and Lewis, Arthur O., eds. **Utopia e Modernita: Teorie e prassi utopiche nell'eta moderna e postmoderna**. Rome: Gangemi Editore, 1989. pp.111-127.

___ Rees, Christine. **Utopian Imagination and Eighteenth Century Fiction**. London: Longman, 1995. 296pp.

___ Relf, Jan. "Utopia the Good Breast: Coming Home to Mother," in: Kumar, Krishan and Bann, Stephen, eds. **Utopias and the Millennium**. London: Reaktion Books, 1993. pp.107-128.

___ Renna, Thomas. "More's **Utopia** and English Medieval Traditions," in: Saccaro Del Buffa, Giuseppa and Lewis, Arthur O., eds. **Utopia e Modernita: Teorie e prassi utopiche nell'eta moderna e postmoderna**. Rome: Gangemi Editore, 1989. pp.739-748.

___ Rielly, Edward J. "Irony in **Gulliver's Travels** and **Utopia**," *Utopian Studies* 3(1): 70-83. 1992.

___ Rode, Silvia A. **Franz Werfels 'Stern der Ungeborenen': die Utopie als Fiktionaler Genrediskurs und Ideengeschichte**. Ph.D. Dissertation, University of California, Los Angeles, 1993. 304pp. (DAI-A 54/03, p. 943. September 1993.)

___ Roemer, Kenneth M. "Domestic Nowheres and Androgynous Voices: The Sentimental Orgins of **Looking Backward**," in: Saccaro Del Buffa, Giuseppa and Lewis, Arthur O., eds. **Utopia e Modernita: Teorie e prassi utopiche nell'eta moderna e postmoderna**. Rome: Gangemi Editore, 1989. pp.641-654.

___ Rosenthal, Rae. "Gaskell's Feminist Utopia: The Cranfordians and the Reign of Goodwill," in: Donawerth, Jane L. and Kolmerten, Carol A., eds. **Utopian and Science Fiction by Women: Worlds of Difference**. Syracuse, NY: Syracuse University Press, 1994. pp.73-92.

___ Saccaro Del Buffa, Giuseppa. "Il II° Congresso Internazionale de Studi sulle Utopia," in: Saccaro Del Buffa, Giuseppa and Lewis, Arthur O., eds. **Utopia e Modernita: Teorie e prassi utopiche nell'eta moderna e postmoderna**. Rome: Gangemi Editore, 1989. pp.13-26.

___ Saccaro Del Buffa, Giuseppa. "Il I° Convegno Internazionale de Studi sulle utopie," in: Saccaro Del Buffa, Giuseppa and Lewis, Arthur O., eds. **Utopie per gli Anni Ottana**. Rome: Gangemi Editore, 1986. pp.35-39.

___ Saccaro Del Buffa, Giuseppa. "Le streghe tra mito e realta: l'utopia del 'gioco'," in: Saccaro Del Buffa, Giuseppa and Lewis, Arthur O., eds. **Utopia e Modernita: Teorie e prassi utopiche nell'eta moderna e postmoderna**. Rome: Gangemi Editore, 1989. pp.599-614.

___ Saccaro Del Buffa, Giuseppa. "Un'utopia dell'autorigenerazione: 'La Crisalide' di Bradbury," in: Saccaro Del Buffa, Giuseppa and Lewis, Arthur O., eds. **Utopie per gli Anni Ottana**. Rome: Gangemi Editore, 1986. pp.427-434.

___ Saccaro Del Buffa, Giuseppa. **Utopie e modernita: teorie e prassi utopiche nell'eta moderna e postmoderna**, by Giuseppa Saccaro Del Buffa and Arthur O. Lewis. Roma: Gangemi, 1989. 2 v., 1196pp.

___ Saccaro Del Buffa, Giuseppa. **Utopie per gli anni ottanta: studi interdisciplinari sui temi, la storia, i progetti**, by Giuseppa Saccaro Del Buffa and Arthur O. Lewis. Roma: Gangemi, 1986. 825pp.

___ Sansone, Gabriele. "Realizzare l'utopia. Le comuni in Italia negli anni settanta," in: Saccaro Del Buffa, Giuseppa and Lewis, Arthur O., eds. **Utopia e Modernita: Teorie e prassi utopiche nell'eta moderna e postmoderna**. Rome: Gangemi Editore, 1989. pp.1135-1151.

___ Sargent, Lyman T. "American Utopianism 1920-1980: Notes Toward a Study," in: Saccaro Del Buffa, Giuseppa and Lewis, Arthur O., eds. **Utopie per gli Anni Ottana**. Rome: Gangemi Editore, 1986. pp.751-762.

___ Sargent, Lyman T. "The Three Faces of Utopianism Revisited," *Utopian Studies* 5(1): 1-37. 1994.

___ Sauter-Bailliet, Theresia. "Marge Piercy: **Woman on the Edge of Time** (1976)," in: Heuermann, Hartmut and Lange, Bernd-Peter, eds. **Die Utopie in der angloamerikanischen Literatur: Interpretationen**. Düsseldorf: Bagel, 1984. pp.349-370.

___ Schaller, Hans-Wolfgang. "B. F. Skinner: **Walden Two** (1948)," in: Heuermann, Hartmut and Lange, Bernd-Peter, eds. **Die Utopie in der angloamerikanischen Literatur: Interpretationen**. Düsseldorf: Bagel, 1984. pp.219-234.

___ Schectman, Aaron H. "Perpetuating Utopia," in: Saccaro Del Buffa, Giuseppa and Lewis, Arthur O., eds. **Utopie per gli Anni Ottana**. Rome: Gangemi Editore, 1986. pp.789-797.

___ Scherer, Rene. "Fourier, la famiglia e le utopie dei Lumi," in: Colombo, Arrigo and Quarta, Cosimo, eds. **Il Destino della Famiglia nell'Utopia**. Bari: Edizione Dedalo, 1991. pp.247-263.

UTOPIA (continued)

___ Schiavone, Giuseppe. "Winstanley, un'utopia familiare nella Rivoluzione inglese," in: Colombo, Arrigo and Quarta, Cosimo, eds. **Il Destino della Famiglia nell'Utopia**. Bari: Edizione Dedalo, 1991. pp.145-166.

___ Schmidt, Jürgen. "George Orwell: **Nineteen Eighty-Four** (1949)," in: Heuermann, Hartmut and Lange, Bernd-Peter, eds. **Die Utopie in der angloamerikanischen Literatur: Interpretationen**. Düsseldorf: Bagel, 1984. pp.235-258.

___ Schültz-Güth, Gudrun. "Doris Lessing: **The Memoirs of a Survivor** (1974)," in: Heuermann, Hartmut and Lange, Bernd-Peter, eds. **Die Utopie in der angloamerikanischen Literatur: Interpretationen**. Düsseldorf: Bagel, 1984. pp.310-327.

___ Schultze, Bruno. "Herbert George Wells: **A Modern Utopia** (1903)," in: Heuermann, Hartmut and Lange, Bernd-Peter, eds. **Die Utopie in der angloamerikanischen Literatur: Interpretationen**. Düsseldorf: Bagel, 1984. pp.161-175.

___ Seeber, Hans-Ulrich. "Utopian Mentality in George Eliot's **Middlemarch** (1871/72) and in D. H. Lawrence's **The Rainbow**," *Utopian Studies* 6(1): 30-39. 1995.

___ Segal, Howard P. **Future Imperfect: The Mixed Blessings of Technology in America**. Amherst: University of Massachusetts Press, 1994. 245pp.

___ Shafi, Monika. **Utopische Entwürfe in der Literatur von Frauen**. Bern: Peter Lang, 1990. 135pp.

___ Shelton, Robert. "The Utopian Film Genre: Putting Shadows on the Silver Screen," *Utopian Studies* 4(2): 18-25. 1993.

___ Shor, Francis. "**The Iron Heel**'s Marginal(ized) Utopia," *Extrapolation* 35(3): 211-229. Fall 1994.

___ Sirianni, Carmen J. "Work and Technology in a Complex Utopia," in: Saccaro Del Buffa, Giuseppa and Lewis, Arthur O., eds. **Utopie per gli Anni Ottana**. Rome: Gangemi Editore, 1986. pp.225-235.

___ Smith, Nicholas D. "Political Activity and Ideal Economics: Two Related Utopian Themes in Aristophanic Comedy," *Utopian Studies* 3(1): 84-94. 1992.

___ Snodgrass, Mary E. **Encyclopedia of Utopian Literature**. Santa Barbara, CA: ABC-CLIO, 1995. 644pp.

___ Snyder, Lillan M. "A Search for Brotherhood, Peace, and Justice: A Description of the Icarian Movement," in: Saccaro Del Buffa, Giuseppa and Lewis, Arthur O., eds. **Utopie per gli Anni Ottana**. Rome: Gangemi Editore, 1986. pp.737-750.

___ Solivetti, Carla. "L'utopia linguistica di Velimir Chlebnikov," in: Saccaro Del Buffa, Giuseppa and Lewis, Arthur O., eds. **Utopie per gli Anni Ottana**. Rome: Gangemi Editore, 1986. pp.51-70.

___ Spies, Bernhard. "Der Anteil der sozialistischen Utopie an der Beendigung der DDR-Literatur. Am Beispiel Christoph Heins," *Germanic Review* 67(3): 112-118. Summer 1992.

___ Springman, Luke. **Comrades, Friends and Companions: Utopian Projections and Social Action in German Literature for Young People, 1926-1934**. New York: P. Lang, 1989. 242pp. [Not seen.]

___ Springman, Luke. **Comrades, Friends and Companions: Utopian Projections and Social Action in German Literature for Young People, 1926-1934**. Ph.D. Dissertation, Ohio State University, 1988. 338pp.

___ Stapleton, Amy L. **Utopias for a Dying World: Contemporary German Science Fiction's Plea for a New Ecological Awareness**. New York: Peter Lang, 1993. 158pp.

___ Steinmüller, Karlheinz. "Das Ende der Utopischen Literatur: Ein themengeschichtlicher Nachruf auf der DDR-Science-Fiction," *Germanic Review* 67(4): 166-173. Fall 1992.

___ Stella, Carmela. "Il marxismo, la rivoluzione russa," in: Colombo, Arrigo and Quarta, Cosimo, eds. **Il Destino della Famiglia nell'Utopia**. Bari: Edizione Dedalo, 1991. pp.357-382.

___ Stillman, Peter S. "A Critique of Ideal Worlds: Hegel and Marx on Modern Utopian Thought," in: Saccaro Del Buffa, Giuseppa and Lewis, Arthur O., eds. **Utopie per gli Anni Ottana**. Rome: Gangemi Editore, 1986. pp.635-674.

___ Stillman, Peter S. "Identity, Complicity, and Resistance in **The Handmaid's Tale**," by Peter S. Stillman and S. Anne Johnson. *Utopian Studies* 5(2): 70-86. 1994.

___ Stoppa, Claudio. "Il kibbuz," in: Colombo, Arrigo and Quarta, Cosimo, eds. **Il Destino della Famiglia nell'Utopia**. Bari: Edizione Dedalo, 1991. pp.339-355.

___ Suksang, Duangrudi. "Equal Partnership: Jane Hume Clapperton's Evolutionist-Socialist Utopia," *Utopian Studies* 3(1): 95-107. 1992.

___ Suksang, Duangrudi. "Overtaking Patriarchy: Crobett's and Dixie's Visions of Women," *Utopian Studies* 4(2): 74-93. 1993.

UTOPIA (continued)

___ Sullivan, E. D. S. "Place in No Place: Examples of the Ordered Society in Literature," in: Sullivan, E. D. S., ed. **The Utopian Vision**. San Diego, CA: San Diego University Press, 1983. pp.29-50.

___ Sullivan, E. D. S., ed. **The Utopian Vision: Seven Essays on the Quincentennial of Sir Thomas More**. San Diego, CA: San Diego University Press, 1983. 265pp.

___ Suvin, Darko. "Locus, Horizon and Orientation: The Concept of Possible Worlds as a Key to Utopian Studies," in: Saccaro Del Buffa, Giuseppa and Lewis, Arthur O., eds. **Utopia e Modernita: Teorie e prassi utopiche nell'eta moderna e postmoderna**. Rome: Gangemi Editore, 1989. pp.47-65.

___ Tafuri, Manfredo. "Un teatro, una 'fontana del Sil' e 'unovago monticello'. Il progetto de Alvise Cornaro per la riconfigurazione del bacino marciano," in: Saccaro Del Buffa, Giuseppa and Lewis, Arthur O., eds. **Utopie per gli Anni Ottana**. Rome: Gangemi Editore, 1986. pp.313-328.

___ Tazzi, Pier L. "Utopia e immaginariio nelle arti vesive degli anni '60 (riasunto)," in: Saccaro Del Buffa, Giuseppa and Lewis, Arthur O., eds. **Utopie per gli Anni Ottana**. Rome: Gangemi Editore, 1986. pp.415-418.

___ Tiger, Virginia. " 'The words had been right and necessary': Doris Lessing's Transformations of Utopian and Dystopian Modalities in **The Marriages Between Zones Three, Four and Five**," *Style* 27(1): 63-80. Spring 1993.

___ Tokarczyk, Roman A. "Polish Utopian Thought: A Historical Survey," *Utopian Studies* 4(2): 128-143. 1993.

___ Trezza, Bruno. "Economia e utopia," in: Saccaro Del Buffa, Giuseppa and Lewis, Arthur O., eds. **Utopia e Modernita: Teorie e prassi utopiche nell'eta moderna e postmoderna**. Rome: Gangemi Editore, 1989. pp.217-224.

___ Trousson, Raymond. "Unia Sintesi Storica," in: Colombo, Arrigo and Quarta, Cosimo, eds. **Il Destino della Famiglia nell'Utopia**. Bari: Edizione Dedalo, 1991. pp.17-31.

___ Tschachler, Heinz. "Ernest Callenbach: **Ecotopia: A Novel about Ecology, People, and Politics in 1999** (1975)," in: Heuermann, Hartmut and Lange, Bernd-Peter, eds. **Die Utopie in der angloamerikanischen Literatur: Interpretationen**. Düsseldorf: Bagel, 1984. pp.328-348.

___ Tundo, Laura. "Fourie: la tansizione verso il nuovo mondo amoroso," in: Colombo, Arrigo and Quarta, Cosimo, eds. **Il Destino della Famiglia nell'Utopia**. Bari: Edizione Dedalo, 1991. pp.265-282.

___ Tzonis, Alexander. "Counterfacts, Counternorms, and Transworld Mental Lines," in: Saccaro Del Buffa, Giuseppa and Lewis, Arthur O., eds. **Utopia e Modernita: Teorie e prassi utopiche nell'eta moderna e postmoderna**. Rome: Gangemi Editore, 1989. pp.71-76.

___ Vanderbilt, Kermit. "Kurt Vonnegut's American Nightmares and Utopias," in: Sullivan, E. D. S., ed. **The Utopian Vision**. San Diego, CA: San Diego University Press, 1983. pp.137-174.

___ Verra, Valerio. "Linee de ricerca sull'utopia: il problema storiografico," in: Saccaro Del Buffa, Giuseppa and Lewis, Arthur O., eds. **Utopia e Modernita: Teorie e prassi utopiche nell'eta moderna e postmoderna**. Rome: Gangemi Editore, 1989. pp.37-46.

___ Wagar, W. Warren. "J. G. Ballard and the Transvaluation of Utopia," *Science Fiction Studies* 18(1): 53-70. March 1991.

___ Wagner, Vivian. "Gender, Technology and Utopia in Faulkner's Airplane Tales," *Arizona Quarterly* 49(4): 79-97. Winter 1993.

___ Warhurst, Christopher. "The End of Another Utopia? The Israeli Kibbutz and Its Industry in a Period of Transition," *Utopian Studies* 5(2): 102-121. 1994.

___ Wegemer, Gerald. "The City of God in Thomas More's **Utopia**," *Renascence* 44(2): 115-136. Winter 1992.

___ Weimer, Annegret. "Utopia and Science Fiction: A Contribution to Their Generic Description," *Canadian Review of Comparative Literature* 19(1/2): 171-200. March/June 1992.

___ Wicken, Jeffrey S. "Evolutionary Constraints on Utopian Thought," in: Saccaro Del Buffa, Giuseppa and Lewis, Arthur O., eds. **Utopia e Modernita: Teorie e prassi utopiche nell'eta moderna e postmoderna**. Rome: Gangemi Editore, 1989. pp.143-156.

___ Widdicombe, Richard T. "Early Histories of Utopian Thought (to 1950)," *Utopian Studies* 3(1): 1-38. 1992.

___ Widdicombe, Toby. "Why Is There Barbed Wire Around Eutopia?," *Extrapolation* 33(2): 145-153. Summer 1992.

___ Wiemer, Annegret J. **The Feminist Science Fiction Utopia: Faces of a Genre, 1820-1897**. Ph.D. Dissertation, University of Alberta, 1991. (Ottawa: National Library of Canada, 1992. 5 microfiche) (DAI-A 53/08, p. 2811. Feb. 1993.)

UTOPIA (continued)

___ Wiemer, Annegret J. "Utopia and Science Fiction: A Contribution to Their Generic Description," *Canadian Review of Comparative Literature* 19(1/2): 171-200. March/June 1992.

___ Williams, Lynn F. "The Clockwork Apple in the Garden of Eden: The Mechanization of the Arcadian Utopia," in: Saccaro Del Buffa, Giuseppa and Lewis, Arthur O., eds. **Utopia e Modernita: Teorie e prassi utopiche nell'eta moderna e postmoderna**. Rome: Gangemi Editore, 1989. pp.655-666.

___ Williams, Lynn F. "Recent Nostalgic Utopias and the New Conservatism," in: Saccaro Del Buffa, Giuseppa and Lewis, Arthur O., eds. **Utopie per gli Anni Ottana**. Rome: Gangemi Editore, 1986. pp.763-788.

___ Wilson, Edmund. "Utopian Aspects of Catholic Social Teachings from Leo XIII to Paul VI," in: Saccaro Del Buffa, Giuseppa and Lewis, Arthur O., eds. **Utopie per gli Anni Ottana**. Rome: Gangemi Editore, 1986. pp.727-734.

___ Winter, Michael. "Utopia in Everyday Politics: Blessing or Nightmare?," in: Saccaro Del Buffa, Giuseppa and Lewis, Arthur O., eds. **Utopia e Modernita: Teorie e prassi utopiche nell'eta moderna e postmoderna**. Rome: Gangemi Editore, 1989. pp.77-86.

___ Wolf, Jack C. "Push-Button Utopias and Square Tomatoes," in: Saccaro Del Buffa, Giuseppa and Lewis, Arthur O., eds. **Utopie per gli Anni Ottana**. Rome: Gangemi Editore, 1986. pp.99-106.

___ Wolmark, Jenny. "Space, Time and Gender: The Impact of Cybernetics on the Feminist Utopia," *Foundation* No. 62: 22-30. Winter 1994/1995.

___ Wu, Dingbo. "Understanding Utopian Literature," *Extrapolation* 34(3): 230-244. Fall 1993.

___ Wu, Quingyun. **Female Rule in Chinese and English Literary Utopias**. Syracuse, NY: Syracuse University Press, 1995. 225pp.; London: Liverpool University Press, 1995. 225pp.

___ Yaari, Monique. "Paul Paon's Sur-surreal Chimera," *Utopian Studies* 5(1): 108-127. 1994.

___ Zaki, Hoda M. **Phoenix Renewed: The Survival and Mutation of Utopian Thought in North American Science Fiction 1965-1982**. Rev. ed. San Bernardino, CA: Borgo Press, 1994. 151pp.

___ Zaki, Hoda M. "Utopia and Ideology in **Daughters of a Coral Dawn** and Contemporary Feminist Utopias," *Women's Studies* 14(2): 119-134. 1987.

___ Zauderer, Naomi B. "Charlotte Perkins Gilman's **Moving the Mountain**: A Response to **Looking Backward**," *Utopian Studies* 3(1): 53-69. 1992.

UTOPIAN STUDIES (MAGAZINE)

___ "*Utopian Studies*: Five Year Index," *Utopian Studies* 5(2): 203-220. 1994.

UTTLEY, ALISON

___ MacIlroy, Barry. "Those Magical Time-Slip Stories," *Souvenir* 21: 14-15. 1992. [Not seen.]

V (TV)

___ Van Hise, James. **Sci Fi TV: From Twilight Zone to Deep Space Nine**. Las Vegas, NV: Pioneer Books, 1993. 160pp. (Reprinted, HarperPrism, 1995. 258pp.)

VALDEZ, LUIS

___ Rangel, Javier. "De lo fantástico a lo alegórico: El llamado a la resistencia en **The Shrunken Head of Pancho Villa**," *Mester* (UCLA) 19(2): 123-136. Fall 1990.

VALHALLA (MOTION PICTURE)

___ "**Valhalla** First Danish Animation to Go Feature Length Since War," *Variety* p. 43. February 27, 1985.

VALLE-INCLAN, RAMON DEL

___ Velasco, Juan. "Lo fantástico y la historia: La polémica entre **La sombra del caudillo y Tirano Banderas**," *Mester* (UCLA) 19(2): 71-82. Fall 1990.

VALUE OF SF

___ "But It's **Star Trek** to the Rescue," *New Scientist* 141(1908): 6. January 15, 1994.

___ "A Modest Proposal From 'The Killer Bees'," *Science Fiction Chronicle* 17(2): 5. December 1995/January 1996.

VALUE OF SF (continued)

___ Bisson, Terry. "Science Fiction and the Post-*Apollo* Blues," *Locus* 32(1): 38-40, 59. January 1994.

___ Bisson, Terry. "Science Fiction and the Post-*Apollo* Blues," *New York Review of Science Fiction* No. 58: 1, 8-11. June 1993.

___ Booker, M. Keith. **The Dystopian Impulse in Modern Literature: Fiction as Social Criticism.** Westport, CT: Greenwood, 1994. 197pp.

___ Bova, Ben. "Why *Science* Fiction?," *Amazing Stories* 67(11): 62-65. February 1993.

___ Bull, Geoff. "Morning Comes Whether You Set the Alarm or Not: Science Fiction, a Genre for the Future," *Orana* (Australia) 31(3): 159-169. August 1995.

___ Caywood, Carolyn. "The Quest for Character," *School Library Journal* 41(3): 152. March 1995.

___ Crisler, Jesse. "Fantasy: A Welcome Alternative," in: Canham, Stephen, ed. **Literature and Hawaii's Children.** Honolulu, HI: University of Hawaii Manoa, 1992. pp.69-75

___ De Canio, Stephen J. "The Future Through Yesterday: Long-Term Forecasting in the Novels of H. G. Wells and Jules Verne," *Centennial Review* 75(1): 75-93. Winter 1994.

___ Dubeck, Leroy W. **Fantastic Voyages: Learning Science Through Science Fiction Films.** New York: American Institute of Physics, 1994. 327pp.

___ Engdahl, Sylvia. "The Mythic Role of Space Fiction," in: Gannon, Susan R. and Thompson, Ruth A., eds. **Work and Play in Children's Literature.** New York: Pace University, 1992. pp.14-19.

___ Ferrell, Keith. "Forum: The Challenges of Science Fiction," *Omni* 14(5): 6. February 1992.

___ Freeman, Judy. "In the Realm of Fantasy," *Instructor* 104(8): 77-82. May 1995.

___ Galen, Russell. "The Near Future Is Perfect," *Writer's Digest* 74(1): 49-50. January 9194.

___ Gardiner, Josephine. "Forward With the Masters of the Sci-Fi Universe," *Times Educational Supplement* 4061: SS2. April 29, 1994.

___ Gough, Noel. **Laboratories in Fiction: Science Education and Popular Media.** Geelong: Deakin University, 1993. 137pp.

___ Gough, Noel. "Neuromancing the Stones: Experience, Intertextuality and Cyberpunk Science Fiction," *Journal of Experiential Education* 16(3): 9-17. December 1993.

___ Harwit, Martin. "Why *Star Trek*?," *Star Trek: The Official Fan Club* No. 89: 9. January/February 1993.

___ Hellman, Mary. "Outta This World," *San Diego (CA) Union* August 1, 1993. in: *NewsBank. Literature.* 75:D6-D8. 1993.

___ Jenkins, Henry. "At Other Times, Like Females: Gender and *Star Trek* Fiction," in: Tulloch, John and Jenkins, Henry, eds. **Science Fiction Audiences: Watching Doctor Who and Star Trek.** New York: Routledge, 1995. pp.196-212.

___ Jenkins, Henry. "How Many Starfleet Officers Does It Take to Change a Lightbulb?: *Star Trek* at MIT," by Henry Jenkins and Greg Dancer. in: Tulloch, John and Jenkins, Henry, eds. **Science Fiction Audiences: Watching Doctor Who and Star Trek.** New York: Routledge, 1995. pp.213-236.

___ Jenkins, Henry. "Infinite Diversity in Infinite Combinations: Genre and Authorship in *Star Trek*," in: Tulloch, John and Jenkins, Henry, eds. **Science Fiction Audiences: Watching Doctor Who and Star Trek.** New York: Routledge, 1995. pp.175-195.

___ Jenkins, Henry. "Out of the Closet and into the Universe: Queers and *Star Trek*," in: Tulloch, John and Jenkins, Henry, eds. **Science Fiction Audiences: Watching Doctor Who and Star Trek.** New York: Routledge, 1995. pp.237-265.

___ Jordan, Anne D. "Future Reading: Science Fiction," *Teaching and Learning Literature* 4(5): 17-23. May/June 1995.

___ Kalade, Linas. "Weaving a Colourful Tapestry," *Viewpoint on Books for Young Adults* 1(2): 8-9. Winter 1993.

___ Kress, Nancy. "An SF Moderate Climbs Cautiously onto the Barricades," *Pulphouse* No. 10: 12-18. July 1992.

___ Lackey, Chad. "Social Science Fiction: Writing Sociological Short Stories to Learn About Social Issues," *Teaching Sociology* 22(2): 166-173. April 1994.

___ Laz, Cheryl. "Science Fiction and Introductory Sociology: The Handmaid in the Classroom," *Teaching Sociology* 24(1): 54-63. January 1995.

___ Lofton, S. C. "Under the Influence," *Lan's Lantern* No. 40: 120-122. September 1992.

___ Marsalek, Kenneth. "Humanism, Science Fiction and Fairy Tales," *Free Inquiry* 15(3): 39-42. Summer 1995.

VALUE OF SF (continued)

___ Mestel, Rosie. "Education: The Final Frontier," *New Scientist* 141(1914): 11. February 26, 1994.

___ Miles, Ian. "Stranger Than Fiction: How Important Is Science Fiction for Futures Studies?," *Futures* 25(3): 315-321. April 1993. (Reprinted: *Engineering Management Review* 21(4): 49-52. Winter 1993.)

___ Nauman, Ann K. "Sci-Fi Science," by Ann K. Nauman and Edward L. Shaw. *Science Activities* 31(3): 18-20. Fall 1994.

___ Pierce, Tamora. "Fantasy: Why Kids Read It, Why Kids Need It," *School Library Journal* 39(10): 50-51. October 1993.

___ Platt, Charles. "Upstream," *Science Fiction Eye* No. 12: 29-34. Summer 1993.

___ Pohl, Frederik. "Science Fiction: Stepchild of Science," *Technology Review* 97(7): 57-61. October 1994.

___ Pohl, Frederik. "The Uses of the Future," *Futurist* 27(2): 9-12. March-April 1993.

___ Rabkin, Eric S. "Imagination and Survival: The Case of Fantastic Literature," *Foundation* No. 56: 84-98. Autumn 1992. (Letter of comment: K. V. Bailey, *Foundation* No. 58: 85-87. Summer 1993.)

___ Renaud, Maurice. "Document in the History of Science Fiction: On the Scientific-Marvellous Novel and Its Influence on the Understanding of Progress," *Science Fiction Studies* 21(3): 397-405. November 1994.

___ Rusch, Kristine K. "Editorial: Science Fiction in the Mainstream," *Magazine of Fantasy and Science Fiction* 87(4/5): 8-10. October 1994.

___ Sandow, Sandra J. "Touch Magic: The Importance of Teaching Folktales to Emotionally Disturbed, Disabled Readers," *Mythlore* 19(4): 56-59. Autumn 1993. (No. 74)

___ Sargent, Pamela. "Writing, Science Fiction, and Family Values," *Amazing Stories* 69(1): 100-111. Spring 1994.

___ Smetak, Jacqueline R. "Summer at the Movies: Steven Spielberg: Gore, Guts, and PG-13," *Journal of Popular Film and Television* 14(1): 4-13. 1986.

___ Stanley, Dick. "Philosophy Teacher Hits Warp Speed; *Star Trek* Boldly Explored in Class," *Austin (TX) American Statesman* Sec. B, pp.1, 6. March 7, 1993.

___ Sutin, Lawrence. "The Case for Science Fiction," *Hungry Mind Review* pp.22-23. Winter 1995/1996.

___ Tulloch, John. "But He's a Time Lord! He's a Time Lord!: Reading Formations, Followers, and Fans," in: Tulloch, John and Jenkins, Henry, eds. **Science Fiction Audiences: Watching Doctor Who and Star Trek.** New York: Routledge, 1995. pp.125-143.

___ Tulloch, John. "But Why Is *Doctor Who* So Attractive?: Negotiating Ideology and Pleasure," in: Tulloch, John and Jenkins, Henry, eds. **Science Fiction Audiences: Watching Doctor Who and Star Trek.** New York: Routledge, 1995. pp.108-124.

___ Tulloch, John. "It's Meant to Be Fantasy: Teenage Audiences and Genre," by John Tulloch and Marian Tulloch. in: Tulloch, John and Jenkins, Henry, eds. **Science Fiction Audiences: Watching Doctor Who and Star Trek.** New York: Routledge, 1995. pp.86-107.

___ Tulloch, John. "Throwing a Little Bit of Poison into Future Generations: *Doctor Who* Audiences and Ideology," in: Tulloch, John and Jenkins, Henry, eds. **Science Fiction Audiences: Watching Doctor Who and Star Trek.** New York: Routledge, 1995. pp.67-85.

___ Tulloch, John. "We're Only a Speck in the Ocean: The Fans as Powerless Elite," in: Tulloch, John and Jenkins, Henry, eds. **Science Fiction Audiences: Watching Doctor Who and Star Trek.** New York: Routledge, 1995. pp.144-172.

___ Webb, Don. "The Mysterious," *Science Fiction Eye* No. 13: 62-66. Spring 1994.

___ Wolf, Milton T. "Science Fiction: Better Than Delphi Studies," *Educom Review* 29(1): 20-34. January/February 1994.

VALUES

___ Colebatch, Hal. "Patterns of Epic: The Re-Affirmation of Western Values in *Star Wars* and **The Lord of the Rings**," *Science Fiction: A Review of Speculative Literature* 11(3): 5-16. 1992. (No. 33)

VAMPIRE IN BROOKLYN (MOTION PICTURE)

___ Persons, Dan. "*A Vampire in Brooklyn*," *Cinefantastique* 27(2): 12-13. November 1995.

VAMPIRES

___ Auerbach, Nina. **Our Vampires, Ourselves.** Chicago: University of Chicago Press, 1995. 231pp.

___ Benefiel, Candace R. "Fangs for the Memories: Vampires in the Nineties," *Wilson Library Bulletin* 69(9): 35-38. May 1995.

VAMPIRES

VAMPIRES (continued)

___ Broeske, Pat H. "Hollywood Goes Batty for Vampires," *New York Times* Sec. 2, p. 15, 22. April 26, 1992.

___ Bunson, Matthew. **The Vampire Encyclopedia**. New York: Crown, 1993. 303pp.

___ Cox, Greg. **The Transylvanian Library: A Consumer's Guide to Vampire Fiction**. San Bernardino, CA: Borgo Press, 1993. 264pp.

___ Dyer, Richard. "Children of the Night: Vampirism as Homosexuality; Homosexuality as Vampirism," in: Radstone, Susannah, ed. **Sweet Dreams: Sexuality, Gender and Popular Fiction**. London: Lawrence & Wishart, 1988. pp.47-72.

___ Dyer, Richard. "*Dracula* and Desire," *Sight and Sound* 3(1): 8-12. January 1993.

___ Guiley, Rosemary E. **The Complete Vampire Companion**. New York: Macmillan, 1994. 258pp.

___ Hendershot, Cyndy. "Vampire and Replicant: The One-Sex Body in a Two-Sex World," *Science Fiction Studies* 22(3): 373-398. November 1995.

___ Hollinger, Veronica. "The Vampire and/as the Alien," *Journal of the Fantastic in the Arts* 5(3): 5-17. 1993. (No. 19)

___ Hunt, Samantha. "Undeathly Literature," *Voice of Youth Advocates* 18(3): 147. August 1995.

___ Johnson, Judith E. "Women and Vampires: Nightmare or Utopia?," *Kenyon Review* 15(1): 72-80. Winter 1993.

___ Joshi, S. T. "Anne Rice: The Philosophy of Vampirism," *Interzone* No. 75: 47-50, 61. September 1993.

___ Kearns, Martha. "Postmodern Images of Sexuality in Vampire Literature," in: Wolf, Milton T. and Mallett, Daryl F., eds. **Imaginative Futures: Proceedings of the 1993 Science Fiction Research Association Conference**. San Bernardino, CA: Jacob's Ladder Books, 1995. pp.147-160.

___ Kendrick, Walter. "Better Undead Than Unread: Have Vampires Lost Their Bite?," *New York Times Book Review* p. 55. October 18, 1992.

___ King, Maureen. "Contemporary Women Writers and the 'New Evil': The Vampires of Anne Rice and Suzy McKee Charnas," *Journal of the Fantastic in the Arts* 5(3): 75-84. 1993. (No. 19)

___ Marigny, Jean. "The Different Faces of Eros in the Vampire Chronicles of Anne Rice," *Paradoxa* 1(3): 352-362. 1995.

___ Marigny, Jean. "Le Vampire dans la science fiction anglo-saxonne [The Vampire in Anglo-Saxon Science Fiction]," *Litteratures* No. 26: 69-85. Spring 1992.

___ Mascetti, Manuela D. **Vampire: The Complete Guide to the World of the Undead**. New York: Viking Studio, 1992. 224pp.

___ McDonald, Beth E. "The Vampire as Trickster Figure in Bram Stoker's *Dracula*," *Extrapolation* 33(2): 128-144. Summer 1992.

___ McNally, Raymond T. **In Search of Dracula: The History of Dracula and Vampires**. Rev. Ed, by Raymond T. McNally and Radu Florescu. Boston, MA: Houghton Mifflin, 1994. 297pp.

___ McSorley, Bonnie S. "Revamping the Vampire in Joan Perucho's **Natural History**," *Studies in Weird Fiction* No. 15: 2-5. Summer 1994.

___ Melton, J. Gordon. **The Vampire Book: The Encyclopedia of the Undead**. Detroit, MI: Visible Ink Press, 1994. 852pp.

___ Nance, Scott. **Bloodsuckers: Vampires at the Movies**. Las Vegas, NM: Pioneer Books, 1992. 149pp.

___ Newman, Kim. "Bloodlines," *Sight and Sound* 3(1): 12-13. January 1993.

___ Noll, Richard. **Vampires, Werewolves, and Demons: Twentieth Century Reports in the Psychiatric Literature**. New York: Brunner, 1992. 244pp.

___ Page, Carol. **Blood Lust: Conversations with Real Vampires**. New York: HarperCollins, 1991. 192pp.; New York: Dell, 1992. 214pp.

___ Sheehan, Henry. "Trust the Teller," *Sight and Sound* 3(1): 14. January 1993.

___ Sinclair, Iain. "Invasion of the Blood," *Sight and Sound* 3(1): 15. January 1993.

___ Skrip, Jack. "I Drink, Therefore I Am: Introspection in the Contemporary Vampire Novel," *Studies in Weird Fiction* No. 14: 3-7. Winter 1994.

___ Taubin, Amy. "Bloody Tales," *Sight and Sound* 5(1): 8-11. January 1995.

___ Wicke, Jennifer. "Vampiric Typewriting: Dracula and Its Media," *ELH* 59(2): 467-494. Summer 1992.

VAMPIRES (MOTION PICTURE)

___ "*Vampires* (Review)," *Variety* p. 12. June 8, 1988.

VAMPYR (1932) (MOTION PICTURE)

___ Hogan, David J. "*Vampyr* (1932) (Review)," *Filmfax* No. 37: 26, 30. February/March 1993.

VAN DAMME, JEAN-CLAUDE

___ Johnson, Kim H. "*Timecop*," in: McDonnell, David, ed. **Starlog's Science Fiction Heroes and Heroines**. New York: Crescent Books, 1995. pp.90-92.

VAN GELDER, RICHARD G.

___ "Van Gelder, Richard G. (Obituary)," *Locus* 32(4): 60. April 1994.

VAN PEEPLES, MARIO

___ Yakir, Dan. "Raising Kane," *Starlog* No. 210: 36-39, 66. January 1995.

VAN VOGT, A. E.

___ "First Fandom Reunion at Archon," *Locus* 35(6): 11. December 1995.

___ Bloom, Harold. "A. E. Van Vogt," in: Bloom, Harold, ed. **Science Fiction Writers of the Golden Age**. New York: Chelsea House, 1995. pp.188-203.

___ Ingebretson, Edward J. "A. E. Van Vogt," in: Bruccoli, Matthew J., ed. **Facts on File Bibliography of American Fiction 1919-1988**. New York: Facts on File, 1991. pp.513-515.

___ Reitz, Bernhard. "A. E. Van Vogt, **Slan** (1940)," in: Heuermann, Harmut, ed. **Der Science Fiction Roman in der angloamerikanischen Literatur: Interpretationen**. Düsseldorf: Bagel, 1986. pp.84-100.

___ Zebrowski, George. "Never Forget the Writers Who Helped Build Yesterday's Tomorrows," *Science Fiction Age* 3(6): 30-36, 100. 1995.

VANCE, JACK

___ "A Jack Vance Chonology," in: Hewett, Jerry and Mallett, Daryl F. **The Work of Jack Vance: An Annotated Bibliography and Guide**. San Bernardino, CA: Borgo, 1994. pp.xv-xxii.

___ Hewett, Jerry. **The Work of Jack Vance: An Annotated Bibliography and Guide**, by Jerry Hewett and Daryl F. Mallett. San Bernardino, CA: Borgo Press, 1994. 293pp. (Issued simultaneously by Underwood-Miller.)

___ Letson, Russell. "Jack Vance," in: Bruccoli, Matthew J., ed. **Facts on File Bibliography of American Fiction 1919-1988**. New York: Facts on File, 1991. pp.511-512.

___ Silverberg, Robert. "Introduction: The World of Jack Vance," in: Hewett, Jerry and Mallett, Daryl F. **The Work of Jack Vance: An Annotated Bibliography and Guide**. San Bernardino, CA: Borgo, 1994. pp.xi-xiii.

___ Temianka, Dan. **The Jack Vance Lexicon: The Coined Words of Jack Vance From Ahulph to Zipangote**. San Bernardino, CA: Borgo Press, 1995. 136pp.

VARDIMAN, GUY

___ Collins, Diana. "Guy Vardiman: Standing in for Data," in: Van Hise, James, ed. **Trek Celebration Two**. Las Vegas, NV: Pioneer, 1994. pp.142-147.

VARLEY, JOHN

___ Delany, Samuel R. "Zelazny/Varley/Gibson--and Quality, Part 1," *New York Review of Science Fiction* No. 48: 1, 10-13. August 1992.

___ Delany, Samuel R. "Zelazny/Varley/Gibson--and Quality, Part 2," *New York Review of Science Fiction* No. 49: 1, 3-7. September 1992.

___ Fischer, Dennis. "**Millennium**: Novel vs. Film," *Lan's Lantern* No. 35: 75-78. December 1990.

___ Hayles, N. Katherine. "The Life Cycle of Cyborgs: Writing the Posthuman," in: Gray, Chris H., ed. **The Cyborg Handbook**. New York: Routledge, 1995. pp.321-335.

___ Hayles, N. Katherine. "The Life Cycle of Cyborgs: Writing the Posthuman," in: Benjamin, Marina, ed. **A Question of Identity: Women, Science, and Literature**. New Brunswick, NJ: Rutgers University Press, 1993. pp.152-170.

___ Howie, Leslie. "A Talk With John Varley," *Science Fiction Eye* No. 11: 96-98. December 1992.

VARMA, DEVENDRA P.

___ "Varma, Devendra (Obituary)," *Science Fiction Chronicle* 16(2): 20. November/December 1994.

___ "Varma, Devendra P. (Obituary)," *Locus* 33(6): 74. December 1994.

VEGAS IN SPACE (MOTION PICTURE)

___ Hoffman, Bill. "The Outer Limits of Taste (Review)," *New York Post* December 10, 1993. in: *NewsBank. Art.* 37:G12. 1993.

___ Persons, Dan. "**Vegas in Space** (Review)," *Cinefantastique* 25(3): 60. June 1994.

VENEZUELA

___ "Radio Caracas to Roll Sci-Fi Series," *Variety* p. 56. February 23, 1983.

VERHEIDEN, MARK

___ Jankiewicz, Pat. "Masks of Time," *Starlog* No. 206: 40-45. September 1994.

VERLANGER, JULIA

___ Macy, Michelle D. **Julia Verlanger: 'grande dame' de la science fiction fran crep**. Master's Thesis, University of South Florida, 1995. 69pp.

VERNE, JULES

___ "Brussels Cancels Verne 'Trip to the Moon'; No Unity of Components--Huisman," *Variety* p. 30. February 4, 1970.

___ "Long-Lost Verne," *Locus* 33(5): 8, 73. November 1994.

___ "Will Jules Verne Win a Hugo?," *Science Fiction Chronicle* 16(1): 5. October 1994.

___ Buard, Jean-Luc. "Verne's 'New' Novel," *Fantasy Commentator* 8(3/4): 269-273. Fall 1995. (Whole No. 47/48)

___ Burgess, Thomas. **Take Me Under the Sea: The Dream Merchants of the Deep**. Salem, OR: Ocean Archives, 1994. 259pp.

___ Crary, David. "Verne's Lost Novel Goes Back to the Future," *Austin (TX) American Statesman* Sec. A, p. 11. October 8, 1994.

___ De Canio, Stephen J. "The Future Through Yesterday: Long-Term Forecasting in the Novels of H. G. Wells and Jules Verne," *Centennial Review* 75(1): 75-93. Winter 1994.

___ Drozdiak, William. "Jules Verne's Crystal Ball," *Washington (DC) Post.* September 24, 1994. in: *NewsBank. Film and Television.* 71:C14-D1. 1994.

___ Evans, Arthur B. "The 'New' Jules Verne," *Science Fiction Studies* 22(1): 35-46. March 1995.

___ Foote, Bud. "Verne's **Paris in the Twentieth Century**: The First Science Fiction Dystopia?," *New York Review of Science Fiction* No. 88: 1, 8-10. December 1995.

___ Hammerton, M. "Verne's Amazing Journeys," in: Seed, David, ed. **Anticipations: Essays on Early Science Fiction and Its Precursors**. Liverpool: Liverpool University Press, 1995. pp.98-110.

___ Jeapes, Ben. "Jules Verne's **Twenty Thousand Leagues Under the Sea**," *Vector* No. 184: 10-12. Summer 1995.

___ Lynch, Lawrence. **Jules Verne**. New York: Twayne, 1992. 127pp.

___ Maertens, James W. "Between Jules Verne and Walt Disney: Brains, Brawn, and Masculine Desire in **20,000 Leagues Under the Sea**," *Science Fiction Studies* 22(2): 209-225. July 1995.

___ Mickel, Emanuel J. "Introduction," in: Verne, Jules. **The Complete Twenty Thousand Leagues Under the Sea**. Bloomington: Indiana University Press, 1991. pp.1-65.

___ Moskowitz, Sam. "Voyagers Through Eternity: A History of Science Fiction From the Beginnings to H. G. Wells; Part XIII, Verne's Greatest Work," *Fantasy Commentator* 7(3): 232-236. Spring 1992. (No. 43)

___ Riding, Alan. "Back to the Present in a Lost Verne Novel," *New York Times* p.B1, B4. September 27, 1994.

___ Taves, Brian. "**Adventures of the Rat Family**: A Verne Expert Brings Fairy Tale to English-Speaking Public," *Library of Congress Information Bulletin* 53(1): 7-11. January 10, 1994.

___ Teeters, Peggy. **Jules Verne: The Man Who Invented Tomorrow**. New York: Walker, 1992. 120pp.

___ Zebrowski, George. "Never Forget the Writers Who Helped Build Yesterday's Tomorrows," *Science Fiction Age* 3(6): 30-36, 100. 1995.

VIAN, BORIS

___ Buffard-O'Shea, Nicolle. "Boris Vian and the Literary Grotesque: The Animated Objects," in: Latham, Robert A. and Collins, Robert A., eds. **Modes of the Fantastic**. Westport, CT: Greenwood, 1995. pp.56-63.

VICTOR GOLLANCZ (PUBLISHER)

___ "Gollancz Sold Again," *Locus* 29(5): 4. November 1992

VIDEO TOASTER

___ Loren, Christalene. "Video Beat: Toasting **Babylon 5**," *Cinefex* No. 57: 11-12. March 1994.

VIDEOCASSETTES

___ "Dealers Ecstatic as Paramount Halves 'Trek II' Tape Tab," *Variety* p. 56. September 1, 1982.

___ "*Star Trek* TV Episode Released by Paramount at $30," *Variety* p. 37. June 2, 1982.

___ "*Star Trek II*: Sales Vs. Rental Fulcrum," *Variety* p. 31-32. October 6, 1982.

VIDEODROME (MOTION PICTURE)

___ "**The Dead Zone** (1983)/**Videodrome** (1984): Interview with David Cronenberg," in: Goldberg, Lee, ed. **The Dreamweavers: Interviews With Fantasy Filmmakers of the 1980s**. Jefferson, NC: McFarland, 1995. pp.58-74.

VIERECK, GEORGE

___ Stableford, Brian. "Yesterday's Bestsellers, 20: **My First Two Thousand Years** by George Viereck and Paul Eldridge," *Interzone* No. 86: 48-52. August 1994.

VIETNAM

___ Franklin, H. Bruce. "*Star Trek* in the Vietnam Era," *Science Fiction Studies* 21(1): 24-34. March 1994.

___ Franklin, H. Bruce. "The Vietnam War as American Science Fiction and Fantasy," in: Irons, Glenwood, ed. **Gender, Language and Myth: Essays on Popular Narrative**. Toronto: University of Toronto Press, 1992. pp.208-230.

___ Haldeman, Joe. "Vietman and Other Alien Worlds," in: Slusser, George and Eric S. Rabkin, eds. **Fights of Fancy: Armed Conflict in Science Fiction and Fantasy**. Athens, GA: University of Georgia Press, 1993. pp.92-102.

___ Olsa, Jaroslav, Jr. "SF in Southeast Asia," *Locus* 34(1) 70. January 1995.

VILLAGE OF THE DAMNED (MOTION PICTURE)

___ Harris, Judith P. "**Village of the Damned** (Review)," *Cinefantastique* 26(6)/27(1): 124. October 1995.

VILLAGE OF THE GIANTS (1965) (MOTION PICTURE)

___ Renzi, Thomas C. **H. G. Wells: Six Scientific Romances Adapted for Film**. Metuchen, NJ: Scarecrow, 1992. 249pp.

VILLIERS D'ISLE-ADAM

___ Gallardo Torrano, Pedro. "**Frankenstein's** French Counterpart: Villiers de l'Isle-Adam's **L'Eve Future**," *Foundation* No. 63: 74-80. Spring 1995.

VINCENT, HARL

___ Gallardo Torrano, Pedro. "Themes and Motifs in a Robot Story: 'Rex' by Harl Vincent," in: Fernández-Corugedo, S. G., ed. **Studia Patriciae Shaw Oblata**. Volumen III. n.p.: University of Oviedo, 1991. pp.214-224.

VINCENT, JOYCE

___ Stone, Graham. "Notes on Australian Science Fiction," *Science Fiction News* (Australia) No. 102: 2-5. March 1987.

VINGE, JOAN D.

___ **Breaking into Writing**. Ann Arbor, MI: Tucker Video, 1994. 1 videocassette, 98 minutes. (Panel Presentation at the 1994 Science Fiction Research Association Conference.)

___ "Joan D. Vinge: The Summer Queen in the Fall," *Locus* 28(3): 5, 76. March 1992.

___ Jacobs, Naomi. "The Frozen Landscape in Women's Utopian and Science Fiction," in: Donawerth, Jane L. and Kolmerten, Carol A., eds. **Utopian and Science Fiction by Women: Worlds of Difference**. Syracuse, NY: Syracuse University Press, 1994. pp.190-202.

VINGE, VERNOR

___ "12th Annual *S. F. Chronicle* Reader Awards," *Science Fiction Chronicle* 14(12): 4. September 1993.

___ "1993 Hugo Awards," *Science Fiction Chronicle* 15(1): 4. October 1993.

___ "1993 Hugo Awards Winners," *Locus* 31(4): 5, 70. October 1993.

VINGE, VERNOR (continued)

___ Davis, Erik. "Techgnosis: Magic, Memory and the Angel of Information," *South Atlantic Quarterly* 92(4): 585-616. Fall 1993. (Reprinted in: Dery, Mark, ed. **Flame Wars: The Discourse of Cyberculture**. Durham, NC: Duke University Press, 1994.)

___ Di Filippo, Paul. "The Man Who Had Too Many Ideas," *Amazing Stories* 69(3): 95-109. Winter 1995.

___ Elliott, Elton. "Interview: Vernor Vinge, Part 1," *Science Fiction Review* No. 8: 10-11, 29-30. March 1992.

___ Kelly, Kevin. "Singular Visionary," *Wired* 3(6): 160-161. June 1995.

VIOLENCE

___ Haldeman, Joe. "Sex and Violence in SF," *The Report: The Fiction Writer's Magazine* No. 9: 1, 3. March 1993.

___ Jones, Alan. "*Judge Dredd*: Wertham Revisited," *Cinefantastique* 26(5): 36. August 1995.

___ Langford, David. "Fun With Senseless Violence," *Vector* No. 170: 15-19. December 1992/January 1993.

___ Moir, Patricia. "Real vs. Reel Terror," *Cinefantastique* 27(3): 40-43. December 1995.

___ Shirley, John. "Violence," *Science Fiction Eye* No. 13: 47-53. Spring 1994.

VIPER (MOTION PICTURE)

___ Pieshel, Bob. "Video Beat: *Viper* Sheds Its Skin," *Cinefex* No. 58: 85-86. June 1994.

VIRTUAL REALITY

___ Bukatman, Scott R. **Terminal Identity: The Virtual Subject in Postmodern Science Fiction**. Durham, NC: Duke University Press, 1993. 404pp.

VIRTUOSITY (MOTION PICTURE)

___ Arnold, Gary. "*Virtuosity* a Lifeless Video Game," *Washington (DC) Times*. August 4, 1995. in: *NewsBank. Film and Television*. 82:C6. 1995.

___ Denerstein, Robert. "Grim *Virtuosity* a Virtual Waste of Time," *(Denver, CO) Rocky Mountain News*. August 4, 1995. in: *NewsBank. Film and Television*. 82:C1. 1995.

___ Hunter, Stephen. "Riding the Information Highway to the Killing Fields," *(Baltimore, MD) Sun*. August 3, 1995. in: *NewsBank. Film and Television*. 82:C2. 1995.

___ Maccarillo, Lisa. "More Than Human," *Sci-Fi Entertainment* 2(2): 62-67, 81. August 1995.

___ Maurstad, Tom. "*Virtuosity*: Hunting for an Original Storyline," *Dallas (TX) Morning News*. August 4, 1995. in: *NewsBank. Film and Television*. 82:C5. 1995.

___ McKay, Niall. "First You Slice Your Leading Man," *New Scientist* 148(2002): 24. November 4, 1995.

___ Medved, Michael. "Virtueless *Virtuosity*," *New York (NY) Post*. August 4, 1995. in: *NewsBank. Film and Television*. 82:C4. 1995.

___ Probst, Chris. "Cyberthriller Comes of Age," *American Cinematographer* 76(10): 88-96. October 1995.

___ Rosenberg, Scott. "Tired *Virtuosity* Rehashes Action Cliches," *San Francisco (CA) Examiner*. August 4, 1995. in: *NewsBank. Film and Television*. 82:B14. 1995.

___ Saunders, Matthew F. "*Virtuosity*," *Cinefantastique* 26(6)/27(1): 66-97. October 1995.

___ Shapiro, Marc. "Virtual Virtuoso," *Starlog* No. 218: 32-35. September 1995.

___ Verniere, James. "*Virtuosity* Creates Virtual Vacuum," *Boston (MA) Herald*. August 4, 1995. in: *NewsBank. Film and Television*. 82:C3. 1995.

VISIONS: THE MAGAZINE OF FANTASY TV, HOME VIDEO AND NEW MEDIA

___ "*Visions: The Magazine of Fantasy TV, Home Video and New Media*," *Science Fiction Chronicle* 16(8): 10. July/August 1995

VISITEURS, LES (MOTION PICTURE)

___ Lowe, Nick. "*Les Visiteurs* (Review)," *Interzone* No. 83: 35-36. May 1994.

VISITOR, NANA

___ Altman, Mark A. "*Star Trek: Deep Space Nine*: Major Kira," *Cinefantastique* 24(3/4): 103. October 1993.

VISITOR, NANA (continued)

___ Altman, Mark A. "*Star Trek: Deep Space Nine*: Visitor on Board," *Cinefantastique* 23(6): 26. April 1993.

___ Spelling, Ian. "Major Player," *Starlog* No. 199: 27-33. February 1994.

___ Spelling, Ian. "Major Player," in: McDonnell, David, ed. **Starlog's Science Fiction Heroes and Heroines**. New York: Crescent Books, 1995. pp.62-65.

VISKOCIL, JOSEPH

___ Duncan, Jody. "Profile: Joseph Viskocil," *Cinefex* No. 50: 23. May 1992.

VISUAL ARTS

___ SEE: ART AND ARTISTS.

VOERMANS, PAUL

___ Paulsen, Steven. "Australian Landscapes: Paul Voermans Interviewed," *Interzone* No. 76: 43-45. October 1993.

VOLLMAN, WILLIAM

___ "Vollman Injured by Land Mine," *Locus* 32(6): 8, 76. June 1994.

VOLTAIRE

___ Davies, Eric L. "Inspector Zadig: Voltaire and the Birth of the Scientific Detective Story," *Fantasy Commentator* 8(3/4): 214-216, 172. Fall 1995. (Whole No. 47/48)

___ Russell, W. M. S. "Voltaire, Science and Fiction: A Tercentenary Tribute," *Foundation* No. 62: 31-46. Winter 1994/1995.

VOLTRON: DEFENDER OF THE UNIVERSE (TV)

___ "Sony Readies 'Voltron' Segs for Vid Market," *Variety* p. 37-38. February 27, 1985.

VON ESCHENBACH, WOLFRAM

___ McConnell, Winder. "The Denial of the Anima in **Parzival**," *Quondam et Futurus* 2(2): 28-40. Summer 1992.

___ Ryan, J. S. "Uncouth Innocence: Some Links Between Chrétien de Troyes, Wolfram von Eschenbach and J. R. R. Tolkien," in: Kranz, Gisbert, ed. **Inklings: Jahrbuch für Literatur und Ästhetik**. 2. Band. [Lüdenscheid, Germany, Stier], 1984. pp.25-41.

VONARBURG, ELISABETH

___ "Aurora Awards Winners," *Locus* 28(2): 7. August 1992.

___ "Aurora Awards Winners, 1992," *Locus* 30(4): 6, 64. April 1993.

___ Bogstad, Janice M. **Gender, Power and Reversal in Contemporary Anglo-American and French Feminist Science Fiction**. Ph.D. Dissertation, University of Wisconsin, Madison, 1992. 229pp. (DAI-A 54/02, p. 509. August 1993.)

___ Wolmark, Jenny. **Aliens and Others: Science Fiction, Feminism, and Postmodernism**. London: Harester Wheatsheaf, 1993. 167pp.; Iowa City: University of Iowa Press, 1994. 167pp.

VONNEGUT, KURT, JR.

___ "Tackle 3-Level Tale; Geller Accepts Writing Challenge of 'Slaughterhouse'," *Variety* p. 5. May 13, 1970.

___ Allen, William R. **Understanding Kurt Vonnegut**. Columbia: University of South Carolina Press, 1992. 192pp.

___ Bland, Michael. "A Game of Black Humor in Vonnegut's **Cat's Cradle**," *Notes on Contemporary Literature* 24(4): 8-9. September 1994.

___ Cubbage, Robert. "Kurt Vonnegut: The Faith of a Skeptic," *National Catholic Reporter* 22: 9-10. May 16, 1986.

___ Drake, Rodney. **The Use, Function and Importance of Kilgore Trout in the Novels of Kurt Vonnegut, Junior**. Master's Thesis, University of Northern Iowa, 1977. 64pp.

___ Droesch, Paul. "Hits and Misses: Kurt Vonnegut's **Harrison Bergeron**," *TV Guide* 43(32): 41. August 12, 1995.

___ Freese, Peter. "Kurt Vonnegut: **Cat's Cradle** (1963)," in: Heuermann, Hartmut and Lange, Bernd-Peter, eds. **Die Utopie in der angloamerikanischen Literatur: Interpretationen**. Düsseldorf: Bagel, 1984. pp.283-309.

___ Freese, Peter. "Kurt Vonnegut, Jr., **The Sirens of Titan** (1959)," in: Heuermann, Harmut, ed. **Der Science Fiction Roman in der angloamerikanischen Literatur: Interpretationen**. Düsseldorf: Bagel, 1986. pp.196-219.

VONNEGUT, KURT, JR. (continued)

___ Freese, Peter. "Surviving the End: Apocalypse, Evolution, and Entropy in Bernard Malamud, Kurt Vonnegut and Thomas Pynchon," *Critique* 36(3): 163-176. Spring 1995.

___ Gilmore, Chris. "Why Is Science Fiction?," *Interzone* No. 62: 48-49. August 1992.

___ Goudas, John N. "Showtime Adapts the Biting Satire of Vonnegut's **Harrison Bergeron**," *Buffalo (NY) News*. August 13, 1995. in: *NewsBank. Film and Television*. 77:D13. 1995.

___ Kaufman, William K. **Mark Twain, Lenny Bruce and Kurt Vonnegut: The Comedian as Confidence Man**. Ph.D. Dissertation, University of Wales, Aberystwyth, 1992. [Not Seen.]

___ Kenny, Glenn. "Kurt Vonnegut's Law of Averages," *TV Guide* 43(32): 31. August 12, 1995.

___ Lee, Luaine. "Welcome to the Monkey House," *San Francisco (CA) Examiner* August 12, 1995. (Cited from the Internet Edition.)

___ Leeds, Marc. **The Vonnegut Encyclopedia: An Authorized Compendium**. Westport, CT: Greenwood, 1995. 693pp.

___ Mayer, Peter C. "Film, Ontology and the Structure of a Novel," *Film Literature Quarterly* 8(3): 204-208. 1980.

___ McCoy, Adrian. "Irreverent Vonnegut Jabs at Status Quo," *Pittsburgh (PA) Press*. March 3, 1992. in: *NewsBank. Literature*. 33: D14. 1992.

___ Morse, Donald E. **Kurt Vonnegut**. Mercer Island, WA: Starmont, 1992. 127pp. (Starmont Reader's Guide, 61)

___ Mustazza, Leonard, ed. **The Critical Response to Kurt Vonnegut**. Westport, CT: Greenwood, 1994. 346pp.

___ Petterson, Bo J. O. **The World According to Kurt Vonnegut: Moral Paradox and Narrative Form**. Ph.D. Dissertation, Abo Akademi (Finland), 1995. 404pp. (DAI-C 56/04, p. 822. Winter 1995.)

___ Puschmann-Nalenz, Barbara. **Science Fiction and Postmodern Fiction: A Genre Study**. New York: Peter Lang, 1992. 268pp. (Trans. of **Science Fiction und Ihre Grenzbereiche**.)

___ Rampton, David. "Into the Secret Chamber: Art and the Artist in Kurt Vonnegut's **Bluebeard**," *Critique* 35(1): 16-26. Fall 1993.

___ Reed, Peter J. "Kurt Vonnegut," in: Bruccoli, Matthew J., ed. **Facts on File Bibliography of American Fiction 1919-1988**. New York: Facts on File, 1991. pp.516-518.

___ Reed, Peter J. "Kurt Vonnegut: A Selected Bibliography, 1985-1992," by Peter J. Reed and Paul Baepler. *Bulletin of Bibliography* 50(2): 123-128. June 1993.

___ Rose, Ellen C. "It's All a Joke: Science Fiction in Kurt Vonnegut's **The Sirens of Titan**," *Literature and Psychology* 29(3): 160-168. 1979.

___ Segal, Howard P. **Future Imperfect: The Mixed Blessings of Technology in America**. Amherst: University of Massachusetts Press, 1994. 245pp.

___ Solomon, Harvey. "Showtime Expands on Vonnegut Satire," *Boston (MA) Herald*. August 12, 1995. in: *NewsBank. Film and Television*. 86:A1. 1995.

___ Stableford, Brian. "Locked in the Slaughterhouse: The Novels of Kurt Vonnegut," in: Stableford, Brian. **Outside the Human Aquarium: Masters of Science Fiction**. San Bernardino, CA: Borgo, 1995. pp.18-27.

___ Vanderbilt, Kermit. "Kurt Vonnegut's American Nightmares and Utopias," in: Sullivan, E. D. S., ed. **The Utopian Vision**. San Diego, CA: San Diego University Press, 1983. pp.137-174.

___ Warren, Tim. "The Write Life: Author Kurt Vonnegut Speaks Freely About Writing," *Baltimore (MD) Sun* December 11, 1991. in: *NewsBank. Literature*. 7:C10-C11. 1992.

VOROS, JUDY

___ "Voros, Judy (Obituary)," *Science Fiction Chronicle* 16(3): 16, 18. January 1995.

VORZIMMER, PETER J.

___ "Vorzimmer, Peter J. (Obituary)," *Science Fiction Chronicle* 17(1): 24. October/November 1995

VOV LE FORT, GERTRUD

___ Kranz, Gisbert. "Stellvertretung bei Williams, Claudel und G. v. le Fort," in: Kranz, Gisbert, ed. **Inklings: Jahrbuch für Literatur und Ästhetik**. 3. Band. [Lüdenscheid, Germany: Stier], 1985. pp.87-108.

VOYAGE HOME (MOTION PICTURE)

___ SEE: STAR TREK IV: THE VOYAGE HOME (MOTION PICTURE).

VOYAGE OF THE ROCK ALIENS (MOTION PICTURE)

___ "*Voyage of the Rock Aliens* (Review)," *Variety* p. 11. February 10, 1988.

VOYAGE TO THE BOTTOM OF THE SEA (TV)

___ Phillips, Mark. "Giant Jellyfish & Alien Invaders (Part 3)," *Starlog* No. 183: 75-81, 72. October 1992.

___ Phillips, Mark. "Giant Jellyfish & Monster Whales (Part 2)," *Starlog* 182: 75-81. September 1992.

___ Phillips, Mark. "Giant Jellyfish and Time-Lost Dinosaurs (Part 1)," *Starlog* 181: 61-66. August 1992.

___ Phillips, Mark. "The Life of Riley," *Starlog* No. 196: 65-69, 79. November 1993.

VOYAGER (TV)

___ SEE: STAR TREK: VOYAGER (TV).

VR.5 (TV)

___ Bellafante, Ginia. "Out of This World," *Time* 145(14): 72. April 3, 1995.

___ Cerone, Daniel H. "*VR.5* Steps into Critical Real World," *Los Angeles (CA) Times*. March 23, 1995. in: *NewsBank. Film and Television*. 51:B13-B14. 1995.

___ Harris, Judith P. "*VR.5* (Review)," *Cinefantastique* 26(6)/27(1): 124. October 1995.

___ Martin, Rick. "Tripping in the Fantasy Zone," *Newsweek* 125(11): 70. March 13, 1995.

___ Millman, Joyce. "*VR5* Virtually Hip But No *X-Files*," *San Francisco (CA) Examiner*. March 10, 1995. in: *NewsBank. Film and Television*. 39: F1-F2. 1995.

___ Solomon, Harvey. "Fox Gets Real, Virtually," *Boston (MA) Herald*. March 9, 1995. in: *NewsBank. Film and Television*. 39:E14. 1995.

___ Soriano, Cesar G. "Fox Series Melds Cyberspace, Sci-Fi," *Washington (DC) Times*. March 10, 1995. in: *NewsBank. Film and Television*. 39:F3. 1995.

WORKSHOPS, WRITER'S

___ "Free From Distractions, They Got Some Writing Done," *Science Fiction Chronicle* 14(7): 6. April 1993.

___ Shockley, W. M. "Workshopping by Computer," *The Report: The Fiction Writer's Magazine* No. 10: 9. Summer 1993.

WAGNER, KARL EDWARD

___ "Wagner, Karl Edward (Obituary)," *Locus* 33(5): 70-72. November 1994.

___ "Wagner, Karl Edward (Obituary)," *Science Fiction Chronicle* 16(2): 20, 22. November/December 1994.

___ Damon, T. Winter. "Karl Edward Wagner Tribute," *Genre Writer's News* 1(7): 6-10. May/June 1995.

WAGNER, LINDSAY

___ Spelling, Ian. "Bionic Breakdown," *Starlog* No. 211: 76-79. February 1995.

WAGNER, RICHARD

___ Shichtman, Martin B. "Wagner and the Arthurian Tradition," in: Fries, Maureen and Watson, Jeanie, eds. **Approaches to the Teaching of the Arthurian Tradition**. New York: Modern Language Association, 1992. pp.139-142.

WAKEFIELD, H. RUSSELL

___ Indick, Ben P. "H. Russell Wakefield: The Man Who Believed in Ghosts," in: Schweitzer, Darrell, ed. **Discovering Classic Horror Fiction I**. Mercer Island, WA: Starmont, 1992. pp.73-93.

WALCOTT, DEREK

___ Willis, Robert J. "**Dream on Monkey Mountain**: Fantasy as Self-Perception," in: Murphy, Patrick D., ed. **Staging the Impossible: The Fantastic Mode in Modern Drama**. Westport, CT: Greenwood, 1992. pp.150-155.

WALDROP, HOWARD

___ Nicholls, Stan. "Howard Waldrop Rides the Rodeo," in: Nicholls, Stan. **Wordsmiths of Wonder: Fifty Interviews with Writers of the Fantastic**. London: Orbit, 1993. pp.182-191.

___ Streitfeld, David. "Ears for Art's Sake," *Washington (DC) Post Book World* p. 15. January 26, 1992.

WALES

___ Bromwich, Rachel, ed. **The Arthur of the Welsh: The Arthurian Legend in Medieval Welsh Literature**, ed. by Rachel Bromwich, A. O. H. Jarman and Brynley F. Roberts. Cardiff: University of Wales Press, 1991. 310pp.

___ Filmer, Kath. "Atseiniau O Ddyddiau Gynt: Welsh Myth and Culture in Contemporary Fantasy," in: Filmer, Kath, ed. **Twentieth-Century Fantasists: Essays in Culture, Society and Belief in Twentieth Century Mythopoeic Literature**. New York: St. Martin's, 1992. pp.108-120.

___ Filmer-Davies, Kath. "Chwedl Gymaeg a Llenyddiaeth Gyfoesol: Welsh Myth and Comtempory Literature," Mythlore 19(3): 53-58. Summer 1993. (No. 73)

___ Jarman, A. O. H. "The Merlin Legend and the Welsh Tradition of Prophecy," in: Bromwich, Rachel, Jarman, A. O. H. and Roberts, Brynley F., eds. **The Arthur of the Welsh**. Cardiff: University of Wales Press, 1991. pp.117-146.

___ Lloyd-Morgan, Ceridwen. "**Breuddwyd Rhonabwy** and Later Arthurian Literature," in: Bromwich, Rachel, Jarman, A. O. H., and Roberts, Brynley F., eds. **The Arthur of the Welsh**. Cardiff: University of Wales Press, 1991. pp.183-208.

___ Lovecy, Ian. "**Historia Peredur ab Efrawg**," in: Bromwich, Rachel, Jarman, A. O. H. and Roberts, Brynley F., eds. **The Arthur of the Welsh**. Cardiff: University of Wales Press, 1991. pp.171-182.

___ Middleton, Roger. "**Chwedl Geraint ab Erbin**," in: Bromwich, Rachel, Jarman, A. O. H. and Roberts, Brynley F., eds. **The Arthur of the Welsh**. Cardiff: University of Wales Press, 1991. pp.147-158.

___ Padel, O. J. "Some South-Western Sites with Arthurian Associations," in: Bromwich, Rachel, Jarman, A. O. H. and Roberts, Brynley F., eds. **The Arthur of the Welsh**. Cardiff: University of Wales Press, 1991. pp.229-248.

___ Roberts, Brynley F. "**Culhwch ac Olwen**, The Triads, Saint's Lives," in: Bromwich, Rachel, Jarman, A. O. H. and Roberts, Brynley F., eds. **The Arthur of the Welsh**. Cardiff: University of Wales Press, 1991. pp.73-96.

___ Roberts, Brynley F. "Geoffrey of Monmouth, **Historia Regum Britanniae** and **Brut y Brenhinedd**," in: Bromwich, Rachel, Jarman, A. O. H. and Roberts, Brynley F., eds. **The Arthur of the Welsh**. Cardiff: University of Wales Press, 1991. pp.97-116.

___ Sims-Williams, Patrick. "The Early Welsh Arthurian Poems," in: Bromwich, Rachel, Jarman, A. O. H. and Roberts, Brynley F., eds. **The Arthur of the Welsh**. Cardiff: University of Wales Press, 1991. pp.33-72.

___ Thomson, R. L. "**Owain: Chwedl Iarlles y Ffynnon**," in: Bromwich, Rachel, Jarman, A. O. H. and Roberts, Brynley F., eds. **The Arthur of the Welsh**. Cardiff: University of Wales Press, 1991. pp.159-170.

WALKER, ALICE

___ McDowell, Elizabeth J. **Power and Environment in Recent Writings by Barbara Kingsolver, Ursula K. Le Guin, Alice Walker and Terry Tempest Williams**. Master's Thesis, University of Oregon, 1992. [Not seen.]

WALKER, PERCY

___ Werning, David H. "The Museum Scene in Walker Percy's **The Last Gentleman**," Renascence 44(3): 203-215. Spring 1992.

WALKER, SAMUEL S.

___ "Walker, Samuel S. (Obituary)," Locus 29(1): 67. July 1992.

___ "Walker, Samuel S. (Obiturary)," Science Fiction Chronicle 13(10): 16. July/August 1992.

WALKER, SULLIVAN

___ Chrissinger, Craig W. "Lessons of Life," Starlog No. 215: 46-49. June 1995.

WALLACE, GEORGE

___ Weaver, Tom. "George Wallace," in: Weaver, Tom. **They Fought the Creature Features: Interviews with 23 Classic Horror, Science Fiction and Serial Stars**. Jefferson, NC: McFarland, 1995. pp.277-287.

WALLACE, JOHN

___ Stone, Graham. "Notes on Australian Science Fiction," Science Fiction News (Australia) No. 102: 2-5. March 1987.

WALPOLE, HORACE

___ Bloom, Harold. "Horace Walpole," in: Bloom, Harold. **Classic Horror Writers**. New York: Chelsea House, 1994. pp.168-180.

WALT DISNEY PICTURES

___ Lyons, Michael. "**Pocahontas**: Animator Glen Keane on the Renaissance of Disney Animation," Cinefantastique 27(3): 50. December 1995.

___ McQuade, Brett. "**Peter Pan**: Disney's Adaptation of J. M. Barrie's Original Work," Mythlore 20(1): 5-9. Winter 1994. (Whole No. 75)

WANDREI, DONALD

___ Frenschkowski, Marco. "Donald Wandrei," Quarber Merkur 30(1): 18-27. June 1992. (No. 77)

WAR

___ Arbur, Rosemarie. "Fights of Fancy: When the 'Better Half' Wins," in: Slusser, George and Eric S. Rabkin, eds. **Fights of Fancy: Armed Conflict in Science Fiction and Fantasy**. Athens, GA: University of Georgia Press, 1993. pp.79-91.

___ Bartter, Martha A. "The Hidden Agenda," in: Slusser, George and Eric S. Rabkin, eds. **Fights of Fancy: Armed Conflict in Science Fiction and Fantasy**. Athens, GA: University of Georgia Press, 1993. pp.155-169.

___ Bretnor, Reginald. "Science Fiction and the Semantics of Conflict," in: Slusser, George and Eric S. Rabkin, eds. **Fights of Fancy: Armed Conflict in Science Fiction and Fantasy**. Athens, GA: University of Georgia Press, 1993. pp.26-34.

___ Caputi, Jane. "Films of the Nuclear Age," Journal of Popular Film and Television 16(3): 100-107. 1988.

___ Clarke, I. F. "20th Century Future-Think: From the Flame Deluge to the Bad Time," Futures 24(6): 605-614. July/August 1992.

___ Clarke, I. F. "20th Century Future-Think: The Shape of Wars to Come," Futures 24(5): 483-492. June 1992.

___ Clarke, I. F. "20th Century Future-Think: World War II; or, What Did the Future Hold?," Futures 26(3): 335-344. April 1994.

___ Clarke, I. F. **The Tale of the Next Great War, 1871-1914: Fictions of Future Warefare and Battles Still-to-Come**. Liverpool: Liverpool University Press, 1995. 382pp.

___ Clarke, I. F. **Voices Prophesying War: Future Wars 1763-3749**. Oxford: Oxford University Press, 1992. 268pp. Revised edition.

___ Clayton, David. "The Apocalyptic Mirage: Violence and Eschatology in **Dhalgren**," in: Slusser, George and Eric S. Rabkin, eds. **Fights of Fancy: Armed Conflict in Science Fiction and Fantasy**. Athens, GA: University of Georgia Press, 1993. pp.132-144.

___ Cooper, Kenneth D. **Fables of the Nuclear Age: Fifty Years of World War III**. Ph.D. Dissertation, Vanderbilt University, 1992. 352pp. (DAI-A 54/01. p. 176. July 1993.)

___ Dalrymple, Scott. "Demonic Therapy: Reading the Holy Word in the Mushroom Cloud," in: Slusser, George and Eric S. Rabkin, eds. **Fights of Fancy: Armed Conflict in Science Fiction and Fantasy**. Athens, GA: University of Georgia Press, 1993. pp.145-154.

___ Davies, Laurence. " 'The Evils of a Long Peace': Desiring the Great War," in: Slusser, George and Eric S. Rabkin, eds. **Fights of Fancy: Armed Conflict in Science Fiction and Fantasy**. Athens, GA: University of Georgia Press, 1993. pp.59-69.

___ Evans-Karastamatis, Joyce A. **Celluloid Mushroom Clouds: Hollywood and the Atomic Bomb**. Ph.D. Dissertation, University of California, San Diego, 1993. 432pp. (DAI-A 54/06, p. 1986. December 1993.)

___ Fitting, Peter. "You're History, Buddy: Postapocalyptic Visions in Recent Science Fiction Film," in: Slusser, George and Eric S. Rabkin, eds. **Fights of Fancy: Armed Conflict in Science Fiction and Fantasy**. Athens, GA: University of Georgia Press, 1993. pp.114-131.

___ Franklin, H. Bruce. "From Realism to Virtual Reality: Images of America's Wars," Georgia Review 48(1): 47-66. Spring 1994.

___ Franklin, H. Bruce. "The Greatest Fantasy on Earth: The Superweapon in Fiction and Fact," in: Morse, Donald E., ed. **The Celebration of the Fantastic**. Westport, CT: Greenwood, 1992. pp.23-38.

___ Franklin, H. Bruce. "**Star Trek** in the Vietnam Era," Science Fiction Studies 21(1): 24-34. March 1994.

___ Gray, Chris H. "There Will Be War: Future War Fantasies and Militaristic Science Fiction in the 1980s," Science Fiction Studies 21(3): 315-336. November 1994.

___ Haldeman, Joe. "Vietman and Other Alien Worlds," in: Slusser, George and Eric S. Rabkin, eds. **Fights of Fancy: Armed Conflict in Science Fiction and Fantasy**. Athens, GA: University of Georgia Press, 1993. pp.92-102.

WAR

WAR (continued)

___ Landon, Brooks. "Solos, Solutions, Info, and Invasion in (and of) Science Fiction Film," in: Slusser, George and Eric S. Rabkin, eds. **Fights of Fancy: Armed Conflict in Science Fiction and Fantasy**. Athens, GA: University of Georgia Press, 1993. pp.194-208.

___ Langford, David. "Fun With Senseless Violence," *Vector* No. 170: 15-19. December 1992/January 1993.

___ Major, Joseph T. "Star Soldiers Are for Star Wars," *Lan's Lantern* No. 38: 33-41. July 1992.

___ Paris, Michael. "Fear of Flying: The Fiction of War, 1886-1916," *History Today* 43: 29-35. June 1993.

___ Pedrotti, Louis. "Warfare Celestial and Terrestrial: Osip Senkovsky's 1833 Russian Science Fantasy," in: Slusser, George and Eric S. Rabkin, eds. **Fights of Fancy: Armed Conflict in Science Fiction and Fantasy**. Athens, GA: University of Georgia Press, 1993. pp.49-58.

___ Rabkin, Eric S. "Reimagining War," in: Slusser, George and Eric S. Rabkin, eds. **Fights of Fancy: Armed Conflict in Science Fiction and Fantasy**. Athens, GA: University of Georgia Press, 1993. pp.12-25.

___ Radisich, Paula R. "Evolution and Salvation: The Iconic Origins of Druillet's Monstrous Combatants of the Night," in: Slusser, George and Eric S. Rabkin, eds. **Fights of Fancy: Armed Conflict in Science Fiction and Fantasy**. Athens, GA: University of Georgia Press, 1993. pp.103-113.

___ Seed, David. "Push-Button Holocaust: Mordecai Roshwald's **Level 7**," *Foundation* No. 57: 68-86. Spring 1993.

___ Slusser, George E. "Third World Fantasies," in: Slusser, George and Eric S. Rabkin, eds. **Fights of Fancy: Armed Conflict in Science Fiction and Fantasy**. Athens, GA: University of Georgia Press, 1993. pp.170-193.

___ Slusser, George E. "Wars Old and New: The Changing Nature of Fictional Combat," by George E. Slusser and Eric S. Rabkin. in: Slusser, George and Eric S. Rabkin, eds. **Fights of Fancy: Armed Conflict in Science Fiction and Fantasy**. Athens, GA: University of Georgia Press, 1993. pp.1-11.

___ Slusser, George E., ed. **Fights of Fancy: Armed Conflict in Science Fiction and Fantasy**, ed. by George E. Slusser and Eric S. Rabkin. Athens, GA: University of Georgia Press, 1993. 223pp.

___ Stableford, Brian. "Future Wars, 1890-1950," in: Stableford, Brian. **Opening Minds: Essays on Fantastic Literature**. San Bernardino, CA: Borgo Press, 1995. pp.111-134.

___ Stableford, Brian. "Yesterday's Bestsellers, 19: **The Battle of Dorking** and Its Aftermath," *Interzone* No. 83: 52-56. May 1994.

___ Turner, Arthur C. "Armed Conflict in the Science Fiction of H. G. Wells," in: Slusser, George and Eric S. Rabkin, eds. **Fights of Fancy: Armed Conflict in Science Fiction and Fantasy**. Athens, GA: University of Georgia Press, 1993. pp.70-78.

___ Westfahl, Gary. "Wrangling Conversation: Linguistic Patterns in the Dialogue of Heroes and Villains," in: Slusser, George and Eric S. Rabkin, eds. **Fights of Fancy: Armed Conflict in Science Fiction and Fantasy**. Athens, GA: University of Georgia Press, 1993. pp.35-48.

___ Wolff, Michael J. "In the Fields of the Fourth Horseman," *Starlog* No. 220: 27-31. November 1995.

___ Worland, Rick. "Captain Kirk: Cold Warrior," *Journal of Popular Film and Television* 16(3): 109-117. 1988.

WAR GAMES (MOTION PICTURE)

___ Lofficier, Randy. "*War Games* (1983): Interview with John Badham," by Randy Lofficier and Jean-Marc Lofficier. in: Goldberg, Lee et al. **Science Fiction Filmmaking in the 1980s**. Jefferson, NC: McFarland, 1995. pp.253-258.

WAR OF THE WORLDS (1953) (MOTION PICTURE)

___ Renzi, Thomas C. **H. G. Wells: Six Scientific Romances Adapted for Film**. Metuchen, NJ: Scarecrow, 1992. 249pp.

___ Weaver, Tom. "In Martian Combat," *Starlog* No. 195: 66-71. October 1993.

WAR OF THE WORLDS (RADIO)

___ "Finnish Radio Drama About *The Next War* Causes a Civil Upset," *Variety* p.1, 145. January 1, 1986.

___ "Welles' 'War' Replayed: Police Alerted, But 31 Years Have Tamed the Drama," *Variety* p. 32. November 5, 1969.

___ Fontrodona, Mariano. "El dia que marte invadio la tierra [The Day That Mars Invaded Earth]," *Historia y Vida* 21(249): 104-109. 1988.

WARGAMES (MOTION PICTURE)

___ Kerman, Judith B. "Virtual Space and Its Boundaries in Science Fiction Film and Television: *Tron*, *Max Headroom*, *War Games*," in: Morse, Donald E., ed. **The Celebration of the Fantastic**. Westport, CT: Greenwood, 1992. pp.191-204.

WARLOCK: THE ARMAGEDDON (MOTION PICTURE)

___ Bacal, Simon. "*Warlock: The Armageddon*," *Cinefantastique* 23(6): 6-7. April 1993.

___ Biodrowski, Steve. "*Warlock: The Armageddon*," *Cinefantastique* 24(3/4): 120-121. October 1993.

___ Harris, Judith P. "*Warlock: The Armageddon*," *Cinefantastique* 24(6)/25(1): 124. February 1994.

WARNER BOOKS

___ "Warner Science Fiction Relaunch," *Locus* 31(5): 6. November 1993.

WARNER, HARRY, JR.

___ "Harry Warner, Jr.," *Science Fiction Chronicle* 14(12): 25. September 1993.

___ "The Hugos (Or, the Empire Strikes Back)," *Science Fiction Chronicle* 17(2): 55-56. December 1995/January 1996.

WARNER, SYLVIA TOWNSEND

___ Russell, R. B. "Alterative Lives in Arthur Machen's 'A Fragment of Life' and Sylvia Townsend Warner's **Lolly Willowes**," *Studies in Weird Fiction* No. 12: 17-19. Spring 1993.

WATCH THE SKIES (MOTION PICTURE)

___ SEE: XTRO 3: WATCH THE SKIES (MOTION PICTURE).

WATCHER (TV)

___ Millman, Joyce. "Acting as Hard as He Can," *San Francisco (CA) Examiner*. April 11, 1995. in: *NewsBank. Film and Television*. 51:C8. 1995.

___ Richmond, Ray. "Kato Gets into the Act Again," *Los Angeles (CA) Daily News*. April 11, 1995. in: *NewsBank. Film and Television*. 51:C7. 1995.

WATCHERS III (MOTION PICTURE)

___ Harris, Judith P. "*Watchers III* (Review)," *Cinefantastique* 26(5): 60. August 1995.

WATERWORLD (MOTION PICTURE)

___ Arroyo, Jose. "*Waterworld* (Review)," *Sight and Sound* 5(9): 62-63. September 1995.

___ Bibby, Patrice. "*Waterworld* Filming Is Awash in Production, Financial Problems," *(Denver, CO) Rocky Mountain News*. March 8, 1995. in: *NewsBank. Film and Television*. 39:F5-F6. 1995.

___ Biodrowski, Steve. "*Waterworld* (Review)," *Cinefantastique* 27(3): 51. December 1995.

___ Campbell, Bob. "H2 Uh-Oh," *(Newark, NJ) Star-Ledger*. July 28, 1995. in: *NewsBank. Film and Television*. 72:G2. 1995.

___ Doherty, Thomas. "*Waterworld*," *Cinefantastique* 26(5): 6-9, 61. August 1995.

___ Dominguez, Robert. "How Do You Sell Tickets on the *Titanic*?," *(New York, NY) Daily News*. July 16, 1995. in: *NewsBank. Film and Television*. 82:D7. 1995.

___ Eller, Claudia. "Plenty of Riptides in *Waterworld* Set," by Claudia Eller and Robert W. Welkos. *Los Angeles (CA) Times*. September 16, 1994. in: *NewsBank. Film and Television*. 117:C10. 1994.

___ Flixman, Ed. "*Waterworld*: Box Office Wild Card," *Sci-Fi Entertainment* 2(2): 50-55, 74. August 1995.

___ Fristoe, Roger. "A Reel Sinking Feeling," *(Louisville, KY) Courier-Journal*. July 23, 1995. in: *NewsBank. Film and Television*. 82:D8-D9. 1995.

___ Harada, Wayne. "*Waterworld* (oops) Dances With Whales," *Honolulu (HI) Advertiser*. February 1, 1995. in: *NewsBank. Film and Television*. 30:G13. 1995.

___ Howard, Scripps. "*Waterworld* Inundated by Hawaiian Lawsuits," *Boston (MA) Herald*. August 2, 1995. in: *NewsBank. Film and Television*. 82:D6. 1995.

___ Hunter, Stephen. "*Waterworld* Isn't Sinking, But It Won't Soar," *(Baltimore, MD) Sun*. August 6, 1995. in: *NewsBank. Film and Television*. 82:D2-D3. 1995.

WATERWORLD (MOTION PICTURE)

WATERWORLD (MOTION PICTURE) (continued)
___ Johnson, Kim H. "Rime of the Future Mariner," *Starlog* No. 218: 40-44. September 1995.
___ Lovell, Glenn. "*Waterworld*: Kevin Costner, Auteur," *Cinefantastique* 26(5): 8. August 1995.
___ Lowe, Nick. "*Waterworld* (Review)," *Interzone* No. 101: 33-34. November 1995.
___ Magid, Ron. "Taking the Plunge on *Waterworld*," *American Cinematographer* 76(12): 73-76. December 1995.
___ Mason, Mary C. "Effects Scene: The Last Hurrah," *Cinefex* No. 63: 117-118. September 1995.
___ Medved, Michael. "Muddy Water," *New York (NY) Post.* July 28, 1995. in: *NewsBank. Film and Television.* 72:G3. 1995.
___ Morrison, Bill. "Costner's Imperfect World," *(Raleigh, NC) News and Observer.* July 28, 1995. in: *NewsBank. Film and Television.* 82:D12. 1995.
___ O'Sullivan, Kevin. "Sinking of *Waterworld*," *(New York, NY) Daily News.* July 16, 1995. in: *NewsBank. Film and Television.* 82:D4-D5. 1995.
___ Odien, Jeff. "On the Water Front," *Cinefex* No. 64: 96-117. December 1995.
___ Rodriguez, Rene. "*Waterworld*," *Miami (FL) Herald.* July 23, 1995. in: *NewsBank. Film and Television.* 72:F12-G1. 1995.
___ Shapiro, Marc. "Storm Gathering," *Starlog* No. 219: 50-53. October 1995.
___ Shapiro, Marc. "Treading Water," *Starlog* No. 217: 67-69. August 1995.
___ Shapiro, Marc. "*Waterworld*," *Starlog* No. 216: 16-17. July 1995.
___ Tittl, Pete. "Anchoring in Kern," *Bakersfield (CA) Californian.* February 3, 1995. in: *NewsBank. Film and Television.* 30:G12. 1995.
___ Truan, Kenneth. "Dancing With Dolphins," *Los Angeles (CA) Times.* July 28, 1995. in: *NewsBank. Film and Television.* 82:D10-D11. 1995.
___ Welkos, Robert W. "Sea Epic's Costs May Bring Wave of Caution," by Robert W. Welkos and Judy Brennan. *Los Angeles (CA) Times.* July 26, 1995. in: *NewsBank. Film and Television.* 82:C13-D1. 1995.
___ Wells, Jerry. "Wettest Movie Ever Made Surfaces for Peek," *(Newark, NJ) Star-Ledger.* January 23, 1995. in: *NewsBank. Film and Television.* 22:G8-G9. 1995.
___ Williams, David E. "An Oceanic Odyssey," *American Cinematographer* 76(8): 40-51. August 1995.
___ Wuntch, Phillip. "A Surprise Viewing of the Priciest Movie in History," *Dallas (TX) Morning News.* May 26, 1995. in: *NewsBank. Film and Television.* 66:D3. 1995.
___ Wuntch, Phillip. "*Waterworld*: Dive into an Old-Fashioned Sloshbuckler," *Dallas (TX) Morning News.* July 28, 1995. in: *NewsBank. Film and Television.* 80:D13. 1995.

WATLING, DEBORAH
___ Airey, Jean. "Victorian Screamer," *Starlog* No. 190: 75-77. May 1993.

WATSON, IAN
___ Crowther, Pete. "Destabilizing Reality: Ian Watson Interviewed," *Interzone* No. 75: 17-24. September 1993.
___ Gomel, Elana. "Mystery, Apocalypse and Utopia: The Case of the Ontological Detective Story," *Science Fiction Studies* 22(3): 343-356. November 1995
___ Schweitzer, Darrell. "*Weird Tales* Talks With Ian Watson," *Weird Tales* 54(2): 54-59. Summer 1993. (No. 307)

WATSON, KEITH
___ "Watson, Keith (Obituary)," *Locus* 32(6): 72. June 1994.

WATT-EVANS, LAWRENCE
___ Murphy, D. Allen. "Crossing All the Borders: An Interview with Lawrence Watt-Evans," *Quantum* No. 42: 25-28. Summer/Fall 1992.
___ Willems, S. F. "Lawrence Watt-Evans Discusses HWA," *Genre Writer's News* 1(7): 11-14. May/June 1995.

WATTLEY, RALPH P.
___ "Wattley, Ralph P. (Obituary)," *Science Fiction Chronicle* 15(1): 16. October 1993.

WAXWORK II: LOST IN TIME (MOTION PICTURE)
___ Biodrowski, Steve. "*Waxwork II: Lost in Time*," *Cinefantastique* 22(6): 48-49. June 1992

WAY OUT (TV)
___ Joseph, Gary. "Inside the Dahl House of Horror," by Gary Joseph and Martin H. Friedenthal. *Filmfax* No. 41: 65-69. October/November 1993.

WE'RE BACK (MOTION PICTURE)
___ Maurstad, Tom. "Even for a Dino Cartoon *We're Back* Is Lightweight (Review)," *Dallas (TX) Morning News.* November 24, 1993. in: *NewsBank. Art.* 38:A4. 1993.

WEAPONS
___ Franklin, H. Bruce. "The Greatest Fantasy on Earth: The Superweapon in Fiction and Fact," in: Morse, Donald E., ed. **The Celebration of the Fantastic**. Westport, CT: Greenwood, 1992. pp.23-38.
___ Lenihan, John H. "Superweapons From the Past," in: Loukides, Paul, ed. **The Material World in American Popular Film**. Bowling Green, OH: Popular Press, 1993. pp.164-174.

WEAVER, SIGOURNEY
___ Jones, Alan. "Queen of Outer Space," *Cinefantastique* 23(4): 6-9. December 1992.
___ Murphy, Kathleen. "The Last Temptation of Sigourney Weaver," *Film Comment* 28(4): 17-20. July/August 1992.
___ Pirani, Adam. "Alien Nemesis," by Adam Pirani and Ian Spelling. in: McDonnell, David, ed. **Starlog's Science Fiction Heroes and Heroines**. New York: Crescent Books, 1995. pp.9-11.

WEBB, RICHARD
___ "Webb, Richard (Obituary)," *Science Fiction Chronicle* 14(10): 16. July 1993.

WEDDELL, ROGER
___ "DUFF's Roger Weddell Dies, Complicating New DUFF Race," *Science Fiction Chronicle* 14(4): 4. January 1993.
___ "Weddell, Roger (Obituary)," *Locus* 30(2): 69. February 1993.

WEINBAUM, STANLEY G.
___ Stableford, Brian. "Creators of Science Fiction, 1: Stanley G. Weinbaum," *Interzone* No. 90: 51-53. December 1994.
___ Stableford, Brian. "The Lost Pioneer: The Science Fiction of Stanley G. Weinbaum," in: Stableford, Brian. **Outside the Human Aquarium: Masters of Science Fiction**. San Bernardino, CA: Borgo, 1995. pp.126-134.

WEINBERG, BOB
___ " 'Cowboy Bob' Revealed," *Science Fiction Chronicle* 13(11/12): 10. August 1992.

WEIRD SCIENCE (TV)
___ "Winter Preview: Unnatural Science," *TV Guide* 42(4): 9. January 22, 1994.

WEIRD TALES (MAGAZINE)
___ "*Weird Tales* Changes Names," *Locus* 32(4): 8. April 1994.
___ "*Weird Tales* Reformats; Other Magazine Changes," *Locus* 29(3): 7, 79. September 1992.
___ "World Fantasy Awards," *Science Fiction Chronicle* 14(3): 4. December 1992.
___ Cockcroft, T. G. L. "An Index to 'The Eyrie'," *Fantasy Commentator* 8(3/4): 217-229. Fall 1995. (Whole No. 47/48)

WEIS, MARGARET
___ "An Interview With Margaret Weis and Tracy Hickman," *Sense of Wonder* p. 1-4. February/March 1994.
___ "Weis and Hickman All Over," *Locus* 33(4): 8, 75. October 1994.
___ Weis, Margaret, ed. **Leaves From the Inn of the Last Home: The Complete Krynn Source Book**, ed. by Margaret Weis and Tracy Hickman. Lake Geneva, WI: TSR, 1993. 255pp.

WEISINGER, MORT
___ "Weisinger, Mort (Obituary)," *Science Fiction News* (Australia) No. 55: 13-14. June 1978.

WEISS, JAN
___ Adamovic, Ivan. "Jan Weiss (1892-1972), Karel Capek's Overlooked Contemporary," *Extrapolation* 36(4): 285-291. Winter 1995.

WEISSMULLER, JOHNNY
___ "Weissmuller, Johnny, 79, Best-Known Screen Tarzan, Dies in Mexico (Obituary)," *Variety* p. 4, 34. January 25, 1984.
___ Fury, David. "Johnny Weissmuller...The Two Career Star," *Burroughs Bulletin* NS. No. 14: 19-28. April 1993.

WELCOME II THE TERRORDOME (MOTION PICTURE)
___ Lowe, Nick. "***Welcome II the Terrordome*** (Review)," *Interzone* No. 93: 32-33. March 1995.

WELDON, FAY
___ Squier, Susan M. "Conceiving Difference: Reproductive Technology and the Construction of Identity in Two Contemporary Fictions," in: Benjamin, Marina, ed. **A Question of Identity: Women, Science, and Literature**. New Brunswick, NJ: Rutgers University Press, 1993. pp.97-115.

WELLES, ORSON
___ "Welles' 'War' Replayed: Police Alerted, But 31 Years Have Tamed the Drama," *Variety* p. 32. November 5, 1969.
___ Fontrodona, Mariano. "El dia que marte invadio la tierra [The Day That Mars Invaded Earth]," *Historia y Vida* 21(249): 104-109. 1988.

WELLMAN, MANLY WADE
___ Schweitzer, Darrell. "Manly Wade Wellman," in: Schweitzer, Darrell. **Speaking of Horror: Interviews With Writers of the Supernatural**. San Bernardino, CA: Borgo, 1994. pp.93-102.

WELLS, H. G.
___ "H. G. Wells," in: Bloom, Harold, ed. **Classic Science Fiction Writers**. New York: Chelsea House, 1995. pp.167-186.
___ "H. G. Wells Conference," *Locus* 35(4): 8. October 1995.
___ "Last H. G. Wells Papers Acquired by the H. G. Wells Archives at Illinois," *Locus* 30(2): 7, 74. February 1993.
___ Aldiss, Brian W. "Introduction to **The War of the Worlds**, Part 1," *New York Review of Science Fiction* No. 50: 1, 8-10. October 1992.
___ Aldiss, Brian W. "Introduction to **The War of the Worlds**, Part 2," *New York Review of Science Fiction* No. 51: 18-22. November 1992.
___ Aldiss, Brian W. "Wells and the Leopard Lady," in: Aldiss, Brian W. **The Detached Retina: Aspects of SF and Fantasy**. Syracuse, NY: Syracuse University Press, 1995. pp.116-127.
___ Allen, Virginia. "Ethos and Marginalization in the Henry James/H. G. Wells Affair," *Extrapolation* 33(4): 317-332. Winter 1992.
___ Allen, Virginia. "The Ethos of English Departments: Henry James and H. G. Wells, Continued," *Extrapolation* 34(4): 305-328. Winter 1993.
___ Bailey, K. V. "Homo Tewler and the Undine: Evolutionary and Mythic Image in Wells's Late Fiction," *Foundation* No. 56: 61-75. Autumn 1992.
___ Battaglia, Beatrice. "L'île comme distinée: **The Island of Doctor Moreau** de H. G. Wells," in: Marimoutou, Jean-Claude, ed. **L'insularité thématique et représentations**. Paris: Editions L'Harmattan, 1995. pp.427-431.
___ Baxter, Stephen. "Further Visions: Sequels to **The Time Machine**," *Foundation* No. 65: 41-50. Autumn 1995.
___ Baxter, Stephen. "Lighting the Future: The Future History of Wells's **The Time Machine**," *Vector* No. 181: 4-6. November/December 1994.
___ Bozzetto, Roger. "L'île bouffonne du Docteur Moreau," in: Marimoutou, Jean-Claude, ed. **L'insularité thématique et représentations**. Paris: Editions L'Harmattan, 1995. pp.441-447.
___ Bozzetto, Roger. "Moreau's Tragi-Farcical Island," *Science Fiction Studies* 20(1): 34-44. March 1993.
___ Caldwell, Larry W. "Wells, Orwell, and Atwood: (EP)Logic and Eu/Utopia," *Extrapolation* 33(4): 333-345. Winter 1992.
___ Coren, Michael. **The Invisible Man: The Life and Liberties of H. G. Wells**. New York: Atheneum, 1993. 240pp.
___ Davies-Morris, Gareth N. **Worlds in Collision: The Dialectic of H. G. Wells's Early Science Fiction**. Master's Thesis, San Diego State University, 1994. 211pp.
___ De Canio, Stephen J. "The Future Through Yesterday: Long-Term Forecasting in the Novels of H. G. Wells and Jules Verne," *Centennial Review* 75(1): 75-93. Winter 1994.
___ Deery, June. "H. G. Wells's **A Modern Utopia** as a Work in Progress," *Extrapolation* 34(3): 216-229. Fall 1993.
___ Derry, Stephen. "The Time Traveller's Utopian Books and His Reading of the Future," *Foundation* No. 65: 16-24. Autumn 1995.
___ Ferrell, Keith. "Forum: The Challenges of Science Fiction," *Omni* 14(5): 6. February 1992.

WELLS, H. G. (continued)
___ Fleissner, Robert F. "H. G. Wells and Ralph Ellison: Need the Effect of One Invisible Man on Another Be *Itself* Invisible?," *Extrapolation* 33(4): 346-350. Winter 1992.
___ Foot, Michael. **H. G.: The History of Mr. Wells**. Washington, DC: Counterpoint, 1995. 318pp.
___ Gilmore, Chris. "Why Is Science Fiction?," *Interzone* No. 62: 48-49. August 1992.
___ Hammond, J. R. "A Checklist of Wells's Short Stories," in: Hammond, J. R. **H. G. Wells and the Short Story**. New York: St. Martin's, 1992. pp.29-39.
___ Hammond, J. R. "The Frontiers of Art," in: Hammond, J. R. **H. G. Wells and the Short Story**. New York: St. Martin's, 1992. pp.19-28.
___ Hammond, J. R. **H. G. Wells and Rebecca West**. New York: St. Martin's, 1991. 280pp.
___ Hammond, J. R. **H. G. Wells and the Short Story**. New York: St. Martin's, 1992. 175pp.
___ Hammond, J. R. "Wells and the Short Story," in: Hammond, J. R. **H. G. Wells and the Short Story**. New York: St. Martin's, 1992. pp.3-18.
___ Harris, Janice H. "Wifely Silence and Speech in Three Marriage Novels by H. G. Wells," *Studies in the Novel* 26(4): 404-419. Winter 1994.
___ Harris-Fain, Darren. **H. G. Wells and the Modernist Revolution**. Ph.D. Dissertation, Kent State University, 1992. 332pp. (DAI-A 53/10. p. 3536. April 1993.)
___ Holt, Philip. "H. G. Wells and the Ring of Gyges," *Science-Fiction Studies* 19(2): 236-247. July 1992.
___ Hunter, Jefferson. "Orwell, Wells, and **Coming Up for Air**," *Modern Philology* 78(1): 38-47. August 1980.
___ Huntington, John. "**The Time Machine** and Wells's Social Trajectory," *Foundation* No. 65: 6-15. Autumn 1995.
___ Lake, David. "Wells, **The First Men in the Moon**, and Lewis's Ransom Trilogy," in: Filmer, Kath, ed. **Twentieth-Century Fantasists: Essays in Culture, Society and Belief in Twentieth Century Mythopoeic Literature**. New York: St. Martin's, 1992. pp.23-33.
___ Lehman, Steven. "The Motherless Child in Science Fiction: **Frankenstein** and Moreau," *Science Fiction Studies* 19(1): 49-58. March 1992.
___ Lowentrout, Peter. "**The War of the Worlds** Revisited: Science Fiction and the Angst of Secularization," *Extrapolation* 33(4): 351-359. Winter 1992.
___ Manlove, C. N. "Charles Kingsley, H. G. Wells, and the Machine in Victorian Fiction," *Nineteenth Century Literature* 48(2): [10pp.] 1995. (Cited from the electronic edition, NCL-E, 48(2), 1995. (http: //sunsite. berkeley. edu:8080/ scan/ncle.482/ articles/ manlove.art482.html)).
___ Meurger, Michel. "Wells's Martians," *Monad* No. 3: 1-34. September 1993.
___ Nardo, Don. **H. G. Wells**. San Diego, CA: Lucent Books, 1992. 111PP.
___ Nardo, Don. **The Importance of H. G. Wells**. San Diego, CA: Lucent Books, 1992. 109pp.
___ Palumbo, Donald E. "The Politics of Entropy: Revolution vs. Evolution in George Pal's 1960 Film Version of H. G. Wells's **The Time Machine**," in: Latham, Robert A. and Collins, Robert A., eds. **Modes of the Fantastic**. Westport, CT: Greenwood, 1995. pp.204-211.
___ Paris, Phyllis. "H. G. Wells: Foreseer of the Future," *Stamps* 252(10): 3. September 2, 1995.
___ Parrinder, Patrick. "From Mary Shelley to **The War of the Worlds**: The Thames Valley Catastrophe," in: Seed, David, ed. **Anticipations: Essays on Early Science Fiction and Its Precursors**. Liverpool: Liverpool University Press, 1995. pp.58-74.
___ Parrinder, Patrick. "H. G. Wells and the Fall of Empires," *Foundation* No. 57: 48-58. Spring 1993.
___ Parrinder, Patrick. **Shadows of the Future: H. G. Wells, Science Fiction and Prophecy**. Liverpool: Liverpool University Press, 1995. 170pp.
___ Philmus, Robert M. "The Strange Case of 'Moreau' Gets Stranger," *Science-Fiction Studies* 19(2): 248-250. July 1992.
___ Renzi, Thomas C. **H. G. Wells: Six Scientific Romances Adapted for Film**. Metuchen, NJ: Scarecrow, 1992. 249pp.
___ Russell, W. M. S. "Time Before and After **The Time Machine**," *Foundation* No. 65: 24-40. Autumn 1995.
___ Scheick, William J., ed. **The Critical Response to H. G. Wells**. Westport, CT: Greenwood, 1995. 194pp.

WELLS, H. G.

___ WELLS, H. G. (continued)

___ Schlutze, Bruno. "Herbert George Wells, **The War of the Worlds** (1898)," in: Heuermann, Harmut, ed. **Der Science Fiction Roman in der angloamerikanischen Literatur: Interpretationen.** Düsseldorf: Bagel, 1986. pp.47-64.

___ Schmitt, Ronald E. **The Reclamation of the Future Dream: Dreams in British Science Fiction (Mary Shelley, H. G. Wells, George Orwell, Michael Moorcock).** Ph.D. Dissertation, University of Rhode Island, 1995. 182pp. (DAI-A 56/09, p. 3598. March 1996.)

___ Schultze, Bruno. "Herbert George Wells: **A Modern Utopia** (1903)," in: Heuermann, Hartmut and Lange, Bernd-Peter, eds. **Die Utopie in der angloamerikanischen Literatur: Interpretationen.** Düsseldorf: Bagel, 1984. pp.161-175.

___ Simpson, Anne B. "H. G. Wells's **Tono-Bungay**: Individualism and Difference," *Essays in Literature* 22(1): 75-86. Spring 1995.

___ Smith, J. Percy , ed. **Bernard Shaw and H. G. Wells.** Toronto: University of Toronto Press, 1995. 242pp.

___ Stableford, Brian. "Opening Minds," in: Stableford, Brian. **Opening Minds: Essays on Fantastic Literature.** San Bernardino, CA: Borgo Press, 1995. pp.23-28.

___ Turner, Arthur C. "Armed Conflict in the Science Fiction of H. G. Wells," in: Slusser, George and Eric S. Rabkin, eds. **Fights of Fancy: Armed Conflict in Science Fiction and Fantasy.** Athens, GA: University of Georgia Press, 1993. pp.70-78.

___ Wells, H. G. **The Annotated H. G. Wells: The Island of Doctor Moreau. A Critical Text of the 1896 London First Edition, with Introduction and Appendices**, edited by Leon Stover. Jefferson, NC: McFarland, 1995. 408pp.

___ Wells, H. G. **The Annotated H. G. Wells: The Time Machine, An Invention. A Critical Text of the 1895 London First Edition, with Introduction and Appendices**, edited by Leon Stover. Jefferson, NC: McFarland, 1995. 269pp.

___ Wells, H. G. **A Critical Edition of the War of the Worlds: H. G. Wells's Scientific Romance.** Bloomington, IN: Indiana University Press, 1992. [CIP, Not seen.]

___ Wells, H. G. **The Island of Dr. Moreau: A Valorum Text**, by H. G. Wells and Robert M. Philmus. Athens, GA: University of Georgia Press, 1993. 240pp.

WELLS, MARTHA

___ Riecher, Anton. "Playing With Fire: Fantasy Author Exercises Vivid Imagination," *Bryan-College Station Eagle* Sec. D, p. 1, 3. August 14, 1994.

WELSH, BO

___ Shapiro, Marc. "Dark Designs," *Starlog* 179: 27-31. June 1992.

WENDELL, LEILAH

___ Davidson, Jane P. "A Golem of Her Own: The Fantastic Art and Literature of Leilah Wendell," in: Wolf, Milton T. and Mallett, Daryl F., eds. **Imaginative Futures: Proceedings of the 1993 Science Fiction Research Association Conference.** San Bernardino, CA: Jacob's Ladder Books, 1995. pp.341-352.

WENDERS, WIM

___ Yakir, Dan. "To the Ends of the Dream World," *Starlog* 177: 38-40, 77. April 1992.

WEREWOLVES

___ Ball, Jerry L. "Guy Endore's **The Werewolf of Paris**: The Definitive Werewolf Novel?," *Studies in Weird Fiction* No. 17: 2-12. Summer 1995.

___ Kies, Cosette. "Never Turn Your Back on a Werewolf," *Voice of Youth Advocates* 18(3): 145-146. August 1995.

___ Noll, Richard. **Vampires, Werewolves, and Demons: Twentieth Century Reports in the Psychiatric Literature.** New York: Brunner, 1992. 244pp.

WERFEL, FRANZ

___ Altmann, Hans. "Franz Werfels 'Stern der Ungeborenen'," in: Kranz, Gisbert, ed. **Inklings: Jahrbuch für Literatur und Ästhetik.** 8. Band. Lüdenscheid, Germany: Stier, 1990. pp.146-160. [Not seen.]

___ Rode, Silvia A. **Franz Werfels 'Stern der Ungeborenen': die Utopie als Fiktionaler Genrediskurs und Ideengeschichte.** Ph.D. Dissertation, University of California, Los Angeles, 1993. 304pp. (DAI-A 54/03, p. 943. September 1993.)

WES CRAVEN'S NEW NIGHTMARE (MOTION PICTURE)

___ Kutzera, Dale. "*Wes Craven's New Nightmare*," *Cinefantastique* 25(4): 6-7, 61. August 1994.

___ Newman, Kim. "*Wes Craven's New Nightmare* (Review)," *Sight and Sound* 5(1): 62-63. January 1995.

WEST, ADAM

___ Nazzaro, Joe. "Bat Attitude," *Starlog* No. 210: 50-53. January 1995.

WEST, NATHANAEL

___ Merrill, Catherine. "Defining the Fantastic Grotesque: Nathanael West's **The Dream Life of Balso Snell**," in: Latham, Robert A. and Collins, Robert A., eds. **Modes of the Fantastic.** Westport, CT: Greenwood, 1995. pp.64-73.

WESTALL, ROBERT

___ "Westall, Robert (Obituary)," *Locus* 30(6): 71. June 1993.

___ "Westall, Robert (Obituary)," *Science Fiction Chronicle* 14(9): 17. June 1993.

___ Newsinger, John. "Futuretracks: The Juvenile Science Fiction of Robert Westall," *Foundation* No. 63: 61-67. Spring 1995.

WESTERN THEME

___ Mogen, David. **Wilderness Visions: The Western Theme in Science Fiction Literature.** 2nd ed., Revised and Expanded. San Bernardino, CA: Borgo Press, 1994. 128pp.

WESTMORE, MICHAEL

___ Maccarillo, Lisa. "In the Lab of the Imagination with Michael Westmore," *Sci-Fi Entertainment* 1(2): 52-54. August 1994.

WESTWORLD (MOTION PICTURE)

___ Telotte, J. P. "**Westworld, Futureworld**, and the World's Obscenity," in: Ruddick, Nicholas, ed. **State of the Fantastic.** Westport, CT: Greenwood, 1992. pp.179-188.

WHALES

___ Wytenbroek, J. R. "Cetacean Consciousness in Katz's **Whalesinger** and L'Engle's **A Ring of Endless Light**," in: Reynolds, Patricia and GoodKnight, Glen H., eds. **Proceedings of the J. R. R. Tolkien Centenary Conference, Keble College, Oxford, 1992.** Altadena, CA: Mythopoeic Press, 1995. pp.435-438. (*Mythlore* Vol. 21, No. 2, Winter 1996, Whole No. 80)

WHARTON, EDITH

___ Burleson, Donald R. "Sabbats: Hawthorne/Wharton," *Studies in Weird Fiction* No. 12: 12-16. Spring 1993.

___ Burleson, Mollie L. "Edith Wharton's Summer: Through the Glass Darkly," *Studies in Weird Fiction* No. 13: 18-20. Summer 1993. [Not seen.]

WHEATLEY, DENNIS

___ "Wheatley, Dennis (Obituary)," *Science Fiction News* (Australia) No. 54: 11. April 1978.

WHEATON, WIL

___ Spelling, Ian. "Guest Star," *Starlog* No. 176: 50-53. March 1992.

WHELAN, MICHAEL

___ "Creative Explorations: An Interview With Michael Whelan," *Hailing Frequencies* (Waldenbooks) No. 9: 2-4. 1993.

___ "Michael Whelan: Breathing Space," *Locus* 30(1): 4, 65. January 1993.

___ McCaffrey, Anne. "Dragon-Master's Dialogue," *Science Fiction Age* 1(6): 78-83. September 1993.

___ McTigue, Maureen. "Man of Wonder: Michael Whelan," *Starlog* No. 197: 32-37, 68. December 1993.

___ Paget, Stephen. "An Interview with Michael Whelan," *Sense of Wonder* (B. Dalton) pp.1-4. October/November 1993.

WHEN WORLDS COLLIDE (MOTION PICTURE)

___ Williams, Wade. "Behind the Scenes with Richard Derr, **When Worlds Collide**," *Filmfax* No. 30: 50-59. December 1991/January 1992.

WHITE DWARF (TV)

WHITE DWARF (TV)
___ Bark, Ed. "*White Dwarf*," *Dallas (TX) Morning News*. May 23, 1995. in: *NewsBank. Film and Television*. 58:A12. 1995.
___ Fischer, Dennis. "*White Dwarf* (Review)," *Cinefantastique* 26(6)/27(1): 124. October 1995.
___ Kenny, Glenn. "Don't Crush That Dwarf," *TV Guide* 43(12): 46. March 25, 1995.
___ Littlefield, Kinney. "A New World for Coppola," (*Santa Ana, CA*) *Orange County Register*. May 23, 1995. in: *NewsBank. Film and Television*. 60:G5. 1995.

WHITE ZOMBIE (MOTION PICTURE)
___ Hogan, David J. "*White Zombie* (1932) (Review)," *Filmfax* No. 35: 18. October/November 1992.
___ Sevastakis, Michael. **Songs of Love and Death: The Classical American Horror Film of the 1930s**. Westport, CT: Greenwood, 1993. 232pp.

WHITE, ANDREW ADAMS
___ "White, Andrew Adams (Drew) (Obituary)," *Locus* 31(3): 82. September 1993.

WHITE, E. B.
___ Griffith, John. **Charlotte's Web: A Pig's Salvation**. New York: Twayne, 1993. 116pp.

WHITE, EDWARD LUCAS
___ Weinstein, Lee. "Edward Lucas White," *Studies in Weird Fiction* No. 11: 15-24. Spring 1992.

WHITE, JAMES
___ "James White: Full-Time Hobbyist," *Locus* 30(3): 4, 73-74. March 1993.

WHITE, T. H.
___ Adderley, C. M. "The Best Thing for Being Sad: Education and Educators in T. H. White's **Once and Future King**," *Quondam et Futurus* 2(1): 55-68. Spring 1992.
___ Hanks, D. Thomas, Jr. "T. H. White's Merlin: More Than Malory Made Him," in: Watson, Jeanie and Fries, Marueen, eds. **The Figure of Merlin in the Nineteenth and Twentieth Centuries**. Lewiston, NY: Mellen, 1989. pp.100-120.
___ Herman, Harold J. "Teaching White, Stewart, and Berger," in: Fries, Maureen and Watson, Jeanie, eds. **Approaches to the Teaching of the Arthurian Tradition**. New York: Modern Language Association, 1992. pp.113-117.
___ Sandler, Florence F. "Family Romance in **The Once and Future King**," *Quondam et Futurus* 2(2): 72-80. Summer 1992.
___ Serrano, Amanda. "T. H. White's Defense of Guenevere: The Portrait of a 'Real' Person," *Mythlore* 21(1): 9-13. Summer 1995. (No. 79)
___ Shippey, Tom. "Tolkien as a Post-War Writer," in: Reynolds, Patricia and GoodKnight, Glen H., eds. **Proceedings of the J. R. R. Tolkien Centenary Conference, Keble College, Oxford, 1992**. Altadena, CA: Mythopoeic Press, 1995. pp.84-93. (*Mythlore* Vol. 21, No. 2, Winter 1996, Whole No. 80)

WHITEHEAD, HENRY S.
___ Frenschkowski, Marco. "Henry S. Whitehead," *Quarber Merkur* 31(2): 55-68. Dezember 1993. (No. 80)
___ Searles, A. Langley. "Henry S. Whitehead: A Retrospection," *Fantasy Commentator* 8(3/4): 186-200. Fall 1995. (Whole No. 47/48)

WHITTLEMORE, EDWARD
___ "Whittlemore, Edward (Obituary)," *Locus* 35(4): 70. October 1995.

WHYTE, ANDREW ADAMS
___ "Whyte, Drew (Obituary)," *Science Fiction Chronicle* 14(12): 12. September 1993.

WIATER, STANLEY
___ Dobbs, G. Michael. "Stanley Wiater: A Conversation with the Interviewer," in: Wiater, Stanley. **Dark Visions: Conversations with the Masters of the Horror Film**. New York: Avon, 1992. pp.1-7.

WIGGINS, MARIANNE
___ Barr, Marleen S. **Lost in Space: Probing Feminist Science Fiction and Beyond**. Chapel Hill, NC: University of North Carolina Press, 1993. 231pp.

WILD PALMS (TV)
___ Altman, Mark A. "*Wild Palms* (Review)," *Cinefantastique* 24(3/4): 123. October 1993.
___ Carlson, Timothy. "The Universe Is Expanding All over the Dial," by Timothy Carlson and Mark Schwed. *TV Guide* 41(1): 16-19. January 2, 1993. (Issue 2075)

WILD, ROBERTA
___ "Wild, Roberta (Obituary)," *Science Fiction Chronicle* 14(6): 16. March 1993.

WILDE, OSCAR
___ Bloom, Harold. "Oscar Wilde," in: Bloom, Harold. **Classic Fantasy Writers**. New York: Chelsea House, 1994. pp.175-187.
___ Jacobs, Susan T. "When Formula Seizes Form: Oscar Wilde's Comedies," in: Murphy, Patrick D., ed. **Staging the Impossible: The Fantastic Mode in Modern Drama**. Westport, CT: Greenwood, 1992. pp.15-29.
___ Ursini, James. **More Things Than Are Dreamt Of: Masterpieces of Supernatural Horror, From Mary Shelley to Stephen King, in Literature and Film**, by James Ursini and Alain Silver. New York: Limelight, 1994. 226pp.

WILDER NAPALM (MOTION PICTURE)
___ Scapperotti, Dan. "*Wilder Napalm*," *Cinefantastique* 23(5): 12-13. February 1993.

WILDER, CHERRY
___ Rousseau, Yvonne. "The Wilder Alien Shores: Or, The Colonials Are Revolting," *Foundation* No. 54: 15-36. Spring 1992.
___ Wilder, Cherry. "The Profession of Science Fiction, 43: Far Fetched," *Foundation* No. 54: 5-15. Spring 1992.

WILDSIDE PRESS
___ "Big Loss at Wildside," *Locus* 35(5): 8. November 1995.
___ "Near Fatal Blow for Wildside Press," *Science Fiction Chronicle* 17(1): 5-6. October/November 1995

WILHELM, KATE
___ Barr, Marleen S. **Lost in Space: Probing Feminist Science Fiction and Beyond**. Chapel Hill, NC: University of North Carolina Press, 1993. 231pp.

WILLIAM L. CRAWFORD MEMORIAL AWARD, 1992
___ "Crawford Award Winners," *Locus* 30(3): 7. March 1993.

WILLIAM L. CRAWFORD MEMORIAL AWARD, 1994
___ "1994 William L. Crawford Memorial Award," *Science Fiction Chronicle* 16(6): 12. May 1995.
___ "Lethem Wins Crawford," *Locus* 34(4): 9. April 1995.

WILLIAM MORRIS SOCIETY
___ Roberts, Helen E. "Commemorating William Morris: Robin Page Arnot and the Early History of the William Morris Society," *Journal of the William Morris Society* 11(2): 33-37. Spring 1995.

WILLIAMS, CHARLES
___ Adderley, C. M. "Preliminary Matters: The Neglected Preludes of Charles Williams' Arthuriad," *Mythlore* 21(1): 23-28. Summer 1995. (No. 79)
___ Baker, Rob. "Tangent: A Modern Metaphor," *Parabola* 17(2): 83-87. May 1992.
___ Beach, Charles F. "Courtesy and Self in the Thought of Charles Williams and C. S. Lewis," *Bulletin of the New York C. S. Lewis Society* 25(3/4): 1-11. January/February 1994.
___ Beach, Charles F. "Courtesy in Charles Williams' **The Greater Trumps**," *Mythlore* 19(1): 16-21. Winter 1993. (No. 71)
___ Beach, Charles F. "The Knight-Poets of Logres: Narrative Voices in Charles Williams' Arthurian Poems," in: Slocum, Sally K., ed. **Popular Arthurian Traditions**. Bowling Green, OH: Popular Press, 1992. pp.173-182.

WILLIAMS, CHARLES (continued)

___ Bloom, Harold. "Charles Williams," in: Bloom, Harold, ed. **Modern Fantasy Writers**. New York: Chelsea House, 1995. pp.180-194.

___ Bosky, Bernadette L. "Charles Williams: Occult Fantasies, Occult Fact," in: Latham, Robert A. and Collins, Robert A., eds. **Modes of the Fantastic**. Westport, CT: Greenwood, 1995. pp.176-185.

___ Christopher, Joe R. "An Inklings Bibliography (45)," by Joe R. Christopher and Wayne G. Hammond. *Mythlore* 18(2): 28-33, 39-40. Spring 1992. (No. 68)

___ Christopher, Joe R. "An Inklings Bibliography (46)," by Joe R. Christopher and Wayne G. Hammond. *Mythlore* 18(3): 49-53. Summer 1992. (No. 69)

___ Christopher, Joe R. "An Inklings Bibliography (47)," by Joe R. Christopher and Wayne G. Hammond. *Mythlore* 18(4): 49-52. Autumn 1992. (No. 70)

___ Christopher, Joe R. "An Inklings Bibliography (48)," by Joe R. Christopher and Wayne G. Hammond. *Mythlore* 19(1): 56-64. Winter 1993. (No. 71)

___ Christopher, Joe R. "An Inklings Bibliography (49)," by Joe R. Christopher and Wayne G. Hammond. *Mythlore* 19(2): 61-65. Spring 1993. (No. 72)

___ Christopher, Joe R. "An Inklings Bibliography (50) (e.g. 51)," by Joe R. Christopher and Wayne G. Hammond. *Mythlore* 19(4): 60-65. Autumn 1993. (No. 74)

___ Christopher, Joe R. "An Inklings Bibliography (50)," by Joe R. Christopher and Wayne G. Hammond. *Mythlore* 19(3): 59-65. Summer 1993. (No. 73)

___ Christopher, Joe R. "An Inklings Bibliography (51)," by Joe R. Christopher and Wayne G. Hammond. *Mythlore* 20(1): 59-62. Winter 1994. (Whole No. 75)

___ Christopher, Joe R. "An Inklings Bibliography (52)," by Joe R. Christopher and Wayne G. Hammond. *Mythlore* 20(2): 32-34. Spring 1994. (Whole No. 76)

___ Christopher, Joe R. "An Inklings Bibliography (54)," by Joe R. Christopher and Wayne G. Hammond. *Mythlore* 20(4): 61-65. Winter 1995. (Whole No. 78)

___ Christopher, Joe R. "An Inklings Bibliography (55)," by Joe R. Christopher and Wayne G. Hammond. *Mythlore* 21(1): 61-65. Summer 1995. (No. 79)

___ Curtis, Jan. "Byzantium and the Matter of Britain: The Narrative Framework of Charles Williams's Later Arthurian Poems," *Quondam et Futurus* 2(1): 28-54. Spring 1992.

___ Curtis, Jan. "Charles Williams: His Reputation in the English-Speaking World from 1917 to 1985," in: Kranz, Gisbert, ed. **Inklings: Jahrbuch für Literatur und Ästhetik**. 9. Band. Lüdenscheid, Germany: Stier, 1991. pp.127-164. [Not seen.]

___ Curtis, Jan. "Charles Williams's 'The Sister of Percivale': Towards a Theology of *Theotokos*," *Quondam et Futurus* 2(4): 56-72. Winter 1992.

___ Dodds, David L. "Magic in the Myths of J. R. R. Tolkien and Charles Williams," in: Kranz, Gisbert, ed. **Jahrbuch für Literatur und Ästhetik**. Lüdenscheid, Germany: Stier, 1992. Band 10, pp.37-60.

___ Duriez, Colin. "Tolkien and the Other Inklings," in: Reynolds, Patricia and GoodKnight, Glen H., eds. **Proceedings of the J. R. R. Tolkien Centenary Conference, Keble College, Oxford, 1992**. Altadena, CA: Mythopoeic Press, 1995. pp.360-363. (*Mythlore* Vol. 21, No. 2, Winter 1996, Whole No. 80)

___ Göller, Karl H. "Die Modernität von Williams' Arthur-Dichtung," in: Kranz, Gisbert, ed. **Inklings: Jahrbuch für Literatur und Ästhetik**. 3. Band. [Lüdenscheid, Germany: Stier], 1985. pp.37-48.

___ Hardie, Colin. "Inklings: British at Oxford and German at Aachen," in: Kranz, Gisbert, ed. **Inklings: Jahrbuch für Literatur und Ästhetik**. 1. Band. Lüdenscheid, Germany: Michael Claren, 1983. pp.15-19.

___ Henry, Richard. "Charles Williams and the Aesthetic Ideal of Friedrich von Schiller," *Extrapolation* 35(4): 271-280. Winter 1994.

___ Hopkins, Lisa. "Female Authority Figures in the Works of Tolkien, C. S. Lewis, and Charles Williams," in: Reynolds, Patricia and GoodKnight, Glen H., eds. **Proceedings of the J. R. R. Tolkien Centenary Conference, Keble College, Oxford, 1992**. Altadena, CA: Mythopoeic Press, 1995. pp.364-366. (*Mythlore* Vol. 21, No. 2, Winter 1996, Whole No. 80)

___ Horne, Brian. "A Peculiar Debt: The Influence of Charles Williams on C. S. Lewis," in: Walker, Andrew and Patric, James, eds. **A Christian for All Christians**. Washington, DC: Regnery, 1992. pp.83-97.

___ King, Roma A., Jr. "Charles William's Merlin: Worker in Time of the Images of Eternity," in: Watson, Jeanie and Fries, Marueen, eds. **The Figure of Merlin in the Nineteenth and Twentieth Centuries**. Lewiston, NY: Mellen, 1989. pp.65-77.

WILLIAMS, CHARLES (continued)

___ Kollmann, Judith. "Eros, Philia, and Agape in Charles Williams' Arthuriad," *Mythlore* 18(4): 9-14. Autumn 1992. (No. 70)

___ Kranz, Gisbert. "Stellvertretung bei Williams, Claudel und G. v. le Fort," in: Kranz, Gisbert, ed. **Inklings: Jahrbuch für Literature und Ästhetik**. 3. Band. [Lüdenscheid, Germany: Stier], 1985. pp.87-108.

___ Kranz, Gisbert, ed. **Inklings: Jahrbuch für Literatur und Ästhetik. 1.Band**. Lüdenscheid: Michael Claren, 1983. 185pp.

___ McKinley, Marlene M. "Viewing 'The Immense Panorama or Futility and Anarchy That Is Contemporary History' in the First Six Novels of Charles Williams," in: Filmer, Kath, ed. **Twentieth-Century Fantasists: Essays in Culture, Society and Belief in Twentieth Century Mythopoeic Literature**. New York: St. Martin's, 1992. pp.71-91.

___ Peckham, Robert W. "Rhetoric and the Supernatural in the Novels of Charles Williams," *Renascence* 45(4): 237-246. Summer 1993.

___ Schneider, Angelika. "Zur Symbolik in Williams' Arthur-Dictung," in: Kranz, Gisbert, ed. **Inklings: Jahrbuch für Literatur und Ästhetik**. 3. Band. [Lüdenscheid, Germany: Stier], 1985. pp.49-70.

___ Schrey, Helmut. "Charles Williams' metaphysische Thriller," in: Kranz, Gisbert, ed. **Inklings: Jahrbuch für Literatur und Ästhetik**. 3. Band. [Lüdenscheid, Germany: Stier], 1985. pp.71-86.

___ Smith, Evans L. "The Mythical Method of **Descent into Hell**," *Mythlore* 20(2): 10-15. Spring 1994. (Whole No. 76)

___ Tilley, Elizabeth S. "Language in Charles Williams's **All Hallows' Eve**," *Renascence* 44(4): 303-319. Summer 1992.

___ Weeks, Dennis L. **Steps Toward Salvation: An Examination of Coinherence and Substitution in the Seven Novels of Charles Williams**. New York: P. Lang, 1991. 116pp.

WILLIAMS, EMLYN

___ Hassler, Donald M. "Machen, Williams, and Autobiography: Fantasy and Decadence," in: Wolf, Milton T. and Mallett, Daryl F., eds. **Imaginative Futures: Proceedings of the 1993 Science Fiction Research Association Conference**. San Bernardino, CA: Jacob's Ladder Books, 1995. pp.319-328.

WILLIAMS, NICK B

___ "Williams, Nick B. (Obituary)," *Locus* 28(2): 65. August 1992.

WILLIAMS, PAUL

___ "Paul Williams Badly Hurt," *Locus* 34(6): 8. June 1995.

WILLIAMS, STEVEN

___ Vitaris, Paula. "**X-Files**: X, the Unknown," *Cinefantastique* 26(6)/27(1): 85-86. October 1995.

WILLIAMS, TAD

___ "Tad Williams: 'Memory, Sorrow, and Thorn' Comes Full Circle," *Hailing Frequencies* (Waldenbooks) No. 6: 9-10. 1993.

___ "Tad Williams: Tailespinner's Song," *Locus* 34(1) 4-5, 73-74. January 1995.

___ Nicholls, Stan. "Facing the Demons," *Starlog* No. 207: 52-57, 72. October 1994.

___ Nicholls, Stan. "Tad Williams Realizes the 'P' Word," in: Nicholls, Stan. **Wordsmiths of Wonder: Fifty Interviews with Writers of the Fantastic**. London: Orbit, 1993. pp.321-331.

___ Nicholls, Stan. "Vegetable Love, Vaster Than Empires: Michael Moorcock and Tad Williams Interviewed," *Interzone* No. 91: 24-30. January 1995.

___ Sinor, Bradley H. "SFC Interviews: Tad Williams: Avoiding Assumptions," *Science Fiction Chronicle* 14(6): 5, 26-28. March 1993.

___ Steele, Colin. "The Limits of Genre: Tad Williams and Greg Bear Interviewed," *SF Commentary* No. 71/72: 25-27. April 1992.

WILLIAMS, TERRY TEMPEST

___ McDowell, Elizabeth J. **Power and Environment in Recent Writings by Barbara Kingsolver, Ursula K. Le Guin, Alice Walker and Terry Tempest Williams**. Master's Thesis, University of Oregon, 1992. [Not seen.]

WILLIAMS, WALTER JON

___ Holliday, Liz. "SFC Interviews: Walter Jon Williams," *Science Fiction Chronicle* 13(11/12): 5, 42. August 1992.

___ Kaveney, Roz. "Walter Jon Williams and Some Problems of Science Fiction Criticism," *Foundation* No. 57: 87-98. Spring 1993.

WOMEN IN SF

WOMEN IN SF (continued)

___ Neuendorf, Fiona T. "Negotiating Feminist and Historicist Concerns: Guinevere in Geoffrey of Monmouth's **Historia Regum Britanniae**," *Quondam et Futurus* 3(2): 26-44. Summer 1993.

___ Parkin-Speer, Diane. "Almost a Feminist: Robert A. Heinlein," *Extrapolation* 36(2): 113-125. Summer 1995.

___ Pharr, Mary. "Partners in the Danse: Women in Stephen King's Fiction," in: Magistrale, Tony, ed. **The Dark Descent: Essays Defining Stephen King's Horrorscape.** Westport, CT: Greenwood, 1992. pp.19-32.

___ Phillips, Julie. "Feminist Sci-Fi: A Brave New World," *Ms.* 5(3): 70-73. November 1994.

___ Reichardt, Mary R. **A Web of Relationship: Women in the Short Stories of Mary Wilkins Freeman.** Jackson: University Press of Mississippi, 1992. 186pp.

___ Reid, Robin A. "Lost in Space Between 'Center' and 'Margin': Some Thoughts on Lesbian-Feminist Discourse, Bisexual Women, and Speculative Fiction," in: Weisser, Susan O., ed. **Feminist Nightmares; Women at Odds: Feminism and the Problem of Sisterhood.** New York: New York University Press, 1994. pp.343-357.

___ Salmonson, Jessica A. "Gender Structuring of Shell Persons in **The Ship Who Sang**," *New York Review of Science Fiction* No. 10: 15-18. June 1989.

___ Simmons, Joe. "Fantasy Art and Warrior Women: An Aesthetic Critique of Feminine Images," *Mythlore* 21(1): 51-54, 65. Summer 1995. (No. 79)

___ Smith, Jeanette C. "The Role of Women in Contemporary Arthurian Fantasy," *Extrapolation* 35(2): 130-144. Summer 1994.

___ Smith, Malaika D. **The African American Heroine in Octavia Butler's Wild Seed and Parable of the Sower.** Master's Thesis, UCLA, 1994. 66pp.

___ Sterling-Hellenbrand, Alexandra. "Women on the Edge in **Parzival**: A Study of the 'Grail Women'," *Quondam et Futurus* 3(2): 56-68. Summer 1993.

___ Tushnet, Rebecca L. **Fire With Firepower: Women in Recent Science Fiction Blockbuster Movies.** Thesis, A. B. Honors in Social Studies, Harvard University, 1995. 153pp.

___ Vaughn, Sue F. "The Female Hero in Science Fiction and Fantasy: 'Carrier Bag' to 'No-Road'," *Journal of the Fantastic in the Arts* 4(4): 82-96. 1991. (No. 16)

___ von Franz, Marie-Louise. **The Feminine in Fairy Tales.** New York: Shambala, 1993. 224pp. (Revised edition of **Problems of the Feminine in Fairy Tales**, 1972.)

___ Webb, Janeen. "Feminism and Science Fiction," *Meanjin* 51(1): 185-198. Autumn 1992.

___ Weller, Greg. "The Masks of the Goddess: The Unfolding of the Female Archetype in Stephen King's **Carrie**," in: Magistrale, Tony, ed. **The Dark Descent: Essays Defining Stephen King's Horrorscape.** Westport, CT: Greenwood, 1992. pp.5-17.

___ Westfahl, Gary. "Superladies in Waiting: How the Female Hero Almost Emerges in Science Fiction," *Foundation* No. 58: 42-62. Summer 1993.

___ Wilcox, Clyde. "The Not-So-Failed Feminism of Jean Auel," *Journal of Popular Culture* 28(3): 63-70. Winter 1994.

___ Wolmark, Jenny. "Space, Time and Gender: The Impact of Cybernetics on the Feminist Utopia," *Foundation* No. 62: 22-30. Winter 1994/1995.

___ Wu, Quingyun. **Female Rule in Chinese and English Literary Utopias.** Syracuse, NY: Syracuse University Press, 1995. 225pp.; London: Liverpool University Press, 1995. 225pp.

___ Yoke, Carl B. "Slaying the Dragon Within: Andre Norton's Female Heroes," *Journal of the Fantastic in the Arts* 4(3): 79-92. 1991. (No. 15)

WOMEN SF WRITERS

___ Albinski, Nan B. "Utopia Reconsidered: Women Novelists and Nineteenth-Century Utopian Visions," *Signs: Journal of Women in Culture and Society* 13(4): 830-841. Summer 1988.

___ Bammer, Angelika. **Visions and Re-visions: The Utopian Impulse in Feminist Fictions.** Ph.D. Dissertation, University of Wisconsin, Madison, 1982. 424pp.

___ Barr, Marleen S. "Blurred Generic Conventions: Pregnancy and Power in Feminist Science Fiction," *Reproductive and Genetic Engineering* 1(2): 167-174. 1988. (Abridged version of an essay from Barr, Marleen. **Alien to Femininity.** 1987.)

___ Barr, Marleen S. "Feminist Fabulation; Or, Playing With Patriarchy vs. the Masculinization of Metafiction," *Women's Studies* 14(2): 187-192. 1987.

WOMEN SF WRITERS (continued)

___ Barr, Marleen S. **Feminist Fabulation: Space/Postmodern Fiction.** Iowa City, IA: University of Iowa Press, 1993. 312pp.

___ Barr, Marleen S. "Immortal Feminist Communities of Women: A Recent Idea in Science Fiction," in: Saccaro Del Buffa, Giuseppa and Lewis, Arthur O., eds. **Utopie per gli Anni Ottana.** Rome: Gangemi Editore, 1986. pp.511-520.

___ Barr, Marleen S. **Lost in Space: Probing Feminist Science Fiction and Beyond.** Chapel Hill, NC: University of North Carolina Press, 1993. 231pp.

___ Bartter, Martha A. "Science, Science Fiction and Women: A Language of (Tacit) Exclusion," *Et Cetera* 49(4): 407-419. Winter 1992.

___ Booker, M. Keith. "Woman on the Edge of a Genre: The Feminist Dystopias of Marge Piercy," *Science Fiction Studies* 21(3): 337-350. November 1994.

___ Cadora, Karen. "Feminist Cyberpunk," *Science Fiction Studies* 22(3): 357-372. November 1995

___ Canty, Joan F. **Does Eugenics = (E)utopia?: Reproductive Control and Ethical Issues in Contemporary North American Feminist Fabulation.** Master's Thesis, California State University, Stanislaus, 1995. 97pp.

___ Capasso, Ruth C. "Islands of Felicity: Women Seeing Utopia in Seventeenth Century France," in: Donawerth, Jane L. and Kolmerten, Carol A., eds. **Utopian and Science Fiction by Women: Worlds of Difference.** Syracuse, NY: Syracuse University Press, 1994. pp.35-53.

___ Carpenter, Sherilee R. "The Re-Emergence of a Feminine and Feminist Mythology in Women's Utopias," in: Saccaro Del Buffa, Giuseppa and Lewis, Arthur O., eds. **Utopie per gli Anni Ottana.** Rome: Gangemi Editore, 1986. pp.477-484.

___ Chien, Ying-Ying. "From Utopian to Dystopian World: Two Faces of Feminism in Contemporary Taiwanese Women's Fiction," *World Literature Today* 68(1): 35-42. Winter 1994.

___ Clark, Robert. "Angela Carter's Desire Machine," *Women's Studies* 14(2): 147-162. 1987.

___ Crosby, Janice C. **Cauldron of Changes: Feminist Spirituality in Contemporary American Women's Fiction.** Ph.D. Dissertation, Louisiana State University, 1994. 221pp. (DAI-A 56/03, p. 928. September 1995.)

___ Dery, Mark. "Reinventing the Future," *Elle* p. 88-89. May 1992.

___ Donawerth, Jane L. "Introduction," by Jane L. Donawerth and Carol A. Kolmerten. in: Donawerth, Jane L. and Kolmerten, Carol A., eds. **Utopian and Science Fiction by Women: Worlds of Difference.** Syracuse, NY: Syracuse University Press, 1994. pp.1-14.

___ Donawerth, Jane L. "Science Fiction by Women in the Early Pulps, 1926-1930," in: Donawerth, Jane L. and Kolmerten, Carol A., eds. **Utopian and Science Fiction by Women: Worlds of Difference.** Syracuse, NY: Syracuse University Press, 1994. pp.137-152.

___ Donawerth, Jane L. "Woman as Machine in Science Fiction by Women," *Extrapolation* 36(3): 210-221. Fall 1995.

___ Donawerth, Jane L., ed. **Utopian and Science Fiction by Women: Worlds of Difference**, ed. by Jane L. Donawerth and Carol A. Kolmerten. Syracuse, NY: Syracuse University Press, 1994. 260pp.

___ Dunne, Linda. "Mothers and Monsters in Sarah Robinson Scott's **Millenium Hall**," in: Donawerth, Jane L. and Kolmerten, Carol A., eds. **Utopian and Science Fiction by Women: Worlds of Difference.** Syracuse, NY: Syracuse University Press, 1994. pp.54-72.

___ Ecker, Gisela. "The Politics of Fantasy in Recent American Women's Novels," *Englishch-Amerikanische Studien* 3: 503-510. 1984.

___ Elgin, Suzette H. "Women's Language and Near Future Science Fiction: A Reply," *Women's Studies* 14(2): 175-182. 1987.

___ Fishburn, Katherine. "Reforming the Body Politic: Radical Feminist Science Fiction," in: Roberts, Sheila, ed. **Still the Frame Holds: Essays on Women Poets and Writers.** San Bernardino, CA: Borgo Press, 1993. pp.29-46.

___ Fitting, Peter. "For Men Only: A Guide to Reading Single-Sex Worlds," *Women's Studies* 14(2): 101-118. 1987.

___ Fitting, Peter. "Reconsiderations of the Separatist Paradigm in Recent Feminist Science Fiction," *Science Fiction Studies* 19(1): 32-48. March 1992.

___ Fowler, Judy. **Exploring How Animals Fare in Worlds Created by Feminist Science Fiction Writers.** Master's Thesis, University of Wisconsin, Whitewater, 1993. 71pp.

WOMEN SF WRITERS (continued)

___ Sargent, Pamela. "Recommended Reading: Science Fiction by Women, 1979-1993," in: Sargent, Pamela, ed. **Women of Wonder: The Contemporary Years; Science Fiction by Women From the 1970s to the 1990s**. Orlando, FL: Harcourt Brace, 1995. pp.405-420.

___ Sargent, Pamela. **Women of Wonder, The Classic Years: Science Fiction by Women From the 1940s to the 1970s**. San Diego, CA: Harcourt Brace, 1995. 438pp.

___ Scheer-Schäzler, Brigitte. "Re-turning the Imagination oder SF&F, ein Abenteuer für Frauen," in: Grabher, Gudrun M. and Devine, Marureen, eds. **Women in Search of Literary Space**. Tübingen: Gunter Narr Verlag, 1992. pp.163-179.

___ Shafi, Monika. **Utopische Entwürfe in der Literatur von Frauen**. Bern: Peter Lang, 1990. 135pp.

___ Simsa, Cyril. "The View From Olympus: Three Czech Women Writers Talk About SF," *Vector* No. 166: 14-16. April/May 1992.

___ Webb, Janeen. "Feminism and Science Fiction," *Meanjin* 51(1): 185-198. Autumn 1992.

___ Wiemer, Annegret J. **The Feminist Science Fiction Utopia: Faces of a Genre, 1820-1897**. Ph.D. Dissertation, University of Alberta, 1991. (Ottawa: National Library of Canada, 1992. 5 microfiche) (DAI-A 53/08, p. 2811. Feb. 1993.)

___ Wiemer, Annegret J. "Foreign L(anguish), Mother Tongue: Concepts of Language in Contemporary Feminist Science Fiction," *Women's Studies* 14(2): 163-184. 1987.

___ Willis, Connie. "The Women SF Doesn't See," *Isaac Asimov's Science Fiction Magazine* 16(11): 4-8. October 1992.

___ Wolstenholme, Susan. **Gothic (Re) Visions: Writing Women as Readers**. Albany: State University of New York Press, 1993. 201pp.

___ Zaki, Hoda M. "Utopia and Ideology in **Daughters of a Coral Dawn** and Contemporary Feminist Utopias," *Women's Studies* 14(2): 119-134. 1987.

WONDERWORKS (TV)

___ "16 Original Hours Plus Pickups Set for **Wonderworks** 3d Stanza," *Variety* p. 76. August 27, 1986.

___ **Wonderworks** has 'Narnia' as 9-Hour Coprod," *Variety* p. 45. June 15, 1988.

WONG, JAMES

___ Spelling, Ian. "**Space: Above and Beyond**," *Starlog* No. 220: 40-45. November 1995.

___ Vitaris, Paula. "Writers," *Starlog* No. 210: 61-64. January 1995.

___ Vitaris, Paula. "**X-Files**: Morgan and Wong," *Cinefantastique* 26(6)/27(1): 62. October 1995.

WOOD, EDWARD D., JR.

___ Grey, Rudolph. **Nightmare of Ecstasy: The Life and Art of Edward D. Wood, Jr.** Los Angeles, CA: Feral House Press, 1992. 231pp.

___ Weaver, Tom. "Man With a Plan (9)," *Starlog* No. 208: 59-67. November 1994.

WOODRUFF, PHILIP

___ Sarjeant, William A. S. "A Forgotten Children's Fantasy: Philip Woodruff's **The Sword of Northumbria**," *Mythlore* 20(4): 30-35. Winter 1995. (Whole No. 78)

WOOLLEY, PERSIA

___ Andresen, Oliver. "An Analysis of **Queen of the Summer Stars** by Use of the Literary Profundity Scale," by Oliver Andresen and Glenn Marin. *Quondam et Futurus* 2(1): 82-97. Spring 1992.

WORDS

___ Westfahl, Gary. "The Words That Could Happen: Science Fiction Neologisms and the Creation of Future Worlds," *Extrapolation* 34(4): 290-304. Winter 1993.

WORK IN SF

___ Hatch, Richard C. "The Ideology of Work and the Architecture of Utopia," in: Saccaro Del Buffa, Giuseppa and Lewis, Arthur O., eds. **Utopia e Modernita: Teorie e prassi utopiche nell'eta moderna e postmoderna**. Rome: Gangemi Editore, 1989. pp.175-186.

WORKSHOPS, WRITER'S

___ "Forum: Writer's Workshops," *Focus* (BSFA) No. 29: 10-13. December 1995/January 1996.

WORKSHOPS, WRITER'S (continued)

___ Smith, David A. "Writer's Workshops," *Quantum* No. 43/44: 32-34, 38. Spring/Summer 1993.

WORKSHOPS, WRITER'S, 1993

___ "26th Clarion SF and Fantasy Workshop Set," *Science Fiction Chronicle* 14(5): 4. February 1993.

WORKSHOPS, WRITER'S, 1995

___ "1995 Clarion and Clarion West SF/Fantasy Workshops Set," *Science Fiction Chronicle* 16(1): 5. October 1994.

WORKSHOPS, WRITER'S, 1996

___ "'96 Clarion Workshop Date Set," *Science Fiction Chronicle* 16(9): 6. August/September 1995.

WORLD DRACULA CONGRESS, 1995

___ "The World Dracula Congress," *Locus* 35(2): 44-45. August 1995.

WORLD FANTASY AWARDS, 1992

___ "1992 World Fantasy Award Jury Empaneled," *Science Fiction Chronicle* 13(4): 5. January 1992.

___ "1992 World Fantasy Awards Judges," *Locus* 28(1): 6. January 1992.

___ "1992 World Fantasy Awards Nominations," *Locus* 29(3): 7. September 1992.

___ "1992 World Fantasy Awards Winners," *Locus* 29(6): 6. December 1992.

___ "World Fantasy Award Nominations," *Science Fiction Chronicle* 14(1): 4. October 1992.

___ "World Fantasy Awards," *Science Fiction Chronicle* 14(3): 4. December 1992.

WORLD FANTASY AWARDS, 1993

___ "1993 World Fantasy Awards Judges Named," *Locus* 29(6): 7. December 1992.

___ "1993 World Fantasy Awards Nominations," *Locus* 31(3): 6. September 1993.

___ "1993 World Fantasy Awards Winners," *Locus* 31(6): 6. December 1993.

___ "Nebula, World Fantasy, Philip K. Dick Award Juries Established," *Science Fiction Chronicle* 14(3): 4-5. December 1992.

___ "World Fantasy Award Nominations," *Science Fiction Chronicle* 14(12): 4. September 1993.

___ "World Fantasy Awards," *Science Fiction Chronicle* 15(2): 4. November/December 1993.

WORLD FANTASY AWARDS, 1994

___ "1994 World Fantasy Awards," *Locus* 33(6): 7, 49. December 1994.

___ "1994 World Fantasy Awards Nominations," *Locus* 33(3): 7. September 1994.

___ "1994 World Fantasy Judges Named," *Locus* 32(1): 6. January 1994.

___ "World Fantasy Award Jury Named," *Science Fiction Chronicle* 15(3): 6. January 1994.

___ "World Fantasy Awards," *Science Fiction Chronicle* 16(2): 4. November/December 1994.

___ "World Fantasy Nominations," *Science Fiction Chronicle* 15(9): 36. August 1994.

WORLD FANTASY AWARDS, 1995

___ "1995 World Fantasy Award Judges Named," *Locus* 34(4): 8. April 1995.

___ "1995 World Fantasy Awards," *Locus* 35(6): 4, 81. December 1995.

___ "1995 World Fantasy Awards Nomination," *Locus* 35(3): 7. September 1995.

___ "World Fantasy Award Jury Named," *Science Fiction Chronicle* 16(5): 4. March/April 1995.

___ "World Fantasy Awards Redux," *Locus* 35(4): 8. October 1995.

___ "World Fantasy Awards, 1995," *Science Fiction Chronicle* 17(2): 5. December 1995/January 1996.

___ "World Fantasy Awards, Final Nominees," *Science Fiction Chronicle* 17(1): 5. October/November 1995

WORLD FANTASY CONVENTION, 1991

___ "1991 World Fantasy Convention," *Locus* 28(1): 36-39, 70. January 1992.

WORLD FANTASY CONVENTION, 1991 (continued)
___ "1991 World Fantasy Convention," *Science Fiction Chronicle* 13(4): 28. January 1992.

WORLD FANTASY CONVENTION, 1992
___ "1992 World Fantasy Convention," *Locus* 30(1): 36-39, 62. January 1993.
___ "World Fantasy Convention, 1992," *Science Fiction Chronicle* 13(9): 26-27. June 1992.

WORLD FANTASY CONVENTION, 1993
___ "1993 World Fantasy Convention," *Locus* 32(1): 34-37. January 1994.
___ Jones, Stephen. "World Fantasy Convention," by Stephen Jones and Jo Fletcher. *Science Fiction Chronicle* 15(4): 30-318. February 1994.

WORLD FANTASY CONVENTION, 1994
___ "World Fantasy Con, 1994," *Locus* 34(1) 40-43. January 1995.
___ Frants, Marina. "Down by the Bayou: The 20th Annual World Fantasy Convention," by Marina Frants and Keith R. A. DeCandido. *Wilson Library Bulletin* 69(5): 51-52. January 1995
___ Jones, Stephen. "World Fantasy Convention 1994: A Short Report," *Science Fiction Chronicle* 16(4): 32-34. February 1995.

WORLD FANTASY CONVENTION, 1995
___ "1995 World Fantasy Convention," *Science Fiction Chronicle* 17(2): 44. December 1995/January 1996.

WORLD HORROR CONVENTION, 1992
___ "1992 World Horror Convention," *Locus* 28(5): 41. May 1992.

WORLD HORROR CONVENTION, 1993
___ "1993 World Horror Convention," *Locus* 30(5): 42-43. May 1993.
___ Jones, Stephen. "World Horror Convention, 1993," by Stephen Jones and Jo Fletcher. *Science Fiction Chronicle* 14(9): 31-32. June 1993.

WORLD HORROR CONVENTION, 1994
___ "1994 World Horror Convention," *Locus* 32(5): 38-39. May 1994.
___ Jones, Stephen. "1994 World Horror Convention Photo Gallery," by Stephen Jones and Jo Fletcher. *Science Fiction Chronicle* 15(7): 28-31. June 1994.

WORLD HORROR CONVENTION, 1995
___ "World Horror Convention, 1995," *Locus* 34(5): 40-42. May 1995.

WORLD OF TOMORROW (MOTION PICTURE)
___ Telotte, J. P. "**The World of Tomorrow** and the 'Secret Goal' of Science Fiction," *Journal of Film and Video* 45(1): 27-39. Spring 1993.

WORLD SCIENCE FICTION CONVENTION, 1941
___ Heinlein, Robert A. "Guest of Honor Speech at the Third World Science Fiction Convention, Denver, 1941," in: Kondo, Yoji, ed. **Requiem: New Collected Works by Robert A. Heinlein and Tributes to the Grand Master.** New York: Tor, 1992. pp.153-167.

WORLD SCIENCE FICTION CONVENTION, 1961
___ Heinlein, Robert A. "Guest of Honor Speech at the XIXth World Science Fiction Convention, Seattle, 1961," in: Kondo, Yoji, ed. **Requiem: New Collected Works by Robert A. Heinlein and Tributes to the Grand Master.** New York: Tor, 1992. pp.168-197.

WORLD SCIENCE FICTION CONVENTION, 1976
___ Heinlein, Robert A. "Guest of Honor Speech at the XXXIVth World Science Fiction Convention, Kansas City, 1976," in: Kondo, Yoji, ed. **Requiem: New Collected Works by Robert A. Heinlein and Tributes to the Grand Master.** New York: Tor, 1992. pp.205-213.

WORLD SCIENCE FICTION CONVENTION, 1989
___ "NorEasCon 3 Videotape Released," *Science Fiction Chronicle* 14(12): 6. September 1993.
___ "NorEasCon Masquerade Video," *Science Fiction Chronicle* 15(1): 6. October 1993.

WORLD SCIENCE FICTION CONVENTION, 1991
___ "Chicon V: 49th World SF Convention," *Science Fiction Chronicle* 13(4): 30-31. January 1992.

WORLD SCIENCE FICTION CONVENTION, 1992
___ "MagiCon," *Locus* 29(5): 36-45, 75-76. November 1992
___ "MagiCon: 1992 World Science Fiction Convention," *Locus* 29(4): 6, 72. October 1992
___ "MagiCon Passes Along $50,000," *Locus* 33(3): 7. September 1994.
___ "MagiCon Profits Give $50,000 to Subsequent Worldcons," *Science Fiction Chronicle* 15(8): 36. June 1994.
___ Madden, J. R. "MagiCon: The 50th World Science Fiction Convention," *Science Fiction Chronicle* 14(2): 30-33. November 1992.
___ Madden, J. R. "MagiCon, the 50th World Science Fiction Convention (Part 2)," *Science Fiction Chronicle* 14(3): 32-36. December 1992.

WORLD SCIENCE FICTION CONVENTION, 1993
___ "1993, 1994 Worldcon Updates," *Science Fiction Chronicle* 14(7): 6. April 1993.
___ "8,365 Members: ConFrancisco Is Second Largest Worldcon Ever," *Science Fiction Chronicle* 15(1): 4. October 1993.
___ "ConFrancisco: 1993 World Science Fiction Convention," *Locus* 31(4): 5, 70. October 1993.
___ "ConFrancisco: More Donations," *Science Fiction Chronicle* 16(4): 5-6. February 1995.
___ "ConFrancisco Refunds $70,000, Spawns Another Worldcon Bid," *Science Fiction Chronicle* 15(7): 5. June 1994.
___ "ConFrancisco Souvenirs," *Science Fiction Chronicle* 15(1): 6. October 1993.
___ "ConFrancisco: The 51st World Science Fiction Convention," *Locus* 31(5): 32-41, 69. November 1993.
___ "ConFrancisco Update," *Locus* 30(3): 7. March 1993.
___ "Last ConFrancisco Update," *Science Fiction Chronicle* 15(5): 5. March 1994.
___ DeCarlo, Tessa. "Tomorrow's Songs Today," *Wall Street Journal* p.A15. November 1, 1993.
___ Frants, Marina. "ConFrancisco, Here We Come: The 51st Annual World Science Fiction Convention," by Marina Frants and Keith R. A. DeCandido. *Wilson Library Bulletin* 68(3): 49-50. November 1993.
___ Hooper, Andrew. "A Report From ConFrancisco, the 51st World Science Fiction Convention," *Science Fiction Chronicle* 15(2): 40-45. November/December 1993.
___ Hooper, Andrew. "A Report From ConFrancisco, The 51st World Science Fiction Convention, Part 2," *Science Fiction Chronicle* 15(3): 26-32. January 1994.
___ Rosenberg, Scott. " 'SF' in S.F.: Not a Mass of Trekkies," *San Francisco (CA) Chronicle* Sec. D, p. 2. September 5, 1993.
___ Rusch, Kristine K. "Editorial: WorldCon," *Magazine of Fantasy and Science Fiction* 86(2): 5-6. February 1994.

WORLD SCIENCE FICTION CONVENTION, 1994
___ "1993, 1994 Worldcon Updates," *Science Fiction Chronicle* 14(7): 6. April 1993.
___ "ConAdian: 1994 World Science Fiction Convention," *Locus* 33(4): 7. October 1994.
___ "ConAdian: 1994 World Science Fiction Convention," *Locus* 33(5): 38-49. November 1994.
___ "ConAdian Update," *Science Fiction Chronicle* 15(6): 7. April/May 1994.
___ DeCarlo, Tessa. "Style: Costuming at the World Con," *Omni* 16(12): 22. September 1994.
___ Flynn, George. "World SF Convention: Business Meeting," *Science Fiction Chronicle* 16(2): 51. November/December 1994.
___ Hertz, John. "Conadian Masquerade Report," *Science Fiction Chronicle* 16(3): 34-36. January 1995.
___ Hull, Elizabeth A. "Highlight of the 1994 Worldcon," *Science Fiction Chronicle* 16(2): 48-50. November/December 1994.
___ Porter, Andrew. "My Conadian Report," *Science Fiction Chronicle* 16(3): 33-34. January 1995.
___ Sweeney, Kate. "Winnipeg Hosts Final Frontier," *Grand Forks (ND) Herald.* September 4, 1994. in: *NewsBank. Film and Television.* 56: D14-E1. 1994.

WORLD SCIENCE FICTION CONVENTION, 1995
___ "1995 World Science Fiction Society Business Meeting," *Science Fiction Chronicle* 17(2): 53. December 1995/January 1996.
___ "1995, 1996 Worldcon Updates," *Science Fiction Chronicle* 16(1): 5. October 1994.
___ "4,800 Attend Glasgow's Intersection; Baltimore Wins 1998 World SF Convention," *Science Fiction Chronicle* 17(1): 6. October/November 1995
___ "Brits Dominate Hugo Awards," *Science Fiction Chronicle* 17(1): 5. October/November 1995
___ "Glasgow, Scotland Wins 1995 World SF Convention," *Science Fiction Chronicle* 14(1): 4. October 1992.
___ "The Hugos (Or, the Empire Strikes Back)," *Science Fiction Chronicle* 17(2): 55-56. December 1995/January 1996.
___ "Intersection Draws 4,800," *Locus* 35(4): 8. October 1995.
___ "Intersection: The 53rd World Science Fiction Convention," *Locus* 35(5): 40-50, 80, 82. November 1995.
___ "Intersection: The 53rd World SF Convention," *Science Fiction Chronicle* 17(2): 24, 48-58. December 1995/January 1996.
___ "Intersection Update," *Science Fiction Chronicle* 16(5): 6. March/April 1995.
___ "Science Fiction: Loving the Alien," *Economist* 336(7930): 82. September 2, 1995.
___ "World Science Fiction Convention Hugo Awards, 1995," *Science Fiction Chronicle* 17(1): 5. October/November 1995

WORLD SCIENCE FICTION CONVENTION, 1996
___ "1995, 1996 Worldcon Updates," *Science Fiction Chronicle* 16(1): 5. October 1994.
___ "4,800 Attend Glasgow's Intersection; Baltimore Wins 1998 World SF Convention," *Science Fiction Chronicle* 17(1): 6. October/November 1995
___ "LACon III Wins 1996 Worldcon," *Science Fiction Chronicle* 15(1): 4-5. October 1993.

WORLD SCIENCE FICTION CONVENTION, 1997
___ "1997, 1998 Worldcon Bids," *Science Fiction Chronicle* 15(1): 26. October 1993.
___ "San Antonio Wins Bid for 1997 Worldcon," *Science Fiction Chronicle* 15(10): 5. September 1994.

WORLD SCIENCE FICTION CONVENTION, 1998
___ "1997, 1998 Worldcon Bids," *Science Fiction Chronicle* 15(1): 26. October 1993.
___ "Baltimore Moves 1998 Worldcon Bid to Early August Date," *Science Fiction Chronicle* 16(1): 5. October 1994.

WORLD SF MEETING, 1992
___ "1992 Eurocon and World SF Meeting Relocate," *Locus* 28(3): 7, 74. March 1992.
___ "Freucon/1992 World SF Meeting," *Locus* 29(6): 46-47. December 1992.

WORLD SF MEETING, 1993
___ "1993 World SF/Helicon," *Locus* 30(6): 49-51. June 1993.

WORLD-WIDE WEB
___ Zeuschner, Bob. "ERB Is Alive and Well on the Information Highway," *Burroughs Bulletin* NS. No. 24: 19-25. October 1995.

WORLDS BEYOND (TV)
___ "Britain's Radnor Rolling 65 Segs of TV Drama on the Supernatural," *Variety* p. 240. April 23, 1986.

WORLDS OF FANTASY AND HORROR (MAGAZINE)
___ "*Weird Tales* Changes Names," *Locus* 32(4): 8. April 1994.

WÖRNER, HANS
___ Munsonius, Jörg M. "Einige Anmerkungern su Hans Wörners SF-Roman **Wir fanden Menschen**," *Quarber Merkur* 33(2): 16-19. December 1995. (No. 84)

WRATH OF KHAN (MOTION PICTURE)
___ SEE: STAR TREK II: THE WRATH OF KHAN (MOTION PICTURE).

WRAY, FAY
___ Harmetz, Aljean. "Kong and Wray: 60 Years of Love," *New York Times* Sec. 2, p. 13. February 28, 1993.
___ Kinnard, Roy. "Queen of Screams," *Starlog* No. 194: 66-69. September 1993.
___ Kinnard, Roy. "Queen of Screams," in: McDonnell, David, ed. **Starlog's Science Fiction Heroes and Heroines.** New York: Crescent Books, 1995. pp.38-40.

WREDE, PATRICIA
___ Ringel, Faye. "The Scribblies: A Shared World," *Extrapolation* 35(3): 201-210. Fall 1994.

WRIGHT, AUSTIN TAPPAN
___ Jacobs, Naomi. "**Islandia**: Plotting Utopian Desire," *Utopian Studies* 6(2): 75-89. 1995.

WRIGHT, HERB
___ Altman, Mark A. "*Star Trek*: Two Wrights Don't Make a Wrong," *Cinefantastique* 23(2/3): 60-61. October 1992.

WRIGHT, S. FOWLER
___ Weinkauf, Mary S. **Sermons in Science Fiction: The Novels of S. Fowler Wright.** San Bernardino, CA: Borgo Press, 1994. 128pp.

WRIGHT, T. M.
___ Proulx, Kevin. **Fear to the World: Eleven Voices in a Chorus of Horror.** Mercer Island, WA: Starmont, 1992. 243pp.

WRITERS OF THE FUTURE CONTEST
___ Verran, James. "If It's Yesterday, This Must Be America!," *Science Fiction News* (Australia) No. 112: 2-4. September 1990.

WRITERS OF THE FUTURE CONTEST, 1992
___ "Hubbard Contest Awards $4000 Prizes," *Locus* 29(4): 8. October 1992

WRITERS OF THE FUTURE CONTEST, 1993
___ "$4,000 for Karawynn Long in Writers of the Future Contest," *Science Fiction Chronicle* 15(2): 6. November/December 1993.
___ "Hubbard Contests Award $4,000 Prizes," *Locus* 31(5): 5. November 1993.

WRITERS OF THE FUTURE CONTEST, 1994
___ "Hubbard Contests Award $4000 Prizes," *Locus* 33(1): 7, 78. July 1994.
___ "Writers of the Future Contest 10th Anniversary," *Locus* 32(4): 8, 63. April 1994.

WRITERS OF THE FUTURE CONTEST, 1995
___ "Hubbard Contests Award $4000 Prizes," *Locus* 35(2): 7, 71. August 1995.

WRITERS, JEWISH
___ Troen, Saul B. **Science Fiction and the Reemergence of Jewish Mythology in a Contemporary Literary Genre.** Ph.D. Dissertation, New York University, 1995. 336pp. (DAI-A 56/05, p. 1762. November 1995.)

WRITING SF AND FANTASY
___ **Breaking into Writing.** Ann Arbor, MI: Tucker Video, 1994. 1 videocassette, 98 minutes. (Panel Presentation at the 1994 Science Fiction Research Association Conference.)
___ "Forum: Characters," *Focus* (BSFA) No. 24: 7-11. June/July 1993.
___ "Forum: Research," *Focus*. (BSFA) No. 28: 3-7. 1995
___ "Forum: Revision," *Focus* (BSFA) No. 26: 5-9. June/July 1994.
___ "Forum: Setting," *Focus* (BSFA) No. 25: 6-8. December/January 1994.
___ "Guidelines (*Analog* and *Asimov's*)," in: Dozois, Gardner, ed. **Writing Science Fiction and Fantasy.** New York: St. Martin's, 1991. pp.259-264.
___ **On Writing Science Fiction and Screenplays.** Alexandra, VA: PBS Adult Learning Satellite Service, 1994. 1 videocassette, 56 minutes.
___ "*Star Trek* Author Complains Her Book Was Rewritten," *Science Fiction Chronicle* 13(7): 4. April 1992.
___ Aiken, Joan. "Writing Ghost Stories," *Writer* 107(1): 9-13. January 1994.

WRITING SF AND FANTASY (continued)

___ Harrison, M. John. "The Profession of Fiction," in: Jakubowski, Maxim and James, Edward, eds. **The Profession of Science Fiction**. New York: St. Martin's, 1992. pp.140-153.

___ Hatch, Daniel. "The Wholesale Planet Warehouse," *SFWA Bulletin* 28(3): 4-17. Winter 1994. (No. 125)

___ Heck, Peter J. "Trends and Genres in Science Fiction: From Space Opera to Steampunk," in: Thompkins, David G., ed. **Science Fiction Writer's Market Place and Source Book**. Cincinnati, OH: Writer's Digest Books, 1994. pp.2-12.

___ Heinlein, Robert A. "On the Writing of Speculative Fiction," in: Dozois, Gardner, ed. **Writing Science Fiction and Fantasy**. New York: St. Martin's, 1991. pp.5-11.

___ Herbert, Brian P. "When Bad Things Happen," *The Report: The Fiction Writer's Magazine* No. 11: 5-8. Summer 1993.

___ Higgins, Stephen. "So, You Want to Be a Horror Writer," *Aurealis* No. 13: 84-85. 1994.

___ Higgins, Stephen. "So, You Want to Be an SF Writer?," *Aurealis* No. 12: 91-92. 1993.

___ Hixon, Celia. "Plotting Science into Science Fiction: Part Four, Human Motivation," *Writers' Journal* 15(1): 8-9. 1993.

___ Hixon, Celia. "Plotting Science into Science Fiction: Part One, Research Methods," *Writers' Journal* 14(4): 9-11. 1993.

___ Hixon, Celia. "Plotting Science into Science Fiction: Part Three, Alien Cultures," *Writers' Journal* 14(6): 9-10. 1993.

___ Hixon, Celia. "Plotting Science into Science Fiction: Part Two, A Star Shopper's Guide," *Writers' Journal* 14(5): 8-9. 1993.

___ Hogan, Ernest. "Guess Who's Killing the Short Story?," *Science Fiction Eye* No. 10: 41-43. June 1992.

___ Holden, Constance. "Bringing More Reality to Fiction," *Science* 263(5144): 176-177. January 14, 1994.

___ Howe, Robert J. "Basic Training: With Pen and Notebook," *The Report: The Fiction Writer's Magazine* No. 10: 20. Summer 1993.

___ Hubbard, L. Ron. "Boos and Taboos," in: Wolverton, Dave, ed. **Writers of the Future, Vol. VIII**. Los Angeles, CA: Bridge, 1992. pp.41-48.

___ Hubert, Hal. "Orbital Mechanics for Science Fiction Writers," *SFWA Bulletin* 26(4): 2-6. Winter 1993. (No. 118)

___ Hubert, Hal. "Orbits, Quibbles, Maps, and Drawing With Satellites," *SFWA Bulletin* 27(2): 6-9. Summer 1993. (No. 120)

___ Ings, Simon. "The Future: Disguising the Real," *Focus* (BSFA) No. 25: 12-13. December/January 1994.

___ Jakubowski, Maxim. "Introduction," by Maxim Jakubowski and Edward James. in: Jakubowski, Maxim and James, Edward, eds. **The Profession of Science Fiction**. New York: St. Martin's, 1992. pp.1-11.

___ Jakubowski, Maxim, ed. **The Profession of Science Fiction: SF Writers on Their Craft and Ideas**, ed. by Maxim Jakubowski and Edward James. New York: St. Martin's, 1992. 208pp.

___ James, E. R. "Shake the Invisible Hand," *Vector* No. 166: 17. April/May 1992.

___ Jones, Diana W. "Aiming for the Moon," *Focus* (BSFA) No. 25: 14-16. December/January 1994.

___ Jones, Gwyneth. "The Effect of Political and Etc. Influences on SF Writers," *Focus* (BSFA) No. 27: 7. December 1994/January 1995.

___ Jones, Gwyneth. "Riddles in the Dark," in: Jakubowski, Maxim and James, Edward, eds. **The Profession of Science Fiction**. New York: St. Martin's, 1992. pp.169-181.

___ Kakutani, Mcihiko. "Making a Literary Lunge into the Future," *New York Times* Sec. C, p. 1. February 21, 1992.

___ Kelly, James P. "You and Your Characters," in: Dozois, Gardner, ed. **Writing Science Fiction and Fantasy**. New York: St. Martin's, 1991. pp.38-49.

___ Kemper, Bart. "Dancing on the Edge," *Writer's Digest* 74(7): 6-7. July 1994.

___ Kessel, John. "The Brother From Another Planet: Science Fiction vs. Mainstream Short Stories," *New York Review of Science Fiction* No. 55: 1, 8-11. March 1993. (Responses: No. 56: 22-23.)

___ Kilworth, Garry. "Confessions of a Bradbury Eater," in: Jakubowski, Maxim and James, Edward, eds. **The Profession of Science Fiction**. New York: St. Martin's, 1992. pp.154-160.

___ King, T. Jackson. "Bookstore Signings: The Good, the Bad, the Ugly," *SFWA Bulletin* 26(3): 10-14. Fall 1992. (No. 117)

___ King, T. Jackson. "Creating Believable Aliens," *SFWA Bulletin* 27(4)/28(1): 32-39. Winter/Spring 1994. (No. 122/123)

___ King, T. Jackson. "Habitable Stars Within 100 Light Years," *The Report: The Fiction Writer's Magazine* No. 9: 9-11. March 1993.

WRITING SF AND FANTASY (continued)

___ Koontz, Dean R. "How To," in: Greenberg, Martin H., Ed Gorman and Bill Munster, eds. **The Dean Koontz Companion**. New York: Berkley, 1994. pp.216-218.

___ Koontz, Dean R. "Keeping the Reader on the Edge of His Seat," in: Greenberg, Martin H., Ed Gorman and Bill Munster, eds. **The Dean Koontz Companion**. New York: Berkley, 1994. pp.219-224.

___ Koontz, Dean R. "Why Novels of Fear Must Do More Than Frighten," in: Greenberg, Martin H., Ed Gorman and Bill Munster, eds. **The Dean Koontz Companion**. New York: Berkley, 1994. pp.225-230.

___ Kress, Nancy. **Beginnings, Middles & Ends**. Cincinnati, OH: Writer's Digest Books, 1993. 149pp.

___ Kress, Nancy. "Plot: Using Coincidence in Your Fiction," in: Thompkins, David G., ed. **Science Fiction Writer's Market Place and Source Book**. Cincinnati, OH: Writer's Digest Books, 1994. pp.30-33.

___ Kress, Nancy. "An SF Moderate Climbs Cautiously onto the Barricades," *Pulphouse* No. 10: 12-18. July 1992.

___ Kube-McDowell, Michael P. "The Quiet Pools," *OtherRealms* No. 27: 4-5. Spring 1990.

___ Langford, David. "Wisdom of the Ancients," *Interzone* No. 55: 43-44. January 1992.

___ Le Guin, Ursula K. "A Citizen of Mondath," in: Jakubowski, Maxim and James, Edward, eds. **The Profession of Science Fiction**. New York: St. Martin's, 1992. pp.73-77.

___ Le Guin, Ursula K. **Earthsea Revisioned**. Madison, NJ: Children's Literature New England, 1993. 26pp.

___ Le Guin, Ursula K. "Talking About Writing," *Writer* 105(12): 9-11, 41. December 1992.

___ Le Guin, Ursula K. "Writing Without Conflict," *Harpers* 279(1666): 35-36. March 1989.

___ Lindskold, Jane M. "The Elements of Fantastic Fiction," *Writer* 106(11): 18-21. September 1993.

___ Lovecraft, H. P. "Notes on Writing Weird Fiction (1932/33)," in: Joshi, S. T., ed. **Miscellaneous Writings: H. P. Lovecraft**. Sauk City, WI: Arkham House, 1995. pp.113-116.

___ Lovecraft, H. P. "Some Notes on Interplanetary Fiction (1934)," in: Joshi, S. T., ed. **Miscellaneous Writings: H. P. Lovecraft**. Sauk City, WI: Arkham House, 1995. pp.117-122.

___ Maddox, Tom. "Reports From the Electronic Frontier: Writing Tools, Part 1," *Locus* 31(1): 11-13, 47 July 1993.

___ Maddox, Tom. "Reports From the Electronic Frontier: Writing Tools, Part 2," *Locus* 31(2): 11, 48. August 1993.

___ Madracki, John. "Writing Your First Novel," *Focus* (BSFA) No. 25: 12-13. December/January 1994.

___ Malzberg, Barry N. "Thus Our Words Unspoken," *Amazing Stories* 67(6): 62-64. September 1992.

___ Manzo, Fred. "The Horror Spot: What Are the Special Ingredients of Outstanding Fiction Writing," *Genre Writer's News* 1(7): 30-31. May/June 1995.

___ Masterson, Graham. "Why Horror?," *Writer* 107(7): 7-9. July 1994.

___ Matracki, John. "Matching Slang," *Focus* (BSFA) No. 27: 9-10. December 1994/January 1995.

___ McComb, Gordon. "The Monogamous Writer," *The Report: The Fiction Writer's Magazine* No. 9: 4. March 1993.

___ McCormack, Thomas. **The Fiction Editor, the Novel, and the Novelist**. New York: St. Martin's, 1994. 202pp.

___ McKillip, Patricia A. "Once Upon a Time Too Often," *Writer* 105(8): 18-20, 44. August 1992.

___ Melia, Sally-Ann. "Writing a First Novel," *Focus* (BSFA) No. 24: 11. June/July 1993.

___ Mitchison, Naomi. "Wonderful Deathless Ditties," in: Jakubowski, Maxim and James, Edward, eds. **The Profession of Science Fiction**. New York: St. Martin's, 1992. pp.34-43.

___ Mosiman, Billie S. "The Sympathetic Killer: Journeying into the Minds of Serial Murderers," *The Report: The Fiction Writer's Magazine* No. 9: 6-7. March 1993.

___ Ochoa, George. **The Writer's Guide to Creating a Science Fiction Universe**. Cincinnati, OH: Writer's Digest, 1993. 314pp.

___ Pace, Sue. "Exploring Your Science Fiction World," *Writer* 106(9): 9-12. September 1993.

___ Palmer, Jerry. **Potboilers: Methods, Concepts and Case Studies in Popular Fiction**. London: Routledge, 1991. 219pp.

___ Palwick, Susan. "Believing (in) Fiction: An Open Letter," *New York Review of Science Fiction* No. 47: 14-15. July 1992. (Replies: No. 50: 18-20. Oct. 1992)

___ Patrouch, Joe. "Rogue Moon and Me," *Lan's Lantern* No. 41: 69-72. July 1993.

WRITING SF AND FANTASY

WRITING SF AND FANTASY (continued)

___ Patterson, Kent. "Confessions of a Mall Rat Writer," *The Report: The Fiction Writer's Magazine* No. 7: 21-22. June 1992.

___ Patton, Charles. **On Writing Science Fiction and Screenplays**, by Charles Patton and Alan D. Foster. Alexandra, VA: PBS Adult Learning Satellite Service, 1994. 1 Videocassette, 30 minutes.

___ Piper, David. "Do SF Writers Have Any Responsibility at All?," *Focus* (BSFA) No. 27: 8-9. December 1994/January 1995.

___ Platt, Charles. "Wrist Voodoo," *Interzone* No. 83: 41-43. May 1994.

___ Pohl, Frederik. "Essay: A SF Grandmaster Explains How Good Ideas Build Better Stories," *Science Fiction Age* 2(6): 34-37. September 1994.

___ Pohl, Frederik. "The Habit of Writing," *SFWA Bulletin* 29(2): 4-6. Summer 1995. (No. 127)

___ Pournelle, Jerry. "The Future Isn't What It Used to Be, But Then, Maybe It Never Was," *Science Fiction Age* 1(1): 22, 70. November 1992.

___ Ptacek, Kathryn. "A Tale of Cash Flow," by Kathryn Ptacek and Ashley McConnell. *The Report: The Fiction Writer's Magazine* No. 11: 9-11. Summer 1993.

___ Rand, Ken. "How to Make Your Tape Recorder Work for You," *The Report: The Fiction Writer's Magazine* No. 10: 21. Summer 1993.

___ Roberson, Jennifer. "Matrimonium Interruptus and Other Roadblocks to Writing," *SFWA Bulletin* 29(2): 14-17. Summer 1995. (No. 127)

___ Robson, Justina. "Politics, Culture, Autobiography: What Responsibilities Have We?," *Focus* (BSFA) No. 27: 7-8. December 1994/January 1995.

___ Rogers, Bruce H. "The Survival Column: Should Writers Be Lovers?," *The Report: The Fiction Writer's Magazine* No. 9: 17-18. March 1993.

___ Royle, Nicholas. "Show and Tell," *Focus* (BSFA) No. 27: 9. December 1994/January 1995.

___ Russo, John. **Scare Tactics: The Art, Craft, and Trade Secrets of Writing, Producing, and Directing Chillers and Thrillers**. New York: Dell, 1992. 241pp.

___ Ryan, William F. "The Genesis of the Techno-Thriller," *Virginia Quarterly Review* 69(1): 24-40. Winter 1993.

___ Salmonson, Jessica A. "Letter to a Friend on the Pursuit of Writing," *Quantum* No. 41: 16-17. Winter/Spring 1992.

___ Sargent, Pamela. "The Historical Novelist and History," *Paradoxa* 1(3): 363-374. 1995.

___ Sargent, Pamela. "Traps," *Astromancer Quarterly* 2(1): 28-35. February 1993.

___ Sargent, Pamela. "The Writer as Nomad," in: Jakubowski, Maxim and James, Edward, eds. **The Profession of Science Fiction**. New York: St. Martin's, 1992. pp.111-119.

___ Sargent, Pamela. "Writing, Science Fiction, and Family Values," *Amazing Stories* 69(1): 100-111. Spring 1994.

___ Schmeidler, Lucy. "Subjective Strange," *New York Review of Science Fiction* No. 73: 16-17. September 1994.

___ Schmidt, Stanley. **Aliens and Alien Societies**. Cincinnati, OH: Writer's Digest Books, 1995. 226pp.

___ Schmidt, Stanley. "Authors vs. Editors," in: Dozois, Gardner, ed. **Writing Science Fiction and Fantasy**. New York: St. Martin's, 1991. pp.236-249.

___ Schmidt, Stanley. "Editorial: Nouveaux Clichés," *Analog* 113(12): 4-10. October 1993.

___ Schmidt, Stanley. "Editorial: Prime Directive," *Analog* 114(10): 4-10. August 1994.

___ Schmidt, Stanley. "Editorial: The Manuscript That Never Was," *Analog* 113(3): 4-12. February 1993.

___ Schmidt, Stanley. "Good Writing Is Not Enough," in: Dozois, Gardner, ed. **Writing Science Fiction and Fantasy**. New York: St. Martin's, 1991. pp.81-104.

___ Schmidt, Stanley. "Hypertext as a Writing Tool," *SFWA Bulletin* 26(2): 6-10. Summer 1992. (No. 116)

___ Schmidt, Stanley. "The Ideas That Wouldn't Die," in: Dozois, Gardner, ed. **Writing Science Fiction and Fantasy**. New York: St. Martin's, 1991. pp.200-207.

___ Schmidt, Stanley. "Seeing Your Way to Better Stories," in: Dozois, Gardner, ed. **Writing Science Fiction and Fantasy**. New York: St. Martin's, 1991. pp.50-61.

___ Schweitzer, Darrell. "Style: Knock Out Weak Verbs!," in: Thompkins, David G., ed. **Science Fiction Writer's Market Place and Source Book**. Cincinnati, OH: Writer's Digest Books, 1994. pp.25-29.

WRITING SF AND FANTASY (continued)

___ Sedgewick, Cristina. "The Fork in the Road: Can Science Fiction Survive in Postmodern, Megacorporate America?," *Science Fiction Studies* 18(1): 11-52. March 1991.

___ Seidman, Michael. "Choosing Your Genre: The Fantasy," *Writer's Digest* 72(9): 37. September 1992.

___ Seidman, Michael. "Choosing Your Genre: The Horror Novel," *Writer's Digest* 72(10): 35. October 1992.

___ Seidman, Michael. "Choosing Your Genre: The Science Fiction Novel," *Writer's Digest* 72(8): 40. August 1992.

___ Service, Pamela F. "On Writing Sci Fi and Fantasy for Kids," *ALAN Review* 19(3): 16-18. Spring 1992.

___ Shaw, Bob. "How to Write Science Fiction," *Interzone* No. 67: 17-24. January 1993.

___ Shaw, Bob. **How to Write Science Fiction**. London: Allison & Busby, 1993. 158pp.

___ Sherman, Fraser. "Off to See the Wizards," *Writer* 107(11): 18-20. November 1994.

___ Sherman, Josepha. "Creating Superheroes in Science Fiction and Fantasy," *Writer* 108(7): 13-14. July 1995.

___ Sherman, Josepha. "An Open Letter to Fantasy Writers," *Writer* 106(5): 13-15. May 1993.

___ Shockley, W. M. "Workshopping by Computer," *The Report: The Fiction Writer's Magazine* No. 10: 9. Summer 1993.

___ Sleator, William. "From Interstellar Pigs to Spirit Houses," *ALAN Review* 19(3): 10-12, 15. Spring 1992.

___ Slonczewski, Joan. "Science in Science Fiction: Making It Work," *Writer* 107(4): 14-17. April 1994.

___ Smith, David A. "How I Write," *Quantum* No. 42: 15-16. Summer/Fall 1992.

___ Smith, David A. "Writer's Workshops," *Quantum* No. 43/44: 32-34, 38. Spring/Summer 1993.

___ Smith, Dean W. "A Short Horror Story," *The Report: The Fiction Writer's Magazine* No. 11: 1, 3. Summer 1993.

___ Smith, Sherwood. "Writing for Adults vs. Writing for Children," *Focus* (BSFA) No. 29: 13-14. December 1995/January 1996.

___ Spinrad, Norman. "Building a Starfaring Age," in: Dozois, Gardner, ed. **Writing Science Fiction and Fantasy**. New York: St. Martin's, 1991. pp.185-199.

___ Spinrad, Norman. "Where I Get My Crazy Ideas," in: Jakubowski, Maxim and James, Edward, eds. **The Profession of Science Fiction**. New York: St. Martin's, 1992. pp.95-100.

___ Stableford, Brian. "How Should a Science Fiction Story End?," *New York Review of Science Fiction* No. 78: 1, 8-15. February 1995.

___ Stableford, Brian. "Writing Fantasy and Horror, Part One," *Focus* (BSFA) No. 25: 10-11. December/January 1994.

___ Stableford, Brian. "Writing Fantasy and Horror, Part Two," *Focus* (BSFA) No. 26: 3-4. June/July 1994.

___ Stableford, Brian. "Writing Science Fiction," *Focus* (BSFA) No. 24: 12. June/July 1993.

___ Starzl, R. F. "The Fantastic Science Market," *Fantasy Commentator* 8(3/4): 161-165, 257. Fall 1995. (Whole No. 47/48)

___ Strock, Ian R. "Market Listings," in: Dozois, Gardner, ed. **Writing Science Fiction and Fantasy**. New York: St. Martin's, 1991. pp.250-258.

___ Thomas, Sue. "Self-Censorship: The Three Dots...," *Focus* (BSFA) No. 29: 3-4. December 1995/January 1996.

___ Thomas, Sue. "Should Writers Teach Writing?," *Focus* (BSFA) No. 25: 12. December/January 1994.

___ Tompkins, David G., ed. **Science Fiction Writer's Marketplace and Sourcebook**. Cincinnati, OH: Writer's Digest, 1994. 486pp.

___ Van Belkom, Edo. "Novelizations," *SFWA Bulletin* 27(3): 4-10. Fall 1993. (No. 121)

___ Van Belkom, Edo. "What's in a Name?," *SFWA Bulletin* 27(2): 10-15. Summer 1993. (No. 120)

___ Vonarburg, Elisabeth. "So You Want to Be a Science Fiction Writer?," *New York Review of Science Fiction* No. 57: 1, 3-5. May 1993.

___ Westfahl, Gary. "The Words That Could Happen: Science Fiction Neologisms and the Creation of Future Worlds," *Extrapolation* 34(4): 290-304. Winter 1993.

___ Westfahl, Gary. "Writing for No Fun and No Profit: A Practical Guide to an Impractical Profession," *The Report: The Fiction Writer's Magazine* No. 10: 14-15. Summer 1993.

___ Williamson, Jack. "The Way It Was, 1933-1937," in: Jakubowski, Maxim and James, Edward, eds. **The Profession of Science Fiction**. New York: St. Martin's, 1992. pp.12-25.

WRITING SF AND FANTASY (continued)

___ Willis, Connie. "Learning to Write Comedy, or Why It's Impossible and How to Do It," in: Dozois, Gardner, ed. **Writing Science Fiction and Fantasy**. New York: St. Martin's, 1991. pp.76-88.

___ Wolfe, Gene. "The Profession of Science Fiction," in: Jakubowski, Maxim and James, Edward, eds. **The Profession of Science Fiction**. New York: St. Martin's, 1992. pp.131-139.

___ Wu, William F. "Lacks 'Oriental' Flavor," *Monad* No. 2:3-16. March 1992.

___ Yep, Laurence. "A Garden of Dragons," *ALAN Review* 19(3): 6-8. Spring 1992.

___ Yolen, Jane. " 'Oh God, Here Come the Elves," in: Ruddick, Nicholas, ed. **State of the Fantastic**. Westport, CT: Greenwood, 1992. pp.3-14.

___ Yolen, Jane. "Turtles All the Way Down," in: Dozois, Gardner, ed. **Writing Science Fiction and Fantasy**. New York: St. Martin's, 1991. pp.62-75.

___ York, J. Steven. "Computer Disasters: Ten Computer Disasters That Will Happen to You (And What to Do About Them)," *The Report: The Fiction Writer's Magazine* No. 11: 19-22. Summer 1993.

___ Zaharoff, Howard. "The Four Rules of SF Humor," *Amazing Stories* 67(10): 60-61. January 1993.

___ Zelazny, Roger. "The Parts That Are Only Glimpsed: Three Reflexes," *SFWA Bulletin* 29(2): 7-8. Summer 1995. (No. 127)

WRITING SF AND FANTASY, BUSINESS ASPECTS

___ "GEnie Round Table on Agents," *SFWA Bulletin* 27(1): 38-46. Spring 1993. (No. 119)

___ "Writers and Electronic Rights," *Locus* 33(6): 9, 79. December 1994.

___ Banks, Michael A. "Attending Science Fiction Conventions for Fun and Profit," in: **1991 Novel and Short Story Writers Market**. Cincinnati, OH: Writer's Digest Books, 1991. pp.55-58.

___ Barnes, John. "Publications in the Bucket: Threat, Menace, Hidden Subsidy, or Just a Thing?," *SFWA Bulletin* 28(2): 6-13. Summer 1994. (No. 124)

___ Better, Cathy. "Open Doors at These Houses of Horror (Part 1)," *Writer's Digest* 73(5): 56-59. May 1993.

___ Better, Cathy. "Open Doors at These Houses of Horror (Part 2)," *Writer's Digest* 73(6): 54-55. June 1993.

___ Brin, David. "Agent-Author (Pre-Nuptial) Agreements," *SFWA Bulletin* 26(1): 34-35. Spring 1992. (No. 115)

___ Cherryh, C. J. "From Disk to Typesetter," *SFWA Bulletin* 26(3): 15-17. Fall 1992. (No. 117)

___ Copobianco, Michael. "Interview With Paul Rosenzweig," *SFWA Bulletin* 28(2): 19-20. Summer 1994. (No. 124)

___ Costikyan, Greg. "Short Fiction Market Response Times," *Science Fiction and Fantasy Writers of America Bulletin* 25(4): 27. Winter 1992. (No. 114)

___ Curtis, Richard. "Agent's Corner: Author? What's an Author?," *Locus* 28(2): 11. February 1992.

___ Curtis, Richard. "Agent's Corner: Author? What's an Author?," *Locus* 28(4): 11, 49-50. April 1992.

___ Curtis, Richard. "Agent's Corner: Last Chance," *Locus* 28(1): 11, 13, 61. January 1992.

___ Di Fate, Vincent. "Sketches: Now Might Be the Right Time to Donate That Painting!," *Science Fiction Chronicle* 13(7): 25-26. April 1992.

___ Feist, Raymond E. "Contract Article IV: Advances, Payment & Royalties, and a Few Other Things," *SFWA Bulletin* 25(4): 15-20. Winter 1992. (No. 114)

___ Feist, Raymond E. "Contract Article IX: Editorial Courtesy," *SFWA Bulletin* 27(1): 47-53. Spring 1993. (No. 119)

___ Feist, Raymond E. "Contract Article V: A Little More Money; Sub-Rights," *SFWA Bulletin* 26(1): 50-57. Spring 1992. (No. 115)

___ Feist, Raymond E. "Contract Article VI: Options and Miscellany," *SFWA Bulletin* 26(2): 20-27. Summer 1992. (No. 116)

___ Feist, Raymond E. "Contract Article VII: Agency Clause, Agents, and Other Writers," *SFWA Bulletin* 26(3): 23-28. Fall 1992. (No. 117)

___ Feist, Raymond E. "Contract Article VIII: Negotiations," *SFWA Bulletin* 26(4): 12-15. Winter 1993. (No. 118)

___ Feist, Raymond E. "Contract Article X: Packagers," *SFWA Bulletin* 27(2): 19-24. Summer 1993. (No. 120)

___ Feist, Raymond E. "Contract Article XI: The Law Is an Ass," *SFWA Bulletin* 27(3): 19-25. Fall 1993. (No. 121)

___ Feist, Raymond E. "Contract Article XII: Changes, Part 1," *SFWA Bulletin* 28(2): 21-26. Summer 1994. (No. 124)

WRITING SF AND FANTASY, BUSINESS ASPECTS (continued)

___ Feist, Raymond E. "Contract Article XIII: Changes, Part 2," *SFWA Bulletin* 28(3): 23-27. Winter 1994. (No. 125)

___ Feist, Raymond E. "Contract Article XIV: Model Contracts," *SFWA Bulletin* 29(1): 44-52. Spring 1995. (No. 126)

___ Galen, Russell. "Finding and Getting the Most Out of a Science Fiction Agent," in: Thompkins, David G., ed. **Science Fiction Writer's Market Place and Source Book**. Cincinnati, OH: Writer's Digest Books, 1994. pp.286-292.

___ Galen, Russell. "Writing in a Fantasy World," *Writer's Digest* 73(5): 53-55. May 1993.

___ Gee, Robin. "Marketing Your Science Fiction Novel," in: Thompkins, David G., ed. **Science Fiction Writer's Market Place and Source Book**. Cincinnati, OH: Writer's Digest Books, 1994. pp.182-192.

___ Gee, Robin. "Marketing Your Short Story," in: Thompkins, David G., ed. **Science Fiction Writer's Market Place and Source Book**. Cincinnati, OH: Writer's Digest Books, 1994. pp.35-38.

___ Gilliam, Richard. "The Science Fiction Anthology Market," by Richard Gilliam and Martin H. Greenberg. in: Thompkins, David G., ed. **Science Fiction Writer's Market Place and Source Book**. Cincinnati, OH: Writer's Digest Books, 1994. pp.173-180.

___ Hordern, Kate. "Selling SF and Fantasy Translation Rights in Eastern Europe and Russia," *SFWA Bulletin* 29(2): 28-31. Summer 1995. (No. 127)

___ King, T. Jackson. "How to Market Your Novel," *SFWA Bulletin* 26(1): 24-28. Spring 1992. (No. 115)

___ Knight, Damon. "Dell Magazine Contract," *SFWA Bulletin* 28(2): 2-4. Summer 1994. (No. 124)

___ Knight, Damon. "Dell Magazines Contract Update," *SFWA Bulletin* 28(3): 2. Winter 1994. (No. 125)

___ Kogelman, David. "Writing and the Law: Advantages of Individual Copyright Registration," *Locus* 33(6): 9, 76. December 1994.

___ Kozak, Ellen M. "Negotiating the Maze That Is GATT," *SFWA Bulletin* 29(2): 26-27. Summer 1995. (No. 127)

___ Mason, Cyn. "Business: Taxes for Writers," *SFWA Bulletin* 27(3): 12-17. Fall 1993. (No. 121)

___ McGarry, Terry. "A Writer's Guide to Understanding the Copy Editor," *SFWA Bulletin* 29(1): 53-56. Spring 1995. (No. 126)

___ Oltion, Jerry. "PROfessional Writers & CONventions," *The Report: The Fiction Writer's Magazine* No. 7: 6-7. June 1992.

___ Peck, Brooks. "On-Demand Printing and Other Dirty Words," *SFWA Bulletin* 29(2): 21-22. Summer 1995. (No. 127)

___ Rusch, Kristine K. "Anatomy of a Sale: 'Mom's Little Friends' to *The Magazine of Fantasy and Science Fiction*," in: Thompkins, David G., ed. **Science Fiction Writer's Market Place and Source Book**. Cincinnati, OH: Writer's Digest Books, 1994. pp.344-357.

___ Ryan, Charles C. "Anatomy of a Sale: 'Due Process' to *Aboriginal Science Fiction*," in: Thompkins, David G., ed. **Science Fiction Writer's Market Place and Source Book**. Cincinnati, OH: Writer's Digest Books, 1994. pp.320-330.

___ Schmidt, Stanley. "Anatomy of a Sale: 'From the Corner of the Eye' to *Analog Science Fiction Science Fact*," in: Thompkins, David G., ed. **Science Fiction Writer's Market Place and Source Book**. Cincinnati, OH: Writer's Digest Books, 1994. pp.331-343.

___ Schmidt, Stanley. "Editorial: The Manuscript That Never Was," *Analog* 113(3): 4-12. February 1993.

___ Shockley, W. M. "Macro-Desiacs, and Five Other Time (Savers) Wasters," *The Report: The Fiction Writer's Magazine* 2(6): 29-31. April 1992. (No. 59)

___ Sperry, Ralph A. "Three Nasty Problems," *SFWA Bulletin* 26(3): 21-22. Fall 1992. (No. 117)

___ Stith, John E. "SFWA Model Author-Agent Contract, First Cut," *SFWA Bulletin* 27(4)/28(1): 40-43. Winter/Spring 1994. (No. 122/123)

___ Thomas, G. W. "The Gaming Market: Writing Role-Playing Games," in: Thompkins, David G., ed. **Science Fiction Writer's Market Place and Source Book**. Cincinnati, OH: Writer's Digest Books, 1994. pp.276-283.

___ Thomas, G. W. "An Untapped Market: Writing Role-Playing Games," *Writer's Digest* 73(6): 38-41. June 1993.

___ Weisskopf, Toni. "Anatomy of a Sale: 'Sleipnir' to Baen Books," in: Thompkins, David G., ed. **Science Fiction Writer's Market Place and Source Book**. Cincinnati, OH: Writer's Digest Books, 1994. pp.358-374.

___ Williams, Sheila. "The Mechanics of Submission," in: Dozois, Gardner, ed. **Writing Science Fiction and Fantasy**. New York: St. Martin's, 1991. pp.211-220.

___ Yarbro, Chelsea Q. "Copyright Infringement, Part 2," *SFWA Bulletin* 26(3): 19-20. Fall 1992. (No. 117)

WRITING SF AND FANTASY, BUSINESS ASPECTS (continued)
___ York, Christina F. "Keeping the Faith," *The Report: The Fiction Writer's Magazine* 2(6): 26-28. April 1992. (No. 59)

WRITING SF AND FANTASY, GAMES
___ Koke, Jak. "Writing for Gaming Companies: A Personal Experience," *The Report: The Fiction Writer's Magazine* No. 10: 8-9. Summer 1993.

WRITING SF AND FANTASY, TV AND MOVIES
___ Adams, Max. "Max Adams' Crash Course in Film Development," *The Report: The Fiction Writer's Magazine* No. 10: 1, 3-4. Summer 1993.
___ Altman, Mark A. "*Star Trek: Deep Space Nine*: Scripting the Adventures," *Cinefantastique* 23(6): 40-42. April 1993.
___ Altman, Mark A. "*Star Trek: The Next Generation*: The Board and the Art of the Pitch," *Cinefantastique* 24(3/4): 52-55. October 1993.
___ Hull, Peter R. "Dreams Come True," *Star Trek: The Official Fan Club* No. 94: 46-47. February/March 1994.
___ Kingston, F. Colin. "*White Dwarf*: Bruce Wagner on Writing Science Fiction for Television," *Cinefantastique* 26(5): 10-11, 61. August 1995.
___ Perry, Steve. "Old Enough to Know Better: The Mating Ritual of the Sand Hill Cranes," *The Report: The Fiction Writer's Magazine* 2(6): 5-9. April 1992. (No. 59)
___ Rubenstein, Steve. "Scotty, Beam Up Some New Aliens," *San Francisco (CA) Chronicle* Sec. C, p. 20. September 12, 1992.

WURTS, JANNY
___ "Janny Wurts: The Best of Both Worlds," *Hailing Frequencies* (Waldenbooks) No. 11: 1-3. 1994.
___ "Maitz, Wurts Paintings Stolen," *Science Fiction Chronicle* 17(2): 5-6. December 1995/January 1996.

WYATT, JANE
___ Weaver, Tom. "Jane Wyatt," in: Weaver, Tom. **They Fought the Creature Features: Interviews with 23 Classic Horror, Science Fiction and Serial Stars.** Jefferson, NC: McFarland, 1995. pp.289-302.

WYLIE, JONATHAN
___ Nicholls, Stan. "Adding the Flesh and Blood: Jonathan Wylie Interviewed," *Interzone* No. 74: 45-47. August 1993.
___ Nicholls, Stan. "Jonathan Wylie Proves Two into One Will Go," in: Nicholls, Stan. **Wordsmiths of Wonder: Fifty Interviews with Writers of the Fantastic.** London: Orbit, 1993. pp.311-320.

WYLIE, PHILIP
___ DuPriest, Margaret D. "Philip Wylie," in: Bruccoli, Matthew J., ed. **Facts on File Bibliography of American Fiction 1919-1988.** New York: Facts on File, 1991. pp.561-562.
___ Reinhart, Werner. "Philip Wylie and Edwin Balmer, **When Worlds Collide** (1933)," in: Heuermann, Harmut, ed. **Der Science Fiction Roman in der angloamerikanischen Literatur: Interpretationen.** Düsseldorf: Bagel, 1986. pp.65-83.
___ Seed, David. "The Postwar Jeremiads of Philip Wylie," *Science Fiction Studies* 22(2): 234-251. July 1995.

WYNDHAM, JOHN
___ "Cuckoo in Wrong Nest," *Locus* 33(1): 9, 75. July 1994.
___ "Eric Frank Russell, Wyndam Collections to UK's SF Foundation," *Science Fiction Chronicle* 15(6): 5-6. April/May 1994.
___ Wymer, Rowland. "How 'Safe' Is John Wyndham? A Closer Look at His Work, With Particular Reference to **The Chrysalids**," *Foundation* No. 55: 25-36. Summer 1992.

X-FILES (COMIC)
___ Florence, Bill. "The X-Comics," *Starlog* No. 212: 58-60. March 1995.

X-FILES (TV)
___ Adalian, Josef. "*X-Files* Space Aliens Abduct Weekend Lineup," *Washington (DC) Times*. September 30, 1994. in: *NewsBank. Film and Television.* 117:G3. 1994.
___ Butko, Tatiana. "*X-Files* Fans Gather at Pasadena Center," *San Gabriel Valley Tribune (West Covina, CA)*. August 27, 1995. in: *NewsBank. Film and Television.* 82:F4. 1995.
___ Cerone, Daniel H. "A Surreal *X-Files* Captures Earthlings," *Los Angeles (CA) Times*. October 28, 1994. in: *NewsBank. Film and Television.* 127:A1-A2. 1994.

X-FILES (TV) (continued)
___ Coe, Steve. "Television of the Weird: Networks Take a Walk on Weird Side," *Broadcasting and Cable* 125(44): 56-57. October 30, 1995.
___ Counts, Kyle. "Scientific American," *Starlog* No. 201: 76-79. April 1994.
___ Counts, Kyle. "True Disbeliever," in: McDonnell, David, ed. **Starlog's Science Fiction Heroes and Heroines.** New York: Crescent Books, 1995. pp.70-72.
___ Dworin, Diana. "*X-Files* Exchange: Television Show's Fans Meet to Swap Stories, Ideas," *Austin (TX) American Statesman* Sec. B, p. 1, 5. November 20, 1995.
___ Florence, Bill. "Keeper of Secrets," *Starlog* No. 211: 28-30, 74. February 1995.
___ Garcia, Frank. "Prince of Darkness," *Starlog* No. 220: 76-79. November 1995.
___ Genge, N. E. **The Unofficial X-Files Companion.** New York: Crown, 1995. 227pp.
___ Grant, James. "Red Hot Right Now: David Duchovny," *Cosmopolitan* 219(4): 144. October 1995.
___ Harris, Judith P. "**The X-Files** (Review)," *Cinefantastique* 24(6)/25(1): 124. February 1994.
___ Infusino, Divina. "Paranoid About the Paranormal," *TV Guide* 42(3): 20-21. January 15, 1994.
___ Kushman, Rick. "Believe It (or Not)," *Sacramento (CA) Bee*. August 4, 1995. in: *NewsBank. Film and Television.* 82:F1-F3. 1995.
___ Kutzera, Dale. "*X-Files*," *Cinefantastique* 26(2): 52-53. February 1995.
___ Lee, Julianne. "X Heroine," *Starlog* No. 213: 32-35. April 1995.
___ Lee, Julianne. "X-Symbol," *Starlog* No. 215: 27-30, 71. June 1995.
___ Littlefield, Kinney. "X-Factor," *(Santa Ana, CA) Orange County Register*. May 11, 1994. in: *NewsBank. Film and Television.* 61:A12-a13. 1994.
___ Lowry, Brian. **The Truth Is Out There: The Official Guide to The X-Files.** New York: HarperCollins, 1995. 277pp.
___ Maccarillo, Lisa. "The Truth Is Out There," *Sci-Fi Entertainment* 2(3): 54-58. October 1995.
___ Maccarillo, Lisa. "*X-Files*," *Sci-Fi Entertainment* 1(4): 74-77. December 1994.
___ Martinez, Cal. "The Man Who Eats Livers: A Visit to an *X-Files* Convention in Pasadena," *Los Angeles (CA) Times* p.B3. August 29, 1995.
___ Millman, Joyce. "*VR5* Virtually Hip But No *X-Files*," *San Francisco (CA) Examiner*. March 10, 1995. in: *NewsBank. Film and Television.* 39: F1-F2. 1995.
___ Nicholaas, Joseph. "X-Rated: **The X-Files**," *Matrix* No. 115: 12-13. June/July 1995.
___ Pallmeyer, Karl. "The Truth Is Out There: *X-Files* Merchandise Is Hot," *Austin (TX) Business Journal* November 17, 1995. in: *NewsBank. Film and Television* FTV 107: C11. 1995.
___ Peet, Judy. "2000 'Philes' Trek to Convention," *Newark (NJ) Star-Ledger*. November 25, 1995. in: *NewsBank. Film and Television.* 107: C12. 1995.
___ Probst, Chris. "Darkness Descends on **The X-Files**," *American Cinematographer* 76(6): 28-32. June 1995.
___ Richmond, Ray. "Chris' X-ellent Adventure," *Los Angeles (CA) Daily News*. August 24, 1995. in: *NewsBank. Film and Television.* 82:E12-E14. 1995.
___ Schwed, Mark. "On the Horizon: Whole New Worlds," *TV Guide* 41(30): 29-31. July 24, 1993.
___ Shapiro, Marc. "Devil's Advocate," *Starlog* No. 202: 46-49. May 1994.
___ Shrieves, Linda. "Fox's Cult Favorite Edges Toward Mainstream Popularity," *Orlando (FL) Sentinel*. October 14, 1994. in: *NewsBank. Film and Television.* 117:F14. 1994.
___ Solomon, Harvey. "*X-Files* Conquers Earth," *Boston (MA) Herald*. September 23, 1994. in: *NewsBank. Film and Television.* 106:G6. 1994.
___ Swallow, James. "X-aminations," *Starlog* No. 221: 30-33, 64. December 1995.
___ Turnquist, Kristi. "'Files': Eerie 'X' Out-Twilights the T-Zone," *Portland (OR) The Oregonian*. February 3, 1995. in: *NewsBank. Film and Television.* 31:B8. 1995.
___ Ventura, Michael. "The Truth Is Out There," *Los Angeles (CA) Times*. September 10, 1995. in: *NewsBank. Film and Television.* 91:F6-F10. 1995.
___ Vitaris, Paula. "Writers," *Starlog* No. 210: 61-64. January 1995.

X-FILES (TV)

X-FILES (TV) (continued)

___ Vitaris, Paula. "*X-Files*: Boy's Club," *Cinefantastique* 26(6)/27(1): 88. October 1995.

___ Vitaris, Paula. "*X-Files*: Cancer Man," *Cinefantastique* 26(6)/27(1): 67-68. October 1995.

___ Vitaris, Paula. "*X-Files*: Casting Call," *Cinefantastique* 26(6)/27(1): 35-36. October 1995.

___ Vitaris, Paula. "*X-Files*: Chris Carter, Creator," *Cinefantastique* 26(6)/27(1): 19-20. October 1995.

___ Vitaris, Paula. "*X-Files*: Cinematography," *Cinefantastique* 26(6)/27(1): 37-38. October 1995.

___ Vitaris, Paula. "*X-Files*: 'Colony' and 'End Game'," *Cinefantastique* 26(6)/27(1): 32-33. October 1995.

___ Vitaris, Paula. "*X-Files*: Computer Graphics," *Cinefantastique* 26(6)/27(1): 71-72. October 1995.

___ Vitaris, Paula. "*X-Files*: David Nutter," *Cinefantastique* 26(6)/27(1): 29-30. October 1995.

___ Vitaris, Paula. "*X-Files*: Deep Throat," *Cinefantastique* 26(6)/27(1): 45-46. October 1995.

___ Vitaris, Paula. "*X-Files*: Episode Guide," *Cinefantastique* 26(6)/27(1): 18-26, 41-42, 49-50, 57-63, 73-74, 81-89. October 1995.

___ Vitaris, Paula. "*X-Files*: F. B. I. Box Skinner," *Cinefantastique* 26(6)/27(1): 77-78. October 1995.

___ Vitaris, Paula. "*X-Files*: F. B. I. Judas," *Cinefantastique* 26(6)/27(1): 75-76. October 1995.

___ Vitaris, Paula. "*X-Files*: Family Ties," *Cinefantastique* 26(6)/27(1): 43-44. October 1995.

___ Vitaris, Paula. "*X-Files*: Fixing It in Post," *Cinefantastique* 26(6)/27(1): 27-28. October 1995.

___ Vitaris, Paula. "*X-Files*: Howard Gordon," *Cinefantastique* 26(6)/27(1): 48-49. October 1995.

___ Vitaris, Paula. "*X-Files*: Making Humbug," *Cinefantastique* 26(6)/27(1): 64-66. October 1995.

___ Vitaris, Paula. "*X-Files*: Monster Maker," *Cinefantastique* 26(6)/27(1): 39-40. October 1995.

___ Vitaris, Paula. "*X-Files*: Morgan and Wong," *Cinefantastique* 26(6)/27(1): 62. October 1995.

___ Vitaris, Paula. "*X-Files*: Mulder and Scully," *Cinefantastique* 26(6)/27(1): 23-24. October 1995.

___ Vitaris, Paula. "*X-Files*: Music of the Night," *Cinefantastique* 26(6)/27(1): 79-81. October 1995.

___ Vitaris, Paula. "*X-Files*: Production Design," *Cinefantastique* 26(6)/27(1): 59-61. October 1995.

___ Vitaris, Paula. "*X-Files*: R. W. Goodwin," *Cinefantastique* 26(6)/27(1): 21-22. October 1995.

___ Vitaris, Paula. "*X-Files*: Rob Bowman," *Cinefantastique* 26(6)/27(1): 83. October 1995.

___ Vitaris, Paula. "*X-Files*: Serial Killer," *Cinefantastique* 26(6)/27(1): 53-54. October 1995.

___ Vitaris, Paula. "*X-Files*: Special Effects," *Cinefantastique* 26(6)/27(1): 55-56. October 1995.

___ Vitaris, Paula. "*X-Files*: Staff Writer," *Cinefantastique* 26(6)/27(1): 51-52. October 1995.

___ Vitaris, Paula. "*X-Files*: The Cliffhanger," *Cinefantastique* 26(6)/27(1): 47. October 1995.

___ Vitaris, Paula. "*X-Files*: The Lone Gunmen," *Cinefantastique* 26(6)/27(1): 69-70. October 1995.

___ Vitaris, Paula. "*X-Files*: X, the Unknown," *Cinefantastique* 26(6)/27(1): 85-86. October 1995.

___ Vitaris, Paula. "*X-Files*," *Cinefantastique* 26(5): 48-49. August 1995.

___ Vitaris, Paula. "*X-Files*," *Cinefantastique* 26(6)/27(1): 16-86. October 1995.

XTRO II: THE SECOND ENCOUNTER (MOTION PICTURE)

___ Harris, Judith P. "*Xtro II* (Review)," *Cinefantastique* 23(1): 61. August 1992.

XTRO (MOTION PICTURE)

___ "*Xtro* Wins Paris Sci-Fi Fest," *Variety* p. 7. December 7, 1983.

XTRO-3: WATCH THE SKIES (MOTION PICTURE)

___ van Hise, James. "*Xtro-3: Watch the Skies*: Creature Effects," *Cinefantastique* 27(2): 48-49. November 1995.

___ van Hise, James. "*Xtro-3: Watch the Skies*: Series Auteur," *Cinefantastique* 27(2): 50. November 1995.

___ van Hise, James. "*Xtro-3: Watch the Skies*," *Cinefantastique* 27(2): 46-51, 61. November 1995.

YOUNG ADULT SF AND FANTASY

YAGHER, KEVIN

___ Beeler, Michael. "*Hellraiser IV: Bloodline*: Kevin Yagher, Director," *Cinefantastique* 26(3): 34. April 1995.

___ Derro, Marc. "Profile: Kevin Yagher," *Cinefex* No. 58: 103-104. June 1994.

___ Wiater, Stanley. "Yagher, Kevin," in: Wiater, Stanley. **Dark Visions: Conversations with the Masters of the Horror Film**. New York: Avon, 1992. pp.199-208.

YAHUA, WEI

___ Clements, Jonathan. "Flesh and Metal: Marriage and Female Emancipation in the Science Fiction of Wei Yahua," *Foundation* No. 65: 61-80. Autumn 1995.

YARBRO, CHELSEA QUINN

___ "Fine Awards to Bloch, Yarbro," *Locus* 30(4): 9. April 1993.

___ Kies, Cosette. **Presenting Young Adult Horror Fiction**. New York: Twayne, 1991. 203pp.

___ Proulx, Kevin. **Fear to the World: Eleven Voices in a Chorus of Horror**. Mercer Island, WA: Starmont, 1992. 243pp.

YEATS, WILLIAM BUTLER

___ Lapisardi, Frederick S. "A Task Most Difficult: Staging Yeats's Mystical Dramas at the Abbey," in: Murphy, Patrick D., ed. **Staging the Impossible: The Fantastic Mode in Modern Drama**. Westport, CT: Greenwood, 1992. pp.30-43.

YEAWORTH, IRVIN S., JR.

___ Weaver, Tom. "Birth of the **Blob**," *Starlog* No. 214: 59-65. May 1995.

YEFREMOV, IVAN

___ SEE: EFREMOV, IVAN.

YEOLAND, SALLY

___ Yeoland, Sally. "Sally and John: The Early Years," by Sally Yeoland and John Bangsund. *Metaphysical Review* No. 22/23: 17-44. November 1995.

YEP, LAURENCE

___ Burnson, Patrick. "In the Studio With Laurence Yep," *Publishers Weekly* 241(20): 25-26. May 16, 1994.

___ Erstein, Hap. "**Dragonwings** Lift Youngsters to Joys of Books," *Washington (DC) Times*. October 20, 1992. in: *NewsBank. Names in the News*. 157:B11. 1992.

___ Yep, Laurence. "A Garden of Dragons," *ALAN Review* 19(3): 6-8. Spring 1992.

YERBY, FRANK

___ "Yerby, Frank (Obituary)," *Locus* 28(2): 68. February 1992.

YOLEN, JANE

___ "1993 Mythopoeic Fiction Awards," *Locus* 31(3): 77. September 1993.

___ May, Jill P. "Jane Yolen's Literary Fairy Tales: Legends, Folktales, and Myths Remade," *Journal of Children's Literature* 21(1): 74-78. Spring 1995.

___ Weil, Ellen R. "The Door to Lilith's Cave: Memory and Imagination in Jane Yolen's Holocaust Novels," *Journal of the Fantastic in the Arts* 5(2): 90-104. 1993. (No. 18)

___ Yolen, Jane. "In the Spirit of Angels," *Catholic Library World* 63(2): 94-97. October/December 1991.

___ Yolen, Jane. " 'Oh God, Here Come the Elves," in: Ruddick, Nicholas, ed. **State of the Fantastic**. Westport, CT: Greenwood, 1992. pp.3-14.

___ Yolen, Jane. "The Route to Story," *New Advocate* 4(3): 143-149. Summer 1991.

YONGDEN, LAMA

___ Schweitzer, Darrell. "When Is a Fantasy Novel Not a Fantasy Novel?," *Studies in Weird Fiction* No. 11: 29-31. Spring 1992.

YOUNG ADULT SF AND FANTASY

___ "Best Science Fiction, Fantasy, & Horror: 1993," *Voice of Youth Advocates* 17(1): 7-10. April 1994.

___ "Young Adult Horror Bright Spot in Market," *Locus* 31(3): 7, 83. September 1993.

YOUNG INDIANA JONES CHRONICLES (TV) (continued)
___ Manson, Chris. "Video Beat: Chronicling Young Indy," *Cinefex* No. 54: 77-78. May 1993.
___ Mink, Eric. "Do or Die for Young Indy: ABC Decides Fate As Show's Plot Deepens," *Boston (MA) Herald*. April 8, 1992. in: *NewsBank. Film and Television*. 48:B5. 1992.
___ Rosenthal, Phil. "No Feeling of Doom for Young Indy (Review)," *Los Angeles (CA) Daily News*. March 1, 1992. in: *NewsBank. Film and Television*. 37:G7-G8. 1992.
___ Rosenthal, Phil. "***Young Indiana Jones*** Doesn't Live Up to Big Screen Brother (Review)," *Los Angeles (CA) Daily News*. March 1, 1992. in: *NewsBank. Film and Television*. 37:G9. 1992.
___ Spelling, Ian. "Young Indy & the First Crusade," *Starlog* No. 183: 33-36. October 1992.
___ Stephens, Lynne. "The Old Indiana Jones Chronicles," *Starlog* 185: 45-48, 65. December 1992.
___ Warren, Bill. "Chronicling ***The Young Indiana Jones***," *Starlog* 178: 52-55, 69. May 1992.
___ Zurawik, David. "Young Indy Explodes onto the Small Screen in a Sprawling, Exciting Yarn (Review)," *Baltimore (MD) Sun*. March 4, 1992. in: *NewsBank. Film and Television*. 27:C3. 1992.

YOUNGS, ISAAC NEWTON
___ Matarese, Susan. "The Artisan as Individual and Communitarian: The Life of Brother Isaac Newton Youngs," by Susan Matarese, Paul G. Salmon and Glendyne R. Wergland. *Utopian Studies* 6(2): 35-51. 1995.

YOUR SISTER IS A WEREWOLF (MOTION PICTURE)
___ SEE: HOWLING II: YOUR SISTER IS A WEREWOLF (MOTION PICTURE).

YUZNA, BRIAN
___ Wiater, Stanley. "Yuzna, Brian," in: Wiater, Stanley. **Dark Visions: Conversations with the Masters of the Horror Film**. New York: Avon, 1992. pp.209-218.

ZAHN, TIMOTHY
___ Grebe, Coralee. "Heir to the Wars," *Starlog* No. 186: 56-58. January 1993.

ZALLINGER, RUDOLPH
___ "Zallinger, Rudolph (Obituary)," *Science Fiction Chronicle* 16(9): 24. August/September 1995.

ZAMIATIN, EVENGII
___ "Zamiatin, Evangii Ivanovich," in: Vronskaya, Jeanne, ed. **A Biographical Dictionary of the Soviet Union 1917-1988**. London: K. G. Sauer, 1989. pp.482.
___ Booker, M. Keith. **The Dystopian Impulse in Modern Literature: Fiction as Social Criticism**. Westport, CT: Greenwood, 1994. 197pp.
___ Browning, William G. **Anti-Utopian Fiction: Definition and Standards for Evaluation**. Ph.D. Dissertation, Louisiana State University, 1966. 145pp.
___ Myers, Alan. "Zamyatin in Newcastle," *Foundation* No. 59: 70-78. Autumn 1993.
___ Rabkin, Eric S. "What Makes **We** a Science Fiction Classic? What Makes a Classic?," *Foundation* No. 65: 50-61. Autumn 1995.
___ Russell, Robert. **Evgeny Zamyatin**. s.l.: Bristol Press, 1992. 196pp.
___ Wegner, Phillip. "On Zamyatin's **We**: A Critical Map of Utopia's Possible Worlds," *Utopian Studies* 4(2): 94-116. 1993.

ZASTUPNEVICH, PAUL
___ Clark, Mike. "Designing Man," *Starlog* No. 187: 75-81, 69. February 1993.

ZELAZNY, ROGER
___ "Roger Zelazny, 1937-1995 (Appreciations)," *Locus* 35(2): 39-43, 72-73. August 1995.
___ "Zelazny, Roger (Obituary)," *Locus* 35(1): 7, 63. July 1995.
___ "Zelazny, Roger (Obituary)," *Science Fiction Chronicle* 16(8): 20-21. July/August 1995
___ "Zelazny, Roger, 1937-1995 (Obituary)," *Matrix* No. 115: 5. June/July 1995.
___ "Zelazny, Roger, 1937-1995 (Obituary)," *Starlog* No. 220: 16. November 1995.
___ "Zelazny, Roger, 58, Science Fiction Novelist (Obituary)," *New York Times* p.10. June 17, 1995.

ZELAZNY, ROGER (continued)
___ Brown, Tanya. "This Immortal: Roger Zelazny (1937-1995)," *Vector* No. 184: 4-7. Summer 1995.
___ Delany, Samuel R. "Zelazny/Varley/Gibson--and Quality, Part 1," *New York Review of Science Fiction* No. 48: 1, 10-13. August 1992.
___ Delany, Samuel R. "Zelazny/Varley/Gibson--and Quality, Part 2," *New York Review of Science Fiction* No. 49: 1, 3-7. September 1992.
___ Krulik, Theodore. **The Complete Amber Sourcebook**. New York: Avon, 1995. 494pp.
___ Lance, Donna. "Science Fiction and Mythology: Creatures of Light and Darkness," in: Kellogg, Judith and Crisler, Jesse, eds. **Literature & Hawaii's Children: Stories as Bridges to Many Realms**. Honolulu, HI: University of Hawaii at Manoa, 1994. pp.125-132.
___ Lindskold, Jane M. "Pervasive Influence of Poetry in the Works of Roger Zelazny," *Extrapolation* 33(1): 41-58. Spring 1992.
___ Lindskold, Jane M. **Roger Zelazny**. New York: Twayne, 1993. 166pp.
___ Stephens, Christopher P. **A Checklist of Roger Zelazny**. Hastings-on-Hudson, NY: Ultramarine, 1993. 47pp.
___ Yoke, Carl B. "Roger Zelazny," in: Bruccoli, Matthew J., ed. **Facts on File Bibliography of American Fiction 1919-1988**. New York: Facts on File, 1991. pp.566-567.
___ Yoke, Carl B. "With a Splash of Brilliant Images," *Amazing Stories* 67(5): 29-31. August 1992.
___ Yoke, Carl B. "Zelazny's Black: The Sidekick as Second Self," in: Ruddick, Nicholas, ed. **State of the Fantastic**. Westport, CT: Greenwood, 1992. pp.115-120.
___ Zelazny, Roger. "How I Spent My Last Thirty Years," *Amazing Stories* 67(5): 4, 8. August 1992.

ZELDES, MARILYN
___ "Zeldes, Marilyn (Obituary)," *Science Fiction Chronicle* 16(4): 16. February 1995.

ZETTEL, SARAH
___ Klein, Jay K. "Biolog: Sarah Zettel," *Analog* 114(10): 121, 126. August 1994.

ZIMMER, EVELYN CONKLIN
___ "Zimmer, Evelyn Conklin (Obituary)," *Locus* 32(6): 72. June 1994.

ZIMMERMAN, HERMAN
___ Altman, Mark A. "***Star Trek: Deep Space Nine***: Herman Zimmerman, Production Designer," *Cinefantastique* 23(6): 28-29. April 1993.

ZINDELL, DAVID
___ "David Zindell: The Quest for Transcendence," *Locus* 31(2): 5, 65. August 1993.

ZOLINE, PAMELA
___ Hewitt, Elizabeth. "Generic Exhaustion and the 'Heat Death' of Science Fiction," *Science Fiction Studies* 21(3): 289-301. November 1994.

ZUNI INDIANS
___ Reno, Shaun. "The Zuni Indian Tribe: A Model for **Stranger in a Strange Land**'s Martian Culture," *Extrapolation* 36(2): 151-158. Summer 1995.

Author Index

ABBOTT, JOE
___ "The Monster Reconsidered: *Blade Runner's* Replicant as Romantic Hero," *Extrapolation* 34(4): 340-350. Winter 1993.
___ "They Came From Beyond the Center: Ideology and Political Textuality in the Radical Science Fiction Films of James Cameron," *Literature/Film Quarterly* 22(1): 21-27. 1994.

ABRAMS, JANET
___ "Escape From Gravity," *Sight and Sound* 5(5): 14-19. May 1995.

ABRASH, MERRITT
___ "Dick and SF Scholarship: A Failure of Scholarship," in: Mullen, R. D., ed. **On Philip K. Dick: 40 Articles From Science-Fiction Studies.** Terre Haute, IN: SF-TH Inc., 1992. pp.123-124.
___ "Dick and SF Scholarship: In Response to George Slusser," in: Mullen, R. D., ed. **On Philip K. Dick: 40 Articles From Science-Fiction Studies.** Terre Haute, IN: SF-TH Inc., 1992. pp.129-130.
___ " 'Man Everywhere in Chains': Dick, Rousseau, and **The Penultimate Truth**," in: Umland, Samuel J., ed. **Philip K. Dick: Contemporary Critical Interpretations**. Westport, CT: Greenwood, 1995. pp.157-168.

ACKERMAN, FORREST J.
___ **Famous Monsters of Filmland, Vol. 2 (Issues 51-100)**. Universal City, CA: Hollywood Publishing, 1991. 162pp.
___ "Introduction: New Eves and New Genesis: The Extraordinary Women Who Write Science Fiction and the Women They Write About," by Janrae Frank, Jean Stine and Forrest J Ackerman. in: Frank, Janrae, Stine, Jean, and Ackerman Forrest J, eds. **New Eves: Science Fiction About the Extraordinary Women of Today and Tomorrow**. Stamford, CT: Longmeadow, 1994. pp.vii-xvi.

ADALIAN, JOSEF
___ "Dead Pretending to Be Lively Drama," *Washington (DC) Times.* June 9, 1994. in: *NewsBank. Film and Television.* 64:D12. 1994.
___ "Nixed Generation," *Washington (DC) Times.* May 22, 1994. in: *NewsBank. Film and Television.* 59:B9-B11. 1994.
___ "Stereotypes Populate **Earth 2** Series," *Washington (DC) Times.* November 6, 1994. in: *NewsBank. Film and Television.* 119:F11. 1994.
___ "**X-Files** Space Aliens Abduct Weekend Lineup," *Washington (DC) Times*. September 30, 1994. in: *NewsBank. Film and Television.* 117: G3. 1994.

ADAMOVIC, IVAN
___ **Encyklopedie fantastického filmu**. Praha: Cinema, 1994. 224pp. [Not seen; OCLC record.]
___ "Jan Weiss (1892-1972), Karel Capek's Overlooked Contemporary," *Extrapolation* 36(4): 285-291. Winter 1995.
___ "SF in the Czech Republic," *Locus* 34(4): 38-39. April 1995.
___ "SF in the Czech Republic in 1993," *Locus* 33(1): 45-46. July 1994.

ADAMS, DAVID A.
___ "Carnivora, or, Lord Greystoke, Cooked and Raw in **Tarzan & the Jewels of Opar**," *Burroughs Bulletin* NS. No. 21: 10-15. January 1995.
___ "Jungle Tales of Tarzan," *Burroughs Bulletin* NS. No. 23: 13-17. July 1995.
___ "Major Burroughs in a Minor Gothic Tale: A Study of **The Oakdale Affair**," *Burroughs Bulletin* NS. No. 24: 3-7. October 1995.

ADAMS, JOHN R.
___ **Good, Evil and Alien: Outer Space and the New World in the European Enlightenment**. Ph.D. Dissertation, University of Texas, Austin, 1992. 275pp. (DAI-A 53/12. p. 4436. June 1993.)

ADAMS, LEITH
___ (ed.) **Graven Images: The Best of Horror, Fantasy, and Science Fiction Film Art from the Collection of Ronald V. Borst**, ed. by Ronald V. Borst, Keith Burns and Leith Adams. New York: Grove Press, 1992. 240pp.

ADAMS, MARUEEN B.
___ **Feminine Mythic Patterns in Doris Lessing's The Summer Before the Dark and The Memoirs of a Survivor**. Master's Thesis, Lehigh University, 1977. 114pp.

ADAMS, MAX
___ "*Ed Wood*: *Plan 10 From Outer Space*," *Cinefantastique* 25(5): 45. October 1994.
___ "*Halloween VI*," *Cinefantastique* 26(6)/27(1): 10-15, 125. October 1995.
___ "Max Adams' Crash Course in Film Development," *The Report: The Fiction Writer's Magazine* No. 10: 1, 3-4. Summer 1993.

ADAMS, THELMA
___ "Don't Take a **Powder**," *New York (NY) Post.* October 27, 1995. in: *NewsBank. Film and Television.* 97:G2. 1995.
___ "A Fiennes Madness," *New York (NY) Post.* October 6, 1995. in: *NewsBank. Film and Television.* 99:C13. 1995.
___ "You'll 'Tank' Yourself," *New York (NY) Post.* March 31, 1995. in: *NewsBank. Film and Television.* 39:A1. 1995.

ADDERLEY, C. M.
___ "The Best Thing for Being Sad: Education and Educators in T. H. White's **Once and Future King**," *Quondam et Futurus* 2(1): 55-68. Spring 1992.
___ "Preliminary Matters: The Neglected Preludes of Charles Williams' Arthuriad," *Mythlore* 21(1): 23-28. Summer 1995. (No. 79)

ADORISIO, ILIO
___ "L'utopia ed i segni dell'economia," in: Saccaro Del Buffa, Giuseppa and Lewis, Arthur O., eds. **Utopie per gli Anni Ottana**. Rome: Gangemi Editore, 1986. pp.185-195.
___ "Ucronia in Oiconomia. Considerazioni sulla cronofagia della societa industriale," in: Saccaro Del Buffa, Giuseppa and Lewis, Arthur O., eds. **Utopia e Modernita: Teorie e prassi utopiche nell'eta moderna e postmoderna**. Rome: Gangemi Editore, 1989. pp.237-276.

AERTSON, HENK
___ (ed.) **Companion to Middle English Romance**, ed. by Henk Aertson and Alasdair A. MacDonald. Amsterdam: VU University Press, 1990. 209pp.

AGOY, NILS I.
___ "Quid Hinieldus cum Christo? New Perspectives on Tolkien's Theological Dilemma and His Sub-Creation Theory," in: Reynolds, Patricia and GoodKnight, Glen H., eds. **Proceedings of the J. R. R. Tolkien Centenary Conference, Keble College, Oxford, 1992**. Altadena, CA: Mythopoeic Press, 1995. pp.31-38. (*Mythlore* Vol. 21, No. 2, Winter 1996, Whole No. 80)

AHEARN, CATHERINE
___ "An Archetype of Pain: From Plath to Atwood and Musgrave," in: Roberts, Sheila, ed. **Still the Frame Holds: Essays on Women Poets and Writers**. San Bernardino, CA: Borgo Press, 1993. pp.137-156.

AIEX, PATRICK K.
___ **Reflections on Science Fiction in Light of Today's Global Concerns**. Position Paper, ERIC ED 364 904. 7pp.

AIKEN, JOAN
___ "Writing Ghost Stories," *Writer* 107(1): 9-13. January 1994.

AIRAUDI, JESSE T.
___ "Fantasia for Sewercovers and Drainpipes: T. S. Eliot, Abram Tertz, and the Surreal Quest for Pravda," in: Latham, Robert A. and Collins, Robert A., eds. **Modes of the Fantastic**. Westport, CT: Greenwood, 1995. pp.21-27.

AIRD, CATHERINE
___ "It Was the Cat!," in: Dale, Alzina S., ed. **Dorothy L. Sayers: The Centenary Celebration**. New York: Walker, 1993. pp.79-86.

AIREY, JEAN
___ "Alien Aboard," *Starlog* No. 188: 38-41, 68. March 1993.
___ "Forest Psychotic," *Starlog* No. 188: 47-49. March 1993.
___ "Lost in Babylon," by Jean Airey and Kim H. Johnson. *Starlog* No. 214: 32-35, 70. May 1995.
___ "The Man Who Killed Robin Hood," *Starlog* No. 175: 91-93, 82. February 1992.
___ "Marian of Sherwood," *Starlog* 180: 56-58. July 1992.
___ "Students of Sherwood," *Starlog* No. 195: 39-42. October 1993.
___ "Victorian Screamer," *Starlog* No. 190: 75-77. May 1993.

AL-RAHEB, HANI
___ "Five Patterns of the Fantastic in an Arabic Saga," *Journal of the Fantastic in the Arts* 5(4): 42-54. 1993. (No. 20)
___ "Religious Satire in Rushdie's **Satanic Verses**," *Journal of the Fantastic in the Arts* 6(4): 330-340. 1995.

ALAMA, PAULINE J.
___ "A Woman in King Arthur's Court: Wendy Mnookin's **Guenevere Speaks**," *Quondam et Futurus* 2(2): 81-88. Summer 1992.

ALAZRAKI, JAIME
___ "Qué es lo neofantástico?," *Mester* (UCLA) 19(2): 21-34. Fall 1990. [Not seen.]

ALBERT, WALTER
___ "Science Fiction Illustration," by Walter Albert and Neil Barron. in: Barron, Neil, ed. **Anatomy of Wonder 4**. New York: Bowker, 1995. pp.651-672.

ALBINSKI, NAN B.
___ "Australia in the 1890s; Depression, Socialism, Utopia," in: Saccaro Del Buffa, Giuseppa and Lewis, Arthur O., eds. **Utopia e Modernita: Teorie e prassi utopiche nell'eta moderna e postmoderna**. Rome: Gangemi Editore, 1989. pp.1019-1032.
___ "Utopia Reconsidered: Women Novelists and Nineteenth-Century Utopian Visions," *Signs: Journal of Women in Culture and Society* 13(4): 830-841. Summer 1988.

ALBRECHT, DONALD
___ "**Blade Runner** Cuts Deep into American Culture," *New York Times* Sec. 2, p. 19. September 20, 1992.

ALDISS, BRIAN W.
___ "The Adjectives of Erich Zann: A Tale of Horror," in: Aldiss, Brian W. **The Detached Retina: Aspects of SF and Fantasy**. Syracuse, NY: Syracuse University Press, 1995. pp.128-130.
___ "All Those Big Machines: The Theme SF Does Not Discuss," *New York Review of Science Fiction* No. 86: 16-19. October 1995.
___ "All Those Big Machines--the Theme Science Fiction Does Not Discuss," *Journal of the Fantastic in the Arts* 7(1): 83-91. 1996.
___ "The Atheist's Tragedy Revisited," in: Aldiss, Brian W. **Detached Retina: Aspects of SF and Fantasy**. Syracuse, NY: Syracuse University Press, 1995. pp.170-176.
___ "Between Privy and Universe: Aldous Huxley (1894-1963)," *New York Review of Science Fiction* No. 74: 19-21. October 1994.
___ "Between Privy and Universe: Aldous Huxley (1894-1963)," in: Aldiss, Brian W. **The Detached Retina: Aspects of SF and Fantasy**. Syracuse, NY: Syracuse University Press, 1995. pp.31-36.

ALDISS, BRIAN W. (continued)
___ "Campbell's Soup," in: Aldiss, Brian W. **The Detached Retina: Aspects of SF and Fantasy**. Syracuse, NY: Syracuse University Press, 1995. pp.145-149.
___ "Culture: Is It Worth Losing Your Balls For?," in: Aldiss, Brian W. **The Detached Retina: Aspects of SF and Fantasy**. Syracuse, NY: Syracuse University Press, 1995. pp.106-115.
___ "Cy Endfield: An Appreciation," *Locus* 34(6): 66-67. June 1995.
___ "Decadence and Development," in: Aldiss, Brian W. **The Detached Retina: Aspects of SF and Fantasy**. Syracuse, NY: Syracuse University Press, 1995. pp.187-191.
___ **The Detached Retina: Aspects of SF and Fantasy**. Syracuse, NY: Syracuse University Press, 1995. 224pp.
___ "Dick's Maledictory Web: About and Around **The Martian Time-Slip**," in: Mullen, R. D., ed. **On Philip K. Dick: 40 Articles From Science-Fiction Studies**. Terre Haute, IN: SF-TH Inc., 1992. pp.37-40.
___ "The Downward Journey: Orwell's **1984**," in: Aldiss, Brian W. **The Detached Retina: Aspects of SF and Fantasy**. Syracuse, NY: Syracuse University Press, 1995. pp.92-100.
___ "Elsewhere, Elsewhat?," *New York Review of Science Fiction* No. 67: 12-13. March 1994.
___ "Fantasy: U.S. Versus U.K.," *Monad* No. 2: 17-24. March 1992.
___ "'im," in: Salwak, Dale, ed. **Kingsley Amis in Life and Letters**. New York: St. Martin's, 1990. pp.40-50.
___ "The Immanent Will Returns-2," in: Aldiss, Brian W. **The Detached Retina: Aspects of SF and Fantasy**. Syracuse, NY: Syracuse University Press, 1995. pp.37-43.
___ "Introduction to **The War of the Worlds**, Part 1," *New York Review of Science Fiction* No. 50: 1, 8-10. October 1992.
___ "Introduction to **The War of the Worlds**, Part 2," *New York Review of Science Fiction* No. 51: 18-22. November 1992.
___ "Jekyll," in: Aldiss, Brian W. **The Detached Retina: Aspects of SF and Fantasy**. Syracuse, NY: Syracuse University Press, 1995. pp.131-132.
___ "Kafka's Sister," in: Aldiss, Brian W. **The Detached Retina: Aspects of SF and Fantasy**. Syracuse, NY: Syracuse University Press, 1995. pp.137-144.
___ "Kaliyuga, or Utopia at a Bad Time," in: Aldiss, Brian W. **The Detached Retina: Aspects of SF and Fantasy**. Syracuse, NY: Syracuse University Press, 1995. pp.159-169.
___ "Living in Catastrophe (Interview, 1988)," in: Ingersoll, Earl G., ed. **Doris Lessing: Conversations**. Princeton, NJ: Ontario Review Press, 1994. pp.169-172.
___ "One Hump or Two?," in: Aldiss, Brian W. **The Detached Retina: Aspects of SF and Fantasy**. Syracuse, NY: Syracuse University Press, 1995. pp.133-136.
___ "One Hump or Two?," in: Latham, Robert A. and Collins, Robert A., eds. **Modes of the Fantastic**. Westport, CT: Greenwood, 1995. pp.173-175.
___ "The Pale Shadow of Science," in: Aldiss, Brian W. **The Detached Retina: Aspects of SF and Fantasy**. Syracuse, NY: Syracuse University Press, 1995. pp.177-186.
___ "Peep," in: Aldiss, Brian W. **The Detached Retina: Aspects of SF and Fantasy**. Syracuse, NY: Syracuse University Press, 1995. pp.101-105.
___ "A Personal Parabola," in: Aldiss, Brian W. **The Detached Retina: Aspects of SF and Fantasy**. Syracuse, NY: Syracuse University Press, 1995. pp.199-212.
___ "Remembrance of Lives Past," *Science Fiction Studies* 21(2): 129-133. July 1994.
___ "A Robot Tended Your Remains," in: Aldiss, Brian W. **The Detached Retina: Aspects of SF and Fantasy**. Syracuse, NY: Syracuse University Press, 1995. pp.16-30.
___ "Science Fiction's Mother Figure," in: Aldiss, Brian W. **The Detached Retina: Aspects of SF and Fantasy**. Syracuse, NY: Syracuse University Press, 1995. pp.52-86.
___ "Some Early Men in the Moon," in: Aldiss, Brian W. **The Detached Retina: Aspects of SF and Fantasy**. Syracuse, NY: Syracuse University Press, 1995. pp.150-158.
___ "Sturgeon: The Cruelty of the Gods," in: Aldiss, Brian W. **The Detached Retina: Aspects of SF and Fantasy**. Syracuse, NY: Syracuse University Press, 1995. pp.87-91.
___ "Thanks for Drowning the Ocelot," in: Aldiss, Brian W. **The Detached Retina: Aspects of SF and Fantasy**. Syracuse, NY: Syracuse University Press, 1995. pp.8-15.
___ "Utopia: Dream or Pipe Dream?," *Locus* 32(5): 41, 66. May 1994.

ALTMAN, MARK A. (continued)

___ "*The Next Generation*: *Star Trek*'s Unification," *Cinefantastique* 23(2/3): 47-50. October 1992.

___ "*The Next Generation*: Data Entry," *Cinefantastique* 23(2/3): 64-66. October 1992.

___ "*The Next Generation*: Ensign Ro Laren," *Cinefantastique* 23(2/3): 96-98. October 1992.

___ "*The Next Generation*: Inside the Writing Staff," *Cinefantastique* 23(2/3): 42. October 1992.

___ "*The Next Generation*: Next Generation's Piller of Strength," *Cinefantastique* 23(2/3): 44-45. October 1992.

___ "*The Next Generation*: Q-Where?," *Cinefantastique* 23(2/3): 63, 125. October 1992.

___ "*The Next Generation*: Quiet on the Set," *Cinefantastique* 23(2/3): 87-89. October 1992.

___ "*The Next Generation*: Reincarnating Denise Crosby," *Cinefantastique* 23(2/3): 34. October 1992.

___ "*The Next Generation*: Shooting *Star Trek*," *Cinefantastique* 23(2/3): 55-58. October 1992.

___ "*The Next Generation*: Tackling Gay Rights," *Cinefantastique* 23(2/3): 71-74. October 1992.

___ "*The Next Generation*: The Making of 'The First Duty'," *Cinefantastique* 23(2/3): 52-53. October 1992.

___ "*The Shadow*: Production Design by Joe Nemec III," *Cinefantastique* 25(4): 31, 61. August 1994.

___ "*The Shadow*: Russell Mulcahy, Genre Stylist," *Cinefantastique* 25(4): 18. August 1994.

___ "*The Shadow*: Screenwriter David Koepp," *Cinefantastique* 25(4): 23. August 1994.

___ "*The Shadow*: The Origin of the Shadow," *Cinefantastique* 25(4): 19. August 1994.

___ "*The Shadow*," *Cinefantastique* 25(4): 16-43. August 1994.

___ "*Space Rangers*," *Cinefantastique* 23(6): 48-49. April 1993.

___ "*Star Trek*: Building for the Future," *Cinefantastique* 23(2/3): 84-85. October 1992.

___ "*Star Trek*: Cinematographer Marvin Rush," *Cinefantastique* 23(2/3): 68-69. October 1992.

___ "*Star Trek*: Fashion in the 24th Century," *Cinefantastique* 23(2/3): 76-77. October 1992.

___ "*Star Trek*: Paramount Turned Down Captain Kirk's Spec Script," *Cinefantastique* 23(4): 5. December 1992.

___ "*Star Trek*: Rick Berman, Trek's New Great Bird," *Cinefantastique* 23(2/3): 36-37. October 1992.

___ "*Star Trek*: Two Wrights Don't Make a Wrong," *Cinefantastique* 23(2/3): 60-61. October 1992.

___ "*Star Trek: Deep Space Nine*: Behind the Scenes, A Day on the Set," *Cinefantastique* 24(3/4): 96-98. October 1993.

___ "*Star Trek: Deep Space Nine*: Casting the Space Station Ensemble," *Cinefantastique* 23(6): 20-21. April 1993.

___ "*Star Trek: Deep Space Nine*: 'Emissary': Creating the Pilot," *Cinefantastique* 24(3/4): 100-101. October 1993.

___ "*Star Trek: Deep Space Nine*: Episode Guide, the First Season," *Cinefantastique* 24(3/4): 91-110. October 1993.

___ "*Star Trek: Deep Space Nine*: Filming on the New Frontier," *Cinefantastique* 23(6): 24-25. April 1993.

___ "*Star Trek: Deep Space Nine*: Herman Zimmerman, Production Designer," *Cinefantastique* 23(6): 28-29. April 1993.

___ "*Star Trek: Deep Space Nine*: Major Kira," *Cinefantastique* 24(3/4): 103. October 1993.

___ "*Star Trek: Deep Space Nine*: Michael Piller, Series Co-Creator," *Cinefantastique* 23(6): 23. April 1993.

___ "*Star Trek: Deep Space Nine*: Odo," *Cinefantastique* 24(3/4): 95. October 1993.

___ "*Star Trek: Deep Space Nine*: Quark," *Cinefantastique* 24(3/4): 90. October 1993.

___ "*Star Trek: Deep Space Nine*: Rick Berman, Trek's Major Domo," *Cinefantastique* 23(6): 18. April 1993.

___ "*Star Trek: Deep Space Nine*: Scripting the Adventures," *Cinefantastique* 23(6): 40-42. April 1993.

___ "*Star Trek: Deep Space Nine*: Shooting on the New Space Station," *Cinefantastique* 24(3/4): 92-93. October 1993.

___ "*Star Trek: Deep Space Nine*: Spin-Off Series Preview," *Cinefantastique* 23(2/3): 80-83. October 1992.

___ "*Star Trek: Deep Space Nine*: The Pilot, Behind the Scenes," *Cinefantastique* 23(6): 32-34. April 1993.

___ "*Star Trek: Deep Space Nine*: Visitor on Board," *Cinefantastique* 23(6): 26. April 1993.

ALTMAN, MARK A. (continued)

___ "*Star Trek: Deep Space Nine*," *Cinefantastique* 23(4): 4-5. December 1992.

___ "*Star Trek: Deep Space Nine*," *Cinefantastique* 23(6): 16-43. April 1993.

___ "*Star Trek: Deep Space Nine*," *Cinefantastique* 24(3/4): 88-110. October 1993.

___ "*Star Trek: The Next Generation*: *Star Trek*'s Next Spin-Off," *Cinefantastique* 24(3/4): 18. October 1993.

___ "*Star Trek: The Next Generation*: Brent Spiner on Data," *Cinefantastique* 24(3/4): 42. October 1993.

___ "*Star Trek: The Next Generation*: Chain of Command," *Cinefantastique* 24(3/4): 39-41. October 1993.

___ "*Star Trek: The Next Generation*: Episode Guide, Sixth Season," *Cinefantastique* 24(3/4): 16-87. October 1993.

___ "*Star Trek: The Next Generation*: Guess Q's Coming to Dinner?," *Cinefantastique* 24(3/4): 47-49. October 1993.

___ "*Star Trek: The Next Generation*: Heading for the Big Screen," *Cinefantastique* 24(3/4): 31-34. October 1993.

___ "*Star Trek: The Next Generation*: Jeri Taylor, Script Supervisor," *Cinefantastique* 24(3/4): 36-37. October 1993.

___ "*Star Trek: The Next Generation*: Marina Sirtis, Betazoid Beauty," *Cinefantastique* 24(3/4): 64-66. October 1993.

___ "*Star Trek: The Next Generation*: Michael Piller, Trek's Secret Weapon," *Cinefantastique* 24(3/4): 28-29. October 1993.

___ "*Star Trek: The Next Generation*: Rene Eschevarria, Waiter Cum Writer," *Cinefantastique* 24(3/4): 68-69. October 1993.

___ "*Star Trek: The Next Generation*: Rick Berman, Keeper of the Flame," *Cinefantastique* 24(3/4): 20-21. October 1993.

___ "*Star Trek: The Next Generation*: Ron Moore and Brannon Braga," *Cinefantastique* 24(3/4): 60-61. October 1993.

___ "*Star Trek: The Next Generation*: Stephen Hawking's *Star Trek* cameo," *Cinefantastique* 24(3/4): 63. October 1993.

___ "*Star Trek: The Next Generation*: Technobabble's Main Man," *Cinefantastique* 24(3/4): 76-77. October 1993.

___ "*Star Trek: The Next Generation*: The Acting Ensemble," *Cinefantastique* 24(3/4): 44-45. October 1993.

___ "*Star Trek: The Next Generation*: The Board and the Art of the Pitch," *Cinefantastique* 24(3/4): 52-55. October 1993.

___ "*Star Trek: The Next Generation*: The Making of 'Birthright'," *Cinefantastique* 24(3/4): 71-74. October 1993.

___ "*Star Trek: The Next Generation*: The Making of 'Relics'," *Cinefantastique* 24(3/4): 22-27. October 1993.

___ "*Star Trek: The Next Generation*: The Making of 'Tapestry'," *Cinefantastique* 24(3/4): 56-57. October 1993.

___ "*Star Trek: The Next Generation*: Will Riker, to Be or Not to Be?," *Cinefantastique* 24(3/4): 58. October 1993.

___ "*Star Trek: The Next Generation*," *Cinefantastique* 23(2/3): 32-102. October 1992.

___ "*Star Trek: The Next Generation*," *Cinefantastique* 24(3/4): 16-87. October 1993.

___ "*Star Trek VI*: Bridging the Generation Gap," *Cinefantastique* 22(5): 52-53. April 1992.

___ "*Star Trek VI*: Gene Roddenberry and the Other Great Birds," *Cinefantastique* 22(5): 39-42. April 1992.

___ "*Star Trek VI*: Mutiny on the *Enterprise*," *Cinefantastique* 22(5): 36-37. April 1992.

___ "*Star Trek VI*: The Importance of Being Valeris," *Cinefantastique* 22(5): 44-45. April 1992.

___ "*Star Trek VI*: The Making of 'The Undiscovered Country'," *Cinefantastique* 22(5): 24-55. April 1992.

___ "*Star Trek VI*: The Search for Saavik," *Cinefantastique* 22(5): 31. April 1992.

___ "*Star Trek VI*: The Undiscovered Prologue," *Cinefantastique* 22(5): 26. April 1992.

___ "*Star Trek VI*: The Unmaking of Starfleet Academy," *Cinefantastique* 22(5): 28-29. April 1992.

___ "Talking Trek," *Star Trek: The Official Fan Club* No. 94: 4-5. November/December 1993.

___ "*Time Trax*," *Cinefantastique* 23(5): 44-45. February 1993.

___ "UFP Law: The Legal Quagmires of the Federation," *Star Trek: The Official Fan Club* No. 93: 2-5. September/October 1993.

___ "*Wild Palms* (Review)," *Cinefantastique* 24(3/4): 123. October 1993.

___ "William Shatner," *Cinefantastique* 22(4): 44-45. February 1992.

ALTMANN, HANS
___ "Franz Werfels 'Stern der Ungeborenen'," in: Kranz, Gisbert, ed. **Inklings: Jahrbuch für Literatur und Ästhetik.** 8. Band. Lüdenscheid, Germany: Stier, 1990. pp.146-160. [Not seen.]

AMIES, CHRIS
___ "Reviewer's Choice: The Best Books of 1991," *Vector* No. 166: 6-9. April/May 1992.

ANDERSON, DAVID
___ "Is Golding's Theology Christian?," in: Biles, Jack I. and Evans, Robert O., eds. **William Golding: Some Critical Considerations.** Lexington, KY: University Press of Kentucky, 1978. pp.1-20.

ANDERSON, DOUGLAS A.
___ **J. R. R. Tolkien: A Descriptive Bibliography,** by Wayne G. Hammond and Douglas A. Anderson. Winchester, UK: St. Paul's Bibliographies, 1992. 434pp.; New Castle, DE: Oak Knoll Books, 1992. 434pp.

ANDERSON, JAMES A.
___ **Out of the Shadows: A Structuralist Approach to Understanding the Fiction of H. P. Lovecraft.** Ph.D. Dissertation, University of Rhode Island, 1992. 187pp. (DAI-A 53/08. p. 2811. February 1993.)

ANDERSON, KATHLEEN
___ "Shaping Self Through Spontaneous Oral Narration in Richard Adam's **Watership Down**," *Journal of the Fantastic in the Arts* 6(1): 25-33. 1993.

ANDERSON, KEVIN J.
___ "Carpal Tunnel Syndrome: When Writing Gets on Your Nerves," by Kevin J. Anderson and Rebecca M. Anderson. *SFWA Bulletin* 26(3): 5-9. Fall 1992. (No. 117)
___ *Futures Past* Magazine," *SFWA Bulletin* 26(4): 16. Winter 1993. (No. 118)

ANDERSON, KRISTINE J.
___ "Feminist Fictional Utopias: A Starter Set," *Collection Management* 18(1/2): 1-10. 1993.

ANDERSON, POUL
___ "Beer Mutterings: John W. Campbell and Anthony Boucher," *Quantum* No. 43/44: 5-6. Spring/Summer 1993.
___ "The Creation of Imaginary Worlds: The World Builder's Handbook and Pocket Companion," in: Dozois, Gardner, ed. **Writing Science Fiction and Fantasy.** New York: St. Martin's, 1991. pp.105-128.
___ "Quatrolude: Epistle to the SFRAns," in: Wolf, Milton T. and Mallett, Daryl F., eds. **Imaginative Futures: Proceedings of the 1993 Science Fiction Research Association Conference.** San Bernardino, CA: Jacob's Ladder Books, 1995. pp.249-262.
___ "RAH: A Memoir," in: Kondo, Yoji, ed. **Requiem: New Collected Works by Robert A. Heinlein and Tributes to the Grand Master.** New York: Tor, 1992. pp.243-251.
___ "Wellsprings of Dream," *Amazing* 68(3): 52-56. June 1993.

ANDERSON, REBECCA M.
___ "Carpal Tunnel Syndrome: When Writing Gets on Your Nerves," by Kevin J. Anderson and Rebecca M. Anderson. *SFWA Bulletin* 26(3): 5-9. Fall 1992. (No. 117)

ANDERSON, VANCE
___ "Eye to Eye with David Wingrove: An Interview," *Science Fiction Eye* No. 10: 44-57. June 1992.

ANDRE-DRIUSSI, MICHAEL
___ "A Closer Look at the Brown Book: Gene Wolfe's Five-faceted Myth," *New York Review of Science Fiction* No. 54: 14-19. February 1993.
___ **Lexicon Urthus: A Dictionary for the Urth Cycle.** San Francisco, CA: Sirius Fiction, 1995. 280pp.

ANDRESEN, OLIVER
___ "An Analysis of **Queen of the Summer Stars** by Use of the Literary Profundity Scale," by Oliver Andresen and Glenn Marin. *Quondam et Futurus* 2(1): 82-97. Spring 1992.

ANDREWS, ARLAN
___ "Science," by Arlan Andrews and Charles Sheffield. *Science Fiction Age* 2(6): 26-32, 38-39. September 1994.
___ "When Earth Has Its First Contact With Alien Beings, Will We Be Ready?," by Arlan Andrews, Yoji Kondo and Charles Sheffield. *Science Fiction Age* 3(2): 22, 24-28, 86. January 1995.

ANDREWS, GRAHAM
___ "Keith Laumer: An Annotated Bibliography," *Interzone* No. 79: 56-60. January 1994.

ANDREWS, SUZANNA
___ "The Man Who Would Be Walt," *New York Times* Sec. 2, p. 1, 20-21. January 26, 1992.

ANDRIANO, JOSEPH
___ "The Masks of Gödel: Math and Myth in Thomas Pynchon's **Gravity's Rainbow**," in: Latham, Robert A. and Collins, Robert A., eds. **Modes of the Fantastic.** Westport, CT: Greenwood, 1995. pp.14-20.

ANGENOT, MARC
___ "The Absent Paradigm: An Introduction to the Semiotics of Science Fiction," *Chung Wai Literary Quarterly* 22(12): May 1994. (Issue not seen; pagination unavailable.) (Reprinted from *Science Fiction Studies*.)

ANGIARI, LUISELLA
___ "Sitges: al supermarket dell'orrore quotidiano [Sitges: At the Daily Horror Supermarket, the 27th International Science Fiction Film Festival]," by Sergiio Giuffrida and Luisella Angiari. *Cineforum* 34(11): 7-9. 1994.

ANGULO, MICHAEL M.
___ **Random Access Memories: Mechanism and Metaphor in the Fiction of William Gibson.** Ph.D. Dissertation, University of Illinois, Urbana-Champaign, 1993. 345pp. (DAI-A 54/11, p. 4086. May 1994.)

ANISFIELD, NANCY
___ "**Godzilla**/Gojiro: Evolution of the Nuclear Metaphor," *Journal of Popular Culture* 29(3): 53-62. Winter 1995.

ANNAS, GEORGE J.
___ "Minerva v. National Health Agency," in: Gray, Chris H., ed. **The Cyborg Handbook.** New York: Routledge, 1995. pp.169-181.

ANNIS, ETHAN
___ **The Utility of Information in William Gibson's Futuristic Science Fiction.** Master's Thesis, University of North Carolina, Chapel Hill, 1992. 38pp.

ANSEN, DAVID
___ "Monsters to Haunt Your Dreams: *Jurassic Park* (Review)," *Newsweek* 121(24): 64-65. June 14, 1993.

ANTHONY, PIERS
___ "The Pun-derful Wizard of Xanth Takes a More Serious Look at Life," *Science Fiction Age* 2(4): 30-32. May 1994.

ANTONUCCI, MIKE
___ "The Final Frontier," *San Jose (CA) Mercury News.* May 22, 1994. in: *NewsBank. Film and Television.* 59:C4. 1994.

ANTOSIK, STANLEY
___ "Utopian Machines: Liebniz's 'Computer' and Hesse's **Glass Bead Game**," *Germanic Review* 67(1): 35-45. Spring 1992.

APPLE, HOPE
___ **To Be Continued: An Annotated Guide to Sequels,** by Merle L. Jacob and Hope Apple. Phoenix, AZ: Oryx, 1995. 364pp.

APPLE, MICHAEL W.
___ **Robot World: An Ethnographic Study of Education, Popular Culture, and Science.** Ph.D. Dissertation, University of Wisconsin, Madison, 1995. 326pp. (DAI-A 56/05, p. 1732. Nov. 1995.)

APPLEBY, ROBIN S.
___ "**Dracula** and Dora: The Diagnosis and Treatment of Alternative Narratives," *Literature and Psychology* 39(3): 16-37. 1993.

APPLEYARD, BRYAN
___ "The Entertainer in Old Age," in: Salwak, Dale, ed. **Kingsley Amis in Life and Letters**. New York: St. Martin's, 1990. pp.1-5.
___ **Understanding the Present: Science and the Soul of Modern Man**. New York: Doubleday, 1992. 269pp.

APRIL, JEAN-PIERRE
___ "Post-SF: du post-modernisme dans la science-fiction québécoise des années 80," *Imagine* No. 61: 75-118. September 1992.

APSELOFF, MARILYN F.
___ "The British Science Fiction of Louise Lawrence," in: Sullivan, C. W., III. **Science Fiction for Young Readers**. Westport, CT: Greenwood, 1993. pp.133-144.

ARAMA, HORIA
___ "Utopias Are Written in Romania as Well," *Utopian Studies* 4(2): 144-149. 1993.

ARAR, YARDENA
___ " 'Addams Family's' Hired Hand," *Los Angeles (CA) Daily News*. November 30, 1991. in: *NewsBank. Film and Television*. 1:A6-A7. 1991
___ "All Ducky on **Batman** Set," *Los Angeles (CA) Daily News*. June 25, 1992. in: *NewsBank. Film and Television*. 67:E11. 1992.
___ "High-Tech Horror No Help in Awkward **Brainscan**," *Los Angeles (CA) Daily News*. April 22, 1994. in: *NewsBank. Film and Television*. 51: F3. 1994.
___ "Mnemonic More Than a Johnny-Come-Lately Thriller," *Los Angeles (CA) Daily News*. May 26, 1995. in: *NewsBank. Film and Television*. 63: A4. 1995.
___ "PG-13 **Jurassic Park** May Be Too Scary for Some Children," *Austin (TX) American Statesman* Sec. B, p. 9. June 14, 1993.
___ "Snipes, Stallone Duke It Out in Engaging 'Demolition' (Review)," *Los Angeles (CA) Daily News* October 8, 1993. in: *NewsBank. Film and Television*. 114:G4. 1993.
___ "**Stargate** Porthole to Thrilling Time Travel," *Los Angeles (CA) Daily News*. October 28, 1994. in: *NewsBank. Film and Television*. 115: G3-G4. 1994.
___ "**Timecop** Takes a Creative Sci-Fi Cue," *Los Angeles (CA) Daily News*. September 16, 1994. in: *NewsBank. Film and Television*. 105:C6. 1994.

ARBITMAN, ROMAN
___ "Vzglyad s 'tsentral 'nogo energoatrona," *Detskaya Lietatura* 5: 6-10. 1993.

ARBUCKLE, NAN
___ "That Hidden Strength: C. S. Lewis' Merlin as Modern Grail," in: Watson, Jeanie and Fries, Marueen, eds. **The Figure of Merlin in the Nineteenth and Twentieth Centuries**. Lewiston, NY: Mellen, 1989. pp.79-99.

ARBUR, ROSEMARIE
___ "Fights of Fancy: When the 'Better Half' Wins," in: Slusser, George and Eric S. Rabkin, eds. **Fights of Fancy: Armed Conflict in Science Fiction and Fantasy**. Athens, GA: University of Georgia Press, 1993. pp.79-91.

ARCHER, SIMON
___ **Gerry Anderson's FAB Facts: Behind the Scenes of TV's Famous Adventures in the 21st Century**. London: HarperCollins, 1993. 94pp.

ARCHER, STEVE
___ **Willis O'Brien: Special Effects Genius**. Jefferson, NC: McFarland, 1993. 239pp.

ARFKEN, DEBORAH E.
___ "Madeleine L'Engle," in: Bruccoli, Matthew J., ed. **Facts on File Bibliography of American Fiction 1919-1988**. New York: Facts on File, 1991. pp.293-294.

ARGYROS, ALEXANDER J.
___ "Chaos Versus Contingency Theory: Epistemological Issues in Orwell's **1984**," *Mosaic* 26(1): 109-120. Winter 1993.

ARLOTT, JOHN
___ "A Frank Man," in: Salwak, Dale, ed. **Kingsley Amis in Life and Letters**. New York: St. Martin's, 1990. pp.31-32.

ARMANI, ELENA P.
___ "Utopia morale e realta sociale nell'assistenza genovese seicentesca: Polivalenze semantiche del primo Albergo dei Poveri italiano," in: Saccaro Del Buffa, Giuseppa and Lewis, Arthur O., eds. **Utopie per gli Anni Ottana**. Rome: Gangemi Editore, 1986. pp.239-246.

ARMSTRONG, DAVID
___ "**Alien 3**: Meat the People," *San Francisco (CA) Examiner*. May 22, 1992. in: *NewsBank. Film and Television*. 49:B11-B12. 1992.
___ "Burrough-ing to Hell (Review)," *San Francisco (CA) Examiner*. January 10, 1992. in: *NewsBank. Film and Television*. 13:G8-G9. 1992.
___ "Mom, Dad Can't Save This Movie (Review)," *San Francisco (CA) Examiner*. July 27, 1992. in: *NewsBank. Film and Television*. 72:B5. 1992.
___ "Violent Nanny Really Knows How to Rock the Cradle (Review)," *San Francisco (CA) Examiner*. January 10, 1992. in: *NewsBank. Film and Television*. 12:B9. 1992.

ARMSTRONG, HELEN
___ "Good Guys, Bad Guys, Fantasy and Reality," in: Reynolds, Patricia and GoodKnight, Glen H., eds. **Proceedings of the J. R. R. Tolkien Centenary Conference, Keble College, Oxford, 1992**. Altadena, CA: Mythopoeic Press, 1995. pp.247-252. (*Mythlore* Vol. 21, No. 2, Winter 1996, Whole No. 80)

ARMSTRONG, MICHAEL A.
___ "Why I Live In Homer, Alaska," *SFWA Bulletin* 29(1): 40-43. Spring 1995. (No. 126)

ARNASON, ELEANOR
___ "On Writing **A Woman of the Iron People**," *Monad* No. 3: 35-64. September 1993.

ARNOLD, GARY
___ "**Alien 3** Lost Is Foggy Plotting and Misdirection," *Washington (DC) Times*. May 22, 1992. in: *NewsBank. Film and Television*. 49:C10. 1992.
___ "**Body Snatchers**: Just a Lifeless Remake," *Washington (DC) Times*. February 19, 1994. in: *NewsBank. Film and Television*. 21: C3. 1994.
___ "**Death**: Plot Sickens While It Thickens (Review)," *Washington (DC) Times*. July 31, 1992. in: *NewsBank. Film and Television*. 68:G4. 1992.
___ "Defective Alien Has Origin in Bad Taste," *Washington (DC) Times*. July 7, 1995. in: *NewsBank. Film and Television*. 81:A8. 1995.
___ "**Dr. Giggles** Proves to Be a Real Cut-Up (Review)," *Washington (DC) Times*. October 26, 1992. in: *NewsBank. Film and Television*. 101:A5. 1992.
___ "**Dracula** Anemic Offspring in the Bloodline," *Washington (DC) Times*. November 13, 1992. in: *NewsBank. Film and Television*. 111: B13-B14. 1992.
___ "Erase From Memory **Johnny Mnemonic**," *Washington (DC) Times*. May 26, 1995. in: *NewsBank. Film and Television*. 55:B8. 1995.
___ "The Farces of Darkness," *Washington (DC) Times*. February 19, 1993. in: *NewsBank. Film and Television*. 20:C14. 1993
___ "Harder Edge and Well-Placed Cuts Make This **Blade Runner** Much Shaper," *Washington (DC) Times*. September 11, 1992. in: *NewsBank. Film and Television*. 87:F12-13. 1992.
___ "Holy Sequel! Burton Lays an Egg Big as Gotham," *Washington (DC) Times*. June 19, 1992. in: *NewsBank. Film and Television*. 67:F7-F8. 1992.
___ "Honey, I Shortchanged the Sequel (Review)," *Washington (DC) Times*. July 17, 1992. in: *NewsBank. Film and Television*. 70:E5. 1992.
___ "Mower Cuts Swath of Diabolical Silliness (Review)," *Washington (DC) Times*. March 7, 1992. in: *NewsBank. Film and Television*. 33: A10. 1992.
___ "Nothing's Bogus in Bill and Ted's New Outing," *Washington (DC) Times*. July 19, 1991. in: *NewsBank. Film and Television*. 65:F7. 1991.
___ "Picard and Co. Engage the Cinema," *Washington (DC) Times*. November 18, 1994. in: *NewsBank. Film and Television*. 125:D14. 1994.
___ "Rebecca DeMornay: Right at Home in Peyton('s) Place (Review)," *Washington (DC) Times*. January 17, 1992. in: *NewsBank. Film and Television*. 12:B7. 1992.

ARNOLD, GARY (continued)
___ "Sci-Fi Film Gets by on Allusion, Illusions," *Washington (DC) Times.* October 28, 1994. in: *NewsBank. Film and Television.* 115: G14. 1994.
___ "*Sneakers* Moves With Playfulness and Bounce (Review)," *Washington (DC) Times.* September 10, 1992. in: *NewsBank. Film and Television.* 96:D11. 1992.
___ "*Tank Girl* Flattens All Potential," *Washington (DC) Times.* March 31, 1995. in: *NewsBank. Film and Television.* 50:C7. 1995.
___ "*Virtuosity* a Lifeless Video Game," *Washington (DC) Times.* August 4, 1995. in: *NewsBank. Film and Television.* 82:C6. 1995.

ARNZEN, MICHAEL A.
___ "Behold the Funhole: Post-Structuralist Theory and Kathe Koja's **The Cipher**," *Paradoxa* 1(3): 342-351. 1995.
___ "Who's Laughing Now? The Postmodern Splatter Film," *Journal of Popular Film and Television* 21(4): 176-814. Winter 1993.

ARONSTEIN, SUSAN
___ " 'Not Exactly a Knight': Arthurian Narrative and Recuperative Politics in the *Indiana Jones* Trilogy," *Cinema Journal* 34(4): 3-30. Summer 1995.

ARRINGTON, ROBERT
___ "The Illustrated Shiel," in: **Shiel in Diverse Hands: A Collection of Essays.** Cleveland, OH: Reynolds Morse Foundation, 1983. pp.171-174.

ARROUYE, JEAN
___ "Rapsodie ropsienne," in: Bozzetto, Roger, ed. **Eros: Science & Fiction Fantastique.** Aix-en-Provence: Universite de Provence, 1991. pp.93-105.

ARROYO, JOSE
___ "*Waterworld* (Review)," *Sight and Sound* 5(9): 62-63. September 1995.

ARS-CARAS
___ "The Last Long Lost Tales," *Lembas Extra.* [Leiden]: Tolkien Genootschap Unquendor, 1991. [Not seen, cf. *Mythlore.*]

ASAKURA, HISASHI
___ "Judith Merril in Japan," *Aloud* (Toronto) 2(7): 3. October 1992.

ASHE, GEOFFREY
___ "The Origins of the Arthurian Legend," *Arthuriana* 5(3): 1-24. Fall 1995.

ASHERMAN, ALLAN
___ **The Star Trek Compendium.** 3rd rev. ed. London: Titan, 1993. 182pp.

ASHLEY, MIKE
___ "The *Amazing* Story: Part 1, The Twenties, By Radio to the Stars," *Amazing Stories* 66(9): 55-59. January 1992.
___ "The *Amazing* Story: Part 2, The Thirties, Escape From Oblivion," *Amazing Stories* 66(10): 64-67. February 1992.
___ "The *Amazing* Story: Part 3, The Forties, 'Gimme Bang-Bang' ," *Amazing Stories* 66(11): 58-63. March 1992.
___ "The *Amazing* Story: Part 4, The Fifties, Dream Worlds," *Amazing Stories* 67(1): 49-54. April 1992.
___ "The *Amazing* Story: Part 5, The Sixties; The Gooseflesh Factor," *Amazing Stories* 67(2): 59-64. May 1992.
___ "The *Amazing* Story: Part 6, The Seventies: Sex and Drugs and Rock and Roll," *Amazing Stories* 67(3): 52-56. June 1992.
___ "The *Amazing* Story: Part 7, The Eighties: Son of *Fantastic*," *Amazing Stories* 67(4): 47-56. July 1992.
___ "Behind the Realities: The Fantasies of John Brunner," *Weird Tales* 53(3): 80-84. Spring 1992. (No. 304)
___ "Blood Brothers: The Supernatural Fiction of A. C., R. H., and E. F. Benson," in: Schweitzer, Darrell, ed. **Discovering Classic Horror Fiction I.** Mercer Island, WA: Starmont, 1992. pp.100-113.
___ "Castaway," in: Jones, Stephen, ed. **James Herbert: By Horror Haunted.** London: New English Library, 1992. pp.69-74.
___ "The Galactic Emancipator: Remembering Homer Eon Flint," *Fantasy Commentator* 8(3/4): 258-267. Fall 1995. (Whole No. 47/48)
___ "A History of *Amazing Stories* Magazine," *Futures Past* No. 2: 6-11. April 1992.

ASHLEY, MIKE (continued)
___ "*Interzone*: A Bridge So Far," *Interzone* No. 57: 45-47. March 1992.
___ "Oliver Onions: The Man at the Edge," in: Schweitzer, Darrell, ed. **Discovering Classic Horror Fiction I.** Mercer Island, WA: Starmont, 1992. pp.120-126.
___ "The Rocket Man: Memories of Philip Cleator," *Fantasy Commentator* 8(3/4): 166-172. Fall 1995. (Whole No. 47/48)
___ "Science Fiction in the Depression," *Fantasy Commentator* 8(1/2): 95-102. Winter 1993/1994. (Whole No. 45/46)
___ **The Supernatural Index: A Listing of Fantasy, Supernatural, Weird, and Horror Anthologies.** Westport, CT: Greenwood Press, 1995. 952pp.
___ "Tell Them I Meant Well: A Tribute to William F. Temple," *Foundation* No. 55: 5-24. Summer 1992.
___ **The Work of William F. Temple: An Annotated Bibliography and Guide.** San Bernardino, CA: Borgo Press, 1994. 112pp.

ASHTON, ROBERT
___ **L'Utopia nella Storia: la Rivoluzione inglese**, by Arrigo Colombo, Giuseppe Schiavone and Robert Ashton. Bari: Edizioni Dedalo, 1992. 294pp. [Not seen.]

ASIMOV, ISAAC
___ **Asimov's Chronology of Science and Discovery.** New York: Harper, 1989. 707pp.
___ "Dialog," in: Dozois, Gardner, ed. **Writing Science Fiction and Fantasy.** New York: St. Martin's, 1991. pp.33-37.
___ "Farewell," *Magazine of Fantasy and Science Fiction* 83(2): 163. August 1992.
___ **I, Asimov: A Memoir.** New York: Doubleday, 1994. 562pp.
___ "New Writers," in: Dozois, Gardner, ed. **Writing Science Fiction and Fantasy.** New York: St. Martin's, 1991. pp.231-235.
___ "Plotting," in: Dozois, Gardner, ed. **Writing Science Fiction and Fantasy.** New York: St. Martin's, 1991. pp.28-32.
___ "Revisions," in: Dozois, Gardner, ed. **Writing Science Fiction and Fantasy.** New York: St. Martin's, 1991. pp.221-225.
___ "Science: Essay 400--A Way of Thinking," by Isaac Asimov and Janet Asimov. *Magazine of Fantasy and Science Fiction* 87(6): 114-131. December 1994.
___ "Writing for Young People," in: Dozois, Gardner, ed. **Writing Science Fiction and Fantasy.** New York: St. Martin's, 1991. pp.226-230.

ASIMOV, JANET
___ "Guest Editorial: Isaac Himself," *Asimov's Science Fiction Magazine* 17(4/5): 4-10. April 1993.
___ "Science: Essay 400--A Way of Thinking," by Isaac Asimov and Janet Asimov. *Magazine of Fantasy and Science Fiction* 87(6): 114-131. December 1994.

ASIMOV, STANLEY
___ (ed.) **Yours, Isaac Asimov.** New York: Doubleday, 1995. 332pp.

ATKIN, DENNY
___ "The Science of *Star Trek*," *Omni* 17(8): 46-53. Fall 1995.

ATKINS, PETER
___ **The Hellraiser Chronicles.** London: Titan, 1992. unpaged.
___ "Other Shelves, Other Shadows: A Conversation With Clive Barker," in: Golden, Christopher, ed. **Cut! Horror Writers on Horror Film.** New York: Berkley, 1992. pp.11-24.

ATKINSON, MICHAEL
___ "*The Mask* (Review)," *Sight and Sound* 4(10): 48-49. October 1994.
___ "Son of Apes," *Film Comment* 31(5): 62-66. September/October 1995.

ATKINSON, MIKE
___ "Delirious Inventions," *Sight and Sound* 5(7): 12-16. July 1995.

ATLAS, JAMES
___ "Burgeoning Burgess," *Vanity Fair* 50: 110-111. March 1987.

ATTEBERY, BRIAN
___ "The Closing of the Final Frontier: Science Fiction After 1960," in: Sanders, Joe, ed. **Functions of the Fantastic.** Westport, CT: Greenwood, 1995. pp.205-213.

ATTEBERY, BRIAN (continued)
___ "Fantasy and the Narrative Transaction," in: Ruddick, Nicholas, ed. **State of the Fantastic**. Westport, CT: Greenwood, 1992. pp.15-27.
___ "Gender, Fantasy, and the Authority of Tradition," *Journal of the Fantastic in the Arts* 7(1): 51-60. 1996.
___ "Godmaking in the Heartland: The Backgrounds of Orson Scott Card's American Fantasy," in: Morse, Donald E., ed. **The Celebration of the Fantastic**. Westport, CT: Greenwood, 1992. pp.61-69.
___ "Pilgrim Award Presentation Speech, 1995," *SFRA Review* No. 219: 25-27. September/October 1995.
___ "The Politics of Fantasy," in: Latham, Robert A. and Collins, Robert A., eds. **Modes of the Fantastic**. Westport, CT: Greenwood, 1995. pp.1-13.
___ **Strategies of Fantasy**. Bloomington: University of Indiana Press, 1992. 152pp.
___ **Teacher's Guide to the Norton Book of Science Fiction**. New York: Norton, 1993. 129pp.

ATTEBERY, JENNIFER E.
___ "The Trolls of Fiction: Ogres or Warm Fuzzies," *Journal of the Fantastic in the Arts* 7(1): 61-74. 1996.

ATWILL, WILLIAM D.
___ **Fire and Power: The American Space Program as Postmodern Narrative**. Athens, GA: The University of Georgia Press, 1994. 172pp.

ATWOOD, MARGARET
___ "Ode to Judith Merril," *Aloud* (Toronto) 2(7): 3. October 1992.

AUERBACH, JONATHAN
___ "The Nation Organized: Utopian Importance in Edward Bellamy's **Looking Backward**," *American Literary History* 6(1): 24-47. Spring 1994.

AUERBACH, NINA
___ **Our Vampires, Ourselves**. Chicago: University of Chicago Press, 1995. 231pp.
___ (ed.) **Forbidden Journeys: Fairy Tales and Fantasies**, ed. by Nina Auerbach and U. C. Knoepflmacher. Chicago: University of Chicago Press, 1992. 373pp.

AUFFRET-BOUCÉ, HÉLÈNE
___ "Babel des étoiles," *Corps Ecrit* No. 36: 151-156. 1990.

AVENI, ANTHONY F.
___ **Conversing with the Planets: How Science and Myth Invented the Cosmos**. New York: Times Books, 1992. 255pp.

AVINGER, CHARLES
___ "Do Science Fiction and Fantasy Writers Have Postmodern Dreams?," by Jeff Cupp and Charles Avinger. *LIT: Literature Interpretation Theory* 4(3): 175-184. 1993.

AXSOM, MARGO
___ "Border Crossings: The Emergence of Feminist Science Fiction as a Genre. Chapter 3: Frankenstein Evolves," [9 pp.] 1996. (Cited from the Internet. (http: //www-admrec. sonoma.edu /A&R /STAFF /axsom .dissertation.html)). (Chapter 3 of a dissertation in progress.)

AYERS, DAVID
___ "'Politics Here Is Death': William Burroughs's **Cities of the Red Night**," in: Kumar, Krishan and Bann, Stephen, eds. **Utopias and the Millennium**. London: Reaktion Books, 1993. pp.90-106.

AYRES, SUSAN
___ "The Straight Mind in Russ's **The Female Man**," *Science Fiction Studies* 22(1): 22-34. March 1995.

BACAL, SIMON
___ "Clive Barker's Triple Threat: **Lord of Illusions**, a Fable of Death and Resurrection," *Sci-Fi Entertainment* 1(5): 28-31. February 1995.
___ "The Cosmic Slide," *Sci-Fi Entertainment* 2(1): 48-49. June 1995.
___ "The Giant Buffalo of Rick Lazzarini's Character Shop," *Cinefantastique* 23(1): 58-59. August 1992.
___ "The Sci-Fi Worlds of Gerry Anderson," *Sci-Fi Entertainment* 2(2): 68-71. August 1995.

BACAL, SIMON (continued)
___ "**Warlock: The Armageddon**," *Cinefantastique* 23(6): 6-7. April 1993.

BACAS, P.
___ "Science Fiction Comes to the Classroom: Maelstrom II," by M. J. Martin-Diaz, A. Pizarro, P. Bacas, J. P. Garcia and F. Perera. *Physics Education* 27(1): 18-23. January 1992.

BACH, CALEB
___ "The Inventions of Adolfo Bioy Casares," *Americas* 45(6): 14-19. November 1993.

BACHMAN, DEBBIE
___ **The Outsider in '50s' Science Fiction**. Master's Thesis, S. U. N. Y. College at Brockport, 1994. 119pp.

BACKMAN, LISA
___ "Movie's Story Line Disputed," *Tampa (FL) Tribune*. July 28, 1992. in: *NewsBank. Film and Television*. 74:F14. 1992.

BACON-SMITH, CAMILLE
___ **Enterprising Women: Television Fandom and the Creation of Popular Myth**. Philadelphia: University of Pennsylvania Press, 1992. 338pp.

BADENHAUSEN, RICHARD
___ "Fear and Trembling in Literature of the Fantastic: Edgar Allan Poe's 'The Black Cat'," *Studies in Short Fiction* 29(4): 487-498. Fall 1992.

BADLEY, LINDA
___ **Film, Horror, and the Body Fantastic**. Westport, CT: Greenwood, 1995. 199pp.

BAEHR, STEPHEN L.
___ **The Paradise Myth in Eighteenth-Century Russia: Utopian Patterns in Early Secular Russian Literature and Culture**. Stanford, CA: Stanford University Press, 1991. 308pp.

BAEN, JIM
___ "Jim Baen's RAH Story," in: Kondo, Yoji, ed. **Requiem: New Collected Works by Robert A. Heinlein and Tributes to the Grand Master**. New York: Tor, 1992. pp.252-254.

BAEPLER, PAUL
___ "Kurt Vonnegut: A Selected Bibliography, 1985-1992," by Peter J. Reed and Paul Baepler. *Bulletin of Bibliography* 50(2): 123-128. June 1993.

BAGGESEN, SOREN
___ **Natur/videnskab/fortælling: Om science fiction som civilisationskritik**. s.l.: Odense Universitetsforlag, 1993. 120pp.

BAHN, LINDA B.
___ **A Comparative Study Between The Lord of the Rings and Das Nibelungenlied**. Master's Thesis, Pennsylvania State University, 1977. 131pp.

BAILEY, K. V.
___ "Alien or Kin? Science Fiction and Poetry," *Fantasy Commentator* 8(1/2): 32-39. Winter 1993/1994. (Whole No. 45/46)
___ "Bright Day-Dreadful Night: Metaphoric Polarities in Fantasy and Science Fiction," *Foundation* No. 54: 36-52. Spring 1992.
___ "Homo Tewler and the Undine: Evolutionary and Mythic Image in Wells's Late Fiction," *Foundation* No. 56: 61-75. Autumn 1992.
___ "Masters, Slaves, and Rebels: Dystopia as Defined and Defied by John Christopher," in: Sullivan, C. W., III. **Science Fiction for Young Readers**. Westport, CT: Greenwood, 1993. pp.97-112.
___ "Spindly Mazes, Dead Men and Doppels: Frederik Pohl's Gateway Creations," *Foundation* No. 63: 40-55. Spring 1995.
___ "We, Old as History Now...," *Vector* No. 180: 15-16. August/ September 1994.

BAILEY, RICHARD W.
___ **Images of English: A Cultural History of the Language**. Ann Arbor: University of Michigan Press, 1992. 329pp. (See section: 'Imaginary English,' pp.215-176.)

BAILLOU, CHARLES
___ "Two Black Film Makers Ripped Off?," *Amsterdam News* p. 72. October 3, 1992.

BAINES, PAUL
___ " 'Able Mechanick': **The Life and Adventures of Peter Wilkins** and the Eighteenth Century Fantastic Voyage," in: Seed, David, ed. **Anticipations: Essays on Early Science Fiction and Its Precursors.** Liverpool: Liverpool University Press, 1995. pp.1-25.

BAKER, ERIC T.
___ "With a Roll of the Dice, *Metascape* Provides Superior Space Opera Thrills," *Science Fiction Age* 2(4): 84-86. May 1994.
___ "The Worlds of Williams and Effinger Come Alive in *Cyberpunk 2020*," *Science Fiction Age* 1(6): 90-92. September 1993.

BAKER, LESLIE
___ "Morris and Music," *Journal of the William Morris Society* 10(3): 6-9. Autumn 1993.
___ "Romantic Realities," *Journal of the William Morris Society* 10(1): 10-13. Autumn 1992.

BAKER, ROB
___ "Tangent: A Modern Metaphor," *Parabola* 17(2): 83-87. May 1992.

BAKER, WAYNE
___ "Community Service, the Final Frontier for the Klingon Fleet," *Chicago Tribune* p. 18D. January 31, 1993.

BAKER-SMITH, DOMINIC
___ **More's Utopia.** New York: HarperCollins Academic, 1991. 269pp.

BALCZERZAK, EWA
___ **Stanislaw Lem.** Warsaw: Pantswowy Instytut Wydawniczy, 1973. (Not seen. Cf. *Science-Fiction Studies*, Nov. 1992.)

BALDERSON, DANIEL
___ **Out of Context: Historical Reference and the Representation of Reality in Borges.** Durham, NC: Duke University Press, 1993. 216pp.

BALDINI, ENZO
___ **Utopia e distopia.** Nuova ed., by Enzo Baldini and Arrigo Colombo. Bari: Edizioni Dedalo, 1993. 373pp. [Not seen.]

BALDRY, CHERITH
___ "A Hand Held out in the Dark: Some Relationships in the Science Fiction of Ursula Le Guin," *Vector* No. 168: 6-8. August/September 1992.
___ "Magic in Narnia," *Vector* No. 176: 16-17. December 1993/January 1994.

BALDWIN, MARC
___ "F. Scott Fitzgerald's 'One Trip Abroad': A Metafantasy of the Divided Self," *Journal of the Fantastic in the Arts* 4(3): 69-78. 1991. (No. 15)

BALL, JERRY L.
___ "Guy Endore's **The Werewolf of Paris**: The Definitive Werewolf Novel?," *Studies in Weird Fiction* No. 17: 2-12. Summer 1995.

BALLARD, J. G.
___ "From Shanghai to Shepperton," in: Jakubowski, Maxim and James, Edward, eds. **The Profession of Science Fiction.** New York: St. Martin's, 1992. pp.44-72.
___ "The Widest Windows onto the New," *Aloud* (Toronto) 2(7): 12. October 1992.

BALSAMO, ANNE
___ "Feminism for the Incurably Informed," *South Atlantic Quarterly* 92(4): 681-712. Fall 1993.
___ "Signal to Noise: On the Meaning of Cyberpunk Subculture," in: Wolf, Milton T. and Mallett, Daryl F., eds. **Imaginative Futures: Proceedings of the 1993 Science Fiction Research Association Conference.** San Bernardino, CA: Jacob's Ladder Books, 1995. pp.217-228.

BALTAKE, JOE
___ "Poe's Subtle Horror Shines in *Evil Eyes* (Review)," *Sacramento (CA) Bee.* December 12, 1991. in: *NewsBank. Film and Television.* 8: E3. 1992.
___ "Raider of Our Lost Youth: With *Hook*, Steven Spielberg Charts His Return to the World of Childhood Fantasy," *Sacramento (CA) Bee.* December 15, 1991. in: *NewsBank. Film and Television.* 7:C4-C6. 1992. also in: *NewsBank. Names in the News.* NIN 8: B6-B8. 1992.

BAMMER, ANGELIKA
___ **Partial Visions: Feminism and Utopianism in the 1970s.** New York: Routledge, 1991. 198pp.
___ **Visions and Re-visions: The Utopian Impulse in Feminist Fictions.** Ph.D. Dissertation, University of Wisconsin, Madison, 1982. 424pp.

BANGSUND, JOHN
___ "Sally and John: The Early Years," by Sally Yeoland and John Bangsund. *Metaphysical Review* No. 22/23: 17-44. November 1995.

BANKS, IAIN
___ "Escape From the Laws of Physics," *New Scientist* 138(1865): 38-39. March 20, 1993.

BANKS, MICHAEL A.
___ "Attending Science Fiction Conventions for Fun and Profit," in: **1991 Novel and Short Story Writers Market.** Cinncinati, OH: Writer's Digest Books, 1991. pp.55-58.

BANN, STEPHEN
___ (ed.) **Utopias and the Millennium**, ed. by Krishan Kumar and Stephen Bann. London: Reaktion Books, 1993. 164pp.

BANSAK, EDMUND G.
___ **Fearing the Dark: The Val Lewton Career.** Jefferson, NC: McFarland, 1995. 571pp.

BARDESCHI, MARCO D.
___ "Il restauro come utopia (riassunto)," in: Saccaro Del Buffa, Giuseppa and Lewis, Arthur O., eds. **Utopie per gli Anni Ottana.** Rome: Gangemi Editore, 1986. pp.395-396.

BARFIELD, OWEN
___ "Entweder--Oder (Über Coleridge)," in: Kranz, Gisbert, ed. **Inklings: Jahrbuch für Literatur und Ästhetik.** 7. Band. Lüdenscheid, Germany: Stier, 1989. pp.25-52. [Not seen.]

BARGREEN, MELINDA
___ "Drawing on Memory Banks," *Seattle (WA) Times.* January 12, 1992. in *NewsBank. Literature.* 8:B2-B3. 1992.

BARK, ED
___ "If Not Excellent, At Least It's Entertaining," *Dallas (TX) Morning News.* November 18, 1994. in: *NewsBank. Film and Television.* 125: D11-12. 1994.
___ "Is the World Ready for Young Indy? That's What Worries George Lucas as His TV Series' Debut Approaches," *Dallas (TX) Morning News.* March 1, 1992. in: *NewsBank. Film and Television.* 22:F13-F14. 1992.
___ "Light Years From Genius," *Dallas (TX) Morning News.* November 6, 1994. in: *NewsBank. Film and Television.* 119:F9. 1994.
___ "Vice-Nasty But Nice," *Dallas (TX) Morning News.* November 12, 1995. in: *NewsBank. Film and Television.* 104:G2. 1995.
___ "*White Dwarf*," *Dallas (TX) Morning News.* May 23, 1995. in: *NewsBank. Film and Television.* 58:A12. 1995.

BARKER, CLIVE
___ "At the Threshold: Some Thoughts on the Razorline Imprint," *Comics Buyer's Guide* No. 1024: 26-28, 32, 40. July 2, 1993.
___ "The History of the Devil: A Play in Two Acts," in: Brown, Michael, ed. **Pandemonium: Further Explorations into the Worlds of Clive Barker.** Staten Island, NY: Eclise, 1991. pp.i-liv.
___ "James Herbert: Afterword," in: Jones, Stephen, ed. **James Herbert: By Horror Haunted.** London: New English Library, 1992. pp.299-301.
___ "Trance of Innocence," *Sight and Sound* 5(12): 59. December 1995.

BARKER, LYNN
___ "Klushantsev: Russia's Wizard of *Fantastika*, Part One," by Lynn Barker and Robert Skotak. *American Cinematographer* 75(6): 78-83. June 1994.
___ "Klushantsev: Russia's Wizard of *Fantastika*, Part Two," by Lynn Barker and Robert Skotak. *American Cinematographer* 75(7): 77-82. July 1994.

BARKER, MARTIN
___ "Seeing How Far You Can See: On Being a Fan of 2000 A.D.," in: Buckingham, D., ed. **Reading Audiences: Young People and the Media**. Manchester, Eng.: Manchester University Press, 1993. pp.159-183.
___ "Waiting for Dredd," by Martin Barker and Kate Brooks. *Sight and Sound* 5(8): 16-19. August 1995.

BARKLEY, CHRISTINE
___ "Point of View in Tolkien," in: Reynolds, Patricia and GoodKnight, Glen H., eds. **Proceedings of the J. R. R. Tolkien Centenary Conference, Keble College, Oxford, 1992**. Altadena, CA: Mythopoeic Press, 1995. pp.256-262. (*Mythlore* Vol. 21, No. 2, Winter 1996, Whole No. 80)
___ "The Realm of Faërie," in: Reynolds, Patricia and GoodKnight, Glen H., eds. **Proceedings of the J. R. R. Tolkien Centenary Conference, Keble College, Oxford, 1992**. Altadena, CA: Mythopoeic Press, 1995. pp.253-255. (*Mythlore* Vol. 21, No. 2, Winter 1996, Whole No. 80)

BARLEY, TONY
___ "Prediction, Programme and Fantasy in Jack London's **The Iron Heel**," in: Seed, David, ed. **Anticipations: Essays on Early Science Fiction and Its Precursors**. Liverpool: Liverpool University Press, 1995. pp.153-171.

BARLOW, ROBERT H.
___ **On Lovecraft and Life**. West Warwick, RI: Necronomicon, 1992. 25pp.

BARNARD, ALAN
___ "Tarzan and the Lost Races: Parallels Between Anthropology and Early Science Fiction," in: Archetti, Eduardo P., ed. **Exploring the Written: Anthropology and the Multiplicity of Writing**. Stockholm: Scandinavian University Press, 1994. pp.231-257.

BARNES, JOHN
___ "Demand, Response, Reaction: A Troubleshooting Technique for Dialogue," *The Report: The Fiction Writer's Magazine* No. 10: 5-7. Summer 1993.
___ "How to Build a Future," in: Dozois, Gardner, ed. **Writing Science Fiction and Fantasy**. New York: St. Martin's, 1991. pp.147-184.
___ "Information and Unfictionable Science," *Information Technology and Libraries* 14(4): 247-250. December 1995. (Cited from *IAC Insite* on-line service.)
___ "On Deconstruction: A Partial Reply to Bruce Sterling," *Monad* No. 2: 43-50. March 1992.
___ "Publications in the Bucket: Threat, Menace, Hidden Subsidy, or Just a Thing?," *SFWA Bulletin* 28(2): 6-13. Summer 1994. (No. 124)

BARNES, SARAH
___ "Movie Scares up Dinosaur Toy Sales," *Austin (TX) American Statesman* Sec. E, p. 1. June 22, 1993.

BARNSTONE, WILLIS
___ **With Borges on an Ordinary Evening in Buenos Aires: A Memoir**. Urbana: University of Illinois Press, 1993. 198pp.

BARON, DAVID
___ "Future Shocker," *New Orleans (LA) Times-Picayune*. May 7, 1994. in: *NewsBank. Film and Television*. 58:A12. 1994.
___ "*Timecop* Stands Still as Van Damme Star Vehicle," *New Orleans (LA) Times-Picayune*. September 16, 1994. in: *NewsBank. Film and Television*. 105:D2. 1994.

BARR, MARLEEN S.
___ "Blurred Generic Conventions: Pregnancy and Power in Feminist Science Fiction," *Reproductive and Genetic Engineering* 1(2): 167-174. 1988. (Abridged version of an essay from Barr, Marleen. **Alien to Femininity**. 1987.)

BARR, MARLEEN S. (continued)
___ "Feminist Fabulation; Or, Playing With Patriarchy vs. the Masculinization of Metafiction," *Women's Studies* 14(2): 187-192. 1987.
___ **Feminist Fabulation: Space/Postmodern Fiction**. Iowa City, IA: University of Iowa Press, 1993. 312pp.
___ "Goodnight, Gynesis; Goodnight, Gyn/Ecology," *Extrapolation* 36(3): 181-183. Fall 1995.
___ "Immortal Feminist Communities of Women: A Recent Idea in Science Fiction," in: Saccaro Del Buffa, Giuseppa and Lewis, Arthur O., eds. **Utopie per gli Anni Ottana**. Rome: Gangemi Editore, 1986. pp.511-520.
___ **Lost in Space: Probing Feminist Science Fiction and Beyond**. Chapel Hill, NC: University of North Carolina Press, 1993. 231pp.
___ "**Searoad Chronicles of Klatsand** as a Pathway Toward New Directions in Feminist Science Fiction: Or, Who's Afraid of Connecting Ursula Le Guin to Virginia Woolf?," *Foundation* No. 60: 58-67. Spring 1994.
___ "Working at Loving: The Postseparatist Feminist Utopia," in: Bozzetto, Roger, ed. **Eros: Science & Fiction Fantastique**. Aix-en-Provence: Universite de Provence, 1991. pp.179-199.

BARRETT, DAVID V.
___ "Music and Magic: Gael Baudino Interviewed," *Interzone* No. 90: 19-22. December 1994.

BARRETT, MIKE
___ "A Primate of Pure Prose (With: The Short Stories of M. P. Shiel: A Chronological Listing)," in: **Shiel in Diverse Hands: A Collection of Essays**. Cleveland, OH: Reynolds Morse Foundation, 1983. pp.133-143.

BARRETT, ROBERT R.
___ "Animal Fashion Plates: Charles Livingston Bull (1874-1932)," *Burroughs Bulletin* NS. No. 15: 22-25. July 1993.
___ "Burroughs, Kline and Henry Herbert Knibbs: Another Opinion," *Burroughs Bulletin* NS No. 9: 27-32. January 1992.
___ "Edgar Rice Burroughs to Zane Grey: Stockton Mulford (1886-?)," *Burroughs Bulletin* NS. No. 16: 16-19. October 1993.
___ "ERB's Ur: A Speculation," *Burroughs Bulletin* NS. No. 24: 8-14. October 1995.
___ "Fortunino Mattania, R. I.: The Last Victorian," *Burroughs Bulletin* NS No. 10: 16-22. April 1992.
___ "The Indian Is Not an Apache!: Paul Stahr (1883-1953)," *Burroughs Bulletin* NS. No. 12: 15-18. October 1992.
___ "Joe Jusko's Edgar Rice Burroughs Collection," *Burroughs Bulletin* NS. No. 22: 3-5. April 1995.
___ "Richard Hescox: Penetrating the Cloud Cover," *Burroughs Bulletin* NS No. 9: 3-7. January 1992.
___ "Tarzan's Third Great Comic Strip Artist: Russell G. Manning (1929-1981)," *Burroughs Bulletin* NS. No. 13: 11-21. January 1993.
___ "To Bora-Bora and Back Again: The Story of Armstrong W. Sperry," *Burroughs Bulletin* NS No. 11: 3-8. July 1992.

BARRICELLI, JEAN-PIERRE
___ "Afterword: The Morigny Conference," in: Mullen, R. D., ed. **On Philip K. Dick: 40 Articles From Science-Fiction Studies**. Terre Haute, IN: SF-TH Inc., 1992. pp.236.

BARRON, NEIL
___ "Author Studies," by Michael A. Morrison and Neil Barron. in: Barron, Neil, ed. **Anatomy of Wonder 4**. New York: Bowker, 1995. pp.547-611.
___ "A Critical Survey of Fantastic Literature and Film Scholarship in 1990," by Neil Barron and Michael Klossner. in: Collins, Robert A. and Latham, Robert, eds. **Science Fiction and Fantasy Book Review Annual 1991**. Westport, CT: Greenwood, 1994. pp.205-239.
___ "General Reference Works," in: Barron, Neil, ed. **Anatomy of Wonder 4**. New York: Bowker, 1995. pp.462-482.
___ "Science Fiction Illustration," by Walter Albert and Neil Barron. in: Barron, Neil, ed. **Anatomy of Wonder 4**. New York: Bowker, 1995. pp.651-672.
___ "Science Fiction Publishing and Libraries," in: Barron, Neil, ed. **Anatomy of Wonder 4**. New York: Bowker, 1995. pp.455-461.
___ (ed.) **Anatomy of Wonder 4: A Critical Guide to Science Fiction**. New York: Bowker, 1995. 912pp.
___ (ed.) **What Do I Read Next? A Reader's Guide to Current Genre Fiction**. Detroit: Gale Research, 1992. 608pp.

BARRY, NORA
___ "Beyond Words: The Impact of Rhythm as Narrative Technique in **The Left Hand of Darkness**," by Nora Barry and Mary Prescott. *Extrapolation* 33(2): 154-165. Summer 1992.

BARSHAY, ROBERT
___ "Ethnic Stereotypes in **Flash Gordon**," *Journal of Popular Film and Television* 3(1): 15-30. 1974.

BARTHOLOMEW, FRANK M.
___ "The Russian Utopia," in: Sullivan, E. D. S., ed. **The Utopian Vision**. San Diego, CA: San Diego University Press, 1983. pp.69-92.

BARTLETT, KAREN J.
___ "Subversive Desire: Sex and Ethics in Delany's **Dahlgren**," *New York Review of Science Fiction* No. 75: 1, 3-7. November 1994.

BARTLETT, SALLY A.
___ "Fantasy and Mimesis in **Doctor Faustus**," *Journal of the Fantastic in the Arts* 5(3): 18-27. 1993. (No. 19)

BARTOLOMMEI, SERGIO
___ "Le 'gocce del passato vivente': Simone Weil e l'utopia della tradizione," in: Saccaro Del Buffa, Giuseppa and Lewis, Arthur O., eds. **Utopie per gli Anni Ottana**. Rome: Gangemi Editore, 1986. pp.705-726.

BARTON-KRIESE, PAUL
___ "Exploring Divergent Realities: Using Science Fiction to Teach Introductory Political Science," *Extrapolation* 34(3): 209-215. Fall 1993.

BARTONE, RICHARD C.
___ "Variations on Arthurian Legend in **Lancelot du Lac** and **Excalibur**," in: Slocum, Sally K., ed. **Popular Arthurian Traditions**. Bowling Green, OH: Popular Press, 1992. pp.144-155.

BARTTER, MARTHA A.
___ "The Hidden Agenda," in: Slusser, George and Eric S. Rabkin, eds. **Fights of Fancy: Armed Conflict in Science Fiction and Fantasy**. Athens, GA: University of Georgia Press, 1993. pp.155-169.
___ "Science, Science Fiction and Women: A Language of (Tacit) Exclusion," *Et Cetera* 49(4): 407-419. Winter 1992.

BASNEY, LIONEL
___ "Tolkien and the Ethical Function of 'Escape' Literature," *Mosaic* 13(2): 24-35. 1980.

BASTIEN, LOUIS A.
___ **Green Fire and the Legacy of the Dragon: Science Fiction, Fantasy and Cultural Ideology**. Ph.D. Dissertation, University of Connecticut, 1992. 238pp. (DAI-A 54/04. p. 1359. October 1993.)

BATTAGLIA, BEATRICE
___ "L'île comme distinée: **The Island of Doctor Moreau** de H. G. Wells," in: Marimoutou, Jean-Claude, ed. **L'insularité thématique et représentations**. Paris: Editions L'Harmattan, 1995. pp.427-431.
___ "L'utopia vittoriana," in: Colombo, Arrigo and Quarta, Cosimo, eds. **Il Destino della Famiglia nell'Utopia**. Bari: Edizione Dedalo, 1991. pp.173-189.

BATTENFELD, ROBERT L.
___ **Walter M. Miller, Jr.: A Bio-Bibliography**, by William H. Roberson and Robert L. Battenfeld. Westport, CT: Greenwood, 1992. 149pp.

BATTISTA, ANNA M.
___ "Intoduzione alle utopie," in: Saccaro Del Buffa, Giuseppa and Lewis, Arthur O., eds. **Utopie per gli Anni Ottana**. Rome: Gangemi Editore, 1986. pp.15-24.

BATTISTI, EUGENIO
___ "L'utopia nell'incertezza," in: Saccaro Del Buffa, Giuseppa and Lewis, Arthur O., eds. **Utopia e Modernita: Teorie e prassi utopiche nell'eta moderna e postmoderna**. Rome: Gangemi Editore, 1989. pp.205-211.
___ "Una citta sperimentale del '700: San Leucio," in: Saccaro Del Buffa, Giuseppa and Lewis, Arthur O., eds. **Utopie per gli Anni Ottana**. Rome: Gangemi Editore, 1986. pp.343-368.

BAUER, HANNSPETER
___ "Anmerkungen zu Tolkiens Wortschatz," in: Kranz, Gisbert, ed. **Jahrbuch für Literatur und Ästhetik**. Lüdenscheid, Germany: Stier, 1992. Band 10, pp.103-109.

BAUGH, E. SUSAN
___ "The Electronic Book in Future Information Access," in: Wolf, Milton T. and Mallett, Daryl F., eds. **Imaginative Futures: Proceedings of the 1993 Science Fiction Research Association Conference**. San Bernardino, CA: Jacob's Ladder Books, 1995. pp.53-60.

BAUGHMAN, JUDITH S.
___ (ed.) **Facts on File Bibliography of American Fiction 1919-1988**, ed. by Matthew J. Bruccoli and Judith S. Baughman. New York: Facts on File, 1991. 2 v.

BAUMBOLD, JULIE
___ "A Graveyard Smash," *Esquire* 123(1): 120, 118. January 1995.

BAXTER, STEPHEN
___ "**Apollo 13**," *Vector* No. 184: 8-9. Summer 1995.
___ "Cheaper, Faster--Better? The Future of America in Space," *Matrix* No. 115: 14-16. June/July 1995.
___ "Cross-Reference and Context: Future Histories in SF," *Vector* No. 179: 26-27. June/July 1994.
___ "Further Visions: Sequels to **The Time Machine**," *Foundation* No. 65: 41-50. Autumn 1995.
___ "Lighting the Future: The Future History of Wells's **The Time Machine**," *Vector* No. 181: 4-6. November/December 1994.
___ "The Profession of Science Fiction, 47: Inspiration and Research," *Foundation* No. 63: 56-60. Spring 1995.
___ "Thinking Out of the Box," *Focus* (BSFA) No. 27: 8. December 1994/January 1995.

BAZIN, NANCY T.
___ "Madness, Mysticism, and Fantasy: Shifting Perspectives of the Novels of Doris Lessing, Bessie Head, and Nadine Gordimer," *Extrapolation* 33(1): 73-87. Spring 1992.
___ "Women and Revolution in Dystopian Fiction: Nadine Gordimer's **July's People** and Margaret Atwood's **The Handmaid's Tale**," in: Crafton, John M., ed. **Selected Essays: International Conference on Representing Revolution, 1989**. n.p.: West Georgia College International Conference, 1991. pp.115-128.

BEACH, CHARLES F.
___ "C. S. Lewis, Courtly Love, and Chaucer's **Troilus and Criseyde**," *Bulletin of the New York C. S. Lewis Society* 26(4/5): 1-10. February/March 1995.
___ "Courtesy and Self in the Thought of Charles Williams and C. S. Lewis," *Bulletin of the New York C. S. Lewis Society* 25(3/4): 1-11. January/February 1994.
___ "Courtesy in Charles Williams' **The Greater Trumps**," *Mythlore* 19(1): 16-21. Winter 1993. (No. 71)
___ "The Knight-Poets of Logres: Narrative Voices in Charles Williams' Arthurian Poems," in: Slocum, Sally K., ed. **Popular Arthurian Traditions**. Bowling Green, OH: Popular Press, 1992. pp.173-182.

BEACH, SARAH
___ "Breaking the Pattern: Alan Garner's **The Owl Service** and the **Mabinogion**," *Mythlore* 20(1): 10-14. Winter 1994. (Whole No. 75)
___ "Harriet in Rehearsal: Hilary Thorpe in **The Nine Tailors**," *Mythlore* 19(3): 37-39, 65. Summer 1993. (No. 73)
___ "Loss and Recompense: Responsibilities in **Beowulf**," *Mythlore* 18(2): 55-65. Spring 1992. (No. 68)

BEAHM, GEORGE
___ **The Stephen King Companion**. Revised edition. Kansas City, MO.: Andrews and McMeel, 1995. 3112pp.

BEAL, REBECCA S.
___ "Arthur as the Bearer of Civilization: **The Alliterative Morte Arthure** 11.901-19," *Arthuriana* 5(4): 32-44. Winter 1995.
___ "C. J. Cherryh's Arthurian Humanism," in: Slocum, Sally K., ed. **Popular Arthurian Traditions**. Bowling Green, OH: Popular Press, 1992. pp.56-67.

BEALE, LEWIS
___ "*Star Wars* Starting Up Again," *(New York, NY) Daily News*. August 22, 1995. in: *NewsBank. Film and Television*. 81:B2. 1995.

BEAR, GREG
___ "Remembering Robert Heinlein," in: Kondo, Yoji, ed. **Requiem: New Collected Works by Robert A. Heinlein and Tributes to the Grand Master**. New York: Tor, 1992. pp.255-258.
___ "State of the Art: Contact in the Classroom," *Analog* 112(1/2): 228-237. January 1992.

BEARD, WILLIAM
___ "The Canadianness of David Cronenberg," *Mosaic* 27(2): 113-133. June 1994.

BEAUCHAMP, GORMAN
___ "Biotechnics and Utopia," in: Saccaro Del Buffa, Giuseppa and Lewis, Arthur O., eds. **Utopie per gli Anni Ottana**. Rome: Gangemi Editore, 1986. pp.73-88.
___ "Eros in Utopia," in: Saccaro Del Buffa, Giuseppa and Lewis, Arthur O., eds. **Utopia e Modernita: Teorie e prassi utopiche nell'eta moderna e postmoderna**. Rome: Gangemi Editore, 1989. pp.625-640.

BEAUDRY, MARY L.
___ "Lignum Vitae in the Two-Year College," in: Fries, Maureen and Watson, Jeanie, eds. **Approaches to the Teaching of the Arthurian Tradition**. New York: Modern Language Association, 1992. pp.122-126.

BECKER, ALLIENNE R.
___ **The Lost Worlds Romance: From Dawn Till Dusk**. Westport, CT: Greenwood, 1992. 184pp.

BECKER, LUCILLE F.
___ "Science and Detective Fiction: Complementary Genres on the Margins of French Literature," *French Literature Series* 20: 119-125. 1993.

BECKER, MURIEL R.
___ "Clifford D. Simak," in: Bruccoli, Matthew J., ed. **Facts on File Bibliography of American Fiction 1919-1988**. New York: Facts on File, 1991. pp.457-458.
___ "The Year in Young Adult Science Fiction, Fantasy and Horror: 1990," in: Collins, Robert A. and Latham, Robert, eds. **Science Fiction and Fantasy Book Review Annual 1991**. Westport, CT: Greenwood, 1994. pp.138-168.

BECKER, SIEGFRIED
___ "Konjunkturen des Phantastischen: Anmerkungen zu den Karrieren von Science Fiction, Fantasy und Marchen sowie verwandtne Formen," by Siegfried Becker and Gerd Hallenberger. *Zeitschrift fur Literaturwissenschaft und Linguistik* No. 92: 141-155. 1993.

BECKWITH, HENRY L. P.
___ "Lovecraft's Xenophobia and Providence Between the Wars," in: Joshi, S. T., ed. **The H. P. Lovecraft Centennial Conference Proceedings**. West Warwick, RI: Necronomicon, 1991. pp.10.

BEELER, MICHAEL
___ "Clive Barker: Horror Visionary," *Cinefantastique* 26(3): 16-31. April 1995.
___ "Clive Barker Producing Horror in Hollywood," *Cinefantastique* 26(3): 28-29. April 1995.
___ "Clive Barker: Surrealist Artist," *Cinefantastique* 26(3): 18. April 1995.
___ "Clive Barker: The Thief of Always," *Cinefantastique* 26(3): 20-21. April 1995.
___ "Clive Barker's *Hellraiser IV: Bloodline*," *Cinefantastique* 26(2): 10-11, 60. February 1995.
___ "Clive Barker's *Hellraiser IV: Bloodline*," *Cinefantastique* 26(3): 32-38. April 1995.
___ "Clive Barker's *Hellraiser IV: Bloodline*," *Cinefantastique* 27(2): 14-15. November 1995.
___ "Clive Barker's *Lord of Illusions*," *Cinefantastique* 26(2): 6-7. February 1995.
___ "Clive Barker's *Lord of Illusions*," *Cinefantastique* 26(3): 23-26. April 1995.

BEELER, MICHAEL (continued)
___ "*The Flintstones*: Building Bedrock," *Cinefantastique* 25(3): 23. June 1994.
___ "*The Flintstones*: Jim Henson's Creature Shop," *Cinefantastique* 25(3): 15-18. June 1994.
___ "*The Flintstones*: The Script Debacle," *Cinefantastique* 25(3): 10. June 1994.
___ "*The Flintstones*," *Cinefantastique* 25(3): 8-23. June 1994.
___ "*Ghost in the Machine*," *Cinefantastique* 24(2): 6-7. August 1993.
___ "*Ghost in the Machine*," *Cinefantastique* 25(2): 56-57. April 1994.
___ "*Hellraiser IV: Bloodline*: Kevin Yagher, Director," *Cinefantastique* 26(3): 34. April 1995.
___ "*Hellraiser IV: Bloodline*: Makeup Effects," *Cinefantastique* 26(3): 39. April 1995.
___ "*Hellraiser IV: Bloodline*: Pin Head Speaks," *Cinefantastique* 26(3): 36-37. April 1995.
___ "Henson's New, Lean, Mean Green Machine," *Cinefantastique* 23(5): 10-11. February 1993.
___ "The Horror Meister," *Cinefantastique* 25(2): 12-13. April 1994.
___ "*Lord of Illusions*," *Cinefantastique* 26(5): 12-13. August 1995.
___ "*Lord of Illusions*," *Cinefantastique* 26(6)/27(1): 90-91. October 1995.
___ "O Lucky Man: Malcolm McDowell on His Career Revival," *Cinefantastique* 27(3): 26-29. December 1995.
___ "*The Puppet Masters*," *Cinefantastique* 25(6)/26(1): 40-43. December 1994.
___ "*The Stand*: Dead Bodies," *Cinefantastique* 25(2): 15. April 1994.
___ "*The Stand*: Working With Stephen King," *Cinefantastique* 25(2): 16-17. April 1994.
___ "*The Stand*: Joe Bob Biggs," *Cinefantastique* 25(3): 29. June 1994.
___ "*The Stand*: Miniseries Review," *Cinefantastique* 25(3): 27. June 1994.
___ "*The Stand*: The Book vs. the Miniseries," *Cinefantastique* 25(2): 10-11. April 1994.
___ "*The Stand*: Working With Stephen King," *Cinefantastique* 25(3): 30-31. June 1994.
___ "*The Stand*," *Cinefantastique* 25(2): 8-22. April 1994.
___ "*Star Trek: Generations*: El-Curian Heavy," *Cinefantastique* 26(2): 23. February 1995.
___ "*Star Trek: Generations*: Feature vs. Series," *Cinefantastique* 26(2): 24-25. February 1995.
___ "*Star Trek: Generations*: John Alonzo," *Cinefantastique* 26(2): 27. February 1995.
___ "*Star Trek: Generations*: Keep On Trekkin'," *Cinefantastique* 26(2): 41. February 1995.
___ "*Star Trek: Generations*: The Star Trek Curse," *Cinefantastique* 26(2): 26. February 1995.
___ "*Star Trek: Generations*: Two Captains," *Cinefantastique* 26(2): 18. February 1995.
___ "*Star Trek: Generations*," *Cinefantastique* 25(5): 4-5. October 1994.
___ "*Star Trek: Generations*," *Cinefantastique* 25(6)/26(1): 20-23. December 1994.
___ "*Star Trek: Generations*," *Cinefantastique* 26(2): 16-30, 40. February 1995.
___ "Stephen King: *The Stand*," *Cinefantastique* 25(3): 24-30. June 1994.
___ "*Witchboard*," *Cinefantastique* 24(2): 48-49. August 1993.

BEER, STAFFORD
___ "Hi-Fi Sci-Fi," *Aloud* (Toronto) 2(7): 11. October 1992.

BEETZ, KIRK H.
___ (ed.) **Beacham's Guide to Literature for Young Adults. Volume 4, Science Fiction and Mystery**. Washington, DC: Beacham, 1991. 1 v.
___ (ed.) **Beacham's Guide to Literature for Young Adults. Volume 5, Fantasy and Gothic**. Washington, DC: Beacham, 1991. 1 v.

BEGGS, DELORES G.
___ "Algis Budrys Talks About Science Fiction," *Quantum* No. 43/44: 9-11. Spring/Summer 1993.

BEGHTOL, CLARE
___ **The Classification of Fiction: The Development of a System Based on Theoretical Principles**. Metuchen, NJ: Scarecrow, 1994. 365pp.

BEGLEY, SHARON

___ "Here Come the DNAsaurs," *Newsweek* 121(24): 56-61. June 14, 1993.

BEHRENDS, STEVE

___ "Spinning in the Night Land: A Footnote to William Hope Hodgson," *Studies in Weird Fiction* No. 13: 35-36. Summer 1993. [Not seen.]

BEKE-BRAMKAMP, RALF

___ "The Meaning of Utopia in the Reception of Premarxist Socialism After Nineteen Sixty," *Utopian Studies* 4(1): 55-63. 1993.

BELL, ANDREA

___ "**Desde Júpiter**: Chile's Earliest Science Fiction Novel," *Science Fiction Studies* 22(2): 187-197. July 1995.

BELL, LYDIA

___ "Writer Stumbled into Success," *New Orleans (LA) Times-Picayune* Sec. OTL, p. 1. May 20, 1993.

BELL-METEREAU, REBECCA

___ "*Altered States* and the Popular Myth of Self-Discovery," *Journal of Popular Film and Television* 9(4): 171-179. 1982.

BELLAFANTE, GINIA

___ "Out of This World," *Time* 145(14): 72. April 3, 1995.

BEN-CHORIN, SCHALOM

___ "Joy Davidman und C. S. Lewis zu alttestamentlichen Texten," in: Kranz, Gisbert, ed. **Inklings: Jahrbuch für Literatur und Ästhetik.** 1. Band. Lüdenscheid, Germany: Michael Claren, 1983. pp.89-102.

BEN-TOV, SHARONA

___ **The Artificial Paradise: Science Fiction and American Reality.** Ann Arbor: University of Michigan Press, 1995. 201pp.

BENEFIEL, CANDACE R.

___ "Fangs for the Memories: Vampires in the Nineties," *Wilson Library Bulletin* 69(9): 35-38. May 1995.

BENFORD, GREGORY

___ "Imagining the Real," *Magazine of Fantasy and Science Fiction* 84(1): 47-59. January 1993.

___ "Interplanetary Pioneer," *Science Fiction Age* 3(3): 86-91. March 1995.

___ "A Lyrical Hardness," *Science Fiction Age* 2(4): 78-83. May 1994.

___ "Real Science, Imaginary Worlds," *New York Review of Science Fiction* No. 65: 1, 8-12. January 1994.

___ "Real Science, Imaginary Worlds," in: Hartwell, David G. and Kathryn Cramer, eds. **The Ascent of Wonder: The Evolution of Hard SF.** New York: Tor, 1994. pp.15-23.

___ "Science Fiction, Rhetoric, and Realities: Words to the Critic," in: Slusser, George E. and Shippey, Tom, eds. **Fiction 2000: Cyberpunk and the Future of Narrative.** Athens: University of Georgia Press, 1992. pp.223-229.

___ "Style, Substance, and Other Illusions," in: Slusser, George E. and Rabkin, Eric S., eds. **Styles of Creation: Aesthetic Technique and the Creation of Fictional Worlds.** Athens: University of Georgia Press, 1992. pp.47-57.

___ "There Is Nothing Wrong With Playing in Each Other's SF Universes," *Science Fiction Age* 3(4): 34-37. May 1995.

___ "Time and **Timescape**," *Science Fiction Studies* 20(2): 184-190. July 1993.

BENISON, JONATHAN

___ "Science Fiction and Postmodernity," in: Barker, Francis, et al., eds. **Postmodernism and the Re-Reading of Modernity.** Manchester, Eng.: Manchester University Press, 1992. pp.138-158.

BENN, ALVIN

___ "Tilley Gets Leading Role in Selma Filming," *Montgomery (AL) Journal and Advertiser.* February 4, 1992. in: *NewsBank. Film and Television.* 17:G2. 1992.

BENNETT, BETTY T.

___ (ed.) **Selected Letters of Mary Wollstonecraft Shelley.** Baltimore, MD: Johns Hopkins University Press, 1995. 391pp.

BENNETT, J. A. W.

___ "From: **The Humane Medievalist**," in: Watson, George, ed. **Critical Essays on C. S. Lewis.** Hants, Eng.: Scolar Press, 1992. pp.52-76.

BENNETT, JAMES R.

___ **Hiroshima, Nagazaki, and the Bomb: A Bibliography of Literature and the Arts,** by James R. Bennett and Karen Clark. Pullman, WA: International Society for the Study of Nuclear Texts and Contexts, 1989. 24pp. (Monograph Series, No. 1)

BENNETT, ROD

___ "I Sing the Image Electric: Ray Bradbury Goes to Hollywood," by Brad Linaweaver and Rod Bennett. *Wonder: The Children's Magazine for Grown-Ups* No. 8: 10-17. 1995.

___ "Inside Darkest Ackerman," by Lint Hatcher and Rod Bennett. *Wonder* No. 7: 4-11, 52-53. 1993.

___ "Monster Fan 2000," by Lint Hatcher and Rod Bennett. *Wonder* No. 7: 39-43, 54-56. 1993.

___ "One Man's Passion, or, How I Got My Tape of *The Bride of Frankenstein*," *Wonder: The Children's Magazine for Grown-Ups* No. 8: 32-39, 51-54. 1995.

BENREKASSA, GEORGES

___ "Utopie et fracture revolutionnaire: Senancour et la critique du discours utopique," in: Saccaro Del Buffa, Giuseppa and Lewis, Arthur O., eds. **Utopia e Modernita: Teorie e prassi utopiche nell'eta moderna e postmoderna.** Rome: Gangemi Editore, 1989. pp.903-918.

BENSON, GORDON, JR.

___ **Andre Norton: Grand Master of the Witch World, a Working Bibliography,** by Phil Stephensen-Payne and Gordon Benson, Jr. Albuquerque, NM: Galactic Central, 1992. 83pp.; San Bernardino, CA: Borgo Press, 1993. 83pp.

___ **Edgar Pangborn: The Persistent Wonder, a Working Bibliography,** by Phil Stephensen-Payne and Gordon Benson, Jr. Albuquerque, NM: Galactic Central, 1993. 26pp.

___ **Gene Wolfe: Urth-Man Extraordinary, a Working Bibliography,** by Phil Stephensen-Payne and Gordon Benson, Jr. Albuquerque, NM: Galactic Central, 1992. 62pp.

___ **H. Beam Piper, Emperor of Paratime: A Working Bibliography.** 4th edition, by Phil Stephensen-Payne and Gordon Benson, Jr. Albuquerque, NM: Galactic Central, 1994. 31pp.

___ **Keith Laumer: Ambassador to Space, a Working Bibliography.** 2nd revised edition, by Phil Stephensen-Payne and Gordon Benson, Jr. Albuquerque, NM: Galactic Central, 1990. 41pp.

___ **Philip Kindred Dick: Metaphysical Conjurer, a Working Bibliography,** by Phil Stephensen-Payne and Gordon Benson, Jr. Albuquerque, NM: Galactic Central, 1995. 154pp. (4th Revised Ed.)

___ **William Tenn: High Klass Talent, a Working Bibliography,** by Phil Stephensen-Payne and Gordon Benson, Jr. Albuquerque, NM: Galactic Central, 1993. 31pp.

___ **Wilson 'Bob' Tucker, Wild Talent: A Working Bibliography,** by Phil Stephensen-Payne and Gordon Benson, Jr. Albuquerque, NM: Galactic Central, 1994. 38pp. 4th. Edition.

BENTON, JILL

___ **Naomi Mitchison: A Century of Experiment in Life and Letters.** London: Pandora, 1992. 192pp.

BENTON, MIKE

___ **Masters of Imagination: The Comic Book Artists Hall of Fame.** Dallas, TX: Taylor, 1994. 176pp.

___ **Science Fiction Comics: The Illustrated History.** Dallas, TX: Taylor, 1992. 150pp.

___ **Superhero Comics: The Illustrated History.** Dallas, TX: Taylor, 1992. 224pp. (Spine title: **Superhero Comics of the Silver Age.**)

BERENBAUM, MAY R.

___ "Life History Strategies and Population Biology in Science Fiction Films," by May R. Berenbaum and Richard J. Leskosky. *Bulletin of the Ecological Society of America* 73(4): 236-240. December 1992.

BERES, STANISLAW

___ **Rozmony ze Stanislawem Lemem** (Conversations with Stanislaw Lem). Cracow: Wydawnictwo Literackie, 1987. (Not seen. Cf. *Science-Fiction Studies*, Nov. 1992.)

BERESFORD, ANNE
___ "Memories of David Jones," in: Kranz, Gisbert, ed. **Inklings: Jahrbuch für Literatur und Ästhetik.** 9. Band. Lüdenscheid, Germany: Stier, 1991. pp.187-192. [Not seen.]

BERGEN, JAMES A., JR.
___ **Price and Reference Guide to Books Written by Edgar Rice Burroughs.** Beaverton, OR: Golden Lion Books, 1991. 214pp.

BERGER, ALBERT I.
___ **The Magic That Works: John W. Campbell and the American Response to Technology.** San Bernardino, CA: Borgo Press, 1993. 231pp.

BERGGREN, DAN
___ "The Sins of the Writer," *The Report: The Fiction Writer's Magazine* No. 9: 21. March 1993.

BERKENKAMP, LAURI
___ "Reading, Writing and Interpreting: Stephen King's **Misery**," in: Magistrale, Tony, ed. **The Dark Descent: Essays Defining Stephen King's Horrorscape.** Westport, CT: Greenwood, 1992. pp.203-211.

BERKMAN, MEREDITH
___ "Trek's Appeal," *Mademoiselle* 100(12): 85. December 1994.

BERKS, JOHN
___ "What Alice Does: Looking Otherwise at **The Cat People**," *Cinema Journal* 32(1): 26-42. Fall 1992.

BERMAN, EMANUEL
___ "Psychoanalysis, Rescue, and Utopia," *Utopian Studies* 4(2): 44-56. 1993.

BERNARD, JAMI
___ "Bat O' Nine Tales," *New York (NY) Post.* June 19, 1992. in: *NewsBank. Film and Television.* 62:F12-F13. 1992.
___ "Buffy: Rough Fluff Just Enough," *New York (NY) Post.* July 31, 1992. in: *NewsBank. Film and Television.* 68:A13. 1992
___ "**Death** Is Full of Femmes Fatales (Review)," *New York (NY) Post.* July 31, 1992. in: *NewsBank. Film and Television.* 68:G3. 1992.
___ "**Dreams** Is a Nightmare (Review)," *New York (NY) Post.* April 15, 1992. in: *NewsBank. Film and Television.* 43:B10. 1992.
___ "**Fatal Attraction**(s) (Review)," *New York (NY) Post.* March 12, 1992. in: *NewsBank. Film and Television.* 31:B2. 1992.
___ "Film Forum Fest Fulfills Fantasy, Horror, and Sci-Fi," *The New York (NY) National.* August 5, 1994. in: *NewsBank. Film and Television.* 93: C8. 1994.
___ "Glad to Meet Chew (Review)," *New York (NY) Post.* April 3, 1992. in: *NewsBank. Film and Television.* 40:G1. 1992.
___ "The Invasion of the Family Snatcher (Review)," *New York (NY) Post.* January 10, 1992. in: *NewsBank. Film and Television.* 12:B14. 1992.
___ "Island of Ah! In Sea of Blah (Review)," *New York (NY) Post.* December 24, 1991. in: *NewsBank. Film and Television.* 8:E6. 1992.
___ "Nothing Alien to Her Is Human," *New York (NY) Post.* May 22, 1992. in: *NewsBank. Film and Television.* 49:C9. 1992.
___ "Out for the Count," *New York (NY) Post.* November 13, 1992. in: *NewsBank. Film and Television.* 111:B10. 1992.
___ "Peter Pan, M. B. A. (Review)," *New York (NY) Post.* December 11, 1991. in: *NewsBank. Film and Television.* 3:F11. 1992.
___ "**Puppet Masters** Is UFOh So Entertaining," *(New York, NY) Daily News.* October 21, 1994. in: *NewsBank. Film and Television.* 114:F10. 1994.
___ "Whisper a Happy Goon," *New York (NY) Post.* February 19, 1993 in: *NewsBank. Film and Television.* 20:C13. 1993

BERNARDI, DANIEL
___ "Infinite Diversity in Infinite Combinations: Diegetic Logics and Racial Articulations in the Originial **Star Trek**," *Film & History* 24(1/2): 60-74. February/May 1994.

BERNARDI, WALTER
___ "Morelly e Deschamps: modelli dell'illuminismo francese," in: Colombo, Arrigo and Quarta, Cosimo, eds. **Il Destino della Famiglia nell'Utopia.** Bari: Edizione Dedalo, 1991. pp.167-172.

BERNARDIN, MARC
___ "Praying **M. A. N. T. I. S.**," by Ian Spelling and Marc Bernardin. *Starlog* No. 208: 27-30. November 1994.

BERNARDO, SUSAN M.
___ "Recycling Victims and Villains in **Batman Returns**," *Literature/Film Quarterly* 22(1): 16-20. 1994.

BERNHARDT, PETER
___ "Theatre of the Fantastic: A Choice of Shadows," *Riverside Quarterly* 9(3): 151-153. June 1995. (Whole No. 35)
___ "Theatre of the Fantastic: Genius Squashed?," *Riverside Quarterly* 9(2): 94-95. August 1993. (Whole No. 34)

BERNSTEIN, ABBIE
___ "Little John in Space," *Starlog* 179: 32-35, 89. June 1992.

BERRESSEM, HANJO
___ **Pynchon's Poetics: Interfacing Theory and Text.** Urbana: University of Illinois Press, 1993. 273pp.

BERTELLI, LUCIO
___ "Esperienze urbanistiche nella costruzione della 'citta ideale' greca," in: Saccaro Del Buffa, Giuseppa and Lewis, Arthur O., eds. **Utopie per gli Anni Ottana.** Rome: Gangemi Editore, 1986. pp.291-312.
___ "Platone," in: Colombo, Arrigo and Quarta, Cosimo, eds. **Il Destino della Famiglia nell'Utopia.** Bari: Edizione Dedalo, 1991. pp.33-48.

BERTELSEN, EVE
___ "Acknowledging a New Frontier (Interview, 1984)," in: Ingersoll, Earl G., ed. **Doris Lessing: Conversations.** Princeton, NJ: Ontario Review Press, 1994. pp.120-145.

BERTHA, CSILLA
___ "Csontváry, the Painter of the 'Sun's Path'," in: Morse, Donald E., ed. **The Celebration of the Fantastic.** Westport, CT: Greenwood, 1992. pp.151-164.
___ "The Harmony of Reality and Fantasy: The Fantastic in Irish Drama," *Journal of the Fantastic in the Arts* 4(3): 2-24. 1991. (No. 15)
___ "The Symbolic Versus the Fantastic: The Example of a Hungarian Painter," *Journal of the Fantastic in the Arts* 6(4): 295-311. 1995.
___ (ed.) **The Celebration of the Fantastic: Selected Papers From the Tenth Anniversary International Conference on the Fantastic in the Arts**, ed. by Donald E. Morse, Marshall B. Tymn and Csilla Bertha. Westport, CT: Greenwood, 1992. 309pp.
___ (ed.) **More Real Than Reality: The Fantastic in Irish Literature and the Arts**, ed. by Donald E. Morse and Csilla Bertha. Westport, CT: Greenwood, 1992. 266pp.

BERTINETTI, ROBERTO
___ **L'infondazione di Babele: l'antiutopia.** Milan: F. Angeli, 1983. 164pp.

BERTOLO, AMEDEO
___ "L'immaginario sovversivo. Considerazioni anarchiche sull'utopia," in: Saccaro Del Buffa, Giuseppa and Lewis, Arthur O., eds. **Utopie per gli Anni Ottana.** Rome: Gangemi Editore, 1986. pp.145-166.

BERUBE, MICHAEL
___ "Urban Renewal," *Village Voice* 40(23): SS8-SS10. June 6, 1995.

BESAS, PETER
___ "Full Roster of New Pics; Retros Set for Sitges Fantasy Festival," *Variety* p. 7. September 24, 1986.
___ "Sitges Fest Stays on Course for Quality Pic; Financial Woes Felt," *Variety* p. 4, 18. October 17, 1984.

BESWICK, NORMAN
___ "Being Unfair to Asimov," *Vector* No. 167: 6-7. June/July 1992
___ "The Machineries of Hokum, in Space Opera and Elsewhere," *Vector* No. 171: 16-18. February/March 1993.

BETANCOURT, JOHN G.
___ "**Shadowrun's** Second Edition Cyberfantasy Is Bigger and Better Than Ever," *Science Fiction Age* 1(4): 66, 71. May 1993.

BETHKE, BRUCE

BETHKE, BRUCE
___ "The Contrapunk Manifesto," *OtherRealms* No. 24: 18. Spring 1989.

BETTER, CATHY
___ "Open Doors at These Houses of Horror (Part 1)," *Writer's Digest* 73(5): 56-59. May 1993.
___ "Open Doors at These Houses of Horror (Part 2)," *Writer's Digest* 73(6): 54-55. June 1993.

BEVERSLUIS, JOHN
___ "Surprised by Freud: A Critical Appraisal of A. N. Wilson's Biography of C. S. Lewis," *Christianity and Literature* 41(2): 179-195. Winter 1992.

BEYETTE, BEVERLY
___ "Monster Collection: Los Angeles Man, 75, Amasses Treasures of Horror and Sci-Fi Films," *Houston (TX) Chronicle* Sec. B, p. 3. January 4, 1993.

BHAT, YASHODA
___ **Aldous Huxley and George Orwell: A Comparative Study of Satire in Their Novels**. New Delhi: Sterling, 1991. 172pp.

BIANCO, LUCIO
___ "Scienza e tecnologia per lo sviluppo," in: Saccaro Del Buffa, Giuseppa and Lewis, Arthur O., eds. **Utopia e Modernita: Teorie e prassi utopiche nell'eta moderna e postmoderna**. Rome: Gangemi Editore, 1989. pp.187-198.

BIANCO, ROBERT
___ "A Good Night for Good Fright," *Boston (MA) Herald*. October 30, 1993. in: *NewsBank. Film and Television,* 123:A6. 1993.

BIANCULLI, DAVID
___ "Babblin' Babylon: Spaced-Out Sci-Fi Show Has No Future," *New York (NY) Post*. February 25, 1992 in: *NewsBank. Film and Television*. 20:D7. 1993
___ "Explorers Finds Nothing New," *(New York, NY) Daily News*. January 18, 1995. in: *NewsBank. Film and Television*. 19:B10. 1995.

BIBBY, PATRICE
___ "**Waterworld** Filming Is Awash in Production, Financial Problems," *(Denver, CO) Rocky Mountain News*. March 8, 1995. in: *NewsBank. Film and Television*. 39:F5-F6. 1995.

BICCHIERI, SARAH N.
___ **Quantum Physics and Annie Dillard: Parallels in Science and Literature**. Master's Thesis, Central Washington University, 1993. 85pp.

BICK, ILSA J.
___ "Boys in Space: *Star Trek*, Latency, and the Neverending Story," *Cinema Journal* 35(2): 43-60. Winter 1996.
___ "The Look Back in *E. T.* ," *Cinema Journal* 31(4): 25-41. Summer 1992.

BIDDICK, KATHLEEN
___ "Humanist History and the Haunting of Virtual Worlds: Problems of Memory and Rememoration," *Genders* No. 18: 47-66. Winter 1993.

BIDDLE, ARTHUR W.
___ "The Mythic Journey in 'The Body'," in: Magistrale, Tony, ed. **The Dark Descent: Essays Defining Stephen King's Horrorscape**. Westport, CT: Greenwood, 1992. pp.83-97.

BIDDLE, FREDERIC M.
___ "Voyager Breathes New Life into Stellar Franchise," *Boston (MA) Herald*. January 16, 1995. in: *NewsBank. Film and Television*. 21:D8. 1995.

BIEDERMAN, MARCIA
___ "Genre Writing: It's Entertaining, But Is It Art?," *Poets and Writers Magazine* 20(1): 21-25. January/February 1992.

BIERBAUM, TOM
___ "Keeping a Lid on *Star Wars*," *Variety* p. 29, 40. December 29, 1982.

BIODROWSKI, STEVE

BIERBAUM, TOM (continued)
___ "Stan Lee's Imperfect Heroes Lifted Marvel to Top of the Heap," *Variety* p. 81, 88. September 17, 1986.
___ "TV Reviews: *Deadly Games*," *Variety* 360(5): 31. September 4, 1995.

BIERMAN, JUDAH
___ "The Metaphor Utopia: Notes Towards a Study of 'The Idea of Utopia, Its Myth and Its Literature'," in: Saccaro Del Buffa, Giuseppa and Lewis, Arthur O., eds. **Utopia e Modernita: Teorie e prassi utopiche nell'eta moderna e postmoderna**. Rome: Gangemi Editore, 1989. pp.553-568.

BIFFLE, KENT
___ "Canonizing the Creator of Conan," *Dallas Morning News* p. 41A, 43A. June 21, 1992.

BIGSBY, CHRISTOPHER
___ "The Need to Tell Stories (Interview, 1980)," in: Ingersoll, Earl G., ed. **Doris Lessing: Conversations**. Princeton, NJ: Ontario Review Press, 1994. pp.70-85.

BIKMAN, MINDA
___ "Creating Your Own Demand (Interview, 1980)," in: Ingersoll, Earl G., ed. **Doris Lessing: Conversations**. Princeton, NJ: Ontario Review Press, 1994. pp.57-63.

BILES, JACK I.
___ "William Golding: Bibliography of Primary and Secondary Sources," in: Biles, Jack I. and Evans, Robert O., eds. **William Golding: Some Critical Considerations**. Lexington, KY: University Press of Kentucky, 1978. pp.237-280.
___ (ed.) **William Golding: Some Critical Considerations**, ed. by Jack I. Biles and Robert O. Evans. Lexington, KY: University Press of Kentucky, 1978. 283pp.

BILIJA, KSENIJA
___ "From Golem to Plastisex: An Analytical Survey of Spanish American Fantastic Literature," *Journal of the Fantastic in the Arts* 7(2/3): 201-214. 1995.

BILLINGS, HAROLD
___ "Gene Wolfe," in: Bruccoli, Matthew J., ed. **Facts on File Bibliography of American Fiction 1919-1988**. New York: Facts on File, 1991. pp.547-548.
___ "The Shape of the Shiel (Notes on the Early Years)," in: **Shiel in Diverse Hands: A Collection of Essays**. Cleveland, OH: Reynolds Morse Foundation, 1983. pp.77-108.

BING, JONATHAN
___ "PW Interviews: Dennis Cooper," *Publishers Weekly* 241(12): 48-49. March 21, 1994.

BINOTTO, THOMAS
___ "Ist Utopia eine Utopie?," in: Kranz, Gisbert, ed. **Inklings: Jahrbuch für Literatur und Ästhetik**. 8. Band. Lüdenscheid, Germany: Stier, 1990. pp.125-144. [Not seen.]

BIODROWSKI, STEVE
___ "*Army of Darkness*," *Cinefantastique* 22(6): 22-23. June 1992
___ "*Army of Darkness*," *Cinefantastique* 23(1): 24-52. August 1992.
___ "*Basket Case 3: The Progeny* (Review)," *Cinefantastique* 23(1): 60. August 1992.
___ "*Batman Forever* (Review)," *Cinefantastique* 27(3): 57. December 1995.
___ "*Batman Forever*," *Cinefantastique* 26(4): 4-5, 61. June 1995.
___ "*Body Bags*: The Horror Games," *Cinefantastique* 24(3/4): 114. October 1993.
___ "*Body Bags*," *Cinefantastique* 24(3/4): 112-115. October 1993.
___ "*Bram Stoker's Dracula*: Francis Ford Coppola on Adapting Stoker's Gothic Masterpiece for the '90s," *Cinefantastique* 23(6): 54. April 1993.
___ "*Casper* (Review)," *Cinefantastique* 27(3): 52. December 1995.
___ "Coppola's *Dracula*: Adapting Bram Stoker," *Cinefantastique* 23(4): 36-38. December 1992.
___ "Coppola's *Dracula*: Directing the Horror Epic," *Cinefantastique* 23(4): 32-34. December 1992.

BIODROWSKI, STEVE (continued)

___ "Coppola's **Dracula**: Filming Lo-Tech Gothic," *Cinefantastique* 23(4): 52-54. December 1992.

___ "Coppola's **Dracula**: The Vampire Brides," *Cinefantastique* 23(4): 48-49. December 1992.

___ "Coppola's **Dracula**: Vampire Effects," *Cinefantastique* 23(4): 40-42. December 1992.

___ "Coppola's **Dracula**," *Cinefantastique* 23(4): 24-55. December 1992.

___ "Coppola's Horror Roots," *Cinefantastique* 23(4): 44-46. December 1992.

___ "**Death Becomes Her** (Review)," *Cinefantastique* 23(4): 60. December 1992.

___ "Director Wes Craven on the Politics of Horror," *Cinefantastique* 22(5): 58. April 1992.

___ "Directors Dave Borthwick and Peter Capladi on **The Secret Adventures of Tom Thumb** and **Franz Kafka's It's a Wonderful Life**," *Cinefantastique* 27(3): 58-59. December 1995.

___ "**Dracula**: The Oft-Told Story," *Cinefantastique* 23(4): 27-30. December 1992.

___ "**Dracula**: The Untold Story," *Cinefantastique* 23(2/3): 12-13. October 1992.

___ "**Evil Dead III**: Introvision Comes of Age," *Cinefantastique* 23(1): 44-45. August 1992.

___ "**Evil Dead III**: KNB's Army of Darkness," *Cinefantastique* 23(1): 42. August 1992.

___ "**Evil Dead III**: Production Design," *Cinefantastique* 23(1): 34. August 1992.

___ "**Evil Dead III**: The Makeup World of Ash," *Cinefantastique* 23(1): 32-33. August 1992.

___ "**Fantastic Four**: Optic Nerve Makeups," *Cinefantastique* 24(3/4): 10. October 1993.

___ "**Fantastic Four**," *Cinefantastique* 24(3/4): 8-11. October 1993.

___ "**Franz Kafka's It's a Wonderful Life** (Review)," *Cinefantastique* 27(3): 59. December 1995.

___ "**Freddy's Dead**," *Cinefantastique* 22(4): 56, 60. February 1992.

___ "Futuristic Musclemen: Jean Claude Van Damme, Dolph Lundgren Flex It in Carolco's **Universal Soldier**," *Cinefantastique* 23(1): 12-13. August 1992.

___ "**Guilty as Charged**," *Cinefantastique* 22(4): 52-53. February 1992.

___ "Guilty Director," *Cinefantastique* 23(6): 53. April 1993.

___ "H. P. Lovecraft's **The Resurrected**," *Cinefantastique* 22(6): 4-6. June 1992

___ "**Hideous Mutant Freekz**," *Cinefantastique* 23(6): 14-15. April 1993.

___ "**Honey, I Blew Up the Kid** (Review)," *Cinefantastique* 23(4): 61. December 1992.

___ "**House IV** (Review)," *Cinefantastique* 22(6): 54-55. June 1992

___ "**The Hunted** (Review)," *Cinefantastique* 27(3): 52-53. December 1995.

___ "**Jurassic Park**: **Carnosaur**," *Cinefantastique* 24(2): 23, 60. August 1993.

___ "**Jurassic Park**: Coordinating the Effects," *Cinefantastique* 24(2): 18-19. August 1993.

___ "**Jurassic Park**: Dinosaurs Attack!," *Cinefantastique* 24(2): 15, 60. August 1993.

___ "**Jurassic Park**: Filming the Dinosaurs," *Cinefantastique* 24(2): 14-16. August 1993.

___ "**Jurassic Park**: Michael Crichton," *Cinefantastique* 24(2): 11-13. August 1993.

___ "**Jurassic Park** (Review)," *Cinefantastique* 24(3/4): 123. October 1993.

___ "**Jurassic Park**: Stan Winston," *Cinefantastique* 24(2): 29-30. August 1993.

___ "**Jurassic Park**: Stop Motion's Extinction," *Cinefantastique* 24(2): 13. August 1993.

___ "**Lord of Illusions** (Review)," *Cinefantastique* 27(3): 55-56, 60. December 1995.

___ "Lovecraft Special Effects," *Cinefantastique* 22(6): 7. June 1992

___ "**Mant**," *Cinefantastique* 24(1): 58. June 1993.

___ "**Matinee**," *Cinefantastique* 23(6): 46-47. April 1993.

___ "**Memoirs of an Invisible Man**," *Cinefantastique* 22(4): 10-11. February 1992.

___ "**Mom and Dad Save the World**," *Cinefantastique* 23(2/3): 22-23. October 1992.

___ "**The Net** (Review)," *Cinefantastique* 27(3): 53. December 1995.

BIODROWSKI, STEVE (continued)

___ "**The Prophecy** (Review)," *Cinefantastique* 27(3): 53. December 1995.

___ "Sam Raimi's **Evil Dead III**," *Cinefantastique* 22(5): 4-5. April 1992.

___ "Sam Raimi's **Evil Dead III**," *Cinefantastique* 23(5): 14-15. February 1993.

___ "**The Secret Adventures of Tom Thumb** (Review)," *Cinefantastique* 27(3): 59. December 1995.

___ "**The Secret of Roan Inish** (Review)," *Cinefantastique* 27(3): 34. December 1995.

___ "**Sleepwalkers** (Review)," *Cinefantastique* 23(1): 61. August 1992.

___ "Slight of Hand: **The Addams Family**," *Cinefantastique* 22(5): 56. April 1992.

___ "**Species** (Review)," *Cinefantastique* 27(3): 53. December 1995.

___ "Stallone: **Demolition Man**," *Cinefantastique* 24(3/4): 4-6. October 1993.

___ "**Universal Soldier** (Review)," *Cinefantastique* 23(4): 61. December 1992.

___ "**Warlock: The Armageddon**," *Cinefantastique* 24(3/4): 120-121. October 1993.

___ "**Waterworld** (Review)," *Cinefantastique* 27(3): 51. December 1995.

___ "**Waxwork II: Lost in Time**," *Cinefantastique* 22(6): 48-49. June 1992

BIRKNER, GERD

___ "Francis Bacon **New Atlantis** (1627)," in: Heuermann, Hartmut and Lange, Bernd-Peter, eds. **Die Utopie in der angloamerikanischen Literatur: Interpretationen**. Düsseldorf: Bagel, 1984. pp.32-59.

BISCHOFF, DAVID

___ "Behind the Scenes of **Star Trek: Deep Space Nine**," *Omni* 15(5): 34-40, 84-85. February/March 1993.

___ "Essaying," *Quantum* No. 43/44: 30-32. Spring/Summer 1993.

___ "The New **Outer Limits**," *Omni* 17(7): 34-43. April 1995.

___ "**Star Trek: Voyager**," *Omni* 17(5): 38-43. February 1995.

BISHOP, ELLEN R.

___ **Feminism, Postmodernism, and Science Fiction: Gender and Ways of Thinking Otherwise**. Ph.D. Dissertation, University of Pittsburgh, 1995. 307pp. (DAI-A 56/05, p. 1768. November 1995.)

BISHOP, MICHAEL

___ "Children Who Survive: An Autobiographical Meditation on Horror Fiction," *Quantum* No. 41: 5-8. Winter/Spring 1992.

___ "Goodbye Thrust, Farewell Quantum: A Personal Retrospective," *Quantum* No. 43/44: 49-50, 66. Spring/Summer 1993.

___ "James Morrow and **Towing Jehovah**," *New York Review of Science Fiction* No. 67: 1, 8-11. March 1994.

___ "James Tiptree, Jr., Is Racoona Sheldon Is Alice B. Sheldon Is...," *Quantum* No. 42: 5-8. Summer/Fall 1992.

BISHOP, NORMA

___ "Utopia and Dystopia in American Folksongs," in: Saccaro Del Buffa, Giuseppa and Lewis, Arthur O., eds. **Utopia e Modernita: Teorie e prassi utopiche nell'eta moderna e postmoderna**. Rome: Gangemi Editore, 1989. pp.1003-1012.

BISSETTE, STEPHEN R.

___ "Higher Ground: Moral Transgressions, Tanscendent Fantasies," in: Golden, Christopher, ed. **Cut! Horror Writers on Horror Film**. New York: Berkley, 1992. pp.25-56.

___ (ed.) **Comic Book Rebels: Conversations With the Creators of the New Comics**, ed. by Stanley Wiater and Stephen R. Bissette. New York: Donald I. Fine, 1993. 312pp.

BISSON, TERRY

___ "Kitchen Sink's *Flesh Crawlers* Brings Back SF's Bug-eyed Monsters," *Science Fiction Age* 2(1): 86-89. November 1993.

___ "Science Fiction and the Post-*Apollo* Blues," *Locus* 32(1): 38-40, 59. January 1994.

___ "Science Fiction and the Post-*Apollo* Blues," *New York Review of Science Fiction* No. 58: 1, 8-11. June 1993.

BITTNER, DREW

___ "Comics of the Beast," *Starlog* No. 188: 32-37, 67. March 1993.

___ "Dragonlady of Pern," *Starlog* No. 190: 40-45. May 1993.

___ "The Storyteller's Song," *Starlog* No. 206: 54-58. September 1994.

BIZONY, PIERS

___ "**2001** at 25," *Omni* 15(7): 42-50. May 1993.

BIZUP, JOSEPH

___ "Hopkins' Influence on Percy's **Love in the Ruins**," *Renascence* 46(4): 247-260. Summer 1994.

BLACK, D. S.

___ "**Blade Runner** Revisited," *PKDS Newsletter* No. 28: 7-8. March 1992.

___ **The Man Who Sold America: Heinlein in Dementia**. San Francisco, CA: Atlantis Express, 1988. 28pp.

BLACK, KENT

___ "The Operatives Behind **Sneakers**," *Los Angeles (CA) Times*. September 15, 1992. in: *NewsBank. Film and Television*. 96:C13-C14. 1992.

BLACKFORD, RUSSELL

___ "Hi-Tech, Samuel R. Delany, and the Transhuman Condition," *New York Review of Science Fiction* No. 74: 1, 3-6. October 1994.

___ "Tiger in the Prison House: Damien Broderick," *Science Fiction: A Review of Speculative Literature* 13(1): 3-9. 1995(?). (No. 37)

BLACKMORE, TIM

___ "The Hunchbacked Hero in the Fiction of A. J. Budrys," *Extrapolation* 33(3): 230-244. Fall 1992.

___ "Talking the Talk, Walking the Walk: The Role of Discourse in Joe Haldeman's 'The Monster' and Lucius Shepard's 'Delta Sly Honey'," *Journal of the Fantastic in the Arts* 6(2/3): 191-202. 1994.

___ "Talking with **Strangers**: Interrogating the Many Texts That Became Heinlein's **Stranger in a Strange Land**," *Extrapolation* 36(2): 136-150. Summer 1995.

___ "Warring Stories: Fighting for Truth in the Science Fiction of Joe Haldeman," *Extrapolation* 34(2): 131-146. Summer 1993.

BLACKWOOD, STEVEN

___ "Atwood's **Wilderness** Has a Sense of Canada," *Milwaukee (WI) Journal*. January 5, 1992. in *NewsBank. Literature*. 8:B4. 1992.

BLAKE, IAN

___ "Lovecraft and the Dark Grail," *Lovecraft Studies* No. 26: 16-18. Spring 1992.

BLAKE, MICHAEL F.

___ "The Dark Duo: Tod Browning and Lon Chaney, Sr.," *Filmfax* No. 43: 50-57, 97. February/March 1994.

___ **Lon Chaney: The Man Behind the Thousand Faces**. Vestal, NY: Vestal Press, 1990. 394pp.

___ "The Man Behind the Thousand Faces," *Filmfax* No. 38: 42-49, 78-82, 94-96. April/May 1993.

___ "Master of Early Movie Makeup: Lon Chaney," *Filmfax* No. 39: 85-63, 98. June/July 1993.

BLANCH, ROBERT J.

___ "Gawain on Film," by Robert J. Blanch and Julian N. Wasserman. in: Harty, Kevin J., ed. **Cinema Arthuriana: Essays on Arthurian Film**. New York: Garland, 1991. pp.57-70.

___ "Hollywood's Myopic Medievalism: **Excalibur** and Malory's **Morte d'Arthur**," by Liam O. Purdon and Robert J. Blanch. in: Slocum, Sally K., ed. **Popular Arthurian Traditions**. Bowling Green, OH: Popular Press, 1992. pp.156-161.

BLANCHARD, JAYNE M.

___ "Bat Vibes: The Dark Comedy of Gotham City's Conflicted Crusader," *Washington (DC) Times*. June 14, 1992. in: *NewsBank. Film and Television*. 62:D10-D11. 1992.

BLAND, MICHAEL

___ "A Game of Black Humor in Vonnegut's **Cat's Cradle**," *Notes on Contemporary Literature* 24(4): 8-9. September 1994.

BLANK, ED

___ "**Two Evil Eyes** Could be Good with Poe Stories, But Just Too Cheesy (Review)," *Pittsburgh (PA) Press*. December 7, 1991. in: *NewsBank. Film and Television*. 8:E4. 1992.

BLEILER, EVERETT F.

___ "Dime Novel Science-Fiction," *AB Bookmans Weekly* 96(17): 1542-1550. October 23, 1995.

___ "In the Early, Early Days: Collecting and Dealing in Science Fiction," *AB Bookmans Weekly* 94(17): 1638-1644. October 24, 1994.

___ "M. P. Shiel 1865-1947," in: **Shiel in Diverse Hands: A Collection of Essays**. Cleveland, OH: Reynolds Morse Foundation, 1983. pp.123-131.

___ "M. P. Shiel: Humorist?," in: **Shiel in Diverse Hands: A Collection of Essays**. Cleveland, OH: Reynolds Morse Foundation, 1983. pp.132.

BLISH, JAMES

___ "The Development of a Science Fiction Writer," in: Jakubowski, Maxim and James, Edward, eds. **The Profession of Science Fiction**. New York: St. Martin's, 1992. pp.26-33.

BLIZNAKOV, MILKA

___ "The Dynamic Egalitarian City: Twentieth Century Designs for Urban Development in Russia and Their Utopian Sources," in: Saccaro Del Buffa, Giuseppa and Lewis, Arthur O., eds. **Utopia e Modernita: Teorie e prassi utopiche nell'eta moderna e postmoderna**. Rome: Gangemi Editore, 1989. pp.401-466.

BLOCH, ROBERT

___ **The Eighth Stage of Fandom**. Newark, NJ: Wildside Press, 1992. 208pp. (Reprint of the 1962 edition.)

___ "Introduction: An Open Letter to H. P. Lovecraft," in: Weinberg, Robert E. and Greenberg, Martin H., eds. **Lovecraft's Legacy**. New York: TOR, 1996. pp.ix-xvi.

___ **Once Around the Bloch: An Unauthorized Autobiography**. New York: Tor, 1993. 416pp.

BLOCH-HANSEN, PETER

___ "Classic Captain," by Peter Bloch-Hansen and Ian Spelling. *Starlog* No. 212: 36-37, 70. March 1995.

___ "**Cybertech P. D.**," *Starlog* No. 221: 70-73. December 1995.

___ "Declaring **TekWar**," *Starlog* No. 199: 46-49, 73. February 1994.

___ "Electric Fuzz Television," *Starlog* No. 202: 52-55, 67. May 1994.

___ "Forever and a Knight," *Starlog* No. 212: 50-53, 72. March 1995.

___ "Heroic Immortal," *Starlog* No. 186: 48-51. January 1993.

___ "Perfect Mating," *Starlog* No. 197: 58-61. December 1993.

___ "Robo Partner," *Starlog* No. 204: 36-39. July 1994.

___ "Tek Hero," *Starlog* No. 213: 44-47. April 1995.

___ "TekNologies," *Starlog* No. 212: 38-39. March 1995.

___ "This Year's **Robocop**," *Starlog* No. 201: 41-44, 66. April 1994.

___ "Unlife to Live," *Starlog* No. 215: 54-57. June 1995.

BLOOM, HAROLD

___ "A. E. Van Vogt," in: Bloom, Harold, ed. **Science Fiction Writers of the Golden Age**. New York: Chelsea House, 1995. pp.188-203.

___ "A. Merritt," in: Bloom, Harold, ed. **Modern Fantasy Writers**. New York: Chelsea House, 1995. pp.110-122.

___ "Alfred Bester," in: Bloom, Harold, ed. **Science Fiction Writers of the Golden Age**. New York: Chelsea House, 1995. pp.47-62.

___ "Algernon Blackwood," in: Bloom, Harold. **Modern Horror Writers**. New York: Chelsea House, 1995. pp.32-47.

___ "Ambrose Bierce," in: Bloom, Harold. **Classic Horror Writers**. New York: Chelsea House, 1994. pp.1-13.

___ "Andrew Lang," in: Bloom, Harold. **Classic Fantasy Writers**. New York: Chelsea House, 1994. pp.124-136.

___ "Ann Radcliffe," in: Bloom, Harold. **Classic Horror Writers**. New York: Chelsea House, 1994. pp.107-120.

___ "Arthur C. Clarke," in: Bloom, Harold, ed. **Science Fiction Writers of the Golden Age**. New York: Chelsea House, 1995. pp.94-109.

___ "Arthur Machen," in: Bloom, Harold. **Modern Horror Writers**. New York: Chelsea House, 1995. pp.155-170.

___ "Beatrix Potter," in: Bloom, Harold. **Classic Fantasy Writers**. New York: Chelsea House, 1994. pp.164-174.

___ "Bram Stoker," in: Bloom, Harold. **Classic Horror Writers**. New York: Chelsea House, 1994. pp.152-167.

___ "C. L. Moore & Henry Kuttner," in: Bloom, Harold, ed. **Science Fiction Writers of the Golden Age**. New York: Chelsea House, 1995. pp.141-156.

___ "C. S. Lewis," in: Bloom, Harold, ed. **Modern Fantasy Writers**. New York: Chelsea House, 1995. pp.85-97.

___ "Charles Brockden Brown," in: Bloom, Harold. **Classic Horror Writers**. New York: Chelsea House, 1994. pp.14-26.

BLOOM, HAROLD (continued)

___ "Charles Robert Maturin," in: Bloom, Harold. **Classic Horror Writers**. New York: Chelsea House, 1994. pp.73-85.

___ "Charles Williams," in: Bloom, Harold, ed. **Modern Fantasy Writers**. New York: Chelsea House, 1995. pp.180-194.

___ "Clark Ashton Smith," in: Bloom, Harold, ed. **Modern Fantasy Writers**. New York: Chelsea House, 1995. pp.151-164.

___ "David Lindsay," in: Bloom, Harold, ed. **Modern Fantasy Writers**. New York: Chelsea House, 1995. pp.98-109.

___ "E. F. Benson," in: Bloom, Harold. **Modern Horror Writers**. New York: Chelsea House, 1995. pp.16-31.

___ "E. R. Eddison," in: Bloom, Harold, ed. **Modern Fantasy Writers**. New York: Chelsea House, 1995. pp.43-56.

___ "Edgar Allan Poe," in: Bloom, Harold. **Classic Horror Writers**. New York: Chelsea House, 1994. pp.86-106.

___ "Frederik Pohl," in: Bloom, Harold, ed. **Science Fiction Writers of the Golden Age**. New York: Chelsea House, 1995. pp.157-172.

___ "Fritz Leiber," in: Bloom, Harold, ed. **Modern Fantasy Writers**. New York: Chelsea House, 1995. pp.71-84.

___ "Fritz Leiber," in: Bloom, Harold, ed. **Science Fiction Writers of the Golden Age**. New York: Chelsea House, 1995. pp.126-140.

___ "George MacDonald," in: Bloom, Harold. **Classic Fantasy Writers**. New York: Chelsea House, 1994. pp.137-149.

___ "H. P. Lovecraft," in: Bloom, Harold. **Modern Horror Writers**. New York: Chelsea House, 1995. pp.138-154.

___ "H. Rider Haggard," in: Bloom, Harold. **Classic Fantasy Writers**. New York: Chelsea House, 1994. pp.82-95.

___ "Henry James," in: Bloom, Harold. **Classic Horror Writers**. New York: Chelsea House, 1994. pp.27-42.

___ "Horace Walpole," in: Bloom, Harold. **Classic Horror Writers**. New York: Chelsea House, 1994. pp.168-180.

___ "Introduction," in: Bloom, Harold, ed. **George Orwell's 1984**. New York: Chelsea House, 1987. pp.1-8.

___ "Isaac Asimov," in: Bloom, Harold, ed. **Science Fiction Writers of the Golden Age**, New York: Chelsea House, 1995. pp.17-46.

___ "J. R. R. Tolkien," in: Bloom, Harold, ed. **Modern Fantasy Writers**. New York: Chelsea House, 1995. pp.165-179.

___ "James Blish," in: Bloom, Harold, ed. **Science Fiction Writers of the Golden Age**. New York: Chelsea House, 1995. pp.63-78.

___ "James Branch Cabell," in: Bloom, Harold. **Classic Fantasy Writers**. New York: Chelsea House, 1994. pp.27-39.

___ "John Collier," in: Bloom, Harold, ed. **Modern Fantasy Writers**. New York: Chelsea House, 1995. pp.16-28.

___ "Joseph Sheridan LeFanu," in: Bloom, Harold. **Classic Horror Writers**. New York: Chelsea House, 1994. pp.43-58.

___ "Kenneth Grahame," in: Bloom, Harold. **Classic Fantasy Writers**. New York: Chelsea House, 1994. pp.71-81.

___ "L. Frank Baum," in: Bloom, Harold. **Classic Fantasy Writers**. New York: Chelsea House, 1994. pp.1-13.

___ "L. P. Hartley," in: Bloom, Harold. **Modern Horror Writers**. New York: Chelsea House, 1995. pp.79-92.

___ "L. Sprague de Camp and Fletcher Pratt," in: Bloom, Harold, ed. **Modern Fantasy Writers**. New York: Chelsea House, 1995. pp.29-42.

___ "Lafcadio Hearn," in: Bloom, Harold. **Classic Fantasy Writers**. New York: Chelsea House, 1994. pp.96-109.

___ "Lewis Carroll," in: Bloom, Harold. **Classic Fantasy Writers**. New York: Chelsea House, 1994. pp.40-55.

___ "Lord Dunsany," in: Bloom, Harold. **Classic Fantasy Writers**. New York: Chelsea House, 1994. pp.56-70.

___ "M. P. Shiel," in: Bloom, Harold, ed. **Modern Fantasy Writers**. New York: Chelsea House, 1995. pp.137-150.

___ "M. R. James," in: Bloom, Harold. **Modern Horror Writers**. New York: Chelsea House, 1995. pp.124-137.

___ "Mary Shelley," in: Bloom, Harold. **Classic Horror Writers**. New York: Chelsea House, 1994. pp.121-137.

___ "Matthew Gregory Lewis," in: Bloom, Harold. **Classic Horror Writers**. New York: Chelsea House, 1994. pp.59-72.

___ "Mervyn Peake," in: Bloom, Harold, ed. **Modern Fantasy Writers**. New York: Chelsea House, 1995. pp.123-136.

___ "Oscar Wilde," in: Bloom, Harold. **Classic Fantasy Writers**. New York: Chelsea House, 1994. pp.175-187.

___ "Poul Anderson," in: Bloom, Harold, ed. **Science Fiction Writers of the Golden Age**. New York: Chelsea House, 1995. pp.1-16.

___ "Ray Bradbury," in: Bloom, Harold, ed. **Modern Fantasy Writers**. New York: Chelsea House, 1995. pp.1-15.

___ "Ray Bradbury," in: Bloom, Harold, ed. **Science Fiction Writers of the Golden Age**. New York: Chelsea House, 1995. pp.78-93.

BLOOM, HAROLD (continued)

___ "Richard Matheson," in: Bloom, Harold. **Modern Horror Writers**. New York: Chelsea House, 1995. pp.171-185.

___ "Robert A. Heinlein," in: Bloom, Harold, ed. **Science Fiction Writers of the Golden Age**. New York: Chelsea House, 1995. pp.110-125.

___ "Robert Aickman," in: Bloom, Harold. **Modern Horror Writers**. New York: Chelsea House, 1995. pp.1-15.

___ "Robert Bloch," in: Bloom, Harold. **Modern Horror Writers**. New York: Chelsea House, 1995. pp.48-63.

___ "Robert E. Howard," in: Bloom, Harold, ed. **Modern Fantasy Writers**. New York: Chelsea House, 1995. pp.57-70.

___ "Robert Louis Stevenson," in: Bloom, Harold. **Classic Horror Writers**. New York: Chelsea House, 1994. pp.138-151.

___ "Rudyard Kipling," in: Bloom, Harold. **Classic Fantasy Writers**. New York: Chelsea House, 1994. pp.110-123.

___ "Shirley Jackson," in: Bloom, Harold. **Modern Horror Writers**. New York: Chelsea House, 1995. pp.108-123.

___ "Theodore Sturgeon," in: Bloom, Harold, ed. **Science Fiction Writers of the Golden Age**. New York: Chelsea House, 1995. pp.173-187.

___ "Walter de la Mare," in: Bloom, Harold. **Modern Horror Writers**. New York: Chelsea House, 1995. pp.64-78.

___ "William Beckford," in: Bloom, Harold. **Classic Fantasy Writers**. New York: Chelsea House, 1994. pp.14-26.

___ "William Hope Hodgson," in: Bloom, Harold. **Modern Horror Writers**. New York: Chelsea House, 1995. pp.93-107.

___ "William Morris," in: Bloom, Harold. **Classic Fantasy Writers**. New York: Chelsea House, 1994. pp.150-163.

___ (ed.) **Classic Fantasy Writers**. New York: Chelsea House, 1994. 187pp.

___ (ed.) **Classic Horror Writers**. New York: Chelsea House, 1994. 180pp.

___ (ed.) **Classic Science Fiction Writers**. New York: Chelsea House, 1995. 186pp.

___ (ed.) **George Orwell's 1984**. New York: Chelsea House, 1987. 135pp.

___ (ed.) **Modern Fantasy Writers**. New York: Chelsea House, 1995. 194pp.

___ (ed.) **Modern Horror Writers**. New York: Chelsea House, 1995. 185pp.

___ (ed.) **Science Fiction Writers of the Golden Age**. New York: Chelsea House, 1995. 203pp.

BLOSSER, FRED

___ "From Cross Plains to the Stars: Robert E. Howard's Science Fiction," *The Dark Man: The Journal of Robert E. Howard Studies* No. 3: 1-8. April 1993.

BLUMBERG, JANE

___ **Mary Shelley's Early Novels**. Iowa City: University of Iowa Press, 1993. 257pp.

BLY, JAMES I.

___ **Structure and Theme in Burgess's *Honey for the Bears, A Clockwork Orange*, and *Tremor of Intent***. Ph.D. Dissertation, University of Northern Colorado, 1978. 372pp. (DAI 39:4954A. Feb. 1979.)

BOARDMAN, PHILLIP C.

___ "Teaching the Moderns in an Arthurian Course," in: Fries, Maureen and Watson, Jeanie, eds. **Approaches to the Teaching of the Arthurian Tradition**. New York: Modern Language Association, 1992. pp.81-87.

BOCHM, GUDRUN

___ "Mary W. Shelley, **Frankenstein, or the Modern Prometheus** (1818)," in: Heuermann, Harmut, ed. **Der Science Fiction Roman in der angloamerikanischen Literatur: Interpretationen**. Düsseldorf: Bagel, 1986. pp.15-30.

BODE, ROBERT F.

___ "A Back-(To the Future)-Formation," by Alan R. Slotkin and Robert F. Bode. *American Speech* 68(3): 323-327. Fall 1993.

BODEI, REMO
___ "Utopie paradossali: utopia del presente, eternita futura, centralita del marginale," in: Saccaro Del Buffa, Giuseppa and Lewis, Arthur O., eds. **Utopia e Modernita: Teorie e prassi utopiche nell'eta moderna e postmoderna.** Rome: Gangemi Editore, 1989. pp.951-958.

BOEDEKER, HAL
___ "New Trek Is Light Years From Perfection," *Miami (FL) Herald.* January 16, 1995. in: *NewsBank. Film and Television.* 21:D10-D11. 1995.

BOEREM, R.
___ "Other Elements in 'The Color out of Space'," in: Joshi, S. T., ed. **The H. P. Lovecraft Centennial Conference Proceedings.** West Warwick, RI: Necronomicon, 1991. pp.37-39.

BOGSTAD, JANICE M.
___ **Gender, Power and Reversal in Contemporary Anglo-American and French Feminist Science Fiction.** Ph.D. Dissertation, University of Wisconsin, Madison, 1992. 229pp. (DAI-A 54/02, p. 509. August 1993.)

BOIVIN, AURELIEN
___ **Bibliographie analytique de la science fiction et du fantastique Quebecois: 1960-1985**, by Aurelien Boivin, Maurice Emond and Michel Lord. Quebec: Nuit blanche editeur, 1992. 577pp.

BOJARSKI, RICHARD
___ **The Complete Films of Bela Lugosi.** New York: Carol Publishing, 1992. 256pp. (Reissue of **The Films of Bela Lugosi**, 1980.)

BOKAMPER, JERRY
___ "*Puppet Masters* Terror Is Too Predictable," *Dallas (TX) Morning News.* October 24, 1994. in: *NewsBank. Film and Television.* 114:F11. 1994.

BÖKER, UWE
___ "Isaac Asimov, **Foundation-Tetralogie** (1951ff)," in: Heuermann, Harmut, ed. **Der Science Fiction Roman in der angloamerikanischen Literatur: Interpretationen.** Düsseldorf: Bagel, 1986. pp.118-143.

BOLHAFNER, J. STEPHEN
___ "Guide to Cyberspace," *Starlog* No. 200: 72-74, 87. March 1994.

BOND, CHRISTOPHER J.
___ **I. Sir James Frazer's 'Homeopathy' and a 'Contagion' as Archetypal and Structural Principles in William Faulkner's 'Go Down Moses.' II. The Auditory Dimension in Arnold's Search for a Distinctive Poetic Voice. III. Images of Women in Recent Speculative Fiction.** Ph.D. Dissertation, Rutgers University, 1974. 201pp. (DAI 35: 3725A.)

BOND, JONATHAN
___ "Sexual Etiquette at Conventions," by Jonathan Bond and Jak Koke. *The Report: The Fiction Writer's Magazine* No. 7: 11-12. June 1992.

BONKO, LARRY
___ "Final Trek," *Norfolk (VA) Virginian-Pilot.* May 28, 1994. in: *NewsBank. Film and Television.* 59:B6-B8. 1994.

BONNER, FRANCES J.
___ "Separate Development: Cyberpunk in Film and TV," in: Slusser, George E. and Shippey, Tom, eds. **Fiction 2000: Cyberpunk and the Future of Narrative.** Athens: University of Georgia Press, 1992. pp.191-207.
___ **Stories of What Is to Come: The Future in Film and Television, 1959-1989.** Ph.D. Dissertation, Open University (Great Britain), 1991. 284pp. (DAI-A 53/09, p. 3028. March 1993.)

BOOE, MARTIN
___ "Gag! It's **Ren and Stimpy**," *Washington (DC) Post.* August 11, 1992. in: *NewsBank. Film and Television.* 83:C11-C14. 1992.
___ "The Monster Maven: Forrest Ackerman, Sci-Fi's Founding Fan," *Washington (DC) Post* Sec. G, p. 1. May 28, 1993.

BOOKER, M. KEITH
___ **The Dystopian Impulse in Modern Literature: Fiction as Social Criticism.** Westport, CT: Greenwood, 1994. 197pp.
___ **Dystopian Literature: A Theory and Research Guide.** Westport, CT: Greenwood Press, 1994. 424pp.
___ "Technology, History, and the Postmodern Imagination: The Cyberpunk Fiction of William Gibson," *Arizona Quarterly* 50(4): 63-87. Winter 1994.
___ "Woman on the Edge of a Genre: The Feminist Dystopias of Marge Piercy," *Science Fiction Studies* 21(3): 337-350. November 1994.

BOONE, TROY
___ "He Is English and Therefore Adventurous: Politics, Decadence and **Dracula**," *Studies in the Novel* 25(1): 76-91. Spring 1993.

BORCHARDT, EDITH
___ "The 'Asralis' poem by Novalis as Creation Myth," in: Latham, Robert A. and Collins, Robert A., eds. **Modes of the Fantastic.** Westport, CT: Greenwood, 1995. pp.129-136.
___ "Caricature, Parody, Satire: Narrative Masks as Subversion of the Picaro in Patrick Süskind's **Perfume**," in: Ruddick, Nicholas, ed. **State of the Fantastic.** Westport, CT: Greenwood, 1992. pp.97-103.
___ "Criminal Artists and Artisans in Mysteries by E. T. A. Hoffman, Dorothy Sayers, Ernesto Sábato, Patrick Süskind, and Thomas Harris," in: Sanders, Joe, ed. **Functions of the Fantastic.** Westport, CT: Greenwood, 1995. pp.125-134.

BORGMEIER, RAIMUND
___ "Brian W. Aldiss, **Frankenstein Unbound** (1973)," in: Heuermann, Harmut, ed. **Der Science Fiction Roman in der angloamerikanischen Literatur: Interpretationen.** Düsseldorf: Bagel, 1986. pp.331-345.

BORGWALD, JAMES M.
___ "Classroom Analysis of Rotating Space Vehicles in *2001: A Space Odyssey*," by James M. Borgwald and Serge Schreiner. *Physics Teacher* 31(7): 406-409. October 1993.

BORST, RONALD V.
___ (ed.) **Graven Images: The Best of Horror, Fantasy, and Science Fiction Film Art from the Collection of Ronald V. Borst**, ed. by Ronald V. Borst, Keith Burns and Leith Adams. New York: Grove Press, 1992. 240pp.

BOSKY, BERNADETTE L.
___ "Amateur Press Associations: Intellectual Society and Social Intellectualism," in: Sanders, Joe, ed. **Science Fiction Fandom.** Westport, CT: Greenwood, 1994. pp.181-196.
___ "Charles Williams: Occult Fantasies, Occult Fact," in: Latham, Robert A. and Collins, Robert A., eds. **Modes of the Fantastic.** Westport, CT: Greenwood, 1995. pp.176-185.
___ "Choice, Sacrifice, Destiny, and Nature in **The Stand**," in: Magistrale, Tony, ed. **A Casebook on The Stand.** San Bernardino, CA: Borgo Press, 1992. pp.123-142.
___ "Haunting and Healing: Memory and Guilt in the Fiction of Peter Straub," *New York Review of Science Fiction* No. 73: 1, 8-13. September 1994.
___ "Playing the Heavy: Weight, Appetite, and Embodiment in Three Novels by Stephen King," in: Magistrale, Tony, ed. **The Dark Descent: Essays Defining Stephen King's Horrorscape.** Westport, CT: Greenwood, 1992. pp.137-156.

BOSS, JUDITH E.
___ "Finding the Facts in Science Fiction Films," by Leroy W. Dubeck, Suzanne E. Moshier, Matthew H. Bruce and Judith E. Boss. *Science Teacher* 60(4): 46-48. April 1993.
___ "Using Science Fiction Films to Teach Science at the College Level," by Leroy W. Dubeck, Suzanne E. Moshier and Judith E. Boss. *Journal of College Science Teaching* 25(1): 46-50. September/October 1995

BOSS, KIT
___ "Reigning Cat and Dog Nickelodeon Has a Hit in **Ren and Stimpy Show** (Review)," *Seattle (WA) Times.* August 13, 1992. in: *NewsBank. Film and Television.* 83:D3-D4. 1992.

BOSSE, JAN
___ "Unquendor, Its Sense and Nonsense," *Lembas Extra.* [Leiden]: Tolkien Genootschap Unquendor, 1991. [Not seen, cf. *Mythlore*.]

BOSWELL, JACKSON C.
___ **Sir Thomas More in the English Renaissance: An Annotated Catalogue**. Binghamton, NY: Medieval & Renaissance Texts & Studies, 1994. 362pp.

BOSWELL, THOM
___ **The Costumemaker's Art: Cloaks of Fantasy, Masks of Revelation**. Asheville, NC: Lark Books, 1992. 144pp.

BOTTERO, MARIA
___ "Il mito dell'autosufficienza nella letteratura utopistica inglese," in: Saccaro Del Buffa, Giuseppa and Lewis, Arthur O., eds. **Utopie per gli Anni Ottana**. Rome: Gangemi Editore, 1986. pp.207-224.

BOUCHARD, ALEXANDER J. L.
___ "Robert A. Heinlein: An Appreciation," *Lan's Lantern* No. 38: 31-32. July 1992.

BOUCHARD, GUY
___ **Images feministes du futur**. Quebec: Groupe de recherches en analyse des discours de l'Universite Laval, 1992. 153pp.
___ **Les 42210 univers de la science-fiction**. Sainte-Foy, Quebec: Le Passeur, 1993. 338pp.
___ "Sexisme et utopie," *Imagine* No. 61: 11-57. September 1992.

BOULTER, AMANDA
___ "Alice James Raccoona Tiptree Sheldon Jr.: Textual Personas in the Short Fiction of Alice Sheldon," *Foundation* No. 63: 5-31. Spring 1995.

BOURASSA, ALAIN
___ "Deaths of *The Immortal*, Part Two," by Alain Bourassa and Mark Phillips. *Starlog* No. 186: 67-72, 74. January 1993.
___ "Lives of *The Immortal*, Part One," by Mark Phillips and Alain Bourassa. *Starlog* 185: 58-62. December 1992.

BOVA, BEN
___ **The Craft of Writing Science Fiction That Sells**. Cincinnati, OH: Writer's Digest, 1994. 218pp.
___ "Future Di Fate," *Science Fiction Age* 2(3): 70-75. March 1994.
___ "On a Clear Day You Can See Mars," *Lan's Lantern* No. 41: 23-25. July 1993.
___ "Why *Science* Fiction?," *Amazing Stories* 67(11): 62-65. February 1993.

BOWEN, J. HARTLEY, JR.
___ "Recalling Robert Anson Heinlein," in: Kondo, Yoji, ed. **Requiem: New Collected Works by Robert A. Heinlein and Tributes to the Grand Master**. New York: Tor, 1992. pp.259-260.

BOWMAN, DAVID
___ "The Strange Odyssey of Helen Chandler," *Filmfax* No. 35: 67-72. October/November 1992.
___ "They Called Him 'Herr Doktor': Edward Van Sloan," *Filmfax* No. 35: 63-66. October/November 1992.
___ "A Tragically Miscast Comedian: Dwight Frye," *Filmfax* No. 35: 73-78. October/November 1992.

BOWMAN, JON
___ "*Demolition Man* Movie Version of an Action-Packed Comic Book (Review)," *(Santa Fe, NM) New Mexican* October 15, 1993. in: *NewsBank. Film and Television.* 115:A3. 1993.
___ "Van Damme Gets His Kicks in *Timecop*," *(Santa Fe, NM) New Mexican*. September 23, 1994. in: *NewsBank. Film and Television.* 105: D7. 1994.

BOWMAN, TANYA F.
___ "Cautionary Tales of Immortality," *Science Fiction: A Review of Speculative Literature* 13(1): 19-21. 1995(?). (No. 37)

BOYERS, ROBERT H.
___ "Introduction: Classic Fantasy," by Robert H. Boyers and Kenneth J. Zahorski. in: Boyer, Robert H. and Zahorski, Kenneth J., eds. **Visions and Imaginings: Classic Fantasy Fiction**. Chicago: Academy Chicago, 1992. pp.xiii-xxvi.

BOYLE, TED E.
___ "Golding's Existential Vision," in: Biles, Jack I. and Evans, Robert O., eds. **William Golding: Some Critical Considerations**. Lexington, KY: University Press of Kentucky, 1978. pp.21-38.

BOZZETTO, ROGER
___ "Dick in France: A Love Story," in: Mullen, R. D., ed. **On Philip K. Dick: 40 Articles From Science-Fiction Studies**. Terre Haute, IN: SF-TH Inc., 1992. pp.153-160.
___ "L'île bouffonne du Docteur Moreau," in: Marimoutou, Jean-Claude, ed. **L'insularité thématique et représentations**. Paris: Editions L'Harmattan, 1995. pp.441-447.
___ "L'Invitation au château. Mélanges Maurice Levy," in: *Les cahiers du CERLI*. Nouvelle série. No. 6: 53-61. Mars 1995. [Not seen; cf. author.]
___ **L'Obscur Objet d'un Savoir: Fantastique et Science-fiction: deux littératures de l'imagination**. Marseille, France: Universite de Provence, 1991. 280pp.
___ "Moreau's Tragi-Farcical Island," *Science Fiction Studies* 20(1): 34-44. March 1993.
___ "William Burroughs, le scribe étasunien halluciné," in: Terramorsi, Bernard, ed. **Américana**. Paris: Université de la Réunion/Éditions l'Harmattan, 1994. pp.201-215. (*Cahiers CRLH Ciraoi* No. 9, 1994)
___ (ed.) **Eros: Science & Fiction Fantastique**, ed. by Roger Bozzetto, Max Duperray and Alain Chareyre-Mejan. Aix-en-Provence: Universite de Provence, 1991. 220pp.

BRADBURY, RAY
___ "About Theodore Sturgeon," in: Sturgeon, Theodore. **The Ultimate Egoist, Vol. 1: The Complete Stories of Theodore Sturgeon**, ed. by Paul Williams. Berkeley, CA: North Atlantic Books, 1994. pp.ix-xii.
___ "Beyond 1984: The People Machines," in: Bradbury, Ray. **Yestermorrow: Obvious Answers to Impossible Futures**. Santa Barbara, CA: Capra Press, 1991. pp.155-174.
___ "Blueprinter of Our Future: Robert McCall," *Science Fiction Age* 1(1): 62-67. November 1992.
___ "Burning Bright: A Foreword," in: Bradbury, Ray. **Fahrenheit 451: The 40th Anniversary Edition**. New York: Simon & Schuster, 1993. pp.11-21.
___ **Green Shadows, White Whale**. New York: Knopf, 1992. 271pp.
___ **Yestermorrow: Obvious Answers to Impossible Futures**. Santa Barbara, CA: Capra Press, 1991. 240pp.

BRADLEY, MARION Z.
___ "Essay: Science Fiction Conventions," *Science Fiction Age* 1(2): 22, 71. January 1993.

BRADLEY, MATTHEW R.
___ "And in the Beginning Was the Word...: An Interview With Screenwriter Richard Matheson," *Filmfax* No. 42: 40-44, 78-80, 98. December 1993/January 1994.
___ "Momma's Boy: A Conversation With Robert Bloch," *Filmfax* No. 40: 78-82. August/September 1993.

BRADLEY, WENDY
___ "*The Tomorrow People* (Review)," *Interzone* No. 69: 40, 49. March 1993.

BRADSHAW, DAVID
___ "A New Bibliography of Aldous Huxley's Work and Its Reception, 1912-1937," *Bulletin of Bibliography* 51(3): 237-256. September 1994.

BRADY, CHARLES A.
___ "A Vaudeville for Mozart," *Buffalo (NY) News*. January 19, 1992. in: *NewsBank. Literature.* 8:G9. 1992

BRADY, JAMES
___ "In Step With: Patrick Stewart," *Austin (TX) American Statesman. Parade Magazine* p. 12. April 5, 1992.

BRADY, MARTIN
___ "Dancing With Both Sexes, Atwood Style," *Chicago (IL) Sun Times*. December 8, 1991. in *NewsBank. Literature.* 1:C8-C9. 1992.

BRAINE, F. S.
___ "Technological Utopias: The Future of the Next Generation," *Film & History* 24(1/2): 1-18. February/May 1994.

BRANDE, DAVID J.
___ **Technologies of Postmodernity: Ideology and Desire in Literature and Science (Pynchon, Thomas; Gibson, William; Butler, Octavia; Acker, Kathy).** Ph.D. Dissertation, University of Washington, 1995. 228pp. (DAI-A 56/07, p. 2677. January 1996.)

BRANDENBURG, SANDRA
___ "Image of the Spider," by Debora Hill and Sandra Brandenburg. *Starlog* 182: 40-41. September 1992.
___ "Things in That Forest: A Profile of Lisa Goldstein," by Sandra Brandenburg and Debora Hill. *Science Fiction Eye* No. 11: 110-113.113. December 1992.
___ "A Time of Fantasies," by Sandra Brandenburg and Debora Hill. *Starlog* 179: 70-72, 90. June 1992.

BRANDNER, GARY
___ "No, But I Saw the Movie," in: Golden, Christopher, ed. **Cut! Horror Writers on Horror Film.** New York: Berkley, 1992. pp.57-66.

BRANDON, CARL
___ "*Alien 3*: A Review of the Work in Progress," *Cinefantastique* 22(6): 20-21. June 1992

BRANDT, JAMES B.
___ "**Street Fighter**," *Cinefantastique* 26(2): 56-57. February 1995.

BRANDT, RICHARD
___ "Fritzish Thoughts," *Lan's Lantern* No. 38: 14-16. July 1992.

BRANSON, DAVID A.
___ "Arthurian Elements in **That Hideous Strength**," *Mythlore* 19(4): 20-21. Autumn 1993. (No. 74)

BRANWYN, GARETH
___ "Compu-sex: Erotica for Cybernauts," *South Atlantic Quarterly* 92(4): 779-791. Fall 1993.

BRATMAN, DAVID
___ "A Corrigenda to the **Lord of the Rings**," *The Tolkien Collector* 6: 17-25. 1994.

BRAUN, GUNTER
___ "Stasi-Akten-phantastiche Literatur?," by Johanna Braun and Gunter Braun. *Quarber Merkur* 32(1): 41-43. June 1994. (Whole No. 81)

BRAUN, JOHANNA
___ "Stasi-Akten-phantastiche Literatur?," by Johanna Braun and Gunter Braun. *Quarber Merkur* 32(1): 41-43. June 1994. (Whole No. 81)

BRAXTON, T. S.
___ "The 'Q' Question," in: Van Hise, James, ed. **Trek Celebration Two.** Las Vegas, NV: Pioneer, 1994. pp.57-70.

BREAM, JON
___ "Mystery Science Project," *TV Guide* 43(28): 19-21. July 15, 1995.
___ "**Mystery Science Theater 3000** Switcheroo," *TV Guide* 41(30): 26-28. July 24, 1993.

BREDEHOFT, THOMAS A.
___ "The Gibson Continuum: Cyberspace and Gibson's Mervyn Kihn Stories," *Science Fiction Studies* 22(2): 252-263. July 1995.

BRENNAN, JUDY
___ "Sea Epic's Costs May Bring Wave of Caution," by Robert W. Welkos and Judy Brennan. *Los Angeles (CA) Times.* July 26, 1995. in: *NewsBank. Film and Television.* 82:C13-D1. 1995.

BRÈQUE, JEAN-DANIEL
___ "Between Entropy and Renaissance: SF in France," by André Ruaud and Jean-Daniel Brèque. *Vector* No. 168: 28-29. August/September 1992.

BRETNOR, REGINALD
___ **Of Force and Violence and Other Imponderables; Essays on War, Politics, and Government.** San Bernardino, CA: Borgo Press, 1992. 144pp.

BRETNOR, REGINALD (continued)
___ "Science Fiction and the Semantics of Conflict," in: Slusser, George and Eric S. Rabkin, eds. **Fights of Fancy: Armed Conflict in Science Fiction and Fantasy.** Athens, GA: University of Georgia Press, 1993. pp.26-34.

BREUER, HANS-PETER
___ **Samuel Butler: An Annotated Bibliography of Writings About Him.** New York: Garland, 1990. 497pp.

BREWER, WILLIAM D.
___ "Mary Shelley on Dreams," *Southern Humanities Review* 29(2): 105-126. Spring 1995.

BRICE, WILLIAM C.
___ "Geology Teaching and Science Fiction," *Journal of Geological Education* 29(2): 105-107. March 1980.

BRICKHOUSE, THOMAS C.
___ "Socrates the Anti-Utopian," by Thomas C. Brickhouse and Nicholas D. Smith. in: Saccaro Del Buffa, Giuseppa and Lewis, Arthur O., eds. **Utopia e Modernita: Teorie e prassi utopiche nell'eta moderna e postmoderna.** Rome: Gangemi Editore, 1989. pp.717-726.

BRIDGMAN, JOAN
___ "The Significance of Myth in **Watership Down**," *Journal of the Fantastic in the Arts* 6(1): 7-24. 1993.

BRIGG, PETER
___ "J. G. Ballard: Time Out of Mind," *Extrapolation* 35(1): 43-59. Spring 1994.
___ "Maggots, Tropes, and Metafictional Challenge: John Fowles' **A Maggot**," in: Wolf, Milton T. and Mallett, Daryl F., eds. **Imaginative Futures: Proceedings of the 1993 Science Fiction Research Association Conference.** San Bernardino, CA: Jacob's Ladder Books, 1995. pp.293-306.

BRIGGS, BILL
___ "**Aliens 3** Jumps Back on Treadmill," *Denver (CO) Post.* May 22, 1992. in: *NewsBank. Film and Television.* 49:B13. 1992.

BRIGGS, SCOTT D.
___ "Robert Aickman: Sojourns into the Unknown," *Studies in Weird Fiction* No. 12: 7-12. Spring 1993.
___ " 'So Much Mystery...': The Fiction of William Peter Blatty," *Studies in Weird Fiction* No. 9: 13-18. Spring 1991.

BRILL, LOUIS M.
___ "Special Venues: Inside the Luxor Pyramid," *Cinefex* No. 61: 23-28. March 1995.

BRIN, DAVID
___ "Agent-Author (Pre-Nuptial) Agreements," *SFWA Bulletin* 26(1): 34-35. Spring 1992. (No. 115)
___ "Extraterrestrial Nightmares," *Omni* 16(9): 4. June 1994.
___ "Only Science Fiction Can Solve the Perplexing Problem of Gun Control," *Science Fiction Age* 2(5): 30-33. July 1994.
___ "A Shaman's View," in: Jakubowski, Maxim and James, Edward, eds. **The Profession of Science Fiction.** New York: St. Martin's, 1992. pp.161-168.
___ "Waging War With Reality," in: Slusser, George E. and Rabkin, Eric S., eds. **Styles of Creation: Aesthetic Technique and the Creation of Fictional Worlds.** Athens: University of Georgia Press, 1992. pp.24-29.

BRITTON, BONNIE
___ "A Broody, Moody **Batman**," *Indianapolis (IN) Star.* June 19, 1992. in: *NewsBank. Film and Television.* 62:F6-F7. 1992.
___ "Holy Cash Registers: **Batman Returns** Generates Merchandising Flurry as Sequel of Gimmicky Movie Heads for Local Theaters," *Indianapolis (IN) Star.* June 17, 1992. in: *NewsBank. Film and Television.* 62:D14-E1. 1992.
___ "Lori Petty Best Part of **Tank Girl**," *Indianapolis (IN) Star.* March 31, 1995. in: *NewsBank. Film and Television.* 50:C2. 1995.
___ "**Next Generation** Cast Inherits Big-Screen Time," *Indianapolis (IN) Star.* November 18, 1994. in: *NewsBank. Film and Television.* 125:D4-D5. 1994.

BRITTON, BONNIE (continued)
___ "Splashy *Hook* Deserves a Look (Review)," *Indianapolis (IN) Star*. December 11, 1991. in: *NewsBank. Film and Television*. 3:F5-F6. 1992.
___ "Van Damme Lives in Past as *Timecop*," *Indianapolis (IN) Star*. September 16, 1994. in: *NewsBank. Film and Television*. 105:D1. 1994.

BRODERICK, DAMIEN
___ "Minds, Modes, Models, Modules," *New York Review of Science Fiction* No. 74: 1, 8-10. October 1994.
___ "The Multiplicity of Worlds, of Others," *Foundation* No. 55: 66-81. Summer 1992.
___ "The Object of Science Fiction," *New York Review of Science Fiction* No. 59: 16-18. July 1993.
___ "The Profession of Science Fiction, 44: The Semi-Detached Sci-Fi Life of an Almost Famous Writer," *Foundation* No. 59: 5-16. Autumn 1993.
___ **Reading By Starlight: Postmodern Science Fiction**. London and New York: Routledge, 1995. 197pp.
___ "Reading by Starlight: Science Fiction as a Reading Protocol," *Science Fiction: A Review of Speculative Literature* 11(2): 5-16. 1991. (No. 32)
___ "Reading SF as a Mega-Text," *New York Review of Science Fiction* No. 47: 1, 8-11. July 1992.
___ "SF as Genetic Engineering," *Foundation* No. 59: 16-28. Autumn 1993.
___ "SF as Modular Calculus," *Southern Review: Literary and Interdisciplinary Essays (Australia)* 24(1): 43-53. March 1991.
___ "Transmitters," *Science Fiction: A Review of Speculative Literature* 13(1): 10-11. 1995(?). (No. 37)
___ "Transreality: Beyond Imagination," *New York Review of Science Fiction* No. 81: 1, 8-11. May 1995.

BRODERICK, MICK
___ "Surviving Armageddon: Beyond the Imagination of Disaster," *Science Fiction Studies* 20(3): 342-382. November 1993.

BRODIE, JOHN
___ "Is Futuristic Realistic?," *Variety* 394(4): 17, 20. November 16, 1992.

BRODMAN, MARIAN M.
___ "*Terra Mater-Luxuria* Iconography and the *Caradoc* Serpent Episode," *Quondam et Futurus* 2(3): 38-45. Fall 1992.

BROESKE, PAT H.
___ "Hollywood Goes Batty for Vampires," *New York Times* Sec. 2, p. 15, 22. April 26, 1992.

BROICH, ULRICH
___ "James Blish, **A Case of Conscience** (1958)," in: Heuermann, Harmut, ed. **Der Science Fiction Roman in der angloamerikanischen Literatur: Interpretationen**. Düsseldorf: Bagel, 1986. pp.166-181.

BROMWICH, RACHEL
___ "The **Tristan** of the Welsh," in: Bromwich, Rachel, Jarman, A. O. H., and Roberts, Brynley F., eds. **The Arthur of the Welsh**. Cardiff: University of Wales Press, 1991. pp.209-228.
___ "First Transmission to England and France," in: Bromwich, Rachel, Jarman, A. O. H., and Roberts, Brynley F., eds. **The Arthur of the Welsh**. Cardiff: University of Wales Press, 1991. pp.273-298.
___ (ed.) **The Arthur of the Welsh: The Arthurian Legend in Medieval Welsh Literature**, ed. by Rachel Bromwich, A. O. H. Jarman and Brynley F. Roberts. Cardiff: University of Wales Press, 1991. 310pp.

BROOKS, KATE
___ "Waiting for Dredd," by Martin Barker and Kate Brooks. *Sight and Sound* 5(8): 16-19. August 1995.

BROOKS, LAWRENCE
___ "**Stepfather III: Father's Day**," *Cinefantastique* 22(5): 22-23. April 1992.

BROSCH, ROBERT
___ **Horror Science Fiction Fantasy Movie Posters & Lobby Cards**. Allen Park, MI: Archival Photography, 1993. 79pp.

BROWN, BILL
___ "Science Fiction, the World's Fair, and the Prosthetics of Empire 1910-1915," in: Kaplan, Amy and Pease, Donald, eds. **Cultures of United States Imperialism**. Durham, NC: Duke University Press, 1993. pp.129-163.

BROWN, CARROLL
___ "The Flame in the Heart of the Wood: The Integration of Myth and Science in Robert Holdstock's **Mythago Wood**," *Extrapolation* 34(2): 158-172. Summer 1993.
___ "SFC Interviews: Robert Holdstock," *Science Fiction Chronicle* 16(2): 5, 44-48. November/December 1994.

BROWN, CHARLES N.
___ "1991 Magazine Summary," by Scott Winnett and Charles N. Brown. in: Brown, Charles N. and Contento, William G. **Science Fiction, Fantasy, & Horror: 1991**. Oakland, CA: Locus Press, 1992. pp.428-432.
___ "1992 Magazine Summary," by Scott Winnett and Charles N. Brown. *Locus* 30(2): 44-46. February 1993.
___ "1993 Book Summary," by Scott Winnett and Charles N. Brown. *Locus* 32(2): 43-45, 73-76. February 1994.
___ "1993 Magazine Summary," by Scott Winnett and Charles N. Brown. *Locus* 32(2): 44-48, 51. February 1994.
___ "25 Years of *Locus*," *Locus* 30(4): 34-35. April 1993.
___ "Hugo Awards Ceremony, 1995," *Locus* 35(4): 40-42. October 1995.
___ "NASFIC/Dragon Con," *Locus* 35(3): 50-51. September 1993.
___ **Science Fiction, Fantasy, & Horror: 1991**, by Charles N. Brown and William G. Contento. Oakland, CA: Locus Press, 1992. 482pp.

BROWN, DWIGHT
___ "The Cadigan Interviews: Interviews with, Yup, Pat Cadigan," *Nova Express* 3(1): 9-19. Fall 1989. (Whole No. 9)

BROWN, GILLIAN
___ "The Poetics of Extinction," in: Rosenheim, Shawn and Rachman, Stephen, ed. **The American Face of Edgar Allan Poe**. Baltimore: Johns Hopkins University Press, 1995. pp.330-344.

BROWN, GREGORY S.
___ "Critical Responses to Utopian Writings in the French Enlightenment: Three Periodicals as Case Studies," *Utopian Studies* 5(1): 48-71. 1994.

BROWN, JULIE
___ "Our Ladies of Perpetual Hell: Witches and Fantastic Virgins in Margaret Atwood's **Cat's Eye**," *Journal of the Fantastic in the Arts* 4(3): 40-52. 1991. (No. 15)

BROWN, MICHAEL
___ "Raising Hell With Peter Atkins," in: Brown, Michael, ed. **Pandemonium: Further Explorations into the Worlds of Clive Barker**. Staten Island, NY: Eclise, 1991. pp.27-42.
___ "Revelations: Barker on Barker," in: Brown, Michael, ed. **Pandemonium: Further Explorations into the Worlds of Clive Barker**. Staten Island, NY: Eclise, 1991. pp.5-26.
___ (ed.) **Pandemonium: Further Explorations into the Worlds of Clive Barker**. Staten Island, NY: Eclipse Books, 1991. 018, LIV pp.

BROWN, RICH
___ "Glossary of Fanspeak," by Joe L. Sanders and Rich Brown. in: Sanders, Joe, ed. **Science Fiction Fandom**. Westport, CT: Greenwood, 1994. pp.265-270.
___ "Post-Sputnik Fandom (1957-1990)," in: Sanders, Joe, ed. **Science Fiction Fandom**. Westport, CT: Greenwood, 1994. pp.75-102.
___ "Sci-Fi Unveils Schedule for September Debut," *Broadcasting* p. 21. July 20, 1992.

BROWN, TANYA
___ "This Immortal: Roger Zelazny (1937-1995)," *Vector* No. 184: 4-7. Summer 1995.

BROWNE, MALCOLM W.
___ "Chemists Succumb to Fantasy's Lure," *New York Times* p. 21. April 12, 1992.
___ "Dinosaurs Alive: High Tech Tricks Build *Jurassic Park*," *Austin (TX) American Statesman* Sec. B, p. 10. June 7, 1993.

BROWNE, MALCOLM W. (continued)
___ "Scientists Fret About *Jurassic Park* Message," *New York Times* p.B1. May 11, 1993.

BROWNING, TONYA J.
___ **Mapping the Unknown and Leaving No Footprints: Feminism and Hard Science Fiction.** Master's Report, The University of Texas at Austin, 1993. 87pp.

BROWNING, WILLIAM G.
___ **Anti-Utopian Fiction: Definition and Standards for Evaluation.** Ph.D. Dissertation, Louisiana State University, 1966. 145pp.

BROWNWORTH, VICTORIA A.
___ "Battling Back," *Lambda Book Report* 4(7): 6-7. November/ December 1994. [Not seen.]

BRUCCOLI, MATTHEW J.
___ "Raymond Chandler," in: Bruccoli, Matthew J., ed. **Facts on File Bibliography of American Fiction 1919-1988.** New York: Facts on File, 1991. pp.126-127.
___ (ed.) **Facts on File Bibliography of American Fiction 1919-1988**, ed. by Matthew J. Bruccoli and Judith S. Baughman. New York: Facts on File, 1991. 2 v.

BRUCE, MATTHEW H.
___ "Finding the Facts in Science Fiction Films," by Leroy W. Dubeck, Suzanne E. Moshier, Matthew H. Bruce and Judith E. Boss. *Science Teacher* 60(4): 46-48. April 1993.

BRUMLIK, JOAN
___ "The Knight, The Lady, and The Dwarf in Chrétien's **Erec**," *Quondam et Futurus* 2(2): 54-72. Summer 1992.

BRUNET, ROBIN
___ "Stay Tooned, Chuck Jones," *Cinefantastique* 23(2/3): 112-113. October 1992.
___ "**Stay Tuned**," *Cinefantastique* 23(1): 14-15. August 1992.
___ "**Timecop**," *Cinefantastique* 25(4): 14-15, 61. August 1994.
___ "**Timecop**," *Cinefantastique* 25(5): 6-7. October 1994.

BRUNNER, JOHN
___ "In Our Pharmaceutical Future, the Cure May Be Worse Than the Disease," *Science Fiction Age* 3(1): 34-40. November 1994.
___ "Sometime in the Recent Future...," *New Scientist* 138(1868): 28-31. April 10, 1993.
___ "Sometime in the Recent Future...," *Science Fiction Chronicle* 15(5): 30-31. March 1994.

BRUNSDALE, MITZI
___ **Dorothy L. Sayers: Solving the Mystery of Wickedness.** Dover, NH: Berg, 1991. 256pp.

BRUSCHINI, ANTONIO
___ **Mondi Incredibili: Il Cinema Fantastico-Avvneturoso Italiano,** by Antonio Bruschini and Antonio Tentori. Bologna: Granta Press, 1995. 173pp.

BRUZZI, STELLA
___ "Space Looks: Space Costumes," *Sight and Sound* 5(9): 10-11. September 1995.

BRYAN, ELIZABETH J.
___ "Truth and the Round Table in Lawman's **Brut**," *Quondam et Futurus* 2(4): 27-35. Winter 1992.

BRYANT, EDWARD
___ "King Richard, Conqueror of Space," *Science Fiction Age* 3(6): 82-87. September 1995.

BRYANT, ERIC
___ "*Century*," *Library Journal* 120(13): 127. August 1995.

BRZEZINSKI, ANTHONY
___ "Paulian Technique," *Futures Past* No. 3:33. September 1992.

BUARD, JEAN-LUC
___ "Verne's 'New' Novel," *Fantasy Commentator* 8(3/4): 269-273. Fall 1995. (Whole No. 47/48)

BUCHANAN, CARL
___ " 'The Music of Erich Zann': A Psychological Interpretation (Or Two)," *Lovecraft Studies* No. 27: 10-13. Fall 1992.
___ " 'The Outsider' as an Homage to Poe," *Lovecraft Studies* No. 31: 12-14. Fall 1994.
___ " 'The Terrible Old Man': A Myth of the Devouring Father," *Lovecraft Studies* No. 29: 19-30. Fall 1993. [Not seen.]

BUCK, JERRY
___ "*Star Trek* Opened Gates for McFadden," *Austin (TX) American Statesman. Show World* p. 8. July 12, 1992.

BUCKRICH, JUDITH R.
___ "Past, Future and Present: Australian Science Fiction; An Interview with Sean McMullen and Lucy Sussex," *Overland* (Australia) 133: 8-14. Summer 1993.

BUDD, LOUIS J.
___ (ed.) **On Poe: The Best From *American Literature***, ed. by Louis J. Budd and Edwin H. Cady. Durham, NC: Duke University Press, 1993. 270pp.

BUDRYS, ALGIS
___ "Naming Characters and Why," in: Wolverton, Dave, ed. **Writers of the Future, Vol. VIII.** Los Angeles, CA: Bridge, 1992. pp.107-111.
___ "Writing: The Basics," in: Thompkins, David G., ed. **Science Fiction Writer's Market Place and Source Book.** Cincinnati, OH: Writer's Digest Books, 1994. pp.14-17.
___ "Writing, Part 1: How to Do It," *Tomorrow: Speculative Fiction* 1(1): 36-.38 January 1993. [Not seen.]
___ "Writing, Part 2," *Tomorrow: Speculative Fiction* 1(2): 27-29. April 1993.
___ "Writing, Part 3," *Tomorrow: Speculative Fiction* 1(3): 32-33. July 1993.
___ "Writing, Part 4," *Tomorrow: Speculative Fiction* 1(4): 33-35. August 1993.
___ "Writing, Part 5," *Tomorrow: Speculative Fiction* 1(5): 23. October 1993.
___ "Writing, Part 6," *Tomorrow: Speculative Fiction* 1(6): 27-28. December 1993.
___ "Writing, Part 7: Agents; The Good, the Bad, and the Mediocre," *Tomorrow: Speculative Fiction* 2(1): 38-39. 1994. [Not seen; data supplied by Budrys.]
___ "Writing, Part 8," *Tomorrow: Speculative Fiction* 2(8): 77-79. April 1994.
___ "Writing, Part 9, Review," *Tomorrow: Speculative Fiction* 2(4): 61-62. August 1994. (No. 10)

BUETTNER, JOHN A.
___ "H. P. Lovecraft: The Mythos of Scientific Materialism," *Strange Magazine* No. 11: 8-9, 51. Spring/Summer 1993.

BUFALINO, JAMIE
___ "Coming on Strong," *TV Guide* 43(28): 16-18. July 16, 1995.

BUFFARD-O'SHEA, NICOLLE
___ "Boris Vian and the Literary Grotesque: The Animated Objects," in: Latham, Robert A. and Collins, Robert A., eds. **Modes of the Fantastic.** Westport, CT: Greenwood, 1995. pp.56-63.

BUFFINGTON, NANCY
___ "What About Bob? Doubles and Demons in *Twin Peaks*," in: Sanders, Joe, ed. **Functions of the Fantastic.** Westport, CT: Greenwood, 1995. pp.101-106.

BUFKIN, E. C.
___ "**The Spire**: The Image of the Book," in: Biles, Jack I. and Evans, Robert O., eds. **William Golding: Some Critical Considerations.** Lexington, KY: University Press of Kentucky, 1978. pp.136-150.

BUHLER, STEPHEN M.
___ " 'Who Calls Me Villian?': Blank Verse and the Black Hat," *Extrapolation* 36(1): 18-27. Spring 1995.

BUJOLD, LOIS M.
___ "Getting Started," in: Wolverton, Dave, ed. **Writers of the Future, Vol. VIII.** Los Angeles, CA: Bridge, 1992. pp.229-236.

BUKATMAN, SCOTT R.
___ "Amidst These Fields of Data: Allegory, Rhetoric, and the Paraspace," *Critique* 33(3): 199-219. Spring 1992.
___ "Bataille y la nueva carnalidad," *Revista de Occidente* No. 153: 113-140. 1994.
___ "Fractal Geographies," *Artforum* 31(4): 6-7. December 1992.
___ "Gibson's Typewriter," *South Atlantic Quarterly* 92(4): 627-645. Fall 1993.
___ **Terminal Identity: The Virtual Subject in Postmodern Science Fiction.** Durham, NC: Duke University Press, 1993. 404pp.
___ **Terminal Identity: The Virtual Subject in Postmodern Science Fiction.** Ph.D. Dissertation, New York University, 1992. 492pp. (DAI-A 53/08, p. 2579. February 1993.)

BULGER, THOMAS
___ "The Utopic Structure of **The Tempest**," *Utopian Studies* 5(1): 38-47. 1994.

BULL, GEOFF
___ "Morning Comes Whether You Set the Alarm or Not: Science Fiction, a Genre for the Future," *Orana* (Australia) 31(3): 159-169. August 1995.

BULLARD, THOMAS E.
___ "UFO Abduction Reports: The Supernatural Kidnap Narrative Returns in Technological Guise," *Journal of American Folklore* 102(404): 147-170. April/June 1989.

BULLARO, GRACE R.
___ "**Blade Runner**: The Subversion and Redefinition of Catagories," *Riverside Quarterly* 9(2): 102-108. August 1993. (Whole No. 34)

BULYCHEV, KIR
___ "Letter From Moscow," *Locus* 28(2): 47-48. August 1992.
___ "Letter From Moscow," *Locus* 30(4): 41-43, 62. April 1993.
___ "Letter From Moscow," *Locus* 31(6): 37-38, 44. December 1993.

BUMAS, E. SHASKAN
___ "The Utopian States of America: The People, the Republic, and Rock and Roll in Thomas Pynchon's **Vineland**," *Arizona Quarterly* 51(3): 149-175. Autumn 1995.

BUNCUGA, FRANCO
___ "Amargi o la Natura Madre," in: Saccaro Del Buffa, Giuseppa and Lewis, Arthur O., eds. **Utopia e Modernita: Teorie e prassi utopiche nell'eta moderna e postmoderna.** Rome: Gangemi Editore, 1989. pp.87-94.
___ "Utopia totale e territorio," in: Saccaro Del Buffa, Giuseppa and Lewis, Arthur O., eds. **Utopie per gli Anni Ottana.** Rome: Gangemi Editore, 1986. pp.369-378.

BUNNELL, JOHN C.
___ "Copyright Notices: Threat or Menace?," *SFWA Bulletin* 26(4): 7-9. Winter 1993. (No. 118)

BUNSON, MATTHEW
___ **The Vampire Encyclopedia.** New York: Crown, 1993. 303pp.

BURDEN, MARTIN
___ "After 390 Books, Sci-Fi's Isaac Asimov Tries a Movie," in: *NewsBank. Literature* LIT 56: C4-C5. 1988.
___ "Boys and a Hood (Review)," *New York (NY) Post.* February 21, 1992. in: *NewsBank. Film and Television.* 24:G7. 1992.
___ "Current Event Tale Fizzles (Review)," *New York (NY) Post.* January 29, 1992. in: *NewsBank. Film and Television.* 12:A13. 1992.
___ "The Cutting Edge for Sci-Fi Fans (Review)," *New York (NY) Post.* March 6, 1992. in: *NewsBank. Film and Television.* 43:A11. 1992.
___ "**Encino Man** Belongs Back on Ice (Review)," *New York (NY) Post.* May 22, 1992. in: *NewsBank. Film and Television.* 52:D2. 1992.
___ "**Invisible** Sight Gags (Review)," *New York (NY) Post.* February 28, 1992. in: *NewsBank. Film and Television.* 23:D9. 1992.

BURELBACK, FREDERICK M.
___ "Totemic Animals in Some Shakespeare Plays," in: Latham, Robert A. and Collins, Robert A., eds. **Modes of the Fantastic.** Westport, CT: Greenwood, 1995. pp.155-160.

BURGER, PHILLIP R.
___ "ERB and the Educated Man: A Reply," *Burroughs Bulletin* NS. No. 24: 15-17. October 1995.
___ **Glimpses of a World Past: Edgar Rice Burroughs, the West, and the Birth of an American Writer.** Master's Thesis, Utah State University, 1987. 158pp.
___ "Knocking About the Neocene: Some Thoughts on **The Eternal Lover**," *Burroughs Bulletin* NS. No. 12: 3-9. October 1992.
___ "Mesas, Mormons, and Martians: The Possible Origins of Barsoomian History," *Burroughs Bulletin* NS. No. 16: 3-7. October 1993.
___ "Of Burroughs and Businessmen," *Burroughs Bulletin* NS. No. 18: 12-15. April 1994.
___ "Whatever Happened to Perry Rhodan, Riding the Space Trails Alone?," *Burroughs Bulletin* NS. No. 22: 12-17. April 1995.
___ " 'Whatever It Is It Gets You and Me': Some Thoughts on **The Return of the Mucker**," *Burroughs Bulletin* NS No. 10: 3-7. April 1992.

BURGESS, ANTHONY
___ "Ingsoc Considered," in: Bloom, Harold, ed. **George Orwell's 1984.** New York: Chelsea House, 1987. pp.35-46.

BURGESS, MARY A.
___ **The Work of Katherine Kurtz: An Annotated Bibliography & Guide,** by Boden Clarke and Mary A. Burgess. San Bernardino, CA: Borgo Press, 1993. 128pp.

BURGESS, MICHAEL
___ **Reference Guide to Science Fiction, Fantasy, and Horror.** Littleton, CO: Libraries Unlimited, 1992. 403pp.
___ **The Work of Robert Reginald: An Annotated Bibliography and Guide** 2nd ed., revised and enlarged. San Bernardino, CA: Borgo Press, 1992. 176pp.

BURGESS, THOMAS
___ **Take Me Under the Sea: The Dream Merchants of the Deep.** Salem, OR: Ocean Archives, 1994. 259pp.

BURGHEIM, MANFRED G.
___ "Philip K. Dicks **Ubik** und Thomas Pynchons **Die Versteigerung von No. 49**: Zwei romane, ein epistemologisches Modell," *Quarber Merkur* 33(2): 25-29. December 1995. (No. 84)

BURKE, RUSTY
___ "The Active Voice: Robert E. Howard's Personae," *The Dark Man: The Journal of Robert E. Howard Studies* No. 3: 22-26. April 1993.
___ "The Old Deserted House: Images of the South in Howard's Fiction," *The Dark Man: The Journal of Robert E. Howard Studies* No. 2: 13-22. July 1991.

BURLESON, DONALD R.
___ "Bierce's 'The Damned Thing': A Nietzschean Allegory," *Studies in Weird Fiction* No. 13: 8-10. Summer 1993. [Not seen.]
___ "Connings: Bradbury/Oates," *Studies in Weird Fiction* No. 11: 24-29. Spring 1992.
___ "Irony and Self-Difference in Robert Bloch's 'Beetles'," *Studies in Weird Fiction* No. 16: 25-28. Winter 1995.
___ "Lovecraft and Adjectivitis: A Deconstructionist View," *Lovecraft Studies* No. 31: 22-24. Fall 1994.
___ "Lovecraft and Gender," *Lovecraft Studies* No. 27: 21-25. Fall 1992.
___ "Lovecraft: Textual Keys," *Lovecraft Studies* No. 32: 27-30. Spring 1995.
___ "Lovecraft's **The Color out of Space**," *Explicator* 52(1): 48-50. Fall 1993.
___ "Lovecraft's 'The Unknown': A Sort of Runic Rhyme," *Lovecraft Studies* No. 26: 19-21. Spring 1992.
___ " 'Midnight Express': Alfred Noyes at the Borderlands of Self-Reference," *Studies in Weird Fiction* No. 17: 18-22. Summer 1995.
___ "On Dunsany's 'Probable Adventure of the Three Literary Men'," *Studies in Weird Fiction* No. 10: 23-26. Fall 1991.
___ "On Lovecraft's 'The Ancient Track'," *Lovecraft Studies* No. 28: 17-20. Fall 1992.

BURLESON, DONALD R.

CAINE, BARRY

BURLESON, DONALD R. (continued)
___ "On Mary Elizabeth Counselman's 'Twister'," *Studies in Weird Fiction* No. 15: 16-18. Summer 1994.
___ "Prismatic Heroes: The Colour out of Dunwich," *Lovecraft Studies* No. 25: 13-18. Fall 1991.
___ "Providence and Lovecraft's Fiction," in: Joshi, S. T., ed. **The H. P. Lovecraft Centennial Conference Proceedings**. West Warwick, RI: Necronomicon, 1991. pp.10-12.
___ "Sabbats: Hawthorne/Wharton," *Studies in Weird Fiction* No. 12: 12-16. Spring 1993.
___ "Scansion Problems in Lovecraft's 'Mirage'," *Lovecraft Studies* No. 24: 18-19, 21. Spring 1991.
___ "The Thing: On the Doorstep," *Lovecraft Studies* No. 33: 14-18. Fall 1995.

BURLESON, MOLLIE L.
___ "Edith Wharton's Summer: Through the Glass Darkly," *Studies in Weird Fiction* No. 13: 18-20. Summer 1993. [Not seen.]
___ "Mirror, Mirror: Sylvia Plath's 'Mirror' and Lovecraft's 'The Outsider'," *Lovecraft Studies* No. 31: 10-12. Fall 1994.

BURMEISTER, KLAUS
___ (ed.) **Streifzüge ins Übermorgen: Science Fiction und Zukunftsforschung**, ed. by Klaus Burmeister and Karlheinz Steinmüller. Weinheim: Beltz, 1992. 328pp.

BURNETT, CATHY
___ (ed.) **Spectrum: The Best in Contemporary Fantastic Art (First Annual Collection)**, ed. by Cathy Burnett, Arnie Fenner and Jim Loehr. Grass Valley, CA: Underwood Books, 1994. 204pp.

BURNFIELD, STEVE
___ "The Butt From Another Planet," *New York (NY) Post*. May 3, 1994. in: *NewsBank. Film and Television*. 58:G2. 1994.

BURNS, CRAIG W.
___ " 'It's That Time of the Month': Representations of the Goddess in the Work of Clive Barker," *Journal of Popular Culture* 27(3): 35-40. Winter 1993.

BURNS, GRANT
___ **The Nuclear Present: A Guide to Recent Books on Nuclear War, Weapons, the Peace Movement, and Related Issues, With a Chronology of Nuclear Events, 1789-1991**. Metuchen, NJ: Scarecrow, 1992. 654pp.

BURNS, JOHN E.
___ "One for the Books: Using Literature-Based Science Lessons," *Science Teacher* 61(7): 38-41. October 1994.

BURNS, JOHN F.
___ "A Science Fiction Writer's Long-ago Voyage to a Quieter World, Far Away," *New York Times* p. A4. November 28, 1994.

BURNS, KEITH
___ (ed.) **Graven Images: The Best of Horror, Fantasy, and Science Fiction Film Art from the Collection of Ronald V. Borst**, ed. by Ronald V. Borst, Keith Burns and Leith Adams. New York: Grove Press, 1992. 240pp.

BURNS, MARJORIE J.
___ "Eating, Devouring, Sacrifice and Ultimate Just Desserts," in: Reynolds, Patricia and GoodKnight, Glen H., eds. **Proceedings of the J. R. R. Tolkien Centenary Conference, Keble College, Oxford, 1992**. Altadena, CA: Mythopoeic Press, 1995. pp.108-114. (*Mythlore* Vol. 21, No. 2, Winter 1996, Whole No. 80)
___ "Echoes of William Morris's **Icelandic Journals** in J. R. R. Tolkien," *Studies in Medievalism* 3(3): 367-373. Winter 1991.

BURNSON, PATRICK
___ "In the Studio With Laurence Yep," *Publishers Weekly* 241(20): 25-26. May 16, 1994.

BURRELL, EVEREIT
___ "The Alien Masters of **Babylon 5**," by John Vulich and Evereit Burrell. *Sci-Fi Entertainment* 1(2): 38-42. August 1994.

BUSBY, F. M.
___ "Fan Clubs: An Example," in: Sanders, Joe, ed. **Science Fiction Fandom**. Westport, CT: Greenwood, 1994. pp.143-148.

BUSBY, KEITH
___ (ed.) **The Arthurian Yearbook I**. New York: Garland, 1991. 234pp.

BUSBY, LAURIE
___ "Serling's Intensity Drove Him into a Twilight Zone in His Personal Life," *Santa Ana (CA) Orange County Register*. November 26, 1992. in: *NewsBank. Film and Television*. 118:G10. 1992.

BUSCHINGER, DANIELLE
___ "Les Problèmes de la Traduction des Textes Médiévaux Allemands dans les Langues Modernes," *Arthuriana* 4(3): 224-232. Fall 1994.

BUTKO, TATIANA
___ "**X-Files** Fans Gather at Pasadena Center," *San Gabriel Valley Tribune (West Covina, CA)*. August 27, 1995. in: *NewsBank. Film and Television*. 82:F4. 1995.

BUTLER, ANDREW M.
___ "You Know, You Might As Well Give Up Now," *Focus* (BSFA) No. 27: 7. December 1994/January 1995.

BUTLER, DAVID W.
___ "Usher's Hypochondriasis: Mental Alienation and Romantic Idealism in Poe's Gothic Tales (1976)," in: Budd, Louis J. and Cady, Edwin H., eds. **On Poe**. Durham, NC: Duke University Press, 1993. pp.185-196.

BUTSCH, RICHARD J.
___ **Personal Perception in Scientific and Medieval World Views: A Comparative Study of Fantasy Literature**. Ph.D. Dissertation, Rutgers University, 1975. 95pp. (DAI 35: 2518B.)

BUTVIN, SUSAN M.
___ "**The Final Encyclopedia** Gordon R. Dickson's Creative Universe," *Extrapolation* 36(4): 360-368. Winter 1995.

BYFIELD, BRUCE
___ "Fritz Leiber," in: Bruccoli, Matthew J., ed. **Facts on File Bibliography of American Fiction 1919-1988**. New York: Facts on File, 1991. pp.291-292.

CADDEN, MICHAEL
___ "The Illusion of Control: Narrative Authority in Robin McKinley's **Beauty** and **The Blue Sword**," *Mythlore* 20(2): 16-19, 31. Spring 1994. (Whole No. 76)

CADORA, KAREN
___ "Feminist Cyberpunk," *Science Fiction Studies* 22(3): 357-372. November 1995

CADY, DICK
___ "Instinct Overdoes the Thrills and Kills," *Indianapolis (IN) Star* March 20, 1992 in: *NewsBank. Film and Television*. 29:B4-B5. 1992.

CADY, EDWIN H.
___ (ed.) **On Poe: The Best From *American Literature***, ed. by Louis J. Budd and Edwin H. Cady. Durham, NC: Duke University Press, 1993. 270pp.

CAERWYN WILLIAMS, J. E.
___ "Brittany and the Arthurian Legend," in: Bromwich, Rachel, Jarman, A. O. H., and Roberts, Brynley F., eds. **The Arthur of the Welsh**. Cardiff: University of Wales Press, 1991. pp.249-272.

CAHIR, LINDA C.
___ "Narratological Parallels in Joseph Conrad's **Heart of Darkness** and Francis Ford Coppola's **Apocalypse Now**," *Literature/Film Quarterly* 20(3): 181-187. 1992.

CAINE, BARRY
___ "**No Escape** Full of Comic-Book Action, Violence," *Oakland (CA) Tribune*. April 29, 1994. in: *NewsBank. Film and Television*. 58:A9. 1994.

CAINE, BARRY (continued)
___ "Stallone's **Demolition Man** Pretty Bizarre, But Fascinating (Review)," *Oakland (CA) Tribune* October 9, 1993. in: *NewsBank. Film and Television.* 114:G5-G6. 1993.
___ "**Timecop** Isn't Great, But It Has It's Moments," *Oakland (CA) Tribune.* September 16, 1994. in: *NewsBank. Film and Television.* 105: C5. 1994.

CALCAGNO, GIAN C.
___ "Ingegneria genetica, famiglia, utopia," in: Colombo, Arrigo and Quarta, Cosimo, eds. **Il Destino della Famiglia nell'Utopia**. Bari: Edizione Dedalo, 1991. pp.405-432.

CALCRAFT, L. G. A.
___ "Aldous Huxley and the Sheldonian Hypothesis," *Annals of Science* 37657-671. 1980.

CALDWELL, LARRY W.
___ "Wells, Orwell, and Atwood: (EPI)Logic and Eu/Utopia," *Extrapolation* 33(4): 333-345. Winter 1992.

CALFEE-MOYE, ROBIN
___ "Rediscovery and Exploration: The Legend of Prince Madoc ap Owain Gwynedd," *Journal of the Fantastic in the Arts* 5(3): 85-97. 1993. (No. 19)

CALHOUN, JOHN
___ "**The Journey Inside**," *TCI* 28(8): 78. October 1994.

CALLAHAN, TIM
___ "Censoring the World Riddle," *Mythlore* 20(1): 15-21. Winter 1994. (Whole No. 75)

CAMERON, ELEANOR
___ "**The Owl Service**: A Study," *Wilson Library Bulletin* 44(4): 425-433. December 1969.

CAMERON, JAMES
___ "Effects Scene: Technology and Magic," *Cinefex* No. 51: 5-7. August 1992.

CAMINERO-SANTANGELO, MARTA
___ "Moving Beyond 'The Blank White Spaces': Atwood's Gilead, Postmodernism, and Strategic Resistance," *Studies in Canadian Literature* 19(1): 20-42. 1994.

CAMMAROTA, RICHARD S.
___ "**The Spire**: A Symbolic Analysis," in: Biles, Jack I. and Evans, Robert O., eds. **William Golding: Some Critical Considerations**. Lexington, KY: University Press of Kentucky, 1978. pp.151-175.

CAMPBELL, BOB
___ "**Afraid of the Dark** Suffers Double Vision," *Newark (NJ) Star-Ledger.* July 24, 1992. in: *NewsBank. Film and Television.* 67:B1. 1992.
___ "**Alien 3** Environment Is No More Healthy for Humans This Time Around," *Newark (NJ) Star-Ledger.* May 22, 1992. in: *NewsBank. Film and Television.* 49:C7-C8. 1992.
___ "**Basic Instinct** More Kinky Than Primal Thriller," *Newark (NJ) Star-Ledger* March 20, 1992 in: *NewsBank. Film and Television.* 29:B9-B10. 1992.
___ "**Bram Stoker's Dracula** a Shocker to Count On," *Newark (NJ) Star-Ledger.* November 13, 1992. in: *NewsBank. Film and Television.* 111: B9. 1992.
___ "Brooding Teen Turns into Mega Hitman on Computer," *(Newark, NJ) Star-Ledger.* April 22, 1994. in: *NewsBank. Film and Television.* 41: B8. 1994.
___ "**Buffy the Vampire Slayer** Plays Its Horror Tooth in Cheek as Wry Reanimated Feature," *Newark (NJ) Star-Ledger.* July 31, 1992. in: *NewsBank. Film and Television.* 68:A12. 1992
___ "Confused **Radio Flyer** Lands Short of Runway (Review)," *Newark (NJ) Star-Ledger.* February 21, 1992. in: *NewsBank. Film and Television.* 24:G6. 1992.
___ "Dauntless Captain Kirk Claims Humor Has Kept Starship *Enterprise* in Orbit," *Newark (NJ) Star-Ledger.* December 15, 1991. in: *NewsBank. Film and Television.* 7:A12-A13. 1992.

CAMPBELL, BOB (continued)
___ "**Death Becomes Her** Falls Victim to Overkill (Review)," *Newark (NJ) Star-Ledger.* July 31, 1992. in: *NewsBank. Film and Television.* 68:G2. 1992.
___ "**Demolition Man** Self Destructs Before Our Eyes (Review)," *Newark (NJ) Star-Ledger* October 8, 1993. in: *NewsBank. Art.* 28:B14. 1993.
___ "Disney Fashions a Tall Tale for Little Ones In High-Giggle **Honey, I Blew Up the Kid** (Review)," *Newark (NJ) Star-Ledger.* July 17, 1992. in: *NewsBank. Film and Television.* 70:E2. 1992.
___ "A Dizzy, Dire Delirium Puts Mind-Blowing Spin on De Palma's **Raising Cain** (Review)," *Newark (NJ) Star-Ledger.* August 7, 1992. in: *NewsBank. Film and Television.* 83:A14. 1992.
___ "GI Corpse Tries to Escape Second Hitch as Robot Soldier (Review)," *Newark (NJ) Star-Ledger.* July 10, 1992. in: *NewsBank. Film and Television.* 74:G6. 1992.
___ "Grisly **Army of Darkness**: A Medieval Monster Mash," *Newark (NJ) Star-Ledger.* February 19, 1993 in: *NewsBank. Film and Television.* 30: D13. 1993
___ "H2 Uh-Oh," *(Newark, NJ) Star-Ledger.* July 28, 1995. in: *NewsBank. Film and Television.* 72:G2. 1995.
___ "Heinlein's Vintage Sci-Fi Still Gives the Chills," *(Newark, NJ) Star-Ledger.* October 21, 1994. in: *NewsBank. Film and Television.* 124:B10. 1994.
___ "Invisible Man Fantasies Have Seen Better Days (Review)," *Newark (NJ) Star Ledger.* February 28, 1992. in: *NewsBank. Film and Television.* 23:D8. 1992.
___ "Jagger's Edge Sharpens Dull Script of **Freejack** (Review)," *Newark (NJ) Star-Ledger.* January 21, 1992. in: *NewsBank. Film and Television.* 11:D9. 1992.
___ "**Johnny Mnemonic** Plays Mind Games in Cyberspace," *(Newark, NJ) Star-Ledger.* May 26, 1995. in: *NewsBank. Film and Television.* 55: B6. 1995.
___ "Jokey Creepshow Guilty of Cinematic Malpractice (Review)," *Newark (NJ) Star-Ledger.* October 27, 1992. in: *NewsBank. Film and Television.* 101:A3. 1992.
___ "Latest Star Trek Mission to Save the World (or 2)," *(Newark, NJ) Star-Ledger.* November 18, 1994. in: *NewsBank. Film and Television.* 125:D7. 1994.
___ "**Meteor Man** a Starry-Eyed Ghetto Fantasy (Review)," *Newark (NJ) Star-Ledger.* August 6, 1993. in: *NewsBank. Art.* 18:E3. 1993.
___ "Modern Fairy Tale's a Rehumanizing Experience (Review)," *Newark (NJ) Star-Ledger.* July 10, 1992. in: *NewsBank. Film and Television.* 73:C10. 1992.
___ "**No Escape** Traps Itself in Outdated Sci-Fi Plot," *(Newark, NJ) Star-Ledger.* April 29, 1994. in: *NewsBank. Film and Television.* 46:E6. 1994.
___ "No Laughs to Be Seen in **Invisible Man**; It's Depressingly Dull (Review)," *Minneapolis (MN) Star and Tribune.* February 28, 1992. in: *NewsBank. Film and Television.* 23:D7. 1992.
___ "Not Creepy Enough to Be a Classic," *Newark (NJ) Star-Ledger.* February 4, 1994. in: *NewsBank. Film and Television.* 21: B14. 1994.
___ "Redford and Company Keep **Sneakers** in Stride (Review)," *Newark (NJ) Star-Ledger.* September 11, 1992. in: *NewsBank. Film and Television.* 96:D8. 1992.
___ "Review," *Newark (NJ) Star-Ledger.* July 29, 1992. in: *NewsBank. Film and Television.* 72:B8. 1992.
___ "Sci-Fi Cop Tries to Change the 'Curse' of History," *(Newark, NJ) Star-Ledger.* September 17, 1994. in: *NewsBank. Film and Television.* 105:D5. 1994.
___ "Spacey Sci-Fi Odyssey Is Metaphysically Far Out (Review)," *Newark (NJ) Star-Ledger.* December 26, 1991. in: *NewsBank. Film and Television.* 8:E5. 1992.
___ "**Stargate** Version of Sci-Fi an Earthbound Melodrama," *Newark (NJ) Star-Ledger.* October 28, 1994. in: *NewsBank. Film and Television.* 115: G13. 1994.
___ "Stodgy, Droning Parody," *(Newark, NJ) Star-Ledger.* June 30, 1995. in: *NewsBank. Film and Television.* 63:A14. 1995.
___ "**Tank Girl** Comes Loaded With Macho Swagger," *(Newark, NJ) Star-Ledger.* March 31, 1995. in: *NewsBank. Film and Television.* 38: G14. 1995.

CAMPBELL, JOHN W.
___ **Collected Editorial From Analog**. Garden City, NY: Doubleday, 1996. 251pp.

CAMPBELL, LAURA E.
___ "Dickian Time in **The Man in the High Castle**," *Extrapolation* 33(3): 190-201. Fall 1992.

CAMPBELL, PATTY
___ "The Sand in the Oyster," *Horn Book* 70(2): 234-238. March/April 1994.

CAMPBELL, RAMSEY
___ "Notes Towards a Reappraisal," in: Jones, Stephen, ed. **James Herbert: By Horror Haunted**. London: New English Library, 1992. pp.289-298.
___ "The Quality of Terror," in: Golden, Christopher, ed. **Cut! Horror Writers on Horror Film**. New York: Berkley, 1992. pp.67-74.

CANAAN, HOWARD
___ "All Hell into His Knapsack: The Spirit of Play in Two Fairy Tales," *Mythlore* 19(4): 41-45. Autumn 1993. (No. 74)

CANNADY, MARILYN
___ **Bigger Than Life: The Creator of Doc Savage**. Bowling Green, OH: Popular Press, 1990. 201pp.

CANNON, JOANN
___ "Literary Signification: An Analysis of Calvino's Trilogy," *Symposium* 34(1): 3-12. Spring 1980.

CANNON, PETER
___ "Frank Belknap Long: When Was He Born and Why Was Lovecraft Wrong?," *Studies in Weird Fiction* No. 17: 33-34. Summer 1995.

CANTO, CHRISTOPHE
___ **The History of the Future: Images of the 21st Century**, by Christophe Canto and Odile Faliu. New York and Paris: Flammarion, 1993. 159pp.

CANTOR, JOANNE
___ "Children's Emotional Reactions to Technological Disasters Conveyed by the Mass Media," in: Wober, J. Mallory, ed. **Television and Nuclear Power: Making the Public Mind**. Norwood, NJ: Ablex, 1992. pp.31-54.

CANTOR, NORMAN F.
___ **Inventing the Middle Ages: The Lives, Works and Ideas of the Great Medievalists of the Twentieth Century**. New York: Morrow, 1991. 477pp.

CANTU, FRANCESCA
___ "Scoperta del nuovo Mondo e visiione utopica nel cinquecento," in: Saccaro Del Buffa, Giuseppa and Lewis, Arthur O., eds. **Utopia e Modernita: Teorie e prassi utopiche nell'eta moderna e postmoderna**. Rome: Gangemi Editore, 1989. pp.749-775.

CANTY, JOAN F.
___ **Does Eugenics = (E)utopia?: Reproductive Control and Ethical Issues in Contemporary North American Feminist Fabulation**. Master's Thesis, California State University, Stanislaus, 1995. 97pp.

CAPANNA, PABLO
___ **El mundo de la ciencia ficcion: Sentido e historia**. Buenos Aires: Ediciones Letra Buena, 1992. 192pp.

CAPASSO, RUTH C.
___ "Islands of Felicity: Women Seeing Utopia in Seventeenth Century France," in: Donawerth, Jane L. and Kolmerten, Carol A., eds. **Utopian and Science Fiction by Women: Worlds of Difference**. Syracuse, NY: Syracuse University Press, 1994. pp.35-53.

CAPEK, KAREL
___ "Edgar Allan Poe: The Unparalleled Adventure of One Hans Pfall," *Studies in Weird Fiction* No. 14: 8-9. Winter 1994.

CAPONE, GLAUCO
___ "L'annunzio evangelico," in: Colombo, Arrigo and Quarta, Cosimo, eds. **Il Destino della Famiglia nell'Utopia**. Bari: Edizione Dedalo, 1991. pp.49-78.

CAPPIO, JAMES
___ "A Long Guide to K. W. Jeter," *New York Review of Science Fiction* No. 44: 1, 8-14. April 1992.

CAPUTI, ANTHONY
___ "The Refrain in Poe's Poetry (1953)," in: Budd, Louis J. and Cady, Edwin H., eds. **On Poe**. Durham, NC: Duke University Press, 1993. pp.92-101.

CAPUTI, JANE
___ "Films of the Nuclear Age," *Journal of Popular Film and Television* 16(3): 100-107. 1988.

CARD, ORSON S.
___ "Characters in Science Fiction," in: Thompkins, David G., ed. **Science Fiction Writer's Market Place and Source Book**. Cincinnati, OH: Writer's Digest Books, 1994. pp.18-24.

CARDUCCI, MARK
___ "**Ed Wood** Cult Legend," *Cinefantastique* 25(5): 20-45. October 1994.
___ "**Ed Wood**: Deadringer for Tor," *Cinefantastique* 25(5): 26-27. October 1994.
___ "**Ed Wood**: Flying Saucer Myths," *Cinefantastique* 25(5): 31. October 1994.
___ "**Ed Wood**: Hollywood Rat Race," *Cinefantastique* 25(5): 38-39. October 1994.
___ "**Ed Wood**: Makeup," *Cinefantastique* 25(5): 28-29, 61. October 1994.
___ "**Ed Wood**," *Cinefantastique* 25(2): 4-5. April 1994.

CARDWELL, ANNETTE
___ "Positive Message Found in **Powder**," *Boston (MA) Herald*. October 27, 1995. in: *NewsBank. Film and Television*. 97:F14. 1995.

CARETTI, VINCENZO
___ "Ronald Laing e la demistificazione della famiglia interiorizzata," in: Colombo, Arrigo and Quarta, Cosimo, eds. **Il Destino della Famiglia nell'Utopia**. Bari: Edizione Dedalo, 1991. pp.309-320.

CARLIN, RUSSELL
___ "The Hero Who Was Thursday: A Modern Myth," *Mythlore* 19(3): 27-30. Summer 1993. (No. 73)

CARLSON, RICHARD C.
___ **2020 Visions: Long View of a Changing World**, by Richard C. Carlson and Bruce Goldman. Stanford, CA: Stanford Alumni Association, 1991. 252pp.

CARLSON, TIMOTHY
___ "The Universe Is Expanding All over the Dial," by Timothy Carlson and Mark Schwed. *TV Guide* 41(1): 16-19. January 2, 1993. (Issue 2075)

CARMAN, TIM
___ "Van Damme's **Timecop** Is Fast, Dumb, So Don't Dare Blink and Don't Dare Think," *Houston (TX) Post*. September 16, 1994. in: *NewsBank. Film and Television*. 105:D10. 1994.

CARMODY, DEIRDRE
___ "Dell Buys Four Noted Fiction Magazines," *New York Times* Sec. D, p. 5. January 24, 1992.

CARONE, DANIEL
___ "Roddenberry Spirit Molds Latest Spinoff, **Deep Space Nine**," *Austin (TX) American Statesman* Sec. B, p. 4. January 5, 1993.

CARPENTER, PHIL
___ "Commercial Spot: Cola Bears," *Cinefex* No. 60: 27-28. December 1994.
___ "Commercial Spot: Sci-Fi Pest Control," *Cinefex* No. 53: 73-74. February 1993.
___ "**Robocop** Redux," *Cinefex* No. 56: 70-83. November 1993.

CARPENTER, SHERILEE R.
___ "The Re-Emergence of a Feminine and Feminist Mythology in Women's Utopias," in: Saccaro Del Buffa, Giuseppa and Lewis, Arthur O., eds. **Utopie per gli Anni Ottana**. Rome: Gangemi Editore, 1986. pp.477-488.

CARR, JAY
___ "A Walk on the Wired Side," *Boston (MA) Globe*. October 13, 1995. in: *NewsBank. Film and Television*. 99:C7-C8. 1995.

CARRERE, EMMANUEL
___ **Je suis vivant et vous etes morts: Philip K. Dick, 1928-1982**. Paris: Editions du Seuil, 1993. 358pp.

CARROLL, JERRY
___ "Sci-Fi Is Big Business," *San Francisco (CA) Chronicle* December 17, 1994. (Cited from the Internet Edition.)
___ "Tapping Dickens for Clues for the Future: New Sci-Fi Master Neal Stephenson Pens a Follow-Up to Cult Hit **Snow Crash**," *San Francisco (CA) Chronicle* February 1, 1995. (Cited from the Internet edition.)

CARTER, CASSIE
___ "The Metacolonization of Dick's **The Man in the High Castle**: Mimicry, Parasitism, and Americanism in the PSA," *Science Fiction Studies* 22(3): 333-342. November 1995

CARTER, GARY M.
___ **The Overstreet Comic Book Grading Guide**. First edition, by Robert M. Overstreet and Gary M. Carter. New York: Avon, 1992. 303pp.

CARTER, LIN
___ **Lovecraft: A Look Behind the Cthulhu Mythos; The Background of a Myth That Has Captured a Generation**. San Bernardino, CA: Borgo Press, 1992. 198pp.

CARTER, PAUL A.
___ "From 'Nat' to 'Nathan': The Liberal Arts Odyssey of a Pulpmaster," in: Slusser, George E. and Rabkin, Eric S., eds. **Styles of Creation: Aesthetic Technique and the Creation of Fictional Worlds**. Athens: University of Georgia Press, 1992. pp.58-78.
___ "From the Golden Age to the Atomic Age: 1940-1963," in: Barron, Neil, ed. **Anatomy of Wonder 4**. New York: Bowker, 1995. pp.115-221.

CARTER, REON
___ "Holy Cow! **Batman** Booty Is Here Again," *Cincinnati (OH) Enquirer*. June 11, 1992. in: *NewsBank. Film and Television*. 62:E2. 1992.

CARTER, STEVEN
___ "Avatars of the Turtles," *Journal of Popular Film and Television* 18(3): 94-102. 1990.

CARTIER, EDD
___ "Notes to the New Artist," in: Wolverton, Dave, ed. **Writers of the Future, Vol. VIII**. Los Angeles, CA: Bridge, 1992. pp.167-175.

CARTON, SHARON
___ "The Law of the Federation: Images of Law, Lawyers, and the Legal System in **Star Trek: The Next Generation**," by Paul Joseph and Sharon Carton. *University of Toledo Law Review* 24(1): 43-85. Fall 1992.
___ "Perry Mason in Space: A Call for More Inventive Lawyers in Television Science Fiction Series," by Paul Joseph and Sharon Carton. in: Wolf, Milton T. and Mallett, Daryl F., eds. **Imaginative Futures: Proceedings of the 1993 Science Fiction Research Association Conference**. San Bernardino, CA: Jacob's Ladder Books, 1995. pp.307-318.

CARY, CATIE
___ "Brian Stableford Interviewed," *Vector* No. 172: 6-10. April/May 1993.
___ "A Conversation With Graham Joyce," *Vector* No. 180: 5-11. August/September 1994.
___ "Katharine Kerr Interviewed," *Vector* No. 168: 16. August/September 1992.
___ "Magic in the Real World: Lisa Tuttle Interviewed," *Vector* No. 168: 16-19. August/September 1992.
___ "Robert Holdstock: Interviewed," *Vector* No. 175: 3-6. October/November 1993.

CASEBEER, EDWIN F.
___ "Dialogue Within the Archetypal Community of **The Stand**," in: Magistrale, Tony, ed. **A Casebook on The Stand**. San Bernardino, CA: Borgo Press, 1992. pp.173-188.
___ "The Ecological System of Stephen King's **The Dark Half**," *Journal of the Fantastic in the Arts* 6(2/3): 126-142. 1994.
___ "The Three Genres of **The Stand**," in: Magistrale, Tony, ed. **The Dark Descent: Essays Defining Stephen King's Horrorscape**. Westport, CT: Greenwood, 1992. pp.47-59.

CASELLA, ELAINE
___ "Apeman, Arab, Ancient Alien: A Synopsis of Gene Roddenberry's Tarzan Script," *Burroughs Bulletin* NS. No. 22: 26-31. April 1995.
___ "A Lion Is Still a Lion," *Burroughs Bulletin* NS. No. 23: 24-30. July 1995.
___ "Two Sequels to **Greystoke**," *Burroughs Bulletin* NS. No. 14: 34-38. April 1993.

CASEY, JOHN J.
___ **An Apostate Instauration: Religion, Moral Vision and Humanism in Modern Science Fiction**. Ph.D. Dissertation, University of Strathclyde, 1991. 2 Vols., 620pp. (DAI 52A: 2147-2148.)

CASEY, TIMOTHY
___ "Selected Basic References in the Philosophy of Technology," by Carl Mitcham and Timothy Casey. in: Greenberg, Mark L. and Schachterle, Lance, eds. **Literature and Technology**. Bethlehem, PA: Lehigh University Press, 1992. pp.307-309.
___ "Toward an Archeology of the Philosophy of Technology and Relations with Imaginative Literature," by Carl Mitcham and Timothy Casey. in: Greenberg, Mark L. and Schachterle, Lance, eds. **Literature and Technology**. Bethlehem, PA: Lehigh University Press, 1992. pp.31-64.

CASPER, MONICA J.
___ "Fetal Cyborgs and Technomoms on the Reproductive Frontier: Which Way to the Carnival?," in: Gray, Chris H., ed. **The Cyborg Handbook**. New York: Routledge, 1995. pp.183-201.

CASSIDAY, BRUCE
___ **Modern Mystery, Fantasy and Science Fiction Writers**. New York: Continuum, 1993. 673pp.

CASSIDY, BELLE C.
___ "Psychobiography of a City Man," *Fantasy Commentator* 7(4): 250-254. Fall 1992. (Whole No. 44)

CASSUTO, LEONARD
___ "The 'Power of Blackness' in **The Stand**," in: Magistrale, Tony, ed. **A Casebook on The Stand**. San Bernardino, CA: Borgo Press, 1992. pp.69-88.

CASTEIN, HANNE
___ "Mit der Reichbahn ins Weltall: Zur Science-Fiction der DDR," in: Goodbody, Axel and Tate, Dennis, eds. **Geist und Macht: Writers and the State in the DDR**. Amsterdam and Atlanta, GA: Rodopi, 1992. pp.81-89. (German Monitor, No. 29)

CASTRIOTA, DAVID
___ "Fantasy and Metonymy in the Ancient Near Eastern Imagery of the Sacred Tree," in: Latham, Robert A. and Collins, Robert A., eds. **Modes of the Fantastic**. Westport, CT: Greenwood, 1995. pp.143-154.

CASTRO, ADAM-TROY
___ "Barry Windsor-Smith Trades in a Barbarian for an Alien Vampire," *Science Fiction Age* 2(3): 76-78. March 1994.
___ "Conquer the Desert Planet Arrakis as Frank Herbert's **Dune** Novels Come to Life," *Science Fiction Age* 2(1): 92-95. November 1993.

CASWELL, BRIAN
___ "The Fantasy Phenomenon," *Orana* 30(4): 256-267. November 1994.

CATSOS, GREGORY J. M.
___ "Priceless: A Farewell Interview With Vincent Price," *Filmfax* No. 42: 45-49. December 1993/January 1994.

CATSOS, GREGORY J. M. (continued)
___ "The Wonderful Witch: A Lost Interview with Margaret Hamilton," *Filmfax* No. 41: 50-57. October/November 1993.

CATTARINUSSI, BERNARDO
___ "L'organization sociale en Utopie," in: Saccaro Del Buffa, Giuseppa and Lewis, Arthur O., eds. **Utopia e Modernita: Teorie e prassi utopiche nell'eta moderna e postmoderna**. Rome: Gangemi Editore, 1989. pp.675-692.

CAVALIERO, GLEN
___ **The Supernatural and English Fiction**. Oxford: Oxford University Press, 1995. 273pp.

CAVE, HUGH B.
___ **Magazines I Remember: Some Pulps, Their Editors, and What It Was Like to Write for Them**. Chicago, IL: Tattered Pages Press, 1994. 174pp.

CAVELL, STANLEY
___ "Being Odd, Getting Even (Descartes, Emerson, Poe)," in: Rosenheim, Shawn and Rachman, Stephen, ed. **The American Face of Edgar Allan Poe**. Baltimore: Johns Hopkins University Press, 1995. pp.3-37.

CAVEN, PATRICIA
___ "A Talk With Charles de Lint," *Worlds of Fantasy and Horror* 1(2): 51-55. Spring 1995. (No. 2)

CAVENDER, CHARLOTTE
___ "Holy Cash Register! Batman Selling Out More Than the Movie," *Charleston (WV) Daily Mail*. June 19 1992. in: *NewsBank. Film and Television*. 62:E9-E10. 1992.

CAYWOOD, CAROLYN
___ "Cyberpunk," *Voice of Youth Advocates* 15(1): 14. April 1992.
___ "The Quest for Character," *School Library Journal* 41(3): 152. March 1995.
___ "Tales of the Dark Side," *School Library Journal* 41(7): 31. July 1995.

CAZZATO, VINCENZO
___ "Il 'Profeta' e il suo Monte. Davide Lazzaretti e la 'Nuova Sion' sul Monte Labbro," in: Saccaro Del Buffa, Giuseppa and Lewis, Arthur O., eds. **Utopia e Modernita: Teorie e prassi utopiche nell'eta moderna e postmoderna**. Rome: Gangemi Editore, 1989. pp.1035-1086.

CECCATO, SILVIO
___ "Utopia, futurologia e scienza. L'utopia e l'uomo del futuro," in: Saccaro Del Buffa, Giuseppa and Lewis, Arthur O., eds. **Utopia e Modernita: Teorie e prassi utopiche nell'eta moderna e postmoderna**. Rome: Gangemi Editore, 1989. pp.199-204.

CERASINI, MARC A.
___ " 'Come Back to Valusia Ag'in, Kull Honey!': Robert E. Howard and Mainstream American Literature," *The Dark Man: The Journal of Robert E. Howard Studies* No. 2: 22-23. July 1991.
___ **How to Write Horror and Get It Published**. Brooklyn Heights, NY: Romantic Times, 1989. 210pp.

CERONE, DANIEL H.
___ "Ending of **Next Generation** Spawns New Films, Series," *Austin (TX) American Statesman* Sec. B, p. 6. April 7, 1994.
___ "Interactive Jones: George Lucas Dreams of Multimedia Adventures for **Young Indiana Jones**," *Los Angeles (CA) Times*. March 4, 1992. in: *NewsBank. Film and Television*. 33:B10. 1992.
___ "The Kindest Cut: Laser Discs Give Directors a Second Chance at Their Films," *Los Angeles (CA) Times*. December 18, 1991. in: *NewsBank. Film and Television*. 1:A8-A10. 1991.
___ "Parting of **Ren and Stimpy** and Its Creator," *Los Angeles (CA) Times/Orange County Edition*. September 28, 1992. in: *NewsBank. Film and Television*. 95:A1. 1992.
___ "**Ren and Stimpy** Creator Fired," *Los Angeles (CA) Times*. September 26, 1992. in: *NewsBank. Film and Television*. 106:F1. 1992.
___ "Sci-Fi Channel on the Launching Pad," *Los Angeles (CA) Times* Sec. F, p. 16. September 5, 1992.

CERONE, DANIEL H. (continued)
___ "**Seaquest** Comes Up for Repairs," *Los Angeles (CA) Times*. April 30, 1994. in: *NewsBank. Film and Television*. 58:F14-G1. 1994.
___ "Space Team Shooting for the Moon," *Los Angeles (CA) Times* Sec. F, p. 1. December 8, 1992.
___ "Star Trek Only a Show? Is This Guy Serious?," *Los Angeles (CA) Times*. November 13, 1994. in: *NewsBank. Film and Television*. 10:D8-D12. 1995.
___ "A Surreal **X-Files** Captures Earthlings," *Los Angeles (CA) Times*. October 28, 1994. in: *NewsBank. Film and Television*. 127:A1-A2. 1994.
___ "Toontown Terrors: Two Twisted Characters and Their Anarchistic Animator Have Made Cable's **Ren & Stimpy** a Ready for Prime Time Phenomenon," *Los Angeles (CA) Times*. August 9, 1992. in: *NewsBank. Film and Television*. 83:C5-C10. 1992.
___ "**VR.5** Steps into Critical Real World," *Los Angeles (CA) Times*. March 23, 1995. in: *NewsBank. Film and Television*. 51:B13-B14. 1995.
___ "Where KCOP Has Not Gone Before," *Los Angeles (CA) Times* Sec. F, p. 1. March 2, 1993.
___ "Why Director Adrian Lyne Went for the Jugular," *Los Angeles (CA) Times*. February 18, 1992. in: *NewsBank. Film and Television*. 19:E4. 1992.

CERSOWSKY, PETER
___ "Varianten phantastischer Lyrik: Edgar Allan Poe und Georg Trakl," in: Kranz, Gisbert, ed. **Inklings: Jahrbuch für Literatur und Ästhetik**. 9. Band. Lüdenscheid, Germany: Stier, 1991. pp.165-186. [Not seen.]

CERUTTI GULDBERG, HORACIO
___ **Ensayos de Utopia**. Toluca: Universidad Atonoma del Estado de Mexico, 1989. 3 v. [Not seen.]

CHADWICK, TONY
___ "Alain Robbe-Grillet and the Fantastic," by Tony Chadwick and Virginia Harger-Grinling. in: Ruddick, Nicholas, ed. **State of the Fantastic**. Westport, CT: Greenwood, 1992. pp.91-96.
___ "The Fantastic Robbe-Grillet," by Tony Chadwick and Virginia Harger-Grinling. in: Harger-Grinling, Virginia and Chadwick, Tony, eds. **Robbe-Grillet and the Fantastic**. Westport, CT: Greenwood, 1994. pp.1-10.
___ (ed.) **Robbe-Grillet and the Fantastic: A Collection of Essays**, ed. by Virginia Harger-Grinling and Tony Chadwick. Westport, CT: Greenwood, 1994. 168pp.

CHALIKOVA, VICTORIA
___ "A Russian Preface to George Orwell," in: Rose, Jonathan, ed. **The Revised Orwell**. East Lansing, MI: Michigan State University Press, 1992. pp.5-12.

CHALIN, MICHAEL
___ "Shazam! Comic Book Heroes Invade the Electronic Frontier," *PC Novice* 5(8): 60-62. August 1994.

CHALKER, JACK L.
___ "On Publishing and Personalities," *Pulphouse* No. 10: 42-45. July 1992.
___ "On Publishing and Personalities," *Pulphouse* No. 11: 53-57. August 1992.
___ **The Science Fantasy Publishers: A Critical and Bibliographic History**, by Jack L. Chalker and Mark Owings. Westminster, MD: Mirage, 1992. 744pp. (Revised Fourth Printing)
___ **The Science Fantasy Publishers: Supplement One, July 1991-June 1992**, by Jack L. Chalker and Mark Owings. Westminster, MD: Mirage Press, 1992. 130pp.

CHALMERS, ALAN D.
___ **Jonathan Swift and the Burden of the Future**. Newark, NJ: University of Delaware Press, 1995. 175pp.

CHALPIN, LILA
___ **Dystopias as Viewed by Social Scientists and Novelists**. Ph.D. Dissertation, Boston University, 1977. 232pp. (DAI 38: 5383A.)

CHAMPLIN, CHARLES
___ **George Lucas, the Creative Impulse: Lucasfilm's First Twenty Years**. New York: Abrams, 1992. 207pp.

CHANCE, JANE
___ **The Lord of the Rings: The Mythology of Power**. New York: Twayne, 1992. 130pp.
___ "Power and Knowledge in Tolkien: The Problem of Difference in 'The Birthday Party'," in: Reynolds, Patricia and GoodKnight, Glen H., eds. **Proceedings of the J. R. R. Tolkien Centenary Conference, Keble College, Oxford, 1992**. Altadena, CA: Mythopoeic Press, 1995. pp.115-120. (*Mythlore* Vol. 21, No. 2, Winter 1996, Whole No. 80)

CHANDLER, DAVID L.
___ "Isaac Asimov's Fiction Brought Facts to Life," *Boston (MA) Globe* p. 57. April 7, 1992.

CHANDLER, DIXON H.
___ **The Sounds of Dissension: Science Fiction Programming on American Popular Radio Through Dimension X (1950/1)**. Master's Thesis, Bowling Green State University, 1992. 194pp.

CHANG, CHRIS
___ "Let Us Play," *Film Comment* 31(6): 6-7. November 1995.

CHANG, KENNY
___ "Capitalism and the Concept of the Other: The Social Significance of Contemporary Hollywood Science Fiction Cinema," *Chung Wai Literary Quarterly* 22(12): May 1994. (Issue not seen; pagination unavailable.)

CHAPMAN, DOUGLAS
___ "The Lovecraft Paradox," by Mark Chorvinsky and Douglas Chapman. *Strange Magazine* No. 11: 4-7, 52-53. Spring/Summer 1993.

CHAPMAN, EDGAR L.
___ "An Ironic Deflation of the Superman Myth: Literary Influence and Science Fiction Tradition in **Dying Inside**," in: Elkins, Charles L. and Greenberg, Martin H., eds. **Robert Silverberg's Many Trapdoors: Critical Essays on His Science Fiction**. Westport, CT: Greenwood, 1992. pp.39-57.
___ " 'Seeing' Invisibility: Or Invisibility as Metaphor in Thomas Berger's **Being Invisible**," *Journal of the Fantastic in the Arts* 4(2): 65-93. 1992. (No. 14)

CHAPMAN, MIKE
___ "Glenn Morris: Tarzan Number Eight," *Burroughs Bulletin* NS. No. 16: 8-15. October 1993.

CHAPMAN, VERA
___ "Reminiscences: Oxford in 1920, Meeting Tolkien and Becoming an Author at 77," in: Reynolds, Patricia and GoodKnight, Glen H., eds. **Proceedings of the J. R. R. Tolkien Centenary Conference, Keble College, Oxford, 1992**. Altadena, CA: Mythopoeic Press, 1995. pp.12-14. (*Mythlore* Vol. 21, No. 2, Winter 1996, Whole No. 80)

CHAREYRE-MEJAN, ALAIN
___ (ed.) **Eros: Science & Fiction Fantastique**, ed. by Roger Bozzetto, Max Duperray and Alain Chareyre-Mejan. Aix-en-Provence: Universite de Provence, 1991. 220pp.

CHARLES, NICK
___ "Cosmic Relief," *(New York, NY) Daily News*. November 8, 1994. in: *NewsBank. Film and Television*. 119:D3. 1994.

CHARLES-EDWARDS, THOMAS
___ "The Arthur of History," in: Bromwich, Rachel, Jarman, A. O. H., and Roberts, Brynley F., eds. **The Arthur of the Welsh**. Cardiff: University of Wales Press, 1991. pp.15-32.

CHARNAS, SUZY M.
___ "A Case for Fantasy," *ALAN Review* 19(3): 20-22. Spring 1992.
___ "Post-Holocaust Themes in Feminist SF (Transcript of the Panel at NorEasCon 2)," by Elizabeth Lynn, Chelsea Q. Yarbro, Suzy M. Charnas and Jeanne Gomoll. *Janus* 6(2): 25-28. Winter 1980. (Whole No. 18)

CHARNON-DEUTSCH, LOU
___ "**Las Vírgenes Locas** as Product of the Unconscious," *Monographis Review* 3(1/2): 49-57. 1987.

CHATELAIN, DANIELE
___ "Spacetime Geometries: Time Travel and the Modern Geometrical Narrative," by George E. Slusser and Daniele Chatelain. *Science Fiction Studies* 22(2): 161-186. July 1995.

CHEEVER, LEONARD A.
___ "Epistemological Chagrin: The Literary and Philosophical Antecedents of Stanislaw Lem's Romantic Misanthrope," *Extrapolation* 35(4): 319-329. Winter 1994.
___ "Fantasies of Sexual Hell: Manuel Puig's **Pubis Angelical** and Margaret Atwood's **The Handmaid's Tale**," in: Latham, Robert A. and Collins, Robert A., eds. **Modes of the Fantastic**. Westport, CT: Greenwood, 1995. pp.110-121.

CHEREWATUK, KAREN
___ "The Saint's Life of Sir Lancelot: Hadiography and the Conclusion of Malory's **Morte Darthur**," *Arthuriana* 5(1): 62-78. Spring 1995.

CHERNIAK, LAURA R.
___ **Calling in Question: Science Fiction and Cultural Studies**. Ph.D. Dissertation, University of California, Santa Cruz, 1995. 257pp. (DAI-A 56/04, p. 1554. October 1995.)

CHERNIAVSKY, EVA
___ "(En)gendering Cyberspace in **Neuromancer**: Postmodern Subjectivity and Virtual Motherhood," *Genders* No. 18: 32-46. Winter 1993.
___ "Revivification and Utopian Time: Poe Versus Stowe," in: Rosenheim, Shawn and Rachman, Stephen, ed. **The American Face of Edgar Allan Poe**. Baltimore: Johns Hopkins University Press, 1995. pp.121-139.

CHERNOFSKY, JACOB L.
___ "Isaac Asimov: The Peculiar Life of an Obsessive Writer," *AB Bookman's Weekly* 90(17): 1438-1446. October 26, 1992.

CHERRYH, C. J.
___ "From Disk to Typesetter," *SFWA Bulletin* 26(3): 15-17. Fall 1992. (No. 117)

CHESTERTON, G. K.
___ "Das ungeborene Kind spricht," in: Kranz, Gisbert, ed. **Inklings: Jahrbuch für Literatur und Ästhetik**. 8. Band. Lüdenscheid, Germany: Stier, 1990. pp.145. [Not seen.]

CHETTA, PETER N.
___ "Multiplicities of Illusion in Tom Stoppard's Plays," in: Murphy, Patrick D., ed. **Staging the Impossible: The Fantastic Mode in Modern Drama**. Westport, CT: Greenwood, 1992. pp.127-136.

CHIARELLO, BARBARA
___ "The Utopian Space of a Nightmare: **The Diary of Anne Frank**," *Utopian Studies* 5(1): 128-140. 1994.

CHICHESTER, ANA G.
___ "Metamorphosis in Two Short Stories of the Fantastic by Virgilio Peñera and Felisberto Hernández," *Studies in Short Fiction* 31(3): 385-395. Summer 1994.

CHIEN, YING-YING
___ "From Utopian to Dystopian World: Two Faces of Feminism in Contemporary Taiwanese Women's Fiction," *World Literature Today* 68(1): 35-42. Winter 1994.

CHOLFIN, BRYAN G.
___ "No One Will Be Watching Us: The Complaints of a Small Press Publisher," *New York Review of Science Fiction* No. 57: 17-20. May 1993.

CHOLLET, LAWRENCE
___ "His Stories Operate on Several Levels," *(Hackensack, NJ) Record*. August 7, 1992. in: *NewsBank. Film and Television*. 76:A14. 1992

CHORVINSKY, MARK
___ "The Lovecraft Paradox," by Mark Chorvinsky and Douglas Chapman. *Strange Magazine* No. 11: 4-7, 52-53. Spring/Summer 1993.

CHRISSINGER, CRAIG W.
___ "Alien Ideas," *Starlog* No. 189: 54-58, 64. April 1993.
___ "Brave New World," *Starlog* No. 209: 42-47. December 1994.
___ "Company Man," *Starlog* No. 212: 76-79. March 1995.
___ "Earth Mother," *Starlog* No. 214: 36-39, 69. May 1995.
___ "Frontier Doctor," *Starlog* No. 213: 48-51, 70. April 1995.
___ "Leaps and Bounds," *Starlog* No. 199: 34-36. February 1994.
___ "Lessons of Life," *Starlog* No. 215: 46-49. June 1995.
___ "Man of Time," *Starlog* No. 189: 34-37. April 1993.
___ "Mechanically Inclined," *Starlog* No. 210: 32-35, 66. January 1995.
___ "Mind Reader," *Starlog* No. 209: 55-58, 66. December 1994.
___ "Sky Pilot," *Starlog* No. 216: 67-70. July 1995.
___ "Station Log," *Starlog* No. 198: 52-55. January 1994.
___ "Time Piece," *Starlog* No. 191: 32-34. June 1993.
___ "Time Police," *Starlog* No. 187: 32-35, 72. February 1993.
___ "Undiscovered Writer," *Starlog* No. 205: 76-81. August 1994.
___ "Warrior Pilot," *Starlog* No. 213: 50-52. April 1995.
___ "Wilderness Leader," *Starlog* No. 211: 36-39, 70. February 1995.

CHRISTENSEN, BRYCE J.
___ "The Family in Utopia," *Renascence* 44(1): 31-44. Fall 1991.

CHRISTENSEN, PETER G.
___ "Abraham Rothberg's **The Sword of the Golem**: The Use of the Fantastic in Defense of Judaism," *Journal of the Fantastic in the Arts* 7(2/3): 163-176. 1995.

CHRISTIANSON, GALE E.
___ "Autobiography as Science Fiction: The Strange Case of Loren Eiseley," in: Morse, Donald E., ed. **The Celebration of the Fantastic**. Westport, CT: Greenwood, 1992. pp.113-119.

CHRISTIE, JOHN
___ "Of Als and Others: William Gibson's Transit," in: Slusser, George E. and Shippey, Tom, eds. **Fiction 2000: Cyberpunk and the Future of Narrative**. Athens: University of Georgia Press, 1992. pp.171-182.

CHRISTOPHER, JOE R.
___ "Biographies and Bibliographies on C. S. Lewis," in: Walker, Andrew and Patric, James, eds. **A Christian for All Christians**. Washington, DC: Regnery, 1992. pp.216-222.
___ "C. S. Lewis' Linguistic Myth," *Mythlore* 21(1): 41-50. Summer 1995. (No. 79)
___ "The Fragmentary Lord Peter," *Mythlore* 19(3): 23-26. Summer 1993. (No. 73)
___ "An Inklings Bibliography (45)," by Joe R. Christopher and Wayne G. Hammond. *Mythlore* 18(2): 28-33, 39-40. Spring 1992. (No. 68)
___ "An Inklings Bibliography (46)," by Joe R. Christopher and Wayne G. Hammond. *Mythlore* 18(3): 49-53. Summer 1992. (No. 69)
___ "An Inklings Bibliography (47)," by Joe R. Christopher and Wayne G. Hammond. *Mythlore* 18(4): 49-52. Autumn 1992. (No. 70)
___ "An Inklings Bibliography (48)," by Joe R. Christopher and Wayne G. Hammond. *Mythlore* 19(1): 56-64. Winter 1993. (No. 71)
___ "An Inklings Bibliography (49)," by Joe R. Christopher and Wayne G. Hammond. *Mythlore* 19(2): 61-65. Spring 1993. (No. 72)
___ "An Inklings Bibliography (50) (e.g. 51)," by Joe R. Christopher and Wayne G. Hammond. *Mythlore* 19(4): 60-65. Autumn 1993. (No. 74)
___ "An Inklings Bibliography (50)," by Joe R. Christopher and Wayne G. Hammond. *Mythlore* 19(3): 59-65. Summer 1993. (No. 73)
___ "An Inklings Bibliography (51)," by Joe R. Christopher and Wayne G. Hammond. *Mythlore* 20(1): 59-62. Winter 1994. (Whole No. 75)
___ "An Inklings Bibliography (52)," by Joe R. Christopher and Wayne G. Hammond. *Mythlore* 20(2): 32-34. Spring 1994. (Whole No. 76)
___ "An Inklings Bibliography (54)," by Joe R. Christopher and Wayne G. Hammond. *Mythlore* 20(4): 61-65. Winter 1995. (Whole No. 78)
___ "An Inklings Bibliography (55)," by Joe R. Christopher and Wayne G. Hammond. *Mythlore* 21(1): 61-65. Summer 1995. (No. 79)
___ "J. R. R. Tolkien and the Clerihew," in: Reynolds, Patricia and GoodKnight, Glen H., eds. **Proceedings of the J. R. R. Tolkien Centenary Conference, Keble College, Oxford, 1992**. Altadena, CA: Mythopoeic Press, 1995. pp.263-271. (*Mythlore* Vol. 21, No. 2, Winter 1996, Whole No. 80)
___ "The Moral Epiphanies in **The Lord of the Rings**," in: Reynolds, Patricia and GoodKnight, Glen H., eds. **Proceedings of the J. R. R. Tolkien Centenary Conference, Keble College, Oxford, 1992**. Altadena, CA: Mythopoeic Press, 1995. pp.121-125. (*Mythlore* Vol. 21, No. 2, Winter 1996, Whole No. 80)

CHRISTOPHER, JOE R. (continued)
___ "No Fish for the Phoenix," *CSL: The Bulletin of the New York C. S. Lewis Society* 23(9): 1-7. July 1992.
___ "On Future History as a Basic S-F Literary Form," *Riverside Quarterly* 9(1): 26-31. August 1992. (No. 33)
___ "A Second View of **Castleview**," *Quondam et Futurus* 3(3): 66-76. Fall 1993.

CHRISTOPHERSEN, BILL
___ **The Apparition in the Glass: Charles Brockden Brown's American Gothic**. Athens: University of Georgia Press, 1994. 208pp.

CHUTE, DAVID
___ **The Making of Judge Dredd**, by Jane Killick, David Chute and Charles M. Lippincott. London: Boxtree, 1995; New York: Hyperion, 1995. 192pp.

CHWAST, SEYMOUR
___ **Jackets Required: An Illustrated History of American Book Jacket Design, 1920-1959**, by Steven Heller and Seymour Chwast. San Francisco, CA: Chronicle Books, 1995. 144pp.

CIESLUK, ANNA B.
___ "Stanislaw Lems **Solaris** in deutschen Übersetzungen. Eine sprachliche Analyse aus polnischer Sicht, 2. Teil," *Quarber Merkur* 30(1): 3-17. June 1992. (No. 77)

CITRO, JOSEPH A.
___ "Foreword: *The King and I*," in: Magistrale, Tony, ed. **The Dark Descent: Essays Defining Stephen King's Horrorscape**. Westport, CT: Greenwood, 1992. pp.xi-xiv.

CLAEYS, GREGORY
___ "Utopianism, Property, and the French Revolution Debate in Britain," in: Kumar, Krishan and Bann, Stephen, eds. **Utopias and the Millennium**. London: Reaktion Books, 1993. pp.46-62.
___ **Utopias of the British Enlightenment**. Oxford: Oxford University Press, 1994. 305pp.

CLANCY, TOM
___ "Speech: Robert A. Heinlein," in: Kondo, Yoji, ed. **Requiem: New Collected Works by Robert A. Heinlein and Tributes to the Grand Master**. New York: Tor, 1992. pp.220-223.

CLARESON, THOMAS D.
___ "The Emergence of Science Fiction: The Beginnings Through 1915," in: Barron, Neil, ed. **Anatomy of Wonder 4**. New York: Bowker, 1995. pp.3-61.
___ "Introduction," in: Elkins, Charles L. and Greenberg, Martin H., eds. **Robert Silverberg's Many Trapdoors: Critical Essays on His Science Fiction**. Westport, CT: Greenwood, 1992. pp.1-13.

CLARK, JOHN R.
___ **The Modern Satiric Grotesque and Its Traditions**. Lexington, KY: University Press of Kentucky, 1991. 212pp.

CLARK, KAREN
___ **Hiroshima, Nagazaki, and the Bomb: A Bibliography of Literature and the Arts**, by James R. Bennett and Karen Clark. Pullman, WA: International Society for the Study of Nuclear Texts and Contexts, 1989. 24pp. (Monograph Series, No. 1)

CLARK, KATERINA
___ "The Changing Image of Science and Technology in Soviet Literature," in: Graham, Loren R., ed. **Science and the Soviet Social Order**. Cambridge: Harvard University Press, 1990. pp.259-298.

CLARK, MIKE
___ "Designing Man," *Starlog* No. 187: 75-81, 69. February 1993.
___ "The Master of Disaster," *Starlog* No. 176: 58-61. March 1992.
___ "Space Station Blues," *Starlog* No. 205: 48-51, 70. August 1994.

CLARK, ROBERT
___ "Angela Carter's Desire Machine," *Women's Studies* 14(2): 147-162. 1987.

CLARK, STEPHEN R. L.
___ "Alien Dreams: Kipling," in: Seed, David, ed. **Anticipations: Essays on Early Science Fiction and Its Precursors**. Liverpool: Liverpool University Press, 1995. pp.172-194.
___ "Extraterrestrial Intelligence: The Neglected Experiment," *Foundation* No. 61: 50-65. Summer 1994.
___ **How to Live Forever: Science Fiction and Philosophy**. London, New York: Routledge, 1995. 223pp.

CLARKE, ADELE
___ "Modernity, Postmodernity, and Reproductive Processes, ca. 1890-1990, or, 'Mommy, Where Do Cyborgs Come From Anyway?'," in: Gray, Chris H., ed. **The Cyborg Handbook**. New York: Routledge, 1995. pp.139-155.

CLARKE, AMY M.
___ **A Woman Writing: Feminist Awareness in the Work of Ursula K. Le Guin**. Ph.D. Dissertation, University of California, Davis, 1992. 290pp. (DAI-A 54/01. p. 176. July 1993.)

CLARKE, ARTHUR C.
___ "About Theodore Sturgeon," in: Sturgeon, Theodore. **The Ultimate Egoist, Vol. 1: The Complete Stories of Theodore Sturgeon**, ed. by Paul Williams. Berkeley, CA: North Atlantic Books, 1994. pp.xii-xiv.
___ "Robert Heinlein," in: Kondo, Yoji, ed. **Requiem: New Collected Works by Robert A. Heinlein and Tributes to the Grand Master**. New York: Tor, 1992. pp.261-264.

CLARKE, BODEN
___ **The Work of Katherine Kurtz: An Annotated Bibliography & Guide**, by Boden Clarke and Mary A. Burgess. San Bernardino, CA: Borgo Press, 1993. 128pp.

CLARKE, I. F.
___ "20th Century Future-Think: All Our Yesterdays," *Futures* 24(3): 251-260. April 1992.
___ "20th Century Future-Think: And Now for the Good News," *Futures* 25(9): 898-996. November 1993.
___ "20th Century Future-Think: From the Flame Deluge to the Bad Time," *Futures* 24(6): 605-614. July/August 1992.
___ "20th Century Future-Think: Infinite Space and Life Everlasting," *Futures* 24(7): 821-830. September 1992.
___ "20th Century Future-Think: Rediscovering Original Sins," *Futures* 24(4): 388-396. May 1992.
___ "20th Century Future-Think: The City: Heaven on Earth or the Hell to Come?," *Futures* 24(7): 701-710. September 1992.
___ "20th Century Future-Think: The Future Formula; or, Are There Lessons in History?," *Futures* 25(10): 1094-1102. December 1993.
___ "20th Century Future-Think: The Future Is Not What It Used to Be," *Futures* 25(7): 792-800. September 1993.
___ "20th Century Future-Think: The Shape of Wars to Come," *Futures* 24(5): 483-492. June 1992.
___ "20th Century Future-Think: World War II; or, What Did the Future Hold?," *Futures* 26(3): 335-344. April 1994.
___ **The Tale of the Next Great War, 1871-1914: Fictions of Future Warefare and Battles Still-to-Come**. Liverpool: Liverpool University Press, 1995. 382pp.
___ **Voices Prophesying War: Future Wars 1763-3749**. Oxford: Oxford University Press, 1992. 268pp. Revised edition.

CLARKE, JEREMY
___ "Jan Svankmajer Puppetry's Dark Poet," *Cinefantastique* 26(3): 54-57. April 1995.

CLARKE, ROBERT
___ "The Actor From Planet X," *Starlog* No. 219: 27-31, 66. October 1995.

CLAUSON, KATHY
___ "The Veil of Time," *US Art* 11(4): 39-44. May/June 1992

CLAYTON, DAVID
___ "The Apocalyptic Mirage: Violence and Eschatology in **Dhalgren**," in: Slusser, George and Eric S. Rabkin, eds. **Fights of Fancy: Armed Conflict in Science Fiction and Fantasy**. Athens, GA: University of Georgia Press, 1993. pp.132-144.

CLEMENT, HAL
___ "The Creation of Imaginary Beings," in: Dozois, Gardner, ed. **Writing Science Fiction and Fantasy**. New York: St. Martin's, 1991. pp.129-146.
___ "Discussing Hard SF," by Gerald Feinberg, Hal Clement, Kathryn Cramer and David G. Hartwell. *New York Review of Science Fiction* No. 46: 19-21. June 1992.
___ "Whatever Happened to the Science in Science Fiction?," *Science Fiction Age* 1(6): 30-33. September 1993.

CLEMENTS, JONATHAN
___ "Flesh and Metal: Marriage and Female Emancipation in the Science Fiction of Wei Yahua," *Foundation* No. 65: 61-80. Autumn 1995.
___ "The Mechanics of the US Anime and Manga Industry," *Foundation* No. 64: 32-44. Summer 1995.

CLEMIT, PAMELA
___ **The Godwinian Novel: The Rational Fictions of Godwin, Brockden Brown, Mary Shelley**. Oxford: Clarendon Press, 1993. 254pp.

CLERY, E. J.
___ **The Rise of Supernatural Fiction, 1762-1800**. Cambridge: Cambridge University Press, 1995. 222pp.

CLOIS, WILLIAM L.
___ "An Interview with Sheri S. Tepper," by William L. Clois and Catherine Mintz. *Quantum* No. 43/44: 35-38. Spring/Summer 1993.

CLORE, DAN
___ "Loss and Recuperation: A Model for Reading Clark Ashton Smith's 'Xeethra'," *Studies in Weird Fiction* No. 13: 15-17. Summer 1993. [Not seen.]
___ "Metonyms of Alterity: A Semiotic Interpretation of **Fungi From Yuggoth**," *Lovecraft Studies* No. 30: 21-32. Spring 1994.

CLOVER, CAROL J.
___ "Her Body, Himself: Gender in the Slasher Film," in: Irons, Glenwood, ed. **Gender, Language and Myth: Essays on Popular Narrative**. Toronto: University of Toronto Press, 1992. pp.253-302.
___ **Men, Women, and Chain Saws: Gender in the Modern Horror Film**. Princeton, NJ: Princeton University Press, 1992. 260pp.

CLUTE, JOHN
___ "Aldous Huxley," in: Clute, John. **Look at the Evidence: Essays and Reviews**. Liverpool: Liverpool University Press, 1995. pp.435-438.
___ **The Encyclopedia of Science Fiction**. CD-ROM Edition. New York: Grolier, 1995. 1 CD-ROM.
___ **The Encyclopedia of Science Fiction**, by John Clute and Peter Nicholls. New York: St. Martin's, 1993. 1370pp.
___ "Gustav Meyrink," in: Clute, John. **Look at the Evidence: Essays and Reviews**. Liverpool: Liverpool University Press, 1995. pp.438-443.
___ "Herbert Rosendorfer," in: Clute, John. **Look at the Evidence: Essays and Reviews**. Liverpool: Liverpool University Press, 1995. pp.443-447.
___ "James Tiptree, Jr.," in: Clute, John. **Look at the Evidence: Essays and Reviews**. Liverpool: Liverpool University Press, 1995. pp.447-453.
___ "Karel Capek," in: Clute, John. **Look at the Evidence: Essays and Reviews**. Liverpool: Liverpool University Press, 1995. pp.427-430.
___ **Look at the Evidence: Essays and Reviews**. Liverpool: Liverpool University Press, 1995. 465pp.
___ "M. John Harrison," in: Clute, John. **Look at the Evidence: Essays and Reviews**. Liverpool: Liverpool University Press, 1995. pp.430-435.
___ "Marrying Out: The Year in SF, 1992," *New York Review of Science Fiction* No. 64: 1, 8-10. December 1993.
___ "Necessary Golems," in: Clute, John. **Look at the Evidence: Essays and Reviews**. Liverpool: Liverpool University Press, 1995. pp.3-7.
___ "On the Arthur C. Clarke Award 1993," *Vector* No. 173: 3-4. June/July 1993.
___ "Pilgrim Award Acceptance Speech," in: Clute, John. **Look at the Evidence: Essays and Reviews**. Liverpool: Liverpool University Press, 1995. pp.8-11.
___ **Science Fiction: The Illustrated Encyclopedia**. London: Dorling, 1995. 312pp.

CLUTE, JOHN (continued)
___ "Something About an Old Encyclopedia, and a Word About a New," *Foundation* No. 58: 96-99. Summer 1993.
___ "When the Wheel Stops," *New Statesman and Society* 6(283): 61-62. December 17, 1993.
___ "Year Roundup from **Nebula Awards 28**," in: Clute, John. **Look at the Evidence: Essays and Reviews**. Liverpool: Liverpool University Press, 1995. pp.355-361.
___ "Year Roundup from **New Worlds 1**," in: Clute, John. **Look at the Evidence: Essays and Reviews**. Liverpool: Liverpool University Press, 1995. pp.195-205.
___ "Year Roundup from **New Worlds 3**," in: Clute, John. **Look at the Evidence: Essays and Reviews**. Liverpool: Liverpool University Press, 1995. pp.275-287.
___ "Year Roundup from **The Orbit Science Fiction Yearbook 1**," in: Clute, John. **Look at the Evidence: Essays and Reviews**. Liverpool: Liverpool University Press, 1995. pp.17-27.
___ "Year Roundup from **The Orbit Science Fiction Yearbook 2**," in: Clute, John. **Look at the Evidence: Essays and Reviews**. Liverpool: Liverpool University Press, 1995. pp.75-84.
___ "Year Roundup from **The Orbit Science Fiction Yearbook 3**," in: Clute, John. **Look at the Evidence: Essays and Reviews**. Liverpool: Liverpool University Press, 1995. pp.139-148.

CLYNES, MANFRED E.
___ "Cyborg II: Sentic Space Travel," in: Gray, Chris H., ed. **The Cyborg Handbook**. New York: Routledge, 1995. pp.35-41.
___ "Cyborgs and Space," by Manfred E. Clynes and Nathan S. Kline. in: Gray, Chris H., ed. **The Cyborg Handbook**. New York: Routledge, 1995. pp.29-33.

COATS, GARY
___ "Stone Soup: Utopia, Gift Exchange, and the Aesthetics of the Self-Consuming Artifact," in: Saccaro Del Buffa, Giuseppa and Lewis, Arthur O., eds. **Utopia e Modernita: Teorie e prassi utopiche nell'eta moderna e postmoderna**. Rome: Gangemi Editore, 1989. pp.287-310.

COBLENTZ, STANTON A.
___ **Adventures of a Freelancer: The Literary Exploits and Autobiography of Stanton A. Coblentz**, by Stanton A. Coblentz and Jeffrey M. Elliot. San Bernardino, CA: Borgo Press, 1993. 160pp.

COCKCROFT, T. G. L.
___ "An Index to 'The Eyrie'," *Fantasy Commentator* 8(3/4): 217-229. Fall 1995. (Whole No. 47/48)

COE, STEVE
___ "Television of the Weird: Networks Take a Walk on Weird Side," *Broadcasting and Cable* 125(44): 56-57. October 30, 1995.

COGSWELL, THEODORE R.
___ (ed.) **PITFCS: Proceedings of the Institute for Twenty-First Century Studies**. Chicago: Advent: Publishers, 1992. 374pp.

COHEN, AMY J.
___ "LeVar Burton: The Vision of Georgi LaForge," *Star Trek: The Official Fan Club* No. 94: C-D, 1. November/December 1993.
___ "More Than Just a Country Doctor," *Star Trek: The Official Fan Club* No. 96: 41-45. April/May 1994.
___ "Rene Auberjonois, the Morphing Man," *Star Trek: The Official Fan Club Magazine* No. 92: 2-6. July/August 1993.

COHEN, AVNER
___ "Marx and the Abolition of Labor: End of Utopia or Utopia as an End," *Utopian Studies* 6(1): 40-50. 1995.

COHEN, CHARLES E.
___ "The Trek to Tek," *TV Guide* 42(3): 16-17. January 15, 1994.

COHN, LAWRENCE
___ "Filmers Resort to Old Scare Tactics: Horror Film Resurgence Boosted by Video," *Variety* p. 1, 24. June 8, 1988.
___ "Horrid Year for Horror Pix at B. O.," *Variety* p. 3, 36. January 25, 1984.
___ "Par Backs Nimoy, 'Trek' to Hilt; Talks Going Re Possible Part IV," *Variety* p. 5, 26. June 6, 1984.

COLAS-CHARPENTIER, HELENE
___ "Four Quebecois Dystopias, 1963-1972," *Science Fiction Studies* 20(3): 383-393. November 1993.

COLE, ADRIAN
___ "Season of the Rat," in: Jones, Stephen, ed. **James Herbert: By Horror Haunted**. London: New English Library, 1992. pp.99-104.

COLE, ALLAN
___ "Magic Brush," *Science Fiction Age* 4(1): 84-89. November 1995.

COLEBATCH, HAL
___ "Patterns of Epic: The Re-Affirmation of Western Values in **Star Wars** and **The Lord of the Rings**," *Science Fiction: A Review of Speculative Literature* 11(3): 5-16. 1992. (No. 33)
___ **Return of the Heroes: The Lord of the Rings, Star Wars, and Contemporary Culture**. Perth, Aust.: Australian Institute for Public Policy, 1990. 104pp.

COLEMAN, STEPHEN
___ "William Morris and Education Toward Revolution," *Journal of the William Morris Society* 11(1): 49-58. Autumn 1994.

COLIN, MARIELLA
___ "Du fantastique en tant que genre litteraire pour les enfants in Italie," in: Perrot, Jean, ed. **Culture, texte et Juene Lecteur. Actes du Xe Congres de l'International Research Society for Children's Literature, Paris, September 1991**. Nancy: Presses Universitaires, 1993. pp.43-49

COLL, STEVE
___ "Arthur C. Clarke's Red Thumb," *Washington (DC) Post* Sec. B, p. 1. March 9, 1992.

COLLINS, DAVID
___ **J. R. R. Tolkien: Master of Fantasy**. Minneapolis, MN: Lerner/First Avenue Editions, 1993. 112pp.

COLLINS, DIANA
___ "Guy Vardiman: Standing in for Data," in: Van Hise, James, ed. **Trek Celebration Two**. Las Vegas, NV: Pioneer, 1994. pp.142-147.
___ "Jonathan Frakes: Will Riker Speaks," in: Van Hise, James, ed. **Trek Celebration Two**. Las Vegas, NV: Pioneer, 1994. pp.122-133.

COLLINS, MICHAEL J.
___ "The Body in the Work of the Body: Physio-Textuality in Contemporary Horror," *Journal of the Fantastic in the Arts* 5(3): 28-35. 1993. (No. 19)

COLLINS, MONICA
___ "Black Superhero Will Help Fox Answer Stereotyping Charges," *Boston (MA) Herald*. August 26, 1994. in: *NewsBank. Film and Television*. 91:A1-A2. 1994.

COLLINS, NANCY A.
___ "The Place of Dreams," in: Golden, Christopher, ed. **Cut! Horror Writers on Horror Film**. New York: Berkley, 1992. pp.75-82.

COLLINS, ROBERT A.
___ (ed.) **Modes of the Fantastic: Selected Essays from the Twelfth International Conference on the Fantastic in the Arts**, ed. by Robert A. Latham and Robert A. Collins. Westport, CT: Greenwood, 1995. 234pp.
___ (ed.) **Science Fiction and Fantasy Book Review Annual 1991**, ed. by Robert A. Collins and Robert A. Latham. Westport, CT: Greenwood, 1994. 880pp.

COLLINS, ROBERT L.
___ "When Disaster Strikes," *The Report: The Fiction Writer's Magazine* No. 11: 25. Summer 1993.

COLOMBO, ARRIGO
___ "Famiglia, utopia, societa fraterna," in: Colombo, Arrigo and Quarta, Cosimo, eds. **Il Destino della Famiglia nell'Utopia**. Bari: Edizione Dedalo, 1991. pp.5-13.
___ **L'Utopia nella Storia: la Rivoluzione inglese**, by Arrigo Colombo, Giuseppe Schiavone and Robert Ashton. Bari: Edizioni Dedalo, 1992. 294pp. [Not seen.]

COLOMBO, ARRIGO (continued)
___ "Le ragioni della dissoluzione: Fourier," in: Colombo, Arrigo and Quarta, Cosimo, eds. **Il Destino della Famiglia nell'Utopia**. Bari: Edizione Dedalo, 1991. pp.223-245.
___ **Utopia e distopia**. Nuova ed., by Enzo Baldini and Arrigo Colombo. Bari: Edizioni Dedalo, 1993. 373pp. [Not seen.]
___ (ed.) **Il Destino della Famiglia nell'Utopia**, ed. by Arrigo Colombo and Cosimo Quarta. Bari: Edizioni Dedalo, 1991. 454pp.

COLOMBO, EDUARDO
___ "L'amputation de la dimension utopique dans l'homme moderne," in: Saccaro Del Buffa, Giuseppa and Lewis, Arthur O., eds. **Utopia e Modernita: Teorie e prassi utopiche nell'eta moderna e postmoderna**. Rome: Gangemi Editore, 1989. pp.95-110.

COLOMBO, JOHN R.
___ "Favorite Canadian Works," *Sol Rising* (Toronto) No. 10: 3-4. May 1994.

COMO, JAMES
___ "The Centrality of Rhetoric to an Understanding of C. S. Lewis," *Bulletin of the New York C. S. Lewis Society* 25(1): 1-7. November 1993.
___ "A Seeing Eye," *Bulletin of the New York C. S. Lewis Society* 25(9/11): 3-6. July/September 1994.
___ "Shadowlands IV," *CSL: The Bulletin of the New York C. S. Lewis Society* 24(6): 1-7. April 1993.

COMPTON, D. G.
___ "By Chance Out of Conviction," in: Jakubowski, Maxim and James, Edward, eds. **The Profession of Science Fiction**. New York: St. Martin's, 1992. pp.101-110.

COMRADA, NORMA
___ "Golem and Robot: The Search for Connections," *Journal of the Fantastic in the Arts* 7(2/3): 244-254. 1995.

CONCANNON, TIM
___ "The Cops and Hackers Can Go to Hell: Bruce Sterling Interviewed," *Interzone* No. 83: 25-29. May 1994.

CONEY, MICHAEL
___ "Thank You for the Music," in: Jakubowski, Maxim and James, Edward, eds. **The Profession of Science Fiction**. New York: St. Martin's, 1992. pp.120-130.

CONGER, SYNDY M.
___ **Mary Wollstonecraft and the Language of Sensibility**. Rutherford, NJ: Fairleigh Dickinson University Press, 1994. 214pp.

CONGREVE, BILL
___ "The Rise of Australian Fantasy," *Aurealis* No. 12: 43-48. 1993.

CONLEY, LAWRENCE V.
___ "Where Empires Touch," *Starlog* 182: 34-39, 71. September 1992.

CONLON, D. J.
___ (ed.) **G. K. Chesterton: The Critical Judgments, Part 1: 1900-1937**. Antwerp, Belgium: Antwerp Studies in English Literature, 1976. 555pp. [Not seen.]

CONNER, JAMES A.
___ "Strategies for Hyperreal Travelers," *Science Fiction Studies* 20(1): 69-79. March 1993.

CONNOLLY, JOHN
___ "A Progressive End: Arthur C. Clarke and Teilhard de Chardin," *Foundation* No. 61: 66-76. Summer 1994.

CONQUEST, ROBERT
___ "Profile," in: Salwak, Dale, ed. **Kingsley Amis in Life and Letters**. New York: St. Martin's, 1990. pp.11-17.

CONSARELLI, BRUNA
___ "La Congiura degli Eguali: utopia o progetto politico?," in: Saccaro Del Buffa, Giuseppa and Lewis, Arthur O., eds. **Utopie per gli Anni Ottana**. Rome: Gangemi Editore, 1986. pp.591-634.

CONSARELLI, BRUNA (continued)
___ "Per una lettura politica dell'utopia di Cyrano di Bergerac," in: Saccaro Del Buffa, Giuseppa and Lewis, Arthur O., eds. **Utopia e Modernita: Teorie e prassi utopiche nell'eta moderna e postmoderna**. Rome: Gangemi Editore, 1989. pp.837-876.

CONSIDINE, J. B.
___ "English Comics *Tank Girl* May Have Most Yanks Yawning," *(Baltimore, MD) Sun*. March 31, 1995. in: *NewsBank. Film and Television*. 50:B12. 1995.

CONSTABLE, JOHN
___ "C. S. Lewis: From Magdalen to Magdalene," in: Watson, George, ed. **Critical Essays on C. S. Lewis**. Hants, Eng.: Scolar Press, 1992. pp.47-51.

CONTENTO, WILLIAM G.
___ **Science Fiction, Fantasy, & Horror: 1991**, by Charles N. Brown and William G. Contento. Oakland, CA: Locus Press, 1992. 482pp.

COOGAN, PETER M.
___ "Science Fiction Comics," in: Barron, Neil, ed. **Anatomy of Wonder 4**. New York: Bowker, 1995. pp.673-689.

COOK, PAM
___ "*Dracula* (Review)," *Sight and Sound* 3(2): 47-48. February 1993.

COOK, SEBASTIAN
___ "Editing the Stars: An Interview With Jane Johnson," *Focus* (BSFA) No. 26: 15-16. June/July 1994.

COOKE, BRETT
___ "Sociobiology, Science Fiction and the Future," *Foundation* No. 60: 42-51. Spring 1994.

COOLEY, DENNIS
___ "Nearer by Far: The Upset 'I' in Margaret Atwood's Poetry," in: Nicholson, Colin, ed. **Margaret Atwood: Writing and Subjectivity: New Critical Essays**. New York: St. Martin's, 1994. pp.68-93.

COOMBS, CHARLES I.
___ "Martian Memories," *Burroughs Bulletin* NS No. 11: 21-23. July 1992.

COOMBS, JENNY
___ "A Physics of Middle-Earth," by Jenny Coombs and Marc Read. in: Reynolds, Patricia and GoodKnight, Glen H., eds. **Proceedings of the J. R. R. Tolkien Centenary Conference, Keble College, Oxford, 1992**. Altadena, CA: Mythopoeic Press, 1995. pp.323-329. (*Mythlore* Vol. 21, No. 2, Winter 1996, Whole No. 80)

COOPER, BOB
___ "How a Classic Newspaper Strip Became a Comic Book Series: The Story Behind a Comic Book Series," *Lucasfilm Fan Club* No. 20: 6, 27. Fall 1993.

COOPER, KENNETH D.
___ **Fables of the Nuclear Age: Fifty Years of World War III**. Ph.D. Dissertation, Vanderbilt University, 1992. 352pp. (DAI-A 54/01. p. 176. July 1993.)

COOPMAN, JEREMY
___ "Sales of Marvel Comics Move Up Fast in Britain," *Variety* p. 83. September 17, 1986.

COOTE, STEPHEN
___ **William Morris: His Life and Work**. Godalming, U.K.: Sutton, 1995. 224pp.

COPOBIANCO, MICHAEL
___ "Interview With Paul Rosenzweig," *SFWA Bulletin* 28(2): 19-20. Summer 1994. (No. 124)

CORBETT, J. MARTIN
___ "Celluloid Projections: Images of Technology and Organizational Futures in Contemporary Science Fiction Film," *Organization* 2(3/4): 467-488. August/November 1995

CORBETT, LIONEL
___ (ed.) **Psyche's Stories: Modern Jungian Interpretations of Fairy Tales**, ed. by Murray Stein and Lionel Corbett. Wilmette, IL: Chiron, 1991. 166pp.

CORCOS, CHRISTINE
___ **Women's Rights and Women's Images in Science Fiction: A Selected Bibliography.** Cleveland, OH: Case Western Reserve University, Law Library, 1994. 17pp.

COREN, MICHAEL
___ **The Invisible Man: The Life and Liberties of H. G. Wells.** New York: Atheneum, 1993. 240pp.
___ **The Man Who Created Narnia: The Story of C. S. Lewis.** Toronto: Lester, 1994. 140pp.

CORIELL, RITA
___ "The Coriell Years of Burroughs Fandom," *Burroughs Bulletin* NS. No. 12: 31-33. October 1992.

CORIELL, VERNELL
___ "*The Son of Tarzan*: The Movie," *Burroughs Bulletin* NS. No. 18: 3-5. April 1994.

CORKERY, P. J.
___ "*Basic Instinct* Toned Down: Two Scenes Reportedly Cut From Costly, Controversial Film in Effort to Win R Rating," *San Francisco (CA) Examiner.* February 12, 1992 in: *NewsBank. Film and Television.* 17:D2. 1992.

CORLISS, RICHARD
___ "The King of Creep," *Time* 139(17): 62-63. April 27, 1992.
___ "Play MST for Me," *Film Comment* 31(4): 26-35. July 1995.

CORLISS, WILLIAM R.
___ "Teleoperators and Human Augmentation," by Edwin G. Johnson and William R. Corliss. in: Gray, Chris H., ed. **The Cyborg Handbook**. New York: Routledge, 1995. pp.83-92.

CORNELL, PAUL
___ **The New Trek Programme Guide,** by Paul Cornell, Martin Day and Keith Topping. London: Virgin, 1995. 378pp.

CORRADO, ADRIANA
___ **Da un'isola all'alltra: il pensiero utopico nella narrativa inglese da Thomas More ad Aldous Huxley.** Napoli: Scientifiche Italiane, 1988. 189pp. [Not seen.]
___ **William Morris, News From Nowhere: cent'anni dopo.** Napoli: Guida Editori, 1992. 133pp. [Not seen.]

CORSALETTI, LOUIS T.
___ "Television Show 'Peaks' Interest," *Seattle (WA) Times.* April 7, 1992. in: *NewsBank. Film and Television.* 47:D3. 1992.

CORYDON, BENT
___ **L. Ron Hubbard: Messiah or Madman?** (Revised, expanded and updated edition). Fort Lee, NJ: Barricade Books, 1992. 459pp.

COSTELLO, JOHN H.
___ "American SF in Russian," *Locus* 35(3): 54. September 1993.

COSTELLO, MATTHEW J.
___ "Films, Television, and Dean Koontz," in: Greenberg, Martin H., Ed Gorman and Bill Munster, eds. **The Dean Koontz Companion.** New York: Berkley, 1994. pp.101-146.
___ **How to Write Science Fiction.** 2nd ed. New York: Marlowe, 1995. 144pp.
___ **How to Write Science Fiction.** New York: Paragon House, 1992. 144pp.

COSTIKYAN, GREG
___ "Short Fiction Market Response Times," *Science Fiction and Fantasy Writers of America Bulletin* 25(4): 27. Winter 1992. (No. 114)

COULOMBE, CHARLES A.
___ "Hermetic Imagination: The Effects of the Golden Dawn on Fantasy Literature," in: Reynolds, Patricia and GoodKnight, Glen H., eds. **Proceedings of the J. R. R. Tolkien Centenary Conference, Keble College, Oxford, 1992.** Altadena, CA: Mythopoeic Press, 1995. pp.345-356. (*Mythlore* Vol. 21, No. 2, Winter 1996, Whole No. 80)

COULSON, JUANITA
___ "Why Is a Fan?," in: Sanders, Joe, ed. **Science Fiction Fandom.** Westport, CT: Greenwood, 1994. pp.1-10.

COULSON, ROBERT
___ "Fandom as a Way of Life," in: Sanders, Joe, ed. **Science Fiction Fandom.** Westport, CT: Greenwood, 1994. pp.11-14.

COUNIHAN, ELIZABETH
___ "The Film or the Book?," *Vector* No. 166: 13. April/May 1992.
___ "The Worst Possible Thing: Lois McMaster Bujold Interviewed," *Interzone* No. 101: 20-23. November 1995.

COUNTS, KYLE
___ "Character Music," *Starlog* No. 183: 55-57, 70. October 1992.
___ "Join **Demolition Man** Sylvester Stallone on the Set of His Near Future SF Thriller," *Science Fiction Age* 2(1): 20-22, 90. November 1993.
___ "Life Beyond the Battlestars," *Starlog* No. 196: 32-37. November 1993.
___ "Living Doll in Giant Land," *Starlog* 181: 27-31, 60. August 1992.
___ "Magic Time," *Starlog* No. 194: 32-37. September 1993.
___ "Scientific American," *Starlog* No. 201: 76-79. April 1994.
___ "Serious Heavy," *Starlog* No. 188: 54-58, 68. March 1993.
___ "A Time to Remember," *Starlog* 180: 32-35, 66. July 1992.
___ "Time Traveler," *Starlog* 179: 38-41, 84. June 1992.
___ "True Disbeliever," in: McDonnell, David, ed. **Starlog's Science Fiction Heroes and Heroines**. New York: Crescent Books, 1995. pp.70-72.
___ "The UFO Incident," *Starlog* No. 206: 28-32, 69. September 1994.
___ "Views of the Wars," *Starlog* No. 191: 41-45. June 1993.

COVEN, LAURENCE
___ "King Turns to Other Worlds for Epic Tales," *Los Angeles (CA) Daily News.* January 5, 1992. in: *NewsBank. Literature.* 11:B6. 1992.

COVERT, COLLIN
___ "Days a Reach That Loses Its Grasp," *Minneapolis (MN) Star And Tribune.* October 13, 1995. in: *NewsBank. Film and Television.* 99: C12.1995.

COVILLE, BRUCE
___ "About Tomorrow: Learning with Literature," *Instructor* 101(9): 20, 22-23. May/June 1992.

COVINGTON, VERONICA
___ "The Science Fiction Research Collection at Texas A&M University," *Popular Culture in Libraries* 2(1): 81-87. 1994.

COWAN, LISA
___ "Kathy Tyers' Most Enjoyable Assignment: **Star Wars: The Mission at Bakura**," *Lucasfilm Fan Club* No. 21: 32-33. Winter 1994.

COWAN, RON
___ "Man Behind **Candyman**," *Salem (OR) Statesman-Journal.* December 8, 1992. in *NewsBank. Literature.* 1:C6. 1993.

COWART, DAVID
___ "Attenuated Postmodernism: Pynchon's **Vineland**," in: Trachtenberg, Stanley, ed. **Critical Essays on American Postmodernism**. New York: G. K. Hall, 1995. pp.182-191.
___ **History and the Contemporary Novel**. Carbondale: Southern Illinois University Press, 1989. 245pp.

COWPER, RICHARD
___ "Backwards Across the Frontier," in: Jakubowski, Maxim and James, Edward, eds. **The Profession of Science Fiction**. New York: St. Martin's, 1992. pp.78-94.

CROWE, EDITH L.

___ "Power in Arda: Sources, Uses and Misuses," in: Reynolds, Patricia and GoodKnight, Glen H., eds. **Proceedings of the J. R. R. Tolkien Centenary Conference, Keble College, Oxford, 1992.** Altadena, CA: Mythopoeic Press, 1995. pp.272-277. (*Mythlore* Vol. 21, No. 2, Winter 1996, Whole No. 80)

CROWTHER, IAN
___ **G. K. Chesterton**. London: Claridge Press, 1991. 101pp. [Not seen.]

CROWTHER, PETE
___ "Destabilizing Reality: Ian Watson Interviewed," *Interzone* No. 75: 17-24. September 1993.

CRUM, RICHARD M.
___ "News Flash: Alien From Another Planet?," *National Geographic World* 231: 17-91. November 1994.

CSICSERY-RONAY, ISTVAN, JR.
___ "Antimancere: Cybernetics and Art in Gibson's **Count Zero**," *Science Fiction Studies* 22(1): 63-86. March 1995.
___ "Futuristic Flu, or, The Revenge of the Future," in: Slusser, George E. and Shippey, Tom, eds. **Fiction 2000: Cyberpunk and the Future of Narrative**. Athens: University of Georgia Press, 1992. pp.26-45.
___ "Pilgrims in Pandemonium: Philip K. Dick and the Critics," in: Mullen, R. D., ed. **On Philip K. Dick: 40 Articles From Science-Fiction Studies**. Terre Haute, IN: SF-TH Inc., 1992. pp.v-xviii.
___ "The Sentimental Futurist: Cybernetics and Art in William Gibson's **Neuromancer**," *Critique* 33(3): 221-240. Spring 1992.

CUBBAGE, ROBERT
___ "Kurt Vonnegut: The Faith of a Skeptic," *National Catholic Reporter* 22: 9-10. May 16, 1986.

CULLEN, ROBERT J.
___ **Words and a Yarn: Language and Narrative Technique in the Works of Thomas Pynchon**. Ph.D. Dissertation, University of California, Los Angeles, 1981. 222pp.

CUMMINGS, MICHAEL S.
___ "Practicing Utopia in the Twilight of Capitalism," in: Saccaro Del Buffa, Giuseppa and Lewis, Arthur O., eds. **Utopie per gli Anni Ottana**. Rome: Gangemi Editore, 1986. pp.125-144.

CUMMINS, ELIZABETH
___ "Judith Merril: A Link With the New Wave, Then and Now," *Extrapolation* 36(3): 198-209. Fall 1995.
___ "Judith Merril: Scouting SF," *Extrapolation* 35(1): 5-14. Spring 1994.
___ "Short Fiction by Judith Merril," *Extrapolation* 33(3): 202-214. Fall 1992.

CUMMISKEY, GARY
___ **The Changing Face of Horror: A Study of the Nineteenth Century French Fantastic Short Story**. New York: Peter Lang, 1992. 170pp.

CUNNEFF, TOM
___ "Star Trip," *People Weekly* 42(17): 37. October 24, 1994.

CUPP, JEFF
___ "Do Science Fiction and Fantasy Writers Have Postmodern Dreams?," by Jeff Cupp and Charles Avinger. *LIT: Literature Interpretation Theory* 4(3): 175-184. 1993.

CURL, ROBERT
___ "The Metaphors of Cyberpunk: Ontology, Epistemology, and Science Fiction," in: Slusser, George E. and Shippey, Tom, eds. **Fiction 2000: Cyberpunk and the Future of Narrative**. Athens: University of Georgia Press, 1992. pp.230-245.

CURRAN, RONALD T.
___ "Complex, Archetype, and Primal Fear: King's Use of Fairy Tales in **The Shining**," in: Magistrale, Tony, ed. **The Dark Descent: Essays Defining Stephen King's Horrorscape**. Westport, CT: Greenwood, 1992. pp.33-46.

CURREY, LLOYD W.
___ "Facing Troubled Times: The Science Fiction Specialist Dealer," *AB Bookman's Weekly* 92(16): 1449-1460. October 18, 1993.
___ "A Select List of Reference Books: Science Fiction, Fantasy and Horror Literature," *AB Bookmans Weekly* 94(17): 1648-1657. October 24, 1994.
___ "Work in Progress: Dan Simmons," *New York Review of Science Fiction* No. 41: 23. January 1992.
___ "Work in Progress: Michael Bishop," *New York Review of Science Fiction* No. 42: 22-23. February 1992.

CURRIE, PHILIP J.
___ "Dinosaurs of Pellucidar," *Burroughs Bulletin* NS. No. 17: 5-9. January 1994.
___ "On Mahars, Gryfs and the Paleontology of ERB," *Burroughs Bulletin* NS. No. 16: 21-24. October 1993.

CURRY, JAYSON
___ "Formal Synthesis in **Deathbird Stories**: Harlan Ellison's Stacked Deck," *Foundation* No. 56: 23-35. Autumn 1992.

CURRY, PATRICK
___ " 'Less Noise and More Green': Tolkien's Ideology for England," in: Reynolds, Patricia and GoodKnight, Glen H., eds. **Proceedings of the J. R. R. Tolkien Centenary Conference, Keble College, Oxford, 1992**. Altadena, CA: Mythopoeic Press, 1995. pp.126-138. (*Mythlore* Vol. 21, No. 2, Winter 1996, Whole No. 80)

CURTIS, JAN
___ "Byzantium and the Matter of Britain: The Narrative Framework of Charles Williams's Later Arthurian Poems," *Quondam et Futurus* 2(1): 28-54. Spring 1992.
___ "Charles Williams: His Reputation in the English-Speaking World from 1917 to 1985," in: Kranz, Gisbert, ed. **Inklings: Jahrbuch für Literatur und Ästhetik**. 9. Band. Lüdenscheid, Germany: Stier, 1991. pp.127-164. [Not seen.]
___ "Charles Williams's 'The Sister of Percivale': Towards a Theology of *Theotokos*," *Quondam et Futurus* 2(4): 56-72. Winter 1992.

CURTIS, RICHARD
___ "Agent's Corner: Author? What's an Author?," *Locus* 28(2): 11. February 1992.
___ "Agent's Corner: Author? What's an Author?," *Locus* 28(3): 11, 13, 61. March 1992.
___ "Agent's Corner: Author? What's an Author?," *Locus* 28(4): 11, 49-50. April 1992.
___ "Agent's Corner: Farewell," *Locus* 28(5): 11, 13. May 1992.
___ "Agent's Corner: Last Chance," *Locus* 28(1): 11, 13, 61. January 1992.
___ **Fool for an Agent**. Eugene, OR: Pulphouse, 1992. 99pp.

CUSHMAN, CAROLYN
___ "1995 *Locus* Survey Results," *Locus* 35(3): 56-58, 84. September 1993.

CUTSINGER, JAMES S.
___ "Angels and Inklings," *Mythlore* 19(2): 57-60. Spring 1993. (No. 72)

CZIRAKY, DAN
___ "**Ed Wood**: Vampira," by Al Ryan and Dan Cziraky. *Cinefantastique* 25(5): 40-41, 61. October 1994.
___ "**Guyver**," *Cinefantastique* 22(4): 46. February 1992.

D'ALESSANDRO, KATHRYN C.
___ **Mixed Competence: The Tendency Toward Hybridization in Post-1976 Science Fiction Films**. Ph.D. Dissertation, University of Wisconsin, Madison, 1992. 308pp. (DAI-A 3/03, p. 649-650. 1992.)

D'AMMASSA, ALGERNON
___ "**Jurassic Park**: The Tip of the Cane," *Lan's Lantern* No. 42: 100-102. May 1994.

D'AMMASSA, DON
___ "Before the Hugos: The H. G. Awards (1921-1956)," *Science Fiction Chronicle* 13(10): 30-31. July/August 1992.
___ "The Best SF, Fantasy and Horror Novels of 1991," *Science Fiction Chronicle* 13(6): 20, 22. March 1992.

D'AMMASSA, DON (continued)
___ "The Best SF, Fantasy and Horror Novels of 1994," *Science Fiction Chronicle* 16(4): 7, 29-30. February 1995.
___ "The Best SF, Fantasy and Horror Novels of the Year," *Science Fiction Chronicle* 15(4): 5, 28-30. February 1994.
___ "The Best SF, Fantasy, and Horror Novels of the Year, 1992," *Science Fiction Chronicle* 14(5): 5, 22-24. February 1993.

D'ANGELO, CARR
___ "Bride of the Fly," by Anthony Timpone and Carr D'Angelo. in: McDonnell, David, ed. **Starlog's Science Fiction Heroes and Heroines**. New York: Crescent Books, 1995. pp.47-49.

D'ORSO, MIKE
___ "*Batman* Movie Ain't Kids' Stuff," *Norfolk (VA) Virginian-Pilot*. June 23, 1992. in: *NewsBank. Film and Television*. 67:F3. 1992.

DAEM, ALEXANDRE O.
___ "Gedanken über die stille beim lesen: Die künstlichen Schricten in Tolkiens *Herrn der Ringe*: Versuch einer Beschreibung," in: Kranz, Gisbert, ed. **Jahrbuch für Literatur und Ästhetik**. Lüdenscheid, Germany: Stier, 1992. Band 10, pp.177-189.

DAEMON, SHIRA
___ "Three Views of Two Guys: *Two Guys From the Future* and Other Plays; An Evening of Science Fiction Theater," by Peter J. Heck, Greg Cox and Shira Daemon. *New York Review of Science Fiction* No. 47: 1, 3-6. July 1992.

DAHLIN, ROBERT
___ "PW Interviews: Norman Spinrad," *Publishers Weekly* 219(1): 8-9. January 2, 1981.

DAILY, GARY W.
___ "Toni Morrison's **Beloved**: Rememory, History, and the Fantastic," in: Morse, Donald E., ed. **The Celebration of the Fantastic**. Westport, CT: Greenwood, 1992. pp.141-148.

DALE, ALZINA S.
___ "A Brief Biography of Dorothy L. Sayers," in: Dale, Alzina S., ed. **Dorothy L. Sayers: The Centenary Celebration**. New York: Walker, 1993. pp.151-152.
___ "**Thrones, Dominations**: Unfinished Testament to Friendship?," in: Dale, Alzina S., ed. **Dorothy L. Sayers: The Centenary Celebration**. New York: Walker, 1993. pp.67-78.
___ (ed.) **Dorothy L. Sayers: The Centenary Celebration**. New York: Walker, 1993. 167pp.

DALEY, BRIAN
___ **Star Wars: The Empire Strikes Back: The National Public Radio Dramatization**. New York: Del Rey, 1995. 309pp.
___ **Star Wars: The National Public Radio Dramatization**. New York: Del Rey, 1994. 346pp.

DALKIN, GARY
___ "*Babylon 5* (Review)," *Interzone* No. 97: 17. July 1995.
___ "Happy Centenary, *Interzone*," *Vector* No. 185: 3. September/October 1995.
___ "Sciphobia: Some Reflections on the Way the Mainstream Sees SF," *Vector* No. 186: 5-7. December 1995.
___ "Some Looking Glass Reflections on the Mainstream Perception of SF: Part 1, the C4 Sci-Fi Weekend," *Vector* No. 185: 9-10. September/October 1995.

DALMYN, TONY
___ "Some Thoughts on Walter Miller's **A Canticle for Leibowitz**," *Winding Numbers* No. 2: 4-8. Winter 1975-1976.

DALRYMPLE, SCOTT
___ "Demonic Therapy: Reading the Holy Word in the Mushroom Cloud," in: Slusser, George and Eric S. Rabkin, eds. **Fights of Fancy: Armed Conflict in Science Fiction and Fantasy**. Athens, GA: University of Georgia Press, 1993. pp.145-154.

DAMERON, J. LASLEY
___ "Poe's Pym and Scoresby on Polar Cataracts," *Resources for American Literary Study* 21(2): 258-260. 1995.

DAMICO, NATALIE W.
___ **The Other: Duality in the Science Fiction of Ursula K. Le Guin**. Master's Thesis, Indiana University of Pennsylvania, 1977. 82pp.

DAMON, T. WINTER
___ "Karl Edward Wagner Tribute," *Genre Writer's News* 1(7): 6-10. May/June 1995.

DANCER, GREG
___ "How Many Starfleet Officers Does It Take to Change a Lightbulb?: *Star Trek* at MIT," by Henry Jenkins and Greg Dancer. in: Tulloch, John and Jenkins, Henry, eds. **Science Fiction Audiences: Watching Doctor Who and Star Trek**. New York: Routledge, 1995. pp.213-236.

DANIEL, DENNIS
___ "The Girl, the Gillman and the Great White One-Piece: An Interview with Julie Adams," *Filmfax* No. 37: 50-56. February/March 1993.

DANIEL, JERRY
___ "The Taste of the Pineapple: A Basis for Literary Criticism," *CSL: The Bulletin of the New York C. S. Lewis Society* 23(2): 1-12. December 1991.

DANIELS, LES
___ **DC Comics: Sixty Years of the World's Favorite Comic Book Heroes**. Boston, MA: Little, Brown, 1995. 256pp.

DANN, JACK
___ "**The Memory Cathedral**," *New York Review of Science Fiction* No. 82: 1, 8-10. June 1995.
___ "The Profession of Science Fiction, 45: Sparks in the Dark," *Foundation* No. 61: 5-35. Summer 1994.

DANSKY, RICHARD E.
___ "Transgression, Spheres of Influence, and the Use of the Utterly Other in Lovecraft," *Lovecraft Studies* No. 30: 5-14. Spring 1994.

DARGIS, MANOHLA
___ "*Batman Forever* (Review)," *Sight and Sound* 5(7): 40-41. August 1995.
___ "Cyber Johnny," *Sight and Sound* 5(7): 6-7. July 1995.

DARKE, CHRIS
___ "It All Happened in Paris," *Sight and Sound* 4(7): 10-13. July 1994.

DARLINGTON, ANDREW
___ "Our Eyes Have Seen Great Wonders: The Lost World of Arthur Conan Doyle," *Fantasy Commentator* 7(3): 181-188. Spring 1992. (No. 43)

DAVEY, JOHN
___ **Michael Moorcock: A Reader's Guide**. London: John Davey, 1992. 35pp. Revised and Updated Edition.

DAVID, JOHN S.
___ "What Is *Star Trek* Today?," *Star Trek: The Official Fan Club Magazine* No. 84: 13. March/April 1992.

DAVID, PETER
___ "A Bad Day in Oblivion," *Starlog* No. 205: 36-39, 70. August 1994.

DAVIDS, HOLLACE
___ "Behind the Creative Impulse," *LucasFilms Fan Club* No. 18: 2-6. 1993.

DAVIDSMEYER, JO
___ "An Illustrious Pair," *Strange New Worlds* No. 7: 6-8. April/May 1993.

DAVIDSON, CLIVE
___ "Catch up on Minsky's Missing Chapters," *Guardian* Sec. 2, p. 17. March 25, 1993. [Not seen.]

DAVIDSON, HOWARD L.
___ "Virtual Reality and Other Electronic Intimacies," in: Wolf, Milton T. and Mallett, Daryl F., eds. **Imaginative Futures: Proceedings of the 1993 Science Fiction Research Association Conference**. San Bernardino, CA: Jacob's Ladder Books, 1995. pp.15-30.

DAVIDSON, JANE P.
___ "A Golem of Her Own: The Fantastic Art and Literature of Leilah Wendell," in: Wolf, Milton T. and Mallett, Daryl F., eds. **Imaginative Futures: Proceedings of the 1993 Science Fiction Research Association Conference.** San Bernardino, CA: Jacob's Ladder Books, 1995. pp.341-352.
___ "Golem--**Frankenstein**--Golem of Your Own," *Journal of the Fantastic in the Arts* 7(2/3): 228-243. 1995.

DAVIDSON, JIM
___ "*The Thing* About Filmmaker Christian Nyby," *Filmfax* No. 34: 36-46. August/September 1992.

DAVIDSON, KEAY
___ "To Fly in the Face of Physics," *San Francisco (CA) Examiner.* December 10, 1991. in: *NewsBank. Film and Television.* 7:D1-D3. 1992.

DAVIDSON, LALE
___ "Daughters of Eurydice in Absentia: The Feminine Heroic Quest for Presence in **Housekeeping**," *Journal of the Fantastic in the Arts* 4(4): 19-36. 1991. (No. 16)

DAVIES, ERIC L.
___ "Inspector Zadig: Voltaire and the Birth of the Scientific Detective Story," *Fantasy Commentator* 8(3/4): 214-216, 172. Fall 1995. (Whole No. 47/48)
___ "Remembering R. F. Starzl: A Conversation with Dr. Thomas E. Starzl," *Fantasy Commentator* 8(3/4): 150-160, 163-165. Fall 1995. (Whole No. 47/48)

DAVIES, LAURENCE
___ " 'The Evils of a Long Peace': Desiring the Great War," in: Slusser, George and Eric S. Rabkin, eds. **Fights of Fancy: Armed Conflict in Science Fiction and Fantasy.** Athens, GA: University of Georgia Press, 1993. pp.59-69.

DAVIES, RUSSELL
___ **Ronald Searle: A Biography.** London: Sinclair-Stevenson, 1990. 192pp.

DAVIES-MORRIS, GARETH N.
___ **Worlds in Collision: The Dialectic of H. G. Wells's Early Science Fiction.** Master's Thesis, San Diego State University, 1994. 211pp.

DAVIN, ERIC L.
___ "The Good Doctor at St. Vincent," *Fantasy Commentator* 7(4): 244-249. Fall 1992. (Whole No. 44)
___ "Pioneer Publisher: An Interview With Lloyd Eshbach," *Fantasy Commentator* 8(1/2): 121-134. Winter 1993/1994. (Whole No. 45/46)

DAVIS, BEN
___ **History, Race and Gender in the Science Fiction of Octavia Estelle Butler.** Master's Thesis, Ohio State University, 1992. 89pp.

DAVIS, DAY
___ "Appearance of a World," *New York Review of Science Fiction* No. 45: 16-17. May 1992.

DAVIS, ERIK
___ "The Imperial Race," *Village Voice* 38(47): 35-40. November 23, 1993.
___ "Techgnosis: Magic, Memory and the Angel of Information," *South Atlantic Quarterly* 92(4): 585-616. Fall 1993. (Reprinted in: Dery, Mark, ed. **Flame Wars: The Discourse of Cyberculture.** Durham, NC: Duke University Press, 1994.)

DAVIS, HAZEL K.
___ (ed.) **Presenting William Sleator**, ed. by James E. Davis and Hazel K. Davis. New York: Twayne, 1992. 131pp.

DAVIS, IVOR
___ "The Maitre'd of Limbo (Review)," *Boston (MA) Herald.* February 27, 1992. in: *NewsBank. Film and Television.* 24:B10. 1992.
___ "Spielberg Finds Contemporary *Hook*," *Boston (MA) Herald.* December 6, 1991. in: *NewsBank. Film and Television.* 3:E9-E10. 1992.

DAVIS, J. C.
___ "Formal Utopia/Informal Millennium: The Struggle Between Form and Substance as a Context for Seventeenth-Century Utopianism," in: Kumar, Krishan and Bann, Stephen, eds. **Utopias and the Millennium.** London: Reaktion Books, 1993. pp.17-32.

DAVIS, JAMES E.
___ "Attracting Middle-School Readers With William Sleator's **Strange Attractors**," by James E. Davis and Alison Smalley. *College English* 55(2): 76-77. February 1993.
___ (ed.) **Presenting William Sleator**, ed. by James E. Davis and Hazel K. Davis. New York: Twayne, 1992. 131pp.

DAVIS, JONATHAN
___ **Stephen King's America.** Mercer Island, WA: Starmont House, 1992.

DAVIS, KERRA
___ "Out of This World (**Star Wars** Collectibles)," *Antiques & Collecting Hobbies* 97: 24-25. July 1992. [Not seen.]

DAVIS, MARIAN
___ "Cuchulainn and Women: A Jungian Perspective," *Mythlore* 20(2): 23-26. Spring 1994. (Whole No. 76)

DAVIS, RAY
___ "Delany's Dirt," *New York Review of Science Fiction* No. 84: 1, 8-13. August 1995.
___ "Five Stories by Martha Soukup," *New York Review of Science Fiction* No. 60: 15-17. August 1993.

DAVIS, SALLY O.
___ "George Lucas Goes for Broke in His TV Debut--the Time Traveling, Globe-Trotting **Young Indiana Jones Chronicles** (Review)," *Boston (MA) Herald.* March 1, 1992. in: *NewsBank. Film and Television.* 37: G10-G11. 1992. also in: *NewsBank. Names in the News* 71:G2-G3. 1992.

DAVIS, VIRGINIA
___ "Morris and Indigo Darkness," *Journal of the William Morris Society* 11(3): 8-18. Autumn 1995.

DAVIS, WILLIAM A.
___ "Hobbit Forming," *Boston (MA) Globe.* December 29, 1991. in: *NewsBank. Names in the News.* 18:E7-E10. 1992.

DAVISON, PETER
___ "George Orwell: Dates and Origins," *The Library* 13(2): 137-150. June 1991. [Not seen.]

DAWES, AMY
___ "It's Just a Movie...Or Is It?," *Los Angeles (CA) Daily News.* October 15, 1995. in: *NewsBank. Film and Television.* 99:B13-B14. 1995.

DAWIDZIAK, MARK
___ "Anne Rice: The Universe Interview," *Sci-Fi Universe* No. 3: 19-27. October/November 1994.
___ "Native Clevelander Shaped Mysterious Return of Batman," *Akron (OH) Beacon Journal.* June 18, 1992. in: *NewsBank. Film and Television.* 62:D3-D4. 1992.
___ "**Nightmare Cafe**," *Cinefantastique* 22(6): 46-47, 61. June 1992
___ "**Young Indiana Jones**," *Cinefantastique* 22(6): 30-31. June 1992

DAWSON, CARL
___ **Lafcadio Hearn and the Vision of Japan.** Baltimore: Johns Hopkins University Press, 1992. 187pp.

DAWSON, W. H.
___ "Forecasts of the Future in Modern Literature," *Science Fiction News* (Australia) No. 91: 2-12. July 1992.

DAY, BRADFORD M.
___ **The Checklist of Fantastic Literature in Paperbound Books.** Revised and enlarged edition. Hillsville, VA: Bradford M. Day, 1994. 890pp.

DAY, DAVID D.
___ "Monty Python and the Medieval Other," in: Harty, Kevin J., ed. **Cinema Arthuriana: Essays on Arthurian Film**. New York: Garland, 1991. pp.83-92.

DAY, MARTIN
___ **The New Trek Programme Guide**, by Paul Cornell, Martin Day and Keith Topping. London: Virgin, 1995. 378pp.

DAY, MILDRED L.
___ "Joseph Campbell and the Power of Arthurian Myth," in: Slocum, Sally K., ed. **Popular Arthurian Traditions**. Bowling Green, OH: Popular Press, 1992. pp.80-84.
___ (ed.) **King Arthur Through the Ages**, ed. by Valerie M. Lagorio and Mildred L. Day. New York: Garland, 1990. 2 v.

DAYAN, JOAN
___ "Amorous Bondage: Poe, Ladies, and Slaves," in: Rosenheim, Shawn and Rachman, Stephen, ed. **The American Face of Edgar Allan Poe**. Baltimore: Johns Hopkins University Press, 1995. pp.179-210.

DE ALMEIDA TOLEDO NETO, SILVIO
___ "**Liuro de Josep ab Aramatia** and the Works of Rober de Boron," *Quondam et Futurus* 3(3): 36-45. Fall 1993.

DE ARMAS, FREDERICK A.
___ "Gyges' Ring: Invisibility in Plato, Tolkien, and Lope de Vega," *Journal of the Fantastic in the Arts* 3(4): 120-138. 1994.
___ "Interpolation and Invisibility: From Herodotus to Cervantes's **Don Quixote**," *Journal of the Fantastic in the Arts* 4(2): 8-28. 1992. (No. 14)

DE CAMP, CATHERINE CROOK
___ "Speech: Robert A. Heinlein," in: Kondo, Yoji, ed. **Requiem: New Collected Works by Robert A. Heinlein and Tributes to the Grand Master**. New York: Tor, 1992. pp.235-238.

DE CAMP, L. SPRAGUE
___ "Speech: Robert A. Heinlein," in: Kondo, Yoji, ed. **Requiem: New Collected Works by Robert A. Heinlein and Tributes to the Grand Master**. New York: Tor, 1992. pp.224-226.

DE CANIO, STEPHEN J.
___ "The Future Through Yesterday: Long-Term Forecasting in the Novels of H. G. Wells and Jules Verne," *Centennial Review* 75(1): 75-93. Winter 1994.

DE LINT, CHARLES
___ "The Heart of the Ticktock Man," in: Greenberg, Martin H., Ed Gorman and Bill Munster, eds. **The Dean Koontz Companion**. New York: Berkley, 1994. pp.75-100.
___ "Recommended Reading for 1990 and 1991," *Pulphouse* 1(12/13): 70-71. September/October 1992.

DE MONTREMY, JEAN-MAURICE
___ "A Writer Is Not a Professor (Interview, 1990)," in: Ingersoll, Earl G., ed. **Doris Lessing: Conversations**. Princeton, NJ: Ontario Review Press, 1994. pp.193-199.

DE SOUSA CAUSO, ROBERTO
___ "Science Fiction, a Global Community: Brazil," *Locus* 32(4): 40-41. April 1994.
___ "SF in Argentina," by Horacio Moreno and Roberto de Sousa Causo. *Locus* 33(1): 48-49. July 1994.
___ "SF in Brazil," *Locus* 28(4): 37, 65. April 1992.
___ "SF in Brazil," *Locus* 29(6): 48. December 1992.
___ "SF in Brazil," *Locus* 31(6): 36, 70. December 1993.
___ "SF in Brazil," *Locus* 33(1): 47. July 1994.
___ "SF in Brazil," *Locus* 34(1) 72. January 1995.
___ "SF in Brazil," *Locus* 34(4): 35, 38. April 1995.
___ "SF in Brazil," *Locus* 35(3): 52-53. September 1993.

DE TORRE GRACIA, EMILIO E.
___ "La ciencia ficción en la poesía de José Hierro," *Monographis Review* 3(1/2): 100-106. 1987.

DE WEEVER, JACQUELINE
___ "Morgan and the Problem of Incest," in: Harty, Kevin J., ed. **Cinema Arthuriana: Essays on Arthurian Film**. New York: Garland, 1991. pp.145-156.

DEAN, JOHN
___ "The Sick Hero Reborn: Two Versions of the Philoctetes Myth," *Comparative Literature Studies* 17(3): 334-340. September 1980.

DEAN, MICHAEL
___ "Writing as Time Runs Out (Interview, 1980)," in: Ingersoll, Earl G., ed. **Doris Lessing: Conversations**. Princeton, NJ: Ontario Review Press, 1994. pp.86-93.

DeARMOND, WILLIAM D.
___ **Ray Bradbury and Oral Interpretation: An Interpreters Theatre Adaptation of Fahrenheit 451**. Ph.D. Dissertation, Southern Illinois University, Carbondale, 1981. 193pp.

DeBELLIS, JACK
___ " 'The Awful Power': John Updike's Use of Kubrick's **2001: A Space Odyssey** in **Rabbit Redux**," *Literature/Film Quarterly* 21(3): 209-217. 1993.

DeCANDIDO, KEITH R. A.
___ "ConFrancisco, Here We Come: The 51st Annual World Science Fiction Convention," by Marina Frants and Keith R. A. DeCandido. *Wilson Library Bulletin* 68(3): 49-50. November 1993.
___ "Down by the Bayou: The 20th Annual World Fantasy Convention," by Marina Frants and Keith R. A. DeCandido. *Wilson Library Bulletin* 69(5): 51-52. January 1995

DeCARLO, TESSA
___ "Style: Costuming at the World Con," *Omni* 16(12): 22. September 1994.
___ "Tomorrow's Songs Today," *Wall Street Journal* p.A15. November 1, 1993.

DeCHICK, JOE
___ "**Alien 3**: Sci-Fi Shocker That Broke All of the Mainstream Rules Spawns a Third Thriller," *Cincinnati (OH) Enquirer*. May 20, 1992. in: *NewsBank. Film and Television*. 49:C12-C13. 1992.
___ "**Brainscan** Tries to Deliver Too Much," *Cincinnati (OH) Enquirer*. April 22, 1994. in: *NewsBank. Film and Television*. 41:B9. 1994.

DEER, HARRIET
___ "Kubrick and the Structures of Popular Culture," by Harriet Deer and Irving Deer. *Journal of Popular Film and Television* 3(3): 232-244. 1974.

DEER, IRVING
___ "Kubrick and the Structures of Popular Culture," by Harriet Deer and Irving Deer. *Journal of Popular Film and Television* 3(3): 232-244. 1974.

DEERY, JUNE
___ "Ectopic and Utopic Reproduction: **He, She and It**," *Utopian Studies* 5(2): 36-49. 1994.
___ "H. G. Wells's **A Modern Utopia** as a Work in Progress," *Extrapolation* 34(3): 216-229. Fall 1993.
___ "Technology and Gender in Aldous Huxley's Alternative (?) Worlds," *Extrapolation* 33(3): 258-273. Fall 1992.

DEIST, THOMAS
___ "Laßt die Puppen tanzen! Eine möglicher neuer Impuls im Horror-Genre und seine Geschichte," *Science Fiction Times* (Germany) 34(1): 12-16. January 1992.

DeKOVEN, MARIANNE
___ "Utopia Limited: Post-Sixties and Postmodern American Fiction," *Modern Fiction Studies* 41(1): 75-98. Spring 1995.

DEL OLMO, FRANK
___ "Donde muy pocos Latinos han ido," *Los Angeles (CA) Times* p.M5. March 19, 1995.

DEL VECCHIO, DEBORAH
___ **Peter Cushing: The Gentle Man of Horror and His 91 Films**, by Deborah Del Vecchio and Tom Johnson. Jefferson, NC: McFarland, 1992. 496pp.

DELANY, SAMUEL R.
___ "Anthony Davis, a Conversation," in: Delany, Samuel R. **Silent Interviews on Language, Race, Sex, Science Fiction and Some Comics.** Hanover, NH: Wesleyan University Press, 1994. pp.289-311.
___ "The Future of the Body: And Science Fiction and Technology," *New York Review of Science Fiction* No. 51: 1, 3-5. November 1992.
___ "Introduction: Reading and the Written Interview," in: Delany, Samuel R. **Silent Interviews on Language, Race, Sex, Science Fiction and Some Comics.** Hanover, NH: Wesleyan University Press, 1994. pp.1-20.
___ "Reading Modern American Science Fiction," in: Kostelanetz, Richard, ed. **American Writing Today.** Troy, NY: Whitston, 1991. pp.517-528.
___ **Silent Interviews on Language, Race, Sex, Science Fiction and Some Comics.** Hanover, NH: Wesleyan University Press, 1994. 322pp.
___ "Zelazny/Varley/Gibson--and Quality, Part 1," *New York Review of Science Fiction* No. 48: 1, 10-13. August 1992.
___ "Zelazny/Varley/Gibson--and Quality, Part 2," *New York Review of Science Fiction* No. 49: 1, 3-7. September 1992.

DELBAERE-GARANT, JEANNE
___ "Rhythm and Expansion in **Lord of the Flies**," in: Biles, Jack I. and Evans, Robert O., eds. **William Golding: Some Critical Considerations.** Lexington, KY: University Press of Kentucky, 1978. pp.72-86.

DELEAULT, ARTHUR R.
___ "Perceptions: Campbell/Burleson," *Studies in Weird Fiction* No. 15: 18-19. Summer 1994.

DELEUZE, GILLES
___ **The Logic of Sense.** New York: Columbia University Press, 1990. 393pp.

DELL'ERBA, ROSMARIA
___ "Un'utopia del socialismo gentile sopravvissuta: la tradizione de Charles Robert Ashbee (1863-1942) in Puglia," in: Saccaro Del Buffa, Giuseppa and Lewis, Arthur O., eds. **Utopia e Modernita: Teorie e prassi utopiche nell'eta moderna e postmoderna.** Rome: Gangemi Editore, 1989. pp.1125-1134.

DELLAVALLE, RENATO
___ "Horror a basso costo," *Cineforum* 30(11): 67-78. 1990.

DELLEPIANE, ANGELA B.
___ "Critical Notes on Argentinian Science Fiction Narrative," *Monographis Review* 3(1/2): 19-32. 1987.

DELLINGER, PAUL
___ "Bimbos, Zombies & Fans," *Starlog* 182: 50-51. September 1992.

DELMENDO, SHARON
___ " 'Born of **Misery**': Stephen King's (En)Gendered Text," in: Slusser, George E. and Rabkin, Eric S., eds. **Styles of Creation: Aesthetic Technique and the Creation of Fictional Worlds.** Athens: University of Georgia Press, 1992. pp.172-180.

DELVILLE, MICHEL
___ "The Moorcock/Hawkwind Connection: Science Fiction and Rock'n'Roll Culture," *Foundation* No. 62: 64-63. Winter 1994/1995.

DEMALINE, JACKIE
___ "Body Language (Review)," *Albany (NY) Times Union.* July 26, 1992. in: *NewsBank. Film and Television.* 68:F9-F10. 1992.

DEMARINIS, G.
___ "Ai bordi dello Sprawl: Macchine di scrittura [Aboard the Sprawl: William Gibson, David Cronenberg, Marshall McLuhan and Muses on Fantasy and Science Fiction]," *Cineforum* 33(1/2): 41-46. 1993.

DEMPSEY, JOHN
___ "Hey! That's My Ghost, Buster," *Variety* p.65. August 28, 1985.

DEMPSEY, JOHN (continued)
___ "**Rocket Boy** a Bit Too Hip," *Variety* p. 109, 130. February 13, 1985.
___ "Sci-Fi and Horror Leading the Way," *Variety* p. 481, 508. February 24, 1988.

DENDLE, BRIAN J.
___ "Spain's First Novel of Science Fiction: A Nineteenth Century Voyage to Saturn," *Monographis Review* 3(1/2): 43-48. 1987.

DENERSTEIN, ROBERT
___ "Dredd Yawningly Familiar," (Denver, CO) *Rocky Mountain News.* June 30, 1995. in: *NewsBank. Film and Television.* 70:B3. 1995.
___ "Grim *Virtuosity* a Virtual Waste of Time," (Denver, CO) *Rocky Mountain News.* August 4, 1995. in: *NewsBank. Film and Television.* 82:C1. 1995.

DENTITH, SIMON
___ "Imagination and Inversion in Nineteenth-Century Utopian Writing," in: Seed, David, ed. **Anticipations: Essays on Early Science Fiction and Its Precursors.** Liverpool: Liverpool University Press, 1995. pp.137-152.

DEPEW, DAVID J.
___ "Aristotle's Critique of Plato's Ideal States," in: Saccaro Del Buffa, Giuseppa and Lewis, Arthur O., eds. **Utopia e Modernita: Teorie e prassi utopiche nell'eta moderna e postmoderna.** Rome: Gangemi Editore, 1989. pp.727-738.

DERLETH, AUGUST
___ "Two Notes on Shiel's Style," in: **Shiel in Diverse Hands: A Collection of Essays.** Cleveland, OH: Reynolds Morse Foundation, 1983. pp.145-146.

DERRO, MARC
___ "Profile: Kevin Yagher," *Cinefex* No. 58: 103-104. June 1994.
___ "Quick Cuts: Animal House," *Cinefex* No. 61: 101-102. March 1995.
___ "Video Beat: Midair Morphing," *Cinefex* No. 58: 29-30. June 1994.

DERRY, STEPHEN
___ "The Time Traveller's Utopian Books and His Reading of the Future," *Foundation* No. 65: 16-24. Autumn 1995.

DERY, MARK
___ "Black to the Future: Interviews with Samuel R. Delany, Greg Tate, and Tricia Rose," *South Atlantic Quarterly* 92(4): 735-788. Fall 1993. (Reprinted in: Dery, Mark, Ed. **Flame Wars: The Discourse of Cyberculture.** Durham, NC: Duke University Press, 1994.)
___ "Cyberculture," *South Atlantic Quarterly* 91 (3): 501-523. Summer 1992.
___ "Reinventing the Future," *Elle* p. 88-89. May 1992.

DeSMET, KATE
___ "Trekkers Chase Future with a Religious Zeal," *Detroit (MI) News.* March 13, 1995. in: *NewsBank. Film and Television.* 38:E7. 1995.

DESMOND, JOHN E.
___ "Walker Percy's Triad: Science, Literature, and Religion," *Renascence* 47(1): 3-10. Fall 1994.

DESRIS, JOE
___ "**Batman**: Comic Co-Creator Bill Finger," *Cinefantastique* 24(6)/25(1): 27. February 1994.
___ "**Batman**: Comic Creator Bob Kane," *Cinefantastique* 24(6)/25(1): 21. February 1994.
___ "**Batman**: Episode Guide," *Cinefantastique* 24(6)/25(1): 8-63. February 1994.
___ "**Batman**: From Comics to TV," *Cinefantastique* 24(6)/25(1): 62-63. February 1994.

DETTMAN, BRUCE
___ "Children and Chills," *Filmfax* No. 31: 34-37. February/March 1992.

DEVER, SEAN
___ "Quick Cuts: Cinematic Cyberspace," *Cinefex* No. 62: 17-18. June 1995.

DeVORE, HOWARD
___ "A Science Fiction Collector," in: Sanders, Joe, ed. **Science Fiction Fandom**. Westport, CT: Greenwood, 1994. pp.221-228.

DEWAN, PAULINE
___ "Patterns of Enclosure in Morris' Early Stories," *Journal of the William Morris Society* 11(2): 9-10. Spring 1995.

DEWEY, PATRICK R.
___ **Fan Club Directory: 2000 Fan Clubs and Fan Mail Addresses in the United States and Abroad**. Jefferson, NC: McFarland, 1993. 104pp.

DEXTER, BRUCE
___ "Burgess Celebrates Mozart's Life With Keen Delight," *San Diego (CA) Union*. January 12, 1992. in: *NewsBank. Literature*. 8:G8. 1992

DI FATE, VINCENT
___ "Creature Capsules," *Science Fiction Chronicle* 13(11/12): 38-42. August 1992.
___ "Gadget Artists Return," by Vincent Di Fate and Roger Reed. *Science Fiction Age* 2(5): 70-75. July 1994.
___ "Persistent Vision: Unforgettable Poster Art From the Golden Age of Science Fiction Movies," by Bob Stephens and Vincent Di Fate. *Sci-Fi Entertainment* 1(2): 48-51. August 1994.
___ "A Short History of SF Art in Paperback," *Science Fiction Chronicle* 16(5): 12, 36-38. March/April 1995.
___ "Sketches: Now Might Be the Right Time to Donate That Painting!," *Science Fiction Chronicle* 13(7): 25-26. April 1992.

DI FILIPPO, PAUL
___ "Eye to Eye with Thomas M. Disch: An Interview," *Science Fiction Eye* No. 11: 39-48. December 1992.
___ "Hugo Winner Alan Moore Takes a Genre-Bending Time Warp Back to 1963," *Science Fiction Age* 1(6): 84-86. September 1993.
___ "The Man Who Had Too Many Ideas," *Amazing Stories* 69(3): 95-109. Winter 1995.
___ "Plumage From Pegasus: Not the Encyclopedia of Science Fiction," *Magazine of Fantasy and Science Fiction* 87(3): 73-79. September 1994.
___ "Sci-Fi Goobers Invent an Intergalactic Game Show That's Anything But Trivial," *Science Fiction Age* 3(4): 94-97. May 1995.
___ "Selling Books, Touching Lives," *Science Fiction Eye* No. 10: 22-26. June 1992.
___ "Topps Returns to Its Cult Classic as *Mars Attacks...Again*," *Science Fiction Age* 2(5): 82-84. July 1994.
___ "Who Are the 50 Most Powerful People in Science Fiction?," *Science Fiction Age* 1(5): 24-27. July 1993.
___ "You Are Not Your Genes!," *Science Fiction Eye* No. 11: 18-22. December 1992.

DICK, ANNE R.
___ **Search for Philip K. Dick, 1928-1982: A Memoir and Biography of the Science Fiction Writer**. Lewiston, NY: Mellen, 1995. 374pp.

DICK, PHILIP K.
___ "3 By PKD: Venom," *PKDS Newsletter* No. 29: 5. September 1992.
___ "A Clarification," in: Mullen, R. D., ed. **On Philip K. Dick: 40 Articles From Science-Fiction Studies**. Terre Haute, IN: SF-TH Inc., 1992. pp.73.
___ "The Different Stages of Love: A Previously Unpublished Passage From **Flow My Tears, the Policeman Said**," *PKDS Newsletter* No. 28: 3-5. March 1992.
___ "Fantasy," *PKDS Newsletter* No. 29: 7. September 1992.
___ "I Hope I Shall Arrive Soon," in: Gray, Chris H., ed. **The Cyborg Handbook**. New York: Routledge, 1995. pp.307-319.
___ "A Letter to Anthony Boucher/A Letter From Anne Dick," *PKDS Newsletter* No. 30: 1-4. December 1992.
___ "Pessimism," *PKDS Newsletter* No. 29: 6. September 1992.
___ **The Selected Letters of Philip K. Dick, Volume 4: 1975-1976**. Lancaster, PA: Underwood-Miller, 1992. 351pp.
___ **The Selected Letters of Philip K. Dick, Volume 5, 1977-1979**. Lancaster, PA: Underwood-Miller, 1993. 260pp.
___ "Universe Makers... and Breakers," *Radio Free P.K.D.* No. 1: 1,8. February 1993.
___ "Unpublished Foreword to **The Preserving Machine**," in: Mullen, R. D., ed. **On Philip K. Dick: 40 Articles From Science-Fiction Studies**. Terre Haute, IN: SF-TH Inc., 1992. pp.16-17.

DICKENS, DAVID B.
___ "Rings, Belts, and a Bird's Nest: Invisibility in German Literature," *Journal of the Fantastic in the Arts* 4(2): 29-48. 1992. (No. 14)

DICKERSON, MARY J.
___ "Stephen King Reading William Faulkner: Memory, Desire, and Time in the Making of *IT*," in: Magistrale, Tony, ed. **The Dark Descent: Essays Defining Stephen King's Horrorscape**. Westport, CT: Greenwood, 1992. pp.171-186.

DICKERSON, VANESSA D.
___ "The Ghost of a Self: Female Identity in Mary Shelley's **Frankenstein**," *Journal of Popular Culture* 27(3): 79-91. Winter 1993.

DICKSON, GORDON R.
___ "Robert Heinlein," in: Kondo, Yoji, ed. **Requiem: New Collected Works by Robert A. Heinlein and Tributes to the Grand Master**. New York: Tor, 1992. pp.265-271.

DICKSON, L. L.
___ **The Modern Allegories of William Golding**. Tampa: University of South Florida Press, 1990. 163pp.

DIENER, ASTRID
___ "An Interview with Owen Barfield: Poetic Diction--Between Conception and Publication," *Mythlore* 20(4): 14-19. Winter 1995. (Whole No. 78)

DIETRICH, BRYAN
___ "**Prince of Darkness**, Prince of Light: From Faust to Physicist," *Journal of Popular Film and Television* 19(2): 91-96. 1991.

DIETZ, FRANK
___ "Back From the Garden: Urban Vision in Contemporary American Utopias," *New York Review of Science Fiction* No. 43: 1, 8-10. March 1992.
___ "Robert Silverberg's **The World Inside** as an Ambiguous Dystopia," in: Elkins, Charles L. and Greenberg, Martin H., eds. **Robert Silverberg's Many Trapdoors: Critical Essays on His Science Fiction**. Westport, CT: Greenwood, 1992. pp.95-105.

DiGIACOMO, FRANK
___ "Naughty and Rice: Author Porn to Be Wild," *New York (NY) Post*. November 24, 1992. in: *NewsBank. Literature*. 105:C7-C8. 1992.

DILLARD, J. M.
___ **Star Trek: Where No One Has Gone Before, a History in Pictures**. New York: Pocket Books, 1994. 239pp.

DINALLO, ANTONELLA
___ " 'I racconti di Samuele Weller': di Giuseppe Mezzanotte: le fantasie scientifiche (Con inedito). [Giuseppe Mezzanotte i 'Racconti de Samuele Weller': Science Fiction Including a Previously Unpublished Text, gli 'Amanti Siderati'," *Critica Letteraria* 21(3): 537-562. 1993.

DINGBO, WU
___ "Fandom in China," in: Sanders, Joe, ed. **Science Fiction Fandom**. Westport, CT: Greenwood, 1994. pp.133-136.

DINGLEY, ROBERT
___ "Meaning Everything: The Image of Pan at the Turn of the Century," in: Filmer, Kath, ed. **Twentieth-Century Fantasists: Essays in Culture, Society and Belief in Twentieth Century Mythopoeic Literature**. New York: St. Martin's, 1992. pp.47-59.

DINGUS, ANNE
___ "Br-u-u-ce!," *Texas Monthly* 23(12): 28. December 1995.

DISCH, THOMAS M.
___ "Big Ideas and Dead-End Thrills," *Atlantic* 269(2): 86-94. February 1992.
___ "My Life as a Child, Part One," *Amazing Stories* 67(7): 8-12. October 1992. (No. 575)
___ "My Life as a Child, Part Two," *Amazing Stories* 67(8): 66-70. November 1992.
___ "Newt's Futurist Brain Trust," by Thomas M. Disch and Michah I. Sifry. *Nation* 260(8): 266-270. February 27, 1995.

DiTOMMASO, LORENZO
___ "History and Historical Effect in Frank Herbert's **Dune**," *Science-Fiction Studies* 19(3): 311-325. November 1992.

DOBBS, G. MICHAEL
___ "Stanley Wiater: A Conversation with the Interviewer," in: Wiater, Stanley. **Dark Visions: Conversations with the Masters of the Horror Film.** New York: Avon, 1992. pp.1-7.

DODDS, DAVID L.
___ "Magic in the Myths of J. R. R. Tolkien and Charles Williams," in: Kranz, Gisbert, ed. **Jahrbuch für Literatur und Ästhetik.** Lüdenscheid, Germany: Stier, 1992. Band 10, pp.37-60.

DOENSE, JAN
___ "*Alien 3*: Design Genius H. R. Giger," *Cinefantastique* 22(6): 10. June 1992

DOHERTY, THOMAS
___ "*Alien 3*," *Cinefantastique* 23(2/3): 6-7, 124. October 1992.
___ "*Basic Instinct* (Review)," *Cinefantastique* 23(1): 60. August 1992.
___ "*Basic Instinct*," *Cinefantastique* 23(2/3): 4-5. October 1992.
___ "*Batman Returns*," *Cinefantastique* 23(2/3): 8-11. October 1992.
___ "*Blade Runner*," *Cinefantastique* 23(5): 56-57. February 1993.
___ "*Bram Stoker's Dracula*: Reviving an Undead Career," *Cinefantastique* 23(6): 59. April 1993.
___ "*Cool World* (Review)," *Cinefantastique* 23(4): 60. December 1992.
___ "*Freddy's Dead: The Final Nightmare* (Review)," *Cinefantastique* 22(4): 57. February 1992.
___ "*Groundhog Day* (Review)," *Cinefantastique* 24(2): 57. August 1993.
___ "*Innocent Blood*," *Cinefantastique* 23(6): 52-53. April 1993.
___ "*Lawnmower Man* (Review)," *Cinefantastique* 23(1): 57. August 1992.
___ "*Matinee* (Review)," *Cinefantastique* 24(1): 59. June 1993.
___ "*Pet Sematary Two* (Review)," *Cinefantastique* 23(5): 54, 61. February 1993.
___ "Peter Pan: Steven Spielberg's *Hook*," *Cinefantastique* 22(6): 44-45. June 1992
___ "*Prelude to a Kiss* (Review)," *Cinefantastique* 23(4): 57. December 1992.
___ "*Radio Flyer* (Review)," *Cinefantastique* 23(1): 58-59. August 1992.
___ "*Raising Cain* (Review)," *Cinefantastique* 23(4): 61. December 1992.
___ "*Silence of the Lambs*: Hannibal Lector's Horror Pedigree," *Cinefantastique* 22(4): 36-37. February 1992.
___ "*Single White Female* (Review)," *Cinefantastique* 23(4): 61. December 1992.
___ "*Sleepwalkers* (Review)," *Cinefantastique* 23(2/3): 121. October 1992.
___ "*Waterworld*," *Cinefantastique* 26(5): 6-9, 61. August 1995.

DOLAN, CARRIE
___ "Translating the Bible into Klingon Stirs Cosmic Debate; Some Favor a Literal Tack, Others Find That Alien; Help for the Lutherans," *Wall Street Journal* p.A1. June 13, 1994.

DOLGOFF, STEPHANIE
___ "What Do Hieroglyphs Really Sound Like," *New York Times* p.H24. October 23, 1994.

DOLPHIN, RIC
___ "Master of the Virtual World," *Maclean's* 105: 44. December 14, 1992. [Not seen.]

DOMINGUEZ, ROBERT
___ "How Do You Sell Tickets on the *Titanic*?," *(New York, NY) Daily News*. July 16, 1995. in: *NewsBank. Film and Television.* 82:D7. 1995.

DONAHOO, ROBERT
___ "Lewis Shiner and the 'Good' Anarchist," by Robert Donahoo and Chuck Etheridge. in: Slusser, George E. and Shippey, Tom, eds. **Fiction 2000: Cyberpunk and the Future of Narrative.** Athens: University of Georgia Press, 1992. pp.183-190.
___ "Moving With the Mainstream: A View of Postmodern American Science Fiction," in: Trachtenberg, Stanley, ed. **Critical Essays on American Postmodernism.** New York: G. K. Hall, 1995. pp.152-165.

DONALD, RALPH R.
___ "The *Mary Ann*, the *Ruptured Duck* and the *Enterprise*: Character Relationships with Air and Space Craft as Metaphors for Human Affinities," in: Loukides, Paul and Fuller, Linda K., eds. **Beyond the Stars III: The Material World in American Popular Film.** Bowling Green, OH: Popular Press, 1993. pp.123-133.

DONATON, SCOTT
___ "New Sci Fi Magazine Will Launch This Fall," *Advertising Age* 63(35): 29. August 31, 1992.

DONAWERTH, JANE L.
___ "Introduction," by Jane L. Donawerth and Carol A. Kolmerten. in: Donawerth, Jane L. and Kolmerten, Carol A., eds. **Utopian and Science Fiction by Women: Worlds of Difference.** Syracuse, NY: Syracuse University Press, 1994. pp.1-14.
___ "Science Fiction by Women in the Early Pulps, 1926-1930," in: Donawerth, Jane L. and Kolmerten, Carol A., eds. **Utopian and Science Fiction by Women: Worlds of Difference.** Syracuse, NY: Syracuse University Press, 1994. pp.137-152.
___ "Woman as Machine in Science Fiction by Women," *Extrapolation* 36(3): 210-221. Fall 1995.
___ (ed.) **Utopian and Science Fiction by Women: Worlds of Difference**, ed. by Jane L. Donawerth and Carol A. Kolmerten. Syracuse, NY: Syracuse University Press, 1994. 260pp.

DONLON, BRIAN
___ "Harve Bennett Makes 'Trax' With Sci-Fi Trek to the Past," *USA Today* Sec. D, p. 3. March 30, 1993.
___ "Sci-Fi Channel Nears a Full Launch," *USA Today* Sec. D., p. 1. May 4, 1992.
___ "Sci-Fi Is Trekking into Prime-Time TV," *USA Today* Sec. D, p. 1. December 22, 1992.

DONNELLY, KATHLEEN
___ "Out of the Closet, a Basic Backlash Hits the Streets," *San Jose (CA) Mercury News* March 20, 1992 in: *NewsBank. Film and Television.* 28: G13. 1992.

DOOLEY, PATRICIA
___ "Earthsea Patterns," *Children's Literature Association.* Quarterly 4(2): 1-4. Summer 1979.

DOPP, JAMIE
___ "Subject-Position as Victim-Position in **The Handmaid's Tale**," *Studies in Canadian Literature* 19(1): 43-57. 1994.

DORFLES, GILLO
___ "L'utopia della omoglossia e il ritorno a un linguaggio prebabelico," in: Saccaro Del Buffa, Giuseppa and Lewis, Arthur O., eds. **Utopie per gli Anni Ottana.** Rome: Gangemi Editore, 1986. pp.45-50.
___ "L'utopia medievaleggiante della 'Heroic Fantasy'," in: Saccaro Del Buffa, Giuseppa and Lewis, Arthur O., eds. **Utopia e Modernita: Teorie e prassi utopiche nell'eta moderna e postmoderna.** Rome: Gangemi Editore, 1989. pp.667-671.

DORSETT, LYLE W.
___ "Researching C. S. Lewis," in: Walker, Andrew and Patric, James, eds. **A Christian for All Christians.** Washington, DC: Regnery, 1992. pp.213-215.

DORSEY, CANDAS J.
___ "All This--And Also Dancing," *Aloud* (Toronto) 2(7): 5, 10. October 1992.

DOTY, GENE
___ "A Clockwork Evil: Guilt and Coincidence in 'The Monkey'," in: Magistrale, Tony, ed. **The Dark Descent: Essays Defining Stephen King's Horrorscape.** Westport, CT: Greenwood, 1992. pp.129-136.

DOTY, KAY
___ "The Primary Bridge Crews of the *Enterprise*," in: Van Hise, James, ed. **Trek Celebration Two.** Las Vegas, NV: Pioneer, 1994. pp.71-75.
___ "Sarek of Vulcan," in: Van Hise, James, ed. **Trek Celebration Two.** Las Vegas, NV: Pioneer, 1994. pp.40-52.

DOUGHAN, DAVID
___ "Tolkien, Sayers, Sex and Gender," in: Reynolds, Patricia and GoodKnight, Glen H., eds. **Proceedings of the J. R. R. Tolkien Centenary Conference, Keble College, Oxford, 1992**. Altadena, CA: Mythopoeic Press, 1995. pp.356-359. (*Mythlore* Vol. 21, No. 2, Winter 1996, Whole No. 80)

DOUGLASS, REBECCA M.
___ "Missed Masses: Absence and the Functions of the Liturgical Year in **Sir Gawain and the Green Knight**," *Quondam et Futurus* 2(2): 20-27. Summer 1992.

DOVER, CAROL
___ "The Split-Shield Motif in the Old French Prose **Lancelot**," in: Busby, Keith, ed. **The Arthurian Yearbook I**. New York: Garland, 1991. pp.43-62.

DOWD, FRANCES A.
___ "Is There a Typical YA Fantasy? A Content Analysis," by Frances A. Dowd and Lisa C. Taylor. *Journal of Youth Services in Libraries* 5(2): 175-183. Winter 1992.

DOWD, MAUREEN
___ "Newt's Potboiler," *New York Times Magazine* pp.44-46. December 4, 1994.

DOWLER, ANDREW
___ "Join William Shatner on the Set of **Tekwar**, His Newest SF Series," *Science Fiction Age* 2(3): 20-23, 79. March 1994.

DOWLIN, C. EDWIN
___ "The Wondrous Williamson Collection," *Popular Culture in Libraries* 1(2): 79-85. 1993.

DOWLING, TERRY
___ "SF in Australia," by Sean McMullen and Terry Dowling. *Locus* 33(1): 46. July 1994.
___ "SF in Australia," by Sean McMullen and Terry Dowling. *Locus* 34(1) 71. January 1995.

DOWNEY, GARY L.
___ "Cyborg Anthropology," by Gary L. Downey, Joseph Dumit and Sarah Williams. in: Gray, Chris H., ed. **The Cyborg Handbook**. New York: Routledge, 1995. pp.341-346.
___ "Human Agency in CAD/CAM Technology," in: Gray, Chris H., ed. **The Cyborg Handbook**. New York: Routledge, 1995. pp.363-370.

DOWNING, DAVID C.
___ **Planets in Peril: A Critical Study of C. S. Lewis's Ransom Trilogy**. Amherst: University of Massachusetts Press, 1992. 186pp.

DOWNING, PAULA E.
___ "Pros and Cons of Being a Writer Couple," by T. Jackson King and Paula E. Downing. *SFWA Bulletin* 25(4): 7-14. Winter 1992. (No. 114)
___ "Writing Science Fiction: Where to Begin," *Writer* 105(5): 18-20, 45. May 1992

DOZOIS, GARDNER
___ "Living the Future: You Are What You Eat," in: Dozois, Gardner, ed. **Writing Science Fiction and Fantasy**. New York: St. Martin's, 1991. pp.12-27.
___ "Summation 1992," in: Dozois, Gardner, ed. **The Year's Best Science Fiction: Tenth Annual Collection**. New York: St. Martin's, 1993. pp.xi-xxxvi.
___ (ed.) **Writing Science Fiction and Fantasy: Twenty Dynamic Essays by Today's Top Professionals**. New York: St. Martins, 1993. 261pp.

DRAKE, BARBARA
___ "Two Utopias: Marge Piercy's **Women on the Edge of Time** and Ursula K. Le Guin's **The Dispossessed**," in: Roberts, Sheila, ed. **Still the Frame Holds: Essays on Women Poets and Writers**. San Bernardino, CA: Borgo Press, 1993. pp.109-128.

DRAKE, DAVID
___ "Hickmania," *Science Fiction Age* 2(1): 80-85. November 1993.

DRAKE, DAVID (continued)
___ "Intolerence," *New York Review of Science Fiction* No. 82: 21. June 1995.

DRAKE, DAVID A.
___ "The New King (Shiel's Final Novel): An Appreciation," in: **Shiel in Diverse Hands: A Collection of Essays**. Cleveland, OH: Reynolds Morse Foundation, 1983. pp.329-330.

DRAKE, RODNEY
___ **The Use, Function and Importance of Kilgore Trout in the Novels of Kurt Vonnegut, Junior**. Master's Thesis, University of Northern Iowa, 1977. 64pp.

DREHER, RON
___ "Be Sure to Beam Yourself up to **Deep Space Nine** (Review)," *Washington (DC) Times*. January 4, 1993. in: *NewsBank. Art.* 1:C4. 1993.
___ "Fox's Batman Pioneers a Genre: Toon Noir," *Washington (DC) Times*. September 5, 1992. in: *NewsBank. Film and Television*. 87:D8. 1992.

DREWER, CECELIA
___ "Symbolism of Style in 'The Strange High House in the Mist'," *Lovecraft Studies* No. 31: 17-21. Fall 1994.

DREXLER, DOUG
___ **The Star Trek Encyclopedia: A Reference Guide to the Future**, by Michael Okuda, Denise Okuda, Debbie Mirek and Doug Drexler. New York: Pocket Books, 1994. 396pp.

DRISCOLL, MATTHEW J.
___ "The Cloak of Fidelity: **Skikkjurimur**, a Late-Medieval Icelandic Version of **Le Mantel Mautaillie**," in: Busby, Keith, ed. **The Arthurian Yearbook I**. New York: Garland, 1991. pp.107-134.

DRISCOLL, ROBERT W.
___ "Engineering Man for Space: The Cyborg Study," in: Gray, Chris H., ed. **The Cyborg Handbook**. New York: Routledge, 1995. pp.75-81.

DROESCH, PAUL
___ "Hits and Misses: **Science Fiction: A Journey into the Unknown**," *TV Guide* 42(50): 53. December 10, 1994.
___ "Hits and Misses' **The Invaders**," *TV Guide* 43(45): 55. November 11, 1995.
___ "Hits and Misses: Kurt Vonnegut's **Harrison Bergeron**," *TV Guide* 43(32): 41. August 12, 1995.
___ "Hits and Misses: The New Explorers," *TV Guide* 43(2): 45. January 14, 1995.

DROR, YUVAL
___ "Social Education: Bridging Between Education and Social Systems: Owen's Utopian Education and Kibbutz Education Today; A Comparison," *Utopian Studies* 5(2): 87-102 1994.

DROZDIAK, WILLIAM
___ "Jules Verne's Crystal Ball," *Washington (DC) Post*. September 24, 1994. in: *NewsBank. Film and Television*. 71:C14-D1. 1994.

DRUMMOND, RON
___ "Steve Erickson...," *Science Fiction Eye* No. 12: 69-73. Summer 1993.

DRUSE, JUDY
___ "Easy Talking: Horror," *Voice of Youth Advocates* 16(1): 11-15, 21. April 1993.

DU MONT, MARY J.
___ "Images of Women in Young Adult Science Fiction and Fantasy, 1970, 1980, and 1990: A Comparative Content Analysis," *Voice of Youth Advocates* 16(1): 11-15, 21. April 1993.

DUBECK, LEROY W.
___ **Fantastic Voyages: Learning Science Through Science Fiction Films**. New York: American Institute of Physics, 1994. 327pp.

DUBECK, LEROY W. (continued)
___ "Finding the Facts in Science Fiction Films," by Leroy W. Dubeck, Suzanne E. Moshier, Matthew H. Bruce and Judith E. Boss. *Science Teacher* 60(4): 46-48. April 1993.
___ "Science and Science Fiction Films," *Journal of College Science Teaching* 11(2): 111-113. November 1981.
___ "Using Science Fiction Films to Teach Science at the College Level," by Leroy W. Dubeck, Suzanne E. Moshier and Judith E. Boss. *Journal of College Science Teaching* 25(1): 46-50. September/October 1995

DUDLEY, JOSEPH M.
___ "Transformational SF Religions: Philip Jose Farmer's **Night of Light** and Robert Silverberg's **Downward to the Earth**," *Extrapolation* 35(4): 342-351. Winter 1994.

DUE, TANANARIVE
___ "Anne Rice: Queen of the Night (Interview)," *Miami (FL) Herald*. November 19, 1992. in: *NewsBank. Literature.* 105:C5-C6. 1992.

DUMARS, DENISE
___ "Writer-Director Clive Barker on Launching Harry D'Amour as a Horror Hero Franchise," *Cinefantastique* 27(3): 55-56. December 1995.

DUMAS, ALAN
___ "Philip Dick Fans Are Seeking Out Fort Morgan Plot," *Denver (CO) Rocky Mountain News*. December 8, 1992. in: *NewsBank. Literature.* 2:E8-E9. 1992.

DUMIT, JOSEPH
___ "Brain-Mind Machines and American Technological Dream Marketing: Towards an Ethnography of Cyborg Envy," in: Gray, Chris H., ed. **The Cyborg Handbook**. New York: Routledge, 1995. pp.347-362.
___ "Cyborg Anthropology," by Gary L. Downey, Joseph Dumit and Sarah Williams. in: Gray, Chris H., ed. **The Cyborg Handbook**. New York: Routledge, 1995. pp.341-346.

DUMONT, JEAN-NOËL
___ "Between Faith and Melancholy: Irony and the Gnostic Meaning of Dick's 'Divine Trilogy'," in: Mullen, R. D., ed. **On Philip K. Dick: 40 Articles From Science-Fiction Studies**. Terre Haute, IN: SF-TH Inc., 1992. pp.240-242.

DUNAWAY, DAVID K.
___ **Aldous Huxley Recollected: An Oral History**. New York: Carroll & Graf, 1995. 225pp.

DUNCAN, JODY
___ "The Beauty in the Beasts," *Cinefex* No. 55: 42-95. August 1993.
___ "Blowing Up Baby," *Cinefex* No. 52: 22-53. November 1992.
___ "Borrowed Flesh," *Cinefex* No. 49: 24-39. February 1992.
___ "**Broken Arrow**: Stealth Effects," *Cinefex* No. 64: 13-14. December 1995.
___ "Commercial Spot: Evolutionary Auto," *Cinefex* No. 55: 105-106. August 1993.
___ "Commercial Spot: They Keep Going and Going," *Cinefex* No. 59: 83-84. September 1994.
___ "Commercial Spot: Thoroughbred Animation," *Cinefex* No. 54: 15-16. May 1993.
___ "Fire and Ice," *Cinefex* No. 57: 42-69. March 1994.
___ "From Zero to Hero," *Cinefex* No. 60: 46-65. December 1994.
___ "Gorilla Warfare," *Cinefex* No. 62: 34-53. June 1995.
___ "The Making of a Blockbuster," *Cinefex* No. 58: 34-65. June 1994.
___ **The Making of Jurassic Park**, by Don Shay and Jody Duncan. New York: Ballantine, 1993. 195pp.
___ "**Money Train**: Training Film," *Cinefex* No. 64: 25-30, 134. December 1995.
___ "Profile: Joseph Viskocil," *Cinefex* No. 50: 23. May 1992.
___ "Profile: Katherine Kean," *Cinefex* No. 51: 12. August 1992.
___ "Profile: Peter Kuran," *Cinefex* No. 54: 88. May 1993.
___ "Quick Cuts: A Crash in the Andes," *Cinefex* No. 55: 117-118. August 1993.
___ "Quick Cuts: Bonnie and Clyde," *Cinefex* No. 63: 53-54. September 1995.
___ "Quick Cuts: Clause and Effects," *Cinefex* No. 61: 17-18. March 1995.

DUNCAN, JODY (continued)
___ "Quick Cuts: Cowboys and Indians," *Cinefex* No. 63: 27-28. September 1995.
___ "Quick Cuts: Crime and Banishment," *Cinefex* No. 58: 11-12. June 1994.
___ "Quick Cuts: Making the Crow Fly," *Cinefex* No. 58: 23-24. June 1994.
___ "Quick Cuts: Maximum Speed," *Cinefex* No. 59: 89-92. September 1994.
___ "Quick Cuts: Terminal Effects," *Cinefex* No. 59: 17-18. September 1994.
___ "Quickcuts: The Ghost and Mr. Muren," *Cinefex* No. 63: 13-16. September 1995.
___ "Special Venues: MGM's Grand EFX," *Cinefex* No. 63: 21-22. September 1995.
___ "Special Venues: Moon Shot," *Cinefex* No. 59: 11-12. September 1994.
___ "Video Beat: Making Movie Magic," *Cinefex* No. 56: 97-98. November 1993.

DUNN, THOM
___ "Growing Home: The Triumph of Youth in the Novels of H. M. Hoover," by Thom Dunn and Karl Hiller. in: Sullivan, C. W., III. **Science Fiction for Young Readers**. Westport, CT: Greenwood, 1993. pp.121-131.

DUNNE, LINDA
___ "Mothers and Monsters in Sarah Robinson Scott's **Millenium Hall**," in: Donawerth, Jane L. and Kolmerten, Carol A., eds. **Utopian and Science Fiction by Women: Worlds of Difference**. Syracuse, NY: Syracuse University Press, 1994. pp.54-72.

DUPERRAY, MAX
___ "Lord Dunsany Revisited," *Studies in Weird Fiction* No. 13: 10-14. Summer 1993. [Not seen.]
___ (ed.) **Eros: Science & Fiction Fantastique**, ed. by Roger Bozzetto, Max Duperray and Alain Chareyre-Mejan. Aix-en-Provence: Universite de Provence, 1991. 220pp.

DuPLESSIS, RACHEL B.
___ "The Feminist Apologies of Lessing, Piercy, and Russ," *Frontiers* 4(1): 1-8. 1979.

DuPRIEST, MARGARET D.
___ "Philip Wylie," in: Bruccoli, Matthew J., ed. **Facts on File Bibliography of American Fiction 1919-1988**. New York: Facts on File, 1991. pp.561-562.

DURDEN, DOUGLAS
___ "**Star Trek** Brings Message of Hope," *Richmond (VA) Times-Dispatch*. February 27, 1992. in: *NewsBank. Film and Television.* 26: A3. 1992.

DURHAM, SCOTT
___ "From the Death of the Subject to a Theology of Late Capitalism," in: Mullen, R. D., ed. **On Philip K. Dick: 40 Articles From Science-Fiction Studies**. Terre Haute, IN: SF-TH Inc., 1992. pp.188-198.

DURIEZ, COLIN
___ **The J. R. R. Tolkien Handbook**. Grand Rapids, MI: Baker House, 1992. 316pp.
___ **The Tolkien and Middle Earth Handbook**. Tunbridge Wells, U.K.: Monarch, 1992. 316pp.
___ "Tolkien and the Other Inklings," in: Reynolds, Patricia and GoodKnight, Glen H., eds. **Proceedings of the J. R. R. Tolkien Centenary Conference, Keble College, Oxford, 1992**. Altadena, CA: Mythopoeic Press, 1995. pp.360-363. (*Mythlore* Vol. 21, No. 2, Winter 1996, Whole No. 80)

DUTKA, ELAINE
___ "Crichton Stays Busy Straddling Worlds of Film, Fiction," *Austin (TX) American Statesman* Sec. B, p. 9. June 14, 1993.

DUTTA, MARY B.
___ " 'Very Bad Poetry, Captain': Shakespeare in **Star Trek**," *Extrapolation* 36(1): 38-45. Spring 1995.

EBY, DOUGLAS (continued)
___ "Tom Holland: Directing Stephen King," *Cinefantastique* 26(5): 52-53. August 1995.

ECKER, GISELA
___ "The Politics of Fantasy in Recent American Women's Novels," *Englishch-Amerikanische Studien* 3: 503-510. 1984.

ECKERN, CLAUDE
___ "La Science-fiction de Jean-Pierre April," *Imagine* No. 61: 119-156. September 1992.

ECKERSLEY, ADRIAN
___ "A Theme in the Early Work of Arthur Machen: 'Degeneration'," *English Literature in Transition* 35(3): 277-287. 1992.

ECKERT, HANS
___ "The Impact of Morris and the Kelmscott Press in Germany," *Journal of the William Morris Society* 11(2): 20-23. Spring 1995.

ECKSTEIN, ARTHUR M.
___ "The Classic Heritage of Airstrip One," in: Rose, Jonathan, ed. **The Revised Orwell**. East Lansing, MI: Michigan State University Press, 1992. pp.97-116.
___ "George Orwell's Second Thoughts on Capitalism," in: Rose, Jonathan, ed. **The Revised Orwell**. East Lansing, MI: Michigan State University Press, 1992. pp.191-206.

EDELSTEIN, ART
___ "Vermont Struggles with Film Policy," *Vermont Business Magazine (Brattleboro, VT)*. February 1,1994. in: NewsBank. Film and Television. 23:D6-D9. 1994.

EDER, RICHARD
___ "Atwood's Anger Shows in Explosive Short Stories," *Miami (FL) Herald*. December 15, 1991. in NewsBank. Literature. 1:C6. 1992.

EDGAR, ROBERT
___ "The Nature of Survival in the 21st Century: The Survival of Concern in 1995," *Vector* No. 185: 5-8. September/October 1995.

EDGE, PEGGY
___ "WLB Biography: Madeleine L'Engle," *Wilson Library Bulletin* 36(9): 766. May 1962.

EGLASH, RON
___ "African Influences in Cybernetics," in: Gray, Chris H., ed. **The Cyborg Handbook**. New York: Routledge, 1995. pp.17-27.
___ "An Interview With Patricia Cowings," in: Gray, Chris H., ed. **The Cyborg Handbook**. New York: Routledge, 1995. pp.93-99.

EHRENSTEIN, DAVID
___ "One From the Art," *Film Comment* 29(1): 27-30. January/February 1993.

EISENHART, MARY
___ "Text: The Ultimate VR Tool? An Electronic Interview with **Snow Crash** Author Neal Stephenson," *Microtimes* No. 112: 91, 231-233. August 23, 1993.

EISENMANN, STEPHEN
___ **Designing Utopia: The Art of William Morris and His Circle: Katonah Museum of Art, February 16 through April 12, 1992**. Katonah, NY: Katonah Museum of Art, 1992. 39pp.

EISNER, JOEL
___ "Throne of Villainy," *Starlog* No. 190: 52-55, 72. May 1993.

ELFLANDSSON, GALAD
___ "Arcturus Revisited: David Lindsay and the Quest for Muspel-Fire," *AB Bookman's Weekly* pp.2131-2146. October 1, 1984.

ELGIN, SUZETTE H.
___ "Women's Language and Near Future Science Fiction: A Reply," *Women's Studies* 14(2): 175-182. 1987.

ELKINS, AARON
___ "The Art of Framing Lies: Dorothy L. Sayers on Mystery Fiction," in: Dale, Alzina S., ed. **Dorothy L. Sayers: The Centenary Celebration**. New York: Walker, 1993. pp.99-108.

ELKINS, CHARLES L.
___ "Isaac Asimov's 'Foundation' Novels: Historical Materialism Distorted into Cyclical Psycho-History," *Chung Wai Literary Quarterly* 22(12): May 1994. (Issue not seen; pagination unavailable.) (Reprinted from *Science Fiction Studies*.)
___ (ed.) **Robert Silverberg's Many Trapdoors: Critical Essays on His Science Fiction**, ed. by Charles L. Elkins and Martin H. Greenberg. Westport, CT: Greenwood, 1992. 154pp.

ELLER, CLAUDIA
___ "Plenty of Riptides in **Waterworld** Set," by Claudia Eller and Robert W. Welkos. *Los Angeles (CA) Times*. September 16, 1994. in: NewsBank. Film and Television. 117:C10. 1994.

ELLER, JON R.
___ "The Stories of Ray Bradbury: An Annotated Finding List (1938-1991)," *Bulletin of Bibliography* 49(1): 72-51. March 1992.

ELLERBEE, LINDA
___ "Movie Offers a Dose of Reality," *Austin (TX) American Statesman* Sec. A, p. 13. June 18, 1993.

ELLIOT, JEFFREY M.
___ **Adventures of a Freelancer: The Literary Exploits and Autobiography of Stanton A. Coblentz**, by Stanton A. Coblentz and Jeffrey M. Elliot. San Bernardino, CA: Borgo Press, 1993. 160pp.

ELLIOTT, DAVID
___ "**No Escape** Is One Action Fest Fully in Touch With Its Male Side," *San Diego (CA) Union*. April 28, 1994. in: NewsBank. Film and Television. 46:E1. 1994.
___ "Van Damme a Model **Timecop**," *The San Diego (CA) Union-Tribune*. September 15, 1994. in: NewsBank. Film and Television. 105: C7. 1994.

ELLIOTT, ELTON
___ "Interview: Vernor Vinge, Part 1," *Science Fiction Review* No. 8: 10-11, 29-30. March 1992.

ELLIS, MARK
___ **Philosophical Romance: Theories of Time and Their Relationship to Genre in the Fiction of John Crowley**. Master's Thesis, University of Manitoba (Canada), 1990. 101pp. (Master's Abstracts 31/02, p. 566. Summer 1993.)

ELLIS, R. J.
___ "Are You a Fucking Mutant?: **Total Recall**'s Fantastic Hesitations," *Foundation* No. 65: 81-97. Autumn 1995.

ELLISON, HARLAN
___ **The Harlan Ellison Hornbook**. New York: Penzler, 1990. 418pp.
___ "Me 'N' Isaac at the Movies: A Brief Memoir of Citizen Calvin," *Science Fiction Age* 3(1): 78-83. November 1994.
___ **Sleepless Nights in a Procrustean Bed**. San Bernardino, CA: Borgo, 1990. 192pp.
___ "Toiling in the Dreamtime," *Science Fiction Age* 1(3): 28-33, 79. March 1993.

ELLISON, JOHN
___ "Baggins Remembered," in: Reynolds, Patricia and GoodKnight, Glen H., eds. **Proceedings of the J. R. R. Tolkien Centenary Conference, Keble College, Oxford, 1992**. Altadena, CA: Mythopoeic Press, 1995. pp.394-395. (*Mythlore* Vol. 21, No. 2, Winter 1996, Whole No. 80)

ELLISON, RUTH
___ "The Saga of Jón Jónsson Saddelsmith of Lithend-Cot," *Journal of the William Morris Society* 10(1): 21-30. Autumn 1992.

ELMER, JONATHAN
___ "Terminate or Liquidate? Poe, Sensationalism, and the Sentimental Tradition," in: Rosenheim, Shawn and Rachman, Stephen, ed. **The American Face of Edgar Allan Poe**. Baltimore: Johns Hopkins University Press, 1995. pp.91-120.

ELMER-DEWITT, PHILIP
___ "Cyberpunk," *Time* 141(6): 59-65. February 8, 1993.

ELMS, ALAN C.
___ "Cordwainer Smith," in: Bruccoli, Matthew J., ed. **Facts on File Bibliography of American Fiction 1919-1988**. New York: Facts on File, 1991. pp.461-462.

ELPHINSTONE, MARGARET
___ "Contemporary Feminist Fantasy in the Scottish Literary Tradition," in: Latham, Robert A. and Collins, Robert A., eds. **Modes of the Fantastic**. Westport, CT: Greenwood, 1995. pp.84-92.

ELY, KATHLEEN
___ "Transforming the Myth: The Use of Arthurian Material in the Church Universal and Triumphant," in: Slocum, Sally K., ed. **Popular Arthurian Traditions**. Bowling Green, OH: Popular Press, 1992. pp.132-143.

EMERSON, JIM
___ "Interview: A Look Back With Jack Williamson," *Futures Past* No. 3: 46-47. September 1992.
___ "Profile: Jack Williamson," *Futures Past* No. 3:40-43. September 1992.

EMOND, MAURICE
___ **Bibliographie analytique de la science fiction et du fantastique Quebecois: 1960-1985**, by Aurelien Boivin, Maurice Emond and Michel Lord. Quebec: Nuit blanche editeur, 1992. 577pp.

ENDE, DAGMAR
___ "Untersuchungen zum Menschen- und Gesellschaftsbild in ausgewählten Science-Fiction-Werken Stanislaw Lems und zu deren Aufnahme durch del Literaturkritik der DDR 1954-1990," *Quarber Merkur* 30(2): 3-13. December 1992. (No. 78)

ENG, STEVE
___ "John Gawsworth...on M. P. Shiel: A Selection," in: **Shiel in Diverse Hands: A Collection of Essays**. Cleveland, OH: Reynolds Morse Foundation, 1983. pp.395-405.
___ "M. P. Shiel and Arthur Machen," in: **Shiel in Diverse Hands: A Collection of Essays**. Cleveland, OH: Reynolds Morse Foundation, 1983. pp.233-247.
___ "M. P. Shiel and Secret Societies," in: **Shiel in Diverse Hands: A Collection of Essays**. Cleveland, OH: Reynolds Morse Foundation, 1983. pp.223-232.
___ "The Speculative Muse: An Introduction to Science Fiction Poetry," in: Barron, Neil, ed. **Anatomy of Wonder 4**. New York: Bowker, 1995. pp.378-392.

ENGDAHL, SYLVIA
___ "The Mythic Role of Space Fiction," in: Gannon, Susan R. and Thompson, Ruth A., eds. **Work and Play in Children's Literature**. New York: Pace University, 1992. pp.14-19.

ENGEL, JOEL
___ **Gene Roddenberry: The Myth and the Man Behind Star Trek**. New York: Hyperion, 1994. 283pp.

ENGELBERGER, JOSEPH F.
___ "Commentary: Robotics in the 21st Century," *Scientific American* 273(3): 166. September 1995.

ENGH, M. J.
___ "Guidelines for Non-Sexist Writing," *The Report: The Fiction Writer's Magazine* 2(6): 11-12, 21-22. April 1992. (No. 59)

ENGHOLM, AHRVID
___ "SF in the Nordic Countries," *Locus* 34(4): 39. April 1995.

ENGLISH, DAVID
___ "The Making of *Babylon 5*," by David Sears and David English. *Compute* 16(7): p.68-74. July 1994. (Cited from *IAC Insite* on-line service.)

ENGLISH, GEORGE
___ "Tripping the Light Fantastic: Terry Pratchett," *Language and Learning* pp.33-35. September/October 1994.

ENSOR, ALLISON
___ "The Magic of Fol-de-Rol: Mark Twain's Merlin," in: Watson, Jeanie and Fries, Marueen, eds. **The Figure of Merlin in the Nineteenth and Twentieth Centuries**. Lewiston, NY: Mellen, 1989. pp.51-63.

EPSTEIN, GRACE A.
___ "Out of the Blue Water: Dream Flight and Narrative Construction in the Novels of Toni Morrison," in: Ruddick, Nicholas, ed. **State of the Fantastic**. Westport, CT: Greenwood, 1992. pp.141-148.

EPSTEIN, WARREN
___ "Beam 'em Up, Scotty: *Star Trek* Convention Puts Ardent Fans into a World of Their Own," *Colorado Springs (CO) Gazette Telegraph*. May 8, 1992. in: *NewsBank. Film and Television*. 59:A4-A5. 1992.

ERAMO, STEVEN
___ "Beautiful Companion," *Starlog* No. 221: 56-58. December 1995.
___ "Cockney Companion," *Starlog* No. 198: 60-61. January 1994.
___ "Girl of Tomorrow," *Starlog* No. 219: 54-55. October 1995.
___ "Space Refugee," *Starlog* No. 221: 47-51, 64. December 1995.
___ "Teenager of Tomorrow," *Starlog* No. 221: 76-78. December 1995.
___ "Traveling Man," *Starlog* No. 215: 58-61. June 1995.
___ "Who's Companion," *Starlog* No. 202: 50-51, 67. May 1994.

ERB, CYNTHIA
___ "Another World or the World of an Other? The Space of Romance in Recent Versions of *Beauty and the Beast*," *Cinema Journal* 34(4): 50-70. Summer 1995.

ERICKSON, JOHN
___ "The Ghost in the Machine: Gilliam's Postmodern Response in *Brazil* to the Orwellian Dystopia of **Nineteen Eighty-Four**," *Utopian Studies* 4(2): 26-34. 1993.

ERICKSON, STEVE
___ "Arc d'X," *Science Fiction Eye* No. 12: 74-76. Summer 1993.

ERISAN, WENDY E.
___ "Inverting the Ideal World: Carnival and the Carnivalesque in Contemporary Utopian Science Fiction," *Extrapolation* 36(4): 331-344. Winter 1995.

ERISMAN, FRED
___ "Zenna Henderson and the Not-So-Final Frontier," *Western American Literature* 30(3): 275-285. November 1995.

ERLICH, RICHARD D.
___ **Clockworks: A Multimedia Bibliography of Works Useful for the Study of the Human/Machine Interface in SF**. Westport, CT: Greenwood Press, 1993. 344pp.

ERRERA, ROBERT
___ "Ellen Datlow Interview," *2AM Magazine* 5(3): 45-46, 50. Spring 1992.

ERSTEIN, HAP
___ "*Dragonwings* Lift Youngsters to Joys of Books," *Washington (DC) Times*. October 20, 1992. in: *NewsBank. Names in the News*. 157:B11. 1992.

ERZGRÄBER, WILLI
___ "Aldous Huxley: **Brave New World** (1932)," in: Heuermann, Hartmut and Lange, Bernd-Peter, eds. **Die Utopie in der angloamerikanischen Literatur: Interpretationen**. Düsseldorf: Bagel, 1984. pp.196-218.

ESCOMEL, GLORIA
___ **Mythes et inquietude metaphysique dans le fantastique et la science fiction**. Ph.D. Dissertation, University of Montreal, 1979. [Not seen.]

ESKIN, LEAH
___ "Sci-fi's a Smash," *Chicago Tribune* Sec. 7, p. 18. July 23, 1993.

ESSELBORN, HANS
___ "Science Fiction als Lehr- und Forschungsgegenstand interkultureller Deutschstudien," *Jahrbuch Deutsch als Fremdsprache* 18: 87-107. 1992.

ESTREN, MARK J.
___ **Horrors Within and Without: A Psychoanalytic Study of Edgar Allan Poe and Howard Phillips Lovecraft**. Ph.D. Dissertation, State University of New York at Buffalo, 1978. 250pp. (DAI 39: 1565A.)

ETHERIDGE, CHUCK
___ "Lewis Shiner and the 'Good' Anarchist," by Robert Donahoo and Chuck Etheridge. in: Slusser, George E. and Shippey, Tom, eds. **Fiction 2000: Cyberpunk and the Future of Narrative**. Athens: University of Georgia Press, 1992. pp.183-190.

ETHRIDGE, GARETH M.
___ "The Company We Keep: Comic Function in M. G. Lewis's **The Monk**," in: Sanders, Joe, ed. **Functions of the Fantastic**. Westport, CT: Greenwood, 1995. pp.63-90.

EVANS, ARTHUR B.
___ "The 'New' Jules Verne," *Science Fiction Studies* 22(1): 35-46. March 1995.
___ "The Fantastic Science Fiction of Maurice Renard," *Science Fiction Studies* 21(3): 380-396. November 1994.
___ "Optograms and Fiction: Photo in a Dead Man's Eye," *Science Fiction Studies* 20(3): 341-361. November 1993.

EVANS, CHRISTOPHER
___ "On the Receiving End," *Interzone* No. 92: 31-33. February 1995.

EVANS, GREG
___ "Indies Head of Genre Pic Middle Ground," *Variety* 359(4): 7, 22. May 22, 1995.

EVANS, GWENTH
___ "Harps and Harpers in Contemporary Fantasy," *Lion and the Unicorn* 16(2): 199-209. December 1992.

EVANS, MARK
___ "Versions of History: **The Handmaid's Tale** and Its Dedicatees," in: Nicholson, Colin, ed. **Margaret Atwood: Writing and Subjectivity: New Critical Essays**. New York: St. Martin's, 1994. pp.177-188.

EVANS, ROBERT O.
___ "**The Inheritors**: Some Inversions," in: Biles, Jack I. and Evans, Robert O., eds. **William Golding: Some Critical Considerations**. Lexington, KY: University Press of Kentucky, 1978. pp.87-102.
___ (ed.) **William Golding: Some Critical Considerations**, ed. by Jack I. Biles and Robert O. Evans. Lexington, KY: University Press of Kentucky, 1978. 283pp.

EVANS, RUSH
___ "CDs Preserve 'Trek' Stars for Eternity," *Austin (TX) American Statesman* Sec. E, p. 11. November 20, 1995.

EVANS, WALTER
___ "Monster Movies and Rites of Initiation," *Journal of Popular Film and Television* 4(2): 124-142. 1975.

EVANS-KARASTAMATIS, JOYCE A.
___ **Celluloid Mushroom Clouds: Hollywood and the Atomic Bomb**. Ph.D. Dissertation, University of California, San Diego, 1993. 432pp. (DAI-A 54/06, p. 1986. December 1993.)

EVENSON, LAURA
___ "Author Jeff Noon's Psychedelic Visions," *San Francisco (CA) Chronicle* February 15, 1996. (Cited from the Internet Edition.)

EVERETT, BARBARA
___ "Kingsley Amis: Devils and Others," in: Salwak, Dale, ed. **Kingsley Amis in Life and Letters**. New York: St. Martin's, 1990. pp.89-99.

EVERMAN, WELCH D.
___ **Cult Science Fiction Films: From the Amazing Colossal Man to Yog, the Monster From Space**. Secaucus, NJ: Carol Publishing Group, 1995. 255pp.

EWART, GAVIN
___ "Kingsley Amis: An Appreciation," in: Salwak, Dale, ed. **Kingsley Amis in Life and Letters**. New York: St. Martin's, 1990. pp.57-64.

EYMAN, SCOTT
___ "Bradbury Goes for Blarney," *West Palm Beach (FL) Post*. July 26, 1992. in: *NewsBank. Literature*. 64:E12. 1992

FAIG, KENNETH W., JR.
___ "Lovecraft's Parents," in: Joshi, S. T., ed. **The H. P. Lovecraft Centennial Conference Proceedings**. West Warwick, RI: Necronomicon, 1991. pp.24-25.

FAIRCHILD, B. H.
___ "An Event Sociologique: *Close Encounters*," *Journal of Popular Film and Television* 6(4): 342-349. 1978.

FALIU, ODILE
___ **The History of the Future: Images of the 21st Century**, by Christophe Canto and Odile Faliu. New York and Paris: Flammarion, 1993. 159pp.

FALK, LORNE
___ "The Conversion of Pere Version," by Lorne Falk and Mireille Perron. in: Gray, Chris H., ed. **The Cyborg Handbook**. New York: Routledge, 1995. pp.445-452.

FALK, SALLY
___ "Talent and Death Take a Holiday in Oddball Film (Review)," *Indianapolis (IN) Star*. July 31, 1992. in: *NewsBank. Film and Television*. 78:D6-D7. 1992.

FALLER, JAMES M.
___ "*Birds II: Land's End* (Review)," *Cinefantastique* 25(5): 59. October 1994.
___ "*Brainscan* (Review)," *Cinefantastique* 25(5): 59. October 1994.
___ "*Cronos* (Review)," *Cinefantastique* 25(4): 59. August 1994.
___ "*Faust* (Review)," *Cinefantastique* 26(4): 59. June 1995.
___ "*The Flintstones* (Review)," *Cinefantastique* 25(6)/26(1): 122. December 1994.
___ "*Heavenly Creatures* (Review)," *Cinefantastique* 26(4): 59. June 1995.
___ "*Leprechaun 2* (Review)," *Cinefantastique* 25(5): 60. October 1994.
___ "*No Escape* (Review)," *Cinefantastique* 25(6)/26(1): 122. December 1994.
___ "*The Shadow* (Review)," *Cinefantastique* 25(6)/26(1): 123. December 1994.
___ "*Unborn II* (Review)," *Cinefantastique* 26(2): 59. February 1995.

FALSANI, TERESA B.
___ "Parke Godwin's Guenevere: An Archetypal Transformation," *Quondam et Futurus* 3(3): 55-65. Fall 1993.

FARINOTTI, PINO
___ **Dizionarion dei film de fantascienza e horror**. Carnago, Italy: SugarCo, 1993. 174pp.

FARMER, PHILIP J.
___ "**Hayy ibn Yaqzan**, by Abu ibn Tufayl: An Arabic Mowgli," *Journal of the Fantastic in the Arts* 3(3): 72-78. 1994.

FAROLINO, AUDREY
___ "Dud Dudes: Bill and Ted Get Bogus," *New York (NY) Post*. July 19, 1991. in: *NewsBank. Film and Television*. 65:F4. 1991.
___ "Jumpin' *Freejack* Flash (Review)," *New York (NY) Post*. January 21, 1992. in: *NewsBank. Film and Television*. 11:D10. 1992.

FARR, RUSSELL B.

FARR, RUSSELL B.
___ "An Interview With Pat Cadigan and Ellen Datlow," *Science Fiction: A Review of Speculative Literature* 13(1): 13-18. 1995(?). (No. 37)

FARRAND, PHIL
___ **The Nitpicker's Guide for Classic Trekkers**. London: Titan, 1994. 393pp.

FARRELL, JOHN ALOYSIUS
___ "The Smithsonian Goes Trekkie," *Boston (MA) Globe*. February 29, 1992. in: *NewsBank. Film and Television.* 26:A2. 1992.

FARRIS, JOHN
___ "A User's Guide to Hollywood Horror (As Told to Kelley Wilde)," in: Golden, Christopher, ed. **Cut! Horror Writers on Horror Film**. New York: Berkley, 1992. pp.83-90.

FASOLINO, GREG
___ "Lestat of the Art: The Dark Gift Discussed," *Reflex* No. 29: 42-46. 1992.

FAULKNER, PETER
___ "Dark Days in Hammersmith: Lily Yates and the Morrises," *Journal of the William Morris Society* 11(3): 22-25. Autumn 1995.
___ "Morris and the Study of English," *Journal of the William Morris Society* 11(1): 26-30. Autumn 1994.

FAUSETT, DAVID
___ **Writing the New World: Imaginary Voyages and Utopias of the Great Southern Land**. Syracuse, NY: Syracuse University Press, 1993. 237pp.

FAVRET, MARY A.
___ "A Woman Writes the Fiction of Science: The Body in **Frankenstein**," *Genders* No. 14: 50-65. Fall 1992.

FEEHAN, ELLEN
___ "Frank Herbert and the Making of Myths: Irish History, Celtic Mythology, and IRA Ideology in **The White Plague**," *Science-Fiction Studies* 19(3): 289-310. November 1992.
___ "An Interview With John Kessel," *Science Fiction Studies* 20(1): 94-107. March 1993.

FEEHAN, MICHAEL
___ "Chinese Finger-Traps or 'A Perturbation in the Reality Field': Paradox as Conversion in Philip K. Dick's Fiction," in: Umland, Samuel J., ed. **Philip K. Dick: Contemporary Critical Interpretations**. Westport, CT: Greenwood, 1995. pp.197-206.

FEELEY, GREGORY
___ "Raters of the Graustark: Science Fiction Criticism and Its Critics," *SFWA Bulletin* 29(1): 35-39. Spring 1995. (No. 126)

FEHN, ANN
___ (ed.) **Neverending Stories: Toward a Critical Narratology**, ed. by Ann Fehn, Ingeborg Hoesterey and Maria Tatar. Princeton, NJ: Princeton University Press, 1992. 274pp.

FEHRENBACHER, RICHARD
___ "The Domestication of Merlin in Malory's **Morte Dauthur**," *Quondam et Futurus* 3(4): 1-16. Winter 1993.

FEIMER, JOEL N.
___ "Biblical Typology in Le Guin's **The Eye of the Heron**: Character, Structure and Theme," *Mythlore* 19(4): 13-19. Autumn 1993. (No. 74)

FEIN, DAVID C.
___ "Laser Revolution: Harryhausen Cornucopia," *Cinefex* No. 53: 81-82. February 1993.
___ "Quick Cuts: Once More into the **Abyss**," *Cinefex* No. 55: 29-30. August 1993.

FEINBERG, GERALD
___ "Discussing Hard SF," by Gerald Feinberg, Hal Clement, Kathryn Cramer and David G. Hartwell. *New York Review of Science Fiction* No. 46: 19-21. June 1992.

FEIST, RAYMOND E.
___ "Contract Article IV: Advances, Payment & Royalties, and a Few Other Things," *SFWA Bulletin* 25(4): 15-20. Winter 1992. (No. 114)
___ "Contract Article IX: Editorial Courtesy," *SFWA Bulletin* 27(1): 47-53. Spring 1993. (No. 119)
___ "Contract Article V: A Little More Money; Sub-Rights," *SFWA Bulletin* 26(1): 50-57. Spring 1992. (No. 115)
___ "Contract Article VI: Options and Miscellany," *SFWA Bulletin* 26(2): 20-27. Summer 1992. (No. 116)
___ "Contract Article VII: Agency Clause, Agents, and Other Writers," *SFWA Bulletin* 26(3): 23-28. Fall 1992. (No. 117)
___ "Contract Article VIII: Negotiations," *SFWA Bulletin* 26(4): 12-15. Winter 1993. (No. 118)
___ "Contract Article X: Packagers," *SFWA Bulletin* 27(2): 19-24. Summer 1993. (No. 120)
___ "Contract Article XI: The Law Is an Ass," *SFWA Bulletin* 27(3): 19-25. Fall 1993. (No. 121)
___ "Contract Article XII: Changes, Part 1," *SFWA Bulletin* 28(2): 21-26. Summer 1994. (No. 124)
___ "Contract Article XIII: Changes, Part 2," *SFWA Bulletin* 28(3): 23-27. Winter 1994. (No. 125)
___ "Contract Article XIV: Model Contracts," *SFWA Bulletin* 29(1): 44-52. Spring 1995. (No. 126)
___ "Everything I Know Is Wrong," *SFWA Bulletin* 29(2): 18-20. Summer 1995. (No. 127)

FEKETE, JOHN
___ "The Transmigration of Philip K. Dick," in: Mullen, R. D., ed. **On Philip K. Dick: 40 Articles From Science-Fiction Studies**. Terre Haute, IN: SF-TH Inc., 1992. pp.119-122.

FELCHNER, WILLIAM J.
___ "Science Fiction Movie Posters," *Antiques & Collecting Magazine* 99(9): 40-43. November 1994.

FELGENHAUER, H. S.
___ "Bradbury at Harper," *Fantasy Commentator* 8(3/4): 182-185. Fall 1995. (Whole No. 47/48)
___ "Pages and Pages of Pohl," *Fantasy Commentator* 8(1/2): 4-13. Winter 1993/1994. (Whole No. 45/46.)

FELPERIN, LESLIE
___ "Animated Dreams," *Sight and Sound* 4(12): 26-29. December 1994.
___ "**Mortal Kombat** (Review)," *Sight and Sound* 5(11): 47-48. November 1995.
___ "**Neverending Story III** (Review)," *Sight and Sound* 5(1): 50-51. January 1995.
___ "**Pagemaster** (Review)," *Sight and Sound* 5(2): 49-50. February 1995.
___ "**Tank Girl** (Review)," *Sight and Sound* 5(7): 54-55. July 1995.

FENNER, ARNIE
___ "Punchatz: A Barnstormer in Texas," *Shayol* No. 6: 20-27. 1982.
___ "Roger Stine," *Shayol* No. 7: 24-31. 1985.
___ (ed.) **Spectrum: The Best in Contemporary Fantastic Art (First Annual Collection)**, ed. by Cathy Burnett, Arnie Fenner and Jim Loehr. Grass Valley, CA: Underwood Books, 1994. 204pp.

FENNESSY, CLARE
___ "Fair Dinkum at Dragonsdawn: Or, How to Turn Australians, and Especially, Australian SF Readers, into Paranoid Androids," by Norman Talbot and Clare Fennessy. *Australian Science Fiction Review* 5(3): 12-15. Spring 1990. (Whole No. 25)

FENTON, BARRY J.
___ "Barney B. Clark, DDS: A View From the Medical Service," by F. Andrew Gaffney and Barry J. Fenton. in: Gray, Chris H., ed. **The Cyborg Handbook**. New York: Routledge, 1995. pp.157-160.

FERCHLAND, JUTTA
___ "**Solaris**. Der Film von Andrej Tarkovskij im Vergleich zu Lems roman," *Quarber Merkur* 32(2): 34-42. December 1994. (Whole No. 82)

FERGUSON, MALCOLM
___ "On Digging Shiel," in: **Shiel in Diverse Hands: A Collection of Essays**. Cleveland, OH: Reynolds Morse Foundation, 1983. pp.69-74.

FERN, YVONNE
___ **Gene Roddenberry: The Last Conversation.** Berkeley: University of California Press, 1994. 228pp.

FERNANDEZ, ELIZABETH
___ "S. F. Furor Over Film Offensive to Gays," *San Francisco (CA) Examiner* March 18, 1992 in: *NewsBank. Film and Television.* 28:G11-G12. 1992.

FERNS, CHRIS
___ "The Value/s of Dystopia: **The Handmaid's Tale** and the Anti-Utopian Tradition," *Dalhousie Review* 69(3): 373-382. Fall 1989.

FERRANTE, A. C.
___ "Jungle Fever: **The Lion King** (Review)," *Sci-Fi Universe* No. 3: 72-73. October/November 1994.
___ "Roland's Gate," *Sci-Fi Universe* No. 3: 28-37. October/November 1994.

FERRELL, KEITH
___ "Forum: The Challenges of Science Fiction," *Omni* 14(5): 6. February 1992.
___ "How to Build an Alien," *Omni* 14(9): 50-57, 111. October 1992.

FICKEY, PIERRETTE
___ "Louis Aragon: The Fantastic in Collage and Poetry," in: Latham, Robert A. and Collins, Robert A., eds. **Modes of the Fantastic.** Westport, CT: Greenwood, 1995. pp.38-47.

FIDDES, PAUL S.
___ "C. S. Lewis the Myth-Maker," in: Walker, Andrew and Patric, James, eds. **A Christian for All Christians.** Washington, DC: Regnery, 1992. pp.132-155.

FIEDLER, HEIKO
___ "Magie und Realität in Malcolm Bradburys Roman **Rates of Exchange**," *Quarber Merkur* 33(1): 15-26. June 1995. (No. 83)

FIELD, MICHELE
___ "PW Interviews: Doris Lessing," *Publishers Weekly* 241(38): 47-48. September 19, 1994.

FIELD, P. J. C.
___ "Caxton's Roman War," *Arthuriana* 5(2): 31-73. Summer 1995.

FIEROBE, CLAUDE
___ "Eros médusé," in: Bozzetto, Roger, ed. **Eros: Science & Fiction Fantastique.** Aix-en-Provence: Universite de Provence, 1991. pp.9-19.

FIGUEROA-SARRIERA, HEIDI J.
___ "Children of the Mind With Disposable Bodies: Metaphors of Self in a Text on Artificial Intelligence and Robotics," in: Gray, Chris H., ed. **The Cyborg Handbook.** New York: Routledge, 1995. pp.127-135.
___ "Introduction: Constructing the Knowledge of Cybernetic Organisms," by Chris H. Gray, Steven Mentor and Heidi J. Figueroa-Sarriera. in: Gray, Chris H., ed. **The Cyborg Handbook.** New York: Routledge, 1995. pp.1-14.

FIKE, MATTHEW A.
___ "Nature as Supernature: Donaldson's Revision of Spenser," *Mythlore* 18(2): 17-20, 22. Spring 1992. (No. 68)

FILMER, KATH
___ "Atseiniau O Ddyddiau Gynt: Welsh Myth and Culture in Contemporary Fantasy," in: Filmer, Kath, ed. **Twentieth-Century Fantasists: Essays in Culture, Society and Belief in Twentieth Century Mythopoeic Literature.** New York: St. Martin's, 1992. pp.108-120.
___ "Dreaming Each Other: The Discourse of Fantasy in Contemporary News Media," in: Filmer, Kath, ed. **Twentieth-Century Fantasists: Essays in Culture, Society and Belief in Twentieth Century Mythopoeic Literature.** New York: St. Martin's, 1992. pp.193-206.
___ **The Fiction of C. S. Lewis: Mask and Mirror.** New York: St. Martin's, 1992. 153pp.; Basingstoke: Macmillan, 1993. 153pp. [Not seen; cf. OCLC.]

FILMER, KATH (continued)
___ "Introduction," in: Filmer, Kath, ed. **Twentieth-Century Fantasists: Essays in Culture, Society and Belief in Twentieth Century Mythopoeic Literature.** New York: St. Martin's, 1992. pp.1-7.
___ "A Place in Deep Heaven: Figurative Language in **Out of the Silent Planet**," in: Kranz, Gisbert, ed. **Inklings: Jahrbuch für Literatur und Ästhetik.** 3. Band. [Lüdenscheid, Germany: Stier], 1985. pp.187-196.
___ **Scepticism and Hope in Twentieth Century Fantasy Literature.** Bowling Green, OH: Bowling Green State University Popular Press, 1992. 160pp.
___ (ed.) **Twentieth-Century Fantasists: Essays on Culture, Society and Belief in Twentieth Century Mythopoeic Literature.** New York: St. Martin's, 1992. 212pp.

FILMER-DAVIES, KATH
___ "Chwedl Gymaeg a Llenyddiaeth Gyfoesol: Welsh Myth and Comtempory Literature," *Mythlore* 19(3): 53-58. Summer 1993. (No. 73)

FINEMAN, MARK
___ "Arthur C. Clarke's Space Odyssey Didn't End With 2001--His New Dream Is Gardening on Mars," *Los Angeles (CA) Times* p. E1, E4. January 24, 1992.
___ "Out of This World," *Los Angeles (CA) Times* Sec. E, p. 1. January 24, 1992.

FINNE, JACQUES
___ "Du fantastique érotique au gore pornographique," in: Bozzetto, Roger, ed. **Eros: Science & Fiction Fantastique.** Aix-en-Provence: Universite de Provence, 1991. pp.85-90.

FINNEY, KATHE D.
___ "Science Fiction and the Discourse of Power: The American Failure 1910-1930," *European Contributions to American Studies* [Netherlands] 10: 178-188. 1986.

FIRPO, LUIGI
___ "Per una definizione de Utopia," in: Saccaro Del Buffa, Giuseppa and Lewis, Arthur O., eds. **Utopie per gli Anni Ottana.** Rome: Gangemi Editore, 1986. pp.801-811.

FISCHER, DENNIS
___ "The Amicus Empire: An Interview With Milton Subotsky," *Filmfax* No. 42: 54-61, 96-97. December 1993/January 1994.
___ **The Birds II: Land's End** (Review)," *Cinefantastique* 26(4): 59. June 1995.
___ "Charles Band: Full Moon Mogul," *Cinefantastique* 26(4): 16-49. June 1995.
___ "**Congo**: Director Frank Marshall on Filming the Bestseller," *Cinefantastique* 26(5): 56-57, 61. August 1995.
___ "**Congo** (Review)," *Cinefantastique* 26(6)/27(1): 123. October 1995.
___ "**Congo**," *Cinefantastique* 26(4): 12-13. June 1995.
___ **The Fire Next Time** (Review)," *Cinefantastique* 24(3/4): 123. October 1993.
___ "Full Moon Effects: Creature Creators," *Cinefantastique* 26(4): 47-49. June 1995.
___ "Full Moon Preview: **Castle Freak**," *Cinefantastique* 26(4): 32-34. June 1995.
___ "Full Moon Preview: **The Primedals**," *Cinefantastique* 26(4): 20-22. June 1995.
___ "Full Moon Profile: Albert Band," *Cinefantastique* 26(4): 28-30. June 1995.
___ "**Indian in the Cupboard**," *Cinefantastique* 26(5): 46-47. August 1995.
___ "**Innocent Blood** (Review)," *Cinefantastique* 23(5): 59. February 1993.
___ "**Lawrence of Arabia** Meets **Star Wars** in **Stargate**," *Science Fiction Age* 2(6): 18-24. September 1994.
___ "**Millennium**: Novel vs. Film," *Lan's Lantern* No. 35: 75-78. December 1990.
___ "Moonbeam Preview: **Josh Kirby, Time Warrior**," *Cinefantastique* 26(4): 24-26. June 1995.
___ "Moonbeam Preview: **Magic Island**," *Cinefantastique* 26(4): 36-37. June 1995.
___ "**Mystery of Rampo** (Review)," *Cinefantastique* 26(6)/27(1): 123. October 1995.
___ "**New Eden** (Review)," *Cinefantastique* 26(2): 59. February 1995.
___ "**Oblivion**," *Cinefantastique* 25(4): 56-57, 61. August 1994.

FLIXMAN, ED
___ "*Judge Dredd, Casper*, and *Congo* Top a Bumper Crop of Genre Blockbusters," *Science Fiction Age* 3(4): 18-23. May 1995.
___ "Man and Machine," *Sci-Fi Entertainment* 2(3): 48-53. October 1995.
___ "The Once and Future Kirk," *Sci-Fi Entertainment* 1(4): 47. December 1994.
___ "*Star Trek: Deep Space Nine*; Beyond the Wormhole," *Sci-Fi Entertainment* 1(4): 56-61. December 1994.
___ "This Fall's SF Television Season Promises to Be Full of Cosmic Excitement," *Science Fiction Age* 3(1): 18-24, 42-43. November 1994.
___ "*Waterworld*: Box Office Wild Card," *Sci-Fi Entertainment* 2(2): 50-55, 74. August 1995.
___ "William Shatner: Back to the Future," *Sci-Fi Entertainment* 1(5): 56-59, 72. February 1995.

FLODSTROM, JOHN H.
___ "Personal Identity in the Majipoor Trilogy, **To Live Again**, and **Downward to Earth**," in: Elkins, Charles L. and Greenberg, Martin H., eds. **Robert Silverberg's Many Trapdoors: Critical Essays on His Science Fiction**. Westport, CT: Greenwood, 1992. pp.73-94.

FLORENCE, BILL
___ "Alien Dreams," *Starlog* No. 194: 50-53. September 1993.
___ "An Alien With Style," *Starlog* No. 219: 32-36, 66. October 1995.
___ "Captain's Lady," *Starlog* No. 220: 54-57. November 1995.
___ "Colors of a Chameleon," *Starlog* No. 191: 56-57. June 1993.
___ "His Pilgrim Soul," *Starlog* No. 215: 75-81. June 1995.
___ "Homeward Bound," *Starlog* No. 213: 64-65. April 1995.
___ "Keeper of Secrets," *Starlog* No. 211: 28-30, 74. February 1995.
___ "The Magic Man," *Starlog* No. 189: 30-33, 68. April 1993.
___ "Robert Silverberg's Alien," *Starlog* No. 219: 34-35. October 1995.
___ "Tomorrow's Story," *Starlog* No. 194: 62-64, 81. September 1993.
___ "Trek World," *Starlog* 182: 56-58, 72. September 1992.
___ "Trials and Errors," *Starlog* 177: 42-45, 68. April 1992.
___ "The X-Comics," *Starlog* No. 212: 58-60. March 1995.

FLORESCU, RADU
___ **In Search of Dracula: The History of Dracula and Vampires**. Rev. Ed, by Raymond T. McNally and Radu Florescu. Boston, MA: Houghton Mifflin, 1994. 297pp.

FLYNN, CAROLINE
___ "Doris Lessing: An Overview," *Science Fiction: A Review of Speculative Literature* 11(2): 17-22. 1991. (No. 32)

FLYNN, GEORGE
___ "World SF Convention: Business Meeting," *Science Fiction Chronicle* 16(2): 51. November/December 1994.

FLYNN, JOHN L.
___ **Cinematic Vampires: The Living Dead on Film and Televison, From** *The Devil's Castle* **(1896) to** *Bram Stoker's Dracula* **(1992)**. Jefferson, NC: McFarland, 1992. 328pp.

FLYNN, ROCHELLE O.
___ "*Boris and Natasha* Is Just Bad Enough," *Boston (MA) Herald*. April 17, 1992. in: *NewsBank. Film and Television*. 39:B10. 1992.

FONDANÈCHE, DANIEL
___ "Dick, the Libertarian Prophet," in: Mullen, R. D., ed. **On Philip K. Dick: 40 Articles From Science-Fiction Studies**. Terre Haute, IN: SF-TH Inc., 1992. pp.161-169.

FONSTAD, KAREN W.
___ **The Atlas of Middle-Earth** Rev. ed. New York: Houghton Mifflin, 1992. 210pp.

FONTRODONA, MARIANO
___ "El dia que marte invadio la tierra [The Day That Mars Invaded Earth]," *Historia y Vida* 21(249): 104-109. 1988.

FOOT, MICHAEL
___ **H. G.: The History of Mr. Wells**. Washington, DC: Counterpoint, 1995. 318pp.

FOOTE, BUD
___ "Assuming the Present in SF: Sarte in a New Dimension," in: Sanders, Joe, ed. **Functions of the Fantastic**. Westport, CT: Greenwood, 1995. pp.161-168.
___ "A Conversation with Kim Stanley Robinson," *Science Fiction Studies* 21(1): 51-60. March 1994.
___ "Kim Stanley Robinson: Premodernist," in: Wolf, Milton T. and Mallett, Daryl F., eds. **Imaginative Futures: Proceedings of the 1993 Science Fiction Research Association Conference**. San Bernardino, CA: Jacob's Ladder Books, 1995. pp.329-340.
___ "Notes on Kim Stanley Robinson's **Red Mars**," *Science Fiction Studies* 21(1): 61-66. March 1994.
___ "Verne's **Paris in the Twentieth Century**: The First Science Fiction Dystopia?," *New York Review of Science Fiction* No. 88: 1, 8-10. December 1995.

FOOTE, DONNA
___ "Coming to a Toy Store Near You," by Jeff Giles and Donna Foote. *Newsweek* 121(24): 64-65. June 14, 1993.

FOOTE, STEPHANIE
___ "Annals of Humanism: We Have Met the Alien and It Is Us," *Humanist* 52(2):21-24, 33. March/April 1992.

FORD, PAUL F.
___ **Companion to Narnia**. 4th ed. San Francisco, CA: Harper, 1994. 460pp.

FORD, RON
___ "The Next Generation Speaks: Dwight D. Frye, the Son of Dracula's Servant," *Filmfax* No. 35: 78-81. October/November 1992.

FORDE, NIGEL
___ "Reporting From the Terrain of the Mind (Interview, 1992)," in: Ingersoll, Earl G., ed. **Doris Lessing: Conversations**. Princeton, NJ: Ontario Review Press, 1994. pp.214-218.

FORMICHETTI, G.
___ "Manoscritti ed immagini di Tommaso Campanella. Orientamenti de recerca," by G. Formichetti, O. Lucchesi, P. Sagi and F. Troncarelli. in: Saccaro Del Buffa, Giuseppa and Lewis, Arthur O., eds. **Utopie per gli Anni Ottana**. Rome: Gangemi Editore, 1986. pp.587-590.

FORREST, LINDA A.
___ "Young Adult Fantasy and the Search for Gender-Fair Genres," *Journal of Youth Services in Libraries* 7(1): 37-42. Fall 1993.

FORRY, STEVEN E.
___ **Hideous Progenies: Dramatizations of Frankenstein From Mary Shelley to the Present**. Philadelphia: University of Pennsylvania Press, 1990. 311pp.

FORSHAW, BARRY
___ "Freighting It In: Gregory Benford Interviewed," *Interzone* No. 102: 27-29. December 1995.

FORSTER, JEAN-PAUL
___ **Jonathan Swift: The Fictions of the Satirist**. New York: Peter Lang, 1991. 248pp.

FORTUNATI, VITA
___ " 'It Makes No Difference': A Utopia of Simulation and Transparency," in: Bloom, Harold, ed. **George Orwell's 1984**. New York: Chelsea House, 1987. pp.109-120.
___ "The Metamorphosis of the Apocalyptic Myth: From Utopia to Science Fiction," in: Kumar, Krishan and Bann, Stephen, eds. **Utopias and the Millennium**. London: Reaktion Books, 1993. pp.81-89.

FOSTER, ALAN D.
___ **On Writing Science Fiction and Screenplays**, by Charles Patton and Alan D. Foster. Alexandra, VA: PBS Adult Learning Satellite Service, 1994. 1 Videocassette, 30 minutes.
___ "Science Fiction and the Root of All Evil," *SFWA Bulletin* 29(1): 29-34. Spring 1995. (No. 126)

FOSTER, DENNIS A.
___ "J. G. Ballard's Empire of the Senses: Perversion and the Failure of Authority," *PMLA* 108(3): 519-532. May 1993.

FOSTER, NATALIE
___ "Science and the Final Frontier: Chemistry and *Star Trek*," *Chemistry and Industry* No. 24: 18-20. December 21, 1992.

FOSTER, STEPHEN W.
___ "Prince Zaleski and Count Stenbock," in: **Shiel in Diverse Hands: A Collection of Essays**. Cleveland, OH: Reynolds Morse Foundation, 1983. pp.175-177.

FOSTER, THOMAS
___ "Incurably Informed: The Pleasures and Dangers of Cyberpunk," *Genders* No. 18: 1-10. Winter 1993.
___ "Meat Puppets or Robopaths? Cyberpunk and the Question of Embodiment," *Genders* No. 18: 11-31. Winter 1993.

FOWLER, CHRISTOPHER J.
___ "Brite Now! Poppy Z. Brite Interviewed," *Interzone* No. 84: 23-27. June 1994.
___ "A Detective Fiction of the Heart: The First London Interview with M. John Harrison," *Foundation* No. 58: 5-26. Summer 1993.
___ "On the Edge: The Last Holmfirth Interview with M. John Harrison," *Foundation* No. 57: 7-25. Spring 1993.

FOWLER, JUDY
___ **Exploring How Animals Fare in Worlds Created by Feminist Science Fiction Writers**. Master's Thesis, University of Wisconsin, Whitewater, 1993. 71pp.

FOX, ROBERT E.
___ **The Mirrors of Caliban: A Study of the Fiction of LeRoi Jones (Imamu Amiri Baraka), Ishmael Reed, and Samuel R. Delany**. Ph.D. Dissertation, State University of New York at Buffalo, 1974. 407pp. (DAI 37: 5121A.)

FRANCAVILLA, JOSEPH
___ "Repetition With Reversal: Robert Silverberg's Ironic Twist Endings," in: Elkins, Charles L. and Greenberg, Martin H., eds. **Robert Silverberg's Many Trapdoors: Critical Essays on His Science Fiction**. Westport, CT: Greenwood, 1992. pp.59-72.

FRANCAVUALLA, JOSEPH
___ "The Concept of the Divided Self and Harlan Ellison's 'I Have No Mouth and I Must Scream' and 'Shatterday'," *Journal of the Fantastic in the Arts* 6(2/3): 107-125. 1994.

FRANCESCATO, DONATA
___ "Le comuni familiari: riflessioni dopo un decennio," in: Colombo, Arrigo and Quarta, Cosimo, eds. **Il Destino della Famiglia nell'Utopia**. Bari: Edizione Dedalo, 1991. pp.399-404.

FRANCIS, DIANA P.
___ "Social Robotics: Constructing the Ideal Woman from Used Ideological Parts," *Journal of the Fantastic in the Arts* 7(1): 92-101. 1996.

FRANCKE, LIZZIE
___ "**Attack of the 50 Ft. Woman** (Review)," *Sight and Sound* 4(10): 35. October 1994.

FRANK, FREDERICK S.
___ **Guide to the Gothic II: An Annotated Bibliography of Criticism, 1983-1993**. Lanham, MD: Scarecrow, 1995. 542pp.

FRANK, JANE
___ "Bio of a Space Artist," *Science Fiction Age* 1(5): 62-67. July 1993.
___ "Should I Buy It?," *Strange New Worlds* No. 7: 4-5, 13. April/May 1993.

FRANK, JANRAE
___ "Introduction: New Eves and New Genesis: The Extraordinary Women Who Write Science Fiction and the Women They Write About," by Janrae Frank, Jean Stine and Forrest J Ackerman. in: Frank, Janrae, Stine, Jean, and Ackerman Forrest J, eds. **New Eves: Science Fiction About the Extraordinary Women of Today and Tomorrow**. Stamford, CT: Longmeadow, 1994. pp.vii-xvi.

FRANK, LYNDSEY M.
___ **From Nautilus to Neuromancer: The Human-Machine Relationship in Science Fiction Literature From the Victorian Era to the 1980s**. Honor's Thesis, Linfield College, 1995. 80pp.

FRANKE, LIZZIE
___ "**Apollo 13** (Review)," *Sight and Sound* 5(9): 42-43. September 1995.
___ "Virtual Fears," *Sight and Sound* 5(12): 6-9. December 1995.

FRANKLIN, H. BRUCE
___ "From Realism to Virtual Reality: Images of America's Wars," *Georgia Review* 48(1): 47-66. Spring 1994.
___ **Future Perfect: American Science Fiction of the Nineteenth Century**. Revised and Expanded Edition. New Brunswick, NJ: Rutgers University Press, 1995. 395pp.
___ "The Greatest Fantasy on Earth: The Superweapon in Fiction and Fact," in: Morse, Donald E., ed. **The Celebration of the Fantastic**. Westport, CT: Greenwood, 1992. pp.23-38.
___ "*Star Trek* in the Vietnam Era," *Film & History* 24(1/2): 36-46. February/May 1994.
___ "*Star Trek* in the Vietnam Era," *Locus* 33(4): 43-45. October 1994.
___ "*Star Trek* in the Vietnam Era," *Science Fiction Studies* 21(1): 24-34. March 1994.
___ "The Vietnam War as American Science Fiction and Fantasy," in: Irons, Glenwood, ed. **Gender, Language and Myth: Essays on Popular Narrative**. Toronto: University of Toronto Press, 1992. pp.208-230.

FRANKO, CAROL
___ "Dialogical Twins: Post-patriarchal Topology in Two Stories by Kim Stanley Robinson," *Science Fiction Studies* 22(3): 305-322. November 1995
___ "Working the 'In Between': Kim Stanley Robinson's Utopian Fiction," *Science Fiction Studies* 21(2): 191-211. July 1994.

FRANTS, MARINA
___ "ConFrancisco, Here We Come: The 51st Annual World Science Fiction Convention," by Marina Frants and Keith R. A. DeCandido. *Wilson Library Bulletin* 68(3): 49-50. November 1993.
___ "Down by the Bayou: The 20th Annual World Fantasy Convention," by Marina Frants and Keith R. A. DeCandido. *Wilson Library Bulletin* 69(5): 51-52. January 1995

FRASER, CHRISTINA L.
___ **The Structure of Creativity: Building a Novel**. Honor's Thesis, St. Mary's of San Antonio, TX, 1993. 101pp.

FRASER, JOHN
___ "The Dark Domain," in: Jones, Stephen, ed. **James Herbert: By Horror Haunted**. London: New English Library, 1992. pp.151-159.

FRATZ, DOUG
___ "Index: *Thrust/Quantum*, No. 1, February 1973-No. 43/44, May 1993," *Quantum* No. 43/44: 67-69. Spring/Summer 1993.
___ "The Twenty-Year Spree: A Personal History of *Thrust/Quantum*," *Quantum* No. 43/44: 51-66. Spring/Summer 1993.

FRAZER, ROGER
___ "A Guide to *The Avon Fantasy Reader*," *Wayfarer II* pp.17-35. n.d.

FRAZIER, KENDRICK
___ "A Celebration of Isaac Asimov: A Man for the Universe," *Skeptical Inquirer* 17(1): 30-47. Fall 1992.

FRAZIER, PAUL M.
___ **Patterns in Recent Science Fiction Drama**. Ph.D. Dissertation, Bowling Green State University, 1992. 196pp.

FREAS, FRANK K.
___ "The Story Between the Words," *Analog* 112(5): 84-89. April 1992.

FREEDMAN, CARL
___ "Editorial Introduction: Dick and Criticism," in: Mullen, R. D., ed. **On Philip K. Dick: 40 Articles From Science-Fiction Studies**. Terre Haute, IN: SF-TH Inc., 1992. pp.145-152.
___ "In Search of Dick's Boswell," in: Mullen, R. D., ed. **On Philip K. Dick: 40 Articles From Science-Fiction Studies**. Terre Haute, IN: SF-TH Inc., 1992. pp.257-261.
___ "Style, Fiction, Science Fiction: The Case of Philip K. Dick," in: Slusser, George E. and Rabkin, Eric S., eds. **Styles of Creation: Aesthetic Technique and the Creation of Fictional Worlds**. Athens: University of Georgia Press, 1992. pp.30-45.
___ "Towards a Theory of Paranoia: The Science Fiction of Philip K. Dick," in: Mullen, R. D., ed. **On Philip K. Dick: 40 Articles From Science-Fiction Studies**. Terre Haute, IN: SF-TH Inc., 1992. pp.111-118.
___ "Towards a Theory of Paranoia: The Science Fiction of Philip K. Dick," in: Umland, Samuel J., ed. **Philip K. Dick: Contemporary Critical Interpretations**. Westport, CT: Greenwood, 1995. pp.7-18.

FREEMAN, JOHN
___ "Discourse on More's **Utopia**: Pretext/Postscript," *ELH* 59(2): 289-312. Summer 1992.
___ "More's Place in 'No Place': The Self-Fashioning Transaction in **Utopia**," *Texas Studies in Literature and Language* 34(2): 197-217. Summer 1992.

FREEMAN, JUDY
___ "In the Realm of Fantasy," *Instructor* 104(8): 77-82. May 1995.

FREEMAN, PAUL
___ "Ears Have it as Rock Stars Roll In *End of the World* Film (Review)," *Washington (DC) Times*. February 16, 1992. in: *NewsBank. Film and Television*. 26:F13. 1992.

FREESE, PETER
___ "Kurt Vonnegut: **Cat's Cradle** (1963)," in: Heuermann, Hartmut and Lange, Bernd-Peter, eds. **Die Utopie in der angloamerikanischen Literatur: Interpretationen**. Düsseldorf: Bagel, 1984. pp.283-309.
___ "Kurt Vonnegut, Jr., **The Sirens of Titan** (1959)," in: Heuermann, Harmut, ed. **Der Science Fiction Roman in der angloamerikanischen Literatur: Interpretationen**. Düsseldorf: Bagel, 1986. pp.196-219.
___ "Surviving the End: Apocalypse, Evolution, and Entropy in Bernard Malamud, Kurt Vonnegut and Thomas Pynchon," *Critique* 36(3): 163-176. Spring 1995.

FREIBERT, LUCY M.
___ "The Role of the Artist in the Commune," in: Saccaro Del Buffa, Giuseppa and Lewis, Arthur O., eds. **Utopie per gli Anni Ottana**. Rome: Gangemi Editore, 1986. pp.397-414.

FRENCH, LAWRENCE
___ "*Bram Stoker's Dracula*: Matte Artistry," *Cinefantastique* 23(6): 55-58. April 1993.
___ "*Ed Wood*: Cinematography," *Cinefantastique* 25(6)/26(1): 16-17. December 1994.
___ "*Ed Wood*: Lugosi's Makeup," *Cinefantastique* 25(6)/26(1): 112-113. December 1994.
___ "*Ed Wood*: Playing Bela Lugosi," *Cinefantastique* 25(5): 34-35. October 1994.
___ "*Ed Wood*: Production Design," *Cinefantastique* 25(6)/26(1): 116-117. December 1994.
___ "*Ed Wood*: Writing the Script," *Cinefantastique* 25(6)/26(1): 12-13. December 1994.
___ "*Ed Wood: The Haunted World of Edward D. Wood, Jr.*," *Cinefantastique* 25(6)/26(1): 120-121. December 1994.
___ "*Jurassic Park*: Dennis Muren," *Cinefantastique* 24(2): 26-28. August 1993.
___ "*Jurassic Park*: Dinosaur Movements," *Cinefantastique* 24(2): 20-21. August 1993.
___ "*Jurassic Park*: Phil Tippett, Dinosaur," *Cinefantastique* 24(2): 16-17. August 1993.
___ "*Naked Lunch*: Special Effects," *Cinefantastique* 22(5): 15-19. April 1992.
___ "*Robocop*: The Ride," *Cinefantastique* 25(3): 58. June 1994.

FRENCH, LAWRENCE (continued)
___ "*Tall Tales*," *Cinefantastique* 26(3): 8-9. April 1995.
___ "Tim Burton's *Ed Wood*," *Cinefantastique* 25(5): 32-34. October 1994.
___ "Tim Burton's *Ed Wood*," *Cinefantastique* 25(6)/26(1): 10-18, 112-121. December 1994.
___ "*Toy Story*: Art Direction," *Cinefantastique* 27(2): 32-33. November 1995.
___ "*Toy Story*: Beginnings," *Cinefantastique* 27(2): 36. November 1995.
___ "*Toy Story*: CGI Director," *Cinefantastique* 27(2): 20-21. November 1995.
___ "*Toy Story*: CGI Production," *Cinefantastique* 27(2): 28-29 November 1995.
___ "*Toy Story*: Licensing," *Cinefantastique* 27(2): 26. November 1995.
___ "*Toy Story*: Pixar," *Cinefantastique* 27(2): 23-25. November 1995.
___ "*Toy Story*: Renderman," *Cinefantastique* 27(2): 18-19. November 1995.
___ "*Toy Story*: Scanning," *Cinefantastique* 27(2): 34-35. November 1995.
___ "*Toy Story*: Voices," *Cinefantastique* 27(2): 31. November 1995.
___ "*Toy Story*," *Cinefantastique* 26(6)/27(1): 8-9, 125. October 1995.
___ "*Toy Story*," *Cinefantastique* 27(2): 16-37. November 1995.
___ "Vampire Girl," *Cinefantastique* 27(2): 44-45, 61. November 1995.

FRENCH, TODD
___ "*Candyman 2*: Interview with the Master," *Cinefantastique* 26(3): 42. April 1995.
___ "Clive Barker's *Candyman 2*," *Cinefantastique* 26(2): 8-9. February 1995.
___ "Clive Barker's *Candyman 2*," *Cinefantastique* 26(3): 40-43. April 1995.
___ "*Reflecting Skin*," *Cinefantastique* 23(2/3): 117-118. October 1992.

FRENSCHKOWSKI, MARCO
___ " 'Alles is Ufer. Ewig ruft das Meer': Maritime Symbolik in zwei Ersählungen von R. H. Barlow und Ramsey Campbell," *Quarber Merkur* 33(2): 48-59. December 1995. (No. 84)
___ "Bis ins dunkelste Herz des Meeres. Maritime Symbolik als Ausdruck des Unheimlichen in Erzählungen von W. H. Hodgson und H. P. Lovecraft," *Quarber Merkur* 32(2): 42-69. December 1994. (Whole No. 82)
___ "Donald Wandrei," *Quarber Merkur* 30(1): 18-27. June 1992. (No. 77)
___ "H. P. Lovecrafts 'The Transition of Juan Romero': eine Interpretation," *Quarber Merkur* 32(1): 43-50. June 1994. (Whole No. 81)
___ "Henry S. Whitehead," *Quarber Merkur* 31(2): 55-68. Dezember 1993. (No. 80)
___ "Machenalia. Neue Veröffentlichungen von und über Arthur Machen," *Quarber Merkur* 31(1): 35-40. June 1993. (No. 79)

FRICK, THOMAS
___ "Caged by the Experts (Interview, 1987)," in: Ingersoll, Earl G., ed. **Doris Lessing: Conversations**. Princeton, NJ: Ontario Review Press, 1994. pp.155-168.

FRIEDENTHAL, MARTIN H.
___ "Inside the Dahl House of Horror," by Gary Joseph and Martin H. Friedenthal. *Filmfax* No. 41: 65-69. October/November 1993.

FRIEDMAN, ELI A.
___ "ISAO Proffers a Marvelous Cover for Acting out Fantasies," in: Gray, Chris H., ed. **The Cyborg Handbook**. New York: Routledge, 1995. pp.167-168.

FRIEDMAN, LAWRENCE S.
___ **William Golding**. New York: Continuum, 1993. 191pp.

FRIEDMAN, REGIEN-MIHAL
___ "Capitals of Sorrow: From **Metropolis** to **Brazil**," *Utopian Studies* 4(2): 35-43. 1993.

FRIEDMAN, WILLIAM F.
___ "Edgar Allan Poe, Cryptographer (1936)," in: Budd, Louis J. and Cady, Edwin H., eds. **On Poe**. Durham, NC: Duke University Press, 1993. pp.40-54.

FRIEDRICH, HANS-EDWIN
___ **Science Fiction in der deutschsprachigen Literatur: Ein Referat zur Forschung bis 1993**. Tubigen: Max Niemeyer Verlag, 1995. 493pp.

FRIES, MAUREEN
___ "Female Heroes, Heroines and Counter-Heroes: Images of Women in Arthurian Tradition," in: Slocum, Sally K., ed. **Popular Arthurian Traditions**. Bowling Green, OH: Popular Press, 1992. pp.5-17.
___ "From the Lady to the Tramp: The Decline of Morgan le Fay in Medieval Romance," *Arthuriana* 4(1): 1-18. Spring 1994.
___ "The Labyrinthe Ways: Teaching the Arthurian Tradition," in: Fries, Maureen and Watson, Jeanie, eds. **Approaches to the Teaching of the Arthurian Tradition**. New York: Modern Language Association, 1992. pp.33-50.
___ "Readings for Students and Teachers," in: Fries, Maureen and Watson, Jeanie, eds. **Approaches to the Teaching of the Arthurian Tradition**. New York: Modern Language Association, 1992. pp.18-30.
___ "Texts for Teaching," in: Fries, Maureen and Watson, Jeanie, eds. **Approaches to the Teaching of the Arthurian Tradition**. New York: Modern Language Association, 1992. pp.3-18.
___ "Women in Arthurian Literature," in: Fries, Maureen and Watson, Jeanie, eds. **Approaches to the Teaching of the Arthurian Tradition**. New York: Modern Language Association, 1992. pp.155-158.
___ (ed.) **Approaches to the Teaching of the Arthurian Tradition**, ed. by Maureen Fries and Jeanie Watson. New York: Modern Language Association, 1992. 195pp.
___ (ed.) **The Figure of Merlin in the Nineteenth and Twentieth Centuries**, ed. by Jeanie Watson and Maureen Fries. Lewiston, NY: Edwin Mellin Press, 1989. 197pp.

FRIESNER, ESTHER M.
___ "One of the Good Guys," *Science Fiction Age* 3(5): 82-87. July 1995.
___ "There's Nothing Funny About Mixing Humor and SF," *Science Fiction Age* 4(1): 36-40. November 1995.

FRISTOE, ROGER
___ "Designs on Hollywood," *(Louisville, KY) Courier-Journal*. July 2, 1995. in: *NewsBank. Film and Television*. 71:G13. 1995.
___ "A Reel Sinking Feeling," *(Louisville, KY) Courier-Journal*. July 23, 1995. in: *NewsBank. Film and Television*. 82:D8-D9. 1995.

FRONGIA, TERRI
___ "Merlin's Fathers: The Sacred and the Profane," *Children's Literature Association Quarterly* 18(3): 120-125. Fall 1993.
___ "Tales of Old Prague: Of Ghettos, Passover, and the Blood Libel," *Journal of the Fantastic in the Arts* 7(2/3): 146-162. 1995.
___ " 'We're on the Eve of 2000': Writers and Critics Speak Out on Cyberpunk, Hypercard, and the (New?) Nature," by Terri Frongia and Alida Allision. in: Slusser, George E. and Shippey, Tom, eds. **Fiction 2000: Cyberpunk and the Future of Narrative**. Athens: University of Georgia Press, 1992. pp.279-292.

FROST, GORDON W.
___ "*Return of the Texas Chainsaw Massacre*," *Cinefantastique* 27(3): 12-13. December 1995.

FROST, TERRY
___ "Four Days at Thylacon," *Metaphysical Review* No. 22/23: 49-51. November 1995.
___ "Four Days in Another Con," *Metaphysical Review* No. 22/23: 45-49. November 1995.

FROW, EDMUND
___ "Morris on Working Folk and the Future of Art," by Edmund Frow and Ruth Frow. *Journal of the William Morris Society* 11(3): 2-5. Autumn 1995.

FROW, RUTH
___ "Morris on Working Folk and the Future of Art," by Edmund Frow and Ruth Frow. *Journal of the William Morris Society* 11(3): 2-5. Autumn 1995.

FRY, CARROL L.
___ "The Goddess Ascending: Feminist Neo-Pagan Witchcraft in Marion Zimmer Bradley's Novels," *Journal of Popular Culture* 27(1): 67-80. Summer 1993.

FUCHS, CYNTHIA J.
___ " 'Death Is Irrelevant': Cyborgs, Reproduction, and the Future of Male Hysteria," *Genders* No. 18: 113-133. Winter 1993. Also in: Gray, Chris H., ed. **The Cyborg Handbook**. New York: Routledge, 1995. pp.281-300.

FULLER, EDWARD
___ "The Christian Spaceman--C. S. Lewis," *Bulletin of the New York C. S. Lewis Society* 27(1/2): 9-15. November/December 1995. (Reprinted from *Horizon* Vol. 1, No. 5, May, 1959.)

FULTON, HELEN
___ "A Woman's Place: Guinevere in the Welsh and French Romances," *Quondam et Futurus* 3(2): 1-25. Summer 1993.

FULTON, VALERIE
___ "The Other Frontier: Voyaging West with Mark Twain and **Star Trek**'s Imperial Subject," *Postmodern Culture* 4(3): [14pp.]. May 1994. (Electronic Journal: pmc@jefferson.village.virginia.edu).

FULWEILER, HOWARD W.
___ "The Other Missing Link: Owen Barfield and the Scientific Imagination," *Renascence* 46(1): 39-54. Fall 1993.

FULWILER, WILLIAM
___ "E. R. B. and H. P. L.," in: Price, Robert M., ed. **Black Forbidden Things**. Mercer Island, WA: Starmont, 1992. pp.60-65.

FUNK, DAVID A.
___ "Explorations into the Psyche of Dwarves," in: Reynolds, Patricia and GoodKnight, Glen H., eds. **Proceedings of the J. R. R. Tolkien Centenary Conference, Keble College, Oxford, 1992**. Altadena, CA: Mythopoeic Press, 1995. pp.330-334. (*Mythlore* Vol. 21, No. 2, Winter 1996, Whole No. 80)

FURTADO, ANTONIO L.
___ " 'Arthur Had An Affair With an Amazon': Says Senator Carucius," *Quondam et Futurus* 2(3): 31-37. Fall 1992.
___ "From Alexander of Macedonia to Arthur of Britain," *Arthuriana* 5(3): 70-86. Fall 1995.
___ "A Source in Babylon," *Quondam et Futurus* 3(1): 38-59. Spring 1993.

FURY, DAVID
___ "Burroughs Spotlight on Rudy Sigmund," *Burroughs Bulletin* NS. No. 21: 24-26. January 1995.
___ "Interview with the Tarzan Man, Mr. Denny Miller," *Burroughs Bulletin* NS. No. 17: 25-29. January 1994.
___ "Johnny Weissmuller...The Two Career Star," *Burroughs Bulletin* NS. No. 14: 19-28. April 1993.
___ **Kings of the Jungle: An Illustrated Reference to 'Tarzan' on Screen and Television**. Jefferson, NC: McFarland, 1993. 272pp.
___ "Maureen O'Sullivan: A Jewel of a Jane," *Burroughs Bulletin* NS. No. 15: 3-10. July 1993.

FUSSELL, BETTY
___ "Kingsley's Rituals," in: Salwak, Dale, ed. **Kingsley Amis in Life and Letters**. New York: St. Martin's, 1990. pp.33-35.

FUSSELL, PAUL
___ **The Anti-Egotist: Kingsley Amis, Man of Letters**. Oxford: Oxford University Press, 1994. 206pp.
___ "Kingsley, As I Know Him," in: Salwak, Dale, ed. **Kingsley Amis in Life and Letters**. New York: St. Martin's, 1990. pp.18-23.

GABILLIET, JEAN-PAUL
___ "Cultural and Mythical Aspects of a Superhero: *The Silver Surfer* 1968-1970," *Journal of Popular Culture* 28(2): 203-213. Fall 1994.

GABILONDO, JOSEBA
___ **Cinematic Hyperspace: New Hollywood Cinema and Science Fiction Film: Image Commodification in Late Capitalism**. Ph.D. Dissertation, University of California, San Diego, 1992. (DAI-A 53/01, p. 5. July 1992.)
___ "Postcolonial Cyborgs: Subjectivity in the Age of Cybernetic Reproduction," in: Gray, Chris H., ed. **The Cyborg Handbook**. New York: Routledge, 1995. pp.423-432.

GADALLAH, LESLIE
___ "On Hard SF," *ON SPEC* 6(1): 89-90. Spring 1994.

GADBERRY, GREG
___ "The Making of a Miniseries: *The Langoliers*," (Portland, ME) *Maine Sunday Telegram*. September 4, 1994. in: *NewsBank. Film and Television*. 100:D4. 1994.

GAFFNEY, F. ANDREW
___ "Barney B. Clark, DDS: A View From the Medical Service," by F. Andrew Gaffney and Barry J. Fenton. in: Gray, Chris H., ed. **The Cyborg Handbook**. New York: Routledge, 1995. pp.157-160.

GAFFORD, SAM
___ " 'The Shadow Over Innsmouth': Lovecraft's Melting Pot," *Lovecraft Studies* No. 24: 6-13. Spring 1991.
___ "Writing Backward: The Novels of William Hope Hodgson," *Studies in Weird Fiction* No. 11: 12-15. Spring 1992.

GAGLIANO, WILLIAM D.
___ "SFC Interviews: Matt Costello's Journey," *Science Fiction Chronicle* 14(9): 5, 29-30. June 1993.

GAILLARD, ROGER
___ **Bienvenue en Utopie**, by Roger Gaillard and Felicie Girardin. Yverdon-les-Bains, Switzerland: Maison d'Ailleurs, 1991. 183pp. [Not seen.]

GAIMAN, NEIL
___ "The Craft," in: Jones, Stephen, ed. **James Herbert: By Horror Haunted**. London: New English Library, 1992. pp.79-91.

GALBRAITH, STUART, IV.
___ "*Godzilla*'s American Cousin: The Eclectic Career of Henry G. Saperstein," *Filmfax* No. 45: 59-63. June/July 1994.
___ "The How to of Making a Monster Movie: An Interview with AIP Producer Herman Cohen," *Filmfax* No. 37: 43-49. February/March 1993.
___ **Japanese Science Fiction, Fantasy and Horror Films: A Critical Analysis and Filmography of 103 Features Released in the United States, 1950-1992**. Jefferson, NC: McFarland, 1994. 424pp.

GALEN, RUSSELL
___ "Finding and Getting the Most Out of a Science Fiction Agent," in: Thompkins, David G., ed. **Science Fiction Writer's Market Place and Source Book**. Cincinnati, OH: Writer's Digest Books, 1994. pp.286-292.
___ "The Near Future Is Perfect," *Writer's Digest* 74(1): 49-50. January 9194.
___ "Writing in a Fantasy World," *Writer's Digest* 73(5): 53-55. May 1993.

GALLAGHER, STEPHEN
___ "Herbert, **Haunted**, and the Integrity of Bestsellerdom," in: Jones, Stephen, ed. **James Herbert: By Horror Haunted**. London: New English Library, 1992. pp.181-188.

GALLARDO TORRANO, PEDRO
___ "**Frankenstein's** French Counterpart: Villiers de l'Isle-Adam's **L'Eve Future**," *Foundation* No. 63: 74-80. Spring 1995.
___ "Themes and Motifs in a Robot Story: 'Rex' by Harl Vincent," in: Fernández-Corugedo, S. G., ed. **Studia Patriciae Shaw Oblata**. Volumen III. n.p.: University of Oviedo, 1991. pp.214-224.

GALLIGAN, JOHN
___ "They Came From Outer Space--And Moved to the 'Burbs," by John Galligan and Jon Haber. *Boston (MA) Globe* Sec. B, p. 29. July 25, 1993.

GALLOWAY, STAN
___ "The Feral Child," *Burroughs Bulletin* NS. No. 18: 27-29. April 1994.

GALVAN, DAVE
___ "Comic Book Heroes: From Panel to Screen," *Sci-Fi Entertainment* 1(6): 42-47, 73. April 1995.

GAMBOA, SUZANNE
___ "Guest of Honor at **Star Trek** Event Urges Support for NASA Space Station," *Austin (TX) American Statesman* Sec. B, p. 1, 3. June 7, 1993.

GAMMONS, NEIL G.
___ "**Till We Have Faces**: A Key-Word Concordance, Part 1," *CSL: The Bulletin of the New York C. S. Lewis Society* 23(10/11): 11-16. August/September 1992.
___ "**Till We Have Faces**: A Key-Word Concordance, Part 2," *CSL: The Bulletin of the New York C. S. Lewis Society* 23/24(No.12/No. 1): 11-16. October/November 1992.

GARBER, ERIC
___ "The Best of Gay Sci-Fi and Fantasy," in: Dynes, Wayne R., ed. **Homosexual Themes in Literary Studies**. New York: Garland, 1992. pp.145-151.

GARCIA Y ROBERTSON, R.
___ "Write From the Heart," in: Wolverton, Dave, ed. **Writers of the Future, Vol. VIII**. Los Angeles, CA: Bridge, 1992. pp.293-297.

GARCIA, BOB
___ "The Animated Adventures: *Batman*," *Cinefantastique* 24(6)/25(1): 68-70, 75-111. February 1994.
___ "*Batman*: Alan Burnett, Script Supervisor," by Bob Garcia and Nancy Garcia. *Cinefantastique* 24(6)/25(1): 84-85. February 1994.
___ "*Batman*: Andrea Romano, Voice Doctor," by Bob Garcia and Nancy Garcia. *Cinefantastique* 24(6)/25(1): 90-93, 125. February 1994.
___ "*Batman*: Batmusic," *Cinefantastique* 24(6)/25(1): 37, 61. February 1994.
___ "*Batman*: Bruce Timm, Series Co-Creator," by Bob Garcia and Nancy Garcia. *Cinefantastique* 24(6)/25(1): 79-80. February 1994.
___ "*Batman*: Building the Batmobile," *Cinefantastique* 24(6)/25(1): 28-31. February 1994.
___ "*Batman*: Catwoman," *Cinefantastique* 24(6)/25(1): 18-19. February 1994.
___ "*Batman*: Composing Music for Animation," by Bob Garcia and Nancy Garcia. *Cinefantastique* 24(6)/25(1): 108-110. February 1994.
___ "*Batman*: Costumes," *Cinefantastique* 24(6)/25(1): 38-40. February 1994.
___ "*Batman*: Directing the Cartoon Action," by Bob Garcia and Nancy Garcia. *Cinefantastique* 24(6)/25(1): 95-97. February 1994.
___ "*Batman*: Episode Guide," by Bob Garcia and Nancy Garcia. *Cinefantastique* 24(6)/25(1): 70-111. February 1994.
___ "*Batman*: Eric Radomski, Series Co-Creator," by Bob Garcia and Nancy Garcia. *Cinefantastique* 24(6)/25(1): 76-77. February 1994.
___ "*Batman*: Lorenzo Semple, Guru of Camp," *Cinefantastique* 24(6)/25(1): 44-45. February 1994.
___ "*Batman*: Making the Original Movie," *Cinefantastique* 24(6)/25(1): 55-58. February 1994.
___ "*Batman*: Paul Dini, Cartoon Criminology," by Bob Garcia and Nancy Garcia. *Cinefantastique* 24(6)/25(1): 87-88. February 1994.
___ "*Batman*: Producing the Presentation Reel," by Bob Garcia and Nancy Garcia. *Cinefantastique* 24(6)/25(1): 100-101. February 1994.
___ "*Batman*: Series Creator," *Cinefantastique* 24(6)/25(1): 12-13. February 1994.
___ "*Batman*: The Batcycle," *Cinefantastique* 24(6)/25(1): 60-61. February 1994.
___ "*Batman*: The Joker," *Cinefantastique* 24(6)/25(1): 42. February 1994.
___ "*Batman*: The Origin of Batgirl," *Cinefantastique* 24(6)/25(1): 32-34. February 1994.
___ "*Batman*: The Origin of Egghead," *Cinefantastique* 24(6)/25(1): 52-53. February 1994.
___ "*Batman*: The Penguin," *Cinefantastique* 24(6)/25(1): 10. February 1994.
___ "*Batman*: The Riddler," *Cinefantastique* 24(6)/25(1): 15-16. February 1994.
___ "*Batman*: Things to Come, Second Season," by Bob Garcia and Nancy Garcia. *Cinefantastique* 24(6)/25(1): 103-105. February 1994.
___ "*Batman*: Comic Book Art Direction," *Cinefantastique* 24(6)/25(1): 22-25. February 1994.
___ "*Batman*: Comic Book Makeup," *Cinefantastique* 24(6)/25(1): 48-50. February 1994.
___ "*Batman*," *Cinefantastique* 24(6)/25(1): 8-63. February 1994.
___ "*Batman: Mask of the Phantasm*, the Animated Movie," *Cinefantastique* 24(6)/25(1): 71-74, 125. February 1994.

GARCÍA, FERNANDO
___ "Burroughs in Argentina," by Fernando García and Hernán Ostuni. *Burroughs Bulletin* NS. No. 17: 10-17. January 1994.
___ "Tarzan, King of the Pampa," by Fernando García and Hernán Ostuni. *Burroughs Bulletin* NS. No. 18: 20-22. April 1994.

GARCIA, FRANK
___ "***The Outer Limits***," *Starlog* No. 214: 54-57. May 1995.
___ "Prince of Darkness," *Starlog* No. 220: 76-79. November 1995.

GARCIA, J. P.
___ "Science Fiction Comes to the Classroom: Maelstrom II," by M. J. Martin-Diaz, A. Pizarro, P. Bacas, J. P. Garcia and F. Perera. *Physics Education* 27(1): 18-23. January 1992.

GARCIA, NANCY
___ "***Batman***: Alan Burnett, Script Supervisor," by Bob Garcia and Nancy Garcia. *Cinefantastique* 24(6)/25(1): 84-85. February 1994.
___ "***Batman***: Andrea Romano, Voice Doctor," by Bob Garcia and Nancy Garcia. *Cinefantastique* 24(6)/25(1): 90-93, 125. February 1994.
___ "***Batman***: Bruce Timm, Series Co-Creator," by Bob Garcia and Nancy Garcia. *Cinefantastique* 24(6)/25(1): 79-80. February 1994.
___ "***Batman***: Composing Music for Animation," by Bob Garcia and Nancy Garcia. *Cinefantastique* 24(6)/25(1): 108-110. February 1994.
___ "***Batman***: Directing the Cartoon Action," by Bob Garcia and Nancy Garcia. *Cinefantastique* 24(6)/25(1): 95-97. February 1994.
___ "***Batman***: Episode Guide," by Bob Garcia and Nancy Garcia. *Cinefantastique* 24(6)/25(1): 70-111. February 1994.
___ "***Batman***: Eric Radomski, Series Co-Creator," by Bob Garcia and Nancy Garcia. *Cinefantastique* 24(6)/25(1): 76-77. February 1994.
___ "***Batman***: Paul Dini, Cartoon Criminology," by Bob Garcia and Nancy Garcia. *Cinefantastique* 24(6)/25(1): 87-88. February 1994.
___ "***Batman***: Producing the Presentation Reel," by Bob Garcia and Nancy Garcia. *Cinefantastique* 24(6)/25(1): 100-101. February 1994.
___ "***Batman***: Things to Come, Second Season," by Bob Garcia and Nancy Garcia. *Cinefantastique* 24(6)/25(1): 103-105. February 1994.

GARCIA, ROBERT T.
___ "The Amazing Colossal Movies: Inspiration and Legal Hassles," *Cinefantastique* 23(1): 21. August 1992.
___ "***Mortal Kombat***: The TV Commercial," *Cinefantastique* 26(5): 44. August 1995.
___ "***Mortal Kombat***," *Cinefantastique* 26(5): 40-44. August 1995.
___ "Robert A. Heinlein," *Cinefantastique* 25(6)/26(1): 42, 125. December 1994.

GARCÍA-SÁNCHEZ, FRANKLIN B.
___ "Ubicación genérica de **El Caballero Encantado** (1909) de Benito Pérez Galdós," *Monographis Review* 3(1/2): 71-80. 1987.

GARDINER, JOSEPHINE
___ "Forward With the Masters of the Sci-Fi Universe," *Times Educational Supplement* 4061: SS2. April 29, 1994.

GARDINER, JUDITH K.
___ **Rhys, Stead, Lessing, and the Politics of Empathy**. Bloomington: Indiana University Press, 1989. 186pp.

GARDINER, MICHAEL
___ "Bakhtin's Carnival: Utopia as Critique," *Utopian Studies* 3(2): 21-49. 1992.
___ "Utopia and Everyday Life in French Social Thought," *Utopian Studies* 6(2): 90-123. 1995.

GARDINER-SCOTT, TANYA
___ "Game as Fantasy in Crucifixion Drama," *Journal of the Fantastic in the Arts* 3(3): 50-61. 1994.

GARDNER, CRAIG S.
___ "Blood and Laughter: The Humor in Horror Film," in: Golden, Christopher, ed. **Cut! Horror Writers on Horror Film**. New York: Berkley, 1992. pp.91-100.

GARDNER, HELEN
___ "British Academy Obituary: C. S. Lewis," in: Watson, George, ed. **Critical Essays on C. S. Lewis**. Hants, Eng.: Scolar Press, 1992. pp.10-21.

GARDNER, JOHN
___ "**The Silmarillion**, by J. R. R. Tolkien," in: Gardner, John. **On Writers and Writing**. Reading, MA: Addison-Wesley, 1994. pp.140-144.

GARDNER, LAUREL J.
___ "Pornography as a Matter of Power in **The Handmaid's Tale**," *Notes on Contemporary Literature* 24(5): 5-7. November 1994.

GARDNER, STEVE
___ "The Mechanics of Dragons: An Introduction to the Study of Their 'Ologies," by Angela Surtees and Steve Gardner. in: Reynolds, Patricia and GoodKnight, Glen H., eds. **Proceedings of the J. R. R. Tolkien Centenary Conference, Keble College, Oxford, 1992**. Altadena, CA: Mythopoeic Press, 1995. pp.411-418. (*Mythlore* Vol. 21, No. 2, Winter 1996, Whole No. 80)

GARGAN, EDWARD A.
___ "For Arthur Clarke, Sri Lanka Is a Link to Space," *New York Times* Sec. C, p. 13. April 7, 1993.

GARLICK, BARBARA
___ "**The Handmaid's Tale**: Narrative Voice and the Primacy of the Tale," in: Filmer, Kath, ed. **Twentieth-Century Fantasists: Essays in Culture, Society and Belief in Twentieth Century Mythopoeic Literature**. New York: St. Martin's, 1992. pp.161-171.

GARNER, JACK
___ "Movie Is Too Scary for Youngsters," *Austin (TX) American Statesman* Sec. E, p. 1. June 10, 1993.

GARNO, DIANA M.
___ "Gender Dilemmas: Equality and Rights for Icarian Women," *Utopian Studies* 6(2): 52-74. 1995.

GAROFALO, CHARLES
___ "Chariots of the Old Ones?," by Robert M. Price and Charles Garofalo. in: Price, Robert M., ed. **Black Forbidden Things**. Mercer Island, WA: Starmont, 1992. pp.86-87.

GARRATT, PETER
___ "Unstoppable Fate: Tanith Lee Interview," *Interzone* No. 64: 23-25. October 1992.

GARREAU, JOEL
___ "Cyberspaceman: Sci-Fi Writer William Gibson, Far Flung and Back Again," *Washington (DC) Post* p.D1. October 18, 1993.

GARRETT, GREG
___ "Objecting to Objectification: Re-viewing the Feminine in **The Silence of the Lambs**," *Journal of Popular Culture* 27(4): 1-12. Spring 1994.

GARRETT, JOHN C.
___ **Hope or Disillusion: Three Versions of Utopia: Nathaniel Hawthorne, Samuel Butler, George Orwell**. Christchurch, NZ: University of Canterbury Publications Committee, 1984. 69pp.

GARRISON, GREG
___ "Storyteller Sees Religion in Many Hues," *Birmingham (AL) News*. January 31, 1992. in: *NewsBank. Names in the News*. 37:D10-D11. 1992.

GARRON, BARRY
___ "*Voyager* Revives Space Pioneer Spirit of Original Trek," *Austin (TX) American Statesman* Sec. B, p. 8. January 21, 1995

GARSAULT, A.
___ "Strougakski, Arcadi and Strougatski, Boris, Russian Science Fiction Writers," *Positif* No. 247: 15. October 1981.

GARTON, RAY
___ "On Kids and **Cat People**," in: Golden, Christopher, ed. **Cut! Horror Writers on Horror Film**. New York: Berkley, 1992. pp.101-112.

GASPARINI, ALBERTO

GASPARINI, ALBERTO
___ "Utopia e carisma nell'organizzazione. Discorsi sulle asimmetrie tra ambiente e Nomadelfia e sulla loro proiezioine al futuro," in: Saccaro Del Buffa, Giuseppa and Lewis, Arthur O., eds. **Utopia e Modernita: Teorie e prassi utopiche nell'eta moderna e postmoderna**. Rome: Gangemi Editore, 1989. pp.1087-1124.

GATLING, CLOVER H.
___ "Echoes of Epic in Lewis' **The Great Divorce**," *Bulletin of the New York C. S. Lewis Society* 26(3): 1-8. January 1995.

GATTEGNO, JEAN
___ **La Science-Fiction**. Paris: Presses Universitaires de France, 1992. 128pp. 5th ed.

GAUGHAN, JACK
___ "An Apprenticeship: Artist," in: Sanders, Joe, ed. **Science Fiction Fandom**. Westport, CT: Greenwood, 1994. pp.207-210.

GAYFORD, NORMAN R.
___ "Lovecraft's Narrators," in: Joshi, S. T., ed. **The H. P. Lovecraft Centennial Conference Proceedings**. West Warwick, RI: Necronomicon, 1991. pp.32-33.

GAYLORD, ALAN T.
___ "Arthur and the Green World," in: Fries, Maureen and Watson, Jeanie, eds. **Approaches to the Teaching of the Arthurian Tradition**. New York: Modern Language Association, 1992. pp.56-60.

GEARY, ROBERT F.
___ "The Corpse in the Dung Cart: *The Night Side of Nature* and the Victorian Supernatural Tale," in: Sanders, Joe, ed. **Functions of the Fantastic**. Westport, CT: Greenwood, 1995. pp.47-54.
___ "**The Exorcist**: Deep Horror?," *Journal of the Fantastic in the Arts* 5(4): 55-63. 1993. (No. 20)
___ "M. G. Lewis and Later Gothic Fiction: The Numinous Dissipated," in: Ruddick, Nicholas, ed. **State of the Fantastic**. Westport, CT: Greenwood, 1992. pp.75-81.
___ **The Supernatural in Gothic Fiction: Horror, Belief and Literary Change**. Lewiston, NY: Mellen, 1992. 151pp.

GEE, ROBIN
___ "Marketing Your Science Fiction Novel," in: Thompkins, David G., ed. **Science Fiction Writer's Market Place and Source Book**. Cincinnati, OH: Writer's Digest Books, 1994. pp.182-192.
___ "Marketing Your Short Story," in: Thompkins, David G., ed. **Science Fiction Writer's Market Place and Source Book**. Cincinnati, OH: Writer's Digest Books, 1994. pp.35-38.

GEIER, MANFRED
___ " 'Eden': Elemente einer 'außerirdischen' Semiologie," *Quarber Merkur* 31(2): 15-33. Dezember 1993. (No. 80)
___ "Stanislaw Lem's Fantastic Ocean: Toward a Semantic Interpretation of **Solaris**," *Science-Fiction Studies* 19(2): 192-218. July 1992.

GELMAN, MORRIE
___ "Sunbow Takes to Marvel Like Duck to Water in Animation," *Variety* p. 81, 98. September 17, 1986.

GENGE, N. E.
___ **The Unofficial X-Files Companion**. New York: Crown, 1995. 227pp.

GENOVESE, E. N.
___ "Paradise and the Golden Age: Ancient Origins of the Heavenly Utopia," in: Sullivan, E. D. S., ed. **The Utopian Vision**. San Diego, CA: San Diego University Press, 1983. pp.9-28.

GENTRY, CHRIS
___ **Greenberg's Guide to Star Trek Collectibles**, by Chris Gentry and Sally Gibson-Downs. Sykesville, MD: Greenberg, 1992. 3 vols.; 190, 172, 192pp.

GEOGHEGAN, VINCENT
___ "The Utopian Past: Memory and History in Edward Bellamy's **Looking Backward** and William Morris's **News From Nowhere**," *Utopian Studies* 3(2): 75-90. 1992.

GERBER, ERNST
___ **The Photo Journal Guide to Comic Books**, by Ernst Gerber and Mary Gerber. Minden, NV: Gerber Publishing, 1989. 856pp.

GERBER, MARY
___ **The Photo Journal Guide to Comic Books**, by Ernst Gerber and Mary Gerber. Minden, NV: Gerber Publishing, 1989. 856pp.

GERNSBACK, HUGO
___ "How to Write 'Science' Stories," *Science Fiction Studies* 21(2): 268-272. July 1994. (Reprinted from *Writer's Digest* 10: 27-29. February 1930.)

GERSTEL, JUDY
___ "Play of Images Is the Thing in Transformation of Shakespeare's **Tempest** (Review)," *Detroit (MI) Free Press*. November 27, 1991. in: *NewsBank. Film and Television*. 6:D6. 1992.

GESS, RICHARD
___ "Notes on Hypertext: One Artist's Slate, 1992-1994," *New York Review of Science Fiction* No. 72: 1, 8-9. August 1994.

GIBBERMAN, SUSAN R.
___ **Star Trek: An Annotated Guide to Resources on the Development, the Phenomenon, the People, the Television Series, the Films, the Novels and the Recordings**. Jefferson, NC: McFarland, 1991. 434pp.

GIBSON, WILLIAM
___ "Notes on a Process: Novel into Film," *Wired* 3(6): 157-159. June 1995.

GIBSON-DOWNS, SALLY
___ **Greenberg's Guide to Star Trek Collectibles**, by Chris Gentry and Sally Gibson-Downs. Sykesville, MD: Greenberg, 1992. 3 vols.; 190, 172, 192pp.

GIES, JOSEPH
___ "Looking Forward to Utopia," *VocEd* 57(1): 30-31. January/February 1982.

GILBERT, ELLIOTT L.
___ "Upward, Not Northward," *English Literature in Transition* 34(4): 391-404. 1991.

GILBERT, JOHN
___ "The Devil You Know," in: Jones, Stephen, ed. **James Herbert: By Horror Haunted**. London: New English Library, 1992. pp.235-241.
___ "Haunted by Success," in: Jones, Stephen, ed. **James Herbert: By Horror Haunted**. London: New English Library, 1992. pp.189-198.
___ "Horror of **The Rats**," in: Jones, Stephen, ed. **James Herbert: By Horror Haunted**. London: New English Library, 1992. pp.105-107.

GILBERT, MICHAEL
___ "A Personal Memoir: Dorothy L. Sayers," in: Dale, Alzina S., ed. **Dorothy L. Sayers: The Centenary Celebration**. New York: Walker, 1993. pp.15-22.

GILES, JEFF
___ "Coming to a Toy Store Near You," by Jeff Giles and Donna Foote. *Newsweek* 121(24): 64-65. June 14, 1993.

GILES, STACIE L. M.
___ **Russian Science Fiction: Window into Which Future?**. Master's Thesis, University of California, Los Angeles, 1995. 126pp.

GILET, P.
___ "Folk Tales and Science Fiction: Testing a Thesis," *Australian Folklore* 8: 142-145. August 1993.

GILLESPIE, BRUCE
___ "Jonathan Carroll, Storyteller," *SF Commentary* No. 71/72: 28-33. April 1992.
___ "The Non-Fiction Novels of Philip K. Dick," *Science Fiction: A Review of Speculative Literature* 12(2): 3-14. 1993. (No. 35)

GOLDBORT, ROBERT C.
___ "Science, Technology, and Popular Literature: (Re)visionary Symbioses," *National Forum: Phi Kappa Phi Journal* 74(4): 5-6. Fall 1994.

GOLDEN, CATHERINE
___ **The Captive Imagination: A Casebook on 'The Yellow Wallpaper'.** New York: Feminist Press, 1992. 341pp.

GOLDEN, CHRISTOPHER
___ "Introduction: First Cut," in: Golden, Christopher, ed. **Cut! Horror Writers on Horror Film.** New York: Berkley, 1992. pp.1-9.
___ (ed.) **Cut! Horror Writers on Horror Film.** New York: Berkley, 1992. 297pp.

GOLDEN, JOANNE M.
___ **A Schema for Analyzing Response to Literature Applied to the Responses of Fifth and Eighth Graders to Realistic and Fantasy Short Stories.** Ph.D. Dissertation, Ohio State University, 1978. 195pp. (DAI 39: 5996A. Apr. 1978.)

GOLDMAN, BRUCE
___ **2020 Visions: Long View of a Changing World,** by Richard C. Carlson and Bruce Goldman. Stanford, CA: Stanford Alumni Association, 1991. 252pp.

GOLDMAN, LOWELL
___ **2001: A Space Odyssey**: Gary Lockwood," *Cinefantastique* 25(3): 47. June 1994.
___ **2001: A Space Odyssey**: Kier Dullea," *Cinefantastique* 25(3): 34. June 1994.

GOLDMAN, MICHAEL R.
___ "Big Bucks Planted in 'Mnemonic'," *Variety* 357(4): 83. November 21, 1994.

GOLDMAN, STEPHEN H.
___ "Frederik Pohl," in: Bruccoli, Matthew J., ed. **Facts on File Bibliography of American Fiction 1919-1988.** New York: Facts on File, 1991. pp.403-405.
___ "Isaac Asimov," in: Bruccoli, Matthew J., ed. **Facts on File Bibliography of American Fiction 1919-1988.** New York: Facts on File, 1991. pp.59-68.

GOLDSMITH, MARLENE H.
___ **Video Values Education: Star Trek as Modern Myth.** Ph.D. Dissertation, University of Minnesota, 1981. 303pp.

GOLDSMITH, SARAH S.
___ "Isaac Asimov Pushes Books," *Baton Rouge (LA) Morning Advocate* July 9, 1989. in: *NewsBank. Names in the News* NIN 236: D5. 1989.

GOLDSMITH, STEVEN
___ "Takei Takes Helm in Autobiography," *Austin (TX) American Statesman* Sec. E, p. 11. October 15, 1994.

GOLDSTINE, LISA
___ "Bilude: The Imaginative Future," in: Wolf, Milton T. and Mallett, Daryl F., eds. **Imaginative Futures: Proceedings of the 1993 Science Fiction Research Association Conference.** San Bernardino, CA: Jacob's Ladder Books, 1995. pp.75-82.

GOLDSWORTHY, PETER
___ "Honk If You Love Science," *Island Magazine* 54: 40-43. Fall 1993.

GOLDWATER, WALTER
___ "Shiel, Van Vechten and the Question of Color," in: **Shiel in Diverse Hands: A Collection of Essays.** Cleveland, OH: Reynolds Morse Foundation, 1983. pp.75-76.

GOLFFING, FRANCIS
___ **Possibility: An Essay in Utopian Vision.** New York: P. Lang, 1991. 157pp. [Not seen.]

GÖLLER, KARL H.
___ "Die Modernität von Williams' Arthur-Dichtung," in: Kranz, Gisbert, ed. **Inklings: Jahrbuch für Literatur und Ästhetik.** 3. Band. [Lüdenscheid, Germany: Stier], 1985. pp.37-48.

GOMEL, ELANA
___ "Mystery, Apocalypse and Utopia: The Case of the Ontological Detective Story," *Science Fiction Studies* 22(3): 343-356. November 1995
___ "The Poetics of Censorship: Allegory as Form and Ideology in the Novels of Arkady and Boris Strugatsky," *Science Fiction Studies* 22(1): 87-105. March 1995.

GOMOLL, JEANNE
___ "Out of Context: Post-Holocaust Themes in Feminist Science Fiction," *Janus* 6(2): 14-17. Winter 1980. (Whole No. 18)
___ "Post-Holocaust Themes in Feminist SF (Transcript of the Panel at NorEasCon 2)," by Elizabeth Lynn, Chelsea Q. Yarbro, Suzy M. Charnas and Jeanne Gomoll. *Janus* 6(2): 25-28. Winter 1980. (Whole No. 18)

GONZALES, DOREEN
___ **Madeleine L'Engle: Author of A Wrinkle in Time.** New York: Dillon Press, 1991. 112pp.

GONZALES, JENNIFER
___ "Envisioning Cyborg Bodies: Notes From Current Research," in: Gray, Chris H., ed. **The Cyborg Handbook.** New York: Routledge, 1995. pp.267-279.

GONZÁLES-MILLÁN, JUAN
___ "Fantasía y parodia: la subversión del texto narrativo en **Las crónicas del sochantre,**" *Monographis Review* 3(1/2): 81-99. 1987.

GOOD, LEE
___ "Interview: Bill Ransom," by Lenora Rain and Lee Good. *Westwind* No. 183: 13-16. December 1993.

GOODERHAM, DAVID
___ "Children's Fantasy Literature: Toward an Anatomy," *Children's Literature in Education* 26(3): 171-183. September 1995.

GOODKNIGHT, GLEN H.
___ "Is Children's Literature Childish?," *Mythlore* 19(4): 4-5. Autumn 1993. (No. 74)
___ "J. R. R. Tolkien in Translation," *Mythlore* 18(3): 61-69. Summer 1992. (No. 69)
___ "Tolkien Centenary Banquet Address," in: Reynolds, Patricia and GoodKnight, Glen H., eds. **Proceedings of the J. R. R. Tolkien Centenary Conference, Keble College, Oxford, 1992.** Altadena, CA: Mythopoeic Press, 1995. pp.15-16. (*Mythlore* Vol. 21, No. 2, Winter 1996, Whole No. 80)
___ "Twenty-Five Years With the Mythopoeic Society: A Personal Reprise," *Mythlore* 19(1): 29-30. Winter 1993. (No. 71)
___ (ed.) **Proceedings of the J. R. R. Tolkien Centenary Conference, Keble College, Oxford, 1992,** ed. by Patricia Reynolds and Glen H. Goodknight. Altadena, CA: Mythopoeic Press, 1995. 458pp.

GOODMAN, DENISE
___ "Creator of Strange Tale Haunts Stephen King," *Boston (MA) Globe.* August 21, 1992. in: *NewsBank. Literature.* 74:G8-G9. 1992.

GOODMAN, MARGARET
___ "Posthumous Journeys: **The Great Divorce** and Other Travels to Eternity," *Bulletin of the New York C. S. Lewis Society* 27(1/2): 1-8. November/December 1995.

GOODMAN, MICHAEL B.
___ "William S. Burroughs," in: Bruccoli, Matthew J., ed. **Facts on File Bibliography of American Fiction 1919-1988.** New York: Facts on File, 1991. pp.111-114.
___ **William S. Burroughs: A Reference Guide.** New York: Garland, 1990. 270pp.

GOVIER, KATHERINE
___ "Q&Q Interview: Margaret Atwood; 'There's Nothing in the Book That Hasn't Already Happened'," *Quill and Quire* pp.66-67. September 1985.

GOYNE, JO
___ "Parataxis and Causality in the Tale of Sir Launcelot du Lake," *Quondam et Futurus* 2(4): 36-48. Winter 1992.

GRACE, DOMINICK M.
___ "Rereading Lester del Rey's 'Helen O'Loy'," *Science Fiction Studies* 20(1): 45-51. March 1993.

GRACE, SHERRILL
___ "Gender as Genre: Atwood's Autobiographical 'I'," in: Nicholson, Colin, ed. **Margaret Atwood: Writing and Subjectivity: New Critical Essays**. New York: St. Martin's, 1994. pp.189-203.

GRAFF, BENNETT
___ **Horror in Evolution: Determinism, Materialism, and Darwinism in the American Gothic (Edgar Allan Poe, Frank Norris, Jack London, H. P. Lovecraft)**. Ph.D. Dissertation, City University of New York, 1995. 282pp. (DAI-A 56/05, p. 1777. November 1995.)

GRAFF, ERIC S.
___ "The Three Faces of Faërie in Tolkien's Shorter Fiction: Niggle, Smith and Giles," *Mythlore* 18(3): 15-18. Summer 1992. (No. 69)

GRAHAM, DOUGLAS F.
___ "Sci-Fi Art: No Alien Concept," *Washington (DC) Times* Sec. B, p. 1. July 4, 1992.

GRAHAM, HARRY L.
___ "How the Gaonas Flew With Tarzan in the Comics," *Burroughs Bulletin* NS. No. 18: 17-19. April 1994.

GRAHNKE, LON
___ **Stay Tuned** Mocks TV, But the Joke's on Ritter (Review)," *Chicago (IL) Sun Times*. August 17, 1992. in: *NewsBank. Film and Television*. 84:A7. 1992.

GRANT, BARRY K.
___ "Looking Upwards: Reason and the Visible in Science Fiction Film," in: Irons, Glenwood, ed. **Gender, Language and Myth: Essays on Popular Narrative**. Toronto: University of Toronto Press, 1992. pp.185-207.
___ "Taking Back *The Night of the Living Dead*: George Romero, Feminism and the Horror Film," *Wide Angle* 14(1): 64-77. January 1992.

GRANT, CHARLES L.
___ "Black and White, in Color," in: Golden, Christopher, ed. **Cut! Horror Writers on Horror Film**. New York: Berkley, 1992. pp.117-122.

GRANT, GLENN
___ "Channeling Horny Jellyfish in an Anyon Field," *New York Review of Science Fiction* No. 67: 7. March 1994.

GRANT, JAMES
___ "Red Hot Right Now: David Duchovny," *Cosmopolitan* 219(4): 144. October 1995.

GRANT, RICHARD
___ "Get Along, Little Robot," in: Jakubowski, Maxim and James, Edward, eds. **The Profession of Science Fiction**. New York: St. Martin's, 1992. pp.182-199.

GRASSO, ELSA
___ "Le professeur et la sirène," in: Bozzetto, Roger, ed. **Eros: Science & Fiction Fantastique**. Aix-en-Provence: Universite de Provence, 1991. pp.167-176.

GRAY, CHRIS H.
___ "The Cyborg Body Politic: Version 1.2," by Chris H. Gray and Steven Mentor. in: Gray, Chris H., ed. **The Cyborg Handbook**. New York: Routledge, 1995. pp.453-467.
___ "An Interview With Jack E. Steele," in: Gray, Chris H., ed. **The Cyborg Handbook**. New York: Routledge, 1995. pp.61-69.

GRAY, CHRIS H. (continued)
___ "An Interview With Manfred E. Clynes," in: Gray, Chris H., ed. **The Cyborg Handbook**. New York: Routledge, 1995. pp.43-53.
___ "Introduction: Constructing the Knowledge of Cybernetic Organisms," by Chris H. Gray, Steven Mentor and Heidi J. Figueroa-Sarriera. in: Gray, Chris H., ed. **The Cyborg Handbook**. New York: Routledge, 1995. pp.1-14.
___ "Science Fiction Becomes Science Fact," in: Gray, Chris H., ed. **The Cyborg Handbook**. New York: Routledge, 1995. pp.104-106.
___ "There Will Be War: Future War Fantasies and Militaristic Science Fiction in the 1980s," *Science Fiction Studies* 21(3): 315-336. November 1994.
___ (ed.) **The Cyborg Handbook**. New York: Routledge, 1995. 540pp.

GRAY, LOUISE
___ "*Meteor Man* (Review)," *Sight and Sound* 4(2): 57-58. February 1994.

GRAY, STEPHEN
___ "Breaking Down These Forms (Interview, 1983)," in: Ingersoll, Earl G., ed. **Doris Lessing: Conversations**. Princeton, NJ: Ontario Review Press, 1994. pp.109-119.

GRAY, W. RUSSELL
___ "Science Fiction Detectives, (or, Stick 'em Up! I Picked Your Pocket With My Invisible Third Hand After You Handcuffed Me)," *Mid-Atlantic Almanack: Journal of the Mid Atlantic Popular American Culture Association* 2: 46-53. 1993.
___ " 'That Frightful Torrent of Trash': Crime/Detective Fiction and **Nineteen Eighty-Four**," in: Rose, Jonathan, ed. **The Revised Orwell**. East Lansing, MI: Michigan State University Press, 1992. pp.117-130.

GREBE, CORALEE
___ "Heir to the Wars," *Starlog* No. 186: 56-58. January 1993.
___ "Tarot Card Symbolism in the *Star Wars* Films," *Mythlore* 20(2): 27-31. Spring 1994. (Whole No. 76)

GREEN, CAROL A.
___ "Only a Girl: Heroines in the Work of Anne McCaffrey and Marion Zimmer Bradley," *Vector* No. 172: 16-17. April/May 1993.
___ "Pretty Bloody Happy! Nicola Griffith Interviewed," *Vector* No. 173: 7-10 June/July 1993.
___ "Women of Color: The Female Protagonists in the Novels of Octavia Butler," *Vector* No. 176: 14-15. December 1993/January 1994.

GREEN, ERNEST J.
___ "The Social Functions of Utopian Architecture," *Utopian Studies* 4(1): 1-13. 1993.

GREEN, MICHELLE G.
___ "There Goes the Neighborhood: Octavia Butler's Demand for Diversity in Utopias," in: Donawerth, Jane L. and Kolmerten, Carol A., eds. **Utopian and Science Fiction by Women: Worlds of Difference**. Syracuse, NY: Syracuse University Press, 1994. pp.166-189.

GREEN, ROCKNE
___ "Thuvia's Secret," *Burroughs Bulletin* NS. No. 16: 26. October 1993.

GREEN, ROGER L.
___ **C. S. Lewis: A Biography**. Revised Edition, by Roger L. Green and Walter Hooper. San Diego, CA: Harcourt Brace, 1994. 320pp.

GREEN, SCOTT E.
___ **Isaac Asimov: An Annotated Bibliography of the Asimov Collection at Boston University**. Westport, CT: Greenwood Press, 1995. 146pp.

GREEN, STEVE
___ "All in Colour for a Dime: A Profile of Stan Lee," *Interzone* No. 59: 43-47. May 1992.
___ "Of Midwich, Moonmen and Monoliths: A Brief Guide to British SF & F Cinema in the Sixties," *Lan's Lantern* No. 41: 64-68. July 1993.
___ "The Shadow of the Torturer: Peter Atkins Interviewed," *Interzone* No. 81: 43-45. March 1994.

GREENBERG, HARVEY R.
___ "Fembo: *Aliens'* Intentions," *Journal of Popular Film and Television* 15(4): 164-171. 1988.

GREENBERG, JAMES
___ "ABC Pics Expects *Day After* to Hit Top 10 Foreign Grossers in 1984; Estimates $50-Mil B. O.," *Variety* p. 3, 38. April 4, 1984.

GREENBERG, MARK L.
___ "Introduction: Literature and Technology," by Mark L. Greenberg and Lance Schachterle. in: Greenberg, Mark L. and Schachterle, Lance, eds. **Literature and Technology**. Bethlehem, PA: Lehigh University Press, 1992. pp.13-24.
___ "Romantic Technology: Books, Printing, and Blake's **Marriage of Heaven and Hell**," in: Greenberg, Mark L. and Schachterle, Lance, eds. **Literature and Technology**. Bethlehem, PA: Lehigh University Press, 1992. pp.154-176.
___ "Selected Bibliography of Works Devoted to Literature and Technology," by Mark L. Greenberg and Lance Schachterle. in: Greenberg, Mark L. and Schachterle, Lance, eds. **Literature and Technology**. Bethlehem, PA: Lehigh University Press, 1992. pp.310-317.
___ (ed.) **Literature and Technology**, ed. by Mark L. Greenberg and Lance Schachterle. Bethlehem, PA: Lehigh University Press, 1992. 322pp.

GREENBERG, MARTIN H.
___ "The Science Fiction Anthology Market," by Richard Gilliam and Martin H. Greenberg. in: Thompkins, David G., ed. **Science Fiction Writer's Market Place and Source Book**. Cincinnati, OH: Writer's Digest Books, 1994. pp.173-180.
___ (ed.) **The Dean Koontz Companion**, ed. by Martin H. Greenberg, Ed Gorman and Bill Munster. New York: Berkley, 1994. 312pp.
___ (ed.) **Robert Silverberg's Many Trapdoors: Critical Essays on His Science Fiction**, ed. by Charles L. Elkins and Martin H. Greenberg. Westport, CT: Greenwood, 1992. 154pp.

GREENBERGER, ROBERT
___ "Rebel Princess," in: McDonnell, David, ed. **Starlog's Science Fiction Heroes and Heroines**. New York: Crescent Books, 1995. pp.15-18.
___ "The Roots of Dredd," *Sci-Fi Entertainment* 2(1): 34-35. June 1995.

GREENE, DEIDRE
___ "Higher Argument: Tolkien and the Tradition of Vision, Epic and Prophecy," in: Reynolds, Patricia and GoodKnight, Glen H., eds. **Proceedings of the J. R. R. Tolkien Centenary Conference, Keble College, Oxford, 1992**. Altadena, CA: Mythopoeic Press, 1995. pp.45-52. (*Mythlore* Vol. 21, No. 2, Winter 1996, Whole No. 80)
___ "Tolkien's Dictionary Poetics: The Influence of the OED's Defining Style on Tolkien's Fiction," in: Reynolds, Patricia and GoodKnight, Glen H., eds. **Proceedings of the J. R. R. Tolkien Centenary Conference, Keble College, Oxford, 1992**. Altadena, CA: Mythopoeic Press, 1995. pp.195-199. (*Mythlore* Vol. 21, No. 2, Winter 1996, Whole No. 80)

GREENE, DOUGLAS G.
___ **John Dickson Carr: The Man Who Explained Miracles**. New York: Penzler, 1995. 537pp.

GREENE, ERIC
___ **Planet of the Apes as American Myth: Race and Politics in the Films and Television Series**. Jefferson, NC: McFarland, 1995. 264pp.

GREENE, GAYLE
___ **Doris Lessing: The Poetics of Change**. Ann Arbor: University of Michigan Press, 1994. 283pp.
___ "Doris Lessing's **Landlocked**: A New Kind of Knowledge," *Contemporary Literature* 28(1): 82-103. Spring 1987.

GREENFIELD, ADAM
___ "New Romancer: Interview with William Gibson," *Spin* 4: 96-99, 119. December 1988.

GREENLAND, COLIN
___ **Michael Moorcock: Death Is No Obstacle**. Manchester, Eng.: Savoy, 1992. 146pp.

GREENMAN, DAVID
___ "Aeneidic and Odyssean Pattern of Escape and Return in Tolkien's 'Fall of Gondolin' and **The Return of the King**," *Mythlore* 18(2): 4-9. Spring 1992. (No. 68)

GREGORY, SINDA
___ "The Semiology of Silence: The *Science Fiction Studies* Interview," by Sinda Gregory and Larry McCaffery. in: Delany, Samuel R. **Silent Interviews on Language, Race, Sex, Science Fiction and Some Comics**. Hanover, NH: Wesleyan University Press, 1994. pp.21-58.

GREIFF, LOUIS K.
___ "Soldier, Sailor, Surfer, Chef: Conrad's Ethics and the Margins of **Apocalypse Now**," *Literature/Film Quarterly* 20(3): 188-197. 1992.

GRELLNER, MARY A.
___ "Arthuriana and Popular Culture," in: Fries, Maureen and Watson, Jeanie, eds. **Approaches to the Teaching of the Arthurian Tradition**. New York: Modern Language Association, 1992. pp.159-162.
___ "Two Films That Sparkle: *The Sword in the Stone* and *Camelot*," in: Harty, Kevin J., ed. **Cinema Arthuriana: Essays on Arthurian Film**. New York: Garland, 1991. pp.71-83.

GRENIER, CHRISTIAN
___ **La science-fiction, lectures d'avenir?**. Nancy: Presses Universitaires de Nancy, 1994. 169pp.

GREPPI, MICHELE
___ "*Alien Nation* Lost in Space," *New York (NY) Post*. October 10, 1995. in: *NewsBank. Film and Television*. 92:A14. 1995.

GRESH, LOIS H.
___ "Digital Pistil," in: Gray, Chris H., ed. **The Cyborg Handbook**. New York: Routledge, 1995. pp.301-306.

GREY, RUDOLPH
___ **Nightmare of Ecstasy: The Life and Art of Edward D. Wood, Jr**. Los Angeles, CA: Feral House Press, 1992. 231pp.

GRIBBIN, JOHN
___ "Fact 'n Fiction 'n Me," *Concatenation* No. 7: 10. 1993.

GRIEST, STEPHANIE
___ "*Mortal Kombat*'s Bloodless Coup," *Washington (DC) Post*. August 28, 1995. in: *NewsBank. Film and Television*. 79:B12-B13. 1995.

GRIFFIN, DOMINIC
___ "Brain Dead at 21," *Sci-Fi Universe* No. 3: 44-46. October/November 1994.

GRIFFIN, SCOTT T.
___ "The Bronze Age Revival," *Burroughs Bulletin* NS. No. 17: 31-34. January 1994.
___ "Why Do We Need Tarzan?," *Burroughs Bulletin* NS. No. 20: 32-33. October 1994.
___ "Woody Strode: An Epic Life Remembered," *Burroughs Bulletin* NS. No. 22: 18-25. April 1995.

GRIFFIN, WILLIAM
___ "In Search of the Real C. S. Lewis," *Bulletin of the New York C. S. Lewis Society* 25(9/11): 18-26. July/September 1994.

GRIFFITH, JOHN
___ **Charlotte's Web: A Pig's Salvation**. New York: Twayne, 1993. 116pp.

GRIFFITHS, NICK
___ "The Cult of Loving Kindness: Paul Park Interview," *Interzone* No. 61: 18-21. July 1992

GRIGORIEVA, NATALIA
___ "Problems of Translating into Russian," in: Reynolds, Patricia and GoodKnight, Glen H., eds. **Proceedings of the J. R. R. Tolkien Centenary Conference, Keble College, Oxford, 1992**. Altadena, CA: Mythopoeic Press, 1995. pp.200-205. (*Mythlore* Vol. 21, No. 2, Winter 1996, Whole No. 80)

GRIMM, KEVIN T.
___ "Editing Malory: What's at (the) Stake?," *Arthuriana* 5(2): 5-14. Summer 1995.
___ "The Reception of Malory's **Morte D'Arthur** Medieval and Modern," *Quondam et Futurus* 2(3): 1-14. Fall 1992.

GRIVET, CHARLES
___ **Fantastique-Fiction**. Paris: Presses universitaires francaises, 1993. 255pp.

GRIXTI, JOSEPH
___ "Consumed Identities: Heroic Fantasy and the Trivialization of Selfhood," *Journal of Popular Culture* 28(3): 207-227. Winter 1994.

GROEBEN, NORBERT
___ "Frauen--Science Fiction--Utopie: Vom Ende aller Utopie(n) zue Neugeburt einer literarischen Gattung?," *Internationales Archiv für Sozialgeschicte der Deutschen Literatur* 19(2): 173-206. 1994.

GROSS, EDWARD
___ **Captain's Logs: The Complete Star Trek Voyages**, by Edward Gross and Mark A. Altman. London: Boxtree, 1993. 269pp. [Not seen.]
___ **Captain's Logs: The Unauthorized Complete Trek Voyages**, by Edward Gross and Mark A. Altman. Boston, MA: Little, Brown, 1995. 361pp.
___ "Fables of the Beast," *Starlog* 179: 62-65, 86. June 1992.
___ "The Klingon Per-Cent Solution," *Starlog* 177: 46-50. April 1992.
___ **The Making of the Trek Films**. 2nd rev. ed., by Edward Gross and Mark A. Altman. East Meadow, NY: Image Publishing, 1992. 162pp.
___ "The New Illustrated Man," *Starlog* 185: 75-79. December 1992.
___ "The Savage Beast," by Marc Shapiro and Edward Gross. in: McDonnell, David, ed. **Starlog's Science Fiction Heroes and Heroines**. New York: Crescent Books, 1995. pp.66-69.

GROSS, GREGORY W.
___ "Secret Rules: Sex, Confession, and Truth in **Sir Gawain and the Green Knight**," *Arthuriana* 4(2): 146-174. Summer 1994.

GROSS, LARRY
___ "Big and Loud," *Sight and Sound* 5(8): 6-11. August 1995.

GROSS, ROSLYN K.
___ "Diana Wynne Jones: An Overview," *SF Commentary* No. 71/72: 34-37. April 1992.

GROSS, RUTH V.
___ (ed.) **Critical Essays on Franz Kafka**. Boston, MA: G. K. Hall, 1990. 281pp.

GROSSMAN, KATHRYN M.
___ "The Ideal Community of George Sand's **La Petite Fadette**," *Utopian Studies* 6(1): 19-29. 1995.
___ "Woman as Temptress: The Way to (Br)otherhood in Science Fiction Dystopias," *Women's Studies* 14(2): 135-146. 1987.
___ "Woman as Temptress: The Way to (Br)otherhood in Science Fiction Dystopias," in: Saccaro Del Buffa, Giuseppa and Lewis, Arthur O., eds. **Utopie per gli Anni Ottana**. Rome: Gangemi Editore, 1986. pp.489-498.

GROSSMAN, LAURIE M.
___ "Marketing: Well, It's in Orbit, But Will It Fly?," *Wall Street Journal* Sec. B, p. 1. September 25, 1992.

GROSSMAN, SUSAN
___ "The Susan Grossman Interview," in: Delany, Samuel R. **Silent Interviews on Language, Race, Sex, Science Fiction and Some Comics**. Hanover, NH: Wesleyan University Press, 1994. pp.250-268.

GROTTA, DANIEL
___ **The Biography of J. R. R. Tolkien: Architect of Middle-Earth**. Philadelphia, PA: Running Press, 1992. 197pp.

GROUT, VINCENT T.
___ **World Without End: The Science Fiction Mind in the Marketplace of Belief**. Master's Thesis, Roosevelt University, 1992. 118pp.

GRUBBS, PETE
___ "Rock Music as Science Fiction," *Lan's Lantern* No. 42: 20-29. May 1994.

GRUESSER, JOHN
___ "Pauline Hopkin's **Of One Blood**: Creating an Afrocentric Fantasy for a Black Middle Class Audience," in: Latham, Robert A. and Collins, Robert A., eds. **Modes of the Fantastic**. Westport, CT: Greenwood, 1995. pp.74-83.

GRUSHETSKIY, VLADIMIR
___ "How Russians See Tolkien," in: Reynolds, Patricia and GoodKnight, Glen H., eds. **Proceedings of the J. R. R. Tolkien Centenary Conference, Keble College, Oxford, 1992**. Altadena, CA: Mythopoeic Press, 1995. pp.221-225. (*Mythlore* Vol. 21, No. 2, Winter 1996, Whole No. 80)

GUARDAMAGNA, DANIELA
___ **Analisi dell'incubo: l'utopia negativa da Swift alla fantascienza**. Roma: Bulzoni, 1980. 237pp. [Not seen.]
___ **La Narrativa di Aldous Huxley**. Bari: Adriatica Editrice, 1989. 252pp. [Not seen.]

GUARINO, BETTYANN
___ "Things You Wanted to Know About the Chesleys: But Were Afraid to Ask," *ASFA Quarterly* 10(1): 6-13. Spring 1992.

GUARNERI, CARL J.
___ "The Americanization of Utopia: Fourierism and the Dilemma of Utopian Dissent in the United States," *Utopian Studies* 5(1): 72-88. 1994.

GUBBINS, TERESA
___ "*Tank Girl*: Generation X Marks the Spot, But This One Missed by a Mile," *Dallas (TX) Morning News*. March 31, 1995. in: *NewsBank. Film and Television*. 50:C6. 1995.

GUILEY, ROSEMARY E.
___ **The Complete Vampire Companion**. New York: Macmillan, 1994. 258pp.
___ **The Encyclopedia of Witches and Witchcraft**. New York: Facts on File, 1989. 421pp.

GUILLAUD, LAURIC
___ "From Bachelor Machines to 'Cybernetic Fiction': 'Eternity Machines' in Science Fiction and Fantasy," *New York Review of Science Fiction* No. 75: 12-17. November 1994.
___ "Paranormal Detectives: Sherlock Holmes in the House of Usher," *Paradoxa* 1(3): 301-319. 1995.

GUILLEMETTE, AUREL
___ **The Best in Science Fiction: Winners and Nominees of the Major Awards in Science Fiction**. Aldershot, Eng.: Scolar Press, 1993. 379pp.

GUILLERME, JACQUES
___ "Teleghaphe el territoire; notes sur l'imaginaire del reseaux," in: Saccaro Del Buffa, Giuseppa and Lewis, Arthur O., eds. **Utopie per gli Anni Ottana**. Rome: Gangemi Editore, 1986. pp.329-342.

GUINN, JOHN
___ "Genius Comes in Multiple Servings," *Detroit (MI) News and Free Press*. December 15, 1991. in: *NewsBank. Literature*. 2:A8. 1992

GUNDERLOY, MIKE
___ **The World of Zines: A Guide to the Independent Magazine Revolution**. New York: Penguin Books, 1992. 181pp.

GUNN, JAMES E.
___ "The Academic Viewpoint," in: Gunn, James E. **Inside Science Fiction: Essays on Fantastic Literature**. San Bernardino, CA: Borgo, 1992. pp.73-78.
___ "The Automated City in Fiction," in: Grenander, M. E., ed. **Proceedings of Apollo Agonistes: The Humanities in a Computerized World**. Albany, NY: State University of New York, Albany, n.d. Volume One. pp.242-250.

GUNN, JAMES E. (continued)
___ "The City and the Critics," in: Gunn, James E. **Inside Science Fiction: Essays on Fantastic Literature**. San Bernardino, CA: Borgo, 1992. pp.92-98.
___ "Dreams Written Out: Libraries in Science Fiction," *Wilson Library Bulletin* 69(6): 26-29. February 1995.
___ "The Education of a Science Fiction Teacher," in: Gunn, James E. **Inside Science Fiction: Essays on Fantastic Literature**. San Bernardino, CA: Borgo, 1992. pp.9-15.
___ "Fifty Amazing, Astounding, Wonderful Years," in: Gunn, James E. **Inside Science Fiction: Essays on Fantastic Literature**. San Bernardino, CA: Borgo, 1992. pp.60-64.
___ "From the Pulps to the Classroom: The Strange Journey of Science Fiction," in: Gunn, James E. **Inside Science Fiction: Essays on Fantastic Literature**. San Bernardino, CA: Borgo, 1992. pp.16-29.
___ "The Gatekeepers," in: Gunn, James E. **Inside Science Fiction: Essays on Fantastic Literature**. San Bernardino, CA: Borgo, 1992. pp.52-59.
___ "The Great Science Fiction Radio Show," in: Gunn, James E. **Inside Science Fiction: Essays on Fantastic Literature**. San Bernardino, CA: Borgo, 1992. pp.118-120.
___ **Inside Science Fiction: Essays on Fantastic Literature**. San Bernardino, CA: Borgo Press, 1992. 176pp.
___ "Looking Backward at *2001*," in: Gunn, James E. **Inside Science Fiction: Essays on Fantastic Literature**. San Bernardino, CA: Borgo, 1992. pp.121-123.
___ "Science Fiction and the Future," in: Gunn, James E. **Inside Science Fiction: Essays on Fantastic Literature**. San Bernardino, CA: Borgo, 1992. pp.150-153.
___ "Science Fiction and the Mainstream," in: Gunn, James E. **Inside Science Fiction: Essays on Fantastic Literature**. San Bernardino, CA: Borgo, 1992. pp.30-51.
___ "Science Fiction and the Nineties," in: Gunn, James E. **Inside Science Fiction: Essays on Fantastic Literature**. San Bernardino, CA: Borgo, 1992. pp.154-160.
___ "Science Fiction as Literature," in: Gunn, James E. **Inside Science Fiction: Essays on Fantastic Literature**. San Bernardino, CA: Borgo, 1992. pp.79-91.
___ "Science Fiction Scholarship Revisited," *Foundation* No. 60: 5-9. Spring 1994.
___ "SF the British Way," *Amazing* 68(2): 54-60. May 1993.
___ "Shapechangers and Fearmongers," in: Gunn, James E. **Inside Science Fiction: Essays on Fantastic Literature**. San Bernardino, CA: Borgo, 1992. pp.146-149.
___ "A Short History of the Space Program; or, a Funny Thing Happened on the Way to the Moon," in: Gunn, James E. **Inside Science Fiction: Essays on Fantastic Literature**. San Bernardino, CA: Borgo, 1992. pp.134-145.
___ "Teaching Science Fiction Revisited," in: Gunn, James E. **Inside Science Fiction: Essays on Fantastic Literature**. San Bernardino, CA: Borgo, 1992. pp.67-72.
___ "Television and *The Immortal*," in: Gunn, James E. **Inside Science Fiction: Essays on Fantastic Literature**. San Bernardino, CA: Borgo, 1992. pp.113-117.
___ "The Tinsel Screen," in: Gunn, James E. **Inside Science Fiction: Essays on Fantastic Literature**. San Bernardino, CA: Borgo, 1992. pp.101-112.
___ "Trilude: Imagining the Future," in: Wolf, Milton T. and Mallett, Daryl F., eds. **Imaginative Futures: Proceedings of the 1993 Science Fiction Research Association Conference**. San Bernardino, CA: Jacob's Ladder Books, 1995. pp.125-135.
___ "The Uses of Space," in: Gunn, James E. **Inside Science Fiction: Essays on Fantastic Literature**. San Bernardino, CA: Borgo, 1992. pp.127-133.
___ "The Worldview of Science Fiction," *Extrapolation* 36(2): 91-95. Summer 1995.

GUNTER, BARRIE
___ "The Impact of Nuclear Fiction in Britain: **The Day After** and **Threads**," by Barrie Gunter and M. Svennevig. in: Wober, J. Mallory, ed. **Television and Nuclear Power: Making the Public Mind**. Norwood, NJ: Ablex, 1992. pp.55-66.

GUSSMAN, NEIL
___ "Translations of Latin, Greek and French Phrases From **Studies in Medieval and Renaissance Literature** and **The Pilgrim's Regress**," *Bulletin of the New York C. S. Lewis Society* 25(12): 1-5. October 1994.

GUSTAFSON, JON
___ "Gene Roddenberry: A Man and Our Art," *Science Fiction Review* No. 8: 47. March 1992.

GUSTERSON, HUGH
___ "*Short Circuit*: Watching Television With a Nuclear-Weapons Scientist," in: Gray, Chris H., ed. **The Cyborg Handbook**. New York: Routledge, 1995. pp.107-117.

GÜTH, GUDRUN
___ "Doris Lessing, **Canopus in Argos: Archives** (1979ff)," by Gudrun Güth and Jürgen Schmidt-Güth. in: Heuermann, Harmut, ed. **Der Science Fiction Roman in der angloamerikanischen Literatur: Interpretationen**. Düsseldorf: Bagel, 1986. pp.375-399.

GUTJAHR, PAUL
___ "Stoker's **Dracula**," *Explicator* 52(1): 36-38. Fall 1993.

GUTTMACHER, PETER
___ **Legendary Horror Films: Essential Genre History; Offscreen Anecdotes; Special Effects Secrets; Ghoulish Facts and Photographs**. New York: Metro Books, 1995. 128pp.

GUY, PAT
___ "*Time* Special Issue Includes Fiction," *USA Today* Sec. B, p. 4. September 28, 1992.

HABER, JON
___ "They Came From Outer Space--And Moved to the 'Burbs," by John Galligan and Jon Haber. *Boston (MA) Globe* Sec. B, p. 29. July 25, 1993.

HACKETT, LARRY
___ "Feeding Hollywood's Kitty," *New York (NY) Daily News*. June 23, 1992. in: *NewsBank. Film and Television*. 62:D2. 1992.

HACKLETON, MATT
___ "Season Six: A Quick Look Back," in: Van Hise, James, ed. **Trek Celebration Two**. Las Vegas, NV: Pioneer, 1994. pp.29-39.

HADDER, RICHARD N.
___ **Techniques of Social-Science-Fiction (With Original Writing)**. Master's Thesis, University of North Texas, 1995. 53pp. (Master's Abstracts 34/01, p. 61. February 1996.)

HADOMI, LEAH
___ [Between Hope and Doubt: The Story of Utopia]. Israel: Hakibbutz Hameuchad Publishing House, 1989. 208pp. (In Hebrew) [Not seen.]
___ "Islands of the Living: Death and Dying in Utopian Fiction," *Utopian Studies* 6(1): 85-101. 1995.

HAEFER, TODD
___ "Happy 100th, J. R. R.," *Oshkosh (WI) Northwestern*. January 30, 1992. in: *NewsBank. Names in the News*. 59:D2-D3. 1992.

HAGENLOCHER, WILL C.
___ "Joe Jusko: An Interview," *Burroughs Bulletin* NS. No. 23: 19-23. July 1995.

HAGGERTY, GEORGE E.
___ **Gothic Fiction/Gothic Form**. University Park: Pennsylvania State University Press, 1989. 194pp.

HAHM, OSCAR
___ "Trayectoria del cuento fantástico hispanoamericano," *Mester* (UCLA) 19(2): 35-46. Fall 1990.

HAINES, JOHN F.
___ "Confessions of a Fantasy Versaholic," *Fantasy Commentator* 7(4): 304-306. Fall 1992. (Whole No. 44)

HAINING, PETER
___ **Doctor Who, A Celebration: Two Decades Through Time and Space**. London: Virgin/Doctor Who Books, 1995. 256pp.

HALBERT, MARTIN
___ "Database Visualization and Future Innovations in Information Retrieval," in: Wolf, Milton T. and Mallett, Daryl F., eds. **Imaginative Futures: Proceedings of the 1993 Science Fiction Research Association Conference.** San Bernardino, CA: Jacob's Ladder Books, 1995. pp.31-52.

HALDEMAN, JOE
___ "Architect of Space," *Science Fiction Age* 2(6): 78-83. September 1994.
___ "Robert A. Heinlein and Us," in: Kondo, Yoji, ed. **Requiem: New Collected Works by Robert A. Heinlein and Tributes to the Grand Master.** New York: Tor, 1992. pp.272-274.
___ "Sex and Violence in SF," *The Report: The Fiction Writer's Magazine* No. 9: 1, 3. March 1993.
___ "Vietman and Other Alien Worlds," in: Slusser, George and Eric S. Rabkin, eds. **Fights of Fancy: Armed Conflict in Science Fiction and Fantasy.** Athens, GA: University of Georgia Press, 1993. pp.92-102.
___ "Why I Live Everywhere Except Gainesville and Boston," *SFWA Bulletin* 29(2): 11-13. Summer 1995. (No. 127)

HALIO, JAY L.
___ "**Free Fall**: Golding's Modern Novel," in: Biles, Jack I. and Evans, Robert O., eds. **William Golding: Some Critical Considerations.** Lexington, KY: University Press of Kentucky, 1978. pp.117-136.

HALL, DEBRA K.
___ **A New Synthesis for Science Fiction: The Fiction of Octavia Butler.** Master's Thesis, Eastern New Mexico University, 1992. 75pp.

HALL, HAL W.
___ **Science Fiction and Fantasy Book Review Index, Volume 18, 1987.** San Bernardino, CA: Borgo Press, 1992. 70pp.
___ **Science Fiction and Fantasy Book Review Index, Volume 19, 1988.** Bryan, TX: SFFBRI, 1992. 87pp.; San Bernardino, CA: Borgo Press, 1992. 85pp.
___ **Science Fiction and Fantasy Book Review Index, Volume 20, 1989.** San Bernardino, CA: Borgo Press, 1993. 90pp.; Bryan, TX: SFFBRI, 1993. 90pp.
___ **Science Fiction and Fantasy Book Review Index, Volume 21, 1990.** Bryan, TX: SFFBRI, 1994. 105pp.
___ **Science Fiction and Fantasy Reference Index, 1985-1991: An International Author and Subject Index to History and Criticism.** Englewood, CO: Libraries Unlimited, 1993. 677pp.
___ **Science Fiction and Fantasy Research Index, Volume 10.** San Bernardino, CA: Borgo Press, 1994. 153pp.
___ **Science Fiction and Fantasy Research Index, Volume 9.** San Bernardino, CA: Borgo Press, 1992. 97pp.

HALL, JOHN S.
___ "Lister, American Style," *Starlog* No. 221: 67-69. December 1995.

HALL, JOHN T.
___ "Bestselling Fantasies," *Starlog* No. 209: 38-41, 68. December 1994.

HALL, MIA M.
___ "Love Kills: Another Look at *Fatal Attraction*," in: Golden, Christopher, ed. **Cut! Horror Writers on Horror Film.** New York: Berkley, 1992. pp.123-130.

HALL, STEVE
___ "Sixth Film a Fine End to Trek Series," *Indianapolis (IN) Star.* December 6, 1991. in: *NewsBank. Film and Television.* 7:D14. 1992.

HALLAB, MARY Y.
___ "Carter and Blake: The Dangers of Innocence," in: Sanders, Joe, ed. **Functions of the Fantastic.** Westport, CT: Greenwood, 1995. pp.177-184.

HALLENBERGER, GERD
___ "Konjunkturen des Phantastischen: Anmerkungen zu den Karrieren von Science Fiction, Fantasy und Marchen sowie verwandtne Formen," by Siegfried Becker and Gerd Hallenberger. *Zeitschrift fur Literaturwissenschaft und Linguistik* No. 92: 141-155. 1993.

HAMBURG, VICTORIA
___ "The King of Cyberpunk," *Interview* 19: 84-86, 91-92. January 1989.

HAMILTON, RUTH E.
___ "Teaching Arthur at a Summer Institute for Secondary School Teachers," in: Fries, Maureen and Watson, Jeanie, eds. **Approaches to the Teaching of the Arthurian Tradition.** New York: Modern Language Association, 1992. pp.118-121.

HAMMELL, TIM
___ "*Reboot* (Review)," *Cinefantastique* 26(4): 60. June 1995.

HAMMER, STEPHANIE
___ "Camouflage and Sabotage: Satiric Maneuvers in the Fantastic Fiction of the German Democratic Republic," in: Slusser, George E. and Rabkin, Eric S., eds. **Styles of Creation: Aesthetic Technique and the Creation of Fictional Worlds.** Athens: University of Georgia Press, 1992. pp.143-152.

HAMMERTON, M.
___ "Prehistoric Science Fiction," *Foundation* No. 54: 87-88. Spring 1992.
___ "Verne's Amazing Journeys," in: Seed, David, ed. **Anticipations: Essays on Early Science Fiction and Its Precursors.** Liverpool: Liverpool University Press, 1995. pp.98-110.

HAMMOND, J. R.
___ "A Checklist of Wells's Short Stories," in: Hammond, J. R. **H. G. Wells and the Short Story.** New York: St. Martin's, 1992. pp.29-39.
___ "The Frontiers of Art," in: Hammond, J. R. **H. G. Wells and the Short Story.** New York: St. Martin's, 1992. pp.19-28.
___ **H. G. Wells and Rebecca West.** New York: St. Martin's, 1991. 280pp.
___ **H. G. Wells and the Short Story.** New York: St. Martin's, 1992. 175pp.
___ "Wells and the Short Story," in: Hammond, J. R. **H. G. Wells and the Short Story.** New York: St. Martin's, 1992. pp.3-18.

HAMMOND, TONY
___ "Selling a Bestseller," by Nick Sayers, Ian Hughes, David Singer and Tony Hammond. in: Jones, Stephen, ed. **James Herbert: By Horror Haunted.** London: New English Library, 1992. pp.199-207.

HAMMOND, WAYNE G.
___ "The Critical Response to Tolkien's Fiction," in: Reynolds, Patricia and GoodKnight, Glen H., eds. **Proceedings of the J. R. R. Tolkien Centenary Conference, Keble College, Oxford, 1992.** Altadena, CA: Mythopoeic Press, 1995. pp.226-232. (*Mythlore* Vol. 21, No. 2, Winter 1996, Whole No. 80)
___ "An Inklings Bibliography (45)," by Joe R. Christopher and Wayne G. Hammond. *Mythlore* 18(2): 28-33, 39-40. Spring 1992. (No. 68)
___ "An Inklings Bibliography (46)," by Joe R. Christopher and Wayne G. Hammond. *Mythlore* 18(3): 49-53. Summer 1992. (No. 69)
___ "An Inklings Bibliography (47)," by Joe R. Christopher and Wayne G. Hammond. *Mythlore* 18(4): 49-52. Autumn 1992. (No. 70)
___ "An Inklings Bibliography (48)," by Joe R. Christopher and Wayne G. Hammond. *Mythlore* 19(1): 56-64. Winter 1993. (No. 71)
___ "An Inklings Bibliography (49)," by Joe R. Christopher and Wayne G. Hammond. *Mythlore* 19(2): 61-65. Spring 1993. (No. 72)
___ "An Inklings Bibliography (50) (e.g. 51)," by Joe R. Christopher and Wayne G. Hammond. *Mythlore* 19(4): 60-65. Autumn 1993. (No. 74)
___ "An Inklings Bibliography (50)," by Joe R. Christopher and Wayne G. Hammond. *Mythlore* 19(3): 59-65. Summer 1993. (No. 73)
___ "An Inklings Bibliography (51)," by Joe R. Christopher and Wayne G. Hammond. *Mythlore* 20(1): 59-62. Winter 1994. (Whole No. 75)
___ "An Inklings Bibliography (52)," by Joe R. Christopher and Wayne G. Hammond. *Mythlore* 20(2): 32-34. Spring 1994. (Whole No. 76)
___ "An Inklings Bibliography (54)," by Joe R. Christopher and Wayne G. Hammond. *Mythlore* 20(4): 61-65. Winter 1995. (Whole No. 78)
___ "An Inklings Bibliography (55)," by Joe R. Christopher and Wayne G. Hammond. *Mythlore* 21(1): 61-65. Summer 1995. (No. 79)
___ **J. R. R. Tolkien: A Descriptive Bibliography,** by Wayne G. Hammond and Douglas A. Anderson. Winchester, UK: St. Paul's Bibliographies, 1992. 434pp.; New Castle, DE: Oak Knoll Books, 1992. 434pp.

HAMMOND, WAYNE G. (continued)
___ **J. R. R. Tolkien: Artist and Illustrator**, by Wayne G. Hammond and Christina Scull. Boston, MA: Houghton Mifflin, 1995. 208pp.
___ "Seraphim, Cherubim and Virtual Unicorns: Order and Being in Madeline L'Engle's Time Quartet," *Mythlore* 20(4): 41-45. Winter 1995. (Whole No. 78)

HANANIA, JOSEPH
___ "Isaac Asimov Looks into Our Future and Finds an Underground World," *New York (NY) Tribune* May 16, 1988. in: *NewsBank. Names in the News* NIN 163: B3-B4. 1988.

HAND, ELIZABETH
___ "Writing Literary Science Fiction," *Writer* 108(1): 11-13. January 1995.

HANKE, KEN
___ **A Critical Guide to Horror Film Series**. New York: Garland, 1991. 341pp.
___ "Tod Slaughter: Demon Barber of Great Britain," *Filmfax* No. 45: 31-35, 98. June/July 1994.

HANKS, D. THOMAS, JR.
___ "Foil and Forecast: Dinadan in **The Book of Sir Tristam**," in: Busby, Keith, ed. **The Arthurian Yearbook I**. New York: Garland, 1991. pp.149-164.
___ "Malory's **Book of Sir Tristram**: Focusing on **Le Morte Dearthur**," *Quondam et Futurus* 3(1): 14-31. Spring 1993.
___ "Malory, Dialogue and Style," *Quondam et Futurus* 3(3): 24-35. Fall 1993.
___ "T. H. White's Merlin: More Than Malory Made Him," in: Watson, Jeanie and Fries, Marueen, eds. **The Figure of Merlin in the Nineteenth and Twentieth Centuries**. Lewiston, NY: Mellen, 1989. pp.100-120.

HANNAHAM, JAMES
___ "Wild Planet," *Village Voice* 39(3): 56-57. January 18, 1994.

HANNAY, MARGARET
___ "The Mythology of **Out of the Silent Planet**," *Mythlore* 20(2): 20-22. Spring 1994. (Whole No. 76)

HANSEN, OLAF
___ "Edward Bellamy: **Looking Backward: 2000-1887** (1888)," in: Heuermann, Hartmut and Lange, Bernd-Peter, eds. **Die Utopie in der angloamerikanischen Literatur: Interpretationen**. Düsseldorf: Bagel, 1984. pp.103-119.

HANSEN, REGINA
___ "Forms of Friendship in **The Roots of the Mountains**," *Journal of the William Morris Society* 11(3): 19-21. Autumn 1995.

HANSON, ALAN
___ "The Edgar Rice Burroughs Amateur Press Association," *Burroughs Bulletin* NS No. 11: 27-30. July 1992.
___ "ERB and the Educated Man," *Burroughs Bulletin* NS. No. 17: 19-24. January 1994.

HANSON, CARTER F.
___ "1920's Yellow Peril Science Fiction: Political Appropriations of the Asian Racial 'Alien'," *Journal of the Fantastic in the Arts* 6(4): 312-329. 1995.

HANSON, PHILIP
___ "Horror and Ethnic Identity in 'The Jewbird'," *Studies in Short Fiction* 30(3): 359-366. Summer 1993.

HANSOT, ELISABETH
___ "Selves, Survival and Resistance in **The Handmaid's Tale**," *Utopian Studies* 5(2): 56-69. 1994.

HARADA, WAYNE
___ "**Waterworld** (oops) Dances With Whales," *Honolulu (HI) Advertiser*. February 1, 1995. in: *NewsBank. Film and Television*. 30:G13. 1995.

HARBOTTLE, PHILIP
___ **British Science Fiction Paperbacks and Magazines, 1949-1956: An Annotated Bibliograhy and Guide**, by Philip Harbottle and Stephen Holland. San Bernardino, CA: Borgo Press, 1994. 232pp.
___ **Vultures of the Void: A History of British Science Fiction Publishing 1946-1956**, by Philip Harbottle and Stephen Holland. San Bernardino, CA: Borgo Press, 1992. 128pp.

HARDAWAY, DONNA J.
___ "Cyborgs and Symbionts: Living Together in the New World Order," in: Gray, Chris H., ed. **The Cyborg Handbook**. New York: Routledge, 1995. pp.xi-xx.

HARDESTY, JOHN J.
___ "Illusions of Endless Affluence," in: Sullivan, E. D. S., ed. **The Utopian Vision**. San Diego, CA: San Diego University Press, 1983. pp.51-68.

HARDIE, COLIN
___ "Inklings: British at Oxford and German at Aachen," in: Kranz, Gisbert, ed. **Inklings: Jahrbuch für Literatur und Ästhetik**. 1. Band. Lüdenscheid, Germany: Michael Claren, 1983. pp.15-19.

HARDY, PHIL
___ **The Overlook Film Encyclopedia: Science Fiction**. Woodstock, NY: Overlook Press, 1994. 478pp.
___ (ed.) **The Overlook Film Encyclopedia: Horror**. Second edition. Woodstock, NY: Overlook, 1994. 496pp.
___ (ed.) **The Overlook Film Encyclopedia: Science Fiction**. Third edition. Woodstock, NY: Overlook, 1995. 512pp.

HARGER-GRINLING, VIRGINIA
___ "Alain Robbe-Grillet and the Fantastic," by Tony Chadwick and Virginia Harger-Grinling. in: Ruddick, Nicholas, ed. **State of the Fantastic**. Westport, CT: Greenwood, 1992. pp.91-96.
___ "The Fantastic Robbe-Grillet," by Tony Chadwick and Virginia Harger-Grinling. in: Harger-Grinling, Virginia and Chadwick, Tony, eds. **Robbe-Grillet and the Fantastic**. Westport, CT: Greenwood, 1994. pp.1-10.
___ (ed.) **Robbe-Grillet and the Fantastic: A Collection of Essays**, ed. by Virginia Harger-Grinling and Tony Chadwick. Westport, CT: Greenwood, 1994. 168pp.

HARGREAVES, MATHEW D.
___ **Anne Inez McCaffrey: Forty Years of Publishing, An International Bibliograpy**. Seattle, WA: Mathew Hargreaves, 1992. 338pp.

HARGREAVES, STELLA
___ "The SF Kick: Terry Pratchett Interviewed," *Interzone* No. 81: 25-28. March 1994.

HARKINS, PATRICIA
___ "Family Magic: Invisibility in Jamaica Kincaid's **Lucy**," *Journal of the Fantastic in the Arts* 4(3): 53-68. 1991. (No. 15)
___ "Myth in Action: The Trials and Transformation of Menolly," in: Sullivan, C. W., III. **Science Fiction for Young Readers**. Westport, CT: Greenwood, 1993. pp.157-166.
___ "Speaking Dead in the Medieval Romance **Sir Amadace and the White Knight**," *Journal of the Fantastic in the Arts* 3(3): 62-71. 1994.
___ " 'Spells of Darkness': Invisibility in **The White Witch of Rosehall**," *Journal of the Fantastic in the Arts* 4(2): 49-64. 1992. (No. 14)

HARMETZ, ALJEAN
___ "Kong and Wray: 60 Years of Love," *New York Times* Sec. 2, p. 13. February 28, 1993.

HARMON, AMY
___ "Crossing Cyberpunk's Threshold: William Gibson," *Los Angeles (CA) Times* p.D1. May 24, 1995.

HARMON, GARY L.
___ "Jung and **Star Trek**: The Coincidentia Oppositorum and Images of the Shadow," by Louis A. Woods and Gary L. Harmon. *Journal of Popular Culture* 28(2): 169-183. Fall 1994.

HARRIS, ROY
___ "The Misunderstanding of Newspeak," in: Bloom, Harold, ed. **George Orwell's 1984**. New York: Chelsea House, 1987. pp.87-94.

HARRIS-FAIN, DARREN
___ **H. G. Wells and the Modernist Revolution**. Ph.D. Dissertation, Kent State University, 1992. 332pp. (DAI-A 53/10. p. 3536. April 1993.)

HARRISON, HARRY
___ "Allen E. Nourse: An Appreciation," *Locus* 29(4): 66. October 1992
___ "Amis vs. SF," in: Salwak, Dale, ed. **Kingsley Amis in Life and Letters**. New York: St. Martin's, 1990. pp.51-56.

HARRISON, IRENE R.
___ **Andre Norton: A Primary and Secondary Bibliography**. Revised edition, by Roger C. Schlobin and Irene R. Harrison. Framingham, MA: NESFA Press, 1994. 92pp.

HARRISON, JAMES
___ **Salman Rushie**. Boston, MA: Twayne, 1992. 147pp.

HARRISON, M. JOHN
___ "The Profession of Fiction," in: Jakubowski, Maxim and James, Edward, eds. **The Profession of Science Fiction**. New York: St. Martin's, 1992. pp.140-153.

HARRISON, MITCHELL
___ "The Burroughs Pre-Pubs," *Burroughs Bulletin* NS. No. 14: 29-32. April 1993.

HART, ALDEN W.
___ **The Poetry of Edgar Allan Poe**. Ph.D. Dissertation, University of Oregon, 1972. 260pp. (DAI 33: 2326A. Nov/Dec. 1972.)

HART, CAROLYN G.
___ "**Gaudy Night**: Quintessential Sayers," in: Dale, Alzina S., ed. **Dorothy L. Sayers: The Centenary Celebration**. New York: Walker, 1993. pp.45-50.

HART, MARA K.
___ "Walkers in the City: George Willard Kirk and Howard Phillips Lovecraft in New York City, 1924-1926," *Lovecraft Studies* No. 28: 2-17. Fall 1992.

HARTL, JOHN
___ "Lots of Bang for a Plot That Fizzles," *Seattle (WA) Times*. October 13, 1995. in: *NewsBank. Film and Television*. 99:D3. 1995.
___ "Their Looks Rock Cradle (Review)," *New York (NY) Daily News*. January 5, 1992. in: *NewsBank. Film and Television*. 12:B5-B6. 1992.

HARTLEY, EEYAN
___ "Morris & Co. in a Baroque Setting," *Journal of the William Morris Society* 11(2): 5-8. Spring 1995.

HARTLEY, MATTHEW R.
___ **The Image of Space in Soviet Literature**. Master's Thesis, University of Massachusetts at Amherst, 1993. 71pp.

HARTNETT, JAMES R.
___ "Black Power in Utopia," in: Saccaro Del Buffa, Giuseppa and Lewis, Arthur O., eds. **Utopie per gli Anni Ottana**. Rome: Gangemi Editore, 1986. pp.435-442.

HARTWELL, DAVID G.
___ "Aspects of Hard Science Fiction," *New York Review of Science Fiction* No. 66: 11-21. February 1994.
___ "Discussing Hard SF," by Gerald Feinberg, Hal Clement, Kathryn Cramer and David G. Hartwell. *New York Review of Science Fiction* No. 46: 19-21. June 1992.
___ "The Golden Age of Science Fiction Is Twelve (Excerpt from **Age of Wonders**)," *Futures Past* No. 2: 49-57. April 1992.
___ "Hard Science Fiction," *New York Review of Science Fiction* No. 62: 1, 8-13. October 1993.
___ "Hard Science Fiction," in: Hartwell, David G. and Kathryn Cramer, eds. **The Ascent of Wonder: The Evolution of Hard SF**. New York: Tor, 1994. pp.30-40.

HARTWELL, DAVID G. (continued)
___ "Introduction," in: Hartwell, David G., ed. **The Dark Descent**. New York: Tor, 1987. pp.1-11.
___ "Introduction to **The Purple Cloud**," in: **Shiel in Diverse Hands: A Collection of Essays**. Cleveland, OH: Reynolds Morse Foundation, 1983. pp.115-122.

HARTY, KEVIN J.
___ "Appendix: An Alphabetical Filmography," in: Harty, Kevin J., ed. **Cinema Arthuriana: Essays on Arthurian Film**. New York: Garland, 1991. pp.245-247.
___ "A Bibliography on Arthurian Film," in: Harty, Kevin J., ed. **Cinema Arthuriana: Essays on Arthurian Film**. New York: Garland, 1991. pp.203-243.
___ "Camelot Twice Removed: *Knightriders* and the Film Versions of **A Connecticut Yankee in King Arthur's Court**," in: Harty, Kevin J., ed. **Cinema Arthuriana: Essays on Arthurian Film**. New York: Garland, 1991. pp.105-120.
___ "**The Knights of the Square Table**: The Boy Scouts and Thomas Edison Make an Arthurian Film," *Arthuriana* 4(4): 313-323. Winter 1994.
___ "Teaching Arthurian Film," in: Fries, Maureen and Watson, Jeanie, eds. **Approaches to the Teaching of the Arthurian Tradition**. New York: Modern Language Association, 1992. pp.147-150.
___ (ed.) "The Arthurian Legend on Film: An Overview," in: Harty, Kevin J., ed. **Cinema Arthuriana: Essays on Arthurian Film**. New York: Garland, 1991. pp.3-28.
___ (ed.) **Cinema Arthuriana: Essays on Arthurian Film**. New York: Garland, 1991. 255pp.

HARVEY, CHARLES
___ "William Morris and the Royal Commission on Technical Instruction, 1881-84," by Charles Harvey and Jon Press. *Journal of the William Morris Society* 11(1): 31-43. Autumn 1994.

HARVEY, JESSICA G.
___ **Are We Not Men Too? Women and the Sex-Gender Role Reversal Motif in Science Fiction**. Master's Thesis, Acadia University, 1993. 160pp. (Master's Abstracts 32/03, p. 804. June 1994.)

HARVEY, RICH
___ "Indiana Jones and the Paperback Crusades," *Starlog* 179: 59-61, 90. June 1992.

HARWIT, MARTIN
___ "Why **Star Trek**?," *Star Trek: The Official Fan Club* No. 89: 9. January/February 1993.

HASCHAK, PAUL G.
___ **Utopian/Dystopian Literature: A Bibliography of Literary Criticism**. Metuchen, NJ: Scarecrow, 1994. 370pp.

HASSLER, DONALD M.
___ "Arthur Machen and Genre: Filial and Fannish Alternatives," *Extrapolation* 33(2): 115-127. Summer 1992.
___ "Machen, Williams, and Autobiography: Fantasy and Decadence," in: Wolf, Milton T. and Mallett, Daryl F., eds. **Imaginative Futures: Proceedings of the 1993 Science Fiction Research Association Conference**. San Bernardino, CA: Jacob's Ladder Books, 1995. pp.319-328.
___ "Swift, Pohl, and Kornbluth: Publicists Anatomize Newness," *Extrapolation* 34(3): 245-250. Fall 1993.
___ "Urban Pastoral and Labored Ease of Samuel R. Delany," in: Hakutani, Yoshinobu and Butler, Robert, eds. **The City in African-American Literature**. Rutherford, NJ: Fairleigh Dickinson University Press, 1995. pp.227-235.
___ "Working on SF: Observation With Extensive View," *Foundation* No. 60: 10-13. Spring 1994.
___ (ed.) **Arthur Machen and Montgomery Evans: Letters of a Literary Friendship, 1923-1947**, ed. by Sue S. Hassler and Donald M. Hassler. Kent, OH: Kent State University Press, 1994. 195pp.

HASSLER, SUE S.
___ (ed.) **Arthur Machen and Montgomery Evans: Letters of a Literary Friendship, 1923-1947**, ed. by Sue S. Hassler and Donald M. Hassler. Kent, OH: Kent State University Press, 1994. 195pp.

HASSOLD, CRIS
___ "The Double and Doubling in Modern and Postmodern Art," *Journal of the Fantastic in the Arts* 6(2/3): 253-274. 1994.

HASUMI, SHIGEHIKO
___ "Über die Nichtexistenz des SF-Films," *Quarber Merkur* 33(2): 21-24. December 1995. (No. 84)

HATCH, DANIEL
___ "The Wholesale Planet Warehouse," *SFWA Bulletin* 28(3): 4-17. Winter 1994. (No. 125)

HATCH, JIM
___ "*Cutthroat Island*: Getting Away With Murder," *Cinefex* No. 64: 49-50, 133. December 1995.

HATCH, RICHARD C.
___ "The Ideology of Work and the Architecture of Utopia," in: Saccaro Del Buffa, Giuseppa and Lewis, Arthur O., eds. **Utopia e Modernita: Teorie e prassi utopiche nell'eta moderna e postmoderna.** Rome: Gangemi Editore, 1989. pp.175-186.

HATCHER, LINT
___ "Enter: The Ackermansion," *Wonder* No. 7: 24-26. 1993.
___ "Inside Darkest Ackerman," by Lint Hatcher and Rod Bennett. *Wonder* No. 7: 4-11, 52-53. 1993.
___ "Monster Fan 2000," by Lint Hatcher and Rod Bennett. *Wonder* No. 7: 39-43, 54-56. 1993.

HATFIELD, LEN
___ "From Master to Brother: Shifting the Balance of Authority in Ursula K. Le Guin's **Farthest Shore** and **Tehanu**," *Children's Literature* 21: 43-65. 1993.
___ "Getting a Kick Out of Chaos: 'Fortunate Failure' in Greg Bear's Future Histories," in: Ruddick, Nicholas, ed. **State of the Fantastic.** Westport, CT: Greenwood, 1992. pp.133-140.
___ "Growing Up in SF: A Profile of Greg Bear," in: Collins, Robert A. and Latham, Robert, eds. **Science Fiction and Fantasy Book Review Annual 1991.** Westport, CT: Greenwood, 1994. pp.36-48. (pp.44-48: Telephone interview with Bear, 1991.)
___ "Legitimate Sequels: Character Structures and the Subject in Greg Bear's Sequence Novels," in: Morse, Donald E., ed. **The Celebration of the Fantastic.** Westport, CT: Greenwood, 1992. pp.237-250.

HATHERLEY, FRANK
___ **A Is for Brian: A 65th Birthday Present for Brian W. Aldiss From His Family, Friends, Colleagues and Admirers.** London: Avernus, 1990. 122pp.

HAUCK, DENNIS W.
___ **Captain Quirk: The Unauthorized Biography of William Shatner.** New York: Pinnacle, 1995. 298pp.
___ **William Shatner: A Bio-Bibliography.** Westport, CT.: Greenwood Press, 1994. 324pp.

HAUGHTON, JOHN
___ "Augustine and the Ainulindale," *Mythlore* 21(1): 4-13. Summer 1995. (No. 79)

HAUPT, ARTHUR
___ "Vanishing Stars: A Retrospective Look at Bester's **The Stars My Destination**," *Quantum* No. 42: 17-19. Summer/Fall 1992.

HAUSER, EVA
___ "Biopunk: A New Literary Movement for Post-Totalitarian Regimes," *Vector* No. 174: 15-16. August/September 1993.
___ "Science Fiction in the Czech Republic and the Former Czechoslovakia: The Pleasures and the Disappointments of the New Cosmopolitanism," *Science Fiction Studies* 21(2): 133-140. July 1994.

HAUTALA, RICK
___ "Bram Stoker Weekend," *Science Fiction Chronicle* 14(12): 26-28. September 1993.
___ "H. R. Giger's Alien Nightmares Invade Your Computer in *Darkseed*," *Science Fiction Age* 1(5): 74, 80. July 1993.

HAVERCROFT, BARBARA
___ "Fluctuations of Fantasy: The Combination and Subversion of Literary Genres in **Djinn**," in: Harger-Grinling, Virginia and Chadwick, Tony, eds. **Robbe-Grillet and the Fantastic.** Westport, CT: Greenwood, 1994. pp.101-124.

HAWK, PAT
___ **Hawk's Author's Pseudonyms for Book Collectors: A Collector's Reference of Modern Author's Pseudonyms.** Southlake, TX: Pat Hawk, 1993. 290pp.

HAWKINS, HARRIETT
___ **Classics and Trash: Traditions and Taboos in High Literature and Popular Modern Genres.** Toronto: University of Toronto Press, 1990. 219pp. [Not seen.]

HAWKINS, ROBERT J.
___ "*Knights* in Shining, Cyborg Armor (Review)," *San Diego (CA) Union* November 25, 1993. in: *NewsBank. Film and Television.* 128: F12-F13. 1993.

HAY, GEORGE
___ "Shiel Versus the Renegade Romantic," in: **Shiel in Diverse Hands: A Collection of Essays.** Cleveland, OH: Reynolds Morse Foundation, 1983. pp.109-113.

HAYCOCK, KATE
___ **Science Fiction Films.** New York: Crestwood House, 1992. 32pp.

HAYES, NANCY V.
___ "An Interview With Octavia E. Butler," *Science Fiction Eye* No. 13: 99-100. Spring 1994.

HAYLES, N. KATHERINE
___ "The Life Cycle of Cyborgs: Writing the Posthuman," in: Gray, Chris H., ed. **The Cyborg Handbook.** New York: Routledge, 1995. pp.321-335.
___ "The Life Cycle of Cyborgs: Writing the Posthuman," in: Benjamin, Marina, ed. **A Question of Identity: Women, Science, and Literature.** New Brunswick, NJ: Rutgers University Press, 1993. pp.152-170.

HAYNES, ROSLYNN D.
___ **From Faust to Strangelove: Representations of the Scientist in Western Literature.** Baltimore: Johns Hopkins University Press, 1994. 417pp.
___ "Science, Myth and Utopia," in: Filmer, Kath, ed. **Twentieth-Century Fantasists: Essays in Culture, Society and Belief in Twentieth Century Mythopoeic Literature.** New York: St. Martin's, 1992. pp.8-22.

HAZEL, FAYE R.
___ "Some Strange New England Mortuary Practices: Lovecraft Was Right," *Lovecraft Studies* No. 29: 13-18. Fall 1993. [Not seen.]

HECK, PETER J.
___ "Three Views of Two Guys: *Two Guys From the Future* and Other Plays; An Evening of Science Fiction Theater," by Peter J. Heck, Greg Cox and Shira Daemon. *New York Review of Science Fiction* No. 47: 1, 3-6. July 1992.
___ "Trends and Genres in Science Fiction: From Space Opera to Steampunk," in: Thompkins, David G., ed. **Science Fiction Writer's Market Place and Source Book.** Cincinnati, OH: Writer's Digest Books, 1994. pp.2-12.

HEESZEL, MARLYS
___ **The Worlds of TSR: A Pictorial Journey Through the Landscape of the Imagination.** Lake Geneva, WI: TSR, 1994. 142pp.

HEGARTY, EMILY
___ "Some Suspect of Ill: Shakespeare's Sonnets and 'The Perfect Mate'," *Extrapolation* 36(1): 55-64. Spring 1995.

HEIDEMAN, ERIC M.
___ "Fritz Leiber," *Lan's Lantern* No. 38: 6-7. July 1992.

HEILBRONER, ROBERT
___ **Visions of the Future: The Distant Past, Yesterday, Today, Tomorrow.** New York: Oxford University Press, 1995. 133pp.

HEILBRUN, CAROLYN G.
___ "Dorothy L. Sayers: Biography Between the Lines," in: Dale, Alzina S., ed. **Dorothy L. Sayers: The Centenary Celebration.** New York: Walker, 1993. pp.1-14.

HEINLEIN, ROBERT A.
___ "Guest of Honor Speech at the Third World Science Fiction Convention, Denver, 1941," in: Kondo, Yoji, ed. **Requiem: New Collected Works by Robert A. Heinlein and Tributes to the Grand Master.** New York: Tor, 1992. pp.153-167.
___ "Guest of Honor Speech at the XIXth World Science Fiction Convention, Seattle, 1961," in: Kondo, Yoji, ed. **Requiem: New Collected Works by Robert A. Heinlein and Tributes to the Grand Master.** New York: Tor, 1992. pp.168-197.
___ "Guest of Honor Speech at the XXXIVth World Science Fiction Convention, Kansas City, 1976," in: Kondo, Yoji, ed. **Requiem: New Collected Works by Robert A. Heinlein and Tributes to the Grand Master.** New York: Tor, 1992. pp.205-213.
___ "Guest of Honor Speech: Rio de Janeiro Movie Festival, 1969," in: Kondo, Yoji, ed. **Requiem: New Collected Works by Robert A. Heinlein and Tributes to the Grand Master.** New York: Tor, 1992. pp.198-204.
___ "Letter to Theodore Sturgeon, February 11, 1955," *New York Review of Science Fiction* No. 84: 1, 3-5. August 1995.
___ "On the Writing of Speculative Fiction," in: Dozois, Gardner, ed. **Writing Science Fiction and Fantasy.** New York: St. Martin's, 1991. pp.5-11.
___ "Shooting *Destination Moon*," in: Kondo, Yoji, ed. **Requiem: New Collected Works by Robert A. Heinlein and Tributes to the Grand Master.** New York: Tor, 1992. pp.117-131.
___ "This I Believe," in: Kondo, Yoji, ed. **Requiem: New Collected Works by Robert A. Heinlein and Tributes to the Grand Master.** New York: Tor, 1992. pp.218-220.
___ **Tramp Royale.** New York: Ace, 1992. 372pp.

HEINLEIN, VIRGINIA
___ "Preface: Requiem," in: Kondo, Yoji, ed. **Requiem: New Collected Works by Robert A. Heinlein and Tributes to the Grand Master.** New York: Tor, 1992. pp.1-5.

HEINZE, THEODOR T.
___ "Science/Fiction, hin und zurück: Mensch, Maschine, Mythos im *Blade Runner*," in: Heinze, Theodor T., ed. **Subjektivität als Fiktion: Zur literarisch psychologischen Konstruktion des Modernen Menschen.** Pfaffenweiler: Gentaurus, 1993. pp.129-158.
___ (ed.) **Subjektivität als Fiktion: zur literarisch psychologischen Konstruktion des modernen Menschen.** Pfaffenweiler: Centaurus, 1993. 172pp.

HEISER, JAMES
___ "C. S. Lewis as Media Critic," *Intercollegiate Review* 27(2): 51-54. Spring 1992.

HELDRETH, LEONARD G.
___ "Conference Report, ICFA XIII," *IAFA Newsletter* 5(2): 7-20. Summer 1992.
___ "Films, Film Fantasies, and Fantasies: Spinning Reality From the Self in *Kiss of the Spider Woman*," *Journal of the Fantastic in the Arts* 3(4): 93-106. 1994.
___ "The Ghost and the Self: The Supernatural Fiction of Henry James," in: Morse, Donald E., ed. **The Celebration of the Fantastic.** Westport, CT: Greenwood, 1992. pp.133-140.
___ "ICFA Converses With 1992 G. O. H. Ursula K. Le Guin," *IAFA Newsletter* 5(2): 24-27. Summer 1992.

HELDRETH, LILLIAN
___ "The Mercy of the Torturer: The Paradox of Compassion in Gene Wolfe's World of the New Sun," in: Latham, Robert A. and Collins, Robert A., eds. **Modes of the Fantastic.** Westport, CT: Greenwood, 1995. pp.186-194.

HELFORD, ELYCE R.
___ "Reading Masculinities in the 'Postpatriarchal' Space of *Red Dwarf*," *Foundation* No. 64: 20-31. Summer 1995.
___ **Reading Space Fictions: Representations of Gender, Race and Species in Popular Culture.** Ph.D. Dissertation, University of Iowa, 1993. (DAI-A 53/11, p. 3908. May 1993.)
___ "We Are Only Seeking Man: Gender, Psychoanalysis, and Stanislaw Lem's *Solaris*," *Science-Fiction Studies* 19(2): 167-177. July 1992.
___ " 'Would You Really Rather Die Than Bear My Young?': The Construction of Gender, Race, and Species in Octavia E. Butler's **Bloodchild**," *African American Review* 28(2): 259-271. Summer 1994.

HELLEKSON, KAREN
___ "Never Never Underpeople: Cordwainer Smith's Humanity," *Extrapolation* 34(2): 123-130. Summer 1993.

HELLER, ARNO
___ "Anthony Burgess, *A Clockwork Orange* (1962)," in: Heuermann, Harmut, ed. **Der Science Fiction Roman in der angloamerikanischen Literatur: Interpretationen.** Düsseldorf: Bagel, 1986. pp.236-252.

HELLER, STEVEN
___ **Jackets Required: An Illustrated History of American Book Jacket Design, 1920-1959,** by Steven Heller and Seymour Chwast. San Francisco, CA: Chronicle Books, 1995. 144pp.

HELLER, TAMAR
___ **Dead Secrets: Wilkie Collins and the Female Gothic.** New Haven, CT: Yale University Press, 1992. 201pp.

HELLMAN, MARY
___ "Outta This World," *San Diego (CA) Union* August 1, 1993. in: *NewsBank. Literature.* 75:D6-D8. 1993.

HELM, JOAN
___ "Erec, the Hebrew Heritage: Urban Tigner Holmes Vindicated," *Quondam et Futurus* 2(1): 1-16. Spring 1992.

HELM, LESLIE
___ "Selling Hollywood in Japan," *Los Angeles (CA) Times.* September 21, 1992. in: *NewsBank. Film and Television.* 87:D6-D7. 1992

HEMINGWAY, LLOYD
___ "Toto, We're Back: The *Cottonwood Review* Interview," by Lloyd Hemingway and Johan Heye. in: Delany, Samuel R. **Silent Interviews on Language, Race, Sex, Science Fiction and Some Comics.** Hanover, NH: Wesleyan University Press, 1994. pp.59-82.

HEMPHILL, JIM
___ "*Dr. Giggle* (Review)," *Cinefantastique* 23(6): 60. April 1993.

HENDEE, J. C.
___ "The Race for Success: An Interview With Brian Herbert," *Quantum* No. 43/44: 24-26. Spring/Summer 1993.

HENDERSHOT, CYNDY
___ "Vampire and Replicant: The One-Sex Body in a Two-Sex World," *Science Fiction Studies* 22(3): 373-398. November 1995

HENDERSON, ED
___ "The Big Green Guy," *Starlog* 180: 29-31, 73. July 1992.

HENDERSON, JAN A.
___ "Where No Show Has Gone Before," *American Cinematographer* 73(1): 34-40. January 1992.

HENDERSON, MARY
___ "Professional Women in *Star Trek*, 1964-1969," *Film & History* 24(1/2): 47-59. February/May 1994.

HENDIN, JOSEPHINE
___ "The Capacity to Look at a Situation Coolly (Interview, 1972)," in: Ingersoll, Earl G., ed. **Doris Lessing: Conversations.** Princeton, NJ: Ontario Review Press, 1994. pp.41-56.

HENDRIX, HOWARD V.

HENDRIX, HOWARD V.
___ "Memories of the Sun, Perceptions of Eclipse," *New York Review of Science Fiction* No. 46: 13-15. June 1992.
___ "The Things of a Child: Coming Full Circle With Alan E. Nourse's **Raiders From the Rings**," in: Sullivan, C. W., III. **Science Fiction for Young Readers**. Westport, CT: Greenwood, 1993. pp.87-96.

HENDRIX, LAUREL L.
___ "A World of Glass: The Heroine's Quest for Identity in Spenser's **Faerie Queene** and Stephen R. Donaldson's **Mirror of Her Dreams**," in: Sanders, Joe, ed. **Functions of the Fantastic**. Westport, CT: Greenwood, 1995. pp.91-100

HENENLOTTER, FRANK
___ "Films From Under the Floorboards," *Sci-Fi Entertainment* 1(6): 52-57. April 1995.

HENIGHNA, TOM
___ "The Cyclopean City: A Fantasy Image of Decadence," *Extrapolation* 35(1): 68-76. Spring 1994.

HENLY, CAROLYN P.
___ "Escape From the **Twilight Zone**: Reading and Writing 'At-Risk' Students," *ALAN Review* 19(3): 31-32, 35, 37. Spring 1992.

HENNESSY, JOAN
___ "King Books 'Off Limits' for Middle School Kids," *Jacksonville (FL) Times-Union*. March 12, 1992. in: *NewsBank. Literature.* 29:D14. 1992.

HENRY, RICHARD
___ "Charles Williams and the Aesthetic Ideal of Friedrich von Schiller," *Extrapolation* 35(4): 271-280. Winter 1994.

HENTERLY, MEGHAN
___ "Kenner Banks on the Caped Crusader," *Cincinati (OH) Enquirer* June 22, 1992. in: *NewsBank. Film and Television.* 62:E3-E4. 1992.

HERBERT, BRIAN P.
___ "When Bad Things Happen," *The Report: The Fiction Writer's Magazine* No. 11: 5-8. Summer 1993.

HERBERT, ISOLDE K.
___ "Nature and Art: Morris's Conception of Progress," *Journal of the William Morris Society* 10(1): 4-9. Autumn 1992.

HERBERT, JAMES
___ "Bowled Over by the Beast: Me and My Car," in: Jones, Stephen, ed. **James Herbert: By Horror Haunted**. London: New English Library, 1992. pp.39-42.
___ "Comic Relief," in: Jones, Stephen, ed. **James Herbert: By Horror Haunted**. London: New English Library, 1992. pp.65-67.
___ "The Fog," in: Jones, Stephen, ed. **James Herbert: By Horror Haunted**. London: New English Library, 1992. pp.109-111.
___ **James Herbert's Dark Places: Locations and Legends**. London: HarperCollins, 1993. 168pp.
___ "My Ten Favorite Books," in: Jones, Stephen, ed. **James Herbert: By Horror Haunted**. London: New English Library, 1992. pp.75-78.
___ "Swamp Thing," in: Jones, Stephen, ed. **James Herbert: By Horror Haunted**. London: New English Library, 1992. pp.231-233.

HERD, VALERIE
___ "Introduction: Speaking of **Star Trek**," in: Van Hise, James, ed. **Trek Celebration Two**. Las Vegas, NV: Pioneer, 1994. pp.13-15.

HERMAN, HAROLD J.
___ "Teaching White, Stewart, and Berger," in: Fries, Maureen and Watson, Jeanie, eds. **Approaches to the Teaching of the Arthurian Tradition**. New York: Modern Language Association, 1992. pp.113-117.

HERNANDEZ, LEA
___ "Japanimation's Rising Sun," *Sci-Fi Entertainment* 1(1): 30-33. June 1994.

HERRICK, JIM
___ "C. S. Lewis and Narrative Argument in **Out of the Silent Planet**," *Mythlore* 18(4): 15-22. Autumn 1992. (No. 70)

HERRON, DON
___ "The Mysteries of M. P. Shiel," in: **Shiel in Diverse Hands: A Collection of Essays**. Cleveland, OH: Reynolds Morse Foundation, 1983. pp.179-194.
___ On Howardian Fairyland. *The Dark Man: The Journal of Robert E. Howard Studies* No. 2: 24. July 1991.
___ (ed.) **The Selected Letters of Philip K. Dick, 1977-1979**. Lancaster, PA: Underwood-Miller, 1993. 260pp.

HERTZ, JOHN
___ "Conadian Masquerade Report," *Science Fiction Chronicle* 16(3): 34-36. January 1995.

HERTZBERG, HENDRIK
___ "Cookie Monster," *New Yorker* 71(20): 6-7. July 17, 1995.

HESS, KATHLEEN
___ "The Bittersweet Vine: Fairy Tales and Nursery Rhymes," *Mythlore* 19(2): 54-56, 60. Spring 1993. (No. 72)

HESSON, ELIZABETH C.
___ "Ionesco and **L'insolite**," by Elizabeth C. Hesson and Ian M. Hesson. in: Murphy, Patrick D., ed. **Staging the Impossible: The Fantastic Mode in Modern Drama**. Westport, CT: Greenwood, 1992. pp.87-107.

HESSON, IAN M.
___ "Ionesco and **L'insolite**," by Elizabeth C. Hesson and Ian M. Hesson. in: Murphy, Patrick D., ed. **Staging the Impossible: The Fantastic Mode in Modern Drama**. Westport, CT: Greenwood, 1992. pp.87-107.

HETTINGA, DONALD R.
___ **Presenting Madeleine L'Engle**. New York: Macmillan/Twayne, 1993. 169pp.

HEUERMANN, HARTMUT
___ "Daniel Keyes, **Flowers for Algernon** (1966)," in: Heuermann, Harmut, ed. **Der Science Fiction Roman in der angloamerikanischen Literatur: Interpretationen**. Düsseldorf: Bagel, 1986. pp.275-294.
___ "Ray Bradbury: **Fahrenheit 451** (1953)," in: Heuermann, Hartmut and Lange, Bernd-Peter, eds. **Die Utopie in der angloamerikanischen Literatur: Interpretationen**. Düsseldorf: Bagel, 1984. pp.259-282.
___ (ed.) **Der Science Fiction Roman in der angloamerikanischen Literatur**. Düsseldorf: Bagel, 1986. 399pp.
___ (ed.) **Die Utopie in der Angloamerikanischen Literatur: Interpretationen**, ed. by Hartmut Heuermann and Bernd-Peter Lange. Düsseldorf: Bagel, 1984. 370pp.

HEWETT, JERRY
___ **The Work of Jack Vance: An Annotated Bibliography and Guide**, by Jerry Hewett and Daryl F. Mallett. San Bernardino, CA: Borgo Press, 1994. 293pp. (Issued simultaneously by Underwood-Miller.)

HEWITT, ELIZABETH
___ "Generic Exhaustion and the 'Heat Death' of Science Fiction," *Science Fiction Studies* 21(3): 289-301. November 1994.

HEYE, JOHAN
___ "Toto, We're Back: The *Cottonwood Review* Interview," by Lloyd Hemingway and Johan Heye. in: Delany, Samuel R. **Silent Interviews on Language, Race, Sex, Science Fiction and Some Comics**. Hanover, NH: Wesleyan University Press, 1994. pp.59-82.

HEYNE, ERIC
___ "**Gateway** to an Erotics of Narrative," *Extrapolation* 35(4): 298-311. Winter 1994.

HEYWOOD, ANDREW
___ "Morris and Early Music: The Shaw/Dolmetsch Connection," *Journal of the William Morris Society* 10(4): 13-19. Spring 1994.

HICKMAN, TRACY
___ (ed.) **Leaves From the Inn of the Last Home: The Complete Krynn Source Book**, ed. by Margaret Weis and Tracy Hickman. Lake Geneva, WI: TSR, 1993. 255pp.

HIGGINS, STEPHEN
___ "So, You Want to Be a Horror Writer," *Aurealis* No. 13: 84-85. 1994.
___ "So, You Want to Be an SF Writer?," *Aurealis* No. 12: 91-92. 1993.

HILBRAND, DAVID
___ "Picks and Pans: **Earth 2**," *People Weekly* 42(21): 17, 19. November 21, 1994.

HILL, DARCI
___ " 'The Church Militant' Resurrected: Mythic Elements in George Herbert's **The Temple**," *Mythlore* 21(1): 29-32. Summer 1995. (No. 79)

HILL, DEBORA
___ "Image of the Spider," by Debora Hill and Sandra Brandenburg. *Starlog* 182: 40-41. September 1992.
___ "Things in That Forest: A Profile of Lisa Goldstein," by Sandra Brandenburg and Debora Hill. *Science Fiction Eye* No. 11: 110-113.113. December 1992.
___ "A Time of Fantasies," by Sandra Brandenburg and Debora Hill. *Starlog* 179: 70-72, 90. June 1992.

HILL, DOUGLAS
___ "Writing SF for Kids," *Books for Keeps* 83: 24-25. 1993.

HILL, MARY A.
___ **Charlotte Perkins Gilman: A Feminist Paradox**. Ph.D. Dissertation, McGill University, 1975. 273pp.
___ **Charlotte Perkins Gilman: The Making of a Radical Feminist, 1860-1896**. Philadelphia, PA: Temple University Press, 1980. 362pp.

HILLER, KARL
___ "Growing Home: The Triumph of Youth in the Novels of H. M. Hoover," by Thom Dunn and Karl Hiller. in: Sullivan, C. W., III. **Science Fiction for Young Readers**. Westport, CT: Greenwood, 1993. pp.121-131.

HILLGÄRTNER, RÜDIGER
___ "William Morris: **News from Nowhere; Or, an Epoch of Rest, Being Some Chapters from a Utopian Romance** (1890)," in: Heuermann, Hartmut and Lange, Bernd-Peter, eds. **Die Utopie in der angloamerikanischen Literatur: Interpretationen**. Düsseldorf: Bagel, 1984. pp.120-138.

HILTBRAND, DAVID
___ "Picks and Pans: **Akira**," *People Weekly* 44(8): 13. August 21, 1995.
___ "Picks and Pans: **Alien Nation**," *People Weekly* 42(17): 17, 15. October 24, 1994.
___ "Picks and Pans: **The Adventures of Captain Zoom in Outer Space**," *People Weekly* 44(9): 14. August 28, 1995.

HINES, SUSAN C.
___ "What's Academic About Trek?," *Extrapolation* 36(1): 5-9. Spring 1995.

HIRSCH, CONNIE
___ "Amidst Endless Superheroes, *Illegal Alien* Is as Ambitious as the Best SF," *Science Fiction Age* 3(1): 84-87. November 1994.
___ "Harlan Ellison Rides a Dark Horse to Invade His Personal *Dream Corridors*," *Science Fiction Age* 3(3): 18. March 1995.

HIRSCH, DAVID
___ "Music for **Robocop**," *Starlog* No. 196: 58-63. November 1993.
___ "Symphony for Klingon," *Starlog* 180: 76-80. July 1992.

HITE, MOLLY P.
___ **Ideas of Order in the Novels of Thomas Pynchon**. Ph.D. Dissertation, University of Washington, 1981. 269pp.
___ "Optics and Autobiography in Margaret Atwood's **Cat's Eye**," *Twentieth Century Literature* 41(2): 135-159. Summer 1995.

HIXON, CELIA
___ "Plotting Science into Science Fiction: Part Four, Human Motivation," *Writers' Journal* 15(1): 8-9. 1993.
___ "Plotting Science into Science Fiction: Part One, Research Methods," *Writers' Journal* 14(4): 9-11. 1993.
___ "Plotting Science into Science Fiction: Part Three, Alien Cultures," *Writers' Journal* 14(6): 9-10. 1993.

HIXON, CELIA (continued)
___ "Plotting Science into Science Fiction: Part Two, A Star Shopper's Guide," *Writers' Journal* 14(5): 8-9. 1993.

HLAVATY, ARTHUR D.
___ "The Politics of Glory: The New SF Grand Masters," *New York Review of Science Fiction* No. 80: 1, 6-9. April 1995.

HOBBS, COLLEEN
___ "Reading the Symptoms: An Exploration of Repression and Hysteria in Mary Shelley's **Frankenstein**," *Studies in the Novel* 25(2): 152-169. Summer 1993.

HOBBY, PATRICK
___ "**Alien 3**," *Cinefantastique* 22(6): 8-21. June 1992

HOBERG, TOM
___ "In Her Own Right: The Guenevere of Parke Godwin," in: Slocum, Sally K., ed. **Popular Arthurian Traditions**. Bowling Green, OH: Popular Press, 1992. pp.68-79.

HOBERMAN, J.
___ "Paranoia and the Pods," *Sight and Sound* 4(5): 28-31. May 1994.

HOBSON, LINDA W.
___ "Walker Percy," in: Bruccoli, Matthew J., ed. **Facts on File Bibliography of American Fiction 1919-1988**. New York: Facts on File, 1991. pp.398-400.

HOCHMAN, DAVID
___ "Playing Doctor," *US* 200: 66-67. September 1994.

HODGES, LAURA F.
___ "Steinbeck's Adaptation of Malory's Launcelot: A Triumph of Realism over Supernaturalism," *Quondam et Futurus* 2(1): 69-81. Spring 1992.
___ "Syngne, Conysaunce, Deuys: Three pentangles in **Sir Gawain and the Green Knight**," *Arthuriana* 5(4): 22-31. Winter 1995.

HODGES, SHARI
___ "A Pedagogically Useful Comparison of **Star Trek II** and **Paradise Lost**," *CEA Forum* 24(2): 4-7. Summer 1994.

HODGSON, JEFFREY
___ "FEATURE-Sci-Fi Writer Wins Awards With Focus on Human Soul," *Reuters* August 12, 1996. (Cited from **The Electric Library** on-line service.)

HODSON, LEIGHTON
___ "**The Scorpion God**: Clarity, Technique, and Communication," in: Biles, Jack I. and Evans, Robert O., eds. **William Golding: Some Critical Considerations**. Lexington, KY: University Press of Kentucky, 1978. pp.188-202.

HOESTEREY, INGEBORG
___ (ed.) **Neverending Stories: Toward a Critical Narratology**, ed. by Ann Fehn, Ingeborg Hoesterey and Maria Tatar. Princeton, NJ: Princeton University Press, 1992. 274pp.

HOFFMAN, BILL
___ "The Outer Limits of Taste (Review)," *New York Post* December 10, 1993. in: *NewsBank*. Art. 37:G12. 1993.

HOFFMAN, CHARLES
___ "Cosmic Filth: Howard's View of Evil," *The Dark Man: The Journal of Robert E. Howard Studies* No. 3: 9-16. April 1993.

HOFFMAN, DONALD L.
___ "Isotta di Rimini: Gabriele D'Annunzio's Use of the Tristan Legend in His **Da Rimini**," *Quondam et Futurus* 2(3): 46-54. Fall 1992.
___ "Mark's Merlin: Magic vs. Technology in **A Connecticut Yankee in King Arthur's Court**," in: Slocum, Sally K., ed. **Popular Arthurian Traditions**. Bowling Green, OH: Popular Press, 1992. pp.46-55.
___ "Pomorex: Arthurian Tradition in Barthelme's **The King**, Acker's **Don Quixote**, and Reed's **Flight to Canada**," *Arthuriana* 4(4): 376-386. Winter 1994.

HOFMANN, ROBERTA
___ "Realism in the Tarzan Novels," *Burroughs Bulletin* NS. No. 20: 29-31. October 1994.

HOFSTEDE, DAVID
___ **Hollywood and the Comics: Film Adaptations of Comic Books and Scripts**. Las Vegas, NV: Zanne-3, 1991. 198pp.

HOGAN, DAVID J.
___ "Art of the Fright: Celebrating the Life of Vincent Price," *Filmfax* No. 42: 32-39, 94-95. December 1993/January 1994.
___ "*Cat Women of the Moon* (Review)," *Filmfax* No. 34: 18, 20. August/September 1992.
___ "*Fangs* (Review)," *Filmfax* No. 35: 18, 20. October/November 1992.
___ "*Four-Sided Triangle* (1953) (Review)," *Filmfax* No. 33: 18, 20. June/July 1992.
___ "*Mars Needs Women* (1956) (Review)," *Filmfax* No. 38: 20, 30. April/May 1993.
___ "*The Munsters*: 'My Fair Munster' (Review)," *Filmfax* No. 33: 18. June/July 1992.
___ "*My Living Doll* (Review)," *Filmfax* No. 31: 20, 22. February/March 1992.
___ "*Night Tide* (Review)," *Filmfax* No. 34: 18. August/September 1992.
___ "*Quatermass and the Pit* (Review)," *Filmfax* No. 37: 19-20. February/March 1993.
___ "*The Quatermass Experiment* (Review)," *Filmfax* No. 37: 18-19. February/March 1993.
___ "*Vampyr* (1932) (Review)," *Filmfax* No. 37: 26, 30. February/March 1993.
___ "*White Zombie* (1932) (Review)," *Filmfax* No. 35: 18. October/November 1992.

HOGAN, ERNEST
___ "Greasy Kid Stuff From Outer Space," *Science Fiction Eye* No. 11: 35-37. December 1992.
___ "Guess Who's Killing the Short Story?," *Science Fiction Eye* No. 10: 41-43. June 1992.

HOGAN, JEANNE
___ "Operation *Enterprise*," *Star Trek: The Official Fan Club Magazine* No. 92: 1, 34. July/August 1993.
___ "Where Faith and Glory Lead: *U. S. S. Enterprise* (CVAN/CN-65) Association Honors Jimmy Doohan for World War II Heroism," *Star Trek: The Official Fan Club* No. 94: 42. February/March 1994.

HOGLE, LINDA F.
___ "Tales From the Cryptic: Technology Meets Organism in the Living Cadaver," in: Gray, Chris H., ed. **The Cyborg Handbook**. New York: Routledge, 1995. pp.203-216.

HOHNE, KAREN A.
___ "The Power of the Spoken Word in the Works of Stephen King," *Journal of Popular Culture* 28(2): 93-103. Fall 1994.
___ "The Voice of Cthulhu: Language Interaction in Contemporary Horror Fiction," in: Slusser, George E. and Rabkin, Eric S., eds. **Styles of Creation: Aesthetic Technique and the Creation of Fictional Worlds**. Athens: University of Georgia Press, 1992. pp.79-87.

HOLDEN, CONSTANCE
___ "Bringing More Reality to Fiction," *Science* 263(5144): 176-177. January 14, 1994.

HOLDER, KEITH
___ "*Body Snatchers*: The New Invasion," *Cinefantastique* 23(4): 10-11. December 1992.
___ "*Body Snatchers*," *Cinefantastique* 24(1): 4-5. June 1993.
___ "*Body Snatchers*," *Cinefantastique* 24(2): 56. August 1993.
___ "*The New Invasion*," *Cinefantastique* 24(1): 5. June 1993.

HOLDER, NANCY
___ "Why *The Haunting* Is So Damn Scary," in: Golden, Christopher, ed. **Cut! Horror Writers on Horror Film**. New York: Berkley, 1992. pp.131-140.

HOLLAMBY, EDWARD
___ "Address at the Birthday Party, 1993," *Journal of the William Morris Society* 10(3): 10-12. Autumn 1993.

HOLLAND, STEPHEN
___ **British Science Fiction Paperbacks and Magazines, 1949-1956: An Annotated Bibliograhy and Guide**, by Philip Harbottle and Stephen Holland. San Bernardino, CA: Borgo Press, 1994. 232pp.
___ **An Index to Mellifont Press: A Working Bibliography**. Leeds, Eng: Galactic Central, 1995. 76pp.
___ **The Mushroom Jungle: A History of Postwar Paperback Publishing**. Westbury, Eng.: Zeon Books, 1993. 196pp.
___ **Vultures of the Void: A History of British Science Fiction Publishing 1946-1956**, by Philip Harbottle and Stephen Holland. San Bernardino, CA: Borgo Press, 1992. 128pp.

HOLLAND-TOLL, LINDA J.
___ "Community in Horror Fiction: As American as God, Mother, and Apple Pie," *Studies in Weird Fiction* No. 17: 12-18. Summer 1995.
___ "Contemporary Tragedy: Stephen King's **Pet Sematary**," *Studies in Weird Fiction* No. 16: 28-33. Winter 1995.

HOLLÄNDER, HANS
___ "Notizen zur Illustration 'phantastischer Literatur'. Anläßlich der Asgabe von MacDonalds **Phantastes** mit den Bildern von Fritz Hechelmann," in: Kranz, Gisbert, ed. **Inklings: Jahrbuch für Literatur und Ästhetik**. 1. Band. Lüdenscheid, Germany: Michael Claren, 1983. pp.139-149.

HOLLIDAY, LIZ
___ "Last of the Old Guard? Liz Holliday Meets Arthur C. Clarke and His Biographer, Neil McAleer," *Interzone* No. 66: 43-46. December 1992.
___ "Master of the Alien: Phillip Mann," *Interzone* No. 68: 41-43. February 1993.
___ "On the Sharing of Worlds: George R. R. Martin Interviewed," *Interzone* No. 70: 44-47. April 1993.
___ "SFC Interviews: Carol Emshwiller," *Science Fiction Chronicle* 14(4): 5, 26-27. January 1993.
___ "SFC Interviews: Larry Niven and Steven Barnes," *Science Fiction Chronicle* 13(6): 6, 22, 24-25. March 1992.
___ "SFC Interviews: Paul J. McAuley," *Science Fiction Chronicle* 13(9): 5, 27-28. June 1992.
___ "SFC Interviews: Terry Pratchett," *Science Fiction Chronicle* 13(7): 5, 26-27. April 1992.
___ "SFC Interviews: Walter Jon Williams," *Science Fiction Chronicle* 13(11/12): 5, 42. August 1992.

HOLLINGER, VERONICA
___ "The Charisma Leak: A Conversation With William Gibson and Bruce Sterling," by Daniel Fischlin, Veronica Hollinger and Andrew Taylor. *Science Fiction Studies* 19(1): 1-16. March 1992.
___ **Future Presence: Intersections of Science Fiction and Postmodernism**. Ph.D. Dissertation, Concordia University, 1994. 248pp. (DAI-A 56/07, p. 2676. January 1996.)
___ "Playing at the End of the World: Postmodern Theater," in: Murphy, Patrick D., ed. **Staging the Impossible: The Fantastic Mode in Modern Drama**. Westport, CT: Greenwood, 1992. pp.182-196.
___ "Specular SF: Postmodern Allegory," in: Ruddick, Nicholas, ed. **State of the Fantastic**. Westport, CT: Greenwood, 1992. pp.29-39.
___ "Travels in Hyperreality: Jean Baudrillard's **America** and J. G. Ballard's **Hello America**," in: Sanders, Joe, ed. **Functions of the Fantastic**. Westport, CT: Greenwood, 1995. pp.185-194.
___ "The Vampire and/as the Alien," *Journal of the Fantastic in the Arts* 5(3): 5-17. 1993. (No. 19)

HOLM, JAN
___ "The Old Grumbler of Runnymede," *Journal of the William Morris Society* 10(2): 17-21. Spring 1993.

HOLMBERT, JOHN-HENRI
___ "Letter From Sweden," *Science Fiction Chronicle* 17(2): 6. December 1995/January 1996.

HOLMEN, RACHEL E.
___ "Interview With Diana L. Paxson and Adrienne Martine-Barnes," *Marion Zimmer Bradley's Fantasy Magazine* No. 28: 47-50. Summer 1995.
___ "Interview With Elizabeth Ann Scarborough," *Marion Zimmer Bradley's Fantasy Magazine* No. 21: 42-47. Fall 1993.
___ "Interview With Katherine Kurtz," *Marion Zimmer Bradley's Fantasy Magazine* No. 24: 40-44. Summer 1994.

HOLT, G. WESLEY
___ "**The Invisible Man** (1933) (Review)," *Filmfax* No. 37: 24, 26. February/March 1993.

HOLT, PHILIP
___ "H. G. Wells and the Ring of Gyges," *Science-Fiction Studies* 19(2): 236-247. July 1992.

HOLT, WESLEY G.
___ "**Frankenstein** (1931) (Review)," *Filmfax* No. 35: 24, 26, 30. October/November 1992.
___ "**Nosferatu** (Prana Films, 1922) (Review)," *Filmfax* No. 38: 25-26. April/May 1993.

HOLTER, RICK
___ "Sci-Fi Film's Promise Turns into a Poor Excuse," *Dallas (TX) Morning News.* July 7, 1995. in: *NewsBank. Film and Television.* 72:A5. 1995.

HOLTSMARK, ERLING B.
___ "Tarzan: Projects Past and Future," *Burroughs Bulletin* NS No. 9: 8-14. January 1992.

HOLWAY, LOWELL H.
___ "Ursula K. Le Guin at SJSU: The Future Is a Metaphor," *San Jose Studies* 20(1): 54-71. Winter 1994.

HOME, W. SCOTT
___ "The Rose Beyond the Thunders and the Whirlpools," in: **Shiel in Diverse Hands: A Collection of Essays.** Cleveland, OH: Reynolds Morse Foundation, 1983. pp.343-355.

HONIGSBERG, DAVID M.
___ "Rava's Golem," *Journal of the Fantastic in the Arts* 7(2/3): 137-145. 1995.
___ "*RoboRally* and *Edge City* Transport Board Games to an Exciting Tomorrow," *Science Fiction Age* 3(3): 98-101. March 1995.
___ "*Star Riders* Sends up SF With Serious Space Opera Silliness," *Science Fiction Age* 2(6): 90-93. September 1994.

HOOD, EDWARD W.
___ **La ficción de Gabriel García Márquez: Repetición e intertextualidad.** New York: Peter Lang, 1994. 229pp.

HOOD, GWENYTH
___ "The Earthly Paradise in Tolkien's **The Lord of the Rings**," in: Reynolds, Patricia and GoodKnight, Glen H., eds. **Proceedings of the J. R. R. Tolkien Centenary Conference, Keble College, Oxford, 1992.** Altadena, CA: Mythopoeic Press, 1995. pp.139-144. (*Mythlore* Vol. 21, No. 2, Winter 1996, Whole No. 80)
___ "Nature and Technology: Angelic and Sacrificial Strategies in Tolkien's **The Lord of the Rings**," *Mythlore* 19(4): 6-12. Autumn 1993. (No. 74)

HOOD, LEROY
___ "Could **Jurassic Park** Happen?," *Atlanta Constitution* Sec. A, p. 15. June 23, 1993.

HOOPER, ANDREW
___ "A Report From ConFrancisco, the 51st World Science Fiction Convention," *Science Fiction Chronicle* 15(2): 40-45. November/December 1993.
___ "A Report From ConFrancisco, The 51st World Science Fiction Convention, Part 2," *Science Fiction Chronicle* 15(3): 26-32. January 1994.

HOOPER, KENT W.
___ "Wassily Kandinsky's Stage Composition **Yellow Sound**: The Fantastic and the Symbolic Mode of Communication," in: Murphy, Patrick D., ed. **Staging the Impossible: The Fantastic Mode in Modern Drama.** Westport, CT: Greenwood, 1992. pp.56-86.

HOOPER, WALTER
___ **C. S. Lewis: A Biography.** Revised Edition, by Roger L. Green and Walter Hooper. San Diego, CA: Harcourt Brace, 1994. 320pp.

HOOVER, BOB
___ "Insights into Canadian Identity," *Pittsburgh (PA) Post Gazette.* January 27, 1992. in *NewsBank. Literature.* 9:E9. 1992.

HOOVER, KENNETH R.
___ "Mondragon's Answers to Utopia's Problems," *Utopian Studies* 3(2): 1-20. 1992.

HOPKINS, CHRIS
___ "Tolkien and Englishness," in: Reynolds, Patricia and GoodKnight, Glen H., eds. **Proceedings of the J. R. R. Tolkien Centenary Conference, Keble College, Oxford, 1992.** Altadena, CA: Mythopoeic Press, 1995. pp.278-280. (*Mythlore* Vol. 21, No. 2, Winter 1996, Whole No. 80)

HOPKINS, LISA
___ "Bilbo Baggins as a Burglar," in: Kranz, Gisbert, ed. **Jahrbuch für Literatur und Ästhetik.** Lüdenscheid, Germany: Stier, 1992. Band 10, pp.93-101.
___ "Female Authority Figures in the Works of Tolkien, C. S. Lewis, and Charles Williams," in: Reynolds, Patricia and GoodKnight, Glen H., eds. **Proceedings of the J. R. R. Tolkien Centenary Conference, Keble College, Oxford, 1992.** Altadena, CA: Mythopoeic Press, 1995. pp.364-366. (*Mythlore* Vol. 21, No. 2, Winter 1996, Whole No. 80)

HOPKINS, MARIANE S.
___ (ed.) **Fandom Directory, No. 14: 1992-1993 Edition.** Springfield, VA: Fandata, 1992. 544pp.
___ (ed.) **Fandom Directory, No. 15, 1995-1996.** Springfield, VA: Fandata Publications, 1995. 607pp.

HOPPENSTAND, GARY
___ **Clive Barker's Short Stories: Imagination as Metaphor in the Books of Blood and Other Works.** Jefferson, NC: McFarland, 1994. 231pp.
___ "Robots of the Past: Fitz-james O'Brien's 'The Wondersmith'," *Journal of Popular Culture* 27(4): 13-30. Spring 1994.
___ "The Secret Self in Clive Barker's Imaginative Fiction," in: Brown, Michael, ed. **Pandemonium: Further Explorations into the Worlds of Clive Barker.** Staten Island, NY: Eclise, 1991. pp.91-96.

HOPWOOD, LYLE
___ "The Mad Scientist Confronts the Witch Doctor," *Science Fiction Eye* No. 12: 51-54. Summer 1993. (Response, p. 55-59.)

HORDERN, KATE
___ "Selling SF and Fantasy Translation Rights in Eastern Europe and Russia," *SFWA Bulletin* 29(2): 28-31. Summer 1995. (No. 127)

HORI, MOTOKAZU
___ "Artificial Liver: Present and Future," in: Gray, Chris H., ed. **The Cyborg Handbook.** New York: Routledge, 1995. pp.163-166.

HORN, JOHN
___ "**Jurassic Park** Devours **Batman** Record," *Austin (TX) American Statesman* Sec. F, p. 6. June 15, 1993.

HORNE, BRIAN
___ "A Peculiar Debt: The Influence of Charles Williams on C. S. Lewis," in: Walker, Andrew and Patric, James, eds. **A Christian for All Christians.** Washington, DC: Regnery, 1992. pp.83-97.

HORNE, LINNETTE
___ "SF in New Zealand," *Locus* 34(1) 72. January 1995.

HORNE, PHILIP
___ "I Shopped With a Zombie," *Critical Quarterly* 34(4): 97-110. Winter 1992.

HORNIG, SUSANNA
___ "Digital Delusions: Intelligent Computers in Science Fiction Film," in: Loukides, Paul and Fuller, Linda K., eds. **Beyond the Stars III: The Material World in American Popular Film.** Bowling Green, OH: Popular Press, 1993. pp.207-215.

HORNIGK, FRANK
___ "Die Literatur bliebt zuständig: Ein Versuch über das Verhältnis on Literatur, Utopie und Politik in der DDR--am Ende der DDR," *Germanic Review* 67(3): 99-105. Summer 1992.

HORSTMANN, ULRICH
___ "Walter M. Miller, **A Canticle for Leibowitz** (1959)," in: Heuermann, Harmut, ed. **Der Science Fiction Roman in der angloamerikanischen Literatur: Interpretationen**. Düsseldorf: Bagel, 1986. pp.182-195.

HOSKINSON, KEVIN
___ "**The Martian Chronicles** and **Fahrenheit 451**: Ray Bradbury's Cold War Novels," *Extrapolation* 36(4): 345-359. Winter 1995.

HOSTETTER, CARL F.
___ "A Mythology for England," by Carl F. Hostetter and Arden R. Smith. in: Reynolds, Patricia and GoodKnight, Glen H., eds. **Proceedings of the J. R. R. Tolkien Centenary Conference, Keble College, Oxford, 1992**. Altadena, CA: Mythopoeic Press, 1995. pp.281-290. (*Mythlore* Vol. 21, No. 2, Winter 1996, Whole No. 80)
___ "Stone Towers," by Carl F. Hostetter and Patrick Wynne. *Mythlore* 19(4): 47-55, 65. Autumn 1993. (No. 74)

HOTTOIS, GILBERT
___ " 'Language et technique' ou 'Du site philosophique de la Science-Fiction contemporaine'," in: Saccaro Del Buffa, Giuseppa and Lewis, Arthur O., eds. **Utopia e Modernita: Teorie e prassi utopiche nell'eta moderna e postmoderna**. Rome: Gangemi Editore, 1989. pp.519-528.

HOUGH, PETER
___ **Looking for the Aliens: A Psychological, Imaginative and Scientific Investigation**, by Peter Hough and Jenny Randles. London: Blandford, 1992. 241pp.

HOUGHTON, HAL
___ **Ripley, Believe It or Not: The 'Alien' Trilogy and the Image of Women in Science Fiction Film**. Master's Thesis, Mankato State University, 1993. 106pp.

HOUGRON, ALEXANDRA
___ "La couleur de l'Autre: Le rouge et le vert dans les films de science fiction," *Positif* No. 375: 143-146. May 1992.

HOULAHAN, MARK
___ "Cosmic Hamlets? Contesting Shakespeare in Federation Space," *Extrapolation* 36(1): 28-37. Spring 1995.

HOUPPERMANS, SJEF
___ "Fantastique Angélique," in: Harger-Grinling, Virginia and Chadwick, Tony, eds. **Robbe-Grillet and the Fantastic**. Westport, CT: Greenwood, 1994. pp.77-100.

HOVANA, ION
___ "Visioni urbanistiche ottocentesche in Romania," in: Saccaro Del Buffa, Giuseppa and Lewis, Arthur O., eds. **Utopia e Modernita: Teorie e prassi utopiche nell'eta moderna e postmoderna**. Rome: Gangemi Editore, 1989. pp.385-400.

HOWARD, ROBERT E.
___ "Bill Smalley and the Power of the Human Eye," *The Dark Man: The Journal of Robert E. Howard Studies* No. 2: 25-30. July 1991.

HOWARD, SCRIPPS
___ "*Waterworld* Inundated by Hawaiian Lawsuits," *Boston (MA) Herald*. August 2, 1995. in: *NewsBank. Film and Television*. 82:D6. 1995.

HOWARTH, DAVID A.
___ **The Technoculture of Cyberpunk Science Fiction and Its Publics: A Grounded Theory Analysis**. Master's Thesis, University of Delaware, 1995. 162pp.

HOWE, DAVID J.
___ "A British Phenomenon," in: Jones, Stephen, ed. **James Herbert: By Horror Haunted**. London: New English Library, 1992. pp.169-180.
___ " 'Creed': The Advertisement," in: Jones, Stephen, ed. **James Herbert: By Horror Haunted**. London: New English Library, 1992. pp.243-247.

HOWE, DAVID J. (continued)
___ **Doctor Who: The Sixties**. London: Doctor Who Books, 1992. 159pp.

HOWE, IRVING
___ "**1984**: Enigmas of Power," in: Bloom, Harold, ed. **George Orwell's 1984**. New York: Chelsea House, 1987. pp.95-108.

HOWE, ROBERT J.
___ "Basic Training: With Pen and Notebook," *The Report: The Fiction Writer's Magazine* No. 10: 20. Summer 1993.

HOWELL, CYNTHIA M.
___ **C. S. Lewis and the Twentieth Century: An Analysis of Out of the Silent Planet, Perelandra and That Hideous Strength**. Master's Thesis, Vanderbilt University, 1975. 78pp.

HOWELL, YVONNE H.
___ **Apocalyptic Realism: The Science Fiction of Arkady and Boris Strugatsky**. New York: Peter Lang, 1994. 184pp.
___ **Apocalyptic Realism: The Science Fiction of Arkady and Boris Strugatsky**. Ph.D. Dissertation, University of Michigan, 1990. 232pp.

HOWELLS, CORAL
___ "**Cat's Eye**: Elaine Risley's Retrospective Art," in: Nicholson, Colin, ed. **Margaret Atwood: Writing and Subjectivity: New Critical Essays**. New York: St. Martin's, 1994. pp.204-218.

HOWIE, LESLIE
___ "A Talk With John Varley," *Science Fiction Eye* No. 11: 96-98. December 1992.

HOWLETT, D. R.
___ "The Literary Context of Geoffrey of Monmouth: An Essay on the Fabrication of Sources," *Arthuriana* 5(3): 25-69. Fall 1995.

HRUSCHKA, JOHN
___ "Anne Sexton and Anima Transformations: Transformations as a Critique of the Psychology of Love in Grimm's Fairy Tales," *Mythlore* 20(1): 45-47. Winter 1994. (Whole No. 75)

HUBBARD, JANICE
___ "Commercial Spot: Reflects of the Dead," *Cinefex* No. 50: 82-83. May 1992.
___ "Commercial Spot: Simian Simulation," *Cinefex* No. 52: 9-10. November 1992.
___ "Commercial Spot: True Colors," *Cinefex* No. 53: 14-15. February 1993.

HUBBARD, L. RON
___ "Boos and Taboos," in: Wolverton, Dave, ed. **Writers of the Future, Vol. VIII**. Los Angeles, CA: Bridge, 1992. pp.41-48.

HUBERT, HAL
___ "Orbital Mechanics for Science Fiction Writers," *SFWA Bulletin* 26(4): 2-6. Winter 1993. (No. 118)
___ "Orbits, Quibbles, Maps, and Drawing With Satellites," *SFWA Bulletin* 27(2): 6-9. Summer 1993. (No. 120)

HUCKLE, PATRICIA
___ "Women in Utopia," in: Sullivan, E. D. S., ed. **The Utopian Vision**. San Diego, CA: San Diego University Press, 1983. pp.115-136.

HUFF, MARJORIE L.
___ **The Monomyth Pattern in Ursula K. Le Guin's Earthsea Trilogy**. Master's Thesis, Middle Tennessee State University, 1977. 164pp.

HUGHES, DAVE
___ "At Home With James Herbert," in: Jones, Stephen, ed. **James Herbert: By Horror Haunted**. London: New English Library, 1992. pp.43-46.
___ "The Golden Age of Plastic: Brian D'Amato Interview," *Interzone* No. 72: 39-41. June 1993.
___ "Jim Meets Gray," in: Jones, Stephen, ed. **James Herbert: By Horror Haunted**. London: New English Library, 1992. pp.267-270.
___ "Talking Fowler Language: Christopher Fowler Interview," *Interzone* No. 55: 19-22. January 1992.

HUGHES, IAN
___ "Selling a Bestseller," by Nick Sayers, Ian Hughes, David Singer and Tony Hammond. in: Jones, Stephen, ed. **James Herbert: By Horror Haunted**. London: New English Library, 1992. pp.199-207.

HUGHES, LINDA K.
___ "Illusion and Relation: Merlin as Image of the Artist in Tennyson, Doré, Burene-Jones, and Beardsley," in: Watson, Jeanie and Fries, Marueen, eds. **The Figure of Merlin in the Nineteenth and Twentieth Centuries**. Lewiston, NY: Mellen, 1989. pp.1-33.
___ "Teaching Tennyson: **Idylls of the King** as a Serial Poem," in: Fries, Maureen and Watson, Jeanie, eds. **Approaches to the Teaching of the Arthurian Tradition**. New York: Modern Language Association, 1992. pp.106-112.

HUGHES, MELINDA
___ "Dark Sisters and Light Sisters: Sister Doubles and the Search for Sisterhood in **The Mists of Avalon** and **The White Raven**," *Mythlore* 19(1): 24-28. Winter 1993. (No. 71)

HUGHES, MIKE
___ "Serling's Tales Continue to Haunt Us," *Boston (MA) Herald*. May 19, 1994. in: *NewsBank. Film and Television*. 60:B12. 1994.

HUGHES, MONICA
___ "Science Fiction as Myth and Metaphor," *ALAN Review* 19(3): 2-5. Spring 1992.

HULBERT, DAN
___ "Film Passes Baton to *Enterprise's* Heirs," *(Atlanta, GA) Journal*. November 17, 1994. in: *NewsBank. Film and Television*. 125:C12-C13. 1994.

HULL, ELIZABETH A.
___ "Asimov: Man Thinking," in: Sullivan, C. W., III. **Science Fiction for Young Readers**. Westport, CT: Greenwood, 1993. pp.47-64.
___ "Highlight of the 1994 Worldcon," *Science Fiction Chronicle* 16(2): 48-50. November/December 1994.

HULL, PETER R.
___ "Brannon Braga: First Best Destiny," *Star Trek: The Official Fan Club Magazine* No. 92: 30-31, 34. July/August 1993.
___ "Creation Salutes *Star Trek*, the Grand Slam Show," *Star Trek: The Official Fan Club Magazine* No. 92: 32-33. July/August 1993.
___ "Dreams Come True," *Star Trek: The Official Fan Club* No. 94: 46-47. February/March 1994.
___ "Exclusive Interview: Bob Justman, the Chief Engineer of *Star Trek*," *Star Trek: The Official Fan Club* No. 96: 46-48. April/May 1994.
___ "The Voice of Jeri Taylor: Multipart Harmony," *Star Trek: The Official Fan Club* No. 94: 44-45. February/March 1994.

HULL, RICHARD
___ "The Arthurian Legend in French Cinema: **Lancelot du Lac** and **Perceval la Gallois**," by Jeff Rider, Richard Hull and Christopher Smith. in: Harty, Kevin J., ed. **Cinema Arthuriana: Essays on Arthurian Film**. New York: Garland, 1991. pp.41-56.

HUME, KATHRYN
___ "Calvino's Fictions: Cogito and Cosmos," Oxford: Clarendon, 1992. 212pp.
___ "Repetition and the Construction of Character in **Gravity's Rainbow**," *Critique* 33(4): 243-254. Summer 1992.
___ "Science and Imagination in Calvino's **Cosmicomics**," *Mosaic* 15(4): 47-58. December 1982.

HUMPHREYS, BRIAN
___ " 'The Night Ocean' and the Subtleties of Cosmicism," *Lovecraft Studies* No. 30: 14-21. Spring 1994.
___ "Who or What Was Iranon?," *Lovecraft Studies* No. 25: 10-13. Fall 1991.

HUNGERFORD, EDWARD
___ "Poe and Phrenology (1930)," in: Budd, Louis J. and Cady, Edwin H., eds. **On Poe**. Durham, NC: Duke University Press, 1993. pp.1-23.

HUNT, LEON
___ "A (Sadistic) Night at the Opera: Notes on the Italian Horror Film," *Velvet Light Trap* 30: 65-75. 1992.

HUNT, PETER
___ " 'Coldtongue coldham coldbeef pickled gherkin salad frenchrolls cresssandwige spottedmeat gingerbeer lemonaide sodawater...' Fantastic Foods in the Books of Kenneth Grahame, Jerome K. Jerome, H. E. Bates, and Other Bakers of the Fantasy England," *Journal of the Fantastic in the Arts* 7(1): 5-22. 1996.

HUNT, SAMANTHA
___ "Undeathly Literature," *Voice of Youth Advocates* 18(3): 147. August 1995.

HUNTER, JEFFERSON
___ "Orwell, Wells, and **Coming Up for Air**," *Modern Philology* 78(1): 38-47. August 1980.

HUNTER, STEPHEN
___ "**Alien 3**: The Thrill Is Gone," *Baltimore (MD) Sun*. May 22, 1992. in: *NewsBank. Film and Television*. 49:C3-C4. 1992.
___ "As Cosmic Battles Go, Kombat's Merely Mortal," *(Baltimore, MD) Sun*. August 19, 1995. in: *NewsBank. Film and Television*. 79:B14. 1995.
___ "Boys Play Soldier and Director in Raimi's Juvenile **Army of Darkness**," *Baltimore (MD) Sun*. February 19, 1993 in: *NewsBank. Film and Television*. 20:C12. 1993
___ "**Brainscan** Is a No-Brainer: Don't Bother," *(Baltimore, MD) Sun*. April 22, 1994. in: *NewsBank. Film and Television*. 41:B7. 1994.
___ "Bring on the Apocalypse, But Spare Us the Travail of **Tank Girl**," *(Baltimore, MD) Sun*. March 31, 1995. in: *NewsBank. Film and Television*. 50:C3. 1995.
___ "Devilishly Bad Movie Gives No Reason to **Stay Tuned** (Review)," *Baltimore (MD) Sun*. August 15, 1992. in: *NewsBank. Film and Television*. 84:A8. 1992.
___ "**Dracula**: The Old Boy Never Looked So Good," *Baltimore (MD) Sun*. November 13, 1992. in: *NewsBank. Film and Television*. 111:B5-B6. 1992.
___ "**Encino Man** Is Primitive Entertainment, From Plot to Message (Review)," *Baltimore (MD) Sun*. May 22, 1992. in: *NewsBank. Film and Television*. 52:C13. 1992.
___ "The End Is Not Near Enough," *(Baltimore, MD) Sun*. October 13, 1995. in: *NewsBank. Film and Television*. 99:C5-C6. 1995.
___ "Generations Has Gaps, But Picard and Co. Are Stellar," *(Baltimore, MD) Sun*. November 18, 1994. in: *NewsBank. Film and Television*. 125: D6. 1994.
___ "**The Hand That Rocks the Cradle** (Review)," *Chicago (IL) Sun Times*. January 10, 1992. in: *NewsBank. Film and Television*. 12:B12-B13. 1992.
___ "Hauer Hams His Way Through an Interminable **Split Second** (Review)," *Baltimore (MD) Sun*. May 1, 1992. in: *NewsBank. Film and Television*. 58:G9. 1992.
___ "In **Robocop 3**, This Man of Steel Has Lost His Edge (Review)," *Baltimore (MD) Sun*. November 5, 1993. in: *NewsBank. Art*. 32:E2. 1993.
___ "**Lawnmower Man** Is a Visual Treat (Review)," *Baltimore (MD) Sun*. March 7, 1992. in: *NewsBank. Film and Television*. 33:A5. 1992.
___ "More Jagger, Less Estevez Might Have Pumped More Life into Feeble **Freejack** (Review)," *Baltimore (MD) Sun*. January 21, 1992. in: *NewsBank. Film and Television*. 11:D7. 1992.
___ "**Naked Lunch** Celebrates the Un-hip in a Plain Brown Suit (Review)," *Baltimore (MD) Sun*. February 13, 1992. in: *NewsBank. Film and Television*. 23:G8. 1992.
___ "New Cut of **Blade Runner** Is as Provocative and Befuddling as Before," *Baltimore (MD) Sun*. September 11, 1992. in: *NewsBank. Film and Television*. 87:F10. 1992.
___ "**No Escape** Is a Mad Mix of Too Many Future Fantasy Movie Styles," *(Baltimore, MD) Sun*. April 29, 1994. in: *NewsBank. Film and Television*. 46:E3. 1994.
___ "**The Puppet Masters** Has the Soul of a 1950s Monster B-Movie," *(Baltimore, MD) Sun*. October 25, 1994. in: *NewsBank. Film and Television*. 114:F8. 1994.
___ "Riding the Information Highway to the Killing Fields," *(Baltimore, MD) Sun*. August 3, 1995. in: *NewsBank. Film and Television*. 82:C2. 1995.

HUNTER, STEPHEN (continued)
___ "The Small-Minded *Stargate* Goes Nowhere Fast," *Baltimore (MD) Sun.* October 29, 1994. in: *NewsBank. Film and Television.* 115: G9. 1994.
___ "Spielberg's Dinosaurs Elevate *Jurassic Park* in Classic Monster Movie (Review)," *Baltimore (MD) Sun.* June 10, 1993. in: *NewsBank. Literature.* 15:C12C13. 1993.
___ "Spielberg's Revisonist Look at Peter Pan Isn't Enough *Hook* to Hang a New Movie On (Review)," *Baltimore (MD) Sun.* December 11, 1991. in: *NewsBank. Film and Television.* 3:F7. 1992.
___ "Stallone's Newest Isn't That Good, But Isn't Dreadful," *(Baltimore, MD) Sun.* June 30, 1995. in: *NewsBank. Film and Television.* 63:A13. 1995.
___ "*Star Trek VI* Latest Adventure Soars With Action and Fun," *Baltimore (MD) Sun.* December 6, 1991. in: *NewsBank. Film and Television.* 7:E1-E2. 1992.
___ "Steamy Scenes Fail to Cover Very Thin Plot," *Baltimore (MD) Sun* March 20, 1992 in: *NewsBank. Film and Television.* 29:B6. 1992.
___ "Streep, Hawn Laugh in the Face of Death (Review)," *Baltimore (MD) Sun.* July 31, 1992. in: *NewsBank. Film and Television.* 78:D8. 1992.
___ "Swords Keep Clanking, But Third Time for *Highlander* Is No Charm," *(Baltimore, MD) Sun.* January 28, 1995. in: *NewsBank. Film and Television.* 17:C11. 1995.
___ "*Timecop* Doesn't Really Know What Time It Is," *(Baltimore, MD) Sun.* September 16, 1994. in: *NewsBank. Film and Television.* 105:D3. 1994.
___ "TV Reporter Saves the World from *Hellraisers* in NYC (Review)," *Baltimore (MD) Sun.* September 12, 1992. in: *NewsBank. Film and Television.* 91:A9. 1992.
___ "The Vampire Hasn't Been Born Whose Fangs Are a Match for a Valley Girl," *Baltimore (MD) Sun.* July 31, 1992. in: *NewsBank. Film and Television.* 77:C3. 1992
___ "*Waterworld* Isn't Sinking, But It Won't Soar," *(Baltimore, MD) Sun.* August 6, 1995. in: *NewsBank. Film and Television.* 82:D2-D3. 1995.

HUNTINGTON, JOHN
___ "Authenticity and Insincerity," in: Mullen, R. D., ed. **On Philip K. Dick: 40 Articles From Science-Fiction Studies**. Terre Haute, IN: SF-TH Inc., 1992. pp.170-177.
___ "Newness, **Neuromancer**, and the End of Narrative," in: Slusser, George E. and Shippey, Tom, eds. **Fiction 2000: Cyberpunk and the Future of Narrative**. Athens: University of Georgia Press, 1992. pp.133-141.
___ "**The Time Machine** and Wells's Social Trajectory," *Foundation* No. 65: 6-15. Autumn 1995.

HUNTSINGER, LYNN
___ "The Matrix, Cyberpunk Literature, and the Apolyptic Landscapes of Information Technology," by Paul F. Starrs and Lynn Huntsinger. *Information Technology and Libraries* 14(4): 251-257. December 1995. (Cited from *IAC Insite* on-line service.)

HURST, JASON
___ "Art and Metaphysics at Party-time: SMS Interviewed," by Andy Robertson and Jason Hurst. *Interzone* No. 100: 22-26. October 1995.

HURST, LESLIE J.
___ "Asimov: A Man and His Work," *Vector* No. 167: 8-9. June/July 1992

HUTCHISON, DAVID
___ "**The Muppet's Christmas Carol**," *Starlog* No. 186: 32-34. January 1993.
___ "Rescues at Sea Trek," *Starlog* No. 196: 50-51. November 1993.

HUTTAR, CHARLES A.
___ "Tolkien, Epic Traditions and Golden Age Myths," in: Filmer, Kath, ed. **Twentieth-Century Fantasists: Essays in Culture, Society and Belief in Twentieth Century Mythopoeic Literature**. New York: St. Martin's, 1992. pp.92-107.

HYDE, BOB
___ "The Prez Sez: ERB, You Should Have Been There!," *Burroughs Bulletin* NS. No. 15: 33-36. July 1993.

HYDE, DAVE
___ "Can We All Get Along?," *Radio Free P.K.D.* No. 1: 6-7. February 1993.

HYDE, PAUL N.
___ "Dances With Dusei: A Personal Response to C. J. Cherryh's **The Faded Sun**," *Mythlore* 18(2): 45-53. Spring 1992. (No. 68)
___ "Quenti Lambardillion: Snuffling out Footsteps; A Translation at Risk," *Mythlore* 18(2): 23-27. Spring 1992. (No. 68)
___ "Quenti Lambardillion: The Gondolinic Runes: Another Picture," *Mythlore* 18(3): 20-25. Summer 1992. (No. 69)

HYNES, JOSEPH
___ "Doris Lessing's Briefing as Structural Life and Death," *Renascence* 46(4): 225-246. Summer 1994.

IACCINO, JAMES F.
___ **Psychological Reflections on Cinematic Terror: Jungian Archetypes in Horror Films**. Westport, CT: Praeger, 1994. 217pp.

IKIN, VAN
___ "Clarke as Constructor: Thoughts About Arthur C. Clarke's **Astounding Days** and **The Ghost From the Grand Banks**," *Science Fiction: A Review of Speculative Literature* 12(1): 9-14. 1993. (Whole No. 34)
___ "Here There Be Monsters: Some Idiosyncrasies of Science Fiction Bibliography in Australia," *Bibliographical Society of Australia nad New Zealand Bulletin* 16(4): 149-153. Fourth Quarter 1992.

IMBROSCIO, CARMELINA
___ "Elementi de rovesciamento speculare nella narrativa utopica del settecento francese," in: Saccaro Del Buffa, Giuseppa and Lewis, Arthur O., eds. **Utopia e Modernita: Teorie e prassi utopiche nell'eta moderna e postmoderna**. Rome: Gangemi Editore, 1989. pp.533-540.

IMDIEKE, SANDRA A.
___ **Characters in Time Travel as Historical Guides**, by Sandra A. Imdieke and Lynn Madaus. ERIC ED 305601. 9pp. 1992.

INDICK, BEN P.
___ **George Alec Effinger: From Entrophy to Buyadeen**. San Bernardino, CA: Borgo Press, 1994. 96pp.
___ "H. Russell Wakefield: The Man Who Believed in Ghosts," in: Schweitzer, Darrell, ed. **Discovering Classic Horror Fiction I**. Mercer Island, WA: Starmont, 1992. pp.73-93.
___ "Long, Frank Belknap: In Memoriam," *Lovecraft Studies* No. 30: 3-4. Spring 1994.
___ "Robert Bloch: A Personal Memory," *Studies in Weird Fiction* No. 16: 2-4. Winter 1995.
___ "Villain, Vaudevillian and Saint," in: **Shiel in Diverse Hands: A Collection of Essays**. Cleveland, OH: Reynolds Morse Foundation, 1983. pp.357-368.

INFUSINO, DIVINA
___ "Paranoid About the Paranormal," *TV Guide* 42(3): 20-21. January 15, 1994.

INGEBRETSON, EDWARD J.
___ "A. E. Van Vogt," in: Bruccoli, Matthew J., ed. **Facts on File Bibliography of American Fiction 1919-1988**. New York: Facts on File, 1991. pp.513-515.
___ "Robert A. Heinlein," in: Bruccoli, Matthew J., ed. **Facts on File Bibliography of American Fiction 1919-1988**. New York: Facts on File, 1991. pp.235-237.

INGERSOLL, EARL G.
___ "Describing This Beautiful and Nasty Planet (Interview, 1994)," in: Ingersoll, Earl G., ed. **Doris Lessing: Conversations**. Princeton, NJ: Ontario Review Press, 1994. pp.228-240.
___ "Margaret Atwood's **The Handmaid's Tale**: Echoes of Orwell," *Journal of the Fantastic in the Arts* 5(4): 64-72. 1993. (No. 20)
___ (ed.) **Doris Lessing: Conversations**. Princeton, NJ: Ontario Review Press, 1994. 248pp.

INGLE, STEPHEN
___ **George Orwell: A Political Life**. Manchester, Eng.: Manchester University Press, 1993. 146pp.

INGS, SIMON
___ "The Future: Disguising the Real," *Focus* (BSFA) No. 25: 12-13. December/January 1994.

INNERHOFER, ROLAND
___ "Flugphantasien. Die Luftfahrt bei Jules Verne und im deutschen technischen Zukunftsroman vom ausgehenden 19. Jahrhundert bis 1914. 1. Teil," *Quarber Merkur* 30(1): 47-68. June 1992. (No. 77)
___ "Flugphantasien. Die Luftfahrt bei Jules Verne und im deutschen technischen Zukunftsroman vom ausgehenden 19. Jahrhundert bis 1914. 2. Teil und Schluß," *Quarber Merkur* 30(2): 14-46. December 1992. (No. 78)
___ "Katastrophenbilder," *Quarber Merkur* 31(1): 53-71. June 1993. (No. 79)

IRVING, JAMES A.
___ **The World Makers: Techniques of Fantasy in J. R. R. Tolkien's The Lord of the Rings and Ursula K. Le Guin's Earthsea Trilogy**. Master's Thesis, Acadia University, 1976. 128pp.

IRWIN, JOHN T.
___ "A Clew to the Clue: Locked Rooms and Labyrinths in Poe and Borges," in: Rosenheim, Shawn and Rachman, Stephen, ed. **The American Face of Edgar Allan Poe**. Baltimore: Johns Hopkins University Press, 1995. pp.139-154.

IRWIN, ROBERT
___ "Fantasy Without God," *Times Literary Supplement* 4770: 7. September 2, 1994.
___ "From Science Future to a Fantasy Past," *Antiquity* 69(263): June 1995.

IVANOV, BORIS
___ "SF in Russia," by Yuri Shervatykh and Boris Ivanov. *Locus* 35(3): 54. September 1993.

IWAO, SUMIKO
___ "*The Day After* in Japan," in: Wober, J. Mallory, ed. **Television and Nuclear Power: Making the Public Mind**. Norwood, NJ: Ablex, 1992. pp.67-76.

JACKSON, H. JEROME
___ "Sci-Fi Tales From Octavia E. Butler," *Crisis* (NAACP) 101(3): 4-5. April 1994.

JACKSON, KEVIN
___ "The Good, the Bad, and the Ugly," *Sight and Sound* 2(3): 10-11. July 1992.
___ "Gothic Shadows," *Sight and Sound* 2(7): 16-19. 1992. [Not seen.]
___ "The Trappings of Disaster: Sci-Fi's Bygone Dystopias," *Sight and Sound* 3(5): 38-39. May 1993.

JACKSON, LESLIE
___ **65 Years in Science Fiction, 1928-1993: A Jack Williamson Bibliography**. Portales: NM: Golden Library, Eastern New Mexico University, 1993. 35pp.

JACOB, MERLE L.
___ **To Be Continued: An Annotated Guide to Sequels**, by Merle L. Jacob and Hope Apple. Phoenix, AZ: Oryx, 1995. 364pp.

JACOBS, DAWNELLEN
___ **Enemies of the Rational Soul: Confrontations With the World, the Flesh, and the Devil in Selected Works of Science Fiction, Fantasy, and Literature of the Fantastic**. Ph.D. Dissertation, University of California, Riverside, 1993. 258pp. (DAI-A 54/07, p. 2567. January 1994.)

JACOBS, NAOMI
___ "The Frozen Landscape in Women's Utopian and Science Fiction," in: Donawerth, Jane L. and Kolmerten, Carol A., eds. **Utopian and Science Fiction by Women: Worlds of Difference**. Syracuse, NY: Syracuse University Press, 1994. pp.190-202.
___ "**Islandia**: Plotting Utopian Desire," *Utopian Studies* 6(2): 75-89. 1995.

JACOBS, SUSAN T.
___ "When Formula Seizes Form: Oscar Wilde's Comedies," in: Murphy, Patrick D., ed. **Staging the Impossible: The Fantastic Mode in Modern Drama**. Westport, CT: Greenwood, 1992. pp.15-29.

JACOBS, TOM
___ "Bill & Ted Redux Is Certainly a Blast," *Los Angeles (CA) Daily News*. July 19, 1991. in: *NewsBank. Film and Television*. 65:E8. 1991.
___ "*Hook* and the Child Within Spielberg (Review)," *Los Angeles (CA) Daily News*. December 11, 1991. in: *NewsBank. Film and Television*. 3: E12. 1992.
___ "*Prospero's Books* Should Stir A Tempest of Artistic Acclaim (Review)," *Los Angeles (CA) Daily News*. November 27, 1991. in: *NewsBank. Film and Television*. 6:D1. 1992.

JAGO, WENDY
___ "**A Wizard of Earthsea** and the Charge of Escapism," *Children's Literature in Education* 8: 21-29. July 1972.

JAKAITIS, JAKE
___ "Ridley Scott and Philip K. Dick," in: Mullen, R. D., ed. **On Philip K. Dick: 40 Articles From Science-Fiction Studies**. Terre Haute, IN: SF-TH Inc., 1992. pp.278-282.
___ "Two Cases of Conscience: Loyalty and Race in **The Crack in Space** and **Counter-Clock World**," in: Umland, Samuel J., ed. **Philip K. Dick: Contemporary Critical Interpretations**. Westport, CT: Greenwood, 1995. pp.169-196.

JAKUBOWSKI, MAXIM
___ "Introduction," by Maxim Jakubowski and Edward James. in: Jakubowski, Maxim and James, Edward, eds. **The Profession of Science Fiction**. New York: St. Martin's, 1992. pp.1-11.
___ (ed.) **The Profession of Science Fiction: SF Writers on Their Craft and Ideas**, ed. by Maxim Jakubowski and Edward James. New York: St. Martin's, 1992. 208pp.

JAMES, CARYN
___ "**Batman Returns** With a Capeload of Angst and Ills," *New York Times* Sec. 2, pp.11, 14. June 28, 1992.
___ "Old Hollywood Horror, But With Depth and Flair," *New York Times* Sec. C, p. 3. July 2, 1993.

JAMES, E. R.
___ "Shake the Invisible Hand," *Vector* No. 166: 17. April/May 1992.

JAMES, EDWARD
___ "Introduction," by Maxim Jakubowski and Edward James. in: Jakubowski, Maxim and James, Edward, eds. **The Profession of Science Fiction**. New York: St. Martin's, 1992. pp.1-11.
___ "Science Fiction by Gaslight: An Introduction to English-Language Science Fiction in the Nineteenth Century," in: Seed, David, ed. **Anticipations: Essays on Early Science Fiction and Its Precursors**. Liverpool: Liverpool University Press, 1995. pp.26-45.
___ "Science Fiction Courses in Higher Education in Great Britain: A Preliminary Guide," by Edward James and Farah Mendlesohn. *Foundation* No. 59: 59-69. Autumn 1993.
___ **Science Fiction in the 20th Century**. Oxford, New York: Oxford University Press, 1994. 250pp.
___ (ed.) **The Profession of Science Fiction: SF Writers on Their Craft and Ideas**, ed. by Maxim Jakubowski and Edward James. New York: St. Martin's, 1992. 208pp.

JAMES, KENNETH
___ "The Kenneth James Interview," in: Delany, Samuel R. **Silent Interviews on Language, Race, Sex, Science Fiction and Some Comics**. Hanover, NH: Wesleyan University Press, 1994. pp.233-249.

JAMES, LOUIS
___ "From Robinson to Robina, and Beyond: **Robinson Crusoe** as a Utopian Concept," in: Kumar, Krishan and Bann, Stephen, eds. **Utopias and the Millennium**. London: Reaktion Books, 1993. pp.33-45.

JAMES, MARTIN
___ "Banks Statement," *Melody Maker* 72(37): 10. September 16, 1995.

JAMES, MICHAEL
___ "Protest of **Basic Instinct** Silenced at the Rotunda," *Baltimore (MD) Sun* March 21, 1992 in: *NewsBank. Film and Television.* 29:A4. 1992.

JAMES, NICK
___ "**Judge Dredd** (Review)," *Sight and Sound* 5(9): 55-56. September 1995.

JAMESON, FREDERIC
___ "After Armageddon: Character Systems in **Dr. Bloodmoney**," in: Mullen, R. D., ed. **On Philip K. Dick: 40 Articles From Science-Fiction Studies.** Terre Haute, IN: SF-TH Inc., 1992. pp.26-36.
___ "Generic Discontinuities in SF: Brian Aldiss' **Starship**," *Chung Wai Literary Quarterly* 22(12): May 1994. (Issue not seen; pagination unavailable.)

JAMESON, SARA
___ "Ursula K. Le Guin: A Galaxy of Books and Laurels," *Publishers Weekly* 242(39): 32-33. September 25, 1995.

JANCOVICH, MARK
___ **Horror.** London: Batsford, 1992. 128pp.
___ "Modernity and Subjectivity in **The Terminator**," *Velvet Light Trap* 30: 3-17. 1992. [Not seen.]

JANKIEWICZ, PAT
___ "Auteur of Zetar," *Starlog* 179: 92-95. June 1992.
___ "Baby Boomer," *Starlog* 181: 48-51, 69. August 1992.
___ "Bard of the Black Lagoon," *Starlog* No. 197: 21-24, 81. December 1993.
___ "Bloody Double," *Starlog* No. 209: 59-62. December 1994.
___ "Borg to Be Wild," *Starlog* No. 201: 36-39. April 1994.
___ "Captain of Television," *Starlog* 179: 73-76. June 1992.
___ "Chris Barnes, the Spectacular Spiderman," *Starlog* No. 213: 52-55. April 1995.
___ "Detective Story," *Starlog* No. 198: 50-51. January 1994.
___ "The Gamesters People Play," *Starlog* 180: 51-55. July 1992.
___ "Ghost, the Rapist," *Starlog* No. 216: 36-39. July 1995.
___ "**Godzilla**, American Style," *Starlog* No. 193: 55. August 1993.
___ "The Good, the Bad, and the Plastic," *Starlog* No. 218: 50-51. September 1995.
___ "Incident of the Nine," *Starlog* No. 192: 76-80. July 1993.
___ "Man and Pakled," *Starlog* No. 187: 54-56, 72. February 1993.
___ "Masks of Time," *Starlog* No. 206: 40-45. September 1994.
___ "Most Wanted: The Klingon Kid," *Starlog* No. 194: 58-61. September 1993.
___ "Mr. Expendable," *Starlog* No. 191: 62-64. June 1993.
___ "Pluto's Stepdaughter," *Starlog* No. 220: 50-53. November 1995.
___ "Present at the Creation," *Starlog* No. 191: 75-79. June 1993.
___ "Star of Zetar," *Starlog* No. 199: 58-60. February 1994.
___ "Stunt Alien," *Starlog* No. 209: 64-65. December 1994.
___ "Time of the Green," *Starlog* No. 204: 72-76. July 1994.

JANKUS, HANK
___ "Has Success Spoiled Stephen King?," *Shayol* No. 6: 17-19. 1982.
___ "Interview: Thomas Blackshear," *Shayol* No. 7: 16-18. 1985.

JARMAN, A. O. H.
___ "The Merlin Legend and the Welsh Tradition of Prophecy," in: Bromwich, Rachel, Jarman, A. O. H. and Roberts, Brynley F., eds. **The Arthur of the Welsh.** Cardiff: University of Wales Press, 1991. pp.117-146.
___ (ed.) **The Arthur of the Welsh: The Arthurian Legend in Medieval Welsh Literature**, ed. by Rachel Bromwich, A. O. H. Jarman and Brynley F. Roberts. Cardiff: University of Wales Press, 1991. 310pp.

JARVIS, JEFF
___ "The Couch Critic: **Earth 2**," *TV Guide* 42(50): 12. December 10, 1994.
___ "The Couch Critic: Space," *TV Guide* 43(38): 8. September 23, 1995.
___ "Hits and Misses: **Robocop**," *TV Guide* 42(11): 53. March 12, 1994.
___ "Moon Struck," by Jeff Jarvis, James Reston, Jr., Glenn Kenny and Penelope Patsuris. *TV Guide* 42(29): 10-16. July 16, 1994.

JARZEBSKI, JERZY
___ (ed.) **Lem w oczach krytyki swiatowej** (Lem in the Eyes of World Criticism). Cracow: Wydawnictwo Literackie, 1989. (Not seen. Cf. *Science-Fiction Studies*, Nov. 1992.)

JAWORZYN, STEFAN
___ "Big Climaxes and Movie Bullshit," in: Jones, Stephen, ed. **James Herbert: By Horror Haunted**. London: New English Library, 1992. pp.249-266.

JEAN, LORRAINE A.
___ "Poul Anderson," in: Bruccoli, Matthew J., ed. **Facts on File Bibliography of American Fiction 1919-1988.** New York: Facts on File, 1991. pp.53-55.
___ "Ursula K. Le Guin," in: Bruccoli, Matthew J., ed. **Facts on File Bibliography of American Fiction 1919-1988.** New York: Facts on File, 1991. pp.288-290.

JEAPES, BEN
___ "Jules Verne's **Twenty Thousand Leagues Under the Sea**," *Vector* No. 184: 10-12. Summer 1995.
___ "Orson Scott Card: An Appreciation," *Vector* No. 168: 8-11. August/ September 1992.

JEEVES, TERRY
___ "British Fandom," in: Sanders, Joe, ed. **Science Fiction Fandom**. Westport, CT: Greenwood, 1994. pp.113-118.

JEHMLICH, REIMER
___ "Aldous Huxley, **Ape and Essence** (1948)," in: Heuermann, Harmut, ed. **Der Science Fiction Roman in der angloamerikanischen Literatur: Interpretationen**. Düsseldorf: Bagel, 1986. pp.101-117.

JENKINS, HENRY
___ "At Other Times, Like Females: Gender and **Star Trek** Fiction," in: Tulloch, John and Jenkins, Henry, eds. **Science Fiction Audiences: Watching Doctor Who and Star Trek**. New York: Routledge, 1995. pp.196-212.
___ "Beyond the **Star Trek** Phenomenon: Reconceptualizing the Science Fiction Audience," by Henry Jenkins and John Tulloch. in: Tulloch, John and Jenkins, Henry, eds. **Science Fiction Audiences: Watching Doctor Who and Star Trek**. New York: Routledge, 1995. pp.3-24.
___ "How Many Starfleet Officers Does It Take to Change a Lightbulb?: **Star Trek** at MIT," by Henry Jenkins and Greg Dancer. in: Tulloch, John and Jenkins, Henry, eds. **Science Fiction Audiences: Watching Doctor Who and Star Trek**. New York: Routledge, 1995. pp.213-236.
___ "Infinite Diversity in Infinite Combinations: Genre and Authorship in **Star Trek**," in: Tulloch, John and Jenkins, Henry, eds. **Science Fiction Audiences: Watching Doctor Who and Star Trek**. New York: Routledge, 1995. pp.175-195.
___ "Out of the Closet and into the Universe: Queers and **Star Trek**," in: Tulloch, John and Jenkins, Henry, eds. **Science Fiction Audiences: Watching Doctor Who and Star Trek**. New York: Routledge, 1995. pp.237-265.

JENKINSON, DAVE
___ "Portrait: Welwyn Wilton Katz," *Emergency Librarian* 21(2): 61-62. November/December 1993.
___ "Welwyn Wilton Katz: Author of Award Winning Fantasy," *Emergency Librarian* 21(2): 61-65. November/December 1993.

JENNINGS, LEE B.
___ "Woman as Reality Demarcator in Three Tales of E. T. A. Hoffman," in: Latham, Robert A. and Collins, Robert A., eds. **Modes of the Fantastic**. Westport, CT: Greenwood, 1995. pp.122-127.

JENSEN, ELIZABETH
___ "Aye, Chihuahua! **Ren and Stimpy** to Air New Shows Later This Month," *New York (NY) Daily News*. October 5, 1992. in: *NewsBank. Film and Television.* 106:E13-E14. 1992.
___ "Latest **Star Trek** Spinoff of Spinoff Starts at Warp Speed," *Wall Street Journal* p. B7. January 7, 1993.
___ "Sci-Fi Channel Will Debut in the Fall," by Elizabeth Jensen and George Maksian. *Austin (TX) American Statesman* Sec. B, p. 4. April 2, 1992.

JENSEN, JEFF
___ "Invasion of the Sci-Fi Marketers," *Advertising Age* 65(49): 1-2. November 21, 1994.

JESS, DAVID J.
___ "On Low-Tech Cyborgs," in: Gray, Chris H., ed. **The Cyborg Handbook**. New York: Routledge, 1995. pp.371-377.

JOHNSON, BARBARA
___ "Strange Fits: Poe and Wordsworth on the Nature of Poetic Language," in: Rosenheim, Shawn and Rachman, Stephen, ed. **The American Face of Edgar Allan Poe**. Baltimore: Johns Hopkins University Press, 1995. pp.37-48.

JOHNSON, BARRY
___ "*Basic Instinct*: Fast Cars, Hot Sex Spell Likely Profits, Lesbian Protests," *Portand (OR) The Oregonian*. March 20, 1992 in: *NewsBank. Film and Television*. 29:B11. 1992.
___ "The Bat and the Cat," *Portland (OR) The Oregonian*. June 19, 1992. in: *NewsBank. Film and Television*. 62:F14-G1. 1992.
___ "Captains Courageous," *Portland (OR) The Oregonian*. November 18, 1994. in: *NewsBank. Film and Television*. 125:D9-D10. 1994.
___ "*Delicatessen* a Good Film to Gobble Up (Review)," *Portland (OR) The Oregonian*. May 8, 1992. in: *NewsBank. Film and Television*. 51: G1. 1992.
___ "*Encino Man* Is Like Totally Bogus (Review)," *Portland (OR) The Oregonian*. May 25, 1992. in: *NewsBank. Film and Television*. 52:D3. 1992.
___ "Journey to Nowhere," *Portland (OR) The Oregonian*. October 28, 1994. in: *NewsBank. Film and Television*. 125:E3. 1994.
___ "Protestors Will Follow Instinct," *Portland (OR) The Oregonian* March 21, 1992 in: *NewsBank. Film and Television*. 29:A8. 1992.
___ "*Timecop* Familiar But Smooth Sci-Fi," *Portland (OR) The Oregonian*. September 16, 1994. in: *NewsBank. Film and Television*. 105:D8. 1994.

JOHNSON, BRIAN D.
___ "Mind Games With William Gibson," *Maclean's* 108(23): 60-64. June 5, 1995.

JOHNSON, EDWIN G.
___ "Teleoperators and Human Augmentation," by Edwin G. Johnson and William R. Corliss. in: Gray, Chris H., ed. **The Cyborg Handbook**. New York: Routledge, 1995. pp.83-92.

JOHNSON, JOHN
___ **Fantastic Cinema Subject Guide: A Topical Index to 2500 Horror, Science Fiction, and Fantasy Films**, by Bryan Senn and John Johnson. Jefferson, NC: McFarland, 1992. 682pp.

JOHNSON, JUDITH E.
___ "Women and Vampires: Nightmare or Utopia?," *Kenyon Review* 15(1): 72-80. Winter 1993.

JOHNSON, KIM H.
___ "*Body Snatchers*," *Starlog* 185: 50-53, 72. December 1992.
___ "Bug Hunt," *Starlog* No. 189: 40-43, 64. April 1993.
___ "Conehead Comics," *Starlog* No. 202: 38-39, 68. May 1994.
___ "Down in Front," *Starlog* No. 210: 54-58. January 1995.
___ "Drill Sergeant to the Stars," *Starlog* 182: 52-55. September 1992.
___ "The Fantastic Realist," *Starlog* No. 200: 44-47, 90. March 1994.
___ "*Forever Young*," *Starlog* No. 186: 44-47. January 1993.
___ "Galactica 1995," *Starlog* No. 220: 36-39. November 1995.
___ "Giant Lizards With Big Guns," *Starlog* No. 193: 38-41, 72. August 1993.
___ "Hard Time," *Starlog* No. 207: 32-35. October 1994.
___ "The Human Touch," *Starlog* No. 192: 48-57. July 1993.
___ "In the Light of **The Shadow Moon**," *Starlog* No. 219: 38-41. October 1995.
___ "Knight Shift," *Starlog* No. 214: 78-81. May 1995.
___ "Lost in Babylon," by Jean Airey and Kim H. Johnson. *Starlog* No. 214: 32-35, 70. May 1995.
___ "*Mars Attacks* Again," *Starlog* No. 203: 38-41. June 1994.
___ "Matters of Identity," *Starlog* No. 190: 60-61. May 1993.
___ "Memories Can't Wait," *Starlog* No. 216: 50-53, 64. July 1995.
___ "Mission Control," *Starlog* No. 217: 40-45, 66. August 1995.
___ "Parallel Excitement," *Starlog* No. 215: 32-35. June 1995.

JOHNSON, KIM H. (continued)
___ "Resurrected Warriors," *Starlog* 178: 75-81. May 1992.
___ "Return to *Star Wars*," by Kim H. Johnson and Hank Kanalz. *Starlog* No. 175: 32-35. February 1992.
___ "Rime of the Future Mariner," *Starlog* No. 218: 40-44. September 1995.
___ "Robodirector," *Starlog* 181: 56-58. August 1992.
___ "Rogue Trooper," *Starlog* 182: 42-45. September 1992.
___ "Sleep No More," *Starlog* No. 189: 75-77. April 1993.
___ "Super-Soldier," *Starlog* 181: 36-39. August 1992.
___ "*Tank Girl*," *Starlog* No. 213: 40-43. April 1995.
___ "Tank Mechanic," *Starlog* No. 214: 46-49. May 1995.
___ "Tarzan," *Starlog* 177: 25-27, 71. April 1992.
___ "This Year's **Robocop**," *Starlog* No. 197: 38-41. December 1993.
___ "*Timecop*," in: McDonnell, David, ed. **Starlog's Science Fiction Heroes and Heroines**. New York: Crescent Books, 1995. pp.90-92.
___ "True Documentation," *Starlog* No. 189: 52-53. April 1993.
___ "Universes Lost," *Starlog* No. 210: 27-31, 69. January 1995.

JOHNSON, MALCOLM
___ "Barren **Species** Barely Fit for Survival," *Hartford (CT) Courant*. July 7, 1995. in: *NewsBank. Film and Television*. 72:A2. 1995.
___ "Bill & Ted Yuk It Up With Grim Reaper," *Hartford (CT) Courant*. July 19, 1991. in: *NewsBank. Film and Television*. 65:E12. 1991.
___ "*Cain* Is a Mixed-up Movie About One Confused Guy (Review)," *Hartford (CT) Courant*. August 7, 1992. in: *NewsBank. Film and Television*. 83:A10. 1992.
___ "Coppola's **Dracula** a Flashy but Hollow Version of a Classic," *Hartford (CT) Courant*. November 13, 1992. in: *NewsBank. Film and Television*. 111:A13-A14. 1992.
___ "Cronenberg's **Lunch** Is Intriguing But Mechanical (Review)," *Hartford (CT) Courant*. January 10, 1992. in: *NewsBank. Film and Television*. 13:G12. 1992.
___ "Dark Ages Time-Travel Horror Film Brandishes Action Aplenty to Please 13-Year-Olds," *Hartford (CT) Courant*. February 19, 1993 in: *NewsBank. Film and Television*. 20:C11. 1993
___ "A Delicious Vision of the Future (Review)," *Hartford (CT) Courant*. June 19, 1992. in: *NewsBank. Film and Television*. 63:E3. 1992.
___ " 'Demolition' Roll to a Crash Finish (Review)," *Hartford (CT) Courant*. October 9, 1993. in: *NewsBank. Art*. 28:B13. 1993.
___ "Despite Gems From the Bard, **Trek** May Leave You Bored (Review)," *Hartford (CT) Courant*. December 7, 1991. in: *NewsBank. Film and Television*. 7:D11-D12. 1991.
___ "Despite Good Makeup Job, **Death Becomes Her** an Unflattering Concept (Review)," *Hartford (CT) Courant*. July 31, 1992. in: *NewsBank. Film and Television*. 68:F11-F12. 1992.
___ "**Encino Man**: Just Hope There's Never a Sequel (Review)," *Hartford (CT) Courant*. May 22, 1992. in: *NewsBank. Film and Television*. 52:C11. 1992.
___ "A Giant Leap for Van Damme in **Timecop**," *Hartford (CT) Courant*. September 16, 1994. in: *NewsBank. Film and Television*. 105:C14. 1994.
___ "**Giggles** So Stupid, It's Not Funny (Review)," *Hartford (CT) Courant*. October 24, 1992. in: *NewsBank. Film and Television*. 101:A1. 1992.
___ "High-Flown **Hook** Oft Suffers for Spielberg's Excess (Review)," *Hartford (CT) Courant*. December 11, 1991. in: *NewsBank. Film and Television*. 3:F1. 1992.
___ "Hot, Heavy Instinct Can't Overcome Lack of Credibility, Humor," *Hartford (CT) Courant* March 20, 1992 in: *NewsBank. Film and Television*. 29:A14-B1. 1992.
___ "**Invisible** Special Effects Would Best Be Left Unseen (Review)," *Hartford (CT) Courant*. February 28, 1992. in: *NewsBank. Film and Television*. 23:D1. 1992.
___ "**Johnny Mnemonic** Is a Movie That You Could Remember to Miss," *Hartford (CT) Courant*. May 27, 1995. in: *NewsBank. Film and Television*. 55:B3. 1995.
___ "Low-Budget Splatter Hits High-Tech Fan in **Brainscan**," *Hartford (CT) Courant*. April 22, 1994. in: *NewsBank. Film and Television*. 41:B6. 1994.
___ "**Prelude** Poignant Yet Boring (Review)," *Hartford (CT) Courant*. July 10, 1992. in: *NewsBank. Film and Television*. 73:C3. 1992.
___ "Promising Vampire Slayer Evaporates," *Hartford (CT) Courant*. July 31, 1992. in: *NewsBank. Film and Television*. 68:A9. 1992
___ "**Radio Flyer** a Fantasy Without Any Direction (Review)," *Hartford (CT) Courant*. February 21, 1992. in: *NewsBank. Film and Television*. 24:G3. 1992.

JONES, ALAN (continued)
___ "*The Shadow*," *Cinefantastique* 25(3): 4-5, 61. June 1994.
___ "*Split Second*," *Cinefantastique* 23(1): 54-55. August 1992.
___ "*Tale of a Vampire*," *Cinefantastique* 24(6)/25(1): 116-117.
February 1994.
___ "Those Little Dickens, the Muppets," *Cinefantastique* 23(5): 8-11.
February 1993.
___ "Tim Burton's *Edward Scissorhands*," *Cinefantastique* 25(5): 12-18.
October 1994.

JONES, DIANA W.
___ "Aiming for the Moon," *Focus* (BSFA) No. 25: 14-16. December/
January 1994.
___ "Why Don't You Write Real Books?," *Reading Time* 37(2): 9-11.
May 1993.

JONES, GWYNETH
___ "C. S. Lewis and Tolkien: Writers for Children?," *New York Review of
Science Fiction* No. 87: 1, 8-12. November 1995.
___ "The Effect of Political and Etc. Influences on SF Writers," *Focus*
(BSFA) No. 27: 7. December 1994/January 1995.
___ "The Journey Through Sumatra," *New York Review of Science
Fiction* No. 77: 1, 8-11. January 1995.
___ "The Mystique of Landscape: An Interview With Garry Kilworth,"
Interzone No. 62: 24-28, 47. August 1992.
___ "The North Wind Read This," *New York Review of Science Fiction*
No. 71: 17-19. July 1994.
___ "Riddles in the Dark," in: Jakubowski, Maxim and James, Edward,
eds. **The Profession of Science Fiction**. New York: St. Martin's, 1992.
pp.169-181.

JONES, KATY H.
___ "Interview With Elizabeth Moon," *Marion Zimmer Bradley's Fantasy
Magazine* No. 22: 36-40. Winter 1994.

JONES, KELLIE F. C.
___ **A Pentaperceptual Analysis of Social and Philosophical
Commentary in A Wrinkle in Time by Madeleine L'Engle**. Ph.D.
Dissertation, University of Mississippi, 1977. 177pp. (DAI-A 38(12):
7325. June 1978.)

JONES, LAUREN
___ "Adam Link vs. I, Robot," *Science Fiction News* (Australia) No. 111:
2-6. July 1990. (Comments: No. 112, p.9-12; No. 113, p. 8-18; No. 114,
p.3-6, 23.)

JONES, NEIL
___ "C. J. Cherryh: An Annotated Bibliography," *Interzone* No. 55: 47-
49. January 1992.
___ "*Star Trek: Voyager* (Review)," *Interzone* No. 99: 34-35. September
1995.

JONES, RAYMOND E.
___ "True Myth: Female Archetypes in Monica Hughes's **The Keeper of
the Isis Light**," in: Sullivan, C. W., III. **Science Fiction for Young
Readers**. Westport, CT: Greenwood, 1993. pp.169-178.

JONES, REBECCA
___ "The Tupperware Lady of Science Fiction," *(Denver, CO) Rocky
Mountain News*. Nov. 7, 1994. in: *NewsBank. Film and Television*. 19:
F12-F13. 1995.

JONES, STEPHEN
___ "1992 Horror Writers of America Meeting," by Stephen Jones and Jo
Fletcher. *Science Fiction Chronicle* 13(11/12): 34-38. August 1992.
___ "1994 World Horror Convention Photo Gallery," by Stephen Jones
and Jo Fletcher. *Science Fiction Chronicle* 15(7): 28-31. June 1994.
___ "A Category to Himself," in: Jones, Stephen, ed. **James Herbert:
By Horror Haunted**. London: New English Library, 1992. pp.19-32.
___ **The Illustrated Dinosaur Movie Guide**. London: Titan, 1993.
144pp.
___ "The Man Who Bought Bela Lugosi's Trousers, or, Ghouls Just Want
to Have Fun," *Science Fiction Chronicle* 14(12): 28-29. September
1993.
___ "World Fantasy Convention 1994: A Short Report," *Science Fiction
Chronicle* 16(4): 32-34. February 1995.

JONES, STEPHEN (continued)
___ "World Fantasy Convention," by Stephen Jones and Jo Fletcher.
Science Fiction Chronicle 15(4): 30-318. February 1994.
___ "World Horror Convention, 1993," by Stephen Jones and Jo
Fletcher. *Science Fiction Chronicle* 14(9): 31-32. June 1993.
___ (ed.) **Horror: 100 Best Books**. Revised and updated edition, ed. by
Stephen Jones and Kim Newman. London: Hodder/New English Library,
1992. 368pp.
___ (ed.) **James Herbert: By Horror Haunted**. London: New English
Library, 1992. 320pp.

JONES, STEVE
___ "Hyper-Punk: Cyberpunk and Information Technology," *Journal of
Popular Culture* 28(2): 81-92. Fall 1994.

JONGEWARD, STEVEN
___ "*2001: A Space Odyssey*: Arthur C. Clarke," *Cinefantastique* 25(3):
37. June 1994.

JOPP, KEN
___ "Cyberfetus Rising: The Technoetenous Prospect," *Science Fiction
Eye* No. 13: 39-45. Spring 1994.

JORDAN, A. M.
___ "Three Masterpieces by Cabell," *Lan's Lantern* No. 40: 36-37.
September 1992.

JORDAN, ANNE D.
___ "**Ender's Game**," *Teaching and Learning Literature* 4(5): 26-28.
May/June 1995.
___ "Future Reading: Science Fiction," *Teaching and Learning Literature*
4(5): 17-23. May/June 1995.
___ "Science Fiction: Something for Everyone," *Teaching and Learning
Literature* 4(5): 24-25. May/June 1995.
___ "Tell Me Where Is Fancy Bred: Fantasy," *Teaching and Learning
Literature* 4(4): 16-20. March/April 1995.

JORDAN, CYNTHIA S.
___ "Poe's Re-Vision: The Recovery of the Second Story (1987)," in:
Budd, Louis J. and Cady, Edwin H., eds. **On Poe**. Durham, NC: Duke
University Press, 1993. pp.247-266.

JOSEPH, GARY
___ "Inside the Dahl House of Horror," by Gary Joseph and Martin H.
Friedenthal. *Filmfax* No. 41: 65-69. October/November 1993.

JOSEPH, PAUL
___ "The Law of the Federation: Images of Law, Lawyers, and the Legal
System in *Star Trek: The Next Generation*," by Paul Joseph and
Sharon Carton. *University of Toledo Law Review* 24(1): 43-85. Fall 1992.
___ "Perry Mason in Space: A Call for More Inventive Lawyers in
Television Science Fiction Series," by Paul Joseph and Sharon Carton.
in: Wolf, Milton T. and Mallett, Daryl F., eds. **Imaginative Futures:
Proceedings of the 1993 Science Fiction Research Association
Conference**. San Bernardino, CA: Jacob's Ladder Books, 1995.
pp.307-318.

JOSHI, S. T.
___ "Anne Rice: The Philosophy of Vampirism," *Interzone* No. 75: 47-50,
61. September 1993.
___ "Arthur Machen: Philosophy and Fiction," in: Schweitzer, Darrell,
ed. **Discovering Classic Horror Fiction I**. Mercer Island, WA: Starmont,
1992. pp.1-33.
___ "Campbell: Before and After Lovecraft," in: Joshi, S. T., ed. **The
Count of Thirty: A Tribute to Ramsey Campbell**. West Warwick, RI:
Necronomicon, 1993. pp.27-31.
___ "Clive Barker: Sex, Death, and Fantasy," *Studies in Weird Fiction*
No. 9: 2-13. Spring 1991.
___ "David J. Schow and Splatterpunk," *Studies in Weird Fiction* No.
13: 21-27. Summer 1993. [Not seen.]
___ "Dennis Etchison: Spanning the Genres," *Studies in Weird Fiction*
No. 15: 30-36. Summer 1994.
___ "The Genesis of 'The Shadow out of Time'," *Lovecraft Studies* No.
33: 24-29. Fall 1995.
___ "H. P. Lovecraft and **The Dream-Quest of Unknown Kadath**," in:
Price, Robert M., ed. **Black Forbidden Things**. Mercer Island, WA:
Starmont, 1992. pp.7-17.

JOSHI, S. T. (continued)
___ **An Index to the Fiction and Poetry of H. P. Lovecraft.** West Warwick, RI: Necronomicon Press, 1992. 42pp.
___ "A Literary Tutelate: Robert Bloch and H. P. Lovecraft," *Studies in Weird Fiction* No. 16: 13-25. Winter 1995.
___ **Lord Dunsany: A Bibliography,** by S. T. Joshi and Darrell Schweitzer. Metuchen, NJ: Scarecrow, 1993. 389pp.
___ **Lord Dunsany: Master of the Anglo-Irish Imagination.** Westport, CT: Greenwood, 1995. 230pp.
___ "Lovecraft and the **Regnum Congo**," in: Price, Robert M., ed. **Black Forbidden Things.** Mercer Island, WA: Starmont, 1992. pp.24-29.
___ "Lovecraft on Human Knowledge: An Exchange," by Kieran Setiya and S. T. Joshi. *Lovecraft Studies* No. 24: 22-23. Spring 1991.
___ "Lovecraft's Aesthetic Development: From Classicism to Decadence," *Lovecraft Studies* No. 31: 24-34. Fall 1994.
___ "Ramsey Campbell: The Fiction of Paranoia," *Studies in Weird Fiction* No. 17: 22-33. Summer 1995.
___ "Shirley Jackson: Domestic Horror," *Studies in Weird Fiction* No. 14: 9-28. Winter 1994.
___ "The Sources for 'From Beyond'," in: Price, Robert M., ed. **Black Forbidden Things.** Mercer Island, WA: Starmont, 1992. pp.18-23.
___ "T. E. D. Klein: Urban Horror," *Studies in Weird Fiction* No. 10: 6-18. Fall 1991.
___ "Thomas Ligotti: The Escape From Life," *Studies in Weird Fiction* No. 12: 30-36. Spring 1993.
___ "Thomas Tyron: Rural Horror," *Studies in Weird Fiction* No. 11: 5-12. Spring 1992.
___ "Who Wrote 'The Mound'?," in: Price, Robert M., ed. **Black Forbidden Things.** Mercer Island, WA: Starmont, 1992. pp.3-6.
___ (ed.) **The Count of Thirty: A Tribute to Ramsey Campbell.** West Warwick, RI: Necronomicon, 1993. 54pp.
___ (ed.) **The H. P. Lovecraft Centennial Conference Proceedings.** West Warwick, RI: Necronomicon, 1991. 80pp.
___ (ed.) **H. P. Lovecraft Letters to Robert Bloch,** ed. by David E. Schultz and S. T. Joshi. West Warrick, RI: Necronomicon, 1993. 91pp.
___ (ed.) **Miscellaneous Writings: H. P. Lovecraft.** Sauk City, WI: Arkham House, 1995. 568pp.

JOST, FRANÇOIS
___ "Fragmented Representation," in: Harger-Grinling, Virginia and Chadwick, Tony, eds. **Robbe-Grillet and the Fantastic.** Westport, CT: Greenwood, 1994. pp.125-138.

JOUANNE, EMMANUEL
___ "How 'Dickian' Is the New French Science Fiction?," in: Mullen, R. D., ed. **On Philip K. Dick: 40 Articles From Science-Fiction Studies.** Terre Haute, IN: SF-TH Inc., 1992. pp.232-235.

JOY, DAN
___ "Eye to Eye With Brian Eno," *Science Fiction Eye* No. 12: 60-67. Summer 1993.

JOYCE, GRAHAM
___ "Science, Superstition and Strange Things Like Yeast; Guest of Honor Speech, Novacon 24," *Vector* No. 182: 14-20. Spring 1995.
___ "SFC Interviews: Storm Constantine," *Science Fiction Chronicle* 13(10): 5, 28-30. July/August 1992.

JOYRICH, LYNNE
___ "Feminist Enterprise: *Star Trek: The Next Generation* and the Occupation of Femininity," *Cinema Journal* 35(2): 61-84. Winter 1996.

JUHREN, MARCELLA
___ "The Ecology of Middle-Earth," *Mythlore* 20(2): 5-9. Spring 1994. (Whole No. 76)

JURICH, MARILYN
___ "Mithraic Aspects of Merlin in Mary Stewart's **The Crystal Cave**," in: Morse, Donald E., ed. **The Celebration of the Fantastic.** Westport, CT: Greenwood, 1992. pp.91-102.
___ " 'A Woman's a Two-faced,' or the *Doppelgängerin* Unveiled," *Journal of the Fantastic in the Arts* 6(2/3): 143-165. 1994.

JURKIEWICZ, KENNETH
___ "Giving the Devil More Than His Due: *The Witches of Eastwick* as Fiction and Film," in: Morse, Donald E., ed. **The Celebration of the Fantastic.** Westport, CT: Greenwood, 1992. pp.205-210.

KAGAN, JANET
___ "Mischief in the Spaceways," in: Olson, Mark L., ed. **The Best of James H. Schmitz.** Cambridge, MA: NESFA Press, 1991. pp.v-xi.

KAGLE, STEVEN E.
___ "Beyond Armageddon: Stephen King's **The Stand** and the Post Catastrophic World in Speculative Fiction," in: Magistrale, Tony, ed. **A Casebook on The Stand.** San Bernardino, CA: Borgo Press, 1992. pp.189-209.
___ "Homage to Melville: Ray Bradbury and the Nineteenth-Century American Romance," in: Morse, Donald E., ed. **The Celebration of the Fantastic.** Westport, CT: Greenwood, 1992. pp.279-289.

KAHL, NATHAN W.
___ **The Meeting of Parallel Lines: Science and Fiction and Science Fiction.** Honor's Paper, Duke University, 1992. 76pp.

KAHN, JOSEPH P.
___ "Beamed up in Boston," *Boston (MA) Globe.* October 3, 1992. in: *NewsBank. Film and Television.* 108:A3-A4. 1992.

KAKU, MICHIO
___ **Hyperspace: A Scientific Odyssey Through Parallel Universes, Time Warps, and the Tenth Dimension.** New York: Oxford University Press, 1994. 359pp.

KAKUTANI, MCIHIKO
___ "Making a Literary Lunge into the Future," *New York Times* Sec. C, p. 1. February 21, 1992.

KALADE, LINAS
___ "Weaving a Colourful Tapestry," *Viewpoint on Books for Young Adults* 1(2): 8-9. Winter 1993.

KALER, ANNE K.
___ **The Picara: From Hera to Fantasy Heroine.** Bowling Green, OH: Popular Press, 1991. 215pp.

KALIEN, BEN
___ "Lust in Space," in: Van Hise, James, ed. **Trek Celebration Two.** Las Vegas, NV: Pioneer, 1994. pp.111-116.

KALTENBACH, CHRIS
___ "Disney's **Powder** Is Predictable," *(Baltimore, MD) Sun.* October 27, 1995. in: *NewsBank. Film and Television.* 97:F13. 1995.
___ "A Maryland Actor Saw His Spaceship Come in in an Awful 1959 Film," *(Baltimore, MD) Sun.* July 7, 1994. in: *NewsBank. Film and Television.* 62:E8. 1994.

KAN, KATHARINE L.
___ **Mindscapes II: Science Fiction and Fantasy in Series.** Honolulu, HI: Hawaii State Public Library System, 1993. 37pp.

KANALZ, HANK
___ "Return to *Star Wars*," by Kim H. Johnson and Hank Kanalz. *Starlog* No. 175: 32-35. February 1992.

KANDEL, MICHAEL
___ "Twelve Thoughts, Not All Equally Important, on Reading Maureen F. McHugh's **China Mountain Zhang** and **Half the Day Is Night**," *New York Review of Science Fiction* No. 77: 21-22. January 1995.

KAPLAND, DAVID A.
___ "Believe in Magic," *Newsweek* 121(24): 60-61. June 14, 1993.

KAPPEL, LAWRENCE
___ "Psychic Geography in **Gravity's Rainbow**," *Contemporary Literature* 21(1): 225-251. Winter 1980.

KARLEN, NEAL
___ "Sci-Fi Schlock Is Turned on Its Ear at Convention of Fans," *New York Times* p.B1. September 19, 1994.

KARLOFF, BORIS
___ "Houses I Have Haunted," *Wonder* No. 7: 22-23. 1993.

KARP, ANDREW
___ "The Need for Boundaries: Homer's Critique of the Phaeakian Utopia in the **Odyssey**," *Utopian Studies* 6(2): 25-34. 1995.

KARTER, WOLFGANG
___ "Jack London: **The Iron Heel** (1908)," in: Heuermann, Hartmut and Lange, Bernd-Peter, eds. **Die Utopie in der angloamerikanischen Literatur: Interpretationen**. Düsseldorf: Bagel, 1984. pp.176-195.

KASON, NANCY M.
___ "The Dystopian Vision in **XYZ** by Clemente Palma," *Monographis Review* 3(1/2): 33-42. 1987.

KASPERSEN, FLEMMING
___ "Tech Noir: blod, teknologi og fremtidsvisioner fra 2001 til Sidste Udkald," *Kosmorama* 36(No. 194): 12-16. 1990.

KASTOR, FRANK S.
___ "C. S. Lewis's John Milton: Influence, Presence and Beyond," *Bulletin of the New York C. S. Lewis Society* 24(9/10): 1-11. July/August 1993.

KATOVICH, MICHAEL A.
___ "The Stories Told in Science Fiction and Social Science: Reading **The Thing** and Other Remakes From Two Eras," by Michael A. Katovich and Patrick T. Kinkade. *Sociological Quarterly* 34(4): 619-651. 1993.

KATZ, BILL
___ "Magazines: *Blue Light Red Light: A Periodical of Speculative Fiction and the Arts*," *Library Journal* p.144. July 1991.
___ "Magazines: *Crank!*," *Library Journal* 119(5): 107. March 15, 1994.
___ "*Next Phase*," *Library Journal* 119(13): 144. August 1994.

KATZ, EPHRIAM
___ **The Film Encyclopedia**. 2nd Ed. New York: Harper Perennial, 1994. 1496pp.

KATZ, FRANCIS
___ "Sell-Out Has Trekkies Weeping in the Rain," *Boston (MA) Herald*. November 19, 1994. in: *NewsBank. Film and Television*. 125:C14. 1994.

KAUFFMAN, LINDA S.
___ **Special Delivery: Epistolary Modes in Modern Fiction**. Chicago: University of Chicago Press, 1992. 278pp.

KAUFMAN, DAVE
___ "Lucas Producing Two ABC Cartoons on Ewoks and R2D2," *Variety* p. 145. January 16, 1985.

KAUFMAN, DEBRA
___ "Effects in the Vertical Realm," *Cinefex* No. 54: 30-53. May 1993.

KAUFMAN, WILLIAM K.
___ **Mark Twain, Lenny Bruce and Kurt Vonnegut: The Comedian as Confidence Man**. Ph.D. Dissertation, University of Wales, Aberystwyth, 1992. [Not Seen.]

KAVENEY, ROZ
___ "New New World Dreams: Angela Carter and Science Fiction," in: Sage, Lorna, ed. **Flesh and the Mirror: Essays on the Art of Angela Carter**. London: Virago, 1994. pp.171-188.
___ "Walter Jon Williams and Some Problems of Science Fiction Criticism," *Foundation* No. 57: 87-98. Spring 1993.

KAY, ANN
___ "William Morris and the National Curriculum," by Ann Kay and John Kay. *Journal of the William Morris Society* 11(1): 44-48. Autumn 1994.

KAY, JOHN
___ "William Morris and the National Curriculum," by Ann Kay and John Kay. *Journal of the William Morris Society* 11(1): 44-48. Autumn 1994.

KAYSER, JOHN R.
___ "Golding's **Lord of the Flies**: Pride as Original Sin," by John F. Fitzgerald and John R. Kayser. *Studies in the Novel* 24(1): 78-88. Spring 1992.

KE, FAN
___ "Science Fiction Film Calls for Environmental Protection: *Legend of the Celestial Sphere* Directed by Wei Judang," *Beijing Review* 38(37): 34. September 11, 1995.

KEARNS, MARTHA
___ "Postmodern Images of Sexuality in Vampire Literature," in: Wolf, Milton T. and Mallett, Daryl F., eds. **Imaginative Futures: Proceedings of the 1993 Science Fiction Research Association Conference**. San Bernardino, CA: Jacob's Ladder Books, 1995. pp.147-160.

KEATING, H. R. F.
___ "Dorothy L.'s Mickey Finn," in: Dale, Alzina S., ed. **Dorothy L. Sayers: The Centenary Celebration**. New York: Walker, 1993. pp.129-138.

KEEFER, JANICE K.
___ "Hope Against Hopelessness: Margaret Atwood's **Life Before Man**," in: Nicholson, Colin, ed. **Margaret Atwood: Writing and Subjectivity: New Critical Essays**. New York: St. Martin's, 1994. pp.153-176.

KEELER, GREG
___ "*The Shining*: Ted Kramer Has a Nightmare," *Journal of Popular Film and Television* 8(4): 2-8. 1981.

KEELEY, EDMUND
___ "An I to I Interview about Kingsley Amis," in: Salwak, Dale, ed. **Kingsley Amis in Life and Letters**. New York: St. Martin's, 1990. pp.24-30.

KEENE, LOUISE E.
___ "The Restoration of Language in Middle-Earth," *Mythlore* 20(4): 6-13. Winter 1995. (Whole No. 78)

KEENEY, BRIAN
___ "Company File: Animal Makers," *Cinefex* No. 59: 29-30. September 1994.

KEENY, GLENN
___ "There Is Nothing Wrong With Your Television Set...," *TV Guide* 42(26): 34. June 25, 1994.

KEESEY, DOUGLAS
___ " 'The Face of Mr. Flip': Homophobia in the Horror of Stephen King," in: Magistrale, Tony, ed. **The Dark Descent: Essays Defining Stephen King's Horrorscape**. Westport, CT: Greenwood, 1992. pp.187-201.
___ " 'I Think the Government Stinks!': Stephen King's **Stand** on Politics," in: Magistrale, Tony, ed. **A Casebook on The Stand**. San Bernardino, CA: Borgo Press, 1992. pp.21-36.

KEFFER, SARAH L.
___ "Work-Writing to Create the Fictional Portrait: Tolkien's Inclusion of Lewis in **The Lord of the Rings**," *English Studies in Canada* 18(2): 181-198. June 1992.

KEGLER, ADELHEID
___ "Die Sozialrevolutionäre Ethik George MacDonalds," in: Kranz, Gisbert, ed. **Inklings: Jahrbuch für Literatur und Ästhetik**. 9. Band. Lüdenscheid, Germany: Stier, 1991. pp.71-91. [Not seen.]
___ "Encountering Darkness: The Black Platonism of David Lindsay," *Mythlore* 19(2): 24-33. Spring 1993. (No. 72)
___ "George MacDonald oder die resakralisierung des Wissens," in: Kranz, Gisbert, ed. **Inklings: Jahrbuch für Literatur und Ästhetik**. 2. Band. [Lüdenscheid, Germany: Stier], 1984. pp.85-110.

KEIM, HEINRICH
___ "James Graham Ballard, **Crash!** (1973)," in: Heuermann, Harmut, ed. **Der Science Fiction Roman in der angloamerikanischen Literatur: Interpretationen**. Düsseldorf: Bagel, 1986. pp.346-354.

KEINHORST, ANNETTE
___ "Emancipatory Projection: An Introduction to Women's Critical Utopias," *Women's Studies* 14(2): 91-100. 1987.
___ **Utopien von Frauen in der zeitgenössischen Literatur der USA**. Frankfurt-am-Main: Peter Lang, 1985. 230pp.

KEISER, GEORGE R.

KEISER, GEORGE R.
___ "Malory and the Middle English Romance: A Graduate Course," in: Fries, Maureen and Watson, Jeanie, eds. **Approaches to the Teaching of the Arthurian Tradition.** New York: Modern Language Association, 1992. pp.131-134.

KEITH, W. J.
___ "Interpreting and Misinterpreting 'Bluebeard's Egg': A Cautionary Tale," in: Nicholson, Colin, ed. **Margaret Atwood: Writing and Subjectivity: New Critical Essays.** New York: St. Martin's, 1994. pp.248-577.
___ **Introducing Margaret Atwood's The Edible Woman: A Reader's Guide.** North York, Ont.: EWC Press, 1989. 79pp.

KELLAR, MICHAEL
___ "Solomon and Sorcery," *The Dark Man: The Journal of Robert E. Howard Studies* No. 2: 11-13. July 1991.

KELLEGHAN, FIONA
___ "Ambiguous News From the Heartland: John Kessel's **Good News From Outer Space**," *Extrapolation* 35(4): 281-297. Winter 1994.
___ "Hell's My Destination: Imprisonment in the Works of Alfred Bester," *Science Fiction Studies* 21(3): 351-364. November 1994.
___ "Humor in Science Fiction," in: Wolf, Milton T. and Mallett, Daryl F., eds. **Imaginative Futures: Proceedings of the 1993 Science Fiction Research Association Conference.** San Bernardino, CA: Jacob's Ladder Books, 1995. pp.263-278.

KELLER, CHESTER Z.
___ "Human Nature: Ecosystemic Limits and Techne. Some Utopian Implications," in: Saccaro Del Buffa, Giuseppa and Lewis, Arthur O., eds. **Utopia e Modernita: Teorie e prassi utopiche nell'eta moderna e postmoderna.** Rome: Gangemi Editore, 1989. pp.131-142.
___ "Imitations of Utopia: Some Readings From Nature," in: Saccaro Del Buffa, Giuseppa and Lewis, Arthur O., eds. **Utopie per gli Anni Ottana.** Rome: Gangemi Editore, 1986. pp.89-98.

KELLER, DAVID
___ "The Translation of Philip K. Dick," *Radio Free P K D* No. 5: 7-8. August 1995.

KELLER, J. R. KEITH
___ " 'Navigator' to Wrap in Norway March 1," *Variety* p. 43. February 26, 1986.

KELLER, JAMES R.
___ "Middleton's **The Witch**: Witchcraft and the Domestic Female Hero," *Journal of the Fantastic in the Arts* 4(4): 37-59. 1991. (No. 16)

KELLEY, MIKE
___ "Monster Manse," *Grand Street* 13(1): 224-233. Summer 1994.

KELLEY, ROBERT
___ "A Maze of Twisty Little Passages All Alike: Aesthetics and Teleology in Interactive Computer Fictional Elements," *Science Fiction Studies* 20(1): 52-68. March 1993.

KELLEY, SCOTT
___ "Photo-Utopia and Poetic Representations of the Impossible: The Utopic Figure in Modern Poetic and Photographic Discourse," *Utopian Studies* 6(1): 1-18. 1995.

KELLY, CHRIS
___ "Space Cadets," *Seventeen* 52(12): 60. December 1993.

KELLY, JAMES P.
___ "You and Your Characters," in: Dozois, Gardner, ed. **Writing Science Fiction and Fantasy.** New York: St. Martin's, 1991. pp.38-49.

KELLY, KEVIN
___ "Singular Visionary," *Wired* 3(6): 160-161. June 1995.

KELLY, THOMAS
___ "The World of King Arthur: An Interdisciplinary Course," by Thomas Kelly and Thomas Ohlgren. in: Fries, Maureen and Watson, Jeanie, eds. **Approaches to the Teaching of the Arthurian Tradition.** New York: Modern Language Association, 1992. pp.77-80.

KELNER, STEVE
___ "Mind and Brain: SF and Fact," *Science Fiction Eye* No. 13: 73-81. Spring 1994.

KEMP, PHILIP
___ "**Species** (Review)," *Sight and Sound* 5(10): 60-61. October 1995.

KEMPEN, BERNHARD
___ "Eine Lektion in Misanthropie: Über Octavia Butlers 'schwarze' SF," *Science Fiction Times* (Germany) 34(1): 4-9. January 1992.
___ "Perry Rhodan--Our Man in Space: Transformations of a German SF Phenomenon," *Foundation* No. 56: 5-22. Autumn 1992.

KEMPER, BART
___ "Dancing on the Edge," *Writer's Digest* 74(7): 6-7. July 1994.
___ "Touching the Reader: An Interview With Lois McMaster Bujold," *Quantum* No. 43/44: 17-18. Spring/Summer 1993.

KENDALL, LUKAS
___ "**Star Trek**: Scoring the Final Frontier," *Cinefantastique* 23(2/3): 100-102, 124. October 1992.
___ "**Star Trek: The Next Generation**: The Final Frontier's Musical Discord," *Cinefantastique* 24(3/4): 84-85. October 1993.

KENDRICK, WALTER
___ "Better Undead Than Unread: Have Vampires Lost Their Bite?," *New York Times Book Review* p. 55. October 18, 1992.

KENING, DAN
___ "Gatekeeper to the Universe," *Chicago Tribune* Sec. 18 (Tempo Northwest), p. 1, 4. October 4, 1992.

KENNEDY, J. GERALD
___ "The Limits of Reason: Poe's Deluded Detectives (1975)," in: Budd, Louis J. and Cady, Edwin H., eds. **On Poe.** Durham, NC: Duke University Press, 1993. pp.172-184.

KENNEDY, JOHN
___ "SFC Interviews: John E. Stith," *Science Fiction Chronicle* 14(10): 5, 27-29. July 1993.

KENNEY, CATHERINE M.
___ "The Comedy of Dorothy L. Sayers," in: Dale, Alzina S., ed. **Dorothy L. Sayers: The Centenary Celebration.** New York: Walker, 1993. pp.139-150.
___ **The Remarkable Case of Dorothy L. Sayers.** Kent, OH: Kent State University Press, 1990. 309pp.

KENNY, GLENN
___ "Animania," *TV Guide* 42(21): 42. May 21, 1994.
___ "**Babylon 5** on Course," *TV Guide* 42(45): 32. November 5, 1994.
___ "**Babylon 5**'s Ivanova Lightens Up," *TV Guide* 42(17): 33. April 23, 1994.
___ "Coming on Strong," *TV Guide* 42(47): 42. November 19, 1994.
___ "Don't Crush That Dwarf," *TV Guide* 43(12): 46. March 25, 1995.
___ "Double Time on DS9," *TV Guide* 43(11): 36. March 18, 1995.
___ "The Facts About Dax," *TV Guide* 42(34): 30. August 20, 1994.
___ "The Ghost With the Most," *TV Guide* 42(25): 40. June 18, 1994.
___ "The Great Bird of the Galaxy Lands a TV Bio," *TV Guide* 42(28): 28. July 9, 1994.
___ "Harlan Ellison Sounds Off," *TV Guide* 42(8): 26. February 19, 1994.
___ "He's a Real **Nowhere Man**," *TV Guide* 43(34): 28. August 26, 1995.
___ "It's Showtime for Corman," *TV Guide* 43(23): 50. June 10, 1995.
___ "Knight Moves," *TV Guide* 42(46): 44. November 12, 1994.
___ "Kurt Vonnegut's Law of Averages," *TV Guide* 43(32): 31. August 12, 1995.
___ "Lost in Space, Again," *TV Guide* 42(42): 42. October 15, 1994.
___ " **M. A. N. T. I. S.**: This Year's Model," *TV Guide* 42(37): 34. September 10, 1994.
___ "**Maxx**-ed Out," *TV Guide* 43(8): 42. February 25, 1995.
___ "Moon Struck," by Jeff Jarvis, James Reston, Jr., Glenn Kenny and Penelope Patsuris. *TV Guide* 42(29): 10-16. July 16, 1994.
___ "MST3K's Conventional Wisdom," *TV Guide* 42(30): 28. July 23, 1994.
___ "MTV's Dead-End Kid," *TV Guide* 42(24): 31. June 11, 1994.

KENNY, GLENN (continued)
___ "New Life for a '50s Classic," *TV Guide* 43(35): 20. September 2, 1995.
___ "OscarVision," *TV Guide* 42(12): 58. March 19, 1994.
___ "Phantasia," *TV Guide* 43(11): 36. March 18, 1995.
___ "A Roborave," *TV Guide* 42(11): 42. March 12, 1994.
___ "Sci-Fi Central," *TV Guide* 43(28): 15. July 16, 1995.
___ "Sci-Fi/Fantasy: Earth 2, 3, 4...," *TV Guide* 43(10): 30. March 11, 1995.
___ "The Sounds of Science," *TV Guide* 43(6): 28. February 11, 1995.
___ "Teleporting Teens and a Generation X Hero," *TV Guide* 42(9): 41. February 26, 1994.
___ "Time and Again," *TV Guide* 42(19): 33. May 7, 1994.
___ "TV's Brave New Worlds," *TV Guide* 42(3): 22-24. January 15, 1994.

KENNY, VIRGINIA C.
___ "The Eternal Feminine Reclaimed: Ford Madox Ford's Medieval Fantasies," in: Filmer, Kath, ed. **Twentieth-Century Fantasists: Essays in Culture, Society and Belief in Twentieth Century Mythopoeic Literature.** New York: St. Martin's, 1992. pp.60-70.

KENT, BRIAN
___ "Stephen King and His Readers: A Dirty, Compelling Romance," in: Magistrale, Tony, ed. **A Casebook on The Stand.** San Bernardino, CA: Borgo Press, 1992. pp.37-68.

KENWORTHY, CHRIS
___ "Toy Cars, Teaspoons and Scissors: Nicholas Royle Interviewed," *Interzone* No. 77: 48-51. November 1993.

KEOUGH, TRENT
___ "The Dystopia Factor: Industrial Capitalism in **Sybil** and **The Grapes of Wrath**," *Utopian Studies* 4(1): 38-54. 1993.

KERESEY, GAYLE
___ "Interview with Mercedes," by Rececca Taylor, Gayle Keresey and Margaret Miles. *Voice of Youth Advocates* 15(4): 213-217. October 1992.

KERMAN, JUDITH B.
___ "Uses of the Fantastic in Literature of the Holocaust," *Journal of the Fantastic in the Arts* 5(2): 14-31. 1993. (No. 18)
___ "Virtual Space and Its Boundaries in Science Fiction Film and Television: **Tron, Max Headroom, War Games**," in: Morse, Donald E., ed. **The Celebration of the Fantastic.** Westport, CT: Greenwood, 1992. pp.191-204.

KERMODE, MARK
___ "Endnotes," *Sight and Sound* 4(6): 71. June 1994.
___ "Ghoul School: The Horror Genre," *Sight and Sound* 3(6): 10-12. June 1993.
___ "**Necronomicon** (Review)," *Sight and Sound* 4(9): 42-43. September 1994.
___ "**Robocop 3** (Review)," *Sight and Sound* 4(7): 51-52. July 1994.

KERN, RAIMUND B.
___ "Von der Werklichkeit zum Phantastischen und zurück: Natur und Kultur in den Narnia-büchern von C. S. Lewis," in: Kranz, Gisbert, ed. **Inklings: Jahrbuch für Literatur und Ästhetik.** 8. Band. Lüdenscheid, Germany: Stier, 1990. pp.71-102. [Not seen.]

KESSEL, JOHN
___ "The Brother From Another Planet: Science Fiction vs. Mainstream Short Stories," *New York Review of Science Fiction* No. 55: 1, 8-11. March 1993. (Responses: No. 56: 22-23.)
___ "It's Time to Load the Canon With SF's Most Influential Books," *Science Fiction Age* 3(2): 32-35. January 1995.

KESSLER, CAROL F.
___ "Annotated Bibliography of U.S. Women's Utopian Fiction, 1836-1988," in: Kessler, Carol F., ed. **Daring to Dream: Utopian Fiction by United States Women Before 1950.** Second Edition. Syracuse, NY: Syracuse University Press, 1995. pp.247-304.
___ "Annotated Bibliography: United States Women's Utopian Fiction, 1836-1983," in: Kessler, Carol K., ed. **Daring to Dream: Utopian Stories by United States Women, 1836-1919.** Boston, MA: Pandora Press, 1984. pp.233-266.

KESSLER, CAROL F. (continued)
___ **Charlotte Perkins Gilman: Her Progress Toward Utopia With Selected Writings.** Liverpool: Liverpool University Press, 1995. 316pp.
___ "Consider Her Ways: The Cultural Work of Charlotte Perkins Gilman's Pragmatopian Stories, 1908-1913," in: Donawerth, Jane L. and Kolmerten, Carol A., eds. **Utopian and Science Fiction by Women: Worlds of Difference.** Syracuse, NY: Syracuse University Press, 1994. pp.126-136.
___ "Daring to Dream: Utopian Fiction by United States Women," in: Saccaro Del Buffa, Giuseppa and Lewis, Arthur O., eds. **Utopie per gli Anni Ottana.** Rome: Gangemi Editore, 1986. pp.455-466.
___ **Daring to Dream: Utopian Fiction by United States Women, 1836-1919.** 2nd ed. Syracuse, NY: Syracuse University Press, 1995. 326pp.
___ "Introduction," in: Kessler, Carol F., ed. **Daring to Dream: Utopian Fiction by United States Women Before 1950.** Second Edition. Syracuse, NY: Syracuse University Press, 1995. pp.xiii-xxviii.
___ "Introduction: Feminist Utopias by United States Women," in: Kessler, Carol K., ed. **Daring to Dream: Utopian Stories by United States Women, 1836-1919.** Boston, MA: Pandora Press, 1984. pp.1-25.

KESSON, KATHLEEN
___ **Body and Narrative as Cultural Text: Toward a Curriculum of Continuity and Connection**, by Noel Gough and Kathleen Kesson. ERIC ED 347544. 9pp. 1992. Paper presented at the Annual Meeting of the American Educational Research Association, San Francisco, CA, April 20-24, 1992.

KETTERER, DAVID
___ **Canadian Science Fiction and Fantasy.** Bloomington: Indiana University Press, 1991. 206pp.
___ "The Corrected **Frankenstein**: Twelve Preferred Readings in the Last Draft," *English Language Notes* 33(1): 23-34. September 1995.
___ "The Establishment of Canadian Science Fiction (1958-1983), Part 1," *New York Review of Science Fiction* No. 42: 1, 8-14. February 1992.
___ "The Establishment of Canadian Science Fiction (1958-1983), Part 2," *New York Review of Science Fiction* No. 43: 17-22. March 1992.
___ "**Frankenstein**: The Source of a Name," *Science Fiction Studies* 22(3): 455-456. November 1995
___ "Outside and Inside Views of Rochon's **The Shell**," by David Ketterer and Esther Rochon. *Science Fiction Studies* 19(1): 17-31. March 1992.

KEVENEY, BILL
___ "Until the Next Voyage," *Hartford (CT) Courant.* May 27, 1994. in: *NewsBank. Film and Television.* 59:C5-C6. 1994.

KHANNA, LEE C.
___ "Contemporary Utopian Fiction: New Strategies for Change," in: Saccaro Del Buffa, Giuseppa and Lewis, Arthur O., eds. **Utopia e Modernita: Teorie e prassi utopiche nell'eta moderna e postmoderna.** Rome: Gangemi Editore, 1989. pp.587-595.
___ "Frontiers of Imagination: Women's World," in: Saccaro Del Buffa, Giuseppa and Lewis, Arthur O., eds. **Utopie per gli Anni Ottana.** Rome: Gangemi Editore, 1986. pp.467-476.
___ "The Subject of Utopia," in: Donawerth, Jane L. and Kolmerten, Carol A., eds. **Utopian and Science Fiction by Women: Worlds of Difference.** Syracuse, NY: Syracuse University Press, 1994. pp.15-34.

KIDD, VIRGINIA
___ "The Expatriate," *Aloud* (Toronto) 2(7): 9. October 1992.

KIES, COSETTE
___ "Eeek! They Just Keep Coming! YA Horror Series," *Voice of Youth Advocates* 17(1): 17-19. April 1994.
___ "The Humor in Horror," *Voice of Youth Advocates* 18(3): 143-144. August 1995.
___ "Never Turn Your Back on a Werewolf," *Voice of Youth Advocates* 18(3): 145-146. August 1995.
___ **Presenting Young Adult Horror Fiction.** New York: Twayne, 1991. 203pp.
___ **Supernatural Fiction for Teens: More Than 1300 Good Paperbacks to Read for Wonderment, Fear and Fun.** 2nd Edition. Englewood, CO: Libraries Unlimited, 1992. 267pp.

KIES, DANIEL
___ "Fourteen Types of Passivity: Suppressing Agency in **Nineteen Eighty-Four**," in: Rose, Jonathan, ed. **The Revised Orwell**. East Lansing, MI: Michigan State University Press, 1992. pp.47-60.

KILBY, CLYDE S.
___ "Mythic and Christian Elements in Tolkien," in: Kranz, Gisbert, ed. **Inklings: Jahrbuch für Literatur und Ästhetik**. 1. Band. Lüdenscheid, Germany: Michael Claren, 1983. pp.103-120.

KILBY, DAMIAN
___ "Freed From a Cosmic Zoo, *Moonshadow* Seeks the Secrets of the Universe," *Science Fiction Age* 2(6): 84-86. September 1994.
___ "Vertigo's *Last One* Shows That Immortality May Not Be All It's Cracked Up to Be," *Science Fiction Age* 1(5): 76-78. July 1993.
___ "Welcome to a New Age of Comic Books Thanks to the Latest SF Invasion," *Science Fiction Age* 2(4): 90-93. May 1994.
___ "With Science Fictional Abilities, the Alien Icon Seeks to Bring Racial Harmony to Earth," *Science Fiction Age* 1(4): 68-69. May 1993.

KILGORE, DE WITT D.
___ **Beyond Earth: Popular Science, Science Fiction, and the Cultural Construction of an American Future in Space**. Ph.D. Dissertation, Brown University, 1994. 414pp. (DAI-A 55/07, p. 2018. January 1995.)

KILGOUR, MAGGIE
___ **The Rise of the Gothic Novel**. New York: Routledge, 1995. 280pp.

KILLHEFFER, ROBERT K. J.
___ "Category Close-Up: Science Fiction, Exploring Alternative Worlds," *Publishers Weekly* 240(31):53-56. August 2, 1993. (Reprinted, *Science Fiction Chronicle*, May 1994, pp.44-46.)
___ "Category Closeup: Science Fiction: Exploring New Worlds," *Publishers Weekly* 241(9): 56-60. February 28, 1994.
___ "Inter-Galactic Licensing," *Publishers Weekly* 242(39): 27-31. September 25, 1995.
___ "The Legacy of Columbus: The Lost Races of Edward Myers and Kenneth Morris," *New York Review of Science Fiction* No. 44: 1, 3-6. April 1992.
___ "Mainstreaming the Millennium," *Publishers Weekly* 241(34): 33-38. August 22, 1994.
___ "PW Interview: John Crowley," *Publishers Weekly* 241(35): 53-54. August 29, 1994.
___ "PW Interview: William Gibson," *Publishers Weekly* 240(36):70-71. September 6, 1993.
___ "The Quest for Future Authors," *Publishers Weekly* 240(6): 25-27. February 8, 1993.
___ "Rising From the Grave: Horror," *Publishers Weekly* 240(38): 43-47. September 20, 1993.
___ "Striking a Balance: Robert Silverberg's **Lord of Darkness, Dying Inside** and Others," *New York Review of Science Fiction* No. 12: 1, 12-14. August 1989.
___ "When Opportunity Knocks: SF and Fantasy Small Presses Find New Niches in a Changing Marketplace," *Science Fiction Chronicle* 16(1): 33-38. October 1994. (Revised from original *Publishers Weekly* publication.)

KILLICK, JANE
___ **The Making of *Judge Dredd***, by Jane Killick, David Chute and Charles M. Lippincott. London: Boxtree, 1995; New York: Hyperion, 1995. 192pp.

KILWORTH, GARRY
___ "Confessions of a Bradbury Eater," in: Jakubowski, Maxim and James, Edward, eds. **The Profession of Science Fiction**. New York: St. Martin's, 1992. pp.154-160.
___ "On Animal Fantasy," *Million* 11: 11-15. 1992. [Not seen.]

KIMBER, GARY
___ "Cronenberg: *Naked Lunch*," *Cinefantastique* 22(5): 8-9. April 1992.
___ "*Naked Lunch*: Production Design," *Cinefantastique* 22(5): 18. April 1992.
___ "*Naked Lunch*: William S. Burroughs, Possessed by Genius," *Cinefantastique* 22(5): 12-14. April 1992.
___ "*The Naked Lunch*," *Cinefantastique* 22(4): 12-13, 60. February 1992.

KIMMEL, DAN
___ "Sci-Fi Festival Is a Giant Sit for Mankind," *Variety* 354(4): 38. February 26, 1994.

KIMSEY, JOHN
___ "Dolorous Strokes, or Balin at the Bat: Malamud, Malory and Chrétien," in: Morse, Donald E., ed. **The Celebration of the Fantastic**. Westport, CT: Greenwood, 1992. pp.103-112.

KINCAID, PAUL
___ "The Art of Reading a Review," *Focus* (BSFA) No. 24: 18. June/July 1993.
___ "British SF: An Obituary," *Vector* No. 176: 12. December 1993/ January 1994.
___ "Cognitive Mapping 1: Alternate History," *Vector* No. 186: 3. December 1995.
___ "Defying Rational Chronology: Time and Identity in the Work of Steve Erickson," *Foundation* No. 58: 27-42. Summer 1993.
___ "The Entire Enchilada: Lawrence Sutin Interviewed," *Vector* No. 168: 9-12. August/September 1992.
___ "How Hard Is SF?," *Vector* No. 182: 5-13. Spring 1995.
___ "A Perfectly Mysterious Process: Samuel R. Delany Interviewed," *Vector* No. 186: 8-14. December 1995.
___ "Secret Maps: The Topography of Fantasy and Morality in the Work of Steve Erickson," *Foundation* No. 57: 26-48. Spring 1993.
___ "Touching the Earth: The Fiction of Robert Holdstock," *Vector* No. 175: 7-9. October/November 1993.

KINDRICK, ROBERT L.
___ "Which Malory Should I Teach?," in: Fries, Maureen and Watson, Jeanie, eds. **Approaches to the Teaching of the Arthurian Tradition**. New York: Modern Language Association, 1992. pp.100-105.

KING, JAMES R.
___ **Old Tales and New Truths: Charting the Bright-Shadow World**. Albany: State University of New York Press, 1992. 267pp.

KING, JEANETTE
___ **Doris Lessing**. New York: Edward Arnold, 1990. 117pp. [Not seen.]

KING, MAUREEN
___ "Contemporary Women Writers and the 'New Evil': The Vampires of Anne Rice and Suzy McKee Charnas," *Journal of the Fantastic in the Arts* 5(3): 75-84. 1993. (No. 19)

KING, ROMA A., JR.
___ "Charles William's Merlin: Worker in Time of the Images of Eternity," in: Watson, Jeanie and Fries, Marueen, eds. **The Figure of Merlin in the Nineteenth and Twentieth Centuries**. Lewiston, NY: Mellen, 1989. pp.65-77.

KING, STEPHEN
___ "James Herbert: Introduction," in: Jones, Stephen, ed. **James Herbert: By Horror Haunted**. London: New English Library, 1992. pp.9-17.
___ "On J. K. Potter: The Art of the Morph," *Interzone* No. 77: 23-24. November 1993.

KING, T. JACKSON
___ "Bookstore Signings: The Good, the Bad, the Ugly," *SFWA Bulletin* 26(3): 10-14. Fall 1992. (No. 117)
___ "Creating Believable Aliens," *SFWA Bulletin* 27(4)/28(1): 32-39. Winter/Spring 1994. (No. 122/123)
___ "Habitable Stars Within 100 Light Years," *The Report: The Fiction Writer's Magazine* No. 9: 9-11. March 1993.
___ "How to Market Your Novel," *SFWA Bulletin* 26(1): 24-28. Spring 1992. (No. 115)
___ "Interview: Poul Anderson," *Expanse* No. 3: 34-43. Summer 1994.
___ "Kate Elliott: The Writer as Anthropological Historian," *Mindsparks* 2(1): 29-34. 1994. (Whole No. 4)
___ "Pros and Cons of Being a Writer Couple," by T. Jackson King and Paula E. Downing. *SFWA Bulletin* 25(4): 7-14. Winter 1992. (No. 114)
___ "SFC Interview: Mary Rosenblum," *Science Fiction Chronicle* 16(8): 5, 34-36. July/August 1995
___ "SFC Interview: Robert J. Sawyer," *Science Fiction Chronicle* 14(12): 5, 30-31. September 1993.

KING, T. JACKSON (continued)
___ "SFC Interview: Susan Shwartz," *Science Fiction Chronicle* 16(7): 5, 30-33. June/July 1995.
___ "SFC Interviews: Dave Wolverton," *Science Fiction Chronicle* 16(3): 5, 31-33. January 1995.
___ "SFC Interviews: F. M. Busby," *Science Fiction Chronicle* 15(3): 5, 24-26. January 1994.
___ "SFC Interviews: Judith Tarr," *Science Fiction Chronicle* 14(7): 5, 27-29. April 1993.
___ "SFC Interviews: Katharine Kerr," *Science Fiction Chronicle* 14(11): 5, 31-34. August 1993.
___ "SFC Interviews: Kevin J. Anderson," *Science Fiction Chronicle* 15(5): 5, 28-30. March 1994.
___ "SFC Interviews: Kevin O'Donnell, Jr.," *Science Fiction Chronicle* 15(9): 7, 30-32. August 1994.
___ "SFC Interviews: Martha Soukup," *Science Fiction Chronicle* 15(7): 5, 34-38. June 1994.
___ "SFC Interviews: Vonda N. McIntyre," *Science Fiction Chronicle* 14(8): 5, 30-32. May 1993.

KING, TOM, JR.
___ "SFC Interviews: Jennifer Roberson," *Science Fiction Chronicle* 14(1): 5, 29-30. October 1992.

KINGSTON, F. COLIN
___ "Dreams for Sale," *Starlog* No. 198: 62-65. January 1994.
___ "*Leprechaun 3*," *Cinefantastique* 26(4): 52-53. June 1995.
___ "*White Dwarf*: Bruce Wagner on Writing Science Fiction for Television," *Cinefantastique* 26(5): 10-11, 61. August 1995.

KINKADE, PATRICK T.
___ "The Stories Told in Science Fiction and Social Science: Reading *The Thing* and Other Remakes From Two Eras," by Michael A. Katovich and Patrick T. Kinkade. *Sociological Quarterly* 34(4): 619-651. 1993.

KINNARD, ROY
___ **Horror in the Silent Films: A Filmography, 1896-1929.** Jefferson, NC: McFarland, 1995. 256pp.
___ "Queen of Screams," *Starlog* No. 194: 66-69. September 1993.
___ "Queen of Screams," in: McDonnell, David, ed. **Starlog's Science Fiction Heroes and Heroines.** New York: Crescent Books, 1995. pp.38-40.
___ (ed.) *The Lost World* of Willis O'Brien: The Original Shooting **Script of the 1925 Landmark Special Effects Dinosaur Film, with Photographs.** Jefferson, NC: McFarland, 1993. 176pp.

KIPEN, DAVID
___ "Petty Can't Save Horribly Misconceived *Tank Girl*," *Boston (MA) Herald.* March 31, 1995. in: *NewsBank. Film and Television.* 50:C5. 1995.

KIRK, ELIZABETH D.
___ "Wel Bycommes Such Craft Upon Cristmasse: The Festive and the Hermeneutic in **Sir Gawain and the Green Knight**," *Arthuriana* 4(2): 93-137. Summer 1994.

KIRKHAM, PAT
___ "Making Frankenstein and the Monster," *Sight and Sound* 4(11): 6-11. November 1994.

KIRTZMAN, ANDREW
___ "Gays Bare Film Plot," *New York (NY) Daily News* March 10, 1992 in: *NewsBank. Film and Television.* 29:A6. 1992.

KLARER, MARIO
___ **Frau und Utopie: feministische Literaturtheorie und utopischer Diskurs im angloamerikanischen Roman.** Darmstadt: Wissenschaftliche Buchgesellschaft, 1993. 164pp. [Not seen.]
___ "Gender and 'The Simultaniety Principle': Ursula K. Le Guin's **The Dispossessed**," *Mosaic* 25(2): 107-121. Spring 1992.

KLAUS, H. GUSTAV
___ "Thomas Spence: **Description of Spensonia** (1795)," in: Heuermann, Hartmut and Lange, Bernd-Peter, eds. **Die Utopie in der angloamerikanischen Literatur: Interpretationen.** Düsseldorf: Bagel, 1984. pp.60-79.

KLEIN, GÉRARD
___ "Concerning Pages Arising From Nothingness: A Preface to the Second French Editon of **Flow My Tears, the Policeman Said**," *PKDS Newsletter* No. 28: 1-3. March 1992.
___ "Discontent in American Science Fiction," *Chung Wai Literary Quarterly* 22(12): May 1994. (Issue not seen; pagination unavailable.) (Reprinted from *Science Fiction Studies*.)

KLEIN, JAY K.
___ "Biolog: Jeffery D. Kooistra," *Analog* 113(14): 89, 110. December 1993.
___ "Biolog: A. J. Austin," *Analog* 112(1/2): 75. January 1992.
___ "Biolog: Brian C. Coad," *Analog* 112(11): 73. September 1992.
___ "Biolog: Bud Sparhawk," *Analog* 114(6): 92, 97. May 1994.
___ "Biolog: David J. Strumfels," *Analog* 114(8/9): 158, 178. July 1994.
___ "Biolog: Doug Beason," *Analog* 112(14): 79. December 1992.
___ "Biolog: Doug Larson," *Analog* 114(1/2): 225, 300. January 1994.
___ "Biolog: Gerald David Nordley," *Analog* 114(3): 94, 158. February 1994.
___ "Biolog: Gregory R. Bennett," *Analog* 114(5): 115, 160. April 1994.
___ "Biolog: Jeanne Robinson," *Analog* 114(12): 69, 141. October 1994.
___ "Biolog: Katherine MacLean," *Analog* 115(1/2): 215, 245. January 1995.
___ "Biolog: Kent Patterson," *Analog* 115(10): 161, 174. August 1995.
___ "Biolog: Kevin J. Anderson," *Analog* 112(13): 161, 169. November 1992.
___ "Biolog: Marianne J. Dyson," *Analog* 114(7): 157, 168. June 1994.
___ "Biolog: Mark Rich," *Analog* 114(13): 99, 108. November 1994.
___ "Biolog: Mike Moscoe," *Analog* 115(3): 93, 103. February 1995.
___ "Biolog: Paula Robinson," *Analog* 113(15): 110. Mid-December 1993.
___ "Biolog: Robert J. Sawyer," *Analog* 114(15): 69, 112. mid-December 1994.
___ "Biolog: Sarah Zettel," *Analog* 114(10): 121, 126. August 1994.
___ "Biolog: Stephen L. Burns," *Analog* 113(1/2): 53-54. January 1993.
___ "Biolog: Tina Lee," *Analog* 115(12): 129, 161. October 1995.

KLEIN, JÜRGEN
___ "Samuel Butler **Erewhon** (1872)," by Jürgen Klein and Klaus Zöllner. in: Heuermann, Hartmut and Lange, Bernd-Peter, eds. **Die Utopie in der angloamerikanischen Literatur: Interpretationen.** Düsseldorf: Bagel, 1984. pp.80-102.

KLEINER, ELAINE
___ "Romanian 'Science Fantasy' in the Cold War Era," *Science Fiction Studies* 19(1): 59-68. March 1992.

KLEINER, RHEINHART
___ "After a Decade and the Kalem Club," *Lovecraft Studies* No. 28: 34-35. Fall 1992. (Reprinted from *The Californian*, Fall 1936.)

KLEINSCHMIDT, ERICH
___ " 'Begreif-Weit': Zur fiktionalen Raumregahrung in der deutschen Literatur des 18. Jahrhunderts," *Germanisch-Romanische Monatsschrift* (Berlin) 41(2): 145-152. 1991.

KLIEWER, BRENT
___ "Eek, There's a **Ghost in the Machine**," *(Santa Fe, NM) New Mexican* January 7, 1994. in: *NewsBank. Film and Television* 12: A9. 1994.

KLINE, BARBARA
___ "Duality, Reality and Magic in **Sir Gawain and the Green Knight**," in: Sanders, Joe, ed. **Functions of the Fantastic**. Westport, CT: Greenwood, 1995. pp.107-114.

KLINE, NATHAN S.
___ "Cyborgs and Space," by Manfred E. Clynes and Nathan S. Kline. in: Gray, Chris H., ed. **The Cyborg Handbook**. New York: Routledge, 1995. pp.29-33.

KLINGER, CORNELIA
___ "Radikalfeminismus, Science Fiction und das Verhältnis zur Natur," in: Grabher, Gudrun M. and Devine, Marureen, eds. **Women in Search of Literary Space**. Tübingen: Gunter Narr Verlag, 1992. pp.180-197.

KLINGHOFFER, DAVID
___ "**Freejack**: Movie Is Born Brain-Dead (Review)," *Washington (DC) Times*. January 20, 1992. in: *NewsBank. Film and Television*. 11:D12. 1992.
___ "Murder Thriller a Muddle," *Washington (DC) Times*. March 20, 1992 in: *NewsBank. Film and Television*. 29:B14. 1992.
___ "Will Young Indy Jones Grow Up to Be Himself? (Review)," *Washington (DC) Times*. March 4, 1992. in: *NewsBank. Film and Television*. 27:C4-C5. 1992.

KLOER, PHIL
___ "**M. A. N. T. I. S.** in Current State Doesn't Have a Prayer," *Atlanta (GA) Journal*. August 26, 1994. in: *NewsBank. Film and Television*. 91: A3. 1994.

KLOSSNER, MICHAEL
___ "A Critical Survey of Fantastic Literature and Film Scholarship in 1990," by Neil Barron and Michael Klossner. in: Collins, Robert A. and Latham, Robert, eds. **Science Fiction and Fantasy Book Review Annual 1991**. Westport, CT: Greenwood, 1994. pp.205-239.
___ "Science Fiction in Film, Television, and Radio," in: Barron, Neil, ed. **Anatomy of Wonder 4**. New York: Bowker, 1995. pp.612-650.
___ "Word and Image: A Survey of Fantastic Film & TV Magazines," *SFRA Newsletter* No. 194: 10-15. January/February 1992.

KNAPP, JEFFREY
___ **An Empire Nowhere: England, America, and Literature from Utopia to The Tempest**. Berkeley: University of California Press, 1992. 387pp.

KNECHT, WILLIAM R.
___ "C. S. Lewis and the Apotheosis," *CSL: The Bulletin of the New York C. S. Lewis Society* 23(8): 1-4. June 1992.

KNEE, ADAM
___ "Metamorphosis of **The Fly**," *Wide Angle* 14(1): 20-35. January 1992.

KNIGHT, DAMON
___ "Dell Magazine Contract," *SFWA Bulletin* 28(2): 2-4. Summer 1994. (No. 124)
___ "Dell Magazines Contract Update," *SFWA Bulletin* 28(3): 2. Winter 1994. (No. 125)
___ "The History of the SFWA 1965-1967," *SFWA Bulletin* 26(3): 3-4. Fall 1992. (No. 117)
___ **An R. A. Lafferty Checklist**. New edition. Polk City, IA: Drumm, 1991. 28pp.

KNOEPFLMACHER, U. C.
___ (ed.) **Forbidden Journeys: Fairy Tales and Fantasies**, ed. by Nina Auerbach and U. C. Knoepflmacher. Chicago: University of Chicago Press, 1992. 373pp.

KNOESPEL, KENNETH J.
___ "Gazing on Technology: *Theatrum Mechanorum* and the Assimilation of Renaissance Machinery," in: Greenberg, Mark L. and Schachterle, Lance, eds. **Literature and Technology**. Bethlehem, PA: Lehigh University Press, 1992. pp.99-124.

KNOWLES, TOM W., II.
___ "Writing from the Heart of Time," *Starlog* No. 183: 27-31, 70. October 1992.

KOEBEL, CHUCK
___ "Fantasy in the Mainstream: The Fiction of Italo Calvino," *OtherRealms* No. 24: 7-8. Spring 1989.

KOGELMAN, DAVID
___ "Writing and the Law: Advantages of Individual Copyright Registration," *Locus* 33(6): 9, 76. December 1994.

KOH, TSE-YING
___ "Oh No!... It's... It's... Jurassic Mania!," *Austin (TX) American Statesman* Sec. E, p. 1, 8. June 10, 1993.

KOHL, LEONARD
___ "Flash Back to the Future: From Cosmic Comic Strip to Serial Sci-Fi," *Filmfax* No. 45: 47-58. June/July 1994.

KOHLER, VINCE
___ "OMSI Exhibit Goes Where No Museum Has Gone Before," *Portland (OR) The Oregonian*. January 24, 1992. in: *NewsBank. Film and Television*. 15:C6. 1992.
___ "**Star Trek**: An American Icon at Work," *Portland (OR) The Oregonian*. January 24, 1992. in: *NewsBank. Film and Television*. 15: C5. 1992.

KOKE, JAK
___ "Sexual Etiquette at Conventions," by Jonathan Bond and Jak Koke. *The Report: The Fiction Writer's Magazine* No. 7: 11-12. June 1992.
___ "Writing for Gaming Companies: A Personal Experience," *The Report: The Fiction Writer's Magazine* No. 10: 8-9. Summer 1993.

KOKOT, JOANNA
___ "Cultural Functions Motivating Art: Poems and Their Contexts in **The Lord of the Rings**," in: Kranz, Gisbert, ed. **Jahrbuch für Literatur und Ästhetik**. Lüdenscheid, Germany: Stier, 1992. Band 10, pp.191-207.

KOLKER, ROBERT P.
___ "The Moving Image Reclaimed," *Postmodern Culture* 5(1): [6pp., with imbedded motion picture full-motion clips in MPEG]. September 1994. (Electronic Journal: pmc@jefferson.village.virginia.edu).

KOLLMANN, JUDITH
___ "Eros, Philia, and Agape in Charles Williams' Arthuriad," *Mythlore* 18(4): 9-14. Autumn 1992. (No. 70)

KOLMERTEN, CAROL A.
___ "Frances Wright and the Search for Equality," in: Saccaro Del Buffa, Giuseppa and Lewis, Arthur O., eds. **Utopia e Modernita: Teorie e prassi utopiche nell'eta moderna e postmoderna**. Rome: Gangemi Editore, 1989. pp.987-1002.
___ "Introduction," by Jane L. Donawerth and Carol A. Kolmerten. in: Donawerth, Jane L. and Kolmerten, Carol A., eds. **Utopian and Science Fiction by Women: Worlds of Difference**. Syracuse, NY: Syracuse University Press, 1994. pp.1-14.
___ "Texts and Contexts: American Women Envision Utopia, 1890-1920," in: Donawerth, Jane L. and Kolmerten, Carol A., eds. **Utopian and Science Fiction by Women: Worlds of Difference**. Syracuse, NY: Syracuse University Press, 1994. pp.107-125.
___ "Women Seeing Utopia: Patterns in Utopian Literature, 1880-1915," in: Saccaro Del Buffa, Giuseppa and Lewis, Arthur O., eds. **Utopie per gli Anni Ottana**. Rome: Gangemi Editore, 1986. pp.499-510.
___ (ed.) **Utopian and Science Fiction by Women: Worlds of Difference**, ed. by Jane L. Donawerth and Carol A. Kolmerten. Syracuse, NY: Syracuse University Press, 1994. 260pp.

KONDO, YOJI
___ "Farewell to the Master," by Yoji Kondo and Charles Sheffield. in: Kondo, Yoji, ed. **Requiem: New Collected Works by Robert A. Heinlein and Tributes to the Grand Master**. New York: Tor, 1992. pp.337-341.
___ "When Earth Has Its First Contact With Alien Beings, Will We Be Ready?," by Arlan Andrews, Yoji Kondo and Charles Sheffield. *Science Fiction Age* 3(2): 22, 24-28, 86. January 1995.
___ (ed.) **Requiem: New Collected Works by Robert A. Heinlein and Tributes to the Grand Master**. New York: Tor, 1992. 341pp.

KONDRATIEV, ALEXEI
___ "Tales Newly Told: Tolkien," *Mythlore* 18(2): 10-11. Spring 1992. (No. 68)

KONONENKO, V. O.
___ **Neznani svity fantastyky: rekomendattsiinyi bibliohrafichnyi pokazhchyk**, by V. O. Kononenko and V. M. Loi. Kyiv: Derzhavan biblioteke Ukrainy, 1992. 35pp. [Not seen.]

KOONTZ, DEAN R.
___ "The Coming Blaylockian Age," in: Greenberg, Martin H., Ed Gorman and Bill Munster, eds. **The Dean Koontz Companion**. New York: Berkley, 1994. pp.177-179.

KOONTZ, DEAN R. (continued)
___ "The Day It Rained Frogs," in: Greenberg, Martin H., Ed Gorman and Bill Munster, eds. **The Dean Koontz Companion.** New York: Berkley, 1994. pp.236-239.
___ "A Genre in Crisis," in: Greenberg, Martin H., Ed Gorman and Bill Munster, eds. **The Dean Koontz Companion.** New York: Berkley, 1994. pp.206-215.
___ "Ghost Stories," in: Greenberg, Martin H., Ed Gorman and Bill Munster, eds. **The Dean Koontz Companion.** New York: Berkley, 1994. pp.202-205.
___ "How To," in: Greenberg, Martin H., Ed Gorman and Bill Munster, eds. **The Dean Koontz Companion.** New York: Berkley, 1994. pp.216-218.
___ "Keeping the Reader on the Edge of His Seat," in: Greenberg, Martin H., Ed Gorman and Bill Munster, eds. **The Dean Koontz Companion.** New York: Berkley, 1994. pp.219-224.
___ "Kittens," in: Greenberg, Martin H., Ed Gorman and Bill Munster, eds. **The Dean Koontz Companion.** New York: Berkley, 1994. pp.193-198.
___ "Koontz, Will You Just Shut Up Already," in: Greenberg, Martin H., Ed Gorman and Bill Munster, eds. **The Dean Koontz Companion.** New York: Berkley, 1994. pp.199-201.
___ "Koontzramble," in: Greenberg, Martin H., Ed Gorman and Bill Munster, eds. **The Dean Koontz Companion.** New York: Berkley, 1994. pp.149-154.
___ "The Man Who Does Not Always Mean What He Says," in: Greenberg, Martin H., Ed Gorman and Bill Munster, eds. **The Dean Koontz Companion.** New York: Berkley, 1994. pp.240-244.
___ "The Man Who Knows All About Hippodurkees," in: Greenberg, Martin H., Ed Gorman and Bill Munster, eds. **The Dean Koontz Companion.** New York: Berkley, 1994. pp.163-166.
___ "The Miracle Tree of Burbank," in: Greenberg, Martin H., Ed Gorman and Bill Munster, eds. **The Dean Koontz Companion.** New York: Berkley, 1994. pp.260-265.
___ "Mister Bizarro," in: Greenberg, Martin H., Ed Gorman and Bill Munster, eds. **The Dean Koontz Companion.** New York: Berkley, 1994. pp.182-186.
___ "My First Short Story," in: Greenberg, Martin H., Ed Gorman and Bill Munster, eds. **The Dean Koontz Companion.** New York: Berkley, 1994. pp.187-192.
___ "No One Can Talk to a Horse, of Course," in: Greenberg, Martin H., Ed Gorman and Bill Munster, eds. **The Dean Koontz Companion.** New York: Berkley, 1994. pp.258-259.
___ "Oh, to Be in Cedar Rapids When the Hog Blood Flows," in: Greenberg, Martin H., Ed Gorman and Bill Munster, eds. **The Dean Koontz Companion.** New York: Berkley, 1994. pp.155-162.
___ "Rex Stout and Nero Wolfe," in: Greenberg, Martin H., Ed Gorman and Bill Munster, eds. **The Dean Koontz Companion.** New York: Berkley, 1994. pp.167-172.
___ "Tater Bacon," in: Greenberg, Martin H., Ed Gorman and Bill Munster, eds. **The Dean Koontz Companion.** New York: Berkley, 1994. pp.173-176.
___ "The Truth About Christmas," in: Greenberg, Martin H., Ed Gorman and Bill Munster, eds. **The Dean Koontz Companion.** New York: Berkley, 1994. pp.180-181.
___ "Tweetie, the Parakeet From Hell," in: Greenberg, Martin H., Ed Gorman and Bill Munster, eds. **The Dean Koontz Companion.** New York: Berkley, 1994. pp.245-257.
___ "The Unluckiest Man in the World," in: Greenberg, Martin H., Ed Gorman and Bill Munster, eds. **The Dean Koontz Companion.** New York: Berkley, 1994. pp.266-273.
___ "*Weird World*: The Introduction," in: Greenberg, Martin H., Ed Gorman and Bill Munster, eds. **The Dean Koontz Companion.** New York: Berkley, 1994. pp.233-235.
___ "Why Novels of Fear Must Do More Than Frighten," in: Greenberg, Martin H., Ed Gorman and Bill Munster, eds. **The Dean Koontz Companion.** New York: Berkley, 1994. pp.225-230.
___ "You'll Either Love It or Hate It--Or Just Be Indifferent to It," in: Greenberg, Martin H., Ed Gorman and Bill Munster, eds. **The Dean Koontz Companion.** New York: Berkley, 1994. pp.231-232.

KOOPMAN THURLINGS, MARISKA
___ "Fantastique ludique et érotisme inquiétant dans l'oeuvre de Michel Tournier," in: Bozzetto, Roger, ed. **Eros: Science & Fiction Fantastique.** Aix-en-Provence: Universite de Provence, 1991. pp.135-153.

KOPPEL, T.
___ **Chronography: A Chronological Bibliography of Books by Charles L. Harness.** Polk City, IA: Chris Drumm, 1993. 27pp.

KORDESKI, STANLEY
___ **Anatomy of Fantasy: An Examination of Works of J. R. R. Tolkien and C. S. Lewis.** Master's Thesis, University of Vermont, 1975. 67pp.

KORDIGEL, METKA
___ "Nastansk in razvoj termina znanstvena fantastike na Slovenskem," *Slavisticna Revija* 41(4): 571-580. 1993. [Not seen.]
___ "Poskus Literarnoteoreticne definicije znanstvene fantastike," *Slavisticna Revija* (Slovenia) 40(3): 291-308. July/September 1992. [Not seen.]

KORMAN, KEN
___ "Building a Better Beast," *Video Magazine* 17(8): 56-57, 98, 108. November 1994.
___ **Secrets of Stargate** (Review)," *Video Magazine* 18(10): 65. January 1995.

KOSATIK, PAVEL
___ **Kdo je Kdo v ceské a slovenské science fiction,** by Zdenek Rampas and Pavel Kosatik. Praha, CZ: Ceskoslovenského fandomu, 1994. 84pp. [Not seen.]

KOSELER, MICHAEL
___ "Leo Perutz' **Der Meister des Jüngsten Tages**: Detektion und Verrätselung," *Quarber Merkur* 33(1): 3-15. June 1995. (No. 83)
___ "Phänomenologie des Schreckens," by Clemens Ruthner and Michael Koseler. *Quarber Merkur* 33(2): 30-34. December 1995. (No. 84)

KOSKO, BART
___ "The Future of God," *Free Inquiry* 15(3): 43-44. Summer 1995.

KOTANI, MARI
___ **Joseijo Muishiki: tekunogaineshisu, josei SF-ron josetsu.** [Techno-gynesis: The Political Unconscious of Feminist Science Fiction]. Tokyo: Keiso Shobo, 1994. 283pp. [In Japanese, not seen. cf. OCLC.]

KOTERSKI, JOSEPH W.
___ "C. S. Lewis and Natural Law," *Bulletin of the New York C. S. Lewis Society* 26(6): 1-7. April 1995.

KOTOWSKI, NATHALIE
___ "Frodo, Sam and Aragorn in the Light of C. G. Jung," in: Kranz, Gisbert, ed. **Jahrbuch für Literatur und Ästhetik.** Lüdenscheid, Germany: Stier, 1992. Band 10, pp.145-159.

KOVTUN, E. N.
___ "Tipy i funksii khudozhestvennoi uslovnosti v evropeskoi literature pervoi poloviny XX veka," *Vestnik Moskovskogo Universiteta. Seriia 9: Filologiia* (Moscow) 9(4): 43-50. July/August 1993. [Not seen.]

KOZACHIK, PETE
___ "Stop Motion Without Compromise: **The Nightmare Before Christmas**," *American Cinematographer* 74(12): 37-43. December 1993.

KOZAK, ELLEN M.
___ "Negotiating the Maze That Is GATT," *SFWA Bulletin* 29(2): 26-27. Summer 1995. (No. 127)

KOZLOFF, SARAH R.
___ "Superman as Saviour: Christian Allegory in the Superman Movies," *Journal of Popular Film and Television* 9(2): 78-82. 1981.

KRABBENHOFT, KENNETH
___ "Lem as Moral Theologian," *Science Fiction Studies* 21(2): 212-224. July 1994.

KRACZMAREK, NANCY
___ "Collaboration: The Science in Science Fiction," *The English Record* 42(3): 13-15. 1992.

KRAISKI, GIORGIO
___ "Aspetti dell'utopia dostoievskiana," in: Saccaro Del Buffa, Giuseppa and Lewis, Arthur O., eds. **Utopie per gli Anni Ottana.** Rome: Gangemi Editore, 1986. pp.675-678.

KRAMARAE, CHERIS
___ "Present Problems With the Language of the Future," *Women's Studies* 14(2): 183-186. 1987.

KRAMER, MARY
___ "Atwood's **Wilderness** Is Over Much Too Soon," *Boston (MA) Herald.* December 8, 1991. in *NewsBank. Literature.* 1:C10. 1992.

KRAMER, REINHOLD
___ "Im/maculate: Some Instances of Gnostic Science Fiction," in: Ruddick, Nicholas, ed. **State of the Fantastic.** Westport, CT: Greenwood, 1992. pp.49-58.

KRANZ, GISBERT
___ "Aldous Huxley und C. S. Lewis: Eine vergleichende Studie," in: Kranz, Gisbert, ed. **Inklings: Jahrbuch für Literatur und Ästhetik.** 2. Band. [Lüdenscheid, Germany: Stier], 1984. pp.112-153.
___ "Der heilende Aragorn," in: Kranz, Gisbert, ed. **Inklings: Jahrbuch für Literatur und Ästhetik.** 2. Band. [Lüdenscheid, Germany: Stier], 1984. pp.11-24.
___ "Ein Dinosaurier? C. S. Lewis und die moderne Literatur," in: Kranz, Gisbert, ed. **Inklings: Jahrbuch für Literatur und Ästhetik.** 7. Band. Lüdenscheid, Germany: Stier, 1989. pp.53-62. [Not seen.]
___ "MacDonald, Novalis, Liebe und Tod," in: Kranz, Gisbert, ed. **Inklings: Jahrbuch für Literatur und Ästhetik.** 9. Band. Lüdenscheid, Germany: Stier, 1991. pp.55-70 [Not seen.]
___ "Stellvertretung bei Williams, Claudel und G. v. le Fort," in: Kranz, Gisbert, ed. **Inklings: Jahrbuch für Literatur und Ästhetik.** 3. Band. [Lüdenscheid, Germany: Stier], 1985. pp.87-108.
___ **Tolkien in aller Welt: Eine Ausstellung der Inklings-Gesellschaft anlässlich des 100. Geburtstags von J. R. R. Tolkien und des Internationalen Tolkien-Symposions in Aachen.** Aachen: Öffentliche Bibliothek der Stadt Aachen, 1992. 67pp.
___ "Tolkien und sein sohn Michael," in: Kranz, Gisbert, ed. **Jahrbuch für Literatur und Ästhetik.** Lüdenscheid, Germany: Stier, 1992. Band 10, pp.11-23.
___ "Tolkine und den Inklings auf der Spur," in: Kranz, Gisbert, ed. **Jahrbuch für Literatur und Ästhetik.** Lüdenscheid, Germany: Stier, 1992. Band 10, pp.283-292.
___ (ed.) **Inklings: Jahrbuch für Literatur und Ästhetik. 1.Band.** Lüdenscheid: Michael Claren, 1983. 185pp.

KRASNER, JAMES
___ **The Entangled Eye: Visual Perception and the Representation of Nature in Post-Darwinian Narrative.** New York: Oxford University Press, 1992. 191pp.

KRATZ, DENNIS M.
___ "Teaching Science Fiction," in: Barron, Neil, ed. **Anatomy of Wonder 4.** New York: Bowker, 1995. pp.715-737.

KRAUSE, MAUREEN T.
___ "Appendix: Selective Glossary," *Journal of the Fantastic in the Arts* 7(2/3): 269-271. 1995.
___ "*Bereshit bara Elohim*: A Survey of the Genesis and Evolution of the Golem," *Journal of the Fantastic in the Arts* 7(2/3): 113-136. 1995.

KRAUSS, LAWRENCE M.
___ "Beam Me Up an Einstein, Scotty," *Wired* 3(11): 16-130. November 1995.
___ **The Physics of Star Trek.** New York: Basic Books, 1995. 188pp.

KREEFT, PETER
___ **C. S. Lewis for the Third Millennium: Six Essays on The Abolition of Man.** San Francisco, CA: Ignatius, 1994. 193pp.
___ "How to Save Western Civilisation: C. S. Lewis as Prophet," in: Walker, Andrew and Patric, James, eds. **A Christian for All Christians.** Washington, DC: Regnery, 1992. pp.190-212.
___ "Walker Percy's **Lost in the Cosmos: The Abolition of Man** in Late-night Comedy Format," in: Kreeft, Peter. **C. S. Lewis for the Third Millenium.** San Francisco, CA: Ignatius, 1994. pp.131-164.

KRESS, NANCY
___ **Beginnings, Middles & Ends.** Cincinnati, OH: Writer's Digest Books, 1993. 149pp.
___ "Plot: Using Coincidence in Your Fiction," in: Thompkins, David G., ed. **Science Fiction Writer's Market Place and Source Book.** Cincinnati, OH: Writer's Digest Books, 1994. pp.30-33.
___ "An SF Moderate Climbs Cautiously onto the Barricades," *Pulphouse* No. 10: 12-18. July 1992.

KRIDLER, CHRIS
___ "*Johnny Mnemonic* Boggles Mind," *(Baltimore, MD) Sun.* May 27, 1995. in: *NewsBank. Film and Television.* 55:B4. 1995.

KRIEGER, TODD
___ "Street Creed: *Sci-Fi Universe*," *Wired* 3(2): 144. February 1995.

KRIPS, VALERIE
___ "Finding One's Place in the Fantastic: Susan Cooper's **The Dark Is Rising**," in: Sanders, Joe, ed. **Functions of the Fantastic.** Westport, CT: Greenwood, 1995. pp.169-176.

KRONKE, DAVID
___ "As Far as Idiocy Goes, **Tuned** Matches Up With the Year's Best (Review)," *Los Angeles (CA) Daily News.* August 15, 1992. in: *NewsBank. Film and Television.* 84:A5. 1992.
___ "**Dracula**'s Problem: All Show and No Tell," *Los Angeles (CA) Daily News.* November 13, 1992. in: *NewsBank. Film and Television.* 111:A8-A9. 1992.
___ "For All Its Gadgetry, **Sneakers** Never Accelerates into High Gear (Review)," *Los Angeles (CA) Daily News.* September 9, 1992. in: *NewsBank. Film and Television.* 96:D1. 1992.
___ "He's Back: Is There Cloaked Violence in Caped Crusader's Sequel?," *Los Angeles (CA) Daily News.* June 19, 1992. in: *NewsBank. Film and Television.* 67:E12-E13. 1992.
___ "Instinct Delivers Compelling Roles," *Los Angeles (CA) Daily News* March 20, 1992 in: *NewsBank. Film and Television.* 29:A11. 1992.
___ "King's Latest Victim May Be the Viewer With This Dumb Plot (Review)," *Los Angeles (CA) Daily News.* April 11, 1992. in: *NewsBank. Film and Television.* 46:C7. 1992.
___ "The Marketing of a Monster," *Dallas Morning News* Sec. C., p. 5, 11. June 12, 1993.
___ "Prelude to an Overly Worked But Slightly Funny Comedy (Review)," *Los Angeles (CA) Daily News.* July 10, 1992. in: *NewsBank. Film and Television.* 73:B14. 1992.
___ "**Prospero's Books** a Complicated Read (Review)," *Dallas (TX) Times Herald.* November 27, 1991. in: *NewsBank. Film and Television.* 6:D7. 1992.
___ "Re-released **Blade Runner** Is Original Work of Great Scott," *Los Angeles (CA) Daily News.* September 11, 1992. in: *NewsBank. Film and Television.* 87:F5. 1992.
___ "**Soldier** Surrenders All Pretense of Plot, Credibility (Review)," *Los Angeles (CA) Daily News.* July 28, 1992. in: *NewsBank. Film and Television.* 74:G1. 1992.
___ "Some Laughs, But Bill and Ted Still Bogus," *Dallas (TX) Times Herald.* July 19, 1991. in: *NewsBank. Film and Television.* 65:F6. 1991.
___ "Sometimes, It Does Pay to Be Villainous," *Los Angeles (CA) Daily News.* June 19, 1992. in: *NewsBank. Film and Television.* 67:E14-F1. 1992.
___ "Struck by Frightening: Barker Puts Own Spin on Scary Films, Kids' Book," *Los Angeles (CA) Daily News* October 19, 1992 in: *NewsBank. Film and Television.* 99:B12-B13. 1992
___ "Tossing Caution, Geography to the Wind: **Encino Man** Neatly Sidesteps Namesake City (Review)," *Los Angeles (CA) Daily News.* February 12, 1992. in: *NewsBank. Film and Television.* 30:G13-G14. 1992.
___ "What's Scary Is How **Alien III** Fails to Deliver," *Los Angeles (CA) Daily News.* May 22, 1992. in: *NewsBank. Film and Television.* 49:B10. 1992.

KRUEGER, RICHARD J.
___ **Science and Fiction.** Thesis (M.F.A), University of Notre Dame, 1994. 32pp.

KRUG, JUSTIN
___ "**Batman Returns** Overrated, but It's Worth Seeing Anyway," *Portland (OR) The Oregonian.* June 24, 1992. in: *NewsBank. Film and Television.* 67:F6. 1992.

KRULIK, THEODORE
___ **The Complete Amber Sourcebook**. New York: Avon, 1995. 494pp.

KRUPNIK, JOSEPH
___ "Infinity in a Cigar Box: The Problem of Science Fiction on Stage," in: Murphy, Patrick D., ed. **Staging the Impossible: The Fantastic Mode in Modern Drama**. Westport, CT: Greenwood, 1992. pp.197-219.

KRYWAK, PIOTR
___ **Stanislaw Lem**. Cracow: Panswowe Wydawnictwo Naukowe, 1974. (Not seen. Cf. *Science-Fiction Studies*, Nov. 1992.)

KUBE-McDOWELL, MICHAEL P.
___ "The Encyclopedic Article of Nebula Lists," *SFWA Bulletin* 27(4)/28(1): 23-31. Winter/Spring 1994. (No. 122/123)
___ "The Quiet Pools," *OtherRealms* No. 27: 4-5. Spring 1990.
___ "Report on the 1991 SFWA Membership Profile Project," *SFWA Bulletin* 26(1): 39-42. Spring 1992. (No. 115)

KUBEY, ROBERT W.
___ "U.S. Opinion and Politics Before and After *The Day After*: Television Movie as Rorschach," in: Wober, J. Mallory, ed. **Television and Nuclear Power: Making the Public Mind**. Norwood, NJ: Ablex, 1992. pp.19-30.

KUBINSKI, WOJCIECH
___ "Comprehending the Incomprehensible: On the Pragmatic Analysis of Elvish Texts in **The Lord of the Rings**," in: Kranz, Gisbert, ed. **Inklings: Jahrbuch für Literatur und Ästhetik**. 7. Band. Lüdenscheid, Germany: Stier, 1989. pp.63-82. [Not seen.]

KUCHMENT, MARK
___ "Bridging the Two Cultures: The Emergence of Scientific Prose," in: Graham, Loren R., ed. **Science and the Soviet Social Order**. Cambridge: Harvard University Press, 1990. pp.335-340.

KUELEN, MARGARETE
___ **Radical Imagination: Feminist Conceptions of the Future in Ursula Le Guin, Marge Piercy and Sally Miller Gearhart**. Frankfurt-am-Main/New York: Peter Lang, 1991. 122pp.

KUHN, ANNETTE
___ "Border Crossing," *Sight and Sound* 2(3): 11-12. July 1992.

KUMAR, KRISHAN
___ "The End of Socialism? The End of Utopia? The End of History?," in: Kumar, Krishan and Bann, Stephen, eds. **Utopias and the Millennium**. London: Reaktion Books, 1993. pp.63-80.
___ "A Pilgrimage of Hope: William Morris's Journey to Utopia," *Utopian Studies* 5(1): 89-107. 1994.
___ (ed.) **Utopias and the Millennium**, ed. by Krishan Kumar and Stephen Bann. London: Reaktion Books, 1993. 164pp.

KUNK, DEBORAH J.
___ "Through a Child's Eyes (Review)," *St. Paul (MN) Pioneer Press-Dispatch*. March 3, 1992. in: *NewsBank. Film and Television*. 24:F13. 1992

KUNZLE, DAVID
___ **The History of the Comic Strip, Vol. 2: The Nineteenth Century**. Berkeley: University of California Press, 1990. 391pp.

KURTIS, BILL
___ **The Science of Star Trek**. Chicago, IL: Public Media Video, 1995. 1 videocassette, 60 minutes.

KURYLLO, HELEN A.
___ "Cyborgs, Sorcery, and the Struggle for Utopia," *Utopian Studies* 5(2): 50-55. 1994.

KURZWEIL, EDITH
___ "Unexamined Mental Attitudes Left Behind by Communism (Interview, 1992)," in: Ingersoll, Earl G., ed. **Doris Lessing: Conversations**. Princeton, NJ: Ontario Review Press, 1994. pp.204-213.

KUSCHNIK, ANNE
___ "Zur Neuübersetzung zweier Tolkien-Gedichte," in: Kranz, Gisbert, ed. **Jahrbuch für Literatur und Ästhetik**. Lüdenscheid, Germany: Stier, 1992. Band 10, pp.209-220.

KUSHMAN, RICK
___ "Believe It (or Not)," *Sacramento (CA) Bee*. August 4, 1995. in: *NewsBank. Film and Television*. 82:F1-F3. 1995.

KUTZERA, DALE
___ "**Coneheads**: Stop Motion Garthok," *Cinefantastique* 24(6)/25(1): 121-122. February 1994.
___ "**Coneheads**," *Cinefantastique* 24(6)/25(1): 118-119. February 1994.
___ "**Dr. Giggles**: Horror Director Manny Coto," *Cinefantastique* 23(4): 23. December 1992.
___ "**Dr. Giggles**: Queasy Mix of Humor and Horror Toplines Larry Drake," *Cinefantastique* 23(4): 20-22. December 1992.
___ "The Mutant Ninja Turtles Movie Mutiny," *Cinefantastique* 23(6): 8-11. April 1993.
___ "Quick Cuts: Digital Effects," *Cinefex* No. 57: 75-76. March 1994.
___ "Quick Cuts: Visionary Visuals," *Cinefex* No. 58: 17-18. June 1994.
___ "**Star Trek: Deep Space Nine**: Episode Guide, Second Season," *Cinefantastique* 25(6)/26(1): 96-111. December 1994.
___ "**Star Trek: Deep Space Nine**," *Cinefantastique* 25(6)/26(1): 94-98. December 1994.
___ "**Star Trek: The Next Generation**: All Things Good," *Cinefantastique* 25(6)/26(1): 74-76. December 1994.
___ "**Star Trek: The Next Generation**: Doctor Turns Director," *Cinefantastique* 25(6)/26(1): 83. December 1994.
___ "**Star Trek: The Next Generation**: Episode Guide, 7th Season," *Cinefantastique* 25(6)/26(1): 47-93. December 1994.
___ "**Star Trek: The Next Generation**: Freelance Writers," *Cinefantastique* 25(6)/26(1): 81-82. December 1994.
___ "**Star Trek: The Next Generation**: Making 'Lower Decks'," *Cinefantastique* 25(6)/26(1): 77-80. December 1994.
___ "**Star Trek: The Next Generation**: Troi's Marina Sirtis," *Cinefantastique* 25(6)/26(1): 88-89. December 1994.
___ "**Star Trek: The Next Generation**," *Cinefantastique* 25(6)/26(1): 44-93, 124. December 1994.
___ "**Star Trek: Voyager**," *Cinefantastique* 25(6)/26(1): 104-105, 124. December 1994.
___ "**Star Trek: Voyager**," *Cinefantastique* 26(2): 28-29. February 1995.
___ "**Teenage Mutant Ninja Turtles III**," *Cinefantastique* 23(5): 6-7. February 1993.
___ "Turtles III: Fixing the Franchise," *Cinefantastique* 23(6): 10. April 1993.
___ "**Wes Craven's New Nightmare**," *Cinefantastique* 25(4): 6-7, 61. August 1994.
___ "**X-Files**," *Cinefantastique* 26(2): 52-53. February 1995.

KYLE, DAVID A.
___ "In Memories Yet Green," *Starlog* 181: 32-35, 60. August 1992.

LABOR, EARLE
___ **Jack London**. Revised edition. New York: Twayne, 1994. 186pp.

LACASSIN, FRANCIS
___ **Tarzan ou le Chevalier crispe**. Paris: H. Veyrier, 1982. 223pp. [Revised edition].
___ **Tarzan ou le Chevalier crispe**. Paris: Union Generale d'editions, 1971. 511pp.

LACKEY, CHAD
___ "Social Science Fiction: Writing Sociological Short Stories to Learn About Social Issues," *Teaching Sociology* 22(2): 166-173. April 1994.

LACY, NORRIS J.
___ "Emergent Direct Discourse in the Vulgate Cycle," *Arthuriana* 4(1): 19-29. Spring 1994.
___ "Mythopoeia in *Excalibur*," in: Harty, Kevin J., ed. **Cinema Arthuriana: Essays on Arthurian Film**. New York: Garland, 1991. pp.121-134.
___ "Teaching the King Arthur of History and Chronicle," in: Fries, Maureen and Watson, Jeanie, eds. **Approaches to the Teaching of the Arthurian Tradition**. New York: Modern Language Association, 1992. pp.51-55.

LADD, THYRIL L.
___ "Ray Cummings: A Meeting," in: Cummings, Ray. **The Girl in the Golden Atom**. Westport, CT: Hyperion, 1974. [8 pp., unpaged]. (Originally published in *Fantasy Commentator*, Winter 1948, as 'This Is About Ray Cummings.')

LAFFERTY, R. A.
___ **It's Down the Slippery Cellar Stairs: Essays and Speeches on Fantastic Literature**. San Bernardino, CA: Borgo, 1995. 104pp.

LAGON, MARK P.
___ " 'We Owe It to Them to Interfere': *Star Trek* and U.S. Statecraft in the 1960s and 1990s," *Extrapolation* 34(3): 251-264. Fall 1993.

LAGORIO, VALERIE M.
___ "King Arthur and Camelot, U.S.A. in the Twentieth Century," in: Rosenthal, Bernard and Szarmach, Paul E., eds. **Medievalism in American Culture**. Binghamton, NY: Medieval & Renaissance Texts and Studies, 1989. pp.151-169.
___ (ed.) **King Arthur Through the Ages**, ed. by Valerie M. Lagorio and Mildred L. Day. New York: Garland, 1990. 2 v.

LAIDLAW, MARC
___ "An Open Letter to John Norman From a Reader He Lost Long Ago," *New York Review of Science Fiction* No. 87: 22. November 1995.

LAKE, DAVID
___ "Wells, **The First Men in the Moon**, and Lewis's Ransom Trilogy," in: Filmer, Kath, ed. **Twentieth-Century Fantasists: Essays in Culture, Society and Belief in Twentieth Century Mythopoeic Literature**. New York: St. Martin's, 1992. pp.23-33.

LAKE, KEN
___ "Lois McMaster Bujold Interviewed," *Vector* No. 171: 7-11. February/March 1993.

LAKE, LISA
___ "Rick Baker Meets the Wolfman," *Sci-Fi Entertainment* 1(1): 24-28. June 1994.

LAMB, JOHN B.
___ "Mary Shelley's **Frankenstein** and Milton's Monstrous Myth," *Nineteenth Century Literature* 47(3): [7pp.] 1995. (Cited from the electronic edition, NCL-E, 47(3), 1995. [http: //sunsite. berkeley. edu: 8080/ scan/ncle.473/ articles/ lamb.art473.html]).

LAMBARSKI, TIM
___ "Homeliness, Strangeness, and Receptivity: Paths to Aslan's Country in **The Voyage of the Dawn Treader**," *Bulletin of the New York C. S. Lewis Society* 25(5/6): 6-11. March/April 1994.

LAMBDIN, LAURA
___ "Swinburne's Early Arthurian Poems: Shadows of His Mature Vision," *Quondam et Futurus* 3(4): 63-76. Winter 1993.

LANCASTER, JANE
___ " 'I Could Easily Have Been an Acrobat': Charlotte Perkins Gilman and the Providence Ladies' Gymnasium 1881-1884," *ATQ* 8(1): 33-52. March 1994.

LANCE, DONNA
___ "Science Fiction and Mythology: Creatures of Light and Darkness," in: Kellogg, Judith and Crisler, Jesse, eds. **Literature & Hawaii's Children: Stories as Bridges to Many Realms**. Honolulu, HI: University of Hawaii at Manoa, 1994. pp.125-132.

LANDIS, GEOFFREY A.
___ "Robots, Reality and the Future of Humanity in the 21st Century," *Analog* 114(7): 57-63. June 1994.

LANDON, BROOKS
___ **The Aesthetics of Ambivalence: Rethinking Science Fiction Film in the Age of Electronic (Re) Production**. Westport, CT: Greenwood, 1992. 224pp.

LANDON, BROOKS (continued)
___ "Not What It Used to Be: The Overloading of Memory in Digital Narrative," in: Slusser, George E. and Shippey, Tom, eds. **Fiction 2000: Cyberpunk and the Future of Narrative**. Athens: University of Georgia Press, 1992. pp.153-167.
___ "Solos, Solutions, Info, and Invasion in (and of) Science Fiction Film," in: Slusser, George and Eric S. Rabkin, eds. **Fights of Fancy: Armed Conflict in Science Fiction and Fantasy**. Athens, GA: University of Georgia Press, 1993. pp.194-208.
___ "Styles of Invisibility: Sustaining the Transparent in Contemporary Prose Semblances," in: Slusser, George E. and Rabkin, Eric S., eds. **Styles of Creation: Aesthetic Technique and the Creation of Fictional Worlds**. Athens: University of Georgia Press, 1992. pp.245-258.

LANE, JOEL
___ "Beyond the Light: The Recent Novels of Ramsey Campbell," in: Joshi, S. T., ed. **The Count of Thirty: A Tribute to Ramsey Campbell**. West Warwick, RI: Necronomicon, 1993. pp.46-50.
___ "Negatives in Print: The Early Novels of Ramsey Campbell," in: Joshi, S. T., ed. **The Count of Thirty: A Tribute to Ramsey Campbell**. West Warwick, RI: Necronomicon, 1993. pp.38-45.

LANG, HANS-JOACHIM
___ "Ignatius Donnelly: **Caesar's Column: A Story of the Twentieth Century** (1890)," in: Heuermann, Hartmut and Lange, Bernd-Peter, eds. **Die Utopie in der angloamerikanischen Literatur: Interpretationen**. Düsseldorf: Bagel, 1984. pp.139-160.

LANGBERG, MIKE
___ "Star Tech," *Austin (TX) American Statesman* Sec. D., p. 1, 3. July 12, 1992.

LANGE, BERND-PETER
___ "Edward Bulwer-Lytton, **The Coming Race** (1871)," in: Heuermann, Harmut, ed. **Der Science Fiction Roman in der angloamerikanischen Literatur: Interpretationen**. Düsseldorf: Bagel, 1986. pp.31-46.
___ "Thomas More: **Utopia** (1516)," in: Heuermann, Hartmut and Lange, Bernd-Peter, eds. **Die Utopie in der angloamerikanischen Literatur: Interpretationen**. Düsseldorf: Bagel, 1984. pp.11-31.
___ (ed.) **Die Utopie in der Angloamerikanischen Literatur: Interpretationen**, ed. by Hartmut Heuermann and Bernd-Peter Lange. Düsseldorf: Bagel, 1984. 370pp.

LANGFORD, DAVID
___ "Banned in New York," *Quantum* No. 41: 15. Winter/Spring 1992.
___ "The Dragonhiker's Guide to Battlefield Covenant at Dune's Edge: Odyssey Two," *Australian Science Fiction Review* 5(3): 3-11. Spring 1990. (Whole No. 25)
___ "The Editor My Destination," *Quantum* No. 43/44: 13, 15. Spring/Summer 1993.
___ "Foodies of the Gods," *New York Review of Science Fiction* No. 58: 1, 3-4. June 1993.
___ "Foodies of the Gods: A Brief After-Dinner Speech," *Vector* No. 176: 9-8. December 1993/January 1994.
___ "Fun With Senseless Violence," *Vector* No. 170: 15-19. December 1992/January 1993.
___ "Tell Me the Old, Old Story," *Quantum* No. 42: 9-11. Summer/Fall 1992.
___ "Wisdom of the Ancients," *Interzone* No. 55: 43-44. January 1992.

LANGSBERG, MIKE
___ "Treknology," *Star Trek: The Official Fan Club* No. 94: 32-35. November/December 1993.

LANSDALE, JOE R.
___ "A Hard-On for Horror: Low-Budget Excitement," in: Golden, Christopher, ed. **Cut! Horror Writers on Horror Film**. New York: Berkley, 1992. pp.141-150.

LANZA, LUCIANO
___ "Al di la dell'economia: primi appunti per una concezione utopica dell'economia," in: Saccaro Del Buffa, Giuseppa and Lewis, Arthur O., eds. **Utopie per gli Anni Ottana**. Rome: Gangemi Editore, 1986. pp.167-184.

LANZA, LUCIANO (continued)
___ "Utopia, domminio, economia," in: Saccaro Del Buffa, Giuseppa and Lewis, Arthur O., eds. **Utopia e Modernita: Teorie e prassi utopiche nell'eta moderna e postmoderna**. Rome: Gangemi Editore, 1989. pp.225-236.

LAPERRIERE, MAUREEN C.
___ **The Evolution of Mothering: Images and Impact of the Mother-Figure in Feminist Utopian Science Fiction**. Master's Thesis, McGill University, 1994. 130pp. (Master's Abstracts. 33/04, p. 1076. August 1995.)

LAPISARDI, FREDERICK S.
___ "A Task Most Difficult: Staging Yeats's Mystical Dramas at the Abbey," in: Murphy, Patrick D., ed. **Staging the Impossible: The Fantastic Mode in Modern Drama**. Westport, CT: Greenwood, 1992. pp.30-43.

LARSEN, CORINNE
___ "The Fourth Branch of the Mabinogi: Structural Analysis Illuminates Character Motivation," *Mythlore* 19(4): 36-40. Autumn 1993. (No. 74)

LARSEN, MICHAEL J.
___ "Selected Bibliography (The Double)," *Journal of the Fantastic in the Arts* 6(2/3): 275-277. 1994.

LARSEN, T. E.
___ "From Fiction to Fact: A Technology Postscript to 'Only the Weatherman'," *Analog* 114(4): 74-79. March 1994.

LARSON, RANDALL D.
___ **2001: A Space Odyssey**: The Music," *Cinefantastique* 25(3): 40-42. June 1994.
___ **Film into Books: An Analytical Bibliography of Film Novelizations, Movie and TV Tie-Ins**. Metuchen, NJ: Scarecrow Press, 1995. 608pp.
___ "A Movie Novelizer Speaks: Alan Dean Foster Interviewed," *Interzone* No. 80: 53-55. February 1994.

LASKOWSKI, GEORGE
___ "Fritz Leiber: A Bibliography," *Lan's Lantern* No. 38: 8-13. July 1992.
___ "Isaac Asimov: Recollections of the Good Doctor," *Lan's Lantern* No. 38: 30. July 1992.
___ "Modern Demons and a Twisted Mind: The Fantastic Fiction of Fritz Leiber," *Lan's Lantern* No. 38: 19-25. July 1992.

LASKOWSKI, WILLIAM E., JR.
___ "George Orwell and the Tory-Radical Tradition," in: Rose, Jonathan, ed. **The Revised Orwell**. East Lansing, MI: Michigan State University Press, 1992. pp.149-190.

LASKY, KATHRYN
___ "Shuttling Through Realities: The Warp and the Weft of Fantasy and Nonfiction Writing," *The New Advocate* 6(4): 235-242. Fall 1993.

LASSNER, PHYLLIS
___ "A New World Indeed: Feminist Critique and Power Relations in British Anti-Utopian Literature of the 1930s," *Extrapolation* 36(3): 259-272. Fall 1995.

LATHAM, DAVID
___ **An Annotated Critical Bibliography of William Morris**, by David Latham and Sheila Latham. New York: St. Martin's, 1991. 423pp.
___ "William Morris: An Annotated Bibliography, 1990-1991," by David Latham and Sheila Latham. *Journal of the William Morris Society* 10(3): i-xxvii. Autumn 1993.
___ "William Morris: An Annotated Bibliography, 1992-1993," by David Latham and Sheila Latham. *Journal of the William Morris Society* 11(3): i-xx. Autumn 1995.

LATHAM, ROBERT A.
___ "Collage as Critique and Invention in the Fiction of William S. Burroughs and Kathy Acker," *Journal of the Fantastic in the Arts* 5(3): 46-57. 1993. (No. 19)

LATHAM, ROBERT A. (continued)
___ "Collage as Critique and Invention in the Fiction of William S. Burroughs and Kathy Acker," in: Latham, Robert A. and Collins, Robert A., eds. **Modes of the Fantastic**. Westport, CT: Greenwood, 1995. pp.29-37.
___ "The Men Who Walked on the Moon: Images of America in the 'New Wave' Science Fiction of the 1960s and 1970s," in: Sanders, Joe, ed. **Functions of the Fantastic**. Westport, CT: Greenwood, 1995. pp.195-204.
___ "Some Thoughts on Modernism and Science Fiction (Suggested by Robert Silverberg's **Downward to the Earth**)," in: Morse, Donald E., ed. **The Celebration of the Fantastic**. Westport, CT: Greenwood, 1992. pp.49-60.
___ "Subterranean Suburbia: Underneath the Smalltown Myth in Two Versions of **Invaders From Mars**," *Science Fiction Studies* 22(2): 198-208. July 1995.
___ "Youth Culture and Cybernetic Technologies," in: Wolf, Milton T. and Mallett, Daryl F., eds. **Imaginative Futures: Proceedings of the 1993 Science Fiction Research Association Conference**. San Bernardino, CA: Jacob's Ladder Books, 1995. pp.191-202.
___ (ed.) **Modes of the Fantastic: Selected Essays from the Twelfth International Conference on the Fantastic in the Arts**, ed. by Robert A. Latham and Robert A. Collins. Westport, CT: Greenwood, 1995. 234pp.
___ (ed.) **Science Fiction and Fantasy Book Review Annual 1991**, ed. by Robert A. Collins and Robert A. Latham. Westport, CT: Greenwood, 1994. 880pp.

LATHAM, ROD
___ "Clanker Meets Gulper," *Necrofile: The Review of Horror Fiction* 4: 7-10. Spring 1992.
___ "Cultural Studies and Science Fiction," *SFRA Review* No. 199: 15-22. June 1992.
___ "Inside Outside: Horror in SF Novels, 1960 to the Present," *Scream Factory: The Magazine of Horrors Past, Present and Future* 13: 20-27. Spring 1994.

LATHAM, SHEILA
___ **An Annotated Critical Bibliography of William Morris**, by David Latham and Sheila Latham. New York: St. Martin's, 1991. 423pp.
___ "William Morris: An Annotated Bibliography, 1990-1991," by David Latham and Sheila Latham. *Journal of the William Morris Society* 10(3): i-xxvii. Autumn 1993.
___ "William Morris: An Annotated Bibliography, 1992-1993," by David Latham and Sheila Latham. *Journal of the William Morris Society* 11(3): i-xx. Autumn 1995.

LAURENCE, ROBERT P.
___ "Jones Chronicles Is Lavish, Yet Shallow (Review)," *San Diego (CA) Union*. March 3, 1992. in: *NewsBank. Film and Television*. 27:C2. 1992.
___ "Series Explores Future Hero's Coming of Age (Review)," *San Diego (CA) Union*. March 3, 1992. in: *NewsBank. Film and Television*. 27:B14-C1. 1992.

LAURENT, DIANE M.
___ "Bram Stoker's **Dracula**: The Ultimate Victorian Novel," *Journal of the Dark* No. 5: 40-42. Winter 1995/1996.

LAURENT, JOHN
___ "C. S. Lewis and Animal Rights," *Mythlore* 19(1): 46-51. Winter 1993. (No. 71)

LAURIOLO, PAULO
___ "La vecchiaia nelle utopie del Cinquecento del Seicento," in: Saccaro Del Buffa, Giuseppa and Lewis, Arthur O., eds. **Utopia e Modernita: Teorie e prassi utopiche nell'eta moderna e postmoderna**. Rome: Gangemi Editore, 1989. pp.693-712.

LAWS, STEPHEN
___ "Breaking the Mould," in: Jones, Stephen, ed. **James Herbert: By Horror Haunted**. London: New English Library, 1992. pp.161-164.

LAWSON, TERRY
___ "**Powder** Means Well, But Veers Out of Control," *Detroit (MI) Free Press*. October 27, 1995. in: *NewsBank. Film and Television*. 97:G1. 1995.

LAYTON, DAVID A.
___ "Approaching the Limits: Science in Postmodernist Fiction," Ph.D. Dissertation, University of California, Santa Barbara, 1994. 571pp.
___ "The Barriers of Inner and Outer Space: The Science Fiction of Barry N. Malzberg," *Science Fiction Studies* 18(1): 71-90. March 1991.
___ "Closed Circuits and Monitored Lives: Television as Power in **Doctor Who**," *Extrapolation* 35(3): 241-251. Fall 1994.

LAZ, CHERYL
___ "Science Fiction and Introductory Sociology: The Handmaid in the Classroom," *Teaching Sociology* 24(1): 54-63. January 1995.

LE GUIN, URSULA K.
___ "American SF and the Other," *Chung Wai Literary Quarterly* 22(12): May 1994. (Issue not seen; pagination unavailable.) (Reprinted from *Science Fiction Studies*.)
___ "A Citizen of Mondath," in: Jakubowski, Maxim and James, Edward, eds. **The Profession of Science Fiction**. New York: St. Martin's, 1992. pp.73-77.
___ **Earthsea Revisioned**. Madison, NJ: Children's Literature New England, 1993. 26pp.
___ "My Appointment With the *Enterprise*: An Appreciation," *TV Guide* 42(20): 31-32. May 14, 1994.
___ "Talking About Writing," *Writer* 105(12): 9-11, 41. December 1992.
___ "Writing Without Conflict," *Harpers* 279(1666): 35-36. March 1989.

LEAYMAN, CHARLES D.
___ "**The Dark Half**: Makeup Effects," *Cinefantastique* 24(1): 18. June 1993.
___ "**The Dark Half**: Stephen King," *Cinefantastique* 24(1): 21. June 1993.
___ "**The Dark Half**: Visual Effects by V. C. E.," *Cinefantastique* 24(1): 23. June 1993.
___ "**The Dark Half**," *Cinefantastique* 24(1): 16-23. June 1993.
___ "**Dead Again** (Review)," *Cinefantastique* 22(4): 59, 61. February 1992.
___ "Stephen King's **The Dark Half**," *Cinefantastique* 22(4): 5. February 1992.

LEDERMAN, MARIE J.
___ "**Superman**, Oedipus and the Myth of the Birth of the Hero," *Journal of Popular Film and Television* 7(3): 235-245. 1979.

LEDGER, SALLY
___ "William Morris, Philip Webb, and Mark Rutherford," *Journal of the William Morris Society* 10(1): 14-20. Autumn 1992.

LEDWON, LENORA
___ "The Passion of the Phallus and Angela Carter's **The Passion of New Eve**," *Journal of the Fantastic in the Arts* 5(4): 26-41. 1993. (No. 20)

LEE, DENNIS
___ "Judith Merril Meets Rochdale College," *Aloud* (Toronto) 2(7): 4-5. October 1992.

LEE, JUDITH Y.
___ "The Feminization of Technology: Mechanical Characters in Picture Books," in: Greenberg, Mark L. and Schachterle, Lance, eds. **Literature and Technology**. Bethlehem, PA: Lehigh University Press, 1992. pp.206-224.

LEE, JULIANNE
___ "X Heroine," *Starlog* No. 213: 32-35. April 1995.
___ "X-Symbol," *Starlog* No. 215: 27-30, 71. June 1995.

LEE, LUAINE
___ "Welcome to the Monkey House," *San Francisco (CA) Examiner* August 12, 1995. (Cited from the Internet Edition.)

LEE, NORA
___ "**Terabyss** Takes Audience on Suboceanic Thrill Mission," by George Turner and Nora Lee. *American Cinematographer* 74(8): 59-65. August 1993.

LEEDS, MARC
___ **The Vonnegut Encyclopedia: An Authorized Compendium**. Westport, CT: Greenwood, 1995. 693pp.

LEEPER, MARK R.
___ "An Annotated Filmography of Ray Harryhausen," *Lan's Lantern* No. 41: 33-35. July 1993.
___ "A Brief Filmography of Arthurian Films," *Lan's Lantern* No. 43: 40-42. March 1995.
___ "Commando Cody and His Lost Science Fiction Fan," *Lan's Lantern* No. 40: 8-9. September 1992.
___ "**Dark Intruder** (Review)," *Lan's Lantern* No. 42: 106. May 1994.
___ "**Frankenstein** (Review)," *Lan's Lantern* No. 42: 109. May 1994.
___ "**Mind Benders** (Review)," *Lan's Lantern* No. 42: 105-106. May 1994.
___ "**Quest for Love** (Review)," *Lan's Lantern* No. 42: 106. May 1994.
___ "**Unearthly Stranger** (Review)," *Lan's Lantern* No. 42: 106. May 1994.

LEES, STELLA
___ "Morality Lesson or Hornblower in Space," *Viewpoint on Books for Young Adults* 1(2): 12-13. Winter 1993.

LEFAIVRE, LIANE
___ " 'Hypnerotomachia Poliphili' as an Erotic Architectural Utopia," in: Saccaro Del Buffa, Giuseppa and Lewis, Arthur O., eds. **Utopia e Modernita: Teorie e prassi utopiche nell'eta moderna e postmoderna**. Rome: Gangemi Editore, 1989. pp.615-624.

LEFANU, SARAH
___ "Difference and Sexual Politics in Naomi Mitchison's **Solution Three**," in: Donawerth, Jane L. and Kolmerten, Carol A., eds. **Utopian and Science Fiction by Women: Worlds of Difference**. Syracuse, NY: Syracuse University Press, 1994. pp.153-165.
___ "Popular Writing and Feminist Intervention in Science Fiction," in: Longhurst, Derek, ed. **Gender, Genre and Narrative Pleasure**. Boston, MA: Unwin Hyman, 1989. pp.177-191.
___ "Robots and Romance: The Science Fiction and Fantasy of Tanith Lee," in: Radstone, Susannah, ed. **Sweet Dreams: Sexuality, Gender and Popular Fiction**. London: Lawrence & Wishart, 1988. pp.121-136.

LEHMAN, STEVEN
___ "The Motherless Child in Science Fiction: **Frankenstein** and Moreau," *Science Fiction Studies* 19(1): 49-58. March 1992.

LEHMANN, L.
___ "Science Fiction," *Maatstaf* (Amsterdam, Netherlands) 39(7): 35-36. July 1991.

LEHNERT, GERTRUD
___ "Trauma, Fluchten, Utopien: Wirklichkeit im Spiegel der phantistischen Kinder- und Jungendliteratur," *Fundevogel* No. 88/89: 11-18. 1991.

LEHR, SUSAN
___ "Fantasy: Inner Journeys for Today's Child," *Publishing Research Quarterly* 7(3): 91-101. Fall 1991. [Not seen.]

LEHTI, STEVEN J.
___ "**Doctor Mordrid** (Review)," *Cinefantastique* 24(6)/25(1): 123. February 1994.
___ "**Fortress** (Review)," *Cinefantastique* 24(6)/25(1): 123. February 1994.
___ "**Trancers II** (Review)," *Cinefantastique* 23(2/3): 123. October 1992.

LEIBACHER-OUVRARD, LISE
___ "Subversion and Stasis in the Utopian Journeys of Foigny, Veiras, and Patot," in: Saccaro Del Buffa, Giuseppa and Lewis, Arthur O., eds. **Utopia e Modernita: Teorie e prassi utopiche nell'eta moderna e postmoderna**. Rome: Gangemi Editore, 1989. pp.827-836.

LEIBER, JUSTIN
___ "Fritz Leiber at Bay," *Locus* 29(5): 47-49. November 1992
___ "Fritz Leiber: Swordsman and Philosopher, Part Two, Philosophical Dramatizations," *Riverside Quarterly* 9(1): 36-44. August 1992. (No. 33)

LELAND, JOHN
___ "Clive Barker: The Horror, the Horror," *Spin* 4: 82-83. December 1988.

LEM, STANISLAW
___ "Philip K. Dick: A Visionary Among the Charlatans," in: Mullen, R. D., ed. **On Philip K. Dick: 40 Articles From Science-Fiction Studies**. Terre Haute, IN: SF-TH Inc., 1992. pp.49-62.

LEMAY, J. A. LEO
___ "The Psychology of 'The Murders in the Rue Morgue' (1982)," in: Budd, Louis J. and Cady, Edwin H., eds. **On Poe**. Durham, NC: Duke University Press, 1993. pp.223-246.

LENIHAN, JOHN H.
___ "Superweapons From the Past," in: Loukides, Paul, ed. **The Material World in American Popular Film**. Bowling Green, OH: Popular Press, 1993. pp.164-174.

LENNE, GÉRARD
___ "Une Galaxie de Messies: le mythe messianique dans la S. F. contemporaine," *Revue du Cinema* No. 482: 68-75. 1992

LENT, JOHN A.
___ **Comic Art of Europe: An International Comprehensive Bibliography**. Westport, CT: Greenwood, 1994. 663pp.

LENTZ, HARRIS M., III.
___ **Science Fiction, Horror & Fantasy Film and Television Credits Supplement 2: Through 1993**. Jefferson, NC: McFarland, 1994. 854pp.

LENZ, MILLICENT
___ "Archetypal Images of Otherworlds in Singer's 'Menaseh's Dream' and Tolkien's 'Leaf by Niggle'," *Children's Literature Association Quarterly* 19(1): 3-7. Spring 1994.
___ "**Danger Quotient, Fiskadoro, Riddley Walker**, and the Failure of the Campbellian Monomyth," in: Sullivan, C. W., III. **Science Fiction for Young Readers**. Westport, CT: Greenwood, 1993. pp.113-119.
___ "Raymond Brigg's **When the Wind Blows**: Toward an Ecology of the Mind for Young Readers," in: Sullivan, C. W., III. **Science Fiction for Young Readers**. Westport, CT: Greenwood, 1993. pp.197-204.

LEONARD, ANDREW
___ "Cyberpunks and Techno-hicks: Surfing the Matrix of Novelist William Gibson," *San Francisco (CA) Bay Guardian* 27(46): 31-33. August 18, 1993.

LEOPOLD, GLENN
___ "New Vampire Saga Has Certain Bite to It," *Los Angeles (CA) Daily News*. October 25, 1992. in *NewsBank. Literature*. 95:C1-C2. 1992.

LEPAGE, FRANCOISE
___ "Pour une rhetorique de la representation fantastique (In Search of a Theory of Illustration of Fantastique)," *Canadian Children's Literature* 60: 97-107. 1990. [Not seen.]

LERNER, FRED
___ "Concerning Purely Personal Preferences," *Voice of Youth Advocates* 17(4): 200-201. October 1994.
___ "The Libertarian Ideal in Science Fiction," *Voice of Youth Advocates* 13(1): 17-18. April 1990.
___ "Master of Our Art: Rudyard Kipling," *Voice of Youth Advocates* 16(4): 211-213. October 1993.
___ "The Posthumous Heinlein," *Voice of Youth Advocates* 17(1): 15-16. April 1994.
___ "Science Fiction With Rivets," *Voice of Youth Advocates* 15(1): 19-20. April 1992.
___ "Small Is Beautiful: SF Small Press Publishing," *Voice of Youth Advocates* 14(1): 17-18. April 1991.

LERNER, JESSE
___ "Face the Nation: The Filmic Formulation of National Identity," *Afterimage* 21(5): 8-10. December 1993.

LESKOSKY, RICHARD J.
___ "Life History Strategies and Population Biology in Science Fiction Films," by May R. Berenbaum and Richard J. Leskosky. *Bulletin of the Ecological Society of America* 73(4): 236-240. December 1992.

LESSING, DORIS
___ **Under My Skin: Volume One of My Autobiography, to 1949**. New York: HarperCollins, 1994. 419pp.

LETEMENDIA, V. C.
___ "Revolution on Animal Farm: Orwell's Neglected Commentary," *Journal of Modern Literature* 18(1): 127-137. Winter 1992.

LETSON, RUSSELL
___ "Contributions to the Critical Dialogue: As an Academic Sees It," in: Sanders, Joe, ed. **Science Fiction Fandom**. Westport, CT: Greenwood, 1994. pp.229-234.
___ "Jack Vance," in: Bruccoli, Matthew J., ed. **Facts on File Bibliography of American Fiction 1919-1988**. New York: Facts on File, 1991. pp.511-512.
___ "Robert Silverberg: An Overview," in: Elkins, Charles L. and Greenberg, Martin H., eds. **Robert Silverberg's Many Trapdoors: Critical Essays on His Science Fiction**. Westport, CT: Greenwood, 1992. pp.15-38.

LEVERENZ, DAVID
___ "Poe and Gentry Virginia," in: Rosenheim, Shawn and Rachman, Stephen, ed. **The American Face of Edgar Allan Poe**. Baltimore: Johns Hopkins University Press, 1995. pp.210-236.

LEVI, PETER
___ "Kingsley Amis (21 in 1943)," in: Salwak, Dale, ed. **Kingsley Amis in Life and Letters**. New York: St. Martin's, 1990. pp.167-172.

LEVIDOW, LES
___ "Socializing the Cyborg Self: The Gulf War and Beyond," by Ken Robins and Les Levidow. in: Gray, Chris H., ed. **The Cyborg Handbook**. New York: Routledge, 1995. pp.119-125.

LEVINE, RICHARD S.
___ "The Sustainable City: A Necessary Utopia," in: Saccaro Del Buffa, Giuseppa and Lewis, Arthur O., eds. **Utopia e Modernita: Teorie e prassi utopiche nell'eta moderna e postmoderna**. Rome: Gangemi Editore, 1989. pp.157-174.

LEVINSON, PAUL
___ "Punctuated Equilibria in Dinosaurs and Trilogies," *New York Review of Science Fiction* No. 81: 14-16. May 1995.

LEVITAS, RUTH
___ "Who Holds the Hose: Domestic Labour in the Work of Bellamy, Gilman and Morris," *Utopian Studies* 6(1): 65-84. 1995.

LEVY, MICHAEL M.
___ "A Certain Inherent Kindness: An Interview With Lois McMaster Bujold," *SFRA Review* No. 220: 15-32. November/December 1995.
___ "The New Wave, Cyberpunk, and Beyond: 1963-1994," by Michael M. Levy and Brian Stableford. in: Barron, Neil, ed. **Anatomy of Wonder 4**. New York: Bowker, 1995. pp.222-377.
___ "The Year in Science Fiction, 1990," in: Collins, Robert A. and Latham, Robert, eds. **Science Fiction and Fantasy Book Review Annual 1991**. Westport, CT: Greenwood, 1994. pp.1-26.

LEVY-LEBLOND, JEAN-MARC
___ "The Mirror, the Beauty and the Touchstone: Or, What Can Literature Do for Science?," *Substance* No. 71/72: 7-26. 1993.

LEWES, DARBY
___ "Gynotopia: A Checklist of Nineteenth Century Utopias by American Women," *Legacy* 6(2): 29-41. Fall 1989.
___ "Middle-Class Edens: Women's Nineteenth-Century Utopian Fiction and the Bourgeois Ideal," *Utopian Studies* 4(1): 14-25. 1993.
___ "Nudes From Nowhere: Pornography, Empire, and Utopia," *Utopian Studies* 4(2): 66-73. 1993.

LEWIS, ALEX
___ "Boromir's Journey," in: Kranz, Gisbert, ed. **Jahrbuch für Literatur und Ästhetik**. Lüdenscheid, Germany: Stier, 1992. Band 10, pp.135-144.
___ "Historical Bias in the Making of **The Silmarillion**," in: Reynolds, Patricia and GoodKnight, Glen H., eds. **Proceedings of the J. R. R. Tolkien Centenary Conference, Keble College, Oxford, 1992**. Altadena, CA: Mythopoeic Press, 1995. pp.158-166. (*Mythlore* Vol. 21, No. 2, Winter 1996, Whole No. 80)

LEWIS, ARTHUR O.
___ "1992 Pilgrim Award Presentation and Acceptance," *SFRA Review* No. 199: 11-14. July/August/September 1992.
___ "Directory of Utopian Scholars, Fourth Edition," *Utopian Studies* 3(2): 121-179. 1992.
___ "Directory of Utopian Scholars, Fourth Edition, Supplement 1," *Utopian Studies* 4(2): 255-265. 1993.
___ "Directory of Utopian Scholars, Fourth Edition, Supplement 2," *Utopian Studies* 5(2): 198-202. 1994.
___ "Introduction: English Language Presentations," in: Saccaro Del Buffa, Giuseppa and Lewis, Arthur O., eds. **Utopia e Modernita: Teorie e prassi utopiche nell'eta moderna e postmoderna**. Rome: Gangemi Editore, 1989. pp.27-36.
___ "The Society for Utopian Studies," in: Saccaro Del Buffa, Giuseppa and Lewis, Arthur O., eds. **Utopie per gli Anni Ottana**. Rome: Gangemi Editore, 1986. pp.25-34.
___ **Utopie e modernita: teorie e prassi utopiche nell'eta moderna e postmoderna**, by Giuseppa Saccaro Del Buffa and Arthur O. Lewis. Roma: Gangemi, 1989. 2 v., 1196pp.
___ **Utopie per gli anni ottanta: studi interdisciplinari sui temi, la storia, i progetti**, by Giuseppa Saccaro Del Buffa and Arthur O. Lewis. Roma: Gangemi, 1986. 825pp.

LEWIS, C. S.
___ **The Letters of C. S. Lewis to Arthur Greeves (1914-1963)**, ed. by Walter Hooper. New York: Collier, 1986. 592pp. (Reissue of **They Stand Together**, 1979.)
___ "Two New Letters from C. S. Lewis," *Bulletin of the New York C. S. Lewis Society* 25(9/11): 14-15. July/September 1994.

LEWIS, DANA
___ "They Really Care Who Killed Laura Palmer," *Los Angeles (CA) Times*. June 21, 1992. in: *NewsBank. Film and Television*. 66:E13-E14. 1992.

LEYDON, JOE
___ " 'Demo Man' Full of Surprises (Review)," *Houston (TX) Post*. October 9, 1993. in: *NewsBank. Film and Television*. 115:A6. 1993.
___ "**Heaven Sent** (Review)," *Variety* 359(2): 68. May 8, 1995.
___ "The Man and the Myth: **Hellraiser** Creator Clive Barker's Horrific Demon Shows More Than the Average Pinhead," *Houston (TX) Post*. September 10, 1992. in: *NewsBank. Film and Television*. 87:D2-D3, 1992

LI, YU-CHENG
___ "The Alien Strikes Back," *Chung Wai Literary Quarterly* 22(12): May 1994. (Issue not seen; pagination unavailable.)

LIBERTI, FABRIZIO
___ "I grandi classici della fantascienza," *Cineforum* 34(4): 90-92. 1994.
___ "Pe regie de Roger Corman in vista della **Factory**" [Roger Corman and Science Fiction in **Factory**]. *Cineforum* 31(9): 18-21. 1991.

LICHTENBERG, JACQUELINE
___ **Star Trek Lives!**, by Jacqueline Lichtenberg, Sandra Marshak and Jean Winston. New York: Bantam, 1975. 274pp.

LIEBERMANN, RANDY
___ (ed.) **Blueprint for Space: Science Fiction to Science Fact**, ed. by Frederick I. Ordway, III and Randy Liebermann. Washington, DC: Smithsonian Institution Press, 1992. 224pp.

LIEBFRED, PHILIP
___ "The Cinema Legacy of a Literary Legend: H. Rider Haggard," *Filmfax* No. 30: 67-71. December 1991/January 1992.
___ "H. Rider Haggard on the Screen," *Films in Review* 46(7/8): 20-29. September/October 1995.

LINAWEAVER, BRAD
___ "Corman Unwound," *Wonder* No. 7: 36-38. 1993.
___ "I Sing the Image Electric: Ray Bradbury Goes to Hollywood," by Brad Linaweaver and Rod Bennett. *Wonder: The Children's Magazine for Grown-Ups* No. 8: 10-17. 1995.
___ "The Monster God of Dreams," *Riverside Quarterly* 9(3): 164-173. June 1995. (Whole No. 35)
___ "Ray Bradbury This Way Comes," *Wonder: The Children's Magazine for Grown-Ups* No. 8: 3-6. 1995. (Reprinted from the **World Science Fiction Convention Program Book**, 1986.)

LIND, MICHAEL
___ "New York Diarist: The Nerd Frontier," *New Republic* 213(5): 42. July 31, 1995.

LINDENSTRUTH, GERHARD
___ **Arthur Conan Doyle. Eine illustrierte Bibliographie der Veroffentlichungen in deutschen Sprachraum**. Amsterdam-Giessen: Verlag Munniksma, 1994. 236pp. [Not seen.]

LINDSKOLD, JANE M.
___ "The Elements of Fantastic Fiction," *Writer* 106(11): 18-21. September 1993.
___ "Pervasive Influence of Poetry in the Works of Roger Zelazny," *Extrapolation* 33(1): 41-58. Spring 1992.
___ "Robert Asprin: The Man Behind the Myths," *Extrapolation* 35(1): 60-67. Spring 1994.
___ **Roger Zelazny**. New York: Twayne, 1993. 166pp.

LINDSKOOG, KATHRYN
___ "The Dark Scandal: Science Fiction Forgery," *Quantum* No. 42: 29-30. Summer/Fall 1992.
___ **Light in the Shadow Lands: Protecting the Real C. S. Lewis**. Sisters, OR: Multnomah Press, 1994. 345pp.

LINTON, RICHARD
___ "Profile: Alan Munro," *Cinefex* No. 52: 84. November 1992.

LIPMAN, AMANDA
___ "**Mary Shelley's Frankenstein** (Review)," *Sight and Sound* 4(12): 51-52. December 1994.

LIPP, LINDA
___ "Bradbury Chronicles," *Chicago Tribune* p. 18L. June 20, 1993.
___ "Ray Bradbury Joins Fight for Library," *Chicago Tribune* Sec. 2C, p. 1. March 9, 1992. [Not seen.]

LIPPER, HAL
___ "Hooked on Horror," *St. Petersburg (FL) Times*. September 22, 1992. in: *NewsBank. Film and Television*. 87:C14. 1992
___ "Victim and Villain (Review)," *St. Petersburg (FL) Times*. January 13, 1992. in: *NewsBank. Film and Television*. 12:B1-B2. 1992.

LIPPI, GIUSEPPE
___ "Lovecraft's Dreamworld Revisited," *Lovecraft Studies* No. 26: 23-25. Spring 1992.

LIPPINCOTT, CHARLES M.
___ **The Making of Judge Dredd**, by Jane Killick, David Chute and Charles M. Lippincott. London: Boxtree, 1995; New York: Hyperion, 1995. 192pp.

LITTLEFIELD, HOLLY
___ "Unlearning Patriarchy: Ursula Le Guin's Feminist Consciousness in **The Tombs of Atuan** and **Tehanu**," *Extrapolation* 36(3): 244-258. Fall 1995.

LITTLEFIELD, KINNEY
___ "**Earth 2**? Not Stellar, But Don't Abort Mission Yet," *(Santa Ana, CA) Orange County Register*. Nov. 4, 1994. in: *NewsBank. Film and Television*. 119:F8. 1994.
___ "A New World for Coppola," *(Santa Ana, CA) Orange County Register*. May 23, 1995. in: *NewsBank. Film and Television*. 60:G5. 1995.
___ "X-Factor," *(Santa Ana, CA) Orange County Register*. May 11, 1994. in: *NewsBank. Film and Television*. 61:A12-a13. 1994.

LITTLETON, C. SCOTT
___ "Some Notes on Merlin," by C. Scott Littleton and Linda A. Malcor. *Arthuriana* 5(3): 87-95. Fall 1995.

LITTLETON, CYNTHIA
___ "Television of the Weird: First-run Faces Unreality," *Broadcasting and Cable* 125(44): 57-58. October 30, 1995.

LIU, ALBERT
___ "The Last Days of Arnold Schwarzenegger," *Genders* No. 18: 102-112. Winter 1993.

LIVIA, ANNA
___ "Putting the Abortion Controversy into Deep Freeze," in: Wolf, Milton T. and Mallett, Daryl F., eds. **Imaginative Futures: Proceedings of the 1993 Science Fiction Research Association Conference.** San Bernardino, CA: Jacob's Ladder Books, 1995. pp.245-248.

LJUNGQUIST, KENT P.
___ "Prospects for the Study of Edgar Allan Poe," *Resources for American Literary Study* 21(2): 173-188. 1995.

LLOPIS, RAFAEL
___ "The Cthulhu Mythos," *Lovecraft Studies* No. 27: 13-21. Fall 1992.

LLOYD, ANN
The Films of Stephen King. New York: St. Martin's, 1993. 96pp.

LLOYD, DONALD G.
___ "Renegade Robots and Hard-Wired Heroes: Technology and Morality in Contemporary Science Fiction Films," in: Loukides, Paul and Fuller, Linda K., eds. **Beyond the Stars III: The Material World in American Popular Film.** Bowling Green, OH: Popular Press, 1993. pp.216-228.

LLOYD, SACHS
___ "Witless, Dreary Pulse Drags *Dr. Giggles* to Horror Lows (Review)," *Chicago (IL) Sun Times.* October 26, 1992. in: *NewsBank. Film and Television.* 101:A2. 1992.

LLOYD-MORGAN, CERIDWEN
___ "**Breuddwyd Rhonabwy** and Later Arthurian Literature," in: Bromwich, Rachel, Jarman, A. O. H., and Roberts, Brynley F., eds. **The Arthur of the Welsh.** Cardiff: University of Wales Press, 1991. pp.183-208.

LO CURZIO, MASSIMO
___ "L'utopia della organizzazione industriale delle attivita produttive nella Calabria del '700," in: Saccaro Del Buffa, Giuseppa and Lewis, Arthur O., eds. **Utopie per gli Anni Ottana.** Rome: Gangemi Editore, 1986. pp.199-206.

LOBDELL, JARED C.
___ "The Man Who Didn't Write Fantasy: Lord Dunsany and the Self-Deprecatory Tradition in English Light Fiction," *Extrapolation* 35(1): 33-42. Spring 1994.

LOCKE, GEORGE
___ "The Book Collector and M. P. Shiel," in: **Shiel in Diverse Hands: A Collection of Essays.** Cleveland, OH: Reynolds Morse Foundation, 1983. pp.159-170.
___ **A Spectrum of Fantasy, Volume II: Acquistions to a Collection of Fantastic Literature, 1980-1993, Together with Additional Notes on Titles Covered in the First Volume.** London: Ferrett Fantasy, 1994. 156pp. [Not seen.]

LOCKWOOD, MICHAEL
___ "A Sense of the Spoken: Language in **The Owl Service**," *Children's Literature in Education* 23(2): 83-92. June 1992.

LOEHR, JIM
___ (ed.) **Spectrum: The Best in Contemporary Fantastic Art (First Annual Collection)**, ed. by Cathy Burnett, Arnie Fenner and Jim Loehr. Grass Valley, CA: Underwood Books, 1994. 204pp.

LOFFICIER, JEAN-MARC
___ "**Aliens** (1986): Interview with James Cameron and Gale Ann Hurd," by Randy Lofficier and Jean-Marc Lofficier. in: Goldberg, Lee et al. **Science Fiction Filmmaking in the 1980s.** Jefferson, NC: McFarland, 1995. pp.7-23.
___ "**Blade Runner** (1982): Interviews with Hampton Francher, David Peoples, Ridley Scott and Syd Mead," by Randy Lofficier and Jean-Marc Lofficier. in: Goldberg, Lee et al. **Science Fiction Filmmaking in the 1980s.** Jefferson, NC: McFarland, 1995. pp.23-58.
___ "**Blue Thunder** (1983): Interview with John Badham," by Randy Lofficier and Jean-Marc Lofficier. in: Goldberg, Lee et al. **Science Fiction Filmmaking in the 1980s.** Jefferson, NC: McFarland, 1995. pp.59-72.
___ **The Doctor Who Programme Guide.** 3rd Ed. London: Doctor Who Books, 1994. 271pp.
___ **The Doctor Who Programme Guide.** London: Target, 1989. 177pp.
___ **Doctor Who: The Terrestrial Index.** London: Target, 1992. 247pp.
___ **Doctor Who: The Universal Databank.** London: Doctor Who Books, 1992. 479pp.
___ **The Dreamweavers: Interviews with Fantasy Filmmakers of the 1980s,** by Lee Goldberg, Randy Lofficier, Jean-Marc Lofficier and William Rabkin. Jefferson, NC: McFarland, 1995. 320pp.
___ "**Dune** (1984): Interviews with David Lynch, Raffaella de Laurentiis and Kyle MacLachlan," by Randy Lofficier and Jean-Marc Lofficier. in: Goldberg, Lee et al. **Science Fiction Filmmaking in the 1980s.** Jefferson, NC: McFarland, 1995. pp.79-110.
___ "Interview: David Peoples," by Randy Lofficier and Jean-Marc Lofficier. *Starlog* 184: 40-41. November 1992.
___ "Interview: Hampton Fancher," by Randy Lofficier and Jean-Marc Lofficier. *Starlog* 184: 35-39. November 1992.
___ "Interview: Lawrence G. Paull," by Randy Lofficier and Jean-Marc Lofficier. *Starlog* 184: 46-47, 70. November 1992.
___ "Interview: Ridley Scott," by Randy Lofficier and Jean-Marc Lofficier. *Starlog* 184: 48-51, 69. November 1992.
___ "Interview: Syd Mead," by Randy Lofficier and Jean-Marc Lofficier. *Starlog* 184: 42-45. November 1992.
___ **Into the Twilight Zone: The Rod Serling Programme Guide,** by Jean-Marc Lofficier and Randy Lofficier. London: Virgin, 1995. 296pp.
___ "**Mad Max** Movies (1979-1985): Interview with George Miller, Terry Hayes, George Ogilvie and Mel Gibson," by Randy Lofficier and Jean-Marc Lofficier. in: Goldberg, Lee et al. **Science Fiction Filmmaking in the 1980s.** Jefferson, NC: McFarland, 1995. pp.133-174.
___ "Road Warrior," by Randy Lofficier and Jean-Marc Lofficier. in: McDonnell, David, ed. **Starlog's Science Fiction Heroes and Heroines.** New York: Crescent Books, 1995. pp.12-14.
___ "**Star Trek** Movies (1980-1988): Interviews with Jack Sowards, Nicholas Mayer, Harve Bennett; Leonard Nimoy and William Shatner," by Randy Lofficier and Jean-Marc Lofficier. in: Goldberg, Lee et al. **Science Fiction Filmmaking in the 1980s.** Jefferson, NC: McFarland, 1995. pp.189-236.
___ "**War Games** (1983): Interview with John Badham," by Randy Lofficier and Jean-Marc Lofficier. in: Goldberg, Lee et al. **Science Fiction Filmmaking in the 1980s.** Jefferson, NC: McFarland, 1995. pp.253-258.
___ (ed.) **Science Fiction Filmmaking in the 1980s: Interviews with Actors, Directors, Producers and Writers,** ed. by Lee Goldberg, Randy Lofficier, Jean-Marc Lofficier and William Rabkin. Jefferson, NC: McFarland, 1995. 279pp.

LOFFICIER, RANDY
___ "**Aliens** (1986): Interview with James Cameron and Gale Ann Hurd," by Randy Lofficier and Jean-Marc Lofficier. in: Goldberg, Lee et al. **Science Fiction Filmmaking in the 1980s.** Jefferson, NC: McFarland, 1995. pp.7-23.
___ "**Blade Runner** (1982): Interviews with Hampton Francher, David Peoples, Ridley Scott and Syd Mead," by Randy Lofficier and Jean-Marc Lofficier. in: Goldberg, Lee et al. **Science Fiction Filmmaking in the 1980s.** Jefferson, NC: McFarland, 1995. pp.23-58.
___ "**Blue Thunder** (1983): Interview with John Badham," by Randy Lofficier and Jean-Marc Lofficier. in: Goldberg, Lee et al. **Science Fiction Filmmaking in the 1980s.** Jefferson, NC: McFarland, 1995. pp.59-72.
___ **The Dreamweavers: Interviews with Fantasy Filmmakers of the 1980s,** by Lee Goldberg, Randy Lofficier, Jean-Marc Lofficier and William Rabkin. Jefferson, NC: McFarland, 1995. 320pp.

LOFFICIER, RANDY (continued)
___ "*Dune* (1984): Interviews with David Lynch, Raffaella de Laurentiis and Kyle MacLachlan," by Randy Lofficier and Jean-Marc Lofficier. in: Goldberg, Lee et al. **Science Fiction Filmmaking in the 1980s**. Jefferson, NC: McFarland, 1995. pp.79-110.
___ "Interview: David Peoples," by Randy Lofficier and Jean-Marc Lofficier. *Starlog* 184: 40-41. November 1992.
___ "Interview: Hamption Fancher," by Randy Lofficier and Jean-Marc Lofficier. *Starlog* 184: 35-39. November 1992.
___ "Interview: Lawrence G. Paull," by Randy Lofficier and Jean-Marc Lofficier. *Starlog* 184: 46-47, 70. November 1992.
___ "Interview: Ridley Scott," by Randy Lofficier and Jean-Marc Lofficier. *Starlog* 184: 48-51, 69. November 1992.
___ "Interview: Syd Mead," by Randy Lofficier and Jean-Marc Lofficier. *Starlog* 184: 42-45. November 1992.
___ **Into the Twilight Zone: The Rod Serling Programme Guide**, by Jean-Marc Lofficier and Randy Lofficier. London: Virgin, 1995. 296pp.
___ "*Mad Max* Movies (1979-1985): Interview with George Miller, Terry Hayes, George Ogilvie and Mel Gibson," by Randy Lofficier and Jean-Marc Lofficier. in: Goldberg, Lee et al. **Science Fiction Filmmaking in the 1980s**. Jefferson, NC: McFarland, 1995. pp.133-174.
___ "Road Warrior," by Randy Lofficier and Jean-Marc Lofficier. in: McDonnell, David, ed. **Starlog's Science Fiction Heroes and Heroines**. New York: Crescent Books, 1995. pp.12-14.
___ "*Star Trek Movies* (1980-1988): Interviews with Jack Sowards, Nicholas Mayer, Harve Bennett; Leonard Nimoy and William Shatner," by Randy Lofficier and Jean-Marc Lofficier. in: Goldberg, Lee et al. **Science Fiction Filmmaking in the 1980s**. Jefferson, NC: McFarland, 1995. pp.189-236.
___ "*War Games* (1983): Interview with John Badham," by Randy Lofficier and Jean-Marc Lofficier. in: Goldberg, Lee et al. **Science Fiction Filmmaking in the 1980s**. Jefferson, NC: McFarland, 1995. pp.253-258.
___ (ed.) **Science Fiction Filmmaking in the 1980s: Interviews with Actors, Directors, Producers and Writers**, ed. by Lee Goldberg, Randy Lofficier, Jean-Marc Lofficier and William Rabkin. Jefferson, NC: McFarland, 1995. 279pp.

LOFTON, S. C.
___ "Under the Influence," *Lan's Lantern* No. 40: 120-122. September 1992.

LOFTS, W. O. G.
___ "My Search for Elusive Shiel Material (With: Magazines Containing Works of M. P. Shiel)," in: **Shiel in Diverse Hands: A Collection of Essays**. Cleveland, OH: Reynolds Morse Foundation, 1983. pp.147-157.

LOGAN, MICHAEL
___ "Close Encounters With the Cast of Voyagers," *TV Guide* 43(28): 6-10. July 16, 1995.
___ "Deep Dish," *TV Guide* 41(1): 10-15. January 2, 1993. (Issue 2075)
___ "Fantastic Voyager," *TV Guide* 43(2): 12-24. January 14, 1995.
___ "*TV Guide* Interview: Rick Berman," *TV Guide* 41(30): 10-13. July 24, 1993.
___ "What's Happening With the Hits: Introducing the Defiant," *TV Guide* 42(39): 24-25. September 24, 1994.

LOI, V. M.
___ **Neznani svity fantastyky: rekomendattsiinyi bibliohrafichnyi pokazhchyk**, by V. O. Kononenko and V. M. Loi. Kylv: Derzhavan biblioteke Ukrainy, 1992. 35pp. [Not seen.]

LOMARTIRE, PAUL
___ "West Palm Native *Leaps* into 1968," *West Palm Beach (FL) Post*. October 6, 1992. in: *NewsBank. Film and Television*. 106:B5. 1992.

LOMBARDI, MIA
___ "Il Palazio Cinetico. La danza in un modello del corpo in moviemento," in: Saccaro Del Buffa, Giuseppa and Lewis, Arthur O., eds. **Utopia e Modernita: Teorie e prassi utopiche nell'eta moderna e postmoderna**. Rome: Gangemi Editore, 1989. pp.891-902.

LOMBERG, JON
___ "What Limits," *Aloud* (Toronto) 2(7): 8. October 1992.

LOMETTI, GUY E.
___ "Broadcast Preparations for and Consequences of *The Day After*," in: Wober, J. Mallory, ed. **Television and Nuclear Power: Making the Public Mind**. Norwood, NJ: Ablex, 1992. pp.3-18.

LONDON, BETTE
___ "Mary Shelley, **Frankenstein**, and the Spectacle of Masculinity," *PMLA* 108(2): 253-267. March 1993.

LONDON, JOAN
___ **Jack London and His Daughters**. Berkeley, CA: Heyday Books, 1990. 184pp.

LONDRAVILLE, JANIS
___ "May Morris's Editing of 'So Many Stories Written Here'," *Journal of the William Morris Society* 10(1): 31-34. Autumn 1992.

LONEY, DOUGLAS
___ "C. S. Lewis' Debt to E. M. Forster's **The Celestial Omnibus and Other Stories**," *Mythlore* 21(1): 14-22. Summer 1995. (No. 79)

LONEY, MARK
___ "SF, Genre, and Conservatism," *Science Fiction: A Review of Speculative Literature* 12(1): 3-8. 1993. (Whole No. 34)

LONG, FRANK B.
___ "Lovecraft the Man," in: Joshi, S. T., ed. **The H. P. Lovecraft Centennial Conference Proceedings**. West Warwick, RI: Necronomicon, 1991. pp.29-30.

LONGHURST, DEREK
___ "Science Fiction: The Dreams of Men," in: Longhurst, Derek, ed. **Gender, Genre and Narrative Pleasure**. Boston, MA: Unwin Hyman, 1989. pp.192-212.

LONGO, ROBERT
___ "Cyber Johnny," *Sight and Sound* 5(7): 6-7. July 1995.

LONOFF, SUE
___ "Comprising **Nineteen Eighty-Four**: The Art of Nightmare," in: Rose, Jonathan, ed. **The Revised Orwell**. East Lansing, MI: Michigan State University Press, 1992. pp.25-46.

LOPEZ, DANIEL
___ **Films by Genre: 775 Categories, Styles, Trends and Movements Defined, with a Filmography for Each**. Jefferson, NC: McFarland, 1993. 519pp.

LORANDO, MARK
___ "Shock Cousteau Scheider Makes More Waves," *New Orleans (LA) Times-Picayune*. September 19, 1994. in: *NewsBank. Film and Television*. 103:E12. 1994.
___ "Trekkies Headed for Deep Space," *New Orleans (LA) Times-Picayune* Sec. A, p. 9. January 21, 1992.

LORD, GLENN
___ "The Mystery Titles of Robert E. Howard," *Wayfarer II* pp.13-16. n.d.

LORD, MICHEL
___ **Bibliographie analytique de la science fiction et du fantastique Quebecois: 1960-1985**, by Aurelien Boivin, Maurice Emond and Michel Lord. Quebec: Nuit blanche editeur, 1992. 577pp.

LOREN, CHRISTALENE
___ "Quick Cuts: A Lady in Disguise," *Cinefex* No. 58: 91-92. June 1994.
___ "Video Beat: *Deep Space Nine* Miniatures," *Cinefex* No. 54: 21-22. May 1993.
___ "Video Beat: Deep Space Wormholes," *Cinefex* No. 55: 11-12. August 1993.
___ "Video Beat: Toasting *Babylon 5*," *Cinefex* No. 57: 11-12. March 1994.

LOUIE, ANDREA
___ "Activists Say They'll Disrupt Film Showing," *Akron (OH) Beacon Journal* March 18, 1992 in: *NewsBank. Film and Television*. 29:A7. 1992.

LOVE, WILLIAM F.
___ "Butler, Dabbler, Spy: Jeeves to Wimsey to Bond," in: Dale, Alzina S., ed. **Dorothy L. Sayers: The Centenary Celebration**. New York: Walker, 1993. pp.31-44.

LOVECE, FRANK
___ "Filmmakers See Future: Science Fiction," *Los Angeles (CA) Times* p.F1. November 9, 1994.

LOVECRAFT, H. P.
___ **H. P. Lovecraft: Letters to Richard F. Searight**, edited by S. T. Joshi. West Warwick, RI: Necronomicon, 1992. 90pp.
___ "In Memoriam: Robert Ervin Howard (1936)," in: Joshi, S. T., ed. **Miscellaneous Writings: H. P. Lovecraft**. Sauk City, WI: Arkham House, 1995. pp.123-126.
___ "A Letter from Lovecraft: On the Philosophy of Religion," *The Generalist Papers* 4(6): 1-4. February 1994.
___ "Letter to Myrta Alice Little," *Lovecraft Studies* No. 26: 26-30. Spring 1992.
___ "Lord Dunsany and His Work (1922)," in: Joshi, S. T., ed. **Miscellaneous Writings: H. P. Lovecraft**. Sauk City, WI: Arkham House, 1995. pp.104-112.
___ "Notes on 'Alias Peter Marchall' by A. F. Lorenz," *Lovecraft Studies* No. 28: 20-21. Fall 1992.
___ "Notes on Writing Weird Fiction (1932/33)," in: Joshi, S. T., ed. **Miscellaneous Writings: H. P. Lovecraft**. Sauk City, WI: Arkham House, 1995. pp.113-116.
___ "Plaster-all [Unpublished poem]," *Lovecraft Studies* No. 27: 30-31. Fall 1992.
___ "Some Notes on Interplanetary Fiction (1934)," in: Joshi, S. T., ed. **Miscellaneous Writings: H. P. Lovecraft**. Sauk City, WI: Arkham House, 1995. pp.117-122.
___ **Supernatural Horror in Literature**. Chislehurst, Kent, Eng.: Gothic Society, 1994. 32pp.
___ "The Unknown [Unpublished poem]," *Lovecraft Studies* No. 25: 36. Fall 1991.

LOVECY, IAN
___ "**Historia Peredur ab Efrawg**," in: Bromwich, Rachel, Jarman, A. O. H. and Roberts, Brynley F., eds. **The Arthur of the Welsh**. Cardiff: University of Wales Press, 1991. pp.171-182.

LOVEGROVE, JAMES
___ "From Rutland to the Universe: Peter F. Hamilton Interviewed," *Interzone* No. 96: 28-31. June 1995.
___ "Mythic Templates: Paul McAuley Interviewed," *Interzone* No. 98: 18-21. August 1995.

LOVELL, GLENN
___ "It Came from Cyberspace," *San Jose (CA) Mercury News*. April 22, 1994. in: *NewsBank. Film and Television*. 51:F5. 1994.
___ "Van Dammed: **No Escape** from Gruesomly Familiar Territory," *San Jose (CA) Mercury News*. April 29, 1994. in: *NewsBank. Film and Television*. 58:A10. 1994.
___ "**Waterworld**: Kevin Costner, Auteur," *Cinefantastique* 26(5): 8. August 1995.

LOVETT, RICHARD A.
___ "**Star Trek** Science Exhibit Tours Country," *Science Fiction Age* 1(6): 20-21. September 1993.

LOVETT, VERENA
___ "Bodily Symbolism and the Fiction of Stephen King," in: Longhurst, Derek, ed. **Gender, Genre and Narrative Pleasure**. Boston, MA: Unwin Hyman, 1989. pp.157-176.

LOVETT-GRAFF, BENNETT
___ "Lovecraft: Reproduction and Its Discontents: Degeneration and Detection in 'The Lurking Fear'," *Paradoxa* 1(3): 325-341. 1995.

LOVISI, GARY
___ "H. Beam Piper in Paperback," *Paperback Parade* No. 35: 50-58. August 1993.
___ "**Little Fuzzy**: The 8th Printing," *Paperback Parade* No. 35: 48-49. August 1993.
___ "The Long Lost Fuzzy," *Paperback Parade* No. 35: 40-44. August 1993.

LOWE, NICK
___ "**The Abyss** (Review)," *Interzone* No. 75: 36. September 1993.
___ "**Accion Mutante** (Review)," *Interzone* No. 78: 34-35. December 1993.
___ "**Addams Family Values** (Review)," *Interzone* No. 81: 39. March 1994.
___ "**Alien 3** (Review)," *Interzone* No. 65: 32-33. November 1992.
___ "**Apollo 13** (Review)," *Interzone* No. 102: 35-36. December 1995.
___ "**Attack of the Fifty Foot Woman** (Review)," *Interzone* No. 88: 36. October 1994.
___ "**Batman Forever** (Review)," *Interzone* No. 100: 35. October 1995.
___ "**Batman Returns** (Review)," *Interzone* No. 64: 31-32. October 1992.
___ "**Beyond Bedlam** (Review)," *Interzone* No. 85: 39-40. July 1994.
___ "**Blade Runner: The Director's Cut** (Review)," *Interzone* No. 69: 39-40. March 1993.
___ "**Body Snatchers** (Review)," *Interzone* No. 83: 36. May 1994.
___ "**Brainscan** (Review)," *Interzone* No. 90: 30-32. December 1994.
___ "**Bram Stoker's Dracula** (Review)," *Interzone* No. 70: 59-60. April 1993.
___ "**Casper** (Review)," *Interzone* No. 99: 34. September 1995.
___ "**City of Lost Children** (Review)," *Interzone* No. 101: 34. November 1995.
___ "**Congo** (Review)," *Interzone* No. 99: 32-33. September 1995.
___ "**The Crow** (Review)," *Interzone* No. 84: 38-39. June 1994.
___ "**Death Becomes Her** (Review)," *Interzone* No. 69: 38-39. March 1993.
___ "**Demolition Man** (Review)," *Interzone* No. 81: 38-39. March 1994.
___ "**Ed Wood** (Review)," *Interzone* No. 96: 36-38. June 1995.
___ "**Eraserhead** (Review)," *Interzone* No. 78: 35-36. December 1993.
___ "**Fire in the Sky** (Review)," *Interzone* No. 76: 37. October 1993.
___ "**Flintstones** (Review)," *Interzone* No. 88: 35-36. October 1994.
___ "**Fortress** (Review)," *Interzone* No. 88: 36. October 1994.
___ "**Groundhog Day** (Review)," *Interzone* No. 74: 38-40. August 1993.
___ "**Gunhed** (Review)," *Interzone* No. 84: 39. June 1994.
___ "**Honey, I Blew Up the Kid** (Review)," *Interzone* No. 70: 60. April 1993.
___ "**In the Mouth of Madness** (Review)," *Interzone* No. 99: 33. September 1995.
___ "**Interview With the Vampire** (Review)," *Interzone* No. 92: 28-29. February 1995.
___ "**Judge Dredd** (Review)," *Interzone* No. 100: 34-35. October 1995.
___ "**Jurassic Park** (Review)," *Interzone* No. 77: 31-32. November 1993.
___ "**Last Action Hero** (Review)," *Interzone* No. 76: 36-37. October 1993.
___ "**Les Visiteurs** (Review)," *Interzone* No. 83: 35-36. May 1994.
___ "**Mangler** (Review)," *Interzone* No. 98: 31-32. August 1995.
___ "**Mary Shelley's Frankenstein** (Review)," *Interzone* No. 91: 37-39. January 1995.
___ "**The Mask** (Review)," *Interzone* No. 89: 38-39. November 1994.
___ "**Matinee** (Review)," *Interzone* No. 74: 40. August 1993.
___ "**Meteor Man** (Review)," *Interzone* No. 82: 31. April 1994.
___ "**Necronomicon** (Review)," *Interzone* No. 89: 39. November 1994.
___ "**Nightmare Before Christmas** (Review)," *Interzone* No. 92: 30. February 1995.
___ "**No Escape** (Review)," *Interzone* No. 85: 38-39. July 1994.
___ "**Outbreak** (Review)," *Interzone* No. 97: 33-35. July 1995.
___ "**The Pagemaster** (Review)," *Interzone* No. 92: 29-30. February 1995.
___ "**The Rapture** (Review)," *Interzone* No. 64: 30-31. October 1992.
___ "**Robocop 3** (Review)," *Interzone* No. 87: 24-25. September 1994.
___ "**Roujin Z** (Review)," *Interzone* No. 87: 25. September 1994.
___ "**Species** (Review)," *Interzone* No. 102: 34-35. December 1995.
___ "**Star Trek: Generations** (Review)," *Interzone* No. 95: 35-36. May 1995.
___ "**Stargate** (Review)," *Interzone* No. 93: 31-32. March 1995.
___ "**Stay Tuned** (Review)," *Interzone* No. 72: 34. June 1993.
___ "**Super Mario Bros.** (Review)," *Interzone* No. 75: 35-36. September 1993.
___ "**Tank Girl** (Review)," *Interzone* No. 98: 30-31. August 1995.
___ "**Timecop** (Review)," *Interzone* No. 93: 32. March 1995.
___ "**Toys** (Review)," *Interzone* No. 72: 34. June 1993.
___ "**UFO--The Movie** (Review)," *Interzone* No. 82: 30. April 1994.
___ "**Universal Soldier** (Review)," *Interzone* No. 65: 33. November 1992.
___ "**Waterworld** (Review)," *Interzone* No. 101: 33-34. November 1995.

LOWE, NICK

LYNN, RUTH N.

LOWE, NICK (continued)
___ "*Welcome II the Terrordome* (Review)," *Interzone* No. 93: 32-33. March 1995.

LOWENBERG, SUSAN
___ **C. S. Lewis: A Reference Guide, 1972-1988.** New York: G. K. Hall, 1993. 319pp.

LOWENTROUT, PETER
___ "*Batman* Winging Through the Ruins of the American Baroque," *Extrapolation* 33(1): 25-31. Spring 1992.
___ "**The War of the Worlds** Revisited: Science Fiction and the Angst of Secularization," *Extrapolation* 33(4): 351-359. Winter 1992.

LOWRY, BRIAN
___ "Beloved *Starman*," by Brian Lowry and Christine C. Menefee. in: McDonnell, David, ed. **Starlog's Science Fiction Heroes and Heroines.** New York: Crescent Books, 1995. pp.55-57.
___ "Gen X Marks the Spot," by J. Max Robins and Brian Lowry. *Variety* 358(7): 1, 63. March 20, 1995.
___ "Science Fiction Hero," in: McDonnell, David, ed. **Starlog's Science Fiction Heroes and Heroines.** New York: Crescent Books, 1995. pp.19-23.
___ "Starfleet Siren," by Brian Lowry and Ian Spelling. in: McDonnell, David, ed. **Starlog's Science Fiction Heroes and Heroines.** New York: Crescent Books, 1995. pp.77-79.
___ **The Truth Is Out There: The Official Guide to The X-Files.** New York: HarperCollins, 1995. 277pp.
___ "TV Reviews: *Science Fiction: A Journey into the Unknown*," *Variety* 357(7): 38. December 12, 1994.

LUBACK, ALAN
___ "Acting Out an Old Story: Twentieth-Century Tristan Plays," in: Slocum, Sally K., ed. **Popular Arthurian Traditions.** Bowling Green, OH: Popular Press, 1992. pp.162-172.

LUBEJ-LONGYKA, MARJETA
___ "Prvine Znanstvene fantastike v noveli Jona Brnak Gradisnika," *Jezik in Slovstvo* (Slovenia) 38(7/8): 261-266. May 1992/1993. [Not seen.]

LUCAS, GEORGE
___ "Tardis in a Time-Warp," *Spectator* 271(8628): 26-27. November 20, 1993.

LUCCHESI, O.
___ "Manoscritti ed immagini di Tommaso Campanella. Orientamenti de recerca," by G. Formichetti, O. Lucchesi, P. Sagi and F. Troncarelli. in: Saccaro Del Buffa, Giuseppa and Lewis, Arthur O., eds. **Utopie per gli Anni Ottana.** Rome: Gangemi Editore, 1986. pp.587-590.

LUCKHURST, ROGER
___ "The Many Deaths of Science Fiction: A Polemic," *Science Fiction Studies* 21(1): 35-50. March 1994.
___ "Petition, Repetition, and Autobiography: J. G. Ballard's **Empire of the Sun** and **The Kindness of Women**," *Contemporary Literature* 35(4): 688-708. Winter 1994.
___ "Repetition and Unreadability: J. G. Ballard's **Vermilion Sands**," *Extrapolation* 36(4): 292-304. Winter 1995.

LUDACER, KENNETH
___ "The Heaven and Hell of More's **Utopia**," *CEA Critic* 56(3): 66-73. Spring/Summer 1995.

LUDLOW, GREGORY
___ "Imagining the Future: Mercier's **L'an 2440** and Morris' **News From Nowhere**," *Comparative Literature Studies* 29(1): 20-38. 1992.

LUGOSI, BELA
___ "I Like Playing Dracula," *Wonder* No. 7: 44-45. 1993.

LULING, VIRGINIA
___ "An Anthropologist in Middle-Earth," in: Reynolds, Patricia and GoodKnight, Glen H., eds. **Proceedings of the J. R. R. Tolkien Centenary Conference, Keble College, Oxford, 1992.** Altadena, CA: Mythopoeic Press, 1995. pp.53-57. (*Mythlore* Vol. 21, No. 2, Winter 1996, Whole No. 80)

LUNDIN, STEVEN J.
___ "*Mommy* (Review)," *Cinefantastique* 27(3): 30-31. December 1995.

LUPACK, ALAN
___ "The Arthurian Legend in America: A Moderated Discussion of 'Arthurnet'," *Arthuriana* 4(4): 291-297. Winter 1994.
___ "Beyond the Model: Howard Pyle's Arthurian Books," in: Busby, Keith, ed. **The Arthurian Yearbook I.** New York: Garland, 1991. pp.215-234.
___ "An Enemy in Our Midst: **The Black Knight** and the American Dream," in: Harty, Kevin J., ed. **Cinema Arthuriana: Essays on Arthurian Film.** New York: Garland, 1991. pp.29-40.
___ (ed.) **Modern Arthurian Literature: An Anthology of English and American Arthuriana From the Renaissance to the Present.** New York: Garland, 1992. 494pp.

LUPACK, BARBARA T.
___ "F. Scott Fitzgerald's 'Following of a Grail'," *Arthuriana* 4(4): 324-347. Winter 1994.

LUPOFF, RICHARD A.
___ "Edgar & Otis & Sam & Bob: Consider the Possibilities," *Burroughs Bulletin* NS No. 11: 24-26. July 1992.
___ "Edgar Rice Burroughs and the Maxwell Perkins Syndrome," *Burroughs Bulletin* NS. No. 13: 3-10. January 1993.
___ "Into the Aether, Junior Spacepersons!," in: Sanders, Joe, ed. **Science Fiction Fandom.** Westport, CT: Greenwood, 1994. pp.197-206.
___ "Wright, Van Dine, Vance," *New York Review of Science Fiction* No. 50: 20-23. October 1992.

LUTTRELL, HANK
___ "The Science Fiction Convention Scene," in: Sanders, Joe, ed. **Science Fiction Fandom.** Westport, CT: Greenwood, 1994. pp.149-160.

LUTZ, REINHART
___ "Styles Within Styles, or 'Death of a Hack Writer': **Herovit's World** Reconsidered," in: Slusser, George E. and Rabkin, Eric S., eds. **Styles of Creation: Aesthetic Technique and the Creation of Fictional Worlds.** Athens: University of Georgia Press, 1992. pp.181-191.

LYALL, FRANCIS
___ "Law in Science Fiction: An Introduction," *Foundation* No. 55: 36-57. Summer 1992.

LYKE, M. L.
___ "Terry Brooks and the Importance of Success," *Seattle Post-Intelligencer* Sec. C, p. 1, 3. April 5, 1993.

LYLE, JODY
___ "*The Abyss*: Like a Fish Out of Water," *Jump Cut* No. 38: 9-13. 1993.

LYMAN, DAVID
___ "*Silence of the Lambs* Wins Chicago Awards," *Cincinnati (OH) Post.* March 16, 1992. in: *NewsBank. Film and Television.* 36:C2. 1992.
___ "Wit, Violence Smashing Hits in 'Demo Man' (Review)," *Cincinnati (OH) Enquirer* October 8, 1993. in: *NewsBank. Art.* 28:C1. 1993.

LYNCH, KATHRYN L.
___ "Implementing an Interdisciplinary Course," in: Fries, Maureen and Watson, Jeanie, eds. **Approaches to the Teaching of the Arthurian Tradition.** New York: Modern Language Association, 1992. pp.65-69.

LYNCH, LAWRENCE
___ **Jules Verne.** New York: Twayne, 1992. 127pp.

LYNN, ELIZABETH
___ "Post-Holocaust Themes in Feminist SF (Transcript of the Panel at NorEasCon 2)," by Elizabeth Lynn, Chelsea Q. Yarbro, Suzy M. Charnas and Jeanne Gomoll. *Janus* 6(2): 25-28. Winter 1980. (Whole No. 18)

LYNN, RUTH N.
___ **Fantasy Literature for Children and Young Adults: An Annotated Bibliography.** 4th ed. New York: Bowker, 1995. 1092pp.

LYONS, MICHAEL
___ "*Pocahontas*: Animator Glen Keane on the Renaissance of Disney Animation," *Cinefantastique* 27(3): 50. December 1995.
___ "*Pocahontas* (Review)," *Cinefantastique* 27(3): 49. December 1995.
___ "*Pocahontas*," *Cinefantastique* 27(3): 48, 50, 60. December 1995.

MAASS, DONALD
___ "Is Horror Dead, or Just Resting?," *Science Fiction Chronicle* 13(6): 25-26. March 1992.

MABEE, BARBARA
___ "Astronauts, Angels, and Time Machines: The Fantastic in Recent German Democratic Republic Literature," in: Morse, Donald E., ed. **The Celebration of the Fantastic**. Westport, CT: Greenwood, 1992. pp.221-236.
___ "The Witch as Double: Feminist Doubles in German Literature and Irmtraud Morgner's **Amanda**," *Journal of the Fantastic in the Arts* 6(2/3): 166-190. 1994.

MACAULEY, WILLIAM R.
___ "From Cognitive Pyschologies to Mythologies: Advancing Cyborg Textualities for a Narrative of Resistance," by William R. Macauley and Angel J. Gordo-Lopez. in: Gray, Chris H., ed. **The Cyborg Handbook**. New York: Routledge, 1995. pp.433-443.

MACBAIN, DANIELLE M.
___ "Love Versus Politics: Competing Paradigms of Chivalry in Malory's **Morte D'Arthur**," *Quondam et Futurus* 2(3): 22-31. Fall 1992.

MacCAMBRIDGE, MICHAEL
___ "Another Spielberg Summer: **Jurassic Park** Revives a Blockbuster Tradition (Review)," *Austin (TX) American Statesman* Weekend Section, p. 5. June 11, 1993.

MACCARILLO, LISA
___ "Brave New World," *Sci-Fi Entertainment* 2(3): 38-41. October 1995.
___ "Cyberpunk Heroine **Tank Girl** Plays Tour Guide to a Gritty Tomorrow," *Science Fiction Age* 3(3): 20-22, 92. March 1995.
___ "Cyberpunk Heroine **Tank Girl**," *Sci-Fi Entertainment* 1(6): 28-33. April 1995.
___ "Hardwired Hero," *Sci-Fi Entertainment* 1(5): 46-50, 72. February 1995.
___ "In the Lab of the Imagination with Michael Westmore," *Sci-Fi Entertainment* 1(2): 52-54. August 1994.
___ "Lost Moon," *Sci-Fi Entertainment* 2(2): 56-61, 81. August 1995.
___ "More Than Human," *Sci-Fi Entertainment* 2(2): 62-67, 81. August 1995.
___ "Renaissance Man: An Afternoon With Stan Winston," *Sci-Fi Entertainment* 2(1): 58-63. June 1995
___ "The Truth Is Out There," *Sci-Fi Entertainment* 2(3): 54-58. October 1995.
___ "William Gibson's Cyberpunk Future Is Made Real in **Johnny Mnemonic**," *Science Fiction Age* 3(2): 18, 20, 81. January 1995.
___ "**X-Files**," *Sci-Fi Entertainment* 1(4): 74-77. December 1994.

MacCARTHY, FIONA
___ **William Morris: A Life for Our Times**. New York: Knopf, 1995. 780pp.

MacCOLLOCH, SIMON
___ "Joe R. Lansdale's 'The Nightrunners': The Art of Violence," *Studies in Weird Fiction* No. 12: 2-6. Spring 1993.

MacCULLOCH, SIMON
___ "The Dead Line: Horror and Tragedy," *Studies in Weird Fiction* No. 10: 26-31. Fall 1991.
___ "Glimpses of Absolute Power: Ramsey Campbell's Concept of Evil," in: Joshi, S. T., ed. **The Count of Thirty: A Tribute to Ramsey Campbell**. West Warwick, RI: Necronomicon, 1993. pp.32-37.
___ "Popacateptl Purple: Poppy Z. Brite's **Lost Souls**," *Studies in Weird Fiction* No. 15: 5-12. Summer 1994.

MacDONALD, ALASDAIR A.
___ (ed.) **Companion to Middle English Romance**, ed. by Henk Aertson and Alasdair A. MacDonald. Amsterdam: VU University Press, 1990. 209pp.

MacDONALD, ALEXANDER
___ "The Liveliness of **News From Nowhere**: Structure, Language, and Allusion," *Journal of the William Morris Society* 10(2): 22-26. Spring 1993.

MacDONALD, EDGAR
___ **James Branch Cabell and Richmond-in-Virginia**. Jackson: University of Mississippi Press, 1993. 373pp.

MACDONALD, GEORGE
___ "Geschichten und Gedanken: Erstmals ins Deutsche übersetzt bon Gisbert Kranz," in: Kranz, Gisbert, ed. **Inklings: Jahrbuch für Literatur und Ästhetik**. 9. Band. Lüdenscheid, Germany: Stier, 1991. pp.18-54 [Not seen.]

MacDONOGH, STEVE
___ (ed.) **The Rushdie Letters: Freedom to Speak, Freedom to Write**. Dingle, Ireland: Brandon, 1993. 189pp.

MacGILLIVRAY, SCOTT
___ "Astor Pictures," *Filmfax* No. 43: 36-41. February/March 1994.

MacGREGOR, JEFF
___ "When Being Scared to Death Was Family Fun," *New York Times* p.H29. June 25, 1995.

MacILROY, BARRY
___ "Those Magical Time-Slip Stories," *Souvenir* 21: 14-15. 1992. [Not seen.]

MACKENZIE, ANGUS
___ "Brush Strokes in Blood: An Exclusive Interview with Alan Plent," in: Brown, Michael, ed. **Pandemonium: Further Explorations into the Worlds of Clive Barker**. Staten Island, NY: Eclipse, 1991. pp.43-51.

MACKENZIE, JIM
___ "Reminiscences of Cotswold Craftsmen," *Journal of the William Morris Society* 11(2): 27-31. Spring 1995.

MACKEY, AIDAN
___ "The Christian Influence of G. K. Chesterton on C. S. Lewis," in: Walker, Andrew and Patric, James, eds. **A Christian for All Christians**. Washington, DC: Regnery, 1992. pp.68-82.

MacKILLOP, IAN
___ "Fly Me to the Moon," *New Scientist* 144(1948): 51-52. October 22, 1994.

MACKLIN, F. ANTHONY
___ "Understanding Kubrick: **The Shining**," *Journal of Popular Film and Television* 9(2): 93-95. 1981.

MACKLIN, LISA A.
___ **Feminism in the Selected Science Fiction Novels of Margaret Atwood and Marge Piercy**. Master's Thesis, Texas Woman's University, 1993. 105pp. (Master's Abstracts 32/03, p. 805. June 1994.)

MacLEAN, HEATHER L.
___ **Science Fiction and Surrealism: A Reader's Dream**. Ph.D. Dissertation, University of North Carolina, Chapel Hill, 1994. 186pp. (DAI-A 55/11, p. 3507. May 1995.)

MacLEAN, KATHERINE
___ "Judith Merril vs. Plotto," *Aloud (Toronto)* 2(7): 6. October 1992.

MACLEOD, NORMAN
___ "The Language of Kingsley Amis," in: Salwak, Dale, ed. **Kingsley Amis in Life and Letters**. New York: St. Martin's, 1990. pp.100-129.

MACNAB, GEOFFREY
___ "**U.F.O.** (Review)," *Sight and Sound* 4(2): 60-61. February 1994.

MacNEE, MARIE J.
___ **Science Fiction, Fantasy and Horror Writers**. Detroit, MI: Gale Research, 1995. 2 vols., 432pp.

MacQUEEN, SCOTT
___ " '43 Phantom Found New Formula for Classic Tale," *American Cinematographer* 74(9): 80-85. September 1993.
___ "Effects Scene: Cinematic Archaeology," *Cinefex* No. 55: 123-124. August 1993.
___ "*The Lost World*: Merely Misplaced?," *American Cinematographer* 73(6): 37-44. June 1992.

MacRAE, SUZANNE H.
___ "Berger's Mythical **Arthur Rex**," in: Slocum, Sally K., ed. **Popular Arthurian Traditions**. Bowling Green, OH: Popular Press, 1992. pp.85-95.

MACY, MICHELLE D.
___ **Julia Verlanger: 'grande dame' de la science fiction fran crep**. Master's Thesis, University of South Florida, 1995. 69pp.

MADAUS, LYNN
___ **Characters in Time Travel as Historical Guides**, by Sandra A. Imdieke and Lynn Madaus. ERIC ED 305601. 9pp. 1992.

MADDEN, J. R.
___ "MagiCon: The 50th World Science Fiction Convention," *Science Fiction Chronicle* 14(2): 30-33. November 1992.
___ "MagiCon, the 50th World Science Fiction Convention (Part 2)," *Science Fiction Chronicle* 14(3): 32-36. December 1992.

MADDOX, TOM
___ "Reports From the Electronic Frontier: 1994, The Year in Review," *Locus* 34(1) 13, 53. January 1995.
___ "Reports From the Electronic Frontier: Computers, Freedom and Privacy, Part 3," *Locus* 30(6): 11, 13, 37. June 1993.
___ "Reports From the Electronic Frontier: Cyberspace, Freedom and the Law," *Locus* 30(1): 11, 49-50. January 1993.
___ "Reports From the Electronic Frontier: Electronic Worlds, Paper Texts, Part 1: Digital Mantras," *Locus* 33(2): 13, 57. August 1994.
___ "Reports From the Electronic Frontier: I Sing the Text Electric, Part 1, Hypertext Local and General," *Locus* 29(5): 11, 58. November 1992
___ "Reports From the Electronic Frontier: I Sing the Text Electric, Part 2, Reading Hypertext," *Locus* 29(6): 11-12. December 1992.
___ "Reports from the Electronic Frontier: Introducing Information Spaces, 1," *Locus* 29(3): 11, 64. September 1992.
___ "Reports from the Electronic Frontier: Introducing Information Spaces, 2," *Locus* 29(4): 17, 56. October 1992
___ "Reports from the Electronic Frontier: Life on the Internet, Part 2; Exploring the Datasphere," *Locus* 30(3): 11, 58. March 1993.
___ "Reports From the Electronic Frontier: Net Spiders on the World Wide Web," *Locus* 33(6): 13, 62. December 1994.
___ "Reports From the Electronic Frontier: Online, Offline, On the Road," *Locus* 31(4): 11, 56. October 1993.
___ "Reports From the Electronic Frontier: Public Key Encryption and Pretty Good Privacy," *Locus* 33(1): 13, 62. July 1994.
___ "Reports From the Electronic Frontier: Someone to Watch Over Me," *Locus* 30(5): 13, 53-54. May 1993.
___ "Reports From the Electronic Frontier: The Clipper Chip," *Locus* 32(6): 13, 61. June 1994.
___ "Reports From the Electronic Frontier: The Community Machines," *Locus* 32(3): 13, 15, 59. March 1994.
___ "Reports From the Electronic Frontier: The Dark Side of the Net," *Locus* 32(2): 13, 60-61. February 1994.
___ "Reports From the Electronic Frontier: The Medium and the Message, or, After the Internet, the Deluge," *Locus* 32(1): 11, 47. January 1994.
___ "Reports From the Electronic Frontier: The Q Question," *Locus* 33(3): 13, 64. September 1994.
___ "Reports From the Electronic Frontier: The Year in Review, Part 1," *Locus* 31(5): 11, 52. November 1993.
___ "Reports From the Electronic Frontier: The Year in Review, Part 2," *Locus* 31(6): 11, 58. December 1993.
___ "Reports From the Electronic Frontier: Time, Space, and Modems," *Locus* 30(4): 11, 50-51. April 1993.
___ "Reports From the Electronic Frontier: Writing Tools, Part 1," *Locus* 31(1): 11-13, 47 July 1993.

MADDOX, TOM (continued)
___ "Reports From the Electronic Frontier: Writing Tools, Part 2," *Locus* 31(2): 11, 48. August 1993.

MADLE, ROBERT A.
___ "Fandom up to World War II," in: Sanders, Joe, ed. **Science Fiction Fandom**. Westport, CT: Greenwood, 1994. pp.37-54.

MADRACKI, JOHN
___ "Twilight's Last Gleaming: A Historical Survey of TV SF," *Vector* No. 179: 28-35. June/July 1994.
___ "Writing Your First Novel," *Focus* (BSFA) No. 25: 12-13. December/January 1994.

MADRIGAL, ALIX
___ "A Specialist in the Unexpected," *San Francisco (CA) Chronicle*. Review p. 5. February 2, 1992.

MADSEN, DAN
___ "The Art of Drew Struzan," *LucasFilms Fan Club* No. 18: 10-13. 1993.
___ "Designing **Deep Space Nine**," *Star Trek: The Official Fan Club* No. 89: 2-6. January/February 1993.
___ "Exclusive Interview: Gene Roddenberry: Looking Back at the Legend," *Star Trek: The Official Fan Club Magazine* No. 84: 2-3. March/April 1992.
___ "Exclusive Interview: Richard Arnold; Memories of the Creator," *Star Trek: The Official Fan Club Magazine* No. 84: 13. March/April 1992.
___ "Exclusive Interview: Sean Patrick Flanery; The Further Adventures of **Young Indiana Jones**," *Lucasfilm Fan Club Magazine* No. 16: 2-6. 1992.
___ "Exclusive Interview: William Shatner: The Final Voyage of Captain Kirk," *Star Trek: The Official Fan Club Magazine* No. 85: 2-4. May/June 1992.
___ "The Future of **Star Trek**," *Star Trek: The Official Fan Club Magazine* No. 85: 7-9. May/June 1992.
___ "George Lucas: The Future of the Force," *The LucasFilm Fan Club* No. 17: 2-6. 1993.
___ "Jonathan Del Arco: I, Borg," *Star Trek: The Official Fan Club* No. 93: 33-34. September/October 1993.
___ "Movie Update," *Star Trek: The Official Fan Club* No. 94: 30-31. November/December 1993.
___ "Nichelle Nichols: Remembering Gene," *Star Trek: The Official Fan Club Magazine* No. 84: 12. March/April 1992.
___ "Rick Berman: Interview," *Star Trek: The Official Fan Club Magazine* No. 91: 2-6. May/June 1993.
___ "**Star Trek** Update," *Star Trek: The Official Fan Club* No. 93: 29-31. September/October 1993.
___ "Syndicating **Star Trek**," *Star Trek: The Official Fan Club* No. 93: 1. September/October 1993.
___ "Uncovering the History Behind Young Indy, Part 2," *The LucasFilm Fan Club* No. 17: 10, 13. 1993.
___ "Welcome to **Deep Space Nine**, Part 1," *Star Trek: The Official Fan Club* No. 89: 10-13. January/February 1993.
___ "Welcome to **Deep Space Nine**, Part 2," *Star Trek: The Official Fan Club* No. 90: 11-13. March/April 1993.
___ "Welcome to **Deep Space Nine**, Part 3," *Star Trek: The Official Fan Club Magazine* No. 91: 10-12. May/June 1993.
___ "**The Young Indiana Jones Chronicles**," *Lucasfilm Fan Club Magazine* No. 15: 2-5. 1992.

MAE, JAMES
___ "Discovering the Dyson Sphere," *Star Trek: The Official Fan Club* No. 90: 10-11. March/April 1993.
___ "A Labor of Love: The Making of 'Relics'," *Star Trek: The Official Fan Club* No. 90: 2-4. March/April 1993.
___ "Return to Yesterday: Recreating the Classic *Enterprise* Bridge," *Star Trek: The Official Fan Club* No. 90: 5-7. March/April 1993.

MAERTENS, JAMES W.
___ "Between Jules Verne and Walt Disney: Brains, Brawn, and Masculine Desire in **20,000 Leagues Under the Sea**," *Science Fiction Studies* 22(2): 209-225. July 1995.

MAGANIELLO, DOMINIC
___ "The Neverending Story: Textual Happiness in **The Lord of the Rings**," *Mythlore* 18(3): 5-14. Summer 1992. (No. 69)

MAGDA, JAMES
___ "Majel Barrett Nurses a Role," *Star Trek: The Official Fan Club* No. 94: 14-16, 41. February/March 1994.

MAGGIN, ELLIOT S.
___ "My Amazing Stories: Memoirs of a Time Traveller, Part 1, by Julius Schwartz," *Amazing* 68(2): 48-53. May 1993.

MAGID, RON
___ "After *Jurassic Park*, Traditional Techniques May Become Fossils," *American Cinematographer* 74(12): 58-65. December 1993.
___ "*Alien 3*: Space, They're Still Screaming," *American Cinematographer* 73(7): 52-58. July 1992.
___ "Back to Gotham: *Batman Returns*," *American Cinematographer* 73(7): 34-41. July 1992.
___ "CFC's Effects Give Life to *Mary Shelley's Frankenstein*," *American Cinematographer* 75(12): 42-48. December 1994.
___ "CGI Spearheads Brave New World of Special Effects," *American Cinematographer* 74(12): 26-36. December 1993.
___ "Digital Domain Arranges an *Interview With the Vampire*," *American Cinematographer* 76(1): 53-61. January 1995.
___ "Digital Domain Provides Rocket Fuel for *Apollo 13*," *American Cinematographer* 76(6): 48-60. June 1995.
___ "Dream Quest Adds Lunatic Fringes," *American Cinematographer* 75(12): 57-58. December 1994.
___ "Effects Add Bite to *Bram Stoker's Dracula*," *American Cinematographer* 73(12): 56-64. December 1992.
___ "Effects Army Mobilizes for Megasequel," *American Cinematographer* 73(7): 42-51. July 1992.
___ "Effects Help Expand Batman's World," *American Cinematographer* 76(7): 45-55. July 1995.
___ "Effects Team Brings Dinosaurs Back from Extinction," *American Cinematographer* 74(6): 46-52. June 1993.
___ "Exploring the Future of Special Effects," *American Cinematographer* 75(2): 26-33. February 1994.
___ "ILM Creates New Universe of Effects for *Star Trek: Generations*," *American Cinematographer* 76(4): 78-88. April 1995.
___ "ILM Magic Is Organized Mayhem," *American Cinematographer* 75(12): 50-56. December 1994.
___ "ILM's Digital Dinosaurs Tear up Effects Jungle," *American Cinematographer* 74(12): 46-57. December 1993.
___ "Incredible Shrinking 'Indian' Effects," by Ron Magid and Chris Probst. *American Cinematographer* 76(8): 68-69. August 1995.
___ "Making Strange Faces," *American Cinematographer* 75(12): 59-60. December 1994.
___ " 'Mega City' Architects," *American Cinematographer* 76(12): 69-72. December 1995.
___ "New Look for a Classic Creature," *American Cinematographer* 75(12): 34-40. December 1994.
___ "*The Pterodactyl Woman of Beverly Hills* Takes Wing," *American Cinematographer* 75(12): 61-62. December 1994.
___ "Speeding Up the Screams in *Alien 3*," *American Cinematographer* 73(12): 70-76. December 1992.
___ "*Star Trek VI*: Creature Feature," *Cinefantastique* 22(5): 33-34. April 1992.
___ "*Star Trek VI*: Designing the Final Frontier," *Cinefantastique* 22(5): 55. April 1992.
___ "*Star Trek VI*: Directing the Last Hurrah," *Cinefantastique* 22(5): 47. April 1992.
___ "*Star Trek VI: The Undiscovered Country*: Director Meyer Explores Familiar Country," *American Cinematographer* 73(1): 51-57. January 1992.
___ "*Star Trek VI: The Undiscovered Country*: ILM Gets a Piece of the Action," *American Cinematographer* 73(1): 58-65. January 1992.
___ "*Star Trek VI: The Undiscovered Country*: Narita Leads *Enterprise* Camera Crew," *American Cinematographer* 73(1): 42-50. January 1992.
___ "*Star Trek VI: The Undiscovered Country*: Specialized Departments Add Artistic Touches," *American Cinematographer* 73(1): 66-75. January 1992.
___ "Taking the Plunge on *Waterworld*," *American Cinematographer* 76(12): 73-76. December 1995.
___ "*Wolf* Sheds Light on a Lycanthrope," *American Cinematographer* 75(6): 48-56. June 1994.

MAGISTRALE, TONY
___ "Art Versus Madness in Stephen King's **Misery**," in: Morse, Donald E., ed. **The Celebration of the Fantastic**. Westport, CT: Greenwood, 1992. pp.271-278.
___ **A Casebook on The Stand**. Mercer Island, WA: Starmont, 1992. 210pp.
___ "Defining Stephen King's Horrorscape: An Introduction," in: Magistrale, Tony, ed. **The Dark Descent: Essays Defining Stephen King's Horrorscape**. Westport, CT: Greenwood, 1992. pp.1-4.
___ "Free Will and Sexual Choice in **The Stand**," *Extrapolation* 34(1): 30-38. Spring 1993.
___ "Free Will and Sexual Choice in **The Stand**," in: Magistrale, Tony, ed. **A Casebook on The Stand**. San Bernardino, CA: Borgo Press, 1992. pp.109-122.
___ "Science, Politics, and the Epic Imagination: **The Talisman**," in: Magistrale, Tony, ed. **The Dark Descent: Essays Defining Stephen King's Horrorscape**. Westport, CT: Greenwood, 1992. pp.113-127.
___ **Stephen King, the Second Decade: Danse Macabre to The Dark Half**. New York: Twayne, 1992. 186pp.
___ (ed.) **The Dark Descent: Essays Defining Stephen King's Horrorscape**. Westport, CT: Greenwood, 1992. 227pp.

MAGYAR, MIKI
___ "Science Fiction for Technical Communicators," in: **International Professional Communication Conference 93 Proceedings: The New Face of Technical Communication: People, Processes, Products.** New York: IEEE, 1993. pp.107-111.

MAHAR, TED
___ "Bill & Ted's Adventure Definitely Bogus," *Portland (OR) Oregonian*. July 19, 1991. in: *NewsBank. Film and Television*. 65:F5. 1991.
___ "Blade Gets Shorter, Sharper," *Portland (OR) The Oregonian*. September 11, 1992. in: *NewsBank. Film and Television*. 87:F11. 1992.
___ "Blood-Splattering Mayhem Spurts Out Unintended Satire in **Universal Soldier** (Review)," *Portland (OR) The Oregonian*. July 11, 1992. in: *NewsBank. Film and Television*. 74:G7. 1992.
___ "Brilliant **Naked Lunch** Only for Stout Hearted (Review)," *Portland (OR) The Oregonian*. January 17, 1992. in: *NewsBank. Film and Television*. 23:G10. 1992.
___ "Buffy Goes for the Jugular," *Portland (OR) The Oregonian*. July 31, 1992. in: *NewsBank. Film and Television*. 77:C4. 1992
___ "Clearly **Invisible Man** Is Something to See (Review)," *Portland (OR) The Oregonian*. March 2, 1992. in: *NewsBank. Film and Television*. 23: D10. 1992.
___ "Contrived **Hand That Rocks the Cradle** Offers Thrills by the Number (Review)," *Portland (OR) The Oregonian*. January 10, 1992. in: *NewsBank. Film and Television*. 12:C1. 1992.
___ " 'Death' Deserves a Proper Burial (Review)," *Portland (OR) The Oregonian*. July 31, 1992. in: *NewsBank. Film and Television*. 78:D9. 1992.
___ "Down for the Count: A Dreary **Dracula**," *Portland (OR) The Oregonian*. November 13, 1992. in: *NewsBank. Film and Television*. 111:B11. 1992.
___ "**Dr. Giggles** Brings Nothing But Yawns (Review)," *Portland (OR) The Oregonian*. October 27, 1992. in: *NewsBank. Film and Television*. 101:A4. 1992.
___ "**Freejack**: A Ho-Hum Mix of Old Sci-Fi Tricks (Review)," *Portland (OR) The Oregonian*. January 20, 1992. in: *NewsBank. Film and Television*. 11:D11. 1992.
___ "A Heavy **Hook** (Review)," *Portland (OR) The Oregonian*. December 11, 1991. in: *NewsBank. ilm and Television*. 3:F12-13. 1992.
___ "A Little Clipping Here and There Wouldn't Hurt **Lawnmower Man** (Review)," *Portland (OR) The Oregonian*. March 14, 1992. in: *NewsBank. Film and Television*. 33:A9. 1992.
___ "Oops! That Silly Scientist Dad Is at It Again (Review)," *Portland (OR) The Oregonian*. July 17, 1992. in: *NewsBank. Film and Television*. 70:E3-E4. 1992.
___ "**Raising Cain** Quickly Sinks to Absurd Levels of Contrivance (Review)," *Portland (OR) The Oregonian*. August 7, 1992. in: *NewsBank. Film and Television*. 83:B1. 1992.
___ "Shakespeare in Space: Aging Crew Trades One-Liners With Those Evil Klingons (Review)," *Portand (OR) The Oregonian*. December 6, 1991. in: *NewsBank. Film and Television*. 7:E6. 1992.
___ "**Sneakers** Romps Through High-Tech Fun (Review)," *Portland (OR) The Oregonian*. September 11, 1992. in: *NewsBank. Film and Television*. 96:D10. 1992.

MAHAR, TED (continued)

___ "They Really Are a Scream," (Portland, OR) *The Oregonian.* November 22, 1991. in: *NewsBank. Film and Television.* 1:A4-A5. 1991

___ "Unbelievably, *Prelude to a Kiss* Works (Review)," *Portland (OR) The Oregonian.* July 10, 1992. in: *NewsBank. Film and Television.* 73: C11. 1992.

___ "Wim Wender's Work to Open Film Festival," *Portland (OR) The Oregonian.* February 13, 1992. in: *NewsBank. Film and Television.* 24: F4. 1992.

MAHONEY, DHIRA B.

___ "Malory's **Tale of Gareth** and the Comedy of Class," in: Busby, Keith, ed. **The Arthurian Yearbook I.** New York: Garland, 1991. pp.165-194.

MAHONEY, EVE

___ "A *Forever Knight* Episode Guide," *Journal of the Dark* No. 4: 35-37. Fall 1995.

___ "A *Forever Knight* Episode Guide," *Journal of the Dark* No. 5: 28-30. Winter 1995/1996.

___ "A *Forever Knight* Episode Guide," *Journal of the Dark* No. 6: 16-18. Spring 1995.

MAIER, LINDA S.

___ **Borges and the European Avant-garde.** New York: P. Lang, 1992. 186pp. [Not seen.]

MAINHARDT, RICIA

___ (ed.) **Robert Bloch: Appreciations of the Master,** ed. by Richard Matheson and Ricia Mainhardt. New York: Tor, 1995. 382pp.

MAJERE, TIKA

___ **Leaves From the Inn of the Last Home: The Complete Krynn Sourcebook.** Lake Geneva, WI: TSR, 1993. 255pp.

MAJOR, JOSEPH T.

___ "Lord Kalvan of Otherwriters," *Paperback Parade* No. 35: 72-100. August 1993.

___ "Star Soldiers Are for Star Wars," *Lan's Lantern* No. 38: 33-41. July 1992.

MAKSIAN, GEORGE

___ "Sci-Fi Channel Will Debut in the Fall," by Elizabeth Jensen and George Maksian. *Austin (TX) American Statesman* Sec. B, p. 4. April 2, 1992.

MALCOR, LINDA A.

___ "Some Notes on Merlin," by C. Scott Littleton and Linda A. Malcor. *Arthuriana* 5(3): 87-95. Fall 1995.

MALEKIN, PETER

___ "Knowing about Knowing: Paradigms of Knowledge in the Postmodern Fantastic," in: Ruddick, Nicholas, ed. **State of the Fantastic.** Westport, CT: Greenwood, 1992. pp.41-47.

___ "The Perilous Edge: Strindberg, Madness, and Other Worlds," in: Murphy, Patrick D., ed. **Staging the Impossible: The Fantastic Mode in Modern Drama.** Westport, CT: Greenwood, 1992. pp.44-55.

___ " 'What Dreams May Come?': Relativity of Perception in Doris Lessing's **Briefing for a Descent into Hell,**" in: Morse, Donald E., ed. **The Celebration of the Fantastic.** Westport, CT: Greenwood, 1992. pp.73-80.

MALKKI, TARYA

___ "The Marriage Metaphor in the Works of Ursula K. Le Guin," in: Latham, Robert A. and Collins, Robert A., eds. **Modes of the Fantastic.** Westport, CT: Greenwood, 1995. pp.100-109.

MALLETT, ANNETTE Y.

___ **The Work of Elizabeth Chater: An Annotated Bibliography and Guide,** by Daryl F. Mallett and Annette Y. Mallett. San Bernardino, CA: Borgo Press, 1994. 80pp.

MALLETT, DARYL F.

___ **Reginald's Science Fiction and Fantasy Awards: A Comprehensive Guide to the Awards and Their Winners.** Third revised edition, by Daryl F. Mallett and Robert Reginald. San Bernardino, CA: Borgo Press, 1993. 248pp.

MALLETT, DARYL F. (continued)

___ **The Work of Elizabeth Chater: An Annotated Bibliography and Guide,** by Daryl F. Mallett and Annette Y. Mallett. San Bernardino, CA: Borgo Press, 1994. 80pp.

___ **The Work of Jack Vance: An Annotated Bibliography and Guide,** by Jerry Hewett and Daryl F. Mallett. San Bernardino, CA: Borgo Press, 1994. 293pp. (Issued simultaneously by Underwood-Miller.)

___ (ed.) **Imaginative Futures: Proceedings of the 1993 Science Fiction Research Association Conference,** ed. by Milton T. Wolf and Daryl F. Mallett. San Bernardino, CA: Jacob's Ladder Books/Borgo Press, 1995. 364pp.

MALMGREN, CARL D.

___ "The Languages of Science Fiction: Samuel Delaney's **Babel 17,**" *Extrapolation* 34(1): 5-17. Spring 1993.

___ "Self and Other in SF: Alien Encounters," *Science Fiction Studies* 20(1): 15-33. March 1993.

MALMQUIST, ALLEN

___ "*Pocahontas,*" *Cinefantastique* 26(5): 14-15. August 1995.

___ "*Pocahontas,*" *Cinefantastique* 26(6)/27(1): 118-121. October 1995.

MALONI, KELLY

___ **NetTrek: Your Guide to Trek Life in Cyberspace.** New York: Random House, 1995. 383pp.

MALZBERG, BARRY N.

___ "A Formal Feeling Comes," *Amazing Stories* 68(7): 61-63. November 1993.

___ "From the Heart's Basement: Alice Sheldon," *Pulphouse* No. 10: 30-32. July 1992.

___ "From the Heart's Basment: Isaac Asimov," *Pulphouse* No. 11: 16-18. August 1992.

___ "Some Reflections on Freud, Fantasy, and the Jewish Condition," *New York Review of Science Fiction* No. 45: 1, 3-5. May 1992.

___ "Thus Our Words Unspoken," *Amazing Stories* 67(6): 62-64. September 1992.

MANCHEL, FRANK

___ "What About Jack? Another Perspective on Family Relationships in Stanley Kubrick's **The Shining,**" *Literature/Film Quarterly* 23(1): 68-78. 1995.

MANCINI, ANTONELLA

___ "Paolo Strigini, La salute come utopia e il suo rovescio a Genova tra Medioevo ed eta industrale," in: Saccaro Del Buffa, Giuseppa and Lewis, Arthur O., eds. **Utopie per gli Anni Ottana.** Rome: Gangemi Editore, 1986. pp.275-288.

MANCOFF, DEBRA N.

___ "Rex Quondam Rexque Ens," *Quondam et Futurus* 2(3): 55-68. Fall 1992.

MANDELL, PAUL

___ "Commercial Spot: Byte-Size Cookies," *Cinefex* No. 60: 129-130. December 1994.

___ "Commercial Spot: Kong Reenergized," *Cinefex* No. 58: 97-98. June 1994.

___ "Harryhausen Animates Annual Sci-Tech Awards," *American Cinematographer* 73(5): 73-74. May 1992.

___ "Of Genies and Dragons: The Career of Ray Harryhausen," *American Cinematographer* 73(12): 77-81. December 1992.

___ "Tarzan of the Paperbacks," *Life* 55(22): 11-12. November 29, 1963.

MANELS, ANDY

___ **Star Wars: The Essential Guide to Characters.** New York: Del Rey, 1995. 199pp.

MANGIONI, GINO

___ "Spielberg Team Picks N.M. for Sci-Fi TV Series," by Gino Mangioni and Chuck Mittlestadt. *Albuquerque (NM) Tribune.* April 28, 1994. in: *NewsBank. Film and Television.* 53:F5. 1994.

MANK, GREGORY W.
___ "Colin Clive: Tragic Victim of His Own Monsters," *Filmfax* No. 35: 40-49, 94. October/November 1992.
___ **Hollywood Cauldron: Thirteen Horror Films From the Genre's Golden Age.** Jefferson, NC: McFarland, 1993. 384pp.

MANLOVE, C. N.
___ "Charles Kingsley, H. G. Wells, and the Machine in Victorian Fiction," *Nineteenth Century Literature* 48(2): [10pp.] 1995. (Cited from the electronic edition, NCL-E, 48(2), 1995. (http: //sunsite. berkeley. edu: 8080/ scan/ncle.482/ articles/ manlove.art482.html)).
___ **Christian Fantasy From 1200 to the Present.** Notre Dame, IN: University of Notre Dame Press, 1992. 356pp.
___ **The Chronicles of Narnia: The Patterning of a Fantastic World.** New York: Twayne, 1993. 136pp.
___ "In the Demythologising Business: Angela Carter's **The Infernal Desire Machines of Dr. Hoffman** (1972)," in: Filmer, Kath, ed. **Twentieth-Century Fantasists: Essays in Culture, Society and Belief in Twentieth Century Mythopoeic Literature.** New York: St. Martin's, 1992. pp.148-160.
___ "On Silverberg's **Tom O'Bedlam**," in: Elkins, Charles L. and Greenberg, Martin H., eds. **Robert Silverberg's Many Trapdoors: Critical Essays on His Science Fiction.** Westport, CT: Greenwood, 1992. pp.121-139.
___ "Scottish Fantasy," *Extrapolation* 35(1): 15-32. Spring 1994.
___ **Scottish Fantasy Literature: A Critical Survey.** Edinburgh: Canongate Academic, 1994. 263pp.
___ "Victorian and Modern Fantasy: Some Contrasts," in: Morse, Donald E., ed. **The Celebration of the Fantastic.** Westport, CT: Greenwood, 1992. pp.9-22.

MANSON, CHRIS
___ "Video Beat: Chronicling Young Indy," *Cinefex* No. 54: 77-78. May 1993.

MANSON, MICHAEL
___ "Heroes and Hideousness: **Frankenstein** and Failed Unity," by Michael Manson and Robert S. Stewart. *Substance* No. 71/72: 228-242. 1993.

MANTELL, SUZANNE
___ "Back to the Future With Arthur C. Clarke," *Publishers Weekly* 240(7): 18-19. February 15, 1993.

MANZO, FRED
___ "The Horror Spot: What Are the Special Ingredients of Outstanding Fiction Writing," *Genre Writer's News* 1(7): 30-31. May/June 1995.

MAPPIN, ALF
___ "A Core List: Fantasy," *Literature Base* 3(2): 16-17. June 1992.
___ "Defining Fantasy," *Literature Base* 3(2): 12-15. June 1992.

MARBELLA, JEAN
___ "Nanny Dearest: *Hand That Rocks the Cradle* Strikes a Nerve Among Nannies, Working Mothers (Review)," *Baltimore (MD) Sun.* January 15, 1992. in: *NewsBank. Film and Television.* 12:B3-B4. 1992.

MARCHAND, ERNEST
___ "Poe as Social Critic (1934)," in: Budd, Louis J. and Cady, Edwin H., eds. **On Poe.** Durham, NC: Duke University Press, 1993. pp.24-39.

MARCHESANI, JOSEPH J.
___ "Constellation Prizes: Using Science Fiction for Lesbian, Gay, and Bisexual Issues in College Classes," ED 370 117 (Paper presented at the Annual Meeting of the Conference on College Composition and Communication, 45th, Nashville, TN, March 16-19, 1994.) 1 microfiche.

MARCHESE, JOHN
___ "Cosmic Collectibles," *TV Guide* 41(30): 32-33. July 24, 1993.

MARCHETTI, DOMENICA
___ "Time Warped: Margaret Atwood Uses the Past to Propel Her Short Stories Forward," *Detroit (MI) News.* February 26, 1992. in *NewsBank. Literature.* 25:A14. 1992.

MARCOIN, FRANCIS
___ "**Les Exiles de la terre** d'Andre Laurie," *La Revue des Livres pour Enfants* 146: 61-65. Summer 1992.

MARCONE, JORGE
___ "La tradición oral y el cuento fantástico en 'La cruz del diablo' de G. A. Bécquer," *Mester* (UCLA) 19(2): 47-62. Fall 1990. [Not seen.]

MARCUS, STEVEN J.
___ "Tunnel Vision in Space," *Technology Review* 84(1): 2. October 1981.

MARENCO, FRANCO
___ "Da Blackheath a Canaan. Il cronotopo utopico nella cultura inglese del Cinquecento," in: Saccaro Del Buffa, Giuseppa and Lewis, Arthur O., eds. **Utopia e Modernita: Teorie e prassi utopiche nell'eta moderna e postmoderna.** Rome: Gangemi Editore, 1989. pp.777-784.

MARGINTER, PETER
___ "Tolkiens Phantastik," in: Kranz, Gisbert, ed. **Inklings: Jahrbuch für Literatur und Ästhetik.** 1. Band. Lüdenscheid, Germany: Michael Claren, 1983. pp.121-138.

MARICONDA, STEVEN J.
___ " 'Expect Great Revelations': Lovecraft Criticism in His Centennial Year," *Lovecraft Studies* No. 24: 24-29. Spring 1991.
___ "H. P. Lovecraft: Art, Artifact, and Reality," *Lovecraft Studies* No. 29: 2-12. Fall 1993. [Not seen.]
___ "Introduction: Style and Imagery in Lovecraft," in: Joshi, S. T., ed. **The H. P. Lovecraft Centennial Conference Proceedings.** West Warwick, RI: Necronomicon, 1991. pp.31.
___ "Tightening the Coil: The Revision of 'The Whisperer in Darkness'," *Lovecraft Studies* No. 32: 12-17. Spring 1995.

MARIGNY, JEAN
___ "The Different Faces of Eros in the Vampire Chronicles of Anne Rice," *Paradoxa* 1(3): 352-362. 1995.
___ "Le Vampire dans la science fiction anglo-saxonne [The Vampire in Anglo-Saxon Science Fiction]," *Litteratures* No. 26: 69-85. Spring 1992.
___ "Les différents visages d'Eros dans la trilogie d'Anne Rice, the Vampire Chronicles," in: Bozzetto, Roger, ed. **Eros: Science & Fiction Fantastique.** Aix-en-Provence: Universite de Provence, 1991. pp.71-83.

MARIK, JAROSLAV
___ "Planlingvo kaj scienca fikcio," *Starto* 4(145): 4-6. 1991.

MARIN, GLENN
___ "An Analysis of **Queen of the Summer Stars** by Use of the Literary Profundity Scale," by Oliver Andresen and Glenn Marin. *Quondam et Futurus* 2(1): 82-97. Spring 1992.

MARIN, RICK
___ "Warp Speed Ahead," *TV Guide* 41(30): 21-24. July 24, 1993.

MARIN, STEPHEN
___ "The Frontiers of Utopia," in: Kumar, Krishan and Bann, Stephen, eds. **Utopias and the Millennium.** London: Reaktion Books, 1993. pp.7-16.

MARINACCIO, DAVE
___ **All I Really Need to Know I Learned From Watching Star Trek.** New York: Crown, 1994. 128pp.

MARINO, EUGENE
___ "New *Star Trek* Incarnation Is Anything But Lost in Space," *(Rochester, NY) Democrat and Chronicle.* January 21, 1995. in: *NewsBank. Film and Television.* 21:D13. 1995.

MARINO, FRANK P.
___ "Sex, Death, and Comics," in: Brown, Michael, ed. **Pandemonium: Further Explorations into the Worlds of Clive Barker.** Staten Island, NY: Eclise, 1991. pp.99-104.

MARION, DAVID E.
___ "Using Fiction to Expose a Fundamental Theme in American Public Policy," *Teaching Political Science* 15(2): 44-49. Winter 1988.

MARIZ, GEORGE

MARIZ, GEORGE
___ "The Doctrine of Labor and Social Reconstruction: The Spread of Utopian Ideas in Nineteenth Century Britain," in: Saccaro Del Buffa, Giuseppa and Lewis, Arthur O., eds. **Utopia e Modernita: Teorie e prassi utopiche nell'eta moderna e postmoderna**. Rome: Gangemi Editore, 1989. pp.341-363.

MARKLEY, ROBERT
___ "Robert Boyle, Peter Shaw, and the Reinscription of Technology: Inventing and Reinventing the Air Pump," in: Greenberg, Mark L. and Schachterle, Lance, eds. **Literature and Technology**. Bethlehem, PA: Lehigh University Press, 1992. pp.125-153.

MARKOWITZ, ANDY
___ "**Twelve Monkeys**: Preview," *Cinefantastique* 27(3): 8-9. December 1995.

MARKS, EMERSON R.
___ "Poe as Literary Theorist: A Reappraisal (1961)," in: Budd, Louis J. and Cady, Edwin H., eds. **On Poe**. Durham, NC: Duke University Press, 1993. pp.122-132.

MARKS, PETER
___ "Where He Wrote: Periodicals and the Essays of George Orwell," *Twentieth Century Literature* 41(4): 266-283. Winter 1995.

MARONIE, SAM
___ "Some Gentle Evil," *Starlog* No. 215: 63-67. June 1995.

MARR, MADELEINE
___ "Don't Lose Sleep Over 'Snatchers' (Review)," *San Juan (Puerto Rico) Star* November 18, 1993. in: *NewsBank. Film and Television.* 124:F3. 1993.

MARRONE, CATERINA
___ "Lingue universali e utopie nel pensiero linguistico del secolo XVII," in: Saccaro Del Buffa, Giuseppa and Lewis, Arthur O., eds. **Utopia e Modernita: Teorie e prassi utopiche nell'eta moderna e postmoderna**. Rome: Gangemi Editore, 1989. pp.505-518.

MARSALEK, KENNETH
___ "Humanism, Science Fiction and Fairy Tales," *Free Inquiry* 15(3): 39-42. Summer 1995.
___ "**Star Trek**: Humanism of the Future," *Free Inquiry* 12(4): 53-57. Fall 1992.

MARSH, JAN
___ "A Note on Morris and Van Eyck," *Journal of the William Morris Society* 11(3): 6-7. Autumn 1995.

MARSHAK, SANDRA
___ **Star Trek Lives!**, by Jacqueline Lichtenberg, Sandra Marshak and Jean Winston. New York: Bantam, 1975. 274pp.

MARSHALL, JOYCE
___ "A Romantic Realist," *Aloud* (Toronto) 2(7): 7. October 1992.

MARTANI, MARCO
___ "Horror party con bididi a basso costo [Fantafestival 1992: The 12th International Rome Film Festival of Science Fiction and Horror]," *Cineforum* 32(9): 38-39. 1992.
___ "Roma: Fantafestival; Concorso d'autore senza l'orrore," *Cineforum* 30(7/8): 31-33. 1990.

MARTI, OSCAR R.
___ "Auguste Comte and the Positivist Utopia," in: Sullivan, E. D. S., ed. **The Utopian Vision**. San Diego, CA: San Diego University Press, 1983. pp.93-114.

MARTIN, CARRIE
___ "Crusty **Encino Man** Totally, Like, Major, Mediocre (Review)," *Denver (CO) Post.* May 22, 1992. in: *NewsBank. Film and Television.* 52:C10. 1992.

MARTIN, DIANE
___ "A Post-Holocaust Bibliography," *Janus* 6(2): 30. Winter 1980. (Whole No. 18)

MARTIN, ED
___ "Science Fiction, By the Numbers: **Earth 2** and **Babylon 5** on Course for Programming's Black Hole," *Inside Media* p. 58. November 30, 1994. (Cited from *IAC Insite* on-line service.)

MARTIN, JOHN
___ "C. S. Lewis and Animals: The Road to Whipsnade," *Bulletin of the New York C. S. Lewis Society* 24(11): 1-7. September 1993.

MARTIN, KEVIN H.
___ "Commercial Spot: Track Sold Separately," *Cinefex* No. 56: 23-24. November 1993.
___ "Kirk Out," *Cinefex* No. 61: 62-77. March 1995.
___ "Letting Slip the Dogs of War," *Cinefex* No. 49: 40-59. February 1992.
___ "Life Everlasting," *Cinefex* No. 52: 54-78. November 1992.
___ "Video Beat: Order out of Xaos," *Cinefex* No. 57: 21-22. March 1994.

MARTIN, RICK
___ "**Fahrenheit 451** Burns Even Brighter," *Washington (DC) Times.* May 10, 1992. in: *NewsBank. Literature.* 45:F7-F8. 1992
___ "Tripping in the Fantasy Zone," *Newsweek* 125(11): 70. March 13, 1995.

MARTIN, ROBERT
___ "The Evolution of **Species**," *Sci-Fi Entertainment* 2(1): 36-39, 64. June 1995.
___ "**The Mangler**," *Sci-Fi Entertainment* 1(6): 34-37. April 1995.
___ "Mounting Madness," *Sci-Fi Entertainment* 1(6): 48-50. April 1995.

MARTIN-DIAZ, M. J.
___ "Science Fiction Comes to the Classroom: Maelstrom II," by M. J. Martin-Diaz, A. Pizarro, P. Bacas, J. P. Garcia and F. Perera. *Physics Education* 27(1): 18-23. January 1992.

MARTINCIK, LISA L.
___ **When Concepts Collide: Science Fiction Meets Feminism in the Feminist Utopia**. Honor's Thesis, University of Nebraska, Omaha, 1992. 15pp.

MARTINEZ MONTALBAN, JORGE L.
___ "Entre la ciencia y la ficcion: avatares de un genero cinematografico [Between Science and Fiction: Transformations of a Cinematic Genre (The Science Fiction Film)," *Arbor - Ciencia Pensamiento y Cultura* 145(569): 39-54. May 1993.

MARTINEZ, CAL
___ "Future Special Effects: Recent Advances in **Star Trek**," in: Van Hise, James, ed. **Trek Celebration Two**. Las Vegas, NV: Pioneer, 1994. pp.148-151.
___ "The Man Who Eats Livers: A Visit to an **X-Files** Convention in Pasadena," *Los Angeles (CA) Times* p.B3. August 29, 1995.

MARTINEZ, JULIA A.
___ "The Utopian Vision: A Selective, Annotated Bibliography of Works in English," in: Sullivan, E. D. S., ed. **The Utopian Vision**. San Diego, CA: San Diego University Press, 1983. pp.175-233.

MARTSCH, NANCY
___ "A Tolkien Chronology," in: Reynolds, Patricia and GoodKnight, Glen H., eds. **Proceedings of the J. R. R. Tolkien Centenary Conference, Keble College, Oxford, 1992**. Altadena, CA: Mythopoeic Press, 1995. pp.291-297. (*Mythlore* Vol. 21, No. 2, Winter 1996, Whole No. 80)
___ (ed.) **List of Tolkienalia**. Sherman Oaks, CA: Beyond Bree, 1992. 56pp.

MARTZ, LOUIS L.
___ **Thomas More: The Search for the Inner Man**. New Haven, CT: Yale University Press, 1990. 112pp.

MARVEL, BILL
___ "Sam Houston Meets the Cyberpunks," *Dallas (TX) Morning News.* January 12, 1992. in: *NewsBank. Literature.* 13:G4-G6. 1992.

MARX, DOUG

___ "The Indeterminate Man," *Oregon* 17: 32-34, 93, 96. December 1987.

MASCETTI, MANUELA D.

___ **Vampire: The Complete Guide to the World of the Undead.** New York: Viking Studio, 1992. 224pp.

MASCHI, BOB

___ "Cardboard Spacecraft," *Starlog* No. 191: 35-40. June 1993.

MASELLO, ROBERT

___ "The Write Stuff: Sci-Fi Authors on Sci-Fi TV," *TV Guide* 41(30): 16-19. July 24, 1993.

MASINTON, CHARLES G.

___ "Capturing Life in a Few Pages," *Kansas City (MO) Star.* February 16, 1992. in *NewsBank. Literature.* 15:B1. 1992.

MASLEY, ED

___ "Actor's Chemistry Tricks in *Split Second* (Review)," *Pittsburgh (PA) Press.* April 30, 1992. in: *NewsBank. Film and Television.* 46:B13. 1992.

___ "*The Rapture* Mixes Sex and Religion and Comes Up Looking Blurred (Review)," *Pittsburgh (PA) Press.* February 14, 1992. in: *NewsBank. Film and Television.* 24:G9. 1992.

MASLIN, JANET

___ "*Godzilla* Clomp! Bestrides the Ages," *New York Times* p.H13. March 14, 1993.

___ "Neither *Dracula* Nor Rumor Frightens Coppola," *New York Times* p. 15, 24. November 15, 1992.

MASON, CYN

___ "Business: Taxes for Writers," *SFWA Bulletin* 27(3): 12-17. Fall 1993. (No. 121)

MASON, MARILYNNE S.

___ "Today's Problems Tomorrow: Television's Growing Fleet of Science Fiction Dramas Paint a Brighter--or Darker--Future," *Christian Science Monitor* p. 12-13. March 2, 1993.

MASON, MARY C.

___ "Effects Scene: The Last Hurrah," *Cinefex* No. 63: 117-118. September 1995.

___ "Profile: Jeff Matakovich," *Cinefex* No. 62: 29. June 1995.

___ "Video Beat: Cannon Creations," *Cinefex* No. 62: 139-140. June 1995.

MASON, MICHAEL

___ "A Clearing of Vision: 1843-1962. The Evolution of the Utopian Ideal in Carlyle, Shaw and Huxley," in: Saccaro Del Buffa, Giuseppa and Lewis, Arthur O., eds. **Utopia e Modernita: Teorie e prassi utopiche nell'eta moderna e postmoderna.** Rome: Gangemi Editore, 1989. pp.931-944.

MASON, RICHARD

___ "We Meet Jane!," *Burroughs Bulletin* NS. No. 24: 32-33. October 1995.

MASSÉ, MICHELLE A.

___ **In the Name of Love: Women, Masochism and the Gothic.** Ithaca, NY: Cornell University Press, 1992. 301pp.

MASSON, CHARLES

___ "Jeff Kaake: Boss in Space," *New Orleans (LA) Times-Picayune* Sec. TV, p. 6. January 3, 1993.

MASSON, SOPHIE

___ "The Medieval and the Fantastic," *Magpies: Talking About Books for Children* 10(4): 8-9. September 1995.

MASTERS, JOHN

___ "Hollywood Strains SF Writer's Imagination," *Financial Post* p. S19. August 28, 1993. (Cited from *IAC Insite* on-line service.)

MASTERSON, GRAHAM

___ "Why Horror?," *Writer* 107(7): 7-9. July 1994.

MATARESE, SUSAN

___ "The Artisan as Individual and Communitarian: The Life of Brother Isaac Newton Youngs," by Susan Matarese, Paul G. Salmon and Glendyne R. Wergland. *Utopian Studies* 6(2): 35-51. 1995.

MATASSI, ELIO

___ "L'utopia de Dostoevskji nelle giovani generazioni intellettuali heidelberghesi alla vigilia dello scoppio della Prima Guerra Mondiale: il giovane Lukacs ed il Manoscritto-Dostoevskji," in: Saccaro Del Buffa, Giuseppa and Lewis, Arthur O., eds. **Utopie per gli Anni Ottana.** Rome: Gangemi Editore, 1986. pp.679-692.

MATHESON, RICHARD

___ (ed.) **Robert Bloch: Appreciations of the Master,** ed. by Richard Matheson and Ricia Mainhardt. New York: Tor, 1995. 382pp.

MATHESON, T. J.

___ "Marcuse, Ellul, and the Science-Fiction Film: Negative Responses to Technology," *Science-Fiction Studies* 19(3): 326-339. November 1992.

___ "Triumphant Technology and Minimal Man: **The Technological Society,** Science Fiction Films, and Ridley Scott's *Alien,*" *Extrapolation* 33(3): 215-229. Fall 1992.

MATHEWS, RACE

___ "Whirlaway to *Thrilling Wonder Stories*: Boyhood Reading in Wartime and Postwar Melbourne," *Metaphysical Review* No. 22/23: 5-16. November 1995.

MATHEWS, RICHARD

___ "The Edges of Reality in Tolkien's Tale of Aldarion and Erendis," *Mythlore* 18(3): 27-31. Summer 1992. (No. 69)

MATICS, MARK A.

___ **Louder Than Bombs: Science Fiction and Nuclear Weapons, 1945-1965.** Master's Thesis, Marshall University, 1992. 86pp.

MATRACKI, JOHN

___ "Matching Slang," *Focus* (BSFA) No. 27: 9-10. December 1994/ January 1995.

MATTEOLI, LORENZO

___ "Utopia, Technology and the Future," [9 pp.] 1996 (?). (Cited from the Internet. (http://www. geocities.com/ Athens/3019/)).

MATTHEW, ROBERT

___ **Japanese Science Fiction: A View of a Changing Society.** New York: Routledge, 1989. 259pp.

MAUCERI, J. B.

___ "Rebuilding *Frankenstein,*" *Sci-Fi Entertainment* 1(4): 68-73, 86-88. December 1994.

MAURSTAD, TOM

___ "Even for a Dino Cartoon *We're Back* Is Lightweight (Review)," *Dallas (TX) Morning News.* November 24, 1993. in: *NewsBank. Art.* 38: A4. 1993.

___ "Future Tense," *Dallas (TX) Morning News.* July 30, 1995. in: *NewsBank. Film and Television.* 80:E9-E11. 1995.

___ "An On-Line Uplink to Adventure," *Dallas (TX) Morning News.* May 26, 1995. in: *NewsBank. Film and Television.* 63:A7. 1995.

___ "*Timecop* a Movie With Muscle and Heart," *Dallas (TX) Morning News.* September 16, 1994. in: *NewsBank. Film and Television.* 105:D9. 1994.

___ "*Virtuosity*: Hunting for an Original Storyline," *Dallas (TX) Morning News.* August 4, 1995. in: *NewsBank. Film and Television.* 82:C5. 1995.

MAUTNER, JOSEF

___ **Das Zerbrechliche Leben Erzaehlen: Erzaehlende Literatur und Theologie des Erzaehlens** [To Narrate Fragile Life: Narrative Literature and Theology of Narration.]. DR, Universitaet Salzburg (Austria), 1990. 468pp. (DAI-C 54/01, p. 25. Spring 1993.)

MAY, JILL P.
___ "Jane Yolen's Literary Fairy Tales: Legends, Folktales, and Myths Remade," *Journal of Children's Literature* 21(1): 74-78. Spring 1995.
___ "The Year in Children's Science Fiction and Fantasy, 1990," in: Collins, Robert A. and Latham, Robert, eds. **Science Fiction and Fantasy Book Review Annual 1991**. Westport, CT: Greenwood, 1994. pp.178-204.

MAY, SCOTT A.
___ "Science Fiction CD-ROMs," *Compute* 16(6): 66-70. June 1994.

MAYER, PETER C.
___ "Film, Ontology and the Structure of a Novel," *Film Literature Quarterly* 8(3): 204-208. 1980.

MAYHAR, ARDATH
___ "**Golden Dreams**: Odyssey of an Alien," *Paperback Parade* No. 35: 45-47. August 1993.

MAYO, MIKE
___ "Successful Low-Budget SF Film-making Is Itself an Act of Science Fiction," *Science Fiction Age* 2(4): 20-23, 33-34. May 1994.

MAYRHOFER, MAXIMILIAN
___ "William Gibsons Cyberspace Trilogie. 2. Teil: Abenteuer -- Science Fiction--Krimi. Struktur in Gibsons Werk," *Quarber Merkur* 31(2): 34-54. Dezember 1993. (No. 80)
___ "William Gibsons Cyberspace-Trilogie. 3. Teil: Thematik und Bausteine einer fiktiven Welt," *Quarber Merkur* 32(1): 21-39. June 1994. (Whole No. 81)
___ "William Gibsons Cyberspace-Trilogie. 4. Teil und Schluß: Sprache bei Gibson und die Sprache Gibsons," *Quarber Merkur* 32(2): 3-23. December 1994. (Whole No. 82)
___ "William Gibsons Cyberspace-Trilogie. I: Handlungsverlauf und Charaktere," *Quarber Merkur* 31(1): 41-52. June 1993. (No. 79)

McALEER, NEIL
___ **Odyssey: The Authorised Biography of Arthur C. Clarke**. London: Gollancz, 1992. 430pp. (As: **Arthur C. Clarke: The Authorized Biography**. New York: Contemporary Books, 1992. 430pp.)

McAULEY, PAUL J.
___ "Regooding Us All: Jack Womack Interviewed," *Interzone* No. 69: 46-49. March 1993.

McBRIDE, JON
___ "Speech: Robert A. Heinlein," in: Kondo, Yoji, ed. **Requiem: New Collected Works by Robert A. Heinlein and Tributes to the Grand Master**. New York: Tor, 1992. pp.233-234.

McBRIDE, SAM
___ "C. S. Lewis's **A Preface to Paradise Lost**, the Milton Controversy, and Lewis Scholarship," *Bulletin of Bibliography* 52(4): 317-332. Decenber 1995.

McCAFFERY, LARRY
___ "Graffiti's Rainbow: Toward the Theoretical Frontiers of 'Fiction:' From Metafiction and Cyberpunk Through Avant-Pop," by Takayuki Tatsumi and Larry McCaffery. *Science Fiction Eye* No. 12: 43-49. Summer 1993.
___ "The Semiology of Silence: The *Science Fiction Studies* Interview," by Sinda Gregory and Larry McCaffery. in: Delany, Samuel R. **Silent Interviews on Language, Race, Sex, Science Fiction and Some Comics**. Hanover, NH: Wesleyan University Press, 1994. pp.21-58.
___ "Skating Across Cyberpunk's Brave New Worlds: An Interview with Lewis Shiner," *Critique* 33(3): 177-196. Spring 1992.

McCAFFREY, ANNE
___ **[Anne McCaffrey; Voting Rights of Women in Canada; Sandy Wimer]**. (Collected interviews: Supplied title.). Troy, NY: WAMC Public Radio, 1993. 1 cassette, 25 minutes.
___ "Dragon-Master's Dialogue," *Science Fiction Age* 1(6): 78-83. September 1993.

McCALLISTER, BRIAN
___ "Dinosaurs Walk the Earth Once More in Stephen Spielberg's **Jurassic Park**," *Science Fiction Age* 1(5): 18-21, 28-29. July 1993.

McCARTHY, TODD
___ "Moroder's Redo of **Metropolis** Sparks Spirited Cannes Talk," *Variety* p. 5, 137. May 16, 1984.

McCARTY, JOHN
___ **John McCarty's Official Splatter Movie Guide, Vol. II**. New York: St. Martin's, 1992. 199pp.
___ **Movie Psychos and Madmen: Film Psychopaths From Jekyll and Hyde to Hannibal Lecter**. Secaucus, NJ: Carol, 1993. 255pp.
___ **Psychos: Eighty Years of Mad Movies, Maniacs, and Murderous Deeds**. New York: St. Martin's, 1986. 211pp.

McCARTY, MICHAEL
___ "The View From a Distant Star," by Stan Nicholls and Michael McCarty. *Starlog* No. 192: 59-69. July 1993.

McCAULEY, BARBARA L.
___ "Giraldus 'Silvester' of Wales and His **Prophetic History of Ireland**: Merlin's Role in the **Expungnatio Hebernica**," *Quondam et Futurus* 3(4): 41-62. Winter 1993.

McCLAIN, BUZZ
___ "**Boris and Natasha** Is Nogoodnik Update," *Washington (DC) Times*. April 17, 1992. in: *NewsBank. Film and Television*. 39:B12. 1992.
___ "Brain-Dead **Brainscan** Clicks Twice on Cliche," *Washington (DC) Times*. April 24, 1994. in: *NewsBank. Film and Television*. 41:B13. 1994.

McCLATCHEY, JOSEPH
___ "Teaching Individual Characters and Motifs," in: Fries, Maureen and Watson, Jeanie, eds. **Approaches to the Teaching of the Arthurian Tradition**. New York: Modern Language Association, 1992. pp.70-72.

McCLAY, WILFRED M.
___ "Reappraisal: Edward Bellamy and the Politics of Meaning," *American Scholar* 64(2): 264-271. Spring 1995.

McCLOUD, SCOTT
___ **Understanding Comics: The Invisible Art**. Northhampton, MA: Tundra, 1993. 215pp.

McCOMAS, ALAN
___ "Negating and Affirming Spirit Through Language: The Integration of Character, Magic and Story in **The Lord of the Rings**, Part 1," *Mythlore* 19(2): 4-14. Spring 1993. (No. 72)
___ "Negating and Affirming Spirit Through Language: The Integration of Character, Magic, and Story in **The Lord of the Rings**, Part 2," *Mythlore* 19(3): 40-49. Summer 1993. (No. 73)

McCOMB, GORDON
___ "The Monogamous Writer," *The Report: The Fiction Writer's Magazine* No. 9: 4. March 1993.

McCOMBS, JUDITH
___ "From 'Places, Migrations' to **The Circle Game**: Atwood's Canadian and Female Metamorphoses," in: Nicholson, Colin, ed. **Margaret Atwood: Writing and Subjectivity: New Critical Essays**. New York: St. Martin's, 1994. pp.51-67.

McCONNELL, ASHLEY
___ "A Tale of Cash Flow," by Kathryn Ptacek and Ashley McConnell. *The Report: The Fiction Writer's Magazine* No. 11: 9-11. Summer 1993.

McCONNELL, WINDER
___ "The Denial of the Anima in **Parzival**," *Quondam et Futurus* 2(2): 28-40. Summer 1992.

McCONVILLE, JIM
___ "Sci-Fi Goes Hi-Tech for Fall," *Broadcasting and Cable* 125(33): 20-21. August 14, 1995.

McCORMACK, THOMAS
___ **The Fiction Editor, the Novel, and the Novelist**. New York: St. Martin's, 1994. 202pp.

McCOY, ADRIAN
___ "Irreverent Vonnegut Jabs at Status Quo," *Pittsburgh (PA) Press*. March 3, 1992. in: *NewsBank. Literature*. 33:D14. 1992.

McCREARY, MARK
___ "Portfolio: *Jurassic Park*," *Cinefex* No. 55: 99-101. August 1993.

McCRUMB, SHARYN
___ "Where the Bodies Are Buried: The Real Murder Cases in the Crime Novels of Dorothy L. Sayers," in: Dale, Alzina S., ed. **Dorothy L. Sayers: The Centenary Celebration**. New York: Walker, 1993. pp.87-98.

McCULLEN, MAURICE L.
___ "**Lord of the Flies**: The Critical Quest," in: Biles, Jack I. and Evans, Robert O., eds. **William Golding: Some Critical Considerations**. Lexington, KY: University Press of Kentucky, 1978. pp.203-236.

McCUTCHEON, ELIZABETH
___ "Ten English Translations: Editions of Thomas More's **Utopia**," *Utopian Studies* 3(2): 102-120. 1992.

McDAID, JOHN
___ "Luddism, SF, and the Aesthetics of Electronic Fiction," *New York Review of Science Fiction* No. 69: 1, 8-11. May 1994.

McDONAGH, MAITLAND
___ "The Ultimate Joe Dante Interview," *Sci-Fi Entertainment* 1(1): 42-46, 62. June 1994.

McDONALD, BETH E.
___ "The Vampire as Trickster Figure in Bram Stoker's **Dracula**," *Extrapolation* 33(2): 128-144. Summer 1992.

McDONALD, T. LIAM
___ "The Horrors of Hammer: The House That Blood Built," in: Golden, Christopher, ed. **Cut! Horror Writers on Horror Film**. New York: Berkley, 1992. pp.151-160.

McDONALD, WILLIAM C.
___ **Arthur and Tristan: On the Intersection of Legends in German Medieval Literature**. Lewiston, NY: Mellen, 1991. 296pp.

McDONNELL, DAVID
___ "Klingon Warrior," by David McDonnell and Ian Spelling. in: McDonnell, David, ed. **Starlog's Science Fiction Heroes and Heroines**. New York: Crescent Books, 1995. pp.58-61.
___ "Q & A," by Ian Spelling and David McDonnell. *Starlog* No. 206: 47-51, 70. September 1994.
___ **Starlog's Science Fiction Heroes and Heroines**. New York: Crescent Books, 1995. 93pp.
___ "Starship Captain," in: McDonnell, David, ed. **Starlog's Science Fiction Heroes and Heroines**. New York: Crescent Books, 1995. pp.24-27.

McDOWELL, ELIZABETH J.
___ **Power and Environment in Recent Writings by Barbara Kingsolver, Ursula K. Le Guin, Alice Walker and Terry Tempest Williams**. Master's Thesis, University of Oregon, 1992. [Not seen.]

McDOWELL, RIDER
___ "More Than Just *Superman*'s Serious Sidekick: A Conversation with Phyllis Coates," *Filmfax* No. 36: 70-73. December 1992/January 1993

McFADDEN, CYRA
___ "Diamond in the Wilderness," *San Francisco (CA) Examiner*. December 9, 1991. in *NewsBank. Literature*. 1:C4-C5. 1992.

McGARRY, TERRY
___ "A Writer's Guide to Understanding the Copy Editor," *SFWA Bulletin* 29(1): 53-56. Spring 1995. (No. 126)

McGEE, MARK T.
___ "Full Moon's Effects Master," *Cinefantastique* 23(5): 47-49. February 1993.

McGHAN, HARLAN
___ "SF Awards, 1991," in: Brown, Charles N. and Contento, William G. **Science Fiction, Fantasy, & Horror: 1991**. Oakland, CA: Locus Press, 1992. pp.457-476.

McGILL, MERIDITH L.
___ "Poe, Literary Nationalism, and Authorial Identity," in: Rosenheim, Shawn and Rachman, Stephen, ed. **The American Face of Edgar Allan Poe**. Baltimore: Johns Hopkins University Press, 1995. pp.271-305.

McGILLIS, RODERICK
___ (ed.) **For the Childlike: George MacDonald's Fantasies for Children**. Metuchen, NJ: Scarecrow, 1992. 242pp.

McGOVERN, EUGENE
___ "The Greeves Letters as Seen by Arthur Greeves," *Bulletin of the New York C. S. Lewis Society* 25(9/11): 9-13. July/September 1994.
___ "Lewis and Modern Christian Novels," *CSL: The Bulletin of the New York C. S. Lewis Society* 23(5): 5-8. March 1992.
___ "Lewis and Winston Churchill: A Note Necessarily Short," *CSL: The Bulletin of the New York C. S. Lewis Society* 23(3): 6-7. January 1992.
___ "Lewis, Columbus, and the Discovery of New Worlds," *CSL: The Bulletin of the New York C. S. Lewis Society* 23/24(No.12/No. 1): 1-7. October/November 1992.

McGREW, LYDIA M.
___ "Action and the Passionate Patient in **That Hideous Strength**," *CSL: The Bulletin of the New York C. S. Lewis Society* 23(7): 1-6. May 1992.

McGUIRE, KAREN
___ "Of Artists, Vampires and Creativity," *Studies in Weird Fiction* No. 11: 2-4. Spring 1992.

McGUIRE, PATRICK
___ "Ray Bradbury's IQ Unnecessary," *Australian Science Fiction Review* 5(3): 11. Spring 1990. (Whole No. 25)

McGUIRK, CAROL
___ "The 'New' Romancers: Science Fiction Innovators From Gernsback to Gibson," in: Slusser, George E. and Shippey, Tom, eds. **Fiction 2000: Cyberpunk and the Future of Narrative**. Athens: University of Georgia Press, 1992. pp.109-129.
___ "Nowhere Man: Towards a Poetics of Post-Utopian Characterization," *Science Fiction Studies* 21(2): 141-154. July 1994.

McHALE, BRIAN
___ **Constructing Postmodernism**. London: Routledge, 1992. 342pp.
___ "Difference Engines," *ANQ* 5(4): 220-223. November 1992.
___ "Elements of a Poetics in Cyberpunk," *Critique* 33(3): 149-175. Spring 1992.

McINERNY, RALPH
___ "Unsoothing Sayers," in: Dale, Alzina S., ed. **Dorothy L. Sayers: The Centenary Celebration**. New York: Walker, 1993. pp.123-128.

McINNIS, JOHN
___ "The Call of Cthulhu: An Analysis," *Fantasy Commentator* 7(4): 268-281. Fall 1992. (Whole No. 44)
___ " 'The Color out of Space' as the History of H. P. Lovecraft's Immediate Family," in: Joshi, S. T., ed. **The H. P. Lovecraft Centennial Conference Proceedings**. West Warwick, RI: Necronomicon, 1991. pp.35-37.

McKAY, GEORGE
___ "It's Not 'About' Science, It's 'About' Fiction and It's 'About' About," *Foundation* No. 60: 51-57. Spring 1994.
___ "**Kay Dick's They** and Rudyard Kipling's *They*: Intertextual Politicisation and the Grand End of Narrative," *Foundation* No. 58: 62-75. Summer 1993.
___ "Metapropaganda: Self-reading Dystopian Fiction: Burdekin's **Swastika Night** and Orwell's **Nineteen Eighty-Four**," *Science Fiction Studies* 21(3): 302-314. November 1994.
___ " 'Time Way Back': 'Motivation' and Speculative Fiction," *Critical Quarterly* 34(1): 102-116. Spring 1992.

McKAY, NIALL
___ "First You Slice Your Leading Man," *New Scientist* 148(2002): 24. November 4, 1995.

McKEE, ALAN
___ "Intentional Phalluses: The Male 'Sex' in J. G. Ballard," *Foundation* No. 57: 58-67. Spring 1993.

McKEE, J. S. C.
___ "Science Fact and Science Fiction: Are They Indistinguishable?," *Physics in Canada* 48(4): 247-250. July 1992.

McKENNA, CHRIS
___ "It's Lawman Against Batman," *New York (NY) Post*. June 18, 1992. in: *NewsBank. Film and Television*. 62:E11-E12. 1992.

McKENNEY, MICHAEL
___ "Chumatsky Shlyah: The Ukrainian National SF Convention," *Lan's Lantern* No. 42: 30-31. May 1994.

McKERROW, STEVE
___ "***Demolition Man*** Looks Awfully Familiar (Review)," *Baltimore (MD) Sun* October 9, 1993. in: *NewsBank. Film and Television*. 114:G12. 1993.

McKILLIP, PATRICIA A.
___ "Once Upon a Time Too Often," *Writer* 105(8): 18-20, 44. August 1992.

McKIM, MARK G.
___ "C. S. Lewis on the Disappearance of the Individual," *CSL: The Bulletin of the New York C. S. Lewis Society* 23(5): 1-5. March 1992.
___ "The Poison Brewed in the West," *Bulletin of the New York C. S. Lewis Society* 26(11/12): 1-6. September/October 1995.

McKINLEY, MARLENE M.
___ "Tolkien's Influence in America," in: Kranz, Gisbert, ed. **Jahrbuch für Literatur und Ästhetik**. Lüdenscheid, Germany: Stier, 1992. Band 10, pp.261-274.
___ "Viewing 'The Immense Panorama or Futility and Anarchy That Is Contemporary History' in the First Six Novels of Charles Williams," in: Filmer, Kath, ed. **Twentieth-Century Fantasists: Essays in Culture, Society and Belief in Twentieth Century Mythopoeic Literature**. New York: St. Martin's, 1992. pp.71-91.

McKITTERICK, CHRISTOPHER
___ "James Gunn and **The Dreamers**: Epitomes of an Evolving Science Fiction," *Extrapolation* 36(4): 316-330. Winter 1995.

McLAUGHLIN, SARA P.
___ "**The City of God** Revisited: C. S. Lewis's Debt to Saint Augustine," *CSL: The Bulletin of the New York C. S. Lewis Society* 23(6): 1-9. April 1992.
___ "A Legacy of Truth: The Influence of George MacDonald's **Unspoken Sermons** on C. S. Lewis's **Mere Christianity**," *CSL: The Bulletin of the New York C. S. Lewis Society* 24(4): 1-6. February 1993.

McLELLAN, DENNIS
___ "The Forward Thinker: Gregory Benford," *Los Angeles (CA) Times* p.E1. September 25, 1994.
___ "Science Fiction, Full of Fact: Surfer-Astrophysicist Explains the Galaxy for the Rest of Us," *San Francisco (CA) Chronicle* October 30, 1994. (Cited from the Internet Edition.)

McLOUGHLIN, MARYANN
___ "Female Utopian Writers and the Environment," *CEA Forum* 22(1): 3-6. Winter 1992.

McMAHAN, ROBERT Y.
___ "John Kirkpatrick: A Personal Remembrance of His Last Nine Years, 1983-1991," *CSL: The Bulletin of the New York C. S. Lewis Society* 23(1): 1-8. November 1991.

McMAHON, PATRICIA
___ "A Second Look: **Elidor**," *Horn Book* 56(3): 328-331. June 1980.

McMILLEN, LYNN
___ "Confluence '93: Through the Eyes of a Newcomer," *Lan's Lantern* No. 42: 34-35. May 1994.

McMULLEN, SEAN
___ "A. Bertram Chandler: A Survey," *Science Fiction: A Review of Speculative Literature* 11(1): 3-9. 1991. (No. 31)
___ "The Golden Age of Australian Science Fiction," *Science Fiction: A Review of Speculative Literature* 12(3): 3-28. 1993(?). (No. 36)
___ "The Quest for Australian Fantasy," by Sean McMullen and Steven Paulsen. *Aurealis* No. 13: 35-42. 1994.
___ "SF in Australia," by Sean McMullen and Terry Dowling. *Locus* 33(1): 46. July 1994.
___ "SF in Australia," by Sean McMullen and Terry Dowling. *Locus* 34(1) 71. January 1995.

McMUNN, MERADITH T.
___ "Filming the Tristan Myth: From Text to Icon," in: Harty, Kevin J., ed. **Cinema Arthuriana: Essays on Arthurian Film**. New York: Garland, 1991. pp.169-180.

McNALLY, JOEL
___ "Sci-Fi Novelist Dips His Hand in the Mainstream," *Milwaukee (WI) Journal*. October 25, 1992. in: *NewsBank. Literature*. 89:D1. 1992

McNALLY, OWEN
___ "Futuristic **Freejack** Fizzles By a Furlong (Review)," *Hartfort (CT) Courant*. January 18, 1992. in: *NewsBank. Film and Television*. 11:D4-D5. 1992.
___ "Gore Aplenty Splatters Screen in **Sematary** (Review)," *Hartford (CT) Courant*. August 29, 1992. in: *NewsBank. Film and Television*. 82:G10. 1992.
___ "**Sneakers** Trips as High-Tech Thriller (Review)," *Hartford (CT) Courant*. September 11, 1992. in: *NewsBank. Film and Television*. 96: D2. 1992.
___ "**Soldier** Is No More Than Bloodbath (Review)," *Hartford (CT) Courant*. July 10, 1992. in: *NewsBank. Film and Television*. 74:G3. 1992.
___ "**Stargate** a Barren Desert Trek," *Hartford (CT) Courant*. October 29, 1994. in: *NewsBank. Film and Television*. 115: G7. 1994.

McNALLY, RAYMOND T.
___ **In Search of Dracula: The History of Dracula and Vampires**. Rev. Ed, by Raymond T. McNally and Radu Florescu. Boston, MA: Houghton Mifflin, 1994. 297pp.

McNAMARA, M. EILEEN
___ "Lovecraft's Medical History," in: Joshi, S. T., ed. **The H. P. Lovecraft Centennial Conference Proceedings**. West Warwick, RI: Necronomicon, 1991. pp.26-27.
___ "Winfield Scott Lovecraft's Final Illness," *Lovecraft Studies* No. 24: 14. Spring 1991.

McNELLY, WILLIS E.
___ "The First Time I Met Brian," in: Hatherley, Frank, ed. **A Is for Brian**. London: Avernus, 1990. pp.58-59.
___ "The Manuscripts and Papers at Fullerton," by Willis E. McNelly and Sharon K. Perry. in: Mullen, R. D., ed. **On Philip K. Dick: 40 Articles From Science-Fiction Studies**. Terre Haute, IN: SF-TH Inc., 1992. pp.xviii-xxiiv.
___ "The Science Fiction Collection," in: Vogeler, Albert R. and Arthur A. Hansen, eds. **Very Special Collections: Essays on Library Holdings at California State University, Fullerton**. Fullerton, CA: Patron of the Library, 1992. pp.17-62.

McQUADE, BRETT
___ "**Peter Pan**: Disney's Adaptation of J. M. Barrie's Original Work," *Mythlore* 20(1): 5-9. Winter 1994. (Whole No. 75)

McQUIDDY, A. P.
___ "Eyeball Kicks, Prigogine's Theory and Re-Thinking the World: An Interview With Bruce Sterling and Lewis Shiner," *Texas SF Inquirer* No. 19: 5-26. December 1986.
___ "William Gibson: Hallucinating on the Present: An Interview," *Texas SF Inquirer* No. 22: 2-7. October/November 1987.

McSORLEY, BONNIE S.
___ "Revamping the Vampire in Joan Perucho's **Natural History**," *Studies in Weird Fiction* No. 15: 2-5. Summer 1994.

McTAGGART, MAUREEN
___ "It's Life, Jim, but Not as We've Known It," *Times Educational Supplement* 4139: SS21. October 27, 1995.

McTIGUE, MAUREEN
___ "Man of Wonder: Michael Whelan," *Starlog* No. 197: 32-37, 68. December 1993.

McTYRE, ROBERT E.
___ "Octavia Butler: Black America's First Lady of Science Fiction," *Michigan Chronicle* pp.PG. April 26, 1994. (Cited from **The Electric Library** on-line service.)

McVEIGH, KEV
___ "And He Was... Geoff Ryman: Interview," *Vector* No. 174: 8-11. August/September 1993.
___ "Mike Jefferies Interviewed," *Vector* No. 167: 14-16. June/July 1992
___ "The Red Prophet: Kim Stanley Robinson, an Interview," *Vector* No. 176: 5-8. December 1993/January 1994.

McWHORTER, GEORGE T.
___ "Fire!: A Report on the Fire at ERB, Inc., May 8, 1958," *Burroughs Bulletin* NS. No. 18: 24-26. April 1994.
___ "Historiated Initials in **The Son of Tarzan**," *Burroughs Bulletin* NS. No. 18: 30-31. April 1994.
___ "Larry Schwinger: Ballantine Cover Artist," *Burroughs Bulletin* NS No. 11: 19-20. July 1992.

McWILLIAMS, MICHAEL
___ "Smashing New **Star Trek** Gets a Stellar Send-Off," *Detroit (MI) News*. January 16, 1995. in: *NewsBank. Film and Television.* 21:D12. 1995.

MDLULI, SIBUSISO H.
___ "Thrice Three: Trifunctional Structure in the Third Fitt of **Sir Gawain and the Green Knight**," *Arthuriana* 4(2): 184-195. Summer 1994.

MEANS, SEAN P.
___ "**Plan 10 From Outer Space**: Utah's Alien Invasion," *Salt Lake City (UT) Tribune*. October 30, 1994. in: *NewsBank. Film and Television.* 123:F2-F4. 1994.

MEDVED, MICHAEL
___ "Gore-geous Alien," *New York (NY) Post*. July 7, 1995. in: *NewsBank. Film and Television.* 81:A7. 1995.
___ "Muddy Water," *New York (NY) Post*. July 28, 1995. in: *NewsBank. Film and Television.* 72:G3. 1995.
___ "Star-Crossed Mission," *New York (NY) Post*. November 18, 1994. in: *NewsBank. Film and Television.* 125:D8. 1994.
___ "A Stroke of Genius (Review)," *New York Post*. June 11, 1993. in: *NewsBank. Art.* 15:C8-C9. 1993.
___ "Techno-Tale's Wires Crossed," *New York (NY) Post*. May 26, 1995. in: *NewsBank. Film and Television.* 55:B7. 1995.
___ "Virtueless **Virtuosity**," *New York (NY) Post*. August 4, 1995. in: *NewsBank. Film and Television.* 82:C4. 1995.

MEHREN, ELIZABETH
___ "Children's Author? Christian Author? Don't Try to Label Madeleine L'Engle. At 73, She's Still. . .Following Her Heart," *Los Angeles (CA) Times*. October 12, 1992. in: *NewsBank. Literature.* 92:G3-G5. 1992.

MEINDL, DIETER
___ "Gender and Narrative Perspective in Margaret Atwood's Stories," in: Nicholson, Colin, ed. **Margaret Atwood: Writing and Subjectivity: New Critical Essays**. New York: St. Martin's, 1994. pp.219-229.

MEISLER, ANDY
___ "New **Star Trek** Adrift After Captain Abandons Ship," *Austin (TX) American Statesman* Sec. B, p. 6. September 17, 1994.

MELARA, MIRIELLA
___ "Science, Fiction and Artificial Paradise: Villiers de l'Isle-Adam's **Future Eve**," in: Wolf, Milton T. and Mallett, Daryl F., eds. **Imaginative Futures: Proceedings of the 1993 Science Fiction Research Association Conference**. San Bernardino, CA: Jacob's Ladder Books, 1995. pp.203-216.

MELEHY, HASSAN
___ "Images Without: Deleuzian Becoming, Science Fiction Cinema in the Eighties," *Postmodern Culture* 5(2): [19pp.] January 1995. (Electronic Journal: pmc@jefferson.village.virginia.edu).

MELIA, SALLY-ANN
___ "The Bells of Hell Go Ting-a-Ling-a-Ling: Anne Gay Interviewed," *Interzone* No. 92: 20-23. February 1995.
___ "Fifteen Years of Nothing, Then an Overnight Dose of Success: Simon Green interviewed," *Interzone* No. 74: 26-29. August 1993.
___ "I Write and I Write Good--And That's the Way of It: Algis Budrys Interviewed," *Interzone* No. 95: 23-26. May 1995.
___ "Leaving Reality Behind: Paul Kearney Interviewed," *Interzone* No. 87: 16-19. September 1994.
___ "Mythago-Mania: A Journey into Robert Holdstock's **Mythago Wood**," *Vector* No. 175: 10-11. October/November 1993.
___ "Positively Dangerous to Stand Still: Artist Jim Burns Interviewed," *Interzone* No. 79: 20-24. January 1994.
___ "Power Corrupts: John Brunner Interviewed," *Interzone* No. 97: 18-21. July 1995.
___ "SFC Interviews: Iain Banks: 'Very likely impossible, but oh, the elegance...'," *Science Fiction Chronicle* 16(1): 7, 42-44. October 1994.
___ "SFC Interviews: Simon Green: 15 Years of Nothing, Then Overnight Success," *Science Fiction Chronicle* 16(6): 5, 42-45. May 1995.
___ " 'What If All Science Is Wrong': John Gribbin Interviewed," *Interzone* No. 84: 43-47. June 1994.
___ "Writing a First Novel," *Focus* (BSFA) No. 24: 11. June/July 1993.

MELIS, GIORGIO
___ "Il caso della Cina," in: Colombo, Arrigo and Quarta, Cosimo, eds. **Il Destino della Famiglia nell'Utopia**. Bari: Edizione Dedalo, 1991. pp.383-398.

MELLEY, TIMOTHY
___ "Bodies Incorporated: Scenes of Agency Panic in **Gravity's Rainbow**," *Contemporary Literature* 25(4): 709-738. Winter 1994.

MELTON, J. GORDON
___ **The Vampire Book: The Encyclopedia of the Undead**. Detroit, MI: Visible Ink Press, 1994. 852pp.

MEMMOTT, DAVID
___ "The Witchdoctor and the Mad Scientist: Mechanical Models of Healing and the Challenge of AIDS," *Science Fiction Eye* No. 11: 53-59. December 1992.

MENAGH, MELANIE
___ "A Channel for Science Fiction," by Melanie Menagh and Stephen Mills. *Omni* 14(9): 76-82, 112. October 1992.

MENDELSOHN, JAMES R.
___ **The Brute Fact: The Cultural Authority of Science in Twentieth Century American Literature**. Ph.D. Dissertation, University of Washington, 1992. (DAI 53: 2372A.)

MENDELSON, MICHAEL
___ "**The Wood Beyond the World** and the Politics of Desire," *Essays in Literature* 18(2): 211-234. Fall 1991.

MENDLESOHN, FARAH
___ "Audio Books: A New Medium for SF?," *Foundation* No. 64: 90-96. Summer 1995.
___ "Gender, Power, and Conflict Resolution: 'Subcommittee' by Zenna Henderson," *Extrapolation* 35(2): 120-129. Summer 1994.
___ "The Profession of Science Fiction, 46: Grinding Axes," *Foundation* No. 62: 10-21. Winter 1994/1995.
___ "Science Fiction Courses in Higher Education in Great Britain: A Preliminary Guide," by Edward James and Farah Mendlesohn. *Foundation* No. 59: 59-69. Autumn 1993.

MENEFEE, CHRISTINE C.
___ "Beloved *Starman*," by Brian Lowry and Christine C. Menefee. in: McDonnell, David, ed. **Starlog's Science Fiction Heroes and Heroines**. New York: Crescent Books, 1995. pp.55-57.
___ "Imagining Mars: The New Chronicles," *School Library Journal* 40(12): 38-39. December 1994.

MENEGALDO, GILLES
___ "Quelques substituts et simulacres d'Eros dans le recit fantastique moderne," in: Bozzetto, Roger, ed. **Eros: Science & Fiction Fantastique**. Aix-en-Provence: Universite de Provence, 1991. pp.43-57.

MENOZZI, LUCIANA
___ " 'Utopia del passato': Spazi e riti in una comunita grecanica," in: Saccaro Del Buffa, Giuseppa and Lewis, Arthur O., eds. **Utopie per gli Anni Ottana**. Rome: Gangemi Editore, 1986. pp.521-541.

MENTOR, STEVEN
___ "The Cyborg Body Politic: Version 1.2," by Chris H. Gray and Steven Mentor. in: Gray, Chris H., ed. **The Cyborg Handbook**. New York: Routledge, 1995. pp.453-467.
___ "Introduction: Constructing the Knowledge of Cybernetic Organisms," by Chris H. Gray, Steven Mentor and Heidi J. Figueroa-Sarriera. in: Gray, Chris H., ed. **The Cyborg Handbook**. New York: Routledge, 1995. pp.1-14.

MENTZER, THOMAS L.
___ "The Ethics of Behavior Modification: **A Clockwork Orange** Revisited," *Essays in Arts and Sciences* 9(1): 93-105. May 1980.

MERCHANT, ROBERT
___ "Pope, Council, Bible and/or Self: Lewis and the Question of Authority," *CSL: The Bulletin of the New York C. S. Lewis Society* 23(10/11): 1-10. August/September 1992.

MERCIER, ANDREE
___ "L'Indien de la Science/Fiction (The Indian in Science/Fiction)," *Recerches Amerindiennes au Quebec* (Canada) 17(3): 53-63. 1987.

MERCIER-DAVIS, HELEN E.
___ "Heinlein's Influence," *Lan's Lantern* No. 38: 42-43. July 1992.

MERRIL, JUDITH
___ "Better to Have Loved: From a Memoir-in-Progress, Part 1," *New York Review of Science Fiction* No. 59: 1, 8-14. July 1993.

MERRILL, CATHERINE
___ "Defining the Fantastic Grotesque: Nathanael West's **The Dream Life of Balso Snell**," in: Latham, Robert A. and Collins, Robert A., eds. **Modes of the Fantastic**. Westport, CT: Greenwood, 1995. pp.64-73.

MERRIWETHER, CHIP
___ "Effects Hero," *Cinefantastique* 22(4): 47, 60. February 1992.

MESTEL, ROSIE
___ "Education: The Final Frontier," *New Scientist* 141(1914): 11. February 26, 1994.

METZER, DAVID
___ "Rhetoric and Death in **Thelma and Louise**: Notes Toward a Logic of the Fantastic," *Journal of the Fantastic in the Arts* 4(4): 9-18. 1991. (No. 16)

MEURGER, MICHEL
___ "Wells's Martians," *Monad* No. 3: 1-34. September 1993.

MEYER, CHARLES A.
___ "The Efrafan Hunt for Immortality in **Watership Down**," *Journal of the Fantastic in the Arts* 6(1): 71-87. 1993.
___ "The Power of Myth and Rabbit Survival in Richard Adams' **Watership Down**," *Journal of the Fantastic in the Arts* 3(4): 139-150. 1994.

MEYER, DAVID S.
___ "Star Wars, **Star Wars**, and American Political Culture," *Journal of Popular Culture* 26(2): 99-115. Fall 1992.

MEYERS, JEFFREY
___ **Edgar Allan Poe: His Life and Legacy**. New York: Macmillan, 1992. 348pp.

MEYERS, JOE
___ "**Delicatessen**: Python-Lovers Will Eat It Up (Review)," *Bridgeport (CT) Post*. July 10, 1992. in: *NewsBank. Film and Television*. 68:G5-G6. 1992.
___ "Sharp Acting Saves Second Remake of **Body Snatchers**," *(Bridgeport, CT) Connecticut Post*. August 14, 1994. in: *NewsBank. Film and Television*. 87:B12. 1994.
___ "**Timecop** Better Than Usual Van Damme," *(Bridgeport, CT) Connecticut Post*. September 16, 1994. in: *NewsBank. Film and Television*. 105:C12. 1994.

MEZA, ED
___ "First Command," *Starlog* No. 217: 32-33. August 1995.

MICHAEL, KAY
___ "Parents Oppose Kid's Exposure to Sex on Screen," *Charleston (WV) Daily Mail*. July 20, 1992. in: *NewsBank. Film and Television*. 67:F4. 1992.

MICHAELS, RICHARD
___ "Night Bloomer: The Defiant Fiction of David J. Schow," in: Collins, Robert A. and Latham, Robert, eds. **Science Fiction and Fantasy Book Review Annual 1991**. Westport, CT: Greenwood, 1994. pp.130-137.

MICHAELSON, SCOTT
___ "Twain's **The American Claimant** and the Figure of Frankenstein: A Reading of the Rhetorical Hermeneutics," in: Latham, Robert A. and Collins, Robert A., eds. **Modes of the Fantastic**. Westport, CT: Greenwood, 1995. pp.195-203.

MICHALSON, KAREN
___ **Victorian Fantasy Literature: Literary Battles with Church and Empire**. Lewiston, NY: Edwin Mellen Press, 1990. 292pp.

MICHELINI, ALEX
___ "**Lawnmower** Trim: Stephen King Gets Himself Cut From Film," *New York (NY) Daily News*. July 7, 1992. in: *NewsBank. Film and Television*. 71:B1. 1992.

MICKEL, EMANUEL J.
___ "Introduction," in: Verne, Jules. **The Complete Twenty Thousand Leagues Under the Sea**. Bloomington: Indiana University Press, 1991. pp.1-65.

MIDDLETON, ROGER
___ "Chwedl Geraint ab Erbin," in: Bromwich, Rachel, Jarman, A. O. H. and Roberts, Brynley F., eds. **The Arthur of the Welsh**. Cardiff: University of Wales Press, 1991. pp.147-158.

MIESEL, SANDRA
___ "The Fan as Critic," in: Sanders, Joe, ed. **Science Fiction Fandom**. Westport, CT: Greenwood, 1994. pp.235-242.

MIESZKOWSKI, GRETCHEN
___ "The Prose Lancelot's Glaehot, Malory's Levain, and the Queering of Late Medieval Literature," *Arthuriana* 5(1): 21-51. Spring 1995.

MILAM, MICHAEL C.
___ "Science Fiction and Human Nature," *Humanist* 55(2): 29-32. March/April 1995.

MILES, BARRY
___ **William Burroughs: El Hombre Invisible**. New York: Hyperion, 1993. 263pp.

MILES, IAN
___ "Stranger Than Fiction: How Important Is Science Fiction for Futures Studies?," *Futures* 25(3): 315-321. April 1993. (Reprinted: *Engineering Management Review* 21(4): 49-52. Winter 1993.)

MILES, MARGARET
___ "Interview with Mercedes," by Rececca Taylor, Gayle Keresey and Margaret Miles. *Voice of Youth Advocates* 15(4): 213-217. October 1992.

MILES, SUSAN G.
___ "Young Adult Science Fiction," by Francis J. Molson and Susan G. Miles. in: Barron, Neil, ed. **Anatomy of Wonder 4**. New York: Bowker, 1995. pp.393-352.

MILLAR, JEFF
___ "It's Kombat," *Houston (TX) Chronicle*. August 21, 1995. in: *NewsBank. Film and Television*. 79:C1. 1995.
___ "A Movie That Made Us Dream," *Houston (TX) Chronicle* Sec. Z, p. 9. June 20, 1993.
___ "*Powder*: It's Hard to Like, Hard to Resist," *Houston (TX) Chronicle*. October 27, 1995. in: *NewsBank. Film and Television*. 97:G4. 1995.
___ "*Strange Days* Full of Thrills," *Houston (TX) Chronicle*. October 13, 1995. in: *NewsBank. Film and Television*. 99:D1. 1995.

MILLER, B. DIANE
___ "Claims-Making in Artificial Intelligence Research," in: Wolf, Milton T. and Mallett, Daryl F., eds. **Imaginative Futures: Proceedings of the 1993 Science Fiction Research Association Conference**. San Bernardino, CA: Jacob's Ladder Books, 1995. pp.61-74.

MILLER, CHUCK
___ "1983-84: The Market of SF&F: An Overview," *AB Bookman's Weekly* pp.2149-2152. October 1, 1984.
___ "Science Fiction, Fantasy & Horror: The Year in Review," *AB Bookman's Weekly* 90(17): 1448-1450. October 26, 1992.

MILLER, EDWIN H.
___ **Salem Is My Dwelling Place: A Life of Nathaniel Hawthorne**. Ames: University of Iowa Press, 1992. 596pp.

MILLER, JEFF T.
___ "Commercial Spot: Chevy Hulk," *Cinefex* No. 57: 79-80. March 1994.

MILLER, JOSEPH D.
___ "Just How Frumious Is a Bandersnatch? The Exotic and the Ambiguous in Imaginative Literature," in: Slusser, George E. and Rabkin, Eric S., eds. **Styles of Creation: Aesthetic Technique and the Creation of Fictional Worlds**. Athens: University of Georgia Press, 1992. pp.128-142.

MILLER, MARCUS
___ "Video Beat: Attack of the 80-Foot Stones," *Cinefex* No. 60: 111-112. December 1994.

MILLER, MARK C.
___ "**2001**: A Cold Descent," *Sight and Sound* 4(1): 18-25. January 1994.

MILLER, MIRIAM Y.
___ "J. R. R. Tolkien's Merlin--An Old Man With a Staff: Galdalf and the Magus Tradition," in: Watson, Jeanie and Fries, Marueen, eds. **The Figure of Merlin in the Nineteenth and Twentieth Centuries**. Lewiston, NY: Mellen, 1989. pp.121-142.
___ " 'Of sum mayn merualye, bat he mygt trawe': **The Lord of the Rings** and **Sir Gawain and the Green Knight**," *Studies in Medievalism* 3(3): 345-365. Winter 1991.

MILLER, NICK
___ "Fans Remain Avid As Ever," *Cincinnati (OH) Post*. December 6, 1991. in: *NewsBank. Film and Television*. 7:D6. 1992.

MILLER, RON
___ **The Dream Machines: An Illustrated History of the Spaceship in Art, Science and Literature**. Malabar, FL: Krieger, 1993. 714pp.

MILLMAN, JOYCE
___ "Acting as Hard as He Can," *San Francisco (CA) Examiner*. April 11, 1995. in: *NewsBank. Film and Television*. 51:C8. 1995.
___ "Animated Pandemonium on MTV (Review)," *San Francisco (CA) Examiner*. January 10, 1992. in: *NewsBank. Film and Television*. 14: E8. 1992.
___ "Boris Is Badenov to Be Buried," *San Francisco (CA) Examiner*. April 2, 1992. in: *NewsBank. Film and Television*. 39:B8-B9. 1992.

MILLMAN, JOYCE (continued)
___ "*Joanna May*: Send in the Clones (Review)," *San Francisco (CA) Examiner*. February 29, 1992. in: *NewsBank. Film and Television*. 30: C4. 1992.
___ "*VR5* Virtually Hip But No *X-Files*," *San Francisco (CA) Examiner*. March 10, 1995. in: *NewsBank. Film and Television*. 39:F1-F2. 1995.

MILLS, ALICE
___ "Burning Women in Ursula K. Le Guin's **Tehanu: The Last Book of Earthsea**," *New York Review of Science Fiction* No. 79: 1, 3-7. March 1995.

MILLS, DAVID
___ "The Horror! The Horror! At Fanex, Film Buffs Revel in the Chill of It All," *Washington (DC) Post* Sec. D, 1. August 17, 1992.

MILLS, MICHAEL
___ "Undead and a Hit (Review)," *West Palm Beach (FL) Post*. November 15, 1992. in: *NewsBank. Film and Television*. 112:E6-E7. 1992.

MILLS, STEPHEN
___ "A Channel for Science Fiction," by Melanie Menagh and Stephen Mills. *Omni* 14(9): 76-82, 112. October 1992.

MILNER, JOSEPH O.
___ "Captain Kirk and Dr. Who: Meliorist and Spenglerian World Views in Science Fiction for Young Adults," in: Sullivan, C. W., III. **Science Fiction for Young Readers**. Westport, CT: Greenwood, 1993. pp.187-196.

MILTNER, ROBERT
___ "**Watership Down**: A Genre Study," *Journal of the Fantastic in the Arts* 6(1): 63-70. 1993.

MINEO, ADY
___ "The Reverse of Salem House: The 'Holistic' Process of Education in **News From Nowhere**," *Journal of the William Morris Society* 11(1): 6-15. Autumn 1994.

MINERVA, NADIA
___ "Il lavoro tra peccato e vertu in alcune utopie francesi della fine del secolo XVII," in: Saccaro Del Buffa, Giuseppa and Lewis, Arthur O., eds. **Utopia e Modernita: Teorie e prassi utopiche nell'eta moderna e postmoderna**. Rome: Gangemi Editore, 1989. pp.313-328.

MINK, ERIC
___ "Do or Die for Young Indy: ABC Decides Fate As Show's Plot Deepens," *Boston (MA) Herald*. April 8, 1992. in: *NewsBank. Film and Television*. 48:B5. 1992.

MINTZ, CATHERINE
___ "An Interview with Sheri S. Tepper," by William L. Clois and Catherine Mintz. *Quantum* No. 43/44: 35-38. Spring/Summer 1993.
___ "Poetry, Poets and the Rest of the World: An Interview with Steve Sneyd," *Foundation* No. 63: 68-73. Spring 1995.
___ "Rules of the Game," *Starlog* No. 203: 61-63. June 1994.
___ "SFC Interviews: Kathy Tyers," *Science Fiction Chronicle* 15(2): 5, 39-40. November/December 1993.

MIREK, DEBBIE
___ **The Star Trek Encyclopedia: A Reference Guide to the Future**, by Michael Okuda, Denise Okuda, Debbie Mirek and Doug Drexler. New York: Pocket Books, 1994. 396pp.

MITCHAM, CARL
___ "Selected Basic References in the Philosophy of Technology," by Carl Mitcham and Timothy Casey. in: Greenberg, Mark L. and Schachterle, Lance, eds. **Literature and Technology**. Bethlehem, PA: Lehigh University Press, 1992. pp.307-309.
___ "Toward an Archeology of the Philosophy of Technology and Relations with Imaginative Literature," by Carl Mitcham and Timothy Casey. in: Greenberg, Mark L. and Schachterle, Lance, eds. **Literature and Technology**. Bethlehem, PA: Lehigh University Press, 1992. pp.31-64.

MORA, GABRIELA
___ **"De repente los Lugares Desaparecen** de Patricio Manns: Ciencia Ficción a la Latinoamericana?," *Revista Iberoamericana* 60(No. 168/169): 1039-1049. July/December 1994.

MOREAU, PIERRE-FRANCOIS
___ "L'organization du travail et le socialisme utopique," in: Saccaro Del Buffa, Giuseppa and Lewis, Arthur O., eds. **Utopia e Modernita: Teorie e prassi utopiche nell'eta moderna e postmoderna**. Rome: Gangemi Editore, 1989. pp.329-340.
___ "Le recit utopique et la recit de science fiction," in: Saccaro Del Buffa, Giuseppa and Lewis, Arthur O., eds. **Utopie per gli Anni Ottana.** Rome: Gangemi Editore, 1986. pp.443-453.

MORENO, HORACIO
___ "SF in Argentina," by Horacio Moreno and Roberto de Sousa Causo. *Locus* 33(1): 48-49. July 1994.

MORGAN, CHRIS
___ "Neverending Visions of Space: David A. Hardy, Britain's Leading Space Artist," *Interzone* No. 69: 19-23. March 1993.

MORGAN, GERALD
___ **Sir Gawain and the Green Knight and the Idea of Righteousness**. Blackrock, Dublin: Irish Academic Press, 1991. 173pp.

MORGAN, GWENDOLYN A.
___ "Dualism and Mirror Imagery in Anglo-Saxon Riddles," *Journal of the Fantastic in the Arts* 5(1): 74-85. 1992. (No. 17)
___ "In Search of the Not-One," *Journal of the Fantastic in the Arts* 4(4): 3-8. 1991. (No. 16)

MORIN, LISE
___ "Deux frères siamois: le fantastique canonique et le néo-fantastique," *Imagine* No. 61: 59-68. September 1992.

MORLEY, PAUL
___ "Strange Death of the Future," *Guardian* Sec. 2, p. 7. November 11, 1992. [Not seen.]

MORRIS, ANNE
___ "'Hitchhiker' Author Not Just Along for Ride," *Austin (TX) American Statesman* Sec. C, p. 1. March 4, 1994.

MORRIS, DAVID
___ **The Masks of Lucifer: Technology and the Occult in Twentieth Century Popular Literature**. London: Batsford, 1992. 223pp.

MORRIS, WILLIAM
___ "Thoughts and Education Under Capitalism," *Journal of the William Morris Society* 11(1): 3-5. Autumn 1994.

MORRISH, BOB
___ "Small Press," *Twilight Zone* 8(2): 12-13, 92-93. June 1988.

MORRISON, BILL
___ "Costner's Imperfect World," *(Raleigh, NC) News and Observer*. July 28, 1995. in: *NewsBank. Film and Television.* 82:D12. 1995.

MORRISON, MICHAEL A.
___ "After the Danse: Horror at the End of the Century," *New York Review of Science Fiction* No. 79: 1, 8-14. March 1995.
___ "Author Studies," by Michael A. Morrison and Neil Barron. in: Barron, Neil, ed. **Anatomy of Wonder 4**. New York: Bowker, 1995. pp.547-611.
___ "Dark Streets and Bright Dreams: Rationalism, Technology, and 'Impossible Knowledge' in Stephen King's **The Stand**," in: Magistrale, Tony, ed. **A Casebook on The Stand**. San Bernardino, CA: Borgo Press, 1992. pp.143-172.
___ "The Eidetic Image," in: Jones, Stephen, ed. **James Herbert: By Horror Haunted**. London: New English Library, 1992. pp.165-168.
___ "From the Bygone Ashes: The Legacy of Howard Phillips Lovecraft," by Michael A. Morrison and Stefan Dziemianowicz. *Lovecraft Studies* No. 27: 2-9. Fall 1992.
___ "Horror at the End of the Century: A Reading List," *New York Review of Science Fiction* No. 79: 10-12. March 1995.

MORRISON, MICHAEL A. (continued)
___ "Horror Enters the '90s," by Stefan Dziemianowicz and Michael A. Morrison. in: Collins, Robert A. and Latham, Robert, eds. **Science Fiction and Fantasy Book Review Annual 1991**. Westport, CT: Greenwood, 1994. pp.87-116.
___ "James Herbert and Science Fiction," in: Jones, Stephen, ed. **James Herbert: By Horror Haunted**. London: New English Library, 1992. pp.137-150.
___ "Journey's End: **The Haunting**: From Book to Film," *Studies in Weird Fiction* No. 12: 25-30. Spring 1993.
___ "The Legacy of Howard Phillips Lovecraft," by Michael A. Morrison and Stefan Dziemianowicz. in: Collins, Robert A. and Latham, Robert, eds. **Science Fiction and Fantasy Book Review Annual 1991**. Westport, CT: Greenwood, 1994. pp.117-129.

MORSE, A. REYNOLDS
___ "M. P. Shiel the Author--Still Unknown," in: **Shiel in Diverse Hands: A Collection of Essays**. Cleveland, OH: Reynolds Morse Foundation, 1983. pp.331-342.

MORSE, DONALD E.
___ **Kurt Vonnegut**. Mercer Island, WA: Starmont, 1992. 127pp. (Starmont Reader's Guide, 61)
___ "Masterpieces or Garbage: Martin Tropp and Science Fiction," *The CEA Critic* 43(3): 14-17. March 1981.
___ (ed.) **The Celebration of the Fantastic: Selected Papers From the Tenth Anniversary International Conference on the Fantastic in the Arts**, ed. by Donald E. Morse, Marshall B. Tymn and Csilla Bertha. Westport, CT: Greenwood, 1992. 309pp.
___ (ed.) **More Real Than Reality: The Fantastic in Irish Literature and the Arts**, ed. by Donald E. Morse and Csilla Bertha. Westport, CT: Greenwood, 1992. 266pp.

MORSE, RUTH
___ "Sterile Queens and Questing Orphans," *Quondam et Futurus* 2(2): 41-53. Summer 1992.

MOSHER, MARK R.
___ "Atemporal Labyrinths in Time: J. L. Borges and the New Physicists," *Symposium* 48(1): 51-61. Spring 1994.
___ **Jorge Luis Borges and the New Physics: The Literature of Modern Science and the Science of Modern Literature**. Ph.D. Dissertation, State University of New York, Albany, 1992. (DAI 53: 2392A.)

MOSHIER, SUZANNE E.
___ "Finding the Facts in Science Fiction Films," by Leroy W. Dubeck, Suzanne E. Moshier, Matthew H. Bruce and Judith E. Boss. *Science Teacher* 60(4): 46-48. April 1993.
___ "Using Science Fiction Films to Teach Science at the College Level," by Leroy W. Dubeck, Suzanne E. Moshier and Judith E. Boss. *Journal of College Science Teaching* 25(1): 46-50. September/October 1995

MOSIMAN, BILLIE S.
___ "The Sympathetic Killer: Journeying into the Minds of Serial Murderers," *The Report: The Fiction Writer's Magazine* No. 9: 6-7. March 1993.

MOSKOWITZ, SAM
___ "Bernarr Macfadden and His Obsession With Science Fiction, Part VII: Conclusion," *Fantasy Commentator* 7(3): 189-203. Spring 1992. (No. 43)
___ "Burroughs Returns to *Argosy*," *Burroughs Bulletin* NS. No. 20: 11-15. October 1994.
___ "Burroughs, Kline, Knibbs: A Reply," *Burroughs Bulletin* NS No. 9: 34-39. January 1992.
___ "Collecting: A Form of Residual Research," *Foundation* No. 60: 13-20. Spring 1994.
___ "A Collector's Tale," *Fantasy Commentator* 8(1/2): 22-31. Winter 1993/1994. (Whole No. 45/46)
___ "Correction re Desmond Hall," *Locus* 30(2): 69. February 1993.
___ "The Dark Plots of One Shiel," in: **Shiel in Diverse Hands: A Collection of Essays**. Cleveland, OH: Reynolds Morse Foundation, 1983. pp.57-68.
___ "Edgar Rice Burroughs and *Blue Book*," *Burroughs Bulletin* NS. No. 15: 11-20. July 1993.

MOSKOWITZ, SAM (continued)

___ "Hugo Gernsback and Edgar Rice Burroughs," *Burroughs Bulletin* NS. No. 21: 3-9. January 1995.

___ "I Remember Asimov," *Fantasy Commentator* 7(4): 254-267. Fall 1992. (Whole No. 44)

___ "The Immortal Storm II: A History of Science Fiction Fandom, Part One," *Fantasy Commentator* 8(1/2): 107-120, 13. Winter 1993/1994. (Whole No. 45/46)

___ "The Immortal Storm II: A History of Science Fiction Fandom, Part Two," *Fantasy Commentator* 8(3/4): 278-288. Fall 1995. (Whole No. 47/48)

___ "The Origin of the Term 'Fanzine'," *Fantasy Commentator* 8(3/4): 200-202. Fall 1995. (Whole No. 47/48)

___ "The Origins of Science Fiction Fandom: A Reconstruction," in: Sanders, Joe, ed. **Science Fiction Fandom**. Westport, CT: Greenwood, 1994. pp.17-36.

___ "A Remedy in Book Jackets," *Fantasy Commentator* 8(3/4): 173-181. Fall 1995. (Whole No. 47/48)

___ "The Science Fiction of Nat Schachner, Part 1," *Fantasy Commentator* 7(3): 160-179. Spring 1992. (No. 43)

___ "The Science Fiction of Nat Schachner, Part 2," *Fantasy Commentator* 7(4): 292-303. Fall 1992. (Whole No. 44)

___ "The Science Fiction of Nat Schachner, Part 3," *Fantasy Commentator* 8(1/2): 52-73. Winter 1993/1994. (Whole No. 45/46)

___ "To Barsoom and Back With Edgar Rice Burroughs, Part 1," *Futures Past* No. 3:14-19. September 1992. (Reprinted from: Moskowitz, Sam. **Explorers of the Infinite**. 1958.)

___ "Voyagers Through Eternity: A History of Science Fiction From the Beginnings to H. G. Wells," *Fantasy Commentator* 8(1/2): 135-144. Winter 1993/1994. (Whole No. 45/46)

___ "Voyagers Through Eternity: A History of Science Fiction From the Beginnings to H. G. Wells; Part XIII, Verne's Greatest Work," *Fantasy Commentator* 7(3): 232-236. Spring 1992. (No. 43)

___ "Voyagers Through Eternity: A History of Science Fiction From the Beginnings to H. G. Wells, Part XV," *Fantasy Commentator* 8(3/4): 230-242. Fall 1995. (Whole No. 47/48)

___ "W. C. Morrow: Forgotten Master of Horror; First Phase," in: Schweitzer, Darrell, ed. **Discovering Classic Horror Fiction I**. Mercer Island, WA: Starmont, 1992. pp.127-173.

MOSLEY, ED

___ "Virtual Reality Bites," *Pittsburgh (PA) Post Gazette*. April 22, 1994. in: *NewsBank. Film and Television*. 41:B11. 1994.

MOSS, ROSE

___ "Would Superwoman Fly?," in: Roberts, Sheila, ed. **Still the Frame Holds: Essays on Women Poets and Writers**. San Bernardino, CA: Borgo Press, 1993. pp.101-108.

MOSS, SIDNEY P.

___ "Poe and His Nemesis: Lewis Gaylord Clark (1956)," in: Budd, Louis J. and Cady, Edwin H., eds. **On Poe**. Durham, NC: Duke University Press, 1993. pp.102-121.

MOSSBERG, S. M.

___ "Eccentric Classics of Modern Science Fiction and Fantasy," *Firsts: Collecting Modern First Editions* 3(10): 16-21. October 1993.

MOSVSHOVITZ, HOWIE

___ "Vampires vs. Valley Girls Comedy Clever But Disjointed," *Denver (CO) Post*. July 31, 1992. in: *NewsBank. Film and Television*. 77:B14. 1992

MOULINOUX, NICOLE

___ "**La morte Amoureuse** ou la mise à mort du fantastique," in: Bozzetto, Roger, ed. **Eros: Science & Fiction Fantastique**. Aix-en-Provence: Universite de Provence, 1991. pp.37-42.

MOULTHROP, STUART

___ "Electronic Fictions and 'The Lost Game of Self'," *New York Review of Science Fiction* No. 66: 1, 8-14. February 1994.

MOVSHOVITZ, HOWIE

___ "**Army of Darkness** a Perfect Film for 14-Year Olds," *Denver (CO) Post*. February 19, 1993 in: *NewsBank. Film and Television*. 30:D11. 1993

MOVSHOVITZ, HOWIE (continued)

___ "Blown-Up Kid Lacks Shrunken Ones' Charm (Review)," *Denver (CO) Post*. July 17, 1992. in: *NewsBank. Film and Television*. 70:D11. 1992.

___ "Bogus Journey Strains If You're Over 14," *Denver (CO) Post*. July 19, 1991. in: *NewsBank. Film and Television*. 65:E11. 1991.

___ "Charm of **Star Trek** Survives in 25th Year (Review)," *Denver (CO) Post*. December 6, 1991. in: *NewsBank. Film and Television*. 7:D10. 1992.

___ "**Delicatessen** Bizarre, Original (Review)," *Denver (CO) Post*. May 8, 1992. in: *NewsBank. Film and Television*. 51:F12. 1992.

___ "**End of the World** Explores Technologies of the Future (Review)," *Denver (CO) Post*. February 7, 1992. in: *NewsBank. Film and Television*. 26:G2-G3. 1992.

___ "Events, Sights, Actors All Off-Center in **Naked Lunch** (Review)," *Denver (CO) Post*. January 10, 1992. in: *NewsBank. Film and Television*. 13:G10-G11. 1992.

___ "Holy Hit! **Batman Returns** Is a Stunner," *Denver (CO) Post*. June 19, 1992. in: *NewsBank. Film and Television*. 62:F1. 1992.

___ "**Split Second** Rat Just Hogwash (Review)," *Denver (CO) Post*. May 1, 1992. in: *NewsBank. Film and Television*. 58:G7. 1992.

___ "**Stargate** Needs 50s Spirit," *Denver (CO) Post*. October 28, 1994. in: *NewsBank. Film and Television*. 115: G6. 1994.

___ "Streep Adds Life to **Death**, But It's Too Late (Review)," *Denver (CO) Post*. July 31, 1992. in: *NewsBank. Film and Television*. 78:D3. 1992.

___ "A Taste for the Bizarre," *Denver (CO) Post*. November 13, 1992. in: *NewsBank. Film and Television*. 111:A12. 1992.

___ "**Timecop** a Hint of All-Night Cable Years From Now," *Denver (CO) Post*. September 16, 1994. in: *NewsBank. Film and Television*. 105:C10. 1994.

___ "Yelling Overpowers **No Escape**," *Denver (CO) Post*. April 29, 1994. in: *NewsBank. Film and Television*. 58:A11. 1994.

MOYLAN, THOMAS P.

___ **Figures of Hope: The Critical Utopia of the 1970s. The Revival, Destruction, and Transformation of Utopian Writing in the United States: A Study of the Ideology, Structure , and Historical Context of Representative Texts**. Ph.D. Dissertation, University of Wisconsin, Milwaukee, 1981. 290pp.

___ "Science Fiction Since 1980: Utopia, Dystopia, Cyberpunk, and Beyond," *Chung Wai Literary Quarterly* 22(12): May 1994. (Issue not seen; pagination unavailable.)

___ "Utopia Is When Our Lives Matter: Reading Kim Stanley Robinson's **Pacific Edge**," *Utopian Studies* 6(2): 1-25. 1995.

MOYLE, DAVID

___ "Beyond the Black Hole: The Emergence of Science Fiction Themes in the Recent Work of Martin Amis," *Extrapolation* 36(4): 305-315. Winter 1995.

MOYNIHAN, MARTIN

___ "C. S. Lewis and the Arthurian Tradition," in: Kranz, Gisbert, ed. **Inklings: Jahrbuch für Literatur und Ästhetik**. 1. Band. Lüdenscheid, Germany: Michael Claren, 1983. pp.21-41.

MRKOCKI, IGOR

___ "SF in Croatia," *Locus* 34(1) 71. January 1995.

MUCCI, EGIDIO

___ "Utopia e immaginario nell'architettura degli anni '60," in: Saccaro Del Buffa, Giuseppa and Lewis, Arthur O., eds. **Utopie per gli Anni Ottana**. Rome: Gangemi Editore, 1986. pp.387-394.

MUCILLO, MARIA

___ "Aristotelismo, platonismo ed ermetismo ne 'La citta felice' de Francesco patrizi da Cherso," in: Saccaro Del Buffa, Giuseppa and Lewis, Arthur O., eds. **Utopie per gli Anni Ottana**. Rome: Gangemi Editore, 1986. pp.553-578.

___ "Eta dell'Oro e tempo ciclico in Francesco Partizi," in: Saccaro Del Buffa, Giuseppa and Lewis, Arthur O., eds. **Utopia e Modernita: Teorie e prassi utopiche nell'eta moderna e postmoderna**. Rome: Gangemi Editore, 1989. pp.785-826.

MUELLER, ALLEN

___ "A Wild Surmise," *Fantasy Commentator* 7(4): 282-285. Fall 1992. (Whole No. 44)

MULLEN, R. D.
___ "A Few Words About Science Fiction Criticism," *Foundation* No. 60: 9. Spring 1994.
___ "From Standard Magazines to Pulps and Big Slicks: A Note on the History of US General and Fiction Magazines," *Science Fiction Studies* 22(1): 144-156. March 1995.
___ (ed.) **On Philip K. Dick: 40 Articles From Science-Fiction Studies.** Terre Haute, IN: SF-TH Inc., 1992. 290pp.

MÜLLER, HANS-HARALD
___ **Leo Perutz.** München: Beck, 1992. 138pp.
___ **Leo Perutz: eine bibliographie.** Frankfurt-am-Main: P. Lang, 1991. 153pp.

MÜLLER, ULRICH
___ "Blank, Syberberg, and the German Arthurian Tradition," in: Harty, Kevin J., ed. **Cinema Arthuriana: Essays on Arthurian Film.** New York: Garland, 1991. pp.157-168.

MULLINAX, GARY
___ "Eager Fans Flip for **Batman Returns**," *Wilminton (DE) News-Journal.* June 20, 1992. in: *NewsBank. Film and Television.* 62:C10. 1992.
___ "Film Angers Gay Groups," *Wilmington (DE) News Journal* March 19, 1992 in: *NewsBank. Film and Television.* 28:G14. 1992.

MUÑÓZ, GABRIEL T.
___ **La Ciencia Ficción: Conocimiento y Literatura.** Mexicali, B. C.: Instituto de Cultura de Baja California, 1991. 349pp. [Not seen.]

MUNSONIUS, JÖRG M.
___ "Einige Anmerkungern su Hans Wörners SF-Roman **Wir fanden Menschen**," *Quarber Merkur* 33(2): 16-19. December 1995. (No. 84)

MUNSTER, BILL
___ (ed.) **The Dean Koontz Companion**, ed. by Martin H. Greenberg, Ed Gorman and Bill Munster. New York: Berkley, 1994. 312pp.

MURDOCH, NORMAN H.
___ "Rose Culture and Social Reform: Edward Bellamy's **Looking Backward** (1888) and William Booth's **Darkest England and the Way Out** (1890)," *Utopian Studies* 3(2): 91-101. 1992.

MURPHY, BRIAN
___ "Monster Movies: They Came From Beneath the Fifties," *Journal of Popular Film and Television* 1(1): 31-44. 1972.

MURPHY, D. ALLEN
___ "Crossing All the Borders: An Interview with Lawrence Watt-Evans," *Quantum* No. 42: 25-28. Summer/Fall 1992.

MURPHY, KATHLEEN
___ "The Last Temptation of Sigourney Weaver," *Film Comment* 28(4): 17-20. July/August 1992.

MURPHY, PATRICK D.
___ "Feminism Faces the Fantastic," *Women's Studies* 14(2): 81-90. 1987.
___ "Introduction," in: Murphy, Patrick D., ed. **Staging the Impossible: The Fantastic Mode in Modern Drama.** Westport, CT: Greenwood, 1992. pp.1-14.
___ "Suicide, Murder, Culture, and Catastrophe: Joanna Russ's **We Who Are About to...**," in: Ruddick, Nicholas, ed. **State of the Fantastic.** Westport, CT: Greenwood, 1992. pp.121-132.
___ (ed.) **Staging the Impossible: The Fantastic Mode in Modern Drama.** Westport, CT: Greenwood, 1992. 245pp.

MURPHY, RICHARD J.
___ "Carnival Desire and the Sideshow of Fantasy: Dream, Duplicity and Representational Instability in **The Cabinet of Dr. Caligari**," *Germanic Review* 66(1): 48-56. Winter 1991.

MURPHY, SUZANNE
___ "The Godfather of Sci-Fi," *Westways* 79: 36-38. June 1987.

MURRAY, ROBERT
___ "Sermon at Thanksgiving Service, Keble College Chapel, 23rd August 1992," in: Reynolds, Patricia and GoodKnight, Glen H., eds. **Proceedings of the J. R. R. Tolkien Centenary Conference, Keble College, Oxford, 1992.** Altadena, CA: Mythopoeic Press, 1995. pp.17-20. (*Mythlore* Vol. 21, No. 2, Winter 1996, Whole No. 80)

MURRAY, STEVE
___ "Bill and Ted as Bogus as They Wanna Be," *Atlanta (GA) Journal.* July 19, 1991. in: *NewsBank. Film and Television.* 65:E13. 1991.
___ "Chevy Transparently Chases Good Fun in **Invisible Man** (Review)," *Atlanta (GA) Journal.* February 28, 1992. in: *NewsBank. Film and Television.* 23:D2. 1992.
___ "**Lawnmower Man**: A Cut Below the Average Thriller (Review)," *Atlanta (GA) Journal.* March 6, 1992. in: *NewsBank. Film and Television.* 22:D8. 1992.
___ "Predictable **Freejack** Goes Back to the Future (Review)," *Atlanta (GA) Journal.* January 20, 1992. in: *NewsBank. Film and Television.* 11: D6. 1992.
___ "Revisited Runner a Dazzler," *Atlata (GA) Journal.* September 11, 1992. in: *NewsBank. Film and Television.* 87:F8. 1992.
___ "**Sleepwalkers** Isn't Likely to Be King's Sleeper Hit (Review)," *Atlanta (GA) Journal.* April 13, 1992. in: *NewsBank. Film and Television.* 46:C9. 1992.
___ "**Tank Girl** Is Road Warrior in Fishnet Hose," *(Atlanta, GA) Journal.* March 31, 1995. in: *NewsBank. Film and Television.* 50:C1. 1995.

MURRAY, TIMOTHY
___ "Philosophical Antibodies: Grotesque Fantasy in a French Stoic Fiction," *Yale French Studies* 86: 143-163. 1994.

MURRAY, WILL
___ "Absolute Recall," *Starlog* 177: 34-37, 68. April 1992.
___ "Behind the Mask of Nyarlathotep," *Lovecraft Studies* No. 25: 25-29. Fall 1991.
___ "The First Cthulhu Mythos Poem," in: Price, Robert M., ed. **Black Forbidden Things.** Mercer Island, WA: Starmont, 1992. pp.37-40.
___ "Heroic Artist," *Starlog* No. 198: 43-49, 82. January 1994.
___ "Lovecraft's Arkham Country," in: Joshi, S. T., ed. **The H. P. Lovecraft Centennial Conference Proceedings.** West Warwick, RI: Necronomicon, 1991. pp.15-16.
___ "Lovecraft, Blackwood, and Chambers: A Colloquium of Ghosts," *Studies in Weird Fiction* No. 13: 2-7. Summer 1993. [Not seen.]
___ "Master of Death," *Starlog* No. 205: 27-31. August 1994.
___ "Prehuman Language in Lovecraft," in: Price, Robert M., ed. **Black Forbidden Things.** Mercer Island, WA: Starmont, 1992. pp.41-45.
___ "The Quiet Future," *Starlog* No. 175: 70-74. February 1992.
___ "Riddler of Forever?," *Starlog* No. 218: 27-30. September 1995.
___ "Self-Parody in Lovecraft's Revisions," in: Price, Robert M., ed. **Black Forbidden Things.** Mercer Island, WA: Starmont, 1992. pp.34-36.
___ "Tentacles in Dreamland: Cthulhu Mythos Elements in the Dunsanian Stories," in: Price, Robert M., ed. **Black Forbidden Things.** Mercer Island, WA: Starmont, 1992. pp.30-33.
___ "Where Was Foxfield?," *Lovecraft Studies* No. 33: 18-23. Fall 1995.

MUSSO, JOSEPH
___ "Forty Acres: A History of the RKO Backlot Films," *Burroughs Bulletin* NS. No. 14: 11-16. April 1993.

MUSTAZZA, LEONARD
___ "Fear and Pity: Tragic Horror in King's **Pet Sematary**," in: Magistrale, Tony, ed. **The Dark Descent: Essays Defining Stephen King's Horrorscape.** Westport, CT: Greenwood, 1992. pp.73-82.
___ "The Power of Symbols and the Failure of Virtue: Catholicism in Stephen King's **Salem's Lot**," *Journal of the Fantastic in the Arts* 3(4): 107-119. 1994.
___ "Repaying Service With Pain: The Role of God in **The Stand**," in: Magistrale, Tony, ed. **A Casebook on The Stand.** San Bernardino, CA: Borgo Press, 1992. pp.89-108.
___ (ed.) **The Critical Response to Kurt Vonnegut.** Westport, CT: Greenwood, 1994. 346pp.

MUZZARELLI, MARIA G.
___ "Christine de Pizan," in: Colombo, Arrigo and Quarta, Cosimo, eds. **Il Destino della Famiglia nell'Utopia.** Bari: Edizione Dedalo, 1991. pp.125-143.

MYERS, ALAN
___ "Zamyatin in Newcastle," *Foundation* No. 59: 70-78. Autumn 1993.

MYERS, CAREN
___ "*Lion King* (Review)," *Sight and Sound* 4(10): 47-48. October 1994.

MYERS, DORIS T.
___ **C. S. Lewis in Context**. Kent, OH: Kent State University Press, 1994. 248pp.
___ "Law and Disorder: Two Settings in **That Hideous Strength**," *Mythlore* 19(1): 9-14. Winter 1993. (No. 71)

MYERS, MICHAEL
___ "Visions of Tomorrow: German Science Fiction and Socialist Utopian Novels of the Late Nineteenth Century," *Selecta* (Corvallis) 14: 63-69. 1993.

NADDAFF, SANDRA
___ **Arabesque: Narrative Structure and the Aesthetics of Repetition in the '1001 Nights'**. Evanston, IL: Northwestern University Press, 1991. 156pp.

NAHIN, PAUL J.
___ **Time Machines: Time Travel in Physics, Metaphysics, and Science Fiction**. New York: American Institute of Physics, 1993. 408pp.

NANCE, SCOTT
___ **Bloodsuckers: Vampires at the Movies**. Las Vegas, NM: Pioneer Books, 1992. 149pp.
___ **Trek: Deep Space Nine**. Las Vegas: Pioneer Books, 1993. 127pp.

NARDO, DON
___ **H. G. Wells**. San Diego, CA: Lucent Books, 1992. 111PP.
___ **The Importance of H. G. Wells**. San Diego, CA: Lucent Books, 1992. 109pp.

NASCIMENTO, R. C.
___ (ed.) **Catálogo de Ficçáo Científica Em Língua Portuguesa (1921-1993)**. Sao Paulo, Brazil: Nasciemento, 1994. Part 1 of 6, 80pp. [Not seen.]

NASH, JESSE W.
___ "Gotham's Dark Knight: The Postmodern Transformation of the Arthurian Mythos," in: Slocum, Sally K., ed. **Popular Arthurian Traditions**. Bowling Green, OH: Popular Press, 1992. pp.36-45.

NASSARO, JOE
___ "*Red Dwarf*," *Starlog* No. 186: 75-80. January 1993.

NATHANSON, PAUL
___ **Over the Rainbow: The Wizard of Oz as a Secular Myth of America**. Albany: State University of New York Press, 1991. 432pp.

NAUMAN, ANN K.
___ "Sci-Fi Science," by Ann K. Nauman and Edward L. Shaw. *Science Activities* 31(3): 18-20. Fall 1994.

NAVARETTE, SUSAN J.
___ "The Soul of the Plot: The Aesthetics of Fin de Siècle Literature of Horror," in: Slusser, George E. and Rabkin, Eric S., eds. **Styles of Creation: Aesthetic Technique and the Creation of Fictional Worlds**. Athens: University of Georgia Press, 1992. pp.88-115.

NAZZARO, JOE
___ "Alien Ambassador," *Starlog* No. 202: 41-44, 70. May 1994.
___ "Android Ideas," *Starlog* No. 192: 27-31. July 1993.
___ "Babylon's Finest," *Starlog* No. 203: 77-79. June 1994.
___ "Bat Attitude," *Starlog* No. 210: 50-53. January 1995.
___ "Cats Tale," *Starlog* No. 190: 78-81. May 1993.
___ "Chief Justice," *Starlog* No. 217: 47-51. August 1995.
___ "Computer Print-Out," *Starlog* No. 189: 48-49. April 1993.
___ "Face of Metal," *Starlog* No. 196: 39-42. November 1993.
___ "Forever the Doctor," *Starlog* No. 197: 50-53, 68. December 1993.
___ "Generations Gap," *Starlog* No. 210: 40-45. January 1995.
___ "Heroic Android," by Joe Nazzaro and Marc Shapiro. in: McDonnell, David, ed. **Starlog's Science Fiction Heroes and Heroines**. New York: Crescent Books, 1995. pp.28-30.

NAZZARO, JOE (continued)
___ "Heroic Passings," *Starlog* No. 221: 35-37. December 1995.
___ "Honorable Diplomat," *Starlog* No. 219: 76-79. October 1995.
___ "Intergalactic Blue," *Starlog* No. 208: 37-40. November 1994.
___ "Little Lost Holly," *Starlog* No. 221: 68-69. December 1995.
___ "Master Strokes," *Starlog* No. 195: 27-31, 72. October 1993.
___ "Newcomer Novels," *Starlog* No. 188: 36-37, 67. March 1993.
___ "Once a Commander," by Joe Nazzaro and Sheelagh J. Wells. *Starlog* No. 208: 53-57, 69. November 1994.
___ "Pressures of Command," *Starlog* No. 213: 27-31, 69. April 1995.
___ "Recession Dwarf," *Starlog* No. 201: 46-49. April 1994.
___ "Reunifications," *Starlog* No. 208: 42-45. November 1994.
___ "Slob of the Spaceways," *Starlog* No. 187: 50-53. February 1993.
___ "Sophisticated Evil," *Starlog* No. 218: 72-75, 65. September 1995.
___ "Underwater Thoughts," *Starlog* No. 204: 54-58. July 1994.
___ "Who's Latest," *Starlog* No. 199: 54-57, 73. February 1994.
___ "Who's Stranger," *Starlog* No. 201: 54-57, 70. April 1994.
___ "Working Class Hologram," *Starlog* No. 188: 78-81. March 1993.

NEAMAN, JUDITH S.
___ "Romancing the Past: Statis and Motion in **Yvain** and Vezelay," *Arthuriana* 4(3): 250-270. Fall 1994.

NEBULONI, ROBERTO
___ "I Francofortesi: Pro e contro la freddezza borghese," in: Colombo, Arrigo and Quarta, Cosimo, eds. **Il Destino della Famiglia nell'Utopia**. Bari: Edizione Dedalo, 1991. pp.285-307.

NELLIST, BRIAN
___ "Imagining the Future: Predictive Fiction in the Nineteenth Century," in: Seed, David, ed. **Anticipations: Essays on Early Science Fiction and Its Precursors**. Liverpool: Liverpool University Press, 1995. pp.111-136.

NELSON, CHARLES W.
___ "But Who Is Rose Cotton? Love and Romance in **The Lord of the Rings**," *Journal of the Fantastic in the Arts* 3(3): 6-20. 1994.

NELSON, CRAIG A.
___ **A Content Analysis of Female and Male Authors' Portrayals of Sex Roles in Science Fiction for Children From 1970 to 1990**. Ph.D. Disseration, University of Minnesota, 1991. 235pp.

NELSON, DALE J.
___ "Lovecraft and the Burkean Sublime," *Lovecraft Studies* No. 24: 2-6. Spring 1991.

NEMAN, DANIEL
___ "**Addams Family**: Not Much of Value (Review)," *Richmond (VA) Times-Dispatch*. November 20, 1993. in: *NewsBank. Art* 32:B2. 1993.
___ "**Brainscan** Is Mostly a Brain-Dead Bore," *Richmond (VA) Times-Dispatch*. April 22, 1994. in: *NewsBank. Film and Television*. 41:B12. 1994.
___ "**Highlander III**: The Final Sequel, Please?," *Richmond (VA) Times-Dispatch*. January 28, 1995. in: *NewsBank. Film and Television*. 17: C13. 1995.
___ "**Timecop** Is a Prime Flop," *Richmond (VA) Times-Dispatch*. September 17, 1994. in: *NewsBank. Film and Television*. 105:D11. 1994.

NEMECEK, LARRY
___ **The Star Trek: The Next Generation Companion**. Revised and Updated. New York: Pocket Books, 1995. 339pp.
___ **The Star Trek: The Next Generation Companion**. New York: Pocket Books, 1992. 213pp.

NENSI, SALMAN A.
___ "David Prowse: The Man Behind the Mask," *LucasFilms Fan Club* No. 19: 23-26. Summer 1993.
___ "Exclusive Interview: Jeremy Bulloch, Behind the Mask of Boba Fett," *Lucasfilm Fan Club* No. 21: 2-3. Winter 1994.
___ "Revealing the History of the Future," *Star Trek: The Official Fan Club Magazine* No. 91: 1, 8. May/June 1993.
___ "The Special Effects of **Jurassic Park**," *Lucasfilm Fan Club* No. 20: 28-30. Fall 1993.
___ "Walking in the Footsteps of a Wookie," *LucasFilms Fan Club* No. 19: 2-4. Summer 1993.

NETCOH, DARLENE M.
___ **The Eyes Have It: Hybrid Humans in Postmodern Science Fiction**. Master's Thesis, Rhode Island College, 1992. 122pp.

NEUENDORF, FIONA T.
___ "Negotiating Feminist and Historicist Concerns: Guinevere in Geoffrey of Monmouth's **Historia Regum Britanniae**," *Quondam et Futurus* 3(2): 26-44. Summer 1993.

NEUSTADTER, ROGER
___ "Back From the Future: Childhood as Utopia," *Extrapolation* 35(2): 145-154. Summer 1994.

NEVEROW, VARA
___ "The Politics of Incorporation and Embodiment: **Woman on the Edge of Time** and **He, She and It** as Feminist Epistemologies of Resistance," *Utopian Studies* 5(2): 16-35. 1994.

NEVERS, KEVIN L.
___ **Immovable Objects, Irrestible Forces: The Sublime and the Technological in the Eighteenth Century**. Ph.D. Dissertation, University of Virginia, 1993. 473pp. (DAI-A 54/08, p. 3044. February 1994.)

NEWLOVE, DONALD
___ "Ray Bradbury Is Back in Top Form, Reclaiming Fans With Refreshed Style," *Philadelphia (PA) Inquirer*. July 26, 1992. in: *NewsBank. Literature*. 56:E10. 1992

NEWMAN, KIM
___ "**Addams Family Values** (Review)," *Sight and Sound* 4(2): 44-45. February 1994.
___ "**Army of Darkness** (Review)," *Sight and Sound* 3(6): 46-47. June 1993.
___ "Bloodlines," *Sight and Sound* 3(1): 12-13. January 1993.
___ "**Brainscan** (Review)," *Sight and Sound* 4(11): 40-41. November 1994.
___ "**Candyman 2: Farewell to the Flesh** (Review)," *Sight and Sound* 5(12): 42-43. December 1995.
___ "**Dr. Jekyll and Ms. Hyde** (Review)," *Sight and Sound* 5(12): 44-45. December 1995.
___ "**Hellraiser III: Hell on Earth** (Review)," *Sight and Sound* 3(2): 46-47. February 1993.
___ "**Interview With the Vampire** (Review)," *Sight and Sound* 5(2): 46-47. February 1995.
___ "**Jurassic Park** (Review)," *Sight and Sound* 3(8): 44-45. August 1993.
___ "**Nightmare Before Christmas** (Review)," *Sight and Sound* 4(12): 53-54. December 1994.
___ "**The Shadow** (Review)," *Sight and Sound* 4(11): 52. November 1994.
___ "**Stargate** (Review)," *Sight and Sound* 5(2): 53-54. February 1995.
___ "**Tales From the Crypt: Demon Knight** (Review)," *Sight and Sound* 5(6): 54-55. June 1995.
___ "**Timecop** (Review)," *Sight and Sound* 5(1): 59-60. January 1995.
___ "**Wes Craven's New Nightmare** (Review)," *Sight and Sound* 5(1): 62-63. January 1995.
___ (ed.) **Horror: 100 Best Books**. Revised and updated edition, ed. by Stephen Jones and Kim Newman. London: Hodder/New English Library, 1992. 368pp.

NEWMAN, ROBERT D.
___ "Thomas Pynchon," in: Bruccoli, Matthew J., ed. **Facts on File Bibliography of American Fiction 1919-1988**. New York: Facts on File, 1991. pp.413-414.

NEWQUIST, ROY
___ "Talking as a Person (Interview, 1964)," in: Ingersoll, Earl G., ed. **Doris Lessing: Conversations**. Princeton, NJ: Ontario Review Press, 1994. pp.3-12.

NEWSINGER, JOHN
___ "Futuretracks: The Juvenile Science Fiction of Robert Westall," *Foundation* No. 63: 61-67. Spring 1995.
___ "**Nineteen Eighty-Four** Since the Collapse of Communism," *Foundation* No. 56: 75-84. Autumn 1992.

NEWSOM, TED
___ "The Creature Remake That Never Got Made: An Afternoon with Jack Arnold and Nigel Kneale," *Filmfax* No. 37: 64-67, 82, 98. February/March 1993.

NICHOLAAS, JOSEPH
___ "X-Rated: **The X-Files**," *Matrix* No. 115: 12-13. June/July 1995.

NICHOLLS, PETER
___ **The Encyclopedia of Science Fiction**, by John Clute and Peter Nicholls. New York: St. Martin's, 1993. 1370pp.

NICHOLLS, STAN
___ "Adding the Flesh and Blood: Jonathan Wylie Interviewed," *Interzone* No. 74: 45-47. August 1993.
___ "Alien Art," *Starlog* 179: 19-25. June 1992.
___ "Author of Odysseys," *Starlog* No. 200: 27-31. March 1994.
___ "A Blip on the Way to the Big Crunch: Arthur C. Clarke Interviewed," *Interzone* No. 78: 23-26. December 1993.
___ "Brian Aldiss Buries His Heart on Far Andromeda," in: Nicholls, Stan. **Wordsmiths of Wonder: Fifty Interviews with Writers of the Fantastic**. London: Orbit, 1993. pp.12-24.
___ "Brian Stableford Cottons On," in: Nicholls, Stan. **Wordsmiths of Wonder: Fifty Interviews with Writers of the Fantastic**. London: Orbit, 1993. pp.164-168.
___ "C. J. Cherryh Clears Out the Dead Wood," in: Nicholls, Stan. **Wordsmiths of Wonder: Fifty Interviews with Writers of the Fantastic**. London: Orbit, 1993. pp.43-54.
___ "Chewing the Raccoon: Dan Simmons Interviewed," *Interzone* No. 59: 24-26. May 1992.
___ "Christopher Fowler Won't Breathe Anything He Can't See," in: Nicholls, Stan. **Wordsmiths of Wonder: Fifty Interviews with Writers of the Fantastic**. London: Orbit, 1993. pp.425-431.
___ "Clive Barker Pulls Away the Veils," in: Nicholls, Stan. **Wordsmiths of Wonder: Fifty Interviews with Writers of the Fantastic**. London: Orbit, 1993. pp.379-389.
___ "Colin Greenland Brings Back Plenty," in: Nicholls, Stan. **Wordsmiths of Wonder: Fifty Interviews with Writers of the Fantastic**. London: Orbit, 1993. pp.71-79.
___ "The Colors of Mars," *Starlog* No. 191: 58-67. June 1993.
___ "Comedy Engineering," *Starlog* No. 188: 60-64. March 1993.
___ "Cultural Differences: Iain Banks Interviewed," *Interzone* No. 86: 22-24. August 1994.
___ "Dan Simmons Chews on the Raccoon," in: Nicholls, Stan. **Wordsmiths of Wonder: Fifty Interviews with Writers of the Fantastic**. London: Orbit, 1993. pp.143-154.
___ "Dance of the Supermarionettes," *Starlog* 184: 52-55, 70. November 1992.
___ "David Brin Won't Cop the Rap," in: Nicholls, Stan. **Wordsmiths of Wonder: Fifty Interviews with Writers of the Fantastic**. London: Orbit, 1993. pp.33-42.
___ "David Gemmell Won't Get Out of This Life Alive," in: Nicholls, Stan. **Wordsmiths of Wonder: Fifty Interviews with Writers of the Fantastic**. London: Orbit, 1993. pp.364-376.
___ "David Wingrove Has an Outrageous Idea," in: Nicholls, Stan. **Wordsmiths of Wonder: Fifty Interviews with Writers of the Fantastic**. London: Orbit, 1993. pp.237-247.
___ "Diana Paxson Invents Her Own Religion," in: Nicholls, Stan. **Wordsmiths of Wonder: Fifty Interviews with Writers of the Fantastic**. London: Orbit, 1993. pp.295-302.
___ "The Donaldson Chronicles: Stephen Donaldson Interviewed," *Interzone* No. 60: 43-45. June 1992.
___ "Douglas Adams Will Never Say Never Again, Probably," in: Nicholls, Stan. **Wordsmiths of Wonder: Fifty Interviews with Writers of the Fantastic**. London: Orbit, 1993. pp.169-181.
___ "Dreaming Boy: Robert Sheckley Interviewed," *Interzone* No. 63: 47-49. September 1992.
___ "Dwina Murphy-Gibb Is on the Greatest High in the World," in: Nicholls, Stan. **Wordsmiths of Wonder: Fifty Interviews with Writers of the Fantastic**. London: Orbit, 1993. pp.332-339.
___ "Facing the Demons," *Starlog* No. 207: 52-57, 72. October 1994.
___ "Frederik Pohl Just Wants Everyone to Play Nicely Together," in: Nicholls, Stan. **Wordsmiths of Wonder: Fifty Interviews with Writers of the Fantastic**. London: Orbit, 1993. pp.3-11.
___ "Gardner Dozois Turns Off the TV," in: Nicholls, Stan. **Wordsmiths of Wonder: Fifty Interviews with Writers of the Fantastic**. London: Orbit, 1993. pp.61-70.

NICHOLS, ASHTON
___ "Liberationist Sexuality and Non-Violent Resistance: The Legacy of Blake and Shelley in Morris's **News From Nowhere**," *Journal of the William Morris Society* 10(4): 20-27. Spring 1994.

NICHOLS, NICHELLE
___ **Beyond Uhura: Star Trek and Other Memories**. New York: Putnam, 1995. 323pp.

NICHOLSON, COLIN
___ "Introduction," in: Nicholson, Colin, ed. **Margaret Atwood: Writing and Subjectivity: New Critical Essays**. New York: St. Martin's, 1994. pp.1-10.
___ "Living on the Edges: Constructions of Post-Colonial Subjectivity in Atwood's Early Poetry," in: Nicholson, Colin, ed. **Margaret Atwood: Writing and Subjectivity: New Critical Essays**. New York: St. Martin's, 1994. pp.11-50.
___ (ed.) **Margaret Atwood: Writing and Subjectivity: New Critical Essays**. New York: St. Martin's, 1994. 261pp.

NICHOLSON, MERVYN
___ "Bram Stoker and C. S. Lewis: **Dracula** as a Source for **That Hideous Strength**," *Mythlore* 19(3): 16-22. Summer 1993. (No. 73)

NICKEL, HELMUT
___ "About Arthurian Armings, for War and for Love," *Arthuriana* 5(4): 3-21. Winter 1995.
___ "Arms and Armor in Arthurian Films," in: Harty, Kevin J., ed. **Cinema Arthuriana: Essays on Arthurian Film**. New York: Garland, 1991. pp.181-202.
___ "The King's Arms, the Queen's Legs, and the Cat's Miau: About Humor and Satire in Arthurian Heraldry," *Quondam et Futurus* 3(4): 28-40. Winter 1993.
___ "Notes on Arthurian Heraldry: The Retroactive System in the 'Armagnac' Armorial," *Quondam et Futurus* 3(3): 1-23. Fall 1993.
___ "Surviving Camlann," *Quondam et Futurus* 3(1): 32-37. Spring 1993.

NICOLAZZINI, PIERGIORGIO
___ **Fantascienza, Fantasy and Horror in Italia: 1990**, by Ernesto Vegetti and Piergiorgio Nicolazzini. Milano, Italy: Nicolazzini, 1992?. 142pp. [Not seen.]

NIDEROST, ERIC
___ "Always the Other Man," *Starlog* No. 176: 64-67. March 1992.

NIEWIADOWSKI, ANDRZEJ
___ **Literatura fantastycznonaukowa**. Warsaw: Wydawn. Naukowe PWN, 1992. 371pp. [Not seen.]

NIKOLCHINA, MIGLENA
___ "Love and Automata: From Hoffman to Lem and From Freud to Kristeva," in: Sanders, Joe, ed. **Functions of the Fantastic**. Westport, CT: Greenwood, 1995. pp.77-82.

NILSON, PETER
___ **Rymdljus: en bok om katastrofer och underverk**. Stockholm: Norstedt, 1992. 266pp. [Not seen.]

NIMOY, LEONARD
___ **I Am Spock**. New York: Hyperion, 1995. 342pp.

NISBET, PETER
___ "The Response to Science and Technology in the Visual Arts," in: Graham, Loren R., ed. **Science and the Soviet Social Order**. Cambridge: Harvard University Press, 1990. pp.341-358.

NIVEN, LARRY
___ "The Return of William Proxmire," in: Kondo, Yoji, ed. **Requiem: New Collected Works by Robert A. Heinlein and Tributes to the Grand Master**. New York: Tor, 1992. pp.275-285.

NIXON, NICOLA
___ "Cyberpunk: Preparing the Ground for Revolution or Keeping the Boys Satisfied?," *Science-Fiction Studies* 19(2): 219-235. July 1992.

NOAD, CHARLES E.
___ "Frodo and His Spectre: Blakean Resonances in Tolkien," in: Reynolds, Patricia and GoodKnight, Glen H., eds. **Proceedings of the J. R. R. Tolkien Centenary Conference, Keble College, Oxford, 1992**. Altadena, CA: Mythopoeic Press, 1995. pp.58-62. (*Mythlore* Vol. 21, No. 2, Winter 1996, Whole No. 80)

NOBLE, ANDREW A. J.
___ "Dostoevsky's Anti-Utopianism," in: Butt, J. and Clarke, I. F., eds. **The Victorians and Social Protest: A Symposium**. New York: David and Charles, 1973. pp.133-155.

NOBLE, PETER
___ "Arthur, Anti-Fascist or Pirate King?," *Quondam et Futurus* 3(3): 46-54. Fall 1993.

NODELMAN, PERRY
___ "Reinventing the Past: Gender in Ursula K. Le Guin's **Tehanu** and the Earthsea Trilogy," *Children's Literature* 23: 179-201. 1995.

NOETZEL, MICHAEL
___ "Kobo Abe: Eine betrachtung und posthume Würdigung des Avant-gardisten der modernen japanischen SF," *Quarber Merkur* 33(1): 39-53. June 1995. (No. 83)

NOGUCHI, SHUNCHI
___ "The Winchester Malory," *Arthuriana* 5(2): 15-23. Summer 1995.

NOLAN, WILLIAM F.
___ "Introduction: Logan, a Media History," in: Nolan, William F. **William F. Nolan's Logan: A Trilogy**. Baltimore, MD: Maclay, 1986. pp.7-19.

NOLL, RICHARD
___ **Vampires, Werewolves, and Demons: Twentieth Century Reports in the Psychiatric Literature**. New York: Brunner, 1992. 244pp.

NOLLINGER, MARK
___ "They Came From Outer Space (Again!)," *TV Guide* 43(45): 24-26. November 11, 1995.

NORMAN, FELICITY
___ "J. R. R. Tolkien's **The Hobbit**," *Literature Base* 3(3): 12-13. August 1992.

NORMAN, JOHN
___ "How Far Is Too Far? An Open Letter From John Norman," *New York Review of Science Fiction* No. 83: 1, 10-15. July 1995.

NORTON, BILL
___ "Pandora's Paintbox," *Cinefex* No. 56: 54-69. November 1993.
___ "Video Beat: Piloting to **Earth 2**," *Cinefex* No. 60: 13-14. December 1994.
___ "Zealots and Xenomorphs," *Cinefex* No. 50: 26-53. May 1992.

NORTON, MARY F.
___ "Visions of the Future: Utopian and Apocalyptic Designs," *CEA Forum* 23(2)/24(1): 15-20. Summer/Winter 1993/1994.

NOTKIN, DEBBIE
___ "Science Fiction Conventions: Behind the Scenes," by Tom Whitmore and Debbie Notkin. in: Sanders, Joe, ed. **Science Fiction Fandom**. Westport, CT: Greenwood, 1994. pp.161-171.

NOTTRIDGE, RHODA
___ **Horror Films**. New York: Crestwood House, 1991. 32pp.

NOURSE, ALAN E.
___ "The History of the SFWA, 1967-1968," *SFWA Bulletin* 27(2): 4. Summer 1993. (No. 120)

NUTMAN, PHILIP
___ "The Exploding Family," in: Golden, Christopher, ed. **Cut! Horror Writers on Horror Film**. New York: Berkley, 1992. pp.171-182.

NUTTALL, A. D.
___ "Jack the Giant-Killer," *CSL: The Bulletin of the New York C. S. Lewis Society* 24(2/3): 1-14. December 1992/January 1993.

O'BRIEN, DENNIS
___ "Shoring Fragments: How CBS's *Beauty and the Beast* Adapts Consensus Reality to Shape Its Magical World," in: Sanders, Joe, ed. **Functions of the Fantastic.** Westport, CT: Greenwood, 1995. pp.37-46.

O'BRIEN, EDWARD W., JR.
___ "Bram Stoker's *Dracula*: Eros or Agape?," *Fantasy Commentator* 8(1/2): 75-79. Winter 1993/1994. (Whole No. 45/46)

O'BRIEN, MAUREEN
___ "Christian Publishing SF/F," *Lan's Lantern* No. 43: 43-46. March 1995.

O'CONNER, JOHN J.
___ "It Came From the 60s: The Bridges Family in Sci-fi for a New Generation," *New York Times* p.10. March 25, 1995.

O'DONNELL, KEVIN, JR.
___ "How Thor Power Hammered Publishing," *SFWA Bulletin* 27(1): 30-37. Spring 1993. (No. 119)

O'NEILL, DENNIS
___ "Refractions of Empire: The *Comics Journal* Interview," in: Delany, Samuel R. **Silent Interviews on Language, Race, Sex, Science Fiction and Some Comics.** Hanover, NH: Wesleyan University Press, 1994. pp.83-126.

O'NEILL, JOHN
___ "*McTopia*: Eating Time," in: Kumar, Krishan and Bann, Stephen, eds. **Utopias and the Millennium.** London: Reaktion Books, 1993. pp.129-137.

O'QUINN, KERRY
___ "My Friend, Gene," *Starlog* No. 175: 42. February 1992.

O'SHAUGHNESSEY, MARGARET
___ "Edwin Austin Abbey's Reinterpretation of the Grail Quest: The Boston Public Library Murals," *Arthuriana* 4(4): 298-312. Winter 1994.

O'SULLIVAN, ELEANOR
___ "Streep Smarts," *Neptune (NJ) Asbury Park Press.* July 30, 1992. in: *NewsBank. Film and Television.* 68:F7-F8. 1992.

O'SULLIVAN, GERRY
___ "Inventing Arcadia: An Interview With Frederick Turner," by Gerry O'Sullivan and Carl Pletsch. *Humanist* 53(6): 9-18. November/ December 1993.

O'SULLIVAN, KEVIN
___ "Sinking of *Waterworld*," *(New York, NY) Daily News.* July 16, 1995. in: *NewsBank. Film and Television.* 82:D4-D5. 1995.

OATES, JOYCE C.
___ "One Keeps Coming (Interview, 1972)," in: Ingersoll, Earl G., ed. **Doris Lessing: Conversations.** Princeton, NJ: Ontario Review Press, 1994. pp.33-40.
___ "Reflections on the Grotesque," *New York Review of Science Fiction* No. 66: 1, 3-5. February 1994.

OBERTINO, JAMES
___ "Moria and Hades: Underworld Journeys in Tolkien and Virgil," *Comparative Literature Studies* 30(2): 153-169. 1993.

OBSATZ, SHARYN
___ "*Earth 2* to Leave Santa Fe," *(Santa Fe, NM) New Mexican.* March 18, 1995. in: *NewsBank. Film and Television.* 33:D9. 1995.

OCHOA, GEORGE
___ **The Writer's Guide to Creating a Science Fiction Universe.** Cincinnati, OH: Writer's Digest, 1993. 314pp.

ODIEN, JEFF
___ "On the Water Front," *Cinefex* No. 64: 96-117. December 1995.

ODIEN, W. C.
___ "The Rise and Fall of Norville Barnes," *Cinefex* No. 58: 66-81. June 1994.

OEHLERT, MARK
___ "From Captain America to Wolverine: Cyborgs in Comic Books, Alternative Images of Cybernetic Heroes and Villains," in: Gray, Chris H., ed. **The Cyborg Handbook.** New York: Routledge, 1995. pp.219-231.

OGDEN, D. PETER
___ "Herman Brix (a.k.a.) Bruce Bennett," *Filmfax* No. 32: 34-40. April/ May 1992.

OGIER, MARK
___ "*Roswell* (Review)," *Matrix* No. 115: 13. June/July 1995.

OHLGREN, THOMAS
___ "The World of King Arthur: An Interdisciplinary Course," by Thomas Kelly and Thomas Ohlgren. in: Fries, Maureen and Watson, Jeanie, eds. **Approaches to the Teaching of the Arthurian Tradition.** New York: Modern Language Association, 1992. pp.77-80.

OKUDA, DENISE
___ **Star Trek Chronology: The History of the Future,** by Michael Okuda and Denise Okuda. New York: Pocket Books, 1993. 184pp.
___ **The Star Trek Encyclopedia: A Reference Guide to the Future,** by Michael Okuda, Denise Okuda, Debbie Mirek and Doug Drexler. New York: Pocket Books, 1994. 396pp.

OKUDA, MICHAEL
___ **Star Trek Chronology: The History of the Future,** by Michael Okuda and Denise Okuda. New York: Pocket Books, 1993. 184pp.
___ **The Star Trek Encyclopedia: A Reference Guide to the Future,** by Michael Okuda, Denise Okuda, Debbie Mirek and Doug Drexler. New York: Pocket Books, 1994. 396pp.

OLEKSY, ELZBIETA H.
___ "From Silence and Madness to the Exchange That Multiplies: Walker Percy and the Woman Question," *Southern Quarterly* 31(3): 58-68. Spring 1993.

OLIVER, MYRNA
___ "Finney, Jack: *Body Snatchers* Author Jack Finney, 84, Dies," *Houston (TX) Chronicle* November 16, 1995. (Cited from the Internet Edition.)

OLLIVER, VICTOR
___ "A Life in the Day of James Herbert," in: Jones, Stephen, ed. **James Herbert: By Horror Haunted.** London: New English Library, 1992. pp.33-37.

OLSA, JAROSLAV, JR.
___ "SF in Southeast Asia," *Locus* 34(1) 70. January 1995.

OLSEN, LANCE
___ "Beckett and the Horrific," in: Murphy, Patrick D., ed. **Staging the Impossible: The Fantastic Mode in Modern Drama.** Westport, CT: Greenwood, 1992. pp.116-126.
___ "Cyberpunk and the Crisis of Postmodernity," in: Slusser, George E. and Shippey, Tom, eds. **Fiction 2000: Cyberpunk and the Future of Narrative.** Athens: University of Georgia Press, 1992. pp.142-152.
___ **William Gibson.** Mercer Island, WA: Starmont, 1992. 131pp. (Starmont Reader's Guide, 58)

OLSON, D. H.
___ "An Interview With Jonathan Carroll," *Tales of the Unanticipated* No. 9: 28-34. Fall/Winter 1991/1992.

OLSZANSKI, TADEUSZ A.
___ "Evil and the Evil One in Tolkien's Theology," in: Reynolds, Patricia and GoodKnight, Glen H., eds. **Proceedings of the J. R. R. Tolkien Centenary Conference, Keble College, Oxford, 1992.** Altadena, CA: Mythopoeic Press, 1995. pp.298-300. (*Mythlore* Vol. 21, No. 2, Winter 1996, Whole No. 80)

OLTION, JERRY
___ "PROfessional Writers & CONventions," *The Report: The Fiction Writer's Magazine* No. 7: 6-7. June 1992.

OLTION, KATHY
___ "How to Survive a Convention," *The Report: The Fiction Writer's Magazine* No. 7: 28-29. June 1992.

OPPENHEIMER, JEAN
___ "***Stargate***: Adding Layers in the Outer Limits," *American Cinematographer* 75(12): 30-32. December 1994.

ORDWAY, FREDERICK I., III
___ (ed.) **Blueprint for Space: Science Fiction to Science Fact**, ed. by Frederick I. Ordway, III and Randy Liebermann. Washington, DC: Smithsonian Institution Press, 1992. 224pp.

ORE, REBECCA
___ "Aliens and the Artificial Other," *New York Review of Science Fiction* No. 56: 18-20. April 1993.
___ "The First Time," *New York Review of Science Fiction* No. 88: 15. December 1995.

OREL, HAROLD
___ (ed.) **Critical Essays on Sir Arthur Conan Doyle**. New York: G. K. Hall, 1992. 290pp.

ORMES, MARIE G.
___ **Robert A. Heinlein: A Bibliographical Research Guide to Heinlein's Complete Works**. Ph.D. Dissertation, University of Kentucky, 1993. 272pp. (DAI 54/11, p. 4095. May 1994.)
___ "Surprises in the Heinlein Bibliography," in: Wolf, Milton T. and Mallett, Daryl F., eds. **Imaginative Futures: Proceedings of the 1993 Science Fiction Research Association Conference**. San Bernardino, CA: Jacob's Ladder Books, 1995. pp.95-114.

OROZCO-ALLAN, GLORIA
___ "Lo fantástico y el discurso femenino en **Dos veces Alicia**, de Albalucia Angel," *Mester* (UCLA) 19(2): 137-144. Fall 1990.

ORR, PHILIP
___ "The Anoedipal Mythos of Batman and Catwoman," *Journal of Popular Culture* 27(4): 169-182. Spring 1994.

OSAKO, MASAMICHI
___ "Science Fiction Fandom in Japan," in: Sanders, Joe, ed. **Science Fiction Fandom**. Westport, CT: Greenwood, 1994. pp.137-140.

OSBORNE, ELIZABETH A.
___ "Collecting," *Lan's Lantern* No. 40: 10. September 1992.

OSIF, BONNIE A.
___ "Teaching Tough Stuff: Science Fiction Futures and Bibliographic Instruction," *Research Strategies* 11(2): 116-119. Spring 1993.

OSTROW, JOANNE
___ "History Powers Indy Chronicles," *Denver (CO) Post*. January 26, 1992. in: *NewsBank. Film and Television*. 16:D9. 1992.

OSTUNI, HERNÁN
___ "Burroughs in Argentina," by Fernando García and Hernán Ostuni. *Burroughs Bulletin* NS. No. 17: 10-17. January 1994.
___ "Tarzan, King of the Pampa," by Fernando García and Hernán Ostuni. *Burroughs Bulletin* NS. No. 18: 20-22. April 1994.

OSWALD, INGRID
___ "Sowjetische Science Fiction Literatur als soziologisches Erkenntnismittel," *Osteuropa* 41(4): 393-405. 1991.

OTTEN, KURT
___ **Der englische Roman: Entwurfe der Gegenwart: Ideenroman und Utopie**. Berlin: E. Schmidt, 1990. 243pp. [Not seen.]

OVERSTREET, ROBERT M.
___ **The Overstreet Comic Book Companion: Identification and Price Guide**. 6th edition. New York: Avon, 1992. 591pp.

OVERSTREET, ROBERT M. (continued)
___ **The Overstreet Comic Book Grading Guide**. First edition, by Robert M. Overstreet and Gary M. Carter. New York: Avon, 1992. 303pp.
___ **Overstreet Comic Book Price Guide**. 23rd edition. New York: Avon, 1993. 542pp.

OWENS, FAITH
___ "Sam Spade, Tarzan, and Copyright Law," *SFWA Bulletin* 26(2): 15-17. Summer 1992. (No. 116)

OWER, JOHN
___ "Theology and Evolution in the Short Fiction of Walter M. Miller, Jr.," *Cithara* 25(2): 57-74. May 1986.

OWINGS, MARK
___ **The Science Fantasy Publishers: A Critical and Bibliographic History**, by Jack L. Chalker and Mark Owings. Westminster, MD: Mirage, 1992. 744pp. (Revised Fourth Printing)
___ **The Science Fantasy Publishers: Supplement One, July 1991-June 1992**, by Jack L. Chalker and Mark Owings. Westminster, MD: Mirage Press, 1992. 130pp.

PACCINI, RICCARDO
___ "La 'Fabbrica del Grande Albergo Generale dei Poveri' a Modena (1764-71)," in: Saccaro Del Buffa, Giuseppa and Lewis, Arthur O., eds. **Utopie per gli Anni Ottana.** Rome: Gangemi Editore, 1986. pp.263-274.

PACE, SUE
___ "Exploring Your Science Fiction World," *Writer* 106(9): 9-12. September 1993.

PADEL, O. J.
___ "Some South-Western Sites with Arthurian Associations," in: Bromwich, Rachel, Jarman, A. O. H. and Roberts, Brynley F., eds. **The Arthur of the Welsh**. Cardiff: University of Wales Press, 1991. pp.229-248.

PADOL, LISA
___ "Whose English?: Language in the Modern Arthurian Novel," *Mythlore* 20(4): 20-24. Winter 1995. (Whole No. 78)

PAGE, CAROL
___ **Blood Lust: Conversations with Real Vampires**. New York: HarperCollins, 1991. 192pp.; New York: Dell, 1992. 214pp.

PAGET, STEPHEN
___ "An Interview With Harlan Ellison," *Sense of Wonder* (B. Dalton) pp.10-12. October/November 1993.
___ "An Interview With Harry Harrison," *Sense of Wonder* (B. Dalton) pp.10-12. August/September 1993.
___ "An Interview with Michael Whelan," *Sense of Wonder* (B. Dalton) pp.1-4. October/November 1993.
___ "An Interview With P. N. Elrod," *Sense of Wonder* (B. Dalton) pp.2-4. August/September 1993.

PAGETTI, CARLO
___ "Dick and Meta-SF," in: Mullen, R. D., ed. **On Philip K. Dick: 40 Articles From Science-Fiction Studies**. Terre Haute, IN: SF-TH Inc., 1992. pp.18-25.

PALLMEYER, KARL
___ "The Truth Is Out There: **X-Files** Merchandise Is Hot," *Austin (TX) Business Journal* November 17, 1995. in: *NewsBank. Film and Television* FTV 107: C11. 1995.

PALLY, MARCIA
___ "Moralizing Mars Film's Fantasy (Review)," *Boston (MA) Herald*. May 18, 1992. in: *NewsBank. Film and Television*. 50:E6. 1992.

PALMER, CHRISTOPHER
___ "Philip K. Dick and the Nuclear Family," in: Umland, Samuel J., ed. **Philip K. Dick: Contemporary Critical Interpretations**. Westport, CT: Greenwood, 1995. pp.61-80.
___ "Postmodernism and the Birth of the Author in **VALIS**," in: Mullen, R. D., ed. **On Philip K. Dick: 40 Articles From Science-Fiction Studies**. Terre Haute, IN: SF-TH Inc., 1992. pp.265-274.

PALMER, JERRY
___ **Potboilers: Methods, Concepts and Case Studies in Popular Fiction.** London: Routledge, 1991. 219pp.

PALMER, LORRAINE
___ "Tracking the Monster: **Frankenstein** in an Academic Library," *RSF: Reference Services Review* 20(3): 25-31. Fall 1992.

PALMER, RANDY
___ "Serious Sci-Fi From the British Front: The Quatermass Experience," *Filmfax* No. 37: 68-75. February/March 1993.

PALMER, STEVE
___ "Head over Wheels: Love in SF," *Vector* No. 165: 6-8. February/March 1992

PALUMBO, DONALD E.
___ "The Monomyth in Time Travel Films," in: Morse, Donald E., ed. **The Celebration of the Fantastic.** Westport, CT: Greenwood, 1992. pp.211-218.
___ "The Politics of Entropy: Revolution vs. Evolution in George Pal's 1960 Film Version of H. G. Wells's **The Time Machine,**" in: Latham, Robert A. and Collins, Robert A., eds. **Modes of the Fantastic.** Westport, CT: Greenwood, 1995. pp.204-211.
___ "Psychohistory and Chaos Theory: The 'Foundation Trilogy' and the Fractal Structure of Asimov's Robot--Empire--Foundation," *Journal of the Fantastic in the Arts* 7(1): 23-50. 1996.

PALWICK, SUSAN
___ "Believing (in) Fiction: An Open Letter," *New York Review of Science Fiction* No. 47: 14-15. July 1992. (Replies: No. 50: 18-20. Oct. 1992)
___ "Never Going Home: Failed Fantasy Logic in Kathleen Sidney's **Michael and the Magic Man** and Robert Irwin's **The Limits of Vision,**" *New York Review of Science Fiction* No. 11: 15-17. July 1989.

PANSHIN, ALEXEI
___ "Greater Work and Lesser Work," *New York Review of Science Fiction* No. 42: 16-19. February 1992.
___ "Some Notes on Whig History and Other Approaches to Reality," *New York Review of Science Fiction* No. 41: 15-17. January 1992.
___ "The Sound of Light's Footsteps," *New York Review of Science Fiction* No. 49: 19-23. September 1992.

PAOLINI, LORENZO
___ "L'ereria medevale," in: Colombo, Arrigo and Quarta, Cosimo, eds. **Il Destino della Famiglia nell'Utopia.** Bari: Edizione Dedalo, 1991. pp.79-124.

PAPAJEWSKI, HELMUT
___ "Tolkiens Briefe," in: Kranz, Gisbert, ed. **Inklings: Jahrbuch für Literatur und Ästhetik.** 3. Band. [Lüdenscheid, Germany: Stier], 1985. pp.109-128.

PARADIS, ANDREA
___ "New Dimensions at the National Library," *National Library News* 27(9): 11-14. September 1995.

PARAPETTI, ROBERTO
___ "Restauro e fortuna dell'immaginario: il caso della Torre di Babele," in: Saccaro Del Buffa, Giuseppa and Lewis, Arthur O., eds. **Utopia e Modernita: Teorie e prassi utopiche nell'eta moderna e postmoderna.** Rome: Gangemi Editore, 1989. pp.369-384.

PARENTE, AUDREY
___ **Pulpmaster: The Theodore Roscoe Story.** Mercer Island, WA: Starmont, 1992. 173pp.

PARIS, MICHAEL
___ "Fear of Flying: The Fiction of War, 1886-1916," *History Today* 43: 29-35. June 1993.

PARIS, PHYLLIS
___ "H. G. Wells: Foreseer of the Future," *Stamps* 252(10): 3. September 2, 1995.

PARISI, LUCIANO
___ "Per una storia della fantascienza italiana: Flavia Steno," *Stanford Italian Review* 9(1/2): 105-113. 1990.

PARISI, PAULA
___ "Long Nights and **Strange Days,**" *American Cinematographer* 76(11): 64-68. November 1995.

PARKER, EMMA
___ "You Are What You Eat: The Politics of Eating in the Novels of Margaret Atwood," *Twentieth Century Literature* 41(3): 349-368. Fall 1995.

PARKER, JO A.
___ "Gendering the Robot: Stanislaw Lem's 'The Mask'," *Science-Fiction Studies* 19(2): 178-191. July 1992.

PARKIN-SPEER, DIANE
___ "Almost a Feminist: Robert A. Heinlein," *Extrapolation* 36(2): 113-125. Summer 1995.
___ "Joanna Russ," in: Bruccoli, Matthew J., ed. **Facts on File Bibliography of American Fiction 1919-1988.** New York: Facts on File, 1991. pp.433-434.

PARKS, LOUIS B.
___ "**12 Monkeys:** Plenty of Style, Little Substance," *Houston (TX) Chronicle* January 4, 1996. (Cited from the Internet Edition.)
___ "Adventure Began 30 Years Ago," *Houston (TX) Chronicle.* November 13, 1994. in: *NewsBank. Film and Television.* 125:E1-E2. 1994.
___ "Kirk and Picard Unite for Stellar Enterprise," *Houston (TX) Chronicle.* November 18, 1994. in: *NewsBank. Film and Television.* 125: D13. 1994.
___ "The Long, Great Trek," *Houston (TX) Chronicle* Sec. D, p. 1, 5. September 1, 1992.
___ "Meow! She's the Purr-fect Villain," *Houston (TX) Chronicle.* June 14, 1992. in: *NewsBank. Film and Television.* 62:D12-D13. 1992.
___ "Starfleet Finds New Commander for Series," *Houston (TX) Chronicle* Sec. D, p. 1, 5. September 1, 1992.

PARLA, PAUL
___ "Creature King: From Out of the Black Lagoon, Ben Chapman Walked," by Tom Weaver and Paul Parla. *Starlog* 180: 59-64, 73. July 1992.
___ "The Other Creature," by Tom Weaver and Paul Parla. *Starlog* No. 206: 61-65. September 1994.

PARRINDER, PATRICK
___ "From Mary Shelley to **The War of the Worlds:** The Thames Valley Catastrophe," in: Seed, David, ed. **Anticipations: Essays on Early Science Fiction and Its Precursors.** Liverpool: Liverpool University Press, 1995. pp.58-74.
___ "H. G. Wells and the Fall of Empires," *Foundation* No. 57: 48-58. Spring 1993.
___ "Landscapes of British Science Fiction," in: Slusser, George E. and Rabkin, Eric S., eds. **Styles of Creation: Aesthetic Technique and the Creation of Fictional Worlds.** Athens: University of Georgia Press, 1992. pp.193-204.
___ "Scientists in Science Fiction: Enlightenment and After," *Chung Wai Literary Quarterly* 22(12): May 1994. (Issue not seen; pagination unavailable.) (Reprinted from Garrett, Rhys. ed. **Science Fiction Roots and Branches.** 1990.)
___ **Shadows of the Future: H. G. Wells, Science Fiction and Prophecy.** Liverpool: Liverpool University Press, 1995. 170pp.

PASHKA, LINDA
___ " 'Hunting for Allegories' in the Prose Fantasy of Lord Dunsany," *Studies in Weird Fiction* No. 12: 19-24. Spring 1993.

PASTOURMATZI, DOMNA A.
___ "God as Gameboy: Religion, Science and Creativity," in: Aristotle University of Thessaloniki. **Yearbook of English Studies** n.p.: Aristotle University of Thessaloniki, 1991/1992. pp285-307.
___ **Vivliogrphia epistemonikes phantasias, phantasias, kai tromou, 1960-1993** [Bibliography of Science Fiction, Fantasy and Horror, 1960-1993.]. Athens: Alien, 1995. 245pp.

PATAI, DAPHNE
___ "Gamesmanship and Androcentrism in **Nineteen Eighty-Four**," in: Bloom, Harold, ed. **George Orwell's 1984**. New York: Chelsea House, 1987. pp.47-86.

PATRICK, JAMES
___ "C. S. Lewis and Idealism," in: Walker, Andrew and Patric, James, eds. **A Christian for All Christians**. Washington, DC: Regnery, 1992. pp.156-173.
___ **A Christian for All Christians: Essays in Honor of C. S. Lewis**, by Andrew Walker and James Patrick. Washington, DC: Regnery, 1992. 255pp.

PATROUCH, JOE
___ "Rogue Moon and Me," *Lan's Lantern* No. 41: 69-72. July 1993.

PATSURIS, PENELOPE
___ "Moon Struck," by Jeff Jarvis, James Reston, Jr., Glenn Kenny and Penelope Patsuris. *TV Guide* 42(29): 10-16. July 16, 1994.

PATTERSON, KENT
___ "Confessions of a Mall Rat Writer," *The Report: The Fiction Writer's Magazine* No. 7: 21-22. June 1992.

PATTERSON, NANCY-LOU
___ "A Bloomsbury Blue-Stocking: Dorothy L. Sayers' Bloomsbury Years in Their 'Spatial and Temporal Content'," *Mythlore* 19(3): 6-15. Summer 1993. (No. 73)
___ "Why We Honor the Centenary of Dorothy L. Sayers (1893-1957)," *Mythlore* 19(3): 4-5. Summer 1993. (No. 73)

PATTISON, JIM
___ **Daughter of the Night: A Tanith Lee Bibliography**, by Paul A. Soanes and Jim Pattison. Toronto: Gaffa Press, 1993. 44pp.

PATTON, CHARLES
___ **On Writing Science Fiction and Screenplays**, by Charles Patton and Alan D. Foster. Alexandra, VA: PBS Adult Learning Satellite Service, 1994. 1 Videocassette, 30 minutes.

PAULSEN, STEVEN
___ "Australian Landscapes: Paul Voermans Interviewed," *Interzone* No. 76: 43-45. October 1993.
___ "The Quest for Australian Fantasy," by Sean McMullen and Steven Paulsen. *Aurealis* No. 13: 35-42. 1994.

PAVIA, ROSARIO
___ "Dall'utopia dell'edilizia pubblica: Orgini della cooperazione de abatazione in Italia," in: Saccaro Del Buffa, Giuseppa and Lewis, Arthur O., eds. **Utopie per gli Anni Ottana**. Rome: Gangemi Editore, 1986. pp.379-386.

PAVKOVIC, ALEKSANDAR
___ "Prosperity and Intellectual Needs: The Credibility and Coherence of More's **Utopia**," *Utopian Studies* 4(1): 26-37. 1993.

PAVLAC, DIANA L.
___ "More Than a Bandersnatch: Tolkien as a Collaborative Writer," in: Reynolds, Patricia and GoodKnight, Glen H., eds. **Proceedings of the J. R. R. Tolkien Centenary Conference, Keble College, Oxford, 1992**. Altadena, CA: Mythopoeic Press, 1995. pp.367-374. (*Mythlore* Vol. 21, No. 2, Winter 1996, Whole No. 80)

PAYNE, CRAIG
___ "The Cycle of the Zodiac in John Gardner's Grendel," *Mythlore* 18(4): 61-65. Autumn 1992. (No. 70)
___ "The Redemption of Cain in John Gardner's Grendel," *Mythlore* 18(2): 12-16. Spring 1992. (No. 68)

PAYSON, PATRICIA
___ **Science Fiction: Imagining Worlds**. Tucson, AZ: Zephyr Press, 1994. 84pp. (Zephyr Press Learning Packet)

PEARCY, ROY J.
___ "Fabliau Intervention in Some Mid-Thirteenth Century Arthurian Verse Romances," in: Busby, Keith, ed. **The Arthurian Yearbook I**. New York: Garland, 1991. pp.63-90.

PEARLMAN, CINDY
___ "Captains Quirk," *Chicago* 44(12): December 1995.
___ "Third **Hellraiser** Saga Is a Film for Pinheads (Review)," *Chicago (IL) Sun Times*. September 22, 1992. in: *NewsBank. Film and Television*. 91:A8. 1992.

PECK, BROOKS
___ "On-Demand Printing and Other Dirty Words," *SFWA Bulletin* 29(2): 21-22. Summer 1995. (No. 127)

PECKHAM, ROBERT W.
___ "Rhetoric and the Supernatural in the Novels of Charles Williams," *Renascence* 45(4): 237-246. Summer 1993.

PEDERSEN, MARTIN
___ "Serial From Prodigy to Be Hardcover Book," *Publishers Weekly* 240(7): 18. February 15, 1993.

PEDROTTI, LOUIS
___ "Warfare Celestial and Terrestrial: Osip Senkovsky's 1833 Russian Science Fantasy," in: Slusser, George and Eric S. Rabkin, eds. **Fights of Fancy: Armed Conflict in Science Fiction and Fantasy**. Athens, GA: University of Georgia Press, 1993. pp.49-58.

PEET, JUDY
___ "2000 'Philes' Trek to Convention," *Newark (NJ) Star-Ledger*. November 25, 1995. in: *NewsBank. Film and Television*. 107:C12. 1995.

PEGG, BARRY
___ "Down to Earth: Terrain, Territory, and the Language of Realism in Ursula K. Le Guin's **The Left Hand of Darkness** and **The Dispossessed**," *Michigan Academician* 27(4): 481-492. August 1995.

PEISHEL, BOB
___ "Commercial Spot: Elevator to the Stars," *Cinefex* No. 52: 14-15. November 1992.
___ "Commercial Spot: What's Up, Nike?," *Cinefex* No. 54: 25-26. May 1993.
___ "Quick Cuts: Feline Fabrication," *Cinefex* No. 56: 17-18. November 1993.
___ "Video Beat: **Alien Nation** Revisited," *Cinefex* No. 59: 23-24. September 1994.

PENDERGAST, JOHN S.
___ "A Nation of Hamlets: Shakespeare and Cultural Politics," *Extrapolation* 36(1): 10-17. Spring 1995.

PENDERY, DAVID
___ "Ernest Gimson's Works in Kelmscott," *Journal of the William Morris Society* 10(3): 13-18. Autumn 1993.

PENLEY, CONSTANCE
___ "Sword & Sorcery, S/M, and the Economics of Inadequation: The *Camera Obscura* Interview," by Constance Penley and Sharon Willis. in: Delany, Samuel R. **Silent Interviews on Language, Race, Sex, Science Fiction and Some Comics**. Hanover, NH: Wesleyan University Press, 1994. pp.127-163.

PENNINGTON, JOHN
___ "Alice at the Back of the North Wind, or the Metafictions of Lewis Carroll and George MacDonald," *Extrapolation* 33(1): 59-72. Spring 1992.
___ "Reader Response and Fantasy Literature: The Use and Abuses of Interpretation in **Queen Victoria's Alice in Wonderland**," in: Sanders, Joe, ed. **Functions of the Fantastic**. Westport, CT: Greenwood, 1995. pp.55-66.
___ "Shamanistic Mythmaking: From Civilization to Wilderness in **Watership Down**," *Journal of the Fantastic in the Arts* 6(1): 34-50. 1993.
___ "Textual Doubling and Divided Selves: The Strange Case of Dr. Jekyll and Mary Reilly," *Journal of the Fantastic in the Arts* 6(2/3): 203-216. 1994.

PEPPERS, CATHY
___ "Dialogic Origins and Alien Identities in Butler's **Xenogenesis**," *Science Fiction Studies* 22(1): 47-62. March 1995.

PERCY, WALKER
___ "Walker Percy on Walter M. Miller, Jr.'s **A Canticle for Leibowitz**," in: Madden, David, ed. **Rediscoveries**. New York: Crown, 1971. pp.262-269.

PERENSON, MELISSA J.
___ "Space War," *Sci-Fi Entertainment* 2(3): 66-70. October 1995.

PERERA, F.
___ "Science Fiction Comes to the Classroom: Maelstrom II," by M. J. Martin-Diaz, A. Pizarro, P. Bacas, J. P. Garcia and F. Perera. *Physics Education* 27(1): 18-23. January 1992.

PEREZ, DAN
___ "The **X-Files** Producers Declare Interstellar War With **Space: Above and Beyond**," *Science Fiction Age* 4(1): 22-24, 104. November 1995.
___ "Dan O'Bannon Brings Philip K. Dick's Nightmare Visions to Life in **Screamers**," *Science Fiction Age* 3(6): 18-22, 101. 1995.
___ "FX Wizards Give Dinosaurs Life," *Science Fiction Age* 1(5): 20-21. July 1993.
___ "Spielberg, Ellison, and a New Trek Series Will Bring More SF to TV Viewers," *Science Fiction Age* 1(6): 18-21, 36. September 1993.
___ "**Star Trek**: The Saga Continues," *Science Fiction Age* 2(3): 22-23. March 1994.

PEREZ, YSIDORE R.
___ "The Value of Utopian Thought: A Platonic View," in: Saccaro Del Buffa, Giuseppa and Lewis, Arthur O., eds. **Utopie per gli Anni Ottana**. Rome: Gangemi Editore, 1986. pp.543-552.

PERIGARD, MARK A.
___ " 'TNG' Mission Accomplished," *Boston (MA) Herald*. May 23, 1994. in: NewsBank. Film and Television. 59:B4-B5. 1994.

PERKINS, KEN PARRISH
___ "**Boris and Natasha** Bombs," *Dallas (TX) Morning News*. April 17, 1992. in: NewsBank. Film and Television. 39:B11. 1992.

PEROTTI, STEFANO
___ "Spazio e utopia nelle societa post-industriali," in: Saccaro Del Buffa, Giuseppa and Lewis, Arthur O., eds. **Utopia e Modernita: Teorie e prassi utopiche nell'eta moderna e postmoderna**. Rome: Gangemi Editore, 1989. pp.277-286.

PERRIN, NOEL
___ "A C. S. Lewis Miscellany," *CSL: The Bulletin of the New York C. S. Lewis Society* 23(3): 1-3. January 1992.

PERRON, MIREILLE
___ "The Conversion of Pere Version," by Lorne Falk and Mireille Perron. in: Gray, Chris H., ed. **The Cyborg Handbook**. New York: Routledge, 1995. pp.445-452.

PERRY, ANNE
___ "Dorothy L. Sayers on Dante," in: Dale, Alzina S., ed. **Dorothy L. Sayers: The Centenary Celebration**. New York: Walker, 1993. pp.109-122.

PERRY, BARBARA
___ "Profile: Madeleine L'Engle, a Real Person," *Language Arts* 812-816. October 1977.

PERRY, CLARK
___ "The **Daedalus Encounter** Moves Big-Budget Special Effects Inside Your PC," *Science Fiction Age* 4(1): 100-101. November 1995.

PERRY, JOSEPH W.
___ "Astro Boy: Happy 30th to That Mighty Mechanical Mite," *Filmfax* No. 42: 50-53. December 1993/January 1994.

PERRY, PHYLLIS J.
___ **The World of Water: Linking Fiction to Nonfiction**. Englewood, CO: Teacher Ideas Press, 1995. 149pp.

PERRY, SHARON K.
___ "The Manuscripts and Papers at Fullerton," by Willis E. McNelly and Sharon K. Perry. in: Mullen, R. D., ed. **On Philip K. Dick: 40 Articles From Science-Fiction Studies**. Terre Haute, IN: SF-TH Inc., 1992. pp.xviii-xxiiv.

PERRY, STEVE
___ "Old Enough to Know Better: The Mating Ritual of the Sand Hill Cranes," *The Report: The Fiction Writer's Magazine* 2(6): 5-9. April 1992. (No. 59)

PERRY, THOMAS
___ "Ham and Eggs and Heinlein," *Monad* No. 3: 91-128. September 1993.
___ "Who Broke the Chronoviatmeter," *Monad* No. 2: 51-64. March 1992.

PERSONS, DAN
___ "The **Maxx** (Review)," *Cinefantastique* 26(6)/27(1): 123. October 1995.
___ "**2001: A Space Odyssey**: Post-Production Editing," *Cinefantastique* 25(3): 44-45. June 1994.
___ "**2001: A Space Odyssey**," *Cinefantastique* 25(3): 32-47. June 1994.
___ "**Batman Forever** (Review)," *Cinefantastique* 27(2): 59. November 1995.
___ "**Batman: Mask of the Phantasm** (Review)," *Cinefantastique* 25(3): 60. June 1994.
___ "**Body Snatchers** (Review)," *Cinefantastique* 25(3): 60. June 1994.
___ "**The Bruce Diet** (Review)," *Cinefantastique* 23(2/3): 122. October 1992.
___ "**Buffy the Vampire Slayer** (Review)," *Cinefantastique* 23(4): 60. December 1992.
___ "**Careful** (Review)," *Cinefantastique* 24(6)/25(1): 123. February 1994.
___ "**Careful**," *Cinefantastique* 25(2): 54-55, 61. April 1994.
___ "**Casper**," *Cinefantastique* 26(4): 14-15, 61. June 1995.
___ "Cheap Genius," *Cinefantastique* 23(5): 53. February 1993.
___ "**The Cloning of Joanna May** (Review)," *Cinefantastique* 23(1): 60. August 1992.
___ "**Crumb** (Review)," *Cinefantastique* 26(6)/27(1): 123. October 1995.
___ "**Delicatessen** (Review)," *Cinefantastique* 23(2/3): 122. October 1992.
___ "**Delicatessen** (Review)," *Cinefantastique* 23(4): 59. December 1992.
___ "Dominique Pinon on Clowning in **Delicatessen**," *Cinefantastique* 23(4): 58-59. December 1992.
___ "**Ed Wood** (Review)," *Cinefantastique* 26(3): 59. April 1995.
___ "An Epitaph for **Ren and Stimpy**," *Cinefantastique* 26(6)/27(1): 98-116. October 1995.
___ "**Family Dog** (Review)," *Cinefantastique* 25(2): 59. April 1994.
___ "**The Hudsucker Proxy** (Review)," *Cinefantastique* 25(4): 60. August 1994.
___ "**Johnny Mnemonic** (Review)," *Cinefantastique* 26(6)/27(1): 123. October 1995.
___ "**Judge** (Review)," *Cinefantastique* 26(3): 59-60. April 1995.
___ "**Jumanji**: Book into Film," *Cinefantastique* 27(2): 10. November 1995.
___ "**Jumanji**," *Cinefantastique* 27(2): 8-11. November 1995.
___ "**Kafka**: Steven Soderbergh on Directing," *Cinefantastique* 22(6): 58-59. June 1992
___ "**Kafka**," *Cinefantastique* 22(6): 59. June 1992
___ "**La Blue Girl** (Review)," *Cinefantastique* 27(2): 59. November 1995.
___ "**The Lion King** (Review)," *Cinefantastique* 25(6)/26(1): 122. December 1994.
___ "**Liquid Dreams** (Review)," *Cinefantastique* 23(2/3): 123. October 1992.
___ "**Meteor Man**," *Cinefantastique* 23(6): 12-13. April 1993.
___ "**Mr. Payback** (Review)," *Cinefantastique* 26(5): 59-60. August 1995.
___ "**Naked Lunch**: Cronenberg's Impossible Dream," *Cinefantastique* 22(5): 10-11. April 1992.
___ "**Needful Things** (Review)," *Cinefantastique* 24(6)/25(1): 124. February 1994.
___ "**Nightmare Before Christmas** (Review)," *Cinefantastique* 25(2): 60. April 1994.

PETZOLD, DIETER (continued)
___ "Zwölf Jahre Tolkien-Rezeption in Deutschland, 1980-1991," in: Kranz, Gisbert, ed. **Jahrbuch für Literatur und Ästhetik.** Lüdenscheid, Germany: Stier, 1992. Band 10, pp.241-259.

PEYSER, THOMAS G.
___ "Reproducing Utopia: Charlotte Perkins Gilman and **Herland,**" *Studies in American Fiction* 20(1): 1-16. Spring 1992.

PFAELZER, JEAN
___ "Subjectivity as Feminist Utopia," in: Donawerth, Jane L. and Kolmerten, Carol A., eds. **Utopian and Science Fiction by Women: Worlds of Difference.** Syracuse, NY: Syracuse University Press, 1994. pp.93-106.

PFITZER, GREGORY M.
___ "The Only Good Alien Is a Dead Alien: Science Fiction and the Metaphysics of Indian-Hating on the High Frontier," *Journal of American Culture* 18(1): 51-67. Spring 1995.

PFLUGER, CARL
___ "God vs. the Flying Saucers," *Southwest Review* 78(4): 555-571. Autumn 1993.

PHARR, MARY
___ "Almost Better: Surviving the Plague in Stephen King's **The Stand,**" in: Magistrale, Tony, ed. **A Casebook on The Stand.** San Bernardino, CA: Borgo Press, 1992. pp.1-20.
___ "Different Shops of Horrors: From Roger Corman's Cult Classic to Frank Oz's Mainstream Musical," in: Latham, Robert A. and Collins, Robert A., eds. **Modes of the Fantastic.** Westport, CT: Greenwood, 1995. pp.212-220.
___ "Partners in the Danse: Women in Stephen King's Fiction," in: Magistrale, Tony, ed. **The Dark Descent: Essays Defining Stephen King's Horrorscape.** Westport, CT: Greenwood, 1992. pp.19-32.

PHELPS, GILBERT
___ "The 'Awfulness' of Kingsley Amis," in: Salwak, Dale, ed. **Kingsley Amis in Life and Letters.** New York: St. Martin's, 1990. pp.65-75.

PHILLIPS, JULIE
___ "Feminist Sci-Fi: A Brave New World," *Ms.* 5(3): 70-73. November 1994.

PHILLIPS, MARK
___ "Biology Amok," *Starlog* No. 203: 52-54. June 1994.
___ "Deaths of **The Immortal,** Part Two," by Alain Bourassa and Mark Phillips. *Starlog* No. 186: 67-72, 74. January 1993.
___ "Giant Jellyfish & Alien Invaders (Part 3)," *Starlog* No. 183: 75-81, 72. October 1992.
___ "Giant Jellyfish & Monster Whales (Part 2)," *Starlog* 182: 75-81. September 1992.
___ "Giant Jellyfish and Time-Lost Dinosaurs (Part 1)," *Starlog* 181: 61-66. August 1992.
___ "Good Warrior," *Starlog* No. 174: 68-69. January 1992.
___ "**Immortal** Chaser," *Starlog* No. 188: 20-22, 66. March 1993.
___ "Impossible Magician," *Starlog* No. 218: 69-71. September 1995.
___ "Journeys to Strange Country," *Starlog* No. 206: 66-67. September 1994.
___ "Life in the **Twilight Zone,**" *Starlog* No. 216: 58-61. July 1995.
___ "The Life of Riley," *Starlog* No. 196: 65-69, 79. November 1993.
___ "Lives of **The Immortal,** Part One," by Mark Phillips and Alain Bourassa. *Starlog* 185: 58-62. December 1992.
___ "Nightmares in Color," *Starlog* No. 217: 70-73. August 1995.
___ "Rocket Wrangler," *Starlog* No. 189: 60-62. April 1993.
___ "Space Cadet," *Starlog* No. 212: 62-67. March 1995.
___ "Space Families Found, Part Two," *Starlog* No. 220: 67-72. November 1995.
___ "Space Families Lost, Part One," *Starlog* No. 219: 69-74. October 1995.
___ "Unmasked **Invaders,** Part Two," *Starlog* No. 207: 59-66. October 1994.
___ "Unseen **Invaders,** Part One," *Starlog* No. 206: 21-26, 69. September 1994.
___ "Untouchable Evil," *Starlog* No. 188: 50-53. March 1993.

PHILMUS, ROBERT M.
___ **The Island of Dr. Moreau: A Valorum Text,** by H. G. Wells and Robert M. Philmus. Athens, GA: University of Georgia Press, 1993. 240pp.
___ "The Strange Case of 'Moreau' Gets Stranger," *Science-Fiction Studies* 19(2): 248-250. July 1992.
___ "The Two Faces of Philip K. Dick," *Science Fiction Studies* 18(1): 91-103. March 1991.
___ "The Two Faces of Philip K. Dick," in: Mullen, R. D., ed. **On Philip K. Dick: 40 Articles From Science-Fiction Studies.** Terre Haute, IN: SF-TH Inc., 1992. pp.246-256.

PICCALUGA, GABRIELLA F.
___ "Il pauperismo a Milano nell'eta de Maria Teresa: Utopia e realita," in: Saccaro Del Buffa, Giuseppa and Lewis, Arthur O., eds. **Utopie per gli Anni Ottana.** Rome: Gangemi Editore, 1986. pp.247-262.

PICCOLI, SEAN
___ "How to Run for Congress and Write Sexy Thrillers--Get a Coauthor," *Insight on the News* 11(18): 24. May 8, 1995.
___ "Lock Up the Kids," *Washington (DC) Times.* December 16, 1992. in *NewsBank. Literature.* 1:C7-C8. 1993.

PIERCE, DALE
___ "Horror With a Spanish Twist: Paul Naschy," *Filmfax* No. 33: 68-71, 98. June/July 1992.

PIERCE, HAZEL
___ "Philip K. Dick," in: Bruccoli, Matthew J., ed. **Facts on File Bibliography of American Fiction 1919-1988.** New York: Facts on File, 1991. pp.146-149.

PIERCE, JOHN J.
___ "Introduction: Cordwainer Smith," in: Smith, Cordwainer. **The Rediscovery of Man: The Complete Short Science Fiction of Cordwainer Smith,** ed. by James A. Mann. Framingham, MA: NESFA Press, 1993. pp.viii-xv.
___ "The Literary Experience of Hard Science Fiction," *Science Fiction Studies* 20(2): 176-183. July 1993.
___ **Odd Genre: A Study in Imagination and Evolution.** Westport, CT: Greenwood, 1994. 222pp.

PIERCE, SUSAN
___ "Despite Standard Shock Tactics, **Brainscan** Disturbingly Realistic," *(Little Rock, AR) Arkansas Democrat-Gazette.* April 27, 1994. in: *NewsBank. Film and Television.* 41:B4. 1994.
___ "'Ghost' Full of Used Spooks," *(Little Rock) Arkansas Democrat* pp.1F, 8F. January 5, 1994. in: *NewsBank. Film and Television* 12: A5-A6. 1994.
___ "Giggles, Thrills, a la Stallone," *(Little Rock) Arkasas Democrat.* October 13, 1993. in: *NewsBank. Film and Television.* 114:G2-G3. 1993.
___ "Not Even Liotta's Charm, Skill Can Rescue Violent **No Escape,**" *(Little Rock, AR) Arkansas Democrat-Gazette.* May 4, 1994. in: *NewsBank. Film and Television.* 58:A8. 1994.
___ "Time-Warp Thriller," *(Little Rock AR) Arkansas Democrat-Gazette.* September 21, 1994. in: *NewsBank. Film and Television.* 105:C3. 1994.

PIERCE, TAMORA
___ "Fantasy: Why Kids Read It, Why Kids Need It," *School Library Journal* 39(10): 50-51. October 1993.

PIERCY, MARGE
___ "Telling Stories About Stories," *Utopian Studies* 5(2): 1-3. 1994.

PIESHEL, BOB
___ "Quick Cuts: Hail to the Imposter," *Cinefex* No. 55: 35-36. August 1993.
___ "Video Beat: **Viper** Sheds Its Skin," *Cinefex* No. 58: 85-86. June 1994.

PIFER, ELLEN
___ **The Fifth Child:** Lessing's Subversion of the Pastoral," in: Morse, Donald E., ed. **The Celebration of the Fantastic.** Westport, CT: Greenwood, 1992. pp.123-132.

PIGG, DANIEL
___ "Language as Weapon: The Poetics of Plot in Malory's 'Tale of Sir Gareth'," *Quondam et Futurus* 2(1): 16-27. Spring 1992.

PINSKER, BETH
___ "*Powder*: Offbeat Flick Misses Too Many Beats," *Dallas (TX) Morning News.* October 27, 1995. in: *NewsBank. Film and Television.* 97:G3. 1995.

PINSKY, MICHAEL
___ **Paradise Deferred: Autobiography as Metaphor and the Effacement of Structure in Philip K. Dick.** Master's Thesis, University of South Florida, 1992. 36pp.

PINSKY, MIKE
___ "The Mistaken Mistake: Permutations of the Golem Legend," *Journal of the Fantastic in the Arts* 7(2/3): 215-227. 1995.

PINTARICH, PAUL
___ "Peter Pan Appeal Springs From Ultimate Escape," *Portland (OR) The Oregonian.* December 13, 1991. in: *NewsBank. Film and Television.* 3:E11. 1992.

PIPER, DAVID
___ "Do SF Writers Have Any Responsibility at All?," *Focus* (BSFA) No. 27: 8-9. December 1994/January 1995.

PIRANI, ADAM
___ "An Actor's Life," *Starlog* No. 176: 25-29, 68. March 1992.
___ "Alien Nemesis," by Adam Pirani and Ian Spelling. in: McDonnell, David, ed. **Starlog's Science Fiction Heroes and Heroines.** New York: Crescent Books, 1995. pp.9-11.
___ "In a *Split Second*," *Starlog* 178: 48-51. May 1992.
___ "The New Vulcan Woman," *Starlog* No. 176: 34-37, 68. March 1992.
___ "*Shadowchaser*," *Starlog* 178: 36-39. May 1992.

PISIK, BETSY
___ "Attack of the Brain-Slurping Celluloid," *Washington (DC) Times* Sec. D, p. 1. March 1, 1992.
___ "Batmania! Merchandizers get on Bat-Wagon for Gotham City's Giddy Gold Rush," *Washington (DC) Times.* June 17, 1992. in: *NewsBank. Film and Television.* 62:E7-E8. 1992.

PITMAN, JACK
___ "But Who's Watching Big Brother?," *Variety* p. 2, 84. June 15, 1983.
___ "Perry Sets Remake of Orwell's **1984**," *Variety* p. 4, 27. November 9, 1983.

PITTENGER, MARK
___ "Imagining Genocide in the Progressive Era: The Socialist Science Fiction of George Allan England," *American Studies* 35(1): 91-108. Spring 1994.

PIZARRO, A.
___ "Science Fiction Comes to the Classroom: Maelstrom II," by M. J. Martin-Diaz, A. Pizarro, P. Bacas, J. P. Garcia and F. Perera. *Physics Education* 27(1): 18-23. January 1992.

PIZZELLO, CHRIS
___ "Riding the Movies with Doug Trumbull," *American Cinematographer* 74(8): 53-58. August 1993.

PIZZELLO, STEPHEN
___ "*Batman Forever* Mines Comic-Book Origins," *American Cinematographer* 76(7): 34-44. July 1995.
___ "Energizer Ad Recharges *King Kong*," *American Cinematographer* 75(3): 66-71. March 1994.
___ "*Honey, I Blew Up the Kid*: The Ultimate Baby Boom," *American Cinematographer* 73(9): 68-76. August 1992.
___ "*Interview With the Vampire* Taps New Vein," *American Cinematographer* 76(1): 43-52. January 1995.
___ "TV Sci-Fi Hits Warp Speed With *The Next Generation*," *American Cinematographer* 73(1): 76-87. January 1992.

PLACE, VANESSA
___ "*Jurassic Park*," *Film Comment* 29(5): 8-10. September/October 1993.

PLAMER, RANDY
___ "Hinds Horrors: Forging the Fright Fantastic," *Filmfax* No. 37: 76-81. February/March 1993.

PLANK, ROBERT
___ **George Orwell's Guide Through Hell.** San Bernardino, CA: Borgo, 1995. 136pp.

PLATT, CHARLES
___ "The 'Missing Middle' of Science Fiction," in: Slusser, George E. and Rabkin, Eric S., eds. **Styles of Creation: Aesthetic Technique and the Creation of Fictional Worlds.** Athens: University of Georgia Press, 1992. pp.167-171.
___ "The Carnival of Angst," *Interzone* No. 87: 31-33. September 1994.
___ "Freeze!," *Science Fiction Eye* No. 11: 61-64. December 1992.
___ "In Search of Science Fiction," *Interzone* No. 85: 44-45. July 1994.
___ "Inside Science Fiction: Trading Data With Dead and Digital," *Magazine of Fantasy and Science Fiction* 86(3): 33-39. March 1994.
___ **My Love Affair With Harlan Ellison.** New York: Interactive Systems, 1994. 90pp.
___ "News From the Ghetto: The Teflon Fantasist," *Quantum* No. 43/44: 19-20. Spring/Summer 1993.
___ "The Selling of Science Fiction," *Interzone* No. 89: 46-47. November 1994.
___ "Taking the N out of Entropy," *Science Fiction Eye* No. 13: 30-35. Spring 1994.
___ "The Tenacity of Fiction," *Interzone* No. 91: 44-45. January 1995.
___ "Upstream," *Science Fiction Eye* No. 12: 29-34. Summer 1993.
___ "Who Needs Privacy?," *Science Fiction Eye* No. 10: 69-71. June 1992.
___ "Why Hypertext Doesn't Really Work," *New York Review of Science Fiction* No. 72: 1, 3-5. August 1994.
___ "Wrist Voodoo," *Interzone* No. 83: 41-43. May 1994.

PLATT, DAVID
___ (ed.) **Celluloid Power: Social Film Criticism From *The Birth of a Nation* to *Judgment at Nuremberg*.** Metuchen, NJ: Scarecrow, 1992. 700pp.

PLEITHNER, REGINA
___ "Zwei Mondreisen des 17. Jahrhunderts: Voyages imaginaires oder Reiseutopien? Beitrage zum Kolloquium der Arbeitsgruppe Kultrugeschichte des Barockzeitalters an der Herzog-August-Bibliothek Wolfenbuttle von 10. Bis 12. Juli 1989," in: Pleithner, Regina, ed. **Reisen des Barock: Selbst- und Fremderfahrung und ihre Darstellung.** Bonn: Romanistischer, 1991. pp.75-87.

PLETSCH, CARL
___ "Inventing Arcadia: An Interview With Frederick Turner," by Gerry O'Sullivan and Carl Pletsch. *Humanist* 53(6): 9-18. November/December 1993.

PLOTSKY, RICHARD
___ "News From the Front: The Penultimate Season," in: Van Hise, James, ed. **Trek Celebration Two.** Las Vegas, NV: Pioneer, 1994. pp.156-164.

PLOTZ, RICHARD
___ "Tolkien and I: A Brief Memoir," *Mythlore* 19(1): 41-42. Winter 1993. (No. 71)

POHL, FREDERIK
___ "Edgar Rice Burroughs and the Development of Science Fiction," *Burroughs Bulletin* NS No. 10: 8-14. April 1992.
___ "Essay: A SF Grandmaster Explains How Good Ideas Build Better Stories," *Science Fiction Age* 2(6): 34-37. September 1994.
___ "Extra-Terrestrial Michelangelo," *Science Fiction Age* 1(4): 54-59. May 1993.
___ "The Habit of Writing," *SFWA Bulletin* 29(2): 4-6. Summer 1995. (No. 127)

POHL, FREDERIK (continued)
___ "Monolide: The Imaginative Future," in: Wolf, Milton T. and Mallett, Daryl F., eds. **Imaginative Futures: Proceedings of the 1993 Science Fiction Research Association Conference.** San Bernardino, CA: Jacob's Ladder Books, 1995. pp.9-14.
___ "Pohl Declares a War of the Words," *Chicago Tribune* Sec. 13, p. 5. May 17, 1992.
___ "Pohlemic: Chasing Science," *Science Fiction Chronicle* 14(5): 30-32. February 1993.
___ "Pohlemic: Tender Loving Cons," *Science Fiction Chronicle* 15(10): 36-37. September 1994.
___ "Political Science Fiction," *Locus* 30(1): 32-33, 63-65. January 1993.
___ "The Politics of Prophecy," *Extrapolation* 34(3): 199-208. Fall 1993.
___ "Science Fiction: Stepchild of Science," *Technology Review* 97(7): 57-61. October 1994.
___ "Two-Way Look at the Literature of Change," *New Scientist* 138(1874): 48-49. May 22, 1993
___ "The Uses of the Future," *Futurist* 27(2): 9-12. March-April 1993.
___ "Where Space Travel Went Wrong," *Amazing Stories* 69(1): 88-99. Spring 1994.

POHL, JEANINE
___ "I'm a Doctor, Jim, Not a Television Station Owner," *Juneau (AK) Empire.* January 20, 1995. in: *NewsBank. Film and Television.* 29:F11. 1995.

POINT, MICHAEL
___ "Business on an Astronomical Scale," *Austin (TX) American Statesman* Time Out, p. 5. June 15, 1993.
___ "The Incredible Shrinking Expectations: The Sci-Fi Channel," *Austin (TX) American Statesman.* October 23, 1995. in: *NewsBank. Film and Television.* 98:E10-E11. 1995.

POIVOIR, SALLY
___ "A Sense of Loss in Ten Finely Crafted Stories by Margaret Atwood," *Houston (TX) Chronicle.* December 22, 1991. in *NewsBank. Literature.* 1:C11. 1992.

POLDERVAART, SASKIA
___ "Utopian Socialism in Holland Around 1900: Strategies and Gender," *Utopian Studies* 6(1): 51-64. 1995.

POLLACK, ANDREW
___ "Fantasy Novels About WWII Becoming Popular in Japan," *Austin (TX) American Statesman* Sec. A, p. 17. March 19, 1995.

POLLIN, BURTON R.
___ "Stephen King's Fiction and the Legacy of Poe," *Journal of the Fantastic in the Arts* 5(4): 2-25. 1993. (No. 20)

POLLVOGT, SUSANNAH W.
___ **A Different Sort of Pussycat: Cyborg Subjectivities in Science Fiction Narratives and Their Promise for Feminist Politics.** Thesis (B.A.), Williams College, 1994. 196pp.

PONSEN, ARTI
___ "In a Hole in the Ground: Tolkien and the Emancipation of Fantasy," *Lembas Extra.* [Leiden]: Tolkien Genootschap Unquendor, 1991. [Not seen, cf. *Mythlore.*]

POPE, RANDOLPH D.
___ "Una brecha sobrenatural en **Theoría del conocimiento** de Luis Goytisolo," *Monographis Review* 3(1/2): 129-139. 1987.

POPESCU, GRIGORE A.
___ "Concezioni utopiche verso la meta del l'Ottocento nei Principati Romeni," in: Saccaro Del Buffa, Giuseppa and Lewis, Arthur O., eds. **Utopia e Modernita: Teorie e prassi utopiche nell'eta moderna e postmoderna.** Rome: Gangemi Editore, 1989. pp.919-930.

PORTER, ANDREW
___ "Last of the Big-Time ABA's?," *Science Fiction Chronicle* 15(9): 33-35. August 1994.
___ "Marooned in Miami: The 1993 ABA Convention Report and Photos," *Science Fiction Chronicle* 14(11): 34-37. August 1993.

PORTER, ANDREW (continued)
___ "My Conadian Report," *Science Fiction Chronicle* 16(3): 33-34. January 1995.

PORTER, ANDY
___ "SF Gleanings at the 1992 ABA Convention," *Science Fiction Chronicle* 13(11/12): 44-48. August 1992.

PORTER, LAURENCE M.
___ "Feminist Fantasy and Open Structure in Monique Wittig's **Les Guérillères**," in: Morse, Donald E., ed. **The Celebration of the Fantastic.** Westport, CT: Greenwood, 1992. pp.261-270.
___ "Psychomachia versus Socialism in **Nineteen Eighty-Four**," in: Rose, Jonathan, ed. **The Revised Orwell.** East Lansing, MI: Michigan State University Press, 1992. pp.61-74.

PORTER, RICHARD
___ "Kingsley in Nashville," in: Salwak, Dale, ed. **Kingsley Amis in Life and Letters.** New York: St. Martin's, 1990. pp.36-39.

PORUSH, DAVID
___ "Frothing the Synaptic Bath: What Puts the Punk in Cyberpunk?," in: Slusser, George E. and Shippey, Tom, eds. **Fiction 2000: Cyberpunk and the Future of Narrative.** Athens: University of Georgia Press, 1992. pp.246-261.
___ "Literature as Dissipative Structure: Prigogine's Theory and the Postmodern 'Chaos' Machine," in: Greenberg, Mark L. and Schachterle, Lance, eds. **Literature and Technology.** Bethlehem, PA: Lehigh University Press, 1992. pp.275-306.

POSPISIL, IVO
___ "Horce ironicka science fiction Faddeje Bulgarina," *Svet Literatury: Casopis pro Novoveke Zahranicni Literatury* (Amsterdam, Netherlands) 5: 22-28. 1993.

POST, JONATHAN V.
___ "Future Spacecraft Sensors," *Quantum* No. 41: 23-26. Winter/Spring 1992.
___ "In Space: Past, Present and Possible Futures," by Jonathan V. Post and Donald D. Rose. *Quantum* No. 43/44: 44-48. Spring/Summer 1993.

POULTON, CODY
___ "The Grotesque and the Gothic: Izumi Kyoka's Japan," *Japan Quarterly* 41(3): 324-35. July 1994.

POUNCEY, EDWIN
___ "In the Hall of the Monster King: Music and the Maestro of Horror," in: Jones, Stephen, ed. **James Herbert: By Horror Haunted.** London: New English Library, 1992. pp.209-216.

POURNELLE, JERRY
___ "The Future Isn't What It Used to Be, But Then, Maybe It Never Was," *Science Fiction Age* 1(1): 22, 70. November 1992.
___ "Speech: Robert A. Heinlein," in: Kondo, Yoji, ed. **Requiem: New Collected Works by Robert A. Heinlein and Tributes to the Grand Master.** New York: Tor, 1992. pp.227-228.

POURROY, JANINE
___ "The Board Game Jungle," *Cinefex* No. 64: 54-71. December 1995.
___ "Heart of Darkness," *Cinefex* No. 53: 22-53. February 1993.
___ "Making Gump Happen," *Cinefex* No. 60: 90-107. December 1994.
___ "Quick Cuts: Unfriendly Skies," *Cinefex* No. 54: 9-10. May 1993.

POURTEAU, CHRIS
___ "The Individual and Society: Narrative Structure and Thematic Unity in Stephen King's **Rage**," *Journal of Popular Culture* 27(1): 171-178. Summer 1993.
___ "Lester del Rey," in: Bruccoli, Matthew J., ed. **Facts on File Bibliography of American Fiction 1919-1988.** New York: Facts on File, 1991. pp.142-143.

POWELL, ANTHONY
___ "Amis Country," in: Salwak, Dale, ed. **Kingsley Amis in Life and Letters.** New York: St. Martin's, 1990. pp.6-10.

POWER, DAVID
___ **David Lindsay's Vision.** Nottingham: Pauper's Press, 1991. 36pp.

PRANSKY, JOANNE
___ "Social Adjustments to a Robotic Future," in: Wolf, Milton T. and Mallett, Daryl F., eds. **Imaginative Futures: Proceedings of the 1993 Science Fiction Research Association Conference**. San Bernardino, CA: Jacob's Ladder Books, 1995. pp.137-146.

PRATCHETT, TERRY
___ "Kevins," *The Author* pp.132-133. Winter 1993.
___ "Let There Be Dragons," *Science Fiction Chronicle* 15(1): 5, 28-29. October 1993.
___ "Let There Be Dragons," *The Bookseller* p. 60-62. June 11, 1993.

PRESCOTT, MARY
___ "Beyond Words: The Impact of Rhythm as Narrative Technique in **The Left Hand of Darkness**," by Nora Barry and Mary Prescott. *Extrapolation* 33(2): 154-165. Summer 1992.

PRESS, JON
___ "William Morris and the Royal Commission on Technical Instruction, 1881-84," by Charles Harvey and Jon Press. *Journal of the William Morris Society* 11(1): 31-43. Autumn 1994.

PREUSS, PAUL
___ "Loopholes in the Net: Ruminations on Hard SF; **Furious Gulf** by Gregory Benford," *New York Review of Science Fiction* No. 75: 1, 10-11. November 1994.

PREVOS, ANDRE J. M.
___ "A Comment About the Utopian Character of the Afro-American Blues," in: Saccaro Del Buffa, Giuseppa and Lewis, Arthur O., eds. **Utopia e Modernita: Teorie e prassi utopiche nell'eta moderna e postmoderna**. Rome: Gangemi Editore, 1989. pp.1013-1018.
___ "Planning and Building the Utopian Village: The Icarian Settlements in Iowa, 1853-1898," in: Saccaro Del Buffa, Giuseppa and Lewis, Arthur O., eds. **Utopia e Modernita: Teorie e prassi utopiche nell'eta moderna e postmoderna**. Rome: Gangemi Editore, 1989. pp.971-986.

PRICE, BEVERLY
___ "Sheri S. Tepper and Feminism's Future," *Mythlore* 18(2): 41-44. Spring 1992. (No. 68)

PRICE, MICHAEL
___ "Nimoy Starts Comics Series," *San Francisco (CA) Chronicle* November 19, 1994. (Cited from the Internet Edition.)

PRICE, ROBERT M.
___ "August Derleth: Myth-Maker," in: Price, Robert M., ed. **Black Forbidden Things**. Mercer Island, WA: Starmont, 1992. pp.72-73.
___ "A Biblical Antecedent for 'The Colour out of Space'," *Lovecraft Studies* No. 25: 23-25. Fall 1991.
___ "Chariots of the Old Ones?," by Robert M. Price and Charles Garofalo. in: Price, Robert M., ed. **Black Forbidden Things**. Mercer Island, WA: Starmont, 1992. pp.86-87.
___ "Cosmic Fear and the Fear of the Lord: Lovecraft's Religious Vision," in: Price, Robert M., ed. **Black Forbidden Things**. Mercer Island, WA: Starmont, 1992. pp.78-85.
___ "The Last Vestige of the Derleth Mythos," *Lovecraft Studies* No. 24: 20-21. Spring 1991.
___ **Lin Carter: A Look Behind His Imaginary Worlds**. Mercer Island, WA: Starmont, 1992. 172pp.
___ "Lovecraft and 'Ligeia'," *Lovecraft Studies* No. 31: 15-17. Fall 1994.
___ "Lovecraftianity and the Pagan Revival," in: Price, Robert M., ed. **Black Forbidden Things**. Mercer Island, WA: Starmont, 1992. pp.74-77.
___ "The Pseudo-Intellectula in Weird Fiction," in: Price, Robert M., ed. **Black Forbidden Things**. Mercer Island, WA: Starmont, 1992. pp.69-71.
___ "Randolph Carter, Warlord of Mars," in: Price, Robert M., ed. **Black Forbidden Things**. Mercer Island, WA: Starmont, 1992. pp.66-68.
___ "Thomas Ligotti's Gnostic Quest," *Studies in Weird Fiction* No. 9: 27-31. Spring 1991.
___ (ed.) **Black Forbidden Things: Cryptical Secrets From the Crypt of Cthulhu**. Mercer Island, WA: Starmont, 1992. 199pp.

PRICKETT, STEPHEN
___ "Centering the Margins: Postmodernism and Fantasy," in: Filmer, Kath, ed. **Twentieth-Century Fantasists: Essays in Culture, Society and Belief in Twentieth Century Mythopoeic Literature**. New York: St. Martin's, 1992. pp.183-192.

PRIEST, CHRISTOPHER
___ "Out of the Temple," *Interzone* No. 86: 37-39. August 1994.
___ "Pax Ortygia," *Interzone* No. 88: 52. October 1994.

PRIESTMAN, JUDITH
___ **J. R. R. Tolkien: Life and Legend**. Oxford: Bodleian Library, 1992. 96pp.

PRINGLE, DAVID
___ "Bob Shaw: An Annotated Bibliography," *Interzone* No. 67: 4-5. January 1993.
___ "Fact and Fiction in J. G. Ballard's **The Kindness of Women**," *J G B News* No. 20: 1-6. August 1993.
___ **Imaginary People: A Who's Who of Modern Fictional Characters**. New York: World Almanac, 1987. 509pp.
___ "SF, Fantasy & Horror Movie Novelizations," *Interzone* No. 80: 38-52. February 1994.
___ "The Sonic Sculptor: William Spencer Interviewed," *Interzone* No. 79: 42-46. January 1994.
___ "Sweated Labour? The Women in Fantasy," *Interzone* No. 60: 32. June 1992.
___ **The Ultimate Guide to Science Fiction: An A-Z of Science Fiction Books by Title**. Second edition. Aldershot, Eng.: Scolar Press, 1995. 481pp.

PRINZ, JESSICA
___ "Spalding Gray's **Swimming to Cambodia**: A Performance Gesture," in: Murphy, Patrick D., ed. **Staging the Impossible: The Fantastic Mode in Modern Drama**. Westport, CT: Greenwood, 1992. pp.156-168.

PRITCHARD, WILLIAM H.
___ "Entertaining Amis," in: Salwak, Dale, ed. **Kingsley Amis in Life and Letters**. New York: St. Martin's, 1990. pp.173-182.

PROBST, CHRIS
___ "Cyberthriller Comes of Age," *American Cinematographer* 76(10): 88-96. October 1995.
___ "Darkness Descends on **The X-Files**," *American Cinematographer* 76(6): 28-32. June 1995.
___ "Incredible Shrinking 'Indian' Effects," by Ron Magid and Chris Probst. *American Cinematographer* 76(8): 68-69. August 1995.
___ "**Indian in the Cupboard**'s Cinematic Intimacy," *American Cinematographer* 76(8): 62-67. August 1995.

PROCTOR, MEL
___ **The Official Fan's Guide to The Fugitive**. Stamford, CT: Longmeadow, 1994. 185pp.

PROIETTI, SALVATOR
___ "Frederick Philip Grove's Version of Pastoral Utopianism," *Science-Fiction Studies* 19(3): 361-377. November 1992.

PROKOP, TIM
___ "Closeup: Adding Teeth to **Wolf**," *Cinefex* No. 59: 97-106. September 1994.
___ "Launching **Apollo 13**," *Cinefex* No. 63: 85-85. September 1995.
___ "The Making of a 50-Foot Woman," *Cinefex* No. 57: 26-41. March 1994.
___ "Quick Cuts: A New Twist on Tornadoes," *Cinefex* No. 61: 11-12. March 1995.
___ "**The Shadow**: Making Mr. Shadow," *Cinefantastique* 25(4): 24-25. August 1994.
___ "**The Shadow**: Matte Painting Beyond the Backlot," *Cinefantastique* 25(4): 40-41. August 1994.
___ "**The Shadow**: Miniaturizing New York," *Cinefantastique* 25(4): 42-43. August 1994.
___ "**The Shadow**: Special Effects Computer Graphics," *Cinefantastique* 25(4): 32-32. August 1994.
___ "**The Shadow**: Superhero Merchandising," *Cinefantastique* 25(4): 39. August 1994.
___ "**The Shadow**: The Art of Makeup," *Cinefantastique* 25(4): 36-37. August 1994.
___ "**Star Trek: Deep Space Nine**: Ferengi Stardom," *Cinefantastique* 25(6)/26(1): 110. December 1994.
___ "**Star Trek: Deep Space Nine**: Special Effects," *Cinefantastique* 25(6)/26(1): 99-102. December 1994.

PROKOP, TIM

PROKOP, TIM (continued)
___ "**Star Trek: Deep Space Nine**: The Alternate," *Cinefantastique* 25(6)/26(1): 106-107. December 1994.
___ "**Star Trek: Deep Space Nine**: The Jem'Hadar," *Cinefantastique* 25(6)/26(1): 106-107. December 1994.
___ "**Star Trek: The Next Generation**: Curry's Heroes," *Cinefantastique* 25(6)/26(1): 92-93. December 1994.
___ "**Star Trek: The Next Generation**: Low Tech Effects," *Cinefantastique* 25(6)/26(1): 90-91. December 1994.
___ "**Star Trek: The Next Generation**: Painting for the Future," *Cinefantastique* 25(6)/26(1): 70-73. December 1994.
___ "**Star Trek: The Next Generation**: Shot by Shot," *Cinefantastique* 25(6)/26(1): 64-69. December 1994.
___ "**Star Trek: The Next Generation**: Special Visual Effects," *Cinefantastique* 25(6)/26(1): 52-63, 124. December 1994.
___ "**Stargate**: CGI Effects," *Cinefantastique* 26(3): 50. April 1995.
___ "**Stargate**: Makeup Design," *Cinefantastique* 25(6)/26(1): 30. December 1994.
___ "**Stargate**: Production Design," *Cinefantastique* 25(6)/26(1): 32-33. December 1994.
___ "**Stargate**: Production Design," *Cinefantastique* 26(3): 52-53. April 1995.
___ "**Stargate**: Special Effects," *Cinefantastique* 25(6)/26(1): 35. December 1994.
___ "**Stargate**," *Cinefantastique* 25(5): 46-47. October 1994.
___ "**Stargate**," *Cinefantastique* 25(6)/26(1): 28-35, 125. December 1994.
___ "**Stargate**," *Cinefantastique* 26(3): 48-53. April 1995.

PROTHERO, JAMES
___ "Lewis's Poetry: A Preliminary Exploration," *Bulletin of the New York C. S. Lewis Society* 25(5/6): 2-6. March/April 1994.

PROULX, KEVIN
___ **Fear to the World: Eleven Voices in a Chorus of Horror**. Mercer Island, WA: Starmont, 1992. 243pp.

PROUTY, WILLIAM
___ " **The Tempest**: Shakespeare's Anti-Utopia Tract," in: Saccaro Del Buffa, Giuseppa and Lewis, Arthur O., eds. **Utopie per gli Anni Ottana**. Rome: Gangemi Editore, 1986. pp.579-586.

PTACEK, KATHRYN
___ "A Tale of Cash Flow," by Kathryn Ptacek and Ashley McConnell. *The Report: The Fiction Writer's Magazine* No. 11: 9-11. Summer 1993.
___ "You Are What You Eat/Watch: Cannibalism in Movies," in: Golden, Christopher, ed. **Cut! Horror Writers on Horror Film**. New York: Berkley, 1992. pp.183-188.

PUJADE, ROBERT
___ "Erotisme et fantastique en photographie," in: Bozzetto, Roger, ed. **Eros: Science & Fiction Fantastique**. Aix-en-Provence: Universite de Provence, 1991. pp.107-131.

PUJIA, ROBERTO
___ "La scienza luciferian. Monismo metodologico ed utopia nella epistemologia moderna," in: Saccaro Del Buffa, Giuseppa and Lewis, Arthur O., eds. **Utopie per gli Anni Ottana**. Rome: Gangemi Editore, 1986. pp.107-121.
___ "Scienza, Utopia scientista e satira nell'Inghilterra dell'eta augustea: l'antifilosofia di J. Swift," in: Saccaro Del Buffa, Giuseppa and Lewis, Arthur O., eds. **Utopia e Modernita: Teorie e prassi utopiche nell'eta moderna e postmoderna**. Rome: Gangemi Editore, 1989. pp.877-890.

PURDON, LIAM O.
___ "Hollywood's Myopic Medievalism: *Excalibur* and Malory's **Morte d'Arthur**," by Liam O. Purdon and Robert J. Blanch. in: Slocum, Sally K., ed. **Popular Arthurian Traditions**. Bowling Green, OH: Popular Press, 1992. pp.156-161.

PURINTON, MARJEAN D.
___ "Ideological Revision: Cross-Gender Characterization in Mary Shelley's **Frankenstein**," *CEA Critic* 56(1): 53-64. Fall 1993.

PURKIS, JOHN
___ "Morris and Traditional Storytelling," *Journal of the William Morris Society* 11(1): 16-18. Autumn 1994.

PURTILL, RICHARD L.
___ "Did C. S. Lewis Lose His Faith?," in: Walker, Andrew and Patric, James, eds. **A Christian for All Christians**. Washington, DC: Regnery, 1992. pp.27-62.

PUSCHMANN-NALENZ, BARBARA
___ **Science Fiction and Postmodern Fiction: A Genre Study**. New York: Peter Lang, 1992. 268pp. (Trans. of **Science Fiction und Ihre Grenzberieche**.)

PUTZIER, MARY G.
___ **Mary Wollstonecraft Shelley and the Creation of Science Fiction**. Master's Thesis, Eastern Washington University, 1995. 113pp.

QUARTA, COSIMO
___ "Le regioni della conservazione: Thomas More," in: Colombo, Arrigo and Quarta, Cosimo, eds. **Il Destino della Famiglia nell'Utopia**. Bari: Edizione Dedalo, 1991. pp.193-221.
___ **Thomas More: Testimone della pace e della coscienza**. n.p.: Edizioni Cultura dell Pace, 1993. 231pp. [Not seen.]
___ **Tommaso Moro: una reinterpretazone dell'Utopia'**. Bari: Edizioni Dedalo, 1991. 434pp. [Not seen.]
___ (ed.) **Il Destino della Famiglia nell'Utopia**, ed. by Arrigo Colombo and Cosimo Quarta. Bari: Edizioni Dedalo, 1991. 454pp.

QUARTERMAINE, PETER
___ "Margaret Atwood's **Surfacing**: Strange Familiarity," in: Nicholson, Colin, ed. **Margaret Atwood: Writing and Subjectivity: New Critical Essays**. New York: St. Martin's, 1994. pp.119-132.

QUINN, JULIE
___ "Paul S. Farkas," *Nevada Magazine* 48: 58-50. March/April 1988.

QUINN, MICHELLE
___ "The Fans: Isolated Loonies or Crest of a New Wave (Review)," *Los Angeles (CA) Times*. August 9, 1992. in: *NewsBank. Film and Television*. 83:D1-D2. 1992.

QUISTELLI, ANTONIO
___ "L'utopia nella condizione post-moderna: un commento con immagini di Soleri e di Moebius," in: Saccaro Del Buffa, Giuseppa and Lewis, Arthur O., eds. **Utopie per gli Anni Ottana**. Rome: Gangemi Editore, 1986. pp.11-14.
___ "Una pietra per il futuro," in: Saccaro Del Buffa, Giuseppa and Lewis, Arthur O., eds. **Utopia e Modernita: Teorie e prassi utopiche nell'eta moderna e postmoderna**. Rome: Gangemi Editore, 1989. pp.11-12.

RABIG, ANTHONY
___ **Science Fiction: An Introduction for Librarians**. Master's Thesis, Emporia State College, Kansas, 1974. 127pp.

RABKIN, ERIC S.
___ "Forms of Future Fiction," *ANQ* 5(4): 236-239. November 1992.
___ "Imagination and Survival: The Case of Fantastic Literature," *Foundation* No. 56: 84-98. Autumn 1992. (Letter of comment: K. V. Bailey, *Foundation* No. 58: 85-87. Summer 1993.)
___ "Irrational Expectations: Or, How Economics and the Post-Industrial World Failed Philip K. Dick," in: Mullen, R. D., ed. **On Philip K. Dick: 40 Articles From Science-Fiction Studies**. Terre Haute, IN: SF-TH Inc., 1992. pp.178-187.
___ "The Male Body in Science Fiction," *Michigan Quarterly Review* 33(1): 203-216. Winter 1994.
___ "Reimagining War," in: Slusser, George and Eric S. Rabkin, eds. **Fights of Fancy: Armed Conflict in Science Fiction and Fantasy**. Athens, GA: University of Georgia Press, 1993. pp.12-25.
___ **Science Fiction: The Literature of the Technological Imagination**. Springfield, VA: The Teaching Company, 1994. 2 videocassettes, 380 minutes.
___ "Undecidability and Oxymoronism," in: Slusser, George E. and Shippey, Tom, eds. **Fiction 2000: Cyberpunk and the Future of Narrative**. Athens: University of Georgia Press, 1992. pp.262-278.
___ "The Utopian Paradox: On the Necessity of an Impossible Dream," *Foundation* No. 55: 57-65. Summer 1992.

RABKIN, ERIC S. (continued)
___ "Wars Old and New: The Changing Nature of Fictional Combat," by George E. Slusser and Eric S. Rabkin. in: Slusser, George and Eric S. Rabkin, eds. **Fights of Fancy: Armed Conflict in Science Fiction and Fantasy**. Athens, GA: University of Georgia Press, 1993. pp.1-11.
___ "What Makes **We** a Science Fiction Classic? What Makes a Classic?," *Foundation* No. 65: 50-61. Autumn 1995.
___ (ed.) **Fights of Fancy: Armed Conflict in Science Fiction and Fantasy**, ed. by George E. Slusser and Eric S. Rabkin. Athens, GA: University of Georgia Press, 1993. 223pp.
___ (ed.) **Styles of Creation: Aesthetic Technique and the Creation of Fictional Worlds**, ed. by George E. Slusser and Eric S. Rabkin. Athens: University of Georgia Press, 1992. 271pp.

RABKIN, WILLIAM
___ "*Cocoon* (1985): Interview with Tom Benedek," in: Goldberg, Lee et al. **Science Fiction Filmmaking in the 1980s**. Jefferson, NC: McFarland, 1995. pp.73-78.
___ **The Dreamweavers: Interviews with Fantasy Filmmakers of the 1980s**, by Lee Goldberg, Randy Lofficier, Jean-Marc Lofficier and William Rabkin. Jefferson, NC: McFarland, 1995. 320pp.
___ "*Enemy Mine* (1985): Interview with Wolfgang Petersen," in: Goldberg, Lee et al. **Science Fiction Filmmaking in the 1980s**. Jefferson, NC: McFarland, 1995. pp.111-132.
___ (ed.) **Science Fiction Filmmaking in the 1980s: Interviews with Actors, Directors, Producers and Writers**, ed. by Lee Goldberg, Randy Lofficier, Jean-Marc Lofficier and William Rabkin. Jefferson, NC: McFarland, 1995. 279pp.

RABY, PETER
___ **Samuel Butler: A Biography**. Iowa City: University of Iowa Press, 1991. 334pp.

RACHMAN, STEPHEN
___ " 'Es lasst sich nicht scrieben': Plagiarism and 'The Man in the Crowd'," in: Rosenheim, Shawn and Rachman, Stephen, ed. **The American Face of Edgar Allan Poe**. Baltimore: Johns Hopkins University Press, 1995. pp.49-90.
___ "Introduction: Beyond 'The Problem of Poe'," by Shawn Rosenheim and Stephen Rachman. in: Rosenheim, Shawn and Rachman, Stephen, eds. **The American Face of Edgar Allan Poe**. Baltimore, MD: Johns Hopkins University Press, 1995. pp.ix-xx.
___ (ed.) **The American Face of Edgar Allan Poe**, ed. by Shawn Rosenheim and Stephen Rachman. Baltimore, MD: Johns Hopkins University Press, 1995. 364pp.

RADICE, SOPHIE
___ "A Horror Story at Bedtime," *Guardian* p. G2, G8. January 4, 1994. [Not seen.]

RADIN, DARLENE M.
___ **The Human and Computer Relationship: A Vehicle for Character Metamorphosis in Fictive Literature**. Ph.D. Dissertation, University of Massachusetts, Amherst, 1992. 167pp.

RADISICH, PAULA R.
___ "Evolution and Salvation: The Iconic Origins of Druillet's Monstrous Combatants of the Night," in: Slusser, George and Eric S. Rabkin, eds. **Fights of Fancy: Armed Conflict in Science Fiction and Fantasy**. Athens, GA: University of Georgia Press, 1993. pp.103-113.

RADNER, JOHN B.
___ "The Fall and Decline: **Gulliver's Travels** and the Failure of Utopia," *Utopian Studies* 3(2): 50-74. 1992.

RAFF, MELVIN
___ "The Structure of **A Voyage to Arcturus**," *Studies in Scottish Literature* 15: 262-268. 1980.

RAFFEL, BURTON
___ "Genre to the Rear, Race and Gender to the Fore: The Novels of Octavia E. Butler," *Literary Review* 38(3): 454-461. Spring 1995.
___ "Translating **Yvain** and **Sir Gawain and the Green Knight** for Classroom Use," in: Fries, Maureen and Watson, Jeanie, eds. **Approaches to the Teaching of the Arthurian Tradition**. New York: Modern Language Association, 1992. pp.88-93.

RAGLAND, ELLIE
___ "Psychoanalysis and Courtly Love," *Arthuriana* 5(1): 1-20. Spring 1995.

RAHN, B. J.
___ "Marriage of True Minds," in: Dale, Alzina S., ed. **Dorothy L. Sayers: The Centenary Celebration**. New York: Walker, 1993. pp.51-66.

RAHR, DAVID
___ "Special Effects Overshadow *Timecop* Story," (Santa Fe, NM) *New Mexican*. September 23, 1994. in: *NewsBank. Film and Television*. 105: D6. 1994.

RAIN, LENORA
___ "Interview: Bill Ransom," by Lenora Rain and Lee Good. *Westwind* No. 183: 13-16. December 1993.

RAK, MICHELE
___ "Il modello sporco: la sociata letteraria tra l'invenzione del libro a stampa e i media elettronici," in: Saccaro Del Buffa, Giuseppa and Lewis, Arthur O., eds. **Utopia e Modernita: Teorie e prassi utopiche nell'eta moderna e postmoderna**. Rome: Gangemi Editore, 1989. pp.569-586.

RAMEY, ANTHONY H.
___ **Postmodernism and the Apocalyptic in Bradbury's Fiction Exposing the Eroding Aesthetic**. Master's Thesis, Marshall University, 1995. 73pp.

RAMIREZ, JUAN-ANTONIO
___ "La modernidad perfecta de la Isla-Maquina," in: Saccaro Del Buffa, Giuseppa and Lewis, Arthur O., eds. **Utopia e Modernita: Teorie e prassi utopiche nell'eta moderna e postmoderna**. Rome: Gangemi Editore, 1989. pp.467-500.

RAMPAS, ZDENEK
___ **Kdo je Kdo v ceské a slovenské science fiction**, by Zdenek Rampas and Pavel Kosatik. Praha, CZ: Ceskoslovenského fandomu, 1994. 84pp. [Not seen.]

RAMPTON, DAVID
___ "Into the Secret Chamber: Art and the Artist in Kurt Vonnegut's **Bluebeard**," *Critique* 35(1): 16-26. Fall 1993.

RAMSLAND, KATHERINE
___ "*Angel Heart*: The Journey to Self as the Ultimate Horror," in: Golden, Christopher, ed. **Cut! Horror Writers on Horror Film**. New York: Berkley, 1992. pp.189-198.
___ **The Anne Rice Trivia Book**. New York: Ballantine, 1994. 244pp.
___ **The Vampire Companion: The Official Guide to Anne Rice's The Vampire Chronicles**. Revised edition. New York: Ballantine, 1995. 581pp.
___ **The Vampire Companion: The Official Guide to Anne Rice's The Vampire Chronicles**. New York: Ballantine, 1993. 512pp.
___ **The Witches' Companion: The Official Guide to Anne Rice's Lives of the Mayfair Witches**. New York: Ballantine, 1994. 540pp.

RAND, KEN
___ "Epic Courtship," *Starlog* No. 202: 56-58. May 1994.
___ "How to Make Your Tape Recorder Work for You," *The Report: The Fiction Writer's Magazine* No. 10: 21. Summer 1993.
___ "SFC Interview: Talking With the Real Lois McMaster Bujold," *Science Fiction Chronicle* 17(1): 7, 37-40. October/November 1995

RANDLES, JENNY
___ **Looking for the Aliens: A Psychological, Imaginative and Scientific Investigation**, by Peter Hough and Jenny Randles. London: Blandford, 1992. 241pp.

RANGEL, JAVIER
___ "De lo fantástico a lo alegórico: El llamado a la resistencia en **The Shrunken Head of Pancho Villa**," *Mester* (UCLA) 19(2): 123-136. Fall 1990.

RANSOM, AMY J.
___ **The Feminine as Fantastic in the Conte Fantastique: Visions of the Other.** New York: P. Lang, 1995. 280pp.
___ **Visions of the Other: The Feminine as Fantastic in the Conte Fantastique.** Ph.D. Dissertation, University of Minnesota, 1993. 286pp.

RAO, ELEONORA
___ "Margaret Atwood's **Lady Oracle**: Writing Against Notions of Unity," in: Nicholson, Colin, ed. **Margaret Atwood: Writing and Subjectivity: New Critical Essays.** New York: St. Martin's, 1994. pp.133-152.
___ **Strategies for Identity: The Fiction of Margaret Atwood.** New York: P. Lang, 1993. 203pp.

RAPISARDA, GIUSI M. L.
___ "l'Utopia del saggismo, l'immagine della stanza chiara'". in: Saccaro Del Buffa, Giuseppa and Lewis, Arthur O., eds. **Utopia e Modernita: Teorie e prassi utopiche nell'eta moderna e postmoderna.** Rome: Gangemi Editore, 1989. pp.945-950.
___ "Superuomisnmo macchinista, utopie e mito del moderno nella letteratura europea inizio Novecento," in: Saccaro Del Buffa, Giuseppa and Lewis, Arthur O., eds. **Utopie per gli Anni Ottana.** Rome: Gangemi Editore, 1986. pp.693-704.

RASKIN, JONAH
___ "The Inadequacy of the Imagination (Interview, 1970)," in: Ingersoll, Earl G., ed. **Doris Lessing: Conversations.** Princeton, NJ: Ontario Review Press, 1994. pp.13-18.

RATHBONE, WENDY
___ **Trek: The Encyclopedia.** 'Unofficial and Uncensored', by Hal Schuster and Wendy Rathbone. Las Vegas, NV: Pioneer, 1994. 229pp.
___ **Trek: The Unauthorized A-Z,** by Hal Schuster and Wendy Rathbone. New York: Harper Prism, 1995. 576pp. (Mass market edition of the 1994 Pioneer Books title **Trek: The Encyclopedia**).

RAULET, GERARD
___ "360 Degrees in Time: Postmodern Architecture and the Question of Consensus," **Utopian Studies** 4(2): 57-65. 1993.
___ "Fin de l'utopie ou nouvelle utopie? Reflexions sur la condition post-moderne," in: Saccaro Del Buffa, Giuseppa and Lewis, Arthur O., eds. **Utopia e Modernita: Teorie e prassi utopiche nell'eta moderna e postmoderna.** Rome: Gangemi Editore, 1989. pp.111-127.

RAVENSCROT, ANTHONY
___ "Convention Art Shows: Seen as the East Wing of Hell," *Lan's Lantern* No. 40: 123-124. September 1992.

RAWLS, MELANIE A.
___ "The Verse of J. R. R. Tolkien," *Mythlore* 19(1): 4-8. Winter 1993. (No. 71)

RAYNS, TONY
___ "*Cite des enfants perdus, La* (Review)," *Sight and Sound* 5(9): 48-49. September 1995.

READ, MALCOLM K.
___ **Jorge Luis Borges and His Predecessors, or Notes Towards a Materialist History of Linguistic Idealism.** Chapel Hill: University of North Carolina, Dept. of Romance Languages, 1993. 152pp.

READ, MARC
___ "A Physics of Middle-Earth," by Jenny Coombs and Marc Read. in: Reynolds, Patricia and GoodKnight, Glen H., eds. **Proceedings of the J. R. R. Tolkien Centenary Conference, Keble College, Oxford, 1992.** Altadena, CA: Mythopoeic Press, 1995. pp.323-329. (*Mythlore* Vol. 21, No. 2, Winter 1996, Whole No. 80)

REAVER, J. RUSSELL
___ "From Seed to Fruit: The Doubling of Psychic Landscapes in Algernon Blackwood's **The Centaur**," *The Romantist* No. 4-5: 55-58. 1982.

REDMOND, JAMES
___ "William Morris or Bernard Shaw: Two Faces of Victorian Socialism," in: Butt, J. and Clarke, I. F., eds. **The Victorians and Social Protest: A Symposium.** New York: David and Charles, 1973. pp.156-176.

REED, JILLY
___ "What's a Convention For, Mummy?," *Matrix* No. 116: 10-11. August/September 1995.

REED, PETER J.
___ "Kurt Vonnegut," in: Bruccoli, Matthew J., ed. **Facts on File Bibliography of American Fiction 1919-1988.** New York: Facts on File, 1991. pp.516-518.
___ "Kurt Vonnegut: A Selected Bibliography, 1985-1992," by Peter J. Reed and Paul Baepler. *Bulletin of Bibliography* 50(2): 123-128. June 1993.

REED, ROGER
___ "Gadget Artists Return," by Vincent Di Fate and Roger Reed. *Science Fiction Age* 2(5): 70-75. July 1994.

REED-PHARRR, ROBERT F.
___ "Sex, Race, and Science Fiction: The *Callaloo* Interview," in: Delany, Samuel R. **Silent Interviews on Language, Race, Sex, Science Fiction and Some Comics.** Hanover, NH: Wesleyan University Press, 1994. pp.216-229.

REES, CHRISTINE
___ **Utopian Imagination and Eighteenth Century Fiction.** London: Longman, 1995. 296pp.

REES, DAVID
___ "Alan Garner: Some Doubts," *Horn Book* 55(3): 282-289. June 1979.

REES, ROBERT R.
___ "Driving Rod Serling," *Starlog* No. 203: 27-29. June 1994.
___ "Master in Twilight," *Starlog* No. 203: 30-31. June 1994.

REESMAN, JEANNE C.
___ "Riddle Game: Stephen King's Metafictive Dialogue," in: Magistrale, Tony, ed. **The Dark Descent: Essays Defining Stephen King's Horrorscape.** Westport, CT: Greenwood, 1992. pp.157-170.

REEVES-STEVENS, GARFIELD
___ **The Making of Star Trek: Deep Space Nine,** by Judith Reeves-Stevens and Garfield Reeves-Stevens. New York: Pocket Books, 1994. 319pp.

REEVES-STEVENS, JUDITH
___ **The Making of Star Trek: Deep Space Nine,** by Judith Reeves-Stevens and Garfield Reeves-Stevens. New York: Pocket Books, 1994. 319pp.

REGINALD, ROBERT
___ **Reginald's Science Fiction and Fantasy Awards: A Comprehensive Guide to the Awards and Their Winners.** Third revised edition, by Daryl F. Mallett and Robert Reginald. San Bernardino, CA: Borgo Press, 1993. 248pp.
___ "A Requiem for Starmont House (1976-1993)," *Science Fiction Studies* 20(3): 414-421. November 1993.
___ **Science Fiction and Fantasy Literature 1975-1991: A Bibliography of Science Fiction, Fantasy and Horror Fiction Books and Nonfiction Monographs.** Detroit: Gale Research, 1992. 1512pp.

REICHARDT, MARY R.
___ **A Web of Relationship: Women in the Short Stories of Mary Wilkins Freeman.** Jackson: University Press of Mississippi, 1992. 186pp.

REID, CONSTANCE
___ "New Light on the Work of John Taine," in: Wolf, Milton T. and Mallett, Daryl F., eds. **Imaginative Futures: Proceedings of the 1993 Science Fiction Research Association Conference.** San Bernardino, CA: Jacob's Ladder Books, 1995. pp.115-124.
___ **The Search for E. T. Bell, Also Known as John Taine.** Washington, DC: Mathematical Association of America, Aug. 1993. 372pp.

REID, ROBIN A.
___ "Lost in Space Between 'Center' and 'Margin': Some Thoughts on Lesbian-Feminist Discourse, Bisexual Women, and Speculative Fiction," in: Weisser, Susan O., ed. **Feminist Nightmares; Women at Odds: Feminism and the Problem of Sisterhood**. New York: New York University Press, 1994. pp.343-357.

REID, T. R.
___ "A Monster Hit (Review)," *Washington (DC) Post*. February 2, 1992. in: *NewsBank. Film and Television*. 20:F8-F9. 1992.

REID, THOMAS R.
___ "Cultural Trends in Literature," *The Dark Man: The Journal of Robert E. Howard Studies* No. 2: 30-32. July 1991.

REILLY, PATRICK
___ **Lord of the Flies: Fathers and Sons**. New York: Twayne, 1992. 153pp.

REILLY, ROBERT
___ "Silverberg's Ambiguous Transcendence," in: Elkins, Charles L. and Greenberg, Martin H., eds. **Robert Silverberg's Many Trapdoors: Critical Essays on His Science Fiction**. Westport, CT: Greenwood, 1992. pp.107-119.

REINHART, WERNER
___ "Philip Wylie and Edwin Balmer, **When Worlds Collide** (1933)," in: Heuermann, Harmut, ed. **Der Science Fiction Roman in der angloamerikanischen Literatur: Interpretationen**. Düsseldorf: Bagel, 1986. pp.65-83.

REINHEIMER, DAVID
___ "Ontological and Ethical Allusion: Shakespeare in **The Next Generation**," *Extrapolation* 36(1): 46-54. Spring 1995.

REINKING, VICTOR
___ "A Conversation with Ursula K. Le Guin," by Victor Reinking and David Willingham. *Paradoxa* 1(1): 39-57. 1995.

REISS, EDMUND
___ **Arthurian Legend and Literature: An Annotated Bibliography. Volume 1: The Middle Ages**, by Edmund Reiss, Louise H. Reiss and Beverly Taylor. New York: Garland, 1984. 467pp.
___ **Arthurian Legend and Literature: An Annotated Bibliography. Volume 2.**, by Edmund Reiss, Louise H. Reiss and Beverly Taylor. New York: Garland, 1995. [Not seen.]

REISS, LOUISE H.
___ **Arthurian Legend and Literature: An Annotated Bibliography. Volume 1: The Middle Ages**, by Edmund Reiss, Louise H. Reiss and Beverly Taylor. New York: Garland, 1984. 467pp.
___ **Arthurian Legend and Literature: An Annotated Bibliography. Volume 2.**, by Edmund Reiss, Louise H. Reiss and Beverly Taylor. New York: Garland, 1995. [Not seen.]

REITZ, BERNHARD
___ "A. E. Van Vogt, **Slan** (1940)," in: Heuermann, Harmut, ed. **Der Science Fiction Roman in der angloamerikanischen Literatur: Interpretationen**. Düsseldorf: Bagel, 1986. pp.84-100.

RELF, JAN
___ "Utopia the Good Breast: Coming Home to Mother," in: Kumar, Krishan and Bann, Stephen, eds. **Utopias and the Millennium**. London: Reaktion Books, 1993. pp.107-128.

RELIHAN, CONSTANCE C.
___ "Vivien, Elaine, and the Model's Gaze: Cameron's Reading of **Idylls of the King**," in: Slocum, Sally K., ed. **Popular Arthurian Traditions**. Bowling Green, OH: Popular Press, 1992. pp.111-131.

RENAUD, MAURICE
___ "Document in the History of Science Fiction: On the Scientific-Marvellous Novel and Its Influence on the Understanding of Progress," *Science Fiction Studies* 21(3): 397-405. November 1994.

RENNA, THOMAS
___ "More's **Utopia** and English Medieval Traditions," in: Saccaro Del Buffa, Giuseppa and Lewis, Arthur O., eds. **Utopia e Modernita: Teorie e prassi utopiche nell'eta moderna e postmoderna**. Rome: Gangemi Editore, 1989. pp.739-748.

RENNER, CHARLOTTE
___ "R. U. R. Reborn," *North Atlantic Review* 277(6): 8-13. November/December 1992.

RENO, SHAUN
___ "The Zuni Indian Tribe: A Model for **Stranger in a Strange Land**'s Martian Culture," *Extrapolation* 36(2): 151-158. Summer 1995.

RENZA, LOUIS A.
___ "Ut Pictura Poe: Poetic Politics in 'The Island of the Fay' and 'Morning on the Wissahiccon'," in: Rosenheim, Shawn and Rachman, Stephen, ed. **The American Face of Edgar Allan Poe**. Baltimore: Johns Hopkins University Press, 1995. pp.305-329.

RENZI, THOMAS C.
___ **H. G. Wells: Six Scientific Romances Adapted for Film**. Metuchen, NJ: Scarecrow, 1992. 249pp.

RESNICK, MIKE
___ "The Hugo Awards," *Science Fiction Chronicle* 16(2): 50-51. November/December 1994.
___ "It's Not That Long a Road From New Fan to SF Elder Statesman," *Science Fiction Age* 3(5): 34-36, 101. July 1995.
___ "A Look at Paradise," *OtherRealms* No. 24: 11-12. Spring 1989.
___ "Through Darkest Africa With Book and Resnick," *Science Fiction Chronicle* 13(11/12): 38. August 1992.
___ "Visions and Voyages," *Science Fiction Age* 3(2): 70-75. January 1995.

RESTON, JAMES, JR.
___ "Moon Struck," by Jeff Jarvis, James Reston, Jr., Glenn Kenny and Penelope Patsuris. *TV Guide* 42(29): 10-16. July 16, 1994.

REWA, MICHAEL P.
___ "The Matter of Britain in English and American Popular Music (1966-1990)," in: Slocum, Sally K., ed. **Popular Arthurian Traditions**. Bowling Green, OH: Popular Press, 1992. pp.104-110.

REYNOLDS, BARBARA
___ **Dorothy L. Sayers: Her Life and Soul**. New York: St. Martin's Press, 1993. 398pp.

REYNOLDS, JIM
___ "The Poor Man's Vincent Price (or, A Famous Monster's Fairy Tale)," *Wonder* No. 7: 12. 1993.

REYNOLDS, PATRICIA
___ "Funeral Customs in Tolkien's Fiction," *Mythlore* 19(2): 45-53. Spring 1993. (No. 72)
___ (ed.) **Proceedings of the J. R. R. Tolkien Centenary Conference, Keble College, Oxford, 1992**, ed. by Patricia Reynolds and Glen H. Goodknight. Altadena, CA: Mythopoeic Press, 1995. 458pp.

REYNOLDS, TREVOR
___ "Index to J. R. R. Tolkien in *Mythlore* Issues 1-68," *Mythlore* 18(3): 70-77. Summer 1992. (No. 69)

RHIEL, MARY
___ "The Taming of the Screw: Rohmer's Filming of Kliest's 'Die Marquise von O...'," in: Ruddick, Nicholas, ed. **State of the Fantastic**. Westport, CT: Greenwood, 1992. pp.83-90.

RHODES, JOE
___ "Eeeeyew. . . Gross. Where's My Wooden Stake," *Los Angeles (CA) Times*. July 31, 1992. in: *NewsBank. Film and Television*. 63:A6-A8. 1992
___ "Nimoy and Son (and a Robot)," *TV Guide* 43(28): 13-14. July 16, 1995.

RHODES, RANDALL

RHODES, RANDALL
___ "Death in **Natures Mortes: Vanitas** in French Still Lifes of the Seventeenth Century," in: Latham, Robert A. and Collins, Robert A., eds. **Modes of the Fantastic**. Westport, CT: Greenwood, 1995. pp.161-172.

RICE, ANNE
___ "The Art of Horror in Film (As Told to Katherine Ramsland)," in: Golden, Christopher, ed. **Cut! Horror Writers on Horror Film**. New York: Berkley, 1992. pp.199-210.

RICE, DALE
___ "Imagination: Anne Rice," *Austin (TX) American Statesman* Sec. C, p. 1, 3. October 15, 1993.
___ "Leaving Old Haunts," *Austin (TX) American Statesman* Sec. F, p. 1, 8. August 18, 1995.

RICE, LYNETTE
___ "Boldly Going into Comics: Leonard Nimoy Is Exploring a New Role," *San Francisco (CA) Chronicle* November 14, 1994. (Cited from the Internet Edition.)

RICH, FRANK
___ "Term Limit for the Man of Steel: Yes, It's Time for Him to Go," *New York Times* Sec. 4, p. 1-2. November 22, 1992

RICH, MARK
___ " 'It Was a Wonderful Time': Outtakes: Kornblume: Kronbluthiana: Issues One Through Nine, 13 August 94 to 13 April 95," *New York Review of Science Fiction* No. 88: 1, 3-7. December 1995.

RICHARDS, BETH
___ "Interview With Margaret Atwood," *Prairie Schooner* 67(4): 8-12. Winter 1993.

RICHARDSON, DARRELL C.
___ **J. Allen St. John: An Illustrated Bibliography**. Memphis, TN: Mid-America Publisher, 1991. 111pp.
___ "The Legendary Fenton Ash," *Fantasy Commentator* 8(3/4): 251-252. Fall 1995. (Whole No. 47/48)

RICHMOND, RAY
___ "Chris' X-ellent Adventure," *Los Angeles (CA) Daily News*. August 24, 1995. in: *NewsBank. Film and Television*. 82:E12-E14. 1995.
___ "In Its Return, **Alien** not Alien to Success," *Los Angeles (CA) Times/Orange County Ed.*. Oct. 25, 1994. in: *NewsBank. Film and Television*. 107:A11. 1994.
___ "It Plays 'Games' With Logic But Scores Big in Nuttiness," *Los Angeles (CA) Daily News*. September 5, 1995. in: *NewsBank. Film and Television*. 84:D2. 1995.
___ "Its Final Frontier: **The Next Generation** Heads Off to Film Just Like **Star Trek**," *Los Angeles (CA) Daily News*. May 23, 1994. in: *NewsBank. Film and Television*. 59:B2-B3. 1994.
___ "Kato Gets into the Act Again," *Los Angeles (CA) Daily News*. April 11, 1995. in: *NewsBank. Film and Television*. 51:C7. 1995.
___ "Not for the Uninitiated," *Los Angeles (CA) Daily News*. May 23, 1994. in: *NewsBank. Film and Television*. 59:C3. 1994.
___ "Rule Breaking Proves Winning TV Formula," *Santa Ana (CA) Orange County Register*. April 21, 1992. in: *NewsBank. Film and Television*. 58:A10-A11. 1992.
___ "Serling's 'Lost' Tales Lose Something in 90s Transition," *Los Angeles (CA) Daily News*. May 19, 1994. in: *NewsBank. Film and Television*. 60: B13. 1994.
___ "Voyager: The Next Final Frontier," *Los Angeles (CA) Daily News*. January 16, 1995. in: *NewsBank. Film and Television*. 21:D6-D7. 1995.

RICKMAN, GREGG
___ "Dick, Deception, and Dissociation: A Comment on 'The Two Faces of Philip K. Dick'," in: Mullen, R. D., ed. **On Philip K. Dick: 40 Articles From Science-Fiction Studies**. Terre Haute, IN: SF-TH Inc., 1992. pp.262-264.
___ "The Nature of Dick's Fantasies," in: Mullen, R. D., ed. **On Philip K. Dick: 40 Articles From Science-Fiction Studies**. Terre Haute, IN: SF-TH Inc., 1992. pp.275-277.
___ " 'What Is This Sickness?': 'Schizophrenia' and **We Can Build You**," in: Umland, Samuel J., ed. **Philip K. Dick: Contemporary Critical Interpretations**. Westport, CT: Greenwood, 1995. pp.143-156.

RINGEL, ELEANOR

RIDDELL, PAUL T.
___ "Scleral Rings: Jurassic Fart; Movie Industry, 3,492--Literate SF 0," *Science Fiction Eye* No. 13: 116-119. Spring 1994.
___ **Squashed Armadillocon: Or 'Fear and Loathing in Austin: A Savage Journey into the Heart of the Fanboy Dream'**. Eugene, OR: Hillybilly Press, 1993. 151pp. [Not seen.]

RIDER, JEFF
___ "The Arthurian Legend in French Cinema: **Lancelot du Lac** and **Perceval la Gallois**," by Jeff Rider, Richard Hull and Christopher Smith. in: Harty, Kevin J., ed. **Cinema Arthuriana: Essays on Arthurian Film**. New York: Garland, 1991. pp.41-56.

RIDING, ALAN
___ "Back to the Present in a Lost Verne Novel," *New York Times* pp.B1, B4. September 27, 1994.

RIECHER, ANTON
___ "AggieCon XXII Blasting Off," *Bryan-College Station Eagle* p. C1. March 19, 1992.
___ "Playing With Fire: Fantasy Author Exercises Vivid Imagination," *Bryan-College Station Eagle* Sec. D, p. 1, 3. August 14, 1994.

RIEDER, JOHN
___ "The Metafictive World of **The Man in the High Castle**: Hermeneutics, Ethics, and Political Ideology," in: Mullen, R. D., ed. **On Philip K. Dick: 40 Articles From Science-Fiction Studies**. Terre Haute, IN: SF-TH Inc., 1992. pp.223-231.

RIELLY, EDWARD J.
___ "Irony in **Gulliver's Travels** and **Utopia**," *Utopian Studies* 3(1): 70-83. 1992.

RIEMENSCHNEIDER, CHRIS
___ "Kombat Set to Battle New Terrain--And Critics," *Los Angeles (CA) Times*. August 24, 1995. in: *NewsBank. Film and Television*. 79:B8. 1995.

RIEMER, JAMES D.
___ **The Fantasies of James Branch Cabell**. Ph.D. Dissertation, Bowling Green State University, 1982. 179pp.

RIGELSFORD, ADRIAN
___ **Classic Who: The Hinchcliffe Years; Seasons 12-14**. London: Boxtree, 1995. 128pp.
___ **The Doctors: 30 Years of Time Travel**. London: Boxtree, 1995. 192pp.

RILEY, PHILIP J.
___ **MagicImage Filmbooks Presents Dracula: The Original 1931 Shooting Script**. Absecon, NJ: MagicImage Filmbooks, 1990. 287pp.

RINGEL, ELEANOR
___ "Au Pair Scare: Frightening Cradle Really Rocks (Review)," *Atlanta (GA) Journal*. January 10, 1992. in: *NewsBank. Film and Television*. 12: B11. 1992.
___ "Biting into **Naked Lunch** (Review)," *Atlanta (GA) Journal*. January 10, 1992. in: *NewsBank. Film and Television*. 13:G13-G14. 1992
___ "**Cain** Not So Able; De Palma Can't Get Back on Track (Review)," *Atlanta (GA) Journal*. August 7, 1992. in: *NewsBank. Film and Television*. 83:A11. 1992.
___ "Cannibal House: This **Delicatessen** Dishes Up Hilarious Helpings of Dark Farce (Review)," *Atlanta (GA) Journal*. May 29, 1992. in: *NewsBank. Film and Television*. 51:F13-F14. 1992.
___ "A Giant Letdown (Review)," *Atlanta (GA) Journal*. July 17, 1992. in: *NewsBank. Film and Television*. 70:D12. 1992.
___ "**Hook**, Line and Stinker (Review)," *Atlanta (GA) Journal*. December 11, 1991. in: *NewsBank. Film and Television*. 3:F2-F3. 1992.
___ "Just Call It Her 'Death' By Vanity (Review)," *Atlanta (GA) Journal*. July 31, 1992. in: *NewsBank. Film and Television*. 78:D4. 1992.
___ "New Blood," *Atlanta (GA) Journal*. November 13, 1992. in: *NewsBank. Film and Television*. 111:B1-B2. 1992.
___ "Pfeiffer's Feline Flair Steals the Spotlight in a Better Balanced and Wittier Sequel," *Atlanta (GA) Journal*. June 19, 1992. in: *NewsBank. Film and Television*. 62:F4. 1992.

RINGEL, ELEANOR (continued)
___ "***Sneakers*** Hits All the Right Buttons (Review)," *Atlanta (GA) Journal*. September 11, 1992. in: *NewsBank. Film and Television*. 96:D3-D4. 1992.
___ "This Lasts ***Until the End of the World*** (Review)," *Atlanta (GA) Journal*. March 20, 1992. in: *NewsBank. Film and Television*. 37:D5. 1992.

RINGEL, FAYE
___ "The Scribblies: A Shared World," *Extrapolation* 35(3): 201-210. Fall 1994.

RIOS, DELIA M.
___ "Brent Spiner Explores His and Data's Future," *Dallas (TX) Morning News*. September 14, 1992. in: *NewsBank. Film and Television*. 96:E4-E6. 1992.

RISCO, ANTONIO
___ "Los autómatas de Holmberg," *Mester* (UCLA) 19(2): 63-70. Fall 1990.
___ "Notas para un estudio de la leteratura fantástica hispánica del siglo XX," *Monographis Review* 3(1/2): 58-70. 1987.

RISCO, MARY
___ "Awakening In Fairyland: The Journey of a Soul in George MacDonald's **The Golden Key**," *Mythlore* 20(4): 46-51. Winter 1995. (Whole No. 78)

RITCHIE, HARRY
___ "An Outrageous Talent," in: Salwak, Dale, ed. **Kingsley Amis in Life and Letters**. New York: St. Martin's, 1990. pp.183-187.

RIVERA, C. J.
___ "Props to the Stars," in: Van Hise, James, ed. **Trek Celebration Two**. Las Vegas, NV: Pioneer, 1994. pp.152-155.

RIZZO, FRANK
___ "Director Learns to Make Art Move in Mnemonic," *Hartford (CT) Courant*. May 21, 1995. in: *NewsBank. Film and Television*. 55:B1-B2. 1995.
___ "***Split Second*** Is One Mess of a Movie (Review)," *Hartford (CT) Courant*. May 2, 1992. in: *NewsBank. Film and Television*. 58:G8. 1992.

ROAZEN, PAUL
___ "Orwell, Freud, and **1984**," in: Bloom, Harold, ed. **George Orwell's 1984**. New York: Chelsea House, 1987. pp.19-34.

ROBERSON, JENNIFER
___ "Matrimonium Interruptus and Other Roadblocks to Writing," *SFWA Bulletin* 29(2): 14-17. Summer 1995. (No. 127)

ROBERSON, WILLIAM H.
___ **Walter M. Miller, Jr.: A Bio-Bibliography**, by William H. Roberson and Robert L. Battenfeld. Westport, CT: Greenwood, 1992. 149pp.

ROBERTS, BETTE B.
___ "The Strange Case of **Mary Reilly**," *Extrapolation* 34(1): 39-47. Spring 1993.

ROBERTS, BRYNLEY F.
___ "**Culhwch ac Olwen**, The Triads, Saint's Lives," in: Bromwich, Rachel, Jarman, A. O. H. and Roberts, Brynley F., eds. **The Arthur of the Welsh**. Cardiff: University of Wales Press, 1991. pp.73-96.
___ "Geoffrey of Monmouth, **Historia Regum Britanniae** and **Brut y Brenhinedd**," in: Bromwich, Rachel, Jarman, A. O. H. and Roberts, Brynley F., eds. **The Arthur of the Welsh**. Cardiff: University of Wales Press, 1991. pp.97-116.
___ (ed.) **The Arthur of the Welsh: The Arthurian Legend in Medieval Welsh Literature**, ed. by Rachel Bromwich, A. O. H. Jarman and Brynley F. Roberts. Cardiff: University of Wales Press, 1991. 310pp.

ROBERTS, HELEN E.
___ "Commemorating William Morris: Robin Page Arnot and the Early History of the William Morris Society," *Journal of the William Morris Society* 11(2): 33-37. Spring 1995.

ROBERTS, JACK
___ "Voices of Terror," *Filmfax* No. 45: 36-45, 96-97. June/July 1994.

ROBERTS, MARIE M.
___ "The Male Scientist, Man-Midwife, and Female Monster: Appropriation and Transmutation in **Frankenstein**," in: Benjamin, Marina, ed. **A Question of Identity: Women, Science, and Literature**. New Brunswick, NJ: Rutgers University Press, 1993. pp.59-73.

ROBERTS, ROBIN
___ "It's Still Science Fiction: Strategies of Feminist Science Fiction Criticism," *Extrapolation* 36(3): 184-197. Fall 1995.
___ "Matthew Arnold's 'Dover Beach', Gender, and Science Fiction," *Extrapolation* 33(3): 245-257. Fall 1992.
___ **A New Species: Gender and Science in Science Fiction**. Urbana: University of Illinois Press, 1993. 170pp.

ROBERTS, SHEILA
___ (ed.) **Still the Frame Holds: Essays on Women Poets and Writers**. San Bernardino, CA: Borgo Press, 1993. 216pp.

ROBERTS, TOM
___ "Tarzan: The Marvel Way! An Interview with John Buscema," *Burroughs Bulletin* NS. No. 15: 26-32. July 1993.

ROBERTSON, ANDY
___ "Art and Metaphysics at Party-time: SMS Interviewed," by Andy Robertson and Jason Hurst. *Interzone* No. 100: 22-26. October 1995.
___ "Barrington J. Bayley: An Annotated Bibliography," *Interzone* No. 71: 52-53. May 1993.

ROBILLARD, DOUGLAS
___ "Eric Temple Bell and John Taine," *Fantasy Commentator* 8(1/2): 17-21, 134. Winter 1993/1994. (Whole No. 45/46.)

ROBINETT, JANE
___ **This Rough Magic: Technology in Latin American Fiction**. New York: P. Lang, 1993. 284pp.

ROBINS, J. MAX
___ "Gen X Marks the Spot," by J. Max Robins and Brian Lowry. *Variety* 358(7): 1, 63. March 20, 1995.

ROBINS, KEN
___ "Socializing the Cyborg Self: The Gulf War and Beyond," by Ken Robins and Les Levidow. in: Gray, Chris H., ed. **The Cyborg Handbook**. New York: Routledge, 1995. pp.119-125.

ROBINSON, FRANK M.
___ "Cinema Summary 1991," in: Brown, Charles N. and Contento, William G. **Science Fiction, Fantasy, & Horror: 1991**. Oakland, CA: Locus Press, 1992. pp.433-436.
___ "Cinema Summary, 1991," *Locus* 28(2): 40, 72-73. February 1992.
___ "Cinema Summary, 1992," *Locus* 30(2): 47-48, 73. February 1993.
___ "Cinema Summary, 1993," *Locus* 32(2): 49-51. February 1994.

ROBINSON, KIM S.
___ "Dick and SF Scholarship: Whose Failure of Scholarship?," in: Mullen, R. D., ed. **On Philip K. Dick: 40 Articles From Science-Fiction Studies**. Terre Haute, IN: SF-TH Inc., 1992. pp.125-126.
___ "Pentalude: Science Fiction as Fantasy," in: Wolf, Milton T. and Mallett, Daryl F., eds. **Imaginative Futures: Proceedings of the 1993 Science Fiction Research Association Conference**. San Bernardino, CA: Jacob's Ladder Books, 1995. pp.353-358.

ROBINSON, SPIDER
___ "Rah Rah RAH!," in: Kondo, Yoji, ed. **Requiem: New Collected Works by Robert A. Heinlein and Tributes to the Grand Master**. New York: Tor, 1992. pp.286-309.
___ "Robert," in: Kondo, Yoji, ed. **Requiem: New Collected Works by Robert A. Heinlein and Tributes to the Grand Master**. New York: Tor, 1992. pp.310-321.

ROBLEY, LES P.
___ "***The Abyss***: Special Edition (Review)," *Cinefantastique* 24(2): 59. August 1993.

ROOKE, GILLIAN
___ "Fossils or Figments?," *Vector* No. 167: 12-13. June/July 1992

ROONEY, DAVID
___ "Eye on the Future," *Variety* 358(5): 47. March 6, 1995.

ROSE, ANNE
___ "Profile: Joan Aiken," *Language Arts* 66(7): 784-790. November 1989.

ROSE, CHARLES J.
___ **The Passionate Observer: Martin Scorcese.** Master's Thesis, University of Southern California, 1980. 175pp.

ROSE, DONALD D.
___ "In Space: Past, Present and Possible Futures," by Jonathan V. Post and Donald D. Rose. *Quantum* No. 43/44: 44-48. Spring/Summer 1993.

ROSE, ELLEN C.
___ "It's All a Joke: Science Fiction in Kurt Vonnegut's **The Sirens of Titan**," *Literature and Psychology* 29(3): 160-168. 1979.

ROSE, JANE A.
___ "Images of Self: The Example of Rebecca Harding Davis and Charlotte Perkins Gilman," *English Language Notes* 29(4): 70-78. June 1992.

ROSE, JONATHAN
___ "Eric Blair's School Days," in: Rose, Jonathan, ed. **The Revised Orwell.** East Lansing, MI: Michigan State University Press, 1992. pp.75-96.
___ "The Invisible Sources of **Nineteen Eighty-Four**," *Journal of Popular Culture* 26(1): 93-107. Summer 1992.
___ "The Invisible Sources of **Nineteen Eighty-Four**," in: Rose, Jonathan, ed. **The Revised Orwell.** East Lansing, MI: Michigan State University Press, 1992. pp.131-148.
___ (ed.) **The Revised Orwell.** East Lansing, MI: Michigan State University Press, 1992. 263pp.

ROSE, RITA
___ "Controversial **Thelma** Is Sexist? Nah. (Review)," *Indianapolis (IN) Star.* January 10, 1992. in: *NewsBank. Film and Television.* 15:F6-F7. 1992.

ROSEBURY, BRIAN
___ **Tolkien: A Critical Assessment.** London: Macmillan, 1992. 167pp.; New York: St. Martin's, 1993. 167pp.

ROSEN, STEPHEN
___ "De Palma's **Raising Cain** Is De-lightful (Review)," *Denver (CO) Post.* August 7, 1992. in: *NewsBank. Film and Television.* 83:A9. 1992.

ROSENBERG, ALAN
___ "Journey's End," *(Providence, RI) Journal-Bulletin.* May 22, 1994. in: *NewsBank. Film and Television.* 59:B12-B13. 1994.

ROSENBERG, BETTY
___ **Genreflecting: A Guide to Reading Interests in Genre Fiction.** Englewood, CO: Libraries Unlimited, 1991. 345pp. 3rd. ed.

ROSENBERG, SCOTT
___ "Batman," *San Francisco (CA) Examiner.* June 19, 1992. in: *NewsBank. Film and Television.* 62:E13-E14. 1992.
___ "**Blade Runner**: Back to the Future," *San Francisco (CA) Examiner.* September 11, 1992. in: *NewsBank. Film and Television.* 87:F6-F7. 1992.
___ "Carnal Gnawledge," *San Francisco (CA) Examiner.* November 13, 1992. in: *NewsBank. Film and Television.* 111:A10-A11. 1992.
___ "A Feminist Nightmare in the Year 2042 (Review)," *San Francisco (CA) Examiner.* February 12, 1993. in: *NewsBank. Art.* 7:C4-C5. 1993.
___ "Honey, I Think I Blew It (Review)," *San Francisco (CA) Examiner.* July 17, 1992. in: *NewsBank. Film and Television.* 70:D9-D10. 1992.
___ "Johnny Aims High, Almost Hits Mark," *San Francisco (CA) Examiner.* May 26, 1995. in: *NewsBank. Film and Television.* 63:A5. 1995.

ROSENBERG, SCOTT (continued)
___ "Knight and the Living Dead," *San Francisco (CA) Examiner.* February 19, 1993 in: *NewsBank. Film and Television.* 30:D9-D10. 1993
___ "**Prelude to a Kiss**: She's Not the Woman He Married, But There's More Here Than Meets the Eye (Review)," *San Francisco (CA) Examiner.* July 10, 1992. in: *NewsBank. Film and Television.* 73:C1-C2. 1992.
___ "A Psychological London Thriller Sheds Little Light on Its Subject," *San Francisco (CA) Examiner.* August 14, 1992. in: *NewsBank. Film and Television.* 76:B2. 1992
___ "Punk Heroine Hits Screen With a Bang," *San Francisco (CA) Examiner.* March 31, 1995. in: *NewsBank. Film and Television.* 50:B13. 1995.
___ "Read My Liposuction: **Death Becomes Her** Goes for Vanity Fare (Review)," *San Francisco (CA) Examiner.* July 31, 1992. in: *NewsBank. Film and Television.* 78:D1-D2. 1992.
___ "Saved By the Belle," *San Francisco (CA) Examiner.* July 31, 1992. in: *NewsBank. Film and Television.* 77:B12-13. 1992
___ "'SF' in S.F.: Not a Mass of Trekkies," *San Francisco (CA) Chronicle* Sec. D, p. 2. September 5, 1993.
___ "**Stargate** Open Portal to a Confusing Universe," *San Francisco (CA) Examiner.* October 28, 1994. in: *NewsBank. Film and Television.* 115: G5. 1994.
___ "**Timecop** in Plot Warp," *San Francisco (CA) Examiner.* September 16, 1994. in: *NewsBank. Film and Television.* 105:C8. 1994.
___ "Tired **Virtuosity** Rehashes Action Cliches," *San Francisco (CA) Examiner.* August 4, 1995. in: *NewsBank. Film and Television.* 82:B14. 1995.
___ "Unable to Raise **Cain** (Review)," *San Francisco (CA) Examiner.* August 7, 1992. in: *NewsBank. Film and Television.* 83:A7-A8. 1992.
___ "Virtual Banality," *San Francisco (CA) Examiner.* April 22, 1994. in: *NewsBank. Film and Television.* 51:F4. 1994.

ROSENFELD, MEGAN
___ "Spielberg in Neverland: Where the Movies Cost Millions and the Moguls Never Grow Up," *Washington (DC) Post.* December 15, 1991. in: *NewsBank. Film and Television.* 7:B13-C3. 1992. also in: *NewsBank. Names in the News* 8:B9. 1992.

ROSENHEIM, SHAWN
___ "Detective Fiction, Psychoanalysis, and the Analytic Sublime," in: Rosenheim, Shawn and Rachman, Stephen, ed. **The American Face of Edgar Allan Poe.** Baltimore: Johns Hopkins University Press, 1995. pp.153-178.
___ "Extraterrestrial: Science Fictions in **A Brief History of Time** and **The Incredible Shrinking Man**," *Film Quartrely* 48(4): 15-21. Summer 1995.
___ "Introduction: Beyond 'The Problem of Poe'," by Shawn Rosenheim and Stephen Rachman. in: Rosenheim, Shawn and Rachman, Stephen, eds. **The American Face of Edgar Allan Poe.** Baltimore, MD: Johns Hopkins University Press, 1995. pp.ix-xx.
___ (ed.) **The American Face of Edgar Allan Poe**, ed. by Shawn Rosenheim and Stephen Rachman. Baltimore, MD: Johns Hopkins University Press, 1995. 364pp.

ROSENTHAL, BRUCE
___ "**Sea Quest's** Spin-off," *Sea Frontiers* 40(1): 8. January 1994.

ROSENTHAL, PHIL
___ "No Feeling of Doom for Young Indy (Review)," *Los Angeles (CA) Daily News.* March 1, 1992. in: *NewsBank. Film and Television.* 37:G7-G8. 1992.
___ "**Young Indiana Jones** Doesn't Live Up to Big Screen Brother (Review)," *Los Angeles (CA) Daily News.* March 1, 1992. in: *NewsBank. Film and Television.* 37:G9. 1992.

ROSENTHAL, RAE
___ "Gaskell's Feminist Utopia: The Cranfordians and the Reign of Goodwill," in: Donawerth, Jane L. and Kolmerten, Carol A., eds. **Utopian and Science Fiction by Women: Worlds of Difference.** Syracuse, NY: Syracuse University Press, 1994. pp.73-92.

ROSS, ANDREW
___ **Strange Weather: Culture, Science, and Technology in the Age of Limits.** London: Verso, 1991. 275pp.

ROSS, BILL
___ "The 1995 ERB Chain of Friendship Gathering," *Burroughs Bulletin* NS. No. 24: 28-31. October 1995.

ROSS, BILL

ROSS, BILL (continued)
___ "The Tenth Annual E. C. O. F. Gathering," *Burroughs Bulletin* NS. No. 12: 21-30. October 1992.

ROSS, PATRICIA
___ "**Boxing Helena**," *Cinefantastique* 24(1): 6-7. June 1993.
___ "*Freejack*," *Cinefantastique* 22(6): 56, 61. June 1992
___ "**Pet Sematary II**: Makeup Effects," *Cinefantastique* 23(2/3): 26. October 1992.
___ "**Pet Sematary II**," *Cinefantastique* 23(1): 6-7. August 1992.
___ "**Pet Sematary II**," *Cinefantastique* 23(2/3): 24-26. October 1992.
___ "**Pet Sematary II**," *Cinefantastique* 23(5): 55. February 1993.

ROSSENBERG, RENÉ VAN
___ **Hobbits in Holland: Leven en werk van J. R. R. Tolkien (1892-1973)**. Den Hag: Koninklijke Bibliotheek, 1992. 99pp. [Not seen.]

ROSSI, UMBERTO
___ "Images From the Disaster Area: An Apocalyptic Reading of Urban Landscapes in Ballard's **The Drowned World** and **Hello America**," *Science Fiction Studies* 21(1): 81-97. March 1994.

ROSSIGNOL, ROSALYN
___ "The Holiest Vessel: Maternal Aspects of the Grail," *Arthuriana* 5(1): 52-61. Spring 1995.

ROTH, ELLEN S.
___ **The Rhetoric of First-Person Point of View in the Novel and Film Forms: A Study of Anthony Burgess' A Clockwork Orange and Henry James' A Turn of the Screw and Their Film Adaptations**. Ph.D. Dissertation, New York University, 1978. 308pp. (DAI 39: 4558A. Feb. 1979.)

ROTHMAN, CHUCK
___ "Larry Niven's Ringworld Novels Spawn a Fun and Challenging Computer Sequel," *Science Fiction Age* 3(1): 88-91. November 1994.

ROTTENSTEINER, FRANZ
___ "Hinweis auf **Fantasia**, Verkaufsangebote," *Quarber Merkur* 33(2): 47. December 1995. (No. 84)

ROUSSEAU, FRANCOIS-OLIVIER
___ "The Habit of Observing (Interview, 1985)," in: Ingersoll, Earl G., ed. **Doris Lessing: Conversations**. Princeton, NJ: Ontario Review Press, 1994. pp.146-154.

ROUSSEAU, YVONNE
___ "The Wilder Alien Shores: Or, The Colonials Are Revolting," *Foundation* No. 54: 15-36. Spring 1992.

ROUSSINEAU, GILLES
___ "Tradition Littéraire et Culture Populaire dans L'Histoire de Troïlus et de Zellandine (**Perceforest**, Troisième partie), Version Ancienne du Conte de la Belle au Bois Dormant," *Arthuriana* 4(1): 30-45. Spring 1994.

ROVANO, MARCELAINE W.
___ "The Angel as a Fantasy Figure in Classic and Contemporary Film," *Journal of the Fantastic in the Arts* 5(3): 56-74. 1993. (No. 19)

ROVIN, JEFF
___ **Aliens, Robots, and Spaceships**. New York: Facts on File, 1995. 372pp.

ROWE, MARGARET M.
___ **Doris Lessing**. New York: St. Martin's, 1994. 137pp.

ROWEN, NORMA
___ "The Making of Frankenstein's Monster: Post-Golem, Pre-Robot," in: Ruddick, Nicholas, ed. **State of the Fantastic**. Westport, CT: Greenwood, 1992. pp.169-177.
___ "Reinscribing **Cinderella**: Jane Austen and the Fairy Tale," in: Sanders, Joe, ed. **Functions of the Fantastic**. Westport, CT: Greenwood, 1995. pp.29-36.

ROY, JOHN F.
___ "The Many Tongues of Pellucidar," *Wayfarer II* pp.4-6. n.d.

ROYLE, NICHOLAS
___ "Show and Tell," *Focus* (BSFA) No. 27: 9. December 1994/January 1995.

RUAUD, ANDRÉ.
___ "Between Entropy and Renaissance: SF in France," by André Ruaud and Jean-Daniel Brèque. *Vector* No. 168: 28-29. August/September 1992.

RUBENS, GODFREY
___ "A Response to Godfrey Rubens," *Journal of the William Morris Society* 11(2): 26-27. Spring 1995.

RUBENSTEIN, STEVE
___ "Scotty, Beam Up Some New Aliens," *San Francisco (CA) Chronicle* Sec. C, p. 20. September 12, 1992.

RUBIN, STEVEN J.
___ "**Goldeneye**: 007: The Best of Bond," *Cinefantastique* 27(3): 21. December 1995.
___ "**Goldeneye**: Recreating Bond for the '90s," *Cinefantastique* 27(3): 19-20. December 1995.
___ "When Saucers Were Young," *Sci-Fi Entertainment* 1(1): 34-37. June 1994.

RUBINSTEIN, MITCHELL
___ "**The Next Generation**: Special Visual Effects," *Cinefantastique* 23(2/3): 38-41. October 1992.

RUCK, E. H.
___ **An Index of Themes and Motifs in Twelfth-Century French Arthurian Poetry**. Rochester, NY: D. S. Brewer, 1991. 176pp. [Not seen.]

RUDDICK, NICHOLAS
___ "Ballard/**Crash**/Baudrillard," *Science-Fiction Studies* 19(3): 354-360. November 1992.
___ **British Science Fiction, 1478-1990: A Chronology**. Westport, CT: Greenwood, 1992. 296pp.
___ "Putting the Bits Together: Information Theory, **Neuromancer**, and Science Fiction," *Journal of the Fantastic in the Arts* 3(4): 84-92. 1994.
___ **Ultimate Island: On the Nature of British Science Fiction**. Westport, CT: Greenwood, 1993. 202pp.
___ (ed.) **State of the Fantastic: Studies in the Theory and Practice of Fantastic Literature and Film**. Westport, CT: Greenwood, 1992. 210pp.

RUDELL, MICHAEL I.
___ "Entertainment Law: Possessory and 'Based Upon' Credits," *New York Law Journal* p. 2, 4. October 23, 1992.

RUDISHINA, T.
___ "O trudnykh i legkikh voposakn zhezni," *Detskaya Literatura* 5: 74-76. May 1991. [Not seen.]

RUEHLMANN, BILL
___ "Ever the Enterprising Helmsman: It's Sulu to the Rescue of **Trek** Crew (Review)," *Norfolk (VA) Virginian-Pilot*. January 21, 1992. in: *NewsBank. Film and Television*. 15:E2-E3. 1992.

RULE, PATTY
___ "Monsters Take over TNT Saturdays," *USA Today* Sec. D, p. 3. June 4, 1993.

RUSCH, KRISTINE K.
___ "Anatomy of a Sale: 'Mom's Little Friends' to *The Magazine of Fantasy and Science Fiction*," in: Thompkins, David G., ed. **Science Fiction Writer's Market Place and Source Book**. Cincinnati, OH: Writer's Digest Books, 1994. pp.344-357.
___ "Editorial: *Sci-Fi Buzz*," *Magazine of Fantasy and Science Fiction* 86(6): 5-8. June 1994.
___ "Editorial: Magazine Readership," *Magazine of Fantasy and Science Fiction* 89(1): 6-8. July 1995.
___ "Editorial: New Readers," *Magazine of Fantasy and Science Fiction* 87(2): 5-7. August 1994.
___ "Editorial: Reader Survey," *Magazine of Fantasy and Science Fiction* 88(2): 5-7. February 1995.

RUSCH, KRISTINE K. (continued)
___ "Editorial: Science Fiction in the Mainstream," *Magazine of Fantasy and Science Fiction* 87(4/5): 8-10. October 1994.
___ "Editorial: Science Fiction Readership," *Magazine of Fantasy and Science Fiction* 89(3): 5-7. September 1995.
___ "Editorial: WorldCon," *Magazine of Fantasy and Science Fiction* 86(2): 5-6. February 1994.

RUSDY, ASHRAF H. A.
___ "Families of Orphans: Relation and Disrelation in Octavia Butler's **Kindred**," *College English* 55(2): 135-157. February 1993.

RUSHDIE, SALMAN
___ "Angela Carter, 1940-1992: A Very Good Wizard, a Very Dear Friend," *New York Times Book Review* p. 5. March 8, 1992.

RUSHING, JAMES A., JR.
___ "Adventure and Iconography: Ywain Picture Cycles and the Literarization of Vernacular Narrative," in: Busby, Keith, ed. **The Arthurian Yearbook I**. New York: Garland, 1991. pp.91-106.

RUSS, JOANNA
___ **To Write Like a Woman: Essays in Feminism and Science Fiction**. Bloomington: Indiana University Press, 1995. 181pp.

RUSSELL, ELIZABETH
___ "Katherine Burdekin's **Swastika Night**: The Search for Truths and Texts," *Foundation* No. 55: 36-43. Summer 1992.

RUSSELL, PETER
___ "Tolkien and the Imagination," in: Kranz, Gisbert, ed. **Jahrbuch für Literatur und Ästhetik**. Lüdenscheid, Germany: Stier, 1992. Band 10, pp.77-91.

RUSSELL, R. B.
___ "Alterative Lives in Arthur Machen's 'A Fragment of Life' and Sylvia Townsend Warner's **Lolly Willowes**," *Studies in Weird Fiction* No. 12: 17-19. Spring 1993.

RUSSELL, ROBERT
___ **Evgeny Zamyatin**. s.l.: Bristol Press, 1992. 196pp.

RUSSELL, W. M. S.
___ "Time Before and After **The Time Machine**," *Foundation* No. 65: 24-40. Autumn 1995.
___ "Voltaire, Science and Fiction: A Tercentenary Tribute," *Foundation* No. 62: 31-46. Winter 1994/1995.

RUSSO, JOHN
___ **Scare Tactics: The Art, Craft, and Trade Secrets of Writing, Producing, and Directing Chillers and Thrillers**. New York: Dell, 1992. 241pp.

RUTHERFORD, BRETT
___ "Maker of Monsters, Maker of Gods," *Lovecraft Studies* No. 30: 2-3. Spring 1994.

RUTHNER, CLEMENS
___ "Phänomenologie des Schreckens," by Clemens Ruthner and Michael Koseler. *Quarber Merkur* 33(2): 30-34. December 1995. (No. 84)
___ "Verfolgte Gespenster. Die deutschsprachige Phantastik und der literarische Kanon," *Quarber Merkur* 32(1): 50-68. June 1994. (Whole No. 81)

RUUD, JAY
___ "Teaching the 'Hoole' Tradition Through Parallel Passages," in: Fries, Maureen and Watson, Jeanie, eds. **Approaches to the Teaching of the Arthurian Tradition**. New York: Modern Language Association, 1992. pp.73-76.

RYAN, AL
___ "**Ed Wood**: Vampira," by Al Ryan and Dan Cziraky. *Cinefantastique* 25(5): 40-41, 61. October 1994.

RYAN, CHARLES C.
___ "Anatomy of a Sale: 'Due Process' to *Aboriginal Science Fiction*," in: Thompkins, David G., ed. **Science Fiction Writer's Market Place and Source Book**. Cincinnati, OH: Writer's Digest Books, 1994. pp.320-330.

RYAN, DESMOND
___ "Could Violent Games Make Teens Kill?," *Philadelphia (PA) Inquirer*. April 23, 1994. in: *NewsBank. Film and Television*. 41:B10. 1994.
___ "Off the Beaten Trek," *Philadelphia (PA) Inquirer*. December 8, 1991. in: *NewsBank. Film and Television*. 7:A14-B1. 1992. also in: *NewsBank. Names in the News*. 1:F13-F14. 1992.

RYAN, J. S.
___ "Uncouth Innocence: Some Links Between Chrétien de Troyes, Wolfram von Eschenbach and J. R. R. Tolkien," in: Kranz, Gisbert, ed. **Inklings: Jahrbuch für Literatur und Ästhetik**. 2. Band. [Lüdensceid, Germany, Stier], 1984. pp.25-41.

RYAN, JAMES
___ "Designing a Deadly Alien Who's Both Beauty, Beast," *Los Angeles (CA) Daily News*. July 7, 1995. in: *NewsBank. Film and Television*. 81: A4-A5. 1995.

RYAN, MARIE-LAURE
___ **Possible Worlds, Artificial Intelligence, and Narrative Theory**. Bloomington: Indiana University Press, 1991. 291pp.

RYAN, WILLIAM F.
___ "The Genesis of the Techno-Thriller," *Virginia Quarterly Review* 69(1): 24-40. Winter 1993.

RYMAN, GEOFF
___ "High Noon: Jeff Noon Interviewed," *Interzone* No. 88: 25-27. October 1994.

RYURIKOV, YURY
___ "Depicting the New Communist World in Science Fiction," *Current Digest of the Soviet Press* 12(10):13-17. April 6, 1990. (Abstracted from *Novy Mir* No. 12, December 1959, pp.228-245.)

SABELLA, ROBERT
___ "Fritz Leiber: A Chronology," *Lan's Lantern* No. 38: 17. July 1992.
___ "The Lost Worlds of Science Fiction: A. Merritt," *Lan's Lantern* No. 40: 34-35. September 1992.
___ "The Lost Worlds of Science Fiction: Murray Leinster," *Lan's Lantern* No. 42: 32-33. May 1994.

SACCARO DEL BUFFA, GIUSEPPA
___ "Il II° Congresso Internazionale de Studi sulle Utopia," in: Saccaro Del Buffa, Giuseppa and Lewis, Arthur O., eds. **Utopia e Modernita: Teorie e prassi utopiche nell'eta moderna e postmoderna**. Rome: Gangemi Editore, 1989. pp.13-26.
___ "Il I° Convegno Internazionale de Studi sulle utopie," in: Saccaro Del Buffa, Giuseppa and Lewis, Arthur O., eds. **Utopie per gli Anni Ottana**. Rome: Gangemi Editore, 1986. pp.35-39.
___ "Le streghe tra mito e realta: l'utopia del 'gioco'," in: Saccaro Del Buffa, Giuseppa and Lewis, Arthur O., eds. **Utopia e Modernita: Teorie e prassi utopiche nell'eta moderna e postmoderna**. Rome: Gangemi Editore, 1989. pp.599-614.
___ "Un'utopia dell'autorigenerazione: 'La Crisalide' di Bradbury," in: Saccaro Del Buffa, Giuseppa and Lewis, Arthur O., eds. **Utopie per gli Anni Ottana**. Rome: Gangemi Editore, 1986. pp.427-434.
___ **Utopie e modernita: teorie e prassi utopiche nell'eta moderna e postmoderna**, by Giuseppa Saccaro Del Buffa and Arthur O. Lewis. Roma: Gangemi, 1989. 2 v., 1196pp.
___ **Utopie per gli anni ottanta: studi interdisciplinari sui temi, la storia, i progetti**, by Giuseppa Saccaro Del Buffa and Arthur O. Lewis. Roma: Gangemi, 1986. 825pp.

SACHS, LLOYD
___ "Animated Batman Fights New Foe in **Mask of the Phantasm** (Review)," *Chicato (IL) Sun Times*. December 27, 1993. in: *NewsBank. Art* 36:G2. 1993.
___ "**Basic Instinct** Debate: Removing the Element of Risk from the Movies," *Chicago (IL) Sun Times* March 22, 1992 in: *NewsBank. Film and Television*. 29:A2-A3. 1992.

SACHS, LLOYD (continued)
___ " 'Death' Has Grave Flaws (Review)," *Chicago (IL) Sun Times.* July 31, 1992. in: *NewsBank. Film and Television.* 78:D5. 1992.
___ "Despite Riley's Heroics, **Alien 3** Lacks the Old Bite," *Chicago (IL) Sun Times.* May 22, 1992. in: *NewsBank. Film and Television.* 49:C1-C2. 1992.
___ "**Raising Cain** Isn't Able to Save De Palma (Review)," *Chicago (IL) Sun Times.* August 7, 1992. in: *NewsBank. Film and Television.* 83: A12. 1992.
___ "Timid **Encino Man** Skimps on Teen Spirit (Review)," *Chicago (IL) Sun Times.* May 22, 1992. in: *NewsBank. Film and Television.* 52:C12. 1992.

SADLER, GLENN E.
___ "**A Wrinkle in Time**: A Life-Fantasy of Tessering Through Space," *Teaching and Learning Literature* 4(5): 29-33. May/June 1995.

SADLER, TOM
___ "An Appreciation of Fritz Leiber's Fiction," *Lan's Lantern* No. 38: 3-5. July 1992.
___ "Thoughts on Fritz Leiber," *Lan's Lantern* No. 38: 26. July 1992.

SAGE, LORNA
___ "Doris Lessing," in: Sage, Lorna. **Women in the House of Fiction: Post-War Women Novelists.** New York: Routledge, 1992. pp.13-23.
___ "In Full Spate: The Fertility and Generosity of Anthony Burgess," *Times Literary Supplement* No. 4733: 26. December 17, 1993.
___ "Margaret Atwood," in: Sage, Lorna. **Women in the House of Fiction: Post-War Women Novelists.** New York: Routledge, 1992. pp.161-168.
___ (ed.) **Flesh and the Mirror: Essays on the Art of Angela Carter.** London: Virago, 1994. 358pp.

SAGI, P.
___ "Manoscritti ed immagini di Tommaso Campanella. Orientamenti de recerca," by G. Formichetti, O. Lucchesi, P. Sagi and F. Troncarelli. in: Saccaro Del Buffa, Giuseppa and Lewis, Arthur O., eds. **Utopie per gli Anni Ottana.** Rome: Gangemi Editore, 1986. pp.587-590.

SAIDMAN, ANNE
___ **Stephen King: Master of Horror.** Minneapolis, MN: Lerner, 1992. 56pp.

SAINT-GELAIS, RICHARD
___ "Détections science-fictionnelles," *Tangence* (Canada) No. 38: 74-84. December 1992.

SALDA, MICHAEL N.
___ "Caxton's Print vs. the Winchester Manuscript: An Introduction to the Debate on Editing Malory's **Morte Darthur**," *Arthuriana* 5(2): 1-4. Summer 1995.
___ "William Faulkner's Arthurian Tale: **Mayday**," *Arthuriana* 4(4): 348-375. Winter 1994.

SALES, IAN
___ "Policing Virtual Reality," *Vector* No. 172: 11-12. April/May 1993.

SALMON, NICHOLAS
___ "The Revision of **A Dream of John Ball**," *Journal of the William Morris Society* 10(2): 15-16. Spring 1993.
___ "Tropical Realism in **The Tables Turned**," *Journal of the William Morris Society* 11(2): 11-19. Spring 1995.

SALMON, PAUL G.
___ "The Artisan as Individual and Communitarian: The Life of Brother Isaac Newton Youngs," by Susan Matarese, Paul G. Salmon and Glendyne R. Wergland. *Utopian Studies* 6(2): 35-51. 1995.

SALMONSON, JESSICA A.
___ **Bibliography: Jessica Amanda Salmonson.** Polk City, IA: Drumm, 1992. [15pp.] [Bound with, inverted: her **Sorceries and Sorrows (Early Poems)**.] [21pp.]
___ "Fanciful Dreams of the Author," *Science Fiction Eye* No. 13: 101. Spring 1994.
___ "Gender Structuring of Shell Persons in **The Ship Who Sang**," *New York Review of Science Fiction* No. 10: 15-18. June 1989.

SALMONSON, JESSICA A. (continued)
___ "Journal Notes on Censorship," *Quantum* No. 43/44: 14-15. Spring/Summer 1993.
___ "Letter to a Friend on the Pursuit of Writing," *Quantum* No. 41: 16-17. Winter/Spring 1992.
___ "A True Tale of Horror: Striving to Break the Rules of the Genre Game," *Quantum* No. 42: 13-14. Summer/Fall 1992.

SALTER, DAVID I.
___ "**Babylon 5**: Alien Makeups," *Cinefantastique* 23(5): 32-33. February 1993.
___ "**Babylon 5**: Costume Design," *Cinefantastique* 23(5): 34. February 1993.
___ "**Babylon 5**: The Future of CGI," *Cinefantastique* 23(5): 39. February 1993.
___ "**The Next Generation**: Alien Makeups," *Cinefantastique* 23(2/3): 103-105. October 1992.
___ "**The Next Generation**: Building the *U. S. S. Enterprise*," *Cinefantastique* 23(2/3): 95. October 1992.
___ "**Skinner**," *Cinefantastique* 25(2): 52-53. April 1994.
___ "**Star Trek**: 24th-Century Techs," *Cinefantastique* 23(2/3): 92-93. October 1992.
___ "**Star Trek: Deep Space Nine**: Alien Makeups," *Cinefantastique* 23(6): 31. April 1993.
___ "**Star Trek: Deep Space Nine**: Conceptual Artist Richard Delgado," *Cinefantastique* 23(6): 36-37. April 1993.
___ "**Star Trek: Deep Space Nine**: Designing Aliens," *Cinefantastique* 24(3/4): 106. October 1993.
___ "**Star Trek: Deep Space Nine**: Effects," *Cinefantastique* 24(3/4): 105. October 1993.
___ "**Star Trek: Deep Space Nine**: Shape-Shifting Security Chief," *Cinefantastique* 23(6): 39. April 1993.
___ "**Star Trek: The Next Generation**: Alien Makeups," *Cinefantastique* 24(3/4): 50. October 1993.
___ "**Star Trek: The Next Generation**: Special Visual Effects," *Cinefantastique* 24(3/4): 79-82. October 1993.

SAMMON, PAUL M.
___ "Effects Scene: The Perigee of Apogee," *Cinefex* No. 54: 83-84. May 1993.
___ "Quick Cuts: That Other T-rex," *Cinefex* No. 56: 87-88. November 1993.
___ "Quick Cuts: Wood Works," *Cinefex* No. 61: 107-110. March 1995.
___ "The Salacious Gaze: Sex, the Erotic Trilogy and the Decline of David Lynch," in: Golden, Christopher, ed. **Cut! Horror Writers on Horror Film.** New York: Berkley, 1992. pp.211-236.

SAMMONS, TODD H.
___ "Science Fiction and Mythology: An Overview," in: Kellogg, Judith and Crisler, Jesse, eds. **Literature & Hawaii's Children: Stories as Bridges to Many Realms.** Honolulu, HI: University of Hawaii at Manoa, 1994. pp.117-124.

SAMUELSON, DAVID N.
___ "Modes of Extrapolation: The Formulas of Hard Science Fiction," *Science Fiction Studies* 20(2): 191-240. July 1993.
___ "Necessary Constraints: Samuel R. Delany on Science Fiction," *Foundation* No. 60: 21-41. Spring 1994.
___ "On Hard Science Fiction: A Bibliography," *Science Fiction Studies* 20(2): 149-156. July 1993.
___ "On Hard Science Fiction: Introduction," *Science Fiction Studies* 20(2): 145-148. July 1993.

SÁNCHEZ RON, JOSÉ M.
___ "Lovecraft, la ciencia y los terrores espacio-temporales," *Revista de Occidente* No. 115: 57-76. December 1990.

SANDER, GORDON
___ **Serling: The Rise and Twilight of Television's Last Angry Man.** New York: Penguin/Dutton, 1992. 284pp.

SANDERS, JOE L.
___ "Breaking the Circle: Heinlein's **The Door into Summer**," *New York Review of Science Fiction* No. 60: 1, 10-13. August 1993.
___ "**Edge of Darkness** as Transhuman Thriller," *Journal of the Fantastic in the Arts* 5(4): 83-91. 1993. (No. 20)

SANDERS, JOE L. (continued)
___ **Functions of the Fantastic: Selected Essays from the Thirteenth International Conference on the Fantastic in the Arts**. Westport, CT: Greenwood, 1995. 230pp.
___ "Glossary of Fanspeak," by Joe L. Sanders and Rich Brown. in: Sanders, Joe, ed. **Science Fiction Fandom**. Westport, CT: Greenwood, 1994. pp.265-270.
___ "Pioneer Award Presentation Speech, 1995," *SFRA Review* No. 219: 23-25. September/October 1995.
___ "**Raising Arizona**: Not Quite Ozzie and Harriet Meet the Biker From Hell," *Journal of the Fantastic in the Arts* 6(2/3): 217-233. 1994.
___ "Science Fiction Magazines," in: Barron, Neil, ed. **Anatomy of Wonder 4**. New York: Bowker, 1995. pp.690-714.
___ "Space Opera Reconsidered," *New York Review of Science Fiction* No. 82: 1, 3-6. June 1995.
___ (ed.) **Science Fiction Fandom**. Westport, CT: Greenwood, 1994. 293pp.

SANDLER, ADAM
___ "TV Reviews: *Sliders*," *Variety* 358(7): 30. March 20, 1995.

SANDLER, FLORENCE F.
___ "Family Romance in **The Once and Future King**," *Quondam et Futurus* 2(2): 72-80. Summer 1992.

SANDOR, ANDRAS
___ "Myths and the Fantastic," *New Literary History* 22(2): 339-358. Spring 1991.

SANDOVAL, CHELA
___ "New Sciences: Cyborg Feminism and the Methodology of the Oppressed," in: Gray, Chris H., ed. **The Cyborg Handbook**. New York: Routledge, 1995. pp.407-421.

SANDOVAL, CHRISTINE
___ "Gordon Smith: Seeking Silicone Solutions," *Cinefex* No. 64: 19-20, 128. December 1995.

SANDOW, SANDRA J.
___ "Touch Magic: The Importance of Teaching Folktales to Emotionally Disturbed, Disabled Readers," *Mythlore* 19(4): 56-59. Autumn 1993. (No. 74)

SANDRIN, KATHLEEN
___ "*Wagon Train* of the Future Keeps on Rolling," *(Santa Fe, NM) New Mexican*. January 27, 1995. in: *NewsBank. Film and Television*. 25: E10. 1995.

SANFORD, JAY A.
___ "Boris Korloff's Classic TV Series *Thriller*, Part Two," *Filmfax* No. 30: 79-85. 1992.
___ "An Interview with Russell Johnson," *Filmfax* No. 33: 62-67, 77. June/July 1992.

SANJEK, DAVID
___ "The Hysterical Imagination: The Horror Films of Oliver Stone," *Post Script* 12(1): 47-60. Fall 1992.

SANSONE, GABRIELE
___ "Realizzare l'utopia. Le comuni in Italia negli anni settanta," in: Saccaro Del Buffa, Giuseppa and Lewis, Arthur O., eds. **Utopia e Modernita: Teorie e prassi utopiche nell'eta moderna e postmoderna**. Rome: Gangemi Editore, 1989. pp.1135-1151.

SANSWEET, STEPHEN J.
___ "Scouting the Galaxy: Collecting **Star Wars** Memoribilia," *Lucasfilm Fan Club* No. 21: 30-31. Winter 1994.
___ **Star Wars: From Concept to Screen to Collectible**. San Francisco, CA: Chronicle Books, 1992. 131pp.
___ **The World of Star Wars: The Creation of a Phenomenon**. San Francisco, CA: Chronicle Books, 1992. [Not seen.]

SARGENT, LYMAN T.
___ "American Utopianism 1920-1980: Notes Toward a Study," in: Saccaro Del Buffa, Giuseppa and Lewis, Arthur O., eds. **Utopie per gli Anni Ottana**. Rome: Gangemi Editore, 1986. pp.751-762.

SARGENT, LYMAN T. (continued)
___ "The Three Faces of Utopianism Revisited," *Utopian Studies* 5(1): 1-37. 1994.

SARGENT, PAMELA
___ "The Historical Novelist and History," *Paradoxa* 1(3): 363-374. 1995.
___ "Introduction," in: Sargent, Pamela, ed. **Women of Wonder: The Classic Years, Science Fiction by Women from the 1940s to the 1970s**. San Diego, CA: Harcourt, 1995. pp.1-20.
___ "Introduction: Women of Wonder," in: Sargent, Pamela, ed. **Women of Wonder: The Contemporary Years; Science Fiction by Women From the 1970s to the 1990s**. Orlando, FL: Harcourt Brace, 1995. pp.1-20.
___ "Recommended Reading: Science Fiction by Women, 1818-1978," in: Sargent, Pamela, ed. **Women of Wonder: The Classic Years, Science Fiction by Women from the 1940s to the 1970s**. San Diego, CA: Harcourt, 1995. pp.426-438.
___ "Recommended Reading: Science Fiction by Women, 1979-1993," in: Sargent, Pamela, ed. **Women of Wonder: The Contemporary Years; Science Fiction by Women From the 1970s to the 1990s**. Orlando, FL: Harcourt Brace, 1995. pp.405-420.
___ "Science Fiction, Women, and Feminism," *Chung Wai Literary Quarterly* 22(12): May 1994. (Issue not seen; pagination unavailable.)
___ "Traps," *Astromancer Quarterly* 2(1): 28-35. February 1993.
___ **Women of Wonder, The Classic Years: Science Fiction by Women From the 1940s to the 1970s**. San Diego, CA: Harcourt Brace, 1995. 438pp.
___ "The Writer as Nomad," in: Jakubowski, Maxim and James, Edward, eds. **The Profession of Science Fiction**. New York: St. Martin's, 1992. pp.111-119.
___ "Writing, Science Fiction, and Family Values," *Amazing Stories* 69(1): 100-111. Spring 1994.

SARJEANT, WILLIAM A. S.
___ "A Forgotten Children's Fantasy: Philip Woodruff's **The Sword of Northumbria**," *Mythlore* 20(4): 30-35. Winter 1995. (Whole No. 78)
___ "The Geology of Middle-Earth," in: Reynolds, Patricia and GoodKnight, Glen H., eds. **Proceedings of the J. R. R. Tolkien Centenary Conference, Keble College, Oxford, 1992**. Altadena, CA: Mythopoeic Press, 1995. pp.334-339. (*Mythlore* Vol. 21, No. 2, Winter 1996, Whole No. 80)
___ "Where Did the Dwarves Come From?," *Mythlore* 19(1): 43, 64. Winter 1993. (No. 71)

SARNYA, COUNT
___ "*The Lad and the Lion* in Films: 1917-1937," *Burroughs Bulletin* NS. No. 14: 3-10. April 1993.

SARRACINO, CARMINE
___ "Natural Law and the Monster," *Connecticut Review* 15(1): 23-32. Spring 1993.

SARROCCO, CLARA
___ "Whittaker Chambers on Christians," *CSL: The Bulletin of the New York C. S. Lewis Society* 23(7): 6-7. May 1992.

SAUNDERS, MATTHEW F.
___ "God's Army," *Cinefantastique* 27(2): 52-53. November 1995.
___ **Star Trek as Modern Myth**. Master's Thesis, Colorado State University, 1994. 142pp.
___ "*Virtuosity*," *Cinefantastique* 26(6)/27(1): 66-97. October 1995.

SAUNDERS, MICHAEL
___ "The Parallel Universes of *Star Trek*," *Boston (MA) Globe*. November 13, 1994. in: *NewsBank. Film and Television*. 10:E1-E4. 1995.

SAUTER-BAILLIET, THERESIA
___ "Joanna Russ, **The Female Man** (1975)," in: Heuermann, Harmut, ed. **Der Science Fiction Roman in der angloamerikanischen Literatur: Interpretationen**. Düsseldorf: Bagel, 1986. pp.355-374.
___ "Marge Piercy: **Woman on the Edge of Time** (1976)," in: Heuermann, Hartmut and Lange, Bernd-Peter, eds. **Die Utopie in der angloamerikanischen Literatur: Interpretationen**. Düsseldorf: Bagel, 1984. pp.349-370.

SAUTTER, DIANE
___ "Erotic and Existential Paradoxes of the Golem: Marge Piercy's **He, She and It**," *Journal of the Fantastic in the Arts* 7(2/3): 255-268. 1995.

SAVADA, ELIAS
___ "Dark Carnival: The Secret World of Tod Browning (Book Excerpt)," by David J. Skal and Elias Savada. *Cinefantastique* 27(3): 36-38. December 1995.

SAWA, HUBERT
___ "Short History of the Territorial Development of the Dwarves' Kingdom in the Second and Third Ages of Middle-Earth," in: Reynolds, Patricia and GoodKnight, Glen H., eds. **Proceedings of the J. R. R. Tolkien Centenary Conference, Keble College, Oxford, 1992.** Altadena, CA: Mythopoeic Press, 1995. pp.396-410. (*Mythlore* Vol. 21, No. 2, Winter 1996, Whole No. 80)

SAWICKI, STEPHEN
___ "**Leprechaun 2** (Review)," *Cinefantastique* 27(2): 60. November 1995.

SAWYER, ANDY
___ "Correspondence Course: Sue Thomas Interviewed," *Vector* No. 167: 10-11. June/July 1992
___ "More Than Metaphor: Double Vision in Lang's **Metropolis**," *Foundation* No. 64: 70-81. Summer 1995.

SAYER, GEORGE
___ **Jack: A Life of C. S. Lewis**. 2nd ed. Wheaton, IL: Crossway, 1994. 457pp.
___ "Recollections of J. R. R. Tolkien," in: Reynolds, Patricia and GoodKnight, Glen H., eds. **Proceedings of the J. R. R. Tolkien Centenary Conference, Keble College, Oxford, 1992.** Altadena, CA: Mythopoeic Press, 1995. pp.21-25. (*Mythlore* Vol. 21, No. 2, Winter 1996, Whole No. 80)

SAYERS, NICK
___ "Selling a Bestseller," by Nick Sayers, Ian Hughes, David Singer and Tony Hammond. in: Jones, Stephen, ed. **James Herbert: By Horror Haunted**. London: New English Library, 1992. pp.199-207.

SBRAGIA, ALBERT
___ "Italo Calvino's Ordering of Chaos," *Modern Fiction Studies* 39(2): 283-306. Summer 1993.

SCAPPEROTTI, DAN
___ "**Candyman**," *Cinefantastique* 23(4): 18-19. December 1992.
___ "**The Crow** (Review)," *Cinefantastique* 25(4): 59. August 1994.
___ "**Dr. Jekyll and Ms. Hyde**," *Cinefantastique* 26(3): 10-11. April 1995.
___ "**Flesh Gordon Meets the Cosmic Cheerleaders** (Review)," *Cinefantastique* 25(2): 59-60. April 1994.
___ "**Fortress**," *Cinefantastique* 24(2): 4-5. August 1993.
___ "**Highlander III: The Magician**," *Cinefantastique* 26(2): 54-55, 60. February 1995.
___ "King Effect: Computer Graphics by Image Design," *Cinefantastique* 26(5): 55. August 1995.
___ "**Midnight Kiss** (Review)," *Cinefantastique* 24(6)/25(1): 123-124. February 1994.
___ "**Model By Day** (Review)," *Cinefantastique* 25(3): 60. June 1994.
___ "The Plan 9 Companion," *Cinefantastique* 25(5): 43. October 1994.
___ "**Preying Mantis** (Review)," *Cinefantastique* 24(6)/25(1): 124. February 1994.
___ "**Prospero's Books**," *Cinefantastique* 22(6): 52-53. June 1992
___ "Runaway Brain," *Cinefantastique* 27(2): 56-57. November 1995.
___ "**The Secret of Roan Inish** (Review)," *Cinefantastique* 26(5): 60. August 1995.
___ "**The Secret of Roan Inish**," *Cinefantastique* 27(3): 3235. December 1995.
___ "**The Shadow**: Movie and Serial Adventures," *Cinefantastique* 25(4): 27-29. August 1994.
___ "**Sherlock Holmes and the Incident at Victoria Falls** (Review)," *Cinefantastique* 23(1): 60. August 1992.
___ "Stephen King's **The Langoliers**," *Cinefantastique* 26(5): 50-54, 61. August 1995.
___ "**Tainted Blood** (Review)," *Cinefantastique* 24(2): 59. August 1993.
___ "**Tank Girl**," *Cinefantastique* 26(4): 50-51. June 1995.

SCAPPEROTTI, DAN (continued)
___ "**Wilder Napalm**," *Cinefantastique* 23(5): 12-13. February 1993.

SCHAAF, BARBARA
___ "Richard Adams: The Early Years," *Chicago (IL) Sun Times*. August 4, 1991. in *NewsBank. Arts and Literature*. 28:A2. 1991

SCHACHTERLE, LANCE
___ "Introduction: Literature and Technology," by Mark L. Greenberg and Lance Schachterle. in: Greenberg, Mark L. and Schachterle, Lance, eds. **Literature and Technology**. Bethlehem, PA: Lehigh University Press, 1992. pp.13-24.
___ "Pynchon and the Civil Wars of Technology," in: Greenberg, Mark L. and Schachterle, Lance, eds. **Literature and Technology**. Bethlehem, PA: Lehigh University Press, 1992. pp.253-274.
___ "Selected Bibliography of Works Devoted to Literature and Technology," by Mark L. Greenberg and Lance Schachterle. in: Greenberg, Mark L. and Schachterle, Lance, eds. **Literature and Technology**. Bethlehem, PA: Lehigh University Press, 1992. pp.310-317.
___ (ed.) **Literature and Technology**, ed. by Mark L. Greenberg and Lance Schachterle. Bethlehem, PA: Lehigh University Press, 1992. 322pp.

SCHAEFFER, SIRIKANYA B.
___ "Award Winning Science Fiction Editor Speaks at LC," *Library of Congress Information Bulletin* 51(13): 289. June 29, 1992.

SCHAEFFER, STEPHEN
___ "Hollywood Goes to Hell," *Boston (MA) Herald*. August 29, 1993. in: *NewsBank. Film and Television*. 104:F1-F2. 1993.
___ "An Instinct for Trouble," *Boston (MA) Herald* March 20, 1992 in: *NewsBank. Film and Television*. 29:A5. 1992.
___ "**Johnny Mnemonic**," *Boston (MA) Herald*. May 26, 1995. in: *NewsBank. Film and Television*. 55:B5. 1995.
___ "Nimoy Ready to Pack Up His Pointed Ears," *Boston (MA) Herald*. December 6, 1991. in: *NewsBank. Names in the News*. 1:D6. 1992.

SCHAFER, WILLIAM J.
___ "The Imagination of Catastrophe," *North American Review* 268(3): 61-66. September 1983.

SCHAFFER, CARL
___ "Leivick's **The Golem** and the Golem Legend," in: Murphy, Patrick D., ed. **Staging the Impossible: The Fantastic Mode in Modern Drama**. Westport, CT: Greenwood, 1992. pp.137-149.

SCHAKEL, PETER J.
___ "Elusive Birds and Narrative Nets: The Appeal of Story in C. S. Lewis' **Chronicles of Narnia**," in: Walker, Andrew and Patric, James, eds. **A Christian for All Christians**. Washington, DC: Regnery, 1992. pp.116-131.

SCHALLER, HANS-WOLFGANG
___ "B. F. Skinner: **Walden Two** (1948)," in: Heuermann, Hartmut and Lange, Bernd-Peter, eds. **Die Utopie in der angloamerikanischen Literatur: Interpretationen**. Düsseldorf: Bagel, 1984. pp.219-234.

SCHECHTER, HAROLD
___ "The Bloody Chamber: Terror Films, Fairy Tales, and Taboo," in: Irons, Glenwood, ed. **Gender, Language and Myth: Essays on Popular Narrative**. Toronto: University of Toronto Press, 1992. pp.233-251.

SCHECTMAN, AARON H.
___ "Perpetuating Utopia," in: Saccaro Del Buffa, Giuseppa and Lewis, Arthur O., eds. **Utopie per gli Anni Ottana**. Rome: Gangemi Editore, 1986. pp.789-797.

SCHEER-SCHÄZLER, BRIGITTE
___ "Re-turning the Imagination oder SF&F, ein Abenteuer für Frauen," in: Grabher, Gudrun M. and Devine, Marureen, eds. **Women in Search of Literary Space**. Tübingen: Gunter Narr Verlag, 1992. pp.163-179.

SCHEICK, WILLIAM J.
___ (ed.) **The Critical Response to H. G. Wells**. Westport, CT: Greenwood, 1995. 194pp.

SCHELDE, PER
___ **Androids, Humanoids, and Other Science Fiction Monsters: Science and Soul in Science Fiction Films**. New York: New York University Press, 1993. 279pp.

SCHELLBACH, RICHARD J.
___ "The Twilight Zone: Tower of Terror," *Sci-Fi Entertainment* 1(5): 52-53, 55. February 1995.

SCHELLY, BILL
___ **The Golden Age of Comic Fandom**. Seattle, WA: Hamster Press, 1995. 144pp.

SCHENKEL, ELMAR
___ "John Cowper Powys und die Ursprünge der Phantasie," in: Kranz, Gisbert, ed. **Inklings: Jahrbuch für Literatur und Ästhetik**. 7. Band. Lüdenscheid, Germany: Stier, 1989. pp.121-138. [Not seen.]
___ "Phantasie und Bewußtseinsgeschichte: Zur Philosophie von Owen Barfields," in: Kranz, Gisbert, ed. **Inklings: Jahrbuch für Literatur und Ästhetik**. 9. Band. Lüdenscheid, Germany: Stier, 1991. pp.111-126. [Not seen.]
___ "Utopie und Phantastik in den Kinderbüchern von E. Nesbit," in: Kranz, Gisbert, ed. **Inklings: Jahrbuch für Literatur und Ästhetik**. 8. Band. Lüdenscheid, Germany: Stier, 1990. pp.103-124. [Not seen.]
___ "Visions From the Verge: Terror and Play in G. K. Chesterton's Imagination," in: Filmer, Kath, ed. **Twentieth-Century Fantasists: Essays in Culture, Society and Belief in Twentieth Century Mythopoeic Literature**. New York: St. Martin's, 1992. pp.34-46.

SCHERER, RENE
___ "Fourier, la famiglia e le utopie dei Lumi," in: Colombo, Arrigo and Quarta, Cosimo, eds. **Il Destino della Famiglia nell'Utopia**. Bari: Edizione Dedalo, 1991. pp.247-263.

SCHIAVONE, GIUSEPPE
___ **L'Utopia nella Storia: la Rivoluzione inglese**, by Arrigo Colombo, Giuseppe Schiavone and Robert Ashton. Bari: Edizioni Dedalo, 1992. 294pp. [Not seen.]
___ "Winstanley, un'utopia familiare nella Rivoluzione inglese," in: Colombo, Arrigo and Quarta, Cosimo, eds. **Il Destino della Famiglia nell'Utopia**. Bari: Edizione Dedalo, 1991. pp.145-166.

SCHICKE, ULRIKE
___ "Individuum und gesellschaft in Ursula K. Le Guins **The Dispossessed**, 1. Teil," *Quarber Merkur* 31(1): 23-34. June 1993. (No. 79)
___ "Individuum und Gesellschaft in Ursula K. Le Guins **The Dispossessed**, 2. Teil," *Quarber Merkur* 31(2): 3-13. Dezember 1993. (No. 80)
___ "Individuum und Gesellschaft in Ursula Le Guins **The Dispossessed**. 3. Teil und Schluß," *Quarber Merkur* 32(1): 3-20. June 1994. (Whole No. 81)

SCHIMEL, LAWRENCE
___ "Be Prepared to Save Tomorrow's Ecology in *Jump Raven's* Complex Future," *Science Fiction Age* 2(5): 76-78. July 1994.

SCHINDLER, RICHARD A.
___ "Canceled on TV? Comic Books to the Rescue!," *TV Guide* 41(30): 25. July 24, 1993.
___ "Joseph Noel Paton's Fairy Paintings: Fantasy Art as Victorian Narrative," *Scotia: Interdisciplinary Journal of Scottish Studies* 14: 13-29. 1990.

SCHLEIER, CURT
___ "Bradbury's Irish Stew of a Story Is Flavored Just Right," *Detroit (MI) News*. May 6, 1992. in: *NewsBank. Literature*. 45:F9. 1992

SCHLEIFER, PAUL C.
___ "Fear of the 'Other' in Melissa Scott's **Dreamships**," *Extrapolation* 35(4): 312-318. Winter 1994.

SCHLOBIN, ROGER C.
___ "Andre Norton," in: Bruccoli, Matthew J., ed. **Facts on File Bibliography of American Fiction 1919-1988**. New York: Facts on File, 1991. pp.382-384.

SCHLOBIN, ROGER C. (continued)
___ **Andre Norton: A Primary and Secondary Bibliography**. Revised edition, by Roger C. Schlobin and Irene H. Harrison. Framingham, MA: NESFA Press, 1994. 92pp.
___ "Andre Norton: The Author Becomes Her Fiction and Creates Life," in: Collins, Robert A. and Latham, Robert, eds. **Science Fiction and Fantasy Book Review Annual 1991**. Westport, CT: Greenwood, 1994. pp.172-177.
___ "The Artisan in Modern Fantasy," *Journal of the Fantastic in the Arts* 6(4): 285-294. 1995.
___ "The Craving for Meaning: Explicit Allegory in the Non-Implicit Age," *Journal of the Fantastic in the Arts* 5(1): 3-12. 1992. (No. 17)
___ "The Formulaic and Rites of Transformation in Andre Norton's Magic Series," in: Sullivan, C. W., III. **Science Fiction for Young Readers**. Westport, CT: Greenwood, 1993. pp.37-45.
___ "Pagan Survival: Why the Shaman in Modern Fantasy?," in: Morse, Donald E., ed. **The Celebration of the Fantastic**. Westport, CT: Greenwood, 1992. pp.39-48.

SCHLOSSBERG, HOWARD
___ "Science Fiction Writer Has Bad News From the Front," *Marketing News* 26(9): 15. April 27, 1992.

SCHLUETER, PAUL
___ "Supplement to 'Trends in Orwell Criticism, 1968-1984' (Through 1990)," *Bulletin of Bibliography* 49(2): 115-126. June 1992.

SCHLUTZE, BRUNO
___ "Herbert George Wells, **The War of the Worlds** (1898)," in: Heuermann, Harmut, ed. **Der Science Fiction Roman in der angloamerikanischen Literatur: Interpretationen**. Düsseldorf: Bagel, 1986. pp.47-64.

SCHMEIDLER, LUCY
___ "Subjective Strange," *New York Review of Science Fiction* No. 73: 16-17. September 1994.

SCHMERTZ, JOHANNA
___ "On Reading the Politics of **Total Recall**," *Post Script* 12(3): 34-42. Summer 1993.

SCHMIDT, JÜRGEN
___ "George Orwell: **Nineteen Eighty-Four** (1949)," in: Heuermann, Hartmut and Lange, Bernd-Peter, eds. **Die Utopie in der angloamerikanischen Literatur: Interpretationen**. Düsseldorf: Bagel, 1984. pp.235-258.

SCHMIDT, STANLEY
___ **Aliens and Alien Societies**. Cincinnati, OH: Writer's Digest Books, 1995. 226pp.
___ "Anatomy of a Sale: 'From the Corner of the Eye' to *Analog Science Fiction Science Fact*," in: Thompkins, David G., ed. **Science Fiction Writer's Market Place and Source Book**. Cincinnati, OH: Writer's Digest Books, 1994. pp.331-343.
___ "Authors vs. Editors," in: Dozois, Gardner, ed. **Writing Science Fiction and Fantasy**. New York: St. Martin's, 1991. pp.236-249.
___ "Editorial: Nouveaux Clichés," *Analog* 113(12): 4-10. October 1993.
___ "Editorial: Prime Directive," *Analog* 114(10): 4-10. August 1994.
___ "Editorial: The Manuscript That Never Was," *Analog* 113(3): 4-12. February 1993.
___ "Good Writing Is Not Enough," in: Dozois, Gardner, ed. **Writing Science Fiction and Fantasy**. New York: St. Martin's, 1991. pp.81-104.
___ "Hypertext as a Writing Tool," *SFWA Bulletin* 26(2): 6-10. Summer 1992. (No. 116)
___ "The Ideas That Wouldn't Die," in: Dozois, Gardner, ed. **Writing Science Fiction and Fantasy**. New York: St. Martin's, 1991. pp.200-207.
___ "Seeing Your Way to Better Stories," in: Dozois, Gardner, ed. **Writing Science Fiction and Fantasy**. New York: St. Martin's, 1991. pp.50-61.

SCHMIDT-GÜTH, JÜRGEN
___ "Doris Lessing, **Canopus in Argos: Archives** (1979ff)," by Gudrun Güth and Jürgen Schmidt-Güth. in: Heuermann, Harmut, ed. **Der Science Fiction Roman in der angloamerikanischen Literatur: Interpretationen**. Düsseldorf: Bagel, 1986. pp.375-399.

SCHWARTZ, JOHN
___ "On the Net's Cutting Edge: **The Diamond Age**, Neal Stephenson's New Science Fiction Novel, Is Turning Him into a Cyber-lebrity," *Washington (DC) Post* p.D1. February 21, 1995.

SCHWARTZ, JULIUS
___ "The Bester Years of My Life: Memoirs of a Time Traveller, Part 2," *Amazing Stories* 68(4): 55-59. July 1993.
___ "Quoth Ray Bradbury: Thank God for Julie: Memoirs of a Time Traveller, Part 3," *Amazing Stories* 68(6): 59-65. September 1993.

SCHWARTZBERG, SHLOMO
___ "***In the Mouth of Madness***," *Cinefantastique* 25(5): 8-9. October 1994.
___ "KNB EFX Madness," *Cinefantastique* 25(5): 11. October 1994.

SCHWARTZKOPFF, FRANCES
___ "Sci-Fi Writer Stretches Outer Limits of Sound," *Atlanta Constitution* Sec. XJ, p. 1. April 1, 1992. [Not seen.]

SCHWED, MARK
___ "On the Horizon: Whole New Worlds," *TV Guide* 41(30): 29-31. July 24, 1993.
___ "The Universe Is Expanding All over the Dial," by Timothy Carlson and Mark Schwed. *TV Guide* 41(1): 16-19. January 2, 1993. (Issue 2075)

SCHWEICHER, ERIC
___ "Aspects of the Fall in **The Silmarillion**," in: Reynolds, Patricia and GoodKnight, Glen H., eds. **Proceedings of the J. R. R. Tolkien Centenary Conference, Keble College, Oxford, 1992**. Altadena, CA: Mythopoeic Press, 1995. pp.167-171. (*Mythlore* Vol. 21, No. 2, Winter 1996, Whole No. 80)

SCHWEIGER, DANIEL
___ "The Amazing Colossal Kid: Low Rent Movie Magic," *Cinefantastique* 23(1): 23. August 1992.
___ "The Amazing Colossal Kid: Tyke Star Temper Tantrums," *Cinefantastique* 23(1): 18. August 1992.
___ "***Brain Dead*** (Review)," *Cinefantastique* 23(5): 59. February 1993.
___ "***Cool World***," *Cinefantastique* 22(6): 32-33, 60. June 1992
___ "***The Hand That Rocks the Cradle*** (Review)," *Cinefantastique* 22(6): 54. June 1992
___ "***Honey, I Blew Up the Kid***," *Cinefantastique* 23(1): 16-22. August 1992.

SCHWEITZER, DARRELL
___ "About 'The Whisperer in Darkness'," *Lovecraft Studies* No. 32: 8-11. Spring 1995.
___ "Brian Lumley," in: Schweitzer, Darrell. **Speaking of Horror: Interviews With Writers of the Supernatural**. San Bernardino, CA: Borgo, 1994. pp.75-80.
___ "Charles L. Grant," in: Schweitzer, Darrell. **Speaking of Horror: Interviews With Writers of the Supernatural**. San Bernardino, CA: Borgo, 1994. pp.47-58.
___ "Chet Williamson," in: Schweitzer, Darrell. **Speaking of Horror: Interviews With Writers of the Supernatural**. San Bernardino, CA: Borgo, 1994. pp.103-112.
___ "Dennis Etchison," in: Schweitzer, Darrell. **Speaking of Horror: Interviews With Writers of the Supernatural**. San Bernardino, CA: Borgo, 1994. pp.37-46.
___ "F. Paul Wilson," in: Schweitzer, Darrell. **Speaking of Horror: Interviews With Writers of the Supernatural**. San Bernardino, CA: Borgo, 1994. pp.113-125.
___ "How Much of Dunsany Is Worth Reading?," *Studies in Weird Fiction* No. 10: 19-23. Fall 1991.
___ "An Interview With Fritz Leiber," *Marion Zimmer Bradley's Fantasy Magazine* No. 15: 7-10. Winter 1992.
___ "Interview With Gahan Wilson," *Marion Zimmer Bradley's Fantasy Magazine* No. 27: 42-46. Spring 1995.
___ "An Interview With Mike Resnick," *Marion Zimmer Bradley's Fantasy Magazine* No. 17: 53-58. Fall 1992.
___ "Interview With Peter Beagle," *Marion Zimmer Bradley's Fantasy Magazine* No. 23: 46-49. Spring 1994.
___ "Interview With Ray Nelson," *Marion Zimmer Bradley's Fantasy Magazine* No. 25: 40-44. Fall 1994.

SCHWEITZER, DARRELL (continued)
___ **Lord Dunsany: A Bibliography**, by S. T. Joshi and Darrell Schweitzer. Metuchen, NJ: Scarecrow, 1993. 389pp.
___ "M. R. James and H. P. Lovecraft: The Ghostly and the Cosmic," *Studies in Weird Fiction* No. 15: 12-16. Summer 1994.
___ "Manly Wade Wellman," in: Schweitzer, Darrell. **Speaking of Horror: Interviews With Writers of the Supernatural**. San Bernardino, CA: Borgo, 1994. pp.93-102.
___ "Ramsey Campbell," in: Schweitzer, Darrell. **Speaking of Horror: Interviews With Writers of the Supernatural**. San Bernardino, CA: Borgo, 1994. pp.23-36.
___ "Richard Middleton: Beauty, Sadness, and Terror," in: Schweitzer, Darrell, ed. **Discovering Classic Horror Fiction I**. Mercer Island, WA: Starmont, 1992. pp.34-40.
___ "Robert Bloch," in: Schweitzer, Darrell. **Speaking of Horror: Interviews With Writers of the Supernatural**. San Bernardino, CA: Borgo, 1994. pp.9-22.
___ "SFC Interview: Kim Newman," *Science Fiction Chronicle* 17(2): 6, 44, 46, 48. December 1995/January 1996.
___ "SFC Interviews: Craig Shaw Gardner," *Science Fiction Chronicle* 15(8): 7, 35-36. June 1994.
___ "SFC Interviews: Marvin Kaye," *Science Fiction Chronicle* 14(2): 5, 27-28. November 1992.
___ "SFC Interviews: Michael Swanwick," *Science Fiction Chronicle* 16(5): 5, 34-36. March/April 1995.
___ **Speaking of Horror: Interviews With Writers of the Supernatural**. San Bernardino, CA: Borgo Press, 1994. 136pp.
___ "Style: Knock Out Weak Verbs!," in: Thompkins, David G., ed. **Science Fiction Writer's Market Place and Source Book**. Cincinnati, OH: Writer's Digest Books, 1994. pp.25-29.
___ "A Talk With Fred Chappell," *Worlds of Fantasy and Horror* 1(1): 40-43. Summer 1994. (No. 1)
___ "Tanith Lee," in: Schweitzer, Darrell. **Speaking of Horror: Interviews With Writers of the Supernatural**. San Bernardino, CA: Borgo, 1994. pp.59-66.
___ "Thomas Ligotti," in: Schweitzer, Darrell. **Speaking of Horror: Interviews With Writers of the Supernatural**. San Bernardino, CA: Borgo, 1994. pp.67-74.
___ "*Weird Tales* Talks With F. Paul Wilson," *Weird Tales* 53(4): 49-56. Winter 1992/1993. (No. 305)
___ "*Weird Tales* Talks With Ian Watson," *Weird Tales* 54(2): 54-59. Summer 1993. (No. 307)
___ "*Weird Tales* Talks With Nina Kiriki Hoffman," *Weird Tales* 54(1): 60-64. Spring 1993. (No. 306)
___ "When Is a Fantasy Novel Not a Fantasy Novel?," *Studies in Weird Fiction* No. 11: 29-31. Spring 1992.
___ "Will the Real Dracula Please Stand Up?," *Sci-Fi Entertainment* 1(1): 56-61, 72. June 1994.
___ "William F. Nolan," in: Schweitzer, Darrell. **Speaking of Horror: Interviews With Writers of the Supernatural**. San Bernardino, CA: Borgo, 1994. pp.81-92.
___ (ed.) **Discovering Classic Horror Fiction I**. Mercer Island, WA: Starmont, 1992. 191pp.

SCOBIE, STEPHEN
___ "What's the Story, Mother?: The Mourning of the Alien," *Science Fiction Studies* 20(1): 80-93. March 1993.

SCOFFHAM, S.
___ "Realms of Fantasy," *Junior Education* pp.22-23. June 1993. [Not seen.]

SCOTT, ELAINE
___ **Movie Magic: Behind the Scenes with Special Effects**. New York: William Morrow, 1995. 95pp.

SCOTT, MELISSA
___ "Fantasy Men," *Lambda Book Report* 4(3): 13-14. March 1994.

SCOTT, RANDALL W.
___ "Comics and Libraries and the Scholarly World," *Popular Culture in Libraries* 1(1): 81-84. 1993.
___ **Comics Librarianship: A Handbook**. Jefferson, NC: McFarland, 1990. 188pp.
___ "Research Libraries of Interest to Fandom," in: Hopkins, Mariane S., ed. **Fandom Directory No. 14**. Springfield, VA: Fandata, 1992. pp.138-148.

SCOTT, RANDALL W.   **SERRANO, AMANDA**

SCOTT, RANDALL W. (continued)
___ "Research Library Collections of Science Fiction," in: Barron, Neil, ed. **Anatomy of Wonder 4.** New York: Bowker, 1995. pp.738-764.

SCOTT, TONY
___ "Reviews: *Babylon 5*," *Variety* 353(12): 69. January 24, 1994.
___ "TV Reviews: *The Outer Limits*," *Variety* 358(7): 30. March 20, 1995.

SCULL, CHRISTINA
___ **J. R. R. Tolkien: Artist and Illustrator**, by Wayne G. Hammond and Christina Scull. Boston, MA: Houghton Mifflin, 1995. 208pp.
___ "Open Minds, Closed Minds in the **Lord of the Rings**," in: Reynolds, Patricia and GoodKnight, Glen H., eds. **Proceedings of the J. R. R. Tolkien Centenary Conference, Keble College, Oxford, 1992.** Altadena, CA: Mythopoeic Press, 1995. pp.151-157. (*Mythlore* Vol. 21, No. 2, Winter 1996, Whole No. 80)

SEABROOK, JACK
___ **Martians and Misplaced Clues: The Life and Work of Fredric Brown.** Bowling Green, OH: Popular Press, 1994. 312pp.

SEAGO, KATE
___ " 'Jurassic' Sells Well at Bookstores, Too," *Los Angeles (CA) Daily News.* May 19, 1993. in: *NewsBank. Literature.* 45:B2. 1993.

SEARLES, A. LANGLEY
___ "Anthology Days: An Interview with E. F. Bleiler," *Fantasy Commentator* 8(3/4): 204-213. Fall 1995. (Whole No. 47/48)
___ "Forgotten Fantasy Verse: I, Arthur Davison Ficke," *Fantasy Commentator* 8(1/2): 14-16. Winter 1993/1994. (Whole No. 45/46.)
___ "Henry S. Whitehead: A Retrospection," *Fantasy Commentator* 8(3/4): 186-200. Fall 1995. (Whole No. 47/48)

SEARS, DAVID
___ "The Making of **Babylon 5**," by David Sears and David English. *Compute* 16(7): p.68-74. July 1994. (Cited from *IAC Insite* on-line service.)

SEBOLD, RUSSELL P.
___ **Bécquer in sus narraciones fantásticas.** Madrid: Taurus, 1989. 217pp.

SEDGEWICK, CRISTINA
___ "The Fork in the Road: Can Science Fiction Survive in Postmodern, Megacorporate America?," *Science Fiction Studies* 18(1): 11-52. March 1991.

SEE, LISA
___ "PW Interviews: Octavia E. Butler," *Publishers Weekly* 240(50): 50-51. December 13, 1993.

SEEBER, HANS-ULRICH
___ "Frank Herbert, **Dune-Trilogie** (1965ff)," in: Heuermann, Harmut, ed. **Der Science Fiction Roman in der angloamerikanischen Literatur: Interpretationen.** Düsseldorf: Bagel, 1986. pp.253-274.
___ "Utopian Mentality in George Eliot's **Middlemarch** (1871/72) and in D. H. Lawrence's **The Rainbow**," *Utopian Studies* 6(1): 30-39. 1995.

SEED, DAVID
___ "Breaking the Bounds: The Rhetoric of Limits in the Works of Edgar Allan Poe, His Contemporaries, and Adaptors," in: Seed, David, ed. **Anticipations: Essays on Early Science Fiction and Its Precursors.** Liverpool: Liverpool University Press, 1995. pp.75-97.
___ "The Postwar Jeremiads of Philip Wylie," *Science Fiction Studies* 22(2): 234-251. July 1995.
___ "Push-Button Holocaust: Mordecai Roshwald's **Level 7**," *Foundation* No. 57: 68-86. Spring 1993.
___ "Take-over Bids: The Power Fantasies of Frederik Pohl and Cyril Kornbluth," *Foundation* No. 59: 42-58. Autumn 1993.
___ (ed.) **Anticipations: Essays on Early Science Fiction and Its Precursors.** Liverpool: Liverpool University Press, 1995. 225pp.

SEELS, JAMES T.
___ "Collecting Dean Koontz," *Firsts: Collecting Modern First Editions* 3(10): 28-36. October 1993.

SEEMAN, CHRIS
___ "Tolkien's Revision of the Romantic Tradition," in: Reynolds, Patricia and GoodKnight, Glen H., eds. **Proceedings of the J. R. R. Tolkien Centenary Conference, Keble College, Oxford, 1992.** Altadena, CA: Mythopoeic Press, 1995. pp.73-83. (*Mythlore* Vol. 21, No. 2, Winter 1996, Whole No. 80)

SEESHOLTZ, MEL
___ "*Homo Electronicus*: Futures of Human-Enhancement, a Pictorial Primer of Probable Possibilities," in: Wolf, Milton T. and Mallett, Daryl F., eds. **Imaginative Futures: Proceedings of the 1993 Science Fiction Research Association Conference.** San Bernardino, CA: Jacob's Ladder Books, 1995. pp.229-244.

SEGAL, HOWARD P.
___ **Future Imperfect: The Mixed Blessings of Technology in America.** Amherst: University of Massachusetts Press, 1994. 245pp.

SEIDEMAN, TONY
___ " 'Raiders' Setting Sales Marks, Paramount Claims 500,000 in Route," *Variety* p. 27-28. November 23, 1983.

SEIDMAN, MICHAEL
___ "Choosing Your Genre: The Fantasy," *Writer's Digest* 72(9): 37. September 1992.
___ "Choosing Your Genre: The Horror Novel," *Writer's Digest* 72(10): 35. October 1992.
___ "Choosing Your Genre: The Science Fiction Novel," *Writer's Digest* 72(8): 40. August 1992.

SELANDER, VICTORIA
___ "Comes the Stranger," *Starlog* No. 188: 75-77. March 1993.

SELLIN, BERNARD
___ "Journeys into Fantasy: The Fiction of David Lindsay and C. S. Lewis," in: Walker, Andrew and Patric, James, eds. **A Christian for All Christians.** Washington, DC: Regnery, 1992. pp.98-115.

SELLIN, CHRISTINE
___ "Quick Cuts: Muppetized Dickens," *Cinefex* No. 53: 9-10. February 1993.

SENF, CAROL A.
___ **The Critical Response to Bram Stoker.** Westport, CT: Greenwood Press, 1993. 216pp.

SENIOR, W. A.
___ "From the Begetting of Monsters: Distortion as Unifier in **A Canticle for Liebowitz**," *Extrapolation* 34(4): 329-339. Winter 1993.
___ "Medieval Literature and Modern Fantasy: Toward a Common Metaphysics," *Journal of the Fantastic in the Arts* 3(3): 32-49. 1994.
___ **Stephen R. Donaldson's Chronicles of Thomas Covenant: Variations on the Fantasy Tradition.** Kent, OH: Kent State University Press, 1995. 275pp.

SENIOR, WILLIAM
___ "Donaldson and Tolkien," *Mythlore* 18(4): 37-43. Autumn 1992. (No. 70)
___ "New Fantasy Writers in 1990," in: Collins, Robert A. and Latham, Robert, eds. **Science Fiction and Fantasy Book Review Annual 1991.** Westport, CT: Greenwood, 1994. pp.70-78.
___ "Oliphaunts in the Perilous Realm: The Function of Internal Wonder in Fantasy," in: Sanders, Joe, ed. **Functions of the Fantastic.** Westport, CT: Greenwood, 1995. pp.115-124.
___ "The Year in Fantasy Literature, 1990," by William Senior and C. W. Sullivan, III. in: Collins, Robert A. and Latham, Robert, eds. **Science Fiction and Fantasy Book Review Annual 1991.** Westport, CT: Greenwood, 1994. pp.49-69.

SENN, BRYAN
___ **Fantastic Cinema Subject Guide: A Topical Index to 2500 Horror, Science Fiction, and Fantasy Films**, by Bryan Senn and John Johnson. Jefferson, NC: McFarland, 1992. 682pp.

SERRANO, AMANDA
___ "T. H. White's Defense of Guenevere: The Portrait of a 'Real' Person," *Mythlore* 21(1): 9-13. Summer 1995. (No. 79)

SERVER, LEE
___ **Danger Is My Business: An Illustrated History of the Fabulous Pulp Magazines 1896-1953**. San Francisco, CA: Chronicle Books, 1993. 144pp.
___ **Over My Dead Body: The Sensational Age of American Paperbacks 1945-1955**. San Francisco, CA: Chronicle Books, 1994. 108pp.

SERVICE, PAMELA F.
___ "On Writing Sci Fi and Fantasy for Kids," *ALAN Review* 19(3): 16-18. Spring 1992.

SESERMAN, SUE
___ "Rebel With a Cause: *Star Wars Rebel Assault*," *LucasFilm Fan Club* No. 21: 4-5. Winter 1994.

SETIYA, KIERAN
___ "Empiricism and the Limits of Knowledge in Lovecraft," *Lovecraft Studies* No. 25: 18-22. Fall 1991.
___ "Lovecraft on Human Knowledge: An Exchange," by Kieran Setiya and S. T. Joshi. *Lovecraft Studies* No. 24: 22-23. Spring 1991.
___ "Lovecraft's Semantics," *Lovecraft Studies* No. 27: 26-30. Fall 1992.
___ "Two Notes on Lovecraft," *Lovecraft Studies* No. 26: 14-16. Spring 1992.

SEVASTAKIS, MICHAEL
___ **Songs of Love and Death: The Classical American Horror Film of the 1930s**. Westport, CT: Greenwood, 1993. 232pp.

SEY, JAMES A.
___ "The *Terminator* Syndrome: Science Fiction, Cinema, and Contemporary Culture," *Liberator: Tydskrif vir Besondere en Vergelykende Taal- en Literatuurstudie* (South Africa) 13(3): 13-19. November 1992.
___ "Trashing the Millenium: Subjectivity and Technology in Cyberpunk Science Fiction," *Liberator: Tydskrif vir Besondere en Vergelykende Taal-en Literatuurstudie* (South Africa) 13(1): 111-117. April 1992.

SEYER, GEOFFREY
___ "'Morris Was a Giant': The Quest of T. E. Lawrence," *Journal of the William Morris Society* 10(4): 48-52. Spring 1994.

SEYMOUR, MIRANDA
___ **Robert Graves: Life on the Edge**. New York: Holt, 1995. 524pp.

SHABERMAN, RAPHAEL B.
___ **George MacDonald: A Bibliographical Study**. Detroit: Omnigraphics, 1990. 176pp.

SHAFI, MONIKA
___ **Utopische Entwürfe in der Literatur von Frauen**. Bern: Peter Lang, 1990. 135pp.

SHAHEEN, JACK
___ "*Aladdin*: Animated Racism," *Cineaste* 20(1): 49. 1993.

SHAMRAY, GERRY
___ "*Double Dragon*," *Cinefantastique* 25(3): 54-55. June 1994.

SHANK, THEODORE
___ "The Shock of the Actual: Disrupting the Theatrical Illusion," in: Murphy, Patrick D., ed. **Staging the Impossible: The Fantastic Mode in Modern Drama**. Westport, CT: Greenwood, 1992. pp.169-181.

SHANKS, EDWARD
___ "**The Purple Cloud** and Its Author (1929)," in: **Shiel in Diverse Hands: A Collection of Essays**. Cleveland, OH: Reynolds Morse Foundation, 1983. pp.23-29.

SHANNON, JEFF
___ "*Encino Man*: Might As Well Roll It Back to the Stone Age (Review)," *Seattle (WA) Times*. May 22, 1992. in: *NewsBank. Film and Television*. 52:D6. 1992.

SHANNON, JOHN
___ "Panic on Liberty Island," *Cinefex* No. 52: 79-80. November 1992.

SHANNON, JOHN (continued)
___ "Quick Cuts: Under Heavy Cetacean," *Cinefex* No. 55: 17-18. August 1993.
___ "Short Intruders," *Cinefex* No. 51: 79-80. August 1992.

SHANNON, L. R.
___ "Science Times: I Left My Heart in the Land of Cyberpunk," *New York Times* Sec. C, p. 8. May 12, 1992.

SHAPIRO, MARC
___ "The Adventures of Socrates Poole," *Starlog* No. 203: 55-58. June 1994.
___ "Another Fine Ferengi," by Sharon Snyder and Marc Shapiro. *Starlog* No. 190: 36-39. May 1993.
___ "Battle of the Immortals," *Starlog* 185: 32-35. December 1992.
___ "Beyond the Dark," *Starlog* No. 207: 46-50, 72. October 1994.
___ "Blood & Shadows," *Starlog* 185: 40-43, 72. December 1992.
___ "Boss of the **Penal Colony**," *Starlog* No. 200: 48-51. March 1994.
___ "Bounty Hunter," *Starlog* No. 204: 27-30. July 1994.
___ "***Coneheads***," *Starlog* No. 194: 43-48. September 1993.
___ "***Cool World***," *Starlog* 178: 32-35, 70. May 1992.
___ "Cosmic Cowboy," *Starlog* No. 197: 63-66. December 1993.
___ "Cosmic Mechanic," *Starlog* No. 189: 27-29, 67. April 1993.
___ "Dark Designs," *Starlog* 179: 27-31. June 1992.
___ "Dark Knight Director," *Starlog* 180: 40-45, 75. July 1992.
___ "Dark Knights in Gotham Again," *Starlog* 178: 40-46. May 1992.
___ "***Demolition Man***," *Starlog* No. 195: 32-37, 72. October 1993.
___ "Demon in the Sewers," *Starlog* No. 183: 38-41. October 1992.
___ "Designer of Tomorrow," *Starlog* No. 193: 75-81. August 1993.
___ "Devil's Advocate," *Starlog* No. 202: 46-49. May 1994.
___ "Dinosaur Safari," *Starlog* No. 175: 94-97. February 1992.
___ "Excellent Adventures?," *Starlog* No. 184: 80-81. November 1992.
___ "Farewell to Spock," *Starlog* No. 174: 30-33, 71. January 1992.
___ "Grand Illusionist," *Starlog* No. 212: 41-44. March 1995.
___ "Hellvision," *Starlog* 181: 76-80. August 1992.
___ "Heroic Android," by Joe Nazzaro and Marc Shapiro. in: McDonnell, David, ed. **Starlog's Science Fiction Heroes and Heroines**. New York: Crescent Books, 1995. pp.28-30.
___ "I'm Invisible and You're Not," *Starlog* 178: 7-9. May 1992.
___ "The Immortal Man," *Starlog* No. 174: 48-51, 71. January 1992.
___ "In Producer Country," *Starlog* 177: 52-55. April 1992.
___ "Independent Data," *Starlog* No. 221: 27-29. December 1995.
___ "Knightmare Master," *Starlog* No. 216: 40-45. July 1995.
___ "The Labors of Hercules," *Starlog* No. 211: 55-58. February 1995.
___ "***Last Action Hero***," *Starlog* No. 192: 39-46. July 1993.
___ "Last Action Man," *Starlog* No. 194: 55-57. September 1993.
___ "Man on Fire," *Starlog* No. 195: 63-65. October 1993.
___ "***Mask*** Maker," *Starlog* No. 205: 32-35. August 1994.
___ "Night of the Cat," *Starlog* No. 183: 42-45. October 1992.
___ "A Passion for Moviemaking," *Starlog* 182: 46-49. September 1992.
___ "Quantum Leaper," by Ian Spelling and Marc Shapiro. in: McDonnell, David, ed. **Starlog's Science Fiction Heroes and Heroines**. New York: Crescent Books, 1995. pp.87-89.
___ "Ranger of Fortune," *Starlog* No. 190: 49-51. May 1993.
___ "Rebel Rouser," *Starlog* No. 176: 54-56. March 1992.
___ "Robin Forever," *Starlog* No. 217: 27-30. August 1995.
___ "The Savage Beast," by Marc Shapiro and Edward Gross. in: McDonnell, David, ed. **Starlog's Science Fiction Heroes and Heroines**. New York: Crescent Books, 1995. pp.66-69.
___ "School's Out," *Starlog* No. 189: 38-39, 68. April 1993.
___ "Second-in-Command," *Starlog* No. 204: 47-50. July 1994. Also in: McDonnell, David, ed. **Starlog's Science Fiction Heroes and Heroines**. New York: Crescent Books, 1995. pp.31-33.
___ "SF's Video Hero," *Starlog* 179: 66-69, 84. June 1992.
___ "Sleeper Cop," *Starlog* No. 196: 27-30. November 1993.
___ "***Star Trek: Deep Space Nine***," *Starlog* No. 186: 40-43. January 1993.
___ "***Stargate***," *Starlog* No. 209: 32-37. December 1994.
___ "Storm Gathering," *Starlog* No. 219: 50-53. October 1995.
___ "Time Keeper," *Starlog* No. 188: 27-31. March 1993.
___ "Time Tripper," by Lee Goldberg and Marc Shapiro. in: McDonnell, David, ed. **Starlog's Science Fiction Heroes and Heroines**. New York: Crescent Books, 1995. pp.84-86.
___ "To Be or Not to Be?," *Starlog* No. 193: 42-46. August 1993.
___ "Treading Water," *Starlog* No. 217: 67-69. August 1995.
___ "Virtual Virtuoso," *Starlog* No. 218: 32-35. September 1995.
___ "***Waterworld***," *Starlog* No. 216: 16-17. July 1995.

SHERMAN, PAUL

___ "Cyberpunk Film Festival Is Pure Sci-Fi Splendor," *Boston (MA) Herald*. March 15, 1994. in: *NewsBank. Film and Television*. 31:G5. 1994.

___ "***Delicatessen*** a Juicy Delight (Review)," *Boston (MA) Herald*. April 17, 1992. in: *NewsBank. Film and Television*. 40:F14. 1992.

___ "***Encino Man*** Is Predictable Teen Comedy (Review)," *Boston (MA) Herald*. May 19, 1992. in: *NewsBank. Film and Television*. 52:C14. 1992.

___ "For Trek Merchandisers, the Sky's No Limit," *Boston (MA) Herald*. November 17, 1994. in: *NewsBank. Film and Television*. 10:A1. 1995.

___ "Futuristic ***Freejack*** Falls Flat on Face (Review)," *Boston (MA) Herald*. January 18, 1992. in: *NewsBank. Film and Television*. 11:D8. 1992.

___ "***Hellraiser III*** Goes Down In Flames (Review)," *Boston (MA) Herald*. September 12, 1992. in: *NewsBank. Film and Television*. 91:A10. 1992.

___ " 'Honey' Sequel's Special Effects Will Grow on You (Review)," *Boston (MA) Herald*. July 17, 1992. in: *NewsBank. Film and Television*. 70:D14. 1992.

___ "***Lawnmower Man*** Is a Seedy Sci-Fi Flick (Review)," *Boston (MA) Herald*. March 6, 1992. in: *NewsBank. Film and Television*. 33:A6. 1992.

___ "Lowest ***Highlander***," *Boston (MA) Herald*. January 28, 1995. in: *NewsBank. Film and Television*. 17:C12. 1995.

___ "***Meteor Man*** a Blast (Review)," *Boston (MA) Herald*. August 6, 1993. in: *NewsBank. Art*. 18:E5. 1993.

___ "***Mom/Dad*** Is Just A ***Bill and Ted*** Reject (Review)," *Boston (MA) Herald*. July 25, 1992. in: *NewsBank. Film and Television*. 72:B7. 1992.

___ "No Escaping It: ***No Escape*** Is Just a Generic Action Flick," *Boston (MA) Herald*. April 29, 1994. in: *NewsBank. Film and Television*. 46:E4-E5. 1994.

___ "Punk Apocalypse Saga Doesn't Always Hit Its Target," *Boston (MA) Herald*. March 31, 1995. in: *NewsBank. Film and Television*. 50:C4. 1995.

___ "***The Puppet Masters*** Is a No Brainer of Sci-Fi," *Boston (MA) Herald*. October 22, 1994. in: *NewsBank. Film and Television*. 114:F9. 1994.

___ "***Reflecting*** More Than Skin Deep Teen Flick (Review)," *Boston (MA) Herald*. January 31, 1992. in: *NewsBank. Film and Television*. 25:A9. 1992.

___ "***Split Second*** Dragged Down (Review)," *Boston (MA) Herald*. May 1, 1992. in: *NewsBank. Film and Television*. 58:G10. 1992.

___ "***Stay Tuned*** Is out of Focus on TV Parody (Review)," *Boston (MA) Herald*. August 15, 1992. in: *NewsBank. Film and Television*. 84:A9. 1992.

___ "Stephen King's Latest Yarn, ***Sleepwalkers***, Is a Yawner (Review)," *Boston (MA) Herald*. April 11, 1992. in: *NewsBank. Film and Television*. 46:C10. 1992.

___ "What a Long, Strange ***Trek*** It's Been," *Boston (MA) Herald*. December 6, 1991. in: *NewsBank. Film and Television*. 7:D4-D5. 1992.

SHERVATYKH, YURI

___ "SF in Russia," by Yuri Shervatykh and Boris Ivanov. *Locus* 35(3): 54. September 1993.

SHICHTMAN, MARTIN B.

___ "Wagner and the Arthurian Tradition," in: Fries, Maureen and Watson, Jeanie, eds. **Approaches to the Teaching of the Arthurian Tradition**. New York: Modern Language Association, 1992. pp.139-142.

SHIEL, M. P.

___ "On Printing," in: **Shiel in Diverse Hands: A Collection of Essays**. Cleveland, OH: Reynolds Morse Foundation, 1983. pp.406.

___ "On Reading and Writing (Revised Version, 1950)," in: **Shiel in Diverse Hands: A Collection of Essays**. Cleveland, OH: Reynolds Morse Foundation, 1983. pp.449-483.

___ "On Reading (First Version, 1909)," in: **Shiel in Diverse Hands: A Collection of Essays**. Cleveland, OH: Reynolds Morse Foundation, 1983. pp.406-447.

SHINER, LEWIS

___ "Inside the Movement: Past, Present, and Future," in: Slusser, George E. and Shippey, Tom, eds. **Fiction 2000: Cyberpunk and the Future of Narrative**. Athens: University of Georgia Press, 1992. pp.17-25.

SHIPIRO, MARC

___ "Some Kind of Mutant," *Starlog* No. 197: 27-30. December 1993.

SHIPPEY, TOM

___ "The Critique of America in Contemporary Science Fiction," *Foundation* No. 61: 36-49. Summer 1994.

___ "The Critique of America in Contemporary Science Fiction," *Interzone* No. 88: 12-17. October 1994.

___ "Heroes and Heroism: Tolkien's Problems, Tolkien's Solutions," *Lembas Extra*. [Leiden]: Tolkien Genootschap Unquendor, 1991. pp.5-17. [Not Seen, cf. *Mythlore*.]

___ **The Road to Middle Earth**. 2nd ed. London: Grafton, 1992. 337pp.

___ "Semiotic Ghosts and Ghostliness in the Work of Bruce Sterling," in: Slusser, George E. and Shippey, Tom, eds. **Fiction 2000: Cyberpunk and the Future of Narrative**. Athens: University of Georgia Press, 1992. pp.208-220.

___ "Tolkien and the Gawain-Poet," in: Reynolds, Patricia and GoodKnight, Glen H., eds. **Proceedings of the J. R. R. Tolkien Centenary Conference, Keble College, Oxford, 1992**. Altadena, CA: Mythopoeic Press, 1995. pp.213-220. (*Mythlore* Vol. 21, No. 2, Winter 1996, Whole No. 80)

___ "Tolkien as a Post-War Writer," in: Reynolds, Patricia and GoodKnight, Glen H., eds. **Proceedings of the J. R. R. Tolkien Centenary Conference, Keble College, Oxford, 1992**. Altadena, CA: Mythopoeic Press, 1995. pp.84-93. (*Mythlore* Vol. 21, No. 2, Winter 1996, Whole No. 80)

___ (ed.) **Fiction 2000: Cyberpunk and the Future of Narrative**, ed. by George E. Slusser and Tom Shippey. Athens: University of Georgia Press, 1992. 303pp.

SHIRLEY, JOHN

___ "The Social Future: An Evolving Essay, Part 3: Completely Unauthorized Possibilities," *Science Fiction Eye* No. 12: 37-41. Summer 1993.

___ "The Social Future, An Evolving Essay, Part 1: Business Ethics, an Oxymoron," *Science Fiction Eye* No. 10: 73-76. June 1992.

___ "The Social Future, An Evolving Essay, Part 2: Deception as Usual...," *Science Fiction Eye* No. 11: 29-34. December 1992.

___ "Violence," *Science Fiction Eye* No. 13: 47-53. Spring 1994.

SHOCKLEY, W. M.

___ "Macro-Desiacs, and Five Other Time (Savers) Wasters," *The Report: The Fiction Writer's Magazine* 2(6): 29-31. April 1992. (No. 59)

___ "Workshopping by Computer," *The Report: The Fiction Writer's Magazine* No. 10: 9. Summer 1993.

SHOOK, KARL

___ "Gentleman Avenger," *Starlog* No. 175: 77-81. February 1992.

SHOR, FRANCIS

___ "**The Iron Heel**'s Marginal(ized) Utopia," *Extrapolation* 35(3): 211-229. Fall 1994.

SHREEVE, JOHN

___ "A Stainless Steel Rap: Harry Harrison Interviewed," *Interzone* No. 72: 23-26. June 1993.

SHRIEVES, LINDA

___ "Fox's Cult Favorite Edges Toward Mainstream Popularity," *Orlando (FL) Sentinel*. October 14, 1994. in: *NewsBank. Film and Television*. 117:F14. 1994.

SHULGASSER, BARBARA

___ "Batman's Happy Medium (Review)," *San Francisco (CA) Examiner*. December 27, 1993. in: *NewsBank. Art* 36:G3. 1993.

___ "Bill & Ted's Latest Is Bogus, But Its Better," *San Francisco (CA) Examiner*. July 19, 1991. in: *NewsBank. Film and Television*. 65:E9-10. 1991.

___ "Director Takes on the Bard but Tempest Fugit (Review)," *San Francisco (CA) Examiner*. November 22, 1991. in: *NewsBank. Film and Television*. 6:D2-D3. 1992.

___ "The Fight of the Living Dead: ***Universal Soldier*** Delivers a Blow to Recycling Programs (Review)," *San Francisco (CA) Examiner*. July 10, 1992. in: *NewsBank. Film and Television*. 74:G2. 1992.

___ "'Giggles' Not Much of a Cutup (Review)," *San Francisco (CA) Examiner*. October 24, 1992. in: *NewsBank. Film and Television*. 100:G14. 1992.

SHULGASSER, BARBARA

SHULGASSER, BARBARA (continued)
___ "Guess Who We're Having for Dinner: French Co-Directors' **Delicatessen** Is a Mouthful, and Full of Belly Laughs (Review)," *San Francisco (CA) Examiner*. April 10, 1992. in: *NewsBank. Film and Television*. 40:F13. 1992.
___ "**Judge Dredd**: It's the (Arm)Pits," *San Francisco (CA) Examiner*. June 30, 1995. in: *NewsBank. Film and Television*. 63:A12. 1995.
___ "King's **Sleepwalkers** Falls Down (Review)," *San Francisco (CA) Examiner*. April 10, 1992. in: *NewsBank. Film and Television*. 46:C8. 1992.
___ "Not With a Bang But a Wenders (Review)," *San Francisco (CA) Examiner*. January 24, 1992. in: *NewsBank. Film and Television*. 26: F14-G1. 1992.
___ "An Old-Fashioned Cop in the Future (Review)," *San Francisco (CA) Examiner* October 8, 1993. in: *NewsBank. Film and Television*. 114:G7. 1993.
___ "Overcome By Gravity: **Radio Flyer** Never Takes Off (Review)," *San Francisco (CA) Examiner*. February 21, 1992. in: *NewsBank. Film and Television*. 24:G1. 1992
___ "**Powder** Is an Inane **E. T.**," *San Francisco (CA) Examiner*. October 27, 1995. in: *NewsBank. Film and Television*. 97:F12. 1995.
___ "**Species**: Return to Sender," *San Francisco (CA) Examiner*. July 7, 1995. in: *NewsBank. Film and Television*. 72:A1. 1995.
___ "**Stay Tuned**: Most Won't to This 3rd-rate Put-down of Television (Review)," *San Francisco (CA) Examiner*. August 15, 1992. in: *NewsBank. Film and Television*. 84:A6. 1992.

SHUTTLEWORTH, SALLY
___ "Science and the Supernatural in the Stories of Margaret Oliphant," in: Benjamin, Marina, ed. **A Question of Identity: Women, Science, and Literature**. New Brunswick, NJ: Rutgers University Press, 1993. pp.173-191.

SHWARTZ, SUSAN
___ "An Interview With Lois McMaster Bujold," *Marion Zimmer Bradley's Fantasy Magazine* No. 16: 14-18. Spring/Summer 1992.

SICLARI, JOE
___ "Science Fiction Fandom: A Selected, Annotated Bibliography," in: Sanders, Joe, ed. **Science Fiction Fandom**. Westport, CT: Greenwood, 1994. pp.245-264.

SIEGEL, LEE
___ "Scientists Have a Bone to Pick with Dinosaur-Cloning Theory," *Austin (TX) American Statesman* Sec. B, p. 10. June 7, 1993.

SIFRY, MICHAH I.
___ "Newt's Futurist Brain Trust," by Thomas M. Disch and Michah I. Sifry. *Nation* 260(8): 266-270. February 27, 1995.

SIGURDSON, KIRK
___ "A Gothic Approach to Lovecraft's Sense of *Outsideness*," *Lovecraft Studies* No. 28: 22-34. Fall 1992.

SILVA, DAVID B.
___ "Keeping Pace With the Master," in: Greenberg, Martin H., Ed Gorman and Bill Munster, eds. **The Dean Koontz Companion**. New York: Berkley, 1994. pp.57-74

SILVA, LOUS F.
___ "SF in Portugal," *Locus* 35(3): 53. September 1993.

SILVER, ALAIN
___ **More Things Than Are Dreamt Of: Masterpieces of Supernatural Horror, From Mary Shelley to Stephen King, in Literature and Film**, by James Ursini and Alain Silver. New York: Limelight, 1994. 226pp.

SILVERBERG, IRA
___ (ed.) **Everything Is Permitted: The Making of Naked Lunch**. London: Grafton, 1992. 128pp.

SILVERBERG, ROBERT
___ "Heinlein," in: Kondo, Yoji, ed. **Requiem: New Collected Works by Robert A. Heinlein and Tributes to the Grand Master**. New York: Tor, 1992. pp.322-327.
___ "The History of the SFWA 1967-1968," *SFWA Bulletin* 27(1): 28-29. Spring 1993. (No. 119)

SILVERBERG, ROBERT (continued)
___ "Introduction," in: Silverberg, Robert. **The Collected Stories of Robert Silverberg**. New York: Bantam, 1992. pp.xi-xviii.
___ "Introduction: The World of Jack Vance," in: Hewett, Jerry and Mallett, Daryl F. **The Work of Jack Vance: An Annotated Bibliography and Guide**. San Bernardino, CA: Borgo, 1994. pp.xi-xiii.
___ "Reflections: Isaac Asimov," *Amazing Stories* 67(3): 5-6. June 1992.
___ "Reflections: Pseudonyms," *Amazing Stories* 67(10): 5-6. January 1993.
___ "The Silverberg Papers: Egypt," *Science Fiction Chronicle* 13(5): 29-32. February 1992.
___ "The Silverberg Papers: The Time of the Great Freeze," *Science Fiction Chronicle* 14(4): 28-29. January 1993.
___ "The Silverberg Papers: The Time of the Great Freeze," *Science Fiction Chronicle* 14(5): 28-29. February 1993.
___ "To Much of the Rest of the World, America *Is* Science Fiction," *Science Fiction Age* 1(4): 22, 37. May 1993.

SIMMONS, JOE
___ "Fantasy Art and Warrior Women: An Aesthetic Critique of Feminine Images," *Mythlore* 21(1): 51-54, 65. Summer 1995. (No. 79)

SIMON, ERIK
___ "Das Quartum Comparatur. Eine Beogbachtung zu Ursula Le Guins Erdsee-Zyklus," *Quarber Merkur* 32(1): 39-41. June 1994. (Whole No. 81)

SIMONS, LESTER E.
___ "Writing and Allied Technologies in Middle-Earth," in: Reynolds, Patricia and GoodKnight, Glen H., eds. **Proceedings of the J. R. R. Tolkien Centenary Conference, Keble College, Oxford, 1992**. Altadena, CA: Mythopoeic Press, 1995. pp.340-343. (*Mythlore* Vol. 21, No. 2, Winter 1996, Whole No. 80)

SIMPSON, ANNE B.
___ "H. G. Wells's **Tono-Bungay**: Individualism and Difference," *Essays in Literature* 22(1): 75-86. Spring 1995.

SIMPSON, ROGER
___ "Merlin and Hull: A Seventeenth Century Prophecy," *Quondam et Futurus* 3(1): 60-65. Spring 1993.
___ "A Minor Road to Camelot: *Once A Week, 1859-1867*," *Arthuriana* 4(1): 46-69. Spring 1994.

SIMS, MICHAEL
___ "William Gibson: The Day After Tomorrow Meets Film Noir in the Imagination of This Writer, Interview," *BookPage* p. 3. August 1993.

SIMS-WILLIAMS, PATRICK
___ "The Early Welsh Arthurian Poems," in: Bromwich, Rachel, Jarman, A. O. H. and Roberts, Brynley F., eds. **The Arthur of the Welsh**. Cardiff: University of Wales Press, 1991. pp.33-72.

SIMSA, CYRIL
___ "The Short Fiction of Henry Slesar," *Foundation* No. 59: 78-87. Autumn 1993.
___ "Two Short Articles About Biopunk," *Vector* No. 174: 12-14. August/September 1993.
___ "The View From Olympus: Three Czech Women Writers Talk About SF," *Vector* No. 166: 14-16. April/May 1992.

SIMSON, MARIA
___ "Halloween Horrors: Books You Can Sink Your Teeth Into," *Publishers Weekly* 239(42): 24-26. September 21, 1992.

SINCLAIR, IAIN
___ "Invasion of the Blood," *Sight and Sound* 3(1): 15. January 1993.

SINGER, DAVID
___ "Selling a Bestseller," by Nick Sayers, Ian Hughes, David Singer and Tony Hammond. in: Jones, Stephen, ed. **James Herbert: By Horror Haunted**. London: New English Library, 1992. pp.199-207.

SINGER, ROBERT
___ "Hellish Contexts: A Study of Hjortsberg's **Falling Angel**," *Studies in Weird Fiction* No. 10: 2-5. Fall 1991.

SINOR, BRADLEY H.
___ "Drawings in the Dark," *Starlog* No. 183: 50-53, 70. October 1992.
___ "Greetings From Ganymede," *Starlog* No. 207: 75-77. October 1994.
___ "Rapier's Edge," *Starlog* No. 203: 49-51. June 1994.
___ "Red Iron Tales," *Starlog* No. 187: 46-49. February 1993.
___ "SFC Interviews: Tad Williams: Avoiding Assumptions," *Science Fiction Chronicle* 14(6): 5, 26-28. March 1993.

SIRCAR, SANJAY
___ "Children's Fantasy Fiction in English: Early Generic Discriminations and Our Modern Critical Inheritance," *Merveilles & Contes* 7(2): 423-449. December 1993.
___ "A Select Bibliography of Woks on Fantasy and Fairytale for Students of Children's Literature," *Papers: Explorations into Children's Literature* 3(3): 131-134. December 1992.

SIRIANNI, CARMEN J.
___ "Work and Technology in a Complex Utopia," in: Saccaro Del Buffa, Giuseppa and Lewis, Arthur O., eds. **Utopie per gli Anni Ottana.** Rome: Gangemi Editore, 1986. pp.225-235.

SISK, DAVID W.
___ **Claiming Mastery over the Word: Transformations of Language in Six Twentieth Century Dystopias.** Ph.D. Dissertation, University of North Carolina, Chapel Hill, 1994. 405pp. (DAI-A 55/07, p. 1972. January 1995.)

SKAL, DAVID J.
___ "The Dance of Dearth: Horror in the Eighties," *New York Review of Science Fiction* No. 52: 1, 10-16. December 1992.
___ "Dark Carnival: The Secret World of Tod Browning (Book Excerpt)," by David J. Skal and Elias Savada. *Cinefantastique* 27(3): 36-38. December 1995.
___ "Drive-Ins Are a Ghoul's Best Friend: Horror in the Fifties," *New York Review of Science Fiction* No. 53: 1, 8-16. January 1993.
___ "The Graveyard Bash: Horror in the Sixties," *New York Review of Science Fiction* No. 56: 1, 8-13. April 1993. (From: **The Monster Show: A Cultural History of Horror.** New York: Norton, 1993.)
___ **The Monster Show: A Cultural History of Horror.** New York: Norton, 1993. 432pp.
___ "The Monsters and Mr. Liveright," *Filmfax* No. 35: 50-62, 98. October/November 1992.
___ "The Spanish *Dracula*," *American Film* 15(12): 38-41. September 1990.

SKEET, MICHAEL
___ "Charles de Lint: On the Border," by Lorna Toolis and Michael Skeet. in: Collins, Robert A. and Latham, Robert, eds. **Science Fiction and Fantasy Book Review Annual 1991.** Westport, CT: Greenwood, 1994. pp.79-86.

SKILTON, DAVID
___ "**The Pyramid** and Comic Social Fiction," in: Biles, Jack I. and Evans, Robert O., eds. **William Golding: Some Critical Considerations.** Lexington, KY: University Press of Kentucky, 1978. pp.176-187.

SKIPP, JOHN
___ "Death's Rich Pageantry, or Skipp and Spector's Handy-Dandy Splatterpunk Guide to the Horrors of Non-Horror Film," by John Skipp and Craig Spector. in: Golden, Christopher, ed. **Cut! Horror Writers on Horror Film.** New York: Berkley, 1992. pp.237-254.

SKLAR, ELIZABETH S.
___ "Thoroughly Modern Morgan: Morgan le Fey in Twentieth-Century Popular Arthuriana," in: Slocum, Sally K., ed. **Popular Arthurian Traditions.** Bowling Green, OH: Popular Press, 1992. pp.24-35.

SKOBLOW, JEFFREY
___ **Paradise Dislocated: Morris, Politics, Art.** Charlottesville: University Press of Virginia, 1993. 221pp.

SKOTAK, ROBERT
___ "Creating the Metaluna Mutant," *Filmfax* No. 33: 56-59. June/July 1992.

SKOTAK, ROBERT (continued)
___ "Creating the Special FX for **This Island Earth**," *Filmfax* No. 33: 78-82, 94-97. June/July 1992.
___ "Klushantsev: Russia's Wizard of **Fantastika**, Part One," by Lynn Barker and Robert Skotak. *American Cinematographer* 75(6): 78-83. June 1994.
___ "Klushantsev: Russia's Wizard of **Fantastika**, Part Two," by Lynn Barker and Robert Skotak. *American Cinematographer* 75(7): 77-82. July 1994.
___ "**This Island Earth**," *Filmfax* No. 33: 50-61. June/July 1992.

SKRIP, JACK
___ "I Drink, Therefore I Am: Introspection in the Contemporary Vampire Novel," *Studies in Weird Fiction* No. 14: 3-7. Winter 1994.

SKUBLICS, HEATHER A.
___ **Naming and Vocation in the Novels of J. R. R. Tolkien, Patricia Kennealy and Anne McCaffrey.** Master's Thesis, McGill University, 1994. 154pp. (Master's Abstracts 33/04, p. 1078. August 1995.)

SLADE, DARREN
___ **Supernatural Spielberg**, by Darren Slade and Nigel Watson. London: Valis, 1992. 136pp.

SLADE, JOSEPH W.
___ "Technology and the Spy Novel," in: Greenberg, Mark L. and Schachterle, Lance, eds. **Literature and Technology.** Bethlehem, PA: Lehigh University Press, 1992. pp.225-252.

SLADE, MARGOT
___ "Ross Perot or Superstoe? Science Fiction Got There First," *New York Times* Sec. 4, p. 4. October 4, 1992.

SLADEK, JOHN
___ "Answers to Questions I Was Not Asked on the Radio," *Monad* No. 2: 65-74. March 1992.

SLATZ, LAURA
___ " '(Horrible to Relate)': Recovering the Body of Marie Roget," in: Rosenheim, Shawn and Rachman, Stephen, ed. **The American Face of Edgar Allan Poe.** Baltimore: Johns Hopkins University Press, 1995. pp.237-270.

SLAVICSEK, BILL
___ **A Guide to the Star Wars Universe.** New York: Del Rey, 1994. 495pp. Revised and Expanded Second Edition.

SLEATOR, WILLIAM
___ "From Interstellar Pigs to Spirit Houses," *ALAN Review* 19(3): 10-12, 15. Spring 1992.

SLEETH, CHARLES R.
___ "Gawain's Judgment Day," *Arthuriana* 4(2): 175-183. Summer 1994.

SLETHAUG, GORDON E.
___ " 'The Discourse of Arrogance,' Popular Power, and Anarchy: The (First) Chronicles of Thomas Covenant the Unbeliever," *Extrapolation* 34(1): 48-63. Spring 1993.
___ **The Play of the Double in Postmodern American Fiction.** Carbondale: Southern Illinois University Press, 1993. 247pp.

SLOCUM, SALLY K.
___ "Arthur the Great Equalizer: Teaching a Course for Graduate and Undergraduate Students," in: Fries, Maureen and Watson, Jeanie, eds. **Approaches to the Teaching of the Arthurian Tradition.** New York: Modern Language Association, 1992. pp.127-130.
___ "Waxing Arthurian: **The Lyre of Orpheus** and **Cold Sassy Tree**," in: Slocum, Sally K., ed. **Popular Arthurian Traditions.** Bowling Green, OH: Popular Press, 1992. pp.96-103.
___ (ed.) **Popular Arthurian Traditions.** Bowling Green, OH: Bowling Green State University Popular Press, 1992. 184pp.

SLONCZEWSKI, JOAN

___ "Bells and Time: A Review of **Doomsday Book,** by Connie Willis," in: Wolf, Milton T. and Mallett, Daryl F., eds. **Imaginative Futures: Proceedings of the 1993 Science Fiction Research Association Conference.** San Bernardino, CA: Jacob's Ladder Books, 1995. pp.161-166.

___ "Science in Science Fiction: Making It Work," *Writer* 107(4): 14-17. April 1994.

SLOTKIN, ALAN R.

___ "A Back-(To the Future)-Formation," by Alan R. Slotkin and Robert F. Bode. *American Speech* 68(3): 323-327. Fall 1993.

SLUSSER, GEORGE E.

___ "Dick and SF Scholarship: Scholars and Pedants," in: Mullen, R. D., ed. **On Philip K. Dick: 40 Articles From Science-Fiction Studies.** Terre Haute, IN: SF-TH Inc., 1992. pp.127-128.

___ "The Frankenstein Barrier," in: Slusser, George E. and Shippey, Tom, eds. **Fiction 2000: Cyberpunk and the Future of Narrative.** Athens: University of Georgia Press, 1992. pp.46-71.

___ "Heinlein's Fallen Futures," *Extrapolation* 36(2): 96-112. Summer 1995.

___ "History, Historicity, Story," in: Mullen, R. D., ed. **On Philip K. Dick: 40 Articles From Science-Fiction Studies.** Terre Haute, IN: SF-TH Inc., 1992. pp.199-222.

___ "Introduction," in: Slusser, George E. and Shippey, Tom, eds. **Fiction 2000: Cyberpunk and the Future of Narrative.** Athens: University of Georgia Press, 1992. pp.1-14.

___ "The Politically Correct Book of Science Fiction: Le Guin's Norton Collection," *Foundation* No. 60: 67-84. Spring 1994.

___ "Reflections on Style and Science Fiction," in: Slusser, George E. and Rabkin, Eric S., eds. **Styles of Creation: Aesthetic Technique and the Creation of Fictional Worlds.** Athens: University of Georgia Press, 1992. pp.3-23.

___ "Spacetime Geometries: Time Travel and the Modern Geometrical Narrative," by George E. Slusser and Daniele Chatelain. *Science Fiction Studies* 22(2): 161-186. July 1995.

___ "Third World Fantasies," in: Slusser, George and Eric S. Rabkin, eds. **Fights of Fancy: Armed Conflict in Science Fiction and Fantasy.** Athens, GA: University of Georgia Press, 1993. pp.170-193.

___ "Wars Old and New: The Changing Nature of Fictional Combat," by George E. Slusser and Eric S. Rabkin. in: Slusser, George and Eric S. Rabkin, eds. **Fights of Fancy: Armed Conflict in Science Fiction and Fantasy.** Athens, GA: University of Georgia Press, 1993. pp.1-11.

___ (ed.) **Fiction 2000: Cyberpunk and the Future of Narrative,** ed. by George E. Slusser and Tom Shippey. Athens: University of Georgia Press, 1992. 303pp.

___ (ed.) **Fights of Fancy: Armed Conflict in Science Fiction and Fantasy,** ed. by George E. Slusser and Eric S. Rabkin. Athens, GA: University of Georgia Press, 1993. 223pp.

___ (ed.) **Styles of Creation: Aesthetic Technique and the Creation of Fictional Worlds,** ed. by George E. Slusser and Eric S. Rabkin. Athens: University of Georgia Press, 1992. 271pp.

SMALLEY, ALISON

___ "Attracting Middle-School Readers With William Sleator's **Strange Attractors,**" by James E. Davis and Alison Smalley. *College English* 55(2): 76-77. February 1993.

SMEDMAN, M. SARAH

___ "The 'Terrible Journey' Past 'Dragons in the Waters' to a 'House Like a Lotus': Faces of Love in the Fiction of Madeleine L'Engle," in: Sullivan, C. W., III. **Science Fiction for Young Readers.** Westport, CT: Greenwood, 1993. pp.65-82.

SMETAK, JACQUELINE R.

___ "Summer at the Movies: Steven Spielberg: Gore, Guts, and PG-13," *Journal of Popular Film and Television* 14(1): 4-13. 1986.

SMILEY, KATHRYN

___ "The Collectible King Arthur," *Firsts: Collecting Modern First Editions* 3(10): 39-41. October 1993.

SMITH, ARDEN R.

___ "Duzen and Ihrzen in the German Translation of **The Lord of the Rings,**" *Mythlore* 21(1): 33-40. Summer 1995. (No. 79)

SMITH, ARDEN R. (continued)

___ "A Mythology for England," by Carl F. Hostetter and Arden R. Smith. in: Reynolds, Patricia and GoodKnight, Glen H., eds. **Proceedings of the J. R. R. Tolkien Centenary Conference, Keble College, Oxford, 1992.** Altadena, CA: Mythopoeic Press, 1995. pp.281-290. (*Mythlore* Vol. 21, No. 2, Winter 1996, Whole No. 80)

SMITH, CHRISTOPHER

___ "The Arthurian Legend in French Cinema: **Lancelot du Lac** and **Perceval la Gallois,**" by Jeff Rider, Richard Hull and Christopher Smith. in: Harty, Kevin J., ed. **Cinema Arthuriana: Essays on Arthurian Film.** New York: Garland, 1991. pp.41-56.

SMITH, CURTIS C.

___ "The Legacy of Mack Reynolds," *Journal of the Fantastic in the Arts* 5(4): 73-82. 1993. (No. 20)

___ **Welcome to the Revolution: The Literary Legacy of Mack Reynolds.** San Bernardino, CA: Borgo, 1995. 136pp.

SMITH, DAVE

___ "Edgar Allan Poe and the Nightmare Ode," *Southern Humanities Review* 29(1): 1-14. Winter 1995.

SMITH, DAVID A.

___ "He, Asimov: The Good Doctor as Seen Through His Late Works, **Forward the Foundation** and **I, Asimov,** Part 1," *New York Review of Science Fiction* No. 75: 1, 8-11. November 1994.

___ "He, Asimov: The Good Doctor as Seen Through His Late Works, **Forward the Foundation** and **I, Asimov,** Part 2," *New York Review of Science Fiction* No. 76: 15-20. December 1994.

___ "How I Write," *Quantum* No. 42: 15-16. Summer/Fall 1992.

___ "Writer's Workshops," *Quantum* No. 43/44: 32-34, 38. Spring/Summer 1993.

SMITH, DEAN W.

___ "A Short Horror Story," *The Report: The Fiction Writer's Magazine* No. 11: 1, 3. Summer 1993.

SMITH, DON G.

___ **Lon Chaney, Jr.: Horror Film Star, 1906-1993.** Jefferson, NC: McFarland, 1995. 272pp.

SMITH, EVANS L.

___ "The Golem and the Garland in Borges and Broch," *Journal of the Fantastic in the Arts* 7(2/3): 177-190. 1995.

___ "The Mythical Method of **Descent into Hell,**" *Mythlore* 20(2): 10-15. Spring 1994. (Whole No. 76)

SMITH, J. PERCY

___ (ed.) **Bernard Shaw and H. G. Wells.** Toronto: University of Toronto Press, 1995. 242pp.

SMITH, JAMES F.

___ "'Everybody Pays. . . Even for Things They Didn't Do': Stephen King's Pay-out in the Bachman Novels," in: Magistrale, Tony, ed. **The Dark Descent: Essays Defining Stephen King's Horrorscape.** Westport, CT: Greenwood, 1992. pp.99-112.

SMITH, JEANETTE C.

___ "The Role of Women in Contemporary Arthurian Fantasy," *Extrapolation* 35(2): 130-144. Summer 1994.

SMITH, KAREN P.

___ **The Fabulous Realm: A Literary-Historical Approach to British Fantasy, 1780-1990.** Metuchen, NJ: Scarecrow, 1993. 532pp.

SMITH, MALAIKA D.

___ **The African American Heroine in Octavia Butler's Wild Seed and Parable of the Sower.** Master's Thesis, UCLA, 1994. 66pp.

SMITH, MARY R.

___ **Dune: More Than Genre Fiction.** Master's Thesis, East Carolina University, 1992. 48pp.

SMITH, NICHOLAS D.

___ "Political Activity and Ideal Economics: Two Related Utopian Themes in Aristophanic Comedy," *Utopian Studies* 3(1): 84-94. 1992.

SMITH, NICHOLAS D. (continued)
___ "Socrates the Anti-Utopian," by Thomas C. Brickhouse and Nicholas D. Smith. in: Saccaro Del Buffa, Giuseppa and Lewis, Arthur O., eds. **Utopia e Modernita: Teorie e prassi utopiche nell'eta moderna e postmoderna.** Rome: Gangemi Editore, 1989. pp.717-726.

SMITH, NIGEL
___ "Gautier, Freud and the Fantastic: Psychoanlysis *avant la lettre?*," in: Sanders, Joe, ed. **Functions of the Fantastic.** Westport, CT: Greenwood, 1995. pp.67-76.

SMITH, RUSSELL
___ "Bridging the Generations Gap," *Austin (TX) American Statesman* p. E1, E8. November 18, 1994.
___ "Gay Groups Tell Hollywood That **Basic Instinct** Is All Bad," *Dallas (TX) Morning News* March 15, 1992 in: *NewsBank. Film and Television.* 29:A9-A10. 1992.
___ "Tribute to a Maker of Monsters," *Dallas (TX) Morning News.* August 7, 1992. in: *NewsBank. Film and Television.* 80:F13-F14. 1992.

SMITH, SARAH
___ "Electronic Fictions: The State of the Art," *New York Review of Science Fiction* No. 63: 1, 8-11. November 1993.

SMITH, SHERWOOD
___ "Writing for Adults vs. Writing for Children," *Focus* (BSFA) No. 29: 13-14. December 1995/January 1996.

SMITH, STARITA
___ "Horror Flicks of Today May Mar Kids Tomorrow," *Austin (TX) American Statesman* Sec. B, p. 1, 8. June 16, 1993.

SMITH, STEPHANIE A.
___ "Morphing, Materialism, and the Marketing of **Xenogenesis**," *Genders* No. 18: 67-86. Winter 1993.

SMITH, SUSAN H.
___ "Atwood Pens Compelling Collection in **Wilderness Tips**," *Pittsburgh (PA) Press.* February 23, 1992. in *NewsBank. Literature.* 15: B2. 1992.

SMYER, RICHARD I.
___ **Animal Farm: Pastoralism and Politics.** Boston, MA: Twayne, 1988. 154pp.

SMYTH, DONNA E.
___ "Words of Space: The Fiction of Sheila Watson and Sharon Riis," in: Roberts, Sheila, ed. **Still the Frame Holds: Essays on Women Poets and Writers.** San Bernardino, CA: Borgo Press, 1993. pp.129-136.

SNEAD, ELIZABETH
___ "His Future Is Closer Than You Think," *USA Today* Sec. D, p. 1. September 2, 1993.

SNEYD, STEVE
___ "Empress of the Stars: A Reassessment of Lilith Lorraine, Pioneering Fantasy Poetess," *Fantasy Commentator* 7(3): 206-229. Spring 1992. (No. 43)
___ "Hearing From the Ion Engineers: A Quarter Century of SF Poetry," *Vector* No. 180: 12-14. August/September 1994.
___ "Michael Moorcock: Interview," *Star Line* 15(1): 3-5. 1992.
___ "Science Fiction and Poetry: An Interview With Duncan Lunan," *Fantasy Commentator* 8(1/2): 84-92. Winter 1993/1994. (Whole No. 45/46)
___ "Space Opera: An Interview With A. C. Evans," *Fantasy Commentator* 8(3/4): 253-256. Fall 1995. (Whole No. 47/48)

SNODGRASS, MARY E.
___ **Encyclopedia of Utopian Literature.** Santa Barbara, CA: ABC-CLIO, 1995. 644pp.

SNYDER, LILLAN M.
___ "A Search for Brotherhood, Peace, and Justice: A Description of the Icarian Movement," in: Saccaro Del Buffa, Giuseppa and Lewis, Arthur O., eds. **Utopie per gli Anni Ottana.** Rome: Gangemi Editore, 1986. pp.737-750.

SNYDER, SHARON
___ "Another Fine Ferengi," by Sharon Snyder and Marc Shapiro. *Starlog* No. 190: 36-39. May 1993.

SOANES, PAUL A.
___ **Daughter of the Night: A Tanith Lee Bibliography,** by Paul A. Soanes and Jim Pattison. Toronto: Gaffa Press, 1993. 44pp.

SOBCHACK, VIVIAN
___ "New Age Mutant Ninja Hackers: Reading *Mondo 2000*," *South Atlantic Quarterly* 92(4): 569-584. Fall 1993.
___ "Pilgrim Award Acceptance Speech, 1995," *SFRA Review* No. 219: 27-29. September/October 1995.

SOLIVETTI, CARLA
___ "L'utopia linguistica di Velimir Chlebnikov," in: Saccaro Del Buffa, Giuseppa and Lewis, Arthur O., eds. **Utopie per gli Anni Ottana.** Rome: Gangemi Editore, 1986. pp.51-70.

SOLMAN, GREGORY
___ "The Illusion of a Future," *Film Comment* 28(2): 32-41. March/April 1992.

SOLOMON, HARVEY
___ "Fox Gets Real, Virtually," *Boston (MA) Herald.* March 9, 1995. in: *NewsBank. Film and Television.* 39:E14. 1995.
___ "Showtime Expands on Vonnegut Satire," *Boston (MA) Herald.* August 12, 1995. in: *NewsBank. Film and Television.* 86:A1. 1995.
___ "**X-Files** Conquers Earth," *Boston (MA) Herald.* September 23, 1994. in: *NewsBank. Film and Television.* 106:G6. 1994.

SORENSEN, PETER
___ "Cyberworld," *Cinefex* No. 50: 54-76. May 1992.

SORIANO, CESAR G.
___ "Fox Series Melds Cyberspace, Sci-Fi," *Washington (DC) Times.* March 10, 1995. in: *NewsBank. Film and Television.* 39:F3. 1995.
___ "**Langoliers** Just Languishes in Its Time Warp," *Washington (DC) Times.* May 13, 1995. in: *NewsBank. Film and Television.* 55:C10. 1995.
___ "Voyager Is Flagship Worthy of New UPN," *Washington (DC) Times.* January 16, 1995. in: *NewsBank. Film and Television.* 21:D14. 1995.

SOTER, TOM
___ "License to Score," *Starlog* No. 199: 41-45. February 1994.

SOUKUP, MARTHA
___ "Climb Aboard an *Iron Dragon* for a Railroad Journey to Adventure," *Science Fiction Age* 3(5): 98-100. July 1995.
___ "Martha Soukup's Walk Your Shoes Off Thumbnail Guide to San Francisco," *Science Fiction Chronicle* 14(11): 29-31. August 1993.

SOYKA, DAVID
___ "Frankenstein and the Miltonic Creation of Evil," *Extrapolation* 33(2): 166-177. Summer 1992.

SPAEMANN, CORDELIA
___ "Phantastische Literatur," in: Kranz, Gisbert, ed. **Jahrbuch für Literatur und Ästhetik.** Lüdenscheid, Germany: Stier, 1992. Band 10, pp.293-308.

SPEAR, THOMAS
___ "Staging the Elusive Self," in: Harger-Grinling, Virginia and Chadwick, Tony, eds. **Robbe-Grillet and the Fantastic.** Westport, CT: Greenwood, 1994. pp.55-76.

SPEARE, MARY J.
___ "Wagnerian and Arthurian Elements in Chausson's **Le Roi Arthus**," in: Busby, Keith, ed. **The Arthurian Yearbook I.** New York: Garland, 1991. pp.195-214.

SPEARING, A. C.
___ "Public and Private Spaces in **Sir Gawain and the Green Knights**," *Arthuriana* 4(2): 138-145. Summer 1994.

SPEARS, MONROE K.
___ "Cosmology and the Writer," *Hudson Review* 47(1): 29-45. Spring 1994.

SPECTOR, CRAIG
___ "Death's Rich Pageantry, or Skipp and Spector's Handy-Dandy Splatterpunk Guide to the Horrors of Non-Horror Film," by John Skipp and Craig Spector. in: Golden, Christopher, ed. **Cut! Horror Writers on Horror Film**. New York: Berkley, 1992. pp.237-254.

SPECTOR, JUDITH A.
___ "Walter Miller's **A Canticle for Leibowitz**: A Parable for Our Time?," *Midwest Quarterly* 22(4): 337-345. Summer 1981.

SPEER, JACK
___ **Up to Now: A History of Fandom as Jack Speer Sees It**. Brooklyn, NY: Richard Newsome, [1996?]. 48pp. (Reprint, originally published in 1939.) [Not seen.]

SPELLER, MAUREEN
___ "Horribly Real: A Conversation With William Gibson," *Vector* No. 179: 12-17. June/July 1994.
___ "A Judges' Summary of the Clarke Award," *Vector* No. 173: 11-13. June/July 1993.

SPELLING, IAN
___ "An *Alien 3* Post-Mortem," *Starlog* No. 196: 71. November 1993.
___ "Actress With Attitude," *Starlog* No. 205: 53-56, 70. August 1994.
___ "Alien Nemesis," by Adam Pirani and Ian Spelling. in: McDonnell, David, ed. **Starlog's Science Fiction Heroes and Heroines**. New York: Crescent Books, 1995. pp.9-11.
___ "Arabian Night Music," *Starlog* No. 186: 52-55. January 1993.
___ "Bashir Grows Up," *Starlog* No. 201: 50-53. April 1994.
___ "Beloved Betazoid," *Starlog* No. 196: 52-57, 80. November 1993.
___ "Bionic Breakdown," *Starlog* No. 211: 76-79. February 1995.
___ "Captain Sulu," *Starlog* No. 174: 43-47. January 1992.
___ "Classic Captain," by Peter Bloch-Hansen and Ian Spelling. *Starlog* No. 212: 36-37, 70. March 1995.
___ "The Colors of Loyalty," *Starlog* No. 213: 36-39, 72. April 1995.
___ "Constable Morph," *Starlog* No. 191: 27-31. June 1993.
___ "Cry of the Warrior," *Starlog* No. 175: 27-31. February 1992.
___ "Deep Thoughts," *Starlog* No. 189: 44-47, 64. April 1993.
___ "Directorial Enterprise," *Starlog* No. 204: 40-45. July 1994.
___ " 'DS9' Pals Live out a Tom Sawyer Fantasy," *Houston (TX) Chronicle* Sec. C, p. 2. June 4, 1994.
___ "Guest Star," *Starlog* No. 176: 50-53. March 1992.
___ "Guide to a New Generation," *Starlog* No. 195: 50-57. October 1993.
___ "The Hero This Time," *Starlog* No. 203: 43-48. June 1994.
___ "Hook's Mate," *Starlog* No. 174: 38-42, 72. January 1992.
___ "Horrors of *Frankenstein*," *Starlog* No. 211: 32-35, 70. February 1995.
___ "I, Nimoy," *Starlog* No. 217: 72-73. August 1995.
___ "In Command," *Starlog* No. 207: 41-44, 70. October 1994.
___ "Intimate Insider," *Starlog* No. 202: 32-36. May 1994.
___ "Jack on the Run," *Starlog* No. 176: 30-33. March 1992.
___ "Klingon Again," *Starlog* No. 219: 42-43. October 1995.
___ "Klingon Warrior," by David McDonnell and Ian Spelling. in: McDonnell, David, ed. **Starlog's Science Fiction Heroes and Heroines**. New York: Crescent Books, 1995. pp.58-61.
___ "Leader of the Space Station," *Starlog* No. 187: 40-45, 70. February 1993.
___ "*Legend* of the West," *Starlog* No. 216: 54-57. July 1995.
___ "Life With Indy," *Starlog* No. 191: 46-49. June 1993.
___ "Like a Phoenix," *Starlog* No. 218: 52-55, 66. September 1995.
___ "Major Player," *Starlog* No. 199: 27-33. February 1994.
___ "Major Player," in: McDonnell, David, ed. **Starlog's Science Fiction Heroes and Heroines**. New York: Crescent Books, 1995. pp.62-65.
___ "Man of Many Parts," *Starlog* 180: 46-50. July 1992.
___ "The Man Who Killed Kirk," *Starlog* No. 213: 75-79, 72. April 1995.
___ "Mayor of Gotham," *Starlog* 181: 52-55. August 1992.
___ "Merchant of Menace," *Starlog* No. 183: 46-49. October 1992.
___ "My Uncle, the Director," *Starlog* No. 204: 64-67. July 1994.
___ "Non Voyager," *Starlog* No. 211: 40-45, 66. February 1995.
___ "The Once and Future Captain," *Starlog* No. 212: 32-35, 70. March 1995.

SPELLING, IAN (continued)
___ "Praying **M. A. N. T. I. S.**," by Ian Spelling and Marc Bernardin. *Starlog* No. 208: 27-30. November 1994.
___ "Q & A," by Ian Spelling and David McDonnell. *Starlog* No. 206: 47-51, 70. September 1994.
___ "Quantum Leaper," by Ian Spelling and Marc Shapiro. in: McDonnell, David, ed. **Starlog's Science Fiction Heroes and Heroines**. New York: Crescent Books, 1995. pp.87-89.
___ "Smoke and Mirrors," *Starlog* No. 216: 27-30, 64. July 1995.
___ "**Space: Above and Beyond**," *Starlog* No. 220: 40-45. November 1995.
___ "Spanning Generations," *Starlog* No. 209: 48-53. December 1994.
___ "Star Quarters," *Starlog* 178: 56-58. May 1992.
___ "Starfleet Siren," by Brian Lowry and Ian Spelling. in: McDonnell, David, ed. **Starlog's Science Fiction Heroes and Heroines**. New York: Crescent Books, 1995. pp.77-79.
___ "Sudden Outbreak," *Starlog* No. 214: 75-77. May 1995.
___ "Swan Songs," *Starlog* No. 204: 32-34. July 1994.
___ "The Trill of It All," *Starlog* No. 188: 42-45, 64. March 1993.
___ "True Believer," *Starlog* No. 189: 50-53, 67. April 1993.
___ "Uhura and Beyond," *Starlog* No. 210: 47-49. January 1995.
___ "Uhura's Mission," *Starlog* No. 175: 36-39, 82. February 1992.
___ "Under Western Skies," *Starlog* No. 217: 76-79. August 1995.
___ "Voyager Captain," *Starlog* No. 212: 27-31, 72. March 1995.
___ "Voyager Captain," in: McDonnell, David, ed. **Starlog's Science Fiction Heroes and Heroines**. New York: Crescent Books, 1995. pp.34-37.
___ "Welcome to **Shatterworld**," *Starlog* No. 205: 58-60. August 1994.
___ "Wildcat Heart," *Starlog* No. 214: 27-30. May 1995.
___ "Young Indy & the First Crusade," *Starlog* No. 183: 33-36. October 1992.

SPENCER, PAUL
___ "The Shadow Over Derleth," in: Schweitzer, Darrell, ed. **Discovering Classic Horror Fiction I**. Mercer Island, WA: Starmont, 1992. pp.114-119.
___ "Shiel Versus Shiel," in: **Shiel in Diverse Hands: A Collection of Essays**. Cleveland, OH: Reynolds Morse Foundation, 1983. pp.31-55.
___ "A Voice From the Past," *The Dark Man: The Journal of Robert E. Howard Studies* No. 2: 32-33. July 1991.

SPERBER, MURRAY
___ "Gazing into the Glass Paperweight: The Structure and Psychology of Orwell's **1984**," *Modern Fiction Studies* 26(2): 213-226. Summer 1980.

SPERRY, RALPH A.
___ "Three Nasty Problems," *SFWA Bulletin* 26(3): 21-22. Fall 1992. (No. 117)

SPIES, BERNHARD
___ "Der Anteil der sozialistischen Utopie an der Beendigung der DDR-Literatur. Am Beispiel Christoph Heins," *Germanic Review* 67(3): 112-118. Summer 1992.

SPIGEL, ERIK J.
___ "An Afterword to 'Kissing Hitler'," *ON SPEC* 5(1): 89-90. Spring 1993.

SPINA, GIORGIO
___ "The Inklings in Italy," in: Kranz, Gisbert, ed. **Inklings: Jahrbuch für Literatur und Ästhetik**. 7. Band. Lüdenscheid, Germany: Stier, 1989. pp.83-92. [Not seen.]

SPINELLI, ERNESTO
___ "Philip K. Dick and the Philosophy of Uncertainty," *PKDS Newsletter* No. 28: 19-22. March 1992.

SPINRAD, NORMAN
___ "Building a Starfaring Age," in: Dozois, Gardner, ed. **Writing Science Fiction and Fantasy**. New York: St. Martin's, 1991. pp.185-199.
___ "If You Love Science Fiction, Then It's Time to Fight Back Against Anti-SF," *Science Fiction Age* 2(1): 32-36. November 1993.
___ "Where I Get My Crazy Ideas," in: Jakubowski, Maxim and James, Edward, eds. **The Profession of Science Fiction**. New York: St. Martin's, 1992. pp.95-100.

SPIVACK, CHARLOTTE
___ **The Company of Camelot: Arthurian Characters in Romance and Fantasy**, by Charlotte Spivack and Roberta L. Staple. Westport, CT: Greenwood, 1994. 161pp.
___ "Morgan le Fey: Goddess or Witch?," in: Slocum, Sally K., ed. **Popular Arthurian Traditions**. Bowling Green, OH: Popular Press, 1992. pp.18-23.
___ "Tolkien's Images of Evil," in: Kranz, Gisbert, ed. **Jahrbuch für Literatur und Ästhetik**. Lüdenscheid, Germany: Stier, 1992. Band 10, pp.23-36.

SPLETT, JÖRG
___ "Der Schmerz und die Freude. C. S. Lewis' christliche Perspektiv," in: Kranz, Gisbert, ed. **Inklings: Jahrbuch für Literatur und Ästhetik**. 1. Band. Lüdenscheid, Germany: Michael Claren, 1983. pp.43-66.

SPONSLER, CLAIRE
___ "Beyond the Ruins: The Geopolitics of Urban Decay and Cybernetic Play," *Science Fiction Studies* 20(2): 251-265. July 1993.
___ "Cyberpunk and the Dilemmas of Postmodern Narrative: The Example of William Gibson," *Contemporary Literature* 33(4): 625-644. December 1992.
___ "William Gibson and the Death of Cyberpunk," in: Latham, Robert A. and Collins, Robert A., eds. **Modes of the Fantastic**. Westport, CT: Greenwood, 1995. pp.47-55.

SPREEN, DIERK
___ "Technotext und Technokörper: Visionen eines neuen Heils," *Quarber Merkur* 33(2): 3-16. December 1995. (No. 84)

SPRINGER, CLAUDIA
___ "Muscular Circuitry: The Invincible Armored Cyborg in Cinema," *Genders* No. 18: 87-101. Winter 1993.
___ "Sex, Memories, and Angry Women," *South Atlantic Quarterly* 92(4): 713-734. Fall 1993.

SPRINGMAN, LUKE
___ **Comrades, Friends and Companions: Utopian Projections and Social Action in German Literature for Young People, 1926-1934**. New York: P. Lang, 1989. 242pp. [Not seen.]
___ **Comrades, Friends and Companions: Utopian Projections and Social Action in German Literature for Young People, 1926-1934**. Ph.D. Dissertation, Ohio State University, 1988. 338pp.

SPRUG, JOSEPH W.
___ **Index to Fairy Tales, 1987-1992: Including 310 Collections of Fairy Tales, Myths and Legends With Significant Pre-1987 Titles Not Previously Indexed**. Metuchen, NJ: Scarecrow, 1994. 587pp.

SPURLOCK, DUANE
___ "Hail and Farewell, Pellucidar: An Interview with Allan Gross," *Burroughs Bulletin* NS. No. 16: 27-31. October 1993.
___ "Where Have All the Fans Gone?: An Interview with Henning Kure," *Burroughs Bulletin* NS. No. 13: 23-35. January 1993.

SQUIER, SUSAN M.
___ "Conceiving Difference: Reproductive Technology and the Construction of Identity in Two Contemporary Fictions," in: Benjamin, Marina, ed. **A Question of Identity: Women, Science, and Literature**. New Brunswick, NJ: Rutgers University Press, 1993. pp.97-115.
___ "Naomi Mitchison: The Feminist Art of Making Things Difficult," in: Mitchison, Naomi. **Solution Three**. New York: Feminist Press, 1995. pp.161-183.

SQUIRES, JOHN D.
___ "Some Contemporary Themes in Shiel's Early Novels: Steel Afloat; M. P. Shiel on Naval Warfare," in: **Shiel in Diverse Hands: A Collection of Essays**. Cleveland, OH: Reynolds Morse Foundation, 1983. pp.303-328.
___ "Some Contemporary Themes in Shiel's Early Novels: The Dragon's Tale; M. P. Shiel on the Emergence of Modern China," in: **Shiel in Diverse Hands: A Collection of Essays**. Cleveland, OH: Reynolds Morse Foundation, 1983. pp.249-301.

SQUIRES, RICHARD D.
___ **Stern Fathers 'neath the Mould: The Lovecraft Family in Rochester**. West Warwick, RI: Necronomicon Press, 1995. 60pp.

SRAGOW, MICHAEL
___ "*Freejack*: If It Only Had a Brain (Review)," *San Francisco (CA) Examiner*. January 18, 1992. in: *NewsBank. Film and Television*. 11:D3. 1992.
___ "*Hook*, Whine and Sinker (Review)," *San Francisco (CA) Examiner*. December 11, 1991. in: *NewsBank. Film and Television*. 3:E13-E14. 1992.
___ "Hype-Point of the Year in Film," *San Francisco (CA) Enquirer* March 20, 1992 in: *NewsBank. Film and Television*. 29:A12-A13. 1992.
___ "It's Not Creepy or Kooky--Just Ooky," *San Francisco (CA) Examiner*. November 22, 1991. in: *NewsBank. Film and Television*. 1: A1-A2. 1991
___ "Last Installment Makes the Case But Is Ultimately Lacking in Pure Logic (Review)," *San Francisco (CA) Examiner*. December 6, 1991. in: *NewsBank. Film and Television*. 7:D8-D9. 1992.

SRPON, VLADO
___ "Dr Gustav Maruricius Reuss: The First Slovak Literary Fantasist," *Foundation* No. 63: 81-84. Spring 1995.

ST. ARMAND, BARTON L.
___ "Roots of Horror in New England," in: Joshi, S. T., ed. **The H. P. Lovecraft Centennial Conference Proceedings**. West Warwick, RI: Necronomicon, 1991. pp.12-14.

ST. CLAIR, GLORIANA
___ "An Overview of the Northern Influences on Tolkien's Work," in: Reynolds, Patricia and GoodKnight, Glen H., eds. **Proceedings of the J. R. R. Tolkien Centenary Conference, Keble College, Oxford, 1992**. Altadena, CA: Mythopoeic Press, 1995. pp.63-67. (*Mythlore* Vol. 21, No. 2, Winter 1996, Whole No. 80)
___ "Tolkien as Reviser: A Case Study," in: Reynolds, Patricia and GoodKnight, Glen H., eds. **Proceedings of the J. R. R. Tolkien Centenary Conference, Keble College, Oxford, 1992**. Altadena, CA: Mythopoeic Press, 1995. pp.145-150. (*Mythlore* Vol. 21, No. 2, Winter 1996, Whole No. 80)
___ "Volsunga Saga and Narn: Some Analogies," in: Reynolds, Patricia and GoodKnight, Glen H., eds. **Proceedings of the J. R. R. Tolkien Centenary Conference, Keble College, Oxford, 1992**. Altadena, CA: Mythopoeic Press, 1995. pp.68-72. (*Mythlore* Vol. 21, No. 2, Winter 1996, Whole No. 80)

ST. CLAIRE, R. T.
___ "Carnivore Knowledge: *Wolf* (Review)," *Sci-Fi Universe* No. 3: 68-69. October/November 1994.

STABLEFORD, BRIAN
___ "Adolf Hitler: His Part in Our Struggle; A Brief Economic History of British SF Magazines," *Interzone* No. 57: 17-20. March 1992.
___ **Algebraic Fantasies and Realistic Romances: More Masters of Science Fiction**. San Bernardino, CA: Borgo Press, 1995 128pp.
___ "C. S. Lewis and the Decline of Scientific Romances," *New York Review of Science Fiction* No. 45: 1, 8-12. May 1992.
___ "The Concept of Mind in Science Fiction," in: Stableford, Brian. **Opening Minds: Essays on Fantastic Literature**. San Bernardino, CA: Borgo Press, 1995. pp.37-52.
___ "Creators of Science Fiction, 1: Stanley G. Weinbaum," *Interzone* No. 90: 51-53. December 1994.
___ "The Creators of Science Fiction, 2: Theodore Sturgeon," *Interzone* No. 93: 43-45, 55. March 1995.
___ "The Creators of Science Fiction, 3: David H. Keller," *Interzone* No. 97: 54-57. July 1995.
___ "The Creators of Science Fiction, 4: Philip K. Dick," *Interzone* No. 101: 54-57. November 1995.
___ "Discotheque for the Devil's Party: Black Metal, Pagan Rock and the Tradition of Literary Shamanism, Part 1," *New York Review of Science Fiction* No. 86: 1, 8-13. October 1995.
___ "Discotheque for the Devil's Party: Black Metal, Pagan Rock and the Tradition of Literary Shamanism, Part 2," *New York Review of Science Fiction* No. 87: 16-20. November 1995.
___ "Edmond Hamilton and Leigh Brackett: An Appreciation," in: Stableford, Brian. **Outside the Human Aquarium: Masters of Science Fiction**. San Bernardino, CA: Borgo, 1995. pp.7-17.
___ "Escape to Reality: A Profile of Bob Shaw," *Interzone* No. 67: 40-43. January 1993.

STABLEFORD, BRIAN

STABLEFORD, BRIAN (continued)
___ "**Frankenstein** and the Origins of Science Fiction," in: Seed, David, ed. **Anticipations: Essays on Early Science Fiction and Its Precursors.** Liverpool: Liverpool University Press, 1995. pp.46-57.
___ "Future Wars, 1890-1950," in: Stableford, Brian. **Opening Minds: Essays on Fantastic Literature.** San Bernardino, CA: Borgo Press, 1995. pp.111-134.
___ "Gernsback's Pessimist: The Futuristic Fantasies of David H. Keller," in: Stableford, Brian. **Outside the Human Aquarium: Masters of Science Fiction.** San Bernardino, CA: Borgo, 1995. pp.108-116.
___ "How Should a Science Fiction Story End?," *New York Review of Science Fiction* No. 78: 1, 8-15. February 1995.
___ "Insoluble Problems: Barry Malzberg's Career in Science Fiction," in: Stableford, Brian. **Outside the Human Aquarium: Masters of Science Fiction.** San Bernardino, CA: Borgo, 1995. pp.28-36.
___ "The Last Chocolate Bar and the Majesty of Truth: Reflections on the Concept of 'Hardness' in Science Fiction, Part 1," *New York Review of Science Fiction* No. 71: 1, 8-12. July 1994.
___ "The Last Chocolate Bar and the Majesty of Truth: Reflections on the Concept of 'Hardness' in Science Fiction, Part 2," *New York Review of Science Fiction* No. 72: 10-16. August 1994.
___ "Little Victories: The Heartfelt Fiction of Philip K. Dick," in: Stableford, Brian. **Outside the Human Aquarium: Masters of Science Fiction.** San Bernardino, CA: Borgo, 1995. pp.99-107.
___ "Locked in the Slaughterhouse: The Novels of Kurt Vonnegut," in: Stableford, Brian. **Outside the Human Aquarium: Masters of Science Fiction.** San Bernardino, CA: Borgo, 1995. pp.18-27.
___ "The Lost Pioneer: The Science Fiction of Stanley G. Weinbaum," in: Stableford, Brian. **Outside the Human Aquarium: Masters of Science Fiction.** San Bernardino, CA: Borgo, 1995. pp.126-134.
___ "Marxism, Science Fiction, and the Poverty of Prophecy: Some Comparisons and Contrasts," in: Stableford, Brian. **Opening Minds: Essays on Fantastic Literature.** San Bernardino, CA: Borgo Press, 1995. pp.99-110.
___ "The Metamorphosis of Robert Silverberg," in: Stableford, Brian. **Outside the Human Aquarium: Masters of Science Fiction.** San Bernardino, CA: Borgo, 1995. pp.37-48.
___ "The Mythology of Man-Made Catastrophe," in: Stableford, Brian. **Opening Minds: Essays on Fantastic Literature.** San Bernardino, CA: Borgo Press, 1995. pp.53-90.
___ "The New Wave, Cyberpunk, and Beyond: 1963-1994," by Michael M. Levy and Brian Stableford. in: Barron, Neil, ed. **Anatomy of Wonder 4.** New York: Bowker, 1995. pp.222-377.
___ "Opening Minds," in: Stableford, Brian. **Opening Minds: Essays on Fantastic Literature.** San Bernardino, CA: Borgo Press, 1995. pp.23-28.
___ **Opening Minds: Essays on Fantastic Literature.** San Bernardino, CA: Borgo Press, 1995. 144pp.
___ **Outside the Human Aquarium: Masters of Science Fiction.** 2nd ed., Revised and Exanded. San Bernardino, CA: Borgo, 1995. 152pp.
___ "Outside the Human Aquarium: The Fantastic Imagination of Clark Ashton Smith," in: Stableford, Brian. **Outside the Human Aquarium: Masters of Science Fiction.** San Bernardino, CA: Borgo, 1995. pp.76-98.
___ "The Plausibility of the Impossible," in: Stableford, Brian. **Opening Minds: Essays on Fantastic Literature.** San Bernardino, CA: Borgo Press, 1995. pp.91-98.
___ "The Politics of Evolution," in: **Shiel in Diverse Hands: A Collection of Essays.** Cleveland, OH: Reynolds Morse Foundation, 1983. pp.369-394.
___ "The Redemption of the Infimal," *New York Review of Science Fiction* No. 52: 1-8. December 1992.
___ "Schemes of Salvation: The Literary Explorations of Theodore Sturgeon," in: Stableford, Brian. **Outside the Human Aquarium: Masters of Science Fiction.** San Bernardino, CA: Borgo, 1995. pp.117-125.
___ "Science Fiction and the Mythology of Progress," in: Stableford, Brian. **Opening Minds: Essays on Fantastic Literature.** San Bernardino, CA: Borgo Press, 1995. pp.29-36.
___ "Science Fiction Between the Wars: 1916-1939," in: Barron, Neil, ed. **Anatomy of Wonder 4.** New York: Bowker, 1995. pp.62-114.
___ "SF: The Nature of the Medium," in: Stableford, Brian. **Opening Minds: Essays on Fantastic Literature.** San Bernardino, CA: Borgo Press, 1995. pp.9-14.

STAPLETON, AMY L.

STABLEFORD, BRIAN (continued)
___ "Utopia--And Afterwards: Socioeconomic Speculation in the SF of Mack Reynolds," in: Stableford, Brian. **Outside the Human Aquarium: Masters of Science Fiction.** San Bernardino, CA: Borgo, 1995. pp.49-75.
___ "William Wilson's Prospectus for Science Fiction, 1851," in: Stableford, Brian. **Opening Minds: Essays on Fantastic Literature.** San Bernardino, CA: Borgo Press, 1995. pp.15-22.
___ "Writing Fantasy and Horror, Part One," *Focus* (BSFA) No. 25: 10-11. December/January 1994.
___ "Writing Fantasy and Horror, Part Two," *Focus* (BSFA) No. 26: 3-4. June/July 1994.
___ "Writing Science Fiction," *Focus* (BSFA) No. 24: 12. June/July 1993.
___ "Yesterday's Bestsellers, 15: F. Anstey and **Vice Versa**," *Interzone* No. 74: 57-60. August 1993.
___ "Yesterday's Bestsellers, 16: Lewis Carroll's Alice Books," *Interzone* No. 76: 56-59. October 1993.
___ "Yesterday's Bestsellers, 17: Mary Shelley's **Frankenstein**," *Interzone* No. 78: 56-58, 68. December 1993.
___ "Yesterday's Bestsellers, 19: **The Battle of Dorking** and Its Aftermath," *Interzone* No. 83: 52-56. May 1994.
___ "Yesterday's Bestsellers, 20: **My First Two Thousand Years** by George Viereck and Paul Eldridge," *Interzone* No. 86: 48-52. August 1994.

STACK, PETER
___ "**12 Monkeys** Is Not Exactly a Barrel of Laughs: Willis, Pitt in Grimy Futuristic Thriller about Killer Virus," *San Francisco (CA) Chronicle* February 5, 1996. (Cited from the Internet Edition.)

STAELS, HILDE
___ "Margaret Atwood's **The Handmaid's Tale**: Resistance Through Narrating," *English Studies* 76(5): 455-467. September 1995.

STAGGS, JEFFREY
___ "**2001**: Space Odyssey of the Mind," *Washington (DC) Times.* April 6, 1993. in: *NewsBank. Film & Television.* 40:A6. 1993.
___ "**No Escape**, Except for the Audience," *Washington (DC) Times.* April 29, 1994. in: *NewsBank. Film and Television.* 58:B1. 1994.

STANLEY, DICK
___ "Philosophy Teacher Hits Warp Speed; **Star Trek** Boldly Explored in Class," *Austin (TX) American Statesman* Sec. B, pp.1, 6. March 7, 1993.

STANLEY, JOHN
___ **The Creature Features Movie Guide Strikes Again: Fourth Revised Edition.** Pacifica, CA: Large Press, 1994. 454pp.
___ "Early Soviet Space-Race Victory," *San Francisco (CA) Chronicle* Sec. DAT, p. 34. April 12, 1992.
___ "An Evening of Androids, Humanoids and Robots," *San Francisco (CA) Chronicle* Sec. C, p. 3. March 13, 1993.
___ "The Fantastic Life of an Ordinary Man, Philip K. Dick," *San Francisco (CA) Chronicle. Datebook.* pp.27-30. September 19, 1993.
___ "New Sci-Fi Show Keeps on Trekking," *San Francisco (CA) Chronicle* Sec. DAT, p. 38. February 21, 1993.
___ "Philip Ridley," *Cinefantastique* 23(2/3): 114-119. October 1992.

STANLEY, T. L.
___ "NBC, Live Entertainment Link TV and Home Vid for Sci-Fi Synergy," *Brandweek* 36(3): 8. January 16, 1995.

STANTON, MICHAEL N.
___ "Some Ways of Reading **The Dead Zone**," in: Magistrale, Tony, ed. **The Dark Descent: Essays Defining Stephen King's Horrorscape.** Westport, CT: Greenwood, 1992. pp.61-72.

STAPLE, ROBERTA L.
___ **The Company of Camelot: Arthurian Characters in Romance and Fantasy**, by Charlotte Spivack and Roberta L. Staple. Westport, CT: Greenwood, 1994. 161pp.

STAPLETON, AMY L.
___ **Future Perspectives: Contemporary German Science Fiction's Contribution to an Ecological Bewesstseinswandel.** Ph.D. Dissertation, University of Wisconsin, Madison, 1992. (DAI-A 52,/11, p. 3947. May 1992.)

STAPLETON, AMY L. (continued)
___ **Utopias for a Dying World: Contemporary German Science Fiction's Plea for a New Ecological Awareness**. New York: Peter Lang, 1993. 158pp.

STARK, SUSAN
___ "Blood Lite: Buffy Sends a Valley Girl on a Comic Sleigh Ride," *Detroit (MI) News*. July 31, 1992. in: *NewsBank. Film and Television*. 68:A11. 1992
___ "The Darker Ages: Raimi's Campy *Army of Darkness* Supplies Special Effects by the Gross," *Detroit (MI) News*. February 19, 1993 in: *NewsBank. Film and Television*. 30:D12. 1993
___ "*Encino Man*'s Missing Links Are Plot and Quality Acting (Review)," *Detroit (MI) News*. May 22, 1992. in: *NewsBank. Film and Television*. 52:D1. 1992.
___ "*Hook*'s Delightful Magic Forgives a Pushy Message (Review)," *Detroit (MI) News*. December 11, 1991. in: *NewsBank. Film and Television*. 3:F9-F10. 1992.
___ "Hurt So Good: *Batman*'s Back, in a Spectacular Clash of Twisted Psyches," *Detroit (MI) News*. June 19, 1992. in: *NewsBank. Film and Television*. 62:F10-F11. 1992.
___ "It's Not All in Your Head: Cyberthrills Add Byte to Terrifying *Strange Days*," *Detroit (MI) News*. October 13, 1995. in: *NewsBank. Film and Television*. 99:C11. 1995.
___ "*Stargate* Shoots for the Moon--and Misses," *Detroit (MI) News*. October 28, 1994. in: *NewsBank. Film and Television*. 115: G12. 1994.
___ "Steep's Spirit Puts Some Life into *Death* (Review)," *Detroit (MI) News*. July 31, 1992. in: *NewsBank. Film and Television*. 68:G1. 1992.
___ "Vanishing Interest: A Transparent Comedy, *Invisible Man* Displays and Excess of F/X, But Little Else (Review)," *Detroit (MI) News*. February 28, 1992. in: *NewsBank. Film and Television*. 23:D6. 1992.
___ "Whoa, Dudes," *Detroit (MI) News*. July 19, 1991. in: *NewsBank. Film and Television*. 65:F2-F3. 1991.

STARR, RICHARD
___ "SFC Interview: John Barnes," *Science Fiction Chronicle* 16(9): 6, 45-47. August/September 1995.
___ "SFC Interviews: A Conversation With Ester Friesner," *Science Fiction Chronicle* 16(4): 5, 30-32. February 1995.
___ "SFC Interviews: A Conversation With Tim Powers," *Science Fiction Chronicle* 15(6): 40-44. April/May 1994.
___ "SFC Interviews: Piers Anthony," *Science Fiction Chronicle* 15(10): 6, 32-36. September 1994.

STARRS, PAUL F.
___ "The Matrix, Cyberpunk Literature, and the Apolyptic Landscapes of Information Technology," by Paul F. Starrs and Lynn Huntsinger. *Information Technology and Libraries* 14(4): 251-257. December 1995. (Cited from *IAC Insite* on-line service.)

STARZL, R. F.
___ "The Fantastic Science Market," *Fantasy Commentator* 8(3/4): 161-165, 257. Fall 1995. (Whole No. 47/48)

STASKOWSKI, ANDREA
___ **Science Fiction Movies**. Minneapolis MN: Lerner, 1992. 80pp.

STAVANS, ILAN
___ "Carlos Fuentes and the Future," *Science Fiction Studies* 20(3): 409-413. November 1993.
___ "El arte de la memoria," *Mester* (UCLA) 19(2): 97-108. Fall 1990.
___ "Introduction: Private Eyes and Time Travelers," *Literary Review* 38(1): 5-20. Fall 1994.

STECHER-HANSEN, MARIANNE
___ "Science Fiction in the Age of Romanticism: Hans Christian Andersen's Futuristic Tales," *Selecta* (Corvallis) 14: 74-78. 1993.

STEELE, ALLEN
___ "Hard Again," *New York Review of Science Fiction* No. 46: 1, 3-5. June 1992.
___ "SF vs. The Thing," *New York Review of Science Fiction* No. 86: 13-16. October 1995.
___ "SF's Cinematic Sentinel," *Science Fiction Age* 3(4): 82-87. May 1995.

STEELE, COLIN
___ "The Limits of Genre: Tad Williams and Greg Bear Interviewed," *SF Commentary* No. 71/72: 25-27. April 1992.

STEELE, JACK E.
___ "How Do We Get There?," in: Gray, Chris H., ed. **The Cyborg Handbook**. New York: Routledge, 1995. pp.55-59.

STEFFEN, NANCY L.
___ **Burgess' World of Words**. Ph.D. Dissertation, Brandeis University, 1977. 469pp. (DAI-A 38(5): 2781. November 1977.)

STEIN, BEN P.
___ "*Star Trek*: Science on the Edge," *Science World* 51(3): 9-13. October 7, 1994.

STEIN, KEVIN
___ **The Guide to Larry Niven's Ringworld**. New York: Baen, 1994. 188pp.

STEIN, LEON
___ "A Holocaust Education in Reverse: Stephen King's 'The Summer of Corruption: Apt Pupil'," *Journal of the Fantastic in the Arts* 5(2): 60-79. 1993. (No. 18)

STEIN, MURRAY
___ (ed.) **Psyche's Stories: Modern Jungian Interpretations of Fairy Tales**, ed. by Murray Stein and Lionel Corbett. Wilmette, IL: Chiron, 1991. 166pp.

STEINER, K. LESLIE
___ "The K. Leslie Steiner Interview," in: Delany, Samuel R. **Silent Interviews on Language, Race, Sex, Science Fiction and Some Comics**. Hanover, NH: Wesleyan University Press, 1994. pp.269-288.

STEINMÜLLER, KARLHEINZ
___ "Das Ende der Utopischen Literatur: Ein themengeschichtlicher Nachruf auf die DDR-Science-Fiction," *Germanic Review* 67(4): 166-173. Fall 1992.
___ (ed.) **Streifzuge ins Übermorgen: Science Fiction und Zukunftsforschung**, ed. by Klaus Burmeister and Karlheinz Steinmüller. Weinheim: Beltz, 1992. 328pp.

STELLA, CARMELA
___ "Il marxismo, la rivoluzione russa," in: Colombo, Arrigo and Quarta, Cosimo, eds. **Il Destino della Famiglia nell'Utopia**. Bari: Edizione Dedalo, 1991. pp.357-382.

STENSTRÖM, ANDERS
___ "A Mythology? for England," in: Reynolds, Patricia and GoodKnight, Glen H., eds. **Proceedings of the J. R. R. Tolkien Centenary Conference, Keble College, Oxford, 1992**. Altadena, CA: Mythopoeic Press, 1995. pp.310-314. (*Mythlore* Vol. 21, No. 2, Winter 1996, Whole No. 80)

STENSTRÖM, BEREGOND A.
___ "Tolkien in Swedish," in: Kranz, Gisbert, ed. **Inklings: Jahrbuch für Literatur und Ästhetik**. 2. Band. [Lüdenscheid, Germany: Stier], 1984. pp.43-49.

STEPHENS, BOB
___ "*Aliens* Finally Busts Out," *San Francisco (CA) Examiner*. February 8, 1992 in: *NewsBank. Film and Television*. 17:A7. 1992
___ "Persistent Vision: Unforgettable Poster Art From the Golden Age of Science Fiction Movies," by Bob Stephens and Vincent Di Fate. *Sci-Fi Entertainment* 1(2): 48-51. August 1994.
___ "*Pet Sematary* Returns Like a Curse (Review)," *San Francisco (CA) Examiner*. August 29, 1992. in: *NewsBank. Film and Television*. 94: D10. 1992.
___ "Pre-tinsel Science Fiction Tales," *San Francisco (CA) Examiner* November 25, 1995. (Cited from the Internet Edition.)
___ "United Artists *Sci-Fi Matinee*," *Films in Review* 46(9/10): 54-60. November/December 1995.

STEPHENS, CHRISTOPHER P.
___ **A Checklist of Fred Brown**. Hastings-on-Hudson, NY: Ultramarine, 1992. 83pp.

STEPHENS, CHRISTOPHER P.

STEPHENS, CHRISTOPHER P. (continued)
___ **A Checklist of John Sladek.** Hastings-on-Hudson, NY: Ultramarine, 1992. 31pp. Revised ed.
___ **A Checklist of Jonathan Carroll.** Hastings-on-Hudson, NY: Ultramarine, 1992. 11pp.
___ **A Checklist of Roger Zelazny.** Hastings-on-Hudson, NY: Ultramarine, 1993. 47pp.
___ **A Checklist of Ultramarine Press.** Hastings-on-Hudson, NY: Ultramarine, 1992. 13pp. Revised ed.

STEPHENS, LYNNE
___ "Bride of Frankenstein," *Starlog* No. 209: 27-30, 68. December 1994.
___ "A Captain's Carol," *Starlog* No. 174: 25-29. January 1992.
___ "Captain's Holiday," *Starlog* No. 186: 35-39, 74. January 1993.
___ "Designing *Hook*," *Starlog* No. 175: 61-65, 85. February 1992.
___ "Miracle Worker," *Starlog* No. 176: 42-45. March 1992.
___ "The Old Indiana Jones Chronicles," *Starlog* 185: 45-48, 65. December 1992.
___ "Raver," *Starlog* No. 190: 24-26. May 1993.
___ "A Study in Starflight," *Starlog* No. 190: 27-29, 69. May 1993.

STEPHENSEN-PAYNE, PHIL
___ **Andre Norton: Grand Master of the Witch World, a Working Bibliography,** by Phil Stephensen-Payne and Gordon Benson, Jr. Albuquerque, NM: Galactic Central, 1992. 83pp.; San Bernardino, CA: Borgo Press, 1993. 83pp.
___ **Bob Shaw, Artist at Ground Zero: A Working Bibliography.** 5th Rev. Ed. Albuquerque, NM: Galactic Central, 1993. 51pp.
___ **C. J. Cherryh: A Working Bibliography.** Albuquerque, NM: Galactic Central, 1992. 36pp.
___ **Charles L. Harness: Attorney in Space, a Working Bibliography.** Albuquerque, NM: Galactic Central, 1992. 15pp.
___ **Edgar Pangborn: The Persistent Wonder, a Working Bibliography,** by Phil Stephensen-Payne and Gordon Benson, Jr. Albuquerque, NM: Galactic Central, 1993. 26pp.
___ **Gene Wolfe: Urth-Man Extraordinary, a Working Bibliography,** by Phil Stephensen-Payne and Gordon Benson, Jr. Albuquerque, NM: Galactic Central, 1992. 62pp.
___ **George R. R. Martin: The Ace From New Jersey.** Albuquerque, NM: Galactic Central, 1989. 22pp. (2nd Revised Edition)
___ **H. Beam Piper, Emperor of Paratime: A Working Bibliography.** 4th edition, by Phil Stephensen-Payne and Gordon Benson, Jr. Albuquerque, NM: Galactic Central, 1994. 31pp.
___ **Keith Laumer: Ambassador to Space, a Working Bibliography.** 2nd revised edition, by Phil Stephensen-Payne and Gordon Benson, Jr. Albuquerque, NM: Galactic Central, 1990. 41pp.
___ **Keith Roberts: Master Craftsman, a Working Bibliography.** Albuquerque, NM: Galactic Central, 1993. 42pp.
___ **Michael Bishop: A Transfigured Talent, a Working Bibliography.** Albuquerque, NM: Galactic Central, 1992. 38pp.
___ **Philip Kindred Dick: Metaphysical Conjurer, a Working Bibliography,** by Phil Stephensen-Payne and Gordon Benson, Jr. Albuquerque, NM: Galactic Central, 1995. 154pp. (4th Revised Ed.)
___ **Robert Heinlein, Stormtrooping Guru: A Working Bibliography.** Albuquerque, NM: Galactic Central, 1993. 100pp.
___ "U.K. Year in SF, 1991," in: Brown, Charles N. and Contento, William G. **Science Fiction, Fantasy, & Horror: 1991.** Oakland, CA: Locus Press, 1992. pp.437-439.
___ **William Tenn: High Klass Talent, a Working Bibliography,** by Phil Stephensen-Payne and Gordon Benson, Jr. Albuquerque, NM: Galactic Central, 1993. 31pp.
___ **Wilson 'Bob' Tucker, Wild Talent: A Working Bibliography,** by Phil Stephensen-Payne and Gordon Benson, Jr. Albuquerque, NM: Galactic Central, 1994. 38pp. 4th. Edition.

STEPHENSON MIMOSA
___ "Proto-Modernism in Tennyson's 'The Holy Grail'," by Will Stephenson and Stephenson Mimosa. *Quondam et Futurus* 2(4): 49-55. Winter 1992.

STEPHENSON, WILL
___ "Proto-Modernism in Tennyson's 'The Holy Grail'," by Will Stephenson and Stephenson Mimosa. *Quondam et Futurus* 2(4): 49-55. Winter 1992.

STERLING, BRUCE
___ "Sneaking for Jesus 2001," *Science Fiction Eye* No. 11: 13-17. December 1992.
___ "A Statement of Principle," *Science Fiction Eye* No. 10: 14-18. June 1992.

STERLING-HELLENBRAND, ALEXANDRA
___ "Women on the Edge in **Parzival**: A Study of the 'Grail Women'," *Quondam et Futurus* 3(2): 56-68. Summer 1993.

STEVENS, CAROL D.
___ **J. R. R. Tolkien,** by David Stevens and Carol D. Stevens. Mercer Island, WA: Starmont, 1992. 178pp. (Starmont Reader's Guide, 54)
___ **J. R. R. Tolkien: The Art of the Myth-Maker.** Revised Ed., by David Stevens and Carol D. Stevens. San Bernardino, CA: Borgo Press, 1993. 178pp.

STEVENS, DAVID
___ **J. R. R. Tolkien,** by David Stevens and Carol D. Stevens. Mercer Island, WA: Starmont, 1992. 178pp. (Starmont Reader's Guide, 54)
___ **J. R. R. Tolkien: The Art of the Myth-Maker.** Revised Ed., by David Stevens and Carol D. Stevens. San Bernardino, CA: Borgo Press, 1993. 178pp.

STEVENS, KEVIN
___ "On a Wing and a Prayer: The Making of *Wing Commander III*," *Sci-Fi Universe* No. 3: 82-83. October/November 1994.
___ "Star Wares," *Sci-Fi Universe* No. 3: 96-97. October/November 1994.

STEVENSON, JAY
___ "*Fist of the North Star* (Review)," *Cinefantastique* 27(3): 29. December 1995.
___ "*Funny Bones* (Review)," *Cinefantastique* 27(3): 52. December 1995.

STEWART, ELIZABETH
___ **Destroying Angels: Messianic Rhetoric in Benjamin, Scholem, Psychoanalysis and Science Fiction.** Ph.D. Dissertation, New York University, 1994. 586pp. (DAI-A 55/09, p. 2820. March 1995.)

STEWART, PATRICK (A.K.A. PICARD, JEAN-LUC).
___ "A Deep Space Diary: Picard Ponders *Star Trek*'s Next Step," *TV Guide* 41(1): 9-10. January 2, 1993. (Issue 2075)

STEWART, ROBERT S.
___ "Heroes and Hideousness: **Frankenstein** and Failed Unity," by Michael Manson and Robert S. Stewart. *Substance* No. 71/72: 228-242. 1993.

STEWIG, JOHN W.
___ "The Witch Woman: A Recurring Motif in Recent Fantasy Writing for Young Readers," *Mythlore* 20(1): 48-52. Winter 1994. (Whole No. 75) (Reprinted: *Children's Literature in Education* 26(2): 119-133. June 1995.)

STILLMAN, PETER S.
___ "A Critique of Ideal Worlds: Hegel and Marx on Modern Utopian Thought," in: Saccaro Del Buffa, Giuseppa and Lewis, Arthur O., eds. **Utopie per gli Anni Ottana.** Rome: Gangemi Editore, 1986. pp.635-674.
___ "Identity, Complicity, and Resistance in **The Handmaid's Tale**," by Peter S. Stillman and S. Anne Johnson. *Utopian Studies* 5(2): 70-86. 1994.

STINE, G. HARRY
___ "Sheldon's Psychohistory," *Analog* 116(5): 100-103. April 1996.

STINE, JEAN
___ "Introduction: New Eves and New Genesis: The Extraordinary Women Who Write Science Fiction and the Women They Write About," by Janrae Frank, Jean Stine and Forrest J Ackerman. in: Frank, Janrae, Stine, Jean, and Ackerman Forrest J, eds. **New Eves: Science Fiction About the Extraordinary Women of Today and Tomorrow.** Stamford, CT: Longmeadow, 1994. pp.vii-xvi.

STITES, RICHARD
___ "World Outlook and Inner Fears in Soviet Science Fiction," in: Graham, Loren R., ed. **Science and the Soviet Social Order.** Cambridge: Harvard University Press, 1990. pp.299-324.

STITH, JOHN E.
___ "SFWA Model Author-Agent Contract, First Cut," *SFWA Bulletin* 27(4)/28(1): 40-43. Winter/Spring 1994. (No. 122/123)

STOCK, LORRAINE K.
___ "Arms and the (Wo)man in Medieval Romance: The Gendered Arming of Female Warriors in the **Roman d'Eneas** and Heldris's **Roman de Silence**," *Arthuriana* 5(4): 56-83. Winter 1995.

STOCKTON, SHARON
___ "The Self Regained: Cyberpunk's Retreat to the Imperium," *Contemporary Literature* 36(4): 588-612. Winter 1995.

STOCKWELL, PETER J.
___ "Do Androids Dream of Electric Sheep? Isomorphic Relations in Reading Science Fiction," *Language and Literature* (England) 1(2): 79-99. 1992. [Not seen.]
___ **The Thinking Machine: Metaphoric Patterns in the Discourse of Science Fiction.** Ph.D. Dissertation, University of Liverpool, 1993. (DAI BRDX97757; 53: 3210A.)

STODDARD, WILLIAM H.
___ "Law and Institutions in the Shire," *Mythlore* 18(4): 4-8. Autumn 1992. (No. 70)

STOFF, ANDRZEJ
___ **Krytyka o pierwszych utworach Stanislawa Lema** (Critical Opinion on the First Works of Stanislaw Lem). Torun: Acta Universitatis Nicolai Copernick, 1975. (Not seen. Cf. *Science-Fiction Studies*, Nov. 1992.)
___ **Lem i inni: Szkice o Polskiej science fiction** (Lem and Others: Sketches on Polish Science Fiction). Bydgoszcz: Pomorze, 1990. (Not seen. Cf. *Science-Fiction Studies*, Nov. 1992.)
___ **Powiesci fantasryczno-naukowe Stanislawa Lema** (The Science Fiction Novels of Stanislaw Lem). Warsaw: Panstwowe Wydawnictwo Naukowe, 1983. (Not seen. Cf. *Science-Fiction Studies*, Nov. 1992.)

STOLER, JOHN A.
___ "Christian Lore and Characters' Names in **A Canticle for Leibowitz**," *Literary Onomastics Studies* 11: 77-91. 1984.

STOLTZFUS, BEN
___ "Fantasy, Metafiction and Desire," in: Harger-Grinling, Virginia and Chadwick, Tony, eds. **Robbe-Grillet and the Fantastic.** Westport, CT: Greenwood, 1994. pp.11-34.

STOLZENBACH, MARY M.
___ "Braid Yorkshire: The Language of Myth? An Appreciation of **The Secret Garden** by Frances Hodgson Burnett," *Mythlore* 20(4): 25-29. Winter 1995. (Whole No. 78)

STONE, ALBERT E.
___ **Literary Aftershocks: American Writers, Readers, and the Bomb.** New York: Twayne, 1994. 204pp.

STONE, GRAHAM
___ "Beginning: Sixty Years of *Amazing Stories*, 1929-1930," *Science Fiction News* (Australia) No. 101: 2-12. February 1987.
___ "Beginning: Sixty Years of *Amazing Stories*, Part 1," *Science Fiction News* (Australia) No. 97: 2-16. April 1986.
___ "Beginning: Sixty Years of *Amazing Stories*, Part 2," *Science Fiction News* (Australia) No. 98: 1-12. May 1986.
___ "Beginning: Sixty Years of *Amazing Stories*, Part 3," *Science Fiction News* (Australia) No. 99: 2-12. June 1986.
___ "Beginnings," *Science Fiction News* (Australia) No. 100: 2-12. November 1986.
___ "Chronology of Australian Science Fiction 1848-1992," *Science Fiction News* (Australia) No. 90: 3-10. July 1992.
___ "Early Days in Sydney SF Activities," *Science Fiction News* (Australia) No. 61: 6-13. June 1979.
___ "Eric North Again," *Science Fiction News* (Australia) No. 117: 10-11. December 1993.

STONE, GRAHAM (continued)
___ "Fifty Years of Science Fiction Groups in Australia," *Science Fiction News* (Australia) No. 108: 2-8. November 1989.
___ "H. M. Crimp--And More," *Science Fiction News* (Australia) No. 116: 19-21. October 1992.
___ "Index to *Science Fiction News* Nos. 59-106, 1979-1987," *Science Fiction News* (Australia) No. 106: 8-17. December 1987.
___ "Looking Backward," *Science Fiction News* (Australia) No. 63: 5-7. 1979.
___ "Notes on Australian Science Fiction," *Science Fiction News* (Australia) No. 102: 2-5. March 1987.
___ "Notes on Australian Science Fiction," *Science Fiction News* (Australia) No. 105: 2-8. October 1987.
___ "Notes on Australian Science Fiction," *Science Fiction News* (Australia) No. 53: 2-5. February 1978.
___ "Notes on Australian Science Fiction," *Science Fiction News* (Australia) No. 67: 2-9. January 1983.
___ "Notes on Australian Science Fiction," *Science Fiction News* (Australia) No. 92: 2-8. February 1985.
___ "Notes on Australian Science Fiction," *Science Fiction News* (Australia) No. 93. 1985. (Not seen; pages not cited.)
___ "Notes on Australian Science Fiction," *Science Fiction News* (Australia) No. 93: 2-11. March 1985.
___ "Notes on Australian Science Fiction," *Science Fiction News* (Australia) No. 94: 2-11. January 1986.
___ "Notes on Australian Science Fiction," *Science Fiction News* (Australia) No. 95: 2-11. February 1986.
___ "Notes on Australian Science Fiction," *Science Fiction News* (Australia) No. 96: 5-9. March 1986.
___ "Notes on Australian Science Fiction: **Out of the Silence**, by Erle Cox," *Science Fiction News* (Australia) No. 62: 6-7. August 1979.
___ "Notes on Australian Science Fiction: **Out of the Silence**, by Erle Cox," *Science Fiction News* (Australia) No. 64: 2-7. 1980.
___ "Notes on Australian Science Fiction: **Out of the Silence**, by Erle Cox and J. Filmore Sherry," *Science Fiction News* (Australia) No. 66: 2-8. September 1982.
___ "Notes on Australian Science Fiction: **Out of the Silence**, by Erle Cox, Part 1," *Science Fiction News* (Australia) No. 58: 18-20. June 1978.
___ "Notes on Australian Science Fiction: **Out of the Silence**, by Erle Cox, Part 2," *Science Fiction News* (Australia) No. 59: 12-16. February 1979.
___ "Notes on Australian Science Fiction: **Out of the Silence**, by Erle Cox, Part 3," *Science Fiction News* (Australia) No. 60: 19-20. April 1979.
___ "Notes on Australian Science Fiction: *The Comet*," *Science Fiction News* (Australia) No. 54: 2-9. April 1978.
___ "Notes on Australian Science Fiction, Or Not, As the Case May Be," *Science Fiction News* (Australia) No. 102: 6-16. March 1987.
___ "Notes on Australian Science Fiction, Or Not, As the Case May Be," *Science Fiction News* (Australia) No. 68: 5-12. January 1983.
___ "Notes on Australian Science Fiction, Or Not, As the Case May Be," *Science Fiction News* (Australia) No. 92: 8-12. February 1985.
___ "Notes on Australian Science Fiction, Or Not, As the Case May Be," *Science Fiction News* (Australia) No. 93: 12. March 1985.
___ "Notes on Australian Science Fiction, Or Not, As the Case May Be," *Science Fiction News* (Australia) No. 94: 11-12. January 1986.
___ "Notes on Australian Science Fiction, Or Not, As the Case May Be," *Science Fiction News* (Australia) No. 95: 11-12. February 1986.
___ "Notes on Australian Science Fiction, Or Not, As the Case May Be," *Science Fiction News* (Australia) No. 96: 10-12. March 1986.
___ "Notes on Australian Science Fiction, Or Not, As the Case May Be, Part 2," *Science Fiction News* (Australia) No. 70: 5-12. April 1983.
___ "Notes on Australian Science Fiction, Or Not, As the Case May Be, Part 3," *Science Fiction News* (Australia) No. 71: 5-8. May 1983.
___ "Notes on Australian Science Fiction, Or Not, As the Case May Be, Part 4," *Science Fiction News* (Australia) No. 72: 6-8. June 1983.
___ "Notes on Australian Science Fiction, Or Not, As the Case May Be, Part 5," *Science Fiction News* (Australia) No. 77: 5-12. June 1983.
___ **Out of the Silence** in Russian--Lost and Found," *Science Fiction News* (Australia) No. 115: 18-20. May 1992.
___ "Report on G. C. Bleeck, Australian Science Fiction Writer," *Science Fiction News* (Australia) No. 118: 1-16. 1995.
___ "Science Fiction in the *Man* Group of Magazines: A Checklist," *Science Fiction News* (Australia) No. 104: 1-18. May 1987. [Not seen.]
___ "Sixty Years of *Amazing Stories*: 1930," *Science Fiction News* (Australia) No. 103: 2-12. March 1987.

STONE, GRAHAM (continued)

___ "Sixty Years of *Amazing Stories*: 1931," *Science Fiction News* (Australia) No. 107: 1-8. 1988.

___ "Sixty Years of *Amazing Stories*: 1931 (Continued)," *Science Fiction News* (Australia) No. 109: 9-16. January 1990.

___ "Sixty Years of *Amazing Stories*: 1932," *Science Fiction News* (Australia) No. 110: 3-13, 16. April 1990.

___ "Sixty Years of *Amazing Stories*: 1933," *Science Fiction News* (Australia) No. 111: 7-16, 20. July 1990.

___ "Sixty Years of *Amazing Stories*: 1934," *Science Fiction News* (Australia) No. 112: 13-16. September 1990.

___ "Sixty Years of *Amazing Stories*: 1934, and The Quarterly, 1931-1934," *Science Fiction News* (Australia) No. 114: 6-23. December 1990.

___ "Sixty Years of *Amazing Stories*: 1935," *Science Fiction News* (Australia) No. 116: 21-24. October 1992.

___ "Sixty Years of *Amazing Stories*: 1935, Continued," *Science Fiction News* (Australia) No. 117: 11-14. December 1993.

___ "Sixty Years of *Amazing Stories*: The Quarterly, 1929-1930," *Science Fiction News* (Australia) No. 105: 8-20. October 1987.

STONE, GRANT

___ "Know the Author: Terry Pratchett," *Magpies* 8(1): 19. March 1993.

STONE, LINDA

___ "A Glimpse of Cyberspace," *Sci-Fi Entertainment* 1(5): 51. February 1995.

STONE, LISA

___ "All Actor: Doug Bradley Is Not Pinhead," *Sci-Fi Entertainment* 1(5): 30-31. February 1995.

___ "*Forever Knight* Has Risen From the Grave," *Sci-Fi Entertainment* 1(5): 34-37, 55. February 1995.

STONE, SANDY

___ "Split Subjects, Not Atoms: or, How I Fell In Love With My Prosthesis," in: Gray, Chris H., ed. **The Cyborg Handbook.** New York: Routledge, 1995. pp.393-406.

STONE-BLACKBURN, SUSAN

___ "Consciousness Evolution and Early Telepathic Tales," *Science Fiction Studies* 20(2): 241-250. July 1993.

___ "Feminist Nurturers and Psychic Healers," in: Wolf, Milton T. and Mallett, Daryl F., eds. **Imaginative Futures: Proceedings of the 1993 Science Fiction Research Association Conference.** San Bernardino, CA: Jacob's Ladder Books, 1995. pp.167-178.

STOPPA, CLAUDIO

___ "Il kibbuz," in: Colombo, Arrigo and Quarta, Cosimo, eds. **Il Destino della Famiglia nell'Utopia.** Bari: Edizione Dedalo, 1991. pp.339-355.

STRACZYNSKI, J. MICHAEL

___ "The Profession of Science Fiction, 48: Approaching Babylon," *Foundation* No. 64: 5-19. Summer 1995.

STRAUSS, BOB

___ "*Alien 3* Is Born: Long Difficult Gestation Finally Reaches an End," *Los Angeles (CA) Daily News.* May 21, 1992. in: *NewsBank. Film and Television.* 49:B7-B9. 1992.

___ "*Basic Instinct*: Survival of the Grittiest?," *Los Angeles (CA) Daily News* March 20, 1992 in: *NewsBank. Film and Television.* 28:G6-G7. 1992.

___ "Captain Doesn't Want to Go Down With His Starship," *Los Angeles (CA) Daily News.* December 6, 1991. in: *NewsBank. Film and Television.* 7:A10-A11. 1992.; *NewsBank. Names in the News.* NIN 1: F11-F12. 1992.

___ "*Charged* Lacks Juice to Pull Off Effective Death Penalty Satire (Review)," *Los Angeles (CA) Daily News.* February 7, 1992. in: *NewsBank. Film and Television.* 21:A9. 1992.

___ "Cradle's Prurient Fun Weakened By Credibility Factor (Review)," *Los Angeles (CA) Daily News.* January 10, 1992. in: *NewsBank. Film and Television.* 12:B8. 1992.

___ "Death and Misery Take on Sick Fascination in *Skin* (Review)," *Los Angeles (CA) Daily News.* December 18, 1991. in: *NewsBank. Film and Television.* 6:E10. 1992.

STRAUSS, BOB (continued)

___ "Finally, It's A-Bat Time: *Batman Returns*, But Don't Expect Too Much," *Los Angeles (CA) Daily News.* June 20, 1992. in: *NewsBank. Film and Television.* 67:F5. 1992.

___ "*Flyer* Is Finally Given Its Wings (Review)," *Los Angeles (CA) Daily News.* February 21, 1992. in: *NewsBank. Film and Television.* 24:F11-F12. 1992

___ "*Freejack*: Back to the Future? (Review)," *Los Angeles (CA) Daily News.* January 19, 1992. in: *NewsBank. Film and Television.* 11:D2. 1992.

___ "Generations," *Los Angeles (CA) Daily News.* November 18, 1994. in: *NewsBank. Film and Television.* 125:C10-C11. 1994.

___ "Generations Sends Originals into Final Frontier," *Los Angeles (CA) Daily News.* November 18, 1994. in: *NewsBank. Film and Television.* 125:D1. 1994.

___ "Ham on Wry at *Deli* (Review)," *Los Angeles (CA) Daily News.* April 10, 1992. in: *NewsBank. Film and Television.* 51:F11. 1992.

___ "*Hook* Stays Afloat at No. 1, But Being Scuttled By Slow Sales," *Los Angeles (CA) Daily News.* December 24, 1991. in: *NewsBank. Film and Television.* 3:E8. 1992.

___ "If Only 'Death' Were as Good as Its Looks (Review)," *Los Angeles (CA) Daily News.* July 31, 1992. in: *NewsBank. Film and Television.* 78:C14. 1992.

___ "Just Call *No Escape* an Apocalypse Man," *Los Angeles (CA) Daily News.* April 29, 1994. in: *NewsBank. Film and Television.* 46:D14. 1994.

___ "Kirk Out?," *Los Angeles (CA) Daily News.* November 26, 1994. in: *NewsBank. Film and Television.* 10:D6-D7. 1995.

___ "*Lawnmower Man* Is Not Exactly Cutting Edge (Review)," *Los Angeles (CA) Daily News.* March 6, 1992. in: *NewsBank. Film and Television.* 33:A4. 1992.

___ "*Naked Lunch* Lays Bare Compulsions and Psychic Powers (Review)," *Los Angeles (CA) Daily News.* December 27, 1991. in: *NewsBank. Film and Television.* 5:F1. 1992.

___ "New Level of Intensity Makes *Strange Days* Strange," *Los Angeles (CA) Daily News.* October 13, 1995. in: *NewsBank. Film and Television.* 99:B12. 1995.

___ "Peploe Fumbles in 'Dark' Trying to Illuminate Life's Fears," *Los Angeles (CA) Daily News.* August 7, 1992. in: *NewsBank. Film and Television.* 76:B1. 1992

___ "*Pet Sematary II* Comes Alive With No Help From King," *Austin (TX) American Statesman* Sec. B, p.5. August 31, 1992.

___ "Peter Pan Takes a Flying Leap: Spielberg Indulges His Love of Flight In New Film," *Los Angeles (CA) Daily News.* December 8, 1991. in: *NewsBank. Film and Television.* 3:E3. 1992.

___ "*Radio Flyer* Has Solid Roles But Never Really Takes Off (Review)," *Los Angeles (CA) Daily News.* February 21, 1992. in: *NewsBank. Film and Television.* 24:F14. 1992

___ "Screenwriter Pleased With Director's Instinct," *Los Angeles (CA) Daily News* March 26, 1992 in: *NewsBank. Film and Television.* 28:G5. 1992.

___ "Skyscraper Sex Thriller With Plot Gives *Dreams* a Lift (Review)," *Los Angeles (CA) Daily News.* June 5, 1992. in: *NewsBank. Film and Television.* 64:F9. 1992.

___ "So Much Wrong With Buffy It Plays Like a Suicide Attempt," *Los Angeles (CA) Daily News.* July 31, 1992. in: *NewsBank. Film and Television.* 77:B11. 1992

___ "Specious *Species* But Old-Fashioned Film," *Los Angeles (CA) Daily News.* July 7, 1995. in: *NewsBank. Film and Television.* 81:A6. 1995.

___ "Spielberg Panning for Gold in *Hook*," *Los Angeles (CA) Daily News.* December 8, 1991. in: *NewsBank. Film and Television.* 3:E4-E7. 1992.

___ "Star Finale: Nimoy Turns in His Ears After 25 Years As Spock," *Los Angeles (CA) Daily News.* December 6, 1991. in: *NewsBank. Names in the News.* 1:D7-D8. 1992.

___ "*Star Trek VI* Ends Film Series By Tearing Down Galactic Walls (Review)," *Los Angeles (CA) Daily News.* December 6, 1991. in: *NewsBank. Film and Television.* 7:D7. 1992.

STRAUSS, WALTER A.

___ "The Golem on the Operatic Stage: Nature's Warning," *Journal of the Fantastic in the Arts* 7(2/3): 191-200. 1995.

STREET, RITA

___ "Toys Will Be Toys," *Cinefex* No. 64: 76-91. December 1995.

STREHLE, SUSAN
___ **Fiction in the Quantum Universe**. Chapel Hill: University of North Carolina Press, 1992. 282pp.

STREITFELD, DAVID
___ "Ears for Art's Sake," *Washington (DC) Post Book World* p. 15. January 26, 1992.
___ "The Human Typewriter," *Washington (DC) Post Book World* p. 15. January 26, 1992.
___ "V. C. Andrews's Afterlife," *Washington (DC) Post Book World* p. 12. May 10, 1992.

STRICK, PHILIP
___ "*Star Trek: Generations* (Review)," *Sight and Sound* 5(3): 55-56. March 1995.

STRICKLAND, DIANE
___ "Favorite Writers of Science Fiction and Fantasy," *English Journal* 82(6): 83-85. October 1993.

STRICKLER, JEFF
___ "Charming Moments Make the Moments in *Prelude to a Kiss* (Review)," *Minneapolis (MN) Star and Tribune*. July 10, 1992. in: *NewsBank. Film and Television*. 73:C9. 1992.
___ " 'Honey' Sequel Has Big Shoes to Fill and Does It Well (Review)," *Minneapolis (MN) Star and Tribune*. July 17, 1992. in: *NewsBank. Film and Television*. 70:E1. 1992.
___ "*Lawnmower Man* Is Just a Cut Above Average Sci-Fi Movies (Review)," *Minneapolis (MN) Star and Tribune*. March 6, 1992. in: *NewsBank. Film and Television*. 33:A7. 1992.
___ "*Naked Lunch* Is a Bizarre Mindbender (Review)," *Minneapolis (MN) Star and Tribune*. February 7, 1992. in: *NewsBank. Film and Television*. 23:G9. 1992.
___ "*Timecop* Is Satisfying Science Fiction Tale," *Minneapolis (MN) Star and Tribune*. September 16, 1994. in: *NewsBank. Film and Television*. 105:D4. 1994.

STROBY, W. C.
___ "Digging Up Stories With Stephen King," *Writer's Digest* 72(3): 22-27. March 1992.

STROCK, IAN R.
___ "Market Listings," in: Dozois, Gardner, ed. **Writing Science Fiction and Fantasy**. New York: St. Martin's, 1991. pp.250-258.

STRUGNELL, JOHN
___ "Hammering the Demons: Sword, Sorcery and Contemporary Society," in: Filmer, Kath, ed. **Twentieth-Century Fantasists: Essays in Culture, Society and Belief in Twentieth Century Mythopoeic Literature**. New York: St. Martin's, 1992. pp.172-182.

STUART, IAN
___ "D. L. S.: An Unsteady Throne?," in: Dale, Alzina S., ed. **Dorothy L. Sayers: The Centenary Celebration**. New York: Walker, 1993. pp.23-30.

STUD BROTHERS
___ "Sci-Fi Fidelity: The Best and Worst SF Motion Pictures," *Melody Maker* 72(32): 36. August 12, 1995.

STURGEON, THEODORE
___ **Argyll: A Memoir**. Glen Ellen, CA: Paul Williams, 1993. 84pp. [Not seen.]

STURGES, ROBERT S.
___ "Chrétien de Troyes in English Translation: A Guide to the Issues," *Arthuriana* 4(3): 205-223. Fall 1994.

SUAREZ, ISABEL CARRERA
___ " 'Yet I Speak, Yet I Exist': Affirmation of the Subject in Atwood's Short Stories," in: Nicholson, Colin, ed. **Margaret Atwood: Writing and Subjectivity: New Critical Essays**. New York: St. Martin's, 1994. pp.230-247.

SUKSANG, DUANGRUDI
___ "Equal Partnership: Jane Hume Clapperton's Evolutionist-Socialist Utopia," *Utopian Studies* 3(1): 95-107. 1992.

SUKSANG, DUANGRUDI (continued)
___ "Overtaking Patriarchy: Crobett's and Dixie's Visions of Women," *Utopian Studies* 4(2): 74-93. 1993.

SULLIVAN, C. W., III.
___ "Cultural Worldview: Marginalizing the Fantastic in the Seventeenth Century," *Paradoxa* 1(3): 287-300. 1995.
___ "Fantasy According to *Mister Roger's Neighborhood* and *In the Night Kitchen*," in: Morse, Donald E., ed. **The Celebration of the Fantastic**. Westport, CT: Greenwood, 1992. pp.183-190.
___ "Heinlein's Juveniles: Growing Up in Outer Space," in: Sullivan, C. W., III. **Science Fiction for Young Readers**. Westport, CT: Greenwood, 1993. pp.21-35.
___ **The Influence of Celtic Myth and Legend on Modern Imaginative Fantasy**. Ph.D. Dissertation, University of Oregon, 1976. 213pp. (DAI 37: 5979A. Mar. 1977.)
___ " 'The Northern Thing' Reconsidered," *Journal of the Fantastic in the Arts* 3(3): 21-31. 1994.
___ **Science Fiction for Young Readers**. Westport, CT: Greenwood, 1993. 214pp.
___ "Tolkien and the Telling of a Traditional Narrative," *Journal of the Fantastic in the Arts* 7(1): 75-82. 1996.
___ "The Year in Fantasy Literature, 1990," by William Senior and C. W. Sullivan, III. in: Collins, Robert A. and Latham, Robert, eds. **Science Fiction and Fantasy Book Review Annual 1991**. Westport, CT: Greenwood, 1994. pp.49-69.

SULLIVAN, DARCY
___ "*Toy Story*," *Starlog* No. 221: 38-45. December 1995.

SULLIVAN, E. D. S.
___ "Place in No Place: Examples of the Ordered Society in Literature," in: Sullivan, E. D. S., ed. **The Utopian Vision**. San Diego, CA: San Diego University Press, 1983. pp.29-50.
___ (ed.) **The Utopian Vision: Seven Essays on the Quincentennial of Sir Thomas More**. San Diego, CA: San Diego University Press, 1983. 265pp.

SULLIVAN, JACK
___ "Clive Barker and the End of the Horror Boom," *Studies in Weird Fiction* No. 14: 2-3. Winter 1994.

SULSKI, JIM
___ "False Futures," *Chicago Tribune* Sec. 5, p. 6. January 7, 1993.
___ "Japanimation, Kitsch Classics No Kids' Stuff," *Chicago Tribune* Sec. 7, p. 61. November 6, 1992.
___ "Moonlighting," *Chicago Tribune* Sec. 5, p. 3. January 12, 1993.

SUMMER, BOB
___ "Graphics Go Literary: Comics Aren't Just for Superheroes Anymore," *Publishers Weekly* 241(38): 20-21. September 19, 1994.

SUMNER, JANE
___ "Rice Has Biting Words for Hollywood (Interview)," *Dallas (TX) Morning News*. November 25, 1992. in: *NewsBank. Literature*. 105:C9-C10. 1992.

SUNDELSON, DAVID
___ "The Dream Therapist and Other Dangers: Jonathan Demme's *The Silence of the Lambs*," *Journal of Popular Film and Television* 21(1): 12-18. Spring 1993.

SURTEES, ANGELA
___ "The Mechanics of Dragons: An Introduction to the Study of Their 'Ologies," by Angela Surtees and Steve Gardner. in: Reynolds, Patricia and GoodKnight, Glen H., eds. **Proceedings of the J. R. R. Tolkien Centenary Conference, Keble College, Oxford, 1992**. Altadena, CA: Mythopoeic Press, 1995. pp.411-418. (*Mythlore* Vol. 21, No. 2, Winter 1996, Whole No. 80)

SUSSMAN, BERNARD J.
___ "Orwell's **1984**," *The Explicator* 38(4): 32-33. Summer 1980.

SUTIN, LAWRENCE
___ "The Case for Science Fiction," *Hungry Mind Review* pp.22-23. Winter 1995/1996.

SUTIN, LAWRENCE (continued)
___ (ed.) **The Shifting Realities of Philip K. Dick: Selected Literary and Philosophical Writings**. New York: Pantheon, 1995. 350pp.

SUTTON, ANNE F.
___ "The Dark Dragon of the Normans: A Creation of Geoffrey of Monmouth, Stephen of Rouen, and Merlin Silvester," by Anne F. Sutton and Livia Visser-Fuchs. *Quondam et Futurus* 2(2): 1-20. Summer 1992.

SUVIN, DARKO
___ "Locus, Horizon and Orientation: The Concept of Possible Worlds as a Key to Utopian Studies," in: Saccaro Del Buffa, Giuseppa and Lewis, Arthur O., eds. **Utopia e Modernita: Teorie e prassi utopiche nell'eta moderna e postmoderna**. Rome: Gangemi Editore, 1989. pp.47-65.
___ "The Opus: Artifice as Refuge and World View (Introductory Reflections)," in: Mullen, R. D., ed. **On Philip K. Dick: 40 Articles From Science-Fiction Studies**. Terre Haute, IN: SF-TH Inc., 1992. pp.2-15.
___ "SF and the Novum," *Chung Wai Literary Quarterly* 22(12): May 1994. (Issue not seen; pagination unavailable.)

SVENNEVIG, M.
___ "The Impact of Nuclear Fiction in Britain: *The Day After* and *Threads*," by Barrie Gunter and M. Svennevig. in: Wober, J. Mallory, ed. **Television and Nuclear Power: Making the Public Mind**. Norwood, NJ: Ablex, 1992. pp.55-66.

SVOBODA, RANDALL A.
___ **Between Private and Public Space: The Problem of Writing Personal History in the Novels of Lessing, Lawrence, Joyce and Fowles**. Ph.D. Dissertation, University of Iowa, 1995. 313pp. (DAI-A 56/06, p. 2253. December 1995.)

SWAIN, ALEX
___ "Zine Scene: Sci-Fi Circuit," *Internet World* 6(9): 50. September 1995.

SWALLOW, JAMES
___ "X-aminations," *Starlog* No. 221: 30-33, 64. December 1995.

SWANWICK, MICHAEL
___ "The Strange Case of Raphael Aloysius Lafferty," *Amazing* 68(7): 51-57. October 1993.
___ "Viewpoint: In the Tradition...," *Asimov's Science Fiction Magazine* 18(12/13): 74-101. November 1994.

SWEENEY, KATE
___ "Winnipeg Hosts Final Frontier," *Grand Forks (ND) Herald*. September 4, 1994. in: *NewsBank. Film and Television.* 56:D14-E1. 1994.

SWEETMAN, DAVID
___ **Mary Renault: A Biography**. New York: Harcourt Brace, 1994. 322pp.

SWIFT, CATHERINE
___ **C. S. Lewis**. Minneapolis, MN: Bethany House, 1989. 127pp.

SWIRES, STEVE
___ "*First Men in the Moon*," *Starlog* No. 205: 62-67. August 1994.
___ "John Carpenter's Guide to Hollywood (In)Visibility," *Starlog* 177: 28-33, 71. April 1992.
___ "Master of the *Time Machine*," in: McDonnell, David, ed. **Starlog's Science Fiction Heroes and Heroines**. New York: Crescent Books, 1995. pp.80-83.
___ "Quartermaster," *Starlog* No. 183: 58-62, 70. October 1992.
___ "Space Mom," by Tom Weaver and Steve Swires. in: McDonnell, David, ed. **Starlog's Science Fiction Heroes and Heroines**. New York: Crescent Books, 1995. pp.44-46.
___ "Vulcan Legend," in: McDonnell, David, ed. **Starlog's Science Fiction Heroes and Heroines**. New York: Crescent Books, 1995. pp.50-54.

SWIRSKI, PETER
___ **Dystopia or Dischtopia: An Analysis of the SF Paradigms in Thomas M. Disch**. Master's Thesis, McGill University, 1990. 123pp. (Master's Abstracts 31/03, p. 1019. Fall 1993.)

SWIRSKI, PETER (continued)
___ "On Games With the Universe: Preconceptions of Science in Stanislaw Lem's **The Invincible**," *Contemporary Literature* 35(2): 324-342. Summer 1994.
___ "Playing a Game of Ontology: A Postmodern Reading of **The Futurological Congress**," *Extrapolation* 33(1): 32-40. Spring 1992.

SYS, JACQUES
___ " 'Look Out! It's Alive!': C. S. Lewis on Doctrine," in: Walker, Andrew and Patric, James, eds. **A Christian for All Christians**. Washington, DC: Regnery, 1992. pp.174-189.

SZARMACH, PAUL E.
___ "Arthurian Archaeology," in: Fries, Maureen and Watson, Jeanie, eds. **Approaches to the Teaching of the Arthurian Tradition**. New York: Modern Language Association, 1992. pp.135-138.

SZEBIN, FREDERICK C.
___ "*Darkman II: Durant Returns*," *Cinefantastique* 25(6)/26(1): 36-37, 125. December 1994.
___ "*Darkman III: Die, Darkman, Die*," *Cinefantastique* 26(6)/27(1): 92-93, 125. October 1995.
___ "*Empire of the Dark* (Review)," *Cinefantastique* 25(2): 59. April 1994.
___ "The New Adventures of **Hercules**," *Cinefantastique* 26(2): 46-51. February 1995.
___ "The Special Effects of **Hercules**," *Cinefantastique* 26(2): 49-50, 60. February 1995.
___ "*The Tourist*: The Hollywood Horror Story of Writer Clair Noto's Unfilmed Masterpiece," *Cinefantastique* 25(4): 46-55. August 1994.

SZEWCZYK, STACEY
___ "Something Is Out There...Maybe," *Sci-Fi Universe* No. 3: 94-95. October/November 1994.

TAFURI, MANFREDO
___ "Un teatro, una 'fontana del Sil' e 'unovago monticello'. Il progetto de Alvise Cornaro per la riconfigurazione del bacino marciano," in: Saccaro Del Buffa, Giuseppa and Lewis, Arthur O., eds. **Utopie per gli Anni Ottana**. Rome: Gangemi Editore, 1986. pp.313-328.

TAKEI, GEORGE
___ **To the Stars: The Autobiography of George Takei, Star Trek's Mr. Sulu**. New York: Pocket Books, 1994. 406pp.
___ **To the Stars: The Autobiography of Star Trek's Mr. Sulu**. New York: Simon & Schuster Audio, 1994. 2 audiocassettes, 3 hours.

TALBOT, MARY
___ " 'It Felt Good to Kill': Schoolboy Dreams in the Novels of James Herbert," *Foundation* No. 62: 47-63. Winter 1994/1995.

TALBOT, NORMAN
___ " 'But He Were King, or Kinges Eyr...': Morris's Retelling of **Havelok**," *Journal of the William Morris Society* 10(4): 28-39. Spring 1994.
___ " 'Escape!': That Dirty Word in Modern Fantasy: Le Guin's Earthsea," in: Filmer, Kath, ed. **Twentieth-Century Fantasists: Essays in Culture, Society and Belief in Twentieth Century Mythopoeic Literature**. New York: St. Martin's, 1992. pp.135-147.
___ "Fair Dinkum at Dragonsdawn: Or, How to Turn Australians, and Especially, Australian SF Readers, into Paranoid Androids," by Norman Talbot and Clare Fennessy. *Australian Science Fiction Review* 5(3): 12-15. Spring 1990. (Whole No. 25)
___ "Where Do Elves Go To? Tolkien and a Fantasy Tradition," in: Reynolds, Patricia and GoodKnight, Glen H., eds. **Proceedings of the J. R. R. Tolkien Centenary Conference, Keble College, Oxford, 1992**. Altadena, CA: Mythopoeic Press, 1995. pp.94-106. (*Mythlore* Vol. 21, No. 2, Winter 1996, Whole No. 80)

TANNENBAUM, JEFFREY A.
___ "Focus on Franchising: Outer Space," *Wall Street Journal* Sec. B, p. 2. April 26, 1993.

TANNER, RON
___ "Toy Robots in America, 1955-75: How Japan Really Won the War," *Journal of Popular Culture* 28(3): 125-154. Winter 1994.

TARRANT, DESMOND
___ "Cabell and James Blish (1921-1975)," *Kalki* 9(4): 133-136. 1991. (No. 36)

TATAR, MARIA
___ **Off With Their Heads: Fairy Tales and the Culture of Childhood**. Princeton, NJ: Princeton University Press, 1992. 295pp.
___ (ed.) **Neverending Stories: Toward a Critical Narratology**, ed. by Ann Fehn, Ingeborg Hoesterey and Maria Tatar. Princeton, NJ: Princeton University Press, 1992. 274pp.

TATE, GREG
___ "Ghetto in the Sky: Samuel Delany's Black Whole," in: Tate, Greg. **Flyboy in the Buttermilk: Essays on Contemporary America**. New York: Simon & Schuster, 1992. pp.159-167.

TATSUMI, TAKAYUKI
___ "Eye to Eye With David Blair: An Interview," *Science Fiction Eye* No. 13: 54-61. Spring 1994.
___ **Gendai SF no retorikku**. [The Rhetoric of Contemporary Science Fiction.]. Tokyo: Iwaanami Shoten, 1992. 266pp. [Not seen.]
___ "Graffiti's Rainbow: Toward the Theoretical Frontiers of 'Fiction:' From Metafiction and Cyberpunk Through Avant-Pop," by Takayuki Tatsumi and Larry McCaffery. *Science Fiction Eye* No. 12: 43-49. Summer 1993.
___ **Japanoido sengen: gendai Nihon Sfo yomu tameni**. Tokyo: Hayakawa Shobo, 1993. 246pp. [Not seen.]
___ "Science Fiction and Criticism: The *Diacritics* Interview," in: Delany, Samuel R. **Silent Interviews on Language, Race, Sex, Science Fiction and Some Comics**. Hanover, NH: Wesleyan University Press, 1994. pp.186-215.
___ "Some Real Mothers: The *SF Eye* Interview," in: Delany, Samuel R. **Silent Interviews on Language, Race, Sex, Science Fiction and Some Comics**. Hanover, NH: Wesleyan University Press, 1994. pp.164-185.

TAUBIN, AMY
___ "Bloody Tales," *Sight and Sound* 5(1): 8-11. January 1995.
___ "Invading Bodies: *Alien 3* and the Trilogy," *Sight and Sound* 2(3): 8-10. 1992. [Not seen.]

TAUTKUS, MARJORIE R.
___ **Salvation at the Cinema: Religious References in American Science Fiction Films of the 1980's**. Master's Thesis, Old Dominion University, 1992. 93pp. (Master's Abstracts, 31/04, p. 1413. Winter 1993.)

TAVARES, BRAULIO
___ (ed.) **Fantastic, Fantasy and Science Fiction Literature Catalog**. Rio de Janeiro, Brasil: Biblioteca Nacional, n.d., ca. 1993. 78pp. (International Publications Series No. 2)

TAVES, BRIAN
___ "**Adventures of the Rat Family**: A Verne Expert Brings Fairy Tale to English-Speaking Public," *Library of Congress Information Bulletin* 53(1): 7-11. January 10, 1994.

TAYLOR, A. J. P.
___ "Intellectual Gaiety," in: Watson, George, ed. **Critical Essays on C. S. Lewis**. Hants, Eng.: Scolar Press, 1992. pp.37-47.

TAYLOR, ANDREW
___ "The Charisma Leak: A Conversation With William Gibson and Bruce Sterling," by Daniel Fischlin, Veronica Hollinger and Andrew Taylor. *Science Fiction Studies* 19(1): 1-16. March 1992.
___ "Cybertheater, Postmodernism, and Virtual Reality: An Interview With Toni Dove and Michael Mackenzie," by Daniel Fischlin and Andrew Taylor. *Science Fiction Studies* 21(1): 1-23. March 1994.
___ "Polishing Up the Pattern: The Ending of **The Owl Service**," *Children's Literature in Education* 23(2): 93-100. June 1992.

TAYLOR, BEVERLY
___ **Arthurian Legend and Literature: An Annotated Bibliography. Volume 1: The Middle Ages**, by Edmund Reiss, Louise H. Reiss and Beverly Taylor. New York: Garland, 1984. 467pp.
___ **Arthurian Legend and Literature: An Annotated Bibliography. Volume 2.**, by Edmund Reiss, Louise H. Reiss and Beverly Taylor. New York: Garland, 1995. [Not seen.]

TAYLOR, BEVERLY (continued)
___ "Using Nineteenth-Century Visual Arts in the Literature Classroom," in: Fries, Maureen and Watson, Jeanie, eds. **Approaches to the Teaching of the Arthurian Tradition**. New York: Modern Language Association, 1992. pp.143-146.

TAYLOR, CLARKE
___ "Animated Asimov: Mr. Sci-Fi (Momentarily) Abandons Books for Film," in: *NewsBank. Film and Television* FTV 27: F4-F5. 1988.

TAYLOR, JENNY B.
___ **In the Secret Theatre of Home: Wilkie Collins, Sensation Narrative, and Nineteenth Century Psychology**. London, New York: Routledge, 1988. 306pp.

TAYLOR, LISA C.
___ "Is There a Typical YA Fantasy? A Content Analysis," by Frances A. Dowd and Lisa C. Taylor. *Journal of Youth Services in Libraries* 5(2): 175-183. Winter 1992.

TAYLOR, MICHAEL
___ "Holy Product Tie-In: The Caped Crusader's New Movie Has Retailers All Aflutter," *Dallas (TX) Morning News*. June 13, 1992. in: *NewsBank. Film and Television*. 62:E5-E6. 1992.

TAYLOR, PHILIP M.
___ **Steven Spielberg: The Man, His Movies, and Their Meaning**. New York: Continuum, 1992. 176pp.

TAYLOR, RECECCA
___ "Interview with Mercedes," by Rececca Taylor, Gayle Keresey and Margaret Miles. *Voice of Youth Advocates* 15(4): 213-217. October 1992.

TAZZI, PIER L.
___ "Utopia e immaginariio nelle arti vesive degli anni '60 (riasunto)," in: Saccaro Del Buffa, Giuseppa and Lewis, Arthur O., eds. **Utopie per gli Anni Ottana**. Rome: Gangemi Editore, 1986. pp.415-418.

TEBBUTT, GLORIE
___ "Reading and Righting: Metafiction and Metaphysics in William Golding's **Darkness Visible**," *Twentieth Century Literature* 39(1): 47-58. Spring 1993.

TEETERS, PEGGY
___ **Jules Verne: The Man Who Invented Tomorrow**. New York: Walker, 1992. 120pp.

TEISSL, VERENA
___ "Der tod in drei asugewählten phantastischen texten der Moderne," *Quarber Merkur* 33(2): 34-46. December 1995. (No. 84)
___ "Die Todestehmatik als ein grundlegendes Muster der Phantastik," *Quarber Merkur* 33(1): 54-65. June 1995. (No. 83)
___ "Paul Leppins **Severins Gang in die Finsternis**. Ein Prager Gespensterroman," *Quarber Merkur* 32(2): 28-32. December 1994. (Whole No. 82)

TEITELBAUM, SHELDON
___ "**The Addams Family**: Creating the Cartoon's Look," *Cinefantastique* 22(4): 50. February 1992.
___ "**The Addams Family**," *Cinefantastique* 22(4): 48-51. February 1992.
___ "**Alien 3**: Development Hell," *Cinefantastique* 22(6): 15-18. June 1992
___ "**Alien 3**: William Gibson's 'Neuroaliens'," *Cinefantastique* 22(6): 12-13. June 1992
___ "**Beauty and the Beast**: The Story Behind the Making of the Fairy Tale," *Cinefantastique* 22(4): 42-43. February 1992.
___ "Disney's **Aladdin**," *Cinefantastique* 23(4): 14-15. December 1992.
___ "**Doppelganger**," *Cinefantastique* 23(5): 40-41. February 1993.
___ "The Mouse Who Sold the Moon: Disney Does Heinlein's **Puppet Masters**," *Sci-Fi Universe* No. 3: 38-43. October/November 1994.
___ "Playing With History," *Los Angeles (CA) Times* Sec. E, p. 1. July 7, 1992.
___ "Scientists Say Asimov Put the Stars in Their Eyes," *Los Angeles (CA) Times*. Sec. E, p. 1. April 8, 1992. in *NewsBank. Literature*. 35: B11-B12. 1992.

TEITELBAUM, SHELDON

TEITELBAUM, SHELDON (continued)
___ "U. F. O. Crash at Roswell," *Cinefantastique* 25(4): 12-13, 61. August 1994.
___ "*Wolf*," *Cinefantastique* 25(2): 6-7. April 1994.

TELOTTE, J. P.
___ "Enframing the Self: The Hardware and Software of **Hardware**," *Science Fiction Studies* 22(3): 323-332. November 1995
___ "In the Realm of the Revealing: The Technological Double in the Contemporary Science Fiction Film," *Journal of the Fantastic in the Arts* 6(2/3): 234-252. 1994.
___ **Replications: A Robotic History of the Science Fiction Film.** Champaign: University of Illinois Press, 1995. 222pp.
___ "**The Terminator**, **Terminator 2**, and the Expanded Body," *Journal of Popular Film and Television* 20(2): 26-34. Summer 1992.
___ "**Westworld**, **Futureworld**, and the World's Obscenity," in: Ruddick, Nicholas, ed. **State of the Fantastic**. Westport, CT: Greenwood, 1992. pp.179-188.
___ "**The World of Tomorrow** and the 'Secret Goal' of Science Fiction," *Journal of Film and Video* 45(1): 27-39. Spring 1993.

TEMIANKA, DAN
___ **The Jack Vance Lexicon: The Coined Words of Jack Vance From Ahulph to Zipangote.** San Bernardino, CA: Borgo Press, 1995. 136pp.

TENTORI, ANTONIO
___ **Mondi Incredibili: Il Cinema Fantastico-Avvneturoso Italiano,** by Antonio Bruschini and Antonio Tentori. Bologna: Granta Press, 1995. 173pp.

TERKEL, STUDS
___ "Learning to Put the Questions Differently (Interview, 1969)," in: Ingersoll, Earl G., ed. **Doris Lessing: Conversations**. Princeton, NJ: Ontario Review Press, 1994. pp.19-32.

TERPENING, JON
___ **Science in Literature: Exploring Fiction, Poetry and Non-Fiction.** Toronto: Harcourt Canada, 1994.

TERRA, RICHARD
___ "Shades of Rose and Red: Nostalgic and Visionary Images of the Human Exploration of Mars," *New York Review of Science Fiction* No. 54: 1, 8-11. February 1993.

TERREL, DENISE
___ "L'Erotisme, un paramètre de définition de la science fiction," in: Bozzetto, Roger, ed. **Eros: Science & Fiction Fantastique**. Aix-en-Provence: Universite de Provence, 1991. pp.191-199.

TERRELL, CARROLL
___ **Stephen King: Man and Artist**. Orono, ME: Northern Lights, 1991. 274pp.

TERRY, CLIFFORD
___ "I Thought I Thaw a Rambo (Review)," *San Jose (CA) Mercury News* October 9, 1993. in: *NewsBank. Film and Television.* 114:G8. 1993.
___ "Set Outperforms Script in 'Escape'," *Richmond (VA) Times-Dispatch*. April 30, 1994. in: *NewsBank. Film and Television.* 58:A14. 1994.

TERRY, R. C.
___ **Robert Louis Stevenson: Interviews and Recollections**. Iowa City: University of Iowa Press, 1995. 216pp.

TESTA, CARLO
___ **Desire and the Devil: Demonic Contracts in French and European Literature**. New York: Peter Lang, 1991. 192pp.

TETEWSKY, LAWRENCE
___ "**Peter Pan**: The Silent Film Version," *Cinefantastique* 22(6): 36-37. June 1992
___ "**Robocop**: The Future of Law Enforcement (Review)," *Cinefantastique* 27(2): 60. November 1995.

THOMPSON, RAYMOND H.

THARP, JULIE
___ "The Transvestite as Monster: Gender Horror in **The Silence of the Lambs** and **Psycho**," *Journal of Popular Film and Television* 19(3): 106-113. 1991.

THARSHER, PAULA C.
___ "**Star Trek** Exhibit Beams You Out of This World," *Atlanta Journal. Leisure Magazine* p. 6. January 30, 1993.

THIEL, JOHN
___ "Fritz Leiber: A Man of Variety," *Lan's Lantern* No. 38: 18. July 1992.

THIHER, ALLEN
___ **Franz Kafka: A Study of the Short Fiction**. Boston, MA: Twayne, 1990. 171pp.

THOMAS, G. W.
___ "The Gaming Market: Writing Role-Playing Games," in: Thompkins, David G., ed. **Science Fiction Writer's Market Place and Source Book**. Cincinnati, OH: Writer's Digest Books, 1994. pp.276-283.
___ "An Untapped Market: Writing Role-Playing Games," *Writer's Digest* 73(6): 38-41. June 1993.

THOMAS, KEVIN
___ "Scare Tactics Don't Work Well in **Pet Sematary II** (Review)," *Newark (NJ) Star-Ledger*. September 1, 1992. in: *NewsBank. Film and Television.* 94:D11. 1992.

THOMAS, MARGARET
___ "Flop Down With a Good Disk," *Juneau (AK) Empire*. January 13, 1994. in: *NewsBank. Film and Television.* 17:A14-B1. 1994.

THOMAS, PASCAL J.
___ "Science Fiction Fandom in Western Europe: A French Perspective," in: Sanders, Joe, ed. **Science Fiction Fandom**. Westport, CT: Greenwood, 1994. pp.119-126.
___ "SF in France," *Locus* 34(4): 34-35. April 1995.

THOMAS, PATRICK M.
___ "**Tristan** and the Avatars of the Lunar Goddess," *Quondam et Futurus* 2(3): 15-22. Fall 1992.

THOMAS, ROY
___ "Tarz and the Apes," *Burroughs Bulletin* NS. No. 21: 16-23. January 1995.

THOMAS, SUE
___ "Self-Censorship: The Three Dots...," *Focus* (BSFA) No. 29: 3-4. December 1995/January 1996.
___ "Should Writers Teach Writing?," *Focus* (BSFA) No. 25: 12. December/January 1994.

THOMAS, TONY
___ **The Best of Universal**. Vestal, NY: Vestal Press, 1990. 102pp.

THOMPSON, LINDA W.
___ **The Image of Nursing in Science Fiction Literature**. Thesis (D.S.N.), University of Alabama at Birmingham School of Nursing, 1993. 297pp. (DAI-B 54/07, p. 3554. January 1994.)

THOMPSON, PAUL
___ **The Work of William Morris**. Third Edition. New York: Viking, 1991. 400pp.

THOMPSON, RAYMOND H.
___ "Anne McCaffrey," in: Bruccoli, Matthew J., ed. **Facts on File Bibliography of American Fiction 1919-1988**. New York: Facts on File, 1991. pp.334-335.
___ "The Comic Sage: Merlin in Thomas Berger's **Arthur Rex**," in: Watson, Jeanie and Fries, Marueen, eds. **The Figure of Merlin in the Nineteenth and Twentieth Centuries**. Lewiston, NY: Mellen, 1989. pp.143-153.
___ "The Ironic Tradition in Arthurian Films Since 1960," in: Harty, Kevin J., ed. **Cinema Arthuriana: Essays on Arthurian Film**. New York: Garland, 1991. pp.93-104.

THOMPSON, RAYMOND H. (continued)
___ "Modern Visions and Revisions of the Matter of Britain," in: Fries, Maureen and Watson, Jeanie, eds. **Approaches to the Teaching of the Arthurian Tradition**. New York: Modern Language Association, 1992. pp.61-64.
___ "Morgause of Orkney, Queen of Air and Darkness," *Quondam et Futurus* 3(1): 1-13. Spring 1993.

THOMPSON, TOM
___ "Interactive Science Fiction for the Mac," *Byte* 19(12): 34-35. December 1994.

THOMSON, R. L.
___ **"Owain: Chwedl Iarlles y Ffynnon,"** in: Bromwich, Rachel, Jarman, A. O. H. and Roberts, Brynley F., eds. **The Arthur of the Welsh**. Cardiff: University of Wales Press, 1991. pp.159-170.

THOMSON, SEDGE
___ "Drawn to a Type of Landscape (Interview, 1989)," in: Ingersoll, Earl G., ed. **Doris Lessing: Conversations**. Princeton, NJ: Ontario Review Press, 1994. pp.178-192.

THONEN, JOHN
___ "Charles Band Filmography," *Cinefantastique* 26(4): 18-49. June 1995.
___ **"Deceit** (Review)," *Cinefantastique* 25(2): 59. April 1994.
___ **"Ed Wood**: Plan 9 Alive! The Musical," *Cinefantastique* 25(5): 36-37. October 1994.
___ **"Ed Wood**: 'Plan 9' Movie Mogul," *Cinefantastique* 25(5): 22. October 1994.
___ **"Evil Toons** (Review)," *Cinefantastique* 23(1): 60. August 1992.
___ **"Screamers** EFX," *Cinefantastique* 27(2): 42. November 1995.
___ **"Screamers,"** *Cinefantastique* 27(2): 40-43. November 1995.
___ **"Star Worms II: Attack of the Pleasure Pods** (Review)," *Cinefantastique* 25(3): 60. June 1994.

THORNHILL, DENICE M.
___ "Boskone 32," *Voice of Youth Advocates* 18(3): 148-149. August 1995.

THORNTON, GINGER
___ "The Weakening of the King: Arthur's Disintegration in **The Book of Sir Tristam**," in: Busby, Keith, ed. **The Arthurian Yearbook I**. New York: Garland, 1991. pp.135-148.

THORPE, DWAYNE
___ "Tolkien's Elvish Craft," in: Reynolds, Patricia and GoodKnight, Glen H., eds. **Proceedings of the J. R. R. Tolkien Centenary Conference, Keble College, Oxford, 1992**. Altadena, CA: Mythopoeic Press, 1995. pp.315-321. (*Mythlore* Vol. 21, No. 2, Winter 1996, Whole No. 80)

THORPE, MICHAEL
___ "Running Through Stories in My Mind (Interview, 1980)," in: Ingersoll, Earl G., ed. **Doris Lessing: Conversations**. Princeton, NJ: Ontario Review Press, 1994. pp.94-101.

THRASHER, PAULA C.
___ **"Star Trek** Exhibit Beams You Out of This World," *Atlanta Journal Constitution* Sec. WL, p. 1. January 30, 1993. [Not seen.]

TIDMARSH, ANDREW
___ "Barry N. Malzberg: An Annotated Bibliography," *Interzone* No. 61: 50-52. July 1992
___ "Dinosaurs, Comics, Conan--and Methphysical Romance: An Interview With Margaret Atwood," *Interzone* No. 65: 23-25. November 1992.
___ "Lawrence Sutin: Interview," *Interzone* No. 56: 26-28. February 1992.
___ "Michael Bishop: An Annotated Bibliography," *Interzone* No. 82: 57-58. April 1994.
___ "R. A. Lafferty: An Annotated Bibliography," *Interzone* No. 64: 44-47. October 1992.

TIEDEMANN, MARK W.
___ "Science Fiction vs. Fantasy: Part IV: Process and Precept: Natural Differences Between Science Fiction and Fantasy," *Quantum* No. 43/44: 43-38. Spring/Summer 1993.

TIGER, VIRGINIA
___ " 'The words had been right and necessary': Doris Lessing's Transformations of Utopian and Dystopian Modalities in **The Marriages Between Zones Three, Four and Five**," *Style* 27(1): 63-80. Spring 1993.

TIGUE, JOHN W.
___ **"Star Wars**, Archetypes, and the Mythic Quest," *The Quest: A Quarterly Journal of Philosophy, Science, Religion and the Arts* 5(1): 22-29. Spring 1992.

TILLEY, ELIZABETH S.
___ "Language in Charles Williams's **All Hallows' Eve**," *Renascence* 44(4): 303-319. Summer 1992.

TILTON, LOIS
___ "Strangling the Baby: Cultural Relativism in Mike Resnick's 'Kirinyaga'," *New York Review of Science Fiction* No. 9: 11-12. May 1989.

TIMPONE, ANTHONY
___ "Bride of the Fly," by Anthony Timpone and Carr D'Angelo. in: McDonnell, David, ed. **Starlog's Science Fiction Heroes and Heroines**. New York: Crescent Books, 1995. pp.47-49.

TIPLER, FRANK J.
___ **The Physics of Immortality**. New York: Doubleday, 1994. 517pp.

TIPTREE, JAMES, JR.
___ "From a Spoken Journal: Thinking About Heinlein, et al., 1971," *New York Review of Science Fiction* No. 60: 1, 3-6. August 1993. (Edited by David G. Hartwell.)
___ "A Genius Darkly: A Letter to Ted White on Philip K. Dick," *New York Review of Science Fiction* No. 63: 16. November 1993.

TITTERINGTON, P. L.
___ "Kubrick and **The Shining**," *Sight and Sound* 50(2): 117-121. Spring 1981.

TITTL, PETE
___ "Anchoring in Kern," *Bakersfield (CA) Californian*. February 3, 1995. in: *NewsBank. Film and Television*. 30:G12. 1995.

TOBENKIN, DAVID
___ "Box-Office Boycotts: **Basic Instinct** Outcry Unlikely to Hurt Results," *Los Angeles (CA) Daily News* March 19, 1992. in: *NewsBank. Film and Television*. 28:G4. 1992.

TOBIN, JEAN
___ "Frank Herbert's **The Heaven Makers**: A Reconsideration, Part 1," *New York Review of Science Fiction* No. 46: 21-23. June 1992.
___ "Frank Herbert's **The Heaven Makers**: A Reconsideration, Part 2," *New York Review of Science Fiction* No. 47: 16-19. July 1992.

TOBIN, LEE A.
___ "Why Change the Arthur Story? Marion Zimmer Bradley's **The Mists of Avalon**," *Extrapolation* 34(2): 147-157. Summer 1993.

TOELLE, KEVIN
___ "Tarzan: The Least Adventure?," *Burroughs Bulletin* NS. No. 23: 31-33. July 1995.

TOHILL, CATHAL
___ **Immoral Tales: European Sex and Horror Movies, 1956-1984**, by Cathal Tohill and Pete Tombs. New York: St. Martin's Griffin, 1995. 272pp.

TOKARCZYK, ROMAN A.
___ "Polish Utopian Thought: A Historical Survey," *Utopian Studies* 4(2): 128-143. 1993.

TOLKIEN, J. R. R.
___ "Letter to Anne Barrett, Houghton Mifflin Co., 30 August 1964, No. 261," in: Watson, George, ed. **Critical Essays on C. S. Lewis**. Hants, Eng.: Scolar Press, 1992. pp.9-10.

TOLKIEN, JOHN
___ **The Tolkien Family Album**, by John Tolkien and Priscilla Tolkien. Boston, MA: Houghton Mifflin, 1992. 90pp.

TOLKIEN, PRISCILLA
___ **The Tolkien Family Album**, by John Tolkien and Priscilla Tolkien. Boston, MA: Houghton Mifflin, 1992. 90pp.

TOLLEY, CLIVE
___ "Tolkien's 'Essay on Man': A Look at *Mythopoeia*," in: Kranz, Gisbert, ed. **Jahrbuch für Literatur und Ästhetik**. Lüdenscheid, Germany: Stier, 1992. Band 10, pp.221-240.

TOLSON, JAY
___ **Pilgrim in the Ruins: A Life of Walker Percy**. New York: Simon & Schuster, 1992. 544pp.

TOMALIN, CLAIRE
___ "Watching the Angry and Destructive Hordes Go By (Interview, 1988)," in: Ingersoll, Earl G., ed. **Doris Lessing: Conversations**. Princeton, NJ: Ontario Review Press, 1994. pp.173-177.

TOMAS, DAVID
___ "Art, Psychasthenic Assimilation, and the Cybernetic Automation," in: Gray, Chris H., ed. **The Cyborg Handbook**. New York: Routledge, 1995. pp.255-266.

TOMASCH, SYLVIA
___ "**Mappae Mundi** and 'The Knight's Tale': The Geography of Power, the Technology of Control," in: Greenberg, Mark L. and Schachterle, Lance, eds. **Literature and Technology**. Bethlehem, PA: Lehigh University Press, 1992. pp.66-98.

TOMBS, PETE
___ **Immoral Tales: European Sex and Horror Movies, 1956-1984**, by Cathal Tohill and Pete Tombs. New York: St. Martin's Griffin, 1995. 272pp.

TOMPKINS, DAVID G.
___ (ed.) **Science Fiction Writer's Marketplace and Sourcebook**. Cincinnati, OH: Writer's Digest, 1994. 486pp.

TOMPSON, RICKY L.
___ "Tolkien's Word-Hoard Onleac," *Mythlore* 20(1): 22-40. Winter 1994. (Whole No. 75)

TONG, TEE KIM
___ "Huang-fan and the Future," *Chung Wai Literary Quarterly* 22(12): May 1994. (Issue not seen; pagination unavailable.)

TOOLIS, LORNA
___ "Charles de Lint: On the Border," by Lorna Toolis and Michael Skeet. in: Collins, Robert A. and Latham, Robert, eds. **Science Fiction and Fantasy Book Review Annual 1991**. Westport, CT: Greenwood, 1994. pp.79-86.

TOOTS, J. M.
___ "There Is **No Escape**," *Sci-Fi Entertainment* 1(1): 52-55. June 1994.

TOPPING, KEITH
___ **The New Trek Programme Guide**, by Paul Cornell, Martin Day and Keith Topping. London: Virgin, 1995. 378pp.

TORRENTS, NISSA
___ "Testimony of Mysticism (Interview, 1980)," in: Ingersoll, Earl G., ed. **Doris Lessing: Conversations**. Princeton, NJ: Ontario Review Press, 1994. pp.64-69.

TORRY, ROBERT
___ " 'You Can't Look Away': Spectacle and Transgression in **King Kong**," *Arizona Quarterly* 49(4): 61-78. Winter 1993.

TORSON, JOHN
___ "**Mom and Dad Save the World** (Review)," *Cinefantastique* 23(4): 61. December 1992.

TOTARO, REBECCA
___ "Regaining Perception: The Ransom Trilogy as a Re-embodiment of the Neoplatonic Model," *CSL: The Bulletin of the New York C. S. Lewis Society* 22(10): 1-11. August 1991.

TOUMEY, CHRISTOPHER P.
___ "The Moral Character of Mad Scientists: A Cultural Critique of Science," *Science, Technology and Human Values* 17(4): 411-437. Autumn 1992.

TOUPONCE, WILLIAM F.
___ "Frank Herbert," in: Bruccoli, Matthew J., ed. **Facts on File Bibliography of American Fiction 1919-1988**. New York: Facts on File, 1991. pp.247-248.

TOWNSEND, EMRU
___ "**Akira**: Anime Comes of Age," *Sci-Fi Entertainment* 2(2): 38-40, 72. August 1995.

TOWNSEND, JOHNNY
___ "Passion vs. Will: Homosexuality in Orson Scott Card's **Wyrms**," *Riverside Quarterly* 9(1): 48-55. August 1992. (No. 33)

TRAMSON, JACQUES
___ "L'ecologie dans la letterature de science fiction," *La Revue des Livres pour Enfants* 147: 96-102. Autumn 1992. [Not seen.]

TRAVERS, PETER
___ "Reel Projections: When Movie-Makers Imagine the Future, the Ending Is Rarely Happy," *House and Garden* 164(1): 94-95. January 1992.

TREGLOWN, JEREMY
___ **Roald Dahl: A Biography**. New York: Farrar, 1994. 322pp.

TREPTOW, KURT W.
___ (ed.) **Dracula: Essays on the Life and Times of Vlad Tepes**. New York: Columbia University Press, 1991. 336pp.

TREZZA, BRUNO
___ "Economia e utopia," in: Saccaro Del Buffa, Giuseppa and Lewis, Arthur O., eds. **Utopia e Modernita: Teorie e prassi utopiche nell'eta moderna e postmoderna**. Rome: Gangemi Editore, 1989. pp.217-224.

TRIMBLE, BJO
___ "Alternative Fandoms," by John Trimble and Bjo Trimble. in: Sanders, Joe, ed. **Science Fiction Fandom**. Westport, CT: Greenwood, 1994. pp.103-109.

TRIMBLE, JOHN
___ "Alternative Fandoms," by John Trimble and Bjo Trimble. in: Sanders, Joe, ed. **Science Fiction Fandom**. Westport, CT: Greenwood, 1994. pp.103-109.

TRISTRAM, PHILIPPA
___ "Golding and the Language of Caliban," in: Biles, Jack I. and Evans, Robert O., eds. **William Golding: Some Critical Considerations**. Lexington, KY: University Press of Kentucky, 1978. pp.39-55.

TROEN, SAUL B.
___ **Science Fiction and the Reemergence of Jewish Mythology in a Contemporary Literary Genre**. Ph.D. Dissertation, New York University, 1995. 336pp. (DAI-A 56/05, p. 1762. November 1995.)

TROIANO, MAUREEN D.
___ **New Physics and the Modern French Novel**. New York: Peter Lang, 1995. 276pp.

TROKHACHEV, SERGEI
___ "Escape to **The High Castle**," *Radio Free P K D* No. 5: 1, 9-11. August 1995.

TRONCARELLI, F.
___ "Manoscritti ed immagini di Tommaso Campanella. Orientamenti de recerca," by G. Formichetti, O. Lucchesi, P. Sagi and F. Troncarelli. in: Saccaro Del Buffa, Giuseppa and Lewis, Arthur O., eds. **Utopie per gli Anni Ottana**. Rome: Gangemi Editore, 1986. pp.587-590.

TROSTER, HORST G.
___ **Science Fiction im Horspiel, 1947-1987**. Frankfurt-am-Main: Rundfunkarchiv, 1993. 750pp.

TROUSSON, RAYMOND
___ "Unia Sintesi Storica," in: Colombo, Arrigo and Quarta, Cosimo, eds. **Il Destino della Famiglia nell'Utopia**. Bari: Edizione Dedalo, 1991. pp.17-31.

TROUT, STEVEN R.
___ "The Expurgated Solomon Kane," *The Dark Man: The Journal of Robert E. Howard Studies* No. 2: 33-37. July 1991.
___ "The Horror Fiction of Robert E. Howard," *The Dark Man: The Journal of Robert E. Howard Studies* No. 2: 2-11. July 1991.

TRUAN, KENNETH
___ "Dancing With Dolphins," *Los Angeles (CA) Times*. July 28, 1995. in: *NewsBank. Film and Television*. 82:D10-D11. 1995.

TRUBOWITZ, RACHEL
___ "The Reenchantment of Utopia and the Female Monarchial Self: Margaret Cavendish's **Blazing World**," *Tulsa Studies in Women's Literature* 11(2): 229-245. Fall 1992.

TRUCHLAR, LEO
___ "Philip K. Dick, **Ubik** (1969)," in: Heuermann, Harmut, ed. **Der Science Fiction Roman in der angloamerikanischen Literatur: Interpretationen**. Düsseldorf: Bagel, 1986. pp.315-330.

TRUDEL, JEAN-LOUIS
___ "French SF and SF in French: A Primer," *New York Review of Science Fiction* No. 88: 12-17. December 1995.
___ "Science Fiction in Francophone Canada (1839-1989)," *Sol Rising* No. 8: 1-5. February 1992.
___ "SF in France," *Locus* 33(1): 47-48. July 1994.

TRULL, ANTHONY
___ "Atlas in Spain: Comparing Nancy Kress' 'Beggars in Spain' with Ayn Rand's **Atlas Shrugged**," *Quantum* No. 42: 31-32. Summer/Fall 1992.

TRUPIA, ROBERT C.
___ "Learning Christian Behavior: The Path of Virtue in **The Chronicles of Narnia**," *Bulletin of the New York C. S. Lewis Society* 24(7/8): 1-5. May/June 1993.

TRUSHELL, JOHN
___ "Return of **Forbidden Planet**?," *Foundation* No. 64: 82-89. Summer 1995.

TSAI, EUGENIE M.
___ **Reconstructing Robert Smithson (Sculpture, Science Fiction)**. Ph.D. Dissertation, Columbia University, 1995. 314pp. (DAI-A 56/06, p. 2022. Dec. 1995.)

TSCHACHLER, HEINZ
___ "Ernest Callenbach: **Ecotopia: A Novel about Ecology, People, and Politics in 1999** (1975)," in: Heuermann, Hartmut and Lange, Bernd-Peter, eds. **Die Utopie in der angloamerikanischen Literatur: Interpretationen**. Düsseldorf: Bagel, 1984. pp.328-348.
___ "Ursula K. Le Guin, **The Left Hand of Darkness** (1969)," in: Heuermann, Harmut, ed. **Der Science Fiction Roman in der angloamerikanischen Literatur: Interpretationen**. Düsseldorf: Bagel, 1986. pp.295-314.

TUCKER, ERNEST
___ "Lifeless Buffy Lacks the Bite of a Good Spoof," *Chicago (IL) Sun Times*. July 31, 1992. in: *NewsBank. Film and Television*. 77:C1-C2. 1992

TULLOCH, JOHN
___ "Beyond the **Star Trek** Phenomenon: Reconceptualizing the Science Fiction Audience," by Henry Jenkins and John Tulloch. in: Tulloch, John and Jenkins, Henry, eds. **Science Fiction Audiences: Watching Doctor Who and Star Trek**. New York: Routledge, 1995. pp.3-24.
___ "But He's a Time Lord! He's a Time Lord!: Reading Formations, Followers, and Fans," in: Tulloch, John and Jenkins, Henry, eds. **Science Fiction Audiences: Watching Doctor Who and Star Trek**. New York: Routledge, 1995. pp.125-143.
___ "But Why Is **Doctor Who** So Attractive?: Negotiating Ideology and Pleasure," in: Tulloch, John and Jenkins, Henry, eds. **Science Fiction Audiences: Watching Doctor Who and Star Trek**. New York: Routledge, 1995. pp.108-124.
___ "The Changing Audiences of Science Fiction," in: Tulloch, John and Jenkins, Henry, eds. **Science Fiction Audiences: Watching Doctor Who and Star Trek**. New York: Routledge, 1995. pp.50-63.
___ "It's Meant to Be Fantasy: Teenage Audiences and Genre," by John Tulloch and Marian Tulloch. in: Tulloch, John and Jenkins, Henry, eds. **Science Fiction Audiences: Watching Doctor Who and Star Trek**. New York: Routledge, 1995. pp.86-107.
___ "Positioning the SF Audience: **Star Trek, Doctor Who** and the Texts of Science Fiction," in: Tulloch, John and Jenkins, Henry, eds. **Science Fiction Audiences: Watching Doctor Who and Star Trek**. New York: Routledge, 1995. pp.25-49.
___ **Science Fiction Audiences: Doctor Who, Star Trek, and Their Fans**. London: Routledge, 1994. 294pp.
___ "Throwing a Little Bit of Poison into Future Generations: **Doctor Who** Audiences and Ideology," in: Tulloch, John and Jenkins, Henry, eds. **Science Fiction Audiences: Watching Doctor Who and Star Trek**. New York: Routledge, 1995. pp.67-85.
___ "We're Only a Speck in the Ocean: The Fans as Powerless Elite," in: Tulloch, John and Jenkins, Henry, eds. **Science Fiction Audiences: Watching Doctor Who and Star Trek**. New York: Routledge, 1995. pp.144-172.

TULLOCH, MARIAN
___ "It's Meant to Be Fantasy: Teenage Audiences and Genre," by John Tulloch and Marian Tulloch. in: Tulloch, John and Jenkins, Henry, eds. **Science Fiction Audiences: Watching Doctor Who and Star Trek**. New York: Routledge, 1995. pp.86-107.

TUMEY, PAUL C.
___ "The First Annual Philip K. Dick Convention: Opening Address," *New York Review of Science Fiction* No. 70: 1, 3-4. June 1994.

TUNDO, LAURA
___ "Fourie: la tansizione verso il nuovo mondo amoroso," in: Colombo, Arrigo and Quarta, Cosimo, eds. **Il Destino della Famiglia nell'Utopia**. Bari: Edizione Dedalo, 1991. pp.265-282.

TUNNELL, MICHAEL O.
___ "The Double-Edged Sword: Fantasy and Censorship," *Language Arts* 71(8): 606-612. December 1994.

TUNNEY, TOM
___ "**Highlander III: The Sorcerer** (Review)'". *Sight and Sound* 5(3): 37-38. March 1995.

TURAJI, KENNETH
___ "**Blade Runner**," *Los Angeles (CA) Times*. September 13, 1992. in: *NewsBank. Film and Television*. 87:E9-F4. 1992.

TURAN, KENNETH
___ "**Blade Runner** 2," *Radio Free P.K.D.* No. 1: 2-3, 9. February 1993.

TURNER, ARTHUR C.
___ "Armed Conflict in the Science Fiction of H. G. Wells," in: Slusser, George and Eric S. Rabkin, eds. **Fights of Fancy: Armed Conflict in Science Fiction and Fantasy**. Athens, GA: University of Georgia Press, 1993. pp.70-78.

TURNER, GEORGE
___ "**Bram Stoker's Dracula**: A Happening Vampire," *American Cinematographer* 73(11): 36-45. November 1992.
___ "**Dracula** Meets the Son of Coppola," *American Cinematographer* 73(11): 46-52. November 1992.

TURNER, GEORGE (continued)
___ "Sailing Back to Skull Island: *The Son of Kong*," *American Cinematographer* 73(8): 67-71. August 1992.
___ "*She*: Empire of the Imagination," *American Cinematographer* 76(6): 103-108. June 1995.
___ "*Terabyss* Takes Audience on Suboceanic Thrill Mission," by George Turner and Nora Lee. *American Cinematographer* 74(8): 59-65. August 1993.

TURNER, MARTHA A.
___ **Mechanism and the Novel: Science in the Narrative Process.** Cambridge: Cambridge University Press, 1993. 199pp.

TURNQUIST, KRISTI
___ " 'Files': Eerie 'X' Out-Twilights the T-Zone," *Portland (OR) The Oregonian*. February 3, 1995. in: *NewsBank. Film and Television.* 31: B8. 1995.

TURTLEDOVE, HARRY
___ "Thank You," in: Kondo, Yoji, ed. **Requiem: New Collected Works by Robert A. Heinlein and Tributes to the Grand Master.** New York: Tor, 1992. pp.328-332.

TUSHER, WILL
___ " 'Jones' Criticism Prompts Valenti to Defend MPAA Rating System," *Variety* p. 5, 24. June 6, 1984.

TUSHNET, REBECCA L.
___ **Fire With Firepower: Women in Recent Science Fiction Blockbuster Movies.** Thesis, A. B. Honors in Social Studies, Harvard University, 1995. 153pp.

TUTTLE, LISA
___ "Memories of Ortygia House," *Interzone* No. 88: 48-51. October 1994.

TWISTE, REGINA
___ **Die Evolutionasthematik in Doris Lessings 'Space Fiction'.** Frankfurt-am-Main: P. Lang, 1994. 357pp.

TYLER, WAT
___ "An Interview with William Morris," *Journal of the William Morris Society* 10(3): 2-5. Autumn 1993.

TYMN, MARSHALL B.
___ (ed.) **The Celebration of the Fantastic: Selected Papers From the Tenth Anniversary International Conference on the Fantastic in the Arts**, ed. by Donald E. Morse, Marshall B. Tymn and Csilla Bertha. Westport, CT: Greenwood, 1992. 309pp.

TYTHERIDGE, ALAN
___ "An Uncrowned Lord of Language (1924)," in: **Shiel in Diverse Hands: A Collection of Essays**. Cleveland, OH: Reynolds Morse Foundation, 1983. pp.1-14.

TZONIS, ALEXANDER
___ "Counterfacts, Counternorms, and Transworld Mental Lines," in: Saccaro Del Buffa, Giuseppa and Lewis, Arthur O., eds. **Utopia e Modernita: Teorie e prassi utopiche nell'eta moderna e postmoderna**. Rome: Gangemi Editore, 1989. pp.71-76.

ULLRICH, ALLAN
___ "Here's Reality: Mower Is Less (Review)," *San Francisco (CA) Examiner*. March 7, 1992. in: *NewsBank. Film and Television.* 33:A8. 1992.
___ "*Split Second* Is a Mindless Rehash (Review)," *San Francisco (CA) Examiner*. May 2, 1992. in: *NewsBank. Film and Television.* 58:G6. 1992.

UMEMOTO, JUNKO
___ "Lafcadio Hearn and Christianity," *Comparitive Literature Studies* 30(4): 388-396. 1993.

UMLAND, REBECCA A.
___ "Unrequited Love in **We Can Build You**," in: Umland, Samuel J., ed. **Philip K. Dick: Contemporary Critical Interpretations**. Westport, CT: Greenwood, 1995. pp.127-142.

UMLAND, SAMUEL J.
___ " 'Faith of Our Fathers': A Comparison of the Original Manuscript with the Published Text," *PKDS Newsletter* No. 29: 12-14. September 1992.
___ "Introduction," in: Umland, Samuel J., ed. **Philip K. Dick: Contemporary Critical Interpretations**. Westport, CT: Greenwood, 1995. pp.1-6.
___ "To Flee From Dionysus: *Euthousiasmos* From 'Upon the Dull Earth' to **VALIS**," in: Umland, Samuel J., ed. **Philip K. Dick: Contemporary Critical Interpretations**. Westport, CT: Greenwood, 1995. pp.81-100.
___ (ed.) **Philip K. Dick: Contemporary Critical Interpretations**. Westport, CT: Greenwood, 1995. 240pp.

UNDERWOOD, ELAINE
___ "Spencer Tests Sci-Fi On-Site TV," *Brandweek* 36(23): 3. June 5, 1995.

UNWIN, RAYNER
___ "Publishing Tolkien," in: Reynolds, Patricia and GoodKnight, Glen H., eds. **Proceedings of the J. R. R. Tolkien Centenary Conference, Keble College, Oxford, 1992**. Altadena, CA: Mythopoeic Press, 1995. pp.26-29. (*Mythlore* Vol. 21, No. 2, Winter 1996, Whole No. 80)

UPCHURCH, MICHAEL
___ "Voice of England, Voice of Africa (Interview, 1992)," in: Ingersoll, Earl G., ed. **Doris Lessing: Conversations**. Princeton, NJ: Ontario Review Press, 1994. pp.219-227.
___ "**Wise Children**," *Seattle (WA) Times*. March 1, 1992. in: *NewsBank. Literature.* 26:B10. 1992

URAM, SUE
___ "*Army of Darkness: Evil Dead III*," *Cinefantastique* 22(4): 41. February 1992.
___ "Beyond Uhura," *Cinefantastique* 26(2): 31. February 1995.
___ "Bruce Campbell: Horror's Rambo," *Cinefantastique* 23(2/3): 31. October 1992.
___ "Dead Auteur: Sam Raimi, Tyro Director," *Cinefantastique* 23(1): 28-29. August 1992.
___ "Dead Hero: Bruce Campbell: Actor/Producer," *Cinefantastique* 23(1): 36-37. August 1992.
___ "*Evil Dead*: 8mm Amateur Origins," *Cinefantastique* 23(1): 26. August 1992.
___ "*Evil Dead*: College Filmmakers Turn Professional," *Cinefantastique* 23(1): 52-53. August 1992.
___ "*Evil Dead*: The Original 16mm Horror," *Cinefantastique* 23(1): 31. August 1992.
___ "*Evil Dead II*: Making the First Sequel," *Cinefantastique* 23(1): 39-41. August 1992.
___ "*Evil Dead II*: Working With Sam Raimi," *Cinefantastique* 23(1): 47. August 1992.
___ "Evil Effects: Tom Sullivan, Gore Auteur," *Cinefantastique* 23(1): 50. August 1992.
___ "*Lunatics*," *Cinefantastique* 22(4): 40-41. February 1992.
___ "*Nightswarm*," *Cinefantastique* 25(5): 56-58. October 1994.
___ "Sam Raimi's *Evil Dead III*," *Cinefantastique* 23(2/3): 28-30. October 1992.
___ "*Star Trek: Generations*: Chekov Makes Captain," *Cinefantastique* 26(2): 32-33. February 1995.
___ "*Star Trek: Generations*: Roddenberry's Legacy," *Cinefantastique* 26(2): 34-39. February 1995.
___ "*Star Trek: Generations*: Spock Speaks," *Cinefantastique* 26(2): 20-21. February 1995.
___ "*Star Trek: Generations*: Where's Captain Sulu," *Cinefantastique* 25(6)/26(1): 22. December 1994.
___ "*Star Trek: Generations*: You're Dead, Jim," *Cinefantastique* 25(6)/26(1): 23. December 1994.

URRACA, BEATRIZ
___ "Angelica Gorodischer's Voyages of Discovery: Sexuality and Historical Allegory in Science Fiction's Cross-Cultural Encounters," *Latin American Literary Review* 23(45): 85-102. January 1995.

URSINI, JAMES
___ **More Things Than Are Dreamt Of: Masterpieces of Supernatural Horror, From Mary Shelley to Stephen King, in Literature and Film**, by James Ursini and Alain Silver. New York: Limelight, 1994. 226pp.

USHER, ROBIN L.
___ "Robert A. Heinlein: Theologist?," *Foundation* No. 54: 70-86. Spring 1992.

VALADA, M. C.
___ "Step Through George R. R. Martin's **Doorways** into Alternate Worlds," *Science Fiction Age* 1(4): 18-21, 72. May 1993.

VALENTINE, MARK
___ **Arthur Machen**. Bridgend, Wales: Seren, 1995. 147pp.

VALLORANI, NICOLETTA
___ "The Body of the City: Angela Carter's **The Passion of the New Eve**," *Science Fiction Studies* 21(3): 365-379. November 1994.

VAN BAKEL, ROGIER
___ "Remembering Johnny," *Wired* 3(6): 154-157. June 1995.

VAN BELKOM, EDO
___ "Editing Anthologies," *SFWA Bulletin* 28(3): 18-21. Winter 1994. (No. 125)
___ "Novelizations," *SFWA Bulletin* 27(3): 4-10. Fall 1993. (No. 121)
___ "What's in a Name?," *SFWA Bulletin* 27(2): 10-15. Summer 1993. (No. 120)

VAN CALENBERGH, HUBERT
___ "The Roots of Horror in **The Golden Bough**," *Lovecraft Studies* No. 26: 21-23. Spring 1992.

VAN CITTERS, ROBERT L.
___ "Artificial Heart and Assist Devices: Directions, Needs, Costs, Societal and Ethical Issues (Abstract)," in: Gray, Chris H., ed. **The Cyborg Handbook**. New York: Routledge, 1995. pp.161-162.

VAN DER SCHAAF, BAUKJE F.
___ "The **Lai de Tyolet** and **Lancelot and the Whitefooted Stag**: Two Romances Based on a Folktale Motif," *Arthuriana* 4(3): 233-249. Fall 1994.

VAN GELDER, GORDON
___ "Let's Go Look at the Natives: Conflicts of Culture in Mike Resnick's 'Kirinyaga'," *New York Review of Science Fiction* No. 9: 11-14. May 1989.

VAN HISE, JAMES
___ **The Deep Space Celebration**. Las Vegas, NV: Pioneer, 1994. 190pp.
___ **The Deep Space Crew Book**. Las Vegas, NV: Pioneer, 1994. 193pp.
___ "*Dragonheart*: Preview," *Cinefantastique* 27(3): 7. December 1995.
___ "Exobiology: Space Medicine at the Time of *Star Trek*," in: Van Hise, James, ed. **Trek Celebration Two**. Las Vegas, NV: Pioneer, 1994. pp.102-110.
___ "Foundation Is *Star Trek*," in: Van Hise, James, ed. **Trek Celebration Two**. Las Vegas, NV: Pioneer, 1994. pp.16-23.
___ **Hot Blooded Dinosaur Movies**. Las Vegas, NV: Pioneer, 1993. 179pp.
___ "An Index to the Reed Crandall Illustrations From the Works of Edgar Rice Burroughs," *Burroughs Bulletin* NS. No. 20: 27-28. October 1994.
___ "Jungle Tales of Tarzan: A Closer Look," *Burroughs Bulletin* NS. No. 23: 3-12. July 1995.
___ **Let's Trek: The Budget Guide to the Klingons 1995**. Las Vegas, NV: Pioneer, 1994. 161pp.
___ "Life in the Mirror Universe," in: Van Hise, James, ed. **Trek Celebration Two**. Las Vegas, NV: Pioneer, 1994. pp.117-121.
___ "A Look at **The Next Generation**," in: Van Hise, James, ed. **Trek Celebration Two**. Las Vegas, NV: Pioneer, 1994. pp.24-28.
___ "The Major Alien Races of *Star Trek*," in: Van Hise, James, ed. **Trek Celebration Two**. Las Vegas, NV: Pioneer, 1994. pp.53-56.
___ **The Man Between the Ears: Star Trek's Leonard Nimoy**. Las Vegas, NV: Pioneer, 1992. 154pp.
___ **The Man Who Created Star Trek: Gene Roddenberry**. Las Vegas, NV: Pioneer Books, 1992. 156pp.
___ "The Music of **The Next Generation**," in: Van Hise, James, ed. **Trek Celebration Two**. Las Vegas, NV: Pioneer, 1994. pp.134-141.
___ **The New Sci Fi TV**. Las Vegas, NV: Pioneer, 1994. 182pp.

VAN HISE, JAMES (continued)
___ **The Next Generation Tribute Book Two**. 'Unauthorized and Uncensored'. Las Vegas, NV: Pioneer, 1994. 171pp.
___ "Reed Crandall: Illustrator of Super Heroes," *Burroughs Bulletin* NS. No. 20: 17-28. October 1994.
___ **Sci Fi TV: From Twilight Zone to Deep Space Nine**. Las Vegas, NV: Pioneer Books, 1993. 160pp. (Reprinted, HarperPrism, 1995. 258pp.)
___ "The Secondary Bridge Crews of the *Enterprise*," in: Van Hise, James, ed. **Trek Celebration Two**. Las Vegas, NV: Pioneer, 1994. pp.89-101.
___ **Stephen King and Clive Barker: Masters of the Macabre II**. Las Vegas, NV: Pioneer Books, 1992. 144pp.
___ **The Trek Celebration Two**. Las Vegas: Pioneer, 1994. 166pp.
___ **Trek in the 24th Century: The Next Generation and Deep Space Nine**. 'Unofficial and Uncensored'. Las Vagas, NV: Pioneer, 1994. 164pp.
___ **Trek: The Next Generation Crew Book**. Las Vegas: Pioneer Books, 1993. 155pp.
___ **Trek: The Next Generation: Third Edition**. Las Vegas: Pioneer, 1994. 268pp.
___ **Trek: The Unauthorized Story of the Movies**, by James Van Hise and Hal Schuster. Las Vegas, NV: Pioneer Books, 1995. 208pp.
___ **The Unauthorized Trek: Deep Space, The Voyage Continues**. Las Vegas, NV: Pioneer, 1994. 198pp.
___ "*Xtro-3: Watch the Skies*: Creature Effects," *Cinefantastique* 27(2): 48-49. November 1995.
___ "*Xtro-3: Watch the Skies*: Series Auteur," *Cinefantastique* 27(2): 50. November 1995.
___ "*Xtro-3: Watch the Skies*," *Cinefantastique* 27(2): 46-51, 61. November 1995.
___ (ed.) **Pulp Heroes of the Thirties**. Yucca Valley, CA: Midnight Graffiti, 1994. 168pp.
___ (ed.) **Trek: The Unauthorized Behind-the-Scenes Story of Trek: The Next Generation**. Las Vegas, NV: Pioneer Books, 1993. 132pp.

VAN MATRE, LYNN
___ "Trekkers Say 'HISlaH' to Klingon Language Lessons," *Austin (TX) American Statesman* Sec. D, p. 6. March 6, 1993.
___ "The Ultimate Foreign Language," *Chicago Tribune* Sec. 5, p. 1. March 2, 1993

VAN ROSSENBERG, RENE
___ "Tolkien's Exceptional Visit to Holland: A Reconstruction," in: Reynolds, Patricia and GoodKnight, Glen H., eds. **Proceedings of the J. R. R. Tolkien Centenary Conference, Keble College, Oxford, 1992**. Altadena, CA: Mythopoeic Press, 1995. pp.301-309. (*Mythlore* Vol. 21, No. 2, Winter 1996, Whole No. 80)

VAN SANT, ANN J.
___ **Eighteenth-Century Sensibility and the Novel: The Senses in Social Context**. Cambridge, Eng.: Cambridge University Press, 1993. 143pp.

VAN VECHTEN, CARL
___ "A Prolegomenon (Introduction to **The Lord of the Sea**, 1924)," in: **Shiel in Diverse Hands: A Collection of Essays**. Cleveland, OH: Reynolds Morse Foundation, 1983. pp.15-21.

VANCHERI, BARBARA
___ "Altogether Ooky Sequel (Review)," *Pittsburgh (PA) Post-Gazette*. November 19, 1993. in: *NewsBank*. Art. 32:B3. 1993.
___ "The Devil Disappoints: *Needful Things* Fails to Shiver (Review)," *Pittsburgh (PA) Post Gazette*. August 27, 1993. in: *NewsBank*. Art. 18: E6. 1993.
___ "Lost in the Jungle," *Pittsburgh (PA) Post Gazette*. April 29, 1994. in: *NewsBank*. Film and Television. 58:A13. 1994.

VANDERBILT, KERMIT
___ "Kurt Vonnegut's American Nightmares and Utopias," in: Sullivan, E. D. S., ed. **The Utopian Vision**. San Diego, CA: San Diego University Press, 1983. pp.137-174.

VANHECKE, JOHAN
___ "Aspects of Christ in Gandalf," *Lembas Extra*. [Leiden]: Tolkien Genootschap Unquendor, 1991. pp.63-75. [Not seen, cf. *Mythlore*.]

VANHECKE, JOHAN (continued)
___ "Tolkien in Dutch: A Study of the Reception of Tolkien's Work in Belgium and the Netherlands," *Mythlore* 18(4): 53-60. Autumn 1992. (No. 70)

VAUGHN, DONALD
___ "A. K. A. Mr. TV: An Interview With William Schallert," *Filmfax* No. 42: 62-69, 98. December 1993/January 1994.

VAUGHN, SUE F.
___ "The Female Hero in Science Fiction and Fantasy: 'Carrier Bag' to 'No-Road'," *Journal of the Fantastic in the Arts* 4(4): 82-96. 1991. (No. 16)

VAUGHN, THOMAS
___ "Voices of Sexual Distortion: Rape, Birth, and Self-Annihilation Metaphors in the *Alien* Trilogy," *Quarterly Journal of Speech* 81(4): 423-435. November 1995.

VAZ, MARK C.
___ "Animation in the Third Dimension," *Cinefex* No. 56: 30-53. November 1993.
___ "*Casino*: The Lights of Las Vegas," *Cinefex* No. 64: 37-38, 140. December 1995.
___ "Dredd World," *Cinefex* No. 62: 58-73. June 1995.
___ "Effects Scene: From Tatooine to Endor," *Cinefex* No. 61: 115-116. March 1995.
___ "Forever a Knight," *Cinefex* No. 63: 90-113. September 1995.
___ "Haunting Creation," *Cinefex* No. 60: 70-85. December 1994.
___ "A Knight at the Zoo," *Cinefex* No. 51: 22-69. August 1992.
___ "Quick Cuts: Shadow World," *Cinefex* No. 60: 33-34. December 1994.
___ "Return to Neverland," *Cinefex* No. 49: 4-23. February 1992.
___ "Special Venues: Deep Earth, Dark Ride," *Cinefex* No. 57: 16-17. March 1994.
___ "Through the *Stargate*," *Cinefex* No. 61: 82-97. March 1995.
___ "Toy Wars," *Cinefex* No. 54: 54-73. May 1993.
___ "Video Beat: McCartney Takes Wing," *Cinefex* No. 57: 85-86. March 1994.

VEDDER, CATHERINE M.
___ **New Woman, Old Science: Readings in Late Victorian Fiction**. Ph.D. Dissertation, Cornell University, 1993. (DAI 54: 537A-538A.)

VEGETTI, ERNESTO
___ **Fantascienza, Fantasy and Horror in Italia: 1990**, by Ernesto Vegetti and Piergiorgio Nicolazzini. Milano, Italy: Nicolazzini, 1992?. 142pp. [Not seen.]

VELASCO, JUAN
___ "Lo fantástico y la historia: La polémica entre **La sombra del caudillo** y Tirano Banderas," *Mester* (UCLA) 19(2): 71-82. Fall 1990.

VELDMAN, MEREDITH
___ **Fantasy, the Bomb, and the Greening of Britain: Romantic Protest, 1945-1980**. Cambridge: Cambridge University Press, 1994. 325pp.

VENTURA, MICHAEL
___ "The Truth Is Out There," *Los Angeles (CA) Times*. September 10, 1995. in: *NewsBank. Film and Television*. 91:F6-F10. 1995.

VERBA, JOAN M.
___ **Boldly Writing: A Trekker Fan and Zine History, 1967-1987**. Minnetonka, MN: FTL Publications, 1996. 100pp.

VERNIERE, JAMES
___ "Bill & Ted's Journey Is a Radical Cool Trip," *Boston (MA) Herald*. July 19, 1991. in: *NewsBank. Film and Television*. 65:F1. 1991.
___ "Bleak to the Future," *Boston (MA) Herald*. October 13, 1995. in: *NewsBank. Film and Television*. 99:C9-C10. 1995.
___ "Buffy Stakes Her Claim," *Boston (MA) Herald*. July 31, 1992. in: *NewsBank. Film and Television*. 68:A10. 1992
___ "Chevy Chase Mixes Laughs, Love in **Invisible Man** (Review)," *Boston (MA) Herald*. February 28, 1992. in: *NewsBank. Film and Television*. 23:D4-D5. 1992.

VERNIERE, JAMES (continued)
___ "De Palma Rebounds With **Raising Cain** (Review)," *Boston (MA) Herald*. August 7, 1992. in: *NewsBank. Film and Television*. 83:A13. 1992.
___ "Death Trap (Review)," *Boston (MA) Herald*. July 31, 1992. in: *NewsBank. Film and Television*. 68:F13-F14. 1992.
___ "Dreadful 'Judge' Is Violent, Dumb," *Boston (MA) Herald*. June 30, 1995. in: *NewsBank. Film and Television*. 70:B6. 1995.
___ "The Final Bleak Chapter of the **Alien** Sci-Fi Saga Gets Lost in Space Movies," *Boston (MA) Herald*. May 22, 1992. in: *NewsBank. Film and Television*. 49:C5-C6. 1992.
___ "**Hook** Should Get the Hook in Neverland Reunion (Review)," *Boston (MA) Herald*. December 11, 1991. in: *NewsBank. Film and Television*. 3:F8. 1992.
___ "In Space, and In Reality, Aliens R Us," *Chicago (IL) Sun Times*. May 24, 1992. in: *NewsBank. Film and Television*. 62:A12-A13. 1992.
___ "**Naked Lunch** a Descent into Drugged-Out Hysteria (Review)," *Boston (MA) Herald*. January 10, 1992. in: *NewsBank. Film and Television*. 14:A2-A3. 1992.
___ "The Never-Ending Voyage," *Boston (MA) Herald*. November 20, 1994. in: *NewsBank. Film and Television*. 10:D13. 1995.
___ "Odd Couple: Light, Romantic Comedy Turns Dark in **Prelude to a Kiss** (Review)," *Boston (MA) Herald*. July 10, 1992. in: *NewsBank. Film and Television*. 73:C7-C8. 1992.
___ "Pain and Pleasure in Gotham," *Boston (MA) Herald*. June 19, 1992. in: *NewsBank. Film and Television*. 62:F8-F9. 1992.
___ " 'Park' Is Might! (Review)," *Boston (MA) Herald*. June 11, 1993. in: *NewsBank. Literature*. 15:C10-C11. 1993.
___ "**Prospero's Books** a Tempest Travesty (Review)," *Boston (MA) Herald*. November 29, 1991. in: *NewsBank. Film and Television*. 6:D5. 1992.
___ "**Radio Flyer's** Attempt at a Childhood Adventure Story Turns into a Fractured Fairy Tale (Review)," *Boston (MA) Herald*. February 21, 1992. in: *NewsBank. Film and Television*. 24:G4-G5. 1992.
___ "Raw Energy Gives Spark to Weird and Wild Plot of **Basic Instinct**," *Boston (MA) Herald* March 20, 1992 in: *NewsBank. Film and Television*. 29:B7-B8. 1992.
___ "Redford's **Sneakers** Comes Untied (Review)," *Boston (MA) Herald*. September 11, 1992. in: *NewsBank. Film and Television*. 96:D6-D7. 1992.
___ "Snatchers Is a Good Update of Attack of the Mod Pod," *Boston (MA) Herald*. February 25, 1994. in: *NewsBank. Film and Television*. 21:B13. 1994.
___ "Space Camp," *Boston (MA) Herald*. October 28, 1994. in: *NewsBank. Film and Television*. 115: G10-G11. 1994.
___ "Spielberg Hopes to Recapture Magic Touch," *Boston (MA) Herald*. December 13, 1991. in: *NewsBank. Film and Television*. 7:B12. 1992.
___ "Super Star (Review)," *Boston (MA) Herald*. December 6, 1991. in: *NewsBank. Film and Television*. 7:E3-E4. 1992.
___ "**Terminator** Ripoff Is a Universal Bore (Review)," *Boston (MA) Herald*. July 10, 1992. in: *NewsBank. Film and Television*. 74:G5. 1992.
___ "Top-Notch Cast Can't Save **Species** From Itself," *Boston (MA) Herald*. July 7, 1995. in: *NewsBank. Film and Television*. 72:A4. 1995.
___ "**Until the End of the World** an Overindulged Megathud (Review)," *Boston (MA) Herald*. January 17, 1992. in: *NewsBank. Film and Television*. 16:B14. 1992.
___ "**Virtuosity** Creates Virtual Vacuum," *Boston (MA) Herald*. August 4, 1995. in: *NewsBank. Film and Television*. 82:C3. 1995.
___ "Visual Feast," *Boston (MA) Herald*. November 13, 1992. in: *NewsBank. Film and Television*. 111:B7-B8. 1992.
___ "Who Took the Wonder out of the Wunderkind," *Boston (MA) Herald*. December 15, 1991. in: *NewsBank. Film and Television*. 7:C7-C8. 1992.

VERRA, VALERIO
___ "Linee de ricerca sull'utopia: il problema storiografico," in: Saccaro Del Buffa, Giuseppa and Lewis, Arthur O., eds. **Utopia e Modernita: Teorie e prassi utopiche nell'eta moderna e postmoderna**. Rome: Gangemi Editore, 1989. pp.37-46.

VERRAN, JAMES
___ "If It's Yesterday, This Must Be America!," *Science Fiction News* (Australia) No. 112: 2-4. September 1990.

VESTER, JOHN
___ "Dean of the Jedi Academy," *Starlog* No. 199: 50-53, 74. February 1994.
___ "Dragonsmith," *Starlog* No. 206: 76-79. September 1994.
___ "In Silken Steel," *Starlog* No. 221: 60-63. December 1995.

VIAUD, DIDIER
___ "Die Zeit als Mittel des Phantastischen in **Zwischen neun und neun und St. Petri Schnee**, 3. Teil," *Quarber Merkur* 31(1): 3-23. June 1993. (No. 79)
___ "Zeit und Phantastik. Die Zeit als Mittel des Phantastischen in den Romanen von Leo Perutz **Zwischen neun und neun** und **Sankt Petri-Schnee**. 2. Teil," *Quarber Merkur* 30(2): 47-60. December 1992. (No. 78)
___ "Zeit und Phantastik. Die Zeit als Mittel des Phantastischen in den Romanen von Leo Perutz **Zwischen neun und neun** und **Sankt Petri-Schnee**, 1. Teil," *Quarber Merkur* 30(1): 28-46. June 1992. (No. 77)

VICKERY, JOHN B.
___ "Alternative Worlds: The Short Stories," in: Salwak, Dale, ed. **Kingsley Amis in Life and Letters**. New York: St. Martin's, 1990. pp.149-166.

VIEIRA, GREGORY C.
___ "No Place for Utopia: Postmodern Theory and **The White Hotel**," *Utopian Studies* 4(2): 117-127. 1993.

VIELHAUER-PFEIFFER, INGE
___ "Merlins Schwester," in: Kranz, Gisbert, ed. **Inklings: Jahrbuch für Literatur und Ästhetik**. 8. Band. Lüdenscheid, Germany: Stier, 1990. pp.161-181. [Not seen.]

VINCE, NICK
___ "Doug Bradley," in: Brown, Michael, ed. **Pandemonium: Further Explorations into the Worlds of Clive Barker**. Staten Island, NY: Eclise, 1991. pp.72-82.
___ "More Than a Face," in: Brown, Michael, ed. **Pandemonium: Further Explorations into the Worlds of Clive Barker**. Staten Island, NY: Eclise, 1991. pp.83-86.
___ "Simon Bamford," in: Brown, Michael, ed. **Pandemonium: Further Explorations into the Worlds of Clive Barker**. Staten Island, NY: Eclise, 1991. pp.87-89.

VINCENT, MAL
___ "Amateurish Animation Fills Dark and Dull Batman (Review)," *Norfolk (VA) Virginian-Pilot*. December 29, 1993. in: *NewsBank. Art* 36: G1. 1993.
___ "A Dune Deal," *Norfolk (VA) Virginian-Pilot*. October 29, 1994. in: *NewsBank. Film and Television*. 115: G1-G2. 1994.
___ "More Technological Brawn With No Brains," *Norfolk (VA) Virginian-Pilot*. April 27, 1994. in: *NewsBank. Film and Television*. 51:F6. 1994.
___ "New **Robocop** Has Hefty Role (Review)," *Norfolk (VA) Virginian-Pilot*. November 4, 1993. in: *NewsBank. Film and Television*. 124:F13-F14. 1993.
___ "Sorcerer of Cinema," *Norfolk (VA) Virginian-Pilot*. February 16, 1992. in: *NewsBank. Film and Television*. 22:G1-G2. 1992. also in: *NewsBank. Names in the News*. 58:D13-D14. 1992.

VINGE, JOAN D.
___ "Introduction to **The Left Hand of Darkness**," *New York Review of Science Fiction* No. 43: 14-16. March 1992.

VINK, RENÉE
___ "Tolkien und Dorothy L. Sayers," in: Kranz, Gisbert, ed. **Jahrbuch für Literatur und Ästhetik**. Lüdenscheid, Germany: Stier, 1992. Band 10, pp.61-76.

VISSER-FUCHS, LIVIA
___ "The Dark Dragon of the Normans: A Creation of Geoffrey of Monmouth, Stephen of Rouen, and Merlin Silvester," by Anne F. Sutton and Livia Visser-Fuchs. *Quondam et Futurus* 2(2): 1-20. Summer 1992.

VITARIS, PAULA
___ "Befriending **Beauty and the Beast**," *Starlog* No. 212: 54-57, 69. March 1995.
___ "**Space: Above and Beyond**," *Cinefantastique* 27(2): 54-55. November 1995.

VITARIS, PAULA (continued)
___ "Writers," *Starlog* No. 210: 61-64. January 1995.
___ "**X-Files**: Boy's Club," *Cinefantastique* 26(6)/27(1): 88. October 1995.
___ "**X-Files**: Cancer Man," *Cinefantastique* 26(6)/27(1): 67-68. October 1995.
___ "**X-Files**: Casting Call," *Cinefantastique* 26(6)/27(1): 35-36. October 1995.
___ "**X-Files**: Chris Carter, Creator," *Cinefantastique* 26(6)/27(1): 19-20. October 1995.
___ "**X-Files**: Cinematography," *Cinefantastique* 26(6)/27(1): 37-38. October 1995.
___ "**X-Files**: 'Colony' and 'End Game'," *Cinefantastique* 26(6)/27(1): 32-33. October 1995.
___ "**X-Files**: Computer Graphics," *Cinefantastique* 26(6)/27(1): 71-72. October 1995.
___ "**X-Files**: David Nutter," *Cinefantastique* 26(6)/27(1): 29-30. October 1995.
___ "**X-Files**: Deep Throat," *Cinefantastique* 26(6)/27(1): 45-46. October 1995.
___ "**X-Files**: Episode Guide," *Cinefantastique* 26(6)/27(1): 18-26, 41-42, 49-50, 57-63, 73-74, 81-89. October 1995.
___ "**X-Files**: F. B. I. Box Skinner," *Cinefantastique* 26(6)/27(1): 77-78. October 1995.
___ "**X-Files**: F. B. I. Judas," *Cinefantastique* 26(6)/27(1): 75-76. October 1995.
___ "**X-Files**: Family Ties," *Cinefantastique* 26(6)/27(1): 43-44. October 1995.
___ "**X-Files**: Fixing It in Post," *Cinefantastique* 26(6)/27(1): 27-28. October 1995.
___ "**X-Files**: Howard Gordon," *Cinefantastique* 26(6)/27(1): 48-49. October 1995.
___ "**X-Files**: Making Humbug," *Cinefantastique* 26(6)/27(1): 64-66. October 1995.
___ "**X-Files**: Monster Maker," *Cinefantastique* 26(6)/27(1): 39-40. October 1995.
___ "**X-Files**: Morgan and Wong," *Cinefantastique* 26(6)/27(1): 62. October 1995.
___ "**X-Files**: Mulder and Scully," *Cinefantastique* 26(6)/27(1): 23-24. October 1995.
___ "**X-Files**: Music of the Night," *Cinefantastique* 26(6)/27(1): 79-81. October 1995.
___ "**X-Files**: Production Design," *Cinefantastique* 26(6)/27(1): 59-61. October 1995.
___ "**X-Files**: R. W. Goodwin," *Cinefantastique* 26(6)/27(1): 21-22. October 1995.
___ "**X-Files**: Rob Bowman," *Cinefantastique* 26(6)/27(1): 83. October 1995.
___ "**X-Files**: Serial Killer," *Cinefantastique* 26(6)/27(1): 53-54. October 1995.
___ "**X-Files**: Special Effects," *Cinefantastique* 26(6)/27(1): 55-56. October 1995.
___ "**X-Files**: Staff Writer," *Cinefantastique* 26(6)/27(1): 51-52. October 1995.
___ "**X-Files**: The Cliffhanger," *Cinefantastique* 26(6)/27(1): 47. October 1995.
___ "**X-Files**: The Lone Gunmen," *Cinefantastique* 26(6)/27(1): 69-70. October 1995.
___ "**X-Files**: X, the Unknown," *Cinefantastique* 26(6)/27(1): 85-86. October 1995.
___ "**X-Files**," *Cinefantastique* 26(5): 48-49. August 1995.
___ "**X-Files**," *Cinefantastique* 26(6)/27(1): 16-86. October 1995.

VIVONA, STEPHEN T.
___ "The Films of Val Lewton and Boris Karloff," *Filmfax* No. 44: 50-56. April/May 1994.

VOEDISCH, LYNN
___ "'Dark' Thriller Has More Than Just Murder in Mind," *Chicago (IL) Sun Times*. September 25, 1992. in: *NewsBank. Film and Television*. 87:A7. 1992
___ "**Enterprise** Takes Sentimental Journey in **Star Trek VI** (Review)," *Chicago (IL) Sun Times*. December 6, 1991. in: *NewsBank. Film and Television*. 7:D13. 1992.
___ "The Trek to Success," *Chicago (IL) Sun Times*. August 7, 1995. in: *NewsBank. Film and Television*. 81:A14. 1995.

VOGER, MARK
___ "The Boy Who Cried 'Woof Woof': An Interview with Butch Patrick," *Filmfax* No. 41: 73-76. October/November 1993.
___ "Clown Prince of Darkness: The Biting Brooklyn Wit of Al Lewis," *Filmfax* No. 41: 70-72. October/November 1993.
___ "Gorilla My Screams; Or, How My Life With Movie Monsters Made a Monkey out of Me," *Filmfax* No. 36: 43-48, 98. December 1992/January 1993.
___ "Mark Goddard: Interview," *Filmfax* No. 33: 72-76. June/July 1992.
___ "The Wily Wit of Jonathan Harris," *Filmfax* No. 32: 44-49, 94. April/May 1992.

VOLAND, JOHN
___ "Giant Imagination Needed to Make 'Honey II' (Review)," *Boston (MA) Herald*. July 16, 1992. in: *NewsBank. Film and Television*. 70:D7-D8. 1992.

VOLLER, JACK G.
___ "Kipling's Myth of Making: Creation and Contradiction in **Puck of Pook's Hill**," in: Morse, Donald E., ed. **The Celebration of the Fantastic**. Westport, CT: Greenwood, 1992. pp.81-90.
___ "Neuromanticism: Cyberspace and the Sublime," *Extrapolation* 34(1): 18-29. Spring 1993.

VOLLPRECHT, SABINE
___ **Science-Fiction fur Kinder in der DDR**. Stuttgart: H.-D. Heinz, 1994. 135pp.

VON FRANZ, MARIE-LOUISE
___ **The Feminine in Fairy Tales**. New York: Shambala, 1993. 224pp. (Revised edition of **Problems of the Feminine in Fairy Tales**, 1972.)

VON GUNDEN, KENNETH
___ **Postmodern Auteurs: Coppola, Lucas, De Palma, Spielberg and Scorcese**. Jefferson, NC: McFarland, 1991. 200pp.

VON MALDER, TOM
___ "Writer Creates a Brave New World," *The Republican Journal* (Maine) Sec. B, p. 2. September 3, 1992.

VON ROSPACH, CHUQ
___ "Reviewing the Reviewers: A Survey of Science Fiction Critics," *OtherRealms* No. 23: 5-7. Winter 1989.

VON SCHWARZKOPF, MARGARETE
___ "Placing Their Fingers on the Wounds of Our Times (Interview, 1981)," in: Ingersoll, Earl G., ed. **Doris Lessing: Conversations**. Princeton, NJ: Ontario Review Press, 1994. pp.102-108.

VONARBURG, ELISABETH
___ "The Reproduction of the Body in Space," in: Ruddick, Nicholas, ed. **State of the Fantastic**. Westport, CT: Greenwood, 1992. pp.59-72.
___ "So Many Children," *Aloud* (Toronto) 2(7): 10. October 1992.
___ "So You Want to Be a Science Fiction Writer?," *New York Review of Science Fiction* No. 57: 1, 3-5. May 1993.

VORBORIL, MARY
___ "The Amazing Asimov," *Miami (FL) Herald* August 20, 1988. in: *NewsBank. Names in the News* NIN 271: B7-B9. 1988.

VORDA, ALLAN
___ "The Forging of Science Fiction: An Interview with Greg Bear," in: Vorda, Allan, ed. **Face to Face: Interviews with Contemporary Novelists**. Houston, TX: Rice University Press, 1993. pp.127-151.

VULICH, JOHN
___ "The Alien Masters of **Babylon 5**," by John Vulich and Evereit Burrell. *Sci-Fi Entertainment* 1(2): 38-42. August 1994.

WACHHORST, WYN
___ "The Dream of Spaceflight: Nostalgia for a Bygone Future," *Massachusetts Review* 36(1): 7-32. Spring 1995.

WADE, JAMES
___ "You Can't Get There From Here: 'How the Old Woman Got Home' and M. P. Shiel as Thinker," in: **Shiel in Diverse Hands: A Collection of Essays**. Cleveland, OH: Reynolds Morse Foundation, 1983. pp.195-203.

WADE, SUSAN
___ "Author Stays Close to Home in East Texas," *Austin (TX) American Statesman* Sec. E, p. 1, 7. September 15, 1995.

WAGAR, W. WARREN
___ "J. G. Ballard and the Transvaluation of Utopia," *Science Fiction Studies* 18(1): 53-70. March 1991.
___ **The Next Three Futures: Paradigms of Things to Come**. Westport, CT: Greenwood, 1991. 164pp.

WAGNER, VIVIAN
___ "Gender, Technology and Utopia in Faulkner's Airplane Tales," *Arizona Quarterly* 49(4): 79-97. Winter 1993.

WAHL, WENDY
___ "Bodies and Technologies: **Dora, Neuromancer**, and Strategies of Resistance," *Postmodern Culture* 3(2): [17pp.]. January 1993. (Electronic Journal: pmc@jefferson.village.virginia.edu).

WAIN, JOHN
___ "C. S. Lewis," in: Watson, George, ed. **Critical Essays on C. S. Lewis**. Hants, Eng.: Scolar Press, 1992. pp.24-36.

WAKE, HELEN
___ "Glad to Be of Use: Bob Shaw Interview," *Interzone* No. 67: 13-16. January 1993.

WALCZUK, ANNA
___ "The Permanent in Lewis and Chesterton," *Chesterton Review* 17(3/4): 313-321. August/November 1991.

WALDEN, JUSTINE
___ "The Political Aesthetic: Nation and Narrativity on the Starship *Enterprise*," [17 pp.] 1994. (Cited from the Internet. HTTP: //remarque.berkeley. edu:8001 /**[tilde]**xcohen /Papers /Walden / walden.toc.html.) (Note: Insert tilde character, delete spaces to use on-line. Typography requirements required these changes.)

WALDO, MARK L.
___ "Mary Shelley's Machines in the Garden: Victor Frankenstein and His Monster," in: Wolf, Milton T. and Mallett, Daryl F., eds. **Imaginative Futures: Proceedings of the 1993 Science Fiction Research Association Conference**. San Bernardino, CA: Jacob's Ladder Books, 1995. pp.179-190.

WALKER, ANDREW
___ **A Christian for All Christians: Essays in Honor of C. S. Lewis**, by Andrew Walker and James Patrick. Washington, DC: Regnery, 1992. 255pp.
___ "Reflections on C. S. Lewis, Apologetics, and the Moral Tradition," by Andrew Walker and Basil Mitchell. in: Walker, Andrew and Patric, James, eds. **A Christian for All Christians**. Washington, DC: Regnery, 1992. pp.7-26.
___ "Under the Russian Cross: A Research Note on C. S. Lewis and the Eastern Orthodox Church," in: Walker, Andrew and Patric, James, eds. **A Christian for All Christians**. Washington, DC: Regnery, 1992. pp.63-67.

WALKER, CHARLOTTE Z.
___ "Marjorie Bradley Kellogg: Creating Spaces, Creating Worlds," *Ms.* 6(3): 91. November 1995.

WALKER, HOLLIS
___ "**Earth 2** Lands in SF," *(Santa Fe, NM) New Mexican*. September 3, 1994. in: *NewsBank. Film and Television*. 97:C12-c13. 1994.

WALKER, MARTIN
___ "*Apollo* and Newt," *Sight and Sound* 5(9): 6-8. September 1995.

WALKER, SUE
___ "Undiscovered Countries: **Milledgeville, Herland** and Beyond," *Connecticut Review* 16(2): 91-100. Fall 1994.

WALSH, MICHAEL
___ "Trekking Onward," by Richard Zoglin and Michael Walsh. *Time* 144(22): 72-79. November 28, 1994.

WALTERS, LORI
___ "The Creation of a Super Romance: Paris, Bibliotheque Nationale, fond francais, MS 1433," in: Busby, Keith, ed. **The Arthurian Yearbook** I. New York: Garland, 1991. pp.3-26.

WANDREI, DONALD
___ "Arthur Machen and **The Hill of Dreams**," *Studies in Weird Fiction* No. 15: 27-30. Summer 1994. (Reprinted from *Minnesota Quarterly*, Spring 1926.)
___ "Bierce," *Studies in Weird Fiction* No. 10: 31-34. Fall 1991. (Reprinted from *Minnesota Quarterly*, Spring 1931.)

WARD, DAVID
___ "**Surfacing**: Separation, Transition, Incorporation," in: Nicholson, Colin, ed. **Margaret Atwood: Writing and Subjectivity: New Critical Essays**. New York: St. Martin's, 1994. pp.94-118

WARD, GEOFF
___ "William Burroughs: A Literary Outlaw?," *Cambridge Quarterly* 22(4): 339-354. 1993.

WARD, RON B.
___ "Review: *Aurealis*, No. 1," *Science Fiction News* (Australia) No. 113: 2-7. December 1990.

WARHURST, CHRISTOPHER
___ "The End of Another Utopia? The Israeli Kibbutz and Its Industry in a Period of Transition," *Utopian Studies* 5(2): 102-121. 1994.

WARNER, HARRY, JR.
___ "Fandom Between World War II and *Sputnik*," in: Sanders, Joe, ed. **Science Fiction Fandom**. Westport, CT: Greenwood, 1994. pp.65-74.
___ "A History of Fanzines," in: Sanders, Joe, ed. **Science Fiction Fandom**. Westport, CT: Greenwood, 1994. pp.175-180.
___ **A Wealth of Fable: An Informal History of Science Fiction Fandom in the 1950s.** Van Nuys, CA: SCIFI Press, 1992. 456pp.

WARREN, ALAN
___ "Full Fathom Five: The Supernatural Fiction of William Hope Hodgson," in: Schweitzer, Darrell, ed. **Discovering Classic Horror Fiction I**. Mercer Island, WA: Starmont, 1992. pp.41-52.
___ **Roald Dahl: From the Gremlins to the Chocolate Factory.** 2nd ed., revised and expanded. San Bernardino, CA: Borgo Press, 1994. 128pp.

WARREN, BILL
___ "Altered Voyages," *Starlog* No. 208: 32-36, 72. November 1994.
___ "The Amazing Colossal Infant Plays Las Vegas," *Starlog* 178: 27-31, 70. May 1992.
___ "Back in Time," *Starlog* No. 198: 56-59. January 1994.
___ "Batman's Batman," *Starlog* No. 215: 50-53, 72. June 1995.
___ "Building the Perfect Beast," *Starlog* No. 214: 41-45, 70. May 1995.
___ "Chronicling **The Young Indiana Jones**," *Starlog* 178: 52-55, 69. May 1992.
___ "The Curator of **Jurassic Park**," *Starlog* No. 192: 32-37, 74. July 1993.
___ "The Deadliest of **Species**," *Starlog* No. 217: 52-56. August 1995.
___ "Deadly Gamesters," *Starlog* No. 219: 45-49. October 1995.
___ "Deadly Rose," *Starlog* No. 221: 52-55. December 1995.
___ "Dinosaur Huntress," in: McDonnell, David, ed. **Starlog's Science Fiction Heroes and Heroines**. New York: Crescent Books, 1995. pp.73-76.
___ "Dinosaur Lunch," *Starlog* No. 194: 38-41, 82. September 1993.
___ "Gorilla Warfare," *Starlog* No. 215: 40-45, 72. June 1995.
___ "Gorillas by Winston," *Starlog* No. 218: 46-49, 66. September 1995.
___ "Hail to the Chief," *Starlog* No. 207: 36-39, 70. October 1994.
___ "The Heroes of **Jurassic Park**," *Starlog* No. 193: 48-54. August 1993.
___ "His Own Man," *Starlog* No. 174: 63-69. January 1992.

WARREN, BILL (continued)
___ "In the Blood," *Starlog* No. 218: 78-81, 66. September 1995.
___ "Jungle Heroine," *Starlog* No. 216: 32-35, 64. July 1995.
___ "Jungle Wizard," *Starlog* No. 217: 35-39, 66. August 1995.
___ "**Jurassic Park**," *Starlog* No. 191: 50-55. June 1993.
___ "Kid Stuff," *Starlog* 181: 40-43, 69. August 1992.
___ "Longhair at Sea," *Starlog* No. 203: 34-37, 66. June 1994.
___ "The Many Faces of Christoper Lloyd," *Starlog* No. 193: 32-36. August 1993.
___ "Other People's Dreams," *Starlog* No. 200: 36-39, 90. March 1994.
___ "Playing Games," *Starlog* No. 220: 46-49. November 1995.
___ "Portals to Elsewhen," *Starlog* No. 189: 78-81. April 1993.
___ "Prepare to Submerge," *Starlog* No. 196: 44-49, 72. November 1993.
___ "Producer in the Cupboard," *Starlog* No. 218: 36-39. September 1995.
___ "Pulling the Strings," *Starlog* No. 208: 46-51, 72. November 1994.
___ "Real Truths," *Starlog* No. 195: 58-61, 72. October 1993.
___ "Self-Made Woman," *Starlog* No. 202: 27-30, 68. May 1994.
___ "Some Call Him Tod," *Starlog* No. 176: 46-49. March 1992.
___ "Spengo's Greatest Director," *Starlog* 177: 63-66. April 1992.
___ "Sub Teen," *Starlog* No. 197: 55-57, 82. December 1993.
___ "Tarzan the Magnificent," *Starlog* No. 187: 27-31. February 1993.
___ "Time Killer," *Starlog* No. 190: 46-48, 69. May 1993.
___ "Underwater Journeyman," *Starlog* No. 199: 37-40, 74. February 1994.
___ "The Vincent Schiavelli Story," *Starlog* No. 187: 36-39, 70. February 1993.
___ "The Young Ted Raimi," *Starlog* No. 198: 38-41. January 1994.

WARREN, TIM
___ "The Write Life: Author Kurt Vonnegut Speaks Freely About Writing," *Baltimore (MD) Sun* December 11, 1991. in: *NewsBank. Literature.* 7: C10-C11. 1992.

WARRICK, PATRICIA S.
___ "The Encounter of Taoism and Fascism in **The Man in the High Castle**," in: Mullen, R. D., ed. **On Philip K. Dick: 40 Articles From Science-Fiction Studies**. Terre Haute, IN: SF-TH Inc., 1992. pp.74-79.
___ "In Memory of Philip K. Dick," in: Mullen, R. D., ed. **On Philip K. Dick: 40 Articles From Science-Fiction Studies**. Terre Haute, IN: SF-TH Inc., 1992. pp.80-91.

WARSH, DAVID
___ "Cyberspace: What Is in It for You?," *Boston (MA) Globe* p. 65. May 30, 1993.

WASHICK, JAMES
___ "The Framed Narrative in **Perelandra**," *Bulletin of the New York C. S. Lewis Society* 25(7/8): 1-4. May/June 1994.

WASHINGTON, JULIE
___ "*Superman* Creator Joe Schuster Dies," *Lan's Lantern* No. 41: 3. July 1993.

WASSERMAN, JULIAN N.
___ "Gawain on Film," by Robert J. Blanch and Julian N. Wasserman. in: Harty, Kevin J., ed. **Cinema Arthuriana: Essays on Arthurian Film**. New York: Garland, 1991. pp.57-70.

WATERS, ELIZABETH
___ "Interview With Mercedes Lackey," *Marion Zimmer Bradley's Fantasy Magazine* No. 19: 50-52. Spring 1993.

WATERSIDE, PAT
___ "Trek Gallery," *Sci-Fi Entertainment* 1(1): 48-51. June 1994.

WATSON, GEORGE
___ "Introduction: **Critical Essays on C. S. Lewis**," *CSL: The Bulletin of the New York C. S. Lewis Society* 24(5): 1-7. March 1993.
___ (ed.) **Critical Essays on C. S. Lewis**. Hants, Eng.: Scolar Press, 1992. 284pp. (Critical Thought Series: 1)

WATSON, GREER
___ "Magic or Make-Believe? Acquiring the Conventions of Witches and Witchcraft," *Journal of the Fantastic in the Arts* 6(4): 341-359. 1995.

WATSON, IAN

___ "Le Guin's **Lathe of Heaven** and the Role of Dick: The False Reality as Mediator," in: Mullen, R. D., ed. **On Philip K. Dick: 40 Articles From Science-Fiction Studies**. Terre Haute, IN: SF-TH Inc., 1992. pp.63-72.

___ "Negentrophy Rules OK: The Refloating of *New Worlds*," *Amazing* 68(1): 48-52. April 1993.

___ "Pratchett Job," *Melody Maker* 72(7): 15. February 18, 1995.

WATSON, JEANIE

___ "Mary Stewart's Merlin: Word of Power," in: Watson, Jeanie and Fries, Marueen, eds. **The Figure of Merlin in the Nineteenth and Twentieth Centuries**. Lewiston, NY: Edwin Mellen Press, 1989. pp.155-174.

___ (ed.) **Approaches to the Teaching of the Arthurian Tradition**, ed. by Maureen Fries and Jeanie Watson. New York: Modern Language Association, 1992. 195pp.

___ (ed.) **The Figure of Merlin in the Nineteenth and Twentieth Centuries**, ed. by Jeanie Watson and Maureen Fries. Lewiston, NY: Edwin Mellin Press, 1989. 197pp.

WATSON, NIGEL

___ **Supernatural Spielberg**, by Darren Slade and Nigel Watson. London: Valis, 1992. 136pp.

WATSON, THOMAS R.

___ "Enlarging Augustinian Systems: C. S. Lewis' **The Great Divorce** and **Till We Have Faces**," *Renascence* 46(3): 163-174. Spring 1994.

WATSON, VICTOR

___ "Snobberies, Sneers, and Narnia: On the Narrowness of C. S. Lewis," *Books for Keeps* 83: 21. November 1994.

WATT-EVANS, LAWRENCE

___ "The Movies Invented Typecasting, But SF Made It an Art," *Science Fiction Age* 3(3): 34-36. March 1995.

___ "SF in the Comic Books," *OtherRealms* No. 27: 27-28. Spring 1990.

WAUGH, ROBERT H.

___ "Documents, Creatures, and History in H. P. Lovecraft," *Lovecraft Studies* No. 25: 2-10. Fall 1991.

___ "Dr. Margaret Murray and H. P. Lovecraft: The Witch-Cult in New England," *Lovecraft Studies* No. 31: 2-10. Fall 1994.

___ "Lovecraft's Documentary Style," in: Joshi, S. T., ed. **The H. P. Lovecraft Centennial Conference Proceedings**. West Warwick, RI: Necronomicon, 1991. pp.34-35.

___ "Perilous Faërie: J. R. R. Tolkien in the Selva Oscura," *Studies in Weird Fiction* No. 15: 20-27. Summer 1994.

___ " 'The Picture in the House': Images of Complicity," *Lovecraft Studies* No. 32: 2-8. Spring 1995.

___ "The Structural and Thematic Unity of **Fungi From Yuggoth**," *Lovecraft Studies* No. 26: 2-14. Spring 1992.

WAXMAN, BARBARA F.

___ "Postextentialism in the Neo-Gothic Mode: Anne Rice's **Interview With the Vampire**," *Mosaic* 25(3): 79-97. Summer 1992.

WEAVER, STEVEN

___ "***Blade Runner***'s Designer Brings His Magic to Your Home Computer With *CyberRace*," *Science Fiction Age* 2(3): 82-85. March 1994.

WEAVER, TOM

___ "Ann Robinson: Interview," in: Weaver, Tom, ed. **Attack of the Monster Movie Makers: Interviews with 20 Genre Giants**. Jefferson, NC: McFarland, 1994. pp.289-308.

___ "Anne Francis," in: Weaver, Tom. **They Fought the Creature Features: Interviews with 23 Classic Horror, Science Fiction and Serial Stars**. Jefferson, NC: McFarland, 1995. pp.161-172.

___ "Ben Chapman: Interview," in: Weaver, Tom, ed. **Attack of the Monster Movie Makers: Interviews with 20 Genre Giants**. Jefferson, NC: McFarland, 1994. pp.31-44.

___ "Betsy Jones-Moreland: Interview," in: Weaver, Tom, ed. **Attack of the Monster Movie Makers: Interviews with 20 Genre Giants**. Jefferson, NC: McFarland, 1994. pp.175-194.

WEAVER, TOM (continued)

___ "Billy Benedict," in: Weaver, Tom. **They Fought the Creature Features: Interviews with 23 Classic Horror, Science Fiction and Serial Stars**. Jefferson, NC: McFarland, 1995. pp.61-72.

___ "Birth of the ***Blob***," *Starlog* No. 214: 59-65. May 1995.

___ "Cameron Mitchell: Interview," in: Weaver, Tom, ed. **Attack of the Monster Movie Makers: Interviews with 20 Genre Giants**. Jefferson, NC: McFarland, 1994. pp.209-228.

___ "Candace Hilligoss: Interview," in: Weaver, Tom, ed. **Attack of the Monster Movie Makers: Interviews with 20 Genre Giants**. Jefferson, NC: McFarland, 1994. pp.145-156.

___ "Captain Marvel's Pal," *Starlog* No. 199: 62-65, 74. February 1994.

___ "Character Star," *Starlog* 184: 57-62, 72. November 1992.

___ "Charles Bennett: Interview," in: Weaver, Tom, ed. **Attack of the Monster Movie Makers: Interviews with 20 Genre Giants**. Jefferson, NC: McFarland, 1994. pp.17-30

___ "Creature King: From Out of the Black Lagoon, Ben Chapman Walked," by Tom Weaver and Paul Parla. *Starlog* 180: 59-64, 73. July 1992.

___ "Director of Dinosaurs," *Starlog* No. 193: 63-68. August 1993.

___ "Don Taylor," in: Weaver, Tom. **They Fought the Creature Features: Interviews with 23 Classic Horror, Science Fiction and Serial Stars**. Jefferson, NC: McFarland, 1995. pp.263-276.

___ "Ed Nelson: Interview," in: Weaver, Tom, ed. **Attack of the Monster Movie Makers: Interviews with 20 Genre Giants**. Jefferson, NC: McFarland, 1994. pp.229-248.

___ "Eugene Lourie," in: Weaver, Tom. **They Fought the Creature Features: Interviews with 23 Classic Horror, Science Fiction and Serial Stars**. Jefferson, NC: McFarland, 1995. pp.201-210.

___ "*Forbidden Planet*," *Starlog* No. 176: 38-41. March 1992.

___ "Friend of **The Thing**," *Starlog* 178: 61-69. May 1992.

___ "George Wallace," in: Weaver, Tom. **They Fought the Creature Features: Interviews with 23 Classic Horror, Science Fiction and Serial Stars**. Jefferson, NC: McFarland, 1995. pp.277-287.

___ "Gotham's Finest," *Starlog* No. 216: 46-49, 63. July 1995.

___ "Harry Spalding: Interview," in: Weaver, Tom, ed. **Attack of the Monster Movie Makers: Interviews with 20 Genre Giants**. Jefferson, NC: McFarland, 1994. pp.319-338.

___ "Herbert Rudley: Interview," in: Weaver, Tom, ed. **Attack of the Monster Movie Makers: Interviews with 20 Genre Giants**. Jefferson, NC: McFarland, 1994. pp.309-318.

___ "Herman Cohen: Interview," in: Weaver, Tom, ed. **Attack of the Monster Movie Makers: Interviews with 20 Genre Giants**. Jefferson, NC: McFarland, 1994. pp.45-84.

___ "In Martian Combat," *Starlog* No. 195: 66-71. October 1993.

___ "It!: The Terror From Beyond Comics," *Starlog* 184: 27-29, 72. November 1992.

___ "Jacques Marquette: Interview," in: Weaver, Tom, ed. **Attack of the Monster Movie Makers: Interviews with 20 Genre Giants**. Jefferson, NC: McFarland, 1994. pp.195-208.

___ "Jane Wyatt," in: Weaver, Tom. **They Fought the Creature Features: Interviews with 23 Classic Horror, Science Fiction and Serial Stars**. Jefferson, NC: McFarland, 1995. pp.289-302.

___ "Jeanne Bates," in: Weaver, Tom. **They Fought the Creature Features: Interviews with 23 Classic Horror, Science Fiction and Serial Stars**. Jefferson, NC: McFarland, 1995. pp.50-60.

___ "Jeff Morrow," in: Weaver, Tom. **They Fought the Creature Features: Interviews with 23 Classic Horror, Science Fiction and Serial Stars**. Jefferson, NC: McFarland, 1995. pp.211-219.

___ "John Agar," in: Weaver, Tom. **They Fought the Creature Features: Interviews with 23 Classic Horror, Science Fiction and Serial Stars**. Jefferson, NC: McFarland, 1995. pp.13-24.

___ "John Archer," in: Weaver, Tom. **They Fought the Creature Features: Interviews with 23 Classic Horror, Science Fiction and Serial Stars**. Jefferson, NC: McFarland, 1995. pp.37-49.

___ "Julie Adams," in: Weaver, Tom. **They Fought the Creature Features: Interviews with 23 Classic Horror, Science Fiction and Serial Stars**. Jefferson, NC: McFarland, 1995. pp.1-11.

___ "June Lockhart," in: Weaver, Tom. **They Fought the Creature Features: Interviews with 23 Classic Horror, Science Fiction and Serial Stars**. Jefferson, NC: McFarland, 1995. pp.187-199.

___ "Kenneth Tobey: Interview," in: Weaver, Tom, ed. **Attack of the Monster Movie Makers: Interviews with 20 Genre Giants**. Jefferson, NC: McFarland, 1994. pp.339-356.

___ "Killer Brains and Giant Women," *Starlog* No. 187: 57-61, 69. February 1993.

___ "Kong Conversations," *Starlog* No. 194: 70-73. September 1993.

WEAVER, TOM (continued)

___ "Lloyd Bridges," in: Weaver, Tom. **They Fought the Creature Features: Interviews with 23 Classic Horror, Science Fiction and Serial Stars**. Jefferson, NC: McFarland, 1995. pp.85-96.

___ "Lori Nelson," in: Weaver, Tom. **They Fought the Creature Features: Interviews with 23 Classic Horror, Science Fiction and Serial Stars**. Jefferson, NC: McFarland, 1995. pp.221-232.

___ "Louise Currie," in: Weaver, Tom. **They Fought the Creature Features: Interviews with 23 Classic Horror, Science Fiction and Serial Stars**. Jefferson, NC: McFarland, 1995. pp.131-143.

___ "Lunar Destiny," *Starlog* No. 202: 60-65. May 1994.

___ "Lupita Tovar: Interview," in: Weaver, Tom, ed. **Attack of the Monster Movie Makers: Interviews with 20 Genre Giants**. Jefferson, NC: McFarland, 1994. pp.357-365.

___ **MagicImage Filmbooks Presents Creature From the Black Lagoon**. Absecon, NJ: MagicImage Filmbooks, 1992. [195pp.]

___ "The Man in the Bubble-Headed Mask," *Starlog* No. 201: 32-35, 66. April 1994.

___ "Man of *The Lost Planet*: Michael Fox Interviewed," *Starlog* No. 198: 67-70, 72. January 1994.

___ "Man of the Seas," *Starlog* 182: 25-29, 66. September 1992.

___ "Man With a Plan (9)," *Starlog* No. 208: 59-67. November 1994.

___ "Mark Goddard," in: Weaver, Tom. **They Fought the Creature Features: Interviews with 23 Classic Horror, Science Fiction and Serial Stars**. Jefferson, NC: McFarland, 1995. pp.173-186.

___ "Merry Anders: Interview," in: Weaver, Tom, ed. **Attack of the Monster Movie Makers: Interviews with 20 Genre Giants**. Jefferson, NC: McFarland, 1994. pp.1-16.

___ "Monkey Business," *Starlog* No. 220: 59-63. November 1995.

___ "The Oldest Living Screenwriter Explains All," *Starlog* No. 193: 57-62, 71. August 1993.

___ "The Other Creature," by Tom Weaver and Paul Parla. *Starlog* No. 206: 61-65. September 1994.

___ "Outrageous Original," *Starlog* No. 198: 32-37, 82. January 1994.

___ **Poverty Row Horrors! Monogram, PRC and Republic Horror Films of the Forties**. Jefferson, NC: McFarland, 1993. 376pp.

___ "The Producer From Lands Unknown (Part Three)," *Starlog* No. 219: 57-64. October 1995.

___ "The Producer From Outer Space (Part One)," *Starlog* No. 217: 57-65. August 1995.

___ "The Producer From the Black Lagoon (Part Two)," *Starlog* No. 218: 57-63, 65. September 1995.

___ "Rex Reason," in: Weaver, Tom. **They Fought the Creature Features: Interviews with 23 Classic Horror, Science Fiction and Serial Stars**. Jefferson, NC: McFarland, 1995. pp.233-243.

___ "Richard Anderson," in: Weaver, Tom. **They Fought the Creature Features: Interviews with 23 Classic Horror, Science Fiction and Serial Stars**. Jefferson, NC: McFarland, 1995. pp.25-36.

___ "Richard Denning," in: Weaver, Tom. **They Fought the Creature Features: Interviews with 23 Classic Horror, Science Fiction and Serial Stars**. Jefferson, NC: McFarland, 1995. pp.145-160.

___ "Ricou Browning," in: Weaver, Tom. **They Fought the Creature Features: Interviews with 23 Classic Horror, Science Fiction and Serial Stars**. Jefferson, NC: McFarland, 1995. pp.97-109.

___ "Robert Cornthwaite," in: Weaver, Tom. **They Fought the Creature Features: Interviews with 23 Classic Horror, Science Fiction and Serial Stars**. Jefferson, NC: McFarland, 1995. pp.111-130.

___ "Robert Day: Interview," in: Weaver, Tom, ed. **Attack of the Monster Movie Makers: Interviews with 20 Genre Giants**. Jefferson, NC: McFarland, 1994. pp.85-97.

___ "Rose Hobart: Interview," in: Weaver, Tom, ed. **Attack of the Monster Movie Makers: Interviews with 20 Genre Giants**. Jefferson, NC: McFarland, 1994. pp.157-174.

___ "Space Duty," *Starlog* No. 190: 30-35, 72. May 1993.

___ "Space Mom," by Tom Weaver and Steve Swires. in: McDonnell, David, ed. **Starlog's Science Fiction Heroes and Heroines**. New York: Crescent Books, 1995. pp.44-46.

___ "Space Patrol," *Starlog* No. 187: 20-22. February 1993.

___ "Susan Hart: Interview," in: Weaver, Tom, ed. **Attack of the Monster Movie Makers: Interviews with 20 Genre Giants**. Jefferson, NC: McFarland, 1994. pp.127-144

___ "Target Earthwoman," *Starlog* No. 201: 59-63. April 1994.

___ **They Fought in the Creature Features: Interviews with 23 Classic Horror, Science Fiction and Serial Stars**. Jefferson, NC: McFarland, 1995. 328pp.

___ "Things Change," *Starlog* No. 174: 35-37, 72. January 1992.

WEAVER, TOM (continued)

___ "Tuhan Bey," in: Weaver, Tom. **They Fought the Creature Features: Interviews with 23 Classic Horror, Science Fiction and Serial Stars**. Jefferson, NC: McFarland, 1995. pp.73-83.

___ "Twilight Testaments," *Starlog* No. 203: 32. June 1994.

___ "Val Guest: Interview," in: Weaver, Tom, ed. **Attack of the Monster Movie Makers: Interviews with 20 Genre Giants**. Jefferson, NC: McFarland, 1994. pp.99-126.

___ "Vincent Price: Interview," in: Weaver, Tom, ed. **Attack of the Monster Movie Makers: Interviews with 20 Genre Giants**. Jefferson, NC: McFarland, 1994. pp.267-288.

___ "William Phipps: Interview," in: Weaver, Tom, ed. **Attack of the Monster Movie Makers: Interviews with 20 Genre Giants**. Jefferson, NC: McFarland, 1994. pp.249-266.

___ "William Schallert," in: Weaver, Tom. **They Fought the Creature Features: Interviews with 23 Classic Horror, Science Fiction and Serial Stars**. Jefferson, NC: McFarland, 1995. pp.245-262.

___ "Woman of the *Forbidden Planet*," *Starlog* No. 186: 27-31. January 1993. Also in: McDonnell, David, ed. **Starlog's Science Fiction Heroes and Heroines**. New York: Crescent Books, 1995. pp.41-43.

___ "Woman of the Apes," *Starlog* No. 213: 57-63. April 1995.

___ "Years After Stillness," *Starlog* No. 211: 24-27, 69. February 1995.

___ (ed.) **Attack of the Monster Movie Makers: Interviews With 20 Genre Giants**. Jefferson, NC: McFarland, 1994. 384pp.

___ (ed.) **Creature From the Black Lagoon**. Absecon, NJ: MagicImage Filmbooks, 1992. unpaged.

WEBB, DON

___ "The Future Book," *New York Review of Science Fiction* No. 72: 5-6. August 1994.

___ "The Mysterious," *Science Fiction Eye* No. 13: 62-66. Spring 1994.

WEBB, JANEEN

___ "Feminism and Science Fiction," *Meanjin* 51(1): 185-198. Autumn 1992.

___ "Post-Romantic Romance: Guy Gavriel Kay's **Tigana** and **A Song for Arbonne**," *New York Review of Science Fiction* No. 77: 17-19. January 1995.

___ "The Quests for Middle-Earth," in: Kranz, Gisbert, ed. **Jahrbuch für Literatur und Ästhetik**. Lüdenscheid, Germany: Stier, 1992. Band 10, pp.161-175.

___ "The Vampire of Shalott," *New York Review of Science Fiction* No. 64: 18-20. December 1993.

WEBB, KENNETH E.

___ **Quest for an American Spirituality: An Analysis of the Sacred Thematic Content in the American Science Fiction Novel, 1980-1989**. Ph.D. Dissertation, Iliff School of Theology and The University of Denver (Colorado Seminary), 1992. 251pp.

WEBB, MARTIN R.

___ "Tailor-Made: An Interview With Peter James," *Vector* No. 182: 3-4. Spring 1995.

WEBB, SARAH JO

___ "Culture as Spiritual Metaphor in Le Guin's **Always Coming Home**," in: Sanders, Joe, ed. **Functions of the Fantastic**. Westport, CT: Greenwood, 1995. pp.155-160.

WEBBER, KEN

___ "Interview With Mike Richardson, Publisher of Dark Horse Comics," *Burroughs Bulletin* NS. No. 21: 27-32. January 1995.

WEBER, KATHARINE

___ "Tessering Through Time," *Connecticut* 51: 76-85. November 1988.

WEEKS, DENNIS L.

___ **Steps Toward Salvation: An Examination of Coinherence and Substitution in the Seven Novels of Charles Williams**. New York: P. Lang, 1991. 116pp.

WEEKS, JANET

___ "Is Faux Violence Less Violent?," *Los Angeles (CA) Daily News*. August 19, 1995. in: *NewsBank. Film and Television*. 79:B10-B11. 1995.

WEGEMER, GERALD
___ "The City of God in Thomas More's **Utopia**," *Renascence* 44(2): 115-136. Winter 1992.

WEGNER, PHILLIP
___ "On Zamyatin's **We**: A Critical Map of Utopia's Possible Worlds," *Utopian Studies* 4(2): 94-116. 1993.

WEIL, ELLEN R.
___ "The Door to Lilith's Cave: Memory and Imagination in Jane Yolen's Holocaust Novels," *Journal of the Fantastic in the Arts* 5(2): 90-104. 1993. (No. 18)

WEIMER, ANNEGRET
___ "Utopia and Science Fiction: A Contribution to Their Generic Description," *Canadian Review of Comparative Literature* 19(1/2): 171-200. March/June 1992.

WEIN, TONI
___ "Wagging the Tail: Margaret Atwood's Historical Notes (**The Handmaid's Tale**)," *Notes on Contemporary Literature* 25(2): 2-3. March 1995.

WEINBERG, ROBERT
___ "The Fan Presses," in: Sanders, Joe, ed. **Science Fiction Fandom**. Westport, CT: Greenwood, 1994. pp.211-220.
___ "Profile: Frank R. Paul," *Futures Past* No. 3:30-32. September 1992. (Reprinted from: Weinberg, Robert. **A Biographical Dictionary of Science Fiction and Fantasy Artists**. 1988.)

WEINER, ANDREW
___ "SF--NOT," *New York Review of Science Fiction* No. 57: 20-22. May 1993.

WEINKAUF, MARY S.
___ **Sermons in Science Fiction: The Novels of S. Fowler Wright**. San Bernardino, CA: Borgo Press, 1994. 128pp.

WEINSTEIN, LEE
___ "Chambers and **The King in Yellow**," in: Schweitzer, Darrell, ed. **Discovering Classic Horror Fiction I**. Mercer Island, WA: Starmont, 1992. pp.57-72.
___ "Edward Lucas White," *Studies in Weird Fiction* No. 11: 15-24. Spring 1992.

WEINSTONE, ANN
___ "Resisting Monsters: Notes on **Solaris**," *Science Fiction Studies* 21(2): 173-190. July 1994.

WEIS, MARGARET
___ (ed.) **Leaves From the Inn of the Last Home: The Complete Krynn Source Book**, ed. by Margaret Weis and Tracy Hickman. Lake Geneva, WI: TSR, 1993. 255pp.

WEISENBURGER, STEVEN
___ **Fables of Subversion: Satire and the American Novel, 1930-1980**. Athens, GA: University of Georgia Press, 1995. 320pp.
___ "Hysteron Proteron in **Gravity's Rainbow**," *Texas Studies in Language and Literature* 34(1): 87-105. Spring 1992.

WEISKIND, RON
___ "Only Shell Is Left," *Pittsburgh (PA) Post Gazette*. February 25, 1994. in: *NewsBank. Film and Television*. 21: C1. 1994.

WEISS, ALLAN
___ "An Interview With Hal Clement," *Sol Rising* (Toronto) No. 10: 4-5. May 1994.

WEISSERT, THOMAS P.
___ "Stanislaw Lem and a Topology of Mind," *Science-Fiction Studies* 19(2): 161-166. July 1992.

WEISSKOPF, TONI
___ "Anatomy of a Sale: 'Sleipnir' to Baen Books," in: Thompkins, David G., ed. **Science Fiction Writer's Market Place and Source Book**. Cincinnati, OH: Writer's Digest Books, 1994. pp.358-374.

WEIST, ANDREW
___ **The Function of Folklore in the Science Fiction of Cordwainer Smith**. Master's Thesis, Bowling Green State University, 1992. 43pp.

WELKOS, ROBERT W.
___ "Director Trims **Basic Instinct** to Get R Rating," *Los Angeles (CA) Times*. February 11, 1992 in: *NewsBank. Film and Television*. 17:C14-D1. 1992.
___ "Plenty of Riptides in **Waterworld** Set," by Claudia Eller and Robert W. Welkos. *Los Angeles (CA) Times*. September 16, 1994. in: *NewsBank. Film and Television*. 117:C10. 1994.
___ "Sea Epic's Costs May Bring Wave of Caution," by Robert W. Welkos and Judy Brennan. *Los Angeles (CA) Times*. July 26, 1995. in: *NewsBank. Film and Television*. 82:C13-D1. 1995.
___ "A Spinner of (Horrific) Tales," *Los Angeles (CA) Times* October 11, 1992 in: *NewsBank. Film and Television*. 99:B9-B11. 1992

WELLER, GREG
___ "The Masks of the Goddess: The Unfolding of the Female Archetype in Stephen King's **Carrie**," in: Magistrale, Tony, ed. **The Dark Descent: Essays Defining Stephen King's Horrorscape**. Westport, CT: Greenwood, 1992. pp.5-17.

WELLS, CURT
___ "**Casper** Has Risen From the Grave," *Sci-Fi Entertainment* 2(1): 50-53. June 1995.
___ "James Herbert Is No **Fluke**," *Sci-Fi Entertainment* 1(6): 58-29, 72. April 1995.
___ "**The Lion King**," *Sci-Fi Entertainment* 1(2): 34-37. August 1994.
___ "Robert Heinlein's Classic **The Puppet Masters** Leaps From Page to Screen at Last!," *Science Fiction Age* 2(5): 18-22, 34. July 1994.

WELLS, EARL
___ "Robert A. Heinlein: EPIC Crusader," *New York Review of Science Fiction* No. 56: 1, 3-7. April 1993.
___ "The Rule of the Game," *New York Review of Science Fiction* No. 47: 6-7. July 1992.

WELLS, H. G.
___ **The Annotated H. G. Wells: The Island of Doctor Moreau. A Critical Text of the 1896 London First Edition, with Introduction and Appendices**, edited by Leon Stover. Jefferson, NC: McFarland, 1995. 408pp.
___ **The Annotated H. G. Wells: The Time Machine, An Invention. A Critical Text of the 1895 London First Edition, with Introduction and Appendices**, edited by Leon Stover. Jefferson, NC: McFarland, 1995. 269pp.
___ **A Critical Edition of the War of the Worlds: H. G. Wells's Scientific Romance**. Bloomington, IN: Indiana University Press, 1992. [CIP, Not seen.]
___ **The Island of Dr. Moreau: A Valorum Text**, by H. G. Wells and Robert M. Philmus. Athens, GA: University of Georgia Press, 1993. 240pp.

WELLS, JERRY
___ "Wettest Movie Ever Made Surfaces for Peek," *(Newark, NJ) Star-Ledger*. January 23, 1995. in: *NewsBank. Film and Television*. 22:G8-G9. 1995.

WELLS, PAUL
___ "The Invisible Man: Shrinking Masculinity in the 1950s Science Fiction B-Movie," in: Kirkham, Pat, and Thumim, Janet, ed. **You Tarzan: Masculinity, Movies, and Men**. New York: St. Martin's, 1993. pp.181-199.

WELLS, SHEELAGH J.
___ "Once a Commander," by Joe Nazzaro and Sheelagh J. Wells. *Starlog* No. 208: 53-57, 69. November 1994.

WELSH, JAMES L.
___ "Ray Bradbury," in: Bruccoli, Matthew J., ed. **Facts on File Bibliography of American Fiction 1919-1988**. New York: Facts on File, 1991. pp.101-103.

WELTON, ANN
___ "Earthsea Revisited: Tehanu and Feminism," *Voice of Youth Advocates* 14(1): 14-16, 18. April 1991.

WENDELL, CAROLYN H.
___ "Alfred Bester," in: Bruccoli, Matthew J., ed. **Facts on File Bibliography of American Fiction 1919-1988**. New York: Facts on File, 1991. pp.89-90.

WERGLAND, GLENDYNE R.
___ "The Artisan as Individual and Communitarian: The Life of Brother Isaac Newton Youngs," by Susan Matarese, Paul G. Salmon and Glendyne R. Wergland. *Utopian Studies* 6(2): 35-51. 1995.

WERNING, DAVID H.
___ "The Museum Scene in Walker Percy's **The Last Gentleman**," *Renascence* 44(3): 203-215. Spring 1992.

WESSEL, KARL
___ "Worlds of Chance and Counterfeit: Dick, Lem, and the Preestablished Cacophony," in: Umland, Samuel J., ed. **Philip K. Dick: Contemporary Critical Interpretations**. Westport, CT: Greenwood, 1995. pp.43-60.

WESTARP, KARLHEINZ
___ "Message to the Lost Self: Percy's Analysis of the Human Situation," *Renascence* 44(3): 215-224. Spring 1992.

WESTBROOK, BRUCE
___ "**2001** Plus 25," *Houston (TX) Chronicle* Sec. Z, p. 8. June 20, 1993.
___ "Bold Journeys: **Wagon Train** Provided a Guide for **Star Trek**," *Houston (TX) Chronicle TV Chronilog* p. 7. January 15-21, 1995.
___ "British Film **Split Second** Targets American Audiences (Review)," *Houston (TX) Chronicle*. May 5, 1992. in: *NewsBank. Film and Television*. 58:G5. 1992.
___ "DS9 Takes a Fresh Approach: Klingon Worf Joins the Crew," *Houston (TX) Chronicle*. October 4, 1995. in: *NewsBank. Film and Television*. 99:B5. 1995.
___ "The Next Voyage: Kate Mulgrew Takes Command of **Star Trek** Role," *Houston (TX) Chronicle TV Chronilog* p. 3-4. January 15-21, 1995.
___ "Re-entering Serling's **Twilight Zone**," *Houston (TX) Chronicle* Sec. C, p. 3. September 4, 1992.
___ "Star Wars," *Houston (TX) Chronicle* Sec. D, p. 1, 6. January 6, 1993.
___ "Third Time's the Charm: Newest **Star Trek** Offers TV Universe a 'Real' Good Time," *Houston (TX) Chronicle. TV Chronilog* pp.3-4. January 3, 1993.
___ "Tonight Marks Series Finale, But Memories Linger," *Houston (TX) Chronicle*. May 23, 1994. in: *NewsBank. Film and Television*. 59:C7. 1994.
___ "Trekkers Plan Farewell Parties," *Houston (TX) Chronicle*. May 23, 1994. in: *NewsBank. Film and Television*. 59:B14. 1994.
___ "Voyager a Hopeful UPN Launch," *Houston (TX) Chronicle*. August 28, 1995. in: *NewsBank. Film and Television*. 81:B1. 1995.

WESTBROOK, DAVID
___ "Video Series Looks Behind the Cameras," *Houston (TX) Chronicle*. March 11, 1992. in: *NewsBank. Film and Television*. 31:B3-B4. 1992.

WESTFAHL, GARY
___ "Academic Criticism of Science Fiction: What It Is, What It Should Be," *Monad* No. 2: 75-96. March 1992.
___ "Beyond Logic and Literacy: The Strange Case of Space Opera," *Extrapolation* 35(3): 176-185. Fall 1994.
___ "The Closely Reasoned Technological Story: The Critical History of Hard Science Fiction," *Science Fiction Studies* 20(2): 157-175. July 1993.
___ "A Convenient Analog System: John W. Campbell, Jr.'s Theory of Science Fiction," *Foundation* No. 54: 52-70. Spring 1992.
___ "The Dark Side of the Moon: Robert A. Heinlein's **Project Moonbase**," *Extrapolation* 36(2): 126-135. Summer 1995.
___ "Dictatorial, Authoritarian, Uncooperative: The Case Against John W. Campbell," *Foundation* No. 56: 36-60. Autumn 1992. (Letter of comment: Alexei Panshin, *Foundation* No. 58: 87-91. Summer 1993; Rejoiner, Westfahl, *Foundation* No. 58: 93-94.)
___ "Extracts From the **The Biographical Encyclopedia of Science Fiction Film**," *Foundation* No. 64: 45-69. Summer 1995.
___ "The Genre That Evolved: On Science Fiction as Children's Literature," *Foundation* No. 62: 70-74. Winter 1994/1995.

WESTFAHL, GARY (continued)
___ " 'The Gernsback Continuum': William Gibson in the Context of Science Fiction," in: Slusser, George E. and Shippey, Tom, eds. **Fiction 2000: Cyberpunk and the Future of Narrative**. Athens: University of Georgia Press, 1992. pp.88-108.
___ "Good Physics, Lousy Engineering: Arthur C. Clarke's **A Fall of Moondust**," *Monad* No. 3: 65-90. September 1993.
___ "In Research of Wonder: The Future of Science Fiction Criticism," in: Wolf, Milton T. and Mallett, Daryl F., eds. **Imaginative Futures: Proceedings of the 1993 Science Fiction Research Association Conference**. San Bernardino, CA: Jacob's Ladder Books, 1995. pp.83-94.
___ "The Jules Verne, H. G. Wells, Edgar Allan Poe Type of Story: Hugo Gernsback's History of Science Fiction," *Science-Fiction Studies* 19(3): 340-353. November 1992.
___ " 'Man Against Man, Brain Against Brain': The Transformation of Melodrama in Science Fiction," in: Redmond, James, ed. **Melodrama**. Cambridge: Cambridge University Press, 1992. pp.193-211.
___ "A New Campaign for Science Fiction," *Extrapolation* 33(1): 6-24. Spring 1992.
___ "Nonsense of Wonder: On Teaching Science Fiction," *Science Fiction Eye* No. 13: 67-71. Spring 1994.
___ "Sequel and Ye Shall Find Well: Book Two in the Chronicles of Westfahl the Critic," *Monad* No. 2: 25-42. March 1992.
___ "The Sequelizer, Or, The Farmer Gone to Hell," *Science Fiction Eye* No. 11: 23-27. December 1992.
___ "Superladies in Waiting: How the Female Hero Almost Emerges in Science Fiction," *Foundation* No. 58: 42-62. Summer 1993.
___ " 'This Unique Document': Hugo Gernsback's **Ralph 124C 41 +** and the Genres of Science Fiction," *Extrapolation* 35(2): 95-119. Summer 1994.
___ "The Undiscovered Country: The Finished and Unfinished Business of Science Fiction Research and Criticism," *Foundation* No. 60: 84-94. Spring 1994.
___ "Wanted: A Symbol for Science Fiction," *Science Fiction Studies* 22(1): 1-21. March 1995.
___ "Words of Wishdom: The Neologisms of Science Fiction," in: Slusser, George E. and Rabkin, Eric S., eds. **Styles of Creation: Aesthetic Technique and the Creation of Fictional Worlds**. Athens: University of Georgia Press, 1992. pp.221-244.
___ "The Words That Could Happen: Science Fiction Neologisms and the Creation of Future Worlds," *Extrapolation* 34(4): 290-304. Winter 1993.
___ "Wrangling Conversation: Linguistic Patterns in the Dialogue of Heroes and Villains," in: Slusser, George and Eric S. Rabkin, eds. **Fights of Fancy: Armed Conflict in Science Fiction and Fantasy**. Athens, GA: University of Georgia Press, 1993. pp.35-48.
___ "Writing for No Fun and No Profit: A Practical Guide to an Impractical Profession," *The Report: The Fiction Writer's Magazine* No. 10: 14-15. Summer 1993.

WESTWOOD, FRANK
___ "Interview with Franco Matania," *Burroughs Bulletin* NS No. 10: 23-28. April 1992.

WEYLAND, JACK
___ **Megapowers: Science Fact vs. Science Fiction**. Toronto: Kids Can Press, 1992. 78pp. (Cf. OCLC)

WHALEN, TERENCE
___ "The Future of a Commodity: Notes Toward a Critique of Cyberpunk and the Information Age," *Science Fiction Studies* 19(1): 75-88. March 1992.

WHALEN, TOM
___ "Romancing Film: Coppola's **Dracula**," *Literature/Film Quarterly* 23(2): 99-101. 1995.

WHARTON, LAWRENCE
___ "**Godzilla** to **Latitude Zero**: The Cycle of the Technological Monster," *Journal of Popular Film and Television* 3(1): 31-38. 1974.

WHEELER, BONNIE
___ "The Masculinity of King Arthur: From Gildas to the Nuclear Age," *Quondam et Futurus* 2(4): 1-27. Winter 1992.

WHITAKER, MURIEL
___ "Arthur for Children," in: Fries, Maureen and Watson, Jeanie, eds. **Approaches to the Teaching of the Arthurian Tradition.** New York: Modern Language Association, 1992. pp.151-154.
___ "Fire, Water, Rock: Elements of Setting in *Excalibur*," in: Harty, Kevin J., ed. **Cinema Arthuriana: Essays on Arthurian Film.** New York: Garland, 1991. pp.135-144.

WHITAKER, ROBERT
___ "Author Leads Armchair Astronauts on 'Voyage' to Mars," *Albany (NY) Times Union* June 6, 1989. in: *NewsBank. Names in the News* NIN 159: D8-D9. 1989.

WHITE, ERIC
___ "The Erotics of Becoming: **Xenogenesis** and *The Thing*," *Science Fiction Studies* 20(3): 394-408. November 1993.

WHITE, JONATHAN
___ "Collectible Science Fiction Magazines," *AB Bookman's Weekly* pp.2109-2130. October 1, 1984.

WHITE, LINDA
___ "Wildmen, Witches, and Wanderlust: No Basque Science Fiction?," in: Wolf, Milton T. and Mallett, Daryl F., eds. **Imaginative Futures: Proceedings of the 1993 Science Fiction Research Association Conference.** San Bernardino, CA: Jacob's Ladder Books, 1995. pp.279-292.

WHITE, MICHAEL
___ **Asimov: The Unauthorized Biography.** London: Orion/Millennium, 1994. 257pp.

WHITE, TAYLOR L.
___ "Batman: Comic Book Vision," *Cinefantastique* 24(6)/25(1): 67. February 1994.
___ "***Batman Returns***," *Cinefantastique* 23(1): 8-11. August 1992.
___ "Creating Catwoman," *Cinefantastique* 23(2/3): 10. October 1992.
___ "Making the Cartoon Classic: Walt Disney's *Peter Pan*," *Cinefantastique* 22(6): 34-45. June 1992

WHITE, TED
___ "My (Last) Column: Prologue and Farewell," *Quantum* No. 43/44: 27-31. Spring/Summer 1993.

WHITE, TIM
___ "William Gibson: Exploring the Newest Frontier," *Mindsparks* 2(1): 35-36. 1994. (Whole No. 4)

WHITMORE, TOM
___ "The Care and Feeding of Reviewers," *The Report: The Fiction Writer's Magazine* 2(6): 22. April 1992. (No. 59)
___ "Science Fiction Conventions: Behind the Scenes," by Tom Whitmore and Debbie Notkin. in: Sanders, Joe, ed. **Science Fiction Fandom.** Westport, CT: Greenwood, 1994. pp.161-171.

WHITTY, STEPHEN
___ "A Journey to No Place Special," *San Jose (CA) Mercury News.* December 2, 1994. in: *NewsBank. Film and Television.* 9:E14. 1995.
___ "Plot a Course, Mr. Sulu: Takei Drops By to Thank the People, Sell Tribbles," *San Jose (CA) Mercury News.* July 3, 1992. in: *NewsBank. Film and Television.* 74:B11-B12. 1992.
___ "Run For Your Life! It's Your Inner Godzilla," *San Jose (CA) Mercury News.* July 8, 1994. in: *NewsBank. Film and Television.* 81:C14. 1994.

WHYDE, JANET M.
___ "Fantastic Disillusionment: Rupturing Narrative and Rewriting Reality in **The Circus of Dr. Lao**," *Extrapolation* 35(3): 230-240. Fall 1994.

WIATER, STANLEY
___ "Barker, Clive," in: Wiater, Stanley. **Dark Visions: Conversations with the Masters of the Horror Film.** New York: Avon, 1992. pp.9-18.
___ "Carpenter, John," in: Wiater, Stanley. **Dark Visions: Conversations with the Masters of the Horror Film.** New York: Avon, 1992. pp.19-28.
___ "Cohen, Larry," in: Wiater, Stanley. **Dark Visions: Conversations with the Masters of the Horror Film.** New York: Avon, 1992. pp.29-38.

WIATER, STANLEY (continued)
___ "Corman, Roger," in: Wiater, Stanley. **Dark Visions: Conversations with the Masters of the Horror Film.** New York: Avon, 1992. pp.39-46.
___ "Craven, Wes," in: Wiater, Stanley. **Dark Visions: Conversations with the Masters of the Horror Film.** New York: Avon, 1992. pp.47-56.
___ "Cronenberg, David," in: Wiater, Stanley. **Dark Visions: Conversations with the Masters of the Horror Film.** New York: Avon, 1992. pp.57-66.
___ "Dark Dreamer," in: Jones, Stephen, ed. **James Herbert: By Horror Haunted.** London: New English Library, 1992. pp.271-282.
___ **Dark Visions: Conversations with the Masters of the Horror Film.** New York: Avon, 1992. 228pp.
___ "Disturbo 13: The Most Disturbing Horror Films Ever Made," in: Golden, Christopher, ed. **Cut! Horror Writers on Horror Film.** New York: Berkley, 1992. pp.255-266.
___ "Englund, Robert," in: Wiater, Stanley. **Dark Visions: Conversations with the Masters of the Horror Film.** New York: Avon, 1992. pp.67-76.
___ "Gordon, Stuart," in: Wiater, Stanley. **Dark Visions: Conversations with the Masters of the Horror Film.** New York: Avon, 1992. pp.77-88.
___ "Hurd, Gale Ann," in: Wiater, Stanley. **Dark Visions: Conversations with the Masters of the Horror Film.** New York: Avon, 1992. pp.89-100.
___ "McDowell, Michael," in: Wiater, Stanley. **Dark Visions: Conversations with the Masters of the Horror Film.** New York: Avon, 1992. pp.101-110.
___ "Munro, Caroline," in: Wiater, Stanley. **Dark Visions: Conversations with the Masters of the Horror Film.** New York: Avon, 1992. pp.111-118.
___ "Nolan, William F.," in: Wiater, Stanley. **Dark Visions: Conversations with the Masters of the Horror Film.** New York: Avon, 1992. pp.119-128.
___ "Price, Vincent," in: Wiater, Stanley. **Dark Visions: Conversations with the Masters of the Horror Film.** New York: Avon, 1992. pp.129-136.
___ "Raimi, Sam," in: Wiater, Stanley. **Dark Visions: Conversations with the Masters of the Horror Film.** New York: Avon, 1992. pp.137-146.
___ "Romero, George A.," in: Wiater, Stanley. **Dark Visions: Conversations with the Masters of the Horror Film.** New York: Avon, 1992. pp.147-158.
___ "Sammon, Paul M.," in: Wiater, Stanley. **Dark Visions: Conversations with the Masters of the Horror Film.** New York: Avon, 1992. pp.219-226.
___ "Savini, Tom," in: Wiater, Stanley. **Dark Visions: Conversations with the Masters of the Horror Film.** New York: Avon, 1992. pp.159-166.
___ "Smith, Dick," in: Wiater, Stanley. **Dark Visions: Conversations with the Masters of the Horror Film.** New York: Avon, 1992. pp.167-178.
___ "Stefano, Joseph," in: Wiater, Stanley. **Dark Visions: Conversations with the Masters of the Horror Film.** New York: Avon, 1992. pp.179-188.
___ "Winston, Stan," in: Wiater, Stanley. **Dark Visions: Conversations with the Masters of the Horror Film.** New York: Avon, 1992. pp.189-198.
___ "Yagher, Kevin," in: Wiater, Stanley. **Dark Visions: Conversations with the Masters of the Horror Film.** New York: Avon, 1992. pp.199-208.
___ "Yuzna, Brian," in: Wiater, Stanley. **Dark Visions: Conversations with the Masters of the Horror Film.** New York: Avon, 1992. pp.209-218.
___ (ed.) **Comic Book Rebels: Conversations With the Creators of the New Comics**, ed. by Stanley Wiater and Stephen R. Bissette. New York: Donald I. Fine, 1993. 312pp.

WICKE, JENNIFER
___ "Vampiric Typewriting: Dracula and Its Media," *ELH* 59(2): 467-494. Summer 1992.

WICKEN, JEFFREY S.
___ "Evolutionary Constraints on Utopian Thought," in: Saccaro Del Buffa, Giuseppa and Lewis, Arthur O., eds. **Utopia e Modernita: Teorie e prassi utopiche nell'eta moderna e postmoderna.** Rome: Gangemi Editore, 1989. pp.143-156.

WIDDER, WILLIAM J.
___ **The Fiction of L. Ron Hubbard: A Comprehensive Bibliography and Reference Guide to Published and Selected Unpublished Works.** Los Angeles, CA: Bridge Publications, 1994. 373pp.

WIDDICOMBE, RICHARD T.
___ "Early Histories of Utopian Thought (to 1950)," *Utopian Studies* 3(1): 1-38. 1992.

WIDDICOMBE, TOBY
___ "Why Is There Barbed Wire Around Eutopia?," *Extrapolation* 33(2): 145-153. Summer 1992.

WIDNER, ART
___ "Wartime Fandom," in: Sanders, Joe, ed. **Science Fiction Fandom.** Westport, CT: Greenwood, 1994. pp.55-64.

WIEMER, ANNEGRET J.
___ **The Feminist Science Fiction Utopia: Faces of a Genre, 1820-1897.** Ph.D. Dissertation, University of Alberta, 1991. (Ottawa: National Library of Canada, 1992. 5 microfiche) (DAI-A 53/08, p. 2811. Feb. 1993.)
___ "Foreign L(anguish), Mother Tongue: Concepts of Language in Contemporary Feminist Science Fiction," *Women's Studies* 14(2): 163-174. 1987.
___ "Utopia and Science Fiction: A Contribution to Their Generic Description," *Canadian Review of Comparative Literature* 19(1/2): 171-200. March/June 1992.

WIGGINS, KAYLA M.
___ "Epic Heroes, Ethical Issues, and Time Paradoxes in **Quantum Leap**," *Journal of Popular Film and Television* 21(3): 111-120. Fall 1993.

WIGNALL, BRENDAN
___ "Tom Holt: Interview," *Interzone* No. 56: 50-53. February 1992.

WILCOX, CLYDE
___ "The Not-So-Failed Feminism of Jean Auel," *Journal of Popular Culture* 28(3): 63-70. Winter 1994.
___ "To Boldly Return Where Others Have Gone Before: Cultural Change and the Old and New **Star Trek**s'," *Extrapolation* 33(1): 88-100. Spring 1992.

WILCOX, RHONDA V.
___ "Dating Data: Miscegenation in **Star Trek: The Next Generation**," *Extrapolation* 34(3): 265-277. Fall 1993.

WILD, FREDRIC M.
___ **A Plank in Reason: Time, Space, and the Perception of the Self in the Modern Novel.** Ph.D. Dissertation, Ohio State University, 1973. 203pp. (DAI 34: 2665A. Nov. 1973.)

WILDER, CHERRY
___ "The Profession of Science Fiction, 43: Far Fetched," *Foundation* No. 54: 5-15. Spring 1992.

WILLEMS, S. F.
___ "Lawrence Watt-Evans Discusses HWA," *Genre Writer's News* 1(7): 11-14. May/June 1995.

WILLENS, MICHELLE
___ "Making Films That Go Straight to Video--By Design," *New York Times* Sec. 2, p. 22. September 19, 1993.

WILLIAMS, CHARLES
___ "Die Region der Sommer-Sterne (I-II)," in: Kranz, Gisbert, ed. **Inklings: Jahrbuch für Literatur und Ästhetik.** 7. Band. s.l.: Stier Verlag, 1989. pp.5-24. [Not seen.]
___ "Die Region der Sommer-Sterne (III-VIII)," in: Kranz, Gisbert, ed. **Inklings: Jahrbuch für Literatur und Ästhetik.** 8. Band. Lüdenscheid, Germany: Stier, 1990. pp.5-46. [Not seen.]

WILLIAMS, DAVID E.
___ "An Oceanic Odyssey," *American Cinematographer* 76(8): 40-51. August 1995.
___ "Time Flop: **Timecop** (Review)," *Sci-Fi Universe* No. 3: 66-67. October/November 1994.

WILLIAMS, DONNA G.
___ "The Moons of Le Guin and Heinlein," *Science Fiction Studies* 21(2): 164-172. July 1994.

WILLIAMS, JOSEPH M.
___ **An Analysis of the Human/Non-Human Opposition in Science Fiction Films: A Research Project.** Master's Thesis, Emerson College, 1988. 67pp.

WILLIAMS, LINDA
___ "Learning to Scream," *Sight and Sound* 4(12): 14-17. December 1994.

WILLIAMS, LUCY C.
___ **The Complete Films of Vincent Price.** New York: Citadel, 1995. 287pp.

WILLIAMS, LYNN F.
___ "The Clockwork Apple in the Garden of Eden: The Mechanization of the Arcadian Utopia," in: Saccaro Del Buffa, Giuseppa and Lewis, Arthur O., eds. **Utopia e Modernita: Teorie e prassi utopiche nell'eta moderna e postmoderna.** Rome: Gangemi Editore, 1989. pp.655-666.
___ "Recent Nostalgic Utopias and the New Conservatism," in: Saccaro Del Buffa, Giuseppa and Lewis, Arthur O., eds. **Utopie per gli Anni Ottana.** Rome: Gangemi Editore, 1986. pp.763-788.
___ "Tolkien of Our Esteem," *Austin (TX) American Statesman* Sec. G, p. 1, 9. January 12, 1992.

WILLIAMS, MADAWC
___ "Tales of Wonder: Science Fiction and Fantasy in the Age of Jane Austen," in: Reynolds, Patricia and GoodKnight, Glen H., eds. **Proceedings of the J. R. R. Tolkien Centenary Conference, Keble College, Oxford, 1992.** Altadena, CA: Mythopoeic Press, 1995. pp.419-430. (*Mythlore* Vol. 21, No. 2, Winter 1996, Whole No. 80)

WILLIAMS, MICHAEL
___ "The 'Language of the Cipher': Interpretation in 'The Gold Bug' (1982)," in: Budd, Louis J. and Cady, Edwin H., eds. **On Poe.** Durham, NC: Duke University Press, 1993. pp.208-222.

WILLIAMS, RAYMOND
___ "George Orwell," in: Bloom, Harold, ed. **George Orwell's 1984.** New York: Chelsea House, 1987. pp.9-18.

WILLIAMS, ROSALIND H.
___ "Jules Romains, **Unanimisme**, and the Poetics of Urban Systems," in: Greenberg, Mark L. and Schachterle, Lance, eds. **Literature and Technology.** Bethlehem, PA: Lehigh University Press, 1992. pp.177-205.
___ **Notes on the Underground: an Essay on Technology, Society, and the Imaginagion.** Cambridge, Mass.: MIT Press, 1990. 265pp. [Not seen.]

WILLIAMS, SARAH
___ "Cyborg Anthropology," by Gary L. Downey, Joseph Dumit and Sarah Williams. in: Gray, Chris H., ed. **The Cyborg Handbook.** New York: Routledge, 1995. pp.341-346.
___ " 'Perhaps Images at One With the World Are Already Lost Forever': Visions of Cyborg Anthropology in Post-Cultural Worlds," in: Gray, Chris H., ed. **The Cyborg Handbook.** New York: Routledge, 1995. pp.379-390.

WILLIAMS, SCOTT
___ "Science Fiction Hottest TV Trend," *Bryan College Station Eagle* p. A12. January 22, 1993.

WILLIAMS, SHEILA
___ "The 1995 Isaac Asimov Award," *Isaac Asimov's Science Fiction Magazine* 19(9): 44-45. August 1995.
___ "Isaac Asimov Award," *Isaac Asimov's Science Fiction Magazine* 17(7): 4-6. June 1993.
___ "Isaac Asimov Award Winners," *Asimov's Science Fiction Magazine* 18(12/13): 152-153. November 1994.
___ "The Mechanics of Submission," in: Dozois, Gardner, ed. **Writing Science Fiction and Fantasy.** New York: St. Martin's, 1991. pp.211-220.

WILLIAMS, TONY
___ "Feminism, Fantasy and Violence: An Interview With Stephanie Rothman," *Journal of Popular Film and Television* 9(2): 84-90. 1981. ('Letter of Correction': 10(3): 137. 1982.)

WILLIAMS, WADE
___ "Behind the Scenes with Richard Derr, **When Worlds Collide**," *Filmfax* No. 30: 50-59. December 1991/January 1992.

WILLIAMSON, JACK
___ "A Long Time Ago, in a Galaxy Not That Far Away, Science Fiction Was Born," *Science Fiction Age* 2(3): 30, 86. March 1994.
___ "The Way It Was, 1933-1937," in: Jakubowski, Maxim and James, Edward, eds. **The Profession of Science Fiction**. New York: St. Martin's, 1992. pp.12-25.
___ "Who Was Robert Heinlein?," in: Kondo, Yoji, ed. **Requiem: New Collected Works by Robert A. Heinlein and Tributes to the Grand Master**. New York: Tor, 1992. pp.333-336.
___ "Wonder Remembered," *Amazing* 68(9): 27-28. Winter 1994.
___ "**Wonder's Child: My Life in Science Fiction**: (Chapter 8), Amazing Stories, 1926-1928," *Futures Past* No. 3:51-54. September 1992. (Reprinted from: Williamson, Jack. **Wonder's Child**. 1984.)

WILLINGHAM, DAVID
___ "A Conversation with Ursula K. Le Guin," by Victor Reinking and David Willingham. *Paradoxa* 1(1): 39-57. 1995.

WILLINGHAM, RALPH A.
___ "Dystopian Vision in the Plays of Elias Canetti," *Science Fiction Studies* 19(1): 69-74. March 1992.
___ **Science Fiction and the Theatre**. Ph.D. Disseration, University of Illinois, Urbana-Champaign, 1991. 382pp.
___ **Science Fiction and the Theatre**. Westport, CT: Greenwood, 1994. 213pp.

WILLIS, CONNIE
___ "**Jurassic Park** and Al Jolson: Thinking About the Information Revolution," *Information Technology and Libraries* 13(1): 51-53. March 1994.
___ "Learning to Write Comedy, or Why It's Impossible and How to Do It," in: Dozois, Gardner, ed. **Writing Science Fiction and Fantasy**. New York: St. Martin's, 1991. pp.76-88.
___ "The Women SF Doesn't See," *Isaac Asimov's Science Fiction Magazine* 16(11): 4-8. October 1992.

WILLIS, MARTIN T.
___ "Scientific Portraits in Magical Frames: The Construction of Preternatural Narrative in the Work of E. T. A. Hoffman and Arthur Machen," *Extrapolation* 35(3): 186-200. Fall 1994.

WILLIS, ROBERT J.
___ "**Dream on Monkey Mountain**: Fantasy as Self-Perception," in: Murphy, Patrick D., ed. **Staging the Impossible: The Fantastic Mode in Modern Drama**. Westport, CT: Greenwood, 1992. pp.150-155.

WILLIS, SHARON
___ "Sword & Sorcery, S/M, and the Economics of Inadequation: The *Camera Obscura* Interview," by Constance Penley and Sharon Willis. in: Delany, Samuel R. **Silent Interviews on Language, Race, Sex, Science Fiction and Some Comics**. Hanover, NH: Wesleyan University Press, 1994. pp.127-163.

WILLMAN, DAVID
___ "Lambs Stew: Battle Over 'Silence' Sequel May Change Hollywood Deal Making," *Los Angeles (CA) Times*. May 29, 1992. in: *NewsBank. Film and Television*. 58:E8-E9. 1992.

WILLS, DEBORAH
___ "The Madwoman in the Matrix: Joanna Russ's **The Two of Them** and the Psychiatric Postmodern," in: Latham, Robert A. and Collins, Robert A., eds. **Modes of the Fantastic**. Westport, CT: Greenwood, 1995. pp.93-99.

WILLSON, ROBERT F., JR.
___ "**The Exorcist** and Multi-Cinema Aesthetics," *Journal of Popular Film and Television* 3(2): 183-187. 1974.

WILMINGTON, MICHAEL
___ "The Rain People (On the Restored Version of **Blade Runner**)," *Film Comment* 28(1): 17-19. 1992.
___ "A Shtick Through the Heart," *Los Angeles (CA) Times*. November 15, 1992. in: *NewsBank. Film and Television*. 111:A5-A7. 1992.

WILSON, BILL
___ "Future Cops," *Starlog* No. 174: 52-55. January 1992.
___ "Gill Man," *Starlog* No. 211: 46-49. February 1995.
___ "I Want My SF-TV," *Starlog* No. 176: 17-21, 71. March 1992.
___ "Mistress of the Sea," *Starlog* No. 216: 74-77. July 1995.
___ "Mutant Hero," *Starlog* No. 214: 50-52, 69. May 1995.
___ "Underwater Cowboy," *Starlog* No. 215: 36-39. June 1995.

WILSON, COLIN
___ "The **Necronomicon**: The Origin of a Spoof," in: Price, Robert M., ed. **Black Forbidden Things**. Mercer Island, WA: Starmont, 1992. pp.88-90.
___ "Why Is Shiel Neglected?," in: **Shiel in Diverse Hands: A Collection of Essays**. Cleveland, OH: Reynolds Morse Foundation, 1983. pp.213-222.

WILSON, EDMUND
___ "Utopian Aspects of Catholic Social Teachings from Leo XIII to Paul VI," in: Saccaro Del Buffa, Giuseppa and Lewis, Arthur O., eds. **Utopie per gli Anni Ottana**. Rome: Gangemi Editore, 1986. pp.727-734.

WILSON, KEITH
___ "Jim, Jake and the Years Between," in: Salwak, Dale, ed. **Kingsley Amis in Life and Letters**. New York: St. Martin's, 1990. pp.76-88.

WILSON, MARY
___ **Balancing Polar Opposites in the Novels of Ursula K. Le Guin**. Master's Thesis, Tennessee Technological University, 1992. 61pp.
___ "The Earthsea Series of Ursula Le Guin: A Successful Example of Modern Fantasy," *Papers: Explorations into Children's Literature* 3(2): 60-74. August 1992. [Not seen.]

WILSON, PATRICIA A.
___ **Conflict and Resolution: The Divergent Roles of Catholic Men of Faith in Science Fiction**. Master's Thesis, University of Regina (Canada), 1992. 108pp. (Master's Abstracts 32/03, p. 805. June 1993.)

WILSON, RAYMOND J., III.
___ "James Blish," in: Bruccoli, Matthew J., ed. **Facts on File Bibliography of American Fiction 1919-1988**. New York: Facts on File, 1991. pp.90-92.

WILSON, SHARON R.
___ **Margaret Atwood's Fairy-Tale Sexual Politics**. Jackson: University Press of Mississippi, 1993. 430pp.

WILT, DAVID
___ "**8 Man** (Review)," *Cinefantastique* 26(5): 59. August 1995.
___ "**Amityville 1992: It's About Time** (Review)," *Cinefantastique* 23(5): 59. February 1993.
___ "**Carnosaur II** (Review)," *Cinefantastique* 27(2): 59. November 1995.
___ "**Children of the Night** (Review)," *Cinefantastique* 23(6): 60. April 1993.
___ "**The Club** (Review)," *Cinefantastique* 25(6)/26(1): 122. December 1994.
___ "**Confessions of a Serial Killer** (Review)," *Cinefantastique* 24(1): 60. June 1993.
___ "**Critters 3** (Review)," *Cinefantastique* 22(6): 54. June 1992
___ "**Critters 4** (Review)," *Cinefantastique* 23(6): 60. April 1993.
___ "**Cthulhu Mansion** (Review)," *Cinefantastique* 23(2/3): 122. October 1992.
___ "**Cyber Ninja** (Review)," *Cinefantastique* 27(2): 59. November 1995.
___ "**Cyber Tracker** (Review)," *Cinefantastique* 26(3): 59. April 1995.
___ "**Cyborg Soldier** (Review)," *Cinefantastique* 27(2): 60. November 1995.
___ "**Die Watching** (Review)," *Cinefantastique* 24(6)/25(1): 123. February 1994.
___ "**Equinox** (Review)," *Cinefantastique* 25(4): 59. August 1994.
___ "**Full Eclipse** (Review)," *Cinefantastique* 25(5): 59. October 1994.

WILT, DAVID (continued)
___ "*Future Shock* (Review)," *Cinefantastique* 25(4): 59. August 1994.
___ "*Ghoulies IV* (Review)," *Cinefantastique* 26(3): 59. April 1995.
___ "*Heartstopper* (Review)," *Cinefantastique* 24(2): 59. August 1993.
___ "*Invisible: The Chronicles of Benjamin Knight* (Review)," *Cinefantastique* 26(2): 59. February 1995.
___ "*Midnight 2: Sex, Death and Videotape* (Review)," *Cinefantastique* 24(2): 59. August 1993.
___ "*Midnight's Child* (Review)," *Cinefantastique* 23(6): 60. April 1993.
___ "*Netherworld* (Review)," *Cinefantastique* 23(4): 61. December 1992.
___ "*Philadelphia Experiment II* (Review)," *Cinefantastique* 25(6)/26(1): 123. December 1994.
___ "*Project: Shadowchaser* (Review)," *Cinefantastique* 23(6): 61. April 1993.
___ "*Prototype X29A* (Review)," *Cinefantastique* 24(2): 59. August 1993.
___ "*Scanners: The Showdown* (Review)," *Cinefantastique* 27(2): 60. November 1995.
___ "*Shatter Dead* (Review)," *Cinefantastique* 26(3): 60. April 1995.
___ "*Silent Night, Deadly Night: The Toymaker*," *Cinefantastique* 23(1): 60. August 1992.
___ "*Slumber Party Massacre 3* (Review)," *Cinefantastique* 23(1): 61. August 1992.
___ "*Sorority House Massacre II* (Review)," *Cinefantastique* 24(1): 61. June 1993.
___ "Stephen King's *Sometimes They Come Back* (Review)," *Cinefantastique* 24(3/4): 123. October 1993.
___ "*Subspecies* (Review)," *Cinefantastique* 22(6): 55. June 1992
___ "*Sundown* (Review)," *Cinefantastique* 22(6): 55. June 1992
___ "*Ticks* (Review)," *Cinefantastique* 26(5): 60. August 1995.
___ "*To Sleep With a Vampire* (Review)," *Cinefantastique* 24(2): 59. August 1993.
___ "*Trancers 4: Jack of Swords* (Review)," *Cinefantastique* 25(4): 60. August 1994.
___ "*Winterbeast* (Review)," *Cinefantastique* 24(1): 61. June 1993.

WIMSATT, W. K., JR.
___ "Poe and the Chess Automaton (1939)," in: Budd, Louis J. and Cady, Edwin H., eds. On Poe. Durham, NC: Duke University Press, 1993. pp.78-91.

WINCHESTER, MARK D.
___ "Comic Strip Theatricals in Public and Private Collections," *Popular Culture in Libraries* 1(1): 67-76. 1993.

WINFREY, LEE
___ "Going Where No Network Has Gone Before: Sci-Fi Channel Debuting Today," *Bryan-College Station Eagle* p. B4. September 24, 1992.

WINGATE, ARTHUR
___ "Working for Morris & Co.," *Journal of the William Morris Society* 11(2): 31-32. Spring 1995.

WINGLER, STEPHEN
___ "Prelude to a Dull Movie (Review)," *Baltimore (MD) Sun*. July 10, 1992. in: *NewsBank. Film and Television*. 73:C5-C6. 1992.

WINGROVE, DAVID
___ "Letter to Catie, with Responses," *Vector* No. 165: 9-15, 23. February/March 1992. (Response to editorial, *Vector* No. 164: 3. December 1991/January 1992.)

WINIKOFF, KENNETH
___ "*Captain Zoom*," *Cinefantastique* 27(2): 38-39, 61. November 1995.
___ "*Hideaway*," *Cinefantastique* 26(3): 14-15, 61. April 1995.
___ "*Outer Limits*," *Cinefantastique* 26(3): 6-7, 61. April 1995.

WINNETT, SCOTT
___ "1991 Book Summary," in: Brown, Charles N. and Contento, William G. Science Fiction, Fantasy, & Horror: 1991. Oakland, CA: Locus Press, 1992. pp.423-427.
___ "1991 Magazine Summary," by Scott Winnett and Charles N. Brown. in: Brown, Charles N. and Contento, William G. Science Fiction, Fantasy, & Horror: 1991. Oakland, CA: Locus Press, 1992. pp.428-432.

WINNETT, SCOTT (continued)
___ "1992 Magazine Summary," by Scott Winnett and Charles N. Brown. *Locus* 30(2): 44-46. February 1993.
___ "1993 Book Summary," by Scott Winnett and Charles N. Brown. *Locus* 32(2): 43-45, 73-76. February 1994.
___ "1993 Magazine Summary," by Scott Winnett and Charles N. Brown. *Locus* 32(2): 44-48, 51. February 1994.

WINSTON, IRIS
___ "Speaking From...Out of This World," *National Library News* (Canada) 27(5): 2-4. May 1995.

WINSTON, JEAN
___ Star Trek Lives!, by Jacqueline Lichtenberg, Sandra Marshak and Jean Winston. New York: Bantam, 1975. 274pp.

WINTER, DOUGLAS E.
___ "Doing It With Style," in: Jones, Stephen, ed. James Herbert: By Horror Haunted. London: New English Library, 1992. pp.47-63.
___ "The Great and Secret Show," in: Brown, Michael, ed. Pandemonium: Further Explorations into the Worlds of Clive Barker. Staten Island, NY: Eclise, 1991. pp.97-98.
___ "Opera of Violence: The Films of Dario Argento," in: Golden, Christopher, ed. Cut! Horror Writers on Horror Film. New York: Berkley, 1992. pp.267-288.
___ "Shadowings: By Any Other Name," *Worlds of Fantasy and Horror* 1(1): 10-14. Summer 1994. (No. 1)

WINTER, KARI J.
___ Subjects of Slavery, Agents of Change: Women and Power in Gothic Novels and Slave Narratives, 1790-1865. Athens: University of Georgia Press, 1992. 172pp.

WINTER, MICHAEL
___ "Utopia in Everyday Politics: Blessing or Nightmare?," in: Saccaro Del Buffa, Giuseppa and Lewis, Arthur O., eds. Utopia e Modernita: Teorie e prassi utopiche nell'eta moderna e postmoderna. Rome: Gangemi Editore, 1989. pp.77-86.

WINTERS, YVOR
___ "Edgar Allan Poe: A Crisis in the History of American Obscurantism (1937)," in: Budd, Louis J. and Cady, Edwin H., eds. On Poe. Durham, NC: Duke University Press, 1993. pp.55-77.

WINTERTON, IAN
___ "Yeti vs. The Bloodsuckers: Alan Moore Interviewed," *Interzone* No. 89: 28-30. November 1994.

WIRTHINGTON, JOHN
___ "'He telleth the number of the stars; he calleth them all by their names': The Lesser Knights of Sir Thomas Malory's Morte Dauthur," *Quondam et Futurus* 3(4): 17-27. Winter 1993.

WISEMAN, GILLIAN
___ "Visions of the Future: The Library in Science Fiction," *Journal of Youth Services in Libraries* 7(2): 191-198. Winter 1994.

WISHNIA, KENNETH
___ "Science Fiction and Magic Realism: Two Openings, Same Space," *Foundation* No. 59: 29-41. Autumn 1993.

WITCHEL, ALEX
___ "Boldly Contemplating Death and the Sequel," *New York Times* p.B1. November 23, 1994.

WOBER, J. MALLORY
___ (ed.) Television and Nuclear Power: Making the Public Mind. Norwood, NJ: Ablex, 1992. 297pp.

WOHLEBER, CURT
___ "The Man Who Can Scare Stephen King," *American Heritage* 46(8): 82-90. December 1995.

WOLANSKY, TARAS
___ "Fantasy vs. Science Fiction: Part III," *Quantum* No. 41: 21-22. Winter/Spring 1992.

WOLF, JACK C.
___ "Push-Button Utopias and Square Tomatoes," in: Saccaro Del Buffa, Giuseppa and Lewis, Arthur O., eds. **Utopie per gli Anni Ottana.** Rome: Gangemi Editore, 1986. pp.99-106.

WOLF, MILTON T.
___ "Science Fiction: Better Than Delphi Studies," *Educom Review* 29(1): 20-34. January/February 1994.
___ (ed.) **Imaginative Futures: Proceedings of the 1993 Science Fiction Research Association Conference,** ed. by Milton T. Wolf and Daryl F. Mallett. San Bernardino, CA: Jacob's Ladder Books/Borgo Press, 1995. 364pp.

WOLFE, GARY K.
___ "ABA 1995," *Locus* 35(1): 8, 36-39, 68. July 1995.
___ "The Dawn Patriot: Sex, Technology, and Irony in Farmer and Ballard," in: Ruddick, Nicholas, ed. **State of the Fantastic.** Westport, CT: Greenwood, 1992. pp.159-167.
___ "History and Criticism," in: Barron, Neil, ed. **Anatomy of Wonder 4.** New York: Bowker, 1995. pp.483-546.
___ "Introduction: Fantasy as Testimony," *Journal of the Fantastic in the Arts* 5(2): 3-10. 1993. (No. 18)
___ "Not Quite Coming to Terms," in: Mullen, R. D., ed. **On Philip K. Dick: 40 Articles From Science-Fiction Studies.** Terre Haute, IN: SF-TH Inc., 1992. pp.237-239.

WOLFE, GENE
___ "About Theodore Sturgeon," in: Sturgeon, Theodore. **The Ultimate Egoist, Vol. 1: The Complete Stories of Theodore Sturgeon,** ed. by Paul Williams. Berkeley, CA: North Atlantic Books, 1994. pp.xiv-xvi.
___ "A Critic at the Crossroads: Gregory Feeley's 'How Far to th' End of the World'," *New York Review of Science Fiction* No. 86: 6-7. October 1995.
___ "The Pirates of Florida, and Other Implausibilities," *Quantum* No. 43/44: 21-23. Spring/Summer 1993.
___ "The Profession of Science Fiction," in: Jakubowski, Maxim and James, Edward, eds. **The Profession of Science Fiction.** New York: St. Martin's, 1992. pp.131-139.

WOLFE, PETER
___ "The Brass Butterfly: Formula for Slow Change.," in: Biles, Jack I. and Evans, Robert O., eds. **William Golding: Some Critical Considerations.** Lexington, KY: University Press of Kentucky, 1978. pp.56-71.
___ "**Walden Two** Twenty-Five Years Later: A Retrospective Look," *Studies in the Literary Imagination* 6(2): 11-26. Fall 1973.

WOLFF, MICHAEL J.
___ "After the Earth Stood Still," *Starlog* No. 211: 19-23, 69. February 1995.
___ "Brain Food," *Starlog* No. 198: 27-31. January 1994.
___ "Extended Engagement," *Starlog* 185: 27-33, 66. December 1992.
___ "Gifts of the New Magi," *Starlog* No. 174: 56-60. January 1992.
___ "In the Fields of the Fourth Horseman," *Starlog* No. 220: 27-31. November 1995.
___ "Metal Dreams," *Starlog* No. 201: 27-31, 64. April 1994.
___ "Nine-Tenths of the Law," *Starlog* No. 190: 56-59. May 1993.
___ "Odysseys of the Mind," *Starlog* No. 194: 27-31, 82. September 1993.
___ "The Season of the Dragons," *Starlog* No. 193: 27-31. August 1993.
___ "Shooting for the Moon," *Starlog* No. 205: 41-45. August 1994.
___ "Time Without Fools," *Starlog* No. 207: 27-30, 69. October 1994.
___ "Universal Relations," *Starlog* No. 206: 35-39, 69. September 1994.
___ "Unseen Possibilities," *Starlog* 177: 56-60. April 1992.

WOLK, ANTHONY
___ "The Swiss Connection: Psychological Systems in the Novels of Philip K. Dick," in: Umland, Samuel J., ed. **Philip K. Dick: Contemporary Critical Interpretations.** Westport, CT: Greenwood, 1995. pp.101-126.

WOLLEN, PETER
___ "Theme Park and Variations," *Sight and Sound* 3(7): 7-10. August 1993.

WOLLEY, JOHN
___ "Tulsa Comics Artist Explodes into Big Time with **Batman Returns**," *Tulsa (OK) World.* September 4, 1992. in *NewsBank. Fine Arts and Architecture.* 49:A8-A9. 1992.

WOLMARK, JENNY
___ **Aliens and Others: Science Fiction, Feminism, and Postmodernism.** London: Harester Wheatsheaf, 1993. 167pp.; Iowa City: University of Iowa Press, 1994. 167pp.
___ "Space, Time and Gender: The Impact of Cybernetics on the Feminist Utopia," *Foundation* No. 62: 22-30. Winter 1994/1995.

WOLSTENHOLME, SUSAN
___ **Gothic (Re) Visions: Writing Women as Readers.** Albany: State University of New York Press, 1993. 201pp.

WOMACK, JACK
___ "The Cannon Are Silent, the Muses Are Drunk," *Science Fiction Eye* No. 11: 67-82. December 1992.

WONG, KIN-YUEN
___ "Rhetoric, History and Interpretation in Chang Hsi-Kuo's The Star Cloud Suite," *Modern Chinese Literature* (Boulder, CO) 6(1/2): 115-132. Spring-Fall 1992.

WOOD, BRENT D.
___ **Cyborgs and Soft Machines: Control and Chaos in Technological Evolution.** Master's Thesis, Trent University, 1995. 263pp. (Master's Abstracts 34/01, p. 124. Feb. 1996.)

WOOD, GARY L.
___ "**Freejack**: Filming 'Immortality Delivered'," *Cinefantastique* 22(4): 14-15. February 1992.
___ "**Lawnmower Man**: Effects by Angel Studios and Xaos, Inc.," *Cinefantastique* 23(1): 56. August 1992.
___ "**The Stand**: Development Movie Hell," *Cinefantastique* 25(2): 19-21. April 1994.
___ "**The Stand**: Stephen King: The Horror Franchise," *Cinefantastique* 25(2): 22-23. April 1994.
___ "Stephen King on Film," *Cinefantastique* 23(4): 12. December 1992.
___ "Stephen King Strikes Again," *Cinefantastique* 22(4): 4-6. February 1992.
___ "Stephen King's **Sleepwalkers**," *Cinefantastique* 22(4): 6. February 1992.
___ "Stephen King's **Sleepwalkers**," *Cinefantastique* 22(5): 20-21. April 1992.
___ "Stephen King's **Sleepwalkers**," *Cinefantastique* 23(2/3): 120. October 1992.
___ "Stephen King's **The Lawnmower Man**," *Cinefantastique* 22(4): 7, 60. February 1992.
___ "Stephen King, Computer Graphic," *Cinefantastique* 22(5): 6-7. April 1992.

WOOD, MARTINE
___ **The Work of Gary Brandner: An Annotated Bibiography and Guide.** San Bernardino, CA: Borgo Press, 1995. 112pp.

WOOD, RALPH C.
___ "Traveling the One Road: **The Lord of the Rings** as a 'Pre-Christian' Classic," *Christian Century* 110(6): 208-211. February 24, 1993.

WOOD, ROBIN
___ "Cat and Dog: Lewis Teague's Stephen King Movies," in: Irons, Glenwood, ed. **Gender, Language and Myth: Essays on Popular Narrative.** Toronto: University of Toronto Press, 1992. pp.303-318.

WOODS, LARRY D.
___ "Speculating on Speculative Fiction," *AB Bookman's Weekly* pp.2153-2154. October 1, 1984.

WOODS, LOUIS A.
___ "Jung and **Star Trek**: The Coincidentia Oppositorum and Images of the Shadow," by Louis A. Woods and Gary L. Harmon. *Journal of Popular Culture* 28(2): 169-183. Fall 1994.

WOODS, RANDY
___ A Typological Analysis of Canadian Science Fiction. Master's Thesis, Carleton University, 1993. 167pp. (Master's Abstracts 32/03, p. 811. June 1994.)

WOOLEY, CHARLES
___ Wolley's History of the Comic Book, 1899-1936: The Origin of the Superhero. Lake Buena Vista, FL: C. Wooley, 1986. [48pp.]

WORCESTER, KENT
___ "Belle of the Blob," Starlog No. 214: 66-67, 70. May 1995.

WORLAND, RICK
___ "Captain Kirk: Cold Warrior," Journal of Popular Film and Television 16(3): 109-117. 1988.
___ "From the New Frontier to the Final Frontier: Star Trek From Kennedy to Gorbachev," Film & History 24(1/2): 19-35. February/May 1994.

WRATHALL, JOHN
___ "Crimson Tide (Review)," Sight and Sound 5(12): 43-44. December 1995.

WRIGHT, BRUCE L.
___ Nightwalkers: Gothic Horror Movies, The Modern Era. Dallas, TX: Taylor Publishing Co., 9195. 171pp.
___ Yesterday's Tomorrows: The Golden Age of the Science Fiction Movie Poster, 1950-1964. Dallas, TX: Taylor, 1993. 184pp.

WRIGHT, MICHELLE R.
___ "Designing the End of History in the Arming of Galahad," Arthuriana 5(4): 45-55. Winter 1995.

WRIGHT, NOLAN
___ "Where's Star Wars 4?," Cinefantastique 22(6): 28-29. June 1992

WU, DINGBO
___ "Understanding Utopian Literature," Extrapolation 34(3): 230-244. Fall 1993.

WU, DUNCAN
___ "Wordsmith in Space: The Fantasies of William S. Burroughs," in: Filmer, Kath, ed. Twentieth-Century Fantasists: Essays in Culture, Society and Belief in Twentieth Century Mythopoeic Literature. New York: St. Martin's, 1992. pp.121-134.

WU, QUINGYUN
___ Female Rule in Chinese and English Literary Utopias. Syracuse, NY: Syracuse University Press, 1995. 225pp.; London: Liverpool University Press, 1995. 225pp.

WU, WILLIAM F.
___ "Lacks 'Oriental' Flavor," Monad No. 2:3-16. March 1992.

WULLSCHLÄGER, JACKIE
___ Inventing Wonderland: The Lives and Fantasies of Lewis Carroll, Edward Lear, J. M. Barrie, Kenneth Grahame and A. A. Milne. New York: Free Press, 1995. 228pp.

WUNDERLICH, RICHARD
___ "De-Radicalizing Pinocchio," in: Sanders, Joe, ed. Functions of the Fantastic. Westport, CT: Greenwood, 1995. pp.19-28.

WUNTCH, PHILLIP
___ "Army of Darkness: Dark Ages Camp Has Relentlessly Messy Fun," Dallas (TX) Morning News. February 19, 1993 in: NewsBank. Film and Television. 30:D14. 1993
___ "Basic Instinct Drama's Cheap Thrills May Be Trashy and Even Campy, but They Do Satisfy," Dallas (TX) Morning News. March 20, 1992 in: NewsBank. Film and Television. 29:B12-B13. 1992.
___ "Blasting Subtley Off the Screen (Review)," Dallas (TX) Morning News. October 9, 1993. in: NewsBank. Film and Television. 115:A5. 1993.
___ "Bram Stoker's Dracula Coppola's Opulence Revives a Classic," Dallas (TX) Morning News. November 13, 1992. in: NewsBank. Film and Television. 111:B12. 1992.

WUNTCH, PHILLIP (continued)
___ "Encino Man: To Find This No-Brainer Funny, You'd Need a Neanderthal Sense of Humor (Review)," Dallas (TX) Morning News. May 22, 1992. in: NewsBank. Film and Television. 52:D4. 1992.
___ "Former TV Tarzan Makes Strong 'Doc'," Dallas Morning News Sec. A, p. 27. June 6, 1975.
___ "Get Ready for an Exhilarating Trip Back to Gotham," Dallas (TX) Morning News. June 19, 1992. in: NewsBank. Film and Television. 62: G2. 1992.
___ "It's Funny; It's Smart; It's Splashy (Review)" (Reprinted from Dallas Morning News). Richmond (VA) Times-Dispatch October 9, 1993. in: NewsBank. Film and Television. 115:A7. 1993.
___ "Jewison Carries the Ball," Dallas Morning News Sec. E, p. 14. June 25, 1975.
___ "Meteor Man: There's a Lot to Like About This Action Hero (Review)," Dallas (TX) Morning News. August 6, 1993. in: NewsBank. Art. 18:E4. 1993.
___ "No Escape: Action Thriller's Characters Seem Familiar," Dallas (TX) Morning News. April 29, 1994. in: NewsBank. Film and Television. 46: E7-E8. 1994.
___ "On the Move With Logan's Run," Dallas Morning News Sec. C, p. 4. July 1, 1975.
___ "The Pod People Make a Witty Comeback," Dallas (TX) Morning News. February 18, 1994. in: NewsBank. Film and Television. 21: C2. 1994.
___ "Road Movie Breaks Down, But Scenery's Great (Review)," Dallas (TX) Morning News. March 6, 1992. in: NewsBank. Film and Television. 37:D6. 1992.
___ "Stay Tuned? On Second Thought, Don't (Review)," Dallas (TX) Morning News. August 15, 1992. in: NewsBank. Film and Television. 84:A10. 1992.
___ "Strange Days: Futuristic Thriller a Strong Dose of Unreality," Dallas (TX) Morning News. October 13, 1995. in: NewsBank. Film and Television. 99:C14. 1995.
___ "A Surprise Viewing of the Priciest Movie in History," Dallas (TX) Morning News. May 26, 1995. in: NewsBank. Film and Television. 66: D3. 1995.
___ "Walk on the Weird Side: Director Tim Burton Leads the Caped Crusader into a Dark, Sexy New Adventure Involving the Penguin and Catwoman," Dallas (TX) Morning News. June 14, 1992. in: NewsBank. Film and Television. 62:D5-D9. 1992.
___ "Waterworld: Dive into an Old-Fashioned Sloshbuckler," Dallas (TX) Morning News. July 28, 1995. in: NewsBank. Film and Television. 80: D13. 1995.

WYMER, ROWLAND
___ "How 'Safe' Is John Wyndham? A Closer Look at His Work, With Particular Reference to The Chrysalids," Foundation No. 55: 25-36. Summer 1992.

WYNNE, FRANK
___ The Making of Tank Girl. London: Titan, 1995. 96pp.

WYNNE, PATRICK
___ "The Growth of Grammar in the Elven Tongues," by Christopher Gilson and Patrick Wynne. in: Reynolds, Patricia and GoodKnight, Glen H., eds. Proceedings of the J. R. R. Tolkien Centenary Conference, Keble College, Oxford, 1992. Altadena, CA: Mythopoeic Press, 1995. pp.187-194. (Mythlore Vol. 21, No. 2, Winter 1996, Whole No. 80)
___ "Stone Towers," by Carl F. Hostetter and Patrick Wynne. Mythlore 19(4): 47-55, 65. Autumn 1993. (No. 74)

WYNNE-TYSON, JON
___ "M. P. Shiel: Right Royal Fantasist," in: Shiel in Diverse Hands: A Collection of Essays. Cleveland, OH: Reynolds Morse Foundation, 1983. pp.208-212.
___ "A Reluctant Monarch," in: Shiel in Diverse Hands: A Collection of Essays. Cleveland, OH: Reynolds Morse Foundation, 1983. pp.205-207.

WYTENBROEK, J. R.
___ "Cetacean Consciousness in Katz's Whalesinger and L'Engle's A Ring of Endless Light," in: Reynolds, Patricia and GoodKnight, Glen H., eds. Proceedings of the J. R. R. Tolkien Centenary Conference, Keble College, Oxford, 1992. Altadena, CA: Mythopoeic Press, 1995. pp.435-438. (Mythlore Vol. 21, No. 2, Winter 1996, Whole No. 80)

WYTENBROEK, J. R. (continued)
___ "The Child as Creature Creator in McCaffrey's **Dragonsong** and **Dragonsinger**," *Lion and the Unicorn* 16(2): 210-214. December 1992.
___ "The Debate Continues: Technology or Nature--A Study of Monica Hughes's Science Fiction Novels," in: Sullivan, C. W., III. **Science Fiction for Young Readers**. Westport, CT: Greenwood, 1993. pp.145-155.
___ "Natural Mysticism in Kenneth Grahame's **The Wind in the Willows**," in: Reynolds, Patricia and GoodKnight, Glen H., eds. **Proceedings of the J. R. R. Tolkien Centenary Conference, Keble College, Oxford, 1992**. Altadena, CA: Mythopoeic Press, 1995. pp.431-434. (*Mythlore* Vol. 21, No. 2, Winter 1996, Whole No. 80)

YAARI, MONIQUE
___ "Paul Paon's Sur-surreal Chimera," *Utopian Studies* 5(1): 108-127. 1994.

YAKIR, DAN
___ "Eternal Beauties," *Starlog* 185: 36-39, 66. December 1992.
___ "Higher Ground," *Starlog* No. 212: 46-49, 72. March 1995.
___ "Raising Kane," *Starlog* No. 210: 36-39, 66. January 1995.
___ "**Strange Days**," *Starlog* No. 220: 32-35. November 1995.
___ "**Super Mario Bros.**," *Starlog* No. 192: 53-58. July 1993.
___ "To the Ends of the Dream World," *Starlog* 177: 38-40, 77. April 1992.
___ " 'Twas the Night Before Halloween," *Starlog* No. 197: 43-48. December 1993.
___ "Two-Fisted Hero," *Starlog* No. 211: 50-53. February 1995.
___ "The Undiscovered Kirk," *Starlog* No. 175: 6-10, 82. February 1992.
___ "Wenders' **End** Looks to Justify the Means (Review)," *Boston (MA) Globe*. January 12, 1992. in: *NewsBank. Film and Television*. 16:B10-B11. 1992.

YAMANO, KOICHI
___ "Japanese SF, Its Originality and Orientation," *Science Fiction Studies* 21(1): 67-80. March 1994. Also in: *Chung Wai Literary Quarterly* 22(12): May 1994. (Issue not seen. Pagination not available.)
___ "Japanese SF, Its Originality and Orientation (1969)," *Chung Wai Literary Quarterly* 22(12): May 1994. (Issue not seen; pagination unavailable.)
___ "Ursula K. Le Guin: Das Mittelalter der Frauenzivilisation," *Quarber Merkur* 33(1): 26-33. June 1995. (No. 83)

YAN, WU
___ "SF in China: A Special Report," *Locus* 33(1): 45. July 1994.

YANCY, GEORGE
___ "Black Woman Pioneers Science Fiction Writing," *Philadelphia Tribune* pp.PG. January 16, 1996. (Cited from **The Electric Library** on-line service.)

YANDELL, STEPHEN
___ "A Pattern Which Our Nature Cries out For: The Medieval Tradition of the Ordered Four in the Fiction of J. R. R. Tolkien," in: Reynolds, Patricia and GoodKnight, Glen H., eds. **Proceedings of the J. R. R. Tolkien Centenary Conference, Keble College, Oxford, 1992**. Altadena, CA: Mythopoeic Press, 1995. pp.375-392. (*Mythlore* Vol. 21, No. 2, Winter 1996, Whole No. 80)

YANO, TETSU
___ "Speech: Robert A. Heinlein," in: Kondo, Yoji, ed. **Requiem: New Collected Works by Robert A. Heinlein and Tributes to the Grand Master**. New York: Tor, 1992. pp.238-239.

YARBRO, CHELSEA Q.
___ "Copyright Infringement, Part 2," *SFWA Bulletin* 26(3): 19-20. Fall 1992. (No. 117)
___ "A Matter of Willful Copyright Infringement," *SFWA Bulletin* 26(2): 11-13. Summer 1992. (No. 116)
___ "On **Freaks**," in: Golden, Christopher, ed. **Cut! Horror Writers on Horror Film**. New York: Berkley, 1992. pp.289-298.
___ "Post-Holocaust Themes in Feminist SF (Transcript of the Panel at NorEasCon 2)," by Elizabeth Lynn, Chelsea Q. Yarbro, Suzy M. Charnas and Jeanne Gomoll. *Janus* 6(2): 25-28. Winter 1980. (Whole No. 18)

YARROW, RALPH
___ "Ambiguity and the Supernatural in Cocteau's **La machine infernale**," in: Murphy, Patrick D., ed. **Staging the Impossible: The Fantastic Mode in Modern Drama**. Westport, CT: Greenwood, 1992. pp.108-115.
___ "Traces of the Trickster," in: Harger-Grinling, Virginia and Chadwick, Tony, eds. **Robbe-Grillet and the Fantastic**. Westport, CT: Greenwood, 1994. pp.35-54.

YATES, JESSICA
___ "Children's Fantasy: A Roundup Review," *Vector* No. 179: 18-22. June/July 1994.
___ "Journeys into Inner Space," *Books For Keeps* No. 83: 26-29. November 1993.
___ "Tolkien the Anti-totalitarian," in: Reynolds, Patricia and GoodKnight, Glen H., eds. **Proceedings of the J. R. R. Tolkien Centenary Conference, Keble College, Oxford, 1992**. Altadena, CA: Mythopoeic Press, 1995. pp.233-245. (*Mythlore* Vol. 21, No. 2, Winter 1996, Whole No. 80)

YEOLAND, SALLY
___ "Sally and John: The Early Years," by Sally Yeoland and John Bangsund. *Metaphysical Review* No. 22/23: 17-44. November 1995.

YEP, LAURENCE
___ "A Garden of Dragons," *ALAN Review* 19(3): 6-8. Spring 1992.

YOGEV, MICHAEL P.
___ "The Fantastic in Holocaust Literature: Writing and Unwriting the Unbearable," *Journal of the Fantastic in the Arts* 5(2): 32-48. 1993. (No. 18)

YOKE, CARL B.
___ "How Do You Get into This Line of Work, Mr. Buonarroti?," *Journal of the Fantastic in the Arts* 3(4): 80-83. 1994.
___ "Poof! Now You See Me, Now You Don't," *Journal of the Fantastic in the Arts* 4(2): 2-7. 1992. (No. 14)
___ "Roger Zelazny," in: Bruccoli, Matthew J., ed. **Facts on File Bibliography of American Fiction 1919-1988**. New York: Facts on File, 1991. pp.566-567.
___ "Slaying the Dragon Within: Andre Norton's Female Heroes," *Journal of the Fantastic in the Arts* 4(3): 79-92. 1991. (No. 15)
___ "With a Splash of Brilliant Images," *Amazing Stories* 67(5): 29-31. August 1992.
___ "Zelazny's Black: The Sidekick as Second Self," in: Ruddick, Nicholas, ed. **State of the Fantastic**. Westport, CT: Greenwood, 1992. pp.115-120.

YOLEN, JANE
___ "Dark Mirrors: The Scholar Guest of Honor Address From the 1993 Mythopoeic Conference," *Mythlore* 20(4): 38-40. Winter 1995. (Whole No. 78)
___ "Foreword: The Rumpelstiltskin Factor," *Journal of the Fantastic in the Arts* 5(2): 11-14. 1993. (No. 18)
___ "In the Spirit of Angels," *Catholic Library World* 63(2): 94-97. October/December 1991.
___ " 'Oh God, Here Come the Elves," in: Ruddick, Nicholas, ed. **State of the Fantastic**. Westport, CT: Greenwood, 1992. pp.3-14.
___ "The Route to Story," *New Advocate* 4(3): 143-149. Summer 1991.
___ "Turtles All the Way Down," in: Dozois, Gardner, ed. **Writing Science Fiction and Fantasy**. New York: St. Martin's, 1991. pp.62-75.

YOO, PAULA
___ "Rice Didn't Become a Nun, But She Did Get the Writing Habit (Interview)," *Seattle (WA) Times*. November 5, 1992. in: *NewsBank. Literature*. 105:C11-C12. 1992.
___ "Science Fiction Author Cranks out Books as If There Were No Tomorrow," *Seattle (WA) Times*. July 14, 1992. in: *NewsBank. Names in the News*. 174:A14-B1. 1992.

YORK, CHRISTINA F.
___ "Keeping the Faith," *The Report: The Fiction Writer's Magazine* 2(6): 26-28. April 1992. (No. 59)
___ "The Secret of Success," *The Report: The Fiction Writer's Magazine* No. 7: 8-10. June 1992.

ZIPES, JACK

ZIPES, JACK (continued)
___ "Recent Trends in the Contemporary American Fairy Tale," in: Sanders, Joe, ed. **Functions of the Fantastic**. Westport, CT: Greenwood, 1995. pp.1-18.

ZOGLIN, RICHARD
___ "Trekking Onward," by Richard Zoglin and Michael Walsh. *Time* 144(22): 72-79. November 28, 1994.

ZÖLLNER, KLAUS
___ "Samuel Butler **Erewhon** (1872)," by Jürgen Klein and Klaus Zöllner. in: Heuermann, Hartmut and Lange, Bernd-Peter, eds. **Die Utopie in der angloamerikanischen Literatur: Interpretationen**. Düsseldorf: Bagel, 1984. pp.80-102.

ZOOK, JIM
___ "Daring Journal of 'SF' Theory," *Chronicle of Higher Education* 40(39): A8. June 1, 1994.

ZOREDA, MARGARET L.
___ "Bakhtin, Blobels and Philip K. Dick," *Journal of Popular Culture* 28(3): 55-61. Winter 1994.

ZUCCOLA, DIANNE
___ "Hits and Misses: **Nowhere Man**," *TV Guide* 43(34): 37. August 26, 1995.

ZUCKERMAN, EDWARD
___ "William Gibson," *People Weekly* 35(22): 103-108. June 10, 1991.

ZURAWIK, DAVID
___ "**Alien Nation** Worth Dropping in On," *(Baltimore, MD) Sun*. October 25, 1994. in: *NewsBank. Film and Television*. 107:A12. 1994.
___ "A Time Warp," *(Baltimore, MD) The Evening Sun*. May 23, 1994. in: *NewsBank. Film and Television*. 59:C1-C2. 1994.
___ "Young Indy Explodes onto the Small Screen in a Sprawling, Exciting Yarn (Review)," *Baltimore (MD) Sun*. March 4, 1992. in: *NewsBank. Film and Television*. 27:C3. 1992.

ZWERDLING, ALEX
___ "Rethinking the Modernist Legacy in **Nineteen Eighty-Four**," in: Rose, Jonathan, ed. **The Revised Orwell**. East Lansing, MI: Michigan State University Press, 1992. pp.13-24.